The American Vision Modern Times

Features and Benefits

Dynamic Instructional Strategies	**. . . present a clear and comprehensive coverage of American History.** • Each engaging section introduction includes Big Ideas, Content and Academic Vocabulary, People and Events, a Reading Strategy, and reading focus prompts. • The Chapter Visual Summary offers a concise outline of important chapter topics and can be used to preview, review, or summarize chapter content.
A Strong Reading Strand	**. . . encourages active reading and learning for students of all reading levels.** • Main Idea and History & You at the beginning of each main heading give students a focus and a reason for reading. • The American Literature Library asks students to analyze poems, biographies, and American fiction. • Reading Checks help students assess their reading comprehension.
Differentiated Instruction	**. . . makes *The American Vision Modern Times* accessible to students of all learning levels.** • *Reading and Study Skills Foldables*™ are 3-D kinesthetic exercises that help students organize and process key concepts as they read. • *American History in Graphic Novel* is one motivating tool among many for differentiating instruction and engaging learners in history.
Standardized Test Preparation	**. . . gives students the opportunity to practice for state and national exams.** • Chapter Assessments are now in standardized test format to provide truly useful standardized test practice. • Prescriptive prompts on each chapter assessment page guide students to where they can revisit the material.
A Variety of History Activities and Features	**. . . are essential for student success and get students excited about history.** • Turning Point features highlight those moments in history that had a huge impact on what came after. • National Geographic's Geography and History helps students understand the impact of geography on events. • Analyzing Supreme Court Cases and Analyzing Primary Sources allow students to apply what they have learned while focusing on interesting topics.
Teacher Resources	**. . . provide convenient strategies to help new and experienced teachers.** • The Teacher Wraparound Edition contains the "Brackets and Letters" system identifying Reading, Differentiated Instruction, Writing Support, Critical Thinking, and Skill Practice activities at *exact* point of use. • Unit Resource Fast Files™ contain a wide variety of reproducible masters organized by unit to save you time.
Technology	**. . . provides time-saving software products to help you creatively engage your students and reduce your prep time.** • *TeacherWorks Plus*™ DVD contains the Interactive Teacher Edition, all ancillaries and transparencies, *editable* blackline masters, and the most powerful and easy-to-use lesson planner. • Presentation Plus! with MindJogger Checkpoint DVD contains a PowerPoint™ presentation of the textbook, all program transparencies, and the interactive MindJogger quiz game. • History Online provides lesson plans, updates, activities, and links to other resources at glencoe.com.

Improving Active Reading and Study Skills

Dinah Zike's

FOLDABLES™

Foldables are easy-to-make, three-dimensional, interactive graphic organizers that students create out of simple sheets of paper. The Teacher Classroom Resources includes *Dinah Zike's High School American History Reading and Study Skills.* This booklet provides you with step-by-step instructions for using Foldables in your classroom. Each Foldable is designed to be used as a study guide for the main ideas and key points presented in a chapter. Foldables can also be used for a more in-depth investigation of a concept, idea, opinion, or event, or people or places studied in a chapter. These unique hands-on tools for study and review were created exclusively for Glencoe by education specialist Dinah Zike.

Why Use Foldables in Social Studies?

Because they:

- organize, display, and arrange information, making it easier for students to grasp social studies concepts, theories, facts, opinions, questions, research, and ideas.

- are student-made study guides that students themselves create as they listen for main ideas, read their textbook, or conduct research.

- provide a multitude of creative formats in which students can present projects, research, interviews, and inquiry-based reports.

- replace teacher-generated writing or photocopied sheets with student-generated print.

- incorporate the use of such skills as comparing and contrasting, recognizing cause-and-effect relationships, and understanding similarities and differences.

- reinforce previously learned vocabulary, concepts, information, generalizations, ideas, and theories, providing students with a strong foundation that they can build upon with new observations, concepts, and knowledge.

- can be used by students or teachers to easily communicate data through graphs, tables, charts, models, and diagrams, including Venn diagrams.

- allow students to make their own journals for recording observations, information, primary and secondary source data, surveys, and so on.

- can be used as alternative assessment tools by teachers to evaluate student progress or by students to evaluate their own progress.

- integrate language arts, the sciences, and mathematics into the study of social studies.

- provide a sense of student ownership or investment in the social studies curriculum.

The AMERICAN VISION

MODERN TIMES

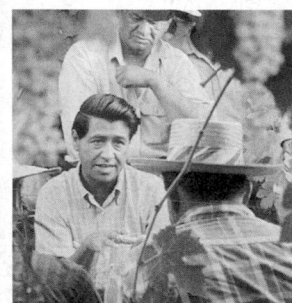

Joyce Appleby, Ph.D.   Alan Brinkley, Ph.D.   Albert S. Broussard, Ph.D.

James M. McPherson, Ph.D.   Donald A. Ritchie, Ph.D.

NATIONAL GEOGRAPHIC

 Glencoe

New York, New York   Columbus, Ohio   Chicago, Illinois   Woodland Hills, California

About the Cover The images on the cover are (from left to right): Construction workers eating lunch on a construction site at Rockefeller Center in New York City; Martin Luther King, Jr. gives his "I Have a Dream" speech in Washington, D.C., in 1963; female U.S. soldier during the Gulf War; Asian American girl holds flags at a Chinese New Year celebration; Harry S. Truman; César Chávez talks to workers in a vineyard; and *Shipping Near the Statue of Liberty* by Christian Cornelius Dommerson.

The McGraw·Hill Companies

 Glencoe

Copyright © 2008 by The McGraw-Hill Companies, Inc. All rights reserved. Except as permitted under the United States Copyright Act, no part of this publication may be reproduced or distributed in any form or by any means, or stored in a database or retrieval system, without the prior permission of the publisher.

The name "National Geographic Society" and the Yellow Border Rectangle are trademarks of the National Geographic Society, and their use, without prior written permission, is strictly prohibited.

TIME Notebook © TIME Inc. Prepared by TIME Learning Ventures in collaboration with Glencoe/McGraw-Hill. TIME and the red border design are trademarks of TIME Inc., and used under license.

Send all inquiries to: Glencoe/McGraw-Hill, 8787 Orion Place, Columbus, OH 43240-4027

ISBN 978-0-07-874524-9   *(Teacher Wraparound Edition)*
MHID 0-07-874524-1   *(Teacher Wraparound Edition)*

ISBN 978-0-07-874523-2   *(Student Edition)*
MHID 0-07-874523-3   *(Student Edition)*

Printed in the United States of America

2 3 4 5 6 7 8 9 10   055/071   11 10 09 08 07

Joyce Appleby, Ph.D., is Professor of History at UCLA. Dr. Appleby's published works include *Inheriting the Revolution: The First Generation of Americans; Capitalism and a New Social Order: The Jeffersonian Vision of the 1790s;* and *Ideology and Economic Thought in Seventeenth-Century England,* which won the Berkshire Prize. She served as president of both the Organization of American Historians and the American Historical Association, and chaired the Council of the Institute of Early American History and Culture at Williamsburg. Dr. Appleby has been elected to the American Philosophical Society and the American Academy of Arts and Sciences, and is a Corresponding Fellow of the British Academy.

Alan Brinkley, Ph.D., is Allan Nevins Professor of American History at Columbia University. His published works include *Voices of Protest: Huey Long, Father Coughlin, and the Great Depression,* which won the 1983 National Book Award; *The End of Reform: New Deal Liberalism in Recession and War; The Unfinished Nation: A Concise History of the American People;* and *Liberalism and Its Discontents.* He received the Levenson Memorial Teaching Prize at Harvard University.

Albert S. Broussard, Ph.D., is Professor of History and Graduate Coordinator at Texas A&M University. Before joining the Texas A&M faculty, Dr. Broussard was Assistant Professor of History and Director of the African American Studies Program at Southern Methodist University. Among his publications are the books *Black San Francisco: The Struggle for Racial Equality in the West, 1900–1954* and *African American Odyssey: The Stewarts, 1853–1963.* Dr. Broussard has also served as president of the Oral History Association.

James M. McPherson, Ph.D., is George Henry Davis Professor of American History at Princeton University. Dr. McPherson is the author of 11 books about the Civil War era. These include *Battle Cry of Freedom: The Civil War Era,* for which he won the Pulitzer Prize in 1989, and *For Cause and Comrades: Why Men Fought in the Civil War,* for which he won the 1998 Lincoln Prize. He is a member of many professional historical associations, including the Civil War Preservation Trust.

Donald A. Ritchie, Ph.D., is Associate Historian of the United States Senate Historical Office. Dr. Ritchie received his doctorate in American history from the University of Maryland after service in the U.S. Marine Corps. He has taught American history at various levels, from high school to university. He edits the Historical Series of the Senate Foreign Relations Committee and is the author of several books, including *Doing Oral History, The Oxford Guide to the United States Government,* and *Press Gallery: Congress and the Washington Correspondents,* which received the Organization of American Historians Richard W. Leopold Prize. Dr. Ritchie has served as president of the Oral History Association and as a council member of the American Historical Association.

The National Geographic Society, founded in 1888 for the increase and diffusion of geographic knowledge, is the world's largest nonprofit scientific and educational organization. Since its earliest days, the Society has used sophisticated communication technologies, from color photography to holography, to convey knowledge to its worldwide membership. The School Publishing Division supports the Society's mission by developing innovative educational programs—ranging from traditional print materials to multimedia programs including CD-ROMs, DVDs, and software.

Contributing Author

Dinah Zike, M.Ed., is an award-winning author, educator, and inventor known for designing three-dimensional hands-on manipulatives and graphic organizers known as Foldables™. Foldables are used nationally and internationally by teachers, parents, and educational publishing companies. Dinah has developed over 150 supplemental educational books and materials. She is the author of *The Big Book of Books and Activities,* which was awarded Learning Magazine's Teachers' Choice Award. In 2004 Dinah was honored with the CESI Science Advocacy Award. Dinah received her M.Ed. from Texas A&M, College Station, Texas.

Academic Consultants

David Berger
Broeklundian Professor of History
Brooklyn College and the Graduate Center
City University of New York
Brooklyn, New York

Paul Cimbala
Professor of History
Fordham University, Rose Hill Campus
Bronx, New York

Linda Clemmons
Assistant Professor of History
Illinois State University
Normal, Illinois

Charles Eagles
Professor of History
University of Mississippi
University, Mississippi

Neil Foley
Associate Professor of History
University of Texas at Austin
Austin, Texas

Allison Gough
Assistant Professor of History
Hawaii Pacific University
Honolulu, Hawaii

K. Austin Kerr
Emeritus Professor of History
The Ohio State University
Columbus, Ohio

Jeffrey Ogbar
Associate Professor of History and Director of
    the Institute for African American Studies
University of Connecticut, Storrs
Storrs, Connecticut

Elizabeth Pleck
Professor of History
University of Illinois at Urbana-Champaign
Urbana, Illinois

William Bruce Wheeler
Emeritus Professor of History
University of Tennessee
Knoxville, Tennessee

Shawn Johansen
Professor of History
Brigham Young University Idaho
Rexburg, Idaho

Teacher Reviewers

Joanna Ackley
John F. Kennedy High School
Taylor, Michigan

Pat Ambrose
Adlai E. Stevenson High School
Lincolnshire, Illinois

Sharon K. Anderson
Cookeville High School
Cookeville, Tennessee

Fred Barnett
Cibola High School
Albuquerque, New Mexico

Shawn Barnum
Tonawanda High School
Tonawanda, New York

Vincent Beasley
Eastern Wayne High School
Goldsboro, North Carolina

Jeremiah Bergan
Baker High School
Baldwinsville, New York

Randy Bishop
Middleton High School
Middleton, Tennessee

Patrick Boyd
Ravenwood High School
Brentwood, Tennessee

Suzanne Brock
Vestavia Hills High School
Vestavia Hills, Alabama

Joyce Brown
LaFayette High School
LaFayette, Georgia

David Chapman
Bentonville High School
Bentonville, Arkansas

Teresa Cooper
Battle Creek Central High School
Battle Creek, Michigan

Timothy Davish
Lakota East High School
Liberty Township, Ohio

Peter DeWolf
First Colonial High School
Virginia Beach, Virginia

Glenn DiTomaso
Norwell High School
Norwell, Massachusetts

Kimberly Dunn
Chase High School
Forest City, North Carolina

Bre England
Warren Central High School
Indianapolis, Indiana

Robert Fenster
Hillsborough High School
Hillsborough, New Jersey

James A. Field
Morgantown High School
Morgantown, West Virginia

Shane Gardner
Freedom High School
Morganton, North Carolina

Diane Gebel
Attica High School
Attica, New York

James Gill
Binghamton High School
Binghamton, New York

Mary Ellen Goergen
Amherst High School
Amherst, New York

Teacher Reviewers

Robert Haley
Cleveland Hill High School
Cheektowaga, New York

Ken Hall
Larkin High School
Elgin, Illinois

Roberta Heath
Capital High School
Charleston, West Virginia

Cliff Hong
Liverpool High School
Liverpool, New York

George Irby
Miami Killian Senior High School
Miami, Florida

JeTaun Jamerson
Lake View High School
Chicago, Illinois

Carol Johnson
Cary High School
Cary, North Carolina

Harry F. Jones
Panther Creek High School
Cary, North Carolina

Shirley Jones
Hillcrest High School
Memphis, Tennessee

Joe Leonard
Southport High School
Indianapolis, Indiana

Tom Long
Buffalo Gap High School
Swoope, Virginia

Rebecca Mabrey
Central Cabarrus High School
Concord, North Carolina

Amy MacIntosh
Fairfield Warde High School
Fairfield, Connecticut

Shannon W. McDonald
Harding University High School
Charlotte, North Carolina

Chad McGee
Warren County High School
McMinnville, Tennessee

Marty McNeil
Akron East High School
Akron, Ohio

Kathryn Merritt
Hillcrest High School
Tuscaloosa, Alabama

Rita Morgan
Beaverton High School
Beaverton, Oregon

Jimmy Neal
Beech High School
Hendersonville, Tennessee

Teresa Pardee
East Mecklenburg High School
Charlotte, North Carolina

Patricia Radigan
Thomas Dale High School
Chester, Virginia

Steven Reeder
Cordova High School
Cordova, Tennessee

Debi Reeves
Liberty High School
Bedford, Virginia

Connie Schlieker
Atherton High School
Louisville, Kentucky

Mark Schuler
North Springs High School
Atlanta, Georgia

Russ Smith
Ashley High School
Wilmington, North Carolina

Mitzi Terry
Franklin High School
Franklin, Tennessee

Dal Tomlinson
Dixon High School
Holly Ridge, North Carolina

Penny Toneatti
Half Hollow Hills High School East
Dix Hills, New York

Lisa Valentine
Harding University High School
Charlotte, North Carolina

Stan Vickers
Westview High School
Martin, Tennessee

Danielle Walsh
Emmaus High School
Emmaus, Pennsylvania

Joshua White
Charlotte High School
Rochester, New York

Gerald Wild II
Alden High School
Alden, New York

Amy Working
Central High School
Memphis, Tennessee

Table of Contents

Unit 1

Table of Contents

NO MOLLY-CODDLING HERE

Unit 3

Table of Contents

Unit 2

The Birth of Modern America 154
1865–1901

Table of Contents

Unit 5

Unit 6

Table of Contents

Appendix

Features

ANALYZING PRIMARY SOURCES

POLITICAL CARTOONS PRIMARY SOURCE

Turning Point

ANALYZING SUPREME COURT CASES

Time Lines

Primary Source Quotes

A variety of quotations and excerpts throughout the text express the thoughts, feelings, and life experiences of people, past and present.

Primary Source Quotes

Primary Source Quotes

Maps

Maps In MOtion See *StudentWorks*™ *Plus* or glencoe.com.

Maps labeled with the In Motion icon have been specially enhanced on the StudentWorks™ Plus DVD and on glencoe.com. These In Motion maps allow you to interact with layers of displayed data and to listen to audio components.

Entries in **blue** are In Motion maps.

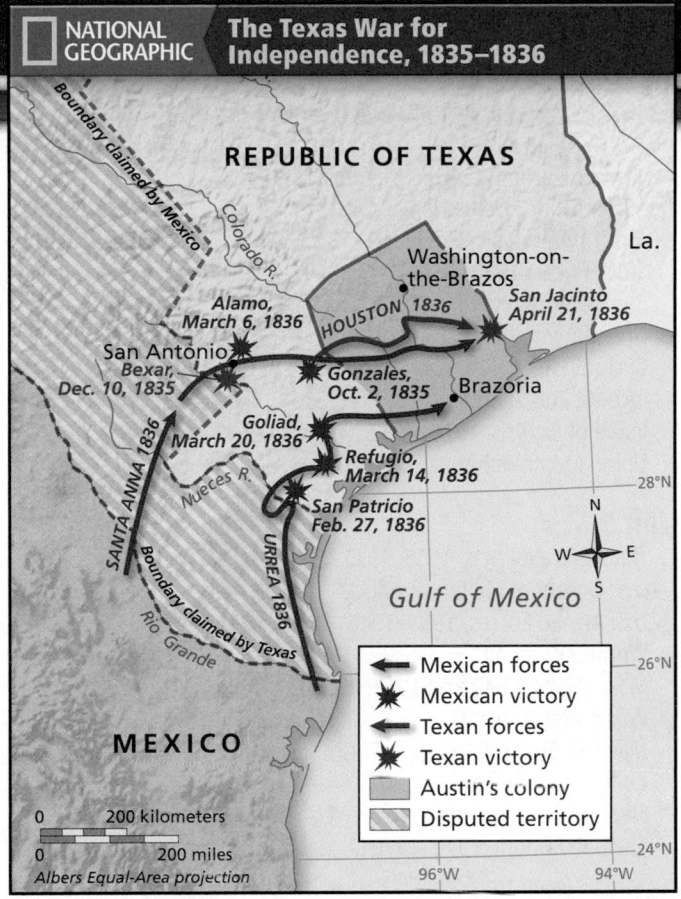

NATIONAL GEOGRAPHIC **The Texas War for Independence, 1835–1836**

REPUBLIC OF TEXAS

La.

Colorado R.

Boundary claimed by Mexico

Washington-on-the-Brazos

Alamo, March 6, 1836

HOUSTON 1836

San Jacinto April 21, 1836

San Antonio
Bexar, Dec. 10, 1835

Gonzales, Oct. 2, 1835

Brazoria

Goliad, March 20, 1836

Nueces R.

Refugio, March 14, 1836

28°N

SANTA ANNA 1836

San Patricio Feb. 27, 1836

URREA 1836

N

W E

S

Gulf of Mexico

MEXICO

Rio Grande

Boundary claimed by Texas

26°N

— Mexican forces
✹ Mexican victory
— Texan forces
✹ Texan victory
  Austin's colony
  Disputed territory

0   200 kilometers
0   200 miles
Albers Equal-Area projection

24°N

96°W   94°W

Charts & Graphs

The American Vision contains a wealth of information. The trick is to know where to look to access all the information in the book. If you go through this scavenger hunt, either alone or with your teacher or parents, you will quickly learn how the textbook is organized and how to get the most out of your reading and study time. Let's get started!

1. How many units and chapters are in the book? 7 units, 24 chapters

2. What is the difference between the glossary and the index? glossary: defines terms; index: lists page numbers for various topics

3. Every chapter contains primary sources—quotes or documents from the era. Where else can you find primary sources in the textbook? in Analyzing Primary Sources features, and in Documents in American History and American Literature Library in the Appendix

4. In what special feature can you find the definition of a physical map, a political map, and a special-purpose map? the Geography Handbook

5. If you want to quickly find all the maps, charts, and graphs about World War II, where in the front do you look? look in the Table of Contents

6. How can you find information about civil rights activist Martin Luther King, Jr.? look in the Index

7. Where can you find an overview of the major events of the Vietnam War discussed in Chapter 19? in the Visual Summary at the end of the chapter

8. Where are the key terms and names for Chapter 8, Section 3 listed, and how are they highlighted in the text? listed in the Guide to Reading and Section Review; boldfaced and highlighted in yellow in the text

9. The Web site for the book is listed seven times in Chapter 16. After finding all seven, list how the Web site can help you. provides previews, additional activities and resources, and practice tests

10. Which of the book's main features will provide you with strategies for improving your studying and writing skills? The Skillbuilder Handbook in the Appendix

THEMES IN THE
AMERICAN VISION: MODERN TIMES

As you read THE AMERICAN VISION: MODERN TIMES, *you will be given help in sorting out all the information you encounter. This textbook organizes the events of your nation's past and present around 10 themes. A theme is a concept, or main idea, that happens again and again throughout history. By recognizing these themes, you will better understand events of the past and how they affect you today.*

Culture and Beliefs

Being aware of cultural differences helps us understand ourselves and others. People from around the world for generations have sung of the "land of the Pilgrims' pride, land where our fathers died," even though their ancestors arrived on these shores long after these events occurred.

Past and Present

Recognizing our historic roots helps us understand why things are the way they are today. This theme includes political, social, religious, and economic changes that have influenced the way Americans think and act.

Geography and History

Understanding geography helps us understand how humans interact with their environment. The United States succeeded in part because of its rich natural resources and its vast open spaces. In many regions, the people changed the natural landscape to fulfill their wants and needs.

Individual Action

Responsible individuals have often stepped forward to help lead the nation. Americans' strong values helped create such individuals. These values spring in part from earlier times when the home was the center of many activities, including work, education, and spending time with one's family.

Group Action

Identifying how political and social groups and institutions operate helps us work together. From the beginning, Americans formed groups and institutions to act in support of their economic, political, social, and religious beliefs.

Government and Society

Understanding the workings of government helps us become better citizens. Abraham Lincoln explained the meaning of democracy as "government of the people, by the people, for the people." Democracy, at its best, is "among" the people.

Science and Technology

Americans have always been quick to adopt innovations. The nation was settled and built by people who gave up old ways in favor of new. Americans' lives are deeply influenced by technology, the use of science, and machines. Perhaps no machine has so shaped modern life as the automobile. Understanding the role of science and technology helps us see their impact on our society and the roles they will play in the future.

Economics and Society

The free enterprise economy of the United States is consistent with the nation's history of rights and freedoms. Freedom of choice in economic decisions supports other freedoms. Understanding the concept of free enterprise is basic to studying American history.

Trade, War, and Migration

Events much bigger than any individual also shape the course of history. Being aware of global interdependence helps us make decisions and deal with the difficult issues we will encounter. Trade, war, and the movement of people between nations have altered the nation's history.

Struggles for Rights

For a democratic system to survive, its citizens must take an active role in government. The foundation of democracy is the right of every person to take part in government and to voice one's views on issues. An appreciation for the struggle to preserve these freedoms is vital to the understanding of democracy.

USING THE BIG IDEAS

You will find Big Ideas at the beginning of every section of every chapter. You are asked questions that help you put it all together to better understand how ideas and themes are connected across time—and to see why history is important to you today.

Correlation of

The American Vision: Modern Times
to the NCSS Thematic Strands

Theme and Performance Expectations	Student Pages
I. *Culture* The study of culture helps students understand similarities and differences within groups of people. By studying a culture's beliefs, values, and traditions, students begin to gain a perspective that helps them relate to different groups. In high school, students can understand and use complex cultural concepts such as adaptation, assimilation, and acculturation to explain how culture and cultural systems function.	
***The American Vision: Modern Times* Related Theme: Culture and Traditions**	
A. Analyze and explain the ways groups, societies, and cultures address human needs and concerns.	4–6, 9–21, 22–29, 34–41, 76–103, 107–116, 230–241, 242–247, 292–314, 376–381, 546–553, 610–616, 622–648, 682–698, 740–745
B. Predict how data and experiences may be interpreted by people from diverse cultural perspectives and frames of reference.	5, 34–41
C. Apply an understanding of culture as an integrated whole that explains the functions and interactions of language, literature, the arts, traditions, beliefs and values, and behavior patterns.	4–6, 8, 34–36, 91, 100, 104–105, 214–219, 222–229, 230–233, 236–239, 240–241, 376–379, 382–387, 388–393, 406–409, 572–574, 576–579, 682–697, 774–777
D. Compare and analyze societal patterns for preserving and transmitting culture while adapting to environmental or social change.	8–13, 16–18, 104–105, 164–165, 166–169, 214–219, 224–229
E. Demonstrate the value of cultural diversity, as well as cohesion, within and across groups.	4–6, 514, 754–759, 788–791
F. Interpret patterns of behavior reflecting values and attitudes that contribute or pose obstacles to cross-cultural understanding.	4–8, 16–21, 94–96, 102–103, 104–105, 214–221, 376–381, 466–473, 582–587, 620–648, 788–798, 808–810
G. Construct reasoned judgments about specific cultural responses to persistent human issues.	R7–R14
H. Explain and apply ideas, theories, and modes of inquiry drawn from anthropology and sociology in the examination of persistent issues and social problems.	4, 231–232, 236–238, 582
II. *Time, Continuity, and Change* Understanding time, continuity, and change involves being knowledgeable about what things were like in the past and how things change and develop over time. Knowing how to read and reconstruct the past helps students gain a historical perspective. In high school, students examine the past's relationship with the present while extrapolating into the future. They also integrate individual stories about people, events, and situations to form a more complete conception, in which continuity and change persist in time and across cultures. Students will use their knowledge of history to make informed choices and decisions in the present.	
***The American Vision: Modern Times* Related Theme: Continuity and Change**	
A. Demonstrate that historical knowledge and the concept of time are socially influenced constructions that lead historians to be selective in the questions they seek to answer and the evidence they use.	24, 114–115, 124, 184, 220–221, 296, 334–335, 426, 432–433, 472–473, 510, 520, 632, 640–641, 792–793, 816
B. Apply key concepts such as time, chronology, causality, change, conflict, and complexity to explain, analyze, and show connections among patterns of historical change and continuity.	7, 24, 81, 96, 102, 124, 132, 142, 145, 160, 184, 246, 278, 296, 326, 350, 392, 426, 428, 478, 510, 520, 556, 584, 612, 626, 632, 756, 809, 816
C. Identify and describe significant historical periods and patterns of change within and across cultures, such as the development of ancient cultures and civilizations, the rise of nation-states, and social, economic, and political revolutions.	4–8, 22–29, 124–139, 140–150, 180–211, 620–651, 686–701, 774–779
D. Systematically employ the processes of critical historical inquiry to reconstruct and reinterpret the past, such as using a variety of sources and checking their credibility, validating and weighing evidence for claims, and searching for causality.	114–115, 220–221, 334–335, 432–433, 472–473, 640–641, 792–793

Theme and Performance Expectations	Student Pages
E. Investigate, interpret, and analyze multiple historical and contemporary viewpoints within and across cultures related to important events, recurring dilemmas, and persistent issues, while employing empathy, skepticism, and critical judgment.	26–27, 114–115, 220–221, 236–237, 272–273, 304–305, 324–325, 334–335, 432–433, 436–437, 472–473, 522–523, 534–535, 640–641, 658–659, 688–689, 748–749, 782–783, 792–793
F. Apply ideas, theories, and modes of historical inquiry to analyze historical and contemporary developments, and to inform and evaluate actions concerning public policy issues.	7, 81, 89, 102, 132, 142, 246, 201,303, 326, 331, 392, 443, 478, 505, 551, 556, 594, 625, 626, 673, 715, 809

III. *People, Places, and Environments*

The study of people, places, and environments will help students as they create their spatial views and geographic perspectives of the world. Students begin to make informed and critical decisions about the relationship between humans and their environment. In high school, geographic concepts become central to students' comprehension of global connections as they expand their knowledge of diverse cultures, both historical and contemporary.

The American Vision: Modern Times **Related Theme: Geography and History**

A. Refine mental maps of locales, regions, and the world that demonstrate understanding of relative locations, direction, size and shape.	GH9, 5, 12, 17, 28, 36, 82, 95, 98, 105, 159, 162, 167, 183, 215, 277, 281, 288, 321, 343, 357, 455, 456, 457, 461, 470, 477, 533, 536, 541, 655, 656, 742, 763, 764, 795, 810
B. Create, interpret, use, and synthesize information from various representations of the earth, such as maps, globes, and photographs.	GH3–GH13, 5, 12, 17, 18, 19, 44, 23, 28, 36, 40, 82, 87, 90–91, 92, 95, 98, 118, 105, 106, 123, 131, 152, 144, 148, 159, 162, 167, 171, 183, 189, 191, 203, 215, 217, 249, 270, 271, 277, 281, 288, 297, 309, 310, 316, 321, 337, 340, 341, 343, 350, 352, 357, 392, 396, 401, 418, 428, 448, 455, 456, 457, 461, 470, 477, 495, 496, 503, 509, 513, 516, 519, 528, 533, 536, 541, 542, 543, 562, 569, 570, 597, 606, 650, 655, 656, 660, 668, 678, 700, 721, 736, 742, 763, 764, 766, 795, 805, 810, 821, 830
C. Use appropriate resources, data sources, and geographic tools such as aerial photographs, satellite images, geographic information systems (GIS), map projections, and cartography to generate, manipulate, and interpret information such as atlases, databases, grid systems, charts, graphs, and maps.	GH3–GH13, 5, 12, 17, 18, 19, 44, 23, 28, 36, 40, 82, 87, 92, 95, 98, 118, 105, 106, 123, 131, 152, 144, 148, 159, 162, 167, 171, 183, 189, 191, 203, 215, 217, 249, 270, 271, 277, 281, 288, 297, 309, 310, 316, 321, 337, 340, 341, 343, 350, 352, 357, 392, 396, 401, 418, 428, 448, 455, 456, 457, 461, 470, 477, 495, 496, 503, 509, 513, 516, 519, 528, 533, 536, 541, 542, 543, 562, 569, 570, 597, 606, 650, 655, 656, 660, 668, 678, 700, 721, 736, 742, 763, 764, 766, 795, 805, 810, 821, 830
D. Calculate distance, scale, area, and density, and distinguish spatial distribution patterns.	36, 167, 191, 215, 217, 396, 760
E. Describe, differentiate, and explain the relationships among various regional and global patterns of geographic phenomena such as landforms, soils, climate, vegetation, natural resources, and population.	4–6, 9–13, 90–93, 104–105, 158–169, 182–183, 730–734
F. Use knowledge of physical system changes such as seasons, climate and weather, and the water cycle to explain geographic phenomena.	168–169, 407, 410–411
G. Describe and compare how people create places that reflect culture, human needs, government policy, and current values and ideals as they design and build specialized buildings, neighborhoods, shopping centers, urban centers, industrial parks, and the like.	222–229, 754–755, 760
H. Examine, interpret, and analyze physical and cultural patterns and their interactions, such as land use, settlement patterns, cultural transmission of customs and ideas, and ecosystem changes.	4–6, 9–21, 90–93, 104–105, 105–107, 158–169, 214–221, 407, 410–411, 730–731, 798
I. Describe and assess ways that historical events have been influenced by, and have influenced, physical and human geographic factors in local, regional, national, and global settings.	4–6, 16–21, 90–93, 104–105, 158–169, 214–221, 242–247, 262–286, 320–327, 407, 410–411, 454–465, 532–547, 602–609, 654–663, 730–731, 794–798, 808–825

Theme and Performance Expectations	Student Pages
J. Analyze and evaluate social and economic effects of environmental changes and crises resulting from phenomena such as floods, storms, and drought.	168–169, 294–295, 407, 410–411, 730–731, 824–825
K. Propose, compare, and evaluate alternative policies for the use of land and other resources in communities, regions, nations, and the world.	158–169, 182–193, 304–305, 407, 410–411, 730–734, 760

IV. Individual Development and Identity

People and culture influence a person's identity. Examining the different forms of human behavior improves one's understanding of social relationships and the development of personal identity. The study of human behavior helps students become aware of how social processes influence a person's identity. In high school, students use methods from the behavioral sciences to examine individuals, societies, and cultures.

The American Vision: Modern Times Related Theme: Individual Action

A. Articulate personal connections to time, place, and social/cultural system.	102–103, 160, 184–185, 200–207, 248–253, 270, 336–345
B. Identify, describe, and express appreciation for the influence of various historical and contemporary cultures on an individual's daily life.	230–239, 292–299, 388–393, 490–501, 496
C. Describe the ways family, religion, gender, ethnicity, nationality, socioeconomic status, and other group and cultural influences contribute to the development of a sense of self.	165, 174, 196–197, 207, 255–256, 296–297
D. Apply concepts, methods, and theories about the study of human growth and development, such as physical endowment, learning, motivation, behavior, perception, and personality.	174, 196–197, 198
E. Examine the interaction of ethnic, national, or cultural influences in specific situations or events.	164–165, 254–259, 269–270, 312–315
F. Analyze the role of perceptions, attitudes, values, and beliefs in the development of personal identity.	206, 300–305, 332–333
G. Compare and evaluate the impact of stereotyping, conformity, acts of altruism, and other behaviors on individuals and groups.	170–175, 255–256, 313, 342–345
H. Work independently and cooperatively within groups and institutions to accomplish goals.	83, 422–431
I. Examine factors that contribute to and damage one's mental health and analyze issues related to mental health and behavioral disorders in contemporary society.	230–239, 299, 729

V. Individuals, Groups, and Institutions

Institutions, such as schools, governments, and churches, influence people and often reflect a society's values. Because of the vital role that institutions play in people's lives, it is important that students know how institutions develop, what controls and influences them, and how humans react to them. High school students must understand the traditions and theories that support social and political traditions.

The American Vision: Modern Times Related Theme: Groups and Institutions

A. Apply concepts such as role, status, and social class in describing the connections and interactions of individuals, groups, and institutions in society.	96–99, 200–207, 301, 440–445
B. Analyze group and institutional influences on people, events, and elements of culture in both historical and contemporary settings.	94–96, 96–99, 91, 100, 105, 111–113, 126–129, 133, 140–144, 145–147, 200–207, 292–299, 388–393, 412–415, 422–431, 440–445, 486–493, 730–733
C. Describe the various forms institutions take, and explain how they develop and change over time.	94–96, 96–99, 100–101, 105–107, 111–113, 126–129, 140–144, 145–147, 201–207, 388–393, 412–415, 422–431
D. Identify and analyze examples of tensions between expressions of individuality and efforts used to promote social conformity by groups and institutions.	91, 100, 133, 140–144, 486–493, 682–685
E. Describe and examine belief systems basic to specific traditions and laws in contemporary and historical movements.	94–96, 105, 111–113, 133, 254–256, 314, 388–393, 440–445, 486–493, 730–733, 740–745
F. Evaluate the role of institutions in furthering both continuity and change.	94–96, 96–99, 105, 126–129, 133, 140–144, 200–207, 292–299, 388–393, 412–415, 422–431, 730–733

Theme and Performance Expectations	Student Pages
G. Analyze the extent to which groups and institutions meet individual needs and promote the common good in contemporary and historical settings.	91, 100, 145–147, 200–207, 292–299, 412–415, 422–431, 730–733
H. Explain and apply ideas and modes of inquiry drawn from behavioral science and social theory in the examination of persistent issues and social problems.	4, 231–232, 236–238, 582

VI. *Power, Authority, and Governance*

Studying structures of power, authority, and governance and their functions in the United States and around the world is important for developing a notion of civic responsibility. Students will identify the purpose and characteristics of various types of government and how people try to resolve conflicts. Students will also examine the relationship between individual rights and responsibilities. High school students study the various systems that have been developed over time to allocate and employ power and authority in the governing process.

The American Vision: Modern Times **Related Theme: Government and Democracy**

A. Examine persistent issues involving the rights, roles, and status of the individual in relation to the general welfare.	22–29, 37–41, 92–93, 96–99, 100–103, 107–116, 132, 140–144, 242–247, 248–253, 292–299, 501–504, 505, 622–647, 682, 697, 740–745
B. Explain the purpose of government and analyze how its powers are acquired, used, and justified.	30–33, 34–41, 46–75, 89, 132, 142, 251, 303, 331, 443, 505, 551, 599, 625, 673, 715
C. Analyze and explain ideas and mechanisms to meet needs and wants of citizens, regulate territory, manage conflict, establish order and security, and balance competing conceptions of a just society.	46–55, 89, 96–99, 100–103, 107–116, 125–139, 140–149, 170–176, 200–208, 242–247, 251, 292–314, 331, 422–439, 443, 505, 551, 599, 622–648, 673, 682–698, 715
D. Compare and analyze the ways nations and organizations respond to conflicts between forces of unity and forces of diversity.	214–221, 376–381, 723–729, 788–793
E. Compare different political systems (their ideologies, structure, institutions, processes, and political cultures) with that of the United States, and identify representative political leaders from selected historical and contemporary settings.	6–13, 105–107, 454–459, 466–473, 532–537, 762–770, 808–819
F. Analyze and evaluate conditions, actions, and motivations that contribute to conflict and cooperation within and among nations.	80–81, 86–88, 94–96, 105–108, 107–116, 140–144, 170–176, 262–286, 320–327, 348–354, 454–479, 532–545, 602–609, 654–675, 762–767, 808–819
G. Evaluate the role of technology in communications, transportation, information-processing, weapons development, or other areas as it contributes to or helps resolve conflicts.	90, 91–93, 128, 160–161, 168, 182–185, 190, 223, 338, 370, 463, 555, 604–605, 754–755, 774–779
H. Explain and apply ideas, theories, and modes of inquiry drawn from political science to the examination of persistent ideas and social problems.	18–20, 20–21, 582, 708
I. Evaluate the extent to which governments achieve their stated ideals and policies at home and abroad.	34–36, 83, 147–149, 175, 342–344, 412–415, 440–445, 454–465, 518–525, 614–615, 670–675, 722–723, 752–753, 762–767
J. Prepare a public policy paper and present and defend it before an appropriate forum in school or community.	317

VII. *Production, Distribution, and Consumption*

Societies try to meet people's needs and wants by trying to answer the basic economic questions: What is to be produced? How should goods be produced? How should goods and services be distributed? How should land, labor, capital, and management be allocated? By studying how needs and wants are met, students learn how trade and government economic policies develop. In high school, students develop economic perspectives and a deeper understanding of key economic concepts and processes.

The American Vision: Modern Times **Related Theme: Economic Factors**

A. Explain how the scarcity of productive resources (human, capital, technological, and natural) requires the development of economic systems to make decisions about how goods and services are to be produced and distributed.	6–21, 90–93, 182–199, 214–221, 262–267, 400–405, 794–797
B. Analyze the role that supply and demand, prices, incentives, and profits play in determining what is produced and distributed in a competitive market system.	16–21, 90–93, 162–163, 194–199, 400–405, 754–755
C. Consider the costs and benefits to society of allocating goods and services through private and public sectors.	16–21, 90–93, 158–169, 182–207, 292–313, 328–335, 400–405, 422–439, 500–507, 610–615, 754–755, 794–797

Theme and Performance Expectations	Student Pages
D. Describe the relationships among the various economic institutions that comprise economic systems such as households, business firms, banks, government agencies, labor unions, and corporations.	147–149, 194–199, 200–207, 320–322, 400–405, 566–571, 746–753, 774–777
E. Analyze the role of specialization and exchange in economic processes.	147–149, 194–199
F. Compare how values and beliefs influence economic decisions in different societies.	4–6, 158–165, 186–187, 202, 362–367, 566–571, 740–745, 762–767, 774–777, 780–787
G. Compare basic economic systems according to how rules and procedures deal with demand, supply, prices, the role of government, banks, labor and labor unions, savings and investments, and capital.	201–207, 242–247, 298–302, 306–307, 310–312, 746–753
H. Apply economic concepts and reasoning when evaluating historical and contemporary social developments and issues.	342
I. Distinguish between the domestic and global economic systems, and explain how the two interact.	158–165, 242–247, 262–267
J. Apply knowledge of production, distribution, and consumption in the analysis of a public issue such as the allocation of health care or the consumption of energy, and devise an economic plan for accomplishing a socially desirable outcome related to that issue.	610–615, 730–733, 780–787, 794–797
K. Distinguish between economics as a field of inquiry and the economy.	362–367, 440–445, 746–753

VIII. *Science, Technology, and Society*

The study of science, technology, and society is ever changing. It raises questions about who will benefit from it and how fundamental values and beliefs can be preserved in a technology-driven society. In high school, students will confront issues that balance the benefits of science and technology against the accompanying social consequences.

The American Vision: Modern Times Related Theme: Science and Technology

A. Identify and describe both current and historical examples of the interaction and interdependence of science, technology, and society in a variety of cultural settings.	6–8, 90–93, 104–105, 161, 168–169, 222–227, 276–283, 368–375, 422–431, 602–607, 630–639, 654–661, 754–759, 774–777
B. Make judgments about how science and technology have transformed the physical world and human society and our understanding of time, space, place, and human-environment interactions.	6–8, 14–15, 90–93, 104–105, 128, 168, 190, 222–227, 284–285, 338, 368–375, 422–431, 463, 554–559, 602–607, 754–759, 774–777
C. Analyze how science and technology influence the core values, beliefs, and attitudes of society, and how core values, beliefs, and attitudes of society shape scientific and technological change.	6–8, 90–93, 368–375, 546–553, 602–607, 754–759, 774–777
D. Evaluate various policies that have been proposed as ways of dealing with social changes resulting from new technologies, such as genetically engineered plants and animals.	284–285, 730–733, 774–777
E. Recognize and interpret varied perspectives about human societies and the physical world using scientific knowledge, ethical standards, and technologies from diverse world cultures.	6–8, 14–15, 794–797
F. Formulate strategies and develop policies for influencing public discussions associated with technology-society issues, such as the greenhouse effect.	730–733, 796–797

IX. *Global Connections*

As countries grow more interdependent, understanding global connections among world societies becomes important. Students will analyze emerging global issues in many different fields. They will also investigate relationships among the different cultures of the world. High school students will address critical issues such as peace, human rights, trade, and global ecology.

The American Vision: Modern Times Related Theme: Global Connections

A. Explain how language, art, music, belief systems, and other cultural elements can facilitate global understanding or cause misunderstanding.	6–8, 9–13, 16–21, 376–393, 554–559, 804–827

Theme and Performance Expectations	Student Pages
B. Explain conditions and motivations that contribute to conflict, cooperation, and interdependence among groups, societies, and nations.	22–26, 83, 86–88, 94–96, 105–108, 122–145, 268–283, 318–353, 450–559, 652–697, 762–767, 808–819
C. Analyze and evaluate the effects of changing technologies on the global community.	91, 92–93, 100, 114–115, 182–193, 382–387, 572–581, 730–736, 774–778
D. Analyze the causes, consequences, and possible solutions to persistent, contemporary, and emerging global issues, such as health, security, resource allocation, economic development, and environmental quality.	420–445, 610–615, 620–647, 680–697, 724–733, 740–745, 802–827
E. Analyze the relationships and tensions between national sovereignty and global interests, in such matters as territory, economic development, nuclear and other weapons, use of natural resources, and human rights concerns.	22–29, 83, 262–283, 320–327, 454–459, 518–525, 530–559, 602–609, 652–663, 706–711, 730–733, 762–768, 808–819
F. Analyze or formulate policy statements demonstrating an understanding of concerns, standards, issues, and conflicts related to universal human rights.	6–8, 16–21, 454–459, 466–471, 622–647, 682–697
G. Describe and evaluate the role of international and multinational organizations in the global arena.	532–537, 538–545, 780–787, 794–797
H. Illustrate how individual behaviors and decisions connect with global systems.	780–787, 794–797, 804–827

X. Civic Ideals and Practices

Understanding civic ideals and practices is crucial to complete participation in society and is the main purpose of social studies. Students will learn about civic participation and the role of the citizen within his or her community, country, and world. High school students learn, through experience, to identify social needs, setting directions for public policy, and working to support both individual dignity and the common good.

The American Vision: Modern Times **Related Theme: Civic Rights and Responsibilities**

A. Explain the origins and interpret the continuing influence of key ideals of the democratic republican form of government, such as individual human dignity, liberty, justice, equality, and the rule of law.	22–24, 30–33, 46–75, 107–11, 596–601, 642–647, 682–697, 724–727, 788–791
B. Identify, analyze, interpret, and evaluate sources and examples of citizens' rights and responsibilities.	22–24, 30–33, 46–75, 107–11, 466–471, 546–553
C. Locate, access, analyze, organize, synthesize, evaluate, and apply information about selected public issues—identifying, describing, and evaluating multiple points of view.	80–81, 107–11, 122–126, 140–144, 546–553, 596–601, 642–647, 664–669
D. Practice forms of civic discussion and participation consistent with the ideals of citizens in a democratic republic.	103, 601, 629, 661, 669, 691, 711, 723, 745, 754, 791, 797, 807, 813
E. Analyze and evaluate the influence of various forms of citizen action and public policy.	102–103, 200–207, 242–247
F. Analyze a variety of public policies and issues from the perspective of formal and informal political actors.	102–103, 200–207, 242–247
G. Evaluate the effectiveness of public opinion in influencing and shaping public policy developments and decision-making.	102–103, 200–207, 242–247
H. Evaluate the degree to which public policies and citizen behaviors reflect or foster the stated ideals of a democratic republican form of government.	80–81, 94–96, 96–103, 104–107, 107–126, 140–149, 200–207, 212–253, 262–267, 276–283, 290–313, 360–393, 398–417, 420–445, 564–587, 594–615, 620–647, 680–697, 704–733, 738–767, 780–787, 802–827
I. Construct a policy statement and an action plan to achieve one or more goals related to an issue of public concern.	103, 659, 661, 669, 691, 745, 754, 791, 797
J. Participate in activities to strengthen the "common good," based upon careful evaluation of possible options for citizen action.	629, 759, 813

To Teachers:

Welcome to the Teacher Wraparound Edition of *The American Vision Modern Times*. We have created this teacher edition based on input from experienced teachers and educational consultants. Our goal is to provide you with teaching strategies and activities that are labeled for you at point-of-use. The following pages will show the structure of the Teacher Wraparound Edition.

Student-Based Instruction

Point-of-Use

- Strategies and activities apply directly to student content.

Differentiated Instruction

- Leveled activities and options for differentiated instruction help meet the needs of all your students, including English language learners.

Review and Reinforcement

- Reading and critical thinking skills are reinforced throughout the lesson.

Assessment and Intervention

- Chapter Assessments provide standardized test practice.
- Assessments gauge student mastery of content.
- Additional resources provide intervention options.

Planning and Teaching the Unit

Planning pages appear at the beginning of each unit.

Pacing Chart

Provides time management suggestions for teaching the unit

Author Note

Highlights author's ideas for teaching the unit

Teacher to Teacher

Includes activities from the classrooms of successful teachers

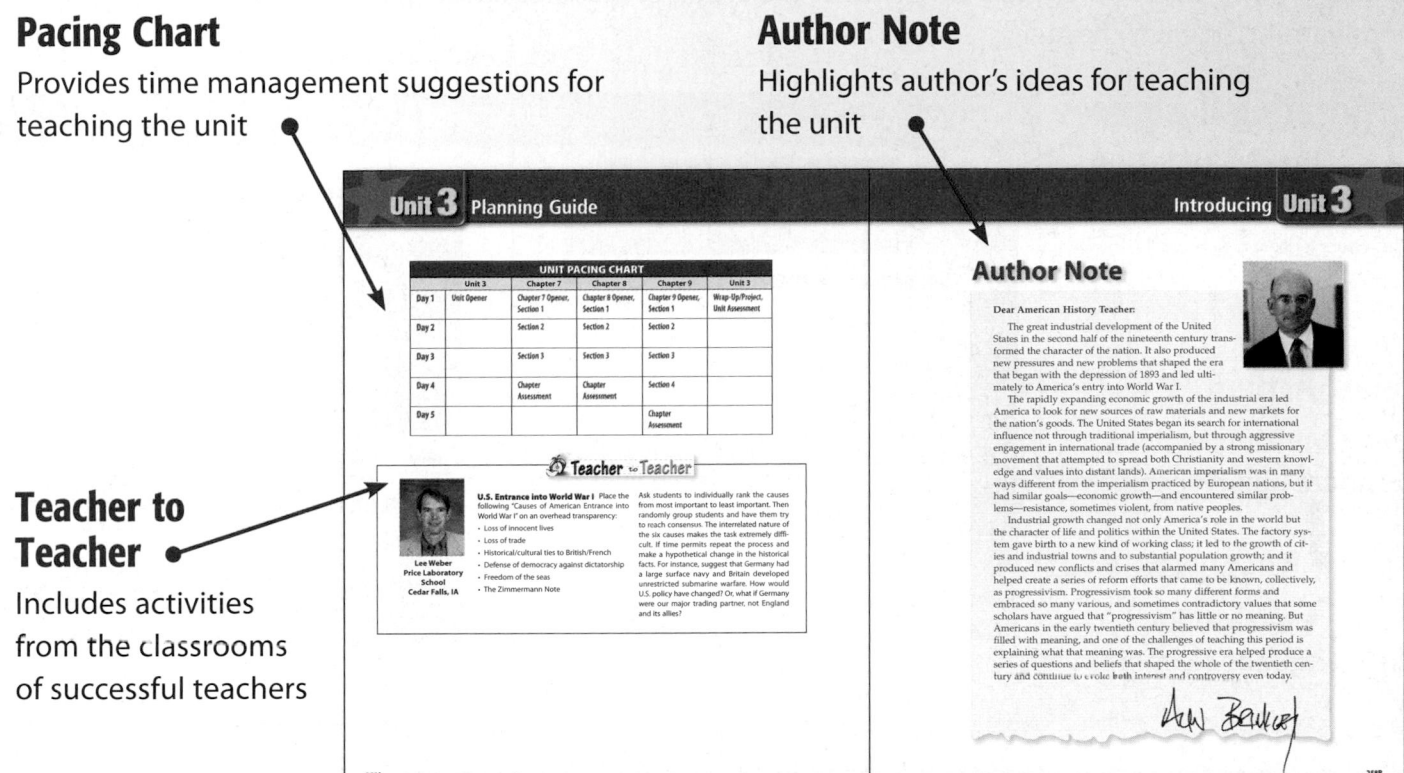

Why It Matters

Provides an activity to help students discover why the events they will study are important

Skill Practice

Point-of-use skill-based activities help students practice historical analysis and geography skills

Team Teaching Activity

Introduce the unit by relating history to other social studies disciplines

Planning the Chapter

Chapter Planning Guides provide a snapshot of the scope of resources available to enhance and extend learning in each chapter.

Incorporating Resources

Utilizes a structured lesson plan to incorporate additional resources

Leveled Activities

Organizes resources by appropriate ability levels

*Spanish Resources

Indicates resources for English language learners

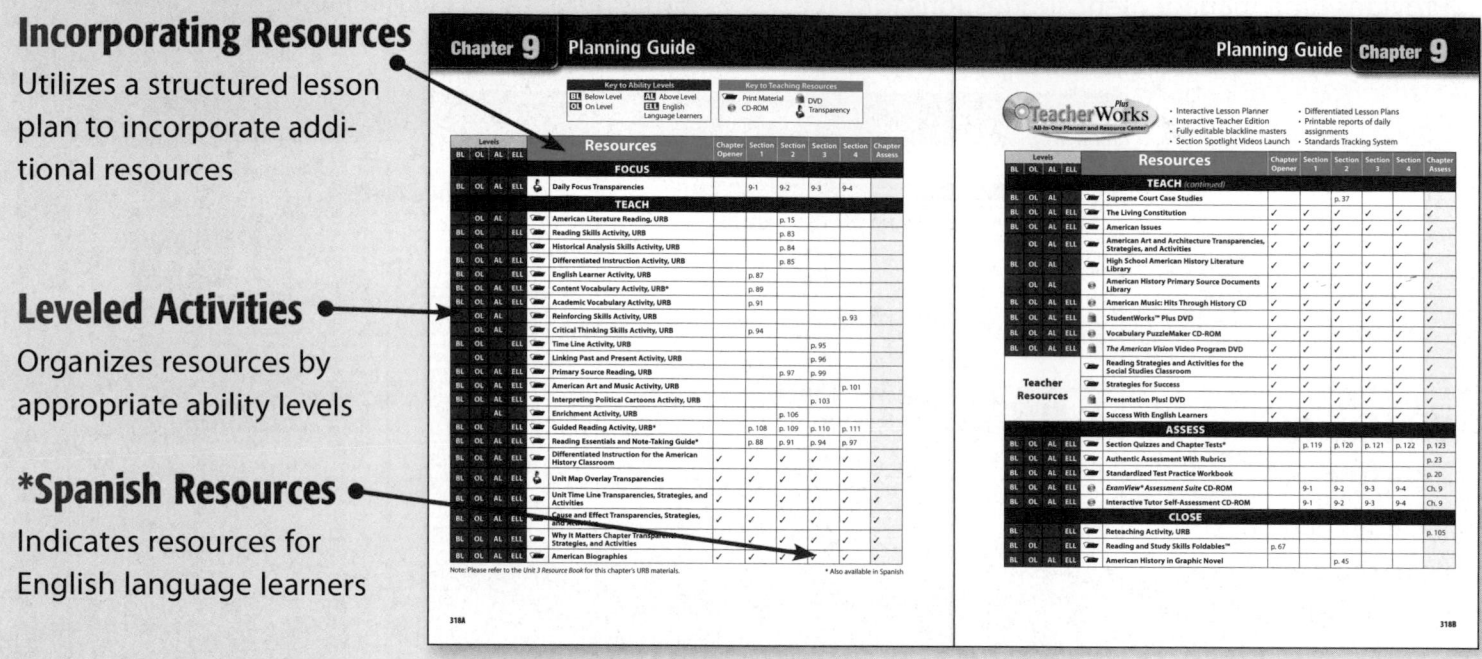

Teaching with Technology

Explains how to incorporate different Glencoe technology resources in the classroom

Online and Downloadable Learning

Engages students and caregivers with online and downloadable content

Additional Resources

Identifies resources for supplementing the chapter

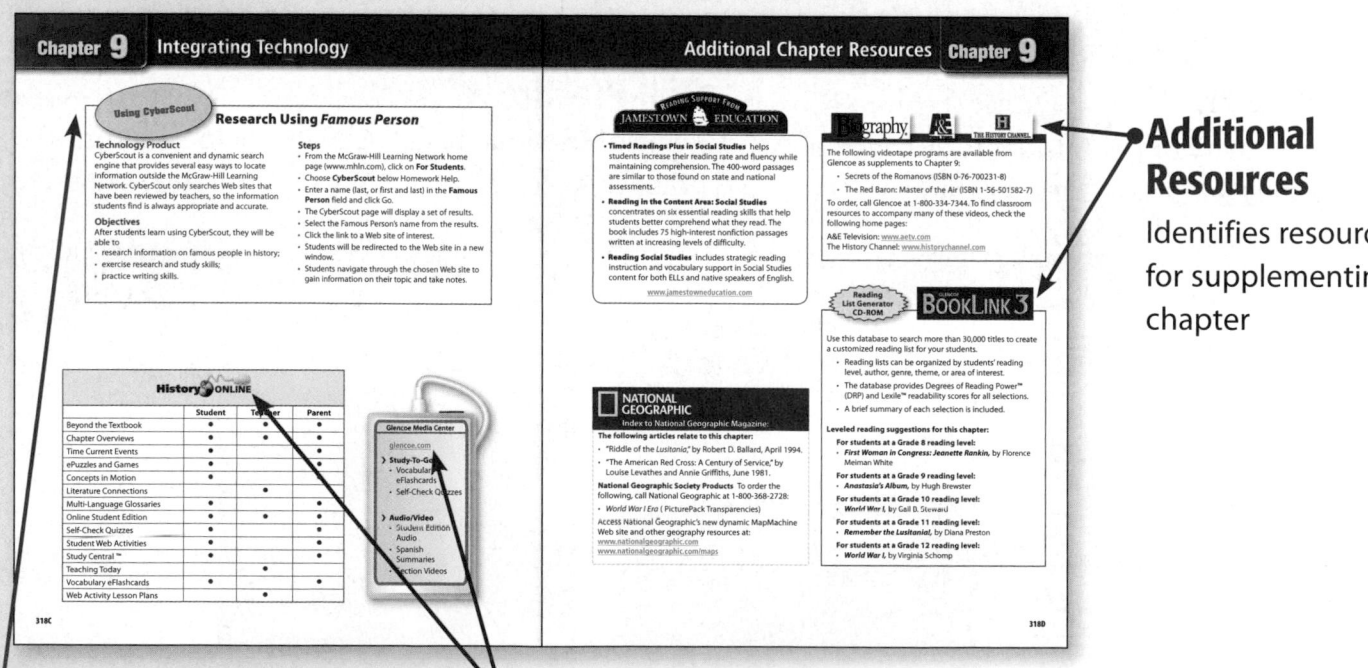

Teaching the Chapter

The Big Ideas and Essential Question at the beginning of the chapter help you teach the most important chapter contents.

Making Connections

Introductory questions lead to an exploration of big ideas. These questions activate students' prior knowledge and lead students to see not only the "big picture," but also the relevancy of what they are learning. These lesson launcher activities compel students to consider the big idea of the chapter.

The Big Ideas

Big Ideas are themes, issues, concepts, questions, or ideas tied to the main concepts of the chapter and of each section. The Essential Question leads to an understanding of Big Ideas. These questions are broad and have no right or wrong answers. Essential Questions are thought-provoking, challenge old assumptions, and stimulate discussion. Student activities throughout the chapter will refer back to the Essential Question, leading to a greater comprehension of chapter themes.

Lesson Structure

Each lesson in *The American Vision Modern Times* is presented in a structured lesson plan: Focus, Teach, Assess, and Close.

FOCUS

Includes a Bellringer activity to help your students think about the lesson topic

Guide to Reading

Provides pre-reading strategies to improve comprehension

Spotlight Video

Engages students with the content using a short BBC video

Resource Manager

Provides a list of teacher edition and supplemental resources that support lesson content and reinforce skills

TEACH

Stimulate learning and interest using leveled activities

ASSESS

Identifies assessment resources

CLOSE

Gauges comprehension of section content

Answers

Lists the answers to Student Edition questions

Understanding the Brackets and Letters

Brackets

Brackets on the reduced Student Edition page correspond to teaching strategies and activities in the Teacher Wraparound Edition. As you teach the section, the brackets show you exactly where to teach these strategies and activities.

Letters*

The letters on the reduced Student Edition page identify the type of strategy or activity. See the key below to learn about the different types of strategies and activities.

KEY for Using the Teacher Wraparound Edition

R **Reading Strategies** activities help you teach reading skills and vocabulary.

C **Critical Thinking** strategies help students apply and extend what they have learned.

D **Differentiated Instruction** activities provide differentiated instruction for students learning to speak English, along with suggestions for teaching various types of learners.

S **Skill Practice** strategies help students practice historical analysis and geography skills.

W **Writing Support** activities provide writing opportunities to help students comprehend the text.

* Letters are followed by a number when there is more than one of the same type of strategy or activity on the page.

Hands-On Chapter Projects

Extend student learning with unique and interactive Hands-On Chapter Projects. These activities allow students to take principles and put them to practical use. Projects progress through each section and culminate in a wrap-up discussion. Students conceptualize, plan, and execute their vision in a hands-on approach that makes people and history come alive.

Steps

Each lesson includes a self-contained activity, with one lesson building on knowledge gained from previous lessons.

Hands-On

Students utilize diverse learning styles and creativity and work cooperatively to create their projects.

Results

The Hands-On project culminates in an interactive discussion where students synthesize what they have learned and draw conclusions.

Differentiated Instruction

Each section of the Teacher Wraparound Edition of *The American Vision Modern Times* provides differentiated instruction activities to meet the diverse needs of every student.

Differentiated Activities

Innovative ideas meet each student's interests and learning styles through point-of-use activities

Additional Resources

Provides suggestions for incorporating additional resources based on students' different learning abilities

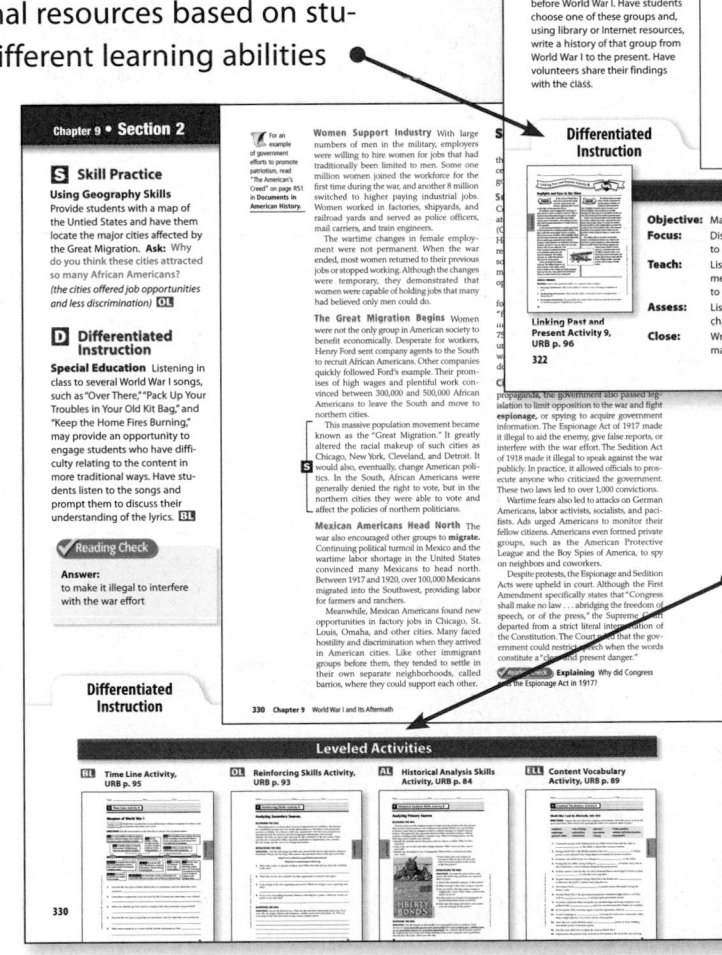

Leveled Activities

Extends instruction beyond the text by suggesting activities related to content on the page

Dynamic Features

Use these creative features to dig deep into the different eras of history covered in the text.

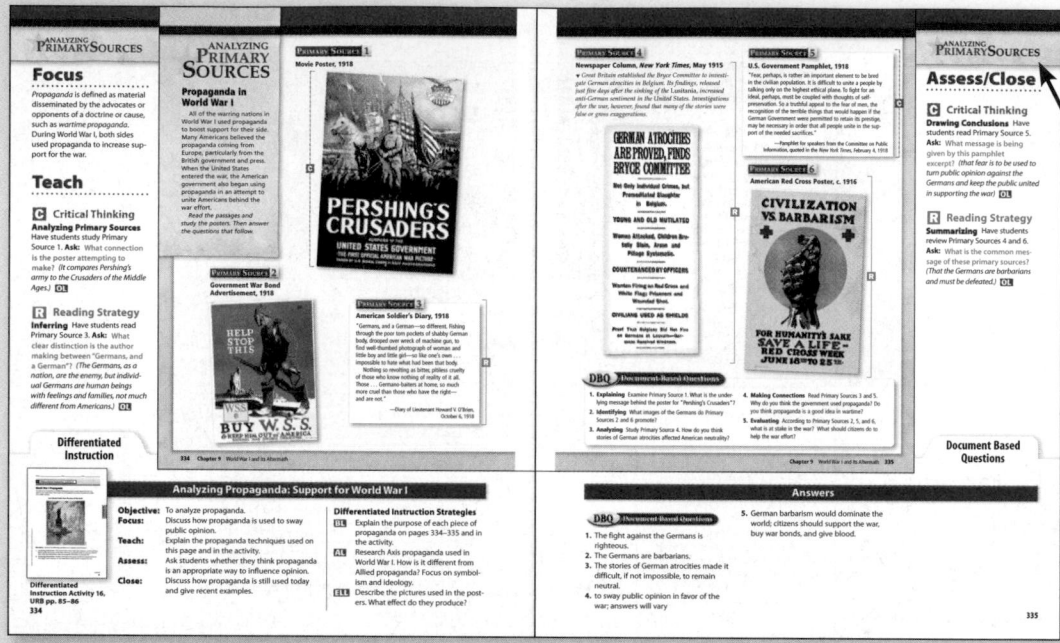

Analyzing Primary Sources

Primary Source readings provide opportunities for historical analysis and discussion

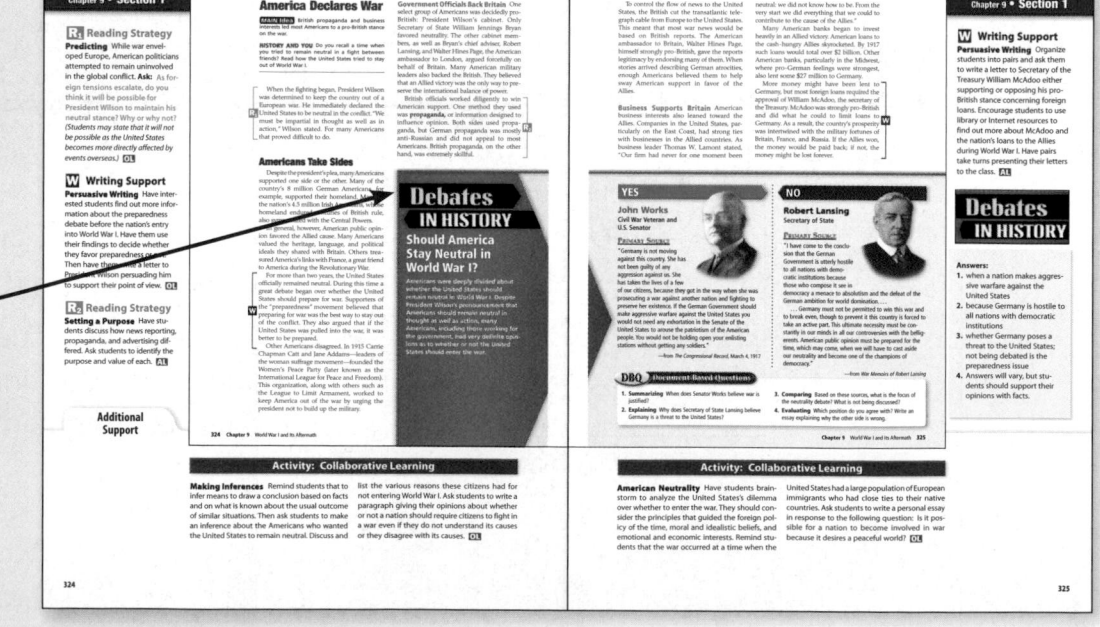

Debates in History

Teaches students to analyze different points-of-view on historical issues

Chapter Summary and Assessment

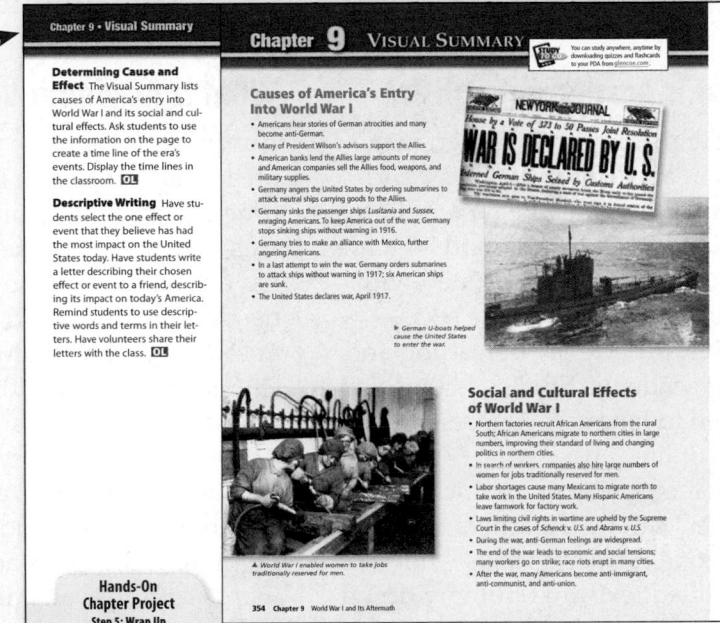

Visual Summary

Summary activities help students to synthesize major chapter themes

Standardized Test Practice

Answers incorporate analysis and identify potential student pitfalls, challenges, distracters, and test-taking strategies

Critical Thinking and Document-Based Questions

Extends answers and analysis through document and graphic assessment

History Online

Provides additional assessment opportunities

Academic Vocabulary

How Can I Help My Students Learn Academic Vocabulary?

What Is Academic English?

Academic English is the language used in academics, business, and courts of law. It is the type of English used in textbooks, and contains linguistic features associated with academic disciplines like social studies. Proficiency in reading and using academic English is especially related to long-term success in all parts of life.

By reinforcing academic English, teachers can help learners to access authentic, academic texts—not simplified texts that dummy down the content. In this way, they can provide information that will help build their students' background knowledge rapidly.

What Is Academic Vocabulary?

Academic vocabulary is based on academic English. By the time children have completed elementary school, they must have acquired the knowledge needed to understand academic vocabulary. How many words should they acquire to be able to access their textbooks? A basic 2,000-word vocabulary of high-frequency words makes up 87% of the vocabulary of academic texts. Eight hundred other academic words comprise an additional 8% of the words. Three percent of the remaining words are technical words. The remaining 2% are low-frequency words. There may be as many as 123,000 low-frequency words in academic texts.

Why Should Students Learn Academic Vocabulary?

English learners who have a basic 2,000-word vocabulary are ready to acquire most general words found in their texts.

Knowledge of academic words and general words can significantly boost a student's comprehension level of academic texts. Students who learn and practice these words before they graduate from high school are likely to master academic material with more confidence and speed. They waste less time and effort in guessing words or consulting dictionaries than those who only know the basic 2,000 words that characterize general conversation.

How Do I Include Academic Vocabulary and Academic English in My Teaching?

Teachers can provide students with academic vocabulary and help students understand the academic English of their text.

To develop academic English, learners must have already acquired basic proficiency in the grammar of everyday English.

Academic English should be taught within contexts that make sense. In terms of instruction, teaching academic English includes providing students with access to core curriculum—in this case Social Studies.

Academic English arises in part from social practices in which academic English is used. The acquisition of academic vocabulary and grammar is necessary to advance the development of academic English.

Tips for Teaching Academic Vocabulary:

✔ **Expose Students to Academic Vocabulary**
You do not need to call attention to words students are learning because they will acquire them subconsciously.

✔ **Do Not Correct Students' Mistakes When Using the Vocabulary Words**
All vocabulary understanding and spelling errors will disappear once the student reads more.

✔ **Help Students Decode the Words Themselves** Once they learn the alphabet, they should be able to decode words. Decoding each word they don't recognize will help them more than trying to focus on sentence structure. Once they can recognize the words, they can read "authentic" texts.

✔ **Do Not Ignore the English Learner in This Process** They can learn academic vocabulary before they are completely fluent in oral English.

✔ **Helping Students Build Academic Vocabulary Leads to Broader Learning** Students who have mastered the basic academic vocabulary are ready to continue acquiring words from the rest of the groups. To help determine which words are in the 2,000-word basic group, refer to *West's General Service List of English Words,* 1953. The list is designed to serve as a guide for teachers and as a checklist and goal list for students. For additional information about the list, visit:

http://www.vuw.ac.nz/lals/research/awl

Guidelines for Teaching Academic Vocabulary

1. Direct and planned instruction	4. Practice
2. Models—that have increasingly difficult language	5. Motivation
3. Attention to form—pointing out linguistic features of words	6. Instructional feedback
	7. Assessment—on a regular basis

Classroom Activity

Writing About Modern America

Give students a brief writing assignment. Ask them to write a short essay about one of the topics listed below in the left column. Have students use as many of the academic vocabulary words in the right column as they can in their essay. When completed, ask student volunteers to share their writing. Note what academic vocabulary words they use.

Topic	Academic Vocabulary
The challenges of reducing poverty in America	sufficient
	minimum
	medical
	income
Recent technological advances	innovate
	technology
	media
	potential
	data
	transmit

Meeting the Diverse Needs of Our Students

by Douglas Fisher, Ph.D.

Today's classroom contains students from a variety of backgrounds with a variety of learning styles, strengths, and challenges. As teachers we are facing the challenge of helping students reach their educational potential. With careful planning, you can address the needs of all students in the social studies classroom. The basis for this planning is universal access. When classrooms are planned with universal access in mind, fewer students require specific accommodations.

What Is a Universal Access Design for Learning?

Universal design was first conceived in architectural studies when business people, engineers, and architects began making considerations for physical access to buildings. The idea was to plan the environment in advance to ensure that everyone had access. As a result, the environment would not have to be changed later for people with physical disabilities, people pushing strollers, workers who had injuries, or others for whom the environment would be difficult to negotiate. The Center for Universal Design at www.design.ncsu.edu/cud defines Universal Design as:

The design of products and environments to be usable by all people, to the greatest extent possible, without the need for adaptation or specialized design.

Universal Design and Access in Education

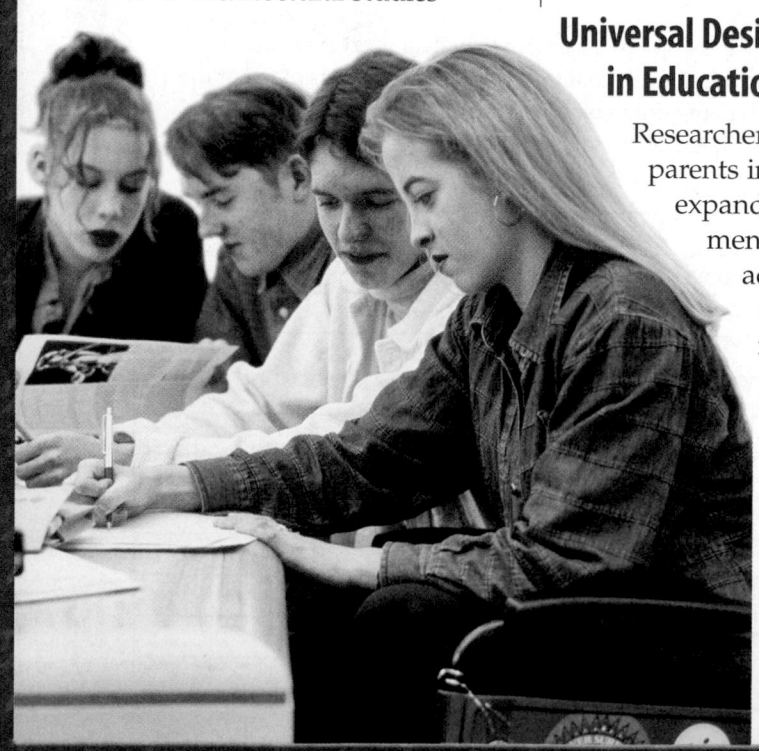

Researchers, teachers, and parents in education have expanded the development of built-in adaptations and inclusive accommodations from architectural space to the educational experience, especially in the area of curriculum.

In 1998, the National Center to Improve the Tools of Educators (NCITE),

with the partnership of the Center for Applied Special Technology (CAST), proposed an expanded definition of universal design focused on education:

In terms of learning, universal design means the design of instructional materials and activities that allows the learning goals to be achievable by individuals with wide differences in their abilities to see, hear, speak, move, read, write, understand English, attend, organize, engage, and remember.

How Does Universal Design Work in Education?

Universal design and access, as they apply to education and schooling, suggest the following:

✔ **Inclusive Classroom Participation**
Curriculum should be designed with all students and their needs in mind. The Glencoe/McGraw-Hill social studies texts and materials were designed with a wide range of students in mind. For example, understanding that English learners and students who struggle with reading would be using this textbook, vocabulary is specifically taught and reinforced. Similarly, the teacher-support materials provide multiple instructional points to be used depending on the needs of the students in the class. Further, the text is written such that main ideas are identified for all learners. Activating prior knowledge is also taken into consideration

by the text. Connections between what students know and think about are made within the text.

✔ **Maximum Text Readability** In universally designed classrooms that provide access for all students, texts use direct language, clear noun-verb agreements, and clear construct-based wording. In addition to these factors, the Glencoe Social Studies text uses embedded definitions for difficult terms, provides for specific instruction in reading skills, uses a number of visual representations, and includes note-taking guides.

✔ **Adaptable and Accommodating** The content in this textbook can be easily translated, read aloud, or otherwise changed to meet the needs of students in the classroom. The section and end-of-chapter assessments provide students with multiple ways of demonstrating their content knowledge while also ensuring that they have practice with thinking in terms of multiple-choice questions. Critical thinking and analysis skills are also practiced.

How Is Differentiated Instruction the Key to Universal Access?

To differentiate instruction, teachers must acknowledge student differences in background knowledge and current reading, writing, and English language skills. They must also consider student learning styles and preferences, interests, and needs, and react accordingly. There are a number of general guidelines for differentiating

instruction in the classroom to reach all students, including:

✔ **Link Assessment With Instruction** Assessments should occur before, during, and after instruction to ensure that the curriculum is aligned with what students do and do not know. Using assessments in this way allows you to plan instruction for whole groups, small groups, and individual students. Backward planning, where you establish the assessment before you begin instruction, is also important.

✔ **Clarify Key Concepts and Generalizations** Students need to know what is essential and how this information can be used in their future learning. In addition, students need to develop a sense of the **Big Ideas**—ideas that transcend time and place.

✔ **Emphasize Critical and Creative Thinking** The content, process, and products used or assigned in the classroom should require that students think about what they are learning. While some students may require support, additional motivation, varied tasks,

materials, or equipment, the overall focus on critical and creative thinking allows for all students to participate in the lesson.

✔ **Include Teacher- and Student-Selected Tasks** A differentiated classroom includes both teacher- and student-selected activities and tasks. At some points in the lesson or day, the teacher must provide instruction and assign learning activities. In other parts of the lesson, students should be provided choices in how they engage with the content. This balance increases motivation, engagement, and learning.

How Do I Support Individual Students?

The vast majority of students will thrive in a classroom based on universal access and differentiated instruction. However, wise teachers recognize that no single option will work for all students and that there may be students who require unique systems of support to be successful.

Classroom Activity

Display a map of westward United States expansion between 1840 and 1860. Discuss with students the general causes of westward expansion during this time period and have them list the different areas of the country settled during this time period.

To differentiate this activity:

- Have students imagine they are living during this period of westward expansion from 1840 to 1860. Have them write a letter to a family member back home about their journey west.
- Have students record the different areas settled during this time period. Have students create a chart of the various destinations of the expansionists.
- Have students compose a song or poem about the hardships of the trail.
- Have students write a three-page paper discussing the risks and rewards these emigrants faced on their journey west.

Tips For Instruction

The following tips for instruction can support your efforts to help all students reach their maximum potential.

✔ Survey students to discover their individual differences. Use interest inventories of their unique talents so you can encourage contributions in the classroom.

✔ Be a model for respecting others. Adolescents crave social acceptance. The student with learning differences is especially sensitive to correction and criticism, particularly when it comes from a teacher. Your behavior will set the tone for how students treat one another.

✔ Expand opportunities for success. Provide a variety of instructional activities that reinforce skills and concepts.

✔ Establish measurable objectives and decide how you can best help students meet them.

✔ Celebrate successes and make note of and praise "work in progress."

✔ Keep it simple. Point out problem areas if doing so can help a student effect change. Avoid overwhelming students with too many goals at one time.

✔ Assign cooperative group projects that challenge all students to contribute to solving a problem or creating a product.

How Do I Reach Students With Learning Disabilities?

✔ Provide support and structure. Clearly specify rules, assignments, and responsibilities.

✔ Practice skills frequently. Use games and drills to help maintain student interest.

✔ Incorporate many modalities into the learning process. Provide opportunities to say, hear, write, read, and act out important concepts and information.

✔ Link new skills and concepts to those already mastered.

✔ If possible, allow students to record answers on audiotape.

✔ Allow extra time to complete assessments and assignments.

✔ Let students demonstrate proficiency with alternative presentations, including oral reports, role plays, art projects, and musical presentations.

✔ Provide outlines, notes, or tape recordings of lecture material.

✔ Pair students with peer helpers, and provide class time for pair interaction.

How Do I Reach Students With Behavioral Challenges?

✔ Provide a structured environment with clear-cut schedules, rules, seat assignments, and safety procedures.

✔ Reinforce appropriate behavior and model it for students.

✔ Cue distracted students back to the task through verbal signals and teacher proximity.

✔ Set goals that can be achieved in the short term. Work for long-term improvement in the big areas.

How Do I Reach Students With Physical Challenges?

✔ Openly discuss with the student any uncertainties you have about when to offer aid.

✔ Ask parents or therapists and students what special devices or procedures are needed and whether any special safety precautions need to be taken.

✔ Welcome students with physical challenges into all activities, including field trips, special events, and projects.

✔ Provide information to assist class members and adults in their understanding of support needed.

How Do I Reach Students with Visual Impairments?

✔ Facilitate independence. Modify assignments as needed.

✔ Teach classmates how and when to serve as visual guides.

✔ Limit unnecessary noise in the classroom if it distracts the student with visual impairments.

✔ Provide tactile models whenever possible.

✔ Foster a spirit of inclusion. Describe people and events as they occur in the classroom. Remind classmates that the student with visual impairments cannot interpret gestures and other forms of nonverbal communication.

✔ Provide taped lectures and reading assignments for use outside the classroom.

✔ Team the student with a sighted peer for written work.

How Do I Reach Students With Hearing Impairments?

✔ Seat students where they can see your lip movements easily and where they can avoid any visual distractions.
✔ Avoid standing with your back to the window or light source.
✔ Use an overhead projector so you can maintain eye contact while writing information for students.
✔ Seat students where they can see speakers.
✔ Write all assignments on the board, or hand out written instructions.
✔ If the student has a manual interpreter, allow both student and interpreter to select the most favorable seating arrangements.
✔ Teach students to look directly at each other when they speak.

How Do I Reach English Learners?

✔ Remember, students' ability to speak English does not reflect their academic abilities.
✔ Try to incorporate the students' cultural experience into your instruction. The help of a bilingual aide may be effective.
✔ Avoid any references in your instruction that could be construed as cultural stereotypes.
✔ Preteach important vocabulary and concepts.
✔ Encourage students to preview text before they begin reading, noting headings.
✔ Remind students not to ignore graphic organizers, photographs, and maps since there is much information in these visuals.
✔ Use memorabilia and photographs whenever possible to build background knowledge and understanding. An example of this would be coins in a foreign currency or a raw cotton ball to reinforce its importance in history.

How Do I Reach Gifted Students?

✔ Make arrangements for students to take selected subjects early and to work on independent projects.
✔ Ask "what if" questions to develop high-level thinking skills. Establish an environment safe for risk taking in your classroom.
✔ Emphasize concepts, theories, ideas, relationships, and generalizations about the content.
✔ Promote interest in the past by inviting students to make connections to the present.
✔ Let students express themselves in alternate ways such as creative writing, acting, debates, simulations, drawing, or music.
✔ Provide students with a catalog of helpful resources, listing such things as agencies that provide free and inexpensive materials, appropriate community services and programs, and community experts who might be called upon to speak to your students.
✔ Assign extension projects that allow students to solve real-life problems related to their communities.

Douglas Fisher is a professor at San Diego State University, San Diego, CA.

Classroom Activity

Students respond eagerly to a subject when they can relate it to their own experiences. With the growing number of students who come from other world regions, explaining history through a global theme can give them a worldwide as well as a regional perspective. Have students use the library or the Internet to research the effect revolution has had around the world and the influence of the American Revolution on revolutions in other countries, such as France and Latin America.
Ask students the following questions:
- What influence has the American Revolution had upon revolutions throughout the world?
- Where have some of these other revolutions occurred?
- How successful have these revolutions and their resulting new governments been as compared to the United States?

Encourage students to do additional research and share what they find with the class.

Backward Mapping

How Can My Instruction Help Students Succeed in a Standards-Based System?

by Emily M. Schell, Ed.D.

Content standards articulate what students should know and be able to do in every social studies classroom. Effective instructional planning based in the standards and maximizing available resources is essential for meaningful teaching and learning of social studies. Planning instruction with educational goals in mind makes for the most effective teaching.

How Do I Map My Curriculum?

Mapping the curriculum from beginning to end, and from the end to the beginning—backward mapping—makes for solid instruction. Mapping out the curriculum allows teachers to achieve several goals. These goals include a better understanding of the standards and content-specific objectives, organization and pacing of the curriculum, and focused assessment related to specific goals and objectives.

✔ **Begin the Process of Curriculum Mapping** To begin, teachers analyze the body of content standards for one grade level. They then compare and contrast these standards to additional sources of information that support effective teaching and learning at that grade level and in that subject area. This process works best with same-grade colleagues who bring varying perspectives and expertise to teaching this subject. As a result of this collaboration, strengths and weaknesses of the standards become apparent. Teachers will have a better understanding of

the standards and identify concerns and questions for follow-up while mapping.

✔ **Analyze the Organization of the Standards-Based Content** Most social studies teachers agree with researchers that history is best taught in chronological order. However, some grade-level standards either do not or cannot present the content in chronological order. Rich discussions about themes and concepts tend to emerge, and teachers identify meaningful methods for presenting complex and overlapping information. In this way students will see the connections that transcend chronology.

✔ **Identify the Content and Order of Teaching** A plan is developed to present certain content first, then second, then third and so on. Folding in content that is either missing from the standards or essential in building background knowledge with students enters the curriculum map as well. Outside resources brought into the classroom are good supplements.

✔ **Separate Overlapping Units** Identify areas of instruction for the topics, themes, big ideas, or

concepts. It is at this stage that backward planning is introduced for the development of instructional units, which will support the grade-level curriculum map. The instruction must support the planned assessment.

✔ **Map Curriculum at Each Grade Level** Curriculum planning should be shared among grade levels. Teachers will have a better understanding of what knowledge and skills students bring to their coursework if they take into consideration what has been learned previously.

How Do I Use Backward Mapping?

After a year-long course of study is mapped out, each unit must be further developed through backward mapping. You will start with the end in mind—knowing your curricular goals and objectives at the outset, which are often found in the content standards and articulated in the curriculum maps. Once goals have been determined, teachers develop assessments that will show progress toward those goals and objectives. In the final step of this backward mapping process, teachers determine meaningful teaching and learning strategies and identify useful resources that support the assessment.

To use backward mapping in developing your units of instruction, consider the following steps:

Step One: Know Your Targets

First, identify exactly what students must know and do in this unit. Analyze content standards and any other resources that support curricular goals and objectives for this unit. As you plan, ask yourself:

- ✔ What do I want my students to know as a result of this unit?
- ✔ What skills will students develop during the course of this unit?
- ✔ How do I describe these goals clearly and concisely to my students so they understand where we should be at the end of this unit?
- ✔ What essential knowledge will students need to access to make sense of this information?
- ✔ Do my instructional goals align with strategies identified in the curriculum map?
- ✔ Have I introduced any Big Ideas that are pertinent to this content?

Step Two: Identify and Develop Assessments

- ✔ Second, consider the multiple forms of formal and informal assessments that will help you determine to what degree each student has achieved the stated goals and objectives seen in Step One. Some assessments are embedded throughout the instructional unit, while others come at the end of the unit. Some assessments are performance-based, while others are not. Some are authentic applications of information and skills, while others require the formal recall of information. Ask yourself:
- ✔ What do I want to know and see from each student?
- ✔ What are the best methods for students to demonstrate what they know and can do based on the goals and objectives?
- ✔ How many assessments do I need to determine what students know and can do?
- ✔ How will I balance informal and formal assessments?
- ✔ How will I assess students with diverse learning styles, skills, and abilities?
- ✔ How can I prepare and support students?
- ✔ How will these assessments promote student progress in social studies?
- ✔ At what time(s) during the unit will I administer these assessments?

Step Three: Develop Meaningful Instruction

After the assessments for the unit have been determined, consider the meaningful and effective teaching strategies that will support learning and student achievement on assessments. While developing lesson plans for instruction, ask yourself:

- ✔ How will students learn what they are expected to know?
- ✔ How will I engage students in the studies of this unit?
- ✔ In what ways might students relate or connect to this information?
- ✔ What research-based strategies will be most effective with my students and in these studies?
- ✔ How will I differentiate my instruction to meet the diverse needs of my students?
- ✔ How will I scaffold or provide access to the curriculum for my English learners?
- ✔ What vocabulary requires attention in this unit?
- ✔ How much time will I have to effectively teach this unit?
- ✔ How will I use the textbook and other resources to support the goals and objectives for this unit?
- ✔ What lessons will I develop?
- ✔ In what sequence will I teach these lessons during this unit?
- ✔ How will these lessons support the assessments from Step Two?

Step Four: Locate and Manage Resources

Effective teaching and learning of social studies requires the use of multiple forms of text and varied resources. Consider what you have available in your classroom, including your textbook, and identify resources you will add in order to teach this unit successfully. Ask yourself:

- ✔ What parts of the textbook are required for the lessons determined in Step Three?
- ✔ What ancillary materials are needed for the lessons in this unit?
- ✔ What Web sites will I recommend to students to support these lessons?
- ✔ Do I need to contact guest speakers or obtain outside resources?
- ✔ What literature resources are available to support this unit?

Emily Schell is Visiting Professor, San Diego State University; and Social Studies Education Director, SDSU City Heights Educational Collaborative, San Diego, CA

Teaching Maps, Graphs, and Charts

How Can I Use Visuals to Improve Students' Reading Comprehension?

Maps, graphs, and charts are visual tools. By using images rather than words, these tools present complex information in an easy-to-understand format. Teach students the following generalized viewing strategies, and encourage them to apply these strategies as they study each chapter.

✔ **Asking Questions** Students should start by looking over the graphic and asking themselves questions, such as "What is my purpose for looking at this image?" Then students can identify questions they hope to answer, such as "What is being compared?" or "What are the most important features?"

✔ **Finding Answers** Next, students should use the graphic's features, such as the title, labels, colors, and symbols, to help them find answers to their questions. If the source of the graphic is available, students should also determine its reliability.

✔ **Drawing Conclusions** After studying the visual, students should summarize its main points and draw conclusions.

✔ **Connecting** Students also should relate what they learned from the visual with what they gained from reading the text selection. Students can examine how the visual supports or extends the meaning of the text.

Maps

Maps show the relative size and location of specific geographic areas. Two of the most common general purpose maps are political maps and physical maps.

Parts of Maps

All maps contain parts that assist in interpreting the information. Help students learn to identify the following map parts.

✔ **Title** The map title identifies the area shown on the visual. The title can also identify a map's special focus.

✔ **Map Key** The map key, or legend, explains the symbols presented on the map, thus unlocking the map's information.

✔ **Compass Rose** A compass rose is a direction marker. It is a symbol that points out where the cardinal directions—north, south, east, and west—are positioned.

✔ **Scale** A measuring line, often called a scale bar, indicates the relationship between the distances on the map and the actual distances on Earth.

✔ **Latitude and Longitude** Mapmakers use lines of latitude and longitude to pinpoint exact locations on maps and globes. The imaginary horizontal lines that circle the globe from east to west are lines of latitude, also called parallels. The imaginary vertical lines are lines of longitude, also called meridians. Both parallels and meridians are measured in degrees.

Europe: Vegetation

Graphs

Graphs are a way of showing numbers or statistics in a clear, easy-to-read way. Because graphs summarize and present information visually, readers have an easier time understanding the data and drawing conclusions. The most common types of graphs are bar graphs, line graphs, circle graphs, and pictographs.

✔ **Bar Graphs** A bar graph shows how two or more subjects or statistics compare. It provides information along two sides or axes. The horizontal axis is the line across the bottom of the graph. The vertical axis is the line along the side. The bars may be either vertical or horizontal. In most cases the labels on one axis show quantity, while the labels on the opposite axis show the categories of data being compared.

✔ **Line Graphs** A line graph shows change over time. Like a bar graph, it organizes information along the horizontal and vertical axes. The horizontal axis usually shows passing time, such as months, years, or decades. The vertical axis usually shows quantity or amount. Sometimes more than one set of data is shown in a line graph. A double-line graph, for instance, plots data for two related quantities, which may be represented in different colors or patterns.

✔ **Circle Graphs** A circle graph, also called a pie graph, shows how each part or percentage relates to the whole. A circle graph enables a viewer to make comparisons between parts and to analyze the relationship of each part to the whole.

✔ **Pictograph** A pictograph uses rows of small symbols or pictures, each representing a particular amount. Like a bar graph, a pictograph is useful for making comparisons.

Charts

While all charts present information or data in a visual way, the type of chart is often dictated by the nature of the information and by the chart-maker's purposes.

✔ **Tables** Tables show information, including numerical data, in columns and rows. This organized arrangement facilitates comparisons between categories of information. Labels are usually located at the top of each column and on the left-hand side of the table.

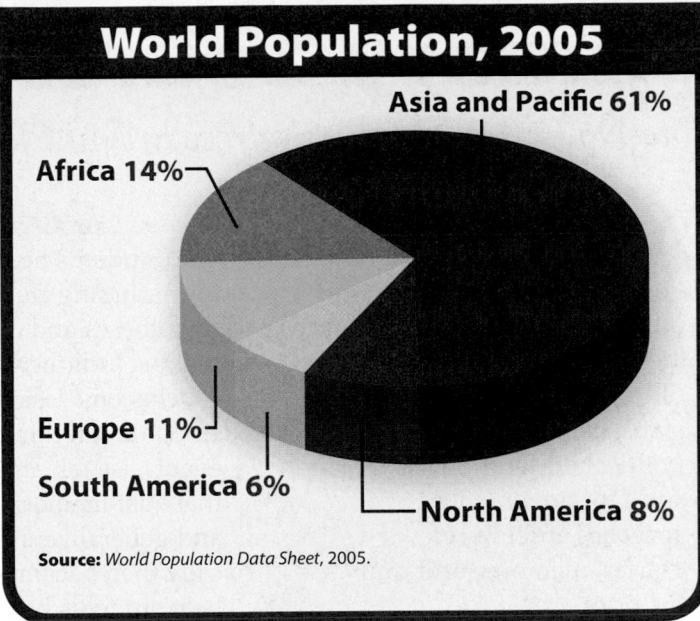

World Population, 2005

Asia and Pacific 61%

Africa 14%

Europe 11%

South America 6%

North America 8%

Source: *World Population Data Sheet*, 2005.

✔ **Diagrams** Diagrams are specialized drawings. They can show steps in a process; point out parts of an object, organization, or idea; or explain how something works. Arrows or lines may join parts of a figure and can show relationships between parts or the flow of steps.

Classroom Activity

Create a Graph

Graphs can be difficult to interpret and understand. Help students by having them create their own graphs. First, separate students into small groups. Then have each group take a survey of classmates and make a graph to show their results. Suggest that students select a bar graph, line graph, circle graph, or pictograph to show their data. To prompt students' thinking, ask the following questions.

- *Do you play on a sports team? Which sport(s)?*
- *What do you plan to do after high school?*
- *About how much time do you spend watching TV each day? About how much time did you spend on TV when you were 10 years old? When you were five years old?*

After students have these graphs completed, invite each group to share its work. Discuss the types of graphs students made and their reasons for choosing them. Each group should then take the graph done by another group and transfer the information to another type of graph.

Primary Source Strategies

How Do I Use Primary Sources in My Classroom?

A primary source is an oral or written account obtained from actual participants in an event. Examples of primary sources include the following:

✔ official documents (records, statistics)
✔ political declarations, laws, and rules for governance
✔ speeches and interviews
✔ diaries, memoirs, and oral histories
✔ autobiographies
✔ recipes and cookbooks
✔ advertisements and posters
✔ letters
✔ physical objects, such as tools, dishes, fine art, photographs, maps, films, and videotapes
✔ songs and audio recordings

Why Use Primary Sources in Your Classroom?

Using primary sources transforms the study of social studies from a passive process to an active one. Students become investigators—finding clues, formulating hypotheses and drawing inferences, making judgments, and reaching conclusions. Using primary sources, students can think critically about events, issues, and concepts rather than just memorizing dates, names, and generalizations. Thinking critically then becomes a habit that can help students become good citizens.

How Do I Introduce Students to Primary Sources?

Carefully explain the nature of primary sources to students. Alert students to the fact that primary sources contain biases and prejudices and must be approached with caution. Every primary source reflects the creator's point of view. Students must consider the authorship and why the primary source was written.

Choosing Primary Sources

Expose students to a variety of sources, including historic photographs, folk or popular music, financial records as well as letters, journals, and historic documents.

When choosing print sources, consider the interests and reading levels of your students. Many texts contain challenging vocabulary and unfamiliar sentence structure. You may need to create a reader's guide that defines key vocabulary and paraphrases the main points of the reading.

Some documents may be too long. Decide whether using an excerpt will provide enough information for students to draw conclusions. You also may need to provide different primary sources to expose students to a variety of perspectives.

Decide how students will access the primary sources: through the Internet, the library, a museum, or other print resources. Consider the possibility of an Internet virtual field trip for students. Students can visit museum sites and other Web pages to view artifacts, interpret data, and read journals, letters, and official documents.

Interpreting a Primary Source

Before students interpret a primary source, they need to know the source's context. Then they can use guidelines, such as those on the next page, to help them analyze and interpret the primary source.

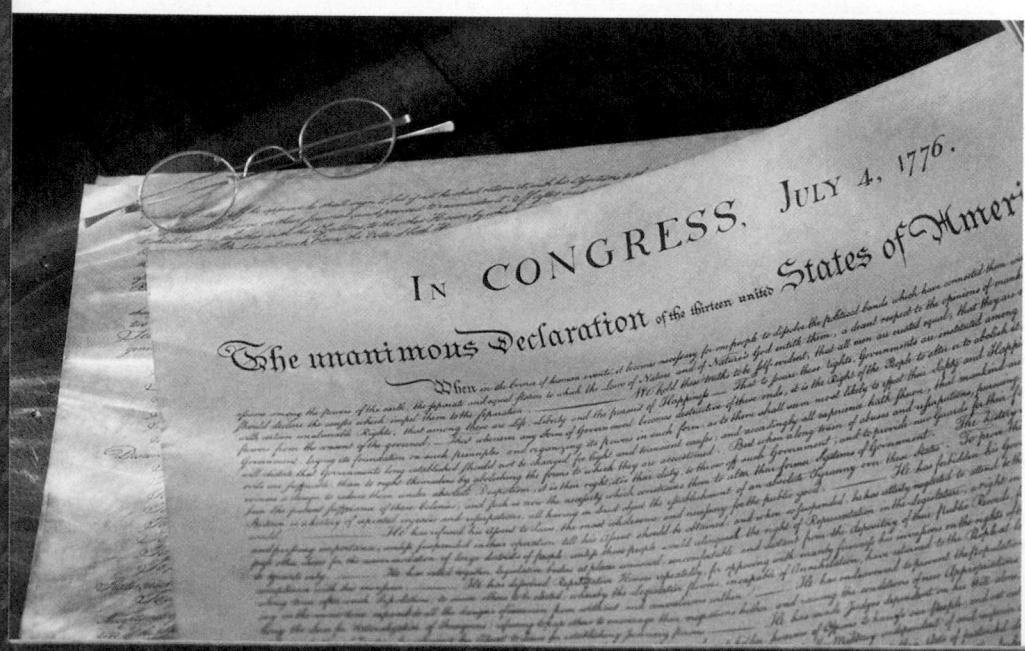

Interpreting a Primary Source

Print Sources

- Who created the source, and what was the purpose for doing so?
- Did the writer personally experience or witness the event(s)?
- Who was the intended audience?
- Was the writer trying to record facts, express an opinion, or persuade others to take action?
- What bias does it reflect?
- What information about the topic can you gather from this document?
- Compare this document with what you know about the topic. Does it confirm those ideas or introduce a new perspective?
- How might other accounts about this topic support or modify the message this source delivers?

Visual Sources

- Who created the source, and what was the purpose for doing so?
- What does the image show?
- Who or what dominates the image or catches your eye?
- How does the view impact the message?
- What is excluded from view?
- What bias does the visual reflect?
- What information about the topic can you gather from this visual?
- How might other visuals about this topic support or modify the message this one delivers?

Audio Sources

- Who created the source? What was the purpose for creating this source?
- What is the main idea of the audio?
- What bias does the audio text reflect?
- What information about the topic can you gather from this audio source?
- Compare the information in this source with what you already know about the topic. Does it confirm those ideas or introduce a new perspective?
- How might other sources about this topic support or modify the message that this one delivers?

Exploring Information

Provide a variety of primary sources related to a topic or time period. Have students compare and contrast the items, analyzing the information, making inferences, and drawing conclusions about the period.

Prereading Activities

Present a primary source for students to study at the beginning of a new chapter or topic. Have students analyze the source, using the questions and guidelines presented above. Then have students make predictions about what they might learn in the upcoming lessons.

Evaluation Activities

Have students evaluate a primary source and tell how it supports or refutes what they learned in the textbook, or have students read a primary source document that provides one perspective on a topic and have students write their own account, presenting another perspective or opinion.

Classroom Activity

Use this activity to explore the use of primary sources. This activity is especially beneficial when a less-proficient reader is paired with a more-proficient reader.

1. Before class make a list of student reading partners. Make sure one of the two is a good reader.
2. Have students read a primary source document, taking turns as they go. They should "mark" any words that they do not understand.
3. After each paragraph, the student pair should stop and restate what it says in their own words.
4. Students should look up unfamiliar words they've marked and create an illustrated dictionary entry for each term.
5. Ask student pairs to present their paraphrased primary source to the rest of the class.

Test-Taking Strategies

How Can I Help My Students Succeed on Tests?

It's not enough for students to learn social studies facts and concepts—they must be able to show what they know in a variety of test-taking situations.

How Can I Help My Students Do Well on Objective Tests?

Objective tests may include multiple choice, true/false, and matching questions. Applying the strategies below can help students do their best on objective tests.

How Can I Help My Students Do Well on Essay Tests?

Essay tests require students to provide well-organized written responses, in addition to telling what they know. Help students use the following strategies on essay tests.

✔ **Analyze** To analyze means to systematically and critically examine all parts of an issue or event.

✔ **Classify or Categorize** To classify or categorize means to put people, things, or ideas into groups, based on a common set of characteristics.

✔ **Compare and Contrast** To compare is to show how things are similar, or alike. To contrast is to show how things are different.

✔ **Describe** To describe means to present a sketch or impression. Rich details, especially details that appeal to the senses, flesh out a description.

✔ **Discuss** To discuss means to systematically write about all sides of an issue or event.

✔ **Evaluate** To evaluate means to make a judgment and support it with evidence.

✔ **Explain** To explain means to clarify or make plain.

✔ **Illustrate** To illustrate means to provide examples or to show with a picture or other graphic.

✔ **Infer** To infer means to read between the lines or to use knowledge and experience to draw conclusions.

✔ **Justify** To justify means to prove or to support a position with specific facts and reasons.

✔ **Predict** To predict means to tell what will happen in the future, based on an understanding of prior events and behaviors.

✔ **State** To state means to briefly and concisely present information.

✔ **Summarize** To summarize means to give a brief overview of the main points of an issue or event.

✔ **Trace** To trace means to present the steps in sequential order.

Objective Tests

Multiple-Choice Questions

- Students should read the directions carefully to learn what answer the test requires—the best answer or the right answer. This is especially important when answer choices include "all of the above" or "none of the above."
- Advise students to watch for negative words in the questions, such as *not, except, unless, never,* and *so forth*. If the question contains a negative, the correct answer choice is the one that does not fit.
- Students should try to mentally answer the question before reading the answer choices.
- Students should read all the answer choices and cross out those that are obviously wrong. Then they should choose an answer from those that remain.

True/False Questions

- It is important that students read the entire question before answering. For an answer to be true, the entire statement must be true. If one part of a statement is false, the answer should be marked False.
- Remind students to watch for words like *all, never, every,* and *always*. Statements containing these words are often false.

Matching Questions

- Students should read through both lists before they mark any answers.
- Unless an answer can be used more than once, students should cross out each choice as they use it.
- Using what they know about grammar can help students find the right answer. For instance, when matching a word with its definition, the definition is often the same part of speech (noun, verb, adjective, and so forth) as the word.

Read the Question

The key to writing successful essay responses lies in reading and interpreting questions correctly. Teach students to identify and underline key words in the questions, and to use these words to guide them in understanding what the question asks. Help students understand the meaning of some of the most common key words, listed on the previous page.

Plan and Write the Essay

After students understand the question, they should follow the writing process to develop their answer. Encourage students to follow the steps below to plan and write their essays.

1. **Map out an answer.** Make lists, webs, or an outline to plan the response.

↓

2. **Decide on an order** in which to present the main points.

↓

3. **Write an opening statement** that directly responds to the essay question.

↓

4. **Write the essay.** Expand on the opening statement. Support key points with specific facts, details, and reasons.

↓

5. **Write a closing statement** that brings the main points together.

↓

6. **Proofread** to check for spelling, grammar, and punctuation.

How Can I Help My Students Prepare for Standardized Tests?

Students can follow the steps below to prepare for standardized assessments they are required to take.

✔ **Read About the Test** Students can familiarize themselves with the format of the test, the types of questions that will be asked, and the amount of time they will have to complete the test. Emphasize that it is very important for students to budget their time during test-taking.

✔ **Review the Content** Consistent study throughout the school year will help students build social studies knowledge and understanding. If there are specific objectives or standards that are tested on the exam, help students review these facts or skills to be sure they are proficient.

✔ **Practice** Provide practice, ideally with real released tests, to build students' familiarity with the content, format, and timing of the real exam. Students should practice all the types of questions they will encounter on the test.

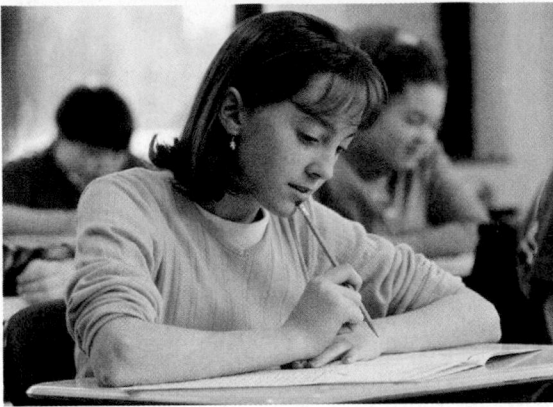

✔ **Pace** Students should pace themselves differently depending on how the test is administered. If the test is timed, students should not allow themselves to become stuck on any one question. If the test is untimed, students should work slowly and carefully. If students have trouble with an item, they should mark it and come back to it later.

✔ **Analyze Practice Results** Help students improve test-taking performance by analyzing their test-taking strengths and weaknesses.

Spend time discussing students' completed practice tests. Help students identify what kinds of questions they had the most difficulty with. Look for patterns in errors and then tailor instruction to review appropriate skills or content.

Classroom Activity

Below is an example of an assessment review activity. Reviewing graded tests is a great way for students to assess their test-taking skills. It also helps teachers teach test-taking strategies and review content. As the class rereads each test question, guide students to think logically about their answer choices. Show students how to:

1. Read each question carefully to determine its meaning.
2. Look for key words in the question to support their answers.
3. Recognize synonyms in the answer choices that may match phrases in the question.
4. Narrow down answer choices by eliminating ones that don't make sense.
5. Anticipate the answer before looking at the answer choices.
6. Circle questions of which they are unsure and go back to them later. Sometimes a clue will be found in another question on the test.

Project CRISS

How Can I Teach My Students How to Learn Social Studies?

by Carol M. Santa, Ph.D.

We all know that teaching social studies involves far more than teaching just course content. We understand that students need to become engaged, confident learners. Achieving that goal means helping them to understand, organize, and retain information.

Teaching Both Content and Skills

In other words, we want our students to have the skills and confidence to be lifelong learners. With its rich content, social studies offer an ideal arena for teaching both content and skills.

✔ **A Dual Responsibility** Let's take a moment to consider why the dual responsibility of teaching both content and skills is so important. Think back to your own middle and high school years. What do you remember about the content you learned? If I recall my experiences, I find I remember remarkably little content. What did I learn in biology or history? What did my textbooks look like? As the years go by, I don't even remember the names of most of my teachers.

✔ **An Inspiring Teacher** Yet I have vivid memories of my eighth-grade social studies teacher, who came out of retirement to fill in for a history teacher who left on maternity leave. I remember how fascinated I became with ancient history; I recall giving oral reports and how she helped me become comfortable speaking before a group. In fact, I remember more from her class than any other I took during high school.

✔ **Teach How to Learn** More important, I now understand that she taught me how to learn to learn. She showed me how to underline, how to organize information using different note-taking formats, and how to write coherent answers on essay tests. She taught me the need to test myself on what I knew. And during that vulnerable, adolescent year, I went from being a mediocre student to being an excellent one. This inspirational teacher did something else for me. At some point during that eighth-grade year, I decided to become a teacher. Later I realized that she had launched me on my professional mission—to spread her wisdom to others. Eventually this led to Project CRISS.

What Is CRISS?

CRISS stands for CReating Independence through Student-owned Strategies. It is a staff development program that I created in collaboration with middle and high school teachers in Kalispell, Montana.

✔ **Origin of CRISS** CRISS had its start 20 years ago in a lunchtime conversation in a teachers' lounge. One of the social studies teachers said, "My students aren't doing a good job of answering chapter questions. In fact, I don't think they even read my assign-ments. My reading assignments are becoming a waste of time!" His words struck a chord. "My students don't have a clue about how to study, and they don't write very well either," another teacher lamented.

✔ **Evolving Strategies** Supported by a state grant, we started working together to find practical ways to help students read, write, and learn content. We met in teams, read professional literature, and designed studies to test class-room strategies. From these efforts, we evolved a project to help students become better readers, writers, and learners. Once the project took shape, we shared our discoveries with other teachers by offering a two- or three-day CRISS workshop to schools and districts in the state.

✔ **Constant Growth** Over the last two decades, Project CRISS has spread from teacher to teacher across this country, into Canada, and to several European countries. The project seems to sell itself. Teachers who use CRISS principles and strategies find that their students attain a deeper understanding of course content and become better readers, writers, and learners at the same time. In fact, data from numerous quantitative studies shows that using CRISS strategies improves student learning. (For the most recent data and for information on CRISS workshops, see www. projectcriss.com)

CRISS Strategies in the Teacher Edition

When the editors of Glencoe/McGraw-Hill asked me and my colleagues to help them integrate CRISS strategies into their social studies texts, we welcomed the opportunity. In this teacher wraparound edition, we offer many references to CRISS strategies. We have packed the pages with strategies that help students gain a deeper understanding of specific content.

CRISS Training

We have one word of caution, however: the integration of CRISS strategies within this teacher wraparound edition does not take the place of a Project CRISS workshop, which provides an in-depth knowledge of CRISS. So, if you haven't yet participated in a CRISS workshop, we encourage you to do so. During a workshop, CRISS trainers take you step-by-step through the philosophy and instructional strategies. Participants are actively involved in all aspects of the program—practicing, adapting, and applying strategies to meet teaching needs.

Long-lasting change occurs when teachers and administrators work together to share, extend ideas, and problem solve. The most effective implementations occur when the initial workshop is supported by follow-up sessions, including a specific follow-up day. At this session, teachers bring examples of strategies they have used since the initial training. Part of this time may be spent in review and in learning new strategies. The rest of the time is for sharing applications. Additional ongoing support can occur in teacher planning periods.

In any case, for those of you unfamiliar with Project CRISS, let's begin with a little background knowledge. In this way you will have some context for the various activities suggested throughout the teacher wraparound edition.

The CRISS Philosophy

The first thing to know is that Project CRISS is more than a collection of learning strategies. Its underlying power rests not on the individual strategies but on the teaching philosophy behind them. This philosophy integrates work from cognitive psychology, social learning theory, and neurological research about how the brain learns. It includes these overlapping principles:

✔ background knowledge and purposeful reading
✔ author's craft
✔ active involvement
✔ discussion
✔ organization
✔ writing
✔ teacher modeling

Let's look at each of these principles in more detail, along with examples of instructional strategies that illustrate them.

Background knowledge and purposeful reading are powerful determinants of reading comprehension.

Teachers involved in Project CRISS often talk about the importance of background knowledge. Readers are far more likely to learn new information when they have some previous knowledge and have a purpose in mind before they read or listen.

✔ **More Than Simply Reading** We warn students not to simply begin reading. We ask them, "What might you already know about the topic? What questions do you have about the topic?" We also remind them to preview the assignment and think about their goals for reading. We often have to be very explicit about the goals. For example, we might tell students, "After reading this selection, you should be able to . . . ," or, "After viewing the video, you should be able to identify . . ."

✔ **KWLH** In the teaching strategies included for each chapter in this book, we offer ideas for helping students tap into their background knowledge. For example, we suggest that students preview their reading assignment and consider what they already know about a topic. Or, we might develop a whole-class KWLH chart (Know, Want to learn, Learned, How to learn more), where students work on this task together. They can generate questions about what they want to learn, and then, after completing the assignment, they can list the new information they have learned and how they can learn more.

K	W	L	H
What I **Know**	What I **Want** to Find Out	What I **Learned**	**How** I Can Learn More

✔ **Reading Goals** We also suggest ways to make sure your students have clear goals for their reading. Each section opener lists reading strategies and main ideas that outline reading goals. Most students will skip over this material and simply start reading. Teachers need to help students understand that the reading goals are important tools for understanding. We tell students, *"Don't ignore your purposes for reading. Take time to think about them before delving into your reading."* Project CRISS also provides hints about how to get students to use these purpose statements to evaluate whether they have understood their reading.

Reading social studies materials has its own special considerations. CRISS specialist Malla S. Kolhoff shares this advice: "As educators, it is our responsibility to set a purpose for historical reading. Students often must struggle to connect history with their own lives. To compare and contrast, establish cause and effect, and sequence events in chronological order presents a challenge for even the best reader. CRISS strategies allow students to move beyond words to the real significance for their society. With CRISS, my students are able to become engaged in the learning process through:

    a. background knowledge
    b. active reading, listening, and learning
    c. discussion
    d. metacognition
    e. writing
    f. organization
    g. understanding

I have found that these strategies help my students attain a higher level of historical thinking and understanding."

Good readers have an intuitive understanding of the author's craft.

When students know how authors craft their writing, they can more readily understand and remember what they read.

✔ **Pay Attention** Good readers and writers know that paying attention to how text is organized—its headings and paragraphs, for example—makes it easier to comprehend its content. Good readers will analyze the author's style of presentation as they read. They might ask themselves, "What is this author doing to help me learn key concepts? How does the writer lead me from one idea to the next?" When students become aware of what the author is doing to impart content, they have a clearer idea of what the author is saying.

✔ **The Walk Through** Walk students through the first lesson of the text. Point out the parts of the lesson to help students discover the author's style of presentation. Point out the surface structure (headings, bold print, color coding of topical headings, italicized words), but also point out main ideas in sample paragraphs to analyze how the author elaborates on key topics.

Effective learners are actively involved when they listen and read.

We learn best when we act on the information presented. We can do this by using a variety of organizing activities that require us to write, talk, and transform the information we are absorbing. None of us learns much from reading alone—it's far too passive.

CRISS strategies encourage active engagement in learning. We might ask students to read a section and describe what they are learning to a partner, or we might be more elaborate and have stu-

dents develop concept maps or write summaries.

Students need many opportunities to talk with one another about what they are learning.

Discussion is critical to learning. The discussions we advocate are different from those in which the teacher remains the authority figure, with students simply reciting answers to questions. If discussion becomes mere recitation and there is little interaction among students, little learning occurs. Thus we focus on how to get students to lead their own discussions about a topic. We want them to understand that it is their discussing, their oral grappling with meaning—not ours—that leads to deeper understanding.

Competent readers know several ways to organize information for learning.

Learning depends on organization. We show students different ways to organize information. They can take notes, underline selectively, develop concept maps, and summarize ideas in charts. Once we have taught students these techniques, we tell them, "You have to do more than just read this assignment. How are you going to organize the information from this assignment? You have to change it, to transform it so that it becomes your own."

For each chapter of this text, we offer ideas for assisting students in organizing information. Once students have learned a variety of organizing systems, we suggest ways to help them apply these structures independently.

Students deserve opportunities to write about what they are learning.

Writing is an integral part of the CRISS project. Writing lets us figure out what we know and what we still need to know. We cannot write about something we do not understand. While we teach students how to write expository papers and essay exams, we also encourage students to write more informally by questioning, speculating, and writing explanations in learning logs. We make sure that students are writing continually about what they are learning.

For each chapter of this text, we offer ideas for assisting students in organizing information. Once students have learned a variety of organizing systems, we suggest ways to help them apply these structures independently.

Teaching involves explanation and modeling.

Our final principle has to do with our own teaching. Students learn to think strategically when we use these processes as part of our instruction. Our demonstrations are especially critical for struggling readers. Most have never been taught how to learn. We have to show them how.

✔ **Take Center Stage** When you introduce a new strategy, you should take the center stage: showing, telling, modeling, demonstrating, and explaining not only the content but the process of active reading. As students learn, gradually release responsibility to them. Strategy instruction involves two overlapping steps. First, we explain what the strategy is and why students should use it. If students do not know why they are performing an activity, they will rarely use the activity on their own. Next, we demonstrate and talk about procedures for carrying out the strategy. We discuss, demonstrate, and think aloud while modeling. Then, students practice under our guidance and feedback.

✔ **A Systematic Approach** Project CRISS is a valuable basis for instruction. It provides a systematic approach for using what we now know about teaching and learning. The following chart lists questions we need to continually ask ourselves while we are teaching. Use this chart to monitor your efforts to incorporate CRISS principles into your teaching.

CRISS Principles	The CRISS Philosophy	Yes	No	Somewhat
Background Knowledge:	Did I assist students in thinking about what they already knew about the topic before beginning the unit? Did I develop necessary concepts before students read?			
Purpose/Setting:	Did my students have a clear purpose about what they were going to learn before beginning the lesson?			
Author's Craft:	Can my students use the author's style of presentation to facilitate their understanding?			
Active Involvement:	Were my students engaged in the topic? Did I help students become actively involved in their learning?			
Discussion:	Did my students have opportunities to talk about what they were learning?			
Organization:	Did my students organize information in a variety of ways?			
Writing:	Did my students write about what they were learning?			
Teacher Modeling:	Did I do enough teacher modeling of learning strategies so that students could begin doing them on their own?			

REFERENCE ATLAS

NATIONAL GEOGRAPHIC

ATLAS KEY

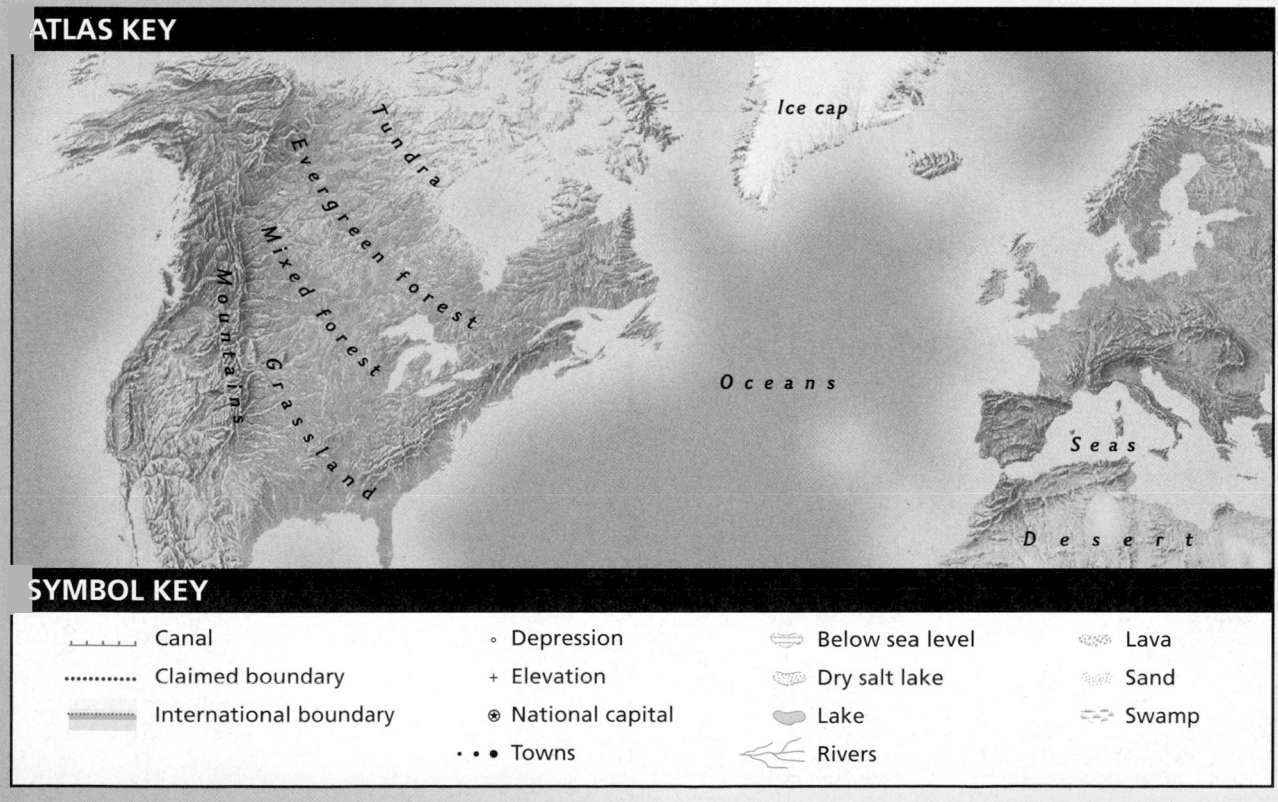

SYMBOL KEY

⌐_⌐	Canal	∘	Depression	⇔	Below sea level	≈	Lava
··········	Claimed boundary	+	Elevation	⌣	Dry salt lake	≈	Sand
▬▬▬	International boundary	⊛	National capital	⬭	Lake	⋖⋗	Swamp
		• • •	Towns	⋖	Rivers		

Cape Flattery
Mt. Olympus
7,965 ft
2,428 m
Seattle

CASCADE RANGE

COLUMBIA PLATEAU

Columbia

Blue Mts.

Clearwater Mts.

Bitterroot Range

Salmon River Mts.

Snake River Plain

Shoshone Falls

Snake

Great Sandy Desert

ROCKY

Absaroka Range

Bighorn Mts.

Wind River Range

Missouri

GREAT

Black Hills

Laramie Mts.

Cape Mendocino

130°W

40°N

SIERRA NEVADA

Lake Tahoe

Central Valley

Great Salt Lake

GREAT BASIN

Wasatch Range

Uinta Mts.

MOUNTAINS

N. Platte

Sand Hills

Missouri

Platte

Denver
14,433 ft
4,399 m
Mt. Elbert

PACIFIC

OCEAN

San Francisco

35°N

Mt. Whitney
14,494 ft
4,418 m

Death Valley
-282 ft, -86 m

Lake Mead

Lake Powell

Colorado

Grand Canyon

Colorado Plateau

San Juan Mts.

Sangre de Cristo Mts.

Arkansas

Point Conception

Mojave Desert

Los Angeles

Channel Islands

San Diego

Salton Sea

Colorado

Phoenix

Sonoran Desert

Sacramento Mts.

Llano Estacado

HIGH PLAINS

Red

Dallas
Brazos

Rio Grande

Edwards Plateau

Rio Grande

CANADA

CO

MEXICO

TROPIC OF CANCER

25°N

ALASKA inset:

ARCTIC OCEAN

Point Barrow

Beaufort Sea

Chukchi Sea

RUSSIA

Bering Strait

North Slope

Brooks Range

ARCTIC CIRCLE

Seward Pen.

St. Lawrence Island

ALASKA

Yukon

Kuskokwim

Tanana

Alaska Range
Mt. McKinley (Denali)
20,320 ft, 6,194 m
Anchorage

CANADA

Nunivak Island

Bering Sea

Bristol Bay

Alaska Peninsula

Kodiak I.

Gulf of Alaska

Alexander Archipelago

ALASKA

0 mi   300
0 km   300

PACIFIC OCEAN

A New Nation, 1787

BRITISH NORTH AMERICA

Claimed by U.S. and Great Britain

Claimed by U.S. and Great Britain

Claimed by N.H. and N.Y.

Part of Mass.

Mississippi

Missouri

NORTHWEST TERRITORY

Ceded by Va. to U.S. 1784

Awarded to Pa. from Conn. 1782

Ceded by Mass. to N.Y. 1786

NEW HAMPSHIRE

MASSACHUSETTS

RHODE ISLAND

Ceded by Mass. to U.S. 1785

CONNECTICUT

New York City (1787–1790)

SPANISH

PA.

NEW JERSEY

Ceded by Conn. to U.S. 1786 & 1800

Wabash

Ohio

MD.

DELAWARE

SPANISH LOUISIANA

Arkansas

NORTH AMERICA

Ceded by New York to U.S. 1782

UNITED STATES

VIRGINIA

ALTA CALIFORNIA

Colorado

Claimed by Virginia

NORTH CAROLINA

Gila

Claimed by North Carolina

SOUTH CAROLINA

Rio Grande

Ceded by S.C. to Ga. 1787

Claimed by Georgia

GEORGIA

BAJA CALIFORNIA

WESTERN INTERIOR PROVINCES

Claimed by Ga., Spain and U.S.

SPANISH FLORIDA

EASTERN INTERIOR PROVINCES

Original 13 states

Land still claimed by states 1787

U.S. territory

British territory

Spanish territory

Disputed boundary

Coming of Age, 1821

Columbia

U.S.–British treaty line of 1818

BRITISH NORTH AMERICA

Claimed by U.S. and Great Britain

RED RIVER BASIN To U.S. 1818

MAINE 1820

OREGON COUNTRY

U.S.–British agreement to joint occupation in 1818

Snake

Mississippi

MICHIGAN TERRITORY

Adams–Onis Treaty line of 1819

UNORGANIZED

Missouri

TERRITORY

INDIANA 1816

ALTA CALIFORNIA

Arkansas

MISSOURI 1821

ILLINOIS 1818

Wabash

Ohio

Washington

ARKANSAS TERRITORY

Red

MEXICO

MISSISSIPPI 1817

ALABAMA 1819

Rio Grande

TEXAS

LOUISIANA 1812

FLORIDA To U.S. 1819

UNITED STATES

TERRITORIAL GROWTH

NATIONAL GEOGRAPHIC

A6   Reference Atlas

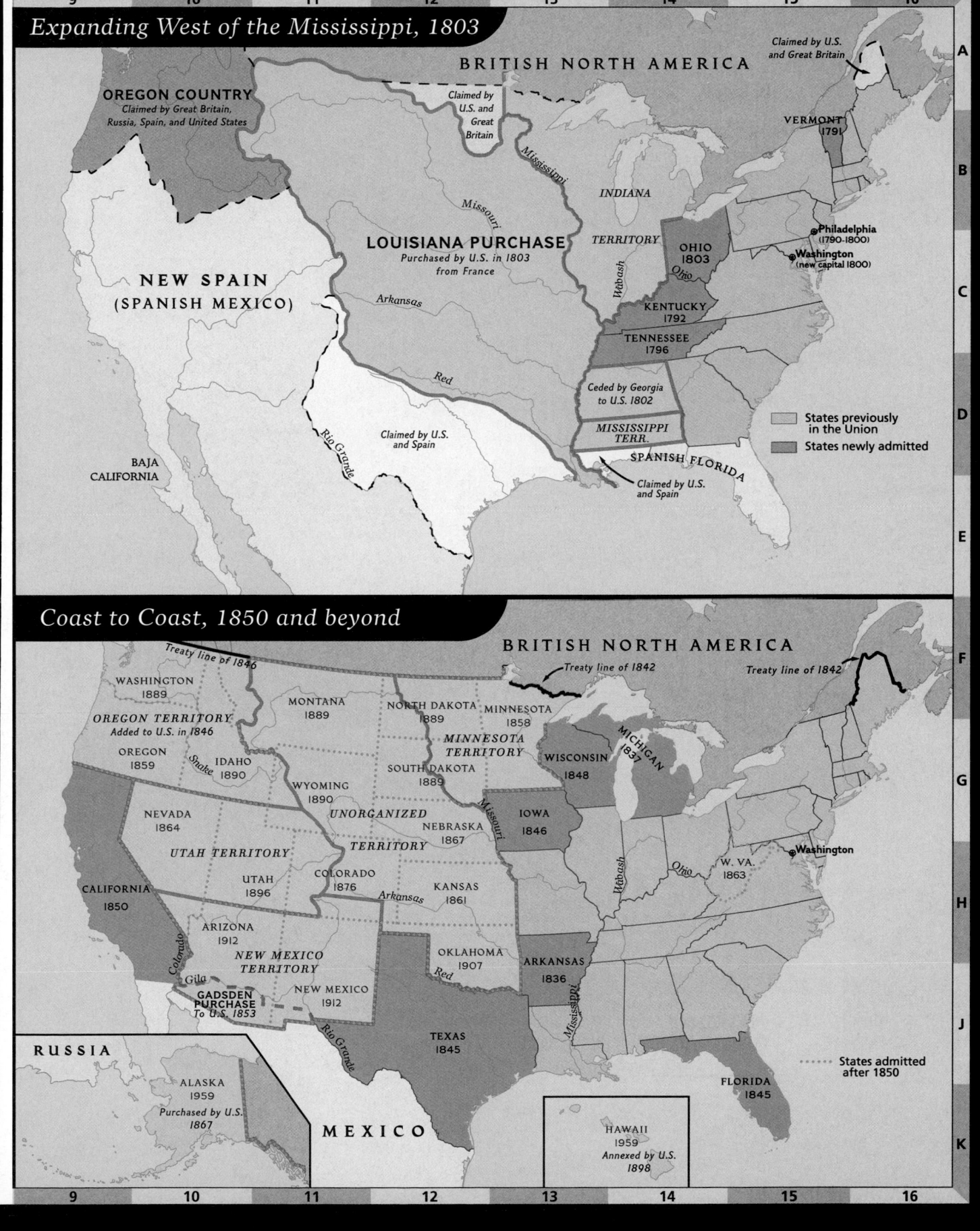

Expanding West of the Mississippi, 1803

BRITISH NORTH AMERICA

Claimed by U.S. and Great Britain

OREGON COUNTRY
Claimed by Great Britain, Russia, Spain, and United States

Claimed by U.S. and Great Britain

VERMONT 1791

NEW SPAIN (SPANISH MEXICO)

INDIANA

Mississippi

Missouri

LOUISIANA PURCHASE
Purchased by U.S. in 1803 from France

TERRITORY

Wabash

OHIO 1803

Ohio

KENTUCKY 1792

TENNESSEE 1796

Arkansas

Philadelphia (1790-1800)

Washington (new capital 1800)

Red

Rio Grande

Claimed by U.S. and Spain

Ceded by Georgia to U.S. 1802

MISSISSIPPI TERR.

SPANISH FLORIDA

BAJA CALIFORNIA

Claimed by U.S. and Spain

☐ States previously in the Union
☐ States newly admitted

Coast to Coast, 1850 and beyond

BRITISH NORTH AMERICA

Treaty line of 1846

Treaty line of 1842

Treaty line of 1842

WASHINGTON 1889

OREGON TERRITORY
Added to U.S. in 1846

MONTANA 1889

NORTH DAKOTA 1889

MINNESOTA 1858

OREGON 1859

Snake

IDAHO 1890

SOUTH DAKOTA 1889

MINNESOTA TERRITORY

MICHIGAN 1837

WISCONSIN 1848

WYOMING 1890

NEVADA 1864

UNORGANIZED

Missouri

IOWA 1846

UTAH TERRITORY

UTAH 1896

COLORADO 1876

TERRITORY

NEBRASKA 1867

Washington

CALIFORNIA 1850

Colorado

ARIZONA 1912

Arkansas

KANSAS 1861

W. VA. 1863

Gila

NEW MEXICO TERRITORY

Ohio

Wabash

GADSDEN PURCHASE
To U.S. 1853

NEW MEXICO 1912

OKLAHOMA 1907

ARKANSAS 1836

Red

Rio Grande

Mississippi

RUSSIA

TEXAS 1845

ALASKA 1959
Purchased by U.S. 1867

MEXICO

FLORIDA 1845

HAWAII 1959
Annexed by U.S. 1898

States admitted after 1850

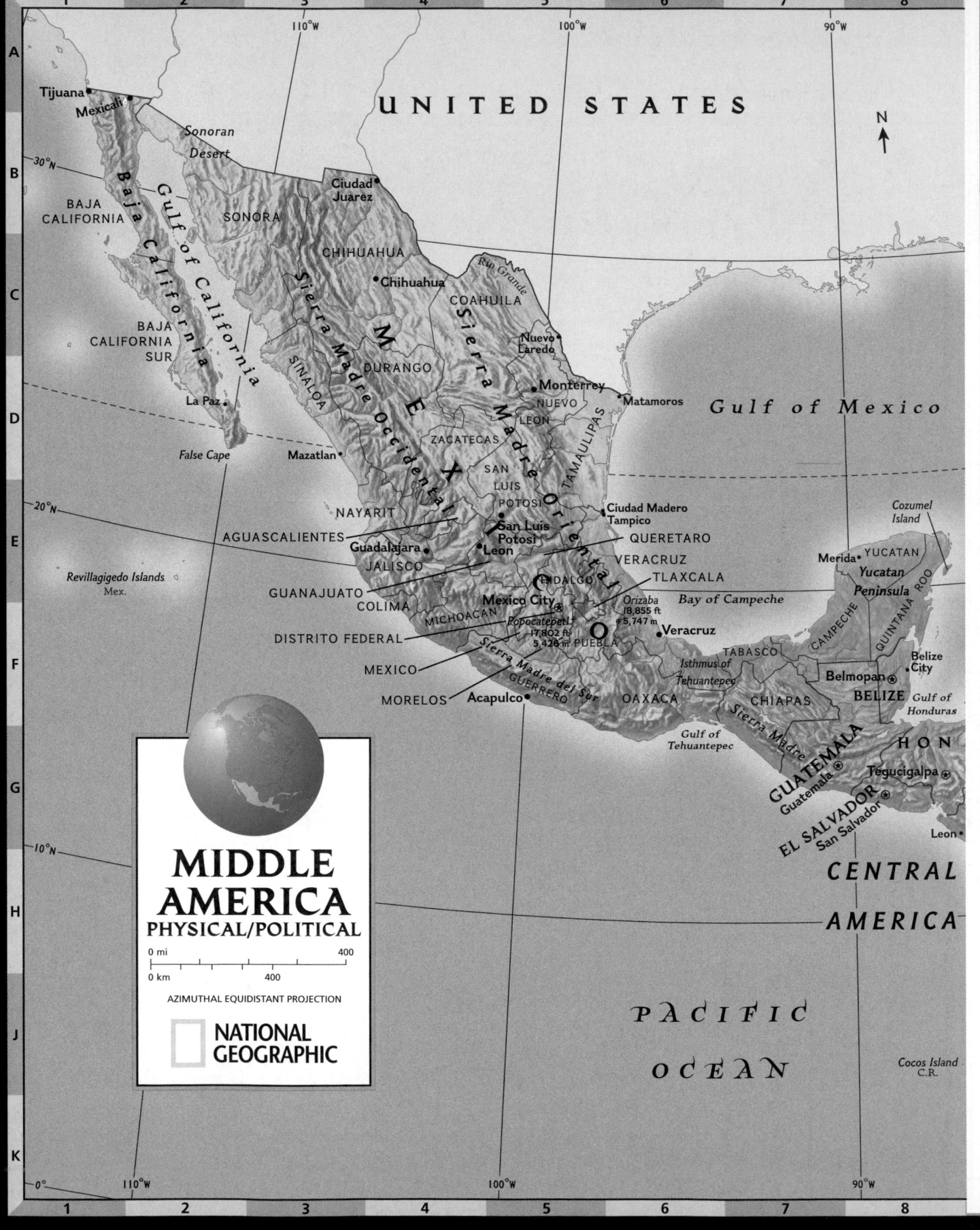

MIDDLE
AMERICA
PHYSICAL/POLITICAL

0 mi — 400
0 km — 400

AZIMUTHAL EQUIDISTANT PROJECTION

NATIONAL
GEOGRAPHIC

UNITED STATES

N

30°N

BAJA
CALIFORNIA

Tijuana
Mexicali

Sonoran
Desert

SONORA

Ciudad
Juarez

CHIHUAHUA

Chihuahua

Rio Grande

COAHUILA

Nuevo
Laredo

Gulf of Mexico

BAJA
CALIFORNIA
SUR

Sierra Madre Occidental

DURANGO

M
E
X
I
C
O

Sierra Madre Oriental

NUEVO
LEON

Monterrey

Matamoros

La Paz

SINALOA

ZACATECAS

TAMAULIPAS

20°N

False Cape

Mazatlan

SAN
LUIS
POTOSI

Ciudad Madero
Tampico

Cozumel
Island

Revillagigedo Islands
Mex.

NAYARIT

AGUASCALIENTES

Guadalajara

JALISCO

San Luis
Potosi

Leon

QUERETARO

VERACRUZ

Merida
Yucatan

YUCATAN

GUANAJUATO

COLIMA

MICHOACAN

HIDALGO

Mexico City

Popocatepetl
17,802 ft
5,426 m

TLAXCALA

Orizaba
18,855 ft
5,747 m

PUEBLA

Bay of Campeche

Yucatan
Peninsula

CAMPECHE

QUINTANA ROO

DISTRITO FEDERAL

MEXICO

MORELOS

Acapulco

Sierra Madre del Sur

GUERRERO

Veracruz

OAXACA

TABASCO

Isthmus of
Tehuantepec

Gulf of
Tehuantepec

Sierra Madre

CHIAPAS

Belmopan

BELIZE

Belize
City

Gulf of
Honduras

GUATEMALA

Guatemala

HON

Tegucigalpa

EL SALVADOR

San Salvador

Leon

CENTRAL

AMERICA

10°N

PACIFIC

OCEAN

Cocos Island
C.R.

0°

110°W

110°W

100°W

100°W

90°W

90°W

A8   Reference Atlas

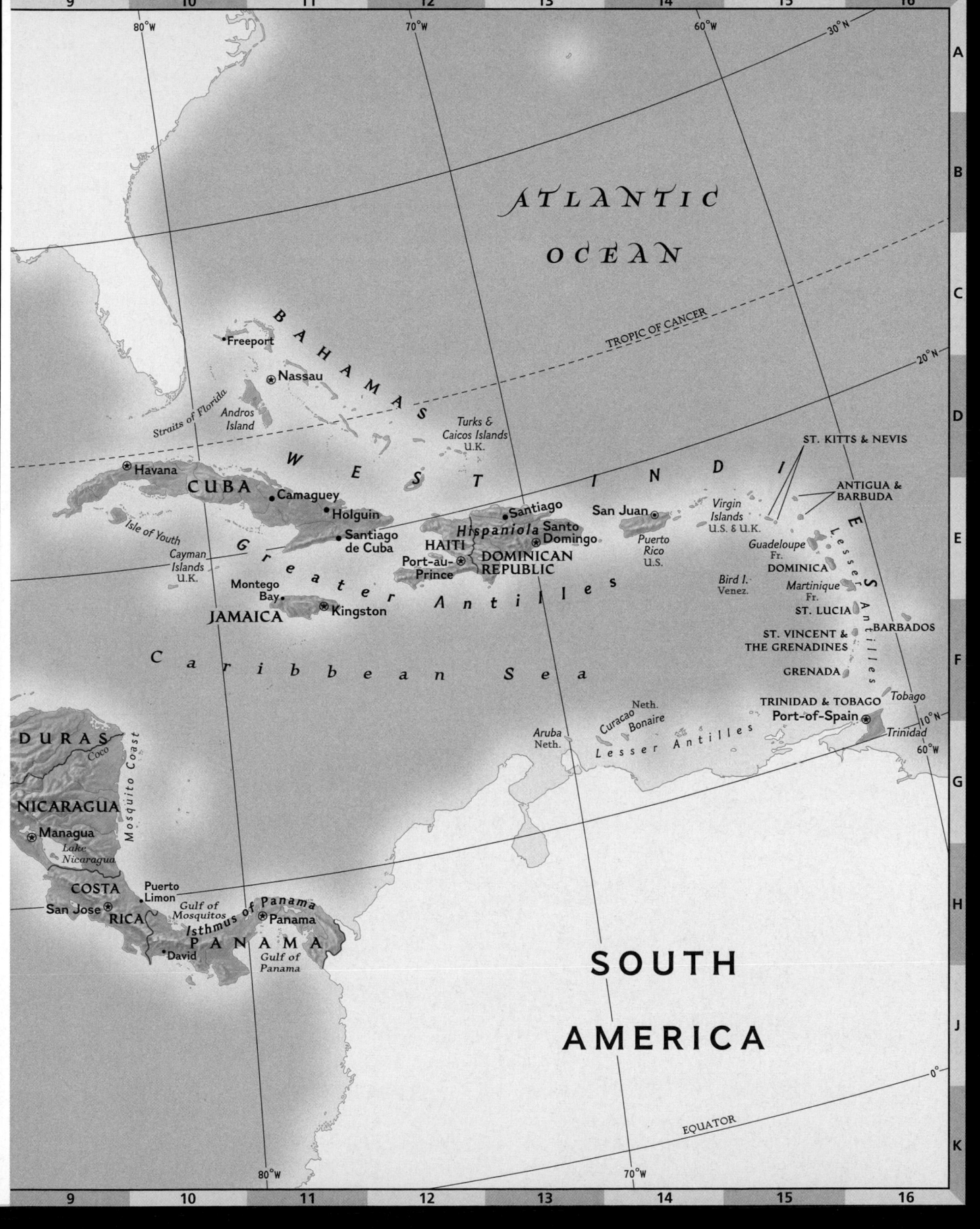

ATLANTIC

OCEAN

TROPIC OF CANCER

20°N

BAHAMAS

Freeport

Nassau

Turks &
Caicos Islands
U.K.

Andros
Island

Straits of Florida

ST. KITTS & NEVIS

W E S T   I N D I E S

ANTIGUA &
BARBUDA

CUBA

Camaguey

Holguin

Santiago

San Juan

Virgin
Islands
U.S. & U.K.

Santiago
de Cuba

Hispaniola

Santo
Domingo

Puerto
Rico
U.S.

Guadeloupe
Fr.

Lesser Antilles

Isle of Youth

HAITI

DOMINICAN
REPUBLIC

DOMINICA

Port-au-
Prince

Cayman
Islands
U.K.

Greater

Bird I.
Venez.

Martinique
Fr.

Montego
Bay

Antilles

ST. LUCIA

JAMAICA

Kingston

BARBADOS

ST. VINCENT &
THE GRENADINES

C a r i b b e a n   S e a

GRENADA

Neth.

TRINIDAD & TOBAGO

Tobago

Curacao
Bonaire

Port-of-Spain

10°N

Aruba
Neth.

Lesser Antilles

Trinidad

60°W

DURAS

Coco

NICARAGUA

Mosquito Coast

Managua

Lake
Nicaragua

SOUTH

COSTA

Puerto
Limon

Isthmus of Panama

San Jose

RICA

Gulf of
Mosquitos

Panama

Panama

AMERICA

PANAMA

David

Gulf of
Panama

0°

EQUATOR

70°W

N

Ellesmere
Island

Devon Island

GREENLAND
(KALAALLIT NUNAAT)
Den.

ICELAND

Baffin
Bay

Melville
Peninsula

Baffin
Island

Foxe
Basin

A V U T

Davis Strait

Southampton
Island

Iqaluit

Hudson Strait

Labrador
Sea

Ungava
Bay

Hudson
Bay

NEWFOUNDLAND
AND LABRADOR

Belcher
Islands

Cartwright

Scheffervlle

Happy Valley-
Goose Bay

Island of
Newfoundland

Smallwood
Reservoir

"Churchill Falls

James Bay

QUEBEC

S H I E L D

Manicouagan
Reservoir
Sept-Iles

St. John's
Avalon
Peninsula

Anticosti I.

St.-Pierre & Miquelon
Fr.

Gulf of
St. Lawrence

ONTARIO

Gaspe
Pen.

PRINCE
EDWARD
ISLAND

Cape Breton I.

ATLANTIC

Lake
Nipigon

Chicoutimi

Charlottetown

NEW
BRUNSWICK

NOVA
SCOTIA

Rouyn-Noranda

Quebec

Thunder
Bay

Lake
Superior

Fredericton
Saint John

St. Lawrence

Halifax

OCEAN

Sudbury

Montreal

Bay of Fundy

Ottawa

Lake
Huron

Lake Michigan

Toronto

L. Ontario

Niagara Falls
London

L. Erie

CANADA
PHYSICAL/POLITICAL

0 mi   400

0 km   400

AZIMUTHAL EQUIDISTANT PROJECTION

NATIONAL
GEOGRAPHIC

80°N
40°W
50°W
60°W
70°W
30°W
20°W
70°N
10°W
60°N
10°W
20°W
30°W
50°N
40°W
40°N
50°N
60°W
70°W
80°W
90°W

EUROPE

Black Sea

40°N

Istanbul
Sea of
Marmara
ANATOLIA

Ankara

Tunis
TURKEY

TUNISIA

Mediterranean Sea
Taurus Mountains

Aleppo

CYPRUS
SYRIA

Tripoli
LEBANON
Damascus
Beirut
Syrian
Desert

30°N
ISRAEL
Jerusalem
Amman

Alexandria
JORDAN

LIBYA
El Giza
Cairo

Sinai
Pen.

See inset below

EGYPT

Nile R.

Hejaz

Eastern Mediterranean Area

30°E

TURKEY

N

Aleppo

CYPRUS
SYRIA

Mediterranean
Sea
LEBANON

Beirut
Damascus

Sea of Galilee
Golan Heights
Jordan River

Aswan
High Dam

SAHARA

Boundary claimed
by Sudan

Red Sea

Tel Aviv–Jaffa
West Bank

Jerusalem
Amman

Gaza Strip
Dead Sea

Suez Canal

ISRAEL
JORDAN

SUDAN

El Giza
Cairo

EGYPT

Nile River
Gulf of Suez
SAUDI
ARABIA

30°N

AFRICA

Gulf of
Aqaba

0 mi   100

0 km   100

Khartoum

Red Sea

30°E

9   10   11   12   13   14   15   16

50°E   60°E   70°E   40°N

Aral Sea

UZBEKISTAN

Tashkent

A

TAJIKISTAN

Dushanbe

B

Caucasus Mountains

GEORGIA

Tbilisi

Yerevan

Baku

Caspian Sea

TURKMENISTAN

A S I A

ARMENIA

Ashkhabad

Kabul

Mt. Ararat
*(16,854 ft.
5,137 m)*

AZERBAIJAN

Mashhad

AFGHANISTAN

C

Elburz Mountains

Tehran

*Plateau
of Iran*

30°N

D

Tigris R.

IRAQ

Baghdad

Zagros Mountains

IRAN

Euphrates R.

Al Basrah

PAKISTAN

E

KUWAIT

Kuwait

*Persian Gulf
(Arabian Gulf)*

F

Manama

BAHRAIN

QATAR

Doha

Abu
Dhabi

Gulf of Oman

TROPIC OF CANCER

*Arabian
Sea*

**SAUDI
ARABIA**

Riyadh

Masqat

**UNITED
ARAB
EMIRATES**

OMAN

20°N

G

*ARABIAN
PENINSULA*

H

Makkah
(Mecca)

A s i r

*Rub al Khali
(Empty Quarter)*

J

N

YEMEN

Sanaa

MIDDLE EAST

PHYSICAL / POLITICAL

0 mi   500

0 km   500

AZIMUTHAL EQUIDISTANT PROJECTION

**NATIONAL
GEOGRAPHIC**

40°E   50°E

Aden

Gulf of Aden

K

9   10   11   12   13   14   15   16

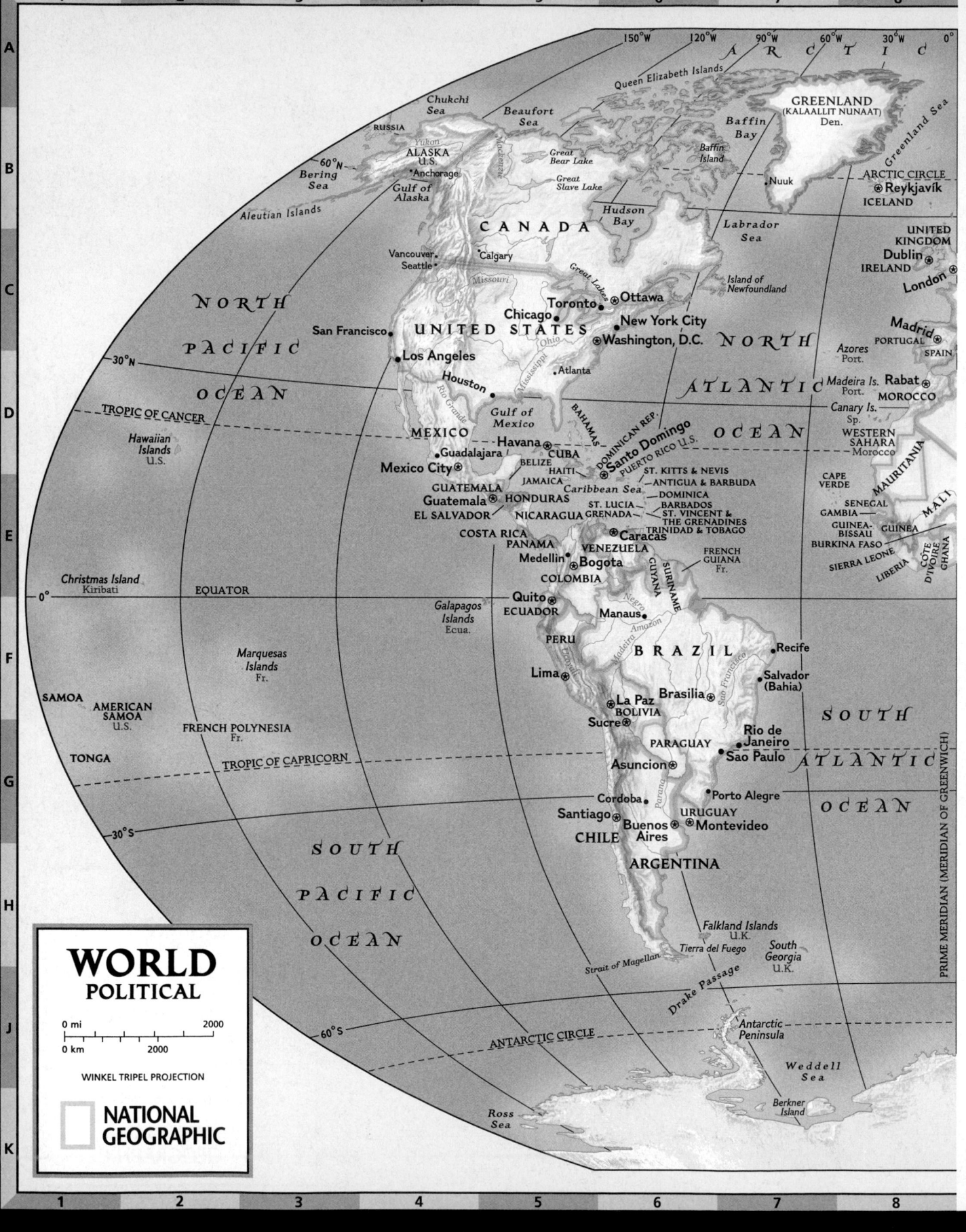

WORLD
POLITICAL

0 mi   2000

0 km   2000

WINKEL TRIPEL PROJECTION

NATIONAL GEOGRAPHIC

ABBREVIATIONS

AUST.	....	AUSTRIA
B.&H.	....	BOSNIA & HERZEGOVINA
BELG.	....	BELGIUM
CROAT.	....	CROATIA
CZECH REP.	....	CZECH REPUBLIC
DEM. REP. OF THE CONGO	....	DEMOCRATIC REPUBLIC OF THE CONGO
EQ. GUINEA	....	EQUATORIAL GUINEA
EST.	....	ESTONIA
HUNG.	....	HUNGARY
LITH.	....	LITHUANIA
MACED.	....	MACEDONIA
MOLD.	....	MOLDOVA
NETH.	....	NETHERLANDS
SERB.	....	SERBIA
MONT.	....	MONTENEGRO
SLOV.	....	SLOVENIA
SWITZ.	....	SWITZERLAND
U.A.E.	....	UNITED ARAB EMIRATES

EUROPE
POLITICAL

0 mi   400

0 km   400

AZIMUTHAL EQUIDISTANT PROJECTION

NATIONAL
GEOGRAPHIC

ICELAND
Reykjavík
Akureyri

ARCTIC CIRCLE

Norwegian Sea

N

Tromso

NORWAY

Are

Trondheim

Alesund

Sundsvall

Gulf of

SWEDEN

Bergen

Oslo

Uppsala

Stockholm

Stavanger

Goteborg

Gotland

Skagerrak

Baltic

Faeroe Islands
Den.
Torshavn

Shetland
Islands

Lerwick

PRIME MERIDIAN (MERIDIAN OF GREENWICH)

Rockall
U.K.

Isle of Lewis

Orkney Islands

Inverness

UNITED
SCOTLAND
Glasgow
Edinburgh
Belfast
NORTHERN
IRELAND
IRELAND
Dublin
Cork
KINGDOM
WALES
ENGLAND
Cardiff
London
Southampton
Land's End
English Channel

Aberdeen

North
Sea

DENMARK
Arhus
Copenhagen
Malmo

Kiel
Hamburg

Gdansk

Berlin

Bydgoszcz

POLAND

Lodz

NETH.
The
Hague
Amsterdam

Irish
Sea

Liverpool
Manchester
Birmingham

Celtic
Sea

Brussels
BELGIUM
Bonn

GERMANY

Frankfurt

Wroclaw

Prague

CZECH REP.

LUX.

Rhine

Le Havre

Brest

Rennes

Paris

Strasbourg

Bratislava

SLOVAKIA

ATLANTIC
OCEAN

Nantes

FRANCE

Munich

Vienna

LIECH.

AUSTRIA

Budapest

La Rochelle

Bay of
Biscay

Limoges

Bordeaux

Zurich
Bern
SWITZERLAND

Geneva
Lyon

ALPS

Milan

Ljubljana

SLOVENIA

HUNGARY

Zagreb

CROATIA

La Coruña

Vigo

Donostia-
San Sebastian

Bilbao

Turin

Genoa

Venice

Adriatic

BOSNIA &
HERZEGOVINA

Porto

Coimbra

Pyrenees

Toulouse

MONACO

Nice

SAN
MARINO

Sea

Sarajevo

Valladolid

ANDORRA

Marseille

PORTUGAL

SPAIN

Madrid

Zaragoza

Barcelona

ITALY

Corsica
Fr.

VATICAN
CITY

Rome

MONTENEGRO
Podgorica

Lisbon

Valencia

Palma

Tiranë
ALBANIA

Cape
St. Vincent

Cordoba

Seville

Murcia

Balearic
Islands
Sp.

Sardinia
It.

Naples

Cadiz

Malaga

Cartagena

Cagliari

Tyrrhenian
Sea

Ionian
Sea

GIBRALTAR
U.K.

Strait of Gibraltar

Mediterranean

Palermo

Messina

Sicily

Catania

AFRICA

Valletta
MALTA

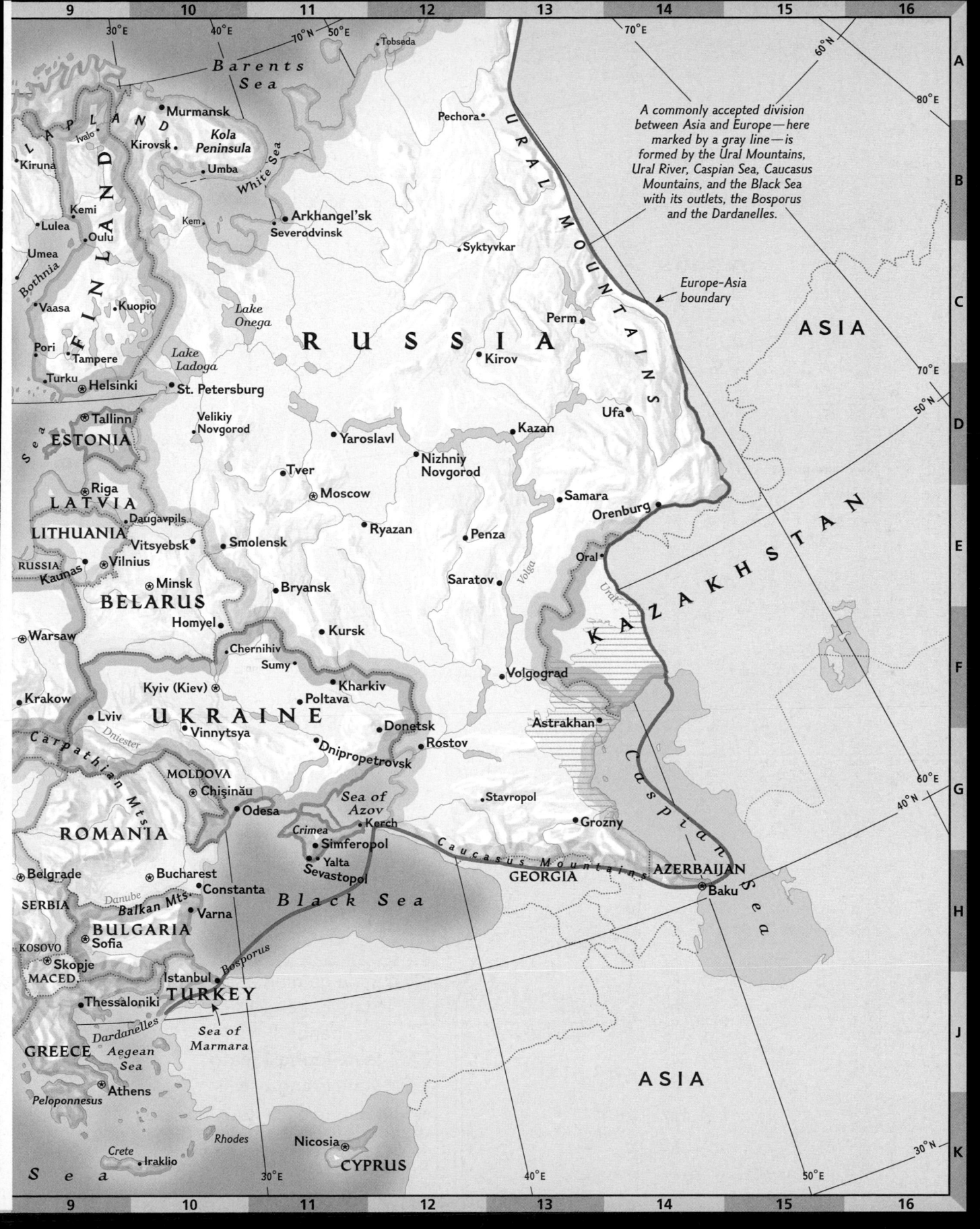

A commonly accepted division between Asia and Europe—here marked by a gray line—is formed by the Ural Mountains, Ural River, Caspian Sea, Caucasus Mountains, and the Black Sea with its outlets, the Bosporus and the Dardanelles.

Europe-Asia boundary

Barents Sea

Tobseda

Murmansk
Kirovsk
Kola Peninsula
Ivalo
Umba
White Sea

Kiruna
Kemi
Lulea
Oulu
Umea
Bothnia
Vaasa
Kuopio
Pori
Tampere
Turku
Helsinki

Pechora

URAL MOUNTAINS

Arkhangel'sk
Severodvinsk
Kem

Syktyvkar

RUSSIA

Perm
Kirov
Ufa
Kazan

ASIA

Lake Onega
Lake Ladoga
St. Petersburg

Tallinn
ESTONIA
Velikiy Novgorod
Yaroslavl
Nizhniy Novgorod
Samara
Orenburg

Riga
LATVIA
Daugavpils
Tver
Moscow
KAZAKHSTAN
Oral
LITHUANIA
Vitsyebsk
Smolensk
Ryazan
Penza
RUSSIA
Vilnius
Kaunas
Minsk
Bryansk
Saratov
Volga
BELARUS
Homyel
Kursk
Volgograd
Warsaw
Chernihiv
Sumy
Astrakhan
Krakow
Kharkiv
Poltava
Caspian Sea
Lviv
UKRAINE
Vinnytsya
Donetsk
Kyiv (Kiev)
Dnipropetrovsk
Rostov
Dniester
MOLDOVA
Chişinău
Stavropol
ROMANIA
Odesa
Sea of Azov
Grozny
Kerch
Crimea
Caucasus Mountains
Belgrade
Bucharest
Simferopol
AZERBAIJAN
Yalta
GEORGIA
Baku
SERBIA
Danube
Constanta
Sevastopol
Black Sea
Balkan Mts.
Varna
BULGARIA
Sofia
KOSOVO
Skopje
Bosporus
MACED.
Istanbul
Thessaloniki
TURKEY
Dardanelles
Sea of Marmara
GREECE
Aegean Sea
Athens
Peloponnesus
ASIA
Crete
Iraklio
Rhodes
Nicosia
Sea
CYPRUS

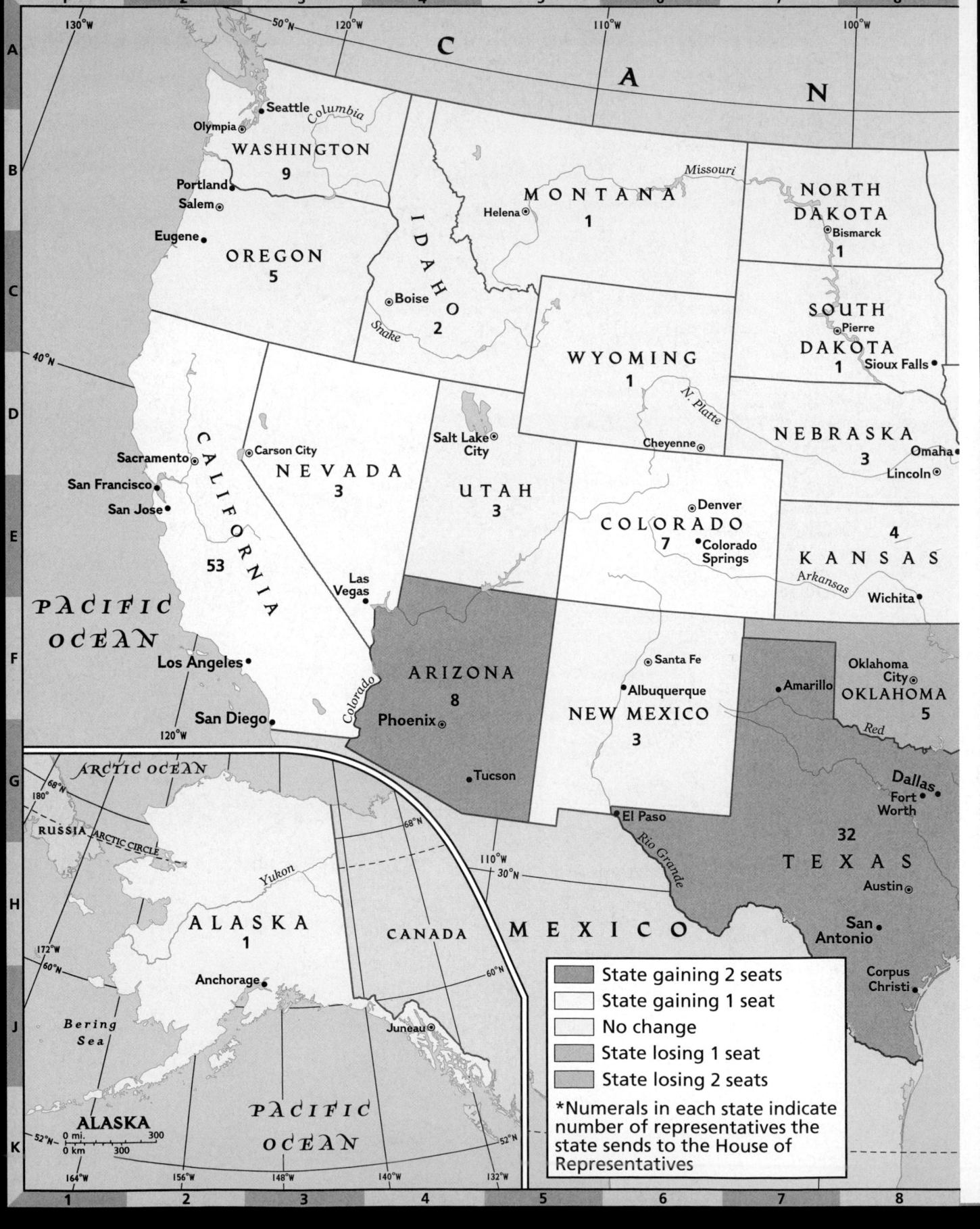

State gaining 2 seats
State gaining 1 seat
No change
State losing 1 seat
State losing 2 seats

*Numerals in each state indicate number of representatives the state sends to the House of Representatives

UNITED STATES
2000 CONGRESSIONAL REAPPORTIONMENT

0 mi.   300
0 km   300
ALBERS CONIC EQUAL-AREA PROJECTION

NATIONAL GEOGRAPHIC

PRINCIPAL HAWAIIAN ISLANDS

0 mi.   100
0 km   100

Geography Skills Handbook

How Do I Study Geography?

Geographers have tried to understand the best way to teach and learn about geography. In order to do this, geographers created the *Five Themes of Geography*. The themes acted as a guide for teaching the basic ideas about geography to students like yourself.

People who teach and study geography, though, thought that the Five Themes were too broad. In 1994, geographers created 18 national geography standards. These standards were more detailed about what should be taught and learned. The Six Essential Elements act as a bridge connecting the Five Themes with the standards.

These pages show you how the Five Themes are related to the Six Essential Elements and the 18 standards.

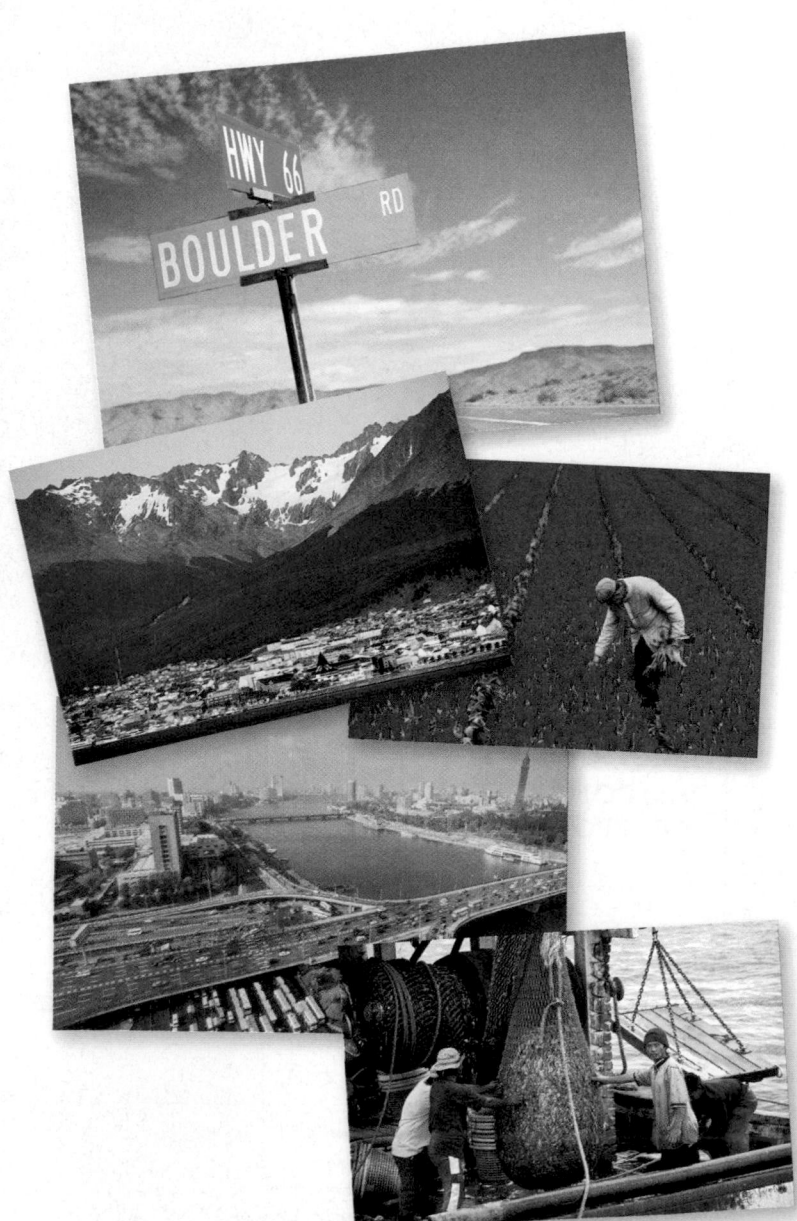

5
Themes of Geography

1 Location
Location describes where something is. Absolute location describes a place's exact position on the Earth's surface. Relative location expresses where a place is in relation to another place.

2 Place
Place describes the physical and human characteristics that make a location unique.

3 Regions
Regions are areas that share common characteristics.

4 Movement
Movement explains how and why people and things move and are connected.

5 Human-Environment Interaction
Human-Environment Interaction describes the relationship between people and their environment.

6
Essential Elements

18
Geography Standards

I. The World in Spatial Terms
Geographers look to see where a place is located. Location acts as a starting point to answer "Where Is It?" The location of a place helps you orient yourself as to where you are.

1 How to use maps and other tools

2 How to use mental maps to organize information

3 How to analyze the spatial organization of people, places, and environments

II. Places and Regions
Place describes physical characteristics such as landforms, climate, and plant or animal life. It might also describe human characteristics, including language and way of life. Places can also be organized into regions. **Regions** are places united by one or more characteristics.

4 The physical and human characteristics of places

5 How people create regions to interpret Earth's complexity

6 How culture and experience influence people's perceptions of places and regions

III. Physical Systems
Geographers study how physical systems, such as hurricanes, volcanoes, and glaciers, shape the surface of the Earth. They also look at how plants and animals depend upon one another and their surroundings for their survival.

7 The physical processes that shape Earth's surface

8 The distribution of ecosystems on Earth's surface

9 The characteristics, distribution, and migration of human populations

10 The complexity of Earth's cultural mosaics

IV. Human Systems
People shape the world in which they live. They settle in certain places but not in others. An ongoing theme in geography is the movement of people, ideas, and goods.

11 The patterns and networks of economic interdependence

12 The patterns of human settlement

13 The forces of cooperation and conflict

14 How human actions modify the physical environment

V. Environment and Society
How does the relationship between people and their natural surroundings influence the way people live? Geographers study how people use the environment and how their actions affect the environment.

15 How physical systems affect human systems

16 The meaning, use, and distribution of resources

VI. The Uses of Geography
Knowledge of geography helps us understand the relationships among people, places, and environments over time. Applying geographic skills helps you understand the past and prepare for the future.

17 How to apply geography to interpret the past

18 How to apply geography to interpret the present and plan for the future

Contents

Geography Skills Handbook

Throughout this text, you will discover how geography has shaped the course of events in United States history. Landforms, waterways, climate, and natural resources all have helped or hindered human activities. Usually people have learned either to adapt to their environments or to transform it to meet their needs. The resources in this handbook will help you get the most out of your textbook—and provide you with skills you will use for the rest of your life.

The study of geography is more than knowing a lot of facts about places. Rather, it has more to do with asking questions about the Earth, pursuing their answers, and solving problems. Thus, one of the most important geographic tools is inside your head: the ability to think geographically.

Globes and Maps

A **globe** is a scale model of the Earth. Because Earth is round, a globe presents the most accurate depiction of geographic information such as area, distance, and direction. However, globes show little close-up detail. A printed **map** is a symbolic representation of all or part of the planet. Unlike globes, maps can show small areas in great detail.

From 3-D to 2-D

Think about the surface of the Earth as the peel of an orange. To flatten the peel, you have to cut it like the globe shown here. To create maps that are not interrupted, mapmakers, or **cartographers**, use mathematical formulas to transfer information from the three-dimensional globe to the two-dimensional map. However, when the curves of a globe become straight lines on a map, distortion of size, shape, distance, or area occurs.

globe accurately shows a great circle route, as indicated on the map below. However, as shown on the flat map, the great circle distance (dotted line) between Tokyo and Los Angeles appears to be far longer than the true direction distance (solid line). In fact, the great circle distance is 345 miles (555 km) shorter.

Great Circle Routes

A straight line of true direction—one that runs directly from west to east, for example—is not always the shortest distance between two points. This is due to the curvature of the Earth. To find the shortest distance, stretch a piece of string around a globe from one point to the other. The string will form part of a *great circle*, an imaginary line the follows the curve of the Earth. Ship captains and airline pilots use these **great circle routes** to reduce travel time and conserve fuel.

The idea of a great circle route is an important difference between globes and maps. A round

---

Practicing SKILLS

1. **Explain** the significance of: globe, map, cartographer, great circle route.

2. **Describe** the problems that arise when the curves of a globe become straight lines on a map.

3. **Use** a Venn diagram like the one below to identify the similarities and differences between globes and maps.

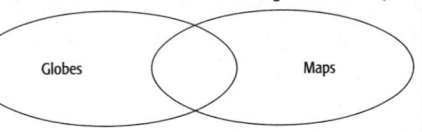

C Critical Thinking

Identifying Central Issues

Ask: Why do map makers use projections? *(Projections help in transferring information from a three-dimensional surface to a two-dimensional surface.)* **OL**

D Differentiated Instruction

Kinesthetic If students are struggling with the concept of projection, give them a large sheet of paper or poster board and a globe. Have students place the paper and the globe in the same physical relationships shown in the illustrations. Check to make sure students can visualize how each projection offers a different approximation of the sphere. **BL**

Projections

C To create maps, cartographers project the round Earth onto a flat surface—making a **map projection**. Distance, shape, direction, or size may be distorted by a projection. As a result, the purpose of the map usually dictates which projection is used. There are many kinds of map projections, some with general names and some named for the cartographers who developed them. Three basic categories of map projections are shown here: **planar**, **cylindrical**, and **conic**.

Planar Projection

A planar projection shows the Earth centered in such a way that a straight line coming from the center to any other point represents the shortest distance. Also known as an azimuthal projection, it is most accurate at its center. As a result, it is often used for maps of the Poles.

Cylindrical Projection

D A cylindrical projection is based on the projection of the globe onto a cylinder. This projection is most accurate near the Equator, but shapes and distances are distorted near the Poles.

Conic Projection

A conic projection comes from placing a cone over part of a globe. Conic projections are best suited for showing limited east-west areas that are not too far from the Equator. For these uses, a conic projection can indicate distances and directions fairly accurately.

Differentiated Instruction

Activity: Creating a Graphic Organizer

Visual/Spatial To help students remember the several different categories and examples of maps discussed in this section, guide them in creating a graphic organizer entitled "Types of Maps." Branching this main head should be three boxes labeled "Political," "Physical," and "Special-Purpose." Have students complete the organizer by taking notes on each of the different types of maps. **OL**

Common Map Projections

Each type of map projection has advantages and some degree of inaccuracy. Four of the most common projections are shown here.

Winkel Tripel Projection

Most general reference world maps are the Winkel Tripel projection. It provides a good balance between the size and shape of land areas as they are shown on the map. Even the polar areas are depicted with little distortion of size and shape.

Goode's Interrupted Equal-Area Projection

An **interrupted projection** resembles a globe that has been cut apart and laid flat. Goode's Interrupted Equal-Area projection shows the true size and shape of Earth's landmasses, but distances are generally distorted.

Robinson Projection

The Robinson projection has minor distortions. The sizes and shapes near the eastern and western edges of the map are accurate, and outlines of the continents appear much as they do on the globe. However, the polar areas are flattened.

Mercator Projection

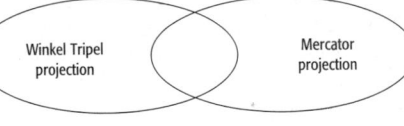

The Mercator projection increasingly distorts size and distance as it moves away from the Equator. However, Mercator projections do accurately show true directions and the shapes of landmasses, making these maps useful for sea travel.

Practicing SKILLS

1. **Explain** the significance of: map projection, planar, cylindrical, conic, interrupted projection.

2. **How** does a cartographer determine which map projection to use?

3. **How** is Goode's Interrupted Equal-Area projection different from the Mercator projection?

4. **Which** of the four common projections described above is the best one to use when showing the entire world? Why?

5. **Use** a Venn diagram like the one below to identify the similarities and differences between the Winkel Tripel and Mercator projections.

| Winkel Tripel projection | Mercator projection |

Geography Handbook   **GH5**

S Skill Practice

Visual Literacy Have students study the selected figures. **Ask:** What are two differences between longitude and latitude? *(Lines of latitude run horizontally and are parallel. Lines of longitude run vertically and intersect at the poles.)* **OL**

D Differentiated Instruction

Logical/Mathematical Have students use the Internet or library resources to determine their exact absolute location. If you have access to GPS equipment, you may wish to let students use it to check their work. **OL**

Hands-On Chapter Project

Determining Location

Geography is often said to begin with the question: *Where?* The basic tool for answering the question is **location.** Lines on globes and maps provide information that can help you locate places. These lines cross one another forming a pattern called a **grid system,** which helps you find exact places on the Earth's surface.

A **hemisphere** is one of the halves into which the Earth is divided. Geographers divide the Earth into hemispheres to help them classify and describe places on Earth. Most places are located in two of the four hemispheres.

Latitude

Lines of **latitude,** or parallels, circle the Earth parallel to the Equator and measure the distance north or south of the Equator in degrees. The Equator is measured at 0° latitude, while the Poles lie at latitudes 90°N (north) and 90°S (south). Parallels north of the Equator are called north latitude. Parallels south of the Equator are called south latitude.

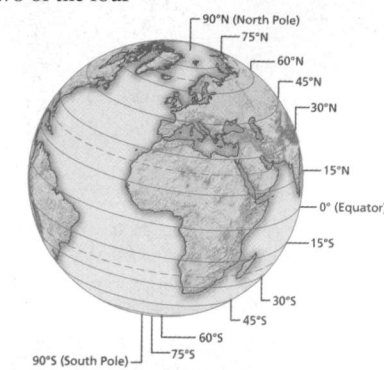

Longitude

Lines of **longitude,** or meridians, circle the Earth from Pole to Pole. These lines measure distance east or west of the **Prime Meridian** at 0° longitude. Meridians east of the Prime Meridian are known as east latitude. Meridians west of the Prime Meridian are known as west longitude. The 180° meridian on the opposite side of the Earth is called the International Date Line.

The Global Grid

Every place has a global address, or **absolute location.** You can identify the absolute location of a place by naming the latitude and longitude lines that cross exactly at that place. For example, Tokyo, Japan, is located at 36°N latitude and 140°E longitude. For more precise readings, each degree is further divided into 60 units called minutes.

Creating a Global Treasure Hunt

Directions Organize students into teams and have each team choose 10 places on Earth to research and study. Students may choose places that are well known or unfamiliar. However, all places should be on land and located at least 50 miles (80 km) from each other. Tell students to make a list of 8–10 interesting facts about each place.

Putting It Together Tell students to "bury" their treasure in each of the locations. Then have students use the facts they learned about the place to create clues for a Treasure Atlas. Clues will be locations, that, when followed, will lead to the buried treasure. The correct response to each clue will be a place name and coordinates that can be easily looked up. Clues should be written on index cards. Students should list all the clues with their answers on a separate sheet of paper. Each correct answer earns another clue to a new location, eventually leading to the buried treasure, so remind students to make sure their clues follow a logical route. **OL**

Northern and Southern Hemispheres

The diagram below shows that the Equator divides the Earth into the Northern and Southern Hemispheres. Everything north of the Equator is in the **Northern Hemisphere.** Everything south of the Equator is in the **Southern Hemisphere.**

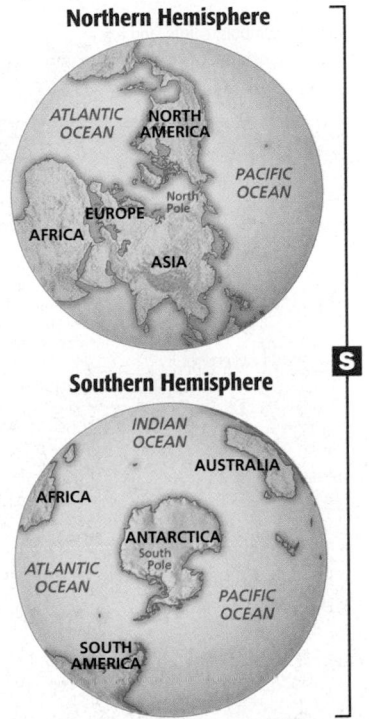

Northern Hemisphere

Southern Hemisphere

Eastern and Western Hemispheres

The Prime Meridian and the International Date Line divide the Earth into the Eastern and Western Hemispheres. Everything east of the Prime Meridian for 180° is in the **Eastern Hemisphere.** Everything west of the Prime Meridian for 180° is in the **Western Hemisphere.**

Eastern Hemisphere

Western Hemisphere

Practicing SKILLS

1. **Explain** the significance of: location, grid system, hemisphere, Northern Hemisphere, Southern Hemisphere, Eastern Hemisphere, Western Hemisphere, latitude, longitude, Prime Meridian, absolute location.
2. **Why** do all maps label the Equator 0° latitude and the Prime Meridian 0° longitude?
3. **Which** lines of latitude and longitude divide the Earth into hemispheres?
4. **Using** the Reference Atlas maps, fill in a chart like the one below by writing the latitude and longitude of three world cities. Have a partner try to identify the cities.
5. **Use** a chart like the one below to identify the continents in each hemisphere. Some may be in more than one hemisphere.

Hemisphere	Continents
Northern	
Southern	
Eastern	
Western	

S Skill Practice

Visual Literacy Point out that most people probably are not used to seeing the globe from these angles. **Ask:** What view do these illustrations show? *(the globe viewed from the top and the bottom)* **Ask:** How do you generally view the globe? *(from the side, along the Equator)* If students still struggle to understand the difference between these views, use an actual globe to show them the view reflected in the illustration. **BL**

C Critical Thinking

Detecting Bias Ask: Since planet Earth has no true top or bottom, why do globes show Europe on the top half of Earth? *(early map makers and explorers were from Europe)* **AL**

PRACTICING SKILLS

Answers

1. location: a specific place on Earth; grid system: pattern formed as the lines of latitude and longitude cross one another; hemisphere: half of a sphere or globe; Northern Hemisphere: everything north of the Equator; Southern Hemisphere: everything south of the Equator; Eastern Hemisphere: everything east of the Prime Meridian for 180°; Western Hemisphere: everything west of the Prime Meridian for 180°

2. They are where the division between north/south (N/S) and east/west (E/W) occur, respectively.

3. Equator and Prime Meridian

4. Answers will vary according to cities chosen.

5. Northern: North America, Asia, Europe, Africa; Eastern: Asia, Europe, Africa, Australia; Southern: Antarctica, Australia, South America, Africa; Western: North America, South America

S Skill Practice

Using Geography Skills Have students use the scale bar on the map to calculate the distance in kilometers between Paris and Stockholm. First, have students use a ruler to measure the distance between the cities on the map in centimeters (4.5 cm). Then, have students measure the map's scale in centimeters. (600 km = 1.7 cm) **Ask:** How can you use this to find the distance between Paris and Stockholm? *(set up a proportion:*

$$\frac{600 \; km}{1.7 \; cm} = \frac{x}{4 \; cm}$$

$$x = \frac{600 \; km \times 4 \; cm}{1.7 \; cm}$$

$$x = 1,412 \; km) \; \boxed{OL}$$

R Reading Strategy

Reading Maps Ask: According to the map, what is the capital of Russia? *(St. Petersburg)* **Ask:** What major city is located southeast of Vienna? *(Budapest)* $\boxed{OL}$

Additional Support

Reading a Map

In addition to latitude and longitude, maps feature other important tools to help you interpret the information they contain. Learning to use these map tools will help you read the symbolic language of maps more easily.

Title
The title tells you what kind of information the map is showing.

Key
The **key** lists and explains the symbols, colors, and lines used on the map. The key is sometimes called a legend.

Scale Bar
The **scale bar** shows the relationship between map measurements and actual distances on the Earth. **S** By laying a ruler along the scale bar, you can calculate how many miles or kilometers are represented per inch or centimeter. The map projection used to create the map is often listed near the scale bar.

Compass Rose
The **compass rose** indicates directions. The four **cardinal directions**—north, south, east, and west—are usually indicated with arrows or the points of a star. The **intermediate directions**—northeast, northwest, southeast, and southwest—may also be shown.

Cities
Cities are represented by a dot. Sometimes the relative sizes of cities are shown using dots of different sizes.

Capitals
National capitals are often represented by a star within a circle.

Boundary Lines
On political maps of large areas, boundary lines highlight the borders between different countries or states.

GH8 Geography Handbook

Activity: Technology Connection

Contrasting Have students use an Internet mapping Web site to help them understand scale. Tell students to find a particular location, such as their school or home address. Then have them use the map's zoom function to help visualize the benefits of increasing and decreasing scale when viewing a location. **Ask:** To find the nearest lake, would you use a distant or a close view? *(distant view)* **Ask:** What view would show the names of neighboring streets? *(closer view)* Point out that a distant view corresponds to an increase in scale: it allows you to view a wider area but you cannot see much detail. Conversely, a close view corresponds to a decrease in scale: detail is increased, but the size of the area is diminished. $\boxed{OL}$

Using Scale

All maps are drawn to a certain scale. **Scale** is a consistent, proportional relationship between the measurements shown on the map and the measurement of the Earth's surface.

W **Small-Scale Maps** A small-scale map, like this political map of France, can show a large area but little detail. Note that the scale bar on this map indicates that about 1 inch is equal to 200 miles.

Large-Scale Maps A large-scale map, like this map of Paris, can show a small area with a great amount of detail. Study the scale bar. Note that the map measurements correspond to much smaller distances than on the map of France.

France: Political

The City of Paris

Absolute and Relative Location

D As you learned on page GH6, absolute location is the exact point where a line of latitude crosses a line of longitude. Another way to indicate location is by **relative location**, or the location of one place in relation to another. To find relative location,

find a reference point—a location you already know—on a map. Then look in the appropriate direction for the new location. For example, locate Paris (your reference point) on the map of France above. The relative location of Lyon can be described as southeast of Paris.

Practicing SKILLS

1. **Explain** the significance of: key, compass rose, cardinal directions, intermediate directions, scale bar, scale, relative location.

2. **Describe** the elements of a map that help you interpret the information displayed on the map.

3. **How** does the scale bar help you determine distances on the Earth's surface?

4. **Describe** the relative location of your school in two different ways.

5. **Use** a Venn diagram to identify the similarities and differences of small-scale maps and large-scale maps.

Small-scale maps ( ) Large-scale maps

Geography Handbook **GH9**

PRACTICING SKILLS

W Writing Support

Narrative Writing Have interested students research and write a story about a physical feature that affected history. Students can explore how mountain ranges and cliffs have served as protection, how frozen lakes and straits allowed for travel, or even how the construction of a canal changed transportation. **AL**

C Critical Thinking

Making Generalizations

Ask: What can relief and elevation tell you about rivers? *(Both elements give a sense of direction: water flows downhill so rivers flow from high elevation to lower elevation.)* **OL**

Physical Maps

W A **physical map** shows the location and the **topography,** or shape of the Earth's physical features. A study of a country's physical features often helps to explain the historical development of the country. For example, mountains may be barriers to transportation, and rivers and streams can provide access into the interior of a country.

Water Features

Physical maps show rivers, streams, lakes, and other water features.

Landforms

C Physical maps may show landforms such as mountains, plains, plateaus, and valleys.

Relief

Physical maps use shading and texture to show general **relief**—the differences in **elevation,** or height, of landforms.

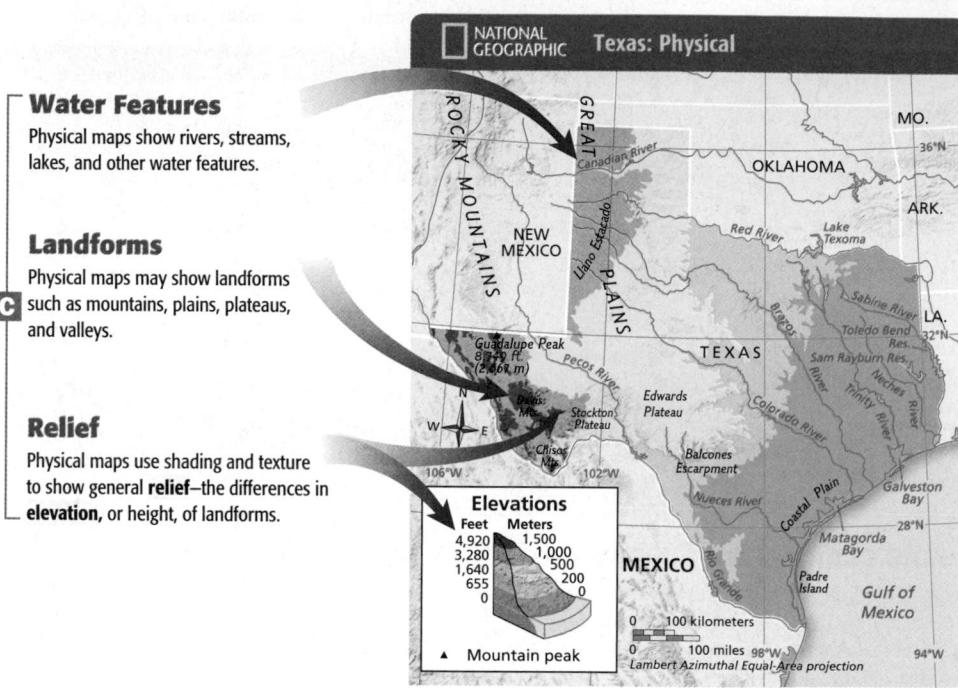

Practicing SKILLS

1. **Explain** the significance of: physical map, topography, relief, elevation.
2. **Complete** a table like the one to the right to explain what you can learn from the map about each of the physical features listed.

Physical Feature	What You Can Learn from the Map
Davis Mountains	
Red River	
Gulf Coastal Plains	

GH10 Geography Handbook

PRACTICING SKILLS

Answers

1. physical map: shows location and topography of Earth's physical features; topography: shape of Earth's physical features; relief: difference in elevation of landforms; elevation: height

2. Davis Mountains: location, elevation, length; Red River: location, length, route; Gulf Coastal Plains: location, elevation, length

Political Maps

A **political map** shows the boundaries and locations of political units such as countries, states, counties, cities, and towns. Many features depicted on a political map are **human-made,** or determined by humans **D** rather than by nature. Political maps can show the networks and links that exist within and between political units.

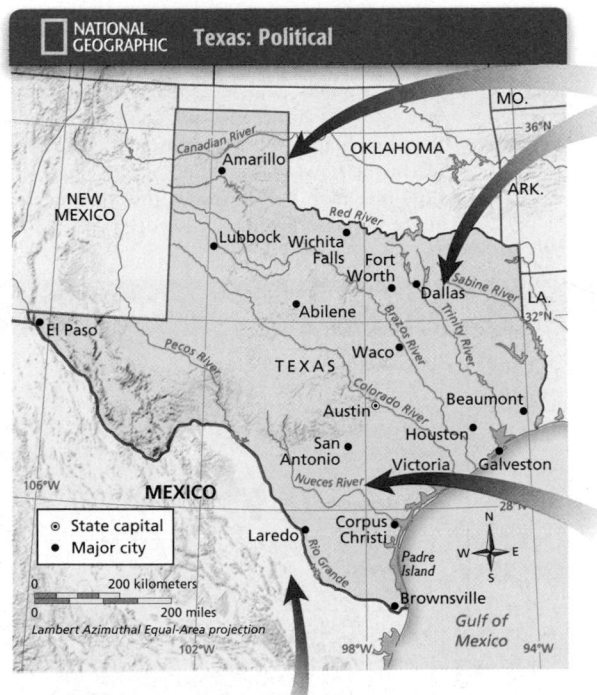

NATIONAL GEOGRAPHIC Texas: Political

Human-Made Features

Political maps show human-made features such as boundaries, capitals, cities, roads, highways, and railroads. **C**

Physical Features

Political maps may show some physical features such as relief, rivers, and mountains.

Nonsubject Area

Areas surrounding the subject area of the map are usually a different color to set them apart. They are labeled to give you a context for the area you are studying.

Practicing SKILLS

1. **Explain** the significance of: political map, human-made.
2. **What** types of information would you find on a political map that would not appear on a physical map?
3. **Complete** a table like the one to the right to explain what you can learn from the map about each of the human-made features listed.

Human-Made Feature	What You Can Learn from the Map
Austin	
El Paso	
Texas state boundary	

Geography Handbook **GH11**

PRACTICING SKILLS

Answers
1. political map: shows boundaries and locations of political units such as countries, states, counties, cities, and towns; human-made: determined by humans rather than nature

2. capitals, cities, roads, highways, railroads

3. Austin: location, that it is the capital city of Texas; El Paso: location; Texas state boundary: what states border Texas, what river forms its southern border

Thematic Maps

Maps that emphasize a single idea or a particular kind of information about an area are called **thematic maps**. There are many kinds of thematic maps, each designed to serve a different need. This textbook includes thematic maps that show exploration and trade, migration of peoples, economic activities, and war and political conflicts.

Qualitative Maps

Maps that use colors, symbols, lines, or dots to show information related to a specific idea are called **qualitative maps**. Such maps are often used to depict historical information. For example, the qualitative map below shows the primary exports of Latin America.

Flow-Line Maps

Maps that illustrate the movement of people, animals, goods, and ideas, as well as physical processes like hurricanes and glaciers, are called **flow-line maps**. Arrows are usually used to represent the flow and direction of movement. The flow-line map below shows the movement of Slavic peoples throughout Europe.

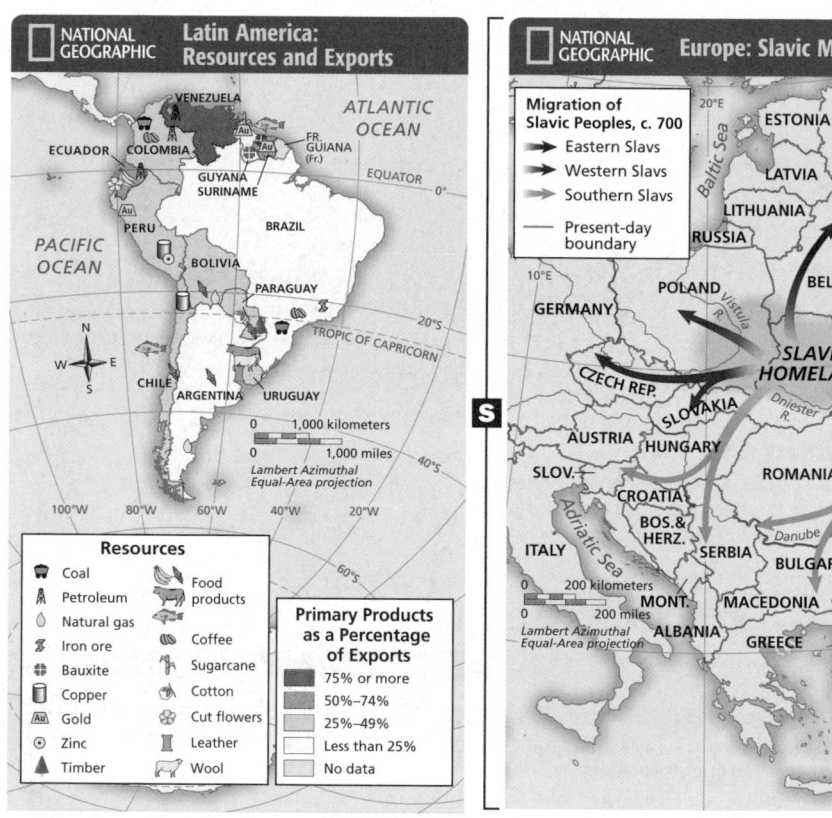

Activity: Collaborative Learning

Making Thematic Maps Divide the class into several groups. Each group will research a theme that interests them and create a thematic map to present to the class. Themes may be national (for example, a U.S. map showing the location of roller coasters or professional football stadiums) or local (for example, a city map displaying the location of public libraries or city parks). After groups choose their themes, each group should designate tasks (research, drawing maps, creating the presentation) among themselves so that each group member participates. Schedule a period for all the groups to present their maps to the class. **OL**

Geographic Information Systems

Modern technology has changed the way maps are made. Most cartographers use computers with software programs called **geographic information systems (GIS)**. A GIS is designed to accept data from different sources—maps, satellite images, printed text, and statistics. The GIS converts the data into a digital code, which arranges it in a database. Cartographers then program the GIS to process the data and produce maps. With GIS, each kind of information on a map is saved as a separate electronic layer.

1 *The first layer of information in a GIS pinpoints the area of interest. This allows the user to see, in detail, the area he or she needs to study. In this case, the area of study is a 5 mile (8 km) radius around Christ Hospital in Jersey City, New Jersey.*

2 *Additional layers of information are added based on the problem or issue being studied. In this case, hospital administrators want to find out about the population living in neighborhoods near the hospital so they can offer the community what it needs. A second layer showing African Americans who live within the 5 mile (8 km) radius has been added to the GIS.*

3 *Complex information can be presented using more than one layer. For example, the hospital's surrounding neighborhoods include other groups in addition to African Americans. A third layer showing whites who live within the 5 mile (8 km) radius has been added to the GIS. Administrators can now use this information to help them make decisions about staffing and services associated with the hospital.*

Practicing SKILLS

1. **Explain** the significance of: thematic map, qualitative maps, flow-line maps.

2. **Which** type of thematic map would best show the spread of Islam during Muhammad's time?

3. **Which** type of thematic map would best show average income per capita in the United States?

4. **How** does GIS allow cartographers to create maps and make changes to maps quickly and easily?

5. **Complete** a chart like the one below by identifying three examples of each type of thematic map found in this textbook. Note the page numbers of each.

Qualitative Maps	Flow-Line Maps

Geography Handbook   GH13

S Skill Practice

Visual Literacy Ask: How could you make GIS maps without a computer? *(You could draw the data on transparencies, and layer the transparencies.)* **OL**

Assess

Summarizing Have students work in pairs to make study cards for the Geography Handbook. Students can use main headings and subheadings to organize the section material. When the cards are finished, have students take turns testing each other on what they have learned. **OL**

Close

Identifying Ask: What are the four main types of maps? *(physical, political, qualitative, and flow-line)*

PRACTICING SKILLS

Answers

1. thematic map: emphasizes a single idea or particular kind of information about an area; qualitative map: uses colors, symbols, lines, or dots to show information related to a specific idea; flow-line map: illustrates movement of people, animals, goods, and ideas, as well as physical processes like hurricanes and glaciers

2. qualitative

3. flow-line

4. by allowing information to be stored and displayed on separate electronic layers

5. Answers will vary. Note that most maps in the text are qualitative maps; most climate maps are qualitative and flow-line.

Geographic Dictionary

Volcano
Mountain peak
Strait
Sound
Valley
Island
Cape
Ocean
Cliff
Isthmus
Bay
Harbor
Peninsula
Gulf
Delta
Seacoast

As you read about the history of the United States, you will encounter the terms listed below. Many of the terms are pictured in the diagram.

absolute location exact location of a place on the earth described by global coordinates

basin area of land drained by a given river and its branches; area of land surrounded by lands of higher elevations

bay part of a large body of water that extends into a shoreline, generally smaller than a gulf

canyon deep and narrow valley with steep walls

cape point of land that extends into a river, lake, or ocean

channel wide strait or waterway between two landmasses that lie close to each other; deep part of a river or other waterway

cliff steep, high wall of rock, earth, or ice

continent one of the seven large landmasses on the earth

cultural feature characteristic that humans have created in a place, such as language, religion, housing, and settlement pattern

delta flat, low-lying land built up from soil carried downstream by a river and deposited at its mouth

divide stretch of high land that separates river systems

downstream direction in which a river or stream flows from its source to its mouth

elevation height of land above sea level

Equator imaginary line that runs around the earth halfway between the North and South Poles; used as the starting point to measure degrees of north and south latitude

glacier large, thick body of slowly moving ice

gulf part of a large body of water that extends into a shoreline, generally larger and more deeply indented than a bay

harbor a sheltered place along a shoreline where ships can anchor safely

highland elevated land area such as a hill, mountain, or plateau

hill elevated land with sloping sides and rounded summit; generally smaller than a mountain

island land area, smaller than a continent, completely surrounded by water

isthmus narrow stretch of land connecting two larger land areas

lake a large inland body of water

latitude distance north or south of the Equator, measured in degrees

longitude distance east or west of the Prime Meridian, measured in degrees

lowland land, usually level, at a low elevation

map drawing of the earth shown on a flat surface

meridian one of many lines on the global grid running from the North Pole to the South Pole; used to measure degrees of longitude mesa broad, flat-topped landform with steep sides; smaller than a plateau

mountain land with steep sides that rises sharply (1,000 feet or more) from surrounding land; generally larger and more rugged than a hill

mountain peak pointed top of a mountain

mountain range a series of connected mountains

mouth (of a river) place where a stream or river flows into a larger body of water

ocean one of the four major bodies of salt water that surround the continents

ocean current stream of either cold or warm water that moves in a definite direction through an ocean

parallel one of many lines on the global grid that circle the earth north or south of the Equator; used to measure degrees of latitude

peninsula body of land jutting into a lake or ocean, surrounded on three sides by water

physical feature characteristic of a place occurring naturally, such as a landform, body of water, climate pattern, or resource

plain area of level land, usually at a low elevation and often covered with grasses

plateau large area of flat or rolling land at a high elevation, about 300–3,000 feet high

Prime Meridian line of the global grid running from the North Pole to the South Pole at Greenwich, England; starting point for measuring degrees of east and west longitude

relief changes in elevation over a given area of land

river large natural stream of water that runs through the land

sea large body of water completely or partly surrounded by land

seacoast land lying next to a sea or ocean

sea level position on land level with surface of nearby ocean or sea

sound body of water between a coastline and one or more islands off the coast

source (of a river) place where a river or stream begins, often in highlands

strait narrow stretch of water joining two larger bodies of water

tributary small river or stream that flows into a larger river or stream; a branch of the river

upstream direction opposite the flow of a river; toward the source of a river or stream

valley area of low land between hills or mountains

volcano mountain created as ash or liquid rock erupts from inside the earth

UNIT PACING CHART

		Unit 1	Chapter 1	Chapter 2	Chapter 3	Unit 1
Day 1	The American Vision Modern Times	Unit Opener	Chapter Opener	Chapter Opener	Chapter Opener	Wrap-Up/Project, Unit Assessment
Day 2	Introduction to The American Vision Modern Times		Section 1	Section 1	Section 1	
Day 3	Introduction to The American Vision Modern Times		Section 2	Section 2	Section 2	
Day 4			Section 3	Section 3	Section 3	
Day 5			Section 4	Section 4	Chapter Assessment	
Day 6			Chapter Assessment	Chapter Assessment		

Teacher to Teacher

**Kelly Baker
Cleveland Hill
High School
Cheektowaga,
New York**

Role Play and Debate Divide your class into two groups. One group will be representatives of Great Britain. The other group will act as leaders of the colony. In this activity, the members of each group will work together to draft a letter to the other side. Britain's representatives will explain to the colonists why they must obey the laws enacted by Parliament. They should outline the benefits of British rule and highlight any sacrifices they made for the benefit of the colony. The group representing colonial leaders should focus on the negative impacts of imperialism on the colonists. They should try to convince Britain to free them. Once the letters have been drafted, each group will present their letters and then debate the issues.

Author Note

Dear American History Teacher,

As you begin to teach this unit, there are themes that recur that you will want to point out to students.

Developments in politics, social life, religion, and the economy laid the foundation for the United States. The significant nation-building acts like declaring independence, winning a war with Great Britain, securing a fair peace treaty, and writing a new constitution are the most salient events in this period. Yet students need to know how ordinary Americans reacted to their new status as Americans rather than subjects of the King of England. For many, the new freedom prompted them to move west. Others, particularly young people, seized opportunities to leave their family farm and take up occupations like teaching school or tending a store. The huge debt incurred in fighting the war and the closure of many trades based in Great Britain affected everyone.

Most observers did not expect that the thirteen original states that formed the Confederation would be able to strengthen the ties that bound them together. Students should realize just how difficult it was to forge the compromises necessary to form a new nation. The Constitution created citizens of the United States and the Bill of Rights made explicit the liberties the Americans had fought for.

Not everyone benefited from these decades of change and innovation. Native Americans were forced to move farther West as white settlers sought land in the unsettled parts of the country. Although the Revolution was fought in the name of natural rights, enslaved men and women, who composed a fifth of the nation's population, did not receive their freedom. Soon, the cultivation of cotton would make slavery's shackles stronger. Women, by and large, had a slightly wider ambit for their ambitions. This is one of the most exciting periods in American history. Students can feel this if they are taught about the daunting challenges the country faced.

Joyce Appleby
Senior Author

Focus

Why It Matters

Have students consider how life might be different if the thirteen colonies had not won the Revolutionary War, but had remained a part of the British Empire. Then have them make generalizations about what their lives would be like today if they lived under British rule. **OL**

Connecting to Past Learning

Have students list the names of any of the nation's Founders on the board. **Ask:** What challenges did these leaders face during the American Revolution and after the American victory? *(Answers may include: the Revolutionary army was untrained; there was no money to pay soldiers; the British army and navy were the most powerful in the world; trade with other countries was cut off; there was no central government in place.)* Tell students that in this unit they will learn about how the United States grew from thirteen colonies to a powerful nation torn by the Civil War. **OL**

Unit Launch Activity

Making Connections Have students brainstorm a list of goods or services that government today provides. List students' answers on the board. Then identify which of these goods and services were not provided by the government in 1776. **Ask:** How would your life have been different without the government supplying these goods or services? *(Answers will vary.)* **OL**

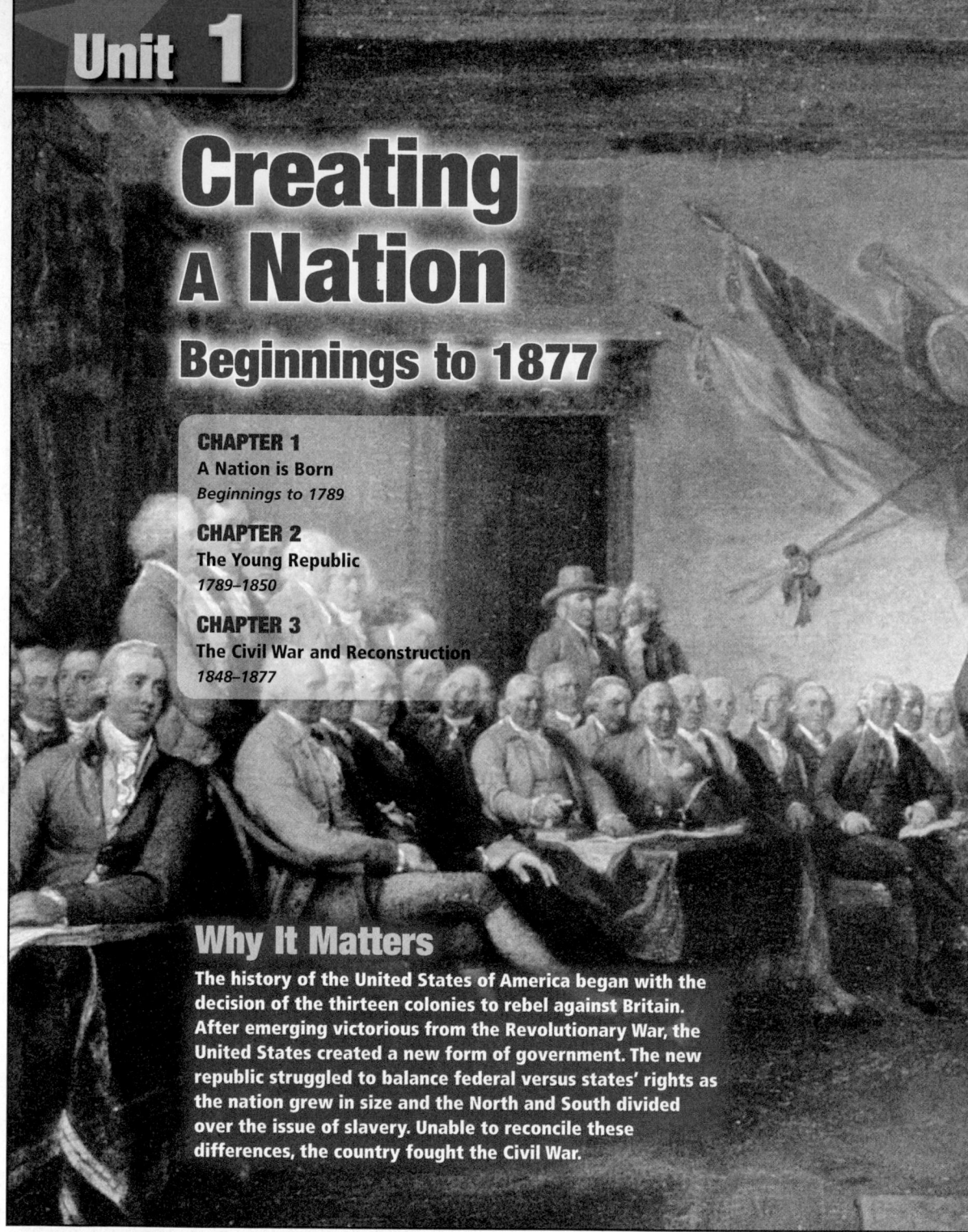

Creating A Nation
Beginnings to 1877

CHAPTER 1
A Nation is Born
Beginnings to 1789

CHAPTER 2
The Young Republic
1789–1850

CHAPTER 3
The Civil War and Reconstruction
1848–1877

Why It Matters

The history of the United States of America began with the decision of the thirteen colonies to rebel against Britain. After emerging victorious from the Revolutionary War, the United States created a new form of government. The new republic struggled to balance federal versus states' rights as the nation grew in size and the North and South divided over the issue of slavery. Unable to reconcile these differences, the country fought the Civil War.

Team Teaching Activity

Economics Have the economics teacher compare and contrast the small family farms of the colonial era with the large agricultural enterprises of today. After the presentation, have a class discussion using the following questions: How are workers treated differently in the two different types of farms? How do the different types of enterprises affect family life? How does the type of farm in which your family might be involved affect where and how you live? **OL**

Signing the Declaration of Independence

1

Teach

S1 Skill Practice

Visual Literacy Have students study the painting. **Ask:** Why do you think the artist, John Trumbull, chose to have Thomas Jefferson holding the Declaration as it is given to John Hancock? *(Jefferson wrote the Declaration.)* **BL**

S2 Skill Practice

Describing Have students again review the painting. **Ask:** What feelings or emotions was the artist attempting to evoke from people who view the painting? *(Answers might include pride, patriotism, and nationalism.)* **OL**

NCLB NO CHILD LEFT BEHIND

Teaching Tip The NCLB Act emphasizes reading. Ask students to write down events and people they will encounter in this unit and keep the list with them as they read. When students find a person or item on the list, they should note the page number and write a brief summary. Students can use this list while studying.

More About the Painting

"The Declaration of Independence," painted by John Trumbull depicts John Adams, Roger Sherman, Robert Livingston, Thomas Jefferson, and Benjamin Franklin presenting the Declaration of Independence to John Hancock, the president of the Continental Congress. The event, as shown, did not actually occur. According to Trumbull, the painting was meant "to preserve the resemblance of the men who were the authors of this memorable act." The 12- by 18-foot painting was commissioned in 1817 and placed in the Capitol Rotunda in 1826.

1

Chapter 1 Planning Guide

Levels (BL OL AL ELL)					Resources	Chapter Opener	Section 1	Section 2	Section 3	Section 4	Chapter Assess
					FOCUS						
BL	OL	AL	ELL	🖨	Daily Focus Skills Transparencies		1-1	1-2	1-3	1-4	
					TEACH						
BL	OL		ELL	📁	Reading Essentials and Note-Taking Guide*		p. 1	p. 4	p. 7	p. 10	
	OL	AL		📁	History Simulations and Problem Solving, URB			p. 9			
BL	OL		ELL	📁	Reading Skills Activity, URB					p. 21	
	OL			📁	Historical Analysis Skills Activity, URB				p. 22		
BL	OL	AL	ELL	📁	Differentiated Instruction Activity, URB				p. 23		
BL	OL		ELL	📁	English Learner Activity, URB					p. 25	
BL	OL	AL	ELL	📁	Content Vocabulary Activity, URB*		p. 27				
BL	OL	AL	ELL	📁	Academic Vocabulary Activity, URB		p. 29				
	OL	AL		📁	Reinforcing Skills Activity, URB				p. 31		
	OL	AL		📁	Critical Thinking Skills Activity, URB					p. 32	
BL	OL		ELL	📁	Time Line Activity, URB				p. 33		
	OL			📁	Linking Past and Present Activity, URB				p. 34		
BL	OL	AL	ELL	📁	Primary Source Reading, URB				p. 35	p. 37	
BL	OL	AL	ELL	📁	American Art and Music Activity, URB				p. 39		
BL	OL	AL	ELL	📁	Interpreting Political Cartoons Activity, URB			p. 41			
		AL		📁	Enrichment Activity, URB					p. 44	
BL	OL		ELL	📁	Guided Reading Activity, URB*		p. 46	p. 47	p. 48	p. 49	
BL	OL	AL	ELL	📁	Differentiated Instruction for the American High School Classroom	✓	✓	✓	✓	✓	✓
BL	OL	AL	ELL	🖨	Unit Map Overlay Transparencies	✓	✓	✓	✓	✓	✓
BL	OL	AL	ELL	📁	Unit Time Line Transparencies, Strategies, and Activities	✓	✓	✓	✓	✓	✓
BL	OL	AL	ELL	📁	Cause and Effect Transparencies, Strategies, and Activities	✓	✓	✓	✓	✓	✓
BL	OL	AL	ELL	📁	Why It Matters Transparencies, Strategies, and Activities	✓	✓	✓	✓	✓	✓
BL	OL	AL	ELL	📁	American Biographies	✓	✓	✓	✓	✓	✓

Note: Please refer to the *Unit 1 Resource Book* for this chapter's URB materials.

* Also available in Spanish

- Interactive Lesson Planner
- Interactive Teacher Edition
- Fully editable blackline masters
- Section Spotlight Videos Launch
- Differentiated Lesson Plans
- Printable reports of daily assignments
- Standards Tracking System

Levels BL OL AL ELL		Resources	Chapter Opener	Section 1	Section 2	Section 3	Section 4	Chapter Assess
TEACH *(continued)*								
BL OL AL ELL	📁	**The Living Constitution**	✓	✓	✓	✓	✓	✓
BL OL AL ELL	📁	**American Issues**	✓	✓	✓	✓	✓	✓
OL AL ELL	📁	**American Art and Architecture Transparencies, Strategies, and Activities**	✓	✓	✓	✓	✓	✓
BL OL AL	📁	**High School American History Literature Library**	✓	✓	✓	✓	✓	✓
OL AL	💿	**American History Primary Source Documents Library**	✓	✓	✓	✓	✓	✓
BL OL AL ELL	💿	**American Music Hits Through History CD**	✓	✓	✓	✓	✓	✓
BL OL AL ELL	💾	**StudentWorks™ Plus DVD**	✓	✓	✓	✓	✓	✓
BL OL AL ELL	💿	**Vocabulary PuzzleMaker CD-ROM**	✓	✓	✓	✓	✓	✓
BL OL AL ELL	💾	***The American Vision* Video Program DVD**	✓	✓	✓	✓	✓	✓
Teacher Resources	📁	**Reading Strategies and Activities for the Social Studies Classroom**	✓	✓	✓	✓	✓	✓
	📁	**Strategies for Success**	✓	✓	✓	✓	✓	✓
	💾	**Presentation Plus! DVD**	✓	✓	✓	✓	✓	✓
	📁	**Success with English Learner**	✓	✓	✓	✓	✓	✓
ASSESS								
BL OL AL ELL	📁	**Section Quizzes and Chapter Tests***		p. 5	p. 6	p. 7	p. 8	p. 9
BL OL AL ELL	📁	**Authentic Assessment With Rubrics**						p. 7
BL OL AL ELL	📁	**Standardized Test Practice Workbook**						p. 1
BL OL AL ELL	💿	***ExamView*® Assessment Suite CD-ROM**		1-1	1-2	1-3	1-4	Ch. 1
BL OL AL ELL	💿	**Interactive Tutor Self-Assessment CD-ROM**		1-1	1-2	1-3	1-4	Ch. 1
CLOSE								
BL ELL	📁	**Reteaching Activity, URB**						p. 43
BL OL ELL	📁	**Reading and Study Skills Foldables™**	p. 45					
BL OL AL ELL	📁	***American History* in Graphic Novel**						p. 1

Using the McGraw-Hill Learning Network

Researching World Book™ Select

Technology Product

World Book Select offers thousands of detailed articles chosen from the *World Book Encyclopedia* and covers all curricular areas. World Book Select allows students to research national and international topics and issues in economics and other curriculum areas.

Objectives

After students learn to use World Book Select, they will be able to
- develop and expand research and study skills;
- practice reading and writing skills.

Steps

Give students the following directions to use World Book Select:
- From the McGraw-Hill Learning Network home page (www.mhln.com), click on **For Students**.
- Choose **World Book Select** below **Homework Help**.

- Click the letter for the encyclopedia volume you want to use.
- On the search page for the volume selected:
  - Click the title of a featured article on the right side of the page; or
  - Click on a topic from the list on the left side of the page; then click on the title of an article of interest on the right.
- Read the article and take notes.

History ONLINE

	Student	Teacher	Parent
Beyond the Textbook	●	●	●
Chapter Overviews	●	●	●
Time Current Events	●		●
ePuzzles and Games	●		●
Concepts in Motion	●		●
Literature Connections		●	
Multi-Language Glossaries	●		●
Online Student Edition	●	●	●
Self-Check Quizzes	●		●
Student Web Activities	●		●
Study Central™	●		●
Teaching Today		●	
Vocabulary eFlashcards	●		●
Web Activity Lesson Plans		●	

Glencoe Media Center

glencoe.com

> **Study-To-Go**
> - Vocabulary eFlashcards
> - Self-Check Quizzes

> **Audio/Video**
> - Student Edition Audio
> - Spanish Summaries
> - Section Videos

- **Timed Readings Plus in Social Studies** helps students increase their reading rate and fluency while maintaining comprehension. The 400-word passages are similar to those found on state and national assessments.

- **Reading in the Content Area: Social Studies** concentrates on six essential reading skills that help students better comprehend what they read. The book includes 75 high-interest nonfiction passages written at increasing levels of difficulty.

- **Reading Social Studies** includes strategic reading instruction and vocabulary support in Social Studies content for both ELLs and native speakers of English.

www.jamestowneducation.com

Index to National Geographic Magazine:

The following articles relate to this chapter:

- "Search for Columbus" by Bob Sacha and Eugene Lyons, January 1992.
- "James Madison: Architect of the Constitution" by Alice J. Hall, September 1987.

National Geographic Society Products To order the following, call National Geographic at 1-800-368-2728:

- *The American Revolution* (PicturePack Transparencies)

Access National Geographic's new, dynamic MapMachine Web site and other geography resources at:

www.nationalgeographic.com
www.nationalgeographic.com/maps

The following videotape programs are available from Glencoe as supplements to Modern Times Chapter 1:

- Christopher Columbus: Explorer of the New World (ISBN 1-56-501667-X)
- The Age of Exploration (ISBN 0-02-822814-6)

To order, call Glencoe at 1-800-334-7344. To find classroom resources to accompany many of these videos, check the following home pages:

A&E Television: www.aetv.com
The History Channel: www.historychannel.com

Reading List Generator CD-ROM

BOOKLINK 3

Use this database to search more than 30,000 titles to create a customized reading list for your students.

- Reading lists can be organized by students' reading level, author, genre, theme, or area of interest.
- The database provides Degrees of Reading Power™ (DRP) and Lexile™ readability scores for all selections.
- A brief summary of each selection is included.

Leveled reading suggestions for this chapter:

For students at a Grade 8 reading level:
- *The Journal of Jesse Smoke: A Cherokee Boy*, by Joseph Bruchac

For students at a Grade 9 reading level:
- *The Rebel*, by John Jakes

For students at a Grade 10 reading level:
- *Abigail Adams: Witness to a Revolution,* by Natalie S. Bober

For students at a Grade 11 reading level:
- *The United States Constitution,* by Kristal Leebrick

For students at a Grade 12 reading level:
- *The Iroquois Constitution,* by Dekanawida

Focus

MAKING CONNECTIONS
Why Do People Rebel?
Ask students to suggest what conditions may cause people to take action against their government, or to move their families to another country they have never seen. **OL**

Teach
The Big Ideas

As students study the chapter, remind them to consider the section-based Big Ideas included in each section's Guide to Reading. The **Essential Questions** in the activities below tie in to the Big Ideas and help students think about and understand important chapter concepts. In addition, the Hands-on Chapter Projects with their culminating activities relate the content from each section to the Big Ideas. These activities build on each other as students progress through the chapter. Section activities culminate in the wrap-up activity on the Visual Summary page.

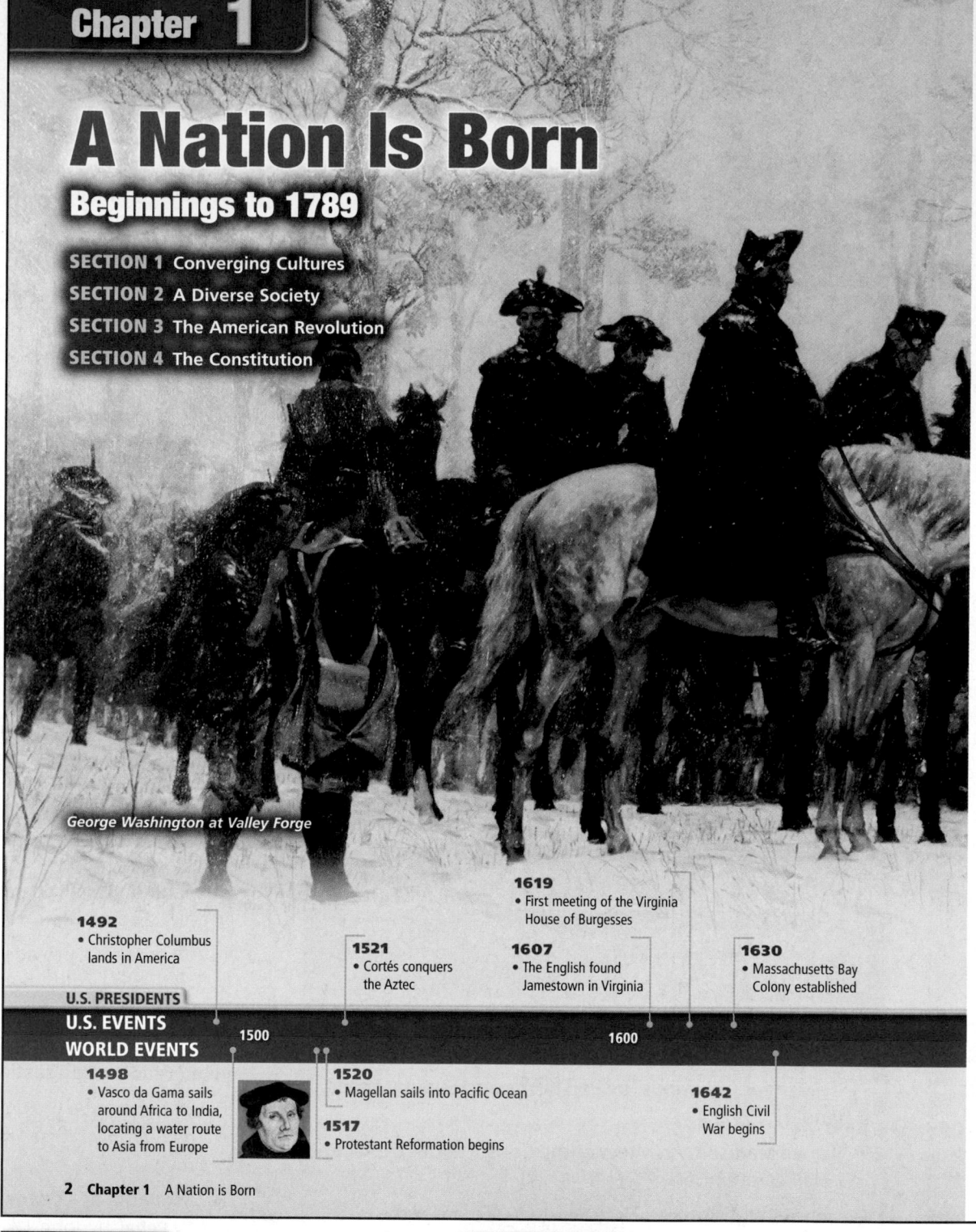

Chapter 1

A Nation Is Born
Beginnings to 1789

SECTION 1 Converging Cultures
SECTION 2 A Diverse Society
SECTION 3 The American Revolution
SECTION 4 The Constitution

George Washington at Valley Forge

1492
• Christopher Columbus lands in America

1521
• Cortés conquers the Aztec

1607
• The English found Jamestown in Virginia

1619
• First meeting of the Virginia House of Burgesses

1630
• Massachusetts Bay Colony established

U.S. PRESIDENTS
U.S. EVENTS
WORLD EVENTS

1500

1600

1498
• Vasco da Gama sails around Africa to India, locating a water route to Asia from Europe

1517
• Protestant Reformation begins

1520
• Magellan sails into Pacific Ocean

1642
• English Civil War begins

2   Chapter 1   A Nation is Born

Section 1

Converging Cultures
Essential Question: How did contact among the cultures of three continents change the society of each culture? Tell students that in this section they will learn about early civilizations that existed in the Americas before European immigrants arrived, as well as the new forms of government the colonists established. **OL**

Section 2

A Diverse Society
Essential Question: How did new ideas and religious fervor brought to the colonies by increased immigration affect settlers' attitudes toward slavery and women's rights? Tell students that in this section they will learn about the effects of increased trade and immigration on the colonies. **OL**

MAKING CONNECTIONS
Why Do People Rebel?

Even today, Americans grow frustrated when the government raises taxes. In the early colonial era, Americans grew accustomed to running their own affairs. So when Britain tried to reestablish control, tensions mounted over taxes and basic rights.

- *Why do you think colonists became angry at Britain?*
- *When do you think it is acceptable to rebel against a government?*

Focus
More About the Art

This famous painting from the Library of Congress is by Percy Moran (1862–1935). It depicts General Washington inspecting the 11,000 members of the Continental Army camped at Valley Forge, Pennsylvania, from December 1777 to June 1778. Because of the suffering they endured there—hungry, poorly clothed, and badly housed—Valley Forge came to symbolize the heroism of the American revolutionaries. Some 2,500 died during the harsh winter. Washington is quoted as having said, "…you might have tracked the army from White Marsh to Valley Forge by the blood of their feet." The troops included free African Americans and Oneida Native Americans.

FOLDABLES

Generalizing on the American Revolution Create a Concept-Map Book Foldable that details the causes and the course of the American Revolutionary War. Select the most important causes of the war and list them inside one-half of the Concept-Map. Use the other half to list the outcomes of battles during the war.

Concept map diagram: °American°Revolution — Causes of the War | Course of the War

History ONLINE Chapter Overview
Visit glencoe.com to preview Chapter 1.

FOLDABLES Study Organizer **Dinah Zike's Foldables**

Dinah Zike's Foldables are three-dimensional, interactive graphic organizers that help students practice basic writing skills, review vocabulary terms, and identify main ideas. Instructions for creating and using Foldables can be found in the Appendix at the end of this book and in the *Dinah Zike's Reading and Study Skills Foldables* booklet.

1788
- Constitution of the United States ratified

1776
- Declaration of Independence signed

Washington 1789–1797

1754
- French and Indian War begins

1700

1800

1688
- Glorious Revolution establishes limited monarchy in England

1748
- Montesquieu's *The Spirit of Laws* published

1776
- Adam Smith's treatise on mercantilism, *Wealth of Nations*, published

1789
- French Revolution begins

Chapter 1 A Nation is Born **3**

Section 3

The American Revolution
Essential Question: What led to the American Revolution and the establishment of the United States? *(A series of restrictions and reprisals established by the British on their American colonies led to increased tensions and rebellion.)* Explain that in Section 3, students will learn how relations between Britain and its colonies deteriorated further, leading to rebellion and the colonists' formation of their own, independent government. **OL**

Section 4

The Constitution
Essential Question: What provisions in the Constitution have made it an enduring framework for government? *(Answers may include checks and balances; a bill of rights)* Point out that in Section 4 students will learn how the Framers of the Constitution compromised to create a new form of government that included a system of checks and balances, and a balance of power between the states and the federal government. **OL**

History ONLINE
Introduce students to chapter content and key terms by having them access the Chapter 1 Overview at glencoe.com.

3

Focus

Bellringer
Daily Focus Transparency 1.1

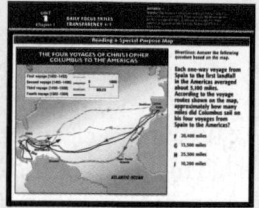

Guide to Reading

Answers:
Students will create an outline using the section headings.

Section Spotlight Video

To generate interest and provide a springboard for class discussion, access the Chapter 1, Section 1 video at glencoe.com or on the video DVD.

Resource Manager

Converging Cultures

Guide to Reading

Big Ideas
Government and Society European settlers established colonies in land inhabited by Native Americans and developed new forms of government.

Content Vocabulary
- joint-stock company *(p. 8)*
- Pilgrim *(p. 8)*
- subsistence farming *(p. 10)*
- proprietary colony *(p. 11)*
- indentured servant *(p. 12)*

Academic Vocabulary
- cultures *(p. 4)*
- immigrate *(p. 8)*

People and Events to Identify
- Jamestown *(p. 8)*
- William Penn *(p. 11)*

Reading Strategy
Taking Notes As you read about the early settlements of America, use the section headings to create an outline similar to the one below.

```
Discovery and Settlement
I.  The Earliest Americans
    A. Early Civilizations in America
    B.
    C.
II. European Exploration
    A.
    B.
    C.
III.
IV.
V.
```

While a number of civilizations flourished in the Americas, Europeans looking for trade routes began settling in the region. Their colonies developed different forms of government, and many depended on slave labor.

The Earliest Americans

MAIN Idea Native Americans adapted to their environments and developed diverse cultures.

HISTORY AND YOU Do you remember getting used to a new school? Read to learn how the first American settlers adapted to their new environments.

No one knows exactly when the first people arrived in America. Scientists have pieced together many clues by studying the Earth's geology and the items left by early humans. Such studies proved that people were here at least 10,000 years ago. More recent research, however, suggests that our ancestors may have arrived much earlier—between 15,000 and 30,000 years ago.

These newcomers to America were probably nomads, people who continually move from place to place. With time, Native Americans learned how to plant and raise crops. The shift to agriculture led to the first permanent villages and to new building methods. As early societies became more complex, civilizations emerged. A civilization is a highly organized society marked by advanced knowledge of trade, government, the arts, science, and, often, written language.

Early Civilizations in America

Anthropologists think the earliest civilization in the Americas arose between 1500 B.C. and 1200 B.C. among the Olmec people in southern Mexico. The Maya and the Aztec later developed their own civilizations in Central America, building impressive temples and pyramids and establishing trade networks. Many anthropologists believe that the agricultural technology of Mesoamerica eventually spread north into the American Southwest and beyond. Around A.D. 300, the Hohokam began farming in what is today Arizona. They and another nearby people, the Anasazi, were able to grow crops in the dry Southwest by building elaborate irrigation systems.

About the time of the early Olmec civilization, the people in North America's eastern woodlands were developing their own **cultures.** The Hopewell built huge geometric earthworks that served as ceremonial centers, observatories, and burial places. Between A.D. 700 and 900, the Mississippian people in the Mississippi River valley created Cahokia, one of the largest early American cities.

R Reading Strategies	**C** Critical Thinking	**D** Differentiated Instruction	**W** Writing Support	**S** Skill Practice
Teacher Edition • Naming, p. 5 • Sequencing, p. 8 • Contrasting, p. 10 • Organizing, p. 11 **Additional Resources** • History Simulations and Prob. Solv. Act., URB p. 9 • Guid. Read. Act., URB p. 46	**Teacher Edition** • Predicting, p. 6 • Analyzing, p. 12 **Additional Resources** • Quizzes/Tests, p. 5	**Teacher Edition** • Kinesthetic, p. 10 • Visual, p. 11	**Teacher Edition** • Personal, p. 8 • Persuasive, p. 13 **Additional Resources** • Content Vocabulary Act., URB p. 27 • Academic Vocabulary Act., URB p. 29	**Teacher Edition** • Drawing Concl., p. 6 • Detecting Bias, p. 7 • Analyzing, p. 9 • Conducting Research, p. 12 **Additional Resources** • Reading Essen., p. 1

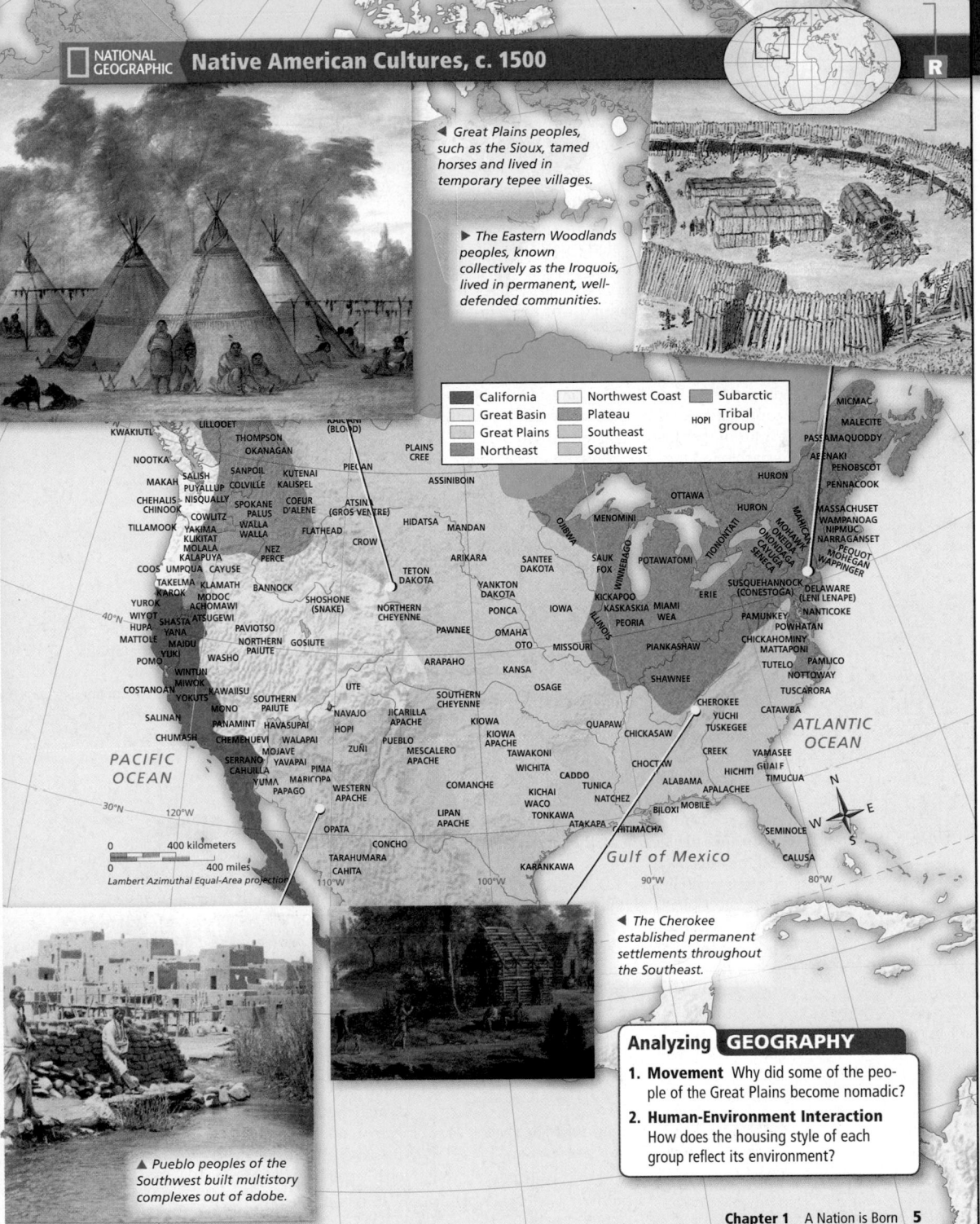

◀ Great Plains peoples, such as the Sioux, tamed horses and lived in temporary tepee villages.

▶ The Eastern Woodlands peoples, known collectively as the Iroquois, lived in permanent, well-defended communities.

California	Northwest Coast	Subarctic
Great Basin	Plateau	Tribal group
Great Plains	Southeast	HOPI
Northeast	Southwest	

KWAKIUTL LILLOOET KAIKANI (BLOOD)
THOMPSON OKANAGAN PLAINS CREE MICMAC
NOOTKA SANPOIL KUTENAI PIEGAN MALECITE
MAKAH SALISH COLVILLE KALISPEL ASSINIBOIN PASSAMAQUODDY
CHEHALIS PUYALLUP NISQUALLY SPOKANE COEUR D'ALENE ATSINA (GROS VENTRE) HURON ABENAKI PENOBSCOT
CHINOOK COWLITZ PALUS HIDATSA MANDAN OTTAWA HURON PENNACOOK
TILLAMOOK YAKIMA WALLA WALLA FLATHEAD MENOMINI MASSACHUSET WAMPANOAG
KLIKITAT MOLALA NEZ PERCE CROW ARIKARA SANTEE DAKOTA OJIBWA WINNEBAGO MAHICAN MOHAWK ONEIDA NIPMUC NARRAGANSET
KALAPUYA COOS UMPQUA CAYUSE TETON DAKOTA SAUK FOX POTAWATOMI ONONDAGA CAYUGA SENECA PEQUOT MOHEGAN WAPPINGER
TAKELMA KLAMATH BANNOCK YANKTON DAKOTA KICKAPOO ERIE SUSQUEHANNOCK (CONESTOGA) DELAWARE (LENI LENAPE)
YUROK KAROK MODOC ACHOMAWI SHOSHONE (SNAKE) NORTHERN CHEYENNE PONCA IOWA KASKASKIA MIAMI WEA NANTICOKE
WIYOT SHASTA ATSUGEWI PAVIOTSO ILLINOIS PEORIA PAMUNKEY POWHATAN
HUPA YANA MAIDU NORTHERN PAIUTE GOSIUTE PAWNEE OMAHA PIANKASHAW CHICKAHOMINY MATTAPONI
MATTOLE YUKI WASHO ARAPAHO OTO MISSOURI TUTELO PAMLICO
POMO WINTUN MIWOK KAWAIISU UTE KANSAS SHAWNEE NOTTOWAY
COSTANOAN YOKUTS SOUTHERN PAIUTE OSAGE CHEROKEE TUSCARORA
SALINAN MONO NAVAJO JICARILLA APACHE SOUTHERN CHEYENNE QUAPAW YUCHI TUSKEGEE CATAWBA
CHUMASH CHEMEHUEVI WALAPAI HOPI KIOWA CHICKASAW CREEK YAMASEE
PACIFIC OCEAN MOJAVE YAVAPAI ZUÑI PUEBLO KIOWA APACHE MESCALERO APACHE TAWAKONI HICHITI GUALE ATLANTIC OCEAN
SERRANO CAHUILLA PIMA WICHITA CADDO ALABAMA TIMUCUA
YUMA MARICOPA PAPAGO WESTERN APACHE COMANCHE KICHAI WACO TUNICA NATCHEZ APALACHEE
LIPAN APACHE TONKAWA BILOXI MOBILE
OPATA ATAKAPA CHITIMACHA SEMINOLE
CONCHO KARANKAWA CALUSA
TARAHUMARA CAHITA Gulf of Mexico

0 400 kilometers
0 400 miles
Lambert Azimuthal Equal-Area projection

120°W 110°W 100°W 90°W 80°W
40°N 30°N

N S E W

◀ The Cherokee established permanent settlements throughout the Southeast.

▲ Pueblo peoples of the Southwest built multistory complexes out of adobe.

Analyzing GEOGRAPHY

1. **Movement** Why did some of the people of the Great Plains become nomadic?
2. **Human-Environment Interaction** How does the housing style of each group reflect its environment?

Teach

R Reading Strategy

Naming Make a game of relating contemporary language to Native American languages. Tell students they will have three minutes to write a list of place names or other words currently in use that derive from Native American words. They may use the map on this page, a dictionary, and their own knowledge to list as many words as possible. After three minutes, have each student read one of the words he or she listed. Everyone who used that word should cross it off his or her list. The person who has the most words on the list that no one else thought of wins the game. **OL**

Analyzing GEOGRAPHY

Answers:
1. They followed their source of food: the buffalo.
2. Each group used local materials, such as hides from buffalo on the plains or wooden houses and stockades in the eastern woodlands.

Hands-On Chapter Project
Step 1

From Colonies to Independence

Step 1: Establishing Colonies in North America Working in small groups, students will list criteria and then research and map the landforms, resources, and people on the east coast of North America to determine where to establish a new colony.
Essential Question: What do colonists need to know about North America to create a successful colony?

Directions Organize students into small groups. Have them assume the role of English people living in about 1600. Using information from the chapter as well as library or Internet resources, each group of students will explore what area of North America is most likely to sustain a colony.

Students should first make a list of criteria for a successful colony. For example, a colony will need a source of water, food, building materials, and be in a defensible location. Next, students should use their research to create a map indicating the locations of the resources on their list of criteria as well as any major landforms. Students should then determine the exact location where they wish to establish their colony.

Summarizing Allow time for the groups to reach an agreement on the location of the colony. Then have representatives for each group share the chosen location with the class and summarize the benefits and challenges of settling there. **OL**
(Chapter Project continued on page 17)

5

C Critical Thinking

Predicting Discuss with the class the personal qualities of explorers. **Ask:** If Cortés, Pizarro, and Columbus were alive today, what do you think they would explore? *(Answers will vary, but may include space, medical research, environmental technologies, and other ideas.)* **OL AL**

S Skill Practice

Drawing Conclusions
Mention several cultures that have disappeared. Have students research them or others to find out why they disappeared. **Ask:** What happened to these cultures? *(Answers will vary, but should demonstrate thorough research and thought.)* **AL**

✓ Reading Check

Answer:
Native Americans living in areas with long growing seasons and fertile soil grew crops and tended to remain in the same areas; those living in harsh climates hunted wildlife, and some became nomadic in order to hunt herds.

Additional Support

History ONLINE
Student Web Activity Visit glencoe.com and complete the activity on American prehistory.

 For an example of Native American storytelling, read the selections on pages R64–R65 in the **American Literature Library.**

Native American Cultural Diversity

In the Eastern Woodlands, most Native Americans combined hunting and fishing with farming. Many different groups lived in the Eastern Woodlands, but most spoke either Algonquian or Iroquoian languages.

In the Southeast, the Cherokee were the largest group. They, along with the Creek, Choctaw, Natchez, and others, generally built wooden stockades around their villages for protection. Women did most of the farming, while men hunted deer, bear, and alligator.

In the Southwest, the Hohokam and the Anasazi eventually disappeared, but their descendants, including the Zuni and the Hopi, continued to farm corn, beans, and cotton. Around the 1500s, two other groups—the Apache and the Navajo—came to the Southwest. The Navajo settled in farming villages, but many of the Apache remained nomadic hunters.

Hunting also sustained the Sioux and other peoples who lived on the western Great Plains. They followed buffalo herds and camped in tepees that they could easily set up, dismantle, and carry.

Along the Pacific Coast, the Northwest was home to fishing peoples like the Kwakiutls and the Chinook. They caught the plentiful salmon, built wooden houses and canoes, and crafted ceremonial totem poles from the trunks of redwood and cedar trees. To the south, in what is today central California, groups such as the Pomo trapped small game and gathered acorns. Farther inland lived other hunter-gatherer groups like the Nez Perce, the Yakima, the Ute, and the Shoshone.

Meanwhile, in the Far North region from Alaska to Greenland, the Inuit and the Aleut hunted seals, walruses, whales, polar bears, and caribou. They adapted to their harsh environment by inventing tools such as the harpoon, kayak, dogsled, and oil lamp.

By the 1500s, Native Americans had established a wide array of cultures and languages. They had also developed economies and lifestyles suited to their particular environments.

✓ Reading Check **Explaining** How did climate and food sources help shape Native American lifestyles?

European Explorations

MAIN Idea European countries began to explore the world and established colonies in the Americas.

HISTORY AND YOU Have you tried new foods from other parts of the world? Read about the exchange of foods after European explorations.

As the people of Europe emerged from the Middle Ages, they became interested in Asia, the source of spices, perfumes, fine silks, and jewels. Rulers of Portugal, Spain, France, and England wanted to find a sailing route to Asia that would bypass the merchants and traders from Italy and the Middle East.

Columbus's Voyages

While Portugal took the lead in searching for a sea route around Africa to Asia in the early 1400s, Spain funded an expedition by Christopher Columbus, an Italian sea captain, to sail west across the Atlantic Ocean. In August 1492 Columbus and his crew set off in three ships—the *Niña*, the *Pinta*, and the *Santa Maria*. After a harrowing voyage, they landed on present-day San Salvador Island and then explored other islands in the Caribbean. Columbus claimed the new lands for Spain, believing all the time that he was in Asia.

When Columbus returned home to Europe with the news he had reached land on the other side of the Atlantic, he triggered a wave of European exploration and settlement of North and South America.

Continuing Expeditions

Europeans soon realized that Columbus had not reached Asia but a part of the globe unknown to Europeans. They named the new continent America in honor of Amerigo Vespucci, who explored the South American coastline for Portugal.

The 1494 Treaty of Tordesillas confirmed Spain's right to most of these newly discovered lands, and conquistadors began building a Spanish Empire in the Americas. With their superior weapons, the Spanish easily conquered the local peoples. Hernán Cortés defeated the Aztec in Mexico in 1521. Francisco Pizarro conquered the Inca in Peru eleven years later. The Spanish also explored parts of North America. Juan Ponce de León claimed

---

Activity: Interdisciplinary Connection

Visual Arts To help students understand the cultures of various early civilizations in the Americas, ask them to list on the chalkboard as many as they can. These may include Maya, Aztec, Toltec, Olmec, Hohokam, Mississippian, Anasazi, Inuit, or any people they may know of who lived in North, Central, or South America before 1492. Have each student choose one of those on the list or research others to create a collage describing the culture chosen. Collages should include photos of artifacts, drawings, and, if possible, maps, plus these headings: "Location"; "Form of Government" (matriarchal, democratic, and so forth); "Food Sources"; "Religion"; "Housing"; "Clothing"; "Other Interesting Facts." **OL**

Turning Point

▶ Although no images of Christopher Columbus exist from his lifetime, this painting from about 1525 is considered to be the closest likeness.

Columbus Arrives in America

Columbus's first voyage to the Americas was a major turning point in world history. For Europeans, it opened up new areas of exploration and discovery and provided vast wealth through trade. The event was devastating, however, for native peoples of the Americas, whose cultures were changed or destroyed by war, disease, and enslavement.

ANALYZING HISTORY Describe one positive and one negative effect of Columbus's voyage to the Americas.

▲ The Landing of Columbus was painted by American artist Albert Bierstadt in 1892, the year of the 400th anniversary of Columbus's arrival in North America. Note that the artist portrayed the indigenous people as shrouded in darkness and shadow, emerging to kneel worshipfully before the Europeans, who bring with them the "light" of civilization. Unfortunately, the arrival of Europeans did more to destroy the indigenous cultures than to enlighten them.

Florida, Francisco Vásquez de Coronado explored the Southwest, and Hernando de Soto explored the Southeast.

The Spanish soon controlled an immense territory stretching from the Florida peninsula to California and into South America. Settlers farmed the land, established mines and ranches, and tried to spread the Catholic faith.

Cultural Changes

The arrival of Europeans in the Americas altered life for everyone. Native Americans introduced the Europeans to new farming methods and foods like corn, potatoes, squash, pumpkins, beans, and chocolate, as well as tobacco and chewing gum. Europeans also adopted many Native American inventions, including canoes, snowshoes, and ponchos.

Meanwhile, the Europeans introduced Native Americans to wheat, rice, coffee, bananas, citrus fruits, and domestic livestock such as chickens, cattle, pigs, sheep, and horses. In addition, Native Americans acquired new technologies, including better metalworking methods. Along with these beneficial imports, however, came deadly ones—germs that cause diseases. Native Americans had never before been exposed to influenza, measles, chicken pox, mumps, typhus, or smallpox. With no immunity, millions of Native Americans died in widespread epidemics. Military conquests also devastated Native Americans, costing them their lands and their traditional ways of life.

✔ Reading Check **Identifying** Why did millions of Native Americans die after contact with Europeans?

Chapter 1 A Nation is Born **7**

Turning Point

Answers:
positive: provided vast wealth for European traders;
negative: killed millions of Native Americans and destroyed their cultures.

S **Skill Practice**

Detecting Bias Tell students that many cultures had developed in the Americas long before Columbus arrived. **Ask:** Why do you think many Americans refer to Columbus as having "discovered" America? (Cultural bias; Euro-centric perspective; failure to consider native cultures equal) **OL**

✔ Reading Check

Answer:
Many died because they had no immunity to European diseases; others were killed in clashes with Europeans.

Additional Support

Activity: Technology Connection

Identifying Tell students that the Renaissance in Europe led to the discovery of new technology used by settlers and explorers. Renewed interest in ancient Greece and Rome led to knowledge of the astrolabe—a navigational device invented by the ancient Greeks and refined by Arab navigators. It uses the sun to determine direction, latitude, and local time. Europeans also acquired the compass from Arab traders who visited China, where it was invented.

Have students find photos of technology and equipment that would have been used by early explorers and settlers, such as a compass, a caravel, an astrolabe, a wooden barrel, a mill, a forge, a windmill (New Netherland colony), or other examples. Save the photos for an upcoming poster activity. **BL** **ELL**

Sequencing Ask students to identify the events that occurred under the heading "Early French and English Settlement" and to place them in the correct sequence, with dates. **BL**

W **Writing Support**

Personal Ask students to imagine how someone their age would feel if their family moved to another continent. **Ask:** Has your family ever moved to a different country or city where you had no friends and did not know what to expect? Have students assume the role of a teenager whose family moved to an American colony. Ask them to write a letter to a friend in their homeland describing their feelings about the move.

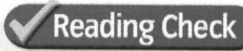
Reading Check

Answer:
Some fled religious persecution; others sought work, land, or mineral wealth.

Additional Support

R **Early French and English Settlement**

MAIN Idea The French and English settled in North America, and English colonists began their own local governments.

W **HISTORY AND YOU** Have you ever wanted to move somewhere new? Why do you think most people move today? Read to learn why the French and English settlers came to North America.

For the complete text of the Mayflower Compact, see page R39 in **Documents in American History.**

Soon after Columbus made his historic voyage, France and England began exploring the eastern part of North America. England sent John Cabot on expeditions in 1497 and 1498. France funded trips by Jacques Cartier and Giovanni da Verrazano in the early 1500s. Yet it was not until the 1600s that the countries succeeded in establishing colonies.

New France

In 1608 French geographer Samuel de Champlain founded the outpost of Quebec. The backers of New France sought profits from fur, and Frenchmen began a brisk trade with Native Americans. Quebec eventually became the capital of New France, a sparsely settled colony of fur traders and Jesuit missionaries.

In the late 1600s, France began expanding the colony. Explorers Louis Jolliet and Jacques Marquette reached the Mississippi River, and René-Robert Cavelier de La Salle followed it to the Gulf of Mexico. The French named the newly claimed region Louisiana. Settlers founded the towns of New Orleans, Biloxi, and Mobile, and they began growing sugar, rice, and tobacco. The French also began importing enslaved Africans to do the hard field work that these labor-intensive crops required.

Jamestown

A year before the French founded Quebec, the English established their first lasting settlement in Virginia. The colony, **Jamestown,** was funded by a **joint-stock company,** a group of private investors who pooled their money to support big projects. These investors, along with others in business and government, saw colonies as sources of raw materials and markets for English goods.

Despite early troubles, the settlers survived with the help of the Powhatan Confederacy, a group of local Native Americans. Within a few years, they began to prosper by growing tobacco. Newcomers arrived, attracted by the promise of land ownership. In 1619 colonists formed an assembly, the House of Burgesses, to make their own laws.

Encouraged by the Virginia Company, more than 4,500 settlers **immigrated** to Virginia by 1622. This expansion alarmed Native Americans, who attacked Jamestown in 1622. An English court blamed the Company's policies for the high death rate and revoked its charter. Virginia became a royal colony run by a governor appointed by the king.

Plymouth Colony

Not all settlers came for economic gain. King James was persecuting a group of Puritans who were called Separatists because they wanted to form their own congregations separate from the Anglican Church, the official church of England. These Separatists hoped to be able to worship freely in America.

In 1620 a small band of Separatists, who came to be known as **Pilgrims,** headed for Virginia on the *Mayflower.* A storm blew their ship off its course. The Pilgrims finally dropped anchor off the coast of Cape Cod, territory without an English government. The settlers drew up a plan for self-government called the Mayflower Compact. They quickly built homes and befriended the local Wampanoag people. The following autumn, the Pilgrims joined with the Wampanoag in a harvest celebration—the first Thanksgiving.

Ten years later, after increasing persecution of Puritans, another group of Puritans arrived in Massachusetts Bay with a charter for a new colony. They founded several towns, including Boston. A depression of England's wool industry drew more people to Massachusetts.

The people of Massachusetts set up a representative government, with an elected assembly to make laws. Government and religion were closely intertwined. The government collected taxes to support the church, and the Puritan leaders of the colony set strict rules for behavior.

Reading Check **Explaining** Why did English colonists come to America?

Activity: Visualizing

Visual/Spatial Help students to fix in their minds the sequence of European settlements by assigning a large-scale time line for display on the wall. Divide the class into small groups and have each group select one of the events from the sequencing activity above. Hang poster paper in a long horizontal shape, using one poster for each step in the sequence. Have each group fill in a poster with dates, photos, drawings, toy boats, Pilgrim hats, Indian corn, and so forth, as well as a sentence stating what the poster depicts, the reason behind the event, and its consequence. As students read succeeding sections in the chapter (or unit), they may add posters to the time line, which will provide a daily, visual review of what they have learned. **OL** **AL** **ELL**

The Thirteen Colonies

MAIN Idea As English settlements grew, colonists developed different forms of government.

HISTORY AND YOU Have you ever been a part of a new organization? What rules did you draw up? Read how colonies established their governments.

The early colonies were only the beginning of English settlements. Over the next century, colonies grew all along the east coast.

The Growth of New England

Puritan efforts in the Massachusetts Bay Colony to suppress other religious beliefs led to other New England colonies. One early dissenter was a minister named Roger Williams. In 1636, after being banned from Massachusetts, Williams headed south, purchased land from the Narraganset people, and founded the town of Providence. There the government had no authority in religious matters.

Like Roger Williams, Anne Hutchinson was exiled from Massachusetts because of her religious views. Hutchinson and a few followers settled near Providence, as did other free-thinking Puritans over the next years. In 1644 Providence joined with neighboring towns to become the colony of Rhode Island and Providence Plantations. Religious freedom, with a total separation of church and state, was a key feature of this new colony.

Some religious dissenters, along with fishers and fur traders, went north instead of south to Rhode Island. In 1679 a large area north of Massachusetts became the royal colony of New Hampshire.

PRIMARY SOURCE
The Causes of English Settlement in America

Three major factors led the English to found colonies in the Americas.

RELIGIOUS PERSECUTION

◄ English Puritans and other non-Anglicans faced prejudice and legal harassment. Many fled to North America where they could worship as they wished.

ECONOMIC CHANGES

▲ The enclosure movement displaced thousands of tenant farmers. Many English leaders thought that having colonies would help absorb England's unemployed people.

RIVALRY WITH SPAIN

◄ The Protestant English wanted to share the riches of the Americas that Catholic Spain was monopolizing.

Analyzing VISUALS

1. **Determining Cause and Effect** How did England's rivalry with Spain drive the nation to establish new colonies in North America?
2. **Explaining** Why did religious groups found colonies?

Chapter 1 A Nation is Born **9**

S Skill Practice
Analyzing Point out that, although one of the reasons settlers emigrated to the colonies was for religious tolerance, they sometimes found—or imposed—the opposite. **Ask:** Why do you think people try to force their beliefs on others? Why do you think some settlers wanted to live in colonies where everyone held the same beliefs, rather than encouraging diversity? Refer students to the Literature Handbook for Chief Red Jacket's views on religious tolerance. **OL**

Analyzing VISUALS

Answers:
1. Because England wanted greater riches to compete with Spain and also naval bases from which to attack Spanish shipping, England was driven to establish new colonies in North America.
2. They wanted to emigrate so that they could worship as they wished.

Additional Support

Activity: Collaborative Activity

Puritan Fashion Organize the class into groups. Have groups create fashion sketches for the typical wardrobe of the Puritans. The sketches should include an ensemble for a woman and one for a man. Encourage students to use library and Internet resources to learn more about clothing in colonial times. Then ask them to use their sketches to write a short paragraph answering this question: How were Puritan values shown in the clothing of the time? *(Answers will vary.)* **AL**

People IN HISTORY

Roger Williams
1603?–1683

Shortly after his arrival in Boston in 1631, Roger Williams declared he was a Separatist and began criticizing Puritan leaders. He served as a minister in Salem, moved briefly to Plymouth Colony in 1632, and then returned to preach at Salem.

When Williams returned to Salem, he continued to criticize Puritan leaders for not making a complete break from the corrupt Anglican Church. He also insisted on greater separation of church and state. Finally, he denounced Massachusetts Bay's charter because it assumed the king had the right to give away land belonging to Native Americans. As Puritan leaders prepared to banish him, Williams fled.

In 1636 he founded Providence—later to be part of Rhode Island—on land he purchased from the Narragansets. In his new colony, Williams created a haven for Quakers, Separatists, Jews, and others whose religious practices or views were not tolerated elsewhere. Most important, Williams championed religious freedom, which later became an important American principle.

What significant contribution to civil rights did Roger Williams make?

Anne Hutchinson
1591–1643

Anne Hutchinson, an experienced midwife and the wife of a prosperous merchant, arrived in Boston in 1634. There, she began to hold meetings with other women to discuss sermons, express her own beliefs, and evaluate the ministers.

Hutchinson stirred up controversy with her discussions of how salvation could be obtained. To most Puritans, this was heresy. In 1637 Hutchinson was tried for sedition by the Massachusetts General Court. Hutchinson did not repent. She said that God "hath let me see which was the clear [correct] ministry and which the wrong. . . ." When asked how God let her know, she replied that God spoke to her "by an immediate revelation." The Court ordered her banished.

Hutchinson, her family, and some of her followers founded a settlement in what is today Rhode Island. After the death of her husband, she moved to Long Island. In 1643 she and all but one of her children were killed in an attack by Native Americans. Some Puritans viewed her tragic death as God's judgment against a heretic.

How did Hutchinson challenge Puritan authority in the Massachusetts Bay Colony?

People IN HISTORY

Answers:

Williams: In his colony of Rhode Island, Williams established the idea of religious freedom, which later became an important American principle.

Hutchinson: Hutchinson challenged Puritan doctrine on how to achieve salvation. Since Puritans ruled Massachusetts, these ideas undermined their authority.

R **Reading Strategy**

Contrasting After students read about Roger Williams, have them research the views of Jonathan Edwards. **Ask: How did Edwards' and Williams' views differ?** Have students write a half-page explanation of the contrasts. **OL**

D **Differentiated Instruction**

Kinesthetic Ask: If you had to grow your own food, what would your diet be like? Interested students may enjoy starting a garden of food they can share with family or classmates, or donate to a local food bank. **ELL**

Additional Support

For an excerpt of the Fundamental Orders of Connecticut, see R40 in **Documents in American History.**

Religion also played a part in the founding of Connecticut. In 1636 the Reverend Thomas Hooker moved his entire congregation from Massachusetts to the Connecticut River valley. Hooker disagreed with the political system that allowed only church members to vote. Three years later, the new colony adopted America's first written constitution, the Fundamental Orders of Connecticut. It allowed all adult men to vote and hold office.

Life in New England New England Puritans valued religious devotion, hard work, and obedience to strict rules regulating daily life. Puritan society revolved around town life. Towns included a meetinghouse (church), a school, and a marketplace around an open public area called the town common. At town meetings, New Englanders discussed local problems and issues. These meetings evolved into the local government, with landowners voting on laws and electing officials to oversee town matters. Yet even residents without property could attend meetings and express their opinions. The colonists grew used to managing their own affairs and came to believe in their right to self-government.

New England's thin and rocky soil was ill suited for cash crops. Instead, from Connecticut to Maine, colonists practiced **subsistence farming** on small farms, raising only enough food to feed their families. The main crop was wheat, but farmers also grew other grains, vegetables, apples, and berries, and they raised dairy cattle, sheep, and pigs.

It was maritime activity, however, that brought prosperity to New England. Fishers sold their catch of cod, mackerel, halibut, and herring to other colonists, people in the Caribbean, and Southern Europeans. Whaling providing blubber for candles and lamp oil.

A thriving lumber industry developed, too. Timber was plentiful, and lumber was in high demand for furniture, building materials, and the barrels that were used to store and ship almost everything in the colonial era. Equally successful was shipbuilding, which was quick and cheap because of forests and sawmills close to the coast. By the 1770s, one of every three British ships had been built in America.

Extending the Content

Who Were the Puritans? The moral character of America was shaped in part by the Puritans—a branch of dissenters who thought the Church of England had been corrupted by politics and human-made doctrines. Many Puritans came to America—mostly New England—to escape religious persecution. They sought religious exclusiveness and attempted to "purify" the church and their lives via strict laws of con- duct. They banished anyone who held opposing views, which led to isolation and repression. In the late 1600s, they jailed more than 200 people and executed 20 others, plus two dogs, for witchcraft in Salem, Massachusetts. Despite such incidents, Puritans advanced the country intellectually. They wrote religious poetry and the first children's books, and studied classic Greek literature. In 1635 they founded the first free public schools in history and the first American college: Harvard.

King Philip's War In 1637 war broke out between the English settlers and the Pequot people of New England. This conflict ended with the near extermination of the Pequot people. In the following decades, however, English settlers and Native Americans lived in relative peace.

In the 1670s, colonial governments began to demand that Native Americans follow English laws and customs. Tensions peaked in 1675 when Plymouth Colony tried and executed three Wampanoag men for murder. This touched off King Philip's War, named after the Wampanoag leader Metacomet, whom the settlers called King Philip. By the time the war ended in 1678, few Native Americans were left in New England.

The Middle Colonies

While the English focused their early settlements on Virginia and New England, the Dutch had claimed much of the land south of Connecticut. In 1609 Henry Hudson, a navigator hired by Dutch merchants, had discovered what is now the Hudson River valley in New York. The Dutch called the region New Netherland and established their main settlement of New Amsterdam on Manhattan Island. Dutch policies encouraged immigration, and by 1664 New Netherland was England's main rival in North America.

New Settlements Charles II, who had become king of England in 1660 after the English Civil War, decided to act. He seized New Netherland from the Dutch and granted the land to his brother, James, the Duke of York. James held onto the largest portion of the land, renaming it New York. The rest of the land became New Jersey, a colony that offered generous land grants, religious freedom, and the right to have a legislative assembly.

In 1681 King Charles gave **William Penn** permission to create a new colony south of New York. Penn regarded Pennsylvania as a "holy experiment" where settlers would have religious freedom and a voice in government. He particularly wanted to help his fellow Quakers escape persecution in England. Quakers objected to obligatory taxes and military service. They also opposed war or violence as a means to settle disputes. A treaty Penn signed in 1682 assured peace with a local group of Native Americans. To give his colony access to the Atlantic Ocean, Penn soon acquired coastal land to the southeast. This land later became the colony of Delaware.

Europe's population growth also brought a new wave of immigrants to America. Many of these newcomers settled particularly in the Middle Colonies, where land was still available.

The Economy The Middle Colonies were blessed with fertile land and a long growing season. Farmers produced bumper crops of rye, oats, barley, and potatoes. Wheat rapidly became the region's main cash crop. In the early and mid-1700s, the demand for wheat soared, thanks to population growth in Europe. Between 1720 and 1770, wheat prices more than doubled in the Middle Colonies. Some people who grew wealthy from the wheat boom invested in new businesses such as glass and pottery works and built large gristmills to produce flour for export.

The Southern Colonies

Farther south, tobacco helped Virginia to thrive. The colony had been joined by Maryland, a **proprietary colony** which began in the 1630s. A proprietary colony was one owned by an individual who could govern it any way he wanted, appointing officials, coining money, imposing taxes, and even raising an army. The owner of the colony was George Calvert, also known as Lord Baltimore. He hoped to make the colony a refuge for Catholics because they, like the Puritans, were persecuted in England. Most settlers, however, were Protestants. Maryland passed the Toleration Act in 1649, granting religious toleration to all Christians in the colony.

New Settlements After the end of the English Civil War, new colonies sprang up south of Virginia. In 1663 King Charles II gave eight friends and political allies a vast tract of land named Carolina. From the start, Carolina developed as two separate regions. A small and scattered population of farmers grew tobacco in North Carolina. North Carolina's coastline made the colony hard to reach, and many more settlers headed to South Carolina. There they established the community of Charles Towne (Charleston), exported deerskins, and grew rice in the tidal swamps.

R Reading Strategy

Organizing Have students use information in this section to create and complete tables like the ones below. OL

New England Colonies

Type of Early Government	Enfranchisement	Economy
town meeting	male property owners	fishing, timber

Middle Colonies

Type of Early Government	Enfranchisement	Economy
some areas proprietary, some assemblies	adult males	wheat, rye, oats, barley, potatoes, glass, pottery, flour exports

Southern Colonies

Type of Early Government	Enfranchisement	Economy
proprietary and assemblies	wealthy plantation owners	tobacco, deerskins, rice

D Differentiated Instruction

Visual Have students create a poster that illustrates the tables they created in the exercise above. BL OL

Additional Support

Activity: Collaborative Learning

Designing a Flag Have students work in small groups to design a flag for one of the colonies mentioned in this section. Have students prepare a drawing of their flag and determine the actual dimensions for the flag. Then have the groups prepare a brief written explanation of the colors and symbols used in the flag. Display the flags around the classroom.

S Skill Practice

Conducting Research Have students use library or Internet resources to prepare a 2-minute oral presentation about James Oglethorpe. **OL**

C Critical Thinking

Analyzing Lead a discussion about whether or not people should be jailed for not paying their debts. Remind students: the average debt of American households with more than one credit card is now more than $8,000; the average American has zero savings. **Ask:** *Why do you think people spend more money than they have?* (Students' answers will vary but should support their opinion.)

Analyzing GEOGRAPHY

Answers:
1. because it gave quicker access to ships for re-supply and the ocean for food
2. Georgia

Additional Support

NATIONAL GEOGRAPHIC **Settling the Thirteen Colonies, 1607–1750**

- Settled by 1660
- Settled by 1700
- Settled by 1760

New York
England took New York from the Dutch in 1664 and continued its focus on trade.

Pennsylvania
William Penn established Pennsylvania in 1681 as a place of religious freedom.

Virginia
The Virginia Company established its colony in 1607 as a money-making venture.

The Carolinas
The Carolina colony was chartered in 1663 as a proprietary colony; its proprietors hoped to make money growing cash crops.

Georgia
James Oglethorpe founded Georgia in 1733 as a refuge for England's poor.

Massachusetts
The Pilgrims arrived in Plymouth in 1620, and the Puritans arrived in Massachusetts Bay 10 years later; both groups fled religious persecution in England.

Rhode Island
Roger Williams founded Providence in 1636 as a place of religious toleration.

Connecticut
Thomas Hooker founded Hartford in 1636 to escape Massachusetts' Puritan political system.

Maryland
Lord Baltimore established Maryland in 1634 as a refuge for Catholics.

Maine (part of Mass.)
N.H. (1623)
N.J. (1664)
Del. (1638)
ATLANTIC OCEAN

0   200 kilometers
0   200 miles
Lambert Azimuthal Equal-Area projection

Analyzing GEOGRAPHY

1. **Location** Why were the earliest settlements on the coast?
2. **Place** Which colony was founded as a haven for debtors?

S Georgia arose south of the Carolinas in 1733, based on an idea of James Oglethorpe. A wealthy member of Parliament, Oglethorpe had been horrified to learn that many English **C** prisoners were jailed simply because they could not pay their debts. Oglethorpe asked King George II for a colony where the poor could start over. The king agreed, realizing that a new Southern colony also would keep Spain from expanding north of Florida.

Life in the South Agriculture was the focus of the Southern economy. In early colonial days, there was plenty of land, but not enough labor to work it. England had the opposite problem—not enough land and high unemployment. The situation led many poor English people to come to America as **indentured servants.** They signed contracts with American colonists, agreeing to work for four or more years in return for paid passage to America

and free food, clothing, and shelter. Southern farmers also relied on the labor of enslaved Africans, a practice that grew dramatically as time passed.

The hard lives of enslaved workers and indentured servants contrasted sharply with the privileged lives of the elite. A small number of wealthy colonists bought most of the land along the rivers and established large plantations. These landholders had enormous economic and political influence. They served in the governing councils and assemblies, commanded the local militias (citizen armies), and became county judges. With few towns or roads in the region, their plantations functioned as self-contained communities.

Although they dominated Southern society, large landowners were few in number. Most Southerners were small farmers living inland in the backcountry. They owned modest plots devoted mostly to subsistence farming.

12 Chapter 1 A Nation is Born

Activity: Interdisciplinary Connection

Mathematics Using a ruler and the map scale for the map "Settling the Thirteen Colonies," have students work in pairs to calculate the distance between one city and the other 13 and list the results in a chart. Then have students do research to find out the average distance a person can travel by horse. Then have students determine how long it would take a person on horseback to travel between their chosen city and the others and add that information to

their chart. Have students conclude by comparing and discussing results with other partners. **Ask:** *What effect might distance have on the development of society, culture, or government in the colonies?* (Students should note that the colonies developed distinct and independent governing bodies, economies, and societies.)

Another group of colonists were tenant farmers—landless settlers who worked fields that they rented.

By the 1660s, Virginia's government was dominated by wealthy planters led by the governor, Sir William Berkeley. Berkeley arranged to restrict voting to property owners, cutting the number of voters in half. He also exempted himself and his councillors from taxation. These actions angered the backcountry farmers and tenant farmers. Yet it was the governor's land policies toward Native Americans that led to a rebellion.

Crisis Over Land

Over time, acquiring land became an important issue for most colonists. Many indentured servants and tenant farmers wanted to own farms eventually. Backcountry farmers wanted to expand their holdings. By the 1670s, most land left was in areas claimed by Native Americans in the Piedmont, the region of rolling hills between the coastal plains and the Appalachians. Most wealthy planters, who lived near the coast, opposed expansion because they did not want to endanger their plantations by risking war with the Native Americans.

In 1675 war broke out between settlers and a Susquehannock group, but Governor Berkeley refused to support further military action. Nathaniel Bacon, a well-to-do but sympathetic planter, took up the cause of outraged backcountry farmers. After organizing a militia to attack the Native Americans, he ran for office and won a seat in the House of Burgesses. The assembly at once authorized another attack. It also restored the right to vote to all free men and took away tax exemptions Berkeley had granted to his supporters. Not satisfied with these reforms, Bacon challenged Berkeley, and a civil war erupted. Bacon's Rebellion ended suddenly the next month, when Bacon, hiding in a swamp, became sick and died. Without his leadership, his army rapidly disintegrated, and Berkeley returned to power.

Bacon's Rebellion convinced many wealthy planters that land should be made available to backcountry farmers. From the 1680s onward, Virginia's government generally supported expanding the colony westward, regardless of the impact on Native Americans.

The rebellion also helped increase Virginia's reliance on enslaved Africans rather than indentured servants. Enslaved workers did not have to be freed and, therefore, would never need their own land. In addition, in 1672 King Charles II granted a charter to the Royal African Company to engage in the slave trade. Planters now found it easier to acquire enslaved people because they no longer had to go through the Dutch or the Portuguese. Earlier purchases had been difficult because English laws limited trade between the English colonies and other countries. Planters also discovered another economic advantage to slavery. Because enslaved Africans, unlike indentured servants, were considered property, planters could use them as collateral to borrow money and expand their plantations.

✔ **Reading Check** **Analyzing** How did the types of settlements influence the way each was governed?

Section 1 REVIEW

Vocabulary
1. **Explain** the significance of: Jamestown, joint-stock company, Pilgrim, subsistence farming, William Penn, proprietary colony, indentured servant.

Main Ideas
2. **Describing** How did geography and climate affect the cultures and traditions of Native American groups?

3. **Explaining** How did the arrival of Europeans affect both Native American and European cultures?

4. **Identifying** How did the Jamestown colony finally prosper?

5. **Analyzing** What role did religion play in the founding of English colonies?

Critical Thinking
6. **Big Ideas** In what ways did early settlers in the English colonies develop new and unique forms of government?

7. **Categorizing** Use a graphic organizer to list the colonies and the reasons for their founding.

Colony	Reason for Founding

8. **Analyzing Visuals** Examine the images on page 9. Summarize the different reasons for English settlement in America.

Writing About History
9. **Descriptive Writing** Take on the role of a settler in Jamestown. Write a letter to someone back in England describing the hardships you faced.

 History ONLINE
Study Central™ To review this section, go to glencoe.com and click on Study Central.

13

✔ **Reading Check**

Answer:
Proprietary colonies were allowed only the type of government the proprietor preferred; some settlements founded by religious groups chose their own governments; some colonies allowed all adult males to vote and hold office, whereas others required property ownership for suffrage and public office.

Assess

 History ONLINE

Study Central™ provides summaries, interactive games, and online graphic organizers to help students review content.

Close

Persuasive Writing Have students write an ad to be placed in a British newspaper seeking to hire indentured servants for an American colony. The ad should include the servant's duties, what provisions the servant will receive, and the duration of the contract. **OL**

Section 1 REVIEW

Answers

1. All definitions can be found in the section and the Glossary.
2. Answers will vary. Students should note how customs and traditions were affected by geography and climate, using examples from the text.
3. Europeans changed Native Americans by taking their land, and bringing new diseases to North America; European culture changed with the new demands for land development, and new crops to produce
4. The Jamestown colonists eventually prospered by growing tobacco.

5. Some colonies were founded by religious sects escaping persecution in Great Britain.
6. Some colonies established town meetings while others offered suffrage for all men.
7. Jamestown: as an investment; Maryland: as a refuge for English Catholics; Plymouth: for religious freedom; Massachusetts Bay: for religious freedom; Rhode Island: for religious freedom; New York: to force the Dutch from the English colonies and remove them as a commercial rival; Pennsylvania: as a place of religious toleration; Georgia: as a place for debtors to start new lives

8. To escape religious persecution in Great Britain or establish religious freedom in a new land; to find land or wealth.
9. Letters will vary, but should mention physical problems of clearing land and building homes; economics—finding work and food sources; the dangers posed by Native Americans already inhabiting land settlers wanted; and problems created by religious intolerance.

Focus

Tell students that the Columbian Exchange had unintended consequences. For example, weeds and germs new to the Americas arrived along with the intended crops and livestock.

Teach

R Reading Skill

Sequencing Have students make charts ordering the events of the Columbian Exchange. *(Possible answer: Europe: brought crops, animals, diseases; took home food, animals. Native Americans: died from diseases. Africa: people enslaved in Americas; food taken to Africa.)* **OL**

C Critical Thinking

Contrasting Have students propose an alternative to enslaved labor. Ask them to consider models that worked at least for a time in other places. *(Possible answers: prisoners in penal colonies, such as Georgia, Australia; indentured servants.)* **OL**

Additional Support

NATIONAL GEOGRAPHIC

GEOGRAPHY & HISTORY

R The Columbian Exchange

The arrival of Europeans in the Americas set in motion a series of complex interactions between peoples and environments. These interactions, called the Columbian Exchange, permanently altered the world's ecosystems and changed nearly every culture around the world.

Native Americans introduced Europeans to new crops. Corn, squash, pumpkins, beans, sweet potatoes, tomatoes, chili peppers, peanuts, chocolate, and potatoes all made their way to Europe, as did tobacco and chewing gum. Perhaps the most significant import for Europeans was the potato. European farmers learned that four times as many people could live off the same amount of land when potatoes were planted instead of grain.

The Europeans introduced Native Americans to wheat, oats, barley, rye, rice, onions, bananas, coffee, and citrus fruits such as lemons and oranges. They also brought over livestock such as cattle, pigs, sheep, and chickens. Perhaps the most important form of livestock was the horse—which dramatically changed life for many Native Americans on the Great Plains.

How Did Geography Shape the Exchange?

C The isolation of the Americas from the rest of the world meant that Native Americans had no resistance to diseases that were common in other parts of the world, such as influenza, measles, chicken pox, mumps, typhus, and smallpox. The consequences were devastating. Epidemics killed millions of Native Americans. This catastrophe also reduced the labor supply available to Europeans, who then turned to the slave trade, eventually bringing millions of Africans to the Americas.

Analyzing GEOGRAPHY

1. **Movement** What new crops were introduced in Europe from the Americas? How did these crops improve the diet of Europeans?
2. **Human-Environment Interaction** How did geography play a role in the spread of diseases?

---

14 Chapter 1 A Nation is Born

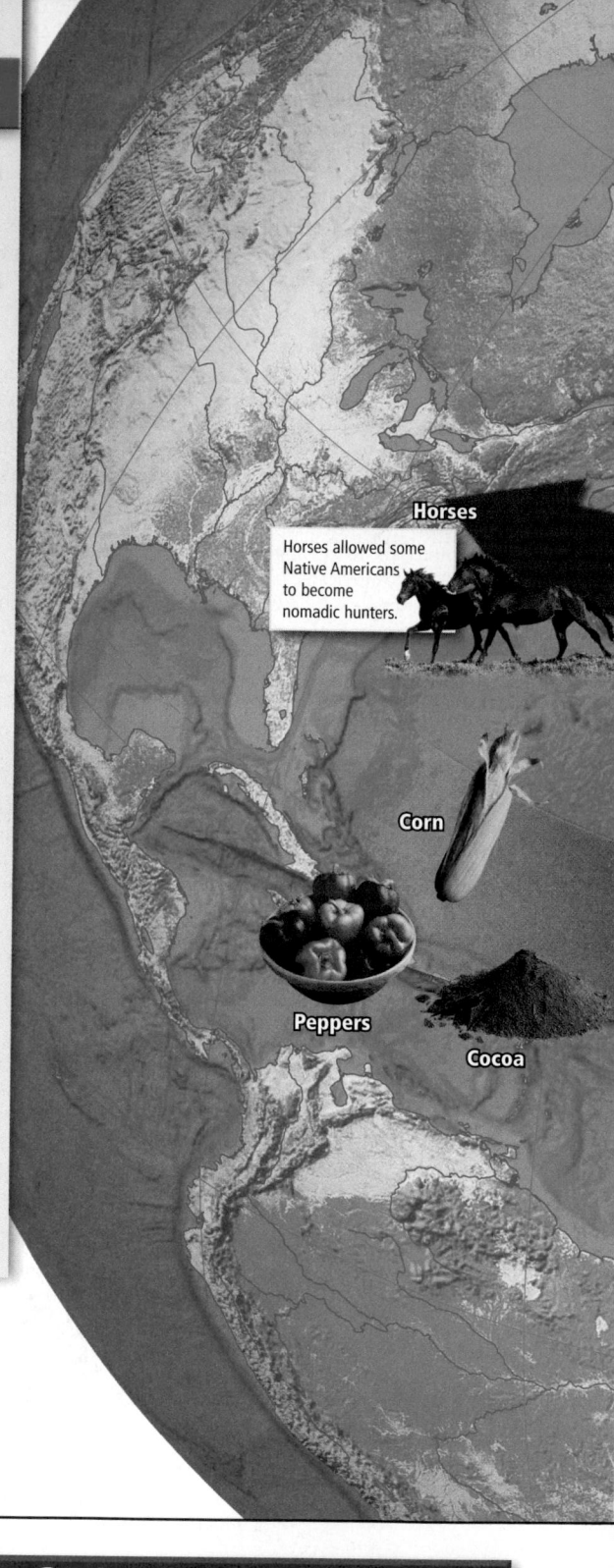

Horses

Horses allowed some Native Americans to become nomadic hunters.

Corn

Peppers

Cocoa

Extending the Content

World Population Growth As a result of the increased number of calories in the European diet produced by the Columbian Exchange, the world population boomed in the years following 1700 at a rate faster than at any time in human history. From 1700 to 1750 the world population jumped from 610 million to 720 million. From 1750 to 1800 total population expanded from 720 million to 900 million. Despite the loss of life due to the spread of diseases, the increased nutrition in diets offset the losses.

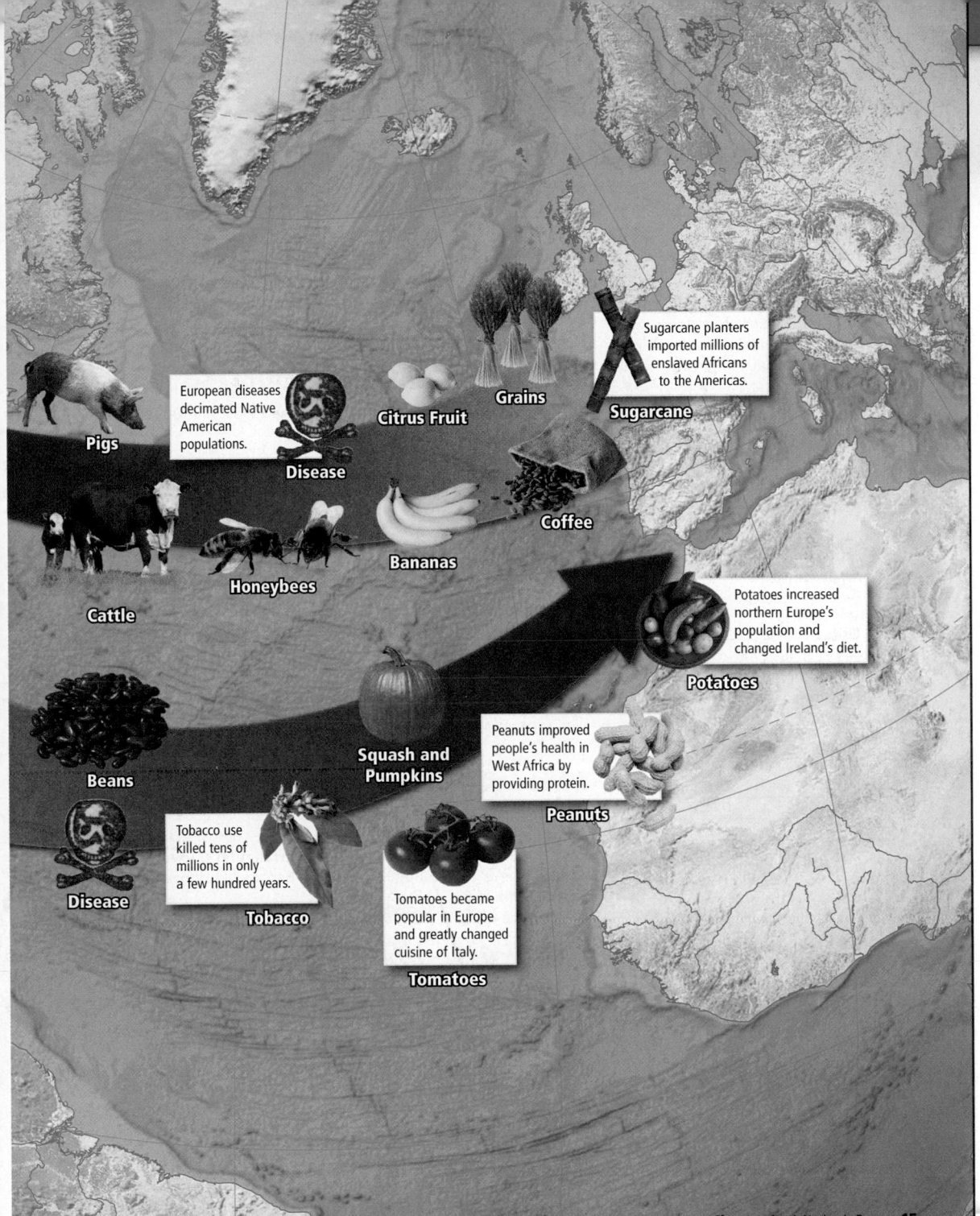

European diseases decimated Native American populations.
Disease

Pigs

Citrus Fruit

Grains

Sugarcane planters imported millions of enslaved Africans to the Americas.

Sugarcane

Coffee

Honeybees

Bananas

Cattle

Potatoes increased northern Europe's population and changed Ireland's diet.

Potatoes

Squash and Pumpkins

Peanuts improved people's health in West Africa by providing protein.

Peanuts

Beans

Tobacco use killed tens of millions in only a few hundred years.

Disease

Tobacco

Tomatoes became popular in Europe and greatly changed cuisine of Italy.

Tomatoes

Assess/Close

D Differentiated Instruction

Naturalist Invite students to choose one of the elements of the Columbian Exchange and use the library or Internet resources to become a specialist on that one aspect. Have them report their findings to the class. **AL**

Analyzing **GEOGRAPHY**

Answers:
1. American crops included corn, squash, pumpkins, beans, sweet potatoes, tomatoes, chili peppers, peanuts, chocolate, and potatoes. Europeans could feed more people off the same amount of land by planting potatoes, and tomatoes changed Italy's cuisine.
2. Because the Americas were isolated, the inhabitants had no resistance to common European diseases. Epidemics killed millions of Native Americans.

Interdisciplinary Connection: Science

Contemporary Exchanges Invite students to find out more about the current situation with invasive species in the United States and to report on efforts to control them. You may wish to divide the class into groups, assigning each group one of the following categories: animals, aquatic species, plants, or microbes. Groups can report on the effects of invasive species on habitats and the economy and on the federal government's response. The USDA Natural Agricultural Library Web site is a good starting point for research.

Focus

Bellringer
Daily Focus Transparency 1.2

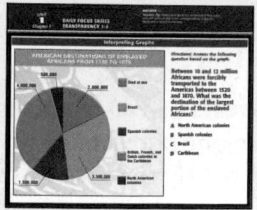

Guide to Reading

Answers:

Germans: Pennsylvania; fled religious wars; **Scots:** Middle Colonies; avoid high taxes, poor harvests, religious persecution; **Jews:** New York, Philadelphia, Charles Town, Savannah, Newport; religious persecution

Section Spotlight Video

To generate interest and provide a springboard for class discussion, access the Chapter 1, Section 2 video at glencoe.com or on the video DVD.

Resource Manager

A Diverse Society

Guide to Reading

Big Ideas
Culture and Beliefs Immigrants from Europe or those brought by force from Africa greatly increased the population of the American colonies in the 1700s.

Content Vocabulary
• triangular trade *(p. 16)*
• slave code *(p. 18)*

Academic Vocabulary
• hierarchy *(p. 16)*

People and Events to Identify
• John Locke *(p. 20)*
• Great Awakening *(p. 21)*

Reading Strategy
Taking Notes As you read about colonial society in the 1700s, complete a graphic organizer similar to the one below by identifying why immigrants settled in the colonies.

Group	Where They Settled	Reasons for Immigrating
Germans		
Scots-Irish		
Jews		

The American colonies experienced rapid population growth. The importation of enslaved Africans continued even as colonists engaged in philosophical and religious discussions about the rights of individuals.

Growth of Colonial America

MAIN Idea The different colonies created new social structures that were more open than those of aristocratic Europe.

HISTORY AND YOU Think about the social structure in your school, from the principal down to you, the student. Read on to learn about the social structure that developed in the growing English settlements.

The population of the American colonies grew rapidly in the eighteenth century. Between 1640 and 1700, the colonial population increased from 25,000 to more than 250,000, and it reached roughly 2.5 million by the time of the American Revolution. High birthrates as well as improved housing and sanitation contributed to this growth. Contagious diseases, however, such as typhoid fever, tuberculosis, cholera, diphtheria, and scarlet fever, remained a threat. The increasing population and a rise in trade changed colonial society. This brought a growth of cities, increased immigration, and changes in status for women and Africans.

Trade and the Rise of Cities

In the early colonial period, settlers produced few goods that England wanted in exchange for the goods they purchased. Instead, colonial merchants developed systems of **triangular trade** involving exchanges of goods among the colonies, England, Caribbean sugar planters, and Africa.

This trade brought great wealth for merchants, who began to build factories. It also fostered the growth of cities in the North. By 1760 the Middle Colonies boasted the two largest cities in America: Philadelphia, with 30,000 people, and New York with 25,000.

In these cities, a new society with distinct social classes developed. At the top of the **hierarchy** were a small number of wealthy merchants who controlled trade. Below them, artisans, or skilled workers, made up nearly half of the urban population in colonial times. Innkeepers and retailers with their own businesses held a similar status. The lower class consisted of people without skills or property. Below them in status were indentured servants and enslaved Africans. Although relatively few enslaved people lived in the North, they made up 10 to 20 percent of the urban population.

R Reading Strategies

Teacher Edition
• Interpreting, p. 18
• Special-Purpose Map, p. 18
• Sequencing, p. 19

Additional Resources
• Guid. Read. Act., URB p. 47

C Critical Thinking

Teacher Edition
• Analyzing, p. 17
• Comparing, p. 19
• Drawing Concl., p. 20

Additional Resources
• Quizzes/Tests, p. 6

D Differentiated Instruction

Additional Resources
• History Simulations and Problem Solving, URB p. 9
• Interpreting Political Cartoons Act., URB p. 41

W Writing Support

Teacher Edition
• Summary Writing, p. 20

Additional Resources
• Foldables, p. 46

S Skill Practice

Additional Resources
• Time Line Act., URB p. 33
• Reading Essen., p. 4

NATIONAL GEOGRAPHIC **Triangular Trade and Rise of Cities**

ATLANTIC OCEAN

GREAT BRITAIN

EUROPE

NORTH AMERICA

BRITISH COLONIES

Manufactured goods, clothes, furniture, luxuries

Lumber, furs, fish, whale oil, grain, naval stores, rice, tobacco, indigo

40°N

Sugar, molasses, fruit

Enslaved persons, money, molasses, sugar

Flour, fish, meat

TROPIC OF CANCER

→ Colonial exports
→ Colonial imports
→ Intercolonial trade

BRITISH WEST INDIES

AFRICA

Rum, cloth, tools

0   600 kilometers
0   600 miles
Miller projection

Enslaved persons (Middle Passage)

EQUATOR

SOUTH AMERICA

Major Cities, c. 1760

Population (thousands)

25 — 23.7
20 — 18.0
15 — 15.6
10 — 8.0 7.5
5
0

Boston New York Philadelphia Charles Town Newport

Source: *Colonial America to 1763.*

Analyzing GEOGRAPHY

1. **Movement** What commodities were shipped from the colonies to West Africa?
2. **Human-Environment Interaction** What types of goods did the American colonies export?

Immigrants

Between 1700 and 1775, hundreds of thousands of free white immigrants streamed in. Most settled in the Middle Colonies, especially Pennsylvania. Among them were Germans fleeing religious wars back home and Scots-Irish escaping high taxes, poor harvests, and religious discrimination in Ireland. Jews migrated to America for religious reasons, too. By 1776 approximately 1,500 Jews lived in the colonies, mainly in the cities of New York, Philadelphia, Charleston, Savannah, and Newport. They were allowed to worship freely, but they could not vote or hold public office.

Women

Women did not have equal rights in colonial America. At first, married women could not legally own property or make contracts or wills. Husbands were the sole guardians of the children and were allowed to physically discipline both their children and their wives. Single women and widows had more rights and could own and manage property, file lawsuits, and run businesses. In the 1700s, the status of married women improved. Despite legal limitations, many women worked outside their homes.

Enslaved Africans

Historians estimate that some 10 to 12 million Africans were enslaved and sent to the Americas between 1450 and 1870. On the way, about 2 million died at sea. Of the 8 to 10 million Africans who reached the Americas, approximately 500,000 were transported to British North America.

Chapter 1 A Nation is Born **17**

Teach

C Critical Thinking

Analyzing Remind students that in colonial times married women could not own property or make contracts or wills, and could be physically disciplined by their husbands. **Ask:** Considering these limitations, why do you think most colonial women married? *(Answers will vary, but may include protection and financial reason.)* OL

Analyzing GEOGRAPHY

Answers:
1. rum, cloth, tools
2. rum, cloth, tools, lumber, furs, fish, whale oil, naval stores, rice, tobacco, indigo, flour, meat, grain

Hands-On Chapter Project
Step 2

From Colonies to Independence

Step 2: Governing the Colony in North America

Directions Returning to their groups, students should review their plans, lists, and map. Using their textbook as a reference, have groups agree on the purpose of their colonies—for example, do they want to achieve religious freedom or make money? They should also determine the type of colony—will it be a joint-stock venture, a proprietary colony, or a royal colony?

Then using the textbook and reference resources, have students create a governing document for their colony, similar to the *Mayflower Compact* (see page R39). As they work to draft their document, students should consider the purpose and type of colony, some basic aspects of English law, ideas about land distribution, as well as the circumstances and the needs of an isolated community.

Putting it Together Have volunteers from each group present the group's governing document to the class. Discuss the strengths and weaknesses of each document as a class. Have groups revise their governing documents, as necessary, based on ideas that came up during the class discussion. OL

(Chapter Project continued on page 25)

Africans had arrived in Virginia as early as 1619, when they were regarded as "Christian servants." By about 1775, these unwilling immigrants and their descendants numbered about 540,000 in all colonies, roughly 20 percent of the colonial population. Laws called **slave codes** kept African captives from owning property, testifying against whites in court, receiving an education, moving about freely, or meeting in large groups.

No group in the American colonies endured lower status or more hardship than enslaved Africans. Most lived on Southern plantations, where they worked long days and were beaten and branded by planters. Planters also controlled enslaved Africans by threatening to sell them away from their families. Family and religion helped enslaved Africans maintain their dignity. Some resisted by escaping to the North, where slavery was not as widespread as in the South; others refused to work hard or lost their tools.

✓ Reading Check **Identifying** What groups faced discrimination in colonial times?

New Ideas

MAIN Idea The ideas of justified revolutions, the Enlightenment, and the Great Awakening made the colonists question their role as English subjects and their limited freedom under mercantilist policies.

HISTORY AND YOU What rights do you have under the Bill of Rights? Read on to learn about the English Bill of Rights.

When Charles II assumed the throne in 1660, he and his advisers were determined to use the colonies to generate wealth for England. Charles asked Parliament to pass the Navigation Acts of 1660, requiring all goods shipped to and from the colonies to be carried on English ships. Specific products, including the major products that earned money for the colonies, could be sold only to England or other English colonies. Three years later, in 1663, Parliament passed another navigation act, the Staple Act. It required all colonial imports to come through England. Merchants bringing foreign goods to the colonies had to stop in England, pay taxes, and then ship the goods out on English ships. This increased the price of the goods in the colonies.

PRIMARY SOURCE
The Atlantic Slave Trade 1500–1800

In 1619 the first Africans arrived in the English colonies, beginning the brutal African slave trade. After a nearly fatal voyage across the Atlantic, known as the Middle Passage, under stifling, dirty, and crowded conditions, those starved and exhausted Africans who managed to survive were sold in markets or at auction.

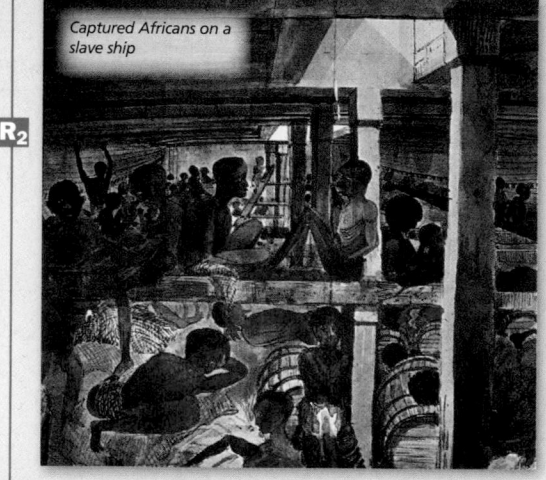

Captured Africans on a slave ship

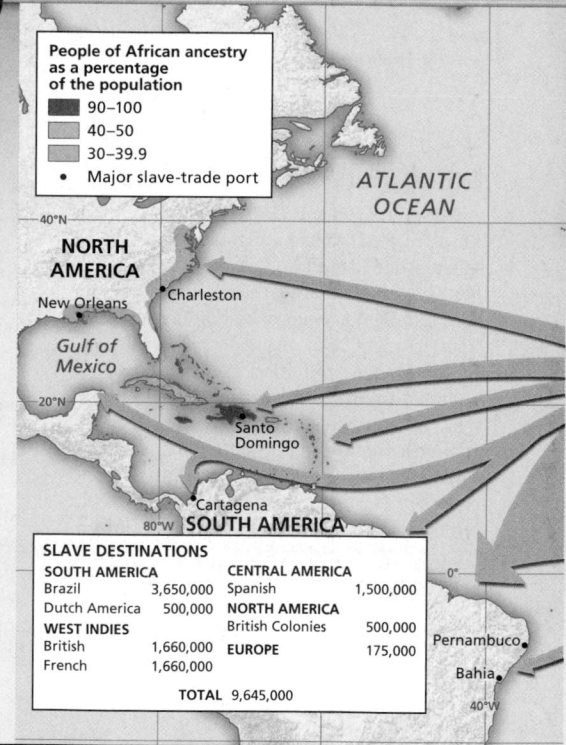

People of African ancestry as a percentage of the population
- 90–100
- 40–50
- 30–39.9
- • Major slave-trade port

ATLANTIC OCEAN

40°N

NORTH AMERICA

New Orleans • Charleston

Gulf of Mexico

20°N

Santo Domingo

Cartagena

80°W SOUTH AMERICA

Pernambuco

Bahia

0°

40°W

SLAVE DESTINATIONS

SOUTH AMERICA		CENTRAL AMERICA	
Brazil	3,650,000	Spanish	1,500,000
Dutch America	500,000	**NORTH AMERICA**	
WEST INDIES		British Colonies	500,000
British	1,660,000	**EUROPE**	175,000
French	1,660,000		
		TOTAL 9,645,000	

Activity: Interdisciplinary Connection

Literature and Folklore Have students use library and Internet resources to learn about traditional storytelling in Africa. **Ask:** How are traditional African folktales the same as or different from American folktales? What are some American folktales with African roots? Encourage students to find English-language translations of African folktales and legends and to compare stories and themes with familiar American folktales and legends. Have students write a short report about their findings. **OL**

Frustration with the Navigation Acts led to many colonial merchants routinely smuggling goods to Europe, the Caribbean, and Africa. To better enforce English law, Charles II deprived Massachusetts of its charter in 1684 and declared it a royal colony. James II, who succeeded his brother Charles to the throne in 1685, went even further by creating a new royal province called the Dominion of New England. At first it included Plymouth, Massachusetts, and Rhode Island, and later Connecticut, New Jersey, and New York. Sir Edmund Andros, the first governor-general of the dominion, quickly made himself unpopular by levying new taxes, rigorously enforcing the Navigation Acts, and attempting to undermine the authority of the Puritan Church.

The Glorious Revolution

While Andros was angering New England colonists, King James II was offending many in England by disregarding Parliament, revoking the charters of many English towns, and practicing Catholicism. The birth of James's son in 1688 led to protests against a Catholic heir. To prevent a Catholic dynasty, Parliament invited James's Protestant daughter Mary and her Dutch husband, William of Orange, to claim the throne. James fled, and William and Mary became the new rulers. This change of power is known as the Glorious Revolution.

Before assuming the throne, William and Mary had to accept the English Bill of Rights. This document, written in 1689, said monarchs could not suspend Parliament's laws or create their own courts, nor could they impose taxes or raise an army without Parliament's consent. The Bill of Rights also guaranteed freedom of speech within Parliament, banned excessive bail and cruel and unusual punishments, and guaranteed every English subject the right to an impartial jury in legal cases.

Almost immediately Boston colonists ousted Governor-General Andros. William and Mary then permitted Rhode Island and Connecticut to resume their previous forms of government, and they issued a new charter for Massachusetts in 1691, granting the right to assemble and freedom of worship.

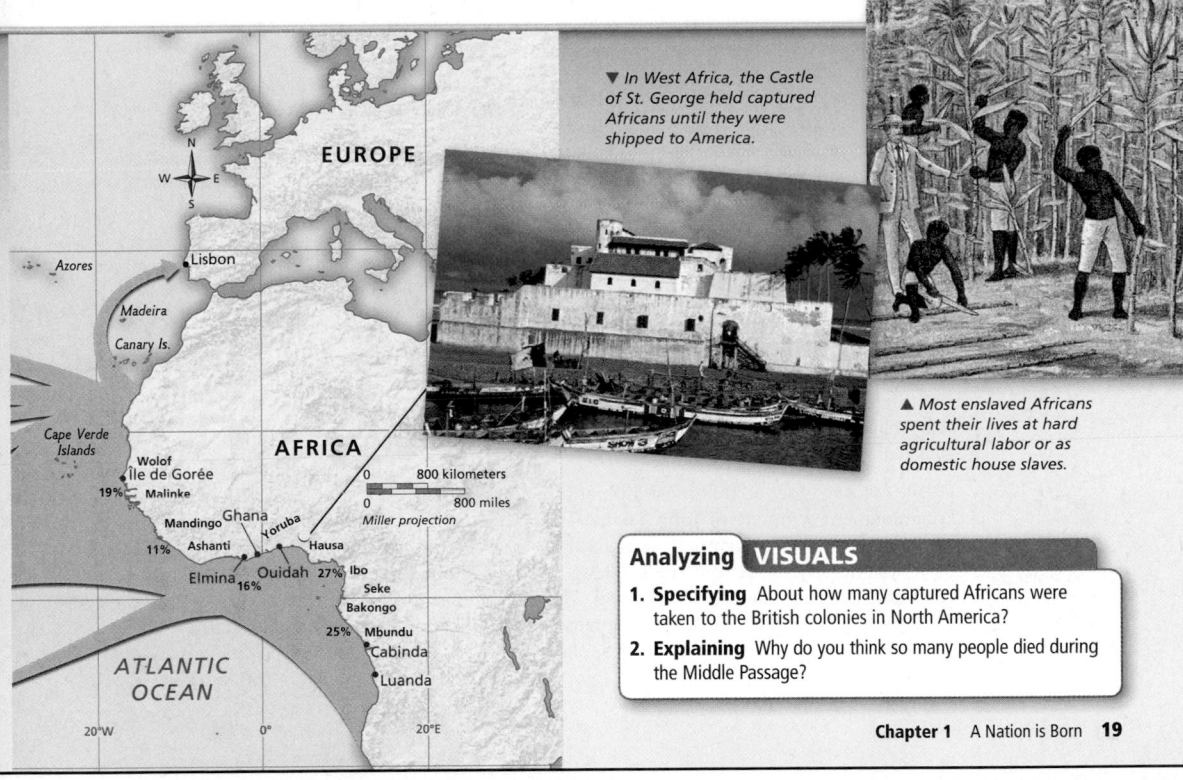

▼ In West Africa, the Castle of St. George held captured Africans until they were shipped to America.

▲ Most enslaved Africans spent their lives at hard agricultural labor or as domestic house slaves.

Analyzing VISUALS
1. **Specifying** About how many captured Africans were taken to the British colonies in North America?
2. **Explaining** Why do you think so many people died during the Middle Passage?

Chapter 1 A Nation is Born **19**

Additional Support

Activity: Technology Connection

The Middle Passage Refer students to the chart and feature on this page. Ask them a series of questions to help them analyze the data. **Ask: To which destination were most enslaved people taken?** *(Brazil)* **Why do you think so many enslaved people were taken to Brazil and so few were taken to Europe?** *(Brazil had a plantation economy that depended on enslaved labor, while Europe did not.)*

Then have students find out more about the Middle Passage, the route between Africa and America aboard the slave trader ships. Tell students of one of the most famous slave revolts that occurred along the Middle Passage on the *Amistad*. In this incident, a group of captives revolted during the voyage across the Atlantic, killing the captain and members of the crew. The *Amistad* captives landed in the United

States, were charged with murder, but were acquitted, and eventually returned to Africa.

Have students work individually or in groups to present their research on the Middle Passage in multimedia or slide show presentations. **OL**

C Critical Thinking

Drawing Conclusions Tell students that Baron Montesquieu was an influential Enlightenment political thinker and social philosopher. Have each student research and write a one-page essay about the continuing influence of Montesquieu on our government. Students should address this question: Why are Montesquieu's ideas important to preserving citizens' freedom? *(He helped provide the basis for the separation of powers in government, which has held the overall power of the federal government in check.)* **OL**

W Writing Support

Summary Writing Have students research other Enlighten-ment thinkers and bring to class a poster that includes a paragraph summarizing the person's life, a paragraph summarizing his or her beliefs and ideas, and a photo. Display the posters in the classroom. As a basis for class discussion of the ideas of the Enlightenment, ask students to read all of the posters. **OL**

Additional Support

People IN HISTORY

John Locke
1632–1704

The Glorious Revolution of 1688 set a very important precedent. It suggested that there were times when revolution was justified. In 1690, John Locke, a philosopher allied with those who had overthrown King James II, wrote *Two Treatises of Government* on this topic.

Locke argued that a government's right to rule came from the people. All people, he said, were born with certain natural rights, including the right to life, liberty, and property. To protect their rights, people created government. In effect, they had made a contract—they agreed to obey the government's laws, and the government agreed to protect their rights. If a ruler violated those rights, the people were justified in rebelling.

Locke's ideas greatly influenced the American colonists because they seemed to fit colonial history. The Mayflower Compact, the Fundamental Orders of Connecticut, and other colonial charters were all agreements between the people and their government. When Locke referred to "natural rights," the colonists understood those to be the specific rights of Englishmen set out in such documents as the Magna Carta and the English Bill of Rights. By the 1770s, the American colonies would put these ideas into practice when they launched their own revolution against Britain.

According to Locke, what is the source of a government's right to rule?

▼ *John Locke wrote* Two Treatises of Government *to justify Parliament's decision to put William and Mary on the throne and require them to accept the English Bill of Rights (shown being presented below).*

📜 For an excerpt from the English Bill of Rights, see page R41 in **Documents in American History.**

The Glorious Revolution and the English Bill of Rights had another important legacy. They suggested that revolution was justified when individual rights were violated. The English Bill of Rights also influenced colonial demands before the American Revolution and helped shape American government.

The Enlightenment

W During the late 1600s and 1700s in Europe, a period known as the Age of Enlightenment, philosophers put forth the theory that both the physical world and human nature operated in an orderly way according to natural laws. They also believed anyone could figure out these laws by using reason and logic.

📜 For an excerpt from the *Second Treatise of Government,* see page R42 in **Documents in American History.**

John Locke One of the most influential Enlightenment writers was **John Locke.** His contract theory of government and natural rights profoundly influenced the thinking of American political leaders. In his work *Two Treatises of Government,* Locke attempted to use reason to discover natural laws that applied to politics and society:

PRIMARY SOURCE

"123. If man in the state of nature be so free . . . why will he part with his freedom . . . ? [T]he enjoyment of property in this state is very unsafe, very insecure. This makes him willing . . . to join in society with others . . . for the mutual preservation of their lives, liberties and estates . . . .

192. For no government can have a right to obedience from a people who have not freely consented to it; which they can never be supposed to do till . . . they are put in a full state of liberty to choose their government. . . ."

—from *Two Treatises of Government*

Locke's ideas struck a chord with American colonists. When Thomas Jefferson drafted the Declaration of Independence in 1776, he relied upon the words and ideas of John Locke. The colonists understood Locke's "natural rights" to be the specific rights English people had developed over the centuries and that were referred to in documents such as the Magna Carta and the English Bill of Rights.

Equally important was Locke's *Essay on Human Understanding.* In this work he argued

---

Extending the Content

Jean-Jacques Rousseau The Enlightenment agenda embodied classic American values: freedom of speech, the press, assembly, and religion, and opposition to the cruelty of unenlightened monarchs, to militarism, and to slavery. An influential French writer of the time, Jean-Jacques Rousseau, (zhahn•ZHAHK ru•SOH) commented on both slavery and the tyranny of monarchs in his famous essay, *The Social*

Contract: "Man is born free and is everywhere in chains….to alienate another's liberty is contrary to the natural order. … the right of slavery is null and void, not only as being illegitimate, but also because it is absurd and meaningless. The words *slave* and *right* contradict each other, and are mutually exclusive. It will always be equally foolish for a man to say to a man or to a people: I make with you a convention

wholly at your expense and wholly to my advantage; I shall keep it as long as I like, and you will keep it as long as I like." Enlightenment writers believed that human reason could be used to combat ignorance, superstition, and tyranny, and to build a better world.

that contrary to what the Church taught, people were not born sinful. Instead their minds were blank slates that society and education could shape for the better. These ideas that all people have rights and that society can be improved became core beliefs in American society.

Rousseau and Montesquieu French thinker Jean-Jacques Rousseau carried Locke's ideas further. In *The Social Contract*, he argued that a government should be formed by the consent of the people, who would then make their own laws. Another influential Enlightenment writer was Baron Montesquieu. In his work *The Spirit of Laws*, published in 1748, Montesquieu suggested that there were three types of political power—executive, legislative, and judicial. These powers should be separated into different branches of the government to protect the liberty of the people. The different branches would provide checks and balances against each other and would prevent the government from abusing its authority.

The Great Awakening

While some Americans turned away from a religious worldview in the 1700s, others renewed their Christian faith. Throughout the colonies, ministers held revivals—large public meetings for preaching and prayer—where they stressed piety and being "born again," or emotionally uniting with God. This widespread resurgence of religious fervor is known as the **Great Awakening.**

The Great Awakening reached its height around 1740 with the fiery preaching of Jonathan Edwards and George Whitefield. Churches soon split into factions over a movement called pietism, which stressed an individual's devoutness. Those who embraced the new ideas—including Baptists, Presbyterians, and Methodists—won many converts, while older, more traditional churches lost members.

In the South, the Baptists gained a strong following among poor farmers. Baptists also welcomed enslaved Africans at their revivals and condemned the brutality of slavery. Hundreds of Africans joined Baptist congregations and listened to sermons that taught that all people were equal before God. Despite violent attempts by planters to break up Baptist meetings, about 20 percent of Virginia's whites and thousands of enslaved Africans had become Baptists by 1775.

A Powerful Legacy

Both the Enlightenment and the Great Awakening emphasized an individualism that inclined American colonists toward political independence. The Enlightenment, along with the Glorious Revolution, provided supporting arguments against British rule. The Great Awakening undermined allegiance to traditional authority.

✔ **Reading Check** **Determining Cause and Effect** How did the Enlightenment and the Great Awakening affect the established order?

Section 2 REVIEW

Vocabulary
1. **Explain** the significance of: triangular trade, slave codes, John Locke, Great Awakening.

Main Ideas
2. **Describing** What was slavery like in the early colonies?

3. **Analyzing** In what ways did the Great Awakening contribute to the independent spirit of American colonists?

Critical Thinking
4. **Big Ideas** What factors and motivations brought people to the American colonies in the 1700s?

5. **Categorizing** Use a graphic organizer similar to the one below to explain the reasons for the population increase in the colonies in the 1700s.

Factors Contributing to Colonial Population Increase

6. **Analyzing Visuals** Study the map on pages 18–19. How did enslaved Africans come to the American colonies? Which destination received the most enslaved people?

Writing About History
7. **Persuasive Writing** Suppose that you are a German immigrant to the colonies in 1725. Write a letter to relatives in Germany explaining what your life in the colonies has been like and encouraging them to join you.

History ONLINE
Study Central™ To review this section, go to glencoe.com and click on Study Central.

21

✔ **Reading Check**

Answer:
The Enlightenment caused many people to question the authority of monarchs and the political power of churches. The Great Awakening also undermined allegiance to traditional authority.

Assess

History ONLINE

Study Central™ provides summaries, interactive games, and online graphic organizers to help students review content.

Close

Analyzing Discuss the American ideal of improving one's social and economic status through hard work and education. **Ask:** Do you think Americans still can do this? Why or why not? Have students research and tell the class about cultures in which people were not able to improve their lot in life, such as seventeenth-century India (caste system) or Britain. **AL** **OL**

Section 2 REVIEW

Answers

1. All definitions can be found in the section and the Glossary.

2. Answers will vary, but may mention hard, forced labor; the break-up of families; the indignity of being treated as inferior and sold as a commodity; the loss of hope inherent in having no access to education or betterment of one's life; physical punishment; and other hardships.

3. Some ministers preached the equality of all men; provided arguments against British rule; supported individualism.

4. The hope of land and livelihood or wealth; ability to pursue their religion; enslaved African labor.

5. Importation of enslaved Africans; founding of new colonies by religious sects; immigration by people seeking land; shipment of British prisoners to the colonies; the promise of work and plentiful natural resources.

6. By boat; Brazil

7. Letters will vary but should mention the freedom to practice their religion and to have a voice in government, as well as the availability of work.

Focus

Section 3

Bellringer

Daily Focus Transparency 1.3

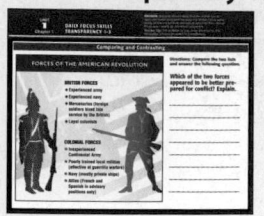

Guide to Reading

Answers:

Proclamation Act of 1763
Customs duties
Stamp Act of 1765
Townshend Acts
Intolerable Acts

Section Spotlight Video

To generate interest and provide a springboard for class discussion, access the Chapter 1, Section 3 video at glencoe.com or on the video DVD.

Resource Manager

Section 3

The American Revolution

Guide to Reading

Big Ideas

Struggles for Rights American colonists became dissatisfied with Britain's rule and fought to gain independence.

Content Vocabulary
• customs duty *(p. 23)*
• committee of correspondence *(p. 25)*
• minutemen *(p. 26)*

Academic Vocabulary
• communicate *(p. 25)*

People and Events to Identify
• Stamp Act *(p. 23)*
• Townshend Acts *(p. 24)*
• Intolerable Acts *(p. 26)*
• Lexington *(p. 26)*
• Concord *(p. 26)*
• George Washington *(p. 26)*
• Yorktown *(p. 29)*

Reading Strategy

Organizing Complete a graphic organizer like the one below to describe the causes that led the colonies to declare their independence.

Causes → Declaration of Independence

Escalating tensions over British control of the colonies resulted in a true revolt against British rule. The colonists established a new government for themselves and won their independence.

Growing Rebelliousness

MAIN Idea Unpopular British laws and taxes led to colonial protests and violence.

HISTORY AND YOU Have you ever read letters to the editor of your local newspaper protesting some local policies? Read on to learn how the colonists began to protest against unpopular taxes.

Britain and France struggled for dominance on the North American continent. Whenever the two countries were at war, their colonies were as well. In 1754 such a conflict began in America.

The French and Indian War

In the 1740s, Great Britain became interested in the Ohio River valley. So did Britain's long-standing rivals, the French. Before long, fighting broke out, and the French, with help from their Native American allies, took temporary control of the region.

From 1754 to 1759, the French and Indian War raged along the North American frontier. The fighting between Great Britain and France also spread to Europe, where it was known as the Seven Years' War. In the end, the British triumphed. The Treaty of Paris of 1763 made Great Britain the dominant power in North America. Its empire now included New France and all of Louisiana east of the Mississippi, except New Orleans. Britain also gained Florida from Spain, which had allied itself with France. However, France gave the Spanish western Louisiana and New Orleans.

Unpopular Regulations

Great Britain's victory left it with steep debts to repay and new territories to govern and defend. Many British leaders thought that the colonies should share in these costs. The American colonists did not like the policies Britain adopted to solve its financial problems.

The first troubles came with passage of the Proclamation Act of 1763. This act tried to halt colonial expansion into Native American lands west of the Appalachian Mountains. King George III wanted to avoid another costly war with the Native Americans, but the colonists who wanted access to the Ohio River valley were enraged.

R Reading Strategies	**C** Critical Thinking	**D** Differentiated Instruction	**W** Writing Support	**S** Skill Practice
Teacher Edition • Sequencing, pp. 23, 24 • Labeling, p. 25 • Identifying, p. 28 **Additional Resources** • Prim. Source Read., URB p. 35 • Guid. Read. Act., URB p. 48	**Teacher Edition** • Identifying Central Issues, p. 25 **Additional Resources** • Linking Past and Present, URB p. 34 • Interpreting Political Cartoons, URB p. 41 • Quizzes/Tests, p. 7	**Teacher Edition** • Organizing, p. 26 **Additional Resources** • Differentiated Instr., URB p. 23 • English Learner Act., URB p. 25 • American Art and Music Act., URB p. 39	**Teacher Edition** • Personal, p. 23 • Creating Pamphlets, p. 26 **Additional Resources** • Enrichment Act., URB p. 44	**Teacher Edition** • Doing Research, p. 24 • Compare/Contrast, p. 28 **Additional Resources** • Hist. Analysis Skill Act., URB p. 22 • Reinforcing Skills Act., URB p. 31 • Time Line Act., URB p. 33 • Reading Essen., p. 7

NATIONAL GEOGRAPHIC The French and Indian War, 1754–1763

JOIN, or DIE.

▲ After developing the Albany Plan, proposing a union of the colonies, Benjamin Franklin drew this cartoon urging the colonies to stand together. A popular legend at the time said that a snake could put itself back together and live if it did so before sunset.

0   200 kilometers
0   200 miles
Albers Equal-Area projection

NEW FRANCE

Sept. 18, 1759: British forces led by Wolfe capture Quebec

July 26, 1758: French surrender Louisbourg

Sept. 8, 1760: French surrender Montreal

July 26, 1759: British troops capture Fort Carillon (Ticonderoga)

August 27, 1758: Fort Frontenac captured by the British

Fall of 1755: Colonial troops are defeated at Crown Point

October, 1755: British deport 6,000 Acadian farmers and disperse them among the colonies

August 9, 1757: British surrender Fort William Henry

Fort Oswego

Fort Niagara

Maine (part of Mass.)

Port Royal

NOVA SCOTIA

ATLANTIC OCEAN

New York

Albany

Boston
Mass.

N.H.

Conn. R.I.

NEWFOUNDLAND

Gulf of St. Lawrence

July 9, 1755: Braddock defeated by French and Indian troops at Fort Duquesne

NEW FRANCE

Pennsylvania

New Jersey

Philadelphia

Maryland

Virginia

Delaware

New York

July 4, 1754: Washington surrenders at Fort Necessity

→ British advance
→ French advance
✴ British victory
✴ French victory
□ Fort

Analyzing GEOGRAPHY
1. **Location** Where did most of the British victories occur?
2. **Movement** From which colonial port did the British fleet sail to conquer Quebec?

▲ High cliffs protected Quebec, the capital of New France. As this painting depicts, British General James Wolfe found a path from the river up the steep cliffs. After defeating the French forces at Quebec, the British captured the city.

While western farmers denounced the Proclamation Act, eastern merchants objected to new tax policies. The British government had learned that the colonists were smuggling goods without paying **customs duties**—taxes on imports and exports. Britain tightened customs control and began introducing other unpopular measures. To bring in new revenue, the Sugar Act of 1764 raised taxes on imports of raw sugar and molasses. It also placed new taxes on silk, wine, coffee, and indigo. To make the colonists contribute to their own defense,

the Quartering Act of 1765 obligated them to provide shelter for British troops.

Nothing, however, outraged the colonists more than the **Stamp Act** of 1765. The act required stamps to be bought and placed on most printed materials, from newspapers to playing cards. This was a direct tax—the first Britain had ever placed on the colonists. Editorials, pamphlets, and speeches poured out against it. Groups calling themselves the Sons of Liberty organized protests and tried to intimidate stamp distributors.

Chapter 1   A Nation is Born   **23**

Teach

W Writing Support
Personal Have students assume the role of a colonist enlisted as a soldier on either the French or British side in the French and Indian War. Each student should write a letter to a relative or friend who lives in another colony. The letter should express how the writer feels about having to be involved in a war the colonists did not start. **OL**

R Reading Strategy
Sequencing Have students use the map to list the battles of the French and Indian War, in sequence. **BL**

Analyzing GEOGRAPHY
Answers:
1. New France
2. Boston

Additional Support

Activity: Collaborative Learning

Determining Cause and Effect Have students work in pairs to summarize the causes of the French and Indian War. *(British competition with France over the Ohio River valley)* **Ask:** Do you agree with Great Britain's opinion that the colonists should share in the costs of the war? Why or why not? *(Answers will vary.)* Have students work independently to write a short paragraph explaining their answers. Then invite volunteers to share what they have written with the class. **OL**

S Skill Practice

Doing Research Remind students that the Sons of Liberty organized one of the first American boycotts. **Ask:** How effective was the boycott? *(very, England saw sales plunge and thousands of workers lost their jobs.)* Have students research the group and write a paragraph about their goals, members, and activities. **OL**

R Reading Strategy

Sequencing Ask students to sequence the events related to the Townshend Acts. **BL**

✔ Reading Check

Answer:
Whether the colonies should help pay for the French and Indian War; whether colonists should pay customs duties; whether printed materials should be taxed; whether Parliament had the right to tax colonists without the approval of colonists' representatives.

Additional Support

In October 1765 representatives from nine colonies met for what became known as the Stamp Act Congress. They issued the Declaration of Rights and Grievances, arguing that only representatives elected by the colonists, not Parliament, had the right to tax them. "No taxation without representation" became a popular catch-phrase.

On November 1, when the Stamp Act took effect, the colonists ignored it and began to boycott all goods made in Britain. Merchants in England saw sales plunge, and thousands of workers lost their jobs. Under pressure, British lawmakers repealed the Stamp Act in 1766.

R The Townshend Acts

With British financial problems worsening, Parliament passed new measures in 1767 to raise money from the colonies. These came to be called the **Townshend Acts,** after Charles Townshend, the head of Britain's treasury. The Townshend Acts put new customs duties on glass, lead, paper, paint, and tea imported into the colonies. They also gave customs officers new powers to arrest smugglers.

The Townshend Acts led to a great outcry. In Massachusetts, Sam Adams and James Otis led the resistance. In Virginia, Patrick Henry, George Washington, and Thomas Jefferson organized opposition. When both colonies passed statements challenging Britain's right to tax them, Parliament dissolved their assemblies.

On March 5, 1770, anger turned to violence in Boston. A crowd of colonists began taunting a British soldier guarding a customs house. He called for help, and during the commotion, the British troops opened fire on the crowd, killing five colonists. The Boston Massacre, as the incident became known, might well have initiated more violence. Within weeks, though, tensions were calmed by news that the British had repealed almost all of the Townshend Acts. Parliament kept one tax—on tea—to uphold its right to tax the colonies. At the same time, it allowed the colonial assemblies to resume meeting. Peace and stability returned to the colonies, at least temporarily.

✔ Reading Check **Summarizing** What disagreements arose between Britain and the colonies in the 1700s?

Countdown to Revolution, 1763–1776

1763
Proclamation of 1763 bans colonists from settling west of the Proclamation Line

1765
Stamp Act Congress issues Declaration of Rights and Grievances

1767
Townshend Acts impose new taxes on trade goods; violators to be tried in vice admiralty courts

1768
Colonial merchants begin nonimportation campaign, refusing to import British goods; Daughters of Liberty help by spinning cloth

1764 | **1766** | **1768** | **1770**

1764
Sugar Act imposes new taxes on trade; James Otis argues that taxation without representation violates colonists' liberties

1765
The Stamp Act imposes taxes on printed materials; Sons of Liberty organize protests and boycotts

1770
British troops shoot colonists at Boston Massacre; most Townshend Acts are repealed

Activity: Collaborative Learning

Creating a Poster Have students work in small groups to research boycotts that have been conducted. Each group should select a boycott and create a poster that educates the class about it. Each poster should include a title, at least one relevant photo, and text that answers these questions: Who? What? Where? When? Why? How? The "How" section should explain how the group organized the boycott and how successful it was. Examples of boycotts might be the national grape boycott led by United Farm Workers Union (1967–1970); the boycott of Jewish businesses in Poland (1935–1945); or the current boycott of Canadian products led by Respect for Animals, protesting seal slaughters; or any other boycott. A list of current boycotts can be found at www.ethicalconsumer.org **OL** **AL**

The Road to War

MAIN Idea When Britain introduced new laws to assert its authority, the colonists decided to declare their independence.

HISTORY AND YOU Have you ever wondered how the colonists must have felt as they decided to defy Parliament? Read on to learn about the growing discontent of the colonists.

The repeal of the Townshend Acts in 1770 brought calm to the colonies for a time. Soon, however, new British policies led American colonists to declare their independence.

The Colonists Defy Britain

After trade with England had resumed, so had smuggling. When some 150 colonists seized and burned the stranded customs ship *Gaspee*, the British gave investigators the authority to bring suspects back to England for trial. Colonists thought this denied them the right to a trial by a jury of their peers. Based on a suggestion by Thomas Jefferson, they created **committees of** **correspondence** to **communicate** with one another and coordinate strategy.

In May 1773, Parliament passed the Tea Act, which created favorable business terms for the struggling British East India Company. American merchants, who feared they would be squeezed out of business, were outraged. That fall, when new shipments of British tea arrived in American harbors, colonists in New York, Philadelphia, and Charleston blocked its delivery. Bostonians went one step further. On the night before the tea was to be unloaded, about 150 men boarded the ships. They dumped 342 chests of tea overboard as several thousand people on shore cheered. The raid came to be called the Boston Tea Party.

The Boston Tea Party outraged the British. In the spring of 1774, Parliament passed new laws known as the Coercive Acts to punish Massachusetts. One law shut down Boston's port until the city paid for the destroyed tea. Other laws banned most town meetings and expanded the powers of the royally appointed governor, General Thomas Gage. To enforce the acts, the king stationed 2,000 troops in New England.

1773
At Boston Tea Party, colonists toss British tea into Boston Harbor

1774
Britain imposes Coercive Acts; First Continental Congress meets, passes the Suffolk Resolves, and issues Declaration of Rights and Grievances

January 1776
Tom Paine publishes *Common Sense*, arguing for independence

July 4, 1776
Congress issues Declaration of Independence

1772 ▶ 1774 ▶ 1776 ▶

1775
British battle colonial militia at Lexington and Concord; Second Continental Congress meets, selects George Washington to head Continental Army

Analyzing TIME LINES

1. **Stating** When and under what circumstances did the concept of "taxation without representation" first appear?
2. **Specifying** Which occurred first—the Boston Tea Party or the battles at Lexington and Concord?

R Reading Strategy

Labeling Tell students that historical events are often called by satirical or euphemistic names. **Ask:** Why do you think a rebellious act was called the "Boston Tea Party"? (*"Tea party" is satirical, ridiculing the well-known British tradition.*) On the board, write: "Satirical," "Euphemistic," and "Actual." Have students fill in the columns with satirical and euphemistic expressions and their actual meanings. **OL** **AL**

C Critical Thinking

Identifying Central Issues Call students' attention to the British reaction to the *Gaspee* incident. **Ask:** Why do you think the colonists supported the right for accused people to be tried by a jury of their peers? (*Answers will vary, but may include that it would help ensure that rights were not violated.*) **OL**

Analyzing TIME LINES

Answers:
1. In 1764, in reaction to the Sugar Act, James Otis argues that taxation without representation violates colonists' rights.
2. Boston Tea Party

Hands-On Chapter Project
Step 3

From Colonies to Independence

Step 3: Understanding Points of View Divide the class into two groups. One group will compile a list of complaints the American colonists had about British rule. The other group will learn more about Parliament and how the British regarded taxation.

Directions Ask the first group: What actions did the king and Parliament take that most angered the colonists? Students will summarize the actions. Students' list of complaints as American colonists should reflect the actions of the king and Parliament. The second group of students will place themselves in the role of the British Prime Minister and respond to the petition written by Group 1.

Composing and Summarizing Members of Group 1 will assume the role of colonists in 1775 and write a letter to King George III explaining their grievances. Students in Group 2 will summarize their actions and reasoning into a governmental action plan. **OL**

(Chapter Project continued on page 35)

W Writing Support

Creating Pamphlets Ask students to write a pamphlet urging other students to join either the Loyalists or the Whigs. Have students share their pamphlets with the class. **OL**

D Differentiated Instruction

Organizing Ask students to write two headings on a sheet of paper: "Britain" and "American colonies." Then have them place each of the following in one of the columns: Tory, Whig, General Gage, Loyalist, Continental Army, John Hancock, minuteman, George Washington, Patriot. **BL**

Additional Support

A few months later the British introduced the Quebec Act, which extended Quebec's boundaries to include much of what is today Ohio, Illinois, Michigan, Indiana, and Wisconsin. Colonists in that territory would have no elected assembly. The Quebec Act, coming so soon after the Coercive Acts, seemed to signal Britain's desire to seize control of colonial governments.

Colonists wasted no time in protesting the **Intolerable Acts,** as the Coercive Acts and the Quebec Act jointly came to be known. In June 1774, the Massachusetts Assembly suggested that representatives from all the colonies meet to discuss the next step. The First Continental Congress met in Philadelphia on September 5. The 55 delegates, who came from each of the 12 colonies except Georgia, debated a variety of ideas. Finally they approved a plan to boycott British goods. They also agreed to hold a second Continental Congress in May 1775 if the crisis remained unresolved.

D The Revolution Begins

Meanwhile, Great Britain had suspended the Massachusetts assembly. Massachusetts lawmakers responded by regrouping and naming John Hancock as their leader. He became, in effect, a rival governor to General Gage. A full-scale rebellion was now under way. The Massachusetts militia began to drill. The town of Concord created a special unit of **minutemen** who were trained and ready to "stand at a minute's warning in case of alarm."

Although many colonists disagreed with Parliament's policies, some still felt a strong sense of loyalty to the king and believed British law should be upheld. These Americans came to be known as Loyalists, or Tories. On the other side were the Patriots, or Whigs, who believed the British had become tyrants. The Patriots dominated in New England and Virginia, while the Loyalists were strong in Georgia, the Carolinas, and New York.

In April 1775, General Gage decided to seize Patriot arms and ammunition being stored in Concord. On the night of April 18, about 700 British troops secretly set out from nearby Boston. Messengers, including Paul Revere, were sent to spread the alarm. When the British reached **Lexington,** a town on the way to Concord, 70 minutemen were waiting for them. No one knows who fired first,

but when the smoke cleared, 8 minutemen lay dead and 10 more were wounded.

The British then headed to **Concord,** only to find most of the military supplies already removed. Colonial militiamen and farmers in the area fired at them from behind trees, stone walls, barns, and houses as they retreated to Boston. As news of the fighting spread, militia raced from all over New England to help. By May 1775, militia troops had surrounded Boston, trapping the British inside.

Three weeks later, the Second Continental Congress met and voted to "adopt" the militia surrounding Boston. **George Washington** became general and commander in chief of this Continental Army. Before Washington could reach his troops, the militia was tested again. It turned back two British advances at the Battle of Bunker Hill before running out of ammunition. The resulting stalemate helped to

Debates IN HISTORY

Should the American Colonies Declare Independence?

Although it may seem like the only natural course today, in 1776 independence was not the obvious choice for the 13 British colonies. While many were fed up with British actions and thought that it was time to institute true self-rule, others felt loyalty to what they considered their mother country and wanted to pursue a resolution of their grievances through political and diplomatic, not military, means. British-born Thomas Paine was one who strongly supported independence, as he discussed in his famous pamphlet, *Common Sense.* American-born John Dickinson, while angered at the behavior of the British, expressed in a speech to the Congress his arguments against splitting from Great Britain.

Cooperative Learning Activity

Discussing a Topic Organize the class into groups of four or five. **Ask:** Was there ever a point during the events discussed in this section when reconciliation between the British and the colonists was possible? When? What would have been required of both parties? After discussion, instruct the groups to take a yes/no vote. One person in each group should report the group's vote, as well as the reasons for it. **OL**

build American confidence. It showed that the largely untrained colonial militia could stand up to one of the world's most feared armies.

Decision for Independence

Many colonists were still not prepared to break away from Great Britain. In July 1775, the Continental Congress sent King George III a document known as the Olive Branch Petition. The petition asserted the colonists' loyalty to the king and urged him to resolve their grievances peacefully. King George not only rejected the petition, but he declared the colonies to be "open and avowed enemies."

With no compromise likely, the fighting spread. The Continental Congress established a navy and began seizing British merchant ships. Patriots invaded Canada and faced off against British and Loyalist troops in Virginia

and the Carolinas. More and more colonists now began to favor a break with Britain.

Thomas Paine helped sway public opinion with his pamphlet *Common Sense,* published in January 1776. Paine argued that King George III, and not Parliament, was responsible for British actions against the colonies. In his view, George III was a tyrant, and it was time to declare independence.

In early July, a committee of the Continental Congress approved a document that Thomas Jefferson had drafted in which the colonies dissolved ties with Britain. On July 4, 1776, the full Congress issued this Declaration of Independence. The colonies now proclaimed themselves the United States of America, and the American Revolution formally began.

History ONLINE
Student Web Activity Visit glencoe.com and complete the activity on the American Revolution.

✔ **Reading Check** **Explaining** Why did the colonies declare their independence?

Debates IN HISTORY

YES	**NO**

Thomas Paine
Writer

PRIMARY SOURCE

"It is the good fortune of many to live distant from the scene of present sorrow; . . . But let our imaginations transport us for a few moments to Boston. . . . The inhabitants of that unfortunate city who but a few months ago were in ease and affluence, have now no other alternative than to stay and starve, or turn out to beg. . . .

Men of passive tempers look somewhat lightly over the offenses of Britain and, still hoping for the best, are apt to call out, *Come, come we shall be friends again for all this.* But examine the passions and feelings of mankind; Bring the doctrine of reconciliation to the touchstone of nature, and then tell me whether you can hereafter love, honour, and faithfully serve the power that hath carried fire and sword into your land?"

—from *Common Sense*

John Dickinson
Delegate, Continental Congress

PRIMARY SOURCE

"Even those Delegates who are not restrained by Instructions [from their legislatures] have no Right to establish an independent separate Government for a Time of Peace. . . . without a full & free Consent of the People plainly exprest [sic]. . . . We are now acting on a principle of the English Constitution in resisting the assumption or Usurpation of an unjust power. We are now acting under that Constitution. Does that Circumstance [support] its Dissolution? But granting the present oppression to be a Dissolution, the Choice of . . . Restoring it, or forming a new one is vested in our Constituents, not in Us. They have not given it to Us. We may pursue measures that will force them into it. But that implies not a Right so to force them."

—from *Letters of Delegates to Congress, 1774–1789*

DBQ **Document-Based Questions**

1. **Finding the Main Idea** What are the main ideas in Paine's argument?
2. **Paraphrasing** Why does Dickinson believe that the Congress has no right to form a new government?
3. **Assessing** Which argument do you think is the most logical? Explain.

Chapter 1 A Nation is Born **27**

Extending the Content

Comparing Cultures Thomas Paine based many of his ideas on his observations of the culture of his Iroquois neighbors. He especially admired these Native American concepts: equal distribution of land; care of the elderly as a responsibility of society; opposition to slavery and capital punishment; public education; and a citizenry characterized by generosity, honesty, humility, courage, caring, and respect. During the writing of the Declaration of Independence,

Paine initiated a major debate over substitution of the phrase "happiness" for "property" in the Declaration. The final wording guarantees every American the right to "life, liberty, and the pursuit of happiness."

R **Reading Strategy**

Identifying Ask students to identify three factors that helped the colonists win the war for independence. *(Local militias' unconventional tactics; Washington's surprise winter attacks in New Jersey; lack of coordination between Generals Howe and Burgoyne; French assistance)* **BL**

S **Skill Practice**

Comparing and Contrasting
Have students research at least three paintings of Washington crossing the Delaware River. Lead a class discussion comparing the styles of the paintings, what each artist tried to convey, and what the details of the paintings say about each artist's intent. **OL**

Analyzing **GEOGRAPHY**

Answers:
1. **north:** British North America, the Great Lakes; **south:** northern Florida; **west:** Mississippi River
2. Britain and Spain

Additional Support

R War for Independence

MAIN Idea With the help of allies, the Americans defeated the British in the Revolutionary War.

HISTORY AND YOU Can you think of wars in which the weaker side defeated a stronger power? Read to learn how the Americans managed to defeat Britain.

The Continental Army could not match the British Army in size, funding, discipline, or experience. However, the Continental Army was fighting on home ground and in every state had help from local militias that used unconventional tactics. Moreover, Britain already faced threats to other parts of its empire and could not afford a long and costly war.

The Northern Campaign

The British under the command of General William Howe were quickly able to seize New York City. Then, in October, Howe led his troops south toward Philadelphia, where the Continental Congress was meeting. George Washington raced to meet him, but both armies were surprised by the early onset of winter weather and set up camp. Nevertheless, Washington decided to try a surprise attack. On the night of December 25, 1776, he led some 2,400 men across the icy Delaware River from Pennsylvania to New Jersey. There they **S** achieved two small victories before they camped for the winter.

By the spring of 1777, both sides were on the move again. General Howe revived his plan to capture Philadelphia and the Continental Congress. On September 11, 1777, he defeated Washington at the Battle of Brandywine Creek. Howe captured Philadelphia, but the Continental Congress escaped.

While General Howe remained in Philadelphia, another British force, led by General John Burgoyne, was marching south from Quebec. Burgoyne expected to link up with Howe in New York but failed to coordinate with him. When he and his 5,000 men reached Saratoga in upstate New York, they

NATIONAL GEOGRAPHIC **North America Following the Treaty of Paris, 1783**

ARCTIC CIRCLE

Hudson Bay

BRITISH NORTH AMERICA

UNITED STATES

SPANISH LOUISIANA

NEW SPAIN

PACIFIC OCEAN

ATLANTIC OCEAN

Gulf of Mexico

TROPIC OF CANCER

British	Spanish	
French	United States	
Russian	Disputed	

0   800 kilometers
0   800 miles
Lambert Azimuthal Equal-Area projection

▲ The British surrender at Yorktown. John Trumbull was not present at the surrender but did his best to depict true likenesses of those he knew personally, such as George Washington, shown on horseback in front of the flag.

Analyzing **GEOGRAPHY**

1. **Location** After the American Revolution, what were the borders of the United States in the north? In the south? In the west?

2. **Regions** Which foreign colonies shared a border with the United States in 1783?

Extending the Content

Surrender Washington is pictured in Trumbull's painting, but he did not receive the British surrender. Cornwallis refused to surrender to Washington, whom he felt was of inferior rank, so he sent his second-in-command, General O'Hara, shown in the red uniform, standing in the center. O'Hara first tried to surrender to the French army commander Rochambeau as more suitable than a lowly colonial general. Rochambeau refused to accept it and sent O'Hara, rightly, to Washington. However, Washington would not accept the surrender from anyone less than Cornwallis, so sent his own subordinate, Major-General Lincoln, who is pictured here on horseback in the center, to accept it from O'Hara. In that way, the surrender finally was accomplished.

were surrounded by a far bigger American army. On October 17, 1777, they surrendered—a stunning victory for the Americans. The victory improved morale and convinced the French to commit troops to the American cause.

While both Spain and France had been secretly aiding the Americans, the French now agreed to fight openly. On February 6, 1778, France signed an alliance, becoming the first country to recognize the United States as an independent nation. In 1779 Spain entered the war as an ally of France.

Fighting on Other Fronts

After losing the Battle of Saratoga, the British suffered other significant losses on the western frontier. In 1779 George Rogers Clark secured American control of the Ohio River valley. American troops also took control of western Pennsylvania, western New York, and Cherokee lands in western Virginia and North Carolina.

In the South, though, the British expected to find more Loyalist support and at first held the upper hand. In December 1778, they captured Savannah, Georgia, and seized control of Georgia's backcountry. Then a massive British force led by General Charles Cornwallis moved on to Charleston, South Carolina. On May 8, 1780, they forced the surrender of nearly 5,500 American troops, the greatest American defeat in the war. The tide finally turned on October 7, 1780, at the Battle of Kings Mountain. After defeating Loyalists, Patriot forces drove the British out of most of the South.

The Americans also fought the British at sea. Since they did not have the resources to assemble a large navy, Congress issued letters of marque, or licenses, to about 2,000 privately owned ships. In addition to winning some naval battles, the Americans were able to seriously harm British trade by attacking merchant ships.

The American Victory

The last major battle of the Revolutionary War was fought in **Yorktown,** Virginia, in the fall of 1781. General Cornwallis became trapped there, with George Washington closing in on land and the French navy blocking escape by sea. On October 19, 1781, Cornwallis and approximately 8,000 British troops surrendered.

After learning of the American victory at Yorktown, Parliament voted to end the war. Peace talks began in early April 1782, and the final settlement, the Treaty of Paris, was signed on September 3, 1783. In this treaty, Britain recognized the United States of America as an independent nation with the Mississippi River as its western border. The British kept Canada, but they gave Florida back to Spain and made other concessions to France. On November 24, 1783, the last British troops left New York City. The Revolutionary War was over, and a new nation began to take shape.

✓ **Reading Check** **Analyzing** Which major battle during the war was a turning point for the Americans?

Section 3 REVIEW

Vocabulary
1. **Explain** the significance of: customs duties, Stamp Act, Townshend Acts, committees of correspondence, Intolerable Acts, minutemen, George Washington, Yorktown.

Main Ideas
2. **Explaining** Why did the British decide to raise taxes to bring in new revenue?
3. **Describing** In July 1775, how did the Continental Congress begin to act like an independent government?
4. **Summarizing** What event convinced the French to openly assist the Americans?

Critical Thinking
5. **Big Ideas** Why were the French at first reluctant to make an alliance with the colonies?
6. **Categorizing** Use a graphic organizer to indicate ways in which colonists defied Britain's attempts at regulation and taxation.

Colonists' Acts of Defiance

7. **Analyzing Visuals** Study the cartoon on page 23. What was the purpose of the cartoon? What did each section of the snake represent?

Writing About History
8. **Persuasive Writing** Suppose that you are a colonial leader during the American Revolution. Write a letter to convince the ruler of a European nation to support the Americans in the war.

History ONLINE
Study Central™ To review this section, go to glencoe.com and click on Study Central.

29

✓ **Reading Check**
Answer:
Kings Mountain

Assess
· · · · · · · · · · · · · · · · · · · ·
History ONLINE
Study Central™ provides summaries, interactive games, and online graphic organizers to help students review content.

Close
· · · · · · · · · · · · · · · · · · · ·
Sequencing Ask students to sequence the major events of the Revolutionary War that led to the American victory. **OL**

Section 3 REVIEW

Answers

1. All definitions can be found in the section and the Glossary.
2. They needed money to pay for the French and Indian War.
3. The Continental Congress established a navy and began seizing British ships.
4. The 1777 American victory at Saratoga, New York
5. They had just fought—and lost—the costly French and Indian War with Britain and were reluctant to enter into another one

openly, although they covertly helped the colonists.
6. smuggled exports without paying customs duties; tried to intimidate stamp-tax distributors; Boston Tea Party; burned the *Gaspee;* formed Continental Congresses; declared independence
7. The cartoon urged the colonies to stand together; each section represented a different colony.
8. Letters will vary, but should include reasons mentioned throughout the section.

THE DECLARATION OF INDEPENDENCE

Focus

MAKING CONNECTIONS

Have students speculate why the nation's Founders thought it was important to formally declare independence from Great Britain and write their suggestions on the board. Then have them skim the Declaration of Independence to determine if Thomas Jefferson, the document's author, gave his readers any reasons. *(Answers will vary, but students may point out that the Declaration justifies independence as an inalienable right that is derived from the consent of the people [the governed]. Jefferson also lists numerous grievances against King George III.)* Discuss with the class how Jefferson's reasons differ from their suggestions.

Teach

D Differentiated Instruction

English Learners Choose a student to read aloud the first paragraph under "Declaration of Natural Rights" on this page. Discuss with students any unfamiliar terms such as *self-evident* and *inalienable*. Then have students close their textbook and write a paraphrase of the first paragraph. **ELL**

Additional Support

What It Means
The Preamble The Declaration of Independence has four parts. The Preamble explains why the Continental Congress drew up the Declaration.

impel *force*

What It Means
Natural Rights The second part, the Declaration of Natural Rights, states that people have certain basic rights and that government should protect those rights. John Locke's ideas strongly influenced this part. In 1690 Locke wrote that government was based on the consent of the people and that people had the right to rebel if the government did not uphold their right to life, liberty, and property.

endowed *provided*

despotism *unlimited power*

What It Means
List of Grievances The third part of the Declaration lists the colonists' complaints against the British government. Notice that King George III is singled out for blame.

30 The Declaration of Independence

In Congress, July 4, 1776. The unanimous Declaration of the thirteen united States of America,

[Preamble]

When in the Course of human events, it becomes necessary for one people to dissolve the political bands which have connected them with another, and to assume among the Powers of the earth, the separate and equal station to which the Laws of Nature and of Nature's God entitle them, a decent respect to the opinions of mankind requires that they should declare the causes which **impel** them to the separation.

[Declaration of Natural Rights]

We hold these truths to be self-evident, that all men are created equal, that they are **endowed** by their Creator with certain unalienable Rights, that among these are Life, Liberty, and the pursuit of Happiness.

That to secure these rights, Governments are instituted among Men, deriving their just powers from the consent of the governed,

That whenever any Form of Government becomes destructive of these ends, it is the Right of the People to alter or to abolish it, and to institute new Government, laying its foundation on such principles and organizing its powers in such form, as to them shall seem most likely to effect their Safety and Happiness. Prudence, indeed, will dictate that Governments long established should not be changed for light and transient causes; and accordingly all experience hath shown, that mankind are more disposed to suffer, while evils are sufferable, than to right themselves by abolishing the forms to which they are accustomed. But when a long train of abuses and usurpations, pursuing invariably the same Object evinces a design to reduce them under absolute **Despotism**, it is their right, it is their duty, to throw off such Government, and to provide new Guards for their future security.

[List of Grievances]

Such has been the patient sufferance of these Colonies; and such is now the necessity which constrains them to alter their former Systems of Government. The history of the

---

Extending the Content

The Real Title Strictly speaking, the title of this famous document is not the "Declaration of Independence," but rather "The Unanimous Declaration of the Thirteen United States of America." The document was not the act by which independence was declared. That had been done on July 2, when the Continental Congress adopted Richard Henry Lee's resolution.

Also, point out to students that their textbook uses the spelling and punctuation from the original document. Thus, in the introduction to the document, for example, the term *united* is not capitalized—just as Jefferson wrote.

present King of Great Britain is a history of repeated injuries and **usurpations**, all having in direct object the establishment of an absolute Tyranny over these States. To prove this, let Facts be submitted to a candid world.

He has refused his Assent to Laws, the most wholesome and necessary for the public good.

He has forbidden his Governors to pass Laws of immediate and pressing importance, unless suspended in their operation till his Assent should be obtained; and when so suspended, he has utterly neglected to attend to them.

He has refused to pass other Laws for the accommodation of large districts of people, unless those people would **relinquish** the right of Representation in the Legislature, a right **inestimable** to them and formidable to tyrants only.

He has called together legislative bodies at places unusual, uncomfortable, and distant from the depository of their Public Records, for the sole purpose of fatiguing them into compliance with his measures.

He has dissolved Representative Houses repeatedly, for opposing with manly firmness his invasions on the rights of the people.

He has refused for a long time, after such dissolutions, to cause others to be elected; whereby the Legislative Powers, incapable of **Annihilation**, have returned to the People at large for their exercise; the State remaining in the mean time exposed to all the dangers of invasion from without, and **convulsions** within.

He has endeavoured to prevent the population of these States; for that purpose obstructing the Laws for **Naturalization of Foreigners**; refusing to pass others to encourage their migrations hither, and raising the conditions of new Appropriations of Lands.

He has obstructed the Administration of Justice, by refusing his Assent to Laws for establishing Judiciary Powers.

He has made Judges dependent on his Will alone, for the **tenure** of their offices, and the amount and payment of their salaries.

He has erected a multitude of New Offices, and sent hither swarms of Officers to harass our people, and eat out their substance.

He has kept among us, in times of peace, Standing Armies without the Consent of our legislature.

He has affected to render the Military independent of and superior to the Civil Power.

He has combined with others to subject us to a jurisdiction foreign to our constitution, and unacknowledged by our laws; giving his Assent to their acts of pretended legislation:

For **quartering** large bodies of troops among us:

For protecting them, by a mock Trial, from Punishment for any Murders which they should commit on the Inhabitants of these States:

usurpations *unjust uses of power*

relinquish *give up*
inestimable *priceless*

annihilation *destruction*

convulsions *violent disturbances*

Naturalization of Foreigners *process by which foreign-born persons become citizens*

tenure *term*

quartering *lodging*

The Declaration of Independence **31**

C **Critical Thinking**

Comparing and Contrasting
The Declaration lists many accusations against King George III.
Ask: Why would Great Britain have been opposed to allowing more immigrants to come to the colonies? *(An influx of immigrants would increase the power of the colonies; by restricting immigration, Britain could restrict the size of the colonial militias.)* Ask students to research the current U.S. policy on immigration. Have them write a one-page report explaining how today's immigration regulations compare with the restrictions placed on immigration to the colonies by the British before the Revolutionary War. **AL**

R **Reading Strategy**

Summarizing Have students read the list of grievances against King George III. Then have them select five of the complaints and summarize them in their own words. **OL**

Additional Support

Extending the Content

The Original Document The most frequently reproduced version of the Declaration of Independence is taken from the engraving made by printer William J. Stone in 1823. The original Declaration, now shown in the Rotunda for the Charters for Freedom in Washington, D.C., has faded badly—largely because of poor preservation techniques during the nineteenth century. Today, this priceless document is cared for using the most exacting archival conditions possible.

S Skill Practice

Organizing Organize the class into small groups. Assign each group one or two of the grievances listed in the Declaration of Independence. Have the groups use their textbooks, the Internet, or library resources to find specific events, acts, or statements made by the king or Parliament that relate to the grievance. Have students read aloud the grievances that they were assigned and state the information that relates to the grievance. **OL**

W Writing Support

Persuasive Writing Tell students to write an editorial about the Declaration of Independence to an influential Loyalist newspaper in Boston. Point out that their editorials should support the position of the newspaper and therefore should explain why the colonists should remain loyal to Great Britain. **AL**

Additional Support

---

render *make*

abducted *given up*

perfidy *violation of trust*

insurrections *rebellions*

petitioned for redress *asked formally for a correction of wrongs*

unwarrantable jurisdiction *unjustified authority*

consanguinity *originating from the same ancestor*

For cutting off our Trade with all parts of the world:

For imposing taxes on us without our Consent:

For depriving us in many cases, of the benefits of Trial by Jury:

For transporting us beyond Seas to be tried for pretended offences:

For abolishing the free System of English Laws in a neighbouring Province, establishing therein an Arbitrary government, and enlarging its Boundaries so as to **render** it at once an example and fit instrument for introducing the same absolute rule into these Colonies:

For taking away our Charters, abolishing our most valuable Laws, and altering fundamentally the Forms of our Governments:

For suspending our own Legislature, and declaring themselves invested with Power to legislate for us in all cases whatsoever.

He has **abdicated** Government here, by declaring us out of his Protection and waging War against us.

He has plundered our seas, ravaged our Coasts, burnt our towns, and destroyed the lives of our people.

He is at this time transporting large armies of foreign mercenaries to compleat the works of death, desolation and tyranny, already begun with circumstances of Cruelty & **perfidy** scarcely paralleled in the most barbarous ages, and totally unworthy the Head of a civilized nation.

He has constrained our fellow Citizens taken Captive on the high Seas to bear Arms against their Country, to become the executioners of their friends and Brethren, or to fall themselves by their Hands.

He has excited domestic **insurrections** amongst us, and has endeavoured to bring on the inhabitants of our frontiers, the merciless Indian Savages, whose known rule of warfare, is an undistinguished destruction of all ages, sexes and conditions.

In every stage of these Oppressions We have **Petitioned for Redress** in the most humble terms: Our repeated Petitions have been answered only by repeated injury. A Prince, whose character is thus marked by every act which may define a Tyrant, is unfit to be the ruler of a free People.

Nor have We been wanting in attention to our British brethren. We have warned them from time to time of attempts by their legislature to extend an **unwarrantable jurisdiction** over us. We have reminded them of the circumstances of our emigration and settlement here. We have appealed to their native justice and magnanimity, and we have conjured them by the ties of our common kindred to disavow these usurpations, which, would inevitably interrupt our connections and correspondence. They too have been deaf to the voice of justice and of **consanguinity**. We must, therefore, acquiesce in the necessity, which denounces our Separation, and hold them, as we hold the rest of mankind, Enemies in War, in Peace Friends.

32 The Declaration of Independence

Extending the Content

Jefferson and the Declaration In June 1776, Thomas Jefferson was assigned to a committee to draft the Declaration of Independence. Jefferson found it difficult to work in his current lodgings in the heart of Philadelphia, so he rented rooms in the home of Jacob Graff. The Graff home, located on the outskirts of the city, provided the peace and quiet Jefferson needed to write. He was able to complete the Declaration in less than three weeks.

The Graff home was torn down in 1883, but photographs of the site enabled the National Park Service to build a faithful recreation of the original building in 1975. Today, the rebuilt house includes a recreation of the rooms Jefferson rented on the second floor furnished with period furnishings.

[Resolution of Independence by the United States]

We, therefore, the Representatives of the united States of America, in General Congress, Assembled, appealing to the Supreme Judge of the world for the **rectitude** of our intentions, do, in the Name, and by Authority of the good People of these Colonies, solemnly publish and declare, That these United Colonies are, and of Right ought to be Free and Independent States; that they are Absolved from all Allegiance to the British Crown, and that all political connection between them and the State of Great Britain, is and ought to be totally dissolved; and that as Free and Independent States, they have full Power to levy War, conclude Peace, contract Alliances, establish Commerce, and to do all other Acts and Things which Independent States may of right do.

And for the support of this Declaration, with a firm reliance on the Protection of Divine Providence, we mutually pledge to each other our Lives, our Fortunes and our sacred Honor.

John Hancock
President from
Massachusetts

Georgia
Button Gwinnett
Lyman Hall
George Walton

North Carolina
William Hooper
Joseph Hewes
John Penn

South Carolina
Edward Rutledge
Thomas Heyward, Jr.
Thomas Lynch, Jr.
Arthur Middleton

Maryland
Samuel Chase
William Paca
Thomas Stone
Charles Carroll
of Carrollton

Virginia
George Wythe
Richard Henry Lee
Thomas Jefferson
Benjamin Harrison
Thomas Nelson, Jr.
Francis Lightfoot Lee
Carter Braxton

Pennsylvania
Robert Morris
Benjamin Rush
Benjamin Franklin
John Morton
George Clymer
James Smith
George Taylor
James Wilson
George Ross

Delaware
Caesar Rodney
George Read
Thomas McKean

New York
William Floyd
Philip Livingston
Francis Lewis
Lewis Morris

New Jersey
Richard Stockton
John Witherspoon
Francis Hopkinson
John Hart
Abraham Clark

New Hampshire
Josiah Bartlett
William Whipple
Matthew Thornton

Massachusetts
Samuel Adams
John Adams
Robert Treat Paine
Elbridge Gerry

Rhode Island
Stephen Hopkins
William Ellery

Connecticut
Samuel Huntington
William Williams
Oliver Wolcott
Roger Sherman

What It Means Resolution of Independence The final section declares that the colonies are "Free and Independent States" with the full power to make war, to form alliances, and to trade with other countries.

rectitude *rightness*

What It Means Signers of the Declaration The signers, as representatives of the American people, declared the colonies independent from Great Britain. Most members signed the document on August 2, 1776.

The Declaration of Independence **33**

Assess

C Critical Thinking
Analyzing Primary Sources
Have students create a chart listing the four sections of the Declaration of Independence and providing a brief summary and explanation of the purpose of each section. **OL**

S Skill Practice
Making Oral Presentations
Organize the class into groups. Assign each group one of the following: the French Revolution, Latin American independence movements, or the breakup of the Soviet Union. Have groups use library or Internet resources to learn about their assigned movement and the effects that the Declaration of Independence had on the movement. Have groups prepare an oral report on their findings. **OL**

Close
Organizing Information
Have students list the powers that the newly independent states planned to claim. **OL**

Additional Support

Extending the Content

John Hancock The signature of John Hancock on the Declaration of Independence is the most flamboyant and easily recognizable of all. In the colonial era, few figures were better known or more popular than John Hancock from Boston. He played an instrumental role in bringing about the American Revolution.

John Hancock was admired by his enemies as well as by his friends. As a populist leader, he had great confidence in the ability of the common people. He was also contemptuous of unreasonable authority. For example, the British had issued a decree in early 1776 offering a large reward for the capture of several leading Revolutionary figures. Hancock was one of them. On signing the Declaration he commented, "The British ministry can read that name without spectacles; let them double their reward."

Focus

Bellringer
Daily Focus Transparency 1.4

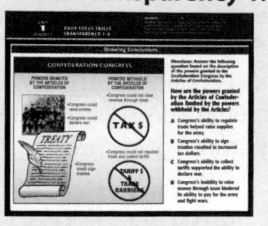

Guide to Reading

Answers:
Column 2: merchants, artisans, farmers dependent on trade, large landowners; goals: to get Constitution ratified **Column 3:** western farmers, less wealthy people, and people concerned about the balance of power between the states and the federal government; goals: to block ratification or add a Bill of Rights

Section Spotlight Video

To generate interest and provide a springboard for class discussion, access the Chapter 1, Section 4 video at glencoe.com or on the video DVD.

Resource Manager

Section 4

The Constitution

Guide to Reading

Big Ideas
Government and Society American leaders created a new Constitution based on compromise that promised a Bill of Rights.

Content Vocabulary
• popular sovereignty (p. 37)
• federalism (p. 37)
• separation of powers (p. 38)
• checks and balances (p. 38)
• veto (p. 38)
• ratification (p. 39)

Academic Vocabulary
• framework (p. 35)
• interpret (p. 38)
• revise (p. 39)

People and Events to Identify
• Federalist (p. 39)
• Anti-Federalist (p. 39)

Reading Strategy
Categorizing Complete a graphic organizer similar to the one below by listing the supporters and goals of the Federalists and Anti-Federalists.

	Federalists	Anti-Federalists
Source of Support		
Goals		

S tates adopted individual constitutions that called for government with powers divided among three different branches. They rejected the Articles of Confederation and ratified the national Constitution after many compromises and the promise of a Bill of Rights.

The Young Nation

MAIN Idea The states created constitutions that gave people more rights, but the national framework could not address all the problems of the new nation.

HISTORY AND YOU If you had lived in the colonies under British rule, what kind of government would you have created? Read on to learn how the American leaders at first created a weak central government.

When American leaders created the United States of America, they were very much aware that they were creating something new. They made a deliberate choice to replace royal rule with a republic. In a republic, power resides with citizens who are entitled to vote. The power is exercised by elected officials who are responsible to the citizens and must govern according to laws or a constitution.

In an ideal republic, all citizens are equal under the law, regardless of their wealth or social class. These ideas conflicted with many traditional beliefs, including ideas about slavery, about women not being allowed to vote or own property, and about certain families being "better" than others. Despite these contradictions, republican ideas began to change American society after the war.

New State Constitutions

Before the war ended, each state had drawn up its own written constitution. Virginia's, written in 1776, and Massachusetts's, drafted in 1780, became models for other states to follow. Their constitutions called for a separation of powers among the executive, legislative, and judicial branches of government. They set up bicameral, or two-house, legislatures, with a senate to represent people of property and an assembly to protect the rights of the common people. They also included a list of rights guaranteeing essential freedoms.

Other states varied in their constitutions. Perhaps most democratic was that of Pennsylvania. Rather than simply limiting the power of the governor, the Pennsylvania constitution eliminated the position entirely, along with the upper house. Instead, the state would be governed by a one-house legislature in which representatives would be elected annually.

R Reading Strategies	**C** Critical Thinking	**D** Differentiated Instruction	**W** Writing Support	**S** Skill Practice
Teacher Edition • Reading Graphs, p. 35 • Skimming, p. 39 **Additional Resources** • Reading Skills Act., URB p. 21 • Prim. Source Read., URB p. 37 • Guid. Read. Act., URB p. 49	**Teacher Edition** • Analyzing Info., p. 36 • Making Inferences, p. 37 • Analyzing, p. 38 **Additional Resources** • Crit. Think. Skills Act., URB p. 32 • Quizzes/Tests, p. 8	**Teacher Edition** • Visual/Spatial, p. 40 **Additional Resources** • English Learner Act., URB p. 25	**Teacher Edition** • Persuasive Writing, pp. 37, 39	**Additional Resources** • Reteaching Act., URB p. 43 • Reading Essen., p. 10

PRIMARY SOURCE

The Revolution Changes Government

Wealth of Elected Officials

Northern States

1765–1775   1783–1790

Southern States

1765–1775   1783–1790

☐ Over £ 5,000   ■ £ 2,000–£ 5,000   ▨ Under £ 2,000

Source: "Government by the People: The American Revolution and the Democratization of the Legislatures."

Analyzing VISUALS

1. **Analyzing** In the North after the Revolution, how much did the percentage of wealthy officeholders increase?

2. **Specifying** In which region did the greater number of middle-class people enter public office after the Revolution?

▲ *After the Revolution, voting rights expanded. In New Jersey, between 1790 and 1807, even women were able to vote. However, the percentage of wealthy people who actually held office increased.*

Teach

R Reading Strategy

Reading Graphs Have students study the graph about the wealth of elected officials. Ask them to summarize the changes in each region by comparing the percentage of wealthy elected officials before and after the American Revolution. **OL**

Analyzing VISUALS

1. about 45 percent
2. the South

Changes in Society

The concern for individual liberty led, among other things, to greater separation of church and state. For example, the Virginia Statute for Religious Freedom, passed in 1786, declared that Virginia no longer had an official church and that the state could not collect taxes to support churches.

Voting rights also expanded. Many states allowed any white male taxpayer to vote, whether or not he owned property. Property restrictions on running for office were also relaxed, and more people of modest means became eligible to serve in government.

Women and African Americans continued to be denied political rights, but they made some advances. Women gained greater access to education and could more easily obtain a divorce. For African Americans, emancipation, or freedom from enslavement, became a major issue. Thousands of enslaved people achieved freedom during the Revolution in return for their military service. Several Northern states,

such as Massachusetts, even took steps to abolish slavery gradually. In the South enslaved labor remained crucial to the economy, and little changed.

A Weak National Government

American leaders now worked to plan a central government for the new nation. On March 2, 1781, the **framework** they created took effect. The Articles of Confederation loosely unified the states under a single governing body, the Congress. There were no separate branches of government, and Congress had only limited powers. After fighting to free themselves from Britain's domineering rule, the states did not want to create a new government that might become tyrannical.

Under the Articles, each state had one vote in Congress. Congress could act only in certain arenas. It could negotiate with other nations, raise armies, and declare war, but it had no authority to regulate trade or impose taxes.

Chapter 1   A Nation is Born   **35**

Hands-On Chapter Project
Step 4

From Colonies to Independence

Step 4: Justifying the War Have students choose a role to take—either a member of the British army or a member of the Continental Army. Students will research the advantages and disadvantages of each opposing side at the beginning of the war.

Directions As a member of the chosen army, students will write a letter home

describing why they are fighting and why they believe that they will win this war.

Justifying Students will use facts to justify their arguments in a written letter. **OL**
(Chapter Project continued on the Visual Summary page)

C Critical Thinking

Analyzing Information Ask:

Why might settlers have wanted to move to the Northwest Territory? *(They might have wanted the independence and adventure of moving to a new region. They might also have been attracted by the exclusion of slavery and by freedom of religion, property rights, and right to trial by jury.)*

Analyzing GEOGRAPHY

1. 6 miles square
2. the income from section 16 in a township was set aside to fund public schools.

Reading Check

Answer:

unable to resolve inconsistent state trade policies; could not compel states to honor agreements with other countries; inability to tax or control currency damaged economy

Additional Support

Despite its weaknesses, the Congress was able to pass the Northwest Ordinance of 1787, a plan for selling and then governing the new lands west of the Appalachian Mountains and north of the Ohio River. The ordinance spelled out how states would be created from the Northwest Territory. It also guaranteed residents certain rights, including freedom of religion and freedom from slavery.

Congress lacked the power to effectively handle other challenges. Trade problems arose because states did not have uniform trade policies, and Congress had no authority to intervene. Foreign relations suffered because Congress could not compel the states to honor its agreements with other countries. The country sank into a severe recession, or economic slowdown, because without the power to tax,

Congress could not raise enough money to pay its war debts or its expenses. It could not even stop the states from issuing their own currency, which rapidly lost value and further weakened the economy.

Among those hardest hit by the recession were poor farmers. Their discontent turned violent in January 1787, when a bankrupt Massachusetts farmer named Daniel Shays led some 1,200 followers in a protest of new taxes. Shays's Rebellion was put down by the state militia, but the incident showed the weakness of the Congress to solve the nation's problems. Increasingly, many people began to call for a stronger central government.

✔ Reading Check **Explaining** In what ways was the Confederation Congress ineffective?

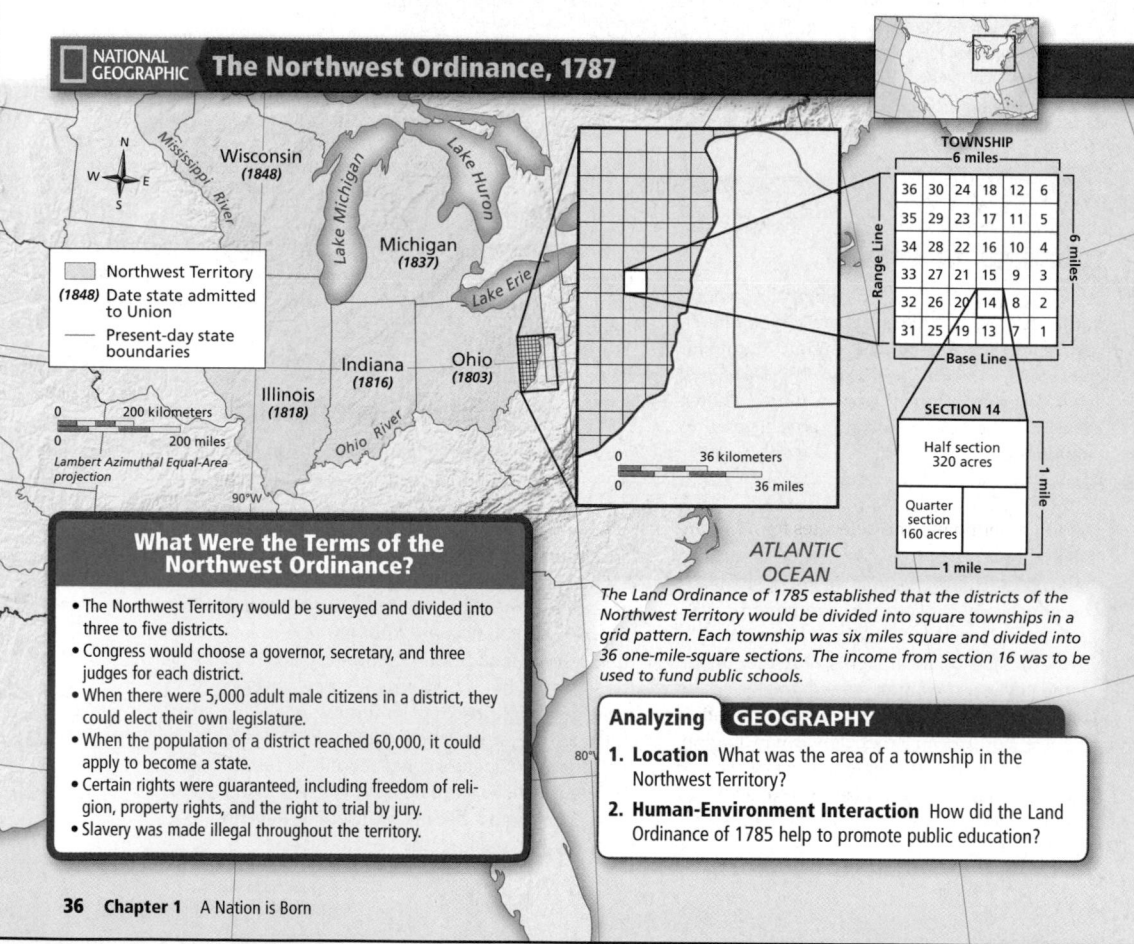

NATIONAL GEOGRAPHIC The Northwest Ordinance, 1787

Legend:
- Northwest Territory
- (1848) Date state admitted to Union
- — Present-day state boundaries

Wisconsin (1848)
Michigan (1837)
Indiana (1816)
Ohio (1803)
Illinois (1818)

0 200 kilometers
0 200 miles
Lambert Azimuthal Equal-Area projection

ATLANTIC OCEAN

TOWNSHIP
6 miles

36	30	24	18	12	6
35	29	23	17	11	5
34	28	22	16	10	4
33	27	21	15	9	3
32	26	20	14	8	2
31	25	19	13	7	1

Base Line
Range Line
6 miles

SECTION 14

Half section 320 acres

Quarter section 160 acres

1 mile

0 36 kilometers
0 36 miles

The Land Ordinance of 1785 established that the districts of the Northwest Territory would be divided into square townships in a grid pattern. Each township was six miles square and divided into 36 one-mile-square sections. The income from section 16 was to be used to fund public schools.

What Were the Terms of the Northwest Ordinance?

- The Northwest Territory would be surveyed and divided into three to five districts.
- Congress would choose a governor, secretary, and three judges for each district.
- When there were 5,000 adult male citizens in a district, they could elect their own legislature.
- When the population of a district reached 60,000, it could apply to become a state.
- Certain rights were guaranteed, including freedom of religion, property rights, and the right to trial by jury.
- Slavery was made illegal throughout the territory.

Analyzing GEOGRAPHY

1. **Location** What was the area of a township in the Northwest Territory?
2. **Human-Environment Interaction** How did the Land Ordinance of 1785 help to promote public education?

Extending the Content

Shays's Rebellion This rebellion, led by Daniel Shays, took place in Massachusetts from August 1786 to February 1787. Poor farmers, deep in debt, rebelled against high taxes and difficult economic conditions they were suffering in the wake of the Revolutionary War. In January 1787, Shays and his followers attacked a federal arsenal at Springfield, but their attack failed. On February 4, 1787, the state militia suppressed the rebellion. As a result of the rebellion, the Massachusetts legislature passed laws to improve the economic condition of those in debt.

A New Constitution

MAIN Idea American leaders created a new constitution based on compromise.

HISTORY AND YOU Have you ever come up with new rules to a game because the old ones did not work? Read on to learn why the Constitution replaced the Articles of Confederation.

The political and economic problems facing the United States in 1787 worried many American leaders. They believed that the new nation would not survive without a strong national government and that the Articles of Confederation had to be revised.

In May 1787 every state except Rhode Island sent delegates to Philadelphia "for the sole purpose of revising the Articles of Confederation." Instead of changing the Articles, though, the delegates quickly decided to abandon the Articles and write a brand-new framework of government. The meeting, attended by 55 of America's most distinguished leaders, is therefore known as the Constitutional Convention. The majority were attorneys, and most of the others were planters or merchants. Most had experience in colonial, state, or national government. The delegates chose George Washington as their presiding officer. Other notable delegates included Benjamin Franklin, Alexander Hamilton, and James Madison.

Debate and Compromise

All the delegates supported a stronger national government with the power to levy taxes and make laws that would be binding upon the states. The delegates also accepted the idea of dividing the government into executive, legislative, and judicial branches.

On other points, the delegates found themselves split. One contentious question was how each state should be represented in Congress. The larger states insisted that representation in Congress should be based on population. The smaller states feared that the larger states would outvote them under such a system and instead wanted each state to have an equal vote. The convention appointed a special committee to find a compromise. Ben Franklin, one of the committee members, warned the delegates what would happen if they failed to agree:

PRIMARY SOURCE

"[You will] become a reproach and by-word down to future ages. And what is worse, mankind may hereafter, from this unfortunate instance, despair of establishing governments by human wisdom, and leave it to chance, war, and conquest."

—from *Debates on the Adoption of the Federal Constitution*

The committee's solution was based on a suggestion by Roger Sherman from Connecticut. Congress would be divided into two houses. In one, the House of Representatives, the number of a state's representatives would depend on its population. In the other, the Senate, each state would have equal representation. The voters in each state would elect members to the House of Representatives, but the state legislatures would choose senators. This proposal came to be known as the Great Compromise or the Connecticut Compromise.

The Connecticut Compromise sparked a fresh controversy: whether to count enslaved people when determining how many representatives each state would have in the House. The matter was settled by the Three-Fifths Compromise. Every five enslaved people would count as three free persons for determining both representation and taxation.

In another compromise, the delegates dealt with the power of Congress to regulate trade. Delegates agreed that the new Congress could not tax exports. They also agreed that it could not ban the slave trade until 1808 or impose high taxes on the import of enslaved persons.

Framework of Government

With the major disputes behind them, the delegates now focused on the details of the new government. The new Constitution they crafted was based on the principle of **popular sovereignty** (SAH·vuhrn· tee), or rule by the people. Rather than a direct democracy, it created a representative system of government in which elected officials speak for the people.

To strengthen the central government but still preserve the rights of the states, the Constitution created a system known as **federalism.** Under federalism, power is divided between the federal, or national, government and the state governments.

C Critical Thinking

Making Inferences Print out for students or write on the board this quotation from Daniel Webster: "We may be tossed upon an ocean where we can see no land—nor, perhaps, the sun or stars. But there is a chart and a compass for us to study, to consult, and to obey. That chart is the Constitution." **Ask: What did he mean by this statement?** *(In uncertain times, the Constitution can provide guidance for all citizens.)* Ask interested students to locate other quotations by Daniel Webster, bring them to class, and explain their relevance today. **BL**

W Writing Support

Persuasive Writing Have students reread the information about the Great Compromise and write a speech by Roger Sherman, in which he sets forth his arguments for the Great Compromise. Their speeches should directly address the fears and concerns of the delegates. **AL**

Additional Support

Activity: Collaborative Learning

Doing Research Tell students that, besides being a political theorist, Ben Franklin was also an author, politician, printer, scientist, inventor, civic activist, and diplomat. Divide the class into small groups. Ask them to use library or Internet resources to learn about his life. Each group should jointly write a half-page description of one of his accomplishments—preferably one they think the rest of the class will not know about. One member of each group should give a short presentation to the class. Another member should bring in related photos.

C Critical Thinking

Analyzing Call students' attention to the areas covered by the Articles of Confederation in the infographic. **Ask:** Why were each of the changes made when the Framers wrote the new Constitution? *(Answers may include to make the federal government stronger and more effective, to eliminate some of the problems that occurred under the Articles of Confederation, and organize the government.)* Have students review previous sections to find the answers. **AL**

Analyzing VISUALS

Answers:

1. Members of the House of Representatives were elected by voters; members of Congress were appointed by state legislatures.
2. It gave the federal government the power to regulate both interstate and foreign trade.

Additional Support

The Constitution also provided for a **separation of powers** in the new government by dividing power among three branches. The two houses of Congress would compose the legislative branch of the government. They would make the laws. The executive branch, headed by a president, would implement and enforce the laws Congress passed. The president would perform other duties as well, such as proposing legislation, appointing judges, putting down rebellions, and serving as commander in chief of the armed forces. The judicial branch—a system of federal courts—would hear all cases arising under federal law and the Constitution, **interpret** federal laws, and render judgment in cases involving those laws. To keep the branches separate, no one serving in one branch could serve in the other branches at the same time.

Checks and Balances

In addition to giving each of the three branches of government separate powers, the framers of the Constitution created a system of **checks and balances** to prevent any one of the three branches from becoming too powerful. Each branch would have some ability to limit the power of the other two.

The president could check Congress by deciding to **veto,** or reject, a proposed law. The legislature would need a two-thirds vote in both houses to override a veto. The Senate also had the power to approve or reject presidential

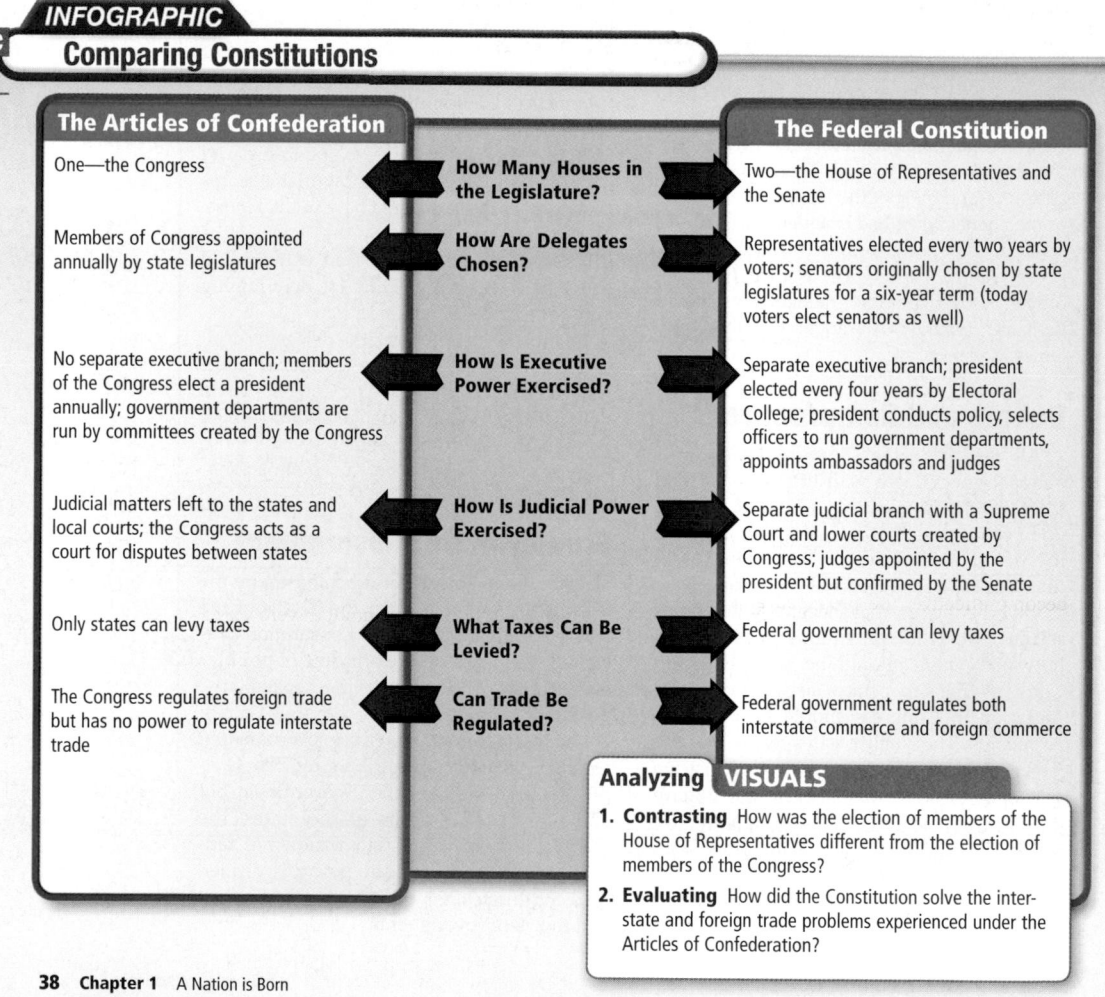

INFOGRAPHIC

C Comparing Constitutions

The Articles of Confederation		The Federal Constitution
One—the Congress	**How Many Houses in the Legislature?**	Two—the House of Representatives and the Senate
Members of Congress appointed annually by state legislatures	**How Are Delegates Chosen?**	Representatives elected every two years by voters; senators originally chosen by state legislatures for a six-year term (today voters elect senators as well)
No separate executive branch; members of the Congress elect a president annually; government departments are run by committees created by the Congress	**How Is Executive Power Exercised?**	Separate executive branch; president elected every four years by Electoral College; president conducts policy, selects officers to run government departments, appoints ambassadors and judges
Judicial matters left to the states and local courts; the Congress acts as a court for disputes between states	**How Is Judicial Power Exercised?**	Separate judicial branch with a Supreme Court and lower courts created by Congress; judges appointed by the president but confirmed by the Senate
Only states can levy taxes	**What Taxes Can Be Levied?**	Federal government can levy taxes
The Congress regulates foreign trade but has no power to regulate interstate trade	**Can Trade Be Regulated?**	Federal government regulates both interstate commerce and foreign commerce

Analyzing VISUALS

1. **Contrasting** How was the election of members of the House of Representatives different from the election of members of the Congress?
2. **Evaluating** How did the Constitution solve the interstate and foreign trade problems experienced under the Articles of Confederation?

38 Chapter 1 A Nation is Born

Activity: Collaborative Learning

Imagining Divide students into four groups. Have each group imagine that they are writing a constitution for a new nation. They should list the areas they want to cover, such as individual rights, trade, and so forth, and then decide how these should be handled in the ideal country. Together, they should write a short constitution for a fictional nation, and present it to the class. The class should vote on which of the fictional nations they would prefer to live in, and explain why. When the vote has been taken, have the class compare and contrast the chosen constitution with the U.S. Constitution written by the Framers. **OL**

appointees to the executive branch and had to consent to any treaties the president negotiated. Congress also had the power of the purse. All bills involving taxes or the spending of government money had to originate in the House of Representatives. If any branch of government became too powerful, the House could always refuse to fund it. In addition, Congress could impeach, or formally accuse of misconduct, the president and other high-ranking officials in the executive or judicial branch and, if convicted, remove them from office.

Members of the judicial branch could hear all cases arising under federal laws and the Constitution. The powers of the judiciary were counterbalanced by the other two branches. The president had the power to nominate judges, including a chief justice of the United States, and the Senate had to confirm or reject such nominations. Once appointed, however, federal judges would serve for life to ensure their independence from the other branches.

Amending the Constitution

The delegates recognized that the Constitution they wrote in the summer of 1787 might need to be **revised** over time. To ensure this could happen, they created a clear system for making amendments, or changes, to the Constitution. To prevent the government from being changed constantly, they made it difficult for amendments to be adopted.

The delegates established a two-step process for amending the Constitution: proposal and ratification. An amendment could be proposed by a vote of two-thirds of the members of both houses of Congress. Alternatively, two-thirds of the states could call a constitutional convention to propose new amendments. To become effective, the proposed amendment would then have to be ratified by three-fourths of the state legislatures or by conventions in three-fourths of the states. **R**

The success of the Philadelphia Convention in creating a government that reflected the country's many different viewpoints was, in Washington's words, "little short of a miracle." The convention, John Adams declared, was "the single greatest effort of national deliberation that the world has ever seen."

✔ **Reading Check** **Summarizing** What compromises did the delegates agree on during the convention?

Ratification

MAIN Idea The promise of a Bill of Rights guaranteed the ratification of the Constitution.

HISTORY AND YOU Have you ever had to convince a friend to agree to something? Read on to learn how the states agreed to ratify the Constitution.

On September 28, Congress voted to submit the Constitution to the states. Each state would hold a convention to vote on it. To go into effect, the Constitution required the **ratification,** or approval, of 9 of the 13 states.

Delaware became the first state to ratify the new Constitution, on December 7, 1787. Pennsylvania, New Jersey, Georgia, and Connecticut quickly followed suit. However, the most important battles still lay ahead. Arguments broke out among Americans, who debated whether the Constitution should be ratified at all.

Debating the Constitution

In fact, debate over ratification began at once—in state legislatures, mass meetings, newspapers, and everyday conversations. Supporters of the new Constitution began calling themselves **Federalists.** They chose the name to emphasize that the Constitution would create a federal system—one with power divided between a central government and state governments.

Many Federalists were large landowners who wanted the property protection that a strong central government could provide. Supporters also included merchants and artisans in large coastal cities and farmers who depended on trade. They all believed it would help their businesses to have an effective federal government that could impose taxes on foreign goods or regulate interstate trade consistently. **W**

Opponents of the Constitution were called **Anti-Federalists,** although they were not truly against federalism. They accepted the need for a national government, but they were determined to protect the powers of the states and concerned about whether the federal or state governments would be supreme. Some Anti-Federalists also believed that the new Constitution needed a bill of rights. Many Anti-Federalists were western farmers living far from the coast. These people considered themselves self-sufficient and were suspicious of the wealthy and powerful.

Chapter 1 A Nation is Born **39**

Chapter 1 • **Section 4**

R Reading Strategy

Skimming Ask: Why did the Framers allow for changing the Constitution, and why did they make it a difficult process? *(to keep government from constantly changing)* **BL**

W Writing Support

Persuasive Writing Have students take on the role of a Federalist or an Anti-Federalist. Each student should write a speech attempting to persuade either Patrick Henry or James Madison to vote for or against the Constitution. **OL**

✔ **Reading Check**

Answers:
A bicameral congress—state representation for one body determined by population and for the other, 2 per state; the Three-Fifths Compromise on counting enslaved persons for representation; taxing of exports; not banning the slave trade until 1808; not imposing high taxes on the importation of slaves.

Additional Support

Activity: Interdisciplinary Connection

Language Arts Ask a language arts teacher to instruct students on the elements of a persuasive essay. Then ask students to assume the role of a colonist just after the Constitution was ratified. Have each student write a one-page amendment that he or she would want to have made at that time. The page should include a title, such as "Amendment 1: Ban of Slavery," background and reasons why it should be adopted, and the exact wording of the amendment. **OL**

D Differentiated Instruction

Visual/Spatial Have students select a point made by Federalists or Anti-Federalists and draw a cartoon illustrating the point made. Suggest that they look at a variety of political cartoons to get ideas.
ELL **OL**

Analyzing GEOGRAPHY

Answers:

1. Many people were merchants and favored federal control of trade to protect their economic interests.
2. Delaware

Did You Know?

Patrick Henry, a fiery speaker often called "the voice of the American Revolution," did not attend the Constitutional Convention because he believed the states should have more power than the federal government, but he fought for inclusion of the Bill of Rights.

Additional Support

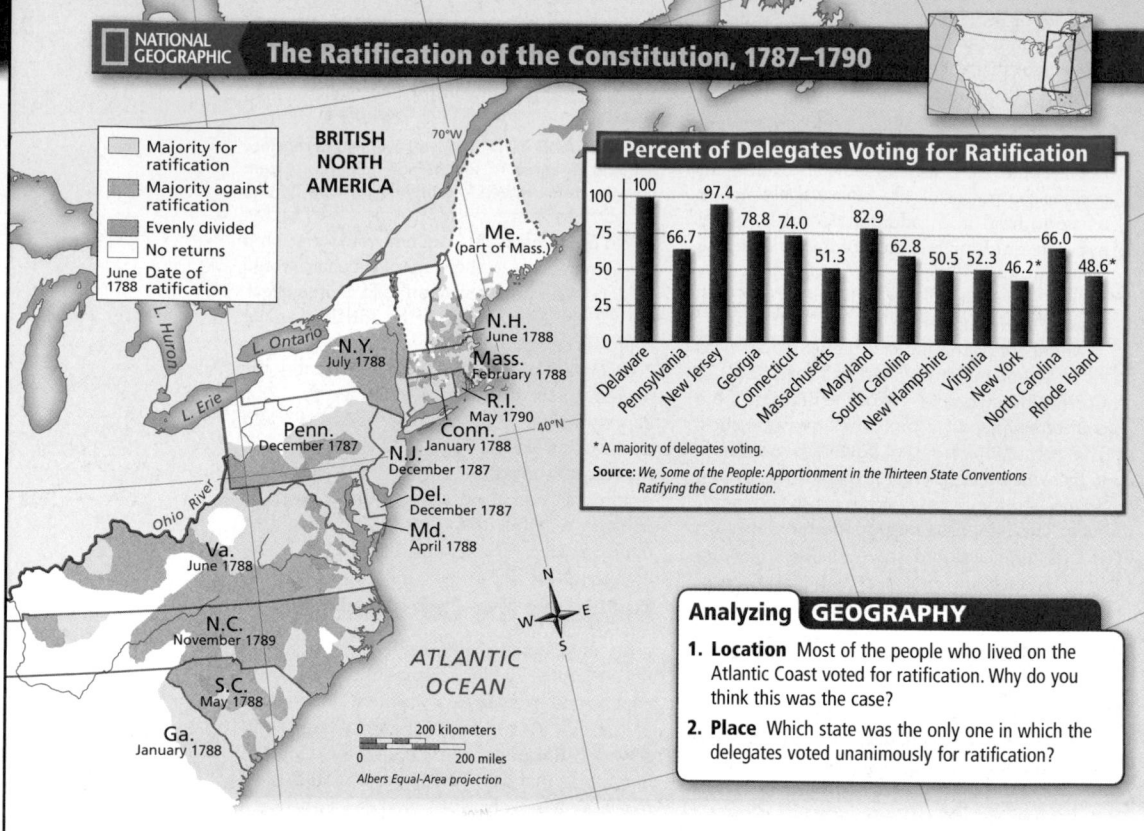

NATIONAL GEOGRAPHIC The Ratification of the Constitution, 1787–1790

Legend:
- Majority for ratification
- Majority against ratification
- Evenly divided
- No returns
- June 1788 Date of ratification

BRITISH NORTH AMERICA

Me. (part of Mass.)
N.H. June 1788
N.Y. July 1788
Mass. February 1788
R.I. May 1790
Conn. January 1788
Penn. December 1787
N.J. December 1787
Del. December 1787
Md. April 1788
Va. June 1788
N.C. November 1789
S.C. May 1788
Ga. January 1788

ATLANTIC OCEAN

0 200 kilometers
0 200 miles
Albers Equal-Area projection

Percent of Delegates Voting for Ratification

State	Percent
Delaware	100
Pennsylvania	66.7
New Jersey	97.4
Georgia	78.8
Connecticut	74.0
Massachusetts	51.3
Maryland	82.9
South Carolina	62.8
New Hampshire	50.5
Virginia	52.3
New York	46.2*
North Carolina	66.0
Rhode Island	48.6*

* A majority of delegates voting.

Source: *We, Some of the People: Apportionment in the Thirteen State Conventions Ratifying the Constitution.*

Analyzing GEOGRAPHY

1. **Location** Most of the people who lived on the Atlantic Coast voted for ratification. Why do you think this was the case?
2. **Place** Which state was the only one in which the delegates voted unanimously for ratification?

As the states prepared for ratification, both sides knew the decision could go either way. Those in favor of the Constitution summarized their arguments in *The Federalist*—a collection of 85 essays written by James Madison, Alexander Hamilton, and John Jay. Federalist No. 1, the first essay in the series, tried to set the framework for the debate:

PRIMARY SOURCE

"After an unequivocal experience of the inefficacy of the subsisting Foederal [sic] Government, you are called upon to deliberate on a new Constitution for the United States of America. . . . It has been frequently remarked that it seems to have been reserved to the people of this country, by their conduct and example, to decide the important question, whether societies of men are really capable or not of establishing good government from reflection and choice, or whether they are forever destined to depend for their political constitutions on accident and force."

—from *The Independent Journal*, October 27, 1787

The essays were extremely influential. Even today, judges, lawyers, legislators, and historians rely upon them to help interpret the intention of the framers of the Constitution.

Massachusetts

In Massachussetts opponents of the proposed Constitution held a clear majority. They included Samuel Adams, who had signed the Declaration of Independence but now strongly **D** believed the Constitution endangered the independence of the states and failed to safeguard Americans' rights.

Federalists quickly promised to attach a bill of rights to the Constitution once it was ratified. They also agreed to support an amendment that would reserve for the states or the people all powers not specifically granted to the federal government. These Federalist promises and the support of artisans guaranteed Massachusetts's approval. In 1791 the

---

Activity: Technology Connection

Creating a Demographic Database Have students use library or Internet resources to find more demographic information about Americans in various states during this period, such as statistics about population, occupation, education, newspaper circulation, and so on. Then have them use graphic design software to create bar graphs and other visual representation of the data they acquire. Students with access to page-making software may create a booklet with both text and graphics. **OL**

promises led to the adoption of the first ten amendments to the Constitution, which came to be known as the Bill of Rights. The amendments guaranteed the freedoms of speech, press, and religion; protection from unreasonable searches and seizures; and the right to a trial by jury.

Maryland easily ratified the Constitution in April 1788, followed by South Carolina in May. On June 21, New Hampshire became the ninth state to ratify the Constitution. The Federalists had now reached the minimum number of states required to put the new Constitution into effect. Virginia and New York, however, still had not ratified. Together, Virginia and New York represented almost 30 percent of the nation's population. Without the support of these states, many feared the new government would not succeed.

Virginia and New York

At the Virginia convention in June, George Washington and James Madison presented strong arguments for ratification. Patrick Henry, Richard Henry Lee, and other Anti-Federalists argued against it. Madison's promise to add a bill of rights won the day for the Federalists—but barely. The Virginia convention voted 89 in favor of the Constitution and 79 against.

In New York, two-thirds of the members elected to the state convention were Anti-Federalists. The Federalists, led by Alexander Hamilton and John Jay, managed to delay the final vote until news arrived that New Hampshire and Virginia had voted to ratify the Constitution and that the new federal government was now in effect. If New York refused to ratify, it would have to operate independently of all of the surrounding states that had accepted the Constitution. This argument convinced enough Anti-Federalists to change sides. The vote was very close, 30 to 27, but the Federalists won.

By July 1788, all the states except Rhode Island and North Carolina had ratified the Constitution. Because ratification by nine states was all that the Constitution required, the members of the Confederation Congress prepared to proceed without them. In mid-September 1788, they established a timetable for electing the new government. The new Congress would hold its first meeting on March 4, 1789.

The two states that had held out finally ratified the Constitution after the new government was in place. North Carolina waited until November 1789 after a bill of rights had actually been proposed. Rhode Island, still nervous about losing its independence, did not ratify the Constitution until May 1790.

The United States now had a new government, but no one knew if the Constitution would work any better than the Articles of Confederation. Many expressed great confidence, however, because George Washington had been chosen as the first president under the new Constitution.

Reading Check **Examining** Why was it important for Virginia and New York to ratify the Constitution, even after the required nine states had done so?

Section 4 REVIEW

Vocabulary
1. **Explain** the significance of: popular sovereignty, federalism, separation of powers, checks and balances, veto, ratification, Federalist, Anti-Federalist.

Main Ideas
2. **Explaining** What did the Northwest Ordinance accomplish?

3. **Describing** How was the Constitution written as a flexible framework of government?

4. **Analyzing** How did the Federalists attempt to assure ratification of the Constitution?

Critical Thinking
5. **Big Ideas** What do you think was the most serious flaw of the Articles of Confederation? Explain.

6. **Categorizing** Use a graphic organizer to list the compromises reached at the Constitutional Convention.

Compromises Reached

7. **Analyzing Visuals** Study the map of the Northwest Ordinance on page 36. What significant provision of this law would contribute to dividing the nation?

Writing About History
8. **Persuasive Writing** Take on the role of a Federalist or an Anti-Federalist at a state ratifying convention. Write a speech in which you try to convince your audience to either accept or reject the new constitution.

History ONLINE
Study Central™ To review this section, go to glencoe.com and click on Study Central.

41

Reading Check
Answer:
Virginia and New York represented almost 30 percent of the nation's population and many feared that, without their support, the new government would not succeed.

Assess
. . . .

History ONLINE

Study Central™ provides summaries, interactive games, and online graphic organizers to help students review content.

Close
. . . .

Evaluating Ask students to make two lists: provisions in the Constitution that they think make it the envy of other nations, and rights it did not include as originally written. *(Answers will vary but may include: 1. representative government, checks and balances, balance of power; 2. freedom and suffrage for all)*

Section 4 REVIEW

Answers

1. All definitions can be found in the section and the Glossary.
2. Surveying and dividing the territory into governable districts; banning slavery in the territory; providing population benchmarks for forming a legislature and for statehood.
3. Provision was made for amending it.

4. By promising a Bill of Rights would be attached once it was ratified.
5. Answers will vary, but may include the inability to negotiate with other nations, raise armies, declare war, regulate trade, or impose taxes. Students' choices should be supported by details.

6. Bicameral legislature; Connecticut or Great Compromise; Three-Fifths Compromise; delay of slavery ban until 1808; non-taxation of exports.
7. Ban on slavery.
8. Students' speeches will vary but should address the concerns of their audience.

Chapter 1 VISUAL SUMMARY

Drawing Conclusions Have students research William Penn's Quaker beliefs. Ask students to do research on Penn and write a half-page essay describing how his beliefs shaped his approach to governing Pennsylvania. **AL**

Reviewing Suggest that students review the causes of the American Revolution in order to answer this question. **Ask:** In what ways did the colonists rebel against Britain's measures to control the colonies, and which ones were the most successful? *(Answers may include: protests, boycotts, petitions, destruction of British property)* **OL**

Visual/Spatial Have interested students research the flag in use at the time of the American Revolution and bring to class information about its design, its maker, and other interesting facts. **ELL BL**

Causes of European Colonization

- The wealth Spain acquired from conquering the Aztec and mining gold encourages others to consider creating colonies.
- The Protestant Reformation in England leads to the rise of Puritans who are persecuted by the English government, as are Catholics and others who disagree with the Anglican Church.
- Puritans, Catholics, and other religious dissenters, such as the Quakers, seek religious freedom by migrating to America.
- The growth of trade and the rising demand for English wool leads to landowners evicting peasants so as to raise sheep. Some of the peasants migrate to America to escape poverty and obtain land.

▲ Trading ships like these vessels of the Dutch East India Company carried goods around the world.

▲ The British surrender at Saratoga. The victory at Saratoga boosted morale and helped Americans gain the support of France and Spain.

Causes of the American Revolution

- Defending the colonies in the French and Indian War costs Britain a great deal of money; Britain seeks ways to cover the costs incurred.
- Britain issues the Proclamation Act of 1763 banning colonists from moving west of the Proclamation line.
- The British crack down on smuggling by enforcing customs duties and creating a vice-admiralty court to try smugglers.
- The Sugar Act is attacked by colonists as taxation without representation.
- The Currency Act banning paper money angers farmer and artisans.
- The 1765 Stamp Act leads to widespread colonial protests.
- The 1767 Townshend Acts lead to further protests.
- The Boston Massacre convinces many that the British are tyrants.
- In 1773 British efforts to help the East India Company lead to the Boston Tea party and other protests against the tea shipments.
- Britain bans Massachusetts town meetings, closes Boston's port, and begins quartering troops in private homes.
- Neither King George nor British officials agree to compromise with the Continental Congress, and Congress orders a boycott of British goods.
- British troops fire on militia at Lexington and Concord; the revolution begins; and the Declaration of Independence is issued, July 4, 1776.

42 Chapter 1 A Nation is Born

Hands-On Chapter Project
Step 4: Wrap Up

From Colonies to Independence

Step 4: Understanding the New Republic Have students read the text, but also use other library and internet sources to research state constitutions and the provisions included in them.

Directions Students will list the provisions that they believe must be included in their state's new constitution.

Making Generalizations Students will support their opinions with evidence and generalize why the provisions that they have included in their state's constitution will result in a strong state and nation. **OL**

ASSESSMENT

STANDARDIZED TEST PRACTICE

TEST-TAKING

As you read each question, be sure to look for main ideas. A main idea or a key word repeated in an answer choice may be a clue that it is the right answer.

Reviewing Vocabulary

Directions: Choose the word or words that best complete the sentence.

1. Because Pennsylvania was owned by William Penn, it was considered
   A a charter colony.
   B a joint-stock company.
   C a proprietary colony.
   D part of the headright system.

2. Who signed individual contracts with American colonists agreeing to work for paid passage to America?
   A serfs
   B indentured servants
   C mercantilists
   D subsistence farmers

3. Massachusetts towns formed militia groups known as _____ in case of British aggression.
   A committees
   B minutemen
   C privateers
   D the Sons of Liberty

4. Which Enlightenment writer influenced American political leaders with his contract theory of government and natural rights?
   A Baron Montesquieu
   B Jean-Jacques Rousseau
   C Thomas Paine
   D John Locke

Reviewing Main Ideas

Directions: Choose the best answer for each of the following questions.

Section 1 *(pp. 4–13)*

5. How was the Massachusetts Bay Colony similar to Jamestown?
   A Both were founded by individuals escaping religious persecution.
   B Tobacco was the primary source of income.
   C The earliest settlers were mainly single men.
   D Each established a local government for the area.

6. Bacon's Rebellion began because
   A farmers wanted to expand their land west into Native American territories.
   B farmers were tired of paying high taxes.
   C farmers were restricted from voting.
   D Virginia's governor was exempt from paying taxes.

Section 2 *(pp. 16–21)*

7. In the 1700s the English colonies were affected by a resurgence of religious zeal known as
   A the Enlightenment.
   B the Glorious Revolution.
   C the Renaissance.
   D the Great Awakening.

Section 3 *(pp. 22–29)*

8. King George III issued the Proclamation of 1763 to
   A make peace with the French and Spanish.
   B give more lands to the colonists.
   C make peace with Native Americans.
   D punish the port of Boston.

Need Extra Help?								
If You Missed Questions . . .	1	2	3	4	5	6	7	8
Go to Page . . .	11	12	26	20	8	13	21	22

Answers and Analyses
Reviewing Vocabulary

1. C Proprietary colonies were owned by a single person, or proprietor. Since Pennsylvania was owned by a single person, students should be able to immediately eliminate *B*, because a joint-stock company is composed of more than one person. Charter colonies were started with the granting of a charter usually to a group of people. The headright system is not related to ownership of colonies.

2. B Students should be able to eliminate *C* and *D* immediately. Choosing between *A* & *B* may be difficult, but students should know the difference between serfs and indentured servants.

3. B Minutemen were supposed to be ready at a minute's notice. A good trick to remember that Massachusetts militiamen were called minutemen is to focus on the shared first letter, M.

4. D John Locke's theory of a social contract between government and the governed became one of the foundations of the movement supporting independence from Britain. According to the social contract theory, people have the right to overthrow an unjust government, because government serves at the will of the people.

Reviewing Main Ideas

5. D This question can be answered using process of elimination. The Massachusetts Bay Colony was founded by people escaping religious persecution, but Jamestown was a joint-stock colony. Tobacco was the primary source of income in Jamestown. Only Jamestown was settled by single men. Mass. Bay and Virginia, however, both had representative assemblies.

6. A The farmers in the backcountry wanted to take more land from Native Americans, but they were not supported in this by the wealthy planters, who did not want to be involved in a fight with Native Americans.

7. D Of the movements mentioned in the answer choices, only the Great Awakening was a religious movement. Point out that the Enlightenment and Renaissance were social movements, and that the Glorious Revolution was political.

8. C The Proclamation of 1763 came about in response to Pontiac's War and had long-lasting effects on the relationship between the colonies and Great Britain because it put a limit on Western settlement.

9. A Remind students that the Coercive Acts were part of the Intolerable Acts (which also included the Quebec Act). A good mnemonic to help students remember that the First Continental Congress was formed in reaction to the Coercive acts is to remember the letter c: the "**c**ause" of the **C**ontinental **C**ongress was the **C**oercive Acts.

10. D Review each answer choice in turn with students. Great Britain was a major world power with an empire. Therefore, it is not reasonable that it did not have funds for the war. In addition, Great Britain did have a large, well-trained army, and part of this was capable officers. Remind students that one significant advantage of the colonists in the Revolution was knowledge of the land.

11. B Hopefully, students will be able to eliminate *C* and *D*. Settlers had not yet explored or reached the Rockies or the Pacific. Students may be tempted to choose the Appalachian Mountains, but remind them that settlers had already expanded west of the Appalachians by the time of the Revolution.

12. B The Northwest Ordinance was one of the few successes of Congress under the Articles of Confederation. It set guidelines for statehood and guaranteed freedom to those who settled there. Students should relate the Ordinance to the Northwest *Territory*. It applied to land, not to ratification of the Constitution or negotiating treaties. The Ordinance banned slavery in the territory, so *D* cannot be correct.

13. D To amend means "to change." The Framers wanted to create a "living" document; that is, they wanted to make the Constitution adaptable so that it would continue to be relevant as times changed. They did not want the document to be replaced. The

9. The First Continental Congress was formed in reaction to the

  A Intolerable Acts.

  B Tea Act.

  C Townshend Acts.

  D Stamp Act.

10. Which of the following was one disadvantage the British faced during the Revolution?

  A They did not have enough money to support the war effort.

  B They had a large, well-trained army.

  C They had few officers capable of leading.

  D They were in a strange land with long distances between supplies.

11. Under the Treaty of Paris, which ended the Revolution, the western boundary of the United States would become the

  A Appalachian Mountains.

  B Mississippi River.

  C Rocky Mountains.

  D Pacific Ocean.

Section 4 *(pp. 34–41)*

12. The Northwest Ordinance outlined the process for

  A ratifying the Constitution.

  B achieving statehood.

  C negotiating international treaties.

  D extending slavery north of the Ohio River.

13. The Framers ensured that the Constitution could evolve over time by

  A establishing a process for replacing it.

  B establishing a bill of rights.

  C establishing that the states could veto federal laws.

  D establishing a process for amending it.

Critical Thinking

Directions: Choose the best answers to the following questions.

Base your answers to questions 14 and 15 on the map below and on your knowledge of Chapter 1.

Settlement of the Colonies, 1587–1700

Settled by 1660
Settled by 1700
Settled by 1760

14. Which of the following colonies had the largest settled areas by 1660?

  A Massachusetts

  B North Carolina

  C New Hampshire

  D Virginia

15. Most colonial cities were located close to

  A the Appalachian Mountains.

  B the Great Lakes.

  C the Atlantic Ocean.

  D the Piedmont.

Need Extra Help?							
If You Missed Questions . . .	9	10	11	12	13	14	15
Go to Page . . .	26	28	29	36	39	R15	R15

GO ON

Bill of Rights is composed of the first Ten Amendments, but the Bill of Rights did not make the document adaptable. *C* would not contribute to the evolution of the Constitution.

Critical Thinking

14. A Careful reading of the map makes map questions easy to answer. The question specifically asks for areas settled by 1660. According to the key, areas settled by 1660 are shaded in the darkest gray. Massachusetts has the high-

est concentration of gray when compared to the other answer choices.

15. C Review the map with students, pointing out each city shown on the map. These cities are closest to the Atlantic Ocean.

16. The Framers provided for a separation of powers in the federal government by

   A establishing executive, legislative, and judicial branches.

   B giving the president the power to command the army.

   C making the Supreme Court the most important court in the nation.

   D establishing a process of changing the Constitution.

Analyze the cartoon and answer the questions that follow. Base your answers on the cartoon and on your knowledge of Chapter 1.

17. To what does the cartoonist compare the states that have ratified the Constitution?

   A pillars supporting the nation

   B storm clouds of controversy

   C stepping-stones to ratification

   D a woven basket of unity

18. Which state is the "ninth and sufficient" state?

   A Massachusetts

   B Virginia

   C New York

   D New Hampshire

Document-Based Questions

Directions: Analyze the document and answer the short-answer questions that follow the document.

In this excerpt from his 1789 textbook, *The American Geography,* the Reverend Jedediah Morse discusses the defects of the Articles of Confederation:

> "[The Articles of Confederation] were framed during the rage of war, when a principle of common safety supplied the place of a coercive power in the government. . . .
> When resolutions were passed in Congress, there was no power to compel obedience. . . . Had one State been invaded by its neighbour, the Union was not constitutionally bound to assist in repelling the invasion. . . ."
>
> —from *The American Geography*

19. What defects in the Articles does Morse mention?

20. Why does Morse think that the Articles were effective during the American Revolution, but not afterwards?

Extended Response

21. The Constitutional Convention met in 1787 to address weaknesses in the Articles of Confederation. Soon the delegates agreed that the Articles had failed and that the Confederation should be replaced with a new form of government. In an essay, explain the three most important changes that the delegates made from the Articles to the Constitution. Explain the change in detail and why it was an improvement. Your essay should include an introduction, at least three paragraphs, and a conclusion.

History ONLINE

For additional test practice, use Self-Check Quizzes— Chapter 1 at glencoe.com.

Need Extra Help?

If You Missed Questions . . .	16	17	18	19	20	21
Go to Page . . .	38	R18	R18	R19	R19	R13

Document-Based Questions

19. Congress did not have the power to enforce laws.

20. During the war, the need for unity against a common enemy compelled states to cooperate; during peace there was nothing that compelled cooperation.

Extended Response

21. Students' essays will vary, but must include what the student believes to be the three most important changes from the Articles to the Constitution. Examples might include federalism, which delegated power to the federal government; the power of Congress to regulate trade and levy taxes; and the power to make laws that were binding. Accept all reasonable answers that are well-supported.

16. A The concept of separation of powers is attributed to Enlightenment thinker Baron Montesquieu. The Framers used this concept in structuring the U.S. government. The other answer choices are true but not correct in terms of the question.

17. A Examine the cartoon with students. There is a row of pillars, labeled with the names of states that had ratified the Constitution. The phrase "United we stand—Divided we fall" and the hand adding one of the pillars supports the idea that the pillars support the nation. In addition, the title of the cartoon includes the word "pillar."

18. D The title of the Cartoon is "The Ninth and Sufficient Pillar Raised." Tell students that in written English at the time, a lower-case "s" looked like an "f." This may help them decipher the title. Counting from the left, New Hampshire is the ninth pillar. Nine states was the minimum needed to ratify the Constitution for it to take effect.

History ONLINE

Have students visit the Web site at glencoe.com to review Chapter 1 and take the Self-Check Quiz.

Need Extra Help?

Have students refer to the pages listed if they miss any of the questions.

Focus

Making Connections Have students speculate why they think it might be important for a nation to have a written constitution and write their ideas on the board.

Ask: What might happen if a nation did not have a written constitution? *(Answers will vary, but students might note that laws would not be clear; the government might assume too much power; people would not know their civil rights.)* **OL**

Guide to Reading

Answers to Graphic:
I. Major Principles
  A. Popular Sovereignty and Republicanism
  B. Limited Government
  C. Federalism
  D. Separation of Powers
  E. Checks and Balances
  F. Individual Rights

Students should complete the outline by including all heads in the section.

Additional Support

THE CONSTITUTION HANDBOOK

Guide to Reading

Big Ideas
Government and Society A written contract between the people and their government can preserve natural rights and allow for change over time.

Content Vocabulary
• popular sovereignty *(p. 46)*
• federalism *(p. 46)*
• enumerated powers *(p. 47)*
• reserved powers *(p. 47)*
• concurrent powers *(p. 48)*
• impeach *(p. 49)*
• bill *(p. 50)*
• cabinet *(p. 51)*
• judicial review *(p. 53)*
• due process *(p. 53)*

Academic Vocabulary
• grant *(p. 47)*
• responsive *(p. 55)*

Reading Strategy
Taking Notes As you read about the Constitution, use the major headings of the handbook to fill in an outline.

I. Major Principles
  A.
  B.
  C.
  D.
  E.
  F.
II.

Serving as the framework of national government and the source of American citizens' basic rights, the Constitution is the most important document of the United States. To preserve self-government, all citizens need to understand their rights and responsibilities.

Major Principles

MAIN Idea The Constitution's basic principles assure people's rights and provide for a balance among the different branches of government.

HISTORY AND YOU If you had to create the rules for a new organization, would you give all members an equal voice? Read on to learn how the Constitution reflects representative government.

The principles outlined in the Constitution were the Framers' solution to the complex problems of a representative government. The Constitution rests on seven major principles of government: (1) **popular sovereignty,** (2) republicanism, (3) limited government, (4) **federalism,** (5) separation of powers, (6) checks and balances, and (7) individual rights.

Popular Sovereignty and Republicanism

The opening words of the Constitution, "We the people," reinforce the idea of popular sovereignty, or "authority of the people." In the Constitution, the people consent to be governed and specify the powers and rules by which they shall be governed.

The Articles of Confederation's government had few powers, and it was unable to cope with the many challenges facing the nation. The new federal government had greater powers, but it also had specific limitations. A system of interlocking responsibilities kept any one branch of government from becoming too powerful.

Voters are sovereign, that is, they have ultimate authority in a republican system. They elect representatives and give them the responsibility to make laws and run the government. For most Americans today, the terms republic and representative democracy mean the same thing: a system of limited government where the people are the final source of authority.

Extending the Content

Constitutions The United States has the oldest written national constitution still in effect. Compared to other written constitutions, it might be characterized as succinct. The average federal constitution contains about 26,500 words, while the U.S. Constitution with its 27 amendments has fewer than 7,500 words.

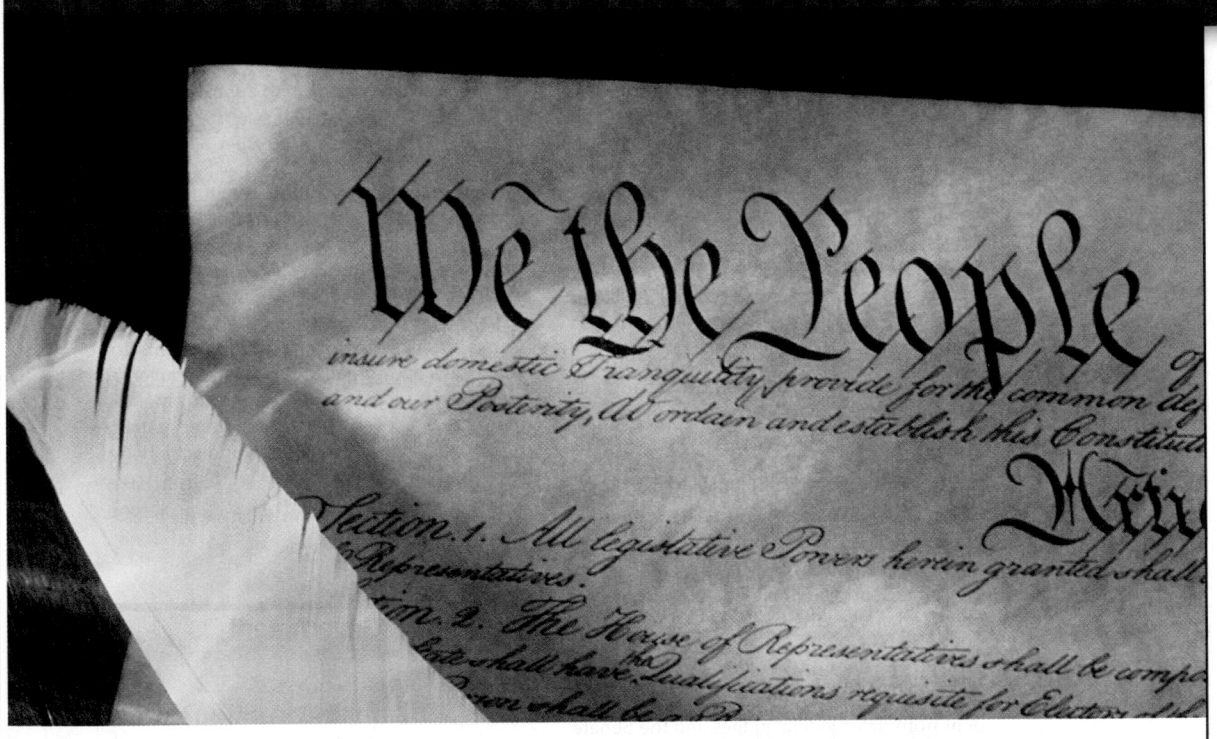

Limited Government

Although the Framers agreed that the nation needed a stronger central authority, they feared misuse of power. They wanted to prevent the government from using its power to give one group special advantages or to deprive another group of its rights. By creating a limited government, they restricted the government's authority to specific powers **granted** by the people.

The delegates to the Constitutional Convention were very specific about the powers granted to the new government. Their decision to provide a written outline of the government's structure also served to show what they intended. Articles I, II and III of the Constitution describe the powers of the federal government and the limits on those powers. Other limits are set forth in the Bill of Rights, which guarantees certain rights to the people.

Federalism

In establishing a strong central government, the Framers did not deprive states of all authority. The states gave up some powers to the national government but retained others. This principle of shared power is called federalism. The federal system allows the people of each state to deal with their needs in their own way, but at the same time, it lets the states act together to deal with matters that affect all Americans.

The Constitution defines three types of government powers. Certain powers belong only to the federal government. These **enumerated powers** include the power to coin money, regulate interstate and foreign trade, maintain the armed forces, and create federal courts (Article I, Section 8).

The second kind of powers are those retained by the states, known as **reserved powers,** including the power to establish schools, set marriage and divorce laws, and regulate trade within the state. Although reserved powers are not specifically listed in the Constitution, the Tenth Amendment says that all powers not granted to the federal government "are reserved to the States."

The Constitution Handbook **47**

Teach

. . . .

C1 **Critical Thinking**

Identifying Central Issues
Have students read through and define in their own words each of the Constitution's major underlying principles. Students should then locate at least one part of the Constitution that addresses each principle. **Ask:** Which constitutional principle affects your life the most today? *(Answers will vary.)* **OL**

C2 **Critical Thinking**

Making Inferences Write the enumerated powers of the federal government on the board. **Ask:** Why do you think the Framers thought it was important to list the powers of the federal government? *(Students may suggest that the Framers wanted to avoid confusion over what the federal government could and could not do.)* **OL**

Additional Support

Extending the Content

Independence Hall The red brick building in which the Framers met to draw up the Constitution is now known as Independence Hall. Several important events took place there, including the meeting of the First and Second Continental Congresses and Jefferson's reading of the Declaration of Independence. On July 4, 2003, the National Constitution Center opened a few blocks from Independence Hall.

This museum explains the importance of the Constitution and its role in the history of the United States.

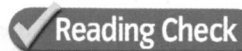
✔ Reading Check

Answer:
making law

Additional Support

 All members of Congress have the responsibility to represent their constituents, the people of their home states and districts. As a constituent, you can expect your senators and **R** representative to promote national and state interests. Thousands of **bills**—proposed laws—are introduced in Congress every year. Because individual members of Congress cannot possibly study all these bills carefully, both houses use committees of selected members to evaluate proposed legislation.

Standing committees are permanent committees in both the House and the Senate that specialize in a particular topic, such as agriculture, commerce, or veterans' affairs. These committees are usually divided into subcommittees that focus on a particular aspect of an issue. The House and the Senate also form temporary select committees to deal with issues requiring special attention. These committees meet only until they complete their task.

Occasionally the House and the Senate form joint committees with members from both houses. These committees meet to consider specific issues. One type of joint committee, a conference committee, has a special function. If the House and the Senate pass different versions of the same bill, a conference committee meets to work out a compromise bill acceptable to both houses.

Once a committee in either house of Congress approves a bill, it is sent to the full Senate or House for debate. After debate the bill may be passed, rejected, or returned to the committee for further changes. When both houses pass a bill, it goes to the president. If the president approves the bill and signs it, the bill becomes law. If the president vetoes the bill, it does not become law unless Congress takes it up again and votes to override the veto.

✔ Reading Check **Analyzing** What is the most important power of the legislative branch?

INFOGRAPHIC

How a Bill Becomes Law

The legislative process is complex. It begins with a representative in Congress introducing a bill and eventually works its way to the president who either signs the bill into law or vetoes it.

How a Bill Becomes Law

1. A legislator introduces a bill in the House or Senate, where it is referred to a committee for review.

2. After review, the committee decides whether to shelve it or to send it back to the House or Senate with or without revisions.

3. The House or Senate then debates the bill, making revisions if desired. If the bill is passed, it is sent to the other house.

4. If the House and Senate pass different versions of the bill, the houses must meet in a conference committee to decide on a compromise version.

5. The compromise bill is then sent to both houses.

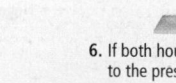

6. If both houses pass the bill, it is sent to the president to sign.

7. If the president signs the bill, it becomes law.

8. The president may veto the bill, but if two-thirds of the House and Senate vote to approve it, it becomes law without the president's approval.

Extending the Content

Congressional Debate A *filibuster* is an attempt to delay for as long as possible or stop altogether the passage of a bill through the Senate. A filibuster exploits the long-held tradition in the Senate of not limiting debate. A senator can hold the floor as long as he or she wants to, as long as he or she continues talking. The Senate can halt a filibuster by passing a vote of cloture to force a vote.

The Executive Branch

MAIN Idea As the nation's leader, the president carries out laws with the help of executive offices, departments, and agencies.

HISTORY AND YOU What would you do if you were the student council president? Read on to learn about the roles of the U.S. president.

The executive branch of government includes the president, the vice president, and various executive offices, departments, and agencies. The executive branch executes, or carries out, the laws that Congress passes.

The President's Roles

The president plays a number of different roles in government. These roles include serving as the nation's chief executive, chief diplomat, commander in chief of the military, chief of state, and legislative leader.

▲ *President Bush signs the Voting Rights Act of 2006.*

Analyzing VISUALS

1. **Describing** What is the role of a conference committee?
2. **Analyzing** How can a bill become law without the approval of the president?

Chief Executive As chief executive, the president is responsible for carrying out the nation's laws. As chief diplomat, the president directs foreign policy, appoints ambassadors, and negotiates treaties with other nations.

Commander in Chief As commander in chief of the armed forces, the president can give orders to the military and direct its operations. The president cannot declare war; only Congress holds this power. The president can send troops to other parts of the world for up to 60 days but must notify Congress when doing so. The troops may remain longer only if Congress gives its approval or declares war.

Chief of State As chief of state, the president is symbolically the representative of all Americans. The president fulfills this role when receiving foreign ambassadors or heads of state, visiting foreign nations, or honoring Americans.

Legislative Leader The president serves as a legislative leader by proposing laws to Congress and working to see that they are passed. In the annual State of the Union address, the president presents his goals for legislation in the upcoming year.

The Executive at Work

Many executive offices, departments, and independent agencies help the president carry out and enforce the nation's laws. The Executive Office of the President (EOP) is made up of individuals and agencies that directly assist the president. Presidents rely on the EOP for advice and for gathering information needed for decision making.

The executive branch has 15 executive departments, each responsible for a different area of government. For example, the Department of State carries out foreign policy, and the Department of the Treasury manages the nation's finances. The department heads have the title of secretary, and are members of the president's **cabinet.** The cabinet helps the president set policies and make decisions.

Reading Check **Explaining** What are the major roles of the president?

The Constitution Handbook **51**

R **Reading Strategy**

Evaluating Have students review the key roles of the president: chief executive and chief diplomat, commander in chief, chief of state, and legislative leader. **Ask: Which of these roles is most important? Why?** *(Students should cite evidence or examples to logically support their opinions.)* **OL**

Analyzing VISUALS

Answers:
1. resolves differences between versions of bills passed by the Senate and the House
2. If the president vetoes a bill and two-thirds of the House and Senate override the veto, the bill becomes law without the president's approval.

Reading Check

Answer:
Chief Executive, Commander in Chief, Chief of State, Legislative leader

Additional Support

Extending the Content

Washington and His Cabinet George Washington's first cabinet included some of the nation's most influential founding fathers. Thomas Jefferson, the primary writer of the Declaration of Independence, served as Secretary of State; Alexander Hamilton, one of the writers of *The Federalist* and tireless champion of Constitutional ratification, served as Secretary of the Treasury. Henry Knox, Secretary of War, was a general from the American Revolution and had served as Secretary of War under the Articles of Confederation. Edmund Randolph, the former governor of Virginia, became the Attorney General. Like Hamilton and Washington, he was a delegate to the Constitutional Convention, and presented the Virginia Plan.

Did You Know?

Careful Selection Of the approximately 7,000 cases that get sent to the U.S. Supreme Court every year, the Court agrees to hear only 160 or so. Many cases are rejected simply because they were improperly filed.

Additional Support

The Judicial Branch

MAIN Idea The judicial branch consists of different federal courts that review and evaluate laws and interpret the Constitution.

HISTORY AND YOU The Constitution did not specifically give the judicial branch the power to review laws. Do you think it is a reasonable task? Read to learn about the role of federal judges and the Supreme Court.

Article III of the Constitution calls for the creation of a Supreme Court and "such inferior [lower] courts as Congress may from time to time ordain and establish." Today the judicial branch consists of three main categories of courts, including:

District and Appellate Courts

United States district courts are the lowest level of the federal court system. These courts consider criminal and civil cases that come under federal authority, such as kidnapping, federal tax evasion, claims against the federal government, and cases involving constitutional rights, such as free speech. There are 91 district courts, with at least one in every state.

The appellate courts, or appeals courts, consider district court decisions in which the losing side has asked for a review of the verdict. If an appeals court disagrees with the lower court's decision, it can overturn the verdict or order a retrial. There are 14 appeals courts, one for each of 12 federal districts, one military appeals court, and an appellate court for the federal circuit.

The Supreme Court

The Supreme Court is the final authority in the federal court system. It consists of a chief justice and eight associate justices. Most of the Supreme Court's cases come from appeals of lower court decisions. Only cases involving foreign ambassadors or disputes between states can begin in the Supreme Court. **W**

INFOGRAPHIC
The Federal Court System

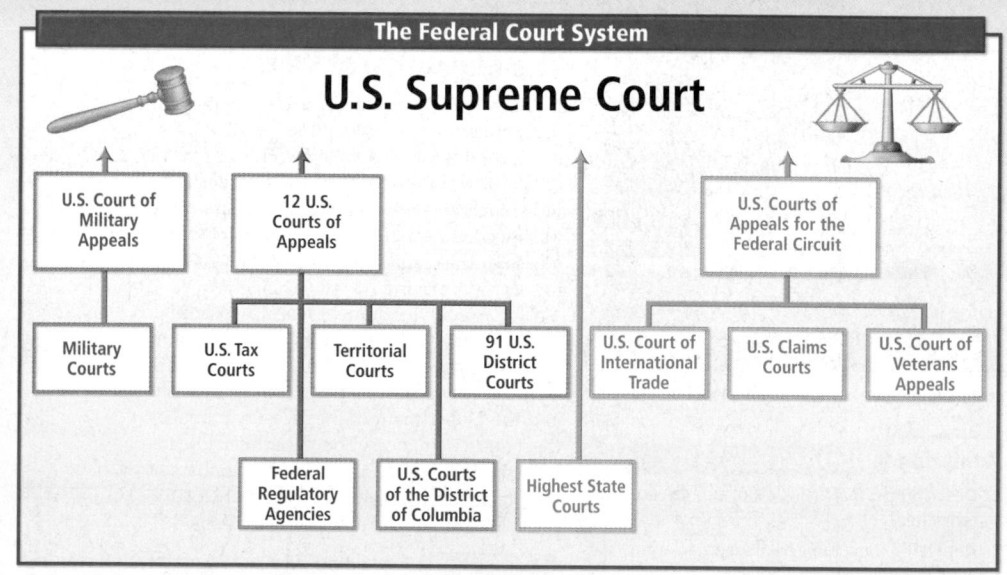

The Federal Court System

U.S. Supreme Court

U.S. Court of Military Appeals • 12 U.S. Courts of Appeals • U.S. Courts of Appeals for the Federal Circuit

Military Courts • U.S. Tax Courts • Territorial Courts • 91 U.S. District Courts • U.S. Court of International Trade • U.S. Claims Courts • U.S. Court of Veterans Appeals

Federal Regulatory Agencies • U.S. Courts of the District of Columbia • Highest State Courts

52 The Constitution Handbook

Extending the Content

Washington and the First Justices
As the first president, George Washington had the responsibility of appointing the first six justices, as specified in the Judiciary Act of 1789. In naming the first justices, Washington paid close attention to their politics, which essentially meant loyalty to the new Constitution. Of his six original appointees, three attended the Constitutional Convention in Philadelphia and the other three supported the document's ratification. John Jay, the first chief justice, was coauthor with James Madison and Alexander Hamilton of *The Federalist*, a series of articles that supported the Constitution. During his two terms of office, Washington appointed five other Supreme Court justices—for a record total of eleven appointments to the Court.

Washington also considered geographical balance in his appointments. Among his first six appointees were three northerners and three southerners.

Supreme Court Independence The president appoints the Court's justices for life, and the Senate confirms the appointments. The public has no input. The Framers hoped that by appointing judges, they would be free to evaluate the law with no concern for pleasing voters.

Judicial Review The role of the judicial branch is not described in detail in the Constitution, but the role of the courts has grown as powers implied in the Constitution have been put into practice. In 1803 Chief Justice John Marshall expanded the power of the Supreme Court by striking down an act of Congress in the case of *Marbury* v. *Madison.* Although not mentioned in the Constitution, judicial review has become a major power of the judicial branch. **Judicial review** gives the Supreme Court the ultimate authority to interpret the meaning of the Constitution.

✔ **Reading Check** **Analyzing** How does the Supreme Court protect the Constitution?

▲ *The U.S. Supreme Court, front row, left to right, Justices Anthony Kennedy and John Paul Stevens, Chief Justice John Roberts, Justices Antonin Scalia and David Souter; back row, left to right, Justices Stephen Breyer, Clarence Thomas, Ruth Bader Ginsburg, Samuel Alito*

Analyzing **VISUALS**

1. **Interpreting** How many routes to the U.S. Supreme Court are depicted in the chart?
2. **Analyzing** How would a case originating in Puerto Rico be appealed to the U.S. Supreme Court?

Rights and Responsibilities

MAIN Idea The Constitution and the Bill of Rights provide Americans with protection and freedoms.

HISTORY AND YOU How do you think the Constitution protects your rights as a student? Read on to find out about the major rights of Americans.

All American citizens have certain basic rights, but they also have specific responsibilities. Living in a system of self-government means ultimately that every citizen is partly responsible for how their society is governed and for the actions the government takes on their behalf.

The Rights of Americans

The rights of Americans fall into three broad categories: the right to be protected from unfair actions of the government, to receive equal treatment under the law, and to retain certain basic freedoms.

Protection from Unfair Actions Parts of the Constitution and the Bill of Rights protect all Americans from unfair treatment by the government or the law. Among these rights are the right to a lawyer when accused of a crime and the right to trial by jury when charged with a crime. In addition, the Fourth **S** Amendment protects us from unreasonable searches and seizures. This provision requires police to have a court order before searching a person's home for criminal evidence. To obtain this, the police must have a very strong reason to suspect the person of committing a crime.

Equal Treatment All Americans, regardless of race, religion, or political beliefs, have the right to be treated the same under the law. The Fifth Amendment states that no person shall "be deprived of life, liberty, or property, without due process of law." **Due process** means that the government must follow procedures established by law and guaranteed by the Constitution, treating all people equally. The Fourteenth Amendment requires every state to grant its citizens "equal protection of the laws."

The Constitution Handbook **53**

Basic Freedoms The basic freedoms are described in the First Amendment—freedom of speech, freedom of religion, freedom of the press, freedom of assembly, and the right to petition. In a democracy, power rests in the hands of the people. Therefore, citizens in a democratic society must be able to exchange ideas freely. The First Amendment allows citizens to criticize the government, in speech or in the press, without fear of punishment.

In addition, the Ninth Amendment states that the rights of Americans are not limited to those in the Constitution. This has allowed Americans to assert other basic rights over the years that have been upheld in court, or assured by amending the Constitution.

Limits on Rights The rights of Americans are not absolute. They are limited based on the principle of respecting everyone's rights equally. For example, many cities and towns require groups to obtain a permit to march on city streets. Such laws do limit free speech, but they also protect the community by ensuring that the march will not endanger other people.

In this and other cases, the government balances an individual's rights, the rights of others, and the community's health and safety. Most Americans are willing to accept some limitations on their rights to gain these protections as long as the restrictions are reasonable and apply equally to all. A law banning all marches would violate the First Amendment rights of free speech and assembly and be unacceptable. Similarly, a law preventing only certain groups from marching would be unfair because it would not apply equally to everyone.

Citizens' Responsibilities

Citizens in a democratic society have both duties and responsibilities. Duties are actions required by law. Responsibilities are voluntary actions. Fulfilling both your duties and your responsibilities helps ensure good government and protects your rights.

Duties One basic duty of all Americans is to obey the law. Laws serve three important functions. They help maintain order; they protect

INFOGRAPHIC
Amending the Constitution

Article V of the Constitution enables Congress and the states to amend, or change, the Constitution.

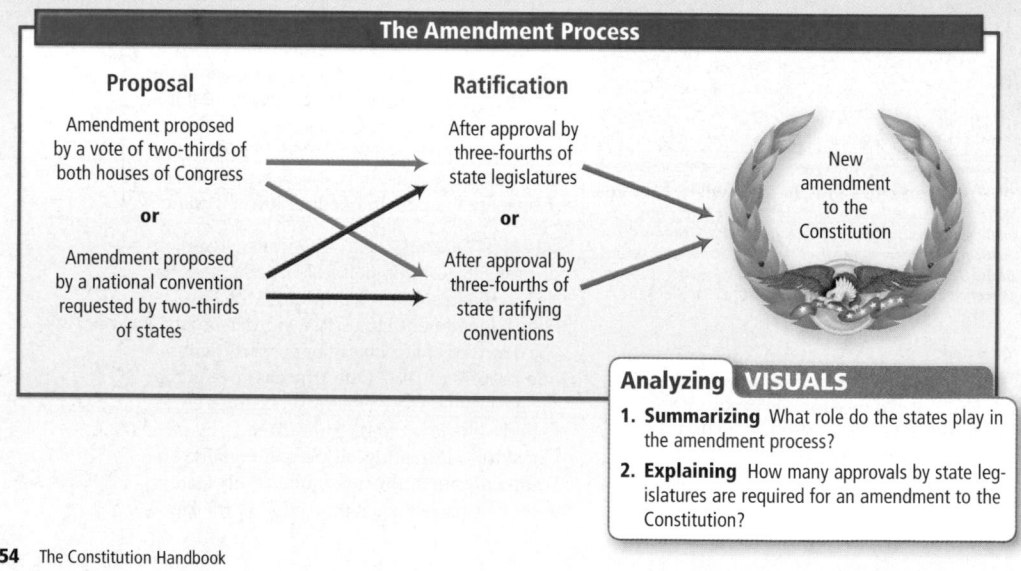

The Amendment Process

Proposal
Amendment proposed by a vote of two-thirds of both houses of Congress

or

Amendment proposed by a national convention requested by two-thirds of states

Ratification
After approval by three-fourths of state legislatures

or

After approval by three-fourths of state ratifying conventions

New amendment to the Constitution

Analyzing VISUALS
1. **Summarizing** What role do the states play in the amendment process?
2. **Explaining** How many approvals by state legislatures are required for an amendment to the Constitution?

54 The Constitution Handbook

Activity: Cooperative Learning

Debating Rights Organize the class into five groups, one for each of the five rights incorporated into the First Amendment. Tell students they will have 10 minutes to prepare an outline about the right assigned to their group. Also tell them they will have five minutes to persuade the class that the right they represent is more important than the other four. Tell them to include as many factual details and real-life scenarios as possible. After each group has presented, have the class vote on which right they think is most important.

the health, safety, and property of all citizens; and they make it possible for people to live together peacefully. If you believe a law is wrong, you can work through your representatives to change it.

Americans also have a duty to pay taxes. The government uses tax money to defend the nation, to build roads and bridges, and to assist people in need. Americans benefit from services provided by the government. Another duty of citizens is to defend the nation. All males aged 18 and older must register with the government in case the nation needs to call on them for military service. Military service is not automatic, but a war could make it necessary.

The Constitution guarantees all Americans the right to a trial by a jury of their equals. For this reason, you may be called to jury duty when you reach the age of 18. Having a large group of jurors on hand is necessary to guarantee the right to a fair and speedy trial. You also have a duty to serve as a trial witness if called to do so.

Most states require you to attend school until a certain age. School is where you gain the knowledge and skills needed to be a good citizen. In school you learn to think more clearly, to express your opinions more accurately, and to analyze the ideas of others. These skills will help you make informed choices when you vote.

Responsibilities The responsibilities of citizens are not as clear-cut as their duties, but they are as important because they help maintain the quality of government and society. One important responsibility is to be well informed. You need to know what is happening in your community, your state, your country, and the world. Knowing what your government is doing and expressing your thoughts about its actions helps to keep it **responsive** to the wishes of the people. You also need to be informed about your rights and to assert them when necessary. Knowing your rights helps preserve them. Other responsibilities include accepting responsibility for your actions, and supporting your family.

To enjoy your rights to the fullest, you must be prepared to respect the rights of others. Respecting the rights of others also means respecting the rights of people with whom you disagree. Respecting and accepting others regardless of race, religion, beliefs, or other differences is essential in a democracy.

Vote, Vote, Vote! Perhaps the most important responsibility of American citizens is to vote when they reach the age of 18. Voting allows you to participate in government and to guide its direction. When you vote for people to represent you in government, you will be exercising your right of self-government. If you disapprove of the job your representatives are doing, it will be your responsibility to help elect other people in the next election. You can also let your representatives know what you think about issues through letters, telephone calls, and petitions and by taking part in public meetings or political rallies.

Reading Check **Describing** What are the major rights and responsibilities of an American citizen?

Vocabulary

1. **Explain** the significance of: popular sovereignty, federalism, enumerated powers, reserved powers, concurrent powers, impeach, bill, cabinet, judicial review, due process.

Main Ideas

2. **Explaining** What are the provisions of the First Amendment?

3. **Summarizing** How are popular sovereignty and voting connected?

Critical Thinking

4. **Big Ideas** What is the difference between a duty and a responsibility?

5. **Organizing** Use a graphic organizer similar to the one below to list reasons why the framers of the Constitution provided for separation of powers.

Separation of Powers

6. **Analyzing Visuals** Study the photograph on page 53. How has the composition of the Supreme Court changed over time?

Writing About History

7. **Expository Writing** Working with a partner, choose one of the constitutional rights listed below. Write a report that traces the right's historical development, from the time the Constitution was ratified to the present.

> suffrage
> freedom of speech
> freedom of religion
> equal protection of law

History ONLINE
Study Central™ To review this section, go to glencoe.com and click on Study Central.

The Constitution Handbook **55**

Assess

History ONLINE

Study Central™ provides summaries, interactive games, and online graphic organizers to help students review content.

Close

Summarizing Ask: In what ways does the Constitution protect our rights? *(Answers will vary, but students should note that the Constitution is designed to prevent any one branch from becoming too powerful; also, the Bill of Rights and the other amendments protect our rights.)* OL

Constitution Handbook REVIEW

Answers

1. All definitions can be found in the section and the Glossary.

2. freedom of speech, religion, and the press; right of assembly; and right to petition

3. The people express their wishes through voting.

4. Duties are actions required by law; responsibilities are voluntary.

5. to prevent one branch of government from becoming too powerful; to provide a system for each branch of government to check and balance the others; to protect individual rights

6. Women and African Americans are now represented on the Court.

7. Reports will vary, but students should use historically accurate information.

Focus

Making Connections Have students suggest ways in which they think the U.S. Constitution affects their daily life and write their ideas on the board. **Ask:** Why is it important to know about the Constitution's main provisions? *(Answers will vary, but students might note that good citizens know about how their nation is governed; citizens would better understand if any laws passed by state or local governments might be unconstitutional.)* **OL**

Teach

D Differentiated Instruction

English Learners Ask students to read the Preamble and help students understand any difficult words or terms. Then have them identify which purpose is most important to them personally. **ELL**

Additional Support

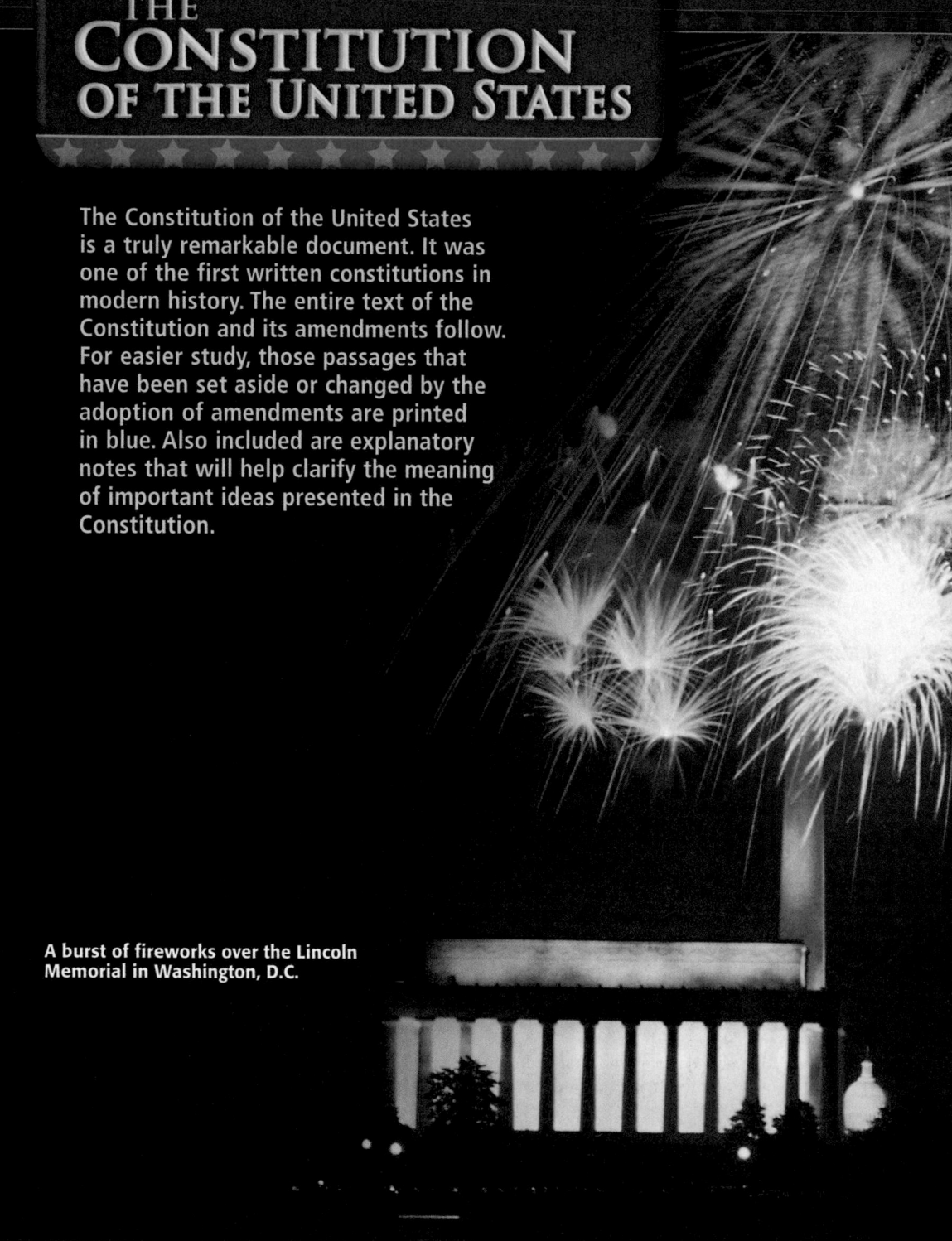

THE CONSTITUTION OF THE UNITED STATES

The Constitution of the United States is a truly remarkable document. It was one of the first written constitutions in modern history. The entire text of the Constitution and its amendments follow. For easier study, those passages that have been set aside or changed by the adoption of amendments are printed in blue. Also included are explanatory notes that will help clarify the meaning of important ideas presented in the Constitution.

A burst of fireworks over the Lincoln Memorial in Washington, D.C.

Extending the Content

Sergeants-at-Arms House and Senate sergeants-at-arms are the police officers of Congress. They enforce the rules and maintain order. When they walk down the aisle of the legislature, carrying the ceremonial staff called a mace, Congress must be orderly. Any member of Congress who persists in disorderly conduct is guilty of contempt. The sergeants-at-arms also maintain security within the Capitol and associated buildings and supervise the Capitol police force. Sometimes the sergeants-at-arms round up members for floor votes, personally escorting any member who refuses to attend.

Preamble

We the People of the United States, in Order to form a more perfect Union, establish Justice, insure domestic Tranquility, provide for the common defence, promote the general Welfare, and secure the Blessings of Liberty to ourselves and our Posterity, do ordain and establish this **Constitution** for the United States of America. **D**

Article I

Section 1

All legislative Powers herein granted shall be vested in a Congress of the United States, which shall consist of a Senate and House of Representatives.

Section 2

[1.] The House of Representatives shall be composed of Members chosen every second Year by the People of the several States, and the Electors in each State shall have the Qualifications requisite for Electors of the most numerous Branch of the State Legislature.

[2.] No person shall be a Representative who shall not have attained to the Age of twenty five Years, and been seven Years a Citizen of the United States, and who shall not, when elected, be an Inhabitant of that State in which he shall be chosen.

[3.] Representatives and direct Taxes shall be apportioned among the several States which may be included within this Union, according to their respective Numbers, which shall be determined by adding to the whole Number of free Persons, including those bound to Service for a Term of Years, and excluding Indians not taxed, three fifths of all other Persons. The actual **Enumeration** shall be made within three Years after the first Meeting of the Congress of the United States, and within every subsequent Term of ten Years, in such Manner as they shall by Law direct. **C** The Number of Representatives shall not exceed one for every thirty Thousand, but each State shall have at Least one Representative; and until such enumeration shall be made, the State of New Hampshire shall be entitled to chuse three; Massachusetts eight, Rhode-Island and Providence Plantations one, Connecticut five, New-York six, New Jersey four, Pennsylvania eight, Delaware one, Maryland six, Virginia ten, North Carolina five, South Carolina five, and Georgia three.

[4.] When vacancies happen in the Representation from any State, the Executive Authority thereof shall issue Writs of Election to fill such Vacancies.

[5.] The House of Representatives shall chuse their Speaker and other Officers; and shall have the sole Power of **Impeachment**.

The Preamble introduces the Constitution and sets forth the general purposes for which the government was established. The Preamble also declares that the power of the government comes from the people.

The printed text of the document shows the spelling and punctuation of the parchment original.

Article I. The Legislative Branch

The Constitution contains seven divisions called articles. Each article covers a general topic. For example, Articles I, II, and III create the three branches of the national government—the legislative, executive, and judicial branches. Most of the articles are divided into sections.

> ### Section 1. Congress
> **Lawmaking** The power to make laws is given to a Congress made up of two chambers to represent different interests: the Senate to represent the states and the House to be more responsive to the people's will.

> ### Section 2.
> **House of Representatives**
> **Division of Representatives Among the States** The number of representatives from each state is based on the size of the state's population. Each state is entitled to at least one representative. The Constitution states that each state may specify who can vote, but the Fifteenth, Nineteenth, Twenty-fourth, and Twenty-sixth Amendments have established guidelines that all states must follow regarding the right to vote. *What are the qualifications for members of the House of Representatives?*

Vocabulary

preamble: *introduction*
constitution: *principles and laws of a nation*
enumeration: *census or population count*
impeachment: *bringing charges against an official*

C Critical Thinking

Analyzing Information Have students research data from the 1990 and 2000 censuses. Students should create a chart of the populations of each state and the number of representatives each state had in 1990. Then students should list the populations each state had in 2000 and whether that state lost or gained representation in the House of Representatives. Have students identify which states gained the most seats and speculate as to why those states gained population. **OL**

Answer: A member of the House of Representatives must be at least 25 years old, be a citizen for at least seven years, and be an inhabitant of the state from which he or she was elected.

Additional Support

Extending the Content

Committee of Style The delegates to the Constitutional Convention appointed five of their members—William Samuel Johnson, Alexander Hamilton, Gouverneur Morris, James Madison, and Rufus King—to write the final draft of the Constitution. The members completed the task in four days and presented their version to the delegates on September 12, 1787. Some additional changes were made before the Constitution was adopted on September 17, 1787.

C1 Critical Thinking

Analyzing Primary Sources
Write on the board the following, which George Washington supposedly said to Thomas Jefferson in defense of the Senate: "We pour legislation into the senatorial saucer to cool it." **Ask:** What do you think Washington meant by this? *(The Senate was the more deliberative of the two houses of Congress.)* **OL**

C2 Critical Thinking

Making Generalizations
Call on students to list the qualifications for serving in Congress as set forth in the Constitution. Then ask students what other qualifications, if any, they think should be applied to members of Congress. Discuss with students whether they would like to serve in Congress. (Note: For information on serving in the House, see Article I, Section 2, on page 131.) **OL**

Answer: The Senate has the power to remove impeached officials from office and disqualify them from holding office in the future.

Additional Support

Section 3. The Senate
Voting Procedure Originally, senators were chosen by the legislators of their own states. The Seventeenth Amendment changed this, so that senators are now elected by their state's people. There are 100 senators, 2 from each state.

What Might Have Been
Electing Senators South Carolina delegate Charles Pinckney suggested during the Convention that the members of the Senate come from four equally proportioned districts within the United States and that the legislature elect the executive every seven years.

Section 3. The Senate
Trial of Impeachments One of Congress's powers is the power to impeach—to accuse government officials of wrongdoing, put them on trial, and, if necessary, remove them from office. The House decides if the offense is impeachable. The Senate acts as a jury, and when the president is impeached, the Chief Justice of the United States serves as the judge. A two-thirds vote of the members present is needed to convict impeached officials. What punishment can the Senate give if an impeached official is convicted?

Vocabulary

president pro tempore: *presiding officer of Senate who serves when the vice president is absent*
quorum: *minimum number of members that must be present to conduct sessions*
adjourn: *to suspend a session*

58 The Constitution Handbook

Section 3

[1.] The Senate of the United States shall be composed of two Senators from each State, chosen by the Legislature thereof, for six Years; and each Senator shall have one Vote.
[2.] Immediately after they shall be assembled in Consequence of the first Election, they shall be divided as equally as may be into three Classes. The Seats of the Senators of the first Class shall be vacated at the Expiration of the second Year, of the second Class at the Expiration of the fourth Year, and of the third Class at the Expiration of the sixth Year, so that one third may be chosen every second Year; and if Vacancies happen by Resignation, or otherwise, during the Recess of the Legislature of any State, the Executive thereof may make temporary Appointments until the next Meeting of the Legislature, which shall then fill such Vacancies.
[3.] No Person shall be a Senator who shall not have attained to the Age of thirty Years, and been nine Years a Citizen of the United States, and who shall not, when elected, be an Inhabitant of that State for which he shall be chosen.
[4.] The Vice President of the United States shall be President of the Senate, but shall have no Vote, unless they be equally divided.
[5.] The Senate shall chuse their other Officers, and also a **President pro tempore,** in the Absence of the Vice-President, or when he shall exercise the Office of the President of the United States.
[6.] The Senate shall have the sole Power to try all Impeachments. When sitting for that Purpose, they shall be on Oath or Affirmation. When the President of the United States is tried, the Chief Justice shall preside: And no Person shall be convicted without the Concurrence of two thirds of the Members present.
[7.] Judgment in Cases of Impeachment shall not extend further than to removal from Office, and disqualification to hold and enjoy any Office of honor, Trust or Profit under the United States: but the Party convicted shall nevertheless be liable and subject to Indictment, Trial, Judgment and Punishment, according to Law.

Section 4

[1.] The Times, Places and Manner of holding Elections for Senators and Representatives, shall be prescribed in each State by the Legislature thereof; but the Congress may at any time by Law make or alter such Regulations, except as to the Places of chusing Senators.
[2.] The Congress shall assemble at least once in every Year, and such Meeting shall be on the first Monday in December, unless they shall by Law appoint a different Day.

Section 5

[1.] Each House shall be the Judge of the Elections, Returns and Qualifications of its own Members, and a Majority of each shall constitute a **Quorum** to do Business; but a smaller Number may **adjourn** from day to day, and may be

---

Extending the Content

Female Representatives Republican and pacifist Jeannette Rankin of Montana was the first woman elected to the House of Representatives in 1916. In 1917 she and 49 House colleagues voted against entering World War I. In 1941 she was the only member of Congress to vote against declaring war on Japan.

In 2007 Nancy Pelosi of California became the first female Speaker of the House of Representatives.

authorized to compel the Attendance of absent Members, in such Manner, and under such Penalties as each House may provide.

[2.] Each House may determine the Rules of its Proceedings, punish its Members for disorderly Behaviour, and, with the **Concurrence** of two thirds, expel a Member.

[3.] Each House shall keep a Journal of its Proceedings, and from time to time publish the same, excepting such Parts as may in their Judgment require Secrecy; and the Yeas and Nays of the Members of either House on any question shall, at the Desire of one fifth of those Present, be entered on the Journal.

[4.] Neither House, during the Session of Congress, shall, without the Consent of the other, adjourn for more than three days, nor to any other Place than that in which the two Houses shall be sitting.

Section 6

[1.] The Senators and Representatives shall receive a Compensation for their Services, to be ascertained by Law, and paid out of the Treasury of the United States. They shall in all Cases, except Treason, Felony and Breach of the Peace, be privileged from Arrest during their Attendance at the Session of their respective Houses, and in going to and returning from the same; and for any Speech or Debate in either House, they shall not be questioned in any other Place.

[2.] No Senator or Representative shall, during the Time for which he was elected, be appointed to any civil Office under the Authority of the United States, which shall have been created, or the **Emoluments** whereof shall have been encreased during such time; and no Person holding any Office under the United States, shall be a Member of either House during his Continuance in Office.

Section 7

[1.] All Bills for raising **Revenue** shall originate in the House of Representatives; but the Senate may propose or concur with Amendments as on other **Bills.**

[2.] Every Bill which shall have passed the House of Representatives and the Senate, shall, before it become a Law, be presented to the President of the United States; If he approve he shall sign it, but if not he shall return it, with his Objections to that House in which it shall have originated, who shall enter the Objections at large on their Journal, and proceed to reconsider it. If after such Reconsideration two thirds of that House shall agree to pass the Bill, it shall be sent, together with the Objections, to the other House, by which it shall likewise be reconsidered, and if approved by two thirds of that House, it shall become a Law. But in all such Cases the Votes of both Houses shall be determined by yeas and Nays, and the Names of the Persons voting for and against the Bill shall be entered on the Journal of each House respectively. If any Bill shall not be returned by the President within ten Days (Sundays excepted) after it shall have been presented to him, the Same shall be a Law, in like Manner as if he had signed it, unless the Congress by their Adjournment prevent its Return, in which Case it shall not be a Law.

W

Vocabulary

concurrence: *agreement*
emoluments: *salaries*
revenue: *income raised by government*
bill: *draft of a proposed law*

Section 6. Privileges and Restrictions
Pay and Privileges To strengthen the federal government, the Founders set congressional salaries to be paid by the United States Treasury rather than by members' respective states. Originally, members were paid $6 per day. In 2002, all members of Congress received a base salary of $150,000.

Section 7. Passing Laws
Revenue Bill All tax laws must originate in the House of Representatives. This ensures that the branch of Congress that is elected by the people every two years has the major role in determining taxes.

Section 7. Passing Laws
How Bills Become Laws A bill may become a law only by passing both houses of Congress and by being signed by the president. The president can check Congress by rejecting—vetoing—its legislation. How can Congress override the president's veto?

R Reading Strategy
Using Context Clues Have students work in pairs to create a study card for each vocabulary word listed on this page. Instruct students to write the term on one side of a blank note card. Have students use the other side to write an explanation of how the term relates to the Constitution. Have students take turns quizzing each other using their study cards. **OL**

W Writing Support
Expository Writing Point out that because of the heavy volume of legislation, both houses of Congress have committees that do much of the work in preparing bills. Each committee deals with a particular issue, such as banking, foreign affairs, or natural resources. Encourage students to write letters asking representatives and senators from your state about the committees on which they serve. Invite volunteers to share the replies they receive. **OL**

Answer: A bill can become law, despite not being signed by the president, if two-thirds of the House of Representatives and two-thirds of the Senate approve the bill.

Additional Support

Extending the Content

Congressional Salaries Wanting to reduce the influence of the states, the Framers decided the members of Congress would be paid from the United States treasury, rather than by the individual states. In 1789 members of Congress received $6.00 per day. The chart shows the increase of congressional pay.

Selected Years	Congressional Salary*	Selected Years	Congressional Salary*	Selected Years	Congressional Salary*
1789	$1,500	1932	$9,000	1983	$69,800
1817	$2,000	1935	$10,000	1990	$96,600
1855	$3,000	1947	$12,500	1991	$125,100
1865	$5,000	1955	$22,500	1998	$136,700
1874	$5,000	1965	$30,000	2001	$145,100
1907	$7,500	1975	$44,600	2003	$154,700
1925	$10,000	1977	$57,500	2007	$168,000

*Daily rates have been converted to an annual salary, based on a hypothetically possible 250-day session.

Analyzing Information
Inform students that one political scientist has called the supremacy clause (Article VI, Section 2) "the most important single provision of the Constitution." **Ask:** Why do you think this might be so? *(This clause made it clear that the national Constitution and laws are supreme over state constitutions.)*
OL

Did You Know?

Ratification The first five states to ratify the Constitution—Delaware, Pennsylvania, New Jersey, Georgia, and Connecticut—did so quickly and by large majorities. The last two of the original thirteen states ratified the Constitution after George Washington had been inaugurated as the first president on April 30, 1789—North Carolina on November 21, 1789, and Rhode Island on May 29, 1790.

Additional Support

Article VI. Constitutional Supremacy
Article VI contains the "supremacy clause." This clause establishes that the Constitution, laws passed by Congress, and treaties of the United States "shall be the supreme Law of the Land." The "supremacy clause" recognizes the Constitution and federal laws as supreme when in conflict with those of the states.

Article VII. Ratification
Article VII addresses ratification and states that, unlike the Articles of Confederation, which required approval of all thirteen states for adoption, the Constitution would take effect after it was ratified by nine states.

---

that no Amendment which may be made prior to the Year One thousand eight hundred and eight shall in any Manner affect the first and fourth Clauses in the Ninth Section of the first Article; and that no State, without its Consent, shall be deprived of its equal Suffrage in the Senate.

Article VI

[1.] All Debts contracted and Engagements entered into, before the Adoption of this Constitution, shall be as valid against the United States under this Constitution, as under the Confederation.

[2.] This Constitution, and the Laws of the United States which shall be made in Pursuance thereof; and all Treaties made, or which shall be made, under the Authority of the United States, shall be the supreme Law of the Land; and the Judges in every State shall be bound thereby, any Thing in the Constitution or Laws of any State to the Contrary notwithstanding.

[3.] The Senators and Representatives before mentioned, and the Members of the several State Legislatures, and all executive and judicial Officers, both of the United States and of the several States, shall be bound by Oath or Affirmation, to support this Constitution; but no religious Test shall ever be required as a Qualification to any Office or public Trust under the United States.

Article VII

The Ratification of the Conventions of nine States, shall be sufficient for the Establishment of this Constitution between the States so ratifying the same.

Done in Convention by the Unanimous Consent of the States present the Seventeenth Day of September in the Year of our Lord one thousand seven hundred and Eighty seven and of the Independence of the United States of America the Twelfth. In witness whereof We have hereunto subscribed our Names,

---

Signers

George Washington, **President and Deputy from Virginia**	**New York** Alexander Hamilton	**Delaware** George Read Gunning Bedford, Jr. John Dickinson Richard Bassett Jacob Broom	**North Carolina** William Blount Richard Dobbs Spaight Hugh Williamson
New Hampshire John Langdon Nicholas Gilman	**New Jersey** William Livingston David Brearley William Paterson Jonathan Dayton		**South Carolina** John Rutledge Charles Cotesworth Pinckney Charles Pinckney Pierce Butler
Massachusetts Nathaniel Gorham Rufus King	**Pennsylvania** Benjamin Franklin Thomas Mifflin Robert Morris George Clymer Thomas FitzSimons Jared Ingersoll James Wilson Gouverneur Morris	**Maryland** James McHenry Daniel of St. Thomas Jenifer Daniel Carroll	**Georgia** William Few Abraham Baldwin
Connecticut William Samuel Johnson Roger Sherman		**Virginia** John Blair James Madison, Jr.	**Attest:** William Jackson, Secretary

---

Extending the Content

Signers of the Constitution Of the 55 delegates who attended the Constitutional Convention, only 39 signed the document. The thirty-ninth signature—that of John Dickinson—was written by George Read at Dickinson's request. Elbridge Gerry of Massachusetts and Edmund Randolph and George Mason of Virginia refused to sign while 13 other delegates left the convention early.

Amendment I

Congress shall make no law respecting an establishment of religion, or prohibiting the free exercise thereof; or abridging the freedom of speech, or of the press; or the right of the people peaceably to assemble, and to petition the Government for a redress of grievances.

Amendment II

A well regulated Militia, being necessary to the security of a free State, the right of the people to keep and bear Arms, shall not be infringed.

Amendment III

No Soldier shall, in time of peace be **quartered** in any house, without the consent of the Owner, nor in time of war, but in a manner to be prescribed by law.

Amendment IV

The right of the people to be secure in their persons, houses, papers, and effects, against unreasonable searches and seizures, shall not be violated, and no **Warrants** shall issue, but upon **probable cause,** supported by Oath or affirmation, and particularly describing the place to be searched, and the persons or things to be seized.

Amendment V

No person shall be held to answer for a capital, or otherwise infamous crime, unless on a presentment or indictment of a Grand Jury, except in cases arising in the land or naval forces, or in the Militia, when in actual service in time of War or public danger; nor shall any person be subject for the same offence to be twice put in jeopardy of life or limb; nor shall be compelled in any criminal case to be a witness against himself, nor be deprived of life, liberty, or property, without due process of law; nor shall private property be taken for public use without just compensation.

Amendment VI

In all criminal prosecutions, the accused shall enjoy the right to a speedy and public trial, by an impartial jury of the State and district wherein the crime shall have been committed, which district shall have been previously ascertained by law, and to be informed of the nature and cause of the accusation; to be confronted with the witnesses against him; to have compulsory process for obtaining Witnesses in his favor, and to have the assistance of counsel for his defence.

Amendment VII

In Suits at common law, where the value in controversy shall exceed twenty dollars, the right of trial by jury shall be preserved, and no fact tried by a jury, shall be otherwise reexamined in any Court of the United States, than according to the rules of **common law.**

The Amendments

This part of the Constitution consists of changes and additions. The Constitution has been amended 27 times throughout the nation's history. **R**

The Bill of Rights

The first 10 amendments are known as the Bill of Rights (1791). These amendments limit the powers of the federal government. The First Amendment protects the civil liberties of individuals in the United States. The amendment freedoms are not absolute, however. They are limited by the rights of other individuals. What freedoms does the First Amendment protect?

Vocabulary

quarter: *to provide living accommodations*

warrant: *document that gives police particular rights or powers*

probable cause: *police must have a reasonable basis to believe a person is linked to a crime*

Amendment 5

Rights of the Accused This amendment contains important protections for people accused of crimes. One of the protections is that government may not deprive any person of life, liberty, or property without due process of law. This means that the government must follow proper constitutional procedures in trials and in other actions it takes against individuals. According to Amendment V, what is the function of a grand jury?

Amendment 6

Right to Speedy and Fair Trial A basic protection is the right to a speedy, public trial. The jury must hear witnesses and evidence on both sides before deciding the guilt or innocence of a person charged with a crime. This amendment also provides that legal counsel must be provided to a defendant. In 1963, in *Gideon* v. *Wainwright*, the Supreme Court ruled that if a defendant cannot afford a lawyer, the government must provide one to defend him or her. Why is the right to a "speedy" trial important?

Vocabulary

common law: *law established by previous court decisions*

The Constitution Handbook **67**

Amendment 25 Presidential Disability and Succession The Twenty-fifth Amendment (1967) established a process for the vice president to take over leadership of the nation when a president is disabled. It also set procedures for filling a vacancy in the office of vice president.

This amendment was used in 1973, when Vice President Spiro Agnew resigned from office after being charged with accepting bribes. President Richard Nixon then appointed Gerald R. Ford as vice president in accordance with the provisions of the Twenty-fifth Amendment. A year later, President Nixon resigned during the Watergate scandal, and Ford became president. President Ford then had to fill the vice presidency, which he had left vacant upon assuming the presidency. He named Nelson A. Rockefeller as vice president. Thus individuals who had not been elected held both the presidency and the vice presidency. Whom does the president inform if he or she cannot carry out the duties of the office?

Section 2
The Congress shall have power to enforce this article by appropriate legislation.

Amendment XXV
Section 1
In case of the removal of the President from office or his death or resignation, the Vice President shall become President.

Section 2
Whenever there is a vacancy in the office of the Vice President, the President shall nominate a Vice President who shall take the office upon confirmation by a majority vote of both Houses of Congress.

Section 3
Whenever the President transmits to the President pro tempore of the Senate and the Speaker of the House of Representatives his written declaration that he is unable to discharge the powers and duties of his office, and until he transmits to them a written declaration to the contrary, such powers and duties shall be discharged by the Vice President as Acting President.

Section 4
Whenever the Vice President and a majority of either the principal officers of the executive departments or of such other body as Congress may by law provide, transmit to the President pro tempore of the Senate and the Speaker of the House of Representatives their written declaration that the President is unable to discharge the powers and duties of his office, the Vice President shall immediately assume the power and duties of the office of Acting President.

Thereafter, when the President transmits to the President pro tempore of the Senate and the Speaker of the House of Representatives his written declaration that no inability exists, he shall resume the powers and duties of his office unless the Vice President and a majority of either the principal officers of the executive department or of such other body as Congress may by law provide, transmit within four days to the President pro tempore of the Senate and the Speaker of the House of Representatives their written declaration that the President is unable to discharge the powers and duties of his office. Thereupon Congress shall decide the issue, assembling within forty-eight hours for that purpose if not in session. If the Congress, within twenty-one days after receipt of the latter written declaration, or, if Congress is not in session, within twenty-one days after Congress is required to assemble, determines by two-thirds vote of both Houses that the President is unable to discharge the powers and duties of his office, the Vice President shall continue to discharge the same as Acting President; otherwise, the President shall resume the power and duties of his office.

Amendment XXVI

Section 1
The right of citizens of the United States, who are eighteen years of age or older, to vote shall not be denied or abridged by the United States or by any State on account of age.

Section 2
The Congress shall have power to enforce this article by appropriate legislation.

Amendment XXVII

No law, varying the compensation for the services of Senators and Representatives, shall take effect, until an election of representatives shall have intervened.

Amendment 26
Voting Age of 18 The Twenty-sixth Amendment (1971) lowered the voting age in both federal and state elections to 18.

Amendment 27
Congressional Salary Restraints The Twenty-seventh Amendment (1992) makes congressional pay raises effective during the term following their passage. James Madison offered the amendment in 1789, but it was never adopted. In 1982 Gregory Watson, then a student at the University of Texas, discovered the forgotten amendment while doing research for a school paper. Watson made the amendment's passage his crusade.

Extending the Content

Key to Ability Levels

BL Below Level **AL** Above Level
OL On Level **ELL** English Language Learners

Key to Teaching Resources

Print Material DVD
CD-ROM Transparency

Levels				Resources	Chapter Opener	Section 1	Section 2	Section 3	Section 4	Chapter Assess
BL	OL	AL	ELL							
FOCUS										
BL	OL	AL	ELL	Daily Focus Skills Transparencies		2-1	2-2	2-3	2-4	
TEACH										
BL	OL		ELL	Reading Essentials and Note-Taking Guide*		p. 13	p. 16	p. 19	p. 22	
BL	OL		ELL	Reading Skills Activity, URB				p. 53		
	OL			Historical Analysis Skills Activity, URB			p. 54			
BL	OL	AL	ELL	Differentiated Instruction Activity, URB					p. 55	
BL	OL		ELL	English Learner Activity, URB					p. 57	
BL	OL	AL	ELL	Content Vocabulary Activity, URB*		p. 59				
BL	OL	AL	ELL	Academic Vocabulary Activity, URB				p. 61		
	OL	AL		Reinforcing Skills Activity, URB					p. 63	
	OL	AL		Critical Thinking Skills Activity, URB			p. 64			
BL	OL		ELL	Time Line Activity, URB			p. 65			
	OL			Linking Past and Present Activity, URB				p. 66		
BL	OL	AL	ELL	Primary Source Reading, URB		p. 67		p. 69		
BL	OL	AL	ELL	American Art and Music Activity, URB		p. 71				
BL	OL	AL	ELL	Interpreting Political Cartoons Activity, URB					p. 73	
		AL		Enrichment Activity, URB			p. 76			
BL	OL		ELL	Guided Reading Activity, URB*		p. 78	p. 79	p. 80	p. 81	
BL	OL	AL	ELL	Differentiated Instruction for the American High School Classroom	✓	✓	✓	✓	✓	✓
BL	OL	AL	ELL	Unit Map Overlay Transparencies	✓	✓	✓	✓	✓	✓
BL	OL	AL	ELL	Unit Time Line Transparencies, Strategies, and Activities	✓	✓	✓	✓	✓	✓
BL	OL	AL	ELL	Cause and Effect Transparencies, Strategies, and Activities	✓	✓	✓	✓	✓	✓
BL	OL	AL	ELL	Why It Matters Transparencies, Strategies, and Activities	✓	✓	✓	✓	✓	✓
BL	OL	AL	ELL	American Biographies	✓	✓	✓	✓	✓	✓
BL	OL	AL		Supreme Court Case Studies		p. 1	p. 3	p. 9	p. 11	
BL	OL	AL	ELL	The Living Constitution	✓	✓	✓	✓	✓	✓

Note: Please refer to the *Unit 1 Resource Book* for this chapter's URB materials.

* Also available in Spanish

- Interactive Lesson Planner
- Interactive Teacher Edition
- Fully editable blackline masters
- Section Spotlight Videos Launch
- Differentiated Lesson Plans
- Printable reports of daily assignments
- Standards Tracking System

Levels					Resources	Chapter Opener	Section 1	Section 2	Section 3	Section 4	Chapter Assess
TEACH *(continued)*											
BL	OL	AL	ELL		American Issues	✓	✓	✓	✓	✓	✓
	OL	AL	ELL		American Art and Architecture Transparencies, Strategies, and Activities	✓	✓	✓	✓	✓	✓
BL	OL	AL			High School American History Literature Library	✓	✓	✓	✓	✓	✓
	OL	AL			American History Primary Source Documents Library	✓	✓	✓	✓	✓	✓
BL	OL	AL	ELL		American Music Hits Through History CD	✓	✓	✓	✓	✓	✓
BL	OL	AL	ELL		StudentWorks™ Plus DVD	✓	✓	✓	✓	✓	✓
BL	OL	AL	ELL		Vocabulary PuzzleMaker CD-ROM	✓	✓	✓	✓	✓	✓
BL	OL	AL	ELL		*The American Vision* Video Program DVD	✓	✓	✓	✓	✓	✓
Teacher Resources					Reading Strategies and Activities for the Social Studies Classroom	✓	✓	✓	✓	✓	✓
					Strategies for Success	✓	✓	✓	✓	✓	✓
					Presentation Plus! DVD	✓	✓	✓	✓	✓	✓
					Success with English Learner	✓	✓	✓	✓	✓	✓
ASSESS											
BL	OL	AL	ELL		Section Quizzes and Chapter Tests*		p. 17	p. 18	p. 19	p. 20	p. 21
BL	OL	AL	ELL		Authentic Assessment With Rubrics						p. 9
BL	OL	AL	ELL		Standardized Test Practice Workbook						p. 3
BL	OL	AL	ELL		*ExamView®* Assessment Suite CD-ROM		2-1	2-2	2-3	2-4	Ch. 2
BL	OL	AL	ELL		Interactive Tutor Self-Assessment CD-ROM		2-1	2-2	2-3	2-4	Ch. 2
CLOSE											
BL			ELL		Reteaching Activity, URB						p. 75
BL	OL		ELL		Reading and Study Skills Foldables™	p. 51					
BL	OL	AL	ELL		*American History* in Graphic Novel					p. 23	

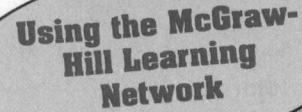

Using the McGraw-Hill Learning Network

Presentation Builder

Technology Product

Presentation Builder is a convenient and dynamic McGraw-Hill Learning Network tool to create online presentations. Use the Presentation Builder to
- create your own presentation slides;
- insert graphics from your Glencoe textbook;
- distribute presentations to students using **Assignments** from the *Classroom Tools*.

Steps

- On the McGraw-Hill Learning Network home page (www.mhln.com), log in as a member.
- Choose **Presentation Builder** under **Resources**.
- Click the **New Presentation** button.
- Enter a title in the **Presentation Title** box, then follow the prompts to select colors and fonts.
- Click the **Next** button and select a slide. Follow the prompts to insert information and complete the

slide. The text boxes automatically adjust in size to accommodate the length of each question.
- Click the **Add Slide** button if you have additional presentation information and follow the prompts.
- Click **Review Presentation** when you are done.
- Click **View Presentation** to review the presentation in a pop-up window.
- Click on an underlined slide title to edit slides; use the drop-down keys to change the order of the slides; push the **Delete** button to delete a slide; and press **Insert Slide** to add a slide.
- Click the **Save** button when you are satisfied with your presentation. The presentation is saved to your **File Cabinet** and can be distributed to students through **Assignments**.

History ONLINE

	Student	Teacher	Parent
Beyond the Textbook	●	●	●
Chapter Overviews	●	●	●
Time Current Events	●		●
ePuzzles and Games	●		●
Concepts in Motion	●		●
Literature Connections		●	
Multi-Language Glossaries	●		●
Online Student Edition	●	●	●
Self-Check Quizzes	●		●
Student Web Activities	●		●
Study Central™	●		●
Teaching Today		●	
Vocabulary eFlashcards	●		●
Web Activity Lesson Plans		●	

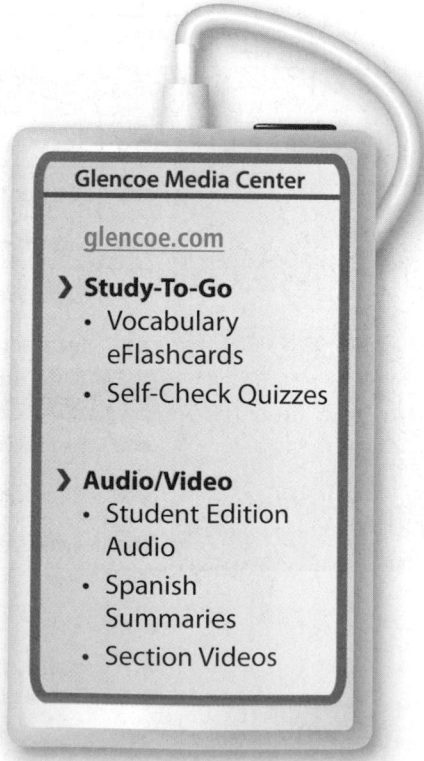

Glencoe Media Center

glencoe.com

❯ **Study-To-Go**
- Vocabulary eFlashcards
- Self-Check Quizzes

❯ **Audio/Video**
- Student Edition Audio
- Spanish Summaries
- Section Videos

READING SUPPORT FROM JAMESTOWN EDUCATION

- **Timed Readings Plus in Social Studies** helps students increase their reading rate and fluency while maintaining comprehension. The 400-word passages are similar to those found on state and national assessments.

- **Reading in the Content Area: Social Studies** concentrates on six essential reading skills that help students better comprehend what they read. The book includes 75 high-interest nonfiction passages written at increasing levels of difficulty.

- **Reading Social Studies** includes strategic reading instruction and vocabulary support in Social Studies content for both ELLs and native speakers of English.

www.jamestowneducation.com

NATIONAL GEOGRAPHIC

Index to National Geographic Magazine:

The following articles relate to this chapter:

- "Lewis and Clark's lost Missouri: a mapmaker re-creates the river of 1804 and changes the course of history" by Cathy Riggs Salter, April 2002.

- "Wide Open Wyoming" by Thomas J. Abercrombie, January 1993.

National Geographic Society Products To order the following, call National Geographic at 1-800-368-2728:

- *Immigration* (CD-ROM)

Access National Geographic's new, dynamic MapMachine Web site and other geography resources at:

www.nationalgeographic.com
www.nationalgeographic.com/maps

The following videotape programs are available from Glencoe as supplements to Modern Times Chapter 2:

- Lewis and Clark (ISBN 1-56-501592-4)
- Andrew Jackson: A Man for the People (ISBN 1-56-501647-5)

To order, call Glencoe at 1-800-334-7344. To find classroom resources to accompany many of these videos, check the following home pages:

A&E Television: www.aetv.com
The History Channel: www.historychannel.com

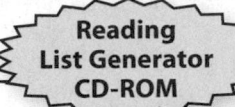

Reading List Generator CD-ROM — GLENCOE BOOKLINK 3

Use this database to search more than 30,000 titles to create a customized reading list for your students.

- Reading lists can be organized by students' reading level, author, genre, theme, or area of interest.
- The database provides Degrees of Reading Power™ (DRP) and Lexile™ readability scores for all selections.
- A brief summary of each selection is included.

Leveled reading suggestions for this chapter:

For students at a Grade 8 reading level:
- *Thomas Jefferson*, by Lucia Raatma

For students at a Grade 9 reading level:
- *Many Thousand Gone: African-Americans from Slavery to Freedom,* by Virginia Hamilton

For students at a Grade 10 reading level:
- *Eli Whitney: Cotton Gin Genius,* by Kaye Patchett

For students at a Grade 11 reading level:
- *James K. Polk: 11th President of the United States,* by Miriam Greenblatt

For students at a Grade 12 reading level:
- *The Mexican War: "Mr. Polk's War,"* by Charles W. Carey

Focus

MAKING CONNECTIONS
How Do Nations Grow?

Discuss the two questions on page 77 with students. Activate students' prior knowledge by prompting students to make generalized statements about what society was like in the North and the South. Also, remind students how small the United States was in 1787 compared to its size on the eve of the Civil War. Westward expansion ultimately caused great conflict between the North and the South. **OL**

Teach
The Big Ideas

As students study the chapter, remind them to consider the section-based Big Ideas included in each section's Guide to Reading. The **Essential Questions** in the activities below tie in to the Big Ideas and help students think about and understand important chapter concepts. In addition, the Hands-on Chapter Projects with their culminating activities relate the content from each section to the Big Ideas. These activities build on each other as students progress through the chapter. Section activities culminate in the wrap-up activity on the Visual Summary page.

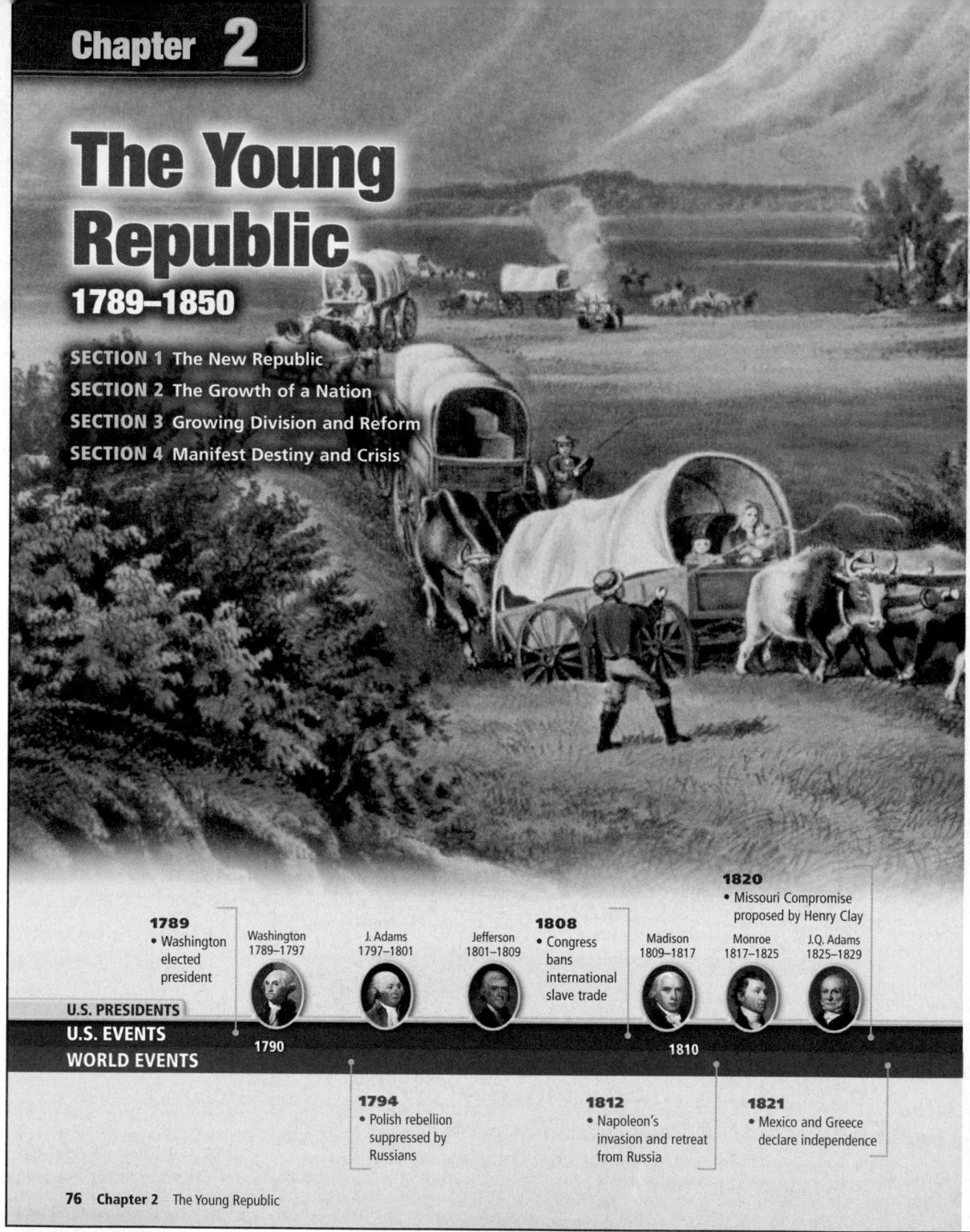

Chapter 2

The Young Republic
1789–1850

SECTION 1 The New Republic

SECTION 2 The Growth of a Nation

SECTION 3 Growing Division and Reform

SECTION 4 Manifest Destiny and Crisis

1789
• Washington elected president

Washington 1789–1797

J. Adams 1797–1801

Jefferson 1801–1809

1808
• Congress bans international slave trade

Madison 1809–1817

Monroe 1817–1825

J.Q. Adams 1825–1829

1820
• Missouri Compromise proposed by Henry Clay

U.S. PRESIDENTS

U.S. EVENTS

1790

1810

WORLD EVENTS

1794
• Polish rebellion suppressed by Russians

1812
• Napoleon's invasion and retreat from Russia

1821
• Mexico and Greece declare independence

76   Chapter 2   The Young Republic

Section 1

The New Republic
Essential Question: What steps did the United States take to establish a stable and lasting national government? *(The First Congress prepared the Bill of Rights; the First Bank of the United States was established; a peaceful transfer of political power occurred; and the nation defended itself in the War of 1812.)* Point out that in Section 1 students will learn about the rise of political parties and the first transfer of political power. **OL**

Section 2

The Growth of a Nation
Essential Question: How did nationalism affect the development of the United States? *(The federal government established the Second Bank of the United States. The judicial system, through Supreme Court rulings, gave the federal courts power over the state courts. The U.S. sought to assert itself internationally.)* Point out that in Section 2 students will learn that nationalism promoted federal authority over state authority. **OL**

MAKING CONNECTIONS
How Do Nations Grow?

The young republic saw the growth of the federal government and nationalism. Sectional disputes began as industry developed in the North while Southern agriculture depended on slavery. As the nation expanded west, sectional conflict continued to escalate.

- *How did economic differences between North and South cause tensions?*
- *How do you think the migration of settlers to the West affected the North and South?*

More About the Painting

Visual Literacy The idea of Manifest Destiny captivated not only the westward bound settlers but also the artists of the era. The painting "Wild West" by Frances F. Palmer (1812–1876) shows a romantic view of the West that was popular in art at the time—the epic, peaceful occupation of an empty continent. None of the forbidding dangers of the journey are represented. The wagon train is following the banks of a gentle stream in a lush setting, while benevolent Native Americans watch from the far bank.

FOLDABLES

Analyzing Events Create a Trifold Book Foldable listing what happened, how it influenced events leading to the Civil War, and what might have happened if the event had turned out differently. Choose one of the following events to complete the Foldable: the Fugitive Slave Act, the Dred Scott Decision, the Lincoln-Douglas Debates, the Missouri Compromise, the Kansas-Nebraska Act, or John Brown's Raid.

FOLDABLES Study Organizer **Dinah Zike's Foldables**

Dinah Zike's Foldables are three-dimensional, interactive graphic organizers that help students practice basic writing skills, review vocabulary terms, and identify main ideas. Instructions for creating and using Foldables can be found in the Appendix at the end of this book and in the *Dinah Zike's Reading and Study Skills Foldables* booklet.

Timeline:

1832
- Democrats hold their first presidential nominating convention

1846
- United States begins war with Mexico

1850
- Compromise of 1850 adopted in an attempt to ease sectional tensions

Jackson 1829–1837

Van Buren 1837–1841

W. Harrison 1841

Tyler 1841–1845

Polk 1845–1849

Taylor 1849–1850

1830

1850

1832
- Male voting rights expanded in England

1842
- China opened by force to foreign trade

1848
- Karl Marx and Friedrich Engels's *The Communist Manifesto* published

1859
- Darwin's *Origin of Species* published

History ONLINE Chapter Overview
Visit glencoe.com to preview Chapter 2.

Chapter 2 The Young Republic **77**

History ONLINE
Introduce students to chapter content and key terms by having them access the Chapter 2 Overview at glencoe.com.

Section 3

Growing Division and Reform
Essential Question: How did the Missouri Compromise seek to address growing sectionalism? *(The Missouri Compromise sought to maintain the balance of power in Congress, dividing the Senate equally between slave and free states, by admitting Missouri to the Union as a slave state and Maine as a free state.)* Point out that in Section 3 students will learn about the sectional dispute over slavery. **OL**

Section 4

Manifest Destiny and Crisis
Essential Question: Why did westward expansion make sectional tensions worse? *(The settlement of new territories and their admittance as states repeatedly threatened to upset the balance between free states and slave states; annexation of Texas and the war with Mexico added vast new lands that could have potentially become slave states.)* Point out that in Section 4 students will see sectional tensions intensify and become violent. **OL**

Focus

Bellringer

Daily Focus Transparency 2.1

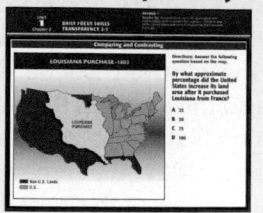

Guide to Reading

Answers:
Congress organized executive branch by creating departments; organized judicial branch; adopted the Bill of Rights; financed government by imposing tariff and tonnage; created national bank; and accepted debt of Continental Congress at full value to establish credit.

Section Spotlight Video

To generate student interest and provide a springboard for class discussion, access the Chapter 2, Section 1 video at glencoe.com or on the video DVD.

Resource Manager

The New Republic

Differences over how to make the government function effectively became the basis for two new political parties. The growth of the nation, along with the War of 1812, gave Americans a strong sense of national pride.

Guide to Reading

Big Ideas
Government and Society An important Supreme Court decision asserted that the Court had the power to decide whether laws passed by Congress are constitutional.

Content Vocabulary
• cabinet (p. 78)
• Bill of Rights (p. 78)
• enumerated powers (p. 79)
• implied powers (p. 79)
• judicial review (p. 83)

Academic Vocabulary
• constitutional (p. 78)

People and Events to Identify
• District of Columbia (p. 80)
• Louisiana Territory (p. 83)
• Louisiana Purchase (p. 83)

Reading Strategy
Sequencing Complete a graphic organizer similar to the one below by indicating the tasks completed by the first Congress under the Constitution.

Tasks of Congress

The Early Years of the Republic

MAIN Idea The United States established a federal government, created a Bill of Rights, and witnessed the first political parties.

HISTORY AND YOU Of all the freedoms that are granted to Americans, which do you consider most precious, and why? Read on to learn about the ratification of the Bill of Rights, which guarantees basic freedoms to all Americans.

The newly elected members of Congress met even before the Constitution had been ratified. Americans were confident, though, because they knew George Washington would be the first president.

One of the first tasks of President Washington and Congress was to organize the government itself. In the summer of 1789, Congress created three executive departments: the Department of State, the Department of the Treasury, and the Department of War, along with the Office of the Attorney General. Washington then chose his **cabinet**—the individuals who would head these departments and advise him. His appointments included Thomas Jefferson as Secretary of State and Alexander Hamilton as Treasury Secretary.

Congress also organized the judicial branch. The Judiciary Act of 1789 outlined the makeup of the Supreme Court and established lower federal courts. Washington chose John Jay as the first Chief Justice of the United States.

The Bill of Rights

One of the most important acts of Congress in 1789 was to propose amendments to the Constitution. During the campaign to ratify the Constitution, the Federalists had promised to add a bill of rights detailing the rights of American citizens.

In September 1789, Congress agreed on 12 **constitutional** amendments. They were then sent to the states, but only 10 were approved. These 10 went into effect and are generally referred to as the **Bill of Rights.** Eight of the amendments protect the rights of individuals against the government. The Ninth Amendment states that the people have other rights not listed in the Constitution. The Tenth Amendment adds that any powers not specifically given to the federal government are reserved for the states.

R **Reading Strategies**	C **Critical Thinking**	D **Differentiated Instruction**	W **Writing Support**	S **Skill Practice**
Teacher Edition • Summarizing, p. 80 **Additional Resources** • Content Vocabulary Activity, URB p. 59 • Prim. Source Reading, URB p. 67	**Teacher Edition** • Analyz. Prim. Sources, p. 80 **Additional Resources** • Reteaching Activity, URB p. 75 • Supreme Court Case Studies, p. 1 • Quizzes and Tests, p. 17	**Additional Resources** • Am. Art/Music Activity, URB p. 71	**Teacher Edition** • Descriptive Writing, p. 81	**Teacher Edition** • Creating a Presentation, p. 79 • Using Geography, p. 82 **Additional Resources** • Guided Reading Activity, URB p. 78 • Reading Essen., p. 13

INFOGRAPHIC
Origins of the Bill of Rights

Basic Rights	Magna Carta (1215)	English Bill of Rights (1689)	Virginia Declaration of Rights (1776)	Virginia Statute for Religious Freedom (1786)	American Bill of Rights (1791)
No state religion				●	●
Freedom of worship		● limited	●	●	●
Freedom of speech		●	●		●
Right to petition		● limited			●
Right to bear arms					●
No quartering troops in private homes without permission					●
No searches and seizures without a specific search warrant	●		●		●
Government cannot take away life, liberty, or property unless it follows proper court procedures (due process)	●	●	●		●
Right to a speedy public trial by jury and to a lawyer	●	●	●	●	●
No excessive bail, fines, or cruel and unusual punishment	●	●	●		●

Steps to the Bill of Rights

In creating the Bill of Rights, the first ten amendments to the Constitution, James Madison drew on the great founding documents of English legal history and tradition: the Magna Carta, the English Bill of Rights, the Virginia Declaration of Rights, and the Virginia Statute for Religious Freedom. Beginning in 1215, these and other documents had established protections of individual rights and freedoms designed to safeguard citizens from oppression and tyrannical government.

Analyzing VISUALS

1. **Specifying** Which right was established in the Magna Carta and appears in all subsequent documents?
2. **Explaining** Which two rights are the only ones unique to the American Bill of Rights, and why do you think that is?

Tackling Financial Troubles

With the bureaucracy up and running, the most pressing concerns involved the economy. The federal government had inherited a huge debt from the Continental Congress. Secretary of the Treasury Alexander Hamilton proposed a plan to pay off all debts. He also wanted the federal government to accept responsibility for the states' outstanding debts. Hamilton called for the creation of a national bank to manage the country's finances.

Thomas Jefferson, James Madison, and others favored less government interference in the economy. They also pointed out that establishing a bank was not one of the federal government's **enumerated powers**—the powers specifically mentioned in the Constitution. Hamilton rebuffed this criticism by citing Article I, Section 8, which gives the federal government the power "to make all laws which shall be necessary and proper" to fulfill its responsibilities. The "necessary and proper" clause, he said, created **implied powers**—powers not explicitly listed in the Constitution but necessary for the government to do its job. A national bank, Hamilton argued, was indeed necessary so that the government could collect taxes, regulate trade, and provide for the common defense.

Teach

S Skill Practice
Creating a Presentation
Organize the class into 10 groups. Assign each group one amendment from the Bill of Rights. Each group should research the amendment and then give an oral presentation in which students explain why it was important to Americans in 1789. **OL**

Analyzing VISUALS

Answers:
1. the right to a speedy trial by jury and to a lawyer
2. The two amendments include the right to bear arms and no quartering of soldiers in private homes. Answers will vary, but most students will assume that this right grew out of the dependence of the colonies on citizen militias at the beginning of the Revolution, and also the fact that the Framers were not comfortable with the concept of a standing army.

Hands-On Chapter Project
Step 1

Presidential Customs

Step 1: Precedents Set by Washington
Students will work individually to research the presidential customs initiated by President George Washington.

Directions Point out that as the first United States President under the federal Constitution, George Washington set the precedent for many customs of the office. Have students research the presidency of Washington. Have each student list three examples of such precedents.

Interpreting Information Students will need to research online or print sources to find descriptions of the Washington presidency. They will then determine which of Washington's actions influenced the presidency. **OL**

(Chapter Project continued on page 87)

R **Reading Strategy**

R **Reading Strategy**

Summarizing Students should learn the basic philosophical differences between the Federalists and Democratic-Republicans.
Ask: What were the major differences of opinion between the Federalists and Democratic-Republicans? *(Possible response: The Federalists believed in a strong national government, which would exercise firm control over the economy. The Democratic-Republicans favored a weaker national government because they feared a powerful national government would abuse its power.)* **OL**

C **Critical Thinking**

Analyzing Primary Sources
Have students read Federalist No. 10 on page R44 and Washington's Farewell Address on page R46.
Ask: How does George Washington's view of political parties compare with those expressed in Federalist No. 10? *(Washington expresses concern about the rise of regional political parties; Federalist 10 assumes parties would represent economic interests but, given the size of the nation, no one party would be able to dominate government.)* **AL**

Additional Support

Hamilton eventually won approval for his financial program after promises to Southern congressmen that the nation's capital would be moved to the **District of Columbia** on land donated by Virginia and Maryland. With that settled, the Bank of the United States was established in 1791 for a 20-year period.

The same year, Congress enacted a high tax on whiskey. The new tax brought in needed revenue, but it proved extremely unpopular among Western farmers who resisted the tax by terrorizing tax collectors, robbing mail, and destroying whiskey-making stills of those who paid the tax. In August 1794, President Washington sent nearly 13,000 troops to crush the Whiskey Rebellion.

**History ONLINE
Student Web Activity** Visit glencoe.com and complete the activity on political parties.

The Rise of Political Parties

The handling of the Whiskey Rebellion intensified the tensions that had arisen over Hamilton's financial program. By 1794 the factions in Congress had solidified into rival political parties.

Hamilton's supporters called themselves Federalists. They favored a strong national government led by the "rich, well born, and able." The Federalist Party included many manufacturers, merchants, and bankers, especially in the urban Northeast who believed that manufacturing and trade were the basis of national wealth and power.

R Their opponents, led by Madison and Jefferson, took the name Democratic-Republicans, although most people at the time referred to them as Republicans. They favored strict limits on the federal government's power and protection of states' rights. They also believed that the strength of the United States was its independent, land-owning farmers and thus supported agriculture over commerce and trade. The party had a strong base among farmers in the rural South and West.

For an excerpt from "Washington's Farewell Address," see page R46 in **Documents in American History.**

Tough Times for Adams

C After two terms as president, a weary George Washington left office. His Farewell Address to the American people warned of the dangers of party politics and sectionalism—pitting North against South, or East against West. Washington also urged Americans "to steer clear of permanent alliances with any portion of the foreign world."

Washington's successor as president was a fellow Federalist, John Adams. One of Adams's most urgent challenges was averting war with France. France was enraged by a treaty between the United States and Britain and had begun seizing American ships at sea. The two nations soon were fighting an undeclared war at sea until negotiations finally brought an end to hostilities in 1800.

Meanwhile, the division between the two political parties had been deepening. The Federalists resented the harsh Republican criticism. Using their majority in Congress, they passed the Alien and Sedition Acts in 1798. One of these laws made it a crime to utter or print anything "false, scandalous, and malicious" against the federal government or any federal official. The other laws were directed at aliens—foreigners living in the country—who often were anti-British and tended to vote Republican once they became citizens. The new laws made it harder for them to gain citizenship and left them vulnerable to deportation without trial.

Many Americans denounced the Alien and Sedition Acts as an infringement on people's freedoms. In 1798 and 1799, Kentucky and Virginia passed resolutions challenging the laws' constitutionality. At the time, few states accepted the premise behind the resolutions that states had a right to decide on the validity of federal laws. Many years later, states used these ideas to defend their interests.

The Election of 1800

Although John Adams hoped to win reelection in 1800, he faced an uphill battle. The Alien and Sedition Acts had angered many people, as had new taxes on houses, land, and enslaved Africans. The Republican nominees, Thomas Jefferson for president and Aaron Burr for vice president, campaigned against the taxes and the national bank. They accused the Federalists of favoring monarchy and discouraging political participation.

The election was very close, and it revealed a flaw in the system for selecting the president. The Constitution does not let citizens vote directly for the chief executive. Instead, each state chooses electors—the same number as it has senators and representatives. This group, known as the Electoral College, then votes for the president.

Activity: Collaborative Learning

Persuasive Writing Divide the class into groups and ask students to write a position paper in which they explain whether or not they think the Alien and Sedition Acts were unconstitutional. Responses should be supported by a logical explanation for the position taken. Encourage students to review the Constitution Handbook before taking their position. **AL**

Turning Points

The Election of 1800

The election of 1800 was a major turning point in American political history. This is because it was the first transfer of power between parties under the federal Constitution, and, despite the enormous political and personal hatred between the party members, it was accomplished peacefully. It demonstrated the commitment on all sides to the Constitution and to a democratic republic despite partisan passions.

ANALYZING HISTORY What made the election of 1800 so significant in American political history?

▲ This cartoon reveals the emotions in American politics and the divisive nature of the relationship between the parties in the early years of the nation. The scene depicts a fight in the House of Representatives in 1798, begun when Federalist Roger Griswold of Connecticut assaulted Republican Matthew Lyon of Vermont.

Presidential Election of 1800

Map labels: NH 6, VT 4, MA 16, NY 12, RI 4, PA 8, NJ 7, CT 9, KY 4, VA 21, MD 3, DE, TN 3, NC 4, SC 8, GA 4

Presidential Candidate	Popular Votes	% of Popular Vote	Electoral Votes
Jefferson	*	*	73
Adams	*	*	65

*Electors were not chosen by popular vote, but by state legislatures.

According to the original terms of the Constitution, each elector in the Electoral College voted for two people in a presidential election. The person receiving the most votes became president, and the person receiving the second-highest number of votes became vice president. Under this system a tie was possible, as happened in the case of the tie between Thomas Jefferson and Aaron Burr in 1800. The House of Representatives then elected Jefferson after 35 rounds of voting in which there was no clear winner. To prevent such confusion in the future, the Twelfth Amendment was added to the Constitution in 1804. The amendment stipulates that electoral votes for president and vice president are counted and listed separately.

The Constitution called for each elector in the Electoral College to vote for two people. The normal practice was for an elector to cast one vote for his party's presidential candidate and another for the vice presidential candidate. To avoid a tie between Jefferson and Burr, the Republicans had intended for one elector to refrain from voting for Burr, but when the votes were counted, Jefferson and Burr each had 73. Since no candidate had a majority, the Federalist-controlled House of Representatives had to choose a president.

The divided House took days to reach a decision. Many Federalists distrusted Jefferson and refused to vote for him. Historians think Jefferson may have promised he would not dis-

mantle Hamilton's financial system because eventually one Federalist cast a blank ballot enabling Jefferson to become president. The election of 1800 was an important turning point in American history. At the time, the Federalists controlled the army and the government, and were powerful enough to overthrow the Constitution. Instead they stepped down, establishing that power could be peacefully transferred despite strong disagreements. The election also led to the Twelfth Amendment in 1804, providing for separate ballots for the president and vice president.

Reading Check **Examining** What is the difference between enumerated powers and implied powers?

Chapter 2 The Young Republic **81**

W **Writing Support**

Descriptive Writing Have students write a job description for the position of President of the United States in 1800. The job descriptions should include a list of duties and qualifications. Encourage students to use help wanted ads in local newspapers or on the Internet as references. **OL**

Turning Point

Answer:
It was a peaceful transfer of power between deeply hostile political parties, so it demonstrated a commitment to the Constitution and to a republican form of government.

Reading Check

Answer:
enumerated powers: specifically mentioned in Constitution; implied: not specifically listed in Constitution.

Additional Support

Extending the Content

Additional Background By the election of 1800, a number of crises had led to deep divisions in the country. Both the Republican and Federalist parties were concerned that the other party, if it obtained power, would betray the ideals of the Revolution and overthrow the Constitution. During the balloting, many feared that civil war might erupt if the vote remained deadlocked. According to one eyewitness, over 100,000 people filled the streets of Washington, anxiously waiting for a winner to be declared.

In his inaugural address of March 4, 1801, Jefferson said: "Let us, then, fellow citizens, unite with one heart and one mind. Let us restore to social intercourse that harmony and affection without which liberty and even life itself are but dreary things. . . . We have called by different names brethren of the same principle. We are all Republicans, we are all Federalists." **Ask:** To what "same principle" is Jefferson referring in his inaugural address? *(Possible response: the principle of representative government)* **OL** **BL**

S Skill Practice

Using Geography Skills Have students study the arrows showing the origin, path, and ending point of each expedition and identify the territories and regions through which each expedition passed. **Ask:** In what ways did the routes of the expeditions differ from each other? *(Much of the Lewis and Clark expedition was generally in a northwestern direction, following, for long distances, the courses of rivers—the Missouri and the Columbia. The Pike expedition followed a more circuitous route—west, south, and then northeast again.)* **BL**

Analyzing GEOGRAPHY

Answers:
1. St. Louis
2. the Rio Grande and the Brazos River

Additional Support

Republicans in Power

MAIN Idea During the Jefferson administration, the Supreme Court established judicial review, and the country doubled in size.

HISTORY AND YOU Are there times when you feel especially patriotic? Read on to learn about the War of 1812, which generated a new spirit of patriotism.

President Jefferson attempted to limit federal powers, while the country expanded in size and faced a war with Great Britain.

Jefferson in Office

Thomas Jefferson took office committed to limiting the scope of government. He began paying off the federal debt, cut government spending, eliminated the hated whiskey tax, and trimmed the armed forces.

Weakening the Federalists' control of the judiciary was another aim of the new administration. On his last day in office, President Adams had appointed dozens of new Federalist judges and court officers. Jefferson asked the incoming Republican Congress to abolish some of the new positions and to withhold the paperwork confirming other appointments. One of those who didn't receive his documents, William Marbury, took the matter to the Supreme Court. The Court sympathized with Marbury but ruled in 1803 that it could not issue an enforcement order. According to Chief Justice John Marshall and his colleagues, the law that authorized the Court to write such orders actually was unconstitutional and invalid.

NATIONAL GEOGRAPHIC **The Louisiana Purchase, 1803**

0 200 kilometers
0 200 miles
Lambert Azimuthal Equal-Area projection

BRITISH TERRITORY

Ft. Clatsop, winter quarters 1805–1806

OREGON TERRITORY

Columbia R.

Ft. Mandan, winter quarters 1804–1805

Lewis
Clark

Snake R.

50°N
40°N
120°W

Missouri R.

LOUISIANA PURCHASE

Colorado R.

Pikes Peak

Santa Fe

Arkansas R.

Indiana Territory

St. Louis

Ohio

Ohio R.

Pa.

Va.

Kentucky

Tenn.

N.C.

S.C.

Ga.

Red R.

Mississippi Territory

Brazos R.

SPANISH TERRITORY

Natchitoches

30°N

Rio Grande

Chihuahua

New Orleans

Gulf of Mexico

Spanish Florida

ATLANTIC OCEAN

90°W

80°W

N
W E
S

100°W

Lewis and Clark's expedition
Zebulon Pike's expedition
United States, 1803

▲ Meriwether Lewis and William Clark with their Native American guide, Sacagawea.

Analyzing GEOGRAPHY

1. **Location** Where did Lewis and Clark begin their expedition?
2. **Movement** What two rivers in Spanish territory did Pike cross during his explorations?

82 Chapter 2 The Young Republic

Activity: Interdisciplinary Connection

Art Have interested students work alone or with a partner to learn more about one of the expeditions mentioned in this section. After they conduct their research, have students create a poster illustrating the highlights of the expedition. The posters might include drawings, maps, and a summary of the explorers' discoveries. Encourage students to find and include excerpts from the explorers' journals as well. Finally, have them make a presentation to the class about the expedition. **OL**

With the case of *Marbury* v. *Madison,* the Court asserted its right of **judicial review,** the power to decide whether laws are constitutional and to strike down those that are not. During more than 30 years as Chief Justice, John Marshall continued to build the Supreme Court into a powerful, independent branch of government.

Westward Expansion

Under Jefferson, the size of the country increased considerably. The Treaty of Paris of 1783 had already established the Mississippi River as the western border of the United States. After the defeat of Native Americans in the Northwest Territory and the Treaty of Greenville in 1795, more settlers poured into the region. During Washington's term, Kentucky and Tennessee had become new states, and Ohio followed suit in 1803.

In 1800 Spain had given Louisiana back to France. To finance his plans for European conquest, the French leader, Napoleon Bonaparte, now offered to sell all of the **Louisiana Territory,** as well as New Orleans, to the United States. Congress overwhelmingly approved the **Louisiana Purchase** of April 30, 1803. The United States paid $11.25 million and also agreed to take on French debts of about $3.75 million owed to American citizens. With the purchase, the United States had more than doubled its size.

The War of 1812

A foreign relations crisis loomed when Republican James Madison became president in 1809. The British regularly seized American ships at sea and often practiced impressment, kidnapping sailors to serve in the British navy. Americans in the West also accused Britain of inciting Native Americans to attack white settlers. President Jefferson had tried economic sanctions with the Embargo Act of 1807, but the actions mostly hurt the United States.

Like Jefferson, President Madison first responded with economic measures. After several attempts, the measures finally began to have the desired effect; unfortunately, word of British cooperation came too late—Congress had already declared war.

At the beginning of the War of 1812, conquering Canada was the primary objective of the United States. American forces on Lake Erie and Lake Champlain were victorious but could not prevent the British from setting fire to both the White House and the Capitol in Washington, D.C. The British, however, had to abandon their attack on Baltimore after bombarding the city's harbor throughout the night of September 13. The sight of the American flag still flying at dawn inspired Francis Scott Key to pen "The Star-Spangled Banner," which later became the national anthem.

With battles still raging, peace talks began in the European city of Ghent. The Treaty of Ghent, signed on December 24, 1814, restored prewar boundaries but did not mention neutral rights or impressment. Still, it increased the nation's prestige overseas and generated a new spirit of patriotism. The American victory also destroyed the Federalist Party, which had strongly opposed the war.

✓ Reading Check **Explaining** Why is the Supreme Court decision *Marbury* v. *Madison* important?

Section 1 REVIEW

Vocabulary
1. **Explain** the significance of: cabinet, Bill of Rights, enumerated powers, implied powers, judicial review, District of Columbia, Louisiana Territory, Louisiana Purchase.

Main Ideas
2. **Summarizing** How was the election of 1800 different from previous elections? What resulted from the election?

3. **Explaining** Why did Napoleon sell Louisiana to the United States?

Critical Thinking
4. **Big Ideas** How did the Supreme Court decision in *Marbury* v. *Madison* strengthen the federal judiciary?

5. **Categorizing** Use a graphic organizer similar to the one below to list the first political parties in the United States, their supporters, and the issues they promoted.

Political Party	Supporters	Issues Supported

6. **Analyzing Visuals** Study the map of the Louisiana Purchase on page 82. In what territory did Lewis and Clark make their 1805–1806 winter camp during their expedition?

Writing About History
7. **Persuasive Writing** Take on the role of an American citizen in 1798. Write a speech to persuade others not to support Alexander Hamilton's financial program.

History ONLINE
Study Central™ To review this section, go to glencoe.com and click on Study Central.

83

✓ Reading Check

Answer:
It established the Supreme Court's right of judicial review, the power to decide whether laws passed by Congress are constitutional.

Assess

History ONLINE

Study Central™ provides summaries, interactive games, and online graphic organizers to help students review content.

Close

Summarizing Students should understand the major political developments in the new republic. **Ask: What were two major accomplishments of the Jefferson administration?** *(possible answers: territorial expansion through the Louisiana Purchase, trying to keep the United States out of war)* **OL**

Section 1 REVIEW

Answers

1. All definitions can be found in the section and the Glossary.
2. The election initially resulted in a tie between Jefferson and his running mate, Burr. It also marked the first transfer of power from one political party to another; Jefferson became president
3. France needed the money for its conquest of Europe.
4. The Supreme Court asserted the power of judicial review.
5. Federalist supporters included merchants, manufacturers, and bankers; issues included strong national government, manufacturing, and trade. Democratic-Republican supporters included farmers in the South and West; issues included agriculture and states' rights.
6. the Oregon Territory
7. Speeches should use persuasive language, appeal to the intended audience, and draw on Madison's actual beliefs.

Focus

C Critical Thinking

Making Inferences Have students read the rules of civil behavior and restate them in modern language. Ask volunteers to share their versions. **Ask:** Which of these rules are still widely observed today? *(Possible answers include: do not put your hands on any part of the body that is usually covered; stay awake when people are speaking to you; do not take glee in the misfortunes of others; think before you speak.)* **OL** **BL**

Teach

W Writing Support

Descriptive Writing Have student read Lucy Flucker Knox's quotation in the Verbatim section and the statistics in the Numbers section. Divide the class into groups and have students research the lives of women and children in the late 1700s. Have students write a description of what daily life was like. **OL**

Additional Support

TIME N O T E B O O K

HULTON GETTY

Profile

GEORGE WASHINGTON *At the age of 16, George Washington carefully transcribed in his own hand the* Rules of Civility and Decent Behaviour in Company and Conversation. *Among the rules our first president lived by:*

- Every action done in company ought to be with some sign of respect to those that are present.
- When in company, put not your hands to any part of the body, not usually [un]covered.
- Put not off your clothes in the presence of others, nor go out your chamber half dressed.
- Sleep not when others speak.
- Spit not in the fire, nor stoop low before it. Neither put your hands into the flames to warm them, nor set your feet upon the fire, especially if there is meat before it.
- Shake not the head, feet or legs. Roll not the eyes. Lift not one eyebrow higher than the other. Wry not the mouth, and bedew no man's face with your spittle, by approaching too near him when you speak.
- Show not yourself glad at the misfortune of another though he were your enemy.
- Be not hasty to believe flying reports to the disparagement of any.
- Think before you speak.
- Cleanse not your teeth with the Table Cloth.

VERBATIM

WAR'S END

❝ I hope you will not consider yourself as commander-in-chief of your own house, but be convinced, that there is such a thing as equal command. ❞

LUCY FLUCKER KNOX,
to her husband Henry Knox, upon his return as a hero from the Revolutionary War

❝ The American war is over, but this is far from being the case with the American Revolution. Nothing but the first act of the drama is closed. ❞

BENJAMIN RUSH,
signer of the Declaration of Independence and member of the Constitutional Convention

❝ You could not have found a person to whom your schemes were more disagreeable. ❞

GEORGE WASHINGTON,
to Colonel Lewis Nicola, in response to his letter urging Washington to seize power and proclaim himself king

❝ It appears to me, then, little short of a miracle that the delegates from so many states . . . should unite in forming a system of national government. ❞

GEORGE WASHINGTON,
in a letter to the Marquis de Lafayette at the close of the Constitutional Convention

❝ It astonishes me to find this system approaching to near perfection as it does; and I think it will astonish our enemies. ❞

LEONARD DESELVA/CORBIS

BENJAMIN FRANKLIN,
remarking on the structure of the new United States government

---

Activity: Collaborative Learning

Creating a Magazine Spread Organize the class into small groups. Assign each group one of the decades in the 1700s and ask them to create their own two-page magazine spread for the decade. Encourage students to use elements similar to those that appear in the Time Notebook but to be creative as they select information that is of particular interest. Students should look at current magazines and books for ideas about page design. This activity can be completed using desktop publishing software or the more traditional cut-and-paste method. **OL**

Annual Salaries

Annual federal employee salaries, 1789

President (he refused it)	$25,000
Vice President	$5,000
Secretary of State	$3,500
Chief Justice	$4,000
Senator	$6 per day
Representative	$6 per day
Army Captain	$420
Army Private	$48

CORBIS

1780s WORD PLAY

Dressing the "Little Pudding Heads"

Can you match these common items of Early American clothing with their descriptions?

1. clout
2. stays
3. surcingle
4. pilch
5. pudding cap

a. a band of strong fabric wrapped around a baby to suppress the navel
b. a diaper
c. the wool cover worn over a diaper
d. a head covering for a child learning to walk to protect its brain from falls
e. a garment worn by children to foster good posture, made from linen and wood or baleen splints

answers: 1.b; 2.e; 3.a; 4.c; 5.d

Milestones

SETTLED, 1781. LOS ANGELES, by a group of 46 men and women, most of whom are of Native American and African descent.

CALLED, 1785. LEMUEL HAYNES, as minister to a church in Torrington, Connecticut. Haynes, who fought at Lexington during the Revolutionary War, is the first African American to minister to a white congregation. A parishioner insulted Haynes by refusing to remove his hat in church, but minutes into the sermon, the parishioner was so moved that the hat came off. He is now a prayerful and loyal member of the congregation.

PUBLISHED, 1788. THE ELEMENTARY SPELLING BOOK, by Noah Webster, a 25-year-old teacher from Goshen, N.Y. The book standardizes American spelling and usage that differs from the British.

NUMBERS

5 Number of years younger average American bride compared to her European counterpart

6 Average number of children per family to survive to adulthood

7 Average number of children born per family

8 Number of Daniel Boone's surviving children

68 Number of Daniel Boone's grandchildren

$5 Average monthly wage for male agricultural laborer, 1784

$3 Average monthly wage for female agricultural laborer, 1784

PIX/FPG

CRITICAL THINKING

1. Contrasting Benjamin Rush made a distinction between the American war and the American Revolution. What do you think he meant by his statement?

2. Making Inferences Based on the rules George Washington lived by, how would you describe his character?

Critical Thinking Answers:
1. Possible response: The revolution to come would be a change in thinking about the proper role of the government.
2. Possible response: He was modest, considerate, polite, and open-minded.

Assess/Close

Summarizing Ask students to discuss which part of the feature they found most interesting, entertaining, or surprising.
Ask: How do these details give you a better picture of life during the period? *(Answers will vary.)* **OL**

Visit the **TIME** Web site at www.time.com for up-to-date news, weekly magazine articles, editorials, on-line polls, and an archive of past magazine and Web articles.

Activity: Interdisciplinary Connection

Language Arts Tell students that many of the concerns of the people of the time—both in government and in private life—were similar to the ones they have today. Invite students to choose one of the quotations in the Verbatim section. Have them identify contemporary issues in government and international relations similar to the ones addressed by the speakers. For example, the quotation by George Washington could be related to contemporary issues of presidential authority. Ask students to write brief synopses of these contemporary issues and then share these with the class. **OL**

Focus

Bellringer
Daily Focus Transparency 2.2

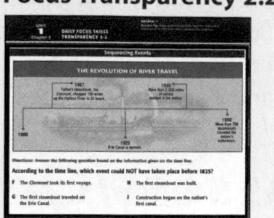

Guide to Reading

Answers:

creation of a new national bank, imposition of protective tariff, decisions by the Supreme Court established dominance of the nation over the states, proclamation of the Monroe Doctrine

Section Spotlight Video

To generate student interest and provide a springboard for class discussion, access the Chapter 2, Section 2 video at glencoe.com or on the video DVD.

Resource Manager

Section 2

The Growth of a Nation

Guide to Reading

Big Ideas
Science and Technology New technologies reshaped American industry.

Content Vocabulary
• revenue tariff (p. 87)
• protective tariff (p. 87)
• labor union (p. 92)

Academic Vocabulary
• transportation (p. 86)

People and Events to Identify
• "Era of Good Feelings" (p. 86)
• John C. Calhoun (p. 87)
• McCulloch v. Maryland (p. 88)
• Monroe Doctrine (p. 88)
• Industrial Revolution (p. 90)

Reading Strategy
Organizing Complete a graphic organizer similar to the one below by listing actions that strengthened the federal government after the War of 1812.

The United States entered an "Era of Good Feelings" after the War of 1812. The national government began building the national road, defended its authority to regulate interstate commerce, and declared the Western Hemisphere off-limits for future colonization.

Growth of American Nationalism

MAIN Idea The surge of nationalism and the survival of only one political party made it possible to make economic and judicial decisions that strengthened the national government.

HISTORY AND YOU Do you know of any Supreme Court decisions that had a significant national impact? Read on to learn about Supreme Court decisions that strengthened the power of the federal government.

After the War of 1812, a sense of nationalism swept the United States. More and more Americans began to consider themselves to be part of a whole, rather than identifying with a state or region. The *Columbian Centinel,* a Boston newspaper, called this time the **"Era of Good Feelings."** Riding this wave of nationalism was Republican James Monroe, the nation's fifth president.

Partisan infighting had largely ended in national politics because only one major political party—the Republicans—remained. The Federalist Party rapidly lost political influence after the War of 1812. At the same time, the war taught Republican leaders that a stronger federal government was necessary. This new perspective allowed many who might have been Federalists in the past to now join the Republicans instead. As a result, James Monroe won the presidency in 1816 with 83 percent of the electoral vote. By the election of 1820, the Federalist Party was gone. All the presidential candidates were members of the Republican Party.

Economic Nationalism

As Monroe's presidency began, focus shifted from world affairs to national growth. The Republicans quickly set out to strengthen the American financial system, protect manufacturers, and to improve the **transportation** system.

The Second Bank Republicans traditionally had opposed the idea of a national bank. They had blocked the charter renewal of the First Bank of the United States in 1811 and offered nothing in its place. The results were disastrous. State-chartered banks and other private banks greatly expanded their lending with bank notes that were used

---

R Reading Strategies	C Critical Thinking	D Differentiated Instruction	W Writing Support	S Skill Practice
Teacher Edition • Determining Import., p. 87 • Making Connections, p. 88 **Additional Resources** • Enrichment Activity, URB p. 76 • Guided Reading Activity, URB p. 79	**Teacher Edition** • Det. Cause/Effect, p. 90 • Compare/Contrast, p. 92 **Additional Resources** • Critical Thinking Skills, URB p. 64 • Supreme Court Case Studies, p. 3 • Quizzes and Tests, p. 18	**Teacher Edition** • Visual/Spatial, pp. 87, 91	**Teacher Edition** • Descriptive Writing, p. 90 • Narrative Writing, p. 91	**Additional Resources** • Historical Analysis Activity, URB p. 54 • Time Line Activity, URB p. 65 • Reading Essen., p. 16

Building the National Road, 1811–1838

▶ Conestoga wagons carried pioneers west

- National Road
- 1820 boundary

In 1806 Congress funded the building of a major east-west highway to connect the eastern United States to St. Louis and the Missouri River, the gateway to the territory of the new Louisiana Purchase. In 1811 laborers started cutting the roadbed westward from Cumberland, Maryland. The 32-foot-wide bed had a surface of sand and gravel. By the 1820s the National Road was a heavily traveled superhighway for its time. It was completed to Vandalia, Illinois, when funding ceased. The National Road turned out to be the only great federally funded transportation project of its time. President Madison vetoed a bill to fund further roads and canals. He did not think the Constitution gave the federal government the authority to make "internal improvements."

Analyzing GEOGRAPHY

1. **Location** Where did the National Road begin and end?
2. **Movement** How long was the stretch of National Road that was federally funded?

Teach

D Differentiated Instruction

Visual/Spatial Ask students to select one of the common means of transportation used in the early 1800s. Have students create a model of their choice. Encourage students to explain the materials used to construct the model and how it worked. Have students show their models to the class. **BL ELL**

R Reading Strategy

Determining Importance Have students read the section and study the map on this page. Then, ask them to write a paragraph explaining how the transportation revolution changed how people lived during this period. **OL**

Analyzing GEOGRAPHY

Answers:
1. National Road began in Cumberland, Maryland; ended in Vandalia, Illinois
2. about 500 miles

---

as money. Without a national bank to regulate currency, prices rose rapidly during the War of 1812. When the government borrowed money to pay for the war, it had to pay high interest rates on the loans.

Because of these problems, many Republicans changed their minds after the war. In 1816 Representative **John C. Calhoun** of South Carolina introduced a bill proposing the Second Bank of the United States. With the support of Henry Clay of Kentucky and Daniel Webster of Massachusetts, the bill passed in 1816. This legislation gave the bank the power to issue notes that would serve as a national currency and to control state banks.

The Protective Tariff Protection of manufacturers from foreign competition was another part of the Republican program. During the War of 1812, an embargo had prevented Americans from buying British goods. American manufacturers had increased their output to meet the demand. Once the war was over, however, British goods flowed into the United States at

such low prices that they threatened to put American manufacturers out of business.

Congress responded with the Tariff of 1816. Unlike earlier **revenue tariffs,** which provided income for the federal government, this tariff was a **protective tariff,** designed to protect American manufacturers by taxing imports to drive up their prices. New England shippers and Southern farmers opposed the tariff and the higher prices it caused, but they could not block its passage.

Transportation The Republicans also wanted to improve the nation's transportation system. In 1816 Calhoun sponsored a federal internal improvement plan that included building roads and canals, but President Madison vetoed it, arguing that spending money to improve transportation was not expressly granted in the Constitution. Nevertheless, road and canal construction soon began, with private businesses and state and local governments funding much of the work.

D

Hands-On Chapter Project
Step 2

Presidential Customs

Step 2: The Legacy of George Washington Students will share their research (from Step 1) in groups.

Directions Divide the class into small groups. Each student will share his or her three examples of presidential precedents set by George Washington. Groups will work together to describe the origins of these precedents and how they have had an impact on the presidency.

Causes and Effects Students will determine why certain presidential customs and procedures are in place. **OL**

(Chapter Project continued on page 95)

R Reading Strategy

Making Connections The Monroe Doctrine was announced in 1823, less than 50 years after the nation declared its independence from Great Britain.

Ask: How does the Monroe Doctrine reflect American attitudes about colonization? *(It showed that Americans still desired to keep European influences away from the United States.)* **OL**

✓ Reading Check

Answer:

Martin v. *Hunter's Lessee* established the Supreme Court as the court of final appeal. *McCulloch* v. *Maryland* prohibited states from interfering with agencies of the federal government exercising its constitutional powers within a state's borders. *Gibbons* v. *Ogden* defined interstate commerce broadly and granted control of it to the federal government.

Additional Support

Judicial Nationalism

The judicial philosophy of the Chief Justice of the United States, John Marshall, provided another boost to postwar nationalism. In several important cases between 1816 and 1824, Marshall interpreted the Constitution broadly to support federal power.

🏛 For further information on the cases of *Martin* v. *Hunter's Lessee* and *Gibbons* v. *Ogden*, see page R59 in **Supreme Court Case Summaries.**

Martin v. Hunter's Lessee In 1816 the Court decided in *Martin* v. *Hunter's Lessee* that it had the authority to hear all appeals of state court decisions in cases involving federal statutes and treaties. In this case, Denny Martin, a British subject, tried to sell land in Virginia inherited from his uncle, Lord Fairfax, a British Loyalist during the war. However, Virginia law stated that no "enemy" could inherit land. The Supreme Court ruled that Virginia's law conflicted with Jay's Treaty, which protected land belonging to Loyalists before the war. The decision helped establish the Supreme Court as the nation's court of final appeal.

McCulloch v. Maryland The 1819 case of ***McCulloch v. Maryland*** involved Maryland's attempt to tax the Baltimore branch of the Second Bank of the United States. Before addressing Maryland's right to tax the national bank, the Supreme Court first ruled on the federal government's right to create a national bank in the first place. In the Court's opinion, written by John Marshall, the Constitution gave the federal government the power to collect taxes, to borrow money, to regulate commerce, and to raise armies and navies. The national bank helped the federal government exercise these powers. Marshall concluded that the "necessary and proper" clause allowed the federal government to use its powers in any way not specifically prohibited by the Constitution.

📜 For the text of the Monroe Doctrine, see page R48 in **Documents in American History.**

Marshall went on to argue that the federal government was "supreme in its own sphere of action." This meant that a state government could not interfere with an agency of the federal government exercising its specific constitutional powers within a state's borders.

Gibbons v. Ogden The Court ruled in another case, *Gibbons* v. *Ogden*, that states could regulate commerce only within their

---

borders, but that control of interstate commerce was a federal right. Defenders of states' rights attacked many of Marshall's decisions, which helped make the "necessary and proper" clause and the interstate commerce clause vehicles for expanding federal power.

Nationalist Diplomacy

Postwar nationalism also influenced foreign affairs. During the early 1800s, Spanish-held Florida was a source of frustration for Southerners. Many runaway slaves hid there, and the Seminole, a Native American group, often clashed with American settlers across the border in Georgia. When Spain was unable to control the border, Secretary of War John C. Calhoun sent troops under the command of Andrew Jackson into Florida. Secretary of State John Quincy Adams then put pressure on Spain concerning ongoing border questions. Occupied with problems throughout its Latin American empire, Spain gave in and ceded all of Florida to the United States in the Adams-Onís Treaty of 1819.

Spain had good reason to worry about Latin America. In 1809 rebellions began to erupt in Spain's colonies, and by 1824 all of Spain's colonies on the American mainland had declared independence. Meanwhile, some European monarchies expressed their interest in helping Spain suppress these Latin American revolutions. However, neither Great Britain nor the United States wanted Spain to regain control of its colonies.

At the same time, Russia's growing presence on North America's Pacific Coast also worried the American government. Russia already claimed Alaska, and in 1821 it announced that its empire extended south into the Oregon Country between Russian Alaska and the western United States.

Under these circumstances, Monroe decided to issue a statement in December 1823. In the **Monroe Doctrine,** the president declared that the American continents were "henceforth not to be considered as subjects for future colonization by any European powers." He specifically advised Europe to respect the sovereignty of new Latin American nations. **R**

✓ Reading Check **Analyzing** How did the decisions of the Marshall Court strengthen the federal government?

Activity: Collaborative Learning

Identifying Central Issues Have students work in pairs to recreate the arguments of one of the cases in this section. Have the pairs work together to decide which side of the issue each of them will present. Have them research the case and present a summary of the arguments to the class. Encourage the pairs to pretend that they are arguing their case before the Supreme Court. Allow the class, acting as the Court, to ask questions of each person. **AL**

What Does "Necessary and Proper" Mean?

★ *McCulloch v. Maryland*, 1819

Background to the Case

In 1816, President James Madison and Congress worked to establish the Second Bank of the United States. Two years later, the state of Maryland passed legislation imposing a tax on the Second Bank. The cashier at the Second Bank's branch in Baltimore, Maryland, James McCulloch, refused to pay the tax, and the matter went to the Supreme Court.

How the Court Ruled

In a unanimous decision the Court found that, under the "necessary and proper" clause, the federal government did have the unenumerated power to establish a national bank and that, while the states had the power to tax, they could not interfere with instruments of the federal government, and the tax was construed to be interference. This established the supremacy of the federal government over the governments of the states.

▲ *The Second Bank of the United States was located in Philadelphia. The Supreme Court held with the McCulloch v. Maryland ruling that the federal government had the right to establish a national bank and that the states could not tax it or otherwise interfere in any federal enterprise.*

PRIMARY SOURCE

The Court's Opinion

Can the Federal Government Create a Bank?

"...Although, among the enumerated powers of government, we do not find the word 'bank' or 'incorporation,' we find the great powers, to lay and collect taxes; to borrow money; to regulate commerce; to declare and conduct a war; and to raise and support armies and navies.... But it may with great reason be contended, that a government, entrusted with such ample powers ... must also be entrusted with ample means for their execution.

... To its enumeration of powers is added, that of making 'all laws which shall be necessary and proper, for carrying into execution the foregoing powers, and all other powers vested by this constitution, in the government of the United States, or in any department thereof.'... [I]t is the unanimous and decided opinion of this Court, that the act to incorporate the Bank of the United States is ... constitutional."

Can a State Tax a Federal Agency or Activity?

"... the power to tax involves the power to destroy.... If the states may tax one instrument, employed by the government ... they may tax all the means employed by the government, to an excess which would defeat all the ends of government.... The result is a conviction that the states have no power, by taxation or otherwise, to retard, impede, burden, or in any manner control, the operations of the constitutional laws enacted by congress to carry into execution the powers vested in the general government. This is, we think, the unavoidable consequence of that supremacy which the constitution has declared."

—Chief Justice John Marshall writing for the Court in *McCulloch v. Maryland*

DBQ Document-Based Questions

1. **Specifying** What two questions did the decision in *McCulloch v. Maryland* address?
2. **Describing** How did Marshall interpret the "necessary and proper" clause in this case?
3. **Summarizing** How did Marshall's decision establish the authority of the federal government over the states?

More About the Case

This ruling established the basis for the expansive authority of Congress. The Supreme Court held that the necessary and proper clause allows Congress to do more than the Constitution specifically authorizes it to do.

DBQ Document Based Questions

Answers:
1. Does the federal government have the power to establish a national bank? Do the states have the authority to interfere in the operations of the federal government?
2. He interpreted "necessary and proper" to mean whatever may be convenient to fulfill the functions of the federal government, not only what is strictly necessary.
3. The decision states that laws or instruments established under the Constitution have supremacy over any other level of government, and that, therefore, state government may not in any way control or interfere with the operations of the federal government.

Additional Support

Extending the Content

Chief Justice Marshall John Marshall served as Chief Justice of the Supreme Court from 1801 to 1835. During his long tenure, he strengthened the power of the federal government over the states and expanded and defined the authority of the federal judiciary. Two of the most significant cases he presided over were *Marbury* v. *Madison* (1803) and *McCulloch* v. *Maryland* (1819). In *Marbury* v. *Madison*, the Court asserted the power of judicial review, or the power to decide whether laws are constitutional and to strike down those laws that are not. In *McCulloch* v. *Maryland*, the Court upheld the doctrine of "implied powers" that allowed Congress more flexibility to enact "necessary and proper" legislation.

W Writing Support

Descriptive Writing Ask interested students to use the library and Internet sources to write a one-page essay describing how Robert Fulton's steamboat changed travel and commerce along the nation's waterways. **OL**

C Critical Thinking

Determining Cause and Effect Write *Industrial Revolution* on the chalkboard. Ask students to list the causes and effects of the Industrial Revolution. For example, one cause was "division of labor" and its effect was "the rise of labor unions." Have students discuss whether they think this would have happened without industrialization. **OL**

A Growing Nation

MAIN Idea New industries and railroads transformed the North in the early 1800s, while slavery expanded in the South.

HISTORY AND YOU What kinds of businesses generate the most wealth in the United States today? Read on to learn about the critical role that farming and industry played during the early 1800s.

The early 1800s were a time of rapid change in the United States. Transportation greatly improved access to different regions, while the Industrial Revolution began transforming the North into a manufacturing center. The South, meanwhile, continued to rely on agriculture.

Transportation Revolution

With the United States expanding rapidly, Americans sought new ways to connect the distant regions of the country. The first steps came in 1806, when Congress funded the National Road. Soon afterward, states, localities, and private businesses began laying hundreds of miles of toll roads.

Rivers offered a more efficient and cheaper way to move goods than did early roads.

Loaded boats and barges, however, could usually travel only downstream, as trips against the current with heavy cargoes were impractical. The invention of the steamboat changed all that. The first successful steamboat was the *Clermont*, developed by Robert Fulton and promoted by Robert R. Livingston. By 1850 more than 700 steamboats, also called riverboats, traveled the Mississippi, the Great Lakes, and other waterways.

Railroads also appeared in the early 1800s. A wealthy, self-educated industrialist named Peter Cooper built the *Tom Thumb*, a tiny but powerful locomotive based on engines originally developed in Great Britain. Perhaps more than any other kind of transportation, trains helped settle the West and expand trade among the nation's different regions.

Industrialization

Along with changes in transportation, a revolution occurred in industry. The **Industrial Revolution,** which began in Britain in the middle 1700s, spread to the United States. Businesses began large-scale manufacturing using complex machines and organized workforces in factories. Manufacturers sold their wares nationwide or abroad instead of just

---

TECHNOLOGY & HISTORY

New technologies in the early 1800s revolutionized transportation, communications, manufacturing, and agriculture. They began transforming the North into an industrial society and contributed to the spread of the cotton plantation in the South.

▲ **The Steamboat**
Paddle-wheeled steamboats, such as Robert Fulton's *Clermont*, made river travel easier and more reliable.

▲ **The Railroad Locomotive**
The *Tom Thumb* was the first American locomotive. Railroads transformed the nation, allowing people and goods to move quickly from city to city and helping to encourage settlement in the West.

90 Chapter 2 The Young Republic

Additional Support

Activity: Collaborative Learning

Writing a Script Organize students into small groups. Have the groups research the lives of children who worked in the textile mills. Based on their research, have the groups write a script of an event that might have occurred in the life of such a child. Examples include an encounter between a foreman and a worker who has fallen asleep, a dialogue with another worker as they are on the way home from a day's work, or a monologue of the child's thoughts as he or she walks to work on a hot summer day. Encourage groups to perform the script for the class. **OL**

locally. These developments transformed not only the economy, but society as well.

The United States industrialized quickly for several reasons. Perhaps the key factor was the American system of free enterprise based on private property rights. People could acquire and use capital without strict governmental controls. At the same time, competition between companies encouraged them to try new technologies. The era's low taxes also meant that entrepreneurs had more money to invest. In addition, beginning in the 1830s, many states promoted industrialization by passing general incorporation laws that made it much easier to form businesses.

Industrialization began in the Northeast, **D** where many swift-flowing streams provided factories with waterpower. The region was also home to many entrepreneurs who were willing to invest in British technology. Soon textile mills sprung up throughout the Northeast. The use of interchangeable parts, or standard components, popularized by a New Englander named Eli Whitney, led to factories producing lumber, shoes, leather, wagons, and other products. The sewing machine allowed inexpensive clothes to be mass produced, and canning allowed foods to be stored and transported without fear of spoilage.

In 1832 a major improvement in communications took place when Samuel F.B. Morse began perfecting the telegraph and developing Morse code. Journalists began using the telegraph to speedily relay news. By 1860 more than 50,000 miles of telegraph wire connected most parts of the country.

Immigration

Between 1815 and 1860, over 5 million foreigners journeyed to America. While thousands of newcomers, particularly Germans, became farmers in the rural West, many others settled in cities, providing a steady source of **W** cheap labor. A large number of Irish—over 44,000—arrived in 1845, after a devastating potato blight caused widespread famine in their homeland.

Not all Americans welcomed the new immigrants. Some had feelings of nativism, a preference for native-born people and a desire to limit immigration. Several societies sprang up to keep foreign-born persons and Catholics—the main religion of the Irish and many Germans—from holding public office. In 1854 delegates from some of these groups formed the American Party. This party came to be called the Know-Nothings.

W **Writing Support**
Narrative Writing Invite students to write a brief story from the point of view of an immigrant who escaped the potato famine in Ireland. Remind students to include the character's name; the reason he or she immigrated; where he or she now lives and why he or she moved there; what he or she does; and his or her impressions of the area. **AL**

D **Differentiated Instruction**
Visual/Spatial Have students work together in small groups to create posters or pamphlets, from the perspective of a factory owner looking for more workers, which are intended to convince rural Americans to move to large cities. Display their creations around the classroom. **OL** **ELL**

Analyzing **VISUALS**

Answers:
1. Railroads were generally quicker and did not have to go only where there were waterways.
2. Answers will vary.

Additional Support

◀ **The Water Frame**
The water frame allowed cotton fibers to be easily spun into cotton thread.

▲ **The Cotton Gin**
In 1793, Eli Whitney built a device that removed the seeds of cotton and increased the profitability of cotton and the need for enslaved laborers.

The Telegraph ▶
The first modern breakthrough in communications was the telegraph and Morse code. Suddenly, news and other information could be sent via telegraph keys over long distances nearly instantly.

Analyzing **VISUALS**
1. **Making Connections** What were the advantages to traveling by railroad rather than steamboat?
2. **Discussing** Which invention do you think was the most significant? Why?

Chapter 2 The Young Republic **91**

Extending the Content

The Lowell Mills The American textile industry took a huge step forward when entrepreneur Francis C. Lowell began opening a series of mills in northeastern Massachusetts in 1814. Using machinery he had built after touring British textile mills, Lowell introduced mass production of cotton cloth to the United States. In Waltham, Massachusetts, the site of the first mill, his Boston Manufacturing Company built residences for workers. The company employed thousands of workers—mostly women and children, who would work for lower wages than men. By 1840 dozens of textile mills had been built in the Northeast. Industrialists also began applying factory techniques to the production of lumber, shoes, leather, wagons, and other products.

C Critical Thinking

Comparing and Contrasting
Remind students of their earlier reading about the economy of the North. Have students make a two-column chart to compare and contrast the economies of the North and South during this period in history. Discuss the results as a class. **OL**

Analyzing GEOGRAPHY

Answers:

1. The Appalachian Mountains in Kentucky and Virginia are full of coal.

2. The states with the greatest percentages of enslaved people in their populations are those states with economies based on cotton.

Additional Support

Rise of Labor Unions

By 1860, factory workers numbered roughly 1.3 million. They included many women and children, who would accept lower wages than men. Not even men were well paid, however, and factory workers typically toiled for 12 or more drudgery-filled hours a day. Hoping to gain higher wages or shorter workdays, some workers began to organize in **labor unions**—groups of workers who press for better working conditions and member benefits. During the late 1820s and early 1830s, about 300,000 men and women belonged to these organizations. Early labor unions had little power. Most employers refused to bargain with them, and the courts often saw them as unlawful conspiracies that limited free enterprise.

Importance of Agriculture

C Despite the trend toward urban and industrial growth, agriculture remained the country's leading economic activity. Until the late 1800s, farming employed more people and produced more wealth than any other kind of work. Northern farmers produced enough to sell their surplus in the growing eastern cities and towns.

Farming was even more important in the South, which had few cities and less industry. The South thrived on the production of several major cash crops, including tobacco, rice, and sugarcane. No crop, however, played a greater role in the South's fortunes during this period than cotton, which was grown in a wide belt stretching from inland South Carolina west into Texas.

Removing cotton seeds by hand from the fluffy bolls was so tedious that it took a worker an entire day to separate a pound of cotton lint. In 1793 Eli Whitney invented the cotton gin—"gin" being short for engine—that quickly and efficiently removed cotton seeds from bolls, or cotton pods. Cotton production soared, and by 1860 Southern cotton accounted for nearly two-thirds of the total export trade of the United States. Southerners began saying, rightly, "Cotton is King."

NATIONAL GEOGRAPHIC An Economy Built on Enslaved Labor, c. 1850

Distribution of Slave Labor

- Rice, Sugar, Hemp 10%
- Tobacco 10%
- Mining, Lumbering, Industry, Construction 10%
- Domestic Servants 15%
- Cotton 55%

Legend:
- Cotton
- Rice
- Sugarcane
- Tobacco
- Coal
- Iron
- Lumber

0 — 200 kilometers
0 — 200 miles
Albers Equal-Area projection

Analyzing GEOGRAPHY

1. **Regions** Why do you think the use of enslaved miners was more common in Virginia and Kentucky?

2. **Human-Environment Interaction** How does the information on the map relate to the percentage of slave labor used in farming?

Maps In MOtion See *StudentWorks*™ *Plus* or glencoe.com.

92 Chapter 2 The Young Republic

Activity: Interdisciplinary Connection

Music Encourage interested students to research the African American music of the antebellum era. Ask them to share examples of the music, lyrics, and tunes with the class. Students may either perform the music or bring recordings. Have students explain the meaning of the lyrics of the songs they have chosen. **OL BL**

While agriculture brought prosperity to Southern states, they lagged behind the North in industrialization. Compared to the many textile mills and factories in the North, the Southern region had only scattered iron works, textile mills, and coal, iron, salt, and copper mines. Together, these accounted for only 16 percent of the nation's total manufacturing.

Enslaved and Free African Americans

The spread of cotton plantations boosted the Southern economy, but it also made the demand for slave labor skyrocket. Congress had outlawed the foreign slave trade in 1808, but a high birthrate among enslaved women—encouraged by slaveholders—kept the population growing. Between 1820 and 1850, the number of enslaved persons in the South rose from about 1.5 million to nearly 3.2 million, to account for almost 37 percent of the total Southern population.

The overwhelming majority of enslaved African Americans toiled in the fields on small farms. Some became house servants, while others worked in trades. All enslaved persons, no matter how well treated, suffered indignities. State slave codes forbade enslaved men and women from owning property, leaving a slave-holder's premises without permission, or testifying in court against a white person. Laws even banned them from learning to read and write. Frederick Douglass, who rose from slavery to become a prominent leader of the antislavery movement, recalled how life as an enslaved person affected him:

PRIMARY SOURCE

"My natural elasticity was crushed; my intellect languished; the disposition to read departed; the cheerful spark that lingered about my eye died; the dark night of slavery closed in upon me, and behold a man transformed to a brute."

—from *Narrative of the Life of Frederick Douglass*

Music helped many African Americans endure the horrors of slavery. Songs also played a key role in religion, one of the most important parts of African American culture.

Many enslaved men and women found ways to actively resist the dreadful lifestyle forced on them. Some quietly staged work slow-downs. Others broke tools or set fire to houses and barns. Still others risked beatings or mutilations by running away. Some enslaved persons turned to violence, killing their owners or plotting revolts.

Free African Americans occupied an ambiguous position in Southern society. In cities like Charleston and New Orleans, some were successful enough to become slaveholders themselves. Almost 200,000 free African Americans lived in the North, where slavery had been outlawed, but they were not embraced there either. Still, in the North free African Americans could organize their own churches and voluntary associations. They also were able to earn money from the jobs they held.

 Reading Check Describing How did the Industrial Revolution change American society?

Section 2 REVIEW

Vocabulary
1. **Explain** the significance of: "Era of Good Feelings," John C. Calhoun, revenue tariff, protective tariff, *McCulloch* v. *Maryland*, Monroe Doctrine, Industrial Revolution, labor union.

Main Ideas
2. **Summarizing** What did the Marshall Court interpret the "necessary and proper" clause to mean?

3. **Determining Cause and Effect** How did the invention of the cotton gin help to increase the importance of cotton as a cash crop in the South?

Critical Thinking
4. **Big Ideas** How did interchangeable parts revolutionize the manufacturing process?

5. **Organizing** Use a graphic organizer similar to the one below to list the effects of some of the technological advances of the early 1800s.

Technological Advances	Effects
Steamboat	
Railroad	

6. **Analyzing Visuals** Study the circle graph on the distribution of slave labor on page 92. After those who worked to produce cotton, what was the next largest group of enslaved workers?

Writing About History
7. **Expository Writing** Suppose that you are a European visitor to the South in 1830. Write a newspaper article explaining your impressions of life in this region.

 History ONLINE
Study Central™ To review this section, go to glencoe.com and click on Study Central.

93

 Reading Check

Answer:
The North became a manufacturing center; a transportation revolution occurred; cities grew and immigration increased; and the cotton gin created more demand for slave labor.

Assess

History ONLINE

Study Central™ provides summaries, interactive games, and online graphic organizers to help students review content.

Close

Determining Importance Ask students which event in the history of the young republic they consider to be the most important and have them explain their answer. **OL**

Section 2 REVIEW

Answers

1. All definitions can be found in the section and the Glossary.
2. It held that the "necessary and proper" clause meant that the government could use any method that was convenient for carrying out its powers, as long as the method was not expressly forbidden by the Constitution.
3. The cotton gin made it much easier to clean cotton, so cotton became "king" in the South.
4. It allowed complex products to be made in stages by unskilled workers.

5. Steamboat: made river transportation reliable and extended the range of transportation in both directions; Railroad: helped settle the West, created national markets, and expanded trade among the nation's regions; Factories and textile mills mass produced clothing and other items.
6. After working to produce cotton, the next largest group of enslaved people worked as domestic servants.

7. Students' articles will vary, but should include descriptive language and details from the section.

Focus

Bellringer
Daily Focus Transparency 2.3

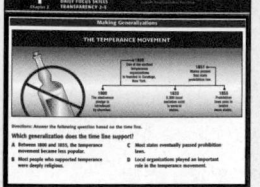

Guide to Reading

Answers:
slavery, states' rights, interpretation of the Constitution, national bank, tariffs

Section Spotlight Video

To generate student interest and provide a springboard for class discussion, access the Chapter 2, Section 3 video at glencoe.com or on the video DVD.

Resource Manager

Section 3
Growing Division and Reform

Guide to Reading

Big Ideas
Government and Society The American political system became more democratic during the Jacksonian era.

Content Vocabulary
• spoils system *(p. 97)*
• secede *(p. 97)*
• benevolent societies *(p. 100)*
• temperance *(p. 100)*
• emancipation *(p. 102)*

Academic Vocabulary
• controversy *(p. 95)*
• exposure *(p. 99)*

People and Events to Identify
• Missouri Compromise *(p. 95)*
• Tariff of Abominations *(p. 97)*
• Trail of Tears *(p. 99)*
• Whigs *(p. 99)*
• Second Great Awakening *(p. 100)*
• Frederick Douglass *(p. 103)*

Reading Strategy
Organizing Complete a graphic organizer similar to the one below by listing the divisive political issues of the 1820s.

Divisive Issues of the 1820s

Sectional differences continued to divide free and slave states as new states joined the Union. While Native Americans were forced to move west, reform movements focused on social issues and the rights of women and African Americans.

The Resurgence of Sectionalism

MAIN Idea Sectionalism increased after the War of 1812, while voting rights expanded for American citizens.

HISTORY AND YOU What do you see as the defining characteristics of your state and region? Read on to learn why conflicts between different sections of the United States arose in the early and mid-1800s.

The Louisiana Purchase and improved transportation spurred new settlement in the West. Soon some of the territories grew large enough to apply for statehood. The matter of statehood for Missouri stirred up passionate disagreements. Increasingly, sectional disputes came to divide Americans.

The Missouri Compromise

The Monroe administration's Era of Good Feelings could not ward off the nation's growing sectional disputes and the passionately differing opinions over slavery. Tensions rose to the boiling point in 1819, when Missouri's application for statehood stirred up the country's most divisive issue: whether slavery should expand westward.

In 1819 the Union consisted of 11 free and 11 slave states. While the House of Representatives already had a majority of Northerners, admitting any new state, either slave or free, would upset the balance of political power in the Senate and touch off a bitter struggle over political power. Many Northerners opposed extending slavery into the western territories because they believed that human bondage was morally wrong. The South feared that if slavery could not expand, new free states would eventually give the North enough votes in the Senate to outlaw slaveholding.

Missouri's territorial government requested admission into the Union as a slave state in 1819. The House of Representatives then passed a resolution banning slaveholders from bringing enslaved people into Missouri as a condition of statehood. Southern Senators angrily blocked the proposal. The next year, Maine, then a part of Massachusetts, sought statehood. The Senate decided to combine Maine's request with Missouri's, and it voted to admit Maine as a free state and Missouri as a slave state. The Senate added an

---

 R Reading Strategies	 **C** Critical Thinking	 **D** Differentiated Instruction	 **W** Writing Support	 **S** Skill Practice
Teacher Edition • Making Connections, pp. 97, 98, 100, 101 • Activate Prior Knowl., p. 100 **Additional Resources** • Academic Vocabulary Activity, URB p. 61 • Prim. Source Reading, URB p. 69 • Guided Reading, URB p. 80	**Teacher Edition** • Det. Cause/Effect, p. 99 • Draw. Concl., p. 102 **Additional Resources** • Linking Past and Present Activity, URB p. 66 • Inter. Pol. Cartoons Activity, URB p. 73 • Supreme Court Case Studies, p. 9 • Quizzes and Tests, p. 19	**Teacher Edition** • Gifted and Talented, p. 102	**Teacher Edition** • Persuasive Writing, p. 96	**Teacher Edition** • Analyz. Info., p. 95 • Creating a Map, p. 96 • Oral Presentations, p. 103 **Additional Resources** • Reading Skills Act., URB p. 53 • Reading Essen., p. 19

NATIONAL GEOGRAPHIC The Missouri Compromise

Slave state/territory
Free state/territory
Territory opened to slavery by the Missouri Compromise
Closed to slavery by the Missouri Compromise

0   400 kilometers
0   400 miles
Albers Equal-Area projection

Maine
Admitted as free state in 1820

CANADA

N.H.

Vt.

Michigan Territory

N.Y.
Mass.
Conn.
R.I.
40°N

Unorganized Territory

Pa.

N.J.
Del.
Md.

Ill. Ind. Ohio

Mo.
Admitted as slave state in 1821

Va.

Ky.

Missouri Compromise Line 36°30'N

Tenn.

N.C.

Arkansas Territory

S.C.

ATLANTIC OCEAN

30°N

Miss. Ala. Ga.

NEW SPAIN

La.

Fla.

Gulf of Mexico

N
W   E
S

90°W   80°W

Voting for the Compromise

Maine

Missouri

House of Representatives, 1820

Vote yes to Missouri as slave state and Maine as free state and for compromise line

Vote yes to Missouri and Maine, but no for compromise line

Votes no on Missouri and Maine, but yes on compromise line

Votes no on Missouri and Maine, and no to compromise line

Analyzing GEOGRAPHY

1. **Regions** Most representatives from which region of the country voted for both provisions of the Missouri Compromise?

2. **Place** Which state came into the Union as a slave state, and which came in as a free state?

Teach

S Skill Practice

Analyzing Information Ask students to review the main provisions of the Missouri Compromise. **Ask:** Do you think the Missouri Compromise adequately resolved the dispute over the expansion of slavery? *(It only temporarily settled the issue.)* **OL**

Analyzing GEOGRAPHY

Answers:
1. the South
2. Missouri entered as a slave state; Maine as a free state

amendment to prohibit slavery in the rest of the Louisiana Territory north of Missouri's southern boundary. This would allow slavery **S** to expand into Arkansas territory south of Missouri, but it would keep it out of the rest of the Louisiana Purchase. Southerners agreed, viewing this Northern region as unsuitable for farming anyway.

Henry Clay carefully steered the **Missouri Compromise** through the House of Representatives, which passed it by a close vote in March 1820. The next year, Missouri became the twenty-fourth state, and the Missouri Compromise temporarily settled the dispute over the westward expansion of slavery. Like Jefferson, however, many leaders feared more trouble ahead.

Once the issue was settled, a new problem developed. Pro-slavery members of the Missouri constitutional convention added a clause to the proposed state constitution prohibiting free African Americans from entering the state. This new **controversy** threatened final approval of Missouri's admission to the Union. Clay again engineered a solution by getting the Missouri legislature to state that they would not honor the spirit of the clause's wording.

Despite Clay's efforts, many leaders feared that the Missouri Compromise was only a temporary solution. "I take it for granted," John Quincy Adams wrote, "that the present question is a mere preamble—a title page to a great tragic volume." The Compromise merely postponed a debate over the future of slavery.

Chapter 2 The Young Republic **95**

Hands-On Chapter Project
Step 3

Presidential Customs

Step 3: The Presidency Today Students will research the procedures and customs of the presidency today.

Directions Divide the class into the small groups established in previous steps of the Chapter project. Groups will divide research topics among their members. For example, one group member may research the procedures and customs of presidents in the area of foreign policy; another may research

presidential customs in the area of organizing the executive department, and so on.

Comparing and Contrasting Students will gather with the results of their independent research to compare notes. They should compare the customs and procedures of the presidency today with the actions taken by the nation's first president. **OL**

(Chapter Project continued on page 105)

W Writing Support

Persuasive Writing Have students imagine they live in one of the states that is considering changing the voting requirements, but they do not own property. Ask them to write a letter to their state representative explaining why the requirements should be changed so that they have the right to vote. **OL**

S Skill Practice

Creating a Map Provide students with an outline map of the United States. Have students research to find out which candidates in the 1824 election won which states. Then, have students assign each candidate a color and shade in the map appropriately. As a follow-up, ask students to speculate about why individual candidates drew more support in some regions of the country and less in others. **OL**

Additional Support

A Disputed Election

S Although the Republicans remained the only official political party, sectional tensions were strong in the election campaign of 1824. On Election Day, four Republicans ran for president. Andrew Jackson of Tennessee led in the popular vote and in the Electoral College, but he did not win the necessary majority of electoral votes. In accordance with constitutional procedure, the decision went to the House of Representatives, whose members would select the president from the top three with the most votes.

Henry Clay of Kentucky, who had placed fourth, was eliminated. As the Speaker of the House, Clay enjoyed tremendous influence, and he threw his support to John Quincy Adams of Massachusetts. On February 9, 1825, Adams won the House election easily, with 13 votes to Jackson's 7 and William Crawford's 4.

Upon taking office, the new president named Clay as his secretary of state. Jackson's supporters immediately accused the pair of striking a "corrupt bargain," whereby Clay had secured votes for Adams in return for a cabinet post. Adams and Clay denied any wrongdoing, and no evidence of a deal ever emerged. Still,

Jackson's outraged supporters decided to break with the faction of the party allied with Adams. The Jacksonians called themselves Democratic Republicans, later shortened to Democrats. Adams and his followers became known as National Republicans.

A New Era in Politics

Throughout the first decades of the 1800s, hundreds of thousands of white males gained the right to vote. This was largely because many states lowered or eliminated property ownership as a voting qualification. They did so partly to reflect the ideals of the Declaration of Independence and the social equality of frontier life. In addition, as cities and towns grew, the percentage of working people who did not own property increased. These people paid taxes and had an interest in the political affairs of their communities, so they wanted a say in electing those who represented them. The expansion of voting rights was very much in evidence by 1828. That year, more than 1.13 million citizens voted for president, compared with about 355,000 in 1824. **W**

The campaign that year pitted John Quincy Adams against Andrew Jackson, who believed

PAST & PRESENT

1844

Choosing a President

Today, nearly all American citizens age 18 and older are eligible to vote. This was not the case in the early 1800s. Under the state constitutions adopted at the time of the American Revolution, the right to vote was usually limited to white males who owned property. Over the next few decades, however, states began lowering or eliminating property requirements for voters. Women could not vote, nor could the overwhelming majority of African American men, even those living in the North who met other requirements for voting. Still, changes in the Jacksonian era meant many more Americans could participate in presidential elections.

The rise of national nominating conventions also changed the process of choosing a president. Rather than congressional party leaders deciding on the party's candidate, delegates from the states could participate in the decision at a nominating convention.

Today, parties still hold national conventions in presidential election years, but voting to choose the party's nominee for president has become largely symbolic. The party's nominee has generally been decided in advance, through state primaries and state caucuses.

▲ Men crowd around the ballot boxes at a New York City polling station, waiting for their chance to vote in the presidential election of 1844.

Extending the Content

Jackson's Inauguration When Andrew Jackson was inaugurated in 1829, he broke a long tradition by inviting the public to his reception. In *The First Forty Years of Washington Society*, one attendee recounts the events of the day:

"The majesty of the people had disappeared, and a rabble, a mob, of boys, . . . women, children—[were] scrambling, fight-

ing, romping. . . . The President, after having been *literally* nearly pressed to death and almost suffocated and torn to pieces by the people in their eagerness to shake hands with Old Hickory, had retreated through the back way. . . . Cut glass and china to the amount of several thousand dollars had been broken in the struggle to get refreshments. . . . Ladies and gentlemen only had

been expected at this levee, not the people *en masse*. But it was the people's day, and the people's President, and the people would rule."

that the presidency had been unjustly denied him four years earlier. The candidates resorted to mudslinging, attacking each other's personalities and morals. When the results came in, Jackson had 56 percent of the popular vote and 178 of the 261 electoral votes, a clear victory. Much of his support came from the West and South, where rural and small-town residents, many voting for the first time, saw Jackson as the candidate most likely to represent their interests.

As president, Jackson actively tried to make the government more inclusive. In an effort to strengthen democracy, he vigorously utilized the **spoils system,** the practice of appointing people to government jobs based on party loyalty and support. In his view, he was getting rid of a permanent office-holding class and opening up the government to more ordinary citizens.

Jackson's supporters also moved to make the political system—specifically, the way in which presidential candidates were chosen—more democratic. At that time, political parties used the caucus system to select presidential candidates. The members of the party who served in Congress would hold a closed meeting, or caucus, to choose the party's nominee.

Jackson's supporters believed that such a method restricted access to office to mainly the elite and well connected. The Jacksonians replaced the caucus with the national nominating convention, where delegates from the states gathered to decide on the party's presidential nominee.

The Nullification Crisis

Jackson had not been in office long before he had to focus on a national crisis. It centered on South Carolina, but it also highlighted the growing rift between the nation's Northern and Southern regions.

In the early 1800s, South Carolina's economy began to decline. Many of the state's residents blamed this situation on the nation's tariffs—the taxes the United States charged other countries to bring their goods into the country. Because it had few industries, South Carolina purchased many of its manufactured goods from England, but tariffs made them extremely expensive. When Congress levied yet another new tariff in 1828—which critics called the **Tariff of Abominations**—many South Carolinians threatened to **secede,** or withdraw, from the Union.

2004

▲ George W. Bush accepts the presidential nomination at the Republican National Convention in 2004.

▲ Today, electronic voting is becoming common. Nearly all U.S. citizens older than 18 years of age may vote.

MAKING **CONNECTIONS**

1. **Contrasting** How is the electorate different today than it was in the early 1800s?
2. **Synthesizing** How have national party conventions changed since the early 1800s?

Activity: Economics Connection

Federal Reserve System Explain to students that over time it became apparent to the nation's financial and political leaders that a central bank or banking system was, indeed, necessary for the economic well being of the country. Have students research and write a report on the roots, structure, and main functions of the Federal Reserve System. In their reports, students should also compare the Federal Reserve to the Second National Bank. **OL**

R Reading Strategy

Making Connections The proposition that states could reject a federal law should not sound new to students. **Ask:** In what prior context was it proposed that states could challenge the validity of a federal law? *(passage of the Kentucky and Virginia Resolutions criticizing the Alien and Sedition Acts)* **OL**

Did You Know?

Andrew Jackson's first biographer, James Parton, described him as follows: "He was one of the greatest of generals and wholly ignorant of the art of war. A writer, brilliant, elegant, eloquent, without being able to compose a correct sentence or spell words of four syllables. . . . A democratic autocrat. An urbane savage. An atrocious saint."

Analyzing GEOGRAPHY

Answers:
1. the Sauk and Fox
2. Fort Gibson, Indian Territory

Additional Support

The growing turmoil particularly troubled Vice President John C. Calhoun, who was from South Carolina. Calhoun felt torn between upholding the country's policies and helping his fellow Carolinians. Rather than support secession, Calhoun put forth the idea of nullification. He argued that because the states had created the federal union, they had the right to declare a federal law null, or not valid.

The issue of nullification intensified in January 1830, when Senators Robert Hayne of South Carolina and Daniel Webster of Massachusetts confronted each other on the Senate floor. Hayne, asserting that the Union was no more than a voluntary association of states, advocated "liberty first and Union afterward." Webster countered that neither liberty nor the Union could survive without binding federal laws. He ended his speech with a stirring call: "Liberty *and* Union, now and for ever, one and inseparable!"

The war of words intensified in 1832 when Congress passed yet another tariff law. Enraged, a special session of South Carolina's legislature voted to nullify the law. President Jackson considered nullification an act of treason and sent a warship to Charleston. As tensions rose, Senator Henry Clay managed to defuse the crisis. At Clay's insistence, Congress passed a bill that would lower tariffs gradually until 1842. South Carolina then repealed its nullification of the tariff law.

NATIONAL GEOGRAPHIC Effects of the Indian Removal Act, 1831–1842

In 1832 Sauk and Fox warriors led by Chief Black Hawk fought to reclaim territory east of the Mississippi River, but were defeated.

▲ Cherokee travel the Trail of Tears.

The Cherokee took their refusal to move to the Supreme Court—and won. Federal troops forced them to leave in 1838.

Chief Osceola led the Seminole in rebellion.

Multi-group removal route
Trail of Tears
■ Fort
1840 border

0   400 kilometers
0   400 miles
Albers Equal-Area projection

Analyzing GEOGRAPHY

1. **Movement** Name two Native American groups in the northern half of the United States that were forced to relocate.
2. **Location** Where did the Trail of Tears end?

Maps In Motion See *StudentWorks™ Plus* or glencoe.com.

98   Chapter 2   The Young Republic

Extending the Content

Jackson Battles the National Bank To make the Bank an issue in the 1832 election, President Jackson's opponents in Congress introduced a bill extending the Bank's charter for another 20 years. Congress passed the bill, but Jackson vetoed it. It quickly became clear that most Americans supported Jackson as he went on to easily win a second term.

Jackson took his reelection as a directive from the people to destroy the Bank at once, even though its charter did not run out until 1836. He removed the government's deposits from the Bank and placed them in state banks. The removal of the deposits greatly weakened the bank, causing a slow death. Jackson had won a major political victory by attacking the Bank. Later, however, critics would charge that destroying the Bank contributed significantly to the financial woes that plagued the country in the years ahead.

Native American Removal

Although slavery remained a divisive question, President Jackson decided to focus on other matters, including Native Americans. While Jackson wanted to ensure the survival of Native American peoples, he accelerated the effort of moving them out of the way of white settlers. In 1830 Jackson signed the Indian Removal Act, which helped the states relocate Native Americans to largely uninhabited regions west of the Mississippi River.

The Cherokee in Georgia fought back by appealing to the Supreme Court, hoping to gain legal recognition of their territorial rights. Chief Justice Marshall supported this right in two decisions, *Cherokee Nation* v. *Georgia* (1831) and *Worcester* v. *Georgia* (1832). Jackson refused to carry out the decision. "Marshall has made his opinion," the president reportedly said, "now let him enforce it."

In 1838 Martin Van Buren, Jackson's successor, sent in the army to forcibly move the Cherokee. Roughly 2,000 Cherokee died in camps while waiting for the westward march. On the journey, known to the Cherokee as the **Trail of Tears,** about 2,000 others died of starvation, disease, and **exposure.**

Missionary-minded religious groups and a few members of Congress, like Henry Clay, declared that Jackson's policies toward Native Americans stained the nation's honor. Most citizens, however, supported them. By 1838 the majority of Native Americans still living east of the Mississippi had been forced onto government reservations.

A New Party Emerges

President Jackson also decided to dismantle the Second Bank of the United States. He resented the power of its wealthy stockholders. Jackson vetoed a bill that would have extended the Bank's charter for 20 years. Then, by withdrawing the federal government's deposits, he forced the Bank to end.

Opposition to Jackson By the mid-1830s, those who criticized Jackson's decision had formed a new political party, the **Whigs.** Led by former National Republicans like Henry Clay, John Quincy Adams, and Daniel Webster, the Whigs wanted to expand the federal government, encourage industrial and commercial development, and create a centralized economy. Such policies differed from those of the Democrats, who favored a limited federal government. The Whigs ran three candidates for president in the election of 1836. Jackson's continuing popularity, however, helped assure victory for his handpicked successor, Democrat Martin Van Buren.

Economic Crisis Shortly after Van Buren took office, a crippling economic crisis hit the nation. The roots of the crisis stretched back to the end of Jackson's term, a period in which investment in roads, canals, and railroads boomed, prompting a wave of land speculation and bank lending. This heavy spending pushed up inflation, which Jackson feared eventually would render the nation's paper currency worthless. Just before leaving office, therefore, Jackson issued the Specie Circular, which ordered that all payments for public lands must be made in the form of silver or gold.

Jackson's directive set off the Panic of 1837. With easy paper credit no longer available, land sales plummeted and economic growth slowed. In addition, the National Bank, which could have helped stabilize the economy, no longer existed. As a result, many banks and businesses failed, and thousands of farmers lost their land through foreclosures. Van Buren, a firm believer in his party's philosophy of limited federal government, did little to ease the crisis.

The Whigs and Tyler With Van Buren clearly vulnerable, the Whigs easily won the 1840 election by nominating General William Henry Harrison, a hero of the battle against Native Americans at Tippecanoe in 1811. Harrison, who spoke at his inauguration for two hours in bitter cold without coat or hat, died one month later of pneumonia. Vice President John Tyler, a Southerner and former Democrat who had left his party in protest over the nullification issue, then took over.

Tyler's ascension to the presidency dismayed Whig leaders. Tyler sided with the Democrats on numerous key issues, refusing to support a higher tariff or a new national bank. The new president did win praise, however, for the 1842 Webster-Ashburton Treaty, which established a firm boundary between the United States and Canada.

✓ Reading Check **Summarizing** What caused the nullification crisis?

C Critical Thinking
Determining Cause and Effect Before discussing the Panic of 1837, ask the economics teacher to explain the conditions that can cause a bank panic. Include the problems caused by individual banks printing their own money and the results of bank panics, such as bank collapses. Based on the discussion, have students create cause-and-effect charts to explain the economic impact of bank panics. **OL**

✓ Reading Check

Answer:
the imposition of tariffs that hurt an already struggling South Carolina economy

Additional Support

Activity: Interdisciplinary Connection

Geography In groups, have student discuss the removal of the Cherokee from Georgia to what is now Oklahoma. **Ask:** How is the geography of Oklahoma different from the geography of Georgia and how do you think the differences affected Cherokee culture after the relocation? *(Possible answer: Not only did the Cherokee suffer being torn from homelands they had occupied for centuries, they also had to leave a landscape of forested hills with streams for one of flat, arid plains. This probably destroyed many of their traditional methods of producing food and other ways of life.)* **AL**

D Differentiated Instruction

Gifted and Talented Invite students to take on the role of an abolitionist and prepare a speech, poster, or pamphlet supporting the abolition of slavery. **AL**

C Critical Thinking

Drawing Conclusions Point out to students that it was against the law to help enslaved people escape, and that the law required runaway slaves to be returned to their masters. Nonetheless, many abolitionists broke such laws. **Ask:** Are there some situations in which breaking the law is an acceptable form of protest? *(Answers will vary.)* **OL**

Answer:
Answers will vary, but students should cite examples from the feature and the text to describe Garrison's role in starting the abolitionist movement of the 1830s.

Additional Support

Turning Point

The Abolitionist Movement Begins

Since colonial times many Americans had believed slavery was immoral. The Second Great Awakening and the general spirit of reform in the period of the 1830s, however, created an environment in which abolition began to gain widespread support. William Lloyd Garrison sparked the movement by publishing *The Liberator,* through which he spread his ideas, and by founding the American Anti-Slavery Society. Garrison's energy, moral certitude, and strong rhetoric attracted fellow activists, as well as new converts, and gave the movement momentum on a national scale.

ANALYZING HISTORY How did William Lloyd Garrison start the abolitionist movement of the 1830s?

▶ *Major leaders of the early abolitionist movement included William Lloyd Garrison (above left), sisters Angelina Grimké (above center) and Sarah Grimké (above right), as well as Frederick Douglass (shown seated left of the table) and Theodore Weld (seated in front).*

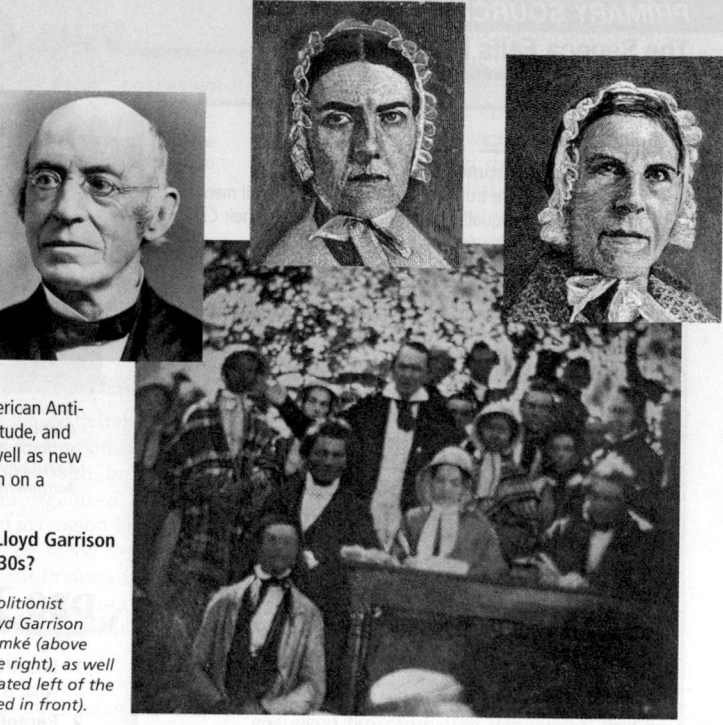

The Abolitionist Movement

Of all the reform movements that began in the early 1800s, the movement calling for abolition, or the immediate end to slavery, was the most divisive. It polarized the nation and helped bring about the Civil War.

Early Opposition Many of the country's founders knew that the nation would have difficulty remaining true to its ideals of liberty and equality if it continued to enslave human **C** beings. Quakers and Baptists in both North and South argued that slavery was a sin. After the Revolution, Baptists in Virginia called for "every legal measure to [wipe out] this horrid evil from the land."

Early antislavery societies advocated gradualism, the idea that slavery should be ended gradually. First they would stop slave traders. Then they would end slavery in phases, first in the North, then in the upper South, and finally in the lower South. They believed this strategy would give the South time to adjust.

One example of antislavery efforts in the early 1800s was the formation of the American Colonization Society (ACS) in 1816. This group, supported by such prominent figures as President James Monroe and Chief Justice John Marshall, encouraged African Americans to resettle in Africa. The privately funded ACS chartered ships and helped relocate between 12,000 and 20,000 African Americans along the west coast of Africa in what became the nation of Liberia. Still, there were more than 1.5 million enslaved persons in the United States in 1820. Many of them, already two or three generations removed from Africa, strongly objected to the idea of resettlement.

New Abolitionists The antislavery movement gained new momentum in the 1830s, thanks largely to William Lloyd Garrison. In his newspaper, the *Liberator,* Garrison called for the immediate **emancipation,** or freeing, of **D** enslaved persons. Garrison went on to found the New England Antislavery Society in 1832 and the American Antislavery Society in 1833.

Extending the Content

Additional Background Slave narratives first appeared in the mid-1700s, nearly a century before the one that became the most famous of the genre, *Narrative of the Life of Frederick Douglass.* Many of them were dictated to abolitionists who encouraged enslaved people and former slaves to tell their stories in order to call attention to the abolitionist cause. In the 1930s, over 2,000 first-person accounts from surviving individuals who had been born into slavery were collected as part of the Federal Writer's Project of the Works Progress Administration. **Ask:** Why did abolitionists collect and publish the life stories of enslaved people? *(To provide testimony of slavery's injustice and cruelty from people who experienced it; to counter slaveholders' assertions that most enslaved people were content.)* **OL**

Many women supported abolitionism. Lucretia Mott, a strong advocate of women's rights, spoke out in favor of abolition. Some Southern women, such as the South Carolina sisters Sarah and Angelina Grimké, also joined the crusade.

African American Abolitionists Not surprisingly, free African Americans took a prominent role in the abolitionist movement. The most famous was **Frederick Douglass,** who had escaped from slavery in Maryland. He published his own anti-slavery newspaper, the *North Star,* and an autobiography. Another important African American abolitionist was Sojourner Truth. She gained freedom in 1827 when New York freed all remaining enslaved persons in the state. Although she lacked a formal education, her eloquent and deeply religious antislavery speeches attracted huge crowds.

Northern Opposition Some Northerners objected to abolitionism because they considered it a dangerous threat to the existing social system. Some whites, including many prominent businesspeople, warned that it would produce a destructive war between the North and the South. Others feared it might bring a great influx of freed African Americans to the North, overwhelming the labor and housing markets. Many Northerners also had no desire to see the South's economy crumble. If that happened, they might lose the huge sums Southern planters owed to Northern banks as well as the Southern cotton that fed Northern textile mills.

Southern Reaction To most Southerners, slavery was a "peculiar institution," one that was distinctive and vital to the Southern way of life. The South had remained mostly agricultural, becoming increasingly tied to cotton and the enslaved people who planted and picked it. Southerners responded to the growing attacks against slavery by vehemently defending the institution. South Carolina's governor called it a "national benefit," while Thomas Dew, a leading academic of the South, claimed that most enslaved persons had no desire for freedom, as they enjoyed a close and beneficial relationship with their slaveholders. "We have no hesitation in affirming," he declared, "that . . . the slaves of good [slaveholders] are his warmest, most constant, and most devoted friends."

In 1831, when a slave rebellion left more than 50 white Virginians dead, Southerners were outraged. They cracked down on enslaved persons throughout the region and railed against the North. Further, they demanded the suppression of abolitionist material as a condition for remaining in the Union. Southern postal workers refused to deliver abolitionist newspapers. In 1836, under Southern pressure, the House of Representatives passed a "gag rule" providing that all abolitionist petitions be shelved without debate. Such measures did not deter abolitionists. While their movement was still relatively small, it continued to cause an uproar.

 Reading Check Comparing How did Northerners' views on abolition differ from those of Southerners?

Section 3 REVIEW

Vocabulary
1. **Explain** the significance of: Missouri Compromise, spoils system, Tariff of Abominations, secede, Trail of Tears, Whigs, Second Great Awakening, benevolent societies, temperance, emancipation, Frederick Douglass.

Main Ideas
2. **Describing** How was the nullification crisis resolved?

3. **Explaining** On what document did the Seneca Falls Convention base the "Declaration of Sentiments"?

Critical Thinking
4. **Big Ideas** In what ways did the United States become more democratic during Jackson's administration?

5. **Categorizing** Use a graphic organizer similar to the one below to list the major areas of reform in the mid-1800s.

Areas of Reform

6. **Analyzing Visuals** Study the map of the effects of Indian removal on page 98. Which groups tried to keep their lands through armed resistance?

Writing About History
7. **Persuasive Writing** Think of one social reform you think is needed in the United States today. Write a letter to a legislator expressing reasons why the reform is needed and how it might be achieved. Give examples of specific problems in your community or state to support your argument.

Study Central™ To review this section, go to glencoe.com and click on Study Central.

103

S **Skill Practice**
Giving an Oral Presentation
Have students prepare a short oral presentation about one of the abolitionists mentioned in this section. Encourage students to use library and Internet sources to learn more about their subjects. **OL**

✓**Reading Check**

Answer:
In the North, there was some support, some opposition, and some indifference. Abolition was widely opposed in the South.

Assess

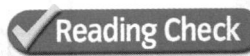

Study Central™ provides summaries, interactive games, and online graphic organizers to help students review content.

Close

Determining Cause and Effect Ask students to explain how nullification intensified the sectional divisions. **OL**

Section 3 REVIEW

Answers

1. All definitions can be found in the section and the Glossary.
2. Henry Clay pushed through Congress a bill that would lower the nation's tariffs gradually until 1842. In response, South Carolina repealed its nullification of the tariff law.
3. the Declaration of Independence
4. More adult white males, regardless of wealth or class, participated in government through voting and government jobs.
5. women's rights, abolition, temperance, prison conditions, education
6. the Sauk and Fox, and the Seminole
7. Students' letters will vary, but should focus on a problem that has an impact on your state or community today.

People IN HISTORY

Answers:

Tubman: Tubman felt so changed by freedom that she felt like she was a new person.

Stowe: The novel created sympathy for people living in slavery and increased Northern hostility to slavery.

Additional Background:

Born in the South into slavery, Harriet Tubman ran away to freedom and then repeatedly returned to the South to help others to escape. Her success can be attributed to several clever ploys, including beginning her journeys on Saturdays because runaway notices were not published in the papers until Mondays.

In contrast, Harriet Beecher Stowe's experience with slavery was second-hand. Coming from a reform-minded, prominent New England family, however, her moral outrage at slavery and skill as a writer led her to pen a novel that evoked tremendous sympathy for people living under slavery.

Additional Support

People IN HISTORY

Harriet Tubman
1820–1913

Known as "Moses" for her courage in leading enslaved people to freedom as Moses had led the Hebrews out of slavery in Egypt, Harriet Tubman was a heroine of the antislavery movement. Tubman was born into slavery in Maryland and struggled early against the system's brutality. At age 13, she tried to save another enslaved person from punishment, and an overseer fractured her skull. Miraculously, she recovered, but she suffered from occasional blackouts for the rest of her life.

Tubman escaped to freedom in 1849. About crossing into Pennsylvania, she later wrote, "I looked at my hands to see if I was the same person. There was such a glory over everything. The sun came up like gold through the trees, and I felt like I was in Heaven."

Her joy inspired others. After Congress passed the Fugitive Slave Act, Tubman returned to the South 19 times to guide enslaved people along the Underground Railroad to freedom.

Tubman became notorious in the eyes of slaveholders, but despite a large reward offered for her capture, no one ever betrayed her whereabouts. Furthermore, in all her rescues, she never lost a "passenger." Tubman's bravery and determination made her one of the most important figures in the antislavery movement.
What do you think Tubman meant when she wrote, "I looked at my hands to see if I was the same person?"

Harriet Beecher Stowe
1811–1896

Daughter of reformer-minister Lyman Beecher, Harriet Beecher Stowe was born into a family of high achievers. Unlike many young women of the time, Stowe received a good education, including teacher training in Hartford, Connecticut. In 1832 Stowe moved to Cincinnati, Ohio. There, Stowe began writing and teaching. She spent 18 years in Ohio—right across the river from the slave state of Kentucky. During this period, she met fugitive slaves, employed a former enslaved woman, and learned about slavery from Southern friends.

In 1850 Stowe moved with her husband to Maine. There, in reaction to the Fugitive Slave Law, she began writing *Uncle Tom's Cabin*, based on what she had learned while in Ohio and antislavery materials she had read. The novel, which humanized the plight of the enslaved, was an instant sensation and further hardened the positions of both abolitionists and slaveholders. When President Lincoln met Stowe, so the story goes, he exclaimed, "So you're the little woman who wrote the book that started this Great War!"

Stowe went on to write many more novels, stories, and articles but is today best known for the novel that so fanned the sectional flames over slavery that it contributed to the start of the Civil War.
What was the effect of Uncle Tom's Cabin on the slavery debate?

The Underground Railroad One reason why so many African Americans could escape from the South was the **Underground Railroad.** This informal but well-organized network of abolitionists helped thousands of enslaved persons flee north. "Conductors" transported runaways in secret, gave them shelter and food along the way, and saw them to freedom in the Northern states or Canada. The most famous conductor was **Harriet Tubman,** herself a runaway. Again and again, she journeyed into the slave states to bring out men, women, and children.

Another important conductor was Levi Coffin, who allowed runaways to stay at his homes in Indiana and Ohio where several Underground Railroad routes converged. Some 3,300 African Americans stayed with Coffin while traveling north to freedom.

For an excerpt from *Uncle Tom's Cabin*, see pages R68–R69 in **American Literature Library.**

Uncle Tom's Cabin A major stop on the railroad was Cincinnati, Ohio, where author Harriett Beecher Stowe resided. Her exposure to runaway slaves and the tragic reports she heard later about victims of the Fugitive Slave Law inspired her to "write something that would make this whole nation feel what an accursed thing slavery is."

Stowe's book, *Uncle Tom's Cabin*, was first published in 1852. Stowe's depiction of the enslaved hero, Tom, and the villainous overseer, Simon Legree, aroused passionate antislavery sentiment in the North. Despite Southern outrage, the book eventually sold millions of copies. It had such a dramatic impact on public opinion that many historians consider it a cause of the Civil War.

New Territorial Troubles

The opening of the Oregon country and the admission of California to the Union brought further problems as the nation expanded.

Many people became convinced of the need for a transcontinental railroad to promote growth in the territories along the route. The

---

Activity: Collaborative Learning

Creating a Thematic Map Organize students into small groups to create a thematic map showing the major Underground Railroad routes. Have students use library and Internet sources to learn more about the extensive network routes traveled by African Americans as they escaped slavery. Make arrangements to display the maps. **OL**

choice of the railroad's eastern starting point was contentious. Many Southerners favored the southern route, from New Orleans to San Diego. Since part of that route would lead through northern Mexico, the United States purchased the necessary land for $10 million.

Democratic Senator Stephen A. Douglas of Illinois wanted the eastern starting point to be in Chicago. He knew that any route from the north would run through the unsettled lands west of Missouri and Iowa and prepared a bill to organize the region into a new territory to be called Nebraska. Key Southern committee leaders prevented this bill from coming to a vote in the Senate. They made it clear that before Nebraska could be organized, Congress had to repeal part of the Missouri Compromise and allow slavery in the new territory.

Kansas-Nebraska Act At first, Douglas tried to gain Southern support for his bill by saying that any states organized in the new Nebraska territory would be allowed to exercise popular sovereignty with regard to slavery. When this failed, Douglas agreed to repeal the antislavery provision of the Missouri Compromise and to divide the region into two territories. Nebraska, adjacent to the free state of Iowa, appeared to become a free state, while Kansas, located west of the slave state of Missouri, would become a slave state. Warned that the South might secede without such concessions, President Pierce eventually gave his support to the bill. Despite opposition, Congress passed the **Kansas-Nebraska Act** in May 1854.

"Bleeding Kansas" Hordes of Northerners hurried into Kansas to create an antislavery majority. Before the March elections of 1855, however, thousands of armed Missourians—called "border ruffians" in the press—crossed the border to vote illegally, helping to elect a pro-slavery legislature. Furious antislavery settlers countered by drafting their own constitution that prohibited slavery. By March 1856, Kansas had two governments, one opposed to slavery and the other supporting it. As more Northern settlers arrived, border ruffians began attacks. "Bleeding Kansas," as newspapers dubbed the territory, had become the scene of a territorial civil war.

✓ Reading Check **Analyzing** Why did the Compromise of 1850 fail to end sectional division?

The Crisis Deepens

MAIN Idea The slavery controversy shook up political parties and accelerated the crisis between North and South.

HISTORY AND YOU Do you know of Supreme Court cases that have sparked major debates? Read to learn how the Dred Scott case divided the nation.

The Kansas-Nebraska Act enraged many opponents of slavery because it reopened the territories to slavery and made obsolete the delicate balance previously maintained by the Missouri Compromise. While a few people struck back with violence, others worked for change through the political system.

Changes in Political Parties

The repeal of the Missouri Compromise had a dramatic effect on the political system. Pro-slavery Southern Whigs and antislavery Northern Whigs had long battled for control of their party, but now the party began to fall apart.

During the congressional elections of 1854, many Northern Whigs joined forces with Free-Soilers and a few antislavery Democrats to organize the Republican Party. Their main goal was to stop Southern planters from becoming an aristocracy that controlled the government. Republicans did not agree on whether slavery should be abolished, but they did agree that it had to be kept out of the territories. A large majority of Northern voters shared this view, enabling the Republicans to make great strides in the elections.

At the same time, public anger against the Northern Democrats enabled the American Party—also known as the Know-Nothings—to make gains. The American Party was an anti-Catholic and nativist party. It opposed immigration. Prejudice and fears that immigrants would take away jobs enabled the Know-Nothings to win many seats in Congress and the state legislatures in 1854. The party began to come apart when Know-Nothings from the Upper South split with Know-Nothings from the North over their support for the Kansas-Nebraska Act. Most Americans considered slavery a far more important issue than immigration. Eventually, the Republican Party absorbed the Northern Know-Nothings.

S Skill Practice
Identifying Points of View
Organize students into groups to create presentations about the transcontinental railroad. Have half of the groups create presentations that describe the northern route and its benefits. Have the other half of the groups present the southern route and its benefits. Remind students to include information such as major cities, safety, and topology in their presentations. Then have the students vote on a proposal for the railroad based on what they have heard in the presentations. **OL**

✓ Reading Check

Answer:
Northerners were opposed to the Fugitive Slave Act; the admission of California as a free state upset the balance of slave/free states in the Senate; repeal of the Missouri Compromise meant more slave states might be created.

Additional Support

Activity: Collaborative Learning

Recognizing Cause and Effect Copy the following headings on the board:

CAUSES→EVENT→EFFECTS

Under "Event," write *Kansas-Nebraska Act, 1854.* Then call on students to complete the chain by adding the causes and effects related to passage of the Kansas-Nebraska Act. *(Cause: desire to organize new territories; desire to resolve the* *issue of expanding slavery; Effects: Northern anger over the spread of slavery to "free" land; outbreak of violence in Kansas.)* **OL**

R Reading Strategy

Predicting Copy the chart below onto the board.
Ask: Which justices were likely to side with Dred Scott and which were not? *(Curtis and McLean dissented.)* **OL**

Justice	Home State When Appointed to the Court
John A. Campbell	Alabama
John Catron	Tennessee
Benjamin R. Curtis	Massachusetts
Peter V. Daniel	Virginia
Robert C. Grier	Pennsylvania
John McLean	Ohio
Samuel Nelson	New York
Roger B. Taney	Maryland
James M. Wayne	Georgia

Analyzing VISUALS

Answers:
1. He is portrayed as a kind, dignified, wronged martyr.
2. The cartoonist is implying that justice was denied to Brown when he was executed.

Additional Support

POLITICAL CARTOONS PRIMARY SOURCE
John Brown Becomes a Martyr

Issued in the North in 1863, in the middle of the Civil War, this print depicts John Brown being led to his execution. The symbols in the print show how John Brown had become a martyr to many Northerners.

A figure wearing a tri-cornered hat of the American Revolution with the number *76* emblazoned on it looks on with concern.

A statue of Justice is shown with her arms and scales broken.

The flag says *Sic Semper Tyrannis*—Latin for "as always with tyrants" and refers to the idea that tyrants must be killed.

Brown is shown standing upright, unhurt, and uncowed as he is led to his death.

Brown's jailers look malevolent, with angry snarls and hands on weapons.

According to tradition, Brown kissed an enslaved child as he was led to the scaffold. This enslaved child and its mother are portrayed in a way that would remind viewers of paintings of Jesus and his mother Mary.

Analyzing VISUALS

1. **Identifying Central Issues** How is John Brown portrayed in this image?
2. **Drawing Conclusions** Why do you think that the statue of Justice is depicted as broken?

The 1856 Election The presidential campaign pitted Republican John C. Frémont, Democrat James Buchanan, and former president Millard Fillmore, the Know-Nothing candidate, against each other. Buchanan had not taken a public stand on the Kansas-Nebraska Act and campaigned on the idea that only he could save the Union. When the votes were counted, Buchanan had won.

Sectional Divisions Grow

Just two days after Buchanan's inauguration, the Supreme Court ruled in a landmark case involving slavery, *Dred Scott* v. *Sandford*. **Dred Scott** was a Missouri slave who had been taken north to work in free territory for several years. After he returned with his slaveholder to Missouri, Scott sued to end his slavery, arguing that living in free territory had made him a free man. His case went all the way to the Supreme Court. On March 6, 1857, Chief Justice Roger B. Taney delivered the majority opinion. Taney ruled against Scott because, he claimed, African Americans were not citizens and therefore

could not sue in the courts. Taney then addressed the Missouri Compromise's ban on slavery in territory north of Missouri's southern border:

PRIMARY SOURCE

"It is the opinion of the court that the Act of Congress which prohibited a citizen from holding and owning [enslaved persons] in the territory of the United States north of the line therein mentioned is not warranted by the Constitution and is therefore void."

—from *Dred Scott* v. *Sandford*

While Democrats cheered the *Dred Scott* decision, Republicans called it a "willful perversion" of the Constitution. They argued that if Dred Scott could not legally bring suit, then the Supreme Court should have dismissed the case without considering the constitutionality of the Missouri Compromise.

After the *Dred Scott* decision, the conflict in "Bleeding Kansas" intensified. Hoping to end the troubles, Buchanan urged the territory to apply for statehood. The pro-slavery legislature

112 Chapter 2 The Young Republic

Activity: Technology Connection

Preparing and Filming a Script Have interested students write a script for a "You Are There" radio program on the reaction to the *Dred Scott* decision. Suggest that the scripts include an introduction that provides background information and interviews with lawyers, Dred Scott, Harriet Scott (his wife who also filed suit for freedom), John F. A. Sanford, other eyewitnesses at the court, and various experts on the Supreme Court. Encourage students to "broadcast" their scripts for the rest of the class on the Web, DVDs, or other presentation tools. **OL**

scheduled an election for delegates to a constitutional convention, but antislavery Kansans boycotted it. The resulting constitution, drafted in 1857 in the town of Lecompton, legalized slavery in the territory.

An antislavery majority then voted down the Lecompton constitution in a territory-wide referendum, or popular vote on an issue. Although the Senate approved the vote, Republicans and Northern Democrats in the House blocked the measure, arguing that it ignored the people's will. Finally, in 1858, President Buchanan and Southern leaders in Congress agreed to allow another referendum in Kansas. Again the voters in Kansas overwhelmingly rejected the Lecompton constitution. Not until 1861 did Kansas become a state—a free one.

John Brown's Raid

About a year after the second rejection of the Lecompton constitution, national attention shifted to John Brown, a fervent abolitionist who opposed slavery not with words but with violence. After pro-slavery forces sacked the town of Lawrence in the Kansas Territory, Brown took revenge by abducting and murdering five pro-slavery settlers living near Pottawatomie Creek.

In 1859 Brown decided to seize the federal arsenal at Harpers Ferry, Virginia (today in West Virginia), free and arm the enslaved people of the area, and begin an insurrection, or rebellion, against slaveholders. On the night of October 16, 1859, Brown and 18 followers seized the arsenal. To the terrified night watchman, he announced, "I have possession now of the United States armory, and if the citizens interfere with me I must only burn the town and have blood." A contingent of U.S. Marines, commanded by Colonel Robert E. Lee, rushed from Washington, D.C., to Harpers Ferry. Outnumbered, Brown surrendered, and a Virginia court sentenced him to death. In his last words, Brown, repenting nothing, declared:

PRIMARY SOURCE

"I believe that to have interfered as I have done, as I have always freely admitted I have done in behalf of [God's] despised poor, I did no wrong, but right. Now if it is deemed necessary that I should forfeit my life for the furtherance of the ends of justice and mingle my blood . . . with the blood of millions in this slave country whose rights are disregarded by wicked, cruel and unjust enactments, I say, let it be done!"

—from *The Life and Letters of Captain John Brown*

Many Northerners saw Brown as a martyr in a noble cause. The execution, Henry David Thoreau predicted, would strengthen abolitionism in the North. "He is not old Brown any longer," Thoreau declared, "he is an angel of light." For most Southerners, however, Brown's raid proved that Northerners were actively plotting the murder of slaveholders. "Defend yourselves!" cried Georgia senator Robert Toombs. "The enemy is at your door!"

Reading Check **Evaluating** How did the issue of Kansas statehood reflect the growing division between North and South?

Section 4 REVIEW

Vocabulary
1. **Explain** the significance of: Manifest Destiny, James K. Polk, Treaty of Guadalupe Hidalgo, popular sovereignty, secession, Compromise of 1850, Underground Railroad, Harriet Tubman, Kansas-Nebraska Act, Dred Scott.

Main Ideas
2. **Identifying** How did Britain and the United States divide the Oregon Territory?

3. **Explaining** Why did Kansas become an area of civil war?

4. **Synthesizing** How did the ruling in *Dred Scott* v. *Sandford* increase sectional division?

Critical Thinking
5. **Big Ideas** What new problem did the additional territories cause for the United States?

6. **Categorizing** Use a graphic organizer similar to the one below to list the provisions of the Treaty of Guadalupe Hidalgo.

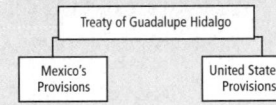

Treaty of Guadalupe Hidalgo	
Mexico's Provisions	United States's Provisions

7. **Analyzing Visuals** Study the image of John Brown's martyrdom on page 112. What do you think is the significance of the figure in the tri-cornered hat?

Writing About History
8. **Expository Writing** Suppose that you are a reporter for a Southern or Northern newspaper in the 1850s. Write an article on the reaction to *Uncle Tom's Cabin*.

History ONLINE
Study Central™ To review this section, go to glencoe.com and click on Study Central.

113

Reading Check

Answer:
Kansas struggled to become a state for four years while the pro-slavery legislature battled the antislavery majority.

Assess
. . . .

History ONLINE

Study Central™ provides summaries, interactive games, and online graphic organizers to help students review content.

Close
. . . .

Summarizing Ask students to identify and write one sentence about each of the events that increased sectional tensions in the late 1850s. **OL**

Section 4 REVIEW

Answers

1. All definitions can be found in the section and the Glossary.
2. Britain and the United States agreed to divide Oregon along the 49th parallel. Britain took the Canadian province of British Columbia, and the Americans received the land that later became the states of Oregon, Washington, and Idaho.
3. The Kansas-Nebraska Act organized Kansas based on popular sovereignty to determine if it would allow slavery. Southerners responded by hurrying into the territory

intent on creating a slavery majority. Antislavery forces also rushed into the territory and a struggle for control of the territory ensued, leading to violence.

4. Southerners viewed the decision as a victory; Northerners feared it meant slavery could not be kept out of the territories and that slavery would expand.

5. The admission of new territories as free states or slave states might change the balance of power in Congress.

6. Mexico: ceded over 500,000 square miles (1,295,000 sq. km) of territory, accepted Rio Grande as Texas border; United States: paid Mexico $15 million and claimed $3.25 million in Mexican debt

7. Possible answer: He represents the spirit of liberty and freedom and other principles for which the American Revolution was fought.

8. Students' articles should be well organized with a clear outline, introduction, body, and conclusion.

Focus

Analyzing Primary Sources

Have students examine the advertisement in Source 2. **Ask:** What other items are to be sold the same day as the three slaves? *(ten slaves for rent, rice, gram, paddy, books, muslins, needles, pins, ribbons, and a celebrated English horse called Blucher)* What does this advertisement show about the way slaves were treated? *(They were sold like crops, goods, and animals.)* What else do you notice about the advertisement? *(The slaves were listed by their first names only, and some of the goods to be sold were of interest to women.)* **OL**

Synthesizing Ask: Why might songs have been an important part of the enslaved African American culture? *(Songs helped pass time during the workday, provided enjoyment, expressed their hopes and desire for freedom, and were used in religious services.)* **OL**

Additional Support

ANALYZING PRIMARY SOURCES

Living Under Slavery

Enslaved persons were not free. That fundamental fact meant they could be sold and separated from their families. They could not legally marry or leave their slaveholder's property without permission. Slaveholders held such power that they controlled access to basic life necessities and could physically punish, even kill, the people they held in slavery without breaking the law.

Study these primary sources and answer the questions that follow.

PRIMARY SOURCE 1

Autobiography, 1845

"The men and women slaves received, as their monthly allowance of food, eight pounds of pork, or its equivalent in fish, and one bushel of corn meal. Their yearly clothing consisted of two coarse linen shirts, one pair of linen trousers, like the shirts, one jacket, one pair of trousers for winter, made of coarse negro cloth, one pair of stockings, and one pair of shoes; the whole of which could not have cost more than seven dollars. The allowance of the slave children was given to their mothers, or the old women having the care of them. The children unable to work in the field had neither shoes, stockings, jackets, nor trousers, given to them; their clothing consisted of two coarse linen shirts per year. When these failed them, they went naked until the next allowance-day. Children from seven to ten years old, of both sexes, almost naked, might be seen at all seasons of the year.

There were no beds given the slaves, unless one coarse blanket be considered such, and none but the men and women had these. This, however, is not considered a very great privation. They find less difficulty from the want of beds, than from the want of time to sleep; for when their day's work in the field is done, the most of them having their washing, mending, and cooking to do, and having few or none of the ordinary facilities for doing either of these, very many of their sleeping hours are consumed in preparing for the field the coming day; and when this is done, old and young, male and female, married and single, drop down side by side, on one common bed,—the cold, damp floor,—each covering himself or herself with their miserable blankets; and here they sleep till they are summoned to the field by the driver's horn."

—from *Narrative of the Life of Frederick Douglass, an American Slave*

PRIMARY SOURCE 2

Advertisement, 1829

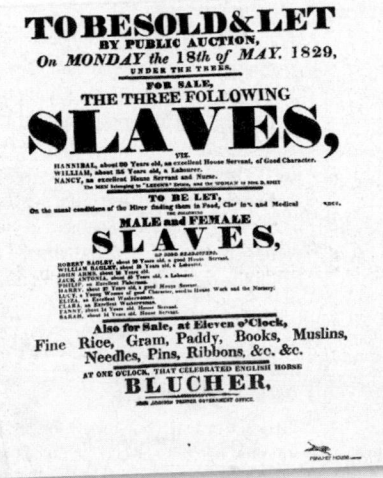

PRIMARY SOURCE 3

Photograph, 1863

▼ *Gordon escaped from his slaveholder in Mississippi during the Civil War. In this photograph, he shows the scars from a brutal whipping.*

Extending the Content

Celebrations Enslaved persons broke the monotony of their everyday lives by holding occasional celebrations on weekends and special holidays. These "parties" usually included a meal followed by singing, dancing, and storytelling. Some planters tried to stop these parties, but others encouraged them. As Frederick Douglass noted, the "parties were among the most effective means in the hands of the slaveholders of keeping down the spirit of insurrection among the slaves." Without this outlet, Douglass continued, "the slave would have been forced to a dangerous desperation."

PRIMARY SOURCE 4

Autobiography, 1861

"I once saw two beautiful children playing together. One was a fair white child; the other was her slave, and also her sister. When I saw them embracing each other, and heard their joyous laughter, I turned sadly away from the lovely sight. I foresaw the inevitable blight that would fall on the little slave's heart. I knew how soon her laughter would be changed to sighs. The fair child grew up to be a still fairer woman. From childhood to womanhood her pathway was blooming with flowers, and overarched by a sunny sky. Scarcely one day of her life had been clouded when the sun rose on her happy bridal morning.

How had those years dealt with her slave sister, the little playmate of her childhood? She, also, was very beautiful; but the flowers and sunshine of love were not for her. She drank the cup of sin, and shame, and misery, whereof her persecuted race are compelled to drink."

—from *Incidents in the Life of a Slave Girl*

PRIMARY SOURCE 5

Painting, c. 1852

Slave Auction of African Family

PRIMARY SOURCE 6

Photograph, 1858

► *Louisa, an enslaved teenager from St. Louis, Missouri, is shown photographed with her slaveholders' son.*

DBQ Document-Based Questions

1. **Analyzing** What does Source 1 reveal about the daily lives of enslaved persons?

2. **Interpreting** Examine Sources 2 and 3. What do these images demonstrate about the status and treatment of enslaved persons?

3. **Comparing and Contrasting** Read Source 4. How were the lives of the two girls similar when they were young but different when they became young women?

4. **Analyzing Visuals** Look at Source 5 and examine the people in the painting. Write a paragraph describing what you see going on in this scene.

5. **Speculating** Study Source 6. How do you think Louisa felt about taking care of this young boy? How might slavery complicate personal relationships?

DBQ Document Based Questions

Answers:

1. Daily life was harsh. They lacked sufficient clothing and food. There were no beds and poor blankets. They worked for endless hours in the fields.

2. They were bought and sold like property and were subject to whatever punishment the slaveholder gave out. Slaves were not protected from abuse by laws.

3. Both seemed to enjoy a happy childhood together. However, the enslaved child faced an adulthood of sin, shame, and misery while the white child's happiness continued into adulthood.

4. An African American family is being sold at an auction attended by well-dressed plantation owners. Most likely, the family will be separated and never see one another again.

5. Louisa's feelings about taking care of the boy may depend on how well she is treated by the child's parents. Louisa may love the boy like her own, because her own children may have been sold away. She may see the boy she loved as a child grow up to reject her because of her place in society.

Chapter 2 VISUAL SUMMARY

Summarizing Divide students into small groups. Each group should select a section of the Visual Summary, for example, a group might select "Political Developments." Then each group should select two bullet points under the section head and create a cause-and-effect diagram around the topic. Each group should share their cause-and-effect diagrams in a whole-class discussion. **OL**

Creating a Time Line As a chapter summary activity, have students work individually or in small groups to use the information from the Visual Summary to create a chapter time line. The time line can be as simple as a paper and pencil graphic organizer or as complex as a multimedia presentation with images found on–line or from the textbook. **OL**

A Growing Nation

Political Developments
- Washington creates the first cabinet; Supreme Court is established.
- The Bill of Rights is added to the Constitution.
- The first political parties develop; the convention system emerges.
- Voting rights are widely extended to free adult men.
- Women begin to seek voting rights.
- United States fights the War of 1812 against Britain.
- Supreme Court asserts power to overturn laws in *Marbury* v. *Madison*.
- The U.S. issues the Monroe Doctrine.

Economic Change
- Canals, railroads, and roads are built linking the nation together.
- Factories open in the North; cotton farming spreads across the South.

Territorial Growth
- The Louisiana Purchase doubles size of the nation.
- United States obtains Florida from Spain.
- The U.S. annexes Texas and divides Oregon with Britain.
- U.S. acquires the Southwest and California after the War with Mexico.

An Emerging National Culture
- Religious revivalism triggers movements to reform education, prisons, asylums, and reduce alcohol consumption.
- New American literature is written.

The U.S. experienced rapid economic growth in the 1800s as new industries opened in the North and cotton farming spread across the South.

135,000 SETS, 270,000 VOLUMES SOLD.

UNCLE TOM'S CABIN

FOR SALE HERE.

AN EDITION FOR THE MILLION, COMPLETE IN 1 Vol, PRICE 37 1/2 CENTS.
• " IN GERMAN, IN 1 Vol, PRICE 50 CENTS.
• " IN 2 Vols, CLOTH, 6 PLATES, PRICE $1.50
SUPERB ILLUSTRATED EDITION, IN 1 Vol, WITH 153 ENGRAVINGS,
PRICES FROM $2.50 TO $5.00.

The Greatest Book of the Age.

The Dred Scott decision and the publication of Uncle Tom's Cabin *fueled the bitter section struggle over slavery.*

A Divided Nation

Economic Differences
- North's economy is based on small family farms, trade, and small-scale industrial production.
- South's economy is based on enslaved labor on plantations and farms.

Political Conflict
- Missouri Compromise divides territories into areas where slavery is and is not permitted.
- Jackson threatens to use force to ensure federal authority over South Carolina in the Nullification Crisis.
- Abolitionism emerges in the North; Southern anxiety grows.
- Underground Railway develops to help enslaved people escape North.
- *Uncle Tom's Cabin* builds support for abolition but enrages the South.
- Compromise of 1850 angers both North and South.
- Northerners openly defy the Fugitive Slave Law.
- Kansas-Nebraska Act leads to fighting between proslavery and anti-slavery settlers.
- Dred Scott ruling allows slavery in territories, angering Northerners.
- John Brown's Raid terrifies and angers Southerners.

Hands-On Chapter Project
Step 5: Wrap Up

Presidential Customs

Step 5: Wrap Up Students will write a brief essay summarizing the chapter project.

Directions After all of the groups have presented, have students write a brief essay. In their essay, students should select one presidential custom or procedure still in place today and explain Washington's legacy in relation to that precedent. Students should describe why the precedent is important.

Drawing Conclusions Students will explain their conclusions on why certain presidential procedures or customs are important to the nation today.

ASSESSMENT

STANDARDIZED TEST PRACTICE

TEST-TAKING TIP

When a question stem contains a negative, try to reword the sentence or phrase to make it positive.

Reviewing Vocabulary

Directions: Choose the word or words that best complete the sentence.

1. Washington set a precedent when he met regularly with his _____ to review issues within the executive departments.

    A secretary

    B speculators

    C cabinet

    D generals

2. The Tariff of 1816 was a _____, unlike earlier measures.

    A promotional tariff

    B protective tariff

    C revenue tariff

    D state tariff

3. Under the guidance of religious leaders, associations known as _____ began to address social problems.

    A benevolent societies

    B penitentiaries

    C asylums

    D seminaries

4. To spare Congress from continued fighting over slavery, Senator Lewis Cass proposed the idea of _____, which would allow each territory to decide if it wanted to allow slavery or not.

    A martial law

    B popular sovereignty

    C abolition

    D insurrection

Reviewing Main Ideas

Directions: Choose the best answer for each of the following questions.

Section 1 *(pp. 78–83)*

5. One of the most important acts of the first U.S. Congress under the Constitution was to

    A elect George Washington as the first president.

    B establish a federal banking system.

    C pass the Tariff of 1789.

    D add a Bill of Rights to the Constitution.

6. The Supreme Court decision in *Marbury* v. *Madison* established the principle of

    A judicial review.

    B democratic republicanism.

    C nullification.

    D constitutionality.

Section 2 *(pp. 86–93)*

7. Which of the following cases established the Supreme Court as the final court of appeal?

    A *Commonwealth* v. *Hunt*

    B *Martin* v. *Hunter's Lessee*

    C *McCulloch* v. *Maryland*

    D *Gibbons* v. *Ogden*

8. What began the United States long-term policy of preventing other powers from intervening in Latin American affairs?

    A Monroe Doctrine

    B Adams-Onís Treaty

    C The Missouri Compromise

    D The "corrupt bargain"

Need Extra Help?								
If You Missed Questions . . .	1	2	3	4	5	6	7	8
Go to Page . . .	78	87	100	107	78	83	88	88

 GO ON

Answers and Analyses
Reviewing Vocabulary

1. C Washington's cabinet consisted of the heads of the Departments of State, Treasury, and War and the office of the Attorney General. This tradition continues today, although the cabinet has expanded over the years.

2. B The Tariff of 1816 was enacted in order to *protect* American businesses by placing a tax on imported goods. Import taxes raise the prices of foreign goods, which causes consumers to buy the less expensive, American-made goods.

3. A Tell students that benevolent means kind or compassionate. So, a compassionate society would care for others and try to improve society. Penitentiaries are prisons. Asylums housed the mentally ill. Seminaries are religious schools.

4. B Popular means "of the public" and sovereignty means "freedom from external control." The concept of popular sovereignty means people can determine for themselves how they are ruled. Rather than the federal government deciding whether or not slavery was allowed, territories would decide for themselves.

5. D Remind students of the Federalist vs. Anti-Federalist debate regarding ratification of the Constitution. The Anti-Federalists were convinced to support ratification on the condition that a bill of rights be added to the Constitution. These men wanted to ensure that they retained certain civil liberties.

6. A Here, students may become confused by choice *D*, because *Marbury* v. *Madison* established judicial review, or the review of the constitutionality of laws. It is vital that students grasp the concept of judicial review, which was born out of one of the judicial branch's checks.

7. B As chapters progress, students may have trouble remembering increasing numbers of Supreme Court cases. Encourage students to begin keeping a chart or making flashcards of all the Supreme Court cases they encounter in reading, which will serve as an effective study aid. In this case, students may be distracted by choice *A*, so reinforce the importance of remembering the names of each case.

8. A President Monroe's statement that the Americas were "henceforth not to be considered as subjects for future colonization by any European powers" became known as the Monroe Doctrine. Explain to students that this doctrine would provide a basis for foreign relations regarding the Americas well into the future.

9. B To remember that the Tariff of Abominations caused SC to threaten to secede, tell students that abominations are outrages or atrocities. It makes sense that something atrocious would have to happen to force a state to do something as drastic as threatening to secede from the U.S.

10. B The Seneca Falls Convention was focused on women's rights and is considered the beginning of the women's rights movement. Stanton did propose that women should fight for the vote.

11. C The concept of Manifest Destiny is uniquely applied to the expansion of the United States. This should help students eliminate *A* and *B*. *D* does concern the United States, but is opposite of the meaning of Manifest Destiny.

12. B The Supreme Court decision said that Congress did not have the power to prohibit slaveholders from taking their slave "property" into the territories.

Critical Thinking

13. B Part of the reason for the "good feelings" was a decrease in political disagreement, due to the fact that only the Republican Party was still intact. There was no competing party, so partisan politics were suspended for a bit.

14. D Reading the graph, the bar that represents the National Republican Party is by far the shortest on the graph.

15. C The Whigs, formed in opposition to Jackson, were not successful in defeating Jackson in 1836, but they did succeed in 1840 with Harrison.

Section 3 *(pp. 94–103)*

9. In 1828, passage of which piece of legislation caused South Carolinians to threaten to secede from the Union?

  A the charter for the Second Bank of the United States

  B the Tariff of Abominations

  C the Force Bill

  D the Indian Removal Act

10. At the Seneca Falls Convention in 1848, attendees were shocked when Elizabeth Cady Stanton

  A wore pants to all the meetings.

  B proposed that women seek the right to vote.

  C insisted that African Americans be admitted.

  D announced that she would run for Congress.

Section 4 *(pp. 104–113)*

11. The term "Manifest Destiny" describes the idea that

  A European nations have no right to establish new colonies in the Western Hemisphere.

  B Protestantism should be the official religion of the United States.

  C the United States should control all of North America.

  D Native Americans should be allowed to retain all their original lands.

12. In the *Dred Scott* decision, the Supreme Court determined that it was unconstitutional to

  A allow slavery in the territories.

  B prohibit slavery in the territories.

  C free slaves in the United States.

  D bring enslaved people from one state to another.

Critical Thinking

Directions: Choose the best answers to the following questions.

13. Which of the following was a characteristic of the Era of Good Feelings?

  A a decrease in national pride

  B a one-party political system

  C a decrease in urban populations

  D an increase in state power

Base your answers to questions 14 and 15 on the graph below and your knowledge of Chapter 2.

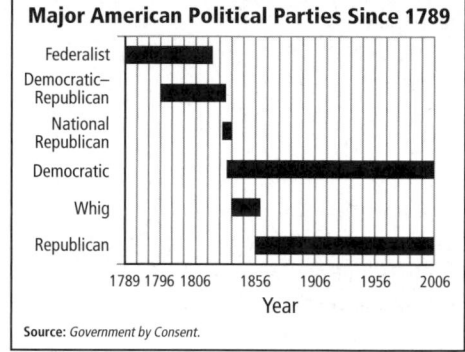

Major American Political Parties Since 1789

Source: *Government by Consent.*

14. What party shown had the shortest life span?

  A Federalist

  B Democratic-Republican

  C Whig

  D National Republican

15. Which party emerged to oppose Andrew Jackson and his policies?

  A Democratic

  B Federalist

  C Whig

  D Republican

Need Extra Help?							
If You Missed Questions . . .	9	10	11	12	13	14	15
Go to Page . . .	97	101–102	104	112	86	R16	R16

GO ON

16. Which of the following was an element of the Compromise of 1850?

  A The Fugitive Slave Act was passed.

  B California was admitted as a slave state.

  C Slavery was banned in Washington, D.C.

  D Slavery was permitted in Oregon.

Analyze the cartoon and answer the question that follows. Base your answer on the cartoon and on your knowledge of Chapter 2.

17. What does Jackson appear to be trampling underfoot?

  A Presidential veto orders

  B Declaration of Independence

  C Articles of Confederation

  D United States Constitution

Document-Based Questions

Directions: Analyze the document and answer the short-answer questions that follow the document.

In her 1861 memoir, Harriet Ann Jacobs recounted what life was like under enslavement. In the excerpt below, she describes circumstances experienced by her enslaved maternal grandmother:

> "She was the daughter of a planter . . . who, at his death, left her mother and his three children free, with money to go to St. Augustine. . . . It was during the Revolutionary War; and they were captured. . . . She was a little girl when she was captured and sold to the keeper of a large hotel. . . . But as she grew older she evinced so much intelligence, and was so faithful, that her master and mistress could not help seeing it was for their interest to take care of such a valuable piece of property. She became an indispensable personage in the household, officiating in all capacities, from cook and wet nurse to seamstress. She was much praised for her cooking; . . . In consequence of numerous requests . . . she asked permission of her mistress to bake crackers at night, after all the household work was done; and she obtained leave to do it, provided she would clothe herself and her children from the profits."
>
> —from *Incidents in the Life of a Slave Girl*

18. In what ways was Jacobs's grandmother treated like property and not a person?

19. Why does the grandmother's mistress give her permission to bake crackers at night?

Extended Response

20. Even at the time, many Americans questioned the motives and goals of the war with Mexico, while others felt it was necessary to fulfill America's Manifest Destiny and the needs of the developing nation. Do you think that the war was justified or not? Choose to support or oppose the war with Mexico. Write a persuasive essay that includes an introduction and at least three paragraphs that support your position.

STOP

History ONLINE

For additional test practice, use Self-Check Quizzes—Chapter 2 at glencoe.com.

Need Extra Help?

If You Missed Questions . . .	16	17	18	19	20
Go to Page . . .	108–109	R18	R19	R19	R10

19. The mistress would lose nothing by giving her permission, since the grandmother baked on her own time. Since the grandmother would pay for her own and her children's clothes with the money she earned, it was one less expense for the mistress.

Extended Response

20. Students' essays will vary, but should provide a clear and reasoned argument to support the viewpoint they choose. Students should not waver from their chosen viewpoint. Essays must follow the format of a persuasive essay and include sufficient support from the text.

16. A If students have difficulty with this question, ask them to review the feature on the Compromise of 1850 on pages 108 and 109.

17. D Study the cartoon with students. Under Jackson's right foot is a piece of paper that says "Constitution of the United States." He is holding the veto in his hand, not stepping on it.

Document-Based Questions

18. Jacobs's grandmother was given her freedom, and then captured and sold as a child. She had to work at various tasks for her master and mistress. She had to ask permission to earn extra money. She had to use the money she made to buy clothes for herself and her enslaved family.

History ONLINE

Have students visit the Web site at glencoe.com to review Chapter 2 and take the Self-Check Quiz.

Need Extra Help?

Have students refer to the pages listed if they miss any of the questions.

Key to Ability Levels	
BL Below Level	**AL** Above Level
OL On Level	**ELL** English Language Learners

Key to Teaching Resources	
Print Material	DVD
CD-ROM	Transparency

Levels					Resources	Chapter Opener	Section 1	Section 2	Section 3	Chapter Assess
BL	OL	AL	ELL							
FOCUS										
BL	OL	AL	ELL	🖥 Daily Focus Skills Transparencies			3-1	3-2	3-3	
TEACH										
BL	OL		ELL	📁 Reading Essentials and Note-Taking Guide*		p. 25	p. 28	p. 31	
BL	OL		ELL	📁 Reading Skills Activity, URB		p. 85			
BL	OL	AL	ELL	📁 Differentiated Instruction Activity, URB		p. 87			
BL	OL		ELL	📁 English Learner Activity, URB		p. 89			
BL	OL	AL	ELL	📁 Content Vocabulary Activity, URB*				p. 91	
BL	OL	AL	ELL	📁 Academic Vocabulary Activity, URB				p. 93	
	OL	AL		📁 Reinforcing Skills Activity, URB	p. 95				
	OL	AL		📁 Critical Thinking Skills Activity, URB				p. 96	
BL	OL		ELL	📁 Time Line Activity, URB				p. 97	
	OL			📁 Linking Past and Present Activity, URB			p. 98		
BL	OL	AL	ELL	📁 Primary Source Reading, URB		p. 99		p. 101	
BL	OL	AL	ELL	📁 American Art and Music Activity, URB	p. 103				
BL	OL	AL	ELL	📁 Interpreting Political Cartoons Activity, URB				p. 105	
		AL		📁 Enrichment Activity, URB			p. 109		
BL	OL		ELL	📁 Guided Reading Activity, URB*		p. 112	p. 113	p. 114	
BL	OL	AL	ELL	📁 Differentiated Instruction for the American High School Classroom	✓	✓	✓	✓	✓
BL	OL	AL	ELL	🖥 Unit Map Overlay Transparencies	✓	✓	✓	✓	✓
BL	OL	AL	ELL	📁 Unit Time Line Transparencies, Strategies, and Activities	✓	✓	✓	✓	✓
BL	OL	AL	ELL	📁 Cause and Effect Transparencies, Strategies, and Activities	✓	✓	✓	✓	✓
BL	OL	AL	ELL	📁 Why It Matters Transparencies, Strategies, and Activities	✓	✓	✓	✓	✓
BL	OL	AL	ELL	📁 American Biographies	✓	✓	✓	✓	✓
BL	OL	AL		📁 Supreme Court Case Studies		p. 13			
BL	OL	AL	ELL	📁 The Living Constitution	✓	✓	✓	✓	✓

Note: Please refer to the *Unit 1 Resource Book* for this chapter's URB materials.

* Also available in Spanish

- Interactive Lesson Planner
- Interactive Teacher Edition
- Fully editable blackline masters
- Section Spotlight Videos Launch
- Differentiated Lesson Plans
- Printable reports of daily assignments
- Standards Tracking System

Levels					Resources	Chapter Opener	Section 1	Section 2	Section 3	Chapter Assess
BL	OL	AL	ELL							
TEACH *(continued)*										
BL	OL	AL	ELL	📁	**American Issues**	✓	✓	✓	✓	✓
	OL	AL	ELL	📁	**American Art and Architecture Transparencies, Strategies, and Activities**	✓	✓	✓	✓	✓
BL	OL	AL		📁	**High School American History Literature Library**	✓	✓	✓	✓	✓
	OL	AL		💿	**American History Primary Source Documents Library**	✓	✓	✓	✓	✓
BL	OL	AL	ELL	💿	**American Music Hits Through History CD**	✓	✓	✓	✓	✓
BL	OL	AL	ELL	🔒	**StudentWorks™ Plus DVD**	✓	✓	✓	✓	✓
BL	OL	AL	ELL	💿	**Vocabulary PuzzleMaker CD-ROM**	✓	✓	✓	✓	✓
BL	OL	AL	ELL	🔒	*The American Vision* **Video Program DVD**	✓	✓	✓	✓	✓
Teacher Resources				📁	**Reading Strategies and Activities for the Social Studies Classroom**	✓	✓	✓	✓	✓
				📁	**Strategies for Success**	✓	✓	✓	✓	✓
				🔒	**Presentation Plus! DVD**	✓	✓	✓	✓	✓
				📁	**Success with English Learner**	✓	✓	✓	✓	✓
ASSESS										
BL	OL	AL	ELL	📁	**Section Quizzes and Chapter Tests***		p. 29	p. 30	p. 31	p.33
BL	OL	AL	ELL	📁	**Authentic Assessment With Rubrics**					p. 11
BL	OL	AL	ELL	📁	**Standardized Test Practice Workbook**		p. 5			
BL	OL	AL	ELL	💿	*ExamView®* **Assessment Suite CD-ROM**		3-1	3-2	3-3	Ch. 3
BL	OL	AL	ELL	💿	**Interactive Tutor Self-Assessment CD-ROM**		3-1	3-2	3-3	Ch. 3
CLOSE										
BL			ELL	📁	**Reteaching Activity, URB**					p. 107
BL	OL		ELL	📁	**Reading and Study Skills Foldables™**	p. 56				
BL	OL	AL	ELL	📁	*American History* **in Graphic Novel**		p. 31			

Using the Glencoe Web Site

Chapter Overviews

Technology Product

The Glencoe Web site offers in-depth overviews that summarize the content of each chapter. The overviews consist of brief chapter summaries and separate overviews for each section. The chapter overviews

- summarize and reinforce chapter content;
- provide discussion points to use in class.

Objectives

The overviews help students

- prepare for better understanding chapter content;
- practice reading and comprehension skills.

Steps

- Provide students with the following steps to complete the activities:
- Locate the Web page for the textbook being studied on the Glencoe Web site glencoe.com.

- Click on **Student Center** under the textbook title.
- Once you are in the Student Center, select a unit from the Unit Resources menu and a chapter from the Chapter Activities menu using the drop-down arrows.
- Click on the **Chapter Overviews** link.
- Have students read the chapter overview in preparation for a reading assignment or activity.

History ONLINE

	Student	Teacher	Parent
Beyond the Textbook	●	●	●
Chapter Overviews	●	●	●
Time Current Events	●		●
ePuzzles and Games	●		●
Concepts in Motion	●		●
Literature Connections		●	
Multi-Language Glossaries	●		●
Online Student Edition	●	●	●
Self-Check Quizzes	●		●
Student Web Activities	●		●
Study Central™	●		●
Teaching Today		●	
Vocabulary eFlashcards	●		●
Web Activity Lesson Plans		●	

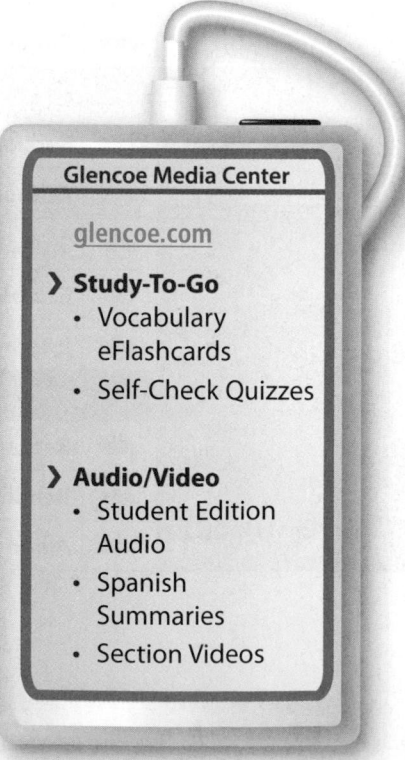

Glencoe Media Center

glencoe.com

❯ **Study-To-Go**
- Vocabulary eFlashcards
- Self-Check Quizzes

❯ **Audio/Video**
- Student Edition Audio
- Spanish Summaries
- Section Videos

READING SUPPORT FROM
JAMESTOWN EDUCATION

- **Timed Readings Plus in Social Studies** helps students increase their reading rate and fluency while maintaining comprehension. The 400-word passages are similar to those found on state and national assessments.

- **Reading in the Content Area: Social Studies** concentrates on six essential reading skills that help students better comprehend what they read. The book includes 75 high-interest nonfiction passages written at increasing levels of difficulty.

- **Reading Social Studies** includes strategic reading instruction and vocabulary support in Social Studies content for both ELLs and native speakers of English.

www.jamestowneducation.com

NATIONAL GEOGRAPHIC
Index to National Geographic Magazine:

The following articles relate to this chapter:

- "Fields of Honor: Pivotal Battles of the Civil War" By Thomson Gale, June 2006.
- "Civil War Battlefields: Saving the Landscapes of America's Deadliest War" By Adam Goodheart, April 2005.

National Geographic Society Products To order the following, call National Geographic at 1-800-368-2728:

- *The Civil War* (CD-ROM)

Access National Geographic's new, dynamic MapMachine Web site and other geography resources at:

www.nationalgeographic.com
www.nationalgeographic.com/maps

The following videotape programs are available from Glencoe as supplements to Modern Times Chapter 3:

- Civil War Battlefields (ISBN 0-76-704083-X)
- Frederick Douglass (ISBN 0-76-700120-6)

To order, call Glencoe at 1-800-334-7344. To find classroom resources to accompany many of these videos, check the following home pages:

A&E Television: www.aetv.com
The History Channel: www.historychannel.com

Reading List Generator CD-ROM

GLENCOE
BOOKLINK 3

Use this database to search more than 30,000 titles to create a customized reading list for your students.

- Reading lists can be organized by students' reading level, author, genre, theme, or area of interest.
- The database provides Degrees of Reading Power™ (DRP) and Lexile™ readability scores for all selections.
- A brief summary of each selection is included.

Leveled reading suggestions for this chapter:

For students at a Grade 8 reading level:
- *Gentle Annie: The True Story of a Civil War Nurse*, by Mary Francis Shura

For students at a Grade 9 reading level:
- *The Battle of Gettysburg: Turning Point of the Civil War*, by Gina DeAngelis

For students at a Grade 10 reading level:
- *A Yankee Girl at Gettysburg,* by Alice Turner Curtis

For students at a Grade 11 reading level:
- *To Hold this Ground: A Desperate Battle at Gettysburg*, by Susan Provost Beller

For students at a Grade 12 reading level:
- *Outrageous Women of Civil War Times*, by Mary Rodd Furbee

Focus

MAKING CONNECTIONS
How Do Nations Fight and Recover from War?

Ask students to recall how the battles of the Revolutionary War were fought. Then, activate prior knowledge by asking them about what battle was like in the Civil War. Students may recall the massive casualties of major battles, the horrors of medical amputations, and trench warfare. **OL**

Teach

The Big Ideas

As students study the chapter, remind them to consider the section-based Big Ideas included in each section's Guide to Reading. The **Essential Questions** in the activities below tie in to the Big Ideas and help students think about and understand important chapter concepts. In addition, the Hands-on Chapter Projects with their culminating activities relate the content from each section to the Big Ideas. These activities build on each other as students progress through the chapter. Section activities culminate in the wrap-up activity on the Visual Summary page.

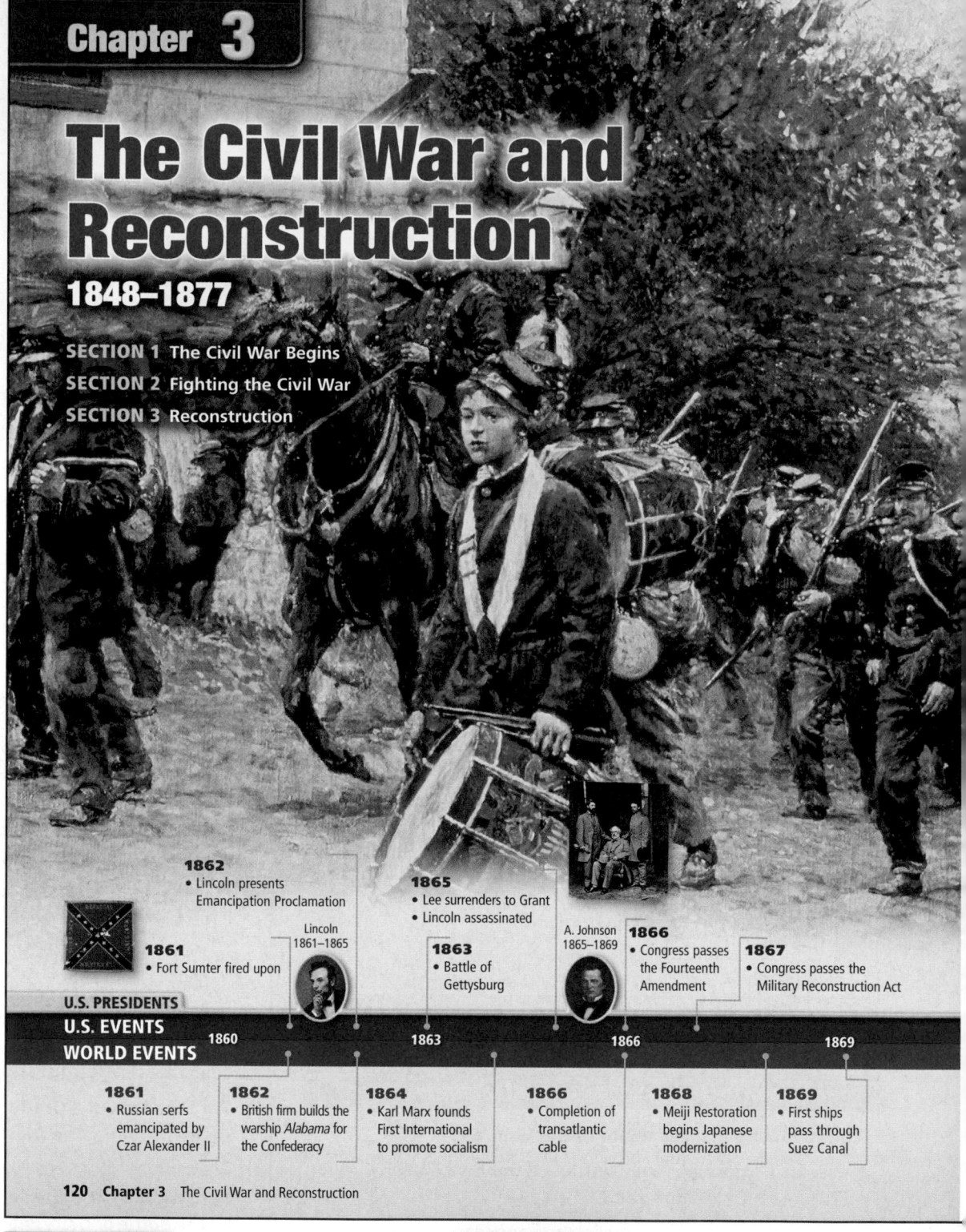

Chapter 3

The Civil War and Reconstruction
1848–1877

SECTION 1 The Civil War Begins
SECTION 2 Fighting the Civil War
SECTION 3 Reconstruction

1862
• Lincoln presents Emancipation Proclamation

1865
• Lee surrenders to Grant
• Lincoln assassinated

Lincoln 1861–1865

A. Johnson 1865–1869

1861
• Fort Sumter fired upon

1863
• Battle of Gettysburg

1866
• Congress passes the Fourteenth Amendment

1867
• Congress passes the Military Reconstruction Act

U.S. PRESIDENTS

U.S. EVENTS 1860 1863 1866 1869

WORLD EVENTS

1861
• Russian serfs emancipated by Czar Alexander II

1862
• British firm builds the warship *Alabama* for the Confederacy

1864
• Karl Marx founds First International to promote socialism

1866
• Completion of transatlantic cable

1868
• Meiji Restoration begins Japanese modernization

1869
• First ships pass through Suez Canal

120   **Chapter 3**   The Civil War and Reconstruction

Section 1

The Civil War Begins
Essential Question: What advantages and disadvantages did the North and the South have at the start of the Civil War? *(The North had a better transportation network, more factories, and a larger population; the South had valuable export crops and many top military leaders.)* Point out that in Section 1 students will learn how the Civil War began and how the fighting differed from earlier wars. **OL**

Section 2

Fighting the Civil War
Essential Question: How did the Emancipation Proclamation change the Civil War? *(By putting the abolition of slavery at the heart of the Union's war effort, the Emancipation Proclamation gave it a new moral dimension.)* Point out that in Section 2 students will learn about the naval war, Lee's invasion of the North, and the reasons that Lincoln issued the Emancipation Proclamation. **OL**

MAKING CONNECTIONS
How Do Nations Fight and Recover From War?

The Civil War was in many respects the first modern war. Both sides fielded large armies, and hundreds of thousands of soldiers were killed. Following the war, the nation faced major problems. American leaders had to find a way to reconcile Northerners and Southerners, restore Southern governments, and protect the rights of the formerly enslaved.

• *Why was the North able to defeat the South?*
• *What did the United States do to reconstruct the South?*

More About the Photo

Visual Literacy The Third Minnesota Infantry Regiment saw action in two different conflicts in the early 1860s. In July 1862, it took part in the campaign for Murfreesboro, Tennessee, during which it surrendered to Confederate forces. Shortly thereafter, however, the regiment was released and allowed to return to Minnesota to put down an uprising among the Sioux known as the Dakota War of 1862. This painting depicts the Third Minnesota Regiment in September 1863, back in the campaign against the Confederacy.

FOLDABLES Study Organizer **Dinah Zike's Foldables**

Dinah Zike's Foldables are three-dimensional, interactive graphic organizers that help students practice basic writing skills, review vocabulary terms, and identify main ideas. Instructions for creating and using Foldables can be found in the Appendix at the end of this book and in the *Dinah Zike's Reading and Study Skills Foldables* booklet.

FOLDABLES

Outlining Compromise Efforts Create a Half-Book Foldable that lists the failure of compromise efforts before the Civil War. Complete the chart by showing the series of compromises attempted. Describe each compromise effort on the left-hand column. In the right-hand column, describe the outcome of each compromise.

History ONLINE Chapter Overview
Visit glencoe.com to preview Chapter 3.

1870 • Fifteenth Amendment ratified

Grant 1869–1877

1875 • "Whiskey Ring" scandal breaks

1877 • Compromise of 1877 ends Reconstruction efforts

Hayes 1877–1881

1872 — 1875 — 1878

1871 • Germany is unified; the German Empire proclaimed

1874 • First Impressionist art exhibit opens in Paris

Chapter 3 The Civil War and Reconstruction **121**

History ONLINE
Introduce students to chapter content and key terms by having them access the Chapter 3 Overview at glencoe.com.

Section 3
Reconstruction
Essential Question: What key issues caused disagreements about how Reconstruction should take place? *(Under what conditions Southern states could organize state governments; oaths of loyalty; amnesty for high-ranking Confederates; protection of formerly enslaved African Americans' rights.)* Tell students that in this section they will learn about three plans for handling these issues, over which there was much debate. **OL**

Focus

Bellringer
Daily Focus Transparency 3.1

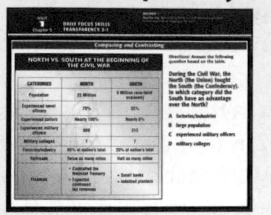

Guide to Reading

Answers:
Students' outlines should begin with the following points:
The Civil War Begins
The Union Dissolves
  I. The Election of 1860
    A. The Democrats Split
    B. Lincoln Is Elected
    C. Secession Begins
  II. Compromise Fails

Students should complete the outline by including all the heads in the section.

Section Spotlight Video

To generate student interest and provide a springboard for class discussion, access the Chapter 3, Section 1 video at glencoe.com or on the video DVD.

Resource Manager

Section 1

The Civil War Begins

Guide to Reading

Big Ideas
Struggles for Rights After Lincoln's election to the presidency, many Southerners placed state loyalty above loyalty to the Union.

Content Vocabulary
• martial law *(p. 126)*
• habeas corpus *(p. 128)*
• attrition *(p. 129)*

Academic Vocabulary
• sufficient *(p. 127)*
• implement *(p. 129)*

People and Events to Identify
• Crittenden's Compromise *(p. 124)*
• Jefferson Davis *(p. 125)*
• Confederacy *(p. 125)*
• Fort Sumter *(p. 125)*
• Robert E. Lee *(p. 126)*
• Anaconda Plan *(p. 129)*

Reading Strategy
Taking Notes Use the major headings in this section to record information about the events that led to the Civil War and the status of the opposing sides.

```
The Union Dissolves
I. The Election of 1860
    A.
    B.
    C.
II.
```

I n the end, all attempts at compromise between the North and South over slavery failed. The outcome of the 1860 election triggered the first shots of the long, bloody Civil War.

The Union Dissolves

MAIN Idea The election of Abraham Lincoln led the Southern states to secede from the Union.

HISTORY AND YOU Think of a time when you were unable to compromise over an issue. Read on to learn why Southern states refused to compromise in 1861 and instead decided to secede from the Union, sparking a bloody civil war.

John Brown's raid on Harpers Ferry became a turning point for the South. Many Southerners were terrified and enraged by the idea that Northerners would deliberately try to arm enslaved people and encourage them to rebel. Although Republican leaders quickly denounced Brown's raid, many Southern newspapers and politicians blamed Republicans for the attack. To many Southerners, the key point was that both the Republicans and Brown opposed slavery.

The Election of 1860

In April 1860, with the South still in an uproar, Democrats from across the United States gathered in Charleston, South Carolina, to choose their nominee for president.

The Democrats Split Southern Democrats wanted their party to uphold the *Dred Scott* decision and defend slaveholders' rights in the territories. Northern Democrats, led by Stephen Douglas, preferred to continue supporting popular sovereignty. When Northerners also rebuffed the idea of a federal slave code in the territories, 50 Southern delegates stormed out of the convention. The walkout meant that neither Douglas nor anyone else could muster the two-thirds majority needed to become the party's nominee.

In June 1860, the Democrats reconvened in Baltimore. Again, Southern delegates walked out. The remaining Democrats then chose Stephen Douglas as their candidate. The Southerners who had bolted organized their own convention in Richmond and nominated John C. Breckinridge of Kentucky, the sitting vice president.

Meanwhile, many former Whigs and others were alarmed at the prospect of Southern secession. They created a new party, the Constitutional Union Party, and chose former Tennessee senator John Bell to run for president. The party took no position on issues dividing

---

R Reading Strategies	**C** Critical Thinking	**D** Differentiated Instruction	**W** Writing Support	**S** Skill Practice
Teacher Edition • Organizing, p. 125 • Academic Vocab., p. 127 • Simulating, p. 128 **Additional Resources** • Reading Skills Act., URB p. 85 • Guide. Read. Act., URB p. 112	**Teacher Edition** • Identifying Central Issues, p. 126 **Additional Resources** • Supreme Court Case Studies, p. 13 • Quizzes/Tests, p. 29	**Teacher Edition** • Gifted/Talented, p. 123 • Interpersonal, p. 128 **Additional Resources** • Differentiated Instr. Act., URB p. 87 • English Learner Act., URB p. 89	**Teacher Edition** • Persuasive Writing, p. 124 **Additional Resources** • Prim. Source Read., URB p. 99 • Foldables, p. 55	**Teacher Edition** • Paraphrasing, p. 124 • Identifying Point of View, p. 125 • Creating a Circle Graph, p. 127 **Additional Resources** • RENTG, p. 25

POLITICAL CARTOONS PRIMARY SOURCE
The Election of 1860

After the slavery issue split the Democratic Party, the election of 1860 evolved into a four-way race. In the cartoon, the artist implies that Lincoln won because he had the best bat, which is labeled "equal rights and free territories," while the other candidates were for compromise or the extension of slavery.

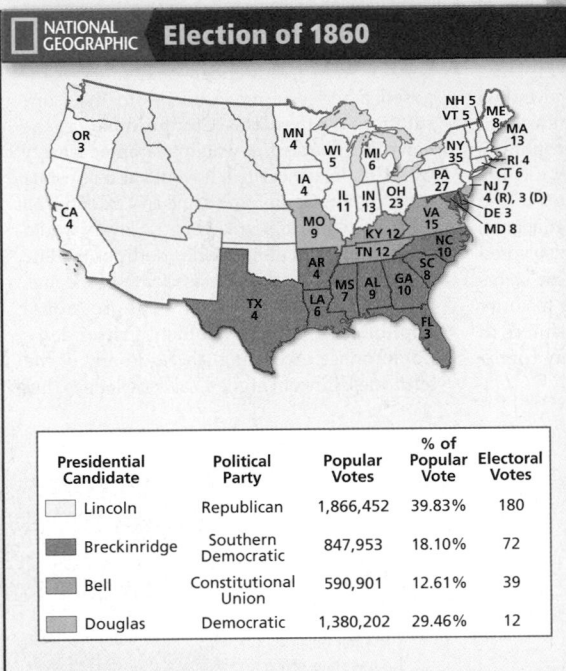

NATIONAL GEOGRAPHIC **Election of 1860**

Presidential Candidate	Political Party	Popular Votes	% of Popular Vote	Electoral Votes
Lincoln	Republican	1,866,452	39.83%	180
Breckinridge	Southern Democratic	847,953	18.10%	72
Bell	Constitutional Union	590,901	12.61%	39
Douglas	Democratic	1,380,202	29.46%	12

Stephen Douglas holds a bat labeled "Non-intervention" and blames Lincoln's rail for his loss.

John Breckinridge's bat is labeled "slavery extension" and his belt says Disunion Club.

John Bell's bat is labeled "Fusion" and his belt says Union Club.

Abraham Lincoln, the winner, stands on home base holding a rail labeled "Equal Rights and Free Territory."

Analyzing VISUALS DBQ

1. **Interpreting** How does the map show that Lincoln was a sectional candidate?
2. **Identifying Points of View** Do you think that the artist was sympathetic to abolition or not? Explain.

North and South. Their purpose, they said, was to uphold the Constitution and the Union.

Lincoln Is Elected The Republicans, realizing they stood no chance in the South, needed a candidate who could sweep most of the North. The most prominent Republican at the time was Senator William Seward from New York, but many Republicans did not think Seward had a wide enough appeal. Instead, they nominated Abraham Lincoln, who had gained a national reputation during his debates

with Douglas. Although he was not an abolitionist, Lincoln believed that slavery was morally wrong, and he opposed its spread into the western territories.

During the campaign the Republicans remained true to their free-soil principles, but they reaffirmed the right of the Southern states to preserve slavery within their borders. They also supported higher tariffs to protect manufacturers and workers, a new homestead law for settlers in the West, and federal funds for a transcontinental railroad. **D**

Teach

D Differentiated Instruction

Gifted and Talented Ask students to use library and Internet sources to research information about the political platforms and principles of the Republican Party between 1854 and 1876 and the party's principles today. Based on their research, have students write a three-page report comparing the party then and now. **AL**

Analyzing VISUALS

Answers:
1. He won no states south of the Ohio River.
2. Possible answer: Yes. The artist labels Lincoln's larger "bat" with the words "equal rights and free territory," and adds the words "wide awake" on Lincoln's belt. Also, Lincoln is saying that you need a "good bat," to hit a "fair ball." All these words are positive. Lincoln is standing tall and the others look somewhat ridiculous.

Hands-On Chapter Project
Step 1

Art Show on the Civil War and Reconstruction

Step 1: Researching the Topics
Essential Question: What events occurred during the Civil War and Reconstruction, and how can they be captured in images?

Directions Explain to students that they are going to create an art show of perhaps 10 images that they will hang in the classroom, a school hall, or foyer, complete with a title, a brief introduction near the beginning, and

the accompanying explanatory tags that will identify the images. In this step, two teams of students will: a) depict events of the Civil War and Reconstruction; and b) depict themes of the Civil War and Reconstruction. Teams will discuss how to depict events and themes of the Civil War and Reconstruction using images. (Students may choose to use graphic organizers, maps, charts, paintings, or drawings. Students may create their own images or find historical images online or in the library.)

Putting It Together After the two teams have selected four or five images, they should share them and see how they fit together. Each team should finalize their selections, and then begin creating them. **OL**
(Chapter Project is continued on page 131)

W **Writing Support**

Persuasive Writing Ask students to imagine that they are President-elect Abraham Lincoln in the winter of 1860–1861. Have students write an essay explaining what they, as Lincoln, think Congress should do to keep the Union together. **OL**

S **Skill Practice**

Paraphrasing Have students read the poster on the time line. Ask them to paraphrase its message. Then, ask students to speculate about what group or individual may have written and posted this message. **OL**

The Republican proposals angered many Southerners, but with the Democrats divided, Lincoln won the election by winning the electoral votes of all the free states except New Jersey, whose votes he split with Douglas.

Secession Begins Many Southerners viewed Lincoln's election as a threat to their society and culture, even their lives. They saw no choice but to secede. The dissolution of the Union began with South Carolina. Shortly after Lincoln's election, the state legislature called for a convention. On December 20, 1860, amid marching bands, fireworks, and militia drills, the convention voted unanimously to repeal the state's ratification of the Constitution and dissolve its ties to the Union.

By February 1, 1861, six more states in the Lower South—Mississippi, Florida, Alabama, Georgia, Louisiana, and Texas—had also voted to secede. Although a minority in these states did not want to leave the Union, the majority of Southerners viewed secession as similar to the American Revolution—a necessary course of action to uphold people's rights.

Compromise Fails

W

Although Lincoln was elected president in November 1860, he would not be inaugurated until the following March. The Union's initial response to secession was the responsibility of President Buchanan. Declaring that the government had no authority to forcibly preserve the Union, Buchanan urged Congress to be conciliatory.

Crittenden's Compromise In December, Senator John J. Crittenden of Kentucky proposed a series of amendments to the Constitution. **Crittenden's Compromise,** as the newspapers called it, would guarantee slavery where it already existed. It would also reinstate the Missouri Compromise line and extend it all the way to the California border. Slavery would be prohibited in all territories north of the line and protected in all territories south of the line.

At Lincoln's request, congressional Republicans voted against Crittenden's Compromise. Accepting slavery in any of the territories, Lincoln argued, "acknowledges that

Steps to Civil War, 1846–1860

▲ David Wilmot

1846
Wilmot Proviso proposing to ban slavery in Mexican cession enrages Southerners

1848
Free-Soil Party is founded by Northern antislavery Whigs, Democrats, and members of the Liberty Party

1850
Compromise of 1850 allows California to enter Union as a free state, giving free states a Senate majority, but the new Fugitive Slave law enrages Northerners

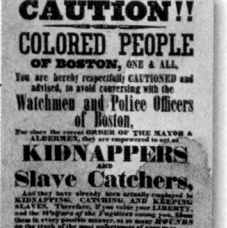

S

1846   **1848**   **1850**   **1852**

1847
Vice President George Dallas proposes popular sovereignty; Democrat Lewis Cass popularizes the idea, angering Northern antislavery Democrats

1849
California Gold Rush brings flood of settlers; California applies for statehood

1852
Uncle Tom's Cabin is published

Extending the Content

Abolition Abraham Lincoln opposed the expansion of slavery into new territories, but did not propose to abolish slavery. In his election campaign of 1860, he promised not to interfere with slavery where it already legally existed (the Southern states). Indeed, even after he won the election, he wrote to future vice president of the Confederacy, Alexander H. Stephens: "Do the people of the South really entertain fears that a Republican administration would, *directly,* or *indirectly,* interfere with their slaves, or with them, about their slaves? If they do, I wish to assure you, as once a friend, and still, I hope, not an enemy, that there is no cause for such fears."

Additional Support

slavery has equal rights with liberty, and surrenders all we have contended for."

Founding the Confederacy On February 8, 1861, delegates from the seceding states met in Montgomery, Alabama, where they declared themselves to be a new nation—the Confederate States of America. They drafted a constitution similar to the U.S. Constitution but with major changes. The Confederate Constitution acknowledged the independence of each state, guaranteed slavery in Confederate territory, banned tariffs, and limited the president to a single six-year term.

The convention delegates chose former Mississippi senator **Jefferson Davis** to be president. In his inaugural address, Davis declared, "The time for compromise has now passed." He then called on the remaining Southern states to join the **Confederacy.**

The Civil War Begins

In his inaugural address on March 4, 1861, President Lincoln again promised not to inter-

fere with slavery where it existed but insisted that "the Union of these States is perpetual." Lincoln encouraged reconciliation:

PRIMARY SOURCE

"In your hands, my dissatisfied countrymen, and not in mine is the momentous issue of civil war. The government will not assail you. You can have no conflict, without yourselves being the aggressors. . . . We must not be enemies. Though passion may have strained, it must not break our bonds of affection."

—from Lincoln's First Inaugural Address

Fort Sumter Falls In April Lincoln announced that he intended to resupply **Fort Sumter** in Charleston Harbor, one of the few federal military bases that Southerners had not already seized. Confederate President Jefferson Davis now faced a problem. To tolerate U.S. troops in the South's most vital Atlantic harbor seemed unacceptable for a sovereign nation. However, firing on the supply ship would undoubtedly provoke war. Jefferson decided to demand the surrender of Fort Sumter before the supply ship arrived.

1854
Kansas-Nebraska Act crafted by Stephen Douglas repeals Missouri Compromise; Republican Party is founded

1856
Charles Sumner is caned in the Senate

1858
Abraham Lincoln wins national attention during Lincoln-Douglas debates

1859
John Brown raids Harpers Ferry

1860
Lincoln is elected; secession begins

1854 1856 1858 1860

1856
Border ruffians attack antislavery settlers in Lawrence, Kansas; John Brown leads attack on pro-slavery settlers in Pottawatomie Creek, Kansas

1857
Dred Scott decision allowing slavery in all federal territories enrages Northerners

▲ Antislavery settlers in Kansas

Analyzing TIME LINES

1. **Specifying** How many years elapsed between the Compromise of 1850 and the beginning of the Civil War?
2. **Identifying** Which came first—the *Dred Scott* decision or the Wilmot Proviso?

R Reading Strategy

Organizing Have students create a chart listing the states in one of three categories: *Free States, Slave States that Seceded,* and *Slave States That Did Not Secede.* **OL**

S Skill Practice

Identifying Point of View
Ask students to read Lincoln's First Inaugural Address and then write a few paragraphs explaining the quote. **Ask:** What message is Lincoln sending to the seceding states? What is his tone? *(He is reminding the South that despite differences, the United States must remain united; his tone is conciliatory.)* **OL**

Analyzing TIME LINES

Answers:
1. 10 years until Lincoln is elected; 11 years until the first shots are fired
2. the Wilmot Proviso

Additional Support

Activity: Connecting with the United States

Comparing and Contrasting Provide students with a copy of the Constitution of the Confederate States of America (available online from the Library of Congress at http://memory.loc.gov/ammem/amlaw/lwcc.html) and ask them to compare it to the Constitution of the United States of America in their textbook. Have students prepare an outline that lists the points upon which the two documents agree and

disagree. **Ask: On which points do the two documents agree? On which points are the two documents different?** *(Similarities: Students should note that the basic framework for government is the same and presented in the same order. Direct students to Article I, Section 9 and Article 6, Section 5 of the Confederate Constitution and ask them to compare these sections to the Bill of Rights. **Differences:** In addition to replac-*

ing "United States" with "Confederate States," the Constitution of the Confederacy uses the term slave while the U.S. Constitution uses "other persons." Direct students to examine closely those sections of the Confederate Constitution that deal with slavery and the rights of slaveholders.) **AL**

C Critical Thinking

Identifying Central Issues
Tell students that under martial law, anyone supporting secession—or suspected of supporting secession—could be arrested and held without trial. **Ask: What rights do you think people in Maryland referred to in their objections?** (Students might mention either individual rights guaranteed in the Bill of Rights or the interference of the federal government in states' rights.) **OL**

Did You Know?

Northwestern Virginians—mostly owners of small farms—did not see why they should leave the Union to protect the rights of plantation slaveholders. In 1861, the northwestern counties applied for statehood as West Virginia.

✓ Reading Check

Answer:
Northern Democrats supported popular sovereignty to decide the issue of slavery in the territories.

Additional Support

The fort's commander, U.S. Army Major Robert Anderson, refused. Confederate forces then bombarded Fort Sumter for 33 hours on April 12 and 13, until Anderson and his exhausted men gave up. No one had been killed, but the Civil War had begun.

The Upper South Secedes After the fall of Fort Sumter, President Lincoln called for 75,000 volunteers to serve in the military for 90 days. Lincoln's action created a crisis in the Upper South. Many people in those states did not want to secede, but they were not willing to take up arms against fellow Southerners. Between April 17 and June 8, 1861, four more states chose to leave the Union—Virginia, Arkansas, North Carolina, and Tennessee. The Confederate Congress then established Richmond, Virginia, as the capital.

Holding the Border States With the Upper South gone, Lincoln could not afford to lose the slaveholding border states as well. Delaware seemed safe, but Lincoln worried about Kentucky, Missouri, and particularly Maryland. Virginia's secession had placed a Confederate state across the Potomac River from the nation's capital. If Maryland joined the South, Washington, D.C., would be surrounded by Confederate territory. To prevent Maryland's secession, Lincoln imposed **martial law**—military rule—in Baltimore, where angry mobs had already attacked federal troops. Although many people objected to this suspension of their rights, Maryland stayed in the Union.

Kentucky initially declared neutrality in the conflict, but when Confederate troops occupied part of Kentucky, the state declared war on the Confederacy, and Lincoln sent troops to help. In Missouri, despite strong public support for the Confederacy, the state convention voted to stay in the Union. Federal troops then ended fights between the pro-Union government and secessionists.

The war shattered old loyalties and made enemies of former friends. For the next several years, the bloody war between the states divided Americans and resulted in hundreds of thousands of casualties.

✓ Reading Check **Explaining** Why did Southern Democrats walk out of the Democratic Convention?

The Opposing Sides

MAIN Idea The North and South each had distinct advantages and disadvantages at the beginning of the Civil War.

HISTORY AND YOU Do you believe limiting civil liberties during wartime is justified? Read on to learn how President Lincoln decided to suspend writs of habeas corpus during the Civil War.

On the same day that he learned his home state of Virginia had voted to secede from the Union, **Robert E. Lee**—one of the best senior officers in the United States Army—received an offer from General Winfield Scott to command Union troops. Although Lee had spoken against secession and considered slavery "a moral and political evil," he refused to fight against the South. Instead, he offered his services to the Confederacy.

Lee was one of hundreds of military officers who resigned to join the Confederacy. In 1860 seven of the nation's eight military colleges were in the South. These colleges provided the region with a large number of trained officers to quickly organize an effective fighting force.

Just as the South had a strong military tradition, the North had a strong naval tradition. More than three-quarters of the Navy's officers came from the North, and the crews of American merchant ships were almost entirely from the North. They provided a large pool of trained sailors for the Union navy as it expanded.

The Opposing Economies

Although the South had many experienced officers to lead its troops in battle, the North had several economic advantages. In 1860 the population of the North was about 22 million, while the South had about 9 million people. The North's larger population gave it a great advantage in raising an army and in supporting the war effort.

Industry The North's industries also gave the region an important economic advantage over the South. In 1860 almost 90 percent of the nation's factories were located in the Northern states. The North could provide its troops with ammunition and other supplies more easily. In addition, the South had only half as many miles of railroad track as the North and had only one line—from Memphis

---

Activity: Technology Connection

Synthesizing Have students consider how the Civil War would have been reported using modern communications methods. **Ask: Do you think modern reporting might have gained the South the international diplomatic support it sought? Why or why not?** Have students consider how the Civil War might be covered today via media such as international satellite broadcasts, instant electronic communications, and Internet blogs. Then, ask students to predict whether more intense international coverage of the war would have won more or less support for the Confederate cause. (Answers will vary.) **OL**

INFOGRAPHIC
The Opposing Sides

▲ Confederate soldiers of the 3rd Georgia Infantry (above) fought under Lee's command during the Peninsula campaign. The Confederacy had fewer soldiers but many of the nation's best officers.

▲ Men of the 110th Pennsylvania Infantry Regiment at Falmouth, Virginia, April 1863. Union troops were generally better equipped than Confederate forces.

Analyzing VISUALS

1. **Interpreting** Based on the graph, what were the North's greatest advantages over the South?

2. **Assessing** Which of the North's advantages do you think were most important in winning the war? Why?

Resources of the Union and of the Confederacy

	Union	Confederacy
Population	71%	29%
Manufactured goods	92%	8%
Exports	56%	44%
Merchant ships	90%	10%
Miles of railroad track	72%	28%
Number of farms	67%	33%
Iron production	94%	6%
Banking capital	82%	18%

Source: *Historical Statistics of the United States.*

to Chattanooga—connecting the western states of the Confederacy to the east. This made it much easier for Northern troops to disrupt the Southern rail system and prevent the movement of supplies and troops.

Financing the War The Union also controlled the national treasury and could expect continued revenue from tariffs. Many Northern banks also held large reserves of cash, which they lent the government by purchasing bonds.

In order to make more money available for emergency use, Congress also passed the Legal Tender Act, creating a national currency and allowing the government to issue paper money. The paper money came to be known as greenbacks, because of its color.

In contrast to the Union, the Confederacy's financial situation was poor, and it became worse over time. Most Southern planters were in debt and unable to buy bonds. Southern banks were small and had few cash reserves; as a result, they could not buy many bonds either. The best hope for the South to raise money was by taxing trade. Then, shortly after the war began, the Union Navy blockaded Southern ports, which reduced trade and, as a result, tax revenues. The Confederacy had to resort to direct taxation of its people, but many Southerners refused to pay.

Lacking **sufficient** money from taxes or bonds, the Confederacy was forced to print paper money to pay its bills. This caused rapid inflation in the South, and Confederate paper money eventually became almost worthless. By the end of the war, the South had experienced 9,000 percent inflation, compared to only 80 percent in the North.

Chapter 3 The Civil War and Reconstruction **127**

Activity: Collaborative Learning

R Reading Strategy

Simulating Have students take on the role of an army recruiter addressing potential soldiers. Have students write newspaper articles listing five reasons to enlist in the Union Army. **OL**

D Differentiated Instruction

Interpersonal Ask students if they know anyone who has served in the military or Peace Corps. Ask how that person kept in touch with family and friends. Then, encourage students to consider how Civil War soldiers communicated with their families. **OL BL**

Analyzing VISUALS

Answers:
1. Hot air balloons made it possible to view the location of the enemy's troops, enabling military leaders to plan more elaborate strategies for attack.
2. Generals learned the results of battles and could transmit orders long distance almost immediately.

Additional Support

The Political Situation

Although many Republicans wanted to end slavery, Lincoln wanted to preserve the Union, even if it meant allowing slavery to continue. The president also had to contend with the Democrats. A faction known as the War Democrats supported a war to save the Union but opposed ending slavery. Peace Democrats wanted to negotiate instead of fighting a war.

One major disagreement between Republicans and Democrats concerned conscription—or forcing people through a draft into military service. In 1862, Congress passed a militia law requiring states to use conscription if they could not recruit enough volunteers, but many Democrats opposed it.

Criticism also greeted President Lincoln's decision to suspend writs of **habeas corpus.** A writ of habeas corpus is a court order that requires the government to charge an imprisoned person with a crime or let the person go free. When writs of habeas corpus are suspended, a person can be imprisoned indefinitely without trial. In this case, President Lincoln suspended the writ for anyone who openly supported the rebels or encouraged others to resist the militia draft. "Must I shoot a simple-minded soldier boy who deserts," the president asked, "while I must not touch a hair of a wily agitator who induces him to desert?

Although the South had no organized opposition party, Confederate president Jefferson Davis also faced political problems. The Confederate constitution protected states' rights and limited the central government's power. This interfered with Davis's ability to conduct the war. Some Southern leaders opposed Davis when he supported conscription and established martial law early in 1862. They also opposed the suspension of writs of habeas corpus, which the South, like the North, had introduced.

D TECHNOLOGY & HISTORY

Civil War Technology Military conflict often leads to the use of new technologies. The Civil War was no exception. New weapons, ships and means of communication greatly changed the nature of warfare.

▲ **Conoidal Bullets**
These new bullets made gunfire more accurate at greater ranges and increased the number of casualties.

▲ **Telegraph**
Invented before the war, the telegraph let generals learn the results of battles almost immediately, and change their strategy and give new orders quickly.

▲ **Balloons**
The Civil War marked the first time aerial reconnaissance was used in war. Both sides used balloons to observe enemy troops.

◄ **Ironclads**
To operate on enemy rivers and coast lines guarded by shore-based cannon, both sides built armor-plated steamships. Ironclads marked the beginning of the shift from wooden ships to steel ships.

Analyzing VISUALS

1. **Explaining** How did balloons change warfare?
2. **Describing** How did the telegraph help both sides fight the war?

Activity: Interdisciplinary Connection

Science Invite a physics teacher or physicist to explain the science behind the effectiveness of the conoidal bullet. Ask the speaker to use and define scientific terminology and to demonstrate the applicable laws of physics. **OL**

The outbreak of the Civil War put the major governments of Europe in a difficult situation. The Union government did not want the Europeans interfering in the war, but Southern leaders wanted them to recognize the Confederacy and provide it with military aid. Southern leaders knew that European textile factories depended on Southern cotton. To pressure the British and French, many Southern planters agreed to stop selling their cotton in these markets until the Europeans recognized the Confederacy. Despite these efforts, both countries chose not to go to war against the United States.

The First Modern War

The North and South were about to embark on what was, in many respects, the first modern war. Unlike earlier European wars, the Civil War involved huge armies that consisted mostly of civilian volunteers and required vast amounts of supplies.

Military Technology By the 1850s, French and American inventors had developed an inexpensive conoidal—or cone-shaped—bullet that was accurate at much greater distances. At the same time, instead of standing in a line, troops defending positions began to use trenches and barricades to protect themselves. This resulted in much higher casualties. **Attrition**—the wearing down of one side by the other through exhaustion of soldiers and resources—also played a critical role as the war dragged on.

The South's Strategy Early in the war, Jefferson Davis imagined a struggle similar to the American war for independence. Southern generals would pick their battles carefully, attacking and retreating when necessary to avoid heavy losses. By waging a defensive war of attrition, Davis believed the South could force the Union to spend its resources until it became tired of the war and agreed to negotiate. Although this strategy made sense, Davis felt great pressure to strike for a quick victory. Many Southerners believed that their military traditions made them superior fighters. In the war, Southern troops went on the offensive in eight battles, suffering 20,000 more casualties than the Union by charging enemy lines. These were heavy losses the South could not afford.

The Union's Anaconda Plan The general in chief of the United States, Winfield Scott, suggested that the Union blockade Confederate ports and send gunboats down the Mississippi River to divide the Confederacy in two. The South, thus separated, would gradually run out of resources and surrender. Many Northerners rejected the strategy, which they called the **Anaconda Plan,** after a snake that slowly strangles its prey to death. They thought it was too slow and indirect for certain victory. Lincoln eventually agreed to **implement** Scott's suggestions and imposed a blockade of Southern ports. He and other Union leaders realized that only a long war that focused on destroying the South's armies had any chance of success.

✔ **Reading Check** **Comparing** In what areas did the opposing sides have advantages and disadvantages?

Section 1 REVIEW

Vocabulary
1. **Explain** the significance of: Crittenden's Compromise, Jefferson Davis, Confederacy, Fort Sumter, martial law, Robert E. Lee, habeas corpus, attrition, Anaconda Plan.

Main Ideas
2. **Identifying** Where and under what circumstances did the American Civil War begin?

3. **Explaining** Why did the South resort to using paper money during the war?

Critical Thinking
4. **Big Ideas** How did the Southerners' belief in states' rights hamper the Confederate government during the war?

5. **Organizing** Using a graphic organizer similar to the one below, list the military innovations of the Civil War era.

Military Innovations

6. **Analyzing Visuals** Examine the conoidal bullets shown on page 128. How did conoidal bullets affect the war effort? What other innovations made the Civil War the first "modern" war?

Writing About History
7. **Persuasive Writing** Suppose you are living in one of the border states at the beginning of the Civil War. Write a letter to a relative explaining why you are planning to join either the Union or Confederate army.

History ONLINE
Study Central™ To review this section, go to glencoe.com and click on Study Central.

129

✔ **Reading Check**

Answer:
The South had a strong military tradition, no organized opposition party, a smaller population, and weaker economy. The North had a strong naval tradition, a larger population, and more industry; controlled the national treasury; and had to deal with political turmoil.

Assess
· · · · · · · · · · · · · · · · · · · ·

History ONLINE

Study Central™ provides summaries, interactive games, and online graphic organizers to help students review content.

Close
· · · · · · · · · · · · · · · · · · · ·

Contrasting Have students contrast the effects of the war on the economies of the North and the South. **OL**

Section 1 REVIEW

Answers

1. All definitions can be found in the section and the Glossary.

2. The Confederacy attacked Fort Sumter in Charleston Harbor, which belonged to the United States, forcing the Union troops there to surrender.

3. The Confederacy was unable to raise sufficient funds from taxes or bonds.

4. The South lacked a strong central government needed to coordinate the war effort.

5. huge armies, civilian volunteers, conoidal bullets, trenches and barricades

6. Conoidal bullets caused high casualty rates; other innovations included quick-loading rifles, new defensive strategies such as trenches and barricades.

7. Students' letters will vary, but should offer plausible scenarios about the decision to join one side or the other.

Focus

Bellringer
Daily Focus Transparency 3.2

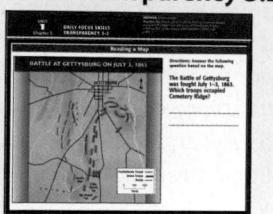

Guide to Reading

Answers:
First Battle of Bull Run: Confederate victory; Battle of Shiloh: Union victory, both sides suffered high casualties; Seven Days' Battle: no decisive victory, heavy casualties, Union retreated; Second Battle of Bull Run: Confederate victory, invasion of Maryland; Antietam: Bloodiest one-day battle in American history, Lee retreated due to such high casualties

Section Spotlight Video

To generate student interest and provide a springboard for class discussion, access the Chapter 3, Section 2 video at glencoe.com or on the video DVD.

Resource Manager

Fighting the Civil War

Guide to Reading

Big Ideas
Individual Action In the final year of the war, Grant refused to let up the pressure the Union forces were putting on Lee's weary troops.

Content Vocabulary
- blockade runner (p. 130)
- siege (p. 134)
- mandate (p. 137)

Academic Vocabulary
- crucial (p. 133)
- guarantee (p. 137)

People and Events to Identify
- "Stonewall" Jackson (p. 130)
- Ulysses S. Grant (p. 131)
- Battle of Antietam (p. 133)
- Emancipation Proclamation (p. 133)
- Gettysburg (p. 134)
- William Tecumseh Sherman (p. 136)
- Thirteenth Amendment (p. 137)

Reading Strategy
Categorizing Complete a graphic organizer similar to the one below by filling in the results of each battle listed.

Battle	Results
First Battle of Bull Run	
Battle of Shiloh	
Seven Days' Battle	
Second Battle of Bull Run	
Antietam	

Despite early losses, with the help of key victories at Vicksburg and Gettysburg, the North defeated the South after four long years of fighting. Debate over slavery continued until President Lincoln decided that the time was right for emancipation.

The Early Stages

MAIN Idea With Union casualties rising, President Lincoln issued the Emancipation Proclamation.

HISTORY AND YOU Do you know someone who experienced rationing during World War II? Read on to learn how the war affected daily life.

Soon after the Civil War began, President Lincoln approved an assault on Confederate troops gathered near Manassas Junction, Virginia, only 25 miles (40 km) south of Washington, D.C. The First Battle of Bull Run, as it came to be called, started well for the Union as it forced Confederate troops to retreat. Then the tide turned when reinforcements under the command of **Thomas J. "Stonewall" Jackson** helped the Confederates defeat the Union forces. This outcome made it clear that the North would need a large, well-trained army to prevail against the South.

Lincoln had originally called for 75,000 men to serve for three months. The day after Bull Run, he signed a bill for the enlistment of 500,000 men for three years. The North initially tried to encourage voluntary enlistment by offering a bounty—a sum of money given as a bonus—to individuals who promised three years of military service. Eventually both the Union and the Confederacy instituted the draft.

The Naval War

While the Union and Confederacy mobilized their armies, President Lincoln proclaimed a blockade of all Confederate ports in an effort to cut Confederate trade with the world. Although the blockade became increasingly effective as the war dragged on, Union vessels were thinly spread and found it difficult to stop all the **blockade runners**—small, fast vessels the South used to smuggle goods past the blockade. The South could ship at least some of its cotton to Europe in exchange for shoes, rifles, and other supplies.

As part of its effort to close Southern ports, the Union navy decided to seize New Orleans—the South's largest city and a center of the cotton trade. In April 1862, forty-two warships under the command of Admiral David G. Farragut fought their way up the Mississippi to New Orleans and unloaded some 15,000 Union troops. Six days later, the troops took control of the city.

R Reading Strategies	**C** Critical Thinking	**D** Differentiated Instruction	**W** Writing Support	**S** Skill Practice
Teacher Edition • Outlining, p. 134 • Determining Importance, p. 135 • Using Context Clues, p. 135 **Additional Resources** • Guide. Read. Act., URB p. 113	**Teacher Edition** • Evaluating, p. 137 **Additional Resources** • Linking Past and Present, URB p. 98 • Quizzes/Tests, p. 30	**Teacher Edition** • Verbal/Linguistic, p. 132 • Visual/Spatial, p. 136 **Additional Resources** • Enrichment Act., URB p. 109	**Teacher Edition** • Descriptive, p. 133 **Additional Resources** • Foldables, p. 56	**Teacher Edition** • Visual Literacy, p. 132 • Identifying Point of View, p. 134 **Additional Resources** • RENTG, p. 23

NATIONAL GEOGRAPHIC **The Early Years of the Civil War, 1861–1863**

Union states
Confederate states
Union blockade
Union forces
Confederate forces
Union victory
Confederate victory
Inconclusive battle

▲ The Battle of Shiloh resulted in enormous casualties.

ATLANTIC OCEAN

0   200 kilometers
0   200 miles
Albers Equal-Area projection

Analyzing GEOGRAPHY

1. **Location** Name four battles that occurred along the eastern seaboard.
2. **Movement** What purpose did the North have in fighting so many battles along the coasts?

Teach

Did You Know?

Union Blockade
Historians disagree over whether or not the Union blockade of the Confederacy was a success. Although most blockade runners made it through the blockade, their impact on the war's outcome remains questionable. By the end of the war, the Confederacy was suffering from a lack of supplies, weakening its ability to continue fighting.

Analyzing GEOGRAPHY

Answers:
1. Answers may include Hampton Roads, Roanoke Island, Cape Hatteras, Fort Sumter, Port Royal, and Ft. Pulaski.
2. The North wanted to control the coastline to cut off supplies headed for the Confederacy.

The War in the West

In February 1862, as Farragut prepared for his attack on New Orleans, Union general **Ulysses S. Grant** began a campaign to seize control of the Cumberland and Tennessee Rivers. Control of these rivers would cut Tennessee in two and provide the Union with a river route deep into Confederate territory.

All of Kentucky and most of western Tennessee fell into Union hands. Grant next headed up the Tennessee River to attack

Corinth, Mississippi. Seizing Corinth would cut the Confederacy's only rail line connecting Mississippi and western Tennessee to the east. Early on April 6, 1862, Confederate forces launched a surprise attack on Grant's troops, near a small church named Shiloh. The Union won the Battle of Shiloh the following day, but both sides paid an enormous cost. Twenty thousand troops had been killed or wounded. When newspapers demanded Grant be fired because of the high casualties, Lincoln refused, saying, "I can't spare this man; he fights."

Chapter 3 The Civil War and Reconstruction **131**

Hands-On Chapter Project
Step 2

Art Show on the Civil War and Reconstruction

Step 2: Selecting the Paintings for the Art Exhibit Essential Question:
What art best represents the Civil War and Reconstruction, and why?

Directions Student teams will continue to create their images. In this step, students will determine which members of their team will create the informational tags that will accompany the images in the art

show. The informational tags should be typed sheets that include the following information:

- Image title
- Brief summary of how the image relates to the Civil War and/or Reconstruction
- Media (oil, watercolor, drawing, and so on)
- Date of completion
- Any other pertinent information

Putting It Together In one or two sittings, students should review the submissions and decide which will be hung in the exhibit. (School policy and space may determine if this ends up being an actual exhibit or a virtual exhibit.) **OL**

(Chapter Project is continued on page 141)

Turning Point

▲ President Lincoln meets General George McClellan (left center, facing Lincoln) after the Battle of Antietam.

◀ With their backs to Antietam Creek, Union troops under the command of General McClellan attack Confederate positions, September 17, 1862.

The Battle of Antietam and the Emancipation Proclamation

The Battle of Antietam marked an important turning point in the war. The Union's victory kept Britain from recognizing the Confederacy as a separate nation. If Britain had taken this action, the balance in the struggle might have tipped in favor of the Confederacy. Also, the victory at Antietam and the terribly high casualties brought President Lincoln to the decision that the time had come to end slavery in the South by issuing the Emancipation Proclamation. The Proclamation was the first step toward finally outlawing slavery throughout the United States.

ANALYZING HISTORY How did emancipation change the war? Write a brief essay explaining your opinion.

▲ Lincoln reads the Emancipation Proclamation to members of his cabinet. Left of Lincoln are Secretary of War Edwin M. Stanton and Secretary of the Treasury Salmon P. Chase. In front of the table sits Secretary of State William Seward.

For the text of the Emancipation Proclamation, see page R49 in **Documents in American History.**

The War in the East

While Grant fought in the West, Union General George B. McClellan's forces set out to capture Richmond, Virginia, the Confederate capital. In late June 1862, Confederate General Robert E. Lee began a series of attacks on McClellan's forces that became known as the Seven Days' Battle. Lee's attacks forced the Union troops to retreat. Together the two sides suffered over 30,000 casualties.

As McClellan's forces withdrew, Lee marched toward Union forces defending Washington. The maneuver led to another battle at Bull Run.

The South again forced the North to retreat, leaving the Confederates only 20 miles (32 km) from Washington, D.C. Soon after, Lee's forces invaded Maryland.

Both Lee and Jefferson Davis believed that an invasion would convince the North to accept the South's independence. They also thought that a victory on Northern soil might help the South win recognition from the British and help the Peace Democrats gain control of Congress in the upcoming elections. Lee could also feed his troops from Northern farms and draw Union troops out of Virginia during harvest season.

132 **Chapter 3** The Civil War and Reconstruction

On September 17, 1862, Lee's forces met Union troops under the command of General McClellan at Antietam (an·TEE·tuhm) Creek. The fight was the bloodiest one-day battle in American history, ending with over 6,000 men killed and another 16,000 wounded. McClellan did not break Lee's lines, but he inflicted so many casualties that Lee decided to retreat to Virginia.

The **Battle of Antietam** was a **crucial** victory for the Union. The British government had been ready to intervene in the war as a mediator if Lee's invasion had succeeded. Britain also had begun making plans to recognize the Confederacy should the North reject mediation. Now the British decided to wait and see how the war progressed. With this decision, the South lost its best chance at gaining international recognition and support. The South's defeat at Antietam had an even more important political impact in the United States. It convinced Lincoln that the time had come to end slavery in the South.

Proclaiming Emancipation

Most Democrats opposed any move to end slavery, while Republicans were divided on the issue. With Northern casualties rising, however, many Northerners began to agree that slavery had to end, in part to punish the South and in part to make the soldiers' sacrifices worthwhile. On September 22, 1862, encouraged by the Union victory at Antietam, Lincoln publicly announced that he would issue the **Emancipation Proclamation**—a decree freeing all enslaved persons in states still in rebellion after January 1, 1863.

Because the Proclamation freed enslaved African Americans only in states at war with the Union, it did not address slavery in the border states. Short of a constitutional amendment, Lincoln could not end slavery in the border states, nor did he want to endanger their loyalty. The Proclamation, by its very existence, transformed the conflict over preserving the Union into a war of liberation.

Life During the Civil War

As the war intensified, the economies of the North and South went in different directions. By the end of 1862, the South's economy had begun to suffer greatly. The collapse of its transportation system and the presence of Union troops in several important agricultural regions led to severe food shortages in the winter of 1862. In several communities, food shortages led to riots. Hearing of such hardships, many Confederate soldiers deserted to return home to help their families.

In contrast, the North actually experienced an economic boom because of the war. With its large, well-established banking industry, the North raised money for the war more easily than the South. Its growing industries also supplied Union troops with clothes, munitions, and other necessities.

Daily Life Both Union and Confederate soldiers endured a hard life with few comforts. They faced the constant threat of disease and extreme medical procedures if injured in battle. Life for prisoners of war was just as difficult, especially in Southern prisons that faced food shortages.

Innovations in agriculture helped minimize the loss of labor as men left to fight. Greater use of mechanical reapers and mowers made farming possible with fewer workers, many of whom were women. Women also filled labor shortages in various industries, particularly in clothing and shoemaking factories.

African Americans While the war brought hardship to many Americans, it offered new opportunities for African Americans. The Emancipation Proclamation officially permitted African Americans to enlist in the Union army and navy. Almost immediately, thousands of African Americans rushed to join the military.

Women Women helped in the war effort at home by managing family farms and businesses. Perhaps their most important contribution to the Civil War was in serving as nurses to the wounded. One of the most prominent war nurses was Clara Barton, who left her job in a Washington patent office to aid soldiers on the battlefield. The Civil War was a turning point for the American nursing profession. The courage shown by women helped break down the belief that women were emotionally weaker than men.

Reading Check **Analyzing** Why do you think African Americans were willing to volunteer to fight?

History ONLINE Student Web Activity Visit glencoe.com and complete the activity on Civil War letters.

W Writing Support
Descriptive Have students imagine themselves as a soldier in the 54th Massachusetts regiment, an African American unit. **Ask:** What does it mean to you to participate in the war? What are your goals as a soldier and free African American? Have students write a journal entry answering the question. **OL**

Reading Check
Answer:
Answers will vary. One possible answer is that African Americans saw volunteering to fight in the war as a way to ensure their freedom from enslavement.

Additional Support

Activity: Interdisciplinary Activity

Health Ask a health care professional to speak to the class about first aid and infection prevention. Have students describe to the professional some of the unsanitary conditions that existed in battlefield hospitals during the Civil War. Then ask the speaker to describe how modern facilities and techniques would have prevented many of the diseases and infections (and amputations and deaths) that occurred. **OL BL**

R Reading Strategy

Outlining As students read about "The Turning Point," have them take notes using the headings found in the text. Students may want to use an outline to help them organize the information. Remind students that although they do not have to write complete sentences, they should be able to understand what they have written. After students read the section, ask questions about what they have read. Students should use their notes to help answer the questions.
OL **BL** **ELL**

S Skill Practice

Identifying Point of View Tell students to imagine that they are newspaper reporters covering the Battle of Gettysburg. Have each student write two accounts of the battle, one for a Northern newspaper, and one for a Southern newspaper. **OL**

Additional Support

R The Turning Point

MAIN Idea Key victories at Vicksburg and Gettysburg helped the North defeat the South.

HISTORY AND YOU Recall a time when you faced a situation you had been dreading. Did the outcome surprise you? Read on to learn about Confederate General Robert E. Lee's surrender to Ulysses S. Grant.

As 1863 began, there was no end to the war in sight. More than two years of battle lay ahead for Americans, and the casualties would continue to rise steeply. Still, 1863 marked the turning point of the war. Three major Union victories put the Confederacy on the defensive and set the stage for its surrender.

Vicksburg

Gaining control of the Mississippi River was a vital element of the Union strategy for winning the Civil War. If the Union could capture Vicksburg, Mississippi, the last major Confederate stronghold on the river, then the North could cut the South in two.

In May 1863, Grant launched two assaults on Vicksburg, but the city's defenders repulsed both attacks and inflicted high casualties. Grant decided to put the city under **siege**—to cut off its food and supplies and bombard it until its defenders gave up. On July 4, 1863, with his troops starving, the Confederate commander at Vicksburg surrendered.

Gettysburg   S

Meanwhile, in Virginia, Lee had been able to defeat Union forces at Fredericksburg and Chancellorsville. Emboldened by these victories, Lee decided in June 1863 to launch another invasion of the North. At the end of June, as Lee's army foraged in the Pennsylvania countryside, some of his troops headed into **Gettysburg,** hoping to seize a supply of shoes. When they arrived near the town, they discovered two brigades of Union cavalry. On July 1,

PRIMARY SOURCE
The Gettysburg Address

The bloody victory at Gettysburg was a major turning point in the Civil War. It kept Britain out of the war, inflicted serious losses on the Confederacy and helped restore Union morale. In November 1863 Lincoln went to Gettysburg to dedicate part of the battlefield as a cemetery. His speech, the Gettysburg Address, became one of the best-known orations in American history.

▼ On July 3, 1863, the Confederate forces launched an attack known later as Pickett's Charge. Charging up Cemetery Ridge into withering cannon fire, the Confederates suffered nearly 7,000 casualties in less than two hours. Soon after the attack failed, General Lee ordered Southern forces to withdraw.

Extending the Content

Military Terms The Civil War was the first war in which strictly military terms were passed into widespread usage. Many of these terms are still used in common speech today, including: *K.P.* (kitchen police), *AWOL* (absent without leave), *pup tents* (originally known as dog tents), and *shoddy* (uniforms made from recycled woolen fibers known as shoddy, which came to denote any article of inferior quality.)

1863, as Confederates pushed the Union troops out of the town, the main forces of both armies hurried to the scene of the fighting.

On July 2, Lee attacked, but the Union troops held their ground. The following day, Lee ordered nearly 15,000 men under the command of General George E. Pickett and General A.P. Hill to make a massive assault. The attack, known as Pickett's Charge, caused 7,000 casualties in less than half an hour, but failed to break the Union lines. "It is all my fault," said Lee. "It is I who have lost this fight." Lee's troops retreated to Virginia. At Gettysburg, the Union suffered 23,000 casualties, the South an estimated 28,000, more than one-third of Lee's entire force.

The disaster at Gettysburg proved to be the turning point of the war in the East. The Union's victory strengthened the Republicans politically and ensured once again that the British would not recognize the Confederacy. For the remainder of the war, Lee's forces remained on the defensive, slowly giving ground to the advancing Union army.

Grant Secures Tennessee

After the Union's major victories at Vicksburg and Gettysburg, fierce fighting erupted in Tennessee near Chattanooga. Chattanooga was a vital railroad junction. Both sides knew that if the Union forces captured Chattanooga, they would control a major railroad running south to Atlanta. Following several battles, Union forces under the command of General Grant succeeded in scattering the Confederate soldiers who blocked the way to the city.

By the spring of 1864, Grant's capture of **R1** Vicksburg had given the Union control of the Mississippi River, while his victory at Chattanooga had secured eastern Tennessee and cleared the way for an invasion of Georgia. Lincoln rewarded Grant by appointing him general in chief of the Union forces and promoting him to lieutenant general, a rank no one had held since George Washington. The president had finally found a general he trusted to win the war.

R2

PRIMARY SOURCE

"Four score and seven years ago our fathers brought forth on this continent a new nation, conceived in Liberty, and dedicated to the proposition that all men are created equal.

Now we are engaged in a great civil war, testing whether that nation, or any nation so conceived and so dedicated, can long endure. We are met on a great battle-field of that war. We have come to dedicate a portion of that field, as a final resting place for those who here gave their lives that that nation might live. It is altogether fitting and proper that we should do this.

But, in a larger sense, we cannot dedicate—we cannot consecrate—we cannot hallow—this ground. The brave men, living and dead, who struggled here, have consecrated it, far above our poor power to add or detract. The world will little note, nor long remember what we say here, but it can never forget what they did here. It is for us the living, rather, to be dedicated here to the unfinished work which they who fought here have thus far so nobly advanced. It is rather for us to be here dedicated to the great task remaining before us—that from these honored dead we take increased devotion to that cause for which they gave the last full measure of devotion—that we here highly resolve that these dead shall not have died in vain—that this nation, under God, shall have a new birth of freedom—and that government of the people, by the people, for the people, shall not perish from the earth."

—The Gettysburg Address, November 19, 1863

▲ More than 50,000 Americans were killed or wounded during the Battle of Gettysburg.

DBQ Document-Based Questions

1. **Specifying** To what event is Lincoln referring that occurred "fourscore and seven years ago"?
2. **Identifying Central Issues** What does Lincoln say is the main purpose of the Civil War and the reason for the sacrifices at Gettysburg?

Chapter 3 The Civil War and Reconstruction **135**

Activity: Interdisciplinary Connection

Language Arts Tell students that Stephen Crane's novel *The Red Badge of Courage* presents a realistic view of the war. Select a few passages from the book that demonstrate how Crane paints a picture of the war. Then, tell students that Crane did not actually fight in the Civil War. He based his book on war stories told by veterans and on the photographs taken by Mathew Brady, a famous Civil War photographer. Discuss the difference between participating in an event and having the event described by others. **OL BL**

Analyzing VISUALS

Answers:
1. World War II and World War I
2. the North

Additional Support

PRIMARY SOURCE
The Cost of the Civil War

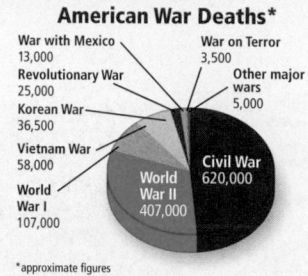

▲ Robert E. Lee surrenders to General Grant at Appomattox Courthouse on April 9, 1865.

▲ The war devastated the South. Hundreds of thousands of people were dead, and several major cities, including Richmond (above), lay in ruins.

Casualties of the Civil War

Troops (thousands) — North / South

	Total Deaths	Battle-related deaths	Non-battle deaths
North	360	110	250
South	258	94	164

Source: *For the Common Defense.*

American War Deaths*

- War with Mexico 13,000
- Revolutionary War 25,000
- Korean War 36,500
- Vietnam War 58,000
- World War I 107,000
- War on Terror 3,500
- Other major wars 5,000
- Civil War 620,000
- World War II 407,000

*approximate figures
Sources: United States Civil War Center; For the Common Defense

Analyzing VISUALS

1. **Identifying** The Civil War cost more American lives than any other conflict. What were the next two most deadly wars?
2. **Specifying** Which region suffered the highest number of battle-related deaths?

Grant Versus Lee

"Whatever happens, there will be no turning back," Grant promised Lincoln. He was determined to march southward, attacking Lee's forces relentlessly, regardless of the cost, until the South surrendered.

Grant kept his forces on the move and gave Lee's troops no time to recover. He attacked them first in the Wilderness, a densely forested area near Fredericksburg, Virginia, then at Spotsylvania Courthouse, then at Cold Harbor, a strategic crossroads northeast of Richmond. He then put the town of Petersburg under siege knowing that once it fell, Richmond, Virginia, would be cut off from supplies.

Sherman's March to the Sea

General Grant had put his most trusted subordinate, **William Tecumseh Sherman,** in charge of Union operations in the west while he headed east to fight Lee. In early August 1864, Sherman marched into Georgia, heading toward the city of Atlanta. After capturing the city, Sherman's troops set fires to destroy its railroads, warehouses, mills, and factories. The fires spread, however, destroying more than one-third of Atlanta.

On November 15, 1864, Sherman led his troops east across Georgia in what became known as the March to the Sea. The purpose of the march was to make Southern civilians

D

Activity: Interdisciplinary Connection

Art Although Mathew Brady revolutionized the artistic documentation of the Civil War through his photography, many artists of the time captured this historic era through fine art. For example, Winslow Homer's paintings *Veteran in a New Field* and *Prisoners from the Front* were completed from sketches he drew from the field. Have students research a painting that stirs up personal feelings about the Civil War. Then, ask students to present and explain the painting to the class. **OL** **BL** **ELL**

understand the horrors of war and to pressure them into giving up the struggle. Sherman's troops cut a path of destruction through Georgia that was at times 60 miles (97 km) wide. By December 21, 1864, they had reached the coast and seized the city of Savannah. Sherman now turned north and headed into South Carolina, the state that many people believed had started the Civil War.

The South Surrenders

The capture of Atlanta revitalized Northern support for the war and for Lincoln, who was elected president to another term. Lincoln interpreted his reelection as a **mandate** to end slavery permanently by amending the Constitution. On January 31, 1865, with the help of Democrats opposed to slavery, the **Thirteenth Amendment** to the Constitution, banning slavery in the United States, passed the House of Representatives and was sent to the states for ratification.

Appomattox Courthouse Meanwhile, Lee knew that time was running out. On April 1, 1865, Union troops led by Philip Sheridan cut the last rail line into Petersburg at the Battle of Five Forks. The following night, Lee's troops withdrew from their positions near the city and raced west.

Lee's desperate attempt to escape Grant's forces failed when Sheridan's cavalry got ahead of Lee's troops and blocked the road at Appomattox Courthouse. With his ragged and battered troops surrounded and outnumbered, Lee surrendered to Grant on April 9, 1865. Grant's generous terms of surrender **guaranteed** that the United States would not prosecute Confederate soldiers for treason. When Grant agreed to let Confederates take their horses home "to put in a crop to carry themselves and their families through the next winter," Lee thanked him, adding that the kindness would "do much toward conciliating our people."

Lincoln's Assassination With the war over, Lincoln delivered a speech describing his plan to restore the Southern states to the Union. In the speech, he mentioned including African Americans in Southern state governments. One listener, actor John Wilkes Booth, sneered to a friend, "That is the last speech he will ever make."

Although his advisers had repeatedly warned him not to appear unescorted in public, Lincoln went to Ford's Theater with his wife to see a play on the evening of April 14, 1865. Just after 10 P.M., Booth slipped quietly behind the president and shot him in the back of the head. Lincoln died the next morning.

The North's victory in the Civil War saved the Union and strengthened the power of the federal government over the states. It transformed American society by ending slavery, but it also left the South socially and economically devastated, and many questions unresolved. Americans from the North and the South tried to answer these questions in the years following the Civil War—an era known as Reconstruction.

C

✔ **Reading Check** **Examining** Why did General Sherman march his army to the sea?

Section 2 REVIEW

Vocabulary
1. **Explain** the significance of: "Stonewall" Jackson, blockade runner, Ulysses S. Grant, Battle of Antietam, Emancipation Proclamation, siege, Gettysburg, William Tecumseh Sherman, mandate, Thirteenth Amendment.

Main Ideas
2. **Identifying Central Issues** What was the significance of the Battle of Antietam for the South?

3. **Explaining** Why was capturing Vicksburg important to the Union?

Critical Thinking
4. **Big Ideas** How did northern military strategy change after Ulysses S. Grant took command of the Union Army.

5. **Organizing** Using a graphic organizer, list the results of the Battle of Gettysburg. Make sure that you consider both the Union and the Confederacy.

Battle of Gettysburg

6. **Analyzing Visuals** Examine the graphs of war deaths on page 136. What would account for the thousands of noncombat deaths?

Writing About History
7. **Descriptive Writing** Take on the role of a reporter living in Georgia during Sherman's March to the Sea. Write a brief article describing the Union's actions and their effects on the people.

History ONLINE
Study Central™ To review this section, go to glencoe.com and click on Study Central.

137

C Critical Thinking
Evaluating Have students search the Web for articles about Abraham Lincoln. Ask students to print out the home page of each site and write a brief explanation of whether or not they rate the site as authoritative. **OL**

✔ **Reading Check**

Answer:
Sherman wanted to make Southern civilians understand the horrors of war and pressure them into surrendering.

Assess
· · · · · · · · · · · · · · · · · · · ·
History ONLINE

Study Central™ provides summaries, interactive games, and online graphic organizers to help students review content.

Close
· · · · · · · · · · · · · · · · · · · ·
Explaining Ask students to explain the importance of Union victories in Virginia and the Deep South. **OL**

Section 2 REVIEW

Answers

1. All definitions can be found in the section and the Glossary.

2. It kept Great Britain from joining the Confederacy when it was poised to do so, and led to the Emancipation Proclamation.

3. It cut the South in two by giving the Union control of the Mississippi River.

4. It became focused on relentlessly attacking the Confederate troops and making life very difficult for Southern civilians.

5. strengthened Republicans politically, very high casualties, put Confederacy on the defensive, ended the South's hope for help from Britain

6. disease spread rapidly in military camps leading to death from disease, conditions were difficult for civilians too

7. Students' articles will vary, but should be based on facts, not on the writer's opinion.

Focus

Thirty years after the war ended, Congress made Gettysburg a National Military Park in tribute to the armies that fought there. Each summer, historical reenactors have recreated the battle. Today National Park Service rangers also provide information to visitors.

Teach

C Critical Thinking

Comparing and Contrasting
Tell students that the Union and Confederate armies were similar in many ways. For example, both armies used similar weapons. Have students use the library or Internet resources to identify other ways in which the two armies were alike and different. You may recommend the National Park Service Web site as a starting point for their research. **OL**

Additional Support

NATIONAL GEOGRAPHIC

GEOGRAPHY & HISTORY

The Battle of Gettysburg

The Confederate invasion of the North in 1863 was a bold stroke. By moving north, General Robert E. Lee gained access to the rich farms and other resources of Pennsylvania. When his troops arrived in Gettysburg on July 1, they forced Union troops to flee to the hills south of the town. Had Confederate forces attacked the Union troops in the hills immediately, they might have won. The decision not to attack enabled Union troops to reinforce their position and build a formidable defensive line.

How Did Geography Shape the Battle?

The Union line stretched from Culp's Hill and Cemetery Hill in the north, south along Cemetery Ridge to another hill called Little Round Top. The Union forces controlled the high ground and were deployed in such a way that troops could easily be moved from one part of the line to another depending on where the enemy attacked.

On July 2, Lee tried to seize Little Round Top. Controlling the hill would have let his artillery fire down the length of the Union line. After savage fighting, his attack was repulsed, but Lee believed the Union had shifted so many troops south to hold Little Round Top that it had left its line on Cemetery Ridge vulnerable to attack.

On July 3, Lee ordered some 12,500 troops to attack Cemetery Ridge in what became known as Pickett's Charge. Union artillery ripped holes in the Confederate line as it advanced. When the Confederates neared the crest of the ridge, Union troops, protected by trenches and barricades they had built, unleashed volley after volley. Firing at point-blank rage, stabbing with bayonets, and battering with rifle butts, the Union soldiers drove the Confederates back. Lee knew he had been beaten. The next day he began his retreat to Virginia.

Analyzing GEOGRAPHY

1. **Place** Why was the Union army in such a strong position in the Battle of Gettysburg?
2. **Movement** What made Pickett's charge so difficult? Why did Lee think it would succeed?

Town of Gettysburg

Culp's Hill

Seminary Ridge

Army of Northern Virginia
Robert E. Lee

Extending the Content

The Hero of Little Round Top The extreme left flank of the Union lines at Gettysburg—a hill called Little Round Top—was commanded by Colonel Joshua Lawrence Chamberlain, a college professor who had taken leave from teaching to fight in the war. Chamberlain knew that if the Confederates took Little Round Top, they would have a view of the whole Union line. Although greatly outnumbered, Chamberlain's forces withstood numerous attacks. Finally, Chamberlain led his troops in a bayonet charge that drove the Confederates from the field. Chamberlain received the Medal of Honor for his bravery at Gettysburg.

On July 3, Lee ordered some 12,500 men to attack Cemetery Ridge. The Confederates marched three-quarters of a mile across open fields and then uphill toward Union lines. Although the attack is known as Pickett's Charge, General Pickett's troops made up only about one-third of the Confederate force that attacked.

Pennsylvania
Carlisle
Chambersburg
Wrightsville
Gettysburg
MEADE
Frederick Baltimore
West Virginia
Winchester
Maryland
Front Royal
HOOKER
Washington, D.C.
Virginia
Fredericksburg
Chancellorsville
LEE
Chesapeake Bay
Richmond
Rappahannock R.

← Union advance
← Confederate advance

0   40 kilometers
0   40 miles
Albers Equal-Area projection

N
W   E
S

Cemetery Ridge

Army of the Potomac
General George G. Meade

Little Round Top

The Devil's Den

Peach Orchard

On July 2, Lee ordered Longstreet to attack the Union lines near the hill named Little Round Top. Savage fighting erupted in the Peach Orchard, on the slopes of Little Round Top, and near a jumble of boulders called the Devil's Den. The Union forces held Little Round Top and drove back the Confederates.

S

Chapter 3   The Civil War and Reconstruction   **139**

S Skill Practice

Reading Maps Have students identify the landforms on the image and explain how the armies used those landforms. **OL**

Analyzing GEOGRAPHY

Answers:
1. The Union army controlled high ground, allowing them to fire down on Confederate troops, and they could move troops easily from one part of the line to another.
2. Pickett's Charge was difficult because the Union troops were protected by barricades and trenches and could fire at the Confederate soldiers as they advanced. Lee believed it would succeed because he thought the Union army had shifted most of the troops to hold Little Round Top, leaving Cemetery Ridge vulnerable.

Activity: Collaborative Learning

Newspaper Page Organize the class into groups to create a newspaper page highlighting the details from the Battle of Gettysburg. Have each group choose whether to describe the Northern or Southern view of the battle. Have students research the Battle of Gettysburg using their book, the Internet, and other sources. Groups should illustrate their newspaper page with drawings depicting a scene from the battle. Have each group compose its newspaper page on a computer using desktop publishing software.

Focus

Bellringer
Daily Focus Transparency 3.3

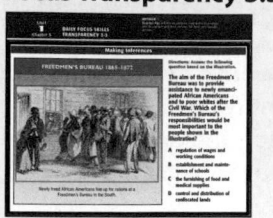

Guide to Reading

Answers:

black codes: severely limited rights of African Americans in the South; Civil Rights Act of 1866: allowed African Americans to own property and stated that they were to be treated equally in court; Fourteenth Amendment: guaranteed all citizens equal protection of the laws; Fifteenth Amendment: guaranteed the right to vote to all adult male citizens.

Section Spotlight Video

To generate student interest and provide a springboard for class discussion, access the Chapter 3, Section 3 video at glencoe.com or on the video DVD.

Resource Manager

Section 3

Reconstruction

Guide to Reading

Big Ideas
Economics and Society After Reconstruction, the South tried to build a new economy, but many problems remained.

Content Vocabulary
• amnesty (p. 140)
• pocket veto (p. 142)
• black codes (p. 143)
• carpetbagger (p. 145)
• scalawag (p. 145)
• sharecropper (p. 149)

Academic Vocabulary
• commissioner (p. 145)
• infrastructure (p. 147)

People and Events to Identify
• Reconstruction (p. 140)
• Radical Republicans (p. 140)
• Freedmen's Bureau (p. 142)
• Fourteenth Amendment (p. 143)
• Fifteenth Amendment (p. 145)
• Compromise of 1877 (p. 148)

Reading Strategy
Organizing Complete a graphic organizer similar to the one below to explain how each piece of legislation listed affected African Americans.

Legislation	Effect
black codes	
Civil Rights Act of 1866	
Fourteenth Amendment	
Fifteenth Amendment	

President Lincoln, moderate Republicans, and Radical Republicans had different ideas about how to rebuild the South and to secure the rights of African Americans. As Democrats regained power in the South, Reconstruction ended.

Reconstruction Begins

MAIN Idea In the months after the Civil War, the nation began the effort to rebuild and reunite.

HISTORY AND YOU Think of a war you have studied in a history course. What were the terms of the peace treaty, and who benefited? Read on to learn about President Lincoln's policies after Union victory in the Civil War.

Helping freed African Americans find their way as citizens of the United States was only one of a myriad of problems the nation faced. At the end of the Civil War, the South was a defeated region with a devastated economy. While some Southerners were bitter over the Union military victory, for many rebuilding their land and their lives was more important. Meanwhile, the president and Congress grappled with the difficult task of **Reconstruction,** or rebuilding the nation after the war.

Lincoln and the Radical Republicans

In December 1863, President Lincoln set forth his moderate plan for reuniting the country in the Proclamation of Amnesty and Reconstruction. Lincoln wanted to reconcile the South with the Union instead of punishing it for treason. He offered a general **amnesty,** or pardon, to all Southerners who took an oath of loyalty to the United States and accepted the Union's proclamations concerning slavery. When 10 percent of a state's voters in the 1860 presidential election had taken this oath, they could organize a new state government. Certain people, such as Confederate government officials and military officers, could not take the oath or be pardoned.

Resistance to Lincoln's plan surfaced at once among a group of Republicans in Congress known as **Radical Republicans.** Led by Representative Thaddeus Stevens of Pennsylvania and Senator Charles Sumner of Massachusetts, the radicals wanted to prevent the leaders of the Confederacy from returning to power after the war. They also wanted the Republican Party to become a powerful institution in the South. Finally, and perhaps most importantly, they wanted the federal government to help African Americans achieve political equality by guaranteeing their right to vote in the South.

R Reading Strategies	**C** Critical Thinking	**D** Differentiated Instruction	**W** Writing Support	**S** Skill Practice
Teacher Edition • Organizing, p. 141 • Questioning, p. 145 • Academic Vocabulary, p. 147 **Additional Resources** • Prim. Source Read., URB p. 101 • Guide. Read. Act., URB p. 114	**Teacher Edition** • Analyzing Information, p. 143 • Predicting Consequences, p. 144 **Additional Resources** • Crit. Think. Skills Act., URB p. 96 • Quizzes/Tests, p. 31	**Teacher Edition** • Visual/Spatial, p. 143 • Gifted/Talented, p. 146 • Verbal/Linguistic, p. 148 **Additional Resources** • Interpreting Political Cartoons, URB p. 105	**Teacher Edition** • Persuasive Writing, p. 141 • Expository Writing, p. 142 **Additional Resources** • Content Voc. Act., URB p. 91 • Academic Voc. Act., URB p. 93	**Teacher Edition** • Sequencing Information, pp. 144, 148 • Evaluating, p. 145 • Conduct. Research, p. 146 • Drawing Concl., pp. 147, 149 **Additional Resources** • Time Line Act., URB p. 97 • Reteacing Act., URB p. 107 • RENTG, p. 31

INFOGRAPHIC
Three Plans for Reconstruction

After the Civil War, three plans were proposed to restore the South to the Union. The political struggle that resulted revealed that sectional tensions had not ended with the Civil War.

1. Lincoln's Plan for Reconstruction

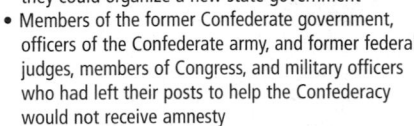

- Amnesty to all but a few Southerners who took an oath of loyalty to the United States and accepted its proclamations concerning slavery
- When 10 percent of a state's voters in the 1860 presidential election had taken the oath, they could organize a new state government
- Members of the former Confederate government, officers of the Confederate army, and former federal judges, members of Congress, and military officers who had left their posts to help the Confederacy would not receive amnesty

Analyzing VISUALS

1. **Identifying** Which plan made the most provisions for formerly enslaved African Americans?
2. **Specifying** Which plan was most forgiving of former Confederate political and military leaders?

2. Congressional Reconstruction

- Passed the Fourteenth and Fifteenth Amendments
- Military Reconstruction Act divided the South into five military districts
- New state constitutions required to guarantee voting rights
- Military rule protected voting rights for African Americans
- Empowered African Americans in government and supported their education

▲ *Thaddeus Stevens*

▶ *Charles Sumner*

3. Johnson's Plan for Reconstruction

- Amnesty for those taking an oath of loyalty to the United States; excluded high-ranking Confederates and those with property over $20,000, but they could apply for pardons individually
- Required states to ratify the Thirteenth Amendment abolishing slavery

W

Congressional Republicans knew that the abolition of slavery would give the South more seats in the House of Representatives. Before the Civil War, enslaved people had only counted in Congress as three-fifths of a free person. Now that African Americans were free, the South was entitled to more seats in Congress. This would endanger Republican control of Congress unless Republicans could find a way to protect African American voting rights in the South.

Although the radicals knew that giving African Americans in the South the right to vote would help the Republican Party win elections, most were not acting cynically. Many

of them had been abolitionists before the Civil War and had pushed Lincoln into making emancipation a goal of the war. They believed in a right to political equality for all Americans, regardless of their race.

The Wade-Davis Bill   **R**

Many moderate Republicans considered Lincoln too lenient, but they also thought the radicals were going too far in their support for African American equality and voting rights. By the summer of 1864, the moderates and radicals had come up with a plan for Reconstruction that they could both support.

Chapter 3 The Civil War and Reconstruction **141**

(Chapter Project is continued on Visual Summary page)

Teach

W Writing Support
Persuasive Writing Have students assume the role of a former Confederate officer and write a letter to the president requesting a pardon. Remind students that those receiving amnesty must sign a loyalty oath. **OL**

R Reading Strategy
Organizing Have students complete a two-column chart listing the components of Lincoln's plan for Reconstruction and the Wade-Davis Bill. **Ask:** What points make the Wade-Davis Bill harsher than Lincoln's plan? *(The Wade-Davis Bill forbade all former Confederate government officials and military officers to vote or hold office and required the majority of white males to pledge allegiance to the Union.)* **OL**

Analyzing VISUALS
Answers:
1. Congress's plan
2. Johnson's plan

Hands-On Chapter Project
Step 3

Art Show on the Civil War and Reconstruction

Step 3: Hanging the Show Essential **Question:** How should the images best be presented to illustrate the Civil War and Reconstruction?

Directions The final job is to hang the show, but this requires decisions about the best order in which to present the images for the audience. Students may choose to hang the images by chronological order,

by date of the artwork, by the artists, or by a perceived theme in the images. Another task is to review the informational tags that will accompany the images. Will the tags give the audience enough information to understand the Civil War and Reconstruction?

Putting It Together If there is space for the show to actually be hung, getting the materials to hang it is the last step. Students from other classes might view it and review it. **OL**

W Writing Support

Expository Writing Andrew Johnson had been vice president for less than six weeks when President Lincoln was assassinated. He then faced the formidable challenge of reuniting the nation. Inform students that Johnson had no formal schooling and remained unable to read well or write until he was almost 20. In pairs, have students research Johnson's background and write a personality profile that tries to explain how his early life was reflected in his plans for Reconstruction. **OL**

Answer:
The Fourteenth Amendment expanded federal power over the states; its equal protection clause has been used to extend civil rights.

Additional Support

This alternative to Lincoln's plan was the Wade-Davis Bill of 1864, which required the majority of the adult white males in a former Confederate state to take an oath of allegiance to the Union. The state could then hold a constitutional convention to create a new state government. The people chosen to attend the constitutional convention had to take an "iron-clad" oath asserting that they had never fought against the Union or supported the Confederacy in any way. Each state's convention would then have to abolish slavery, reject all debts the state had acquired as part of the Confederacy, and deprive all former Confederate government officials and military officers of the right to vote or hold office.

Although Congress passed the Wade-Davis Bill, Lincoln blocked it with a **pocket veto.** Although Lincoln sympathized with some of the radicals' goals, he believed that imposing a harsh peace would only alienate many whites in the South.

The Freedmen's Bureau

History ONLINE
Student Web Activity Visit glencoe.com and complete the activity on Southern Reconstruction.

Lincoln realized that the South was already in chaos, with thousands unemployed, homeless, and hungry. At the same time, the victorious Union armies had to try to help the large numbers of African Americans who flocked to Union lines as the war progressed. As Sherman marched through Georgia and South Carolina, thousands of freed African Americans—now known as freedmen—began following his troops seeking food and shelter.

In March 1865, Congress established the Bureau of Refugees, Freedmen, and Abandoned Lands, better known as the **Freedmen's Bureau.** The Bureau was directed to feeding and clothing war refugees in the South using surplus army supplies. Beginning in September 1865, it issued nearly 30,000 rations a day for the next year.

The Bureau helped formerly enslaved people find work on plantations and negotiated labor contracts with planters. Many Northerners argued that people who had been enslaved should receive land to support themselves now that they were free. To others, however, taking land from plantation owners and giving it to freedmen seemed to violate the nation's commitment to individual property rights. As a result, Congress refused to confirm the right of African Americans to own the lands that had

---

been seized from plantation owners and given to them.

Johnson Takes Office

Shortly after Congress established the Freedmen's Bureau, Lincoln was assassinated. Although his successor, Vice President Andrew Johnson, was a Democrat from Tennessee, he had remained loyal to the Union. Like Lincoln, he believed in a moderate policy to bring the South back into the Union.

In the summer of 1865, with Congress in recess, Johnson began implementing his reconstruction plan. He offered to pardon all former citizens of the Confederacy who took an oath of loyalty to the Union and to return their property. He excluded from the pardon the same people Lincoln had excluded. Like Lincoln, Johnson required Southern states to ratify the Thirteenth Amendment. **W**

The former Confederate states, for the most part, met Johnson's conditions. They then organized new governments and held elections. By the time Congress gathered for its next session in December 1865, Johnson's plan was well underway. Many members of

Turning Point

The Fourteenth Amendment

The passage of the Fourteenth Amendment was a turning point in American political and legal history. Since its ratification, the amendment has been used to expand federal power over the states and to extend civil rights through its equal protection clause. It also provided the foundation for the doctrine of incorporation—the concept that the rights and protections in the Bill of Rights apply to the states. This doctrine was first upheld by the Supreme Court in *Gitlow* v. *New York* in 1925. In the 1950s and 1960s, the Warren Court used the clause extensively to extend civil rights in cases such as *Brown* v. *Board of Education, Gideon* v. *Wainwright,* and *Reynolds* v. *Sims,* among others.

ANALYZING HISTORY What is significant about the ratification of the Fourteenth Amendment? Write a brief essay to explain your answer.

Turning Point

Additional Background The Fourteenth Amendment was formally proposed on June 13, 1866. By July 1868, enough had ratified it for the amendment to be added to the Constitution. Other states continued to ratify it, however, for many years to come. On March 18, 1976, Kentucky ratified the amendment, 109 years after first rejecting it. Ohio's position on the amendment long remained open to legal questions. The Ohio General Assembly ratified the amendment in 1867; after an intervening election, a new legislature voted to rescind approval in 1868. To settle the issue, the Ohio General Assembly again voted to ratify the Fourteenth Amendment in 2003. **Ask:** What are the three main provisions of the Fourteenth Amendment? *(1. grants citizenship to all persons born or naturalized in the United States; 2. forbids states from depriv-ing persons of life, liberty, or property without due process of law; 3. ensures equal protection of the laws)*

Congress were astonished and angered when they realized that Southern voters had elected dozens of Confederate leaders to Congress. Moderate Republicans joined with the Radical Republicans and voted to reject the new Southern members of Congress.

Congressional Republicans were also angry that the new Southern legislatures had passed laws, known as **black codes,** which seemed to be intended to keep African Americans in a condition similar to slavery. They required **D** African Americans to enter into annual labor contracts. Those who did not could be arrested for vagrancy and forced into involuntary servitude. Several codes established specific hours of labor and also required them to get licenses to work in nonagricultural jobs.

Radical Reconstruction

With the election of former Confederates to office and the introduction of the black codes, more and more moderate Republicans joined the radicals. Finally, in late 1865, House and Senate leaders created a Joint Committee on Reconstruction to develop their own program for rebuilding the Union.

The Fourteenth Amendment In March 1866, congressional Reconstruction began with the passage of an act intended to override the black codes. The Civil Rights Act of 1866 granted citizenship to all persons born in the United States except for Native Americans. The act guaranteed the rights of African Americans to own property and stated that they were to be treated equally in court. It also gave the federal government the power to sue people who violated those rights. Johnson vetoed the act, arguing it was unconstitutional and would "[cause] discord among the races." The veto convinced the remaining moderate **C** Republicans to join the radicals in overriding Johnson's veto, and the act became law.

Fearing that the Civil Rights Act might later be overturned in court, however, the radicals introduced the **Fourteenth Amendment** to the Constitution. This amendment granted citizenship to all persons born or naturalized in the United States and declared that no state could deprive any person of life, liberty, or property "without due process of law." It also declared that no state could deny any person "equal protection of the laws." In 1868, the amendment was ratified.

The Fourteenth Amendment
"No State shall make or enforce any law which shall abridge the privileges or immunities of citizens of the United States; nor shall any State deprive any person of life, liberty, or property, without due process of law; nor deny to any person within its jurisdiction the equal protection of the laws."

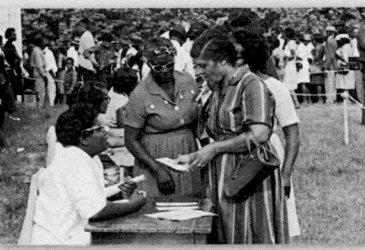

▲ In 1964, in Reynolds v. Sims, the Court used the Fourteenth Amendment's equal protection clause to ensure that state voting districts were of equal size.

◄ Clarence Gideon

► Ernesto Miranda

▲ In two major cases, Gideon v. Wainwright in 1963 and Miranda v. Arizona in 1966, the Court clarified that the Fifth and Sixth Amendments of the Bill of Rights had to be upheld by the states.

► In 1925, in Gitlow v. New York, the Supreme Court began using the Fourteenth Amendment to apply the Bill of Rights to the states. In this case, it held that state laws had to protect free speech.

▲ Benjamin Gitlow

◄ In 1954 the Supreme Court based its decision ending school segregation, Brown v. Board of Education, on the Fourteenth Amendment's equal protection clause.

Teacher Tip

Suggest that one group choose the Supreme Court's ruling in *Bush v. Gore* (2000). It should produce an interesting class discussion of contemporary application of the equal protection clause.

Activity: Collaborative Learning

Understanding the Fourteenth Amendment Divide the class into three groups. Have each group research a Supreme Court case based on the Fourteenth Amendment. They may use one of the cases mentioned on this page or any other case they find. Students will assume the role of attorneys arguing the case before the Court—in this case, the rest of the class. One member of the group should present a brief background of the case. The rest of the group should be divided into two teams—one for each side of the argument. Each of the members should present one point for or against the plaintiff's case. After the presentations, the class should render a decision for each case. **OL**

S Skill Practice

Sequencing Information

Have students use library and Internet resources to research the presidency of Andrew Johnson. Then write the title "Reconstruction During Andrew Johnson's Presidency" on the board and draw a time line that begins with 1865 and ends with 1868. Call on volunteers to come to the board and enter the major events that occurred during these years. Ask students to use information on the time line to write a chronological summary of Reconstruction up to the presidential election of 1868. **OL** **BL**

C Critical Thinking

Predicting Consequences

Write the phrase "Military Reconstruction" on the board. Ask students to predict the response of people living in the former Confederate states to being placed under the charge of a Union general. *(anger or resentment at living under Northern control)* **OL**

Analyzing GEOGRAPHY

1. Tennessee
2. 5 years

Additional Support

NATIONAL GEOGRAPHIC Military Reconstruction, 1867

What Are the Provisions of the Reconstruction Amendments?

The 13th Amendment (1865)
• Slavery is illegal.

The 14th Amendment (1868)
• All people born or naturalized in the United States are citizens.
• The states may not deny anyone the equal protection of the laws.
• Leaders of the Confederacy cannot serve in the U.S. government or military without a two-thirds vote by Congress.

The 15th Amendment (1870)
• The rights of citizens to vote shall not be denied on account of race, color, or previous condition of servitude.

Military Districts and Commanders
1 General John Schofield
2 General Daniel Sickles
3 General John Pope
4 General Edward Ord
5 General Philip Sheridan
1868 Date of readmission to Union

Analyzing GEOGRAPHY

1. **Location** Which former Confederate state was not part of a military district?
2. **Movement** How many years after the war ended was the last Southern state readmitted to the United States?

Maps In MOtion See *StudentWorks™ Plus* or glencoe.com.

President Johnson attacked the Fourteenth Amendment and made it the major issue of the 1866 congressional elections. He hoped Northerners would vote out the Radical Republicans and elect representatives who supported his plan for Reconstruction. Instead, the Republicans won approximately a three-to-one majority in Congress. They now could override any presidential veto and could claim that they had a mandate, or command, to enact their own Reconstruction program in place of Johnson's plan.

Military Reconstruction Begins In March 1867, Congress passed the Military Reconstruction Act, which essentially nullified Johnson's programs. The act divided the former Confederacy, except for Tennessee—which had ratified the Fourteenth Amendment in 1866—into five military districts. A Union general was placed in charge of each district with orders to maintain peace and "protect the rights of persons and property."

In the meantime, each former Confederate state had to hold another constitutional convention to design a constitution acceptable to Congress. The new state constitutions had to give the right to vote to all adult male citizens, regardless of race. Each state also had to ratify the Fourteenth Amendment before it would be allowed to elect people to Congress.

Johnson's Impeachment Republicans knew that they had the votes to override presidential vetoes, but they also knew that President Johnson could still refuse to enforce the laws they passed. To restrict Johnson, Congress passed two new laws: the Command of the Army Act and the Tenure of Office Act. The Command of the Army Act required all orders from the president to go through the headquarters of the General of the Army. This

144 Chapter 3 The Civil War and Reconstruction

Extending the Content

Section 2 of the Fourteenth Amendment introduces the word "male" into the Constitution for the first time. Although many woman suffragists also supported civil rights for African Americans, the Fourteenth Amendment caused a split in the women's movement between those who supported ratification despite the exclusion of women and those who opposed ratification of an amendment that enshrined gender discrimination in the Constitution.

was the headquarters of General Grant, whom the Republicans trusted. The Tenure of Office Act required the Senate to approve the removal of any official whose appointment had required the Senate's consent.

In order to challenge the Tenure of Office Act, Johnson fired Secretary of War Edwin M. Stanton, who supported the Radical Republicans. Three days later, the House of Representatives voted to impeach Johnson, **R** meaning that they charged him with "high crimes and misdemeanors" in office. They accused Johnson of breaking the law by refusing to uphold the Tenure of Office Act.

As provided in the Constitution, the Senate then put the president on trial. If two-thirds of the senators found the president guilty of the charges, he would be removed from office. In **S** May 1868, the Senate voted 35 to 19 that Johnson was guilty of high crimes and misdemeanors. This was just one vote short of the votes needed for conviction.

Although Johnson remained in office, he finished his term quietly and did not run for election in 1868. That year, the Republicans nominated Ulysses S. Grant. During the campaign, Union troops in the South enabled African Americans to vote in large numbers. As a result, Grant won six Southern states and most Northern states. The Republicans also retained large majorities in Congress.

The Fifteenth Amendment With their majority secure, and a trusted president in office, congressional Republicans moved rapidly to expand their Reconstruction program. Recognizing the importance of African American suffrage, Congress passed the **Fifteenth Amendment.** This amendment declared that the right to vote "shall not be denied . . . on account of race, color, or previous condition of servitude." By March 1870, the amendment had been ratified.

Radical Reconstruction had a dramatic impact on the South, particularly in the short term. It brought hundreds of thousands of African Americans into the political process for the first time. It also began to change Southern society. As it did so, it angered many white Southerners, who began to fight back against the federal government's policies.

✓Reading Check **Analyzing** Why did congressional Republicans pass amendments to the Constitution?

Republican Rule

MAIN Idea As African Americans entered politics, some white Southerners began to resist Republican reforms.

HISTORY AND YOU Have you heard of recent activities of the Ku Klux Klan? Read on to find out when and why the KKK was founded.

By late 1870, all former Confederate states had rejoined the Union. With many issues unresolved, reunification did little to restore harmony between the North and South.

Carpetbags and Scalawags

During Reconstruction, a large number of Northerners traveled to the South. Many were eventually elected or appointed to positions in the new state governments. Southerners, particularly supporters of the Democratic Party, called these newcomers **carpetbaggers** because some arrived with their belongings in suitcases made of carpet fabric. Local residents saw them as intruders seeking to exploit the South for their own gain.

Some white Southerners did work with the Republicans and supported Reconstruction. Other Southerners called them **scalawags**— an old Scots-Irish term for weak, underfed, worthless animals. The scalawags were a diverse group. Some were former Whigs who had grudgingly joined the Democratic Party before the war. Others were owners of small farms who did not want the wealthy planters to regain power. Some were business people who favored Republican economic plans.

African Americans

Having gained the right to vote, African American men entered into politics with great enthusiasm. They served as legislators and administrators for nearly all levels of government. Hundreds served as delegates to the conventions that created the new state constitutions. They also won election to many local offices, from mayor to police chief to school **commissioner.** Dozens served in the South's state legislatures, 14 were elected to the House of Representatives, and two, Hiram Revels and Blanche K. Bruce, were elected to the Senate.

R Reading Strategy

Questioning Only Andrew Johnson and Bill Clinton have been impeached. **Ask:** For what offenses do you think a president should be impeached? *(Answers will vary, but may include breaking the law, treason, and other reasonable answers.)* **OL**

S Skill Practice

Evaluating Organize students into several small groups. **Ask:** If you had been a member of the House of Representatives in 1868, would you have voted for or against the impeachment of Johnson? Why? *(Answers will vary.)* After groups discuss the issue, call on representatives to present their responses.

✓**Reading Check**

Answer:
to make former slaves citizens of the United States with equal rights, to give voting rights to African American men, who were more likely to vote Republican and would help the Republicans control Congress

Additional Support

Activity: Collaborative Learning

Analyzing Primary Sources In groups, have students read the following excerpt from a letter written by Jourdon Anderson (who had escaped slavery) in response to an invitation to work for his former slaveholder after the Civil War:

"Sir: . . . . I want to know particularly what the good chance is you propose to give me. I am doing tolerably well here [in Dayton,

Ohio]. I get twenty-five dollars a month, with victuals and clothing; have a comfortable home for Mandy,—the folks call her Mrs. Anderson,—and the children . . . go to school and are learning well. . . . [W]e have decided to test your sincerity by asking you to send us our wages for the time we served you. . . . Add to this the interest for the time our wages have been kept back, and deduct what you paid for our clothing . . . and the

balance will show what we are in justice entitled to. . . .

Say howdy to George Carter, and thank him for taking the pistol from you when you were shooting at me." (See URB pp. 101–102 for a longer excerpt from the letter.) **Ask:** What aspects of freedom does Anderson most value? *(economic independence, being treated with respect, education for his children)*

145

S Skill Practice

Conducting Research Have students research and then write a short profile of one of the African Americans who served in Congress during Reconstruction. Encourage students to use library and Internet resources to conduct their research.

D Differentiated Instruction

Gifted and Talented Invite interested students to use historical statistical abstracts to find data on African American enrollment in schools from 1860 to 1900. Have students report on what they find and present the information in a bar or line graph. Display the graphs in the classroom. **AL**

Analyzing VISUALS

Answers:
1. Under slavery, they had had no power to control their own lives. Voting and holding public office gave them political power.
2. They are seated on the sidelines, not among the men at the table, indicating their status as nonvoters and their lack of political power.

Additional Support

PRIMARY SOURCE
African Americans Enter Politics

Reconstruction provided African Americans with new opportunities to participate in politics. Many took part in the state constitutional conventions and were elected to state legislatures—achieving a majority in South Carolina's state assembly—and to local offices.

▲ This drawing from 1867 depicts the primary groups that became political leaders of the South's African American community—artisans (shown with tools), the middle class, and Union soldiers.

▲ This sketch from 1868 shows African Americans campaigning. African Americans were excited to participate in politics. The sketch shows women and children as well, suggesting that the entire community regarded political issues as important, even though only adult males could vote.

Analyzing VISUALS

1. **Identifying Central Issues** Why do you think African Americans were so enthusiastic about participating in politics?
2. **Explaining** What about the illustration above indicates the political position of women?

▲ The sketch above from the 1870s shows South Carolina's legislature—the only state legislature with an African American majority during Reconstruction.

S As formerly enslaved people entered Southern politics, many white Southerners claimed that "Black Republicanism" ruled the South. Such claims were greatly exaggerated. No African American ever served as governor. In South Carolina, where African Americans were a majority of the population, they did gain control of the legislature, but it lasted for only one term. African Americans participated in government, but they did not control it.

Many African Americans wanted an education, something they had been denied under slavery. As Reconstruction began, the Freedmen's Bureau, with the help of Northern charities, established schools for African Americans across the South. In the 1870s, Reconstruction governments built a public school system in D the South, and by 1876 about 40 percent of all African American children (roughly 600,000 students) attended school.

Formerly enslaved people across the South also began building their own churches. Churches frequently served as the center of many African American communities, as they housed schools and hosted social events and political gatherings.

146   Chapter 3   The Civil War and Reconstruction

Extending the Content

Historically Black Colleges After the Civil War, African American institutions of higher education were established in the South. These included Fisk University in Tennessee and Atlanta University and Morehouse College in Georgia. The institution that would become Howard University was founded in 1867 in Washington, D.C., by a group of Congregationalists who wanted to establish a seminary for African American ministers. Soon the idea expanded to the creation of an entire university, named for one of the founders and head of the Freedmen's Bureau, General Oliver Howard. Howard University quickly expanded to include the first law school for African Americans established in 1869. The Hampton Institute was started in 1868 in Virginia to teach African Americans a trade or agricultural techniques. In 1881, after Reconstruction, Spelman College—the first college for African American women—and the Tuskegee Institute, now Tuskegee University, were founded. The first teacher at Tuskegee was Booker T. Washington, who later became an important African American leader.

Republican Reforms

Because of past disloyalty, some Southern whites were barred from participating in the new Southern governments, and many others simply refused to do so. Republicans did have the support of many poor white farmers, who resented the planters and Democratic Party that had dominated the South before the war. This enabled a coalition of poor Southern-born whites, African Americans, and Northern carpetbaggers to elect Republican candidates.

R The Republican governments in the South instituted a number of reforms. They repealed the black codes, and established state hospitals and institutions for orphans. To improve the **infrastructure,** they rebuilt roads, railways, and bridges damaged during the Civil War and provided funds for the construction of new railroads and industries in the South.

Many white Southerners scorned these reforms, which did not come without cost. Many state governments had to borrow money and impose high property taxes to pay for the repairs and new programs. Many landowners, unable to pay these new taxes, lost their land.

Southern Resistance

Unable to strike openly at the Republicans running their states, some Southern opponents of Reconstruction organized secret societies to undermine Republican rule. The largest of these groups was the Ku Klux Klan. Started in 1866 by former Confederate soldiers in Pulaski, Tennessee, the Klan spread rapidly throughout the South. Hooded, white-robed Klan members rode in bands at night terrorizing African Americans, white Republicans, carpetbaggers, teachers in African American schools, and others who supported the Republican governments. Republicans and African Americans responded by organizing their own militias to fight back.

As the violence increased, Congress passed three Enforcement Acts in 1870 and 1871, one of which outlawed the activities of the Klan. Although local authorities and federal agents arrested more than 3,000 Klan members, only about 600 were convicted, and fewer still served any time in prison.

✔ **Reading Check** **Explaining** Why did only some Southerners support Republican reforms?

Reconstruction Ends

MAIN Idea Reconstruction ended as Democrats regained power in the South and in Congress.

HISTORY AND YOU What values and policies do you associate with the Republican and Democratic parties? Read to learn about the roles these parties played during the Reconstruction period.

As commander of the Union forces, Ulysses S. Grant had led the North to victory in the Civil War. His reputation had then carried him into the White House in the election of 1868. Unfortunately, Grant had little experience in politics. He believed that the president's role was to carry out the laws and leave the development of policy to Congress. This approach pleased the Radical Republicans in Congress, but it left the president weak and ineffective when dealing with other issues. Eventually, Grant's lack of political experience helped to divide the Republican Party and to undermine public support for Reconstruction.

During his first term, Ulysses S. Grant faced a growing number of Republicans who were concerned that interests in making money and selling influence were beginning to dominate the Republican Party. These **S** critics also argued that the economic policies most Republicans supported, such as high tariffs, favored the rich over the poor. In 1872, these critics, known as Liberal Republicans, split from the Republican Party and nominated their own candidate, the influential newspaper publisher Horace Greeley. Despite this split, Grant easily won reelection to a second term.

During Grant's second term, a series of scandals damaged his reputation. In addition, the nation endured a staggering and long-lasting economic crisis that began during Grant's second term. After a powerful banking firm declared bankruptcy, a wave of fear known as the Panic of 1873 quickly spread through the nation's financial community. The panic soon set off a full-fledged depression that lasted until almost the end of the decade.

The scandals in the Grant administration and the nation's deepening economic depression hurt the Republicans politically. In the 1874 midterm elections, the Democrats won back control of the House of Representatives and made gains in the Senate.

Chapter 3 The Civil War and Reconstruction **147**

R **Reading Strategy**

Academic Vocabulary A prefix is a word part that comes before a base word, or root, and modifies the meaning of the word. Discuss how knowing the meaning of a prefix helps students decipher the meaning of words such as *infrastructure*.
OL **BL** **ELL**

S **Skill Practice**

Drawing Conclusions Have students research Ulysses S. Grant's background. **Ask:** How did Grant's background improve or deter his effectiveness as president? *(military experience: leadership; lack of political experience: unable to gain backing for programs, stop corruption, or choose reliable cabinet members; lack of financial background to deal with the Panic of 1873.)* **OL**

✔ **Reading Check**

Answer:
Poor white farmers and African Americans supported the reforms; others opposed giving rights to African Americans and having to pay for programs.

Additional Support

Activity: Collaborative Learning

Debating Show students an electoral map of the 1876 presidential election, including the states where the outcome was in dispute. Inform students that the Democrat, Samuel Tilden, won 51% of the popular vote compared to 48% for Republican Rutherford B. Hayes—but Tilden lost the election. Remind students that there is no provision in the U.S. Constitution for popular election of the president; technically, citizens have no right under the Constitution to cast a vote for president. The Electoral College elects the president and the manner for selecting electors in the Electoral College is decided by individual states. Divide the class into two teams and ask them to do research on the Electoral College. Then have them debate the topic "The Electoral College Should Be Abolished." In making the assignment, mention the concept of One Person, One Vote. **OL** **AL**

D Differentiated Instruction

Verbal Linguistic Help students review the section by speculating about the problems that 4 million enslaved people would confront when they were suddenly set free but had no money, housing, education, or jobs. **BL**

S Skill Practice

Sequencing Information
Have students reread the section on the Compromise of 1877. Ask them to create a list of the events leading to the compromise. **BL**

Analyzing VISUALS

Answers:
1. North Carolina, South Carolina, Georgia
2. Possible answer: The South still had fertile land, the know-how to do it, and African Americans who, while technically free, were still available and with sharecropping could be forced to farm the land.

Additional Support

The New South was a blend of the old and the new. Industry began to develop, but agriculture remained vital to the economy. By the 1890s, the South was exporting more cotton, rice, and tobacco than before the Civil War. Although slavery had ended, many African Americans were poor sharecroppers who harvested crops for landowners.

Sharecropping in the South, 1880

Percentage of sharecropped farms by county
- 34.2% to 81.0%
- 25.8% to 34.1%
- 19.6% to 25.7%
- 12.7% to 19.5%
- 0% to 12.6%

Albers Equal-Area projection

▲ The industry of the "New South" was still driven by agricultural products, such as tobacco. The workers shown above are processing tobacco in a Richmond tobacco factory in 1899.

Analyzing VISUALS

1. **Specifying** In which three states was sharecropping most common?
2. **Explaining** Why do you think the South's economy remained so dependent on agriculture after Reconstruction?

▲ Sharecroppers harvest cotton in Georgia in 1898.

The Compromise of 1877

The rising power of the Democrats in Congress and Republican concerns over scandals made enforcing Reconstruction more difficult. At the same time, many Northerners were becoming more concerned about the economy than the situation in the South.

In the 1870s, Democrats began to regain power in the South. They did so in part through intimidation and fraud, and in part by defining elections as a struggle between whites and African Americans. They also won back support by promising to cut the high taxes the Republicans had imposed and by accusing

Republicans of corruption. Southern Democrats viewed their efforts to regain power as a crusade to help save the South from Republican rule. By 1876, the Democrats had taken control of all but three Southern state legislatures.

That year, the nation's presidential election pitted Republican Rutherford B. Hayes, a former governor of Ohio, against Democrat Samuel Tilden, a wealthy corporate lawyer and former governor of New York. On Election Day, twenty electoral votes were disputed. Nineteen of the votes were in the three Southern states controlled by Republicans. As a result, congressional leaders worked out a deal known as the **Compromise of 1877.**

Activity: Economics Connection

Trends in the Labor Force Invite the economics teacher to describe the labor force and how jobs are classified into agricultural, manufacturing, or service sector jobs. Ask students to estimate what the trends in each category have been from the Civil War to the present. Then, have students use resources such as *Historical Statistics of the United States* to research the trends over time in the number of people employed in agriculture, manufacturing, and the service sector. Help them create line charts using the data to see if their estimations about the trends were accurate. **AL**

Historians are not sure if a deal really took place or what its exact terms were. The Compromise of 1877 reportedly included a promise by the Republicans to pull federal troops out of the South, if Hayes was elected, and that is in fact what happened within a month of Hayes taking office. However, it is also true that the nation was tired of the politics of Reconstruction and that Republican leaders were ready to end Reconstruction. Indeed, President Grant had pulled troops out of Florida even before Hayes took office.

A "New South" Arises

Many Southern leaders realized the South could never return to the pre–Civil War agricultural economy dominated by the planter elite. Instead, they called for the creation of a "New South"—a phrase coined by Henry Grady, editor of the *Atlanta Constitution*. They believed the region had to develop a strong industrial economy.

An alliance between powerful white Southerners and Northern financiers brought great economic changes to some parts of the South. Northern capital helped to build railroads, and by 1890, almost 40,000 miles of railroad track crisscrossed the South—nearly four times the amount there in 1860. Southern industry also grew. A thriving iron and steel industry developed around Birmingham, Alabama. In North Carolina, tobacco processing became big business, and cotton mills appeared in numerous small towns.

In other ways, however, the South changed little. Despite its industrial growth, the region remained agrarian. As late as 1900, only 6 percent of the Southern labor force worked in manufacturing. For many African Americans in particular, the end of Reconstruction meant a return to the "Old South," where they had little political power and were forced to labor under difficult and unfair conditions.

The collapse of Reconstruction ended African American hopes of being granted their own land in the South. Instead, many returned to plantations owned by whites, where they either worked for wages or became tenant farmers, paying rent for the land they farmed. Most tenant farmers eventually became **share-croppers.** Sharecroppers did not pay their rent in cash. Instead, they paid a share of their crops—often as much as one-half to two-thirds—to cover their rent as well as the cost of the seed, fertilizer, tools, and animals they needed.

Many sharecroppers needed more seed and supplies than their landlords could provide. Local suppliers, known as furnishing merchants, provided the supplies on credit, but at interest rates as high as 40 percent. To make sure sharecroppers paid their debts, laws allowed merchants to put liens on their crops. This meant the merchant could take crops to cover the debts. The crop lien system and high interest rates trapped sharecroppers on the land because they could not pay off their debts and leave, nor could they declare bankruptcy. Failure to pay off debts could lead to imprisonment or forced labor. The Civil War had ended slavery, but Reconstruction had left many African Americans trapped in poverty.

✔ Reading Check **Explaining** What major issue was settled by the Compromise of 1877?

S

Section 3 REVIEW

Vocabulary
1. **Explain** the significance of: Reconstruction, amnesty, Radical Republicans, pocket veto, Freedmen's Bureau, black codes, Fourteenth Amendment, Fifteenth Amendment, carpet-baggers, scalawags, Compromise of 1877, sharecroppers.

Main Ideas
2. **Identifying Points of View** What was President Lincoln's attitude toward the Reconstruction goals of the Radical Republicans?

3. **Explaining** What was the goal of one of the Enforcement Acts, passed in 1870–1871?

4. **Determining Cause and Effect** What was the cause and effect of the Panic of 1873?

Critical Thinking
5. **Big Ideas** What factors contributed to the improving economy of the South after Reconstruction?

6. **Organizing** Use a graphic organizer similar to the one below to identify the problems faced by Grant's administration.

Problems Faced by Grant's Administration

7. **Analyzing Visuals** Review the map on page 144. In what year were most southern states readmitted to the Union, and which states were they?

Writing About History
8. **Expository Writing** Write a short essay explaining what you consider to be the three most important events of Reconstruction and why you chose them.

History ONLINE
Study Central™ To review this section, go to glencoe.com and click on Study Central.

149

S **Skill Practice**
Drawing Conclusions Write on the board: "Difficult Problem" and "Difficult Solution." Ask students to list the problems they think were the most difficult for the South to solve during Reconstruction—and why. Then have the class vote on the most difficult. **OL**

✔ Reading Check

Answer:
the outcome of the presidential election of 1876

Assess
. . . .

History ONLINE

Study Central™ provides summaries, interactive games, and online graphic organizers to help students review content.

Close
. . . .

Summarizing Ask students how conditions changed for African Americans in the South from before the war to after Reconstruction. *(They were free, but rights gained initially were lost after Reconstruction.)*

Section 3 REVIEW

Answers

1. All definitions can be found in the section and the Glossary.
2. He sympathized with some of their views, but did not want to alienate Southerners with a harsh peace.
3. to outlaw the activities of the Ku Klux Klan
4. cause: A major banking firm declared bankruptcy; effect: a major economic depression that lasted for nearly the entire decade
5. investment by Northerners, growth of new industries

6. perception that wealthy Americans had too much influence, a series of scandals, the Panic of 1873
7. 1868; Arkansas, Florida, North Carolina, Louisiana, South Carolina, Alabama
8. Essays should include three events and an explanation for each.

You can study anywhere, anytime by downloading quizzes and flashcards to your PDA from glencoe.com.

Analyzing Have students research the point of view that someone in one of the following groups might have had about the war: Southern farmers, Southern shopkeepers, Southern merchant ship owners, Northern farmers, free Northern African American laborers, or Northern textile mill owners. Tell students to then write an essay explaining how a person in one of these groups might have felt about the war once it was over and why. Have students share their essays in class, and have classmates evaluate whether each essay accurately portrays the point of view of the person selected. **AL**

▲ *Jefferson Davis meets with his cabinet and General Lee.*

▲ *After the Battle of Antietam (above), Lincoln issued the Emancipation Proclamation.*

North v. South

1861
- Lincoln orders a blockade of Southern ports.
- The Confederacy organizes its government.
- The South wins the First Battle of Bull Run.
- Both sides begin building up their forces.

1862
- Farragut captures New Orleans.
- After the Battles of Shiloh and Murfreesboro, the Union gains control of western Tennessee.
- Led by McClellan, Union troops land in Virginia to begin the Peninsula Campaign; after a series of battles with Lee's forces, McClellan's forces withdraw.
- Lee invades the North but is defeated at the Battle of Antietam.

1863: The Turning Point
- Lincoln issues the Emancipation Proclamation.
- Grant captures Vicksburg after a long siege and cuts the Confederacy in two.
- After winning the battles of Fredericksburg and Chancellorsville, Lee invades the north but is defeated at the Battle of Gettysburg.
- After losing the Battle of Chickamauga, Union forces drive back Southern forces at the Battle of Chattanooga.
- Grant is given command of all Union forces.

1864
- Grant battles Lee's forces in northern Virginia; Lee retreats into Petersburg, which Grant puts under siege.
- Sherman captures Atlanta, then begins his March to the Sea across Georgia.

1865
- Lee attempts to escape from Petersburg but is surrounded by Grant's forces and surrenders at Appomattox Courthouse; other Confederate forces surrender as well.
- Lincoln is assassinated.

▼ *The capture of New Orleans (below) gave the Union control of the mouth of the Mississippi River.*

▼ *The failure of Pickett's Charge convinced Lee to withdraw from Gettysburg. It was the turning point of the war.*

▼ *Mourners surround Lincoln's hearse in Philadelphia in April 1865.*

150 Chapter 3   The Civil War and Reconstruction

Hands-On Chapter Project
Step 4: Wrap Up

Art Show on the Civil War and Reconstruction

Step 4: Wrap Up After students have hung the presentation, they will acquire feedback and learn from it.

Directions Ask viewers of the exhibit for their feedback. (You may want to put comment cards out.) As a class, review the comments and discuss your own reactions to the show. Ask the following questions to start the discussion:

- What was good about the show?
- Did the images illustrate the Civil War and/or Reconstruction clearly? Why or why not?
- How could the show have been improved?
- What would you do differently if you did this project again?

Putting It Together Have students write a brief summary of their reactions to the project, explaining how it illustrated the Civil War and Reconstruction and whether the project helped them review the chapter. **OL**

ASSESSMENT

STANDARDIZED TEST PRACTICE

TEST-TAKING TIP

Be sure to read each question carefully to identify any key words that may help you to either choose the correct answer choice or eliminate incorrect answer choices.

Reviewing Vocabulary

Directions: Choose the word or words that best complete the sentence.

1. Abraham Lincoln declared _____ in Baltimore to prevent Maryland's secession.
   A martial law
   B abolition
   C habeas corpus
   D popular sovereignty

2. Because of the effectiveness of the Union Navy, the Confederacy often used _____ to get needed supplies.
   A ironclads
   B blockade runners
   C cavalry
   D British warships

3. General Ulysses S. Grant employed a strategy known as a _____ to capture the city of Vicksburg.
   A battle
   B blockade
   C siege
   D charge

4. Northerners who came to the South during Reconstruction were called _____ by Southerners who believed the Northerners were exploiting the South's misfortune for personal gain.
   A scalawags
   B sharecroppers
   C carpetbaggers
   D furnishing merchants

Reviewing Main Ideas

Directions: Choose the best answer for each of the following questions.

Section 1 *(pp. 122–129)*

5. The Civil War began when
   A Lincoln refused to send troops into Kentucky.
   B Fort Sumter fell to the Confederacy.
   C Virginia seceded from the Union.
   D Army officers imprisoned many suspected secessionists.

6. Which of the following was part of the Union's Anaconda Plan for defeating the Confederacy?
   A a blockade of Southern ports
   B a quick ground offensive
   C the assassination of Jefferson Davis
   D a defensive war of attrition

Section 2 *(pp. 130–137)*

7. One result of the Battle of Antietam was that
   A Lincoln issued the Emancipation Proclamation.
   B the Confederacy was split in two.
   C Great Britain decided to support the Confederacy.
   D David Farragut became a hero in the North.

8. The institution of slavery was formally abolished in the United States by the
   A Compromise of 1850.
   B Emancipation Proclamation of 1863.
   C ratification of the Thirteenth Amendment.
   D creation of the Freedman's Bureau in 1865.

Need Extra Help?

If You Missed Questions . . .	1	2	3	4	5	6	7	8
Go to Page . . .	126	130	134	145	125	129	133	137

GO ON

Answers and Analyses
Reviewing Vocabulary

1. A Martial law is when the military takes over for local government and people's civil rights are suspended. Abolition is to end something, and does not make sense. Habeas corpus was suspended during the war, not declared. Lincoln did not declare popular sovereignty.

2. B Three of the answers are types of ships, which may confuse students. However, the Union navy used blockades, which means they sealed off Southern harbors and cut them off to trade. Blockade runners literally ran (moved) through the blockades to smuggle supplies.

3. C Students should think of a siege as an all-out attack. Grant cut off the food supply and troops bombarded the city. Battle and charge are too general to work in the blank. A blockade cuts off food and supplies, but does not involve a coordinated attack to devastate a city.

4. C Carpetbaggers were called so because of their bags made of carpet remnants. A scalawag was a white Southerner who supported Reconstruction. Furnishing merchant is a distracter based on similarity to "carpet."

Reviewing Main Ideas

5. B Students can approach this question in a chronological way. Fort Sumter fell before the events in the other answer choices happened. Virginia seceded right after Sumter fell. Army officers imprisoned suspected secessionists during martial law in Maryland. Shortly after that, Lincoln refused to send troops into Kentucky.

6. A Remind students that an anaconda is a snake that kills its prey by strangulation. The Anaconda plan included a blockade, *A*, in addition to splitting the Confederacy by taking the Mississippi. This would slowly "strangle" the South.

7. A Lincoln had not emancipated enslaved African Americans at the beginning of the war, for fear of alienating border states. However, after Antietam, the issuance of the Proclamation added a new motivation to the war: freeing enslaved people.

8. C Students may be tempted to choose *B*, but remind them that the Proclamation only declared free those enslaved persons residing in areas still in rebellion against the United States. The Thirteenth Amendment formally ended slavery.

151

9. D Grant's capture of Vicksburg and victory at Chattanooga proved his military skill and leadership.

10. A This question can be answered using the process of elimination. *B* is incorrect, because under the Bill, once all white men in the state had taken an oath of allegiance, they could then hold a constitutional convention. *C* is the opposite of one of the provisions, which stated the constitutions must ban all former Confederate leaders from voting. *D* was not a provision of the Wade-Davis Bill.

11. D The Compromise of 1877 was the name given to the election of Hayes. Although the details of a compromise, if there indeed was one, are murky, it was said that Hayes promised to remove federal troops from the South. Federal troops were removed from the South shortly after Hayes became president, which confirmed for some that a compromise had taken place.

12. C The culture of the South during Reconstruction makes choices *A, B,* and *D* highly unlikely. Black codes limited the rights of Southern African Americans.

Critical Thinking

13. B Choices *A, C,* and *D* are untrue. The largest weapons factories were in the North. It cannot be said that most people in the country agreed with the Southern states, given the number of states that stayed with the Union. The Confederacy failed in its efforts to gain support from Great Britain and France.

14. D General McClellen was a Union General. Have students trace the black arrow, which according to the key represents the Union advance. Have students trace their finger along the line.

---

9. After the successful capture of Chattanooga, Lincoln

  A recalled General Sherman to Washington, D.C.

  B issued the Emancipation Proclamation.

  C began negotiations for peace with the Confederacy.

  D made General Grant general in chief of the Union.

Section 3 *(pp. 140–149)*

10. Which of the following was a provision of the Wade-Davis Bill for readmitting Southern states to the Union?

  A The majority of white men in the state had to take an oath of allegiance to the United States.

  B Each state could hold a constitutional convention.

  C All former Confederate political and military leaders would be given the right to vote.

  D Freed African Americans had to be provided with "forty acres and a mule."

11. In the Compromise of 1877, supposedly Rutherford B. Hayes was made president if he would do which of the following once in office?

  A free all enslaved African Americans in the Southern states

  B ensure the passage of the Enforcement Acts

  C pardon members of President Grant's administration

  D remove all federal troops from the Southern states

12. Following the Civil War, many Southern states enacted Black Codes to

  A provide free farmland for African Americans.

  B guarantee equal civil rights for African Americans.

  C restrict the rights of formerly enslaved persons.

  D support the creation of the Freedmen's Bureau.

Critical Thinking

Directions: Choose the best answers to the following questions.

13. One advantage that the Confederacy held during the Civil War was that

  A it received military and financial support from the British and French.

  B many battles occurred on lands with which Southerners were more familiar.

  C the largest weapons factories were located in the South.

  D most people in the country agreed with the position of the Southern states.

Base your answers to questions 14 and 15 on the map below and your knowledge of Chapter 3.

Peninsula Campaign, April–May 1862

14. How did General McClellan move his troops to Virginia?

  A by railroad.

  B by wagon.

  C by land.

  D by water.

15. The object of the Peninsula campaign for the Union was to

  A capture Richmond.

  B capture Yorktown.

  C beat Magruder to Fredericksburg.

  D blockade Chesapeake Bay.

Need Extra Help?							
If You Missed Questions . . .	9	10	11	12	13	14	15
Go to Page . . .	135	141–142	148–149	143	132–133	R15	R15

GO ON

---

15. A Even without knowledge from the chapter, it is evident from the map that all of the Union and Confederate paths move toward a convergence at Richmond.

16. After the Civil War, many formerly enslaved African Americans earned a living by becoming

A railroad workers in the West.

B sharecroppers on Southern farms.

C workers in Northern factories.

D gold miners in California.

Analyze the cartoon and answer the question that follows. Base your answer on the cartoon and on your knowledge of Chapter 3.

17. This cartoon features Peace Democrats, called "Copperheads," and the main idea is that they are

A helpful to the Union cause.

B a threat to the Union cause.

C frightening to many people.

D peaceful and caring.

Document-Based Questions

Directions: Analyze the document and answer the short-answer questions that follow the document.

At the beginning of the Civil War, Robert E. Lee wrote a letter to his sister, Anne Marshall, explaining his decision to resign from the U.S. Army. Below is an excerpt from that letter:

> "My Dear Sister:
>
> . . . With all my devotion to the Union and the feeling of loyalty and duty of an American citizen, I have not been able to make up my mind to raise my hand against my relatives, my children, my home. I have, therefore, resigned my commission in the Army, and, save in defense of my native state . . . I hope I may never be called on to draw my sword. I know you will blame me; but you must think as kindly of me as you can. . . ."
>
> —from *Personal Reminiscences, Anecdotes, and Letters of General Robert E. Lee*

18. Why did Robert E. Lee think it was necessary to resign from the U.S. Army at the start of the war?

19. What do you think Lee's feelings were about the war?

Extended Response

20. President Lincoln suspended writs of habeas corpus during the Civil War to prevent interference with the draft. In a persuasive essay, explain your views on the suspension of civil liberties in this case, and in general. Do you think that the suspension of civil liberties is justified in some situations? In your essay, include an introduction and at least three paragraphs with details from the chapter to support your views.

STOP

ONLINE

For additional test practice, use Self-Check Quizzes— Chapter 3 at glencoe.com.

Need Extra Help?					
If You Missed Questions . . .	16	17	18	19	20
Go to Page . . .	149	R18	R19	R19	R12

19. Answers will vary. Possible answer: He probably thought it was a terrible tragedy, and he could not fight a war against his own family.

Extended Response

20. Students' essays must present a clear position, either for or against the suspension of writs of habeas corpus during war and in other circumstances. Arguments must be focused and well-reasoned. Essays must include supporting details from the text, as well as an introduction, conclusion, and at least three body paragraphs.

16. B Many formerly enslaved African Americans became sharecroppers, which left them little better off than they had been when they were enslaved. Sharecroppers were tied to the land because they were constantly working to pay off debts that could never be repaid; they were essentially economically enslaved.

17. B Help students analyze the cartoon. The woman, carrying a shield that says "Union" represents the Union. This is a play on the traditional Lady Liberty figure. The Copperheads are clearly advancing on the woman in a threatening way. *A* and *D* do not fit with the threatening nature of the Copperheads. *C* is too general to describe the cartoon.

Document-Based Questions

18. Lee did not want to stay in the Union Army and fight fellow Virginians. Lee, like hundreds of other Southern military men, did not want to break up the Union, but his loyalty to his "countrymen" would not permit him to take up arms against them.

ONLINE

Have students visit the Web site at glencoe.com to review Chapter 3 and take the Self-Check Quiz.

Need Extra Help?

Have students refer to the pages listed if they miss any of the questions.

UNIT PACING CHART

	Unit 2	Chapter 4	Chapter 5	Chapter 6	Unit 2
Day 1	Unit Opener	Chapter 4 Opener, Section 1	Chapter 5 Opener, Section 1	Chapter 6 Opener, Section 1	Wrap-Up/Project, Unit Assessment
Day 2		Sections 2 & 3	Section 2	Section 2	
Day 3		Chapter Assessment	Section 3	Section 3	
Day 4			Section 4	Section 4	
Day 5			Chapter Assessment	Section 5	
Day 6				Chapter Assessment	

Teacher to Teacher

**Teresa Squires Osborne
Reynolds High School
Troutdale, OR**

Immigration Panel Create a panel of students, from your class and/or from the school, made up of first and second generation immigrants to the United States. After panel members have shown their country of origin on a map, have the student panel address the following information:

1. What is the story of your family's arrival here? Where and when did you or your parents arrive in the United States?

2. Why did your family choose to leave your native country?

3. What is different or similar about life in the United States compared to your family's native country?

4. How would your life be different if you or your parents had remained?

Have students compare the answers of the panel with the experiences of earlier immigrant groups.

Author Note

Dear American History Teacher,

Each of the chapters in this unit focuses on one of the three major developments in the United States during the generation after the Civil War. The Union victory removed the conflict between slavery and freedom that had entangled westward expansion before 1861, and loosened dynamic forces of expansion that filled up a million square miles of the West and brought 10 new states into the Union. Five transcontinental railroads built during these years connected the western half of the country to the rest in a continental economy of unprecedented proportions. Cattle ranching and mining became dominant features of this new West. But if for white Americans (and some African Americans) the West represented frontiers of opportunity, for Native Americans these decades spelled the doom of their once vital independent culture as they were squeezed onto smaller and smaller reservations.

All kinds of industry grew exponentially after the Civil War. A distant second to Britain in world industrial production in 1860, the United States surpassed Britain in the 1880s and, by 1900, American factories produced as much as those of Britain and Germany combined. But this growth produced a widening gap between rich and poor and violent conflict between capital and labor that at times seemed to threaten the very fabric of American society.

So did the growth of American cities, fed by large-scale immigration. The United States became a multi-ethnic and multi-cultural nation where various nationalities and languages co-existed uneasily in burgeoning cities whose institutions and infrastructures failed to keep pace with this rapid growth.

At the local, state, and national levels, government seemed unable to cope with these multiple dimensions of spatial, industrial, and population growth. All of these developments climaxed in what historians have described as "the crisis of the 1890s." Not until the post-1890s generation would the American polity begin to get a grip on these problems.

James M. McPherson
Senior Author

Focus

Why It Matters

Have students consider the changes that have occurred in their lifetimes as a result of technological advances. Then have them make generalizations about the effects of technological change on peoples' lives. **OL**

Connecting to Past Learning

Have students recall social and economic conditions after the Civil War. **Ask:** How were conditions in the North different from conditions in the South? *(The infrastructure of the North was intact and manufacturing industries were growing; the South was in ruins.)* Tell students that in this unit they will learn about the rapid industrialization that took place after the Civil War, as well as reform movements that developed in response to industrialization. **OL**

Unit Launch Activity

Making Connections Have students brainstorm a list of inventions or new technologies that they did not have five or ten years ago. List students' answers on the board. **Ask:** How is your life different with these inventions or new technologies? *(Answers will vary, but students might note that communication is faster; downloading music or video is easier.)* Discuss with the class how inventions and new technologies changed the lives of the people living after the Civil War. **OL**

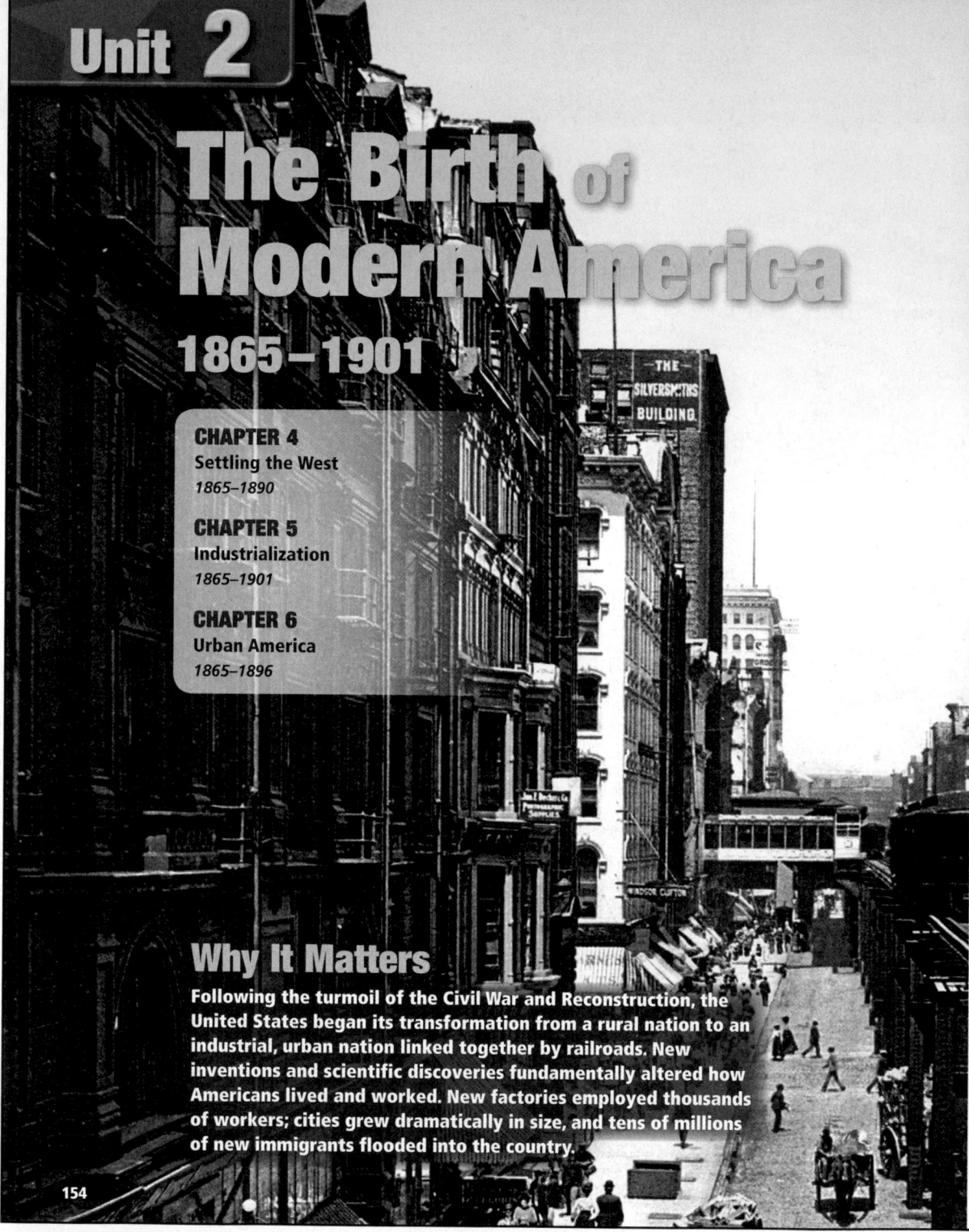

Unit 2
The Birth of Modern America
1865–1901

CHAPTER 4
Settling the West
1865–1890

CHAPTER 5
Industrialization
1865–1901

CHAPTER 6
Urban America
1865–1896

Why It Matters

Following the turmoil of the Civil War and Reconstruction, the United States began its transformation from a rural nation to an industrial, urban nation linked together by railroads. New inventions and scientific discoveries fundamentally altered how Americans lived and worked. New factories employed thousands of workers; cities grew dramatically in size, and tens of millions of new immigrants flooded into the country.

154

Team Teaching Activity

Economics Have the economics teacher compare and contrast small, entrepreneurial businesses with big businesses, and family farms with large agricultural enterprises. After the presentation, have a class discussion using the following questions: How are workers treated differently in different types of enterprises? How is family life affected by various enterprises? How does the type of enterprise in which your family is involved affect where and how you live? What effect do economic changes such as recessions have on these types of enterprises? **OL**

Wabash Avenue and the elevated railroad in downtown Chicago, 1900.

155

More About the Photo

Visual Literacy Because of its location, Chicago grew to be a transportation hub. To help the city's growing population move around, the city built elevated commuter rail lines, which have become known as the "L." The first line was completed in 1888.

Teach

Skill Practice

Visual Literacy Have students study the unit photograph. **Ask:** What types of transportation are shown in the photograph? *(elevated rail lines, horse-drawn-cart)* Based on the photograph, have students make a generalization about Chicagoans' lives at the time. *(Answers will vary, but students should note that it was a time of great change.)* **BL**

Skill Practice

Describing Have students again review the unit photograph. **Ask:** Based on the photograph, what concerns or issues might some citizens have? *(Answers might include overcrowding, noise pollution, air pollution, unsanitary conditions.)* Given the list of issues, have students describe what concerned citizens might do. *(Organize reform movements.)* **OL**

NO CHILD LEFT BEHIND

Teaching Tip The NCLB Act emphasizes reading. Ask students to write down events and people they will encounter in this unit and keep the list with them as they read. When students find a person or item on the list, they should note the page number and write a brief summary. Students can use this list while studying.

Levels BL	OL	AL	ELL		Resources	Chapter Opener	Section 1	Section 2	Section 3	Chapter Assess
					FOCUS					
BL	OL	AL	ELL	🖋	Daily Focus Transparencies		4-1	4-2	4-3	
					TEACH					
	OL	AL		📁	American Literature Reading, URB		p. 13		p. 15	
BL	OL		ELL	📁	Reading Skills Activity, URB			p. 21		
	OL			📁	Historical Analysis Skills Activity, URB		p. 22			
BL	OL	AL	ELL	📁	Differentiated Instruction Activity, URB				p. 23	
BL			ELL	📁	English Learner Activity, URB		p. 25			
BL	OL	AL	ELL	📁	Content Vocabulary Activity, URB*		p. 27			
BL	OL	AL	ELL	📁	Academic Vocabulary Activity, URB		p. 29			
	OL	AL		📁	Reinforcing Skills Activity, URB			p. 31		
	OL	AL		📁	Critical Thinking Skills Activity, URB				p. 32	
BL	OL		ELL	📁	Time Line Activity, URB				p. 33	
	OL			📁	Linking Past and Present Activity, URB		p. 34			
BL	OL	AL	ELL	📁	Primary Source Reading, URB				p. 35	p. 37
BL	OL	AL	ELL	📁	American Art and Music Activity, URB		p. 39			
BL	OL	AL	ELL	📁	Interpreting Political Cartoons Activity, URB				p. 41	
		AL		📁	Enrichment Activity, URB				p. 45	
BL	OL		ELL	📁	Guided Reading Activity, URB*		p. 48	p. 49	p. 50	
BL	OL	AL	ELL	📁	Reading Essentials and Note-Taking Guide*		p. 34	p. 37	p. 40	
BL	OL	AL	ELL	📁	Differentiated Instruction for the American History Classroom	✓	✓	✓	✓	✓
BL	OL	AL	ELL	🖋	Unit Map Overlay Transparencies	✓	✓	✓	✓	✓
BL	OL	AL	ELL	📁	Unit Time Line Transparencies, Strategies, and Activities	✓	✓	✓	✓	✓
BL	OL	AL	ELL	📁	Cause and Effect Transparencies, Strategies, and Activities	✓	✓	✓	✓	✓
BL	OL	AL	ELL	📁	Why It Matters Chapter Transparencies, Strategies, and Activities	✓	✓	✓	✓	✓

Note: Please refer to the *Unit 2 Resource Book* for this chapter's URB materials.

* Also available in Spanish

- Interactive Lesson Planner
- Interactive Teacher Edition
- Fully editable blackline masters
- Section Spotlight Videos Launch
- Differentiated Lesson Plans
- Printable reports of daily assignments
- Standards Tracking System

Levels BL OL AL ELL		Resources	Chapter Opener	Section 1	Section 2	Section 3	Chapter Assess
BL OL AL ELL		**American Biographies**				✓	
BL OL AL ELL		**Supreme Court Case Studies**			p. 21		
BL OL AL ELL		**The Living Constitution**	✓	✓	✓	✓	✓
BL OL AL ELL		**American Issues**	✓	✓	✓	✓	✓
OL AL ELL		**American Art and Architecture Transparencies, Strategies, and Activities**	✓	✓	✓	✓	✓
BL OL AL		**High School American History Literature Library**	✓	✓	✓	✓	✓
OL AL		**American History Primary Source Documents Library**	✓	✓	✓	✓	✓
BL OL AL ELL		**American Music: Hits Through History CD**	✓	✓	✓	✓	✓
BL OL AL ELL		**StudentWorks™ Plus DVD**	✓	✓	✓	✓	✓
BL OL AL ELL		**Vocabulary PuzzleMaker CD-ROM**	✓	✓	✓	✓	✓
BL OL AL ELL		*The American Vision* **Video Program DVD**	✓	✓	✓	✓	✓
Teacher Resources		**Reading Strategies and Activities for the Social Studies Classroom**	✓	✓	✓	✓	✓
		Strategies for Success	✓	✓	✓	✓	✓
		Presentation Plus! DVD	✓	✓	✓	✓	✓
		Success With English Learners	✓	✓	✓	✓	✓

ASSESS

Levels BL OL AL ELL		Resources	Chapter Opener	Section 1	Section 2	Section 3	Chapter Assess
BL OL AL ELL		**Section Quizzes and Chapter Tests***		p. 49	p. 50	p. 51	p. 53
BL OL AL ELL		**Authentic Assessment With Rubrics**					p. 13
BL OL AL ELL		**Standardized Test Practice Workbook**					p. 8
BL OL AL ELL		*ExamView®* **Assessment Suite CD-ROM**		4-1	4-2	4-3	Ch. 4
BL OL AL ELL		**Interactive Tutor Self-Assessment CD-ROM**		4-1	4-2	4-3	Ch. 4

CLOSE

Levels BL OL AL ELL		Resources	Chapter Opener	Section 1	Section 2	Section 3	Chapter Assess
BL ELL		**Reteaching Activity, URB**					p. 43
BL OL ELL		**Reading and Study Skills Foldables™**	p. 59				
BL OL AL ELL		*American History* **in Graphic Novel**		p. 23			

Using CyberScout

Research Using *Subject Area*

Technology Product

CyberScout is a convenient and dynamic search engine that provides several easy ways to locate information outside the McGraw-Hill Learning Network. CyberScout only searches Web sites that have been reviewed by teachers, so the information students find is always appropriate and accurate.

Objectives

After students learn using CyberScout, they will be able to

- research topics and issues in history using CyberScout;
- exercise research and study skills;
- practice writing skills.

Steps

- From the McGraw-Hill Learning Network home page (www.mhln.com), click on **For Students.**
- Choose **CyberScout** below **Homework Help.**

- Click on a subject area link to narrow the search.
- The CyberScout page will display a set of results.
- Drill down by continuing to click result links until you find a Web site of interest.
- Click on the link to reach the Web site.
- Students will be redirected to the Web site in a new window.
- Students navigate through the chosen Web site to gain information on their topic and take notes.

	Student	Teacher	Parent
Beyond the Textbook	●	●	●
Chapter Overviews	●	●	●
Time Current Events	●		●
ePuzzles and Games	●		●
Concepts in Motion	●		●
Literature Connections		●	
Multi-Language Glossaries	●		●
Online Student Edition	●	●	●
Self-Check Quizzes	●		●
Student Web Activities	●		●
Study Central™	●		●
Teaching Today		●	
Vocabulary eFlashcards	●		●
Web Activity Lesson Plans		●	

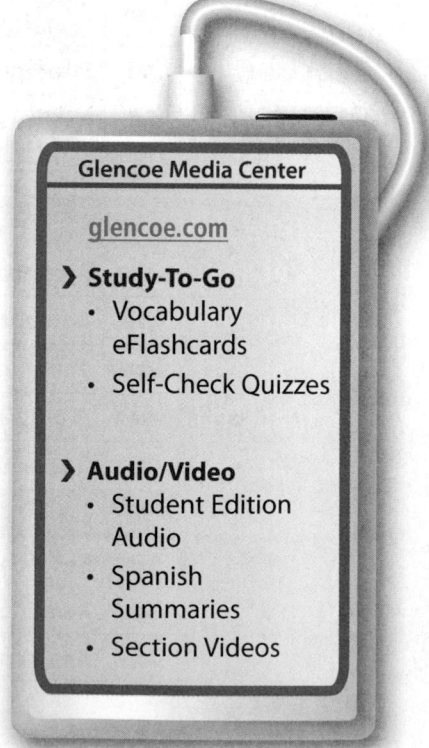

Glencoe Media Center

glencoe.com

❯ **Study-To-Go**
- Vocabulary eFlashcards
- Self-Check Quizzes

❯ **Audio/Video**
- Student Edition Audio
- Spanish Summaries
- Section Videos

- **Timed Readings Plus in Social Studies** helps students increase their reading rate and fluency while maintaining comprehension. The 400-word passages are similar to those found on state and national assessments.

- **Reading in the Content Area: Social Studies** concentrates on six essential reading skills that help students better comprehend what they read. The book includes 75 high-interest nonfiction passages written at increasing levels of difficulty.

- **Reading Social Studies** includes strategic reading instruction and vocabulary support in Social Studies content for both ELLs and native speakers of English.

www.jamestowneducation.com

The following videotape programs are available from Glencoe as supplements to Chapter 4:

- Buffalo Bill: Showman of the West (ISBN 1-56-501940-7)
- Sitting Bull: Chief of the Lakota Nation (ISBN 1-56-501684-X)

To order, call Glencoe at 1-800-334-7344. To find classroom resources to accompany many of these videos, check the following home pages:

A&E Television: www.aetv.com
The History Channel: www.historychannel.com

Index to National Geographic Magazine:

The following articles relate to this chapter:

- "The American Prairie: Roots of the Sky," by Douglas H. Chadwick and Jim Brandenbur, October 1993.

- "Custer and the warriors of the plains; Ghosts on the Little Bighorn. (George Armstrong Custer)," by Robert Paul Jordan, December 1986.

National Geographic Society Products To order the following, call National Geographic at 1-800-368-2728:

- *The Westward Movement* (CD-ROM).

Access National Geographic's new dynamic MapMachine Web site and other geography resources at:
www.nationalgeographic.com
www.nationalgeographic.com/maps

Use this database to search more than 30,000 titles to create a customized reading list for your students.

- Reading lists can be organized by students' reading level, author, genre, theme, or area of interest.

- The database provides Degrees of Reading Power™ (DRP) and Lexile™ readability scores for all selections.

- A brief summary of each selection is included.

Leveled reading suggestions for this chapter:

For students at a Grade 8 reading level:
- *Laura Ingalls Wilder: Young Pioneer,* by Beatrice Gromley

For students at a Grade 9 reading level:
- *The Story of the Little Bighorn,* by R. Conrad Stein

For students at a Grade 10 reading level:
- *Wild West,* by Mike Stotter

For students at a Grade 11 reading level:
- *Sod Houses on the Great Plains,* by Glen Rounds

For students at a Grade 12 reading level:
- *In the Days of the Vaqueros: America's First True Cowboys,* by Russell Freedman

Focus

MAKING CONNECTIONS
Why Did Settlers Move West? Ask: For what reasons might Americans have wanted to move west after the Civil War? Might the reasons have been different for white Americans and for African Americans? *(Possible answer: Students might conclude that both white Americans and African Americans sought new lives and new economic opportunities. White settlers, however, had not been enslaved, while many formerly enslaved African American settlers moved west to escape from the sharecropping system that developed in the South after the Civil War.)* **OL**

Teach

Big Ideas

As students study the chapter, remind them to consider the section-based Big Ideas included in each section's Guide to Reading. Focusing on these ideas will help them understand the important concepts in each section and in the chapter as a whole. In addition, the Hands-on Chapter Projects with their culminating activities relate the content from each section to the Big Ideas. These activities build on each other as students progress through the chapter. Section activities culminate in the wrap-up activity on the Visual Summary page.

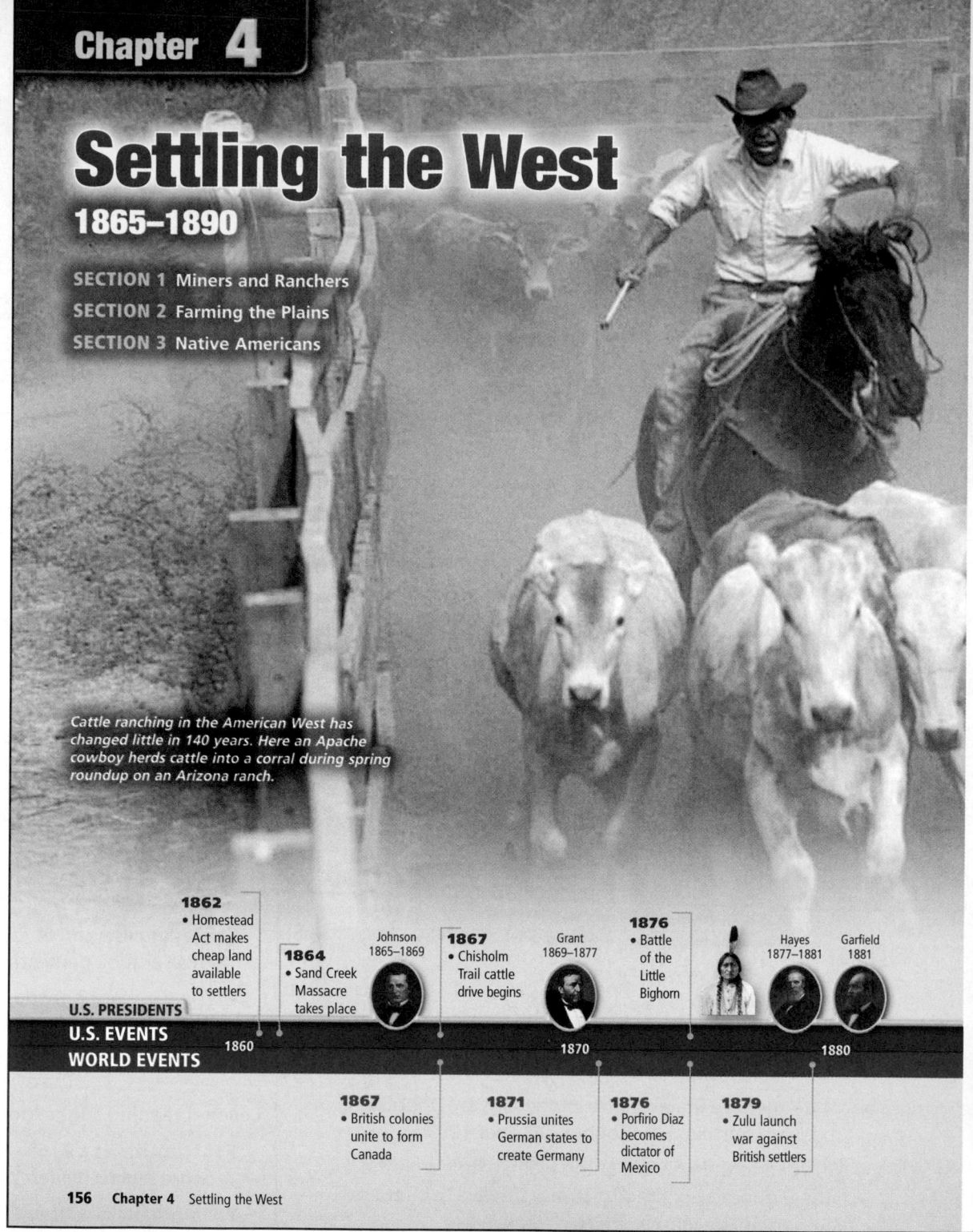

Chapter 4

Settling the West
1865–1890

SECTION 1 Miners and Ranchers
SECTION 2 Farming the Plains
SECTION 3 Native Americans

Cattle ranching in the American West has changed little in 140 years. Here an Apache cowboy herds cattle into a corral during spring roundup on an Arizona ranch.

U.S. PRESIDENTS
U.S. EVENTS
WORLD EVENTS

1862
• Homestead Act makes cheap land available to settlers

1864
• Sand Creek Massacre takes place

Johnson 1865–1869

1867
• Chisholm Trail cattle drive begins

Grant 1869–1877

1876
• Battle of the Little Bighorn

Hayes 1877–1881

Garfield 1881

1860

1870

1880

1867
• British colonies unite to form Canada

1871
• Prussia unites German states to create Germany

1876
• Porfirio Diaz becomes dictator of Mexico

1879
• Zulu launch war against British settlers

156 Chapter 4 Settling the West

Section 1

Miners and Ranchers
Ask: What economic opportunities did miners and ranchers seek? *(Miners sought to strike it rich quickly; ranchers saw their ranches as a long-term economic investment.)* Point out that in Section 1 students will learn about the impact of miners and ranchers on Western settlement. **OL**

Section 2

Farming the Plains
Ask: What difficulties might farmers have faced as they worked the new land? *(hard soil that was difficult to plow; lack of rain; few trees from which to build cabins for shelter)* Point out that in Section 2 students will learn how land once called "The Great American Desert" became the most productive farmland in the world. **OL**

MAKING CONNECTIONS
Why Did Settlers Move West?

After the Civil War, many American settlers continued migrating to the western frontier. The lives of western miners, farmers, and ranchers were filled with hardships.

- *Why do you think settlers continued migrating west when life on the Great Plains was so difficult?*
- *When the frontier closed what effect do you think this had on American society?*

1887
- Dawes Act eliminates communal ownership of Native American reservations

Arthur 1881–1885

Cleveland 1885–1889

Harrison 1889–1893

Cleveland 1893–1897

McKinley 1897–1901

1890

1900

1886
- Gold is discovered in South Africa

1891
- Russia begins Trans-Siberian railway and many settlers head east to Siberia

FOLDABLES™

Summarizing Displacement Make a Sentence Strips Foldable to represent how the arrival of settlers changed the American West. Choose an event and create a flip book. On the front of each strip write the event and its location. Write a brief explanation of how the event changed the West.

History ONLINE Chapter Overview
Visit glencoe.com to preview Chapter 4.

Chapter 4 Settling the West **157**

More About the Photo

Visual Literacy Despite the success of ranching in the late 1800s, cowboys received little of the profits. Cattle hands who endured the grueling 800 mile drive from Texas to Kansas earned only $30 dollars a month. Because of this, most cowboys were young men looking for temporary work. Many other drivers were African Americans, who were barred from other types of jobs and found a sense of freedom on the trails.

FOLDABLES™ Study Organizer Dinah Zike's Foldables

Dinah Zike's Foldables are three-dimensional, interactive graphic organizers that help students practice basic writing skills, review vocabulary terms, and identify main ideas. Instructions for creating and using Foldables can be found in the Appendix at the end of this book and in the Dinah Zike's Reading and Study Skills Foldables booklet.

Section 3

Native Americans

Ask: Why did conflicts arise between Native Americans and the settlers? *(Miners, ranchers, and farmers took Native Americans' land and destroyed their sources of food.)* Point out that in Section 3 students will learn about how the American government tried to settle the conflicts between the Native Americans and the settlers. **OL**

History ONLINE
Introduce students to chapter content and key terms by having them access the Chapter 4 Overview at glencoe.com.

Focus

Bellringer

Daily Focus Transparency 4.1

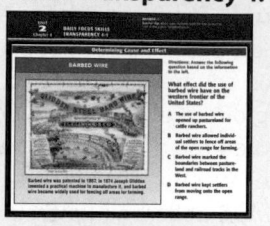

Guide to Reading

Answers may include: silver in Nevada (Comstock Lode), lead and silver in Leadville, Colorado, gold in Colorado, gold in Dakota Territory, copper in Montana, copper in Arizona

Section Spotlight Video

To generate student interest and provide a springboard for class discussion, access the Chapter 4, Section 1 video at glencoe.com or on the video DVD.

Resource Manager

Section 1

Miners and Ranchers

Guide to Reading

Big Ideas
Geography and History Miners and ranchers settled large areas of the West.

Content Vocabulary
• vigilance committee (p. 159)
• hydraulic mining (p. 161)
• open range (p. 162)
• long drive (p. 163)
• hacienda (p. 164)
• barrios (p. 165)

Academic Vocabulary
• extract (p. 160)
• adapt (p. 162)
• prior (p. 162)

People and Events to Identify
• Henry Comstock (p. 158)
• boomtown (p. 158)

Reading Strategy
Organizing As you read about the development of the mining industry, complete a graphic organizer listing the locations of mining booms and the discoveries made there.

Mining Booms & Discoveries

Mining and ranching attracted settlers to western territories that soon had populations large enough to qualify for statehood. People mined for gold, silver, and lead, or shipped longhorn cattle to the East.

Growth of the Mining Industry

MAIN Idea The discovery of gold, silver, and other minerals attracted thousands of settlers who established new states on the frontier.

HISTORY AND YOU Do you remember reading about the 1849 California gold rush? Read on to learn how mineral discoveries shaped the settlement of the West.

Mining played an important role in the settling of the American West. Beginning with the California gold rush, and continuing throughout the late 1800s, wave after wave of prospectors came to the region hoping to strike it rich mining gold, silver, and other minerals. Demand for minerals rose dramatically after the Civil War as the United States changed from a farming nation to an industrial nation. Mining in the West also encouraged the building of railroads to connect the mines to factories back east.

Boomtowns

In 1859 a prospector named **Henry Comstock** staked a claim in Six-Mile Canyon, near Virginia City, Nevada. Frustrated by his failure to find any gold, Comstock sold his claim a few months later. He had not realized that the sticky, blue-gray clay that made mining in the area difficult was in fact nearly pure silver ore.

News of the Comstock Lode, as the strike came to be called, brought a flood of eager prospectors to Virginia City. So many people arrived that, in 1864, Nevada was admitted as the 36th state. The Comstock Lode generated more than $230 million and helped the Union finance the Civil War.

The story of the Comstock Lode was replayed many times in the American West. News of a mineral strike would start a stampede of prospectors. Almost overnight, tiny frontier towns were transformed into small cities. Virginia City, for example, grew from a town of a few hundred people to nearly 30,000 in just a few months. It had an opera house, shops with furniture and fashions from Europe, several newspapers, and a six-story hotel.

These quickly growing towns were called **boomtowns.** Using the word "boom" this way began in the late 1800s. It refers to a time of rapid economic growth.

R Reading Strategies	**C** Critical Thinking	**D** Differentiated Instruction	**W** Writing Support	**S** Skill Practice
Teacher Edition • Using Context Clues, p. 162 • Read Prim. Sources, p. 164 **Additional Resources** • Guided Read. Act., URB p. 48 • Am. History in Graphic Novel, p. 23	**Teacher Edition** • Making Gen., p. 160 • Identify. Central Issues, p. 163 • Predict. Conseq., p. 164 **Additional Resources** • Link. Past and Present, URB p. 34 • Quizzes and Tests, p. 49	**Teacher Edition** • Visual/Spatial, p. 160 • Kinesthetic, p. 165 **Additional Resources** • Eng. Learner Act., URB p. 25 • Foldables, p. 59 • Am. Art and Music Act., URB p. 39	**Teacher Edition** • Descrip. Writing, pp. 161, 162 **Additional Resources** • Content Vocab. Act., URB p. 27 • Acad. Vocab. Act., URB p. 29	**Teacher Edition** • Reading a Graph, p. 387 **Additional Resources** • Hist. Analysis Skills Act., URB p. 22 • RENTG, p. 34

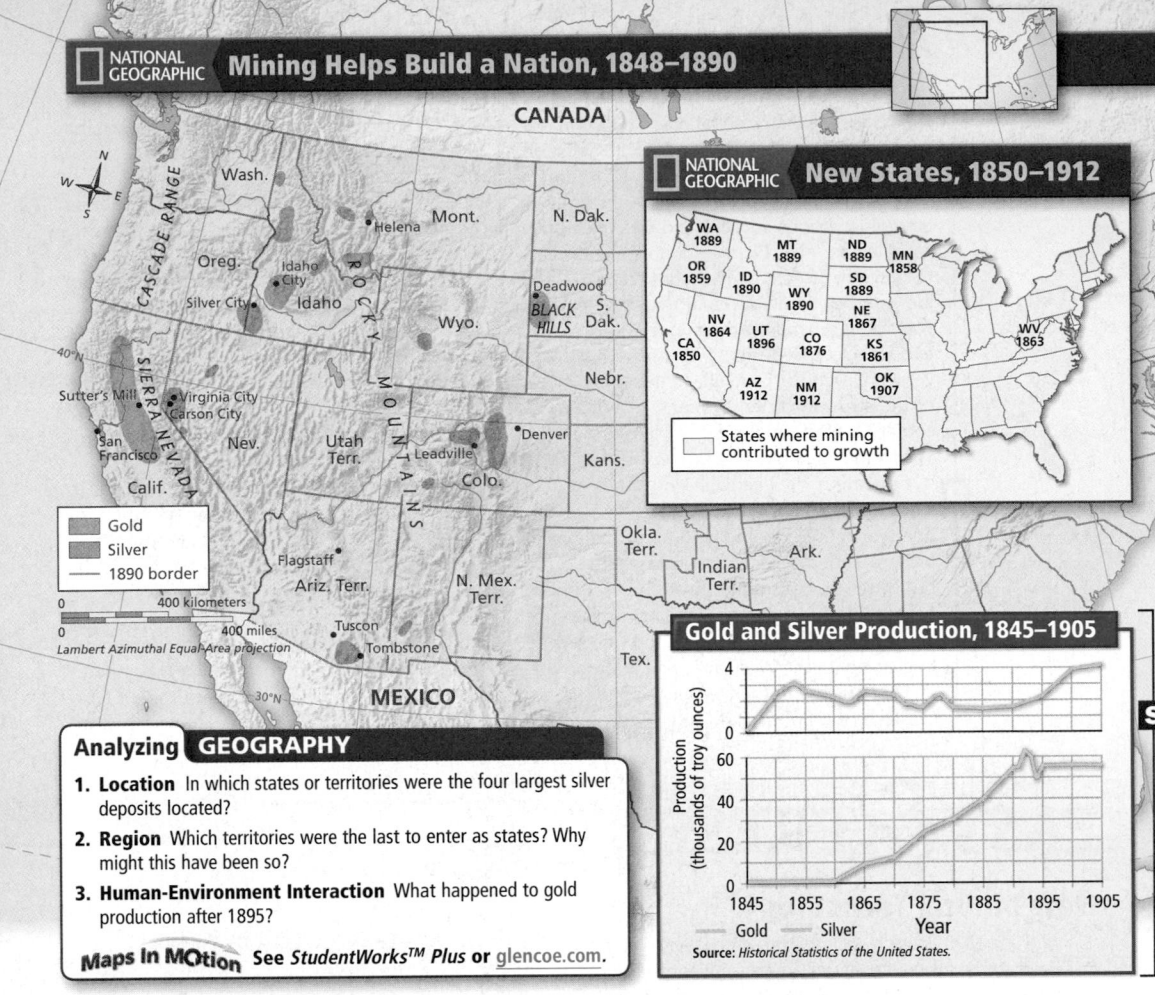

Mining Helps Build a Nation, 1848–1890

NATIONAL GEOGRAPHIC

CANADA

New States, 1850–1912

NATIONAL GEOGRAPHIC

WA 1889	MT 1889	ND 1889	MN 1858
OR 1859	ID 1890	SD 1889	
	WY 1890	NE 1867	
NV 1864	UT 1896	CO 1876	KS 1861	WV 1863
CA 1850	AZ 1912	NM 1912	OK 1907

☐ States where mining contributed to growth

Gold
Silver
1890 border

0   400 kilometers
0   400 miles
Lambert Azimuthal Equal-Area projection

MEXICO

Analyzing GEOGRAPHY

1. **Location** In which states or territories were the four largest silver deposits located?

2. **Region** Which territories were the last to enter as states? Why might this have been so?

3. **Human-Environment Interaction** What happened to gold production after 1895?

Maps In MOtion See *StudentWorks™ Plus* or glencoe.com.

Gold and Silver Production, 1845–1905

Production (thousands of troy ounces)

1845 1855 1865 1875 1885 1895 1905
Year

Gold   Silver

Source: *Historical Statistics of the United States.*

Teach

S **Skill Practice**

Reading a Graph Ask: Compare the number of troy ounces of gold produced in 1885 with the number of troy ounces of silver in that same year. How do you think the differing outputs affected the value of the two metals? *(About 1.5 thousand troy ounces of gold were produced in 1885; about 40 thousand troy ounces of silver were produced the same year. Gold was more scarce than silver and was thus much more valuable.)* **AL**

Analyzing GEOGRAPHY

Answers:

1. Nevada, Idaho, Arizona Territory, Colorado

2. Arizona and New Mexico; Answers will vary but may include climate, location of deposits near border with Mexico, in the case of New Mexico few deposits would have attracted fewer settlers.

3. It increased

Boomtowns were rowdy places. Prospectors fought over claims, and thieves haunted the streets and trails. Often, "law and order" was enforced by **vigilance committees**— self-appointed volunteers who would track down and punish wrongdoers. In some cases, they punished the innocent or let the guilty go free, but most people respected the law and tried to deal firmly but fairly with the accused.

Men were usually first to arrive at a mining site, but women soon followed. Many found work in laundries or as cooks. Others worked at "hurdy-gurdy" houses (named after the mechanical violin), where they waited on tables and danced with men for the price of a drink. Some women became property owners and community leaders.

Boomtowns could not last forever because, eventually, the mines that supported the economy would be used up. A few boomtowns were able to survive when the mines closed, but many did not. Instead, they went "bust"— a term borrowed from card games that refers to players losing all of their money. In Virginia City, for example, the mines were exhausted by the late 1870s, and the economy collapsed. Most residents moved on; by 1930, Virginia City had only 500 residents. Other towns were completely abandoned, becoming "ghost-towns."

Chapter 4 Settling the West **159**

Hands-On Chapter Project
Step 1

Making the Move West

Step 1: Planning your Move Pairs of students will make a list of items to take with them as they prepare to move to the Great Plains to begin a new farm.

Essential Question What resources, types of soil, weather, and people will be encountered on the Great Plains?

Directions Write the Big Idea on the board and ask pairs of students to assume the role of small farmers living in upstate New York.

They have decided to sell their farm to seek new opportunities on the Great Plains.

First, each pair of students should use the maps in this chapter, as well as library or Internet resources, to determine exactly where they will move. Remind students to consider the climate and geography of the region under consideration. Students should also plan what type or types of transportation they will need to get to their new farm, and at what cities and towns they will stop as they move west. After each pair of students has

made their decisions, they should plot their route on an outline map of the United States, labeling the cities and towns along the way and the distances between each place.

Summarizing Allow time for pairs to share their decisions and what they have learned about their destination as well as the places along their route. Students may also include pictures of the places where they will stop along the way. **OL** (Chapter Project continued on page 167)

C Critical Thinking

Making Generalizations
Have students reread this paragraph. Note that it states that unsuccessful miners "headed home." Have them think about what other actions unsuccessful miners might have taken. Have students write a paragraph describing an alternate action. **OL**

D Differentiated Instruction

Visual/Spatial Have students work in small groups to create a thematic map showing important mining towns in Colorado, the Dakota Territory, and Montana. Encourage students to use library and Internet resources to locate the information needed to construct their maps. Display the maps throughout the classroom. **OL**

Additional Support

Mining Leads to Statehood

C Mining also spurred the development of Colorado, Arizona, the Dakotas, and Montana. After gold was discovered in 1858 in Colorado near Pikes Peak, miners rushed to the area, declaring "Pikes Peak or Bust." Many panned for gold without success and headed home, complaining of a "Pikes Peak hoax."

In truth, the Colorado mountains contained plenty of gold and silver, although much of it was hidden beneath the surface and hard to **extract.** Deep deposits of lead mixed with silver were found at Leadville in the 1870s. News of the strike attracted as many as 1,000 newcomers a week, making Leadville one of the West's most famous boomtowns.

D Operations at Leadville and other mining towns in Colorado yielded more than $1 billion worth of silver and gold (many billions in today's money). This bonanza spurred the building of railroads through the Rocky Mountains and transformed Denver, the supply point for the mining areas, into the second largest city in the West, after San Francisco.

Three railroads, the Denver and Rio Grande Western, the South Park and Pacific, and the Colorado Midland all made stops at towns in the mining region.

The discovery of gold in the Black Hills of the Dakota Territory and copper in Montana drew miners to the region in the 1870s. When the railroads were completed, many farmers and ranchers settled the area. In 1889 Congress admitted three new states: North Dakota, South Dakota, and Montana.

In the Southwest, the Arizona Territory followed a similar pattern. Miners had already begun moving to Arizona in the 1860s and 1870s to work one of the nation's largest copper deposits. When silver was found at the town of Tombstone in 1877, however, it set off a boom that attracted a huge wave of prospectors to the territory.

The boom lasted less than 10 years, but in that time, Tombstone became famous for its lawlessness. Marshall Wyatt Earp and his brothers gained their reputations during the famous gunfight at the O. K. Corral there in 1881. Although Arizona did not grow as quickly as Colorado, Nevada, or Montana, by 1912 it had enough people to apply for statehood, as did the neighboring territory of New Mexico.

PAST & PRESENT

1866

New Mining Technology

In the late 1800s, mining companies developed a new technology—hydraulic mining—to remove large quantities of earth and process it for minerals. Miners generated a high-pressure spray by directing water from nearby rivers into narrower and narrower channels, through a large canvas hose and out a giant iron nozzle called a monitor. Using a powerful high-pressure blast of water, "a handful of men," as one journalist wrote, "took out the very heart of a mountain."

Although hydraulic mining is no longer used in the United States, the invention of earth-moving machines such as bulldozers and excavators has made it possible to continue to dig for minerals by removing large quantities of earth. This kind of mining is called open-pit mining or strip mining. It has many of the same problems faced by hydraulic miners. Specifically, something has to be done with the leftovers. The processed ore is usually pumped to a pond, where the water evaporates. These ponds can often be toxic because of the chemicals and minerals that are left after the ore is removed.

▲ The high-pressure water washed the loose earth into large sluices, or ditches that carried the water and earth into riffle boxes. The boxes agitated the water, causing the silver or gold to settle out. The leftover debris, called tailings or "slickens," was then washed into a nearby stream.

Activity: Collaborative Learning

Constructing a Plan Organize students into several groups and ask groups to construct a plan for a late-1800s Western town. Students should use their book, the Internet, and other sources to find examples of how towns were organized in the West and the types of buildings and amenities that were located in towns. Suggest that groups consider the following points in preparing their plans: the buildings they will include and their location; the building materials, energy sources, and landscaping they want to use; and the public facilities they will include. Have each group draw a pictorial map of their town and accompany it with a short report explaining the choices they made in planning.

Mining Technology

Extracting minerals from the rugged mountains of the American West required ingenuity and patience. Early prospectors extracted shallow deposits of ore in a process called placer mining, using simple tools like picks, shovels, and pans.

Other prospectors used sluice mining. Sluices were used to search riverbeds more quickly than the panning method. A sluice diverted the current of a river into trenches. The water was directed to a box with metal "riffle" bars that caused heavier minerals to settle to the bottom of the box. A screen at the end of the box prevented the minerals from escaping with the water and sediment.

When deposits near the surface ran out, miners began **hydraulic mining** to remove large quantities of earth and process it for minerals. Miners sprayed water at very high pressure against the hill or mountain they were mining. The water pressure washed away the dirt, gravel, and rock, and exposed the minerals beneath the surface.

Hydraulic mining began in California, near Nevada City. It effectively removed large quantities of minerals and generated a lot of tax money for local and state governments. Unfortunately, it also had a devastating effect on the local environment. Millions of tons of silt, sand, and gravel were washed into local rivers. The sediment raised the riverbed, and the rivers began overflowing their banks, causing major floods that wrecked fences, destroyed orchards, and deposited rocks and gravel on what had been good farm soil.

In the 1880s farmers fought back by suing the mining companies. In 1884 federal judge Lorenzo Sawyer ruled in favor of the farmers. He declared hydraulic mining a "public and private nuisance" and issued an injunction stopping the practice.

Congress eventually passed a law in 1893 allowing hydraulic mining if the mining company created a place to store the sediment. By then most mining companies had moved to quartz mining—the kind of mining familiar to people today—in which deep mine shafts are dug, and miners go underground to extract the minerals. **W**

✓ Reading Check **Explaining** What role did mining play in the development of the American West?

August 1995

▼ *Mining is still very important to the western economy. The Kennecott Copper Mine in Bingham Canyon, Utah, is the largest human-made excavation in the world. The mine is 2½ miles wide and ¾ mile deep. It supplies approximately 15% of all copper used in the United States.*

▲ *An example of the problems of open-pit mining can be seen at the Berkeley Pit copper mine in Montana (above). When the mine closed, groundwater flooded the pit. The water passed through mineral deposits and became very acidic and contaminated with chemicals. Cleanup is scheduled for 2018 once a treatment plant has been built.*

MAKING CONNECTIONS

1. **Comparing** How was mining in the 1880s similar to mining today?
2. **Problem-Solving** How might mining companies avoid damaging the environment and still extract the minerals they need?

Activity: Collaborative Learning

Creating a Thematic Map Ask: What effects did the mining industry have upon the West? *(Possible answers: populated the West, led to statehood for western territories)* Divide students into small groups. Have the groups create thematic maps showing the locations mentioned under the heading "Growth of the Mining Industry." Some of the locations that should be included are: Virginia City, NV; Leadville, CO; Black Hills, Dakota Territory; Montana; Arizona Territory. **OL**

R Reading Strategy

Using Context Clues Have students reread the first two paragraphs on this page. Using clue words and phrases such as "cattle from the East could not survive" and "these cattle had been allowed to run wild and, slowly, a new breed—the longhorn—emerged," ask students to define the term *adapted*. Students should note that the term means, "to change to fit a new purpose." **BL**

W Writing Support

Descriptive Writing Ask students to find books in the library about the long drives. Then have students write letters describing to family members their experiences during a cattle drive. Students should include details such as daily routines, problems they had to solve, and wildlife they may have encountered. **OL**

Additional
Support

Ranching and Cattle Drives

MAIN Idea Ranchers built vast cattle ranches on the Great Plains and shipped their cattle on railroads to eastern markets.

HISTORY AND YOU What images come to mind when you think of cowboys? Read on to learn about the realities of life as a cowboy in the West.

R While many Americans headed to the Rocky Mountains to mine gold and silver, others began herding cattle on the Great Plains. Americans had long believed it was impossible to raise cattle in the region. Water was scarce, and cattle from the East could not survive on the tough prairie grasses. In Texas, however, lived a breed of cattle that had **adapted** to the Great Plains—the Texas longhorn.

The longhorn was descended from Spanish cattle introduced two centuries earlier. These cattle had been allowed to run wild and, slowly, a new breed—the longhorn—had emerged.

Lean and rangy, the longhorn could easily survive the harsh climate of the Plains. By 1865, some 5 million roamed the Texas grasslands.

Cattle ranching also prospered on the Plains because of the **open range,** a vast area of grassland that the federal government owned. The open range covered much of the Great Plains and provided land where ranchers could graze their herds free of charge and unrestricted by private property.

The Long Drive Begins

Prior to the Civil War, ranchers had little incentive to round up the longhorns. Beef prices were low, and moving cattle to eastern markets was not practical. The Civil War and the coming of the railroads changed this situation. During the Civil War, eastern cattle were slaughtered in huge numbers to feed the armies of the Union and the Confederacy. After the war, beef prices soared and ranchers looked for a way to round up the longhorns and sell them to eastern businesses.

NATIONAL GEOGRAPHIC Cattle Ranching and the Long Drive, c. 1870

W

Cattle trails
Railroads
1890 border

0   200 kilometers
0   200 miles
Lambert Azimuthal
Equal-Area projection

PRIMARY SOURCE

Charles Goodnight and Oliver Loving carved out the Goodnight-Loving Trail from Texas to Colorado, New Mexico, and Wyoming. Goodnight spoke of the dangers of a night stampede:

"The cattle were nervous and easily frightened, and the slightest noise might startle them into running. The heat developed by a large drove of cattle during a stampede was surprising . . . . Animal heat seems to attract electricity, especially when the cattle are wet, and after a storm I have seen the faces of men riding with a herd scorched as if some furnace blast had blazed against them."

—from *The West*

Activity: Interdisciplinary Connection

Mathematics: Longhorns, Long Drives, Long Distances To make a profit, the ranchers of South Texas had to get their huge herds of cattle to market. This lengthy process included the long drive—taking herds of cattle north to be loaded onto railway cars and then shipping the cattle to slaughterhouses in cities such as Chicago. Using the map key on the map on this page, have students calculate the approximate distance from Fort Concho to Cheyenne and then from Cheyenne to Chicago. *(800 miles (approximately 1287 km); 800 miles (approximately 1287 km))* Then have students determine the approximate distance of the Shawnee Trail and then the approximate distance from Kansas City to Chicago. *(600 miles (approximately 965 km); just less than 400 miles (approximately 644 km))* **Ask:** Why might ranchers choose one route over another? *(Answers may include: Ranchers would have started the long drive from near their ranch; some routes may have been less likely to be attacked by Native Americans.)* **OL**

By the 1860s, railroads had reached the Great Plains. Lines ended at Abilene and Dodge City in Kansas and at Sedalia in Missouri. Ranchers and livestock dealers realized that if they could move the cattle as far as the railroad, the longhorns could be sold for a huge profit and shipped east to market.

In 1866 ranchers began rounding up the longhorns and drove about 260,000 of them to Sedalia, Missouri. Most of the cattle did not survive this first **long drive,** but those that survived sold for 10 times the price they would have brought in Texas. Other trails soon opened. The route to Abilene, Kansas, became the major route north. Between 1867 and 1871, cowboys drove nearly 1.5 million head of cattle up the Chisholm Trail from southern Texas to Abilene. As the railroads expanded in the West, other trails reached from Texas to more towns in Kansas, Nebraska, Montana, and Wyoming.

A long drive was a spectacular sight. In the spring, ranchers met with their cowboys to round up cattle from the open range. Stock from many different owners made up these herds. Cowboys from major ranches went north with the herds. The only way to tell them apart was by the brands burned onto their hides by branding irons. Stray calves without brands were called mavericks. These were divided and branded. The herds could number anywhere from 2,000 to 5,000 cattle.

Ranching Becomes Big Business

Cowboys drove millions of cattle north from Texas to Kansas and points beyond. Some of the longhorns went straight to slaughterhouses, but others were sold to ranchers who were building up herds in Wyoming, Montana, and other territories. Sheep herders moved their flocks onto the range and farmers settled there, blocking the trails. "Range wars" broke out among groups competing for land. Eventually, after much loss of life, hundreds of square miles were fenced cheaply and easily with a new invention—barbed wire.

At first, ranchers did not want to abandon open grazing and complained when farmers put up barriers that prevented the ranchers' livestock from roaming. Soon, however, ranchers used barbed wire to shut out those competing with them for land and to keep their animals closer to sources of food and water. For cowboys, however, barbed wire ended the adventure of the long cattle drive.

The fencing of the range was not the only reason the long drives ended. Investors from the East and from Britain had poured money into the booming cattle business, causing an oversupply of animals on the market. Prices plummeted in the mid-1880s and many ranchers went bankrupt. Then, in the winter of 1886–1887, blizzards buried the Plains in deep snow, and temperatures dropped as low as 40 degrees below zero. Massive numbers of cattle froze or starved to death.

The cattle industry survived this terrible blow, but it was changed forever. The day of the open range had ended. From that point on, herds were raised on fenced-in ranches. New European breeds replaced longhorns, and the cowboy became a ranch hand.

✔ **Reading Check** **Analyzing** How did heavy investment in the cattle industry affect the industry as a whole?

▼ *Women help rope and brand cattle at the J. W. Lough ranch in Kansas, 1891.*

Analyzing VISUALS   DBQ

1. **Explaining** What were two by-products of a cattle stampede?
2. **Analyzing** Why did the cattle trails north stop where they did?

Chapter 4 Settling the West **163**

Activity: Interdisciplinary Connection

C **Critical Thinking**

Predicting Consequences
Remind students that thousands of Mexicans became American citizens when the United States acquired the Mexican Cession in 1848. **Ask: What were some of the characteristics of these new citizens?** *(spoke Spanish, were Roman Catholic)* Have students write an essay predicting how these new citizens might interact with the English-speaking settlers who moved into these lands. **AL**

R **Reading Strategy**

Reading Primary Sources
Have students reread the primary source on this page and summarize the skills of the vaquero. **OL**

Analyzing VISUALS

Answers:
1. He may be a performer. His colorful, decorated clothing is not suitable for ranching.
2. All ages/families worked farms; all had to work to support the family because as white settlers moved in, the status of Mexican Americans fell.

Additional Support

Settling the Hispanic Southwest

MAIN Idea The arrival of new settlers changed life for Hispanics in the Southwest.

HISTORY AND YOU Do you remember reading about New Spain? Read on to learn how the Hispanic community changed when the Southwest became part of the United States.

For centuries, much of what is today the American Southwest belonged to Spain's empire. After Mexico won its independence, the region became the northern territories of the Republic of Mexico. When the United States defeated Mexico in 1848 and took control of the region, it acquired the Spanish-speaking population living there. According to the Treaty of Guadalupe Hidalgo ending the war, the region's residents retained their property rights and became American citizens.

In California, the Spanish mission system had collapsed by the early 1800s. In its place, a society dominated by a landholding elite had emerged. These landowners owned vast **haciendas**—huge ranches that covered thousands of acres. The heavy influx of "Forty-Niners" during the California gold rush, however, changed this society dramatically. California's population grew from 14,000 to 100,000 in two years. Suddenly, Hispanic Californians were vastly outnumbered.

Some Hispanic Californians welcomed the newcomers and the economic growth that resulted. Others distrusted the English-speaking prospectors, who tried to exclude them from the mines. When California achieved statehood in 1850, Hispanics served in many state and local offices. Increasingly, however, the original Hispanic population found their status diminished and, frequently, they were relegated to lower-paying and less desirable jobs.

As they had done with Native Americans, settlers from the East clashed with Mexican Americans over land. Across the region, many Hispanics lost their land to the new settlers.

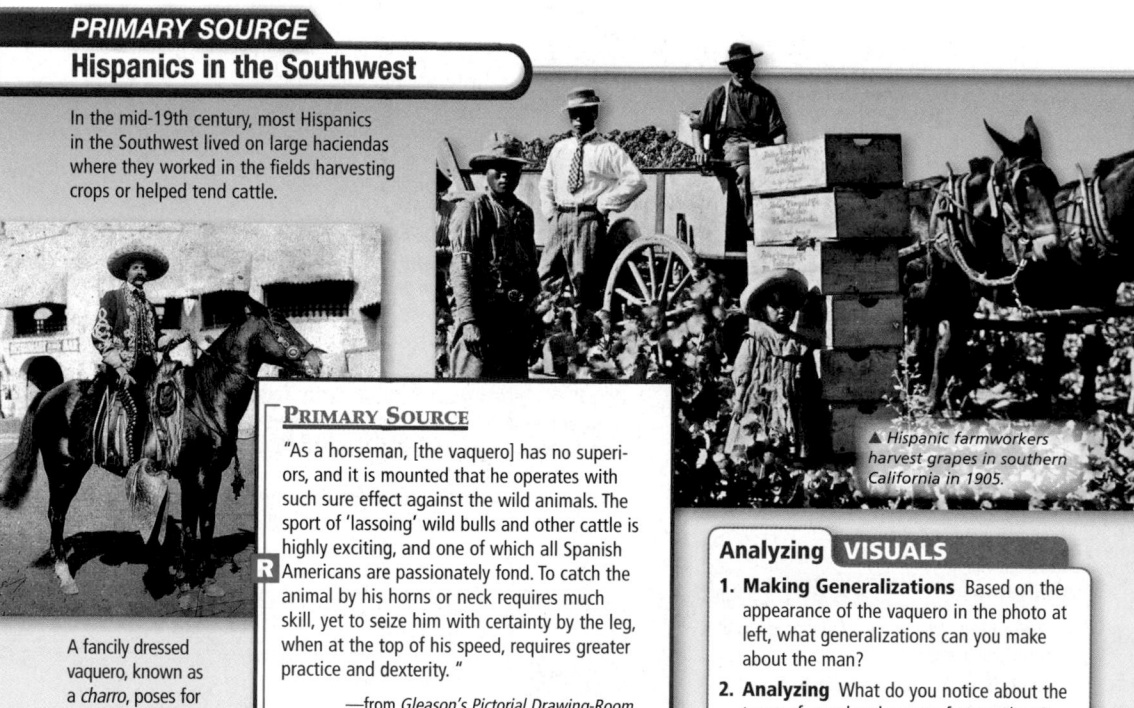

PRIMARY SOURCE

Hispanics in the Southwest

In the mid-19th century, most Hispanics in the Southwest lived on large haciendas where they worked in the fields harvesting crops or helped tend cattle.

A fancily dressed vaquero, known as a *charro*, poses for a photo in 1890.

PRIMARY SOURCE

"As a horseman, [the vaquero] has no superiors, and it is mounted that he operates with such sure effect against the wild animals. The sport of 'lassoing' wild bulls and other cattle is highly exciting, and one of which all Spanish Americans are passionately fond. To catch the animal by his horns or neck requires much skill, yet to seize him with certainty by the leg, when at the top of his speed, requires greater practice and dexterity. "

—from *Gleason's Pictorial Drawing-Room Companion*, 1852

▲ *Hispanic farmworkers harvest grapes in southern California in 1905.*

Analyzing VISUALS

1. **Making Generalizations** Based on the appearance of the vaquero in the photo at left, what generalizations can you make about the man?
2. **Analyzing** What do you notice about the types of people who were farmworkers? Why might this be so?

164 Chapter 4 Settling the West

Activity: Collaborative Learning

Land Ownership In the Treaty of Guadalupe Hidalgo, the United States promised that Hispanics living on the territory the United States gained could retain their property and became American citizens. As settlers moved into the area, they also claimed territory. American courts frequently sided with settlers and revoked Mexican American property rights. **Ask: How might the Hispanics living in the western territories have reacted to becoming American citizens?** *(Possible Answers: some may have been happy, others frightened or angry)* Have students split into small groups. Have each group use library or Internet resources to find out how life changed for Mexican Americans living in the West. Pretending they are Mexican Americans whose property rights have been revoked, students should write a persuasive letter to the president requesting that their property rights be reinstated. **AL**

Mexican American claims to the land often dated back to Spanish land grants. These grants were hundreds of years old and defined the boundaries of property in vague terms. When ownership of a property was claimed by more than one person, American courts frequently held that the old land grants were insufficient proof of ownership. This allowed others to stake claim to the property. In some instances, outright fraud was used to take land illegally from Mexican Americans.

The cattle boom of the 1870s and 1880s had a tremendous impact on Hispanics in the Southwest, where many had long worked as vaqueros (the Spanish word for "cowboys"). Vaqueros developed the tools and techniques for managing cattle. They taught American cowboys their trade and enriched the English language with words of Spanish origin, including "lariat," "lasso," and "stampede."

With the increasing demand for beef in the eastern United States, English-speaking ranchers wanted to expand their herds and claimed large tracts of land of Mexican origin. In some cases, the Hispanic population fought back. In New Mexico, residents of the town of Las Vegas were outraged when English-speaking ranchers tried to fence in land that had long been used by the community to graze livestock. In 1889 a group of Hispanic New Mexicans calling themselves *Las Gorras Blancos* (white caps) raided ranches owned by English-speakers, tore down their fences, and burned their barns and houses. The raids finally ended in 1890 when the governor threatened to call in federal troops.

Despite the influx of English-speaking settlers, the Hispanic population of New Mexico remained more influential in public affairs than did their counterparts in California and Texas. Hispanics remained the majority, both in population and in the state legislature. In addition, a Hispanic frequently served as New Mexico's territorial delegate to Congress.

As more railroads were built in the 1880s and 1890s, the population of the Southwest continued to swell. The region not only attracted Americans and European immigrants, but also immigrants from Mexico. Mexican immigrants worked mainly in agriculture and on the railroads. In the growing cities of the Southwest—such as El Paso, Albuquerque, and Los Angeles— **D** Hispanics settled in neighborhoods called **barrios.** Barrios had Spanish-speaking businesses and Spanish-language newspapers and they helped keep Hispanic cultural and religious traditions alive. As native Californian Mariano Guadalupe Vallejo explained in 1890:

<u>PRIMARY SOURCE</u>

"No class of American citizens is more loyal than the Spanish Californians, but we shall always be especially proud . . . to honor the founders of our ancient families, and the saints and heroes of our history since the days when Father Junipero planted the cross at Monterey."

—quoted in *Foreigners in Their Native Land*

✔ Reading Check **Describing** How did vaqueros contribute to the cattle industry in the West?

Section 1 REVIEW

Vocabulary
1. **Explain** the significance of: Henry Comstock, boomtown, vigilance committee, hydraulic mining, open range, long drive, hacienda, barrios.

Main Ideas
2. **Explaining** How did hydraulic mining affect the environment?

3. **Stating** What caused the decline of the cattle business in the late 1800s?

4. **Describing** How did the gold rush change society in California?

Critical Thinking
5. **Big Ideas** How did mining contribute to the development of the West?

6. **Organizing** Use a graphic organizer similar to the one below to list the ways barbed wire was used and the result of using barbed wire on the Great Plains.

7. **Analyzing Visuals** Sketch a map of the western cattle trails. Then compare your map to the one on page 162, and list the differences between the two maps.

Writing About History
8. **Descriptive Writing** Write a summary for a story line for a Hollywood movie. Your script should realistically portray the life of either a miner or rancher in the West in the mid- to late 1800s.

History ONLINE
Study Central™ To review this section, go to glencoe.com and click on Study Central.

D **Differentiated Instruction**

Kinesthetic Have students create a map of the Southwestern United States today, showing present-day state boundaries. Students should find out the current percentage of the Hispanic population of each state and display this data on the map. **BL**

✔ **Reading Check**

Answer:
developed tools and techniques for managing cattle

Assess

History ONLINE

Study Central™ provides summaries, interactive games, and online graphic organizers to help students review content.

Close

Summarizing Ask: *Why did miners and ranchers move to the Great Plains? (They sought new economic opportunities.)* **OL**

Section 1 REVIEW

Answers

1. All definitions can be found in the section and the Glossary.
2. Millions of tons of silt, sand, and gravel were washed into local rivers.
3. An oversupply of cattle drove down prices, and the winter of 1886 to 1887 killed a large number of cattle.
4. More settlers moved into the state. Spanish-speaking people became the minority, and their status diminished.

5. People moved west, towns sprung up, and railroads expanded.

6.

Barbed Wire		
Purposes		Result
keep out competitors	keep animals closer to food and water supplies	keep livestock from roaming freely
		ended the long cattle drives

7. Maps should include rail lines, towns, and trails. Students' list should correctly note any differences.
8. Students' summaries will vary but should reflect facts found in the section.

Focus

Bellringer
Daily Focus Transparency 4.2

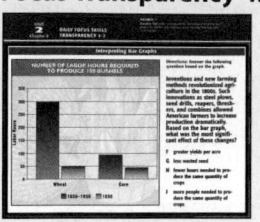

Guide to Reading
Answers:
offered 160 acres of land to settlers under Homestead Act; later legislation increased size of land given to settlers; opened Oklahoma Territory for settlement

Section Spotlight Video

To generate student interest and provide a springboard for class discussion, access the Chapter 4, Section 1 video at glencoe.com or on the video DVD.

Resource Manager

Farming the Plains

Guide to Reading

Big Ideas
Group Action After 1865 settlers staked out homesteads and began farming the Great Plains.

Content Vocabulary
• homestead (p. 167)
• dry farming (p. 168)
• sodbuster (p. 168)
• bonanza farm (p. 169)

Academic Vocabulary
• prospective (p. 166)
• innovation (p. 168)

People and Events to Identify
• Great Plains (p. 166)
• Stephen Long (p. 166)
• Homestead Act (p. 167)
• Wheat Belt (p. 169)

Reading Strategy
Organizing As you read about the settlement of the Great Plains, complete a graphic organizer similar to the one below by listing the ways the government encouraged settlement.

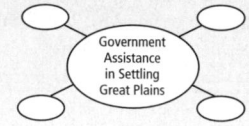

Government Assistance in Settling Great Plains

The Homestead Act encouraged settlers to move to the Great Plains. Although life was difficult, settlers discovered that wheat could be grown on the Great Plains using new technologies. By 1890 there was no longer a true frontier in the United States.

The Beginnings of Settlement

MAIN Idea Settlers staked out homesteads and began farming the region.

HISTORY AND YOU Would you move to a region with extreme weather such as drought and blizzards? Read on to learn how settlers coped with the harsh environment of the Great Plains.

The population of the **Great Plains** grew steadily in the decades after the Civil War. Land once thought to be worthless for farming was transformed into America's wheat belt. Homesteaders faced many challenges. Without trees to use as timber, many early settlers built their homes from chunks of sod, densely packed soil held together by grass roots. To obtain water, they had to drill wells more than 100 feet deep and operate the pump by hand. Nothing was wasted. Homesteader Charley O'Kieffe recalled eating weeds from the garden, as well as the vegetables, joking that he was obeying the rule, "If you can't beat 'em, eat 'em."

O'Kieffe and his neighbors were early settlers on the Great Plains. This region extends westward to the Rocky Mountains from around the 100th meridian—a line of longitude running north and south from the central Dakotas through western Texas. It is dry grassland where trees grow naturally only along rivers and streams. For centuries this open country had been home to vast herds of buffalo that grazed on the prairie grasses. Nomadic Native American groups had hunted the buffalo for food and used buffalo hides for clothing and shelter.

Major **Stephen Long,** who explored the region with an army expedition in 1819, called it the "Great American Desert" and concluded that it was "almost wholly unfit for cultivation." He predicted that the scarcity of wood and water would prove to be "an insuperable obstacle in … settling the country."

During the late 1800s, several developments undermined the assumption that the region was uninhabitable. One important factor was the construction of the railroads. Railroad companies sold land along the rail lines at low prices and provided credit to **prospective** settlers. Pamphlets and posters spread the news to city dwellers across Europe and America that cheap farm land was theirs to claim if they were willing to move.

R Reading Strategies	C Critical Thinking	D Differentiated Instruction	W Writing Support	S Skill Practice
Additional Resources • Read. Skills Act., URB p. 21 • Guided Read. Act., URB p. 49	**Teacher Edition** • Draw. Concl., p. 169 **Additional Resources** • Supreme Court Case Studies, p. 21 • Quizzes and Tests, p. 50	**Teacher Edition** • English Learners, p. 167	**Teacher Edition** • Expository Writing, p. 168 • Persuasive Writing, p. 168	**Additional Resources** • Reinforcing Skills Act., URB p. 31 • RENTG, p. 37

NATIONAL GEOGRAPHIC — Farming the American West, 1870–1900

Corn
Cotton
Wheat
Cattle

PACIFIC OCEAN

0   200 kilometers
0   200 miles
Lambert Azimuthal Equal-Area projection

TROPIC OF CANCER

▲ A family stands outside their sod house on the Great Plains in 1880. There were very few trees on the Great Plains, and wood was expensive because it had to be shipped to the region. So settlers cut chunks of earth from the ground to build their homes.

What Was the Homestead Act?

The Homestead Act of 1862 created a procedure for people who wanted to settle on federal land in the West.

Requirements of the Act
- Settlers had to be 21 years of age.
- Settlers had to be head of a household.
- Settlers had to pay a $10 filing fee and $2 commission to the land agent to be given 160 acres of land.
- To gain title to the land, settlers had to live on it for five years, and make improvements such as building a house and clearing land for farming.
- Alternatively, settlers could buy the land for $1.25 per acre after six months.

Analyzing GEOGRAPHY

1. **Human-Environment Interaction** What were the similarities and differences in land use between Iowa and California?
2. **Region** In what region of the country were both cattle raised and cotton grown?

A Nebraskan coined the slogan "Rain follows the plow" to sell the idea that cultivating the Plains would increase rainfall. The weather seemed to cooperate. For more than a decade beginning in the 1870s, rainfall on the Plains was well above average. The lush green of the plains contradicted assertions that the region was a desert.

In 1862 the government encouraged settlement on the Great Plains by passing the **Homestead Act.** For a $10 registration fee, an individual could file for a **homestead**—a tract of public land available for settlement. A homesteader could claim up to 160 acres of land and could receive title to that land after living there for five years. Later government legislation increased the size of the tracts available. With

their property rights assured, more settlers moved to the Plains.

Settlers often found life very difficult on the Plains. In addition to building sod houses and drilling deep wells for water, they faced summer temperatures greater than 100°F. Prairie fires were a frequent danger. Sometimes swarms of grasshoppers swept over farms and destroyed the crops. In winter there were terrible blizzards and extreme cold. Despite these challenges and hardships, most homesteaders persisted and gradually learned how to live in the difficult environment.

✓**Reading Check** **Analyzing** What is the relationship between private property rights and the settlement of the Great Plains?

Teach

D Differentiated Instruction

English Learners Have students work together in small groups to create posters or pamphlets convincing Americans to move to the Great Plains. Display the pamphlets and posters around the classroom. Have students vote on which ones are most convincing and explain why they think so. **BL**

Analyzing GEOGRAPHY

Answers:
1. Both raised cattle. Iowa also grew corn.
2. Texas

Reading Check

Answer:
The government promised land to settlers who stayed for five years, thus encouraging settlers to come to the Great Plains.

Hands-On Chapter Project
Step 2

Making the Move West

Step 2: Preparing for the Trip Pairs of students continue to plan their trip west to begin a new farm on the Great Plains.

Directions Write the Big Idea on the board. Tell the pairs of students that they will make a list of the items they will need to take with them as they move west. Based on the information in the text, as well as library and Internet sources, students should first identify the items needed for survival in the Great

Plains. Remind students to consider what resources they might find in their new locale as well as weather conditions. Next have pairs review their chosen route and the methods of transportation they will use. Have the pairs review their lists to determine if all the items can be taken with them given their proposed methods of transportation. Remind students that, in addition to personal items such as clothing, they will likely need to bring tools and farm implements. They may also consider bringing some live-

stock or other farm animals with them. Have students consider the weight, bulk, and portability of the items on their list. Also, have them consider if any items on their list will spoil during the trip west. Pairs should prepare a final list based on their research.

Putting it Together Ask volunteers to explain what they are going to pack and why. Next have pairs share what they have learned about the Big Idea while preparing for the trip. **OL**

(Chapter Project continued on page 171)

W₁ **Writing Support**

Expository Writing Have students find out details about the process of dry farming, and write a one-page essay describing the process. **OL**

W₂ **Writing Support**

Persuasive Writing Ask students to find books in the library about the lives of farmers in the Great Plains between the 1860s and 1890s. Have them use information from their books to assume the point of view of a settler and write a persuasive letter to a family member back East. The letter should encourage the family member to move to the Great Plains and should describe the settler's daily life, challenges, and successes. **OL**

Analyzing VISUALS

Answers:
1. wind
2. horses

The Wheat Belt

History ONLINE
Student Web Activity Visit glencoe.com and complete the activity on settling the West.

MAIN Idea As a result of new farming methods and machinery, settlers on the Great Plains were able to produce large amounts of wheat.

HISTORY AND YOU Do you remember learning about the way the cotton gin changed Southern life? Read on to learn how agricultural practices changed life on the Plains.

Many new farming methods and inventions in the nineteenth century revolutionized agriculture. One approach, called **dry farming,** was to plant seeds deep in the ground, where there was enough moisture for them to grow. By the 1860s farmers on the Plains were using plows, seed drills, reapers, and threshing machines. These new steel machines made dry farming possible. Unfortunately, soil on the plains could blow away during a dry season. Many **sodbusters,** as those who plowed the Plains were called, eventually lost their homesteads through the combined effects of drought, wind erosion, and overuse of the land.

Large landholders could invest in mechanical reapers and steam tractors that made it easier to harvest a large crop. Threshing machines knocked kernels loose from the stalks. Mechanical binders tied the stalks into bundles for collection. These **innovations** were well suited for harvesting wheat, a crop that could endure the dry conditions of the Great Plains.

During the 1880s many farmers from the Midwest moved to the Great Plains to take advantage of the inexpensive land and the new

TECHNOLOGY & HISTORY

Farm Machinery Farmers are indebted to the inventions of John Deere and Cyrus McCormick. Deere's steel plow broke through the hard ground. McCormick's mechanical reaper did the work of five men. Later inventions included a mechanical harrow to help prepare the ground for seeds and a grain drill to plant seeds.

▼ *Technology made farming the vast open plains of America feasible. Here, horse-drawn binders are being used to gather hay in the late 1800s.*

▼ *Windmills were vital to settling the Great Plains where farmers faced one major problem: a lack of water. There were few rivers, and it rarely rained. To get water, settlers drilled deep wells and used windmills to pump the water to the surface. The strong winds on the flat, treeless plains were an ideal power source.*

The tail keeps the rotor oriented into the wind.

In the 1870s, the rotor was made of wooden blades. In high winds, the sections could tilt open to let wind through and protect the rotor from damage.

The pump is run by a crank in the gear box that is connected to a shaft in the tower.

STAR MILL
FLINT & WALLING
KENDALLVILLE, IND.

Analyzing VISUALS

1. **Identifying** What was used to power the windmill?
2. **Analyzing Visuals** In addition to field hands, what else did farmers using mechanical harvesting machines need?

Differentiated Instruction

Reinforcing Skills Activity 4

Sequencing Events

Organizing Information: Sequencing Events

Objective: Read a newspaper article and outline the sequence of events described.

Focus: Choose an article from a recent newspaper or newsmagazine. Read the article.

Teach: Circle words that show the chronological structure of the event or events described.

Assess: Make a list of circled words. Discuss what each word tells about the order of events.

Close: Draw a time line or diagram and order the event or events from the article.

Differentiated Instruction Strategies

BL Read the news article and determine words that show chronological order.

AL Write a short essay predicting why the farming techniques used on the Great Plains were harmful to the region's ecosystem.

ELL Write a few sentences about your daily activities. Use as many words that indicate chronological order as you can.

farming technology. The **Wheat Belt** began at the eastern edge of the Great Plains and encompassed much of the Dakotas and parts of Nebraska and Kansas. The new machines allowed a single family to bring in a substantial harvest on a wheat farm covering several hundred acres. Some wheat farms covered up to 50,000 acres. These were called **bonanza farms** because they yielded big profits. Like mine owners, bonanza farmers formed companies, invested in property and equipment, and hired laborers as needed.

Farmers Fall on Hard Times

The bountiful harvests in the Wheat Belt helped the United States become the world's leading exporter of wheat by the 1880s. Then things began to go wrong. A severe drought struck the Plains in the late 1880s, destroying crops and turning the soil to dust. In addition, competition from farmers in other countries began to increase. By the 1890s a glut of wheat on the world market caused prices to drop. Some farmers tried to make it through these difficult times by mortgaging their land—that is, they borrowed money based on the value of their land. If they failed to meet their mortgage payments, they forfeited the land to the bank. Some who lost their land continued to work it as tenant farmers, renting the land from its new owners. By 1900 tenants cultivated about one-third of the farms on the Plains.

Closing the Frontier

On April 22, 1889, the government opened one of the last large territories for settlement. Within hours, more than 10,000 people raced to stake claims in an event known as the Oklahoma Land Rush. The next year, the Census Bureau reported that there was no longer a true frontier left in America. In reality, there was still a lot of unoccupied land, and new settlement continued into the 1900s, but the "closing of the frontier" marked the end of an era. It worried many people, including historian Frederick Jackson Turner. Turner believed that the frontier had provided a "safety-valve of social discontent." It was a place where Americans could always make a fresh start.

Most settlers did indeed make a fresh start, adapting to the difficult environment of the Plains. Water from their deep wells enabled them to plant trees and gardens. Railroads brought lumber and brick to replace sod as a building material, as well as coal for fuel. They also brought manufactured goods from the East, such as clothes and household goods. Small-scale farmers rarely became wealthy, but they could be self-sufficient. Typical homesteaders raised cattle, chickens, and a few crops. The real story of the West was not one of limitless opportunity, nor one in which heroes rode off into the sunset. It was about ordinary people who settled down and built homes and communities through great effort.

✔**Reading Check** **Identifying** What technological innovations helped farmers cultivate the Plains?

Section 2 REVIEW

Vocabulary
1. **Explain** the significance of: Great Plains, Stephen Long, Homestead Act, homestead, dry farming, sodbuster, Wheat Belt, bonanza farm.

Main Ideas
2. **Identifying** How did the Homestead Act encourage settlement of the Plains?

3. **Explaining** What factors contributed to the making of the Wheat Belt in the Great Plains and then to troubled times for wheat farmers in the 1890s?

Critical Thinking
4. **Big Ideas** What challenges did Plains farmers face?

5. **Organizing** Make a graphic organizer similar to the one below that lists the effects of technology on farming in the Great Plains.

Invention	Advantage for Farmers

6. **Analyzing Visuals** Examine the photograph on page 168 of farmers using machinery. Based on the terrain and the type of work they needed to do, what other types of technology would have helped farmers on the Plains?

Writing About History
7. **Persuasive Writing** Write an advertisement to persuade people from the East and Europe to establish homesteads on the Great Plains.

History ONLINE
Study Central™ To review this section, go to glencoe.com and click on Study Central.

169

C Critical Thinking
Drawing Conclusions Historian Frederick Jackson Turner believed the spirit of the United States was tied to westward expansion. When the frontier closed, he concluded that the period that had fostered individualism and economic opportunity had ended. Have students write an essay defending or refuting Turner's ideas. **AL**

✔**Reading Check**

Answer:
the mechanical reaper, steam tractor, threshing machines

Assess

History ONLINE

Study Central™ provides summaries, interactive games, and online graphic organizers to help students review content.

Close

Summarizing Ask: What caused economic hardship for farmers? *(severe drought, a wheat glut, and competition from foreign countries)* **OL**

Section 2 REVIEW

Answers

1. All definitions can be found in the section and the Glossary.

2. Individuals could file for 160 acres of public land and would receive the title after living and making improvements on the land for five years.

3. the Homestead Act, new farming techniques and equipment; good harvests and world competition led to a glut that caused prices to drop

4. difficult climate: hot summers and harsh cold winters; lack of wood for homes; had to dig deep wells for water; drought; grasshoppers; prairie fires

5.

Invention	Advantage for Farmers
mechanical reapers	speeded harvesting
mechanical binders	tied stalks
threshing machines	knocked kernels loose

6. Answers may include telegraph for communication.

7. Advertisements will vary but should reflect information presented in the section.

Focus

Bellringer
Daily Focus Transparency 4.3

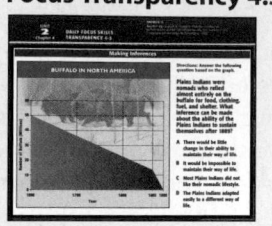

Guide to Reading

1862-Dakota Sioux Uprising: deaths of settlers and Native Americans
1864-Sand Creek Massacre: formation of the Indian Peace Commission
1866-Fetterman's Massacre: U.S. Army defeat
1876-Battle of Little Big Horn: Native American victory
1890-Wounded Knee: about 200 Lakota died

Section Spotlight Video

To generate student interest and provide a springboard for class discussion, access the Chapter 4, Section 3 video at glencoe.com or on the video DVD.

Resource Manager

Section 3

Native Americans

Guide to Reading

Big Ideas
Culture and Beliefs Settling the West dramatically changed the way of life of the Plains Indians.

Content Vocabulary
- nomad *(p. 170)*
- annuity *(p. 170)*
- assimilate *(p. 175)*
- allotment *(p. 175)*

Academic Vocabulary
- relocate *(p. 170)*
- ensure *(p. 172)*
- approximately *(p. 175)*

People and Events to Identify
- Sand Creek Massacre *(p. 172)*
- Indian Peace Commission *(p. 172)*
- George A. Custer *(p. 173)*
- Chief Joseph *(p. 174)*
- Dawes Act *(p. 175)*

Reading Strategy
Sequencing As you read about the crises facing Native Americans during the late 1800s, complete a time line to record the battles between Native Americans and the United States government and the results of each.

As settlers entered Native American lands on the Great Plains, clashes grew more common. Conflicts continued as the government tried to force Native Americans onto reservations and encouraged them to assimilate into the culture of the United States.

Struggles of the Plains Indians

MAIN Idea The settlement of the West dramatically altered the way of life of the Plains Indians.

HISTORY AND YOU Can you recall a situation in which someone broke a promise to you? Do you remember your reaction? Read on to learn how Native Americans responded when the federal government broke treaties.

For centuries the Great Plains were home to many groups of Native Americans. Some lived in communities as farmers and hunters, but many were **nomads** who roamed vast distances, following their main source of food—the buffalo.

The groups of Plains Indians were similar in many ways. Plains Indian nations were divided into bands consisting of up to 500 people. A governing council headed each band, but most members participated in making decisions. Most lived in extended family groups and believed in the spiritual power of the natural world.

The ranchers, miners, and farmers who moved onto the Plains deprived Native Americans of their hunting grounds, broke treaties guaranteeing certain lands to the Plains Indians, and often forced them to **relocate** to new territory. Native Americans resisted by attacking wagon trains, stagecoaches, and ranches. Occasionally, an entire group would go to war against nearby settlers and troops.

The Dakota Sioux Uprising

The first major clash began in 1862, when the Dakota people (also known as the Sioux) launched a major uprising in Minnesota. The Sioux had agreed to live on a reservation in exchange for **annuities,** or annual payments from the government. The annuities, however, frequently got caught up in bureaucracy and corruption and never reached them. By 1862 many lived in desperate poverty and faced possible starvation. When Chief Little Crow asked local traders to provide food on credit, one replied, "If they are hungry, let them eat grass or their own dung." Two weeks later, when the Dakota took up arms, that trader was found dead with his mouth stuffed with grass.

Little Crow reluctantly agreed to lead this uprising. He wanted to wage war against soldiers, not civilians, but he was unable to keep

---

R Reading Strategies	**C** Critical Thinking	**D** Differentiated Instruction	**W** Writing Support	**S** Skill Practice
Additional Resources • Guided Read. Act., URB p. 50 • Primary Source Reading Act., URB p. 35	**Teacher Edition** • Draw. Concl., p. 173 • Analy. Info., p. 174 • Comparing, p. 175 **Additional Resources** • Interp. Pol. Cartoons, URB p. 41 • Quizzes and Tests, p. 51 • Authentic Assess. p. 13	**Teacher Edition** • Advanced Learners, p. 171 • Visual/Spatial, p. 172 **Additional Resources** • Diff. Instruction Act., URB p. 23 • Enrich. Act., URB p. 45	**Teacher Edition** • Narrative Writing, p. 171 • Persuasive Writing, p. 172 • Descriptive Writing, p. 173	**Additional Resources** • Critical Thinking Skills Act., URB p. 32 • Time Line Act., p. 33 • RENTG, p. 40

NATIONAL GEOGRAPHIC Native American Battles and Reservations, 1860–1890

CANADA

Wash.

Bear Paw Mountain 1877

Oreg.

Mont.
Little Bighorn 1876

Idaho

N. Dak.

Fetterman Massacre 1866
Ft. Kearney
BLACK HILLS

Dakota Sioux Uprising 1862

S. Dak.

Minn.

Wyo.

Wounded Knee 1890

Iowa

Fort Laramie Treaties:
1851: Native Americans agree to the construction of roads and forts on their lands
1868: The Sioux agree to move to a reservation in the Black Hills

Ft. Laramie

Nebr.

Nev.

Utah Terr.

Colo.

Ft. Lyon

Sand Creek 1864

Kans.

Mo.

Medicine Lodge

NO MAN'S LAND

Calif.

Ft. Defiance

Ariz. Terr.

N. Mex. Terr.

BOSQUE REDONDO (1863–1868)

Ft. Sumner

CHEYENNE AND ARAPAHO

UNASSIGNED LANDS

CHEROKEE OUTLET

OSAGE
CHEROKEE
CREEK
SEMINOLE
CHOCTAW

Ark.

Treaty of Medicine Lodge, 1867:
Southern Plains Indians agree to move to Indian Territory

Miss.

Texas

CHICKASAW
COMANCHE, KIOWA, AND APACHE

La.

Skeleton Canyon, 1886:
Apache leader Geronimo surrenders

Reservation in 1890
Route of Chief Joseph and the Nez Perce, 1877
Battle
Fort
Treaty Site
1890 border

0   400 kilometers
0   400 miles
Lambert Azimuthal Equal-Area projection
120°W   110°W

MEXICO

Native American Population

Population
500,000
400,000
300,000
200,000
100,000

1850 1860 1870 1880 1890 1900
Year

Sources: *Nations Within a Nation*; U.S. Census Bureau.

Analyzing VISUALS

1. **Analyzing** What happened to the Native American population between 1850 and 1900?

2. **Locating** From what state to what state did the Nez Perce travel in 1877? Through what other states did they pass?

Maps In Motion See *StudentWorks™ Plus* or glencoe.com.

angry Dakota from slaughtering hundreds of settlers in the area.

After the rebellion was suppressed, a military tribunal sentenced 307 Dakota to death. After reviewing the evidence, President Lincoln reduced the number to 38. Others fled the reservation when federal troops arrived and became exiles in a region that bore their name—the Dakota Territory.

Red Cloud's War

The Dakota Territory was home to another Sioux tribe, the Lakota. The Lakota were a nomadic tribe who fought hard to keep control

of their hunting grounds, which extended from the Black Hills westward to the Bighorn Mountains. They had battled rival groups for this country and did not intend to let settlers have it. Leading them were chiefs Red Cloud, Crazy Horse, and Sitting Bull.

The army suffered a major defeat during "Red Cloud's War" of 1866–1868. The army was constructing forts along the Bozeman Trail, the path used to reach the Montana gold mines. In December 1866, Crazy Horse, a religious leader and war chief, tricked the fort's commander into sending Captain William Fetterman and about 80 soldiers out to pursue what they thought was a small raiding party.

W **D**

Chapter 4   Settling the West   **171**

Teach

D Differentiated Instruction

Advanced Learners Have students research the geography and mineral resources of the Black Hills. Have students use their findings to write a one-page essay explaining why white settlers wanted to remove Native Americans from the Black Hills. **AL**

W Writing Support

Narrative Writing Have students find out about one leading Native American chief, such as Red Cloud, Crazy Horse, or Sitting Bull. Have students write a brief narrative describing the life of the leader chosen. **BL**

Analyzing VISUALS

Answers:
1. declined dramatically
2. Oregon to Montana; Idaho and Wyoming

Hands-On Chapter Project
Step 3

Making the Move West

Step 3: Take the Trip Students will describe the various people they will likely meet on their journey westward.

Directions Write the Big Idea on the board. Have the pairs of students refer to the map they created in Step 1. Using information from the textbook, as well as library or Internet resources, students should research the types of people they will likely encounter on their trip westward. For example, as

they move through towns and cities, they might meet merchants, innkeepers, and bankers. As they pass through established farmland, they might meet other small farmers. Finally, as they approach their destination, they might encounter native peoples. Based on their research, students should create brief personal profiles of five different individuals that they will likely meet along the way. Remind pairs to provide a physical description of the people, identify their occupations, and describe

their daily lives. Students should also include how they interacted with each of the five people they profiled.

Putting it Together Ask volunteers to describe the people they have met on their journey westward. **OL**
(Chapter Project continued on the Visual Summary page 176)

Chapter 4 • Section 3

W Writing Support

Persuasive Writing Have interested students assume the role of an assistant to territorial governor John Evans and write a letter to Cheyenne Chief Black Kettle attempting to persuade him to go to Fort Lyon. Remind students to provide solid and compelling reasons to Chief Black Kettle. **OL**

D Differentiated Instruction

Visual/Spatial Have students use their textbooks and library and Internet resources to create two maps of Native American reservations. One map should show the reservations before the formation of the Indian Peace Commission and the other should show the reservations after the Commission. Use the maps to discuss how the federal government tried to gain authority over Native Americans in the Great Plains. **AL**

✓ Reading Check

Answer:
creating two large reservations for the Sioux and for the Southern Plains Indians

Additional Support

Teacher Tip

Collaborative Learning This activity requires students to do research, write, and illustrate. The activity allows students with different levels to work together. As you form groups, consider the needed skills and choose students accordingly.

Hundreds of warriors were waiting in ambush and wiped out the entire unit (an event that became known as Fetterman's Massacre). The Sioux continued to resist any military presence in the region, and in 1868 the army abandoned its posts along the trail.

Sand Creek

In the 1860s tensions began to rise between the miners coming into Colorado in search of silver and gold and the Cheyenne and Arapaho who already lived there. As the number of settlers increased, bands of Native Americans began raiding wagon trains and stealing cattle and horses from ranches. By the summer of 1864, trade had come to a standstill, dozens of homes had been burned, and an estimated 200 settlers had been killed. The territorial governor, John Evans, ordered the Native Americans to surrender at Fort Lyon, where he said they would be given food and protection. Those who failed to report would be subject to attack.

Although several hundred Native Americans surrendered at the fort, many others did not. In November 1864, Chief Black Kettle brought several hundred Cheyenne to the fort, not to surrender but to negotiate a peace deal. The fort's commander did not have the authority to negotiate, and he told Black Kettle to make camp at Sand Creek while he waited for orders. Shortly afterward, Colonel John Chivington of the Colorado Volunteers was ordered to attack the Cheyenne at Sand Creek.

When Chivington stopped at Fort Lyon, he was told that the Native Americans at Sand Creek were waiting to negotiate. Chivington replied that, since the Cheyenne had been attacking settlers, including women and children, there could be no peace. The events that followed became known as the **Sand Creek Massacre.**

What actually happened at Sand Creek is unclear. Some witnesses stated afterward that Black Kettle had been flying both an American flag and a white flag of truce, which Chivington ignored. Others reported that the American troops fired on the unsuspecting Native Americans and then brutally murdered hundreds of women and children. Still others described a savage battle in which both sides fought ferociously for two days. Fourteen soldiers died, but the number of Native Americans reported killed varied from 69 to 600. One general later called Chivington's attack "the foulest and most unjustifiable crime in the annals of America." The truth of what really happened is still debated.

A Doomed Plan for Peace

In light of escalating conflict with Native Americans on the Great Plains, Congress took action. In 1867 Congress formed an **Indian Peace Commission,** which proposed creating two large reservations on the Plains, one for the Sioux and another for Native Americans of the southern Plains. Agents from the federal government's Bureau of Indian Affairs would run the reservations. The army would deal with any groups that refused to report or remain there.

Reservations were not a new idea. Both Puritan and Jesuit missionaries had used them in colonial days to separate Native American nations from one another. The reservations were also intended to encourage Native Americans to adopt white culture. After the American Revolution, the Iroquois (who called themselves the Haudenosaunee) were placed on reservations in western New York. These reservations, however, existed to separate Native Americans and citizens of the United States. Nearly a century later, reservations were based exclusively on keeping the Native Americans separate from American citizens.

The reservation system was again tested after the California gold rush. California, Oregon, and Washington all tried reservations as a way to minimize conflicts between Native Americans and settlers.

The Indian Peace Commission's plan was doomed to failure. Pressuring Native American leaders into signing treaties, as negotiators did at Medicine Lodge Creek in 1867, did not **ensure** that chiefs or their followers would abide by them, nor could they prevent settlers from violating their terms. Those who did move to reservations faced much the same conditions that drove the Dakota Sioux to violence—poverty, despair, and the corrupt practices of American traders.

✓ **Reading Check** **Explaining** What proposal did the Indian Peace Commission present to the Plains Indians?

Activity: Collaborative Learning

Conflicting Evidence Ask: Why are the details of the Sand Creek Massacre still being debated? (*Historians have received conflicting eyewitness accounts; reports of the massacre may have been tarnished by the observers' personal biases.*) Organize the class into small groups. Have each group use library or Internet resources to find different primary sources, eyewitness accounts, or secondary sources of the fateful events surrounding the Sand Creek Massacre. Have each group analyze its findings and write a report on its conclusions. Each group should also illustrate its findings with maps, drawings, or dioramas. **OL**

The Last Native American Wars

MAIN Idea Settlers and Native Americans fought for land and cultural traditions.

HISTORY AND YOU Can you identify parts of the world where development is destroying local cultures? Read how the destruction of the buffalo changed some Native American cultures.

By the 1870s many Native Americans on the southern Plains had left the reservations in disgust. They preferred hunting buffalo on the open plains, so they joined others who had also shunned the reservations. Buffalo, however, were rapidly disappearing as settlers killed off thousands of the animals.

Following the Civil War, professional buffalo hunters invaded the area, seeking buffalo hides for markets in the East. Other hunters killed merely for sport, leaving carcasses to rot. Then railroad companies hired sharpshooters to kill large numbers of buffalo that were obstructing rail traffic and used them to feed the workers.

The army, determined to force Native Americans onto reservations, encouraged buffalo killing. By 1889 very few of the animals remained.

Battle of the Little Bighorn

In 1876 prospectors overran the Lakota Sioux reservation in the Dakota Territory to mine gold in the Black Hills. The Lakota saw no reason they should abide by a treaty that American settlers were violating, so many left the reservation that spring to hunt near the Bighorn Mountains in southeastern Montana.

The government responded by sending an expedition commanded by General Alfred H. Terry. Lieutenant Colonel **George A. Custer** and the Seventh Cavalry were with the expedition. Custer underestimated the fighting capabilities of the Lakota and Cheyenne. On June 25, 1876, ignoring orders, and acting on his own initiative, he launched a three-pronged attack in broad daylight on one of the largest groups of Native American warriors ever assembled on the Great Plains.

POLITICAL CARTOONS PRIMARY SOURCE
Government Native American Policies

▲ This cartoon from 1878 shows Secretary of the Interior Carl Schurz investigating the Indian "bureau."

▲ This cartoon is labeled "The Reason of the Indian Outbreak" and quotes General Miles who said the "Indians are starved into rebellion."

Analyzing VISUALS **DBQ**

1. **Examining** Who does the cartoon on the right blame for the problems of Native Americans?
2. **Analyzing** According to the cartoon on the left, why was the Indian Bureau unable to help Native Americans?

Activity: Collaborative Activity

Newspaper Page Organize the class into groups to create a newspaper page highlighting details from the Battle of Little Bighorn. Have each group choose whether to describe the Native Americans' or the American soldiers' view of the battle. Have students research the Battle of Little Bighorn using their book, the Internet, and other sources. Groups should illustrate their newspaper page with drawings depicting a scene from the battle. Have each group compose their newspaper page on a computer using desktop publishing software.

People IN HISTORY

Answer:

Custer: Custer might persevere despite overwhelming odds
Sitting Bull: Sitting Bull wanted it to be remembered that he was the last Lakota to surrender his rifle.

C Critical Thinking

Analyzing Information

Remind students that the army forced the Nez Perce to move to Oklahoma. **Ask: How did this action by the U.S. government affect the rights of these Native Americans?** *(It denied them basic rights guaranteed under the Constitution.)*

Additional Support

People IN HISTORY

George Custer
1839–1876

George Custer, who graduated at the bottom of his West Point class, became an unlikely hero during the Civil War. During the many cavalry charges he led, 11 horses were shot out from under him. At the age of 23, he became the youngest Union Army general. When Custer later commanded the Seventh Cavalry in the West, the Cheyenne called him "Yellow Hair," because he wore his curly blond hair to his shoulders. Custer wore buckskins for battle, though he wore velveteen uniforms in the camp. He spent many hours studying military tactics and reading military history. He risked his own career to testify against the corruption of the Indian Bureau. In anger at his testimony, President Grant removed him from command. However, the public outcry in favor of Custer led to his return to command, a decision that cost the lives of Custer and all his troops.

How did Custer's actions in the Civil War indicate what he might do in other combat situations?

Sitting Bull
c. 1831–1890

The great Lakota chief Sitting Bull faced his first battle at age 14, in a raid against the Crow tribe. As a young man he joined two groups, a warrior society known as Strong Heart and a group that worked for tribal welfare, Silent Eaters. Sitting Bull became chief when he was 37 years old. A holy man as well as a warrior, Sitting Bull led Native Americans in sun dances and prayers to the Great Spirit. After his victory at the Little Bighorn, Sitting Bull led his people to Canada to avoid the reservation system. In 1881, with his people facing starvation, Sitting Bull led them to Montana. He asked his son to hand the commanding officer of Fort Buford his rifle, hoping to show that "he has become a friend of the Americans." Sitting Bull also asked it to be remembered that "I was the last man of my tribe to surrender my rifle." Four years later, he briefly joined Buffalo Bill's Wild West show. He was killed by a Lakota, as he had seen in a vision five years before: A Lakota policeman shot him in a scuffle trying to keep the great chief from joining a Ghost Dance, which had been outlawed.

How did Sitting Bull wish to be remembered?

The Native American forces first repulsed a cavalry charge from the south. Then they turned on Custer and his 210 soldiers and killed all but one of them. One Lakota warrior recalled the scene afterward: "The soldiers were piled one on top of another, dead, with here and there, an Indian among the soldiers. Horses lay on top of men, and men on top of horses."

Newspaper accounts portraying Custer as a victim of a massacre produced a public outcry in the East, and the army stepped up its campaign against Native Americans on the Plains. Sitting Bull fled with his followers to Canada, but the other Lakota were forced to return to the reservation and give up the Black Hills.

Flight of the Nez Perce

Farther west, the Nez Perce people, led by **Chief Joseph,** refused to be moved to a smaller reservation in Idaho in 1877. When the army came to relocate them, they fled their homes and embarked on a journey of more than 1,300 miles. Finally, in October 1877, Chief Joseph surrendered, and he and his followers were exiled to Oklahoma. His speech summarized the hopelessness of their cause:

PRIMARY SOURCE

"Our chiefs are killed.... The little children are freezing to death. My people ... have no blankets, no food.... Hear me, my chiefs; I am tired; my heart is sick and sad. From where the sun now stands I will fight no more forever."

—quoted in *Bury My Heart at Wounded Knee*

Tragedy at Wounded Knee

Native American resistance came to a final and tragic end on the Lakota Sioux reservation in 1890. Defying the orders of the government, the Lakota continued to perform the Ghost Dance, a ritual that celebrated a hoped-for day of reckoning when settlers would disappear, the buffalo would return, and Native Americans would reunite with their dead ancestors.

Federal authorities had banned the ceremony fearing it would lead to violence. They blamed the latest defiance on Chief Sitting Bull, who had returned from Canada, and sent police to arrest the chief. Sitting Bull's supporters tried to stop the arrest. In the exchange of gunfire that followed, the chief himself was killed.

Leveled Activities

BL Reading Skills Activity 4, URB p. 21

OL Linking Past and Present Activity, URB p. 34

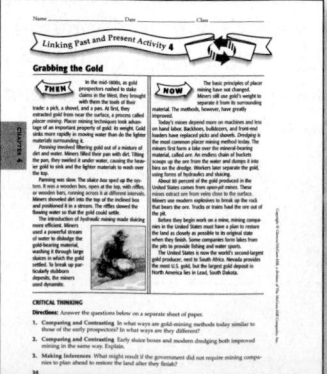

AL Enrichment Activity, URB p. 45

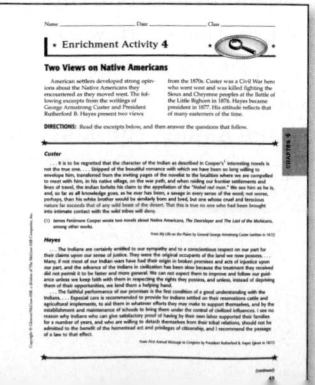

ELL Content Vocabulary Activity, URB p. 27

A group of Ghost Dancers then fled the reservation, and the army went after them. On December 29, 1890, as troops tried to disarm them at Wounded Knee Creek, gunfire broke out. A deadly battle ensued, taking the lives of 25 U.S. soldiers and **approximately** 200 Lakota men, women, and children.

The Dawes Act

Some Americans had long opposed the treatment of Native Americans. In her 1881 book *A Century of Dishonor,* Helen Hunt Jackson detailed the years of broken promises and injustices. Her descriptions of events such as the massacre at Sand Creek sparked new debate on the issue. Some Americans believed the solution was to encourage Native Americans to **assimilate,** or be absorbed, into American society as landowners and citizens. This meant dividing reservations into individual **allotments,** where families could become self-supporting.

This policy became law in 1887 when Congress passed the **Dawes Act.** This act allotted to each head of household 160 acres of reservation land for farming; single adults received 80 acres, and 40 acres were allotted for children. The land that remained after all members had received allotments would be sold to American settlers, with the proceeds going into a trust for Native Americans.

This plan failed to achieve its goals. Some Native Americans succeeded as farmers or ranchers, but many had little training or enthusiasm for either pursuit. Like homesteaders, they often found their allotments too small to be profitable, so they sold them. Some Native American groups had grown attached to their reservations and hated to see them transformed into homesteads for settlers as well as Native Americans.

In the end, the assimilation policy proved a dismal failure. No legislation could provide a satisfactory solution to the Native American issue, because there was no entirely satisfactory solution to be had. The Native Americans were doomed because they were dependent on buffalo for food, clothing, fuel, and shelter. When the herds were wiped out, Native Americans on the Plains had no way to sustain their way of life, and few adopted American settlers' lifestyles in place of their traditional cultures.

The Dawes Act granted citizenship to Native Americans who stayed on their allotments for 25 years. Few qualified, and it was not until 1924 that Congress passed the Citizenship Act, granting all Native Americans citizenship. Some states—Arizona, Maine, and New Mexico—did not grant Native Americans the right to vote until after World War II.

Under Franklin Roosevelt's New Deal, the policies of assimilation and allotments finally ended in 1934. The Indian Reorganization Act reversed the Dawes Act's policy of assimilation. It restored some reservation lands, gave Native American tribes control over those lands, and permitted them to elect tribal governments.

Reading Check **Cause and Effect** What effect did Helen Hunt Jackson's book *A Century of Dishonor* have?

Section 3 REVIEW

Vocabulary

1. **Explain** the significance of: nomad, annuity, Sand Creek Massacre, Indian Peace Commission, George A. Custer, Chief Joseph, assimilate, allotment, Dawes Act.

Main Ideas

2. **Comparing** In what ways were the different groups of the Plains Indians similar?

3. **Discussing** Why do you think the government's policy of assimilation of Native Americans was a failure?

Critical Thinking

4. **Big Ideas** How did Native Americans respond to the loss of land from white settlement of the Great Plains?

5. **Organizing** Use a graphic organizer similar to the one below to list the reasons the government's plans to move the Plains Indians onto reservations failed.

6. **Analyzing Visuals** Examine the map of battle sites and reservations on page 171. Then, from the point of view of a historian, explain the actions taken against Native Americans within the historical context of the time.

Writing About History

7. **Descriptive Writing** Assume the role of a Plains Indian. Write a journal entry describing how you feel about the Dawes Act and how it has affected your life.

History ONLINE

Study Central™ To review this section, go to glencoe.com and click on Study Central.

175

Chapter 4 • **Section 3**

C Critical Thinking

Comparing Have students use library or Internet resources to find more information about the Dawes Act and the Indian Reorganization Act. Have students create a bulletin board display comparing the two laws. **BL**

Assess

History ONLINE

Study Central™ provides summaries, interactive games, and online graphic organizers to help students review content.

Close

Summarizing Ask: Why did settlers and Native Americans come into conflict? (*Native Americans sought to maintain traditional ways of life, while settlers wanted their land*) **OL**

✓ Reading Check

Answer: It sparked debate on the treatment of Native Americans.

Section 3 REVIEW

Answers

1. All definitions can be found in the section and the Glossary.

2. many were nomadic, divided into bands with a governing council heading each band, lived in extended family groups, believed in spiritual power of natural world

3. Answers may include: Native Americans were unwilling or unable to change their way of life. They received no training in farming and their allotments were too small to be profitable.

4. Some attacked wagon trains and ranches, going to war against nearby settlers and troops

5.

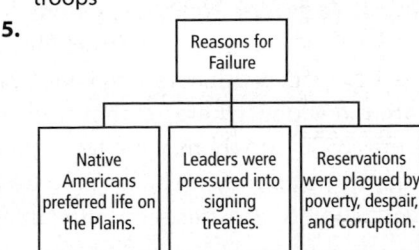

6. Answers may vary. Accept different viewpoints as long as the reasoning is sound and based on facts.

7. Students' journal entries will vary. Entries should be written from the perspective of a Native American.

175

Chapter 4 VISUAL SUMMARY

Determining Cause and Effect The Visual Summary lists the causes and effects of settlers moving west to the Great Plains. Have students use the information provided to create a cause-and-effect flow chart illustrating these events. **BL**

Descriptive Writing Have students select one of the three major occupations that affected the settlement of the Great Plains—mining, ranching, or farming—and write a paragraph describing why a settler might move west to pursue one of those ways of life. **OL**

Causes of Settlers Moving West to the Great Plains

Mining
- Deposits of gold, silver, and copper are discovered.
- New technologies, such as hydraulic mining, make it possible to remove vast quantities of ore.

Ranching
- Wild longhorn cattle, found to survive well on the Plains, are available in large numbers to be rounded up.
- Railroads provide an easy way to ship cattle to eastern markets.

Farming
- Congress passes the Homestead Act in 1862.
- New farming technologies, including new plows, reapers, and drills, make it possible to farm on the Plains.
- Railroads advertise for settlers and bring necessities such as lumber and coal to the Plains.

▶ *Tens of thousands of settlers headed west, lured by the possibility of striking it rich mining gold or silver. This photo shows miners standing beside a stack of silver ingots in Leadville, Colorado, c. 1880.*

▶ *A Plains family stands atop their reaper on their Nebraska farm in the 1890s. Technology such as the reaper made farming the Great Plains practical.*

Effects of Settling the Great Plains

- Miners arrive in such large numbers that Colorado, the Dakotas, Nevada, and Montana are able to become states.
- Hydraulic mining damages the environment in some areas and interferes with farming.
- The Great Plains becomes the nation's Wheat Belt, growing tens of thousands of acres of wheat.
- The arrival of miners, ranchers, and farmers leads to conflict with Native Americans.
- The federal government fights several wars with the Native Americans, establishes reservations, and passes the Dawes Act to assimilate Native Americans.

▲ *Although the Dawes Act was intended to assimilate Native Americans, traditional ways of life persisted. Above, a Cheyenne woman uses a stone mortar and pestle to grind wild cherries outside her home in the 1890s.*

Hands-On Chapter Project
Step 4: Wrap Up

Making the Move West

Step 4: Describing the Trip Students will synthesize what they have learned in Steps 1, 2, and 3.

Directions Write the Essential Question on the board. Have students refer to their maps, their lists, and the personal profiles of the people they encountered on the trip westward. Using this information and what they have learned, students should write a brief paragraph describing the most difficult part

of moving westward. Ask volunteers to share their observations and list them on the board. Discuss their thoughts and observations.

Putting It Together Next, have students write a letter to a neighbor left behind in upstate New York. Students should describe how they decided where to move, what items they took with them, what route they traveled, and who they met along the way. Students should also describe difficulties

they encountered along the way. Finally, they should conclude their letter—either recommending that their neighbor should join them on the Great Plains or recommending that the neighbor stay in upstate New York. **OL**

ASSESSMENT

STANDARDIZED TEST PRACTICE

TEST-TAKING TIP

Look at each question to find clues to support your answer. Try not to get confused by the wording of the question. Then look for an answer that best fits the question.

Reviewing Vocabulary

Directions: Choose the word or words that best completes the sentence.

1. Cattle ranching developed on the Great Plains as a result of the _____, which was a vast area of grassland owned by the government.

A open range

B long drive

C barbed wire

D Chisholm Trail

2. The government promoted settlement in the Great Plains by allowing individuals to file for a _____, which let people claim public land as their own.

A bonanza farm

B mine permit

C homestead

D reservation

3. _____ were yearly payments made by the United States government to Native Americans on reservations.

A Nomads

B Allotments

C Sodbusters

D Annuities

4. In the early 1800s, society in California was dominated by landowners who lived on large

A barrios.

B haciendas.

C bonanza farms.

D homesteads.

Reviewing Main Ideas

Directions: Choose the best answers to the following questions.

Section 1 *(pp. 158–165)*

5. In 1889 the discovery of gold and copper led to the rapid development of the northern Great Plains with the following states being formed:

A Montana, North Dakota, South Dakota.

B Montana, Wyoming, Idaho.

C North Dakota, South Dakota, Iowa.

D North Dakota, South Dakota, Nebraska.

6. The open range was closed to grazing with the use of

A the long drive.

B barbed wire.

C hydraulic mining.

D placer mining.

7. Why did *Las Gorras Blancos* carry out night raids in New Mexico?

A The English-speaking ranchers claimed land used by the community to graze livestock.

B Vaqueros were outlawed by the English-speaking ranchers.

C The English-speaking majority in the legislature closed the barrios.

D The Hispanic minority did not want New Mexico to join the United States.

Need Extra Help?

If You Missed Questions . . .	1	2	3	4	5	6	7
Go to Page . . .	162–163	166–167	170	164	160	162–163	164–165

GO ON ➡

Chapter 4 Settling the West **177**

---

6. B A careful reading of the question should lead students to the correct answer. The key words in the question are "closed to grazing." Barbed wire literally fenced in, or closed, the open range.

7. A English-speaking ranchers began fencing in community land, causing *Las Gorras Blancos* to raid their homes. Students may be tempted to choose *B*, which also mentions English-speaking ranchers. It is important that students read each answer choice carefully to avoid choosing a similar sounding, but incorrect, answer.

Answers and Analyses
Reviewing Vocabulary

1. A Students who are unsure of the answer should look for the answer that is closest in meaning to "vast area of grassland." *B* and *C* are incorrect because neither describes a place. Long drive refers to cattle drives, and barbed wire is an object. The Chisholm Trail was not a vast area of grassland. Only open range makes sense.

2. C Choice *A* is a distracter that may confuse students. Bonanza farms were large wheat farms that made large profits. Homesteads were tracts of land. A homesteader's $10 registration fee could allow them to claim up to 160 acres of land. Thinking about this "purchase" as settlers "buying a home" may help students remember the definition of homestead.

3. D Students who have trouble answering this question will most likely have trouble choosing between "allotments" and "annuities." Remind these students that annuities are yearly, or annual, payments. The shared word root may help them retain the definition of annuities.

4. B Choice *A* is incorrect. *Barrios* are Spanish-speaking neighborhoods. Bonanza farms and homesteads were on the Great Plains, not California. Haciendas were huge ranches in California. If students have trouble with this question, have them review "Settling the Hispanic Southwest" on page 164.

Reviewing Main Ideas

5. A North Dakota, South Dakota, and Montana were admitted as states in 1889. Developing a rhyme or acrostic can help students remember facts like this one. Consider pairing up students to create rhymes or acrostics to share with the class.

8. C Using the process of elimination can help lead students to the correct answer. *A* is incorrect; long cattle drives were a result of settlement, not a cause. The Great Plains do not get large amounts of rainfall, so *B* can be eliminated. It is unlikely that dry, windy weather would provide an incentive to farm. *C* is correct. The Homestead Act allowed people the opportunity to own land and contributed to the expansion of the Plains.

9. D Wind is not a factor that affects growing crops. Students should eliminate *B* and *C* based on what they have learned about the geography of the Plains. Review innovations such as mechanical reapers and steam tractors that helped make wheat farming suitable.

10. B It is important that students understand what the frontier represented to Americans: a place of opportunity that offered the chance of a fresh start. For many, the frontier also represented the ideas of freedom and adventure.

11. C The two proposed reservations were for the Sioux and the Southern Plains Indians. Students should remember that the reservations were based on keeping Native Americans separate from American citizens to keep the peace.

12. D In this question, the correct choice is the one that is opposite the three other choices. *A, B,* and *C* would be positive and respectful to Native Americans. However, the American government was not respectful of Native American lands and culture. White Americans felt superior to Native Americans, and sought to make Native Americans more like Americans of European descent with actions such as the passage of the Dawes Act.

Section 2 *(pp. 166–169)*

8. Which of the following factors provided an incentive for people to farm the Great Plains?

   A long cattle drives

   B large amounts of rainfall

   C the Homestead Act

   D dry, windy weather

9. Why was wheat a suitable crop to grow on the Great Plains?

   A The environment was windy.

   B Wheat needs more water than corn.

   C Wheat requires large amounts of rainfall.

   D New innovations were suited for harvesting wheat.

10. Why were some Americans concerned about the closing of the frontier?

   A People were worried that Native Americans might revolt.

   B People were worried that the idea of Americans traveling west to make a new start had come to an end.

   C Some farmers wanted more land to increase their political power with the federal government.

   D Settlers worried about the cost of supplies with the increased number of homesteaders.

Section 3 *(pp. 170–175)*

11. The Indian Peace Commission was formed to end the conflict with Native Americans on the Great Plains. They proposed

   A a treaty to end the Battle of the Little Bighorn.

   B federal regulations for hunting buffalo.

   C creating two large reservations for the Plains Indians.

   D removing Sitting Bull from power.

12. The aim of the Dawes Act of 1887 was to

   A restore previously taken land to Native American tribes.

   B maintain traditional Native American cultures.

   C end all governmental contact with Native Americans.

   D assimilate Native Americans into American culture.

Need Extra Help?

If You Missed Questions . . .	8	9	10	11	12	13	14	15
Go to Page . . .	166–167	168–169	169	172	174–175	173–175	170–175	173–175

178 Chapter 4 Settling the West

Critical Thinking

Directions: Choose the best answers to the following questions.

13. The Native American wars that occurred between 1860 and 1890 were mainly the result of

   A disputes over the spread of slavery.

   B conflict with Mexico over Texas and California.

   C the search for gold in California.

   D the movement of settlers onto the Great Plains.

Base your answers to questions 14 and 15 on the chart below and your knowledge of Chapter 4.

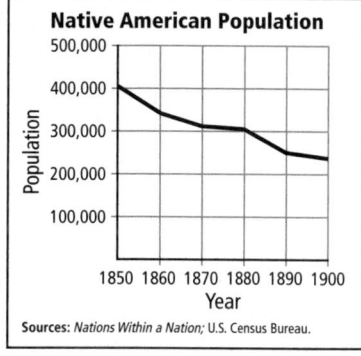

Native American Population

Sources: *Nations Within a Nation*; U.S. Census Bureau.

14. What does the graph indicate about the Native American population between 1850 and 1900?

   A The Native American population was over 400,000 in 1860.

   B The Native American population increased over 50 years.

   C The Native American population declined between 1840 and 1850.

   D The Native American population was less than 300,000 in 1890.

15. What factor caused the Native American population to decline sharply between 1880 and 1890?

   A increase in reservation land

   B conflict with American settlers from the East

   C increase in the number of wild buffalo

   D conflict with Hispanic settlers

GO ON

Critical Thinking

13. D Only choice *D* relates to Native Americans. Point out to students that careful reading of the answer choices reveals that the first three involve disputes or events that had little if nothing to do with Native Americans. The movement of settlers onto the Great Plains displaced the Native Americans who lived there.

14. D Students should examine each choice and compare each one to the graph. The Native American population was between

200,000 and 300,000 according to the graph, so *D* is correct.

15. B Although the graph does show a decline in the Native American population, it does not explain reasons for this decline. Therefore, students must rely on their knowledge of the chapter. *B* is the only choice that makes sense, based on the chapter.

16. Placer mining is a process by which

   A deep mine shafts are dug and miners go underground to extract the minerals.

   B miners use simple tools like picks, shovels, and pans to extract shallow deposits of minerals.

   C a number of men use a high-pressure blast of water to loosen large quantities of earth and remove the minerals.

   D earth-moving machines remove large quantities of earth to remove the minerals.

17. Vigilance committees performed what function?

   A found new lodes

   B ensured that mining companies did not harm the environment

   C supervised the building of western railroads

   D enforced law and order in boomtowns

18. What type of mining allowed sediment into the local rivers, causing them to overflow and flood the area?

   A placer mining

   B quartz mining

   C hydraulic mining

   D panning mining

19. Why did the Dakota Sioux clash with local traders and settlers in 1862?

   A Annuity payments never reached them, resulting in poverty.

   B Other Native American tribes claimed the area as their own.

   C Settlers began to increase in the area, disregarding the local treaties.

   D Buffalo hunters invaded the area and killed the remaining buffalo.

Document-Based Questions

Directions: Analyze the document and answer the short-answer questions that follow the document.

In the late 1860s, the U.S. government adopted a policy of forcing Native Americans onto small reservations. Many Native Americans refused to move and fought to maintain their traditional way of life. In the excerpt that follows, Satanta, a chief of the Kiowa, responds to the government's policy:

> "I have heard that you intend to settle us on a reservation near the mountains. I don't want to settle. I love to roam over the prairies. There I feel free and happy, but when we settle down we grow pale and die. I have laid aside my lance, bow, and shield, and yet I feel safe in your presence. I have told you the truth. I have no little lies hid about me, but I don't know how it is with the commissioners. Are they as clear as I am? A long time ago this land belonged to our fathers; but when I go up to the river I see camps of soldiers on its banks. These soldiers cut down my timber; they kill my buffalo; and when I see that, my heart feels like bursting; I feel sorry . . . . Has the white man become a child that he should recklessly kill and not eat? When the red men slay game, they do so that they may live and not starve."
>
> —quoted in *Bury My Heart at Wounded Knee*

20. What reasons does Satanta give for not wanting to settle on a reservation?

21. How does Satanta view the white settlers' approach to the land and the resources on it?

Extended Response

22. Write an essay comparing two different perspectives of the settlement of the West. Analyze how the views of Native Americans and white settlers differed on settling the Great Plains. How did each group view the government's involvement and the environment? The essay should include an introduction, at least three paragraphs, and a conclusion that supports your position.

History ONLINE

For additional test practice, use Self-Check Quizzes—Chapter 4 at glencoe.com.

Need Extra Help?							
If You Missed Questions . . .	16	17	18	19	20	21	22
Go to Page . . .	160–161	159	160–161	170–171	172–175	172–175	166–175

---

19. A The Dakota Sioux experienced poverty and starvation because their annuities never reached them. They did not clash with other Native American tribes. Local traders refused to help the Sioux, resulting in harsh feelings.

Document-Based Questions

20. Students should state that Satanta enjoyed his nomadic life. Point students to the beginning of the passage, in which he states, "I do not want to settle. I love to roam over the prairies."

21. Students' answers should include: Satanta thinks the white man does not respect his land. He says the white men kill buffalo recklessly.

Extended Response

22. Students' responses will vary, but their answers must address the different views of white settlers and Native Americans. Students must provide adequate support for their claims, as well.

---

16. B Review the section on Mining Technology on page 160 with students. Placer mining is described in the first paragraph as mining with simple tools. Placer mining was only useful for mining on the surface, however. The other answer choices differ from the correct answer in that they describe more advanced mining techniques.

17. D Remind students that vigilance means "watchfulness." Vigilance committees watched over boomtowns, enforcing law and order. *B* is a distracter, but students should be aware that there was no concern for the environment involved in early mining.

18. C The root hydra- is used for water, which may help students recall that hydraulic mining uses water to remove quantities of earth, which students should relate to flooding.

History ONLINE

Have students visit the Web site at glencoe.com to review Chapter 4 and take the Self-Check Quiz.

Need Extra Help?

Have students refer to the pages listed if they miss any of the questions.

Key to Ability Levels
- **BL** Below Level
- **OL** On Level
- **AL** Above Level
- **ELL** English Language Learners

Key to Teaching Resources
- Print Material
- CD-ROM
- DVD
- Transparency

BL	OL	AL	ELL		Resources	Chapter Opener	Section 1	Section 2	Section 3	Section 4	Chapter Assess
					FOCUS						
BL	OL	AL	ELL	🖨	Daily Focus Transparencies		5-1	5-2	5-3	5-4	Ch. 5
					TEACH						
BL	OL	AL		📁	Economics and History Activity, URB		p. 7				
BL	OL		ELL	📁	Reading Skills Activity, URB			p. 53			
	OL			📁	Historical Analysis Skills Activity, URB			p. 54			
BL	OL	AL	ELL	📁	Differentiated Instruction Activity, URB					p. 55	
BL	OL		ELL	📁	English Learner Activity, URB					p. 57	
BL	OL	AL	ELL	📁	Content Vocabulary Activity, URB*		p. 59				
BL	OL	AL	ELL	📁	Academic Vocabulary Activity, URB		p. 61				
	OL	AL		📁	Reinforcing Skills Activity, URB				p. 63		
	OL	AL		📁	Critical Thinking Skills Activity, URB					p. 64	
BL	OL		ELL	📁	Time Line Activity, URB		p. 65				
	OL			📁	Linking Past and Present Activity, URB		p. 66				
BL	OL	AL	ELL	📁	Primary Source Reading, URB			p. 69		p. 67	
BL	OL	AL	ELL	📁	American Art and Music Activity, URB		p. 71				
BL	OL	AL	ELL	📁	Interpreting Political Cartoons Activity, URB				p. 73		
		AL		📁	Enrichment Activity, URB				p. 77		
BL	OL		ELL	📁	Guided Reading Activity, URB*		p. 80	p. 81	p. 82	p. 83	
BL	OL	AL	ELL	📁	Reading Essentials and Note-Taking Guide*		p. 43	p. 46	p. 49	p. 52	
BL	OL	AL	ELL	📁	Differentiated Instruction for the American History Classroom	✓	✓	✓	✓	✓	✓
BL	OL	AL	ELL	🖨	Unit Map Overlay Transparencies	✓	✓	✓	✓	✓	✓
BL	OL	AL	ELL	📁	Unit Time Line Transparencies, Strategies, and Activities	✓	✓	✓	✓	✓	✓
BL	OL	AL	ELL	📁	Cause and Effect Transparencies, Strategies, and Activities	✓	✓	✓	✓	✓	✓
BL	OL	AL	ELL	📁	Why It Matters Chapter Transparencies, Strategies, and Activities	✓	✓	✓	✓	✓	✓
BL	OL	AL	ELL	📁	American Biographies					✓	

Note: Please refer to the *Unit 2 Resource Book* for this chapter's URB materials.

* Also available in Spanish

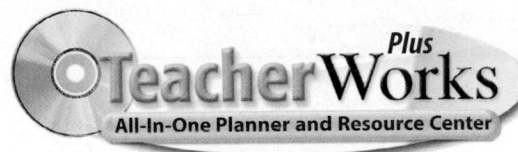

Teacher**Works** *Plus*
All-In-One Planner and Resource Center

- Interactive Lesson Planner
- Interactive Teacher Edition
- Fully editable blackline masters
- Section Spotlight Videos Launch
- Differentiated Lesson Plans
- Printable reports of daily assignments
- Standards Tracking System

Levels					Resources	Chapter Opener	Section 1	Section 2	Section 3	Section 4	Chapter Assess
BL	OL	AL	ELL		**TEACH** *(continued)*						
BL	OL	AL			**Supreme Court Case Studies**		p. 15	p. 21	p. 23	p. 25	
BL	OL	AL	ELL		**The Living Constitution**	✓	✓	✓	✓	✓	✓
BL	OL	AL	ELL		**American Issues**	✓	✓	✓	✓	✓	✓
	OL	AL	ELL		**American Art and Architecture Transparencies, Strategies, and Activities**	✓	✓	✓	✓	✓	✓
BL	OL	AL			**High School American History Literature Library**	✓	✓	✓	✓	✓	✓
	OL	AL			**American History Primary Source Documents Library**	✓	✓	✓	✓	✓	✓
BL	OL	AL	ELL		**American Music: Hits Through History CD**	✓	✓	✓	✓	✓	✓
BL	OL	AL	ELL		**StudentWorks™ Plus DVD**	✓	✓	✓	✓	✓	✓
BL	OL	AL	ELL		**Vocabulary PuzzleMaker CD-ROM**	✓	✓	✓	✓	✓	✓
BL	OL	AL	ELL		*The American Vision* **Video Program DVD**	✓	✓	✓	✓	✓	✓
Teacher Resources					**Reading Strategies and Activities for the Social Studies Classroom**	✓	✓	✓	✓	✓	✓
					Strategies for Success	✓	✓	✓	✓	✓	✓
					Presentation Plus! DVD	✓	✓	✓	✓	✓	✓
					Success With English Learners	✓	✓	✓	✓	✓	✓
					ASSESS						
BL	OL	AL	ELL		**Section Quizzes and Chapter Tests***		p. 61	p. 62	p. 63	p. 64	p. 65
BL	OL	AL	ELL		**Authentic Assessment With Rubrics**						p. 15
BL	OL	AL	ELL		**Standardized Test Practice Workbook**						p. 10
BL	OL	AL	ELL		*ExamView®* **Assessment Suite CD-ROM**		5-1	5-2	5-3	5-4	Ch. 5
BL	OL	AL	ELL		**Interactive Tutor Self-Assessment CD-ROM**		5-1	5-2	5-3	5-4	Ch. 5
					CLOSE						
BL			ELL		**Reteaching Activity, URB**						p. 75
BL	OL		ELL		**Reading and Study Skills Foldables™**	p. 60					

Using ExamView® Assessment

Quick Test

Technology Product

Glencoe's *ExamView® Assessment Suite* includes powerful assessment tools and enables you to quickly create, adapt, and assess tests for your students. *ExamView®* allows you to

- develop online testing materials that focus on the specific skills and competencies of what has been taught in the classroom;
- create several versions of these test materials that are adjusted to meet the different ability levels of your students;
- provide a variety of test formats including Multiple Choice, True/False, Yes/No, Matching, Completion (Fill-in-the-Blank), and Numeric Response.

Steps

- Open the ExamView® Test Generator.
- Select **Create a new test using the QuickTest Wizard** and click **OK.**
- Name the test you are creating.
- From the list, select the *Chapter Banks* you would like to use. Click **Next.**
- Indicate the number of questions you want per question type. Click **Next.**
- Enter number of matching groups. Click **Next.**
- Verify summary of selections and click **Finish.**
- The *QuickTest Wizard* will build your test. Print the test or save it for students to take the test on a computer using the internet.

History ONLINE

	Student	Teacher	Parent
Beyond the Textbook	●	●	●
Chapter Overviews	●	●	●
Time Current Events	●		●
ePuzzles and Games	●		●
Concepts in Motion	●		●
Literature Connections		●	
Multi-Language Glossaries	●		●
Online Student Edition	●	●	●
Self-Check Quizzes	●		●
Student Web Activities	●		●
Study Central ™	●		●
Teaching Today		●	
Vocabulary eFlashcards	●		●
Web Activity Lesson Plans		●	

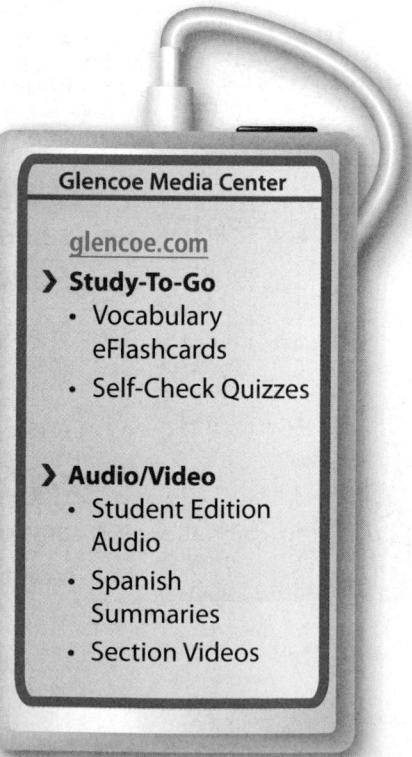

Glencoe Media Center

glencoe.com

❯ **Study-To-Go**
- Vocabulary eFlashcards
- Self-Check Quizzes

❯ **Audio/Video**
- Student Edition Audio
- Spanish Summaries
- Section Videos

- **Timed Readings Plus in Social Studies** helps students increase their reading rate and fluency while maintaining comprehension. The 400-word passages are similar to those found on state and national assessments.

- **Reading in the Content Area: Social Studies** concentrates on six essential reading skills that help students better comprehend what they read. The book includes 75 high-interest nonfiction passages written at increasing levels of difficulty.

- **Reading Social Studies** includes strategic reading instruction and vocabulary support in Social Studies content for both ELLs and native speakers of English.

www.jamestowneducation.com

The following videotape programs are available from Glencoe as supplements to Chapter 5:

- The Transcontinental Railroad (ISBN 1-56-501731-5)
- Legacy of King Coal: Empires of American Industry (ISBN 0-76-700621-6))

To order, call Glencoe at 1-800-334-7344. To find classroom resources to accompany many of these videos, check the following home pages:

A&E Television: www.aetv.com
The History Channel: www.historychannel.com

NATIONAL GEOGRAPHIC

Index to National Geographic Magazine:

The following articles relate to this chapter:

- "Alexander Graham Bell," by Robert V. Bruce and Ira Block, September 1988.
- "Pittsburgh–Stronger than Steele," by Peter Miller, December 1991.

National Geographic Society Products To order the following, call National Geographic at 1-800-368-2728:

- *ZipZapMap! USA Windows* (ZipZapMap! USA)

Access National Geographic's new, dynamic MapMachine Web site and other geography resources at:
www.nationalgeographic.com
www.nationalgeographic.com/maps

Reading List Generator CD-ROM

Use this database to search more than 30,000 titles to create a customized reading list for your students.

- Reading lists can be organized by students' reading level, author, genre, theme, or area of interest.
- The database provides Degrees of Reading Power™ (DRP) and Lexile™ readability scores for all selections.
- A brief summary of each selection is included.

Leveled reading suggestions for this chapter:

For students at a Grade 8 reading level:
- *The Wright Brothers: The Birth of Modern Aviation,* by Anna Sproule

For students at a Grade 9 reading level:
- *The Story of Thomas Alva Edison,* by Margaret Cousins

For students at a Grade 10 reading level:
- *Mother Jones: Fierce Fighter for Workers' Rights,* by Judith Pinkerton Josephson

For students at a Grade 11 reading level:
- *Telephones* by Elaine Marie Alphin

For students at a Grade 12 reading level:
- *The Wright Brothers: How They Invented the Airplane,* by Russell Freedman

Focus

MAKING CONNECTIONS
Did Industry Improve Society?

Ask students to give suggestions as to the ways they think industry has improved society. Students may cite improvements in manufacturing processes, transportation, communication, entertainment, or trade. Activate students' prior knowledge by asking them to name various inventions with which they are familiar. Students may identify a wide variety of items. Discuss how different their lives would be if the items they identified had not been produced by American industries. **OL**

Teach
The Big Ideas

As students study the chapter, remind them to consider the section-based Big Ideas included in each section's Guide to Reading. The **Essential Questions** in the activities below tie in to the Big Ideas and help students think about and understand important chapter concepts. In addition, the Hands-on Chapter Projects with their culminating activities relate the content from each section to the Big Ideas. These activities build on each other as students progress through the chapter.

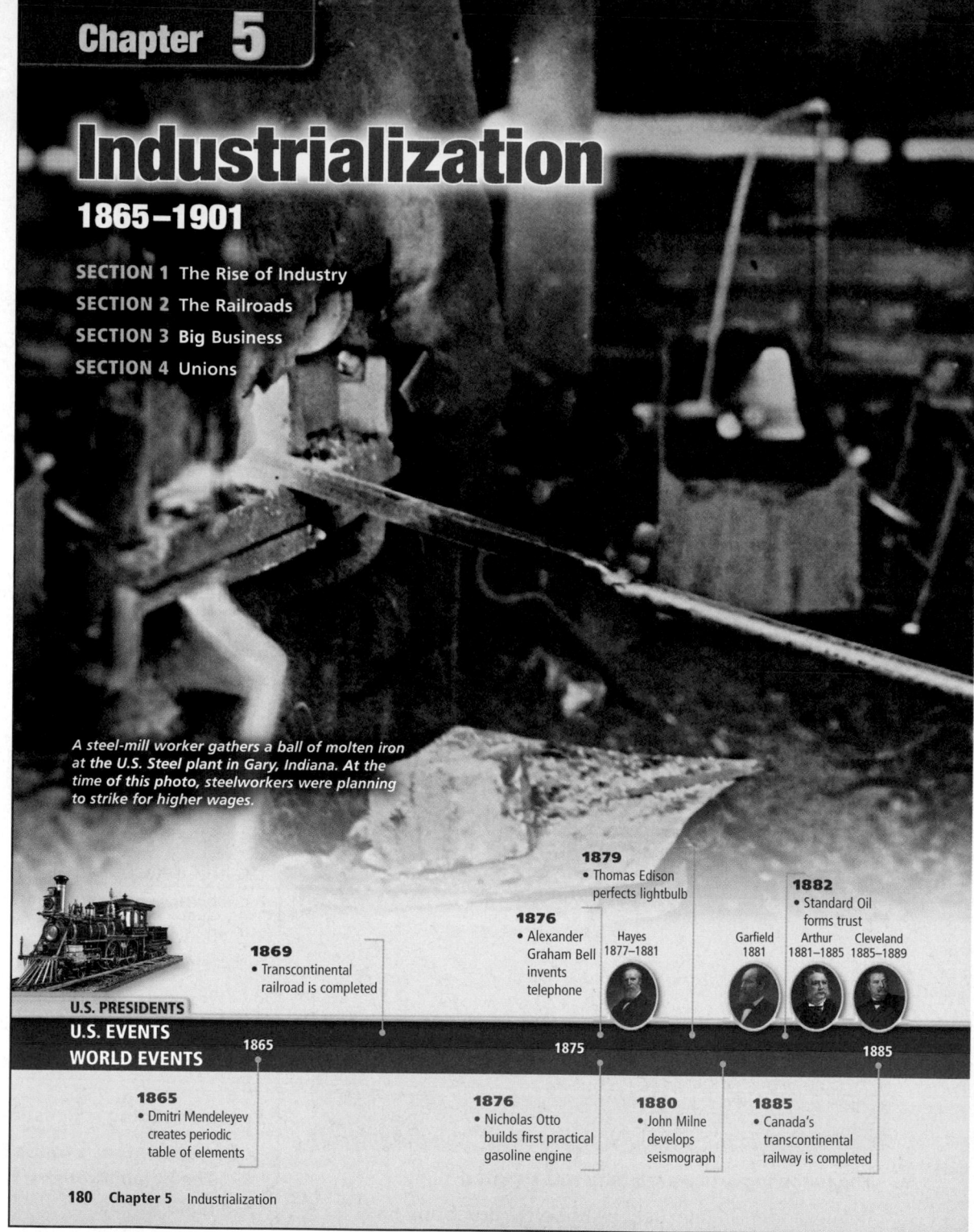

Chapter 5

Industrialization
1865–1901

SECTION 1 The Rise of Industry
SECTION 2 The Railroads
SECTION 3 Big Business
SECTION 4 Unions

A steel-mill worker gathers a ball of molten iron at the U.S. Steel plant in Gary, Indiana. At the time of this photo, steelworkers were planning to strike for higher wages.

1879
• Thomas Edison perfects lightbulb

1882
• Standard Oil forms trust

1876
• Alexander Graham Bell invents telephone

Hayes 1877–1881

Garfield 1881

Arthur 1881–1885

Cleveland 1885–1889

1869
• Transcontinental railroad is completed

U.S. PRESIDENTS
U.S. EVENTS
WORLD EVENTS

1865   1875   1885

1865
• Dmitri Mendeleyev creates periodic table of elements

1876
• Nicholas Otto builds first practical gasoline engine

1880
• John Milne develops seismograph

1885
• Canada's transcontinental railway is completed

180   Chapter 5   Industrialization

Section 1

The Rise of Industry
Essential Question: What economic policies allowed industries to expand after the Civil War? *(Laissez-faire, or "hands-off," economic policies allowed industries to grow rapidly because there was no government interference to restrict growth.)* Point out that in Section 1 students will learn about laissez-faire and other factors that led to the rapid growth of industry in the United States. **OL**

Section 2

The Railroads
Essential Question: How did the railroads encourage the settlement of the Plains and the West? *(The railroads brought settlers and goods west; they transported goods east. Railroads make travel and shipping of goods fast and cheap.)* Point out that in Section 2 students will learn how the railroads accelerated the settlement of the Plains and the West. **OL**

MAKING CONNECTIONS
Did Industry Improve Society?

Many factors promoted industrialization, including cheap labor, new inventions and technology, and plentiful raw materials. Railroads rapidly expanded, while government policies encouraged economic growth.

- *What changes in lifestyle do you think occurred because of industrialization?*
- *How do you think industrialization changed American politics?*

More About the Photo

Visual Literacy Working in a steel mill was dirty. Work conditions were often hazardous, and there was no compensation in case of death or injury. Strikes were often the only tool available to workers as they sought better wages and working conditions.

FOLDABLES Study Organizer **Dinah Zike's Foldables**

Dinah Zike's Foldables are three-dimensional, interactive graphic organizers that help students practice basic writing skills, review vocabulary terms, and identify main ideas. Instructions for creating and using Foldables can be found in the Appendix at the end of this book and in the *Dinah Zike's Reading and Study Skills Foldables* booklet.

History ONLINE
Introduce students to chapter content and key terms by having them access the Chapter 5 Overview at glencoe.com.

Timeline

1886
- Haymarket riot occurs

1892
- Homestead strike occurs

B. Harrison
1889–1893

Cleveland
1893–1897

1894
- Pullman strike begins

McKinley
1897–1901

1901
- J.P. Morgan forms U.S. Steel

1895

1892
- Rudolf Diesel patents diesel engine

1895
- Louis and Auguste Lumière introduce motion pictures

FOLDABLES

Analyzing Organizations Make a Three-Tab Book Foldable to help you analyze how the Civil War transformed the nature of industry. As you read the chapter, write details under the corresponding tab.

Before the Civil War | Both | After the Civil War

INDUSTRIALIZATION

History ONLINE **Chapter Overview**
Visit glencoe.com to preview Chapter 5.

Chapter 5   Industrialization   **181**

Section 3

Big Business
Essential Question: Why did captains of industry such as Andrew Carnegie expand their businesses through new ways of organization? *(They sought to control all aspects of their respective businesses to keep costs low and profits high. They also sought to eliminate competition.)* Point out that in Section 3 students will learn about how big businesses became monopolies. **OL**

Section 4

Unions
Essential Question: Why did workers form unions? *(Workers wanted to form unions because unionization allowed workers to join forces. Forming unions was the only tool available after requests for better wages and working conditions failed.)* Point out that in Section 4 students will learn about how unions were organized and the social and political opposition to unions that prevented them from success. **OL**

Focus

Bellringer
Daily Focus Transparency 5.1

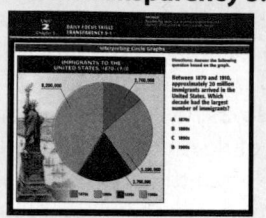

Guide to Reading

Answer: abundance of raw materials; oil production; population increase; free enterprise system; large free trade area; new inventions

Section Spotlight Video

To generate student interest and provide a springboard for class discussion, access the Chapter 5, Section 1 video at glencoe.com or on the video DVD.

Resource Manager

Section 1

The Rise of Industry

Guide to Reading

Big Ideas
Government and Society The United States government adopted a policy of laissez-faire economics, allowing business to expand.

Content Vocabulary
• gross national product (p. 182)
• laissez-faire (p. 186)
• entrepreneur (p. 187)

Academic Vocabulary
• resource (p. 182)
• practice (p. 187)

People and Events to Identify
• Edwin Drake (p. 182)
• Alexander Graham Bell (p. 184)
• Thomas Alva Edison (p. 184)
• Morrill Tariff (p. 187)

Reading Strategy
Organizing As you read about the changes brought about by industrialization, complete a graphic organizer similar to the one below, listing the causes of industrialization.

Causes → United States Becomes an Industrial Nation

American business and industry grew rapidly after the end of the Civil War. Industrialization changed the way people lived and worked.

The United States Industrializes

MAIN Idea Natural resources and a large labor force allowed the United States to industrialize rapidly.

HISTORY AND YOU What natural resources are located in your area? Read to learn how the availability of raw materials encouraged industrialization.

Although the Industrial Revolution reached the United States in the early 1800s, most Americans still lived on farms. Out of a population of over 30 million, only 1.3 million Americans worked in industry when the Civil War began in 1861. After the war, industry rapidly expanded, and millions of Americans left their farms to work in mines and factories. Factories began to replace smaller workshops as complex machinery began to substitute for simpler hand tools.

By the late 1800s, the United States was the world's leading industrial nation. By 1914 the nation's **gross national product** (GNP)—the total value of all goods and services that a country produces—was eight times greater than it had been in 1865 when the Civil War came to an end.

Natural Resources

An abundance of raw materials was one reason for the nation's industrial success. The United States had vast natural **resources,** including timber, coal, iron, and copper. This meant that American companies could obtain them cheaply and did not have to import them from other countries. Many of these resources were located in the American West. The settlement of this region helped accelerate industrialization, as did the transcontinental railroad. Railroads took settlers and miners to the region and carried resources back to factories in the East.

At the same time, people began using a new resource, petroleum. Even before the automotive age, petroleum was in high demand because it could be turned into kerosene. The American oil industry was built on the demand for kerosene, a fuel used in lanterns and stoves. The industry began in western Pennsylvania, where residents had long noticed oil bubbling to the surface of area springs and streams. In 1859 **Edwin Drake** drilled the first oil well near Titusville, Pennsylvania. By 1900 oil fields from Pennsylvania to Texas had been drilled. As oil production rose, it led to economic expansion.

R Reading Strategies	**C** Critical Thinking	**D** Differentiated Instruction	**W** Writing Support	**S** Skill Practice
Teacher Edition • Seq. Info., p. 184 **Additional Resources** • Content Vocab., URB p. 59 • Guided Read., URB p. 80 • RENTG, p. 43	**Teacher Edition** • Analyzing Info., p. 187 **Additional Resources** • Linking Past/Present, URB p. 66 • Economics and History Act., URB p. 7 • Supreme Court Case Studies, p. 15	**Additional Resources** • Enrichment Act., URB p. 77 • Am. Art and Music Act., URB p. 71	**Teacher Edition** • Descrip. Writing, pp. 184, 185, 186 **Additional Resources** • Academic Vocab., URB p. 61	**Teacher Edition** • Analyzing, p. 183 • Explaining, p. 184 **Additional Resources** • Quizzes/Tests, p. 61 • Time Line Act., URB p. 65

NATIONAL GEOGRAPHIC Natural Resource Sites of the United States, c. 1890

Mineral Production, 1865–1900

- Coal (tons)
- Iron (tons)
- Petroleum (barrels)

Source: *Historical Statistics of the United States.*

Legend:
- Coal
- Copper
- Iron
- Limestone
- Petroleum
- Softwood timber
- Other timber

0   400 kilometers
0   400 miles
Lambert Azimuthal Equal-Area projection

Analyzing GEOGRAPHY

1. **Region** For what natural resource were the states of West Virginia, Ohio, and Pennsylvania known?
2. **Human-Environment Interaction** Why do you think the first steel factories were built in Pennsylvania?

Maps In Motion See *StudentWorks™ Plus* or glencoe.com.

Teach

S Skill Practice

Analyzing Ask: In what region of the United States was most softwood timber harvested? What role might the climate and geography have played? *(the southeast; the rich soil and warm climate of this region were essential to the growth of softwood timber.)* **BL**

Analyzing GEOGRAPHY

Answers:
1. coal
2. The nearby coal mines provided coal to fuel the smelting process.

✔ Reading Check

Answer:
It increased economic expansion.

A Large Workforce

The human resources available to American industry were as important as natural resources in enabling the nation to industrialize rapidly. Between 1860 and 1910 the population of the United States nearly tripled. This population growth provided industry with an abundant workforce and also created greater demand for the consumer goods manufactured by factories.

Population growth stemmed from two causes—large families and a flood of immigrants. Because of better living conditions, more children survived and grew to adulthood. American industry began to grow at a time when social and economic conditions in eastern Europe and China convinced many people to immigrate to the United States in search of a better life. Many were also seeking to escape oppressive governments and religious persecution. Between 1870 and 1910, more than 17 million immigrants arrived in the United States. These multitudes entered the growing industrial workforce, helped factories increase production, and became consumers of industrial products.

✔ **Reading Check** **Explaining** How did oil production affect the American economy?

Chapter 5 Industrialization **183**

Hands-On Chapter Project
Step 1

Starting a Business

Step 1: Planning Your Business
Working in small groups, students will determine what business they would like to start and how to organize it to be successful.

Essential Question What resources will the business require to be successful?

Directions Organize students into small groups. Have them assume the role of entrepreneurs. Using information from the chapter as well as library or Internet resources,

each group of students should first determine what their business will be.

Students should then make a list of the resources they will need for their business. Remind students to consider labor or human resources, natural resources, and financial resources, as well as machinery, factories, processing plants, and so on. Using library or Internet resources, students should determine how much capital will be needed to acquire the resources the group identified.

Next, students should create a flowchart

illustrating the processes that will likely be followed in their business. The flowchart should identify where in the process each resource identified by the group will be utilized or consumed.

Summarizing Allow time for groups to share their decisions, what they have learned about their businesses, and the costs of the businesses. Students may also include pictures of the resources or of the processes used in the business. **OL**

(Chapter Project continued in Section 2, p. 189)

R Reading Strategy

Sequencing Information Have students research one of the inventions of the late 1800s. Instruct students to create time lines for significant events related to their chosen invention. For example, a time line for the telephone might include the dates for the invention of the telephone keypad, the cordless telephone, and the cell phone. **OL**

W Writing Support

Descriptive Writing Have students write a paragraph describing how one of the inventions shown on the time line has changed the way people work. Encourage students to share their paragraphs with the class. **BL**

S Skill Practice

Explaining Have interested students research to find out the processes that Bell, Edison, or Westinghouse used when developing their inventions. Encourage students to share their findings with the class. **AL**

Additional Support

New Inventions

MAIN Idea During the late 1800s, inventions such as the telephone and the lightbulb spurred economic development.

HISTORY AND YOU What invention has most changed your daily life? Read about the new inventions of the late 1800s.

Natural resources and labor were essential to America's economic development, but new inventions and technology were important as well. New technology increased the nation's productivity and improved transportation and communications networks. New inventions also resulted in new industries, which in turn produced more wealth and jobs.

Bell and the Telephone

S In 1874 a Scottish immigrant named **Alexander Graham Bell** suggested the idea of a telephone to his assistant, Thomas Watson. Watson recalled, "He had an idea by which he believed it would be possible to talk by telegraph."

Bell began experimenting with ways to transmit sound via an electrical current of varying intensity. In 1876 he succeeded. Picking up the crude telephone, he placed a call to the next room, saying, "Come here, Watson, I want you." Watson heard and came. The telephone revolutionized business and personal communication. In 1877 Bell organized the Bell Telephone Company, which eventually became the American Telephone and Telegraph Company (AT&T).

Edison, Westinghouse, and Electricity

S Perhaps the leading pioneer in new technology was **Thomas Alva Edison.** Curious about the world from an early age, he learned all he could about the mechanical workings of objects. His laboratory at Menlo Park, New Jersey, was the forerunner of the modern research laboratory. Edison set up his lab with money he earned by improving the telegraph system for Western Union. He referred to it as an "invention factory." During the first five years Menlo Park existed, Edison patented an invention almost every

American Inventions, 1865–1895

1872
Elijah McCoy invents automatic lubricator for steam engines, allowing trains to run faster with less maintenance

1877
Thomas Edison develops phonograph

▲ Early Edison phonograph

1886
Josephine Cochrane develops automatic dishwasher; its basic design is still used today

1870   **1875**   **1880**   **1885**

W
R

1873
Christopher Sholes develops typewriter and sells it to Remington and Sons

1876
Alexander Graham Bell invents telephone

▲ Bell's first telephone

1882
Lewis Latimer invents the carbon filament for lightbulbs, allowing them to last much longer

▲ Alexander Graham Bell

▲ Edison's first commercial lightbulb

184   Chapter 5   Industrialization

Activity: Interdisciplinary Connections

Science Invite a science teacher or a representative of a telephone company to demonstrate the science behind the invention of the telephone and discuss the science involved in cellular communications. Encourage students to ask questions. After the presentation, discuss how the standard telephone and cellular telephone have changed the way people communicate with one another. List the advantages and disadvantages of telephone communications. **OL**

month. By the time he died, Edison held more than one thousand patents.

Edison first achieved international fame in 1877 with the invention of the phonograph. Two years later he perfected the electric generator and the lightbulb. Although Edison had expected to produce an inexpensive lightbulb in six weeks, the task took more than a year. His laboratory then went on to invent or improve several other major devices, including the battery, the dictaphone, and the motion picture.

An Edison company began to transform American society in 1882 when it started supplying electric power to New York City. In 1889 several Edison companies merged to form the Edison General Electric Company (today known as GE).

Engineer and industrialist George Westinghouse invented an air-brake system for railroads. Unlike earlier manual systems that required brakes to be applied to each car, Westinghouse's invention provided a continuous braking system, so that all the cars' brakes were applied at the same time. Because the trains could brake rapidly and smoothly, they could safely travel at higher speeds.

Westinghouse also developed an alternating current (AC) system to distribute electricity using transformers and generators. Working with inventor Nikola Tesla, Westinghouse further improved his system. His Westinghouse Electric Company lit Chicago's Columbia Exhibition in 1893. It was also the first to use the hydroelectric power of Niagara Falls to generate electricity for streetcars and lights in Buffalo, New York, 22 miles away.

Technology's Impact

In ways big and small, technology changed the way people lived. Shortly after the Civil War, Thaddeus Lowe invented the ice machine, the basis of the refrigerator. In the early 1870s Gustavus Swift, founder of Swift Meatpacking, hired an engineer to develop a refrigerated railroad car. Swift shipped the first refrigerated load of fresh meat in 1877. The widespread use of refrigeration kept food fresh longer and reduced the risk of food poisoning.

W | **Writing Support**
Descriptive Writing Invite students to use library and Internet resources to write a one-page essay describing the process of how a refrigerated railroad car worked in the 1870s and how it differs today. Encourage students to share their essays with the class. **OL**

Analyzing TIME LINES
Answers:
1. The invention of the phonograph came after the invention of the typewriter.
2. 10 years
3. the automatic dishwasher

1893
Charles and Frank Duryea invent gasoline-powered automobile

▲ *The Wright Flyer lifts off, December 17, 1903.*

1903
Wilbur and Orville Wright make first successful powered flight at Kitty Hawk, North Carolina

1890 1895 1900 1905

1888
George Eastman patents first hand-held camera, the Kodak

Analyzing TIME LINES
1. **Sequencing** Did the invention of the phonograph occur before or after the invention of the typewriter?
2. **Calculating** How much time elapsed between the invention of a gasoline-powered automobile and the first flight of the Wright brothers?
3. **Identifying** For what invention is Josephine Cochrane known?

Chapter 5 Industrialization **185**

Differentiated Instruction

Linking Past and Present Activity, URB p. 66

The Telephone: Past and Present

Objective: To link technological innovations in the late 1800s to technology today.

Focus: Have students relate how Alexander Graham Bell's telephone has impacted their lives today.

Teach: Explain Bell's invention and how it changed Americans' lives.

Assess: Create a time line describing the history of the telephone.

Close: Discuss other inventions from the 1800s and 1900s that have greatly affected our lives today.

Differentiated Instruction Strategies
BL Explain how technology like the telephone improves people's lives.

AL Create a flowchart illustrating how another invention from this period influenced today's technology.

ELL Create a list of all new or unfamiliar terms in the reading. First, guess at the meanings. Then look up the words.

W Writing Support

Descriptive Writing Ask students to find books in the library about the laying of the Atlantic cable. Then have students write a telegram to family members in Europe describing their experiences using one "new" invention of the 1860s or 1870s. Students should include details such as how the invention works and how it affects their daily routines. **OL**

Analyzing VISUALS

Answers:
1. They are being washed away by a flood of foreign goods.
2. In the absence of free trade, the consumer faces higher (inflated) costs.

✓ Reading Check

Answer:
It revolutionized business by opening up entirely new markets for inventions and goods to sell.

Additional Support

The textile industry had long depended on machines to turn fibers into cloth. By the mid-1800s, the introduction of the Northrop automatic loom allowed cloth to be made at a much faster rate. Bobbins, which had to be changed by hand, could now be changed automatically.

Changes also took place in the clothing industry. Standard sizes were used in making ready-made clothes. Power-driven sewing machines and cloth cutters rapidly moved the clothing business from small tailor shops to large factories. Similar changes took place in shoemaking. By 1900 cobblers had nearly disappeared.

W Technology's impact also included improved communications. Cyrus Field laid a telegraph cable across the Atlantic Ocean in 1866. This cable provided instant contact between the United States and Europe.

✓ Reading Check **Explaining** How did the use of electric power affect economic development?

Free Enterprise

MAIN Idea Laissez-faire economics promoted industrialization, but tariffs protected American companies from competition.

HISTORY AND YOU Do you remember how Americans objected to British taxes on trade before the American Revolution? Read how tariffs affected American industries in the late 1800s.

Another important reason the United States was able to industrialize rapidly was its free enterprise system. In the late 1800s, many Americans embraced the idea of **laissez-faire** (leh•say•FARE), a French phrase meaning "let people do as they choose." Supporters of laissez-faire believe the government should not interfere in the economy other than to protect private property rights and maintain peace. They argue that if the government regulates the economy, it increases costs and eventually hurts society more than it helps.

POLITICAL CARTOONS PRIMARY SOURCE
Should Government Regulate the Economy?

◄ Entitled "The Consumer Consumed," this cartoon shows a shopper being told that if he buys domestic goods, he has to pay extra money to trusts (monopolies), and if he buys foreign goods, he has to pay extra money (duties) to the government.

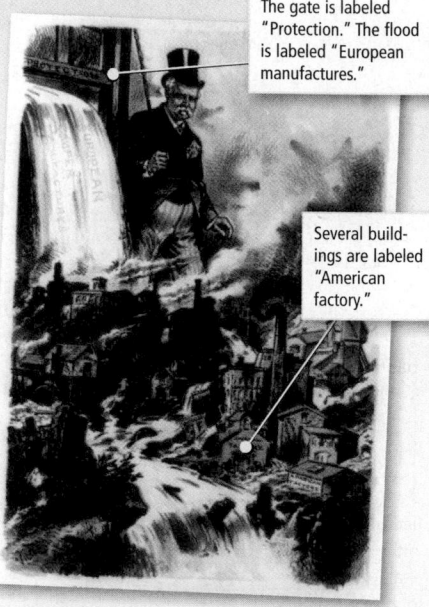

The gate is labeled "Protection." The flood is labeled "European manufactures."

Several buildings are labeled "American factory."

▲ The original caption for this cartoon read "Goods will be so much cheaper—Democratic argument. But what will happen to all the American factories?"

Analyzing VISUALS   DBQ

1. **Interpreting** What is happening to American factories after the protection gate is opened?
2. **Analyzing** What argument does the cartoon on the left give in favor of free trade?

186 Chapter 5 Industrialization

Activity: Collaborative Learning

Survey Divide students into groups. Have each group develop a list of the electrical equipment he or she uses during a typical week. Then have the groups survey one adult between 30 and 40 years old, a second between 40 and 50 years old, and a third between 60 and 70 years old about the electrical equipment they used as teenagers. Have students compare what is the same and different about the lists from each group. Ask students what these lists reflect about changes in technology.

Laissez-faire relies on supply and demand, rather than the government, to regulate wages and prices. Supporters believe a free market with competing companies leads to greater efficiency and creates more wealth for everyone. Laissez-faire advocates also support low taxes and limited government debt to ensure that private individuals, not the government, will make most of the decisions about how the nation's wealth is spent.

In the late 1800s, the profit motive attracted many capable and ambitious people into business. **Entrepreneurs**—people who risk their capital to organize and run businesses—were attracted by the prospect of making money in manufacturing and transportation. Many entrepreneurs from New England, who had accumulated money by investing in trade, fishing, and textile mills, now invested in factories and railroads. An equally important source of private capital was Europe, especially Great Britain. Foreign investors saw great opportunities for profit in the United States.

In many ways, the United States **practiced** laissez-faire economics in the late 1800s. State and federal governments kept taxes and spending low. They did not impose costly regulations on industry or try to control wages and prices. In other ways, however, the government went beyond laissez-faire and introduced policies intended to promote business.

Since the early 1800s, leaders in the Northeast and the South had different ideas about the proper role of the government in the economy. Northern leaders wanted high tariffs to protect manufacturers from foreign competition and also supported federal subsidies for companies building roads, canals, and railroads. Southern leaders opposed subsidies and favored low tariffs to promote trade and to keep the cost of imported goods low.

The Civil War ended the debate. After the Southern states seceded, the Republican-controlled Congress passed the **Morrill Tariff,** which greatly increased tariff rates. By 1865 tariffs had nearly tripled. Congress also gave vast tracts of Western land and nearly $65 million in loans to Western railroads, and sold public lands with mineral resources for much less than their market value.

In the late 1800s, the United States was one of the largest free trade areas in the world. The Constitution bans states from imposing tariffs, and there were few regulations on commerce or immigration. Supporters of laissez-faire say these factors played a major role in the country's tremendous economic growth.

High tariffs, however, contradicted laissez-faire ideas. When the nation raised tariffs on foreign goods, other countries raised their tariffs on American goods. This hurt American companies trying to sell goods abroad, particularly farmers who sold their products overseas. Despite these problems, many business leaders and members of Congress believed tariffs were necessary. Few believed that new American industries could compete with established European factories without tariffs to protect them. Later, in the early 1900s, after American companies had become large and efficient, business leaders began to push for free trade. They believed they could now compete internationally and win sales in foreign markets.

✓ **Reading Check** **Analyzing** Do you think government policies at this time helped or hindered industrialization? Why?

Section 1 REVIEW

Vocabulary

1. **Explain** the significance of: gross national product, Edwin Drake, Alexander Graham Bell, Thomas Alva Edison, laissez-faire, entrepreneur, Morrill Tariff.

Main Ideas

2. **Explaining** How did an abundance of natural resources contribute to economic growth in the United States in the late 1800s?

3. **Organizing** Use a graphic organizer similar to the one below to indicate how the inventions listed affected the nature of American work and business.

Invention	Effects
telephone	
lightbulb	
automatic loom	

4. **Describing** How did the principles of the free enterprise system, laissez-faire, and profit motive encourage the rise of industry?

Critical Thinking

5. **Big Ideas** What role did the federal government play in increasing industrialization after the Civil War?

6. **Analyzing Visuals** Examine the time line on pages 184–185. Choose one invention and explain how it changed society.

Writing About History

7. **Descriptive Writing** Imagine you are a young person living in this country in the late 1800s. Choose one of the inventions discussed in the section and write a journal entry describing its impact on your life.

 History ONLINE
Study Central™ To review this section, go to glencoe.com and click on Study Central.

187

C Critical Thinking

Analyzing Information Ask interested students to use library or Internet resources to find out more about the roles of entrepreneurs in the free enterprise system. **Ask:** Who are entrepreneurs in the United States today? **AL**

Assess
· ·

 History ONLINE

Study Central™ provides summaries, interactive games, and online graphic organizers to help students review content.

Close
· ·

Summarizing Ask: In what ways did the federal government encourage industrialization in the late 1800s? *(Laissez-faire policies; grants to railroads)* **OL**

✓ **Reading Check**

Answer:
Students might mention that while higher tariffs hurt consumers, they spurred industrialization.

Section 1 REVIEW

Answers

1. All definitions can be found in the section and the Glossary.

2. Americans did not have to import resources from other countries, saving resources for internal growth.

3. telephone: better communications; lightbulb: cheap lighting; automatic loom: made cloth faster

4. They put development in the hands of entrepreneurs rather than in the hands of the government.

5. Congress subsidized railroads and sold land for below market value.

6. Answers will vary depending on which invention students select.

7. Students' journal entries will vary. Students should describe the invention and its impact from a firsthand perspective.

Focus

Bellringer
Daily Focus Transparency 5.2

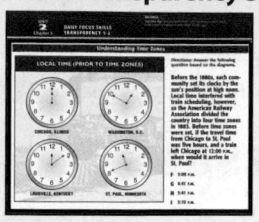

Guide to Reading

Answers: development of time zones; sped long-distance transportation; longer and heavier trains used; rate per mile declined; united America's regions; promoted a national market

Section Spotlight Video

To generate student interest and provide a springboard for class discussion, access the Chapter 5, Section 2 video at glencoe.com or on the video DVD.

Resource Manager

The Railroads

Guide to Reading

Big Ideas
Science and Technology The growth of railroads encouraged development of the Plains and Western regions.

Content Vocabulary
• time zone (p. 191)
• land grant (p. 192)

Academic Vocabulary
• integrate (p. 191)
• investor (p. 192)

People and Events to Identify
• Pacific Railway Act (p. 188)
• Grenville Dodge (p. 188)
• Leland Stanford (p. 189)
• Cornelius Vanderbilt (p. 191)
• Jay Gould (p. 192)
• Crédit Mobilier (p. 192)
• James J. Hill (p. 193)

Reading Strategy
Organizing As you read about the development of a nationwide rail network, complete a graphic organizer similar to the one below, listing the effects of this rail network on the nation.

Major railroads, including the transcontinental railroad, were constructed rapidly after the Civil War ended. Railroads required major capital investment and government land grants. The huge profits to be made, however, led to some corruption as well.

Linking the Nation

MAIN Idea After the Civil War, the rapid construction of railroads accelerated the nation's industrialization and linked the country together.

HISTORY AND YOU How has technology helped unify the United States in recent years? Read to learn how railroads helped connect the nation.

In 1865 the United States had about 35,000 miles of railroad track, almost all of it east of the Mississippi River. After the Civil War, railroad construction expanded dramatically, linking the distant regions of the nation in a transportation network. By 1900 the United States, now a booming industrial power, had more than 200,000 miles of track.

The Transcontinental Railroad

The railroad boom began in 1862, when President Abraham Lincoln signed the **Pacific Railway Act.** This act provided for the construction of a transcontinental railroad by two corporations. To encourage rapid construction, the government offered each company land along its right-of-way. A competition between the two companies developed, as each raced to obtain as much land and money as possible.

The Union Pacific Under the direction of engineer **Grenville Dodge,** a former Union general, the Union Pacific began pushing westward from Omaha, Nebraska, in 1865. The laborers faced blizzards in the mountains, scorching heat in the desert, and, sometimes, angry Native Americans. Labor, money, and engineering problems plagued the supervisors of the project. As Dodge observed:

PRIMARY SOURCE

"Everything—rails, ties, bridging, fastenings, all railway supplies, fuel for locomotives and trains, and supplies for men and animals on the entire work—had to be transported from the Missouri River."

—quoted in *The Growth of the American Republic*

The railroad workers of the Union Pacific included Civil War veterans, newly recruited Irish immigrants, frustrated miners and farmers, cooks, adventurers, and ex-convicts. At the height of the project, the Union

---

R Reading Strategies	C Critical Thinking	D Differentiated Instruction	W Writing Support	S Skill Practice
Teacher Edition • Using Context Clues, p. 191 **Additional Resources** • Guided Read., URB p. 81 • RENTG, p. 46	**Teacher Edition** • Drawing Concl., p. 193 **Additional Resources** • Historical Analysis Skills, URB p. 54 • Supreme Court Case Studies, p. 21	**Teacher Edition** • Visual/Spatial, p. 192 **Additional Resources** • Primary Source Reading, URB p. 69	**Teacher Edition** • Narr. Writing, p. 189 • Descrip. Writing, p. 190	**Teacher Edition** • Kinesthetic, p. 189 **Additional Resources** • Quizzes/Tests, p. 62 • Reading Skills Act., p. 53

HISTORY AND GEOGRAPHY
The Transcontinental Railroad Connects the Nation

NATIONAL GEOGRAPHIC

The two railroads join at Promontory Summit, Utah, 1869.

Wash. Terr.
Oreg.
Mont. Terr.
Idaho Terr.
Wyo. Terr.
Sacramento
Nev.
Calif.
Utah Terr.
Colo. Terr.
Nebr. Omaha
Kans.
Ariz. Terr.
N. Mex. Terr.
Indian Terr.
Tex.
CENTRAL PACIFIC
UNION PACIFIC

S

W

▲ Led by Grenville Dodge (top right), workers built the Union Pacific Railroad from Omaha, across the Great Plains, to Utah. Many Irish immigrants worked on the railroad.

▲ The Union Pacific and Central Pacific met in Utah, where a ceremonial gold spike was driven, joining the two lines.

▲ Led by Theodore Judah (above, left), workers built the Central Pacific Railroad eastward from Sacramento, through the Rocky Mountains to Utah. Many Chinese immigrants worked on the railroad.

Analyzing VISUALS

1. **Analyzing** Based on the map and photos, why do you think Union Pacific workers were able to lay so many more miles of track than Central Pacific workers?

2. **Describing** Based on the photos, why do you think life as a railroad worker was so difficult?

Pacific employed about 10,000 workers. Camp life was rough, dirty, and dangerous, with lots of gambling, hard drinking, and fighting.

The Central Pacific The Central Pacific Railroad began as the dream of engineer Theodore Judah. He sold stock in his fledgling Central Pacific Railroad Company to four Sacramento merchants: grocer **Leland Stanford,** shop owner Charley Crocker, and hardware store owners Mark Hopkins and

Collis P. Huntington. These "Big Four" eventually made huge fortunes, and Stanford became governor of California, served as a United States senator, and founded Stanford University.

Because of a shortage of labor in California, the Central Pacific Railroad hired about 10,000 workers from China and paid them about $1.00 a day. All the equipment—rails, cars, locomotives, and machinery—was shipped from the eastern United States, either around Cape Horn at the tip of South America or over the isthmus of Panama in Central America.

Chapter 5 Industrialization **189**

Teach

S Skill Practice
Kinesthetic Have students create a map of the western United States today, showing the routes of the Transcontinental Railroad, state boundaries, and capital cities. Students should then locate major cities along the route of the railroad. Have students draw conclusions about the impact of the railroad on the settlement of the West. **BL**

W Writing Support
Narrative Writing Have students research the life of a railroad worker. Using their findings, students should write a letter to family members back home describing one day at work. **OL**

Analyzing VISUALS

Answers:
1. The land where the Union Pacific workers laid track was much flatter.
2. little or no shelter from the elements; no conveniences; workers moved as the track was laid

Hands-On Chapter Project
Step 2

Starting a Business

Step 2: Obtaining the Capital

Directions Returning to their groups, students should review the plans, lists, and flowcharts for their business. Using their textbook as well as library or Internet resources, students should find out how business leaders obtain the money necessary to start a business. Students may want to look ahead and refer to the table on page 195. Remind students that a sole proprietorship is usually a small business owned by one person and that a partnership is owned by two or more people who usually invest their own money in the business. Larger businesses, however, require huge amounts of money, or capital. Two of the most common ways businesses obtain the large amounts of capital required are bank loans and the selling of stocks to investors, who then own part of the business. Each group should prepare a chart showing the advantages and disadvantages of these two options. After the charts are complete, a representative from each group should share the group's chart and findings with the class. Next, have students return to their groups and decide the best way for their business to obtain the needed capital.

Putting It Together Have volunteers from each group explain how the group plans to obtain the required capital and why the group chose that particular option. Discuss with the class the likelihood of each business's success in obtaining the necessary capital. **OL**

(Chapter Project continued in Section 3, p. 195)

189

Writing Support

Descriptive Writing Have students find out more about the celebratory events at Promontory Summit, Utah, on May 10, 1869. Then have students use that information to create a newspaper article describing the celebrations for their hometown paper back East. **OL**

Did You Know?

Nearly 50 years after the United States completed its transcontinental railroad, the Russians hammered the final spike into their own cross-country rail line. Begun in 1891 and completed in 1916, the Trans-Siberian Railroad was the longest in the world, running nearly 5,800 miles (9,330 km) from Moscow in the west to Vladivostok on the Sea of Japan (East Sea) in the east. Like the American railroads, the Trans-Siberian line opened up the way for trade and settlement throughout Russia's frontier. A passenger train takes seven days to travel between Moscow to Vladivostok.

Additional Support

TECHNOLOGY & HISTORY

Railroads and the Economy Building the railroad system led to the creation of new technologies and jobs. Economists refer to this as the "multiplier effect." Whenever a new technology becomes widely used, it creates many new jobs in other industries that are needed to support it.

Building railroad engines and cars created many jobs in other industries. For example, textile workers made fabric for seats in passenger cars, glassworkers made the lenses for the lamps, and metalworkers cast the bronze bells.

Railroads greatly increased the demand for coal, both to power locomotives and to melt iron in steel refineries. This created a huge coal-mining industry in Pennsylvania and West Virginia. In 1860, some 36,000 people were coal miners; by 1889, there were more than 290,000.

Railroads created many new jobs. Engineers, firemen, and brakemen were needed to run the trains; mechanics, machinists, oilers, dispatchers, track workers, loaders, and many others were needed to keep the railway running. By 1900, more than 1 million people worked for the railroads.

In 1860 the nation had 30,000 miles of railroad track. By 1890, another 130,000 miles had been laid. Track-laying crews employed thousands of workers. In addition, the lumber industry needed tens of thousands of workers to make railroad ties. Thousands of others worked in iron mines and in the steel industry, helping make rails, engine boilers, and other steel components.

History ONLINE Student Web Activity Visit glencoe.com and complete the activity on industrialization.

The Last Spike Workers completed the Transcontinental Railroad in only four years, despite the physical challenges. Each mile of track required 400 rails; each rail took 10 spikes. The Central Pacific, starting from the west, laid a total of 688 miles of track. The Union Pacific laid 1,086 miles.

On May 10, 1869, hundreds of spectators gathered at Promontory Summit, Utah, to watch dignitaries hammer five gold and silver spikes into the final rails that would join the Union Pacific and Central Pacific. General Grenville Dodge was at the ceremony:

PRIMARY SOURCE

"The trains pulled up facing each other, each crowded with workmen. . . . The officers and invited guests formed on each side of the track. . . . Prayer was offered; a number of spikes were driven in the two adjoining rails . . . and thus the two roads were welded into one great trunk line from the Atlantic to the Pacific."

—from *Mine Eyes Have Seen*

After Leland Stanford hammered in the last spike, telegraph operators sent the news across the nation. Cannons blasted in New York City, Chicago held a parade, and citizens in Philadelphia rang the Liberty Bell.

Railroads Spur Growth

The transcontinental railroad was the first of many lines that began crisscrossing the nation after the Civil War. By linking the nation, railroads increased the markets for many products, spurring American industrial growth. Railroads also stimulated the economy by spending huge amounts of money on steel, coal, timber, and other materials.

Hundreds of small, unconnected railroads had been built before the Civil War. Gradually, however, large rail lines took them over. By 1890, for example, the Pennsylvania Railroad had consolidated 73 smaller companies. Eventually, seven giant systems with terminals in major cities and scores of branches

190   **Chapter 5**   Industrialization

Interdisciplinary Activity: Language Arts

Tell students that most large industries have their own specialized terms that are used on the job. Have interested students create a lexicon of terms used by railroad workers. Tell them that the lexicon should include the pronunciation and solid working definitions for each term. For at least two of the terms, students should also include a drawing or diagram for further explanation. **OL**

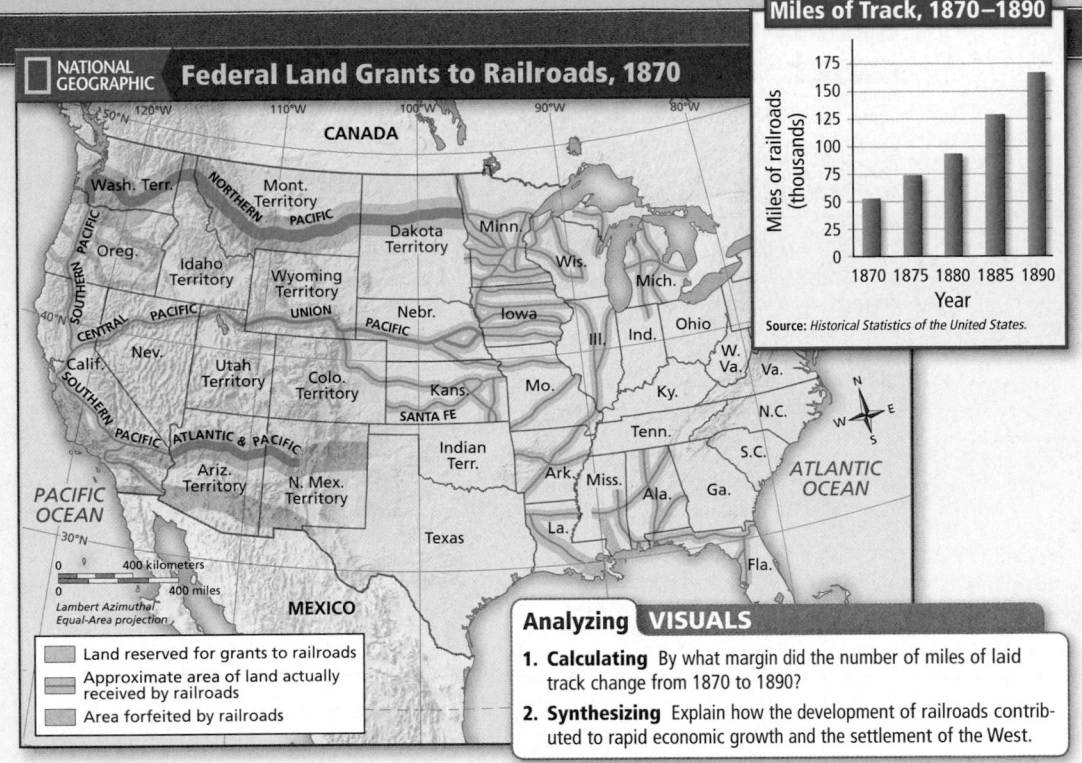

Federal Land Grants to Railroads, 1870

Miles of Track, 1870–1890

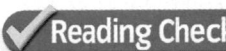

Source: *Historical Statistics of the United States.*

Land reserved for grants to railroads
Approximate area of land actually received by railroads
Area forfeited by railroads

Analyzing VISUALS

1. **Calculating** By what margin did the number of miles of laid track change from 1870 to 1890?

2. **Synthesizing** Explain how the development of railroads contributed to rapid economic growth and the settlement of the West.

Reading Strategy

Using Context Clues Have students reread the first full paragraph in column two on this page. Using clue words and phrases such as "combined" and "railroad systems," ask students to define the term *integrated*. Students should note that the term means "to join together" or "to unify." **BL**

Analyzing VISUALS

Answers:
1. about 110,000
2. Railroads brought settlers and goods west cheaply and efficiently.

Reading Check

Answer:
to make rail service safer and more reliable

reaching into the countryside controlled most rail traffic.

One of the most successful railroad consolidators was **Cornelius Vanderbilt.** By 1869, Vanderbilt had purchased and merged three short New York railroads to form the New York Central, running from New York City to Buffalo. Within four years he had extended his control over lines all the way to Chicago, which enabled him to offer the first direct rail service between New York City and Chicago. In 1871 Vanderbilt began building New York's Grand Central Terminal.

Before the 1880s each community set its clocks by the sun's position at noon. Having many local time zones interfered with train scheduling, however, and at times even threatened passenger safety. When two trains traveled on the same track, collisions could result from scheduling errors caused by variations in time. To make rail service safer and reliable, the American Railway Association divided the country into four **time zones** in 1883. The federal government ratified this change in 1918.

Meanwhile, new locomotive technology and the invention of air brakes enabled railroads to put longer and heavier trains on their lines. When combined with large, **integrated** railroad systems, operations became so efficient that the average rate per mile for a ton of freight dropped from two cents in 1860 to three-quarters of a cent in 1900.

The nationwide rail network also helped unite Americans in different regions. The *Omaha Daily Republican* observed in 1883 that railroads had "made the people of the country homogeneous, breaking through the peculiarities and provincialisms which marked separate and unmingling sections." This was a bit of an overstatement, but it recognized that railroads were changing American society.

Reading Check **Explaining** Why was the country divided into four time zones?

Chapter 5 Industrialization **191**

Extending the Content

Time Zones Opponents of standard time called local time "God's time" because it was based on the laws of nature—the sun's position in the sky—rather than on human criteria. They referred to standard time as "railroad time," and blocked attempts to create time zones. Not until 1918 was Congress able to pass a law that standardized time zones.

Additional Support

D Differentiated Instruction

Visual/Spatial Have interested students use library or Internet resources to research an entrepreneur of today. Have the students use their findings to create a political cartoon satirizing or supporting the entrepreneur's efforts. Display the cartoons in the classroom. **OL**

Analyzing VISUALS

Answers:

1. Banker, inexperienced investor, small operator, and stockbroker; it implies that Gould has manipulated stock prices, which hurt small investors and businesses.
2. The four robber barons are enjoying themselves as they carve up the United States.

Additional Support

Robber Barons

MAIN Idea The government helped finance railroad construction by providing land grants, but this system also led to corruption.

HISTORY AND YOU Have you heard of any recent financial scandals? Read to learn how government grants led to large-scale corruption.

Building railroad lines often required more money than most private **investors** could raise on their own. To encourage railroad construction across the Great Plains, the federal government gave **land grants** to many railroad companies. The railroads then sold the land to settlers, real estate companies, and other businesses to raise money to build the railroad.

During the 1850s and 1860s, the federal land grant system gave railroad companies more than 120 million acres of public land, an area larger than New England, New York, and Pennsylvania combined. Several railroads, including the Union Pacific and Central Pacific, received enough land to cover most of the cost of building their lines.

The great wealth many railroad entrepreneurs acquired in the late 1800s led to accusations that they had built their fortunes by swindling investors and taxpayers, bribing officials, and cheating on their contracts and debts. Infamous for manipulating stock, **Jay Gould** was the most notoriously corrupt railroad owner.

Bribery occurred frequently, partly because government helped fund the railroads. Some investors quickly discovered that they could make more money by acquiring government land grants than by operating a railroad. To get more grants, some investors began bribing members of Congress.

POLITICAL CARTOONS PRIMARY SOURCE
The Robber Barons

▲ Jay Gould bowls on Wall Street with balls labeled "Trickery," and "False Reports." The pins are labeled "Banker," "Inexperienced Investor," "Small Operator," and "Stock Broker."

▲ Railroad owners Jay Gould (lower left), Cornelius Vanderbilt (upper left), Russell Sage (upper right), and Cyrus W. Field (lower right) carve up the United States. The figure in back is lowering an envelope to European royalty labeled "Sealed proposals for the purchase of Europe."

Analyzing VISUALS   DBQ

1. **Analyzing Visuals** What "pins" has Jay Gould managed to knock down, and what does this suggest?
2. **Interpreting** What do the faces and actions of the five men in the cartoon suggest?

Activity: Collaborative Learning

Illustrated Time Lines Organize students into groups. Assign each group one of the following subjects: the development of the steam locomotive in the United States, custom Pullman cars, or the architecture of railroad terminals. Have groups use the Internet and library resources to do research and create an illustrated time line that details important events in the development of their assigned topic. Display the illustrated time lines in the classroom.

The Crédit Mobilier Scandal

Corruption in the railroad industry became public in 1872, when the **Crédit Mobilier** scandal erupted. Crédit Mobilier was a construction company set up by several stockholders of the Union Pacific Railroad, including Oakes Ames, a member of Congress. Acting for both the Union Pacific and Crédit Mobilier, the investors signed contracts with themselves. Crédit Mobilier greatly overcharged Union Pacific and added miles to the railroad construction. Because the same investors controlled both companies, the railroad agreed to pay the inflated bills without questions.

By the time the Union Pacific railroad was completed, these investors had made millions of dollars, but the railroad itself had used up its federal grants and was almost bankrupt. To convince Congress to give the railroad more grants, Ames sold other members of Congress shares in the Union Pacific at a price well below their market value.

During the election campaign of 1872, an angry associate of Ames sent a letter to the *New York Sun* listing the members of Congress who had accepted shares. The scandal led to an investigation that implicated several members of Congress, including Speaker of the House James G. Blaine and Representative James Garfield, who later became president. It also revealed that Vice President Schuyler Colfax had accepted stock from the railroad. Neither criminal nor civil charges were filed against anyone involved with Crédit Mobilier, however, nor did the scandal affect the outcome of the elections.

The Great Northern Railroad

The Crédit Mobilier scandal created the impression that all railroad entrepreneurs were "robber barons"—people who loot an industry and give nothing back. Some, like Jay Gould, deserved this reputation, but others did not.

James J. Hill was clearly no robber baron. Hill built and operated the Great Northern Railroad from Wisconsin and Minnesota in the East to Washington in the West, without any federal land grants or subsidies. He had carefully planned the railroad's route to pass close to established towns in the region.

To increase business, he offered low fares to settlers who homesteaded along his route. Later, he sold homesteads to the Norwegian and Swedish immigrants coming to the region. He then identified American products that were in demand in China, including cotton, textiles, and flour, and arranged to haul those goods to Washington for shipment to Asia. This enabled the railroad to earn money by hauling goods both east and west, instead of simply sending lumber and farm products east and coming back empty, as many other railroads did at that time. The Great Northern became the most successful transcontinental railroad and the only one that was not eventually forced into bankruptcy.

✔ **Reading Check** **Describing** How was the Great Northern different from other railroads of its time?

Section 2 REVIEW

Vocabulary

1. **Explain** the significance of: Pacific Railway Act, Grenville Dodge, Leland Stanford, Cornelius Vanderbilt, time zone, land grant, Jay Gould, Crédit Mobilier, James J. Hill.

Main Ideas

2. **Describing** How did Grenville Dodge contribute to the economic growth of the United States in the late 1800s?

3. **Listing** Use a graphic organizer similar to the one below to list the different ways by which railroads were financed.

Ways Railroads Were Financed

Critical Thinking

4. **Big Ideas** How did railroad expansion lead to industrial growth?

5. **Theorizing** Why might politicians be tempted to accept gifts of railroad stock? Why did Crédit Mobilier become a scandal?

6. **Analyzing Visuals** Examine the map and graph on page 191. Then make up a quiz of at least five questions based on the information presented.

Writing About History

7. **Persuasive Writing** Take on the role of an employee of a major railroad corporation. Your job is to write an advertisement to recruit workers for your corporation. After writing the advertisement, present it to your class.

History ONLINE

Study Central™ To review this section, go to glencoe.com and click on Study Central.

193

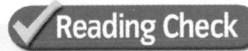

Answers

Focus

Bellringer
Daily Focus Transparency 5.3

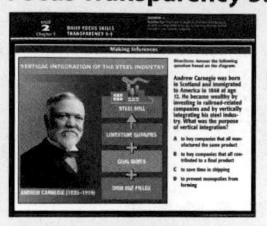

Guide to Reading

Answer: pools; vertical and horizontal integration; holding companies; trusts

Section Spotlight Video

To generate student interest and provide a springboard for class discussion, access the Chapter 5, Section 3 video at glencoe.com or on the video DVD.

Section 3

Big Business

Guide to Reading

Big Ideas
Economics and Society Business people such as Andrew Carnegie developed new ways to expand business.

Content Vocabulary
- corporation (p. 194)
- stock (p. 194)
- economies of scale (p. 194)
- pool (p. 196)
- vertical integration (p. 197)
- horizontal integration (p. 197)
- monopoly (p. 197)
- trust (p. 198)
- holding company (p. 198)

Academic Vocabulary
- distribution (p. 194)
- consumer (p. 196)

People and Events to Identify
- Andrew Carnegie (p. 196)
- John D. Rockefeller (p. 197)

Reading Strategy
Organizing As you read about the rise of corporations in the United States, complete a graphic organizer showing the steps large business owners took to weaken or eliminate competition.

Following the Civil War, large corporations developed that could consolidate various business functions and produce goods more efficiently. Retail stores began using advertising and mail-order catalogs to attract new consumers.

The Rise of Big Business

MAIN Idea Corporations could produce goods more efficiently, which allowed the rise of big business.

HISTORY AND YOU Do you own stock in a corporation or know someone who does? Read to learn why corporations issue stock.

Before the Civil War, most manufacturing enterprises were owned by just a few people working in partnership. Everything had changed by 1900. Big businesses dominated the economy, operating vast complexes of factories, warehouses, and **distribution** facilities.

Big business would not have been possible without the **corporation.** A corporation is an organization owned by many people but treated by law as though it were a person. It can own property, pay taxes, make contracts, and sue and be sued. The people who own the corporation are called stockholders because they own shares of ownership called **stock.** Issuing stock allows a corporation to raise large amounts of money for big projects while spreading out the financial risk.

Before the 1830s there were few corporations, because entrepreneurs had to convince a state legislature to issue them a charter. In the 1830s, however, states began passing general incorporation laws, allowing companies to become corporations and issue stock without charters from the legislature.

With the money they raised from the sale of stock, corporations could invest in new technologies, hire large workforces, and purchase many machines, greatly increasing their efficiency. This enabled them to achieve **economies of scale:** the cost of manufacturing is decreased by producing goods quickly in large quantities.

All businesses have two kinds of costs, fixed costs and operating costs. Fixed costs are costs a company has to pay, whether or not it is operating. For example, a company has to pay its loans, mortgages, and taxes, regardless of whether it is operating. Operating costs are costs that occur when running a company, such as paying wages and shipping costs and buying raw materials and supplies.

The small manufacturers that were common before the Civil War usually had low fixed costs but high operating costs. If sales dropped, it was cheaper to shut down temporarily. Big manufacturers,

---

Resource Manager

R Reading Strategies	**C** Critical Thinking	**D** Differentiated Instruction	**W** Writing Support	**S** Skill Practice
Additional Resources • Guided Read., URB p. 82 • RENTG, p. 49 • Enrichment Act., URB p. 77	**Teacher Edition** • Identify Issues, p. 196 • Draw Concl., p. 198 • Analyze Info., p. 199 **Additional Resources** • Interp. Political Cartoons, URB p. 73	**Additional Resources** • Reinforcing Skills Act., URB p. 63	**Teacher Edition** • Descrip. Writing, p. 195 • Persuas. Writing, pp. 196, 197 **Additional Resources** • Supreme Court Case Studies, p. 23	**Additional Resources** • Quizzes/Tests, p. 63

INFOGRAPHIC
Types of Business Organizations

	Sole proprietorship	Partnership	Corporation
Who owns the business?	One person owns the business and often manages it	Two or more people own and manage the business	All investors who own its stock; managers are hired
How is money raised?	Owner uses savings and borrows money from a bank	Partners each invest some of their own money and borrow money from a bank	Shares of stock are sold to finance business; bank loans are also used
Advantages	Easy to start Low fixed costs, as facilities are usually small and inexpensive to maintain	Partners share responsibility for running the business Low fixed costs	Limited liability for investors Low operating costs; can stay open if economy slows
Disadvantages	Difficult to raise money; limited opportunities for growth; owner has unlimited liability; high operating costs may force business to shut down if the economy is weak	Partners may disagree on direction the company should take; owners have unlimited liability High operating costs	Often have high fixed costs because of size of facilities and equipment needed

W ▶ The rise of corporations whose stock could be sold publicly also led to the rise of stock exchanges, where stockbrokers bought and sold stock for investors. The photo shows the trading floor of the New York Stock Exchange (NYSE) in 1908. By the late 1800s, the NYSE was the nation's most important stock exchange.

U.S. Businesses, 1870–1900

Businesses (thousands): 0, 20, 40, 60, 80, 100, 120
Years: 1870, 1880, 1890, 1900

Source: Historical Statistics of the United States.

Analyzing VISUALS

1. **Making Inferences** After comparing proprietorships and corporations, why do you think both still exist today?
2. **Making Generalizations** Based on the chart, what generalization can you make about the growth of U.S. businesses during those three decades? What explanation can you offer?

however, had the high fixed costs of building and maintaining a factory. Compared to their fixed costs, the operating costs of big businesses were low. Operating costs, such as wages, were such a small part of a corporation's costs that it made sense to continue operating, even in a recession.

In these circumstances, big corporations had several advantages. They could produce more goods cheaply and efficiently. They could continue to operate in poor economic times by cutting prices to increase sales rather than shutting down. Many were also able to negotiate rebates from the railroads, further lowering their operating costs.

Small businesses with high operating costs found it difficult to compete with large corporations, and many were forced out of business. At the time, many people criticized corporations for cutting prices and negotiating rebates. They believed the corporations were behaving unethically by driving small companies out of business. In many cases, it was the changing nature of business organization and the new importance of fixed costs that caused competition to become so severe and led to so many small companies going out of business.

✔ **Reading Check** **Describing** What factors led to the rise of big business in the United States?

Teach

W Writing Support
Descriptive Writing Have students find out about the New York Stock Exchange. Have students write two paragraphs describing the activities on the floor of the exchange. Encourage students to share their descriptions with the class. **BL**

Analyzing VISUALS

Answers:
1. Both sole proprietorships and corporations are viable ways of organizing a business, and each fills a different purpose in the nation's economy.
2. The number of businesses grew quickly between 1870 and 1890, but then the rate of increase slowed. Explanations may include that new restrictions were placed on businesses at the turn of the last century.

✔ Reading Check

Answer:
general incorporation laws and economies of scale

Hands-On Chapter Project
Step 3

Starting a Business

Step 3: Expanding the Business

Directions Returning to their groups, students should review the plans, lists, and flowcharts for their business. They should also assume that they have received the necessary capital and that, so far, their business is successful. Given their business's success, each group of business leaders now wants to expand the business by

becoming more efficient, keeping costs low, and eliminating competition.

Using their textbook as well as library or Internet resources, each group should research what steps might be taken to expand or improve the business. For example, the group might decide that vertical or horizontal integration might be a useful way to expand the business. Alternatively, the group may decide to expand the business by building more factories and hiring more workers.

Each group should make a final recommendation based on members' research.

Putting It Together Have volunteers from each group present the group's recommendation to the class. Discuss with the class the pros and cons of the various recommendations. Have the class hypothesize which recommendations are likely to be the most successful. **OL**

(Chapter Project continued in Section 4, p. 201)

C Critical Thinking

Identifying Central Issues
Remind students that the pools received no support from state legislatures and no protection from American courts. **Ask:** Why did legislatures and the courts see pools as suspect? *(Because pools interfered with competition and property rights.)* **AL**

W Writing Support

Persuasive Writing Have students assume the role of an assistant to Andrew Carnegie and write a memo to Carnegie attempting to persuade him to adopt the Bessemer process. **OL**

Did You Know?

Steel Output In 1898, although Carnegie's steel output had increased three-fold over the previous few years, the number of workers needed to produce the steel had decreased by 400. The use of electricity to drive machinery was largely responsible for the decline in the workforce.

Additional Support

Consolidating Industry W Andrew Carnegie and Steel

MAIN Idea Business leaders devised new and larger forms of business organizations and new ways to promote their products.

HISTORY AND YOU How does advertising reach you today? How has technology created new ways to market and sell goods? Read to learn how an increase in new products led to new selling methods.

Many business leaders did not like the intense competition that had been forced on them. Although falling prices benefited **consumers,** they cut into profits. To stop prices from falling, many companies organized **pools,** or agreements, to keep prices at a certain level.

C American courts and legislatures were suspicious of pools because they interfered with competition and property rights. As a result, companies that formed pools had no legal protection and could not enforce their agreements in court. Pools generally did not last long anyway. They broke apart whenever one member cut prices to steal the market share from another. By the 1870s, competition had reduced many industries to a few large and highly efficient corporations.

The remarkable life of **Andrew Carnegie** illustrates many of the factors that led to the rise of big business in the United States. Born in Scotland, Carnegie was the son of a poor hand weaver who moved to the United States in 1848. At age 12, Carnegie went to work as a bobbin boy in a textile factory earning $1.20 per week. After two years, he became a messenger in a telegraph office, then worked as secretary to Thomas Scott, a superintendent and, later, president of the Pennsylvania Railroad. Carnegie's energy impressed Scott, and when Scott was promoted, Carnegie became the new superintendent.

As a railroad supervisor, Carnegie knew that he could make a lot of money by investing in companies that served the railroad industry. He bought shares in iron mills and factories that made sleeping cars and locomotives. He also invested in a company that built railroad bridges. By his early 30s, he was earning $50,000 per year and decided to quit his job to concentrate on his own business investments.

As part of his business activities, Carnegie frequently traveled to Europe. On one trip, he

INFOGRAPHIC
The Rise of the Steel Industry

Several factors led to the rise of big business in the late 1800s: the use of new technology, the advantages of economies of scale, and the process of vertical and horizontal integration.

Coke, iron ore, and limestone are hoisted to the top of the blast furnace and sprinkled into the furnace. Blasts of super-hot air melt the ore as it falls.

Blast furnace

Coke (from coal)   Iron ore   Limestone

Carnegie's use of a Bessemer converter enabled his steel mills to make large quantities of inexpensive steel. Molten iron is poured into the converter and then air is blown in, separating the impurities, and leaving high grade steel to pour out.

Impurities rise to the top of the molten iron and are skimmed off. The iron drains out the bottom of the furnace and is carried to the Bessemer converter.

Bessemer converter

Activity: Interdisciplinary Connection

Debate Divide students into groups. Have the groups form opinions as to whether big business should or should not be allowed to function without restraints on size, competition, hiring policies, ways of obtaining investment capital, and so on. Have groups do additional research using library sources and the Internet to support the chosen opinion. Have students from opposing sides debate. As a class, decide which group presented the more convincing argument.

met Sir Henry Bessemer, who had invented a new process for making high-quality steel efficiently and cheaply. After meeting Bessemer, Carnegie opened a steel company in Pittsburgh in 1875 and began using the Bessemer process. Carnegie often boasted about how cheaply he could produce steel:

PRIMARY SOURCE

"Two pounds of iron stone mined upon Lake Superior and transported nine hundred miles to Pittsburgh; one pound and one-half of coal mined and manufactured into coke, and transported to Pittsburgh; one-half pound of lime, mined and transported to Pittsburgh; a small amount of manganese ore mined in Virginia and brought to Pittsburgh—and these four pounds of materials manufactured into one pound of steel, for which the consumer pays one cent."

—quoted in *The Growth of the American Republic*

To make his company more efficient, Carnegie began the **vertical integration** of the steel industry. A vertically integrated company owns all of the different businesses on which it depends for its operation. Instead of paying companies for coal, lime, and iron, Carnegie's steel company bought coal mines, limestone quarries, and iron ore fields. Vertical integration saved money and enabled many companies to become even bigger.

Rockefeller and Standard Oil W

Successful business leaders also pushed for **horizontal integration,** or combining firms in the same business into one large corporation. Horizontal integration took place as companies competed. When a company began to lose market share, it would often sell out to competitors to create a larger organization.

Perhaps the most famous industrialist who achieved almost complete horizontal integration of his industry is **John D. Rockefeller.** When oil was discovered in Pennsylvania, many entrepreneurs started drilling for oil, hoping to strike it rich. Rockefeller decided to build oil refineries instead. By 1870, his company, Standard Oil, was the nation's largest oil refiner. He then began buying out his competitors. By 1880, the company controlled about 90 percent of the oil-refining industry in the United States. When a single company achieves control of an entire market, it becomes a **monopoly.**

Vertical Integration

▲ In a vertically integrated industry, a company owns all parts of the industrial process. In this case, a steel company owns the iron and coal mines, the limestone quarries, and the ships and trains that move the materials, as well as the steel mills.

Horizontal Integration

▲ When one company grows by buying up its competitors, it is using horizontal integration to expand.

Analyzing VISUALS

1. **Analyzing Visuals** What enabled entrepreneurs such as Andrew Carnegie to build large steel factories?
2. **Explaining** Why did business owners want to vertically integrate their companies?

Chapter 5 Industrialization **197**

People IN HISTORY

C **Critical Thinking**

Drawing Conclusions Trusts and holding companies became widespread ways of business organization in the 1880s.

Ask: Are trusts and holding companies good for America's consumers? Have students use library or Internet resources to find out more information about trusts and holding companies. Then have them write a brief essay explaining their findings. Remind students that their essay should reach a conclusion supporting their viewpoint. **AL**

People IN HISTORY

Answers:

Rockefeller: Rockefeller invested in the newest, most efficient refining methods; he used ruthless business tactics; he organized the Standard Oil Trust.

Morgan: Morgan tried to make the railroad industry more efficient.

Additional Support

John D. Rockefeller
1839–1937

John Davison Rockefeller was one of the foremost industrialists of the late 1800s. Born in upstate New York, Rockefeller moved with his family to Cleveland, Ohio, as a teenager. As a young man, he established a grain and livestock business that made huge profits during the Civil War.

Meanwhile, Cleveland had emerged as a center for refining the oil extracted from the oil fields of western Pennsylvania. In 1863 Rockefeller used his wartime profits to start an oil-refining company. He then began buying up other oil refineries. In 1870 Rockefeller and some associates founded the Standard Oil Company. Rockefeller invested in the newest and most efficient refining technology. He also became known for using ruthless tactics to get preferential shipping rates from railroad companies and acquire competing oil refineries.

By the early 1880s, Rockefeller had created the Standard Oil Trust. With a near-monopoly on American oil refining, Standard Oil made Rockefeller one of the richest men in the world. Rockefeller later donated much of his wealth to philanthropic causes, most notably funding colleges and universities.

What made Standard Oil so successful?

J. P. Morgan
1837–1913

John Pierpont Morgan, the most powerful and influential financier of his era, built a financial empire that became known as the "House of Morgan." The son of a successful Boston banker, Morgan began his career working in the New York City branch of his father's bank.

Morgan soon developed a reputation for shrewd business sense. He specialized in financing railroads, an industry plagued by cut-throat competition and instability. Before Morgan would agree to rescue a troubled railroad company, he insisted the company reorganize to become more efficient, combine smaller railway lines to create a larger coordinated railroad system, and agree to have a representative from Morgan's firm oversee future decisions.

During the depression of the 1890s, Morgan used his immense fortune to finance a bond to rescue the federal government's depleted gold reserve. In 1901 Morgan made history when he organized the first billion-dollar corporation, U.S. Steel, by merging the Carnegie Steel Company and several other steel companies.

How did Morgan try to help the railroad industry?

New Business Organizations

Many Americans feared monopolies because they believed that a monopoly could charge whatever it wanted for its products. Others, however, believed that monopolies had to keep prices low because raising prices would encourage competitors to reappear and offer the products for a lower price. In some industries, one company had a near-monopoly in the United States but was competing on a global scale. Standard Oil, for example, came very close to having a monopoly in the United States, but international competition forced the company to keep its prices low in the late 1800s and early 1900s.

In the late 1800s, in an effort to stop horizontal integration and the rise of monopolies, many states made it illegal for one company to own stock in another company. It did not take long, however, for companies to discover ways around the laws.

C **Trusts** In 1882 Standard Oil formed the first **trust,** a new way of merging businesses that did not violate such laws. A trust is a legal arrangement that allows one person to man-

age another person's property. The person who manages that property is called a trustee.

Instead of buying a company outright, Standard Oil had stockholders give their stocks to a group of Standard Oil trustees. In exchange, the stockholders received shares in the trust, which entitled them to a portion of the trust's profits. Since the trustees did not own the stock but were merely managing it, they were not violating any laws. The trustees could control a group of companies as if they were one large, merged company.

C **Holding Companies** Beginning in 1889, the state of New Jersey further accelerated the rise of big business with a new general incorporation law. This law allowed corporations chartered in New Jersey to own stock in other businesses without any need for special legislative action. Many companies immediately used the law to create a new organization, the **holding company.** A holding company does not produce anything itself. Instead, it owns the stock of companies that do produce goods. The holding company manages the companies it owns, effectively merging them into one large enterprise.

Activity: Interdisciplinary Connection

Economics Invite a representative from the Small Business Administration to speak to the class about the impact of small businesses on the community. Ask the speaker to address the basics of how one goes about setting up a small business. As a class, discuss the various ways to finance a business.

Investment Banking Another increase in the size of corporations began in the mid-1890s, when investment bankers began to help put new holding companies together. Perhaps the most famous and successful investment banker of the era was J. P. Morgan. John Pierpont Morgan began his career in 1857 as an agent for his father's banking company in New York, America's financial capital. Investment bankers like Morgan specialized in helping companies issue stock. Companies would sell large blocks of stock to investment bankers at a discount. The bankers would then find people willing to buy the stock and sell it for a profit.

In the mid-1890s, investment bankers became interested in selling stock in holding companies that merged many of America's already large corporations. In 1901, J. P. Morgan bought out Andrew Carnegie. Morgan then merged Carnegie Steel with other large steel companies into an enormous holding company called the United States Steel Company. U.S. Steel, worth $1.4 billion, was the first billion-dollar company in American history. By 1904, the United States had 318 holding companies. Together, these giant corporations controlled over 5,300 factories and were worth more than $7 billion.

Selling the Product

The creation of giant manufacturing companies in the United States forced retailers—companies that sell products directly to consumers—to expand in size as well. The vast array of products that American industries produced led retailers to look for new ways to attract consumers. N. W. Ayer and Son, the first advertising company, began creating large illustrated ads instead of relying on the old small print line ads previously used in newspapers. By 1900, retailers were spending over $90 million a year on advertising in newspapers and magazines.

Advertising attracted readers to the newest retail business, the department store. In 1877 advertisements billed John Wanamaker's new Philadelphia department store, the Grand Depot, as the "largest space in the world devoted to retail selling on a single floor." When it opened, only a handful of department stores existed in the United States; soon hundreds sprang up. Department stores provided a huge selection of products in one large, elegant building. The store atmosphere made shopping seem glamorous and exciting.

Chain stores, a group of retail outlets owned by the same company, first appeared in the mid-1800s. In contrast to department stores, which offered many services, chain stores focused on offering low prices. Woolworth's, which opened in 1879, became one of the most successful retail chains in American history. **C**

To reach the millions of people who lived in rural areas far from chain stores or department stores, retailers began issuing mail-order catalogs. Two of the largest mail-order retailers were Montgomery Ward and Sears, Roebuck and Co. Their huge catalogs, widely distributed through the mail, used attractive illustrations and appealing descriptions to advertise thousands of items for sale.

✓**Reading Check** **Explaining** What techniques did corporations use to consolidate their industries?

Section 3 REVIEW

Vocabulary

1. **Explain** the significance of: corporation, stock, economies of scale, pool, Andrew Carnegie, vertical integration, horizontal integration, John D. Rockefeller, monopoly, trust, holding company.

Main Ideas

2. **Stating** Why did the number of corporations increase in the late 1800s?

3. **Comparing** Use a graphic organizer to list ways business leaders in the 1800s tried to eliminate competition.

Attempts to Eliminate Competition

Critical Thinking

4. **Big Ideas** What techniques were used by Carnegie and others to consolidate their industries? How did state governments respond?

5. **Forming an Opinion** Do you think an individual today can rise from "rags to riches" like Andrew Carnegie did? Why or why not?

6. **Analyzing Visuals** Look again at the chart on page 195. During which decade did the number of U.S. businesses increase the most? By how many?

Writing About History

7. **Expository Writing** Write a newspaper editorial in which you explain why entrepreneurs were a positive or a negative force on the U.S. economy in the late 1800s.

History ONLINE
Study Central™ To review this section, go to glencoe.com and click on Study Central.

199

C **Critical Thinking**

Analyzing Information Have students name chain stores and describe the types of items available for sale in those stores. **Ask: How do chain stores serve consumers in their community?** *(Chain stores provide a wide variety of goods in one location.)* **OL**

✓**Reading Check**

Answer:
pools, vertical and horizontal integration, monopolies, trusts, and holding companies

Assess

History ONLINE

Study Central™ provides summaries, interactive games, and online graphic organizers to help students review content.

Close

Identifying Central Issues As a class, discuss how large corporations came to dominate American business. Have students write an essay in which they address whether large corporations have helped or hindered the American economy.

Section 3 REVIEW

Answers

1. All definitions can be found in the section and the Glossary.

2. Companies were allowed to incorporate without getting a state charter; companies sold stock and, with the profits, were able to achieve economies of scale that smaller companies could not.

3. pools; trusts; monopolies; vertical and horizontal integration

4. Pools, trusts, monopolies, vertical and horizontal integration; many states made it illegal for one company to own stock in another company.

5. Students' answers will vary but should be supported.

6. during the 1870s; about 27,000

7. Editorials should incorporate clear arguments.

Focus

Section 4

Bellringer

Daily Focus Transparency 5.4

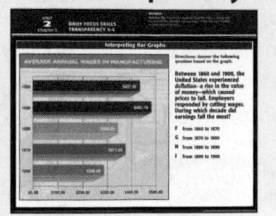

Guide to Reading

Answers:
1877—Great Railroad Strike: involves 80,000 workers; police, state militias, and federal troops break up strike; millions of dollars in damage; more than 100 people killed
1886—Haymarket Riot: weakens the Knights of Labor
1894—Pullman Strike: nearly paralyzes the economy; federal troops force end to strike; federal court issued an injunction to halt the boycott

Section Spotlight Video

To generate student interest and provide a springboard for class discussion, access the Chapter 5, Section 4 video at glencoe.com or on the video DVD.

Resource Manager

Section 4

Unions

Guide to Reading

Big Ideas
Struggles for Rights Unions grew and labor unrest intensified as workers fought for more rights.

Content Vocabulary
• deflation (p. 200)
• trade union (p. 201)
• industrial union (p. 201)
• blacklist (p. 201)
• lockout (p. 202)
• arbitration (p. 204)
• injunction (p. 205)
• closed shop (p. 206)

Academic Vocabulary
• restraint (p. 202)
• constitute (p. 207)

People and Events to Identify
• Marxism (p. 202)
• Knights of Labor (p. 204)
• American Federation of Labor (p. 206)
• Samuel Gompers (p. 206)

Reading Strategy
Sequencing As you read about the increase of American labor unions in the late 1800s, complete a time line similar to the one below by filling in the incidents of labor unrest discussed and the results of each incident.

Workers tried to form unions in the late 1800s, hoping to improve wages, hours, and working conditions. Business leaders were willing to deal with some trade unions but generally opposed industrial unions. Many strikes in this era led to violence, which hurt the image of unions and slowed their growth.

Working in the United States

MAIN Idea Low wages, long hours, and difficult working conditions caused resentment among workers and led to efforts to organize unions.

HISTORY AND YOU Have you ever felt that you were underpaid for an after-school job? Read about the conditions that made workers want to organize.

Life for workers in industrial America was difficult. Many workers had to perform dull, repetitive tasks in working conditions that were often unhealthy and dangerous. Workers breathed in lint, dust, and toxic fumes. Heavy machines lacking safety devices caused many injuries. Despite the difficult working conditions, industrialism led to a dramatic rise in the standard of living. The average worker's wages rose by 50 percent between 1860 and 1890. Nonetheless, the uneven division of income between the wealthy and the working class caused resentment among workers. In 1900 the average industrial worker made 22¢ per hour and worked 59 hours per week.

Deflation, or a rise in the value of money, added to tensions between workers and employers. Between 1865 and 1897, deflation caused prices to fall, which increased the buying power of workers' wages. Although companies cut wages regularly in the late 1800s, prices fell even faster, so that wages were actually still going up in buying power. Workers, however, resented getting less money. Eventually, many concluded that they needed a union to bargain for them in order to get higher wages and better working conditions.

Early Unions

There were two basic types of industrial workers in the United States in the 1800s—craft workers and common laborers. Craft workers had special skills and training. They included machinists, iron molders, stonecutters, shoemakers, printers, and many others. Craft workers received higher wages and had more control over how they organized their time. Common laborers had few skills and received lower wages.

R Reading Strategies	C Critical Thinking	D Differentiated Instruction	W Writing Support	S Skill Practice
Additional Resources • Guided Read., URB p. 83 • RENTG, p. 52 • Supreme Court Cases, p. 25 • Primary Source Reading, URB p. 67	**Teacher Edition** • Compare/Contrast, pp. 202, 206 • Analyz. Pri. Sources, p. 203 • Make Inferences, p. 204 • Analyz. Info., p. 205 **Additional Resources** • Critical Thinking Skills, URB p. 64	**Teacher Edition** • Visual/Spatial, p. 201 **Additional Resources** • Diff. Instruction, URB p. 55 • Reteaching Act., URB p. 75 • English Learner Act., URB p. 57	**Teacher Edition** • Descrip. Writing, pp. 201, 204, 205, 206 • Persuas. Writing, pp. 203, 207 **Additional Resources** • Foldables, p. 62	**Additional Resources** • Quizzes/Tests, p. 64 • Authentic Assess., p. 15 • Test Practice, p. 10

PRIMARY SOURCE
Why Did Workers Want to Organize?

In 1893 a recession hit the United States; by 1894, millions of workers were unemployed and over 750,000 were on strike. A former quarry foreman named Jacob Coxey organized unemployed workers and began a march on Washington to demand jobs on public works projects. The marchers were known as "Coxey's Army."

▲ Whether they were working in Western silver mines (top photo) or handling hot steel at a Pittsburgh foundry (above), workers toiled in unsafe conditions for very little money.

Annual Nonfarm Earnings

Earnings (dollars)

600, 500, 400, 300, 200, 100, 0

1865 1870 1875 1880 1885 1890 1895 1900
Year

— Real wages
— Not adjusted for inflation

Source: *Historical Statistics of the United States.*

Analyzing VISUALS

1. **Analyzing** What do you observe about the working conditions and equipment of the men in both of the inset photos?
2. **Contrasting** What happened to real wages and those not adjusted for inflation between 1865 and 1900? Given this fact, why do you think workers wanted to organize?

In the 1830s, as industrialization began to spread, craft workers began to form **trade unions.** By 1873 there were 32 national trade unions in the United States. Among the largest and most successful were the Iron Molders' International Union, the International Typographical Union, and the Knights of St. Crispin—the shoemakers' union.

Industry Opposes Unions Employers often had to negotiate with trade unions because they represented workers whose skills they needed. However, employers generally viewed unions as conspiracies that interfered with property rights. Business leaders particularly opposed **industrial unions,** which united all workers in a particular industry.

Companies used several techniques to stop workers from forming unions. They required workers to take oaths or sign contracts promising not to join a union. They hired detectives to identify union organizers. Workers who tried to organize a union or strike were fired and placed on a **blacklist**—a list of "troublemakers"—so that no company would hire them.

Teach

D Differentiated Instruction

Visual/Spatial Organize students into groups of four and have each group create a collage of workers today. They should show how working conditions are different or similar to working conditions in the late 1800s. **OL**

W Writing Support

Descriptive Writing Have students find out more about the practices that industries used against unionized workers. Then have students write a letter to the editor explaining why they believe that being blacklisted is unfair. **OL**

Analyzing VISUALS

Answers:
1. Working conditions are poor.
2. Real wages increased even though actual wages decreased. Workers wanted to organize because they were being paid less.

Hands-On Chapter Project
Step 4

Starting a Business

Step 4: Negotiating With a Union

Directions Have students return to their groups. Each group should assume that their business is successful and that the business owners are making a good profit. The business's workers have joined a union and are now asking for improvements such as better benefits, a shorter work week, and higher wages.

Using their textbook as well as library or Internet resources, have each group make a list of their workers' specific demands. Groups should include a rationale from the workers' viewpoint for each request.

Next, each group should review and evaluate the list of the workers' demands; have the group determine if the business will accept, reject, or attempt to compromise on each point. Remind the groups that each worker's demand will likely cost money, thus reducing the profitability of the business. The group should also provide a rationale for each of the business's decisions.

Putting It Together Have a volunteer from each group present to the class the list of workers' demands and the business's responses. Discuss what might happen if a compromise between the business and the workers cannot be reached. After the class discussion, groups may want to reconvene to reevaluate the business's decisions. *(Chapter Project continued on the Visual Summary page.)*

C Critical Thinking

Comparing and Contrasting
Organize students into pairs. Have one student in each pair use library and Internet resources to find out more information about Karl Marx and his views on communism; have the second student in each pair find out more about Adam Smith and capitalism. Have students create a chart comparing and contrasting the differences of each man's philosophy. Have pairs of students present their charts to the class. **AL**

✓ Reading Check

Answer:
They associated unions with immigrants, revolution, and anarchy.

When workers formed a union, companies used **"lockouts"** to break it. They locked workers out of the property and refused to pay them. If the union called a strike, employers would hire replacements, or strikebreakers.

Political and Social Opposition Efforts to **C** break unions often succeeded because there were no laws giving workers the right to form unions or requiring owners to negotiate with them. Courts frequently ruled that strikes were "conspiracies in **restraint** of trade," for which labor leaders might be fined or jailed.

Unions also suffered from the perception that they were un-American. In the 1800s, the ideas of Karl Marx, called **Marxism,** became very influential in Europe. Marx argued that the basic force **C** shaping capitalist society was the class struggle between workers and owners. He believed that workers would eventually revolt, seize control of the factories, and overthrow the government.

Marxists claimed that after the revolution the government would seize all private property and create a socialist society where wealth was evenly divided. Eventually, Marx thought, the state would disappear, leaving a communist society where classes did not exist.

While many labor supporters agreed with Marx, a few supported anarchism. Anarchists **C** believe that society does not need any government. At the time, some believed that with only a few acts of violence they could ignite a revolution to topple the government. In the late 1800s, anarchists assassinated government officials and set off bombs all across Europe, hoping to trigger a revolution.

During the same period, tens of thousands of European immigrants headed to America. Anti-immigrant feelings were already strong in the United States and, as people began to associate immigrant workers with radical ideas, they became suspicious of unions. These fears, and concerns for law and order, often led officials to use the courts, the police, and even the army to crush strikes and break up unions.

✓ Reading Check **Identifying** Why were some Americans suspicious of unions?

Union Membership, 1880–1900

Sources: *New Estimates of Union Membership; The Growth of American Trade Unions.*

INFOGRAPHIC
Working in the United States, 1870–1900

The status of the American economy played an important role in the development of unions. Although union membership rose dramatically by 1900, the willingness of people to join unions at any given time varied depending on how well the economy was doing.

The U.S. Economy, 1870–1900

Source: *The Great Republic.*

202 Chapter 5 Industrialization

Leveled Activities

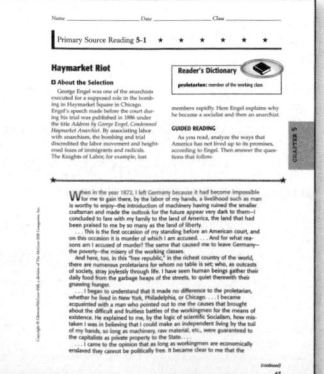

Struggling to Organize

MAIN Idea Workers began to form unions to fight for better wages and working conditions but had few successes.

HISTORY AND YOU Do you sometimes feel that you spend too many hours a day in school? Read to learn how workers sought an eight-hour workday.

Although workers attempted on many occasions to create large industrial unions, they rarely succeeded. In many cases the confrontations with owners and the government led to violence and bloodshed. In 1868 William Sylvis, president of the Iron Molders' Union, wrote to Karl Marx in support of his work and to express his own beliefs:

PRIMARY SOURCE

C

" . . . monied power is fast eating up the substance of the people. We have made war upon it, and we mean to win it. If we can we will win through the ballot box; if not, we will resort to sterner means. A little bloodletting is sometimes necessary in desperate causes."

—quoted in *Industrialism and the American Worker*

The Great Railroad Strike   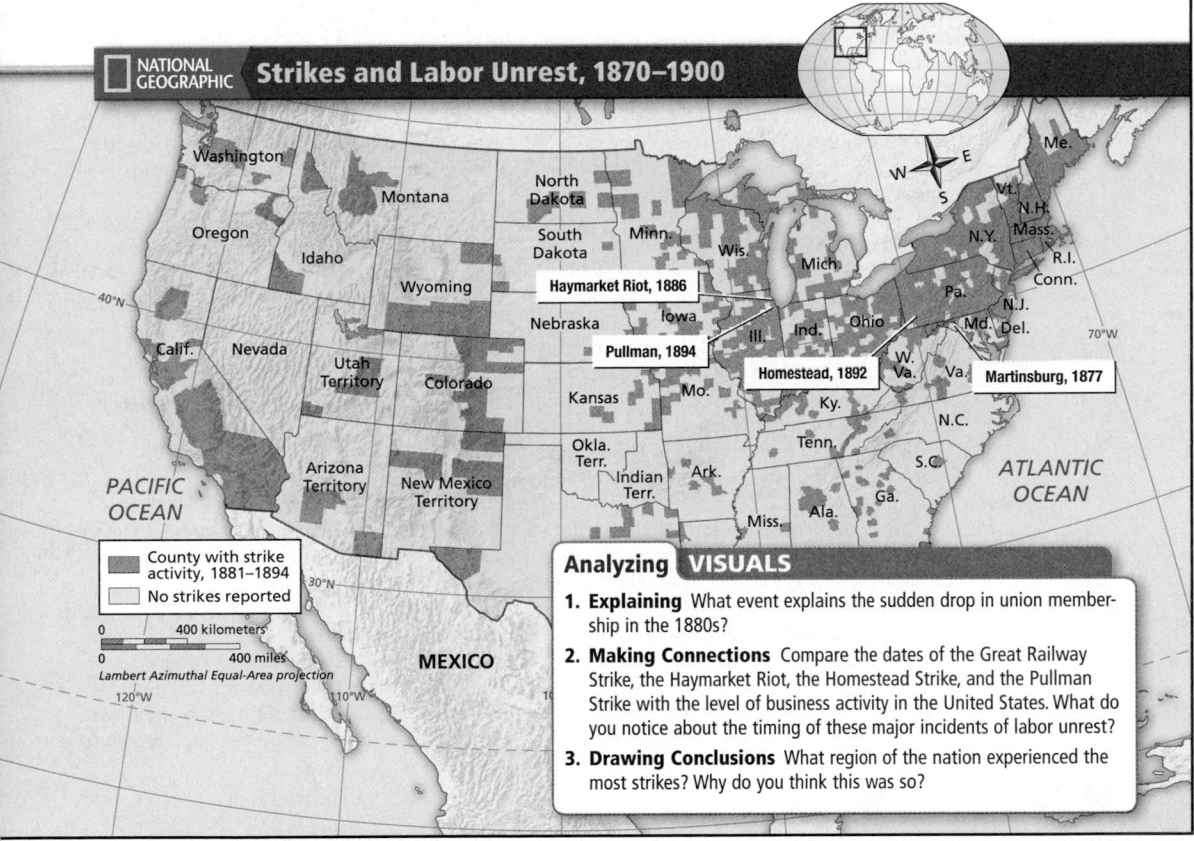W

The panic of 1873 was a severe recession that struck the American economy and forced many companies to cut wages. The economy had still not recovered when, in July 1877, the Baltimore and Ohio Railroad announced it was cutting wages, for the third time. In Martinsburg, West Virginia, workers walked off the job and blocked the tracks.

As word spread, railroad workers across the country walked off the job. The strike eventually involved 80,000 railroad workers and affected two-thirds of the nation's railways. Angry strikers smashed equipment, tore up tracks, and blocked rail service in New York, Baltimore, Pittsburgh, St. Louis, and Chicago. The governors of several states called out their militias. In many places, gun battles erupted between the militia and the strikers.

Declaring a state of "insurrection," President Hayes sent federal troops to Martinsburg, Baltimore, Pittsburgh, and elsewhere. It took 12 bloody days for police, state militias, and

NATIONAL GEOGRAPHIC — Strikes and Labor Unrest, 1870–1900

County with strike activity, 1881–1894

No strikes reported

0   400 kilometers
0   400 miles
Lambert Azimuthal Equal-Area projection

Haymarket Riot, 1886
Pullman, 1894
Homestead, 1892
Martinsburg, 1877

PACIFIC OCEAN

ATLANTIC OCEAN

MEXICO

Analyzing VISUALS

1. **Explaining** What event explains the sudden drop in union membership in the 1880s?

2. **Making Connections** Compare the dates of the Great Railway Strike, the Haymarket Riot, the Homestead Strike, and the Pullman Strike with the level of business activity in the United States. What do you notice about the timing of these major incidents of labor unrest?

3. **Drawing Conclusions** What region of the nation experienced the most strikes? Why do you think this was so?

C Critical Thinking

Analyzing Primary Sources Have students reread the primary source on this page. **Ask:** What methods does Karl Marx indicate that his followers will use to defeat the "monied power?" *(first the ballot, then revolution)* **OL**

W Writing Support

Persuasive Writing Have interested students assume the role of a striking railroad worker and write a one-paragraph letter to the editor of their local newspaper calling on other unionized workers to strike as a show of sympathy. The letters should provide solid reasons why other workers should join the strike. Encourage students to read their letters to the class. **BL**

Analyzing VISUALS

Answers:
1. the Haymarket Riot
2. Labor unrest increased during economic downturns.
3. the Northeast; because it was the most industrialized

Interdisciplinary Activity: Economics

Union Membership Have interested students use library or Internet resources to research the history of union membership from 1870 to the present day. Students should determine union membership at five-year intervals, beginning with 1870. Students should then make a bar graph using their data. Next have students choose one year shown on the graph; using additional resources, have students determine the state of the U.S. economy in that year. **Ask:** Does there seem to be a relationship between union membership and the state of the economy? *(Answers will vary, but in general, union membership tended to increase during times of economic hardship.)* **AL**

C Critical Thinking

Making Inferences Remind students that the Knights of Labor welcomed African American and female workers into its ranks. **Ask:** Why might the Knights of Labor and other early unions include all workers among its members? *(Early unions were looking for support from all workers.)* **AL**

W Writing Support

Descriptive Writing Have interested students use library or Internet resources to find out more about the Haymarket Riot, the Homestead Strike, or the Pullman Strike. Then have students write a one-page essay describing the conditions that caused the workers to strike. **OL**

Additional Support

federal troops to restore order. By the time the strike collapsed, more than 100 people lay dead, and over $10 million in railroad property had been destroyed. The violence of this strike alarmed many Americans and pointed to the need for more peaceful means to settle labor disputes.

The Knights of Labor

The **Knights of Labor,** founded in 1869, took a different approach to labor issues. Its leader, Terrence Powderly, opposed strikes, preferring to use boycotts to pressure employers. The Knights of Labor also supported **arbitration,** a process in which a third party helps workers and employers reach an agreement. The Knights called for an eight-hour workday and supported equal pay for women, the abolition of child labor, and the creation of worker-owned factories. Unlike many organizations of the era, the Knights welcomed women and African Americans as members.

Early Successes In the early 1880s, the Knights began to use strikes and were initially successful. After they convinced one of Jay Gould's railroads to reverse wage cuts in 1885, membership in the union soared. In less than one year, the Knights grew from 100,000 to 700,000 members. Then, in the spring of 1886, an event known as the Haymarket Riot undermined the Knights' reputation.

W The Haymarket Riot In 1886 supporters of the eight-hour workday called for a nationwide strike on May 1st. On that date, strikes took place in many cities. In Chicago, the local Knights of Labor led a march of 80,000 people through the center of the city on that date. Over the next few days, nearly 70,000 workers went on strike across the city.

On May 3, police intervened to stop a fight on the picket line at the McCormick Harvesting Machine Company. The incident turned violent and police fired on the strikers, killing four. Afterward, a local anarchist group organized a meeting in Chicago's Haymarket Square to protest the shooting of the strikers.

On the evening of May 4, about 3,000 people gathered to hear the speeches. As the meeting began to break up, the police moved in to keep order. Someone threw a bomb, killing one officer and wounding six others. The

police opened fire, and workers shot back. About 100 people, including nearly 70 police officers, were injured.

The police arrested eight people for the bombing. Seven were German immigrants and advocates of anarchism. The incident horrified people across the country. Although the evidence was weak, all eight men were convicted, and four were executed.

Critics long opposed to the union movement pointed to the Haymarket riot to claim that unions were dominated by dangerous radicals. One of the men arrested was a member of the Knights of Labor. This association hurt the Knights' reputation and, coupled with lost strikes, led to a steady decline in membership and influence.

W The Homestead Strike

In the summer of 1892, another labor dispute led to bloodshed. A steel mill owned by Andrew Carnegie in Homestead, Pennsylvania, was managed by an anti-union business partner, Henry Clay Frick. The mill's employees belonged to the Amalgamated Association of Iron, Steel, and Tin Workers, the largest craft union in the country. When the union's contract was about to expire, Frick proposed to cut wages by 20 percent. He then locked employees out of the plant and arranged for the Pinkerton Detective Agency to bring in replacement workers.

When the Pinkertons and strikebreakers approached the plant on barges, the strikers refused to let them land. Gunfire followed. After 14 hours, several Pinkertons and strikers were dead, and dozens more were injured. The governor of Pennsylvania then ordered the militia to take control and protect the replacement workers. After four months, the strike collapsed.

W The Pullman Strike

Under the leadership of Eugene V. Debs, railroad employees organized the American Railway Union (ARU) in 1893. As an industrial union, the ARU tried to organize all employees of the railroad industry. Among the workers the union organized were the employees of the Pullman Palace Car Company. The owner, George Pullman, had built a company town, Pullman, just outside of Chicago and required

Activity: Collaborative Learning

Debate For and Against Unions Divide students into two groups. Ask one group to act as the employers and have the group discuss what they would tell employees to keep them from joining a union. Ask the other group to act as union organizers and have the group discuss what they would tell workers about the advantages of joining a union. Have students from each group present their arguments. After the debates, discuss as a class the long-range economic and social effects of unions in the United States. **OL**

INFOGRAPHIC
Comparing Major Strikes

	Homestead Steel Strike, 1892	Pullman Railroad Strike, 1895	Lawrence Textile Strike, 1912
Conditions	Seeking to break the union, the Carnegie Steel Company rejects wage increase and proposes a 20% wage cut	Deep wage cuts without cuts in rent and food prices at company housing and company stores	Very low wages; high mortality among workers (many workers are young girls); extreme poverty among workers; strike begins after new wage cuts
Union	Amalgamated Association of Iron, Steel, and Tin Workers	American Railway Union	International Workers of the World (IWW); strikers mostly female, immigrant textile workers
Tactics	**Workers:** Surround factory with pickets and armed workers to keep it shut down and keep strikebreakers out **Employer:** Locks workers out of the plant; hires Pinkertons to break strike	**Workers:** Refuse to handle any railcars built by Pullman; railroads are tied up nationwide **Employer:** Locks workers out of factory	**Workers:** Picketing; union provides food and money to strikers; gains support by touring child workers around country **Employer:** Uses firehoses on picketing workers
Role of Government	State government sends in militia to end violence between strikers and Pinkertons	Federal government gets court injunction to end strike because it interferes with shipment of U.S. mail; federal troops end strike	Local police and state and local militia make mass arrests, attack picketers; after attack on women and children, strike is publicized; Congress and President Taft investigate
Outcome	Company hires strikebreakers; strike collapses after anarchist tries to kill plant manager	ARU leaders are jailed, strike ends unsuccessfully; ARU membership declines	Employers give in, grant workers' demands

Analyzing VISUALS

1. **Contrasting** How does the Lawrence Textile Strike differ from the others?
2. **Analyzing Visuals** In which instance do federal troops break the strike, and on what grounds?

his workers to live there and to buy goods from company stores. In 1893 the Pullman Company laid off workers and slashed wages. The wage cuts made it difficult for workers to pay their rent and the high prices at the company stores. After the company refused to discuss workers' grievances, a strike began. To show support for the Pullman strikers, other ARU members across the United States refused to handle Pullman cars.

This boycott tied up the railroads and threatened to paralyze the economy. Determined to break the strike, railroad managers arranged for U.S. mail cars to be attached to the Pullman cars. If the strikers refused to handle the Pullman cars, they would be interfering with the U.S. mail, a violation of federal law. President Grover Cleveland then sent in troops, claiming it was his responsibility to keep the mail running. Then a federal court issued an **injunction,** or formal court order, directing the union to halt the boycott. Debs went to jail for violating the injunction, but both the strike at Pullman and the ARU strike collapsed. In the case *In re Debs* (1895), the Supreme Court upheld the right to issue such an injunction. This gave business a powerful tool for dealing with labor unrest.

✔ Reading Check **Summarizing** Why was it difficult for unions to succeed in the 1800s?

Teacher Sidebar (right column)

W Writing Support
Descriptive Writing Have students find out more about one of the major strikes and describe the conditions that led to the strike. **BL**

C Critical Thinking
Analyzing Information
Ask: What are the advantages and disadvantages of living in a company town? *(advantages might include the convenience of living near work; disadvantages might include being too dependent on one's employer.)* **OL**

Analyzing VISUALS
Answers:
1. the employers give in and grant the workers' demands
2. the Pullman Railroad strike because the strike stopped the delivery of the U.S. mail

✔ Reading Check
Answer:
People lost faith in unions after frequent strikes and interference by the authorities.

Critical Thinking Skills Activity, URB p. 64

Identifying the Main Idea

Objective: Identify the main idea from the excerpt of a speech.

Focus: What is Samuel Gompers' message in this speech?

Teach: The main idea of a reading or speech is the "big idea" of the material.

Assess: Paraphrase the excerpt, that is, restate the speech, but in your own words. Is the main idea the same?

Close: Ask: Why did Gompers give this speech?

Differentiated Instruction Strategies

BL Explain how to find the main idea in a paragraph from the textbook.

AL Bring an excerpt to class from a news-magazine, the newspaper, or from an online source. Summarize the article, then state the main idea.

ELL Write the steps to finding a main idea in a flowchart.

205

C Critical Thinking

Comparing Have interested students find out more about the lives of Gompers and Debs.
Ask: What were the similarities and differences between their approaches to union activity? *(Gompers stuck to major issues and tried not to get political; Debs was very politically oriented.)* **OL**

W Writing Support

Descriptive Writing Have students use library or Internet resources to determine the difference between a closed shop and an open shop. Have students write a brief paragraph describing the difference between the two. **BL**

People IN HISTORY

Answers:
Gompers: Students' responses should be supported.
Debs: Students should note that Debs was a member of the Socialist Party, while Gompers distrusted socialism.

Additional Support

New Unions Emerge

MAIN Idea The AFL fought for skilled workers; new unions tried to organize unskilled workers.

HISTORY AND YOU Do you know anyone who belongs to a union? Read on to learn about the different types of unions and how they tried to help their members.

Although workers often shared the same complaints about wage rates and working hours, unions took very different approaches to how they tried to improve workers' lives. Trade unions remained the most common type of labor organization. Of course, most workers were unskilled and unrepresented by trade unions. Thus, new types of unions emerged that tried to reach out to those workers and had different ideas about how to help them.

The Rise of the AFL

The **American Federation of Labor** (AFL) was the dominant union of the late 1800s. In 1886 leaders of several national trade unions came together to create the AFL. From its beginning, the AFL focused on promoting the interests of skilled workers.

Samuel Gompers was the first president of the AFL, a position he held until 1924 (with the exception of one year). While other unions became involved in politics, Gompers tried to steer away from controversy and stay focused on "pure and simple" unionism. That is, he thought it best that the AFL stay focused on "bread and butter" issues—wages, working hours, and working conditions. He was willing to use the strike but preferred to negotiate.

W The AFL had three main goals. First, it tried to convince companies to recognize unions and to agree to collective bargaining. Second, it pushed for **closed shops,** meaning that companies could only hire union members. Third, it promoted an eight-hour workday.

The AFL grew slowly, but by 1900 it was the biggest union in the country, with over 500,000 members. Still, at that time, the AFL represented less than 15 percent of all nonfarm workers. Most AFL members were white men, because the unions discriminated against African Americans, and only a few would admit women.

The IWW

In 1905 a group of labor radicals, many of them socialists, created the Industrial

People IN HISTORY

C

Samuel Gompers
1850–1924

Samuel Gompers was the longest-serving president of the American Federation of Labor. Born in London to a Dutch Jewish family, Gompers quit school at 10 to earn money for his family, working as a cigarmaker. He and his family moved to the United States in 1863.

In 1877 Gompers became president of the Cigarmakers' Union. In 1886 he persuaded other craft unions to form the American Federation of Labor and became its first president. Within four years, the AFL had a quarter of a million members. That number grew to one million during the next two years.

A practical man who distrusted socialism, Gompers avoided political ideas and concentrated on improving working conditions. He believed that a just society was built on a fair labor policy. "Show me the country in which there are no strikes and I will show you that country in which there is no liberty," he said.

Do you agree that a union can try to improve working conditions without becoming involved in politics? Explain your answer.

Eugene V. Debs
1855–1926

Eugene Victor Debs was a prominent labor leader and member of the American Socialist Party. Born in Terre Haute, Indiana, Debs went to work at age 15 as a railroad fireman. He helped found the Brotherhood of Locomotive Firemen.

In 1893 Debs helped organize the American Railway Union (ARU). At the time, railway engineers, firemen, conductors, and switchmen all had separate unions. The ARU tried to organize all railroad employees into one union. Debs was arrested for interfering with the U.S. mail during the ARU's unsuccessful Pullman strike. While in prison, Debs read works by Karl Marx and became very critical of capitalism.

Debs ran for president five times between 1900 and 1920 as the nominee of the American Socialist Party. He waged his last campaign from prison while serving time for speaking against America's involvement in World War I.

What did Debs think about combining politics with union activities? How does this differ from Gompers's approach?

Activity: Collaborative Learning

Strike Negotiation Organize students into groups of four. Have each group write a skit and role-play the pre-strike negotiations among a company representative, two union workers, and a union representative. The dialogue should reflect the attitudes of the characters and should include the vocabulary in the section. Each group member should write the dialogue for his or her character. Have groups present their skits. **OL**

Workers of the World (IWW). Nicknamed "the Wobblies," the IWW wanted to organize all workers according to industry, without making distinctions between skilled and unskilled workers. The IWW endorsed using strikes and believed "The working class and the employing class have nothing in common."

The IWW believed all workers should be organized into "One Big Union." In particular, the IWW tried to organize the unskilled workers who were ignored by most unions.

In 1912 the IWW led a successful strike of textile workers in Lawrence, Massachusetts. After textile companies cut wages, 25,000 workers went on strike. During the strike, the children of strikers were sent out of town—in case things became violent. The companies reversed the wage cuts after ten weeks. The Lawrence strike was the IWW's greatest victory. Most IWW strikes failed.

The IWW never gained a large membership, but its radical philosophy and controversial strikes led many to condemn the organization as subversive.

Working Women

After the Civil War, the number of women wage earners began to increase. By 1900 women made up more than 18 percent of the labor force. The type of jobs women did outside the home reflected society's ideas about what **constituted** "women's work." About one-third of women wage earners worked as domestic servants. Another third worked as teachers, nurses, and sales clerks. The remaining third were industrial workers. Many worked in the garment industry and food-processing plants.

Regardless of the job, women were paid less than men even when they performed the same jobs. It was assumed that a woman had a man helping to support her, and that a man needed higher wages to support a family. Most unions excluded women.

One of the most famous labor leaders of the era was Mary Harris Jones, also known as "Mother Jones." An Irish immigrant, Jones began as a labor organizer for the Knights of Labor, then helped to organize mine workers. Her persuasiveness as a public speaker made her a very successful organizer, leading John D. Rockefeller to label her "the most dangerous woman in America."

In 1900 Jewish and Italian immigrants who worked in the clothing business in New York City founded the International Ladies' Garment Workers Union. The membership, composed mostly of female workers, expanded rapidly in a few years. In 1909 a strike of 20,000 garment workers won union recognition in the industry and better wages and benefits for employees.

In 1903 Mary Kenney O'Sullivan and Leonora O'Reilly decided to establish a separate union for women. With the help of Jane Addams and Lillian Wald, they established the Women's Trade Union League (WTUL), the first national association dedicated to promoting women's labor issues. The WTUL pushed for an eight-hour workday, the creation of a minimum wage, an end to evening work for women, and the abolition of child labor.

 Reading Check **Comparing** How were female industrial workers treated differently from male workers in the late 1800s?

Section 4 REVIEW

Vocabulary

1. **Explain** the significance of: deflation, trade union, industrial unions, blacklist, lockout, Marxism, Knights of Labor, arbitration, injunction, American Federation of Labor, Samuel Gompers, closed shop.

Main Ideas

2. **Identifying** Use a graphic organizer similar to the one below to list the factors that led to an increase in unions in the late 1800s.

Factors Contributing to Unionization

3. **Describing** What groups of workers were represented by the Knights of Labor?

4. **Discussing** How did employers and unions treat women differently from men? What reasons were given for the differences?

Critical Thinking

5. **Big Ideas** Why did industrial unions frequently fail in the late 1800s?

6. **Determining Cause and Effect** Why do you think the rise of unions might have led to increased opposition to immigrants in the United States?

7. **Analyzing Visuals** Look at the map on page 203. In what state did two major disturbances occur? How do you explain this?

Writing About History

8. **Persuasive Writing** Imagine that you are an American worker living in one of the nation's large cities. Write a letter to a friend explaining why you support or oppose the work of labor unions.

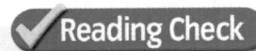

History ONLINE

Study Central™ To review this section, go to glencoe.com and click on Study Central.

207

C Critical Thinking

Drawing Conclusions Review with students the information about the IWW. **Ask:** What is the advantage of organizing workers into "One Big Union?" *(Workers would have more power against businesses than if they were organized into many smaller unions.)*

W Writing Support

Persuasive Writing Have interested students use library or Internet resources to find out more about the Women's Trade Union League (WTUL). Then have students write a persuasive letter to a colleague encouraging him or her to join the league. Encourage students to share their letters with the class. **AL**

Reading Check

Answer:
They were excluded from unions, paid less than men for the same job, and worked in jobs considered appropriate for women.

Section 4 REVIEW

Answers

1. All definitions can be found in the section and the Glossary.

2. concern for working conditions; concern for pay; concern for job security; economic challenges such as deflation

3. industrial workers, trade workers

4. Women were paid less because it was assumed that they were being supported by a man's salary. Women were thought to be good at domestic tasks, so often they did "women's work," which paid less. Most unions excluded women, assuming that a father or husband would express the woman's concerns.

5. confrontations led to violence, courts ruled against them, there were frequent strikes, they fought for many things all at the same time, and blacklisting

6. Many of those in the unions were immigrants and were associated with fears of anarchy and revolution.

7. Illinois; the Chicago area was heavily industrialized and had a large immigrant population.

8. Students' letters will vary but should express and support a point of view.

Chapter 5 VISUAL SUMMARY

Determining Cause and Effect The Visual Summary lists causes of industrialization and the growth of big business, as well as the effects on the workplace. Ask students to use the information on the page to create a time line of the era's events. Students should color code "causes" in blue and "events" in red. Display the time lines in the classroom. **OL**

Causes of Industrialization

- Abundant natural resources
- Cheap immigrant labor force
- High tariffs reduce the import of foreign goods
- National transportation and communication networks

▶ The Central Pacific Railroad Company changed the way companies did business and helped link the nation together.

▲ Blast furnaces of a U.S. Steel plant line the Monongahela River east of Pittsburgh in Braddock, Pennsylvania, in 1905. New technology and new forms of business organization made possible the rise of large-scale industrial factories in the late 1800s.

Causes of the Growth of Big Business

- Little or no government intervention
- Development of pools, trusts, holding companies, and monopolies
- Small businesses could not compete with economies of scale of larger businesses
- Practices of some big businesses sometimes limited competition

Effects on the Workplace

- Rural migration and immigration created large, concentrated workforce
- Low wages, long hours, and dangerous working conditions were common in large-scale industries
- First large unions formed but had little bargaining power against larger companies

▶ Workers fill molds with molten steel at a foundry in 1905. Working conditions of the era led to many industrial accidents and contributed to the rise of unions.

208 Chapter 5 Industrialization

Hands-On Chapter Project
Step 5: Wrap Up

Starting a Business

Step 5: Being an Entrepreneur Students will synthesize what they have learned in Steps 1, 2, 3, and 4.

Directions Have the groups of students review their business, its cost, its growth, and its relationship with its workers. Have students determine which of the general aspects of starting the business was the most difficult. Have each group try to reach a consensus. Have a volunteer from each group share the group's decision with the class. Discuss with the class the difficulty of being a business leader, or entrepreneur. **OL**

ASSESSMENT

STANDARDIZED TEST PRACTICE

TEST-TAKING TIP

Be sure to pay close attention to specific words in a question. Words can change the meaning of the sentence and of the correct answer.

Reviewing Vocabulary

Directions: Choose the word or words that best completes the sentence.

1. _____ are formed by a legal agreement in which one person manages another person's property.

   A Trusts

   B Pools

   C Corporations

   D Monopolies

2. _____ united all craft workers and common laborers in a particular industry.

   A Closed shops

   B Trade unions

   C Industrial unions

   D Blacklists

3. Costs a company has to pay, such as loans, mortgages, and taxes, whether or not it is operating, are called

   A investment funds.

   B economies of scale.

   C fixed costs.

   D operating costs.

4. Supporters of _____ believe that the government should not interfere in the economy other than to protect private property rights.

   A high tariffs

   B laissez-faire

   C industrial regulations

   D high taxes for private individuals

Reviewing Main Ideas

Directions: Choose the best answers to the following questions.

Section 1 *(pp. 182–187)*

5. What factors contributed to industrialization?

   A lack of natural resources

   B free enterprise system

   C limited workforce

   D deteriorating railroad system

6. Laissez-faire relies on

   A the government to regulate wages and prices.

   B high taxes and government debt to fund businesses.

   C high tariffs on foreign goods.

   D supply and demand to regulate wages and prices.

Section 2 *(pp. 188–193)*

7. How did the federal government aid railroad construction in the 1850s and 1860s?

   A advertised overseas to attract immigrants to help build tracks

   B used tax dollars to fund many railroad projects

   C passed laws to legalize railroad monopolies

   D granted public lands to railroads to sell to raise funds

8. The Pacific Railway Act provided for the construction of a railway

   A by offering right-of-way land grants to railroad companies.

   B along the Pacific coast from California north to Canada.

   C by the Union Pacific Railroad company.

   D by the Central Pacific Railroad company.

Need Extra Help?								
If You Missed Questions . . .	1	2	3	4	5	6	7	8
Go to Page . . .	198	201–202	194–195	186–187	186–187	186–187	192	188

GO ON →

4. B Students should realize that one answer choice, *B,* is in opposition to the other answer choices. The other choices all imply government interference or regulation in business. It is government that would impose tariffs, regulations, and taxes.

Reviewing Main Ideas

5. B Choices *A, C,* and *D* are the negatives of factors that contributed to industrialization: an abundance of natural resources, a large potential workforce, and a growing transportation industry. Students who do not carefully read the answer choices may have trouble with this question.

6. D This question presents a good opportunity to reinforce the definition of *laissez-faire.* A solid understanding of the free enterprise system will be beneficial when students eventually learn about other economic systems, such as socialism.

7. D Although immigrants helped build the railroad tracks, the business did not advertise overseas for help, so *A* is not correct. The Pacific Railway Act provided for two corporations to build the Transcontinental Railroad, so the government would not need tax dollars to fund it. The government did not pass laws to legalize any monopolies, so students should eliminate *C.* Review "The Transcontinental Railroad" on page 188 with students who have trouble with this question.

8. A Review the Pacific Railway Act with students who have trouble with this question. Despite the name "Pacific," the act provided for the construction of a *transcontinental* railroad. A misunderstanding of this may lead some students to select *B.* The act provided for *two* corporations to build the railroad, so *C* and *D* are incorrect.

Reviewing Vocabulary

1. A The formation of trusts allowed big businesses to skirt anti-monopoly laws while maintaining monopolistic control of their respective industries. A good method to remember the definition of *trusts* is to think of one business *trusts* another to manage its business. This should help students distinguish trusts from monopolies and corporations.

2. C Closed shops and blacklists were tactics used by management and labor unions in labor disputes. Students may have trouble choosing between trade unions and industrial unions. The key words are "united craft workers and *common laborers.*" Trade unions united skilled workers in the same trade. Industrial unions united all workers in the same *industry,* regardless of skill.

3. C Point out to students who are confused by choice *D* that the question specifies costs a company has to pay "whether or not it is *operating.*" Operating costs pay for the running, or operating, of a company. Fixed costs are *always present.*

209

Chapter 5

9. B Any business can receive federal funds or have a monopoly (until the government breaks it up, at any rate). These are not characteristics limited to corporations. A corporation earns money for its stockholders, not its workers (unless the workers hold stock). Corporations do sell stock, however. A corporation is owned by a number of people, but acts as a single entity.

10. D A discussion of the board game Monopoly® can help reinforce the concept of a monopoly. Remind students that the point of the game is to own all of a certain color or all of the railroads, which *eliminates competition* from the other players. The winner of the game is the person who owns the most "monopolies" and makes the most money. Explain that the other answer choices are all related to labor unions, not business strategies.

11. B Students should eliminate *A*, which suggests that unions help *owners*, not labor. Explain that although unions did fight to prevent lockouts, this is not the reason they were *formed*.

12. C Review the section on the Knights of Labor on page 204 and the Haymarket Riot on page 204, which explain that the Haymarket Riot contributed to the decline of the organization. Those who were opposed to unions used the riot to undermine the reputation of unions and their leaders.

13. B As the United States industrialized, business grew, spurring the growth of a middle class. New industries required workers. Meanwhile, businesses sought to preserve competition by establishing trusts. The lives of workers under large corporations became difficult, leading to the creation of labor unions.

Section 3 *(pp. 194–199)*

9. Corporations are organizations that
 A receive federal funding.
 B sell stock to the public.
 C have a monopoly on a product or service.
 D earn profits for their workers.

10. In the late 1800s, which of the following helped business leaders eliminate competition?
 A strikes
 B labor unions
 C closed shops
 D monopolies

Section 4 *(pp. 200–207)*

11. Labor unions were formed to
 A protect factory owners and improve workers' wages.
 B improve workers' wages and make factories safer.
 C make factories safer and prevent lockouts.
 D prevent lockouts and fight deflation.

12. Which of the following events reduced membership in the Knights of Labor?
 A the Pullman Strike
 B the panic of 1873
 C the Haymarket Riot
 D the Great Railroad Strike of 1877

13. In the last half of the 1800s, which development led to the other three?
 A expansion of the middle class
 B growth of industrialization
 C formation of trusts
 D creation of labor unions

Critical Thinking

Directions: Choose the best answers to the following questions.

14. The slogan "Eight hours for work, eight hours for sleep, eight hours for what we will" was used in the late 1800s to promote a major goal of
 A farmers.
 B politicians.
 C industrialists.
 D organized labor.

Base your answers to questions 15 and 16 on the chart below and your knowledge of Chapter 5.

Steel Production, 1865–1895

Source: *Historical Statistics of the United States.*

15. Between what years did steel production increase the most?
 A 1865–1870
 B 1885–1890
 C 1890–1895
 D 1895–1900

16. How did increased steel production contribute to American industrialization?
 A decreased the number of jobs available for workers
 B discouraged the consolidation of industry
 C improved transportation methods such as railroads
 D encouraged immigration by providing a safe work environment

Need Extra Help?

If You Missed Questions . . .	9	10	11	12	13	14	15	16
Go to Page . . .	194	197–199	200–202	204	200–204	200–207	194–199	196–197

 GO ON

Critical Thinking

14. D Organized labor sought better working conditions and pay, among other reforms in industry. Farmers' workdays and working conditions were dictated by nature. Politicians did not need regulation of their working hours. The slogan was directed at industrialists from members of organized labor. The gist of the slogan is the limiting of the workday to 8 hours.

15. B Between the years of 1885 and 1890, steel production jumped by 3 million tons.

16. C The question asks how steel production *contributed* to industrialization, so students should look for the answer choice that had a *positive effect* on industrialization. Improved transportation allowed industry to grow by providing more efficient and less expensive means of moving goods.

ASSESSMENT

17. Which of the following statements about labor unions in the late 1800s is accurate?

  A Strikes by labor unions usually gained public support.

  B Labor union activities were frequently opposed by the government.

  C Demands by labor unions were usually met.

  D Arbitration was commonly used to end labor unrest.

18. The immigrants who came to the United States between 1870 and 1910 came primarily from

  A eastern Europe and China.

  B northern and western Europe.

  C East Asia.

  D Latin America.

Analyze the cartoon and answer the question that follows. Base your answer on the cartoon and on your knowledge of Chapter 5.

Source: Bernhard Gillam, *Puck*, February 7, 1883

19. What does this cartoon say about Gould and Vanderbilt?

  A They are giving money to the hard-working laborers.

  B They are getting rich at the expense of others' back-breaking work.

  C The ship is slowly crumbling like their empires.

  D The workers are determined to overthrow them.

Document-Based Questions

Directions: Analyze the document and answer the short-answer questions that follow the document.

In the following excerpt from *History of the Standard Oil Company*, Ida Tarbell warns of the effects of Rockefeller's business practices on the nation's morality. Read the excerpt and answer the questions that follow:

> *"Very often people who admit the facts, who are willing to see that Mr. Rockefeller has employed force and fraud to secure his ends, justify him by declaring, 'It's business.' That is, 'It's business' has come to be a legitimate excuse for hard dealing, sly tricks, special privileges. It is a common enough thing to hear men arguing that the ordinary laws of morality do not apply in business.*
>
> *As for the ethical side, there is no cure but in an increasing scorn of unfair play. . . . When the businessman who fights to secure special privileges, to crowd his competitor off the track by other than fair competitive methods, receives the same summary disdainful ostracism by his fellows that the doctor or lawyer who is 'unprofessional,' . . . we shall have gone a long way toward making commerce a fit pursuit for our young men."*
>
> —from *History of the Standard Oil Company*

20. According to Tarbell, what practices had Rockefeller used to establish Standard Oil Company?

21. In what way did Tarbell believe the attitudes of the American people contributed to Rockefeller's business practices?

Extended Response

22. Identify labor unions formed during the late 1800s and early 1900s. Discuss the different views, goals, and activities of each organization. How were these organizations similar to or different from each other? What roles did unions and union members play in industrialization? Write an expository essay that supports your position with relevant facts and details.

History ONLINE

For additional test practice, use Self-Check Quizzes—Chapter 5 at glencoe.com.

Need Extra Help?

If You Missed Questions . . .	17	18	19	20	21	22
Go to Page . . .	201–207	182–187	197–199	197–199	197–199	200–207

---

17. B This is another question in which one answer choice is the opposite of the others. As students read, labor unions struggled to gain the support of the government, the public, and industry. Strikes did not often have public support, and often contributed to a negative public opinion. Demands of unions were often not met, and arbitration was not commonly used in the 1800s. Government opposition in the 1800s, however, was a large obstacle to labor unions.

18. A As a result of social and economic conditions in eastern Europe and China, many people immigrated to the United States in search of a better life.

19. B In the cartoon, laborers are bent over in what looks like painful positions, holding up the ship on their backs. Captains of industry sit on top of the ship. They are not giving money to anyone. There is no evidence that the ship is crumbling.

Document-Based Questions

20. According to Tarbell, Rockefeller used "force and fraud" to establish Standard Oil. This answer can be found in the first sentence of the first paragraph. Tarbell then explains that his excuse was that it was "just business."

21. Tarbell believed that the attitude that "it's just business" was held by the American people, and contributed to Rockefeller's practices. She speaks here of a pervasive attitude that creates an environment of acceptance of Rockefeller's tactics of "force and fraud."

Extended Response

22. Students' essays will vary, but must follow the guidelines for an expository essay. Each essay should include an introduction, body, and a conclusion. Essays should identify at least two labor unions and provide a well thought out comparison of the organizations. A complete essay will also discuss the contributions of unions to industrialization.

History ONLINE

Have students visit the Web site at glencoe.com to review Chapter 5 and take the Self-Check Quiz.

Need Extra Help?

Have students refer to the pages listed if they miss any of the questions.

Key to Ability Levels

BL Below Level   **AL** Above Level
OL On Level   **ELL** English Language Learners

Key to Teaching Resources

Print Material   DVD
CD-ROM   Transparency

Levels (BL OL AL ELL)				Resources	Chapter Opener	Section 1	Section 2	Section 3	Section 4	Section 5	Chapter Assess
FOCUS											
BL	OL	AL	ELL	Daily Focus Transparencies		6-1	6-2	6-3	6-4	6-5	
TEACH											
	OL	AL		Geography and History, URB		p. 3					
	OL	AL		History Simulations and Problem Solving, URB				p. 9			
		AL		American Literature Reading, URB		p. 17					
BL	OL		ELL	Reading Skills Activity, URB						p. 87	
	OL			Historical Analysis Skills Activity, URB		p. 88					
BL	OL	AL	ELL	Differentiated Instruction Activity, URB		p. 89					
BL	OL		ELL	English Learner Activity, URB		p. 91					
BL	OL	AL	ELL	Content Vocabulary Activity, URB		p. 93					
BL	OL	AL	ELL	Academic Vocabulary Activity, URB		p. 95					
	OL	AL		Reinforcing Skills Activity, URB		p. 97					
	OL	AL		Critical Thinking Skills Activity, URB						p. 98	
BL	OL		ELL	Time Line Activity, URB			p. 99				
	OL			Linking Past and Present Activity, URB		p. 100					
BL	OL	AL	ELL	Primary Source Reading, URB			p. 101		p. 103		
BL	OL	AL	ELL	American Art and Music Activity, URB				p. 105			
BL	OL	AL	ELL	Interpreting Political Cartoons Activity, URB		p. 107					
		AL		Enrichment Activity, URB			p. 111				
BL	OL		ELL	Guided Reading Activity, URB		p. 114	p. 115	p. 116	p. 117	p. 118	
BL	OL	AL	ELL	Reading Essentials and Note-Taking Guide		p. 55	p. 58	p. 61	p. 64	p. 67	
BL	OL	AL	ELL	Differentiated Instruction for the American High School Classroom	✓	✓	✓	✓	✓	✓	✓
BL	OL	AL	ELL	Unit Map Overlay Transparencies	✓	✓	✓	✓	✓	✓	✓
BL	OL	AL	ELL	Unit Time Line Transparencies and Activities	✓	✓	✓	✓	✓	✓	✓
BL	OL	AL	ELL	Cause and Effect Transparencies, Strategies, and Activities	✓	✓	✓	✓	✓	✓	✓

Note: Please refer to the *Unit 2 Resource Book* for this chapter's URB materials.

* Also available in Spanish

Plus
TeacherWorks
All-In-One Planner and Resource Center

- Interactive Lesson Planner
- Interactive Teacher Edition
- Fully editable blackline masters
- Section Spotlight Videos Launch

- Differentiated Lesson Plans
- Printable reports of daily assignments
- Standards Tracking System

Levels					Resources	Chapter Opener	Section 1	Section 2	Section 3	Section 4	Section 5	Chapter Assess
BL	OL	AL	ELL									
TEACH *(continued)*												
BL	OL	AL	ELL	📁	Why It Matters Transparencies, Strategies, and Activities	✓	✓	✓	✓	✓	✓	✓
BL	OL	AL	ELL	📁	American Biographies			✓	✓	✓	✓	
BL	OL	AL		📁	Supreme Court Case Studies					p. 15	p. 27	
BL	OL	AL	ELL	📁	The Living Constitution	✓	✓	✓	✓	✓	✓	✓
BL	OL	AL	ELL	📁	American Issues	✓	✓	✓	✓	✓	✓	✓
	OL	AL	ELL	📁	American Art and Architecture Transparenices, Strategies, and Activites	✓	✓	✓	✓	✓	✓	✓
BL	OL	AL		📁	High School American History Literature Library	✓	✓	✓	✓	✓	✓	✓
	OL	AL		💿	American History Primary Source Documents Library	✓	✓	✓	✓	✓	✓	✓
BL	OL	AL	ELL	💿	American Music: Hits Through History CD	✓	✓	✓	✓	✓	✓	✓
BL	OL	AL	ELL	💽	StudentWorks™ Plus DVD	✓	✓	✓	✓	✓	✓	✓
BL	OL	AL	ELL	💿	Vocabulary PuzzleMaker CD-ROM	✓	✓	✓	✓	✓	✓	✓
BL	OL	AL	ELL	💽	*The American Vision* Video Program DVD	✓	✓	✓	✓	✓	✓	✓
Teacher Resources				📁	Strategies for Success	✓	✓	✓	✓	✓	✓	✓
				💽	Presentation Plus! DVD	✓	✓	✓	✓	✓	✓	✓
				📁	Success With English Learners	✓	✓	✓	✓	✓	✓	✓
ASSESS												
BL	OL	AL	ELL	📁	Section Quizzes and Chapter Tests		p. 73	p. 74	p. 75	p. 76	p. 77	p. 79
BL	OL	AL	ELL	📁	Authentic Assessment With Rubrics							p. 17
BL	OL	AL	ELL	📁	Standardized Test Practice Workbook							p. 12
BL	OL	AL	ELL	💿	*ExamView*® Assessment Suite CD-ROM		6-1	6-2	6-3	6-4	6-5	Ch. 6
BL	OL	AL	ELL	💿	Interactive Tutor Self-Assessment CD-ROM		6-1	6-2	6-3	6-4	6-5	Ch. 6
CLOSE												
BL			ELL	📁	Reteaching Activity, URB							p. 109
BL	OL		ELL	📁	Reading and Study Skills Foldables™	pp. 58, 61, 63						

Chapter 6 | Integrating Technology

Using StudentWorks™ Plus CD-ROM

Read and Listen Simultaneously

Technology Product

Glencoe's *StudentWorks™ Plus* CD-ROM contains everything your students need, including the complete Student Edition, text in audio, access to all student workbooks, and links to online activities and resources.

- Students can read chapters with Adobe Acrobat Reader software, which is opened automatically by the *StudentWorks™ Plus* program.
- The complete textbook is available with audio via the *StudentWorks™ Plus* CD-ROM.
- Students can read and listen simultaneously with page-by-page audio, which can improve content comprehension for all your students.
- Use this component with struggling readers or to emphasize an important concept.

Objectives

Using *StudentWorks™ Plus* will help your students
- practice their reading skills;
- improve their listening comprehension.

Steps

Provide students with the following information:
- Launch StudentWorks™ Plus.
- Select **Student Edition with Audio** from the launch screen.
- Use the bookmarks along the left side to navigate to the desired chapter or use the **Page Navigator** link in the bookmarks to link to the exact page number in the Student Edition.
- Click on the audio icon located on each page in the upper left corner to launch the audio.
- Read along with the audio.

History ONLINE

	Student	Teacher	Parent
Beyond the Textbook	●	●	●
Chapter Overviews	●	●	●
Time Current Events	●		●
ePuzzles and Games	●		●
Concepts in Motion	●		●
Literature Connections		●	
Multi-Language Glossaries	●		●
Online Student Edition	●	●	●
Self-Check Quizzes	●		●
Student Web Activities	●		●
Study Central ™	●		●
Teaching Today		●	
Vocabulary eFlashcards	●		●
Web Activity Lesson Plans		●	

Glencoe Media Center

glencoe.com

❯ **Study-To-Go**
- Vocabulary eFlashcards
- Self-Check Quizzes

❯ **Audio/Video**
- Student Edition Audio
- Spanish Summaries
- Section Videos

212C

- **Timed Readings Plus in Social Studies** helps students increase their reading rate and fluency while maintaining comprehension. The 400-word passages are similar to those found on state and national assessments.

- **Reading in the Content Area: Social Studies** concentrates on six essential reading skills that help students better comprehend what they read. The book includes 75 high-interest nonfiction passages written at increasing levels of difficulty.

- **Reading Social Studies** includes strategic reading instruction and vocabulary support in Social Studies content for both ELLs and native speakers of English.

www.jamestowneducation.com

Index to National Geographic Magazine:

The following articles relate to this chapter:

- "New Life for Ellis Island," by Alice J. Hall, September 1990.
- "Boston's North Enders," by Erla Zwingle, October 2000.

National Geographic Society Products To order the following, call National Geographic at 1-800-368-2728:

- *Immigration* (CD-ROM)

Access National Geographic's new, dynamic MapMachine Web site and other geography resources at:
www.nationalgeographic.com
www.nationalgeographic.com/maps

The following videotape programs are available from Glencoe as supplements to Chapter 6:

- Ellis Island (ISBN 0-76-700005-6)
- Ellis Island DVD (ISBN 0-76-704451-7)

To order, call Glencoe at 1-800-334-7344. To find classroom resources to accompany many of these videos, check the following home pages:

A&E Television: www.aetv.com
The History Channel: www.historychannel.com

Reading List Generator CD-ROM

Use this database to search more than 30,000 titles to create a customized reading list for your students.

- Reading lists can be organized by students' reading level, author, genre, theme, or area of interest.
- The database provides Degrees of Reading Power™ (DRP) and Lexile™ readability scores for all selections.
- A brief summary of each selection is included.

Leveled reading suggestions for this chapter:

For students at a Grade 8 reading level:
- *The Great Wheel,* by Robert Lawson

For students at a Grade 9 reading level:
- *If Your Name Was Changed at Ellis Island,* by Ellen Levine

For students at a Grade 10 reading level:
- *My Antonia,* by Willa Cather

For students at a Grade 11 reading level:
- *Irish Immigrants: 1840–1920,* by Megan O'Hara

For students at a Grade 12 reading level:
- *We Are Americans: Voices of the Immigrant Experience,* by Dorothy Hoobler and Thomas Hoobler

Focus

MAKING CONNECTIONS
Why Do People Migrate?

Have students brainstorm the reasons people move to other countries and list their answers on the chalkboard. Discuss with students the reasons, if any, for which they might move to another country. Then discuss how they think life would be different in a new country. **OL** **BL**

Teach

The Big Ideas

As students study the chapter, remind them to consider the section-based Big Ideas included in each section's Guide to Reading. The **Essential Questions** in the activities below tie in to the Big Ideas and help students think about and understand important chapter concepts. In addition, the Hands-on Chapter Projects with their culminating activities relate the content from each section to the Big Ideas. These activities build on each other as students progress through the chapter. Section activities culminate in the wrap-up activity on the Visual Summary page.

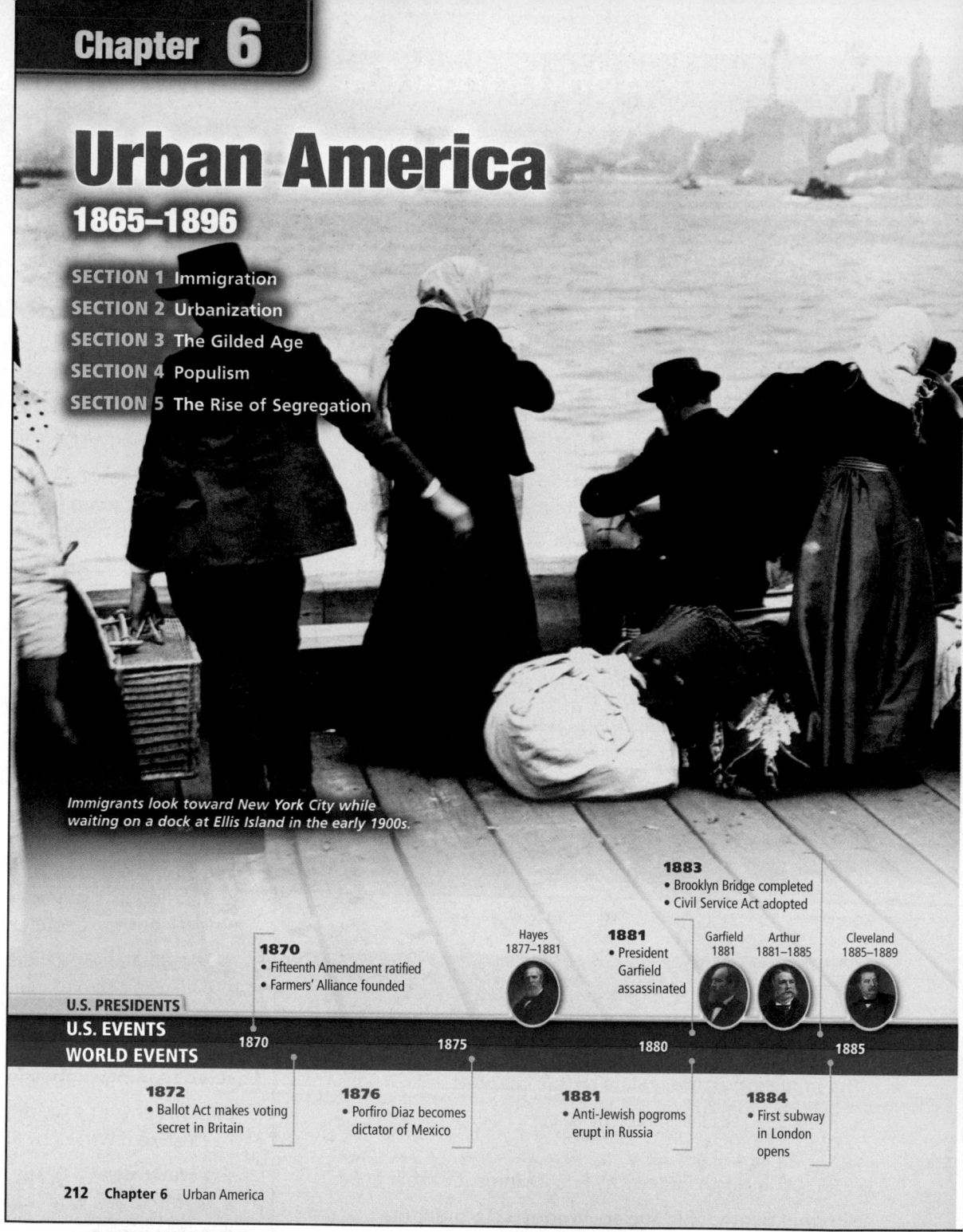

Chapter **6**

Urban America
1865–1896

SECTION 1 Immigration
SECTION 2 Urbanization
SECTION 3 The Gilded Age
SECTION 4 Populism
SECTION 5 The Rise of Segregation

Immigrants look toward New York City while waiting on a dock at Ellis Island in the early 1900s.

U.S. PRESIDENTS

U.S. EVENTS
WORLD EVENTS

1870
• Fifteenth Amendment ratified
• Farmers' Alliance founded

Hayes
1877–1881

1881
• President Garfield assassinated

1883
• Brooklyn Bridge completed
• Civil Service Act adopted

Garfield
1881

Arthur
1881–1885

Cleveland
1885–1889

1870   1875   1880   1885

1872
• Ballot Act makes voting secret in Britain

1876
• Porfiro Diaz becomes dictator of Mexico

1881
• Anti-Jewish pogroms erupt in Russia

1884
• First subway in London opens

212 **Chapter 6** Urban America

Section 1

Immigration

Essential Question: Why did Europeans come to America in the late 1900s? *(better economic opportunities, new freedoms, peace)* Tell students that in this section they will learn why millions of people came to the United States and how they changed America. **OL**

Section 2

Urbanization

Essential Question: What are some of the characteristics of cities? *(Answers might include large populations, density of buildings, noise, pollution, traffic, cultural amenities, access to public services.)* Tell students that this section will focus on how the growth of cities changed the United States. **OL**

Section 3

The Gilded Age

Essential Question: What were the characteristics of the Gilded Age? *(growth of big business, the idea of individualism, new social reforms)* Tell students that in Section 3 they will learn about the Gilded Age in the United States, as well as how society and culture changed during that time. **OL**

More About the Photo

Visual Literacy More than 12 million immigrants passed through the Ellis Island Immigration Station between 1892 and 1954, and the vast majority of them were allowed to enter the United States. Most immigrants were poor and traveled in steerage, one of the lowest decks on a ship. Steerage lacked privacy and toilet facilities were limited.

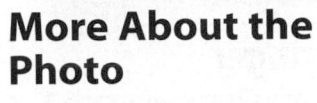 **Dinah Zike's Foldables**

Dinah Zike's Foldables are three-dimensional, interactive graphic organizers that help students practice basic writing skills, review vocabulary terms, and identify main ideas. Instructions for creating and using Foldables can be found in the Appendix at the end of this book and in the Dinah Zike's Reading and Study Skills Foldables booklet.

Introduce students to chapter content and key terms by having them access the Chapter 6 Overview at glencoe.com.

MAKING CONNECTIONS
Why Do People Migrate?

European and Asian immigrants arrived in the United States in great numbers during the late 1800s. Providing cheap labor, they made rapid industrial growth possible. They also helped populate the growing cities.

- *How do you think life in big cities was different from life on farms and in small towns?*
- *How do you think the immigrants of the late 1800s changed American society?*

FOLDABLES

Analyzing Information Make a Folded Table Foldable to clarify your understanding of how immigration and urbanization are related. As you read the chapter, list the causes and effects of immigration and urbanization. In each cell, list as many causes and effects as possible and include approximate dates where appropriate.

1888
- First electric trolley line opens in Richmond, Virginia

1890
- Sherman Antitrust Act passed

Harrison 1889–1893

1895
- Booker T. Washington gives Atlanta Compromise speech

Cleveland 1893–1897

1896
- *Plessey v. Ferguson* establishes "separate but equal" doctrine

1890   1895

1888
- Brazil ends slavery

1889
- Eiffel Tower completed for Paris World Exhibit

1896
- Athens hosts first modern Olympic games

History ONLINE Chapter Overview
Visit glencoe.com to preview Chapter 6.

Chapter 6 Urban America **213**

Section 4

Populism
Essential Question: What is populism and how did it affect the United States? *(A reform movement that started with the nation's farmers; the movement brought attention to the plight of farmers, and farmers organized to increase their political power.)* Tell students that this section will cover the rise of the Populist Movement and its impact on the nation. **OL**

Section 5

The Rise of Segregation
Essential Question: What is racial segregation? Why is it inherently wrong? *(Separation of racial groups based on skin color; it is wrong because it violates the founding principles of the United States.)* Tell students that this section will focus on the increase of racial segregation in the late 1800s and the passing of laws that legalized racial separation. **OL**

Focus

Bellringer
Daily Focus Transparency 6.1

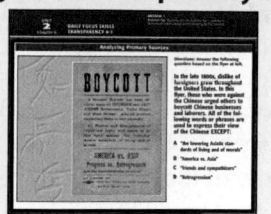

Guide to Reading

Answers to Graphic:

Reasons for Immigrating	
Push Factors	Pull Factors
Farm poverty and worker uncertainty	Plenty of land and plenty of work
Wars and compulsory military service	Higher standard of living
Political Tyranny	Democratic political system
Religious oppression	Opportunity for social advancement
Population pressure	

Section Spotlight Video

To generate student interest and provide a springboard for class discussion, access the Chapter 6, Section 1 video at glencoe.com or on the video DVD.

Resource Manager

Section 1

Immigration

Guide to Reading

Big Ideas
Trade, War, and Migration Many people from Europe came to the United States to escape war, famine, or persecution or to find better jobs.

Content Vocabulary
• steerage (p. 215)
• nativism (p. 218)

Academic Vocabulary
• immigrant (p. 214)
• ethnic (p. 216)

People and Events to Identify
• Ellis Island (p. 215)
• Jacob Riis (p. 216)
• Angel Island (p. 217)
• Chinese Exclusion Act (p. 219)

Reading Strategy
Categorizing Complete a graphic organizer similar to the one below by filling in the reasons people left their homelands to immigrate to the United States.

Reasons for Immigrating	
Push Factors	Pull Factors

In the late nineteenth century, a major wave of immigration began. Most immigrants settled in cities, where distinctive ethnic neighborhoods emerged. Some Americans, however, feared that the new immigrants would not adapt to American culture or might be harmful to American society.

Europeans Flood Into America

MAIN Idea Immigrants from Europe came to the United States for many reasons and entered the country through Ellis Island.

HISTORY AND YOU Have you ever been to an ethnic neighborhood where residents have re-created aspects of their homeland? Read on to learn how immigrants adjusted to life in the United States.

Between 1865—the year the Civil War ended—and 1914—the year World War I began—nearly 25 million Europeans immigrated to the United States. By the late 1890s, more than half of all **immigrants** in the United States were from eastern and southern Europe, including Italy, Greece, Austria-Hungary, Russia, and Serbia. This period of immigration is known as "new" immigration. The "old" immigration, which occurred before 1890, had been primarily of people from northern and western Europe. More than 70 percent of these new immigrants were men; they were working either to be able to afford to purchase land in Europe or to bring family members to America.

Europeans immigrated to the United States for many reasons. Many came because American industries had plenty of jobs available. Europe's industrial cities, however, also offered plenty of jobs, so economic factors do not entirely explain why people migrated. Many came in the hope of finding better jobs that would let them escape poverty and the restrictions of social class in Europe. Some moved to avoid forced military service, which in some nations lasted for many years. In some cases, as in Italy, high food prices encouraged people to leave. In Poland and Russia, population pressure led to emigration. Others, especially Jews living in Russia and the Austro-Hungarian Empire, fled to escape religious persecution.

In addition, most European states had made moving to the United States easy. Immigrants were allowed to take their savings with them, and most countries had repealed old laws forcing peasants to stay in their villages and banning skilled workers from leaving the country. At the same time, moving to the United States offered a chance to break away from Europe's class system and move to a democratic nation where people had the opportunity to move up the social ladder.

R Reading Strategies	**C** Critical Thinking	**D** Differentiated Instruction	**W** Writing Support	**S** Skill Practice
Teacher Edition • Using Word Parts, p. 218 **Additional Resources** • American Lit. Read.,URB p. 17 • Acad. Vocab, URB p. 95 • Guided Read, URB p. 114	**Teacher Edition** • Determining Cause and Effect, p. 215 • Contrasting, p. 217 • Assessing, p. 218 **Additional Resources** • Link. Past and Present, URB p. 100 • Quizzes and Tests, p. 73 • Interpreting Pol. Cartoons, URB p. 107	**Teacher Edition** • Interpersonal, p. 216 **Additional Resources** • Diff Instruction Act., URB p. 89 • English Learner Act., URB p. 91 • Foldables, pp. 58, 61, 63	**Teacher Edition** • Personal Writing, p. 216 **Additional Resources** • Cont. Vocab, URB p. 93	**Teacher Edition** • Analyzing Visuals, p. 215 • Reading Charts, p. 217 **Additional Resources** • Historical Analysis Skills Act., URB p. 88 • Reinforce Skills Act., URB p. 97 • RENTG, p. 55

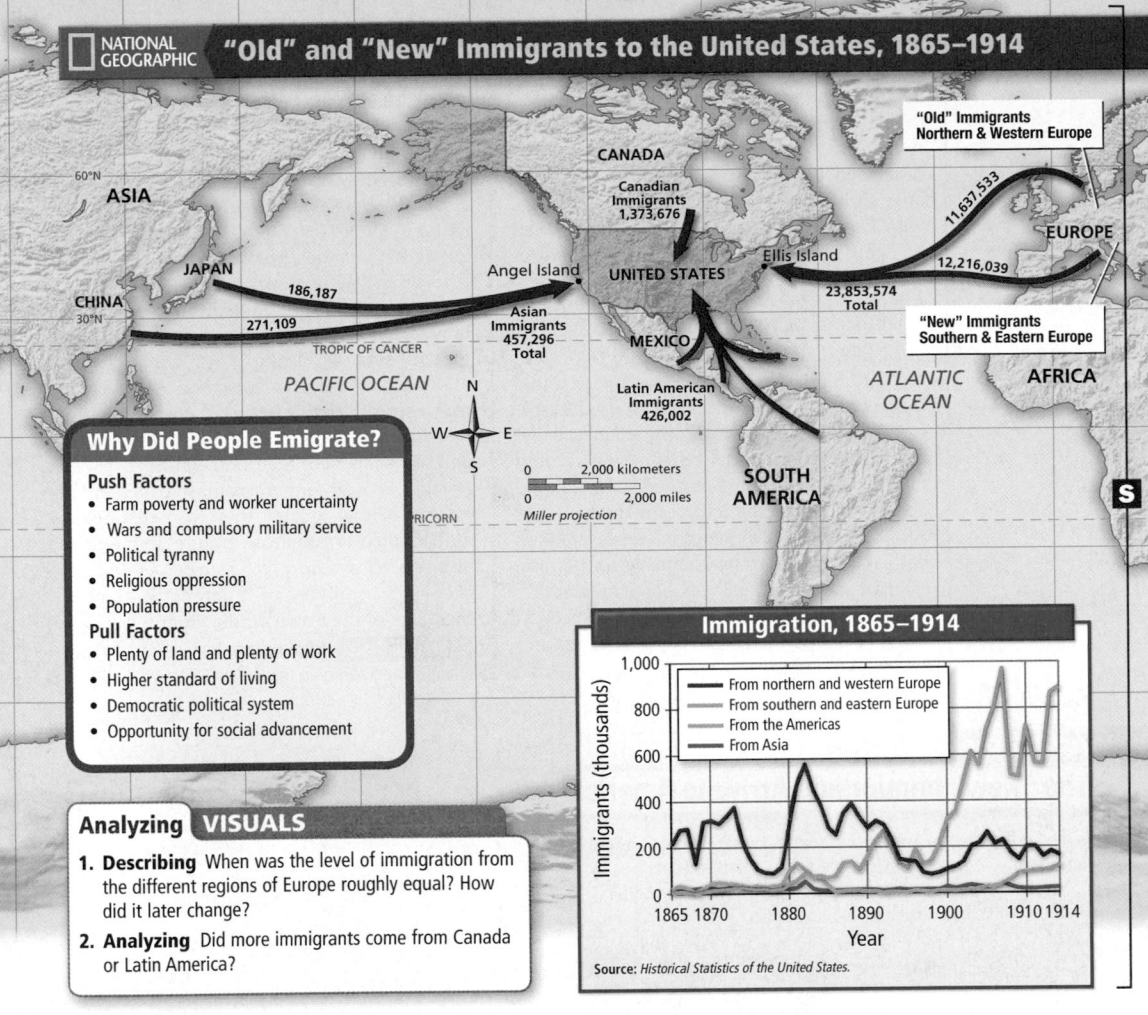

NATIONAL GEOGRAPHIC "Old" and "New" Immigrants to the United States, 1865–1914

Why Did People Emigrate?

Push Factors
- Farm poverty and worker uncertainty
- Wars and compulsory military service
- Political tyranny
- Religious oppression
- Population pressure

Pull Factors
- Plenty of land and plenty of work
- Higher standard of living
- Democratic political system
- Opportunity for social advancement

Analyzing VISUALS

1. **Describing** When was the level of immigration from the different regions of Europe roughly equal? How did it later change?
2. **Analyzing** Did more immigrants come from Canada or Latin America?

Immigration, 1865–1914

Immigrants (thousands)
- From northern and western Europe
- From southern and eastern Europe
- From the Americas
- From Asia

Source: *Historical Statistics of the United States.*

The Atlantic Voyage

The voyage to the United States was often very difficult. Most immigrants booked passage in **steerage,** the cheapest accommodations on a steamship. Edward Steiner, an Iowa clergyman who posed as an immigrant in order to write a book on immigration, described the miserable quarters:

PRIMARY SOURCE

"Narrow, steep and slippery stairways lead to it. Crowds everywhere, ill smelling bunks, uninviting washrooms—this is steerage. The odors of scattered orange peelings, tobacco, garlic and disinfectants meeting but not blending. No lounge or chairs for comfort, and a continual babble of tongues—this is steerage. The food, which is miserable, is dealt out of huge kettles into the dinner pails provided by the steamship company."

—quoted in *World of Our Fathers*

At the end of a 14-day journey, the passengers usually disembarked at **Ellis Island,** a tiny island in New York Harbor. There, a huge three-story building served as the processing center for many of the immigrants arriving from Europe after 1892.

Chapter 6 Urban America **215**

W Writing Support

Personal Writing Explain that immigrants were sometimes denied entrance, which separated families. People then had to decide whether all would return to their homeland or some would remain. Have students write a personal response to the inspection process. **AL**

D Differentiated Instruction

Interpersonal Ask: How did ethnic neighborhoods both help and hinder immigrants? *(Answers will vary. Possible response: People could communicate more easily and feel more comfortable; however, this comfort may have made some less willing to learn new customs, language, and ideas.)* **BL**

✔ Reading Check

Answer:
The population became more ethnically diverse, especially in the urban areas.

Additional Support

Ellis Island

Most immigrants passed through Ellis Island in about a day. They would not soon forget their hectic introduction to the United States. A medical examiner who worked there later described how "hour after hour, ship load after ship load ... the stream of human beings with its kaleidoscopic variations was ... hurried through Ellis Island by the equivalent of 'step lively' in every language of the earth." About 12 million immigrants passed through Ellis Island between 1892 and 1954.

W In Ellis Island's enormous hall, crowds of immigrants filed past the doctor for an initial inspection. "Whenever a case aroused suspicion," an inspector wrote, "the alien was set aside in a cage apart from the rest ... and his coat lapel or shirt marked with colored chalk" to indicate the reason for the isolation. About one out of five newcomers was marked with an "H" for heart problems, "K" for hernias, "Sc" for scalp problems, or "X" for mental disability. Newcomers who failed the inspection might be separated from their families and returned to Europe.

Ethnic Cities

Many of those who passed these inspections settled in the nation's cities. By the 1890s, immigrants made up a large percentage of the population of major cities, including New York, Chicago, Milwaukee, and Detroit. **Jacob Riis**, a Danish-born journalist, observed in 1890 that a map of New York City, "colored to designate nationalities, would show more stripes than on the skin of a zebra."

D In the cities, immigrants lived in neighborhoods that were often separated into **ethnic** groups, such as "Little Italy" or the Jewish "Lower East Side" in New York City. There they spoke their native languages and re-created the churches, synagogues, clubs, and newspapers of their homelands.

How well immigrants adjusted depended partly on how quickly they learned English and adapted to American culture. Immigrants also tended to adjust well if they had marketable skills or money, or if they settled among members of their own ethnic group.

✔ **Reading Check** **Explaining** How did immigration affect demographics in the United States?

PRIMARY SOURCE
The "New" Immigrants Arrive in America

In the late 1800s, the number of immigrants coming from northwest Europe began to decline, while "new immigrants," fleeing war, poverty, and persecution, began to arrive in large numbers from southern and eastern Europe, and from Asia.

▲ Many Italian immigrants took jobs as construction workers, bricklayers, and dockworkers in urban areas, but this group is building a railroad, c. 1900.

▲ Jewish people migrated to the United States from all across Europe seeking an opportunity to better their lives. Many Jews from Eastern Europe (such as those above) were also fleeing religious persecution.

◄ Many Chinese came to America to escape poverty and civil war. Many helped build railroads. Others set up small businesses. These children were photographed in San Francisco's Chinatown, c. 1900.

216 Chapter 6 Urban America

Activity: Interdisciplinary Connection

Civics Ask: How did you become a United States citizen? *(Answers will vary. Some students may respond that they were born in the United States. Others may say they were born abroad but to American parents. Others may volunteer that they have undergone the naturalization process.)* Have students work with a partner to list the requirements immigrants must meet before they can apply for U.S. citizenship. Students can obtain this information by taking the U.S. Immigration Service online quiz at www.uscitizenship.info/en_US/citizenship/home.html. Then ask partners to research the naturalization process on the Internet at www.uscitizenship.info/ins-citizenship-process.htm. Have partners create a poster that could be displayed in your community, informing immigrants of the application requirements and naturalization process. Display the posters in your school. **OL**

Asian Immigration

MAIN Idea Asian immigrants arrived on the West Coast, where they settled mainly in cities.

HISTORY AND YOU Do you know someone who has moved to the United States from Asia? What motivated that person to come here? Read on to learn about the experiences of earlier generations of Asian immigrants.

In the mid-1800s, China's population reached about 430 million, and the country was suffering from severe unemployment, poverty, and famine. Then, in 1850, the Taiping Rebellion erupted in China. This insurrection caused such suffering that thousands of Chinese left for the United States. In the early 1860s, as construction began on the Central Pacific Railroad, the demand for railroad workers led to further Chinese immigration.

Chinese immigrants settled mainly in western cities, where they often worked as laborers or servants or in skilled trades. Others became merchants. Because native-born Americans kept them out of many businesses, some Chinese immigrants opened their own.

Japanese also began immigrating to the United States. Although some came earlier, the number of Japanese immigrants soared upward between 1900 and 1910. As Japan industrialized, economic problems caused many Japanese to leave their homeland for new economic opportunities.

Until 1910 Asian immigrants arriving in San Francisco first stopped at a two-story shed at the wharf. As many as 500 people at a time were often squeezed into this structure, which Chinese immigrants from Canton called *muk uk,* or "wooden house." In January 1910 California opened a barracks on **Angel Island** **C** for Asian immigrants. Most were young men in their teens or twenties, who nervously awaited the results of their immigration hearings. The wait could last for months. On the walls of the barracks, several immigrants wrote anonymous poems in pencil or ink.

✔ **Reading Check** **Making Generalizations** Why did Chinese immigrants come to the United States?

Immigration Settlement Patterns

NATIONAL GEOGRAPHIC

Legend: China, Germany, Ireland, Italy, Japan, Mexico, Poland, Russia, Scandinavia
Settlement figures in thousands

New York: 480, 425, 182, 165, 66, 42, 7
Massachusetts: 249, 32, 28, 26
Wisconsin: 242, 61, 30, 23
Illinois: 332, 129, 64, 28, 23
Ohio: 204, 55
Pennsylvania: 212, 205, 72, 66, 50
California: 72, 44, 40, 10, 8
Texas: 72, 48

Analyzing VISUALS

1. **Analyzing Visuals** To which state did most Russian immigrants come to live?
2. **Contrasting** How would you contrast the immigration settlement patterns of Texas and Ohio?

Why Did Immigrants Come to America? / Typical Occupations in America

Why Did Immigrants Come to America?	Typical Occupations in America
Italians • cholera epidemic in 1880s • land shortage for peasants; landlords charge high rent • food shortages • poverty, unemployment	**Italians** • unskilled labor—dock work, construction, railroads • some skilled labor, such as bricklayers, stonemasons, and other trades
East Europeans • Russians, Poles: land shortages for peasants, unemployment, high taxes; long military draft • Jews: discrimination, poverty, and recurring pogroms	**East Europeans** • Poles: farmers, coal miners, steel and textile millworkers; meatpacking • Jews: laborers, garment workers, merchants
Chinese • famine • land shortage for peasants • civil war (Taiping rebellion)	**Chinese** • railroad and construction workers; some skilled labor • merchants, small businesses

Skill Practice

Reading Charts Ask: What push factor did the three groups of immigrants have in common? *(land shortage for peasants)* **ELL**

Critical Thinking

Contrasting Ask: How did the immigration process at Angel Island differ from that at Ellis Island? *(Immigrants had to wait longer at Angel Island.)* **OL**

Analyzing VISUALS

1. New York
2. Unlike the two fairly equal groups in Texas, one immigrant group far outnumbered the other in Ohio.

Reading Check

Answer:
high unemployment; poverty and famine in China; Taiping Rebellion; availability of railroad jobs in the United States

Extending the Content

Chinese Immigration During the 1906 San Francisco earthquake, most immigration records in the city burned. This helped the Chinese bring others from China into America. Because no records were available, the Chinese already living in the United States could claim they were born here, which automatically made them citizens. This entitled them to bring their children from China. As children of citizens, they too were automatically citizens.

Nativism Resurges

MAIN Idea Economic concerns and religious and ethnic prejudices led some Americans to push for laws restricting immigration.

HISTORY AND YOU In what ways does immigration affect the area in which you live? Read on to learn why nativists tried to stop immigration.

Eventually the wave of immigration led to increased feelings of nativism on the part of many Americans. **Nativism** is an extreme dislike of immigrants by native-born people. It had surfaced during the heavy wave of Irish immigration in the 1840s and 1850s. In the late 1800s, anti-immigrant feelings focused mainly on Asians, Jews, and eastern Europeans.

Nativists opposed immigration for many reasons. Some feared that the influx of Catholics from countries such as Ireland, Italy, and Poland would swamp the mostly Protestant United States. Many labor unions also opposed immigration, arguing that immigrants undermined

American workers because they would work for low wages and accept jobs as strikebreakers.

Prejudice Against Catholics

Increased feelings of nativism led to the founding of anti-immigrant organizations. The American Protective Association, founded by Henry Bowers in 1887, was an anti-Catholic organization. Its members vowed not to hire or vote for Catholics.

The Irish were among the immigrants who suffered most from the anti-Catholic feeling. Arriving to escape famine and other hardships, many were illiterate and found only the lowest-paying work as miners, dockhands, ditch-diggers, and factory workers. Irish women worked as cooks, servants, and mill-workers. The dominant Protestant, British culture in America, which considered Irish poverty to be the result of laziness, superstition, and ignorance, had no use for the Catholic Irish.

Although several presidents vetoed legislation that would have limited immigration, prejudice

---

POLITICAL CARTOONS PRIMARY SOURCE
Prejudice Against Catholic Immigrants

Anti-Catholic prejudice was strong in the United States for most of the 1800s. Many Americans tried to prevent Catholic immigration to the United States, fearing Catholic beliefs were incompatible with American values.

THE AMERICAN RIVER GANGES.

▲ Catholic priests crawl ashore as children are tossed to them by New York politicians in this 1871 cartoon criticizing New York's decision to fund Catholic schools.

218   Chapter 6   Urban America

PRIMARY SOURCE

"We unite to protect our country and its free institutions against the secret, intolerant, and aggressive efforts . . . by a certain religious political organization to control the government of the United States. . . .

. . . We have men born in several countries remote from this that are as loyal as any native, but they are not Romanists [Catholics]. American loyalty consists in devotion to our Constitution, laws, institutions, flag, and, above all, our public schools, for without intelligence this representative republic will go to pieces. . . . We are opposed to priests and prelates as such 'taking part in elections' and voting their laity as a unit in the interests of a foreign corporation . . ."

—from the platform of the American Protective Association, 1894

DBQ Document-Based Questions

1. **Explaining** What does the American Protective Association believe is incompatible with American citizenship? To what power does the statement refer?
2. **Detecting Bias** How does the cartoon express hostility toward Catholicism? Why might the cartoonist have depicted the public school on the hill in ruins?

Researching Immigration and Political Ads

Step 1: Researching German and Irish Immigration, 1815–1860
Essential Question: When did Irish and German immigrate in this period and where did they settle?

Directions Explain to students that they will create a poster display of the dominant groups that immigrated in this period. Students

should research historical census figures using library books and the Internet. Student teams can focus on different elements for the final product: numbers of German and Irish immigrants by decade or half-decade; maps of their migration routes (even narrowing in on the area of the "home country" if possible) and copies of art or visuals that represent the time period, immigrants' backgrounds, and so on.

Putting It Together When the teams meet, they can sift through their data and determine how to best display it on a white board or poster. German and Irish immigrant information might be presented in a side-by-side format if the data is comparable, or on separate posters. **OL**

(Chapter Project continued on page 226)

against immigrants stimulated the passage of a new federal law. Enacted in 1882, the law banned convicts, paupers, and the mentally disabled from immigrating to the United States. The law also placed a 50¢ per head tax on each newcomer.

Restrictions on Asian Immigration

In the West, anti-Chinese sentiment sometimes led to racial violence. Denis Kearney, himself an Irish immigrant, organized the Workingman's Party of California in the 1870s to fight Chinese immigration. The party won seats in California's legislature and pushed to cut off Chinese immigration.

In 1882 Congress passed the **Chinese Exclusion Act.** The law barred Chinese immigration for 10 years and prevented the Chinese already in the country from becoming citizens. The Chinese in the United States organized letter-writing campaigns, petitioned the president, and even filed suit in federal court, but their efforts failed. Congress renewed the law in 1892 and made it permanent in 1902. It was not repealed until 1943.

On October 11, 1906, in response to rising Japanese immigration, the San Francisco Board of Education ordered "all Chinese, Japanese and Korean children" to attend the racially segregated "Oriental School" in the city's Chinatown neighborhood. (Students of Chinese heritage had been forced to attend racially segregated schools since 1859.) The directive caused an international incident. Japan took great offense at the insulting treatment of its people.

In response, Theodore Roosevelt invited school board leaders to the White House. He proposed a deal. He would limit Japanese immigration, if the school board would rescind its segregation order. Roosevelt then carried out his end of the deal. He began talks with Japan, and negotiated an agreement whereby Japan agreed to curtail the emigration of Japanese to the continental United States. The San Francisco school board then revoked its segregation order. This deal became known as the "Gentleman's Agreement" because it was not a formal treaty and depended on the leaders of both countries to uphold the agreement.

The Literacy Debate

In 1905 Theodore Roosevelt commissioned a study on how immigrants were admitted to the nation. The commission recommended an English literacy test. Two years later, another commission suggested literacy tests—in any language—for immigration. These recommendations reflected the bias of people against the "new immigrants," who were thought to be less intelligent than the "old immigrants." Although Presidents Taft and Wilson both vetoed legislation to require literacy from immigrants, the legislation eventually passed in 1917 over Wilson's second veto. The purpose of the law was to reduce immigration from southeastern European nations.

✔ Reading Check **Explaining** Why did the federal government pass the Chinese Exclusion Act?

Section 1 REVIEW

Vocabulary
1. **Explain** the significance of: steerage, Ellis Island, Jacob Riis, Angel Island, nativism, Chinese Exclusion Act.

Main Ideas
2. **Listing** Why did European immigrants come to the United States?

3. **Describing** What caused the increase in Chinese immigration in the 1860s?

4. **Organizing** Complete a graphic organizer by listing the reasons nativists opposed immigration to the United States.

Critical Thinking
5. **Big Ideas** Where did most immigrants settle in the late 1800s? How did this benefit ethnic groups?

6. **Interpreting** Why did some Americans blame immigrants for the nation's problems?

7. **Analyzing Visuals** Select one of the people featured in any photo in this section. Write a journal entry about his or her experience, based on what you see in the photo.

Writing About History
8. **Descriptive Writing** Imagine that you are an immigrant who arrived in the United States in the 1800s. Write a letter to a relative in your home country describing your feelings during processing at either Ellis Island or Angel Island.

History ONLINE
Study Central™ To review this section, go to glencoe.com and click on Study Central.

219

✔ Reading Check

Answer:
to limit Chinese immigration; It was a reaction to violence against Chinese immigrants in California and a reflection of the era's prejudice.

Assess

History ONLINE

Study Central™ provides summaries, interactive games, and online graphic organizers to help students review content.

Close

Identifying **Ask:** What government actions limited Asian immigration? *(Chinese Exclusion Act, Gentleman's Agreement, required literacy tests)* **OL**

Section 1 REVIEW

Answers

1. Significant terms, people, and events are boldfaced and highlighted in the section.
2. The United States had few immigration restrictions. There were plenty of available jobs. It was a way to escape poverty, forced military service, and religious persecution.
3. severe unemployment, poverty, famine, war, job opportunities

4.
- influx of Catholics would give the Roman Catholic Church too much power
- immigrants would weaken unions
- Reasons Nativists Opposed Immigration
- immigrants would take jobs from Americans

5. large cities; more available jobs, easier access to transportation, and greater ability to be part of a community

6. Answers will vary. Possible responses: Immigrants took jobs from native-born Americans. The large influx of immigrants caused cities to spend money to upgrade public utilities and law enforcement.
7. Journals will vary but should accurately reflect the experience of one of the individuals pictured in this section.
8. Letters will vary but should incorporate details from the text about the Ellis and Angel Island processing centers.

ANALYZING PrimarySOURCES

Focus

Chinese immigrants who could prove they were children of American fathers were automatically American citizens. Because "paper sons and daughters" bought false documents to claim citizenship, all were carefully questioned before being admitted. **Ask:** How might this have affected processing at Angel Island? *(slowed the process)*

Teach

S Skill Practice

Visual Literacy Ask:

According to the cartoon, what push factors drew immigrants to the United States? *(no oppressive taxes, no expensive kings, no compulsory military service, no knouts or dungeons)* **BL**

C Critical Thinking

Predicting Consequences

Ask: What may have happened as a result of the eye examinations? *(Answers will vary but could include that immigrants received eye injuries and infections from the examinations.)* **OL**

Differentiated Instruction

Primary Source Reading, URB p. 101

ANALYZING PRIMARY SOURCES

Immigration

The United States is a nation of immigrants. In the late nineteenth century, more immigrants arrived on American shores than ever before. Some came from places such as the British Isles and Germany, from which many earlier immigrants had arrived. Others came from southern and eastern Europe, Asia, and other parts of the Americas. As the United States welcomed this mixture of ethnicities, religions, and languages, immigration became a subject of heated political debate.

Study these primary sources and answer the questions that follow.

PRIMARY SOURCE 2

Photograph, 1905

▼ *Immigrants are checked for trachoma and other contagious eye diseases at Ellis Island. The inspector is using a buttonhook, normally used to fasten ladies' gloves, to lift this woman's eyelid. The instrument was "cleaned" between inspections by wiping it on the towel hanging nearby.*

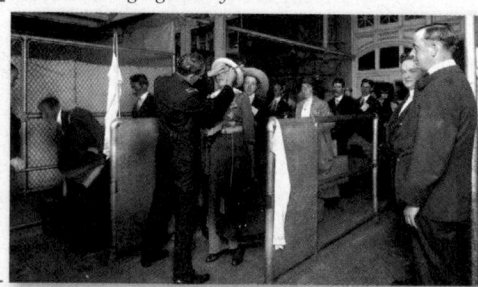

220 **Chapter 6** Urban America

PRIMARY SOURCE 1

Political Cartoon, 1880

▼ *"Welcome to All, " by J. Keppler, Puck (1880)*

PRIMARY SOURCE 3

Memoir Reflecting on Arrival at Ellis Island

"A group of Slovenian immigrants, of which this writer was one, arrived in New York from . . . Austria. . . . It was a beautiful morning in May 1906. After leaving the French ship LA TOURAINE, we were transported to Ellis Island for landing and inspection. There we were 'sorted out' as to the country we came from and placed in a 'stall' with the letter 'A' above us. ('A' was for Austria.)

There were at least a hundred Slovenian immigrants. We separated ourselves, as was the custom at home—men on the right and women and children on the left. All of us were waiting to leave for all parts of the United States.

The day was warm and we were very thirsty. An English-speaking immigrant asked the near-by guard where we could get a drink of water. The guard withdrew and returned shortly with a pail of water, which he set before the group of women. Some men stepped forward quickly to have a drink, but the guard pushed them back saying: 'Ladies first!' When the women learned what the guard had said, they were dumbfounded, for in Slovenia . . . women always were second to men. . . . Happy at the sudden turn of events, one elderly lady stepped forward, holding a dipper of water, and proposed this toast:

'Živijo Amerika, kjer so ženske prve!'
(Long live America, where women are first!)"

—Marie Priesland, recalling her arrival in the United States

Primary Source Reading

Objective: Read to learn why political machines like Tammany Hall appealed to immigrants.

Focus: Discern why the civil service system is inefficient according to this political machine leader.

Assess: Summarize the content of this excerpt in 2 to 3 sentences.

Close: Create an advertisement aimed at recruiting workers to the political machine.

Differentiated Learning Strategies

BL Describe what's wrong with the civil service law according to Plunkett.

AL Write a brief counterpoint to Plunkett's argument.

ELL Work with a partner to paraphrase the excerpt (using your own words.)

PRIMARY SOURCE 4

Magazine Article, 1903

"When I went to work for that American family I could not speak a word of English, and I did not know anything about housework. The family consisted of husband, wife and two children. They were very good to me and paid me $3.50 a week, of which I could save $3.

"I did not understand what the lady said to me, but she showed me how to cook, wash, iron, sweep, dust, make beds, wash dishes, clean windows, paint and brass, polish the knives and forks, etc., by doing the things herself and then overseeing my efforts to imitate her. . . . In six months I had learned how to do the work of our house quite well, and . . . I had also learned English. . . . I worked for two years as a servant . . . . and I was now ready to start in business."

—Chinese immigrant Lee Chew, reflecting on his first years in America

PRIMARY SOURCE 5

Questions Asked Immigrants, c. 1907

U.S. IMMIGRATION SERVICE		
1	Calling or Occupation?	farmer
2	Able to Read?	yes
3	Able to Write?	yes
4	Nationality?	Germany
5	Whether having a ticket to final destination?	yes
6	By whom was passage paid?	father
7	Whether in possession of $50, and if less, how much?	$20
8	Whether going to join a relative or friend?	friend
9	Ever in prison or almshouse or institution for care or treatment of the insane or supported by charity?	no
10	Whether a Polygamist?	no
11	Whether an Anarchist?	no
12	Whether coming by reason of any offer, solicitation, promise, or agreement, express or implied, to labor in the United States? Condition of Health, Mental and Physical?	no, no health problem
13	Deformed or Crippled. Nature, length of time and cause	no

PRIMARY SOURCE 6

Political Cartoon, 1896

"The Immigrant: The Stranger at Our Gate,"
The Ram's Horn *(April 25, 1896)*
Emigrant: "Can I come in?"
Uncle Sam: "I 'spose you can; there's no law to keep you out."

THE STRANGER AT OUR GATE.
EMIGRANT.—Can I come in?   UNCLE SAM.—I 'spose you can; there's no law to keep you out.

DBQ Document-Based Questions

1. **Analyzing Visuals** Compare the political cartoons in Sources 1 and 6. How do the two depictions differ on the reasons why immigrants left their homeland and why they came to the United States?

2. **Making Inferences** Why did immigrants have to undergo health inspections? What do you suppose happened when an immigrant was found to have a contagious illness?

3. **Interpreting** Why do you think the author of Source 3 remembered Ellis Island so clearly decades later?

4. **Evaluating** According to Lee Chew in Source 4, what were some factors that helped him adapt as an immigrant and become a small business owner?

5. **Making Inferences** Study the questions listed in Source 5. Why do you think immigrants were required to answer these questions?

Assess/Close

Have students work in pairs to research the symbolism of the Statue of Liberty. Ask students to draw a new statue to attract immigrants in the twenty-first century.

DBQ Document Based Questions

Answers:

1. Source 1: a U.S. free from the problems of immigrants' homelands, eager to welcome them; Source 6: reluctance to accept immigrants who brought with them poverty, disease, and different religious and political beliefs.

2. Some came from homelands where disease was epidemic, such as Italy. Most of the sick were denied entrance.

3. Answers will vary. Perhaps coming to America meant a great deal to her, especially since the author is a woman.

4. He was able to save a large portion of his wages, learn skills and English.

5. The idea that a healthy, literate immigrant could be self-supporting.

Additional Support

Activity: Collaborative Learning

Immigration Skit Ask: Were all immigrants glad they had moved to the United States? *(Responses may vary. Explain that a number of immigrants regretted leaving their homelands and moved back.)* **Ask:** Why did immigrants have different views of their new homeland? *(Responses may vary, but should include age, gender, and personal experiences.)* Have the students form "family" groups consisting of a grandparent, two parents, a daughter, and a son. Suggest that students choose one of the homelands discussed in this chapter. Have the groups discuss how age, gender, and experiences influenced how immigrants felt about living in the United States. Have each group perform a skit in which family members evaluate their decision to move to the United States. Encourage students to include details from the text about problems that "pushed" the family from its homeland.
OL ELL

Focus

Bellringer
Daily Focus Transparency 6.2

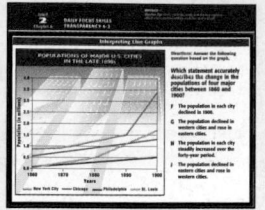

Guide to Reading

Answers to Graphic: crime, violence, disease, pollution, fire

Section Spotlight Video

To generate student interest and provide a springboard for class discussion, access the Chapter 6, Section 2 video at glencoe.com or on the video DVD.

Resource Manager

Section 2
Urbanization

Guide to Reading

Big Ideas
Government and Society The growth of and problems in major cities led to political machines that controlled local politics.

Content Vocabulary
• skyscraper (p. 222)
• tenement (p. 225)
• political machine (p. 227)
• party boss (p. 227)
• graft (p. 227)

Academic Vocabulary
• incentive (p. 222)
• trigger (p. 227)

People and Events to Identify
• Louis Sullivan (p. 223)
• George Plunkitt (p. 227)
• William "Boss" Tweed (p. 227)

Reading Strategy
Organizing As you read about urbanization in the United States in the late 1800s, complete a graphic organizer similar to the one below by filling in the problems the nation's cities faced.

Native-born Americans and immigrants were drawn to cities by the jobs available in America's growing industries. The new, modern cities had skyscrapers, public transportation systems, and neighborhoods divided by social class. In many cities, political machines controlled city government.

Americans Migrate to the Cities

MAIN Idea Rural Americans and immigrants moved to the cities where skyscrapers and mass transit were developed to deal with congestion.

HISTORY AND YOU Have you ever ridden the bus, subway, or railway system? How do you think your ride to school or the store would be different without mass transportation? Read on to learn why cities developed mass transportation systems.

After the Civil War, the urban population of the United States grew from around 10 million in 1870 to more than 30 million in 1900. New York City, which had more than 800,000 inhabitants in 1860, grew to almost 3.5 million by 1900. During the same period, Chicago swelled from 109,000 residents to more than 1.6 million. The United States had only 131 cities with populations of 2,500 or more residents in 1840; by 1900, there were more than 1,700 such urban areas.

Most of the immigrants who poured into the United States in the late 1800s lacked both the money to buy farms and the education to obtain higher-paying jobs. Thus, they settled in the nation's growing cities, where they toiled long hours for little pay in the rapidly expanding factories of the United States. Despite the harshness of their new lives, most immigrants found that the move had improved their standard of living.

Rural Americans also began moving to the cities at this time. Farmers moved to cities because urban areas offered more and better-paying jobs than did rural areas. Cities had much to offer, too—bright lights, running water, and modern plumbing, plus attractions such as museums, libraries, and theaters.

The physical appearance of cities also changed dramatically. As city populations grew, demand raised the price of land, creating the **incentive** to build upward rather than outward. Soon, tall, steel frame buildings called **skyscrapers** began to appear. Chicago's ten-story Home Insurance Building, built in 1885, was the first skyscraper, but other buildings quickly dwarfed it. New York City, with its business district on the narrow island of Manhattan, boasted more skyscrapers than any other city in the world. With limited space, New Yorkers had to build up, not out.

R Reading Strategies	C Critical Thinking	D Differentiated Instruction	W Writing Support	S Skill Practice
Teacher Edition • Making Connections, p. 226 • Organizing, p. 227 **Additional Resources** • Prim. Source Read., URB p. 101 • Guided Reading Act., URB p. 115	**Teacher Edition** • Contrasting, p. 223 • Drawing Conclusions, p. 224 • Speculating, p. 225 • Making Inferences, p. 226 **Additional Resources** • Quizzes and Tests, p. 74	**Teacher Edition** • Visual/ Spatial, p. 224 • Kinesthetic, p. 225 **Additional Resources** • Enrichment Act., URB p. 111	**Teacher Edition** • Persuasive Writing, p. 224	**Additional Resources** • Time Line Act., URB p. 99 • RENTG, p. 58

TECHNOLOGY & HISTORY

The Technology of Urbanization

Before the mid-1800s, few buildings exceeded four or five stories. To make wooden and stone buildings taller required enormously thick walls in the lower levels. This changed when steel companies began mass-producing cheap steel girders and steel cable.

Completed in 1913, the Woolworth Building is 792 feet high. It was the tallest building in the world until 1930.

A steel frame carries the weight, allowing the building to be much taller than stone or wood structures.

With steel beams instead of walls supporting the building, windows could be larger.

▲ Steel Cable

Steel also changed the way bridges were built. Engineers could now suspend bridges from steel towers using thick steel cables. Using this technique, engineer John Roebling designed New York's Brooklyn Bridge—the world's largest suspension bridge at the time. It was completed in 1883.

▶ Elevators

Elisha Otis invented the safety elevator in 1852. By the late 1880s, the first electric elevators had been installed, making tall buildings practical.

Analyzing VISUALS

1. **Theorizing** What other technologies were necessary in order to build modern skyscrapers?
2. **Predicting** What long-term effects do you think the new building technologies had on cities?

No one contributed more to the design of skyscrapers than Chicago's **Louis Sullivan.** "What people are within, the buildings express without," explained Sullivan, whose lofty structures featured simple lines and spacious windows using new, durable plate glass.

To move people around cities quickly, various kinds of mass transit developed. At first, almost all cities relied on the horsecar, a railroad car pulled by horses. In 1890 horsecars moved about 70 percent of urban traffic in the United States.

More than 20 cities, beginning with San Francisco in 1873, installed cable cars, which were pulled along tracks by underground cables. Then, in 1887, engineer Frank J. Sprague developed the electric trolley car. The country's first electric trolley line opened the following year in Richmond, Virginia.

In the largest cities, congestion became so bad that engineers began looking for ways to move mass transit off the streets. Chicago responded by building an elevated railroad, while Boston, followed by New York, built the first subway systems.

✓ Reading Check **Summarizing** What new technologies helped people in the late 1800s get to and from work?

Teach

C Critical Thinking

Contrasting **Ask:** How did Chicago's and Boston's mass transit systems differ? *(Chicago's is aboveground; Boston's is underground.)* **BL**

Analyzing VISUALS

Answers:
1. mass production of steel; elevators; durable plate glass
2. Answers will vary but could include the idea of unlimited future expansion.

✓ Reading Check

Answer:
cable cars, electric trolley cars, elevated railroads, subways

Differentiated Instruction

Leveled Activities

BL Academic Vocabulary Activity 6, pp. 95–96	**OL** Time Line Activity 6, p. 99	**AL** Enrichment Activity 6, p. 111	**ELL** Content Vocabulary Activity 6, p. 93

Separation by Class

MAIN Idea In the cities, society was separated by classes, with the upper, middle, and working classes living in different neighborhoods.

HISTORY AND YOU Do you know the history of certain neighborhoods in your city or town? Can you see where the classes were divided? Read on to learn how each class lived in the cities.

In the growing cities, the wealthy people and the working class lived in different parts of town. So, too, did members of the middle class. The boundaries between neighborhoods were quite definite and can still be seen in many American cities today.

High Society

During the last half of the 1800s, the wealthiest families established fashionable districts in the heart of a city. Americans with enough money could choose to construct homes in the style of a feudal castle, an English manor house, a French château, a Tuscan villa, or a Persian pavilion. In Chicago, merchant and real estate developer Potter Palmer chose a castle. In New York, Cornelius Vanderbilt's grandson commissioned a $3 million French château with a two-story dining room, a gymnasium, and a marble bathroom.

As their homes grew larger, wealthy women managed an increasing number of servants, such as cooks, maids, butlers, coachmen, nannies, and chauffeurs, and spent a great deal of money on social activities. In an age in which many New Yorkers lived on $500 a year, socialite hostess Cornelia Sherman Martin spent $360,000 on a dance.

Middle-Class Gentility

American industrialization also helped expand the middle class. The nation's rising middle class included doctors, lawyers, engineers, managers, social workers, architects, and teachers. Many people in the middle class moved away from the central city so as to escape the crime and pollution and be able to afford larger homes. Some took advantage of the new commuter rail lines to move to "streetcar suburbs."

PRIMARY SOURCE
Urban Society

Urban industrial society in the late 1800s was divided into social classes. The upper class and middle class lived well, but conditions for the working class and poor were often abysmal.

THE UPPER CLASS

THE MIDDLE CLASS

▲ The upper class could afford elaborate mansions and many servants. Men typically owned or managed large businesses. Women almost never worked. Clothing was elaborate and expensive. Events, such as afternoon tea in their garden (above), required formal dress and shows they had substantial leisure time.

▲ Middle class families could generally afford their own homes and better quality clothing. Women rarely worked—and if they did it was usually because they wanted a career, not out of necessity. Many families had at least one servant (shown above in back holding the baby) and enough money left over to buy luxuries, such as the new gramophone shown above.

224 Chapter 6 Urban America

In the late nineteenth century, most middle class families had at least one live-in servant. This gave the woman of the house more time to pursue activities outside the home. "Women's clubs" became popular. At first, these clubs focused on social and educational activities. Over time, however, "club women" became very active in charitable and reform activities. In Chicago, for example, the Women's Club helped establish juvenile courts and exposed the terrible conditions at the Cook County Insane Asylum.

The Working Class

Few families in the urban working class could hope to own a home. Most spent their lives in crowded **tenements,** or apartment buildings. The first tenement in the United States was built in 1839. In New York, three out of four residents squeezed into tenements, dark and crowded multi-family apartments. To supplement the average industrial worker's annual income of $445, many families rented precious space to a boarder. Zalmen Yoffeh, a journalist, lived in a New York tenement as a child. He recalled:

PRIMARY SOURCE

"With . . . one dollar a day [our mother] fed and clothed an ever-growing family. She took in boarders. Sometimes this helped; at other times it added to the burden of living. Boarders were often out of work and penniless; how could one turn a hungry man out? She made all our clothes. She walked blocks to reach a place where meat was a penny cheaper, where bread was a half cent less. She collected boxes and old wood to burn in the stove."

—quoted in *How We Lived*

History ONLINE
Student Web Activity Visit glencoe.com and complete the activity on tenement life.

The Family Economy

Within the working class, some people were better off than others. White native-born men earned higher wages than African American men, immigrants, and women.

One economist estimated that 64 percent of working class families relied on more than one wage earner in 1900. In some cases, the whole family worked, including the children. The dangerous working conditions faced by child workers, and the fact that they were not in school, alarmed many reformers.

THE WORKING CLASS

▲ *Most working class families lived in apartments, often only a single room in size. They had no servants, and often husbands and wives both had to work.*

WORKING WOMEN

▶ *Many young women, such as this one making a straw hat in a factory, worked long hours for little pay.*

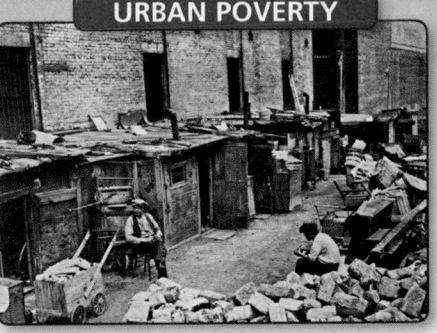

URBAN POVERTY

▲ *Unable to afford homes, the urban poor slept on the street or built shacks in back alleys like these in New York City in the early 1900s.*

Analyzing VISUALS

1. **Comparing and Contrasting** What do the upper class and middle class have in common compared to the working class and poor?
2. **Drawing Conclusions** How effective was industrial society at meeting people's needs?

Chapter 6 Urban America **225**

D Differentiated Instruction

Kinesthetic Have students form "families" of eight. Block window light. Have students cooking, playing, studying, and sleeping in a small area. Have "families" describe their reactions to "tenement life." **BL**

C Critical Thinking

Speculating Ask: Why did the woman accept nonpaying boarders? *(Answers will vary but may assert that the woman knew how poverty felt.)* **OL**

Analyzing VISUALS

Answers:
1. The upper and middle classes owned homes; the working class rented apartments, and the poor were homeless.
2. Most students will answer that the needs of only the top two classes were met.

Additional Support

Activity: Economics Connection

Budgeting Ask: What factors do you consider before buying something? *(Answers may include the price, affordability, or need for an item.)* Have students work in pairs to develop a household budget. Allow class time for partners to compare their itemized budgets and add expenditures they had not considered. Then ask partners to interview a family member or other adult about the costs of each budget item for a family of four. Have students calculate the income of two working adults, assuming 40-hour workweeks at minimum wage. Ask partners to calculate the shortfall between income and expenses and then list ways in which their shortfall can be addressed (such as deleting recreational and luxury items, working additional jobs, and so on). As a class, discuss the challenges of "making ends meet" and the emotional repercussions of not being able to meet the needs of the family. **OL**

C Critical Thinking

Making Inferences Ask: Why do you think social isolation was a result of domestic service? *(The upper and middle classes regarded domestic servants as social inferiors and did not associate with them.)* **AL**

R Reading Strategies

Making Connections Remind students that there was no compensation for maimed or killed workers during this time period. **Ask:** How are disabled or injured workers or families of killed workers protected today? *(Workers' compensation, disability and work-related life insurance.)* **OL**

DBQ Document Based Questions

Answers:
1. His men notify him.
2. Plunkitt receives their votes.

✔ Reading Check

Answer:
doctors, lawyers, engineers, managers, social workers, teachers; streetcar suburbs

Hands-On Chapter Project
Step 2

A growing number of women took jobs outside the home. Native-born white women typically had more years of education than other women. Thus, many used their literacy to work as teachers or do clerical work.

The largest source of employment for women, however, remained domestic service. Immigrant women often worked as domestic **C** servants in the North; African American women usually worked as domestic servants in the South. Such work involved long hours, low wages, and social isolation.

When people were physically unable to work, they had to rely on family members or charity. When a worker was maimed or killed on the job, there was usually no compensation. **R** Most older Americans lived with family members. Nearly 70 percent of those 65 or older lived with their grown children. A growing number, however, lived independently or in homes for the aged.

✔ Reading Check **Explaining** Who was in the "middle class" in the late 1800s? Where did they live?

POLITICAL CARTOONS **PRIMARY SOURCE**
Were Political Machines Bad for Cities?

Critics of political machines said that they took bribes and gave contracts to friends, robbing cities of resources. Defenders argued that they provided services and kept the city running.

EMPTY. "WHAT ARE YOU GOING TO DO ABOUT IT?" FULL.

EMPTY TO THE WORKMEN.   THE FOUR MASTERS THAT EMPTIED IT.

▲ Workers in New York find the city treasury empty, while behind the scenes, Boss Tweed and other city politicians enjoy a sumptuous feast.

226   Chapter 6   Urban America

Urban Problems

MAIN Idea Major problems plagued the cities; political machines provided help for some residents but were frequently corrupt.

HISTORY AND YOU What kinds of programs are used in your area to deal with urban problems? Read about political machines and how they ran city government.

City living posed the risks of crime, violence, fire, disease, and pollution. The rapid growth of cities only made these problems worse and complicated the ability of urban governments to respond to these problems.

Crime and Pollution

Crime was a growing problem in American cities. Minor criminals, such as pickpockets, swindlers, and thieves, thrived in crowded urban living conditions. Major crimes multiplied as well. From 1880 to 1900, the murder rate jumped sharply from 25 per million people to more than 100 per million people.

PRIMARY SOURCE

New York "Boss" George W. Plunkitt explains the benefits of the political machines:

"The poor are the most grateful people in the world, and, let me tell you, they have more friends in their neighborhoods than the rich have in theirs.

If there's a family in my district in want I know it before the charitable societies do, and me and my men are first on the ground.... The consequence is that the poor look up to George W. Plunkitt ... and don't forget him on election day.

Another thing, I can always get a job for a deservin' man.... I know every big employer in the district and in the whole city, for that matter, and they ain't in the habit of sayin' no to me when I ask them for a job."

—quoted in William L. Riordan,
Plunkitt of Tammany Hall

DBQ Document-Based Questions

1. **Analyzing Primary Sources** How does Plunkitt say he learns of people in need in his district?
2. **Determining Cause and Effect** What is the result of Plunkitt's care for the needy in his district?

Researching Immigration and Political Ads

Step 2: Compiling Data on Hispanic Immigration, 1960–2005 Essential Question: When did Hispanic groups immigrate in this period to the United States and where did they settle?

Directions Explain to students that they will create a poster display of Hispanic immigration to the United States in recent decades. They can use figures and graphs from their textbook, historical census figures, library books and the Internet. Student teams can focus on different elements for the final product: numbers of immigrants by decade or half-decade; maps of their migration route (even targeting the area of their home country, if possible) and copies of art or visuals that illustrate important points; e.g., the class background of most immigrants.

Putting It Together When the teams meet they can sift through their data and determine how to best display it on a white board or poster. Information and visuals might include other text to explain any particular forces impelling emigration from Mexico and Central and South America. **OL**
(Chapter Project continued on page 236)

Alcohol contributed to violent crime, both inside and outside the home. Danish immigrant Jacob Riis, who documented slum life in his 1890 book *How the Other Half Lives,* accused saloons of "breeding poverty," corrupting politics, bringing suffering to the wives and children of drunkards, and fostering "the corruption of the child" by selling beer to minors.

Disease and pollution posed even bigger threats. Improper sewage disposal contaminated city drinking water and **triggered** epidemics of typhoid fever and cholera. Though flush toilets and sewer systems existed in the 1870s, pollution remained a severe problem as horse manure was left in the streets, smoke belched from chimneys, and soot and ash accumulated from coal and wood fires.

Machine Politics

The **political machine,** an informal political group designed to gain and keep power, came about partly because cities had grown much faster than their governments. New city dwellers needed jobs, housing, food, heat, and police protection. In exchange for votes, political machines and the **party bosses** who ran them eagerly provided these necessities.

Graft and Fraud The party bosses who ran the political machines also controlled the city's finances. Many machine politicians grew rich as the result of fraud or **graft**—getting money through dishonest or questionable means. **George Plunkitt,** one of New York City's most powerful party bosses, defended what he called "honest graft." For example, a politician might find out in advance where a new park was to be built and buy the land near the site. The politician would then sell the land to the city for a profit. As Plunkitt stated, "I see my opportunity, and I take it."

Outright fraud occurred when party bosses accepted bribes from contractors who were supposed to compete fairly to win contracts to build streets, sewers, and buildings. Corrupt bosses also sold permits to their friends to operate public utilities, such as railroads, waterworks, and power systems.

Tammany Hall Tammany Hall, the New York City Democratic political machine, was the most infamous such organization. **William "Boss" Tweed** was its leader during the 1860s and 1870s. Tweed's corruptness led to a prison sentence in 1874.

City machines often controlled all the city services, including the police department. In St. Louis, the "boss" never feared arrest when he called out to his supporters at the police-supervised voting booth, "Are there any more repeaters out here that want to vote again?"

Opponents of political machines, such as political cartoonist Thomas Nast, blasted bosses for their corruption. Defenders, though, argued that machines provided necessary services and helped to assimilate the masses of new city dwellers.

☑ Reading Check **Evaluating** Why did political machines help city dwellers in the late 1800s?

Section 2 REVIEW

Vocabulary
1. **Explain** the significance of: skyscraper, Louis Sullivan, tenement, political machine, party boss, graft, George Plunkitt, William "Boss" Tweed.

Main Ideas
2. **Identifying** What technologies made the building of skyscrapers possible?

3. **Comparing** How did the living conditions of the upper, middle, and the working classes in the late 1800s compare?

4. **Organizing** Complete the graphic organizer below by listing the effects of many Americans moving from rural to urban areas in the late 1800s.

Critical Thinking
5. **Big Ideas** How did political machines respond to the needs of the people?

6. **Synthesizing** Why were pollution and sewage a problem in American cities in the late 1800s?

7. **Analyzing Visuals** Look at the photos on pages 224–225. How did industrialization affect the class structure in the United States?

Writing About History
8. **Persuasive Writing** Take on the role of an urban planner in a major city in the late 1800s. Write a letter to members of the city government listing specific reasons for the importance of setting aside city land for parks and recreational areas.

History ONLINE
Study Central™ To review this section, go to glencoe.com and click on Study Central.

227

Answers

1. Significant terms, places, and people are boldfaced and highlighted in the section.
2. steel frames, elevators, durable plate glass
3. The wealthy lived in grand homes in fashionable areas, the middle class lived in comfortable homes in streetcar suburbs, and the working class lived in tenements.

4.

5. Political machines provided jobs, housing, food, heat, and police protection.

6. They contaminated drinking water and triggered epidemics of typhoid fever and cholera, as well as other health problems.
7. Answers will vary but may include: expanded the middle class; separated classes into distinctly different neighborhoods.
8. Letters will vary but should include specific reasons for parks and recreational areas.

Focus

Tell students that the first settlement house was founded in New York City in 1886. Settlement houses helped immigrants adjust to life in America. Italians coming to the United States would be able to learn English, send their children to school, enjoy recreational activities, and have access to health services.

Teach

R Reading Strategy

Reading Maps **Ask:** What other ethnic group had a large presence in New York City? *(Chinese, in Chinatown)* BL

C Critical Thinking

Drawing Conclusions **Ask:** Why did people from different parts of Italy live on different New York City streets? *(Dialects and customs changed from village to village in Italy and people were more likely to live near those they have connections with.)* OL

Additional Support

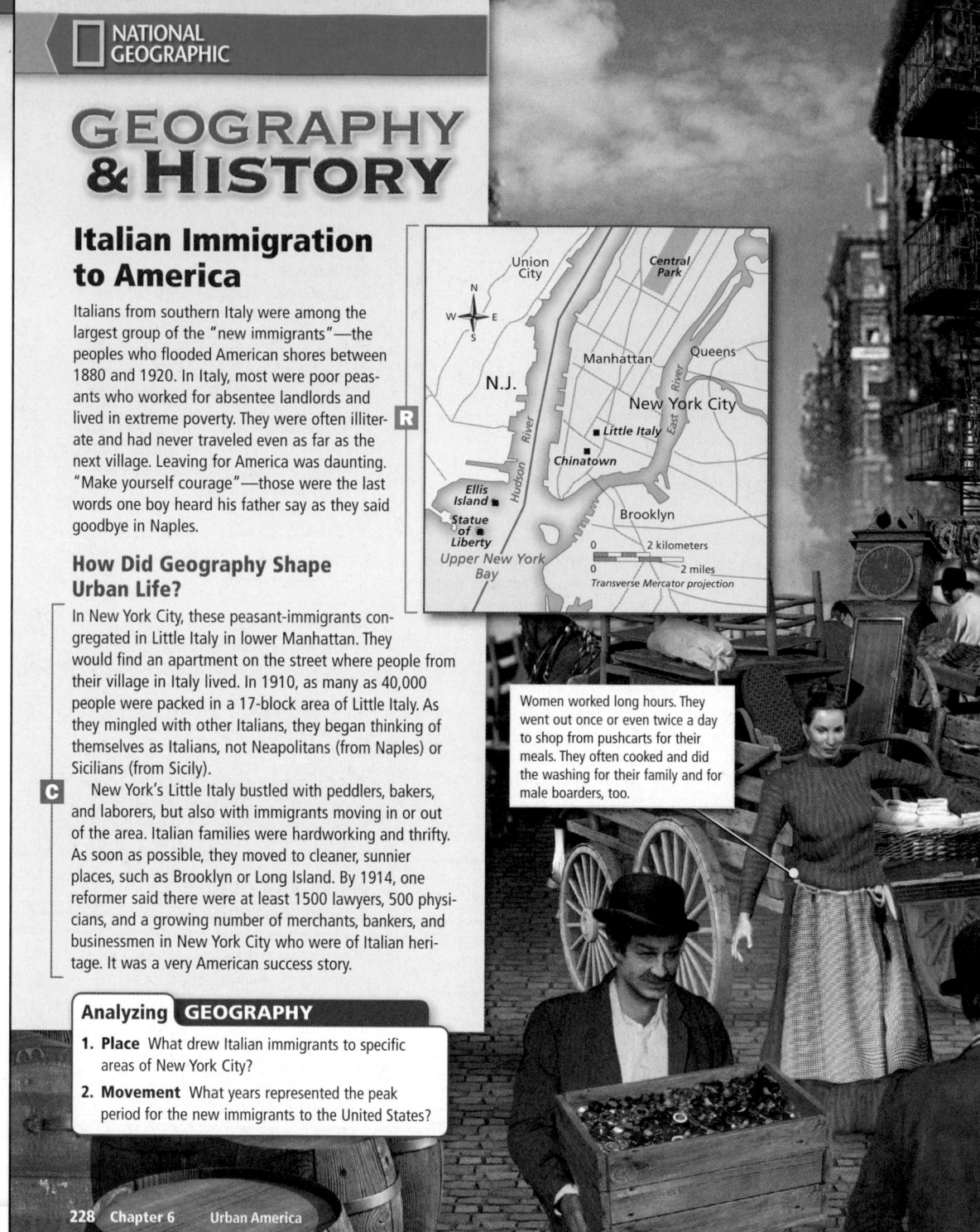

NATIONAL GEOGRAPHIC

GEOGRAPHY & HISTORY

Italian Immigration to America

Italians from southern Italy were among the largest group of the "new immigrants"—the peoples who flooded American shores between 1880 and 1920. In Italy, most were poor peasants who worked for absentee landlords and lived in extreme poverty. They were often illiterate and had never traveled even as far as the next village. Leaving for America was daunting. "Make yourself courage"—those were the last words one boy heard his father say as they said goodbye in Naples. R

How Did Geography Shape Urban Life?

In New York City, these peasant-immigrants congregated in Little Italy in lower Manhattan. They would find an apartment on the street where people from their village in Italy lived. In 1910, as many as 40,000 people were packed in a 17-block area of Little Italy. As they mingled with other Italians, they began thinking of themselves as Italians, not Neapolitans (from Naples) or Sicilians (from Sicily).

C New York's Little Italy bustled with peddlers, bakers, and laborers, but also with immigrants moving in or out of the area. Italian families were hardworking and thrifty. As soon as possible, they moved to cleaner, sunnier places, such as Brooklyn or Long Island. By 1914, one reformer said there were at least 1500 lawyers, 500 physicians, and a growing number of merchants, bankers, and businessmen in New York City who were of Italian heritage. It was a very American success story.

Map labels: Union City, Central Park, N.J., Manhattan, Queens, New York City, Little Italy, East River, Chinatown, Hudson River, Ellis Island, Statue of Liberty, Brooklyn, Upper New York Bay, N W E S, 0 2 kilometers, 0 2 miles, Transverse Mercator projection

Women worked long hours. They went out once or even twice a day to shop from pushcarts for their meals. They often cooked and did the washing for their family and for male boarders, too.

Analyzing GEOGRAPHY

1. **Place** What drew Italian immigrants to specific areas of New York City?
2. **Movement** What years represented the peak period for the new immigrants to the United States?

228 Chapter 6 Urban America

Activity: Collaborative Learning

Learn About Little Italy Divide the class into small groups. Ask each group to select a major city in the United States known to have a Little Italy or other ethnic neighborhood. (San Diego, San Francisco, Cleveland, and Chicago all have a Little Italy.) Have each group use library or Internet resources to research that city's unique contributions. Ask each group to use its findings to prepare a presentation for the class. Presentations should include visual elements such as photographs, maps, and illustrations. OL

Mulberry Street was the heart of Little Italy. Neapolitans (people from Naples) tended to settle on Mulberry Street, while Sicilians crowded the tenements on Elizabeth Street two blocks away.

Around 1900, roughly 4,300 tenement apartments were occupied by large families who lived in just a few rooms.

Street vendors often sold foods that were popular in Italy. They were very busy during holidays. In Little Italy, one of the biggest holidays was the feast of Saint Gennaro, patron saint of Naples—still celebrated in Little Italy in New York today.

Bread was often sold on the streets because tenement ovens could not produce the traditional Italian crust. Young children ran many errands, like buying food and gathering wood for fuel.

Assess/Close

Have students assume the role of the young person whose father told him to "Make yourself courage." Have them write a letter back to their family in Italy telling them about life in New York's Little Italy. **OL**

Analyzing GEOGRAPHY

Answers:
1. Italian immigrants moved to neighborhoods in New York where other people from their home villages lived.
2. between 1880 and 1920

Additional Support

Activity: Economics Connection

Migrant Workers and the Law The young Italian males who came to the United States often intended to work for one or two seasons before returning to Italy. They generally did not speak English, and relied on labor bosses to find them jobs in construction. The padrones, as they were called, sometimes cheated the young workers. Have students find contemporary examples of similar situations that migrant workers or other immigrants face. Lead a discussion of how this justice issue might be resolved. **OL**

Focus

Bellringer
Daily Focus Transparency 6.3

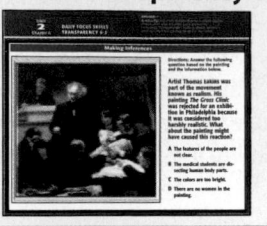

Guide to Reading

Answers To Graphic:

Theory or Movement	Main Idea
Social Darwinism	survival of the fittest
Laissez-Faire	no government interference in business
Gospel of Wealth	the wealthy use philanthropy to create conditions that help people help themselves
Realism	portray the world realistically

Section Spotlight Video

To generate student interest and provide a springboard for class discussion, access the Chapter 6, Section 3 video at glencoe.com or on the video DVD.

Resource Manager

Section 3

The Gilded Age

Guide to Reading

Big Ideas
Past and Present Ideas about wealth during the last part of the 1800s continue to affect society today.

Content Vocabulary
- individualism (p. 230)
- Social Darwinism (p. 231)
- philanthropy (p. 232)
- settlement house (p. 239)
- Americanization (p. 239)

Academic Vocabulary
- evolution (p. 231)
- publish (p. 233)

People and Events to Identify
- Gilded Age (p. 230)
- Gospel of Wealth (p. 232)
- Mark Twain (p. 233)
- Social Gospel (p. 238)
- Jane Addams (p. 239)

Reading Strategy
Categorizing Complete a graphic organizer similar to the one below by filling in the main idea of each of the theories and movements listed.

Theory or Movement	Main Idea
Social Darwinism	
Laissez-Faire	
Gospel of Wealth	
Realism	

The industrialization of the United States led to new art and literature and new ideas about government's role in society. Social Darwinists believed society developed through "survival of the fittest." Other Americans thought steps needed to be taken to help the less fortunate.

Social Darwinism

MAIN Idea Individualism and Social Darwinism shaped Americans' attitudes toward industrial society.

HISTORY AND YOU Do you think each individual person should be left on his or her own to succeed, or should people help those who fall behind? Read to learn about people who applied the notion of "survival of the fittest" to human society.

In 1873 Mark Twain and Charles Warner wrote a novel entitled *The Gilded Age: A Tale of Today.* Historians later adopted the term and applied it to the era in American history that began about 1870 and ended around 1900. The era was in many ways a time of marvels. Amazing new inventions led to rapid industrial growth. Cities expanded to sizes never seen before. Masses of workers thronged the streets. Skyscrapers reached to the sky, electric lights banished the darkness, and wealthy entrepreneurs built spectacular mansions.

By calling this era the **Gilded Age,** Twain and Warner were sounding an alarm. Something is gilded if it is covered with gold on the outside but made of cheaper material inside. A gilded age might appear to sparkle, but critics pointed to corruption, poverty, crime, and great disparities in wealth between the rich and the poor.

Whether the era was golden or merely gilded, it was certainly a time of great cultural activity. Industrialism and urbanization altered the way Americans looked at themselves and their society, and these changes gave rise to new values, new art, and new entertainment.

The Idea of Individualism

One of the strongest beliefs of the era—and one that remains strong today—was the idea of **individualism.** Many Americans firmly believed that no matter how humble their origins, they could rise in society and go as far as their talents and commitment would take them. No one expressed the idea of individualism better than Horatio Alger, who wrote more than 100 "rags-to-riches" novels. In his books, a poor person goes to the big city and, through a combination of hard work and luck,

---

R Reading Strategies	C Critical Thinking	D Differentiated Instruction	W Writing Support	S Skill Practice
Teacher Edition • Academic Vocab., p. 232 • Using Context Clues, p. 234 • Activ. Prior Knowledge, pp. 235, 236, 238 • Paraphrasing, p. 237 **Additional Resources** • Guided Reading Act., URB p. 116	**Teacher Edition** • Predicting Consequences, p. 234 • Making Inferences, p. 233 • Cause/Effect, p. 235 • Explaining, p. 236 **Additional Resources** • History Simulations, URB p. 9 • Quizzes and Tests, p. 75	**Teacher Edition** • Auditory/Musical, p. 232 **Additional Resources** • Am. Art and Music Act., URB p. 105	**Teacher Edition** • Personal Writing, pp. 231, 238	**Teacher Edition** • Analyzing Visuals, p. 233 **Additional Resources** • RENTG, p. 61

PRIMARY SOURCE
Social Darwinism and Society

PRIMARY SOURCE

The Gospel of Wealth

"In bestowing charity, the main consideration should be to help those who will help themselves; to provide part of the means by which those who desire to improve may do so; to give those who desire to rise the aids by which they may rise; to assist, but rarely or never to do all. Neither the individual nor the race is improved by almsgiving. Those worthy of assistance, except in rare cases, seldom require assistance. The really valuable men of the race never do, except in cases of accident or sudden change.... He is the only true reformer who is as careful and as anxious not to aid the unworthy as he is to aid the worthy, and, perhaps, even more so, for in almsgiving more injury is probably done by rewarding vice than by relieving virtue.... "

—Andrew Carnegie, quoted in *The North American Review*, June 1889

W

PRIMARY SOURCE

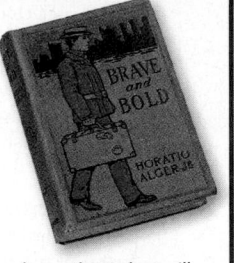

"Robert was very different. He inherited from his father an unusual amount of courage and self-reliance, and if one avenue was closed to him, he at once set out to find another. It is of this class that successful men are made, and we have hopes that Robert will develop into a prosperous and successful man."

—from Horatio Alger, *Brave and Bold*

DBQ Document-Based Questions

1. **Analyzing Primary Sources** What does Carnegie believe is the way to dignify the lives of rich people?

2. **Describing** On what does Alger base Robert's chances of success? Do you agree with his criteria? Why or why not?

becomes successful. His popular books convinced many young people that no matter how many obstacles they faced, success was possible.

Social Darwinism

Another powerful idea of the era was **Social Darwinism.** This philosophy, loosely derived from Darwin's theories, strongly reinforced the idea of individualism.

Herbert Spencer British philosopher Herbert Spencer applied Charles Darwin's theory of **evolution** and natural selection to human society. In his 1859 book *On the Origin of Species by Means of Natural Selection*, Darwin argued that plant and animal life had evolved over the years by a process he called natural selection. In this process, those species that cannot adapt to the environment in which they live gradually die out, while those that do adapt thrive and live on.

Spencer took this theory intended to explain developments over millions of years and argued that human society also evolved through competition and natural selection. He argued that society progressed and became better because only the fittest people survived. Spencer and others, such as American scholar William Graham Sumner, who shared his views, became known as Social Darwinists, and their ideas became known as Social Darwinism. "Survival of the fittest" became the catchphrase of their philosophy.

Social Darwinism also paralleled the economic doctrine of laissez-faire that opposed any government programs that interfered with business. Not surprisingly, industrial leaders heartily embraced the theory. John D. Rockefeller maintained that survival of the fittest, as demonstrated by the growth of huge businesses like his own Standard Oil, was "merely the working out of the law of nature and the law of God."

Chapter 6 Urban America **231**

Teach

W Writing Support

Personal Writing Have students write letters to Andrew Carnegie, agreeing or disagreeing with his philosophy. **OL**

DBQ Document Based Questions

Answers:
1. using their power to help others
2. courage, self-reliance, and perseverance; Answers will vary but should contain supporting evidence for the opinion.

Additional Support

Activity: Interdisciplinary Connection

Science Ask: In the natural world, which animals survive and which do not? *(Answers may include that the physically weak, sick, injured, or small animals may not survive predation or environmental factors, such as extreme climate and drought.)* Invite a science teacher to talk with students about "survival of the fittest" in the animal world. Ask the teacher to describe how animals adapt to improve their chances of survival. After the presentation, have students form groups to list ways in which immigrants adapt to improve their chances of physical, economic, and social survival. Have groups create a "Tips for Survival" poster that will help a new immigrant succeed in today's United States. Display the posters and discuss them as a class. **Ask:** Does adapting to fit into American society threaten an immigrant's chances of retaining his or her cultural heritage? Can an individual live successfully within two cultures? **OL**

R Reading Strategy

Academic Vocabulary Explain that the Greek *philos* means "loving" and *anthropos* means "human being." **Ask:** From these word parts, what is philanthropy? *(a desire to help humanity, especially through charitable activities)* **OL**

D Differentiated Instruction

Auditory/Musical Read aloud the excerpt from *Huckleberry Finn.* **Ask:** What conclusions can you reach about Huck by listening to him speak? *(Answers will vary but may include that he is poorly educated and lives in a different time or place.)* **BL**

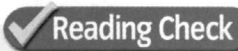

Reading Check

Answer:
Human society evolves through competition and natural selection, or survival of the fittest.

Additional Support

Darwinism and the Church For many devout Christians, however, Darwin's conclusions were upsetting and offensive. They rejected the theory of evolution because they believed it contradicted the Bible's account of creation. Some ministers, however, concluded that evolution may have been God's way of creating the world. One of the most famous ministers of the era, Henry Ward Beecher, called himself a "Christian evolutionist."

Carnegie's Gospel of Wealth Andrew Carnegie advocated a gentler version of Social Darwinism that he called the **Gospel of Wealth.** This philosophy held that wealthy Americans should engage in **philanthropy** and use their great fortunes to create the conditions that would help people help themselves. Building schools and hospitals, for example, was better than giving handouts to the poor. Carnegie himself helped fund the creation of public libraries in cities across the nation because libraries provided the information people needed to get ahead in life.

Reading Check **Summarizing** What was the main idea of Social Darwinism?

PRIMARY SOURCE
Realism in Art and Literature

Realist writers and artists did not want to portray people and the world idealistically. Instead they sought to present things as accurately as possible.

> **PRIMARY SOURCE**
>
> "'Say, who is you? Whar is you? Dog my cats ef I didn' hear sumf'n. Well, I know what I's gwyne to do: I's gwyne to set down here and listen tell I hears it agin.'"
>
> So he set down on the ground betwixt me and Tom. He leaned his back up against a tree, and stretched his legs out till one of them most touched one of mine. My nose begun to itch. It itched till the tears come into my eyes. But I dasn't scratch. Then it begun to itch on the inside. Next I got to itching underneath. I didn't know how I was going to set still. This miserableness went on as much as six or seven minutes; but it seemed a sight longer than that."
>
> —from *The Adventures of Huckleberry Finn* by Mark Twain

A Changing Culture

MAIN Idea Artists and writers began portraying life in America more realistically, and cities offered new forms of entertainment.

HISTORY AND YOU Have you read Mark Twain's *The Adventures of Huckleberry Finn*? Read to learn about how Twain portrayed American life in a realistic way.

The late 1800s was a period of great cultural change for writers and artists, and for many urban Americans who sought new forms of entertainment.

Realism

A new movement in art and literature called realism began in the 1800s. Just as Darwin tried to explain the natural world scientifically, artists and writers tried to portray the world realistically. European realists included Edgar Degas and Edouard Manet. Perhaps the best known American realist painter was Thomas Eakins. In realistic detail, he painted young men rowing and athletes playing baseball, and he showed surgeons and scientists in action.

▲ *Realist painters did not generally choose heroic or historical topics for their art. Instead they preferred to depict ordinary people doing ordinary things. Thomas Eakins, perhaps the best-known American realist, depicted various aspects of American life, including a carriage ride by the wealthy (above) or a professional baseball game (right).*

Activity: Technology Connection

Using Technology to Create Realist Art Ask: What images would you choose to realistically portray American life to a prospective immigrant? *(Students may name game systems, popular foods, sports teams, and so on.)* Have students work in pairs with a computer presentation program to create a slide show of images that realistically represent various facets of American life today, such as home life, school, work, recreation, communities, politics, and organizations. Encourage students to use their imaginations. Suggest that they incorporate music into their presentations. Have partners present their slide shows to the class. During the presentations, ask class members to note particularly effective and realistic images. At the end of the presentations, discuss memorable images with the class. **Ask:** Did some presentations give conflicting views of American life? Why might one person's "reality" differ from another's? **OL**

Writers also attempted to capture the world as they saw it. In several novels, William Dean Howells presented realistic descriptions of American life. For example, his novel *The Rise of Silas Lapham* (1885) described the attempts of a self-made man to enter Boston society. Also an influential literary critic, Howells was the first to declare **Mark Twain** an incomparable American genius.

Twain, whose real name was Samuel Clemens, **published** his masterpiece, *The Adventures of Huckleberry Finn,* in 1884. In this novel, the title character and his friend Jim, an escaped slave, float down the Mississippi River on a raft. Twain wrote in local dialect with a lively sense of humor. He had written a true American novel, in which the setting, subject, characters, and style were clearly American.

Popular Culture

Popular culture changed considerably in the late 1800s. Industrialization improved the standard of living for many people, enabling them to spend money on entertainment and recreation. Increasingly, urban Americans divided their lives into separate units—that of

Analyzing **VISUALS** **DBQ**

1. **Analyzing** How does Twain's writing reflect a realist approach to writing?
2. **Making Inferences** Why might Realist art have become popular in the late 1800s?

work and that of home. People began "going out" to public entertainment.

The Saloon In cities, saloons often outnumbered groceries and meat markets. As a place for social gathering, saloons played a major role in the lives of male workers. Saloons offered drinks, free toilets, water for horses, and free newspapers for customers. They even offered the first "free lunch": salty food that made patrons thirsty and eager to drink more. Saloons also served as political centers and saloonkeepers were often key figures in political machines.

Amusement Parks and Sports Working-class families and single adults could find entertainment at new amusement parks such as New York's Coney Island. Amusements such as water slides and railroad rides cost only a nickel or dime.

Watching professional sports also became popular during the late 1800s. Formed in 1869, the first professional baseball team was the Cincinnati Red Stockings. Other cities soon fielded their own teams. In 1903 the first official World Series was played between the Boston Red Sox and the Pittsburgh Pirates. Football also gained in popularity and by the late 1800s had spread to public colleges.

As work became less strenuous, many people looked for activities involving physical exercise. Tennis, golf, and croquet became popular. In 1891 James Naismith, athletic director for a college in Massachusetts, invented a new indoor game called basketball.

S **Vaudeville and Ragtime** Adapted from French theater, vaudeville took on an American flavor in the early 1880s with its hodgepodge of animal acts, acrobats, and dancers. The fast-paced shows went on continuously all day and night.

Like vaudeville, ragtime music echoed the hectic pace of city life. Its syncopated rhythms **C** grew out of the music of riverside honky-tonks, saloon pianists, and banjo players, using the patterns of African American music. Scott Joplin, one of the most important African American ragtime composers, became known as the "King of Ragtime." He wrote his most famous piece, "The Maple Leaf Rag," in 1899.

✓ Reading Check **Describing** What was the importance of the saloon in city life?

For examples of literature from the Gilded Age, read excerpts from the writings of Mark Twain and Carl Sandburg on pages R70–71 in **American Literature Library.**

Chapter 6 Urban America **233**

Additional Support

Politics in Washington

MAIN Idea The two major parties were closely competitive in the late 1800s; tariff rates and big business regulation were hotly debated political issues.

HISTORY AND YOU Have you ever considered getting a job working for the government once you graduate? Read to learn why you will have to take an examination if you want a government job.

After President James A. Garfield was elected in 1880, many of his supporters tried to claim the "spoils of office"—the government jobs that are handed out following an election victory. President Garfield did not believe in the spoils system. One of these job seekers made daily trips to the White House in the spring of 1881 asking for a job. He was repeatedly rejected. Reasoning that he would have a better chance for a job if Vice President Chester A. Arthur were president, this man shot President Garfield on July 2, 1881. Weeks later, Garfield died from his wounds.

Civil Service Reform

For many, Garfield's assassination highlighted the need to reform the political system. Traditionally, under the spoils system, elected politicians extended patronage—the power to reward supporters by giving them government jobs. Many Americans believed the system made government inefficient and corrupt. In the late 1870s, reformers had begun pushing him for an end to patronage.

When Rutherford B. Hayes became president in 1877, he tried to end patronage by firing officials who had been given their jobs because of their support of the party and replacing them with reformers. His actions divided the Republican Party between "Stalwarts" (who supported patronage) and the "Halfbreeds" (who opposed it), and no reforms were passed. In 1880 the Republicans nominated James Garfield, a "Halfbreed," for president and Chester A. Arthur, a "Stalwart," for vice president. Despite the internal feud over patronage, the Republicans managed to win the election, only to have Garfield assassinated a few months later.

Garfield's assassination turned public opinion against the spoils system. In 1883 Congress responded by passing the Pendleton Act. This law required that some jobs be filled by competitive written examinations, rather than through patronage. This marked the beginning of professional civil service—a system where most government workers are given jobs based on their qualifications rather than on their political affiliation. Although only about 10 percent of federal jobs were made civil service positions in 1883, the percentage steadily increased over time.

The Election of 1884

In 1884 the Democratic Party nominated Grover Cleveland, the governor of New York, for president. Cleveland was a reformer with a reputation for honesty. The Republican Party nominated James G. Blaine, a former Speaker of the House rumored to have accepted bribes. Some Republican reformers were so unhappy with Blaine that they supported Cleveland. They became known as "Mugwumps," from an Algonquian word meaning "great chief." If Blaine was their party's candidate, declared the Mugwumps, they would vote for Cleveland, "an honest Democrat."

Blaine hoped to make up for the loss of the Mugwumps by courting Catholic voters. Shortly before the election, however, Blaine met with a Protestant minister who denounced the Democrats for having ties to Catholicism. When Blaine was slow to condemn the remark, he lost many Catholic votes. Cleveland narrowly won the election.

As the first elected Democratic president since 1856, Grover Cleveland faced a horde of supporters who expected him to reward them with jobs. Mugwumps, on the other hand, expected him to increase the number of jobs protected by the civil service system. Cleveland chose a middle course and angered both sides. Economic issues, however, soon replaced the debate about patronage reform.

The Interstate Commerce Commission Many Americans were concerned by the power of large corporations. Small businesses and farmers had become particularly angry at the railroads. While large corporations such as Standard Oil were able to negotiate rebates and lower rates because of the volume of goods they shipped, others were forced to pay much higher rates. Although the high fixed costs and low operating costs of railroads caused much

234 **Chapter 6** Urban America

Activity: Economics Connection

National Budget Divide the class into groups. Have each group research the nation's budget surpluses and deficits since 1860. Based on the information, groups should create a line graph showing the changing trends. At each point where the trend shows a change of direction, identify the events that might have brought about the change. Have students write a paragraph stating how political leaders have contributed to surpluses and deficits and whether their decisions have helped or hurt the country. **OL** **AL**

POLITICAL CARTOONS PRIMARY SOURCE
Political Debates of the Gilded Age

▲ Senator Pendleton is congratulated for his civil service bill; behind him a trash bin overflows with papers saying reform is impossible.

JOHN BULL AND HIS FRIEND CLEVELAND.

▲ John Bull, symbol of Britain, thanks Grover Cleveland for free trade because it keeps British workers employed even if everyone else starves.

Analyzing VISUALS

1. **Analyzing** Does the cartoon on the right say free trade is a good idea? How do you know?

2. **Explaining** Did the artist who drew the cartoon on the left favor civil service reform? How does he indicate his opinion?

of this problem, many Americans believed railroads were gouging customers.

Neither party moved quickly at the federal level to address these problems. Both believed that government should not interfere with corporations' property rights, which courts had held to be the same as those of individuals. Many states, however, passed laws regulating railroad rates; in 1886 the Supreme Court ruled in the case of *Wabash, St. Louis, and Pacific Railway* v. *Illinois* that states could not regulate railroad rates for traffic between states because only the federal government could regulate interstate commerce.

R Public pressure forced Congress to respond to the Wabash ruling. In 1887 Cleveland signed the Interstate Commerce Act. This act, which created the Interstate Commerce Commission (ICC), was the first federal law to regulate **C** interstate commerce. The legislation limited railroad rates to what was "reasonable and just," forbade rebates to high-volume users, and made it illegal to charge higher rates for shorter hauls. The commission was not very

effective in regulating the industry, however, because it had to rely on the courts to enforce its rulings.

Debating Tariffs Another major economic issue concerned tariffs. Many Democrats thought that Congress should cut tariffs because these taxes had the effect of raising the price of manufactured goods. Although it may have made sense to protect weak domestic manufacturing after the Civil War, many questioned the need to maintain high tariffs in the 1880s, when large American companies were fully capable of competing internationally. High tariffs also forced other nations to respond in kind, making it difficult for farmers to export their surpluses.

In December 1887 President Cleveland proposed lowering tariffs. The House, with a Democratic majority, passed moderate tariff reductions, but the Republican-controlled Senate rejected the bill. With Congress deadlocked, tariff reduction became a major issue in the election of 1888.

Chapter 6 Urban America **235**

Activity: Economics Connection

R Reading Strategies

Activating Prior Knowledge
Remind students that Harrison won the electoral vote, but not the popular vote. **Ask:** Why was Harrison ruled the winner of the 1888 election if he did not receive the majority of the popular vote? *(The electoral vote, not the popular vote, decides the presidency.)* **OL**

C Critical Thinking

Explaining Ask: Why were trusts powerful? *(Trusts consolidated similar businesses, giving them monopolies; without competition, they could set prices as high as they wished.)* **OL**

Reading Check

Answer: created the Interstate Commerce Commission and passed the Sherman Antitrust Act

Hands-on Chapter Project
Step 3

Researching Immigration and Political Ads

Step 3: Comparing Immigration in 19th and 20th Centuries Essential Question: Has immigration differed in basic ways in the past nearly 200 years?

Directions Students can compare their work from Steps 1 and 2 and formulate questions that will focus on what may differ. For example: Are the numbers vastly different? Have the reasons for migration

Republicans Regain Power

R The Republicans and their presidential candidate, Benjamin Harrison, received large campaign contributions in 1888 from industrialists who benefited from high tariffs. Cleveland and the Democrats campaigned against high tariff rates. In one of the closest races in American history, Harrison lost the popular vote but won the electoral vote.

The McKinley Tariff The election of 1888 gave the Republicans control of both houses of Congress as well as the White House. Using this power, the party passed legislation to address points of national concern. In 1890 Representative William McKinley of Ohio pushed through a tariff bill that cut tobacco taxes and tariff rates on raw sugar but greatly increased rates on other goods, such as textiles, to discourage people from buying those imports.

The McKinley Tariff was intended to protect American industry from foreign competition and encourage consumers to buy American goods. Instead, it helped to trigger a steep rise in the prices of all goods, which angered many Americans and may have contributed to President Harrison's defeat in the 1892 election.

The Sherman Antitrust Act Congress also responded to popular pressure to do something about the power of the large business combinations known as trusts. In 1890 Congress passed the Sherman Antitrust Act, which prohibited any "combination . . . or conspiracy, in restraint of trade or commerce among the several States." The law, however, was vaguely worded, poorly enforced, and C weakened by judicial interpretation. Most significantly, the Supreme Court ruled the law did not apply to manufacturing, holding that manufacturing was not interstate commerce. Thus the law had little impact. In the 1890s businesses formed trusts and combinations at a great rate. Like the ICC, the Sherman Antitrust Act was more important for establishing a precedent than for its immediate impact.

Reading Check **Summarizing** What actions did Congress take to regulate big business?

The Rebirth of Reform

MAIN Idea Reformers developed new methods and philosophies for helping the urban poor.

HISTORY AND YOU Have you ever been to a YMCA? What activities can you do there? Read on to find out the origin of the YMCA and other community centers.

The tremendous changes that industrialism and urbanization brought triggered a debate over how best to address society's problems. While many Americans embraced the ideas of individualism and Social Darwinism, others disagreed, arguing that society's problems could be fixed only if Americans and their government began to take a more active role in regulating the economy and helping those in need.

Debates IN HISTORY

Is Social Darwinism the Best Approach for Ensuring Progress and Economic Growth?

The social problems that came with industrialization led to a debate over government's role in the economy. Some believed that government should intervene to help the poor and solve problems while others argued that leaving things alone was the best solution.

changed? Students may find that their earlier research is helpful here, even if it was not reflected on the poster. Encourage students to consider the political and social conditions in both the home countries and in the United States in, say 1860 compared to 2000.

Putting It Together Students may want to create a bulleted list or another poster to illustrate their comparative findings with charts, tables, or other visuals. **OL**
(Chapter Project continued on page 244)

Challenging Social Darwinism

In 1879 journalist Henry George published *Progress and Poverty*, a discussion of the American economy that quickly became a national bestseller. In his book George observed, "The present century has been marked by a prodigious increase in wealth-producing power." This should, he asserted, have made poverty "a thing of the past." Instead, he claimed, the "gulf between the employed and the employer is growing wider; social contrasts are becoming sharper." In other words, laissez-faire economics was making society worse—the opposite of what Social Darwinists believed.

Most economists now argue that George's analysis was flawed. Industrialism did make some Americans very wealthy, but it also improved the standard of living for most others as well. At the time, however, in the midst of poverty, crime, and harsh working conditions, many Americans did not believe things were improving. George's economic theories encouraged other reformers to challenge the assumptions of the era.

Lester Frank Ward In 1883 Lester Frank Ward published *Dynamic Sociology,* in which he argued that humans were different from animals because they had the ability to make plans to produce the future outcomes they desired.

Ward's ideas came to be known as Reform Darwinism. People, he insisted, had succeeded in the world because of their ability to cooperate; competition was wasteful and time-consuming. Government, he argued, could regulate the economy, cure poverty, and promote education more efficiently than competition in the marketplace could.

R Reading Strategies

Paraphrasing Ask: In your own words, what was the main idea of Ward's *Dynamic Sociology*? *(Government is better able to fix social and economic problems because it represents a cooperative effort on the part of everyone.)* **AL**

Debates IN HISTORY

YES

William Graham Sumner
Professor

PRIMARY SOURCE

"The moment that government provided work for one, it would have to provide work for all, and there would be no end whatever possible. Society does not owe any man a living. In all the cases that I have ever known of young men who claimed that society owed them a living, it has turned out that society paid them—in the State prison ... The fact that a man is here is no demand upon other people that they shall keep him alive and sustain him. He has got to fight the battle with nature as every other man has; and if he fights it with the same energy and enterprise and skill and industry as any other man, I cannot imagine his failing—that is, misfortune apart."

—testimony before the U.S. House of Representatives, 1879

NO

Lester Frank Ward
Sociologist

PRIMARY SOURCE

"The actions of men are a reflex of their mental characteristics. Where these differ so widely the acts of their possessors will correspondingly differ. Instead of all doing the same thing they will do a thousand different things. The natural and necessary effect of this is to give breadth to human activity. Every subject will be looked at from all conceivable points of view, and no aspect will be overlooked or neglected. It is due to this multiplicity of viewpoints, growing out of natural inequalities in the minds of men, that civilization and culture have moved forward along so many lines and swept the whole field of possible achievement."

—from "Social Classes in the Light of Modern Sociological Theory," 1908

Answers:
1. There would be no end to government assistance; society does not owe people a living.
2. Because people look at things differently, civilization and culture will advance.
3. the need for personal struggle vs. the creation of a society in which each person can develop his or her own talents
4. Answers should contain supporting evidence.

DBQ Document-Based Questions

1. **Summarizing** What argument does Professor Sumner make against government assisting people?
2. **Paraphrasing** How does Professor Ward believe that different abilities aid society?
3. **Contrasting** How can you contrast the ideas of the two men?
4. **Evaluating** Which opinion do you agree with? Write a brief essay explaining your ideas.

Additional Support

Activity: Interdisciplinary Connection

Civics A supporter of *laissez-faire*, William Graham Sumner objected to government regulation of the economy, social legislation, and trade unions. When asked by a congressman whether government could hire workers who had lost their jobs to mechanization, Sumner said the worker must make the best of the situation and rely on his own resourcefulness. In contrast, Ward felt that a kind government could meet the needs of its citizens. He believed in equality for all, regardless of class, race, or gender. Universal education, Ward thought, was the key to establishing full equality. **Ask: In what way are both men's ideas similar?** *(Both believed people are capable of examining a situation and taking action.)* **OL**

People IN HISTORY

People IN HISTORY

Jane Addams
1860–1935

After visiting a settlement house in London, England, Jane Addams decided to open Hull House in 1889 to assist poor immigrants in Chicago.

That assistance took on many forms: day care, kindergartens, libraries, an art gallery, an employment agency, and a meeting place for trade unions. The women who worked at Hull House, many of them college-educated in social work, pushed for protective legislation for children and women, which was enacted first in Illinois and then nationally.

Addams wrote books about her experiences at Hull House, giving an example to many others throughout the nation who also founded settlement houses. She favored woman suffrage and supported the founding of the American Civil Liberties Union and the National Association for the Advancement of Colored People. She was active in the peace movement, serving as first president of the organization that became the Women's International League for Peace and Freedom. For her efforts, she was awarded the Nobel Peace Prize in 1931.

What kind of assistance did Hull House provide immigrants?

▲ *Children stand in front of Hull House in 1905.*

Looking Backward Writer Edward Bellamy promoted another alternative to Social Darwinism and laissez-faire economics. In 1888 he published *Looking Backward,* a novel about a man who falls asleep in 1887 and awakens in the year 2000 to find that the nation **R** has become a perfect society with no crime, poverty, or politics. In this fictional society, the government owns all industry and shares the wealth equally with all Americans. Bellamy's ideas were essentially a form of socialism. His book became a bestseller and helped to shape the thinking of some American reformers.

Naturalism in Literature Criticism of industrial society also appeared in literature in a new style of writing known as naturalism. Social Darwinists argued that people could make choices to improve their situation. Naturalists challenged this idea by suggesting **W** that some people failed in life simply because they were caught up in circumstances they could not control. Sometimes people's lives were destroyed through no fault of their own.

Among the most prominent naturalist writers were Stephen Crane, Jack London, and Theodore Dreiser. Stephen Crane's novel

Maggie, A Girl of the Streets (1893), told the story of a girl's descent into prostitution and death. Jack London's tales of the Alaskan wilderness demonstrated the power of nature over civilization. Theodore Dreiser's novels, such as *Sister Carrie* (1900), painted a world where people sinned without punishment and where the pursuit of wealth and power often destroyed their character.

Helping the Urban Poor

The plight of the urban poor prompted some reformers to find new ways to help. Their efforts gave rise to the Social Gospel movement, the Salvation Army, the YMCA, and settlement houses.

The Social Gospel The **Social Gospel** movement worked to better conditions in cities according to the biblical ideals of charity and justice. Washington Gladden, a minister, was an early advocate who popularized the movement in writings such as *Applied Christianity* (1887). Walter Rauschenbusch, a Baptist minister from New York, became the leading voice in the Social Gospel movement.

Activity: Interdisciplinary Connection

Sociology The eighth of nine children in a prosperous family, Jane Addams was valedictorian of her college graduating class. Although she attempted to study medicine, poor health forced her to stop. Upon recovery, Addams toured Europe with her friend Ellen G. Starr. There they visited Toynbee Hall, a settlement house in London's East End. Convinced they could open a similar place in the United States, Addams and Starr leased a large house in Chicago, made speeches to raise money, convinced young women of wealthy families to volunteer their time and services, took care of children, nursed the sick, and listened to the troubles of people who came for help. By its second year, Hull House saw over 2,000 people every week. **Ask:** Would Jane Addams have been as successful today? *(Answers will vary but should be supported with sound reasoning.)* **OL**

The Church, he argued, must "demand protection for the moral safety of the people." The Social Gospel movement inspired many churches to take on new community functions. Some churches built gyms and provided social programs and child care. Others focused exclusively on helping the poor.

The Salvation Army and the YMCA The Salvation Army and the YMCA also combined faith and an interest in reform. The Salvation Army offered practical aid and religious counseling to the urban poor. The Young Men's Christian Association (YMCA) tried to help industrial workers and the urban poor by organizing Bible studies, citizenship training, and group activities. YMCAs, or "Ys," offered libraries, gymnasiums, auditoriums, and low-cost hotel rooms available on a temporary basis to those in need.

The head of the Chicago YMCA, Dwight L. Moody, was a gifted preacher who founded his own church, today known as Moody Memorial Church. By 1867, Moody had begun to organize revival meetings in other American cities, which drew thousands of people. Moody rejected both the Social Gospel and Social Darwinism. He believed the way to help the poor was not by providing them with services but by redeeming their souls and reforming their character.

The Settlement House Movement The **settlement house** movement began as an offshoot of the Social Gospel movement. In the late 1800s idealistic reformers—including many college-educated women—established settlement houses in poor, often heavily immigrant neighborhoods. A settlement house was a community center where reformers resided and offered everything from medical care and English classes to kindergartens and recreational programs. **Jane Addams** opened the famous Hull House in Chicago in 1889. Her work inspired others, including Lillian Wald, who founded the Henry Street Settlement in New York City.

Public Education As the United States became increasingly industrialized and urbanized, it needed more workers who were trained and educated. The number of public schools increased dramatically after the Civil War. The number of children attending school rose from 6,500,000 in 1870 to 17,300,000 in 1900. Public schools were often crucial to the success of immigrant children. At public schools, immigrant children were taught English and learned about American history and culture, a process known as **Americanization.**

Schools also tried to instill discipline and a strong work ethic. Grammar schools divided students into grades and drilled them in punctuality, neatness, and efficiency—necessary habits for the workplace. At the same time, vocational education in high schools taught skills required in specific trades.

Not everyone had access to school. Cities were far ahead of rural areas. Many African Americans also did not have equal educational opportunities. Some African Americans started their own schools, following the example of Booker T. Washington, who founded the Tuskegee Institute in 1881.

✔ **Reading Check** **Explaining** What was the purpose of a settlement house?

Section 3 REVIEW

Vocabulary
1. **Explain** the significance of Gilded Age, individualism, Social Darwinism, Gospel of Wealth, philanthropy, Mark Twain, Social Gospel, settlement house, Jane Addams, Americanization.

Main Ideas
2. **Defining** What were the defining characteristics of the Gilded Age?

3. **Describing** How did changes in art and literature reflect the issues and characteristics of the late 1800s?

4. **Explaining** Why was the Sherman Antitrust Act ineffective?

5. **Categorizing** Complete a chart like the one below by listing the names and goals of reform movements that arose in the late 1800s to help the urban poor.

Reform Movement	Goals

Critical Thinking
6. **Big Ideas** Do you think the idea of the Gospel of Wealth is still alive today? Why or why not?

7. **Analyzing Visuals** Look at the cartoon on the right on page 235. What do the figures in the background suggest?

Writing About History
8. **Descriptive Writing** Imagine that you are a newspaper editor in the late 1800s. Write an editorial in which you support or oppose the philosophy of Social Darwinism.

History **ONLINE**
Study Central™ To review this section, go to glencoe.com and click on Study Central.

239

✔ **Reading Check**

Answer: a community center where reformers offered medical care, English classes, kindergartens, and recreational programs

Assess

History **ONLINE**

Study Central™ provides summaries, interactive games, and online graphic organizers to help students review content.

Close

Determining Importance
Ask: Why were reformers important in the Gilded Age? *(They exposed and worked to cure social ills, such as poverty and illiteracy which were otherwise ignored by a society experiencing newly increasing wealth.)*

Section 3 REVIEW

Answers

1. Significant terms are boldfaced and highlighted throughout the section.
2. individualism; urbanization; new values, art, and forms of entertainment
3. Art and literature became more realistic as artists and writers depicted the changing values of industrializing America.
4. The enforcing courts judged the legislation too vague and refused to rule against big companies.

5.
Reform Movement	Goals
Social Gospel	better conditions in cities according to biblical ideals of charity and justice
Revivalism	help the poor by redeeming their souls
Settlement house	improve living conditions of the poor

6. Answers will vary but should be backed up by examples of and/or statistics on philanthropy of wealthy individuals.
7. disgruntled, out-of-work Americans whose factory is no longer producing, while the British factory continues to operate
8. Editorials will vary but should accurately express the philosophy of Social Darwinism.

Focus

Ask: Why is the author appalled at the number of children? *(Answers may vary but may include the idea that tenements were unsafe for children.)* What is the irony in the water and beer reference? *(While the second floor of the tenement has no running water, immigrants spend their money on beer.)*

Teach

C Critical Thinking

Assessing Ask: The author says the immigrant is *sullen*, or resentful. Does the immigrant have any choices? *(Answers will vary but could reflect that the immigrant does not have to buy beer.)* **OL**

S Skill Practice

Calculating Ask: What percentage of monthly income is spent on charitable donations? *(just under 2%)* **AL**

Additional Support

BROWN BROTHERS

Eyewitness

In his exposé of urban poverty, How the Other Half Lives *(1890),* **JACOB RIIS** *documented the living conditions in New York City tenements:*

C "The statement once made a sensation that between seventy and eighty children had been found in one tenement. It no longer excites even passing attention, when the sanitary police report counting 101 adults and 91 children in a Crosby Street house, one of twins, built together. The children in the others, if I am not mistaken, numbered 89, a total of 180 for two tenements! Or when midnight inspection in Mulberry Street unearths a hundred and fifty "lodgers" sleeping on filthy floors in two buildings. In spite of brown-stone fittings, plate-glass and mosaic vestibule floors, the water does not rise in summer to the second story, while the beer flows unchecked to the all-night picnics on the roof. The saloon with the side-door and the landlord divide the prosperity of the place between them, and the tenant, in sullen submission, foots the bill."

VERBATIM

❝Tell 'em quick, and tell 'em often.❞

WILLIAM WRIGLEY,
*soap salesman and promoter of chewing gum,
on his marketing philosophy*

❝A pushing, energetic, ingenious person, always awake and trying to get ahead of his neighbors.❞

HENRY ADAMS,
historian, describing the average New Yorker or Chicagoan

❝We cannot all live in cities, yet nearly all seem determined to do so.❞
HORACE GREELEY,
newspaper editor

INDICATORS:
Livin' in the City

Moving off the farm for a factory job? Sharpen your pencil. You'll need to budget carefully to buy all you will need.

Here are the numbers for a Georgia family of four in 1890. The husband is a textile worker, and the wife works at home. There is one child, age 4, and a boarder. They share a two-room, wood-heated, oil-lighted apartment.

INCOME: (annual)

husband's income	$312.00
boarder's rent	10.00
TOTAL INCOME	**$322.00**

EXPENSES: (annual)

medical	$65.00
furniture	46.90
clothing	46.00
rent	21.00
flour/meal	25.00
hog products	17.00
other meat	13.00
vegetables	13.00
lard	6.50
S potatoes	6.40
butter	5.00
sugar	4.00
charitable donations	6.10
vacation	3.25
alcohol	3.25
tobacco	3.00
molasses	2.00
other food	27.80
miscellaneous	68.20
TOTAL EXPENSES	**$382.40**

Extending the Content

The Woman Suffrage Movement Years before Susan B. Anthony began her suffrage work, President John Adams' wife, Abigail, reminded him to "remember the ladies" as he and others met to write the Declaration of Independence in 1776. Sarah Grimké lent her speaking talent to the cause of both women's suffrage and abolition. In 1848, the first women's rights convention was held in Seneca Falls, New York. Another dynamic speaker, former slave Sojourner Truth delivered her famous "Ain't I a Woman" speech at a similar convention in Ohio in 1851. Anthony became more vocal as she and Elizabeth Cady Stanton formed the American Equal Rights Association with both male and female membership. At the same time Anthony was jailed in New York, Sojourner Truth was denied a ballot at a polling booth in Michigan. It wasn't until 1912 that the first political party—Teddy Roosevelt's Bullmoose Party—supported women's suffrage. Although World War I slowed down suffrage efforts, the 19th Amendment was finally ratified in 1920, marking almost 150 years of effort.

Milestones

ON THE RUN, 1881. THE JESSE JAMES GANG, after robbing a Chicago, Rock Island, and Pacific train near Winston, Missouri, and killing the conductor and a passenger.

OVERTURNED, 1878. BY THE SUPREME COURT, a Louisiana court decision that awarded damages to an African American woman who had been refused admission to a steamship stateroom reserved for whites.

PLAGUED BY GRASSHOPPERS, 1874. THE AMERICAN GREAT PLAINS. Insect swarms a mile wide blot out the midday sun. Two inches deep on the ground, they leave "nothing but the mortgage," as one farmer put it.

CELEBRATED IN EUROPE, 1887. ANNIE OAKLEY, star of Buffalo Bill's Wild West Show. Oakley shot a cigarette from the lips of Crown Prince Wilhelm of Germany. Years later, when the U.S. goes to war against Kaiser Wilhelm, Oakley will quip: "I wish I'd missed that day!"

Jesse James

REMOVED, 1884. IDA B. WELLS, journalist and former slave, from a ladies coach on a train. Wells refused to move to the smoking car where African Americans were to be seated.

ARRESTED, 1872. SUSAN B. ANTHONY, for casting a ballot in Rochester, New York. Anthony argued that the Fourteenth and Fifteenth Amendments applied to women.

Susan B. Anthony

NUMBERS

1 in 12 Americans living in cities of 100,000 or more in 1865

A crowded New York City street

1 in 5 Americans living in cities in 1896

522 Inhabitants in a one-acre area in the Bowery, New York City

$2 Daily wage for a farm laborer, New York, 1869

$4 Daily wage for a plumber, New York City, 1869

50¢ Price of a pair of boy's knee pants, a parasol, button boots, or a necktie (1870s)

$8 Price of a "Fine All-Wool Suit," 1875

25¢ Admission to "Barnum's American Museum" (featuring the smallest pair of human beings ever seen!), 1896

CRITICAL THINKING

1. Analyzing Visuals Look at the Jacob Riis photo of an urban family and the photo of a New York City street. What do the pictures tell you about urban life in the 1890s?

2. Comparing What character traits do you think Ida B. Wells and Susan B. Anthony may have shared?

R Reading Strategies

Identifying Ask: Whose civil rights did Wells and Anthony work to establish? *(The rights of African Americans and women)*
ELL

C Critical Thinking

Inferring Ask: Why do you think plumbers were paid twice as much as farm laborers in 1889? *(With the rapid growth of cities, plumbers were in demand. There was no shortage of farm laborers.)* **OL**

Assess/Close

Have students explain the connection between Greeley's comment and the tenement conditions described by Riis.

Critical Thinking Answers:

1. Urban life was crowded and filled with poverty.
2. determination, courage, a sense of justice.

Visit the TIME Web site at www.time.com for up-to-date news, weekly magazine articles, editorials, online polls, and an archive of past magazine and Web articles.

Additional Support

Activity: Collaborative Activity

Congressional Debate Ask: Why is it important that all Americans have the right to vote? *(Answers will vary but may include the ideas that all citizens should have a voice in their government, that universal suffrage lends varied perspectives and a balanced approach to decision-making, and that crucial legislation affecting women and minority groups may not have passed without universal suffrage.)* Tell students they are members of the House of Representatives and are considering a bill that would require women, as well as men, to register for the draft. Have students form groups of four or five by gender (all male, all female) and list the merits or disadvantages of the bill. Ask groups to share their lists while you note their points on the board. Place a star by comments proffered by females. Ask students to volunteer how perspectives might differ because of gender. As a class, vote on the bill. **OL**

1 Focus

Bellringer

Daily Focus Transparency 6.4

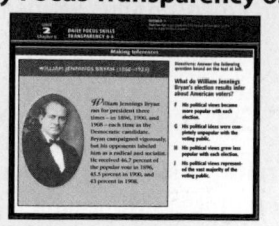

Guide to Reading

Answers to Graphic:

Populism
I. Unrest in Rural America
   A. The Money Supply
   B. The Grange Takes Action
   C. The Farmers' Alliance
II. The Rise of Populism
   A. The Subtreasury Plan
   B. A Populist Runs for President
III. The Election of 1896
   A. Bryan's Campaign
   B. The Front Porch Campaign

Section Spotlight Video

To generate student interest and provide a springboard for class discussion, access the Chapter 6, Section 4 video at glencoe.com or on the video DVD.

Resource Manager

Populism

Guide to Reading

Big Ideas
Economics and Society The Populist movement and its presidential candidate William Jennings Bryan strongly supported silver as the basis for currency.

Content Vocabulary
- populism *(p. 242)*
- greenbacks *(p. 242)*
- inflation *(p. 242)*
- deflation *(p. 242)*
- cooperatives *(p. 243)*
- graduated income tax *(p. 245)*

Academic Vocabulary
- bond *(p. 242)*
- currency *(p. 243)*
- strategy *(p. 244)*

People and Events to Identify
- Farmers' Alliance *(p. 244)*
- People's Party *(p. 245)*
- William Jennings Bryan *(p. 246)*
- William McKinley *(p. 247)*

Reading Strategy
Taking Notes As you read about the emergence of populism in the 1890s, use the major headings of the section to create an outline similar to the one below.

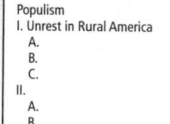

Populism
I. Unrest in Rural America
   A.
   B.
   C.
II.
   A.
   B.

After the Civil War, falling crop prices and deflation made it hard for farmers to make a living. Farmers tried to overcome these problems by forming organizations such as the Grange and the Farmers' Alliance. In the 1890s, many farmers joined the Populist Party.

Unrest in Rural America

MAIN Idea Deflation, low crop prices, and tariffs hurt farmers economically.

HISTORY AND YOU What can you buy for a dollar today? Read on to learn how the value of a dollar has changed over time.

Populism was a movement to increase farmers' political power and to work for legislation in their interest. Farmers joined the Populist movement because they were in the midst of an economic crisis. New technology enabled farmers to produce more crops, but the greater supply had caused prices to fall. High tariffs also made it hard for farmers to sell their goods overseas. Farmers also felt they were victimized by large and faraway entities: the banks from which they obtained loans and the railroads that set their shipping rates.

The Money Supply

Some farmers thought adjusting the money supply would solve their economic problems. During the Civil War, the federal government had expanded the money supply by issuing millions of dollars in **greenbacks**—paper currency that could not be exchanged for gold or silver coins. This increase in the money supply without an increase in goods for sale caused **inflation,** or a decline in the value of money. As the paper money lost value, the prices of goods soared.

After the Civil War ended, the United States had three types of currency in circulation—greenbacks, gold and silver coins, and national bank notes backed by government **bonds.** To get inflation under control, the federal government stopped printing greenbacks and began paying off its bonds. In 1873 Congress also decided to stop making silver into coins. These decisions meant that the money supply was not large enough for the country's growing economy. In 1865, for example, there was about $30 in circulation for each person. By 1895, there was only about $23. As the economy expanded, **deflation**—or an increase in the value of money and a decrease in prices—began. As money increased in value, prices fell.

Deflation hit farmers especially hard. Most farmers had to borrow money for seed and other supplies to plant their crops. Because

---

R Reading Strategies	**C** Critical Thinking	**D** Differentiated Instruction	**W** Writing Support	**S** Skill Practice
Teacher Edition • Using Word Parts, p. 243 • Using Context Clues, p. 244 • Sequencing Info, p. 246 **Additional Resources** • Guided Reading Act., URB p. 117 • Primary Source Reading, URB p. 103	**Teacher Edition** • Det. Cause/Effect, p. 244 • Explaining, p. 245 **Additional Resources** • Supreme Court Case Stud., URB p. 15 • Quizzes and Tests, p. 76	**Teacher Edition** • Logical/Math., p. 245		**Teacher Edition** • Reading Graphs, p. 243 • Analyzing Maps, p. 246 **Additional Resources** • RENTG, URB p. 64

PRIMARY SOURCE
Why Were Farmers Having Problems?

New technology, such as this McCormick grain binder, allowed more land to be farmed, but more food on the market drove down prices and profits.

Farm Prices, 1870–1900

Source: *Historical Statistics of the United States.*

Farmers had to buy seed and supplies and pay railroads to ship their harvest. They also had to pay their mortgage. As food prices fell and interest rates stayed high, farmers were caught in the middle.

Analyzing VISUALS

1. **Analyzing** Which crop declined in price the most by 1900? Which region would be most affected by this decline?

2. **Explaining** How did technology contribute to the decline in farm prices?

---

money was in short supply, interest rates began to rise, which increased the amount farmers owed. Rising interest rates also made mortgages more expensive, but falling prices meant the farmers sold their crops for less, and they still had to make the same mortgage payments to the banks.

Realizing that their problems were partly caused by a shortage of **currency,** many farmers concluded that Eastern bankers had pressured Congress into reducing the money supply. Some farmers called for the printing of more greenbacks. Others, particularly those in the West where new silver mines had been found, wanted the government to mint silver coins. They referred to the decision to stop minting silver as "The Crime of '73."

The Grange Takes Action

In 1866 the Department of Agriculture sent Oliver H. Kelley to tour the rural South and report on the condition of the region's farmers. Realizing how isolated farmers were from each other, Kelley founded the first national farm organization, the Patrons of Husbandry, better known as the Grange, in 1867.

At first Grangers met largely for social and educational purposes. Then, in 1873, the nation plunged into a severe recession, and farm income fell sharply. Farmers looking for help joined the Grange in large numbers. By 1874, the Grange had between 800,000 and 1.5 million members.

Grangers responded to the crisis by pressuring state legislatures to regulate railroad and warehouse rates. They also tried to create **cooperatives**—marketing organizations that try to increase prices and lower costs for their members.

One of the reasons farmers could not charge higher prices for their crops was that there were so many farmers in competition. If a farmer raised prices, a buyer could always go elsewhere and pay less. Cooperatives pooled farmers' crops and held them off the market in order to force up prices. Because a cooperative controlled a large quantity of farm products, it could also negotiate better shipping rates with the railroads.

Chapter 6 Urban America **243**

Teach

S Skill Practice

Reading Graphs Ask: Which crop price was least affected by technology? *(wheat)* **ELL**

R Reading Strategies

Using Word Parts Ask: How does the base word in *cooperatives* explain how these organizations work? *(Members cooperate to improve the profits for all.)* **BL**

Analyzing VISUALS

Answers:
1. wheat; Great Plains
2. Technology enhanced production. Overproduction created surpluses, which lowered prices.

Differentiated Instruction

Primary Source Reading, URB pp. 103–104

The Farmers' Plight

Objective: Interpret a primary source to determine the concerns of farmers in the late 1800s.

Focus: Students should underline or circle all of the causes of suffering by the farmers.

Teach: Summarize the farmers' plight in one sentence.

Assess: Create a Problem-Solution chart (graphic organizer) by listing the problems and the proposed solutions.

Close: Draft a (legislative) bill that would address the farmers' concerns raised in this excerpt.

Differentiated Instruction Strategies

BL Characterize this excerpt. Is it a positive or negative message? Why do you think so?

AL Compare the plight of the farmers of the late 1800s with the plight of farmers today. Do any similarities exist?

ELL Two words are defined in the Reader's Dictionary. Add at least three other words to this list and definitions.

243

Analyzing VISUALS

Answers:
1. Farmers suffer while railroads prosper.
2. big business and Congress

✔ Reading Check

Answer:
by forming large cooperatives to
force prices up and to make low-
interest loans to farmers

None of the **strategies** the Grangers
employed improved farmers' economic conditions. Several Western states passed "Granger
laws" that set maximum rates and prohibited
railroads from charging more for short hauls
than for long ones. The railroads fought back
by cutting services and refusing to lay new
track. Then, in 1886, the Supreme Court ruled
in *Wabash* v. *Illinois* that states could not regulate railroads or any commerce that crossed
state lines.

The Grange's cooperatives also failed, partly
because they were too small to have any effect
on prices, and partly because Eastern businesses and railroads considered them to be
similar to unions—illegitimate conspiracies
that restricted trade—so they refused to do
business with them. By the late 1870s, farmers
began to leave the Grange for organizations
they hoped would address their problems.

The Farmers' Alliance

As the Grange began to fall apart, a new
organization, known as the **Farmers' Alliance,**
began to form. By 1890, the Alliance had
between 1.5 and 3 million members, with
strong support in the South and on the Great
Plains, particularly in Kansas, Nebraska, North
Dakota, and South Dakota.

When Charles W. Macune became the leader
of the Alliance, he announced a plan to organize
very large cooperatives, which he called
exchanges. Macune hoped these exchanges
would be big enough to force farm prices up and
to make loans to farmers at low interest rates.
The exchanges had some success. The Texas
Exchange successfully marketed cotton at prices
slightly higher than those paid to individual
farmers, while the Illinois Exchange negotiated
slightly better railroad rates for wheat farmers.

Ultimately, the large cooperatives failed.
Many overextended themselves by lending too
much money at low interest rates that was
never repaid. In many cases, wholesalers, railroads, and bankers discriminated against them,
making it difficult for them to stay in business.
They also failed because they were still too
small to affect world prices for farm products.

✔ **Reading Check** **Explaining** How did the Farmers'
Alliance try to help farmers?

POLITICAL CARTOONS PRIMARY SOURCE
Who Is to Blame for Farmers' Problems?

▲ *A farmer wearing a Granger hat tries
to warn people about the railroad.*

▲ *A thin farmer is
an unwelcome guest
at the Congressional
kitchen, where
businessmen are
enjoying their meals.*

Analyzing VISUALS

1. **Analyzing** What is the cartoon on the left
implying about the railroad's relationship to
farmers?
2. **Explaining** Who does the cartoon on the
right blame for the problems facing farmers?

Hands-on Chapter Project
Step 4

Researching Immigration and Political Ads

**Step 4: Determining the Winning
Messages in the 1896 Election**
Essential question: What turned the tide
in the historic 1896 election?

Directions Explain to students that they
will use their imagination for this project,
pretending that McKinley and Bryan, the
Republican and Democratic candidates,
had access to television campaigning. Two

teams will be working, one for the Democrats and one for the Republicans. Their
product will be the scripts and ideas for
visuals for three short TV ads directed at different groups of voters.

Putting It Together Each team must
research the planks of their respective candidate and what part of the body politic
he needed to persuade. At the end of this
stage, they can meet to share their information and refine it. **OL**
(Chapter Project continued on page 252)

The Rise of Populism

MAIN Idea Farmers started the People's Party to fight for their interests and attracted many supporters when a depression hit in the 1890s.

HISTORY AND YOU Do you remember reading about the creation of the Republican Party in the 1850s? Read how another new party, the Populists, shook up politics in the 1890s.

By 1890 the Alliance's lack of success had started a debate in the organization. Some Alliance leaders, particularly in the western states, wanted to form a new party and push for political reforms. Members of the Kansas Alliance formed the **People's Party,** also known as the Populists, and nominated candidates to run for Congress and the state legislature. Alliances in Nebraska, South Dakota, and Minnesota quickly followed Kansas's example.

Most Southern leaders of the Alliance opposed the idea of a third party. They did not want to undermine the Democrats' control of the South. Instead, they suggested that the Alliance produce a list of demands and promise to vote for candidates who supported those demands. They hoped this would force Democrats to adopt the Alliance program.

The Subtreasury Plan

To get Southern Democrats to support the Alliance, Charles Macune introduced the subtreasury plan, which called for the government to set up warehouses called subtreasuries. Farmers would store their crops in the warehouses, and the government would provide low-interest loans to the farmers.

Macune believed the plan would enable farmers to hold their crops off the market in large enough quantities to force prices up. The Alliance also called for the free coinage of silver, an end to protective tariffs and national banks, tighter regulation of the railroads, and direct election of senators by voters.

Macune's strategy seemed to work at first. In 1890 the South elected four governors, all Democrats, who had pledged to support the Alliance program. Several Southern legislatures now had pro-Alliance majorities, and more than 40 Democrats who supported the Alliance program were elected to Congress.

A Populist Runs for President

Meanwhile, the new People's Party did equally well in the West. Populists took control of the Kansas and Nebraska legislatures. Populists also held the balance of power in Minnesota and South Dakota. Eight Populist representatives and two Populist senators were elected to the United States Congress.

At first, Southern members of the Alliance were excited over their success in electing so many pro-Alliance Democrats to Congress and to Southern state legislatures, but over the next two years, their excitement turned into frustration. Despite their promises, few Democrats followed through in their support of the Alliance program.

In May 1891 Western populists met with some labor and reform groups in Cincinnati. There, they endorsed the creation of a new national People's Party to run candidates for president. The following year, many Southern farmers had reached the point where they were willing to break with the Democratic Party and join the People's Party.

In July 1892 the People's Party held its first national convention in Omaha, Nebraska. James B. Weaver was nominated to run for president. The Omaha convention endorsed a platform that denounced the government's refusal to coin silver as a "vast conspiracy against mankind" and called for a return to unlimited coinage of silver at a ratio that gave 16 ounces of silver the same value as one ounce of gold. It also called for federal ownership of railroads and a **graduated income tax,** one that taxed higher earnings more heavily.

Populists also adopted proposals designed to appeal to organized labor. The Omaha platform also called for an eight-hour workday and immigration restrictions, but workers found it hard to identify with a party focused on rural problems and the coinage of silver. The Populists had close ties to the Knights of Labor, but that organization was in decline, and the fast-growing American Federation of Labor had steered clear of an alliance with them. As a result, most urban workers continued to vote for the Democrats, whose candidate, Grover Cleveland, won the election.

Reading Check **Summarizing** What was the main outcome of the Populist campaign in the elections of 1892?

D Differentiated Instruction

Logical/Mathematical
Ask: Why would keeping crops off the market drive prices up? *(People are willing to pay more for goods that are scarce.)* **BL**

C Critical Thinking

Explaining Ask: What impact did immigration restrictions have on labor unions? *(Fewer immigrants meant fewer workers willing to work for low wages which, in turn, boosted unions' bargaining power.)* **OL**

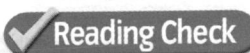

Answer:
The Populist candidate lost the election.

Additional Support

Activity: Economics Connection

Scarcity and Choice Ask: How do you determine what you are willing to pay for an item while you're shopping? *(Answers will vary but may include an evaluation of need or want, item availability, and price.)* Discuss each consideration and relate them to the situation in which crop farmers found themselves in the 1890s. Have students work in pairs to design an item they wish to "sell" to classmates. Allow student partners to decide quantity and price (ranging from $5 to $25). Reconvene the class, giving each student $25 in play money. Ask each student pair to auction their item after providing a verbal description of what they are selling. When the auction concludes, ask students why they purchased particular items. **Ask:** Which items appealed to you because supply was limited? **OL**

Focus

Bellringer
Daily Focus Transparency 6.5

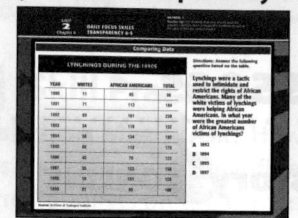

Guide to Reading

Answers to Graphic: poll tax, literacy test, grandfather clause, Jim Crow laws

Section Spotlight Video

To generate student interest and provide a springboard for class discussion, access the Chapter 6, Section 5 video at glencoe.com or on the video DVD.

Resource Manager

Section 5

The Rise of Segregation

Guide to Reading

Big Ideas
Individual Action Several prominent African Americans led the fight against racial discrimination.

Content Vocabulary
• poll tax *(p. 250)*
• segregation *(p. 250)*
• Jim Crow laws *(p. 250)*
• lynching *(p. 252)*

Academic Vocabulary
• discrimination *(p. 250)*

People and Events to Identify
• Ida B. Wells *(p. 252)*
• Booker T. Washington *(p. 253)*
• W. E. B. Du Bois *(p. 253)*

Reading Strategy
Organizing As you read, complete a web diagram listing ways that states disenfranchised African Americans and legalized discrimination.

Factors Contributing to Discrimination

After Reconstruction ended, Southern states began passing laws that eroded the rights of African Americans by introducing segregation and denying voting rights. African American leaders struggled to protect civil rights and improve quality of life but could not always agree on the most effective strategy.

Resistance and Repression

MAIN Idea Many African Americans fled the South, but some stayed and joined the Populist Party.

HISTORY AND YOU Do you remember reading about the rise of sharecropping after the Civil War? Read how African American farmers tried to work together in the late 1800s.

After Reconstruction, many African Americans in the rural South lived in conditions of grinding poverty. Most were sharecroppers, landless farmers who gave their landlords a large portion of their crops as rent, rather than paying cash. Sharecropping usually left farmers in chronic debt. Many eventually left farming and sought jobs in Southern towns or headed west to claim homesteads.

The Exodusters Head to Kansas

In the mid-1870s, Benjamin "Pap" Singleton, a former slave, became convinced that African Americans would never be given a chance to get ahead in the South. He began urging African Americans to move west, specifically to Kansas, and form their own independent communities where they could help each other get ahead. His ideas soon set in motion a mass migration. In the spring of 1879, African American communities in Louisiana, Mississippi, and Texas were swept with a religious enthusiasm for moving to Kansas—seeing it as a new promised land. In less than two months, approximately 6,000 African Americans left their homes in the rural South and headed to Kansas. The newspapers called it "an Exodus," like the Hebrews' escape from Egyptian bondage. The migrants themselves came to be known as "Exodusters."

One of the migrants to Kansas later explained why they went: "The whole South—every State in the South—had got into the hands of the very men that held us as slaves." The first Exodusters, many possessing little more than hope and the clothes on their backs, arrived in Kansas in the spring of 1879. A journalist named Henry King described the scene:

R Reading Strategies	**C** Critical Thinking	**D** Differentiated Instruction	**W** Writing Support	**S** Skill Practice
Teacher Edition • Activ. Prior Knowledge, pp. 249, 252 • Academic Vocab., p. 250 **Additional Resources** • Guided Reading Act., URB p. 118	**Teacher Edition** • Predict Consequences, p. 250 • Speculating, p. 252 **Additional Resources** • Critical Thinking Skills Act., URB p. 98 • Quizzes and Tests, p. 77	**Additional Resources** • Auth. Assess, p. 17 • Reteaching Act., URB p. 109	**Additional Resources** • Supreme Court Case Stud., p. 27	**Teacher Edition** • Reading Maps, p. 249 **Additional Resources** • Reading Skills Act., URB p. 87 • RENTG, p. 67

PRIMARY SOURCE
The Exodusters

NATIONAL GEOGRAPHIC — The Exodus to Kansas

Legend:
- State abandoned by Exodusters
- State where Exodusters settled
- Route of migration

▲ In 1879, soon after Reconstruction ended, an estimated 6,000–15,000 African Americans left the rural South and headed to Kansas where they hoped to build a better life for themselves.

Analyzing VISUALS

1. **Analyzing** According to the map, which states were departure points for the Exodusters?
2. **Making Connections** What earlier events in American history would have made the Exodusters think Kansas was a good place to settle?

PRIMARY SOURCE

"One morning in April, 1879, a Missouri steamboat arrived at Wyandotte, Kansas, and discharged a load of negro men, women and children, with . . . barrels, boxes, and bundles of household effects. . . . [T]heir garments were incredibly patched and tattered . . . and there was not probably a dollar in money in the pockets of the entire party. . . . They looked like persons coming out of a dream. And, indeed, such they were . . . . for this was the advance guard of the Exodus."

—quoted in *Eyewitness: The Negro in History*

Forming a Separate Alliance

While some African Americans fled the South, others joined with poor white farmers who had created the Farmers' Alliance. Alliance leaders urged African Americans to form a similar organization. In 1886 African American farmers established the Colored Farmers' National Alliance. By 1890, the organization had about 1.2 million members.

When the Populist Party formed in 1891, many African American farmers joined the new organization. This posed a major challenge to the Democratic Party in the South. If poor whites left the party and joined with African Americans in voting for the Populists, the coalition might be unbeatable.

To win back the poor white vote, Democratic leaders began appealing to racism, warning whites that support for Populism would return the South to "Black Republican" rule, similar to Reconstruction. In addition, election officials began using various methods to make it harder and harder for African Americans to vote. As one Democratic leader in the South told a reporter, "Some of our people, some editors especially, deny that [African Americans] are hindered from voting; but what is the good of lying? They are interfered with, and we are obliged to do it, and we may as well tell the truth."

✓ **Reading Check** **Examining** Who were the Exodusters, and why did they migrate to Kansas?

Chapter 6 Urban America **249**

Teach

S Skill Practice

Reading Maps Ask: Where did the Exodusters settle? *(Kansas)* **ELL**

R Reading Strategies

Summarizing Ask: What tactics did Democrats use to win the vote of poor whites in the South? *(appeals to racism; conjuring memories, fear, and anger associated with Reconstruction)* **OL**

Analyzing VISUALS

Answers:
1. North Carolina, Georgia, Louisiana, Texas, Florida
2. "Bleeding Kansas" was an antislavery battleground.

✓ Reading Check

Answers:
African Americans who migrated from the rural South to Kansas; to escape discrimination

Additional Support

Extending the Content

Exodusters Benjamin Singleton's association—the Edgefield Real Estate and Homestead Association in Tennessee—had scouted out land and had carefully planned the movement, but by 1879, the sheer number of African Americans heading to Kansas overwhelmed his efforts. In total, more than 20,000 African American migrants headed for Kansas between 1877 and 1879.

C Critical Thinking

Predicting Consequences

Ask: What results when a group of people are denied the vote? *(Answers will vary but may include that they are denied rights; have no one to represent them and their rights and interests.)* **OL**

R Reading Strategies

Academic Vocabulary Ask: What synonym can be used for *poll* in the term *poll tax*? *(voting)* **OL**

✔ Reading Check

Answers:

It upheld segregation and expressed a new legal doctrine endorsing "separate but equal" facilities for African Americans.

Additional Support

Imposing Segregation

MAIN Idea Southern states passed laws that imposed segregation and denied African American men their voting rights.

HISTORY AND YOU Can you think of a rule that is unfairly or unevenly enforced? Read about the tactics used to disfranchise African Americans.

After Reconstruction ended in 1877, the rights of African Americans were gradually undermined. Attempts to unify whites and African Americans politically and economically failed. Instead, a movement to diminish the civil rights of African Americans gained momentum as the century ended.

Taking Away the Vote

The Fifteenth Amendment prohibits states from denying citizens the right to vote on the basis of "race, color, or previous condition of servitude," but it does not bar states from denying the right to vote on other grounds. In the late 1800s, Southern states began imposing restrictions that, while not mentioning race, were designed to make it difficult or impossible for African Americans to vote.

In 1890 Mississippi began requiring all citizens registering to vote to pay a **poll tax** of $2, a sum beyond the means of most poor African Americans. Mississippi also instituted a literacy test, requiring voters to read and understand the state constitution. Few African Americans born after the Civil War had been able to attend school and those who had grown up under slavery were largely illiterate. Even those who knew how to read often failed the test because officials deliberately picked passages that few people could understand.

Other Southern states adopted similar restrictions. In Louisiana the number of African Americans registered to vote fell from about 130,000 in 1890 to around 5,300 in 1900. In Alabama the number fell from about 181,000 to about 3,700.

Election officials were far less strict in applying the poll tax and literacy requirements to whites, but the number of white voters also fell significantly. To let more whites vote, Louisiana introduced the "grandfather clause," which allowed any man to vote if he had an ancestor who could vote in 1867. This provision, which was adopted in several Southern states, exempted most whites from voting restrictions such as literacy tests.

Legalizing Segregation

African Americans in the North were often barred from public places, but **segregation,** or the separation of the races, was different in the South. Southern states passed laws that enforced **discrimination**. These laws became known as **Jim Crow laws.** The term probably refers to the song "Jump Jim Crow," which was popular in minstrel shows of the day.

Civil Rights Cases In 1883 the Supreme Court set the stage for legalized segregation when it overturned the Civil Rights Act of 1875. That law had prohibited keeping people out of public places on the basis of race and barred racial **discrimination** in selecting jurors. The 1883 Supreme Court decision, however, said that the Fourteenth Amendment provided only that "no state" could deny citizens equal protection under the law. Private organizations—such as hotels, theaters, and railroads—were free to practice segregation.

Encouraged by the Supreme Court's ruling and by the decline of congressional support for civil rights, Southern states passed a series of laws that established racial segregation in virtually all public places. Southern whites and African Americans could no longer ride together in the same railroad cars, eat in the same dining halls, or even drink from the same fountains.

Plessy* v. *Ferguson In 1892 an African American named Homer Plessy challenged a Louisiana law that forced him to ride in a separate railroad car from whites. He was arrested for riding in a "whites-only" car. In 1896 the Supreme Court, in *Plessy* v. *Ferguson*, upheld the Louisiana law and set out a new doctrine of "separate but equal" facilities for African Americans. The ruling established the legal basis for discrimination in the South for more than 50 years. While public facilities for African Americans in the South were always separate, they were far from equal. In many cases, they were inferior.

✔ **Reading Check** **Summarizing** How did the Supreme Court help to legalize segregation?

Activity: Collaborative Learning

Recognizing Bias Ask: What required tests do Americans take in order to gain the right to do something? *(Answers will vary but may include driver's tests, blood tests for marriage licenses, drug tests for employment, and so on.)* Remind students that literacy tests required of African Americans in the South were designed to ensure failure so African Americans could not vote. Have students form groups. Tell students for the purpose of this exercise that the school now requires students to pass a test in order to attend dances, athletic events, and other extracurricular activities. Have groups decide what qualifications students should meet in order to be allowed to attend these events. Ask them to use these qualifications to design a screening test. Ask groups to share their tests with the class. Discuss differences and similarities and the fairness of criteria and questions. **OL**

ANALYZING SUPREME COURT CASES

Do states have the right to segregate citizens by race?

★ *Plessy* v. *Ferguson*, 1896

Background to the Case

When Homer Adolph Plessy, a light-skinned man who was one-eighth African American, took a seat in the whites-only section of an East Louisiana Railway train and refused to move, he was arrested. Convicted of breaking a Louisiana law enacted in 1890, Plessy appealed his case to the Louisiana Supreme Court, then to federal Supreme Court. The incident was planned in advance to test the statute, using Plessy, who appeared to be white, to show the folly of the law. Although the words "separate but equal" do not appear in the court responses, the term came to describe a condition that persisted until 1954.

How the Court Ruled

The Court upheld the right of states to make laws that sustained segregation. The majority of justices wanted to distinguish between political rights guaranteed by the Fourteenth and Fifteenth Amendments and social rights.

PRIMARY SOURCE

The Court's Opinion

"The object of the [Fourteenth] amendment was undoubtedly to enforce the absolute equality of the two races before the law, but . . . it could not have been intended to abolish distinctions based upon color, or to enforce social, as distinguished from political equality, or a commingling of the two races upon terms unsatisfactory to either. Laws permitting, and even requiring, their separation in places where they are liable to be brought into contact do not necessarily imply the inferiority of either race to the other . . . We cannot say that a law which authorizes or even requires the separation of the two races in public conveyances is unreasonable."

—Justice Henry Billings Brown writing for the Court in
Plessy v. *Ferguson*

▲ *A conductor orders Homer Plessy to leave the white section of the railroad car.*

PRIMARY SOURCE

Other Views

"Our constitution is color-blind, and neither knows nor tolerates classes among citizens. In respect of civil rights, all citizens are equal before the law. . . . We boast of the freedom enjoyed by our people above all other peoples. But it is difficult to reconcile that boast with a state of law which, practically, puts the brand of servitude and degradation upon a large class of our fellow citizens—our equals before the law. The thin disguise of 'equal' accommodations for passengers in railroad coaches will not mislead any one, nor atone for the wrong this day done."

—Justice John Marshall Harlan writing the lone dissent in
Plessy v. *Ferguson*

DBQ Document-Based Questions

1. **Analyzing Primary Sources** What distinction does Justice Brown make about the rights of citizens?
2. **Identifying Points of View** How does Justice Harlan regard the Court's decision?
3. **Evaluating** What rights do you think all states should extend to their citizens? Why do you think so?

More About the Case

What arguments did Homer Plessy make to the courts?

- He said the Separate Car Act violated his civil rights under the 13th and 14th Amendments.
- He said that, since he was only one-eighth black and looked white, he should have a white man's rights.

The three lower courts upheld the Act, since equal accommodations were available. Although the Supreme Court agreed, it found the issue of Plessy's race important but not properly placed in this case.

DBQ Document Based Questions

Answers:
1. He distinguishes between civil/political and social rights.
2. He sees it as wrong and argues that the Constitution is color-blind.
3. Answers will vary but should support choices.

Differentiated Instruction

(Continued)

Analyzing a Supreme Court Case

Objective: Learn why "separate but equal" was ruled to be unconstitutional.

Focus: Identify the central issue of the case.

Teach: Discuss the Court's opinion.

Assess: Explain the importance of the case (segregation was outlawed).

Close: Write a paragraph summarizing the case.

Case Study 37: *Brown v. Board of Education of Topeka, KS*, p. 73

Differentiated Instruction Strategies

BL List two methods people use to fight discrimination.

AL Create a time line that shows the impact of the *Brown* decision.

ELL Explain the difference between the *Plessy* decision and the *Brown* decision.

252

R Reading Strategies

Activating Prior Knowledge
Ask: Which Bill of Rights amendment supports Wells' demand?
(Fifth) **OL**

C Critical Thinking

Speculating Ask: Why do you think Harrison was unwilling to publicly condemn lynching?
(Answers will vary but may include the idea that he would lose voter support in the South.) **BL**

People IN HISTORY

Answers:
Washington: He founded the Tuskegee Institute, and organized the Negro Business League.
Du Bois: He focused on legal and voting rights while Washington promoted economic gains.

Hands-on Chapter Project:
Step 5

Researching Immigration and Political Ads

Step 5: Comparing Campaigns
Essential Question: Are today's presidential campaigns less substantive and more sensationalized than nineteenth-century and early twentieth-century campaigns?

Directions Each team should review what they learned about the McKinley-Bryan campaign in Step 4, as well as previous campaigns they have studied. Then ask the

---

The African American Response

MAIN Idea Some African American leaders focused on practical vocational education, while others pushed for full civil rights and educational opportunities.

HISTORY AND YOU How would your life be different without an education? Read on to learn why some early civil rights leaders focused on access to education.

The African American community responded to violence and discrimination in several ways. Ida B. Wells used the press to end violence, while Mary Church Terrell worked in education. Booker T. Washington proposed that African Americans focus on achieving economic goals, rather than political goals. W. E. B. Du Bois argued African Americans should demand equal rights immediately.

Ida B. Wells

In the late 1800s, mob violence increased in the United States, particularly in the South. Between 1890 and 1899, there was an average of 187 **lynchings**—hangings without proper court proceedings—each year.

In 1892 **Ida B. Wells,** a fiery young African American woman from Tennessee, launched a fearless crusade against lynching. After a mob drove Wells out of town, she settled in Chicago and continued her campaign. In 1895 she published a book denouncing mob violence and demanding "a fair trial by law for those accused of crime, and punishment by law after honest conviction." Although Congress rejected an anti-lynching bill, the number of lynchings decreased significantly in the 1900s, due in great part to the efforts of activists such as Wells.

Mary Church Terrell

One lynching victim had been a close friend of Mary Church Terrell, a college-educated woman who'd been born during the Civil War. This death, and President Harrison's refusal to publicly condemn lynching, started Terrell on her lifelong battle against lynching, racism, and sexism.

Terrell also worked with woman suffrage workers such as Jane Addams and Susan B. Anthony. In addition to helping found the

People IN HISTORY

Booker T. Washington
1856–1915

Born into slavery on a plantation in Virginia, Booker T. Washington spent his childhood working in the coal mines of West Virginia. At age 16, he heard about the Hampton Institute in Virginia, where African Americans could learn farming or a trade. With little money in his pockets, Washington left home and walked nearly 500 miles to the school, where he was able to work as a janitor to pay for his education.

When the Alabama legislature decided in 1881 to begin a school to train black leaders, Washington was recommended for the job. He borrowed money to buy an abandoned plantation; the students built classrooms, a chapel, and dormitories. The Tuskegee Institute became well-known, attracting prominent scholars such as George Washington Carver to the faculty.

Washington used his influence with white businessmen to raise money for the school. He encouraged the development of black-owned businesses, and he organized the National Negro Business League in 1900. He was a nationally known spokesperson for the African American community and advised presidents William Howard Taft and Theodore Roosevelt on political appointments.
What were Booker T. Washington's most important achievements?

W.E.B. Du Bois
1868–1963

W. E. B. Du Bois was born in Massachusetts a few years after the end of the Civil War. After graduating from Fisk University, Du Bois earned a Ph.D. from Harvard. As a professor at Atlanta University, Du Bois focused his research on race relations in the United States.

The Souls of Black Folk, Du Bois's 1903 collection of essays, had a major impact on its readers. In them, Du Bois directly criticized Booker T. Washington for being too cautious and conservative on civil rights issues. Du Bois believed African Americans needed to insist upon equal treatment and voting rights. He also helped to found the Niagara Movement, the forerunner of the NAACP. In 1910 he began publishing *The Crisis,* the official magazine of the NAACP.

In his later years, Du Bois turned to socialism and became active in the peace movement. This led to political censure and the State Department's refusal to allow Du Bois to travel outside the country. When he was permitted to leave, he went to Ghana, where he became a citizen the year he died.
How did W. E. B. Du Bois's approach to civil rights differ from Washington's approach?

---

teams to conduct research on recent presidential elections and compare and contrast these aspects of the candidates' campaigns: the types of communication used, major issues stressed, voter segments they tried to reach, and campaign strategies that defeated the losing candidate or won the White House. **OL**

(Chapter Project continued on the Visual Summary page)

National Association of Colored Women and the National Association for the Advancement of Colored People, Terrell formed the Women Wage-Earners Association, which assisted African American nurses, waitresses, and domestic workers.

Terrell led a boycott against department stores in Washington, D.C., that refused to serve African Americans. In an address to the National American Women's Suffrage Association Terrell said, "With courage, born of success achieved in the past, with a keen sense of the responsibility which we shall continue to assume, we look forward to a future large with promise and hope. Seeking no favors because of our color, nor patronage because of our needs, we knock at the bar of justice, asking an equal chance."

Calls for Compromise

The most famous African American of the late nineteenth century was the influential educator **Booker T. Washington.** He proposed that African Americans concentrate on achieving economic goals rather than political ones. In 1895 Washington summed up his views in a speech before a mostly white audience in Atlanta. Known as the Atlanta Compromise, the speech urged African Americans to postpone the fight for civil rights and instead concentrate on preparing themselves educationally and vocationally for full equality:

PRIMARY SOURCE

"The wisest among my race understand that the agitation of questions of social equality is the extremest folly, and that the enjoyment of all the privileges that will come to us must be the result of severe and constant struggle rather than of artificial forcing. . . . It is important and right that all privileges of the law be ours, but it is vastly more important that we be prepared for the exercise of these privileges. The opportunity to earn a dollar in a factory just now is worth infinitely more than the opportunity to spend a dollar in an opera-house."

—adapted from *Up From Slavery*

Du Bois Rejects Compromise

The Atlanta Compromise speech provoked a strong challenge from **W. E. B. Du Bois,** the leader of a new generation of African American activists. In his 1903 book *The Souls of Black Folk,* Du Bois explained why he saw no advantage in giving up civil rights, even temporarily. He was particularly concerned with protecting and exercising voting rights. "Negroes must insist continually, in season and out of season," he wrote, "that voting is necessary to proper manhood, that color discrimination is barbarism." In the years that followed, many African Americans worked to win the vote and end discrimination. The struggle, however, would prove to be a long one.

✔ **Reading Check** **Describing** How did Ida B. Wells try to stop the practice of lynching?

Section 5 REVIEW

Vocabulary

1. **Explain** the significance of: poll tax, segregation, Jim Crow laws, lynching, Ida B. Wells, Booker T. Washington, W. E. B. Du Bois.

Main Ideas

2. **Describing** Under what kind of conditions did many African Americans in the South live in after Reconstruction?

3. **Identifying** How did Southern states restrict African American voting in the 1890s?

4. **Organizing** Use a graphic organizer similar to the one below to list the responses of some prominent African Americans to racial discrimination.

African American	Response to Discrimination
Ida B. Wells	
Booker T. Washington	
W.E.B. Du Bois	

Critical Thinking

5. **Big Ideas** How did Booker T. Washington's answer to racial discrimination differ from that of W. E. B. Du Bois?

6. **Analyzing Visuals** Look at the cartoon on page 251. How does the cartoonist play into white fears?

Writing About History

7. **Expository Writing** Imagine that you are living in the 1890s. Write a letter to the editor of the local newspaper explaining your view of the Supreme Court ruling in *Plessy v. Ferguson.*

History ONLINE
Study Central™ To review this section, go to glencoe.com and click on Study Central.

253

Answer:
She wrote newspaper articles and a book denouncing lynching.

Assess

History ONLINE

Study Central™ provides summaries, interactive games, and online graphic organizers to help students review content.

Close

Summarizing Ask: How did African Americans work to end violence and discrimination? *(They wrote news articles and books, formed associations such as the NAACP and NACW, and worked to educate others about the evils of prejudice.)* **OL**

Section 5 REVIEW

Answers

1. Sentences should use vocabulary words according to their definitions in the section and in the Glossary.

2. Conditions were little better than slavery because African Americans owned no property and gained little or no economic freedom as sharecroppers.

3. poll taxes, literacy tests, grandfather clause

4.

African American	Response to Discrimination
Ida B. Wells	wrote against lynching
Booker T. Washington	urged African Americans to prepare educationally and vocationally for equality
W.E.B. Du Bois	campaigned for civil and voting rights and helped found the Niagara Movement

5. Washington concentrated on achieving economic goals rather than legal and political ones. Du Bois was concerned with protecting legal and voting rights.

6. By portraying a prosperous African American sitting while a white woman stands, the cartoonist suggests that African Americans are usurping the social, economic, and political power of whites.

7. Letters will vary but should clearly state a position on the *Plessy v. Ferguson* ruling with logical supporting evidence.

Chapter 6 VISUAL SUMMARY

Assessing Ask: How might political machines have done more good than harm? *(Answers will vary but may include that, although machines manipulated voters for the selfish motives of party bosses and their associates, the practical help they gave new immigrants made it possible for immigrants to survive in their new homeland.)*

In what way are today's voters similar to those of the late nineteenth century? *(Answers will vary but may include that voters often choose candidates who promise programs and legislation that benefit their constituents.)* **OL**

Synthesizing Ask: Why were artistic realism and naturalism natural outcomes of the times? *(Answers will vary but could include the fact that the American experience was rapidly changing and that artists wanted to capture the reality of those changes. Writers and artists also wanted to depict the problems that arose with industrialization.)* **AL**

Hands-On Chapter Project

Step 6:

Researching Immigration and Political Ads

Step 6: Creating the Ads **Essential Question:** In a 60-90 second television time-slot, what will get a candidate's message across to a specific group?

Directions Students may have new ideas about campaign strategies after completing Step 5. In Step 6 they should review the

Effects of Industrialization:

1. Immigration and Urbanization

- Rise of large factories greatly increases the demand for labor in the United States, encouraging immigrants to move to America in large numbers.
- The increase in industrial jobs encourages large numbers of Americans and immigrants to settle in cities.
- As cities grow large, pollution, crime, disease, and fire become serious problems.
- New industrial technology allows cities to grow even larger with the development of the skyscraper, the elevator, and the trolley car.
- Large urban areas change the nature of politics creating corrupt urban political "machines" such as Tammany Hall in New York.

▲ A crowded immigrant community in New York in the early 1900s

Effects of Industrialization:

2. Farm Problems

- Industrialization and new technology increases farm production and creates the ability to ship farm products across the country.
- Farmers produce huge surpluses, driving down food prices, while a money shortage leads to high interest rates; farmers grow deeper in debt while income falls.
- High railroad rates in the West combine with high rents for tenant farmers in the South to create a crisis for farmers.
- Farmers form the Grange, the Alliance, and the Populist Party to help address their concerns.

▲ Sharecroppers in the South were often trapped in poverty and debt.

Effects of Industrialization:

3. Changes in Culture

- Industrial society initially leads to a strong belief in individualism; Social Darwinism emerges as the idea that government should not interfere in society.
- Ongoing social problems caused by industrialization lead to Reform Darwinism and the emergence of reformers who want to use government to help solve society's problems and regulate the economy.
- New forms of realist and naturalist art and literature depict industrial life in serious and realistic ways.

▲ Settlement houses, such as Hull House (above), helped poor immigrants educate their children and adapt to life in the United States.

254 Chapter 6 Urban America

scripts they began earlier. They will probably need to throw out some of their ideas as they realize that a message to one group might result in a negative reaction from another group. Their final product of 3 short ads can be in different forms—a written script and sketches of visuals, digital camera shots—whatever a given class can access.

Putting It Together The Democratic and Republican teams can meet to review the work of the other team, comparing notes about the process and offering ideas for improvement or revision. **OL**

STANDARDIZED TEST PRACTICE

TEST-TAKING TIP

Read the questions carefully. From the wording of each question, you can see that some have two or three concepts in common. Find the one choice that best answers each question.

Reviewing Vocabulary

Directions: Choose the word or words that best completes the sentence.

1. _____ was a philosophy that believed wealthy Americans bore the responsibility of using their fortunes to further social progress.

   A Social Darwinism

   B Realism

   C Gospel of Wealth

   D Individualism

2. Immigrant children became knowledgeable about American culture at public schools—a process known as

   A Americanization.

   B nativism.

   C Social Darwinism.

   D individualism.

3. The rapid increase in the money supply without an increase in the amount of goods for sale caused _____, or the decline in the value of money.

   A goldbugs

   B silverites

   C deflation

   D inflation

4. The _____ was an informal political group that provided city services in return for votes and political power.

   A party bosses

   B political machine

   C Populists

   D Grange

Reviewing Main Ideas

Directions: Choose the best answers to the following questions.

Section 1 *(pp. 214–219)*

5. In the late nineteenth century, many labor unions opposed immigration, arguing that immigrants

   A would work for higher wages.

   B eased financial drains on social services.

   C assimilated into American culture.

   D would accept jobs as strikebreakers.

6. What was the major reason for Chinese immigration to the United States in the early nineteenth century?

   A Many Chinese were escaping severe unemployment and famine.

   B Many Chinese were escaping religious persecution.

   C Many Chinese left to avoid required military service.

   D Many Chinese left to escape the class system and move up the social ladder.

Section 2 *(pp. 222–227)*

7. Working class individuals residing in cities usually lived

   A in the streetcar suburbs.

   B in tenements.

   C in fashionable downtown districts.

   D away from the central city.

8. Who was the leader of Tammany Hall during the 1860s and 1870s?

   A Thomas Nast

   B James Pendergast

   C William Tweed

   D Thomas Pendergast

Need Extra Help?

If You Missed Questions . . .	1	2	3	4	5	6	7	8
Go to Page . . .	231–232	239	242–243	227	218	217	225	227

Reviewing Vocabulary

1. C Social Darwinism was the application of survival of the fittest to society. Realism was an artistic movement. Individualism was a philosophy that prized success by individual effort. The Gospel of Wealth was coined by Andrew Carnegie. He believed those who had money should use it to help people help themselves.

2. A This is a good place to discuss the suffix *–ization*, which means a process or the result of making something. So, Americanization means the process of making someone American.

3. D Students may have trouble choosing between inflation and deflation. An **in**crease in the money supply leads to **in**flation. (A decrease in the money supply can lead to **de**flation.) Goldbugs and silverites are not economic terms.

4. B Party bosses, such as the infamous Boss Tweed in New York, "ran" political machines. The Populists grew out of the Grange movement, and both are associated with democratic ideals, not corruption.

Reviewing Main Ideas

5. D *A, B,* and *C* are incorrect, because they inaccurately represent the feelings of many labor unions toward immigrants. In reality, immigrants' willingness to work for *lower* wages worried unions. In addition, increased immigration placed increasing strains on social services. Immigrants did not immediately assimilate into American culture, which caused prejudice against them.

6. A The answer choices all list push factors that cause immigration, but only one applies to Chinese immigrants. Review the

---

chart "Why Did the Immigrants Come to America?" on page 217.

7. B Students will hopefully eliminate A, since suburbs are not cities. Immigrants were poor, so they would not live in the fashionable district downtown; they lived in the inner city. The term *inner city* is still used today to describe economically depressed urban areas. Tenement buildings housed working-class people in cities in extremely tight quarters.

8. C William "Boss" Tweed led Tammany Hall. Thomas Nast was a cartoonist who opposed political machines. James Pendergast ran a huge political machine in Kansas City, MO. Thomas was his brother.

9. C Each answer choice describes a nineteenth-century philosophy. Students should connect Social Darwinism with Darwin's theory of survival of the fittest, which is described in C. A describes socialism. B and D describe communism.

10. D The federal government began regulating the railroads due to the type of problems described in the first three answer choices.

11. C The Populist Party was closely tied to economic goals and principles, so C makes the most sense.

12. C *Plessy* v. *Ferguson* established the concept of "separate but equal" facilities for whites and African Americans. This concept was based on the Fourteenth Amendment.

Critical Thinking

13. A The People's Party originated with farmers, and the subtreasury plan was introduced by Charles Macune to help farmers raise crop prices. The other answer choices were opposite of Populist goals.

14. D Wheat prices decreased significantly during this ten-year period, while cotton prices decreased gradually.

Section 3 *(pp. 230–239)*

9. The nineteenth-century philosophy of Social Darwinism maintained that

A the government should have control over the means of production and the marketplace.

B all social class distinctions in American society should be eliminated.

C economic success comes to those who are the hardest working and most competent.

D wealth and income should be more equally distributed.

10. The Interstate Commerce Act (1887) was designed to regulate interstate commerce by requiring

A railroads to increase rebates to high-volume users.

B railroads to charge higher rates for short hauls.

C states to regulate interstate railroad traffic.

D the federal government to regulate railroad rates.

Section 4 *(pp. 242–247)*

11. The Populist Party supported government ownership of railroads and telegraph lines because government ownership would

A increase railroad and telegraph lines across rural areas.

B make these services more reliable.

C keep prices more stable.

D provide enough revenue to allow the government to eliminate the graduated income tax.

Section 5 *(pp. 248–253)*

12. The ruling from *Plessy* v. *Ferguson* (1896) was based on the Supreme Court's interpretation of the

A necessary and proper clause from Article I, Section 8 of the U.S. Constitution.

B free speech provision of the First Amendment.

C equal protection clause in the Fourteenth Amendment.

D voting rights provision in the Fifteenth Amendment.

Critical Thinking

Directions: Choose the best answers to the following questions.

13. In 1890 the Populists formed the People's Party and supported

A the subtreasury plan where farmers could store crops in warehouses to force prices up.

B limited governmental regulations for the railroad companies.

C the election of senators by state legislatures.

D the free coinage of gold.

Base your answer to question 14 on the chart below and your knowledge of Chapter 6.

14. What happened to crop prices between 1870 and 1880?

A The price of cotton increased as the price of wheat and corn decreased.

B The price of wheat, corn, and cotton increased.

C The price of cotton, wheat, and corn stayed the same following an initial increase.

D The price of wheat significantly decreased as the price of cotton decreased steadily.

Need Extra Help?						
If You Missed Questions . . .	9	10	11	12	13	14
Go to Page . . .	230–231	234–235	245	250	245	243

GO ON

15. Which of the following concepts is associated with the Gospel of Wealth?

   A survival of the fittest

   B laissez-faire

   C unregulated competition

   D philanthropy

Analyze the cartoon and answer the question that follows. Base your answer on the cartoon and on your knowledge of Chapter 6.

16. What does the cartoon express about immigrants coming to the United States?

   A Immigrants were welcome to the United States.

   B Immigrants had to pass by dogs to gain entry.

   C Anarchists, Socialists, and Communists were welcome.

   D Anarchists, Socialists, and Communists were not welcome.

17. The "new immigrants" to the United States between 1890 and 1915 came primarily from

   A southern and eastern Europe.

   B northern and western Europe.

   C East Asia.

   D Latin America.

Document-Based Questions

Directions: Analyze the document and answer the short-answer questions that follow the document.

Reaction in the United States to "old" immigration was generally more favorable than reaction to "new" immigration. The following excerpt from an 1882 editorial in the *Commercial and Financial Chronicle* addresses the effects of immigration on the nation:

> *"In the very act of coming and traveling to reach his destination, he [the immigrant] adds ... to the immediate prosperity and success of certain lines of business. Not only do the ocean steamers ... get very large returns in carrying passengers of this description, but in forwarding them to the places chosen by the immigrants as their future homes the railroad companies also derive great benefit and their passenger traffic is greatly swelled....*
>   *... These immigrants not only produce largely, ... but, having wants which they cannot supply themselves, create a demand for outside supplies.... Thus it is that the Eastern manufacturer finds the call upon him for his wares and goods growing more urgent all the time, thus the consumption of coal keeps on expanding notwithstanding the check to new railroad enterprises, and thus there is a more active and larger interchange of all commodities. "*
>   —from *Commercial and Financial Chronicle*

18. According to the editorial, what effect did immigration have on the nation's economy?

19. How is the editorial's view of the effects of immigration different from that of the nativists?

Extended Response

20. Identify how events during the late 1800s and early 1900s, such as urbanization and immigration, influenced social change, and evaluate the extent to which reform movements were successful in bringing about change. Write an expository essay that supports your answer with relevant facts, examples, and details.

STOP

History ONLINE

For additional test practice, use Self-Check Quizzes—Chapter 6 at glencoe.com.

Need Extra Help?						
If You Missed Questions . . .	15	16	17	18	19	20
Go to Page . . .	231–232	230–233	214–215	218–219	218–219	236–239

"by the very act of coming and traveling [to the U.S.]" immigrants lend success to certain businesses.

19. The editorial views immigration in a positive light and focuses on the economic benefits. Nativists opposed immigration and worried about cultural and economic threats they thought immigration presented.

Extended Response

20. Responses will vary. Answers must address and evaluate the effectiveness of the different reform movements during the period. Essays should include Social Darwinism, nativist response, populism, and changes in cities.

15. D Philanthropy was associated with the Gospel of Wealth, but not with survival of the fittest—a central Social Darwinist theory. Unregulated competition is a feature of laissez faire.

16. D In the cartoon, lady liberty is signaling figures representing Anarchists, Communists, and Socialists to halt by holding up her hand. In addition, she is holding guard dogs to help keep them at bay.

17. A Have students who incorrectly answer this question refer to the map on page 215. Although it covers a longer time period, it should help students in answering the question.

Document-Based Questions

18. Immigration had a positive effect by increasing prosperity for ocean steamers, railroads, and manufacturing. Editorial states that

History ONLINE

Have students visit the Web site at glencoe.com to review Chapter 6 and take the Self-Check Quiz.

Need Extra Help?

Have students refer to the pages listed if they miss any of the questions.

UNIT PACING CHART

	Unit 3	Chapter 7	Chapter 8	Chapter 9	Unit 3
Day 1	Unit Opener	Chapter 7 Opener, Section 1	Chapter 8 Opener, Section 1	Chapter 9 Opener, Section 1	Wrap-Up/Project, Unit Assessment
Day 2		Section 2	Section 2	Section 2	
Day 3		Section 3	Section 3	Section 3	
Day 4		Chapter Assessment	Chapter Assessment	Section 4	
Day 5				Chapter Assessment	

Teacher to Teacher

**Lee Weber
Price Laboratory
School
Cedar Falls, IA**

U.S. Entrance into World War I Place the following "Causes of American Entrance into World War I" on an overhead transparency:

- Loss of innocent lives
- Loss of trade
- Historical/cultural ties to British/French
- Defense of democracy against dictatorship
- Freedom of the seas
- The Zimmermann Note

Ask students to individually rank the causes from most important to least important. Then randomly group students and have them try to reach consensus. The interrelated nature of the six causes makes the task extremely difficult. If time permits repeat the process and make a hypothetical change in the historical facts. For instance, suggest that Germany had a large surface navy and Britain developed unrestricted submarine warfare. How would U.S. policy have changed? Or, what if Germany were our major trading partner, not England and its allies?

Author Note

Dear American History Teacher:

The great industrial development of the United States in the second half of the nineteenth century transformed the character of the nation. It also produced new pressures and new problems that shaped the era that began with the depression of 1893 and led ultimately to America's entry into World War I.

The rapidly expanding economic growth of the industrial era led America to look for new sources of raw materials and new markets for the nation's goods. The United States began its search for international influence not through traditional imperialism, but through aggressive engagement in international trade (accompanied by a strong missionary movement that attempted to spread both Christianity and western knowledge and values into distant lands). American imperialism was in many ways different from the imperialism practiced by European nations, but it had similar goals—economic growth—and encountered similar problems—resistance, sometimes violent, from native peoples.

Industrial growth changed not only America's role in the world but the character of life and politics within the United States. The factory system gave birth to a new kind of working class; it led to the growth of cities and industrial towns and to substantial population growth; and it produced new conflicts and crises that alarmed many Americans and helped create a series of reform efforts that came to be known, collectively, as progressivism. Progressivism took so many different forms and embraced so many various, and sometimes contradictory values that some scholars have argued that "progressivism" has little or no meaning. But Americans in the early twentieth century believed that progressivism was filled with meaning, and one of the challenges of teaching this period is explaining what that meaning was. The progressive era helped produce a series of questions and beliefs that shaped the whole of the twentieth century and continue to evoke both interest and controversy even today.

Alan Brinkley

Focus

Why It Matters

Tell students that today many people consider the United States the world's only superpower. Ask students if they agree with that assessment and why or why not. **OL**

Connecting to Past Learning

Have students identify nations that they think are powerful. **Ask:** What makes a nation powerful? *(Answers might include a strong military, a robust economy, industry, and political influence.)* Tell students that in this unit they will learn about how the United States became a world power and became increasingly involved in world events. **OL**

Unit Launch Activity

Making Connections Have students brainstorm a list of weapons used in warfare today. List students' answers on the board. **Ask:** Which of these weapons existed at the beginning of the twentieth century? *(Answers will vary.)* Discuss with the class how new weaponry has changed warfare since the early 1900s. **OL**

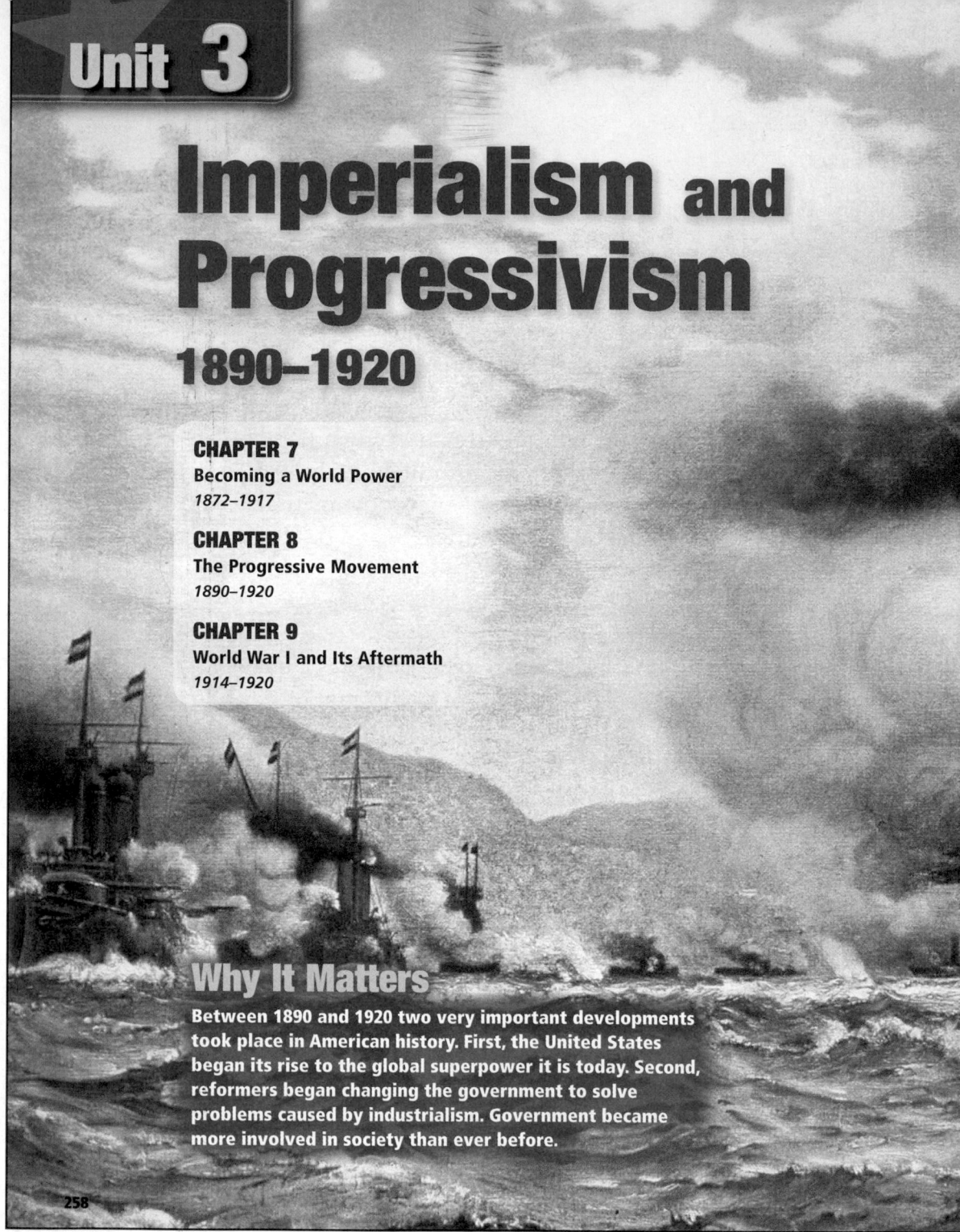

Unit 3

Imperialism and Progressivism
1890–1920

CHAPTER 7
Becoming a World Power
1872–1917

CHAPTER 8
The Progressive Movement
1890–1920

CHAPTER 9
World War I and Its Aftermath
1914–1920

Why It Matters

Between 1890 and 1920 two very important developments took place in American history. First, the United States began its rise to the global superpower it is today. Second, reformers began changing the government to solve problems caused by industrialism. Government became more involved in society than ever before.

258

Team Teaching Activity

Sociology Read to the students the following lines written by poet Sarah Cleghorn in the early 1900s: "The golf links lie so near the mill/That almost every day/The laboring children can look out/And see the men at play." **Ask:** What do you think this quote tells you about the economic and social conditions in the United States in 1900? *(There were no child labor laws; children worked in factories; wealthy men played golf.)* Have the economics teacher come and explain the evolution of child labor laws and their impact on the business world. **OL**

Teach

S1 Skill Practice

Visual Literacy Have students study the unit painting. **Ask: What impression or feeling is the artist trying to convey in this painting?** *(The United States is militarily strong; the Spanish fleet is weak.)* **BL**

S2 Skill Practice

Concluding Have students again review the unit painting. **Ask: What is the topic of the painting?** *(America's military power)* Discuss with the class why reformers might be opposed to the nation's growing military power at the beginning of the twentieth century. **OL**

S₁ S₂

U.S. warships battle the Spanish off the coast of Cuba, 1898.

259

More About the Photo

The U.S. fleet set out for Havana Harbor during the Spanish-American War. The quick American victory in that war made the nation an imperialist power.

NCLB NO CHILD LEFT BEHIND

Teaching Tip The NCLB Act emphasizes reading. Have students make a time line that begins with 1872 and ends with 1919. Have them keep the time line with them and add key events as they read the unit. Students can use the time line while studying to help understand the sequence of events.

Key to Ability Levels

BL Below Level	**AL** Above Level
OL On Level	**ELL** English Language Learners

Key to Teaching Resources

Print Material   DVD
CD-ROM   Transparency

Levels					Resources	Chapter Opener	Section 1	Section 2	Section 3	Chapter Assess
BL	OL	AL	ELL							
					FOCUS					
BL	OL	AL	ELL		Daily Focus Skills Transparencies		7-1	7-2	7-3	
					TEACH					
BL	OL		ELL		Reading Essentials and Note-Taking Guide*		p. 70	p. 73	p. 76	
	OL				Historical Analysis Skills Activity, URB				p. 20	
BL	OL		ELL		Guided Reading Activities, URB*		p. 46	p. 47	p. 48	
BL	OL	AL	ELL		Content Vocabulary Activity, URB*		p. 25			
BL	OL	AL	ELL		Academic Vocabulary Activity, URB		p. 27			
	OL	AL			Critical Thinking Skills Activity, URB				p. 30	
BL	OL		ELL		Reading Skills Activity, URB		p. 19			
BL			ELL		English Learner Activity, URB			p. 23		
	OL	AL			Reinforcing Skills Activity, URB			p. 29		
BL	OL	AL	ELL		Differentiated Instruction Activity, URB				p. 21	
BL	OL		ELL		Time Line Activity, URB				p. 31	
	OL				Linking Past and Present Activity, URB		p. 32			
BL	OL	AL	ELL		American Art and Music Activity, URB			p. 37		
BL	OL	AL	ELL		Interpreting Political Cartoons Activity, URB				p. 39	
		AL			Enrichment Activity, URB			p. 43		
BL	OL	AL	ELL		American Biographies			✓		
BL	OL	AL	ELL		Primary Source Reading, URB		p. 35	p. 33		
BL	OL	AL	ELL		The Living Constitution*	✓	✓	✓	✓	✓
	OL	AL			American History Primary Source Documents Library	✓	✓	✓	✓	✓
BL	OL	AL	ELL		Unit Map Overlay Transparencies	✓	✓	✓	✓	✓
BL	OL	AL	ELL		Differentiated Instruction for the American High School Classroom	✓	✓	✓	✓	✓
BL	OL	AL	ELL		StudentWorks™ Plus DVD	✓	✓	✓	✓	✓
BL	OL	AL	ELL		Vocabulary PuzzleMaker CD-ROM	✓	✓	✓	✓	✓

Note: Please refer to the *Unit 3 Resource Book* for this chapter's URB materials.

* Also available in Spanish

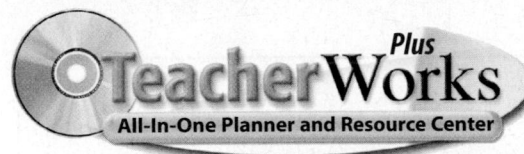

- Interactive Lesson Planner
- Interactive Teacher Edition
- Fully editable blackline masters
- Section Spotlight Videos Launch

- Differentiated Lesson Plans
- Printable reports of daily assignments
- Standards Tracking System

Levels					Resources	Chapter Opener	Section 1	Section 2	Section 3	Chapter Assess
BL	OL	AL	ELL							
TEACH *(continued)*										
BL	OL	AL	ELL	💿	American Music Hits Through History CD	✓	✓	✓	✓	✓
BL	OL	AL	ELL	📁	Unit Time Line Transparencies and Activities	✓	✓	✓	✓	✓
BL	OL	AL	ELL	📁	Cause and Effect Transparencies, Strategies, and Activities	✓	✓	✓	✓	✓
BL	OL	AL	ELL	📁	Why It Matters Transparencies, Strategies, and Activities	✓	✓	✓	✓	✓
BL	OL	AL	ELL	📁	American Issues	✓	✓	✓	✓	✓
	OL	AL	ELL	📁	American Art and Architecture Transparencies, Strategies, and Activities	✓	✓	✓	✓	✓
BL	OL	AL		📁	High School American History Literature Library	✓	✓	✓	✓	✓
BL	OL	AL	ELL	🔒	*The American Vision* Video Program DVD	✓	✓	✓	✓	✓
Teacher Resources				📁	Strategies for Success	✓	✓	✓	✓	✓
				📁	Success with English Learner	✓	✓	✓	✓	✓
				📁	Studies Classroom	✓	✓	✓	✓	✓
				🔒	Presentation Plus! DVD	✓	✓	✓	✓	✓
ASSESS										
BL	OL	AL	ELL	📁	Section Quizzes and Chapter Tests*		p. 95	p. 96	p. 97	p. 99
BL	OL	AL	ELL	📁	Authentic Assessment With Rubrics					p. 19
BL	OL	AL	ELL	📁	Standardized Test Practice Workbook					p. 15
BL	OL	AL	ELL	💿	*ExamView®* Assessment Suite CD-ROM		7-1	7-2	7-3	Ch. 7
BL	OL	AL	ELL	💿	Interactive Tutor Self-Assessment CD-ROM		7-1	7-2	7-3	Ch. 7
CLOSE										
BL			ELL	📁	Reteaching Activity, URB					p. 41
BL	OL		ELL	📁	Reading and Study Skills Foldables™	p. 64				

Using Interactive Tutor Self Assessment

Electronic Quiz

Technology Product

Glencoe's Interactive Tutor Self Assessment software allows students to assess their mastery of chapter content, taking as much time as they need to review each section of a chapter. The Interactive Tutor Self Assessment

- contains quizzes for individual section of chapters, with section overviews covering important concepts and keywords;
- allows students to read overviews based on sections, chapters, or units before starting quizzes;
- lets students check their answers, receive feedback and hints, and identify content areas for review;
- permits student to move back and forth among the questions during a quiz;
- generate performance reports and graphs to monitor student progress section by section.

Objectives

Using the Interactive Tutor Self Assessment allows students to assess their mastery of chapter content; identify chapter content they need to review.

Steps

- Install Interactive Tutor Self-Assessment.
- Register yourself and create classes.
- Register new students/users in the database, organized by classes. Assign individual passwords to students.
- Save student records to a location easily accessible to students.
- Assign section quizzes to students.
- Generate performance reports and graphs for individual students and classes.

History ONLINE

	Student	Teacher	Parent
Beyond the Textbook	●	●	●
Chapter Overviews	●	●	●
Time Current Events	●		●
ePuzzles and Games	●		●
Concepts in Motion	●		●
Literature Connections		●	
Multi-Language Glossaries	●		●
Online Student Edition	●	●	●
Self-Check Quizzes	●		●
Student Web Activities	●		●
Study Central™	●		●
Teaching Today		●	
Vocabulary eFlashcards	●		●
Web Activity Lesson Plans		●	

Glencoe Media Center

glencoe.com

❯ **Study-To-Go**
- Vocabulary eFlashcards
- Self-Check Quizzes

❯ **Audio/Video**
- Student Edition Audio
- Spanish Summaries
- Section Videos

- **Timed Readings Plus in Social Studies** helps students increase their reading rate and fluency while maintaining comprehension. The 400-word passages are similar to those found on state and national assessments.

- **Reading in the Content Area: Social Studies** concentrates on six essential reading skills that help students better comprehend what they read. The book includes 75 high-interest nonfiction passages written at increasing levels of difficulty.

- **Reading Social Studies** includes strategic reading instruction and vocabulary support in Social Studies content for both ELLs and native speakers of English.

www.jamestowneducation.com

The following videotape programs are available from Glencoe as supplements to Chapter 7:

- The Panama Canal (ISBN 1-56-501243-7)
- Teddy Roosevelt: An American Lion (0-76-705176-9)

To order, call Glencoe at 1-800-334-7344. To find classroom resources to accompany many of these videos, check the following home pages:

A&E Television: www.aetv.com

The History Channel: www.historychannel.com

Index to National Geographic Magazine:

The following articles relate to this chapter:

- "Remember the *Maine*," by Thomas B. Allen, February 1998
- "Panama's rite of passage. (Panama receives control of the Panama Canal Zone from the US)," by Lewis M. Simons. November, 1999.

National Geographic Society Products To order the following, call National Geographic at 1-800-368-2728:

- *ZipZapMap! USA* (ZipZapMap!)

Access National Geographic's new, dynamic MapMachine Web site and other geography resources at:
www.nationalgeographic.com
www.nationalgeographic.com/maps

Reading List Generator CD-ROM

GLENCOE BOOKLINK 3

Use this database to search more than 30,000 titles to create a customized reading list for your students.

- Reading lists can be organized by students' reading level, author, genre, theme, or area of interest.
- The database provides Degrees of Reading Power™ (DRP) and Lexile™ readability scores for all selections.
- A brief summary of each selection is included.

Leveled reading suggestions for this chapter:

For students at a Grade 8 reading level:
- *Theodore Roosevelt,* by Clara Ingram Judson

For students at a Grade 9 reading level:
- *Bully for You, Teddy Roosevelt,* by Jean Fritz

For students at a Grade 10 reading level:
- *The Spanish-American War,* by Kerry A. Graves

For students at a Grade 11 reading level:
- *The Panama Canal,* by Leslie A. DuTemple

For students at a Grade 12 reading level:
- *Mornings on Horseback,* by David McCullough

Focus

MAKING CONNECTIONS
How Are Empires Built?

Essential Question: What geographic considerations might have played a role in where the United States built its empire? *(Latin America was located just to the south of the United States; East Asia, located due west across the Pacific Ocean, was also being exploited by European powers. Both areas were accessible to the U.S. Navy.)* **Essential Question:** Why do some experts say that today the United States is the world's sole superpower? *(Today, the United States is one of the world's richest nations; it has more military power than any other nation.)* **OL**

Teach

Big Ideas

As students study the chapter, remind them to consider the Big Ideas presented at the beginning of each section. The **Essential Questions** in the activities below tie in to the Big Ideas and help students think about and understand important chapter concepts. In addition, the Hands-on Chapter Project relates the content from each section to the Big Ideas. The steps in each section build on each other and culminate in the Wrap-up activity on the Visual Summary page.

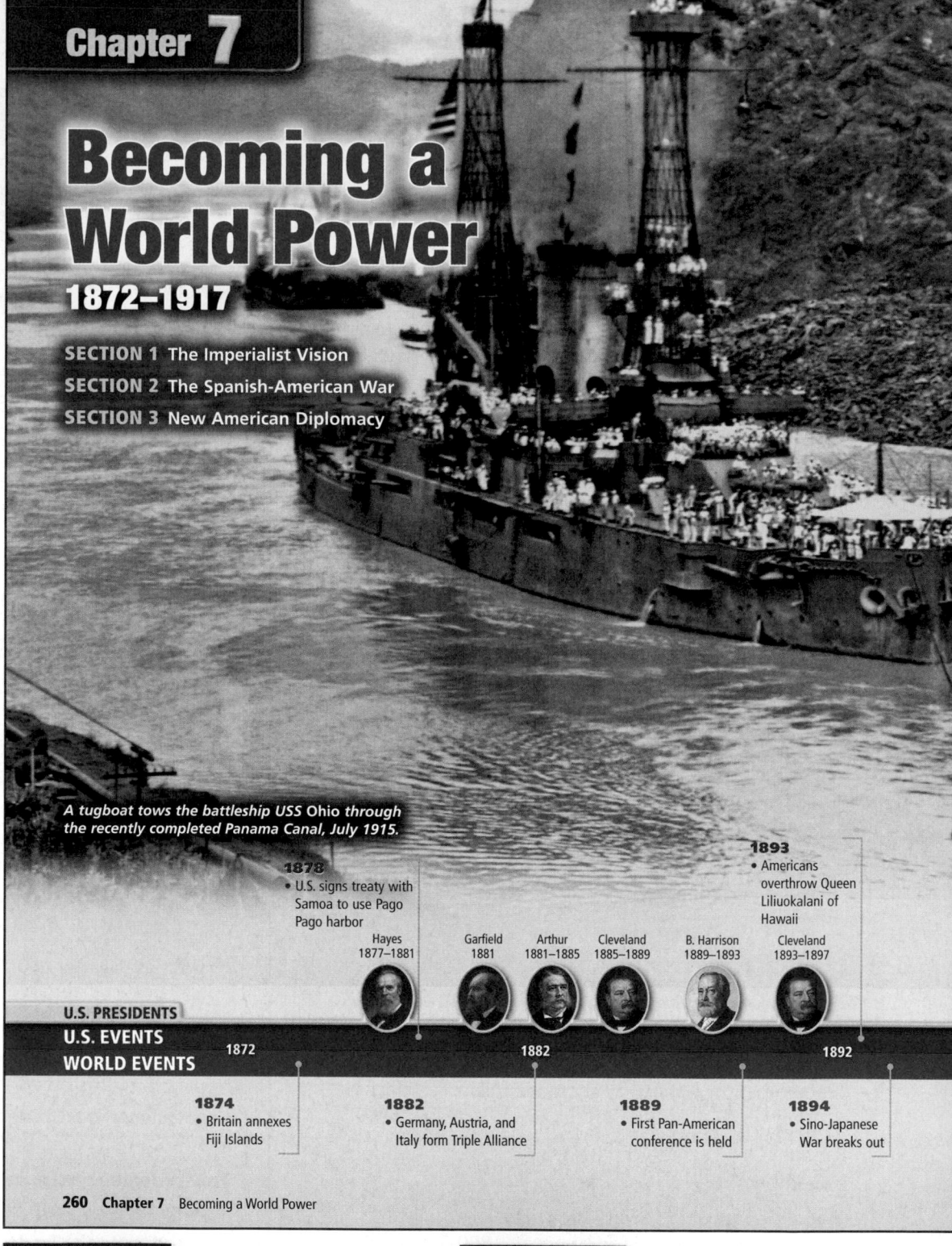

Chapter 7

Becoming a World Power
1872–1917

SECTION 1 The Imperialist Vision
SECTION 2 The Spanish-American War
SECTION 3 New American Diplomacy

A tugboat tows the battleship USS Ohio through the recently completed Panama Canal, July 1915.

1878
• U.S. signs treaty with Samoa to use Pago Pago harbor

1893
• Americans overthrow Queen Liliuokalani of Hawaii

Hayes 1877–1881
Garfield 1881
Arthur 1881–1885
Cleveland 1885–1889
B. Harrison 1889–1893
Cleveland 1893–1897

U.S. PRESIDENTS
U.S. EVENTS
WORLD EVENTS

1872
1882
1892

1874
• Britain annexes Fiji Islands

1882
• Germany, Austria, and Italy form Triple Alliance

1889
• First Pan-American conference is held

1894
• Sino-Japanese War breaks out

260 Chapter 7 Becoming a World Power

Section 1

The Imperial Vision
Essential Question: Why did the United States seek to become an imperialist power? *(National pride; an extension of Manifest Destiny; businesses sought new markets for their products)* Point out that in Section 1 students will learn about why the United States began an imperialist foreign policy. **OL**

Section 2

The Spanish-American War
Essential Question: Was sympathy for the Cuban people or economic expansion the major reason why the United States declared war on Spain? *(Students' answers will vary, but they should point out that the causes of the war were intertwined.)* Point out that in Section 2 students will learn the causes of the Spanish-American War. **OL**

MAKING CONNECTIONS
How Are Empires Built?
International economic and military competition convinced the United States it must become a world power. In the late 1800s, the United States increased its trade and military presence in East Asia and Latin America, and by the early 1900s, it had created an American empire.

- *Why do you think the United States focused on East Asia and Latin America?*
- *What factors make a nation a world power?*

More About the Photo

Visual Literacy The chapter opening photograph was taken on July 16, 1915. It shows the tugboat *Tavernela* towing the battleship USS *Ohio* through the Gaillard Cut of the Panama Canal.

FOLDABLES **Dinah Zike's**
Study Organizer **Foldables**

Dinah Zike's Foldables are three-dimensional, interactive graphic organizers that help students practice basic writing skills, review vocabulary terms, and identify main ideas. Instructions for creating and using Foldables can be found in the Appendix at the end of this book and in the *Dinah Zike's Reading and Study Skills Foldables* booklet.

History ONLINE
Introduce students to chapter content and key terms by having them access the Chapter 7 Overview at glencoe.com.

1898
- U.S. declares war on Spain

McKinley
1897–1901

T. Roosevelt
1901–1909

1904
- Panama Canal construction begins
- Roosevelt Corollary is issued

Taft
1909–1913

1902

1912

1899
- John Hay sends Open Door notes

1900
- Boxer Rebellion begins in China

1904
- Russo-Japanese War begins

FOLDABLES

Taking Notes Create a Concept-Map Book Foldable to help you take basic notes about the relationship between economic and military power. As you read the chapter, write details under each tab and be careful to note the years in which events and developments occurred.

U.S. Expansion
Economic Power | Military Power

History ONLINE Chapter Overview
Visit glencoe.com to preview Chapter 7.

Chapter 7 Becoming a World Power **261**

Section 3

New American Diplomacy
Essential Question: Why did the United States use diplomacy to achieve its economic objectives in Asia? *(Diplomacy, rather than war, allowed the United States as well as the European powers access to Asian markets.)* Point out that in Section 3 students will learn about the success of the Open Door Policy in Asia. **OL**

Focus

Bellringer

Daily Focus Transparency 7.1

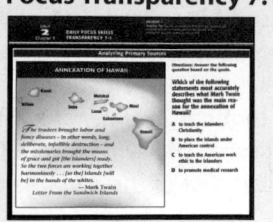

Guide to Reading

Answers:

I. Building Support for Imperialism
    A. A Desire for New Markets
    B. A Feeling of Superiority
    C. Building a Modern Navy
II. American Expansion in the Pacific
    A. Perry Opens Japan
    B. Annexing Hawaii
III. Diplomacy in Latin America

Section Spotlight Video

To generate student interest and provide a springboard for class discussion, access the Chapter 7, Section 1 video at glencoe.com or on the video DVD.

Resource Manager

Section 1

The Imperialist Vision

During the late 1800s, the desire to find new markets, increase trade, and build a powerful navy caused the United States to become more involved in international affairs.

Guide to Reading

Big Ideas
Economics and Society In the late 1800s, many Americans wanted the United States to expand its military and economic power overseas.

Content Vocabulary
• imperialism (p. 262)
• protectorate (p. 262)

Academic Vocabulary
• expansion (p. 263)
• conference (p. 267)

People and Events to Identify
• Anglo-Saxonism (p. 264)
• Matthew C. Perry (p. 265)
• Queen Liliuokalani (p. 266)
• Pan-Americanism (p. 267)

Reading Strategy
Organizing As you read about the development of the United States as a world power, use the major headings of the section to create an outline similar to the one below.

> The Imperialist Vision
> I. Building Support for Imperialism
>   A.
>   B.
>   C.
> II.
>   A.
>   B.

Building Support for Imperialism

MAIN Idea A desire for world markets and belief in the superiority of Anglo-Saxon culture led the United States to assert itself as a world power.

HISTORY AND YOU Do you remember what role George Washington thought the United States should play in world affairs? Read to learn why Americans' opinions changed in the 1880s.

In the years immediately following the Civil War, most Americans showed little interest in expanding their nation's territory outside the United States or increasing its international influence. Instead, they focused on reconstructing the South, building up the nation's industries, and settling the West. Beginning in the 1880s, however, economic and military competition from other nations, as well as a growing feeling of cultural superiority, convinced many Americans that the United States should become a world power.

A Desire for New Markets

Several European nations were already expanding overseas, a development known as the New Imperialism. **Imperialism** is the economic and political domination of a strong nation over weaker ones. Europeans expanded their power overseas for many reasons. Factories depended on raw materials from all over the world. No country had all of the resources its economy needed. In addition, by the late 1800s, most industrialized countries had placed high tariffs against each other. These tariffs were intended to protect a nation's industries from foreign competition. The tariffs reduced trade between industrialized countries, forcing companies to look for other markets overseas.

At the same time, the growth of investment opportunities in Western Europe had slowed. Most of the factories, railroads, and mines that Europe's economy needed had been built. Increasingly, Europeans began looking overseas for places to invest their capital. They started to invest in industries located in other countries, particularly in Africa and Asia.

To protect their investments, European nations began exerting control over those territories. Some areas became colonies. Many others became protectorates. In a **protectorate,** the imperial power

---

R Reading Strategies	**C** Critical Thinking	**D** Differentiated Instruction	**W** Writing Support	**S** Skill Practice
Additional Resources • Guided Read. Act., URB p. 46 • Content Vocab. Act., URB p. 25 • Prim. Source Read., URB p. 35	**Teacher Edition** • Draw. Concl., p. 264 • Identify. Central Issues, p. 266 **Additional Resources** • Link. Past/Present, URB p. 32 • Quizzes and Tests, p. 95	**Additional Resources** • Foldables, p. 64 • Academic Vocab. Act., URB p. 27	**Teacher Edition** • Persuas. Writing, pp. 263, 264 • Descrip. Writing, p. 265	**Teacher Edition** • Inferring, p. 263 **Additional Resources** • RENTG, p. 70 • Reading Skills Act., URB p. 19

PRIMARY SOURCE
Causes of American Imperialism

American imperialism had three main causes:

1. The belief in the superiority of American culture
2. The belief that the nation needed a large navy for security, with bases overseas
3. The belief that the economy needed overseas markets

1. ANGLO-SAXONISM

S

"The work which the English race began when it colonized North America is destined to go on until every land . . . that is not already the seat of an old civilization shall become English in its language, in its religion, in political habits and traditions, and to a predominant extent in the blood of its people."
—John Fiske, quoted in *The Expansionists of 1898*

2. MILITARY BASES

". . . [T]he ships of war of the United States, in war, will be like land birds, unable to fly far from their own shores. To provide resting-places for them, where they can coal and repair, would be one of the first duties of a government proposing to itself the development of the power of the nation at sea."
—Alfred Thayer Mahan, *The Influence of Sea Power Upon History*

3. OVERSEAS MARKETS

"[W]e are raising more than we can consume, . . . making more than we can use. Therefore we must find new markets for our produce…"
—Albert Beveridge, quoted in *The Meaning of the Times and Other Speeches*

Exports and Imports, 1865–1900

Trade (millions of dollars) — Exports / Imports

1,500 1,200 900 600 300

1865 1870 1875 1880 1885 1890 1895 1900

Source: *Historical Statistics of the United States.*

DBQ Document-Based Questions

1. **Interpreting** Based on the quote above, how do you think Albert Beveridge would use the data shown in the graph to support his argument?
2. **Comparing** What is the difference between Fiske's support for expanding American power overseas and Mahan's support for establishing military bases overseas?

allowed the local rulers to stay in control and protected them against rebellions and invasion. In exchange, the local rulers usually had to accept advice from the Europeans on how to govern their countries.

The United States noticed the **expansion** of European power overseas. As the United States industrialized, many Americans took an interest in the new imperialism. Until the late 1800s, the United States had expanded by settling more territory in North America. Now, with settlers finally filling up the western frontier, many Americans concluded that the nation needed new overseas markets to keep its economy strong.

A Feeling of Superiority

In addition to economic concerns, certain other key ideas convinced many Americans to encourage their nation's expansion overseas. Many supporters of Social Darwinism argued that nations competed with each other politically, economically, and militarily, and that only the strongest would survive. To them, this idea justified increasing American influence abroad. **W**

Teach

S Skill Practice

Inferring Ask: Based on the quotation by John Fiske, what can you infer about his views of other cultures and peoples? *(Fiske believed that English-speaking white Christians were superior to all others.)* **AL**

DBQ Document Based Questions

Answers:
1. Exports were growing rapidly.
2. Fiske supports imperialism to bring American culture and civilization to other parts of the world; Mahan is interested in building military bases so that warships can be refueled or repaired.

W Writing Support

Persuasive Writing Invite interested students to write an essay supporting or opposing Social Darwinism as justification for the United States to pursue its imperialist foreign policy. **AL**

Hands-On Chapter Project
Step 1

Preparing a Multimedia Presentation

Step 1: Research American Areas of Interest

Directions Divide the class into small groups, assigning each group one of the following categories: Cuba, China, Japan, the Philippines, Puerto Rico, and Guam. Have students use Internet and library resources, as well as their textbooks, to locate and analyze information about the reasons for and the effects of imperialism in their assigned country. Encourage students to use both primary and secondary resources in their research.

Tell students to focus on the following causes and effects of imperialism: economics, naval power, national pride, Manifest Destiny, loss of autonomy, increased development, and war and other conflicts.

Putting It Together Give students a tutorial on the software they will be using to develop their presentations. Encourage students to ask questions about aspects of the program they find confusing. If necessary, pair students who have experience using the program with those who do not. **OL**

(Chapter Project continued on page 269)

C Critical Thinking

Drawing Conclusions Ask:
How might a strong navy support Fiske's idea of Anglo-Saxonism? *(A strong navy would militarily support the spread of Anglo-Saxonism to other places.)* `OL`

W Writing Support

Persuasive Writing Have interested students write a letter to Senator Lodge or Senator Beveridge advocating or opposing a big navy. Encourage students to share their essays with the class. `BL`

Reading Check

Answer:
More people believed it was America's destiny to spread its civilization overseas.

Additional Support

Many Americans, such as the well-known writer and historian John Fiske, took this idea even further. Fiske argued that English-speaking nations had superior character, ideas, and systems of government.

Fiske's ideas, known as **Anglo-Saxonism,** were popular in Britain and the United States. Many Americans linked it with the idea of Manifest Destiny. They believed the nation's destiny had been to expand westward to the Pacific Ocean. Now they believed the United States was destined to expand overseas and spread its civilization to other people.

Another influential advocate of Anglo-Saxonism was Josiah Strong, a popular American minister in the late 1800s. Strong linked Anglo-Saxonism to Christian missionary ideas. His ideas influenced many Americans. "The Anglo-Saxon," Strong declared, "[is] divinely commissioned to be, in a peculiar sense, his brother's keeper." By linking missionary work with Anglo-Saxonism, Strong convinced many Americans to support an expansion of American power overseas.

Building a Modern Navy

As imperialism and Anglo-Saxonism gained support, the United States became increasingly assertive in foreign affairs. Three international crises illustrated this new approach. In 1888 the country risked war to prevent Germany from taking control of Samoa in the South Pacific. Three years later, when a mob in Chile attacked American sailors in the port of Valparaíso, the United States threatened to go to war unless Chile paid reparations. Then, in 1895, the United States backed Venezuela against Great Britain in a border dispute with British Guiana. After Britain rejected an American ultimatum, many newspapers and members of Congress called for war. All three crises were eventually resolved peacefully.

As Americans became increasingly willing to risk war to defend American interests overseas, support for building a large modern navy began to grow. Supporters argued that if the United States did not build up its navy and acquire bases overseas, European nations would shut it out of foreign markets.

Captain Alfred T. Mahan, an officer in the U.S. Navy who taught at the Naval War College, best expressed this argument. In 1890 Mahan published his lectures in a book called *The*

Influence of Sea Power upon History, 1660–1783. In this book Mahan pointed out that many prosperous peoples in the past, such as the British and Dutch, had built large fleets of merchant ships to trade with the world. He then suggested that a nation also needed a large navy to protect its merchant ships and to defend its right to trade with other countries.

Mahan's book became a best-seller, helping to build public support for a big navy. Two powerful senators, Henry Cabot Lodge and Albert J. Beveridge, pushed for constructing a new navy. In the executive branch, Benjamin Tracy, secretary of the navy under President Harrison, and John D. Long, secretary of the navy under President McKinley, strongly supported Mahan's ideas. **W**

By the 1890s, several different ideas had come together in the United States. Business leaders wanted new markets overseas. Anglo-Saxonism had convinced many Americans of their destiny to dominate the world. Growing European imperialism threatened America's security. Combined with Mahan's theories, these ideas convinced Congress to authorize the construction of a large, modern navy.

Reading Check **Summarizing** How did Americans' opinions about overseas expansion change in the late 1800s?

PRIMARY SOURCE
Perry Arrives in Japan

In 1853 Japan was a closed society. Its rulers had deliberately ended contact with the outside world, permitting only a small amount of trade with the Dutch and the Chinese. They were largely unaware of the changes the industrial revolution had brought to Europe and the United States. Perry's black steamships, belching smoke, and moving without any visible sails, were something the Japanese had never seen before.

The Japanese had cannons and guns, but Perry's ships carried 65 large cannons—a staggering number that represented immense power—and a direct threat to Japan's many coastal castles and towns. Perry's arrival carried different meanings for people living in the two countries, as shown in the two images to the right—one from Japan and the other from the United States.

Activity: Technology Connection

Shipbuilding Organize interested students into two groups. Have one group use library or Internet resources to find out more information about the Great White Fleet. Students should find out at what shipyards the ships were built; the size, length, and displacement of the ships; and how the ships were powered. Have the other group find out the same types of information about recently built ships. Each group should make posters detailing their findings. Have a spokesperson from each group present their findings to the class. Then ask the entire class to write a brief paragraph comparing one aspect of shipbuilding in the early 1900s with modern-day shipbuilding. `OL`

American Expansion in the Pacific

MAIN Idea The desire for new markets led to trade with Japan and the annexation of Hawaii.

HISTORY AND YOU What products do you use that are made in Japan? Read how the United States and Japan first became trading partners.

From the earliest days of the Republic, Americans had expanded their nation by moving westward. When Americans began looking overseas for new markets in the 1800s, therefore, they naturally tended to look toward the Pacific. Even before imperialist ideas became popular, American businesses had begun sending ships to trade in East Asia.

Perry Opens Japan

Many American business leaders believed that the United States would benefit from trade with Japan, as well as with China. Japan's rulers, however, who believed that excessive contact with the West would destroy their culture, allowed only the Chinese and Dutch to trade with their nation. In 1852, after receiving several petitions from Congress, President Millard Fillmore decided to force Japan to trade with the United States. He ordered Commodore **Matthew C. Perry** to take a naval expedition to Japan to negotiate a trade treaty.

On July 8, 1853, four American warships under Perry's command entered Edo Bay (today known as Tokyo Bay). The display of American technology and firepower impressed the Japanese, who had never before seen steamships. Realizing that they could not resist modern Western technology and weapons, the Japanese agreed to sign the Treaty of Kanagawa. In addition to granting the United States permission to trade at two ports in Japan, the treaty called for peace between the two countries; promised help for any American ships and sailors shipwrecked off the Japanese coast; and gave American ships permission to buy supplies such as wood, water, food, and coal in the Japanese ports.

The American decision forcing Japan to open trade played an important role in Japanese history. Japanese leaders concluded that it was time to remake their society. They adopted Western technology and launched their own industrial revolution. By the 1890s, the Japanese had a powerful navy and had begun building their own empire in Asia.

▶ American painter James Evans entitled his work "Commodore Perry Carrying the Gospel of God to the Heathen, 1853."

W

▼ This Japanese color print depicts one artist's perspective of Perry's "black ships" that arrived in Japan in 1853.

U.S. JAPAN FLEET, Comt PERRY, carrying the 'GOSPEL of GOD', to the HEATHEN, 1853.

Analyzing VISUALS

1. **Comparing** What elements did both the American and Japanese artists depict the same way? Which were different?
2. **Making Inferences** What impression of the Americans does the Japanese image convey? What is the American painting communicating about Perry's mission?

W Writing Support

Descriptive Writing Have students compare the two paintings of Commodore Perry's ships shown on this page. Then have students write a paragraph describing how the two artists portrayed the ships. Encourage students to share their essays with the class. **BL**

Analyzing VISUALS

Answers:
1. same: smoke, smokestacks, sails, waves; different: shape of the ship, Asian elements on the Japanese print are not shown on the American painting
2. The Japanese print makes the Americans look aggressive and threatening; the American painting makes the ship appear majestic and the mission divinely inspired.

Differentiated Instruction

Time Line Activity 7, URB p. 31

Illustrating Expansion: Make a Map

Objective: Create a map to show the expansion of U.S. territory from 1872–1912.

Focus: Give each student a copy of a world map.

Teach: Make a list of the states, countries, and territories that were involved in events that led to U.S. expansion.

Assess: Identify which areas became new parts of the U.S.

Close: Draw a new map or color the world map to show the expansion of U.S. territory.

Differentiated Instruction Strategies

BL Write a list of the states that joined the Union from 1872 to 1912.

AL Research each of the states that joined the Union from 1872 to 1912. Find out their size and determine in square miles how much territory was added during this time period.

ELL Based on the time line, make a list of the years in which new states were added to the Union.

People IN HISTORY

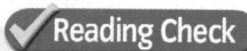

Answer:
Planters revolted against Liliuokalani because they wanted Hawaii to become part of the United States.

C Critical Thinking

Identifying Central Issues

Ask students to review the conflict between the Hawaiian rulers and the planters. **Ask:** What is the main issue at the root of the conflict between these two groups? *(who would be the ruler of the Hawaiian Islands)* OL

✓ Reading Check

Answer:
It led them to annex Hawaii and to open trade with Japan.

Additional Support

People IN HISTORY

Queen Liliuokalani
1838–1917

Queen Liliuokalani was the last ruling monarch of the Hawaiian Islands. A group of white sugar planters had forced her predecessor to accept a new constitution that minimized the power of the monarchy, gave voting rights to Americans and Europeans, and denied voting rights to most Hawaiians and all Asians.

As queen, Liliuokalani was determined to regain royal power and reduce the power of foreigners. On January 14, 1893, she issued a new constitution, which restored the power of the monarchy and the rights of the Hawaiian people. In response, a group of planters led by Sanford B. Dole launched a revolt. Under protest, Liliuokalani surrendered her throne on January 17. After supporters led a revolt in an attempt to restore her to power in 1895, Liliuokalani was placed under house arrest for several months. After her release, she lived out her days in Washington Palace in Honolulu.
Why did sugar planters lead a revolt against Queen Liliuokalani?

▲ *Sanford B. Dole gives Hawaii, represented as the bride, to Uncle Sam.*

For an example of American views on annexing Hawaii read "President Harrison on Hawaiian Annexation" on page R51 in **Documents in American History.**

Annexing Hawaii

As trade with Asia grew during the 1800s, Americans began seeking ports where they could refuel and resupply while crossing the Pacific Ocean. Pago Pago, in the Samoan Islands, had one of the finest harbors in the South Pacific. In 1878 the United States negotiated permission to open a base there.

More important was Hawaii. Whaling ships and merchant vessels crossing the Pacific often stopped there to rest and to take on supplies. In 1819 missionaries from New England arrived in Hawaii. American settlers found that sugarcane grew well in Hawaii's climate and soil. By the mid-1800s, businessmen had established many plantations on the islands.

A severe recession struck Hawaii in 1872. Three years later, worried that the economic crisis might force the Hawaiians to turn to the British or French for help, the United States signed a treaty exempting Hawaiian sugar from tariffs. When the treaty came up for renewal several years later, the Senate insisted that Hawaii grant the United States exclusive rights to a naval base at Pearl Harbor.

The treaty led to a boom in the Hawaiian sugar industry and wealth for the planters. In 1887 prominent planters pressured the Hawaiian king into accepting a constitution that limited the king's authority. As tensions mounted between the planters and Hawaiians, Congress passed a new tariff in 1890 that gave subsidies to sugar producers in the United States. The subsidies made Hawaiian sugar more expensive than American sugar. Unable to sell much sugar, planters concluded that the only way to increase sales was to have Hawaii become part of the United States.

In 1891 **Queen Liliuokalani** ascended the Hawaiian throne. Liliuokalani disliked the influence that American settlers had gained in Hawaii. In January 1893 she tried to impose a new constitution reasserting her authority as ruler of Hawaii. In response, a group of planters tried to overthrow the monarchy. Supported by the marines from the *USS Boston*, they forced the queen to step down. Then they set up a provisional government and asked the United States to annex Hawaii. **C**

President Cleveland strongly opposed imperialism. He withdrew the annexation treaty from the Senate and tried to return Liliuokalani to power. Hawaii's new leaders refused to restore the queen and decided to wait until Cleveland left office. Five years later, the United States annexed Hawaii.

✓ Reading Check **Explaining** How did the search for new markets push the United States to become a world power?

Extending the Content

American Samoa In the mid-nineteenth century, islands across the Pacific attracted the interest of imperialist nations. In the South Pacific, the Samoan Islands drew the attention of Germany, Britain, and the United States, all of which laid claim to parts of Samoa. The Samoan Islands attracted attention because the islands lay in a strategic position in the Pacific, could serve as coaling stations to refuel ships, and offered new markets for imperialist powers. The United States signed a "treaty of friendship and commerce" with Samoa in 1878 that granted the U.S. a coaling and naval station in the port of Pago Pago. In 1899 Germany and the United States signed the Treaty of Berlin, by which the United States annexed the eastern islands of Samoa and Germany annexed the western islands. Today the residents of American Samoa elect one nonvoting congressperson to the U.S. House of Representatives.

Diplomacy in Latin America

MAIN Idea The United States worked to increase trade with Latin America.

HISTORY AND YOU What products have you used that come from Latin America? Read to learn how the United States tried to expand its trade relations with Latin America.

The Pacific was not the only region where the United States sought to increase its influence in the 1800s. It also focused on Latin America. Although the United States bought raw materials from this region, Latin Americans bought most of their manufactured goods from Europe. American business leaders and government officials wanted to increase the sale of American products to the region. They also wanted the Europeans to understand that the United States was the dominant power in the region.

James G. Blaine, who served as secretary of state in three administrations in the 1880s, led early efforts to expand American influence in Latin America. "What we want," Blaine explained, "are the markets of these neighbors of ours that lie to the south of us. . . . With these markets secured new life would be given to our manufacturers, the product of the western farmer would be in demand, the reasons for and inducements to strikers, with all their attendant evils, would cease." Blaine proposed that the United States invite the Latin American nations to a **conference** in Washington, D.C. The conference would discuss ways in which the American nations could work together to support peace and to increase trade. The idea that the United States and Latin America should work together came to be called **Pan-Americanism.**

On October 2, 1889, Washington, D.C., hosted the first modern Pan-American conference, which all Latin American nations except the Dominican Republic attended. Blaine had two goals for the conference. First, he wanted to create a customs union between Latin America and the United States. He also wanted to create a system for American nations to work out their disputes peacefully.

A customs union would require all of the American nations to reduce their tariffs against each other and to treat each other equally in trade. Blaine hoped that a customs union would turn the Latin Americans away from European products and toward American products. He also hoped that a common system for settling disputes would keep the Europeans from meddling in American affairs.

Although the warm reception they received in the United States impressed the Latin American delegates to the conference, they rejected both of Blaine's ideas. They did agree, however, to create the Commercial Bureau of the American Republics, an organization that worked to promote cooperation among the nations of the Western Hemisphere. In 1920 the name was changed to the International Bureau of the American Republics. This organization was later known as the Pan-American Union and is today called the Organization of American States (OAS).

Reading Check **Summarizing** How did Secretary of State Blaine attempt to increase American influence in Latin America?

Section 1 REVIEW

Vocabulary

1. **Explain** the significance of: imperialism, protectorate, Anglo-Saxonism, Matthew C. Perry, Queen Liliuokalani, Pan-Americanism.

Main Ideas

2. **Listing** Use a graphic organizer to list the factors that led the United States to adopt an imperialist policy in the 1890s.

Factors Leading to U.S. Imperialist Policy

3. **Describing** Why and how did the Americans force the Japanese to trade with the United States?

4. **Explaining** Why did Secretary of State James G. Blaine convene the Pan-American conference in 1889?

Critical Thinking

5. **Big Ideas** Do you think the United States should have supported the planters in their attempt to overthrow Queen Liliuokalani of Hawaii? Why or why not?

6. **Evaluating** How did trade with the United States change Japanese society?

7. **Analyzing Visuals** Study the two images of Perry's ship on page 265. How do the artists' perspectives vary? Do you think the artists show any bias in their representations? Why or why not?

Writing About History

8. **Persuasive Writing** Imagine that you are living in the United States in the 1890s. Write a letter to the president persuading him to support or oppose an imperialist policy for the United States.

History ONLINE
Study Central™ To review this section, go to glencoe.com and click on Study Central.

Reading Check

Answer:
He wanted to create a customs union between Latin America and the United States. He also wanted to create a system for American nations to work out their disputes peacefully.

Assess

History ONLINE

Study Central™ provides summaries, interactive games, and online graphic organizers to help students review content.

Close

Summarizing Ask: Why did the United States become an imperial power? *(to spread American culture and civilization; to find new economic opportunities and markets; to compete with European powers)* **OL**

Section 1 REVIEW

Answers

1. All definitions can be found in the section and the Glossary.

2. feeling of superiority, interest in expanding trade, need for strategic military bases, European competition

3. Pressured by Congress, which in turn had been pressured by American businessmen, President Millard Fillmore sent Matthew C. Perry and a naval expedition to Tokyo to open Japan. The Japanese were impressed by modern ships and technology, against which they could not compete.

4. He convened the conference to support peace and increase trade among the nations in the Americas.

5. Students' answers will vary. Students should be able to defend their points of view.

6. Many Japanese leaders determined that it was time to remake and modernize their society. They launched an industrial revolution and built a navy, and then they began to build an empire.

7. Each artist depicts the ship from his own point of view. Both artists are biased in their representations because each is expressing the viewpoint of his or her nation.

8. Letters should express a clear point of view.

Focus

Bellringer
Daily Focus Transparency 7.2

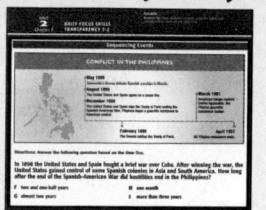

Guide to Reading

Answers to Graphic Organizer:
sinking of the *Maine*; sympathy for Cuban revolution; need to protect American investments in Cuba

Section Spotlight Video

To generate student interest and provide a springboard for class discussion, access the Chapter 7, Section 2 video at <u>glencoe.com</u> or on the video DVD.

Resource Manager

The Spanish-American War

During the Spanish-American War, the United States defeated Spanish troops in Cuba and the Philippines. Afterward, the United States annexed the Philippines and became an imperial power.

The Coming of War

MAIN Idea In support of the Cuban rebellion and in retaliation for the loss of the USS *Maine*, the United States declared war on Spain.

HISTORY AND YOU Do you remember what led the American colonists to declare their independence from Britain? Read about another colony that fought for independence from a colonial ruler.

By 1898 Cuba and Puerto Rico were Spain's last remaining colonies in the Western Hemisphere. Cubans had periodically revolted against Spanish rule, and many Americans regarded the Spanish as tyrants. Ultimately, the United States issued a declaration of war. Although the fighting lasted only a few months, the "splendid little war," as Secretary of State John Hay described it, dramatically altered the position of the United States on the world stage.

The Cuban Rebellion Begins

Cuba was one of Spain's oldest colonies in the Americas. Its sugarcane plantations generated considerable wealth for Spain and produced nearly one-third of the world's sugar in the mid-1800s. Until Spain abolished slavery in 1886, about one-third of the Cuban population was enslaved and forced to work for wealthy landowners on the plantations.

In 1868 Cuban rebels declared independence and launched a guerrilla war against Spanish authorities. Lacking internal support, the rebellion collapsed a decade later. Many Cuban rebels then fled to the United States. One of the exiled leaders was **José Martí,** a writer and poet. While living in New York City in the 1880s, Martí brought together Cuban exile groups living in the United States. The groups raised funds, purchased weapons, and trained troops in preparation for an invasion of Cuba.

By the early 1890s, the United States and Cuba had become closely linked economically. Cuba exported much of its sugar to the United States, and Americans had invested approximately $50 million in Cuba's sugar plantations, mines, and railroads. These economic ties created a crisis in 1894, when the United States imposed a new tariff on sugar that devastated Cuba's economy. With Cuba in financial

Guide to Reading

Big Ideas
Trade, War, and Migration The United States defeated Spain in a war, acquired new overseas territories, and became an imperial power.

Content Vocabulary
• yellow journalism *(p. 269)*
• autonomy *(p. 270)*
• jingoism *(p. 271)*

Academic Vocabulary
• intervene *(p. 270)*
• volunteer *(p. 272)*

People and Events to Identify
• José Martí *(p. 268)*
• William Randolph Hearst *(p. 269)*
• Joseph Pulitzer *(p. 269)*
• Emilio Aguinaldo *(p. 272)*
• Platt Amendment *(p. 274)*
• Foraker Act *(p. 275)*

Reading Strategy
Organizing As you read about the Spanish-American War, complete a graphic organizer like the one below by listing the circumstances that contributed to war with Spain.

Factors Contributing to Declaration of War

R Reading Strategies	C Critical Thinking	D Differentiated Instruction	W Writing Support	S Skill Practice
Teacher Edition • Using Contxt. Clues, p. 270 • Inferring, p. 274 **Additional Resources** • Guided Read. Act., URB p. 47 • Prim. Source Read., URB p. 33	**Teacher Edition** • Analy. Prim. Sources, p. 269 • Making Infer., p. 271 • Draw. Concl., p. 272 • Comparing, p. 274 **Additional Resources** • Quizzes and Tests, p. 96	**Teacher Edition** • Visual/Spatial, p. 270 **Additional Resources** • Am. Art and Music Act., URB p. 37 • Enrich. Act., URB p. 43 • English Learner Act., URB p. 23	**Teacher Edition** • Persuasive Writing, pp. 269, 273	**Additional Resources** • RENTG, p. 73 • Reinforcing Skills Act., URB p. 29

Causes of the Spanish-American War

The Spanish-American War had four main causes:

1. The Cuban Rebellion against Spain
2. American desire to protect its investments in Cuba
3. Yellow journalism that intensified public anger at Spain
4. The explosion of the USS *Maine*

CUBANS REBEL AGAINST SPAIN

◄ Spanish oppression of the Cuban people triggered a rebellion that earned the sympathy of many Americans, some of whom began providing arms and money to the rebels.

U.S. Investment in Cuba, 1897

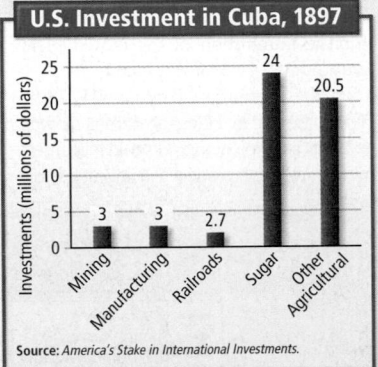

Investments (millions of dollars)

Mining 3
Manufacturing 3
Railroads 2.7
Sugar 24
Other Agricultural 20.5

Source: *America's Stake in International Investments.*

◄ With $30 to $50 million invested in Cuba and nearly $100 million in annual trade, American business leaders wanted Spain out of Cuba and an end to the rebellion.

YELLOW JOURNALISM

NEW YORK JOURNAL
AND ADVERTISER

DESTRUCTION OF THE WAR SHIP MAINE WAS THE WORK OF AN ENEMY

$50,000! $50,000 REWARD! For the Detection of the Perpetrator of the Maine Outrage!

Assistant Secretary Roosevelt Convinced the Explosion of the War Ship Was Not an Accident.

$50,000! $50,000 REWARD! For the Detection of the Perpetrator of the Maine Outrage!

The Journal Offers $50,000 Reward for the Conviction of the Criminals Who Sent 258 American Sailors to Their Death. Naval Officers Unanimous That the Ship Was Destroyed

▲ Dramatic and emotional stories in newspapers owned by Hearst and Pulitzer described Spanish atrocities in Cuba and enraged the American people, some of whom began to call for war.

THE *MAINE* EXPLODES, 1898

▲ President McKinley sent the battleship Maine to Cuba to help Americans evacuate. When the ship exploded, an enraged nation blamed Spain, and "Remember the Maine!" became the battle cry for war.

Analyzing VISUALS

1. **Interpreting** What do you think contributed to American sympathy with the Cubans?
2. **Identifying Central Issues** What role did economics play in the lead-up to war with Spain?

Teach

C Critical Thinking

Analyzing Primary Sources Have students study the Primary Source feature on this page. **Ask:** What events caused American public opinion to favor the Cubans? What event caused the United States to declare war on Spain? *(the Cuban revolution, yellow journalism, and U.S. economic involvement; the sinking of the* Maine*)*

Analyzing VISUALS

Answers:
1. the oppression of the Cuban people by the Spanish
2. The United States had money invested in Cuba in the late 1890s and sought to protect those economic interests.

W Writing Support

Persuasive Writing Have students write a letter to the editor of the *New York Journal* supporting or opposing the newspaper's views on the uprising in Cuba. **BL**

distress, Martí's followers launched a new rebellion in February 1895. Although Martí died during the fighting, the rebels seized control of eastern Cuba, declared independence, and formally established the Republic of Cuba in September 1895.

America Supports Cuba

When the uprising in Cuba began, President Grover Cleveland declared the United States neutral. Outside the White House, however, many people openly supported the rebels. Some citizens compared the Cubans' struggle to the American Revolution. A few sympathetic Americans even began smuggling guns from Florida to the Cuban rebels.

What caused most Americans to support the rebels were the stories of Spanish atrocities reported in two of the nation's major newspapers, the *New York Journal* and the *New York World*. The *Journal*, owned by **William Randolph Hearst,** and *The World,* owned by **Joseph Pulitzer,** competed with each other to increase their circulation. The *Journal* reported outrageous stories of the Spanish feeding Cuban prisoners to sharks and dogs. Not to be outdone, *The World* described Cuba as a place with "blood on the roadsides, blood in the fields, blood on the doorsteps, blood, blood, blood!" This kind of sensationalist reporting, in which writers often exaggerated and even made up stories to attract readers, became known as **yellow journalism.**

Hands-On Chapter Project
Step 2

Preparing a Multimedia Presentation

Step 2: Organizing Information on the Presentation Groups begin to create and organize their presentations.

Directions Have students meet in their groups with the notes they have taken on their assigned country. Have groups discuss how they want to organize the information they've gathered. Suggest the options of chronology, cause-and-effect, or organization by subcategory.

Once groups have determined the format, have them begin assembling the information they want to include in their presentations. Encourage students to use primary source quotes, informational text, diagrams, photographs, or even drawings they've created. Students may also use propaganda from the period.

Putting It Together Have students review their presentation once they have entered their information to verify the accuracy of the information and to make sure nothing has been left out. **OL**

(Chapter Project continued on page 277)

270

R Reading Strategy

Using Context Clues Have students reread the first paragraph under "Calls for War" on this page. Using clue words and phrases such as "believing it would cost too many lives," "hurt the economy," and "asked the Spanish if the United States could help negotiate an end to the conflict," ask students to define the term *intervene*. Students should note that the term means "to get involved or to interfere." **BL**

D Differentiated Instruction

Visual/Spatial Have interested students create a map of Cuba. Using library or Internet resources, students should show the location of the battles that occurred during the Spanish-American War and the position of the American navy around the island. Display the maps in the classroom. **BL**

Additional Support

Although the press invented sensational stories, Cubans indeed suffered horribly. The Spanish sent nearly 200,000 troops to the island to put down the rebellion and appointed General Valeriano Weyler as governor. Weyler's harsh policies quickly earned him the nickname "*El Carnicero*" ("The Butcher").

The Cuban rebels staged hit-and-run raids, burned plantations and sugar mills, tore up railroad tracks, and attacked supply depots. Knowing that many American businesses had investments in Cuba, the rebels hoped that the destruction of American property would lead to American intervention in the war.

To prevent Cuban villagers from helping the rebels, Weyler herded hundreds of thousands of rural men, women, and children into "reconcentration camps," where tens of thousands died of starvation and disease. News reports of these camps enraged Americans.

Calls for War

R   In 1897 Republican William McKinley became president of the United States. The new president did not want to **intervene** in the war, believing it would cost too many lives and hurt the economy. In September 1897, he asked the Spanish if the United States could R help negotiate an end to the conflict. He made it clear that if the war did not end soon, the United States might have to intervene.

Spain removed Weyler from power and offered the Cubans **autonomy**—the right to their own government—but only if Cuba remained part of the Spanish empire. The Cuban rebels refused to negotiate.

Spain's concessions enraged many Spanish loyalists in Cuba. In January 1898, the loyalists rioted in Havana. Worried that Americans in Cuba might be attacked, McKinley sent the battleship USS *Maine* to Havana in case the Americans had to be evacuated.

On February 9, 1898, the *New York Journal* printed a letter intercepted by a Cuban agent. Written by Enrique Dupuy de Lôme, the Spanish ambassador to the United States, the letter described McKinley as "weak and a bidder for the admiration of the crowd." The nation erupted in fury over the insult.

Then, on the evening of February 15, 1898, while the *Maine* sat in Havana Harbor, it was ripped apart by an explosion and sank. No one is sure why the *Maine* exploded. An investigation

PRIMARY SOURCE
The Spanish-American War

When the United States declared war on Spain, the U.S. Army had approximately 25,000 soldiers. Spain had roughly 200,000 in Cuba alone. To expand its forces, the government called into service soldiers from the state militias and also enlisted 20,000 volunteers in the army. Among those volunteers was the First Volunteer Cavalry, nicknamed the Rough Riders, under the command of Colonels Leonard Wood and Theodore Roosevelt.

U.S. Deaths in the Spanish-American War

Battle 385

Food Poisoning and Disease 2,061

Source: *The Nystrom Atlas of United States History.*

NATIONAL GEOGRAPHIC The Battle for Cuba, 1898

0   100 kilometers
0   100 miles
Miller projection

← U.S. forces
← Spanish forces
⚓ U.S. naval blockade
✱ Major battle

Tampa
UNITED STATES
Key West
Bahamas U.K.
ATLANTIC OCEAN
Havana
CUBA
SHAFTER
20°N
MILES
Santiago de Cuba
Jamaica U.K.
CERVERA
HAITI
Caribbean Sea
80°W

On Feb. 15, 1898, the USS *Maine* sinks.

On July 3, 1898, the Spanish fleet tries to flee but is destroyed.

Battle of San Juan Heights
On July 1, 1898, Teddy Roosevelt and the Rough Riders go into battle.

D

Extending the Content

The Rough Riders When Congress called for raising three cavalry units, Assistant Secretary of the Navy Theodore Roosevelt leapt at the opportunity to recruit his diverse acquaintances. The background of these recruits reflected Roosevelt's affluent background and interests as an outdoorsman and hunter, as he later recounted:

"We drew recruits from Harvard, Yale, Princeton ... from clubs like the Somerset, of Boston, and Knickerbocker, of New York ... Four of the policemen who had served under me while I was President of the New York Police Board ... the high jumper ... the football players ... the steeple-chase rider ... the crack polo player ... the cowboy, the hunter, and the mining prospector ... From the Indian Territory there came a number of Indians—Cherokees, Chickasaws, Choctaws, and Creeks."

in the 1970s suggested that the spontaneous combustion of a coal bunker aboard the ship caused the explosion, but a study in the 1990s concluded that a mine could have done the damage. In 1898, however, many Americans believed it was an act of sabotage by Spanish agents. "Remember the *Maine*!" became the rallying cry for those demanding a declaration of war against Spain.

In response, Congress authorized McKinley to spend $50 million for war preparations. McKinley faced tremendous pressure to go to war. Within the Republican Party, **jingoism**—aggressive nationalism—was very strong. Many Democrats also demanded war, and Republicans feared that if McKinley did not go to war, the Democrats would win the elections in 1900. Finally, on April 11, 1898, McKinley asked Congress to authorize the use of force.

On April 19, Congress proclaimed Cuba independent, demanded that Spain withdraw from the island, and authorized the president to use armed force if necessary. In response, on April 24, Spain declared war on the United States. For the first time in 50 years, the United States was at war with another nation.

Reading Check **Examining** What conditions led to the Cuban rebellion in 1895?

A War on Two Fronts

MAIN Idea The United States fought and defeated Spain in both the Caribbean and the Pacific.

HISTORY AND YOU Have you ever had to plan a trip or an event? Read to learn about the problems American troops encountered in the war of 1898.

The United States Navy was ready for war with Spain. The navy's North Atlantic Squadron blockaded Cuba, and Commodore George Dewey, commander of the American naval squadron based in Hong Kong, was ordered to attack the Spanish fleet based in the Philippines. The Philippines was a Spanish colony, and American naval planners wanted to prevent the Spanish fleet based there from sailing east to attack the United States.

The Battle of Manila Bay

A short time after midnight, on May 1, 1898, Dewey's squadron entered Manila Bay in the Philippines. As dawn broke, four American ships in the squadron opened fire and rapidly destroyed all eight of the severely outgunned Spanish warships.

C Critical Thinking

Making Inferences Point out to students that, at first, President McKinley was reluctant to go to war with Spain but eventually asked Congress for a declaration of war. **Ask:** Did McKinley yield to political pressure when he asked Congress to declare war on Spain? *(Students might infer that because many Republicans and some Democrats favored war, McKinley felt he had no choice but to ask Congress for war.)* **OL**

Reading Check

Answer:
Spanish oppression, Spanish economic exploitation

Analyzing GEOGRAPHY

Answers:
1. near Santiago and Manila
2. Both are islands, and the American navy was much stronger than the Spanish navy.

Additional Support

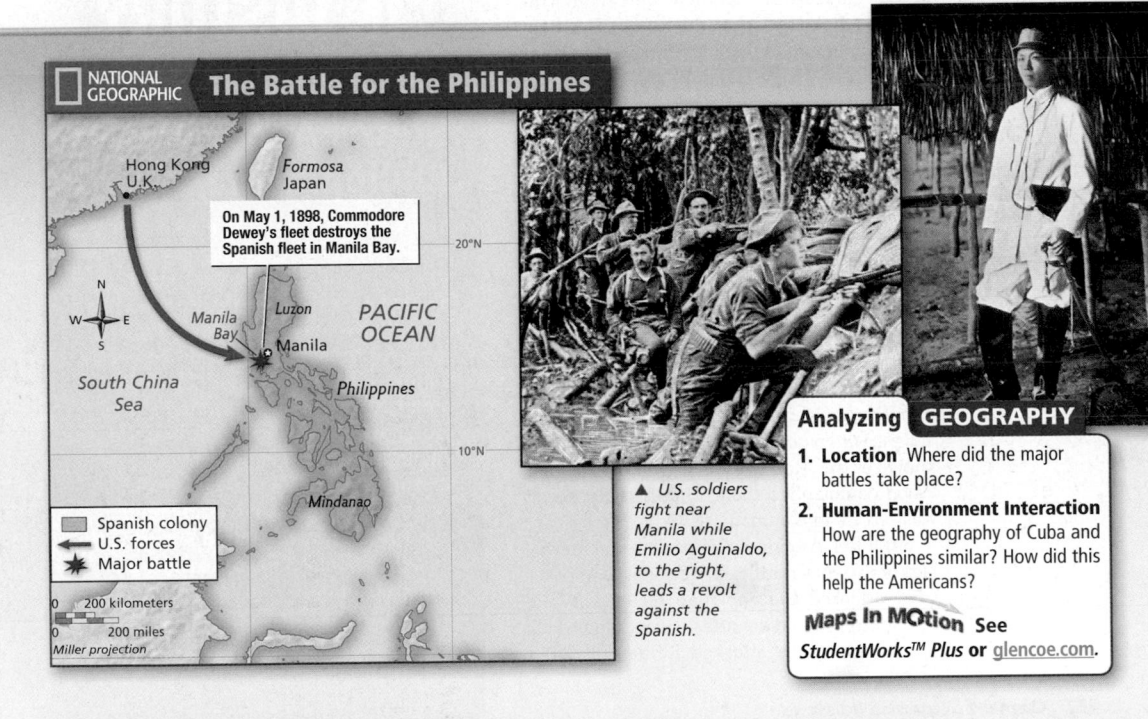

NATIONAL GEOGRAPHIC **The Battle for the Philippines**

Hong Kong U.K. · Formosa Japan

On May 1, 1898, Commodore Dewey's fleet destroys the Spanish fleet in Manila Bay.

20°N

Manila Bay · Luzon · Manila · PACIFIC OCEAN

South China Sea · Philippines

10°N

Mindanao

- Spanish colony
- ← U.S. forces
- ★ Major battle

0 200 kilometers
0 200 miles
Miller projection

▲ U.S. soldiers fight near Manila while Emilio Aguinaldo, to the right, leads a revolt against the Spanish.

Analyzing GEOGRAPHY

1. **Location** Where did the major battles take place?
2. **Human-Environment Interaction** How are the geography of Cuba and the Philippines similar? How did this help the Americans?

Maps In Motion See *StudentWorks™ Plus* or glencoe.com.

Activity: Collaborative Learning

Writing a Feature Article Organize the students into groups of four. Have each student in the group write a feature article about the causes of the Spanish-American War from one of the following points of view: a U.S. soldier, a yellow journalist, a wife of a crew member of the USS *Maine,* or a Cuban who had been forced to live in a reconcentration camp. Have the group review and critique each feature article.

Then have the groups combine the articles into a small newspaper. Encourage students to share their newspapers with others in the class. **OL**

C Critical Thinking

Drawing Conclusions The text states that both the Spanish and American militaries believed that the war would be decided at sea. **Ask:** What factors would lead military planners to that conclusion? *(The Americans did not have a large navy at the beginning of the war, but they still needed to send troops to Cuba or other Spanish-controlled areas. The Spanish fleet, however, was old; yet the Spanish needed to send new troops to Cuba to reinforce those already there, who were tired and strained from fighting the Cuban rebels.)* **AL**

✔ Reading Check

Answer:
Although at first poorly prepared in comparison to the U.S. Navy, the U.S. Army created a plan to attack around Santiago, frightening the Spanish fleet out of the harbor and into battle with the American navy.

Differentiated Instruction

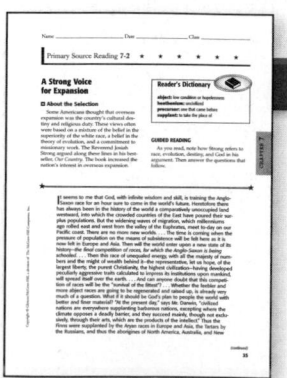

**Primary Source Reading,
URB pp. 35–36**

Dewey's quick victory took McKinley and his advisers by surprise. The army was not yet ready to send troops to help Dewey. Hastily, the army assembled 20,000 troops to sail from San Francisco to the Philippines. On the way, the Americans also seized the island of Guam, another Spanish possession in the Pacific.

While waiting for the American troops to arrive, Dewey contacted **Emilio Aguinaldo,** a Filipino revolutionary leader who had staged an unsuccessful uprising against the Spanish in 1896. Aguinaldo quickly launched a new rebellion against the Spanish. While the rebels took control of most of the islands, American troops seized the Philippine capital of Manila.

American Forces in Cuba

The Spanish in Cuba were not prepared for war. Tropical diseases and months of fighting rebels had weakened their soldiers. Their warships were old and their crews poorly trained. Both sides knew that the war would ultimately be decided at sea. If the United States could defeat the Spanish fleet, Spain would not be able to supply its troops in Cuba. Eventually, they would have to surrender.

The United States Army was not prepared for war either. Although there were many **volunteers,** the army lacked the resources to train and equip them. In many training camps, conditions were so unsanitary that epidemics broke out, and hundreds died—far more than would be killed in battle with the Spanish.

Finally, on June 14, 1898, a force of about 17,000 troops landed east of the city of Santiago, Cuba. The Spanish fleet, well-protected by powerful shore-based guns, occupied Santiago Harbor. American military planners wanted to capture those guns to drive the Spanish fleet out of the harbor and into battle with the American fleet waiting nearby.

Among the American troops advancing toward Santiago was a volunteer cavalry unit from the American west. They were a flamboyant mix of cowboys, miners, and law officers known as the "Rough Riders." Colonel Leonard Wood commanded them. Theodore Roosevelt was second in command.

On July 1, American troops attacked the village of El Caney northeast of Santiago. Another force attacked the San Juan Heights. While one group of soldiers attacked San Juan Hill, the Rough Riders attacked Kettle Hill. After

---

seizing Kettle Hill, Roosevelt and his men assisted in the capture of San Juan Hill.

The all-black 9th and 10th Cavalry Regiments accompanied the Rough Riders up Kettle Hill. Roughly one-fourth of the American troops fighting in Cuba were African Americans, four of whom received the Medal of Honor for their bravery during the war.

The Spanish commander in Santiago panicked after the American victories at El Caney and the San Juan Heights and ordered the Spanish fleet in the harbor to flee. As they exited the harbor on July 3, American warships attacked them, sinking or beaching every Spanish vessel. Two weeks later, the Spanish troops in Santiago surrendered. Soon afterwards, American troops occupied the nearby Spanish colony of Puerto Rico as well.

✔ Reading Check **Comparing** How prepared was the U.S. Army as compared to the U.S. Navy to fight a war against Spain?

Debates IN HISTORY

Should the United States Annex the Philippines?

In the Treaty of Paris of 1898, Spain ceded control of the Philippine Islands to the United States. Americans were divided over whether the United States should give the Filipinos their independence or become an imperial power by annexing the Philippines. Supporters of annexation argued the United States would benefit economically and the Filipinos would benefit from exposure to American values and principles. Opponents, however, considered it hypocritical for the United States, with its own colonial past, to become an imperial nation.

Primary Source Readings: Recognizing Bias

Objective: Read to identify bias in primary sources.

Focus: Read the primary source in support of expansionism.

Teach: Define bias and discuss how it can affect students' understanding of history.

Assess: Identify instances of bias in the selection and highlight the passages.

Differentiated Instruction Strategies

BL Identify two instances of bias in the selection.

AL Search magazines and newspapers for articles that show bias. Discuss how the bias influences the information presented in the article.

ELL Define each vocabulary word in the selection using glossaries or dictionaries.

An American Empire

MAIN Idea In defeating Spain, the United States acquired an overseas empire.

HISTORY AND YOU Do you think Puerto Rico should become the 51st state? Read how Puerto Rico became an American territory.

As American and Spanish leaders met to discuss the terms for a peace treaty, Americans debated what to do about their newly acquired lands. Cuba would receive its independence as promised, and Spain had agreed to the U.S. annexation of Guam and Puerto Rico. The big question was what to do with the Philippines. The United States faced a difficult choice—remain true to its republican ideals or become an imperial power that ruled a foreign country without the consent of its people. The issue sparked an intense political debate.

The Debate Over Annexation

Many people who supported annexing the Philippines emphasized the economic and military benefits of taking the islands. They would provide the United States with another Pacific naval base, a stopover on the way to China, and a large market for American goods.

Other supporters believed America had a duty to help "less civilized" peoples. "Surely this Spanish war has not been a grab for empire," commented a New England minister, "but a heroic effort [to] free the oppressed and to teach the millions of ignorant, debased human beings thus freed how to live."

Not all Americans supported annexation. Anti-imperialists included William Jennings Bryan, industrialist Andrew Carnegie, social worker Jane Addams, writer Samuel Clemens (Mark Twain), and Samuel Gompers, leader of the American Federation of Labor.

W

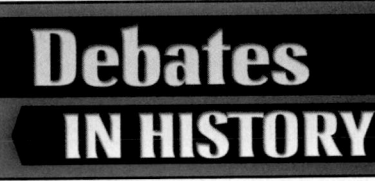

Debates IN HISTORY

YES

Albert J. Beveridge
United States Senator

PRIMARY SOURCE

"The Opposition tells us that we ought not to govern a people without their consent. I answer, The rule of liberty that all just government derives its authority from the consent of the governed, applies only to those who are capable of self-government. We govern the Indians without their consent, we govern our territories without their consent, we govern our children without their consent. . . . Would not the people of the Philippines prefer the just, humane, civilizing government of this Republic to the savage, bloody rule of pillage and extortion from which we have rescued them?"
—from *The Meaning of the Times*

NO

William Jennings Bryan
Presidential Candidate

PRIMARY SOURCE

"It is not necessary to own people in order to trade with them. We carry on trade today with every part of the world, and our commerce has expanded more rapidly than the commerce of any European empire. . . . A harbor and coaling station in the Philippines would answer every trade and military necessity and such a concession could have been secured at any time without difficulty.
. . . Imperialism finds no warrant in the Bible. The command 'Go ye into all the world and preach the gospel to every creature' has no Gatling gun attachment. . . ."
—from *Speeches of William Jennings Bryan*

DBQ Document-Based Questions

1. **Making Inferences** According to Albert Beveridge, why is annexation of the Philippines an honorable decision?

2. **Recognizing Bias** What does Beveridge think of the people of the Philippines?

3. **Analyzing** What are William Jennings Bryan's two main criticisms of imperialism?

4. **Drawing Conclusions** After studying both sides of the issue, who do you think was right? Explain.

Chapter 7 Becoming a World Power **273**

Activity: Technology Connection

Preparing a Multimedia Presentation
Divide students into groups and have them use library or Internet resources to learn more about the debate over annexation of the Philippines. Have students create a computer-based multimedia presentation to portray both sides of the debate. Groups should depict the views of one imperialist and one anti-imperialist. Encourage students to include quotes from their chosen debaters as well as background information on their lives. Have groups conclude their presentations by imagining the reaction of both parties to McKinley's decision to annex the islands. **AL**

R **Reading Strategy**

Inferring Have students reread the Primary Source quote from President McKinley. **Ask:** What can you infer about McKinley's views of the Filipino people? *(He thought they were not Christians, when in fact, most Filipinos were Catholic.)* OL

C **Critical Thinking**

Comparing Review with students the status of the Philippines and Cuba after the 1898 peace treaty and the passage of the Platt Amendment. **Ask:** How did the status of the Philippines and Cuba differ? *(The Philippines were a territory of the United States; Cuba was nominally independent.)* OL

Analyzing VISUALS

Answers:
1. McKinley is supporting imperialism while Bryan is attacking imperialism.
2. Uncle Sam is going to choose several items from the "menu." Uncle Sam states that he can't decide which to order first.

Differentiated Instruction

POLITICAL CARTOONS PRIMARY SOURCE
The Debate Over Empire

▲ President McKinley raises the American flag over the Philippines while William Jennings Bryan tries to chop it down.

▲ President McKinley (the waiter) prepares to take Uncle Sam's order. The menu posted on the wall shows three regions of choice: the Cuba steak, the Porto [Puerto] Rico pig; and the Philippines and Sandwich Islands (Hawaii) in the Pacific.

Analyzing VISUALS

1. **Identifying Central Issues** Based on the cartoon on the left, what do you think McKinley is trying to accomplish? What about Bryan?
2. **Making Inferences** What does the cartoon on the right suggest that Uncle Sam is going to do? On what basis do you infer that?

History ONLINE Student Web Activity Visit glencoe.com and complete the activity on American imperialism.

Andrew Carnegie argued that the cost of an empire far outweighed the economic benefits it provided. Gompers worried that competition from cheap Filipino labor would drive down American wages. Addams, Clemens, and others believed imperialism violated American principles. Despite the objections of the anti-imperialists, President McKinley ultimately decided to annex the islands. He later explained his reasoning as follows:

PRIMARY SOURCE

R "And one night late it came to me this way. . . (1) that we could not give them back to Spain—that would be cowardly and dishonorable; (2) that we could not turn them over to France or Germany. . . that would be bad for business and discreditable; (3) that we could not leave them to themselves—they were unfit for self-government. . . and (4) that there was nothing left for us to do but to take them all, and to educate the Filipinos, and uplift and civilize and Christianize them."

—A Diplomatic History of the American People

On December 10, 1898, the United States and Spain signed the Treaty of Paris. Under the treaty, Cuba became an independent nation, and the United States acquired Puerto Rico and Guam and agreed to pay Spain $20 million for the Philippines. After an intense debate, the Senate ratified the treaty in February 1899. The United States had become an imperial power.

The Platt Amendment

Although the United States had promised to grant Cuba its independence, President McKinley took steps to ensure that Cuba would remain tied to the United States. He allowed the Cubans to prepare a new constitution for their country but attached conditions. The **Platt Amendment,** submitted by Senator Orville Platt, specified the following: (1) Cuba could not make any treaty with another nation that would weaken its independence; (2) Cuba had to allow the United States to buy or lease naval stations in Cuba; (3) Cuba's debts had to be kept low to prevent foreign countries from landing troops to enforce payment; and (4) the United States would have the right to intervene to protect Cuban independence and keep order. C

Leveled Activities

BL **Guided Reading Activity, URB p. 47**

OL **American Art and Music, URB p. 37**

AL **Enrichment Activity, URB p. 43**

ELL **Reading Essentials and Note-Taking Guide, p. 73**

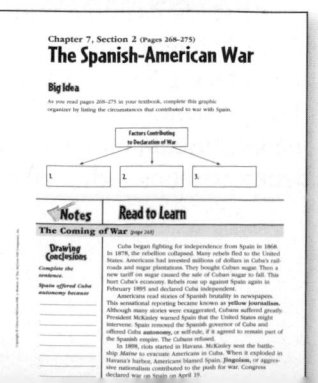

Reluctantly, the Cubans added the amendment to their constitution. The Platt Amendment, which effectively made Cuba an American protectorate, remained in effect until its repeal in 1934.

Governing Puerto Rico

Another pressing question was how to govern Puerto Rico. In 1900 Congress passed the **Foraker Act,** establishing a civil government for the island. The law provided for an elected legislature, but also called for a governor and executive council, to be appointed by the president, who held final authority. Supreme Court rulings subsequently held that Puerto Ricans were not American citizens and so did not possess the constitutional rights of citizens.

Congress gradually allowed Puerto Ricans greater self-government. In 1917 it granted Puerto Ricans American citizenship. Thirty years later, islanders were allowed to elect their own governor. At this time a debate began over whether Puerto Rico should become a state, become independent, or continue as a self-governing commonwealth of the United States. This debate over Puerto Rico's status continues today.

Rebellion in the Philippines

The United States quickly learned that controlling its new empire would not be easy. Emilio Aguinaldo called the American decision to annex his homeland a "violent and aggressive seizure" and ordered his troops to attack American soldiers. The Philippine-American war, or Philippine Insurrection as it was referred to at the time, lasted for more than three years. Approximately 126,000 American soldiers were sent to the Philippines to fight the insurgency. More than 4,300 American soldiers died, either from combat or disease, as did an estimated 50,000–200,000 Filipinos.

To fight the Filipino guerrillas, the United States military adopted many of the same policies that America had condemned Spain for using in Cuba. Reconcentration camps were established to separate Filipino guerrillas from civilians. Consequently, thousands of people died from disease and starvation, just as they had in Cuba.

While American troops fought the guerrillas, the first U.S. civilian governor of the islands, William Howard Taft, tried to win over the Filipinos by improving education, transportation, and health care. Railroads and bridges were built. Public schools were set up, and new health-care policies virtually eliminated diseases such as cholera and smallpox. These reforms slowly reduced Filipino hostility.

In March 1901, American troops captured Aguinaldo. A month later, Aguinaldo called on the guerrillas to surrender. On July 4, 1902, the United States declared the war over. Eventually the United States allowed the Filipinos a greater role in governing their own country. By the mid-1930s, they were permitted to elect their own congress and president. Finally, in 1946, the United States granted independence to the Philippines.

✔ **Reading Check** **Explaining** What were the arguments for and against establishing an American empire?

Section 2 REVIEW

Vocabulary
1. **Explain** the significance of: José Martí, William Randolph Hearst, Joseph Pulitzer, yellow journalism, autonomy, jingoism, Emilio Aguinaldo, Platt Amendment, Foraker Act.

Main Ideas
2. **Explaining** Why did many Americans blame Spain for the explosion of the USS *Maine*?

3. **Identifying** How did the U.S. fight the Spanish-American War on two fronts?

4. **Categorizing** Complete the table by summarizing the effects of the United States annexing lands obtained after the Spanish-American War.

Lands Annexed	Effects

Critical Thinking
5. **Big Ideas** How has the government of Puerto Rico changed since the Foraker Act was passed in 1900?

6. **Evaluating** Why did Filipinos feel betrayed by the U.S. government after the Spanish-American War?

7. **Analyzing Visuals** Study the circle graph on page 270. What caused the most casualties during the war? Explain.

Writing About History
8. **Descriptive Writing** Imagine that you are a Filipino living during the time of the U.S. annexation of the Philippine Islands. Write a journal entry in which you describe your feelings about American control of the islands.

History ONLINE
Study Central™ To review this section, go to glencoe.com and click on Study Central.

275

✔ **Reading Check**

Answer:
for: a naval base in Asia and a market for American goods, a chance to teach people who were regarded as less fortunate; against: cost, competition, violated American principles, cheap labor might drive down American wages

Assess
· ·
History ONLINE

Study Central™ provides summaries, interactive games, and online graphic organizers to help students review content.

Close
· ·
Summarizing Ask: Why did the United States go to war with Spain? *(public opinion favored Cuban uprising; to protect American economic interests in Cuba; public swayed by yellow journalism; sinking of the battleship USS Maine)* **OL**

Section 2 REVIEW

Answers

1. All definitions can be found in the section and the Glossary.
2. Cuba was fighting Spain for its independence, and many Americans saw the Spanish as tyrants.
3. The navy's North Atlantic Squadron blockaded Cuba. The American fleet based in Hong Kong attacked the Spanish fleet in the Philippines to prevent the ships from sailing east to attack the United States. While waiting for the army to arrive with reinforcements, the navy cooperated with Filipino revolutionaries.

4. Puerto Rico: U.S. control of its government, Puerto Ricans become U.S. citizens after 1917; Philippines: some improvements in Filipino schools, roads, and healthcare.
5. Under the Foraker Act, Puerto Ricans had no constitutional rights or power of self-government. Over time, Puerto Ricans were made citizens and allowed to elect their own governor. Debate continues over whether the commonwealth should become a state, become an independent nation, or remain as it is.

6. The Filipinos believed that the United States was helping them achieve independence from Spain, and so they were disappointed to be made part of an empire. The United States attempted to gain support by improving education, transportation, and health care. These efforts were somewhat successful.
7. Food poisoning and disease caused the most deaths. Sanitary conditions were poor.
8. Journal entries will vary but should express a Filipino's point of view.

Focus

Bellringer
Daily Focus Transparency 7.3

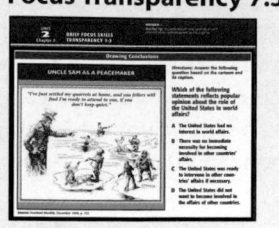

Guide to Reading

Answers to Graphic Organizer:
save time, save money, help the United States remain a world power

Section Spotlight Video

To generate student interest and provide a springboard for class discussion, access the Chapter 7, Section 3 video at glencoe.com or on the video DVD.

Resource Manager

Section 3

New American Diplomacy

Guide to Reading

Big Ideas
Trade, War, and Migration Under President Theodore Roosevelt, the United States increased its power on the world stage.

Content Vocabulary
• sphere of influence (p. 276)
• Open Door policy (p. 277)
• dollar diplomacy (p. 281)
• guerrilla (p. 283)

Academic Vocabulary
• access (p. 277)
• tension (p. 280)

People and Events to Identify
• Boxer Rebellion (p. 278)
• Hay-Pauncefote Treaty (p. 280)
• Roosevelt Corollary (p. 280)
• Victoriana Huerta (p. 283)
• Pancho Villa (p. 283)

Reading Strategy
Organizing As you read about American diplomacy complete a graphic organizer by listing the reasons the U.S. wanted a canal through Central America.

Reasons to Build Canal

Succeeding President McKinley, President Theodore Roosevelt mediated disputes in Asia and Latin America and acquired the Panama Canal Zone. Presidents Taft and Wilson worked to increase American trade and influence in Latin America.

American Diplomacy in Asia

MAIN Idea The United States pursued an Open Door policy to allow all nations access to China's markets.

HISTORY AND YOU Do you remember reading about a trade agreement with Japan in the 1850s? Read to learn about America's efforts to keep trade open with China in the 1900s.

In 1899 the United States was a major power in Asia, with naval bases all across the Pacific. Operating from those bases, the United States Navy—by then the third-largest navy in the world—could exert American power anywhere in East Asia. The nation's primary interest in Asia, however, was not conquest but commerce. Between 1895 and 1900, American exports to China increased fourfold. Although China bought only about two percent of American exports, the vast Chinese markets excited American business leaders, especially those in the textile, oil, and steel industries.

The Open Door Policy

In 1894 war erupted between China and Japan over Korea, which at that time was part of the Chinese empire. Western observers were astonished when Japan easily defeated China's massive military. In the peace treaty, China granted Korea independence and gave Japan territory in Manchuria. The war showed that Japan had mastered Western technology and industry. It also demonstrated that China was far weaker than anyone had thought.

The Russians were concerned about Japan's rising power. They did not want Japan to acquire the territory in Manchuria, because it bordered Russia. Backed by France and Germany, Russia forced Japan to return the Manchurian territory it had acquired. Then, in 1898, Russia demanded China lease the territory to Russia instead.

Leasing a territory meant that it would still belong to China, even though a foreign government would maintain overall control. Soon Germany, France, and Britain demanded "leaseholds" in China as well. Each "leasehold" became the center of a country's **sphere of influence,** an area where a foreign nation controlled economic development such as railroad construction and mining.

R Reading Strategies	**C** Critical Thinking	**D** Differentiated Instruction	**W** Writing Support	**S** Skill Practice
Teacher Edition • Inferring, p. 277 **Additional Resources** • Guided Read. Act., URB p. 48 • Read. Skills Act., URB p. 19	**Teacher Edition** • Comparing, p. 279 • Identify. Central Issues, p. 279 • Draw. Concl., p. 280 • Analyz. Info., p. 281 **Additional Resources** • Inter. Pol. Cartoons Act., URB p. 39 • Quizzes and Tests, p. 97 • Critical Thinking Skills Act., URB p. 30	**Teacher Edition** • Visual/Spatial, pp. 278, 280 • Advanced Learners, p. 282 **Additional Resources** • Diff. Instr. Act., URB p. 21 • Authentic Assess., p. 33 • Reteach. Act., URB p. 41	**Teacher Edition** • Persuasive Writing, pp. 277, 281 • Descrip. Writing, p. 283	**Additional Resources** • RENTG, p. 76 • Historical Analysis Skills Act., URB p. 20 • Time Line Act., URB p. 31

NATIONAL GEOGRAPHIC The Open Door Policy and the Boxer Rebellion

In June 1900, Boxer rebels attack foreign compounds in Peking and Tientsin.

Empire
- British
- French
- Japanese
- Russian
- German

Sphere of Influence

0   1000 kilometers
0   1000 miles
Miller projection

What Was the Open Door Policy?

1. Within its sphere of influence, each power agreed not to interfere with any existing business interests or port treaties of other powers.

2. Existing Chinese tariffs would remain unchanged in all spheres of influence and would be collected by the Chinese government.

3. Within each sphere of influence, harbor fees and railroad charges would be the same for all countries, giving no special rates to the countries whose businesses owned and operated the harbors and railroads.

▲ Secretary of State John Hay

Analyzing VISUALS

1. **Interpreting** What do you think Britain was attempting with the locations of their spheres of influence?

2. **Analyzing** Based on the map, which country do you believe had the most influence?

▲ International soldiers pose in Tianjin after rescuing their besieged delegations during the Boxer Rebellion. The American is second from left.

Politicians and businessmen in the United States worried about these events. President McKinley and Secretary of State John Hay both supported what they called an **Open Door policy,** in which all countries would be allowed to trade with China. In 1899 Hay sent notes to countries with leaseholds in China asking them not to discriminate against other nations wanting to do business in their sphere of influence. Each of the nations responded by saying they accepted the Open Door policy but would not act on it unless all of the others agreed. Once Hay had received assurances from all of the nations with leaseholds, he declared that the United States expected the other powers to uphold the policy.

The Boxer Rebellion

While foreign countries debated **access** to China's market, secret Chinese societies organized to fight foreign control. Westerners referred to one such group, the Society of Harmonious Fists, as the Boxers. In 1900 the group decided to destroy both the "foreign devils" and their Chinese Christian converts, whom they believed were corrupting Chinese society.

Teach

R Reading Strategy

Inferring Ask: Based on the text, what was the United States's motivation for putting forth the Open Door Policy? *(The United States wanted access to all of China's markets.)* **OL**

W Writing Support

Persuasive Writing Ask interested students to write a letter to the governments of Great Britain, France, Germany, and Russia persuading them to accept the Open Door Policy. **AL**

Analyzing VISUALS

Answers:
1. keep the French sphere of influence from expanding
2. Students may say Britain or Russia because of the amount of territory they control bordering China and the size of their spheres of influence.

Hands-On Chapter Project
Step 3

Preparing a Multimedia Presentation

Step 3: Editing the Presentation Groups will edit their presentations for accuracy, content, and mechanics.

Directions Have groups run through their presentations to make sure that links to other pages are working properly and that all information is displayed correctly. Students should also edit their presentations for grammar, punctuation, and sentence structure. Encourage students to pair up with another group and review each other's presentations. Tell students that presentations should be coherent and easily understood.

Putting It Together Once students have reviewed their presentations, they should make any necessary changes, additions, or corrections. **OL**
(Chapter Project continued on the Visual Summary page)

278

D Differentiated Instruction

Visual/Spatial Have interested students locate the parts of Beijing and Tianjin that were under siege by the Boxers. Then have the students create maps of the cities showing the areas of fighting. **OL**

✓ Reading Check

Answer:
to ensure that all nations had access to China's markets

Additional Support

In what became known as the **Boxer Rebellion,** the Boxers, supported by some Chinese troops, besieged foreign embassies in Beijing and Tianjin, killing more than 200 foreigners and taking others prisoner. After the German ambassador to China was killed, eight nations—Germany, Austria-Hungary, Britain, France, Italy, Japan, Russia, and the United States—decided to intervene. A large international force of nearly 50,000 troops, including 3,400 Americans, landed in China to rescue the foreigners and smash the rebellion.

During the crisis, Secretary of State John Hay worked with British diplomats to persuade the other powers not to partition China. In a second set of Open Door notes, Hay convinced the participating powers to accept compensation from China for damages caused by the rebellion. After some discussion, the powers agreed not to break up China into European-controlled colonies. The United States retained access to China's lucrative trade in tea, spices, and silk and maintained an increasingly larger market for its own goods.

✓ Reading Check **Explaining** What was the purpose of the Open Door policy?

Roosevelt's Diplomacy

MAIN Idea Presidents Roosevelt and Taft continued to support a policy of expanding United States influence in foreign countries.

HISTORY AND YOU Do you know of a country that is trying to expand its influence today? Read to find out about expansion of United States influence in the early 1900s.

The election of 1900 once again pitted President McKinley against William Jennings Bryan. Bryan, an anti-imperialist, attacked the Republicans for their support of imperialism in Asia. McKinley, who chose war hero Theodore Roosevelt as his running mate, focused on the country's increased prosperity and ran on the slogan "Four Years More of the Full Dinner Pail." He won the election by a wide margin.

On September 6, 1901, while visiting Buffalo, New York, President McKinley was attacked by Leon Czolgosz, an anarchist who opposed all forms of government. Czolgosz fired two shots and hit the president. A few days later, McKinley died from his wounds. Theodore Roosevelt took over the presidency.

PAST & PRESENT

The Great White Fleet

In 1907 President Theodore Roosevelt sent 16 new battleships on a voyage around the world to showcase the nation's ability to project power to any place in the world. Painted white, the ships became known as the "Great White Fleet." The tour made a stop in Japan to demonstrate that the United States would uphold its interests in Asia. The visit did not help ease the growing tensions between the United States and Japan.

The use of naval power to send a diplomatic message continues today. Just as the battleship symbolized naval power in 1900, so too today does the aircraft carrier symbolize the power and global reach of the United States Navy. In March 1996, for example, a strike force led by the aircraft carrier *Kitty Hawk* was sent to the Taiwan Straits. This show of force came after China tested missiles in the area. The carrier sent the message to China that the United States would protect Taiwan from aggression.

1907

▲ *The Great White Fleet gets underway in December 1907.*

Great White Fleet

◄ *The Great White Fleet circumnavigated the globe.*

278 Chapter 7 Becoming a World Power

Activity: Economics Connection

The Open Door Policy Ask students to use library and Internet resources to identify the products that were traded between countries involved with China. Have students use what they learn to create a chart showing the trading relationships among the various nations. Then ask students to write a position paper supporting or opposing the Open Door Policy. Discuss students' positions on the Open Door Policy. **AL**

Theodore Roosevelt, just 42 years old at the time, was the youngest person ever to become president. Republican leaders had asked him to run for vice president because his charisma and status as a war hero would win votes, but they had hoped the relatively powerless position of vice president would keep him from causing political problems. Now they cringed at the thought of him in the White House. Ohio Republican senator Mark Hanna exclaimed,"Now look, that . . . cowboy is president of the United States!"

Roosevelt favored increasing American power on the world stage. He warned Americans not to become "an assemblage of well-to-do hucksters who care nothing for what happens beyond." Roosevelt also accepted some of Anglo-Saxonism's ideas. He believed that the United States had a duty to shape the "less civilized" corners of the earth.

Balancing Power in East Asia

As president, Theodore Roosevelt supported the Open Door policy in China and worked to prevent any single nation from monopolizing trade there. This concern prompted Roosevelt to help negotiate an end to the war between Japan and Russia that had broken out in 1905. At a peace conference in Portsmouth, New Hampshire, Roosevelt convinced the Russians to recognize Japan's territorial gains and persuaded the Japanese to stop fighting and to seek no further territory. For his efforts in ending the war, Roosevelt won the Nobel Peace Prize in 1906.

In the years after the peace treaty, relations between the United States and Japan grew steadily worse. As the two nations vied for greater influence in Asia, they held each other in check through a series of agreements. They pledged to respect each other's territorial possessions, to uphold the Open Door policy, and to support China's independence.

The Panama Canal

Theodore Roosevelt believed in a strong global military presence. He insisted that displaying American power to the world would make nations think twice about fighting, and thus promote peace. He often expressed this belief with a West African saying, "Speak softly and carry a big stick."

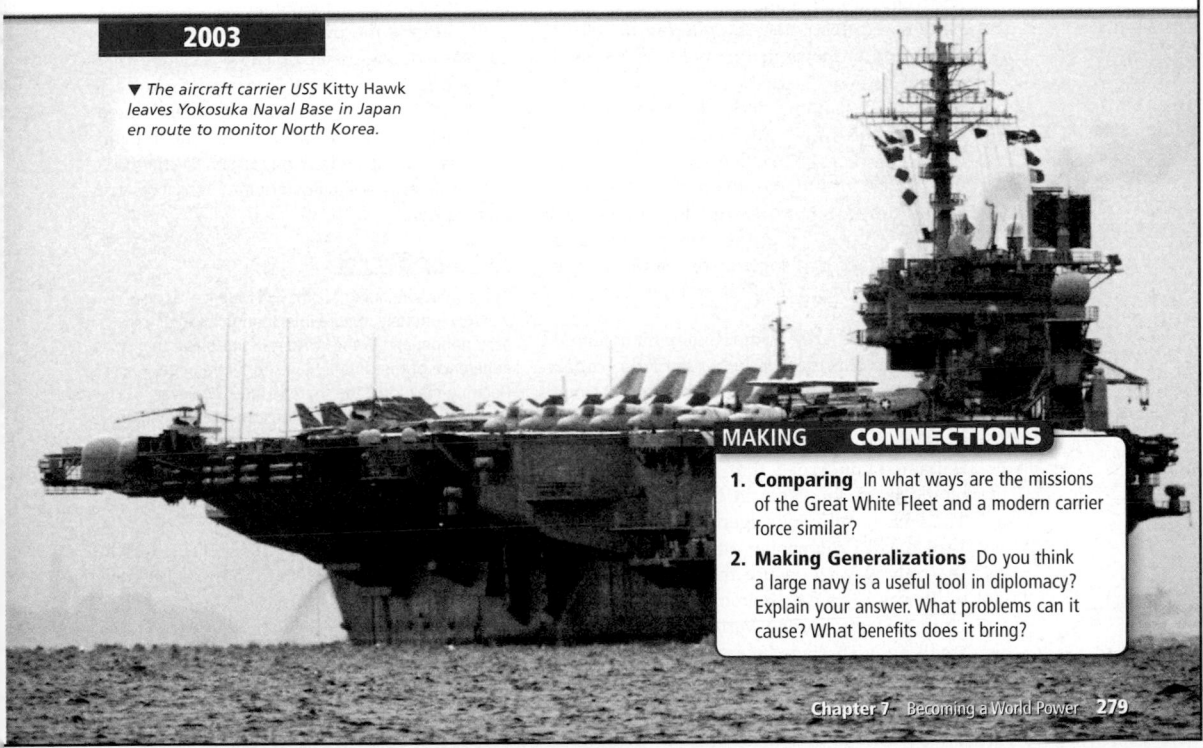

2003

▼ *The aircraft carrier USS Kitty Hawk leaves Yokosuka Naval Base in Japan en route to monitor North Korea.*

MAKING CONNECTIONS

1. **Comparing** In what ways are the missions of the Great White Fleet and a modern carrier force similar?
2. **Making Generalizations** Do you think a large navy is a useful tool in diplomacy? Explain your answer. What problems can it cause? What benefits does it bring?

Chapter 7 Becoming a World Power **279**

D Differentiated Instruction

Visual/Spatial Provide students with a world map. Have them trace the water route from San Francisco to New York City around Cape Horn, using the map's scale to calculate the approximate distance. *(about 13,000 miles)* Next have students trace the route by ship from San Francisco to New York City via the Panama Canal and calculate the distance. *(about 5,200 miles)* Have students write a paragraph explaining how the Panama Canal improved United States trade and business. **OL**

C Critical Thinking

Drawing Conclusions Tell students that President Roosevelt bragged, "I took the Canal Zone and let Congress debate; and while the debate goes on, the canal does also." **Ask:** Were President Roosevelt's actions in the Panama revolt justified? *(Answers will vary, but students should defend their opinions.)* **AL**

Differentiated Instruction

Roosevelt's "big stick" policy was perhaps most evident in the Caribbean. There the world witnessed one of the most dramatic acts of his presidency—the acquisition and construction of the Panama Canal. Roosevelt and others believed that having a canal through Central America was vital to American power in the world. A canal would save time and money for both commercial and military shipping.

Acquiring the Canal Zone As early as 1850, the United States and Great Britain had agreed not to build a canal without the other's participation. In 1901 the United States and Great Britain signed the **Hay-Pauncefote Treaty,** which gave the United States the exclusive right to build any proposed canal through Central America.

A French company had begun digging a canal through Panama in 1881. By 1889, however, it abandoned its efforts because of bankruptcy and terrible losses from disease among the workers. The company was reorganized in 1894, but it hoped only to sell its rights to dig the canal.

The United States had long considered two possible canal sites, one through Nicaragua and one through Panama. The French company eased this choice by offering to sell its rights and property in Panama to the United States.

In 1903 Panama was Colombia's most northern province. Secretary of State Hay offered Colombia $10 million and a yearly rent of $250,000 for the right to construct the canal and to control a narrow strip of land on either side of it. Considering the price too low and afraid of losing control of Panama, the Colombian government refused the offer.

Panama Revolts Some Panamanians feared losing the commercial benefits of the canal. Panama had opposed Colombian rule since the mid-1800s, and the canal issue added to the **tension.** In addition, the French company remained concerned that the United States would build the canal in Nicaragua instead. The French company's agent, Philippe Bunau-Varilla, and Panamanian officials decided that the only way to ensure the canal would be built was to make their own deal with the United States. Bunau-Varilla arranged for a small army to stage an uprising in Panama.

Meanwhile, to prevent Colombian interference, President Roosevelt ordered U.S. warships to the area.

On November 3, 1903, with ten U.S. warships looming offshore, Bunau-Varilla's forces revolted. Within a few days, the United States recognized Panama's independence, and the two nations soon signed a treaty allowing the canal to be built.

Protesters in the United States and throughout Latin America condemned Roosevelt's actions as unjustifiable aggression. The president countered that he had advanced "the needs of collective civilization" by building a canal that shortened the distance between the Atlantic and the Pacific by about 8,000 nautical miles (14,816 km).

The Roosevelt Corollary

By the early 1900s, American officials had become very concerned about the size of the debts Latin American nations owed to European banks. In 1902, after Venezuela defaulted on its debts, Great Britain, Germany, and Italy blockaded Venezuelan ports. The crisis was resolved peacefully after the United States intervened and put pressure on both sides to reach an agreement.

To address the problem, Roosevelt gave an address to Congress in which he declared what came to be known as the **Roosevelt Corollary** to the Monroe Doctrine. The corollary stated that the United States would intervene in Latin American affairs when necessary to maintain economic and political stability in the Western Hemisphere:

PRIMARY SOURCE

"Chronic wrongdoing . . . may, in America, as elsewhere, ultimately require intervention by some civilized nation, and in the Western Hemisphere the adherence of the United States to the Monroe Doctrine may force the United States, however reluctantly, in flagrant cases of such wrongdoing or impotence, to the exercise of an international police power."

—quoted in *The Growth of the United States*

The goal of the Roosevelt Corollary was to prevent European powers from using the debt problems of Latin America to justify intervening in the region. The United States first applied the Roosevelt Corollary in the

Leveled Activities

BL Guided Reading Activity, URB p. 48

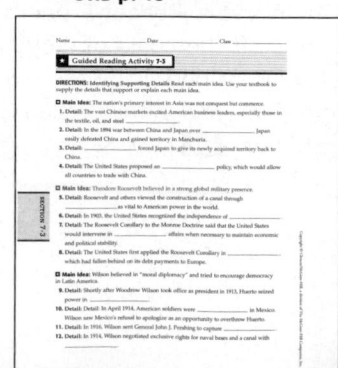

OL Differentiated Instruction, URB p. 21

AL Interpreting Political Cartoons, URB p. 39

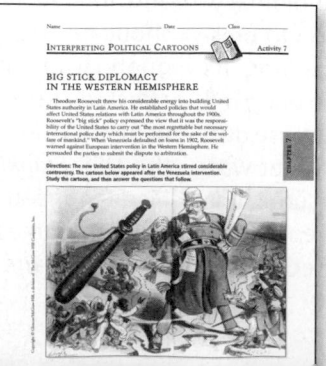

ELL Reading Essentials and Note-Taking Guide, p. 76

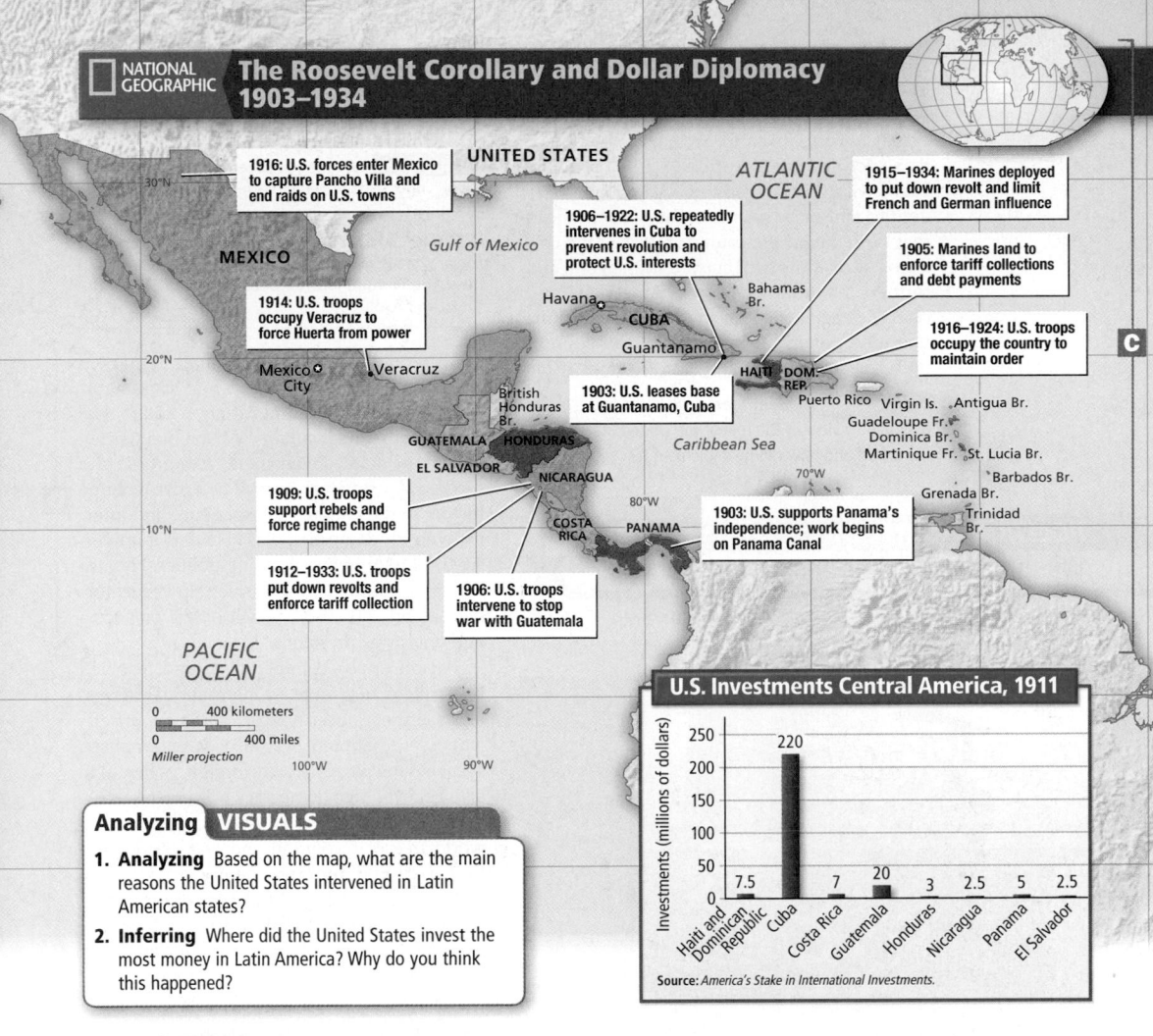

The Roosevelt Corollary and Dollar Diplomacy 1903–1934

1916: U.S. forces enter Mexico to capture Pancho Villa and end raids on U.S. towns

UNITED STATES

ATLANTIC OCEAN

1915–1934: Marines deployed to put down revolt and limit French and German influence

1906–1922: U.S. repeatedly intervenes in Cuba to prevent revolution and protect U.S. interests

1905: Marines land to enforce tariff collections and debt payments

MEXICO

Gulf of Mexico

1914: U.S. troops occupy Veracruz to force Huerta from power

Havana
Bahamas Br.
CUBA
Guantanamo

1916–1924: U.S. troops occupy the country to maintain order

Mexico City
Veracruz

HAITI
DOM. REP.
Puerto Rico
Virgin Is.
Antigua Br.

British Honduras Br.

1903: U.S. leases base at Guantanamo, Cuba

Guadeloupe Fr.
Dominica Br.
Martinique Fr.
St. Lucia Br.

GUATEMALA
HONDURAS

Caribbean Sea

EL SALVADOR

Barbados Br.

NICARAGUA

Grenada Br.
Trinidad Br.

1909: U.S. troops support rebels and force regime change

COSTA RICA
PANAMA

1903: U.S. supports Panama's independence; work begins on Panama Canal

1912–1933: U.S. troops put down revolts and enforce tariff collection

1906: U.S. troops intervene to stop war with Guatemala

PACIFIC OCEAN

0   400 kilometers
0   400 miles
Miller projection

U.S. Investments Central America, 1911

Investments (millions of dollars)

Haiti and Dominican Republic	7.5
Cuba	220
Costa Rica	7
Guatemala	20
Honduras	3
Nicaragua	2.5
Panama	5
El Salvador	2.5

Source: *America's Stake in International Investments.*

Analyzing VISUALS

1. **Analyzing** Based on the map, what are the main reasons the United States intervened in Latin American states?

2. **Inferring** Where did the United States invest the most money in Latin America? Why do you think this happened?

Dominican Republic, which had fallen behind on its debt payments to European nations. In 1905 the United States assumed the responsibility of collecting customs tariffs in the Dominican Republic, using the United States Marine Corps as its agent.

Dollar Diplomacy

Latin American nations resented the growing American influence in the region, but Roosevelt's successor, William Howard Taft, continued his policies. Taft placed much less emphasis on military force and more on helping Latin American industry. He believed that

if American business leaders supported Latin American development, everyone would benefit. American businesses would increase their trade and profits, and countries in Latin America would rise out of poverty and social disorder. Taft's policy came to be called **dollar diplomacy.**

Administration officials also worked hard to replace European loans with loans from American banks. The goal of this policy was to give the Europeans fewer reasons to intervene in Latin American affairs. During Taft's administration, American bankers took over debts that Honduras owed to Britain and took control of Haiti's national bank.

Chapter 7 Becoming a World Power **281**

Activity: Interdisciplinary Connection

281

D Differentiated Instruction

Advanced Learners Have students determine the level of education achieved by U.S. presidents. Then have students find out how historians have rated the presidents. Based on the information, they should write a paper analyzing the relationship between education and success in the presidency. **AL**

Analyzing VISUALS

Answers:

1. The cartoonist is indicating that Wilson believes he is smarter than the leaders of the Latin American countries.

2. The cartoon implies that Mexico favors revolution and may be spreading it to other countries.

✓ Reading Check

Answer:

"Speak softly and carry a big stick." Using diplomacy to settle problems, while openly displaying U.S. military might.

Additional Support

Although Taft described his brand of diplomacy as "substituting dollars for bullets," in Nicaragua he used both. American bankers began making loans to Nicaragua to support its shaky government in 1911. The following year, civil unrest forced the Nicaraguan president to appeal for greater assistance. American marines entered the country, replaced the collector of customs with an American agent, and formed a committee of two Americans and one Nicaraguan to control the customs commissions. American troops stayed to support both the government and customs until 1925.

✓ **Reading Check** **Summarizing** What was Roosevelt's view of the role of the United States in the world and how did he implement it?

POLITICAL CARTOON   PRIMARY SOURCE
Wilson and Mexico

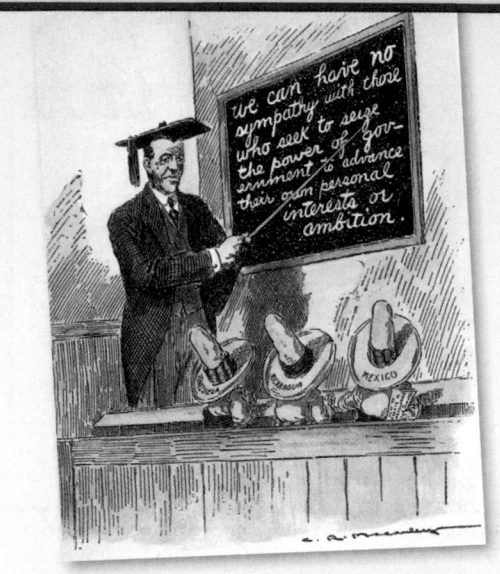

▲ President Wilson (who had a Ph.D.) is shown teaching Venezuela, Nicaragua, and Mexico that revolution for personal gain is wrong, while Mexico is shown hiding a note labeled "How to create a revolution."

Analyzing VISUALS

1. **Analyzing** In what ways is the cartoon making fun of President Wilson?

2. **Inferring** What is the cartoon implying about Mexico?

Woodrow Wilson's Diplomacy in Mexico

MAIN Idea Wilson believed in "moral diplomacy" and tried to encourage democracy in Latin America.

HISTORY AND YOU Can you think of a country today that is going through a long civil war? Read how the United States became involved in the Mexican Revolution.

"It would be the irony of fate," remarked Woodrow Wilson just before he was inaugurated in 1913, "if my administration had to deal chiefly with foreign affairs." Wilson had written books on state government, Congress, and George Washington, as well as a five-volume history of the nation. His experience and interest were in domestic policy. He was a university professor before entering politics. He also was a committed progressive. However, foreign affairs did absorb much of Wilson's time and energy as president.

Wilson opposed imperialism and resolved to "strike a new note in international affairs" and see that "sheer honesty and even unselfishness . . . should prevail over nationalistic self-seeking in American foreign policy." He also believed that democracy was essential to a nation's stability and prosperity. To ensure a world free of revolution and war, the United States should promote democracy. During Wilson's presidency, however, other forces frustrated his hope to lead the world by moral example. In fact, Wilson's first international crisis was awaiting him when he took office.

The Mexican Revolution

For more than 30 years, Porfirio Díaz ruled Mexico as a dictator. During his reign, Mexico became much more industrialized, but foreign investors owned and financed the new railroads and factories that were built. Most Mexican citizens remained poor and landless. In 1911 widespread discontent erupted into revolution.

Francisco Madero, a reformer who appeared to support democracy, constitutional government, and land reform, led the revolution. Madero, however, proved to be an unskilled administrator. Worried about Madero's plans for land reform, conservative forces plotted

---

Extending the Content

Eyewitness to Revolution On the night of April 21, 1914, Edith O'Shaughnessy wrote of her fears of a pending U.S.-Mexican conflict in her diary, later published as *A Diplomat's Wife in Mexico*:

"I can't sleep. National and personal potentialities are surging through my brain. Three stalwart railroad men came to the Embassy this evening. They brought reports of a plan for the massacre of Americans in the street to-night, but, strange and wonderful thing, a heavy rain is falling. It is my only experience of a midnight rain in Mexico... rain is as potent as shell-fire in clearing the streets... Providence seems to keep an occasional unnatural shower on hand for Mexican crises."

Neither the rain shower nor Providence could stop what O'Shaughnessy feared. On April 22, she recorded: "We are at war. American and Mexican blood flowed in the streets of Vera Cruz today."

against him. In February 1913, General **Victoriano Huerta** seized power; Madero was murdered, presumably on Huerta's orders.

Huerta's brutality repulsed Wilson, who refused to recognize the new government. Instead, Wilson announced a new policy. Groups that seized power in Latin America would have to set up "a just government based upon law, not upon arbitrary or irregular force," in order to win American recognition. Wilson was convinced that, without the support of the United States, Huerta soon would be overthrown. Meanwhile, Wilson ordered the navy to intercept arms shipments to Huerta's government. He also permitted Americans to arm Huerta's opponents.

Wilson Sends Troops Into Mexico

In April 1914, American sailors visiting the city of Tampico were arrested after entering a restricted area. Although they were quickly released, their American commander demanded an apology. The Mexicans refused. Wilson saw the refusal as an opportunity to overthrow Huerta. He asked Congress to authorize the use of force, and shortly after Congress passed the resolution, he learned that a German ship was unloading weapons at the Mexican port of Veracruz. Wilson immediately ordered American warships to shell the Veracruz harbor and then sent marines to seize the city.

Although the president expected the Mexican people to welcome his action, anti-American riots broke out. Wilson then accepted international mediation to settle the dispute. Venustiano Carranza, whose forces had acquired arms from the United States, became Mexico's president.

Mexican forces opposed to Carranza were not appeased, and they conducted raids into the United States, hoping to force Wilson to intervene. In March 1916, **Pancho Villa** (VEE•yah) and a group of **guerrillas**—an armed band that uses surprise attacks and sabotage rather than open warfare—burned the town of Columbus, New Mexico, and killed 16 Americans. Wilson responded by sending 6,000 troops under General John J. Pershing across the border to find and capture Villa. The expedition dragged on with no success. Wilson's growing concern over the war raging in Europe finally caused him to recall Pershing's troops in 1917.

Wilson's Mexican policy damaged U.S. foreign relations. The British ridiculed the president's attempt to "shoot the Mexicans into self-government." Latin Americans regarded his "moral imperialism" as no improvement over Theodore Roosevelt's "big stick" diplomacy. In fact, Wilson followed Roosevelt's example in the Caribbean. In 1914 he negotiated exclusive rights for naval bases and a canal with Nicaragua. In 1915 he sent marines into Haiti to put down a rebellion. The marines remained there until 1934. In 1916 he sent troops into the Dominican Republic to preserve order and to set up a government he hoped would be more stable and democratic than the current regime.

✓ Reading Check **Examining** Why did President Wilson intervene in Mexico?

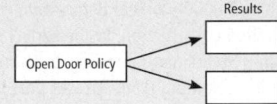

Section 3 REVIEW

Vocabulary

1. **Explain** the significance of: sphere of influence, Open Door policy, Boxer Rebellion, Hay-Pauncefote Treaty, Roosevelt Corollary, dollar diplomacy, Victoriano Huerta, Pancho Villa, guerrilla.

Main Ideas

2. **Summarizing** Use a graphic organizer to list the results of the Open Door policy.

| Open Door Policy | → | Results |
| | → | |

3. **Identifying** Why did President Theodore Roosevelt want to increase U.S. influence overseas?

4. **Specifying** How did Latin Americans view Wilson's "moral imperialism"?

Critical Thinking

5. **Big Ideas** Why did the United States decide to build a canal through Panama? How did Roosevelt assist Panama in becoming independent?

6. **Analyzing** How did the Roosevelt Corollary and dollar diplomacy affect U.S. relations with other countries?

7. **Analyzing Visuals** Study the map on page 281. To which countries did the U.S. send troops most often?

Writing About History

8. **Expository Writing** Imagine that you are a Mexican citizen during Wilson's presidency. Write a radio news broadcast expressing your feelings about American actions in Mexico.

History ONLINE
Study Central™ To review this section, go to glencoe.com and click on Study Central.

W **Writing Support**
Descriptive Writing Have students find out more information about the American occupation of Veracruz. Then have students write an essay describing the Americans' actions and the response of the people of Veracruz. **OL**

✓ Reading Check

Answer:
first to help support the overthrow of Huerta; later to suppress Villa

Assess

History ONLINE

Study Central™ provides summaries, interactive games, and online graphic organizers to help students review content.

Close

Summarizing Ask: How did America's diplomacy affect its role as a world power? (*America's diplomacy required it to build up its power.*) **OL**

Section 3 REVIEW

Answers

1. All definitions can be found in the section and the Glossary.

2. all countries could trade with China; prevented warfare among competing nations

3. He felt the United States should become involved in world events and become a world power. Believing in some of the ideas of Anglo-Saxonism, he also felt it was the United States's duty to help other "less fortunate" nations.

4. Students' answers will vary. Possible answers: The Latin-American nations wanted the right of self-determination. They knew that America would act in its own interests, not in the interests of Latin-American countries.

5. A canal would save time and money in commercial and military shipping. Panama was chosen over Nicaragua because a French company sold its rights and property in Panama. Roosevelt sent ships to Panama and recognized that nation's independence from Colombia.

6. Many nations resented America's policies.

7. Nicaragua, Cuba

8. Students' broadcasts will vary. Broadcasts should be based on information from the chapter.

Focus

Tell students that the Spanish, as early as the 1500s, were the first to imagine a canal to connect the Atlantic and Pacific Oceans. The American interest in such a waterway developed only after the Civil War. Businessman Cornelius Vanderbilt attempted to build a canal through Nicaragua, but without success. During the 1840s both Britain and the United States wanted to build the canal, but it was the same French company that built the Suez Canal that actually began the work. The attempt bankrupted the company.

Teach

R Reading Strategy

Activating Prior Knowledge
Ask students to identify some historical events that might have motivated interest in a canal through Central America. *(Students may suggest the California Gold Rush, Civil War battles, or the Spanish American War.)* **OL**

Additional Support

NATIONAL GEOGRAPHIC

GEOGRAPHY & HISTORY

The Panama Canal

The idea of a canal connecting the Atlantic and Pacific oceans had been around for a long time before a French company began digging a canal across Panama in 1882. Disease and mud slides killed more than 20,000 workers before financial setbacks halted construction. In the early 1900s, the United States negotiated rights to build the canal with Colombia (Panama was part of Colombia at that time), but Colombia's Senate refused to ratify the treaty. With the support of the United States, Panama declared independence from Colombia and signed a treaty giving the United States a perpetual lease on the canal site in exchange for $10 million and annual payments. Construction resumed in 1904, and the canal was opened in 1914.

How Does Geography Affect the Canal?

Before the canal opened, ships sailing from New York to San Francisco traveled 12,600 miles (20,277 km) around the treacherous tip of South America. Afterwards, the trip was only 4,900 miles (7,886 km) and could be completed in less than half the time. Panama's geography made building the canal a challenge because the center of the country was much higher than sea level. Engineers built a series of lakes and concrete locks to raise and lower ships as they traveled the 51-mile canal. In each chamber of the locks, some 26 million gallons of water are pumped in or drained out in only 7 minutes to raise or lower a ship. At the artificial Gatun Lake, a dam generates electricity that powers the locks while gravity adjusts the water level.

San Francisco · New York City · ATLANTIC OCEAN
4,900 miles · Panama Canal
12,600 miles · PACIFIC OCEAN

Ships transit the canal more than 14,000 times each year, generating over $1 billion in tolls.

Pacific Ocean
Panama City •

Analyzing GEOGRAPHY

1. **Human-Environment Interaction** How were the geographical features of Panama used or overcome in order to build the canal?

2. **Location** Why do you think the Panama site was ultimately selected for the canal?

Interdisciplinary Connection

Health About 6,000 workers died while the United States built the canal. Many of them succumbed to yellow fever or malaria, diseases carried by mosquitoes. Ask students to find out more about the challenges due to diseases that Panama Canal workers faced and how those challenges were met. Have them present their findings to the class as a radio or newscast. **OL**

Atlantic
Ocean

Pacific
Ocean

**Miraflores
Locks**

**Pedro Miguel
Lock**

Lake Gatún

**Gatún
Locks**

Atlantic
Ocean

Cross Section of the Panama Canal

Gatún Dam created Lake Gatún—one of the largest artificial lakes in the world. A hydroelectric station at the dam generates power to run the pumps and gates of the locks.

Gatún Locks has 3 chambers for each direction. Together they raise ships at sea level up 86 feet to the level of Lake Gatún.

Lake Gatún

• Colón

▲ The Miraflores locks (above) are one of three sets of locks on the Panama Canal, and the first set for ships entering from the Pacific. After a ship enters a lock chamber, water is pumped in raising the ship up 27 feet to the next level. The ship then moves to the next chamber and is raised another 27 feet.

Chapter 7   Becoming a World Power   285

GEOGRAPHY & HISTORY

Assess/Close

D Differentiated Instruction

Visual/Spatial Invite students to make a sketch or a three-dimensional model of the three locks that allow passage through the Panama Canal. **OL**

Analyzing GEOGRAPHY

Answers:
1. The center of the country was higher than sea level, so engineers built a series of locks and canals to raise and lower ships going through the 51-mile canal.
2. Panama offered the shortest distance across Central America.

Technology Connection

Investigate Primary Sources Several Web sites offer extensive information and primary resources on the building of the Panama Canal. Ask students to select three articles from different sites and summarize their contents. The following sites are possible starting points:

Smithsonian Institute, Make the Dirt Fly!
PBS's American Experience
American Treasures of the Library of Congress

Chapter 7 VISUAL SUMMARY

Creating a Time Line The Visual Summary lists the causes of American imperialism, the effects of the Spanish-American War, and the events in which the United States demonstrated its might as a world power. Have students choose six events from the Visual Summary and create a time line, placing the events in the correct chronological order. **BL**

Causes of American Imperialism

- The United States wanted new markets for its products, particularly its manufactured goods.
- Many Americans believed it was the destiny of the United States to spread its power and civilization to other parts of the world.
- American leaders believed that having a powerful navy and controlling trade were key to being a world power.

► USS Texas docks in port in 1896

▲ American soldiers in Cuba cheer the news that the city of Santiago, Cuba, has surrendered during the Spanish-American War, 1898.

Effects of the Spanish-American War

- Cuba officially became an independent nation, although the United States claimed control over its foreign relations and exerted influence over internal politics.
- The United States acquired Puerto Rico, Guam, and the Philippines.
- Americans debated the morality and wisdom of becoming an imperial nation.
- The United States fought a three-year war to secure control over the Philippines.

The United States Acts As a World Power

- The United States used diplomatic means to establish the Open Door policy in China.
- President Theodore Roosevelt negotiated a peace agreement between Russia and Japan.
- The United States completed construction of the Panama Canal.
- The United States intervened, with the intent to provide stability, in the affairs of several Caribbean nations.
- The United States twice intervened in the lengthy Mexican Revolution.

▲ After supporting a revolution in Panama, the United States begins construction of the Panama Canal.

286 Chapter 7 Becoming a World Power

Hands-On Chapter Project
Step 4: Wrap Up

Preparing a Multimedia Presentation

Step 4: Sharing the Presentation Groups will share their presentations with the class.

Directions Tell students to develop a narrative to go along with their presentations. The narrative should compliment their presentations and explain the causes and effects of imperialism in their assigned nation. Once all groups have presented, encourage students to individually take a closer look at any of the presentations that intrigued them.

Next have students critique the presentations on quality of information, ease of use, and creativity. Encourage students to share aspects of their own presentations they found interesting or challenging.

Putting It Together Have students discuss each of the six countries presented: Cuba, China, Japan, the Philippines, Puerto Rico, and Guam. Ask students to draw a conclusion about the effects of imperialism on other nations. **Ask:** Was imperialism beneficial or harmful for these nations? **OL**

ASSESSMENT

STANDARDIZED TEST PRACTICE

TEST-TAKING TIP

Note that in some cases you are asked to choose the BEST answer. This means that in some instances there will be more than one possible answer. Be sure to read all the choices carefully before selecting your answer.

Reviewing Vocabulary

Directions: Choose the word or words that best complete the sentence.

1. The major European powers each had a(n) _____ in China.
   - **A** protectorate
   - **B** sphere of influence
   - **C** Open Door policy
   - **D** tariff policy

2. Taft's policies in Latin America were called
   - **A** "big stick" diplomacy.
   - **B** open door diplomacy.
   - **C** missionary diplomacy.
   - **D** dollar diplomacy.

3. Support for the war against Spain came in part from the _____ practiced by some newspapers.
   - **A** anti-Americanism
   - **B** objectivity
   - **C** yellow journalism
   - **D** sphere of influence

4. Local rulers are permitted to retain some power in a
   - **A** protectorate.
   - **B** monarchy.
   - **C** republic.
   - **D** dictatorship.

Reviewing Main Ideas

Directions: Choose the best answers to the following questions.

Section 1 *(pp. 262–267)*

5. Which of the following was a major contributor to the growth of American imperialism in the late 1800s?
   - **A** curiosity about other cultures
   - **B** need for spices from the East Indies
   - **C** the end of the Civil War
   - **D** desire for new markets for American goods

6. What effect did Commodore Matthew C. Perry have on Japan?
   - **A** Japan began building an army.
   - **B** Japan began to westernize.
   - **C** Japan ended its trade with China.
   - **D** Japan refused to negotiate with the United States.

7. A major goal of the Pan-American conference in 1889 was to
   - **A** create a customs union for nations in the Americas.
   - **B** end trade with the nations of Europe.
   - **C** free Cuba from Spanish control.
   - **D** decide on a route for a canal through Central America.

Section 2 *(pp. 268–275)*

8. The effect of yellow journalism on the Cuban rebellion was
   - **A** unimportant to people in the United States.
   - **B** helpful in changing McKinley's mind about going to war with Spain.
   - **C** critical to raising public support for war against Spain.
   - **D** harmful to American businesses in Cuba.

Need Extra Help?

If You Missed Questions . . .	1	2	3	4	5	6	7	8
Go to Page . . .	276	281	269	262–263	262–264	265	267	269

 GO ON

6. B Commodore Matthew Perry's visit to Japan caused Japan to modernize, because Japan realized the need to compete with Western technology. Therefore, Japan began to Westernize. This led to cooperation between the two nations. However, remind students that before Perry and the American warships arrived in Japan, Japan had refused contact. The U.S. forced contact by sending Perry.

7. A This is a good opportunity to discuss *pan* as prefix from the Greek that means "all." Although the Pan-American conference did not include Canada, this information should help students remember that only nations in the Americas would be involved in the Pan-American conference.

8. C The fact that journalism is intended to reach the masses should help students figure out this answer. Increased public support for the war was a direct consequence of yellow journalism.

Reviewing Vocabulary

1. B A sphere of influence was an area in China in which a foreign nation controlled economic development. These spheres were held by the major European powers, and worried the U.S. A protectorate was a territory that maintained local rulers, but was protected by and had to take advice from other nations. The Open Door Policy was instated as a reaction to spheres of influence.

2. D Taft's policies in Latin America were a form of economic imperialism. This allowed the U.S. to control events without creating protectorates or colonies. These economic policies were called dollar diplomacy.

3. C Yellow journalism was sensationalist reporting, which often used exaggeration and untruths to provoke an emotional response. The response provoked helped rally Americans to support a war against Spain.

4. A A monarchy is a system of government ruled by monarchs, or a royal family. A republic is a system of representative government. A dictatorship is a form of government in which one person holds all of the power. In a protectorate, a nation allows another nation to influence its policies in exchange for protection.

Reviewing Main Ideas

5. D The Industrial Revolution led to a massive increase in manufacturing. Leaders soon realized that more money could be made if there were expanded markets for goods. Remind students who are distracted by choice *B* that the need for spices motivated European exploration in the 15th century.

287

Chapter 7

9. D Review the section "American Forces in Cuba" if students have trouble with this question. San Juan Hill and Kettle Hill were both captured by the U.S. in battle, but this happened before the surrender. Guam is a different island from Cuba. It may be helpful to have students create a time line of events of the war.

10. A If students read each answer choice carefully, only *A* makes sense. Sugarcane production was an issue in Hawaii. Students may be tempted to choose *C* because they relate an amendment with the Bill of Rights. However, remind students that the Bill of Rights only applies to American citizens and (now) citizens of Puerto Rico. It would not make sense for the U.S. to allow European nations to buy or lease naval stations in Cuba, since it is so close to the U.S.

11. D To remember that the Open Door Policy ensured trading rights for all nations, students should think of an open door as allowing everything through. Leaseholds were what created spheres of influence. However, spheres of influence are what *caused* the U.S. to push for the Open Door Policy: to combat the Europeans' spheres of influence. The Boxer Rebellion was a response to the Open Door Policy. A cause-and-effect chart might help students understand this chain of events.

---

9. Spanish resistance in Cuba ended with the surrender of
   A San Juan Hill.
   B Kettle Hill.
   C Guam.
   D Santiago.

10. What effect did the Platt Amendment have on Cuba?
    A It effectively made Cuba a protectorate of the United States.
    B It cut sugarcane production so Cuba could not compete with production in the United States.
    C It guaranteed all the freedoms of the Bill of Rights to Cubans.
    D It gave Cuba the right to allow European countries to buy or lease naval stations in Cuba.

Section 3 (pp. 276–283)

11. The purpose of the Open Door policy in China was to
    A end the Boxer Rebellion.
    B gain leaseholds.
    C establish spheres of influence.
    D ensure trading rights for all nations.

12. What was the Roosevelt Corollary to the Monroe Doctrine?
    A It provided for the purchase of land to build a canal across Panama.
    B It warned the nations of Europe not to impose high tariffs on goods from the Americas.
    C It stated that the United States would intervene in Latin American affairs as needed for political and economic stability.
    D It reinforced the policy of isolationism of the United States in world affairs.

Need Extra Help?						
If You Missed Questions . . .	9	10	11	12	13	14
Go to Page . . .	272	274–275	276–277	280–281	271–274	271–274

Critical Thinking

Directions: Choose the best answers to the following questions.

Base your answers to questions 13 and 14 on the map below and your knowledge of Chapter 7.

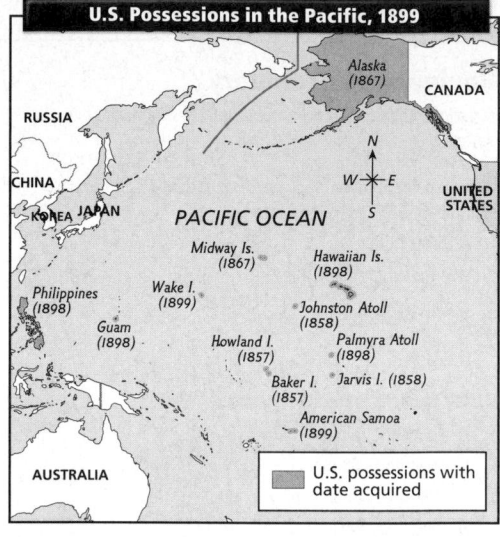

U.S. Possessions in the Pacific, 1899

13. Which of the following became a U.S. territory before the Spanish-American War?
    A Wake Island
    B Howland Island
    C American Samoa
    D Guam

14. Which U.S. possession is the Philippines nearest to?
    A Alaska
    B Hawaii
    C Midway Islands
    D Guam

GO ON

---

12. C The Monroe Doctrine informed Europe that the Americas were no longer open to European colonization. If students remember this, it is not a stretch to remember that the Roosevelt Corollary was basically an extension of this: its purpose was to protect American interests in Latin America. Instead of ending colonization, however, it banned European interference in Latin American affairs.

Critical Thinking

13. B The U.S. acquired Howland Island in 1857.

14. D Students should be able to answer this question by simply glancing at the map. Among the choices given, Guam is clearly the closest to the Philippines. Midway is the next closest but is between Guam and Hawaii.

15. The "big stick" policy and dollar diplomacy were attempts to

　A　increase United States power in Latin America.

　B　contain the spread of communism in eastern Europe.

　C　protect free trade on the Asian continent.

　D　strengthen political ties with Western Europe.

Analyze the cartoon and answer the question that follows. Base your answer on the cartoon and on your knowledge of chapter 7.

16. What does the cartoon demonstrate?

　A　It disagrees with of Taft's dollar diplomacy.

　B　It shows Theodore Roosevelt's "big stick" policy in the Caribbean.

　C　It shows the effect of John Jay's Open Door policy.

　D　It demonstrates the difficulty of finding land for a canal.

17. The sugarcane planters in Hawaii revolted against Queen Liliuokalani because

　A　she taxed the sugarcane plantations too heavily.

　B　she wanted a constitution that returned her to power as the ruler of Hawaii.

　C　they wanted to overturn the McKinley Tariff.

　D　they hoped to open Asian markets to sugarcane from Hawaii.

Document-Based Questions

Directions: Analyze the document and answer the short-answer questions that follow the document.

After the Spanish-American War, Carl Schurz, the leader of the liberal wing of the Republican Party, opposed American expansion abroad. In the following excerpt, Schurz attacks the arguments for taking over the Philippine Islands:

> "Many imperialists admit that our trade with the Philippines themselves will not nearly be worth its cost; but they say that we must have the Philippines as a foothold, a sort of power station, for the expansion of our trade on the Asiatic continent, especially in China. Admitting this, for argument's sake, I ask what kind of a foothold we should really need. Coaling stations and docks for our fleet, and facilities for the establishment of commercial houses and depots. That is all. And now I ask further, whether we could not easily have had these things if we had, instead of making war upon the Filipinos, favored the independence of the islands. Everybody knows that we could. We might have those things now for the mere asking if we stopped the war and came to a friendly understanding with the Filipinos tomorrow. . . ."
>
> —quoted in *The Policy of Imperialism*

18. What does Schurz believe is necessary to establish a foothold in trade with Asia?

19. What action other than annexation does Schurz suggest the United States could have taken to obtain trade with Asia?

Extended Response

20. Discuss U.S. foreign policy during the late 1800s and early 1900s. How were the various countries and regions of the world changed by the policies of the United States? Write an expository essay that includes an introduction, several paragraphs, and a conclusion that supports your position.

STOP

History ONLINE

For additional test practice, use Self-Check Quizzes—Chapter 7 at **glencoe.com**.

Document-Based Questions

18. Shurtz believes coaling stations, docks, and facilities for commercial houses and depots are all that is necessary to establish a foothold in trade with Asia. Shurtz is arguing against war with the Philippines. He believes these few needs could have been met by supporting Philippine independence.

19. Shurtz believes the U.S. could have supported Philippine independence and kept open communication. He does not argue against the benefits of having strategic footholds in the Philippines, but he doesn't feel force was needed in achieving this goal.

Extended Response

20. Students' essays will vary, but must demonstrate a strong grasp of the imperialist policies of the United States. Essays should describe the effects of these policies on the people and the lands that were affected by U.S. imperialism. Students may discuss, for example, the Panama Canal, the Spanish-American War, the annexation of Hawaii, or relations with Asian nations. Essays must include an introduction and a conclusion.

---

15. A It is important that students understand the motivations behind the "big stick" policy and dollar diplomacy and can relate them to Latin America. The United States practiced economic imperialism in Latin America—these policies did not concern Europe or Asia.

16. B Students should be able to identify the figure of Theodore Roosevelt in this cartoon by his uniform, glasses, and mustache. He is striding over the islands of Latin America, and he carries a big stick that actually says "Big Stick" on it. From these clues, C is the obvious choice.

Make sure students are comfortable analyzing images.

17. B The sugarcane planters in Hawaii were not native Hawaiians; they were American businessmen. Therefore, their best interest would be served if Hawaii were part of the United States. If the Queen reasserted her power, this would not happen, so the planters revolted.

History ONLINE

Have students visit the Web site at **glencoe.com** to review Chapter 7 and take the Self-Check Quiz.

Need Extra Help?

Have students refer to the pages listed if they miss any of the questions.

Key to Ability Levels	
BL Below Level	**AL** Above Level
OL On Level	**ELL** English Language Learners

Key to Teaching Resources	
Print Material	DVD
CD-ROM	Transparency

Levels BL	OL	AL	ELL		Resources	Chapter Opener	Section 1	Section 2	Section 3	Chapter Assess
FOCUS										
BL	OL	AL	ELL	🖋	Daily Focus Skills Transparencies		8-1	8-2	8-3	
TEACH										
	OL	AL		📁	Geography and History, URB			p. 3		
	OL	AL		📁	History Simulations and Problem Solving, URB		p. 9			
	OL	AL		📁	American Literature Reading, URB		p. 13			
BL	OL		ELL	📁	Reading Essentials and Note-Taking Guide*		p. 79	p. 82	p. 85	
	OL			📁	Historical Analysis Skills Activity, URB		p. 52			
BL	OL		ELL	📁	Guided Reading Activities, URB*		p. 78	p. 79	p. 80	
BL	OL	AL	ELL	📁	Content Vocabulary Activity, URB*		p. 57			
BL	OL	AL	ELL	📁	Academic Vocabulary Activity, URB		p. 59			
	OL	AL		📁	Critical Thinking Skills Activity, URB			p. 62		
BL	OL		ELL	📁	Reading Skills Activity, URB		p. 51			
BL			ELL	📁	English Learner Activity, URB		p. 55			
	OL	AL		📁	Reinforcing Skills Activity, URB		p. 61			
BL	OL	AL	ELL	📁	Differentiated Instruction Activity, URB		p. 53			
BL	OL		ELL	📁	Time Line Activity, URB		p. 63			
	OL			📁	Linking Past and Present Activity, URB			p. 64		
BL	OL	AL	ELL	📁	American Art and Music Activity, URB				p. 69	
BL	OL	AL	ELL	📁	Interpreting Political Cartoons Activity, URB		p. 71			
BL	OL	AL		📁	Economics and History Activity, URB		p. 7			
		AL		📁	Enrichment Activity, URB				p. 75	
BL	OL	AL	ELL	📁	American Biographies	✓	✓	✓	✓	✓
BL	OL	AL	ELL	📁	Primary Source Reading, URB		p. 67	p. 65		
BL	OL	AL	ELL	📁	Supreme Court Case Studies		p. 33	p. 29		
BL	OL	AL	ELL	📁	The Living Constitution*	✓	✓	✓	✓	✓
	OL	AL		💿	American History Primary Source Documents Library	✓	✓	✓	✓	✓
BL	OL	AL	ELL	🖋	Unit Map Overlay Transparencies	✓	✓	✓	✓	✓
BL	OL	AL	ELL	📁	Differentiated Instruction for the American High School Classroom	✓	✓	✓	✓	✓

Note: Please refer to the *Unit 3 Resource Book* for this chapter's URB materials.

* Also available in Spanish

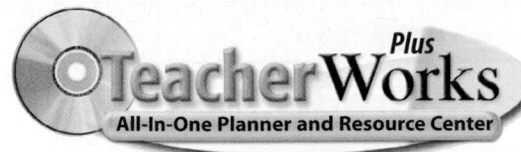

All-In-One Planner and Resource Center

- Interactive Lesson Planner
- Interactive Teacher Edition
- Fully editable blackline masters
- Section Spotlight Videos Launch

- Differentiated Lesson Plans
- Printable reports of daily assignments
- Standards Tracking System

Levels					Resources	Chapter Opener	Section 1	Section 2	Section 3	Chapter Assess
BL	OL	AL	ELL							
TEACH (continued)										
BL	OL	AL	ELL	💾	StudentWorks™ Plus DVD	✓	✓	✓	✓	✓
BL	OL	AL	ELL	💿	Vocabulary PuzzleMaker CD-ROM	✓	✓	✓	✓	✓
BL	OL	AL	ELL	💿	American Music Hits Through History CD	✓	✓	✓	✓	✓
BL	OL	AL	ELL	📁	Unit Time Line Transparencies and Activities	✓	✓	✓	✓	✓
BL	OL	AL	ELL	📁	Cause and Effect Transparencies, Strategies, and Activities	✓	✓	✓	✓	✓
BL	OL	AL	ELL	📁	Why It Matters Transparencies, Strategies, and Activities	✓	✓	✓	✓	✓
BL	OL	AL	ELL	📁	American Issues	✓	✓	✓	✓	✓
	OL	AL	ELL	📁	American Art and Architecture Transparencies, Strategies, and Activities	✓	✓	✓	✓	✓
BL	OL	AL		📁	High School American History Literature Library	✓	✓	✓	✓	✓
BL	OL	AL	ELL	💾	*The American Vision* Video Program DVD	✓	✓	✓	✓	✓
Teacher Resources				📁	Strategies for Success	✓	✓	✓	✓	✓
				📁	Success with English Learner	✓	✓	✓	✓	✓
				📁	Studies Classroom	✓	✓	✓	✓	✓
				💾	Presentation Plus! DVD	✓	✓	✓	✓	✓
ASSESS										
BL	OL	AL	ELL	📁	Section Quizzes and Chapter Tests*		p. 107	p. 108	p. 109	p. 111
BL	OL	AL	ELL	📁	Authentic Assessment With Rubrics					p. 21
BL	OL	AL	ELL	📁	Standardized Test Practice Workbook					p. 18
BL	OL	AL	ELL	💿	*ExamView*® Assessment Suite CD-ROM		8-1	8-2	8-3	Ch. 8
BL	OL	AL	ELL	💿	Interactive Tutor Self-Assessment CD-ROM		8-1	8-2	8-3	Ch. 8
CLOSE										
BL			ELL	📁	Reteaching Activity, URB					p. 73
BL	OL		ELL	📁	Reading and Study Skills Foldables™	pp. 65–66				
BL	OL	AL	ELL	📁	*American History* in Graphic Novel		p. 15			

Using StudentWorks™ Plus

Daily Assignments and Grade Logs

Technology Product

Glencoe's *StudentWorks™ Plus* CD-ROM contains everything your students need, including the complete Student Edition and access to all student workbooks. *StudentWorks™ Plus* also includes a Daily Assignment and Activity Log that allows students to

- record and track progress on their daily assignments and responsibilities;
- log results achieved, including their grades;
- sort assignments alphabetically or by category;
- view and print the assignment and grade log in a table or calendar format.

Objectives

Using *StudentWorks™ Plus* will help your students

- take responsibility for their individual tasks;
- improve independent study skills.

Steps

Provide students with the following information:

- Launch *StudentWorks™ Plus*.
- Select the **Daily Assignments and Grade Log** button at the bottom of the launch screen.
- Create a new file or open an existing one. The log is organized as a table, with a row of information for each assignment.
- Add information for each assignment, including the date of the assignment, the name, additional comments, the due date, and the grade.
- Edit rows as assignment information is provided or changed. Add a new row to the log for each new assignment.

History ONLINE

	Student	Teacher	Parent
Beyond the Textbook	●	●	●
Chapter Overviews	●	●	●
Time Current Events	●		●
ePuzzles and Games	●		●
Concepts in Motion	●		●
Literature Connections		●	
Multi-Language Glossaries	●		●
Online Student Edition	●	●	●
Self-Check Quizzes	●		●
Student Web Activities	●		●
Study Central™	●		●
Teaching Today		●	
Vocabulary eFlashcards	●		●
Web Activity Lesson Plans		●	

Glencoe Media Center

glencoe.com

❯ **Study-To-Go**
- Vocabulary eFlashcards
- Self-Check Quizzes

❯ **Audio/Video**
- Student Edition Audio
- Spanish Summaries
- Section Videos

- **Timed Readings Plus in Social Studies** helps students increase their reading rate and fluency while maintaining comprehension. The 400-word passages are similar to those found on state and national assessments.

- **Reading in the Content Area: Social Studies** concentrates on six essential reading skills that help students better comprehend what they read. The book includes 75 high-interest nonfiction passages written at increasing levels of difficulty.

- **Reading Social Studies** includes strategic reading instruction and vocabulary support in Social Studies content for both ELLs and native speakers of English.

www.jamestowneducation.com

The following videotape programs are available from Glencoe as supplements to Chapter 8:

- Susan B. Anthony: Rebel for the Cause (ISBN 1-56-501646-7)

- Woodrow Wilson: Reluctant Warrior (ISBN 0-76-700101-X)

To order, call Glencoe at 1-800-334-7344. To find classroom resources to accompany many of these videos, check the following home pages:

A&E Television: www.aetv.com

The History Channel: www.historychannel.com

Use this database to search more than 30,000 titles to create a customized reading list for your students.

- Reading lists can be organized by students' reading level, author, genre, theme, or area of interest.

- The database provides Degrees of Reading Power™ (DRP) and Lexile™ readability scores for all selections.

- A brief summary of each selection is included.

Leveled reading suggestions for this chapter:

For students at a Grade 8 reading level:
- *Alice Paul*, by Elizabeth Raum

For students at a Grade 9 reading level:
- *The Story of Susan B. Anthony*, by Susan Clinton

For students at a Grade 10 reading level:
- *Susan B. Anthony: Daring to Vote*, by Barbara Keevil Parker

For students at a Grade 11 reading level:
- *Forward Into the Light: The Struggle for Women's Suffrage*, by Madeleine Meyers

For students at a Grade 12 reading level:
- *Failure Is Impossible: Susan B. Anthony in Her Own Words*, by Lynn Sherr

Index to National Geographic Magazine:

The following articles relate to this chapter:

- "Roosevelt country: T.R.'s wilderness legacy," by John L. Eliot and Farrell Grehan. September 1982.

- "Time Machine: Yosemite in Photos Then and Now," by Claire Stanford, October 2005.

National Geographic Society Products To order the following, call National Geographic at 1-800-368-2728:

- *ZipZapMap! USA* (ZipZapMap!)

Access National Geographic's new, dynamic MapMachine Web site and other geography resources at:

www.nationalgeographic.com
www.nationalgeographic.com/maps

Focus

MAKING CONNECTIONS
Can Politics Fix Social Problems?

Ask students to suggest ways that they think today's society might be improved and list their suggestions on the board. Discuss how these suggestions could be implemented and who would be responsible for them. **OL**

Teach
The Big Ideas

As students study the chapter, remind them to consider the section-based Big Ideas included in each section's Guide to Reading. The **Essential Questions** in the activities below tie in to the Big Ideas and help students think about and understand important chapter concepts. In addition, the Hands-on Chapter Projects with their culminating activities relate the content from each section to the Big Ideas. These activities build on each other as students progress through the chapter. Section activities culminate in the wrap-up activity on the Visual Summary page.

290

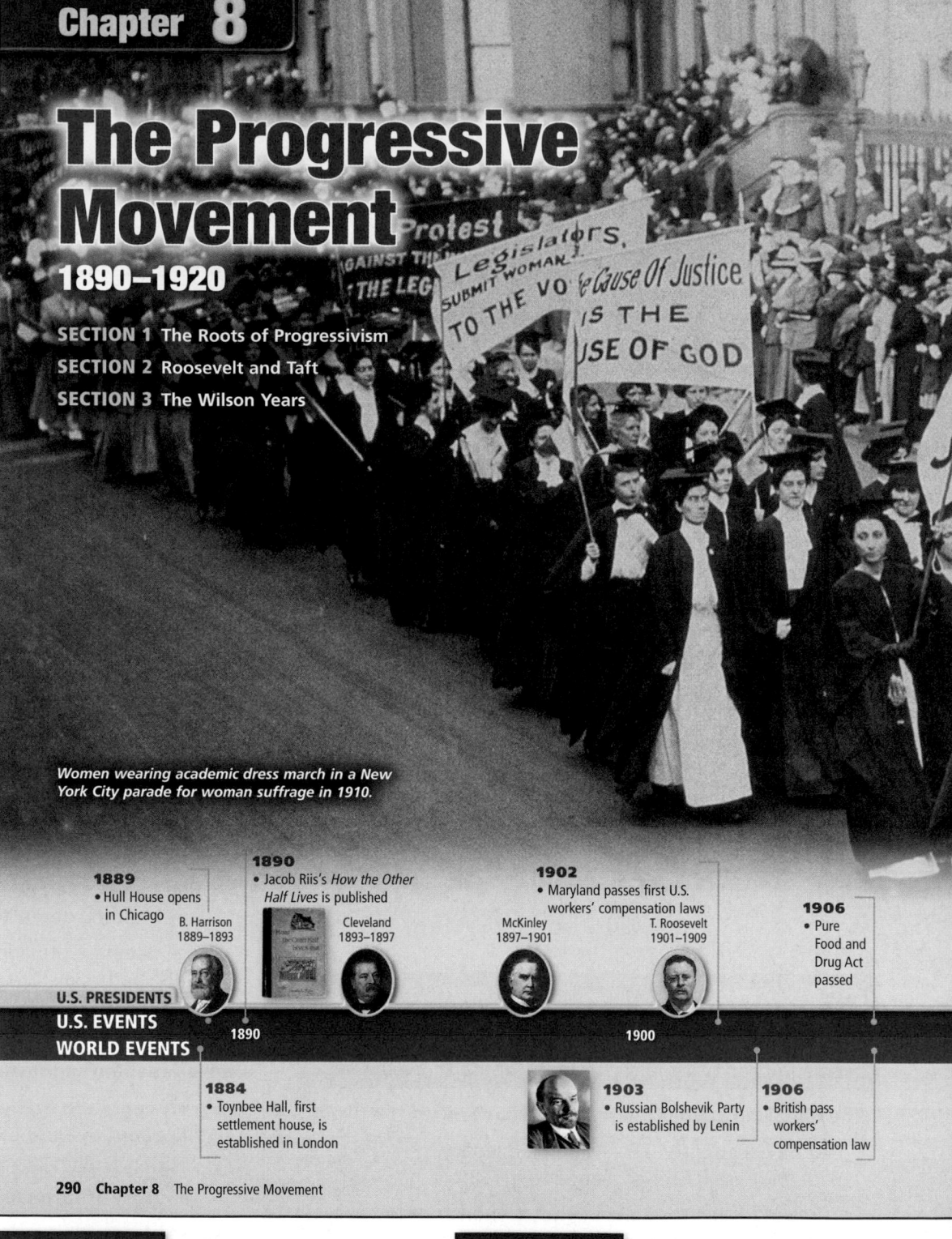

Chapter 8

The Progressive Movement
1890–1920

SECTION 1 The Roots of Progressivism
SECTION 2 Roosevelt and Taft
SECTION 3 The Wilson Years

Women wearing academic dress march in a New York City parade for woman suffrage in 1910.

1889
• Hull House opens in Chicago

B. Harrison 1889–1893

1890
• Jacob Riis's *How the Other Half Lives* is published

Cleveland 1893–1897

1902
• Maryland passes first U.S. workers' compensation laws

McKinley 1897–1901

T. Roosevelt 1901–1909

1906
• Pure Food and Drug Act passed

U.S. PRESIDENTS
U.S. EVENTS   1890   1900
WORLD EVENTS

1884
• Toynbee Hall, first settlement house, is established in London

1903
• Russian Bolshevik Party is established by Lenin

1906
• British pass workers' compensation law

290   Chapter 8   The Progressive Movement

Section 1

The Roots of Progressivism
Essential Question: Why did many citizens call for reforms? *(Some citizens wanted to restrict the power of big business; others wanted to improve living conditions in the cities; women sought the right to vote; others wanted to improve society overall.)* Tell students that in this section they will learn about the social reforms that were carried out in the early 1900s. **OL**

Section 2

Roosevelt and Taft
Essential Question: What were the policies and achievements of the Roosevelt and Taft presidencies? *(Answers might include the breaking up of the trusts, increased consumer protection, and better conservation of resources.)* Tell students that this section will focus on the reforms achieved during the Roosevelt and Taft administrations. **OL**

MAKING CONNECTIONS

Can Politics Fix Social Problems?

Industrialization changed American society. Cities were crowded, working conditions were often bad, and the old political system was breaking down. These conditions gave rise to the Progressive movement. Progressives campaigned for both political and social reforms.

- *What reforms do you think progressives wanted to achieve?*
- *Which of these reforms can you see in today's society?*

More About the Photo

Visual Literacy Before the ratification of the Nineteenth Amendment in 1920, women's voting rights varied by state. Most Western states had granted full suffrage to women well before 1920. In other states, mainly in the Midwest, women had partial suffrage which meant that women could vote for some political offices—such as president, city mayor, or school board members—but not all. Most states in the South and the East had granted no voting rights to women before 1920. In this photograph from 1910, members of the Collegiate Equal Suffrage League, wearing caps and gowns, participate in a suffrage demonstration in New York City. In 1917 New York granted full suffrage to women.

Taft 1909–1913

1910
- Mann-Elkins Act passed

Wilson 1913–1921

1913
- Seventeenth Amendment requires direct election of senators

1920
- Nineteenth Amendment gives women voting rights

1910 — 1920

1908
- Germany limits working hours for children and women

1911
- British create national health insurance program

1914
- World War I begins in Europe

1917
- Russian Revolution begins

FOLDABLES

Analyzing Reform Programs Create a Pocket Book Foldable that divides the Progressive agenda into political reforms and social reforms. Take notes on a wide range of reforms, placing each one in the proper column of the Foldable.

Progressive Political Reform / *Progressive Social Reforms*

History ONLINE Chapter Overview
Visit glencoe.com to preview Chapter 8.

Chapter 8 The Progressive Movement **291**

FOLDABLES **Dinah Zike's**
Study Organizer **Foldables**

Dinah Zike's Foldables are three-dimensional, interactive graphic organizers that help students practice basic writing skills, review vocabulary terms, and identify main ideas. Instructions for creating and using Foldables can be found in the Appendix at the end of this book and in the *Dinah Zike's Reading and Study Skills Foldables* booklet.

History ONLINE
Introduce students to chapter content and key terms by having them access the Chapter 8 Overview at glencoe.com.

Section 3

The Wilson Years

Essential Question: What reforms did President Wilson undertake? *(tariff reforms, antitrust actions, and new business regulations)* Tell students that in Section 3 they will learn about President Wilson's policies during the first part of his administration. **OL**

Focus

Bellringer
Daily Focus Transparency 8.1

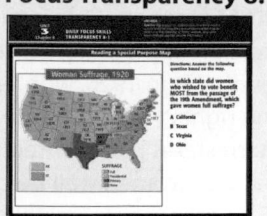

Guide to Reading

Answers:
Progressive Beliefs:
Industrialization and urbanization created social problems; Free market unable to fix social problems; Government should address social problems; Government should be reformed; Business should be regulated; Scientific principles useful in fixing social problems

Section Spotlight Video

To generate student interest and provide a springboard for discussion, access the Chapter 8, Section 1 video at glencoe.com or on the video DVD.

Resource Manager

Section 1

The Roots of Progressivism

Guide to Reading

Big Ideas
Group Action The progressives sought to improve life in the United States with social, economic, and political reforms.

Content Vocabulary
- muckraker (p. 293)
- direct primary (p. 294)
- initiative (p. 295)
- referendum (p. 295)
- recall (p. 295)
- suffrage (p. 296)
- prohibition (p. 299)

Academic Vocabulary
- legislation (p. 295)
- advocate (p. 299)

People and Events to Identify
- Jacob Riis (p. 293)
- Robert M. La Follette (p. 294)
- Carrie Chapman Catt (p. 297)

Reading Strategy
Organizing As you read about the beginnings of progressivism, complete a graphic organizer similar to the one below by filling in the beliefs of progressives.

The Progressive Era was a time when many Americans tried to improve their society. They tried to make government honest, efficient, and more democratic. The movement for women's suffrage gained more support, as did efforts to limit child labor and reduce alcohol abuse.

The Rise of Progressivism

MAIN Idea Progressives tried to solve the social problems that arose as the United States became an urban, industrialized nation.

HISTORY AND YOU What areas of public life do you believe need to be reformed? Read on to learn about a movement that tried to fix many of society's problems.

Progressivism was a collection of different ideas and activities. It was not a tightly organized political movement with a specific set of reforms. Rather, it was a series of responses to problems in American society that had emerged from the growth of industry. Progressives had many different ideas about how to fix the problems they saw in American society.

Who Were the Progressives?

Progressivism was partly a reaction against laissez-faire economics and its emphasis on an unregulated market. Progressives generally believed that industrialization and urbanization had created many social problems. After seeing the poverty of the working class and the filth and crime of urban society, reformers began doubting the free market's ability to address those problems.

Progressives belonged to both major political parties. Most were urban, educated, middle-class Americans. Among their leaders were journalists, social workers, educators, politicians, and members of the clergy. Most agreed that government should take a more active role in solving society's problems. At the same time, they doubted that the government in its present form could fix those problems. They concluded that government had to be fixed before it could be used to fix other problems.

One reason progressives thought they could improve society was their strong faith in science and technology. The application of scientific knowledge had produced the lightbulb, the telephone, and the automobile. It had built skyscrapers and railroads. Science and technology had benefited people; thus, progressives believed using scientific principles could also produce solutions for society.

R Reading Strategies	**C** Critical Thinking	**D** Differentiated Instruction	**W** Writing Support	**S** Skill Practice
Teacher Edition • Organizing Info p. 293 • Setting Purpose p. 294 • Monitoring p. 298 • Summarizing p. 298 **Additional Resources** • Guided Read., URB p. 78 • Prim. Source, URB p. 67 • Am. History in Graphic Novel, p. 15 • Historical Analysis Skills Act., URB p. 52	**Teacher Edition** • Making Inferences p. 294 • Pred. Consequences p. 296 **Additional Resources** • Hist. Sim., URB p. 9 • Inter. Pol. Cartoons, URB p. 71 • Quizzes and Tests, p. 107	**Teacher Edition** • Gifted Talented pp. 295, 299 **Additional Resources** • Diff. Instr., URB p. 53 • Academic Vocab. Act., URB p. 59 • Eng. Learner Act., URB p. 55 • Foldables, pp. 65–66	**Teacher Edition** • Personal Writing p. 296 **Additional Resources** • Supreme Court Case Studies, p. 33 • Econ. and History Act., URB p. 7 • Content Vocab. Act., URB p. 57	**Teacher Edition** • Reading a Time Line p. 297 **Additional Resources** • RENTG, p. 79 • Reinf. Skills Act., URB p. 61 • Read. Skills Act., URB p. 51 • Time Line Act., URB p. 63

The Photojournalism of Jacob Riis

Photography offered a new tool in combating injustice. One of the most famous early photojournalists was Jacob Riis, whose book, *How the Other Half Lives*, helped stir progressives to action:

PRIMARY SOURCE

"Look into any of these houses, everywhere the same piles of rags, of malodorous bones and musty paper. . . . Here is a 'flat' or 'parlor' and two pitch-dark coops called bedrooms. Truly, the bed is all there is room for. The family teakettle is on the stove, doing duty for the time being as a wash-boiler. By night it will have returned to its proper use again, a practical illustration of how poverty in 'the Bend' makes both ends meet. One, two, three beds are there, if the old boxes and heaps of foul straw can be called by that name; a broken stove with crazy pipe from which the smoke leaks at every joint, a table of rough boards propped up on boxes, piles of rubbish in the corner. The closeness and smell are appalling. How many people sleep here? The woman with the red bandanna shakes her head sullenly, but the bare-legged girl with the bright face counts on her fingers—five, six!"

—from *How the Other Half Lives*

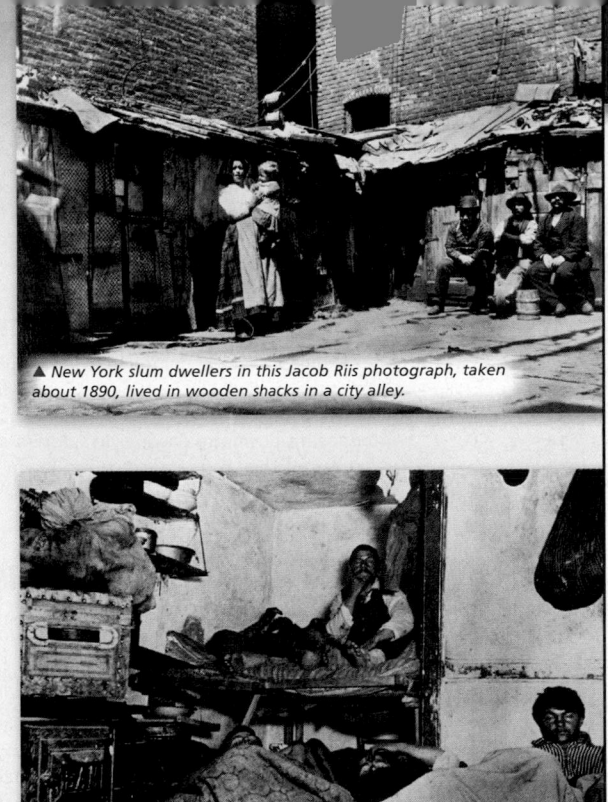

▲ New York slum dwellers in this Jacob Riis photograph, taken about 1890, lived in wooden shacks in a city alley.

▲ Riis took this photograph of a crowded one-room apartment in a New York tenement in 1885.

DBQ Document-Based Questions

1. **Analyzing Visuals** What effect do Riis's photos convey?
2. **Making Inferences** Based on the quotation above, how could you summarize Riis's views on changing life in the slums?

The Muckrakers

Among the first people to articulate progressive ideas was a group of crusading journalists who investigated social conditions and political corruption. President Theodore Roosevelt nicknamed these writers "**muckrakers.**" The term referred to a character in John Bunyan's book *Pilgrim's Progress*, who single-mindedly scraped up the filth on the ground, ignoring everything else. These journalists, according to Roosevelt, were obsessed with scandal and corruption. Widely circulated, cheap newspapers and magazines helped to spread the muckrakers' ideas.

Muckrakers uncovered corruption in many areas. Some concentrated on exposing the unfair practices of large corporations. In *Everybody's Magazine*, Charles Edward Russell attacked the beef industry. In *McClure's*, Ida Tarbell published a series of articles critical of the Standard Oil Company. Other muckrakers targeted government and social problems. Lincoln Steffens reported on vote stealing and other corrupt practices of urban political machines. These articles were later collected into a book, *The Shame of the Cities*.

Still other muckrakers concentrated on social problems. In his influential book, *How the Other Half Lives* (1890), **Jacob Riis** published photographs and descriptions of the poverty, disease, and crime that afflicted many immigrant neighborhoods in New York City. By raising public awareness of these problems, the muckrakers stimulated calls for reform.

📗 Read literature from the era on pages R72–R73 in the **American Literature Library.**

✓ Reading Check **Describing** How did the muckrakers help spark the Progressive movement?

Teach

R Reading Strategy
Organizing Information
Have students create a chart listing progressive actions discussed in this section, the social causes they represented, and their approaches to solving the problems. **OL**

DBQ Document Based Questions

Answers:
1. the hardships of poverty
2. Slums are filthy, appalling places that are unfit for people to live in and society must find a way to improve living conditions in poor neighborhoods.

✓ Reading Check

Answer:
Muckrakers raised awareness about corruption and social problems through their writing.

Hands-On Chapter Project
Step 1

Learning How Government Affects People's Lives

Step 1: Becoming a Progressive In the first of four activities for this chapter, students will relate their knowledge of the problems the progressives addressed to contemporary community issues. They will identify a community problem and suggest a solution.

Directions Have students review Section 1, noting the types of issues reformers tackled. Each student will then identify a problem in his or her community that affects citizens' lives today.

Identifying Problems and Solutions Students will either present to the class or write an analysis of the problem that includes these points: problem description, explanation of why they think the problem exists, and a statement about whether or how they believe government should go about solving the problem. If they believe the problem should not or cannot be solved by government, students should explain why and what other resources should be used. **OL**

(Project continued on page 306)

History ONLINE
**Student Web
Activity** Visit
glencoe.com
and complete the
activity on the
Progressive
movement.

Reforming Government

MAIN Idea Progressives tried to make government more efficient and more responsive to citizens.

HISTORY AND YOU How do you use your time and resources wisely? Read on to learn how progressives tried to make the government more efficient.

Progressivism included a wide range of reform activities. Different issues led to different approaches, and progressives even took opposing positions on how to address some problems. They condemned corruption in government but did not always agree on the best way to fix the problem.

Making Government Efficient

One group of progressives focused on making government more efficient by using ideas from business. Theories of business efficiency first became popular in the 1890s. Books such as Frederick W. Taylor's *The Principles of Scientific Management* (1911) described how a company could increase efficiency by managing time, breaking tasks down into small parts, and using standardized tools. In his book, Taylor argued that this "scientific method" of managing businesses optimized productivity and provided more job opportunities for unskilled workers. Many progressives argued that managing a modern city required the use of business management techniques.

R Progressives saw corruption and inefficiency in municipal government where, in most cities, the mayor or city council chose the heads of city departments. Traditionally, they gave these jobs to political supporters and friends, who often knew little about managing city services.

Progressives supported two proposals to reform city government. The first, a commission plan, divided city government into several departments, each one under an expert commissioner's control. The second approach was a council-manager system. The city council would hire a city manager to run the city instead of the mayor. In both systems, experts play a major role in managing the city. Galveston, Texas, adopted the commission system in 1901. Other cities soon followed.

Democratic Reforms

Another group of progressives focused on making the political system more democratic and more responsive to citizens. Many believed that the key to improving government was to make elected officials more responsive and accountable to the voters.

La Follette's Laboratory of Democracy
Led by Republican governor **Robert M. La Follette,** Wisconsin became a model of progressive reform. La Follette attacked the way political parties ran their conventions. Party bosses controlled the selection of convention delegates, which meant they also controlled the **C** nomination of candidates. La Follette pressured the state legislature to pass a law requiring parties to hold a **direct primary,** in which all party members could vote for a candidate to run in the general election. This and other successes earned Wisconsin a reputation as the "laboratory of democracy." La Follette later recalled:

PRIMARY SOURCE
New Types of Government

The most deadly hurricane in United States history slammed into Galveston, Texas, on September 8, 1900, killing about 6,000 people. Because the political machine running the city was incapable of responding to the disaster, local business leaders convinced the state to allow them to take control. The following April, Galveston introduced the commission system of local government, which replaced the mayor and city council with five commissioners. Sometimes referred to as the Galveston Plan, its constitutionality was confirmed and took effect.

Four of those commissioners were local business leaders. Reformers in other cities were impressed by the city's rapid recovery. Clearly, the city benefited from dividing the government into departments under the supervision of an expert commissioner. Soon, other cities adopted either the commission or council-manager systems of government.

▶ *A house sits on its side after a hurricane ripped through Galveston, Texas, in September 1900.*

PRIMARY SOURCE

"It was clear to me that the only way to beat boss and ring rule was to keep the people thoroughly informed. Machine control is based upon misrepresentation and ignorance. Democracy is based upon knowledge. It is of first importance that the people shall know about their government and the work of their public servants."

—from La Follette's *Autobiography*

Wisconsin's use of the direct primary soon spread to other states, but to force legislators to listen to the voters, progressives also pushed for three additional reforms: the initiative, the referendum, and the recall. The **initiative** permitted a group of citizens to introduce **legislation** and required the legislature to vote on it. The **referendum** allowed citizens to vote on proposed laws directly without going to the legislature. The **recall** provided voters an option to demand a special election to remove an elected official from office before his or her term had expired.

Direct Election of Senators Progressives also targeted the Senate. As originally written, the federal constitution directed each state legislature to elect two senators. Political machines and business interests often influenced these elections. Some senators, once elected, repaid their supporters with federal contracts and jobs.

To counter Senate corruption, progressives called for direct election of senators by the state's voters. In 1912, Congress passed a direct-election amendment. Although the direct election of senators was intended to end corruption, it also removed one of the state legislatures' checks on federal power. In 1913 the amendment was ratified and became the Seventeenth Amendment to the Constitution.

✓ **Reading Check** **Evaluating** What was the impact of the Seventeenth Amendment? What problem was it intended to solve?

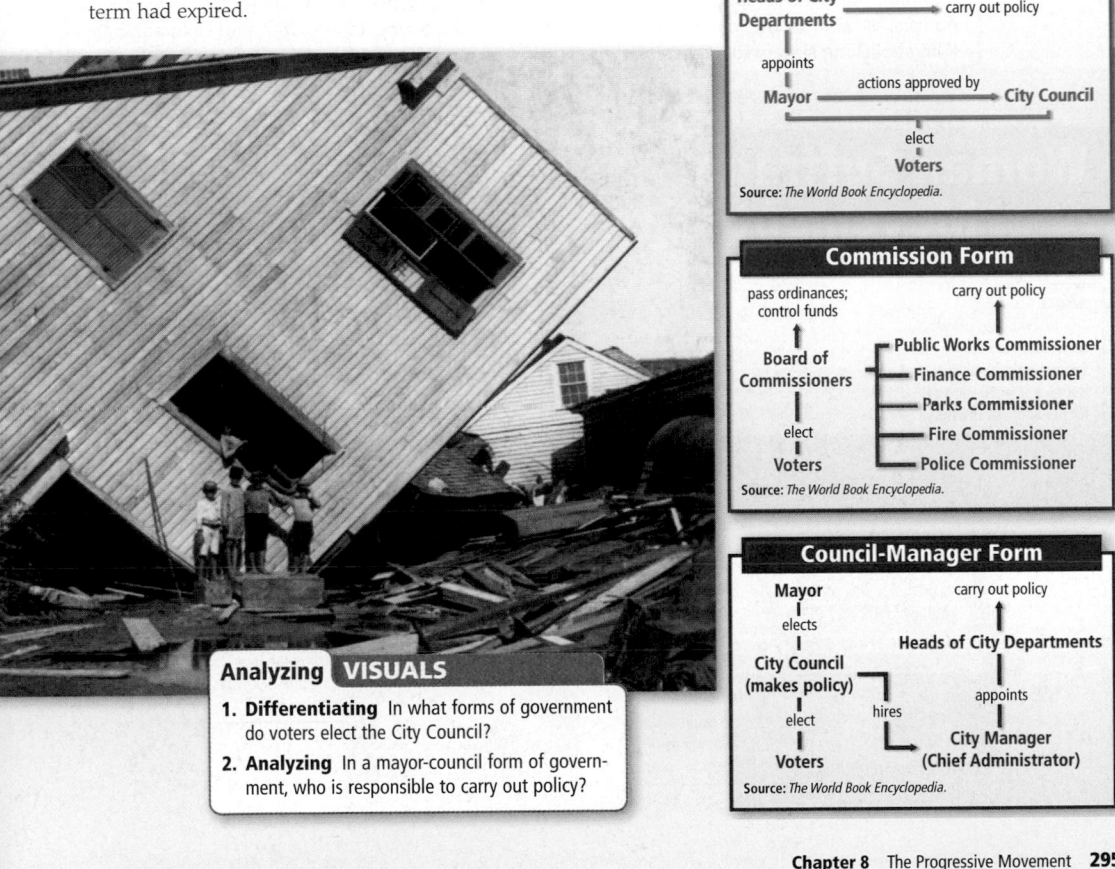

Mayor-Council Form

Heads of City Departments → carry out policy

appoints

Mayor — actions approved by → City Council

elect

Voters

Source: *The World Book Encyclopedia.*

Commission Form

pass ordinances; control funds   carry out policy

Board of Commissioners
- Public Works Commissioner
- Finance Commissioner
- Parks Commissioner
- Fire Commissioner
- Police Commissioner

elect

Voters

Source: *The World Book Encyclopedia.*

Council-Manager Form

Mayor   carry out policy
elects
City Council (makes policy)   Heads of City Departments
elect   hires   appoints
Voters   City Manager (Chief Administrator)

Source: *The World Book Encyclopedia.*

Analyzing VISUALS

1. **Differentiating** In what forms of government do voters elect the City Council?
2. **Analyzing** In a mayor-council form of government, who is responsible to carry out policy?

D **Differentiated Instruction**

Gifted and Talented Have students research and write a report about a referendum issue. They should describe the referendum, present both sides of the issue, and report on the result of the vote. **AL**

✓ **Reading Check**

Answer:
It led to the direct election of senators and was intended to counter Senate corruption.

Analyzing VISUALS

Answers:
1. Mayor-Council and Council-Manager forms
2. Heads of city departments

Additional Support

Activity: Collaborative Learning

Drafting an Initiative Divide the class into groups of three or four students and have the students work to identify a social or political problem they wish the legislature to address. After identifying a problem, the group should develop a proposal for the problem's solution. Next, have group members write the text of their initiative, as it would be presented to legislators. Have groups read their initiatives to the class. Encourage the class to discuss how effective the initiatives might be in addressing the problems they seek to solve. **Ask:** How does an initiative differ from a referendum? *(An initiative is presented to legislators to be voted on, referendums are voted on directly by citizens.)* **OL**

296

W Writing Support

Personal Writing Ask students to write a few paragraphs about whether abolition should have been given a higher priority than woman suffrage. Have students explain their reasoning. **OL**

C Critical Thinking

Predicting Consequences

Ask: Do you think American women might have gained suffrage sooner if the group agreed on a strategy? *(Students' answers will vary.)* **OL**

For an example of the early woman suffrage movement read "The Seneca Falls Declaration" on page R48 in **Documents in American History.**

Suffrage

MAIN Idea Many progressives joined the movement to win voting rights for women.

HISTORY AND YOU Do you remember reading about the Seneca Falls Convention in 1848? Read about the momentum of the women's rights movement in the 1910s.

At the first women's rights convention in Seneca Falls, New York, in 1848, Elizabeth Cady Stanton convinced the delegates that their first priority should be the right to vote. Decades later, universal woman **suffrage**—the right to vote—still had not been granted. It became a major goal for women progressives.

Early Problems

W The woman suffrage movement got off to a slow start. Some people threatened women suffragists and said they were unfeminine and immoral. Many of its supporters were abolitionists, as well. In the years before the Civil War, abolishing slavery took priority.

After the Civil War, Congress introduced the Fourteenth and Fifteenth Amendments to grant citizenship to African Americans and voting rights to African American men. Leaders of the woman suffrage movement wanted these amendments to give women the right to vote, as well. They were disappointed when Republicans refused.

The debate over the Fourteenth and Fifteenth Amendments split the suffrage movement into two groups: the New York City–based National Woman Suffrage Association, which Elizabeth Cady Stanton and Susan B. Anthony founded in 1869, and the Boston-based American Woman Suffrage Association, which Lucy Stone and Julia Ward Howe led.

The first group wanted to focus on passing a constitutional amendment. The second group believed that the best strategy was convincing state governments to give women voting rights **C** before trying to amend the Constitution. This split weakened the movement, and by 1900 only Wyoming, Idaho, Utah, and Colorado had granted women full voting rights.

THE Woman Suffrage Movement

1848
The first women's rights convention is held in Seneca Falls, New York, and issues a "Declaration of Rights and Sentiments"

1872
Susan B. Anthony votes illegally in the presidential election in Rochester, New York, claiming the Fourteenth Amendment gives her that right; she is arrested and found guilty

▲ Susan B. Anthony

1850   **1870**   **1890**

▲ Women voting in Cheyenne, Wyoming, 1869

1869
Territory of Wyoming becomes the first state or territory to grant women the right to vote

1890
Elizabeth Cady Stanton becomes president of the National American Woman Suffrage Association

▲ Elizabeth Cady Stanton

296   **Chapter 8**   The Progressive Movement

Additional Support

Activity: Collaborative Learning

Analyzing Primary Sources Have students work in groups to search the Internet for primary documents concerning woman suffrage. For each event on the Woman Suffrage Movement time line, have student groups find a pertinent quote from a primary source such as a speech, article, book, or song. Have each group recreate the time line using the quotes they selected for each date. Remind students to identify the speaker and source of each quote on their time line. Have groups present their time lines and compare the quotes they selected. **Ask:** What do the quotes tell you about attitudes toward woman suffrage? **OL**

Building Support

In 1890 the two groups united to form the National American Woman Suffrage Association (NAWSA) but still had trouble convincing women to become politically active. As the Progressive movement gained momentum, however, many middle-class women concluded that they needed the vote to promote the reforms they favored. Many working-class women also wanted the vote to pass labor laws protecting women.

As the movement grew, women began lobbying lawmakers, organizing marches, and delivering speeches on street corners. On March 3, 1913, the day before President Wilson's inauguration, suffragists marched on Washington, D.C.

Alice Paul, a Quaker social worker who headed NAWSA's congressional committee, had organized the march. Paul wanted to use protests to confront Wilson on suffrage. Other members of NAWSA who wanted to negotiate with Wilson were alarmed. Paul left NAWSA and formed the National Woman's Party. Her supporters picketed the White House, blocked sidewalks, chained themselves to lampposts, and went on hunger strikes if arrested.

In 1915 **Carrie Chapman Catt** became NAWSA's leader and tried to mobilize the suffrage movement in one final nationwide push. She also threw NAWSA's support behind Wilson's reelection campaign.

As more states granted women the right to vote, Congress began to favor a constitutional amendment. In 1918 the House of Representatives passed a women's suffrage amendment. The Senate voted on the amendment, but it failed by two votes.

During the midterm elections of 1918, Catt used NAWSA's resources to defeat two antisuffrage senators. In June 1919 the Senate passed the amendment by slightly more than the two-thirds vote needed. On August 26, 1920, after three-fourths of the states had ratified it, the Nineteenth Amendment, guaranteeing women the right to vote, went into effect.

✓ Reading Check **Evaluating** How successful were women in lobbying for the Nineteenth Amendment?

▲ *Women and children march in a 1912 suffrage parade in New York City.*

1910 ▸ **1920**

1913
Alice Paul and Lucy Burns found the Congressional Union for Woman Suffrage (later the National Woman's Party), which uses civil disobedience to promote women's suffrage

1920
Nineteenth Amendment, granting women the right to vote, is ratified

Woman Suffrage, 1869–1920

WA 1910	
OR 1912	
ID 1896	
MT 1914	ND
SD 1918	MN
WY 1869	WI
NV 1914	NE
CA 1911	UT 1870	CO 1893	IA
AZ 1912	NM	KS 1912	MO
	OK 1918	AR
TX	LA

VT NH ME
NY 1917 MA RI CT
MI 1918 PA NJ
IL IN OH DE MD
WV VA
KY
TN NC
SC
MS AL GA
FL

- ☐ Full woman suffrage before 1920, with date granted
- ☐ Partial woman suffrage before 1920
- ☐ No woman suffrage until ratification of Nineteenth Amendment

Analyzing TIME LINES

1. **Identifying** In what state or territory were women first granted the right to vote?
2. **Analyzing** What region of the nation seemed most willing to grant woman suffrage without a national amendment?

S

Chapter 8 The Progressive Movement **297**

Activity: Interdisciplinary Connection

Art Tell students that the 1913 suffrage parade in Washington, D.C., was filled with posters and pageantry. Gowned women rode horseback, and young girls carried posters with slogans such as "Votes for us when we are women!" Have students work in groups to research photographs of the parade. Then have each group create their own suffrage posters inspired by images they found through their research. **Ask:** Which symbols convey the most powerful message? Have groups share their posters with the class. **BL** **OL**

R₁ Reading Strategy

Monitoring Ask: What influenced states to pass child labor laws? *(books such as* The Bitter Cry of the Children*)* **BL**

R₂ Reading Strategy

Summarizing Have students write a short summary of adult working conditions and the influence of progressives and unions on labor laws. **OL**

R₁ Reading Strategy

Monitoring Ask: What influenced states to pass child labor laws? *(books such as* The Bitter Cry of the Children*)* **BL**

R₂ Reading Strategy

Summarizing Have students write a short summary of adult working conditions and the influence of progressives and unions on labor laws. **OL**

Analyzing VISUALS

Answers:
1. Students may note that the spray from fire hoses barely reaches top floor and people are trapped in the building looking for help.
2. the protest signs mention Hebrew trades, some of the background signs are in other languages.

Additional Support

Reforming Society

MAIN Idea Many progressives focused on social welfare problems such as child labor, unsafe working conditions, and alcohol abuse.

HISTORY AND YOU Have you heard of companies using "sweatshop" labor in foreign countries? Read on to learn how progressives tried to ban child labor and make factories safer for workers.

History ONLINE
Student Skill Activity To learn how to create and modify a database, visit glencoe.com and complete the skill activity.

While many progressives focused on reforming the political system, others focused on social problems. These social-welfare progressives created charities to help the poor and disadvantaged. They also pushed for new laws they hoped would fix social problems.

Child Labor

Probably the most emotional progressive issue was the campaign against child labor. Children had always worked on family farms, but mines and factories presented more dangerous and unhealthy working conditions. Muckraker John Spargo's 1906 book, *The Bitter Cry of the Children,* presented detailed evidence of child labor conditions. It told of coal mines that hired thousands of 9- or 10-year-old "breaker boys" to pick slag out of coal, paying them 60 cents for a 10-hour day. It described the way that the work bent their backs permanently and often crippled their hands.

Reports like these convinced states to pass laws that set a minimum age for employment and established other limits on child labor, such as maximum hours children could work.

Health and Safety Codes

Many adult workers also labored in difficult conditions. When workers were injured or killed on the job, they and their families received little or no compensation. Progressives joined union leaders to pressure states for workers' compensation laws. These laws established insurance funds that employers financed. Workers injured in accidents received payments from the funds.

In two cases, *Lochner* v. *New York* (1905) and *Muller* v. *Oregon* (1908), the Supreme Court addressed government's authority to regulate business to protect workers. In the Lochner case, the Court ruled that a New York law forbidding bakers to work more than 10 hours a day was unconstitutional. The state did not have the right to interfere with the liberty of

PRIMARY SOURCE
A Tragedy Brings Reform

Fire broke out on the top floors of the Triangle Shirtwaist Company on March 25, 1911. Young women struggled against locked doors to escape. A few women managed to get out using the fire escape before it collapsed. The single elevator stopped running. Some women jumped from windows on the ninth floor to their death, while others died in the fire. Nearly 150 of the 500 employees lost their lives in the blaze.

The Triangle factory was a nonunion shop. Health and safety issues were a major concern for unions. The disaster illustrated that fire precautions and inspections were inadequate. Exit doors were kept locked, supposedly to prevent theft. As a result of the fire and loss of life, New York created a Factory Investigating Commission. Between 1911 and 1914, the state passed 36 new laws reforming the labor code.

▲ Firemen fight Triangle Shirtwaist fire, March 25, 1911.

▲ Trade union members march in support of the women who died.

Analyzing VISUALS
1. **Analyzing** What do you observe about the efforts at fighting the fire in the photo at left?
2. **Interpreting** What clues in the photo at right suggest that at least some of the women who died were immigrants?

Activity: Technology Connection

Discussing Working Conditions Divide students into groups of 4 or 5. Have them use the Internet to research industrial accidents and unsafe conditions in such cases as the Wal-Mart Lock-Ins, 2003; Imperial Foods Fire, 1991; and the Kader Industrial Fire, 1993. Ask groups to write a report summarizing the accident or working conditions they researched. Have students include in their report the impact, if any, of the incident on labor laws and working conditions. Students should share their reports with the class. **Ask:** What basic rights and working conditions do you think workers should be guaranteed? **OL AL**

employers and employees. In the case of women working in laundries in Oregon, however, the Court upheld the state's right to limit hours. The different judgments were based on gender differences. The Court stated that healthy mothers were the state's concern and, therefore, the limits on women's working hours did not violate their Fourteenth Amendment rights.

Some progressives also favored zoning laws as a method of protecting the public. These laws divided a town or city into zones for commercial, residential, or other development, thereby regulating how land and buildings could be used. Building codes set minimum standards for light, air, room size, and sanitation, and required buildings to have fire escapes. Health codes required restaurants and other facilities to maintain clean environments for their patrons.

The Prohibition Movement

Many progressives believed alcohol explained many of society's problems. Settlement house workers knew that hard-earned wages were often spent on alcohol and that drunkenness often led to physical abuse and sickness. Some employers believed drinking hurt workers' efficiency. The temperance movement—which **advocated** that people stop, or at least moderate, their alcohol consumption—emerged from these concerns.

For the most part, women led the temperance movement. In 1874 a group of women formed the Woman's Christian Temperance Union (WCTU). By 1911 the WCTU had nearly 250,000 members. In 1893 evangelical Protestant ministers formed another group, the Anti-Saloon League. When the temperance movement began, it concentrated on reducing alcohol consumption. Later it pressed for **prohibition**—laws banning the manufacture, sale, and consumption of alcohol.

Progressives Versus Big Business

Many progressives agreed that big business needed regulation. Some believed the government should break up big companies to restore competition. This led to the Sherman Antitrust Act in 1890. Others argued that big business was the most efficient way to organize the economy. They pushed for government to regulate big companies and prevent them from abusing their power. The Interstate Commerce Commission (ICC), created in 1887, was an early example of this kind of thinking.

Some progressives went even further and advocated socialism—the idea that the government should own and operate industry for the community. They wanted the government to buy up large companies, especially industries that affected everyone, such as utilities. At its peak, socialism had some national support. Eugene V. Debs, the former American Railway Union leader, won nearly a million votes as the American Socialist Party candidate for president in 1912. Most progressives and most Americans, however, believed the American system of free enterprise was superior.

Reading Check **Comparing** In what ways were progressive efforts to end child labor and impose safety codes similar?

Section 1 REVIEW

Vocabulary
1. **Explain** the significance of: muckraker, Jacob Riis, Robert M. La Follette, direct primary, initiative, referendum, recall, suffrage, Carrie Chapman Catt, prohibition.

Main Ideas
2. **Organizing** Use a graphic organizer similar to the one below to list the kinds of problems that muckrakers exposed.

```
Problems Exposed
by Muckrakers
```
```
☐  ☐  ☐  ☐  ☐  ☐
```

3. **Summarizing** How did initiative, referendum, and recall change democracy in the United States?

4. **Stating** What key provision did the Nineteenth Amendment make?

5. **Describing** Explain the various zoning laws and codes favored by progressives.

Critical Thinking
6. **Big Ideas** Identify the different social issues associated with progressives. How do these ideals influence society today?

7. **Analyzing Visuals** Study the charts on page 295. Which system gives voters the most control over department heads? How?

Writing About History
8. **Expository Writing** Create a database of progressive ideas of the period. Then write a one-page report using a word processor to summarize the progressive ideals.

History ONLINE
Study Central™ To review this section, go to glencoe.com and click on Study Central.

299

D **Differentiated Instruction**

Gifted and Talented Have students prepare a report on the Sherman Antitrust Act of 1890. Have them describe the conditions that contributed to the act, the support and opposition it faced, and what resulted from its enactment. **AL**

Assess

History ONLINE

Study Central™ provides summaries, interactive games, and online graphic organizers to help students review content.

Close

Summarizing Have students summarize the influences progressives had on society during this period in history.

Reading Check

Answer:
both wanted to reduce injuries; both wanted to limit work hours; both reflected the belief that women and children needed protection

Section 1 REVIEW

Answers

1. Definitions for the vocabulary terms are found in the section and the Glossary.

2. Problems Exposed by Muckrakers: unfair practices by big business, corrupt government, inefficient government, poverty, child labor practices, adult labor conditions.

3. Initiatives permitted citizens to introduce legislation that lawmakers were required to vote on. Referendums allowed citizens to vote directly on proposed laws. Recall provided voters with a way to remove politicians from office before their terms ended.

4. The Nineteenth Amendment granted women the right to vote.

5. Zoning laws divided areas into commercial or residential areas to regulate building and land use. Building codes regulated room size and required fire escapes.

6. Progressives were concerned with issues of social justice including poverty, fair labor practices, and reining in big business. These concerns are still with us today and are major topics of public debate.

7. The commission form of government gives voters the most control over department heads because voters elect them directly.

8. Reports will vary but should give reasons for a clearly stated position.

Focus

Bellringer
Daily Focus Transparency 8.2

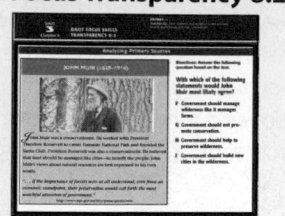

Guide to Reading

Answers:
Roosevelt and Taft
1. Roosevelt Revives the Presidency
A. Roosevelt Takes on the Trusts
B. The Coal Strike of 1902
C. Regulating Big Business
D. Consumer Protection
II. Conservation
A. Western Land Development
B. Gifford Pinchot
C. Roosevelt's Legacy

Section Spotlight Video

To generate student interest and provide a springboard for discussion, access the Chapter 8, Section 2 video at glencoe.com or on the video DVD.

Resource Manager

Section 2

Roosevelt and Taft

Guide to Reading

Big Ideas
Individual Action Presidents Theodore Roosevelt and William Taft worked to improve labor conditions, control big business, and support conservation.

Content Vocabulary
• Social Darwinism (p. 306)
• arbitration (p. 301)
• insubordination (p. 307)

Academic Vocabulary
• regulate (p. 302)
• environmental (p. 304)

People and Events to Identify
• Square Deal (p. 300)
• United Mine Workers (p. 301)
• Hepburn Act (p. 302)
• Upton Sinclair (p. 302)
• Meat Inspection Act (p. 302)
• Pure Food and Drug Act (p. 302)
• Gifford Pinchot (p. 304)
• Richard A. Ballinger (p. 306)
• Children's Bureau (p. 307)

Reading Strategy
Notes As you read about the Roosevelt and Taft administrations, use the headings of the section to create an outline similar to the one below.

```
Roosevelt and Taft
I. Roosevelt Revives the Presidency
   A.
   B.
   C.
   D.
II.
```

As president, Theodore Roosevelt extended the federal government's ability to curb the power of big business and to conserve natural resources. His successor, William Howard Taft, was less popular with progressives.

Roosevelt Revives the Presidency

MAIN Idea Theodore Roosevelt, who believed in progressive ideals for the nation, took on big business.

HISTORY AND YOU How much do you think a president's personal beliefs should shape national policy? Read on to learn how Theodore Roosevelt used his ideas to change trusts and big business.

Theodore Roosevelt became president at age 42—the youngest person ever to take office. Roosevelt was intensely competitive, strong-willed, and extremely energetic. In international affairs, Roosevelt was a Social Darwinist. He believed the United States was in competition with the other nations of the world and that only the fittest would survive. Domestically, however, Roosevelt was a committed progressive, who believed that government should actively balance the needs of competing groups in American society.

"I shall see to it," Roosevelt declared in 1904, "that every man has a square deal, no less and no more." His reform programs soon became known as the **Square Deal.** To Roosevelt, it was not inconsistent to believe in **Social Darwinism** and progressivism at the same time.

Roosevelt Takes on the Trusts

Roosevelt believed that trusts and other large business organizations were very efficient and part of the reason for America's prosperity. Yet Roosevelt remained concerned that the monopoly power of some trusts hurt the public interest. His goal was to ensure that trusts did not abuse their power. When the *New York Sun* declared that Roosevelt was "bringing wealth to its knees," the president disagreed. "We draw the line against misconduct," he declared, "not against wealth."

Roosevelt decided to make an example out of major trusts that he believed were abusing their power. His first target was J. P. Morgan's railroad holding company, Northern Securities. Established in 1901, the company proposed, through an exchange of stock, to merge existing railroad systems to create a monopoly on railroad traffic in the Northwest. As a monopoly, Northern Securities would have no competition. Farmers and business owners feared it would raise rates and hurt their profits. In 1902 the president ordered the attorney

---

R Reading Strategies	**C** Critical Thinking	**D** Differentiated Instruction	**W** Writing Support	**S** Skill Practice
Teacher Edition • Monitoring p. 305 • Det. Importance p. 306 • Academic Vocab. p. 307 **Additional Resources** • Guided Reading, URB p. 79 • Prim. Source Read., URB p. 65	**Teacher Edition** • Det. Cause/Effect p. 301 • Drawing Con. pp. 302, 304 **Additional Resources** • Quizzes and Tests, p. 108 • Crit. Think. Skills Act., URB p. 62 • Linking Past/Present, URB p. 64	**Teacher Edition** • Gifted/Talented p. 302	**Teacher Edition** • Persuasive Writing p. 304 **Additional Resources** • Geo. and History, URB p. 3 • Supreme Court Case Studies, p. 29	**Teacher Edition** • Visual Literacy p. 301 **Additional Resources** • RENTG, p. 82

POLITICAL CARTOONS PRIMARY SOURCE
Roosevelt Versus the Trusts

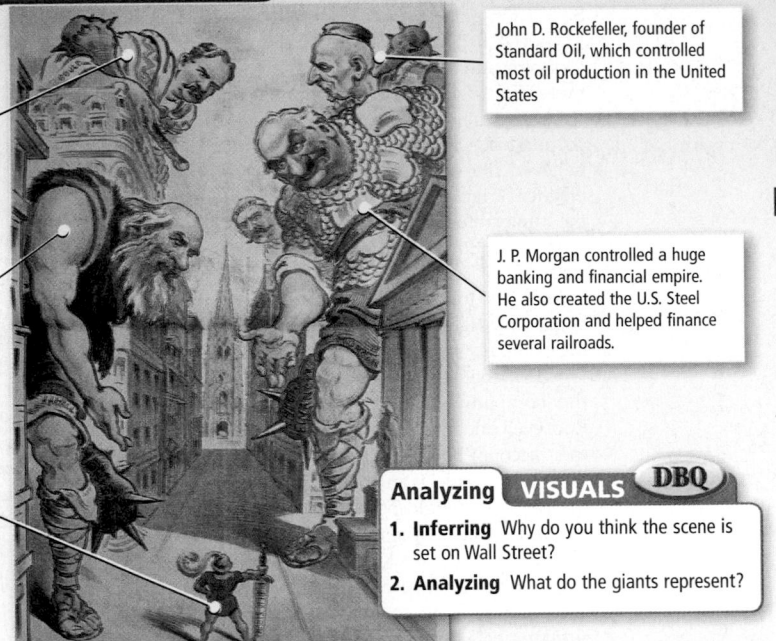

Jay Gould was a well-known railroad speculator who had been involved in many scandals. At one point, he controlled the four largest western railroads, including the Union Pacific.

James J. Hill, founder of the Great Northern Railway Company and a partner with J. P. Morgan in Northern Securities

Theodore Roosevelt, shown standing in the middle of Wall Street carrying a sword labeled "Public Service"

John D. Rockefeller, founder of Standard Oil, which controlled most oil production in the United States

J. P. Morgan controlled a huge banking and financial empire. He also created the U.S. Steel Corporation and helped finance several railroads.

S

Analyzing VISUALS DBQ

1. **Inferring** Why do you think the scene is set on Wall Street?
2. **Analyzing** What do the giants represent?

general to file suit under the Sherman Antitrust Act, charging the company was a "combination in restraint of trade."

Roosevelt's action baffled J. P. Morgan. Expecting to resolve the suit without legal action, he inquired what could be done to "fix it up." Unmoved, Roosevelt proceeded with the case. In 1904, in *Northern Securities* v. *United States*, the Supreme Court ruled that Northern Securities had indeed violated the Sherman Antitrust Act. Roosevelt proclaimed, "The most powerful men in the country were held to accountability before the law." Newspapers hailed Roosevelt as a "trustbuster," and his popularity with the American public soared.

The Coal Strike of 1902

As president, Roosevelt regarded himself as the nation's head manager. He believed it was his job to keep society operating efficiently by mediating conflicts between different groups and their interests. In the fall of 1902, he put these beliefs into practice.

The previous spring, the **United Mine Workers** (UMW) had launched a strike by the anthracite (hard coal) miners of eastern Pennsylvania. Nearly 150,000 workers walked out, demanding increased pay, reduced work hours, and union recognition. Coal prices began to rise. Roosevelt viewed it as another example of groups pursuing their private interests at the nation's expense. If the strike dragged on too long, the country would face a coal shortage that could shut down factories and leave many homes unheated.

Roosevelt urged the union and the owners to accept **arbitration**—a settlement negotiated by an outside party. The union agreed; the mine owners did not. The mine owners' stubbornness infuriated Roosevelt, as well as the public. Roosevelt threatened to order the army to run the mines. Fearful of this, the mine owners finally accepted arbitration. By intervening in the dispute, Roosevelt took the first step toward establishing the federal government as an honest broker between powerful groups in society.

C

Chapter 8 The Progressive Movement **301**

Activity: Interdisciplinary Connection

Literature Have student groups select a passage from *The Jungle* to present as a reading to the class. Ask groups to select a section in which there is both description and characters speaking dialogue. Have each group select a student to be the narrator and read descriptions; assign the characters to other students. Have each group practice reading their sections clearly and with feeling. When groups are ready, have them present their readings to the class. Encourage the class to discuss their reactions to the novel. **Ask:** If you wanted to influence changes in today's society, what would you write about? **AL**

C **Critical Thinking**

C **Critical Thinking**

Drawing Conclusions

Ask: When the ICC limited competition among railroads and began setting rates to ensure industry profits, was it betraying its original mission? Why or why not? *(Student responses will vary.)* `OL` `AL`

D **Differentiated Instruction**

Gifted and Talented Have students research early 20th century ads for patent medicines and compare them to ads for present-day medicines. How are they similar and different? `AL`

✔ **Reading Check**

Answer:
Roosevelt's policies were called a "Square Deal." This term was accurate because he attempted to protect all Americans through industry regulation.

Additional Support

Regulating Big Business

Despite his lawsuit against Northern Securities and his role in the coal strike, Roosevelt believed most trusts benefited the economy and that breaking them up would do more harm than good. Instead, he proposed creating a new federal agency to investigate corporations and publicize the results. He believed the most effective way to keep big business from abusing its power was to keep the public informed.

In 1903 Roosevelt convinced Congress to create the Department of Commerce and Labor. The following year, this department began investigating U.S. Steel, a gigantic holding company that had been created in 1901. Worried about a possible antitrust lawsuit, the company's leaders met privately with Roosevelt and offered a deal. They would open their account books and records for examination. In exchange, if any problems were found, the company would be advised privately and allowed to correct them without having to go to court.

Roosevelt accepted this "gentlemen's agreement," as he called it, and soon made similar deals with other companies. These arrangements gave Roosevelt the ability to **regulate** big business without having to sacrifice economic efficiency by breaking up the trusts.

In keeping with his belief in regulation, Roosevelt pushed the **Hepburn Act** through Congress in 1906. This act was intended to strengthen the Interstate Commerce Commission (ICC) by giving it the power to set railroad rates. At first, railroad companies were suspicious of the ICC and tied up its decisions by challenging them in court. Eventually, the railroads realized that they could work with the ICC to set rates and regulations that limited competition and prevented new competitors from entering the industry. Over time, the ICC became a supporter of the railroads' interests, and by 1920 it had begun setting rates at levels intended to ensure the industry's profits.

Consumer Protection

By 1905 consumer protection had become a national issue. That year, a journalist named Samuel Hopkins Adams published a series of articles in *Collier's* magazine describing the patent medicine business.

Many companies patented and marketed potions they claimed would cure a variety of ills. Many of these medicines were little more than alcohol, colored water, and sugar. Others contained caffeine, opium, cocaine, and other dangerous compounds. Consumers had no way to know what they were taking, nor did they receive any assurance that the medicines worked as claimed. Adams's articles pointed out that these supposed cures could cause health problems. The articles in *Collier's* outraged many Americans.

Many Americans were equally concerned about the food they ate. Dr. W. H. Wiley, chief chemist at the United States Department of Agriculture, had issued reports documenting the dangerous preservatives being used in what he called "embalmed meat." Then, in 1906, **Upton Sinclair** published his novel *The Jungle*. Based on Sinclair's close observations of the slaughterhouses of Chicago, the powerful book featured appalling descriptions of conditions in the meatpacking industry:

PRIMARY SOURCE

"[T]here would come all the way back from Europe old sausage that had been rejected, and that was [moldy] and white—it would be dosed with borax and glycerine, and dumped into the hoppers, and made over again for home consumption. . . . There would be meat stored in great piles in rooms; and the water from leaky roofs would drip over it, and thousands of rats would race about [upon] it."

—from *The Jungle*

Sinclair's book was a best-seller. It made consumers ill—and angry. Many became vegetarians after reading the book. Roosevelt and Congress responded with the **Meat Inspection Act,** passed in 1906. It required federal inspection of meat sold through interstate commerce and required the Agriculture Department to set standards of cleanliness in meatpacking plants. The **Pure Food and Drug Act,** passed on the same day in 1906, prohibited the manufacture, sale, or shipment of impure or falsely labeled food and drugs.

✔ Reading Check **Identifying** What term was used to describe Roosevelt's policies and how accurate was it?

Activity: Collaborative Learning

Comparing and Contrasting National Parks Divide students into small groups. Have each group research and create a guide for a national park. Guides should include a general history of the park, the park's mission, and points of interest. Ask students to include photographs of the park in their guides. Students may produce their guides as a pamphlet, slide show, or live presentation. Encourage groups to share their guides with the class. Ask students to compare the features of various parks. **Ask:** In what ways are the parks similar and different? `BL` `OL`

Can Government Regulate Business Activity?

★ *Northern Securities* v. *United States,* 1904

Background to the Case

In 1901 three powerful businessmen, J. P. Morgan, James J. Hill, and Edward H. Harriman, created Northern Securities—a holding company that owned the majority of the stock in several major railroads. The government sued the company for violating the Sherman Antitrust Act, and a court ordered the company broken up.

How the Court Ruled

The Constitution gives the federal government the power to regulate interstate commerce—but did "commerce" mean all business activity, or just the movement of goods across state lines? The owners of Northern Securities argued that their company was a holding company set up to buy stock. It had been created legally under New Jersey law, and federal laws should not apply because the company itself did not engage in interstate commerce. In a 5-4 decision, the Court concluded that the commerce clause allows the federal government to regulate the ownership of companies.

NO MOLLY-CODDLING HERE

▲ *President Roosevelt once said "Speak softly and carry a big stick." This cartoon shows Roosevelt swinging his stick and knocking down the trusts—and everything else, as well.*

PRIMARY SOURCE

The Court's Opinion

"No state can, by merely creating a corporation . . . project its authority into other states, and across the continent, so as to prevent Congress from exerting the power it possesses under the Constitution over interstate and international commerce. . . .

. . . Every corporation created by a state is necessarily subject to the supreme law of the land. . . . In short, the court may make any order necessary to bring about the dissolution or suppression of an illegal combination that restrains interstate commerce. All this can be done without infringing in any degree upon the just authority of the states."

—Justice John Marshall Harlan, writing for the Court

PRIMARY SOURCE

Dissenting Views

"Commerce depends upon population, but Congress could not, on that ground, undertake to regulate marriage and divorce. If the act before us is to be carried out according to what seems to me the logic of the argument . . . I can see no part of the conduct of life with which . . . Congress might not interfere.

. . . This act is construed by the Government to affect the purchasers of shares in two railroad companies because of the effect it may have . . . upon the competition of these roads. If such a remote result of the exercise of an ordinary incident of property and personal freedom is enough to make that exercise unlawful, there is hardly any transaction concerning commerce between the States that may not be made a crime by the finding of a jury or a court."

—Justice Oliver Wendell Holmes, dissenting

DBQ Document-Based Questions

1. **Interpreting** How does Justice Harlan view the rights of states and the authority of Congress?
2. **Defining** How does Justice Harlan refer to the Sherman Antitrust Act?
3. **Analyzing** What does Justice Holmes fear in narrowly applying a law?

Teach

Five months into his presidency, Roosevelt took on the richest man in the country, J. Pierpont Morgan. Morgan was an international investment banker who made his money from the many trusts he ran. He used his wealth to support and influence politicians. When Roosevelt brought suit against his railroad company, Northern Securities, Morgan was surprised and furious. Morgan wanted to settle things quietly between himself and the president. Roosevelt said no because he believed the public interest had to be protected.

DBQ Document Based Questions

Answers:
1. The authority of Congress supercedes the rights of states.
2. as a Constitutional power
3. Congress could interfere in all areas of life.

Differentiated Instruction

Analyzing a Supreme Court Decision

Objective: Learn how the Constitution is applied to a Supreme Court case.

Focus: Identify the central issue of the case.

Teach: Discuss the Court's opinion.

Assess: Explain the importance of the case (broad interpretation of Congressional power).

Close: Write a paragraph summarizing the case.

Differentiated Instruction Strategies

BL Restate the constitutional issue at stake in your own words.

AL According to the decision, Congress was allowed and not allowed to take certain actions. Create a graphic organizer that details this.

ELL Explain to a partner the issue that brought the case to the Supreme Court and its resolution.

C Critical Thinking

Drawing Conclusions

Ask: How did Roosevelt's personal experience influence his environmental policies? *(As an enthusiastic outdoorsman, he placed a great value on protecting the environment.)* **OL**

W Writing Support

Persuasive Writing Write a paragraph that supports or disputes the idea that because it is in the best interest of lumber companies to conserve forests, the government should stay out of regulating forest conservation. Use facts to support your position. **OL AL**

Conservation

MAIN Idea New legislation gave the federal government the power to conserve natural resources.

HISTORY AND YOU Have you ever visited a national park or forest? Read on to find out how Roosevelt made some national parks and forests possible.

Roosevelt put his stamp on the presidency most clearly in the area of **environmental** conservation. Realizing that the nation's bountiful natural resources were being used up at an alarming rate, Roosevelt urged Americans to conserve those resources.

An enthusiastic outdoorsman, Roosevelt valued the country's minerals, animals, and rugged terrain. He cautioned against unregulated exploitation of public lands and believed in conservation to manage the nation's resources. Roosevelt argued that the government must distinguish "between the man who skins the land and the man who develops the country. I am going to work with, and only with, the man who develops the country."

Western Land Development

Roosevelt quickly applied his philosophy in the dry Western states, where farmers and city dwellers competed for scarce water. In 1902 Roosevelt supported passage of the Newlands Reclamation Act, authorizing the use of federal funds from public land sales to pay for irrigation and land development projects. The federal government thus began transforming the West's landscape and economy on a large scale.

Gifford Pinchot

Roosevelt also backed efforts to save the nation's forests through careful management of the timber resources of the West. He appointed his close friend **Gifford Pinchot** to head the United States Forest Service established in 1905. "The natural resources," Pinchot said, "must be developed and preserved for the benefit of the many and not merely for the profit of a few."

As progressives, Roosevelt and Pinchot both believed that trained experts in forestry and resource management should apply the same

scientific standards to the landscape that others were applying to managing cities and industry. They rejected the laissez-faire argument that the best way to preserve public land was to sell it to lumber companies, who would then carefully conserve it because it was the source of their profits. With the president's support, Pinchot's department drew up regulations controlling lumbering on federal lands. Roosevelt also added over 100 million acres to the protected national forests and established five new national parks and 51 federal wildlife reservations.

Roosevelt's Legacy

President Theodore Roosevelt changed the role of the federal government and the nature of the presidency. He used his power in the

Debates IN HISTORY

Should Resources Be Preserved?

The origins of the environmentalist movement can be traced back to the Progressive Era. Then, as now, people disagreed over the best approach to the environment. Their disagreements were represented in the differing views of John Muir, founder of the Sierra Club, who worked with Roosevelt to create Yosemite National Park, and Gifford Pinchot, head of the U.S. Forest Service under Theodore Roosevelt. Muir was a preservationist, hoping that wild places could be left as they were. Pinchot was a conservationist who believed in managing the use of land for the benefit of the nation's citizens.

Differentiated Instruction

Yellowstone National Park: A Natural Treasure

Objective: Understand a result of the conservation movement.

Focus: Describe the features of Yellowstone National Park and why it has been preserved.

Teach: Explain how Yellowstone National Park set a precedent for future national parks.

Assess: Explain why conservation is important.

Close: Cite other examples of "national treasures."

Differentiated Instruction Strategies

BL Research to find or draw diagrams of the hydrothermal features found at Yellowstone National Park.

AL Describe a scenario in which Yellowstone is not a national park.

ELL Research to find a "Did You Know" fun fact about Yellowstone National Park.

White House to present his views, calling it his "bully pulpit." Increasingly, Americans began looking to the federal government to solve the nation's economic and social problems.

Under Roosevelt, the power of the executive branch of government had dramatically increased. The Hepburn Act gave the Interstate Commerce Commission the power to set rates, the Meat Inspection Act stated that the Agriculture Department could inspect food, the Department of Commerce and Labor could monitor business, the Bureau of Corporations could investigate corporations and issue reports, and the attorney general could rapidly bring antitrust lawsuits under the Expedition Act.

Reading Check **Examining** How did Roosevelt's policies help the conservation of natural resources?

Taft's Reforms

MAIN Idea William Howard Taft broke with progressives on tariff and conservation issues.

HISTORY AND YOU Have you ever been judged in comparison with the accomplishments of a sibling or friend? Read on to learn how Taft had to deal with comparisons with Roosevelt.

Roosevelt believed William Howard Taft to be the ideal person to continue his policies. Taft had worked closely with Roosevelt. He had served as a judge, as governor of the Philippines, and as Roosevelt's secretary of war. Taft easily received his party's nomination. His victory in the general election in November 1908 was a foregone conclusion. The Democratic candidate, William Jennings Bryan, lost for a third time.

R Reading Strategy

Monitoring Ask: During Roosevelt's presidency, which bureau was charged with inspecting food? (the Agriculture Department) **BL**

✓ Reading Check

Answer:
He regulated use of public lands and supported conservation acts such as the Newlands Reclamation Act.

Debates IN HISTORY

Answers:
1. Muir believed that wild places should be left as they are. Pinchot believed in managing the use of land to benefit citizens.
2. Students should back up their positions.
3. Most students will say that ranchers and farmers would likely support the idea of managing natural resources because their livelihoods depended on access to land and water.

Additional Support

YES

John Muir
Sierra Club Founder

PRIMARY SOURCE

"The making of gardens and parks goes on with civilization all over the world, and they increase both in size and number as their value is recognized.

Everybody needs beauty as well as bread, places to play in and pray in, where Nature may heal and cheer and give strength to body and soul alike. . . . Nevertheless, like anything else worth while . . . they have always been subject to attack by despoiling gainseekers . . . eagerly trying to make everything immediately and selfishly commercial, with schemes disguised in smug-smiling philanthropy, industriously, shampiously crying, 'Conservation, conservation, panutilization,' that man and beast may be fed and the dear Nation made great."

—from *The Yosemite*

NO

Gifford Pinchot
Chief of U.S. Forest Service

PRIMARY SOURCE

"The first principle of conservation is development, the use of the natural resources now existing on this continent for the benefit of the people who live here now. There may be just as much waste in neglecting the development and use of certain natural resources as there is in their destruction. . . .

Conservation stands emphatically for the development and use of water power now, without delay. It stands for the immediate construction of navigable waterways . . . as assistants to the railroads. . . .

In addition . . . natural resources must be developed and preserved for the benefit of the many, and not merely for the profit of the few."

—from *The Fight for Conservation*

DBQ Document-Based Questions

1. **Contrasting** How do the two men differ in their views about nature?

2. **Making Connections** Which view do you think is more common today? Why do you think so?

3. **Speculating** Which viewpoint do you think was more likely to be held by ranchers and farmers in California in the early twentieth century?

Chapter 8 The Progressive Movement **305**

Extending the Content

Conservationists Gifford Pinchot and John Muir were friends who shared a love of nature. But their friendship ended in a bitter disagreement over Yosemite National Park in the Sierra Nevada mountains of California.

The dispute focused on the desire of some to dam a river in the park to supply drinking water for San Francisco, California. Muir argued that it was the right of all Americans to enjoy the undisturbed beauty of nature. Pinchot felt that natural resources should be used wisely to meet the needs of people. In 1913 Congress decided the issue by passing the Raker Act, which allowed the dam to be built.

PRIMARY SOURCE
Campaigning Against Child Labor

In 1900, 18 percent of children were employed. Mary Harris Jones, "Mother" Jones, as she was called, campaigned against child labor. After working with children in an Alabama cotton mill, she wrote, "Little girls and boys . . . reaching thin little hands into the machinery to repair snapped threads. They replaced spindles all day long; all night through . . . six-year-olds with faces of sixty did an eight-hour shift for ten cents a day . . ."

Using posters like the one shown at right to build public support, the campaign against child labor made steady progress. Between 1880 and 1910, 36 states passed laws on the minimum age for manufacturing workers.

Analyzing VISUALS

1. **Analyzing** What in the photo indicates that the children could easily be injured?
2. **Hypothesizing** What effect do you think the images on the inset poster may have had on people in the early 1900s?

▲ *At a Georgia cotton mill in 1909, two boys keep a spinning machine running by repairing broken thread and replacing bobbins as they are filled.*

The Payne-Aldrich Tariff

Like many progressives, Taft believed high tariffs limited competition, hurt consumers, and protected trusts. Roosevelt had warned him to stay away from tariff reform because it would divide the Republican Party. Taft, however, called Congress into special session to lower tariff rates.

As Roosevelt predicted, the tariff debate divided progressives, who favored tariff reduction, and conservative Republicans who wanted to maintain high tariffs. In the prolonged negotiations on the bill, Taft's support for tariff reductions wavered, and then collapsed. In the end, Taft signed into law the Payne-Aldrich Tariff, which cut tariffs hardly at all and actually raised them on some goods.

Progressives felt outraged by Taft's decision: "I knew the fire had gone out of [the progressive movement]," recalled the head of the U.S. Forest Service, Gifford Pinchot, after Roosevelt left office. "Washington was a dead town. Its leader was gone, and in his place [was] a man whose fundamental desire was to keep out of trouble."

Ballinger Versus Pinchot

With Taft's standing among Republican progressives deteriorating, a sensational controversy broke out late in 1909 that helped permanently destroy Taft's popularity with reformers. Many progressives were unhappy when Taft replaced Roosevelt's secretary of the interior, James R. Garfield, an aggressive conservationist, with **Richard A. Ballinger,** a more conservative corporate lawyer. Suspicion of Ballinger grew when he tried to make nearly a million acres of public forests and mineral reserves available for private development.

In the midst of this mounting concern, Gifford Pinchot charged the new secretary **R** with having once plotted to turn over valuable public lands in Alaska to a private business group for personal profit. Taft's attorney general investigated the charges and decided they

306 Chapter 8 The Progressive Movement

were groundless. Not satisfied, Pinchot leaked the story to the press and asked Congress to investigate. Taft fired Pinchot for **insubordination,** or disobedience to authority. The congressional investigation cleared Ballinger.

By the second half of his term of office, many Americans believed that Taft had "sold the Square Deal down the river." Popular indignation was so great that the congressional elections of 1910 resulted in a sweeping Democratic victory, with Democrats taking the majority in the House, and Democrats and progressive Republicans grabbing control of the Senate from conservative Republicans.

Taft's Achievements

Despite his political problems, Taft also had several successes. Although Roosevelt was nicknamed the "trustbuster," Taft was a strong opponent of monopoly and actually brought twice as many antitrust cases in four years as his predecessor had in seven. In other areas, too, Taft pursued progressive policies. Taft established the **Children's Bureau** in 1912, an agency that investigated and publicized the problems of child labor. The agency exists today, and deals with issues such as child abuse prevention, adoption, and foster care.

The Ballinger-Pinchot controversy aside, Taft was also a dedicated conservationist. His contributions in this area actually equaled or surpassed those of Roosevelt. He set up the Bureau of Mines in 1910 to monitor the activities of mining companies, expand the national forests, and protect waterpower sites from private development. Most of the new and emerging technologies in the minerals field were partly made possible by the existence of the Bureau of Mines.

After Taft took office in 1909, Roosevelt left for a big-game hunt in Africa, followed by a tour of Europe. He did not return to the United States until June 1910. Although disturbed by stories of Taft's "betrayal" of progressivism, Roosevelt at first refused to criticize the president.

In October 1911 Taft announced an antitrust lawsuit against U.S. Steel, claiming that the company's decision to buy the Tennessee Coal and Iron Company in 1907 had violated the Sherman Antitrust Act. The lawsuit was the final straw for Roosevelt. As president, he had approved U.S. Steel's plan to buy the company.

Roosevelt believed Taft's focus on breaking up trusts was destroying the carefully crafted system of cooperation and regulation that Roosevelt had established with big business. In November 1911 Roosevelt publicly criticized Taft's decision. Roosevelt argued that the best way to deal with the trusts was to allow them to exist while continuing to regulate them.

After Roosevelt broke with Taft, it was only a matter of time before progressives convinced him to reenter politics. In late February 1912, Roosevelt announced that he would enter the presidential campaign of 1912 and attempt to replace Taft as the Republican nominee for president.

✓ Reading Check **Evaluating** How did Taft's accomplishments regarding conservation and trust-busting compare to Roosevelt's?

Section 2 REVIEW

Vocabulary

1. **Explain** the significance of: Square Deal, Social Darwinism, United Mine Workers, arbitration, Hepburn Act, Upton Sinclair, Meat Inspection Act, Pure Food and Drug Act, Gifford Pinchot, Richard A. Ballinger, insubordination, Children's Bureau.

Main Ideas

2. **Explaining** What was the intent of the Hepburn Act?

3. **Describing** How did Roosevelt's policies change the Western landscape?

4. **Discussing** How did Taft help conservation efforts and child labor problems?

Critical Thinking

5. **Big Ideas** How did Upton Sinclair contribute to involving the federal government in protecting consumers?

6. **Organizing** Use a graphic organizer to list Taft's progressive reforms.

Taft's Progressive Reforms

7. **Analyzing Visuals** Study the photo on page 306. Could this photo be used to rally the cause against child labor? Explain the dangerous elements of the job.

Writing About History

8. **Expository Writing** Suppose that you are living in the early 1900s and have just read Sinclair's *The Jungle*. Write a letter to a friend summarizing the plot and how it characterizes the Progressive Era.

History ONLINE
Study Central™ To review this section, go to glencoe.com and click on Study Central.

Academic Vocabulary Have students demonstrate their understanding of the word *insubordination* by using it correctly in a sentence. **OL**

✓ **Reading Check**

Answer:
Taft brought more antitrust cases than Roosevelt, and his conservation efforts at least equaled those of Roosevelt.

Assess

History ONLINE

Study Central™ provides summaries, interactive games, and online graphic organizers to help students review content.

Close

Summarizing Ask: What was the response of progressives to presidents Roosevelt and Taft? *(Roosevelt was very popular with progressives. Taft was not popular with progressives despite his accomplishments regarding antitrust and conservation.)* **OL**

Section 2 REVIEW

Answers

1. Definitions for the vocabulary terms are found in the section and the Glossary.

2. It was intended to strengthen the Interstate Commerce Commission by giving it the authority to set railroad rates.

3. Roosevelt supported passage of the Newland Reclamation Act, which authorized use of federal funds from sale of public lands for irrigation and land development projects.

4. Taft set up the Bureau of Mines to monitor mining companies, expanded national forests, and protected waterpower sites. He established the Children's Bureau to investigate and publicize problems of child labor.

5. He wrote a novel about the meatpacking industry called *The Jungle*. It publicized disgusting industry practices.

6. Taft's Progressive Reforms: Children's Bureau, Bureau of Mines, antitrust lawsuit against U.S. Steel

7. This photo could be used to rally against child labor. Children could easily get hurt on the job because their small hands were used to fix machines. Also, child laborers worked long hours with little pay.

8. Writing will vary but should explain that Sinclair's investigation of the meatpacking industry spurred people to work for change.

Focus

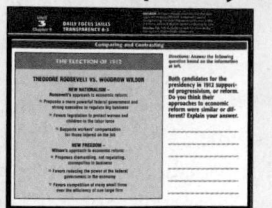
Guide to Reading

Answers:
Economic Reforms
Lowered tariffs
Taxed earnings
Established federal reserve system
Created Federal Trade
Commission
Social Reforms
Attempted to regulate child labor
Established 8-hour day for railroad
workers
Provided farmers with low-interest
loans

Section Spotlight Video

To generate student interest and
provide a springboard for discussion, access the Chapter 8,
Section 3 video at glencoe.com
or on the video DVD.

Resource Manager

Section 3

The Wilson Years

Guide to Reading

Big Ideas
Individual Action Woodrow Wilson
increased the control of the government
over business.

Content Vocabulary
• income tax (p. 310)
• unfair trade practices (p. 311)

Academic Vocabulary
• academic (p. 308)
• unconstitutional (p. 312)

People and Events to Identify
• Progressive Party (p. 308)
• New Nationalism (p. 309)
• New Freedom (p. 309)
• Federal Reserve Act (p. 311)
• Federal Trade Commission (p. 311)
• Clayton Antitrust Act (p. 311)
• National Association for the Advancement of Colored People (p. 313)

Reading Strategy
Organizing As you read about progressivism during the Wilson administration, complete a chart similar to the
one below by listing Wilson's progressive economic and social reforms.

Economic Reforms	Social Reforms

Woodrow Wilson, a progressive Democrat, won
the election of 1912. While in office, he supported
lower tariffs, more regulation of business, and creation of
a federal reserve banking system.

The Election of 1912

MAIN Idea Woodrow Wilson was elected after Republican voters split
between Taft and Roosevelt.

HISTORY AND YOU Do you remember a catchy slogan from a political
campaign? Read about the competing slogans and platforms in the
1912 election.

The 1912 presidential campaign featured a current president, a
former president, and an **academic** who had entered politics only
two years earlier. The election's outcome determined the path of the
Progressive movement.

Picking the Candidates

Believing that President Taft had failed to live up to progressive
ideals, Theodore Roosevelt informed seven state governors that he
was willing to accept the Republican nomination. "My hat is in the
ring!" he declared. "The fight is on."

The struggle for control of the Republican Party reached its climax
at the national convention in Chicago in June 1912. Conservatives
rallied behind Taft. Most of the progressives supported Roosevelt.
When it became clear that Taft's delegates controlled the nomination, Roosevelt decided to leave the party and campaign as an
independent.

Declaring himself "fit as a bull moose," Roosevelt became the
presidential candidate for the newly formed **Progressive Party,**
which quickly became known as the Bull Moose Party. Because
Taft had alienated so many groups, the election of 1912 became a
contest between two progressives: Roosevelt and the Democratic
candidate, Woodrow Wilson.

After a university teaching career that ended in his becoming
the president of Princeton University, Woodrow Wilson entered
politics as a firm progressive. As governor of New Jersey, he pushed
through one progressive reform after another. He signed laws that
introduced the direct primary, established utility regulatory boards,
and allowed cities to adopt the commissioner form of government.
In less than two years, New Jersey became a model of progressive
reform.

R Reading Strategies	**C** Critical Thinking	**D** Differentiated Instruction	**W** Writing Support	**S** Skill Practice
Teacher Edition • Skimming, p. 310 • Monitoring, p. 311 • Identifying, p. 312 **Additional Resources** • Guided Reading, URB p. 80	**Teacher Edition** • Det. Cause/Effect p. 310 **Additional Resources** • Quizzes and Tests, p. 109	**Teacher Edition** • Gifted/Talented p. 311 **Additional Resources** • Enrich. Act., URB p. 75 • Amer. Art/Music, URB p. 69 • Authentic Assessment Act., p. 21 • Reteaching Act., URB p. 73	**Teacher Edition** • Expository Writing p. 313	**Teacher Edition** • Reading a Chart, p. 309 **Additional Resources** • RENTG, p. 85

New Nationalism Versus New Freedom

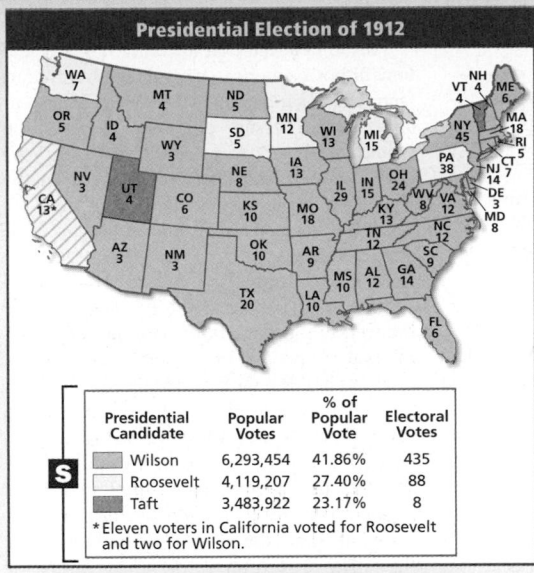

Presidential Election of 1912

Presidential Candidate	Popular Votes	% of Popular Vote	Electoral Votes
Wilson	6,293,454	41.86%	435
Roosevelt	4,119,207	27.40%	88
Taft	3,483,922	23.17%	8

*Eleven voters in California voted for Roosevelt and two for Wilson.

DBQ Document-Based Questions

1. **Analyzing Visuals** From which state did Roosevelt gain the most Electoral College votes?
2. **Analyzing Primary Sources** How do Wilson and Roosevelt differ on trusts?
3. **Making Generalizations** What can you generalize about the two men based solely on their appearance in giving a speech?

Maps In Motion See *StudentWorks™ Plus* or glencoe.com.

WILSON'S NEW FREEDOM

"I am perfectly willing that [a business] should beat any competitor by fair means . . . But there must be no squeezing out the beginner . . . no secret arrangements against him. All the fair competition you choose, but no unfair competition of any kind. . . . A trust is an arrangement to get rid of competition. . . . A trust does not bring efficiency . . . it *buys efficiency out of business.* I am for big business, and I am against the trusts . . . any man who can put others out of business by making the thing cheaper to the consumer . . . I take off my hat to . . . "

—from *The New Freedom*

ROOSEVELT'S NEW NATIONALISM

"Combinations in industry [trusts] are the result of an imperative economic law which cannot be repealed by political legislation. . . . The way out lies, not in attempting to prevent such combinations, but in completely controlling them in the interest of the public welfare. . . . The absence of an effective state, and, especially national, restraint upon unfair money getting has tended to create a small class of enormously wealthy and economically powerful men. . . . The prime need is to change the conditions which enable these men to accumulate power."

—from *The New Nationalism*

Wilson Versus Roosevelt

The election of 1912 was a contest between two progressives with different approaches to reform. Roosevelt accepted the large trusts as a fact of life and set out proposals to increase regulation. Roosevelt also outlined a complete program of reforms. He favored legislation to protect women and children in the labor force and supported workers' compensation for those injured on the job. Roosevelt called his program the **New Nationalism.**

Wilson countered with what he called the **New Freedom.** He criticized Roosevelt's New Nationalism for supporting "regulated monopoly." Monopolies, he believed, should be destroyed, not regulated. Wilson argued that

Roosevelt's approach gave the federal government too much power in the economy and did nothing to restore competition. Freedom, in Wilson's opinion, was more important than efficiency. "The history of liberty," Wilson declared, "is the history of the limitation of governmental power. . . . If America is not to have free enterprise, then she can have freedom of no sort whatever."

As expected, Roosevelt and Taft split the Republican voters, enabling Wilson to win the Electoral College with 435 votes and the election, even though he received less than 42 percent of the popular vote.

✓ **Reading Check** Summarizing Who were the major candidates in the election of 1912?

Teach

S Skill Practice

Reading a Chart Ask: Did most of the electorate vote for Woodrow Wilson or for other candidates? *(Though Wilson received the most votes [6,294,345 votes], most of the electorate voted for the other two candidates [a total of 7,603,129 votes])* **BL** **OL**

DBQ Document Based Questions

Answers:
1. Pennsylvania
2. Wilson is completely against trusts; Roosevelt wants to control them.
3. Wilson is more reserved while Roosevelt is larger than life.

✓ Reading Check

Summarizing
William Howard Taft, Theodore Roosevelt, and Woodrow Wilson

Hands-On Chapter Project
Step 3

Learning how Government Affects People's Lives

Step 3: Presentations Students will work in groups to present the community problem they researched or their conservation posters.

Directions Have students work together as a team to present a community problem and its resolution to the class. Students may also choose to present their conservation posters.

Representing Information Give students time to prepare for their presentations. They may role play or use media other than their posters to present the information. Encourage students to state the topic clearly, describe it, and summarize the information. **OL**

(Project continued on the Visual Summary page)

R Reading Strategy

Skimming Have students glance at the text under the heading "Wilson's Reforms." **Ask:** About what key issues do you expect to learn? *(tariff and tax reform)* **BL**

C Critical Thinking

Determining Cause and Effect **Ask:** What effect did Wilson believe lowering tariffs would produce? *(improved products and lower prices)* **OL**

Additional Support

Wilson's Reforms

MAIN Idea President Wilson reformed tariffs and banks and oversaw the creation of the Federal Trade Commission.

HISTORY AND YOU Are you aware of recent economic concerns and presidential responses to them? Read to learn of Wilson's economic actions after his election.

R   The new chief executive lost no time in embarking on his program of reform. "The president is at liberty, both in law and conscience, to be as big a man as he can," Wilson had once written. "His capacity will set the limit." During his eight years as president, Wilson demonstrated his executive power as he crafted reforms affecting tariffs, the banking system, trusts, and workers' rights.

Reforming Tariffs

Five weeks after taking office, Wilson appeared before Congress, the first president to do so since John Adams. He had come to present his bill to reduce tariffs. Wilson per-

sonally lobbied members of Congress to support the tariff reduction bill. Not even Roosevelt had taken such an active role in promoting legislation.

   Wilson believed that lowering tariffs would benefit both American consumers and manufacturers. If tariff rates were lowered, he reasoned, the pressure of foreign competition would lead American manufacturers to improve their products and lower their prices. In the long term, businesses would benefit from the "constant necessity to be efficient, economical, and enterprising." **C**

   In 1913 Congress passed the Underwood Tariff, and Wilson signed it into law. This law reduced the average tariff on imported goods to about 30 percent of the value of the goods, or about half the tariff rate of the 1890s.

   An important section of the Underwood Tariff Act provided for levying an **income tax,** or a direct tax on the earnings of individuals. The Constitution originally prohibited direct taxes on individuals. Ratification of the Sixteenth Amendment in 1913, however, gave the federal government the power to tax the income of individuals directly.

INFOGRAPHIC
Progressives Reform the Economic System

During Wilson's presidency, Congress passed several major reforms affecting the nation's economy. The Federal Reserve and the Federal Trade Commission were created, federal income tax was introduced, and unions were legalized.

The Federal Reserve

Why Was the Federal Reserve Created?
- to create national supervision of the banking industry
- to decentralize banking institutions and access to credit
- to prevent recurring "panics," such as the Panic of 1907
- to allow the demands of business to control the expanding and contracting of currency

What Does the Federal Reserve Do?
- controls the money supply and credit policies
- raises interest rates to member banks in times of plenty so that people won't borrow or spend too much money
- lowers interest rates to member banks during recessions so that people can more easily obtain needed credit
- supervises and supports Federal Reserve banks in twelve regions
- buys and sells government bonds and other securities

NATIONAL GEOGRAPHIC   **Federal Reserve System**

Seattle, Portland, Helena, 9, Minneapolis, Salt Lake City, 12, San Francisco, Denver, 10, Omaha, Kansas City, 7, Chicago, Cleveland, Detroit, Cincinnati, 8, St. Louis, Louisville, 4, 3, Pittsburgh, Buffalo, 2, Philadelphia, New York, 1, Boston, Baltimore, Richmond, Nashville, 5, Memphis, Charlotte, Los Angeles, Oklahoma City, Little Rock, Birmingham, Atlanta, 6, El Paso, Dallas, 11, Houston, San Antonio, New Orleans, Jacksonville, Miami, 12, 12

- **6** Federal Reserve District
- ★ Federal Reserve Bank
- • Federal Reserve Branch Bank

Activity: Economics Connection

Analyzing the Federal Reserve Have students find a current news article about the Federal Reserve. Ask them to write a brief summary of the news story. Then have students list actions taken by the Federal Reserve in the news story. Have students match those actions with the functions of the Federal Reserve listed in the infographic "Progressives Reform the Economic System." Encourage volunteers to share their summaries and action lists. **Ask:** What are the intended consequences of the actions taken by the Federal Reserve? **OL** **AL**

Reforming the Banks

The United States had not had a central bank since the 1830s. During the economic depressions that hit the country periodically after that time, hundreds of small banks collapsed, wiping out the life savings of many of their customers.

To restore public confidence in the banking system, President Wilson supported the establishment of a federal reserve system. Banks would have to keep a portion of their deposits in a regional reserve bank, which would provide a financial cushion against unanticipated losses. The **Federal Reserve Act** of 1913 created 12 regional banks to be supervised by a Board of Governors, appointed by the president. This allowed national supervision of the banking system. The Board could set the interest rates the reserve banks charged other banks, thereby indirectly controlling the interest rates of the entire nation and the amount of money in circulation. The Federal Reserve Act became one of the most significant pieces of legislation in American history.

Other Reforms

Why Was the Federal Trade Commission Created?
- to advise business people on the legality of their actions
- to protect consumers from false advertising
- to investigate unfair trade practices

What Was the Clayton Antitrust Act?
- outlawed unfair trade practices
- made it illegal for a company to hold stock in another, if by doing so, it reduced competition
- made owners and directors of businesses guilty of violating antitrust laws criminally liable
- allowed private parties who had been injured by trusts to collect any damages in legal suits
- banned use of injunctions against strikes
- farm and labor organizations could no longer be considered illegal combinations in restraint of trade

Analyzing VISUALS

1. **Analyzing** What do the Federal Trade Commission and the Clayton Antitrust Act have in common?
2. **Identifying** What do you notice about the Western states and the locations of the Federal Reserve Banks? Why do you think this pattern exists?

Antitrust Action

During his campaign, Wilson had promised to restore competition to the economy by breaking up monopolies. Roosevelt had argued this was unrealistic, because big businesses were more efficient and unlikely to be replaced by smaller, more competitive firms. Once in office, Wilson's opinion shifted and he came to agree with Roosevelt. Progressives in Congress, however, continued to demand action against big business.

In the summer of 1914, at Wilson's request, Congress created the **Federal Trade Commission** (FTC) to monitor American business. The FTC had the power to investigate companies and issue "cease and desist" orders against companies engaging in **unfair trade practices,** or those that hurt competition. The FTC could be taken to court if a business disagreed with its rulings.

Wilson did not want the FTC to break up big business. Instead, it was to work toward limiting business activities that unfairly limited competition. He deliberately appointed conservative business leaders to serve as the FTC's first commissioners.

Unsatisfied by Wilson's approach, progressives in Congress responded by passing the **Clayton Antitrust Act** in 1914. The act outlawed certain practices that restricted competition. For example, it forbade agreements that required retailers who bought from one company to stop selling a competitor's products. It also banned price discrimination. Businesses could not charge different customers different prices. Manufacturers could no longer give discounts to some retailers who bought a large volume of goods, but not to others. Farm and labor organizations could no longer be considered illegal combinations in restraint of trade. The passing of the Clayton Antitrust Act corrected deficiencies in the Sherman Antitrust Act of 1890, which was the first federal antitrust law.

Before the Clayton act passed, labor unions lobbied Congress to exempt unions from antitrust legislation. The Clayton Antitrust Act specifically declared that its provisions did not apply to labor organizations or agricultural organizations. When the bill became law, Samuel Gompers, the head of the American Federation of Labor, called the act the workers' "Magna Carta" because it gave unions the right to exist.

R Reading Strategy

Monitoring Ask: Why did the Federal Reserve Act require banks to keep a portion of their deposits in a regional reserve bank? *(to provide a financial cushion against unanticipated losses)* **BL OL**

D Differentiated Instruction

Gifted and Talented Have students research the Clayton Antitrust Act and the Sherman Antitrust Act and list their similarities and differences. **AL**

Analyzing VISUALS

Answers:
1. They regulate big business to promote fair competition.
2. There are fewer Federal Reserve Banks in the West (District 12) because the West had a smaller population.

Additional Support

Activity: Collaborative Learning

Locating Information Tell students that Samuel Gompers was one of the founders of the American Federation of Labor. Gompers was also active in the effort to persuade Congress to exempt unions from antitrust legislation. Break the class up into groups and have them research Gompers' life. Assign groups areas of research including: Gompers' early life, his work with the Cigar Makers' Union, formation of the American Federation of Labor, his political involvement with the Democratic Party, and his death and legacy. Have groups prepare a short report from their research and present it to the class. **OL AL**

R Reading Strategy

Identifying Ask: Why did the Supreme Court declare the Keating-Owen Child Labor Act unconstitutional? *(Child labor was not interstate commerce and therefore only states could regulate it.)* BL OL

✓ Reading Check

Answer:
The Sixteenth Amendment made it legal for the federal government to directly tax individual income.

DBQ Document Based Questions

Answers:
1. The magazine took the name "The Crisis" to reflect that it was a critical time in history.
2. One of peace and goodwill among all races

Differentiated Instruction

Regulating Business

Despite his accomplishments, Wilson was not guaranteed reelection. In the congressional elections of 1914, Democrats suffered major losses. The Republican Party was also not likely to be divided as it had been in the election of 1912.

In 1916 Wilson signed the first federal law regulating child labor. The Keating-Owen Child Labor Act prohibited the employment of children under the age of 14 in factories producing goods for interstate commerce. In 1918 the Supreme Court declared the law **unconstitutional** on the grounds that child labor was not interstate commerce and therefore only states could regulate it. Wilson's effort, however, helped his reputation with progressive voters. Wilson also supported the Adamson Act, which established the eight-hour workday for railroad workers, and the Federal Farm Loan Act, which helped provide farmers with loans at low interest rates.

✓ Reading Check **Evaluating** What was the impact of the passage of the Sixteenth Amendment?

PRIMARY SOURCE
Founding of the NAACP

W.E.B. Du Bois was one of six founders of the NAACP. In *The Crisis*, the journal of the NAACP, Du Bois wrote:

PRIMARY SOURCE

"The object of this publication is to set forth those facts and arguments which show the danger of race prejudice. . . . It takes its name from the fact that the editors believe that this is a critical time in the history. . . . Catholicity and tolerance, reason and forbearance can today make the world-old dream of human brotherhood approach realization: while bigotry and prejudice, emphasized race consciousness and force can repeat the awful history of the contact of nations and groups in the past. We strive for this higher and broader vision of Peace and Good Will."
—from *The Crisis*, November 1910

▲ W.E.B. Du Bois works with his staff in the office of The Crisis.

▲ The first issue of The Crisis, *November 1910*

DBQ Document-Based Questions

1. **Analyzing** According to Du Bois, why was the magazine given its name?
2. **Analyzing Primary Sources** What "vision" does Du Bois recommend to his readers?

Progressivism's Legacy and Limits

MAIN Idea Progressivism changed many people's ideas about the government's role in social issues.

HISTORY AND YOU Do you believe that groups of people have been left out of "the American dream"? Read on to find out about progressivism's failures and successes.

During his presidency, Wilson had built upon Roosevelt's foundation. He expanded the role of the federal government and the power of the president.

A New Kind of Government

Progressivism made important changes in the political life of the United States. Before this era, most Americans did not expect the government to pass laws protecting workers or regulating big business. In fact, many courts had previously ruled the passage of such laws unconstitutional.

312 Chapter 8 The Progressive Movement

Leveled Activities

BL Reading Skills Activity, URB p. 51

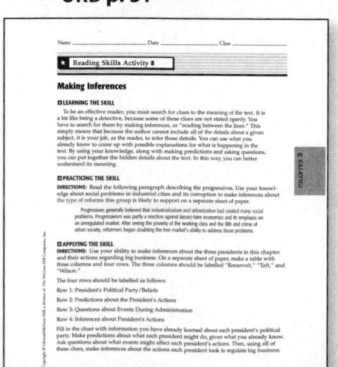

OL American Literature Reading, URB pp. 13–14

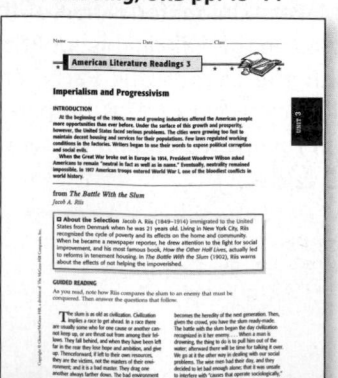

AL Economics and History Activity, URB pp. 7–8

ELL English Learner Activity, URB pp. 55–56

By the end of the Progressive Era, however, both legal and public opinion had shifted. Increasingly, Americans expected the government, particularly the federal government, to play a more active role in regulating the economy and solving social problems.

The Limits of Progressivism

The most conspicuous limit to progressivism was its failure to address racial and religious discrimination. African Americans themselves, however, were absorbing the reform spirit, which fueled their longstanding desire for advancement.

In 1905 W.E.B. Du Bois and 28 other African American leaders met at Niagara Falls to demand full rights for African Americans. They met on the Canadian side of the falls because no hotel on the American side would accept them. There, they launched what became known as the Niagara Movement. This meeting was one of many steps leading to the founding of the **National Association for the Advancement of Colored People** (NAACP) in 1909. Du Bois and other NAACP founders believed that voting rights were essential to end lynching and racial discrimination. "The power of the ballot we need in sheer self-defense," Du Bois said, "else what shall save us from a second slavery? Freedom too, the long-sought we still seek,—the freedom of life and limb, the freedom to work and think, the freedom to love and aspire. Work, culture, liberty,—all these we need, not singly, but together."

In 1908 race riots in Springfield, Illinois, shocked many people, including Mary White Ovington, a settlement house worker. She had been studying African Americans in New York, determined to do something to improve their situation. Other progressives, including Jane Addams of Hull House, and muckrakers Ida Wells-Barnett and Lincoln Steffens, joined Ovington in calling for change. Capitalizing on Springfield as Lincoln's hometown and his centennial birthday on February 12, 1909, they organized a national conference to take stock of the progress in emancipation. At a second conference the following year, the NAACP was born. Through Du Bois, the members learned of the Niagara Movement, and the two groups eventually merged.

African Americans were not the only minority group facing discrimination. Jewish people also lived in fear of mob violence. In 1913 Leo Frank, a Jew being tried in Atlanta for a murder he did not commit, was sentenced to death. Although his sentence was changed to life imprisonment, a mob lynched him two years later.

In this context, lawyer Sigmund Livingston started the Anti-Defamation League (ADL) to combat stereotypes and discrimination. The ADL worked to remove negative portrayals of Jews in movies, in print, and on stage. For example, the League protested an army manual published during World War I that targeted Jews as likely to pretend to be sick to escape work or battle. When the ADL complained, President Wilson had the manual recalled.

✓ **Reading Check** **Evaluating** How did progressivism change American beliefs about the federal government?

Section 3 REVIEW

Vocabulary
1. **Explain** the significance of: Progressive Party, New Nationalism, New Freedom, income tax, Federal Reserve Act, Federal Trade Commission, unfair trade practices, Clayton Antitrust Act, National Association for the Advancement of Colored People.

Main Ideas
2. **Discussing** Explain how Wilson won the presidency without winning the popular vote.

3. **Identifying** Why did Wilson propose the Federal Reserve system?

4. **Organizing** Use a graphic organizer similar to the one below to list the effects progressivism had on American society.

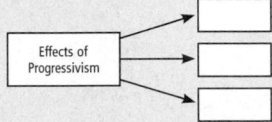

Critical Thinking
5. **Big Ideas** What new federal agencies increased the government's power to regulate the economy?

6. **Forming an Opinion** Which of Wilson's reforms do you consider to be most important? Why?

7. **Analyzing Visuals** Study the chart on page 310. What was the purpose of the Federal Reserve?

Writing About History
8. **Expository Writing** Suppose that you are a newspaper editor during Wilson's administration. Write an article about the failure of Progressives to address African American reform issues.

History ONLINE
Study Central™ To review this section, go to glencoe.com and click on Study Central.

313

W **Writing Support**
Expository Writing Have students research a progressive figure (such as Jane Addams, Lincoln Steffens, or Sigmund Livingston) and write a short report on his or her life and accomplishments.
OL **AL**

✓**Reading Check**

Answer:
expanded democracy and raised expectations of the federal government's role in the economy and society

Assess
....
History ONLINE

Study Central™ provides summaries, interactive games, and online graphic organizers to help students review content.

Close
....
Summarizing Ask: **What economic reforms did President Wilson institute?** *(Wilson lowered tariffs, created the Federal Reserve and the Federal Trade Commission.)*
OL

Section 3 REVIEW

Answers

1. Definitions for the vocabulary terms are found in the section and the Glossary.

2. Although Wilson did not win a majority of the popular vote, he won in the Electoral College.

3. to restore public confidence in the banking system

4. expanded democracy, improved quality of life, expanded role of government, increased regulation of business and banking

5. Federal Reserve System, Federal Trade Commission

6. Students' answers will vary but should include a reasonable argument.

7. The purpose of the Federal Reserve was to require banks to set aside a portion of their deposits in a regional bank to protect against unanticipated losses.

8. Students' editorials will vary but should point out specific shortcomings and suggest ways that the progressives could have addressed these social problems.

Chapter 8 VISUAL SUMMARY

Summarizing Ask: Which progressive reforms were attempts to lessen problems from laissez-faire economic practices? *(labor laws, health and safety codes, antitrust laws, government oversight agencies, consumer protection laws, conservation efforts, tariff reforms)* **OL**

Expository Writing The Children's Bureau was established in 1912 by President Taft. The agency is still in existence. Research the agency and write a short report of its history. **Ask:** How has the mission of the Children's Bureau changed since it was established in 1912? **OL** **AL**

Causes of the Progressive Movement

- People thought progress in science and knowledge could improve society.
- People thought immigration, urbanization, and industrialization had created social problems.
- People thought laissez-faire economics and an unregulated market led to social problems and that government could fix them.
- Political corruption prevented the government from helping its citizens.

▶ In 1910 a young boy works in a glass factory, an example of the type of child labor progressive reformers wanted to end.

Effects on Business and Society

- Interstate Commerce Commission is strengthened.
- Consumer protection laws are passed.
- Federal Trade Commission is created.
- Federal Reserve System is created to regulate the money supply.
- Clayton Antitrust Act grants labor unions more rights.
- Zoning laws and building codes improve urban housing.
- Child labor laws are passed, regulating time and conditions for minors to work.
- Workers' compensation laws are passed.
- Temperance movement begins seeking limitations on the production and consumption of alcohol.

▲ Trade unions begin their march honoring victims of the Triangle Shirtwaist Factory fire.

Effects on Politics

- Cities begin adopting commission and city-manager forms of government.
- States begin to adopt the direct primary system, allowing voters to choose candidates for office.
- States begin to allow initiatives, referendums, and recall votes.
- Seventeenth Amendment is ratified, requiring direct election of senators.
- Nineteenth Amendment is ratified, guaranteeing women the right to vote.

PRESIDENT WILSON SAYS: "This is the time to support Woman Suffrage."

▶ Women march in 1916 in support of Woodrow Wilson's efforts to grant women the right to vote.

314 Chapter 8 The Progressive Movement

Hands-On Chapter Project
Step 4: Wrap Up

Learning how Government Affects People's Lives

Step 4: Wrap Up This activity will synthesize the causes of the Progressive Movement and its effects on people's lives by personalizing the issues.

Directions Divide the class into six teams. Each team should select one presenter to take on the role of an individual whose life was affected by the Progressive Movement (such as a former child laborer now enrolled in school, a woman voting for the first time, and so on). To avoid duplication among the teams, have each team announce which role their presenter will play. If there are duplicates, assign another role to one of the teams. Be sure at least one team covers the effects of progressivism on some aspect of business, society, and politics.

Analyzing Information Team members will collaboratively write a journal page from the perspective of the presenter. Each journal page should describe vividly the person's life before and after the reform resulting from progressives' efforts. It should also mention the legislation or other action that made the reform possible. Presenters will read the group's journal page to the class. The rest of the class may want to ask the presenters questions. To make the presentations more lively and memorable, presenters may wish to carry relevant signs, dress in costumes, or hold up photos. **OL**

ASSESSMENT

STANDARDIZED TEST PRACTICE

TEST-TAKING TIP

You can eliminate some answers by using your own knowledge and common sense. Read through each option and decide if it fits with what you know; if it does not, discard it.

Reviewing Vocabulary

Directions: Choose the word or words that best complete each sentence.

1. The term "muckraker" was used in the early 1900s to describe
   A street sweepers.
   B investigative journalists.
   C farmers.
   D garden designers.

2. Women spent more than 70 years actively seeking _____, or the right to vote.
   A initiative
   B petition
   C recall
   D suffrage

3. The temperance movement was linked to the _____ of alcohol.
   A prohibition
   B production
   C reduction
   D requisition

4. When Gifford Pinchot leaked a story to the press against William Taft's will, the president fired him for
   A arbitration.
   B prohibition.
   C insubordination.
   D initiation.

Reviewing Main Ideas

Directions: Choose the best answers to the following questions.

Section 1 *(pp. 292–299)*

5. Progressivism used the principles of science to solve problems resulting from
   A industrialization and urbanization.
   B global warming and fossil fuel use.
   C the outbreak of war and proliferation of weapons.
   D epidemic diseases and plagues.

6. Which of the following allowed proposed legislation to be placed on the ballot for voter approval?
   A direct primary
   B referendum
   C initiative
   D veto

7. What did the Nineteenth Amendment accomplish?
   A It required colleges to accept women.
   B It guaranteed child care for workers' children.
   C It granted women the right to vote.
   D It guaranteed equal pay for equal work.

Section 2 *(pp. 300–307)*

8. Theodore Roosevelt became known as a trustbuster for his actions against
   A the Northern Securities company.
   B the United Mine Workers.
   C the automobile industry.
   D national parks.

Need Extra Help?

If You Missed Questions . . .	1	2	3	4	5	6	7	8
Go to Page . . .	293	296–297	299	306–307	304	295	296–297	300–301

GO ON

Answers and Analyses
Reviewing Vocabulary

1. B Muckrakers brought to light urban and social problems by writing about them in newspapers, magazines, and books. They were called muckrakers by President Roosevelt. Muck is another word for dirt. These writers exposed the dirt and corruption.

2. D Suffrage is the right to vote. Initiative, petition, and recall are political ways that people can affect legislation or remove elected officials from office.

3. A It is important that students connect the temperance movement with the prohibition of alcohol. Temperance means restraint. Those in favor of temperance did not just want to reduce alcohol, they wanted to eliminate it. Production is the opposite of the correct answer. Requisition is to acquire something.

4. C A subordinate is someone of lower status than someone else. For example, an employee is a subordinate of a boss. Insubordination is when a subordinate rebels against the superior. In this case, Taft, the boss, fired Pinchot, the subordinate, for disobeying orders.

5. A Progressives sought to make social *progress*. That means they wanted to solve problems, as the question states. During the late nineteenth century, industrialization and urbanization were the driving forces behind society's problems.

6. B Review with students these important political terms. The direct primary allows all members of a political party to vote for candidates to run in the general election. Referendum allows proposed legislation to be submitted to the voters, initiative allowed citizens to introduce legislation that the legislature was required to vote on, and veto is the power to reject a bill.

7. C The Nineteenth Amendment granted women the right to vote.

8. A To answer this question, students should be aware of the dominance of the railroad industry at the time. Roosevelt's busting of J.P. Morgan's Northern Securities led newspapers to hail him as a trustbuster.

9. B The easiest way for students to remember that *The Jungle* dealt with the meatpacking industry is to remember that there are animals in the jungle, and animals are used for meat. None of the other answer choices deal with animals.

10. D Taft was warned by Roosevelt to stay away from tariff reform, because of the problems it would cause, but Taft did not listen and it hurt him politically.

11. A The establishment of the Federal Reserve System had far-reaching significance. This is a good opportunity to discuss the role the Federal Reserve took in regulating the economy, and to discuss the role it plays today in setting monetary policy.

12. C The NAACP believed voting rights were essential, because if African Americans could not vote and take part in government, how could they change it? Discuss with students how this was similar to the colonists wanting the right to vote and have a say in legislation governing them.

13. B La Follette's requiring political parties to hold direct primaries caused a monumental change in party politics.

14. C Students should locate the state in each answer choice and make note of the date listed. Reformers came to power in Washington in 1889.

15. A States in which reformers controlled state legislatures are shaded in the lightest gray. These states are concentrated in the Pacific Northwest, Great Plains, and South.

316

---

9. Upton Sinclair's novel *The Jungle* was instrumental in exposing which industry?

A steel

B meatpacking

C oil

D alcohol

10. President Taft broke with Roosevelt and progressives over

A unions.

B child labor.

C trust-busting.

D tariffs.

Section 3 *(pp. 308–313)*

11. How did President Wilson attempt to reform the banking industry?

A He created the Federal Reserve System.

B He vetoed the Underwood Tariff Act.

C He opposed the Sixteenth Amendment.

D He refused to break up monopolies.

12. What did Du Bois and other NAACP founders believe was essential to end racial violence?

A establishment of African American colleges

B higher-paying jobs for low-income citizens

C voting rights for African Americans

D private schools for African American children

Critical Thinking

Directions: Choose the best answers to the following questions.

13. How did Wisconsin governor Robert M. La Follette help to expand democracy in the United States?

A by favoring women's suffrage

B by requiring political parties to hold a direct primary

C by allowing recall elections to remove elected officials from office before the end of his or her term

D by providing for absentee ballots to voters

Need Extra Help?							
If You Missed Questions . . .	9	10	11	12	13	14	15
Go to Page . . .	302	306	311	313	294–295	294–295	294–295

Base your answers to questions 14 and 15 on the map below and on your knowledge of Chapter 8.

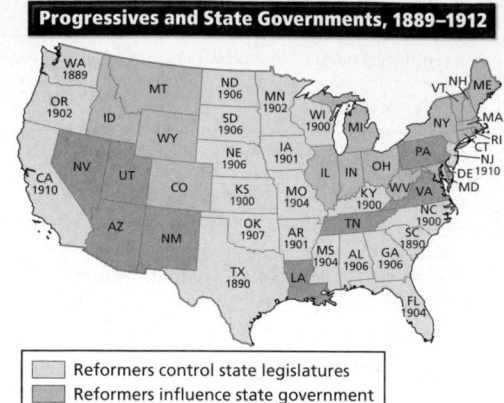

Progressives and State Governments, 1889–1912

Reformers control state legislatures
Reformers influence state government
Reformers not effective
1900 Date reformers came to power

14. Which state came under the control of reformers before Wisconsin?

A Florida

B Oregon

C Washington

D Nebraska

15. According to the map, what generalization can you make about progressives in state governments?

A Progressives were most active in the Pacific Northwest, the Great Plains, and the South.

B They had no influence in the New England states.

C Reformers controlled few state legislatures by 1910.

D Reformers had little success in the Deep South.

GO ON

16. The Progressive movement strengthened the cause of woman suffrage by

   A drawing attention to child labor.

   B encouraging trust-busting.

   C making government more efficient.

   D showing women they needed the vote to get the reforms they wanted.

Analyze the cartoon and answer the question that follows. Base your answer on the cartoon and on your knowledge of Chapter 8.

Source: S.D. Ehrhart, *Puck*, February 24, 1909

17. How does the cartoon portray William Howard Taft?

   A as eager to see Roosevelt leave the White House

   B as Roosevelt's equal in every way

   C as a servant walking off with Roosevelt's big stick

   D as a nursemaid to the baby, Roosevelt's policies

Document-Based Questions

Directions: Analyze the document and answer the short-answer questions that follow the document.

Lucy Haessler writes of her childhood memories surrounding the woman suffrage movement:

> *"The suffragettes had a big headquarters in downtown Washington. My mother would take me up there on Saturdays when she volunteered to help out with mailings. The backbone of the suffrage movement was composed of well-to-do, middle-class women, both Republicans and Democrats. There weren't many working-class women in the movement. . . .*
> *The suffragettes organized pickets and marches and rallies. I was only ten years old the first time I went to a march with my mother. She told me, 'Oh, you're too young, you can't go.' But I said, 'I am going, because you're going to win the right to vote and I'm going to vote when I'm grown-up.' So she let me march. . . . The more marches that were held, the more you could feel the movement just building and building. . . ."*
> —quoted in *The Century for Young People*

18. Who does Haessler say were the backbone of the movement? Why do you think working-class women were not involved?

19. Why did Haessler want to march when she was only ten years old?

Extended Response

20. Upton Sinclair and other muckrakers took on the social ills of their day, forcing passage of legislation such as the Pure Food and Drug Act. Select one social problem of modern life and write a persuasive essay that suggests legislation to address the issue. The essay should include an introduction, several paragraphs, and a conclusion that supports your position.

 STOP

History ONLINE

For additional test practice, use Self-Check Quizzes—Chapter 8 at glencoe.com.

Need Extra Help?					
If You Missed Questions . . .	16	17	18	19	20
Go to Page . . .	294–297	305–307	296–297	296–297	293–299

Extended Response

20. Answers will vary. Students must select and focus on one social problem. Essays must follow proper format for a persuasive essay and include support from the text. Some possible social problems are global warming, poverty, education inequalities, and racism. Accept any problem a student chooses to write about that is appropriate and pertains to the topic.

16. D Showing women they needed the vote to get the reforms they wanted.

17. D Review the cartoon with students. Roosevelt is standing on the steps, smiling and taking the baby (with a blanket titled "my policies") from Taft. The baby represents Roosevelt's policies. Taft is dressed as a nursemaid (note the frilly cap and apron). Taft is the nursemaid to Roosevelt's policies.

Document Based Questions

18. The backbone of the movement was well-to-do, middle-class women. Working-class women may have lacked the time to get involved and may have been less educated about political issues.

19. She wants to march because she expects her mother and the suffragettes to succeed and looks forward to being able to vote herself.

History ONLINE

Have students visit the Web site at glencoe.com to review Chapter 8 and take the Self-Check Quiz.

Need Extra Help?

Have students refer to the pages listed if they miss any of the questions.

317

Key to Ability Levels
- BL Below Level
- OL On Level
- AL Above Level
- ELL English Language Learners

Key to Teaching Resources
- Print Material
- CD-ROM
- DVD
- Transparency

Levels (BL OL AL ELL)	Resources	Chapter Opener	Section 1	Section 2	Section 3	Section 4	Chapter Assess
FOCUS							
BL OL AL ELL	Daily Focus Transparencies		9-1	9-2	9-3	9-4	
TEACH							
OL AL	American Literature Reading, URB			p. 15			
BL OL ELL	Reading Skills Activity, URB			p. 83			
OL	Historical Analysis Skills Activity, URB			p. 84			
BL OL AL ELL	Differentiated Instruction Activity, URB			p. 85			
BL OL ELL	English Learner Activity, URB		p. 87				
BL OL AL ELL	Content Vocabulary Activity, URB*		p. 89				
BL OL AL ELL	Academic Vocabulary Activity, URB		p. 91				
OL AL	Reinforcing Skills Activity, URB					p. 93	
OL AL	Critical Thinking Skills Activity, URB		p. 94				
BL OL ELL	Time Line Activity, URB				p. 95		
OL	Linking Past and Present Activity, URB				p. 96		
BL OL AL ELL	Primary Source Reading, URB		p. 97	p. 99			
BL OL AL ELL	American Art and Music Activity, URB					p. 101	
BL OL AL ELL	Interpreting Political Cartoons Activity, URB				p. 103		
AL	Enrichment Activity, URB			p. 106			
BL OL ELL	Guided Reading Activity, URB*		p. 108	p. 109	p. 110	p. 111	
BL OL AL ELL	Reading Essentials and Note-Taking Guide*		p. 88	p. 91	p. 94	p. 97	
BL OL AL ELL	Differentiated Instruction for the American History Classroom	✓	✓	✓	✓	✓	✓
BL OL AL ELL	Unit Map Overlay Transparencies	✓	✓	✓	✓	✓	✓
BL OL AL ELL	Unit Time Line Transparencies, Strategies, and Activities	✓	✓	✓	✓	✓	✓
BL OL AL ELL	Cause and Effect Transparencies, Strategies, and Activities	✓	✓	✓	✓	✓	✓
BL OL AL ELL	Why It Matters Chapter Transparencies, Strategies, and Activities	✓	✓	✓	✓	✓	✓
BL OL AL ELL	American Biographies	✓	✓	✓	✓	✓	✓

Note: Please refer to the *Unit 3 Resource Book* for this chapter's URB materials.

* Also available in Spanish

Plus
TeacherWorks
All-In-One Planner and Resource Center

- Interactive Lesson Planner
- Interactive Teacher Edition
- Fully editable blackline masters
- Section Spotlight Videos Launch
- Differentiated Lesson Plans
- Printable reports of daily assignments
- Standards Tracking System

Levels					Resources	Chapter Opener	Section 1	Section 2	Section 3	Section 4	Chapter Assess
BL	OL	AL	ELL		**TEACH** (continued)						
BL	OL	AL		📁	**Supreme Court Case Studies**			p. 37			
BL	OL	AL	ELL	📁	**The Living Constitution**	✓	✓	✓	✓	✓	✓
BL	OL	AL	ELL	📁	**American Issues**	✓	✓	✓	✓	✓	✓
	OL	AL	ELL	📁	**American Art and Architecture Transparencies, Strategies, and Activities**	✓	✓	✓	✓	✓	✓
BL	OL	AL		📁	**High School American History Literature Library**	✓	✓	✓	✓	✓	✓
	OL	AL		💿	**American History Primary Source Documents Library**	✓	✓	✓	✓	✓	✓
BL	OL	AL	ELL	💿	**American Music: Hits Through History CD**	✓	✓	✓	✓	✓	✓
BL	OL	AL	ELL	💽	**StudentWorks™ Plus DVD**	✓	✓	✓	✓	✓	✓
BL	OL	AL	ELL	💿	**Vocabulary PuzzleMaker CD-ROM**	✓	✓	✓	✓	✓	✓
BL	OL	AL	ELL	💽	***The American Vision* Video Program DVD**	✓	✓	✓	✓	✓	✓
				📁	**Reading Strategies and Activities for the Social Studies Classroom**	✓	✓	✓	✓	✓	✓
Teacher Resources				📁	**Strategies for Success**	✓	✓	✓	✓	✓	✓
				💽	**Presentation Plus! DVD**	✓	✓	✓	✓	✓	✓
				📁	**Success With English Learners**	✓	✓	✓	✓	✓	✓
					ASSESS						
BL	OL	AL	ELL	📁	**Section Quizzes and Chapter Tests***		p. 119	p. 120	p. 121	p. 122	p. 123
BL	OL	AL	ELL	📁	**Authentic Assessment With Rubrics**						p. 23
BL	OL	AL	ELL	📁	**Standardized Test Practice Workbook**						p. 20
BL	OL	AL	ELL	💿	***ExamView®* Assessment Suite CD-ROM**		9-1	9-2	9-3	9-4	Ch. 9
BL	OL	AL	ELL	💿	**Interactive Tutor Self-Assessment CD-ROM**		9-1	9-2	9-3	9-4	Ch. 9
					CLOSE						
BL			ELL	📁	**Reteaching Activity, URB**						p. 105
BL	OL		ELL	📁	**Reading and Study Skills Foldables™**	p. 67					
BL	OL	AL	ELL	📁	**American History in Graphic Novel**			p. 45			

Using CyberScout

Research Using *Famous Person*

Technology Product

CyberScout is a convenient and dynamic search engine that provides several easy ways to locate information outside the McGraw-Hill Learning Network. CyberScout only searches Web sites that have been reviewed by teachers, so the information students find is always appropriate and accurate.

Objectives

After students learn using CyberScout, they will be able to
- research information on famous people in history;
- exercise research and study skills;
- practice writing skills.

Steps

- From the McGraw-Hill Learning Network home page (www.mhln.com), click on **For Students**.
- Choose **CyberScout** below Homework Help.
- Enter a name (last, or first and last) in the **Famous Person** field and click Go.
- The CyberScout page will display a set of results.
- Select the Famous Person's name from the results.
- Click the link to a Web site of interest.
- Students will be redirected to the Web site in a new window.
- Students navigate through the chosen Web site to gain information on their topic and take notes.

History ONLINE

	Student	Teacher	Parent
Beyond the Textbook	●	●	●
Chapter Overviews	●	●	●
Time Current Events	●		●
ePuzzles and Games	●		●
Concepts in Motion	●		●
Literature Connections		●	
Multi-Language Glossaries	●		●
Online Student Edition	●	●	●
Self-Check Quizzes	●		●
Student Web Activities	●		●
Study Central ™	●		●
Teaching Today		●	
Vocabulary eFlashcards	●		●
Web Activity Lesson Plans		●	

Glencoe Media Center

glencoe.com

❯ **Study-To-Go**
- Vocabulary eFlashcards
- Self-Check Quizzes

❯ **Audio/Video**
- Student Edition Audio
- Spanish Summaries
- Section Videos

- **Timed Readings Plus in Social Studies** helps students increase their reading rate and fluency while maintaining comprehension. The 400-word passages are similar to those found on state and national assessments.

- **Reading in the Content Area: Social Studies** concentrates on six essential reading skills that help students better comprehend what they read. The book includes 75 high-interest nonfiction passages written at increasing levels of difficulty.

- **Reading Social Studies** includes strategic reading instruction and vocabulary support in Social Studies content for both ELLs and native speakers of English.

www.jamestowneducation.com

The following videotape programs are available from Glencoe as supplements to Chapter 9:

- Secrets of the Romanovs (ISBN 0-76-700231-8)
- The Red Baron: Master of the Air (ISBN 1-56-501582-7)

To order, call Glencoe at 1-800-334-7344. To find classroom resources to accompany many of these videos, check the following home pages:

A&E Television: www.aetv.com
The History Channel: www.historychannel.com

Index to National Geographic Magazine:

The following articles relate to this chapter:

- "Riddle of the *Lusitania*," by Robert D. Ballard, April 1994.
- "The American Red Cross: A Century of Service," by Louise Levathes and Annie Griffiths, June 1981.

National Geographic Society Products To order the following, call National Geographic at 1-800-368-2728:

- *World War I Era* (PicturePack Transparencies)

Access National Geographic's new dynamic MapMachine Web site and other geography resources at:
www.nationalgeographic.com
www.nationalgeographic.com/maps

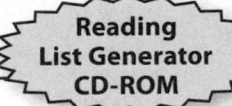

Use this database to search more than 30,000 titles to create a customized reading list for your students.

- Reading lists can be organized by students' reading level, author, genre, theme, or area of interest.
- The database provides Degrees of Reading Power™ (DRP) and Lexile™ readability scores for all selections.
- A brief summary of each selection is included.

Leveled reading suggestions for this chapter:

For students at a Grade 8 reading level:
- ***First Woman in Congress: Jeanette Rankin,*** by Florence Meiman White

For students at a Grade 9 reading level:
- ***Anastasia's Album,*** by Hugh Brewster

For students at a Grade 10 reading level:
- ***World War I,*** by Gail B. Steward

For students at a Grade 11 reading level:
- ***Remember the Lusitania!,*** by Diana Preston

For students at a Grade 12 reading level:
- ***World War I,*** by Virginia Schomp

Focus

MAKING CONNECTIONS
Why Do Nations Go to War?

Have students brainstorm the reasons nations go to war and list their answers on the chalkboard. Discuss with students if they think any of the reasons listed are valid and have them consider if the reasons might be different today than they were in 1914. **OL**

Teach

The Big Ideas

As students study the chapter, remind them to consider the section-based Big Ideas included in each section's Guide to Reading. The **Essential Questions** in the activities below tie in to the Big Ideas and help students think about and understand important chapter concepts. In addition, the Hands-on Chapter Projects with their culminating activities relate the content from each section to the Big Ideas. These activities build on each other as students progress through the chapter. Section activities culminate in the wrap-up activity on the Visual Summary page.

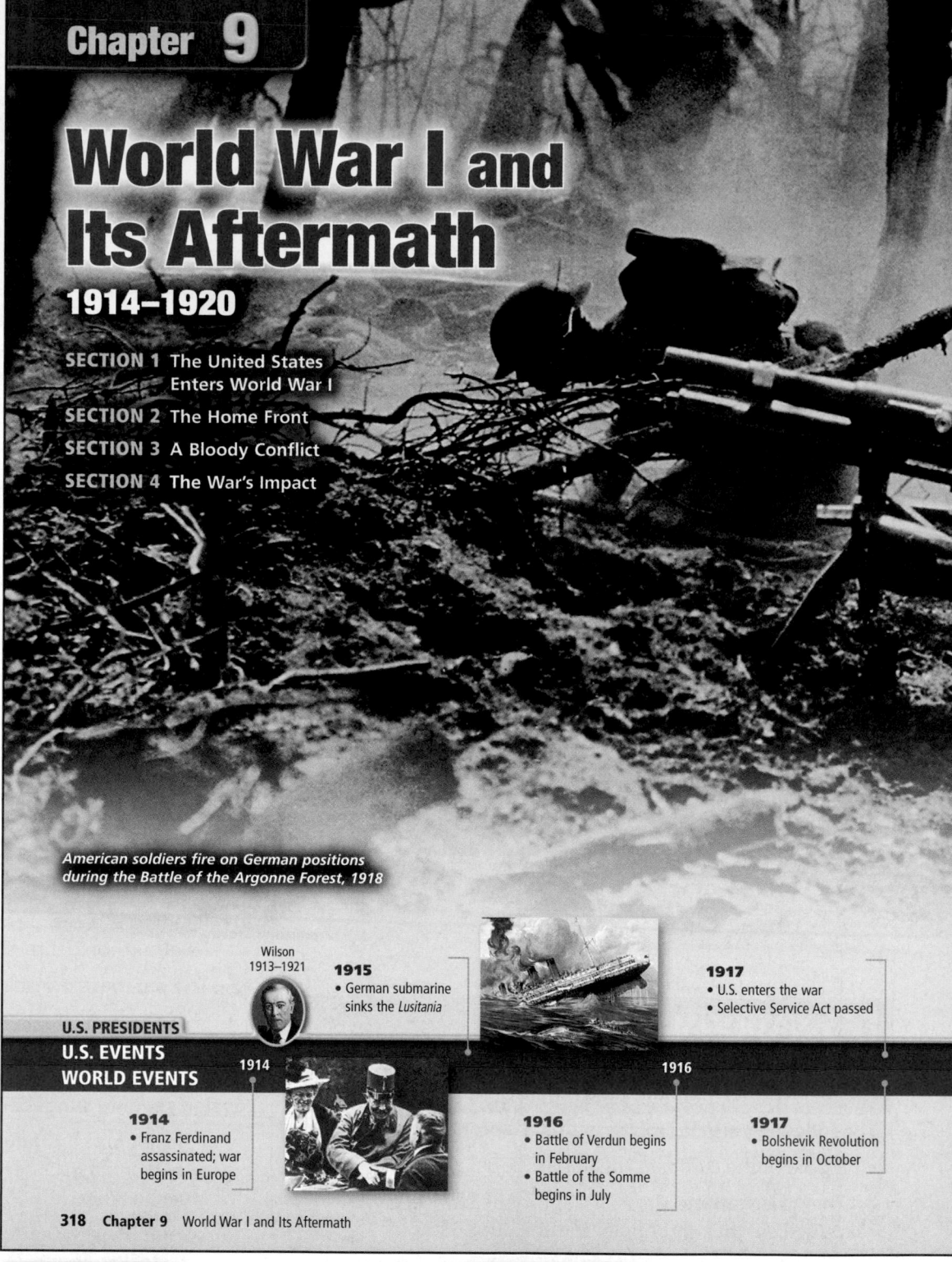

Chapter 9

World War I and Its Aftermath
1914–1920

SECTION 1 The United States Enters World War I

SECTION 2 The Home Front

SECTION 3 A Bloody Conflict

SECTION 4 The War's Impact

American soldiers fire on German positions during the Battle of the Argonne Forest, 1918

Wilson
1913–1921

U.S. PRESIDENTS

U.S. EVENTS

WORLD EVENTS

1914

1914
• Franz Ferdinand assassinated; war begins in Europe

1915
• German submarine sinks the *Lusitania*

1916

1916
• Battle of Verdun begins in February
• Battle of the Somme begins in July

1917
• U.S. enters the war
• Selective Service Act passed

1917
• Bolshevik Revolution begins in October

318 **Chapter 9** World War I and Its Aftermath

Section 1

The United States Enters World War I
Essential Question: What is neutrality? *(supporting neither side in a quarrel or war)* When would you remain neutral in a conflict with friends, and what would cause you to intervene? Tell students that in this section they will learn how the United States attempted to remain neutral in World War I and the events that finally led to U.S. involvement. **OL**

Section 2

The Home Front
Essential Question: If the United States were currently preparing for war, what needs would be different from its needs in preparing for World War I? What needs would be the same? *(Answers will vary, but students should support their answers with examples.)* Have students discuss what a country would need in order to be prepared for war. Tell them that this section will focus on how the United States mobilized for World War I. **OL**

MAKING CONNECTIONS
Why Do Nations Go to War?

World War I was the first time in American history that the United States sent troops to fight in Europe. This decision ended the long-standing policy of remaining neutral in Europe's wars.

- *Why do you think the United States changed its policy and sent troops to Europe?*
- *Do you think it was a difficult decision?*

More About the Photo

Visual Literacy The 23rd Infantry participated in six campaigns during World War I: Aisne, Lorraine, Île de France, Aisne-Marne, St. Mihiel, and Meuse-Argonne.

FOLDABLES Study Organizer **Dinah Zike's Foldables**

Dinah Zike's Foldables are three-dimensional, interactive graphic organizers that help students practice basic writing skills, review vocabulary terms, and identify main ideas. Instructions for creating and using Foldables can be found in the Appendix at the end of this book and in the *Dinah Zike's Reading and Study Skills Foldables* booklet.

Timeline

1918
- Congress passes Sedition Act
- Armistice ends fighting on November 11

1919
- Race riots and strikes take place in Northern cities

1920
- Red scare and Palmer Raids

1918 — 1920

1918
- Treaty of Brest-Litovsk ends Russian-German war

1919
- Versailles Peace Conference begins

FOLDABLES

Organizing Information As you read the chapter, write information under each tab, listing which country is in the alliance, why it joined the alliance, or what reasons it had for disagreeing with the countries in the opposing alliance.

| Central Powers | Allied Powers |
World War I

History ONLINE
Introduce students to chapter content and key terms by having them access the Chapter 9 Overview at glencoe.com.

History ONLINE Chapter Overview
Visit glencoe.com to preview Chapter 9.

Section 3

A Bloody Conflict
Essential Question: What are some synonyms for *reparations*? *(compensation, restitution, amends)* In what situations are people required to make reparations? *(replacing a damaged item, paying for repairs when causing a car accident, court cases)* Tell students that in Section 3 they will learn about the reparations Germany was forced to make after World War I. **OL**

Section 4

The War's Impact
Essential Question: How does a strike affect consumers? *(services become unavailable, costs rise)* Have students discuss reasons that workers go on strike. *(poor working conditions, lack of benefits, low wages)* Tell students that this section will cover some of the strikes that resulted from the economic upheaval following World War I. **OL**

Focus

Guide to Reading

Answers may include: Balkan crisis, alliance system, naval race, assassination of Franz Ferdinand

Section Spotlight Video

To generate student interest and provide a springboard for class discussion, access the Chapter 9, Section 1 video at glencoe.com or on the video DVD.

Resource Manager

Section 1

The United States Enters World War I

Militarism, alliances, imperialism, and nationalism led to World War I in Europe. Attacks on U.S. ships and American support for the Allies eventually caused the United States to enter the war.

Guide to Reading

Big Ideas
Trade, War, and Migration Although the United States tried to stay neutral, events pushed the nation into war.

Content Vocabulary
- militarism (p. 321)
- nationalism (p. 322)
- propaganda (p. 324)
- contraband (p. 326)

Academic Vocabulary
- emphasis (p. 322)
- erode (p. 326)

People and Events to Identify
- Balkans (p. 322)
- Franz Ferdinand (p. 322)
- Sussex pledge (p. 327)
- Zimmermann telegram (p. 327)

Reading Strategy
Organizing Complete the graphic organizer shown below by identifying the factors that contributed to the conflict.

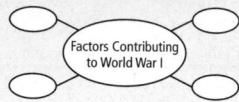

Factors Contributing to World War I

World War I Begins

MAIN Idea Old alliances and nationalist sentiments among European nations set the stage for World War I.

HISTORY AND YOU Does your school have a long-standing rivalry with another school? Read how European nations formed political alliances that brought most of the continent into war.

Despite more than 40 years of general peace, tensions among European nations were building in 1914. Throughout the late 1800s and early 1900s, a number of factors created problems among the powers of Europe and set the stage for a monumental war.

Militarism and Alliances

The roots of World War I date back to the 1860s. In 1864, while Americans fought the Civil War, the German kingdom of Prussia launched the first of a series of wars to unite the various German states into one nation. By 1871 Prussia had united Germany and proclaimed the birth of the German Empire. The new German nation rapidly industrialized and quickly became one of the most powerful nations in the world.

The creation of Germany transformed European politics. In 1870, as part of their plan to unify Germany, the Prussians had attacked and defeated France. They then forced the French to give up territory along the German border. From that point forward, France and Germany were enemies. To protect itself, Germany signed alliances with Italy and with Austria-Hungary, a huge empire that controlled much of southeastern Europe. This became known as the Triple Alliance.

The new alliance alarmed Russian leaders, who feared that Germany intended to expand eastward into Russia. Russia and Austria-Hungary were also competing for influence in southeastern Europe. Many of the people of southeastern Europe were Slavs—the same ethnic group as the Russians—and the Russians wanted to support them against Austria-Hungary. As a result, Russia and France had a common interest in opposing Germany and Austria-Hungary. In 1894 they signed the Franco-Russian Alliance, promising to come to each other's aid in a war with the Triple Alliance.

R Reading Strategies	**C** Critical Thinking	**D** Differentiated Instruction	**W** Writing Support	**S** Skill Practice
Teacher Edition • Predicting, p. 324 • Setting a Purpose, p. 324 • Act. Prior Know., p. 326 • Using Word Parts, p. 326 • Sequencing Info., p. 327 **Additional Resources** • Guid. Read. Act, URB p. 108	**Teacher Edition** • Drawing Con., p. 322 **Additional Resources** • Crit. Think. Skills Act., URB p. 94 • Quizzes and Tests, p. 119	**Teacher Edition** • Visual/Spatial, p. 326 **Additional Resources** • Eng. Learner Act., URB p. 87 • Foldables, p. 67	**Teacher Edition** • Persuasive Writing, pp. 324, 325 • Narrative Writing, p. 322 **Additional Resources** • Content Vocab. Act., URB p. 89 • Academic Vocab. Act., URB p. 91	**Teacher Edition** • Analyzing Visuals, p. 321 • Using Geo. Skills, p. 323 **Additional Resources** • RENTG, p. 88

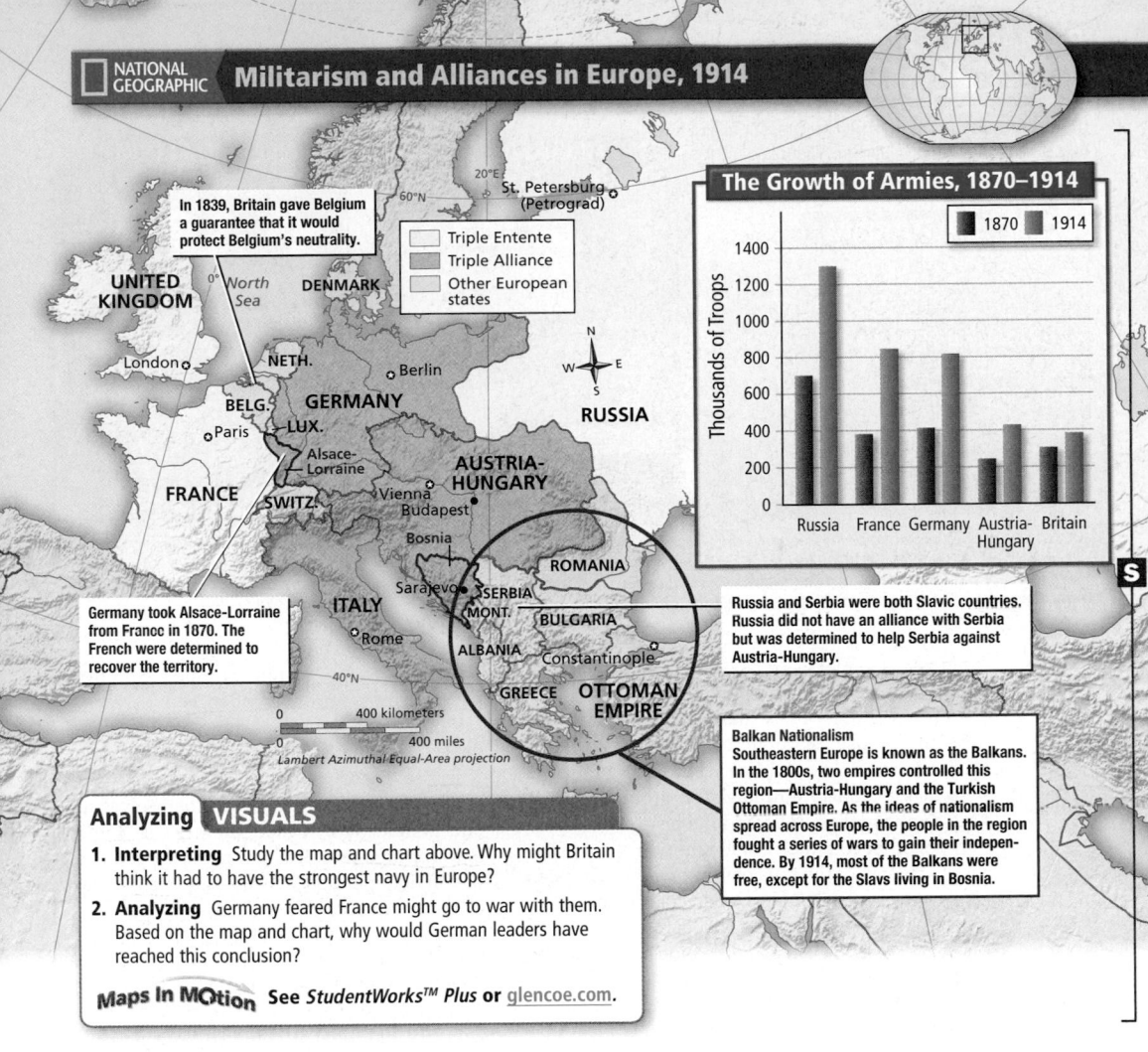

NATIONAL GEOGRAPHIC Militarism and Alliances in Europe, 1914

In 1839, Britain gave Belgium a guarantee that it would protect Belgium's neutrality.

Triple Entente
Triple Alliance
Other European states

UNITED KINGDOM

DENMARK

London
NETH.
Berlin
BELG.
GERMANY
LUX.
Paris
Alsace-Lorraine
FRANCE
SWITZ.
AUSTRIA-HUNGARY
Vienna
Budapest
Bosnia
ITALY
Rome
ROMANIA
Sarajevo
SERBIA
MONT.
BULGARIA
ALBANIA
Constantinople
GREECE
OTTOMAN EMPIRE

St. Petersburg (Petrograd)

RUSSIA

20°E
60°N
North Sea
40°N

0   400 kilometers
0   400 miles
Lambert Azimuthal Equal-Area projection

Germany took Alsace-Lorraine from France in 1870. The French were determined to recover the territory.

Russia and Serbia were both Slavic countries. Russia did not have an alliance with Serbia but was determined to help Serbia against Austria-Hungary.

The Growth of Armies, 1870–1914

1870 1914

Thousands of Troops

1400
1200
1000
800
600
400
200
0

Russia   France   Germany   Austria-Hungary   Britain

Balkan Nationalism
Southeastern Europe is known as the Balkans. In the 1800s, two empires controlled this region—Austria-Hungary and the Turkish Ottoman Empire. As the ideas of nationalism spread across Europe, the people in the region fought a series of wars to gain their independence. By 1914, most of the Balkans were free, except for the Slavs living in Bosnia.

Analyzing VISUALS

1. **Interpreting** Study the map and chart above. Why might Britain think it had to have the strongest navy in Europe?

2. **Analyzing** Germany feared France might go to war with them. Based on the map and chart, why would German leaders have reached this conclusion?

Maps In Motion See *StudentWorks™ Plus* or glencoe.com.

The system of alliances in Europe encouraged **militarism**—the aggressive build-up of armed forces to intimidate and threaten other nations. German militarism eventually forced Britain to become involved in the alliance system. Britain's policy was to support weaker countries against stronger ones so as to make sure no country conquered all of Europe. By the late 1800s, it was clear that Germany had become the strongest nation in Europe.

In 1898 Germany began building a large modern navy as well. A strong German navy threatened the British, who depended on their naval strength to protect their island from invasion. By the early 1900s, an arms race had begun between Great Britain and Germany, as both nations raced to build warships.

The naval race greatly increased tensions between Germany and Britain and convinced the British to establish closer relations with France and Russia. The British still refused to sign a formal alliance, so their new relationship with the French and Russians became known as an entente cordiale—a friendly understanding. Britain, France, and Russia became known as the Triple Entente.

Chapter 9   World War I and Its Aftermath   **321**

R Reading Strategy

Making Connections Write the terms *nationalism* and *imperialism* on the board. Then have students list the ways in which the ideas of nationalism and imperialism were opposed to each other. Discuss with students the roles that these opposing ideas played in World War I. **AL**

W Writing Support

Narrative Writing Have students write a newspaper article from the point of view of a reporter who witnessed the assassination of Archduke Franz Ferdinand. Instruct students to use narrative and descriptive techniques in their articles. Encourage students to share their articles with the class. **BL**

C Critical Thinking

Drawing Conclusions Have students list the peoples who were pushing for independence before World War I. Have students choose one of these groups and, using library or Internet resources, write a history of that group from World War I to the present. Have volunteers share their findings with the class.

Differentiated Instruction

Linking Past and Present Activity 9, URB p. 96

322

PRIMARY SOURCE
Causes of World War I

Use the acronym MAIN to remember the four main causes of World War I: Militarism, Alliances, Imperialism, Nationalism.

MILITARISM

▲ Warships of the German Imperial fleet are shown anchored near Kiel, Germany in 1911. The naval race between Britain and Germany caused tension in Europe prior to World War I.

ALLIANCES

France
Austria-Hungary
Germany   Italy

▲ An 1883 British cartoon illustrates the Triple Alliance.

IMPERIALISM

▲ Franz Joseph, Emperor of Austria-Hungary, and Wilhelm II, Emperor of Germany, salute during a parade in Berlin in 1889.

Imperialism and Nationalism

By the late 1800s, **nationalism,** or a feeling of intense pride in one's homeland, had become a powerful idea in Europe. Nationalists place primary **emphasis** on promoting their homeland's culture and interests above those of other countries. Nationalism was one of the reasons for the tensions among the European powers. Each nation viewed the others as competitors, and many people were willing to go to war to expand their nation at the expense of others.

One of the basic ideas of nationalism is the right to self-determination—the idea that people who share a national identity should have their own country and government. In the 1800s nationalism led to a crisis in southeastern Europe in the region known as the **Balkans.** Historically, the Ottoman Empire and the Austro-Hungarian Empire had ruled the Balkans. Both of these empires were made up of many different nations.

Imperialism—the idea that a country can increase its power and wealth by controlling other peoples—had convinced the major European powers to build empires in the 1700s and 1800s. Nationalism ran counter to imperialism. As the idea of nationalism spread in the late 1800s and early 1900s, the different national groups within Europe's empires began to press for independence.

Among the groups pushing for independence were the Serbs, Bosnians, Croats, and Slovenes. These people all spoke similar languages and had come to see themselves as one people. They called themselves South Slavs, or Yugoslavs. The first of these people to obtain independence were the Serbs, who formed a nation called Serbia between the Ottoman and Austro-Hungarian Empires. Serbs believed their nation's mission was to unite the South Slavs.

Russia supported the Serbs, while Austria-Hungary did what it could to limit Serbia's growth. In 1908 Austria-Hungary annexed Bosnia, which had belonged to the Ottoman Empire. The Serbs were furious. They wanted Bosnia to be part of their nation. The annexation demonstrated to the Serbs that Austria-Hungary had no intention of letting the Slavic people in its empire become independent.

A Terrorist Attack Brings War

In late June 1914 the heir to the Austro-Hungarian throne, the Archduke **Franz Ferdinand,** visited the Bosnian capital of Sarajevo. As he and his wife rode through the city, a Bosnian revolutionary named Gavrilo

322   Chapter 9   World War I and Its Aftermath

Writing a Narrative Essay

Objective: Make decisions on budget priorities.

Focus: Discuss how budgets require decision-makers to prioritize needs and wants.

Teach: List rounded prices for each type of aircraft mentioned in the reading. Give a set amount to spend on aircraft.

Assess: List how many of each kind of aircraft to purchase. Make sure to stay within the budget.

Close: Write a paragraph explaining the decisions made in spending the budget.

Differentiated Instruction Strategies

BL With a partner, make a time line that shows the progression of the ways aircraft were used in World War I.

AL Choose one part of the most recent U.S. budget and explain the priorities of that particular department.

ELL Write the definition of each of the italicized words in the reading using context clues and other resources.

NATIONALISM

▲ *Serbian nationalist Gavrilo Princip is dragged into police headquarters in Sarajevo shortly after killing Archduke Franz Ferdinand, heir to the Austro-Hungarian throne.*

Analyzing VISUALS

1. **Interpreting** What point is the cartoonist trying to make about the Triple Alliance?
2. **Explaining** How did Austrian imperialism and Balkan nationalism contribute to the outbreak of World War I?

Princip rushed their open car and shot the couple to death. The assassin was a member of a Serbian nationalist group nicknamed the "Black Hand." The assassination took place with the knowledge of Serbian officials who hoped to start a war that would bring down the Austro-Hungarian Empire.

The Alliances Are Triggered The Austro-Hungarian government blamed Serbia for the attack and decided the time had come to crush Serbia in order to prevent Slavic nationalism from undermining its empire. Knowing an attack on Serbia might trigger a war with Russia, the Austrians asked their German allies for support. Germany promised to support Austria-Hungary if war erupted.

Austria-Hungary then issued an ultimatum to the Serbian government. The Serbs counted on Russia to back them up, and the Russians, in turn, counted on France. French leaders were worried that they might someday be caught alone in a war with Germany, so they promised to support Russia if war began.

On July 28 Austria-Hungary declared war on Serbia. Russia immediately mobilized its army, including troops stationed on the German border. On August 1 Germany declared war on Russia. Two days later, it declared war on France. World War I had begun.

Germany's Plan Fails Germany had long been prepared for war against France and Russia. It immediately launched a massive invasion of France, hoping to knock the French out of the war. It would then be able to send its troops east to deal with the Russians.

The German plan had one major problem. **S** It required the German forces to advance through neutral Belgium in order to encircle the French troops. The British had guaranteed Belgium's neutrality. When German troops crossed the Belgian frontier, Britain declared war on Germany.

Those fighting for the Triple Entente were called the Allies. France, Russia, and Great Britain formed the backbone of the Allies along with Italy, which joined them in 1915 after the other Allies promised to cede Austro-Hungarian territory to Italy after the war. What remained of the Triple Alliance—Germany and Austria-Hungary—joined with the Ottoman Empire and Bulgaria to form the Central Powers.

The German plan seemed to work at first. German troops swept through Belgium and headed into France, driving back the French and British forces. Then, to the great surprise of the Germans, Russian troops invaded Germany. The Germans had not expected Russia to mobilize so quickly. They were forced to pull some of their troops away from the attack on France and send them east to stop the Russians. This weakened the German forces just enough to give the Allies a chance to stop them. The Germans drove to within 30 miles (48 km) of Paris, but stubborn resistance by British and French troops at the Battle of the Marne finally stopped the German advance. Because the swift German attack had failed to defeat the French, both sides became locked in a bloody stalemate along hundreds of miles of trenches that would barely change position for the next three years.

The Central Powers had greater success on the Eastern Front. German and Austro-Hungarian forces stopped the Russian attack and then went on the offensive. They swept across hundreds of miles of territory and took hundreds of thousands of prisoners. Russia suffered 2 million killed, wounded, or captured in 1915 alone, but it kept fighting.

✓ **Reading Check** **Explaining** What incident triggered the beginning of World War I?

S Skill Practice

Using Geography Skills
Provide students with a topographical map of Europe. Instruct them to research the path Germany hoped to take through Belgium and eventually to Paris. Have students trace the path and then mark the location where British and French troops stopped the German advance. **OL**

Analyzing VISUALS

Answers:
1. The Triple Alliance is poised to attack France.
2. Austria was determined to maintain its influence and control in the Balkans; the people of the Balkans were just as determined to establish independent nations and rule themselves.

✓ Reading Check

Answer:
the assassination of Austrian Archduke Franz Ferdinand, the heir to the Austro-Hungarian throne

Additional Support

Activity: Collaborative Learning

Explaining Causes Write the following terms on the chalkboard: *imperialism, nationalism, militarism,* and *balance of power.* Have students define each term. Using the text and additional research, ask them to explain how each contributed to the war in Europe. Ask if students think that any one nation or group of nations was primarily responsible for World War I. Ask each student to present evidence to support his or her opinion. **OL**

R₁ **Reading Strategy**

Predicting While war enveloped Europe, American politicians attempted to remain uninvolved in the global conflict. **Ask:** As foreign tensions escalate, do you think it will be possible for President Wilson to maintain his neutral stance? Why or why not? *(Students may state that it will not be possible as the United States becomes more directly affected by events overseas.)* **OL**

W Writing Support

Persuasive Writing Have interested students find out more information about the preparedness debate before the nation's entry into World War I. Have them use their findings to decide whether they favor preparedness or not. Then have them write a letter to President Wilson persuading him to support their point of view. **OL**

R₂ **Reading Strategy**

Setting a Purpose Have students discuss how news reporting, propaganda, and advertising differed. Ask students to identify the purpose and value of each. **AL**

Additional Support

America Declares War

MAIN Idea British propaganda and business interests led most Americans to a pro-British stance on the war.

HISTORY AND YOU Do you recall a time when you tried to remain neutral in a fight between friends? Read how the United States tried to stay out of World War I.

When the fighting began, President Wilson was determined to keep the country out of a European war. He immediately declared the United States to be neutral in the conflict. "We must be impartial in thought as well as in action," Wilson stated. For many Americans that proved difficult to do.

Americans Take Sides

Despite the president's plea, many Americans supported one side or the other. Many of the country's 8 million German Americans, for example, supported their homeland. Many of the nation's 4.5 million Irish Americans, whose homeland endured centuries of British rule, also sympathized with the Central Powers.

In general, however, American public opinion favored the Allied cause. Many Americans valued the heritage, language, and political ideals they shared with Britain. Others treasured America's links with France, a great friend to America during the Revolutionary War.

For more than two years, the United States officially remained neutral. During this time a great debate began over whether the United States should prepare for war. Supporters of the "preparedness" movement believed that preparing for war was the best way to stay out of the conflict. They also argued that if the United States was pulled into the war, it was better to be prepared.

Other Americans disagreed. In 1915 Carrie Chapman Catt and Jane Addams—leaders of the woman suffrage movement—founded the Women's Peace Party (later known as the International League for Peace and Freedom). This organization, along with others such as the League to Limit Armament, worked to keep America out of the war by urging the president not to build up the military.

Government Officials Back Britain One select group of Americans was decidedly pro-British: President Wilson's cabinet. Only Secretary of State William Jennings Bryan favored neutrality. The other cabinet members, as well as Bryan's chief adviser, Robert Lansing, and Walter Hines Page, the American ambassador to London, argued forcefully on behalf of Britain. Many American military leaders also backed the British. They believed that an Allied victory was the only way to preserve the international balance of power.

British officials worked diligently to win American support. One method they used was **propaganda,** or information designed to influence opinion. Both sides used propaganda, but German propaganda was mostly anti-Russian and did not appeal to most Americans. British propaganda, on the other hand, was extremely skillful.

Debates IN HISTORY

Should America Stay Neutral in World War I?

Americans were deeply divided about whether the United States should remain neutral in World War I. Despite President Wilson's pronouncement that Americans should remain neutral in thought as well as action, many Americans, including those working for the government, had very definite opinions as to whether or not the United States should enter the war.

Activity: Collaborative Learning

Making Inferences Remind students that to infer means to draw a conclusion based on facts and on what is known about the usual outcome of similar situations. Then ask students to make an inference about the Americans who wanted the United States to remain neutral. Discuss and list the various reasons these citizens had for not entering World War I. Ask students to write a paragraph giving their opinions about whether or not a nation should require citizens to fight in a war even if they do not understand its causes or they disagree with its causes. **OL**

To control the flow of news to the United States, the British cut the transatlantic telegraph cable from Europe to the United States. This meant that most war news would be based on British reports. The American ambassador to Britain, Walter Hines Page, himself strongly pro-British, gave the reports legitimacy by endorsing many of them. When stories arrived describing German atrocities, enough Americans believed them to help sway American support in favor of the Allies.

Business Supports Britain American business interests also leaned toward the Allies. Companies in the United States, particularly on the East Coast, had strong ties with businesses in the Allied countries. As business leader Thomas W. Lamont stated, "Our firm had never for one moment been

neutral: we did not know how to be. From the very start we did everything that we could to contribute to the cause of the Allies."

Many American banks began to invest heavily in an Allied victory. American loans to the cash-hungry Allies skyrocketed. By 1917 such loans would total over $2 billion. Other American banks, particularly in the Midwest, where pro-German feelings were strongest, also lent some $27 million to Germany.

More money might have been lent to Germany, but most foreign loans required the approval of William McAdoo, the secretary of the Treasury. McAdoo was strongly pro-British and did what he could to limit loans to Germany. As a result, the country's prosperity was intertwined with the military fortunes of Britain, France, and Russia. If the Allies won, the money would be paid back; if not, the money might be lost forever. **W**

W **Writing Support**
Persuasive Writing Organize students into pairs and ask them to write a letter to Secretary of the Treasury William McAdoo either supporting or opposing his pro-British stance concerning foreign loans. Encourage students to use library or Internet resources to find out more about McAdoo and the nation's loans to the Allies during World War I. Have pairs take turns presenting their letters to the class. **AL**

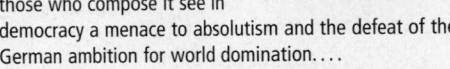

Debates IN HISTORY

YES

John Works
Civil War Veteran and U.S. Senator

PRIMARY SOURCE

"Germany is not moving against this country. She has not been guilty of any aggression against us. She has taken the lives of a few of our citizens, because they got in the way when she was prosecuting a war against another nation and fighting to preserve her existence. If the German Government should make aggressive warfare against the United States you would not need any exhortation in the Senate of the United States to arouse the patriotism of the American people. You would not be holding open your enlisting stations without getting any soldiers."

—from *The Congressional Record*, March 4, 1917

NO

Robert Lansing
Secretary of State

PRIMARY SOURCE

"I have come to the conclusion that the German Government is utterly hostile to all nations with democratic institutions because those who compose it see in democracy a menace to absolutism and the defeat of the German ambition for world domination....

... Germany must not be permitted to win this war and to break even, though to prevent it this country is forced to take an active part. This ultimate necessity must be constantly in our minds in all our controversies with the belligerents. American public opinion must be prepared for the time, which may come, when we will have to cast aside our neutrality and become one of the champions of democracy."

—from *War Memoirs of Robert Lansing*

DBQ Document-Based Questions

1. **Summarizing** When does Senator Works believe war is justified?
2. **Explaining** Why does Secretary of State Lansing believe Germany is a threat to the United States?
3. **Comparing** Based on these sources, what is the focus of the neutrality debate? What is not being discussed?
4. **Evaluating** Which position do you agree with? Write an essay explaining why the other side is wrong.

Answers:
1. when a nation makes aggressive warfare against the United States
2. because Germany is hostile to all nations with democratic institutions
3. whether Germany poses a threat to the United States; not being debated is the preparedness issue
4. Answers will vary, but students should support their opinions with facts.

Activity: Collaborative Learning

American Neutrality Have students brainstorm to analyze the United States's dilemma over whether to enter the war. They should consider the principles that guided the foreign policy of the time, moral and idealistic beliefs, and emotional and economic interests. Remind students that the war occurred at a time when the United States had a large population of European immigrants who had close ties to their native countries. Ask students to write a personal essay in response to the following question: Is it possible for a nation to become involved in war because it desires a peaceful world? **OL**

Moving Toward War

Although most Americans supported the Allies and hoped for their victory, they did not want to join the conflict. However, a series of events gradually **eroded** American neutrality and drew the nation into the war.

German Submarines Go Into Action

Shortly after the war began, the British declared a blockade of German ports and began intercepting neutral merchant ships sailing to Europe. They forced the ships to land at British ports where they were inspected for **contraband,** or goods prohibited from shipment to Germany and its allies.

Although Britain's decision to intercept neutral ships, including American ships, led to protests from the U.S. government, the German response angered Americans even more. Britain and France depended on food, equipment, and other supplies from both the United States and their overseas empires. To stop those shipments, Germany deployed submarines known as U-boats—from the German word *Unterseeboot* ("underwater boat"). In February 1915, the Germans announced that they would sink without warning any ship they found in the waters around Britain.

Germany's announcement triggered outrage in the United States and elsewhere. Germany had signed an international treaty that banned attacks on civilian ships without warning. The Germans claimed that their U-boats would be placed at great risk if they had to surface and give a warning before firing.

The Germans Sink the *Lusitania* The issue reached a crisis on May 7, 1915, when the British passenger ship *Lusitania* entered the war zone. A German submarine sunk the ship, killing nearly 1,200 passengers—including 128 Americans. The attack outraged Americans who saw the sinking as a terrorist attack on civilians, including women and children, not as a legitimate act of war.

Wilson tried to defuse the crisis. He refused to threaten Germany with war saying that the United States was "too proud to fight." Instead, he sent several official protests to Germany insisting that it stop endangering the lives of noncombatants in the war zone.

Late in March 1916, Wilson's policy was tested when a U-boat torpedoed the French passenger ship *Sussex*, injuring several Americans on board. Although Wilson's closest advisers favored breaking off diplomatic relations with Germany, the president chose

Turning Points

The Sinking of the *Lusitania*

When World War I began, many Americans supported one side or the other, but most agreed the United States should stay out of the war. Eight months later, when the German submarine U-20 sank the *Lusitania*, killing 1,195 people, including 128 Americans, attitudes began to shift.

The attack seemed to prove that Germany was acting in an uncivilized way and it gave credibility to British propaganda. Even though the United States would not enter the war for nearly two more years, the attack on the *Lusitania* marked a turning point in the war because it changed American attitudes and set the stage for the American entry into the war.

ANALYZING HISTORY Do you think the use of submarines in World War I was justified? Write a brief essay explaining your opinion.

▲ A mass funeral for Lusitania *victims was held in Queenston, Ireland, on May 23, 1915. How do you think people reacted when they saw photos like this in the newspaper?*

▲ *After the sinking, the Boston Committee of Public Safety issued this poster showing a drowning woman and baby and urging Americans to prepare for war by building up the military.*

to issue one last warning. He demanded that the German government abandon its methods of submarine warfare or risk war with the United States.

Germany did not want to strengthen the Allies by drawing the United States into the war. It promised with certain conditions to sink no more merchant ships without warning. The **Sussex Pledge,** as it was called, met the foreign-policy goals of both Germany and President Wilson by keeping the United States out of the war a little longer.

Wilson's efforts to keep American soldiers at home played an important part in his reelection bid in 1916. Campaigning as the "peace" candidate, his campaign slogan, "He kept us out of the war," helped Wilson win a narrow victory over the Republican nominee, Charles Evans Hughes.

The United States Declares War

Following Wilson's reelection, events quickly brought the country to the brink of war. In January 1917, a German official named Arthur Zimmermann sent a telegram to the German ambassador in Mexico asking him to make an offer to the Mexican government: If Mexico agreed to become an ally of Germany in a war with the United States, Germany promised Mexico would regain its "lost territory in Texas, New Mexico, and Arizona" after the war. British intelligence intercepted the **Zimmermann telegram.** Shortly afterward, it was leaked to American newspapers. Furious, many Americans now concluded war with Germany was necessary.

R

Then, on February 1, 1917, Germany resumed unrestricted submarine warfare. German military leaders believed that they could starve Britain into submission in four to six months if their U-boats began sinking all ships on sight. Although they knew this decision might draw the United States into the war, they did not believe the Americans could raise an army and transport it to Europe in time. Between February 3 and March 21, German U-boats sank six American ships. Finally roused to action, President Wilson appeared before a special session of Congress on April 2, 1917. Declaring that "the world must be made safe for democracy," Wilson asked Congress to declare war on Germany.

PRIMARY SOURCE

"It is a fearful thing to lead this great peaceful people into war. . . . But the right is more precious than peace, and we shall fight for the things which we have always carried nearest to our hearts—for democracy, for the right of those who submit to authority to have a voice in their own governments, for the rights and liberties of small nations. . . ."

—quoted in the Congressional Record, 1917

After a debate, the Senate passed the resolution on April 4 by a vote of 82 to 6. The House concurred 373 to 50 on April 6, and Wilson signed the resolution. America was at war.

 Summarizing How did Germany's use of unrestricted submarine warfare bring America into World War I?

Vocabulary

1. **Explain** the significance of: militarism, nationalism, Balkans, Franz Ferdinand, propaganda, contraband, Sussex Pledge, Zimmermann telegram.

Main Ideas

2. **Identifying** Name the two alliances in Europe at the start of World War I, and list the members of each alliance.

3. **Explaining** Why did many Americans support the British in the war even though the United States was officially neutral?

Critical Thinking

4. **Big Ideas** How did trade and economics contribute to America's entry into World War I?

5. **Organizing** Use a graphic organizer similar to the one below to identify the events that led the United States to enter World War I.

Events → U.S. Enters World War I

6. **Analyzing Visuals** Examine the images on page 326. How did images like these contribute to America's eventual entry into the war?

Writing About History

7. **Expository Writing** Imagine you are an American survivor of the sinking of the *Lusitania.* Write a letter to President Wilson about what you think he should do.

History ONLINE
Study Central™ To review this section, go to glencoe.com and click on Study Central.

327

R **Reading Strategy**
Sequencing Information
Have students create a time line that highlights the events that led the United States to enter World War I. Display the time lines in the classroom. **OL**

Assess

History ONLINE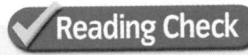

Study Central™ provides summaries, interactive games, and online graphic organizers to help students review content.

Close

Summarizing Ask: What were the main causes of World War I? *(militarism, alliances, imperialism, and nationalism)* **OL**

✓ Reading Check

Answer:
With the resumption of unrestricted submarine warfare, German U-boats sank six American ships between February 3 and March 21. Wilson asked Congress to declare war.

Section 1 REVIEW

Answers

1. All definitions can be found in the section and the Glossary.

2. Triple Alliance: Germany, Austria-Hungary, Italy; Triple Entente: France, Great Britain, Russia

3. They believed that Allied victory was the only way to preserve the international balance of power, had greater financial and business ties to the Alliance countries, and they cited the close historical ties with Great Britain and France.

4. The economy of the United States was deeply intertwined with the economies of the Allies.

5. unrestricted submarine warfare; the Zimmermann telegram

6. images turned public opinion against Germany

7. Letters will vary, but students should use information from the textbook in their letters.

Focus

Bellringer

Daily Focus Transparency 9.2

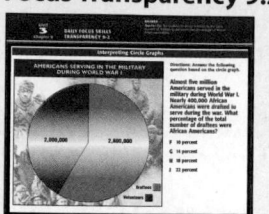

Guide to Reading

Answers:

> **The Home Front**
> I. Organizing the Economy
>   A. Wartime Agencies
>   B. Mobilizing the Workforce
>   C. Shaping Public Opinion
> II. Building the Military

Students should complete the outline by using all the heads in this section.

Section Spotlight Video

To generate student interest and provide a springboard for class discussion, access the Chapter 9, Section 2 video at glencoe.com or on the video DVD.

Resource Manager

Section 2

The Home Front

Guide to Reading

Big Ideas
Government and Society To successfully fight the war, the United States government had to mobilize the entire nation.

Content Vocabulary
• victory garden (p. 328)
• espionage (p. 330)

Academic Vocabulary
• migrate (p. 330)
• draft (p. 332)

People and Events to Identify
• War Industries Board (p. 328)
• National War Labor Board (p. 329)
• Committee on Public Information (p. 330)
• selective service (p. 332)

Reading Strategy
Taking Notes Use the major headings of this section to create an outline similar to the one below.

> The Home Front
> I. Organizing the Economy
>   A.
>   B.
>   C.
> II.
>   A.
>   B.

To fight World War I, the American government used progressive ideas and new government agencies to mobilize the population and organize the economy.

Organizing the Economy

MAIN Idea The government used progressive ideas to manage the economy and pay for the war.

HISTORY AND YOU How do you help conserve food or fuel resources? Read how Americans made sacrifices to aid the war effort.

When the United States entered the war in April 1917, progressives controlled the federal government. Rather than abandon their ideas during wartime, they applied progressive ideas to fighting the war. Their ideas about planning and scientific management shaped how the American government organized the war effort.

Wartime Agencies

To efficiently manage the relationship between the federal government and private companies, Congress created new agencies to coordinate mobilization and ensure the efficient use of national resources. These agencies emphasized cooperation between big business and government, not direct government control. Business executives, managers, and government officials staffed the new agencies.

Managing the Economy Perhaps the most important of the new agencies was the **War Industries Board** (WIB), established in July 1917 to coordinate the production of war materials. At first, the WIB's authority was limited, but problems with production convinced Wilson to expand its powers and appoint Bernard Baruch, a Wall Street stockbroker, to run it. The WIB told manufacturers what they could produce, allocated raw materials, ordered the construction of new factories, and, in a few instances, set prices.

Perhaps the most successful agency was the Food Administration, run by Herbert Hoover. This agency was responsible for increasing food production while reducing civilian consumption. Using the slogan "Food Will Win the War—Don't Waste It," it encouraged families to conserve food and grow their own vegetables in **victory gardens.** By having Wheatless Mondays, Meatless Tuesdays, and Porkless Thursdays, families would leave more food for the troops.

While Hoover managed food production, the Fuel Administration, run by Harry Garfield, tried to manage the nation's use of coal and oil.

R Reading Strategies	**C** Critical Thinking	**D** Differentiated Instruction	**W** Writing Support	**S** Skill Practice
Teacher Edition • Understanding Vocab., p. 332 **Additional Resources** • Prim. Source Read., URB p. 97 • Guid. Read. Act., URB p. 109 • Am. History in Graphic Novel, p. 45	**Additional Resources** • Enrichment Act., URB p. 106 • Supreme Court Case Studies, p. 37 • Quizzes and Tests, p. 120	**Teacher Edition** • Special Ed., p. 330 • Verbal/Ling., p. 332 **Additional Resources** • Diff. Instr. Act., URB p. 85	**Teacher Edition** • Narrative Writing, p. 333 **Additional Resources** • Enrichment Act., URB p. 106	**Teacher Edition** • Making Conn., p. 329 • Using Geo. Skills, p. 330 **Additional Resources** • Hist. Analysis Skills Act., URB p. 84 • RENTG, p. 91 • Reading Skills Act., URB p. 83

PRIMARY SOURCE
Raising Money for World War I

▶ The actor Douglas Fairbanks urges Americans to buy Liberty Bonds at a rally held in New York City in 1918.

"SHALL WE BE MORE TENDER WITH OUR DOLLARS THAN WITH THE LIVES OF OUR SONS?"

BUY A UNITED STATES GOVERNMENT BOND OF THE
2ND LIBERTY LOAN OF 1917

REMEMBER!
THE FLAG OF LIBERTY SUPPORT IT!

BUY U.S. Government Bonds
3rd LIBERTY LOAN

Paying for World War I

Billions of dollars

First Liberty Loan	2.0
Second Liberty Loan	3.8
Third Liberty Loan	4.2
Fourth Liberty Loan	7.0
Victory Loan	4.5
Other Loans	3.1
Taxation	7.3

Analyzing VISUALS

To pay for World War I, the U.S. government increased taxes and issued bonds. Progressives liked bonds because they were voluntary and Americans could buy them based on their financial situation. Officials worried, however, that the war had so divided Americans that few would buy them. To get people to buy bonds, the government printed posters, organized parades, and asked movie stars to promote them.

1. **Analyzing** What was the total revenue raised by loans? What percentage of the cost of the war was paid by taxes?

2. **Interpreting** What point is the poster for the 2nd Liberty Loan making? What group of people does the poster for the 3rd Liberty Loan address?

To conserve energy, Garfield introduced daylight savings time and shortened workweeks for factories that did not make war materials. He also encouraged Americans to observe Heatless Mondays.

Paying for the War By the end of the war, the United States had spent about $32 billion. To fund the war effort, Congress raised income tax rates, placed new taxes on corporate profits, and imposed an extra tax on the profits of arms factories.

Taxes, however, did not cover the entire cost of the war. The government also borrowed over $20 billion through the sale of Liberty Bonds and Victory Bonds. Americans who bought bonds were lending money to the government that would be repaid with interest in a specified number of years.

Mobilizing the Workforce

The success of the war effort also required the cooperation of workers. To prevent strikes from disrupting the war effort, the government established the **National War Labor Board** (NWLB) in March 1918. Chaired by William Howard Taft and Frank Walsh, a prominent labor attorney, the NWLB attempted to mediate labor disputes that might otherwise lead to strikes.

The NWLB often pressured industry to improve wages, adopt an eight-hour workday, and allow unions the right to organize and bargain collectively. In exchange, labor leaders agreed not to disrupt war production with strikes or other disturbances. As a result, membership in unions increased by just over one million between 1917 and 1919.

History ONLINE
Student Web Activity Visit glencoe.com and complete the activity on wartime propaganda.

Teach

S Skill Practice

Making Connections Have students review the photograph, posters, and chart on this page. **Ask:** In what way are they connected? *(The photograph and the posters are appeals for money to support the war; the chart illustrates the results of those appeals.)* **Ask:** How does national unity help a nation win a war? *(National unity helps direct all the nation's resources to the common goal of winning the war.)* **OL**

Analyzing VISUALS

Answers:
1. about $25 billion; about 23% came from taxes
2. The poster for 2nd Liberty Loan appeals to Americans to make sure there are enough funds to equip and support soldiers properly. The poster for 3rd Liberty Loan appeals to immigrants who recently came to the United States.

Hands-On Chapter Project
Step 2

Presenting World War I

Step 2: Presenting the Home Front at the Start of the War Ask: What actions did the United States take to mobilize for the war?

Directions Explain to students that they will create one to three multimedia slides or screens to explain the actions the United States took to mobilize for war. Divide students into two teams. The first team should focus on the mobilization of the military. The second team should focus on the mobilization of industry and the workforce. (In both groups, further division might be made between those responsible for boiling down the literal explanation and those finding graphic/visual elements.)

Putting It Together When the two teams meet to finalize the choices for the slides, they will determine how the selected slides demonstrate the preparations of the United States for war. **OL**

(Chapter Project continued on page 337)

S Skill Practice

Using Geography Skills
Provide students with a map of the Untied States and have them locate the major cities affected by the Great Migration. **Ask:** Why do you think these cities attracted so many African Americans? *(the cities offered job opportunities and less discrimination)* **OL**

D Differentiated Instruction

Special Education Listening in class to several World War I songs, such as "Over There," "Pack Up Your Troubles in Your Old Kit Bag," and "Keep the Home Fires Burning," may provide an opportunity to engage students who have difficulty relating to the content in more traditional ways. Have students listen to the songs and prompt them to discuss their understanding of the lyrics. **BL**

✔ Reading Check

Answer:
to make it illegal to interfere with the war effort

Differentiated Instruction

For an example of government efforts to promote patriotism, read "The American's Creed" on page R51 in **Documents in American History.**

Women Support Industry With large numbers of men in the military, employers were willing to hire women for jobs that had traditionally been limited to men. Some one million women joined the workforce for the first time during the war, and another 8 million switched to higher paying industrial jobs. Women worked in factories, shipyards, and railroad yards and served as police officers, mail carriers, and train engineers.

The wartime changes in female employment were not permanent. When the war ended, most women returned to their previous jobs or stopped working. Although the changes were temporary, they demonstrated that women were capable of holding jobs that many had believed only men could do.

The Great Migration Begins Women were not the only group in American society to benefit economically. Desperate for workers, Henry Ford sent company agents to the South to recruit African Americans. Other companies quickly followed Ford's example. Their promises of high wages and plentiful work convinced between 300,000 and 500,000 African Americans to leave the South and move to northern cities.

This massive population movement became known as the "Great Migration." It greatly altered the racial makeup of such cities as Chicago, New York, Cleveland, and Detroit. It would also, eventually, change American politics. In the South, African Americans were generally denied the right to vote, but in the northern cities they were able to vote and affect the policies of northern politicians.

Mexican Americans Head North The war also encouraged other groups to **migrate.** Continuing political turmoil in Mexico and the wartime labor shortage in the United States convinced many Mexicans to head north. Between 1917 and 1920, over 100,000 Mexicans migrated into the Southwest, providing labor for farmers and ranchers.

Meanwhile, Mexican Americans found new opportunities in factory jobs in Chicago, St. Louis, Omaha, and other cities. Many faced hostility and discrimination when they arrived in American cities. Like other immigrant groups before them, they tended to settle in their own separate neighborhoods, called barrios, where they could support each other.

Shaping Public Opinion

Progressives did not think that organizing the economy was enough to ensure the success of the war effort. They also believed the government needed to shape public opinion.

Selling the War Eleven days after asking Congress to declare war, President Wilson created the **Committee on Public Information** (CPI) to "sell" the war to the American people. Headed by George Creel, a journalist, the CPI recruited advertising executives, artists, authors, songwriters, entertainers, public speakers, and motion picture companies to help sway public opinion in favor of the war.

The CPI distributed pamphlets and arranged for thousands of short patriotic talks, called "four-minute speeches," to be delivered at movie theaters and other public places. Some 75,000 speakers, known as Four-Minute Men, urged audiences to support the war in various ways, from buying war bonds to reporting draft dodgers to the authorities.

Civil Liberties Curtailed Besides using propaganda, the government also passed legislation to limit opposition to the war and fight **espionage,** or spying to acquire government information. The Espionage Act of 1917 made it illegal to aid the enemy, give false reports, or interfere with the war effort. The Sedition Act of 1918 made it illegal to speak against the war publicly. In practice, it allowed officials to prosecute anyone who criticized the government. These two laws led to over 1,000 convictions.

Wartime fears also led to attacks on German Americans, labor activists, socialists, and pacifists. Ads urged Americans to monitor their fellow citizens. Americans even formed private groups, such as the American Protective League and the Boy Spies of America, to spy on neighbors and coworkers.

Despite protests, the Espionage and Sedition Acts were upheld in court. Although the First Amendment specifically states that "Congress shall make no law . . . abridging the freedom of speech, or of the press," the Supreme Court departed from a strict literal interpretation of the Constitution. The Court ruled that the government could restrict speech when the words constitute a "clear and present danger."

✔ Reading Check **Explaining** Why did Congress pass the Espionage Act in 1917?

Leveled Activities

Can Government Limit Free Speech?

★ *Schenck* v. *United States*, 1919
★ *Abrams* v. *United States*, 1919

Background to the Cases

In the fall of 1917, Charles Schenck mailed pamphlets to draftees telling them the draft was wrong and urging them to write protest letters. In August 1918, Jacob Abrams wrote pamphlets denouncing the war and criticizing the decision to send troops to Russia to fight communist forces. Both men were convicted of violating the Espionage Act. Both appealed their convictions all the way to the Supreme Court.

How the Court Ruled

The Schenck and Abrams cases raised the question: Are there some circumstances in which the First Amendment's protection of free speech no longer applies? In both cases, the Supreme Court upheld the Espionage Act, concluding that under certain circumstances, the government can indeed limit free speech. In the Schenck case, the Supreme Court decision was unanimous, but in the Abrams case, the Court split 7-2 in their decision.

▲ Eugene Debs, leader of the American Socialist Party, delivers a speech protesting the war in Canton, Ohio, in 1918. Debs was arrested for making the speech and convicted under the Espionage Act. He appealed to the Supreme Court, but the Court upheld his conviction, citing the *Schenck* case as the precedent.

PRIMARY SOURCE

The Court's Opinion

"The most stringent protection of free speech would not protect a man in falsely shouting fire in a theatre and causing a panic.... The question in every case is whether the words used are used in such circumstances and are of such a nature as to create a clear and present danger that they will bring about the substantive evils that Congress has a right to prevent. It is a question of proximity and degree. When a nation is at war, many things that might be said in time of peace are such a hindrance to its effort that their utterance will not be endured so long as men fight, and that no Court could regard them as protected by any constitutional right."

—Justice Oliver Wendell Holmes writing for the Court in *Schenck* v. *U.S.*

PRIMARY SOURCE

Dissenting Views

"It is only the present danger of immediate evil or an intent to bring it about that warrants Congress in setting a limit to the expression of opinion where private rights are not concerned.... Now nobody can suppose that the surreptitious publishing of a silly leaflet by an unknown man, without more, would present any immediate danger that its opinions would hinder the success of the government arms....

... the ultimate good desired is better reached by free trade in ideas—that the best test of truth is the power of the thought to get itself accepted in the competition of the market ..."

—Justice Oliver Wendell Holmes dissenting in *Abrams* v. *U.S.*

Teach

Use the library or Internet to find a copy of the speech delivered by Eugene V. Debs that led to his arrest and conviction under the Espionage Act. Make copies and distribute them to students. Ask students to read the speech and highlight the passages that they think might have been considered to be in violation of the Espionage Act. Then, ask students to write an essay explaining whether or not they believe Debs broke the law.

DBQ Document Based Questions

Answers:
1. when the nation is at war
2. Being able to discuss ideas and opinions openly; answers will vary.
3. Schenck's pamphlets were a direct attempt to undermine the American war effort; Abrams was expressing his opinions of the war and criticizing a government decision.

DBQ Document-Based Questions

1. **Explaining** When does Holmes think the government can restrict speech?
2. **Analyzing** What does Holmes mean by referring to the "free trade in ideas?" Do you think the government should ever be allowed to restrict free speech? Why or why not?
3. **Making Inferences** Why do you think Holmes regarded *Schenck* as a much more immediate danger than *Abrams*? What was the difference between their actions?

Extending the Content

Defending Free Speech Not all Americans were caught up in the wartime frenzy. Some spoke out against the espionage and sedition laws and what they considered violations of free speech. Senator Robert La Follette and Professor Zechariah Chafee, Jr., of Harvard Law School, openly defended Americans' rights to exercise freedom of speech with regard to war. The newly formed Civil Liberties Union assisted pacifists and conscientious objectors who had been subjected to ridicule and abuse. Professor Chafee explained that he believed that the Framers of the First Amendment intended "to wipe out the common law of sedition, and make further prosecutions for criticism of the government, without any incitement to law breaking, forever impossible in the United States of America." Most Americans, however, gave little thought to restrictions on speech and supported the war without questioning the rights they were giving up.

Building the Military

MAIN Idea The United States instituted a draft for military service, and African Americans and women took on new roles.

HISTORY AND YOU Describe a time you were required to do something that you might not have done otherwise. Read on to learn about the selective service system.

Progressives did not abandon their ideas when it came to building up the military. Instead, they applied their ideas and developed a new system for recruiting a large army.

Volunteers and Conscripts

When the United States entered the war in 1917, the army and National Guard together had slightly more than 300,000 troops. Many men volunteered after war was declared, but many more were still needed.

R **Selective Service** Many progressives believed that conscription—forced military service—was a violation of democratic and republican principles. Believing a **draft** was necessary, however, Congress, with Wilson's support, created a new conscription system called **selective service.**

Instead of having the military run the draft from Washington, D.C., the Selective Service Act of 1917 required all men between 21 and 30 to register for the draft. A lottery randomly determined the order in which they were called before a local draft board in charge of selecting or exempting people from military service.

The thousands of local boards were the heart of the system. The members of the draft boards were civilians from local communities. Progressives believed local people, understanding community needs, would know which men to draft and would do a far better job than a centralized government bureaucracy. Eventually about 2.8 million Americans were drafted.

Volunteers for War Not all American soldiers were drafted. Approximately 2 million men volunteered for military service. Some had heard stories of German atrocities and wanted to fight back. Others believed democracy was at stake. Many believed they had a duty to respond to their nation's call. They had **D**

PRIMARY SOURCE
African Americans in World War I

During World War I, the U.S. Army kept most African American soldiers out of combat, assigning them to work as cooks, laborers, and laundrymen. The 369th Regiment, however, was assigned to the French Army and was sent to frontline trenches almost immediately. Nicknamed the "Harlem Hell-Fighters," the entire 369th was awarded the French Croix de Guerre ("war cross"), for gallantry in combat. The regiment spent 191 days in the trenches, much longer than many other units, and suffered 1,500 casualties.

▼ *African American soldiers march near Verdun, France, November 1918.*

▲ *A 1918 poster commemorates the 369th Regiment—the first Americans to see combat in World War I.*

Analyzing VISUALS

1. **Theorizing** Why do you think the French were willing to use African Americans in combat?
2. **Analyzing** Why do you think the poster includes a quote from Abraham Lincoln?

Activity: Collaborative Learning

Planning Promotional Campaigns
Organize students into four groups. Have one group create a plan to promote conscription; another group plan to promote food conservation; a third group to rouse support for the war effort among business and labor organizations; and a fourth group to plan to promote pacifism or opposition to the war. Have each group research its topic and then choose a spokesperson to present the plan. Make sure students find an appropriate way to divide and complete the work. **OL BL**

grown up listening to stories of the Civil War and the Spanish-American War. They saw World War I as a great adventure and wanted to fight for their country.

Although the horrors of war soon became apparent to the American troops, their morale remained high, helping to ensure victory. More than 50,000 Americans died in combat and over 200,000 were wounded. Another 60,000 soldiers died from disease, mostly from the influenza epidemic of 1918 and 1919.

The flu epidemic was not limited to the battlefield. It spread around the world and made more than a quarter of all Americans sick. The disease killed an estimated 25–50 million people worldwide, including more than 500,000 Americans.

African Americans in the War Of the nearly 400,000 African Americans who were drafted, about 42,000 served overseas as combat troops. African American soldiers encountered discrimination and prejudice in the army, where they served in racially segregated units, almost always under the supervision of white officers.

Despite these challenges, many African American soldiers fought with distinction. For example, the African American 92nd and 93rd Infantry Divisions fought in bitter battles along the Western Front. Many of them won praise from both the French commander, Marshal Henri Pétain, and the United States commander, General John Pershing.

Women Join the Military

World War I was the first war in which women officially served in the armed forces, although only in noncombat positions. As the military prepared for war in 1917, it faced a severe shortage of clerical workers because so many men were assigned to active duty. Early in 1917, the navy authorized the enlistment of women to meet its clerical needs.

Women serving in the navy wore a standard uniform and were assigned the rank of yeoman. By the end of the war, over 11,000 women had served in the navy. Although most performed clerical duties, others served as radio operators, electricians, pharmacists, chemists, and photographers.

Unlike the navy, the army refused to enlist women. Instead, it began hiring women as temporary employees to fill clerical jobs. The only women to actually serve in the army were in the Army Nursing Corps.

Women nurses had served in both the army and navy since the early 1900s, but as auxiliaries. They were not assigned ranks, and were not technically enlisted in the army or navy. Army nurses were the only women in the military sent overseas during the war. More than 20,000 nurses served in the Army Nursing Corps during the war, including more than 10,000 overseas.

✓ Reading Check **Describing** How did Congress ensure that the United States would have enough troops to serve in World War I?

Section 2 REVIEW

Vocabulary
1. **Explain** the significance of: War Industries Board, victory gardens, National War Labor Board, Committee on Public Information, espionage, selective service.

Main Ideas
2. **Examining** How did government efforts to ensure public support for the war conflict with ideas about civil rights?

3. **Describing** What were the contributions of African Americans during the war?

Critical Thinking
4. **Big Ideas** How did progressives use their ideas to mobilize both the economy and the American people during the war?

5. **Organizing** Use a graphic organizer similar to the one below to identify the effects of the war on the American workforce.

U.S. Groups	Effects
Women	
African Americans	
Hispanics	

6. **Analyzing Visuals** Examine the graph on page 329. How much did World War I cost? Do you think the government should rely on taxes or loans to fund a war? Explain.

Writing About History
7. **Persuasive Writing** Imagine that you are working for the Committee on Public Information. Write text for an advertisement or lyrics to a song in which you attempt to sway public opinion in favor of the war.

History ONLINE
Study Central™ To review this section, go to glencoe.com and click on Study Central.

333

Writing Support
Narrative Writing Have students write a one-page paper that describes the gains for women due to World War I and the limitations they still faced. **OL**

Assess

History ONLINE

Study Central™ provides summaries, interactive games, and online graphic organizers to help students review content.

Close

Summarizing Ask: How did World War I affect America on the home front? *(the government managed the economy; civil liberties were curtailed; African Americans moved to northern cities; many Mexicans migrated to the United States)* **OL**

✓ **Reading Check**

Answer:
The United States initiated the draft.

Section 2 REVIEW

Answers

1. All definitions can be found in the section and the Glossary.

2. The government passed the Espionage and Sedition Acts. These acts made it illegal to print information opposed to the war or speak against the war publicly. These provisions curtailed First Amendment freedoms.

3. Most African Americans served in support services, but some served alongside French troops against the Germans. At home, African Americans supported the war effort by working in factories.

4. Progressives established agencies such as the War Industries Board and the National War Labor Board and created the Committee on Public Information to sell the war.

5. women: worked in jobs that had been traditionally held by men, joined the navy, served as army nurses; African Americans: moved to Northern cities for more opportunities, served in the military; Hispanics: migrated to the United States and Mexican Americans moved to industrial cities.

6. About $32 billion; answers will vary, but students should support their opinions with examples.

7. Students' advertisements or lyrics will vary.

ANALYZING PRIMARY SOURCES

Focus

Propaganda is defined as material disseminated by the advocates or opponents of a doctrine or cause, such as *wartime propaganda*. During World War I, both sides used propaganda to increase support for the war.

Teach

C Critical Thinking

Analyzing Primary Sources
Have students study Primary Source 1. **Ask:** What connection is the poster attempting to make? *(It compares Pershing's army to the Crusaders of the Middle Ages.)* **OL**

R Reading Strategy

Inferring Have students read Primary Source 3. **Ask:** What clear distinction is the author making between "Germans, and a German"? *(The Germans, as a nation, are the enemy, but individual Germans are human beings with feelings and families, not much different from Americans.)* **OL**

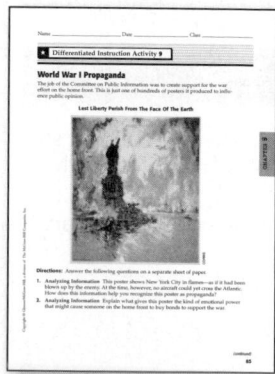

Differentiated Instruction

Differentiated Instruction Activity 16, URB pp. 85–86

ANALYZING PRIMARY SOURCES

Propaganda in World War I

All of the warring nations in World War I used propaganda to boost support for their side. Many Americans believed the propaganda coming from Europe, particularly from the British government and press. When the United States entered the war, the American government also began using propaganda in an attempt to unite Americans behind the war effort.

Read the passages and study the posters. Then answer the questions that follow.

PRIMARY SOURCE 2

Government War Bond Advertisement, 1918

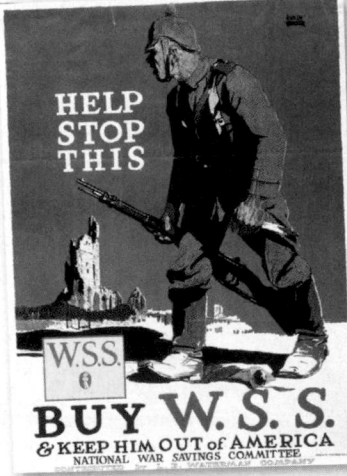

PRIMARY SOURCE 1

Movie Poster, 1918

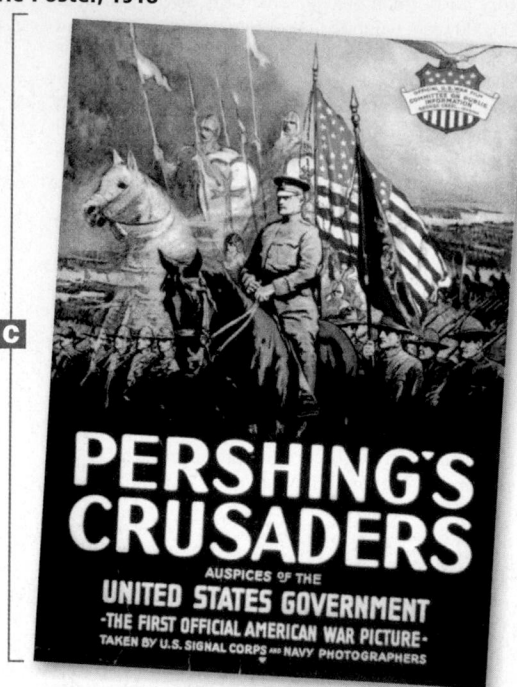

PRIMARY SOURCE 3

American Soldier's Diary, 1918

"Germans, and a German—so different. Fishing through the poor torn pockets of shabby German body, drooped over wreck of machine gun, to find well-thumbed photograph of woman and little boy and little girl—so like one's own . . . impossible to hate what had been that body.

Nothing so revolting as bitter, pitiless cruelty of those who know nothing of reality of it all. Those . . . Germano-baiters at home, so much more cruel than those who have the right—and are not."

—Diary of Lieutenant Howard V. O'Brien, October 6, 1918

Analyzing Propaganda: Support for World War I

Objective: To analyze propaganda.

Focus: Discuss how propaganda is used to sway public opinion.

Teach: Explain the propaganda techniques used on this page and in the activity.

Assess: Ask students whether they think propaganda is an appropriate way to influence opinion.

Close: Discuss how propaganda is still used today and give recent examples.

Differentiated Instruction Strategies

BL Explain the purpose of each piece of propaganda on pages 334–335 and in the activity.

AL Research Axis propaganda used in World War I. How is it different from Allied propaganda? Focus on symbolism and ideology.

ELL Describe the pictures used in the posters. What effect do they produce?

PRIMARY SOURCE 4

Newspaper Column, *New York Times*, May 1915

▼ *Great Britain established the Bryce Committee to investigate German atrocities in Belgium. Its findings, released just five days after the sinking of the Lusitania, increased anti-German sentiment in the United States. Investigations after the war, however, found that many of the stories were false or gross exaggerations.*

GERMAN ATROCITIES ARE PROVED, FINDS BRYCE COMMITTEE

Not Only Individual Crimes, but Premeditated Slaughter in Belgium.

YOUNG AND OLD MUTILATED

Women Attacked, Children Brutally Slain, Arson and Pillage Systematic.

COUNTENANCED BY OFFICERS

Wanton Firing on Red Cross and White Flag; Prisoners and Wounded Shot.

CIVILIANS USED AS SHIELDS

Proof That Belgians Did Not Fire on Germans at Louvain—Germans Received Kindness.

PRIMARY SOURCE 5

U.S. Government Pamphlet, 1918

"Fear, perhaps, is rather an important element to be bred in the civilian population. It is difficult to unite a people by talking only on the highest ethical plane. To fight for an ideal, perhaps, must be coupled with thoughts of self-preservation. So a truthful appeal to the fear of men, the recognition of the terrible things that would happen if the German Government were permitted to retain its prestige, may be necessary in order that all people unite in the support of the needed sacrifices."

—Pamphlet for speakers from the Committee on Public Information, quoted in the *New York Times*, February 4, 1918

PRIMARY SOURCE 6

American Red Cross Poster, c. 1916

CIVILIZATION VS. BARBARISM

FOR HUMANITY'S SAKE SAVE A LIFE - RED CROSS WEEK JUNE 18TH TO 25TH.

DBQ Document-Based Questions

1. **Explaining** Examine Primary Source 1. What is the underlying message behind the poster for "Pershing's Crusaders"?

2. **Identifying** What images of the Germans do Primary Sources 2 and 6 promote?

3. **Analyzing** Study Primary Source 4. How do you think stories of German atrocities affected American neutrality?

4. **Making Connections** Read Primary Sources 3 and 5. Why do you think the government used propaganda? Do you think propaganda is a good idea in wartime?

5. **Evaluating** According to Primary Sources 2, 5, and 6, what is at stake in the war? What should citizens do to help the war effort?

Assess/Close

C Critical Thinking

Drawing Conclusions Have students read Primary Source 5. **Ask:** What message is being given by this pamphlet excerpt? *(that fear is to be used to turn public opinion against the Germans and keep the public united in supporting the war)* **OL**

R Reading Strategy

Summarizing Have students review Primary Sources 4 and 6. **Ask:** What is the common message of these primary sources? *(That the Germans are barbarians and must be defeated.)* **OL**

Document Based Questions

Answers

DBQ Document Based Questions

1. The fight against the Germans is righteous.
2. The Germans are barbarians.
3. The stories of German atrocities made it difficult, if not impossible, to remain neutral.
4. to sway public opinion in favor of the war; answers will vary

5. German barbarism would dominate the world; citizens should support the war, buy war bonds, and give blood.

Focus

Section 3

Bellringer

Daily Focus Transparency 9.3

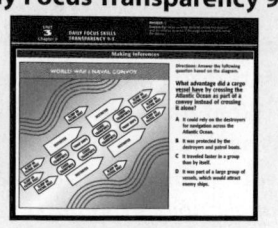

Guide to Reading

Answers may include: airplanes, poison gas, machine guns, trenches, tanks

Section Spotlight Video

To generate student interest and provide a springboard for class discussion, access the Chapter 9, Section 3 video at glencoe.com or on the video DVD.

Resource Manager

Section 3

A Bloody Conflict

Guide to Reading

Big Ideas
Individual Action American troops played a major role in helping end the war.

Content Vocabulary
• convoy *(p. 339)*
• armistice *(p. 341)*
• national self-determination *(p. 342)*
• reparations *(p. 344)*

Academic Vocabulary
• network *(p. 336)*
• adequately *(p. 339)*
• resolve *(p. 342)*

People and Events to Identify
• no-man's-land *(p. 336)*
• John J. Pershing *(p. 340)*
• Treaty of Versailles *(p. 342)*
• Fourteen Points *(p. 342)*
• League of Nations *(p. 343)*

Reading Strategy
Organizing Complete a graphic organizer similar to the one below by listing the kinds of warfare and technology used in the fighting.

Technology caused both sides to lose millions of men during World War I. The arrival of American troops helped the Allies win, but the peace treaty set the stage for another war to come.

Combat in World War I

MAIN Idea New technologies made World War I the first modern war.

HISTORY AND YOU What new technologies have been developed or proposed in your lifetime? Read on to learn about the weapons that World War I personnel faced.

By the spring of 1917, World War I had devastated Europe. Old-fashioned strategies and new technologies resulted in terrible destruction. Many Americans believed, however, that their troops would make a difference and quickly bring the war to an end.

Trench Warfare

Early offensives in 1914 demonstrated that warfare had changed. Powerful artillery guns were placed several miles behind the front lines. From there, they hurled huge explosive shells onto the battlefield. More people were killed by artillery fire than by any other weapon in World War I. Artillery fire produced horrific scenes of death and destruction, as one American noted in his diary:

PRIMARY SOURCE

"Many dead Germans along the road. One heap on a manure pile. . . . Devastation everywhere. Our barrage has rooted up the entire territory like a ploughed field. Dead horses galore, many of them have a hind quarter cut off—the Huns [Germans] need food. Dead men here and there."

—quoted in *The American Spirit*

To protect themselves from artillery, troops began digging trenches. On the Western Front—where German troops confronted French, British, and Belgian forces—the troops dug a **network** of trenches that stretched from the English Channel to the Swiss border. To prevent the enemy from overrunning the trenches, troops relied upon a new weapon, the machine gun, to hold off the attackers. The space between opposing trenches was called **no-man's-land.** It was a rough barren landscape filled with craters from artillery fire. To prevent troops from crossing no-man's-land, both sides built barbed wire entanglements and obstacles in front of their trenches.

R Reading Strategies	**C** Critical Thinking	**D** Differentiated Instruction	**W** Writing Support	**S** Skill Practice
Teacher Edition • Analyzing, p. 337 • Analyzing Text Structure, p. 338 **Additional Resources** • Guid. Read. Act., URB p. 110 • Primary Source Reading, URB p. 99	**Teacher Edition** • Drawing Conclusions, p. 344 • Det. Cause and Effect, p. 339 • Making Inferences, pp. 340, 344 **Additional Resources** • Quizzes and Tests, p. 121 • Linking Past and Present, URB p. 96	**Teacher Edition** • Visual/Spatial, p. 343 **Additional Resources** • Interpreting Pol. Cartoons, URB p. 103	**Teacher Edition** • Narrative Writing, p. 341 • Descriptive Writing, pp. 338, 340, 343 • Expository Writing, pp. 339, 342	**Teacher Edition** • Visual Literacy, p. 340 • Ident. Point of View, p. 345 **Additional Resources** • Time Line Act., URB p. 95 • RENTG, p. 94

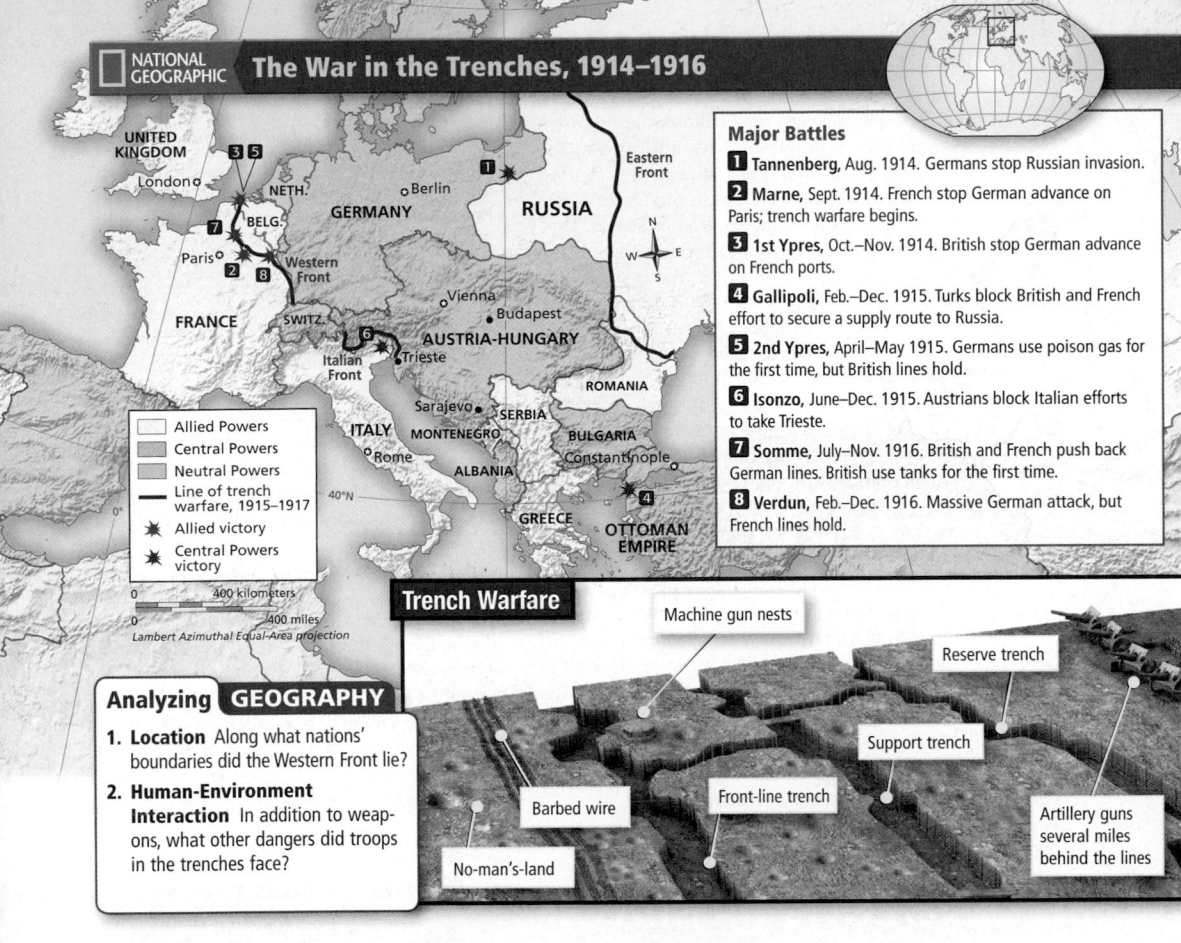

NATIONAL GEOGRAPHIC The War in the Trenches, 1914–1916

Major Battles

1 **Tannenberg,** Aug. 1914. Germans stop Russian invasion.

2 **Marne,** Sept. 1914. French stop German advance on Paris; trench warfare begins.

3 **1st Ypres,** Oct.–Nov. 1914. British stop German advance on French ports.

4 **Gallipoli,** Feb.–Dec. 1915. Turks block British and French effort to secure a supply route to Russia.

5 **2nd Ypres,** April–May 1915. Germans use poison gas for the first time, but British lines hold.

6 **Isonzo,** June–Dec. 1915. Austrians block Italian efforts to take Trieste.

7 **Somme,** July–Nov. 1916. British and French push back German lines. British use tanks for the first time.

8 **Verdun,** Feb.–Dec. 1916. Massive German attack, but French lines hold.

Allied Powers
Central Powers
Neutral Powers
Line of trench warfare, 1915–1917
Allied victory
Central Powers victory

400 kilometers
400 miles
Lambert Azimuthal Equal-Area projection

Analyzing GEOGRAPHY

1. **Location** Along what nations' boundaries did the Western Front lie?

2. **Human-Environment Interaction** In addition to weapons, what other dangers did troops in the trenches face?

Trench Warfare

Machine gun nests

Reserve trench

Support trench

Front-line trench

Artillery guns several miles behind the lines

Barbed wire

No-man's-land

To break through enemy lines, the attacker would begin with a massive artillery barrage. Soldiers would then scramble out of their trenches, race across no-man's-land while enemy machine guns fired at them, and try to capture the enemy's trenches.

Before charging enemy trenches, troops fixed bayonets—long knives—to their rifles. For those troops that made it across no-man's-land, fighting in the trenches was brutal. Troops threw grenades—small bombs—at each other, and used bayonets, rifle butts, knives, axes, pistols and even rocks and fists to kill the enemy.

The results of this kind of warfare were horrific. In major battles, both sides often lost hundreds of thousands of men, yet neither side was able to break through the other's lines.

New Technology

New technologies were needed to break through enemy lines. In April 1915, the Germans first used poison gas in the Second Battle of Ypres. The fumes caused vomiting, blindness, and suffocation. Soon afterward the Allies also began using gas. To counter gas attacks, both sides developed gas masks.

In late 1915, the British introduced the armored tank into battle. These tanks were slow and mechanically unreliable, but they could crush barbed wire and cross trenches. Unfortunately, there were not enough of them. The tanks could support the troops, but they did not revolutionize warfare in World War I. By the time World War II broke out, however, tanks had replaced cavalry in most modern armies and made trench warfare obsolete.

Chapter 9 World War I and Its Aftermath **337**

Teach

R **Reading Strategy**

Analyzing Tell students to read the description of trench warfare. **Ask:** Why were casualty rates so high in World War I? *(Troops crossing the open spaces between trenches known as "no-man's land" were easily gunned down by enemy fire.)* **BL**

Did You Know?

Corpses left in trenches, as well as food scraps, attracted many rats. Since rats propagate rapidly (one pair of rats can produce 880 offspring in a year), the trenches soon became infested. The rats became large and bold and would even eat a wounded man if he could not defend himself.

Analyzing GEOGRAPHY

Answers:

1. France, Germany, and Belgium

2. disease; poor sanitary conditions; weather exposure

Hands-On Chapter Project
Step 3

Presenting World War I

Step 3: Presenting the Battles and Victories of World War I
Ask: What were the crucial factors that led to a victory in the war?

Directions Explain to students that they will create one to three multimedia slides or screens to describe the factors that led to an Allied victory in the war. Divide students into two teams. The first team should focus on the battles and the factors that led to

military victories. The second team should focus on the victory and the peace that followed. (In both groups, further division might be made between those responsible for boiling down the literal explanation and those finding graphic/visual elements.)

Putting It Together When the two teams meet to finalize the choices for the slides, they will determine how to illustrate the battles of the war and the peace that followed. **OL**

(Chapter Project continued on page 349)

W Writing Support

Descriptive Writing Have students use library or Internet resources to find out more about one of the weapons first used in World War I. Then have students write a paragraph describing this weapon in use as if they are seeing it for the first time. **BL**

R Reading Strategy

Analyzing Text Structures
Ask students to define the word *convoy* as both a noun and a verb. (noun: a group of cars, trucks, or ships traveling together; verb: to escort or guide) **Ask:** Where do you typically see convoys today? (*trucks traveling together on the highway*) **BL**

✔ Reading Check

Answer:
poison gas, tanks, zeppelins, airplanes

Additional Support

World War I also marked the first use of aircraft in war. In addition, it was the first and last time that zeppelins were used in combat. Zeppelins are giant rigid balloons, also known as blimps or dirigibles. Early in the war, the Germans sent squadrons of zeppelins to drop bombs on British warships in the North Sea.

At first, airplanes were used as scouts. They flew over enemy territory, as well as the English Channel and the North Sea, spying on enemy troops and ships. Before long, however, the Allies equipped them with machine guns to attack the German zeppelin fleet. The machine guns were timed to fire through the aircraft's propeller as it spun so that the bullets did not hit the propeller. A few airplanes even carried rockets to destroy the zeppelins. Others carried small bombs to drop on enemy lines.

As technology advanced, aircraft were used to shoot down other aircraft. Battles between aircraft became known as dogfights. Early military aircraft were difficult to fly and easy to destroy. The wings and body frame were covered in cloth and easily caught fire. Pilots did not carry parachutes. The average life expectancy of a combat pilot in World War I was about two weeks.

✔ **Reading Check** **Describing** What new technologies were introduced in World War I?

The Americans Arrive

MAIN Idea The arrival of Americans changed the course of the war and helped the Allies win.

HISTORY AND YOU Have you ever had to boost someone's morale? Read on to learn about Americans who helped the Allies win World War I.

Waves of American troops marched into this bloody stalemate—nearly 2 million before the war's end. Although the "doughboys," as American soldiers were nicknamed, were inexperienced, they were fresh and eager to fight. Their presence boosted the morale of Allied forces. It also demoralized the German soldiers, who now faced large numbers of fresh troops. As the Americans began to arrive, many in Germany concluded that the war was lost.

Winning the War at Sea

No American troopships were sunk on their way to Europe thanks to the efforts of American Admiral William S. Sims. The British preferred to fight German submarines by sending warships to find them, while merchant ships would race across the Atlantic individually. This approach enabled German submarines to inflict heavy losses on British shipping. Sims

TECHNOLOGY & HISTORY

New Weapons World War I is often called the first modern war because troops used new technology that is still widely used in warfare today. Much of this new technology developed in response to trench warfare.

◄ **Artillery Forces Troops into Trenches**
Australian soldiers load an artillery shell during the Battle of Passchendaele in 1917. Powerful long-range artillery fire from guns like this forced troops to build trenches for protection.

▲ **Machine Guns Defend Trenches**
Machine guns made it very difficult to capture enemy trenches. They could fire thousands of bullets per minute. A small team with a machine gun could down hundreds of troops crossing open terrain. This photo shows a German machine gun crew.

338

Extending the Content

Flying Aces Three pilots who flew bombers in World War I were among the best-known fighters of the war. American Eddie Rickenbacker shot down 22 planes during the war. Using a daring method, Rickenbacker flew extremely close to enemy planes before firing his guns. He often returned from dogfights with his own plane riddled with bullets. After the war, Rickenbacker settled into the automobile industry and started the Rickenbacker Motor Company.

Flying aces from other countries also became famous. Manfred von Richthofen of Germany, known as the "Red Baron," was credited with 80 victories. As von Richthofen's fame spread he increasingly became the target of Allied warplanes, and on April 21, 1918, he was shot down and killed. His body was recovered by British forces, who buried him with full military honors.

Frenchman René Fonck was credited with 75 victories in World War I. He closely studied the methods of enemy pilots and strictly conserved ammunition during fights—tactics that aided him in his victories. After the war, Fonck worked as a demonstration pilot and an inspector of fighter aviation within the French Air Force.

proposed that merchant ships and troop transports be gathered into groups, called **convoys.** Small highly maneuverable warships called destroyers would protect and escort the convoys across the Atlantic.

Convoys also saved lives. If a ship was sunk, other ships in the convoy could rescue survivors. The system worked. Convoys greatly reduced shipping losses and ensured that a large number of American troops arrived safely in Europe in time to help stop Germany's last great offensive on the Western Front.

Russia Leaves the War

In March 1917, riots broke out in Russia over the government's handling of the war and the scarcity of food and fuel. Czar Nicholas II, the leader of the Russian Empire, abdicated his throne. This marked the beginning of the Russian Revolution.

Political leadership in Russia passed to a provisional, or temporary, government. The leaders of the provisional government wanted Russia to stay in the war. However, the government was unable to deal **adequately** with the major problems afflicting the nation, such as food shortages. The Bolshevik Party, led by Vladimir Lenin, overthrew the provisional government and established a Communist government in November 1917.

Germany's military fortunes improved with the Bolshevik takeover of Russia. Lenin's first act after seizing power was to pull Russia out of the war and concentrate on establishing a Communist state. Lenin agreed to the Treaty of Brest-Litovsk with Germany on March 3, 1918. Under this treaty, Russia lost substantial territory. It gave up the Ukraine, its Polish and Baltic territories, and Finland.

With the Eastern Front settled, Germany could now concentrate its forces in the west. German leaders knew this was their last chance to win. If the troops transferred from Russia could not break Allied lines, it was only a matter of time before Germany would have to surrender.

Americans Enter Combat

At the time World War I began, many Americans knew that the French had helped the United States during the American Revolution. American school children still learned the story of the Marquis de Lafayette, who had brought French officers to America to help train American soldiers and who had served on George Washington's staff during the Revolutionary War. Many Americans regarded the French people as friends and believed the nation owed the French a debt for their help in the revolution.

◀ **Poison Gas vs. Trenches** To break through trench lines, both sides began using poison gas. To protect against gas attacks, troops were forced to carry gas masks similar to those shown here worn by American soldiers in France in 1917.

▲ **Airplanes Bomb Trenches** Airplanes offered both sides a way to counter trench warfare. Several types of aircraft, including the British Sopwith Camel shown above, could carry 4–5 small bombs to drop on enemy artillery and trenches. They also attacked troops using their machine guns.

Tanks vs. Trenches ▶ To help capture trenches, the Allies built tanks that were immune to machine gun fire and able to smash through barbed wire. Tanks had tracks instead of wheels, enabling them to cross the mud and craters of no-man's-land.

Analyzing VISUALS
1. **Analyzing** Modern militaries do not use trench warfare. Which weapons pictured eventually ended the use of trenches?
2. **Synthesizing** Explain how the different technologies of World War I worked together to kill so many people.

339

Extending the Content

Gas Masks During World War I, soldiers were equipped with gas masks to protect them against poison gas attacks. So, too, were their horses. In his war diary, Lieutenant Robert Casey of the 124th Field Artillery described his experience:

"The horses wear gas masks also. . . . Neat little bundle perched atop the nose and soaked every time the animal takes a drink. A horse without a gas mask can live about five minutes. With a gas mask he can live about five minutes. It takes only about eleven minutes to convince the horse that he ought to wear the gas mask. And there you are."

C Critical Thinking

Making Inferences Remind students that almost all American troops who fought in World War I remained under American, rather than foreign, command. **Ask:** Why was it important for American troops to answer to American generals during the war? *(Answers will vary, but students might note that it helped build public support at home and gave U.S. commanders independence.)* **AL**

W Writing Support

Descriptive Writing Have students use library or Internet resources to find out more information about the Battle of Cantigny. Then have students assume the role of a newspaper reporter and write an article about the battle. **OL**

S Skill Practice

Visual Literacy Have students refer back to the photo of the Argonne Forest on pages 318 and 319. **Ask:** What conditions do you observe that would make fighting difficult? *(Answers might include fog, mud, and lack of cover.)* **OL**

Additional Support

When General **John J. Pershing,** commander of the American Expeditionary Force (AEF), arrived in Paris on July 4, 1917, he and his officers headed to Picpus Cemetery where Lafayette was buried. One of Pershing's officers, Colonel Charles E. Stanton, raised his hand in salute and proclaimed, "Lafayette, we are here!" France had helped the United States gain its freedom. Now American soldiers would help the French to preserve theirs.

When American troops began arriving in France, the British and French commanders wanted to integrate them into their armies under British and French command. Pershing refused, and President Wilson supported him. Pershing insisted that American soldiers fight in American units under American command.

Despite French and British pleas that they needed American soldiers to replace their own losses, Pershing held firm with one exception. The 93rd Infantry Division—an African American unit—was transferred to the French. Its soldiers became the first Americans to enter combat.

Germany's Last Offensive On March 21, 1918, the Germans launched a massive attack along the Western Front, beginning with gas attacks and a huge artillery bombardment. German forces, strengthened by reinforcements from the Russian front, pushed deep into Allied lines. By early June, they were less than 40 miles (64 km) from Paris.

American troops played an important role in containing the German offensive. In late May, as the German offensive continued, the Americans launched their first major attack, quickly capturing the village of Cantigny. On June 1, American and French troops blocked the German drive on Paris at the town of Château-Thierry. On July 15, the Germans launched one last massive attack in an attempt to take Paris, but American and French troops held their ground.

The Battle of the Argonne Forest With the German drive stalled, French Marshal Ferdinand Foch, supreme commander of the Allied forces, ordered massive counterattacks. In mid-September, American troops drove back German forces at the battle of Saint-Mihiel. Next, an American offensive was launched in the region between the Meuse River and the Argonne Forest. General Pershing

NATIONAL GEOGRAPHIC U.S. Battles, 1918

- Allied Powers
- Central Powers
- Neutral Powers
- ★ Allied victory
- → German spring offensive, 1918
- - - Limit of German advance, 1918
- — Line of trench warfare, 1915–1917
- — Armistice Line, 1918
- → American advances

assembled over 600,000 American troops, 40,000 tons of supplies, and roughly 4,000 artillery pieces for the most massive attack in American history.

The attack began on September 26, 1918. German positions slowly fell to the advancing American troops. The Germans inflicted heavy casualties, but by early November the Americans had shattered German defenses and opened a hole on the eastern flank of the German lines. Soon after, all across the Western Front, the Germans began to retreat.

American Heroes

Although the brutal trench warfare of World War I led to many acts of astonishing bravery, the actions of two Americans, Corporal Alvin York and Captain Eddie Rickenbacker, captured the nation's imagination.

Alvin York Born in 1887, Alvin York grew up poor in the mountains of Tennessee, where he learned to shoot by hunting wild game. Opposed to war, he initially tried to avoid the draft as a conscientious objector—a person who refuses to obey the law because of his moral or religious beliefs. As a Christian, York

---

Activity: Interdisciplinary Connection

Literature Explain that German author Erich Maria Remarque (1898–1970) served in the front line trenches during the Great War. In his 1929 novel *All Quiet on the Western Front,* he wrote of the devastation and cruelty of the war and life in the trenches. Have students read the following quote and ask them to paraphrase Remarque's words. **OL**

"The sun goes down, night comes, the shells whine, life is at an end.

Still the little piece of convulsed earth in which we lie is held. We have yielded no more than a few hundred yards of it as a prize to the enemy. But on every yard there lies a dead man."

PRIMARY SOURCE

Alvin York and the Battle of the Argonne Forest

October 8th 1918, Argonne Forest, France.

"So on the morning of the 8th, just before daylight, we started for the hill of Chattel Chehery. So before we got there it got light, and the Germans sent over a heavy barrage and also gas, and we put on our gas masks and just pressed right on through those shells and got to the top of hill 223.... [A]t the zero hour ... we done went over the top.... The Germans ... jes stopped us in our tracks. Their machine guns were up there on the heights overlooking us and well hidden, and we couldn't tell for certain where the terrible heavy fire was coming from.... So we decided to try and get them by a surprise attack in the rear.... So there was 17 of us boys went around on the left flank to see if we couldn't put those guns out of action."

—from *Sergeant York*

Map legend:
- town
- hill
- American advances
- Alvin York's unit
- U.S. lines, Oct. 4, 1918
- U.S. lines, Oct. 13, 1918
- German position that fired on York's men

Aincreville, Cunel Heights, Meuse River, Grandpré, Romagne Heights, Aisne R., Châtel-Chéhéry, Hill 223, Apremont, Aire R., Montfaucon, Varennes, Argonne Forest

0 4 kilometers
0 4 miles

DBQ Document-Based Questions

1. **Extrapolating** Why was the American victory in the Argonne Forest important?

2. **Explaining** What made capturing enemy positions in the Argonne Forest so difficult?

Maps In MOtion See *StudentWorks™ Plus* or glencoe.com.

believed he was not allowed to kill anyone. Eventually, he decided that he could fight in a war if the cause was just.

On October 8, 1918, during the Battle of the Argonne Forest, German machine guns on a fortified hill fired on York's platoon and killed nine men. York took command and charged the machine guns. By the end of the battle, York had killed between 9 and 25 Germans, captured the machine guns, and taken 132 prisoners. For his actions, he received the Medal of Honor and the French Croix de Guerre. After returning home, he used his fame to raise money for the Alvin York Institute—a school for poor Tennessee children.

Eddie Rickenbacker Born in Columbus, Ohio, Eddie Rickenbacker was a famous race car driver before the war. Rickenbacker's car-racing reflexes served him well as a combat pilot. He was named commander of the 94th Aero Squadron, the first all-American squadron to enter combat. In all, he fought in 134 air battles and shot down 26 aircraft, becoming the top American combat pilot. In one battle, he single-handedly fought seven

German aircraft—a feat for which he was later awarded the Congressional Medal of Honor.

The War Ends

While fighting raged along the Western Front, a revolution engulfed Austria-Hungary. In October 1918, Poland, Hungary, and Czechoslovakia declared independence. By early November, the governments of the Austro-Hungarian Empire and the Ottoman Empire had surrendered to the allies.

On November 3, sailors in Kiel, the main base of the German fleet, mutinied. Within days, groups of workers and soldiers seized power in other German towns. As the revolution spread, the German emperor decided to step down. On November 9, Germany became a republic. Two days later the government signed an **armistice**—a truce, or an agreement to stop fighting. At the 11th hour on the 11th day of the 11th month, 1918, the fighting stopped.

Reading Check **Interpreting** Why would Pershing want to keep U.S. soldiers in their own units?

W Writing Support

Narrative Writing Have interested students use library or Internet resources to find out more information about the abdication of the German emperor. Then have them write a one-page paper telling why he stepped down and fled to the Netherlands. Encourage volunteers to read their papers to the class. **OL**

DBQ Document Based Questions

Answers:
1. It caused the Germans to begin their final retreat.
2. The land was hilly and the forest was thick; the Germans also used gas.

✓ Reading Check

Answer:
to be sure the troops were following American commanders' orders

Additional Support

Extending the Content

Veterans Day The holiday that is now celebrated as Veterans Day originated in efforts to commemorate the armistice of November 11, 1918 that ended World War I. The first Armistice Day was observed the following year. On November 11, 1919, President Woodrow Wilson delivered the following address:

"The war showed us the strength of great nations acting together for high purposes, and the victory of arms foretells the enduring conquests which can be made in peace when nations act justly and in furtherance of the common interests of men. To us in America, the reflections of Armistice Day will be filled with solemn pride in the heroism of those who died in the country's service and with gratitude for the victory, both because of the thing from which it has freed us and because of the opportunity it has given

America to show her sympathy with peace and justice in the councils of the nations."

Most states designated November 11 as a legal holiday. In 1938, Armistice Day became a federal holiday. To extend recognition to the veterans of World War II and the Korean War, President Eisenhower signed into law a bill in 1954 that changed the name of the holiday to Veterans Day.

Read Wilson's "Fourteen Points" on page R52 in **Documents in American History.**

W Writing Support

Expository Writing Have interested students use library or Internet resources to create a database of the four leaders of the Allied nations. Instruct students to include the number of years each served as leader and any information on other international conflicts in which they were involved. Have students use the facts they gather to write a paragraph about the leader they feel was the most experienced. **AL**

C Critical Thinking

Making Inferences Have students define, in their own words, the idea of national self-determination. Discuss with the class how national self-determination played a role in Wilson's Fourteen Points and in the treaties that ended World War I. **Ask:** What groups today seek national self-determination? *(Answers will vary, but students might note the Kurds, Palestinians, Basques, Taiwanese, and the people of Kosovo.)*

Additional Support

A Flawed Peace

MAIN Idea The United States Senate refused to ratify the Treaty of Versailles and rejected the League of Nations.

HISTORY AND YOU How might your feelings toward a peace plan differ if you lived in a defeated country compared to a victorious country? Read on to learn why the U.S. Senate did not ratify the Treaty of Versailles.

Although the fighting stopped in November 1918, World War I was not over. A peace treaty had to be negotiated and signed. In January 1919, delegates from 27 countries traveled to France to attend the peace conference. The conference took place at the Palace of Versailles, near Paris, and the treaty with Germany that resulted came to be called the **Treaty of Versailles.** The conference also negotiated the Treaty of Saint-Germain, ending the war with Austria-Hungary.

Negotiations on the Treaty of Versailles lasted five months. The most important participants were the so-called "Big Four" of the Allies: President Wilson of the United States, British Prime Minister David Lloyd George, French Premier Georges Clemenceau, and Italian Prime Minister Vittorio Orlando.

Representatives from Russia were not invited to the conference. Wilson and the other Allied leaders refused to recognize Lenin's government as legitimate. At the time of the peace conference, a civil war was raging in Russia between communist and non-communist forces. In mid-1918, the United States, Great Britain, and Japan had sent troops to Russia to help the anti-communist forces. Nearly 15,000 American troops remained in Russia—which had been renamed the Soviet Union by the Bolsheviks—until the spring of 1920. By that time, it had become clear that the Bolsheviks had won the civil war.

The Fourteen Points

When President Wilson arrived in Paris in January 1919, he brought with him a peace plan known as the **Fourteen Points.** Wilson had presented the plan to Congress in January 1918 to explain the goals of the United States in the war. The president believed that if the Fourteen Points were implemented, they would establish the conditions for a lasting peace in Europe.

What Did President Wilson Want?

The Fourteen Points

1. End secret treaties and secret diplomacy among nations.
2. Guarantee freedom of navigation on the seas for all nations.
3. Create free trade among nations.
4. Reduce armed forces as much as possible consistent with domestic safety.
5. Settle all colonial claims fairly taking into account the views of both the colonial peoples and the imperial nations.
6. Evacuate German troops from Russia and restore all conquered territory.
7. Restore Belgium's independence.
8. Restore all French territory occupied by Germany, including Alsace-Lorraine.
9. Adjust Italy's borders based on where Italians live.
10. Divide Austria-Hungary into new nations for each ethnic group.
11. Base borders of the Balkan states on nationality.
12. Break up the Ottoman Empire and make Turkey a separate country.
13. Create an independent Poland.
14. Create a League of Nations.

The Fourteen Points were based on "the principle of justice to all peoples and nationalities." In the first five points, Wilson proposed to eliminate the causes of the war through free trade, freedom of the seas, disarmament, an impartial adjustment of colonial claims, and open diplomacy instead of secret agreements.

The next eight points addressed the right of **national self-determination.** This is the idea that the borders of countries should be based on ethnicity and national identity. A group of people who feel that they are a nation should be allowed to have their own country. Wilson and other supporters of national self-determination believed that when borders are not based on national identity, border disputes will occur and nations are more likely to go to war to **resolve** them.

The principle of national self-determination also meant that no nation should be allowed to keep territory taken from another nation. Wilson's Fourteen Points required the Central Powers to evacuate all of the countries invaded during the war. Wilson also wanted the territory

---

Activity: Collaborative Learning

Negotiating Have students hold a peace conference. Organize the class into four groups. Each group should participate as one of the Big Four nations. Structure the negotiations around Woodrow Wilson's Fourteen Points (see page R52). Tell students that they have the power to accept, amend, or reject each point and should confer within their group before negotiating with the other groups' members. **OL**

What Did the Allies Agree to Do?

Treaty of Versailles (peace with Germany)
- German troops will return all captured territory to Belgium, Russia, and France.
- Germany will be divided in two; some German territory will be given to Denmark, France, Poland, Czechoslovakia, and Belgium.
- Germany will be held responsible for all wartime losses and must pay reparations.
- Germany's army and navy will be limited in size. Germany cannot have an air force, and cannot have military forces west of the Rhine.

Treaty of Saint-Germain (peace with Austria)
- The Austro-Hungarian Empire is dissolved and replaced by the nation of Austria.
- Four new nations are recognized: Czechoslovakia, Hungary, Poland, and Yugoslavia.
- Austria may not unite with Germany; its army is limited to 30,000 men.

The Covenant of the League of Nations (included in both peace treaties above)
- Members agree to reduce armaments.
- Members agree to protect each other against aggression.
- Colonies of the Central Powers will now be supervised by League members.
- Parts of the Ottoman Empire will be made independent under League supervision.

NATIONAL GEOGRAPHIC **Changes in Europe, 1919**

Former Austria-Hungary boundary
Former German boundary
Former Russian boundary

0   500 kilometers
0   500 miles
Lambert Azimuthal Equal-Area projection

Analyzing VISUALS

1. **Comparing** How many of the Fourteen Points were accepted at the Paris Peace Conference?
2. **Analyzing** What nations received territory from the Austro-Hungarian Empire?

Maps In MOtion See *StudentWorks™ Plus* or glencoe.com.

of Alsace-Lorraine that Germany had taken in 1871 restored to France.

The fourteenth point was most important to Wilson. It called for the creation of a "general association of nations" that would later be called the **League of Nations.** The League's member nations would help preserve peace by pledging to respect and protect each other's territory and political independence. Wilson was so determined to get agreement on the League of Nations that he was willing to give up other goals in the Fourteen Points in exchange for support for the League.

The Treaty of Versailles

Wilson received an enthusiastic reception from crowds in Paris and other national capitals that he visited. Many people believed that the American intervention had brought an end to four grim years of war. Wilson's popularity in Europe put him in a strong negotiating position. He was delighted when the peace conference decided to use the Fourteen Points as the basis for negotiations.

Not everyone was impressed by President Wilson's ideas. Premier Clemenceau of France, in particular, wanted to punish the Germans for the suffering they had inflicted on the French people. He was also determined to end the German threat once and for all. Other Allied governments tended to agree.

Despite Wilson's hopes, the peace terms were harsh. The Treaty of Versailles, reluctantly signed by Germany on June 28, 1919, included many terms designed to punish and weaken Germany. Germany's armed forces were greatly reduced in size and Germany was not allowed to put troops west of the Rhine River—the region near the French border. The treaty also specifically blamed Germany for the war, stating that it had been caused by "the aggression of Germany."

W Writing Support

Descriptive Writing Have students find out more about the Treaty of Versailles. Ask students to use what they have learned to write one paragraph describing the terms of the treaty. Encourage students to include whether they believe the terms are fair or not. **BL**

D Differentiated Instruction

Visual/Spatial Distribute two outline maps of Europe to each member of the class. On one map, have students draw the boundaries of European nations in 1914, before World War I, and on the other map have students draw the boundaries in 1919, after the Treaty of Versailles. After students have completed their maps, discuss the changes in the borders. **AL**

Analyzing VISUALS

Answers:
1. nine
2. Austria, Hungary, Czechoslovakia, Poland, Romania, Yugoslavia, and Italy

Additional Support

Activity: Interdisciplinary Connection

Literature Ask interested students to use library and Internet resources to learn more about Wilson's trip to Paris in 1919 and the triumphant greeting he received. Be sure students identify the people who accompanied Wilson on this trip. Based on this information, students may write a one-act play depicting Wilson's arrival in Paris. After the play is complete, have students enact the play. **AL**

C₁ Critical Thinking

Drawing Conclusions Review with students the new nations that were created after World War I. **Ask: Is it important for all people of one ethnic group to have their own country?** *(Students might note that having common customs, traditions, religion, and language help unify people and prevent dissent.)* **OL**

C₂ Critical Thinking

Making Inferences Remind students that Wilson was not successful in getting the Allies to include freedom of the seas or free trade in the Treaty of Versailles. **Ask: Given Wilson's position at the peace conference, could he have pushed to get these issues addressed?** *(Answers will vary.)* **AL**

Analyzing VISUALS

Answers:
1. The Treaty of Versailles was beaten up and defeated.
2. International agreement will help maintain peace.

Additional Support

When the German government signed the treaty, it, in effect, acknowledged that Germany was guilty of causing the war. This allowed the Allies to demand that Germany pay **reparations**—monetary compensation for all of the war damage it had caused. A commission set up after the treaty was signed decided that Germany owed the Allies approximately $33 billion. This sum was far more than Germany could pay all at once and was intended to keep Germany's economy weak for a long time.

Wilson had somewhat better success in promoting national self-determination. Four empires were dismantled as a result of World War I and the peace negotiations: the Austro-Hungarian Empire, the Russian Empire, the German Empire, and the Ottoman Empire. The various peace treaties signed after the war created nine new nations in Europe: Austria, Czechoslovakia, Estonia, Finland, Hungary, Latvia, Lithuania, Poland and Yugoslavia. In general, the majority of people in these new countries were from one ethnic group.

National self-determination was not, however, applied to Germany. Both Poland and Czechoslovakia were given territory where the majority of the people were German. Germany was even split in two in order to give Poland access to the Baltic Sea. By leaving a large number of Germans living outside Germany, the Treaty of Versailles helped set the stage for a new series of crises in the 1930s.

The Treaty of Versailles did not address several of Wilson's Fourteen Points. It did not mention freedom of the seas or free trade. It also ignored Wilson's goal of a fair settlement of colonial claims. No colonial people in Asia or Africa were granted independence. Germany's colonies in Africa and the Middle East were placed under the supervision of Britain and France. Japan was given responsibility for Germany's colonies in East Asia.

The treaty also stated that new countries were to be created from the Ottoman Empire. In 1920 the Ottoman Empire was divided into the nations of Turkey, Syria (including Lebanon), Iraq, Palestine, and Transjordan. Syria was put under French supervision and Iraq, Palestine, and Transjordan were put under British supervision.

Although disappointed with many parts of the Treaty of Versailles, Wilson achieved his

---

POLITICAL CARTOONS PRIMARY SOURCE
Debating the Treaty of Versailles

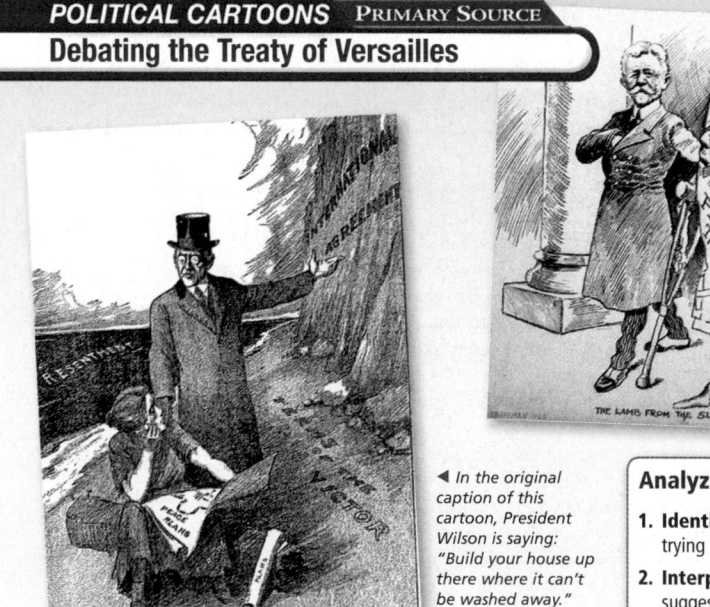

◄ Senator Henry Cabot Lodge escorts the peace treaty out of the Senate.

◄ In the original caption of this cartoon, President Wilson is saying: "Build your house up there where it can't be washed away."

Analyzing VISUALS — DBQ

1. **Identifying** What point is the cartoon on the right trying to make?
2. **Interpreting** Why does the cartoon on the left suggest that international agreement on a peace treaty is important?

344 Chapter 9 World War I and Its Aftermath

Activity: Interdisciplinary Connection

Art Have interested students use library and Internet resources to find other political cartoons about the Treaty of Versailles and have them make a poster collage of the cartoons—highlighting either the "Irreconcilable" or the "Reservationist" point of view. Then have students draw their own political cartoon to include in the collage. Be sure students write a caption describing their poster. Display the posters in the classroom. **AL**

primary goal. The treaty called for the creation of a League of Nations. League members promised to reduce armaments, to submit all disputes that endangered the peace to arbitration, and to come to the aid of any member who was threatened with aggression by another state.

The U.S. Senate Rejects the Treaty

President Wilson was confident the American people would support the Treaty of Versailles, but he had badly underestimated the opposition in Congress. All treaties signed by the United States must be ratified by two-thirds of the Senate, and in November 1918, the Democratic Party had lost control of the Senate. Even though he needed Republican support to ratify the treaty, Wilson refused to take any Republican leaders with him to the peace conference. This ensured that Wilson's views prevailed, but it also meant that Republican concerns were not addressed.

Opposition in the Senate focused on the League of Nations. One group of senators, nicknamed the "Irreconcilables," refused to support the treaty under any circumstances. They assailed the League as the kind of "entangling alliance" that the Founders had warned against. A larger group of senators, known as the "Reservationists," was led by the powerful chairman of the Foreign Relations committee, Henry Cabot Lodge. The Reservationists were willing to support the treaty if certain amendments were made to the League of Nations.

The Reservationists pointed out that the Constitution requires Congress to declare war. Yet the League of Nations could require member states to aid any member who was attacked. The Reservationists argued that this might force the United States into a war without Congressional approval. They agreed to ratify the treaty if it was amended to say that any military action by the United States required the approval of Congress. Wilson refused, fearing the change would undermine the League's effectiveness.

To overcome Senate opposition, Wilson decided to take his case directly to the American people. If public support for the treaty was strong enough, the senators would back down. Starting in September 1919, Wilson traveled 8,000 miles and made over 30 major speeches in three weeks. On September 25, the president collapsed from the physical strain and soon afterward suffered a stroke. Bedridden, Wilson ignored the advice of his wife and Democratic leaders and refused to compromise on the treaty.

The Senate finally voted in November 1919. It voted again in March 1920. Both times it refused to ratify the treaty. After Wilson left office in 1921, the United States negotiated separate peace treaties with each of the Central Powers. The League of Nations, the foundation of President Wilson's plan for lasting world peace, took shape without the United States.

✓ Reading Check **Examining** What was national self-determination and why did Wilson think it would help prevent war?

Section 3 REVIEW

Vocabulary
1. **Explain** the significance of: no-man's-land, convoy, John J. Pershing, armistice, Treaty of Versailles, Fourteen Points, national self-determination, League of Nations, reparations.

Main Ideas
2. **Explaining** How did technology change the way World War I was fought?

3. **Analyzing** What impact did John J. Pershing and the Battle of the Argonne Forest have on World War I?

4. **Organizing** Use a graphic organizer to list the results of World War I.

Critical Thinking
5. **Big Ideas** Why did President Wilson propose his Fourteen Points?

6. **Analyzing** What countries were involved in the Paris peace conference in 1919? Which country was not invited to participate? Why?

7. **Analyzing Maps and Charts** Examine the map and chart on page 343. Prepare a quiz with questions based on information from both. Give the quiz to some of your classmates.

Writing About History
8. **Descriptive Writing** Imagine that you are an American soldier fighting in Europe during World War I. Write a letter home describing your situation and how you feel about fighting there.

History ONLINE
Study Central™ To review this section, go to glencoe.com and click on Study Central.

345

S Skill Practice

Identifying Point of View
Ask students to summarize the opinions of the "Irreconcilables" and "Reservationists" toward the Treaty of Versailles. **OL**

Assess

History ONLINE

Study Central™ provides summaries, interactive games, and online graphic organizers to help students review content.

Close

Summarizing Ask: Was World War I the "war to end all wars?" *(No; in fact the peace terms ending World War I laid the foundation for World War II.)* **OL**

✓ Reading Check

Answer:
each group of people, or nation, should govern itself, Wilson believed it would lessen border disputes and international conflict

Section 3 REVIEW

Answers

1. All definitions can be found in the section and the Glossary.

2. Tanks could crush barbed wire and roll over trenches; poison gas was used by both sides, killing troops or rendering them unable to fight; airplanes were used as scouts and later battles took place in the air.

3. General Pershing directed the AEF attack which broke through German lines.

4. answers may include: League of Nations, dissolution of four empires, nine new

European countries, Germany pays reparations

5. He wanted to prevent future wars.

6. the United States, Great Britain, France, and Italy; Russia was not invited because the allies refused to recognize Lenin's government

7. Answers will vary; quizzes should be accurate.

8. Answers will vary; students should use descriptive terms in their letters.

TIME NOTEBOOK

Focus

Ask: After reading the information on these pages, what do you think were the major issues or topics of the era? *(World War I; communism)* **Ask:** Why is Jeanette Rankin pictured? *(She was the first woman elected to Congress.)* **Ask:** What items does a doughboy need and how much is the cost? How does the cost then likely compare to the cost of outfitting a soldier today? *(A doughboy required 107 pieces of fighting equipment, 50 articles of clothing, eating utensils, and 11 cooking implements, which cost $156.30. Today the cost of outfitting a soldier is likely to run into the thousands of dollars.)* **OL**

Teach

C Critical Thinking

Analyzing Primary Sources
Have students read the quote by Woodrow Wilson. **Ask:** Why does Wilson think applauding his speech is odd? *(because his request for war against Germany will result in the deaths of thousands of young American soldiers)* **AL**

Additional Support

American soldiers set sail for Europe.

World War Firsts

Human ingenuity goes to work in the service of war:

AERIAL COMBAT, 1914. War takes to the air. Two Allied aircraft chase two German planes across Britain.

GAS ATTACKS, 1915. The German High Command admits to using chlorine gas bombs and shells on the field of combat. Deadly mustard gas is used in 1917.

GAS MASKS. Issued to Allied soldiers in 1915.

DONKEY'S EARS. A new trench periscope enables soldiers to observe the battleground from the relative safety of a trench without risking sniper fire.

BIG BERTHA. Enormous howitzer gun bombards Paris. "Big Bertha," named after the wife of its manufacturer, is thought to be located nearly 63 miles behind German lines. Moving at night on railroad tracks, the gun is difficult for the Allies to locate.

Color My World

Some bright spots in a dark decade:

- Color newspaper supplements (1914)
- 3-D films (1915)
- Nail polish (1916)
- Three-color traffic lights (1918)
- Color photography introduced by Eastman Kodak (1914)

One of the first color photographs

VERBATIM

❝My message was one of death for young men. How odd to applaud that.❞
WOODROW WILSON, C
on returning to the White House after asking Congress for a declaration of war, 1917

❝Food is Ammunition—Don't Waste It ❞
POSTER FROM U.S. FOOD ADMINISTRATION,
administered by Herbert Hoover

❝I have had a hard time getting over this war. My old world died. ❞
RAY STANNARD BAKER,
journalist

❝Let us, while this war lasts, forget our special grievances and close our ranks shoulder to shoulder with our own white fellow citizens and the allied nations that are fighting for democracy. ❞
W.E.B. DU BOIS,
African American scholar and leader, 1918

❝America has at one bound become a world power in a sense she never was before. ❞
BRITISH PRIME MINISTER DAVID LLOYD GEORGE,
on the U.S. entry into World War I, 1917

❝In the camps I saw barrels mounted on sticks on which zealous captains were endeavoring to teach their men how to ride a horse. ❞
THEODORE ROOSEVELT,
on touring U.S. military training facilities, 1917

❝The war was over, and it seemed as if everything in the world were possible, and everything was new, and that peace was going to be all we dreamed about. ❞
FLORENCE HARRIMAN,
Red Cross volunteer, in Paris on Armistice Day, 1918

Background

Stars and Stripes *Stars and Stripes,* the armed forces newspaper staffed entirely by soldiers, was first published in 1918. In addition to being a source of information and morale for soldiers, it provided many young journalists and cartoonists with their first jobs.

Two well-known cartoonists whose work appeared in *Stars and Stripes* were Milt Caniff ("Terry and the Pirates") and Bill Mauldin, who won the Pulitzer Prize in 1945 for his "Willie" and "GI Joe" cartoons.

How to Make a Doughboy
Take one American infantryman.

1. Arm with 107 pieces of fighting equipment, including:
   - rifle
   - rifle cartridges
   - cartridge belt
   - steel helmet
   - clubs
   - knives
   - gas mask
   - wire cutters
   - trench tool
   - bayonet and scabbard
   - grenades
2. Add 50 articles of clothing, including 3 wool blankets and a bedsack.
3. Equip with eating utensils and 11 cooking implements.
4. Train well.

TOTAL COST: $156.30

(not including training and transportation to Europe)

Milestones

SHOT DOWN AND KILLED, APRIL 22, 1918. "THE RED BARON," Manfred von Richthofen, Germany's ace pilot. Von Richthofen destroyed more than 80 Allied aircraft. The English fighter pilot Edward Mannock said, "I hope he roasted all the way down."

Jeannette Rankin

ELECTED, NOVEMBER 7, 1916. JEANNETTE RANKIN of Montana, to the U.S. Congress. The first woman congressional representative explained her victory by saying that women "got the vote in Montana because the spirit of pioneer days was still alive."

Vladimir Lenin

REPATRIATED, APRIL 10, 1917. VLADIMIR ILYICH LENIN, to Russia, after an 11-year absence. The leader of the leftist Bolshevik party hopes to reorganize his revolutionary group.

NUMBERS 1915

$1,040 Average annual income for workers in finance, insurance, and real estate

$687 Average income for industrial workers (higher for union workers, lower for nonunion workers)

$510 Average income for retail trade workers

$355 Average income for farm laborers

$342 Average income for domestic servants

$328 Average income for public school teachers

$11.95 Cost of a bicycle

$1.15 Cost of a baseball

$1 Average cost of a hotel room

39¢ Cost of one dozen eggs

5¢ Cost of a glass of cola

7¢ Cost of a large roll of toilet paper

CRITICAL THINKING

1. **Analyzing** What pioneer qualities was Jeannette Rankin referring to when she said women "got the vote in Montana because the spirit of pioneer days was still alive"?

2. **Drawing Conclusions** How do you think the inventions in "Color My World" kept up spirits on the home front during World War I? Why was this important?

W Writing Support
Narrative Writing Have students reread the Milestone concerning "The Red Baron." Then have students use library or Internet resources to find out more about "The Red Baron" and his role in World War I. Using what they have learned, have students write a British newspaper article announcing the Baron's death. **OL**

Assess/Close

Have students select an item listed under Numbers and find a correlating statistic from today.

Visit the Time Web site at www.time.com for up-to-date news, weekly magazine articles, editorials, online polls, and an archive of past magazines and Web articles.

DBQ Document Based Questions

Answers:
1. individualism, freedom, ruggedness, the desire to explore
2. New inventions meant progress and something to look forward to, good morale on the home front was essential to winning the war.

Additional Support

Activity: Technology Connection

Comparing and Contrasting Have students review the information presented in the TIME Notebook and have students use library or Internet resources to find out more about the topics presented. Then have them make a list of items, issues, or inventions from the World War I era that are still relevant today. **Ask:** How do you think the events, issues, or inventions from the World War I era affect your life today? What inventions are still useful today? Which inventions have been improved upon? What political issues or ideas are still relevant today? *(Answers will vary, but students should cite data from the TIME Notebook and their research to support their ideas.)* **OL**

Focus

The War's Impact

Bellringer

Daily Focus Transparency 9.4

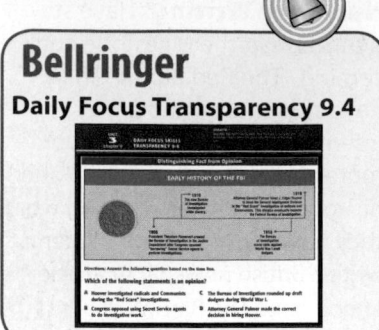

Guide to Reading

Answers:

Effects of World War I on Economy → rapid inflation

Effects of World War I on Economy → mass demand for goods

Effects of World War I on Economy → strikes

Section Spotlight Video

To generate student interest and provide a springboard for class discussion, access the Chapter 9, Section 4 video at glencoe.com or on the video DVD.

Resource Manager

Guide to Reading

Big Ideas

Economics and Society The change from wartime to peacetime caused many economic and social problems.

Content Vocabulary
• cost of living (p. 348)
• general strike (p. 349)
• deport (p. 352)

Academic Vocabulary
• widespread (p. 349)
• authorities (p. 352)

People and Events to Identify
• Calvin Coolidge (p. 349)
• Red Scare (p. 351)
• A. Mitchell Palmer (p. 351)
• J. Edgar Hoover (p. 352)

Reading Strategy

Organizing Complete a graphic organizer similar to the one below to list the effects of the end of World War I on the American economy.

Effects of World War I on Economy →

America's victory overseas led to turmoil at home. The end of the wartime economy led to a depression and fears of communism, as strikes, riots, and bombings took place.

An Economy in Turmoil

MAIN Idea The country suffered economic uncertainty, strikes, and riots in the year after the war.

HISTORY AND YOU Do you know anyone who has participated in a strike? Read why millions of workers went on strike in 1919.

With the war over, Americans welcomed the soldiers back as heroes. Parades were thrown in their honor, and a new organization, the American Legion, was created to support the veterans. But their arrival home was also bittersweet. Two million men now needed to find jobs in an economy that was shutting down its production of war materials and sliding into recession.

When the war ended, government agencies removed their controls from the economy. People raced to buy goods that had been rationed, while businesses rapidly raised prices they had been forced to keep low during the war. The result was rapid inflation. In 1919 prices rose more than 15 percent. Inflation greatly increased the **cost of living**— the cost of food, clothing, shelter, and other essentials that people need to survive. Orders for war materials evaporated, so factories laid off workers. Soldiers returned home looking for civilian employment but found jobs scarce. In short, 1919 was a year of economic turmoil.

Inflation Leads to Strikes

Many companies had been forced to raise wages during the war, but inflation now threatened to wipe out the gains workers had made. While workers wanted higher wages to keep up with inflation, companies resisted because inflation was also driving up their operating costs.

During the war, the number of workers in unions had increased dramatically. By the time the war ended, workers were better organized and much more capable of implementing strikes. Many business leaders, on the other hand, were determined to break the power of the unions and roll back the gains labor had made. These circumstances led to an enormous wave of strikes in 1919. By the end of the year, more than 3,600 strikes involving more than 4 million workers had taken place.

R Reading Strategies	C Critical Thinking	D Differentiated Instruction	W Writing Support	S Skill Practice
Teacher Edition • Categorizing Info., p. 349 • Act. Prior Know., p. 351 **Additional Resources** • Guid. Read. Act., URB p. 111	**Teacher Edition** • Drawing Conclusions, p. 351 • Analyzing Prim. Sources, p. 353 **Additional Resources** • Quizzes and Tests, p. 122 • Auth. Assess., p. 23	**Teacher Edition** • Visual/Spatial, p. 349 **Additional Resources** • English Learner Act., URB p. 87 • Reteach. Act., URB p. 105	**Teacher Edition** • Narrative Writing, pp. 350, 352 • Persuasive Writing, p. 352 **Additional Resources** • American Art and Music, URB p. 101	**Additional Resources** • Reinforcing Skills Act., URB p. 93 • RENTG, p. 97

The Strikes of 1919

▲ National Guard troops get rioting under control in Boston during the Police Strike of 1919

Workers on Strike, 1916–1921

[Line graph. Vertical axis: Thousands of Workers, from 1,000 to 4,500. Horizontal axis: Year, 1916–1921. Values start around 1,500 in 1916, dip near 1,000 in 1917–1918, rise sharply to a peak above 4,000 in 1919, then fall back to around 1,000 by 1921.]

Analyzing VISUALS

1. **Evaluating** Why do you think strikes in 1919 worried the government more than strikes in previous years?

2. **Making Inferences** Why do you think the Boston Police Strike received so much attention? Why were officials willing to use military force in Boston so quickly?

The Seattle General Strike The first major strike took place in Seattle, where some 35,000 shipyard workers walked off the job demanding higher wages and shorter hours. Other unions in Seattle soon joined the shipyard workers and organized a general strike.

A **general strike** is a strike that involves all workers in a community, not just workers in a particular industry. The Seattle general strike involved more than 60,000 people and paralyzed the city for five days. Although the strikers returned to work without making any gains, their actions worried many Americans because the general strike was a common tactic used in Europe by communists and other radical groups.

The Boston Police Strike Perhaps the most famous strike of 1919 took place in Boston, where roughly 75 percent of the police force walked off the job. Riots and looting soon erupted in the city, forcing the governor, **Calvin Coolidge,** to call in the National Guard. When the strikers tried to return to work, the police commissioner then fired the strikers and hired a new police force instead.

Despite protests, Coolidge agreed that the men should be fired, declaring: "There is no

right to strike against the public safety by anybody, anywhere, anytime." Coolidge's response earned him **widespread** public support and convinced the Republicans to make him their vice presidential candidate in the 1920 election.

The Steel Strike Shortly after the police strike ended, one of the largest strikes in American history began when an estimated 350,000 steelworkers went on strike for higher pay, shorter hours, and recognition of their union. Elbert H. Gary, the head of U.S. Steel, refused even to talk to union leaders. Instead, he set out to break the union by using anti-immigrant feelings to divide the workers.

Many steelworkers were immigrants. The company blamed the strike on foreign radicals and called for loyal Americans to return to work. Meanwhile, to keep the mills running, the company hired African Americans and Mexicans as replacement workers. Clashes between company guards and strikers were frequent. In Gary, Indiana, a riot left 18 strikers dead. The strike collapsed in early 1920 and its failure set back the union cause in the steel industry. Steel workers remained unorganized until 1941.

Teach

R Reading Strategy

Categorizing Information
Have students create a graphic organizer with five columns labeled "Who," "What," "Where," "How Many," and "Results." Label the rows with the three major strikes in this section. As students read, have them use this graphic organizer to compare the strikes. **OL**

D Differentiated Instruction

Visual/Spatial Have students create signs that steel workers could have carried during the 1919 strike. Signs can exhibit any effective use of language. **BL**

Analyzing CHARTS

Answers:
1. Many believed communists were behind the strikes.
2. Public officials were not supposed to strike; to prevent further disruption in the city and to keep the peace.

Hands-On Chapter Project
Step 4

Presenting World War I

Step 4: Post-War America Ask:
How did the war influence the economy and society of the United States?

Directions Explain to students that they will create one to three multimedia slides or screens to describe the effect of the war on the United States. Divide students into two teams. The first team should focus on the economy of post-war United States. The

second team should focus on the American society after the war. (In both groups, further division might be made between those responsible for boiling down the literal explanation and those finding graphic/visual elements.)

Putting It Together When the two teams meet to finalize the choices for the slides, they will determine not only how to illustrate the post-war economy and society,

but also how to explain why the war impacted the economy and society. **OL**

(Chapter Project continued on the Visual Summary page)

Racial Unrest

The economic turmoil after the war also contributed to widespread racial unrest. Many African Americans had moved north during the war to take factory jobs. As people began to be laid off and returning soldiers found it hard to find work and affordable housing, many gave in to feelings of racism and blamed African Americans for taking their jobs. Frustration and racism combined to produce violence.

In the summer of 1919, 25 race riots broke out across the nation. African American leader James Weldon Johnson called the summer of 1919, "the red summer" because of the amount of blood that was spilled. The riots began in July, when a mob of angry white people burned shops and homes in an African American neighborhood in Longview, Texas. A week later, in Washington, D.C., gangs of African Americans and whites fought each other for four days before troops got the riots under control.

W The worst violence occurred in Chicago. On a hot July day, African Americans went to a whites-only beach. Both sides began throwing stones at each other. Whites also threw stones at an African American teenager swimming near the beach to prevent him from coming ashore, and he drowned. A full-scale riot then erupted in the city.

Angry African Americans attacked white neighborhoods while whites attacked African American neighborhoods. The Chicago riot lasted for almost two weeks and the government was forced to send in National Guard troops to impose order. By the time the rioting ended, 38 people had been killed—15 white and 23 black—and over 500 had been injured.

The race riots of 1919 disillusioned some African Americans who felt their wartime contributions had been for nothing. For others, however, the wartime struggle for democracy encouraged them to fight for their rights at home.

The race riots of 1919 were different in one respect. For the first time, African Americans organized and fought back against the white mobs. Many African Americans also dedicated themselves to fighting for their rights politically. The NAACP surged in membership after the war, and in 1919, it launched a new campaign for a federal law against lynching.

✔ Reading Check **Analyzing** Why did the end of the war lead to race riots?

PAST & PRESENT

Terrorists Attack America

When terrorists attacked the United States on September 11, 2001, many Americans believed the United States was experiencing something new—multiple attacks by a terrorist organization.

It is almost forgotten by the American people that in June 1919, eight bombs exploded in eight American cities within minutes of each other, and another 30 bombs sent through the mail were intercepted before they exploded. In September 1920 an even larger bomb exploded in New York. As it did after 9/11, the United States government created a new federal agency to protect the American people. In 1919 the government created the General Intelligence Division, headed by Herbert Hoover, who later headed the FBI. In 2002 the government created the Department of Homeland Security.

September, 1920

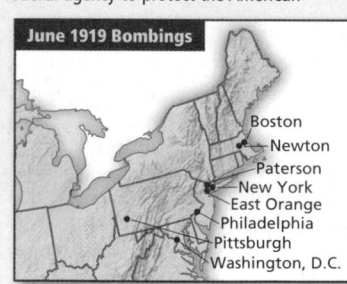

June 1919 Bombings

Boston
Newton
Paterson
New York
East Orange
Philadelphia
Pittsburgh
Washington, D.C.

▲ In September 1920, a bomb made of 100 lbs. of dynamite and 500 lbs. of steel fragments exploded in New York City, killing 38 people and injuring 300 others.

350 Chapter 9 World War I and Its Aftermath

Activity: Interdisciplinary Connection

Literature American writer John Dos Passos published his trilogy *U.S.A.* between 1930 and 1936. The second novel in the series, simply titled *1919*, is set during the tumultuous year that followed World War I. In the trilogy, Dos Passos experimented with unconventional techniques. He interwove the fictional story of his characters with sections that included headlines, news stories, and brief biographies of important or notorious figures from the era.

Provide students with excerpts from *1919* and then ask them to compose an essay in Dos Passos's style in which they present the material from this section of Chapter 9. **AL**

The Red Scare

MAIN Idea Fear of a Communist revolution caused a nationwide panic.

HISTORY AND YOU Many Americans believed the country was in danger in 1919. Read on to see similarities with today's concerns about security.

The wave of strikes in 1919 helped to fuel fears that Communists were conspiring to start a revolution in the United States. Americans had been stunned when Communists seized power in Russia and negotiated a separate peace agreement with Germany. Many Americans viewed this as a betrayal, and hostility toward Communists increased. Communism became associated with disloyalty and treachery.

Americans had long been suspicious of communist ideas. Since the late 1800s, many Americans had accused immigrants of importing radical socialist and communist ideas and blamed them for labor unrest and violence. Events in Russia seemed to justify fears of a Communist revolution. The Soviet establishment of the Communist International in 1919—an organization for coordinating Communist parties in other countries—appeared to be further proof of a growing threat.

The strikes of 1919 fueled fears that Communists, or "reds," as they were called, might seize power. This led to a nationwide panic known as the **Red Scare.** Many people were particularly concerned about workers using strikes to start a revolution. Seattle's mayor, Ole Hanson, for example, claimed that the Seattle general strike was part of an attempt to "take possession of our American government and try to duplicate the anarchy of Russia."

In April, the postal service intercepted more than 30 parcels containing homemade bombs addressed to prominent Americans. In May, union members, socialists, and communists organized a parade in Cleveland to protest the jailing of American Socialist Party leader Eugene Debs. The parade turned into a series of riots. By the time police and army units got the violence under control, two people were dead and another 40 were injured.

In June, eight bombs in eight cities exploded within minutes of one another, suggesting a nationwide conspiracy. One of them damaged the home of United States Attorney General **A. Mitchell Palmer.** Most people believed the bombings were the work of radicals trying to destroy the American way of life.

September, 2001

▼ Firefighters search for victims in the rubble of the World Trade Center in September 2001.

MAKING CONNECTIONS

1. **Comparing** How was the government's response to the 1919 and 1920 attacks similar to its response to the attacks of September 11, 2001? How was it different?

2. **Synthesizing** How do you think the government should have responded to the bombings of 1919 and 1920? In what ways were the government's policies inappropriate?

351

W₁ Writing Support

Narrative Writing Have interested students use library or Internet resources to research and write a five-page paper on the early history of the General Intelligence Division. **AL**

W₂ Writing Support

Persuasive Writing Have students imagine that they are the defense attorney for a citizen falsely accused during the Palmer raids. Instruct students to write an argument describing their client's rights that have been violated and why their client should be released. **OL**

Analyzing **GEOGRAPHY**

Answers:
1. the South; the Northeast
2. The West because the people of the West were more opposed to the nation's involvement in international affairs; answers will vary.

Additional Support

HISTORY AND GEOGRAPHY
The End of Progressivism?

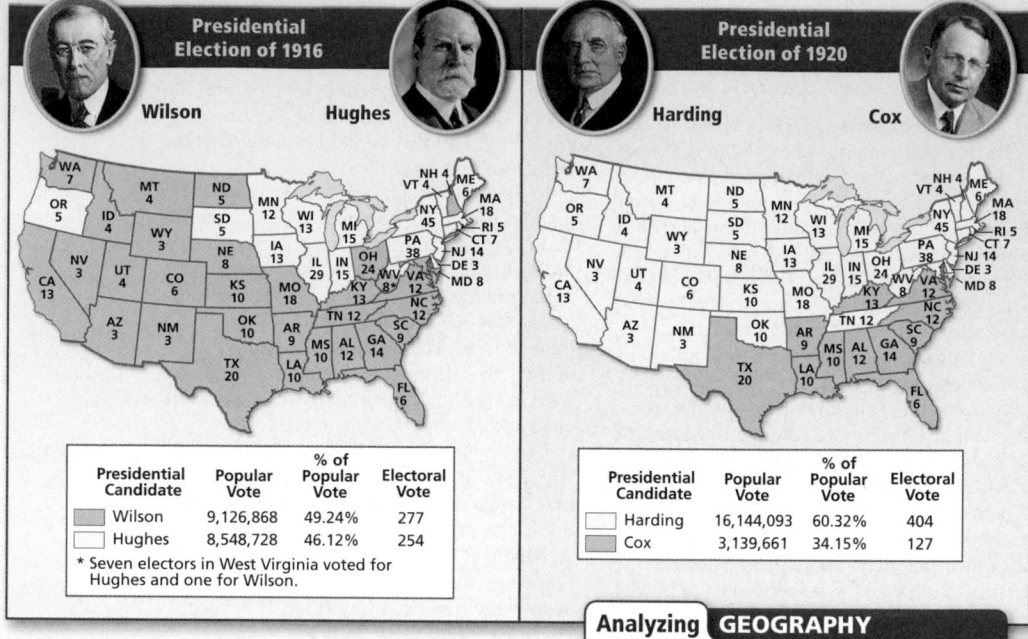

Presidential Candidate	Popular Vote	% of Popular Vote	Electoral Vote
Wilson	9,126,868	49.24%	277
Hughes	8,548,728	46.12%	254

* Seven electors in West Virginia voted for Hughes and one for Wilson.

Presidential Candidate	Popular Vote	% of Popular Vote	Electoral Vote
Harding	16,144,093	60.32%	404
Cox	3,139,661	34.15%	127

Many political historians used to think of the election of 1920 as the end of the Progressive Era. It is true that the 1920 election represented a dramatic shift from the progressive Woodrow Wilson to the much more traditionally conservative Warren Harding. But did the election really show a great change in voting habits throughout the country?

Analyzing **GEOGRAPHY**

1. **Region** Which region voted for the Democrats in both elections? Which region voted Republican in both elections?
2. **Region** What region of the country changed its vote between 1916 and 1920? Why do you think this happened? Does this change suggest people's views of progressivism had changed?

The Palmer Raids

Declaring that a "blaze of revolution" was "burning up the foundations of society," Palmer took action. He established a special division within the Justice Department, the General Intelligence Division. This division, headed by **J. Edgar Hoover,** eventually became the Federal Bureau of Investigation (FBI).

Although evidence pointed to no single group as the bombers, Palmer's agents targeted the foreign-born. On November 7, 1919, Palmer ordered a series of raids on offices of the Union of Russian Workers in 12 cities. Less than seven weeks later, a transport ship left New York for Russia carrying 249 immigrants who had been deported, or expelled from the country.

In January 1920, Palmer ordered another series of raids, this time on the headquarters of various radical organizations. Nearly 6,000 people were arrested. That same month, the New York state legislature expelled five members of the Socialist Party who had been elected to the legislature. Over the next few months, 32 states passed sedition laws making it illegal to join groups advocating revolution. Palmer's raids continued until the spring of 1920. **Authorities** detained thousands of suspects and nearly 600 people were **deported.**

352 Chapter 9 World War I and Its Aftermath

Activity: Interdisciplinary Connection

Language Arts Remind students that the Palmer raids took place at the same time that several major strikes were taking place. Have students discuss what daily life was like for industrial workers and the effect a major strike might have on businesses and the public. Help students recognize that each major strike caused elements of the public to be less tolerant of strikers, and to blame communist influences. Even though strikers only wanted safer working conditions, public fear of violence and revolution overrode the real strike issues. Finally, have students write a letter from a young steelworker to a parent explaining the situation. **OL BL**

Palmer's agents often ignored the civil liberties of the suspects. Officers entered homes and offices without search warrants. People were mistreated. Some were jailed for indefinite periods of time and were not allowed to talk to their attorneys. Many of the immigrants who were deported were never granted a court hearing to challenge the evidence against them or to contest the deportation order.

For a while, Palmer was regarded as a national hero. His raids, however, failed to turn up any hard evidence of revolutionary conspiracy. When his prediction that violence would rock the nation on May Day 1920—a celebration of workers in Europe—proved wrong, Palmer lost much of his credibility and support.

The Red Scare greatly influenced people's attitudes during the 1920s. Americans often linked radicalism with immigrants, and that attitude led to a call for Congress to limit immigration.

The Election of 1920

Economic problems, labor unrest, and racial tensions, as well as the fresh memories of World War I, all combined to create a general sense of disillusionment in the United States. By 1920 Americans wanted an end to the upheaval.

During the 1920 campaign, Ohio governor James M. Cox and his running mate, Assistant Secretary of the Navy Franklin D. Roosevelt, ran on a platform of progressive ideals. President Wilson tried to convince the Democrats to make the campaign a referendum on the Treaty of Versailles and the League of Nations, but the party chose not to take a strong stand on the issue for fear of alienating voters.

The Republican candidate, Warren G. Harding, called for a return to "normalcy." His vice-presidential running mate, Calvin Coolidge, was chosen because people admired the way he had handled the Boston police strike. Harding argued that what the United States needed was a return to simpler days before the Progressive Era reforms:

PRIMARY SOURCE

C "[Our] present need is not heroics, but healing; not nostrums, but normalcy; not revolution, but [bold] restoration; not agitation, but adjustment; not surgery, but serenity; not the dramatic, but the dispassionate; . . . not submergence in internationality, but sustainment in triumphant nationality."

—quoted in *Portrait of a Nation*

Harding's sentiments struck a chord with voters, and he won the election by a landslide margin of over 7 million votes. Many Americans were weary of more crusades to reform society and the world. They hoped to put the country's racial and labor unrest and economic troubles behind them and build a more prosperous and stable society.

✓ Reading Check **Examining** After World War I, why were Americans suspicious of some union leaders?

Vocabulary
1. **Explain** the significance of: cost of living, general strike, Calvin Coolidge, Red Scare, A. Mitchell Palmer, J. Edgar Hoover, deport.

Main Ideas
2. **Identifying** Use a chart like the one below to list the various causes of labor unrest in 1919.

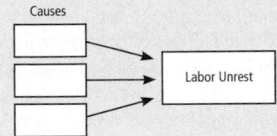

Causes → Labor Unrest

3. **Describing** What events made many Americans believe a revolution was imminent in 1919?

Critical Thinking
4. **Big Ideas** Why did the end of World War I bring such turmoil to the United States?

5. **Analyzing** Provide evidence to explain whether or not the Palmer raids deprived some people of their civil rights.

6. **Analyzing Visuals** Examine the photograph on page 349. What do you notice about the rioters? What does this tell you about the riots?

Writing About History
7. **Persuasive Writing** Imagine that you are a European immigrant working in a factory in the United States in 1919. Write a letter to a relative in Europe describing the feelings of Americans toward you and other immigrants.

History ONLINE
Study Central™ To review this section, go to glencoe.com and click on Study Central.

353

C Critical Thinking
Analyzing Primary Sources
Have students read the quote from candidate Warren G. Harding on this page. **Ask:** What message is the candidate giving? (*The nation needs a period of peace.*)
OL

Assess
· · · · · · · · · · · · · · · · · · ·
History ONLINE

Study Central™ provides summaries, interactive games, and online graphic organizers to help students review content.

Close
· · · · · · · · · · · · · · · · · · ·
Summarizing Ask: How did the end of World War I affect the United States? (*Conversion to a peacetime economy led to strikes and race riots; people grew fearful of communism.*) **OL**

✓ Reading Check

Answer:
They blamed union leaders for causing social unrest through strikes and thought unions were dominated by radicals.

Section 4 REVIEW

Answers

1. All definitions can be found in the section and the Glossary.

2. answers may include: conversion to peacetime economy, inflation, layoffs, lowered wages

3. strikes, race riots, protests, the 1917 Russian Revolution

4. soldiers returned home from the war; shift from a wartime to a peacetime economy; pent-up demand for higher wages to purchase new consumer goods; adjusting to new social climate after the Great Migration

5. Answers will vary, but most students will likely note that the raids did deprive some people of their civil rights.

6. The rioters were mostly white men; they were unarmed. Violence may not have been imminent.

7. Students' letters will vary.

Chapter 9 VISUAL SUMMARY

Determining Cause and Effect The Visual Summary lists causes of America's entry into World War I and its social and cultural effects. Ask students to use the information on the page to create a time line of the era's events. Display the time lines in the classroom. **OL**

Descriptive Writing Have students select the one effect or event that they believe has had the most impact on the United States today. Have students write a letter describing their chosen effect or event to a friend, describing its impact on today's America. Remind students to use descriptive words and terms in their letters. Have volunteers share their letters with the class. **OL**

Causes of America's Entry Into World War I

- Americans hear stories of German atrocities and many become anti-German.
- Many of President Wilson's advisors support the Allies.
- American banks lend the Allies large amounts of money and American companies sell the Allies food, weapons, and military supplies.
- Germany angers the United States by ordering submarines to attack neutral ships carrying goods to the Allies.
- Germany sinks the passenger ships *Lusitania* and *Sussex*, enraging Americans. To keep America out of the war, Germany stops sinking ships without warning in 1916.
- Germany tries to make an alliance with Mexico, further angering Americans.
- In a last attempt to win the war, Germany orders submarines to attack ships without warning in 1917; six American ships are sunk.
- The United States declares war, April 1917.

▶ German U-boats helped cause the United States to enter the war.

▲ World War I enabled women to take jobs traditionally reserved for men.

Social and Cultural Effects of World War I

- Northern factories recruit African Americans from the rural South; African Americans migrate to northern cities in large numbers, improving their standard of living and changing politics in northern cities.
- In search of workers, companies also hire large numbers of women for jobs traditionally reserved for men.
- Labor shortages cause many Mexicans to migrate north to take work in the United States. Many Hispanic Americans leave farmwork for factory work.
- Laws limiting civil rights in wartime are upheld by the Supreme Court in the cases of *Schenck v. U.S.* and *Abrams v. U.S.*
- During the war, anti-German feelings are widespread.
- The end of the war leads to economic and social tensions; many workers go on strike; race riots erupt in many cities.
- After the war, many Americans become anti-immigrant, anti-communist, and anti-union.

354 **Chapter 9** World War I and Its Aftermath

Hands-On Chapter Project
Step 5: Wrap Up

Presenting World War I

Step 5: Wrap Up Students will divide into teams to complete their presentations.

Directions Divide the class into two teams. Each team will complete the presentation by placing all the slides created in Sections 1, 2, 3, and 4 into a unified presentation. Students will need to provide logical transitions between topics, as well as edit the slides prior to presentation day.

Putting It Together Set aside class time for each team to give their presentations. Allow time for a discussion after all presentations have been given. Ask students the following questions:

- What were the main points of the presentation?
- Did the presentation present World War I clearly?
- Were the transitions clear?
- What were the good (and bad) parts of the presentation? How could it be improved? **OL**

ASSESSMENT

STANDARDIZED TEST PRACTICE

TEST-TAKING TIP

> Eliminate answers that do not make sense. For instance, if an answer refers to World War II, you know it cannot be correct.

Reviewing Vocabulary

Directions: Choose the word or words that best complete the sentence.

1. The British used _____ to convince Americans to support the Allied war effort.

   A espionage

   B armistice

   C conscription

   D propaganda

2. The _____ system ensured that American troops arrived safely in Europe.

   A nationalism

   B convoy

   C reparations

   D cost of living

3. British officials ordered a naval blockade to prevent _____, or prohibited materials, from entering Germany.

   A contraband

   B cost of living

   C conscription

   D self-determination

4. Soldiers in World War I dug a complex _____ of trenches to protect themselves.

   A emphasis

   B stability

   C restoration

   D network

Reviewing Main Ideas

Directions: Choose the best answers to the following questions.

Section 1 *(pp. 320–327)*

5. Which of the following was one of the primary causes of World War I?

   A a complex set of alliances among European nations

   B the exile of Mexican General Victoriano Huerta

   C the dissatisfaction of Russian peasants

   D the breakup of the Austro-Hungarian Empire

6. The event that triggered the American entry into World War I was

   A the sinking of the *Lusitania*.

   B the resumption of unrestricted submarine warfare.

   C the invasion of neutral Belgium.

   D the interception of the Zimmermann telegram.

Section 2 *(pp. 328–333)*

7. During World War I, which federal mobilization agency introduced daylight savings time and shortened the work week for some factories?

   A War Industries Board

   B Committee on Public Information

   C National War Labor Board

   D Fuel Administration

8. Both the Espionage Act and the Sedition Act of 1918 were designed to

   A provide plans for rebuilding Germany after the war.

   B help the British and French economies during the war.

   C limit opposition to the war in the United States.

   D protect the rights of German Americans.

Need Extra Help?								
If You Missed Questions . . .	1	2	3	4	5	6	7	8
Go to Page . . .	324	338–339	326	336	320–322	326–327	328–329	330

 GO ON

Answers and Analyses
Reviewing Vocabulary

1. D One strategy to employ with vocabulary questions is to substitute the definition of each answer choice into the blank to find the one that makes the most sense. Propaganda is information that is meant to influence someone's position. The other choices do not fit. Espionage is spying. Armistice is a cease-fire. Conscription is drafting a person into military service.

2. B In a convoy, cargo ships and ships carrying troops were protected by destroyers. Convoy means "fleet" or "procession." Nationalism is feelings of intense national pride. Reparations are payments for damages. Cost of living is an economic term.

3. A Contra- as a prefix means "against" or "contrary." This should help students remember that contraband is goods that are prohibited (*against* the law/rules).

4. D Only *D* makes sense. A network is a system or complex. *A* and *B* do not make sense. Soldiers did not "restore" trenches, they dug new trenches.

Reviewing Main Ideas

5. A European nations developed a system of complex alliances in response to the actions taken during the creation/uniting of Germany and also to the spread of nationalism in Europe. Because of these alliances, one act of aggression triggered many nations to be at odds.

6. B There is never a single cause for a nation entering a war, but there is often a "final straw," that triggers a nation's involvement. Choices *A* and *D* both contributed to American support of going to war, but it was Germany's resumption of unrestricted warfare that finally drew the U.S. into war.

7. D Discuss the purposes/benefits of daylight savings with students. It allows more work to be done during daylight. This, in turn, saves energy. The Fuel Administration is the most likely organization listed to want to conserve energy.

8. C Espionage is spying. Sedition is subversion or treason. The passage of these acts suppressed war opposition. They did not protect rights, they suspended them.

Chapter 9

9. A The use of cannons far pre-dates the use of tanks. Remind students that cannons were used during the Revolutionary War. Aircraft carriers were developed in the early 1900s, but were not used in combat until after WWI. Hot air balloons were developed in eighteenth century.

10. A Remind students of the desire to return to isolationist ways and retreat from world affairs expressed by many at the close of WWI. The Treaty of Versailles was rejected because of the inclusion of the League of Nations. Members of Congress thought the agreement would entangle the U.S. in world affairs.

11. B Communists were called "reds." The Red Scare was a fear of communism that swept through the nation in the years following WWI. Nuclear power was not invented until the WWII era, so *A* and *D* can be eliminated. *C* is not likely.

12. D The General Intelligence Division was formed during the Red Scare in response to a series of bombings that many believed to be the acts of subversives, Communists in particular. Damage to the home of the Attorney General prompted him to form the Division, which later became the FBI. The organization was formed after WWI, so *A* and *B* can be eliminated. Although many believed that unions were involved with communism, the organization was not intended to head off strikes.

Section 3 *(pp. 336–345)*

9. Which of the following technologies was first used during World War I?

   A tanks

   B cannons

   C aircraft carriers

   D hot air balloons

10. Why did the Senate reject the Treaty of Versailles?

    A to keep the United States free from foreign entanglements

    B to express opposition to the harsh sanctions imposed on Germany

    C to avoid the dues for membership in the League of Nations

    D to reduce United States military forces in Europe

Section 4 *(pp. 348–353)*

11. The Red Scare was a fear that

    A nuclear power would result in widespread destruction in the United States.

    B Communists would seize power in the United States.

    C fire would spread quickly through overcrowded American cities.

    D the Soviet Union would develop an atomic bomb.

12. The organization that eventually became the Federal Bureau of Investigation was originally formed to

    A uncover German spies during World War I.

    B spread propaganda within the United States in support of World War I.

    C infiltrate unions to head off strikes.

    D raid the headquarters of radical organizations in order to look for evidence of a Communist conspiracy.

Need Extra Help?

If You Missed Questions . . .	9	10	11	12	13	14
Go to Page . . .	337–339	343–345	351	352	332–333	342–343

Critical Thinking

Directions: Choose the best answers to the following questions.

13. How did Congress ensure that the United States would have enough troops to serve in World War I?

    A Congress allowed women to serve in the armed forces.

    B The Selective Service Act of 1917 required all men ages 21 to 30 to register for the draft.

    C Congress allowed African Americans to serve in the armed forces.

    D Congress offered a free education and cheap land to anyone willing to serve.

Base your answer to question 14 on the map below and your knowledge of Chapter 9.

Europe after WWI

— Former Austria-Hungary boundary
— Former German boundary
— Former Russian boundary
— Current country boundary

14. Which countries lost territory as a result of World War I?

    A Germany, Russia, France

    B Germany, France, England

    C Germany, Italy, Austria-Hungary

    D Germany, Austria-Hungary, Russia

GO ON

Critical Thinking

13. B Women did not serve in combat positions, so *A* can be eliminated. African Americans did serve in the armed forces; but only a small number served in combat. The Selective Service Act required men to sign up for the draft, and the draft ensured that the U.S. would have a large pool of possible troops.

14. D Examine the map with students. Explain that there were three empires broken up at the end of the war: the German Empire, the Russian Empire, and the Austro-Hungarian Empire. France, Italy, and England were part of the "Big Four" present at the Peace Conference. Any answer containing these countries can be eliminated as they were unlikely to lose any territory in the war.

15. President Wilson's Fourteen Points plan called for

A Germany to pay war reparations to the Allies.

B Germany to acknowledge guilt for the outbreak of World War I.

C the creation of the United Nations.

D the creation of the League of Nations.

Analyze the cartoon and answer the question that follows. Base your answers on the cartoon and on your knowledge of Chapter 9.

16. The cartoonist is expressing the opinion that

A England's blockade of Germany was beneficial for neutral shipping.

B England's blockade of the United States hurt neutral shipping.

C England's blockade of the United States hurt American shipping.

D England's blockade of Germany hurt American shipping.

<table>
<tr><td colspan="6">**Need Extra Help?**</td></tr>
<tr><td>If You Missed Questions . . .</td><td>15</td><td>16</td><td>17</td><td>18</td><td>19</td></tr>
<tr><td>Go to Page . . .</td><td>342–343</td><td>324–327</td><td>330</td><td>330</td><td>342–345</td></tr>
</table>

Document-Based Questions

Directions: Analyze the document and answer the short-answer questions that follow the document.

On September 12, 1918, Socialist leader Eugene V. Debs was convicted of violating the Espionage Act. Debs later spoke to the court at his sentencing. The document below is an excerpt from that speech:

> "I look upon the Espionage laws as a despotic enactment in flagrant conflict with democratic principles and with the spirit of free institutions. . . . I am opposed to the social system in which we live. . . . I believe in fundamental change, but if possible by peaceful and orderly means. . . .
>
> I am thinking this morning of the men in the mills and factories, . . . of the women who for a paltry wage are compelled to work out their barren lives; of the little children who in this system are robbed of their childhood and . . . forced into industrial dungeons. . . . In this high noon of our twentieth century Christian civilization, money is still so much more important than the flesh and blood of childhood. In very truth gold is god. . . . "
>
> —from Eugene Debs in *Echoes of Distant Thunder*

17. According to Debs, what were some problems in American society at this time? How did he believe change should be brought about?

18. How did Debs seem to feel about the Espionage Act? Do you agree with him? Why or why not?

Extended Response

19. After World War I, the United States Senate refused to ratify the Treaty of Versailles despite the intense efforts of Woodrow Wilson to convince Americans that ratification would help ensure that the peace would be an enduring one. Choose to either support or oppose the United States's ratification of the Treaty of Versailles. Write a persuasive essay that includes an introduction and at least three paragraphs that support your position.

History ONLINE

For additional test practice, use Self-Check Quizzes—Chapter 9 at glencoe.com.

Document-Based Questions

17. Debs said the problems in American society were the espionage acts, unfair working conditions, and the importance of profit over peoples' lives.

18. Debs felt the espionage laws went against the democratic principles upon which the nation was founded. Answers to the second question will vary. Accept all well-reasoned and relevant answers.

Extended Response

19. Students' essays will vary, but must demonstrate an understanding of the purpose of the League of Nations and of the motivations behind those who opposed it. Essays should take a position for or against the rejection of the Treaty of Versailles and present a balanced argument using information from the chapter as support. Essays should follow proper guidelines for writing a persuasive essay.

15. D Direct students who have trouble with this question to review the chart on page 342 that lists the Fourteen Points. Students should relate President Wilson with the creation of the League of Nations, even if the U.S. eventually failed to join. The United Nations was created at the end of WWII.

16. D Study the cartoon with students. Uncle Sam is chastising England for interfering with those who have the right to trade on the seas, namely, neutral commerce and American shipping, represented by crying children. England is trying to "hit" Germany with the blockade (see writing on the stick/bat). England blockaded Germany, not the United States, so B and C can be eliminated. The children are unhappy about England's actions toward Germany, eliminating choice A.

History ONLINE

Have students visit the Web site at glencoe.com to review Chapter 9 and take the Self-Check Quiz.

Need Extra Help?

Have students refer to the pages listed if they miss any of the questions.

Unit 4 Planning Guide

UNIT PACING CHART					
	Unit 4	**Chapter 10**	**Chapter 11**	**Chapter 12**	**Unit 4**
Day 1	Unit Opener	Chapter 10 Opener, Section 1	Chapter 11 Opener, Section 1	Chapter 12 Opener, Section 1	Wrap-Up/Project, Unit Assessment
Day 2		Section 2	Section 2	Section 2	
Day 3		Sections 3 & 4	Section 3	Section 3	
Day 4		Section 5	Chapter Assessment	Chapter Assessment	
Day 5		Chapter Assessment			

 Teacher to Teacher

**Jennifer G. Lange
Forest Hills High
School
Forest Hills, NY**

The Culture of Slang Provide the students with a list of slang expressions from the Jazz Age. Do not give them the explanations of the slang. Ask students to try to decide what the words mean (some of the expressions we still use today). Ask students to explain how the new vocabulary reflected the culture of the Jazz Age. Ask students to describe the role that slang plays in their lives today. Some slang terms that developed in the period include:

- cat's meow (or cat's pajamas)—something fantastic
- crush—an infatuation with someone
- gatecrasher—someone who "crashes" a party

- blind date—dating someone you never met
- big cheese—the boss
- bump off—murder or kill
- goofy—silly
- gams—a woman's legs
- heebie jeebies—jitters
- high-hat—snub
- flapper—the "new woman" of the 1920s
- gyp—cheat
- darb—something truly wonderful
- gin mill—a speakeasy

Author Note

Dear American History Teacher:

When I teach the period covered in this unit, I try to convey to students the extraordinary character of this period in American history—an economic boom that transformed the nation's landscape and culture, and a catastrophic economic collapse that destabilized not just the United States but much of the world.

The Great Depression of the 1930s was a direct result of some of the economic changes of the 1920s, and of the weaknesses those changes helped to produce. Indeed, the real beginning of the Great Depression came not in the aftermath of the stock market crash of 1929, but with an agricultural depression that had begun several years earlier. And the response to the Great Depression—first by Herbert Hoover and later by Franklin Roosevelt—drew heavily from ideas about the economy that the 1920s boom helped create.

Looming behind the domestic issues that preoccupied the nation during much of the period between the two world wars was a continuing global crisis. The settlement of World War I had not stabilized the international system. On the contrary, the aftermath of the war unleashed new regimes and new ideologies—most notably communism and fascism—that slowly eroded the peace and led to the outbreak of war in China in the mid-1930s, in Europe in 1939, and in the United States in 1941.

The period between the two wars was in many ways a catastrophic time for the world, unleashing forces that produced the greatest and most terrible war in human history. This period marked a fundamental break in history. The United States was ultimately drawn into the war too, but despite the many sacrifices Americans made in World War II, America emerged from the conflict stronger and more stable than it had been in decades.

It is important to introduce students to the contrasts and crises of this period, and to the continuities in American life that tied these years together.

Alan Brinkley
Senior Author

Focus

Why It Matters

Write these terms on the board: *Roaring '20s, Great Depression, New Deal.* Have students describe what images come to mind when they see or hear these terms. Then have them make generalizations about what their lives would be like during each of the time periods described by those terms. **OL**

Connecting to Past Learning

Remind students that in the previous unit they learned about the development of the United States after the Civil War era. **Ask:** What challenges from the recent past might people in the 1920s, 1930s, and 1940s have continued to face? *(Answers may include economic challenges, social change, and racial prejudice.)* Tell students that in this unit they will learn about the Boom and Bust cycles the United States experienced from 1920 until 1941. **OL**

Unit Launch Activity

Making Connections Point out to students that the early part of this unit's time span was a carefree time, seen by some as a decadent period prior to the hardships of economic depression and war. **Ask:** Why do you think the 1920s was a decade of great cultural change? *(Answers will vary, but students might note that new inventions and new styles of music, art, and literature all affected the nation.)* **OL**

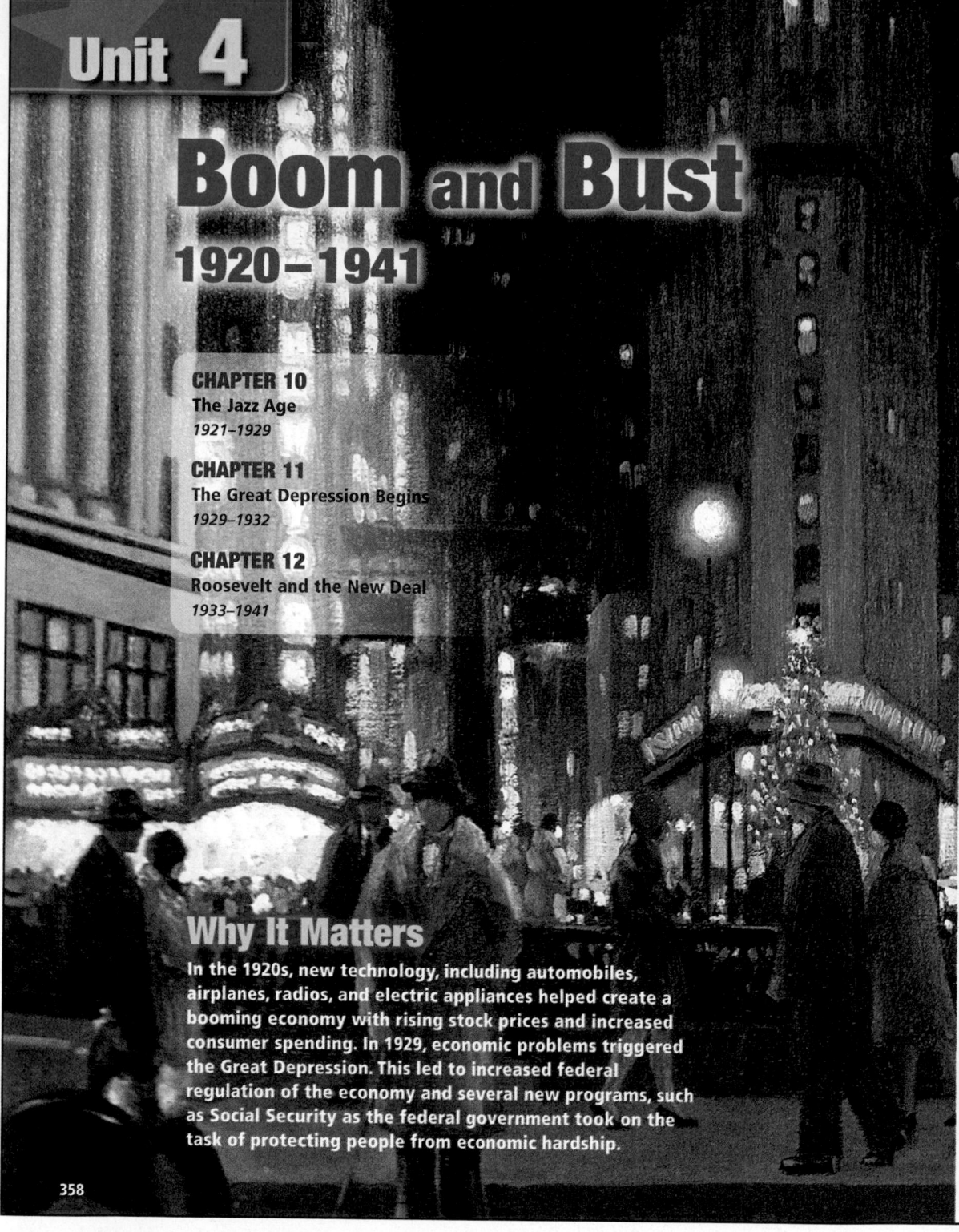

Unit 4

Boom and Bust
1920–1941

CHAPTER 10
The Jazz Age
1921–1929

CHAPTER 11
The Great Depression Begins
1929–1932

CHAPTER 12
Roosevelt and the New Deal
1933–1941

Why It Matters

In the 1920s, new technology, including automobiles, airplanes, radios, and electric appliances helped create a booming economy with rising stock prices and increased consumer spending. In 1929, economic problems triggered the Great Depression. This led to increased federal regulation of the economy and several new programs, such as Social Security as the federal government took on the task of protecting people from economic hardship.

358

Team Teaching Activity

Art Invite the art teacher to your class to explain the Art Deco style and show classic examples of the style. Then have students research your local community for examples of Art Deco architecture, art, and design. If possible, have students take photographs of the examples to present to the class. Have students point out why the samples they have chosen illustrate Art Deco style. **OL**

Teach

S₁ S₂

The Great White Way, Times Square, New York, 1925

359

More About the Painting

Howard Thain Although he was a Texas native, Howard Thain's favorite subject was his adopted home, New York City. Originally an impressionist, he became a modernist painter of urban scenes and portraits. *The Great White Way* (1925) captures the energy of Times Square at night. Obsessed with light, Thain conveys the glitz and excitement of urban nightlife during the period when electric lights first became more common than kerosene lamps and cities became nighttime playgrounds for urbanites with disposable income. Many of his paintings depict the frenzied pursuit of pleasure and diversion associated with the Roaring Twenties.

Key to Ability Levels
- **BL** Below Level
- **OL** On Level
- **AL** Above Level
- **ELL** English Language Learners

Key to Teaching Resources
- Print Material
- CD-ROM
- DVD
- Transparency

Levels (BL OL AL ELL)		Resources	Chapter Opener	Section 1	Section 2	Section 3	Section 4	Section 5	Chapter Assess
FOCUS									
BL OL AL ELL	🖨	Daily Focus Skills Transparencies		10-1	10-2	10-3	10-4	10-5	
TEACH									
OL AL	📁	History Simulations and Problem Solving, URB					p. 9		
AL	📁	American Literature Reading, URB						p. 13	
BL OL ELL	📁	Reading Essentials and Note-Taking Guide*		p. 100	p. 103	p. 106	p. 109	p. 112	
OL	📁	Historical Analysis Skills Activity, URB			p. 22				
BL OL ELL	📁	Guided Reading Activities, URB*		p. 46	p. 47	p. 48	p. 49	p. 50	
BL OL AL ELL	📁	Content Vocabulary Activity, URB*		p. 27					
BL OL AL ELL	📁	Academic Vocabulary Activity, URB		p. 29					
OL AL	📁	Critical Thinking Skills Activity, URB		p. 32					
BL OL ELL	📁	Reading Skills Activity, URB			p. 21				
BL ELL	📁	English Learner Activity, URB		p. 25					
OL AL	📁	Reinforcing Skills Activity, URB				p. 31			
BL OL AL ELL	📁	Differentiated Instruction Activity, URB						p. 23	
BL OL ELL	📁	Time Line Activity, URB			p. 33				
OL	📁	Linking Past and Present Activity, URB						p. 34	
BL OL AL ELL	📁	American Art and Music Activity, URB						p. 39	
BL OL AL ELL	📁	Interpreting Political Cartoons Activity, URB				p. 41			
AL	📁	Enrichment Activity, URB						p. 44	
BL OL AL ELL	📁	American Biographies				✓	✓	✓	
BL OL AL ELL	📁	Primary Source Reading, URB				p. 35		p. 37	
BL OL AL ELL	📁	Supreme Court Case Studies		p. 43		p. 39			
BL OL AL ELL	📁	The Living Constitution*	✓	✓	✓	✓	✓	✓	✓
OL AL	💿	American History Primary Source Documents Library	✓	✓	✓	✓	✓	✓	✓
BL OL AL ELL	🖨	Unit Map Overlay Transparencies	✓	✓	✓	✓	✓	✓	✓

Note: Please refer to the *Unit 4 Resource Book* for this chapter's URB materials.

* Also available in Spanish

TeacherWorks™ Plus
All-In-One Planner and Resource Center

- Interactive Lesson Planner
- Interactive Teacher Edition
- Fully editable blackline masters
- Section Spotlight Videos Launch
- Differentiated Lesson Plans
- Printable reports of daily assignments
- Standards Tracking System

Levels					Resources	Chapter Opener	Section 1	Section 2	Section 3	Section 4	Section 5	Chapter Assess
TEACH *(continued)*												
BL	OL	AL	ELL	📁	Differentiated Instruction for the American High School Classroom	✓	✓	✓	✓	✓	✓	✓
BL	OL	AL	ELL	💿	StudentWorks™ Plus DVD	✓	✓	✓	✓	✓	✓	✓
BL	OL	AL	ELL	💿	Vocabulary PuzzleMaker CD-ROM	✓	✓	✓	✓	✓	✓	✓
BL	OL	AL	ELL	💿	American Music Hits Through History CD	✓	✓	✓	✓	✓	✓	✓
BL	OL	AL	ELL	📁	Unit Time Line Transparencies and Activities	✓	✓	✓	✓	✓	✓	✓
BL	OL	AL	ELL	📁	Cause and Effect Transparencies, Strategies, and Activities	✓	✓	✓	✓	✓	✓	✓
BL	OL	AL	ELL	📁	Why It Matters Transparencies, Strategies, and Activities	✓	✓	✓	✓	✓	✓	✓
BL	OL	AL	ELL	📁	American Issues	✓	✓	✓	✓	✓	✓	✓
	OL	AL	ELL	📁	American Art and Architecture Transparencies, Strategies, and Activities	✓	✓	✓	✓	✓	✓	✓
BL	OL	AL		📁	High School American History Literature Library	✓	✓	✓	✓	✓	✓	✓
BL	OL	AL	ELL	💿	*The American Vision* Video Program DVD	✓	✓	✓	✓	✓	✓	✓
Teacher Resources				📁	Strategies for Success	✓	✓	✓	✓	✓	✓	✓
				📁	Success with English Learner	✓	✓	✓	✓	✓	✓	✓
				📁	Studies Classroom	✓	✓	✓	✓	✓	✓	✓
				💿	Presentation Plus! DVD	✓	✓	✓	✓	✓	✓	✓
ASSESS												
BL	OL	AL	ELL	📁	Section Quizzes and Chapter Tests*		p. 139	p. 140	p. 141	p. 142	p. 143	p. 145
BL	OL	AL	ELL	📁	Authentic Assessment With Rubrics							p. 25
BL	OL	AL	ELL	📁	Standardized Test Practice Workbook							p. 22
BL	OL	AL	ELL	💿	*ExamView®* Assessment Suite CD-ROM		10-1	10-2	10-3	10-4	10-5	Ch. 10
BL	OL	AL	ELL	💿	Interactive Tutor Self-Assessment CD-ROM		10-1	10-2	10-3	10-4	10-5	Ch. 10
CLOSE												
BL			ELL	📁	Reteaching Activity, URB							p. 43
BL	OL		ELL	📁	Reading and Study Skills Foldables™	pp. 68–70						

Using the Glencoe Web Site

Self-Check Quizzes

Objectives
The Self-Check Quizzes help students
- assess their comprehension and recall of chapter content;
- build study skills;
- identify areas for additional study and reinforcement.

Technology
Students can assess their comprehension of chapter content with Self-Check Quizzes on the Glencoe Web site. The Web site provides a 10-question quiz for each chapter.

Focus/Teach
Provide students with the following steps to complete the activities:
- Locate the Web page for the textbook being studied on the Glencoe Web site glencoe.com.
- Click on **Student Center** under the textbook title.
- In the Student Center, select a unit from the Unit Resources menu and a chapter from the Chapter Activities menu using the drop-down arrows.
- Click on the **Self-Check Quizzes** link.

Assess
Have students answer the questions in the chapter quiz and review feedback on incorrect answers.

Close
Provide students an e-mail address to submit their quiz results for analysis and recording.

History ONLINE

	Student	Teacher	Parent
Beyond the Textbook	●	●	●
Chapter Overviews	●	●	●
Time Current Events	●		●
ePuzzles and Games	●		●
Concepts in Motion	●		●
Literature Connections		●	
Multi-Language Glossaries	●		●
Online Student Edition	●	●	●
Self-Check Quizzes	●		●
Student Web Activities	●		●
Study Central™	●		●
Teaching Today		●	
Vocabulary eFlashcards	●		●
Web Activity Lesson Plans		●	

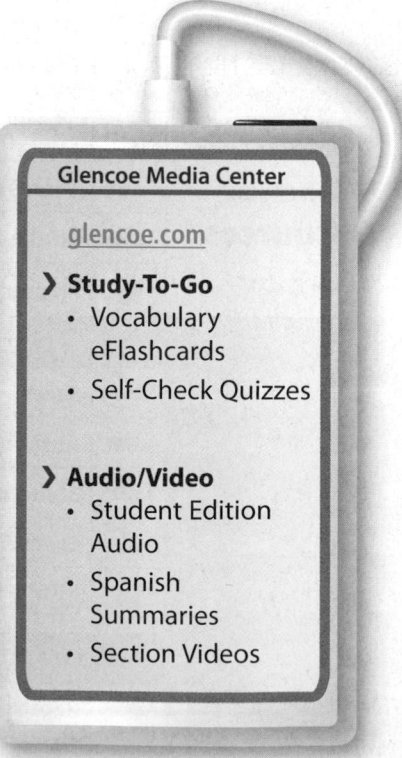

Glencoe Media Center

glencoe.com

❯ **Study-To-Go**
- Vocabulary eFlashcards
- Self-Check Quizzes

❯ **Audio/Video**
- Student Edition Audio
- Spanish Summaries
- Section Videos

- **Timed Readings Plus in Social Studies** helps students increase their reading rate and fluency while maintaining comprehension. The 400-word passages are similar to those found on state and national assessments.

- **Reading in the Content Area: Social Studies** concentrates on six essential reading skills that help students better comprehend what they read. The book includes 75 high-interest nonfiction passages written at increasing levels of difficulty.

- **Reading Social Studies** includes strategic reading instruction and vocabulary support in Social Studies content for both ELLs and native speakers of English.

www.jamestowneducation.com

The following videotape programs are available from Glencoe as supplements to Chapter 10:

- The Prohibition Era (ISBN 0-76-700179-6)
- The Monkey Trial, In Search of History (ISBN 0-76-700609-7)

To order, call Glencoe at 1-800-334-7344. To find classroom resources to accompany many of these videos, check the following home pages:

A&E Television: www.aetv.com
The History Channel: www.historychannel.com

Index to National Geographic Magazine:

The following articles relate to this chapter:
- "Growing up in East Harlem," by Jere Van Dyk, May 1990.
- "Traveling the Blues Highway," by Charles E. Cobb, Jr., April 1999.

National Geographic Society Products To order the following, call National Geographic at 1-800-368-2728:
- ZipZapMap! USA (ZipZapMap!)

Access National Geographic's new, dynamic MapMachine Web site and other geography resources at:

www.nationalgeographic.com
www.nationalgeographic.com/maps

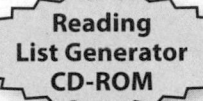

Reading List Generator CD-ROM — GLENCOE BOOKLINK 3

Use this database to search more than 30,000 titles to create a customized reading list for your students.

- Reading lists can be organized by students' reading level, author, genre, theme, or area of interest.
- The database provides Degrees of Reading Power™ (DRP) and Lexile™ readability scores for all selections.
- A brief summary of each selection is included.

Leveled reading suggestions for this chapter:

For students at a Grade 8 reading level:
- *Giants of Jazz*, by Studs Terkel

For students at a Grade 9 reading level:
- *Great African Americans in Jazz*, by Carlotta Hacker

For students at a Grade 10 reading level:
- *Jazz and Blues*, by Roger Thomas

For students at a Grade 11 reading level:
- *Jazz: An American Saga*, by James Lincoln Collier

For students at a Grade 12 reading level:
- *When the Negro Was in Vogue*, by Langston Hughes

Focus

MAKING CONNECTIONS
Why Does Culture Change?

Ask students to explain what their culture is like today. Then ask them how it was different ten years ago. Students may point out that the latest technologies did not exist ten years earlier. Activate students' prior knowledge by asking them to name aspects of their present-day culture that did not exist in the time of their parents' or caregivers' youth. Students may note that cell phones were not common, mp3 players did not exist, and so on. Discuss with students how watching movies or listening to music has changed since the 1920s. **BL** **ELL**

Teach
The Big Ideas

As students study the chapter, remind them to consider the section-based Big Ideas included in each section's Guide to Reading. The **Essential Questions** in the activities below tie in to the Big Ideas and help students think about and understand important chapter concepts. In addition, the Hands-on Chapter Projects with their culminating activities relate the content from each section to the Big Ideas. These activities build on each other as students progress through the chapter. Section activities culminate in the wrap-up activity on the Visual Summary page.

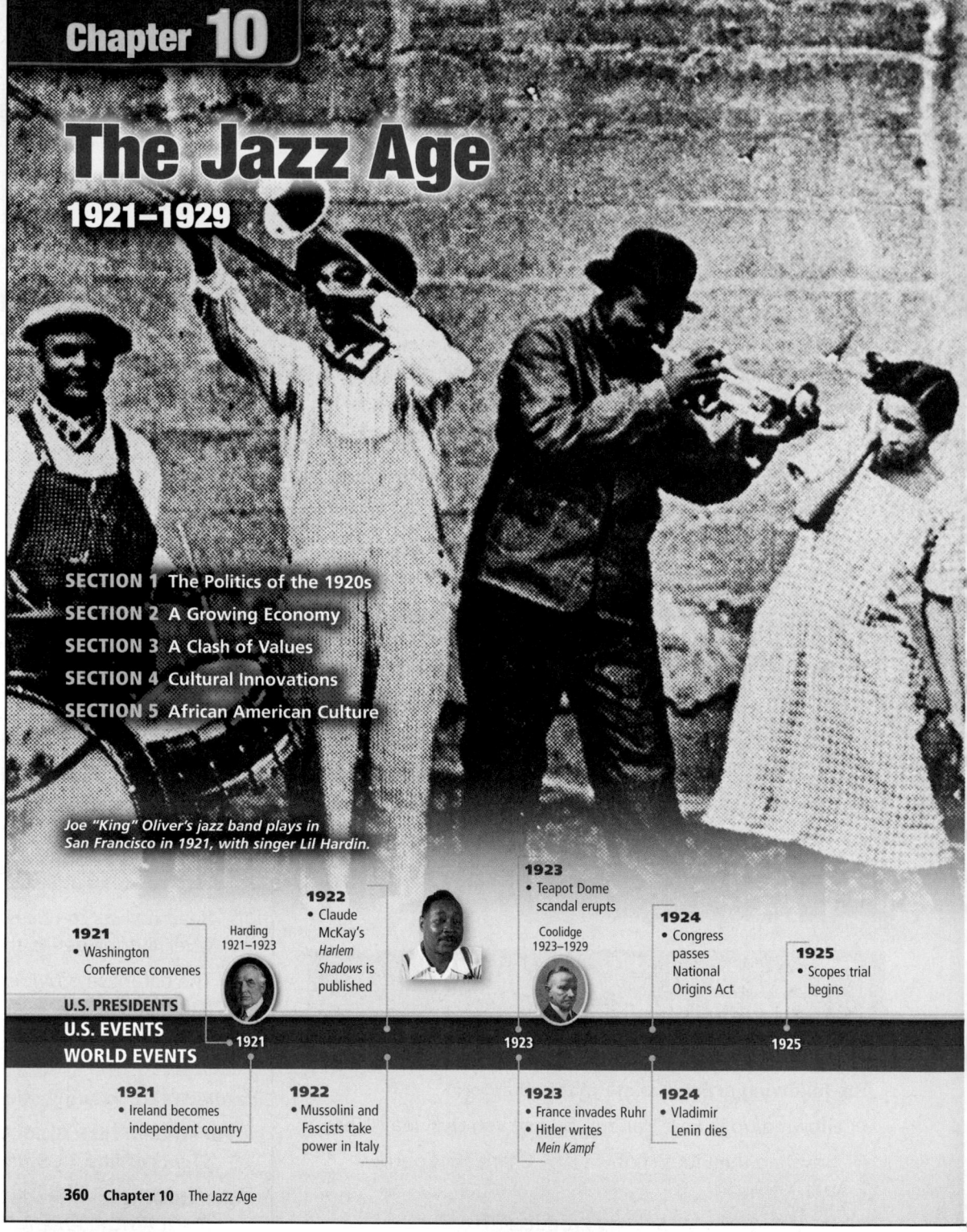

The Jazz Age
1921–1929

SECTION 1 The Politics of the 1920s
SECTION 2 A Growing Economy
SECTION 3 A Clash of Values
SECTION 4 Cultural Innovations
SECTION 5 African American Culture

Joe "King" Oliver's jazz band plays in San Francisco in 1921, with singer Lil Hardin.

U.S. PRESIDENTS

Harding 1921–1923

Coolidge 1923–1929

U.S. EVENTS

1921
• Washington Conference convenes

1921

1922
• Claude McKay's *Harlem Shadows* is published

1923
• Teapot Dome scandal erupts

1923

1924
• Congress passes National Origins Act

1925
• Scopes trial begins

1925

WORLD EVENTS

1921
• Ireland becomes independent country

1922
• Mussolini and Fascists take power in Italy

1923
• France invades Ruhr
• Hitler writes *Mein Kampf*

1924
• Vladimir Lenin dies

360 Chapter 10 The Jazz Age

Section 1

The Politics of the 1920s

Essential Question: Why did the American people want life to return to the way it was before World War I? *(People wanted to put the suffering of the war behind them; they were eager to buy new goods that were not available during the war.)* Point out that in Section 1 students will learn about the scandals of the Harding administration and the successes of the Coolidge Administration. **OL**

Section 2

A Growing Economy

Essential Question: How did new industries contribute to economic growth? *(New industries such as the automobile industry and the airline industry required vast amounts of material from other industries, including the steel, oil, rubber, and glass industries.)* Point out that in Section 2 students will learn how the new industries accelerated economic growth in the 1920s. **OL**

Making Connections
Why Does Culture Change?

In the 1920s, technology spurred economic growth and cultural change. Although not everyone approved, young people adopted new styles of dress, listened to jazz music, and had more independence than earlier generations.

- *What technologies changed life in the 1920s?*
- *How do you think the invention of radio and movies changed popular culture?*

1927
- Lindbergh completes first solo transatlantic flight

1928
- Kellogg-Briand Pact signed

Hoover
1929–1933

1927

1929

1926
- British General Strike paralyzes British economy

1927
- Stalin gains control of Soviet Union

1928
- Chiang Kai-shek becomes leader of China

FOLDABLES

Categorizing the Harlem Renaissance
Create a Trifold Book Foldable to present a brief biography, with artistic works, of major figures in the Harlem Renaissance under the category of writers, poets, and musicians. You may want to expand on your entries by using the Internet.

Writers	Poets	Musicians

History ONLINE Chapter Overview
Visit glencoe.com to preview Chapter 10.

Chapter 10   The Jazz Age   **361**

More About the Photo

Visual Literacy Around 1907, Joe "King" Oliver began his musical career in New Orleans. He later joined the "great migration" of African Americans moving north, settling in Chicago in 1919, and then spent time performing in California. In 1921 he returned to Chicago and formed King Oliver's Creole Jazz Band, which Louis Armstrong later joined.

FOLDABLES Study Organizer **Dinah Zike's Foldables**

Dinah Zike's Foldables are three-dimensional, interactive graphic organizers that help students practice basic writing skills, review vocabulary terms, and identify main ideas. Instructions for creating and using Foldables can be found in the Appendix at the end of this book and in the *Dinah Zike's Reading and Study Skills Foldables* booklet.

History ONLINE
Introduce students to chapter content and key terms by having them access the Chapter 10 Overview at glencoe.com.

Section 3

A Clash of Values
Essential Question: Why did the modern culture of the 1920s cause some people to think that traditional society and morality were under attack? *(Many people were afraid of new beliefs and ways of doing things. In addition, some people were fearful of immigrants.)* Point out that in Section 3 students will learn how some Americans reacted to the culture of the 1920s. **OL**

Section 4

Cultural Innovations
Essential Question: How did popular culture, the arts, and literature change in the 1920s? *(More Americans used their increased leisure time to enjoy popular culture; artists and writers expressed the exuberance as well as the loneliness of the decade.)* Point out that in Section 4 students will learn how popular culture and the arts reflected the moods of the 1920s. **OL**

Section 5

African American Culture
Essential Question: How did African Americans affect American society in the 1920s? *(The Harlem Renaissance led to new African American literature, music, and art; the influx of African Americans to northern cities made them a powerful political voice.)* Point out that in Section 5 students will learn about the contributions of African Americans in the 1920s. **OL**

Focus

Bellringer
Daily Focus Transparency 10.1

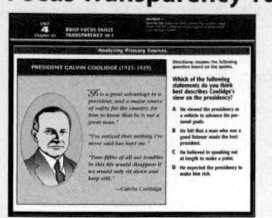

Guide to Reading

Answers may include:

Presidential Politics

I. The Harding Administration

  A. Teapot Dome and Other
     Scandals

  B. "Silent Cal" Takes Over

Students should complete the
outline by including all the heads
in the section.

Section Spotlight Video

To generate student interest and
provide a springboard for class
discussion, access the Chapter 10,
Section 1 video at glencoe.com or
on the video DVD.

Resource Manager

The Politics of the 1920s

Guide to Reading

Big Ideas
Economics and Society Government
policies helped create prosperity in the
1920s.

Content Vocabulary
• supply-side economics (p. 365)
• cooperative individualism (p. 365)
• isolationism (p. 366)

Academic Vocabulary
• investigation (p. 363)
• revelation (p. 364)

People and Events to Identify
• Teapot Dome (p. 363)
• Charles G. Dawes (p. 367)
• Charles Evans Hughes (p. 367)
• Kellogg-Briand Pact (p. 367)

Reading Strategy
Taking Notes As you read about
Presidents Harding and Coolidge, create
an outline similar to the one below.

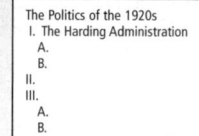

The Politics of the 1920s
  I. The Harding Administration
    A.
    B.
  II.
  III.
    A.
    B.

Warren G. Harding's administration suffered from
corruption and scandals. His successor, Calvin
Coolidge, worked hard to restore the American public's
faith in their government and to promote a healthy
economy.

The Harding Administration

MAIN Idea President Harding staffed his administration with political
friends from Ohio; his presidency was marred by many scandals.

HISTORY AND YOU If you were choosing teammates, would you pick a
friend or a better player? Read on to learn about the problems Harding
created by making poor choices for government appointments.

Warren G. Harding was born in 1865 in Corsica, Ohio. In 1898
voters elected Harding to the Ohio General Assembly, where he fit in
comfortably with the powerful Ohio Republican political machine.
Voters elected him as Ohio's lieutenant governor in 1903 and United
States senator in 1914. After serving one term in the Senate, Harding
ran for and won the presidency in 1920.

Harding's political philosophy fit in well with the times. In his
campaign, he had promised "a return to normalcy," by which he
meant "normal" life after the war. His charm and genial manner
endeared him to the nation, and people applauded when the open,
easygoing atmosphere of the Harding administration replaced the
quiet gloom of President Wilson's last years.

Teapot Dome and Other Scandals

Harding made several distinguished appointments to the cabinet,
including former Supreme Court Justice Charles Evans Hughes as
secretary of state, former Food Administrator Herbert Hoover as secretary of commerce, and business tycoon Andrew Mellon as secretary
of the treasury. All three men would play an important role in supporting and shaping the economic prosperity of the 1920s.

Many of Harding's other appointments, however, were disastrous.
He gave cabinet posts and other high-level jobs to friends and political allies from Ohio. Harding named Harry M. Daugherty, his campaign manager and boss of the Ohio Republican Party, attorney
general. He made his boyhood friend Daniel Crissinger chairman of
the Federal Reserve Board and selected Colonel Charles R. Forbes—
another Ohio acquaintance—to head the Veterans Bureau.

Harding felt more comfortable among his old poker-playing
friends, known as the Ohio Gang, than he did around such sober and

---

R Reading Strategies	**C** Critical Thinking	**D** Differentiated Instruction	**W** Writing Support	**S** Skill Practice
Additional Resources • Guided Read., URB p. 46	**Teacher Edition** • Analyzing Prim. Sources, p. 363 • Making Comparisons, p. 365 • Making Inferences, p. 366 • Analyze Info., p. 367 **Additional Resources** • Quizzes and Tests, p. 139 • Critical Thinking Skills Act., URB p. 32	**Teacher Edition** • Visual/Spatial, p. 366 **Additional Resources** • Foldables, pp. 68–70 • Academic Vocab. Act., URB p. 29 • English Learner Act., URB p. 25	**Teacher Edition** • Persuasive Writing, p. 364 **Additional Resources** • Supreme Court Case Stud., p. 43 • Content Vocab. Act., URB p. 27	**Teacher Edition** • Analyzing, p. 363 **Additional Resources** • RENTG, p. 100

POLITICAL CARTOONS PRIMARY SOURCE
An Administration Plagued by Scandal

▲ This cartoon shows politicians on the slippery "White House Highway" trying to outrun the scandal of Teapot Dome.

▲ "Bargain Day in Washington" shows the U.S. Capitol, the Washington Monument, the army, the White House, and the navy as having been "sold" to the highest bidder.

Analyzing VISUALS DBQ

1. **Drawing Conclusions** What does the cartoon on the left suggest about politicians?
2. **Analyzing** What does the cartoon on the right imply about corruption in the federal government?

serious people as Herbert Hoover. According to Alice Roosevelt Longworth, the White House study resembled a speakeasy.

PRIMARY SOURCE

"The air [would be] heavy with tobacco smoke, trays with bottles containing every imaginable brand of whiskey . . . cards and poker chips at hand—a general atmosphere of waistcoat unbuttoned, feet on desk, and spittoons alongside."
—quoted in *The Perils of Prosperity, 1914–1932*

The Ohio Gang did more than drink, smoke, and play poker with the president. Some members used their positions to sell government jobs, pardons, and protection from prosecution. Forbes sold scarce medical supplies from veterans' hospitals and kept the money for himself, costing the taxpayers about $250 million. When Harding learned what was going on, he complained privately that he had been betrayed. He said that he had no troubles with his enemies, but his friends were a different story: "They're the ones that keep me walking the floor nights!"

In June 1923 Harding left to tour the West. En route from Alaska to California, he became ill with what was probably a heart attack. He died in San Francisco on August 2, shortly before the news of the Forbes scandal broke. Early the next morning, the vice president, Calvin Coolidge, took the oath of office and became president.

The Forbes scandal was only the latest in a series of scandals and accusations that had marked the Harding administration. The most famous scandal, known as **Teapot Dome,** began in early 1922 when Harding's secretary of the interior, Albert B. Fall, secretly allowed private interests to lease lands containing U.S. Navy oil reserves at Teapot Dome, Wyoming, and Elk Hills, California. In return, Fall received bribes from these private interests totaling more than $300,000.

After the *Wall Street Journal* broke the story, the Senate launched an **investigation** that took most of the 1920s to complete. Trials followed; the Supreme Court invalidated the leases in 1927, and in 1929 Secretary Fall became the first cabinet officer in American history to go to prison.

Teach

S Skill Practice

Analyzing Have students study the political cartoons. **Ask:** Why are politicians fearful of scandals? Why do politicians worry about how their actions are perceived in their home districts? *(The hint of scandal or the perception that they are not responsible to their constituents may make them lose the next election.)* **OL**

C Critical Thinking

Analyzing Primary Sources Have students reread the primary source excerpt on this page. **Ask:** What impression does the excerpt describe? *(The excerpt describes a very relaxed, laid-back, casual atmosphere—hardly indicative of leadership.)* **BL**

Analyzing VISUALS

Answers:
1. They are fearful that the scandal will hurt their careers.
2. The government is for sale to the highest bidder.

Hands-On Chapter Project
Step 1

Creating a Memory Book

Step 1: Selecting Memorable Participants Students will skim the chapter and choose a person who played a role in the events of this chapter. Students may choose people mentioned in the chapter or research other people not mentioned, but involved in the events of this period. Students will learn more about him or her in order to contribute a page to a class memory book.

Directions Make a scrapbook with the title "Memories of the Jazz Age" on the cover, and write the title on the board. Ask students to list on the board the names of people they may already know who played active roles in this period, such as Calvin Coolidge, Henry Ford, John T. Scopes, Mary Pickford, or Duke Ellington. Have students read ahead or do research to add as many names to the list as there are class members. Then have each student choose one name from the list.

Analyzing Information Students will identify the role played by each person added to the list. **OL**

(Chapter Project continued on page 369)

Another Harding administration scandal involved Attorney General Harry Daugherty. During World War I, the federal government had seized a German-owned company in the United States as enemy property. To acquire the company and its valuable chemical patents, a German agent bribed a "go-between" politician, and a portion of the bribe ended up in a bank account that Daugherty controlled.

Under investigation by his own Justice Department, Daugherty refused to turn over requested files and bank records. He also refused to testify under oath, claiming immunity, or freedom from prosecution, on the grounds that he had had confidential dealings with the president. Daugherty's actions disgusted the new president, Calvin Coolidge, who demanded his resignation.

"Silent Cal" Takes Over

Calvin Coolidge was very different from Harding. Harding had enjoyed the easy conversation and company of old friends. Coolidge, joked a critic, could be "silent in five languages." Although he quickly distanced himself from the Harding administration, Coolidge asked the most capable cabinet members—Hughes, Mellon, and Hoover—to remain in the cabinet. Coolidge's philosophy of government was simple. He believed that prosperity rested on business leadership and that part of his job as president was to make sure that government interfered with business and industry as little as possible.

In the year following Harding's death and the **revelations** of the scandals, Coolidge avoided crises and adopted policies to help keep the nation prosperous. He easily won the Republican nomination for president in 1924.

The Republicans campaigned using the slogan "Keep Cool with Coolidge." They promised the American people that the policies that had brought prosperity would continue. Coolidge won the election easily, winning more than half the popular vote and 382 electoral votes.

✓ **Reading Check** **Analyzing** What do the scandals of the Harding administration have in common with each other?

PRIMARY SOURCE
Coolidge and Prosperity

Critics have accused Calvin Coolidge of catering to big business and cite his comment that the "business of the American people is business." This quote comes from his 1925 speech to the American Society of Newspaper Editors. Examine the graphs and the speech to assess if his policies benefited business at the expense of the public.

PRIMARY SOURCE

"After all, the chief business of the American people is business. They are profoundly concerned with producing, buying, selling, investing and prospering in the world. . . . In all experience, the accumulation of wealth means the multiplication of schools, the increase of knowledge, the dissemination of intelligence, the encouragement of science, the broadening of outlook, the expansion of liberties, the widening of culture. . . . We make no concealment of the fact that we want wealth, but there are many other things that we want very much more. We want peace and honor, and that charity which is so strong an element of all civilization.

The chief ideal of the American people is idealism. I cannot repeat too often that America is a nation of idealists."

—*New York Times,* January 18, 1925

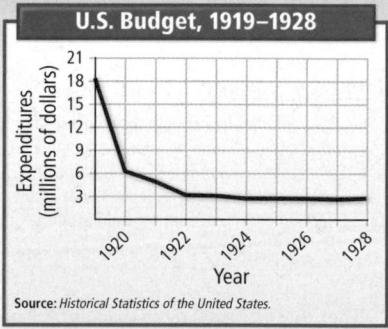

U.S. Budget, 1919–1928

Source: *Historical Statistics of the United States.*

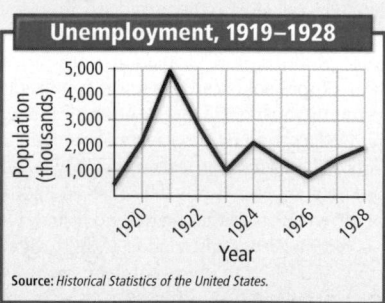

Unemployment, 1919–1928

Source: *Historical Statistics of the United States.*

Extending the Content

Calvin Coolidge In August 1923, Vice President Calvin Coolidge was taking a short vacation at his family's homestead in Vermont. The straitlaced Coolidge went to bed at 9:00 as usual on August 2, but at 2:30 A.M., his father woke him. "I noticed that his voice trembled," Coolidge later wrote. "I knew that something of the gravest nature had occurred." After learning that President Harding was dead, Coolidge dressed hurriedly and went downstairs. Shortly afterward, in a small, sparsely furnished room lit by a flickering kerosene lamp, the elder Coolidge, a farmer and justice of the peace, got out the family Bible and administered the presidential oath of office to his son.

Later, while painting a portrait of the new president, artist Charles Hopkinson asked, "Mr. Coolidge, what was the first thought that came into your mind when you were told that Mr. Harding was dead and the presidency was yours?" Coolidge replied, "I thought I could swing it."

Policies of Prosperity

MAIN Idea During the 1920s, the government cut taxes and spending to encourage economic growth.

HISTORY AND YOU Do you have a sales tax in your state? Do you think taxes are too high? How do you know? Read to learn about changes to American taxes in the 1920s.

Although Harding gave many corrupt friends government jobs, he also selected several highly qualified individuals for his cabinet. Among them were Andrew Mellon and Herbert Hoover. Both of these men were responsible for policies that contributed to the economic growth and prosperity of the 1920s.

At the beginning of the 1920s, the nation had a large national debt, and many people were worried that it would not recover from the postwar recession. Harding chose Andrew Mellon, a successful banker and industrialist, to be secretary of the treasury. Mellon became the chief architect of economic policy and served as secretary of the treasury for three Republican presidents.

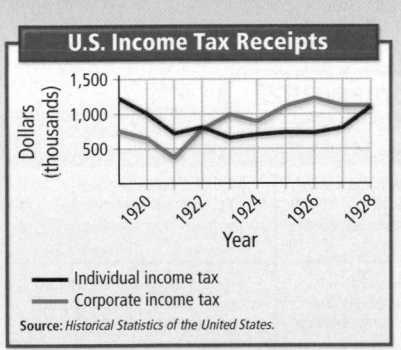

U.S. Income Tax Receipts

— Individual income tax
— Corporate income tax

Source: *Historical Statistics of the United States.*

Analyzing VISUALS **DBQ**

1. **Analyzing Primary Sources** What does Coolidge believe is the point of accumulating wealth? Do you believe that the United States has achieved Coolidge's goals? Explain.

2. **Evaluating** Based on the graphs, what did Coolidge's economic policies achieve in the 1920s?

When Mellon took office, he had three major goals: to balance the budget, to reduce the government's debt, and to cut taxes. He was convinced these policies would promote economic growth and prosperity. He also firmly believed that the government should apply business principles to its operations.

In 1921 Mellon convinced Congress to create both the Bureau of the Budget to prepare a unified federal budget, and the General Accounting Office to track spending. He then began cutting spending. The federal budget fell from $6.4 billion to less than $3 billion in seven years. He also cut tax rates.

Mellon argued that high tax rates actually reduced the amount of tax money the government collected. If taxes were lower, businesses and consumers would spend and invest their extra money, causing the economy to grow. As the economy grew, Americans would earn more money, and the government would actually collect more taxes at a lower rate than it would if it kept tax rates high. This idea is known today as **supply-side economics,** or "trickle-down" economics.

At Mellon's urging, Congress dramatically reduced tax rates. When Mellon took office, most taxpayers paid 4 percent federal income tax, while wealthy Americans in the highest bracket paid 73 percent. By 1928, Congress had reduced the rate most Americans paid to 0.5 percent and cut the rate for the wealthiest Americans to 25 percent.

Secretary of Commerce Herbert Hoover also sought to promote economic growth. He tried to balance government regulation with his own philosophy of **cooperative individualism.** This idea involved encouraging businesses to form trade associations that would voluntarily share information with the federal government. Hoover believed this system would reduce costs and promote economic efficiency.

To assist businesses, Hoover directed the Bureau of Foreign and Domestic Commerce to find new markets for companies. He also established the Bureau of Aviation to regulate and promote the growth of the airline industry and the Federal Radio Commission to help the young radio industry by regulating radio frequencies and the power of transmitters.

✔ **Reading Check** **Summarizing** What strategies did Mellon use to promote economic growth?

C Critical Thinking

Making Comparisons Have students find out Americans' tax rates today. **Ask:** How do the tax rates that Andrew Mellon recommended compare with tax rates today? Why might this be so? *(Rates today are higher overall. Students might point out that the government today pays for many goods and services that it did not in 1928.)* **OL**

DBQ Document Based Questions

Answers:

1. More schools, more knowledge, greater intelligence, development of science, a broadened outlook, expanded liberties, and widened culture; students' responses will vary but should be supported.

2. He increased the government's revenue from taxes.

✔ Reading Check

Answer:
He balanced the budget, reduced the government's debt, and cut taxes.

Differentiated Instruction

Activity: Collaborative Learning

Debate Have students work in groups to research the financial philosophy of Andrew Mellon using their book, the Internet, and library resources. Remind students that Mellon believed that the wealthy should not be penalized in the form of taxes on excess profits, inheritances, and large incomes because such taxes would discourage investment. Hold a class debate in which students discuss whether they agree or disagree with Mellon's philosophy. Students' arguments should be supported by facts gained in their research of Mellon's philosophy.

D **Differentiated Instruction**

Visual/Spatial Have students use library or Internet resources to find political cartoons about isolationism in the 1920s to create a bulletin board display either favoring or opposing an isolationist foreign policy. **OL**

C **Critical Thinking**

Making Inferences Have students review the Infographic on this page. **Ask:** What were these three treaties designed to accomplish? Were the treaties successful? *(The treaties were designed to prevent war; the treaties were not successful.)* Conduct a class discussion focusing on why these treaties were not successful. **AL**

Analyzing VISUALS

Answers:
1. the United States, Great Britain, France, Japan, and Italy
2. The western powers were trying to restrain Japan's aggressive foreign policy and to keep China open to trade.

Additional Support

Trade and Arms Control

MAIN Idea During the 1920s, the United States tried to promote peace and stability through economic policies and arms control agreements.

HISTORY AND YOU Do you remember reading about the Treaty of Versailles and how the United States never ratified it? Read to learn how America initiated other treaties in the 1920s.

Before World War I the United States was a debtor nation. By the end of the war, the situation was reversed. Wartime allies owed the United States more than $10 billion in war debts. By the 1920s, the United States was the dominant economic power in the world. Under the leadership of Secretary of State Charles Evan Hughes, the nation tried to use its economic power to promote peace and stability.

The Myth of Isolationism

D The majority of Americans—tired of being entangled in the baffling, hostile, and dangerous politics of Europe—favored **isolationism.** This is the idea that the United States will be safer and more prosperous if it stays out of world affairs.

To many people at the time, it appeared that the United States had become isolationist. The United States had not ratified the Treaty of Versailles and had not joined the League of Nations. The Permanent Court of International Justice, better known as the World Court, **D** opened in 1921, but the United States refused to join it as well.

Despite appearances, the United States was too powerful and too interconnected with other countries economically to be truly isolationist. Instead of relying on armed force and the collective security of the League of Nations, the United States tried to promote peace by using economic policies and arms control agreements.

The Dawes Plan

America's former allies had difficulty making the payments on their immense war debts. High American tariffs hampered their economic

INFOGRAPHIC

The Washington Conference, November 1921–February 1922

Treaty	Signers	Terms	Weaknesses
Four-Power Treaty	United States, Great Britain, France, Japan	• All agreed to respect the others' territory in the Pacific • Full and open negotiations in the event of disagreements	• Mutual defense of other co-signers not specified
Five-Power Treaty	United States, Great Britain, France, Japan, Italy	• All agreed to freeze naval production at 1921 levels and halt production of large warships for 10 years • U.S. and Great Britain agreed not to build new naval bases in the western Pacific	• No restrictions on the construction of smaller battle craft such as submarines and naval destroyers • Did not place restrictions on the ground forces
Nine-Power Treaty	United States, Great Britain, France, Japan, Italy, Belgium, China, the Netherlands, Portugal	• All agreed to preserve equal commercial rights to China—a reassertion of the Open Door policy	• No enforcement of the terms of the Open Door policy specified

Analyzing VISUALS

1. **Interpreting Charts** Which countries signed the Five-Power Treaty?

2. **Analyzing** Why do you think the terms of the treaties focused on the Pacific region?

Extending the Content

The Washington Naval Conference A major American goal at the Washington Naval Conference was to limit Japanese expansion in East Asia. For this reason, the American delegation proposed that the United States be allowed to have 10 major warships for every 6 that Japan had. The Japanese accepted the proposal but in return the United States had to agree not to fortify its bases in the Philippines or Guam. This decision shifted the balance of power in East Asia. Without fortified bases in the region, the United States had no hope of stopping a Japanese attack. When war erupted in 1941, the Philippines and Guam fell quickly to the Japanese forces, and the United States was forced to begin its campaign against Japan from much further east.

recovery by making it difficult to sell their products in the United States. This meant they could not acquire the money to pay off their war debts. These countries also were receiving reparations—huge cash payments Germany was required to make as punishment for starting the war. These payments, however, were crippling the German economy.

It was vital for the United States that European economies be healthy so that the Europeans could buy American exports and repay their debts. Thus, in 1924, American diplomat **Charles G. Dawes** negotiated an agreement with France, Britain, and Germany by which American banks would make loans to Germany that would enable it to make reparations payments. In exchange, Britain and France would accept less in reparations and pay back more on their war debts.

The Washington Conference

Despite their debts, the major powers were involved in a costly postwar naval arms race. To end the weapons race, the United States invited representatives from eight major countries—Great Britain, France, Italy, China, Japan, Belgium, the Netherlands, and Portugal—to Washington, D.C., to discuss disarmament. The Washington Conference opened on November 12, 1921.

In his address to the delegates, Secretary of State **Charles Evans Hughes** proposed a 10-year moratorium, or halt, on the construction of new warships. He also proposed a list of warships in each country's navy to be destroyed, beginning with some American battleships. The discussions that followed produced the Five-Power Naval Limitation Treaty in which Britain, France, Italy, Japan, and the United States essentially formalized Hughes's proposal.

As a long-term effort to prevent war, the conference had some serious shortcomings. It did nothing to limit land forces. It also angered the Japanese because it required Japan to maintain a smaller navy than either the United States or Great Britain. It did, however, give Americans cause to look forward to a period of peace, recovery, and prosperity.

Abolishing War

The apparent success of the Washington Conference boosted hopes that written agreements could end war altogether. Perhaps the highest expression of that idea occurred when U.S. Secretary of State Frank Kellogg and French Foreign Minister Aristide Briand proposed a treaty to outlaw war. On August 27, 1928, the United States and 14 other nations signed the **Kellogg-Briand Pact.** Although it had no binding force, the pact was hailed as a victory for peace. It stated that all signing nations agreed to abandon war and to settle all disputes by peaceful means. The Kellogg-Briand Pact and the Dawes Plan were perhaps the most notable foreign policy achievements of the Coolidge administration.

✓ Reading Check **Identifying** What problem was the Dawes Plan intended to solve?

Section 1 REVIEW

Vocabulary
1. **Explain** the significance of: Teapot Dome, supply-side economics, cooperative individualism, isolationism, Charles G. Dawes, Charles Evans Hughes, Kellogg-Briand Pact.

Main Ideas
2. **Summarizing** What scandals marred Harding's presidency?

3. **Explaining** What strategies did Andrew Mellon and Herbert Hoover use to stimulate economic growth?

4. **Describing** In what two ways did the United States try to promote peace during the 1920s?

Critical Thinking
5. **Big Ideas** What efforts did the United States make to promote worldwide economic recovery?

6. **Categorizing** Use a graphic organizer like the one below to list the major terms of the treaties resulting from the Washington Conference.

Major Terms of Treaties

7. **Analyzing Visuals** Examine the charts on page 364. What explanation can you offer for the drop in the United States's budget from 1919 to 1928?

Writing About History
8. **Persuasive Writing** Imagine that you are an American business owner or farmer in the 1920s. Write a letter to your representatives in Congress explaining why you think cutting taxes is a good or bad idea.

History ONLINE
Study Central™ To review this section, go to **glencoe.com** and click on Study Central.

367

C Critical Thinking
Analyzing Information Ask students to find out more about the Kellogg-Briand Pact. **Ask:** *Is it possible to outlaw war? (Students should support their opinions.)* **AL**

✓ Reading Check

Answer:
the problem of former Allied nations being unable to pay their war debts and to purchase American-made goods

Assess

History ONLINE

Study Central™ provides summaries, interactive games, and online graphic organizers to help students review content.

Close

Summarizing Ask: In what ways did the federal government encourage a return to "normalcy" in the 1920s? *(decrease of government spending; support for business; attempts to prevent another war)* **OL**

Section 1 REVIEW

Answers

1. All definitions can be found in the section and the Glossary.

2. The Ohio Gang members sold medicine intended for the Veterans Bureau and kept the money, Albert Fall leased private lands to oil interests for a bribe in the Teapot Dome scandal, and Daugherty was accused of accepting bribes.

3. balanced federal budget, reduced government debts, cut taxes, encouraged the development of trade associations to share

information with the government to reduce costs and promote efficiency

4. economic policies and arms control agreements

5. Students' answers should reflect analysis of text information, including the Dawes Plan and the Washington Conference.

6. respect the other nations' territories in the Pacific; full and open negotiations in the event of disagreements; agreed to freeze naval production at 1921 levels and halt

production of large warships for 10 years; the U.S. and Great Britain agreed not to build new naval bases in the western Pacific; agreed to preserve equal commercial rights to China—a reassertion of the Open Door Policy

7. The government was not spending money on war equipment and supplies.

8. Letters should be written from the point of view of a business owner or farmer.

Focus

Guide to Reading

Answers: Industry: air travel, automobiles, consumer goods, radio; Society: consumer-oriented credit, workers shifting from farming to industry, labor-saving devices, growing mobility

Section Spotlight Video

To generate student interest and provide a springboard for class discussion, access the Chapter 10, Section 2 video at glencoe.com or on the video DVD.

Resource Manager

Section 2

A Growing Economy

Guide to Reading

Big Ideas
Economics and Society The United States experienced stunning economic growth during the 1920s.

Content Vocabulary
• mass production (p. 368)
• assembly line (p. 368)
• Model T (p. 368)
• welfare capitalism (p. 374)
• open shop (p. 374)

Academic Vocabulary
• disposable (p. 370)
• credit (p. 372)

People and Events to Identify
• Charles Lindbergh (p. 372)

Reading Strategy
Organizing As you read about the booming era of the 1920s, complete a graphic organizer to analyze the causes of economic growth and prosperity in the 1920s.

Industry   Society

In the 1920s widespread ownership of automobiles, radios, and other innovations changed how Americans lived. The Coolidge administration encouraged business growth and tried to promote stability in international affairs.

The Rise of New Industries

MAIN Idea Mass production and the assembly line allowed new industries, such as automobile and airplane manufacturing, to grow.

HISTORY AND YOU How would businesses, governments, and your family be affected if air travel did not exist? Read to learn how the transportation industry changed during the 1920s and 1930s.

By the 1920s, the automobile had become an accepted part of American life. In a 1925 survey conducted in Muncie, Indiana, 21 out of 26 families who owned cars did not have bathtubs with running water. When asked why her family decided a car was more important than indoor plumbing, a farm wife explained, "You can't ride to town in a bathtub."

The automobile was just one part of a rising standard of living that Americans experienced in the 1920s. Real per capita earnings soared 22 percent between 1923 and 1929. Meanwhile, as Americans' wages increased, their work hours decreased. In 1923 U.S. Steel cut its daily work shift from 12 hours to 8 hours. In 1926 Henry Ford cut the workweek for his employees from six days to five, and International Harvester, a maker of farm machinery, instituted an annual two-week paid vacation for employees. These changes took place because **mass production,** or large-scale manufacturing done with machinery, increased supply and reduced costs. Workers could be paid more and the consumer goods they bought cost less.

The Assembly Line and the Model T

First adopted by carmaker Henry Ford, the moving **assembly line** divided operations into simple tasks and cut unnecessary motion to a minimum. In 1913 Ford installed the first moving assembly line at his plant in Highland Park, Michigan. By the following year, workers were building an automobile every 93 minutes. Before, the task had taken 12 hours. By 1925 a Ford car was rolling off the line every 10 seconds. Ford was the first person to build factories based on the concept of the assembly line.

Ford's assembly-line product was the **Model T**—affectionately called the "Tin Lizzie" or "Flivver." In 1908, the Model T's first year,

---

R Reading Strategies	C Critical Thinking	D Differentiated Instruction	W Writing Support	S Skill Practice
Teacher Edition • Categorizing Info., p. 371 • Act. Prior Know., p. 374 **Additional Resources** • Guided Read., URB p. 47	**Teacher Edition** • Ident. Cent. Issues, p. 370 • Det. Cause and Effect, p. 372 **Additional Resources** • Quizzes and Tests, p. 140	**Teacher Edition** • Visual/Spatial, p. 373 • Verbal/Linguistic, p. 372	**Teacher Edition** • Narrative Writing, p. 369 • Descriptive Writing, p. 370 **Additional Resources** • Time Line Act., URB p. 33	**Teacher Edition** • Chronological Thinking, p. 375 **Additional Resources** • RENTG, p. 103 • Historical Analysis Skills Act., URB p. 22 • Reading Skills Act., URB p. 21

INFOGRAPHIC
The Car Changes America

Many industries that were needed to build cars prospered. Car manufacturers needed steel for the car body, glass for the windows, and rubber for the tires. The automobile also led to changes in society. People moved to the suburbs, but were less isolated from the benefits of the city. At the same time, there was a decline in mass transportation such as railroads and trolleys.

▲ Cars greatly increased the demand for oil, leading to a boom in the oil business, as shown by the forest of oil wells in Signal Hills, California in 1930. To keep cars refueled, roadside gas stations sprang up across the country.

▲ Cars allowed people greater mobility and freedom. These young women drove to the country to have a picnic.

▶ The auto industry spurred a boom in other industries, as well. These workers at Goodyear Tire and Rubber in Akron, Ohio, are removing car tires from curing pits.

▲ The car let people live further out in the suburbs and commute to jobs in the city.

Analyzing VISUALS DBQ

1. **Determining Cause and Effect** How did the automobile help other industries grow? Which industries were most affected?
2. **Drawing Conclusions** Based on the images above, how did the car change people's lives?

---

it sold for $850. In 1914 mass production reduced the price to $490. Three years later, improved assembly-line methods and a high volume of sales brought the price down to $360. By 1924 Model Ts were selling for $295, and Ford sold millions of them. His business philosophy was: lower the cost per car and thereby increase the volume of sales.

The low prices made possible by Ford's mass-production methods not only created an immense market for his cars but also spawned imitators. By the mid-1920s, other car manufacturers, notably General Motors and Chrysler, competed successfully with Ford. The auto industry also spurred growth in other industries, such as rubber, plate glass, nickel, and lead. The auto industry alone consumed 15 percent of the nation's steel and led to a huge expansion of the petroleum industry.

High Wages for Workers Ford also increased his workers' wages in 1914 to $5 a day (doubling their pay) and reduced the workday to eight-hour shifts. Ford took these dramatic steps to build up workers' loyalty and to undercut union organizers.

Teach

W Writing Support
Narrative Writing Have students use library or Internet sources to find out information about the life of a worker in a rubber factory, such as Goodyear Tire and Rubber in Akron, Ohio. Using their findings, students should write a letter to family members back home describing one day at work. Remind students to use details to bring their letters to life. Encourage students to share their letters with the class. OL

Analyzing VISUALS

Answers:
1. The automobile industry helped the steel, rubber, glass, and oil industries grow. Answers will vary, but students will likely identify the oil and steel industries.
2. People had more mobility; they could live farther away from where they worked; they used the automobile for leisure activities.

Hands-On Chapter Project
Step 2

Creating a Memory Book

Step 2: Researching Selected Names
Each student will do research on the name chosen in Step 1.

Directions Have students use library, Internet, or family resources to learn more about the person whose name they chose. They should write a short biography of the person, and select a quotation or short paragraph written by the person, if possible.

Evaluating Information To decide which information to include, students will gain practice in evaluating the reliability of sources and the relevance of the information to the project. OL

(Chapter Project continued on page 377)

C Critical Thinking

Identifying Central Issues
Tell students to imagine that their school has instituted a new policy of home visitations. Explain that you will be coming by their homes regularly to make sure they are eating properly, getting enough sleep, and doing their homework. **Ask: What do you think of this policy? Is it necessary or worthwhile?** *(Answers will vary, but students will likely view such visits as an invasion of their privacy.)* After some discussion, read the paragraph about Ford's Sociological Department. Ask the class to discuss circumstances that made this policy possible. **OL**

W Writing Support

Descriptive Writing Have students reread the paragraph "The Social Impact of the Automobile." Then have them write a paragraph describing how their own lives would be different if the automobile had not been invented. Encourage students to share their paragraphs. **BL**

Additional Support

There were strings attached, however. Ford created a "Sociological Department," which set requirements workers had to meet. For example, renting space in one's home to nonfamily members was strictly forbidden. Investigators visited employees' homes to verify their eligibility and workers who broke the rules could be disqualified from extra pay, suspended, or even fired.

The Social Impact of the Automobile
Cars revolutionized American life. They eased the isolation of rural life and enabled more people to live farther from work. An entirely new kind of worker, the auto commuter, appeared. Since commuters could drive from their homes in suburbia to their workplaces, other forms of urban transportation, such as the trolley, became less popular.

Consumer Goods

In response to rising **disposable** income, many other new goods came on the market. Americans bought such innovations as electric razors, facial tissues, frozen foods, and home hair color.

Companies created many new products for the home. As indoor plumbing became more common, Americans' concern for hygiene led to the development of numerous household cleaning products. By appealing to people's health concerns, advertisers convinced homemakers to buy cleansers in hopes of protecting their families from disease.

New appliances advertised as labor-savers changed the home. Electric irons, vacuum cleaners, washing machines, and refrigerators changed the way people cleaned their homes and prepared meals.

Another lucrative category of consumer products focused on Americans' concern with fashion and youthful appearance. Mouthwash, deodorants, cosmetics, and perfumes became popular products in the 1920s.

Birth of the Airline Industry

In the early 1900s, many people were trying to build the first powered airplane that could

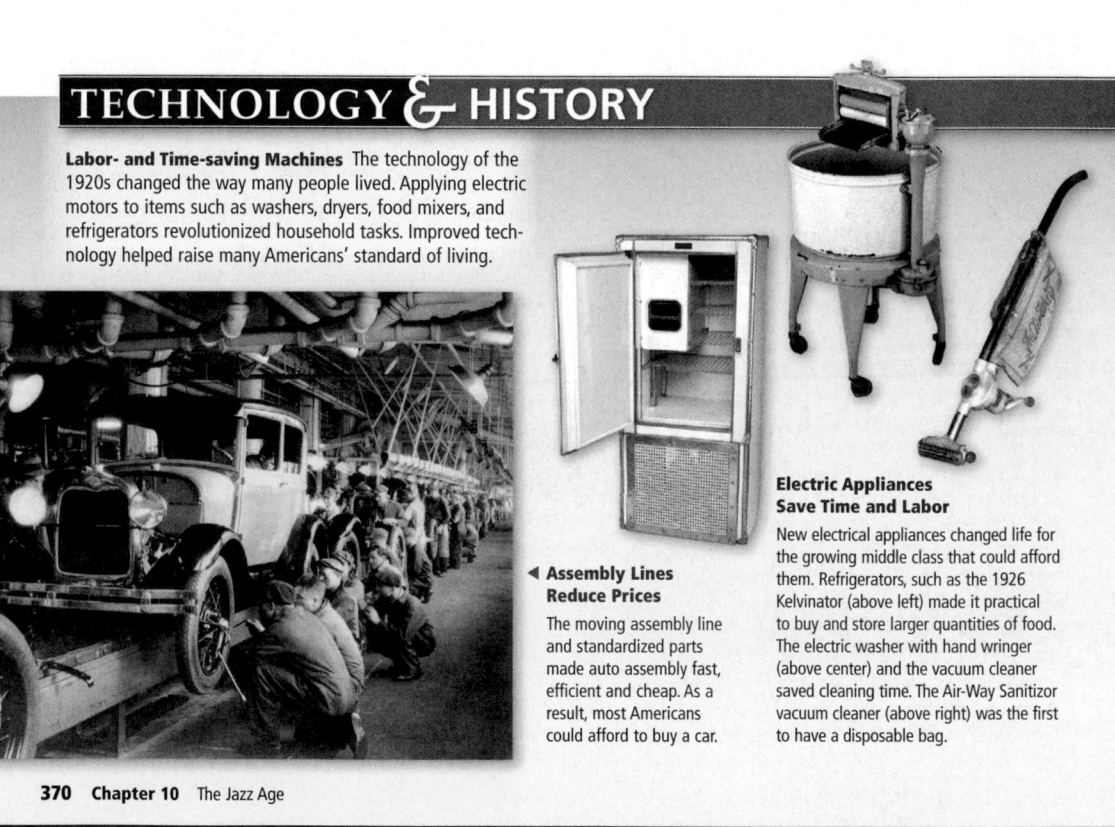

TECHNOLOGY & HISTORY

Labor- and Time-saving Machines The technology of the 1920s changed the way many people lived. Applying electric motors to items such as washers, dryers, food mixers, and refrigerators revolutionized household tasks. Improved technology helped raise many Americans' standard of living.

◀ **Assembly Lines Reduce Prices**
The moving assembly line and standardized parts made auto assembly fast, efficient and cheap. As a result, most Americans could afford to buy a car.

Electric Appliances Save Time and Labor
New electrical appliances changed life for the growing middle class that could afford them. Refrigerators, such as the 1926 Kelvinator (above left) made it practical to buy and store larger quantities of food. The electric washer with hand wringer (above center) and the vacuum cleaner saved cleaning time. The Air-Way Sanitizor vacuum cleaner (above right) was the first to have a disposable bag.

370 Chapter 10 The Jazz Age

Activity: Interdisciplinary Activity

Language Arts Explain to students that many new words were developed to better describe the societal changes that came about because of the automobile. Tell students that a lexicon is a list of words and their meanings. Have interested students create a lexicon of terms that developed in the early 1900s after the automobile was invented and became popular. Tell them that the lexicon should include the pronunciation and solid working definitions for each term. For at least two of the terms, students should also include a drawing or diagram for further explanation. **OL**

carry a human being. Samuel Langley, secretary of the Smithsonian Institution, was perhaps best known for his attempts at the time. Langley had built small model airplanes powered by steam engines, and the War Department had awarded him $50,000 to build an airplane that could carry a person. On December 8, 1903, Langley demonstrated his plane to government officials in Washington, D.C. Unfortunately, his plane broke apart on takeoff and crashed into the Potomac River.

The War Department, in its final report on the Langley project, concluded that "[W]e are still far from the ultimate goal, and it would seem as if years of constant work and study by experts, together with the expenditure of thousands of dollars, would still be necessary before we can hope to produce an apparatus of practical utility on these lines."

Nine days later, Wilbur and Orville Wright, two inventors from Dayton, Ohio, tested the airplane they had built using only $1,000 of their personal savings. The Wright brothers had carefully studied the problems of earlier airplanes and had designed one with better wings, a more efficient propeller, and a strong but very light engine. On December 17, 1903, at Kitty Hawk, North Carolina, Orville made the first crewed, powered flight in history.

After the Wright brothers' successful flight, the aviation industry began developing rapidly. Leading the way was American inventor Glenn Curtiss. Curtiss owned a motorcycle company in Hammondsport, New York. Fascinated by airplanes, he agreed in 1907 to become director of experiments at the Aerial Experiment Association, an organization that Alexander Graham Bell founded. Within a year, Curtiss had invented ailerons—surfaces attached to wings that can be tilted to steer the plane. Ailerons made it possible to build rigid wings and much larger aircraft. They are still used today.

Curtiss's company began building aircraft and sold the first airplanes in the United States. The company grew from a single factory to a huge industrial enterprise during World War I, as orders for his biplanes and engines flooded in from Allied governments. Although Curtiss retired in 1920, his inventions made possible the airline industry that emerged in the 1920s.

R Reading Strategy
Categorizing Information
Have students research the economic impact of the airline industry in the United States during the 1900s. Tell them that they can focus on the revenues generated by the industry or on the number of people employed in the industry. Have students create tables or charts to show the growth of the airline industry and its effects on the American economy. **Ask:** Based on the information and trends identified, can you predict what will happen to the airline industry in the first half of the twenty-first century? *(Answers will vary, depending upon how students have interpreted their data.)* OL

Analyzing VISUALS
Answers:
1. Answers will vary, but students should support their responses with examples.
2. Transportation and communication have become faster, more efficient, and cheaper.

Additional Support

Airlines Speed Travel
The aviation industry developed quickly after the Wright brothers' first successful flight in 1903 (above). Below, passengers are shown boarding a Northwest Orient Airlines Ford Tri-motor. Although seating was cramped (right), passenger airlines carried increasing numbers of people in the 1920s.

Radio Links the Nation Together ▶
Commercial radio grew rapidly in the 1920s. It helped create a national community as people across the country could listen to the same music, sports, news, and entertainment programs. The technicians shown at right are preparing for the first NBC radio show, which was broadcast in 1926.

Analyzing VISUALS · DBQ
1. **Making Connections** Which of the inventions pictured is most important to your life? Which do you think is most important to the nation as a whole?
2. **Making Generalizations** How have advances in transportation and communication changed life in the United States in the past 100 years?

Chapter 10 The Jazz Age **371**

Extending the Content

The *Wright Flyer* The Wright brother's aircraft flown at Kitty Hawk was named the *Wright Flyer*. It was a wood-and-muslin fabric aircraft. After the initial success of the first flight on December 17, 1903, at Kitty Hawk, the Wright brothers continued to improve the designs of their aircraft. The Wright brothers' first planes were difficult to control and frequently crashed.

The *Wright Flyer III* made its first flight at Huffman Prairie in Dayton, Ohio, in 1905. This plane could be steered, make turns, and be controlled in a gust of wind. Soon, the plane was modified to hold a passenger. Later versions of the *Wright Flyer III* reached speeds of 45 miles per hour (72 km/h), soared to an altitude of 360 feet (107.9 m), and covered a distance of 77 miles (124 km).

The *Wright Flyer III* was taken apart and its parts were displayed in many locations. Finally, in 1947, with direction from Orville Wright, the plane was reassembled, although some new parts had to be created. The original *Wright Flyer,* which flew at Kitty Hawk, hangs in the Smithsonian Air and Space Museum in Washington, D.C. The *Wright Flyer III* is on display in Wright Hall at Dayton's Carillon Park.

D Differentiated Instruction

Verbal/Linguistic Invite students to research the development of CBS and NBC from radio broadcasting companies to multimedia corporations. Ask them to prepare written reports that focus on this transformation, and then have them share their findings in a class presentation. **OL**

C Critical Thinking

Determining Cause and Effect The use of credit is commonplace among consumers today, but misuse of this purchasing power remains a problem. **Ask:** How can consumers get into trouble when they buy things on credit? *(Answers may include that consumers may be encouraged to buy more things than they need and borrow more from creditors than they can afford to repay. Remind students to withhold personal details.)* **OL**

Reading Check

Answer:
It allowed people to live further from work and eased rural isolation.

Additional Support

After Curtiss and other entrepreneurs started building practical aircraft, the federal government began to support the airline industry. President Wilson's postmaster general introduced the world's first regular airmail service in 1918 by hiring pilots to fly mail between Washington, D.C., and New York. In 1919 the Post Office expanded airmail service across the continent.

The aviation industry received an economic boost in 1925 when Congress passed the Kelly Act, authorizing postal officials to contract with private airplane operators to carry mail. The following year Congress passed the Air Commerce Act, which provided federal aid for building airports. Former airmail pilot **Charles Lindbergh** made an amazing transatlantic solo flight in 1927, showing the possibilities of commercial aviation. By the end of 1928, 48 airlines were serving 355 American cities.

The Radio Industry

In 1913 Edwin Armstrong, an American engineer, invented a special circuit that made it practical to transmit sound via long-range radio. The radio industry began a few years later. In November 1920 the Westinghouse Company broadcast the news of Harding's landslide election victory from station KDKA in Pittsburgh—one of the first public broadcasts in history. That success persuaded Westinghouse to open other stations.

In 1926 the National Broadcasting Company (NBC) set up a network of stations to broadcast daily programs. By 1927, almost 700 stations dotted the country. Sales of radio equipment grew from $12.2 million in 1921 to $842.5 million in 1929, by which time 10 million radios were in use across the country.

In 1928 the Columbia Broadcasting System (CBS) assembled a coast-to-coast network of stations to rival NBC. The two networks sold advertising time and hired musicians, actors, and comedians from vaudeville, movies, and the nightclub circuit to appear on their shows. Americans experienced the first presidential election campaign to use radio broadcasts in 1928, when the radio networks sold more than $1 million in advertising time to the Republican and Democratic Parties.

Reading Check **Analyzing** How did the automobile change the way people lived?

The Consumer Society

MAIN Idea Consumer credit and advertising helped to create a nation of consumers.

HISTORY AND YOU Have you ever purchased something on credit or bought an item because of advertising? Read to discover the beginnings of the widespread consumer culture in America.

Higher wages and shorter workdays resulted in a decade-long buying spree that kept the economy booming. Shifting from traditional attitudes of thrift and prudence, Americans in the 1920s enthusiastically accepted their new role as consumers.

Easy Consumer Credit

One notable aspect of the economic boom was the growth of individual borrowing. **Credit** had been available before the 1920s, but most Americans had considered debt shameful. Now, however, attitudes toward debt started changing as people began believing in their ability to pay their debts over time. Many

PRIMARY SOURCE
Advertising to Consumers

The early advertising age used techniques that continue to persuade consumers today. Easy credit terms and installment plans, envy of peers and neighbors, and the link of a product with a famous, attractive person all convinced people that they needed the flood of newly available consumer goods.

Extending the Content

Air Travel In the 1920s, airlines attracted an elite group of travelers. Forced to compete with comfortable, affordable rail service and highway travel, early airlines survived on mail delivery, splitting up a few lucrative government contracts. The airmail boom of the early 1930s led to improved airstrips and air traffic control. Meanwhile, the search began for a plane large enough, safe enough, and comfortable enough to attract a profitable number of passengers. The plane would also have to be inexpensive to run and maintain. Aeronautical engineer Donald Douglas set his designers to work on a large, two engine plane that would fly even if an engine, a set of instruments, or the landing gear failed. The result was the DC-1 in 1932 and the improved DC-2 in 1933. In 1935, the new DC-3 became the first profitable plane, carrying passengers for Transcontinental and Western Air (TWA).

listened to the sales pitch "Buy now and pay in easy installments," and racked up debts. Americans bought 75 percent of their radios and 60 percent of their automobiles on the installment plan. Some started buying on credit at a faster rate than their incomes increased.

Mass Advertising

When inventor Otto Rohwedder developed a commercial bread slicer in 1928, he faced a problem common to new inventions: the invention—sliced bread—was something no one knew was needed. To attract consumers, manufacturers turned to advertising, another booming industry in the 1920s.

Advertisers linked products with qualities associated with the modern era, such as progress, convenience, leisure, success, and style. In a 1924 magazine advertisement for deodorant, the headline read, "Flappers they may be—but they know the art of feminine appeal!" An advertisement for a spaghetti product told homemakers that heating is the same as cook-

ing: "Just one thing to do and it's ready to serve." Advertisers also preyed on consumers' fears and anxieties, such as jarred nerves due to the hectic pace of modern life or insecurities about one's status or weight.

The Managerial Revolution

By the early 1920s, many industries had begun to create modern organizational structures. Companies were split into divisions with different functions, such as sales, marketing, and accounting. To run these divisions, businesses needed to hire managers. Managers freed executives and owners from the day-to-day running of the companies.

The managerial revolution in companies created a new career—the professional manager. The large numbers of new managers helped expand the size of the middle class, which in turn added to the nation's prosperity. Similarly, so many companies relied on new technology that engineers were also in very high demand. They, too, joined the ranks of the growing middle class.

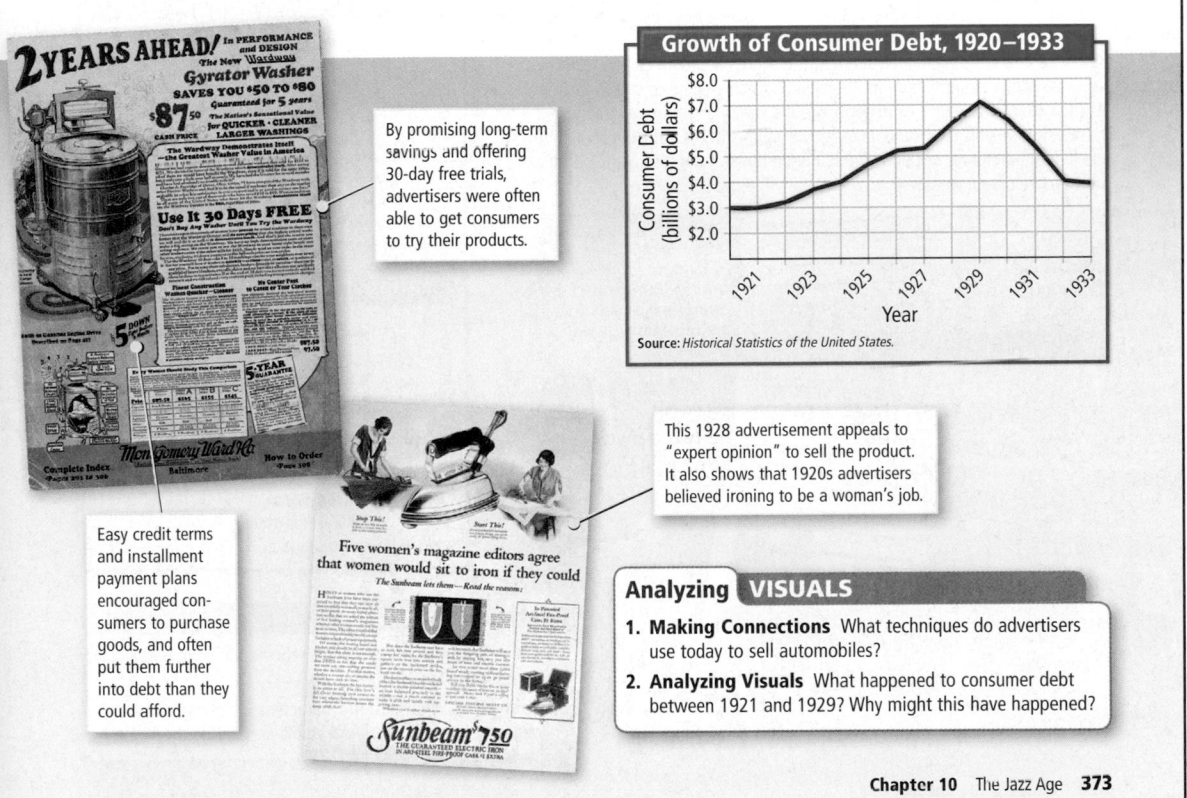

Growth of Consumer Debt, 1920–1933

Source: Historical Statistics of the United States.

By promising long-term savings and offering 30-day free trials, advertisers were often able to get consumers to try their products.

Easy credit terms and installment payment plans encouraged consumers to purchase goods, and often put them further into debt than they could afford.

This 1928 advertisement appeals to "expert opinion" to sell the product. It also shows that 1920s advertisers believed ironing to be a woman's job.

Analyzing VISUALS

1. **Making Connections** What techniques do advertisers use today to sell automobiles?
2. **Analyzing Visuals** What happened to consumer debt between 1921 and 1929? Why might this have happened?

Chapter 10 The Jazz Age **373**

Activity: Economics Connection

Advertising Ask students to create an advertisement with pictures and text promoting a refrigerator, radio, or labor-saving device that was new in the 1920s. Students will have to research one of these developments, think about the potential market for the product, and write accompanying text that rings true for both product and audience. They may also want to research period illustrations and design styles as they create the pictures. Encourage students to present their advertisements on a class Web page. **OL**

R **Reading Strategy**
Activating Prior Knowledge
Remind students that they have studied the terms *welfare*, *capitalist*, and *open shop* in earlier chapters. Review the meanings of these terms and then ask students to apply that knowledge as they determine the meanings of new terms found on this page. **OL**

Analyzing VISUALS

Answers:
1. the South
2. The wages of farm employees remained consistently lower than the wages of non-farm employees.

✓ Reading Check

Answer:
preyed on consumers' fears and anxieties; linked products to progress and success

Welfare Capitalism

Middle-class Americans were not the only members of the new consumer society. Industrial workers also had more disposable income, partly due to rising wages and partly because many corporations introduced what came to be called **welfare capitalism.** Companies allowed workers to buy stock, participate in profit sharing, and receive medical care and pensions.

R **The Decline of Unions** Benefits programs also made unions seem unnecessary to many workers. During the 1920s, unions lost both influence and membership. Employers promoted the **open shop**—a workplace where employees were not required to join a union. With benefits covering some of their basic needs, workers were able to spend more of their income to improve their quality of life. Many purchased consumer goods they previously could not afford.

Uneven Prosperity Not all Americans shared in this economic boom. Thousands of African Americans had factory jobs during World War I. When servicemen returned from the war, they replaced both African Americans and women.

Native Americans were also excluded from prosperity. Although granted citizenship in 1924, they were often isolated on reservations, where there was little productive work.

The majority of immigrants to the United States continued to come from Europe. Even these people often found it difficult to find work; most of them were farmers and factory workers whose wages were pitifully low.

Many people in the Deep South were also left out of the economic boom. The traditional agricultural economic base eroded after the war ended. Farmers in general failed to benefit from the growth of the economy.

✓ **Reading Check** **Analyzing** How did advertisers try to convince Americans to buy their products?

PRIMARY SOURCE
Prosperity for Whom?

Although many people benefited from the economic boom of the 1920s, several groups did not share in the general prosperity, nor did all regions of the country. Members of minority groups, newly arrived immigrants, and farmers often struggled economically. During the 1920s, for example, laborers in manufacturing not only outnumbered farmers but also acquired three times more actual wealth.

▼ *For many African Americans, including this family in rural Georgia, the 1920s was a time of poverty, not prosperity.*

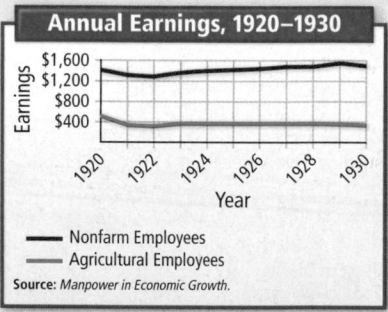

Average Hourly Earnings, 1929

	0.47	0.45		0.47
Earnings			0.31	
	Northeast	Midwest	South	West

$0.50, $0.40, $0.30, $0.20, $0.10, 0

Source: *Manpower in Economic Growth.*

Annual Earnings, 1920–1930

Earnings: $1,600, $1,200, $800, $400
Year: 1920, 1922, 1924, 1926, 1928, 1930

— Nonfarm Employees
— Agricultural Employees
Source: *Manpower in Economic Growth.*

Analyzing VISUALS

1. **Identifying** In what region of the nation were hourly wages lowest in 1929?
2. **Analyzing** What pattern characterizes the gap between wages of farm and nonfarm employees during the 1920s?

374 **Chapter 10** The Jazz Age

Additional Support

Activity: Interdisciplinary Connection

Sociology Have interested students select one group who was left out of the prosperity of the 1920s—African Americans, Native Americans, or farmers—and use library or Internet resources to find out more about the group and why they were excluded. Have students use their findings to write a two-page report describing the group's situation. Tell students to consider the following question as they prepare their reports: Might prejudice and racism have been a factor in determining who enjoyed prosperity and who did not? *(Answers will vary, but students should base their answers on their research findings.)* After students have completed their reports, conduct a class discussion about the connection of prejudice and racism to economic success and prosperity in the United States today. Ask students to provide examples of this connection. **AL**

⑤ The Farm Crisis

MAIN Idea Increases in farm productivity and decreases in foreign markets led to lower prices for farmers.

HISTORY AND YOU Do you remember reading about the platform of the Populist Party in the 1890s? Read to learn about farmers' troubles in the 1920s.

American farmers did not share in the prosperity of the 1920s. On average, they earned less than one-third of the income of workers in the rest of the economy. Technological advances in fertilizers, seed varieties, and farm machinery allowed them to produce more, but higher yields without a corresponding increase in demand meant that they received lower prices. Between 1920 and 1921, corn prices dropped almost 19 percent, and wheat went from $1.83 a bushel to $1.03. The cost of the improved farming technology, meanwhile, continued to increase.

Changing Market Conditions

Many factors contributed to this "quiet depression" in American agriculture. During the war, the government had urged farmers to produce more to meet the great need for food supplies in Europe. Many farmers borrowed heavily to buy new land and new machinery to raise more crops. Sales were strong, prices were high, and farmers prospered. After the war, however, European farm output rose, and the debt-ridden countries of Europe had little money to spend on American farm products. Congress had unintentionally made matters worse when it passed the Fordney-McCumber Act in 1922. This act raised tariffs dramatically in an effort to protect American industry from foreign competition. By dampening the American market for foreign goods, however, it provoked a reaction in foreign markets against American agricultural products. Farmers in the United States could no longer sell as much of their crops overseas, and prices tumbled.

Helping Farmers

Some members of Congress tried to help the farmers sell their surplus. Every year from 1924 to 1928, Senator Charles McNary of Oregon and Representative Gilbert Haugen of Iowa proposed the McNary-Haugen Bill, a plan in which the government would boost farm prices by buying up surpluses and selling them, at a loss, overseas.

Congress passed the bill twice, but President Coolidge vetoed it both times. He argued that with money flowing to farmers under this law, they would be encouraged to produce even greater surpluses. American farmers remained mired in a recession throughout the 1920s.

✔ Reading Check **Synthesizing** What factors led to the growing economic crisis in farming?

Section 2 REVIEW

Vocabulary

1. **Explain** the significance of: mass production, assembly line, Model T, Charles Lindbergh, welfare capitalism, open shop.

Main Ideas

2. **Evaluating** How did the automobile affect American society?

3. **Summarizing** What factors led to the new consumer society in the United States during the 1920s?

4. **Analyzing** What conditions contributed to the tough times farmers faced in the early 1920s?

Critical Thinking

5. **Big Ideas** How did the availability of credit change society?

6. **Organizing** Use a graphic organizer like the one below to list some of the new industries that grew in importance during the 1920s.

New Industries

7. **Analyzing Visuals** Study the Technology & History on pages 370–371. How do appliances, cars, and airplanes differ today? How do you think new products change society today?

Writing About History

8. Write an article for a contemporary newspaper analyzing the impact of Charles Lindbergh's transatlantic flight on the development of aviation in the United States and the world.

History ONLINE
Study Central™ To review this section, go to **glencoe.com** and click on Study Central.

375

---

⑤ Skill Practice

Chronological Thinking Ask students to create a time line that shows the various economic difficulties that farmers faced and the solutions they found before the 1920s. **OL**

Assess

History ONLINE

Study Central™ provides summaries, interactive games, and online graphic organizers to help students review content.

Close

Summarizing Ask: Who benefited and who did not from the growing economy of the 1920s? *(Most consumers benefited from new inventions, new industries, and easy credit; African Americans, Native Americans, and farmers in general did not enjoy the prosperity of the 1920s.)* **OL**

✔ Reading Check

Answer:
a decline in foreign markets and increased productivity

Section 2 REVIEW

Answers

1. All definitions can be found in the section and the Glossary.

2. eased rural isolation, allowed workers to live farther away from work

3. mass production, mass advertising, easy credit, and economic prosperity

4. Higher crop yields led to lower prices, and European markets stopped buying at the same level.

5. Consumers were able to purchase large-ticket items sooner because they did not need to save money for the purchases. Financial institutions made money by offering credit to consumers.

6. airline, automobile, consumer goods, radio

7. Appliances today are more efficient, faster, and use less energy. New products often save time and labor.

8. Students' articles will vary but should include factual information.

Focus

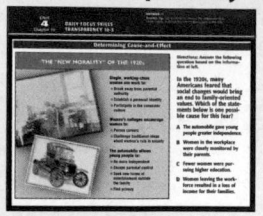

Guide to Reading

Answers may include: Causes: job competition, European immigrant influx, eugenics, economic recession; Effects: return of KKK, Sacco-Vanzetti case, governmental control of immigration

Section Spotlight Video

To generate student interest and provide a springboard for class discussion, access the Chapter 10, Section 3 video at glencoe.com or on the video DVD.

Resource Manager

A Clash of Values

Guide to Reading

Big Ideas
Past and Present The struggles of the 1920s regarding immigration and proper behavior continue to affect current events.

Content Vocabulary
• nativism (p. 376)
• anarchist (p. 376)
• evolution (p. 380)
• creationism (p. 380)
• speakeasy (p. 381)

Academic Vocabulary
• source (p. 378)
• deny (p. 380)

People and Events to Identify
• Emergency Quota Act (p. 378)
• National Origins Act (p. 378)
• Fundamentalism (p. 380)

Reading Strategy
Organizing As you read about Americans' reactions to immigrants during the 1920s, complete a graphic organizer similar to the one below by filling in the causes and effects of anti-immigrant prejudices.

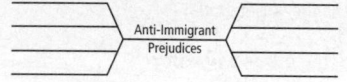

Anti-Immigrant Prejudices

The 1920s are often called the "Roaring Twenties" because to many the decade seemed to be one long party. Urban Americans celebrated the new "modern" culture, but not everyone agreed that the new trends were a good thing. Rural Americans believed traditional society and morality were under attack.

Nativism Resurges

MAIN Idea Nativism and racism increased in the 1920s and led to changes in immigration laws.

HISTORY AND YOU In your school, is there a limit to the number of students in each class? Read to learn why the United States imposed new rules in the 1920s limiting the number of immigrants admitted each year.

The 1920s was a time of economic growth, but it was also a time of cultural turmoil. When the 1920s began, an economic recession, an influx of immigrants, and cultural tensions combined to create an atmosphere of disillusionment and intolerance. The fear and prejudice many felt toward Germans and communists during and after World War I expanded to include all immigrants. This triggered a general rise in racism and **nativism**—a belief that one's native land needs to be protected against immigrants.

During World War I, immigration to the United States had dropped sharply. By 1921, however, it had returned to prewar levels, with the majority of immigrants coming from southern and eastern Europe. Many Americans reacted to the bombings, strikes, and recession of the postwar years by blaming immigrants. Many believed immigrants were taking jobs that would otherwise have gone to soldiers returning home from the war.

The Sacco-Vanzetti Case

The controversial Sacco-Vanzetti case reflected the prejudices and fears of the era. On April 15, 1920, two men robbed and murdered two employees of a shoe factory in Massachusetts. Police subsequently arrested two Italian immigrants, Nicola Sacco and Bartolomeo Vanzetti, for the crime.

The case created a furor when newspapers revealed that the two men were **anarchists,** or people who oppose all forms of government. They also reported that Sacco owned a gun similar to the murder weapon and that the bullets used in the murders matched those in Sacco's gun. The evidence was questionable, but the fact that the accused men were anarchists and foreigners led many people to assume they were guilty, including the jury. On July 14, 1921,

---

R Reading Strategies	**C** Critical Thinking	**D** Differentiated Instruction	**W** Writing Support	**S** Skill Practice
Additional Resources • Guided Read., URB p. 48 • Primary Source Reading Act., URB p. 35	**Teacher Edition** • Analyzing Info., p. 378 • Making Generalizations, p. 380 • Making Inferences, p. 381 **Additional Resources** • Quizzes and Tests, p. 141 • Supreme Court Case Studies, p. 39	**Teacher Edition** • Visual/Spatial, p. 379 **Additional Resources** • Interpreting Pol. Cartoons Act., URB p. 41	**Teacher Edition** • Persuasive Writing, p. 377	**Additional Resources** • RENTG, p. 106 • Reinforcing Skills Act., URB p. 31

POLITICAL CARTOONS PRIMARY SOURCE
Hostility Toward Immigrants

In the 1920s, many Americans believed that immigrants from southern and eastern Europe would not assimilate into American culture. These concerns led to the rise of a new Ku Klux Klan and efforts in Congress to pass legislation that would keep "undesirable" immigrants out.

Men, women, and children participate in a Klan march in Cincinnati, Ohio, in 1925 (left). Membership in the KKK soared in the early 1920s because of its opposition to immigrants. Not everyone agreed with the Klan, however; the cartoon above mocks a proposal to impose a literacy test on immigrants.

European Immigration, 1900–1924

Bar chart — Immigrants (millions) on vertical axis (0 to 5):
- United Kingdom: ~1.5
- Germany: ~0.5
- Eastern Europe: ~3.2
- Southern Europe: ~4.3

Source: *Historical Statistics of the United States.*

Analyzing VISUALS   DBQ

1. **Making Inferences** What does the presence and membership of children in the Klan suggest to others?
2. **Analyzing Visuals** What is the "wall" made of in the cartoon?
3. **Making Connections** From which two regions did the majority of immigrants come? Why were so many people from these regions willing to leave their homelands and come to the United States?

Sacco and Vanzetti were found guilty and sentenced to death. After six years of appeals, Sacco and Vanzetti were executed on August 23, 1927.

Return of the Ku Klux Klan

W At the forefront of the movement to restrict immigration was the Ku Klux Klan, or KKK. The old KKK had flourished in the South after the Civil War and used threats and violence to intimidate newly freed African Americans. The new Klan had other targets as well: Catholics, Jews, immigrants, and other groups said to be "un-American." In the 1920s, the Klan claimed it was fighting for "Americanism."

William J. Simmons founded the new Ku Klux Klan in Georgia, in 1915. A former preacher, Simmons pledged to preserve America's white, Protestant civilization. The Klan attracted few members until 1920, when Simmons began using professional promoters to sell Klan memberships. By 1924 membership had reached nearly 4 million as it spread beyond the South into Northern cities. **W**

The Klan began to decline in the late 1920s, however, largely as a result of scandals and power struggles between its leaders. Membership shrank, and politicians backed by the Klan were voted out of office. In addition, new restrictions on immigration deprived the Klan of one of its major issues.

Read "Sacco and Vanzetti Must Die" by John Dos Passos on pages R74–R75 of the **American Literature Library**.

Teach

W Writing Support
Persuasive Writing Have interested students use library or Internet resources to find out more about the rise of the Ku Klux Klan in the early 1900s, as well as the terror tactics it employed against minorities. Have students use their findings to write a persuasive letter to their member of Congress encouraging him or her to pass legislation to curb or outlaw the Klan's activities. Encourage volunteers to share their letters with the class. **AL**

Analyzing VISUALS

Answers:
1. Their parents are teaching them bigotry and intolerance.
2. a literacy test with pens
3. Most immigrants came from southern and eastern Europe. People from those regions were looking for new economic opportunities and trying to escape war, revolution, and poor economic conditions.

Hands-On Chapter Project
Step 3

Creating a Memory Book

Step 3: Researching Images for Selected Persons Ask students to gather photos and information about the person's background, motivation, and his or her role in the history of this period.

Directions Students will illustrate the biography of the person by finding photographs, related images, or drawing diagrams related to the person. Students should annotate all images with captions or explanations.

Identifying Central Issues Students must identify the central role played by the selected person, and illustrate the biography with images that relate to this role. **OL**

(Chapter Project continued on page 383)

C Critical Thinking

Analyzing Information Have students use library or Internet resources to locate historical immigration statistics for 1890, 1900, 1910, 1920, and 1930. Tell them to select two countries, one from Western Europe and one from Eastern Europe. Have students use the data to construct an immigration chart that shows the effects of the immigration laws of 1921 and 1924. Ask students to write a brief explanation of the significance of their findings. **OL**

✓ Reading Check

Answer:
The Klan of the 1920s targeted Jews, Catholics, immigrants, and anyone else they thought had "un-American" values, as well as the African American community that the earlier Klan had targeted.

Additional Support

Controlling Immigration

American immigration policies changed in response to the postwar recession and nativist pleas to "Keep America American." Even some business leaders, who had favored immigration as a **source** of cheap labor, now saw the new immigrants as radicals.

In 1921 President Harding signed the **Emergency Quota Act.** The act restricted annual admission to the United States to only 3 percent of the total number of people in any ethnic group already living in the nation. Ethnic identity and national origin thus determined **C** admission to the United States.

In 1924 the **National Origins Act** made immigration restriction a permanent policy. The law set quotas at 2 percent of each national group represented in the U.S. Census of 1890. Thus, immigration quotas were based on the ethnic composition of the country more than 30 years earlier—before the heavy wave of immigration from southern and eastern Europe. The new quotas deliberately favored immigrants from northwestern Europe. Although subsequent legislation made some changes in immigration laws, the National Origins Act set the framework for immigration for the next four decades.

Hispanic Immigration

While workers and unions rejoiced at the reduction in competition with European immigrants for jobs, employers desperately needed laborers for agriculture, mining, and railroad work. Mexican immigrants were able to fill this need because the National Origins Act of 1924 exempted natives of the Western Hemisphere from the quota system.

Large numbers of Mexican immigrants had already begun moving to the United States after the passage of the Newlands Reclamation Act of 1902. The act funded irrigation projects in the Southwest and led to the creation of large factory farms that needed thousands of farmworkers. As the demand for cheap farm labor steadily increased, Mexican immigrants crossed the border in record numbers. By the end of the 1920s, nearly 700,000 had migrated to the United States.

✓ Reading Check **Explaining** How was the Ku Klux Klan of the 1920s different from the earlier Klan?

A Clash of Cultures

MAIN Idea Supporters of the new morality in the 1920s clashed with those who supported more traditional values.

HISTORY AND YOU How do you think older generations view your generation? Read about the changes in morality during the 1920s.

Many groups that wanted to restrict immigration also wanted to preserve what they considered to be traditional values. They feared that a "new morality" was taking over the nation. Challenging traditional ways of behaving, the new morality glorified youth and personal freedom and changed American society—particularly the status of women.

Women in the 1920s

Having won the right to vote in 1920, many women sought to break free of the traditional roles and behaviors that were expected of them. Attitudes toward marriage—popularized by magazines and other media—changed considerably. As the loving and emotional aspects of marriage grew in importance, the

PRIMARY SOURCE
Changing Roles for Women

As women achieved greater independence, access to higher education, and professional opportunities in the 1920s, they adopted new clothing styles that expressed their identities.

► *Many young women adopted the flapper style in the 1920s. They stopped wearing corsets, bobbed their hair, and wore short skirts, high heels, and rounded hats with almost no brim. The style expressed the sense of freedom many women felt in the 1920s.*

Extending the Content

Women Voters After 1869, when the Territory of Wyoming granted women the right to vote, woman suffrage expanded unevenly across the nation. By 1920, some states had granted women full voting rights, others had granted women the right to vote for some, but not all, political offices, and other states did not allow women to vote for any political office.

When the Nineteenth Amendment (1920) went into effect, it dramatically expanded the electorate. Many Americans predicted that the addition of so many female voters would transform American politics. They anticipated that women would support progressive candidates who would push for social and labor reform legislation. The 1920s, however, proved to be an era

dominated by political conservatives. As it turned out, factors such as income, ethnicity, and religion influenced the political allegiances of female voters, just as it did their male counterparts.

ideas of romance, pleasure, and friendship became linked to successful marriages.

The popularizing of Sigmund Freud's psychological theories also changed people's ideas about relationships. Freudian psychology emphasized human sexuality and his theories (often oversimplified) became acceptable subjects of public conversation.

The automobile played a role in encouraging the new morality. Cars allowed young people to escape the careful watch of their parents. Instead of socializing at home with the family, many youths could now use cars to "go out" with their friends.

Women in the workforce began to define the new morality. Many working-class women took jobs because they or their families needed the wages but for some young, single women, work was a way to break away from parental authority and establish financial independence. Earning money also allowed women to participate in the consumer culture.

Fashion, too, changed during the 1920s, particularly for women, who "bobbed," or shortened, their hair, wore flesh-colored silk stockings, and copied the glamorous look of movie stars. The flapper personified these changes, even though she was not typical of most women. The flapper smoked cigarettes, drank prohibited liquor, and wore makeup and sleeveless dresses with short skirts.

Women who attended college in the 1920s often found support for their emerging sense of independence. Women's colleges, in particular, encouraged their students to pursue careers and to challenge traditional ideas about women's role in society.

Many professional women made major contributions in science, medicine, law, and literature in the 1920s. In medicine, Florence Sabin's research led to a dramatic drop in death rates from tuberculosis while Edith Wharton, Willa Cather, and Edna Ferber each won a Pulitzer Prize in fiction for their novels.

Public health nurse Margaret Sanger believed that families could improve their standard of living by limiting the number of children they had. She founded the American Birth Control League in 1921 to promote knowledge about birth control. This organization became Planned Parenthood in the 1940s. During the 1920s and 1930s, the use of birth control increased dramatically, particularly among middle-class couples.

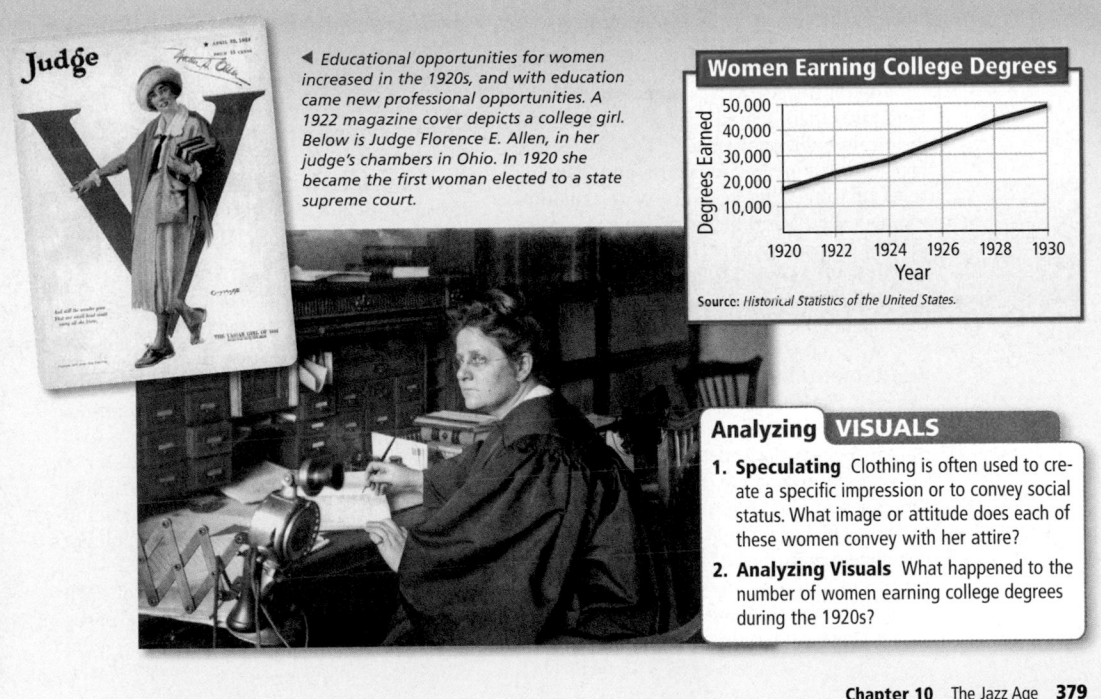

◀ Educational opportunities for women increased in the 1920s, and with education came new professional opportunities. A 1922 magazine cover depicts a college girl. Below is Judge Florence E. Allen, in her judge's chambers in Ohio. In 1920 she became the first woman elected to a state supreme court.

Women Earning College Degrees

Source: Historical Statistics of the United States.

Analyzing VISUALS

1. **Speculating** Clothing is often used to create a specific impression or to convey social status. What image or attitude does each of these women convey with her attire?

2. **Analyzing Visuals** What happened to the number of women earning college degrees during the 1920s?

Chapter 10 The Jazz Age **379**

D **Differentiated Instruction**

Visual/Spatial Have students make a table showing areas where women's roles changed in the 1920s. Ask them to include visuals and examples for each area on the chart. Display the charts in the classroom. **OL**

Analyzing VISUALS

Answers:
1. The flappers are dressed to look free and fun loving; the student is dressed to look smart and sophisticated; the judge is dressed to appear thoughtful and authoritative.
2. increased from about 18,000 to almost 50,000 annually

Additional Support

Activity: Interdisciplinary Connection

Civics Organize the class into teams of two. Have student pairs use library or Internet resources to learn more about Florence Sabin, Edith Wharton, Willa Cather, Edna Ferber, or Margaret Sanger and their contributions to their respective field. Students will use their findings to prepare an oral report for the class. Remind students to incorporate visual aids, such as photos and posters into their presentations.

Once all student pairs have completed their oral reports, conduct a class discussion. **Ask:** What effect do the contributions of these women have on women of the twenty-first century? (Answers will vary, but students should note that the contributions of these women paved the way for successful women since their time.) **OL**

C Critical Thinking

Making Generalizations
Initiate a class discussion about the attempts to control the use of alcohol. **Ask:** What sorts of attempts have been made to limit alcohol consumption in recent years? *(raising the minimum legal age for alcohol purchase, restrictions on hard liquor advertisements on television, warning labels on alcohol products, high alcohol taxes, education programs, MADD, SADD)* Discuss whether students think these attempts have been successful and whether other initiatives should be considered. **OL**

Analyzing VISUALS

Answers:
1. Opponents of Prohibition might have pointed out a connection between the rise of organized crime and the murder rate. Other reasons for the increase in the murder rate might include the economic conditions resulting from the Great Depression.
2. The mother and child are being overshadowed by the alcohol bottle.

Additional Support

The War Against Alcohol

Prohibition supporters argued that it reduced violence, illness, and poverty. Critics argued that it increased violence because gangs fought to control the sale of illegal alcohol, and that it led to illness because many people drank unsafe "moonshine."

The Shadow of Danger

▲ Supporters of Prohibition portrayed the sale of alcohol as a danger to mothers and children.

◀ Prohibition led to the creation of a special federal bureau charged with stopping the sale of illegal alcohol. In this photo, a federal agent cracks open barrels of illegal rum in San Francisco in 1927.

Murder Rate, 1920–1940

*per 100,000 residents
Source: *Historical Statistics of the United States.*

Analyzing VISUALS DBQ

1. **Theorizing** How might opponents of Prohibition use the murder rate in the 1920s and 1930s to support their argument? Can you think of other reasons the murder rate might have fallen in the 1930s?
2. **Analyzing Visuals** How does the poster use emotional appeal to strengthen its argument?

Fundamentalism

While many Americans embraced the new morality, others feared that the country was losing its traditional values. They viewed the consumer culture, relaxed ethics, and changing roles of women as evidence of the nation's moral decline. Many of these people, especially in rural towns, responded by joining a religious movement known as **Fundamentalism,** a name derived from a series of Christian religious pamphlets titled "The Fundamentals."

Fundamentalist Beliefs Fundamentalists believed that the Bible was literally true and without error. They rejected the idea that human beings derived their moral behavior from society and nature, not God. In particular, they rejected Charles Darwin's theory of **evolution,** which said that human beings had developed from lower forms of life over the course of millions of years. Instead, they believed in **creationism**—the belief that God created the world as described in the Bible.

Two popular preachers, Billy Sunday and Aimee Semple McPherson, stirred supporters by preaching in very nontraditional ways. Sunday, a former professional baseball player, drew huge crowds with his showmanship and rapid-fire sermons. McPherson conducted her revivals and faith healings in Los Angeles in a flamboyant theatrical style, using stage sets and costumes that expressed the themes of her highly emotional sermons.

The Scopes Trial In 1925 Tennessee outlawed any teaching that **denied** "the story of the Divine Creation of man as taught in the Bible," or taught that "man descended from a lower order of animals." The American Civil Liberties Union (ACLU) advertised for a teacher willing to be arrested for teaching evolution. John T. Scopes, a biology teacher in Dayton, Tennessee, volunteered. He taught evolution and was arrested.

The trial took place in the summer of 1925. William Jennings Bryan, a three-time presidential candidate, was the prosecutor who

---

Extending the Content

Agents of Prohibition Isador Einstein, known as Izzy, and his partner Moe Smith worked as a team to trap lawbreakers during Prohibition. Masters of disguise, they were a flamboyant pair who used any number of methods to enforce the law. Izzy was particularly adept at going through diverse neighborhoods because he spoke five languages. He once seized an unsuspecting speakeasy owner by disguising himself as a pickle salesman. Together, Izzy and Moe made some 4,000 arrests and hauled in around $15 million worth of alcohol.

represented the creationists. Clarence Darrow, one of the country's most celebrated trial lawyers, defended Scopes. After eight days of trial, Scopes was found guilty and fined $100, although the conviction was later overturned on a technicality. The trial had been broadcast over the radio, and Darrow's blistering cross-examination of Bryan hurt the Fundamentalist cause. Increasingly, Fundamentalists felt isolated and their commitment to political activism declined.

Prohibition

The movement to ban alcohol grew stronger in the early 1900s. People supported the prohibition of alcohol sales for many reasons. Some opposed alcohol consumption for religious reasons; others thought prohibition would reduce unemployment, domestic violence, and poverty. Prohibition supporters achieved their goal when the Eighteenth Amendment went into effect in January 1920.

C Congress passed the Volstead Act, making the U.S. Treasury Department responsible for enforcing Prohibition. Treasury agents had enforced federal tax laws for many years, but police powers—a government's power to control people and property in the interest of public safety, health, welfare, and morals—had generally been reserved for state governments. The Eighteenth Amendment granted federal and state governments the power to enforce Prohibition, marking a dramatic increase in federal police powers.

The Treasury Department struggled to enforce Prohibition. During the 1920s, treasury agents made more than 540,000 arrests, but Americans persisted in blatantly ignoring the law. People flocked to secret bars called **speakeasies,** where they could purchase alcohol. In New York City alone, an estimated 32,000 speakeasies sold liquor illegally. Liquor also was readily available in rural areas, where bootlegging—the illegal production and distribution of liquor—was common.

Organized crime thrived on the illegal trade in alcohol. Huge profits could be made smuggling liquor from Canada and the Caribbean. Crime became big business, and some gangsters had enough money to corrupt local politicians. Al Capone, one of the most successful and violent gangsters of the era, had many police officers, judges, and other officials on his payroll. Capone dominated organized crime in Chicago. Finally, Eliot Ness, the leader of a special Treasury Department task force, brought Capone to justice. More than 70 federal agents were killed while enforcing Prohibition in the 1920s.

The battle to repeal Prohibition began almost as soon as the Eighteenth Amendment was ratified. The Twenty-first Amendment, ratified in 1933, repealed the Eighteenth Amendment and ended Prohibition. Prohibition had reduced alcohol consumption, but it had not improved society in the ways its supporters had hoped.

✓ **Reading Check** **Identifying** What political, social, and economic contributions did women make to American society in the 1920s?

Section 3 REVIEW

Vocabulary

1. **Explain** the significance of: nativism, anarchist, Emergency Quota Act, National Origins Act, Fundamentalism, evolution, creationism, speakeasy.

Main Ideas

2. **Identifying** What two factors influenced the limits on immigration?

3. **Summarizing** What issues caused clashes between traditional and new moralities?

Critical Thinking

4. **Big Ideas** Why did many Americans oppose immigration after World War I? What connections can you make with immigration policies today?

5. **Categorizing** Use a graphic organizer similar to the one below to list the provisions of the immigration acts passed in the 1920s.

Act	Provisions

6. **Analyzing Visuals** Look at the chart on page 377 showing European immigration. How would these figures have affected someone who was a nativist? Why?

Writing About History

7. **Persuasive Writing** Imagine it is the 1920s. Write a letter to your senator persuading him or her either to continue supporting Prohibition or to work for its repeal.

History ONLINE
Study Central™ To review this section, go to glencoe.com and click on Study Central.

C Critical Thinking

Making Inferences Have students find out more about the Volstead Act and write a one-page summary of their findings. **OL**

✓ **Reading Check**

Answer:
Some pursued social freedoms, some entered the workforce, and some contributed to medicine, literature, and science.

Assess

History ONLINE

Study Central™ provides summaries, interactive games, and online graphic organizers to help students review content.

Close

Summarizing **Ask:** Why did some Americans reject the new morality and embrace traditional values? *(They were afraid that consumer culture, relaxed ethics, and growing urbanism symbolized the nation's moral decline.)* **OL**

Section 3 REVIEW

Answers

1. All definitions can be found in the section and the Glossary.
2. post–World War I recession and nativism
3. behavior of women, drinking alcohol, beliefs about the creation of the world
4. People feared immigrants as radicals and as a threat to job security. Students may suggest similar fears exist today, leading to new attempts to secure the border with Mexico.
5. 1921 Emergency Quota Act: limited the number of immigrants to 3 percent of the existing immigrant population based on the 1910 census; 1924 National Origins Act: limited the number of immigrants to 2 percent of the existing immigrant population based on the 1890 census
6. A nativist would be upset because of the large number of immigrants from eastern and southern Europe.
7. Letters should clearly express a point of view.

Focus

Bellringer
Daily Focus Transparency 10.4

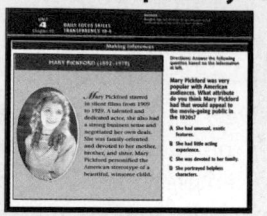

Guide to Reading

Answers: Art: diverse, individual expression influenced by European art movement; Literature: various styles and subject matter, themes of disillusionment and emptiness; Popular Culture: sports heroes, Hollywood allure, radio shows, jazz, and blues

Section Spotlight Video

To generate student interest and provide a springboard for class discussion, access the Chapter 10, Section 4 video at glencoe.com or on the video DVD.

Resource Manager

Section 4

Cultural Innovations

Guide to Reading

Big Ideas
Culture and Beliefs Through sharing in the arts and sports of the time, Americans embraced new ways of thinking.

Content Vocabulary
• bohemian *(p. 382)*
• mass media *(p. 385)*

Academic Vocabulary
• diverse *(p. 382)*
• unify *(p. 385)*

People and Events to Identify
• Carl Sandburg *(p. 383)*
• Willa Cather *(p. 383)*
• Ernest Hemingway *(p. 384)*
• F. Scott Fitzgerald *(p. 384)*
• Edith Wharton *(p. 384)*

Reading Strategy
Organizing As you read about the 1920s, complete a graphic organizer like the one below by filling in the main characteristics of art, literature, and popular culture that reflect the era.

Cultural Movement	Main Characteristics
Art	
Literature	
Popular Culture	

The 1920s was an era of great artistic innovation. Artists and writers experimented with new techniques. Popular culture also changed. Broadcast radio introduced Americans around the country to the latest trends in music and entertainment, and motion pictures became a major leisure-time activity.

Art and Literature

MAIN Idea New York City's Greenwich Village and Chicago's South Side became known as centers for new artistic work.

HISTORY AND YOU Is there a neighborhood with many art galleries in your community? Read about the flowering of the arts during the 1920s in the United States.

During the 1920s, American artists and writers challenged traditional ideas. These artists explored what it meant to be "modern," and they searched for meaning in the emerging challenges of the modern world. Many artists, writers, and intellectuals of the era flocked to Manhattan's Greenwich Village and Chicago's South Side. The artistic and unconventional, or **bohemian,** lifestyle of these neighborhoods allowed young artists, musicians, and writers greater freedom to express themselves.

Modern American Art

European art movements greatly influenced the modernists of American art. Perhaps most striking was the **diverse** range of artistic styles, each attempting to express the individual, modern experience. American painter John Marin drew on nature as well as the urban dynamics of New York for inspiration, explaining, "the whole city is alive; buildings, people, all are alive; and the more they move me the more I feel them to be alive." Painter Charles Scheeler applied the influences of photography and the geometric forms of Cubism to urban and rural American landscapes. Edward Hopper revived the visual accuracy of realism in his haunting scenes. His paintings conveyed a modern sense of disenchantment and isolation. Georgia O'Keeffe's landscapes and flowers were admired in many museums throughout her long life.

Poets and Writers

Poets and writers of the 1920s varied greatly in their styles and subject matter. Chicago poet, historian, folklorist, and novelist **Carl**

R **Reading Strategies**	C **Critical Thinking**	D **Differentiated Instruction**	W **Writing Support**	S **Skill Practice**
Additional Resources • Guided Read. Act., URB p. 49	**Additional Resources** • Quizzes and Tests, p. 142 • Hist. Simulations, URB p. 9		**Teacher Edition** • Descriptive Writing, pp. 383, 384	**Additional Resources** • RENTG, p. 109

Ashcan Realists and the Lost Generation

Many artists and writers focused on the isolation and alienation of modern society. A group of artists who painted urban life became known as the Ashcan Realists. The writers who described modern life as spiritually empty and materialistic became known as the "Lost Generation."

Excerpt from _The Great Gatsby_ (1925)
by F. Scott Fitzgerald

"They were careless people, Tom and Daisy—they smashed up things and creatures and then retreated back into their money or their vast carelessness, or whatever it was that kept them together, and let other people clean up the mess they had made. . . .

I shook hands with him; it seemed silly not to, for I felt suddenly as though I were talking to a child. Then he went into the jewelry store to buy a pearl necklace—or perhaps only a pair of cuff buttons—rid of my provincial squeamishness forever."

Excerpt from "The Hollow Men" (1925)
by T.S. Eliot

We are the hollow men
We are the stuffed men
Leaning together
Headpiece filled with straw. Alas!
Our dried voices, when
We whisper together
Are quiet and meaningless
As wind in dry grass
Or rats' feet over broken glass
In our dry cellar
Shape without form, shade without colour,
Paralysed force, gesture without motion;
Those who have crossed
With direct eyes, to death's other Kingdom
Remember us—if at all—not as lost
Violent souls, but only
As the hollow men
The stuffed men.

◄ Edward Hopper studied with one of the founders of the Ashcan Realist movement. His painting, Automat, (left) expresses the loneliness and isolation many young people felt during the 1920s. An automat was a place where a person could buy food or drinks from vending machines.

W

DBQ Document-Based Questions

1. **Analyzing Primary Sources** How does Fitzgerald characterize Tom and Daisy? What does their attitude say about the culture of the 1920s?

2. **Explaining** Eliot uses the adjectives _hollow_ and _stuffed_ to describe contemporary people. How can both be true?

3. **Analyzing Primary Sources** How is Hopper's painting similar to Eliot's poem and Fitzgerald's novel?

Sandburg used common speech to glorify the Midwest, as did Pulitzer Prize–winner **Willa Cather,** who wrote about life on the Great Plains. In Greenwich Village, another Pulitzer Prize winner, Edna St. Vincent Millay, expressed women's equality and praised a life intensely lived.

Several poets had an important impact on the literary culture. Gertrude Stein, an avant-garde poet of the era, was a mentor to many writers, including Ernest Hemingway. Some poets, including Ezra Pound, Amy Lowell, and William Carlos Williams, used clear, concise images to express moments in time. Others concentrated on portraying what they perceived to be the negative effects of modernism. In "The Hollow Men," for example, T.S. Eliot described a world filled with empty dreams that would end "not with a bang but a whimper."

Among playwrights, one of the most innovative was Eugene O'Neill. His plays, filled with bold artistry and modern themes, portrayed realistic characters and situations, offering a vision of life that sometimes touched on the tragic.

Teach

W Writing Support
Descriptive Writing Have interested students read a work by one of the authors or playwrights mentioned in this section. Have them write a one-page essay describing the main idea of the work. Encourage students to read their essays to the class. **OL**

DBQ Document Based Questions

Answers:

1. Tom and Daisy were careless and rich; they did not care about other people. Their attitude symbolizes the carefree spirit of the 1920s.

2. The men Eliot describes are hollow and unfeeling; they are filled only with dead straw.

3. All three reflect the materialistic nature of the 1920s and the loneliness and desertion felt by many people.

Hands-On Chapter Project
Step 4

Creating a Memory Book

Step 4: Selecting and Researching a Cultural Innovation Ask students to choose a cultural innovation discussed in Section 4. Students will work in teams to design and create a memory page centered on the innovation selected.

Directions Have students either take turns stating their selected topic or write their topics on a class sheet of paper. Then have students divide into groups of two or three to create the memory page.

Analyzing Information Students will need to determine how to illustrate their topic using both images and text. Students will summarize the importance of the innovation through their page design. **OL**
(Chapter Project continued on page 389)

W Writing Support

Descriptive Writing Have students use library or Internet resources to find out more about how people spent their leisure time in the 1920s. Have students write a one-page essay that describes leisure time in the 1920s. Discuss with the class the differences and similarities between how leisure time was spent in the 1920s and how it is spent now. **OL**

Analyzing VISUALS

Answers:

1. There are no live musicians at movies today; moviegoers do not dress up.
2. The crowd appears to be all male; most are wearing suits with jackets, ties, and caps.

Reading Check

Answer:

It offered freedom from the conformity to old ideas.

Additional Support

Many American writers wrote about their disillusionment with World War I. Some, known as the "Lost Generation," moved to Paris or other cities in Europe. There, they often wrote about "heroic antiheroes"—flawed individuals who still had heroic qualities. **Ernest Hemingway** was one such writer. In direct simple prose, he described the experience of war in such novels as *For Whom the Bell Tolls* and *A Farewell to Arms.*

Sinclair Lewis wrote about the absurdities of small-town life in *Main Street* and *Babbitt.* **F. Scott Fitzgerald's** colorful characters chased futile dreams in *The Great Gatsby,* a novel critical of modern society's superficiality. Similarly, **Edith Wharton** used irony and humor to criticize upper-class ignorance and pretensions. Her 1920 novel, *The Age of Innocence,* won the Pulitzer Prize.

✓ Reading Check **Examining** Why did many creative people flock to Greenwich Village during the 1920s?

Popular Culture

MAIN Idea Broadcast radio and "talking" pictures were new forms of popular entertainment.

HISTORY AND YOU What forms of entertainment make up today's popular culture? Read how Americans spent their leisure time in the 1920s.

The economic prosperity of the 1920s provided many Americans with more leisure time and more spending money, which they devoted to making their lives more enjoyable. Millions of Americans eagerly watched sports and enjoyed music, theater, and other forms of popular entertainment. They also fell in love with motion pictures and radio programs.

Movies and Radio Shows

For many Americans in the 1920s, nothing quite matched the allure of motion pictures. Before technology made sound possible in

---

PRIMARY SOURCE
Entertainment Brings Americans Together

Part of what made the 1920s feel "new" and "modern" was the rise of mass culture. Popular entertainment—whether movies or sports—brought Americans together in a shared experience.

W

Professional sports drew huge crowds in the 1920s. Top players such as Babe Ruth (left) and Ty Cobb (above) became celebrities and were among the first to be paid to endorse products in advertisements.

Movies were very popular in the 1920s. Note the live musicians playing music to accompany the silent film. On screen is actress Clara Bow. At left are actors Douglas Fairbanks, Sr., Mary Pickford, Charlie Chaplin, and director D. W. Griffith. They founded the United Artists movie studio in 1919.

Analyzing VISUALS

1. **Making Connections** How does the experience of seeing a movie today compare or contrast with what you observe in the photograph of early filmgoers?
2. **Analyzing** What do you observe about the crowds at the baseball games?

Extending the Content

Nickelodeons and Cinemas Tiny halls and converted shops where motion pictures were projected on a screen were first called nickelodeons because they charged an entrance fee of five cents. By 1907 it was estimated that there were 3,000 nickelodeons in the United States. As larger cinemas were built, however, the older and ill-equipped nickelodeons were replaced. By the mid-1920s the picture palace, with its plush décor and white-gloved ushers, was an accepted and cherished part of American life. Theater openings and movie premiers drew crowds. By the late 1920s, the number of cinemas had grown from about 15,000 in 1915 to more than 20,000. The introduction of sound caused an immediate reduction in the number of buildings, for it proved uneconomic to convert many of the older and more dilapidated silent cinemas.

films, theaters hired piano players to provide music during the feature, while subtitles explained the plot. Audiences thronged to see such stars as Mary Pickford, Charlie Chaplin, Tom Mix, Douglas Fairbanks, Sr., Rudolph Valentino, and Clara Bow. In 1927 the golden age of Hollywood began when the first "talking" picture—*The Jazz Singer*—was produced.

Entertainment programs broadcast over the radio also had a large following during the Jazz Age. Most stations in the 1920s played the popular songs of the day, such as "Yes! We Have No Bananas" and "Ain't We Got Fun." Broadcasts such as *The Eveready Hour* offered everything from classical music to comedy. In one of the most popular shows, *Amos 'n' Andy,* the trials and tribulations of two African American characters (portrayed by white actors) captured the nation's attention every evening.

The **mass media**—radio, movies, newspapers, and magazines aimed at a broad audience—did more than just entertain. Their easy availability to millions helped break down patterns of provincialism, or narrow focus on local interests. They fostered a sense of shared experience that helped **unify** the nation and spread new ideas and attitudes.

Sports

Thanks to motion pictures and radio, sports such as baseball and boxing reached new heights of popularity in the 1920s. Baseball star Babe Ruth became a national hero, famous for hitting hundreds of home runs. As one broadcaster later remarked, "He wasn't a baseball player. He was a worldwide celebrity, an international star, the likes of which baseball has never seen since."

Sports fans also idolized boxer Jack Dempsey. Dempsey held the title of world heavyweight champion from 1919 until 1926, when he lost it to Gene Tunney. When Dempsey attempted to win back the title in 1927, fans' enthusiasm for the rematch reached such a frenzy that one store sold $90,000 worth of radios—an incredible sum at that time—in the two weeks before the event.

Americans eagerly followed other sports and sports figures, too. Newspaper coverage helped generate enthusiasm for college football. One of the most famous players of the 1920s was Red Grange of the University of Illinois. Grange was known as the "Galloping Ghost" because of his speed and ability to evade members of opposing teams.

The triumphs of Bobby Jones, the best golfer of the decade, and tennis players Bill Tilden and Helen Wills, who dominated world tennis, also thrilled sports fans. In 1926 Jones became the first golfer to win the U.S. Open and the British Open in the same year. When swimmer Gertrude Ederle shattered records by swimming the English Channel in a little over 14 hours in 1927, Americans were enchanted.

✓ **Reading Check** **Summarizing** How did the economy of the 1920s affect popular culture?

Section 4 REVIEW

Vocabulary
1. **Explain** the significance of: bohemian, Carl Sandburg, Willa Cather, Ernest Hemingway, F. Scott Fitzgerald, Edith Wharton, mass media.

Main Ideas
2. **Describing** What were the main themes of artists and writers during the 1920s?

3. **Discussing** How did Americans enjoy their leisure time in the 1920s? What made these activities possible?

Critical Thinking
4. **Big Ideas** How did writers, artists, and popular culture of the 1920s affect traditional ideas in the United States?

5. **Organizing** Use a graphic organizer similar to the one below to list the effects of mass media on American culture.

Effects

Mass Media of 1920s

6. **Analyzing Visuals** Look at the painting on page 383. How does Edward Hopper create a sense of alienation in this painting?

Writing About History
7. **Descriptive Writing** Imagine that you have moved to New York's Greenwich Village in the 1920s. Write a letter to a friend describing the atmosphere in your neighborhood.

History ONLINE
Study Central™ To review this section, go to glencoe.com and click on Study Central.

385

✓ **Reading Check**
Answer:
Economic prosperity allowed Americans more leisure time and more spending money to pursue different kinds of popular culture.

Assess
· · · · · · · · · · · · · · · · · · ·
History ONLINE

Study Central™ provides summaries, interactive games, and online graphic organizers to help students review content.

Close
· · · · · · · · · · · · · · · · · · ·
Summarizing Ask: **How did the cultural innovations of the 1920s reflect the spirit and mood of the era?** *(The art and literature reflected the exuberance of the era as well as the desperation and loneliness that some Americans experienced. The increase in leisure time allowed more people to attend sports events and movie theaters.)*

Section 4 REVIEW

Answers

1. All definitions can be found in the section and the Glossary.
2. disenchantment, isolation, disillusionment, and emptiness
3. They enjoyed movies, radio, and sporting events. The increase in income and leisure time made this possible.
4. They helped create a national culture as they broke down local patterns of narrow interest.
5. broke down patterns of provincialism, unified Americans through shared national experience, spread new ideas and attitudes
6. The woman is seated alone, staring at her coffee cup; the background is dark.
7. Letters will vary but should include descriptive details.

Focus

Ask: After reading the information on these pages, what do you think were the major issues or topics of the era? *(jazz, isolationism vs. internationalism; new inventions)* **Ask:** Why is Santa Claus pictured? *(He was being marketed heavily in the 1920s.)* **Ask:** Why is Charles Lindbergh pictured? In what way is he symbolic of the era? *(Lindbergh was the first man to fly solo across the Atlantic Ocean. He became a worldwide celebrity. To many people, he symbolized the 1920s because of his bravery and daring achievement.)*

Teach

R Reading Strategy

Recognizing Bias Have students reread the excerpt from *Pravda.* **Ask:** Do you think the author was fair in his observations? Why or why not? *(Most likely, the writer was biased against America even before his observations in New York City.)* **OL**

Additional Support

TIME NOTEBOOK

Appreciation

LOUIS DANIEL ARMSTRONG *Writer Stanley Crouch remembers Louis Armstrong, a Jazz Age great.*

Pops. Sweet Papa Dip. Satchmo. He had perfect pitch and perfect rhythm. His improvised melodies and singing could be as lofty as a moon flight or as low-down as the blood drops of a street thug dying in the gutter. The extent of his influence across jazz and across American music continues to this day.

Not only do we hear Armstrong in trumpet players who represent the present renaissance in jazz, we can also detect his influence in certain rhythms that sweep from country-and-western music to rap.

Louis Daniel Armstrong was born in New Orleans on August 4, 1901. It was at a home for troubled kids that young Louis first put his lips to the mouthpiece of a cornet and, later, a trumpet.

In 1922 Armstrong went to Chicago, where he joined King Oliver and his Creole Jazz Band. The band brought out the people and all the musicians, black and white, who wanted to know how it was truly done.

When he first played in New York City in 1924, his improvisations set the city on its head. The stiff rhythms of the time were slashed away by his combination of the percussive and the soaring. He soon returned to Chicago, perfected what he was doing, and made one record after another.

Louis Armstrong was so much, in fact, that every school of jazz since has had to address how he interpreted the basics of the idiom—swing, blues, ballads, and Afro-Hispanic rhythms. His freedom, his wit, and his discipline give his music a perpetual position in the wave of the future that is the station of all great art.

VERBATIM

❝The great creators of the government . . . thought of America as a light to the world, as created to lead the world in the assertion of the right of peoples and the rights of free nations. ❞

    WOODROW WILSON, *in defense of the League of Nations, 1920*

❝We seek no part in directing the destinies of the Old World. ❞

    WARREN G. HARDING, *Inaugural Address, 1921*

❝Here was a new generation, . . . dedicated more than the last to the fear of poverty and the worship of success; grown up to find . . . all wars fought, all faiths in man shaken. ❞

F. Scott Fitzgerald

    F. SCOTT FITZGERALD, *author, This Side of Paradise*

❝There has been a change for the worse during the past year in feminine dress, dancing, manners and general moral standards. [One should] realize the serious ethical consequences of immodesty in girls' dress. ❞

from the **PITTSBURGH OBSERVER,** *1922*

❝[In New York] I saw 7,000,000 two-legged animals penned in an evil smelling cage, . . . streets as unkempt as a Russian steppe, . . . rubbish, waste paper, cigar butts. . . . One glance and you know no master hand directs. ❞

article in Soviet newspaper **PRAVDA** *describing New York City in 1925*

Extending the Content

Flapper Style In 1922 psychologist G. Stanley Hall wrote an article for the *Atlantic Monthly* in which he described a typical flapper:

"[H]er gait was swagger and superior.... She wore a knitted hat, with hardly any brim, of a flame or bonfire hue; a henna scarf; two strings of Betty beads, of different colors, twisted together; an open short coat, with ample pockets; a skirt with vertical stripes... On her wrist were several bangles; on her left, of course, a wrist watch. Her shoes were oxfords, with a low broad heel. Her stockings were woolen and of brilliant hue. But most noticeable of all were her high overshoes or galoshes. One seemed to be turned down at the top and entirely unbuckled, while the other was fastened below and flapped about her trim ankle in a way that compelled attention.... She was out to see the world and, incidentally, to be seen of it..."

WHAT'S NEW
Invented This Decade
How did we live without . . .

- push-button elevators
- neon signs
- oven thermostats
- electric razors
- tissues
- spiral-bound notebooks
- motels
- dry ice
- zippers
- pop-up toasters
- flavored yogurt
- car radios
- adhesive tape
- food disposals
- water skiing
- automatic potato peeler
- self-winding wristwatch

BROWN BROTHERS

Milestones

EMBARRASSED, 1920. TEXAS SENATOR MORRIS SHEPPARD, a leading proponent of the Eighteenth Amendment, when a large whiskey still is found on his farm.

ERASED, 1922. THE WORD "OBEY," from the Episcopal marriage ceremony, by a vote of American Episcopal bishops.

DIED, 1923. HOMER MOREHOUSE, 27, in the 87th hour of a record-setting 90-hour, 10-minute dance marathon.

EXONERATED, 1921. EIGHT CHICAGO WHITE SOX PLAYERS charged with taking bribes to throw the 1919 World Series. The players were found "not guilty" when grand jury testimony disappeared. Newly appointed commissioner of baseball Kenesaw Mountain Landis banned the "Black Sox" from baseball.

MAKING A COMEBACK, 1926. SANTA CLAUS, after falling into low favor in the last decade. Aiming at children, advertisers are marketing St. Nick heavily.

CULVER PICTURES

NUMBERS

60,000
Families with radios in 1922

9,000,000
Motor vehicles registered in U.S. in 1920

33.5 Number of hours Charles Lindbergh spent in his nonstop flight from New York to Paris on May 20, 1927

1,800 Tons of ticker tape and shredded paper dropped on Charles Lindbergh in his parade in New York City

$16,000 Cost of cleaning up after the parade

7,000 Job offers received by Lindbergh

3.5 million
Number of letters received by Lindbergh

Charles Lindbergh

BROWN BROTHERS

CRITICAL THINKING

1. Recognizing Bias How does the communist newspaper *Pravda* describe New York City? Why do you think the writer described the city in such negative terms?

2. Making Connections Why do you think Charles Lindbergh's flight caused such excitement among Americans in 1927?

W Writing Support
Descriptive Writing Have students research one of the inventions mentioned and discover what preceded the invention, who invented it, and what improvements were made to the product. Students should also decide if the invention is still relevant today or if it has become obsolete. Students should write a two-page report describing their chosen invention. **OL**

C Critical Thinking
Comparing and Contrasting Have students create two political cartoons, one expressing the popular sentiment about Prohibition and one expressing the concerns over alcohol consumption today. **AL**

Assess/Close

Have students select an item listed under Numbers and find a correlating statistic today.

TIME Visit the Time Web site at www.time.com for up-to-date news, weekly magazine articles, editorials, online polls, and an archive of past magazines and Web articles.

Additional Support

Activity: Technology Connection

Comparing and Contrasting Have students review the information presented in the TIME Notebook and have students use library or Internet resources to find out more about the topics presented. Then have them make a list of items, issues, or inventions from the 1920s that are still relevant today. **Ask:** How do you think the events, issues, or inventions of the 1920s affect your life today? What 1920s inventions are still useful today? Which inventions have been improved upon? What political issues or ideas are still relevant today? *(Answers will vary, but students should cite data from the TIME Notebook and their research to support their ideas.)* **OL**

Focus

Bellringer
Daily Focus Transparency 10.5

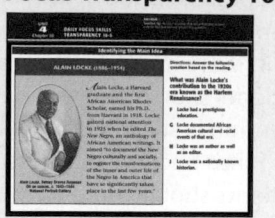

Guide to Reading

Answers may include: Causes: Great Migration and racial pride; Effects: important African American writers, jazz, blues, theater, sparked political change

Section Spotlight Video

To generate student interest and provide a springboard for class discussion, access the Chapter 10, Section 5 video at glencoe.com or on the video DVD.

Resource Manager

Section 5

African American Culture

The Harlem Renaissance was a creative era for African American artists and writers. The growing African American population in the North meant an increasing number of African Americans had meaningful political power to continue the struggle for civil rights.

Guide to Reading

Big Ideas
Group Action The artistic and political contributions of African Americans changed American society.

Content Vocabulary
• jazz (p. 389)
• blues (p. 390)

Academic Vocabulary
• symbolize (p. 390)
• impact (p. 392)
• ongoing (p. 393)

People and Events to Identify
• Great Migration (p. 388)
• Harlem Renaissance (p. 388)
• Claude McKay (p. 388)
• Langston Hughes (p. 388)
• Zora Neale Hurston (p. 388)
• Cotton Club (p. 390)
• Marcus Garvey (p. 393)

Reading Strategy
Organizing As you read about the African American experience in the 1920s, complete a graphic organizer similar to the one below by filling in the causes and effects of the Harlem Renaissance.

Causes   Effects

Harlem
Renaissance

The Harlem Renaissance

MAIN Idea The Harlem Renaissance sparked new trends in literature, music, and art.

HISTORY AND YOU Can you think of any examples of integrating different cultures in today's music and visual arts? Read to learn about the contributions of African Americans to the arts during the 1920s.

During World War I and the 1920s, hundreds of thousands of African Americans joined in the **Great Migration** from the rural South to industrial cities in the North. By moving north, African Americans sought to escape Southern segregation, find economic opportunities, and build better lives. Although job discrimination and economic inequality remained the norm in Northern cities, the North still offered much greater economic opportunities for African Americans compared to the South. After World War I, African American populations swelled in large Northern cities. The cities were full of nightclubs and music, particularly in the New York City neighborhood of Harlem—the heart and soul of the African American renaissance. It was there that African American artistic development, racial pride, and political organization thrived. The result was a flowering of African American arts that became known as the **Harlem Renaissance.**

The Writers

Claude McKay was the first important writer of the Harlem Renaissance. McKay translated the shock of American racism into *Harlem Shadows,* a collection of poetry published in 1922. In such poems as "The Lynching" and "If We Must Die," McKay's eloquent verse expressed a proud defiance and bitter contempt of racism—two striking characteristics of Harlem Renaissance writing. **Langston Hughes** was a prolific, original, and versatile writer. He became a leading voice of the African American experience in America.

Another important Harlem Renaissance author was **Zora Neale Hurston.** Hurston published her first novels, *Jonah's Gourd Vine* and *Their Eyes Were Watching God,* in the 1930s. Hurston's personal and spirited portrayals of rural African American culture were also the

---

R Reading Strategies	**C** Critical Thinking	**D** Differentiated Instruction	**W** Writing Support	**S** Skill Practice
Teacher Edition • Act. Prior Know., p. 389 **Additional Resources** • Guided Read., URB p. 50 • Primary Source Reading, URB p. 37	**Teacher Edition** • Making Inferences, pp. 390, 392 **Additional Resources** • Linking Past and Present Act., URB p. 34 • Quizzes and Tests, p. 143 • Auth Assess, p. 39 • Am. Literature Reading, URB p. 13	**Teacher Edition** • Auditory/Musical, p. 390 **Additional Resources** • Enrich Act, p. 44 • Reteaching Act., URB p. 43 • Differentiated Instruction Act., URB p. 23 • Am. Art and Music Act., URB p. 39	**Teacher Edition** • Narrative Writing, pp. 391, 392 • Persuasive Writing, p. 393	**Additional Resources** • RENTG, p. 112

Voices From the Harlem Renaissance

Excerpt from
Dust Tracks on a Road
by Zora Neale Hurston

"I can look back and see sharp shadows, high lights, and smudgy inbetweens. I have been in Sorrow's kitchen and licked out all the pots. Then I have stood on the peaky mountain wrapped in rainbows, with a harp and a sword in my hands.

"What I had to swallow in the kitchen has not made me less glad to have lived, nor made me want to low-rate the human race . . . It is the graceless acknowledgment of defeat . . . I am in the struggle with the sword in my hands, and I don't intend to run until you run me [away]."

▲ *Zora Neale Hurston*

If We Must Die
By Claude McKay

If we must die—let it not be like hogs
Hunted and penned in an inglorious spot,
While round us bark the mad and hungry dogs,Making their mock at our accursed lot. If we must die—oh, let us nobly die,
So that our precious blood may not be shed
In vain; then even the monsters we defy
Shall be constrained to honor us though dead!
Oh, Kinsmen! We must meet the common foe;
Though far outnumbered, let us show us brave,
And for their thousand blows deal one deathblow!
What though before us lies the open grave?
Like men we'll face the murderous, cowardly pack,
Pressed to the wall, dying, but fighting back!

I, Too, Sing America
by Langston Hughes

I, too, sing America.

I am the darker brother.
They send me to eat in the kitchen
When company comes,
But I laugh,
And eat well,
And grow strong.

Tomorrow,
I'll be at the table
When company comes.
Nobody'll dare
Say to me,
"Eat in the kitchen,"
Then.

Besides,
They'll see how
beautiful I am
And be ashamed—

I, too, am America.

▲ *Langston Hughes stressed racial pride in his poetry. He reminded African Americans that they had their own history and achievements which were in every way as worthy of celebration as those of white people.*

◄ *Originally from Jamaica, Claude McKay wrote both poems and novels. "If We Must Die" was written shortly after World War I when race riots were erupting across the nation.*

DBQ **Document-Based Questions**

1. **Speculating** What might have been some of the "pots" in Sorrow's kitchen for a woman in the Harlem Renaissance?

2. **Comparing and Contrasting** What does McKay's poem have in common with Hurston's excerpt and the poem by Hughes?

---

first major stories featuring African American women as central characters. Other notable writers of the Harlem Renaissance include Countee Cullen, Alain Locke, Dorothy West, and Nella Larsen.

Jazz, Blues, and the Theater

When New Orleans native Louis Armstrong moved to Chicago in 1922, he introduced an improvisational early form of **jazz,** a style of music influenced by Dixieland blues and ragtime, with its syncopated rhythms and improvisational elements. Three years later, Armstrong awed fellow musicians with a series of recordings made with his group, the Hot Five. In these recordings, especially in the song "Cornet Chop Suey," Armstrong broke away from the New Orleans tradition of ensemble or group playing by performing highly imaginative solos. He became the first great cornet and trumpet soloist in jazz music. The artistic freedom of Chicago's South Side gave Armstrong the courage to create his own type of jazz.

History ONLINE
Student Web Activity Visit glencoe.com and complete the activity on the Jazz Age.

Teach

R **Reading Strategy**
Activating Prior Knowledge
Before students begin to take in any new knowledge, prepare them by bringing to mind what they already know about the topic they are about to study. Before beginning this section, ask students what they know about the Harlem Renaissance, including whom it involved and where it began. Use the ideas generated to encourage students to think about the topic in more detail and to share more ideas. As students read the section, point out where the ideas they generated can be found in the text. **BL**

DBQ **Document Based Questions**

Answers:
1. Answers will vary, but should focus on the discrimination blacks experienced even in northern cities.
2. All reflect African American pride.

Hands-On Chapter Project
Step 5

Creating a Memory Book

Step 5: Design a Class Memory Page
Students will collaborate as a class to plan, design, and create a memory page focused on the content of Section 5—African American Culture.

Directions Divide the class into four groups. Each group will sketch a storyboard that depicts, using both images and text, the African American culture of this historical period. After the groups have created their storyboards, bring the class into one discussion. Have group representatives present their ideas, and then decide on a class presentation of the topic. The class will then determine roles for each group to build the memory page.

Synthesizing Information Students will collect information from each group and determine the best way to present the topic using all the ideas presented. **OL** *(Chapter Project continued on Visual Summary page)*

D Differentiated Instruction

Auditory/Musical Have interested students create a presentation titled "Introduction to Jazz." Encourage students to create a multimedia presentation that provides a musical overview of the patterns and themes common in jazz. **OL**

C Critical Thinking

Making Inferences Have interested students research why the Cotton Club, which featured African American performers and was located in the Harlem area of New York City, served only white customers. **Ask:** Based on what you have learned, what can you infer about the racial attitudes and prejudices of the 1920s? *(Answers will vary, but students will likely point out that racial segregation was still the norm at the time.)* **AL**

Additional Support

Ragtime also influenced the composer, pianist, and bandleader Edward "Duke" Ellington, who listened as a teenager to ragtime piano players in Washington, D.C. In 1923 Ellington, also known simply as "Duke," formed a small band, moved to New York, and began playing in speakeasies and clubs. He soon created his own sound, a blend of improvisation and orchestration using different combinations of instruments. In fact, Ellington often did not like to use the word "jazz," since he believed it put a restriction on the general concept of his music. The Ellington style appeared in such hits as "Mood Indigo" and "Sophisticated Lady." Ellington, who had to be forced to practice piano as a child, eventually composed nearly 6,000 musical pieces, about a third of them jazz numbers. He also wrote religious music, the scores for five movies, and a ballet.

Like many other African American entertainers, Ellington got his start at the **Cotton Club,** the most famous nightclub in Harlem (but one that served only white customers). Years later, reflecting on the music of this era, Ellington said, "Everything, and I repeat, every-thing had to swing. And that was just it, those cats really had it; they had that soul. And you know you can't just play some of this music without soul. Soul is very important."

Bessie Smith seemed to **symbolize** soul. Her emotional singing style and commanding voice earned her the title "the Empress of the Blues." Smith sang of unfulfilled love, poverty, and oppression—the classic themes of the **blues,** a soulful style of music that evolved from African American spirituals. Born in Tennessee, Smith started performing in tent shows, saloons, and small theaters in the South. Discovered by Ma Rainey, one of the early great blues singers, Smith later performed with many of the greatest jazz bands of the era, including those of Louis Armstrong, Fletcher Henderson, and Benny Goodman. Her first recorded song, "Down Hearted Blues," became a major hit in 1923.

While jazz and blues filled the air during the Harlem Renaissance, the theater arts were also flourishing. *Shuffle Along,* the first musical written, produced, and performed by African Americans, made its Broadway debut in 1921. The show's success helped launch a number of

PRIMARY SOURCE
Scenes From the Harlem Renaissance

The Harlem Renaissance made both jazz and blues music popular and enabled African American entertainers to reach a wide audience.

▲ Many famous acts got their start at Harlem's Cotton Club. Patrons flocked there to hear the latest jazz music—African American music played by African American musicians—but the audience was limited to whites.

▲ Louis Armstrong and his band, the Hot Five

▶ Duke Ellington and his band at a Chicago nightclub

390 Chapter 10 The Jazz Age

Activity: Interdisciplinary Connection

Music Have interested students listen to recordings of jazz and blues performances by popular artists from the 1920s, such as Duke Ellington or Bessie Smith. Instruct students to use library or Internet resources to learn more about the performer they have selected. Then have students prepare a profile of the life of their chosen performer. Encourage students to include information about their music and their personal lives. Invite students to share their profiles with the class. If possible, arrange to play clips of music from the various jazz and blues performers. **OL**

careers, including those of Florence Mills and Paul Robeson.

Robeson first gained recognition as an athlete at Rutgers University, where he was valedictorian of his class. After graduating from law school, he focused on an acting career. A celebrated singer and actor, Robeson received wide acclaim in the title role of a 1924 New York production of *Emperor Jones,* a play by Eugene O'Neill. Four years later, Robeson gained fame for his work in the musical, *Show Boat.* He also often appeared at the Apollo Theater, another famous club in Harlem.

Perhaps the most daring performer of the era, Josephine Baker transformed a childhood knack for flamboyance into a career as a well-known singer and dancer. Baker performed on Broadway but later moved to Paris and launched an international career.

The Harlem Renaissance succeeded in bringing international fame to African American arts. It also sparked a political transformation in the United States.

Reading Check Analyzing How did African Americans help shape the national identity through the use of music?

African Americans and 1920s Politics

MAIN Idea While the NAACP pursued racial equality through the courts, black nationalists supported independence and separation from whites.

HISTORY AND YOU How does a sense of positive self-esteem help you perform better? Read how African Americans developed a new sense of pride.

In 1919, 1,300 African American veterans of World War I marched through Manhattan to Harlem. The march symbolized the new aspirations of African Americans in the 1920s. W. E. B. Du Bois captured the new sense of dignity and defiance of African Americans:

PRIMARY SOURCE

"We return. We return from fighting. We return fighting. Make way for democracy! We saved it in France, and by the Great Jehovah, we will save it in the United States of America, or know the reason why."

—quoted in *When Harlem Was in Vogue*

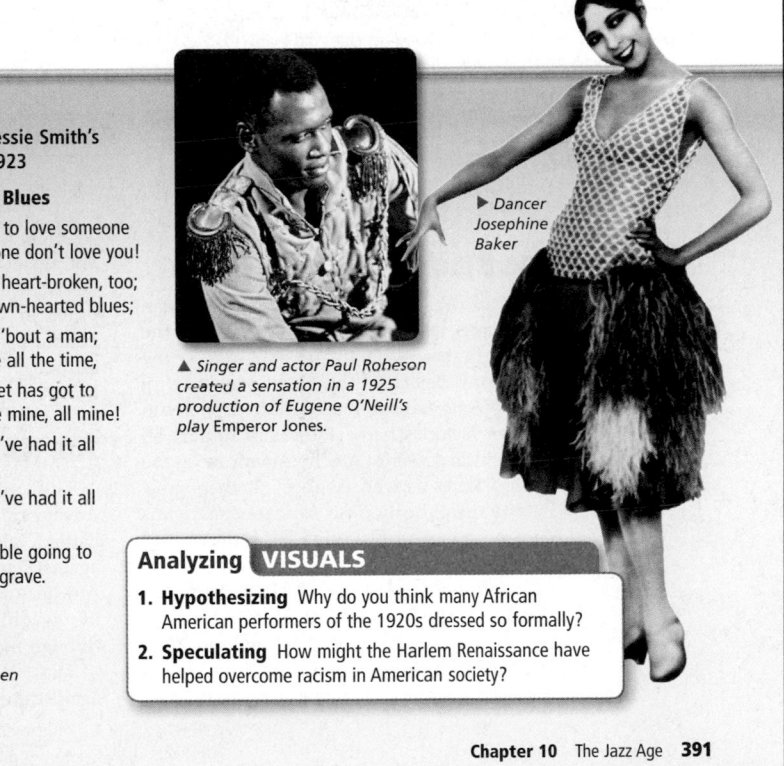

Excerpt from Bessie Smith's first hit song, 1923

Down Hearted Blues

Gee, but it's hard to love someone when that someone don't love you!

I'm so disgusted, heart-broken, too; I've got those down-hearted blues;

Once I was crazy 'bout a man; he mistreated me all the time,

The next man I get has got to promise me to be mine, all mine!

Trouble, trouble, I've had it all my days,

Trouble, trouble, I've had it all my days;

It seems like trouble going to follow me to my grave.

◄ *Bessie Smith was one of the earliest and most famous women blues singers.*

▲ *Singer and actor Paul Robeson created a sensation in a 1925 production of Eugene O'Neill's play* Emperor Jones.

► *Dancer Josephine Baker*

Analyzing VISUALS

1. **Hypothesizing** Why do you think many African American performers of the 1920s dressed so formally?
2. **Speculating** How might the Harlem Renaissance have helped overcome racism in American society?

Chapter 10 The Jazz Age **391**

Extending the Content

Black Swan Records African American musicians were rarely recorded in the early twentieth century. White record companies would buy songs written by African Americans for white singers to record. In 1921 Harry Herbert Pace formed Black Swan Records, the first major African American owned recording company. During its existence, the company, which Pace first ran from his basement in Harlem, recorded for and marketed to African American consumers. During its heyday, Black Swan Records produced and sold some 7,000 recordings daily.

C Critical Thinking

Making Inferences Have students find out more about the Great Migration of the 1920s. **Ask:** How did the influx of large numbers of African Americans affect northern cities? *(Answers will vary, but students should support their answers with findings from their research. They may note that racial tensions increased in some cities as workers competed for jobs. Students may also note that African Americans were able to vote as a bloc, thus gaining political power.)* **AL**

W Writing Support

Narrative Writing Have students use library or Internet resources to find out more about Oscar DePriest. Have students write a one-page narrative of his career, including his early life and his efforts in Congress. **OL**

Analyzing GEOGRAPHY

Answers:
1. St. Louis, Chicago, and Detroit
2. New York and Philadelphia

Additional Support

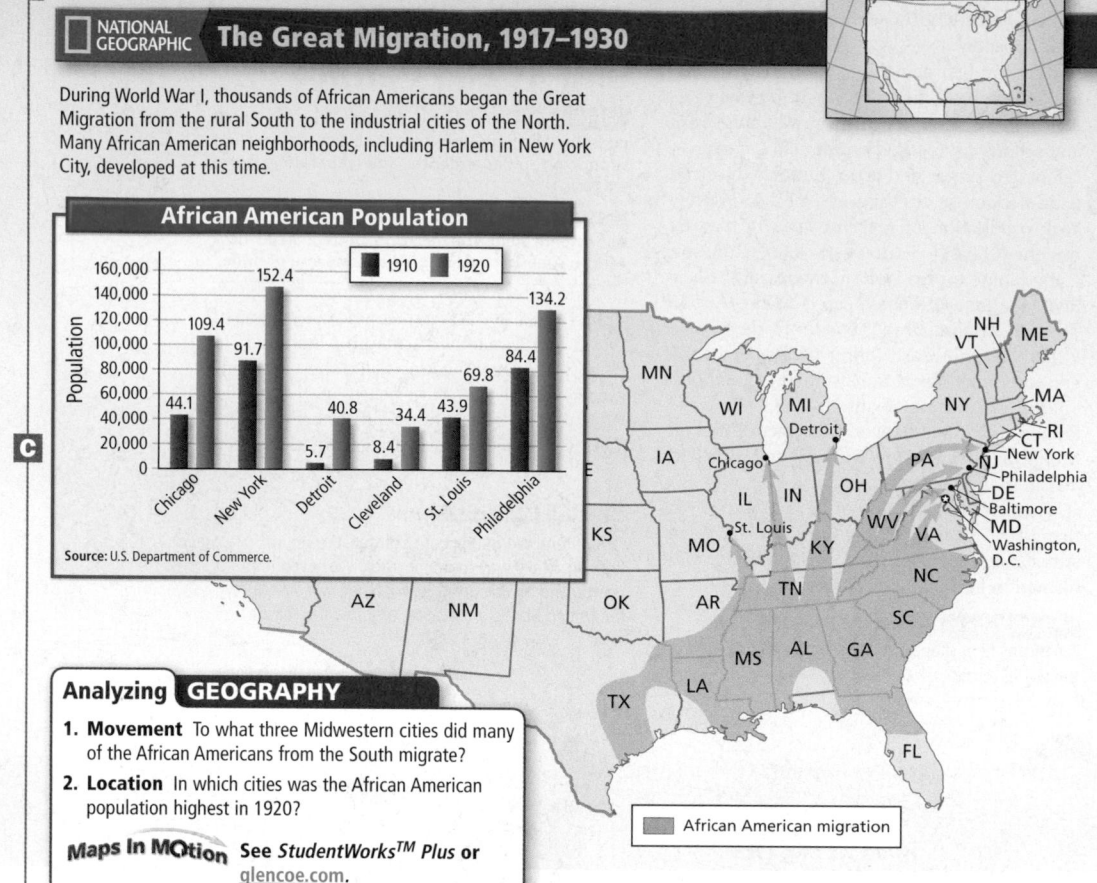

NATIONAL GEOGRAPHIC The Great Migration, 1917–1930

During World War I, thousands of African Americans began the Great Migration from the rural South to the industrial cities of the North. Many African American neighborhoods, including Harlem in New York City, developed at this time.

African American Population

Legend: ■ 1910 ■ 1920

Population (y-axis: 0 to 160,000)

- Chicago: 44.1 / 109.4
- New York: 91.7 / 152.4
- Detroit: 5.7 / 40.8
- Cleveland: 8.4 / 34.4
- St. Louis: 43.9 / 69.8
- Philadelphia: 84.4 / 134.2

Source: U.S. Department of Commerce.

African American migration

Analyzing GEOGRAPHY

1. **Movement** To what three Midwestern cities did many of the African Americans from the South migrate?
2. **Location** In which cities was the African American population highest in 1920?

Maps In MOtion See *StudentWorks™ Plus* or glencoe.com.

The Black Vote in the North

World War I set the stage for African Americans to reenter federal politics in the United States, although perhaps not in the way many expected. The Great Migration of African Americans to the North to take jobs in the war factories had a significant **impact** on the political power of African Americans in the United States as well. As their numbers grew in city neighborhoods, African Americans became a powerful voting bloc that could sometimes sway the outcome of elections.

At election time, most African American voters in the North cast their votes for Republicans, the party of Abraham Lincoln. In 1928 African American voters in Chicago achieved a significant political breakthrough.

Voting as a bloc, they helped elect Oscar DePriest, the first African American representative in Congress from a Northern state. During his three terms in Congress, DePriest introduced laws to oppose racial discrimination and make lynching a federal crime. **W**

The NAACP Battles Injustice

The National Association for the Advancement of Colored People (NAACP) battled valiantly—but often unsuccessfully—against segregation and discrimination against African Americans. Its efforts focused primarily on lobbying public officials and working through the court system.

The NAACP also lobbied and protested against the horrors of lynching. The NAACP's

392 Chapter 10 The Jazz Age

Activity: Economics Connection

The NAACP Have interested students find out more information about the NAACP today. Students should also find out how the NAACP uses its organization to boycott cities or states that allegedly discriminate against minorities. **Ask:** Based on your findings, are the NAACP's economic boycotts successful? What financial impact do the boycotts have on the targeted area? *(Answers will vary, but students should note that the purchasing power of the African American community, especially if a boycott attracts widespread support, could have a major economic impact on an area.)* **OL**

persistent efforts led to the passage of antilynching legislation in the House of Representatives in 1922. The Senate defeated the bill, but the NAACP continued the fight. Its **ongoing** efforts to end lynching kept the issue in the news and probably helped to reduce the number of lynchings that took place.

One of the NAACP's greatest political triumphs occurred in 1930 with the defeat of Judge John J. Parker's nomination to the U.S. Supreme Court. The NAACP joined with labor unions to launch a highly organized national campaign against the North Carolina judge, who allegedly was racist and antilabor. By a narrow margin, the Senate refused to confirm Parker's nomination. His defeat demonstrated that African American voters and lobby groups had finally achieved enough influence to affect national politics and change decisions in Congress.

Black Nationalism and Marcus Garvey

While the NAACP fought for integration and improvement in the economic and political position of African Americans, other groups began to emphasize black nationalism and black pride. Eventually, some began calling for black separation from white society.

A dynamic black leader from Jamaica, **Marcus Garvey,** captured the imagination of millions of African Americans with his "Negro Nationalism," which glorified the black culture and traditions. Inspired by Booker T. Washington's call for self-reliance, Garvey founded the Universal Negro Improvement Association (UNIA), an organization aimed at promoting black pride and unity. The central message of Garvey's Harlem-based movement was that African Americans could gain economic and political power by educating themselves. Garvey also advocated separation and independence from whites. In 1920, at the height of his power, Garvey told his followers they would never find justice or freedom in America, and he proposed leading them to Africa.

The emerging African American middle class and intellectuals distanced themselves from Garvey and his push for racial separation. FBI officials saw UNIA as a dangerous catalyst for black uprisings in urban areas. Garvey also alienated key figures in the Harlem Renaissance by characterizing them as "weak-kneed and cringing . . . [flatterers of] the white man." Convicted of mail fraud in 1923, Garvey served time in prison. In 1927 President Coolidge commuted Garvey's sentence and used Garvey's immigrant status to have him deported to Jamaica.

Despite Garvey's failure to keep his movement alive, he instilled millions of African Americans with a sense of pride in their heritage and inspired hope for the future. That sense of pride and hope survived long after Garvey and his "back to Africa" movement was gone. This pride and hope reemerged strongly during the 1950s and played a vital role in the civil rights movement of the 1960s.

Reading Check Summarizing How did World War I change attitudes among African Americans toward themselves and their country?

Section 5 REVIEW

Vocabulary

1. **Explain** the significance of: Great Migration, Harlem Renaissance, Claude McKay, Langston Hughes, Zora Neale Hurston, jazz, Cotton Club, blues, Marcus Garvey.

Main Ideas

2. **Analyzing** What musical style did Duke Ellington create? How was it different from other styles of music?

3. **Synthesizing** How did the Great Migration affect the political power of African Americans in the North?

Critical Thinking

4. **Big Ideas** What actions did the NAACP take to expand political rights for African Americans?

5. **Organizing** Use a graphic organizer similar to the one below to describe the impact of the Harlem Renaissance on U.S. society.

Impact of Harlem Renaissance

6. **Analyzing Visuals** Look at the photographs of Harlem Renaissance writers on page 389. Select one person and write a description of him or her, based only on what you see in the photo.

Writing About History

7. **Descriptive Writing** Imagine that you witnessed the African American men of the 369th Infantry, who had come back from the war, march through Manhattan and home to Harlem. Write a paragraph describing your feelings upon seeing these men.

History ONLINE
Study Central™ To review this section, go to **glencoe.com** and click on Study Central.

393

W Writing Support
Persuasive Writing Have students find out more about Marcus Garvey and the "Back to Africa" movement and write a letter to President Coolidge giving an opinion about Garvey. **OL**

✔ Reading Check

Answer:
They saw themselves as entitled to all the rights of citizens.

Assess

History ONLINE

Study Central™ provides summaries, interactive games, and online graphic organizers to help students review content.

Close

Summarizing Ask: How did African Americans influence American society in the 1920s? *(They contributed to the arts and gained political power as they moved to northern cities.)* **OL**

Section 5 REVIEW

Answers

1. All definitions can be found in the section and the Glossary.

2. distinctive orchestration and improvisation; Ellington's music had "soul"

3. created a strong voting bloc

4. lobbied and worked through the courts

5. literature, new styles of music, theater, political influence

6. Answers will vary, but descriptions should accurately reflect the image.

7. Students' paragraphs should focus on emotional responses.

Chapter 10 VISUAL SUMMARY

Determining Cause and Effect The Visual Summary lists causes of prosperity and its effects on society. Ask students to use the information on the page to create a time line of the era's events. Display the time lines in the classroom. **OL**

Descriptive Writing Have students select the one characteristic or event that they believe is symbolic of the 1920s. Examples may include Prohibition, the rise of the automobile, jazz, the Harlem Renaissance, Lindbergh's flight, and the arts and literature of the era. Have students write a letter describing their chosen event or characteristic to a friend. Remind students to use descriptive words and terms in their letters. Have volunteers share their letters with the class. **OL**

Causes of Prosperity

Government's Role
- Limits interference with business
- Cuts taxes, debt, and government spending
- Imposes higher tariffs to protect young industries

Business Innovation and Technology
- Mass production creates a wide range of consumer goods sold at low prices.
- Technology such as autos, airplanes, and radio leads to new industries and economic growth.
- Business pays high wages.

New Consumer Society
- People have more disposable income and leisure time
- Credit is more readily available
- Mass advertising begins

▲ Joe "King" Oliver's band, with Louis Armstrong on slide trumpet, performs in Chicago in 1923, introducing the sound of jazz to America.

▲ The moving assembly line, pioneered by Henry Ford, made building automobiles efficient and greatly reduced prices.

A Changing Society

Cultural Changes
- A new youth culture with a "new morality" develops.
- Young people and women gain more independence.
- The working class enjoys more leisure time.
- New mass media in radio, movies, and sports develops.

Changes for African Americans
- Harlem Renaissance begins.
- Literature reveals racial pride and contempt of racism.
- Jazz and blues are popularized.
- Great Migration during the war creates strong African American voting blocs in Northern cities.
- First African American from the North is elected to Congress.
- NAACP battles segregation and discrimination.

Opposition to Change
- Nativists and a new Ku Klux Klan target immigrants, Catholics, Jews, and African Americans.
- Government imposes new quotas on immigration.
- Fundamentalists push for traditional values.
- Prohibition is implemented.

◄ A federal agent enforces Prohibition by dumping barrels of illegal alcohol as neighborhood children watch.

394 Chapter 10 The Jazz Age

Hands-On Chapter Project
Step 6: Wrap Up

Creating a Memory Book

Step 6: Wrap Up Students will use their prior knowledge and the materials they researched to edit and revise the pages of the memory book.

Directions Give each student a page of the memory book. Each student will edit and revise the page as needed to create an attractive, informative page. They may wish to decorate the pages with other appropriate images, as well. The complete book may be used by the class to review the chapter and then displayed in the school.

Analyzing Information Students will determine the main topics presented and clarify the information to best represent the main ideas of the topic. **OL**

ASSESSMENT

STANDARDIZED TEST PRACTICE

TEST-TAKING TIP

Make sure that you can define the chapter's vocabulary terms. You will see these words in questions on standardized tests. By understanding their meanings you can omit incorrect answers through the process of elimination.

Reviewing Vocabulary

Directions: Choose the word or words that best complete each sentence.

1. What economic philosophy encouraged businesses to form trade associations?
   A monopolies
   B cooperative individualism
   C moratorium
   D supply-side economics

2. Companies introduced _____, which were programs that benefited workers by allowing them to participate in profit-sharing and to receive health benefits and pensions.
   A normalcy
   B open shop system
   C supply-side economics
   D welfare capitalism

3. Sacco and Vanzetti were _____, or people who opposed all forms of government.
   A anarchists
   B Communists
   C bohemians
   D creationists

4. Prohibition led to an increase in _____, or bars where people sold liquor illegally.
   A mass media
   B speakeasies
   C police powers
   D bootlegging

Reviewing Main Ideas

Directions: Choose the best answers to the following questions.

Section 1 *(pp. 362–367)*

5. Teapot Dome is an example of a scandal during the administration of
   A Calvin Coolidge.
   B Warren G. Harding.
   C Woodrow Wilson.
   D William Howard Taft.

6. What agreement involved American banks giving loans to Germany to pay war reparations to France and Britain?
   A the Washington Conference
   B Kellogg-Briand Pact
   C the Dawes Plan
   D Four-Power Treaty

Section 2 *(pp. 368–375)*

7. Henry Ford's contribution to manufacturing was the
   A expansion of the petroleum industry.
   B requirement of open shop.
   C idea of mass marketing.
   D adoption of the assembly line.

8. The change in Americans' ideas about _____ resulted in more spending on what had once been luxury goods.
   A mass production
   B consumer credit
   C advertising
   D welfare capitalism

Need Extra Help?

If You Missed Questions . . .	1	2	3	4	5	6	7	8
Go to Page . . .	365	374	376–377	381	362–364	366–367	368–370	372–373

 GO ON

Answers and Analyses
Reviewing Vocabulary

1. B The philosophy of cooperative individualism was suggested by Secretary of Commerce Herbert Hoover, who believed that trade associations would share information with the government. In a trade association, businesses interact and "cooperate" with each other. A monopoly is a type of business, not a philosophy. A moratorium is an action taken. Supply-side economics is a philosophy, which may throw students off, so make sure students understand the difference between the two philosophies.

2. D Welfare means "benefit" or "wellbeing." Therefore, welfare capitalism provides benefits to workers. Help students who have trouble with this question connect welfare with the concept of helping people make improvements.

3. A For students who have trouble with this question, review the definitions of the answer choices. Communists believed in a classless society in which people would share wealth equally, but they did not oppose all forms of government. Creationists are people who believe in the creation story as told in the book of Genesis in the Bible. Bohemians are either people from Bohemia, or, in the context of the chapter, people who lived an unconventional lifestyle.

4. B Students who read the question carefully will have no trouble selecting the correct answer. The question specifies that the missing word is another word for a type of bar. A bar is a place. Choices *A*, *C*, and *D* are not places. Students who do not carefully read the question may select bootlegging as the correct answer, as it is related to Prohibition.

Reviewing Main Ideas

5. B Warren G. Harding's administration was plagued with scandal. Harding was from Ohio, which may help students remember his connection with the Ohio Gang.

6. C The Washington Conference was a meeting, not an agreement. It is unlikely that a treaty would involve loans. The Kellogg-Briand Pact outlawed war. The Dawes Plan is correct. It was suggested by a diplomat named Charles G. Dawes.

7. D Remind students that the assembly line led to the mass production of the Model-T, the first automobile to be accessible to the masses. The use of the assembly line helped Ford keep the cost of the final product down.

8. B Only *B* makes sense in the context of the sentence. The rise in consumer credit resulted from changing American ideals, as a whole. In the past, being in debt was dishonorable. This change in attitude was reflected in the number of Americans using consumer credit to pay off luxury items over time.

395

9. A The Eighteenth Amendment, ratified in 1920, prohibited the sale or consumption of alcohol.

10. B Students may have trouble choosing between the two immigration acts listed in the answer choices: the Emergency Quota Act and the National Origins Act. However, the question asks which act restricted "each *national* group." This should clue students in to the correct answer–the National Origins Act.

11. A As two of the nation's largest cities, Chicago and New York were, of course, centers of industry, politics, and banking. However, the question does not ask about the cities, it asks about neighborhoods within the cities. These neighborhoods provided a nurturing environment for artists, writers, and musicians.

12. D To help students remember this, briefly review the Renaissance with them—explaining the artistic and social strides made in that period. Also explain that a renaissance of any kind is a revitalization or a revival. The Harlem Renaissance was a revival of African American culture. While the other answer choices are related to African Americans during that time period, none is broad enough to encompass all artistic developments of African Americans in the 1920s.

13. B Black nationalism differed from other African American movements in that it supported pride in African American culture, including independence from whites. Integration and political improvement was an idea of the NAACP. Marcus Garvey supported the "back to Africa" idea, not back to Jamaica. He was deported to Jamaica.

Section 3 *(pp. 376–381)*

9. The passage of the Eighteenth Amendment was seen as a victory for
   A opponents of alcohol consumption.
   B supporters of women's suffrage.
   C nativists.
   D Sacco and Vanzetti.

10. What act restricted immigration to 2 percent of each national group represented in the 1890 U.S. Census?
   A Emergency Quota Act
   B National Origins Act
   C Reclamation Act
   D Clayton Antitrust Act

Section 4 *(pp. 382–385)*

11. Chicago's South Side and New York's Greenwich Village were centers for
   A the arts.
   B industry.
   C politics.
   D banking.

Section 5 *(pp. 388–393)*

12. The artistic developments of African Americans in the 1920s were known as the
   A Great Migration.
   B Saint Louis blues.
   C New Orleans sound.
   D Harlem Renaissance.

13. What was an idea of black nationalism?
   A integration and political improvement in society
   B separation and independence from whites
   C emigration from the United States to Jamaica
   D support for the arts as a way to improve African American society

Critical Thinking

Directions: Choose the best answers to the following questions.

14. What effect did greater education and job opportunities for women create?
   A Many women began earning as much money as men did.
   B Women contributed to both scientific and artistic knowledge.
   C More women preferred to remain at home.
   D Most women working outside the home gained leadership positions.

Base your answer to question 15 on the map below and on your knowledge of Chapter 10.

European Immigration Totals, 1890–1920

Number of People Immigrating to U.S. by Region, 1890–1920

488,099	2,135,312
672,223	3,060,151
1,130,656	3,695,828
1,195,628	3,859,297
— 1914 border	

15. Which nation or empire sent the greatest number of immigrants to the United States between 1890 and 1920?
   A Italy
   B Russian Empire
   C German Empire
   D Spain

GO ON

Need Extra Help?

If You Missed Questions . . .	9	10	11	12	13	14	15
Go to Page . . .	381	378	382–384	388	393	378–379	377–378

396 Chapter 10 The Jazz Age

Critical Thinking

14. B Students should approach this question as a cause-and-effect question. Although women had greater education and job opportunities, it did not lead to equality with men in the workplace. Therefore, most women working outside the home did not achieve leadership positions. By the same token, women did not earn as much as men. It does not make sense that greater opportunity would cause more women to remain at home. However, these opportunities allowed women to make scientific and artistic contributions.

15. A Using the key, students should first find the color or pattern that represents the greatest number of immigrants: 3,859,297. They should then find this area on the map. Italy is correct.

16. What written agreement declared war illegal?

  A the Washington Conference

  B the Dawes Plan

  C the Kellogg-Briand Pact

  D the League of Nations Charter

17. What was a principal reason for rapid economic growth in the United States during the 1920s?

  A prosperity of American agriculture

  B increase of American imports

  C development of many new consumer goods

  D increased spending on defense

Analyze the cartoon and answer the question that follows. Base your answer on the cartoon and your knowledge of Chapter 10.

CIRCUS DAYS

18. What does the cartoon imply about Coolidge?

  A He was trying to select which party to support in the next election.

  B He wanted to control the congressional leadership.

  C He wanted to cut back on unnecessary government expenditures.

  D He wanted to increase taxes and government spending.

Document-Based Questions

Directions: Analyze the document and answer the short-answer questions that follow the document.

Charles Lindbergh, who made the first transatlantic flight from New York to Paris in 1927, later wrote a book about the experience. He titled the book after the plane he flew, *The Spirit of St. Louis.* The following excerpt is from that book:

> "What endless hours I worked over this chart in California, measuring, drawing, rechecking each 100-mile segment of its great-circle route, each theoretical hour of my flight. . . . A few lines and figures on a strip of paper, a few ounces of weight, this [map] strip is my key to Europe. With it, I can fly the ocean. With it, that black dot at the other end marked 'Paris' will turn into a famous French city with an aerodrome where I can land. But without this chart, all my years of training, all that went into preparing for this flight, no matter how perfectly the engine runs or how long the fuel lasts, all would be as directionless as those columns of smoke in the New England valleys behind me."
> —from *The Spirit of St. Louis*

19. What does Lindbergh believe is the most valuable tool he has?

20. What conclusions can you draw about Lindbergh as a person, based on this excerpt?

Extended Response

21. The Harding and Coolidge administrations promoted economic prosperity and world peace. Consider how both administrations attempted this difficult task. Write an essay that explains the methods used to accomplish the goal of economic and political stability worldwide. How successful was each administration? Your essay should include an introduction, several paragraphs, and a conclusion. Use relevant facts and details to support your conclusion.

 STOP

History ONLINE

For additional test practice, use Self-Check Quizzes—Chapter 10 at glencoe.com.

19. Lindbergh believes his most valuable tool is the map strips of his journey that he's so carefully drawn and checked. Lindbergh writes that "this map strip is my key to Europe."

20. Lindbergh is careful, detail-oriented, and patient. If students have trouble with this conclusion, read the passage aloud to class, and ask student to brainstorm their impressions and give reasons for them.

Extended Response

21. Students' essays will vary, but must include discussion of both Harding's and Coolidge's administrations and should stay focused on economic improvement and international diplomacy. Students should provide well-reasoned assessments of the success of each administration.

Need Extra Help?						
If You Missed Questions . . .	16	17	18	19	20	21
Go to Page . . .	367	367–372	R18	R19	R19	362–365

16. C The Washington Conference was the impetus for the Kellogg-Briand Pact, which outlawed war. The Dawes Plan was related to helping Germany repay war debts. The League of Nations charter set up the League, but it did not outlaw war.

17. C The development of new goods helped spur growth by raising wages and encouraging consumption. *A, B,* and *D* were not factors for growth.

18. C In the cartoon, Coolidge is making elephants (Republicans) and donkeys (Democrats) jump through hoops labeled economy. *A* and *B* don't make sense as they don't deal with economic issues. *D* doesn't work because jumping through hoops usually implies making something harder, in this case government action. So *C* is the correct answer.

History ONLINE

Have students visit the Web site at glencoe.com to review Chapter 10 and take the Self-Check Quiz.

Need Extra Help?

Have students refer to the pages listed if they miss any of the questions.

Key to Ability Levels
- **BL** Below Level
- **OL** On Level
- **AL** Above Level
- **ELL** English Language Learners

Key to Teaching Resources
- Print Material
- CD-ROM
- DVD
- Transparency

Levels (BL / OL / AL / ELL)		Resources	Chapter Opener	Section 1	Section 2	Section 3	Chapter Assess
		FOCUS					
BL OL AL ELL	(Transparency)	Daily Focus Skills Transparencies		11-1	11-2	11-3	
		TEACH					
OL AL	(Print)	Geography and History, URB				p. 3	
BL OL ELL	(Print)	Reading Essentials and Note-Taking Guide*		p. 115	p. 118	p. 121	
OL	(Print)	Historical Analysis Skills Activity, URB		p. 54			
BL OL ELL	(Print)	Guided Reading Activities, URB*		p. 78	p. 79	p. 80	
BL OL AL ELL	(Print)	Content Vocabulary Activity, URB*		p. 59			
BL OL AL ELL	(Print)	Academic Vocabulary Activity, URB		p. 61			
OL AL	(Print)	Critical Thinking Skills Activity, URB			p. 64		
BL OL ELL	(Print)	Reading Skills Activity, URB			p. 53		
BL ELL	(Print)	English Learner Activity, URB			p. 57		
OL AL	(Print)	Reinforcing Skills Activity, URB		p. 63			
BL OL AL ELL	(Print)	Differentiated Instruction Activity, URB			p. 55		
BL OL ELL	(Print)	Time Line Activity, URB				p. 65	
OL	(Print)	Linking Past and Present Activity, URB			p. 66		
BL OL AL ELL	(Print)	American Art and Music Activity, URB			p. 71		
BL OL AL ELL	(Print)	Interpreting Political Cartoons Activity, URB		p. 73			
BL OL AL	(Print)	Economics and History Activity, URB			p. 7		
AL	(Print)	Enrichment Activity, URB				p. 76	
BL OL AL ELL	(Print)	American Biographies	✓	✓	✓	✓	✓
BL OL AL ELL	(Print)	Primary Source Reading, URB		p. 67	p. 69		
BL OL AL ELL	(Print)	The Living Constitution*	✓	✓	✓	✓	✓
OL AL	(CD-ROM)	American History Primary Source Documents Library	✓	✓	✓	✓	✓
BL OL AL ELL	(Transparency)	Unit Map Overlay Transparencies	✓	✓	✓	✓	✓
BL OL AL ELL	(Print)	Differentiated Instruction for the American High School Classroom	✓	✓	✓	✓	✓
BL OL AL ELL	(DVD)	StudentWorks™ Plus DVD	✓	✓	✓	✓	✓
BL OL AL ELL	(CD-ROM)	Vocabulary PuzzleMaker CD-ROM	✓	✓	✓	✓	✓

Note: Please refer to the *Unit 4 Resource Book* for this chapter's URB materials.

* Also available in Spanish

TeacherWorks *Plus*
All-In-One Planner and Resource Center

- Interactive Lesson Planner
- Interactive Teacher Edition
- Fully editable blackline masters
- Section Spotlight Videos Launch

- Differentiated Lesson Plans
- Printable reports of daily assignments
- Standards Tracking System

Levels					Resources	Chapter Opener	Section 1	Section 2	Section 3	Chapter Assess
BL	OL	AL	ELL							
					TEACH *(continued)*					
BL	OL	AL	ELL	●	**American Music Hits Through History CD**	✓	✓	✓	✓	✓
BL	OL	AL	ELL	📁	**Unit Time Line Transparencies and Activities**	✓	✓	✓	✓	✓
BL	OL	AL	ELL	📁	**Cause and Effect Transparencies, Strategies, and Activities**	✓	✓	✓	✓	✓
BL	OL	AL	ELL	📁	**Why It Matters Transparencies, Strategies, and Activities**	✓	✓	✓	✓	✓
BL	OL	AL	ELL	📁	**American Issues**	✓	✓	✓	✓	✓
	OL	AL	ELL	📁	**American Art and Architecture Transparencies, Strategies, and Activities**	✓	✓	✓	✓	✓
BL	OL	AL		📁	**High School American History Literature Library**	✓	✓	✓	✓	✓
BL	OL	AL	ELL	📀	*The American Vision* **Video Program DVD**	✓	✓	✓	✓	✓
Teacher Resources				📁	**Strategies for Success**	✓	✓	✓	✓	✓
				📁	**Success with English Learner**	✓	✓	✓	✓	✓
				📁	**Studies Classroom**	✓	✓	✓	✓	✓
				📀	**Presentation Plus! DVD**	✓	✓	✓	✓	✓
					ASSESS					
BL	OL	AL	ELL	📁	**Section Quizzes and Chapter Tests***		p. 153	p. 154	p. 155	p. 157
BL	OL	AL	ELL	📁	**Authentic Assessment With Rubrics**					p. 27
BL	OL	AL	ELL	📁	**Standardized Test Practice Workbook**					p. 24
BL	OL	AL	ELL	●	*ExamView®* **Assessment Suite CD-ROM**		11-1	11-2	11-3	Ch. 11
BL	OL	AL	ELL	●	**Interactive Tutor Self-Assessment CD-ROM**		11-1	11-2	11-3	Ch. 11
					CLOSE					
BL			ELL	📁	**Reteaching Activity, URB**					p. 75
BL	OL		ELL	📁	**Reading and Study Skills Foldables™**	p. 71				

Using the Glencoe Web Site

ePuzzles and Games

Technology Product

The Glencoe Web site offers activities that students can perform as they study the chapter content. The activities consist of a variety of puzzles and games that help students test their comprehension and recall and reinforce vocabulary and facts in each chapter.

Objectives

The Student Web Activities help students:
- assess their comprehension of chapter content;
- build study skills;
- identify areas for additional study and reinforcement.

Steps

Provide students with the following steps to complete the activities:
- Locate the Web page for *The American Vision: Modern Times* on the Glencoe Web site glencoe.com.
- Click on **Student Center** under the textbook title.

- In the Student Center, select a unit from the Unit Resources menu and a chapter from the Chapter Activities menu using the drop-down arrows.
- Click on the **ePuzzles and Games** link.
- Click on and complete the featured puzzle or game for the chapter selected.

History ONLINE

	Student	Teacher	Parent
Beyond the Textbook	●	●	●
Chapter Overviews	●	●	●
Time Current Events	●		●
ePuzzles and Games	●		●
Concepts in Motion	●		●
Literature Connections		●	
Multi-Language Glossaries	●		●
Online Student Edition	●	●	●
Self-Check Quizzes	●		●
Student Web Activities	●		●
Study Central™	●		●
Teaching Today		●	
Vocabulary eFlashcards	●		●
Web Activity Lesson Plans		●	

Glencoe Media Center

glencoe.com

> **Study-To-Go**
- Vocabulary eFlashcards
- Self-Check Quizzes

> **Audio/Video**
- Student Edition Audio
- Spanish Summaries
- Section Videos

- **Timed Readings Plus in Social Studies** helps students increase their reading rate and fluency while maintaining comprehension. The 400-word passages are similar to those found on state and national assessments.

- **Reading in the Content Area: Social Studies** concentrates on six essential reading skills that help students better comprehend what they read. The book includes 75 high-interest nonfiction passages written at increasing levels of difficulty.

- **Reading Social Studies** includes strategic reading instruction and vocabulary support in Social Studies content for both ELLs and native speakers of English.

www.jamestowneducation.com

Index to National Geographic Magazine:

The following articles relate to this chapter:

- "The Okies—Beyond the Dust Bowl," by William Howarth, September 1984.

- "Nary a Drop to Spare: Drought Grips the West," by Chris Carroll, July 2005.

National Geographic Society Products To order the following, call National Geographic at 1-800-368-2728:

- ZipZapMap! USA (ZipZapMap!)

Access National Geographic's new, dynamic MapMachine Web site and other geography resources at:
www.nationalgeographic.com
www.nationalgeographic.com/maps

The following videotape programs are available from Glencoe as supplements to Chapter 11:

- The Stock Exchange (ISBN 0-76-700562-7)
- The Great Depression (ISBN 0-76-700859-6)

To order, call Glencoe at 1-800-334-7344. To find classroom resources to accompany many of these videos, check the following home pages:

A&E Television: www.aetv.com
The History Channel: www.historychannel.com

Reading List Generator CD-ROM

GLENCOE BookLink 3

Use this database to search more than 30,000 titles to create a customized reading list for your students.

- Reading lists can be organized by students' reading level, author, genre, theme, or area of interest.
- The database provides Degrees of Reading Power™ (DRP) and Lexile™ readability scores for all selections.
- A brief summary of each selection is included.

Leveled reading suggestions for this chapter:

For students at a Grade 8 reading level:
- *Cat Running,* by Zipha Keatley Snyder

For students at a Grade 9 reading level:
- *A Renaissance in Harlem: Lost Voices of an American Community,* by Lionel C. Bascom

For students at a Grade 10 reading level:
- *Seabiscuit: An American Legend,* by Laura Hillenbrand

For students at a Grade 11 reading level:
- *Children of the Dust Bowl: The True Story of the School at Weedpatch Camp,* by Jerry Stanley

For students at a Grade 12 reading level:
- *Herbert Hoover,* by David M. Holford

Focus

MAKING CONNECTIONS
What Causes Depressions?
Discuss with students the two questions posed on p. 399. If you live in or near a region of the country where many traditional, manufacturing jobs have been lost, use that experience to enhance discussion and give students a sense of the scope of the Great Depression. Invite students to imagine life in their community if one in every four people lost his or her job. **OL** **ELL**

Teach
The Big Ideas

As students study the chapter, remind them to consider the section-based Big Ideas included in each section's Guide to Reading. The **Essential Questions** in the activities below tie in to the Big Ideas and help students think about and understand important chapter concepts. In addition, the Hands-on Chapter Projects, with their culminating activities, relate the content from each section to the Big Ideas. These activities build on each other as students progress through the chapter. Section activities culminate in the wrap-up activity on the Visual Summary page.

The Great Depression Begins
1929–1932

SECTION 1 The Causes of the Great Depression
SECTION 2 Life During the Depression
SECTION 3 Hoover Responds to the Depression

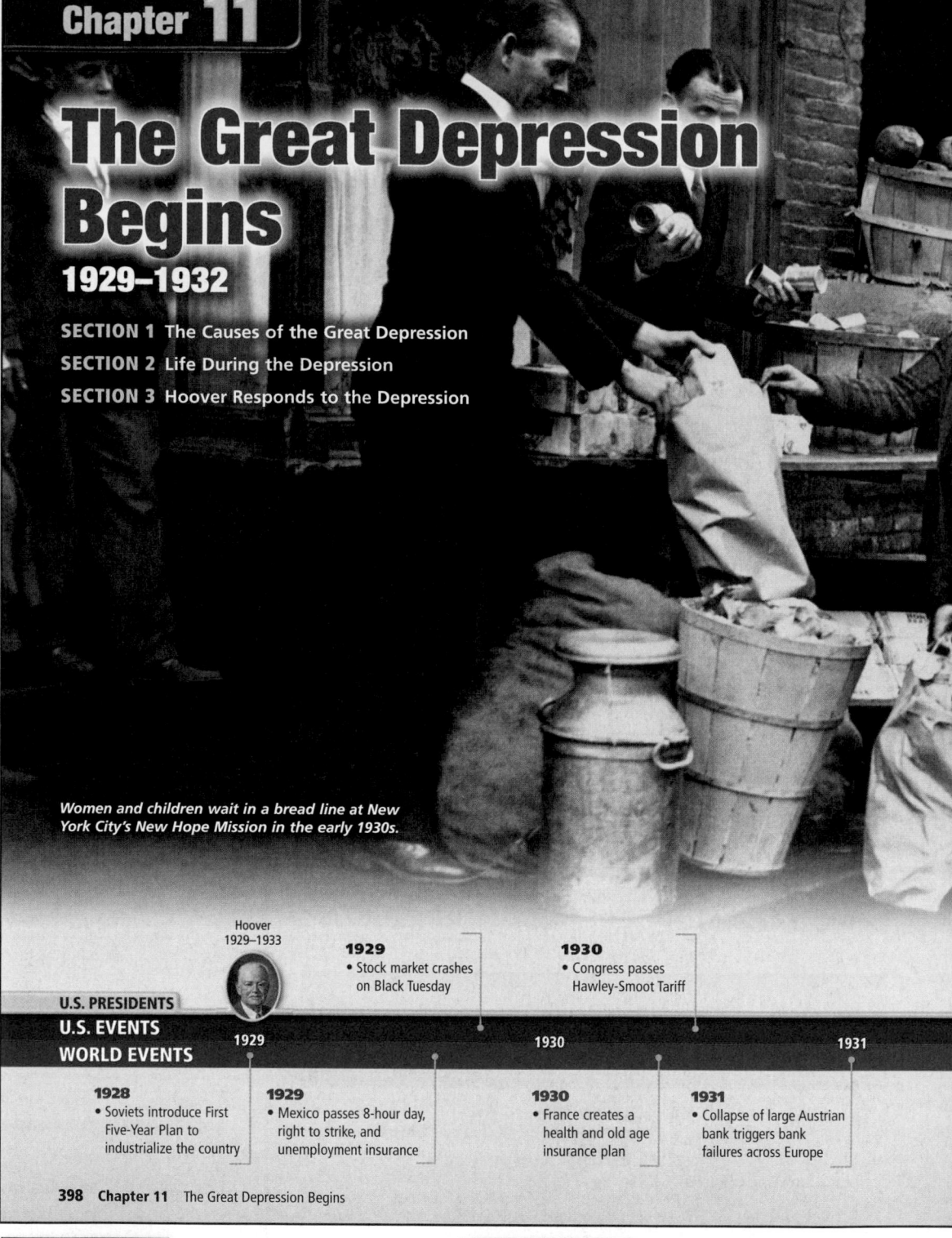

Women and children wait in a bread line at New York City's New Hope Mission in the early 1930s.

Hoover
1929–1933

U.S. PRESIDENTS
U.S. EVENTS
WORLD EVENTS

1929 — **1929** • Stock market crashes on Black Tuesday

1930 — **1930** • Congress passes Hawley-Smoot Tariff

1931

1928 • Soviets introduce First Five-Year Plan to industrialize the country

1929 • Mexico passes 8-hour day, right to strike, and unemployment insurance

1930 • France creates a health and old age insurance plan

1931 • Collapse of large Austrian bank triggers bank failures across Europe

398 Chapter 11 The Great Depression Begins

Section 1

The Causes of the Great Depression
Essential Question: What factors led to the Great Depression? *(inflated stock prices, overproduction, high tariffs, and mistakes by the Federal Reserve Board)* Point out that in Section 1 students will learn about the root causes of the Great Depression. **OL**

Section 2

Life During the Depression
Essential Question: How did people cope with life's struggles during the Great Depression? *(They escaped through movies and popular culture. Some, especially farmers living in the Dust Bowl, went west to seek better jobs.)* Tell students that in Section 2 they will learn about the increased problems during the Depression and how people struggled to survive. **OL**

Making Connections

What Causes Depressions?

In the 1930s, the Great Depression caused high unemployment, business failures, and farm foreclosures. Many people lost their homes and savings and became willing to vote for politicians who offered new approaches to solving the crisis.

- *What kind of political and social problems do you think depressions cause?*
- *Why do you think the Great Depression was worse than other economic slowdowns?*

More About the Photo

Visual Literacy The lyrics to "Brother, Can You Spare a Dime?" were written by E. Y. Harburg in the early 1930s. First recorded by crooner Rudy Vallee in 1932, the song became the signature song of the Great Depression:
"They used to tell me I was building a dream
With peace and glory ahead.
Why should I be standing in line
Just waiting for bread?
"Once I built a railroad, made it run,
Made it race against time.
Once I built a railroad, now it's done,
Brother, can you spare a dime?"

FOLDABLES Study Organizer **Dinah Zike's Foldables**

Dinah Zike's Foldables are three-dimensional, interactive graphic organizers that help students practice basic writing skills, review vocabulary terms, and identify main ideas. Instructions for creating and using Foldables can be found in the Appendix at the end of this book and in the *Dinah Zike's Reading and Study Skills Foldables* booklet.

1931
- National Credit Corporation is created

1932
- Drought begins on Great Plains
- Bonus Marchers arrive in Washington, D.C.

Franklin D. Roosevelt 1933–1945

1932   1933

1931
- Japan invades Manchuria

1932
- Government-induced famine begins in USSR, killing millions
- Unemployment in Germany reaches 6 million

FOLDABLES

Analyzing Popular Culture Create a Two-Tab Book Foldable to research the way people coped with adversity during the Depression. As you read the chapter, list examples of the hardships people endured in real life and the kinds of entertainment that flourished.

Everyday Reality | Escapist Entertainment | Life During the Depression

History ONLINE Chapter Overview
Visit glencoe.com to preview Chapter 11.

History ONLINE
Introduce students to chapter content and key terms by having them access the Chapter 11 Overview at glencoe.com.

Section 3

Hoover Responds to the Depression

Essential Question: How did Hoover's policies attempt to lessen the Great Depression? *(He organized a series of conferences with business leaders and increased funding for public works. He created the National Credit Corporation after the Federal Reserve Board refused his request to put more money into circulation. He set up the Reconstruction Finance*

Corporation to offer businesses loans.) Tell students that in Section 3 they will learn about Hoover's strategies for ending the Great Depression and why they failed. **OL**

Focus

Bellringer
Daily Focus Transparency 11.1

Guide to Reading

Answers: Hoover: Republican, Quaker, engineer, secretary of commerce; Issues: prosperity Smith: Democrat, Catholic, four-time governor of New York; Issues: Catholicism

Section Spotlight Video

To generate student interest and provide a springboard for class discussion, access the Chapter 11, Section 1 video at glencoe.com or on the video DVD.

Resource Manager

Section 1

The Causes of the Great Depression

Although the 1920s were prosperous, speculation in the stock market, risky lending policies, overproduction, and uneven income distribution eventually undermined the economy and led to the Great Depression.

Guide to Reading

Big Ideas
Economics and Society Stock speculation on an unregulated stock market put investors and banks at risk in the 1920s.

Content Vocabulary
• stock market (p. 400)
• bull market (p. 401)
• margin (p. 401)
• margin call (p. 401)
• speculation (p. 401)
• bank run (p. 403)
• installment (p. 405)

Academic Vocabulary
• collapse (p. 400)
• invest (p. 401)
• sum (p. 403)

People and Events to Identify
• Alfred E. Smith (p. 400)
• Black Tuesday (p. 402)
• Hawley-Smoot Tariff (p. 405)

Reading Strategy
Categorizing As you read about the election of 1928, complete a graphic organizer similar to the one below comparing the backgrounds and issues of the presidential candidates.

1928 Presidential Campaign		
Candidate	Background	Issues

The Long Bull Market

MAIN Idea A strong economy helped Herbert Hoover win the 1928 election, but increasing speculation in the stock market set the stage for a crash.

HISTORY AND YOU Have you ever taken a risk while playing a game or sport? How did you decide if the risk was worth it? Read on to learn about the risks people were willing to take in the stock market in the 1920s.

The economic **collapse** that began in 1929 seemed unimaginable only a year earlier. In the 1928 election, both presidential candidates tried to paint a rosy picture of the future. Republican Herbert Hoover declared, "We are nearer to the final triumph over poverty than ever before in the history of any land."

The Election of 1928

When Calvin Coolidge declined to run for reelection in 1928, the Republicans nominated his secretary of commerce, Herbert Hoover. Hoover was well-known to Americans because he had run the Food Administration during World War I. The Democrats chose **Alfred E. Smith,** four-time governor of New York. Smith was the first Roman Catholic to win a major party's nomination for president.

Smith's beliefs became a campaign issue. Some Protestants claimed that the Catholic Church financed the Democratic Party and would rule the United States if Smith became president. These slurs embarrassed Hoover, a Quaker, and he tried to quash them, but the charges damaged Smith's candidacy.

Smith's biggest challenge, however, was the prosperity of the 1920s, for which the Republicans took full credit. Hoover defeated Smith by more than 6 million votes and won the Electoral College in a landslide, 444 to 87. On March 4, 1929, an audience of 50,000 stood in the rain to hear Hoover's inaugural speech. "I have no fears for the future of our country," Hoover said. "It is bright with hope."

The Stock Market Soars

The optimism that swept Hoover into the White House also drove stock prices to new highs. Sometimes the **stock market** experiences

---

R Reading Strategies	**C** Critical Thinking	**D** Differentiated Instruction	**W** Writing Support	**S** Skill Practice
Teacher Edition • Predicting, p. 402 • Analyzing Text Structure, p. 403 • Making Connections, p. 404 • Act. Prior Know., p. 405 **Additional Resources** • Guid. Read. Act., URB p. 78	**Teacher Edition** • Analyzing Prim. Sources, p. 402 **Additional Resources** • Prim. Source Read., URB p. 67 • Intr. Polit. Cartoon, URB p. 73 • Quizzes and Tests, p. 153	**Teacher Edition** • Special Ed., p. 404 **Additional Resources** • Academic Vocab. Act., URB p. 61	**Additional Resources** • Content Vocab. Act., URB p. 59	**Teacher Edition** • Analyzing Maps, p. 401 • Reading Graphs, p. 403 **Additional Resources** • Hist. Analysis Skills, URB p. 54 • Reinforcing Skills Act., URB p. 63 • RENTG, p. 115

PRIMARY SOURCE
Hoover and "Rugged Individualism"

Presidential Election of 1928

Smith   Hoover

[Election map showing states]

WA 7, MT 4, ND 5, MN 12, WI 13, MI 15, NH 4, VT 4, ME 6, MA 18, NY 45, RI 5, CT 7, OR 5, ID 4, WY 3, SD 5, IA 13, IL 29, IN 15, OH 24, PA 38, NJ 14, DE 3, MD 8, NV 3, UT 4, CO 6, NE 8, KS 10, MO 18, KY 13, WV 8, VA 12, NC 12, CA 13, AZ 3, NM 3, OK 10, AR 9, TN 12, SC 9, MS 10, AL 12, GA 14, TX 20, LA 10, FL 6

Presidential Candidate	Popular Vote	% of Popular Vote	Electoral Vote
☐ Hoover	21,392,190	58.18%	444
☐ Smith	15,016,443	40.84%	87

PRIMARY SOURCE

"We were challenged with a peacetime choice between the American system of rugged individualism and a European philosophy of diametrically opposed doctrines—doctrines of paternalism and state socialism.... [T]hese ideas would have meant the destruction of self-government through centralization of government. It would have meant the undermining of ... individual initiative and enterprise ...

"... You cannot extend the mastery of the government over the daily working life of a people without at the same time making it the master of the people's souls and thoughts.... Free speech does not live many hours after free industry and free commerce die.... Every step of bureaucratizing of the business of our country poisons the very roots of liberalism—that is, political equality, free speech, free assembly, free press, and equality of opportunity. It is the road not to more liberty, but to less liberty."

—Herbert Hoover, speech delivered October 22, 1928

DBQ Document-Based Questions

1. **Contrasting** Against what other system does Hoover contrast "rugged individualism"?

2. **Analyzing Primary Sources** What does Hoover believe is at stake if free industry and free commerce die? Do you agree or disagree? Explain your position.

---

a long period of rising stock prices, or a **bull market.** In the late 1920s a prolonged bull market convinced many people to **invest** in stocks. By 1929 approximately 10 percent of American households owned stocks.

As the market continued to soar, many investors began buying stocks on **margin,** making only a small cash down payment (as low as 10 percent of the price). With $1,000, an investor could buy $10,000 worth of stock. The other $9,000 would come as a loan from a stockbroker, who earned both a commission on the sale and interest on the loan. The broker held the stock as collateral.

If the price of the stock kept rising, the investor could make a profit. For example, the investor who borrowed to buy $10,000 worth of stock had only to wait for it to rise to $11,000 in value. The investor could then sell the stock, repay the loan, and make $1,000 in profit. The problem came if the stock price began to fall.

To protect the loan, a broker could issue a **margin call,** demanding the investor repay the loan at once. As a result, many investors were very sensitive to any fall in stock prices. If prices fell, they had to sell quickly, or they might not be able to repay their loans.

Before the late 1920s, the prices investors paid for stocks had generally reflected the stocks' true value. If a company made a profit or had good future sales prospects, its stock price rose; prices fell when earnings dropped. In the late 1920s, however, many investors bid prices up without considering a company's earnings and profits. Buyers, hoping for a quick windfall, engaged in **speculation.** They bet the market would continue to climb, thus enabling them to sell the stock and make money quickly.

✓ Reading Check **Summarizing** What was the stock market like in the 1920s?

Teach

S Skill Practice

Analyzing Maps Point out the 1928 election map in the Primary Source. **Ask:** What section of the nation supported Smith? Why might this be surprising? *(The South supported Smith, which might be surprising because Smith was Catholic, and the Ku Klux Klan, much of which centered in the South, was anti-Catholic.)* OL

DBQ Document Based Questions

Answers:
1. European paternalism and state socialism
2. Free speech and the other freedoms of the Bill of Rights: free assembly, free press, political equality and equality of opportunity; students' opinions will vary but should be supported.

✓ Reading Check

Answer: The stock market was a bull market, a long period of rising stock prices that fueled speculation.

Hands-On Chapter Project
Step 1

Making a Storyboard

Step 1: "Seeing" the Story Have small groups work together to create storyboards for the chapter content.

Essential Question Ask: What was life like during the Depression?

Directions Divide the class into small groups. Tell students that they will be presenting section content in storyboard format, as if they are going to make a short film. Students can create a character who is an omniscient narrator or one who is part of the story and responds to events as they occur. Students can also incorporate historical figures mentioned in the text. Remind students as they read Section 1 to look for events or ideas that can be illustrated.

Putting It Together Suggest that students divide the work according to their skills, with one student doing the drawing, another writing captions, and so on. OL

(Chapter Project continued on page 407)

R **Reading Strategy**

R **Reading Strategy**

Predicting Invite students to predict how the stockbroker and Groucho Marx fared in the Great Depression. *(Students may suggest that a film star would have new opportunities to make another fortune, but a stockbroker during a financial depression would probably not fare well.)* **OL**

C **Critical Thinking**

Analyzing Primary Sources
Have a volunteer read aloud the Primary Source quotation.
Ask: What descriptions show the stockbroker's despair? *(He is sitting with his head in his hands; the floor is messy with ticker tape.)* **BL**

Turning Point

Analyzing **HISTORY**

Students' answers will vary. Students should note that many cities and people needed help, but had nowhere to go for help.

Additional Support

The Great Crash

MAIN Idea Rising stock prices led to risky investment practices; when the stock market crashed, banks were in trouble.

HISTORY AND YOU Have you ever paid more for something than it was worth? Read on to learn why the stock market collapsed in 1929.

The bull market lasted only as long as investors continued putting new money into it. By the latter half of 1929, the market was running out of new customers. In September, professional investors sensed danger and began to sell off their holdings. Prices slipped. Other investors sold shares to pay the interest on their brokerage loans. Prices fell further.

The Stock Market Crash

R On Monday, October 21, 1929, the comedian Groucho Marx was awakened by a telephone call from his broker. "You'd better get down here with some cash to cover your margin," the broker said. The stock market had plunged. The dazed comedian had to pay back the money he had borrowed to buy stocks, which were now selling for far less than he had paid for them. Other brokers made similar margin calls. Nervous customers put their stocks up for sale at a frenzied pace, driving the market into a tailspin.

On October 24, a day that came to be called Black Thursday, the market plummeted fur- **R** ther. Marx was wiped out. He had earned a small fortune from plays and films, but now it was gone, and he was deeply in debt. His son recalled his final visit to the brokerage firm, as Groucho spotted his broker:

PRIMARY SOURCE

"He was sitting in front of the now-stilled ticker-tape machine, with his head buried in his hands. Ticker tape was strewn around him on the floor, and the place . . . looked as if it hadn't been swept out **C** in a week. Groucho tapped [him] on the shoulder and said, 'Aren't you the fellow who said nothing could go wrong?' 'I guess I made a mistake,' the broker wearily replied. 'No, I'm the one who made a mistake,' snapped Groucho. 'I listened to you.'"

—quoted in *1929: The Year of the Great Crash*

The following week, on October 29, a day that was later dubbed **Black Tuesday,** prices took the steepest dive yet. That day, almost 16 million shares of stock were sold; the stock

Turning Point

A Crash Becomes a Depression

When the stock market crashed in October 1929, it exposed many weaknesses in the American economy. By 1932 over 25 percent of American workers were unemployed. Charities could not help all who were in need. Many cities had gone bankrupt and newly created state relief agencies had insufficient funds to help.

The Great Depression prompted major political changes. When Franklin D. Roosevelt ran for president in 1932, he had offered few details about how he would save the economy. Once in office, however, he launched a massive program to rescue the banking system, stabilize industry, and aid the unemployed. By the late 1930s, the federal government had taken on huge new responsibilities for the health of the economy and welfare of American families.

ANALYZING HISTORY Do you think the Great Depression required government intervention to resolve? Write a brief essay explaining your opinion.

Stock Prices, 1920–1932

Price per Share — $400, $300, $200, $100

- Annual High
- Annual Low

Dow-Jones Industrial Averages (1920–1932)

Source: Standard and Poor's *Security Price Index Record*.

▼ *Mayhem erupts on Wall Street after the stock market crash.*

Activity: Economics Connection

Evaluating Businesses wanting to expand during the prosperous 1920s increased the number of stock shares available to the public, feeding the buying frenzy. The number of stockholders of American Telephone and Telegraph (AT&T) increased dramatically. In 1920, there were 139,000 stockholders; ten years later, the number had grown to 567,000. Speculation inflated stocks' value. In 1925 stocks were valued at $27 billion. That figure increased to more than $87 billion by October 1929.

The problems on Wall Street after the crash affected both the unemployed and the employed. Between 1929 and 1931, average working hours per week had dropped from 48 to 38 hours. In addition, wages continued to fall. In 1929 the average weekly salary was $28.50. It fell to $18.46 in 1932. **Ask:** Could government regulation of the stock market have prevented the Wall Street crash? *(Students may say that the economy was headed for a fall, regardless of what the government did.)* **OL** market lost between $10 billion and $15 billion in value. By mid-November, stock prices had dropped by more than one-third. Some $30 billion was lost, a **sum** roughly equal to the total wages Americans earned in 1929. Although the stock market crash was not the major cause of the Great Depression, it undermined the economy's ability to overcome other weaknesses.

Banks Begin to Close

The market crash severely weakened the nation's banks in two ways. First, by 1929 banks had loaned nearly $6 billion to stock speculators. Second, many banks had invested depositors' money in the stock market, hoping for higher returns than they could get by using the money for loans.

When stock values collapsed, banks lost money on their investments, and speculators defaulted on their loans. Having suffered serious losses, many banks cut back drastically on the loans they made. With less credit available, consumers and businesses were not able to borrow as much money. This helped to send the economy into a recession.

Some banks could not absorb the losses they suffered and were forced to close. The government did not insure bank deposits, so if a bank collapsed, customers, including those who did not invest in the stock market, lost their savings. Bank failures in 1929 and 1930 created a crisis of confidence in the banking system.

News of bank failures worried Americans. Some depositors made runs on banks, causing the banks to collapse. A **bank run** takes place when many depositors decide to withdraw their money at one time, usually because of fear that the bank is going to collapse.

Most banks make a profit by lending money received from depositors and collecting interest on the loans. The bank keeps only a fraction of depositors' money in reserve to cover daily business and withdrawals. Usually, that reserve is enough to meet the bank's needs. If too many people withdraw their money, however, the bank will collapse. More than 10 percent of the nation's banks—nearly 3,500—had closed by 1932.

✔ **Reading Check** Determining Cause and **Effect** What chain of events led to the economic crash of 1929?

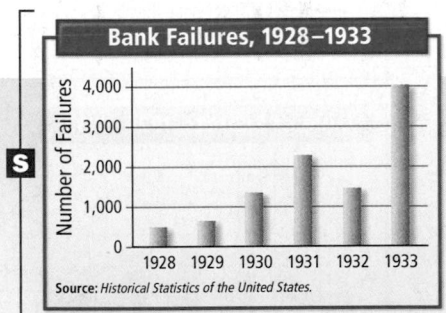

Bank Failures, 1928–1933

Source: *Historical Statistics of the United States.*

◀ *Depositors at a New York bank line up to withdraw their money in 1930.*

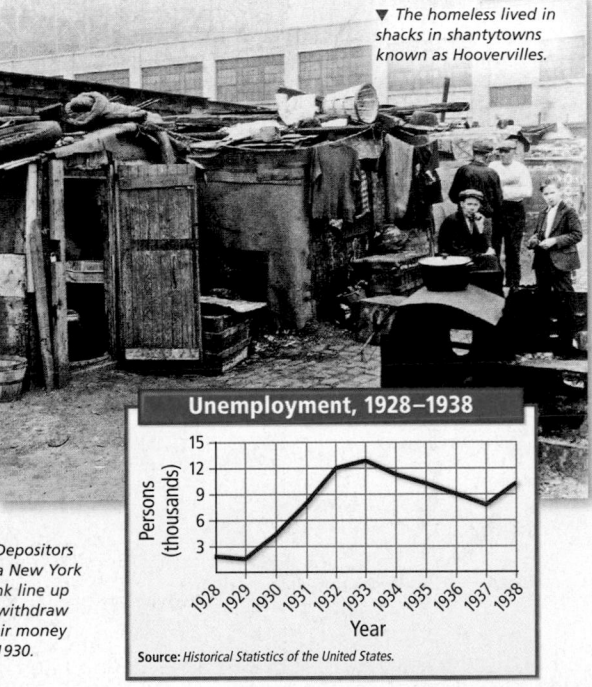

▼ *The homeless lived in shacks in shantytowns known as Hoovervilles.*

Unemployment, 1928–1938

Source: *Historical Statistics of the United States.*

Chapter 11 The Great Depression Begins **403**

R Reading Strategy

Analyzing Text Structure
Have students read the first paragraph under "Banks Begin to Close." Discuss how the text makes the information understandable and clear. *(The text says there are two ways the nation's banks were weakened. The next two sentences begin with the words* First *and* Second.*)* OL

S Skill Practice

Reading Graphs Ask students to look at the graph showing bank failures. **Ask:** Which two years had nearly similar numbers of closings? *(1928 and 1929; 1930 and 1932)* **Ask:** Based on these statistics, why might people have been hopeful in 1932? *(The number of bank closings decreased from 1931 to 1932.)* BL

✔ **Reading Check**

Answer:
Fewer investors entered the market, professional investors sold off their stock holdings, prices fell, others sold shares to pay interest on brokerage loans, prices fell again, market collapsed on Black Thursday and Black Tuesday, and banks collapsed.

Additional Support

Activity: Collaborative Learning

The Stock Market Stock market profits began rising in 1924, gradually at first. The wild bull market did not begin until 1927. Stocks began to double and triple in value, some doing so nearly overnight. Leaders in business and government, as well as economics professors, believed this trend would continue, bringing a golden age of prosperity to all. **As a class discuss the question:** What is a sensible way to invest in the stock market? *(research the company's background and growth before buying stock; invest broadly in several types of companies)* OL

D Differentiated Instruction

Special Education Students with reading difficulties may benefit from making an outline of this section. Have them copy the main heading and subheadings into their notebooks, with room under each head for taking notes about the key events and concepts. Remind students to use the chapter time lines to preview events they will read about. **BL**

R Reading Strategy

Making Connections Have students find out the current statistics on distribution of wealth and disposable income in the United States. Ask them to compare their findings to the information presented for 1929. **AL**

Analyzing VISUALS

1. There was less demand for steel, causing lower wages and unemployment.
2. 1929 and 1930

Additional Support

D The Roots of the Great Depression

MAIN Idea An uneven distribution of income, tariff policies, and the Federal Reserve Board's mistakes contributed to the Great Depression.

HISTORY AND YOU How evenly is wealth distributed in your community? Read about the uneven distribution of income in the late 1920s.

The stock market crash played a major role in putting the economy into a recession. Yet the crash would not have led to a long-lasting depression if other forces had not been at work. The roots of the Great Depression were deeply entangled in the economy of the 1920s.

The Uneven Distribution of Income

Overproduction was one factor contributing to the onset of the Great Depression. More efficient machinery increased the production capacity of both factories and farms. Most Americans, however, did not earn enough to buy up the flood of goods they helped produce. While manufacturing output per person-hour rose 32 percent, the average worker's wage increased only 8 percent. In 1929 the top 5 percent of all American households earned 30 percent of the nation's income. In contrast, about two-thirds of families earned less than $2,500 a year, leaving them with little disposable income. **R**

INFOGRAPHIC
Causes of the Great Depression

What Caused the Economy to Collapse?

- **Low Interest Rates** Federal Reserve kept interest rates low; companies borrowed money and expanded more than necessary.
- **Overproduction** Companies made more goods than could be sold.
- **Uneven Distribution of Wealth** Not everyone who wanted consumer goods could afford them.
- **High Tariffs** Tariffs restricted foreign demand for American goods.
- **Falling Demand** With too many goods unsold, production was cut back and employees were laid off.
- **Stock Market Speculation** Low interest rates encouraged borrowing money to speculate, endangering bank solvency.

Cyclical Effect

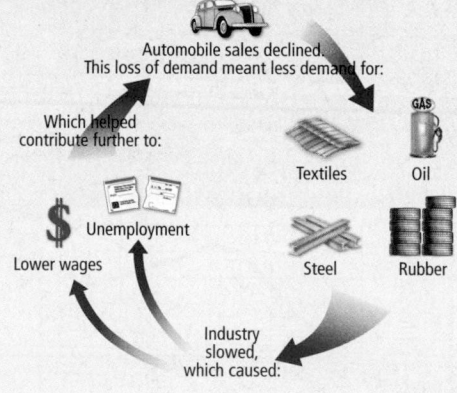

Automobile sales declined. This loss of demand meant less demand for:

Textiles, Oil, Steel, Rubber

Industry slowed, which caused:

Lower wages, Unemployment

Which helped contribute further to:

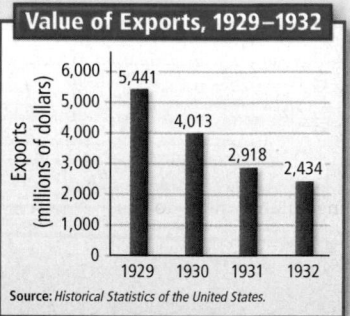

Income and Spending

Source: *Historical Statistics of the United States.*

— Personal Spending
— Personal Income

Value of Exports, 1929–1932

Year	Exports (millions of dollars)
1929	5,441
1930	4,013
1931	2,918
1932	2,434

Source: *Historical Statistics of the United States.*

Analyzing VISUALS **DBQ**

1. **Analyzing** What effect did the decline in automobile sales have on the steel industry?
2. **Calculating** Between what two years was the decrease in the value of exports the greatest?

404 Chapter 11 The Great Depression Begins

Activity: Interdisciplinary Connection

Economics Invite an economics teacher or economist to speak to the class about the safeguards now in place to help prevent a depression as serious as the one during the 1920s and 1930s. Ask the speaker to look at other drops in the market and how these safeguards have worked at these times. Ask the speaker to provide an activity or pretest that the students can complete before he or she comes to speak. **OL**

During the 1920s many Americans had purchased high-cost items, such as refrigerators and cars, on the **installment** plan. Purchasers could make small down payments and pay the remainder of the item's price in monthly installments. Paying off such debts eventually forced some buyers to stop making new purchases. Because of the decrease in sales, manufacturers in turn cut production and laid off employees.

The slowdown in retail sales reverberated throughout the economy. When radio sales slumped, for example, makers cut back on orders for copper wire, wood cabinets, and glass radio tubes. Montana copper miners, Minnesota lumberjacks, and Ohio glass-workers, in turn, lost their jobs. Jobless workers cut back on purchases, further cutting sales. This kind of chain reaction put more and more Americans out of work. Many families had little or no savings. They had nothing to support themselves when they lost their jobs. In 1930 alone, about 26,000 businesses collapsed.

The Loss of Export Sales

R Many jobs might have been saved if American manufacturers had sold more goods abroad. As the bull market of the 1920s sped up, U.S. banks made loans to speculators rather than loans to foreign companies. Foreign countries were also facing a recession after World War I. Many nations did not have the money to buy American-manufactured goods or crops.

In 1929 Hoover wanted to encourage overseas trade by lowering tariffs. Conservative Republicans, however, wanted to protect American industry from foreign competition by raising tariffs. The resulting legislation, the **Hawley-Smoot Tariff,** raised the average tariff rate to the highest level in American history. In the end, it failed to help American businesses, because foreign countries responded by raising their own tariffs. This meant fewer American products were sold overseas. By 1932 exports had fallen to about one-fifth of what they had been in 1929, which hurt both American companies and farmers.

Mistakes by the Federal Reserve

Just as consumers were able to buy more goods on credit, access to easy money propelled the stock market. Instead of raising interest rates to curb excessive speculation, the Federal Reserve Board kept its rates very low throughout the 1920s.

The Board's failure to raise interest rates significantly helped cause the Depression in two ways. First, by keeping rates low, it encouraged member banks to make risky loans. Second, its low interest rates led business leaders to think the economy was still expanding. As a result, they borrowed more money to expand production, a serious mistake because it led to overproduction when sales were falling. When the Depression finally hit, companies had to lay off workers to cut costs. Then the Federal Reserve made another mistake. It raised interest rates, tightening credit. The economy continued to spiral downward.

✔**Reading Check** **Listing** What were three factors that contributed to the Great Depression?

Section 1 REVIEW

Vocabulary
1. **Explain** the significance of: Alfred E. Smith, stock market, bull market, margin, margin call, speculation, Black Tuesday, bank run, installment, Hawley-Smoot Tariff.

Main Ideas
2. **Identifying** What factors contributed to Herbert Hoover's election in 1928?

3. **Examining** How did the stock market collapse affect banks?

4. **Explaining** What effect did tariff policies have on the Great Depression?

Critical Thinking
5. **Big Ideas** How did the practice of buying on margin and speculation cause the stock market to rise?

6. **Organizing** Use a graphic organizer similar to the one below to list the causes of the Great Depression.

Causes → Great Depression

7. **Analyzing Visuals** Look at the graph on page 402. What generalization can you make about the variation in highs and lows of the stock market from 1920 to 1932?

Writing About History
8. **Expository Writing** Write an article for a financial magazine explaining the stock market's rapid decline in 1929 and the reasons for the crash on Black Tuesday.

History ONLINE

Study Central™ To review this section, go to glencoe.com and click on Study Central.

405

R Reading Strategy
Activating Prior Knowledge
Ask students to recall the terms of reparations after World War I and which country might be facing the most severe recession. *(Heavy reparations were placed on Germany.)* **OL**

✔**Reading Check**

Answer: uneven distribution of income, loss of export sales, and mistakes by the Federal Reserve

Assess
....

History ONLINE

Study Central™ provides summaries, interactive games, and online graphic organizers to help students review content.

Close
....

Summarizing **Ask:** How did the stock market crash lead to bank failures? *(Banks lost money when speculators could not repay the money they borrowed to buy stock. Banks had also invested depositors' money in the stock market. Many depositors withdrew their funds.)* **OL**

Section 1 REVIEW

Answers

1. All definitions can be found in the section and the Glossary.

2. apparently strong economy and rising stock market prices

3. Banks had lent money to investors, who lost everything and couldn't repay it; they had also invested depositors' money in the stock market. They lost money on their investments, and debtors defaulted on loans. Some banks had to close and this further eroded consumer confidence.

4. They led to a decrease in export trade, which further hurt the economy.

5. Buying on margin meant that an investor could make a small down payment and borrow the rest of the stocks' cost from the broker. Many people bought stocks on speculation, hoping that the market would continue climbing.

6. uneven distribution of wealth, decline in sales, mistakes by the Federal Reserve

7. The gap between the two wasn't so large until highs began to spike in 1928. The gap remained large until 1932, when highs and lows returned to the distance level of 1920.

8. Students' articles will vary but should include appropriate vocabulary.

Focus

Bellringer

Daily Focus Transparency 11.2

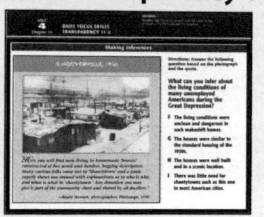

Guide to Reading

Answers:

I. The Depression Worsens
   A. Struggling to Get By
   B. The Dust Bowl

II. Art and Entertainment
   A. Hollywood
   B. On the Air
   C. Literature and Art

Section Spotlight Video

To generate student interest and provide a springboard for class discussion, access the Chapter 11, Section 2 video at glencoe.com or on the video DVD.

Resource Manager

Section 2

Life During the Depression

Guide to Reading

Big Ideas
Past and Present As the Great Depression and the drought worsened, thousands of people tried to find work and shelter in other places.

Content Vocabulary
- bailiff (p. 406)
- hobo (p. 406)
- soap opera (p. 409)

Academic Vocabulary
- suspend (p. 406)
- colleague (p. 408)
- technique (p. 409)

People and Events to Identify
- Dust Bowl (p. 407)
- Walt Disney (p. 408)
- John Steinbeck (p. 409)
- William Faulkner (p. 409)
- Grant Wood (p. 409)

Reading Strategy
Taking Notes As you read about life in the United States during the Great Depression, use the major headings of the section to create an outline similar to the one below.

```
Life During the Depression
I. The Depression Worsens
   A.
   B.
II.
```

The Great Depression caused large numbers of people to lose their jobs and property. To help people escape their misery, popular entertainment offered humorous and optimistic movies and radio programs. Novelists and photographers created more realistic portrayals of American life.

The Depression Worsens

MAIN Idea Hunger and homelessness became severe problems by the early 1930s; then, a terrible drought devastated the Great Plains.

HISTORY AND YOU Have you ever been caught outside in a thunderstorm? Read about the deadly dust storms of the 1930s.

The Depression grew steadily worse during Hoover's administration. In 1930, 1,352 banks **suspended** operations across the nation, more than twice the number of bank failures in 1929. More than 9,000 banks had failed by 1933. In 1932 alone, some 30,000 companies went out of business. By 1933 more than 12 million workers, or roughly one-fourth of the workforce, were unemployed.

Struggling to Get By

People without jobs often went hungry. Whenever possible they stood in bread lines—sometimes blocks long—for free food or lined up outside soup kitchens, which private organizations set up to give the poor meals. New York City's YMCA fed up to 12,000 people daily.

Families or individuals who could not pay their rent or mortgage lost their homes. Some of them, paralyzed by fear and humiliation over their sudden misfortune, simply would not or could not move. Their landlord would then ask the court for an eviction notice. Court officers known as **bailiffs** then ejected the nonpaying tenants, piling their belongings in the street.

Throughout the country, newly homeless people put up shacks on unused or public lands, forming communities called shantytowns. Blaming the president for their plight, people referred to such places as Hoovervilles.

In search of work or a better life, many homeless and unemployed Americans began to wander around the country—walking, hitchhiking, or, most often, "riding the rails." These wanderers, called **hobos,** would sneak past railroad police to slip into open boxcars on freight trains. Hundreds of thousands of people, mostly boys and young men, wandered from place to place in this fashion.

R Reading Strategies	**C** Critical Thinking	**D** Differentiated Instruction	**W** Writing Support	**S** Skill Practice
Teacher Edition • Making Connections, p. 408 **Additional Resources** • Guid. Read. Act., URB p. 79	**Teacher Edition** • Det. Cause/Effect, p. 407 **Additional Resources** • Critical Thinking Skills, URB p. 64 • Quizzes and Tests, p. 154 • Linking Past and Present, URB p. 66	**Teacher Edition** • Logical/Math., p. 408 **Additional Resources** • Differentiated Instr., URB p. 55 • American Art and Music Act., URB p. 71	**Additional Resources** • Primary Source Reading, URB p. 69	**Additional Resources** • RENTG, p. 118 • Reading Skills Act., URB p. 53

PRIMARY SOURCE
Fleeing the Dustbowl

The fierce dust storms of the 1930s destroyed farms and caused many to flee the Great Plains. Below, girls pump water during a dust storm in Springfield, Colorado.

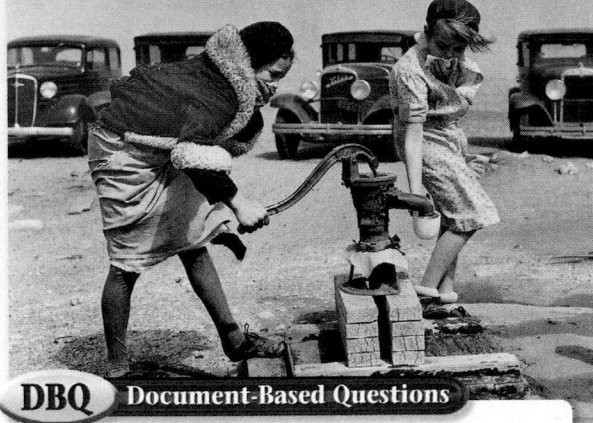

DBQ Document-Based Questions

1. **Analyzing Primary Sources** What advantage does the owner of the fields have when it comes to paying people to work?
2. **Drawing Conclusions** Why might the owners of the fields prefer to get "a fella with kids"?

About 40 percent of migrant farmers who fled the Dust Bowl went to California's San Joaquin Valley to pick cotton and grapes. In his novel *The Grapes of Wrath*, John Steinbeck describes what these migrants found when they arrived to harvest crops:

PRIMARY SOURCE

"Maybe he [the owner of the fields] needs two hunderd men, so he talks to five hunderd, an' they tell other folks, an' when you get to the place, they's a thousan' men. This here fella says, 'I'm payin' twenty cents an hour.' An' maybe half the men walk off. But they's still five hunderd that's so . . . hungry they'll work for nothin' but biscuits. Well, this here fella's got a contract to pick them peaches or—chop that cotton. You see now? The more fellas he can get, an' the hungrier, less he's gonna pay. An' he'll get a fella with kids if he can."

—from *The Grapes of Wrath*

The Dust Bowl

Farmers soon faced a new disaster. Since homesteading had begun on the Great Plains, farmers' plows had uprooted the wild grasses that held the soil's moisture. When crop prices dropped in the 1920s, farmers left many of their fields uncultivated. Then, a terrible drought struck the Great Plains. With neither grass nor wheat to hold the scant rainfall, the soil dried to dust. From the Dakotas to Texas, America's wheat fields became a vast **"Dust Bowl."**

Winds whipped the arid earth, blowing it aloft and blackening the sky for hundreds of miles. When the dust settled, it buried crops and livestock. Humans and animals caught outdoors sometimes died of suffocation when the dust filled their lungs. The number of yearly dust storms grew, from 22 in 1934 to 72 in 1937. Will and Carolyn Henderson farmed in western Oklahoma. Carolyn wrote a series of articles for the *Atlantic Monthly* about their life during the drought.

PRIMARY SOURCE

"At the little country store, after one of the worst of these storms, the candies in the show case all looked alike and equally brown. Dust to eat and dust to breathe and dust to drink. Dust in the beds and in the flour bin, on dishes and walls and windows, in hair and eyes and ears and teeth and throats. . . ."

—from *Dust to Eat: Drought and Depression in the 1930s*

Some Great Plains farmers managed to hold on to their land, but many had no chance. If their withered fields were mortgaged, they had to turn them over to the banks. Then, nearly penniless, many families headed west, hoping for a better life in California. Because many migrants were from Oklahoma, they became known as "Okies." In California, they lived in roadside camps and remained homeless and impoverished.

History ONLINE Student Web Activity Visit **glencoe.com** and complete the activity on hobo life during the Depression.

✔ **Reading Check** **Explaining** What chain of events turned the once-fertile Great Plains into the Dust Bowl?

Teach

C Critical Thinking
Determining Cause and Effect Ask students to read the first column on this page. Have them create graphic organizers showing the cause-and-effect nature of events that led to the Dust Bowl. **BL**

DBQ Document Based Questions

Answers:
1. People are so hungry they will work for food only.
2. If someone with kids is hired, the children will work in the fields too.

✔ Reading Check

Answer:
uprooting the wild grasses, a drop in prices left fields uncultivated, and terrible drought

Hands-On Chapter Project
Step 2

Making a Storyboard

Step 2: Begin Making Drawings

Directions Have students begin making their storyboard drawings based on what they have learned in Section 1. Remind them that working on the drawings as they read can help them comprehend the material. Section 2 is particularly suited for this activity. Encourage students to have fun while using the material in the text as the topics of their drawings.

Putting It Together Allow time for students to share preliminary drawings. Discuss ideas for any key elements in Section 1 they found difficult to illustrate. **OL**

(Chapter Project continued on page 413)

Art and Entertainment

MAIN Idea Movies and radio shows were very popular during the 1930s, a period that also produced new art and literature.

HISTORY AND YOU Has a movie ever helped you get through a difficult time? Read to learn ways that people coped with the Great Depression.

The hard times of the 1930s led many Americans to prefer entertainment that let them escape their worries. For this reason, movies and radio plays grew increasingly popular. Also, in the 1930s, comic books grew rapidly in popularity. The first comic books cheered people by reprinting newspaper comics, but in the late 1930s, the "superhero" genre was born with the printing of the first tales of *Superman* in 1938 and *Batman* in 1939.

Hollywood

During the 1930s more than 60 million Americans went to the movies each week. Child stars such as Shirley Temple and Jackie Coogan delighted viewers. Groucho Marx wisecracked while his brothers amused audiences in such films as *Animal Crackers,* and comedies became very popular because they provided a release from daily worries.

King Kong, first released in 1933, showcased new special effects. Moviegoers also loved cartoons. **Walt Disney,** who brought Mickey Mouse to life in 1928, produced the first feature-length animated film, *Snow White and the Seven Dwarfs,* in 1937.

Even serious films were optimistic. In *Mr. Smith Goes to Washington,* Jimmy Stewart played a naïve scout leader who becomes a senator. He exposes the corruption of some of his **colleagues** and calls upon senators to view American government as a high achievement.

In 1939 MGM produced *The Wizard of Oz,* a colorful musical that lifted viewers' spirits. That same year, Vivien Leigh and Clark Gable thrilled audiences in *Gone with the Wind,* a Civil War epic that won nine Academy Awards. Hattie McDaniel, who won the award for Best Supporting Actress, was the first African American to win an Academy Award.

On the Air

While movies captured the imagination, radio offered information and entertainment as near as the living room. Tens of millions of people listened to the radio daily, and radio comedians such as Jack Benny, George Burns, and Gracie Allen were popular, as were the radio adventures of superheroes such as the Green Hornet and the Lone Ranger.

People IN HISTORY

Margaret Bourke-White
1904–1971

While a student at Columbia University, Margaret Bourke-White took a photography course. She went on to become one of the leading photographers of her time. In 1927 she began photographing architectural and industrial subjects. Her originality led to jobs at major magazines such as *Fortune* and *Life.* During World War II she became the first woman photographer attached to the U.S. armed forces. She covered the Italian campaign and the siege of Moscow. She was among those who photographed concentration camp survivors. Bourke-White traveled to India after the war to document Gandhi's efforts to gain that nation's independence from Great Britain. During the Korean War, she traveled with South Korean troops.

What made Margaret Bourke-White's career and photography unusual for the time?

▲ African American flood victims wait for food and clothing from the Red Cross in 1937 in one of Margaret Bourke-White's most famous photos. The people contrast sharply with the billboard.

Extending the Content

Female Photographer Margaret Bourke-White began her career as a commercial photographer, and her work reflects the importance of American industry. Part of Bourke-White's success was her fearlessness. When photographing steel mills in Cleveland, Ohio, she got so close to the metal being poured that her face turned red and her camera's finish blistered. She climbed on top of New York City's Chrysler Building, perching on a gargoyle to get a shot. She hung out of bomber airplanes. She was the only woman on staff at the launch of *Life* magazine, and a photo of hers was used on the cover of the premiere issue. Bourke-White invented the photographic essay.

Daytime radio dramas carried over their story lines from day to day. Programs such as *The Guiding Light* presented middle-class families confronting illness, conflict, and other problems. The shows' sponsors were often makers of laundry soaps, so the shows were nicknamed **soap operas.** Radio created a new type of community. Even strangers found common ground in discussing the lives of radio characters.

Literature and Art

Literature and art also flourished during the 1930s. Writers and artists tried to portray life around them, using the homeless and unemployed as their subjects in stories and pictures.

Novelist **John Steinbeck** added flesh and blood to journalists' reports of poverty and misfortune. His writing evoked both sympathy for his characters and indignation at social injustice. In *The Grapes of Wrath* (1939), which was awarded the Pulitzer Prize and was made into a movie, Steinbeck tells the story of the Joad family fleeing the Dust Bowl to find a new life in California after losing their farm. The novel was based on Steinbeck's visits to migrant camps and his interviews with migrant families. In one article he described typical housing for the migrants, for which they paid the growers as much as $2.00 daily:

PRIMARY SOURCE

"[They have] one-room shacks usually about 10 by 12 feet, have no rug, no water, no bed. In one corner there is a little iron wood stove. Water must be carried from the faucet at the end of the street."

—from *Dust to Eat: Drought and Depression*

Other novelists developed new writing techniques. In *The Sound and the Fury,* **William Faulkner,** who later won the Nobel Prize for Literature, shows what his characters are thinking and feeling before they speak. Using this stream of consciousness **technique,** he exposes hidden attitudes of Southern whites and African Americans in a fictional Mississippi county.

Although written words remained powerful, images were growing more influential. Photographers roamed the nation with the new 35-millimeter cameras, seeking new subjects. In 1936, *Time* magazine publisher Henry Luce introduced *Life,* a weekly photojournalism magazine that enjoyed instant success. The striking pictures of photojournalists Dorothea Lange and Margaret Bourke-White showed how the Great Depression had affected average Americans.

Painters in the 1930s included Thomas Hart Benton and **Grant Wood,** whose styles were referred to as the regionalist school. Their work emphasized traditional American values, especially those of the rural Midwest and South. Wood's painting that is best-known today is *American Gothic.* The portrait pays tribute to no-nonsense Midwesterners while gently making fun of their severity.

✔ **Reading Check** **Examining** What subjects did artists, photographers, and writers emphasize during the 1930s?

Section 2 REVIEW

Vocabulary

1. **Explain** the significance of: bailiff, hobo, Dust Bowl, Walt Disney, soap opera, John Steinbeck, William Faulkner, Grant Wood.

Main Ideas

2. **Analyzing** What environmental event of the 1930s worsened the Great Depression?

3. **Explaining** How did people try to escape the realities of life during the Great Depression?

Critical Thinking

4. **Big Ideas** How did some Great Plains farmers respond to the loss of their fields to the banks?

5. **Organizing** Use a graphic organizer such as the one below to identify the effects of the Great Depression.

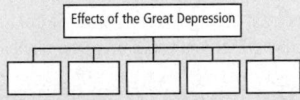

Effects of the Great Depression

6. **Analyzing Visuals** Look at the photo on page 407. What details indicate that this is a severe dust storm?

Writing About History

7. **Descriptive Writing** Imagine you are writing the catalogue for an art show of photographs by Dorothea Lange or Margaret Bourke-White. Write a paragraph describing one of the images in this section or discussing their photographic skill.

History ONLINE
Study Central™ To review this section, go to glencoe.com and click on Study Central.

✔ Reading Check

Answer:
Some work, such as Disney's cartoons, was escapist; other artists focused on the plight of those most clearly affected by the Great Depression and Dust Bowl.

Assess

History ONLINE

Study Central™ provides summaries, interactive games, and online graphic organizers to help students review content.

Close

Summarizing Ask: What forms of entertainment were popular during the Great Depression? *(reading comic books, going to the movies, listening to radio shows and soap operas)* **BL**

Section 2 REVIEW

Answers

1. All definitions can be found in the section and the Glossary.

2. drought and resulting crop failure

3. movies and radio

4. Many farmers headed west, hoping for a better life in California.

5. bank failures, unemployment, hunger, homelessness, and a terrible drought

6. They hold handkerchiefs to cover their mouths and noses. They are wearing hats; one has on a coat to protect herself. The girl holding the cup has it close to the faucet so no sand will blow into it. The wind is whipping their skirts.

7. Students' paragraphs will vary but should focus on one photo in the chapter.

Focus

Tell students that more than 325 dust storms hit between 1930 and 1941. A May, 1934 storm moved perhaps a third of a billion tons of topsoil, dropping it in Boston, Washington, D.C., and on ships hundreds of miles in the Atlantic.

Teach

D Differentiated Instruction

Naturalist Invite students to find out about measures that the government took to conserve the soil and improve farming practices during the Dust Bowl years. Have them take on the role of a worker from the Soil Conservation Service explaining options to the class. **OL**

C Critical Thinking

Predicting Consequences Ask students to imagine what might happen to the land when farmers left for California or other places to find work. *(Possible answer: it reverted back to uninhabited plains)* **OL**

Additional Support

NATIONAL GEOGRAPHIC

GEOGRAPHY & HISTORY

The Dust Bowl

D C In the late nineteenth century, settlers on the Great Plains turned the semiarid region into the breadbasket of America, growing vast fields of wheat and other crops. Intensive farming destroyed the region's native grasses and loosened the soil. At first, this was not a problem, as the Great Plains experienced higher than normal rainfall in the late 1800s. Over time, however, farmers exhausted the soil. When rainfall began to decline and temperatures rose in the 1920s, the soil began to dry out. In 1932, a full-scale drought hit. The fierce heat dried the exhausted soil into fine dustlike particles. The high winds of the open plains easily lifted the dirt into the air creating "dust storms." In 1932 alone, 14 dust storms struck the Great Plains. These storms carried the soil of the Great Plains hundreds of miles. In May 1934, a huge storm dumped piles of dirt in Chicago. Further east, silt from the storm collected on the windows of the White House.

How Did the Dust Bowl Affect Americans?

The "Dust Bowl" is sometimes called a human-made natural disaster. The drought and rising temperatures of the 1930s were a natural disaster. But the dust storms were human-made, the result of decades of overcultivation. These "black blizzards" scoured and buried homes, ruined vehicle engines, and diminished visibility. The blowing dirt could injure eyes and damage lungs; it even suffocated people. As the drought destroyed their livelihood, and the dust storms destroyed their belongings, many farmers abandoned the land, packed up their families, and fled the region in search of work elsewhere.

> **Analyzing GEOGRAPHY**
>
> 1. **Movement** Which states lost population in the 1930s? In which direction did most people fleeing the Dust Bowl move?
>
> 2. **Human-Environment Interaction** Study the image at right. What problems and dangers does the dust storm create?

Map legend:
- Area with severe loss of topsoil
- Area with moderate loss of topsoil
- → Movement of people
- • Destination of Dust Bowl emigrants
- — State with population loss, 1930–1940

Map labels: N. Dak., Fargo, Minn., S. Dak., Minneapolis, Ore., Ida., Wyo., Iowa, Calif., Central Valley, Nev., Grand Junction, Nebr., Omaha, Fresno, Utah, Denver, Colo., Kans., Kansas City, Bakersfield, Flagstaff, Santa Fe, Albuquerque, Oklahoma City, Okla., Tulsa, Los Angeles, PACIFIC OCEAN, Ariz., N. Mex., Dallas, Tex., Houston

0 400 kilometers
0 400 miles
Albers Equal-Area projection
120°W 40°N 30°N

The drought on the Great Plains in the 1930s was the worst ever recorded in U.S. history. Summer temperatures soared above 110 degrees in many locations, setting records that still stand. The lack of water and fierce heat dried the soil to a fine dust. An estimated 200 million acres of land lost some or all of its topsoil.

Extending the Content

Drought Conditions The Dust Bowl of the 1930s was not the only drought in the United States during the 20th century. A drought occurred in Great Plains states and Texas from 1951 until 1956. By 1953, three-quarters of Texas reported below normal amounts of rainfall. By 1957, when the spring rains ended the drought, 244 of Texas's 254 counties had been declared federal drought disaster areas. More than a third of the United States was affected by the drought of 1987 to 1989. There were catastrophic fires in 1988, such as the ones that burned in Yellowstone National Park. During the early years of the 21st century, the Plains states again suffered years of drought.

Dust storms towered thousands of feet in the air and moved rapidly across the open plains. When a storm hit, it became dark outside, and visibility often dropped to only a few feet.

▲ Many farmers in the dust bowl, such as Elmer Thomas and his family of Muskogee, Oklahoma (above), decided to leave the region. Many became migrant workers, traveling from across the west in search of short-term employment.

The fine grit of dust storms could clog car engines and other mechanical devices beyond repair.

People raced for cover when a storm hit. The grit stung the skin and eyes. Breathing the dust could cause dust pneumonia. Many people, especially children and senior citizens, became sick, and many died.

GEOGRAPHY & HISTORY

Assess/Close

R Reading Skill

Making Connections Have students find out about the Green Belt Movement, in which Nobel Prize winner Wangari Maathai began to counter the threat of drought in Africa as a result of deforestation and soil erosion. Allow time for them to report their findings to the class.

Analyzing GEOGRAPHY

Answers:
1. North Dakota, South Dakota, Nebraska, and Kansas all lost population. Most people headed west to California.
2. Dust storms cause a loss of topsoil; create breathing problems, particularly for the aged and children; cause a loss of visibility, and damage equipment such as engines.

Interdisciplinary Connection

Language Arts

Hold a Debate Global warming continues to be a topic of concern to farmers and others. Have students debate the possible solutions to this problem and the role that the United States might take.

Focus

Hoover Responds to the Depression

Bellringer
Daily Focus Transparency 11.3

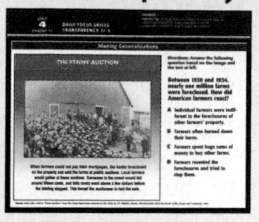

Guide to Reading

Answers: Initiative: Industry was to keep factories open and stop slashing wages; Result: business leaders did not follow through; Initiative: Hoover wanted to increase public works; Result: this had little effect; Initiative: to pump money into the economy; Result: this was too limited and could not reverse the accelerating collapse

Section Spotlight Video

To generate student interest and provide a springboard for class discussion, access the Chapter 11, Section 3 video at glencoe.com or on the video DVD.

Resource Manager

Guide to Reading

Big Ideas
Government and Society President Hoover's ideas about government shaped his response to the Great Depression, making the government slow to respond.

Content Vocabulary
• public works (p. 412)
• relief (p. 414)
• foreclose (p. 415)

Academic Vocabulary
• series (p. 412)
• community (p. 413)

People and Events to Identify
• Reconstruction Finance Corporation (p. 413)
• Bonus Army (p. 415)

Reading Strategy
Categorizing As you read about Herbert Hoover's response to the Depression, create a graphic organizer listing his major initiatives and their results.

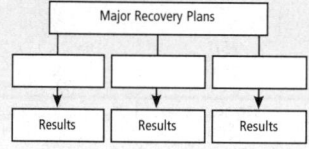

President Hoover tried to fix the economy by providing loans to banks and corporations and by starting public works projects. Later, he reluctantly supported direct aid to impoverished families. By the early 1930s, more Americans were demanding the government's help.

Promoting Recovery

MAIN Idea Hoover encouraged businesses to stop laying off workers and created public works projects.

HISTORY AND YOU What efforts would you have taken to help the economy if you had been president? Read about the public works efforts of the early 1930s.

On Friday, October 25, 1929, the day after Black Thursday, President Herbert Hoover declared that "the fundamental business of the country . . . is on a sound and prosperous basis." On March 7, 1930, he told the press that "the worst effects of the crash upon employment will have passed during the next sixty days." Critics derided his optimism as conditions worsened. Hoover, however, hoped to downplay the public's fears. He wanted to avoid more bank runs and layoffs by urging consumers and business leaders to make rational decisions. In the end, Hoover's efforts failed to inspire the public's confidence, and the economy continued its downward slide.

President Hoover believed that the American system of "rugged individualism" would keep the economy moving. He felt that the government should not step in to help individuals out. After World War I, many European countries had implemented a form of socialism, which Hoover felt contributed to their lack of economic recovery. In 1922 Hoover had written a book, *American Individualism*, which presented arguments for why the American system of individualism was the best social, political, spiritual, and economic system in the world. Thus, it was difficult for Hoover to propose policies that had the government taking more control.

Despite his public statements that the economy was not in trouble, Hoover was worried. To devise strategies for improving the economy, he organized a **series** of conferences, bringing together the heads of banks, railroads, and other big businesses, as well as labor leaders and government officials.

Industry leaders pledged to keep factories open and to stop slashing wages. By 1931, however, they had broken those pledges. Hoover then increased the funding for **public works**, or government-financed building projects. The resulting construction jobs were intended to replace some of those lost in the private sector.

R Reading Strategies	C Critical Thinking	D Differentiated Instruction	W Writing Support	S Skill Practice
Teacher Edition • Analyzing Text Structure, p. 413 **Additional Resources** • Guid. Read. Act., URB p. 80 • RENTG, p. 121 • Reteaching Act., URB p. 75	**Additional Resources** • Quizzes and Tests, p. 155 • Auth. Assess, p. 27	**Teacher Edition** • Visual/Spatial, p. 413 **Additional Resources** • Geography and Hist., URB p. 3 • Enrichment Act., URB p. 76	**Teacher Edition** • Persuasive Writing, p. 414	**Additional Resources** • Interp. Pol. Cartoons, URB p. 73 • Time Line Act, URB p. 65

POLITICAL CARTOONS PRIMARY SOURCE
Can Hoover Fight the Depression?

▲ *While the Democratic Party donkey marches outside singing old songs, Hoover tries to deal with economic problems caused by high tariffs, depression and drought.*

▲ *Herbert Hoover reassures a farmer his scarecrow labeled farm relief will help.*

Analyzing VISUALS DBQ

1. **Analyzing** What does the cartoon on the right suggest about Hoover's plan to help farmers?

2. **Analyzing** How are Hoover and the Democrats portrayed in the cartoon on the left?

Public works projects did create some jobs but for only a small fraction of the millions who were unemployed. The government could create enough new jobs only by massively increasing government spending, which Hoover refused to do.

R Someone had to pay for public works projects. If the government raised taxes to pay for them, consumers would have less money to spend, further hurting already struggling businesses. If the government kept taxes low and ran a budget deficit instead—spending more money than it collected in taxes—it would have to borrow the money. Borrowing would mean less money available for businesses to expand and for consumer loans. Hoover feared that deficit spending would actually delay an economic recovery.

As the 1930 congressional elections approached, most Americans felt threatened by rising unemployment. Citizens blamed the party in power for the ailing economy. The Republicans lost 49 seats and their majority in the House of Representatives; they held on to the Senate by a single vote.

Trying to Rescue the Banks

To get the economy growing again, Hoover focused on expanding the money supply. The government, he believed, had to help banks make loans to corporations, which could then expand production and rehire workers.

The president asked the Federal Reserve Board to put more currency into circulation, but the Board refused. In an attempt to ease the money shortage, Hoover set up the National Credit Corporation (NCC) in October 1931. The NCC created a pool of money that allowed troubled banks to continue lending money in their **communities.** This program, however, failed to meet the nation's needs.

D In 1932 Hoover requested Congress to set up the **Reconstruction Finance Corporation** (RFC) to make loans to businesses. By early 1932 the RFC had lent about $238 million to approximately 160 banks, 60 railroads, and 18 building-and-loan organizations. The RFC was overly cautious, however. It failed to increase its lending sufficiently to meet the need, and the economy continued its decline.

Chapter 11 The Great Depression Begins **413**

Teach

R Reading Strategy
Analyzing Text Structure
Draw students' attention to the second paragraph. Ask them to develop flowcharts showing the options for paying for public works projects. **OL**

D Differentiated Instruction
Visual/Spatial Invite students to create time lines showing the efforts Hoover made to try to keep disaster from occurring. **BL**

Analyzing VISUALS

Answers:

1. The cartoonist pictures Hoover's farm relief as a scarecrow, trying to scare off the birds labeled "hard times."

2. Hoover is shown as a nursemaid trying to quiet the various unhappy "babies," or problems his administration faces. The Democrats are shown as loudly singing about the problems.

Hands-On Chapter Project
Step 3

Making a Storyboard

Step 3: Peer Review Groups will exchange storyboards completed to this point.

Directions Have the groups exchange storyboard projects completed thus far. Ask each group to honestly and fairly evaluate whether the storyboard captures the most important material in Sections 1 and 2. Comments should be constructive and

helpful and should be limited to content, rather than focusing on the quality of the drawings.

Putting It Together Have students incorporate the suggestions they have received for improving their storyboards.

(Chapter Project continued on the Visual Summary page)

W Writing Support

Persuasive Writing Ask students to suppose they are living in 1931 when President Hoover refused to extend federal assistance to those in need. Ask them to write editorials to the local newspaper persuading a local Congressperson to support direct relief to the citizens. Remind them to use facts and reasons to support their argument. **OL**

Analyzing VISUALS

Answers:
1. They had no weapons.
2. Students may suggest they would be dismayed at the loss of good food.

Reading Check

Answer:
He felt that only state and city governments should provide relief.

Additional Support

Direct Help for Citizens

From the start, Hoover strongly opposed the federal government's participation in **relief**—money given directly to impoverished families. He believed that only state and local governments should dole out relief. Any other needs should be met by private charity, not by the federal government. By the spring of 1932, however, state and local governments were running out of money, and private charities lacked the resources to handle the crisis.

That year, political support for a federal relief measure increased, and Congress passed the Emergency Relief and Construction Act in July. Reluctantly, Hoover signed the bill. The new act called for $1.5 billion for public works and $300 million in emergency loans to the states for direct relief. For the first time in United States history, the federal government was supplying direct relief funds, although governors of the states had to apply for the loans. By this time, however, the new program could not reverse the accelerating collapse.

✔ **Reading Check** **Summarizing** Why did Hoover oppose a federal relief program?

In an Angry Mood

MAIN Idea Farmers, veterans, and others who were suffering grew frustrated and demanded the government do something to help.

HISTORY AND YOU Have you ever felt strongly enough about an issue to take part in a protest? Read what happened when veterans of World War I demonstrated in Washington, D.C., in 1932.

In the months after the Wall Street crash, most Americans were resigned to bad economic news. By 1931, however, many people were becoming increasingly discontent.

Hunger Marches and Protests by Farmers

In January 1931 about 500 residents of Oklahoma City looted a grocery store. Crowds began showing up at rallies and "hunger marches" organized by the American Communist Party. On December 5, 1932, in Washington, D.C., a group of about 1,200 hunger marchers chanted, "Feed the hungry, tax the rich." Police herded them into a cul-de-sac

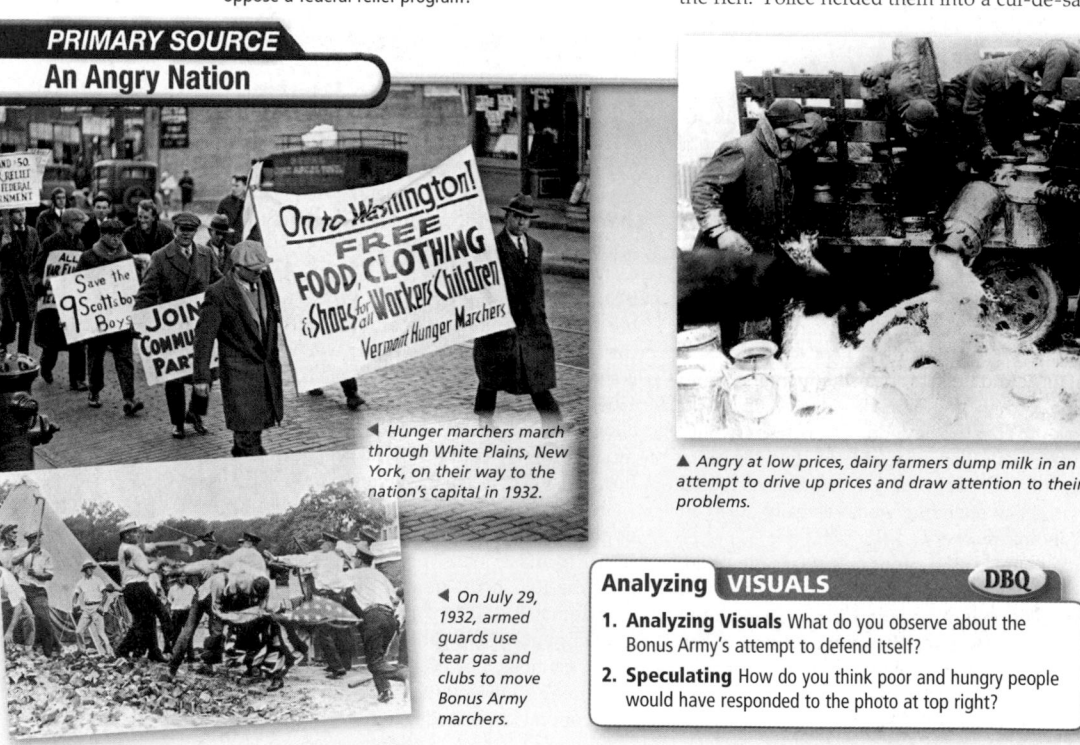

PRIMARY SOURCE
An Angry Nation

◄ Hunger marchers march through White Plains, New York, on their way to the nation's capital in 1932.

◄ On July 29, 1932, armed guards use tear gas and clubs to move Bonus Army marchers.

▲ Angry at low prices, dairy farmers dump milk in an attempt to drive up prices and draw attention to their problems.

Analyzing VISUALS   DBQ

1. **Analyzing Visuals** What do you observe about the Bonus Army's attempt to defend itself?
2. **Speculating** How do you think poor and hungry people would have responded to the photo at top right?

Activity: Interdisciplinary Connection

Language Arts Point out to students that selfless activity is a survival mechanism for groups. Often the most selfless people are those who have the least in terms of material possessions. In *The Grapes of Wrath*, for example, Ma Joad declares, "If you're in trouble or hurt or need—go to poor people. They're the only ones that'll help." Ask students to analyze this statement and then write a paragraph discussing why they feel that acting selflessly might be a group survival mechanism. Have students support their analyses with examples. **AL**

and denied them food and water, until some members of Congress insisted on the marchers' right to petition their government. They were then permitted to march to Capitol Hill.

The hungry poor were not the only people who began to protest conditions during the Depression. During World War I's agricultural boom, many farmers had heavily mortgaged their land to pay for seed, feed, and equipment. After the war, prices sank so low that farmers began losing money. Creditors **foreclosed** on nearly one million farms between 1930 and 1934, taking ownership of the land and evicting the families. Some farmers began destroying their crops, desperately trying to raise prices by reducing the supply. In Nebraska, farmers burned corn to heat their homes. Georgia dairy farmers blocked highways and stopped milk trucks, dumping the milk into ditches.

The Bonus Marchers

After World War I, Congress had enacted a $1,000 bonus for each veteran, to be distributed in 1945. In 1931 Texas congressman Wright Patman introduced a bill that would authorize early payment of these bonuses. In May 1932 several hundred Oregon veterans began marching to Washington to lobby for passage of the legislation. As they moved east, other veterans joined them until they numbered about 1,000. Wearing ragged military uniforms, they trudged along the highways or rode the rails, singing old war songs. The press termed the marchers the **"Bonus Army."**

Once in Washington, the marchers camped in Hoovervilles. More veterans joined them until the Bonus Army swelled to 15,000. President Hoover acknowledged the veterans' right to petition but refused to meet with them. When the Senate voted down the bonus bill, veterans outside the Capitol began to grumble. Many returned home, but some marchers stayed on. Some squatted in vacant buildings downtown.

In late July, Hoover ordered the buildings cleared. The police tried, but when an officer panicked and fired into a crowd, killing two veterans, the city government called in the army. General Douglas MacArthur ignored Hoover's orders to clear the buildings but to leave the camps alone. MacArthur sent in cavalry, infantry, and tanks to clear the camps.

Soon unarmed veterans were running away, pursued by 700 soldiers. The soldiers tear-gassed stragglers and burned the shacks. National press coverage of troops assaulting veterans further harmed Hoover's reputation and hounded the president throughout the 1932 campaign.

Although Hoover failed to resolve the economic crisis, he did more than any prior president to expand the federal government's economic role. The Reconstruction Finance Corporation was the first federal agency created to stimulate the economy during peacetime. The route of the Bonus Army marchers and the lingering Depression, however, tarnished Hoover's public image.

Reading Check **Evaluating** How did Americans react as the Depression continued?

Section 3 REVIEW

Vocabulary
1. **Explain** the significance of: public works, Reconstruction Finance Corporation, relief, foreclose, Bonus Army.

Main Ideas
2. **Identifying** What two major strategies did President Hoover use to promote economic recovery?

3. **Explaining** What did World War I veterans do to try to get their service bonuses early?

Critical Thinking
4. **Big Ideas** How did President Hoover's philosophy of government guide his response to the Depression?

5. **Organizing** Use a graphic organizer similar to the one below to list American reactions to the Great Depression.

American Reactions

6. **Analyzing Visuals** Look at the photo of the Hunger Marchers on page 414. How would you compare their approach and style to protestors today?

Writing About History
7. **Persuasive Writing** Imagine that you are a World War I veteran in 1931. Write a persuasive letter to your congressperson explaining why you need your bonus now, not in 1945.

History ONLINE
Study Central™ To review this section, go to glencoe.com and click on Study Central.

415

Reading Check
Answer:
Reactions included hunger marches, farmers' revolts, and the Bonus Army's march attempting to receive their bonuses early.

Assess

History ONLINE

Study Central™ provides summaries, interactive games, and online graphic organizers to help students review content.

Close

Summarizing **Ask:** What were some of the main events during the Great Depression that led to Hoover's decline in popularity? *(the suffering economy, hunger marchers petitioning the government, protests by farmers, and the Bonus Marchers being assaulted)* **OL**

Section 3 REVIEW

Answers

1. All definitions can be found in the section and the Glossary.

2. He encouraged businesses to stop laying off workers and he created public works projects.

3. They marched to Washington to lobby and camped in Hoovervilles. They stayed outside the Capitol and squatted in vacant buildings.

4. Because he believed in the role of state and local government to assist those in need, he delayed federal intervention until the crisis became enormous.

5. Possible answers include: bonus marchers, discontent, farmers' revolts, hunger marches, squatting, escaping through entertainment

6. The marchers are all men; they are dressed formally in suits, hats, ties, and white shirts; today's protestors are not dressed so formally, but like the Hunger Marchers they carry signs to advocate their demands.

7. Students' letters will vary but should be written from the perspective of a World War I veteran and include reasons for receiving a bonus at that time.

Chapter 11 VISUAL SUMMARY

STUDY TO GO You can study anywhere, anytime by downloading quizzes and flashcards to your PDA from glencoe.com.

Auditory/Musical Play for students a recording of one of the songs popular during the Depression era. Many of these are available online, as well as at libraries. Then invite students to compose a song with lyrics focusing on one of the effects of the Depression. Suggest they use a tune they are already familiar with or compose an alternative tune. **AL**

Descriptive Writing Have students select one of the photographs on this page. Ask them to focus on the elements of the photo and to describe them in such a way that someone who had not seen the photo would understand its impact. **BL**

Causes of the Depression

Long-Range Causes

- Uneven distribution of wealth ensures that many consumers do not have enough income to purchase the goods being produced.
- Interest rates are kept too low by the Federal Reserve, which encourages businesses to borrow money and to expand production beyond market demand.
- Overproduction by business eventually floods the market with goods that cannot be sold. Businesses begin laying off workers and shutting down production.

Immediate Causes

- People and businesses borrow money to invest in the stock market; speculation drives stock prices too high and when they collapse, many people lose all of their money, and many banks collapse when loans are not repaid.
- As companies lay off workers, demand for goods falls as workers lack the income to purchase goods being produced. This in turn causes even more layoffs and a cyclical effect sets in, driving up unemployment.
- In order to protect American companies from competition, Congress raises tariffs. When other countries respond in kind, foreign demand for American goods falls, further hurting American companies.

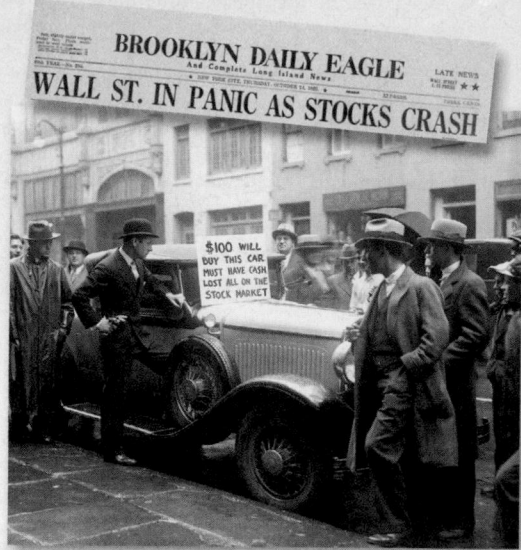

▲ A New York paper trumpets the stock crash. To raise cash to pay their stock debts, people began selling anything of value, including this car.

▲ Shantytowns appeared in many cities during the Depression as homelessness and unemployment rose.

Effects of the Depression

- Unemployment rises to record levels.
- Many people, unable to pay their debts, lose their homes and farms; the homeless create shantytowns, nicknamed Hoovervilles, on the edges of cities.
- Hunger marches, protests by farmers, and marches by veterans seeking their bonuses indicate growing anger among the population at economic conditions.
- The Republican Party rapidly loses political support, enabling the Democrats to take control of Congress.
- The federal government, for the first time, begins providing direct relief to citizens in need.
- Forms of entertainment, including movies, radio shows, and comic books, focus on distracting people from their daily lives.

416 Chapter 11 The Great Depression Begins

Hands-On Chapter Project
Step 4: Wrap Up

Making a Storyboard

Step 4: Complete the Storyboards
Groups finalize the drawings and captions of their storyboards for the chapter.

Directions Have students complete the final frames of the storyboard for Section 3 materials. Allow time for students to present their storyboards to the class. **OL**

ASSESSMENT

STANDARDIZED TEST PRACTICE

TEST-TAKING TIP

If you are not sure of the answer, try to narrow the options. First, eliminate any choices that you know are clearly wrong. Then, if necessary, make a guess among the remaining choices.

Reviewing Vocabulary

Directions: Choose the word or words that best complete the sentence.

1. In the late 1920s, many investors engaged in speculation, or purchasing stock
   - A after considering a company's earnings and profits.
   - B and quickly selling the stock for a profit.
   - C by borrowing money from a stockbroker.
   - D to invest long-term in the future of the company.

2. The Democratic Party's first Roman Catholic candidate for president was
   - A Alfred E. Smith.
   - B Franklin Delano Roosevelt.
   - C Herbert Hoover.
   - D Calvin Coolidge.

3. A _____ most often traveled by hopping a railroad car.
   - A photographer
   - B journalist
   - C novelist
   - D hobo

4. President Hoover opposed _____, or giving money directly to needy families.
   - A foreclosure
   - B relief
   - C public works
   - D unionization

Reviewing Main Ideas

Directions: Choose the best answers to the following questions.

Section 1 *(pp. 400–405)*

5. One of the major problems with the stock market in the late 1920s was the number of people who bought stocks
   - A on margin, with borrowed money.
   - B in companies that they supported.
   - C only after carefully studying a company's history.
   - D without knowing their stockbroker's reputation.

6. Which of the following was a root cause of the Great Depression?
   - A prohibiting the sale of alcohol
   - B giving women the right to vote
   - C uneven distribution of income
   - D the end of federal control of banks

7. Herbert Hoover won the 1928 election in a landslide, in part because of
   - A fears of another world war.
   - B prosperity under Calvin Coolidge.
   - C having been vice president.
   - D his support for unions.

Section 2 *(pp. 406–409)*

8. Drought and _____ brought about the conditions that caused the Dust Bowl.
   - A overgrazing at large cattle farms
   - B the near-extinction of the buffalo
   - C famine
   - D poor farming practices

Need Extra Help?								
If You Missed Questions . . .	1	2	3	4	5	6	7	8
Go to Page . . .	401	400	406	414	400–401	404–405	400	407

 GO ON

Answers and Analyses
Reviewing Vocabulary

1. B Many students may choose C, because borrowing money from a stockbroker was a common practice before the Depression. Remind them this is called buying on the margin. A and D represent good stock-buying strategies and so can be easily dismissed.

2. A This question requires students to recall either the religious affiliations of the candidates mentioned or the attacks on Smith during the 1928 election.

3. D The term *hopping* should be a major clue for students. Most passengers *board* a train; *hopping* denotes a way around tickets and authority, which only a hobo without money would need to do.

4. B Students may associate the other meaning of *relief* to answer this question correctly. Needy families receiving money would feel relief that their basic needs can be met. *Public works* is the next best answer, but it gives job opportunities rather than money directly.

Reviewing Main Ideas

5. A In analyzing this question, students should focus on the term *major problem*. Doing so eliminates both B and C as choices. The stockbroker's reputation could have been a problem, but it was not the major problem.

6. C The term *root cause* is the essential part of the question. Students should remember the great disparity in incomes during the 1920s and correctly identify the answer.

7. B The 1928 election followed a period of postwar prosperity. Students should recall that World War I had ended in 1919 and Americans had returned to isolationism.

8. D None of the other distractors were the issue during the 1930s. The removal of native grasses from the prairies to plant domestic crops, among other practices, hastened the drought.

Chapter 11

9. A Students can associate Hoover, president during the beginning of the Depression, with Hoovervilles to determine the correct answer.

10. C Students should note that the major reason for high movie attendance was that movies provided a temporary escape from daily worries.

11. B To find the correct response, students should recall that social welfare programs are costly. Hoover, a conservative, opposed deficit spending, though he supported public works funded by state and local groups and private charities.

12. D Only two of the responses could be possible. Unhappy voters do not reelect their leaders, nor do they avoid the polls, their only means of expressing displeasure.

13. B Because three of the options are positive actions, the correct answer stands out. Remind students to use this strategy to eliminate distractors.

Critical Thinking

14. D Remind students to look carefully at the map. Although each body of water listed as a possible answer is marked, the dam clearly spans only the Colorado River.

15. B Careful attention to the map is all that is needed to answer this correctly. Utah is easily eliminated, because the map shows no benefit to it. The other two states gained less than half the power that California did.

---

9. The people who lost their homes in the Great Depression sometimes lived in

- **A** shantytowns.
- **B** roadside motels.
- **C** the lawn of the national capital.
- **D** public libraries opened to them.

10. Despite the poverty of the 1930s, more than 60 million people went to the movies weekly. Why were movies so popular?

- **A** The special effects used in movies then were amazing.
- **B** People could not get over the fact that actors talked.
- **C** Movies offered an escape from viewers' hard lives.
- **D** Theaters were air conditioned and offered free popcorn.

Section 3 *(pp. 412–415)*

11. Hoover was slow to respond to the economic crisis because he opposed

- **A** all public works projects.
- **B** deficit spending.
- **C** investing in stocks.
- **D** private charities.

12. How did American citizens respond to the Great Depression in the 1930 midterm election?

- **A** by reelecting Hoover
- **B** by voting for socialist candidates
- **C** by staying away from the polls
- **D** by voting for Democrats

13. What was Hoover's response to the Bonus Army marchers who came to Washington, D.C.?

- **A** He ordered them to be paid their bonuses.
- **B** He had the army remove them.
- **C** He visited them and listened to them.
- **D** He set up soup kitchens to feed them.

Critical Thinking

Base your answers to questions 14 and 15 on the map below and on your knowledge of Chapter 11.

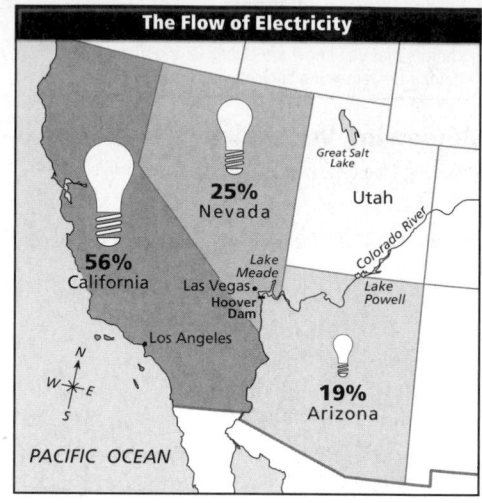

Directions: Choose the best answers to the following questions.

14. The federal government began building Hoover Dam in 1931. What body of water was it designed to control?

- **A** the Pacific Ocean
- **B** Lake Powell
- **C** the Great Salt Lake
- **D** the Colorado River

15. Which state benefited most from the hydroelectric power of Hoover Dam?

- **A** Utah
- **B** California
- **C** Nevada
- **D** Arizona

Need Extra Help?							
If You Missed Questions . . .	9	10	11	12	13	14	15
Go to Page . . .	406	408–409	412–414	413	415	R15	R15

GO ON ➤

ASSESSMENT

16. Why did writers such as John Steinbeck use fiction to draw attention to the Great Depression?

   A Readers could be sympathetic to the characters' situations.

   B Writing fiction meant the authors didn't have to do any research.

   C Nonfiction sales had dropped during the 1920s.

   D Publishers weren't interested in true accounts of national events.

Analyze the cartoon and answer the question that follows. Base your answer on the cartoon and on your knowledge of Chapter 11.

17. What does the cartoon reveal about the character?

   A The man was careless with his money.

   B He saved his money so it would be there in hard times but lost it through no fault of his own.

   C The man should have purchased stocks and bonds rather than put his money in the bank.

   D The man should be more prepared by storing his money under his mattress.

Document-Based Questions

Directions: Analyze the document and answer the short-answer questions that follow the document.

Gordon Parks, who later became a famous photographer, was a young man when the stock market crashed in 1929:

> "The newspapers were full of it, and I read everything I could get my hands on, gathering in the full meaning of such terms as Black Thursday, deflation and depression. I couldn't imagine such financial disaster touching my small world; it surely concerned only the rich. But by the first week of November I too knew differently; along with millions of others across the nation, I was without a job. All that next week I searched for any kind of work that would prevent my leaving school. Again it was, 'We're firing, not hiring.' 'Sorry, sonny, nothing doing here.' Finally, on the seventh of November I went to school and cleaned out my locker, knowing it was impossible to stay on. A piercing chill was in the air as I walked back to the rooming house. The hawk had come. I could already feel his wings shadowing me."
> —from *A Choice of Weapons*

18. Why did Parks at first think he was safe from the effects of the stock market crash? What changed his mind?

19. Why do you think Parks used the image of a hawk to express his feelings about the Great Depression?

Extended Response

20. Write an essay that analyzes the following quote from John Steinbeck's novel *The Grapes of Wrath*. "If you're in trouble or hurt or need—go to poor people. They're the only ones that'll help." Based on your knowledge of the Great Depression, indicate whether you believe the quote to be true or false and why. Support your answer with relevant facts and details.

For additional test practice, use Self-Check Quizzes—Chapter 11 at <u>glencoe.com</u>.

Need Extra Help?

If You Missed Questions . . .	16	17	18	19	20
Go to Page . . .	409	R18	402–404	402–404	406–409

Extended Response

20. Students may say that poor people will help because they understand the need and have learned compassion from dealing with their own problems.

---

16. A Students need only recall books or films they have seen to know the power of empathy with a fictionalized character.

17. B The label on the man indicates he had done the "right" thing by placing his money in a bank for savings. The other possible answers were not wise choices to prepare for the future.

Document-Based Questions

18. He wasn't one of the wealthy people who owned stocks, but a struggling student. He learned differently when he lost his job.

19. Possible answer: Hawks are large birds of prey; they connote the ideas of death and feeding on carrion.

Have students visit the Web site at <u>glencoe.com</u> to review Chapter 11 and take the Self-Check Quiz.

Need Extra Help?

Have students refer to the pages listed if they miss any of the questions.

Key to Ability Levels

BL Below Level		**AL** Above Level	
OL On Level		**ELL** English Language Learners	

Key to Teaching Resources

Print Material
CD-ROM
DVD
Transparency

Levels BL	OL	AL	ELL		Resources	Chapter Opener	Section 1	Section 2	Section 3	Chapter Assess
					FOCUS					
BL	OL	AL	ELL	🖨	Daily Focus Skills Transparencies		12-1	12-2	12-3	
					TEACH					
BL	OL		ELL	📁	Reading Essentials and Note-Taking Guide*		p. 124	p. 128	p. 131	
	OL			📁	Historical Analysis Skills Activity, URB		p. 84			
BL	OL		ELL	📁	Guided Reading Activities, URB*		p. 110	p. 111	p. 112	
BL	OL	AL	ELL	📁	Content Vocabulary Activity, URB*	p. 89				
BL	OL	AL	ELL	📁	Academic Vocabulary Activity, URB	p. 91				
	OL	AL		📁	Critical Thinking Skills Activity, URB		p. 94			
BL	OL		ELL	📁	Reading Skills Activity, URB		p. 83			
BL			ELL	📁	English Learner Activity, URB	p. 87				
	OL	AL		📁	Reinforcing Skills Activity, URB			p. 93		
BL	OL	AL	ELL	📁	Differentiated Instruction Activity, URB			p. 85		
BL	OL		ELL	📁	Time Line Activity, URB					p. 95
	OL			📁	Linking Past and Present Activity, URB		p. 96			
BL	OL	AL	ELL	📁	American Art and Music Activity, URB					p. 101
BL	OL	AL	ELL	📁	Interpreting Political Cartoons Activity, URB		p. 103			
		AL		📁	Enrichment Activity, URB			p. 107		
BL	OL	AL	ELL	📁	American Biographies		✓		✓	
BL	OL	AL	ELL	📁	Primary Source Reading, URB			pp. 97, 99		
BL	OL	AL	ELL	📁	Supreme Court Case Studies		p. 49	p. 51		
BL	OL	AL	ELL	📁	The Living Constitution*	✓	✓	✓	✓	✓
	OL	AL		💿	American History Primary Source Documents Library	✓	✓	✓	✓	✓
BL	OL	AL	ELL	🖨	Unit Map Overlay Transparencies	✓	✓	✓	✓	✓
BL	OL	AL	ELL	📁	Differentiated Instruction for the American High School Classroom	✓	✓	✓	✓	✓
BL	OL	AL	ELL	💿	StudentWorks™ Plus DVD	✓	✓	✓	✓	✓
BL	OL	AL	ELL	💿	Vocabulary PuzzleMaker CD-ROM	✓	✓	✓	✓	✓

Note: Please refer to the *Unit 4 Resource Book* for this chapter's URB materials.

* Also available in Spanish

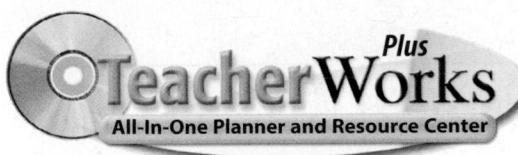

TeacherWorks *Plus*
All-In-One Planner and Resource Center

- Interactive Lesson Planner
- Interactive Teacher Edition
- Fully editable blackline masters
- Section Spotlight Videos Launch

- Differentiated Lesson Plans
- Printable reports of daily assignments
- Standards Tracking System

Levels					Resources	Chapter Opener	Section 1	Section 2	Section 3	Chapter Assess
BL	OL	AL	ELL							
TEACH *(continued)*										
BL	OL	AL	ELL	💿	American Music Hits Through History CD	✓	✓	✓	✓	✓
BL	OL	AL	ELL		Unit Time Line Transparencies and Activities	✓	✓	✓	✓	✓
BL	OL	AL	ELL		Cause and Effect Transparencies, Strategies, and Activities	✓	✓	✓	✓	✓
BL	OL	AL	ELL		Why It Matters Transparencies, Strategies, and Activities	✓	✓	✓	✓	✓
BL	OL	AL	ELL		American Issues	✓	✓	✓	✓	✓
	OL	AL	ELL		American Art and Architecture Transparencies, Strategies, and Activities	✓	✓	✓	✓	✓
BL	OL	AL			High School American History Literature Library	✓	✓	✓	✓	✓
BL	OL	AL	ELL		*The American Vision* Video Program DVD	✓	✓	✓	✓	✓
Teacher Resources					Strategies for Success	✓	✓	✓	✓	✓
					Success with English Learner	✓	✓	✓	✓	✓
					Studies Classroom	✓	✓	✓	✓	✓
					Presentation Plus! DVD	✓	✓	✓	✓	✓
ASSESS										
BL	OL	AL	ELL		Section Quizzes and Chapter Tests*		p. 165	p. 166	p. 167	p. 169
BL	OL	AL	ELL		Authentic Assessment With Rubrics					p. 29
BL	OL	AL	ELL		Standardized Test Practice Workbook					p. 26
BL	OL	AL	ELL	💿	*ExamView® Assessment Suite* CD-ROM		12-1	12-2	12-3	Ch. 12
BL	OL	AL	ELL	💿	Interactive Tutor Self-Assessment CD-ROM		12-1	12-2	12-3	Ch. 12
CLOSE										
BL			ELL		Reteaching Activity, URB					p. 105
BL	OL		ELL		Reading and Study Skills Foldables™	p. 72				
BL	OL	AL	ELL		*American History* in Graphic Novel		p. 49			

Using the Glencoe Web Site

Vocabulary eFlashcards

Technology Product

The Vocabulary eFlashcards on the Glencoe Web site enable students to review vocabulary and their definitions for each chapter. The Vocabulary eFlashcards provide separate card sets for content vocabulary and academic vocabulary, and a separate set for people, places, and events, along with textbook page references. The final set combines all words and terms. Students can print sets of cards to review vocabulary away from the computer.

Objectives

The Vocabulary eFlashcards help students
- practice and reinforce their comprehension of vocabulary and key terms in each chapter;
- identify areas for additional study and reinforcement.

Steps

Provide students with the following steps to work with the Vocabulary eFlashcards:
- Locate the Web page for the textbook being studied on the Glencoe Web site glencoe.com.
- Click on **Student Center** under the textbook title.
- In the Student Center, select a unit from the Unit Resources menu and a chapter from the Chapter Activities menu using the drop-down arrows.
- Click on the **Vocabulary e-Flashcards** link.
- Select and review one of the vocabulary lists for the chapter: Academic; Content; People, Places, Events; or Combined. A new window will open.
- Review vocabulary in one of the three viewing modes: View Terms and Definitions, View Terms, and View Definitions. Click on **Flip Card** to read the relevant term or definition.

History ONLINE

	Student	Teacher	Parent
Beyond the Textbook	●	●	●
Chapter Overviews	●	●	●
Time Current Events	●		●
ePuzzles and Games	●		●
Concepts in Motion	●		●
Literature Connections		●	
Multi-Language Glossaries	●		●
Online Student Edition	●	●	●
Self-Check Quizzes	●		●
Student Web Activities	●		●
Study Central™	●		●
Teaching Today		●	
Vocabulary eFlashcards	●		●
Web Activity Lesson Plans		●	

Glencoe Media Center

glencoe.com

❯ **Study-To-Go**
- Vocabulary eFlashcards
- Self-Check Quizzes

❯ **Audio/Video**
- Student Edition Audio
- Spanish Summaries
- Section Videos

- **Timed Readings Plus in Social Studies** helps students increase their reading rate and fluency while maintaining comprehension. The 400-word passages are similar to those found on state and national assessments.

- **Reading in the Content Area: Social Studies** concentrates on six essential reading skills that help students better comprehend what they read. The book includes 75 high-interest nonfiction passages written at increasing levels of difficulty.

- **Reading Social Studies** includes strategic reading instruction and vocabulary support in Social Studies content for both ELLs and native speakers of English.

www.jamestowneducation.com

Index to National Geographic Magazine:

The following article relates to this chapter:

- "The Okies—Beyond the Dust Bowl," by William Howarth, September 1984.

National Geographic Society Products To order the following, call National Geographic at 1-800-368-2728:

- ZipZapMap! USA (ZipZapMap!)

Access National Geographic's new, dynamic MapMachine Web site and other geography resources at:

www.nationalgeographic.com
www.nationalgeographic.com/maps

The following videotape programs are available from Glencoe as supplements to Chapter 12:

- The Tennessee Valley Authority (ISBN 0-76-700031-5)
- Eleanor Roosevelt: A Restless Spirit (ISBN 1-56-501405-7)

To order, call Glencoe at 1-800-334-7344. To find classroom resources to accompany many of these videos, check the following home pages:

A&E Television: www.aetv.com
The History Channel: www.historychannel.com

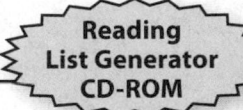

Use this database to search more than 30,000 titles to create a customized reading list for your students.

- Reading lists can be organized by students' reading level, author, genre, theme, or area of interest.
- The database provides Degrees of Reading Power™ (DRP) and Lexile™ readability scores for all selections.
- A brief summary of each selection is included.

Leveled reading suggestions for this chapter:

For students at a Grade 8 reading level:
- *Franklin D. Roosevelt*, by Steve Potts

For students at a Grade 9 reading level:
- *Franklin D. Roosevelt*, by Michael Burgan

For students at a Grade 10 reading level:
- *Empire State Building*, by Elizabeth Mann

For students at a Grade 11 reading level:
- *Eleanor Roosevelt: First Lady of the World*, by Doris Faber

For students at a Grade 12 reading level:
- *Eleanor Roosevelt: A Life of Discovery*, by Russell Freedman

Focus

MAKING CONNECTIONS
Can Government Fix the Economy?
Ask students to give examples of some of the ways that government tries to fix the economy, such as the Federal Reserve Board's regulation of interest rates. Discuss with students the questions listed on p. 421. Challenge students to activate prior knowledge of regulation of any of the economic sectors mentioned. **AL**

Teach

The Big Ideas

As students study the chapter, remind them to consider the section-based Big Ideas included in each section's Guide to Reading. The **Essential Questions** in the activities below tie in to the Big Ideas and help students think about and understand important chapter concepts. In addition, the Hands-on Chapter Projects with their culminating activities relate the content from each section to the Big Ideas. These activities build on each other as students progress through the chapter. Section activities culminate in the wrap-up activity on the Visual Summary page.

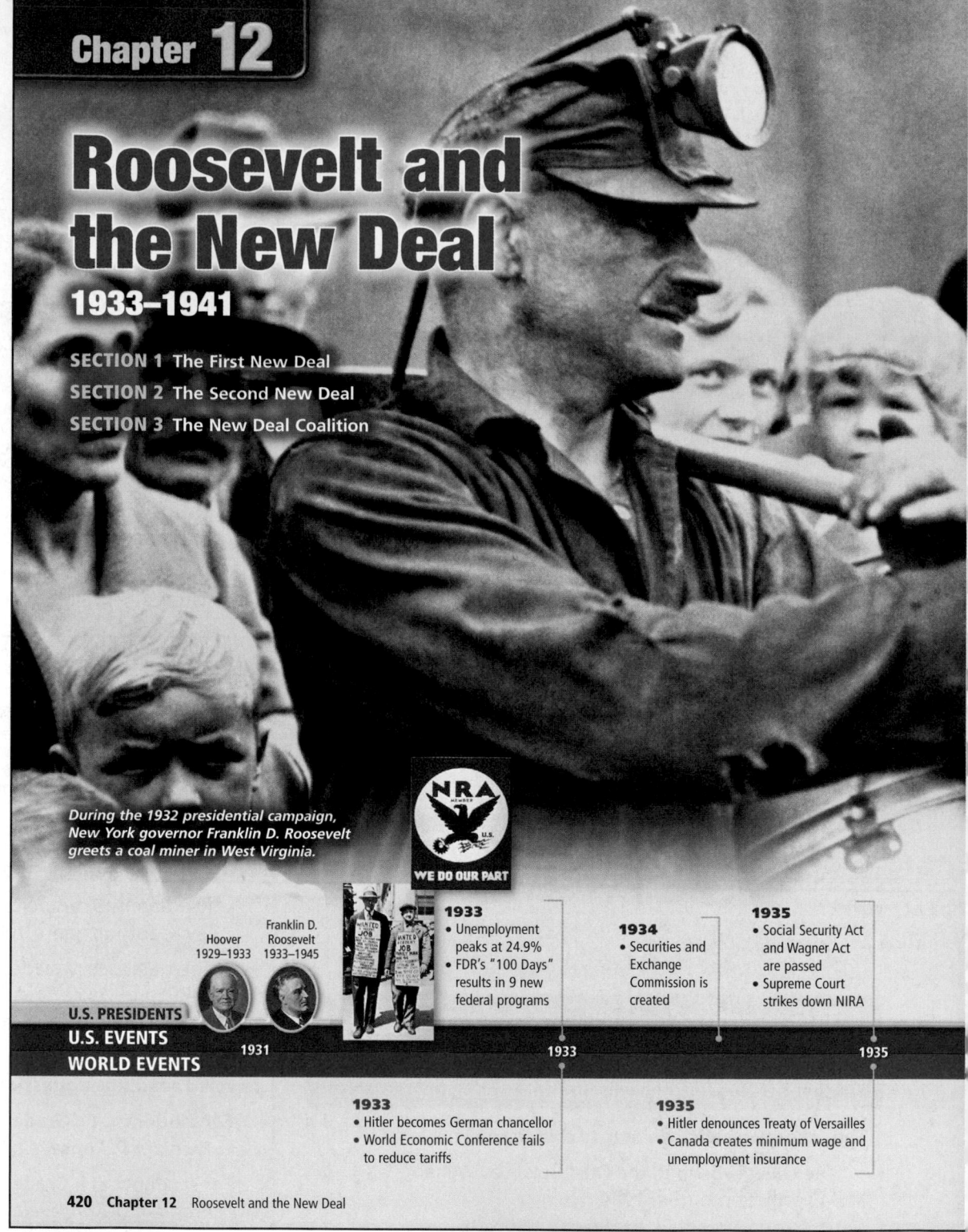

Chapter 12

Roosevelt and the New Deal
1933–1941

SECTION 1 The First New Deal
SECTION 2 The Second New Deal
SECTION 3 The New Deal Coalition

During the 1932 presidential campaign, New York governor Franklin D. Roosevelt greets a coal miner in West Virginia.

NRA
MEMBER
U.S.
WE DO OUR PART

U.S. PRESIDENTS
Hoover 1929–1933
Franklin D. Roosevelt 1933–1945

U.S. EVENTS
1931

WORLD EVENTS

1933
• Unemployment peaks at 24.9%
• FDR's "100 Days" results in 9 new federal programs

1933

1934
• Securities and Exchange Commission is created

1935
• Social Security Act and Wagner Act are passed
• Supreme Court strikes down NIRA

1935

1933
• Hitler becomes German chancellor
• World Economic Conference fails to reduce tariffs

1935
• Hitler denounces Treaty of Versailles
• Canada creates minimum wage and unemployment insurance

420   Chapter 12   Roosevelt and the New Deal

Section 1

The First New Deal
Essential Question: In what areas did the New Deal attempt to make major economic improvements? *(The New Deal targeted banks [FDIC], the stock market [SEC], debt relief for home owners [HOLC], farms [FCA and AAA], industry [NRA], and public works programs to aid the unemployed [CCC, PWA, CWA].)* Tell students that in Section 1 they will learn about many programs that were developed to stimulate the economy. **OL**

Section 2

The Second New Deal
Essential Question: How did the Second New Deal assist unions, the elderly, and the unemployed? *(The Wagner Act gave workers the right to organize in unions. The Social Security Act benefited both the elderly workers and the unemployed.)* Inform students that in this section they will study programs that still exist. **OL**

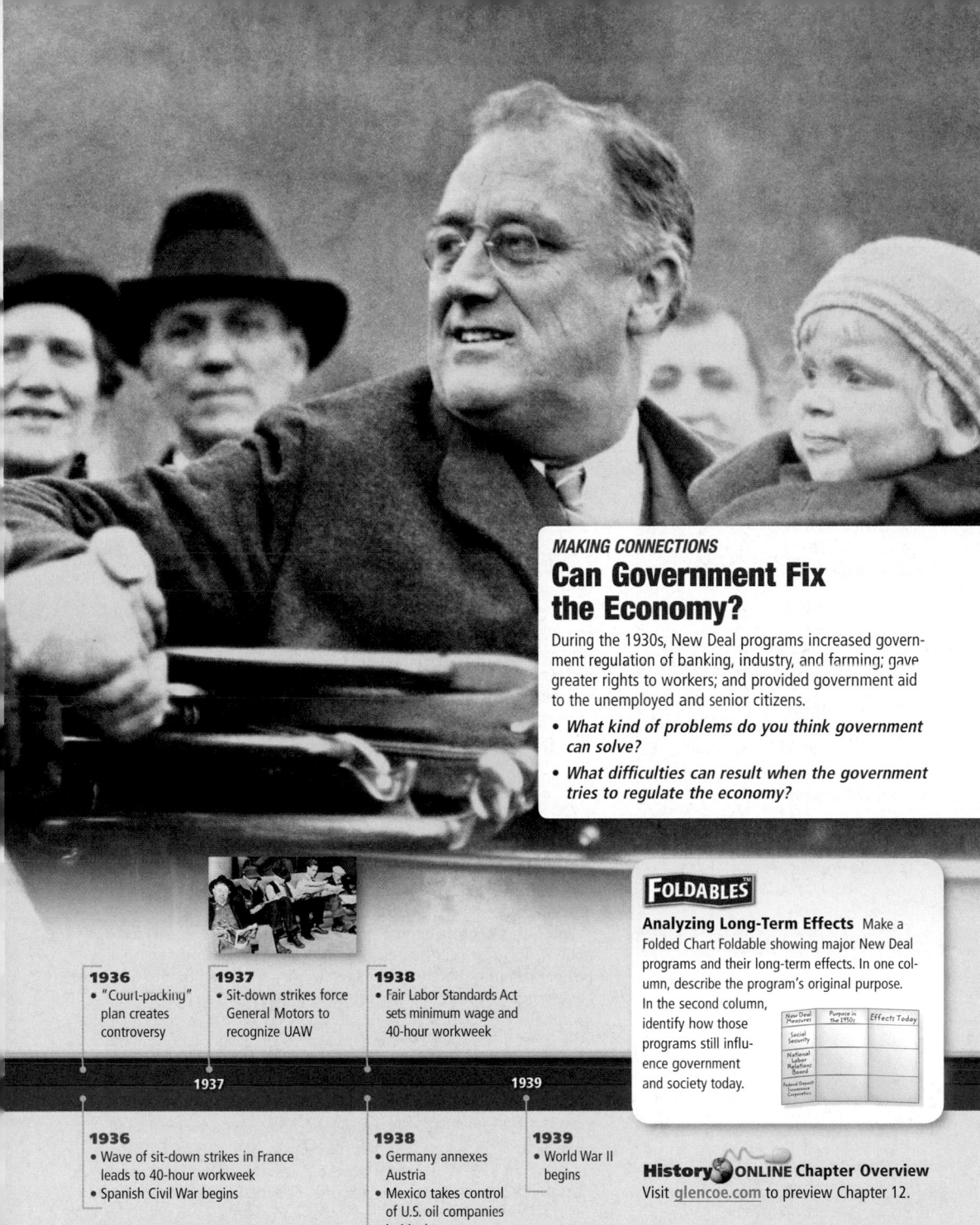

More About the Photo

Visual Literacy After becoming disabled, Roosevelt had a special Model A Ford with hand controls built for his use. Driving that car, he could feel physically independent. During campaigning, however, he often used a driver to free him for greeting voters. During his first campaign, he delivered almost 60 speeches, 27 of them major addresses, to allay fears that he was not physically strong enough to endure the strain of the presidency.

FOLDABLES Study Organizer **Dinah Zike's Foldables**

Dinah Zike's Foldables are three-dimensional, interactive graphic organizers that help students practice basic writing skills, review vocabulary terms, and identify main ideas. Instructions for creating and using Foldables can be found in the Appendix at the end of this book and in the *Dinah Zike's Reading and Study Skills Foldables* booklet.

History ONLINE
Introduce students to chapter content and key terms by having them access the Chapter 12 Overview at glencoe.com.

MAKING CONNECTIONS

Can Government Fix the Economy?

During the 1930s, New Deal programs increased government regulation of banking, industry, and farming; gave greater rights to workers; and provided government aid to the unemployed and senior citizens.

- *What kind of problems do you think government can solve?*
- *What difficulties can result when the government tries to regulate the economy?*

FOLDABLES

Analyzing Long-Term Effects Make a Folded Chart Foldable showing major New Deal programs and their long-term effects. In one column, describe the program's original purpose. In the second column, identify how those programs still influence government and society today.

New Deal Measures	Purpose in the 1930s	Effects Today
Social Security		
National Labor Relations Board		
Federal Deposit Insurance Corporation		

1936
- "Court-packing" plan creates controversy

1937
- Sit-down strikes force General Motors to recognize UAW

1938
- Fair Labor Standards Act sets minimum wage and 40-hour workweek

1937   1939

1936
- Wave of sit-down strikes in France leads to 40-hour workweek
- Spanish Civil War begins

1938
- Germany annexes Austria
- Mexico takes control of U.S. oil companies in Mexico

1939
- World War II begins

History ONLINE Chapter Overview
Visit glencoe.com to preview Chapter 12.

Chapter 12   Roosevelt and the New Deal   **421**

Section 3

The New Deal Coalition
Essential Question: What was the legacy of the New Deal? *(New Deal programs gave many people a stronger sense of stability and security by creating a safety net. It positioned the federal government as conflict mediator in a broker state.)* Tell students that in Section 3 they will learn about the lasting effects of the New Deal. **OL**

Focus

Bellringer
Daily Focus Transparency 12.1

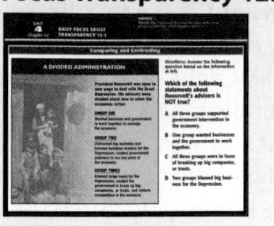

Guide to Reading

Answer: Major problems addressed include bank runs, unprotected bank deposits, stock fraud, and the plight of farmers.

Section Spotlight Video

To generate student interest and provide a springboard for class discussion, access the Chapter 12, Section 1 video at glencoe.com or on the video DVD.

Resource Manager

The First New Deal

Guide to Reading

Big Ideas
Individual Action Franklin Delano Roosevelt's character and experiences prepared him for the presidency.

Content Vocabulary
• polio *(p. 422)*
• gold standard *(p. 424)*
• bank holiday *(p. 424)*
• fireside chats *(p. 425)*

Academic Vocabulary
• apparent *(p. 423)*
• ideology *(p. 424)*
• fundamental *(p. 430)*

People and Events to Identify
• New Deal *(p. 423)*
• Hundred Days *(p. 424)*
• Civilian Conservation Corps *(p. 430)*

Reading Strategy
Sequencing As you read about Roosevelt's first three months in office, complete a time line to record the major problems he addressed during this time.

Franklin Delano Roosevelt was elected president in 1932, following his promise of a "new deal" for Americans. In his first 100 days in office, he let loose a flood of legislation designed to rescue banks, industry, and agriculture and provide jobs for the unemployed.

Roosevelt's Rise to Power

MAIN Idea Franklin D. Roosevelt was governor of New York when he was elected president in 1932, promising a New Deal for the American people.

HISTORY AND YOU Do you believe your past experiences can make you stronger? Read how FDR's experiences helped prepare him to be president.

A distant cousin of Theodore Roosevelt, Franklin Delano Roosevelt grew up in Hyde Park, New York. In his youth he learned to hunt, ride horses, and sail; he also developed a lifelong commitment to conservation and a love of rural America. Roosevelt was educated at Harvard and Columbia Law School. While at Harvard, he became friends with Theodore Roosevelt's niece Eleanor, whom he later married.

Intensely competitive, Roosevelt liked to be in control. He also liked being around people. His charming personality, deep rich voice, and wide smile expressed confidence and optimism. In short, his personality seemed made for a life in politics.

Roosevelt began his political career in 1910, when he was elected to the New York State Senate. Three years later, having earned a reputation as a progressive reformer, he became assistant secretary of the navy in the Wilson administration. In 1920 his reputation (and famous surname) helped him win the vice presidential nomination on the unsuccessful Democratic ticket.

After losing the election, Roosevelt temporarily withdrew from politics. The next year he caught the dreaded paralyzing disease **polio.** Although there was no cure, Roosevelt refused to give in. He began a vigorous exercise program to restore muscle control. Eventually, by wearing heavy steel braces on his legs, he was able to walk short distances by leaning on a cane and someone's arm and swinging his legs forward from his hips.

While recovering from polio, Roosevelt depended on his wife and his aide Louis Howe to keep his name prominent in the New York Democratic Party. Eleanor Roosevelt became an effective public speaker, and her efforts kept her husband's political career alive.

By the mid-1920s, Roosevelt was again active in the Democratic Party. In 1928 he ran for governor of New York. He campaigned hard

---

R Reading Strategies	**C** Critical Thinking	**D** Differentiated Instruction	**W** Writing Support	**S** Skill Practice
Teacher Edition • Taking Notes, p. 424 • Predicting, p. 430 • Act. Prior Know., p. 431 **Additional Resources** • Read Skills Act., URB p. 83 • Guid. Read. Act., URB p. 110	**Teacher Edition** • Ident. Issues, p. 424 • Compare/Contrast, p. 424 • Det. Cause/Effect, p. 426 • Predict. Conseq., p. 428 • Analyzing Info, p. 429 • Making Gen., p. 430 **Additional Resources** • Interp. Pol. Cartoons, URB p. 103 • Quizzes and Tests, p. 165	**Teacher Edition** • Advanced Learners, p. 425 • Logical/Math., p. 427 **Additional Resources** • English Learner Act., URB p. 87 • Am. History in Graphic Novel, p. 49	**Teacher Edition** • Persuasive Writing, p. 428 **Additional Resources** • Supreme Court Case Studies, p. 49	**Teacher Edition** • Reading a Time Line, p. 426 **Additional Resources** • RENTG, p. 124 • Historical Analy., URB p. 84 • Link. Past & Present, URB p. 96 • Crit. Think. Skills, URB p. 94

PRIMARY SOURCE
Roosevelt's First Inaugural Address

March 4, 1933

"This is preeminently the time to speak the truth, the whole truth, frankly and boldly. Nor need we shrink from honestly facing conditions in our country today. This great Nation will endure as it has endured, will revive and will prosper. So, first of all, let me assert my firm belief that the only thing we have to fear is fear itself—nameless, unreasoning, unjustified terror which paralyzes needed efforts to convert retreat into advance.

. . . Restoration calls, however, not for changes in ethics alone. This Nation asks for action, and action now.

. . . Our greatest primary task is to put people to work. This is no unsolvable problem if we face it wisely and courageously. It can be accomplished in part by direct recruiting by the Government itself, treating the task as we would treat the emergency of a war.

. . . Action in this image and to this end is feasible under the form of government which we have inherited from our ancestors. Our Constitution is so simple and practical that it is possible always to meet extraordinary needs by changes in emphasis and arrangement without loss of essential form.

We do not distrust the future of essential democracy. The people of the United States have not failed. In their need they have registered a mandate that they want direct, vigorous action."

—from *The Public Papers and Addresses of Franklin D. Roosevelt*

▲ *Franklin Roosevelt delivers his First Inaugural Address.*

DBQ · Document-Based Questions

1. **Analyzing Primary Sources** Why does Roosevelt think that "nameless, unreasoning, unjustified terror" is such a big problem?

2. **Identifying Central Issues** What unspoken fear does Roosevelt address in the final two paragraphs?

---

to demonstrate that his illness had not slowed him down, and he narrowly won the election. Two years later he was reelected in a landslide. As governor, Roosevelt oversaw the creation of the first state relief agency to aid the unemployed.

Roosevelt's popularity in New York paved the way for his presidential nomination in 1932. Americans saw in him an energy and optimism that gave them hope despite the tough economic times. After Roosevelt became president, his serenity and confidence amazed people. When one aide commented on his attitude, Roosevelt replied, "If you had spent two years in bed trying to wiggle your big toe, after that anything else would seem easy."

In mid-June 1932, with the country deep in the Depression, Republicans gathered in Chicago and nominated Herbert Hoover to run for a second term as president. Later that month, the Democrats also held their national convention in Chicago. When Roosevelt won the nomination, he broke with tradition by flying to Chicago to accept it in person. His speech set the tone for his campaign:

PRIMARY SOURCE

"Let it be from now on the task of our Party to break foolish traditions. . . . It is inevitable that the main issue of this campaign should revolve about . . . a depression so deep that it is without precedent. . . . Republican leaders not only have failed in material things, they have failed in national vision, because in disaster they have held out no hope. . . . I pledge you, I pledge myself, to a new deal for the American people."

—from *The Public Papers and Addresses of Franklin D. Roosevelt*

From that point forward, Roosevelt's policies for ending the Depression became known as the **New Deal.** Roosevelt's confidence that he could make things better contrasted sharply with Herbert Hoover's **apparent** failure to do anything effective. On Election Day, Roosevelt won in a landslide, receiving the electoral vote of all but six states.

✓ **Reading Check** **Interpreting** What events in Roosevelt's life shaped his ideas and character?

Teach

C Critical Thinking
Identifying Central Issues
Ask students to read the Primary Source quotation. **Ask:** What did Roosevelt consider to be the failure of the Republican leaders? *(They failed in national vision and in holding out hope.)* **OL**

DBQ · Document-Based Questions

Answers:
1. It keeps people from taking action to tackle the Depression.
2. that by taking action, the government will somehow overstep its rights given in the Constitution and the nation will lose democracy

✓ Reading Check

Answer:
privileged upbringing, love of outdoors, good marriage, polio, experiences as a state senator, assistant secretary of the Navy, and a governor

Hands-On Chapter Project
Step 1

Writing a Newspaper

Step 1: Identifying American Groups to Watch Small groups of students receive their assignments.

Directions Divide the class into five groups, assigning each group one of the following groups of Americans: women, children, African Americans, Native Americans, and Hispanic Americans. Tell students that they will create a newspaper from the viewpoint of their assigned group during the

1930s. The newspaper will include news stories, editorials, and cartoons. Encourage students to begin a separate section of their notebooks to take notes on the chapter from their assigned viewpoint and to record findings from additional research in the library or on the Internet.

Putting It Together Make sure that students have in-class access to copies of local and national newspapers as a model on which to base their own newspapers. **OL**
(Chapter Project continued on page 435)

C Critical Thinking

Comparing and Contrasting
Ask students to think about the question: How was the New Deal a continuation of the Progressive era? Tell students to write down ways in which the two were alike and different as they read the section. At the end of the section, debate the question. **AL**

R Reading Strategy

Taking Notes Have students create graphic organizers to take notes on the section "A Divided Administration." Suggest they use a three-column chart to jot down the ideas of the three groups within FDR's administration. **BL**

✓ Reading Check

Answer:
One group wanted joint government-business cooperation, another wanted government control of business, and a third group wanted more competition.

Additional Support

Teacher Tip

At the time of the Great Depression, the United States did not have any social programs in place for its citizens. Suggest students use the Internet to find current programs that assist those in need. The government Web site for HUD, for example, offers information on housing.

The Hundred Days

MAIN Idea Upon taking office, FDR launched the New Deal by sending 15 major pieces of legislation to Congress.

HISTORY AND YOU Do you remember reading about the "New Nationalism" and "New Freedom"? Read how those ideas influenced New Deal legislation.

Although Roosevelt won the presidency in November 1932, the country's unemployed and homeless had to endure another winter as they waited for his inauguration on March 4, 1933. All through the winter, unemployment continued to rise and bank runs increased, further threatening the banking system.

Some of the bank runs occurred because people feared that Roosevelt would abandon the **gold standard** and reduce the value of the dollar in order to fight the Depression. Under the gold standard, one ounce of gold equaled a set number of dollars. To reduce the value of the dollar, the United States would have to stop exchanging dollars for gold. Many Americans, and many foreign investors with deposits in American banks, decided to take their money out of the banks and convert it to gold before it lost its value.

Across the nation, people stood in long lines with paper bags and suitcases, waiting to withdraw their money from banks. By March 1933, more than 4,000 banks had collapsed, wiping out nine million savings accounts. In 38 states, governors declared **bank holidays**—closing the remaining banks before bank runs could put them out of business.

By the day of Roosevelt's inauguration, most of the nation's banks were closed. One in four workers was unemployed. The economy seemed paralyzed. Roosevelt knew he had to restore the nation's confidence. "First of all," the president declared in his Inaugural Address, "let me assert my firm belief that the only thing we have to fear is fear itself. . . . This nation asks for action, and action now!"

The New Deal Begins

Roosevelt and his advisers, sometimes called the "brain trust," came into office bursting with ideas about how to end the Depression. Roosevelt had no clear agenda, nor did he have

a strong political **ideology.** The previous spring, during his campaign for the presidential nomination, Roosevelt had revealed the approach he would take as president. "The country needs," Roosevelt explained, "bold, persistent experimentation . . . . Above all, try something."

The new president began to send bill after **C** bill to Congress. Between March 9 and June 16, 1933—which came to be called the **Hundred Days**—Congress passed 15 major acts to resolve the economic crisis, setting a pace for new legislation that has never been equaled. Together, these programs made up what would later be called the First New Deal.

A Divided Administration

To generate new ideas and programs, Roosevelt deliberately chose advisers who disagreed with each other. He wanted to hear many different points of view, and by setting his advisers against one another, Roosevelt ensured that he alone made the final decision on what policies to pursue.

Despite their disagreements, Roosevelt's advisers generally favored some form of government intervention in the economy—although they disagreed over what the government's role should be.

One influential group during the early years of Roosevelt's administration supported the "New Nationalism" of Theodore Roosevelt. These advisers believed that if government **R** agencies worked with businesses to regulate wages, prices, and production, they could lift the economy out of the Depression.

A second group of Roosevelt's advisers went even further. They distrusted big business and blamed business leaders for causing the Depression. These advisers wanted government planners to run key parts of the economy.

A third group in Roosevelt's administration supported the "New Freedom" of Woodrow Wilson. These advisers wanted Roosevelt to support "trust busting" by breaking up big companies and allowing competition to set wages, prices, and production levels. They also thought the government should impose regulations to keep economic competition fair.

✓ Reading Check **Summarizing** What ideas did Roosevelt's advisers support?

424 **Chapter 12** Roosevelt and the New Deal

Activity: Collaborative Learning

Making a Plan Before students begin reading about actual New Deal programs, divide the class into small groups of four or five. Ask each student within each group to concentrate on one of the issues facing Roosevelt: safeguarding bank deposits, providing emergency relief, bolstering business, or creating jobs. Have members of the groups review and refine each oth-

er's ideas. Allow time for groups to present their ideas to the class. **OL**

Eleanor Roosevelt
1884–1962

Orphaned at age 10, Eleanor Roosevelt was raised by relatives and later attended boarding school in England. When she returned home as a young woman, she devoted time to a settlement house on Manhattan's Lower East Side. During this time, she became engaged to Franklin D. Roosevelt, a distant cousin. They were married in 1905. At their wedding, Eleanor's uncle, President Theodore Roosevelt, gave her away.

During FDR's presidency, Eleanor Roosevelt transformed the role of First Lady. Rather than restricting herself to traditional hostess functions, she became an important figure in his administration. She traveled extensively, toured factories and coal mines, and met with factory workers and farmers. She then told her husband what people were thinking. In doing so, she became FDR's "eyes and ears" when his disability made travel difficult.

Eleanor was also a strong supporter of civil rights and prodded her husband to stop discrimination in New Deal programs. When the Daughters of the American Revolution barred African American singer Marian Anderson from performing in its auditorium, Eleanor intervened and arranged for Anderson to perform at the Lincoln Memorial instead.

After FDR's death, Eleanor remained politically active. She continued to write her syndicated newspaper column, "My Day," which she began in 1936, and became a delegate to the United Nations where she helped draft the Universal Declaration of Human Rights.

How might Franklin Roosevelt's political career have been different if Eleanor had not been his wife?

▲ *In this 1935 photo, Eleanor Roosevelt speaks to Geraldine Walker, a five-year-old from Detroit, Michigan, as slums in that city were about to be cleared.*

D Differentiated Instruction

Advanced Learners Invite students to find out the usual amount of time it takes for present-day Congresses to write and pass a bill. Then have them compare that to FDR's request for a banking bill in less than five days, perhaps using a chart to explain their findings to the class. **AL**

People IN HISTORY

Answer: If Eleanor Roosevelt had not been Franklin's wife, his political career may well have ended when he contracted polio. His effectiveness as president would have been less without her unannounced eyewitness observations.

Banks and Debt Relief

MAIN Idea President Roosevelt took steps to strengthen banks and the stock market and to help farmers and homeowners keep their property.

HISTORY AND YOU Have you ever watched a presidential address? Read about Roosevelt's "fireside chats" and how they encouraged optimism that the economy would get better.

As the debate over policies and programs swirled around him, President Roosevelt took office with one thing clear in his mind. Very few of the proposed solutions would work as long as the nation's banks remained closed. The first thing he had to do was restore confidence in the banking system.

D On his very first night in office, Roosevelt told Secretary of the Treasury William H. Woodin that he wanted an emergency banking bill ready for Congress in less than five days. The following afternoon, Roosevelt declared a national bank holiday, temporarily closing all banks, and called Congress into a special session scheduled to begin on March 9, 1933.

When Congress convened, the House of Representatives unanimously passed the Emergency Banking Relief Act after only 38 minutes of debate. The Senate approved the bill that evening, and Roosevelt signed it into law shortly afterward. The new law required federal examiners to survey the nation's banks and issue Treasury Department licenses to those that were financially sound.

On March 12 President Roosevelt addressed the nation by radio. Sixty million people listened to this first of many "**fireside chats,**" direct talks in which Roosevelt let the American people know what he was trying to accomplish. He told people that their money would be secure if they put it back into the banks: "I assure you that it is safer to keep your money in a reopened bank than under the mattress." When banks opened the day after the speech, deposits far outweighed withdrawals. The banking crisis was over.

Chapter 12 Roosevelt and the New Deal **425**

Additional Support

Extending the Content

Eleanor Roosevelt Not used to public speaking, Eleanor Roosevelt experienced stage fright when confronted with an audience. Her knees shook, but she soon became one of the most successful speakers of her time. She was also the first First Lady to hold her own regular press conferences, which offered female reporters the opportunity to find out White House information. When the Second Bonus Army marched on Washington, D.C., Eleanor went down to visit the veterans, who were using an army camp the president had offered them. Even though the bonuses were still not paid, veterans were offered food, medical care, and a navy band. One said, "Hoover sent the army. Roosevelt sent his wife." Eleanor traveled to check on so many government projects that the Secret Service gave her the code name "Rover."

426

C Critical Thinking

Determining Cause and Effect Have students read the section on the FDIC and SEC. Ask them to identify the causes for each provision of the Securities Act and Glass-Steagall Act. *(Securities Act: required companies selling stocks and bonds to give complete and truthful information to investors, because many investors during the 1920s had no reliable information about companies. Glass-Steagall Act: separated commercial and investment banking firms because banks had lent money to play the stock market, putting depositors' funds at risk. It also created the FDIC to insure deposited funds.)* **OL**

S Skill Practice

Reading a Time Line **Ask:** On what days did two major events occur and what were they? *(May 12: Agricultural Adjustment Act signed and Federal Emergency Relief Administration begins making grants to the states; June 16: PWA begins and the NRA begins setting codes for industry)* **OL**

Additional Support

C The FDIC and SEC

Although President Roosevelt had restored confidence in the banking system, many of his advisers urged him to go further. They pushed for new regulations for both banks and the stock market. Roosevelt agreed with their ideas and supported the Securities Act of 1933 and the Glass-Steagall Banking Act.

The Securities Act required companies that sold stocks and bonds to provide complete and truthful information to investors. The following year, Congress created a government agency, the Securities and Exchange Commission (SEC), to regulate the stock market and prevent fraud.

The Glass-Steagall Act separated commercial banking from investment banking. Commercial banks handle everyday transactions. They take deposits, pay interest, cash checks, and lend money for mortgages. Under the Glass-Steagall Act, these banks were no longer allowed to risk depositors' money by using it to speculate on the stock market.

To further protect depositors, the Glass-Steagall Act also created the Federal Deposit Insurance Corporation (FDIC) to provide government insurance for bank deposits up to a certain amount. By protecting depositors in this way, the FDIC greatly increased public confidence in the banking system.

Mortgage and Debt Relief

While some of Roosevelt's advisers believed low prices had caused the Depression, others believed that debt was the main obstacle to economic recovery. With incomes falling, people had to use most of their money to pay their debts and had little left over to buy goods or services. Many Americans, terrified of losing their homes and farms, cut back on their spending to make sure they could pay their mortgages. Roosevelt responded to the crisis by introducing several policies intended to assist Americans with their debts.

The Home Owners' Loan Corporation To help homeowners make their mortgage payments, Roosevelt asked Congress to establish the Home Owners' Loan Corporation (HOLC). The HOLC bought the mortgages of many

THE **First Hundred Days**

March 9
Roosevelt signs the Emergency Banking Relief Act and 3 days later delivers his first fireside chat

▲ *Farmers in Texas receive their AAA checks.*

May 12
The Agricultural Adjustment Act is signed, and farmers soon begin receiving payments to destroy their crops in an effort to push up prices

April 1933　　　　　**May 1933**

S

March 31
The Civilian Conservation Corps is created and soon afterward begins hiring 3 million young men to work in the nation's forests

May 12
The Federal Emergency Relief Administration begins making grants to states to help the unemployed

Activity: Economics Connection

Personal Debt Americans generally have high debt levels and low savings levels. Ask students to use library or Internet resources to find the latest figures on individual and national credit debt. Then have them find recommendations for wise use of credit. Ask them to share their findings with the class via a poster presentation. **Ask:** How can a young person establish credit wisely? *(Students may suggest limiting the number of credit cards and paying off balances each month, as well as choosing cards with low interest rates.)* **OL**

homeowners who were behind in their payments. It then restructured them with longer terms of repayment and lower interest rates. Roughly 10 percent of homeowners received HOLC loans.

The HOLC did not help everyone. It made loans only to homeowners who were not farm owners and who were still employed. When people lost their jobs and could no longer make their mortgage payments, the HOLC foreclosed on their property, just as a bank would have done. Between 1933 and 1936, the three years during which it functioned as a loan source, the HOLC made loans to cover one million mortgages—one out of every ten in the United States.

The Farm Credit Administration Three days after Congress authorized the creation of the HOLC, it authorized the Farm Credit

Administration (FCA) to help farmers refinance their mortgages. Over the next seven months, the FCA lent four times as much money to farmers as the entire banking system had the year before. It was also able to push interest rates substantially lower. These loans saved millions of farms from foreclosure.

Although FCA loans helped many farmers in the short term, their long-term value can be questioned. FCA loans helped less efficient farmers keep their land, but giving loans to poor farmers meant that the money was not available to lend to more efficient businesses in the economy. Although FCA loans may have slowed the overall economic recovery, they did help many desperate and impoverished people hold onto their land.

✔ **Reading Check** Explaining How did the government restore confidence in the banking system?

May 18 Congress creates the Tennessee Valley Authority

June 13 The Home Owners' Loan Corporation is authorized to make low interest mortgage loans to homeowners

June 16 The Public Works Administration is created. Under the leadership of Harold Ickes, it begins spending over $3 billion on public works such as new highways, dams, and public buildings. The agency begins spending.

▲ Workers of the Grand Coulee Dam in Washington.

June 1933

June 16 The National Recovery Administration is authorized to begin setting codes and regulations for industry

Analyzing TIME LINES

1. **Analyzing** What groups of people were targeted for help in the first hundred days of Roosevelt's first term?

2. **Drawing Conclusions** What was Roosevelt's first act after becoming president? Why do you think he chose this as a first step?

Chapter 12 Roosevelt and the New Deal **427**

Activity: Interdisciplinary Connection

Language Arts Have students listen to a recording of one of Roosevelt's fireside chats, which are available at libraries and on the Internet. Then have them view an address by the current president. Discuss how the speeches and delivery compare and contrast. **Ask:** How do the styles of speaking reflect the people in office and the events going on at the time of the speech? *(Answers will vary depending on the speeches that students hear.* **AL**

C Critical Thinking

Predicting Consequences
Have students read only the first paragraph of the section "The AAA." Then ask them to predict what would happen to prices after farmers followed the advice of the AAA. *(They would rise.)* **BL**

W Writing Support

Persuasive Writing Ask students to write a newspaper editorial in favor of or opposed to the policy of slaughtering animals and taking fields out of production during a time of hunger. Remind them to support their ideas with facts. **OL**

Farms and Industry

MAIN Idea New Deal legislation tried to raise crop prices and stabilize industry.

HISTORY AND YOU Can you think of a product that gets more expensive when less of it is available? Read to learn how some New Deal programs tried to raise prices.

Many of Roosevelt's advisers believed that both farmers and businesses were suffering because prices were too low and production too high. Several advisers believed competition was inefficient and bad for the economy. They favored creating federal agencies to manage the economy.

The AAA

To further help the nation's farmers, Secretary of Agriculture Henry Wallace drafted the Agricultural Adjustment Act. President Roosevelt asked Congress to pass the act. This legislation was based on a simple idea—that prices for farm goods were low because farmers grew too much food. Under Roosevelt's

program, the government would pay some farmers *not* to raise certain livestock, and *not* to grow certain crops. Some farmers were also asked *not* to produce dairy products. As the program went into effect, farmers slaughtered 6 million piglets and 200,000 sows and plowed under 10 million acres of cotton—all in an effort to raise prices. The program was administered by the Agricultural Adjustment Administration (AAA).

Over the next two years, farmers withdrew millions more acres from cultivation and received more than $1 billion in support payments. The program accomplished its goal: the farm surplus fell greatly by 1936. Food prices then rose, as did total farm income, which quickly increased by more than 50 percent.

In a nation caught in a Depression, however, raising food prices drew harsh criticism. Furthermore, not all farmers benefited. Large commercial farmers who concentrated on one crop profited more than smaller farmers who raised several products. Worse, thousands of poor tenant farmers, many of them African Americans, became homeless and jobless when landlords took their fields out of production.

PAST & PRESENT

The TVA

The Tennessee Valley Authority (TVA) was a New Deal project that produced visible benefits. The TVA built dams to control floods, conserve forest lands, and bring electricity to rural areas.

Today, TVA power facilities include 17,000 miles of transmission lines, 29 hydroelectric dams, 11 fossil-fuel plants, 4 combustion-turbine plants, 3 nuclear power plants, and a pumped-storage facility. These combine to bring power to nearly 8 million people in a seven-state region.

Since 1998, the TVA has been working to reduce air pollution. Projects are designed to cut harmful emissions released into the air. The TVA is committed to developing programs that protect the environment.

The TVA, 1940

Area served by TVA
✦ Major dam
■ Power plant

0   100 kilometers
0   100 miles
Albers Equal-Area projection

428 **Chapter 12** Roosevelt and the New Deal

Activity: Economics Connection

Supply and Demand Remind students of the economic law of supply and demand in establishing prices. Discuss any current situation in which this law is affecting their lives. For example, bad weather in California or Florida affects the availability of fresh, inexpensive produce. **Ask:** Do you believe it is right to keep fields out of production when people are hungry in order to drive up prices? *(Students' opinions will vary, but may suggest that feeding people is more important than making a profit.)* **OL**

The NRA

The government turned its attention to manufacturing in June 1933, when Roosevelt and Congress enacted the National Industrial Recovery Act (NIRA). The NIRA suspended antitrust laws and allowed business, labor, and government to cooperate in setting up voluntary rules for each industry.

These rules were known as codes of fair competition. Some codes set prices, established minimum wages, and limited factories to two shifts per day so that production could be spread to as many firms as possible. Other codes shortened workers' hours, with the goal of creating additional jobs. Another provision in the law guaranteed workers the right to form unions. The codes also helped businesses develop codes of fair competition within industries.

Under the leadership of Hugh Johnson, the National Recovery Administration (NRA) ran the entire program. Business owners who signed code agreements received signs displaying the National Recovery Administration's symbol—a blue eagle—and the slogan, "We Do Our Part." The NRA had limited power to enforce the codes, but urged consumers to buy goods only from companies that displayed the blue eagle.

The NRA did revive a few American industries, but its gains proved short-lived. Small companies complained, justifiably, that large corporations wrote the codes to favor themselves. American employers disliked codes that gave workers the right to form unions and bargain collectively over wages and hours. They also argued that paying high minimum wages forced them to charge higher prices to cover their costs.

C

The codes were also difficult to administer, and business leaders often ignored them. Furthermore, businesses could choose not to sign code agreements and thus not be bound by their rules. It became obvious that the NRA was failing when industrial production actually fell after the organization was established. By the time the Supreme Court declared the NRA unconstitutional in 1935, it had already lost much of its political support.

✔ **Reading Check** **Examining** What were the goals of the Agricultural Adjustment Act and the National Industrial Recovery Act?

C **Critical Thinking**

Analyzing Information Ask students to analyze why the National Recovery Administration largely failed in its task. Tell them to find at least three reasons for the failure. *(Large companies wrote the codes to favor their interests, employers disliked unions and paying higher wages, and rules were difficult to administer and voluntary.)* **OL**

MAKING **CONNECTIONS**

Answers:
1. Kentucky, Alabama, Virginia, North Carolina, Georgia, and Mississippi
2. eastern Tennessee

✔ **Reading Check**

Answer:

to improve the lot of farmers, set cooperative codes of fair competition, and improve the economy

Additional Support

2006

▼ *This photo shows the completed Cherokee Hydroelectric Dam.*

▲ *Tennessee's Cherokee Dam is today part of the TVA. Workers (upper right) built it in the late 1930s.*

MAKING **CONNECTIONS**

1. **Listing** Look at the map on page 428. What states other than Tennessee benefited from the TVA projects?

2. **Examining** Where were most of the projects located?

Maps In Motion See *StudentWorks™ Plus* or glencoe.com.

Extending the Content

The National Industrial Recovery Act The NIRA was influenced by the work of the War Industries Board that functioned during World War I. Labor and business leaders also offered suggestions. The primary writers of the legislation were General Hugh S. Johnson, who had served on the War Industries Board, and New York senator Robert F. Wagner, later to be known for the act that bears his name. The NIRA also established the Public Works Administration, funding it with $3.3 billion.

R **Reading Strategy**

Predicting Ask students if they think that young people today would be interested in working in a group similar to the Civilian Conservation Corps. Have students explain their reasoning. **BL**

C **Critical Thinking**

Making Generalizations Invite students to generalize the CCC's effect on the morale of each of the groups of workers mentioned in the final paragraph. Ask them to imagine as well the effect on the families of those men. **OL**

Analyzing VISUALS

1. People are tossing quack solutions to Uncle Sam, the dock is collapsing, and pieces of it are hitting Uncle Sam.
2. Congress, shown as a nurse to ailing Uncle Sam

Additional Support

Relief Programs

MAIN Idea Programs such as the CCC, the PWA, and the WPA provided jobs for some unemployed workers.

HISTORY AND YOU Do you know who built your school, post office, or playground? Read about the projects completed by the New Deal workers.

History ONLINE **Student Skill Activity** To learn how to use a word processor, visit glencoe.com and complete the Skill activity.

While many of President Roosevelt's advisers emphasized tinkering with prices and providing debt relief to solve the Depression, others maintained that its **fundamental** cause was low consumption. They thought getting money into the hands of needy individuals would be the fastest remedy. Because neither Roosevelt nor his advisers wanted simply to give money to the unemployed, they supported work programs for the unemployed.

The CCC

The most highly praised New Deal work relief program was the **Civilian Conservation Corps** (CCC). The CCC offered unemployed young men 18 to 25 years old the opportunity to work under the direction of the forestry service planting trees, fighting forest fires, and building reservoirs. To prevent a repeat of the Dust Bowl, the workers planted a line of more than 200 million trees, known as a Shelter Belt, from north Texas to North Dakota.

The young men lived in camps near their work areas and earned $30 a month, $25 of which was sent directly to their families. The average CCC worker returned home after six to twelve months, better nourished and with greater self-respect. CCC programs also taught more than 40,000 of its recruits to read and write. By the time the CCC closed down in 1942, it had put 3 million young men to work outdoors—including 80,000 Native Americans, who helped to reclaim land they had once owned. After a second Bonus Army March on Washington in 1933, Roosevelt added some 250,000 veterans to the CCC as well.

FERA and the PWA

A few weeks after authorizing the CCC, Congress established the Federal Emergency Relief Administration (FERA). Roosevelt chose

---

POLITICAL CARTOONS PRIMARY SOURCE
Did the New Deal Help Americans?

▲ This cartoon, entitled "How Much More Do We Need?" shows Uncle Sam grasping New Deal lifesavers to stay afloat.

► This 1935 cartoon shows FDR as a doctor with a variety of medicines to help ailing Uncle Sam.

Analyzing VISUALS DBQ

1. **Interpeting** In the cartoon at the left, what is happening to the dock, and why?

2. **Analyzing** With whom is President Roosevelt conferring in the cartoon at right?

430 **Chapter 12** Roosevelt and the New Deal

Activity: Interdisciplinary Connection

Science Have interested students use library or Internet resources to find out about current conservation efforts by government agencies. For example, the United States Forestry Service, a division of the Department of Agriculture, manages 193 million acres (78 million ha) of national grasslands and forests. Students may want to start their research by visiting the Forest Service Web site at www.fs.fed.us. Ask students to share their findings with the class during a class discussion. **OL**

Harry Hopkins, a former social worker, to run the agency. FERA did not initially create projects for the unemployed. Instead, it channeled money to state and local agencies to fund their relief projects.

Half an hour after meeting with Roosevelt to discuss his new job, Hopkins set up a desk in the hallway outside of his office. In the next two hours, he spent $5 million on relief projects. When critics charged that some of the projects did not make sense in the long run, Hopkins replied, "People don't eat in the long run—they eat every day."

In June 1933 Congress authorized another relief agency, the Public Works Administration (PWA). One-third of the nation's unemployed were in the construction industry. To put them back to work, the PWA began building highways, dams, sewer systems, schools, and other government facilities. In most cases, the PWA did not hire workers directly but instead awarded contracts to construction companies. By insisting that contractors not discriminate against African Americans, the agency broke down some of the long-standing racial barriers in the construction trades.

The CWA

By the fall of 1933 neither FERA nor the PWA had reduced unemployment significantly. Hopkins realized that unless the federal government acted quickly, a huge number of unemployed citizens would be in severe distress once winter began. After Hopkins explained the situation, President Roosevelt authorized him to set up the Civil Works Administration (CWA).

R Unlike the PWA, the CWA hired workers directly. That winter the CWA employed 4 million people, including 300,000 women. Under Hopkins's direction, the agency built or improved 1,000 airports, 500,000 miles of roads, 40,000 school buildings, and 3,500 playgrounds and parks. The cost of the CWA was huge— the program spent nearly $1 billion in just five months.

Although the CWA helped many people get through the winter, President Roosevelt was alarmed by how quickly the agency was spending money. He did not want Americans to get used to the federal government providing them with jobs. Warning that the CWA would "become a habit with the country," Roosevelt insisted that it be shut down the following spring.

Success of the First New Deal

During his first year in office, Roosevelt convinced Congress to pass an astonishing array of legislation. The programs enacted during the first New Deal did not restore prosperity, but they reflected Roosevelt's zeal for action and his willingness to experiment. Banks were reopened, many more people retained their homes and farms, and more people were employed. Perhaps the most important result of the first New Deal was a noticeable change in the spirit of the American people. Roosevelt's actions had inspired hope and restored Americans' faith in their nation.

✔ **Reading Check** **Identifying** What types of projects did public works programs undertake?

Section 1 REVIEW

Vocabulary

1. **Explain** the significance of: polio, New Deal, gold standard, bank holiday, Hundred Days, fireside chats, Civilian Conservation Corps.

Main Ideas

2. **Describing** What actions did Roosevelt take during the Hundred Days?

3. **Explaining** How did government regulate banks and the stock market in the first Roosevelt administration?

4. **Interpreting** How did the AAA affect farm prices?

5. **Organizing** Use a graphic organizer to list the major organizations of the First New Deal.

Roosevelt's New Agencies

Critical Thinking

6. **Big Ideas** In what ways did FDR's early experiences shape his political ideology?

7. **Analyzing Charts** Look at the time line on pages 426–427. How did the various agencies listed change the role of government?

Writing About History

8. **Expository Writing** Interview a member of your community who lived during the Great Depression. How did the New Deal programs affect your community? Create a one-page report using a word processor to summarize your findings.

History ONLINE
Study Central™ To review this section, go to glencoe.com and click on Study Central.

431

Answers

1. All definitions can be found in the section and the Glossary.

2. FDR began to fix the banks and stock market, help farmers and the unemployed, and assist industry, as well as provide debt relief.

3. Congress created the Securities and Exchange Commission and the Federal Deposit Insurance Corporation.

4. It increased farm prices by providing an incentive to plant and raise less.

5. Answers may include the following: Major organizations: HOLC (Home Owners' Loan Corporation); FCA (Farm Credit Administration); AAA (Agricultural Adjustment Administration); NRA (National Recovery Administration); CCC (Civilian Conservation Corps); FERA (Federal Emergency Relief Administration); PWA (Public Works Administration); CWA (Civil Works Administration); TVA (Tennessee Valley Authority).

6. FDR's privileged upbringing, love of outdoors, good marriage, polio, and various political offices shaped his political ideology.

7. Answers should match text information.

8. Students' journal entries will vary but should reflect a working day for a member of one of the relief agencies.

Focus

Tell students that prior to the New Deal, most Americans had very little contact with the federal government or federal agencies because the government was much smaller. Before the 1930s, the only federal agency with which most Americans had regular contact was the U.S. Postal Service. Ask students to name some federal agencies that individual citizens may come into contact with today.

Teach

R Reading Strategy

Predicting Ask student to read carefully the last paragraph in Source 1. **Ask:** To what other sort of national crisis does President Roosevelt compare the challenge of solving the Depression? *(war)* Based on his speech, what would you expect him to do next? *(take immediate action to solve the nation's economic problems, commit huge government resources and money to the task)* **OL** **AL**

Additional Support

ANALYZING PRIMARY SOURCES

The First New Deal

When FDR took office in 1933, the economy had been getting worse for more than three years. During the first one hundred days of his presidency, he oversaw 15 major pieces of legislation that attempted to revive the nation's economy and provide relief to the unemployed. Never before had the federal government intervened so directly in the economy. Key to stopping the economic downslide was FDR's ability to inspire confidence that the nation's economic problems could be solved.

Study these primary sources and answer the questions that follow.

PRIMARY SOURCE 2

Oral History Interview

"During the whole '33 one-hundred days' Congress, people didn't know what was going on, the public. Couldn't understand these things that were being passed so fast. They knew something was happening, something good for them. They began investing and working and hoping again. . . .

"A Depression is much like a run on a bank. It's a crisis of confidence. People panic and grab their money."

—Raymond Moley, original member of FDR's "brains trust"

Excerpted from *Hard Times: An Oral History of the Great Depression (1970)*

PRIMARY SOURCE 1

Inaugural Address, 1933

"I am certain that my fellow Americans expect that on my induction into the Presidency I will address them with a candor and a decision which the present situation of our nation impels. This is pre-eminently the time to speak the truth, the whole truth, frankly and boldly. . . .

"So, first of all, let me assert my firm belief that the only thing we have to fear is fear itself—nameless, unreasoning, unjustified terror which paralyzes needed efforts to convert retreat into advance. In every dark hour of our national life a leadership of frankness and vigor has met with that understanding and support of the people themselves which is essential to victory. I am convinced that you will again give that support to leadership in these critical days. . . .

"This Nation asks for action, and action now.

R "Our greatest primary task is to put people to work. This is no unsolvable problem if we face it wisely and courageously. It can be accomplished in part by direct recruiting by the Government itself, treating the task as we would treat the emergency of a war, but at the same time, through this employment, accomplishing greatly needed projects to stimulate and reorganize the use of our natural resources."

—President Franklin D. Roosevelt, first inaugural address, delivered March 4, 1933

Excerpted from *The Public Papers and Addresses of Franklin D. Roosevelt*

PRIMARY SOURCE 3

Magazine Cover, 1933

▶ *"The Faces of Victory and Defeat," portrayal of Herbert Hoover and Roosevelt on inauguration day, March 4, 1933*

Activity: Interdisciplinary Connection

Political Science Unlike most Western European nations, the United States did not have any national system of unemployment insurance or retirement benefits before the 1930s. Today, most Americans do not question the need to have at least a basic system of social insurance (for retirees, unemployed workers, persons with disabilities, impoverished children). Using library or Internet sources, have students compare the system of social insurance created by the New Deal with similar programs that existed in the 1930s in another country (suggest Canada, Britain, or Germany). Then, ask them to compare the social policies and programs in their chosen country today with those that exist in the United States today. **AL**

PRIMARY SOURCE 4

New Deal poster for the CCC, c. 1935 ▼

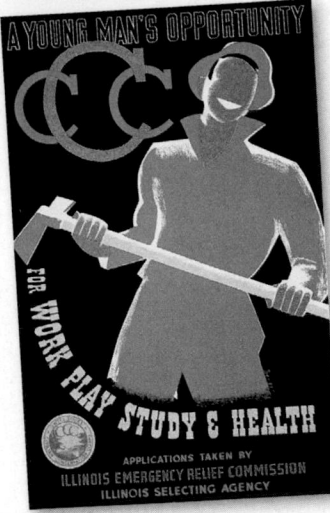

PRIMARY SOURCE 5

Oral History Interview

"What Roosevelt and the New Deal did was to turn about and face the realities. . . . A hundred years from now, when historians look back on it, they will say a big corner was turned. People agreed that old things didn't work. What ran through the whole New Deal was finding a way to make things work.

"Before that, Hoover would loan money to farmers to keep their mules alive, but wouldn't loan money to keep their children alive. This was perfectly right within the framework of classical thinking. If an individual couldn't get enough to eat, it was because he wasn't on the ball. It was his responsibility. The New Deal said: Anybody who is unemployed isn't necessarily unemployed because he's shiftless."

—Economist Gardiner C. Means, economic adviser in the Roosevelt administration

Excerpted from *Hard Times: An Oral History of the Great Depression* (1970)

D

PRIMARY SOURCE 7

Magazine Cover, 1934

▶ *Uncle Sam being tattooed with the initials of New Deal agencies (October 1934).*

PRIMARY SOURCE 6

Contemporary Book, 1934

W

"Even if the government conduct of business could give us the maximum of efficiency instead of least efficiency, it would be purchased at the cost of freedom. It would increase rather than decrease abuse and corruption, stifle initiative and invention, undermine the development of leadership, cripple the mental and spiritual energies of our people and the forces which make progress."

—Former president Herbert Hoover in his book, *The Challenge to Liberty* (1934)

Excerpted from *The Era of Franklin D. Roosevelt, 1933–1945*

DBQ Document-Based Questions

1. **Evaluating** What themes did Roosevelt emphasize in his inaugural address? How would you have responded to this speech if you had been an unemployed worker?

2. **Explaining** Study Sources 2 and 3. How did FDR inspire confidence and optimism? What effect did this have on the economy?

3. **Describing** In Source 4, the poster highlights four opportunities offered by the CCC. Describe some specific ways the CCC provided such opportunities.

4. **Paraphrasing** In Source 5, how does the author define Roosevelt's attitude toward unemployment and Hoover's approach to unemployment?

5. **Evaluating** In Source 6, why does Herbert Hoover object to the New Deal? What programs do you think he found most objectionable?

6. **Speculating** Study the picture in Source 7. How does the artist feel about the New Deal? What symbols are used to convey that message?

Answers

DBQ Document Based Questions

Answers:

1. Themes include truth and honesty, confidence, taking action, using the government to get people back to work. Answers will vary, but should note that most unemployed workers would respond positively to his message of hope.

2. Exerting a positive attitude (compare grinning FDR to dour Hoover) and getting legislation enacted inspired confidence. When people felt more confidence about the economy they were willing to invest and place money in banks again.

3. Answers will vary. Students may draw on examples from the previous section of the chapter.

4. Hoover's approach assumed direct aid, "the dole," to the poor would be bad for their personal character. Roosevelt's New Deal approach recognized farmers and unemployed workers were living in hardship due to forces beyond their control.

5. New Deal gives too much power to government, takes away personal freedom, and is less efficient than letting the free market solve economic problems. NRA and AAA are two good examples of programs that were attacked by conservatives.

6. Artist thinks the New Deal is distorting the nation and or national character. Uncle Sam is being tattooed (possibly disfigured) by a character in graduation cap and gown (likely an attack on the Ivy League idealists in FDR's administration).

433

Focus

Bellringer
Daily Focus Transparency 12.2

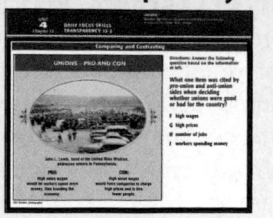

Guide to Reading

Answers may include the following: Legislation: Wagner Act; Provision: Workers had right to organize and to collective bargaining; Legislation: Social Security Act; Provision: security for retired workers, who received monthly checks beginning at age 65, unemployment insurance, and aid for people with certain disabilities and impoverished mothers with dependent children

Section Spotlight Video

To generate student interest and provide a springboard for class discussion, access the Chapter 12, Section 2 video at glencoe.com or on the video DVD.

Resource Manager

Section 2

The Second New Deal

Guide to Reading

Big Ideas
Economics and Society In 1935 Roosevelt introduced new programs to help unions, senior citizens, and the unemployed.

Content Vocabulary
• deficit spending (p. 434)
• binding arbitration (p. 438)
• sit-down strike (p. 438)

Academic Vocabulary
• benefit (p. 435)
• finance (p. 436)
• thereby (p. 437)

People and Events to Identify
• American Liberty League (p. 435)
• Works Progress Administration (p. 436)
• National Labor Relations Board (p. 437)
• Congress of Industrial Organizations (p. 439)
• Social Security Act (p. 439)

Reading Strategy
Organizing As you read about President Roosevelt's Second New Deal, complete a graphic organizer similar to the one below by filling in his main legislative successes during this period.

Legislation	Provisions

I n response to criticisms of the New Deal, President Roosevelt introduced several major pieces of legislation in 1935. These laws created the Works Progress Administration, the National Labor Relations Board, and the Social Security Administration.

Launching the Second New Deal

MAIN Idea By 1935, the New Deal faced political and legal challenges, as well as growing concern that it was not ending the Depression.

HISTORY AND YOU Do you know anyone who can easily convince others to follow his or her ideas? Read about several people who used this power against Roosevelt and his New Deal policies.

Harry Hopkins, head of the Federal Emergency Relief Administration, worked long hours in his Washington office, a bare, dingy room with exposed water pipes. Hopkins also took to the road to explain the New Deal. Once in Iowa, where he was discussing spending programs, someone called out, "Who's going to pay for it?" Hopkins peeled off his jacket, loosened his tie, and rolled up his sleeves, before roaring his response: "You are!"

President Roosevelt appreciated Harry Hopkins's feistiness. He needed effective speakers who were willing to contend with his adversaries. Although Roosevelt had been tremendously popular during his first two years in office, opposition to his policies had begun to grow.

The economy had shown only a slight improvement, even though the New Deal had been in effect for two years. Although the programs had created more than 2 million new jobs, more than 10 million workers remained unemployed, and the nation's total income was about half of what it had been in 1929.

Criticism From Left and Right

Hostility toward Roosevelt came from both the political right and the left. People on the right generally believed the New Deal regulated business too tightly. The right wing also included many Southern Democrats who believed the New Deal had expanded the federal government's power at the expense of states' rights.

The right wing, which had opposed the New Deal from the beginning, increased that opposition by late 1934. To pay for his programs, Roosevelt had started **deficit spending,** abandoning a balanced budget and borrowing money. Many business leaders became greatly alarmed at the government's growing deficit.

R **Reading Strategies**	C **Critical Thinking**	D **Differentiated Instruction**	W **Writing Support**	S **Skill Practice**
Teacher Edition • Academic Vocabulary, p. 435 • Act. Prior Know., p. 438 **Additional Resources** • Prim. Source Read., URB pp. 97, 99 • Guid. Read. Act., URB p. 111	**Teacher Edition** • Ident. Cent. Issues, p. 437 • Analyzing Prim. Sources, p. 438 **Additional Resources** • Supreme Court Case Studies, p. 51 • Quizzes and Tests, p. 166	**Teacher Edition** • Logical/Math, p. 436 **Additional Resources** • Diff. Inst., URB p. 85 • Enrichment Act., URB p. 107	**Teacher Edition** • Expository Writing, p. 436	**Additional Resources** • Reinforcing Skills Act., URB p. 93 • RENTG, p. 128

PRIMARY SOURCE
Opposition to the New Deal

By 1935 some Americans had grown impatient with the New Deal economic recovery. They believed that the reforms did not go far enough and called for wider-ranging change.

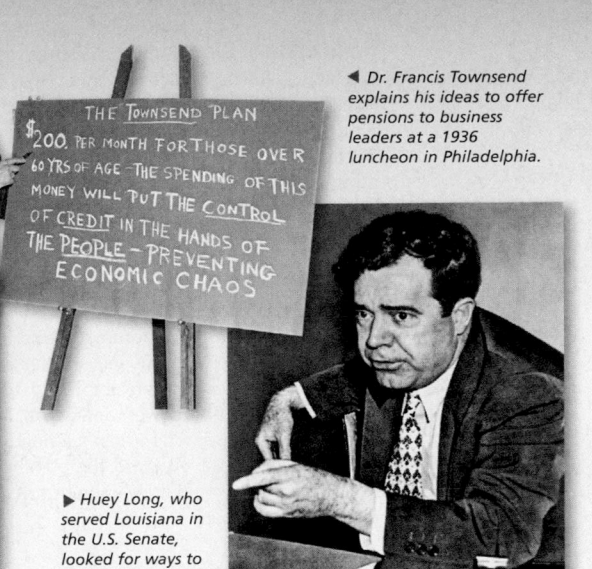

THE TOWNSEND PLAN
$200 PER MONTH FOR THOSE OVER 60 YRS OF AGE – THE SPENDING OF THIS MONEY WILL PUT THE CONTROL OF CREDIT IN THE HANDS OF THE PEOPLE – PREVENTING ECONOMIC CHAOS

◀ Dr. Francis Townsend explains his ideas to offer pensions to business leaders at a 1936 luncheon in Philadelphia.

▶ Huey Long, who served Louisiana in the U.S. Senate, looked for ways to redistribute wealth.

▲ Father Coughlin speaks to a crowd of 6,000 members of the National Union for Social Justice at the Hippodrome in Detroit shortly after the stock market collapse in 1929. By the mid-1930s, Coughlin favored massive taxes.

Analyzing VISUALS

1. **Comparing and Contrasting** What strikes you as the same and different about these three men?
2. **Assessing** Which man do you think would have the largest audience, and why?

In August 1934 business leaders and anti–New Deal politicians from both parties joined together to create the **American Liberty League.** Its purpose was to organize opposition to the New Deal and "teach the necessity of respect for the rights of person and property."

While criticisms from the right threatened to split the Democratic Party and reduce business support for Roosevelt, another serious challenge to the New Deal came from the political left. People on the left believed Roosevelt had not gone far enough. They wanted even more dramatic government economic intervention to shift wealth from the rich to middle-income and poor Americans.

Huey Long Perhaps the most serious threat came from Huey Long of Louisiana. As governor of Louisiana, Long had championed the poor and downtrodden. He had improved schools, colleges, and hospitals, and built roads and bridges. These **benefits** made Long popular, enabling him to build a powerful—but

corrupt—political machine. In 1930 Long was elected to the U.S. Senate.

Long's attacks on the rich were popular in the midst of the Great Depression. He captivated audiences with folksy humor and fiery oratory. By 1934, he had established a national organization, the Share Our Wealth Society, to promote his plan for massive redistribution of wealth. Long announced he would run for president in 1936.

Father Coughlin Roosevelt also faced a challenge from Father Charles Coughlin, a Catholic priest in Detroit. About 30 to 45 million listeners heard his weekly radio show.

Originally an ardent New Deal supporter, Coughlin had become impatient with its moderate reforms. He called instead for inflating the currency and nationalizing the banking system. In 1935 Coughlin organized the National Union for Social Justice, which some Democrats feared would become a new political party.

**History ONLINE
Student Web
Activity** Visit
glencoe.com
and complete the
activity on the
New Deal.

Chapter 12 Roosevelt and the New Deal **435**

Teach

R Reading Strategy
Academic Vocabulary Point out the term *benefits* near the end of the first column. Tell students that the Latin root *bene* means "well." Ask students to brainstorm other words that incorporate this root. *(beneficiary, benevolent, benediction)* **OL**

Analyzing VISUALS

Answers:
1. Students' responses will vary but may mention the more cheerful appearance of Father Coughlin and the different means each man used to spread his message. Each offered specific solutions to the nations problems.
2. Students may say that Father Coughlin had the largest audience because he used the modern medium of radio rather than the more personal approach Townsend used.

Hands-On Chapter Project
Step 2

Writing a Newspaper

Step 2: Write and Plan Newspaper Copy Students begin to write articles and editorials and to draw cartoons based on the content of Section 1.

Directions Remind students to include the basic facts in news stories and to support opinions in editorials and letters to the editor. Have them plan the length of their newspaper and begin to write to fit that length. Encourage students to find templates online or in word processing software that can help them place copy in newspaper format.

Putting It Together Invite a teacher familiar with word processing programs to class to offer a tutorial for students unfamiliar with the software and how to use it.
(Chapter Project continued on page 441)

D Differentiated Instruction

Logical/Mathematical Invite students to depict the information on the WPA's achievements in graph form. Suggest they use a bar or circle graph. **OL**

W Writing Support

Expository Writing Have students use library or Internet resources to find out more about the women and men supported through Federal Number One. Ask students to use their findings to write a short essay describing the artists or their works. **OL**

✔ Reading Check

Answer:
The economy did not improve quickly after two years. Right wing critics of the New Deal felt that it regulated business too tightly. Southern Democrats feared the expansion of the federal government. Business leaders opposed Roosevelt's deficit spending. Critics on the left felt the New Deal had not gone far enough.

Additional Support

The Townsend Plan A third challenge came from Francis Townsend, a California physician. Townsend proposed that the federal government pay citizens over age 60 a pension of $200 a month. Recipients would have to retire and spend their entire pension check each month. He believed the plan would increase spending and remove people from the workforce, freeing up jobs for the unemployed.

Townsend's proposal attracted millions of supporters, especially among older Americans, who mobilized as a political force for the first time. Townsend's program was particularly popular in the West. When combined with Long's support in the Midwest and South, and Coughlin's support among urban Catholics in the Northeast, Roosevelt faced the possibility of a coalition that would draw enough votes to prevent his reelection.

The WPA

Roosevelt was also disturbed by the failure of the New Deal to generate a rapid economic recovery. In 1935 he launched a series of programs now known as the Second New Deal.

D Among these new programs was the **Works Progress Administration** (WPA). Headed by Harry Hopkins, the WPA was the largest public works program of the New Deal. Between 1935 and 1941, the WPA spent $11 billion. Its 8.5 million workers constructed about 650,000 miles of highways, roads, and streets, 125,000 public buildings, and more than 8,000 parks. It built or improved more than 124,000 bridges and 853 airports.

W The WPA's most controversial program was Federal Number One, a program for artists, musicians, theater people, and writers. The artists created thousands of murals and sculptures for public buildings. Musicians established 30 symphony orchestras, as well as hundreds of smaller musical groups. The Federal Theater Project **financed** playwrights, actors, and directors. It also funded writers who recorded the stories of former slaves and others whose voices were not often heard.

The Supreme Court's Role

In May 1935, in *Schechter Poultry Company v. United States*, the Supreme Court unanimously struck down the authority of the National Recovery Administration. The Schechter broth-

ers had been convicted of violating the NRA's poultry code.

The Court ruled that the Constitution did not allow Congress to delegate its legislative powers to the executive branch. Thus, it declared the NRA's codes unconstitutional. Although relieved to be rid of that "awful headache," the NRA, Roosevelt still worried about the ruling. It suggested that the Court could strike down the rest of the New Deal.

Roosevelt knew he needed a new series of programs to keep voters' support. He called congressional leaders to a White House conference. Pounding his desk, he thundered that Congress could not go home until it passed his new bills. That summer, Congress worked busily to pass Roosevelt's programs.

✔ **Reading Check** **Identifying Points of View** What criticisms prompted the Second New Deal?

Debates IN HISTORY

Was the New Deal Socialistic?

Franklin Roosevelt took extraordinary measures to stimulate the economy with his New Deal programs. Many Americans were divided on the issue of increased government intervention in the economy. Some claimed the New Deal was socialistic and a violation of American values. Others thought the New Deal did not do enough to help Americans.

Extending the Content

Federal Writers' Project The Federal Writers' Project was one of four segments of Federal One, which also included components in music, theater, and art. To avoid the controversy that might come from allowing writers to produce works of the imagination, the Federal Writers' Project asked authors to focus on nonfiction. A series of popular guidebooks, the American Guide series, was produced for each state, as well as major counties and cities, interstate highway routes, and areas of the nation. Interviews and oral histories of formerly enslaved persons, farm and mill owners, and others published in *These Are Our Lives* gave new dimensions to American history. At its peak in 1936, the Federal Writers' Project employed 6,700 writers. Some 10,000 writers gained employment through the program, producing more than 1,000 publications.

Reforms for Workers and Senior Citizens

MAIN Idea Roosevelt asked Congress to pass the Wagner Act and Social Security to build support among workers and older Americans.

HISTORY AND YOU Do you have an older relative who has retired from his or her job? Read about benefits created by the Social Security Act.

When the Supreme Court struck down the NRA, it also invalidated the section of the NIRA that gave workers the right to organize. President Roosevelt and the Democrats in Congress knew that the working-class vote was very important in winning reelection in 1936. They also believed that unions could help end the Depression. They thought that high union wages would give workers more money to spend, **thereby** boosting the economy. Opponents disagreed, arguing that high wages forced companies to charge higher prices and hire fewer people. Despite these concerns, Congress pushed ahead with new labor legislation.

The Wagner Act

In July 1935 Congress passed the National Labor Relations Act (also called the Wagner Act after its author, Senator Robert Wagner of New York). The act guaranteed workers the right to organize unions and to bargain collectively. It also set up the **National Labor Relations Board** (NLRB), which organized factory elections by secret ballot to determine whether workers wanted a union.

C Critical Thinking

Identifying Central Issues Have students create word webs to record the provisions of the Wagner Act. Remind them to use these graphic organizers as study aids. **BL**

Debates IN HISTORY

Answers:
1. Students may say that Smith's call for a balanced budget, which was part of the 1932 platform, seems valid.
2. The New Deal accepts the basic institutions and loyalties of the present system, while the Socialist Party wants to replace the system.
3. Students' answers will vary.
4. Students' answers will vary.

YES

Alfred E. Smith
Former Democratic Candidate

PRIMARY SOURCE

"Now what would I have my party do? I would have them re-declare the principles that they put forth in that 1932 platform [reduce the size of government, balance the federal budget] . . .

Just get the platform of the Democratic party and get the platform of the Socialist party and . . . make your mind up to pick up the platform that more nearly squares with the record, and you will have your hand on the Socialist platform. . . .

[I]t is all right with me, if they want to disguise themselves as Karl Marx or Lenin or any of the rest of that bunch, but I won't stand for their allowing them to march under the banner of Jackson or Cleveland."

—speech delivered January 25, 1936

NO

Norman Thomas
Socialist Party Candidate

PRIMARY SOURCE

"All of these leaders or would-be leaders out of our wilderness, however they may abuse one another, however loosely they may fling around the charge of socialism or communism—still accept the basic institutions and loyalties of the present system. A true Socialist is resolved to replace that system. . . .

The New Deal did not say, as socialism would have said, 'Here are so many millions of American people who need to be well fed and well clothed. How much food and cotton do we require?' We should require more, not less. What Mr. Roosevelt said was 'How much food and cotton can be produced for which the exploited masses must pay a higher price?'"

—speech delivered February 2, 1936

DBQ Document-Based Questions

1. **Distinguishing Fact From Opinion** Compare Smith's attack on the New Deal with what you have read about it elsewhere. Does he make any valid points?

2. **Contrasting** According to Thomas, how are the principles of the New Deal and those of the Socialist Party different?

3. **Evaluating** Which speaker do you find more persuasive? Why?

4. **Hypothesizing** Do you think either speaker would be able to persuade someone who did not agree with him to reconsider his or her attitude?

Additional Support

Chapter 12   Roosevelt and the New Deal   **437**

Activity: Interdisciplinary Connection

Language Arts The question of whether the New Deal was socialistic in nature began in light of disillusionment with Roosevelt's policies. The conservatives charged that Roosevelt was considering a fascist dictatorship and later changed their rhetoric to suggest the administration was proposing "absolute communism." The debate grew louder as the 1934 elections approached and has continued among historians to this day. **Ask: How does word choice influence the nature of a debate?** *(Students may note that name calling and labeling inflame opinions but do not clarify issues.)* **If the United States had not vigorously opposed communism and socialism, would labeling something socialistic provoke such intense feelings?** *(Students may suggest that these terms gained power to generate intense feelings primarily based on the Red Scare of 1919. Had the United States not given much attention to the movement, words such as socialism would not be likely to create such intense feelings.)* **OL**

The Wagner Act also set up a process called **binding arbitration** whereby dissatisfied union members could take their complaints to a neutral party who would listen to both sides and decide on the issues. The NLRB could investigate employers' actions and stop unfair practices, such as spying on workers.

The CIO Is Formed The Wagner Act led to a burst of labor activity. John L. Lewis led the United Mine Workers union. He worked with several other unions to organize industrial workers. They formed the Committee for Industrial Organization (CIO) in 1935.

The CIO set out to organize unions that included all workers, skilled and unskilled, in a particular industry. It focused first on the automobile and steel industries—two of the largest industries in which workers were not yet unionized.

Sit-Down Strikes Union organizers used new tactics, such as the **sit-down strike,** in which employees stopped work inside the factory and refused to leave. (This technique prevented management from sending in replacement workers.) First used effectively to organize rubber workers, the sit-down strike became a common CIO tactic for several years.

The United Auto Workers (UAW), a CIO union, initiated a series of sit-down strikes against General Motors. On December 31, 1936, the workers at General Motor's plant in Flint, Michigan, began a sit-down strike. The UAW strikers held the factory for weeks, while spouses, friends, and other supporters passed them food and other provisions through windows. A journalist who was allowed to enter the plant reported on conditions in the factory:

PRIMARY SOURCE

"Beds were made up on the floor of each car, the seats being removed if necessary. . . . I could not see—and I looked for it carefully—the slightest damage done anywhere to the General Motors Corporation. The nearly completed car bodies, for example, were as clean as they would be in the salesroom, their glass and metal shining."

—quoted in *The Great Depression*

Violence broke out in Flint when police launched a tear gas assault on one of the plants. The police wounded 13 strikers, but the strike held. On February 11, 1937, the company gave in and recognized the UAW as its employees' sole bargaining agent. The UAW became one of the most powerful unions in the United States.

PRIMARY SOURCE
The CIO Uses Sit-Down Strikes

▲ *Sit-down strikers at the GM Fisher Body plant in Flint, Michigan, take over the plant on December 30, 1936. Their action led to a national strike that lasted until February 11, 1937.*

Union Membership, 1933–1940

Members (thousands): 10,000 / 8,000 / 6,000 / 4,000 / 2,000 / 0

1933 1934 1935 1936 1937 1938 1939 1940

Source: *Historical Statistics of the United States.*

Analyzing VISUALS

1. **Analyzing** How can you tell from the men's appearance and activities that they intend to stay?
2. **Summarizing** When did union membership increase the most? How can you account for this jump?

Activity: Interdisciplinary Connection

Civics Explain to students that sit-down strikes were a form of nonviolent protest that would be used extensively during the Civil Rights Movement of the 1960s. Invite students to use library or Internet resources to find other instances of the technique as well as the 1930s Supreme Court rulings on the legality of the strikes. Ask students to write a brief summary or create a time line to show their findings. Invite volunteers to share their finished work with the class. **AL**

U.S. Steel, the nation's largest steel producer and a long-standing opponent of unionizing, decided it did not want to repeat the General Motors experience. In March 1937 the company recognized the CIO's steelworkers union. Smaller steel producers did not follow suit and suffered bitter strikes. By 1941, however, the steelworkers union had won contracts throughout the industry.

In the late 1930s, workers in other industries worked hard to gain union recognition from their employers. Union membership tripled from roughly 3 million in 1933 to about 9 million in 1939. In 1938 the CIO changed its name to the **Congress of Industrial Organizations** and became a federation of industrial unions.

Social Security

After passing the Wagner Act, Congress began work on one of America's most important pieces of legislation. This was the **Social Security Act.** Its major goal was to provide some security for older Americans and unemployed workers.

Roosevelt and his advisers spent months preparing the bill, which they viewed primarily as an insurance measure. Workers earned the right to receive benefits because they paid premiums, just as they did in buying a life insurance policy. The premiums were a tax paid to the federal government. The legislation also provided modest welfare payments to other needy people, including those with disabilities and poor mothers with dependent children.

The core of Social Security was the monthly retirement benefit, which people could collect when they stopped working at age 65. Another important benefit, unemployment insurance, supplied a temporary income to unemployed workers looking for new jobs. Some critics did not like the fact that the money came from payroll taxes imposed on workers and employers, but to Roosevelt these taxes were crucial: "We put those payroll contributions there so as to give the contributors a legal, moral, and political right to collect their pensions and their unemployment benefits."

Since the people receiving benefits had already paid for them, he explained, "no . . . politician can ever scrap my social security program." What Roosevelt did not anticipate was that, in the future, Congress would borrow money from the Social Security fund to pay for other programs while failing to raise payroll deductions enough to pay for the benefits.

Although Social Security helped many people, initially it left out many of the neediest—farm and domestic workers. Some 65 percent of all African American workers in the 1930s fell into these two categories. Nevertheless, Social Security established the principle that the federal government should be responsible for those who, through no fault of their own, were unable to work.

✓ **Reading Check** **Explaining** How did the Social Security Act protect workers?

Section 2 REVIEW

Vocabulary
1. **Explain** the significance of: deficit spending, American Liberty League, Works Progress Administration, National Labor Relations Board, binding arbitration, sit-down strike, Congress of Industrial Organizations, Social Security Act.

Main Ideas
2. **Summarizing** How did the ideas of Father Coughlin, Senator Long, and Dr. Townsend differ?

3. **Analyzing** Why was the Social Security Act an important piece of legislation?

Critical Thinking
4. **Big Ideas** How did the New Deal contribute to the growth of industrial unions?

5. **Organizing** Use a graphic organizer similar to the one below to list the political challenges Roosevelt faced in his first term.

Political Challenges

6. **Analyzing Visuals** Look again at the photo of Dr. Townsend on page 435. How does he intend to prevent economic chaos?

Writing About History
7. **Persuasive Writing** Choose one of the figures who criticized the New Deal. Write an editorial to the local newspaper expressing why people should be in favor of or opposed to that person's ideas.

History ONLINE
Study Central™ To review this section, go to glencoe.com and click on Study Central.

Reading Check

Answer:
It provided temporary income to unemployed workers looking for new jobs and a small pension for retired workers.

Assess
· · · · · · · · · · · · · · · · · · · ·

History ONLINE

Study Central™ provides summaries, interactive games, and online graphic organizers to help students review content.

Close
· · · · · · · · · · · · · · · · · · · ·

Summarizing Ask: *What were some of the criticisms of the New Deal? (Some detractors thought that Roosevelt was not doing enough to help the American people, while others feared the plan resembled socialism and did not align with American values. There was also great concern about the growing deficit.)* **OL**

Section 2 REVIEW

Answers

1. All definitions can be found in the section and the Glossary.
2. Coughlin: tax the rich and nationalize the banking system; Long: share the wealth; Townsend: pensions for the elderly
3. It provided a basic social safety net for the elderly, the unemployed, and other vulnerable groups.
4. The Wagner Act encouraged workers to organize unions and set up a process to protect unions as they developed.

5. American Liberty League, left-wing Democrats, the Depression had not ended
6. by putting control of credit in the hands of the people by giving $200 a month to those over 60
7. Students' editorials will vary but should express an opinion and support it.

Focus

Bellringer

Daily Focus Transparency 12.3

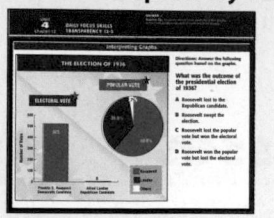

Guide to Reading

The New Deal Coalition
I. Roosevelt's Second Term
   A. The Election of 1936
   B. The Court-Packing Plan
   C. The Recession of 1937
II. The New Deal Ends
   A. The Last New Deal Reforms
   B. The New Deal's Legacy

Section Spotlight Video

To generate student interest and provide a springboard for class discussion, access the Chapter 12, Section 3 video at glencoe.com or on the video DVD.

Resource Manager

The New Deal Coalition

Guide to Reading

Big Ideas
Group Action Backed by a new coalition of voters FDR easily won reelection, but conservative opposition prevented the passage of additional reforms.

Content Vocabulary
- court-packing (p. 442)
- broker state (p. 445)
- safety net (p. 445)

Academic Vocabulary
- recovery (p. 442)
- mediate (p. 445)

People and Events to Identify
- Frances Perkins (p. 441)
- Henry Morgenthau (p. 442)
- John Maynard Keynes (p. 442)

Reading Strategy
Taking Notes As you read, create an outline similar to the one below.

The New Deal Coalition
I. Roosevelt's Second Term
   A.
   B.
   C.
II.
   A.
   B.

President Roosevelt won a landslide reelection victory in 1936. Early in his second term, however, his court-packing plan and a new recession hurt him politically. The Fair Labor Standards Act, the last significant piece of New Deal legislation, provided new protections for workers.

Roosevelt's Second Term

MAIN Idea Roosevelt was easily reelected, but the New Deal lost momentum during his second term due to his court-packing plan and a new recession.

HISTORY AND YOU Does your family rent or own your home? Read how the New Deal started programs that tried to make home ownership more affordable.

Since the Civil War, African Americans had been reliable Republican voters. The Republican Party was the party of both Abraham Lincoln and emancipation. In the 1930s, however, this allegiance unraveled. The Great Depression had hit African Americans hard, and the Republican Party had done little to help. To many African Americans, it seemed their votes were taken for granted. That was certainly the sentiment of Robert L. Vann, editor of the *Pittsburgh Courier,* Pennsylvania's leading African American newspaper. Vann decided it was time for a change and started a campaign to persuade African Americans to join the Democratic Party. "My friends, go turn Lincoln's picture to the wall," he told audiences. "That debt has been paid in full."

The dramatic shift in party allegiance by African Americans was part of a historic political realignment the New Deal triggered. As the election of 1936 approached, millions of voters owed their jobs, mortgages, and bank accounts to the New Deal, and they knew it.

The white South, which had been the core of the Democratic Party, now became just one part of a new coalition that included farmers, industrial workers, African Americans, new immigrants, ethnic minorities, women, progressives, and intellectuals. First Lady Eleanor Roosevelt helped bring about the change in the African American and women's vote. She had demonstrated strong sympathies toward African Americans in her many tours of the country. She recounted her experiences to her husband and persuaded him to address at least some of their problems in his New Deal programs.

African Americans made some modest gains during the New Deal. The president appointed several African Americans to positions in his administration, where they informally became known as the Black Cabinet. FDR also tried to see that public works projects included African Americans.

R Reading Strategies	**C** Critical Thinking	**D** Differentiated Instruction	**W** Writing Support	**S** Skill Practice
Teacher Edition • Act. Prior Know., p. 442 • Read. Prim. Sources, p. 444 • Academic Vocab., p. 445 **Additional Resources** • Guid. Read. Act., URB p. 112	**Teacher Edition** • Drawing Con., p. 442 • Analyzing Info., p. 444 **Additional Resources** • Quizzes and Tests, p. 167	**Teacher Edition** • Visual/Spatial, p. 441 **Additional Resources** • Auth Assess., p. 29 • Reteach. Act., URB p. 105	**Teacher Edition** • Expository Writing, p. 441	**Additional Resources** • RENTG, p. 131 • Time Line Act., URB p. 95

PRIMARY SOURCE
Building the New Deal Coalition

By creating programs that addressed the needs of different groups in American society, the New Deal created a new voting coalition: African Americans, women, and laborers.

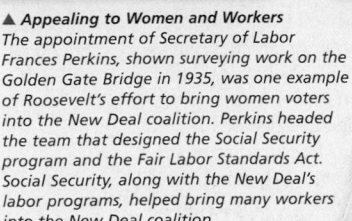

▲ **Appealing to Women and Workers**
The appointment of Secretary of Labor Frances Perkins, shown surveying work on the Golden Gate Bridge in 1935, was one example of Roosevelt's effort to bring women voters into the New Deal coalition. Perkins headed the team that designed the Social Security program and the Fair Labor Standards Act. Social Security, along with the New Deal's labor programs, helped bring many workers into the New Deal coalition.

▲ **New Deal Raises African American Hopes**
Mary McLeod Bethune, shown with Eleanor Roosevelt, was appointed in 1936 as director of the Office of Minority Affairs within the National Youth Association. Bethune became the first black woman to head a federal agency. Roosevelt also relied on an informal advisory group, the "Black Cabinet," also known as the "Black Brain Trust." FDR failed in some areas of civil rights, such as not opposing poll taxes for fear of causing Southern Democrats to block New Deal programs.

Analyzing VISUALS

1. **Analyzing** Look at the photo of Frances Perkins and the workers. What clues do you get that she took her job seriously?

2. **Evaluating** What mood does the photograph of Mary McLeod Bethune and Eleanor Roosevelt convey?

▲ **A New Deal for Native Americans**
Commissioner of Indian Affairs John Collier, shown here consulting with Native American leaders in South Dakota, helped create the Indian Reorganization Act of 1934. The act reversed the Dawes Act's policy of assimilation. It restored some reservation lands, gave Native Americans control over those lands, and permitted them to elect their own governments.

A similar policy guided FDR's approach to women. He appointed the first woman to a cabinet post, Secretary of Labor **Frances Perkins,** and appointed many other women to lower-level posts. He also appointed two female diplomats and a female federal judge. Despite these gains, New Deal programs paid women lower wages than men.

D The Election of 1936

To challenge President Roosevelt's reelection bid, the Republicans nominated Alfred Landon, the governor of Kansas. Although Landon favored some New Deal policies, he declared it was time "to unshackle initiative and free the spirit of American enterprise." Landon was unable to convince the majority of American voters it was time for a change. Roosevelt and the New Deal that he represented remained very popular, and on Election Day, Roosevelt swept to victory in one of the largest landslides in American history. He won more than 60 percent of the popular vote and carried every state except Maine and Vermont.

Chapter 12 Roosevelt and the New Deal **441**

Teach

W Writing Support
Expository Writing Invite students to find out more about the women whom Roosevelt appointed to government posts. Suggest that students focus on one woman or on one arena, such as federal judges or diplomats. Have students write a one-page summary of their findings. **OL**

D Differentiated Instruction
Visual/Spatial Ask students to create election maps of the 1932 and 1936 elections. Remind them to make a key. Ask them to compare the results and report their findings to the class. **OL**

Analyzing VISUALS

Answers:
1. She is wearing a hard hat, intending to be on the construction site rather than just reading or hearing about it.
2. Both are laughing, as is one of the men in the background. There is a sense of a pleasant meeting of friends.

Hands-On Chapter Project
Step 3

Writing a Newspaper

Step 3: Copyedit and Content Edit the Paper Students submit their articles to designated "editors" who evaluate both the content and the grammar of the pieces.

Directions Ask each group to choose a person to be the editor. Then have groups exchange their articles so that an objective, outside reader sees each one. Then have students revise according to the feedback they receive.

Putting It Together Remind students that careful editing involves an attention to detail and to factual accuracy. Encourage editors to find positive comments to make about each piece they edit.
(Chapter Project continued on the Visual Summary page)

C Critical Thinking

Drawing Conclusions

Ask: What have you already learned about Roosevelt that prepares you to read that he was "furious" that the Supreme Court declared the Agricultural Adjustment Act unconstitutional? *(He was intensely competitive; he had held executive office before on the state level and was used to command and power)* Ask students what other steps might Roosevelt have taken instead of his court-packing plan. *(He might have gone to the members individually and talked with them.)* **OL**

R Reading Strategy

Activating Prior Knowledge

Ask students how a house of Congress can "kill" a bill. *(Bills can die in committee or never be brought to the floor for a vote.)* **OL**

Reading Check

Answer:
court-packing plan and recession

**Additional
Support**

The Court-Packing Plan

Although many people supported the New Deal, the Supreme Court saw things differently. In January 1936, in *United States* v. *Butler,* the Court had declared the Agricultural Adjustment Act unconstitutional. With cases pending on Social Security and the Wagner Act, it was possible that the Court would strike down most of the major New Deal programs.

Roosevelt was furious that a handful of jurists, "nine old men" as he called them, were blocking the wishes of a majority of the people. After winning reelection, he decided to try to change the political balance on the Court. In March 1937 he sent Congress a bill to increase the number of justices. It proposed that if any justice had served for 10 years and did not retire within six months after reaching the age of 70, the president could appoint an additional justice to the Court. Since four justices were in their 70s and two more were in their late 60s, the bill, if passed, would allow Roosevelt to quickly appoint as many as six new justices.

The **court-packing** plan, as the press called it, was Roosevelt's first serious political mistake. Although Congress had the power to change the Court's size, the scheme created the impression that the president was trying to undermine the Court's independence.

The issue split the Democratic Party. Many Southern Democrats feared Roosevelt's plan would put justices on the Court who would overturn segregation. At the same time, African American leaders worried that once Roosevelt set the precedent of changing the Court's makeup, a future president might pack the Court with justices opposed to civil rights. Many Americans believed the plan would give the president too much power.

Despite the uproar, Roosevelt's actions appeared to force the Supreme Court to back down. In April 1937, the Court upheld the constitutionality of the Wagner Act by a vote of 5-4 in the case *National Labor Relations Board* v. *Jones and Laughlin Steel Corporation.* In May the Court narrowly upheld the Social Security Act in *Steward Machine Company* v. *Davis.* Shortly afterward, a conservative justice resigned, enabling Roosevelt to appoint a New Deal supporter to the Court.

In mid-July the Senate quietly killed the court-packing bill without bringing it to a vote.

Roosevelt achieved his goal of changing the Court's view of the New Deal. The fight over the court-packing plan, however, hurt his reputation and encouraged conservative Democrats to work with Republicans to block any further New Deal proposals.

The Recession of 1937

In late 1937 Roosevelt's reputation again suffered when unemployment suddenly surged. Early in the year, the economy had seemed on the verge of full **recovery.** Industrial output was almost back to pre-Depression levels, and many people believed the worst was over. Roosevelt decided it was time to balance the budget. Concerned about the dangers of too much debt, Roosevelt ordered the WPA and the PWA to be cut significantly. Unfortunately, Roosevelt cut spending just as the first Social Security payroll taxes removed $2 billion from the economy, which plummeted. By the end of 1937, about 2 million people had been thrown out of work.

The recession of 1937 led to a debate inside Roosevelt's administration. Treasury Secretary **Henry Morgenthau** favored balancing the budget and cutting spending. This would encourage business leaders to invest in the economy. Harry Hopkins, head of the WPA, and Harold Ickes, head of the PWA, both disagreed. They pushed for more government spending using a new theory called Keynesianism to support their arguments.

Keynesianism was based on the theories of an influential British economist named **John Maynard Keynes.** In 1936 Keynes published a book arguing that government should spend heavily in a recession, even if it required deficit spending, to jump-start the economy.

According to Keynesian economics, Roosevelt had done the wrong thing when he cut back programs in 1937. At first, Roosevelt was reluctant to begin deficit spending again. Many critics believed the recession proved the public was becoming too dependent on government spending. Finally, in the spring of 1938, with no recovery in sight, Roosevelt asked Congress for $3.75 billion for the PWA, the WPA, and other programs.

Reading Check **Summarizing** What events weakened Roosevelt's reputation in 1937?

Activity: Economics Connection

Keynesian Economics Invite students to use library or Internet resources to find out more about Keynesian theory and how it affected the New Deal. Suggest that students use charts and graphs to show the economic changes between 1932 and 1941, when the war economy effectively ended the Great Depression. Ask students to determine how effective they believe Keynesian theory was during Roosevelt's time and if it is a valid theory. Have them record their thoughts in a brief essay. **AL**

ANALYZING SUPREME COURT CASES

Can Government Regulate Business

★ *Schechter Poultry v. United States* (1935)
★ *NLRB v. Jones & Laughlin Steel Corp.* (1937)

Background to the Cases

These two cases look at the federal government's right to regulate interstate commerce. In the *Schechter* case, the Court overturned the NIRA and the industrial codes that regulated business. In the *Jones & Laughlin* case, Chief Justice Hughes switched sides from the *Schechter* case and upheld the Wagner Act's labor regulations. The case marks the Supreme Court's shift toward upholding New Deal legislation.

How the Court Ruled

Both cases addressed the question of federal power to regulate interstate commerce. In the *Schechter* case, the Court ruled that the federal government could regulate only business activity that was *directly* related to interstate commerce. In the *NLRB* case, the Court extended congressional power to regulate commerce and upheld the constitutionality of the Wagner Act.

▲ *In this 1937 cartoon, the donkey, a symbol of the Democratic Party, kicks up a storm and the dove of peace flies off, dropping the olive branch, in response to FDR's court-packing plan.*

PRIMARY SOURCE

The Court's Opinion

"The persons employed in slaughtering and selling in local trade are not employed in interstate commerce. Their hours and wages have no direct relation to interstate commerce. The question of how many hours these employees should work and what they should be paid differs in no essential respect from similar questions in other local businesses which handle commodities brought into a state and there dealt in as a part of its internal commerce. . . .

On both the grounds we have discussed, the attempted delegation of legislative power and the attempted regulation of intrastate transactions which affect interstate commerce only indirectly, we hold the code provisions here in question to be invalid."

—Chief Justice Charles E. Hughes
writing for the Court in *Schechter* v. *U.S.*

PRIMARY SOURCE

Dissenting Views

"The fundamental principle is that the power to regulate commerce is the power to enact 'all appropriate legislation' for its 'protection or advancement' . . . Although activities may be intrastate in character when separately considered, if they have such a close and substantial relation to interstate commerce that their control is essential or appropriate to protect that commerce from burdens and obstructions, Congress cannot be denied the power to exercise that control.

When industries organize themselves on a national scale . . . . how can it be maintained that their industrial labor relations constitute a forbidden field into which Congress may not enter when it is necessary to protect interstate commerce from the paralyzing consequences of industrial war?"

—Chief Justice Charles E. Hughes
writing for the Court in *NLRB* v. *Jones & Laughlin Steel Corporation*

DBQ Document-Based Questions

1. **Explaining** In *Schechter*, why does the Court assert that poultry workers are not engaged in interstate commerce?
2. **Analyzing** In the *NLRB* decision, how has the Court's reasoning changed?
3. **Drawing Conclusions** How would you explain the shift in the Court's attitude toward federal labor regulations?

Teach

Sometimes termed the "Sick Chicken Case," *Schechter Poultry* v. *U.S.* brought down the NIRA. Chief Justice Hughes made three arguments against the NIRA:

1. The NIRA gave legislative power to the executive branch.
2. There was no constitutional authority for the legislation.
3. Businesses that were intrastate in nature could not be subjected to federal regulation.

DBQ Document Based Questions

Answers:
1. Their hours and wages have no direct relations to interstate commerce.
2. It decides that because industries organize themselves nationally, industrial labor relations are not a field forbidden to Congress.
3. Students may suggest that the Court had adopted a broader interpretation of the commerce clause or the Court was afraid to knock down a popular New Deal program.

Differentiated Instruction

Identifying Cause-and-Effect: Recession and Depression

Economics and History Activity 4, URB p. 7–8

Objective: Identify the causes and effects of recessions and depressions.

Focus: Read the information on recessions and depressions.

Teach: Define *recession* and *depression* and list the causes and effects of each.

Assess: Make a list of the things that will need to happen to lift the economy out of a recession or depression.

Close: Create a poster illustrating an economic cycle from boom to recession.

Differentiated Instruction Strategies

BL Identify two causes of recession and the resulting effects on businesses.

AL Research unemployment rates during the recession periods and write a short report of the results.

ELL Underline any words that are unclear. Use a dictionary or develop a definition for each word.

R Reading Strategy

Reading Primary Sources
Ask: What does Roosevelt say is the test of progress? *(whether we provide enough for those who have too little)* `OL`

C Critical Thinking

Analyzing Information Ask students to create graphic organizers to note the three final New Deal reforms as they read. *(National Housing Act, Farm Security Administration, Fair Labor Standards Act)* `BL`

Analyzing VISUALS

Answers:
1. the Securities and Exchange Commission
2. Department of Housing and Urban Development

Additional Support

The New Deal Ends

MAIN Idea The New Deal expanded federal power over the economy and established a social safety net.

HISTORY AND YOU Do you think the government should help those in need? Read how people felt about the government as the New Deal came to an end.

In his second Inaugural Address, Roosevelt had pointed out that despite the nation's progress in climbing out of the Depression, many Americans were still poor:

PRIMARY SOURCE

"I see one-third of a nation ill-housed, ill-clad, ill-nourished. . . . The test of our progress is not whether we add more to the abundance of those who have much; it is whether we provide enough for those who have too little."

—from *The Public Papers and Addresses of Franklin D. Roosevelt*

The Last New Deal Reforms

One of the president's goals for his second term was to provide better housing for the nation's poor. Eleanor Roosevelt, who had toured poverty-stricken Appalachia and the rural South, strongly urged the president to do something. Roosevelt responded with the National Housing Act, establishing the United States Housing Authority. This organization received $500 million to subsidize loans for builders willing to provide low-cost housing.

Roosevelt also sought to help the nation's tenant farmers. Before being shut down, the AAA had paid farmers to take land out of production. In doing so, it had inadvertently hurt tenant farmers. Landowners had expelled tenants from the land to take it out of production. As a result, some 150,000 white and 195,000 African American tenants left farming during the 1930s. To stop this trend, Congress created the Farm Security Administration to give loans to tenants so they could purchase farms.

INFOGRAPHIC
What New Deal Programs Still Exist Today?

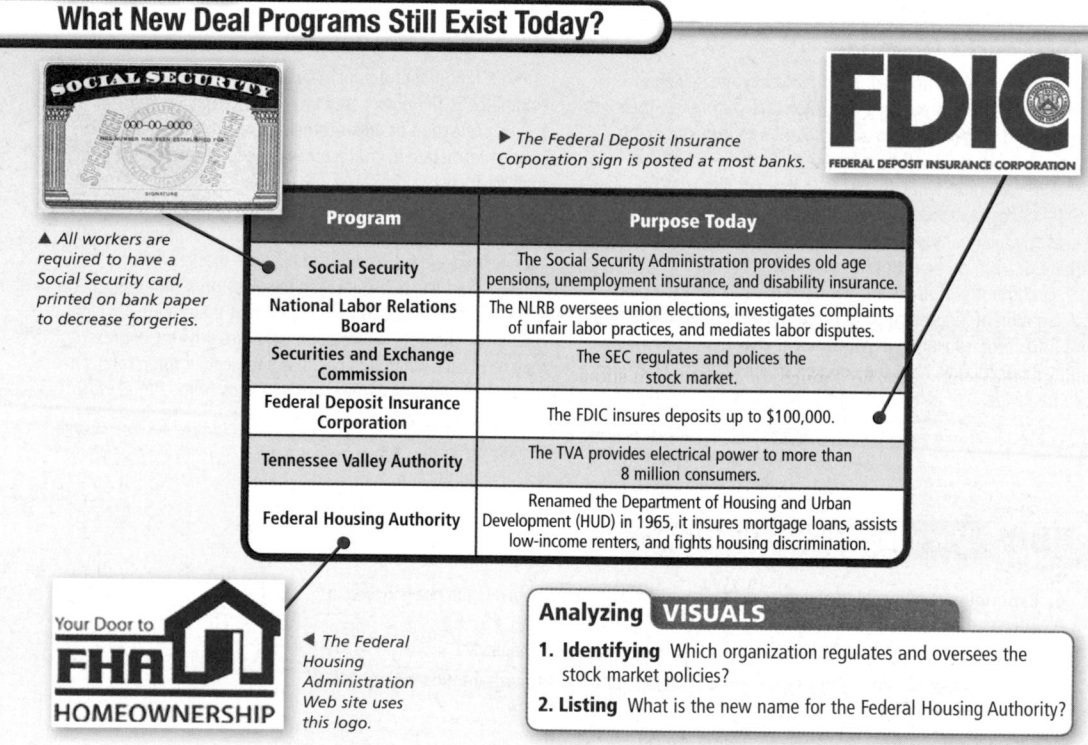

▶ *The Federal Deposit Insurance Corporation sign is posted at most banks.*

▲ *All workers are required to have a Social Security card, printed on bank paper to decrease forgeries.*

Program	Purpose Today
Social Security	The Social Security Administration provides old age pensions, unemployment insurance, and disability insurance.
National Labor Relations Board	The NLRB oversees union elections, investigates complaints of unfair labor practices, and mediates labor disputes.
Securities and Exchange Commission	The SEC regulates and polices the stock market.
Federal Deposit Insurance Corporation	The FDIC insures deposits up to $100,000.
Tennessee Valley Authority	The TVA provides electrical power to more than 8 million consumers.
Federal Housing Authority	Renamed the Department of Housing and Urban Development (HUD) in 1965, it insures mortgage loans, assists low-income renters, and fights housing discrimination.

◀ *The Federal Housing Administration Web site uses this logo.*

Analyzing VISUALS

1. **Identifying** Which organization regulates and oversees the stock market policies?
2. **Listing** What is the new name for the Federal Housing Authority?

Activity: Collaborative Learning

Analyze Roosevelt's Inaugural Addresses Divide the class into four groups, assigning each group one of the four inaugural addresses that Roosevelt gave. Have students look for key thoughts in the speech and determine how Roosevelt fostered hope and vision during difficult times. **Ask:** To what extent did the inaugural address set forth an agenda, or blueprint, to be followed? *(Students' responses will vary depending on the inaugural address they studied.)* `OL`

To further help workers, Roosevelt pushed through Congress the Fair Labor Standards Act, which abolished child labor, limited the workweek to 44 hours for most workers, and set the first federal minimum wage at 25 cents an hour. The Fair Labor Standards Act was the last major piece of New Deal legislation. The recession of 1937 enabled the Republicans to win seats in Congress in the midterm elections of 1938. Together with conservative Southern Democrats, they began blocking further New Deal legislation. By 1939, the New Deal era had come to an end.

The New Deal's Legacy

The New Deal had only limited success in ending the Depression. Unemployment remained high, and economic recovery was not complete until after World War II. Even so, the New Deal gave many Americans a stronger sense of security and stability.

As a whole, the New Deal tended to balance competing economic interests. Business leaders, farmers, workers, homeowners, and others now looked to government to protect their interests. The federal government's ability to take on this new role was enhanced by two important Supreme Court decisions. In 1937, in *NLRB* v. *Jones and Laughlin Steel,* the Court ruled that the federal government had the authority to regulate production within a state. Later, in 1942, in *Wickard* v. *Filburn,* the Court used a similar argument to allow the federal government to regulate consumption in the states. These decisions increased federal power over the economy and allowed it to **mediate** between competing groups.

In taking on this mediating role, the New Deal established what some have called the **broker state,** in which the government works out conflicts among interests. This broker role has continued under the administrations of both parties ever since. The New Deal also brought about a new public attitude toward government. Roosevelt's programs had succeeded in creating a **safety net** for Americans—safeguards and relief programs that protected them against economic disaster. By the end of the 1930s, many Americans felt that the government had a duty to maintain this safety net, even though doing so required a larger, more expensive federal government.

Critics continue to argue that the New Deal made the government too powerful. Thus, another legacy of the New Deal is a continuing debate over how much the government should intervene in the economy or support the disadvantaged. Throughout the hard times of the Depression, most Americans maintained a surprising degree of confidence in the American system. Journalist Dorothy Thompson expressed this feeling in 1940:

PRIMARY SOURCE

"We have behind us eight terrible years of a crisis. . . . Here we are, and our basic institutions are still intact, our people relatively prosperous and most important of all, our society relatively affectionate. . . . No country is so well off."

—from the *Washington Post,* October 9, 1940

✔ **Reading Check** **Summarizing** What was the legacy of Roosevelt's New Deal?

Section 3 REVIEW

Vocabulary

1. **Explain** the significance of: Frances Perkins, court-packing, Henry Morgenthau, John Maynard Keynes, broker state, safety net.

Main Ideas

2. What caused a recession early in Roosevelt's second term?

3. How did the New Deal expand federal power over the economy?

Critical Thinking

4. **Big Ideas** What groups made up the New Deal coalition?

5. **Organizing** Use a chart like the one below to list the achievements and defeats of Roosevelt's second term.

Achievements	Defeats

6. **Analyzing Visuals** Choose one of the photos on page 441 and write a brief account of the day's activities from the viewpoint of one of the people in the photograph.

Writing About History

7. **Persuasive Writing** Imagine that you are a staff member in Roosevelt's cabinet. Write a short paper criticizing or defending FDR's court-packing plan.

History ONLINE
Study Central™ To review this section, go to glencoe.com and click on Study Central.

445

R **Reading Strategy**

Academic Vocabulary Tell students that the Latin root word used in *mediate* means "middle." Ask them for other words that use this same root. *(intermediary, intermediate, medium)* **OL**

✔ **Reading Check**

Answer:
It increased the government's role and fostered the attitude that the government was responsible for a safety net.

Assess

History ONLINE

Study Central™ provides summaries, interactive games, and online graphic organizers to help students review content.

Close

Summarizing Ask: At the end of Roosevelt's second term, how did Americans view the effects of the New Deal? *(Many felt it was a positive plan that provided a safety net against economic disaster.)* **OL**

Section 3 REVIEW

Answers

1. All definitions can be found in the section and the Glossary.

2. The recession was created when Social Security began making payments just as WPA and PWA programs were cut.

3. The New Deal introduced federal regulations in agriculture, industry, banking, and the stock market. It also established a minimum wage.

4. African Americans, farmers, labor, minorities, new immigrants, women, intellectuals, and progressives

5. Achievements: court upholds reforms, National Housing Act, Fair Labor Standards Act; Defeats: Great Depression continued, court-packing plan

6. Students' responses will vary but should be consistent with text material.

7. Students' papers will vary but should take a position on the court-packing plan and defend it.

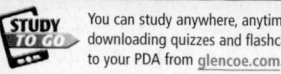

Determining Cause and Effect Invite students to write at least one cause-and-effect statement for each of the four areas covered by the Visual Summary. **Ask:** What was the overall effect of the New Deal? *(Although the New Deal assisted many people, it did not end the Depression. It did, however, expand the role of the federal government and offered a social safety net.)* **OL**

Expository Writing Have students select one of the four categories and write a one-page summary of the provisions and effects of the New Deal in that area. **Ask:** In which area do you think the New Deal had the most lasting and important effect? *(Students' responses will vary but should be supported by reasons.)* **OL**

The New Deal in Action

Banking and Finances

- Emergency Banking Relief Act regulated banks.
- Federal Deposit Insurance Corporation insured bank deposits.
- Farm Credit Administration refinanced farm mortgages.
- Home Owners' Loan Corporation financed homeowners' mortgages.

Agriculture and Industry

- Agricultural Adjustment Administration paid farmers to limit surplus production.
- National Industrial Recovery Act limited industrial production and set prices.
- National Labor Relations Act gave workers the right to organize unions and bargain collectively.
- Tennessee Valley Authority financed rural electrification and helped develop the economy of a seven-state region.

▲ A steel worker labors on the Grand Coulee Dam on the Columbia River in eastern Washington.

Work and Relief

- Civilian Conservation Corps created forestry jobs for young men.
- Federal Emergency Relief Administration funded city and state relief programs.
- Public Works Administration created work programs to build public projects, such as roads, bridges, and schools.

◄ A Civilian Conservation Corps member plants trees.

Social "Safety Net"

- Social Security Act provided
  – income for senior citizens, handicapped, and unemployed
  – monthly retirement benefit for people over 65

▶ In 1935 President Roosevelt signs the Social Security Bill while Secretary of Labor Perkins and legislators observe.

446 Chapter 12 Roosevelt and the New Deal

Hands-On Chapter Project
Step 4: Wrap Up

Writing a Newspaper

Step 4: Produce and Distribute the Paper Have students make enough copies of their newspaper for the class. Allow time for students to read and comment on each other's completed work. Display the completed papers in the classroom.

Putting It Together Use the newspapers as the basis of a classroom display or bulletin board. Enhance the display with photos and maps. **OL**

ASSESSMENT

STANDARDIZED TEST PRACTICE

TEST-TAKING TIP

Questions sometimes ask for the exception, rather than the one right answer. Be sure to read through the question carefully, as well as each response, to see which one does not fit.

Reviewing Vocabulary

Directions: Choose the word or words that best complete the sentence.

1. The purpose of a _____ was to prevent banks from being closed completely because of bank runs.

   A New Deal

   B bank holiday

   C gold standard

   D fireside chat

2. The period of intense congressional activity after FDR took office was known as the

   A Square Deal.

   B Securities and Exchange Commission.

   C New Deal.

   D Hundred Days.

3. _____ involves borrowing money to pay for programs.

   A Deficit spending

   B The gold standard

   C States' rights

   D Binding arbitration

4. Roosevelt ran into major opposition to his _____ plan.

   A broker state

   B gold standard

   C recovery

   D court-packing

Reviewing Main Ideas

Directions: Choose the best answers to the following questions.

Section 1 (pp. 422–431)

5. One of the ways in which Franklin Roosevelt gained political experience before being president was by serving as the

   A U.S. senator for Maine.

   B mayor of Boston.

   C governor of New York.

   D congressional representative from Connecticut.

6. The _____ was created to protect bank deposits.

   A Agricultural Adjustment Act

   B Home Owners' Loan Corporation

   C Securities and Exchange Commission

   D Federal Deposit Insurance Corporation

7. To _____, the Agricultural Adjustment Act paid farmers not to grow certain crops.

   A raise farm prices

   B lower farm prices

   C feed the homeless

   D let farmers relax

8. The _____ provided work for unemployed young men, who planted trees and built reservoirs.

   A Civil Works Administration

   B Public Works Administration

   C Civilian Conservation Corps

   D Federal Emergency Relief Administration

Need Extra Help?								
If You Missed Questions . . .	1	2	3	4	5	6	7	8
Go to Page . . .	424	424	434–435	442	422–423	426	428	430

 GO ON

Answers and Analyses
Reviewing Vocabulary

1. B Although all the terms given as possible answers to this question do relate to the New Deal, only *bank holiday* fully answers the question. The New Deal itself was larger than a bank holiday and not designed only to prevent bank closings. The fear that Roosevelt would take the nation off the gold standard actually provoked some bank runs. The fireside chats were intended to calm the nation in general and to give listeners a sense that they had a friend in the White House.

2. D The Square Deal can be easily eliminated, as it refers to Theodore Roosevelt's agenda. The word *commission* does not refer to a time period; the Securities and Exchange Commission was created to control the activities of Wall Street. The New Deal was a series of broad programs designed to help the nation's economic recovery.

3. A The gold standard demanded that an ounce of gold equaled a certain amount of dollars. States' rights was the insistence on the right of individual states to conduct business without the interference of the federal government. In binding arbitration, two sides in a dispute agree to accept the decision of a neutral party.

4. D By defining each term, students can eliminate distractors.

5. C This question asks students to differentiate from among political offices and locations. They need to remember that Roosevelt was from New York.

6. D Although all the possible answers have to do with programs that the New Deal created, only "the FDIC" completely answers the question. The Agricultural Adjustment Act provided a way to raise farm prices. The Home Owners' Loan Corporation was designed to help homeowners with their mortgage payments. The SEC regulated stock market activities.

7. A The key term in the name of this act is *Adjustment*. Students should recall that farm prices were already very low. Also, remind students that generally in tests, when two possible answers directly contradict each other, one of them is the correct answer and the other distractors can be ignored.

8. C This question asks students to select among various New Deal programs to find the correct answer. The term *conservation* in the correct response should be a clue.

447

Chapter 12

9. D This question requires students to place events in sequence and to recall that 1935 was the year before the 1936 presidential election. Knowing that FDR wanted a second term and that the failure to end the Great Depression stood in his way can help students find the correct response.

10. C The term *benefits* can be a key to finding the right answer to this question. Students can link the word *Security* in the correct response with *benefit* and thus eliminate the other programs mentioned.

11. A Students may recall the cartoon showing the Democratic donkey kicking the fence and thereby remember the uproar created by Roosevelt's court-packing plan.

12. B The possible answers offer a preliminary choice between two options: was the New Deal a state or federal program? Then students must decide if the federal expansion was over economy or the Constitution.

13. D To answer this question, students can frame it as a then/now issue. By doing so, they can see that the major issue was that of providing a safety net for retired or disabled workers, who had suffered deeply during the Great Depression.

14. C By correctly identifying the lighter-colored region on the map as the Northeast, students can answer this question.

15. A Remind students to look carefully at the map to be sure they have not overlooked any state before they answer.

Section 2 *(pp. 434–439)*

9. By 1935 the New Deal was criticized because it
   A had created too many new programs.
   B was focusing only on the Midwest.
   C had spent too much money on the stock market.
   D had not ended the Great Depression.

10. Benefits for older Americans were guaranteed by the
   A Congress of Industrial Organizations.
   B Works Progress Administration.
   C Social Security Act.
   D Wagner Act.

Section 3 *(pp. 440–445)*

11. Roosevelt split his own party by suggesting the need to
   A appoint additional Supreme Court judges.
   B include African Americans in New Deal programs.
   C appoint women to his cabinet.
   D follow Keynesian economics.

12. Part of the New Deal's legacy was an expansion of
   A state power over the courts.
   B federal power over the economy.
   C federal power over the Constitution.
   D state power over social safety nets.

13. The New Deal changed American attitudes toward government and
   A the desire for easy wealth.
   B the challenge of unionization.
   C the duty to regulate industry.
   D the need to provide a safety net.

Critical Thinking

Directions: Choose the best answers to the following questions.

Base your answers to questions 14 and 15 on the map below and on your knowledge of Chapter 12.

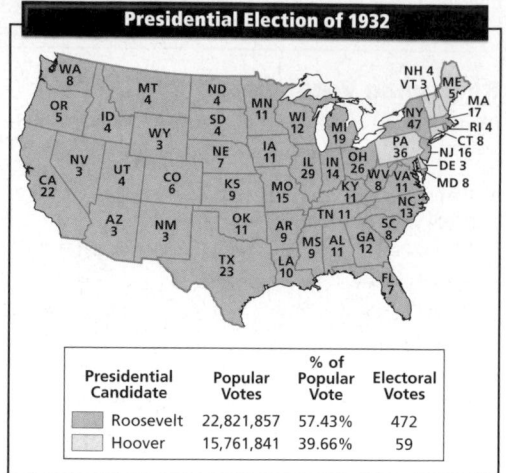

Presidential Election of 1932

Presidential Candidate	Popular Votes	% of Popular Vote	Electoral Votes
Roosevelt	22,821,857	57.43%	472
Hoover	15,761,841	39.66%	59

14. Which of the following regions remained supportive of Republican President Hoover?
   A Midwest
   B South
   C Northeast
   D West

15. Which state gave Hoover the largest number of votes in the Electoral College?
   A Pennsylvania
   B New York
   C Connecticut
   D Texas

Need Extra Help?

If You Missed Questions . . .	9	10	11	12	13	14	15
Go to Page . . .	434–436	439	442	445	440–444	R15	R15

GO ON

ASSESSMENT

16. Social Security was an important piece of legislation because it

   A provided monthly retirement benefits.

   B encouraged state governments to improve schools.

   C forced the federal government to hire the unemployed.

   D mandated that workers be issued safety equipment.

Analyze the cartoon and answer the question that follows. Base your answer on the cartoon and your knowledge of Chapter 12.

17. This cartoon was published just after FDR took office. What message does it send?

   A Republicans are not very happy about the new legislation.

   B Congress is slow and stubborn as a donkey.

   C The new president is not slowed down by being in a wheelchair.

   D The Congress and many people are happy to follow Roosevelt.

Document-Based Questions

Directions: Analyze the document and answer the short-answer questions that follow the document.

Eleanor Roosevelt wrote in her autobiography of her experiences with people around the country:

> "This trip to the mining areas was my first contact with the work being done by the Quakers. I liked the idea of trying to put people to work to help themselves. The men were started on projects and taught to use their abilities to develop new skills. The women were encouraged to revive any household arts they might once have known but which they had neglected in the drab life of the mining village.
>
> This was only the first of many trips into the mining districts but it was the one that started the homestead idea [placing people in communities with homes, farms, and jobs] . . . . It was all experimental work, but it was designed to get people off relief, to put them to work building their own homes and to give them enough land to start growing food."
>
> —from *The Autobiography of Eleanor Roosevelt*

18. Why did Eleanor Roosevelt like the Quaker project?

19. Based on this excerpt, how do you think Eleanor Roosevelt felt about New Deal programs? Explain your answer.

Extended Response

20. Review the various New Deal programs discussed in the chapter. Select one that you think could be used or adapted to a current situation. Explain what group or groups it would help and how it would do so.

 STOP

For additional test practice, use Self-Check Quizzes—Chapter 12 at **glencoe.com**.

16. A Social Security provided monthly retirement checks.

17. D A careful look at the cartoon shows people for as far as the horizon extends, following FDR. Congress is leading the pack. All other distractors are incorrect.

18. It emphasized individual initiative in improving the lives of the miners.

19. She supported the New Deal programs; this is clear because she advised FDR on peoples' needs and visited projects.

20. Answers will vary. Students' answers should involve one specific New Deal program and one current situation to which it might be adapted.

History ONLINE
Have students visit the Web site at glencoe.com to review Chapter 12 and take the Self-Check Quiz.

Need Extra Help?
Have students refer to the pages listed if they miss any of the questions.

449

UNIT PACING CHART

	Unit 5	Chapter 13	Chapter 14	Chapter 15	Chapter 16	Unit 5
Day 1	Unit Opener	Chapter 13 Opener, Section 1	Chapter 14 Opener, Section 1	Chapter 15 Opener, Section 1	Chapter 16 Opener, Section 1	Wrap-Up/Project, Unit Assessment
Day 2		Section 2	Section 2	Section 2	Section 2	
Day 3		Section 3	Section 3	Section 3	Section 3	
Day 4		Section 4	Section 4	Section 4	Chapter Assessment	
Day 5		Chapter Assessment	Section 5	Chapter Assessment		
Day 6			Chapter Assessment			

Teacher to Teacher

**Peter DeWolf
First Colonial
High School
Virginia Beach,
Virginia**

A-Bomb Shelters Divide the students into groups. Each group must come up with a list of items to stock a 12' x 12' bomb shelter with everything a family of four would need to survive for four weeks. Ask the groups to prioritize their list by categories. Upon list completion, each group will share its list with the class. Then the class will discuss how each group made decisions about prioritizing.

• Why did they rank some categories higher than others?

• Did they include provisions for personal hygiene, nutrition, comfort, entertainment, and medical care? Why or why not?

• Why aren't all the lists and the categories the same?

Conclude the activity by discussing:

1. What was the hardest thing about supplying the shelter?

2. How would students feel about spending four weeks in the shelter they had supplied?

Explain that the Cold War forced people to deal with unusual situations that they were not accustomed to. This added to the fear of what may happen. Students should have obtained some awareness and insight into that uncomfortable position by completing this activity.

Author Note

Dear American History Teacher:

As you begin to teach this unit, there are themes that recur throughout the chapters that you will want to point out to students.

In this unit, students will monitor a debate between those Americans who wanted the U.S. to stay out of another war, and those who felt that the U.S. had a responsibility to resist the spread of tyranny. That debate took place in the halls of Congress, on the pages of the newspapers, and in mass public rallies. It ended when Japan attacked Pearl Harbor.

World War II became a total war that affected every citizen. My father was among the millions of Americans who responded to the call to defend their nation. He stood in a long line of recruits whom military personnel were sending, seemingly at random, through different doors. The door that he entered put him in the Coast Guard. Vast numbers of American volunteers and conscripts fought in Africa, Europe, and across the Pacific, while civilians mobilized on the home front. New opportunities opened for women and minorities in the defense industries. Yet Japanese Americans suffered grievous restrictions of their civil liberties.

Victory in World War II was followed closely by a prolonged Cold War in which the United States and its allies confronted the Communist bloc nations. International tensions, especially the anxiety over the threat of nuclear war, spurred investigations of Communist subversion within the United States. For those of us in school at the time, the nuclear threat meant "duck and cover" exercises under our desks and in the hallways. Such drills brought home to us the significance that world events had within our own communities.

By studying these events, your students will be able to consider the links between U.S. foreign policy and its domestic politics, as well as between international affairs and the everyday lives of individuals.

Donald A. Ritchie

Senior Author

Focus

Why It Matters

Have a volunteer read the *Why It Matters* paragraph on this page. Ask students to identify the three results of the United States's involvement in the war. *(emerged as a global power, abandoned isolationism, and began building alliances)* Then have students suggest current examples illustrating each of those results. *(Answers may include leading other nations in fighting terrorism or United Nations and NATO membership.)* **OL**

Connecting to Past Learning

Challenge students to recall the reasons for **both** World War I and the involvement of the United States in that war. *(Germany's military build-up, forming of alliances, assassination of Archduke Ferdinand; the United States entered the war in 1917 because of German submarine attacks on American ships, and growing anti-German sentiment in Wilson's administration and among the public.)*

Unit Launch Activity

Fact Finding Mission Place students in three groups, one for each decade represented in the unit. Challenge the groups to recall or find five facts about their assigned decade within a short period of time. Allow them to skim their textbooks for facts. **OL**

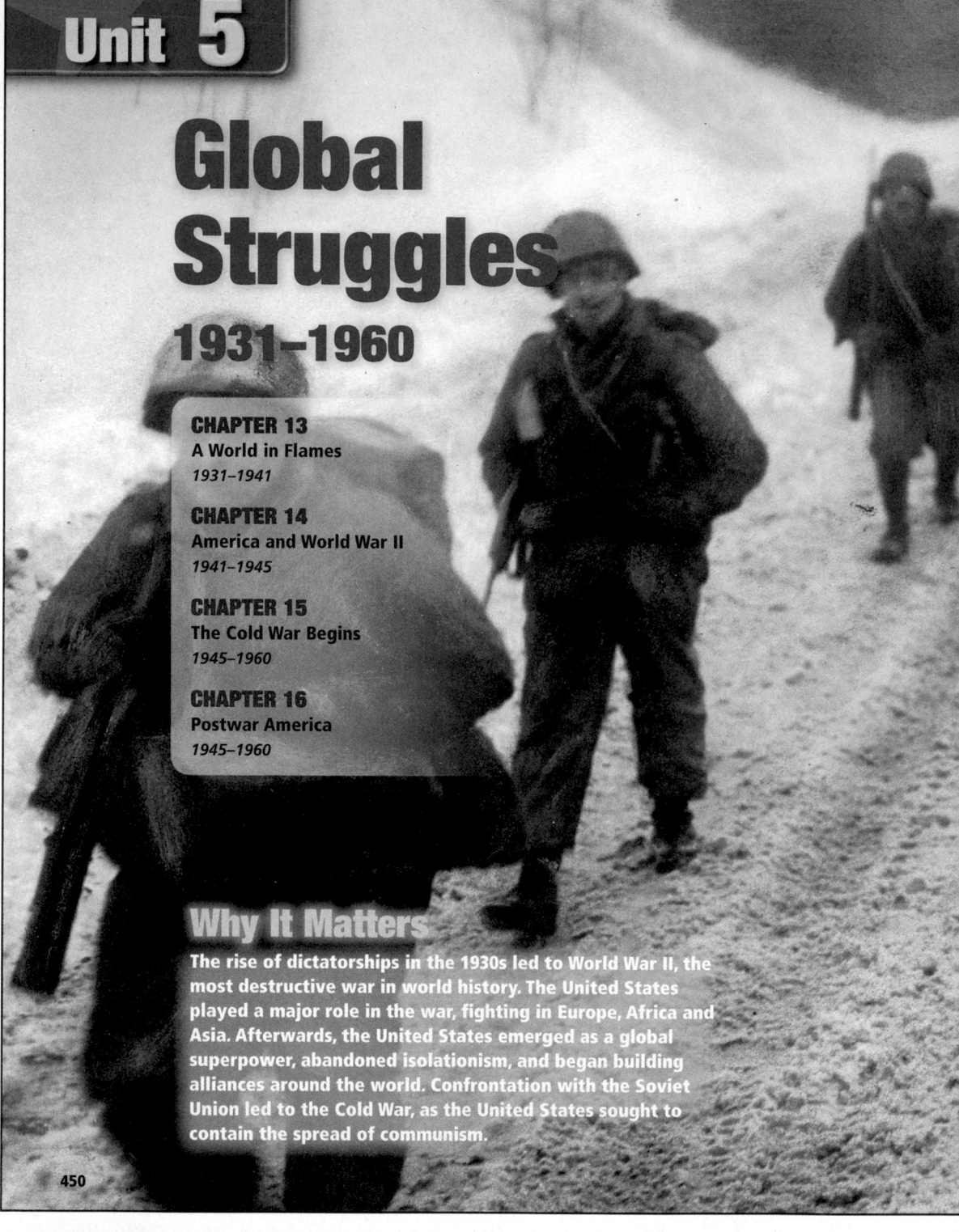

Unit 5

Global Struggles

1931–1960

CHAPTER 13
A World in Flames
1931–1941

CHAPTER 14
America and World War II
1941–1945

CHAPTER 15
The Cold War Begins
1945–1960

CHAPTER 16
Postwar America
1945–1960

Why It Matters

The rise of dictatorships in the 1930s led to World War II, the most destructive war in world history. The United States played a major role in the war, fighting in Europe, Africa and Asia. Afterwards, the United States emerged as a global superpower, abandoned isolationism, and began building alliances around the world. Confrontation with the Soviet Union led to the Cold War, as the United States sought to contain the spread of communism.

450

Team Teaching Activity

Economics Explain to students that the booming postwar economy affected millions of Americans and continues to ripple through today's economy. Cold War military spending, new home construction, and demand for consumer goods each played a role in the healthy U.S. economy. Work with the economics teacher to coordinate the study of the economic trends of postwar America. Then invite the economics teacher to teach a lesson on the topic to your history class. Encourage students to participate in the discussion. **OL**

Despite the fog, American soldiers march in Belgium during the winter of 1944–1945.

451

Teach

Differentiated Instruction

Auditory/Musical Play for students recorded samples of popular music from each decade covered in the unit. Ask students to jot down impressions of the way life must have been during each decade as they listen to the songs. **BL**

Skill Practice

Using Geography Skills Use a large classroom map to pinpoint places of war and conflict between 1941 and 1960. Invite students to place flags or other markers on the locations you mention so that students can visualize the truly global nature of the wars. **OL**

 NO CHILD LEFT BEHIND

Teaching Tip The NCLB Act places an emphasis on reading skills. Review with students the skills of scanning and skimming and when each would be useful in studying this unit.

More About the Photo

Visual Literacy In December 1944, as Allied forces marched through Belgium and northern France toward the German border, Adolf Hitler ordered a massive counterattack. German forces smashed into American lines in Belgium with the goal of splitting Allied forces in two and capturing the city of Antwerp. The attack caught the Americans by surprise, but their lines did not break. Instead, as American forces fell back, the front line "bulged" outward on the map. This is why the engagement became known as the Battle of the Bulge. The troops had to fight in heavy snow in sub-zero conditions. Snowstorms reduced visibility and prevented aircraft from aiding the troops. Some 19,000 Americans were killed during the Battle of the Bulge, making it the deadliest engagement of the war for Americans.

Chapter 13 Planning Guide

Levels (BL OL AL ELL)		Resources	Chapter Opener	Section 1	Section 2	Section 3	Section 4	Chapter Assess
FOCUS								
BL OL AL ELL	Daily Focus Transparencies			13-1	13-2	13-3	13-4	
TEACH								
BL OL AL ELL	Reading Essentials and Note-Taking Guide*			p. 134	p. 137	p. 140	p. 143	
BL OL ELL	Reading Skills Activity, URB			p. 21				
OL	Historical Analysis Skills Activity, URB			p. 22				
BL OL ELL	Guided Reading Activity, URB*			p. 48	p. 49	p. 50	p. 51	
BL OL AL ELL	Differentiated Instruction Activity, URB						p. 23	
BL OL ELL	English Learner Activity, URB		p. 25					
BL OL AL ELL	Content Vocabulary Activity, URB*		p. 27					
BL OL AL ELL	Academic Vocabulary Activity, URB		p. 29					
OL AL	Reinforcing Skills Activity, URB				p. 31			
OL AL	Critical Thinking Skills Activity, URB			p. 32				
BL OL ELL	Time Line Activity, URB					p. 33		
OL	Linking Past and Present Activity, URB							p. 34
BL OL AL ELL	Primary Source Reading, URB			p. 35			p. 37	
BL OL AL ELL	American Art and Music Activity, URB							p. 39
BL OL AL ELL	Interpreting Political Cartoons Activity, URB						p. 41	
AL	Enrichment Activity, URB						p. 45	
BL OL AL ELL	Differentiated Instruction for the American History Classroom	✓	✓	✓	✓	✓	✓
BL OL AL ELL	Unit Map Overlay Transparencies	✓	✓	✓	✓	✓	✓
BL OL AL ELL	Unit Time Line Transparencies, Strategies, and Activities	✓	✓	✓	✓	✓	✓
BL OL AL ELL	Cause and Effect Transparencies, Strategies, and Activities	✓	✓	✓	✓	✓	✓
BL OL AL ELL	Why It Matters Chapter Transparencies, Strategies, and Activities	✓	✓	✓	✓	✓	✓
BL OL AL ELL	American Biographies					✓	

Note: Please refer to the *Unit 5 Resource Book* for this chapter's URB materials.

* Also available in Spanish

TeacherWorks Plus
All-In-One Planner and Resource Center

- Interactive Lesson Planner
- Interactive Teacher Edition
- Fully editable blackline masters
- Section Spotlight Videos Launch
- Differentiated Lesson Plans
- Printable reports of daily assignments
- Standards Tracking System

Levels BL OL AL ELL		Resources	Chapter Opener	Section 1	Section 2	Section 3	Section 4	Chapter Assess
TEACH (continued)								
BL OL AL ELL		The Living Constitution	✓	✓	✓	✓	✓	✓
BL OL AL ELL		American Issues	✓	✓	✓	✓	✓	✓
OL AL ELL		American Art and Architecture Transparencies, Strategies, and Activities	✓	✓	✓	✓	✓	✓
BL OL AL		High School American History Literature Library	✓	✓	✓	✓	✓	✓
OL AL		American History Primary Source Documents Library	✓	✓	✓	✓	✓	✓
BL OL AL ELL		American Music: Hits Through History CD	✓	✓	✓	✓	✓	✓
BL OL AL ELL		StudentWorks™ Plus DVD	✓	✓	✓	✓	✓	✓
BL OL AL ELL		Vocabulary PuzzleMaker CD-ROM	✓	✓	✓	✓	✓	✓
BL OL AL ELL		*The American Vision* Video Program DVD	✓	✓	✓	✓	✓	✓
Teacher Resources		Reading Strategies and Activities for the Social Studies Classroom	✓	✓	✓	✓	✓	✓
		Strategies for Success	✓	✓	✓	✓	✓	✓
		Presentation Plus! DVD	✓	✓	✓	✓	✓	✓
		Success With English Learners	✓	✓	✓	✓	✓	✓
ASSESS								
BL OL AL ELL		Section Quizzes and Chapter Tests*		p. 185	p. 186	p. 187	p. 188	p. 189
BL OL AL ELL		Authentic Assessment With Rubrics						p. 31
BL OL AL ELL		Standardized Test Practice Workbook						p. 28
BL OL AL ELL		*ExamView® Assessment Suite* CD-ROM		13-1	13-2	13-3	13-4	Ch. 13
BL OL AL ELL		Interactive Tutor Self-Assessment CD-ROM		13-1	13-2	13-3	13-4	Ch. 13
CLOSE								
BL ELL		Reteaching Activity, URB						p. 43
BL OL ELL		Reading and Study Skills Foldables™	p. 73					

Using the McGraw-Hill Learning Network

Researching World Book™ Select

Objective
After students learn to use World Book Select, they will be able to
- develop and expand research and study skills;
- practice reading and writing skills.

Technology
World Book Select offers thousands of detailed articles chosen from the *World Book Encyclopedia* and covers all curricular areas. World Book Select allows students to research national and international topics and issues in economics and other curriculum areas.

Focus/Teach
Give students the following direction to use World Book Select:
- From the McGraw-Hill Learning Network home page (www.mhln.com), click on For Students.
- Choose World Book Select below Homework Help.

- Click the letter for the encyclopedia volume you want to use.
- On the search page for the volume selected:
- Click the title of a featured article on the right side of the page; or
- Click on a topic from the list on the left side of the page; then click on the title of an article of interest on the right.
- Read the article and take notes.

History ONLINE	Student	Teacher	Parent
Beyond the Textbook	●	●	●
Chapter Overviews	●	●	●
Time Current Events	●		●
ePuzzles and Games	●		●
Concepts in Motion	●		●
Literature Connections		●	
Multi-Language Glossaries	●		●
Online Student Edition	●	●	●
Self-Check Quizzes	●		●
Student Web Activities	●		●
Study Central ™	●		●
Teaching Today		●	
Vocabulary eFlashcards	●		●
Web Activity Lesson Plans		●	

Glencoe Media Center

glencoe.com

❯ **Study-To-Go**
- Vocabulary eFlashcards
- Self-Check Quizzes

❯ **Audio/Video**
- Student Edition Audio
- Spanish Summaries
- Section Videos

- **Timed Readings Plus in Social Studies** helps students increase their reading rate and fluency while maintaining comprehension. The 400-word passages are similar to those found on state and national assessments.

- **Reading in the Content Area: Social Studies** concentrates on six essential reading skills that help students better comprehend what they read. The book includes 75 high-interest nonfiction passages written at increasing levels of difficulty.

- **Reading Social Studies** includes strategic reading instruction and vocabulary support in Social Studies content for both ELLs and native speakers of English.
www.jamestowneducation.com

Index to National Geographic Magazine:

The following articles relate to this chapter:

- "Pearl Harbor: A Return to the Day of Infamy," by Thomas B. Allen, December 1991.

- "Remembering the Blitz," by Cameron Thomas, July 1991.

National Geographic Society Products To order the following, call National Geographic at 1-800-368-2728:

- World War II Era (PicturePack Transparencies).

Access National Geographic's new, dynamic MapMachine Web site and other geography resources at:

www.nationalgeographic.com
www.nationalgeographic.com/maps

The following videotape programs are available from Glencoe as supplements to Chapter 13:

- FDR: The War Years (ISBN 1-56-501458-8)
- Anne Frank (ISBN 0-76-701409-X)

To order, call Glencoe at 1-800-334-7344. To find classroom resources to accompany many of these videos, check the following home pages:

A&E Television: www.aetv.com

The History Channel: www.historychannel.com

Reading List Generator CD-ROM

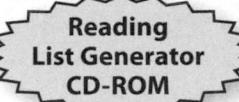

Use this database to search more than 30,000 titles to create a customized reading list for your students.

- Reading lists can be organized by students' reading level, author, genre, theme, or area of interest.

- The database provides Degrees of Reading Power™ (DRP) and Lexile™ readability scores for all selections.

- A brief summary of each selection is included.

Leveled reading suggestions for this chapter:

For students at a Grade 8 reading level:
- *Edith's Story,* by Edith Velmans

For students at a Grade 9 reading level:
- *Anne Frank: The Diary of a Young Girl,* by Anne Frank

For students at a Grade 10 reading level:
- *The Painted Bird,* by Jerzy Kosinski

For students at a Grade 11 reading level:
- *Never to Forget: The Jews of the Holocaust,* by Milton Meltzer

For students at a Grade 12 reading level:
- *The Hidden Children,* by Howard Greenfeld

Introducing Chapter 13

Focus

MAKING CONNECTIONS
Could World War II Have Been Prevented?
Use the two questions as the basis for a class discussion about the inevitability of a second world war. Elicit from students the terms of the Treaty of Versailles, including reparations and land partitions, that might contribute to bad feelings among the nations that lost World War I. Students should also comment on the United States's refusal to join the League of Nations as Wilson requested. **OL**

Teach

The Big Ideas

As students study the chapter, remind them to consider the section-based Big Ideas included in each section's Guide to Reading. The **Essential Questions** in the activities below tie in to the Big Ideas and help students think about and understand important chapter concepts. In addition, the Hands-on Chapter Projects with their culminating activities relate the content from each section to the Big Ideas. These activities build on each other as students progress through the chapter. Section activities culminate in the wrap-up activity on the Visual Summary page.

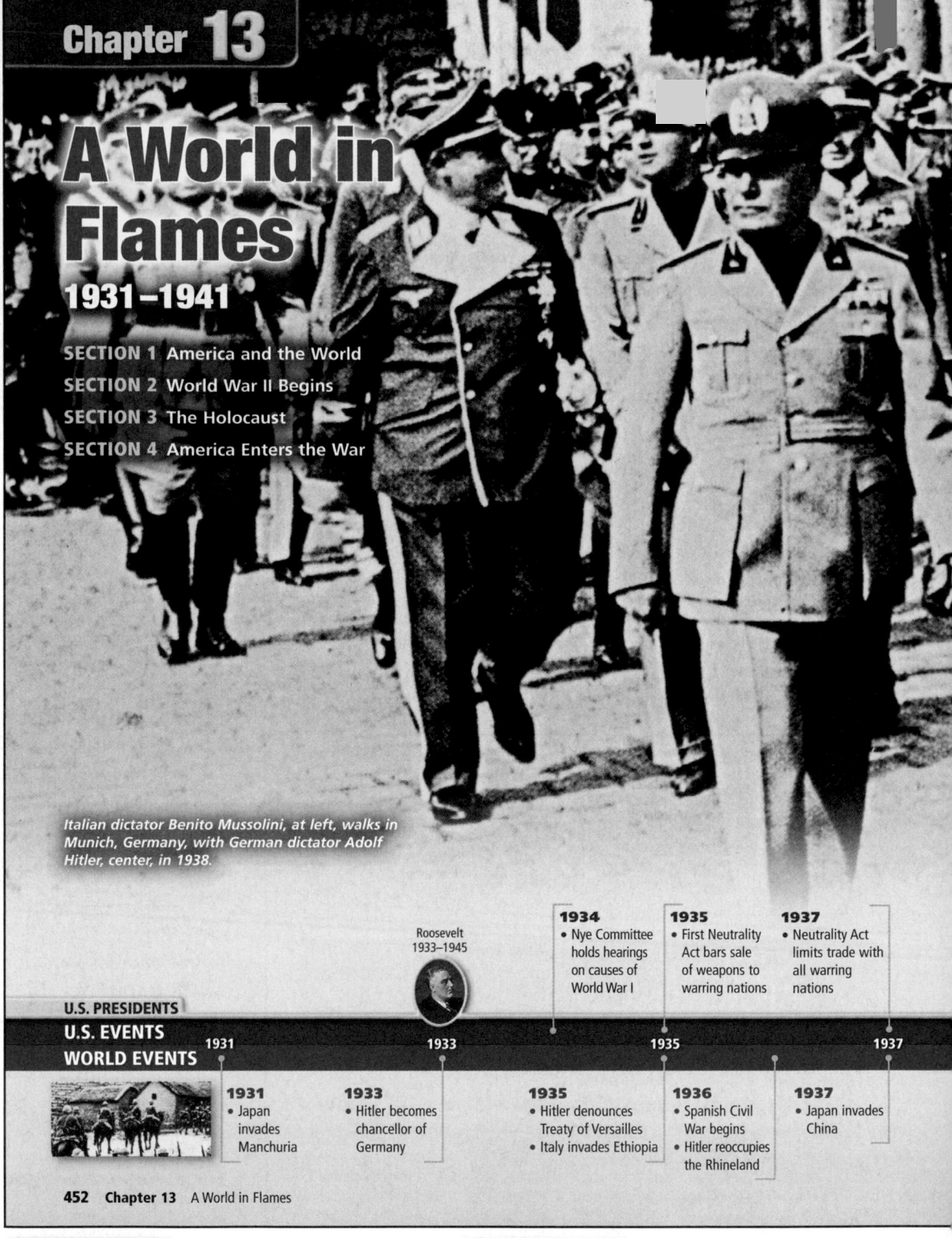

Chapter 13

A World in Flames

1931–1941

SECTION 1 America and the World
SECTION 2 World War II Begins
SECTION 3 The Holocaust
SECTION 4 America Enters the War

Italian dictator Benito Mussolini, at left, walks in Munich, Germany, with German dictator Adolf Hitler, center, in 1938.

U.S. PRESIDENTS

Roosevelt 1933–1945

U.S. EVENTS

1934
• Nye Committee holds hearings on causes of World War I

1935
• First Neutrality Act bars sale of weapons to warring nations

1937
• Neutrality Act limits trade with all warring nations

1931   1933   1935   1937

WORLD EVENTS

1931
• Japan invades Manchuria

1933
• Hitler becomes chancellor of Germany

1935
• Hitler denounces Treaty of Versailles
• Italy invades Ethiopia

1936
• Spanish Civil War begins
• Hitler reoccupies the Rhineland

1937
• Japan invades China

452 Chapter 13 A World in Flames

Section 1

America and the World
Essential Question: How did events after WWI lead to dictatorships and American neutrality? *(Many nations were dissatisfied with the Treaty of Versailles, and worldwide financial depression made people desperate. Americans wanted to avoid another war.)* Tell students that in Section 1 they will learn about events around the world that led to dictatorships even as America retreated into isolation. **OL**

Section 2

World War II Begins
Essential Question: What steps led to war in Europe in the late 1930s? *(Hitler violated the Versailles Treaty, rebuilt Germany's forces, occupied Austria, demanded the Sudetanland from Czechoslovakia. Britain and France tried to appease Hitler but Hitler occupied Czechoslovakia, then invaded Poland.)* Inform students that in this section they will be learning about how World War II began in Europe. **OL**

More About the Photo

Visual Literacy In the 1930s, both Adolf Hitler and Benito Mussolini sought to revitalize their struggling nations by promoting aggressive nationalism. The two nations established a military alliance on May 22, 1939, with the Pact of Steel, an agreement that committed both countries to support the other in the event of war. War came on September 1, 1939, when Nazi Germany invaded Poland. Italy joined the war on June 10, 1940, by declaring war against France and Great Britain. In September 1940, Italy attacked British forces in Egypt, spreading the war to North Africa.

FOLDABLES **Dinah Zike's**
Study Organizer **Foldables**

Dinah Zike's Foldables are three-dimensional, interactive graphic organizers that help students practice basic writing skills, review vocabulary terms, and identify main ideas. Instructions for creating and using Foldables can be found in the Appendix at the end of this book and in the *Dinah Zike's Reading and Study Skills Foldables* booklet.

MAKING CONNECTIONS
Could World War II Have Been Prevented?

In the 1930s, global economic problems brought dictators to power in Europe and Japan, and another world war erupted. Many Americans, disillusioned by World War I, wanted to remain neutral, but when Japan attacked Pearl Harbor, the United States was forced to join the war.

- *What problems do you think World War I created that contributed to the outbreak of World War II?*
- *Do you think different American policies in the 1920s and 1930s could have prevented World War II?*

FOLDABLES

Comparing Totalitarian Dictators Make a Trifold Book Foldable to compare and contrast the dictatorships of Benito Mussolini, Joseph Stalin, and Adolf Hitler. As you read the chapter, add details about each ruler under his name. Use your list as a helpful study guide on their differences and similarities.

1938
- Munich Conference gives Sudetenland to Hitler

1939
- United States denies SS *St. Louis* permission to dock

1939
- Poland invaded; World War II begins

1940
- Roosevelt makes "destroyers-for-bases" deal with Britain

1940
- France surrenders to Germany; Britain wins Battle of Britain

1941
- Congress passes Lend Lease Act
- Japan attacks Pearl Harbor

1939   1941

History ONLINE Chapter Overview
Visit glencoe.com to preview Chapter 13.

Chapter 13   A World in Flames   **453**

Section 3

The Holocaust
Essential Question: How did the Nazis persecute the Jewish people? *(Nuremberg Laws, Kristallnacht, concentration and extermination camps)* Tell students that in this section they will learn about Hitler's attempts to destroy the Jewish people. **OL**

Section 4

America Enters the War
Essential Question: How did the United States become involved in World War II? *(supporting Britain through the Lend-Lease Act and the hemispheric defense zone, embargoing Japan, responding to the attack on Pearl Harbor)* Inform students that in this section they will learn about America's response to and involvement in the war. **OL**

History ONLINE
Introduce students to chapter content and key terms by having them access the Chapter 13 Overview at glencoe.com.

453

Focus

Bellringer
Daily Focus Transparency 13.1

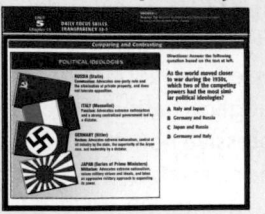

Guide to Reading

Answers may include:
America and the World
I. The Rise of Dictators
   A. Mussolini and Fascism in Italy
   B. Stalin Takes Over the USSR
   C. Hitler and Nazi Germany
   D. Militarists Control Japan
II. American Neutrality
   A. The Nye Committee
   B. Legislating Neutrality
   C. Roosevelt's Internationalism

Section Spotlight Video

To generate student interest and provide a springboard for class discussion, access the Chapter 13, Section 1 video at glencoe.com or on the video DVD.

Resource Manager

Section 1
America and the World

Guide to Reading

Big Ideas
Government and Society In the years following World War I, aggressive and expansionistic governments took power in both Europe and Asia.

Content Vocabulary
- fascism (p. 454)
- collective (p. 455)
- internationalism (p. 459)

Academic Vocabulary
- exploit (p. 454)
- dominate (p. 457)

People and Events to Identify
- Benito Mussolini (p. 454)
- Vladimir Lenin (p. 455)
- Joseph Stalin (p. 455)
- Adolf Hitler (p. 456)
- Manchuria (p. 457)
- Neutrality Act of 1935 (p. 458)
- Axis Powers (p. 459)

Reading Strategy
Taking Notes As you read about the events in Europe and Asia after World War I, use the major headings of the section to create an outline similar to the one below.

```
America and the World
I. The Rise of Dictators
   A.
   B.
   C.
   D.
II.
```

In the years following World War I, aggressive and expansionist governments took power in Europe and Asia. Meanwhile, most Americans did not want to get involved in another foreign war.

The Rise of Dictators

MAIN Idea Dictators took control of the governments of Italy, the Soviet Union, Germany, and Japan.

HISTORY AND YOU Can you think of a country today that is ruled by a dictator? Read about the repressive governments that arose during the 1920s and 1930s.

When World War I ended, President Wilson had hoped that the United States could "aid in the establishment of just democracy throughout the world." Instead, the treaty that ended the war, along with the economic depression that followed, contributed to the rise of antidemocratic governments in both Europe and Asia.

Mussolini and Fascism in Italy

One of Europe's first dictatorships arose in Italy. In 1919 **Benito Mussolini** founded Italy's Fascist Party. **Fascism** was an aggressive nationalistic movement that considered the nation more important than the individual. Fascists believed that order in society would come only through a dictator who led a strong government. They also thought nations became great by building an empire.

Fascism was also strongly anticommunist. After the Russian Revolution, many Europeans feared that communists, allied with labor unions, were trying to bring down their governments. Mussolini **exploited** these fears by portraying fascism as a bulwark against communism. Fascism began to stand for the protection of private property and the middle class. Mussolini also promised the working class full employment and social security. He pledged to return Italy to the glories of the Roman Empire.

Backed by the Fascist militia known as the Blackshirts, Mussolini threatened to march on Rome in 1922, claiming he was coming to defend Italy against a communist revolution. Liberal members of the Italian parliament insisted that the king declare martial law. When he refused, the cabinet resigned. Conservative advisers then persuaded the king to appoint Mussolini as the premier.

Once in office, Mussolini worked quickly to set up a dictatorship. Weary of strikes and riots, many Italians welcomed Mussolini's leadership. With the support of industrialists, landowners, and the Roman

---

R Reading Strategies	C Critical Thinking	D Differentiated Instruction	W Writing Support	S Skill Practice
Teacher Edition • Organizing, p. 456 • Taking Notes, p. 458 **Additional Resources** • Read. Skills Act., URB p. 21 • Prim. Source Read., URB p. 35 • Guid. Read. Act., URB p. 48	**Teacher Edition** • Comp. & Cont., p. 456 • Ident. Cent. Iss., p. 457 **Additional Resources** • Crit. Think. Skills, URB p. 32 • Quizzes and Tests, p. 185	**Teacher Edition** • Advanced Learners, p. 455 • Visual/Spatial, p. 458 **Additional Resources** • English Learn. Act., URB p. 25 • Foldables, p. 73	**Additional Resources** • Cont. Vocab. Act., URB p. 27 • Academic Vocab. Act., URB p. 29	**Teacher Edition** • Using Geography Skills, p. 455 **Additional Resources** • Hist. Analysis Skills, URB p. 22 • RENTG, p. 134

NATIONAL GEOGRAPHIC — The Rise of Dictators, 1922–1933

In 1936 General Francisco Franco launches a military revolt that overthrows Spain's democratic government; Franco then establishes a dictatorship.

In 1933, high unemployment and fears of communism enable Adolf Hitler and the Nazi Party to take power. Hitler imposed a dictatorship, enacted anti-Jewish policies, and began rebuilding the military.

In 1926 Joseph Stalin becomes dictator of the Soviet Union and begins to collectivize agriculture and industrialize the economy. His policies kill millions of rural peasants.

In 1922 fears of communism and economic chaos enable Benito Mussolini to lead the Fascists to power in Italy.

In 1931, the militarist Empire of Japan invades Manchuria; six years later, Japan attacks China. In 1941 General Hideki Tōjō becomes prime minister and led the nation into war with the United States.

Analyzing GEOGRAPHY

1. **Region** In which region of the world did a dictator first come to power, and when?
2. **Human-Environment Interactions** What effect did Stalin's policies have on the Soviet Union?

Catholic Church, Mussolini—who took the title of Il Duce, or "The Leader"—embarked on an ambitious program of bringing order to Italy.

Stalin Takes Over the USSR

After the Russian Revolution, the Communist Party, led by **Vladimir Lenin,** established communist governments throughout the Russian Empire. In 1922 they renamed these territories the Union of Soviet Socialist Republics (USSR). The Communists instituted one-party rule, suppressed individual liberties, and punished opponents.

After Lenin died in 1924, a power struggle began between Leon Trotsky and **Joseph Stalin.** Born with the surname of Dzuhgashvili, Stalin replaced his last name with the Russian word *stal,* meaning "steel." Between 1902 and 1913, he had been imprisoned or exiled seven times, but he always escaped.

By 1926, Stalin had become the new Soviet dictator. He began a massive effort to industrialize his country, using Five-Year Plans. During the first two of these Five-Year Plans, from 1928 to 1937, steel production increased from 4 million to 18 million tons (3.628 to 16.326 million t). At the same time, however, industrial wages declined by 43 percent from 1928 to 1940. Family farms were combined and turned into **collectives,** or government-owned farms. Peasants who resisted by killing livestock or hoarding crops faced show trials or death from starvation. As many as 10 million peasants died in famines during 1932 and 1933.

Stalin tolerated no opposition, targeting not only political enemies but also artists and intellectuals. During the late 1930s, the USSR was a nation of internal terrorism, with public trials that featured forced confessions. A new constitution, passed in 1936, promised many freedoms but was never enforced.

Chapter 13 A World in Flames **455**

Teach

D Differentiated Instruction

Advanced Learners Invite students to learn more about the power struggles that ensued after Lenin's death and Trotsky's fate. Suggest they present their findings to the class as a play or radio drama. **AL**

S Skill Practice

Using Geography Skills Ask students to look at the map and identify what they see as likely difficulties in governing the USSR. *(Students may suggest that the nation's great size would make effective government difficult, especially in the 1920s and 1930s, before improvements in both telecommunications and transportation.)* **OL**

Analyzing VISUALS

Answers:
1. Italy, 1922
2. farms and factories belonged to the state; millions died

Hands-On Chapter Project
Step 1

Creating a World War II Memory Book

Step 1: Selecting Memorable People

Ask: What famous people can you name who were in World War II?

Directions Ask students to list on the board the names of people who played a role in the war. Have students read ahead or do research to add as many names to the list as there are class members. Tell students to choose a name from the list and learn more about him or her in order to contribute a page to a class memory book. Make a scrapbook with the title "Memories of World War II" on the cover.

Putting It Together Students will identify the role played by each person added to the list. When dictators are chosen, students will discuss what conditions in each country allowed the dictators to gain power. **OL**
(Chapter Project continued on page 461)

R Reading Strategy

Organizing Have students create word webs or other graphic organizers to note the beliefs of postwar Germany's Nazi Party. Remind students that these graphic organizers can be helpful study aids. **BL**

C Critical Thinking

Comparing and Contrasting Have students compare Hitler's ideology to the ideas of Stalin and Mussolini. Ask them to identify elements that are similar and elements that are unique to Nazism. *(Hitler, Stalin, and Mussolini all created one-party states ruled by one strong leader; all three used violence to control political opponents; only Hitler had a specific racial component to his ideology)* **OL**

Additional Support

Stalin also used concentration camps; by 1935 some 2 million people were in camps, most of which were located in the Arctic. Prisoners were used as slave labor. Between 8 and 10 million people died as a result of Stalin's rule, which lasted until his death in 1953.

Hitler and Nazi Germany

Adolf Hitler was a fervent anticommunist and an admirer of Mussolini. A native Austrian, Hitler had fought for Germany in World War I. Germany's surrender and the subsequent Treaty of Versailles caused him and many other Germans to hate both the victorious Allies and the German government that had accepted the peace terms.

Postwar Germany's political and economic chaos led to the rise of new political parties. One of these was the National Socialist German Workers' Party, or the Nazi Party. The party was nationalistic and anticommunist, calling for Germany to expand its territory and not abide by the terms of the Treaty of Versailles. It also was anti-Semitic. Using the words *Socialist* and *Workers* in its name, the party

hoped to attract unhappy workers. Adolf Hitler was one of the party's first recruits.

In November 1923, the Nazis tried to seize power by marching on city hall in Munich, Germany. Hitler intended to seize power locally and then march on Berlin, the German capital, but the plan failed. The Nazi Party was banned for a time, and Hitler was arrested.

R While in prison, Hitler wrote *Mein Kampf* ("My Struggle"), in which he called for the unification of all Germans under one government. He claimed that Germans, particularly blond, blue-eyed Germans, belonged to a "master race" called Aryans. He argued that Germans needed more space and called for **C** Germany to expand east into Poland and Russia. According to Hitler, the Slavic peoples of eastern Europe belonged to an inferior race, which Germans should enslave. Hitler's racism was strongest, however, toward Jews. He believed that Jews were responsible for many of the world's problems, especially for Germany's defeat in World War I.

After his release, Hitler changed his tactics. Instead of trying to seize power violently, he focused on getting Nazis elected to the

NATIONAL GEOGRAPHIC — War and Civil War in the 1930s

▼ *Japanese officers targeted resource-rich Manchuria as the first goal in their drive to build an empire.*

Japan Invades Manchuria, 1931

U.S.S.R.
MONGOLIA
MANCHURIA (MANCHUKUO)
Sakhalin
Karafuto
CHINA
Changchun
Mukden
Peking
Dairen
Pyongyang
Seoul
Korea
Sea of Japan
JAPAN
Tokyo
Yellow Sea
Shanghai

→ Japanese invasion of Manchuria

0 400 kilometers
0 400 miles
Miller projection

Italy Invades Ethiopia, 1935

■ Italian-held territory
□ Ethiopia (Abyssinia)
← Italian invasion route

Red Sea
Eritrea
Anglo-Egyptian Sudan
Makale
Dessie
French Somaliland
Gulf of Aden
Dire Dawa
British Somaliland
Addis Ababa
Harar
ETHIOPIA
Italian Somaliland
Neghelli
INDIAN OCEAN
British East Africa

0 200 kilometers
0 200 miles
Miller projection

▲ *Mussolini, the dictator of Italy, wanted to build a new Roman Empire in Africa. In 1935 the Italian army invaded Ethiopia, then known as Abyssinia. The emperor, Haile Selassie, went into exile.*

Extending the Content

Inflation Remind students that inflation occurs when the cost of goods and services goes up and the value of money declines. One of the reasons for Germany's despair and willingness to accept Hitler as a leader can be attributed to the experience Germans had with inflation ten years earlier. In October 1922 the exchange rate was 4,500 German marks for one United States dollar. Eleven months later, the rate was 4.2 trillion marks per dollar. In 1923 a Hershey chocolate bar that sold for five cents in the United States cost 150,000 German marks or almost 33 dollars. Children used bundles of German marks to make building blocks; women used them to light fires. Although Germany got inflation under control, many people lost their savings and lost faith in the government. When the Great Depression hit in the 1930s, many Germans were willing to support Hitler and the Nazi Party because they recalled how badly the government had handled the economy during the time of inflation.

Reichstag, the lower house of the German parliament. When the Great Depression struck Germany, many desperate Germans began to vote for radical parties, including the Nazis and Communists. By 1932, the Nazis were the largest party in the Reichstag. The following year, the German president appointed Hitler as chancellor, or prime minister.

After taking office, Hitler called for new elections. He then ordered the police to crack down on the Socialist and Communist Parties. Storm troopers, as the Nazi paramilitary units were called, began intimidating voters. After the election, the Reichstag, dominated by the Nazis and other right-wing parties, voted to give Hitler dictatorial powers. In 1934 Hitler became president, which gave him control of the army. He then gave himself the new title of Der Führer, or "The Leader."

Militarists Control Japan

In Japan, as in Germany, difficult economic times helped undermine the political system. Japanese industries had to import nearly all of the resources they needed to produce goods.

During the 1920s Japan did not earn enough money from its exports to pay for its imports, which limited economic growth. When the Depression struck, other countries raised their tariffs. This made the situation even worse.

Many Japanese military officers blamed the country's problems on corrupt politicians. Most officers believed that Japan was destined to **dominate** East Asia and saw democracy as "un-Japanese" and bad for the country.

Japanese military leaders and their civilian supporters argued that seizing territory was the only way Japan could get the resources it needed. In September 1931, the Japanese army invaded **Manchuria,** a resource-rich region of northern China. When the Japanese prime minister tried to stop the war by negotiating with China, officers assassinated him. From that point forward, the military controlled the country. Japan's civilian government supported the nationalist policy of expanding the empire and appointed a military officer to serve as prime minister.

✓ Reading Check **Examining** How did postwar conditions contribute to the rise of dictatorships in Europe?

The Spanish Civil War, 1936–1939

In 1936 a civil war broke out in Spain when Fascist General Francisco Franco attempted a military coup. With aid from Hitler and Mussolini, Spain became a testing ground for new military ideas such as air strikes. On April 26, 1937, planes released 100,000 pounds of bombs, destroying 70% of Guernica, shown at left after the bombing. A mere 15 days after the bombing, the artist Pablo Picasso began painting Guernica (above).

Analyzing VISUALS

1. **Comparing** In what way were the three wars shown on the map all a prelude to World War II?
2. **Analyzing** How does Picasso show the terror of the Guernica bombing?

Chapter 13 A World in Flames **457**

Extending the Content

Japan and China Japan had dominated Manchuria since 1905, when Japan defeated both Russia and China. Japan at that time also controlled Korea and Taiwan, then known as Formosa. Japan was the strongest military power in the region and expanded industrially, only to face major losses due to the worldwide economic depression. During the mid-1930s, the Chinese were fighting a civil war between communists and nationalists. The two sides agreed, however, to join forces to defeat Japan. In spite of China's resistance, by 1938 Japan controlled much of eastern China, with puppet governments in both Nanjing and Beijing. The war between these two Asian nations continued until the end of World War II.

Analyzing VISUALS

1. Americans felt the country should have stayed out of World War I.
2. They wanted to avoid another war.

Additional Support

American Neutrality

MAIN Idea Most Americans did not want to get involved in another European war, despite Franklin Roosevelt's emphasis on internationalism.

HISTORY AND YOU Do you think the United States should become involved in the wars of other nations even when it is not under attack? Read to learn about American attitudes during the 1930s.

The rise of dictatorships and militarism discouraged many Americans. The sacrifices they had made during World War I seemed pointless. Once again, Americans began supporting isolationism and trying to avoid involvement in international conflicts.

The Nye Committee

Isolationist ideas became stronger in the early 1930s for two reasons. When the Depression began, many European nations found it difficult to repay money they had borrowed during World War I. In 1934 all of the debtor nations except Finland announced they would no longer repay their war debts.

Meanwhile, dozens of books and articles appeared arguing that arms manufacturers had tricked the United States into entering World War I. In 1934 Senator Gerald P. Nye of North Dakota held hearings to investigate these allegations. The Nye Committee documented the huge profits that arms factories had made during the war. The report created the impression that these businesses influenced the decision to go to war. Coupled with the European refusal to repay their loans, the Nye Committee's findings turned even more Americans toward isolationism.

Legislating Neutrality

Italian and German aggression increased under Mussolini and Hitler. Worried that the actions of these nations might lead to war, Congress passed the **Neutrality Act of 1935.** This legislation—reflecting the belief that arms sales had helped bring the United States into World War I—made it illegal for Americans to sell arms to any country at war.

In 1936 a rebellion erupted in Spain after voters elected a coalition of Republicans, Socialists, and Communists. General Francisco Franco led the rebellion, backed by Spanish Fascists, army officers, landowners, and Catholic Church leaders. The revolt became a civil war and attracted

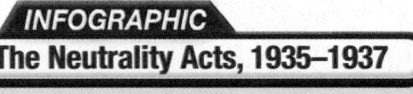

INFOGRAPHIC
The Neutrality Acts, 1935–1937

Causes
- Nye Senate Committee report suggesting that the American arms industry had pushed the nation into World War I for its own profit
- growing belief that America should have stayed out of World War I

The Neutrality Act of 1935
- mandatory embargo on selling or exporting arms, ammunition, or implements of war to nations at war
- discretionary travel restrictions
- set to expire after 6 months

Causes
- Italy's invasion of Ethiopia; FDR encourages a moral embargo against Italy, which he could not enforce

The Neutrality Act of 1936
- arms embargo with countries at war
- discretionary travel restrictions
- ban on loans to nations fighting, but short-term credits exempted
- republics in the Americas exempted

Causes
- Spanish Civil War
- sale of aviation parts to rebels in Spain, which FDR thought unpatriotic
- agreements creating the Axis alliance

The Neutrality Act of 1937
- arms embargo against nations at war
- travel ban on warring nations' ships
- trade with countries at war on a cash-and-carry basis allowed if goods were not contraband or sent on foreign ships

▲ Republican Senator Gerald Nye headed the Senate Munitions Committee, whose findings convinced many that arms makers were "merchants of death" and that the United States should remain neutral.

Analyzing VISUALS

1. **Analyzing** What impact did the Nye Committee's findings have on public opinion?
2. **Evaluating** Why did so many Americans support neutrality?

458 Chapter 13 A World in Flames

Activity: Collaborative Learning

Write a Résumé Have students work together in pairs to create a résumé for one of the major leaders of this period. Tell them to include the leader's education, career experience, political offices held, and major events in which the person participated. Also ask them to include any skills, activities, and memberships that might present a fuller picture. Possible subjects include Adolf Hitler, Benito Mussolini, Joseph Stalin, Hideki Tojo, Winston Churchill, and Franklin Roosevelt. **OL**

worldwide attention. Congress passed a second neutrality act, banning the sale of arms to either side in a civil war.

Shortly after the Spanish Civil War began, Hitler and Mussolini pledged to cooperate on several international issues. Mussolini termed this new relationship the Rome-Berlin Axis. The following month, Japan aligned itself with Germany and Italy when it signed the Anti-Comintern Pact with Germany. The pact required the two countries to exchange information about communist groups. Together, Germany, Italy, and Japan became known as the **Axis Powers,** although they did not formally become military allies until September 1940.

With tensions in Europe worsening, Congress passed the Neutrality Act of 1937. This act not only continued the ban on selling arms to warring nations, but also required them to buy all nonmilitary supplies from the United States on a "cash-and-carry" basis. Countries at war had to send their own ships to the United States to pick up the goods, and they had to pay cash. Loans were not allowed. Isolationists knew that attacks on American ships carrying supplies to Europe had helped bring the country into World War I. They wanted to prevent such attacks from involving the nation in another European war.

Roosevelt's Internationalism

When he took office in 1933, President Roosevelt knew that ending the Great Depression was his first priority. He was not, however, an isolationist. He supported **internationalism,** the idea that trade between nations creates prosperity and helps prevent war. Internationalists also believed that the United States should try to preserve peace in the world. Roosevelt warned that the neutrality acts "might drag us into war instead of keeping us out," but he did not veto the bills.

In July 1937, Japanese forces in Manchuria launched a full-scale attack on China. Roosevelt decided to help the Chinese. Because neither China nor Japan had actually declared war, Roosevelt claimed the Neutrality Act of 1937 did not apply, and he authorized the sale of weapons to China. He warned that the nation should not stand by and let an "epidemic of lawlessness" infect the world:

PRIMARY SOURCE

"When an epidemic of physical disease starts to spread, the community ... joins in a quarantine of the patients in order to protect the health of the community against the spread of the disease.... War is a contagion, whether it be declared or undeclared.... There is no escape through mere isolation or neutrality.... "

—quoted in *Freedom From Fear*

Despite his words, Americans were still not willing to risk another war. "It is a terrible thing," the president said, "to look over your shoulder when you are trying to lead—and find no one there."

✔**Reading Check** **Evaluating** Why did many Americans support isolationism?

Section 1 REVIEW

Vocabulary

1. **Explain** the significance of: Benito Mussolini, fascism, Vladimir Lenin, Joseph Stalin, collectives, Adolf Hitler, Manchuria, Neutrality Act of 1935, Axis Powers, internationalism.

Main Ideas

2. **Identifying** Which nations did dictators govern during the years after World War I?

3. **Analyzing** What events caused Roosevelt to become more of an internationalist?

Critical Thinking

4. **Big Ideas** Why did antidemocratic governments rise to power in postwar Europe and Asia?

5. **Organizing** Use a graphic organizer similar to the one below to compare the governments opposed to democracy in Europe and Asia.

Country	Dictator	Ideology

6. **Analyzing Visuals** Look at the photograph on page 457 of Guernica after it was destroyed. How might both isolationists and internationalists have used the image to win support for their cause?

Writing About History

7. **Persuasive Writing** Write a newspaper editorial supporting either isolationism or internationalism after World War I. Include reasons that support your ideas and that help convince others to embrace your position.

 History ONLINE
Study Central™ To review this section, go to glencoe.com and click on Study Central.

459

Assess

History ONLINE

Study Central™ provides summaries, interactive games, and online graphic organizers to help students review content.

Close

Summarizing **Ask:** How did World War I influence the political destinies of both European nations and the United States? *(In European nations, many were faced with heavy reparations, unemployment, and economic depression and grew desperate for powerful leadership, even at the loss of personal liberties. In the United States, a feeling of betrayal and a return to isolationism produced an unwillingness to become involved in Europe's difficulties.)* **OL**

✔**Reading Check**

Answer: They felt that remaining apart from European conflicts would avoid another war.

Section 1 REVIEW

Answers

1. All definitions can be found in the section and the Glossary.
2. Italy, the USSR, and Germany
3. Japanese invasion of China
4. unhappiness with Treaty of Versailles terms, worldwide economic depression
5. Italy: Mussolini, Fascism; USSR: Stalin, Communism; Germany: Hitler, Nazism; Japan: Japanese military, Japanese militarism

6. Students' responses will vary but students may suggest that isolationists would have depicted the destruction as a reason to stay out of war, while internationalists may have emphasized growing fascism as a reason to increase involvement.
7. Answers will vary but should include text material.

Focus

Bellringer
Daily Focus Transparency 13.2

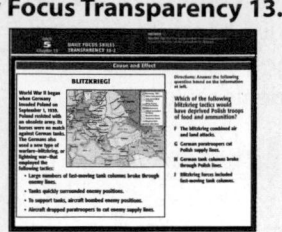

Guide to Reading

Answers:
1937: Hitler calls for German unity; February 1938: Hitler threatens to invade Austria; March 1938: the *Anschluss*; September 1938: Germany claims Sudetenland; October 1938 Germany demands return of Danzig; March 1939: Germany annexes Czechoslovakia; May 1939 Germany invades Poland; August 1939: Nazi-Soviet Nonaggression Pact

Section Spotlight Video

To generate student interest and provide a springboard for class discussion, access the Chapter 13, Section 2 video at glencoe.com or on the video DVD.

Resource Manager

Section 2

World War II Begins

The shadow of World War I loomed large in the minds of European leaders in the late 1930s. Although Nazi Germany appeared increasingly aggressive, Britain and France wanted to avoid another bloody conflict. Efforts to negotiate peaceful agreements with Nazi Germany ultimately failed.

Path to War

MAIN Idea European nations tried to prevent war by giving in to Adolf Hitler's demands.

HISTORY AND YOU Do you remember reading how Europe was divided after World War I? Read to learn how German demands for more territory started World War II.

In 1935 Hitler began to defy the Treaty of Versailles that had ended World War I. He announced that Germany would build a new air force and begin a military draft that would greatly expand its army—actions in direct **violation** of the treaty. Rather than enforce the treaty by going to war, European leaders tried to negotiate with Hitler. At the time, the Nazi **regime** was weaker than it later would become. If European leaders had responded more aggressively, could war have been avoided? Historians still debate this question today.

Europe's leaders had several reasons for believing—or wanting to believe—that a deal could be reached with Hitler and that war could be avoided. First, they wanted to avoid a repeat of the bloodshed of World War I. Second, some thought most of Hitler's demands were reasonable, including his demand that all German-speaking regions be united. Third, many people assumed that the Nazis would be more interested in peace once they gained more territory.

The Austrian *Anschluss*

In late 1937 Hitler again called for the unification of all German-speaking people, including those in Austria and Czechoslovakia. He believed that Germany could expand its territory only by "resort[ing] to force with its attendant risks."

In February 1938 Hitler threatened to invade German-speaking Austria unless Austrian Nazis were given important government posts. Austria's chancellor gave in to this demand, but then tried to put the matter of unification with Germany to a democratic vote. Fearing the outcome, Hitler sent troops into Austria in March and announced the *Anschluss,* or unification, of Austria and Germany.

Guide to Reading

Big Ideas
Trade, War, and Migration World War II officially began with the Nazi invasion of Poland and the French and British declarations of war on Germany in September 1939.

Content Vocabulary
• appeasement *(p. 461)*
• blitzkrieg *(p. 462)*

Academic Vocabulary
• violation *(p. 460)*
• regime *(p. 460)*
• concentrate *(p. 462)*
• transport *(p. 465)*

People and Events to Identify
• *Anschluss (p. 460)*
• Munich Conference *(p. 461)*
• Maginot Line *(p. 462)*
• Winston Churchill *(p. 465)*
• Battle of Britain *(p. 465)*

Reading Strategy
Sequencing As you read about the events leading up to World War II, record them by completing a time line similar to the one below.

R Reading Strategies	**C** Critical Thinking	**D** Differentiated Instruction	**W** Writing Support	**S** Skill Practice
Teacher Edition • Using Word Parts, p. 461 **Additional Resources** • Guid. Read. Act., URB p. 49	**Teacher Edition** • Making Inferences, p. 461 • Drawing Con., p. 462 • Analyzing Info., p. 464 • Det. Cause/Effect, p. 465 **Additional Resources** • Quizzes and Tests, p. 186	**Teacher Edition** • Verbal/Linguistic, p. 463		**Additional Resources** • Reinforcing Skills Act., URB p. 31 • RENTG, p. 137

NATIONAL GEOGRAPHIC **The Causes of World War II in Europe, 1935–1939**

0   200 kilometers
0   200 miles
Lambert Azimuthal
Equal-Area projection

Hitler demands the return of Danzig to Germany, October 1938.

In August 1939, the Nazi-Soviet Pact is signed. One week later, on Sept. 1, Germany invades Poland.

In March 1936, Germany sends troops into the Rhineland, defying the Treaty of Versailles.

Austrian *Anschluss*, 1938—Germany annexes Austria.

▲ At Munich in 1938, Britain's Neville Chamberlain (left), Mussolini (second from left), and Hitler (right) reached a deal that prevented war but required Czechoslovakia to give up the Sudetenland (brown area on the Czech border above) to Germany. Six months later, Germany occupied all of Czechoslovakia.

Analyzing GEOGRAPHY

1. **Region** Why do you think Hitler's first military action was in the Rhineland?
2. **Region** Why might Hitler have welcomed a nonaggression pact with the Soviets?

Maps In MOtion See *StudentWorks*™ *Plus* or glencoe.com.

The Munich Crisis

Hitler next announced German claims to the Sudetenland, an area of Czechoslovakia with a large German-speaking population. The Czechs strongly resisted Germany's demands for the Sudetenland. France threatened to fight if Germany attacked Czechoslovakia, and the Soviet Union also promised aid. Prime Minister Neville Chamberlain pledged Britain's support to France, its ally.

Representatives of Britain, France, Italy, and Germany agreed to meet in Munich to decide Czechoslovakia's fate. At the **Munich**

Conference, on September 29, 1938, Britain and France agreed to Hitler's demands, a policy that came to be known as **appeasement.** In other words, they made concessions in exchange for peace. Supporters of appeasement believed that Hitler had a few limited demands. They felt that if they gave him what he wanted, they could avoid war. Czechoslovakia was told to give up the Sudetenland or fight Germany on its own. When Chamberlain returned home, he promised "a peace with honor . . . peace in our time," but he also began to speed up British rearmament—in case appeasement failed.

Chapter 13 A World in Flames **461**

Teach

R Reading Strategy

Using Word Parts Ask students to identify the root and the suffix in *appeasement.* (*appease* is the root; *-ment* is the suffix) Remind students that the suffix *-ment* means "process or action." **EL**

C Critical Thinking

Making Inferences Point out the final sentence of text on this page. **Ask:** How do you know that Chamberlain did not trust Hitler? (*He began rearming Britain at a faster pace.*) **OL**

Analyzing GEOGRAPHY

Answers:
1. the Rhineland was part of Germany so it was harder to object to his actions there
2. Hitler wanted to free himself for war against Western countries by making sure the Soviets would not halt his expansionism.

Hands-On Chapter Project
Step 2

Creating a World War II Memory Book

Step 2: Researching Selected Names Each student will do research on the name chosen in Step 1.

Directions Have students use library, Internet, or family resources to learn more about the person whose name they chose. Ask students to gather photos and information about the person's background, motivation, and his or her role in the war. They

should also select a quotation or short paragraph written by the person, if possible.

Evaluating Information To decide which information to include, students will gain practice in evaluating the reliability of sources and the relevance of the information to the project. **OL**

(*Chapter Project continued on page 467*)

Did You Know?

The Baltic city of Gdansk (or Danzig in German) has historically been politically free and part of either Poland or German-speaking Prussia. It was part of Prussia until the Treaty of Versailles, when it became free. Identification with Germany has been strong, however; in the 1930s, Nazi officials were voted into the majority of the city assembly.

C Critical Thinking

Drawing Conclusions

Ask: What did Germany and the USSR each stand to gain by this treaty? *(They both would gain some of Poland and other Eastern European lands. Germany would not have to fight on two fronts and could concentrate on defeating Britain and France. The USSR would be safe from German attack.)* **OL**

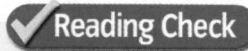

Reading Check

Answer: Austria, Czechoslovakia, Danzig, Poland

Additional Support

Appeasement did fail to preserve the fragile peace. In March 1939, Germany sent troops into Czechoslovakia and divided the country. Slovakia became independent in name, but it was actually under German control. The Czech lands became a German protectorate.

Hitler Demands Danzig

A month after the Munich Conference, Hitler demanded that the city of Danzig be returned to German control. Although Danzig was more than 90 percent German, it had been part of Poland since World War I. Hitler also requested a highway and railroad across the Polish Corridor, an area that separated western Germany from the German state of East Prussia.

Hitler's new demands convinced Britain and France that war was inevitable. On March 31, 1939, Britain announced that if Poland went to war to defend its territory, Britain and France would come to its aid. This declaration encouraged Poland to refuse Hitler's demands. In May 1939, Hitler ordered the German army to prepare to invade Poland. He also ordered his foreign minister to begin negotiations with the USSR. If Germany was going to fight Britain and France, Hitler did not want to have to fight the Soviets, too.

The Nazi-Soviet Pact

When German officials proposed a nonaggression treaty to the Soviets, Stalin agreed. He believed the best way to protect the USSR was to turn the capitalist nations against each other. If the treaty worked, Germany would go to war against Britain and France, and the USSR would be safe.

C The nonaggression pact, signed by Germany and the USSR on August 23, 1939, shocked the world. Communism and Nazism were supposed to be totally opposed to each other. Leaders in Britain and France understood, however, that Hitler had made the deal to free himself for war against their countries and Poland. They did not know that the treaty also contained a secret deal to divide Poland between Germany and the Soviet Union.

Reading Check **Identifying** What regions did Hitler take or demand in the lead-up to the war?

The War Begins

MAIN Idea After Poland and France fell to the Nazis, the British evacuated thousands of trapped troops from Dunkirk.

HISTORY AND YOU Can you think of a contemporary situation in which people acted heroically to save others in danger? Read to learn about the heroism of civilians and soldiers in World War II.

On September 1, 1939, Germany invaded Poland. Two days later, Britain and France declared war on Germany. World War II had begun.

Poland bravely resisted Germany's onslaught, but its army was outdated. The Polish army rode horses and carried lances against German tanks. In addition, the Germans used a new type of warfare called **blitzkrieg**, or "lightning war." Blitzkrieg used large numbers of massed tanks to break through and rapidly encircle enemy positions. To support the tanks, waves of aircraft bombed enemy positions and dropped paratroopers to cut their supply lines. The Polish army could not repel the attack. Warsaw, the Polish capital, fell to the Germans on September 27. By October 5, 1939, the Germans had defeated the Polish military.

The Fall of France

In contrast to the war in Poland, western Europe remained eerily quiet. The Germans referred to this situation as the *sitzkrieg*, or "sitting war." The British called it the "Bore War," while American newspapers nicknamed it the "Phony War." The British had sent troops to France, and both countries remained on the defensive, waiting for the Germans to attack.

After World War I, the French had built a line of concrete bunkers and fortifications called the **Maginot Line** along the German border. Rather than risk their troops by attacking, the French preferred to wait behind the Maginot Line for the Germans to approach. This decision proved to be disastrous for two reasons. First, it allowed Germany to **concentrate** on Poland first before turning west to face the British and French. Second, Hitler decided to go around the Maginot Line, which protected France's border with Germany but not France's border with Belgium.

Activity: Cooperative Learning

Prepare a News Broadcast Divide the class into six small groups. Assign each group one of the following events: the Austrian Anschluss, the Munich Conference, the Nazi-Soviet Nonaggression Pact, the invasion of Poland, the invasion of France, or the evacuation of Dunkirk. Have each group create a brief television newscast covering the event. If possible, allow students to videotape their stories in chronological order and then play the videotape for the class. **OL**

To get around the Maginot Line, the Germans would have to invade the Netherlands, Belgium, and Luxembourg first—which is exactly what they did. On May 10, Hitler launched a new blitzkrieg. While German troops parachuted into the Netherlands, an army of tanks rolled into Belgium and Luxembourg.

The British and French had expected the German attack. As soon as it began, British and French forces raced north into Belgium. This was a mistake. Instead of sending their tanks through the open countryside of central Belgium, the Germans sent their main force through the Ardennes Mountains of Luxembourg and eastern Belgium. The French did not think that large numbers of tanks could move through the mountains, and had left only a few troops to defend that part of the border. The Germans easily smashed through the French lines, and then turned west across northern France to the English Channel. The British and French armies were still in Belgium and could not move back into France quickly enough. They were now trapped in Belgium.

The Miracle at Dunkirk

After trapping the Allied forces in Belgium, the Germans began to drive them toward the English Channel. The only hope for Britain and France was to evacuate their surviving troops by sea, but the Germans had captured all but one port, Dunkirk, in northern France near the Belgian border.

D

D **Differentiated Instruction**

Verbal/Linguistic Invite students to read Paul Gallico's short story "The Snow Goose," which is about a disabled man in England who helps with the evacuation of Dunkirk. Ask them to take notes as they read and prepare a response summarizing the story and describing why they think that so many citizens wanted to contribute to the war effort. **OL**

Analyzing VISUALS

Answers:
1. Students may point out the long line of tanks, the isolated countryside, or the lack of any resistance.
2. Students may suggest snipers, land mines, or other forms of enemy attack, in addition to risk of parachutes not opening.

TECHNOLOGY & HISTORY

Blitzkrieg In 1939 Germany unleashed blitzkrieg—lightning war—on Europe. Blitzkrieg combined several technologies—aircraft, tanks, parachutes, and radios—to produce a highly mobile, fast-moving army that could coordinate multiple attacks, break through lines, and rapidly encircle enemy positions.

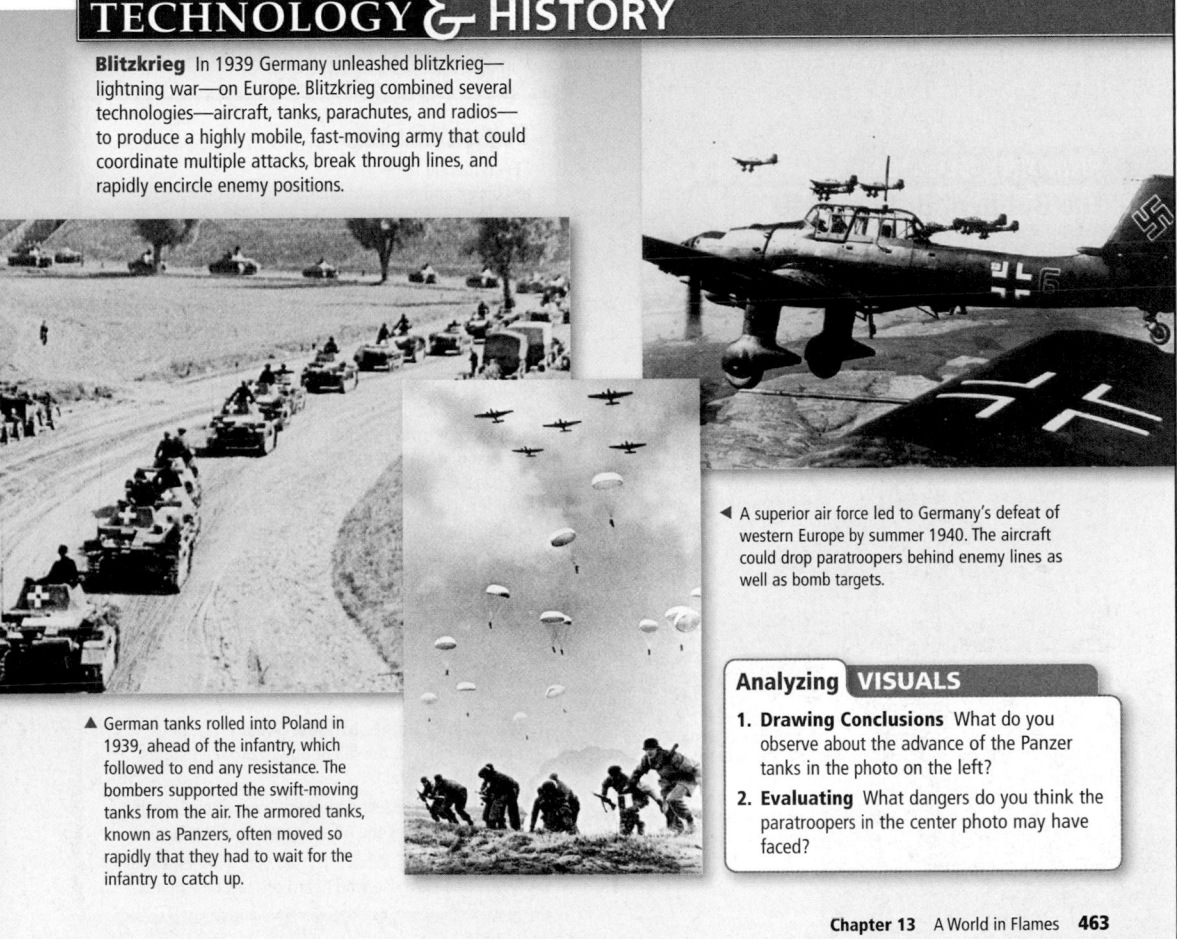

◄ A superior air force led to Germany's defeat of western Europe by summer 1940. The aircraft could drop paratroopers behind enemy lines as well as bomb targets.

▲ German tanks rolled into Poland in 1939, ahead of the infantry, which followed to end any resistance. The bombers supported the swift-moving tanks from the air. The armored tanks, known as Panzers, often moved so rapidly that they had to wait for the infantry to catch up.

Analyzing VISUALS

1. **Drawing Conclusions** What do you observe about the advance of the Panzer tanks in the photo on the left?
2. **Evaluating** What dangers do you think the paratroopers in the center photo may have faced?

Chapter 13 A World in Flames **463**

Additional Support

Extending the Content

Winston Churchill British Prime Minister Neville Chamberlain resigned in May 1940. Winston Churchill, heading a coalition government, took office on May 11. Less than a month later, the evacuation of Dunkirk began. Although the successful evacuation raised morale, Churchill warned members of Parliament that, "Wars are not won by evacuations." The son of an American mother and a British lord, Churchill had attended the British equivalent of West Point and had seen fighting in Cuba, India, Sudan, and South Africa before his service in France during World War I. He was among the first to sense the danger of the Nazi Party.

Critical Thinking

Analyzing Information Draw students' attention to the first paragraph, listing assumed reasons for Hitler's delay in attacking Dunkirk. Ask students to evaluate each reason and determine its validity. **OL**

✔**Reading Check**

Answer: by use of the blitzkrieg, using large numbers of tanks, infantry, and air power in a coordinated attack

DBQ **Document Based Questions**

Answers:
1. None; they are going to fight and defend the island regardless of Nazi successes elsewhere.
2. their confidence and their strength in the air
3. Students' responses will vary but may suggest that it gave his audience determination and hope.

Differentiated Instruction

As German forces closed in on Dunkirk, Hitler suddenly ordered them to stop. No one is sure why he gave this order. Historians know that Hitler was nervous about risking his tank forces, and he wanted to wait until more infantry arrived. Hermann Goering, the head of the German air force, also assured Hitler that aircraft alone could destroy the trapped soldiers. There is also some evidence that Hitler thought that the British would be more willing to accept peace if the Germans did not humiliate them by destroying their forces at Dunkirk.

Whatever Hitler's reasons, his order provided a three-day delay. This gave the British time to strengthen their lines and begin the evacuation. Some 850 ships of all sizes—from navy warships to small sailboats operated by civilian volunteers—headed to Dunkirk from England, many of them making the 48-mile trip multiple times. French, Dutch, and Belgian ships joined British ones in "Operation Dynamo." The British had hoped to rescue about 45,000 troops. Instead, when the evacu-

ation ended on June 4, an estimated 338,000 British and French troops had been saved. This became known as the "Miracle at Dunkirk."

The evacuation had its price, however. Almost all of the British army's equipment remained at Dunkirk—90,000 rifles, 7,000 tons of ammunition, and 120,000 vehicles. If Hitler invaded Britain, it would be almost impossible to stop him from conquering the country.

Three weeks later, on June 22, 1940, Hitler accepted the French surrender in the same railway car in which the Germans had surrendered at the end of World War I. Germany now occupied much of northern France and its Atlantic coastline. To govern the rest of France, Germany installed a puppet government at the town of Vichy and made Marshal Philippe Pétain the new government's figurehead leader. Pétain predicted that Britain "will have her neck wrung like a chicken."

✔**Reading Check** **Explaining** By what means did Hitler overtake both Poland and France?

PRIMARY SOURCE
The Battle of Britain, 1940

During the Battle of Britain, bombs fell around London's St. Paul's Cathedral, a famous architectural treasure as well as a place of worship. Some of the subways no longer ran but were converted to air-raid shelters where people could sleep.

PRIMARY SOURCE

▲ *Winston Churchill*

"Even though large tracts of Europe and many old and famous States have fallen or may fall into the grip of the Gestapo and all the odious apparatus of Nazi rule, we shall not flag or fail, we shall go on to the end, we shall fight in France, we shall fight on the seas and oceans, we shall fight with growing confidence and growing strength in the air, we shall defend our island, whatever the cost may be, we shall fight on the beaches, we shall fight on the landing grounds, we shall fight in the fields and in the streets, we shall fight in the hills; we shall never surrender...."

—Winston Churchill, Speech to Parliament, June 4, 1940

DBQ **Document-Based Questions**

1. **Identifying Points of View** What effect does Churchill suggest the fall of other European states will have on Britain?
2. **Analyzing Primary Sources** What does Churchill expect to grow as the Allied forces fight the Nazis?
3. **Hypothesizing** What effect do you think Churchill's words had on those who heard or read the speech?

Leveled Activities

BL **Critical Thinking Skills Activity, URB p. 32**

OL **American Art and Music Activity, URB p. 40**

AL **Enrichment Activity, URB p. 45**

ELL **Primary Source Reading Activity, URB p. 35**

Britain Remains Defiant

MAIN Idea Despite the bombing of London and other major cities, Britain's Winston Churchill stood firm against the threat of Nazi invasion.

HISTORY AND YOU Think of a time when the odds were against you. How did you react? Read about British resolve when faced with Nazi air raids.

Neither Pétain nor Hitler anticipated the bravery of the British people or the spirit of their leader, **Winston Churchill,** who had replaced Neville Chamberlain as prime minister. Hitler expected Britain to negotiate peace after France surrendered, but on June 4, 1940, Churchill delivered a defiant speech in Parliament, vowing that Britain would never surrender. The speech was intended to rally the British people and to alert the isolationist United States to Britain's plight.

Realizing Britain would not surrender, Hitler ordered his commanders to prepare to invade. Getting across the English Channel, however, posed a major challenge. Germany had few **transport** ships, and the British air force would sink them if they tried to land troops in England. To invade, therefore, Germany first had to defeat the British Royal Air Force.

In June 1940, the German air force, called the *Luftwaffe*, began to attack British shipping in the English Channel. Then, in mid-August, the *Luftwaffe* launched an all-out air battle to destroy the Royal Air Force. This air battle, which lasted into the fall of 1940, became known as the **Battle of Britain.**

On August 23, German bombers accidentally bombed London, the British capital. This attack on civilians enraged the British, who responded by bombing Berlin the following night. For the first time in the war, bombs fell on the German capital. Infuriated, Hitler ordered the *Luftwaffe* to stop its attacks on British military targets and to concentrate on bombing London.

Hitler's goal was to terrorize the British people into surrendering. The British endured, however, taking refuge in cellars and subway stations whenever German bombers appeared.

Although the Royal Air Force was greatly outnumbered, the British had one major advantage. They had developed a new technology called radar. Using radar stations placed along their coast, the British were able to detect incoming German aircraft and direct British fighters to intercept them.

Day after day, the British fighters inflicted more losses on the Germans than they suffered. During the long battle, Germany lost 1,733 aircraft while the British lost 915 fighter planes, along with 449 pilots. The skill of more than 2,000 British and 500 foreign pilots—including many Poles, Canadians, Frenchmen, and a few Americans—successfully thwarted Hitler's plan to invade Britain. These pilots flew as often as five times a day. Praising them, Churchill told Parliament, "Never in the field of human conflict was so much owed by so many to so few." On October 12, 1940, Hitler canceled the invasion of Britain.

✓ Reading Check **Evaluating** How was Britain able to resist Hitler and the Nazis?

Section 2 REVIEW

Vocabulary

1. **Explain** the significance of: *Anschluss*, Munich Conference, appeasement, blitz-krieg, Maginot Line, Winston Churchill, Battle of Britain.

Main Ideas

2. **Explaining** Why did Europe's leaders first try to deal with Hitler through appeasement?

3. **Analyzing** Why was the decision to leave French forces behind the Maginot Line disastrous for Europe?

4. **Summarizing** In what ways did Winston Churchill prove to be an effective leader for Britain as the war began?

Critical Thinking

5. **Big Ideas** What was the new type of warfare used by Germany against Poland? Explain the technique.

6. **Organizing** Use a graphic organizer similar to the one below to list early events of the war in Poland and western Europe.

Events

7. **Analyzing Visuals** Look again at the photograph on page 461. What do you observe about the participants at the Munich Conference?

Writing About History

8. **Expository Writing** Choose one dramatic incident from the beginnings of World War II and write a news story explaining what happened.

History ONLINE
Study Central™ To review this section, go to glencoe.com and click on Study Central.

465

C Critical Thinking

Determining Cause and Effect Ask students to read the material under the subheading "Britain Remains Defiant." Have them make cause-and-effect graphic organizers and use them to show the interaction between Britain and Germany in 1940. **OL**

Assess

Study Central™ provides summaries, interactive games, and online graphic organizers to help students review content.

Close

Summarizing Ask: **What factor encouraged Hitler's aggression in Europe?** *(the reluctance of France and Britain to fight another war)* **OL**

✓ Reading Check

Answer: Germany had few transport ships to send troops across the English Channel; the British had developed radar.

Section 2 REVIEW

Answers

1. All definitions can be found in the section and the Glossary.

2. They believed that Hitler had few demands and that by giving in they could prevent another war.

3. It allowed Germany to concentrate on Poland first; when Germany went around the line, troops were trapped in Belgium.

4. Churchill was determined to prevent the Germans from controlling Britain.

5. The Germans used blitzkrieg, a lightning war in which tanks on the ground supported airstrikes.

6. Answers may include the following: Germany and Soviets invade Poland; Britain and France enter the war; Germany invades Norway, Denmark, Belgium, the Netherlands, Luxembourg, and France

7. No one looks pleased or relaxed, despite the apparent progress in preventing war.

8. Students' news stories will vary but should center on a single event at the beginning of World War II and be written in journalistic style.

Focus

Bellringer
Daily Focus Transparency 13.3

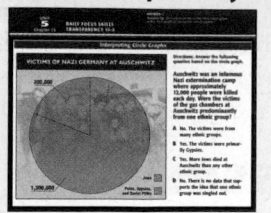

Guide to Reading

Answers:

Answers may include the following: segregated from the rest of the population, lost their jobs, stripped of citizenship, prohibited from voting or holding office, had identifying mark placed on passport, confined to concentration camps, killed in extermination camps

Section Spotlight Video

To generate student interest and provide a springboard for class discussion, access the Chapter 13, Section 3 video at glencoe.com or on the video DVD.

Resource Manager

The Holocaust

Guide to Reading

Big Ideas

Group Action The Nazis believed Jews to be subhuman. They steadily increased their persecution of Jews and eventually set up death camps and tried to kill all the Jews in Europe.

Content Vocabulary
• concentration camp (p. 470)
• extermination camp (p. 470)

Academic Vocabulary
• prohibit (p. 466)
• assume (p. 468)
• virtually (p. 471)

People and Events to Identify
• Shoah (p. 466)
• Nuremberg Laws (p. 466)
• Gestapo (p. 468)
• Wannsee Conference (p. 470)

Reading Strategy

Organizing As you read about the Holocaust, complete a graphic organizer similar to the one below by listing examples of Nazi persecution of European Jews.

Nazis first acted upon their racist ideology when they imposed restrictions on Jews and stripped them of basic rights. Eventually, Nazi Germany created concentration camps and systematically attempted to kill all European Jews and others whom they regarded as inferior.

Nazi Persecution of the Jews

MAIN Idea Nazi laws stripped Jews of citizenship and all fundamental rights; immigration restrictions in other countries made leaving Germany difficult.

HISTORY AND YOU Do you know anyone who came to the United States as a refugee? Read how Jewish refugees were turned away in the late 1930s.

During the Holocaust, the Nazis killed nearly 6 million European Jews. The Nazis also killed millions of people from other groups they considered inferior. The Hebrew term for the Holocaust is **Shoah,** meaning "catastrophe," but it is often used specifically to refer to the Nazi campaign to exterminate the Jews during World War II.

The Nuremberg Laws

Although the Nazis persecuted anyone who dared oppose them, as well as the disabled, Gypsies, homosexuals, and Slavic peoples, they reserved their strongest hatred for the Jews. This loathing went far beyond the European anti-Semitism that was common at the time. Over the centuries, people who were prejudiced against Jews had discriminated against them in many ways. For example, Jews had sometimes been segregated in ghettos or **prohibited** from owning land.

After the Nazis took power, they quickly moved to deprive German Jews of many established rights. In September 1935, the **Nuremberg Laws** took citizenship away from Jewish Germans and banned marriage between Jews and other Germans. Two months later, another decree defined a Jew as a person with at least one Jewish grandparent and barred Jews from holding public office or voting. Another law compelled Jews with German-sounding names to adopt "Jewish" names. Soon the passports of Jews were marked with a red *J* to identify them as Jewish.

By the summer of 1936, at least half of Germany's Jews were jobless, having lost the right to work as civil servants, journalists, farmers, teachers, and actors. In 1938 the Nazis also banned Jews from practicing law and medicine and from operating businesses. With no source of income, life became very difficult.

R Reading Strategies	C Critical Thinking	D Differentiated Instruction	W Writing Support	S Skill Practice
Teacher Edition • Summarizing, p. 467 • Act. Prior Know., p. 469 • Inferring, p. 469 • Using Word Parts, p. 470 • Using Context Clues, p. 470 **Additional Resources** • Guid. Read. Act., URB p. 50	**Teacher Edition** • Analyzing Prim. Sources, p. 467 **Additional Resources** • Quizzes and Tests, p. 187	**Teacher Edition** • Verbal/Linguistic, p. 468		**Teacher Addition** • Creating Charts, p. 468 **Additional Resources** • Time Line Act., URB p. 33 • RENTG, p. 140

The Persecution Begins, 1935–1938

▼ *Nazi storm troopers place warning signs encouraging a boycott on Jewish-owned businesses in 1933.*

▲ *On Kristallnacht, November 7, 1938, roaming bands of Nazi storm troopers destroyed Jewish property and terrorized Jewish families across the Third Reich.*

Analyzing VISUALS

1. **Hypothesizing** What effect do you think the signs might have had on the woman in the photograph on the left?
2. **Making Connections** How do you think publication of the photograph of the synagogue would have affected world opinion toward the Nazis?

Despite worsening conditions, many Jews chose to remain in Germany during the early years of Nazi rule. Well integrated into German society before this time, they were reluctant to leave and give up the lives they had built there. Many also thought that conditions would surely improve after a time. In fact, conditions soon became worse.

Kristallnacht

On November 7, 1938, a young Jewish refugee named Herschel Grynszpan shot and killed a German diplomat in Paris. Grynszpan's father and 10,000 other Jews had been deported from Germany to Poland, and the distraught young man was seeking revenge for this act and for the persecution of the Jews in general.

In retaliation, an infuriated Hitler ordered his minister of propaganda, Joseph Goebbels,

to stage attacks against the Jews that would seem like a spontaneous popular reaction to news of the murder. On the night of November 9, this plan played out in a spree of destruction. In Vienna, a Jewish child named Frederic Morton watched in terror that night as Nazi storm troopers broke into his family's apartment:

PRIMARY SOURCE

"They yanked out every drawer in every one of our chests and cupboards, and tossed each in the air. They let the cutlery jangle across the floor, the clothes scatter, and stepped over the mess to fling the next drawer.... 'We might be back,' the leader said. On the way out he threw our mother-of-pearl ashtray over his shoulder, like confetti. We did not speak or move or breathe until we heard their boots against the pavement."

—quoted in *Facing History and Ourselves*

Chapter 13 A World in Flames **467**

Teach

R Reading Strategy

Summarizing Have students write one-paragraph summaries of the events of *Kristallnacht*. Then place students in pairs to have them proofread each other's summaries. **OL**

C Critical Thinking

Analyzing Primary Sources Draw students' attention to the quotation by Frederic Morton. **Ask:** How did the storm troopers make sure that the family would not rest after they left? (Not only did they create disorder, but they also threatened to return.) **OL**

Analyzing VISUALS

Answers:
1. Students' responses will vary but may suggest that the signs would prevent her from shopping in that store.
2. Students' responses will vary but may suggest that further evidence of aggression would have turned world opinion even more strongly against the Nazis.

Hands-On Chapter Project
Step 3

Creating a World War II Memory Book

Step 3: Researching the Holocaust Students will work in groups to create a page in the Memory Book dedicated to Holocaust survivors.

Directions Have students use library, Internet, or family resources to learn more about the Holocaust and the survivors. Ask students to gather information about how they survived the war and lived their lives

after the war. Students may choose to include primary sources on these pages of the Memory Book.

Putting It Together To decide which information to include, students will gain practice in finding relevant sources and synthesizing information from many sources. **OL**

(Chapter Project continued on page 475)

D Differentiated Instruction

Verbal/Linguistic Albert Einstein was only one of many scientists who left Nazi Germany. Ask students to find out more about these scientists and their contributions to the Allied war effort. Have them present their findings to the class in the character of the scientist, telling his or her own story. **AL**

S Skill Practice

Creating Charts Have students use the information presented in this section to create a chart illustrating the following facts: the number of Jews who fled Germany from 1933 to 1939, the number of immigrants allowed to enter the United States each year, the number of Jews killed at Auschwitz, and the total number of Jews killed in Europe. **OL**

Additional Support

The anti-Jewish violence that erupted throughout Germany and Austria that night came to be called *Kristallnacht,* or "night of broken glass," because broken glass littered the streets afterward. By the following morning, more than 90 Jews were dead, hundreds were badly injured, and thousands more were terrorized. The Nazis had forbidden police to interfere while bands of thugs destroyed 7,500 Jewish businesses and wrecked more than 180 synagogues.

The lawlessness of *Kristallnacht* persisted. Following that night of violence, the **Gestapo,** the government's secret police, arrested at least 20,000 wealthy Jews, releasing them only if they agreed to emigrate and surrender all their possessions. The state also confiscated insurance payments owed to Jewish owners of ruined businesses.

Jewish Refugees Try to Flee

S *Kristallnacht* and its aftermath marked a significant escalation of Nazi persecution against the Jews. Many Jews, including Frederick Morton's family, decided that it was time to leave and fled to the United States. Between 1933, when Hitler took power, and the start of World War II in 1939, some 350,000 Jews escaped Nazi-controlled Germany. These emigrants included prominent scientists, such as Albert Einstein, and business owners like Otto Frank, who resettled his family in **D** Amsterdam in 1933. Otto's daughter Anne kept a diary of her family's life in hiding after the Nazis overran the Netherlands. The "secret annex," as she called their hiding place, has become a museum.

Limits on Jewish Immigration By 1938, one American consulate in Germany had a backlog of more than 100,000 visa applications from Jews trying to leave for the United States. Following the Nazi *Anschluss,* some 3,000 Austrian Jews applied for American visas each day. Many never received visas to the United States or to the other countries where they applied. As a result, millions of Jews remained trapped in Nazi-dominated Europe.

Several factors limited Jewish immigration to the United States. Nazi orders prohibited Jews from taking more than about four dollars out of Germany. American immigration law, however, forbade granting a visa to anyone "likely to become a public charge." Customs officials tended to **assume** that this description

PRIMARY SOURCE
The Holocaust

▼ After World War II broke out, the Nazis methodically deprived Jews of their rights, confining many to overcrowded ghettos. After weeks of fierce resistance, Jews in the Warsaw ghetto in Poland (below) were rounded up for deportation to concentration camps in May 1943.

▲ By 1943, the Nazis had started to implement their plans to exterminate the Jews. The system of ghettos was abandoned in favor of herding men, women, and children onto cattle cars for transport to death camps.

Activity: Interdisciplinary Connection

Language Arts Invite students from a drama class to perform one or two scenes from the play based on *The Diary of Anne Frank*, dramatized by Frances Goodrich and Albert Hackett. After the performance, have students discuss the scenes, including their initial impression and the social and historical importance of the play. **OL**

applied to Jews, because Germany had forced them to leave behind any wealth. High unemployment rates in the 1930s also made immigration unpopular. Few Americans wanted to raise immigration quotas, even to accommodate European refugees. Others did not want to admit Jews because they held anti-Semitic attitudes. The existing immigration policy **R₁** allowed only 150,000 immigrants annually, with a fixed quota from each country. The law permitted no exceptions for refugees or victims of persecution.

International Response At an international conference on refugees in 1938, several European countries, the United States, and Latin America stated their regret that they could not take in more of Germany's Jews without raising their immigration quotas. Meanwhile, Nazi propaganda chief Joseph Goebbels announced that "if there is any country that believes it has not enough Jews, I shall gladly turn over to it all our Jews." Hitler also **R₂** declared himself "ready to put all these criminals at the disposal of these countries . . . even on luxury ships."

As war loomed in 1939, many ships departed from Germany crammed with Jews desperate to escape. Some of their visas, however, had been forged or sold illegally, and Mexico, Paraguay, Argentina, and Costa Rica all denied access to Jews with such documents. So, too, did the United States.

The *St. Louis* Affair On May 27, 1939, the SS *St. Louis* entered the harbor in Havana, Cuba, with 930 Jewish refugees on board. Most of these passengers hoped to go to the United States eventually, but they had certificates improperly issued by Cuba's director of immigration giving them permission to land in Cuba. When the ships arrived in Havana, the Cuban government revoked the certificates and refused to let the refugees come ashore. For several days, the ship's captain steered his ship in circles off the coast of Florida, awaiting official permission to dock at an American port. Denied permission, the ship turned back toward Europe. The passengers finally disembarked in France, Holland, Belgium, and Great Britain. Within two years, the first three of these countries fell under Nazi domination. Many of the refugees brought to these countries perished in the Nazis' "final solution."

✓ **Reading Check** **Analyzing** Why did many Jews stay in Germany despite being persecuted?

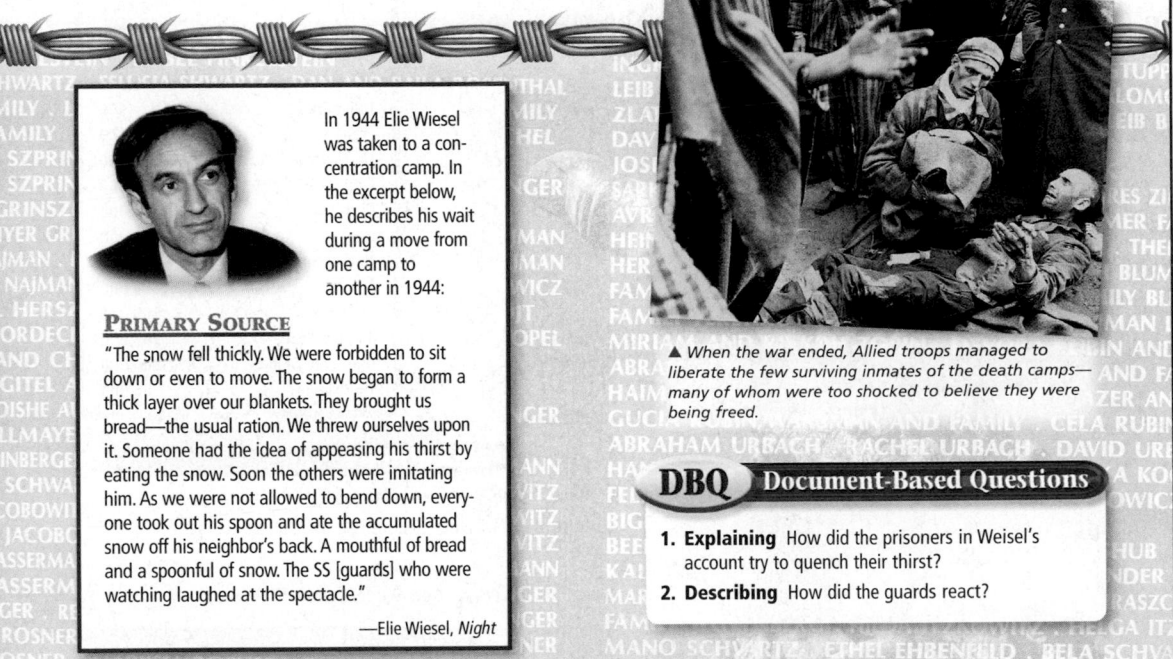

In 1944 Elie Wiesel was taken to a concentration camp. In the excerpt below, he describes his wait during a move from one camp to another in 1944:

PRIMARY SOURCE

"The snow fell thickly. We were forbidden to sit down or even to move. The snow began to form a thick layer over our blankets. They brought us bread—the usual ration. We threw ourselves upon it. Someone had the idea of appeasing his thirst by eating the snow. Soon the others were imitating him. As we were not allowed to bend down, everyone took out his spoon and ate the accumulated snow off his neighbor's back. A mouthful of bread and a spoonful of snow. The SS [guards] who were watching laughed at the spectacle."

—Elie Wiesel, *Night*

▲ *When the war ended, Allied troops managed to liberate the few surviving inmates of the death camps—many of whom were too shocked to believe they were being freed.*

DBQ **Document-Based Questions**

1. **Explaining** How did the prisoners in Weisel's account try to quench their thirst?
2. **Describing** How did the guards react?

Chapter 13 A World in Flames **469**

Activity: Collaborative Learning

Researching Historical Events Divide the class into small groups, assigning each group one of the following topics: *Kristallnacht*, the Warsaw ghetto, German use of slave labor, or stolen artwork, which Germany stole from occupied nations and from the Jews. Have each group present their findings to the class as a panel discussion. **Ask:** What is acceptable behavior in situations of war? *(Students may suggest that basic human rights should be preserved even in conditions of war.)* **OL**

R₁ Reading Strategy

Using Word Parts Point out the terms *concentration* and *extermination*. Ask students to identify the suffix (-*tion*). Remind them that the suffix means "process or act." **BL**

R₂ Reading Strategy

Using Context Clues Draw students' attention to the word *concentration*. Ask them to give multiple meanings for the word. *(a liquid made stronger and thicker by removing water from it; to focus attention or thoughts; to come together in a single place)* Remind students that when faced with an unfamiliar term, they can use the context of the sentence or paragraph to determine the meaning of the word. **OL**

Analyzing GEOGRAPHY

Answers:
1. Poland
2. Poland, Ukrainian SSR, Hungary

Additional Support

The Final Solution

MAIN Idea Nazi atrocities included sending millions of Jews, Gypsies, Slavs, the disabled, and others to concentration camps and extermination camps.

HISTORY AND YOU Can you think of a conflict today where violence is motivated by ethnic or religious hatred? Read to learn how prejudice led to mass murder in Nazi Germany.

On January 20, 1942, Nazi leaders met at the **Wannsee Conference** to determine the "final solution of the Jewish question." Previous "solutions" had included rounding up Jews, Gypsies, Slavs, and others from conquered areas, shooting them, and piling them into mass graves. Another method forced Jews and other "undesirables" into trucks and then piped in exhaust fumes to kill them. These methods, however, had proven too slow and inefficient for the Nazis.

At Wannsee, the Nazis made plans to round up Jews from the vast areas of Nazi-controlled Europe and take them to detention centers known as **concentration camps.** There, healthy individuals would work as slave laborers until they dropped dead of exhaustion, disease, or malnutrition. Most others, including the elderly, the infirm, and young children, would be sent to **extermination camps,** attached to many of the concentration camps, to be executed in massive gas chambers.

NATIONAL GEOGRAPHIC The Holocaust, 1939–1945

Jewish Losses, 1939–1945	
Baltic States	228,000
Belgium	40,000
Bulgaria	14,000
Byelorusian SSR	245,000
Czechoslovakia	155,000
Denmark	500
France	90,000
Germany and Austria	210,000
Greece	54,000
Hungary	450,000
Italy	8,000
Netherlands	195,000
Poland	3,000,000
Romania	300,000
Russian SSR	107,000
Ukrainian SSR	900,000
Yugoslavia	26,000

- ■ Concentration camp
- ■ Extermination camp
- ■ Location of *Einsatzgruppen*
- — International boundary, January 1938

◄ A survivor of the Buchenwald camp drinks water outside the camp barracks, April 1945

Analyzing GEOGRAPHY

1. **Place** Where were most of the extermination camps located?
2. **Region** Which three nations had the highest number of Jewish losses?

Maps In MOtion See *StudentWorks™ Plus* or glencoe.com.

Activity: Interdisciplinary Connection

Civics Have students work in pairs to create charts that compare the U.S. Bill of Rights with the rights that Nazis denied to the Jews. Students may need to conduct outside research to complete their charts. Use the charts as a basis for a class discussion on civil liberties. **Ask:** What effects did Nazi rule have on Jewish civil liberties? *(Jewish civil liberties effectively ceased to exist under the Nazis.)* **OL**

Concentration Camps

The Nazis had established their first concentration camps in 1933 to jail political opponents. After the war began, the Nazis built concentration camps throughout Europe.

Buchenwald, one of the largest concentration camps, was built near the town of Weimar in Germany in 1937. During its operation, more than 200,000 prisoners worked 12-hour shifts as slave laborers in nearby factories. Although Buchenwald had no gas chambers, hundreds of prisoners died there every month from exhaustion and horrible living conditions.

Leon Bass, a young American soldier, saw Buchenwald at the end of the war. A room built to hold 50 people had housed more than 150, with bunk beds built almost to the ceiling. Bass recalled:

PRIMARY SOURCE

"I looked at a bottom bunk and there I saw one man. He was too weak to get up; he could just barely turn his head. He was skin and bones. He looked like a skeleton; and his eyes were deep set. He didn't utter a sound; he just looked at me with those eyes, and they still haunt me today."

—quoted in *Facing History and Ourselves*

Extermination Camps

After the Wannsee Conference, the Nazis built extermination facilities in a number of the concentration camps, mostly in Poland, to kill Jews more efficiently. At these camps, including the infamous Treblinka and Auschwitz, Jews were the Nazis' main victims. Auschwitz alone housed about 100,000 people in 300 prison barracks. Its gas chambers, built to kill 2,000 people at a time, sometimes gassed 12,000 people in a day. Of the estimated 1,600,000 people who died at Auschwitz, about 1,300,000 were Jews. The other 300,000 were Poles, Soviet prisoners of war, and Gypsies.

Upon arrival at Auschwitz, healthy prisoners were selected for slave labor. Elderly or disabled people, the sick, and mothers and children went immediately to the gas chambers, after which their bodies were burned in giant crematoriums.

In only a few years, Jewish culture, which had existed in Europe for over 1,000 years, had been **virtually** obliterated by the Nazis in the lands they conquered. Despite exhaustive debate, there is still great controversy about why and how an event so horrifying as the Holocaust could have occurred. No consensus has been reached, but most historians point to a number of factors: the German people's sense of injury after World War I; severe economic problems; Hitler's control over the German nation; the lack of a strong tradition of representative government in Germany; German fear of Hitler's secret police; and a long history of anti-Jewish prejudice and discrimination in Europe.

✓ Reading Check **Summarizing** How did Hitler try to exterminate Europe's Jewish population?

Section 3 REVIEW

Vocabulary

1. **Explain** the significance of: *Shoah*, Nuremberg Laws, Gestapo, Wannsee Conference, concentration camp, extermination camp.

Main Ideas

2. **Listing** What early steps did Germany take in persecution of Jewish people?

3. **Analyzing** What was the purpose of the Wannsee Conference?

Critical Thinking

4. **Big Ideas** Do you think the German people or other nations could have prevented the Holocaust? Why or why not?

5. **Organizing** Use a graphic organizer similar to the one below to list the methods the Nazis used to try to destroy the Jewish population.

Extermination Methods

6. **Analyzing Visuals** Study the photos on pages 467–468. How do the images show the destruction of Jewish life?

Writing About History

7. **Persuasive Writing** Imagine that you are living in the United States during the 1930s. You believe that more Jewish immigrants should be allowed to come into the country. Write a letter to your representative or senator in Congress to express your point of view.

History ONLINE

Study Central™ To review this section, go to glencoe.com and click on Study Central.

471

Assess

History ONLINE

Study Central™ provides summaries, interactive games, and online graphic organizers to help students review content.

Close

Summarizing Ask: Do you think that greater American involvement in Europe could have prevented or limited the effects of Nazi persecution? *(Responses will vary but may suggest that Hitler was determined and had a powerful army at his disposal to enforce his desires.)* **OL**

✓ Reading Check

Answer: In extermination camps, Jews were immediately killed in gas chambers. In concentration camps, they were worked until they died of disease, starvation, or exhaustion.

Section 3 REVIEW

Answers

1. All definitions can be found in the section and the Glossary.

2. required them to live in ghettos, deprived them of citizenship and the right to vote, identified in passports and through yellow stars as Jewish, and through *Kristallnacht*, the destruction of Jewish areas

3. to determine a "final solution of the Jewish question"

4. Students' answers will vary but should be supported by reasons.

5. gas chambers, malnutrition and starvation, untreated disease, worked to death

6. They show stages of Hitler's campaign, from civil discrimination and violence to deportation to camps.

7. Students' letters will vary, but should use information from the section.

Focus

When people arrived at a concentration camp, their heads were shaved, their clothing and belongings removed, and, at Auschwitz, identification numbers were tattooed on their arms. Those able to work did so 12 hours a day, with little food. Some Nazi officers took pleasure in abusing inmates; the infamous Dr. Josef Mengele conducted experiments on both dead and living prisoners.

Teach

C Critical Thinking

Analyzing Primary Sources

Invite students to read the first Primary Source. Ask them to identify the ways in which both the Nazis and the prisoners were described. (Nazis were brutes, barbarians; prisoners were hordes of people, poor innocents)

Ask: What effect does this word choice have on the account? (Students may say the descriptions make it very clear who is the villain and who is the victim.) **OL**

Differentiated Instruction

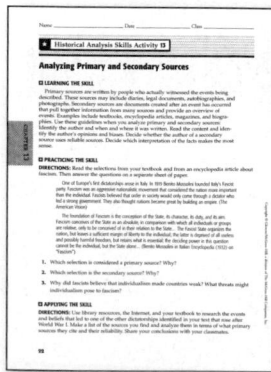

Historical Analysis Activity 13, URB p. 22

ANALYZING
PRIMARY SOURCES

The Holocaust

As the Allies liberated areas from German control in the spring of 1945, they discovered horrifying scenes in Nazi concentration camps. The Nazi regime had systematically murdered six million Jews and killed another six million Poles, Slavs, Gypsies, homosexuals, communists, and mentally disabled persons. Photographs of the newly liberated camps shocked the American public, although the Roosevelt administration and the State Department had evidence of the death camps as early as 1942.

Study these primary sources and answer the questions that follow.

PRIMARY SOURCE 1

Eyewitness Account

"[There] were two barracks: the men stood on one side, the women on the other. They were addressed in a very polite and friendly way: 'You have been on a journey. You are dirty. You will take a bath. Get undressed quickly.' Towels and soap were handed out, and then suddenly the brutes woke up and showed their true faces: this horde of people, these men and women were driven outside with hard blows and forced both summer and winters to go the few hundred metres to the 'Shower Room.' Above the entry door was the word 'Shower'. One could even see shower heads on the ceiling which were cemented in but never had water flowing through them.

These poor innocents were crammed together, pressed against each other. Then panic broke out, for at last they realized the fate in store for them. But blows with rifle butts and revolver shots soon restored order and finally they all entered the death chamber. The doors were shut and, ten minutes later, the temperature was high enough to facilitate the condensation of the hydrogen cyanide for the condemned were gassed with hydrogen cyanide. This was the so-called 'Zyklon B' . . . which was used by the German barbarians. . . . One could hear fearful screams, but a few moments later there was complete silence."

—André Lettich, Jewish prisoner assigned to remove bodies from the gas chambers at Birkenau from *Nazism 1919–1945, Volume 3: Foreign Policy, War and Racial Extermination—A Documentary Reader*

PRIMARY SOURCE 2

Photograph, 1945

▼ *Newly liberated survivors at Dachau concentration camp, May 4, 1945*

PRIMARY SOURCE 3

Nazi Decree, 1941

I (1) Jews over six years of age are prohibited from appearing in public without wearing a Jewish star.
(2) The Jewish star is a yellow piece of cloth with a black border, in the form of a six-pointed star the size of the palm of the hand. The inscription reads "JEW" in black letters. It shall be worn visibly, sewn on the left chest side of the garment.
II Jews are forbidden:
(a) to leave their area of residence without written permission of the local police, carried on their person.
(b) to wear medals, decorations or other insignia.

—Nazi decree issued September 1, 1941 from *Nazism 1919–1945, Volume 3: Foreign Policy, War and Racial Extermination—A Documentary Reader*

Identifying Facts and Opinions: Primary and Secondary Sources

Objective: Read to identify facts and opinions in primary and secondary sources.

Focus: Read the selections from the textbook and from an encyclopedia article on p. 22.

Teach: Define fact and opinion.

Assess: Identify the facts in the selections by underlining them. Identify the opinions by circling them.

Close: Write one or two factual sentences about fascism and one or two opinion sentences.

Differentiated Instruction Strategies

BL Identify one fact and one opinion in each selection.

AL Choose an op-ed piece from a newspaper, and identify the facts and opinions. Discuss how the writer used facts to support his or her opinions.

ELL Flip through the textbook and identify as many primary sources as possible.

PRIMARY SOURCE 4

American Soldier's Diary, 1945

"One thousand Weimar citizens toured the Buchenwald camp in groups of 100. They saw blackened skeletons and skulls in the ovens of the crematorium. In the yard outside, they saw a heap of white human ashes and bones. . . .

The living actually looked worse than the dead. Those who lived wore striped uniforms, with the stripes running up and down. Those who were dead were stripped of their clothing and lay naked, many stacked like cordwood waiting to be burned in the crematory. At one time, 5,000 had been stacked on the vacant lot next to the crematory.

Often . . . the SS wished to make an example of someone in killing him. They hung him on the lot adjacent to the crematory, and all the three sections of the camp witnessed the sight—some 30,000 prisoners. They used what I call hay hooks, catching him under the chin and the other in the back of his neck. He hung in this manner until he died."

—diary of Captain Luther D. Fletcher, from *World War II: From the Battle Front to the Home Front*

PRIMARY SOURCE 5

Photograph, April 17, 1945

◄ *American soldiers force German civilians to view bodies after the liberation of the Buchenwald concentration camp.*

PRIMARY SOURCE 6

Painting

Unable to Work, by Auschwitz survivor David Olère

DBQ — Document-Based Questions

1. **Speculating** How do you suppose soldiers could participate in such barbaric acts?

2. **Analyzing Visuals** What does the appearance of these survivors tell you about conditions in the camps?

3. **Drawing Conclusions** What purpose did the restrictions listed in Source 3 serve?

4. **Drawing Conclusions** Study Sources 5 and 6. How do you think American troops reacted to the horrifying scenes they found in the concentration camps? Why do you think American troops made Germans tour the liberated concentration camps?

5. **Analyzing Visuals** Study the painting in Source 6. What symbols does the artist use to illustrate the fate of those too weak to work?

Assess/Close

Have students read Primary Source 4. Discuss with students the historical value of Primary Source accounts such as diaries and letters written at the time, rather than written after the fact. *(The accounts are not edited nor impressions blurred by the passage of time.)*

Encourage students who have not read Anne Frank's diary to do so, noting that Anne actually kept two accounts, one meant to be public and the other her own.

Document Based Questions

Answers

1. Student answers will vary but may suggest that the soldiers saw these acts as part of their jobs.

2. The extreme thinness of the survivors indicates that life was hard and food was scarce.

3. The restrictions made Jews easily identifiable and served to make life more difficult for them.

4. American troops probably reacted with horror. They wanted Germans to tour the camps to try to get them to see the evil that had been done while they did nothing to stop it.

5. A skeletal figure hovers over the weak ones, indicating coming death.

Focus

Bellringer
Daily Focus Transparency 13.4

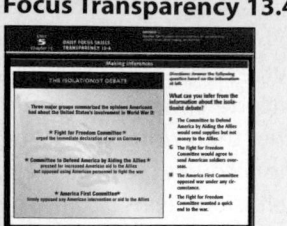

Guide to Reading

Answers:
Britain's struggle with Germany; Japan's attack on Pearl Harbor

Section Spotlight Video

To generate student interest and provide a springboard for class discussion, access the Chapter 13, Section 4 video at glencoe.com or on the video DVD.

Resource Manager

Section 4
America Enters the War

Guide to Reading

Big Ideas
Government and Society After World War II began, the United States attempted to continue its prewar policy of neutrality.

Content Vocabulary
• hemispheric defense zone (p. 476)
• strategic materials (p. 478)

Academic Vocabulary
• revise (p. 474)
• purchase (p. 474)
• underestimate (p. 479)

People and Events to Identify
• America First Committee (p. 475)
• Lend-Lease Act (p. 476)
• Atlantic Charter (p. 477)

Reading Strategy
Organizing As you read about America's efforts to stay neutral, complete a graphic organizer similar to the one below by naming events that shifted American opinion toward helping the Allies.

Events That Shifted American Opinion

As World War II began, the United States remained officially neutral but aided Great Britain considerably in its fight against Germany. In the Pacific, Japan's territorial expansion led to growing tensions with the United States, which peaked when Japan attacked Pearl Harbor.

FDR Supports England

MAIN Idea President Roosevelt favored changes in American neutrality laws, although Americans remained divided about the war and American involvement.

HISTORY AND YOU Have you ever been drawn into an argument when you just wanted to be left alone? Read about the increasing difficulties that the United States faced in trying to stay out of World War II.

President Roosevelt officially proclaimed the United States neutral two days after Britain and France declared war on Germany. Despite this proclamation, however, he was determined to help the two countries as much as possible in their struggle against Hitler.

Destroyers-for-Bases Deal

Soon after the war began, Roosevelt called Congress into a special session to **revise** the neutrality laws. He asked Congress to eliminate the ban on arms sales to nations at war. Public opinion strongly supported the president. Congress passed the new law, but isolationists demanded a price for the revision. Under the Neutrality Act of 1939, warring nations could buy weapons from the United States only on a "cash-and-carry" basis. This law was similar to the 1937 Neutrality Act governing the sale of nonmilitary items to countries that were at war.

In the spring of 1940, the United States faced its first test in remaining neutral. In May, Prime Minister Winston Churchill asked Roosevelt to transfer old American destroyers to Britain, which had lost nearly half its destroyers. To protect its cargo ships from German submarines and to block any German attempt to invade Britain, the nation needed more destroyers.

Determined to give Churchill the destroyers, Roosevelt used a loophole in the neutrality act that required cash for **purchases.** In exchange for the right to build American bases on British-controlled Newfoundland, Bermuda, and islands in the Caribbean, Roosevelt sent 50 old American destroyers to Britain. Because the deal did not involve an actual sale, the neutrality act did not apply.

R Reading Strategies	**C** Critical Thinking	**D** Differentiated Instruction	**W** Writing Support	**S** Skill Practice
Teacher Edition • Act. Prior Know., p. 476 • Inferring, p. 477 • Taking Notes, p. 478 **Additional Resources** • Pri. Source Reading, URB p. 37 • Guid. Read. Act., URB p. 51	**Teacher Edition** • Making Generalizations, p. 475 • Analyzing Prim. Sources, p. 476 • Comparing, p. 478 **Additional Resources** • Interp. Pol. Car., URB p. 41 • Auth Assess, p. 31 • Quizzes and Tests, p. 188	**Additional Resources** • Differentiated Intsr., URB p. 23 • Reteaching Act., URB p. 43 • Enrichment Act., URB p. 45	**Teacher Edition** • Expository Writing, p. 479 **Additional Resources** • Linking Past & Present, URB p. 34	**Teacher Edition** • Using Geo. Skills, p. 477 **Additional Resources** • RENTG, p. 143

The Only Way We Can Save Her

▲ This 1939 cartoon shows Uncle Sam standing guard over Democracy, whose only refuge is America.

▲ Nazi bullets whiz past Uncle Sam and his isolationist policies.

Analyzing VISUALS DBQ

1. **Analyzing Visuals** According to the cartoon at left, what message is Democracy sending to Uncle Sam?

2. **Analyzing Visuals** What do you observe about Uncle Sam's perch in the cartoon above?

The Isolationist Debate

Widespread acceptance of the destroyers-for-bases deal reflected a change in public opinion. By July 1940, most Americans favored offering limited aid to the Allies. That spirit was hardly unanimous, however. In fact, people who wanted greater American involvement in the war and those who felt that the United States should remain neutral began debating the issue in the spring of 1940.

At one extreme was the Fight for Freedom Committee, a group that urged the repeal of all neutrality laws and stronger action against Germany. At the other extreme was the **America First Committee.** It was a staunchly isolationist group opposed to any American intervention or aid to the Allies. The committee's members included aviator Charles Lindbergh and Senator Gerald Nye.

Closer to the center, the Committee to Defend America by Aiding the Allies, which journalist William Allen White headed, pressed for increased American aid to the Allies but opposed armed intervention.

The heated neutrality debate took place during the 1940 presidential election campaign. For months, Americans had wondered whether President Roosevelt would follow the tradition George Washington had set and retire after a second term. With the United States in a precarious position, however, many believed a change of leaders might not be in the country's best interest. Roosevelt decided to run for an unprecedented third term.

During the campaign, FDR steered a careful course between neutrality and intervention. The Republican nominee, Wendell Willkie, did the same, promising he too would assist the Allies but stay out of the war. The voters reelected Roosevelt by a wide margin, preferring to keep a president they knew during this crisis period.

Reading Check Identifying Identify different groups and their positions on U.S. neutrality in the late 1930s.

Teach

C Critical Thinking

Making Generalizations
Ask: What effect do you think it had on people to realize that famous men such as Lindbergh and Nye were part of this group? *(Students may say that men of their fame and stature might sway the opinions of people.)* **OL**

Analyzing VISUALS

Answers:
1. Uncle Sam should stay out of European conflicts.
2. It seems very unsteady and unsafe.

✓ Reading Check

Answer: The America First Committee was isolationist. The Committee to Defend America by Aiding the Allies opposed armed intervention but wanted to aid the Allies. The Fight for Freedom Committee wanted repeal of all neutrality laws.

Hands-On Chapter Project
Step 4

Creating a World War II Memory Book

Step 4: Debating the War Students will create a page in their Memory Book that documents the debate over whether the United States should remain neutral.

Directions Have students use library or Internet sources to find arguments for and against the United States's neutrality in 1940. Students will build a page in the Memory Book that illustrates this debate.

Putting It Together Students will select quotations or summarize arguments for and against neutrality. **OL**
(Chapter Project continued on the Visual Summary page)

R Reading Strategy

Activating Prior Knowledge
Draw students' attention to the "Four Freedoms" Roosevelt identifies. **Ask:** In what American document can the first two Freedoms be found? *(the First Amendment in the Bill of Rights in the United States Constitution)* **OL**

C Critical Thinking

Analyzing Primary Sources
Invite a volunteer to read aloud the fourth freedom that Roosevelt addresses. **Ask:** How much progress do you think the world has made toward this goal since the end of 1945? *(Students' answers will vary but may suggest that nuclear arms and the arms race have not allowed this goal to be accomplished.)* **OL**

Additional Support

Edging Toward War

MAIN Idea In 1940 and 1941, the United States took more steps to provide aid to Great Britain.

HISTORY AND YOU What kinds of aid does America provide other countries today? Why? Read why FDR thought it was important to "lend" Britain some help.

Read "The Four Freedoms" on page R53 in **Documents in American History.**

R With the election over, Roosevelt expanded the nation's role in the war. Britain was fighting for democracy, he said, and the United States had to help. Speaking to Congress, he listed the "Four Freedoms" for which both the United States and Britain stood: freedom of speech, freedom of worship, freedom from want, and freedom from fear.

The Lend-Lease Act

By December 1940, Great Britain had run out of funds to wage its war against Germany. Roosevelt came up with a way to remove the cash requirement of the most recent neutrality act. He proposed the **Lend-Lease Act,** which allowed the United States to lend or lease arms to any country considered "vital to the defense of the United States." The act allowed Roosevelt to send weapons to Britain if the British government promised to return or pay rent for them after the war.

Roosevelt warned that, if Britain fell, an "unholy alliance" of Germany, Japan, and Italy would keep trying to conquer the world. The president argued that the United States should become the "great arsenal of democracy" to keep the British fighting and make it unnecessary for Americans to go to war.

The America First Committee disagreed, but Congress passed the Lend-Lease Act by a wide margin. By the time the program ended, the United States had "lent" more than $40 billion in weapons, vehicles, and other supplies to the Allied war effort.

While shipments of supplies to Britain began at once, lend-lease aid eventually went to the Soviet Union, as well. In June 1941, violating the Nazi-Soviet pact, Hitler invaded the Soviet Union. Although Churchill detested communism and considered Stalin a harsh dictator, he vowed that any person or state "who fights against Nazism will have our aid." Roosevelt, too, supported this policy.

A Hemispheric Defense Zone

Congressional approval of the Lend-Lease Act did not solve the problem of getting American arms and supplies to Britain. German submarines patrolling the Atlantic Ocean were sinking hundreds of thousands of tons of shipments each month; the British Navy did not have enough ships to stop them.

Because the United States was still technically neutral, Roosevelt could not order the U.S. Navy to protect British cargo ships. Instead, he developed the idea of a **hemispheric defense zone.** Roosevelt declared that the entire western half of the Atlantic was part of the Western Hemisphere and, therefore, neutral. He then ordered the U.S. Navy to patrol the western Atlantic and reveal the location of German submarines to the British.

The Atlantic Charter

In August 1941, Roosevelt and Churchill met on board American and British warships anchored near Newfoundland. During these meetings, the two men agreed on the text of

PRIMARY SOURCE
Aiding Britain, 1939–1941

The Four Freedoms

"In the future days, which we seek to make secure, we look forward to a world founded upon four essential human freedoms.

The first is freedom of speech and expression—everywhere in the world.

The second is freedom of every person to worship God in his own way—everywhere in the world.

The third is freedom from want—which . . . will secure to every nation a healthy peacetime life for its inhabitants—everywhere in the world.

The fourth is freedom from fear—which, translated into world terms, means a world-wide reduction of armaments to such a point and in such a thorough fashion that no nation will be in a position to commit an act of physical aggression against any neighbor—anywhere in the world."

—Address to Congress, January 6, 1941

Activity: Collaborative Learning

Analyzing Propaganda Divide the class into three groups. Have each group analyze the propaganda used by both the Axis powers and the Allied powers during World War II. Assign each member of the group one of the following tasks: researching the information, writing descriptions of the information, or analyzing the propaganda. Have group members combine their efforts to make an in-class presentation. **OL**

the **Atlantic Charter.** This agreement committed both nations to a postwar world of democracy, nonaggression, free trade, economic advancement, and freedom of the seas. By late September, an additional 15 anti-Axis nations had signed the charter. Churchill later said that FDR pledged to "force an 'incident' . . . which would justify him in opening hostilities" with Germany.

An incident quickly presented itself. In early September, a German submarine, or U-boat, fired on an American destroyer that had been radioing the U-boat's position to the British. Roosevelt promptly responded by ordering American ships to follow a "shoot-on-sight" policy toward German submarines.

The Germans escalated hostilities the following month, targeting two American destroyers. One of them, the *Reuben James,* sank after being torpedoed, killing 115 sailors. As the end of 1941 drew near, Germany and the United States continued a tense standoff.

✓ Reading Check **Evaluating** How did the Lend-Lease Act help the Allied war effort?

Japan Attacks

MAIN Idea The Japanese attack on Pearl Harbor led the United States to declare war on Japan.

HISTORY AND YOU Do you remember how the United States acquired territory in the Pacific? Read about the threats to American interests as Japan expanded its empire.

Despite the growing tensions in the Atlantic, the Japanese attack on Pearl Harbor finally brought the United States into World War II. Ironically, Roosevelt's efforts to help Britain fight Germany resulted in Japan's decision to attack the United States.

America Embargoes Japan

Roosevelt knew that Britain needed much of its navy in Asia to protect its territories there from Japanese attack. As German submarines sank British ships in the Atlantic, however, the British began moving warships from Southeast Asia, leaving India and other colonial possessions vulnerable.

How Did FDR Help Britain While the U.S. Remained Neutral?

- Neutrality Act of 1939 allowed warring nations to buy weapons from the United States if they paid cash and transported arms on their own ships
- Destroyers-for-bases provided old American destroyers in exchange for the right to build U.S. defense bases in British-controlled Bermuda, Caribbean Islands, and Newfoundland
- Lend-Lease Act permitted U.S. to lend or lease arms to any country "vital to the defense of the United States"
- Hemispheric defense zone established the entire western half of the Atlantic as part of the Western Hemisphere and, therefore, neutral

What Did the Atlantic Charter Declare?

1. The U.S. and Britain do not seek to expand their territories.
2. Neither seeks territorial changes against the wishes of the people involved.
3. Both respect people's right to select their own government.
4. All nations should have access to trade and raw materials.
5. Improved labor standards and economic advances are vital.
6. Both nations hope people will be free from want and fear.
7. Everyone should be able to freely travel the high seas.
8. All nations must abandon the use of force; disarmament is necessary after the war.

NATIONAL GEOGRAPHIC **Sending Aid to Britain, 1939–1941**

September 4, 1941: Attack on the *Greer* prompts FDR's "shoot-on-sight" policy.

EUROPE

NORTH AMERICA

AFRICA

ATLANTIC OCEAN

0   800 kilometers
0   800 miles
Miller projection

SOUTH AMERICA

····· Hemispheric Defense Zone
→ Lend-Lease convoy route
← Area with German submarines

DBQ **Document-Based Questions**

1. **Drawing Conclusions** Why do you think it was important to begin the Atlantic Charter with the first three points?
2. **Analyzing Primary Sources** How does the Atlantic Charter echo FDR's Four Freedoms speech?

Chapter 13 A World in Flames **477**

Reading Strategy

Inferring Draw students' attention to the quotation by Churchill. **Ask:** What does this information tell you about Roosevelt? *(He was committed to assisting Britain and fighting against Germany.)* **OL**

Skill Practice

Using Geography Skills Have students look at the map titled "Sending Aid to Britain, 1939–1941." **Ask:** Where was the largest concentration of German submarines? *(off the coasts of Europe and Africa)* **BL**

DBQ **Document Based Questions**

Answers:
1. Students' responses will vary but may suggest that the Allies wanted to reassure the world that they were not seeking additional territory.
2. It repeats the need for freedom from want and fear.

✓ Reading Check

Answer: It helped by getting arms to the Allies.

Additional Support

Extending the Content

Great Britain was not the only country to receive aid under the Lend-Lease Act of 1941. The Soviet Union, which prior to World War II had little trade with the United States, received over $11 billion dollars in war materials between 1941 and 1945. The Allies wanted to keep the Soviet Union fighting against Germany on the Eastern Front. Aid to civilians in the Soviet Union came through the Red Cross and the U.S. Russian War Relief (a private, nonprofit organization).

Joseph Stalin never told his people how much Lend-Lease and the private aid helped the USSR survive the war. However, at the Yalta Conference at the end of the war he said, "Lend-Lease is one of Franklin Roosevelt's most remarkable and vital achievements in the formation of the anti-Hitler alliance."

R Reading Strategy

Taking Notes Have students create a graphic organizer listing the three actions Roosevelt took in response to the Japanese sending troops to southern Indochina. *(He froze all Japanese assets in the United States, reduced the amount of oil being shipped to Japan, and sent General Douglas MacArthur to the Philippines to build up American defenses there.)* **BL**

C Critical Thinking

Comparing Remind students of the embargo Roosevelt ordered in 1940 against exports of scrap metal to Japan, which later extended to other products that had military uses. Discuss the embargoes or sanctions currently in effect. Discuss whether these are effective in preventing war or accomplishing the goals established by the nations that impose them. **AL**

Answer: Students' responses will vary but should be supported with reasons.

Additional Support

Turning Point

Japan Attacks Pearl Harbor

Pearl Harbor was an important turning point because it not only brought the United States into the war but also decisively marked an end to U.S. isolationism. After the war ended, the nation did not withdraw from its role in international affairs, as it had done following World War I. Involvement in the war signaled the beginning of a global role for the United States that has continued to the present day. With the decision to support the United Nations and efforts to rebuild Europe, the nation became actively involved in international events.

HYPOTHESIZING Do you believe the United States would have entered the war regardless of the attack on Pearl Harbor? Support your ideas with reasons.

▲ Rescue boats approach the burning USS West Virginia *and* USS Tennessee, *which were hit by enemy fire on December 7, 1941. In the photo to the right, President Roosevelt addresses Congress the following day.*

◀ *Although ideas to create a memorial of Pearl Harbor were put forth as early as 1946, not until 1958 did President Eisenhower sign the bill that authorized this memorial, a bridge built over the sunken USS* Arizona. *The completed memorial was dedicated in 1962.*

History ONLINE
Student Web Activity Visit glencoe.com and complete the activity on Pearl Harbor.

History ONLINE
Student Skill Activity To learn how to create multimedia presentations, visit glencoe.com and complete the skill activity.

To hinder Japanese aggression, Roosevelt began applying economic pressure. Japan depended on the United States for many key materials, including scrap iron, steel, and especially oil. At that time, the United States supplied roughly 80 percent of Japan's oil. In July 1940 Congress gave the president the power to restrict the sale of **strategic materials** (materials important for fighting a war). Roosevelt immediately blocked the sale of airplane fuel and scrap iron to Japan. Furious, the Japanese signed an alliance with Germany and Italy, becoming a member of the Axis.

In 1941 Roosevelt began sending lend-lease aid to China. Japan, which had invaded China in 1937, controlled much of the Chinese coast by 1941. Roosevelt hoped that lend-lease aid would enable the Chinese to tie down the Japanese and prevent them from attacking elsewhere. The strategy failed. By July 1941,

R Japan had sent military forces into southern Indochina, posing a direct threat to the British Empire.

Roosevelt responded. He froze all Japanese assets in the United States, reduced the amount of oil being shipped to Japan, and sent General Douglas MacArthur to the Philippines to build up American defenses there.

C Roosevelt made it clear that the oil embargo would end only if Japan withdrew from Indochina and made peace with China. With its war against China in jeopardy because of a lack of oil and other resources, the Japanese military planned to attack the resource-rich British and Dutch colonies in Southeast Asia. They also decided to seize the Philippines and to attack the American fleet at Pearl Harbor. While the Japanese prepared for war, negotiations with the Americans continued, but neither side would back down. In late November

478 Chapter 13 A World in Flames

Extending the Content

Attack on Pearl Harbor Japanese pilots began training for the attack on Pearl Harbor in the spring of 1941. The commander of the Japanese fleet devised a plan that used naval aviation and aircraft carriers on a large scale. Six aircraft carriers and 24 supporting vessels coordinated the attack in addition to submarines intended to sink any warships that survived the attack. The first wave of the surprise attack involved 181 planes. A second wave of 170 planes took off half an hour later. In addition to hitting the fleet anchored in Pearl Harbor, the Japanese also hit two Navy air bases, a Marine air field, and three Army Air Corps fields. By hitting these additional sites, the Japanese hoped to prevent American planes from intercepting the Japanese force. The attack lasted less than two hours. More than 90 percent of the attacking planes survived and returned to the Japanese aircraft carriers.

1941, six Japanese aircraft carriers, two battleships, and several other warships set out for Hawaii.

Japan Attacks Pearl Harbor

The Japanese government appeared to be continuing negotiations with the United States in good faith. American intelligence, however, had decoded Japanese communications that made it clear that Japan was preparing to go to war against the United States.

On November 27, American commanders at the Pearl Harbor naval base received a war warning from Washington, but it did not mention Hawaii as a possible target. Because of the great distance from Japan to Hawaii, officials doubted that Japan would attempt such a long-range attack.

The U.S. military's inability to correctly interpret the information they were receiving left Pearl Harbor an open target. The result was devastating. Japan's surprise attack on December 7, 1941, sank or damaged eight battleships, three cruisers, four destroyers, and six other vessels. The attack also destroyed 188 airplanes and killed 2,403 Americans. Another 1,178 were injured.

That night, a gray-faced Roosevelt met with his cabinet, telling them the country faced the most serious crisis since the Civil War. The next day, he asked Congress to declare war:

PRIMARY SOURCE

"Yesterday, December 7, 1941—a date which will live in infamy—the United States of America was suddenly and deliberately attacked by naval and air forces of the Empire of Japan. . . . No matter how long it may take us . . . the American people in their righteous might will win through to absolute victory."

—from *The Public Papers and Addresses of Franklin D. Roosevelt*

The Senate voted 82 to 0 and the House 388 to 1 to declare war on Japan.

Germany Declares War

Although Japan and Germany were allies, Hitler was not bound to declare war against the United States. The terms of the alliance specified that Germany had to come to Japan's aid only if Japan was attacked, not if it attacked another country. Hitler had grown frustrated with the American navy's attacks on German submarines, however, and he believed the time had come to declare war.

Hitler greatly **underestimated** the strength of the United States. He expected the Japanese to easily defeat the Americans in the Pacific. By helping Japan, he hoped for Japanese support against the Soviet Union after they had defeated the Americans. On December 11, Germany and Italy both declared war on the United States.

✓ Reading Check **Examining** Why did military officials not expect an attack on Pearl Harbor?

Section 4 REVIEW

Vocabulary

1. **Explain** the significance of: America First Committee, Lend-Lease Act, hemispheric defense zone, Atlantic Charter, strategic materials.

Main Ideas

2. **Analyzing** What early efforts did Roosevelt make to help the British?

3. **Explaining** What was the hemispheric defense zone? Why was it developed?

4. **Summarizing** Why was the United States unprepared for Japan's attack on Pearl Harbor?

Critical Thinking

5. **Big Ideas** After Roosevelt's efforts to help Britain, some people accused him of being a dictator. Do you agree or disagree with this label? Explain your answer.

6. **Organizing** Use a graphic organizer similar to the one below to show how Roosevelt helped Britain while remaining officially neutral.

Help to Britain

7. **Analyzing Visuals** Study the images on page 475. Then create a multimedia presentation that traces the Japanese attack on Pearl Harbor.

Writing About History

8. **Expository Writing** Write a letter to the editor of your newspaper explaining why you think the United States should either remain neutral or become involved in World War II.

History ONLINE
Study Central™ To review this section, go to glencoe.com and click on Study Central.

479

W **Writing Strategy**

Expository Writing Have students investigate the Pearl Harbor Memorial and other efforts to preserve the history of the attack. Ask them to present their findings. OL

Assess
• • • • • • • • • • • • • • • • • • • •
History ONLINE

Study Central™ provides summaries, interactive games, and online graphic organizers to help students review content.

Close
• • • • • • • • • • • • • • • • • • • •
Summarizing Ask: How did Americans slowly leave their position of staying out of Europe's wars? *(offered aid to Allies, responded to Japanese aggression, signed agreements such as the Atlantic Charter)* OL

✓ Reading Check

Answer: They did not think that the Japanese would attempt an attack at such a distance.

Section 4 REVIEW

Answers

1. All definitions can be found in the section and the Glossary.

2. destroyers for bases deal, Lend-Lease Act, hemispheric defense zone

3. The hemispheric defense zone was an imaginary division of the Atlantic Ocean to justify patroling for German submarines that were disrupting British shipping.

4. The United States did not expect Japan to attack a target at such a distance. It also failed to correctly interpret military information.

5. Students may say it was important to stop Germany; others will say that Roosevelt violated the Neutrality Act.

6. destroyers for bases deal, Lend-Lease Act, hemispheric defense zone

7. Students' presentations should note that isolationism failed to prevent the attack. Presentations should also contain accurate accounts of the attack.

8. Students' letters will vary but should express a clear and reasoned opinion.

Organizing Divide the class into three groups, assigning each group one of the three nations listed under "Causes of the Rise of Dictators." Invite students to create graphic organizers that link the causes that pertain to their countries to particular effects.

Special Education Help students organize events by having them make a four-column chart. Ask them to label the columns Allied Powers, Axis Powers, Axis-controlled Countries, and Neutral Countries. Students then can use the text and maps to identify and list the countries under the appropriate headings.

Causes of the Rise of Dictators

Italy
- Mussolini's Fascist Party believed in the supreme power of the state.
- In 1922 Mussolini threatened to march on Rome; the king appointed Mussolini as the premier.

Germany
- Hitler's Nazi Party believed in an all-powerful state, territorial expansion, and ethnic purity.
- Hitler believed that Germans needed more living space and called for Germany to expand east into Poland and Russia.
- Germany invaded Poland in 1939, France in 1940, and the USSR in 1941.

Japan
- Military leaders pushed for territorial expansion.
- Japan attacked Manchuria in 1931.
- Japan invaded China in 1937.
- Japan attacked Pearl Harbor in 1941.

▲ German tanks move down a highway near Soissons, France in May 1940.

Effects

Holocaust
- During the Holocaust, the Nazis killed an estimated 6 million Jews.
- Jews were targeted and sent to concentration or extermination camps throughout Europe.

World War II
- Leaders of France and Britain tried to appease Hitler by allowing territorial growth.
- Britain and France declared war on Germany following the invasion of Poland.
- The United States sent aid to the Allied forces through the lend-lease program and cash-and-carry provision.
- France was defeated by the Nazis, who occupied the country in 1940.
- The United States declared war on Japan in 1941, after the bombing of Pearl Harbor.

▲ These survivors of Buchenwald, liberated in 1945, show the horrifying conditions under which they lived.

480 Chapter 13 A World in Flames

Hands-On Chapter Project
Step 5

Creating a World War II Memory Book

Step 5: Wrap Up Students will use their prior knowledge and the materials they researched to complete the pages of the memory book.

Directions Give each student a page of the memory book and ask them to use the photos and information they researched to create an attractive, informative page. They may wish to decorate the pages with other appropriate images, as well. The complete book may be used by the class to review the chapter and then displayed in the school or donated to a local VFW chapter or other group. **OL**

ASSESSMENT

STANDARDIZED TEST PRACTICE

TEST-TAKING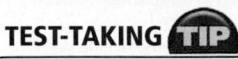

> Look at each question to find clues to support your answer. Try not to get confused by the wording of the question. Then look for an answer that best fits the question.

Reviewing Vocabulary

Directions: Choose the word or words that best complete the sentence.

1. What type of government considered the nation more important than the individual?
   A dictatorship
   B monarchy
   C fascism
   D democracy

2. What did Hitler call Germany's quick air strikes?
   A blitzkrieg
   B *Kristallnacht*
   C *Anschluss*
   D gestapo

3. What were the Nuremberg Laws?
   A regulations passed by Congress that explained when the United States could go to war against Germany
   B regulations passed by Congress that restricted the number of Jewish immigrants allowed into the U.S.
   C regulations passed by the United Nations that outlawed World War II
   D regulations passed by Germany that deprived German Jews of certain rights such as citizenship

4. _____, such as oil, steel, and iron supplies, were used by the United States to put pressure on Japan.
   A Rationed items
   B Strategic materials
   C Lend-Lease goods
   D Cash-and-carry materials

Reviewing Main Ideas

Directions: Choose the best answers to the following questions.

Section 1 *(pp. 454–459)*

5. Which factor encouraged an American policy of neutrality during the 1930s?
   A disillusionment with World War I and its results
   B decline in the military readiness of other nations
   C repeal of Prohibition
   D economic prosperity of the period

6. In the 1930s the United States responded to the rise of fascism in Europe by
   A invading Germany and Italy.
   B forming military alliances.
   C passing a series of neutrality laws.
   D joining the League of Nations.

Section 2 *(pp. 460–465)*

7. What term refers to the German annexation of Austria?
   A *Kristallnacht*
   B *Anschluss*
   C Munich Conference
   D Nazi-Soviet Nonaggression Pact

8. When France fell to the Nazis, the French and British evacuated thousands of troops from
   A Dunkirk.
   B Danzig.
   C Buchenwald.
   D Poland.

Need Extra Help?								
If You Missed Questions . . .	1	2	3	4	5	6	7	8
Go to Page . . .	454	462	466	478	458–459	458	460	462–464

 GO ON

Chapter 13 A World in Flames **481**

Answers and Analyses

1. C The main distractor for students will likely be *A*, because dictatorships and fascism are sometimes associated. Remind students that not all dictatorships are within fascist states, nor do all dictatorships consider the nation of supreme importance.

2. A This question can be confusing because of the number of foreign terms. Point out the key term, *quick,* and help students associate it with *blitz.*

3. D Only one response assigns the laws to Germany. Students may associate Nuremberg with the German city to reach the correct answer.

4. B By recalling that the last two options were directed toward Britain, students can eliminate answers *C* and *D*. No mention has yet been made of rationing, so *B* is the correct answer.

5. A Students may be confused by the distractor *B*. The responses *C* and *D* are clearly irrelevant or false. By recalling that all of the Axis nations were building up their militaries, students can see that *A* is the correct answer.

6. C The key to this question is the date given. Responses *B* and *D* are similar in nature and can be eliminated. Invasions did not occur before Pearl Harbor, so *A* is also false.

7. B Students can eliminate *C* and *D,* because conferences and pacts have nothing to do with invasions. They are left with two German words; it may help to have them associate the letter *A* with the nation, the act of annexing, and the term *Anschluss.*

8. A This question asks students to recall geography and locations. The key to the question is the mention of France. Students may be able to eliminate all distractors simply by analyzing the words as unlikely to be connected to France.

Chapter 13

9. B Suggest that students observe the words *extermination* and *final* to identify the correct response. Camps deprived Jews of any sort of justice, so *A* can be eliminated. Students should also note that *B* is the only answer choice contained in quotations. The question asks the *name* of the Nazi policy, so students should deduce that the correct answer would contain quotation marks.

10. A The key to this question is the date given, 1939, and the term *immediate*, thus eliminating *B*. Because *A* is in contrast to *C*, logically only one of them is the correct response.

11. A The hemispheric defense zone established an imaginary line in the Atlantic Ocean. The western half of the Atlantic was declared neutral to allow U.S. ships to patrol for German subs. Students should remember that the Wannsee Conference was held by Germany and concerned the "final solution," while the Munich Conference was held to appease Hitler. The America First Committee was an isolationist group and thus would not be interested in aiding Britain.

12. B Students should recognize that Pearl Harbor is part of the United States and therefore the bombing demanded a response. Both *A* and *C* involved other nations. They can also eliminate *D*, which occurred in World War I.

Section 3 *(pp. 466–471)*

9. Concentration camps and extermination camps were part of what Nazis called
   A justice for all.
   B the "final solution."
   C population control.
   D the last straw.

Section 4 *(pp. 474–479)*

10. In 1939 the immediate response of the United States to the start of World War II in Europe was to
   A modify its neutrality policy by providing aid to the Allies.
   B declare war on Germany and Italy.
   C strengthen its isolationist position by ending trade with Britain.
   D send troops to the Allied nations to act as advisers.

11. What was one step that America took to aid Great Britain?
   A created a hemispheric defense zone
   B founded the America First Committee
   C called for the Wannsee Conference
   D attended the Munich Conference

12. Why did the United States enter the war in 1941?
   A blitzkrieg over Poland
   B bombing of Pearl Harbor
   C embargo on Japan
   D sinking of the *Lusitania*

Critical Thinking

Directions: Choose the best answers to the following questions.

13. When Roosevelt signed the Lend-Lease Act, he said America must become the "arsenal of democracy" in order to
   A end the Depression.   C remain neutral.
   B help the Axis Powers.   D help Britain.

Base your answers to questions 14 and 15 on the map below and on your knowledge of Chapter 13.

Nazi Concentration and Extermination Camps

14. In which two countries were most of the concentration and extermination camps located?
   A Germany and France
   B Germany and Poland
   C Germany and the Soviet Union
   D Germany and Austria

15. What can you conclude about the extent of the Nazis' concentration and extermination camps?
   A The Nazis constructed camps in every European country.
   B The Nazis constructed camps in countries that Germany conquered.
   C The Nazis constructed camps in Britain.
   D The Nazis constructed camps in the Soviet Union.

Need Extra Help?

If You Missed Questions . . .	9	10	11	12	13	14	15
Go to Page . . .	470–471	474–476	476–477	477–479	476	R15	R15

GO ON ➡

13. D Students should focus on the word "arsenal" to help them answer this question. If they think of weapons in connection with Lend-Lease, they should be able to narrow the choices to *B* and *D*. Students should then recognize that America was against the Axis Powers, leaving only *D* as the correct response.

14. B Remind students to look carefully at the map in answering this question. Although all responses include Germany, the second part of the answer is determinative.

15. B Students should use the map to help them answer the question. The map shows many European countries without concentration camps, so *A* can be eliminated. The map also shows that no camps existed in Britain or the Soviet Union, eliminating *C* and *D*.

16. Why were the British able to prevent the Germans from invading their country?

  A The United States joined the Allied forces.

  B Germany could not penetrate the Maginot Line.

  C France defeated Germany and pushed them back into Belgium.

  D Britain had developed radar stations to detect German aircraft.

Analyze the cartoon and answer the question that follows. Base your answer on the cartoon and on your knowledge of Chapter 13.

17. According to the cartoon, how did Americans feel about assisting the Allies?

  A They sent troops to help make the world safe for democracy.

  B Many Americans were willing to help the British but did not want to sell them arms.

  C Many Americans did not want to help the British fight the Germans.

  D The United States sold arms to Britain and France.

Document-Based Questions

Directions: Analyze the document and answer the short-answer questions that follow the document.

Daniel Inouye earned a Medal of Honor for his service in World War II and later became a United States senator. In 1941, however, he was a teenager living in Hawaii. This is his account of Pearl Harbor:

> "As soon as I finished brushing my teeth and pulled on my trousers, I automatically clicked on the little radio that stood on the shelf above my bed. I remember that I was buttoning my shirt and looking out the window . . . when the hum of the warming set gave way to a frenzied voice. 'This is no test,' the voice cried out. 'Pearl Harbor is being bombed by the Japanese!'"
>
> [The family ran outside to look toward the naval base at Pearl Harbor.]
>
> "And then we saw the planes. They came zooming up out of that sea of gray smoke, flying north toward where we stood and climbing into the bluest part of the sky, and they came in twos and threes, in neat formations, and if it hadn't been for that red ball on their wings, the rising sun of the Japanese Empire, you could easily believe that they were Americans, flying over in precise military salute."
>
> —quoted in *Eyewitness to America*

18. How did Inouye find out about the attack on Pearl Harbor?

19. What made him certain that the planes were Japanese, not American?

Extended Response

20. Could the Holocaust have been avoided if the Allies had intervened? Write an essay that takes a position and defends it. Your essay should include an introduction, several paragraphs, and a conclusion. Use relevant facts and details to support your conclusion.

STOP

History ONLINE

For additional test practice, use Self-Check Quizzes—Chapter 13 at glencoe.com.

Need Extra Help?

If You Missed Questions . . .	16	17	18	19	20
Go to Page . . .	465	R18	R19	R19	R6

---

16. D Students may need to focus on order of events to answer this question correctly. The United States did not join the Allies until after Germany's attempt to invade Britain. Germany went around the Maginot Line. C is clearly false, because Germany defeated France.

17. B Careful examination of the cartoon indicates that Americans wanted only to honor long friendship and ties with Britain, not to provide troops or arms.

18. over the radio

19. the red ball painted on the wings of the planes, representing the rising sun of the Japanese Empire

20. Students' essays will vary but should take a position and support it with relevant facts and details. Essays should include an introduction, multiple paragraphs, and a conclusion.

History ONLINE

Have students visit the Web site at glencoe.com to review Chapter 13 and take the Self-Check Quiz.

Need Extra Help?

Have students refer to the pages listed if they miss any of the questions.

Key to Ability Levels
- **BL** Below Level
- **OL** On Level
- **AL** Above Level
- **ELL** English Language Learners

Key to Teaching Resources
- Print Material
- CD-ROM
- DVD
- Transparency

Levels (BL OL AL ELL)	Resources	Chapter Opener	Section 1	Section 2	Section 3	Section 4	Section 5	Chapter Assess
FOCUS								
BL OL AL ELL	Daily Focus Skills Transparencies		14-1	14-2	14-3	14-4	14-5	
TEACH								
OL AL	Geography and History Activity, URB					p. 3		
OL AL	American Literature Reading, URB		p. 13		p. 15			
BL OL ELL	Reading Essentials and Note-Taking Guide*		p. 146	p. 149	p. 152	p. 155	p. 158	
OL	Historical Analysis Skills Activity, URB		p. 56					
BL OL ELL	Guided Reading Activities, URB*		p. 82	p. 83	p. 84	p. 85	p. 86	
BL OL AL ELL	Content Vocabulary Activity, URB*	p. 61						
BL OL AL ELL	Academic Vocabulary Activity, URB	p. 63						
OL AL	Critical Thinking Skills Activity, URB						p. 66	
BL OL ELL	Reading Skills Activity, URB							p. 55
BL ELL	English Learner Activity, URB					p. 59		
OL AL	Reinforcing Skills Activity, URB					p. 65		
BL OL AL ELL	Differentiated Instruction Activity, URB							p. 57
BL OL ELL	Time Line Activity, URB							p. 67
OL	Linking Past and Present Activity, URB		p. 68					
BL OL AL ELL	American Art and Music Activity, URB							p. 73
BL OL AL ELL	Interpreting Political Cartoons Activity, URB			p. 75				
AL	Enrichment Activity, URB				p. 79			
BL OL AL ELL	American Biographies		✓					
BL OL AL ELL	Primary Source Reading, URB			p. 69	p. 71			
BL OL AL ELL	Supreme Court Case Studies				pp. 61, 63			
BL OL AL ELL	The Living Constitution*	✓	✓	✓	✓	✓	✓	✓
OL AL	American History Primary Source Documents Library	✓	✓	✓	✓	✓	✓	✓
BL OL AL ELL	Unit Map Overlay Transparencies	✓	✓	✓	✓	✓	✓	✓
BL OL AL ELL	Differentiated Instruction for the American High School Classroom	✓	✓	✓	✓	✓	✓	✓

Note: Please refer to the *Unit 5 Resource Book* for this chapter's URB materials.

* Also available in Spanish

TeacherWorks Plus
All-In-One Planner and Resource Center

- Interactive Lesson Planner
- Interactive Teacher Edition
- Fully editable blackline masters
- Section Spotlight Videos Launch
- Differentiated Lesson Plans
- Printable reports of daily assignments
- Standards Tracking System

Levels					Resources	Chapter Opener	Section 1	Section 2	Section 3	Section 4	Section 5	Chapter Assess
TEACH *(continued)*												
BL	OL	AL	ELL		StudentWorks™ Plus DVD	✓	✓	✓	✓	✓	✓	✓
BL	OL	AL	ELL		Vocabulary PuzzleMaker CD-ROM	✓	✓	✓	✓	✓	✓	✓
BL	OL	AL	ELL		American Music Hits Through History CD	✓	✓	✓	✓	✓	✓	✓
BL	OL	AL	ELL		Unit Time Line Transparencies and Activities	✓	✓	✓	✓	✓	✓	✓
BL	OL	AL	ELL		Cause and Effect Transparencies, Strategies, and Activities	✓	✓	✓	✓	✓	✓	✓
BL	OL	AL	ELL		Why It Matters Transparencies, Strategies, and Activities	✓	✓	✓	✓	✓	✓	✓
BL	OL	AL	ELL		American Issues	✓	✓	✓	✓	✓	✓	✓
	OL	AL	ELL		American Art and Architecture Transparencies, Strategies, and Activities	✓	✓	✓	✓	✓	✓	✓
BL	OL	AL			High School American History Literature Library	✓	✓	✓	✓	✓	✓	✓
BL	OL	AL	ELL		*The American Vision* Video Program DVD	✓	✓	✓	✓	✓	✓	✓
Teacher Resources					Strategies for Success	✓	✓	✓	✓	✓	✓	✓
					Success with English Learner	✓	✓	✓	✓	✓	✓	✓
					Studies Classroom	✓	✓	✓	✓	✓	✓	✓
					Presentation Plus! DVD	✓	✓	✓	✓	✓	✓	✓
ASSESS												
BL	OL	AL	ELL		Section Quizzes and Chapter Tests*		p. 197	p. 198	p. 199	p. 200	p. 201	p. 203
BL	OL	AL	ELL		Authentic Assessment With Rubrics							p. 33
BL	OL	AL	ELL		Standardized Test Practice Workbook							p. 31
BL	OL	AL	ELL		*ExamView®* Assessment Suite CD-ROM		14-1	14-2	14-3	14-4	14-5	Ch. 14
BL	OL	AL	ELL		Interactive Tutor Self-Assessment CD-ROM		14-1	14-2	14-3	14-4	14-5	Ch. 14
CLOSE												
BL			ELL		Reteaching Activity, URB							p. 77
BL	OL		ELL		Reading and Study Skills Foldables™	p. 74						

Using the McGraw-Hill Learning Network

Web Site Builder

Technology Product

The Web Site Builder is a convenient and dynamic McGraw-Hill Learning Network tool that helps you build Web sites quickly. The site allows you to include your own images, videos, and text to customize it to your needs. The Web site builder also provides you with a variety of tools to make your Web site inviting. Use the Web Site Builder to

- provide assignments and important dates to your students;
- keep students and parents informed of events in your classroom;
- publish your contact information.

Steps

- On the McGraw-Hill Learning Network home page (www.mhln.com), log in as a member.
- Choose **Web Site Builder** under **Resources**.

- Choose a template from the **Create a new site** pull-down options and follow the prompts on the screen to select a design, insert text, and select fonts, colors, and sizes.
- Create the content students will need to study for a chapter text or post homework assignments.
- Use the navigation buttons on the bottom of the screen to edit, add, and delete information, images, and videos.
- Publish the site and provide the URL to your students.

History ONLINE

	Student	Teacher	Parent
Beyond the Textbook	●	●	●
Chapter Overviews	●	●	●
Time Current Events	●		●
ePuzzles and Games	●		●
Concepts in Motion	●		●
Literature Connections		●	
Multi-Language Glossaries	●		●
Online Student Edition	●	●	●
Self-Check Quizzes	●		●
Student Web Activities	●		●
Study Central ™	●		●
Teaching Today		●	
Vocabulary eFlashcards	●		●
Web Activity Lesson Plans		●	

Glencoe Media Center

glencoe.com

〉 **Study-To-Go**
- Vocabulary eFlashcards
- Self-Check Quizzes

〉 **Audio/Video**
- Student Edition Audio
- Spanish Summaries
- Section Videos

- **Timed Readings Plus in Social Studies** helps students increase their reading rate and fluency while maintaining comprehension. The 400-word passages are similar to those found on state and national assessments.

- **Reading in the Content Area: Social Studies** concentrates on six essential reading skills that help students better comprehend what they read. The book includes 75 high-interest nonfiction passages written at increasing levels of difficulty.

- **Reading Social Studies** includes strategic reading instruction and vocabulary support in Social Studies content for both ELLs and native speakers of English.

www.jamestowneducation.com

The following videotape programs are available from Glencoe as supplements to Chapter 14:

- The Last Days of World War II (ISBN 1-56-501536-3)
- D-Day: The Total Story (ISBN 0-76-700606-2)

To order, call Glencoe at 1-800-334-7344. To find classroom resources to accompany many of these videos, check the following home pages:

A&E Television: www.aetv.com
The History Channel: www.historychannel.com

NATIONAL GEOGRAPHIC
Index to National Geographic Magazine:

The following articles relate to this chapter:

- "The Wings of War: How the Yanks of the Eighth Air Force Helped Turn the Tide in World War II," by Thomas B. Allen, March 1994.
- "Remembering the Blitz," by Cameron Thomas, July 1991.

National Geographic Society Products To order the following, call National Geographic at 1-800-368-2728:

- *World War II Era CD-ROM* (CD-ROM)

Access National Geographic's new, dynamic MapMachine Web site and other geography resources at:

www.nationalgeographic.com
www.nationalgeographic.com/maps

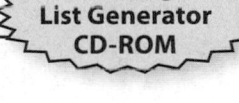

Reading List Generator CD-ROM

BOOKLINK 3

Use this database to search more than 30,000 titles to create a customized reading list for your students.

- Reading lists can be organized by students' reading level, author, genre, theme, or area of interest.
- The database provides Degrees of Reading Power™ (DRP) and Lexile™ readability scores for all selections.
- A brief summary of each selection is included.

Leveled reading suggestions for this chapter:

For students at a Grade 8 reading level:
- *Summer of My German Soldier*, by Bette Greene

For students at a Grade 9 reading level:
- *The Winds of War*, by Herman Wouk

For students at a Grade 10 reading level:
- *Flags of Our Fathers*, by James Bradley and Ron Powers

For students at a Grade 11 reading level:
- *Never to Forget: The Jews of the Holocaust*, by Milton Meltzer

For students at a Grade 12 reading level:
- *America in World War II: 1945*, by Edward F. Dolan

Focus

MAKING CONNECTIONS
What Kind of Sacrifices Does War Require?

Ask students what kind of sacrifices they would be willing to make for their country. Lead a discussion regarding citizens' roles at home during wartime. Discuss different attitudes people have about supporting war. Encourage students to state why World War II inspired patriotism throughout the country. **BL** **OL**

Teach
The Big Ideas

As students study the chapter, remind them to consider the section-based Big Ideas included in each section's Guide to Reading. The **Essential Questions** in the activities below tie in to the Big Ideas and help students think about and understand important chapter concepts. In addition, the Hands-on Chapter Projects with the culminating activities relate the content from each section to the Big Ideas. These activities build on each other as students progress through the chapter. Section activities culminate in the wrap-up activity on the Visual Summary page.

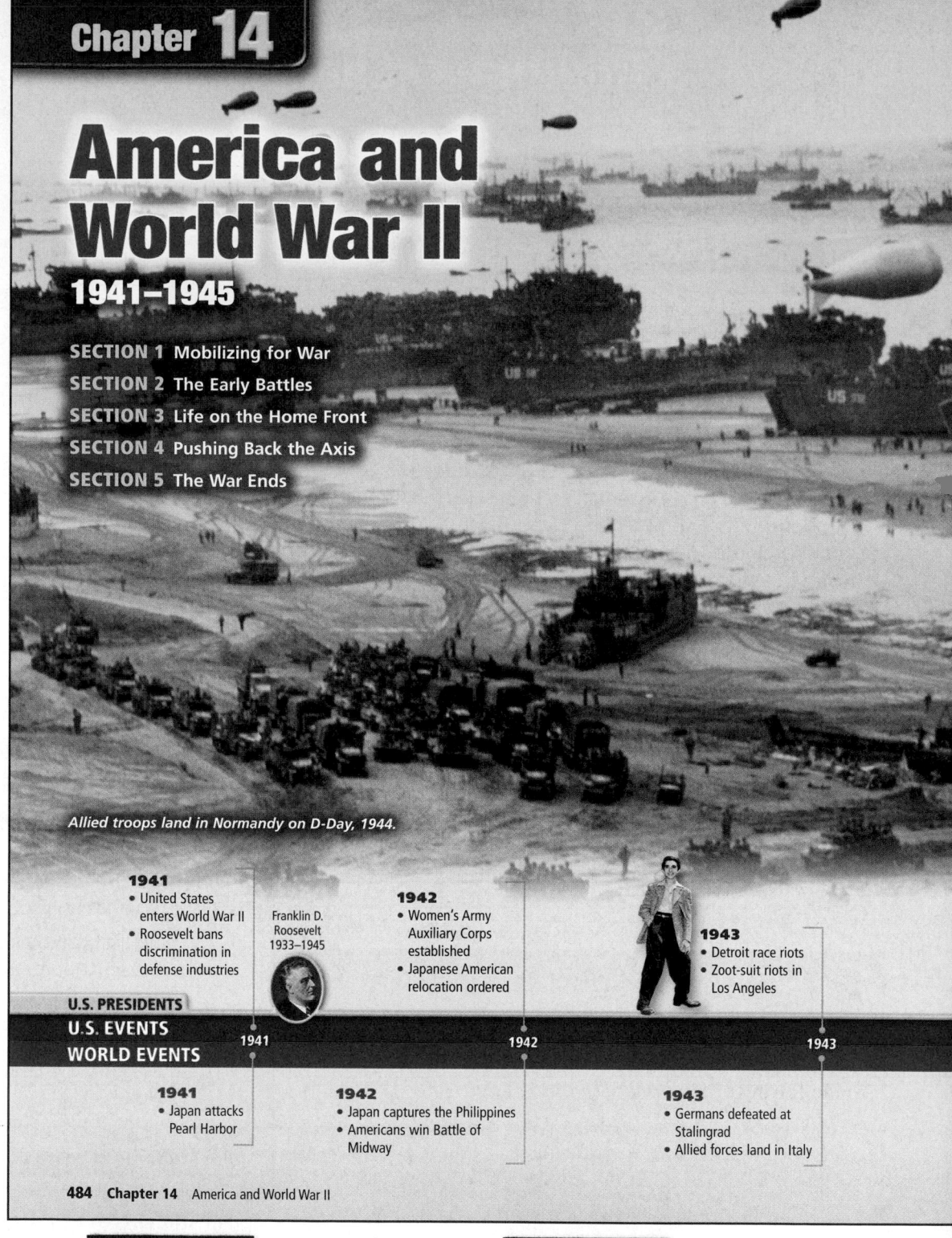

Chapter 14

America and World War II
1941–1945

SECTION 1 Mobilizing for War
SECTION 2 The Early Battles
SECTION 3 Life on the Home Front
SECTION 4 Pushing Back the Axis
SECTION 5 The War Ends

Allied troops land in Normandy on D-Day, 1944.

U.S. PRESIDENTS
Franklin D. Roosevelt 1933–1945

U.S. EVENTS — 1941 — 1942 — 1943
WORLD EVENTS

1941
• United States enters World War II
• Roosevelt bans discrimination in defense industries

1942
• Women's Army Auxiliary Corps established
• Japanese American relocation ordered

1943
• Detroit race riots
• Zoot-suit riots in Los Angeles

1941
• Japan attacks Pearl Harbor

1942
• Japan captures the Philippines
• Americans win Battle of Midway

1943
• Germans defeated at Stalingrad
• Allied forces land in Italy

484 Chapter 14 America and World War II

Section 1
Mobilizing for War
Essential Question: How could the United States increase its productivity in a short period of time? *(Workers must be motivated to work long hours. Materials must be readily available to allow for faster production.)* Tell students that Section 1 describes how Roosevelt and business leaders rapidly mobilized the economy to ensure success in the war. **OL**

Section 2
The Early Battles
Essential Question: What unique decisions did the United States face as a result of fighting a war on two fronts? *(whether to fight both wars with equal strength or to emphasize one front and one enemy over the other)* Inform students that Section 2 will highlight how the U.S. balanced operations against the Japanese and Germany. **OL**

Section 3
Life on the Home Front
Essential Question: How do you think women and African Americans responded to the war? *(They took factory jobs typically held by white men. Some may have protested the war.)* Explain that in Section 3, students will learn about how these groups responded to new opportunities, prejudices, and restrictions. **OL**

MAKING CONNECTIONS
What Kinds of Sacrifices Does War Require?

During World War II, millions of Americans enlisted in the armed forces, risking their lives in the struggle. On the home front, Americans also helped the war effort by giving up goods needed by the military and buying war bonds.

- *Why do you think so many Americans volunteered to fight in World War II?*
- *Should civilians have to make sacrifices in wartime?*

More About the Photo

Visual Literacy On June 6, 1944, American, British, and Canadian troops assaulted five different beach heads in Normandy, France. Known as D-Day, the invasion included nearly 7,000 ships, including battleships and landing craft. Allied troops stormed the beaches in the early morning. Though they suffered heavy losses, with the heaviest casualties at Omaha Beach, they succeeded at pushing the German troops inland.

FOLDABLES Study Organizer — Dinah Zike's Foldables

Dinah Zike's Foldables are three-dimensional, interactive graphic organizers that help students practice basic writing skills, review vocabulary terms, and identify main ideas. Instructions for creating and using Foldables can be found in the Appendix at the end of this book and in the *Dinah Zike's Reading and Study Skills Foldables* booklet.

1944
- Supreme Court rules in *Korematsu* v. *United States* that Japanese American relocation is constitutional

Harry Truman 1945–1953

1945
- Franklin Roosevelt dies in office; Harry S. Truman becomes president

1944   1945

1944
- Eisenhower leads D-Day invasion
- MacArthur's forces land in the Philippines

1945
- U.S. Marines capture Iwo Jima
- United States drops atomic bomb on Japan

FOLDABLES

Summarizing American Life During World War II Make a Pocket Book Foldable to summarize various aspects of daily life that World War II affected. Label the two pockets as Economic and Social. Include general effects as well as specific programs under each pocket.

Economic   Social

History ONLINE Chapter Overview
Visit glencoe.com to preview Chapter 14.

Chapter 14   America and World War II   **485**

History ONLINE
Introduce students to chapter content and key terms by having them access the Chapter 14 Overview at glencoe.com.

Section 4

Pushing Back the Axis
Essential Question: Why were Americans still willing to fight a war with so many American casualties? *(Responses may include the desire to protect America from Hitler, stop the Holocaust, seek revenge for Pearl Harbor.)* Tell students that in Section 4, they will learn about the strategic battles of the war and the large number of casualties. **OL**

Section 5

The War Ends
Essential Question: Why do you think America used atomic weapons against Japan? *(Responses may include to bring about the end of the war with Japan; save the lives of American soldiers fighting in Pacific.)* As you lead a discussion, remind students that this question continues to be debated. Section 5 will cover some of the debate. **OL**

Focus

Mobilizing for War

Bellringer
Daily Focus Transparency 14.1

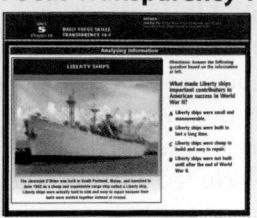

Guide to Reading

Answers:
Government Agencies Created to Mobilize the Economy:
National Defense Advisory Committee
Reconstruction Finance Corporation
War Production Board
Office of War Mobilization

Section Spotlight Video

To generate student interest and provide a springboard for class discussion, access the Chapter 14, Section 1 video at glencoe.com or on the video DVD.

Guide to Reading

Big Ideas
Economics and Society Americans quickly converted to a wartime economy to support the war effort.

Content Vocabulary
• cost-plus *(p. 488)*
• disenfranchised *(p. 491)*

Academic Vocabulary
• vehicle *(p. 489)*
• draft *(p. 490)*

People and Events to Identify
• War Production Board *(p. 489)*
• Office of War Mobilization *(p. 489)*
• "Double V" campaign *(p. 492)*
• Tuskegee Airmen *(p. 492)*
• Oveta Culp Hobby *(p. 493)*
• Women's Army Corps *(p. 493)*

Reading Strategy
Organizing Complete a graphic organizer similar to the one below by filling in the agencies that the U.S. government created to mobilize the nation for war.

Government Agencies Created to Mobilize the Economy

After World War I, America returned to isolationism. When the nation entered World War II in 1941, its armed forces ranked nineteenth in might, behind the tiny European nation of Belgium. Three years later, the United States was producing 40 percent of the world's arms.

Converting the Economy

MAIN Idea The United States quickly mobilized the economy to fight the war.

HISTORY AND YOU Have you ever changed the way you performed a task in order to do it faster or more efficiently? What steps did you take to speed things up? Read on to learn how the United States changed the way factories produced goods during World War II.

Shortly after 1:30 P.M. on December 7, 1941, Secretary of the Navy Frank Knox phoned President Roosevelt at the White House. "Mr. President," Knox said, "it looks like the Japanese have attacked Pearl Harbor." A few minutes later, Admiral Harold Stark, chief of naval operations, phoned and confirmed the attack.

Although President Roosevelt remained calm when he heard the news, he later expressed his concerns to his wife Eleanor: "I never wanted to have to fight this war on two fronts. We haven't got the Navy to fight in both the Atlantic and Pacific. . . . We will have to build up the Navy and the Air Force and that will mean we will have to take a good many defeats before we can have a victory."

Although the difficulties of fighting a global war troubled the president, British prime minister Winston Churchill was not worried. Churchill knew that victory in modern war depended on a nation's industrial power. He compared the American economy to a gigantic boiler: "Once the fire is lighted under it there is no limit to the power it can generate."

Churchill was right. The industrial output of the United States during the war astounded the rest of the world. American workers were twice as productive as German workers and five times more productive than Japanese workers. In 1943 the Soviet leader Joseph Stalin toasted "American production, without which this war would have been lost." American war production turned the tide in favor of the Allies. In less than four years, the United States and its allies achieved what no other group of nations had ever done—they fought and won a two-front war against two powerful military empires, forcing each to surrender.

Resource Manager

R Reading Strategies	**C** Critical Thinking	**D** Differentiated Instruction	**W** Writing Support	**S** Skill Practice
Teacher Edition • Inferring, pp. 487, 490 • Academic Vocab., p. 490 • Paraphrasing, p. 493	**Teacher Edition** • Det. Cause/Effect, p. 487 • Hypothesizing, p. 489 • Evaluating, p. 491 • Making Inf., p. 492	**Teacher Edition** • Visual/Spatial, pp. 488, 489	**Teacher Edition** • Persuasive Writing, p. 492	**Teacher Edition** • Interpreting a Chart, p. 490
Additional Resources • Guide. Reading, URB p. 82	**Additional Resources** • Historical Analysis Skills Act, URB p. 56 • Link. Past/Present Act., URB p. 68 • Quizzes and Tests, p. 197	**Additional Resources** • Acad. Vocab. Act., URB p. 63 • Foldables, p. 74	**Additional Resources** • Content Vocab. Act., URB p. 61	**Additional Resources** • RENTG, p. 146

PRIMARY SOURCE
The Arsenal of Democracy

Analyzing VISUALS

1. **Determining Cause and Effect** When did tank production begin to drop? Why might this be so?
2. **Making Connections** How do you think the workers felt as they watched the tanks rolling out of the factory?

U.S. Output of Military Products

[Line graph showing Products (y-axis: 20,000 to 80,000) vs Year (x-axis: 1941–1945)]

— Combat aircraft   — Ships   — Tanks

Source: *The Big 'L': American Logistics in World War II.*

The United States rapidly increased its war production after the attack on Pearl Harbor. The expansion was possible in part because the government had already begun mobilizing the economy before the country entered the war. When the German blitzkrieg swept into France in May 1940, President Roosevelt declared a national emergency and announced a plan to build 50,000 warplanes a year. Two months later he asked Congress for $4 billion to build a "Two-Ocean" Navy.

R Shocked by the success of the German attack, many Americans were willing to build up the country's defenses. By October 1940, Congress had increased the defense budget to more than $17 billion. The Army-Navy Munitions Board—the military agency in charge of buying equipment—began signing contracts with American companies for new aircraft, ships, and equipment.

Roosevelt believed that government and business had to work together to prepare for war. He created the National Defense Advisory Committee to help mobilize the economy and asked several business leaders to serve on the committee. The president and his advisers believed that giving industry an incentive to move quickly was the best way to rapidly mobilize the economy. As Henry Stimson, the new secretary of war, wrote in his diary: "If you are going to try and go to war, or to prepare for war, in a capitalist country, you have got to let business make money out of the process or business won't work." **C**

Chapter 14 America and World War II **487**

R **Reading Strategy**

Inferring Ask: Why were Americans eager to increase production? *(Answers may include shock at German success; national pride; a desire to build up U.S. defenses.)* **OL**

C **Critical Thinking**

Determining Cause and Effect Ask: Why did Roosevelt provide incentives to businesses that would aid in the war? *(He knew that businesses were better equipped than the government. If they made money, they would work harder.)* **OL**

Analyzing VISUALS

Answers:
1. after 1943; Answers may include steady growth in tank production over 2 years lessened the need for production
2. proud to be helping with the war effort

Additional Support

Activity: Technology Connection

Analyzing Technology Assign students to small groups and have them research new technology that was being used in American tanks and fighter planes in the 1940s (for example, Sherman tanks, Wildcat, Hellcat, and Mustang fighters). Direct them to read about the reasoning for utilizing the new technology, about production information, and about how the tanks and planes fared in actual warfare. Students should write a short report and include photos or other visuals to support their findings. **OL**

D Differentiated Instruction

Visual/Spatial Have students work in pairs to create posters that illustrate information about unemployment, production figures for several industries, and other economic indications from before the war and then again after mobilization. **OL**

✓ Reading Check

Answer:
The cost-plus program encouraged companies to make many products quickly. The RFC made loans to help companies convert to war production.

DBQ Document Based Questions

Answers:
1. to protect herself from getting burned
2. She had to fill in the seams of the ship with hot lead before the welders came in.

Hands-On Chapter Project
Step 1

An Interview with a World War II Veteran

Step 1: Finding a Veteran to Interview and Shaping the Questions
Essential Question: What can we learn from a World War II veteran?

Directions Explain to students that they will document an interview with a World War II veteran (using a CD or DVD). Students should begin by thinking about what they might learn from a veteran. For example,

---

Normally when the government needed military equipment, it would ask companies to bid for the contract, but that system was too slow in wartime. Instead of asking for bids, the government signed **cost-plus** contracts. The government agreed to pay a company whatever it cost to make a product plus a guaranteed percentage of the costs as profit.

Under the cost-plus system, the more a company produced and the faster it did the work, the more money it would make. The system was not cheap, but it did get war materials produced quickly and in quantity.

Cost-plus convinced many companies to convert to war production. Other firms, however, could not afford to reequip their factories to make military goods. To convince more companies to convert, Congress gave new authority to the Reconstruction Finance Corporation (RFC). That government agency, set up during the Depression, could make loans to companies wanting to convert their factories to war production.

✓ **Reading Check** **Analyzing** What government policies helped American industry to produce large quantities of war materials?

PRIMARY SOURCE
Building the Liberty Ships

▲ In this 1942 photograph, workers construct a Liberty ship in San Francisco.

PRIMARY SOURCE

"I took classes on how to weld. I had leather gloves, leather pants, a big hood, goggles and a leather jacket.... They put me forty feet down in the bottom of the ship to be a tacker. I filled the long seams of the cracks in the ship corners full of hot lead and then brushed them good and you could see how pretty it was. The welders would come along and weld it so it would take the strong waves and deep water and heavy weight."

—Katie Grant, World War II riveter at Kaiser Richmond Shipyard, California

---

American Industry Gets the Job Done

MAIN Idea Factories built tanks, airplanes, trucks, and jeeps for military use, as well as safer ships.

HISTORY AND YOU Has a coach or an instructor ever challenged you to improve your speed or efficiency at a task? Read on to learn how American industry helped the war effort.

By the fall of 1941, much had already been done to prepare the economy for war, but it was still only partially mobilized. Although many companies were producing military equipment, most still preferred to make consumer goods. The Great Depression was ending, demand was up, and sales were rising. The Japanese attack on Pearl Harbor, however, changed everything. A flood of orders by the government for war materials began, and by the summer of 1942, almost all major industries and some 200,000 companies had converted to war production. Together they made the nation's wartime "miracle" possible.

DBQ Document-Based Questions

1. **Interpreting** Why would Katie Grant have had to wear leather clothing?
2. **Summarizing** What was her job?

---

students could learn American attitudes in that person's community toward the war, where he or she served, what he or she knew at the time about Europe, how service affected his or her political views. The next and crucial task is to find a veteran to interview. A local VFW group can be helpful (asking other community organizations or churches is also a possibility.) Students may write a letter or phone the veteran to ask for his/her participation.

Putting It Together Once students know the basics about their interviewee (such as the branch of the military and theater of the war involved), they should write out the questions they will ask in a question-and-answer format, organizing the questions in a logical fashion (the person's life before the war, mission during the war, and so on). **OL**

(Chapter Project continued on page 496)

Tanks Replace Cars

The automobile industry was uniquely suited to the mass production of military equipment. Automobile factories began producing trucks, jeeps, and tanks. Mass production was critical in modern warfare, because the country that could move troops and supplies most quickly usually won the battle. As General George C. Marshall, chief of staff for the United States Army, observed:

PRIMARY SOURCE

"The greatest advantage . . . the United States enjoyed on the ground in the fighting was . . . the jeep and the two-and-a-half ton truck. These are the instruments that moved and supplied United States troops in battle, while the German army . . . depended heavily on animal transport. . . . The United States, profiting from the mass production achievements of its automotive industry . . . had mobility that completely outclassed the enemy."

—quoted in *Miracle of World War II*

Automobile factories did not just produce **vehicles.** They also built artillery, rifles, mines, helmets, pontoon bridges, and dozens of other pieces of military equipment. Henry Ford created an assembly line for the enormous B-24 bomber known as the "Liberator" at Willow Run Airport near Detroit. By the end of the war, the factory had built more than 8,600 aircraft. Overall, the auto industry produced nearly one-third of all military equipment manufactured during the war.

Building the Liberty Ships

Ford's remarkable achievement in aircraft production was more than matched by Henry Kaiser's shipyards. Henry Kaiser started in the construction industry, but when World War II began, Kaiser shifted from the construction industry to shipbuilding.

German submarines were sinking American cargo ships at a terrifying rate. The United States had to find a way to build cargo ships as quickly as possible. Kaiser believed that speed was more important than quality and that cost was less important than results. He spent whatever it took to get the job done quickly. To save time, he applied techniques from the construction industry to shipbuilding. Instead of building an entire ship in one place from the keel up, parts were prefabricated and brought to the shipyard for assembly.

Kaiser's shipyards built many different kinds of ships, but they were best known for Liberty ships. The Liberty ship was the basic cargo ship used during the war. Liberty ships were welded instead of riveted. Although welded ships tended to crack, Vice Admiral Emory Land, head of the U.S. Maritime Commission, preferred the Liberty ships:

PRIMARY SOURCE

"Every time a riveted ship goes into dock you have a lot of repairs to do. You do not have them in welded ships. . . . On combat damage, comparing the welded Liberty ships and others, everything is in favor of the Liberty. . . . riveted ships are apt to go to the bottom if they are bombed or mined or torpedoed. . . . Never mind about the fractures or the cracks—[the Liberty ships] get into port."

—quoted in *Miracle of World War II*

When the war began, it took 244 days to build the first Liberty ship. After Kaiser shipyards applied their mass-production techniques, average production time dropped to 41 days. Kaiser's shipyards built 30 percent of all American ships constructed during the war, including nearly 3,000 Liberty ships.

The War Production Board

As American companies converted to war production, many business leaders became frustrated with the mobilization process. Government agencies argued constantly about supplies and contracts and whose orders had the highest priority.

After Pearl Harbor, President Roosevelt tried to improve the system by creating the **War Production Board** (WPB). He gave the WPB the authority to set priorities and production goals and to control the distribution of raw materials and supplies. Almost immediately, the WPB clashed with the military. Military agencies continued to sign contracts without consulting with the WPB. Finally, in 1943, Roosevelt established the **Office of War Mobilization** (OWM) to settle arguments among the different agencies.

✔ **Reading Check** **Explaining** What military need led to the production of Liberty ships?

Chapter 14 • Section 1

D Differentiated Instruction

Visual/Spatial Tell students they are on a committee to design a stamp commemorating the World War II mobilization effort. They must choose between Henry Ford and Henry Kaiser. Have each student draw a picture of their stamp and explain their design. **BL**

C Critical Thinking

Hypothesizing Have students theorize why government agencies and private businesses argued over supplies. *(Students may suggest that government officials may have had previous business relations with companies that they did not want to offend.)* **OL**

✔ **Reading Check**

Answer:
The Germans had been sinking cargo ships regularly, keeping important cargo from reaching U.S. ports. New ships that were cheap, easy to build, and fast were in great demand.

Additional Support

Teacher Tip

Collaborative Learning This activity requires students to research, write, and illustrate. As you form groups, allow students with different levels of academic skills to work together. Assist groups by assigning tasks based on each student's strengths.

Activity: Collaborative Learning

Identifying Central Issues Assign students to small groups. Students will work together to research the Liberty ships. Encourage them to use the Internet to find information as well as photographs of the ships. **Ask:** How important were the ships to the Allied victory in World War II? *(Students may suggest that ships were important in supplying and transporting troops.)* Each group should prepare a report to answer the question. Have groups present their reports and photographs to the class. Discuss students' findings following the presentations. **OL**

489

R₁ Reading Strategy

Academic Vocabulary Have students use context clues and prior knowledge to define the word *draft*. *(choosing individuals for compulsory military service)* **OL**

R₂ Reading Strategy

Inferring Lead students in a discussion about current U.S. policy regarding military preparedness and reinstating the draft. **Ask: Under what circumstances, if any, do you think the United States should reinstate the draft?** *(Answers may include a need for more soldiers in time of war; for national defense in time of war.)* Write a list of pros and cons of reinstating the draft on the board. **OL**

S Skill Practice

Interpreting a Chart Have students look at the chart. **Ask: In which year were the armed forces at a peak?** *(1945)* **at a low?** *(1939–40)* **BL**

Additional Support

Building an Army

MAIN Idea Minorities and women played an important role in the United States armed forces during World War II.

HISTORY AND YOU Do you think the United States should have a military draft? Read to learn about the first peacetime draft in American history.

Converting factories to war production was only part of the mobilization process. To fight and win the war, the United States also needed to build up its armed forces.

Creating an Army

Within days of Germany's attack on Poland in 1939, President Roosevelt expanded the army to 227,000 soldiers. Before the spring of 1940, college students, unions, isolationists, and most members of Congress had opposed a peacetime **draft.** Opinions changed after France surrendered to Germany in June 1940. Two members of Congress introduced the Selective Service and Training Act, a plan for the first peacetime draft in American history. In September, Congress approved the draft by a wide margin.

You're in the Army Now

More than 60,000 men enlisted in the month after the attack on Pearl Harbor. At first, the flood of recruits overwhelmed the army's training facilities. Many recruits had to live in tents rather than barracks. The army also experienced equipment shortages. Troops carried sticks representing guns, threw stones simulating grenades, and practiced maneuvers with trucks labeled "TANK."

New recruits were initially sent to a reception center, where they were given physical exams and injections against smallpox and typhoid. The draftees were then issued uniforms, boots, and whatever equipment was available. The clothing bore the label "G.I.," meaning "Government Issue," which is why American soldiers were called GIs.

After taking aptitude tests, recruits went to basic training for eight weeks. They learned

PRIMARY SOURCE
Creating an American Army

▲ Soldiers from a Mexican-American platoon train at Fort Benning in 1943.

U.S. Armed Forces, 1939–1946

Military personnel (millions)

— Army
— Navy
— Marines

Source: *Historical Statistics of the United States.*

PRIMARY SOURCE

For many Americans, entering the army changed their perspective, as historian Carl Degler recalls:

"Entrance into the Army in August, 1942, widened my horizons literally as well as experientially: for the first time I travelled beyond a 200 mile radius from Newark. I marvelled at the flatness of the prairie in Illinois . . . . Stops at posts in Miami Beach, Florida, and Richmond, Virginia, were my introduction to the American South."

—from *The History Teacher*, vol. 23, 1990

Activity: Collaborative Learning

Diagramming the Draft From 1948 until 1973, during both peacetimes and periods of conflict, men were drafted to fill vacancies in the armed forces that could not be filled through voluntary means. The draft ended in 1973, toward the close of the Vietnam War, and the United States converted to an all-volunteer military. **Ask: Who had to sign up for the draft? Where did they sign up? What happened when they went to sign up? When was the lottery introduced? How were numbers picked?** Have students use the Internet and interview people who were drafted to get answers to these questions. Have students work together to create a flow chart that illustrates the draft process. **OL**

how to handle weapons, load backpacks, read maps, pitch tents, and dig trenches. Trainees drilled and exercised constantly and learned how to work as a team.

Basic training helped to break down barriers between soldiers. Recruits came from all over the country, and training together created a "special sense of kinship," as one soldier noted. "The reason you storm the beaches is not patriotism or bravery. It's that sense of not wanting to fail your buddies."

A Segregated Army

Although basic training promoted unity, most recruits did not encounter Americans from every part of society. At the start of the war, the U.S. military was segregated. White recruits did not train alongside African Americans. African Americans had separate barracks, latrines, mess halls, and recreational facilities. Once trained, African Americans were organized into their own military units, but white officers generally commanded them. Most military leaders also wanted to keep African American soldiers out of combat and assigned them to construction and supply units.

Some African Americans did not want to support the war. As one student at a black college noted: "The Army Jim Crows us. . . . Employers and labor unions shut us out. Lynchings continue. We are **disenfranchised** . . . and spat upon. What more could Hitler do to us than that?" Despite the bitterness, most African Americans agreed with African American writer Saunders Redding that they should support their country:

PRIMARY SOURCE

"There are many things about this war that I do not like . . . yet I believe in the war. . . . [We] know that whatever the mad logic of [Hitler's] New Order there is no hope for us under it. The ethnic theories of the Hitler 'master folk' admit of no chance of freedom. . . . This is a war to keep [people] free. The struggle to broaden and lengthen the road of freedom—our own private and important war to enlarge freedom here in America—will come later. . . . I believe in this war because I believe in America. I believe in what America professes to stand for."

—from "A Negro Looks at This War"

c

A Segregated Army

Although the U.S. armed forces were segregated, discrimination did not prevent minority groups from performing with courage. Two of the best-known examples are the Tuskegee Airmen (right), comprised of African American volunteers, and the 442nd Regimental Combat Team (below), made up of Japanese American volunteers. The 450 Tuskegee Airmen fought in North Africa, Sicily, and Italy. The 442nd Regimental Combat Team became the most decorated unit in U.S. history.

Analyzing VISUALS

1. **Identifying** In what year did the army experience the most rapid growth? Why do you think that is the case?
2. **Evaluating** What do the expressions on the faces of the Tuskegee Airmen convey?

Chapter 14 America and World War II **491**

Activity: Collaborative Learning

Making Connections Assign students to small groups. Have them read about the Tuskegee Airmen. The Tuskegee Airmen were the fighter pilots who opened the door for African American pilots and helped integrate the army. After students have completed their reading, have them create a worksheet about the Tuskegee Airmen with short answer questions, a crossword puzzle, a trivia game, and so on. Have groups exchange and complete each other's worksheets. Then have a class discussion about what students have learned. Encourage volunteers to share worksheet elements they found creative or interesting. **OL**

C Critical Thinking

Making Inferences Partly in response to the Double V campaign, President Roosevelt ordered recruitment of African Americans for combat.

Ask: How do you think both whites and African Americans responded to Roosevelt's new policies toward African American soldiers? *(Answers will vary, but students should note the racial discrimination of the 1940s.)* **OL**

W Writing Support

Persuasive Writing Direct students to write letters to the editor supporting racial integration of the U.S. armed forces during World War II. Have students share their letters with the class. **OL**

Analyzing VISUALS

Answers:
1. Answers may include that they felt women lacked necessary skills and physical strength
2. lacked necessary supplies; overcrowded

Pushing for "Double V" Many African American leaders combined patriotism with protest. In 1941 the National Urban League asked its members to encourage African Americans to join the war effort. It also asked them to make plans for building a better society in the United States after the war. The *Pittsburgh Courier*, a leading African American newspaper, launched the **"Double V" campaign.** The campaign urged African Americans to support the war to achieve a double victory—over both Hitler's racism abroad and the racism at home.

C African Americans in Combat Under pressure from African American leaders, President Roosevelt ordered the army, air force, navy, and marines to recruit African Americans, and he told the army to put African Americans into combat. He also promoted Colonel Benjamin O. Davis, Sr., the highest-ranking African American officer, to the rank of brigadier general.

In early 1941 the air force created its first African American unit, the 99th Pursuit Squadron. The pilots trained in Tuskegee, Alabama, and became known as the **Tuskegee Airmen.** In April 1943, after General Davis urged the military to put African Americans into combat as soon as possible, the squadron was sent to the Mediterranean. Lieutenant Colonel Benjamin O. Davis, Jr., General Davis's son, commanded the squadron and helped win the battle of Anzio in Italy. **W**

In late 1943 Colonel Davis took command of three new squadrons that had trained at Tuskegee. Known as the 332nd Fighter Group, these squadrons were ordered to protect American bombers as they flew to their targets. The 332nd Fighter Group flew 200 such missions and did not lose a single member to enemy aircraft.

African Americans also performed well in the army. The all–African American 761st Tank Battalion was commended for its service during the Battle of the Bulge. Although the

PRIMARY SOURCE
Women in World War II

About 400,000 American women played a major role in the military side of the war effort, if not in direct combat. Sixteen American women were awarded the Purple Heart for being injured as a result of enemy action. More than 400 American military women lost their lives.

◀ In this 1943 photo, Nancy Nesbit checks with the control tower from her plane at Avenger Field in Sweetwater, Texas, where the Women's Auxiliary Ferrying Squadron of the U.S. Army trained.

▲ A doctor and an army nurse tend to a patient at a U.S. Army hospital in Leyte in the Philippines.

Analyzing VISUALS

1. **Inferring** Why might the military have been reluctant to allow women in combat?
2. **Evaluating** What does the photo above suggest about conditions in military hospitals?

Differentiated Instruction

Linking Past and Present Activity, URB p. 68

492

Women With Wings

Objective: Compare the roles of women in the military in World War II with the roles of women in the military today.

Focus: Determine how the necessities of war granted female pilots an opportunity to participate.

Teach: In a bulleted list, describe the risks that female pilots faced during World War II.

Assess: Use a graphic organizer to compare female pilots then and now.

Close: Have students read ahead and list other ways the war enabled women to progress.

Differentiated Instruction Strategies

BL Write a short letter as Jackie Cochran attempting to convince the army chief to start a female pilot training program.

AL Find other instances of women's accounts of their actions in World War II. Share what you find with the class.

ELL Create a list of unfamiliar terms in the reading. Then define the terms.

military did not end all segregation during the war, it did integrate military bases in 1943 and steadily expanded the role of African Americans within the armed forces. These successes paved the way for President Truman's decision to fully integrate the military in 1948.

Other Minorities in the Military Japanese Americans were not allowed to serve in the military at first. As the war progressed, however, second-generation Japanese Americans served in the 100th Infantry Battalion and the 442nd Regimental Combat Team. Almost half had been in internment camps in the American Southwest. Together these units became the most decorated in the history of the United States military. Many Mexican Americans had joined the National Guard during the 1930s and served on the front lines. Most minorities were allowed only in noncombat positions, such as kitchen workers. Native Americans, who were regarded as fierce warriors, were an exception to that policy. One-third of all healthy Native American men aged 18–50 served during the war.

Women Join the Armed Forces

Women joined the armed forces, as they had done during World War I. The army enlisted women for the first time, although they were barred from combat. Many jobs in the army were administrative and clerical. Assigning women to these jobs made more men available for combat.

Congress first allowed women in the military in May 1942, when it established the Women's Army Auxiliary Corps (WAAC) and appointed **Oveta Culp Hobby,** an official with the War Department, to serve as its first director. Although pleased about the establishment of the WAAC, many women were unhappy that it was an auxiliary corps and not part of the regular army. A little over a year later, the army replaced the WAAC with the **Women's Army Corps** (WAC). Director Hobby was assigned the rank of colonel. "You have a debt and a date," Hobby explained to those training to be the nation's first women officers. "A debt to democracy, a date with destiny."

As early as 1939, pilot Jackie Cochran had written to Eleanor Roosevelt suggesting that women pilots could aid the war effort. The following year, Nancy Love wrote to army officials to suggest that women be allowed to deliver planes. (The air force was not yet a separate branch of the military.) Training programs began in 1942; the Women Airforce Service Pilots (WASPs) began the next year. Although the WASPs were no longer needed after 1944, about 300 women pilots made more than 12,000 deliveries of 77 different kinds of planes.

The Coast Guard, the navy, and the marines quickly followed the army and set up their own women's units. In addition to serving in these new organizations, another 68,000 women served as nurses in the army and navy.

✔ **Reading Check** **Summarizing** How did the status of women and African Americans in the armed forces change during the war?

Section 1 REVIEW

Vocabulary

1. **Explain** the significance of: cost-plus, War Production Board, Office of War Mobilization, disenfranchised, "Double V" campaign, Tuskegee Airmen, Oveta Culp Hobby, Women's Army Corps.

Main Ideas

2. **Describing** How did Congress support factories that converted to war production?

3. **Analyzing** What role did the OWM play in the war production effort?

4. **Explaining** How were minorities discriminated against in the military?

Critical Thinking

5. **Big Ideas** How did American industry rally behind the war effort?

6. **Organizing** Use a graphic organizer like the one below to list the challenges facing the United States as it mobilized for war.

7. **Analyzing Visuals** Look again at the photograph on page 488. What do you observe about the construction process?

Writing About History

8. **Expository Writing** Interview a World War II veteran or research your community during the war. How did industry rally behind the war effort? Write a one-page report to summarize your findings.

History ONLINE
Study Central™ To review this section, go to glencoe.com and click on Study Central.

493

R Reading Strategy

Paraphrasing Have students reread the quote by Director Hobby. **Ask:** What did Oveta Culp Hobby mean when she said that women had a date with destiny? *(By serving, they expanded women's equality.)* **OL**

✔ **Reading Check**

Answer:
Each received more and new roles.

Assess
....

History ONLINE

Study Central™ provides summaries, interactive games, and online graphic organizers to help students review content.

Close
....

Summarizing Have students create two columns: businesses and minorities. Have them make a bulleted list of how these groups assisted in war mobilization. **OL**

Section 1 REVIEW

Answers

1. All definitions can be found in the section and in the Glossary.

2. It supported them financially by allowing the Reconstruction Finance Corporation to make loans to companies who wanted to convert their factories to war production.

3. The OWM served as a mediator between different government agencies.

4. Minorities were placed in segregated units, with segregated barracks, mess halls, latrines, and recreational facilities. They were often assigned to non-combat duties such as construction and supply units.

5. Major industries started to rapidly produce trucks, jeeps, tanks, and ships.

6.

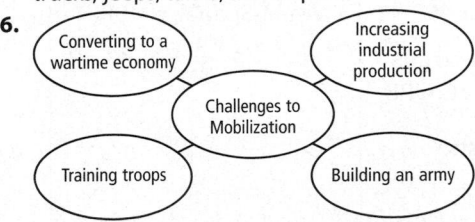

7. The construction appears to take place in stages, like an assembly line. It took a lot of workers to get the job done.

8. Students' reports will vary but should provide factual information about industry's support of the war effort.

Focus

The Early Battles

Bellringer

Daily Focus Transparency 14.2

Guide to Reading

Answers:

April 1942 Doolittle Raid, Allies
April 1942 Philippines, Axis
May 1942 Coral Sea, Allies
June 1942 Midway, Allies
February 1943 Stalingrad, Allies
May 1943 North Africa, Allies

Section Spotlight Video

To generate student interest and provide a springboard for class discussion, access the Chapter 14, Section 2 video at glencoe.com or on the video DVD.

Guide to Reading

Big Ideas

Individual Action Several key people made decisions that changed the course of the war.

Content Vocabulary
• periphery (p. 497)
• convoy system (p. 499)

Academic Vocabulary
• code (p. 496)
• target (p. 498)

People and Events to Identify
• Chester Nimitz (p. 494)
• Douglas MacArthur (p. 494)
• Bataan Death March (p. 495)
• Corregidor (p. 495)
• James Doolittle (p. 495)

Reading Strategy

Organizing Complete a time line similar to the one below to record the major battles discussed and the victor in each.

The early battles of the war on both fronts required changes in strategy from all sides. In the Pacific, the Battle of Midway was a major turning point against the Japanese, while the Battle of the Atlantic and the Battle of Stalingrad made it clear that Germany would not win the war.

Holding the Line Against Japan

MAIN Idea The Japanese continued to win victories in the Pacific until the Battle of Midway.

HISTORY AND YOU Have you ever continued toward a goal even though the odds were against you? Read on to learn about the early battles in the Pacific.

Admiral **Chester Nimitz,** the commander of the United States Navy in the Pacific, began planning operations against the Japanese Navy. Although the Japanese had badly damaged the American fleet at Pearl Harbor, the American aircraft carriers, which were on a mission at sea, were safe. The United States had several carriers in the Pacific, and Nimitz was determined to use them. In the days just after Pearl Harbor, however, he could do little to stop Japan's advance into Southeast Asia.

The Fall of the Philippines

A few hours after bombing Pearl Harbor, the Japanese attacked American airfields in the Philippines. Two days later, they landed troops. The American and Filipino forces defending the Philippines were badly outnumbered. Their commander, General **Douglas MacArthur,** retreated to the Bataan Peninsula. Using the peninsula's rugged terrain, the troops held out for more than three months.

By March, in desperation, the troops ate cavalry horses and mules. The lack of food and supplies, along with diseases such as malaria, scurvy, and dysentery, took their toll. The women of the Army Nurse Corps worked on Bataan in primitive conditions. Patients slept in the open air. One nurse, Rose Meier, reported, "If we needed more room, we got our axes and chopped some bamboo trees down."

Realizing MacArthur's capture would demoralize the American people, President Roosevelt ordered the general to evacuate to Australia. MacArthur promised, "I came through, and I shall return."

On April 9, 1942, the weary defenders of the Bataan Peninsula finally surrendered. Nearly 78,000 prisoners of war were forced

494 Chapter 14 America and World War II

Resource Manager

R Reading Strategies	**C** Critical Thinking	**D** Differentiated Instruction	**W** Writing Support	**S** Skill Practice
Additional Resources • Primary Source Reading, URB p. 69 • Guide. Reading, URB p. 83	**Teacher Edition** • Problem-Solving, p. 495 • Contrasting, p. 497 • Drawing Con., p. 499 **Additional Resources** • Inter. Pol. Car. Act., URB p. 75 • Quizzes and Tests, p. 198	**Teacher Edition** • Gifted and Talented, p. 496 • Visual/Spatial, p. 498	**Teacher Edition** • Expository Writing, p. 495 • Descriptive Writing, p. 498	**Teacher Edition** • Visual Literacy, p. 496 **Additional Resources** • RENTG, p. 149

PRIMARY SOURCE
The Bataan Death March, April 1942

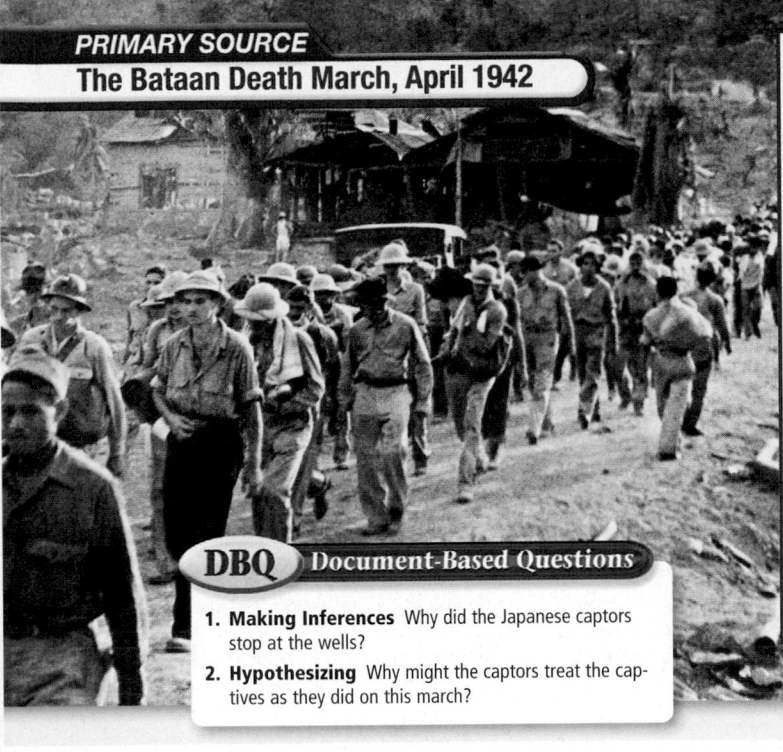

Private Leon Beck was taken prisoner when Bataan surrendered and took part in the Bataan Death March for 13 days before escaping:

LUZON
Camp O'Donnell
South China Sea
Bataan Peninsula
Manila Bay
← Bataan Death March route
120°E 120°30'E 15°N 14°30'N

PRIMARY SOURCE

"They'd halt us in front of these big artesian wells . . . so we could see the water and they wouldn't let us have any. Anyone who would make a break for water would be shot or bayoneted. Then they were left there. Finally, it got so bad further along the road that you never got away from the stench of death. There were bodies laying all along the road in various degrees of decomposition—swollen, burst open, maggots crawling by the thousands. . . ."

—from *Death March: The Survivors of Bataan*

DBQ Document-Based Questions

1. **Making Inferences** Why did the Japanese captors stop at the wells?
2. **Hypothesizing** Why might the captors treat the captives as they did on this march?

---

to march—sick, exhausted, and starving—65 miles (105 km) to a Japanese prison camp. Almost ten thousand troops died on this march, which was later called the **Bataan Death March.** Sixty-six women nurses were also captured and sent to the University of Santo Tomas in Manila. They remained there—with 11 navy nurses and some 3,000 Allied civilians—until early in 1945.

Although the troops in the Bataan Peninsula surrendered, a small force held out on the island of **Corregidor** in Manila Bay. Finally, in May 1942, Corregidor surrendered. The Philippines had fallen to the Japanese.

The Doolittle Raid on Tokyo

Even before the Philippines fell, President Roosevelt was searching for a way to raise the morale of the American people. He wanted to bomb Tokyo, but American planes could reach Tokyo only if an aircraft carrier brought them close enough. Unfortunately, Japanese ships in the North Pacific prevented carriers from getting near Japan.

In early 1942, a military planner suggested replacing the carrier's usual short-range bombers with long-range B-25 bombers that could attack from farther away. The only problem was that, although B-25s could take off from a carrier, the bombers could not land on its short deck. After attacking Japan, they would have to land in China.

President Roosevelt put Lieutenant Colonel **James Doolittle** in command of the mission to bomb Tokyo. At the end of March, a crane loaded sixteen B-25s onto the aircraft carrier *Hornet.* The next day, the *Hornet* headed west across the Pacific. On April 18, American bombs fell on Japan for the first time.

Japan Changes Strategy

While Americans rejoiced in the air force's success, Japanese leaders were aghast at the raid. Those bombs could have killed the emperor, who was revered as a god. The Doolittle raid convinced Japanese leaders to change their strategy.

Chapter 14 America and World War II **495**

Teach

C Critical Thinking
Problem-Solving Have students create a graphic, stating the problem the military had attacking Japan in one box and their solution in another box. *(Problem: could not get planes over Japan for air attack; Solution: used long range bombers (B-25s) instead of short-range bombers; B-25's could reach target)* **OL**

W Writing Support
Expository Writing Have students prepare a one-page report about Lieutenant Colonel James Doolittle. The reports should address how Doolittle contributed to the war effort, the events of the Doolittle Raid, and what he did later in his career. **OL**

DBQ Document Based Questions

Answers:
1. It was a form of torture. Prisoners could see the water, but were not allowed to have any.
2. to demoralize the troops and the civilians back home

Additional Support

Extending the Content

Bataan Death March Of the 78,000 Allied prisoners of war who began the six-day march from Bataan, only 54,000 survived. The Bataan Death March began on April 10, 1942. Any troops who fell behind were executed. Soldiers were beaten, denied food and water, and were forced to sit in the sun. Those who asked for water were executed. Survivors of the March faced starvation and disease as they were transported on "hell ships" to Japan. Prisoners were released after Japan's formal surrender.

D Differentiated Instruction

Gifted and Talented Have students research how the Japanese code was broken. Ask students to discuss the importance of using codes during war, the job code-breakers have, and how code is deciphered in present times. **AL**

S Skill Practice

Visual Literacy Have students organize the information from the map into a time line. Based on their time lines, ask them to identify the point in which the battle seemed to shift toward an Allied victory. *(Answers will vary. Students should note the sinking of three Japanese ships as a significant event.)* **OL**

Before the raid, the Japanese navy had disagreed about the next step. The officers in charge of the navy's planning wanted to cut American supply lines to Australia by capturing the south coast of New Guinea. The commander of the fleet, Admiral Yamamoto, wanted to attack Midway Island—the last American base in the North Pacific west of Hawaii. Yamamoto believed that attacking Midway would lure the American fleet into battle and enable his fleet to destroy it.

After Doolittle's raid, the Japanese war planners dropped their opposition to Yamamoto's idea. The American fleet had to be destroyed to protect Tokyo from bombing. The attack on New Guinea would still go ahead, but only three aircraft carriers were assigned to the mission. All of the other carriers were ordered to assault Midway.

The Battle of the Coral Sea

D The Japanese believed that they could safely proceed with two attacks at once because they thought their operations were secret. What the Japanese did not know was that an American team of code breakers based in Hawaii had already broken the Japanese navy's secret **code** for conducting operations.

In March 1942, decoded Japanese messages alerted the United States to the Japanese attack on New Guinea. In response, Admiral Nimitz sent two carriers, the *Yorktown* and the *Lexington*, to intercept the Japanese in the Coral Sea. There, in early May, carriers from both sides launched all-out airstrikes against each other. Although the Japanese sank the *Lexington* and badly damaged the *Yorktown*, the American attacks prevented the Japanese from landing on New Guinea's south coast and kept the supply lines to Australia open.

The Battle of Midway

Back at Pearl Harbor, the code-breaking team now learned of the plan to attack Midway. With so many ships at sea, Admiral Yamamoto transmitted the plans for the Midway attack by radio, using the same code the Americans had already cracked.

Admiral Nimitz had been waiting for the opportunity to ambush the Japanese fleet. He

NATIONAL GEOGRAPHIC **The Battle of Midway, 1942**

8 June 4, 5:01 P.M. *Yorktown* fliers join *Enterprise* attack on the *Hiryu*, setting it ablaze.

Course of *Yorktown*

Course of *Enterprise* and *Hornet*

9 June 6, 1:31 P.M. Japanese submarine *I-168* torpedoes the *Yorktown*, which sinks the next morning.

Hiryu sinks ✖

Course of Japanese fleet

Akagi sinks
Kaga sinks
Soryu sinks ✖

7 June 4, noon. Planes from the *Hiryu* attack U.S. carriers. *Yorktown* hit. The ship is abandoned but remains afloat.

Yorktown sinks

6 June 4, 10:22-10:28 A.M. U.S. Dive-bombers score direct hits on *Kaga*, *Akagi*, and *Soryu*.

1 June 4, 4:30 A.M. Japanese carriers launch 108 warplanes to strike U.S. base at Midway.

2 June 4, 6:16 A.M. U.S. fighters clash with attackers.

U.S. Dauntless dive-bomber

5 June 4, 9:17 A.M. Japanese planes return. Fleet turns to engage U.S. carriers.

4 June 4, 7:08 A.M. U.S. fliers from Midway begin attacking Japanese fleet.

Line of U.S. submarines stationed 170 miles from Midway.

Kure Atoll (U.S.)

3 June 4, 6:30 A.M. Japanese begin bombing Midway.

Midway Islands (U.S.)

PACIFIC OCEAN

N W E S

● U.S. actions
● Japanese actions

Hands-On Chapter Project
Step 2

An Interview with a World War II Veteran

Step 2: Practicing the Interview
Essential Question: What is the most important information to get?

Directions Students should use the list of questions that they created in Step 1 to conduct mock interviews to get practice in interviewing (especially in being alert to

follow up a question when a discussion gets off the script) and to help decide on the interviewing team. One to two students should be present at the interview. Students should select a location that is informal, yet quiet enough to conduct the interview without disturbances.

Putting It Together As students practice, they should refine their list of questions. Students should note the content of their

questions. (Are they getting the information they want?) They should also note the length of their questions and question list. (Are there enough questions? Are there too many questions?) The interview should not take longer than one hour. **OL**
(Chapter Project continued on page 502)

immediately ordered carriers to take up positions near Midway. Unaware that they were heading into an ambush, the Japanese launched their aircraft against Midway on June 4, 1942. The Americans were ready. The Japanese ran into a blizzard of antiaircraft fire, and 38 planes were shot down.

As the Japanese prepared a second wave to attack Midway, aircraft from the American carriers *Hornet, Yorktown,* and *Enterprise* launched a counterattack. The American planes caught the Japanese carriers with fuel, bombs, and aircraft exposed on their flight decks. Within minutes, three Japanese carriers were reduced to burning wrecks. A fourth was sunk a few hours later, and Admiral Yamamoto ordered his remaining ships to retreat.

The Battle of Midway was a turning point in the war. The Japanese navy lost four large carriers—the heart of its fleet. Just six months after Pearl Harbor, the United States had stopped the Japanese advance. The victory was not without cost, however. The battle killed 362 Americans and 3,057 Japanese.

✓ Reading Check **Explaining** Why was the United States able to ambush the Japanese at Midway?

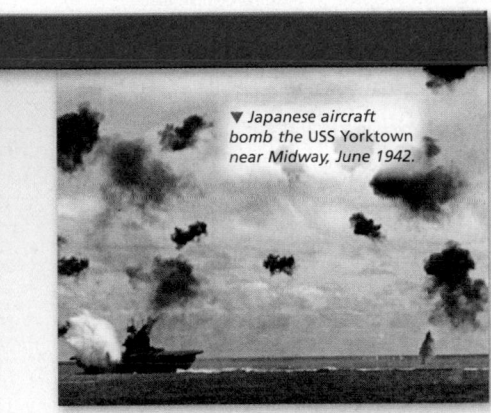

▼ *Japanese aircraft bomb the USS Yorktown near Midway, June 1942.*

Analyzing VISUALS

1. **Interpreting** When did Japan launch the attack on Midway?

2. **Drawing Conclusions** Why were aircraft carriers so vital to the war in the Pacific?

Maps In MOtion See *StudentWorksTM Plus* or glencoe.com.

Stopping the Germans

MAIN Idea The Allies defeated Germany in Africa and in the Battle of the Atlantic. The Soviet victory at Stalingrad was a turning point of the war.

HISTORY AND YOU Have you ever tried something simple before attempting a more challenging problem? Read on to learn about the Allied strategy for attacking the Germans.

In 1942 Allied forces began to win victories in Europe as well. Almost from the moment the United States entered the war, Joseph Stalin, the leader of the Soviet Union, urged President Roosevelt to open a second front in Europe. Stalin appreciated the lend-lease supplies that the United States had sent, but the Soviets were doing most of the fighting. If British and American troops opened a second front by attacking Germany from the west, it would take pressure off the Soviet Union.

Roosevelt wanted to get American troops into battle in Europe, but Prime Minister Churchill urged caution. He did not believe the United States and Great Britain were ready to launch a full-scale invasion of Europe. Instead, Churchill wanted to attack the **periphery,** or edges, of the German empire. Roosevelt agreed, and in July 1942, he ordered the invasion of Morocco and Algeria—two French territories indirectly under German control.

The Struggle for North Africa

Roosevelt decided to invade Morocco and Algeria for two reasons. First, the invasion would give the army some experience without requiring a lot of troops. More important, once American troops were in North Africa, they would be able to help the British troops fight the Germans in Egypt.

Great Britain needed Egypt because the Suez Canal was located there. Most of Britain's empire, including India, Hong Kong, Singapore, Malaya, and Australia, sent supplies to Britain through the canal. General Erwin Rommel—a brilliant leader whose success earned him the nickname "Desert Fox" —commanded the German forces in the area, known as the "Afrika Korps."

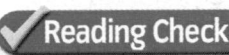

History ONLINE Student Web Activity Visit glencoe.com and complete the activity on America and World War II.

C Critical Thinking

Contrasting Discuss the opposing views of Roosevelt and Churchill regarding a European invasion. **Ask:** Why might Roosevelt have decided to support Churchill's cautious approach? *(Students may suggest that Roosevelt did not want to confront Churchill or perhaps he realized fighting two fronts called for a more guarded approach.)* **OL**

Analyzing VISUALS

Answers:
1. June 4, 1942, 4:30 A.M.
2. reduced distance planes had to fly; reduced amount of fuel they consumed; supplied fuel

✓ Reading Check

Answer:
The U.S. had broken the Japanese code and knew their attack plans.

Additional Support

Activity: Collaborative Learning

Contrasting Assign half the class to research Fleet Admiral Chester W. Nimitz. The other half will research Admiral Isoroku Yamamoto. Have students research details of their education, their commands, major victories in battle, and an overview of their military careers. In addition, students should provide a statement of each man's philosophy. Encourage students to find visuals to use in their reports. Have volunteers share their reports with the class. Then create a Venn diagram for the class to compare the two men. **OL**

498

D Differentiated Instruction

Visual/Spatial Have students draw a map of Africa and use colored pens to show the direction of the separate American forces who tried to trap Rommel. **OL**

W Writing Support

Descriptive Writing Have students imagine they had to dim their lights every evening to protect American ships. Ask students to write how they might feel if they lived in an area that was close to enemy submarines. Ask students to reflect on what they would be willing to give up in order to protect the United States. **OL**

Analyzing VISUALS

Answers:
1. El Alamein was a desert. The terrain was rough, and there was no cover for soldiers. Stalingrad was brutally cold.
2. These two battles were major defeats for the Germans. They also gave confidence to Allied forces.

Additional Support

PRIMARY SOURCE
El Alamein and Stalingrad, November 1942

Just as the Battle of Midway was a turning point in the war in the Pacific, so too were the battles of El Alamein in North Africa and Stalingrad in Europe. The British victory over German General Rommel at El Alamein secured the Suez Canal and kept the Germans away from the oil resources of the Middle East. Germany's defeat at the Battle of Stalingrad was a major turning point by ending Hitler's plans to dominate Europe.

◀ A British tank successfully navigates a wide ditch outside a town in North Africa.

▲ A Soviet gun crew fights against Nazi forces in Stalingrad. Only one day after the Nazis publicly boasted that the city would fall to them, the Red Army turned the tide of battle.

Analyzing VISUALS

1. **Assessing** How do you think the environment made combat at El Alamein and Stalingrad challenging?
2. **Evaluating** Why were the battles shown so important to the Allies?

D Although the British forced Rommel to retreat in November 1942, after a 12-day battle against the coastal city of El Alamein near the Suez Canal, German forces remained a serious threat. Later that month, Americans under General Dwight D. Eisenhower's command invaded North Africa. He planned to trap Rommel between two Allied forces. The American forces in Morocco, led by General George Patton, quickly captured the city of Casablanca, while those in Algeria seized the cities of Oran and Algiers. The Americans then headed east into Tunisia, while British forces headed west into Libya.

When the American troops advanced into the mountains of western Tunisia, they had to fight the German army for the first time. They did not do well. At the Battle of Kasserine Pass, the Americans were outmaneuvered and outfought. They suffered roughly 7,000 casualties and lost nearly 200 tanks. Eisenhower fired the

general who led the attack and put Patton in command. Together, the American and British forces finally pushed the Germans back. On May 13, 1943, the last German troops in North Africa surrendered.

The Battle of the Atlantic

As American and British troops fought the German army in North Africa, the war against German submarines in the Atlantic Ocean intensified. After Germany declared war on the United States, German submarines entered American coastal waters. American cargo ships were easy **targets,** especially at night when the glow from the cities in the night sky silhouetted the vessels. To protect the ships, cities on the East Coast dimmed their lights every evening. People also put up special "blackout curtains" and, if they had to drive at night, did so with their headlights off. **W**

Activity: Collaborative Learning

Sequencing Assign students to small groups and have them research the Allied pursuit of Rommel and the Germans in North Africa. Students should use the Internet, library resources, and their book to make a list of significant events that occurred, including the Allied capture of cities in North Africa such as El Alamein, Casablanca, Oran, and Algiers. Allied losses such as the American defeat at the Battle of Kasserine Pass in Tunisia should also be recorded. Using the information collected, students should create a time line complete with photos, quotes, and other primary sources.

By August 1942, German submarines had sunk about 360 American ships along the East Coast. So many oil tankers were sunk that gasoline and fuel oil had to be rationed. To keep oil flowing, the government built the first long-distance oil pipeline, stretching some 1,250 miles (2,010 km) from Texas to Pennsylvania.

The loss of so many ships convinced the U.S. Navy to set up a **convoy system.** Under this system, cargo ships traveled in groups escorted by navy warships. The convoy system improved the situation dramatically. It made it much more difficult for a submarine to torpedo a cargo ship and escape without being attacked.

The spring of 1942 marked the high point of the German submarine campaign. In May and June alone, over 1.2 million tons of shipping were sunk. Yet in those same two months, American and British shipyards built more than 1.1 million tons of new shipping. From July 1942 onward, American shipyards produced more ships than German submarines managed to sink. At the same time, American airplanes and warships began to use new technology, including radar, sonar, and depth charges, to locate and attack submarines. As the new technology began to take its toll on German submarines, the Battle of the Atlantic turned in favor of the Allies.

The Battle of Stalingrad

In the spring of 1942, before the Battle of the Atlantic turned against Germany, Adolf Hitler was very confident that he would win the war. The German army was ready to launch a new offensive to knock the Soviets out of the war.

Hitler was convinced that only by destroying the Soviet economy could he defeat the Soviet Union. In May 1942, he ordered his army to capture strategic oil fields, factories, and farmlands in southern Russia and Ukraine. The city of Stalingrad, which controlled the Volga River and was a major railroad junction, was the key to the attack. If the German army captured Stalingrad, they would cut off the Soviets from the resources they needed to stay in the war.

When German troops entered Stalingrad in mid-September, Stalin ordered his troops to hold the city at all costs. Retreat was forbidden. The Germans were forced to fight from house to house, losing thousands of soldiers in the process. They were not equipped to fight in the bitter cold, but Soviet troops had quilted undersuits, felt boots, fur hats, and white camouflaged oversuits.

On November 23, Soviet reinforcements arrived and surrounded Stalingrad, trapping almost 250,000 German troops. When the battle ended in February 1943, some 91,000 Germans had surrendered, although only 5,000 of them survived the Soviet prison camps and returned home after the war. Each side lost nearly half a million soldiers. The Battle of Stalingrad was a major turning point in the war. Just as the Battle of Midway put the Japanese on the defensive for the rest of the war, the Battle of Stalingrad put the Germans on the defensive as well.

✔ **Reading Check** **Describing** How did the United States begin winning the Battle of the Atlantic?

Section 2 REVIEW

Vocabulary
1. **Explain** the significance of: Chester Nimitz, Douglas MacArthur, Bataan Death March, Corregidor, James Doolittle, periphery, convoy system.

Main Ideas
2. **Explaining** Briefly explain the causes and effects of the effort to defeat the Japanese in 1942.

3. **Analyzing** Why did Churchill want to defeat the Germans in Africa before staging a European invasion?

Critical Thinking
4. **Big Ideas** Explain the significance of one person whose actions made a difference in the war.

5. **Organizing** Use a graphic organizer like the one below to list the reasons that the Battle of Midway is considered a turning point of the war.

Battle of Midway

6. **Analyzing Visuals** Look again at the map on page 496. How long did the Battle of Midway last?

Writing About History
7. **Expository Writing** Much of the course of wars is determined by the need for supply lines to remain open. Write a brief essay explaining how this need shaped early battles in which the United States was involved.

History ONLINE
Study Central™ To review this section, go to glencoe.com and click on Study Central.

499

C Critical Thinking
Drawing Conclusions **Ask:**
Why did the Soviet army need to hold the city of Stalingrad? *(to keep their supply lines opened.)* What was the result of the Battle of Stalingrad? *(It put the Germans on the defensive.)* **OL**

✔ **Reading Check**

Answer:
They started using a convoy system to protect the cargo ships, and they started using new technology to locate and attack German submarines.

Assess

History ONLINE

Study Central™ provides summaries, interactive games, and online graphic organizers to help students review content.

Close

Summarizing Have students work in groups and review their battle time lines. Have each group take notes while discussing the importance of each battle. **OL**

Section 2 REVIEW

Answers

1. All definitions can be found in the section and in the Glossary.

2. U.S. bombing of Tokyo led to Japanese attack on Midway. The Battle of Midway resulted in a U.S. victory that stopped the Japanese advance.

3. Churchill did not believe the Allied forces were ready to launch a full-scale invasion of Europe.

4. Student choices will vary. Students should support their choice by using specific details from the text.

5.
Battle of Midway
— Japanese lost four carriers
— Stopped Japanese advance in the Pacific
— Ended Japanese offensive

6. June 4 to June 6

7. Essays will vary but should explain the importance of supply lines.

Focus

Bellringer

Daily Focus Transparency 14.3

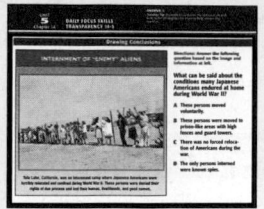

Guide to Reading

Answers:

	Women	African Americans
Before War	few job opportunities, low pay	few opportunities
After War	better job selection	Fair Employment Practices oversight
Still Needed	Answers will vary	Answers will vary

Section Spotlight Video

To generate student interest and provide a springboard for class discussion, access the Chapter 14, Section 3 video at glencoe.com or on the video DVD.

Resource Manager

Section 3

Life on the Home Front

Guide to Reading

Big Ideas
Trade, War, and Migration During World War II, Americans faced demands and new challenges at home.

Content Vocabulary
• Sunbelt *(p. 502)*
• zoot suit *(p. 504)*
• victory suit *(p. 504)*
• rationing *(p. 506)*
• victory garden *(p. 507)*

Academic Vocabulary
• coordinate *(p. 503)*
• justify *(p. 504)*

People and Events to Identify
• A. Philip Randolph *(p. 502)*
• Bracero Program *(p. 502)*
• Great Migration *(p. 503)*
• Office of Price Administration *(p. 506)*

Reading Strategy
Organizing Complete a graphic organizer listing opportunities for women and African Americans before and after the war. Evaluate what progress was still needed after the war.

Opportunities	Before War	After War	Still Needed
Women			
African Americans			

Although women and African Americans gained new work opportunities, Latinos and Japanese Americans faced violence in American cities. To assist with the war effort, the government controlled wages and prices, rationed goods, encouraged recycling, and sold bonds.

Women and Minorities Gain Ground

MAIN Idea With many men on active military duty, women and minorities found factory and other jobs open to them.

HISTORY AND YOU Do you remember reading about the unequal treatment of African American soldiers in World War I? Read on to learn how desegregation of the military began in World War II.

As American troops fought their first battles against the Germans and Japanese, the war began dramatically changing American society at home. In contrast to the devastation that large parts of Europe and Asia experienced, American society gained some benefits from World War II. The war finally ended the Great Depression. Mobilizing the economy created almost 19 million new jobs and nearly doubled the average family's income. For Robert Montgomery, a worker at an Ohio machine tool plant, "one of the most important things that came out of World War II was the arrival of the working class at a new status level in this society. . . . The war integrated into the mainstream a whole chunk of society that had been living on the edge."

The improvement in the economy did not come without cost. American families had to move to where the defense factories were located. Housing conditions were terrible. The pressures and prejudices of the era led to strikes, race riots, and rising juvenile delinquency. Goods were rationed and taxes were higher than ever before. Workers were earning more money, but they were also working an average of 90 hours per week. Despite the hardships, James Covert, whose mother owned a grocery store during the war, was probably right when he said that the war "changed our lifestyle and more important, our outlook. . . . There was a feeling toward the end of the war that we were moving into a new age of prosperity."

When the war began, American defense factories wanted to hire white men. With so many men in the military, however, there simply were not enough white men to fill all of the jobs. Under pressure to produce, employers began to recruit women and minorities.

R Reading Strategies	**C** Critical Thinking	**D** Differentiated Instruction	**W** Writing Support	**S** Skill Practice
Teacher Edition • Act. Prior Know., p. 502 **Additional Resources** • Pri. Source Reading, URB p. 71 • Guide. Reading, URB p. 84	**Teacher Edition** • Compare/Contrast, p. 501 • Recognizing Bias, p. 502 • Det. Cause & Effect, p. 503 • Defending, p. 506 **Additional Resources** • Supreme Court Case Studies, pp. 61, 63 • Quizzes and Tests, p. 199	**Teacher Edition** • Interpersonal, p. 503 • Visual/Spatial, p. 504 • Logical/Math, p. 506 **Additional Resources** • Enrichment Act., URB p. 79	**Teacher Edition** • Descriptive Writing, p. 501 • Persuasive Writing, p. 504	**Additional Resources** • RENTG, p. 152

We Can Do It!

At left, a riveter works on a bomber in Fort Worth, Texas. Posters such as those above and to the right encouraged women to participate in the war effort.

"THE GIRL HE LEFT BEHIND" IS STILL BEHIND HIM

She's a **WOW**

Women Working

Source: *Historical Statistics of the United States.*

Analyzing VISUALS

1. **Listing** During what years did women's employment outside the home hit its highest levels?

2. **Analyzing** How are the women portrayed in the posters?

Women in the Defense Plants

During the Great Depression, many people believed married women should not work outside the home, especially if they took jobs that could go to men trying to support their families. Most working women were young, single, and employed in traditional female jobs such as domestic work or teaching. The wartime labor shortage, however, forced factories to recruit married women for industrial jobs traditionally reserved for men.

Although the government hired nearly 4 million women, primarily for clerical jobs, the women working in the factories captured the public's imagination. The great symbol of the campaign to hire women was "Rosie the Riveter," a character from a popular song by the Four Vagabonds. The lyrics told of Rosie, who worked in a factory while her boyfriend served in the marines. Images of Rosie appeared on posters, in newspapers, and in magazines. Eventually 2.5 million women worked in shipyards, aircraft factories, and other manufacturing plants. Working in a factory changed the perspectives of many middle-class women like Inez Sauer:

PRIMARY SOURCE

"I learned that just because you're a woman and have never worked is no reason you can't learn. The job really broadened me. . . . I had always been in a shell; I'd always been protected. But at Boeing I found a freedom and an independence I had never known. After the war I could never go back to playing bridge again, being a club woman. . . . when I knew there were things you could use your mind for. The war changed my life completely."

—quoted in *The Homefront*

Activity: Interdisciplinary Connection

Art When millions of men took up the uniform, women were recruited to work in factories, performing "men's work." Many women worked in shipyards, especially those owned by Henry Kaiser. This was not work for the weak! Rosie the Riveter was used as a propaganda technique to lure women into these tough industrial jobs. She was tough, loyal, efficient, and of course, patriotic. Rosie the Riveter was also a response to Tokyo Rose and Axis Sally, enemy characters who broadcast anti-Allied propaganda over the radio in the Pacific and in Europe. Have students find the music to the song, "Rosie the Riveter." Then have students work in groups to either sing the song in its original version, perform a new musical rendition of the song, write a poem based on the song lyrics, or create a new Rosie poster. The poster should reflect the strength of the women who worked in shipyards. **OL**

R Reading Strategy

Activating Prior Knowledge
After students read the section "African Americans Demand War Work," ask them to identify other times in which a crisis has provided opportunity for minorities to gain social and economic opportunities. *(Students might mention the slight gains African Americans and women made after World War I and the gains industrial workers gained during the Great Depression.)* **OL**

C Critical Thinking

Recognizing Bias Have students gather more details about the Bracero Program. Have students write a one-page report describing the living conditions of the migrant workers, the pay they received, and what happened to them after the war. **OL**

✓ Reading Check

Answer:
Mobilizing the economy for war production created nearly 19 million new jobs and nearly doubled the average income.

Hands-On Chapter Project
Step 3

An Interview with a World War II Veteran

Step 3: Conducting the Interview
Essential Question: What is the goal of this interview? What information am I trying to get?

Directions Explain to students that only one or at most two people can actually meet with the subject (the second person may want to take notes). It is also a good idea to record the interview. Students should obtain permission to record from the subject. No more than one hour of the interviewee's time should be taken. The interview can be conducted in a home or at school (wherever a computer with a microphone hook-up is available).

Putting It Together After the interview, students should meet to review what happened and discuss it. Was anything missed? Are any answers ambiguous? Are there gaps in what the script had covered? This information will prepare students for Step 4. **OL**

(Chapter Project continued on page 510)

By the end of the war, the number of working women had increased from 12.9 million to 18.8 million. Although most women were laid off or left their jobs voluntarily after the war, their success permanently changed American attitudes about women in the workplace.

African Americans Demand War Work

R Although factories were hiring women, they resisted hiring African Americans. Frustrated by the situation, **A. Philip Randolph,** the head of the Brotherhood of Sleeping Car Porters—a major union for African American railroad workers—decided to take action. He informed President Roosevelt that he was organizing "from ten to fifty thousand [African Americans] to march on Washington in the interest of securing jobs . . . in national defense and . . . integration into the military and naval forces."

In response, Roosevelt issued Executive Order 8802, on June 25, 1941. The order declared, "there shall be no discrimination in the employment of workers in defense industries or government because of race, creed, color, or national origin." To enforce the order, the president created the Fair Employment Practices Commission—the first civil rights agency the federal government had established since the Reconstruction Era.

Mexican Farmworkers

C American citizens were not the only ones who gained in the wartime economy. In 1942 the federal government arranged for Mexican farmworkers to help with the harvest in the Southwest. The laborers were part of the **Bracero Program.** *Bracero* is a Spanish word meaning "worker." More than 200,000 Mexicans came to help harvest fruit and vegetables. Many also helped to build and maintain railroads. The Bracero Program continued until 1964. Migrant farmworkers thus became an important part of the Southwest's agricultural system.

✓ **Reading Check Describing** How did mobilizing the economy help end the Depression?

502   **Chapter 14**   America and World War II

A Nation on the Move

MAIN Idea Millions of Americans relocated during the war to take factory jobs or to settle in less prejudiced areas.

HISTORY AND YOU Has someone in your family moved because of a job transfer? Read on to find out about relocations that resulted from the war.

The wartime economy created millions of new jobs, but the Americans who wanted these jobs did not always live near the factories. To get to the jobs, 15 million Americans moved during the war. The Midwest assembly plants and Northeast and Northwest shipyards attracted many workers. Most Americans, however, headed west and south in search of jobs.

The growth of southern California and the expansion of cities in the Deep South created a new industrial region—the **Sunbelt.** For the first time since the Industrial Revolution began

PRIMARY SOURCE
A Nation on the Move

During the war, millions of Americans flocked to the cities to work in factories. Many immigrants stayed on after the war to become citizens. As a result, populations of Northern cities became more ethnically diverse, and these cities remained more populous after the war.

▼ *Workers at an Iowa arms plant lived in this trailer camp in 1942.*

in the United States, the South and West led the way in manufacturing and urbanization.

The Housing Crisis

In many ways, the most difficult task facing cities with war industries was where to put the thousands of workers arriving in their communities. Tent cities and parks filled with tiny trailers sprang up. Landlords began renting "hot beds." The worker paid 25 cents for eight hours in the bed, then went to work while the bed was rented to another worker.

Anticipating the housing crisis, Congress had passed the Lanham Act in 1940. The act provided $150 million for housing. In 1942 President Roosevelt created the National Housing Agency (NHA) to **coordinate** all government housing programs. By 1943, those programs had been allocated over $1.2 billion. Although prefabricated public housing had tiny rooms, thin walls, poor heating, and almost no privacy, it was better than no housing at all. Nearly 2 million people lived in government-built housing during the war.

Racism Leads to Violence

African Americans left the South in large numbers during World War I, but this "**Great Migration**," as historians refer to it, slowed during the Great Depression. When jobs in war factories opened up for African Americans during World War II, the Great Migration resumed. In the crowded cities of the North and West, however, African Americans were often met with suspicion and intolerance. Sometimes these attitudes led to violence.

The worst racial violence of the war erupted in Detroit on Sunday, June 20, 1943. The weather that day was sweltering. To cool off, nearly 100,000 people crowded into Belle Isle, a park on the Detroit River. Gangs of white and African American teenage girls began fighting. These fights triggered others, and a full-scale riot erupted across the city. By the time the violence ended, 25 African Americans and 9 whites had been killed. Despite the appalling violence in Detroit, African American leaders remained committed to their "Double V" campaign.

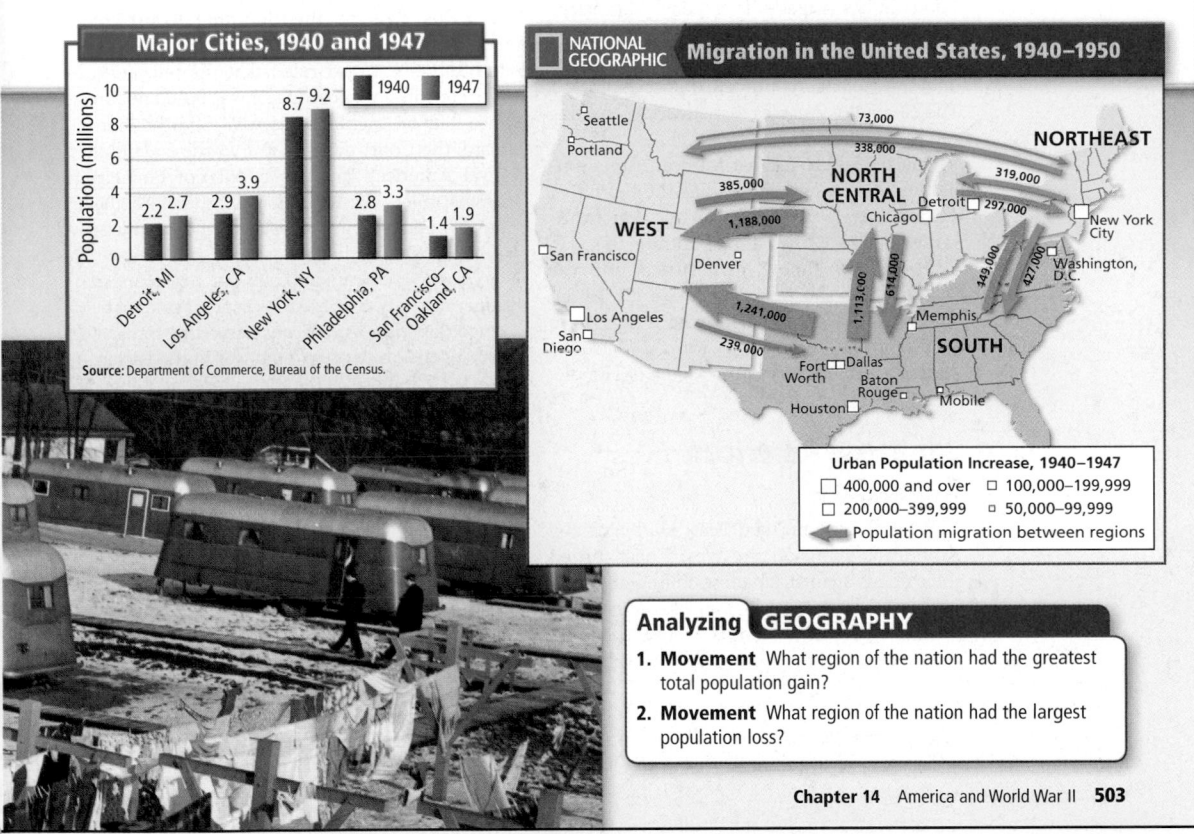

Major Cities, 1940 and 1947

City	1940	1947
Detroit, MI	2.2	2.7
Los Angeles, CA	2.9	3.9
New York, NY	8.7	9.2
Philadelphia, PA	2.8	3.3
San Francisco-Oakland, CA	1.4	1.9

Source: Department of Commerce, Bureau of the Census.

NATIONAL GEOGRAPHIC **Migration in the United States, 1940–1950**

Seattle
Portland
73,000
338,000
NORTHEAST
385,000
NORTH CENTRAL
319,000
1,188,000
Detroit 297,000
Chicago
New York City
WEST
San Francisco
Denver
Washington, D.C.
1,113,600
619,000
449,000
427,000
Los Angeles
San Diego
1,241,000
Memphis
239,000
Fort Worth Dallas
Baton Rouge
SOUTH
Houston
Mobile

Urban Population Increase, 1940–1947
- ☐ 400,000 and over
- ☐ 100,000–199,999
- ☐ 200,000–399,999
- ☐ 50,000–99,999
- ⬅ Population migration between regions

Analyzing GEOGRAPHY

1. **Movement** What region of the nation had the greatest total population gain?
2. **Movement** What region of the nation had the largest population loss?

Chapter 14 America and World War II **503**

Activity: Technology Connection

Identifying Central Issues Assign students to small groups and have them research the 1943 Detroit race riot. Remind students to use reliable sources on the Internet and encourage them to find old newspapers from the library. Have students create their own newspaper, complete with headlines, several articles, photos, captions, editorials, and a small advertisement, perhaps something to do with the war effort. Invite students to present their newspapers to the class. **OL**

D Differentiated Instruction

Visual/Spatial Have students use the library or Internet to find photographs of the zoot suit and victory suit. Challenge them to find other fashions worn during World War II. Have students create posters with the photos they found and display them in the room. **Ask:** Why was it patriotic to wear a victory suit? *(They saved fabric for the war.)* **OL**

W Writing Support

Persuasive Writing Have students research Japanese-American internment camps and Executive Order 9066. Encourage them to read personal narratives during their research. Then have students write a one-page editorial, voicing their opinions about internment camps. **AL**

Reading Check

Answer:
They were looking for job opportunities in factories.

Additional Support

The Zoot Suit Riots

Wartime prejudice boiled over elsewhere as well. In southern California, racial tensions became entangled with juvenile delinquency. Across the nation, the number of crimes committed by young people rose dramatically. In Los Angeles, racism against Mexican Americans and the fear of juvenile crime became linked because of the "zoot suit."

A **zoot suit** had very baggy, pleated pants and an overstuffed, knee-length jacket with wide lapels. Accessories included a wide-brimmed hat and a long key chain. Zoot-suit wearers usually wore their hair long, gathered into a ducktail. The zoot suit angered many Americans. In order to save fabric for the war, most men wore a "**victory suit**"—a suit with no vest, no cuffs, a short jacket, and narrow lapels. To many, the zoot suit was unpatriotic.

In California, Mexican American teenagers adopted the zoot suit. In June 1943, after hearing rumors that zoot-suiters had attacked several sailors, some 2,500 soldiers and sailors stormed into Mexican American neighborhoods in Los Angeles. They attacked Mexican American teenagers, cut their hair, and tore off their zoot suits. The police did not intervene, and the violence continued for several days. The city of Los Angeles responded by banning the zoot suit.

Racial hostility against Mexican Americans did not deter them from joining the war effort. Approximately 500,000 Hispanic Americans served in the armed forces during the war, fighting in Europe, North Africa, and the Pacific. Most—about 400,000—were Mexican American. Another 65,000 were from Puerto Rico. By the end of the war, 17 Mexican Americans had received the Medal of Honor.

Japanese American Relocation

When Japan attacked Pearl Harbor, many Americans living on the West Coast turned their anger against Japanese immigrants and Japanese Americans. Mobs attacked their businesses and homes. Banks would not cash their checks, and grocers refused to sell them food.

Newspapers printed rumors about Japanese spies in the Japanese American community.

Members of Congress, mayors, and many business and labor leaders demanded that all people of Japanese ancestry be removed from the West Coast. They did not believe that Japanese Americans would remain loyal to the United States in the war with Japan.

On February 19, 1942, President Roosevelt signed an order allowing the War Department to declare any part of the United States a military zone and to remove people from that zone. He must have felt **justified** only four days later, when a Japanese submarine surfaced north of Santa Barbara, California, and shelled an oil refinery, or in September of that year, when Japanese bombers twice dropped bombs on an Oregon forest. American fears of a Japanese attack on the West Coast must have seemed reasonable. Secretary of War Henry Stimson declared most of the West Coast a military zone and ordered all people of Japanese ancestry to evacuate to 10 internment camps further inland.

Not all Japanese Americans accepted the relocation without protest. Fred Korematsu argued that his rights had been violated and took his case to the Supreme Court. In December 1944, in *Korematsu* v. *United States,* the Supreme Court ruled that the relocation was constitutional because it was based not on race, but on "military urgency." Shortly afterward, the Court did rule in *Ex parte Endo* that loyal American citizens could not be held against their will. In early 1945, therefore, the government began to release the Japanese Americans from the camps.

Despite the fears and rumors, no Japanese American was ever tried for espionage or sabotage. Japanese Americans served as translators for the army during the war in the Pacific. The all-Japanese 100th Battalion, later integrated into the 442nd Regimental Combat Team, was the most highly decorated unit in World War II.

After the war, the Japanese American Citizens League (JACL) tried to help Japanese Americans who had lost property during the relocation. In 1988 President Ronald Reagan apologized to Japanese Americans on behalf of the U.S. government and signed legislation granting $20,000 to each surviving Japanese American who had been interned.

✔ **Reading Check** **Comparing** Why did millions of people relocate during the war?

Activity: Interdisciplinary Connection

Literature Have students read one of the many personal narratives about the Japanese internment camps. Suggested readings include *The Cross on Castle Rock: A Childhood Memoir* by George Nakagawa, *Looking Like the Enemy* by Mary Matsuda Gruenewald, and *Farewell to Manzanar* by Jeanne Houston. Then have students work in small groups to create short plays about daily life in the internment camps during the war. Have groups present their plays to the rest of the class. As a class, discuss what students have learned about internment camps and their reactions to them. **AL**

Can the Government Limit Civil Liberties in Wartime?

Korematsu v. *United States*, 1944

Background to the Case

During World War II, President Roosevelt's Executive Order 9066 and other legislation gave the military the power to exclude people of Japanese descent from areas that were deemed important to U.S. national defense and security. In 1942, Toyosaburo Korematsu refused to leave San Leandro, California, which had been designated as a "military area," based on Executive Order 9066. Korematsu was found guilty in federal district court of violating Civilian Exclusion Order No. 34. Korematsu petitioned the Supreme Court to review the federal court's decision.

How the Court Ruled

In their decision, the majority of the Supreme Court, with three dissenting, found that, although exclusion orders based on race are constitutionally suspect, the government is justified in time of "emergency and peril" to suspend citizens' civil rights. A request for a rehearing of the case in 1945 was denied.

▲ *Japanese American women and their children talk together at the Heart Mountain Relocation Camp.*

PRIMARY SOURCE

The Court's Opinion

"It should be noted, to begin with, that all legal restrictions which curtail the civil rights of a single racial group are immediately suspect. That is not to say that all such restrictions are unconstitutional. It is to say that courts must subject them to the most rigid scrutiny. Pressing public necessity may sometimes justify the existence of such restrictions; racial antagonism never can. . . . Korematsu was not excluded from the Military Area because of hostility to him or his race. He was excluded because . . . the properly constituted military authorities feared an invasion of our West Coast [by Japan] and felt constrained to take proper security measures, because they decided that the military urgency of the situation demanded that all citizens of Japanese ancestry be segregated from the West Coast temporarily, and finally, because Congress . . . determined that they should have the power to do just this."

—Justice Hugo Black
writing for the court in
Korematsu v. *United States*

PRIMARY SOURCE

Dissenting View

"I dissent, because I think the indisputable facts exhibit a clear violation of Constitutional rights. This is not . . . a case of temporary exclusion of a citizen from an area for his own safety or that of the community, nor a case of offering him an opportunity to go temporarily out of an area where his presence might cause danger to himself or to his fellows. On the contrary, it is the case of convicting a citizen as a punishment for not submitting to imprisonment in a concentration camp, based on his ancestry, and solely because of his ancestry, without evidence or inquiry concerning his loyalty and good disposition towards the United States. If this be a correct statement of the facts disclosed by this record, and facts of which we take judicial notice, I need hardly labor the conclusion that Constitutional rights have been violated."

—Justice Owen J. Roberts, dissenting in
Korematsu v. *United States*

DBQ Document-Based Questions

1. **Explaining** Why did the Supreme Court find in favor of the government in this case, even though the justices were suspicious of exclusion based on race?
2. **Contrasting** Why did Justice Roberts disagree with the majority opinion?
3. **Analyzing** Under what circumstances, if any, do you think the government should be able to suspend civil liberties of all or specific groups of American citizens?

Chapter 14   America and World War II   **505**

Teach

In March 1942, U.S. General John DeWitt, acting under War Department orders, began the evacuation of all persons of Japanese descent from the western parts of Washington, Oregon, and California and the southern part of Arizona. Most of the evacuees had been born in the United States. DeWitt, however, explained the evacuation by saying, "It makes no difference whether a Japanese is theoretically a citizen. He is still Japanese. . . ."

DBQ Document Based Questions

Answers:
1. The majority felt that Korematsu was relocated not due to his race but rather that the United States was in danger of being attacked.
2. He felt the confinements were unconstitutional. He believed it was a clear case of racial discrimination.
3. Answers will vary. Students should support their opinions.

Differentiated Instruction

Supreme Court Case Study 32

The Rights of People of Suspect Ethnic Backgrounds
Korematsu v. *United States*, 1944

[small reproduced worksheet text]

Case Study 32:
Korematsu v. *United States*, p. 63

Analyzing a Supreme Court Decision

Objective:	Learn how the Supreme Court determined whether the relocation program was constitutional.
Focus:	Identify the central issue of the case.
Teach:	Discuss the Court's opinion.
Assess:	Explain the importance of the case (interpretation of War Relocation Authority).
Close:	Write a paragraph summarizing the case.

Differentiated Instruction Strategies

BL Explain how the *Korematsu* and *Endo* decisions are similar or different.

AL Paraphrase the Court's decision. Read your version to the class.

ELL Explain what a relocation camp was.

D Differentiated Instruction

Logical/Mathematical Assign students to small groups and have them explore the effects of inflation on consumer prices. Have the groups research the way in which inflation is measured, in particular the Consumer Price Index (CPI). Ask groups to prepare displays showing the effects of inflation from 1900 to 1999. Encourage groups to link inflation to political and social events. **AL**

C Critical Thinking

Defending Roosevelt used the federal government to regulate wages and prices on certain products. **Ask:** Do you think the government should have such authority? *(Students may suggest the world was different then, but now, such a move by the government would not be acceptable.)* **OL**

Analyzing VISUALS

Answers:

1. They encourage people to act heroically and help them believe they can win.
2. They boosted morale and made the enemy less frightening.

Additional Support

Daily Life in Wartime

MAIN Idea The federal government took steps to stabilize wages and prices, as well as to prevent strikes. Americans supported the war through rationing, growing food, recycling, and buying bonds.

HISTORY AND YOU Have you ever given up something you enjoyed for a short period of time to gain something greater? Read on to learn how Americans sacrificed during the war.

Housing shortages and racial tensions were serious difficulties during the war, but mobilization strained society in other ways as well. Prices rose, materials were in short supply, and the question of how to pay for the war loomed ominously over the war effort.

Wage and Price Controls

D Both wages and prices began to rise quickly during the war because of the high demand for workers and raw materials. The president worried about inflation. To stabilize both wages **C** and prices, Roosevelt created the **Office of Price Administration** (OPA) and the Office of Economic Stabilization (OES). The OES regulated wages and the price of farm products. The OPA regulated all other prices. Despite some problems with labor unions, the OPA and OES kept inflation under control. At the end of the war, prices had risen only about half as much as they had during World War I.

While the OPA and OES worked to control inflation, the War Labor Board (WLB) tried to prevent strikes. In support, most American unions issued a "no strike pledge." Instead of striking, unions asked the WLB to mediate wage disputes. By the end of the war, the WLB had helped to settle more than 17,000 disputes involving more than 12 million workers.

Blue Points, Red Points

The demand for raw materials and supplies created shortages. The OPA began **rationing,** or limiting the purchase of, many products to make sure enough were available for military use. Meat and sugar were rationed. Gasoline was rationed, driving distances were restricted, and the speed limit was set at 35 miles per hour to save gas and rubber.

PRIMARY SOURCE
Hollywood Goes to War

In 1942 President Roosevelt created the Office of War Information (OWI). The OWI's role was to improve the public's understanding of the war and to act as a liaison office with the various media. The OWI established detailed guidelines for filmmakers, including a set of questions to be considered before making a movie, such as, "Will this picture help win the war?"

▲ Movies ranged from a comic Donald Duck cartoon to a serious portrayal of a bombing raid on Germany.

◄ Chaplin, noted as a comic and a director, made this movie in 1940, before the United States entered the war.

Analyzing VISUALS

1. **Interpreting** How would heroic movies like *The Memphis Belle* help win the war?
2. **Analyzing** Why do you think so many movies about Hitler were comedies?

506 Chapter 14 America and World War II

Activity: Interdisciplinary Connection

Daily Life Tell students that women painted seams on their legs to make it look as though they were wearing stockings. During the war, silk was needed to make parachutes, not stockings. Have students pair up and use Internet or library resources to research other items that were rationed.

Encourage students to interview family members or community members to get first-hand accounts of rationing. Finally, have students create a pamphlet that describes and illustrates the information they found. Ask students to present their pamphlets to the class. **OL**

A person from each household picked up a book of ration coupons every month. Blue coupons, called blue points, controlled processed foods. Red coupons, or red points, controlled meats, fats, and oils. Other coupons controlled items such as coffee, shoes, and sugar. Thirteen rationing programs were in effect at the height of the program. When people bought food, they also had to give enough coupon points to cover their purchases. Most rationing ended before the war was over. Sugar and rubber rationing continued after the war; sugar was rationed until 1947.

Victory Gardens and Scrap Drives

Americans also planted gardens to produce more food for the war effort. Any area of land might become a garden—backyards, school yards, city parks, and empty lots. The government encouraged **victory gardens** by praising them in film reels, pamphlets, and official statements.

Certain raw materials were so vital to the war effort that the government organized scrap drives. Volunteers collected spare rubber, tin, aluminum, and steel. They donated pots, tires, tin cans, car bumpers, broken radiators, and rusting bicycles. Oils and fats were so important to the production of explosives that the WPB set up fat-collecting stations. Americans would exchange bacon grease and meat drippings for extra ration coupons. The scrap drives boosted morale and did contribute to the success of American industry during the war.

Paying for the War

The federal government spent more than $300 billion during World War II—more money than it had spent from Washington's administration to the end of Franklin Roosevelt's second term. To raise money, the government raised taxes. Because most Americans opposed large tax increases, Congress refused to raise taxes as high as Roosevelt requested. As a result, the extra taxes collected covered only 45 percent of the war's cost.

The government issued war bonds to make up the difference between what was needed and what taxes supplied. Buying bonds is a way to lend money to the government. In exchange for the money, the government promises to repay the bonds' purchase price plus interest at some future date. The most common bonds during World War II were E bonds, which sold for $18.75 and could be redeemed for $25.00 after 10 years. Individuals bought nearly $50 billion worth of war bonds. Banks, insurance companies, and other financial institutions bought the rest—more than $100 billion worth of bonds.

Despite the hardships, the overwhelming majority of Americans believed the war had to be fought. Although the war brought many changes to the United States, most Americans remained united behind one goal—winning the war.

✓**Reading Check** **Evaluating** How did rationing affect daily life in the United States? How did it affect the economy?

Section 3 REVIEW

Vocabulary
1. **Explain** the significance of: A. Philip Randolph, Bracero Program, Sunbelt, Great Migration, zoot suit, victory suit, Office of Price Administration, rationing, victory garden.

Main Ideas
2. **Assessing** Why were jobs suddenly available to women and minorities?

3. **Evaluating** For what reasons did Americans relocate during the war?

4. **Explaining** How did the federal government control the economy during the war?

Critical Thinking
5. **Big Ideas** What challenges did Americans at home face during the war?

6. **Organizing** Use a graphic organizer like the one below to list the results of increased racial tensions during the war.

7. **Analyzing Visuals** Look again at the photograph on pages 502–503. How does the photographer capture the feeling of people settling into a new area?

Writing About History
8. **Persuasive Writing** Write a newspaper editorial urging fellow citizens to conserve resources so that those resources can be used in the war effort.

History ONLINE
Study Central™ To review this section, go to glencoe.com and click on Study Central.

507

✓**Reading Check**
Answer:
Rationing limited access to many products allowing people to buy them in limited supply. It helped control inflation and ensure there were goods for citizens and military.

Assess

History ONLINE

Study Central™ provides summaries, interactive games, and online graphic organizers to help students review content.

Close

Identifying Central Issues
Have students break into groups and discuss prejudices in society, in the 1940s and today. Have students create two lists: one that shows how people worked together in the 1940s, the other showing modern examples of American unity. **OL**

Section 3 REVIEW

Answers

1. All definitions can be found in the section and in the Glossary.
2. Many of the white men had enlisted in the armed forces. They were fighting the war.
3. to find work in factories; to escape prejudice
4. The government controlled the economy through wage and price controls, rationing, and the selling of bonds to pay for the war.

5. They had to accept rationing, growing their own gardens, living in government housing, recycling of scrap materials, paying higher taxes, and learning to work with minorities.

6.
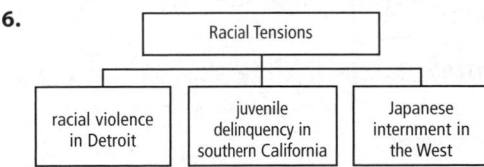

7. The photographer captures how make-shift and temporary the housing was.
8. Editorials will vary but should reflect positive, persuasive techniques.

Focus

Bellringer
Daily Focus Transparency 14.4

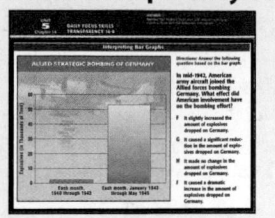

Guide to Reading

Answers:

Pacific: Tarawa Atoll, Gilbert Islands, Allies

Kwajalein Atoll, Marshall Islands, Allies

Guam, Mariana Islands, Allies

Europe: Sicily, Allies

Northern Italy, Allies

D-Day June 1944, Allies

Section Spotlight Video

To generate student interest and provide a springboard for class discussion, access the Chapter 14, Section 4 video at glencoe.com or on the video DVD.

Resource Manager

Section 4

Pushing Back the Axis

After British and American troops won victories over the Axis in North Africa and Italy, Allied leaders made plans for an invasion of Europe. Led by Admiral Nimitz and General MacArthur, American forces steadily advanced across the Pacific.

Striking Germany and Italy

MAIN Idea The Allies stepped up bombing of Germany and invaded Sicily and Italy.

HISTORY AND YOU Have you ever talked over your ideas with a good friend whose opinion you value? Read on to learn about FDR's meetings with Churchill and Stalin.

The Allied invasion of North Africa in November 1942 had shown that a large-scale invasion from the sea was possible. The success of the landings convinced Roosevelt to meet again with Churchill to plan the next stage of the war. In January 1943, FDR headed to Casablanca, Morocco, to meet the prime minister.

At the **Casablanca Conference,** Roosevelt and Churchill agreed to step up the bombing of Germany. The goal of this new campaign was "the progressive destruction of the German military, industrial, and economic system, and the undermining of the morale of the German people." The Allies also agreed to attack the Axis on the island of Sicily. Churchill called Italy the "soft underbelly" of Europe. He was convinced that the Italians would quit the war if the Allies invaded their homeland.

Strategic Bombing

The Allies had been bombing Germany even before the Casablanca Conference. Britain's Royal Air Force had dropped an average of 2,300 tons (2,093 t) of explosives on Germany every month for more than three years. The United States Eighth Army Air Force had dropped an additional 1,500 tons (1,365 t) of bombs during the last six months of 1942. These numbers were small, however, compared to the massive new campaign. Between January 1943 and May 1945, the Royal Air Force and the United States Eighth Army Air Force dropped approximately 53,000 tons (48,230 t) of explosives on Germany every month.

The bombing campaign did not destroy Germany's economy or undermine German morale, but it did cause a severe oil shortage and wrecked the railroad system. It also destroyed so many aircraft factories that Germany's air force could not replace its losses. By the time

Guide to Reading

Big Ideas
Geography and History The Allies slowly pushed back the German and Japanese forces during 1943 and 1944.

Content Vocabulary
• amphtrac (p. 514)
• kamikaze (p. 515)

Academic Vocabulary
• briefly (p. 512)
• intense (p. 512)

People and Events to Identify
• Casablanca Conference (p. 508)
• D-Day (p. 512)
• Omar Bradley (p. 512)
• Guadalcanal (p. 515)

Reading Strategy
Organizing Complete a graphic organizer similar to the one below by filling in the names and battles fought. Indicate whether Allied or Axis forces won the battle.

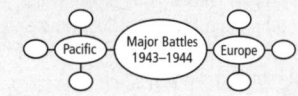

Pacific — Major Battles 1943–1944 — Europe

R Reading Strategies	**C** Critical Thinking	**D** Differentiated Instruction	**W** Writing Support	**S** Skill Practice
Teacher Edition • Identifying, p. 509 • Det. Importance, pp. 510, 514 • Listing, p. 511 • Explaining, p. 513 **Additional Resources** • Guide. Reading, URB p. 85	**Teacher Edition** • Pred. Consequences, p. 510 • Making Decisions, p. 512 • Making Inferences, p. 514 **Additional Resources** • Quizzes and Tests, p. 200	**Teacher Edition** • Visual/Spatial, pp. 512, 513	**Teacher Edition** • Descriptive Writing, p. 515	**Teacher Edition** • Using Geo. Skills, p. 511 **Additional Resources** • RENTG, p. 155 • Reinforcing Skills Act., URB p. 65

NATIONAL GEOGRAPHIC — The War in Europe and North Africa, 1942–1945

Legend:
- Extent of Axis control before World War II
- Extent of Axis control, early Nov. 1942
- Allies
- Neutral nations
- ★ Allied victory
- ✴ Axis victory

0 400 kilometers
0 400 miles
Lambert Azimuthal Equal-Area projection

Important Battles of World War II

1 **El Alamein,** Nov. 1942. British forces defeat German forces commanded by Rommel, preventing German control of North Africa.

2 **Stalingrad,** Nov. 1942. A large German force is defeated at the city of Stalingrad, ending German hopes of defeating the Soviet Union.

3 **Kasserine Pass,** Feb.–May 1943. American troops fight German forces for the first time and are badly beaten.

4 **Leningrad,** Sept. 1941–Jan. 1944. The Russians hold off the Germans besieging the city of Leningrad for 900 days.

5 **Sicily,** July–Aug. 1943. Allies land in Sicily; begin the liberation of Italy.

6 **Anzio,** Jan.–May 1944. U.S. forces land near Rome behind German lines.

7 **D-Day,** June 1944. Allies land at Normandy; begin liberation of France.

8 **Operation Market Garden,** Sept. 1944. Allied troops parachute into the Netherlands to seize bridges across the Rhine, but attack fails.

9 **Battle of the Bulge,** Dec. 1944–Jan. 1945. Last large German counter-attack against American and British troops is halted.

Analyzing GEOGRAPHY

1. **Place** Into what country did the Allies land for Operation Market Garden?
2. **Region** What Allied victories are shown in North Africa?

Maps In MOtion See StudentWorks™ Plus or glencoe.com.

---

the Allies landed in France, they had control of the air, ensuring that their troops would not be bombed.

Striking the Soft Underbelly

R As the bombing campaign against Germany intensified, plans to invade Sicily also moved ahead. General Dwight D. Eisenhower commanded the invasion, with General Patton and the British General Bernard Montgomery head-

ing the ground forces. The invasion began before dawn on July 10, 1943. Despite bad weather, the Allied troops made it ashore with few casualties. A new amphibious truck delivered supplies and artillery to the soldiers on the beach.

Eight days after the troops came ashore, American tanks smashed through enemy lines and captured the western half of the island. Patton's troops then headed east, while the British attacked from the south. By August 18, the Germans had evacuated the island.

Chapter 14 America and World War II **509**

Teach

R Reading Strategy

Identifying Ask: Why did the Allies decide to attack Italy first? *(They thought the Italians would surrender more quickly than the Germans.)* How long did it take Allied troops to take over Sicily? *(about 1 month)* **OL**

Did You Know?

Leaflets signed by Roosevelt and Churchill were dropped onto Rome from Allied planes on June 7, 1943. They read, "The time has come for you, the Italian people, to decide whether Italians should die for Mussolini and Hitler—or live for Italy and civilization."

Analyzing GEOGRAPHY

Answers:
1. the Netherlands
2. Casablanca, El Alamein

Differentiated Instruction

Leveled Activities

BL Reteaching Activity, URB p. 77
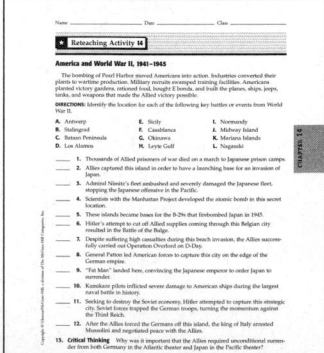

OL Primary Source Reading, URB pp. 66–72
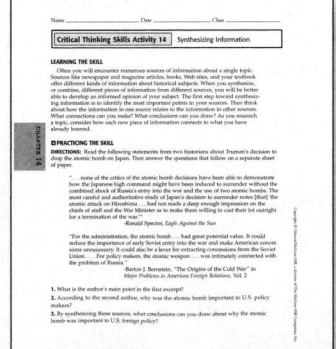

AL Interpreting Political Cartoons, URB pp. 75–76
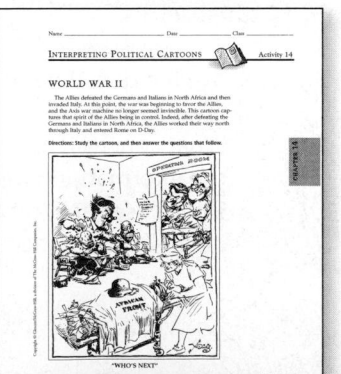

ELL Time Line Activity, URB p. 67

The attack on Sicily created a crisis within the Italian government. The king of Italy, Victor Emmanuel, and a group of Italian generals decided that it was time to depose Mussolini. On July 25, 1943, the king invited the dictator to his palace. "My dear Duce," the king began, "it's no longer any good. Italy has gone to bits. The soldiers don't want to fight anymore. At this moment, you are the most hated man in Italy." The king then arrested Mussolini, and the new Italian government began negotiating a surrender to the Allies.

Following Italy's surrender, however, German troops seized control of northern Italy, including Rome, and returned Mussolini to power. The Germans then took up positions near the heavily fortified town of Cassino. The terrain near Cassino was steep, barren, and rocky. Rather than attack such difficult terrain, the Allies landed at Anzio, behind German lines. Instead of retreating, however, as the Allies had hoped, the Germans surrounded the Allied troops near Anzio.

It took the Allies five months to break through the German lines at Cassino and Anzio. Finally, in late May 1944, the Germans

retreated. Less than two weeks later, the Allies captured Rome. Fighting in Italy continued, however, for another year. The Italian cam-paign was one of the bloodiest in the war, with more than 300,000 Allied casualties.

The Tehran Conference

Roosevelt wanted to meet with Stalin before the Allies invaded France. In late 1943, Stalin agreed, proposing that Roosevelt and Churchill meet him in Tehran, Iran.

The leaders reached several agreements. Stalin promised to launch a full-scale offensive against the Germans when the Allies invaded France in 1944. Roosevelt and Stalin then agreed to divide Germany after the war so that it would never again threaten world peace. **C** Stalin promised that once Germany was defeated, the Soviet Union would help the **R** United States against Japan. He also accepted Roosevelt's proposal of an international peace-keeping organization after the war.

✔ **Reading Check** **Explaining** What effect did the Allied victory in Sicily have on Italy?

Driving Back the Germans, 1943–1944

November 28, 1943
Stalin, Roosevelt, and Churchill meet at the Tehran Conference

January 1943
The British and American air forces begin massive strategic bombing of German industry and infrastructure

Jan. 1943 ⟩ **March 1943** ⟩ **July 1943** ⟩ **Dec. 1943** ⟩

July 10, 1943
Patton and Montgomery land forces on Sicily, begin-ning the invasion of Italy

July 25, 1943
The king of Italy puts Mussolini under arrest and the new Italian government nego-tiates surrender with the Allies

December 4–6, 1943
Roosevelt and Churchill meet in Cairo to plan D-Day. Roosevelt selects Eisenhower to com-mand the invasion

510 **Chapter 14** America and World War II

Landing in France

MAIN Idea The Allies landed a massive force on France's beaches on June 6, 1944, known as D-Day.

HISTORY AND YOU What has been the biggest surprise you ever successfully planned? Read on to find out how the Allies made a surprise landing in France.

After the conference in Tehran, Roosevelt headed to Cairo, Egypt, where he and Churchill continued planning the invasion of France. One major decision still had to be made. The president had to choose the commander for Operation Overlord—the code name for the invasion. Roosevelt selected General Eisenhower.

Planning Operation Overlord

Knowing that the Allies would eventually invade France, Hitler had fortified the coast along the English Channel. The Allies did have the advantage of surprise, because the Germans did not know when or where the Allies would land. The Germans believed the Allies would land in Pas-de-Calais—the area of France closest to Britain. The Allies placed dummy equipment along the coast across from Calais as decoys. The real target was to be further south, at five beaches covering a 60-mile spread along the Normandy coast.

By the spring of 1944, more than 1.5 million American soldiers, 12,000 airplanes, and 5 million tons (4.6 million t) of equipment had been sent to England. Only one thing was left to do—pick the date for the invasion and give the command to go. The invasion had to begin at night to hide the ships crossing the English Channel. The ships had to arrive at low tide so that they could see the beach obstacles. The low tide had to come at dawn so that gunners bombarding the coast could see their targets. Paratroopers, who would be dropped behind enemy lines before the main landing on the beaches, needed a moonlit night to see where to land. Perhaps most important of all, the weather had to be good. A storm would ground the airplanes, and high waves would swamp landing craft.

March 4, 1944
The Allies make their first major daylight bombing raid on Berlin

June 6, 1944
Over 130,000 American, British, and Canadian troops land in Normandy on D-Day, beginning the liberation of France

Jan. 1944   **June 1944**

January 1944
American forces attack Monte Cassino and land at Anzio in an attempt to break through German lines and capture Rome

Analyzing TIME LINES

1. **Identifying** On what date did Allied forces land at Normandy to begin liberating France, and what is the date known as?

2. **Determining Cause and Effect** What effect did the successful Allied invasion of Sicily have on politics in Italy?

Chapter 14   America and World War II   **511**

S Skill Practice

Using Geography Skills Have students locate the coast of Normandy on a map. **Ask:** Why did the Allies choose to land at Normandy rather than at Pas-de-Calais? *(Students may note the element of surprise, the geography of the beaches, and so on.)* **OL**

R Reading Strategy

Listing Have students create two columns: *conditions* and *reasons*. Have students list the conditions required for the invasion and why they were required. *(begin at night—to conceal ships; low tide—to see obstacles; moonlit night—paratroopers could see where to land; good weather—bad weather could ground airplanes and high waves would swamp landing craft.)* **OL**

Analyzing TIME LINES

Answers:
1. June 6, 1944; D-Day
2. Mussolini was arrested, and a new government negotiated with the Allies.

Additional Support

Activity: Technology Connection

Creating a Radio Broadcast Have students work in small groups to prepare a radio broadcast of the D-Day invasion. Remind students that the operation was secretive, so the landing would have been quite a shock. Tell students they can broadcast from the point of view of an Allied radio station or an Axis one. Make sure students include some synthesis of the event. The broadcaster should describe what the invasion means for their side. Students may add music or sound effects, if they choose. Have students enact or perform their broadcasts in class. **OL**

C Critical Thinking

Making Decisions Eisenhower had a difficult decision to make: Should he launch D-Day on June 6 or wait another month? Have students work in pairs and make two lists of reasons: one that supports the launch and the other to postpone it. Ask students what advice they would give Eisenhower if they were on his advisory committee. **OL**

D Differentiated Instruction

Visual/Spatial Have students research and create a chart that documents the number of ships, troops, and aircraft used at each of the five beaches. Have them include number of casualties as well. **OL**

Reading Check

Answer:
The invasion had to begin at night; the ships had to arrive at low tide; and the weather had to be relatively good.

Additional Support

Given all these requirements, there were only a few days each month when the invasion could begin. The first opportunity was from June 5 to 7, 1944. Eisenhower's planning staff referred to the day any operation began by the letter *D*. The date for the invasion, therefore, came to be known as **D-Day.** Heavy cloud cover, strong winds, and high waves made landing on June 5 impossible. The weather was forecast to improve **briefly** a day later. The Channel would still be rough, but the landing ships and aircraft could operate. After looking at forecasts one last time, shortly after midnight on June 6, 1944, Eisenhower gave the final order: "OK, we'll go."

The Longest Day

Nearly 7,000 ships carrying more than 100,000 soldiers headed for Normandy's coast. At the same time, 23,000 paratroopers were dropped inland, east and west of the beaches. Allied fighter-bombers raced up and down the coast, hitting bridges, bunkers, and radar sites. At dawn, Allied warships began a tremendous barrage. Thousands of shells rained down on the beaches, code-named "Utah," "Omaha," "Gold," "Sword," and "Juno."

The American landing at Utah Beach went well. The German defenses were weak, and in less than three hours the troops had captured the beach and moved inland, suffering fewer than 200 casualties. On the eastern flank, the British and Canadian landings also went well. By the end of the day, British and Canadian forces were several miles inland. Omaha Beach, however, was a different story. Under **intense** German fire, the American assault almost disintegrated. Lieutenant John Bentz Carroll was in the first wave that went ashore:

PRIMARY SOURCE

"Two hundred yards out, we took a direct hit.... Somehow or other, the ramp door opened up ... and the men in front were being struck by machine-gun fire. Everyone started to jump off into the water.... The tide was moving us so rapidly.... We would grab out on some of those underwater obstructions and mines built on telephone poles and girders, and hang on. We'd take cover, then make a dash through the surf to the next one, fifty feet beyond."

—from *D-Day: Piercing the Atlantic Wall*

General **Omar Bradley,** commander of the American forces landing at Omaha and Utah, began making plans to evacuate. Slowly, however, the American troops began to knock out the German defenses. More landing craft arrived, ramming their way through the obstacles to get to the beach. Nearly 2,500 Americans were either killed or wounded on Omaha, but by early afternoon, Bradley received this message: "Troops formerly pinned down on beaches . . . [are] advancing up heights behind beaches." By the end of the day, nearly 35,000 American troops had landed at Omaha, and another 23,000 had landed at Utah. More than 75,000 British and Canadian troops were on shore as well. The invasion—the largest amphibious operation in history—had succeeded.

✔ **Reading Check** **Summarizing** What conditions had to be met before Eisenhower could order D-Day to begin?

PRIMARY SOURCE

The United States began island-hopping across the Pacific with the Battle of Tarawa in November 1943. Reporter Robert Sherrod witnessed the savage hand-to-hand fighting:

"A Marine jumped over the seawall and began throwing blocks of fused TNT into a coconut-log pillbox. . . . Two more Marines scaled the seawall, one of them carrying a twin-cylindered tank strapped to their shoulders, the other holding the nozzle of the flame thrower. As another charge of TNT boomed inside the pillbox, causing smoke and dust to billow out, a khaki-clad figure ran out the side entrance. The flame thrower, waiting for him, caught him in its withering stream of intense fire. As soon as it touched him, the [Japanese soldier] flared up like a piece of celluloid. He was dead instantly . . . charred almost to nothingness."

—from *Tarawa: The Story of a Battle*

Activity: Interdisciplinary Connection

Art Storming the Normandy beaches was no small feat. Troops on the ground and in the air had to be prepared. They were going to be exposed to enemy attack on open beachheads. Many soldiers were laden with 70 pounds of gear and had to jump in neck-deep water. **Ask:** What was the typical D-Day soldier carrying when he landed in Normandy? Have students use the Internet and library resources to find the answer to this question. Have students sketch the typical battle gear of the Allied soldiers during the D-Day invasion. Have students write paragraphs to accompany each sketch that describes each item and how they were used during the invasion. Display students' work in class. **BL**

Driving Japan Back

MAIN Idea American troops slowly regained islands in the Pacific that the Japanese had captured.

HISTORY AND YOU Have you ever had to do a project over? Read to learn about American forces that took back Pacific islands from the Japanese.

R While the buildup for invading France was taking place in Britain, American military leaders were also developing a strategy to defeat Japan. The American plan called for a two-pronged attack. The Pacific Fleet, commanded by Admiral Nimitz, would advance through the central Pacific by "hopping" from one island to the next, closer and closer to Japan. Meanwhile, General MacArthur's troops would advance through the Solomon Islands, capture the north coast of New Guinea, and then launch an invasion to retake the Philippines.

Island-Hopping in the Pacific

By the fall of 1943, the navy was ready to launch its island-hopping campaign, but the geography of the central Pacific posed a problem. Many of the islands were coral reef atolls. The water over the coral reef was not always deep enough to allow landing craft to get to the shore. If the landing craft ran aground on the reef, the troops would have to wade to the beach. As some 5,000 United States Marines learned at Tarawa Atoll, wading ashore could cause very high casualties. Tarawa, part of the Gilbert Islands, was the navy's first objective. The Japanese base there had to be captured in order to put air bases in the nearby Marshall Islands. **D**

R **Reading Strategy**

Explaining **Ask:** What was the purpose of "island-hopping" in the Pacific? *(to take over islands in the Pacific, one at a time, in order to establish bases as close as possible to Japan)* **BL**

D **Differentiated Instruction**

Visual/Spatial Have students find photos of coral reef atolls or draw them. Have them explain why these reefs proved difficult for armed forces. **OL**

Analyzing **GEOGRAPHY**

Answers:
1. Tarawa, part of the Gilbert Islands
2. the Japanese

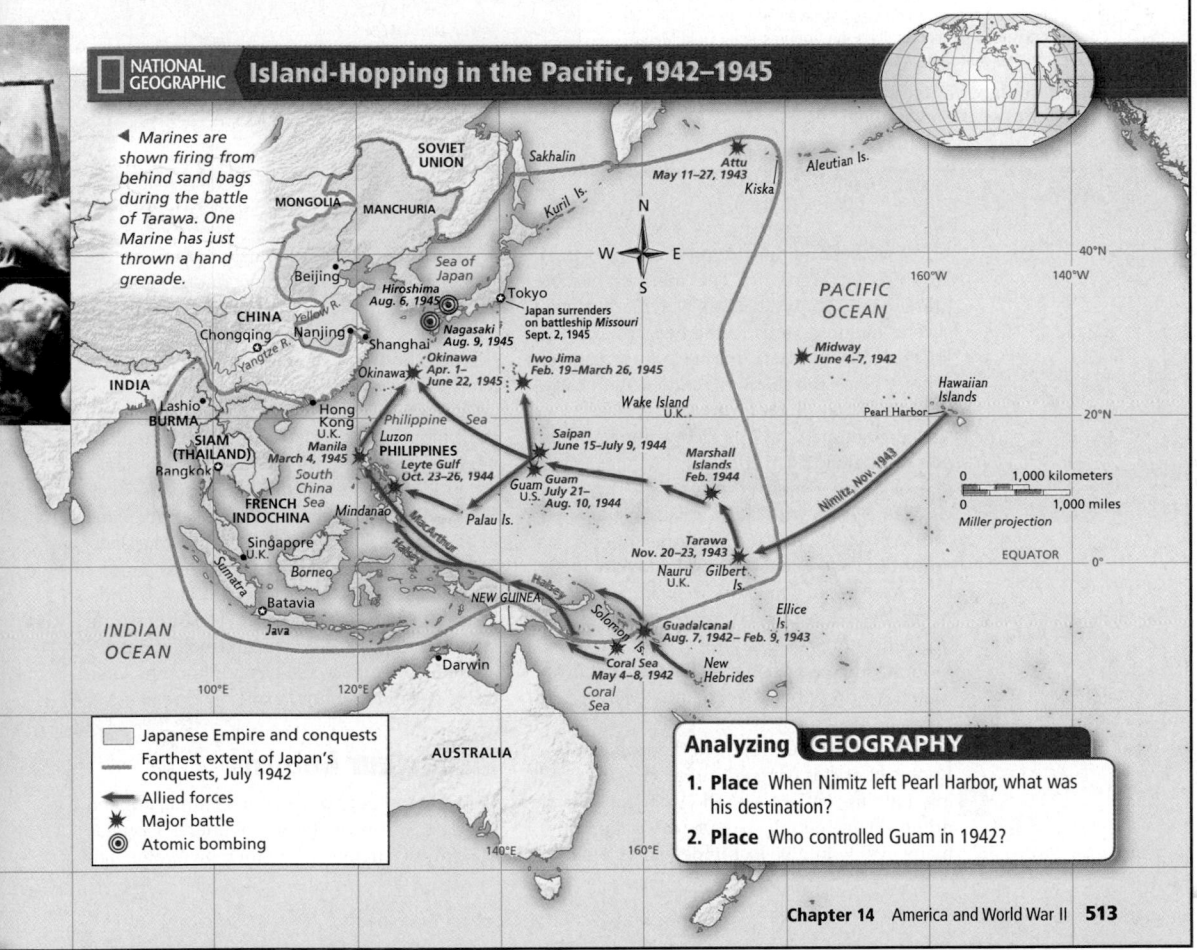

NATIONAL GEOGRAPHIC **Island-Hopping in the Pacific, 1942–1945**

◀ Marines are shown firing from behind sand bags during the battle of Tarawa. One Marine has just thrown a hand grenade.

Attu May 11–27, 1943
Kiska
Aleutian Is.
40°N
160°W   140°W

Hiroshima Aug. 6, 1945
Tokyo
Japan surrenders on battleship Missouri Sept. 2, 1945
Nagasaki Aug. 9, 1945

PACIFIC OCEAN

Midway June 4–7, 1942
Hawaiian Islands
Pearl Harbor
20°N

Iwo Jima Feb. 19–March 26, 1945
Okinawa Apr. 1– June 22, 1945
Wake Island U.K.

Saipan June 15–July 9, 1944
Marshall Islands Feb. 1944

Guam July 21– Aug. 10, 1944 U.S.
Palau Is.

Nimitz, Nov. 1943

Tarawa Nov. 20–23, 1943
Nauru U.K.   Gilbert Is. U.K.

0   1,000 kilometers
0   1,000 miles
Miller projection

EQUATOR   0°

Ellice Is.

Guadalcanal Aug. 7, 1942– Feb. 9, 1943

Coral Sea May 4–8, 1942
New Hebrides

SOVIET UNION
Sakhalin
MONGOLIA   MANCHURIA
Kuril Is.
Beijing
Sea of Japan
CHINA
Chongqing   Nanjing
Yellow R.
Shanghai
Yangtze R.
INDIA
Lashio
BURMA
Hong Kong U.K.
Philippine Sea
Luzon
PHILIPPINES
Manila
Leyte Gulf Oct. 23–26, 1944
March 4, 1945
Bangkok
SIAM (THAILAND)
South China Sea
FRENCH INDOCHINA   Mindanao
Singapore U.K.
Borneo
Sumatra
Batavia
Java
INDIAN OCEAN
100°E   120°E
Darwin
NEW GUINEA
MacArthur
Halmahera
Solomon Is.
Coral Sea
AUSTRALIA
140°E   160°E

Legend:
- Japanese Empire and conquests
- Farthest extent of Japan's conquests, July 1942
- → Allied forces
- ✴ Major battle
- ◎ Atomic bombing

Analyzing **GEOGRAPHY**
1. **Place** When Nimitz left Pearl Harbor, what was his destination?
2. **Place** Who controlled Guam in 1942?

Activity: Collaborative Learning

Summarizing Have partners create a map similar to the one on page 513. Assign pairs major battles in the Pacific. **Ask:** Was there a change in control of an island in the battle you have been assigned during the war? Have each pair discuss their battle and use their maps to show military movement and changes. They may also include a drawing that depicts the battle on their island. After students have finished their maps, make a class list that summarizes the changes on the Pacific islands during the course of the war. **OL**

Additional Support

People IN HISTORY

The Navajo Code Talkers

When American marines stormed an enemy beach, they used radios to communicate. Using radios, however, meant that the Japanese could intercept and translate the messages. In the midst of the battle, however, there was no time to use a code-machine. Acting upon the suggestion of Philip Johnston, an engineer who had lived on a Navajo reservation as a child, the marines recruited Navajos to serve as "code talkers."

The Navajo language had no written alphabet and was known only to the Navajo and a few missionaries and anthropologists. The Navajo recruits developed code words, using their own language, that stood for military terms. For example, the Navajo word *jay-sho,* or "buzzard," was code for *bomber; lotso,* or "whale," meant *battleship;* and *na-ma-si,* or "potatoes," stood for *grenades.*

Code talkers proved invaluable in combat. They could relay a message in minutes that would have taken a code-machine operator hours to encipher and transmit. At the battle of Iwo Jima, code talkers transmitted more than 800 messages during the first 48 hours as the marines struggled to get ashore under intense bombardment. More than 400 Navajo served in the marine corps as code talkers. Sworn to secrecy, their mission was not revealed until 1971. In 2001 Congress awarded the code talkers the Congressional Gold Medal for their unique contribution during the war.

What advantage did the code talkers provide over traditional forms of communication?

▲ *These Navajo code talkers assigned to a Pacific-based marine regiment relay orders using a field radio.*

When the landing craft hit the reef, at least 20 ships ran aground. The marines had to plunge into shoulder-high water and wade several hundred yards to the beach. Raked by Japanese fire, only one marine in three made it ashore. Once the marines reached the beach, the battle was still far from over.

Although many troops died wading ashore, one vehicle had been able to cross the reef and deliver its troops onto the beaches. The vehicle was a boat with tank tracks, nicknamed the "Alligator." This amphibious tractor, or **amphtrac,** had been invented in the late 1930s to rescue people in Florida swamps. It had never been used in combat, and the navy decided to buy only 200 of them in 1941. If more had been available at Tarawa, American casualties probably would have been much lower.

C More than 1,000 marines died on Tarawa. Photos of bodies lying crumpled next to burning landing craft shocked Americans back home. Many people began to wonder how many lives would be lost in defeating Japan.

The next assault—Kwajalein Atoll in the Marshall Islands—went much more smoothly. This time all of the troops went ashore in amphtracs. Although the Japanese resisted fiercely, the marines captured Kwajalein and nearby Eniwetok with far fewer casualties.

After the Marshall Islands, the navy targeted the Mariana Islands. American military planners wanted to use the Marianas as a base for a new heavy bomber, the B-29 Superfortress. The B-29 could fly farther than any other plane in the world. From airfields in the Marianas, B-29s could bomb Japan. Admiral Nimitz **R** decided to invade three of the Mariana Islands: Saipan, Tinian, and Guam. Despite strong Japanese resistance, American troops captured all three by August 1944. A few months later, B-29s began bombing Japan.

MacArthur Returns

As the forces under Admiral Nimitz hopped across the central Pacific, General Douglas MacArthur's troops began their own campaign

Activity: Interdisciplinary Connection

Art and Literature Ask: Why was Douglas MacArthur so important to the war effort? Have students draw a picture of MacArthur, with his famed corncob pipe. Students may either write a brief biography of his life or a poem about him, describing why he is admired and considered a great leader. Have students use library or Internet sources to learn more about his views concerning the use of atomic weapons, as well. **BL**

in the southwest Pacific. The campaign began by invading **Guadalcanal** in the Solomon Islands, east of New Guinea, in August 1942. It continued until early 1944, when MacArthur's troops finally captured enough islands to surround the main Japanese base in the region. In response, the Japanese withdrew their ships and aircraft from the base, although they left 100,000 troops behind to hold the island.

Worried that the navy's advance across the central Pacific was leaving him behind, MacArthur ordered his forces to leap nearly 600 miles (966 km) to capture the Japanese base at Hollandia on the north coast of New Guinea. Shortly after securing New Guinea, MacArthur's troops seized the island of Morotai—the last stop before the Philippines.

To take back the Philippines, the United States assembled an enormous invasion force. In October 1944, more than 700 ships carrying more than 160,000 troops sailed for Leyte Gulf in the Philippines. On October 20, the troops began to land on Leyte, an island on the eastern side of the Philippines. A few hours after the invasion began, MacArthur headed to the beach. Upon reaching the shore, he strode to a radio and spoke into the microphone: "People of the Philippines, I have returned. By the grace of Almighty God, our forces stand again on Philippine soil."

To stop the American invasion, the Japanese sent four aircraft carriers toward the Philippines from the north and secretly dispatched another fleet to the west. Believing the Japanese carriers were leading the main attack, most of the American carriers protecting the invasion left Leyte Gulf and headed north to stop them. Seizing their chance, the Japanese warships to the west raced through the Philippine Islands into Leyte Gulf and ambushed the remaining American ships.

The Battle of Leyte Gulf was the largest naval battle in history. It was also the first time that the Japanese used **kamikaze** attacks. *Kamikaze* means "divine wind" in Japanese. It refers to the great storm that destroyed the Mongol fleet during its invasion of Japan in the thirteenth century. Kamikaze pilots would deliberately crash their planes into American ships, killing themselves but also inflicting severe damage. Luckily for the Americans, just as their situation was becoming desperate, the Japanese commander, believing more American ships were on the way, ordered a retreat.

Although the Japanese fleet had retreated, the campaign to recapture the Philippines from the Japanese was long and grueling. More than 80,000 Japanese were killed; fewer than 1,000 surrendered. MacArthur's troops did not capture Manila until March 1945. The battle left the city in ruins and more than 100,000 Filipino civilians dead. The remaining Japanese retreated into the rugged terrain north of Manila; they were still fighting in August 1945 when word came that Japan had surrendered.

Reading Check **Describing** What strategy did the United States Navy use to advance across the Pacific?

Section 4 REVIEW

Vocabulary
1. **Explain** the significance of: Casablanca Conference, D-Day, Omar Bradley, amphtrac, Guadalcanal, kamikaze.

Main Ideas
2. **Determining Cause and Effect** What event prompted Italy to surrender?
3. **Describing** Why was D-Day's success so vital to an Allied victory?
4. **Summarizing** What was the military goal in the Pacific?

Critical Thinking
5. **Big Ideas** How did the geography of the Pacific affect American strategy?
6. **Organizing** Use a graphic organizer like the one below to explain the importance of each leader listed in the text.

Leader	Significance
Dwight Eisenhower	
George Patton	
George Marshall	
Omar Bradley	
Douglas MacArthur	

7. **Analyzing Visuals** Look at the photo on page 511 of the D-Day landing. What do you observe about the manner of the landing?

Writing About History
8. **Persuasive Writing** Imagine that you are living in Florida and see the potential for the amphtrac in the war. Write a letter to a member of Congress detailing reasons why it would be a good purchase for the marines.

 History ONLINE
Study Central™ To review this section, go to glencoe.com and click on Study Central.

 Writing Support
Descriptive Writing Have students research Kamikaze pilots. Then have students write a poem that compares the pilots to the storm. **OL**

Reading Check
Answer:
island-hopping

Assess

 History ONLINE

Study Central™ provides summaries, interactive games, and online graphic organizers to help students review content.

Close

Summarizing Have groups create five posters that describe five important events that happened between 1941–1945. Students should note how the events affected U.S. and foreign policy. **OL**

Section 4 REVIEW

Answers

1. All definitions can be found in the section and in the Glossary.
2. the successful Allied invasion of Sicily
3. It would force the Germans to fight on two fronts.
4. to move from island to island, recapturing islands that had earlier been lost to the Japanese, to stop the Japanese offensive, and to slowly advance toward Japan
5. Coral reefs around the atolls made it difficult for landing craft to land. They began using amphtracs to land soldiers.
6.

Leader	Significance
Dwight Eisenhower	commanded invasion of Italy and D-Day operations
George Patton	led ground forces in Africa and Italy
George Marshall	planned Operation Overlord
Omar Bradley	commander at Omaha and Utah beaches
Douglas MacArthur	took back the Philippines from the Japanese

7. It looks as though a lot of men had to be landed quickly. For such a large operation, it had to be orchestrated very precisely.
8. Letters will vary but should be persuasive in nature.

Focus

Highlight for students the incredible drama and significance of D-Day, June 6, 1944. Tell them that the Russians had been pressing their American and British allies for a second front since 1942.

Teach

S Skill Practice

Using Geography Skills Have students study the geography of western Europe. Discuss with students why a seaborne attack on western Europe was so difficult and how the Nazis used geography as a defense. **AL**

Analyzing GEOGRAPHY

Answers:
1. firm, flat beaches within range of Allied planes and enough roads and paths to move troops.
2. cliffs and bluff overlooking the beach gave the Germans great defense advantages

Additional Support

NATIONAL GEOGRAPHIC

GEOGRAPHY & HISTORY

The Battle for Omaha Beach

The selection of a site for the largest amphibious landing in history was one of the biggest decisions of World War II. Allied planners considered coastlines from Denmark to Portugal in search of a sheltered location with firm flat beaches within range of friendly fighter planes in England. There also had to be enough roads and paths to move jeeps and trucks off the beaches and to accommodate the hundreds of thousands of American, Canadian, and British troops set to stream ashore following the invasion. An airfield and a seaport that the Allies could use were also needed. Most important was a reasonable expectation of achieving the element of surprise.

How Did Geography Shape the Battle?

Surrounded at both ends by cliffs that rose wall-like from the sea, Omaha Beach was only four miles long. The entire beach was overlooked by a 150-foot high bluff and there were only five ravines leading from the beach to the top of the bluff.

The Germans made full use of the geographic advantage the 150-foot bluff gave them. They dug trenches and built concrete bunkers for machine guns at the top of the cliffs and positioned them to guard the ravines leading to the beach.

Map labels:
American
British
Canadian
BRITAIN
Portsmouth · Dover · Shoreham · Calais
Southampton
Portland
Dartmouth OMAHA
UTAH GOLD JUNO SWORD Straits of Dover
English Channel Cherbourg · Dieppe · Le Havre
St.-Lo · Caen Seine River
NORMANDY FRANCE
0 100 kilometers
0 100 miles
Lambert Azimuthal Equal-Area projection

Once ashore they had to cross 300 yards of open beach to the base of the bluff.

The men had to jump into the water and wade ashore against a strong tide in water that was nearly over their heads.

Analyzing GEOGRAPHY

1. **Location** Why did the Allies choose Normandy as the invasion site?
2. **Human-Environment Interaction** How did geography make the invasion of Omaha Beach difficult?

516 Chapter 14 America and World War II

Extending the Content

"Ducks" on D-Day Photos of the D-Day landing invariably feature the DUKW, the square-shaped vehicle the Allied troops used to land on Omaha Beach. The nickname "duck" came from soldiers, a take-off from the technical name of DUKW (a code acronym that identified that it was amphibian and had front and rear wheel drive). The DUKW was developed by General Motors to withstand difficult amphibious operations. It was first used in 1943 for the Allied invasion of Sicily.

American troops were carried to Omaha Beach in landing craft. Many of the landing craft came under such intense fire that they opened their front ramp doors early.

C Critical Thinking

Comparing Help students learn more about D-Day by comparing it to other military campaigns or battles. Students might choose a battle or campaign from a historic war—the Revolutionary War, the Civil War, or World War I. Once they have chosen a battle or campaign, have students make a list of points to compare it with D-Day. Students' criteria may include: How important was each battle to each war? How did strategy differ? Were a large number of troops involved? Have students discuss their findings. **OL**

Assess/Close

Summarizing **Ask:** What might have happened if the Allies had attacked the Germans from the west sooner than June 1944? *(Students might suggest that the Allied assault would not have been so massive and may have failed. Others might say that it would have been successful.)*

Additional Support

517

Extending the Content

Taking Pointe du Hoc Pointe du Hoc was a piece of land held by the Germans that allowed them to observe the Omaha and Utah beaches. With huge cannons in their heavily reinforced bunkers, the Germans could hit either beach with artillery shells. For that reason, the Allies bombarded the Pointe du Hoc bunkers for weeks before D-Day. They ceased fire when 225 men of the 2nd Ranger Battalion were due to land. Navigational problems and tidal currents made them late, and once they scaled the cliffs with ropes and grappling hooks, the Germans were waiting. The fighting was fierce, and the surviving rangers had to fend off further attack once they took the Pointe, but their determined action played a key role in the events of D-Day.

Focus

Bellringer
Daily Focus Transparency 14.5

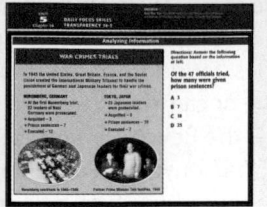

Guide to Reading

Answers:
Students should complete the outline by including all headings in the section.

Section Spotlight Video

To generate student interest and provide a springboard for class discussion, access the Chapter 14, Section 5 video at glencoe.com or on the video DVD.

Resource Manager

Section 5

The War Ends

Guide to Reading

Big Ideas
Individual Action After fierce military campaigns, President Harry S. Truman decided to use atomic weapons against Japan.

Content Vocabulary
• hedgerow (p. 518)
• napalm (p. 521)
• charter (p. 525)

Academic Vocabulary
• despite (p. 520)
• nuclear (p. 523)

People and Events to Identify
• Battle of the Bulge (p. 518)
• V-E Day (p. 519)
• Harry S. Truman (p. 520)
• Iwo Jima (p. 520)
• Manhattan Project (p. 523)
• V-J Day (p. 524)
• United Nations (p. 524)
• Nuremberg Trials (p. 525)

Reading Strategy
Create an outline of the section, using the major headings as the main points. Follow the structure shown below.

```
The War Ends
I. The Third Reich Collapses
   A.
   B.
II.
   A.
   B.
```

Fierce fighting in both Europe and the Pacific during 1945 led to the defeat of the Axis powers. The Allies began war crimes trials and set up a peacekeeping organization to prevent another global war.

The Third Reich Collapses

MAIN Idea The war in Europe ended in spring 1945 after major battles, as the Allies moved west toward Germany.

HISTORY AND YOU Have you ever been in a competition in which you persevered, despite fatigue, to win? Read to learn how the Allies fought in Europe to defeat Germany.

Although D-Day had been a success, it was only the beginning. Surrounding many fields in Normandy were **hedgerows**—dirt walls, several feet thick, covered in shrubbery. The hedgerows had been built to fence in cattle and crops, but they also enabled the Germans to fiercely defend their positions. The battle of the hedgerows ended on July 25, 1944, when 2,500 American bombers blew a hole in the German lines, enabling American tanks to race through the gap.

As the Allies broke out of Normandy, the French Resistance—French civilians who had secretly organized to resist the German occupation of their country—staged a rebellion in Paris. When the Allied forces liberated Paris on August 25, they found the streets filled with French citizens celebrating their victory.

The Battle of the Bulge

As the Allies advanced toward the German border, Hitler decided to stage one last desperate offensive. His goal was to cut off Allied supplies coming through the port of Antwerp, Belgium. The attack began just before dawn on December 16, 1944. Six inches (15 cm) of snow covered the ground, and the weather was bitterly cold. Moving rapidly, the Germans caught the American defenders by surprise. As the German troops raced west, their lines bulged outward, and the attack became known as the **Battle of the Bulge.**

Shortly after the Germans surrounded the Americans, Eisenhower ordered General Patton to rescue them. Three days later, faster than anyone expected in the midst of a snowstorm, Patton's troops slammed into the German lines. As the weather cleared, Allied aircraft began hitting German fuel depots.

On Christmas Eve, out of fuel and weakened by heavy losses, the German troops driving toward Antwerp were forced to halt. Two days later, Patton's troops broke through to the German line. Although

---

R Reading Strategies	C Critical Thinking	D Differentiated Instruction	W Writing Support	S Skill Practice
Teacher Edition • Paraphrasing, p. 520 • Identifying, p. 522 **Additional Resources** • Guide. Reading, URB p. 86	**Teacher Edition** • Defending, p. 521 • Contrasting, p. 522 • Evaluating, p. 524 • Speculating, p. 524 **Additional Resources** • Crit. Think. Skills Act., URB p. 66 • Quizzes and Tests, p. 201	**Teacher Edition** • Gifted and Talented, p. 520 • Naturalist, p. 523 **Additional Resources** • Diff. Instruction Act., URB p. 57 • English Learner Act., URB p. 59 • Authentic Assess., p. 33 • Reteach Act., URB p. 77	**Teacher Edition** • Expository Writing, p. 519 • Descriptive Writing, p. 521	**Additional Resources** • RENTG, p. 158 • Time Line Act., p. 67

INFOGRAPHIC
The War Ends in Europe, 1945

The Axis Before the War, 1939

The Axis at its Peak, 1942

The Axis at German Surrender, 1945

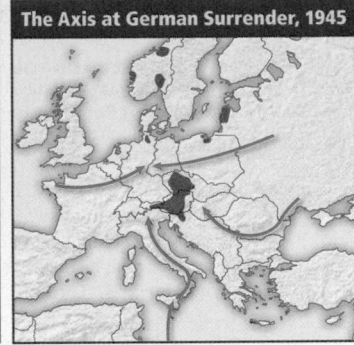

How Many People Died in World War II?		
Country	Military Deaths	Civilian Deaths
USSR	11,000,000	6,700,000
Germany	3,250,000	2,350,000
Japan	1,740,000	393,000
China	1,400,000	8,000,000
Poland	110,000	5,300,000
United States	405,000	2,000
Great Britain	306,000	61,000
Italy	227,000	60,000
France	122,000	470,000

Axis-controlled territory
Allied advances, 1944–45
0   400 kilometers
0   400 miles
Lambert Azimuthal Equal-Area projection

Analyzing VISUALS

1. **Comparing** Which nation had the greatest number of civilian casualties?

2. **Analyzing** Why did the United States have so few civilian deaths?

fighting continued for three weeks, the United States had won the Battle of the Bulge. On January 8, the Germans began to withdraw. They had suffered more than 100,000 casualties and lost many tanks and aircraft. They had very few resources left to prevent the Allies from entering Germany.

The War Ends in Europe

While American and British forces fought to liberate France, the Soviets began a massive attack on German troops in Russia. By the time the Battle of the Bulge ended, the Soviets had driven Hitler's forces out of Russia and back across Poland. By February 1945, Soviet troops were only 35 miles (56 km) from Berlin.

As the Soviets crossed Germany's eastern border, American forces attacked Germany's western border. By the end of February 1945, American troops had fought their way to the Rhine River, Germany's last major line of defense in the west. On March 7, American tanks crossed the Rhine.

As German defenses crumbled, American troops raced east to within 70 miles (113 km) of Berlin. On April 16, Soviet troops finally smashed through the German defenses and reached the outskirts of Berlin five days later.

Deep in his Berlin bunker, Adolf Hitler knew the end was near. On April 30, 1945, he committed suicide. Before killing himself, Hitler chose Grand Admiral Karl Doenitz as his successor. Doenitz tried to surrender to the Americans and British while continuing to fight the Soviets, but Eisenhower insisted on unconditional surrender. On May 7, 1945, Germany accepted the terms. The next day—May 8, 1945—was proclaimed **V-E Day,** for "Victory in Europe."

✔Reading Check **Explaining** Why was the Battle of the Bulge such a disastrous defeat for Germany?

Teach

W Writing Support

Expository Writing Have students research the movements of the Allied and Axis forces at the Battle of the Bulge. Have them write a two-page report. The first page should identify the good and bad strategic moves related to the battle. Encourage students to include a map that shows the movement. The second page will highlight General Patton's contribution. **OL**

✔Reading Check

Answer:
The Germans lost over 100,000 troops and lost many of their tanks and aircraft. They had little left to keep the Allies out of Germany.

Analyzing VISUALS

Answers:
1. China
2. The war was not fought on U.S. soil.

Additional Support

Extending the Content

German Surrender Germany accepted unconditional surrender on May 7, 1945, at a small schoolhouse in France. In Moscow, gigantic rays of light were projected in the air to celebrate. In the United States, the Washington Monument, the Capitol dome, and the Statue of Liberty were lit the very first time since the bombing of Pearl Harbor. After less than a month in office, President Truman reflected on this triumph when he addressed the nation by saying, "This is a solemn but glorious hour. I only wish FDR had lived to witness this day."

R Reading Strategy

Paraphrasing Ask students to offer their interpretation of Truman's words about President Roosevelt. *(Most students will say that Truman was overwhelmed with grief. It seemed as though nothing was right—everything was out of order. Truman had a great weight (the war) to deal with.)* **OL**

D Differentiated Instruction

Gifted and Talented The Battle of Iwo Jima was a heroic victory. The famous photograph boosted American morale. A monument based on this photo was sculpted and stands in the Arlington National Cemetery. Have students research the photographer, the men in the photograph, and the sculptor and create their own montage that symbolizes the importance of this battle. **AL**

Japan Is Defeated

MAIN Idea The United States decided to end the war with Japan by using napalm and atomic bombs.

HISTORY AND YOU When was the last time you had to make a difficult decision, with no really good choice? Read to learn about the decision President Truman made in 1945.

Unfortunately, President Roosevelt did not live to see the defeat of Germany. On April 12, 1945, while vacationing in Warm Springs, Georgia, he died of a stroke. His vice president, **Harry S. Truman,** became president during this difficult time.

The next day, Truman told reporters: "Boys, if you ever pray, pray for me now. . . . When they told me yesterday what had happened, I felt like the moon, the stars, and all the planets had fallen on me." **Despite** his feelings, Truman began at once to make decisions about the war. Although Germany surrendered a few weeks later, the war with Japan continued, and

Truman was forced to make some of the most difficult decisions of the war during his first six months in office.

The Battle of Iwo Jima

On November 24, 1944, bombs fell on Tokyo. Above the city flew 80 B-29 Superfortress bombers that had traveled more than 1,500 miles (2,414 km) from new American bases in the Mariana Islands.

At first the B-29s did little damage because they kept missing their targets. By the time the B-29s reached Japan, they did not have enough fuel left to fix their navigational errors or to adjust for high winds. The pilots needed an island closer to Japan so the B-29s could refuel. American military planners decided to invade **Iwo Jima.**

Iwo Jima was perfectly located, roughly halfway between the Marianas and Japan, but its geography was formidable. At its southern tip was a dormant volcano. The terrain was rugged, with rocky cliffs, jagged ravines, and

Winning the War
Against Japan, 1944–1945

April 1, 1945
American troops land on Okinawa

March 9, 1945
Firebombing destroys most of Tokyo

Feb. 1945 **April 1945** **June 1945**

October 23–24, 1944
Victory in the Battle of Leyte Gulf enables MacArthur to return to the Philippines

February 19, 1945
U.S. Marines land on Iwo Jima; over 6,800 marines are killed before the island is captured

520 **Chapter 14** America and World War II

Hands-On Chapter Project
Step 5

An Interview with a World War II Veteran

Step 5: Presenting the Interview
Essential Question: How should the interview be presented?

Directions Students will determine the final format of the interview presentation. For example, should it be a video presented to the class? Should it be part of a large Web page or presentation? Students should integrate the interview into the final presenta-

tion. Set class time aside for students to present their interviews. Students may also present it to a community group and, certainly, to the veteran who was the subject.

Putting It Together Presenters should be prepared for follow-up questions from their audience. They should be sure that they have researched the topics covered in the interview and are familiar with those mentioned by the subject. **OL**

(Chapter Project continued on the Visual Summary page)

dozens of caves. Volcanic ash covered the ground. Even worse, the Japanese had built a vast network of concrete bunkers connected by miles of tunnels.

On February 19, 1945, some 60,000 Marines landed on Iwo Jima. As the troops leapt from the amphtracs, they sank up to their ankles in the soft ash. Meanwhile, Japanese artillery began to pound the invaders.

The marines crawled inland, using flame-throwers and explosives to attack the Japanese bunkers. More than 6,800 marines were killed capturing the island. Admiral Nimitz later wrote that, on Iwo Jima, "uncommon valor was a common virtue."

Firebombing Japan

While American engineers prepared air-fields on Iwo Jima, General Curtis LeMay, commander of the B-29s based in the Marianas, decided to change strategy. To help the B-29s hit their targets, he ordered them to drop bombs filled with **napalm**—a kind of jellied gasoline. The bombs were designed not only to explode but also to start fires. Even if the B-29s missed their targets, the fires they started would spread to the intended targets.

The use of firebombs was very controversial because the fires would also kill civilians; however, LeMay could think of no other way to destroy Japan's war production quickly. Loaded with firebombs, B-29s attacked Tokyo on March 9, 1945. As strong winds fanned the flames, the firestorm grew so intense that it sucked the oxygen out of the air, asphyxiating thousands. As one survivor later recalled:

PRIMARY SOURCE

"The fires were incredible . . . with flames leaping hundreds of feet into the air. . . . With every passing moment the air became more foul. . . the noise was a continuing crashing roar. . . . Fire-winds filled with burning particles rushed up and down the streets. I watched people . . . running for their lives. . . . The flames raced after them like living things, striking them down. . . . Wherever I turned my eyes, I saw people . . . seeking air to breathe."

—quoted in *New History of World War II*

W **Writing Support**

Descriptive Writing Have students use the details from the text and what they have seen in the movies to write a description of the landing at Iwo Jima from a news reporter's point of view. Allow students to work in groups. **OL**

C **Critical Thinking**

Defending The military started using weapons that were designed to destroy more than military targets. Civilians would be killed. Using napalm was controversial, both in World War II and Vietnam. Have a student read the Primary Source aloud. Then, lead a discussion about the use of such weapons. Write major ideas on the board. **OL**

Analyzing **TIME LINES**

Answers:
1. March 9, 1945
2. three days

September 2, 1945
The Japanese delegation boards the battleship USS *Missouri* in Tokyo Bay for the official surrender ceremony

August 9, 1945
A second atomic bomb is dropped on Japan, destroying the city of Nagasaki

August 1945

August 6, 1945
An atomic bomb destroys the Japanese city of Hiroshima

Analyzing **TIME LINES**
1. **Listing** When was Tokyo destroyed?
2. **Sequencing** How many days lapsed between the dropping of the first and second atomic bombs?

Chapter 14 America and World War II **521**

Additional Support

Activity: Interdisciplinary Connection

Science The B-29s that attacked Tokyo dropped almost 2,000 tons of incendiaries. Large portions of the city were destroyed and nearly 100,000 civilians died. Since many residential areas were constructed from wood, the fires spread quickly. The air filled with lethal gases, superheating the atmosphere, and the firestorm that occurred was like a hurricane of fire. Ten square miles of Tokyo was completely destroyed. Have students write a report that describes the physics behind this phenomenon. Encourage students to use a visual graphic. **AL**

The Tokyo firebombing killed more than 80,000 people and destroyed more than 250,000 buildings. By the end of June 1945, Japan's six most important industrial cities had been fire-bombed, destroying almost half of their total urban area. By the end of the war, the B-29s had firebombed 67 Japanese cities.

The Invasion of Okinawa

Despite the massive damage the firebombing caused, there were few signs in the spring of 1945 that Japan was ready to quit. Many American officials believed the Japanese would not surrender until Japan had been invaded. To prepare for the invasion, the United States needed a base near Japan to stockpile supplies and build up troops. Iwo Jima was small and still too far away. Military planners chose Okinawa—only 350 miles (563 km) from Japan.

American troops landed on Okinawa on April 1, 1945. Instead of defending the beaches, the Japanese troops took up positions in the island's rugged mountains. To dig the Japanese out of their caves and bunkers, the Americans had to fight their way up steep slopes against constant machine gun and artillery fire. More than 12,000 American soldiers, sailors, and marines died during the fighting, but by June 22, 1945, Okinawa had finally been captured.

The Terms for Surrender

Shortly after the United States captured Okinawa, the Japanese emperor urged his government to find a way to end the war. The biggest problem was the American demand for unconditional surrender. Many Japanese leaders were willing to surrender, but on one condition: the emperor had to stay in power.

American officials knew that the fate of the emperor was the most important issue for the Japanese. Most Americans, however, blamed the emperor for the war and wanted him removed from power. President Truman was reluctant to go against public opinion. Furthermore, he knew the United States was almost ready to test a new weapon that might force Japan to surrender without any conditions. The new weapon was the atomic bomb.

The Manhattan Project

In 1939 Leo Szilard, one of the world's top physicists, learned that German scientists had split the uranium atom. Szilard had been the first scientist to suggest that splitting the atom might release enormous energy. Worried that the Nazis were working on an atomic bomb, Szilard convinced the world's best-known physicist, Albert Einstein, to sign a letter Szilard had drafted and send it to President Roosevelt. In the letter, Einstein warned that by using uranium, "extremely powerful bombs of a new type may . . . be constructed."

Roosevelt responded by setting up a scientific committee to study the issue. The committee remained skeptical until 1941, when they met with British scientists who were already working on an atomic bomb. The British research so impressed the Americans that they

Debates IN HISTORY

Should America Drop the Atomic Bomb on Japan?

More than 60 years later, people continue to debate what some historians have called the most important event of the twentieth century—President Truman's order to drop atomic bombs on Japan. Did his momentous decision shorten the war and save American lives, as Truman contended, or was it a barbaric and unnecessary show of superior military technology designed to keep the Soviet Union out of Japan?

Extending the Content

The Bombing of Hiroshima Historians continue this debate, more than 60 years after the bombing. Some historians say the bombing was avoidable and find its use similar to Nazi war crimes. Their argument is that the U.S. could have used blockades, conventional bombing, and waited for the Soviet Union to declare war on the Japanese to force the Japanese to surrender.

On the other side, historians feel that the use of the bomb was a necessary choice. They claim that if the Americans had to invade Japan, the number of American casualties would have been higher than those who died at Hiroshima. Another argument was that the second bomb wasn't necessary. Truman should have waited a few days longer to allow the Japanese to surrender.

convinced Roosevelt to begin a program to build an atomic bomb.

The secret American program to build an atomic bomb was code-named the **Manhattan Project** and was headed by General Leslie R. Groves. The first breakthrough came in 1942, when Szilard and Enrico Fermi, another physicist, built the world's first **nuclear** reactor at the University of Chicago. Groves then organized a team of engineers and scientists to build an atomic bomb at a secret laboratory in Los Alamos, New Mexico. J. Robert Oppenheimer led the team. On July 16, 1945, they detonated the world's first atomic bomb in New Mexico.

Hiroshima and Nagasaki

Even before the bomb was tested, American officials began debating how to use it. Admiral William Leahy, chairman of the Joint Chiefs of Staff, opposed using the bomb because it killed civilians indiscriminately. He believed an economic blockade and conventional bombing would convince Japan to surrender. Secretary of War Henry Stimson wanted to warn the Japanese about the bomb while at the same time telling them that they could keep the emperor if they surrendered. Secretary of State James Byrnes, however, wanted to drop the bomb without any warning to shock Japan into surrendering.

President Truman later wrote that he "regarded the bomb as a military weapon and never had any doubts that it should be used." His advisers had warned him to expect massive casualties if the United States invaded Japan. Truman believed it was his duty as president to use every weapon available to save American lives.

Debates IN HISTORY

YES

Harry S. Truman
President of the United States

PRIMARY SOURCE

"The world will note that the first atomic bomb was dropped on Hiroshima, a military base. . . . If Japan does not surrender, bombs will have to be dropped on her war industries and, unfortunately, thousands of civilian lives will be lost. . . .

Having found the bomb we have used it. We have used it against those who attacked us without warning at Pearl Harbor, against those who have starved and beaten and executed American prisoners of war, against those who have abandoned all pretense of obeying international laws of warfare. We have used it in order to shorten the agony of war, in order to save the lives of thousands and thousands of young Americans."

—from *Public Papers of the Presidents*

NO

William Leahy
Chairman of the Joint Chiefs of Staff

PRIMARY SOURCE

"It is my opinion that the use of this barbarous weapon at Hiroshima and Nagasaki was of no material assistance in our war against Japan. The Japanese were already defeated and ready to surrender because of the effective sea blockade and the successful bombing with conventional weapons. . . .

The lethal possibilities of atomic warfare in the future are frightening. My own feeling was that in being the first to use it, we had adopted an ethical standard common to the barbarians of the Dark Ages. I was not taught to make war in that fashion, and wars cannot be won by destroying women and children."

—from *I Was There*

DBQ Document-Based Questions

1. **Explaining** What reasons does Truman offer to justify the use of the atomic bomb?
2. **Summarizing** Why does Leahy say he was against using the bomb?
3. **Evaluating** Whom do you think makes the more persuasive argument? Explain your answer.

D Differentiated Instruction

Naturalist In July, 1945, atomic tests were also conducted on Bikini Island in the Pacific Ocean. Have students research atomic testing at Bikini Island and create a poster that describes the effects the bomb had on the environment. **OL**

Answers:
1. recompense for the Japanese attacking Pearl Harbor without warning; starving and executing American prisoners of war; refusing to obey international laws of warfare. He also said it would save thousands of American lives.
2. He said the Japanese were already defeated and ready to surrender and that such a lethal weapon is barbaric. It is not honorable for warriors to use such weapons.
3. Responses will vary.

Additional Support

Activity: Collaborative Learning

Summarizing Once the atomic bombs were dropped on Hiroshima and Nagasaki, it was obvious that international controls on atomic weapons and energy were necessary. Who would be able to objectively monitor atomic weapons? In 1946, the United States, who at the time held the secret to atomic bombs, asked the United Nations to establish these controls. Have students work in small groups to research the decision the United Nations made to call for an elimination of atomic weapons and weapons of mass destruction. **Ask:** How was the arms control decision received by the nations, particulary the United States and Russia? Have students write a summary of the UN's resolution, and have them speculate on why no atomic bombs have been used since Hiroshima and Nagasaki. **OL**

C1 Critical Thinking

Evaluating Ask students if they, like Truman, would have threatened to use the bomb. **Ask:** How far would you have gone to end the war in the Pacific? **OL**

C2 Critical Thinking

Speculating Ask: When the Japanese saw the power of the atomic bomb, why do you think they did not surrender? *(Students may suggest that they thought it might be a one-time incident, or perhaps they were so shocked, they could not respond.)* **OL**

✓ Reading Check

Answer:
the potentially massive casualties involved in a ground invasion of Japan and his duty to save American lives

DBQ Document Based Questions

Answers:
1. 21
2. Without the basic human rights listed earlier, an education is worthless.
3. Responses will vary.

Additional Support

The Allies threatened Japan with "prompt and utter destruction" if the nation did not surrender, but the Japanese did not reply. Truman then ordered the military to drop the bomb. On August 6, 1945, a B-29 bomber named *Enola Gay* dropped an atomic bomb, code-named "Little Boy," on Hiroshima, an important industrial city.

C1 The bomb destroyed about 63 percent of the city. Between 80,000 and 120,000 people died instantly, and thousands more died later from burns and radiation sickness. Three days later, on August 9, the Soviet Union declared war on Japan. Later that day, the United States dropped another atomic bomb, code-named "Fat Man," on the city of Nagasaki, killing between 35,000 and 74,000 people.

C2 Faced with such massive destruction and the shock of the Soviets joining the war, the Japanese emperor ordered his government to surrender. On August 15, 1945—**V-J Day**—Japan surrendered. The long war was over.

✓ **Reading Check** **Analyzing** What arguments did Truman consider when deciding whether to use the atomic bomb?

PRIMARY SOURCE
Plans for a Better World

▲ The Nuremberg trials

DBQ Document-Based Questions

1. **Identifying** Which right relates to free elections?
2. **Speculating** Why do you think that the right to an education might be so far down on the list?
3. **Evaluating** Which five of the human rights included in the Declaration do you feel are the most important today? Why?

Building a New World

MAIN Idea The victorious Allies tried to create an organization to prevent future wars.

HISTORY AND YOU What are some of your most noble goals? Read to learn about the goals of the Allied forces after the war.

Well before the war ended, President Roosevelt had begun thinking about what the world would be like after the war. The president had wanted to ensure that war would never again engulf the world.

Creating the United Nations

President Roosevelt believed that a new international political organization could prevent another world war. In 1944, at the Dumbarton Oaks estate in Washington, D.C., delegates from 39 countries met to discuss the new organization, which was to be called the **United Nations** (UN). The delegates at the conference agreed that the UN would have a General Assembly, in which every member

The Universal Declaration of Human Rights
Issued by the United Nations, December 10, 1948

1. All human beings are born free and equal in dignity and rights.
3. Everyone has the right to life, liberty, and security of person.
4. No one shall be held in slavery or servitude . . .
5. No one shall be subjected to torture or to cruel, inhuman or degrading treatment or punishment.
7. All are equal before the law and are entitled without any discrimination to equal protection of the law.
11. Everyone charged with a penal offense has the right to be presumed innocent until proved guilty . . .
13. Everyone has the right to freedom of movement . . .
16. Men and women . . . are entitled to equal rights as to marriage, during marriage and at its dissolution . . .
17. Everyone has the right to own property . . .
18. Everyone has the right to freedom of thought, conscience and religion . . .
19. Everyone has the right to freedom of opinion and expression . . .
20. Everyone has the right to freedom of peaceful assembly and association.
21. The will of the people . . . shall be expressed in periodic and genuine elections which shall be by universal and equal suffrage . . .
23. Everyone has the right to work . . .
25. Everyone has the right to a standard of living adequate for the health and well-being of himself and of his family, including food, clothing, housing and medical care and necessary social services, and the right to security in the event of unemployment, sickness, disability, widowhood, old age or other lack of livelihood . . .
26. Everyone has the right to education . . .

524 Chapter 14 America and World War II

Activity: Interdisciplinary Connection

Health Assign students to small groups. Have them use the library or Internet to research the kind of short- and long-term heath problems the Japanese people suffered after the atomic bomb was dropped. Students should research the different kinds of radiation sickness and how long the effects lasted. Students may also include information about how food, especially crops and livestock, were affected and the consequences of eating contaminated food. **OL**

nation in the world would have one vote. The UN would also have a Security Council with 11 members. Five countries would be permanent members of the Security Council: Britain, France, China, the Soviet Union, and the United States—the five big powers that had led the fight against the Axis. These five permanent members would each have veto power.

On April 25, 1945, representatives from 50 countries came to San Francisco to officially organize the United Nations and design its **charter,** or constitution. The General Assembly was given the power to vote on resolutions, to choose the non-permanent members of the Security Council, and to vote on the UN's budget. The Security Council was responsible for international peace and security. It could investigate any international problem and propose settlements. It could also take action to preserve the peace, including asking its members to use military force to uphold a UN resolution.

Soon after its founding, the UN created a Commission on Human Rights and chose Eleanor Roosevelt to serve as its first chair. The Commission drafted the Universal Declaration of Human Rights, and the UN issued it in 1948. The document strongly reflects the ideas and principles that Eleanor Roosevelt espoused during her life. It lists 30 rights that are said to be universally applicable to all human beings in all societies.

Putting the Enemy on Trial

Although the Allies had declared their intention to punish German and Japanese leaders for war crimes, they did not work out the details until the summer of 1945. In August, the United States, Britain, France, and the Soviet Union created the International Military Tribunal (IMT). The Tribunal held trials in Nuremberg, Germany, where Hitler had staged Nazi Party rallies.

Twenty-two leaders of Nazi Germany were prosecuted at the **Nuremberg Trials.** Three were acquitted and seven were given prison sentences. The remaining 12 were sentenced to death. Trials of lower-ranking officials and military officers continued until April 1949. Those trials led to the execution of 24 more German leaders. Another 107 were given prison sentences.

Similar trials were held in Tokyo. The IMT for the Far East charged 25 Japanese leaders with war crimes. Significantly, the Allies did not indict the Japanese emperor. They feared that any attempt to put him on trial would lead to an uprising by the Japanese people. Eighteen Japanese defendants were sentenced to prison. The rest were sentenced to death by hanging.

The war crimes trials punished many of the people responsible for World War II and the Holocaust, but they were also part of the American plan for building a better world. As Robert Jackson, chief counsel for the United States at Nuremberg, observed in his opening statement to the court: "The wrongs we seek to condemn and punish have been so calculated, so malignant and so devastating, that civilization cannot tolerate their being ignored because it cannot survive their being repeated."

Reading Check Describing How is the United Nations organized?

Section 5 REVIEW

Vocabulary
1. **Explain** the significance of: hedgerow, Battle of the Bulge, V-E Day, Harry S. Truman, Iwo Jima, napalm, Manhattan Project, V-J Day, United Nations, charter, Nuremberg Trials.

Main Ideas
2. **Explaining** What was the significance of the Battle of the Bulge?

3. **Identifying** What was the advantage of using napalm bombs?

4. **Synthesizing** How was the United Nations designed to prevent global wars?

Critical Thinking
5. **Big Ideas** If you had been a member of President Truman's cabinet, what advice would you have given him about dropping the atomic bomb?

6. **Organizing** Using a graphic organizer like the one below, indicate the steps to victory in Europe and over Japan. Add boxes as needed.

```
          Allied Victory
         /              \
Victory in Europe    Victory over Japan
     |                     |
```

7. **Analyzing Visuals** Look at the photo of the Japanese delegation on page 521. What do you observe about the scene?

Writing About History
8. **Descriptive Writing** Imagine that you are in a large American city when news of victory over Japan comes. Describe the celebrations and the mood of the people.

History ONLINE
Study Central™ To review this section, go to glencoe.com and click on Study Central.

525

Reading Check

Answer:
a General Assembly of all member nations and an 11-member Security Council with five permanent members, each of whom has veto power over UN actions

Assess

History ONLINE

Study Central™ provides summaries, interactive games, and online graphic organizers to help students review content.

Close

Identifying Central Issues
Have students work in groups to create a collage that illustrates the major battles that ended World War II. Then have them write several paragraphs that explain the images on their collage. **OL**

Section 5 REVIEW

Answers

1. All definitions can be found in the section and in the Glossary.

2. It weakened the German military enough to allow the Allies to enter Germany.

3. The bombs did not have to hit exact targets. The fires would spread and cause general destruction.

4. If all nations were under the surveillance of an international organization, a country would be less likely to start a war. The Security Council can investigate international problems, propose settlements, and send military forces to uphold a resolution.

5. Answers will vary but should be defensible.

6.

```
          Allied Victory
         /              \
Victory in Europe    Victory over Japan
     |                     |
Battle of the     Battle of Iwo Jima, bombing
Bulge, entry      of Tokyo, invasion of
into Germany      Okinawa; atomic bomb in
                  Hiroshima and Nagasaki
```

7. The Japanese look proud but also somber and defeated. The scene looks very formal.

8. Descriptions will vary but should reflect the exuberance and relief of the people.

Chapter 14 VISUAL SUMMARY

Categorizing Have students create a cluster diagram to list the major campaigns the United States fought in the Pacific and in Europe. **OL**

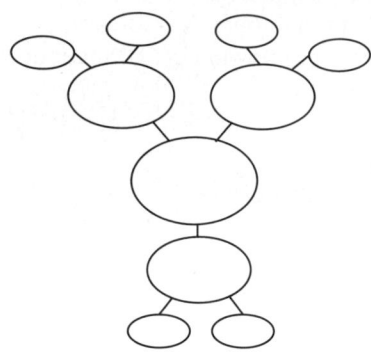

Cause and Effect Have students list and describe five effects World War II had on the social lives of Americans. Then have them list and describe three effects the war had on the economy. **AL**

The Pacific

1941
- Japan attacks Pearl Harbor, Dec. 7

1942
- The United States defeats Japan in the Battles of the Coral Sea and Midway

1943
- The United States begins its island-hopping campaign

1944
- The United States retakes the Philippines

1945
- The United States drops the atomic bomb; Japan surrenders on August 15

Europe and North Africa

1941
- Germany invades the Soviet Union

1942
- The Allies turn the tide in the Battle of the Atlantic

1943
- The Allies invade Italy; German forces in North Africa and Stalingrad surrender to Allies

1944
- The Allies invade Normandy on June 6

1945
- Germany surrenders unconditionally on May 7

The Home Front

1941
- President Roosevelt forbids race discrimination in defense industries

1942
- Congress establishes WAAC; War Department relocates Japanese Americans to internment camps

1943
- Race riots occur in Detroit and Los Angeles; Roosevelt establishes OWM

1944
- Supreme Court hears case of *Korematsu* v. *United States*

1945
- Nearly 40 nations sign the United Nations charter

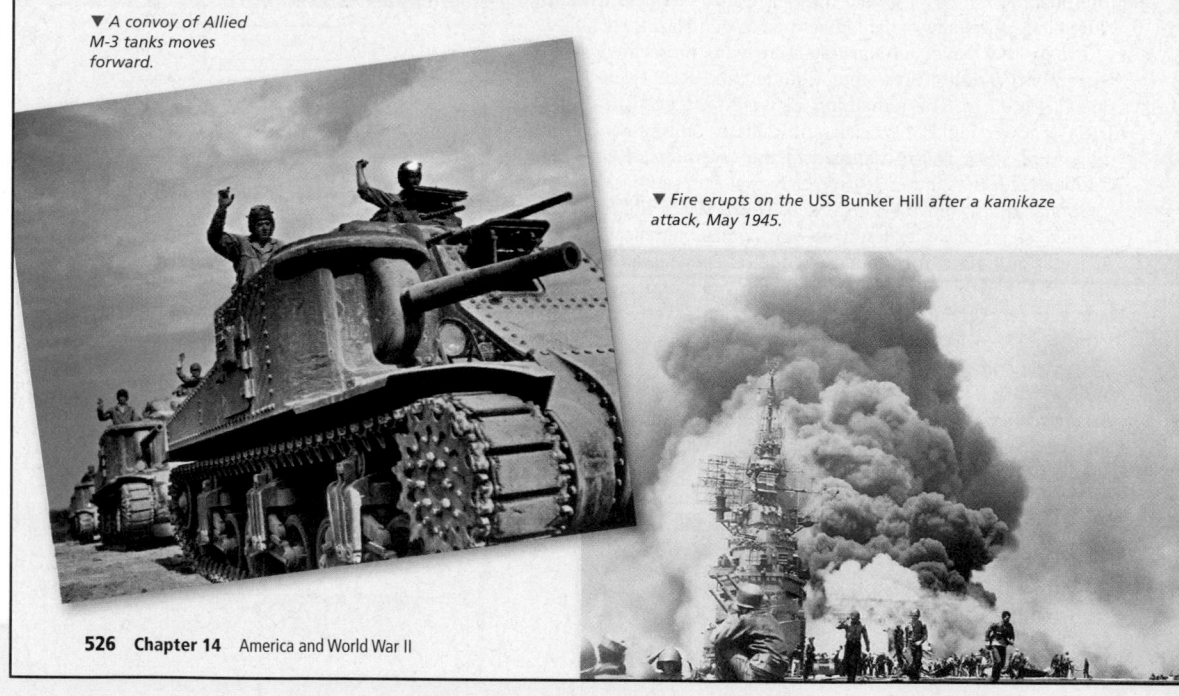

▼ *A convoy of Allied M-3 tanks moves forward.*

▼ *Fire erupts on the USS Bunker Hill after a kamikaze attack, May 1945.*

526 **Chapter 14** America and World War II

Hands-On Chapter Project
Step 6: Wrap Up

An Interview with a World War II Veteran

Step 6: Wrap Up Students will review the presentations and provide an evaluation of their work.

Directions Students follow up their presentations with a self-evaluation of both the project and their work on it. Students should write a brief essay that answers the questions to the right.

- What was the most difficult part of this project? Why?
- What was the best part of this project? Why?
- What could be done to improve the presentation?
- What did I learn about World War II by completing this project?

Putting It Together Students should provide clear essays and succinct answers to each question above. **OL**

ASSESSMENT

STANDARDIZED TEST PRACTICE

TEST-TAKING

Look at each question to find clues to support your answer. Try not to get confused by the wording of the question. Then look for an answer that best fits the question.

Reviewing Vocabulary

Directions: Choose the word or words that best complete the sentence.

1. One complaint of African Americans at the beginning of World War II was that they were
   A integrated.
   B employed.
   C empowered.
   D disenfranchised.

2. Winston Churchill wanted to attack the _____, or edges, of the German Empire.
   A eastern front
   B periphery
   C left flank
   D western front

3. To aid in the war effort, American citizens accepted the _____ of some items.
   A rationing
   B disappearance
   C abundance
   D commandeering

4. Japanese suicide pilots were known as _____ pilots.
   A Shinto
   B Samurai
   C kamikaze
   D amphtrac

Reviewing Main Ideas

Directions: Choose the best answers to the following questions.

Section 1 (pp. 486–493)

5. The Liberty ship was superior to many warships because it was
   A welded instead of riveted.
   B riveted instead of welded.
   C painted in camouflage colors.
   D painted red, white, and blue.

6. African Americans pushed for a _____ victory in the war effort.
   A Tuskegee
   B Triple C
   C Double V
   D Carver

Section 2 (pp. 494–499)

7. The Japanese were determined to destroy the American fleet in the Pacific after
   A they were successful at Pearl Harbor.
   B the Americans surrendered at Bataan.
   C the crew of the *Enola Gay* dropped an atomic bomb on Hiroshima.
   D James Doolittle dropped bombs on Tokyo.

8. To prevent huge shipping losses in the Atlantic, Americans used
   A antisubmarine devices.
   B a convoy system.
   C an air force escort.
   D minesweepers.

Need Extra Help?								
If You Missed Questions . . .	1	2	3	4	5	6	7	8
Go to Page . . .	491	497	506	515	489	492	495–496	499

Chapter 14 America and World War II **527**

Answers and Analyses
Reviewing Vocabulary

1. D Enfranchised means "given the right to vote." The prefix dis- means absence of, deprived of, or not. Therefore, disenfranchised means deprived of the right to vote.

2. B Periphery means edges. Help students remember this by discussing or explaining peripheral vision. Make sure students read vocabulary questions carefully, because often, as in this case, the definition is given in the question.

3. A *C* does not make sense. Students may be distracted by *B,* by equating disappearing with scarcity. Items were not taken over, they were just not available in abundance. Ration means to distribute or allocate. In this case, scarce items were rationed so as not to waste them and so everyone, theoretically, could have some.

4. C Shinto is a religion. Samurai are Japanese warriors who lived by the code of Bushido. They are not pilots. Amphtracs were military vehicles involved in Pacific invasions.

Reviewing Main Ideas

5. A *C* and *D* do not make sense; how a ship is painted would not make it superior to other ships. Welding is the melding of metals with heat. Welded ships required fewer repairs.

6. C Students may be confused by choice *B.* An easy way for students to remember double V is to relate the two As in African American to the double (two) in double V.

7. D If students have trouble with this question, review "Japan Changes Strategy" on page 495. The Japanese decided to destroy the American fleet after they realized the bombs dropped on Tokyo might have killed the emperor. The other answer choices do not make sense, chronologically.

8. B In a convoy, cargo ships traveled with warships, which cut down on losses. It is important that students read the question carefully. The key words in the question are shipping losses.

9. B One meaning of drive, as a noun, is a collection effort. Students are probably familiar with clothing and food drives. Victory gardens, rationing, and war bonds were all ways that citizens could support the war effort, but none involved collecting materials.

10. A Study a map with students who have trouble with this question. Only Sicily is near Italy. Have students identify each answer choice on the map so they can see that, clearly, invading Sicily would most help move troops into Italy.

11. C The D-Day invasion involved amphibious landings on the beaches of the French coastline. Therefore, weather was a huge concern.

12. A This code name is something students must simply commit to memory. Thinking of the building of the bomb as a science project may help trigger students' memories. In addition, the other answer choices all describe military action. Only *A* implies a plan to build something, rather than attack something.

13. B By process of elimination, only *B* can be correct. The Soviet Union had already been involved. *C* is too broad; it is not likely that this was the first successful invasion by sea in all of history. Geographically, *D* does not make sense.

Section 3 *(pp. 500–507)*

9. What did the United States do to encourage the collection of materials that could be used in the war effort?
   A victory gardens
   B scrap drives
   C rationing
   D war bonds

Section 4 *(pp. 508–515)*

10. Where did the Allies begin their invasion of Italy?
    A Sicily
    B Casablanca
    C Tehran
    D Normandy

11. Planning for D-Day was complicated by concerns for the
    A German army.
    B amphtracs.
    C weather.
    D air forces.

Section 5 *(pp. 518–525)*

12. What was the code name for the plan to build the atomic bomb?
    A Manhattan Project
    B Doolittle Raid
    C Operation Overlord
    D V-J Day

Need Extra Help?							
If You Missed Questions . . .	9	10	11	12	13	14	15
Go to Page . . .	507	509–510	511–512	522–523	510	R15	504

528 Chapter 14 America and World War II

Critical Thinking

Directions: Choose the best answers to the following questions.

13. The invasion of Normandy was important because it
    A brought the Soviet Union into the war.
    B forced the Germans to fight a two-front war.
    C marked the first successful invasion by sea.
    D protected the Pacific fleet.

Base your answer to question 14 on the map below and your knowledge of Chapter 14.

Relocation Camps, 1942–1946

14. Most of the relocation camps were located in what region of the United States?
    A the West
    B the Southeast
    C the Deep South
    D the Midwest

15. What was the purpose of the Japanese American Citizens League?
    A to fight the Japanese invasion of California
    B to fight Roosevelt's order to declare the western United States a military zone
    C to help Japanese Americans recover lost property from the relocation
    D to encourage Japanese Americans to join the U.S. armed forces

GO ON

---

14. A Examine the map with students. The relocation camps are marked by white boxes. It is clear that the majority of the centers were located in the West.

15. C Hopefully, students are able to immediately eliminate *A*, which never took place. The JACL helped Japanese Americans who had been held at the centers get back the property they had owned.

16. Women were able to serve in noncombat positions in the military and in factories at home because

A there were not enough men to fill the positions.

B no one else wanted the jobs.

C people realized it was unfair to keep them out.

D women organized, as they did to win the vote.

Analyze the cartoon and answer the question that follows. Base your answer on the cartoon and on your knowledge of Chapter 14.

Illumination for the Shooting Gallery

17. According to the cartoon, why were Americans encouraged to turn out their lights?

A The British could use the lights to create a blockade.

B The lights prevented American ships from seeing the British ships.

C The lights provided a silhouette for ships, making them targets for German submarines.

D The lights used too much electricity, creating city-wide blackouts.

Document-Based Questions

Directions: Analyze the document and answer the short-answer questions that follow the document.

Many historians believe that the civil rights movement of the 1950s and 1960s had its roots in the "Double V" campaign and the march on Washington. Alexander Allen, a member of the Urban League during the war, believed that World War II was a turning point for African Americans.

> *"Up to that point the doors to industrial and economic opportunity were largely closed. Under the pressure of war, the pressures of government policy, the pressures of world opinion, the pressures of blacks themselves and their allies, all this began to change. . . .The war forced the federal government to take a stronger position with reference to discrimination, and things began to change as a result. There was a tremendous attitudinal change that grew out of the war. There had been a new experience for blacks, and many weren't willing to go back to the way it was before."*
>
> —quoted in *Wartime America*

18. How did the war change the status of African Americans in American society?

19. Why do you think the war forced the government to take a stronger position on discrimination in the workplace?

Extended Response

20. At the end of World War I, President Wilson asked Congress to join the League of Nations, but the United States did not join. As World War II ended, the United States hosted a conference to create another International organization, the United Nations. Discuss what had changed so that the American people were willing to participate in the United Nations. Also discuss the likelihood of the UN succeeding. Write an essay that supports your answer with relevant facts, examples, and details.

For additional test practice, use Self-Check Quizzes—Chapter 14 at glencoe.com.

Need Extra Help?					
If You Missed Questions . . .	16	17	18	19	20
Go to Page . . .	501	R18	R19	R19	522–525

Document-Based Questions

18. The new positions and roles African Americans played in industry and the military changed attitudes about African Americans and caused the federal government to take a stronger position on discrimination. The experiences of African Americans made many unwilling to go back to life as it was before the war.

19. Answers will vary. Accept any reasonable, focused answer.

Extended Response

20. Essays must demonstrate an understanding of the motivations behind the refusal of the U.S. to join the League of Nations and motivations to create the United Nations, including the realization that isolationism as practiced between the wars would not work as a means of keeping world peace.

---

16. A When men left for war, they left behind many open positions that needed to be filled. So many men were away at war, that women had to take their places in the workforce. After the war, women lost their jobs as returning men took them over.

17. C In the foreground, a submarine can be seen with its periscope pointed toward the New York skyline (it can be identified by the flag). The glowing lights of the city illuminate the American ships, so the submarine could attack the ships. The message is, turn out your lights to keep us safe.

Have students visit the Web site at glencoe.com to review Chapter 14 and take the Self-Check Quiz.

Need Extra Help?

Have students refer to the pages listed if they miss any of the questions.

Key to Ability Levels
- BL Below Level
- OL On Level
- AL Above Level
- ELL English Language Learners

Key to Teaching Resources
- Print Material
- CD-ROM
- DVD
- Transparency

Levels (BL OL AL ELL)		Resources	Chapter Opener	Section 1	Section 2	Section 3	Section 4	Chapter Assess
FOCUS								
BL OL AL ELL	🖋	Daily Focus Transparencies		15-1	15-2	15-3	15-4	
TEACH								
OL AL	📁	History Simulations and Problem Solving, URB			p. 9			
BL OL AL ELL	📁	Reading Essentials and Note-Taking Guide*		p. 161	p. 164	p. 167	p. 170	
BL OL ELL	📁	Reading Skills Activity, URB			p. 89			
OL	📁	Historical Analysis Skills Activity, URB				p. 90		
BL OL ELL	📁	Guided Reading Activity, URB*		p. 116	p. 117	p. 118	p. 119	
BL OL AL ELL	📁	Differentiated Instruction Activity, URB				p. 91		
BL OL ELL	📁	English Learner Activity, URB			p. 93			
BL OL AL ELL	📁	Content Vocabulary Activity, URB*	p. 95					
BL OL AL ELL	📁	Academic Vocabulary Activity, URB	p. 97					
OL AL	📁	Reinforcing Skills Activity, URB			p. 99			
OL AL	📁	Critical Thinking Skills Activity, URB			p. 100			
BL OL ELL	📁	Time Line Activity, URB						p. 101
OL	📁	Linking Past and Present Activity, URB				p. 102		
BL OL AL ELL	📁	Primary Source Reading, URB				p. 105	p. 103	
BL OL AL ELL	📁	American Art and Music Activity, URB						p. 107
BL OL AL ELL	📁	Interpreting Political Cartoons Activity, URB				p. 109		
AL	📁	Enrichment Activity, URB					p. 113	
BL OL AL ELL	📁	Differentiated Instruction for the American History Classroom	✓	✓	✓	✓	✓	✓
BL OL AL ELL	🖋	Unit Map Overlay Transparencies	✓	✓	✓	✓	✓	✓
BL OL AL ELL	📁	Unit Time Line Transparencies, Strategies, and Activities	✓	✓	✓	✓	✓	✓
BL OL AL ELL	📁	Cause and Effect Transparencies, Strategies, and Activities	✓	✓	✓	✓	✓	✓
BL OL AL ELL	📁	Why It Matters Chapter Transparencies, Strategies, and Activities	✓	✓	✓	✓	✓	✓

Note: Please refer to the *Unit 5 Resource Book* for this chapter's URB materials.

* Also available in Spanish

- Interactive Lesson Planner
- Interactive Teacher Edition
- Fully editable blackline masters
- Section Spotlight Videos Launch
- Differentiated Lesson Plans
- Printable reports of daily assignments
- Standards Tracking System

| Levels | | | | | Resources | Chapter Opener | Section 1 | Section 2 | Section 3 | Section 4 | Chapter Assess |
BL	OL	AL	ELL								
TEACH (continued)											
BL	OL	AL		📁	Supreme Court Case Studies				pp. 69, 75, 77		
BL	OL	AL	ELL	📁	The Living Constitution	✓	✓	✓	✓	✓	✓
BL	OL	AL	ELL	📁	American Issues	✓	✓	✓	✓	✓	✓
	OL	AL	ELL	📁	American Art and Architecture Transparencies, Strategies, and Activities	✓	✓	✓	✓	✓	✓
BL	OL	AL		📁	High School American History Literature Library	✓	✓	✓	✓	✓	✓
	OL	AL		💿	American History Primary Source Documents Library	✓	✓	✓	✓	✓	✓
BL	OL	AL	ELL	💿	American Music: Hits Through History CD	✓	✓	✓	✓	✓	✓
BL	OL	AL	ELL	💿	StudentWorks™ Plus DVD	✓	✓	✓	✓	✓	✓
BL	OL	AL	ELL	💿	Vocabulary PuzzleMaker CD-ROM	✓	✓	✓	✓	✓	✓
BL	OL	AL	ELL	💿	*The American Vision* Video Program DVD	✓	✓	✓	✓	✓	✓
Teacher Resources				📁	Reading Strategies and Activities for the Social Studies Classroom	✓	✓	✓	✓	✓	✓
				📁	Strategies for Success	✓	✓	✓	✓	✓	✓
				💿	Presentation Plus! DVD	✓	✓	✓	✓	✓	
				📁	Success With English Learners	✓	✓	✓	✓	✓	✓
ASSESS											
BL	OL	AL	ELL	📁	Section Quizzes and Chapter Tests*		p. 211	p. 212	p. 213	p. 214	p. 215
BL	OL	AL	ELL	📁	Authentic Assessment With Rubrics						p. 35
BL	OL	AL	ELL	📁	Standardized Test Practice Workbook						p. 34
BL	OL	AL	ELL	💿	*ExamView®* Assessment Suite CD-ROM		15-1	15-2	15-3	15-4	Ch. 15
BL	OL	AL	ELL	💿	Interactive Tutor Self-Assessment CD-ROM		15-1	15-2	15-3	15-4	Ch. 15
CLOSE											
BL			ELL	📁	Reteaching Activity, URB						p. 111
BL	OL		ELL	📁	Reading and Study Skills Foldables™	pp. 75–76					
BL	OL	AL	ELL	📁	American History in Graphic Novel				p. 57		

Online Jumble Puzzles

Technology Product

Glencoe's Vocabulary PuzzleMaker™ 3.1 CD-ROM is an easy-to-use program that lets you create your own puzzles based on the glossary for classroom use. The PuzzleMaker allows you to

- create jumble puzzles based on content vocabulary and academic vocabulary that is specific to what is taught in the classroom;
- create online (LAN-based or local area network) or paper jumble puzzles.

Objectives

After students complete the jumble puzzles, they will be able to

- recall and identify scrambled terms with the help of clues;
- reinforce their understanding of the vocabulary.

Steps

- Run PuzzleMaker™ 3.1. On the main menu, click on Create a New Puzzle.
- From the list of *Puzzle Databases*, select the appropriate database for the vocabulary.
- The *PuzzleMaker Wizard* will take you through selecting a puzzle type and grid type.
- Then select one or more chapters from the list. Indicate whether you want the words selected randomly or manually.
- Select the language and words you wish to use within the maximum for the puzzle. Click Finish.
- Save your jumble puzzle to a location that is easily accessible by your students with PuzzlePlayer™ 3.1, or print copies for your students to complete.
- Use PuzzlePlayer™ 3.1 to review the puzzles after your students have worked on and saved them.

History ONLINE

	Student	Teacher	Parent
Beyond the Textbook	●	●	●
Chapter Overviews	●	●	●
Time Current Events	●		●
ePuzzles and Games	●		●
Concepts in Motion	●		●
Literature Connections		●	
Multi-Language Glossaries	●		●
Online Student Edition	●	●	●
Self-Check Quizzes	●		●
Student Web Activities	●		●
Study Central ™	●		●
Teaching Today		●	
Vocabulary eFlashcards	●		●
Web Activity Lesson Plans		●	

Glencoe Media Center

glencoe.com

❭ **Study-To-Go**
- Vocabulary eFlashcards
- Self-Check Quizzes

❭ **Audio/Video**
- Student Edition Audio
- Spanish Summaries
- Section Videos

READING SUPPORT FROM
JAMESTOWN EDUCATION

- **Timed Readings Plus in Social Studies** helps students increase their reading rate and fluency while maintaining comprehension. The 400-word passages are similar to those found on state and national assessments.

- **Reading in the Content Area: Social Studies** concentrates on six essential reading skills that help students better comprehend what they read. The book includes 75 high-interest nonfiction passages written at increasing levels of difficulty.

- **Reading Social Studies** includes strategic reading instruction and vocabulary support in Social Studies content for both ELLs and native speakers of English.

www.jamestowneducation.com

NATIONAL GEOGRAPHIC

Index to National Geographic Magazine:

The following articles relate to this chapter:

- "DMZ Korea's Dangerous Divide," by Tom O'Neill, July 2003.

- "Douglas MacArthur: An American Soldier," by Geoffrey C. Ward and Cary Wolinsky, March 1992.

National Geographic Society Products To order the following, call National Geographic at 1-800-368-2728:

- *ZipZapMap! USA WIndows* (ZipZapMap! USA).

Access National Geographic's new dynamic MapMachine Web site and other geography resources at:
www.nationalgeographic.com
www.nationalgeographic.com/maps

The following videotape programs are available from Glencoe as supplements to Chapter 15:

- Berlin Airlift: The First Battle of the Cold War (ISBN 0-76-701166-X)

- Harry S. Truman: A New View (ISBN 1-56-501449)

To order, call Glencoe at 1-800-334-7344. To find classroom resources to accompany many of these videos, check the following home pages:

A&E Television: www.aetv.com
The History Channel: www.historychannel.com

Reading List Generator CD-ROM

GLENCOE BOOKLINK 3

Use this database to search more than 30,000 titles to create a customized reading list for your students.

- Reading lists can be organized by students' reading level, author, genre, theme, or area of interest.

- The database provides Degrees of Reading Power™ (DRP) and Lexile™ readability scores for all selections.

- A brief summary of each selection is included.

Leveled reading suggestions for this chapter:

For students at a Grade 8 reading level:
- *Joseph McCarthy and the Cold War,* by Victoria Sherrow

For students at a Grade 9 reading level:
- *I Remember Korea: Veterans Tell Their Stories of the Korean War, 1950–53,* by Linda Granfield

For students at a Grade 10 reading level:
- *The Emperor's General: A Novel,* by James Webb

For students at a Grade 11 reading level:
- *Wild Swans: Three Daughters of China,* by Jung Chang

For students at a Grade 12 reading level:
- *Spectacular Space Travelers,* by Jason Richie

Focus

MAKING CONNECTIONS
How Did the Atomic Bomb Change the World?

Ask students to imagine that a new, powerful weapon has been invented by an enemy nation. This new weapon is so powerful that no one, not even its inventor, knows the extent of the damage that the new weapon might cause. Have students explain what feelings they might have about the use of such a weapon and list them on the board. Explain that many Americans grew fearful of the power of the atomic bomb, especially after the Soviet Union developed a bomb of its own. **OL**

The Big Ideas

As students study the chapter, remind them to consider the section-based Big Ideas included in each section's Guide to Reading. The **Essential Questions** in the activities below tie in to the Big Ideas and help students think about and understand important chapter concepts. In addition, the Hands-on Chapter Projects with their culminating activities relate the content from each section to the Big Ideas. These activities build on each other as students progress through the chapter. Section activities culminate in the wrap-up activity on the Visual Summary page.

Chapter 15

The Cold War Begins
1945–1960

SECTION 1 The Origins of the Cold War
SECTION 2 The Early Cold War Years
SECTION 3 The Cold War and American Society
SECTION 4 Eisenhower's Cold War Policies

The world's first nuclear artillery shell is test fired on May 25, 1953. Such tests were common during the early cold war.

U.S. PRESIDENTS

1945
• Franklin Roosevelt dies

Truman
1945–1953

1947
• Truman Doctrine is declared

1948
• Berlin airlift begins

1950
• McCarthy charges that Communists staff the U.S. State Department
• Korean War begins

1953
• Armistice agreement is reached in Korea

Eisenhower
1953–1961

U.S. EVENTS 1945

WORLD EVENTS

1950

March 1945
• Yalta Conference is held to plan postwar world

July 1945
• Potsdam Conference partitions Germany

1948
• State of Israel is created

1949
• Communists take power in China

530 Chapter 15 The Cold War Begins

Section 1

The Origins of the Cold War
Essential Question: How did the Cold War emerge after World War II? *(Relations between the Soviet Union and the other Allies soured as the Soviets set up Communist governments in Eastern Europe.)* Tell students that in this section they will learn how the Cold War began and how it affected American foreign policy. **OL**

Section 2

The Early Cold War Years
Essential Question: How did President Truman attempt to deter Communism? *(Truman authorized billions of dollars of American aid to devastated European nations as well as to the Allies' former enemies, Germany and Japan.)* Tell students that this section will focus on how American policies controlled the spread of Communism during the Cold War. **OL**

MAKING CONNECTIONS

How Did the Atomic Bomb Change the World?

The destructiveness of the atomic bomb raised the stakes in military conflicts. Growing tensions between the United States and the Soviet Union after World War II led to a constant threat of nuclear war.

• *How did the atomic bomb change relations between nations?*

• *Do you think the invention of the atomic bomb made the world safer?*

More About the Photo

Visual Literacy In the 1950s, nuclear tests were regularly carried out above ground. People did not fully understand the dangerous side effects of nuclear fallout. The United States alone has conducted more than 1,000 nuclear tests, some above ground and some below ground. The Test Ban Treaty of 1963 prohibits nuclear weapons tests "or any other nuclear explosion" in the atmosphere, in outer space, and under water. The treaty does not ban underground testing.

FOLDABLES
Study Organizer
Dinah Zike's Foldables

Dinah Zikes' Foldables are three-dimensional, interactive graphic organizers that help students practice basic writing skills, review vocabulary terms, and identify main ideas. Instructions for creating and using Foldables can be found in the Appendix at the end of this book and in the *Dinah Zike's Reading and Study Skills Foldables* booklet.

1960
• U-2 incident occurs

1955   **1960**

1956
• Hungarians rebel against the Communist government

1957
• Soviet Union launches Sputnik

FOLDABLES
Analyzing Causes Make a Two-Tab Book Foldable that lists the long-term and short-term causes of the Cold War. List the information as you read and review the chapter.

Long-Term Causes

Short-Term Causes

Cold War Causes

History ONLINE Chapter Overview
Visit glencoe.com to preview Chapter 15.

Chapter 15   The Cold War Begins   **531**

History ONLINE
Introduce students to chapter content and key terms by having them access the Chapter 15 Overview at glencoe.com.

Section 3

The Cold War and American Society
Essential Question: How did the Cold War change the nation at home? *(People grew fearful of the possibility of Communists infiltrating the U.S. government; others were afraid that the Soviet Union would attack the United States with nuclear weapons).* Tell students that in Section 3 they will learn about how the Cold War affected all parts of American society. **OL**

Section 4

Eisenhower's Cold War Policies
Essential Question: How did Eisenhower's policies address the Cold War issues? *(Eisenhower believed the United States needed a strong economy as well as a strong military; he also used covert operations to prevent Soviet expansion.)* Tell students that in Section 4 they will learn about how President Eisenhower confronted the Soviet Union during the Cold War. **OL**

531

Focus

Bellringer
Daily Focus Transparency 15.1

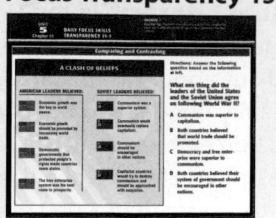

Guide to Reading

Answers:

Conferences	Outcomes
Yalta Conference	Poland's government recognized, free elections for Poland, Declaration of Liberated Europe, Germany divided, German reparations set
Potsdam Conference	German-Polish border established, German reparations to the Soviets reconstructed

Section Spotlight Video

To generate student interest and provide a springboard for class discussion, access the Chapter 15, Section 1 video at glencoe.com or on the video DVD.

Resource Manager

Section 1

The Origins of the Cold War

Guide to Reading

Big Ideas
Government and Society Although World War II was nearly over, personal and political differences among Allied leaders and the peoples they represented led to new global challenges.

Content Vocabulary
- satellite nations (p. 537)
- Iron Curtain (p. 537)

Academic Vocabulary
- liberate (p. 532)
- equipment (p. 534)

People and Events to Identify
- Yalta (p. 532)
- Cold War (p. 534)
- Potsdam (p. 536)

Reading Strategy
Categorizing Complete a graphic organizer similar to the one below by filling in the names of the conferences held among the "Big Three" Allies and the outcomes of each.

Conferences	Outcomes

After the war ended, tensions continued to rise over the amount of freedom the Soviets were going to allow the nations they controlled. Leaders of Britain, the United States, and the Soviet Union held conferences but could not resolve this issue.

The Yalta Conference

MAIN Idea Roosevelt, Churchill, and Stalin met at Yalta to discuss Poland, Germany, and the rights of liberated Europe.

HISTORY AND YOU Do you remember Wilson's idealistic Fourteen Points and how they were changed during negotiations after World War I? Read on to learn how negotiations during and after World War II led to results different from what Roosevelt and Truman wanted.

In February 1945, with the war in Europe almost over, Roosevelt, Churchill, and Stalin met at **Yalta**—a Soviet resort on the Black Sea—to plan the postwar world. Although the conference seemed to go well, several agreements reached at Yalta later played an important role in causing the Cold War.

Poland

The first issue discussed at Yalta was what to do about Poland. Shortly after the Germans invaded Poland, the Polish government fled to Britain. In 1944, however, Soviet troops drove back the Germans and entered Poland. As they **liberated** Poland from German control, the Soviets encouraged Polish Communists to set up a new government. This meant there were now two governments claiming the right to govern Poland: one Communist and one non-Communist.

President Roosevelt and Prime Minister Churchill both argued that the Poles should be free to choose their own government. "This is what we went to war against Germany for," Churchill explained, "that Poland should be free and sovereign."

Stalin quickly responded to Churchill's comments. According to Stalin, because Poland was on the Soviet Union's western border, the need for its government to be friendly was a matter of "life and death" from the Soviet point of view. Every time invaders had entered Russia from the west, they had come through Poland. Eventually, the three leaders compromised. Roosevelt and Churchill agreed to recognize the Polish government set up by the Soviets. Stalin agreed that the government would include members of the prewar Polish government and that free elections would be held as soon as possible.

R	**Reading Strategies**	C	**Critical Thinking**	D	**Differentiated Instruction**	W	**Writing Support**	S	**Skill Practice**

Reading Strategies
Teacher Edition
- Identifying, p. 534
- Det. Importance, p. 536

Additional Resources
- Guided Read., URB p. 116

Critical Thinking
Teacher Edition
- Pred. Consequences, p. 533
- Contrasting, p. 534
- Hypothesizing, p. 535

Additional Resources
- Quizzes/Tests, p. 211

Differentiated Instruction
Teacher Edition
- Visual/Spatial, p. 537

Additional Resources
- Academic Vocab. Act., URB p. 97
- Foldables, pp. 75–76

Writing Support
Teacher Edition
- Personal Writing, p. 534

Additional Resources
- Content Vocab. Act., URB p. 95

Skill Practice
Teacher Edition
- Interpreting a Map, p. 536

Additional Resources
- RENTG, p. 161

PRIMARY SOURCE
The Yalta Conference, 1945

▲ Churchill, Roosevelt, and Stalin at Yalta

The Declaration of Liberated Europe

At Yalta, the Allies issued the Declaration of Liberated Europe. The Soviet Union's failure to uphold the Declaration contributed to the coming of the Cold War. The Declaration contained the following commitments:

• The peoples of Europe will be allowed to create democratic institutions of their own choice, but must destroy all remaining aspects of Nazism and fascism in their societies.

• The United States, Great Britain, and the Soviet Union will help the peoples of Europe to do the following:
  1. Establish peace in their country
  2. Provide aid to people in distress
  3. Form temporary governments that represent all democratic elements of the society and hold free elections to choose a government that responds to the will of the people

• The United States, Great Britain, and the Soviet Union will continue to support the principles expressed in the Atlantic Charter.

NATIONAL GEOGRAPHIC The Division of Germany, 1945

0   100 kilometers
0   100 miles
Albers Equal-Area projection

North Sea
Baltic Sea
POLAND
U.K.
NETH.
Berlin
BELG.
CZECH.
FRANCE
Elbe R.
Rhine R.
Danube R.
SWITZ.
AUSTRIA

Allied Occupation Zones, 1945–1949
- American
- British
- French
- Soviet
- Present-day Germany

0   6 kilometers
0   6 miles
West Berlin
East Berlin

Analyzing VISUALS

1. **Specifying** In the Declaration of Liberated Europe, what three things did the Big Three promise to help the peoples of Europe do?

2. **Locating** In what zone in the divided Germany was Berlin located?

The Declaration of Liberated Europe ⓒ

After reaching a compromise on Poland, Roosevelt, Churchill, and Stalin agreed to issue the Declaration of Liberated Europe. The declaration asserted "the right of all people to choose the form of government under which they will live."

The Allies promised that the people of Europe would be allowed "to create democratic institutions of their own choice." They also promised to create temporary governments that represented "all democratic elements" and pledged "the earliest possible establishment through free elections of governments responsive to the will of the people."

Dividing Germany

After discussing Poland and agreeing to a set of principles for liberating Europe, the conference focused on Germany. Roosevelt, Churchill, and Stalin agreed to divide Germany into four zones. Great Britain, the United States, the Soviet Union, and France would each control one zone. The same four countries would also divide the German capital city of Berlin into four zones, even though it was in the Soviet zone.

Chapter 15 The Cold War Begins **533**

Teach

ⓒ Critical Thinking

Predicting Consequences
Ask: What compromise did Roosevelt, Churchill, and Stalin, reach about Poland? *(Roosevelt and Churchill agreed to accept the Communist government Stalin had set up, and Stalin promised free elections for Poland as soon as possible.)* Based on Stalin's actions, do you think he would honor his word about a liberated Europe? *(probably not; He saw the situation from a "Soviet point of view.")* **OL**

Analyzing VISUALS

Answers:
1. to establish peace in their countries, to provide aid to people in distress, and to form temporary, free governments until a government elected by the people could be formed
2. in the Soviet zone

Additional Support

Activity: Economics Connection

Making Connections Explain to students that after World War II, millions of people were uprooted. After six years of fighting, they had fled their countries, hoping to find a place of refuge. Many large cities were completely devastated, or left in ruins. Have students use library or Internet resources to research the ways in which the United States and Great Britain provided aid to these people in distress. Organize students into three groups to conduct research on the Marshall Plan, the American Red Cross, and UNICEF. Have groups present their findings in a chart showing the main goals of each organization, how aid was given, and the effectiveness of each organization. **OL**

W Writing Support

Personal Writing The Soviets promised that Poland would have free elections, then refused to let the Poles vote. Have students write a journal entry about how they would feel to learn that their country was not liberated and their right to vote was suddenly gone. **OL**

R Reading Strategy

Identifying Ask: What was the Cold War? *(a silent war of hostility and competition between the United States and the Soviet Union.)* **OL**

C Critical Thinking

Contrasting Have students create a T-chart. On one side, have students list Soviet goals after World War II *(to keep Germany weak, to encourage communism in other countries)* and U.S. goals on the other side *(to repair the economies of European countries, to avoid future wars)* **OL**

Additional Support

Although pleased with the decision to divide Germany, Stalin also demanded that Germany pay heavy reparations for the war damage it had caused. Roosevelt agreed, but he insisted reparations be based on Germany's ability to pay. He also suggested, and Stalin agreed, that Germany pay reparations with trade goods and products instead of cash. The Allies would also be allowed to remove industrial machinery, railroad cars, and other **equipment** from Germany as reparations. This decision did not resolve the issue. Over the next few years, arguments about German reparations greatly increased tensions between the United States and the Soviet Union.

Tensions Begin to Rise

The Yalta decisions shaped the expectations of the United States. Two weeks after Yalta, the Soviets pressured the king of Romania into appointing a Communist government. The United States accused the Soviets of violating the Declaration of Liberated Europe.

W Soon afterward, the Soviets refused to allow more than three non-Communist Poles to serve in the 18-member Polish government. There was also no indication that they intended to hold free elections in Poland as promised. On April 1, President Roosevelt informed the Soviets that their actions in Poland were not acceptable.

R Yalta marked a turning point in Soviet-American relations. President Roosevelt had hoped that an Allied victory and the creation of the United Nations would lead to a more peaceful world. Instead, as the war came to an end, the United States and the Soviet Union became increasingly hostile toward each other. This led to an era of confrontation and competition between the two nations that lasted from about 1946 to 1990. This era became known as the **Cold War.**

Soviet Security Concerns

C The tensions between the United States and the Soviet Union led to the Cold War because the two sides had different goals. As the war ended, Soviet leaders became concerned about security. They wanted to keep Germany weak and make sure that the countries between Germany and the Soviet Union were under Soviet control.

Although security concerns influenced their thinking, Soviet leaders were also communists. They believed that communism was a superior economic system that would eventually replace capitalism, and that the Soviet Union should encourage communism in other nations. Soviet leaders also accepted Lenin's theory that capitalist countries would eventually try to destroy communism. This made them suspicious of capitalist nations.

American Economic Issues

While Soviet leaders focused on securing their borders, American leaders focused on economic problems. Many American officials believed that the Depression had caused World War II. Without it, Hitler would never have come to power, and Japan would not have wanted to expand its empire.

Debates IN HISTORY

Did the Soviet Union Cause the Cold War?

Many people have debated who was responsible for the Cold War. Most Americans, including diplomat George Kennan who had served in Russia, believed that it was Soviet ideology and insecurity that brought on the Cold War. On the other side, communist leaders, such as Stalin's adviser Andrei Zhdanov, believed that capitalism and imperialism caused the Cold War.

Activity: Interdisciplinary Connection

Geography Tell students that several nations in Eastern Europe have a long history of being overrun by more powerful nations. Organize students into small groups. Give each group a blank outline map of Eastern Europe today and several overhead transparencies. Have the groups research to show how the boundaries of these countries have changed by creating a series of overlays for the map. Suggest that students show the boundaries at the turn of each century or on other significant dates from 1500 to the present. **OL**

American advisers also thought that the Depression became so severe because nations reduced trade. They believed that when nations stop trading, they are forced into war to get resources. By 1945, Roosevelt and his advisers were convinced that economic growth was the key to peace. They wanted to promote economic growth by increasing world trade.

Similar reasoning convinced American leaders to promote democracy and free enterprise. They believed that democratic governments with protections for people's rights made countries more stable and peaceful. They also thought that the free enterprise system, with private property rights and limited government intervention in the economy, was the best route to prosperity.

C

✓ **Reading Check** **Identifying** What did the Allies decide at Yalta?

Truman Takes Control

MAIN Idea Although President Truman took a firm stand against Soviet aggression, Europe remained divided after the war.

HISTORY AND YOU Have you ever had to say no to someone or insist they do something? Read to learn about President Truman's actions at Potsdam.

Eleven days after confronting the Soviets on Poland, President Roosevelt died and Harry S. Truman became president. Truman was strongly anti-Communist. He also believed that World War II had begun because Britain had tried to appease Hitler. He did not intend to make the same mistake with Stalin. "We must stand up to the Russians," he told Secretary of State Edward Stettinius the day after taking office.

C Critical Thinking

Hypothesizing Ask: How can economic growth prevent a country from going to war? *(If a country is prosperous, has plenty of resources, and its people are gainfully employed, there is no reason for war.)* **OL**

✓ **Reading Check**

Answer: The Allies decided Poland's government, Europeans' right to choose their own governments, the division of Germany and Berlin into four zones, the addition of the Soviets in the war effort against Japan, and reparations from Germany.

Debates IN HISTORY

Answers:
1. antagonistic "capitalist encirclement"
2. to strengthen it in order to hatch an imperialist war, defeat socialism and democracy and support fascism

---

YES

George F. Kennan
American Diplomat

PRIMARY SOURCE

"[The] USSR still [believes] in antagonistic 'capitalist encirclement' with which in the long run there can be no permanent peaceful coexistence. . . . At bottom of [the] Kremlin's neurotic view of world affairs is traditional and instinctive Russian sense of insecurity. . . . And they have learned to seek security only in patient but deadly struggle for total destruction of rival power, never in compacts and compromises with it.

. . . In summary, we have here a political force committed fanatically to the belief that . . . it is desirable and necessary that the internal harmony of our society be disrupted, our traditional way of life be destroyed, the international authority of our state be broken, if Soviet power is to be secure."

—Moscow Embassy Telegram #511, 1946

NO

Andrei Zhdanov
Advisor to Stalin

PRIMARY SOURCE

"The more the war recedes into the past, the more distinct becomes . . . the division of the political forces operating on the international arena into two major camps. . . . The principal driving force of the imperialist camp is the U.S.A. . . . The cardinal purpose of the imperialist camp is to strengthen imperialism, to hatch a new imperialist war, to combat socialism and democracy, and to support reactionary and antidemocratic profascist regimes. . . .

. . . As embodiment of a new and superior social system, the Soviet Union reflects in its foreign policy the aspirations of progressive mankind, which desires lasting peace and has nothing to gain from a new war hatched by capitalism."

—from *For a Lasting Peace for a People's Democracy*, no. 1, November 1947

DBQ Document-Based Questions

1. **Paraphrasing** What belief of the Soviets does Kennan say will prevent "permanent peaceful coexistence" with the United States?

2. **Identifying Central Issues** What does Zhdanov say are the goals of the "imperialist camp" led by the United States?

Chapter 15   The Cold War Begins   **535**

Role-Playing to Demonstrate McCarthyism in Action

Step 1: Researching the Army-McCarthy Hearings of 1954 Essential question: How did Senator Joe McCarthy conduct the Army-McCarthy hearings that were televised in 1954?

Directions Explain to students that they will be re-enacting or improvising the Army-McCarthy hearings that were so influential, and which turned the tide against

McCarthyism. For background, they can consult sources found online or in the library. Students can also research in books on McCarthy or McCarthyism to find direct quotations from the hearings or people who witnessed them.

Putting It Together Students should share their research and then discuss the essential elements they want to convey about McCarthyism in the performance they will do for the class. **OL**

(Chapter Project continued on page 543)

Hands-On Chapter Project
Step 1

R Reading Strategy

Determining Importance
Truman was determined to demonstrate American resolve toward the Soviet Union. **Ask:** Why was President Truman's meeting with Molotov an important turning point in U.S.–Soviet diplomacy? *(Truman stood up to the Soviets. He demanded that Stalin hold free elections in Poland.)* **OL**

S Skill Practice

Interpreting a Map Have students look at the map. **Ask:** With which Communist countries did Austria share a border? *(Yugoslavia, Hungary, and Czechoslovakia)* **BL**

DBQ Document Based Questions

Answers:
1. a political and economic barrier between the Soviet sphere and Western Europe; The image provides a strong division between the world and the Soviets. Churchill wanted to illustrate that the Soviets would be a formidable enemy.
2. the Soviet attempts to establish communism in other countries across Europe

Additional Support

NATIONAL GEOGRAPHIC The Iron Curtain in Europe, 1948

Communist countries
Non-communist countries
— Iron Curtain

PRIMARY SOURCE

"A shadow has fallen upon the scenes so lately light by the Allied victory.... From Stettin in the Baltic to Trieste in the Adriatic, an iron curtain has descended across the continent. Behind that line lie all the capitals of the ancient states of Central and Eastern Europe. Warsaw, Berlin, Prague, Vienna, Budapest, Belgrade, Bucharest and Sofia, all these famous cities and the populations around them lie in what I must call the Soviet sphere, and all are subject in one form or another, not only to Soviet influence, but to a very high and, in some cases, increasing measure of control from Moscow....

The Communist parties, which were very small in all these Eastern States of Europe, have been raised to pre-eminence and power far beyond their numbers and are seeking everywhere to obtain totalitarian control....

In front of the iron curtain which lies across Europe are other causes for anxiety . . . in a great number of countries, far from the Russian frontiers and throughout the world, Communist fifth columns are established and work in . . . absolute obedience to the directions they receive from the Communist center.... I do not believe that Soviet Russia desires war. What they desire is the fruits of war and the indefinite expansion of their power and doctrines."

—Winston Churchill, address to Westminster College, Fulton, Missouri, March 5, 1946

DBQ Document-Based Questions

1. **Finding the Main Idea** What was the "iron curtain," and why do you think Churchill described it in that way?
2. **Identifying Central Issues** What "other causes for anxiety" did Churchill say the Soviets were creating?

R Ten days later, Truman did exactly that during a meeting with Soviet Foreign Minister Molotov. Truman immediately brought up the issue of Poland and demanded that Stalin hold free elections as he had promised at Yalta. Molotov took the unexpectedly strong message back to Stalin. The meeting marked an important shift in Soviet-American relations and set the stage for further confrontations.

The Potsdam Conference

In July 1945 with the war against Japan still raging, Truman finally met Stalin at **Potsdam,** near Berlin. Both men had come to Potsdam primarily to work out a deal on Germany.

Truman was now convinced that industry was critical to Germany's survival. Unless that nation's economy was allowed to revive, the rest of Europe would never recover, and the German people might turn to communism out of desperation.

Stalin and his advisers were equally convinced that they needed reparations from Germany. The war had devastated the Soviet economy. Soviet troops had begun stripping their zone in Germany of its machinery and industrial equipment for use back home, but Stalin wanted Germany to pay much more.

Teacher Tip

Collaborative Learning This activity requires students within each group to participate on some level. Have each group select a leader to help divide the work. A person from each group should be selected to lead the debate.

Activity: Collaborative Learning

Identifying Central Issues Ask students to imagine that they are delegates at the Potsdam Conference. Divide the class into two groups: one representing the Soviet Union, the other the United States. Have each group work together to write a paragraph defending their position on German reparations. Students may use the library or Internet to find primary sources to use in their presentations. Remind students that the Allies were no longer sympathetic toward Stalin. Stalin was worried about the destruction in the Soviet Union. Have a representative from each group engage in a debate. Ask the class to vote on the most convincing argument. **OL**

At the conference, Truman took a firm stand against heavy reparations. He insisted that Germany's industry had to be allowed to recover. Truman suggested that the Soviets take reparations from their zone, while the Allies allowed industry to revive in the other zones. Stalin opposed this idea since the Soviet zone was mostly agricultural. It could not provide all the reparations the Soviets wanted.

To get the Soviets to accept the agreement, Truman offered Stalin a small amount of German industrial equipment from the other zones, but required the Soviets to pay for part of it with food shipments from their zone. He also offered to accept the new German-Polish border the Soviets had established.

Stalin did not like Truman's proposal. At Potsdam, Truman learned that the atomic bomb had been successfully tested, and he hinted to Stalin that the United States had developed a new, powerful weapon. Stalin suspected that Truman was trying to bully him into a deal and that the Americans were trying to limit reparations to keep the Soviets weak.

Despite his suspicions, Stalin had to accept the terms. American and British troops controlled Germany's industrial heartland, and there was no way for the Soviets to get any reparations except by cooperating. Nevertheless, the Potsdam conference marked yet another increase in tensions between the Soviets and the Americans.

The Iron Curtain Descends

Although Truman had won the argument over reparations, he had less success on other issues at Potsdam. The Soviets refused to make any stronger commitments to uphold the Declaration of Liberated Europe. The presence of the Soviet army in Eastern Europe ensured that pro-Soviet Communist governments would eventually be established in Poland, Romania, Bulgaria, Hungary, and Czechoslovakia. "This war is not as in the past," Stalin commented. "Whoever occupies a territory also imposes his own social system. . . . It cannot be otherwise."

The Communist countries of Eastern Europe came to be called **satellite nations** because they were controlled by the Soviets, as satellites are tied by gravity to the planets they orbit. These nations had to remain Communist and friendly to the Soviet Union. They also had to follow policies that the Soviets approved.

After watching the Communist takeover in Eastern Europe, Winston Churchill coined a phrase to describe what had happened. In a 1946 speech delivered in Fulton, Missouri, he referred to an "iron curtain" falling across Eastern Europe. The press picked up the term and, for the next 43 years, when someone referred to the Iron Curtain, they meant the Communist nations of Eastern Europe and the Soviet Union. With the **Iron Curtain** separating the Communist nations of Eastern Europe from the West, the World War II era had come to an end. The Cold War was about to begin.

✓ **Reading Check** **Explaining** How did the Potsdam Conference hurt Soviet-American relations?

Section 1 REVIEW

Vocabulary
1. **Explain** the significance of: Yalta, Cold War, Potsdam, satellite nations, Iron Curtain.

Main Ideas
2. **Identifying** At Yalta, what agreement did the "Big Three" come to about Germany's future after World War II?
3. **Summarizing** What concerns made the Soviets suspicious of the Western Allies?
4. **Explaining** How did the Potsdam Conference help bring about the Cold War?

Critical Thinking
5. **Big Ideas** How did different economic systems cause tensions between the United States and the Soviet Union?
6. **Organizing** Use a graphic organizer similar to the one below to list events that led to the Cold War.

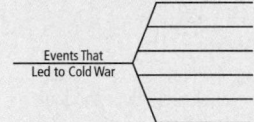

Events That Led to Cold War

7. **Analyzing Visuals** Study the map on page 536. Why did the Soviet Union want to have control over the countries on its western border?

Writing About History
8. **Expository Writing** Suppose that you are an adviser to Truman. Write a report explaining your interpretation of Churchill's "iron curtain" speech.

History ONLINE
Study Central™ To review this section, go to glencoe.com and click on Study Central.

537

Answers

1. All definitions can be found in the section and the Glossary.
2. Germany was divided into four zones controlled by Great Britain, France, the Soviet Union, and the United States.
3. The Soviets were suspicious that the Western Allies wanted to increase economic independence in Europe and establish free governments. They were also unwilling to make the Germans pay large reparations.
4. The conference increased the tension between the Soviet Union and the United

States. It was clear that Truman, with the atomic bomb in his pocket, was not willing to make concessions.

5. The United States wanted to promote strong economic growth throughout Europe. The Soviet Union wanted only to rebuild its own country.

6.

Events That Led to Cold War
- disagreement over Germany
- Soviet refusal to honor Declaration of Liberated Europe
- Soviet actions in Poland
- Potsdam Conference

7. to protect itself from invasion by Germany
8. Reports will vary but should include specific references to Churchill's speech.

Focus

Bellringer
Daily Focus Transparency 15.2

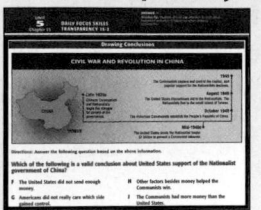

Guide to Reading

Answers:

Answers may include: 1945
Soviet-U.S. division of Korea;
June 1950 North Korea invades
South Korea;
November 1950 China intervenes;
April 1951 MacArthur fired

Section Spotlight Video

To generate student interest and
provide a springboard for class
discussion, access the Chapter 15,
Section 2 video at glencoe.com or
on the video DVD.

Resource Manager

The Early Cold War Years

Guide to Reading

Big Ideas
Trade, War, and Migration As the
Cold War began, the United States
struggled to oppose Communist aggression in Europe and Asia through political, economic, and military measures.

Content Vocabulary
• containment (p. 538)
• limited war (p. 545)

Academic Vocabulary
• insecurity (p. 538)
• initially (p. 541)

People and Events to Identify
• George Kennan (p. 538)
• Long Telegram (p. 538)
• Marshall Plan (p. 540)
• NATO (p. 541)
• SEATO (p. 545)

Reading Strategy
Sequencing Complete a time line
similar to the one below by recording
the major events related to the
Korean War.

President Truman worked to contain communism by
supporting Greece, Iran, and West Germany. When
Communist North Korea invaded South Korea, Truman
and the UN sent troops to aid South Korea.

Containing Communism

MAIN Idea The Truman Doctrine offered aid to any nation resisting
communism; the Marshall Plan aided European countries in rebuilding.

HISTORY AND YOU Is there a conflict in the world today where you think
the United States should intervene? Read on to learn how President Truman
adopted policies designed to stop the spread of communism.

Despite growing tensions with the Soviet Union, many American
officials continued to believe cooperation with the Soviets was possible. In late 1945 the foreign ministers of the former wartime Allies
met first in London, then in Moscow, to discuss the future of Europe
and Asia. Although both British and American officials pushed for
free elections in Eastern Europe, the Soviets refused to budge. "Our
relations with the Russians," the British foreign minister gloomily
concluded, "are drifting into the same condition as that in which we
had found ourselves with Hitler."

The Long Telegram

Increasingly exasperated by the Soviets' refusal to cooperate,
officials at the State Department asked the American Embassy in
Moscow to explain Soviet behavior. On February 22, 1946, diplomat
George Kennan responded with what became known as the **Long
Telegram**, a 5,540-word message explaining his views of the Soviets.

According to Kennan, the Soviets' view of the world came from a
traditional "Russian sense of **insecurity**" and fear of the West, intensified by the communist ideas of Lenin and Stalin. Because communists believed that they were in a long-term historical struggle
against capitalism, Kennan argued, it was impossible to reach any
permanent settlement with them.

Kennan therefore proposed what became the basic American
policy throughout the Cold War: "a long-term, patient but firm and
vigilant **containment** of Russian expansive tendencies." Kennan
explained that, in his opinion, the Soviet system had several major
economic and political weaknesses. If the United States could keep
the Soviets from expanding their power, it would be only a matter of
time before the Soviet system would fall apart. Communism could be
beaten without going to war. The Long Telegram circulated widely in

---

R Reading Strategies	**C** Critical Thinking	**D** Differentiated Instruction	**W** Writing Support	**S** Skill Practice
Teacher Edition • Identifying, p. 540 • Summarizing, p. 542 • Inferring, p. 543 **Additional Resources** • Guided Reading Act., URB p. 117	**Teacher Edition** • Analyzing Prim. Sources, p. 539 • Drawing Con., pp. 540, 544 • Det. Cause/Effect, pp. 542, 545 **Additional Resources** • History Simulations, URB p. 9 • Critical Thinking Skills Activity, URB p. 100	**Teacher Edition** • Visual/Spatial p. 540 **Additional Resources** • English Learner Act., URB p. 93	**Teacher Edition** • Persuasive Writing, p. 541 • Personal Writing, p. 544	**Teacher Edition** • Using Geo. Skills, pp. 539, 543 **Additional Resources** • Reading Skills Act., URB p. 89 • Reinf. Skills Act., URB p. 99 • RENTG, p. 164

PRIMARY SOURCE
The Truman Doctrine

▲ President Truman signs the Foreign Aid Assistance Act, providing aid to Greece and Turkey; the use of aid to support nations resisting Communist pressure became known as the Truman Doctrine.

PRIMARY SOURCE

"The peoples of a number of countries of the world have recently had totalitarian regimes forced upon them against their will. The Government of the United States has made frequent protests against coercion and intimidation, in violation of the Yalta agreement in Poland, Romania, and Bulgaria. At the present moment in world history nearly every nation must choose between alternative ways of life. The choice is too often not a free one. . . . I believe that it must be the policy of the United States to support free peoples who are resisting attempted subjugation by armed minorities or by outside pressures. I believe that we must assist free peoples to work out their own destinies in their own way."

—Truman's address to Congress, March 12, 1947

C

DBQ Document-Based Questions

1. **Finding the Main Idea** What was the stated goal of the Truman Doctrine?
2. **Drawing Conclusions** Which nation received the most aid through the Marshall Plan? Why do you think this might be?

Marshall Plan Aid to Major Countries

Aid (millions)

| 30 | 24 | 18 | 12 | 6 | 0 |

Austria Belg. & Lux. Denmark France Germany Greece U.K. Italy Neth. Norway

Source: *The Marshall Plan Fifty Years Later.*

Teach

Analyzing Primary Sources
Ask students if the United States still practices the policy as set forth by Truman—that the U.S. "must assist free peoples." Have students use current examples to support their statements. **AL**

S Skill Practice
Using Geography Skills
Provide students with a map of Eastern Europe. Ask them to identify the following: Turkey, the straits of Dardanelles, the Black Sea, and the Mediterranean Sea. **Ask:** Why did the Soviet Union want to gain influence over Turkey? *(To secure access to the Mediterranean.)* **BL**

DBQ Document Based Questions

Answers:
1. to support free peoples, fight Soviet aggression, and stop the spread of communism
2. U.K.; It had been bombed and was America's closest ally.

Truman's administration. The administration based its policy of containment—keeping communism within its present territory through the use of diplomatic, economic, and military actions—on this document.

Crisis in Iran

While Truman's administration discussed Kennan's ideas, a series of crises erupted during the spring and summer of 1946. These crises seemed to prove that Kennan was right about the Soviets. The first crisis began in Iran in March 1946.

During World War II, the United States had put troops in southern Iran while Soviet troops occupied northern Iran to secure a supply line from the Persian Gulf. After the war, instead of withdrawing as promised, the Soviet troops remained in northern Iran. Stalin then began demanding access to Iran's oil supplies. To increase the pressure, Soviet troops helped

local Communists in northern Iran establish a separate government.

To American officials, these actions signaled a Soviet push into the Middle East. The secretary of state sent Stalin a strong message demanding that Soviet forces withdraw. At the same time, the battleship USS *Missouri* sailed into the eastern Mediterranean. The pressure seemed to work. Soviet forces withdrew, having been promised a joint Soviet-Iranian oil company, although the Iranian parliament later rejected the plan.

The Truman Doctrine

Frustrated in Iran, Stalin turned northwest to Turkey. There, the straits of the Dardanelles were a vital route from Soviet Black Sea ports to the Mediterranean. For centuries, Russia had wanted to control this strategic route. In August 1946, Stalin demanded joint control of the Dardanelles with Turkey. **S**

For more of the text of Truman's Address to Congress, see page R54 in **Documents in American History**.

Additional Support

Activity: Economics Connection

Analyzing Information The Tripartite Treaty of Alliance of January 29, 1942, was an agreement between Russia, Britain, and Iran. Allied troops agreed to withdraw from Iran within six months after the end of World War II. British and American troops left Iran, but Stalin did not. Iranian Prime Minister Ahmad Qavam tried to persuade Stalin to remove his troops by agreeing to

a Soviet oil concession and a peace agreement with the Azerbeijani Republic, a Soviet puppet republic set in the Soviet military zone in Northern Iran. When the *USS Missouri* arrived and the Soviets finally left Iran, Qavam then reclaimed his concessions. **Ask:** Why was Iran important to the Allies? Why did Stalin refuse to honor the treaty? Have students look at a current map identi-

fying oil and gas production areas. They should then write a one-page report answering the above questions. **OL**

R Reading Strategy

Identifying Ask: How much money did Truman ask Congress to appropriate to fight communism? *($400 million)* Remind students of the value of the dollar in 1947. **Ask:** Why did the United States have to support the Greek government? *(The British did not have the resources to help Greece.)* **BL**

D Differentiated Instruction

Visual/Spatial Have students draw a map of the German zones in 1948. Instruct students to use a transparency to show what West Germany and West Berlin looked like after the United States, Britain, and France merged their zones. **Ask:** Why was this merger not welcomed by the Soviets? *(The Soviets saw this as an attempt to undermine their reparations plan.)* **OL**

Differentiated Instruction

Presidential adviser Dean Acheson saw this move as another move in a Soviet plan to control the Middle East, and he advised Truman to make a show of force. The president declared, "We might as well find out whether the Russians are bent on world conquest." He then ordered the new aircraft carrier *Franklin D. Roosevelt* to join the *Missouri* in protecting Turkey and the eastern Mediterranean.

While the United States supported Turkey, Britain tried to help Greece. In August 1946 Greek Communists launched a guerrilla war against the Greek government. For about six months, British troops helped the Greeks fight the guerrillas. The effort strained Britain's economy, which was still weak from World War II. In February 1947 Britain informed the United States that it could no longer afford to help Greece.

R On March 12, 1947, Truman went before Congress to ask for $400 million to fight Communist aggression in Greece and Turkey. His speech outlined a policy that became known as the Truman Doctrine. Its goal was to aid "free peoples who are resisting attempted subjugation by armed minorities or by outside pressures." Its immediate goal was to stabilize the Greek government and help Turkey resist Soviet demands. In the long run, it pledged the United States to fight the spread of communism worldwide.

The Marshall Plan

Meanwhile, postwar Western Europe faced grave problems. Economies and cities were ruined, people were nearing starvation, and political chaos was at hand. The terrible winter of 1946 made things worse.

In June 1947 Secretary of State George C. Marshall proposed the European Recovery Program, or **Marshall Plan,** which would give European nations American aid to rebuild their economies. Truman saw the Marshall Plan and the Truman Doctrine as "two halves of the same walnut," both essential for containment. Marshall offered help to all nations planning a recovery program:

PRIMARY SOURCE

"Our policy is directed not against any country or doctrine but against hunger, poverty, desperation and chaos. Its purpose should be the revival of a working economy in the world so as to permit the emergence of political and social conditions in which free institutions can exist."

—quoted in *Marshall: Hero for Our Times*

Although the Marshall Plan was offered to the Soviet Union and its satellite nations in Eastern Europe, those nations rejected the offer. Instead, the Soviets developed their own economic program. This action further separated Europe into competing regions. The Marshall Plan pumped billions of dollars worth of supplies, machinery, and food into Western Europe. Western Europe's recovery weakened the appeal of communism and opened new markets for trade.

The Berlin Airlift

President Truman and his advisers believed that Western Europe's prosperity depended on Germany's recovery. The Soviets, however, still wanted Germany to pay reparations to the Soviet Union. Eventually, the dispute over Germany brought the United States and the Soviet Union to the brink of war.

By early 1948, U.S. officials had concluded that the Soviets were deliberately trying to undermine Germany's economy. In response, the United States, Great Britain, and France announced that they were merging their zones in Germany and allowing the Germans to have their own government. They also agreed to **D** merge their zones in Berlin and to make West Berlin part of the new German republic.

The new nation was officially called the Federal Republic of Germany, but it became known as West Germany. The Soviet zone eventually became the German Democratic Republic, also known as East Germany. West Germany was not allowed to have a military, but in most respects, it was independent.

The decision to create West Germany convinced the Soviets that they would never get the reparations they wanted. In late June 1948, Soviet troops cut all road and rail traffic to West Berlin hoping to force the United States to either reconsider its decision or abandon West Berlin. This blockade provoked a crisis. President Truman sent bombers with atomic weapons to bases in Britain and the American commander in Germany warned: "If we mean to hold Europe against communism, then we

---

Leveled Activities

BL **Reading Skills Activity, URB p. 89**

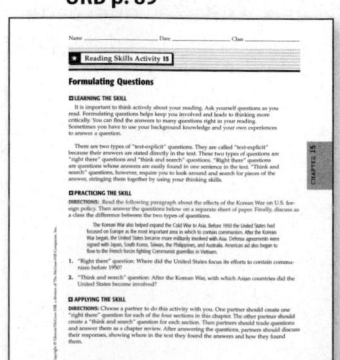

OL **Content Vocabulary Activity, URB p. 95**

AL **Primary Source Reading, URB p. 103**

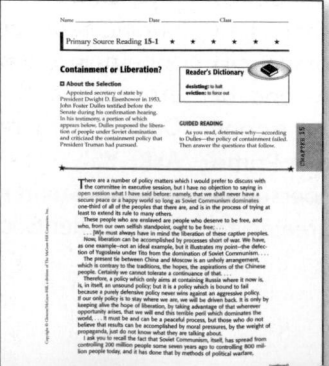

ELL **English Learner Activity, URB, p. 93**

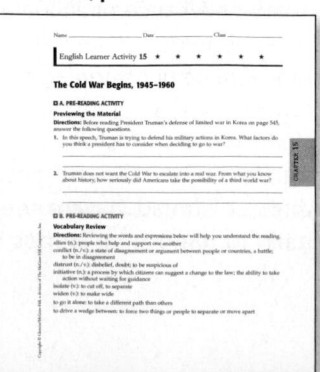

must not budge." The challenge was to keep West Berlin alive without provoking war with the Soviets. Instead of ordering troops to fight their way to Berlin, and thereby triggering war with the Soviet Union, Truman ordered the air force to fly supplies into Berlin instead.

The Berlin airlift began in June 1948 and continued through the spring of 1949, bringing in more than 2 million tons of supplies to the city. Stalin finally lifted the blockade on May 12, 1949. The airlift symbolized American determination to contain communism and not give in to Soviet demands.

NATO

The Berlin blockade convinced many Americans that the Soviets were bent on conquest. The public began to support a military alliance with Western Europe. By April 1949, an agreement had been reached to create the North Atlantic Treaty Organization (NATO)—a mutual defense alliance.

NATO initially included 12 countries: the United States, Canada, Britain, France, Italy, Belgium, Denmark, Portugal, the Netherlands, Norway, Luxembourg, and Iceland. NATO members agreed to come to the aid of any member who was attacked. For the first time in its history, the United States had committed itself to maintaining peace in Europe. Six years later, NATO allowed West Germany to rearm and join its organization. This decision alarmed Soviet leaders. They responded by organizing a military alliance in Eastern Europe known as the Warsaw Pact.

History ONLINE
Student Web Activity Visit glencoe.com and complete the activity on the Berlin Airlift.

W

✔ **Reading Check** **Evaluating** What triggered the beginning of the Berlin airlift?

PRIMARY SOURCE
The Berlin Airlift, 1948–1949

After the Soviet Union blockaded West Berlin, the United States delivered 4,000 tons of food, medicine, coal and other supplies that were needed every day to keep the city functioning. A cargo plane had to land with supplies every three and a half minutes. To keep the airlift running, crews stayed onboard and food was brought to them while the planes were unloaded and refueled. Meanwhile, 20,000 volunteers in Berlin built a third airport, enabling the flow of supplies to increase to 13,000 tons a day.

NATIONAL GEOGRAPHIC **NATO Is Born, 1949**

- Founding members
- Joined 1952
- Joined 1955
- Warsaw Pact

Analyzing VISUALS

1. **Interpreting** Which nations are the founding members of NATO?
2. **Identifying** Which NATO nations shared a border with one or more Warsaw Pact nations?

Chapter 15 The Cold War Begins **541**

Did You Know?

During the Berlin airlift, a plane flew into the city every three minutes. Without the supplies those planes carried, West Berliners would have had to back down.

Analyzing VISUALS

Answers:
1. United Kingdom, France, Italy, Belgium, Denmark, Portugal, the Netherlands, Norway, Luxembourg, and Iceland
2. Greece, Turkey, West Germany

✔ **Reading Check**

Answer: Soviet blockade of West Berlin

Additional Support

Extending the Content

Point Four Program In his 1949 inaugural address, President Harry Truman announced (as the fourth point of his speech) "a bold new program for making the benefits of our scientific advances and industrial progress available for the improvement and growth of underdeveloped areas" around the globe. The program was intended to encourage development and economic growth in poorer countries and thereby diminish the appeal of socialist or communist doctrines. Officially titled the United States Technical Assistance Plan, the Point Four Program focused on providing technical assistance to developing nations.

542

R Reading Strategy

Summarizing Have students state why China suspended its civil war during World War II and what happened at the end of the war. *(Communist forces and the Nationalist government suspended fighting to make sure Japan would not try to invade. Once the war was over, they continued fighting since a resolution was never obtained.)* **OL**

C Critical Thinking

Determining Cause and Effect **Ask:** What happened in China when the United States discontinued financial aid? *(The Chinese Nationalists fled to Taiwan, and China became an established Communist country.)* What effect did this have on American policy and why? *(The new strategy was to help Japan recover quickly from the war, due to its strategic location. The Americans believed that by strengthening Japan, they could fend off communism in the rest of Asia.)* **OL**

Additional Support

The Korean War

MAIN Idea Attempts to keep South Korea free from communism led the United States to military intervention.

HISTORY AND YOU What happens to someone who disobeys a coach, employer, or teacher? Read on to learn what happened to General MacArthur when he criticized the president.

The Cold War eventually spread beyond Europe. Conflicts also emerged in Asia, where events in China and Korea brought about a new attitude toward Japan and sent American troops back into battle in Asia less than five years after World War II had ended.

The Chinese Revolution

In China, Communist forces led by Mao Zedong had been struggling against the Nationalist government led by Chiang Kai-shek since the late 1920s. During World War II, the two sides suspended their war to resist Japanese occupation. With the end of World War II, however, civil war broke out again. Although Mao made great gains, neither side could win nor agree to a compromise.

To prevent a Communist revolution in Asia, the United States sent the Nationalist government $2 billion in aid beginning in the mid-1940s, but the Nationalists squandered this advantage through poor military planning and corruption. By 1949, the Communists had captured the Chinese capital of Beijing, while support for the Nationalists declined.

In August 1949 the U.S. State Department discontinued aid to the Chinese Nationalists. The defeated Nationalists then fled to the small island of Taiwan (Formosa). The victorious Communists established the People's Republic of China in October 1949.

China's fall to communism shocked Americans. To make matters worse, in September 1949 the Soviet Union announced that it had successfully tested its first atomic weapon. Then, early in 1950, the People's Republic of China and the Soviet Union signed a treaty of friendship and alliance. Many Western leaders feared that China and the Soviet Union would support Communist revolutions in other nations.

The United States kept formal diplomatic relations with only the Nationalist Chinese in

▲ **June–September 1950**

North Korean troops invade South Korea, driving South Korean and UN forces south into a small perimeter around Pusan.

0	400 kilometers
0	400 miles

Miller projection

- North Korean-controlled territory
- South Korean-controlled territory
- ← North Korean advance
- ← UN counteroffensive
- — Front line
- ← Chinese counteroffensive
- — Armistice line

Taiwan. It used its veto power in the UN Security Council to keep representatives of the new Communist People's Republic of China out of the UN, allowing the Nationalists to retain their seat.

New Policies in Japan

The Chinese revolution brought about a significant change in American policy toward Japan. At the end of World War II, General Douglas MacArthur had taken charge of occupied Japan. His mission was to introduce democracy and keep Japan from threatening war again. Once the United States lost China as its chief ally in Asia, it adopted policies to encourage the rapid recovery of Japan's industrial economy. Just as

Activity: Collaborative Learning

Contrasting In 1949, Nationalists fled the Chinese mainland to the island of Taiwan. While mainland China became a Communist stronghold, Taiwan remained tied to the West. Have students work in groups and trace the development of China and Taiwan over the last 55 years. Groups should create a time line to document and illustrate main events and crises between China and Taiwan. Have groups present their time lines in class. **Ask:** Why does China want Taiwan? How far will China go to ensure Taiwan does not become independent? What do the Taiwanese people want? **OL**

▲ **September–November 1950**
Led by General MacArthur, UN troops land behind North Korean lines at the port of Inchon. North Korean forces fall back rapidly, and the UN forces head north into North Korea.

▲ **November 1950–January 1951**
As UN forces near the Chinese border, Chinese troops cross into North Korea driving the UN back. MacArthur wants to attack Chinese territory. He publicly argues with Truman and is fired.

▲ **January 1951–July 1953**
Led by U.S. General Matthew Ridgway, the UN forces push the Chinese and North Korean forces out of South Korea. The war bogs down into a stalemate along the 38th parallel.

S

◀ *Soldiers of the U.S. 2nd Infantry Division man a machine gun near the Chongchun River in Korea, December 15, 1950.*

Analyzing GEOGRAPHY

1. **Human-Environment Interaction** What occurred at the port of Inchon in 1950?
2. **Location** What geographical feature forms the border between China and North Korea?

the United States viewed West Germany as the key to defending all of Europe against communism, it saw Japan as the key to defending Asia.

The Korean War Begins

At the end of World War II, American and Soviet forces entered Korea to disarm the Japanese troops stationed there. The Allies divided Korea at the 38th parallel of latitude. Soviet troops controlled the north, while American troops controlled the south.

As the Cold War began, talks to reunify Korea broke down. A Communist Korean government was organized in the north, while an American-backed government controlled the south. Both governments claimed authority over Korea, and border clashes were common. The Soviet Union provided military aid to the North Koreans, who quickly built up an army. On June 25, 1950, North Korean troops invaded the south, rapidly driving back the poorly equipped South Korean forces.

Truman saw the Communist invasion of South Korea as a test of the containment policy and ordered United States naval and air power into action. He then called on the United Nations to act. Truman succeeded because the Soviet delegate was boycotting the UN Security Council over its China policy and was not present to veto the American proposal. With the pledge of UN troops, Truman ordered General MacArthur to send American troops from Japan to Korea.

R

Chapter 15 The Cold War Begins **543**

S Skill Practice

Using Geography Skills Have students look at the map of Korea. Ask them to identify the 38th parallel of latitude. **Ask:** Why did the Allies divide Korea at the 38th parallel? *(It looks like an even division.)* What is the importance of Korea's geographic location? *(It is close to China and the Soviet Union.)* **BL**

R Reading Strategy

Inferring Ask: Why do you think Truman called on the UN to assist the United States troops in Korea? *(Students might suggest that he did not want the world to think the United States was a "military bully." He wanted international approval and support.)* **OL**

Analyzing GEOGRAPHY

Answers:
1. U.N. forces under General MacArthur landed and cut off the North Korean army.
2. the Yalu River

Hands-On Chapter Project
Step 2

Role-Playing to Demonstrate McCarthyism in Action

Step 2: Creating the Roles and the Script Essential question: How much of a hearing can student cast members perform and who will write the script?

Directions From reading about the hearings or even seeing them if a historical video exists, students will create their script and cast different students in the lead and supporting roles. These roles should include Senator McCarthy, army lawyer Joseph Welch, other senators on the committee, and a witness.

Putting It Together Students should meet to finalize the product—a script outline (some improvisation might be allowed), and a definite beginning and an end that will make sense to viewers. **OL**

(Chapter Project continued on page 549)

W Writing Support

Personal Writing Have students write a journal entry expressing what they think about the MacArthur/Truman debate. **Ask:** Should a country use all the military force at its disposal to guarantee a victory, or should a country fight a limited war, hoping to avoid a nuclear war? **OL**

C Critical Thinking

Drawing Conclusions When the Chinese came to the aid of the North Koreans, MacArthur wanted to attack China, but Truman disagreed. **Ask:** Why was Truman against expanding the war to China? *(Truman wanted to fight a limited war. The Chinese would be a formidable enemy. He didn't want to drop another atomic bomb.)* **OL**

Analyzing VISUALS

Answers:
1. the one on the right
2. make decisions reserved for the president

Additional Support

POLITICAL CARTOONS **PRIMARY SOURCE**

Truman vs. MacArthur

W

▲ President Truman, Secretary of State Dean Acheson, and "The Pentagon" are held over the flame of public opinion for firing General MacArthur. "John Q." refers to "John Q. Public," or the American people.

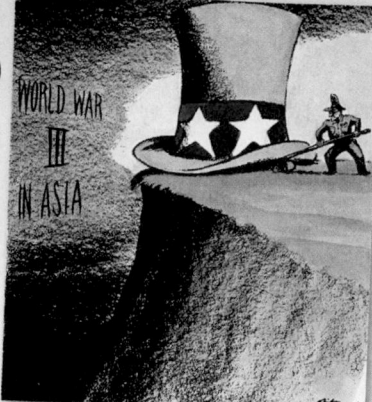

▲ Entitled "Not a General's Job," this cartoon suggests that MacArthur had overstepped his authority in Korea.

Analyzing VISUALS

1. **Identifying Points of View** Which of the cartoons supports President Truman's decision to fire General MacArthur? Explain.
2. **Making Inferences** What does the cartoon on the right imply MacArthur was trying to do in Asia?

The American and South Korean troops were driven back into a small pocket of territory near the port of Pusan. Inside the "Pusan perimeter," as it came to be called, the troops stubbornly resisted the North Korean onslaught, buying time for MacArthur to organize reinforcements.

On September 15, 1950, MacArthur ordered a daring invasion behind enemy lines at the port of Inchon. The Inchon landing took the North Koreans by surprise. Within weeks they were in full retreat back across the 38th parallel. Truman then gave the order to pursue the North Koreans beyond the 38th parallel. MacArthur pushed the North Koreans north to the Yalu River, the border with China.

China Enters the War The Communist People's Republic of China saw the advancing UN troops as a threat and warned the forces to halt their advance. When those warnings were ignored, Chinese forces crossed the Yalu River in November. Hundreds of thousands of Chinese troops flooded across the border, driving the UN forces back across the 38th parallel.

As his troops fell back, an angry MacArthur demanded approval to expand the war against China. He asked for a blockade of Chinese ports, the use of Chiang Kai-shek's Nationalist forces, and the bombing of Chinese cities with atomic weapons.

Truman Fires MacArthur President Truman refused MacArthur's demands because he did not want to expand the war into China or to use the atomic bomb. MacArthur persisted. He publicly criticized the president, arguing that it was a mistake to keep the war limited. "There is no substitute for victory," MacArthur insisted, by which he meant that if the United States was going to go to war, it should use all of its power to win. Keeping a war limited was, in his view, a form of appeasement, and appeasement he argued, "begets new and bloodier war."

Determined to maintain control of policy and to show that the president commanded the military, an exasperated Truman fired MacArthur for insubordination in April 1951. Later, in private conversation, Truman explained:

Activity: Collaborative Learning

Identifying Central Issues A controversy between Harry S. Truman and General Douglas MacArthur began shortly after the outbreak of the Korean War. It reached a climax when the president relieved MacArthur of his command. Truman believed in limited war; MacArthur wanted total victory.

Have students review the Constitutional powers of the president. Then ask students to use the library or the Internet to locate and read the letter from Truman to MacArthur, dated April 11, 1951. Have students work in groups to discuss if President Truman made the correct choice. **Ask:** Do you think President Truman exercised his presidential powers according to the Constitution? Should Truman have dealt differently with MacArthur? After groups have reached their conclusions, lead a class discussion, writing major ideas on the board. **OL**

"I was sorry to have to reach a parting of the way with the big man in Asia, but he asked for it and I had to give it to him."

MacArthur, who remained popular despite being fired, returned home to parades and a hero's welcome. Many Americans criticized the president. Congress and other military leaders, however, supported Truman's decision and his Korean strategy. American policy in Asia remained committed to **limited war**—a war fought to achieve a limited objective, such as containing communism. Truman later explained why he favored limited war in Korea:

PRIMARY SOURCE

"The Kremlin [Soviet Union] is trying, and has been trying for a long time, to drive a wedge between us and the other nations. It wants to see us isolated. It wants to see us distrusted. It wants to see us feared and hated by our allies. Our allies agree with us in the course we are following. They do not believe we should take the initiative to widen the conflict in the Far East. If the United States were to widen the conflict, we might well have to go it alone."

—from "Address to the Civil Defense Conference," May 7, 1951

As Truman also noted, America's allies in Europe were much closer to the Soviet Union. If war broke out, Europe would suffer the most damage and might well be attacked with atomic bombs. This concern—that all-out war in Korea might lead to nuclear war—was the main reason why Truman favored limited war. This concern shaped American foreign policy throughout the Cold War.

Changes in Policy

By mid-1951, the UN forces had pushed the Chinese and North Korean forces back across the 38th parallel. The war then settled down into a series of relatively small battles over hills and other local objectives. In November 1951, peace negotiations began, but an armistice would not be signed until July 1953. More than 33,600 American soldiers died in action in the Korean War, and more than 2,800 died from accidents or disease.

The Korean War marked an important turning point in the Cold War. Until 1950, the United States had preferred to use political pressure and economic aid to contain communism. After the Korean War began, the United States embarked on a major military buildup.

The Korean War also helped expand the Cold War to Asia. Before 1950, the United States had focused on Europe as the most important area in which to contain communism. After the Korean War began, the United States became more militarily involved in Asia. In 1954 the United States signed defense agreements with Japan, South Korea, Taiwan, the Philippines, and Australia, forming the Southeast Asia Treaty Organization (**SEATO**). American aid also began flowing to French forces fighting Communists in Vietnam.

C

✓ Reading Check **Analyzing** How did President Truman view the Communist invasion of South Korea?

Section 2 REVIEW

Vocabulary

1. **Explain** the significance of: George Kennan, Long Telegram, containment, Marshall Plan, NATO, limited war, SEATO.

Main Ideas

2. **Explaining** How did the Truman Doctrine and the Marshall Plan address the spread of communism?

3. **Describing** What originally led to the formation of two Koreas?

Critical Thinking

4. **Big Ideas** How did the Long Telegram influence U.S. foreign policy?

5. **Categorizing** Use a graphic organizer similar to the one below to list early conflicts between the Soviet Union and the United States.

Conflicts Between the USSR and the U.S.

6. **Analyzing Visuals** Study the maps of the Korean War on page 543. When did the United Nations control the most territory in Korea? When did both sides finally agree on an armistice line?

Writing About History

7. **Persuasive Writing** Write a letter to the editor of a newspaper explaining why you agree or disagree with President Truman's firing of General MacArthur.

History ONLINE
Study Central™ To review this section, go to glencoe.com and click on Study Central.

545

C Critical Thinking

Determining Cause and Effect Ask: How did the Korean War change U.S. policy in regard to communism? *(Prior to the Korean War, the U.S. preferred to use political and economic pressures. After Korea, the U.S. turned toward a militaristic approach by building up its army and its arsenals.)* **OL**

✓ Reading Check

Answer: He saw it as a test of the U.S. containment policy.

Assess

History ONLINE

Study Central™ provides summaries, interactive games, and online graphic organizers to help students review content.

Close

Cause and Effect Have students work in groups to create two cause and effect graphic organizers—one for the Cold War and the other for the Korean War. **OL**

Section 2 REVIEW

Answers

1. All definitions can be found in the section and the Glossary.

2. The Truman Doctrine pledged U.S. military involvement to fight the spread of communism, and the Marshall Plan provided economic aid to strengthen resistance to communism.

3. At the end of World War II, the Soviet Union and the United States both entered Korea to disarm Japanese troops. The Soviets took control of Korea north of the 38th parallel, and the U.S. took control south of the 38th

parallel. Talks to unite the country broke down with the Soviets establishing a Communist government in the north and the U.S. organizing a non-Communist government in the south.

4. In the Long Telegram, George Kennan recommended a policy of containment of the Soviet Union's expansion, which became a mainstay of U.S. foreign policy throughout the Cold War.

5. Students should include: Crisis in Iran, Berlin crisis, Korean War, Crisis with Turkey

6. November 1950; July 27, 1953

7. Letters will vary but should express a point of view based on facts.

Focus

Bellringer

Daily Focus Transparency 15.3

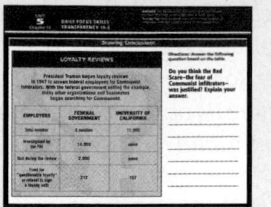

Guide to Reading

Answers: Students should complete the outline by including all headings in the section.

Section Spotlight Video

To generate student interest and provide a springboard for class discussion, access the Chapter 15, Section 3 video at glencoe.com or on the video DVD.

Resource Manager

The Cold War and American Society

Guide to Reading

Big Ideas

Struggles for Rights In the early part of the Cold War, the fear of communism led to a hunt for spies and to intolerance and suspicion of people with radical ideas in the United States.

Content Vocabulary

- subversion (p. 546)
- loyalty review program (p. 546)
- perjury (p. 548)
- censure (p. 550)
- fallout (p. 553)

Academic Vocabulary

- manipulate (p. 547)
- convince (p. 548)

People and Events to Identify

- Red Scare (p. 546)
- Alger Hiss (p. 548)
- McCarran Act (p. 550)
- McCarthyism (p. 550)

Reading Strategy

Summarizing As you read, summarize the section content by using the major headings to create an outline similar to the one below.

The Cold War and American Society
I. A New Red Scare
  A. The Loyalty Review Program
  B.
  C.

Fearing subversive activity, the government tried to root out Communists in government, Hollywood, and labor unions, while Americans learned to live with the threat of nuclear attack.

A New Red Scare

MAIN Idea Public accusations and trials followed in the wake of fears of communism and spies.

HISTORY AND YOU Do you remember reading about the fears of communism during the early twentieth century? Read on to learn of a second major scare in the 1950s.

During the 1950s, thousands of ordinary people—from teachers to autoworkers to high government officials—shared a disturbing experience. Rumors and accusations of Communists in the United States and of Communist infiltration of the government tapped into fears that Communists were trying to take over the world.

The **Red Scare** began in September 1945, when a clerk named Igor Gouzenko walked out of the Soviet Embassy in Ottawa, Canada, and defected. Gouzenko carried documents revealing a massive effort by the Soviet Union to infiltrate organizations and government agencies in Canada and the United States, with the specific goal of obtaining information about the atomic bomb.

The Gouzenko case stunned Americans. It implied that spies had infiltrated the American government. Soon, however, the search for spies escalated into a general fear of Communist **subversion.** Subversion is the effort to weaken a society secretly and overthrow its government.

The Loyalty Review Program

In early 1947, just nine days after his powerful speech announcing the Truman Doctrine, the president established a **loyalty review program** to screen all federal employees. Rather than calm public suspicion, Truman's action seemed to confirm fears that Communists had infiltrated the government and helped to increase the fear of communism sweeping the nation.

Between 1947 and 1951, more than 6 million federal employees were screened for their loyalty—a term difficult to define. A person might become a suspect for reading certain books, belonging to various groups, traveling overseas, or even seeing certain foreign films. About 14,000 employees were subject to scrutiny by the Federal Bureau of Investigation (FBI). Some 2,000 employees quit their jobs

---

R Reading Strategies	**C** Critical Thinking	**D** Differentiated Instruction	**W** Writing Support	**S** Skill Practice
Teacher Edition • Making Connections, pp. 547, 553 • Inferring, p. 547 **Additional Resources** • Pri. Source Reading, URB p. 105 • Guided Reading Act., URB p. 118	**Teacher Edition** • Recognizing Bias, p. 548 • Det. Cause/Effect, p. 549 • Interpreting, p. 550 **Additional Resources** • Supreme Court Case Studies, pp. 69, 75, 77 • Link. Past and Present, URB p. 102 • Interpret. Political Cartoons, URB p. 109 • Quizzes/Tests, p. 213	**Teacher Edition** • Visual/Spatial, pp. 548, 552 • Kinesthetic, p. 549 **Additional Resources** • Differentiated Inst. Act., URB p. 91 • Am. History in Graphic Novel, p. 57	**Teacher Edition** • Descriptive Writing, p. 550	**Teacher Edition** • Visual Literacy p. 552 **Additional Resources** • RENTG., p. 167 • Historical Analysis Skills Act., URB p. 90

PRIMARY SOURCE
The Hunt for Spies, 1947–1954

▲ **Loyalty and Dissent, Oppenheimer, 1953**
Although he had led the effort to develop the atomic bomb, Dr. Robert Oppenheimer's left-wing views and opposition to the hydrogen bomb led to the suspension of his security clearance and controversial public hearings.

▲ **Hiss v. Chambers, 1948**
In 1948, Whittaker Chambers, a *TIME* magazine editor and former Communist Party member, testified that U.S. diplomat Alger Hiss was a Communist. Hiss denied being a spy or a member of the Communist Party. Evidence provided by Chambers led to Hiss being convicted of perjury.

▶ **The Rosenbergs Are Convicted, 1950**
In 1950 the hunt for spies who had given U.S. nuclear secrets to the Soviets led to the arrest of Julius and Ethel Rosenberg. Accused of running a Soviet spy network, the Rosenbergs became the first civilians executed for espionage in 1953. Their case was controversial and led to public protests.

Analyzing VISUALS

1. **Summarizing** What were the Rosenbergs accused of and what was the result?
2. **Explaining** Why was Robert Oppenheimer's security clearance suspended?

---

during the check, many under pressure. Another 212 were fired for "questionable loyalty," although no actual evidence against them was uncovered. **R1**

House Un-American Activities Committee (HUAC)

Although the FBI helped screen federal employees, FBI Director J. Edgar Hoover was not satisfied. In 1947 Hoover went before the House Un-American Activities Committee (HUAC). Formed in 1938 to investigate both Communist and Fascist activities in the United States, HUAC was a minor committee until Hoover expanded its importance.

Hoover urged HUAC to hold public hearings on Communist subversion. The committee, Hoover said, could reveal "the diabolic machinations of sinister figures engaged in un-American activities." Hoover's aim was to expose not just Communists but also "Communist sympathizers" and "fellow travelers." Under Hoover's leadership, the FBI sent agents to infiltrate groups suspected of subversion and wiretapped thousands of telephones.

Hollywood on Trial One of HUAC's first hearings in 1947 focused on the film industry as a powerful cultural force that Communists might **manipulate** to spread their ideas and influence. HUAC's interviews routinely began, "Are you now, or have you ever been, a member of the Communist Party?" Future American president Ronald Reagan was head of the Screen Actors Guild at the time and, when called before HUAC, he testified that there were Communists in Hollywood. **R2**

Teach

R1 Reading Strategy
Making Connections Have students work in small groups and come up with a definition for *loyalty.* Discuss as a class why it is difficult to define an abstraction in absolute terms. **OL**

R2 Reading Strategy
Inferring HUAC was concerned that Communists were using the American film industry to disseminate their ideas. **Ask:** Why did this tactic seem plausible? *(Students might say that films reached large audiences, so many Americans would be exposed to Communist ideas—and it would happen without their knowledge or consent.)* **OL**

Analyzing VISUALS

Answers:
1. They were accused of running a Soviet spy network. They were executed.
2. He opposed the hydrogen bomb and had left-wing views.

Additional Support

Activity: Collaborative Learning

Identifying Points of View Many members of Hollywood were brought before the HUAC; half provided names for the committee to investigate, the other half refused to name names. Nine screenwriters and one director went to jail. Nearly 300 writers, directors, and actors were "blacklisted," or unable to get jobs. One actor, Charlie Chaplin, left the United States. Others changed their names to get work.

Have students work in groups to research HUAC versus Hollywood. They may use actual transcripts or articles, many of which can be found on the Internet. **Ask:** Is it un-American to produce a film that contains Communist propaganda? What films were identified as "Communistic"? Does the entertainment business have the power to manipulate public opinion? Was Hollywood a menace to society? Did HUAC violate citizens' right to free speech? Have students prepare a five minute presentation, offering their views on these questions. Ask students to use specific examples to support their findings. **OL**

D Differentiated Instruction

Visual/Spatial Have students write two newspaper headlines about the execution of the Rosenbergs. One headline should be from the point of view of someone who believes that the Rosenbergs were innocent of the charges, and the other should be from the point of view of someone who is convinced of their guilt. **OL**

C Critical Thinking

Recognizing Bias Ask:
Do you think union members, schools or universities, churches, or businesses have the right to make members divulge information about their political views? Why or why not? *(Responses will vary. Most students will suggest that political views are private and protected under the Constitution.)* **OL**

✔ Reading Check

Answer: to discover Communists who might have infiltrated the U.S. government or areas of American society

Additional Support

During the hearings, ten screenwriters, known as the "Hollywood Ten," used their Fifth Amendment right to protect themselves from self-incrimination and refused to testify. The incident led producers to blacklist, or agree not to hire, anyone who was believed to be a Communist or who refused to cooperate with the committee. In 1950 a pamphlet called *Red Channels* was published, listing 151 blacklisted actors, directors, broadcasters, and screenwriters. The blacklist created an atmosphere of distrust and fear.

Alger Hiss In 1948 Whittaker Chambers, a *TIME* magazine editor and former Communist Party member, testified to HUAC that several government officials were also former Communists or spies.

The most prominent official named by Chambers was **Alger Hiss,** a diplomat who had served in Roosevelt's administration, attended the Yalta conference, and taken part in organizing the United Nations. After Hiss sued him for libel, Chambers testified before a grand jury that, in 1937 and 1938, Hiss had given him secret documents from the State Department. Hiss denied being either a spy or a member of the Communist Party, and he also denied ever having known Chambers.

The committee was ready to drop the investigation until Representative Richard Nixon of California **convinced** his colleagues to continue the hearings to determine whether Hiss or Chambers had lied. Chambers produced copies of secret documents, along with microfilm that he had hidden in a hollow pumpkin on his farm. These "pumpkin papers," Chambers claimed, proved Hiss was lying. A jury agreed and convicted Hiss of **perjury,** or lying under oath.

The Rosenbergs Another sensational spy case centered on accusations that American Communists had sold the secrets of the atomic bomb to the Soviets. Many people did not believe that the Soviet Union could have produced an atomic bomb in 1949 without help. This belief intensified the hunt for spies.

In 1950 the hunt led to a British scientist who admitted sending information to the Soviet Union. After hearing his testimony, the FBI arrested Julius and Ethel Rosenberg, a New York couple who were members of the Communist Party. The government charged them with heading a Soviet spy ring.

The Rosenbergs denied the charges but were condemned to death for espionage. Many people believed that they were not leaders or spies but victims caught up in the wave of anti-Communist frenzy. Appeals, public expressions of support, and pleas for clemency failed, however, and the couple was executed in June 1953.

Project Venona The American public hotly debated the guilt or innocence of individuals, like the Rosenbergs, who were accused of being spies. There was, however, solid evidence of Soviet espionage, although very few Americans knew it at the time. In 1946 American and British cryptographers, working for a project code-named "Venona," cracked the Soviet spy code of the time, enabling them to read approximately 3,000 messages between Moscow and the United States collected during the Cold War.

The messages collected using Project Venona confirmed extensive Soviet spying and an ongoing effort to steal nuclear secrets. The government did not reveal Project Venona's existence until 1995. The Venona documents provided strong evidence that the Rosenbergs were indeed guilty.

The Red Scare Spreads

Following the federal government's example, many state and local governments, universities, businesses, unions, churches, and private organizations began their own efforts to find Communists. The University of California required its 11,000 faculty members to take loyalty oaths and fired 157 who refused to do so. Many Catholic groups became strongly anti-Communist and urged their members to identify Communists within the Church.

The Taft-Hartley Act of 1947 required union leaders to take oaths that they were not Communists, but many union leaders did not object. Instead, they launched their own efforts to purge Communists from their organizations. The president of the CIO called Communist sympathizers "skulking cowards" and "apostles of hate." The CIO eventually expelled 11 unions that refused to remove Communist leaders from their organization.

✔ **Reading Check** **Explaining** What was the purpose of the loyalty review boards and HUAC?

Activity: Interdisciplinary Connection

Civics Many people, including Albert Einstein and Pope Pius XII, urged clemency for the Rosenbergs. Files released after the fall of the Soviet Union seem to indicate that the Rosenbergs were guilty. However, information revealed in a 1996 interview with David Greenglass, Ethel Rosenberg's brother, puts Ethel's guilt in doubt.

Have students research the details of the trial. **Ask:** Who were the Rosenbergs? How did they come under suspicion? Why was the trial so highly publicized? What were the official charges? Why were they sentenced to death? How many people protested their execution? What exactly did the Venona transcripts reveal about them?

Have students write a two-page summary of their findings to present in class. Encourage students to include photos in their reports. **OL**

McCarthyism

MAIN Idea Senator Joseph R. McCarthy used the fear of communism to increase his own power and destroy the reputations of many people.

HISTORY AND YOU Have you ever known anyone who spread untrue stories about others? Read on to find out about the false accusations that Senator McCarthy spread in the early 1950s.

In 1949 the Red Scare intensified even further. In that year, the Soviet Union successfully tested an atomic bomb, and China fell to communism. To many Americans, these events seemed to prove that the United States was losing the Cold War. Deeply concerned, they wanted to know why their government was failing. As a result, many continued to believe that Communists had infiltrated the government and remained undetected.

In February 1950, soon after Alger Hiss's perjury conviction, a little-known Wisconsin senator gave a political speech to a Republican women's group in West Virginia. Halfway through his speech, Senator Joseph R. McCarthy made a surprising statement:

PRIMARY SOURCE

"While I cannot take the time to name all the men in the State Department who have been named as members of the Communist Party and members of a spy ring, I have here in my hand a list of 205 that were known to the Secretary of State as being members of the Communist Party and who nevertheless are still working and shaping the policy of the State Department."

—quoted in *The Fifties*

The Associated Press picked up the statement and sent it to newspapers nationwide. While at an airport, reporters asked McCarthy to see his list of Communists. McCarthy replied that he would be happy to show it to them, but unfortunately, it was in his bag on the plane. In fact, the list never appeared. McCarthy, however, continued to make charges and draw attention.

McCarthy's use of sensationalist charges was not new. When he ran for the Senate in 1946, he accused his opponent, Robert M. La Follette, Jr., of being "communistically inclined." McCarthy did not provide any evidence to support his accusation, but it helped him win the election.

C Critical Thinking

Determining Cause and Effect McCarthy accused people of being Communists with no evidence. **Ask:** Why was McCarthy so successful in getting the press to believe his claims, even though he had no evidence? *(People were extremely fearful.)* **OL**

D Differentiated Instruction

Kinesthetic Illustrate how baseless yet powerful McCarthy was by designating some students as "Communists" for a day. Arbitrarily assign these students to sit in a different part of the class. Do not call on them or let others talk to them. They can only rejoin the group if they identify someone else as a Communist. The accused will join the isolated group. **OL**

Analyzing VISUALS

Answers:
1. he refused to condemn McCarthy
2. Answers will vary. Students should support their choice.

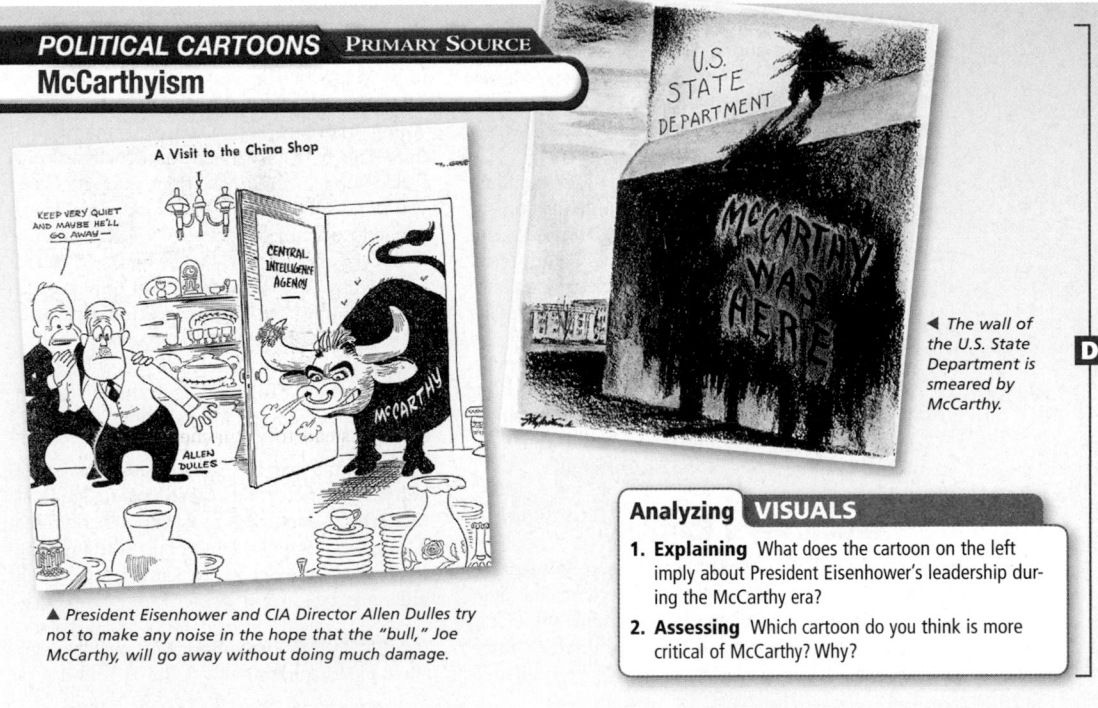

POLITICAL CARTOONS PRIMARY SOURCE
McCarthyism

◀ The wall of the U.S. State Department is smeared by McCarthy.

▲ President Eisenhower and CIA Director Allen Dulles try not to make any noise in the hope that the "bull," Joe McCarthy, will go away without doing much damage.

Analyzing VISUALS

1. **Explaining** What does the cartoon on the left imply about President Eisenhower's leadership during the McCarthy era?
2. **Assessing** Which cartoon do you think is more critical of McCarthy? Why?

Chapter 15 The Cold War Begins **549**

Hands-On Chapter Project
Step 3

Role-Playing to Demonstrate McCarthyism in Action

Step 3: Staging the Hearing **Essential Question: Does the role-play or mock hearing succeed in reflecting what happened and give a sense of why McCarthy ultimately failed?** *(Performers' Perspective)*

Directions Students will perform the role-play before the entire class. Viewers can take notes and ask questions after the performance.

Putting It Together After the performance, the students who created and performed the mock-hearing should meet. They can then decide if they need to revise it in any way based on audience feedback. **OL**

(Chapter Project continued on page 557)

C Critical Thinking

Interpreting Truman vetoed the McCarran Bill stating, "The basic error of this bill is that it moves in the direction of suppressing opinion and belief...that would make a mockery of the Bill of Rights and of our claims to stand for freedom in the world." Ask students if they agree with Truman or Congress, which overrode his veto. **Ask:** Do you think a bill such as the McCarran Act could become law in present times? *(Responses will vary.)* **OL**

W Writing Support

Descriptive Writing

McCarthyism was often called the "Witch Hunt of the 1950s." Have students research and explain the metaphor in a one-page paper. *(Students should compare McCarthyism to the Puritan persecution of women in Salem.)* **AL**

✔ Reading Check

Answer: it ruined many careers, colored political life, and influenced popular culture

Additional Support

After becoming a senator, McCarthy continued to proclaim that Communists were a danger both at home and abroad. To some audiences, he distributed a booklet called "The Party of Betrayal," which accused Democratic Party leaders of corruption and of protecting Communists. Secretary of State Dean Acheson was a frequent target. According to McCarthy, Acheson was incompetent and a tool of Stalin. He also wildly accused George C. Marshall, the former army chief of staff and secretary of state, of disloyalty as a member of "a conspiracy so immense as to dwarf any previous such ventures in the history of man."

McCarthy was not alone in making such charges. In the prevailing mood of anxiety about communism, many Americans were ready to believe them.

The McCarran Act

In 1950, with the Korean War underway and McCarthy and others arousing fears of Communist spies, Congress passed the Internal Security Act, usually called the **McCarran Act.** Declaring that "world Communism has as its sole purpose the establishment of a totalitarian dictatorship in America," Senator Pat McCarran of Nevada offered a way to fight "treachery, infiltration, sabotage, and terrorism." The act made it illegal to "combine, conspire, or agree with any other person to perform any act which would substantially contribute to . . . the establishment of a totalitarian government."

The McCarran Act required all Communist Party and "Communist-front" organizations to publish their records and register with the United States attorney general. Communists could not have passports to travel abroad and, in cases of a national emergency, Communists and Communist sympathizers could be arrested and detained. Unwilling to punish people for their opinions, Truman vetoed the bill, but Congress easily overrode his veto in 1950. Later Supreme Court cases, however, limited the scope of the McCarran Act.

McCarthy's Tactics

After the Republicans won control of Congress in 1952, McCarthy became chairman of the Senate subcommittee on investigations. Using the power of his committee to force government officials to testify about alleged

---

Communist influences, McCarthy turned the investigation into a witch hunt—a search for disloyalty based on flimsy evidence and irrational fears. His tactic of damaging reputations with vague and unfounded charges became known as **McCarthyism.**

McCarthy's sensational accusations drew the attention of the press, which put him in the headlines and quoted him widely. When he questioned witnesses, McCarthy would badger them and then refuse to accept their answers. His tactics left a cloud of suspicion that McCarthy and others interpreted as guilt. Furthermore, people were afraid to challenge him for fear of becoming targets themselves.

McCarthy's Downfall

In 1954 McCarthy began to look for Soviet spies in the United States Army. During weeks of televised Army-McCarthy hearings, millions of Americans watched McCarthy question and bully officers, harassing them about trivial details and accusing them of misconduct. His popular support began to fade.

Finally, to strike back at the army's lawyer, Joseph Welch, McCarthy brought up the past of a young lawyer in Welch's firm who had been a member of a Communist-front organization while in law school. Welch, who was fully aware of the young man's past, now exploded at McCarthy for possibly ruining the young man's career: "Until this moment, I think I never really gauged your cruelty or your recklessness. . . . You have done enough. Have you no sense of decency, sir, at long last? Have you left no sense of decency?"

Spectators cheered. Welch had said aloud what many Americans had been thinking. As Senator Stuart Symington of Missouri commented, "The American people have had a look at you for six weeks. You are not fooling anyone." McCarthy had lost the power to arouse fear. Newspaper headlines repeated: "Have you no sense of decency?"

Later that year, the Senate passed a vote of **censure,** or formal disapproval, against McCarthy—one of the most serious criticisms it can level against a member. Although he remained in the Senate, McCarthy had lost all influence. He died in 1957.

✔ Reading Check **Evaluating** What were the effects of McCarthyism?

Activity: Technology Connection

Identifying Points of View News writers, radio broadcasters, average Americans, and even well-known and respected politicians were afraid to speak out against McCarthy for fear they would be next to face his committee (HUAC). When the McCarthy hearings were televised, it drew national attention. The American people were able to witness the bullying techniques of McCarthy.

When McCarthy began attacking the United States Army, he had gone too far. Those who had remained silent finally spoke up, including Edward R. Murrow, an experienced television broadcaster. On March 9, 1954, Murrow used his television program, *See It Now*, to express his views on McCarthyism. Have students use the Internet and library to discover what Murrow said and how the American public reacted. Have students

work in groups to present a "live" or "prerecorded" TV talk show that reflects Murrow's stance, public reaction, and McCarthy's spin on the broadcast. **AL**

ANALYZING SUPREME COURT CASES

Are There Limits on Congressional Power?

★ *Watkins v. United States*, 1957
Background to the Case

In 1954 labor organizer John Watkins testified before the House Un-American Activities Committee. He agreed to discuss his own connections with the Communist Party and to identify people he knew who were still members, but he refused to give information about those who were no longer members. Watkins received a misdemeanor conviction for refusing to answer questions "pertinent to the question under inquiry." In 1957 he appealed his case to the Supreme Court.

How the Court Ruled

The Watkins case raised the question: Is it constitutional for a congressional committee to ask any question or investigate any topic, whether or not it is directly related to Congress's law-making function? In a 6-to-1 decision—two members did not participate—the Supreme Court held that the activities of HUAC during its investigations were, indeed, beyond the scope of the stated aims of the committee, as well as the authority of congressional powers.

▲ Senator Joseph McCarthy (above) symbolized the fears of the early 1950s, when communist spies were suspected to have infiltrated all aspects of American society. Together, McCarthy's committee in the Senate and the House Un-American Activities Committee used their power to subpoena people to investigate their loyalty. As a result many reputations were smeared and careers ruined.

More About the Case

Watkins, who was an active leader in the labor movement, was identified by witnesses as Communist. Watkins testified freely about his own activities, admitting to participating in some Communist activities and to making contributions. As a union official, he also worked closely with the Communist Party. However, Watkins denied that he was ever a "card carrying member" of the Communist Party, and he refused to answer questions about others who may have been members of the Communist Party, claiming that information was not relevant to the Committee's work.

PRIMARY SOURCE

The Court's Opinion

"The power of the Congress to conduct investigations is inherent in the legislative process. That power is broad. . . . But, broad as is this power of inquiry, it is not unlimited. There is no general authority to expose the private affairs of individuals without justification in terms of the functions of the Congress. . . . Nor is the Congress a law enforcement or trial agency. These are functions of the executive and judicial departments of government. No inquiry is an end in itself; it must be related to, and in furtherance of, a legitimate task of the Congress. Investigations conducted solely for the personal aggrandizement of the investigators or to "punish" those investigated are indefensible."

—Chief Justice Earl Warren, writing for the majority in *Watkins v. United States*

PRIMARY SOURCE

Dissenting View

"It may be that at times the House Committee on Un-American Activities has, as the Court says, "conceived of its task in the grand view of its name." And, perhaps, as the Court indicates, the rules of conduct placed upon the Committee by the House admit of individual abuse and unfairness. But that is none of our affair. So long as the object of a legislative inquiry is legitimate and the questions propounded are pertinent thereto, it is not for the courts to interfere with the committee system of inquiry. To hold otherwise would be an infringement on the power given the Congress to inform itself. . . ."

—Justice Tom Campbell Clark, author of the dissenting opinion in *Watkins v. United States*

DBQ Document-Based Questions

1. **Explaining** On what does Warren say a congressional inquiry must always be based?
2. **Discussing** Why does Clark disagree with the majority opinion?
3. **Making Inferences** What opinion do you think Warren had of HUAC?

DBQ Document Based Questions

1. must be based on the law-making, or legislative duties, of Congress
2. He argued that Congress was pursuing an inquiry on a "legitimate" topic, and the judicial branch should not interfere.
3. Warren appears to have been hostile to HUAC.

Differentiated Instruction

Case Study 38: *Watkins v. United States*, p. 75

Analyzing a Supreme Court Decision

Objective: Learn how judicial review was applied to a refusal to answer questions of the HUAC.

Focus: Identify the central issue of the case: Congressional powers of investigation are not unlimited.

Teach: Discuss the Court's opinion.

Assess: Explain the importance of the case (First and Fifth Amendment rights).

Close: Write a paragraph summarizing the case.

Differentiated Instruction Strategies

BL Define *judicial review* using your own words.

AL Write a brief essay in which you argue against the Court's decision.

ELL Create a list of all of the unfamiliar words in the reading. Then work with a partner to define them.

D Differential Instruction

Visual/Spatial Have students create a chart that includes all the nations that have developed nuclear weapons since 1945. The chart should include the name of the country and the year it conducted its first nuclear test. **OL**

S Skill Practice

Visual Literacy Have students look at the school picture and the bomb shelter. **Ask:** How did people think they were going to survive a nuclear bomb? *(by covering their heads and eyes, hiding underground, eating canned food)* **Ask:** Have you seen any old fallout shelter signs in your community? If so, where are they located? *(Answers will vary.)* **BL**

Analyzing VISUALS

Answers:
1. to protect people from a nuclear bomb blast
2. If a nuclear bomb were dropped, most services would not be available. Each person would have to fend for himself.

Additional Support

Life During the Early Cold War

MAIN Idea Obsessed with fear of a nuclear attack, many Americans took steps to protect themselves.

HISTORY AND YOU Have you ever felt the need to protect yourself from something dangerous or scary? Read to learn more about how Americans tried to deal with their fears during the early 1950s.

The Red Scare and the spread of nuclear weapons had a profound impact on American life in the 1950s. Fear of communism and of nuclear war affected the thinking and choices of many ordinary Americans, as well as their leaders in government. Some Americans responded by preparing to survive a nuclear attack, while others became active in politics in an effort to shape government policy. Writers responded by describing the dangers of atomic war and the threat of communism— sometimes to convince people to take action and sometimes to protest policies they feared might lead to war.

Facing the Bomb

Already upset by the first Soviet atomic test in 1949, Americans were shocked when the Soviets again successfully tested the much more powerful hydrogen bomb, or H-bomb, in 1953. The United States had tested its own H-bomb less than a year earlier.

Americans prepared for a surprise Soviet attack. Schools set aside special areas as bomb shelters. In bomb drills, students learned to

PRIMARY SOURCE

Living with the Bomb in the 1950s

The Cold War convinced many in American society that they needed to be prepared to survive a nuclear attack. While authorities made Civil Defense plans, individuals took it upon themselves to build bomb shelters and stockpile supplies.

▶ In the 1950s school children took part in "duck-and-cover" drills designed to give them a chance at surviving a nuclear blast if they were far enough from the epicenter.

AMERICA CALLING

Take your place in **CIVILIAN DEFENSE**
CONSULT YOUR NEAREST DEFENSE COUNCIL

▲ The Civil Defense Agency set up bomb shelters in cities, and made plans to assist survivors after an attack. Today the Civil Defense Agency is known as FEMA—the Federal Emergency Management Agency.

◀ Some Americans invested in personal bomb shelters stocked with food to allow them to survive a bomb blast and the radiation that would follow.

CANNED FOOD

CANNED WATER

Analyzing VISUALS

1. **Explaining** What was the purpose of the "duck-and-cover" drills and bomb shelters?
2. **Making Inferences** Even if some preparations would not work, why might the government have wanted people to prepare for war?

552 | Chapter 15   The Cold War Begins

Activity: Interdisciplinary Connection

Literature The literature and pop culture of the 1950s reflected themes that were often in conflict with one another. On one side, the view was annihilistic, filled with anti-Communism hysteria and the threat of nuclear war. Ray Bradbury's *The Martian Chronicles* features a doomsday view of the future. Science fiction movies such as *The Invasion of the Body Snatchers* were allegories for communist (alien) subversion.

The other side portrayed an unrealistic view of family life in suburbia. Houses were filled with new appliances and perfect children. Television shows such as *Ozzie and Harriet* and *Leave It To Beaver* portrayed families who were not concerned about bomb shelters or communism.

Have students read some of Bradbury's stories, look at movie posters from the 1950s,

and watch a few episodes of 1950s sitcoms to create a poster with a 1950s theme to be shared with the class. **OL** duck under their desks, turn away from the windows, and cover their heads with their hands. These "duck-and-cover" actions were supposed to protect them from a nuclear bomb blast.

Although "duck-and-cover" might have made people feel safe, it would not have protected them from deadly nuclear radiation. According to experts, for every person killed outright by a nuclear blast, four more would die later from **fallout,** the radiation left over after a blast. To protect themselves, some families built backyard fallout shelters and stocked them with canned food.

Popular Culture in the Cold War

Worries about nuclear war and Communist infiltration filled the public's imagination. Cold War themes soon appeared in films, plays, television, the titles of dance tunes, and popular fiction.

In 1953 Arthur Miller's thinly veiled criticism of the Communist witchhunts, *The Crucible,* appeared on Broadway. The play remains popular today as a cautionary tale about how hysteria can lead to false accusations. Matt Cvetic was an FBI undercover informant who secretly infiltrated the Communist Party in Pittsburgh, Pennsylvania. His story captivated magazine readers in the *Saturday Evening Post* in 1950 and came to movie screens the next year as *I Was a Communist for the FBI.* Another suspense film, *Walk East on Beacon* (1951), features the FBI's activities in an espionage case.

In 1953 television took up the theme with a series about an undercover FBI counterspy who was also a Communist Party official. Each week, *I Led Three Lives* kept television viewers on edge. Popular tunes such as "Atomic Boogie" and "Atom Bomb Baby" played on the radio.

In 1954 author Philip Wylie published *Tomorrow!* This novel describes the horrific effects of nuclear war on an unprepared American city. As an adviser on civil defense, Wylie had failed to convince the federal government to play a strong role in building bomb shelters. Frustrated, he wrote his novel to educate the public about the horrors of atomic war.

One of the most famous and enduring works of this period is John Hersey's nonfiction book *Hiroshima.* Originally published as the entire contents of the August 1946 edition of *The New Yorker* magazine, the book provides the firsthand accounts of six survivors of the U.S. dropping of the atomic bomb on Hiroshima, Japan. Not only did it make some Americans question the use of the bomb, *Hiroshima* also underscored the real and personal horrors of a nuclear attack. **R**

At the same time that these fears were haunting Americans, the country was enjoying postwar prosperity and optimism. That spirit, combined with McCarthyism, fears of Communist infiltration, and the threat of atomic attack, made the early 1950s a time of contrasts. As the 1952 election approached, Americans were looking for someone or something that would make them feel secure.

✓ **Reading Check** **Describing** How did the Cold War affect life in the 1950s?

Section 3 REVIEW

Vocabulary
1. **Explain** the significance of: Red Scare, subversion, loyalty review program, Alger Hiss, perjury, McCarran Act, McCarthyism, censure, fallout.

Main Ideas
2. **Explaining** What was the result of President Truman's loyalty review program?

3. **Analyzing** Hearings to investigate Communist subversion in what organization led to McCarthy's downfall?

4. **Identifying** What event made Americans fearful of a nuclear attack by the Soviets?

Critical Thinking
5. **Big Ideas** How did the Red Scare and McCarthyism change American society and government?

6. **Organizing** Use a graphic organizer similar to the one below to list the causes and effects of the Red Scare of the 1950s.

Causes   Effects

Red Scare

7. **Analyzing Visuals** Study the cartoons on page 549. Which cartoon do you think makes the stronger point? Explain.

Writing About History
8. **Persuasive Writing** Suppose that you are a newspaper editor during the Army-McCarthy hearings. Write an editorial giving reasons why people should support or condemn Senator McCarthy.

History ONLINE
Study Central™ To review this section, go to glencoe.com and click on Study Central.

553

R Reading Strategy

Making Connections Ask: Why would John Hersey's book *Hiroshima* have been so popular during the Cold War? *(It tied together the recent history of using an atomic bomb to people's fears that the U.S. would soon be victims of a nuclear attack.)* **OL**

✓ Reading Check

Answer: Americans prepared for a surprise Soviet attack, worried about a nuclear war, and watched films and read books about Communist infiltration.

Assess
. . . .

History ONLINE

Study Central™ provides summaries, interactive games, and online graphic organizers to help students review content.

Close
. . . .

Identifying Have students break into groups and discuss how American society reflected fears of the nuclear age. **OL**

Section 3 REVIEW

Answers

1. All definitions can be found in the section and the Glossary.
2. Six million federal employees were screened for their loyalty, 2,000 employees quit their jobs, and 212 were fired.
3. the U.S. Army
4. The Soviets successfully tested a hydrogen bomb in 1953.
5. While people were enjoying postwar prosperity and optimism, they feared communism and an atomic attack.

6. Causes: Alger Hiss Trial, Rosenbergs, Russia's successful test of an atomic bomb
Effects: Loyalty Review Program, HUAC, McCarran Act, McCarthyism, fallout shelters, blacklists, duck-and-cover, and so on
7. Responses will vary. Students should support their answers with sound reasoning.
8. Editorials will vary but should reflect a position supported with persuasive reasons.

Focus

Bellringer
Daily Focus Transparency 15.4

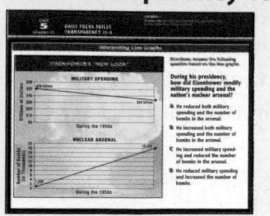

Guide to Reading

Answers:
brinkmanship, covert operations, massive retaliation

Section Spotlight Video

To generate student interest and provide a springboard for class discussion, access the Chapter 15, Section 4 video at glencoe.com or on the video DVD.

Resource Manager

Section 4

Eisenhower's Cold War Policies

Guide to Reading

Big Ideas
Science and Technology Nuclear technology enabled Eisenhower to change U.S. military policy, while new missile technology marked the beginning of the space age.

Content Vocabulary
- massive retaliation (p. 555)
- brinkmanship (p. 555)
- covert (p. 557)
- developing nation (p. 557)
- military-industrial complex (p. 559)

Academic Vocabulary
- imply (p. 558)
- response (p. 559)

People and Events to Identify
- Central Intelligence Agency (p. 557)
- Sputnik (p. 559)

Reading Strategy
Organizing Complete a concept web similar to the one below by filling in aspects of Eisenhower's "New Look."

Eisenhower's "New Look"

President Eisenhower believed developing new technology to deliver nuclear weapons would help prevent war. He also directed the CIA to use covert operations in the struggle to contain communism.

Massive Retaliation

MAIN Idea Eisenhower fought the Cold War by increasing the U.S. nuclear arsenal and using the threat of nuclear war to end conflicts in Korea, Taiwan, and the Suez.

HISTORY AND YOU Do you know anyone who uses threats to get his or her way? Read further to learn about Eisenhower's use of nuclear threats to achieve foreign policy goals.

By the end of 1952, many Americans were ready for a change in leadership. The Cold War had much to do with that attitude. Many people believed that Truman's foreign policy was not working. The Soviet Union had tested an atomic bomb and consolidated its hold on Eastern Europe. China had fallen to communism, and American troops were fighting in Korea.

Tired of the criticism and uncertain he could win, Truman decided not to run again. The Democrats nominated Adlai Stevenson, governor of Illinois. The Republicans chose Dwight D. Eisenhower, the general who had organized the D-Day invasion. Stevenson had no chance against a national hero who had helped win World War II. Americans wanted someone they could trust to lead the nation in the Cold War. Eisenhower won in a landslide.

"More Bang for the Buck"

The Cold War shaped Eisenhower's thinking from the moment he took office. He was convinced that the key to victory in the Cold War was not simply military might but also a strong economy. The United States had to show the world that free enterprise could produce a better society than communism. At the same time, economic prosperity would prevent Communists from gaining support in the United States and protect society from subversion.

As a professional soldier, Eisenhower knew the costs associated with large-scale conventional war. Preparing for that kind of warfare, he believed, was too expensive. "We cannot defend the nation in a way which will exhaust our economy," the president declared. Instead of maintaining a large and expensive army, the nation "must be prepared to use atomic weapons in all forms." Nuclear weapons, he said, gave "more bang for the buck."

R Reading Strategies	**C** Critical Thinking	**D** Differentiated Instruction	**W** Writing Support	**S** Skill Practice
Teacher Edition • Explaining, p. 559 **Additional Resources** • Pri. Source Reading, URB p. 103 • Guided Reading Act., URB p. 119	**Teacher Edition** • Analyzing Info., p. 555 • Speculating, p. 556 • Drawing Con., p. 557 • Evaluating, p. 558 **Additional Resources** • Authentic Assess., p. 35 • Supreme Court Case Studies, p. 77 • Quizzes/Tests, p. 214	**Teacher Edition** • Visual/Spatial, p. 556 • Gifted and Talented, p. 558 **Additional Resources** • Reteaching Act., URB p. 111 • Enrichment Act., URB p. 113 • American Art and Music Act., p. 107		**Teacher Edition** • Using Geo. Skills, p. 557 **Additional Resources** • Time Line Act., URB p. 101 • RENTG, p. 170

TECHNOLOGY & HISTORY

Cold War Technology President Eisenhower's emphasis on nuclear weapons required new technology to deliver them. Eisenhower wanted to make sure that the United States could wage nuclear war even if the Soviets destroyed American bases in Europe or Asia. This required technology that would allow the U.S. to strike the USSR without needing bases in Europe.

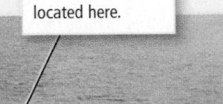

Sixteen missiles were carried in silos located here.

▲ Long-Range Bombers
In 1955 the U.S. Air Force unveiled the huge B-52 bomber (above), which could fly across continents to drop nuclear bombs. The B-52 is still in use today.

▶ ICBMs
Because bombers could be shot down, Eisenhower also approved the development of intercontinental ballistic missiles (ICBMs) that could reach anywhere in the world in less than 30 minutes. The Atlas missile (right) was the first American ICBM. It was also used to launch the first seven U.S. astronauts. It is still used today to launch satellites.

◀ Missile Submarines
Eisenhower also began a program to build submarines capable of launching nuclear missiles from underwater. The Polaris submarine (left) launched in 1960 and carried 16 nuclear missiles.

Analyzing VISUALS

1. **Determining Cause and Effect** How did Eisenhower's nuclear strategy lead to the development of new technologies?
2. **Defining** What is an ICBM and what is its purpose?

The Korean War had convinced Eisenhower that the United States could not contain communism by fighting a series of small wars. Such wars were unpopular and too expensive. Instead, wars had to be prevented from happening in the first place. The best way to do that seemed to be to threaten to use nuclear weapons. This policy came to be called **massive retaliation.**

The new policy enabled Eisenhower to cut military spending from $50 billion to $34 billion. He did this by reducing the size of the army, which was expensive to maintain. At the same time, he increased the U.S. nuclear arsenal from about 1,000 bombs in 1953 to about 18,000 bombs in 1961.

Brinkmanship

President Eisenhower's willingness to threaten nuclear war to maintain peace worried some people. However, Secretary of State John Foster Dulles, the dominant figure in the nation's foreign policy in the 1950s, strongly defended this approach:

PRIMARY SOURCE

"You have to take chances for peace, just as you must take chances in war. Some say that we were brought to the verge of war. Of course we were brought to the verge of war. The ability to get to the verge without getting into the war is the necessary art.... If you try to run away from it, if you are scared to go to the brink, you are lost. We've had to look it square in the face.... We walked to the brink and we looked it in the face. We took strong action."

—quoted in *Rise to Globalism*

Critics called this **brinkmanship**—the willingness to go to the brink of war to force the other side to back down—and argued that it was too dangerous. During several crises, however, President Eisenhower felt compelled to threaten nuclear war.

Chapter 15 The Cold War Begins **555**

Teach

C **Critical Thinking**
Analyzing Information Have students create a T-chart. One column should list the advantages of massive retaliation; the other column should list the disadvantages. Lead a discussion as to whether massive retaliation is a sound policy. **OL**

Analyzing VISUALS

Answers:
1. Nuclear weapons had to be delivered quickly and with little or no harm to Americans. Special planes required new technology—their range had to be longer with an ability to fly higher. Missiles that were launched from land and from submarines were also developed.
2. intercontinental ballistic missile; its purpose was to reach its target within 30 minutes—no pilot required.

Differentiated Instruction

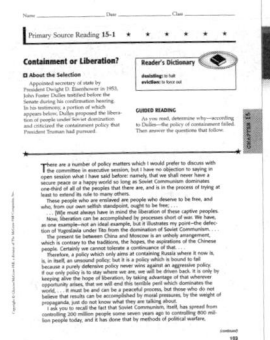

Primary Source Reading, URB p. 103

Writing a Narrative Essay

Objective: Examine a speech regarding the policy of containment.

Focus: Read the speech to determine the message.

Teach: List the reasons Dulles gives to support his argument.

Assess: Write an essay either supporting or contradicting Dulles' opinion.

Close: Ask students: In your opinion, why did containment fail?

Differentiated Instruction Strategies

BL List the examples Dulles gives. Why does he give these examples?

AL Find another primary source about containment.

ELL Outline the speech.

555

C Critical Thinking

Speculating Remind students that during the Korean War, Truman did not want to fight China; MacArthur wanted to use atomic weapons. Eisenhower "hinted" that he would use nuclear bombs, and the Chinese backed off. **Ask: Did Eisenhower do the right thing? Should Truman have used a similar threat?** Write student responses on the board and decide as a class which president took the best approach to end the war. **OL**

D Differentiated Instruction

Visual/Spatial Have students create a time line, listing actions the North Koreans have taken in the last ten years. **Ask: How should the U.S. and the world deal with North Korea?** *(Responses will vary.)* **OL**

Essays will vary but should include an opinion supported with information from the text.

Additional Support

History ONLINE Student Skill Activity To learn how to create a multimedia presentation visit glencoe.com and complete the skill activity.

The Korean War Ends

During his campaign for the presidency, Eisenhower had said, "I shall go to Korea," promising to end the costly and increasingly unpopular war. On December 4, 1952, he kept his promise. Bundled against the freezing Korean winter, the president-elect talked with frontline commanders and their troops.

Eisenhower became convinced that the ongoing battle was costing too many lives and bringing too few victories. He was determined to bring the war to an end. The president then quietly let the Chinese know that the United States might continue the Korean War "under circumstances of our own choosing"—a hint at a nuclear attack.

The threat to go to the brink of nuclear war seemed to work. In July 1953 negotiators signed an armistice. The battle line between the two sides in Korea, which was very near the prewar boundary, became the border between North Korea and South Korea. A "demilitarized zone" (DMZ) separated them. American troops are still based in Korea, helping to defend South Korea's border. There has never been a peace treaty to end the war.

The Taiwan Crisis

Shortly after the Korean War ended, a new crisis erupted in Asia. Although Communists had taken power in mainland China, the Nationalists still controlled Taiwan and several

Turning Point

Sputnik Launches a Space Race

As the United States began to develop ICBMs, Americans were stunned to discover that the Soviet Union already had them. On October 4, 1957, the Soviets demonstrated this technology by launching *Sputnik*, the first artificial satellite to orbit Earth.

Worried that the United States was falling behind, Congress created the National Aeronautics and Space Administration (NASA) to coordinate missile research and space exploration. It also passed the National Defense Education Act (NDEA), which provided funds for education in science, math, and foreign languages.

Sputnik marked the beginning of a new era—the use of satellites in space. Both nations in the Cold War began launching satellites to assist in communications and to spy on the other nation. Today, satellites are a vital part of modern communications and travel. They transmit television and cell phone signals, and the satellites of the Global Positioning System (GPS) help ships and airplanes to navigate. Hikers and drivers can also buy GPS receivers to help determine where they are.

ANALYZING HISTORY Do you think missile and satellite technology helped prevent conflict during the Cold War or made the Cold War worse? Create a multimedia presentation on the Space Race and how it has changed American society.

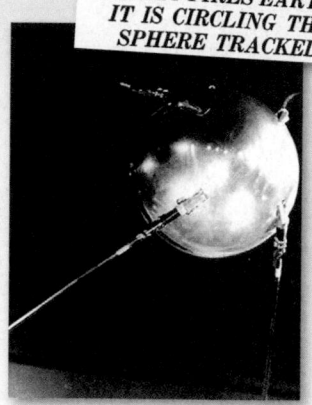

The New York Times.

SOVIET FIRES EARTH SATELLITE INTO SPACE; IT IS CIRCLING THE GLOBE AT 18,000 M. P. H.; SPHERE TRACKED IN 4 CROSSINGS OVER U. S.

▲ *Sputnik (above) was the world's first artificial satellite. It made news around the world and launched the space race.*

▲ *Scientists prepare the first U.S. satellite, Explorer I, for launch in 1958.*

▲ *Sputnik II, launched only a month after Sputnik, carried the first living creature into orbit—an "astro" dog named Laika.*

Extending the Content

Space Race New technology led to planes that could fly across continents at very high altitudes and deliver nuclear bombs. Americans were sure they were ahead of the Russians in the arms race. But *Sputnik* shocked and terrified them.

Then, on November 3, 1957, the Soviets stunned the Americans again when they launched *Sputnik 2* with a live dog on board! America met this challenge head on. On January 31, 1958, *Explorer 1* lifted off from Cape Canaveral, Florida. The United States had just launched its first artificial satellite.

Less than a year after the launch of *Sputnik 1*, Congress approved the creation of the National Aeronautics and Space Administration (NASA). Its mission was to develop an unmanned moon probe, hoping to be the first to the moon. Its goal, however, was a human space exploration program.

small islands along China's coast. In the fall of 1954, China threatened to seize two of the islands. Eisenhower saw Taiwan as part of the "anti-Communist barrier" in Asia that needed to be protected at all costs.

When China began shelling the islands and announced that Taiwan would be liberated, Eisenhower asked Congress to authorize the use of force to defend Taiwan. He then warned the Chinese that any attack on Taiwan would be resisted by U.S. naval forces stationed nearby and hinted that they would use nuclear weapons to stop an invasion. Soon afterward, China backed down.

The Suez Crisis

The following year, a serious crisis erupted in the Middle East. Eisenhower's goal in that region was to prevent Arab nations from aligning with the Soviet Union. To build support among Arabs, Secretary of State Dulles offered to help Egypt finance the construction of a dam on the Nile River.

The deal ran into trouble in Congress, however, because Egypt had bought weapons from Communist Czechoslovakia. Dulles was forced to withdraw the offer. A week later, Egyptian troops seized control of the Suez Canal from the Anglo-French company that had controlled it. The Egyptians intended to use the canal's profits to pay for the dam.

The British and French responded quickly to the Suez Crisis. In October 1956, British and French troops invaded Egypt. Eisenhower was furious with Britain and France. The situation became even more dangerous when the Soviet Union threatened rocket attacks on Britain and France and offered to send troops to help Egypt. Eisenhower immediately put U.S. nuclear forces on alert, noting, "If those fellows start something, we may have to hit them—and if necessary, with everything in the bucket."

Under strong pressure from the United States, the British and French called off their invasion. The Soviet Union had won a major diplomatic victory, however, by supporting Egypt. Soon afterward, other Arab nations began accepting Soviet aid as well.

Reading Check Identifying What was brinkmanship?

Covert Operations

MAIN Idea Eisenhower directed the Central Intelligence Agency to use covert operations to limit the spread of communism and Soviet influence.

HISTORY AND YOU Do you enjoy reading spy novels? Read on to learn of the development and work of a spy agency in the United States.

President Eisenhower relied on brinkmanship on several occasions, but he knew it could not work in all situations. It could prevent war, but it could not, for example, prevent Communists from staging revolutions within countries. To prevent Communist uprisings in other countries, Eisenhower decided to use **covert,** or hidden, operations conducted by the **Central Intelligence Agency (CIA).**

Many of the CIA's operations took place in **developing nations**—nations with primarily agricultural economies. Many of these countries blamed European imperialism and American capitalism for their problems. Their leaders looked to the Soviet Union as a model of how to industrialize their countries. They often threatened to nationalize, or put under government control, foreign businesses operating in their countries.

One way to stop developing nations from moving into the Communist camp was to provide them with financial aid, as Eisenhower had tried to do in Egypt. In some cases, however, where the threat of communism seemed stronger, the CIA ran covert operations to overthrow anti-American leaders and replace them with pro-American leaders.

Iran and Guatemala

Two examples of covert operations that achieved U.S. objectives took place in Iran and Guatemala. By 1953, Iranian Prime Minister Mohammed Mossadegh had already nationalized the Anglo-Iranian Oil Company. He seemed ready to make an oil deal with the Soviet Union. The pro-American Shah of Iran tried to force Mossadegh out of office, but failed and fled into exile. The CIA quickly sent agents to organize street riots and arrange a coup that ousted Mossadegh and returned the shah to power.

C Critical Thinking
Drawing Conclusions First with Korea and then again with Taiwan, Eisenhower "hints" to China that the U.S. may use nuclear weapons. **Ask:** How many times do you think a threat like this will work? Is brinkmanship a good diplomatic tool? *(Answers will vary. Students may suggest that it will only work a few times.)* **OL**

S Skills Practice
Using Geography Skills Have students locate the Suez Canal on a map. **Ask:** What two bodies of water does the Suez Canal connect? *(the Mediterranean Sea and the Red Sea)* **BL**

Reading Check

Answer: Brinkmanship is the willingness to go to the brink of war to force the other side to back down.

Hands-On Chapter Project
Step 4

Role-Playing to Demonstrate McCarthyism in Action

Step 4: Critiquing the Performance
Essential Question: Does the role-play or mock hearing succeed in reflecting what happened and give a sense of why McCarthy ultimately failed? *(Viewers' Perspective)*

Directions Viewers of the performance should divide into groups or meet as whole to critique the performance. Using their notes, viewers should evaluate the performance by answering and discussing the following questions:

• What was the main message of the performance?

• How did the performance compare with the description of McCarthyism in the textbook?

• Why did McCarthy's early targets not challenge him when they stood accused?

• Why did support for McCarthy eventually fade?

Putting It Together After the discussion, have students divide into groups and each choose one of the questions cited above. Give groups a few minutes to agree on an answer. Then have each group recite their answers. **OL**
(Chapter Project continued on the Visual Summary page)

C Critical Thinking

Evaluating Ask: Is secret aggression by the CIA, such as in Guatemala and Eastern Europe justifiable? Why or why not? What events in your lifetime have shaped your answer? *(Responses and examples will vary.)* **OL**

D Differentiated Instruction

Gifted and Talented Have interested students research the cultural, social, and historical factors that affected the Hungarians' reaction to Communist control. Have students present their findings in a brochure form, complete with photos and captions. **AL**

Analyzing VISUALS

Answers:
1. war
2. Because the U-2 flew so high, it might go undetected.

Additional Support

The following year, the CIA intervened in Guatemala. In 1951, with Communist support, Jacobo Arbenz Guzmán was elected president of Guatemala. His land-reform program took over large estates and plantations, including those of the American–owned United Fruit Company. In May 1954, Communist Czechoslovakia delivered arms to Guatemala. The CIA responded by arming the Guatemalan opposition and training them at secret camps in Nicaragua and Honduras. Shortly after these CIA-trained forces invaded Guatemala, Arbenz Guzmán left office.

Trouble in Eastern Europe

Covert operations did not always work as Eisenhower hoped. Stalin died in 1953, and a power struggle began in the Soviet Union. By 1956, Nikita Khrushchev had emerged as the leader of the Soviet Union. That year, Khrushchev delivered a secret speech to Soviet officials. He attacked Stalin's policies and insisted that there were many ways to build a communist society. Although the speech was secret, the CIA obtained a copy of it. With Eisenhower's permission, the CIA arranged for it to be broadcast to Eastern Europe.

Many Eastern Europeans had long been frustrated with Communist rule. Hearing Khrushchev's speech further discredited communism. In June 1956 riots erupted in Eastern Europe. By late October, a full-scale uprising had begun in Hungary. Although Khrushchev was willing to tolerate greater freedom in Eastern Europe, he had never meant to **imply** that the Soviets would tolerate an end to communism in the region. Soon after the uprising began, Soviet tanks rolled into Budapest, the capital of Hungary, and crushed the rebellion.

The Eisenhower Doctrine

The United States was not the only nation using covert means to support its foreign policy. President Gamal Abdel Nasser of Egypt had emerged from the Suez crisis as a hero to the Arab people, and by 1957 he had begun working

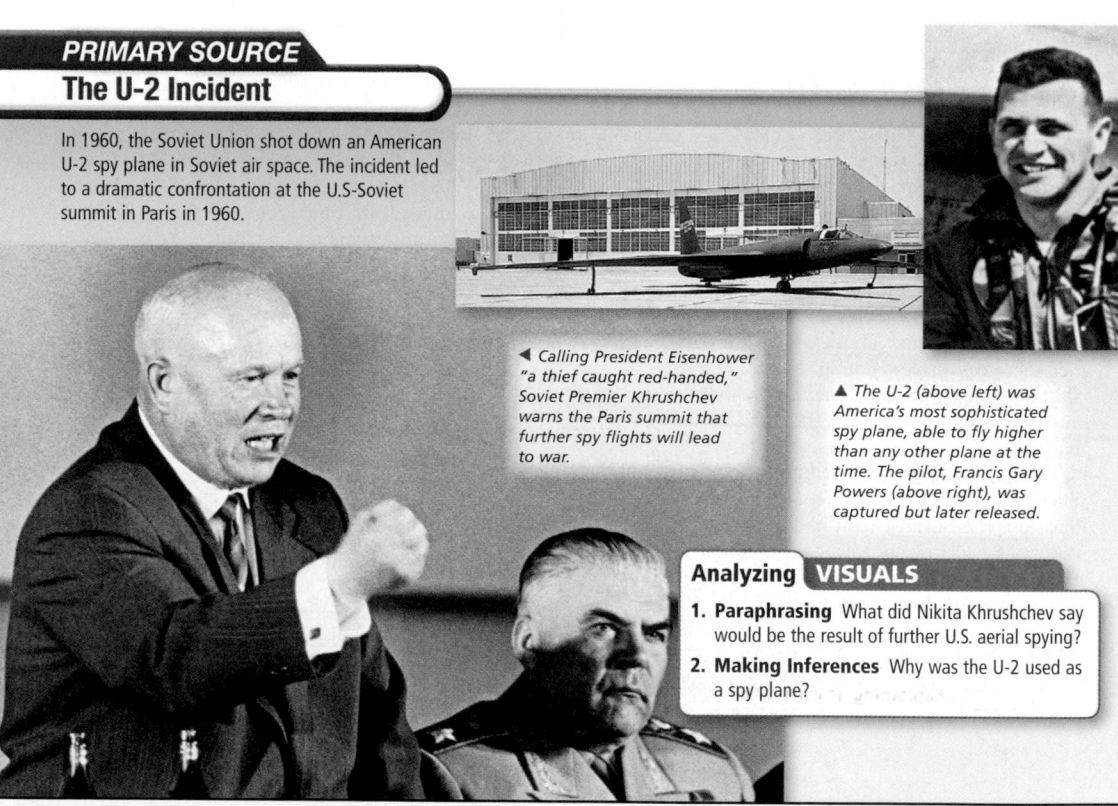

PRIMARY SOURCE
The U-2 Incident

In 1960, the Soviet Union shot down an American U-2 spy plane in Soviet air space. The incident led to a dramatic confrontation at the U.S-Soviet summit in Paris in 1960.

◀ Calling President Eisenhower "a thief caught red-handed," Soviet Premier Khrushchev warns the Paris summit that further spy flights will lead to war.

▲ The U-2 (above left) was America's most sophisticated spy plane, able to fly higher than any other plane at the time. The pilot, Francis Gary Powers (above right), was captured but later released.

Analyzing VISUALS

1. **Paraphrasing** What did Nikita Khrushchev say would be the result of further U.S. aerial spying?
2. **Making Inferences** Why was the U-2 used as a spy plane?

Activity: Collaborative Learning

Determining Cause and Effect In 1959 Premier Khrushchev visited several cities in the United States and met with President Eisenhower. The two leaders agreed to a summit in Paris the following year. The U-2 incident occurred just weeks before the summit. When Eisenhower thought the pilot was dead, he denied the allegations, but he admitted the truth when he learned pilot Francis Gary Powers was alive. Khrushchev left Paris before the meeting and withdrew an invitation to Eisenhower to visit the Soviet Union. The focus of the summit was disarmament. Have students use the Dwight D. Eisenhower Library on the Internet to create a poster of the U-2 incident and write a one-page report about what happened to Powers.

Ask: Do you think Khrushchev overreacted or do you think he was justified in leaving the summit? **OL**

with Jordan and Syria to spread pan-Arabism—the idea that all Arab people should be united into one nation. Eisenhower and Dulles worried about Nasser's links to the Soviets and feared that he was laying the groundwork to take control of the Middle East. In late 1957 Eisenhower asked Congress to authorize the use of military force whenever the president thought it necessary to assist Middle East nations resisting Communist aggression. The policy came to be called the Eisenhower Doctrine. It essentially extended the Truman Doctrine and the policy of containment to the Middle East.

In February 1958 Eisenhower's concerns appeared to be confirmed when left-wing rebels, believed to be backed by Nasser and the Soviet Union, seized power in Iraq. Fearing that his government was next, the president of Lebanon asked the United States for help. Eisenhower immediately ordered 5,000 marines to Lebanon to protect its capital, Beirut. At the same time, British forces went into Jordan at the request of King Hussein to protect his government. Once the situation stabilized, the U.S. forces withdrew.

A Spy Plane Is Shot Down

After the Hungarian uprising, Khrushchev reasserted Soviet power and the superiority of communism. Although he had supported "peaceful coexistence" with capitalism, he began accusing the "capitalist countries" of starting a "feverish arms race." In 1957 after the launch of *Sputnik*, Khrushchev boasted, "We will bury capitalism. . . . Your grandchildren will live under communism."

Late the following year, Khrushchev demanded the withdrawal of Allied troops from West Berlin. Secretary of State Dulles rejected Khrushchev's demands. If the Soviets threatened Berlin, Dulles announced, NATO would respond, "if need be by military force." Brinkmanship worked again, and Khrushchev backed down.

At Eisenhower's invitation, Khrushchev visited the United States in late 1959. After the success of that visit, the two leaders agreed to hold a summit in Paris. A summit is a formal face-to-face meeting of leaders from different countries to discuss important issues.

Shortly before the summit was to begin in 1960, the Soviet Union shot down an American U-2 spy plane. At first, Eisenhower claimed that the aircraft was a weather plane that had strayed off course. Then Khrushchev dramatically produced the pilot. Eisenhower refused to apologize, saying the flights had protected American security. In **response,** Khrushchev broke up the summit.

In this climate of heightened tension, President Eisenhower prepared to leave office. In January 1961 he delivered a farewell address to the nation. In the address, he pointed out that a new relationship had developed between the military establishment and the defense industry. He warned Americans to be on guard against the influence of this **military-industrial complex** in a democracy. Although he had avoided war and kept communism contained, Eisenhower was also frustrated: "I confess I lay down my official responsibility in this field with a definite sense of disappointment. . . . I wish I could say that a lasting peace is in sight." **R**

✔**Reading Check** **Explaining** In what nations did the United States intervene with covert operations?

Section 4 REVIEW

Vocabulary
1. **Explain** the significance of: massive retaliation, brinkmanship, covert, Central Intelligence Agency, developing nation, *Sputnik*, military-industrial complex.

Main Ideas
2. **Summarizing** Why did Eisenhower want to depend on nuclear weapons instead of traditional military approaches to war?

3. **Defining** What was the goal of the Eisenhower Doctrine?

Critical Thinking
4. **Big Ideas** How did technology shape Eisenhower's military policy?

5. **Organizing** Use a graphic organizer similar to the one below to list Eisenhower's strategies for containing communism.

6. **Analyzing Visuals** Study the photograph of Khrushchev on page 558. How does this photograph illustrate the U.S. and Soviet relationship at this point in the Cold War?

Writing About History
7. **Persuasive Writing** Suppose that you are a member of Eisenhower's Cabinet. Defend or attack brinkmanship as a foreign policy tactic. Be sure to provide specific reasons for your opinions.

History ONLINE

Study Central™ To review this section, go to glencoe.com and click on Study Central.

559

R Reading Strategy

Explaining Ask: Why did Eisenhower warn the American people about the military-industrial power? *(He thought a military-industrial power would threaten democracy.)* **OL**

✔ Reading Check

Answer:
Iran, Guatemala, and the countries of Eastern Europe

Assess
. . . .
History ONLINE

Study Central™ provides summaries, interactive games, and online graphic organizers to help students review content.

Close
. . . .
Evaluating Have groups debate the effectiveness of Eisenhower's foreign policy. **OL**

Section 4 REVIEW

Answers

1. All definitions can be found in the section and the Glossary.
2. He thought large-scale conventional wars were too expensive and would exhaust the economy. Nuclear weapons provided "more bang for the buck."
3. to extend military aid to the Middle East in order to contain communism
4. It allowed him to pursue the policy of brinkmanship since the nuclear arsenal was a real threat. It also allowed the U.S. to spy on other nations with satellites and spy planes.

5.
Strategies for Containing Communism

strong economy
nuclear weapons for massive retaliation
brinkmanship
covert operations

6. Khrushchev looks strained and defensive, with his fists clenched, an image that reflects the strained relations between the U.S. and the Soviet Union.
7. Responses will vary but should express an opinion supporting or opposing brinkmanship.

Chapter 15 VISUAL SUMMARY

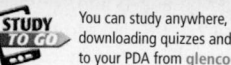

Visual/Spatial Instruct students to use the information on the page and prepare two cause and effect graphic organizers—one for immediate causes of the Cold War and one for long term causes. **OL**

Evaluating Ask students to create a T-chart. In one column, have them identify positive effects of the Cold War (*rebuilding Europe, rebuilding Japan, NATO is created*). In the other column, have them list negative effects (*Germany is divided, China falls to communism, HUAC invades people's private lives, more weapons of mass destruction are built*). **Ask:** Which effects do you think are neutral? (*Responses will vary.*) **OL**

Causes of the Cold War

Long-Range Causes

- Both the United States and the Soviet Union believe their economic and political systems are superior.
- Defeat of Germany creates a power vacuum in Europe and leaves U.S. and Soviet forces occupying parts of Europe.
- The U.S. wants to rebuild Europe's economy and support democratic governments to ensure peace and security.
- The USSR wants Germany weak and believes nations on the Soviet border should have Communist governments.

Immediate Causes

- At Yalta, Soviets promise to allow free elections in Eastern Europe but instead gradually impose Communist regimes.
- At Potsdam, Soviets want German reparations, but the U.S. supports rebuilding Germany's economy.
- Soviet troops help Communists in northern Iran, but U.S. pressure forces a withdrawal.
- George Kennan sends the Long Telegram to U.S. officials, explaining that the Soviets need to be contained.
- Soviets send aid to Communist rebels in Greece and demand Turkey share control of the Dardanelles with the USSR; Truman issues the Truman Doctrine and sends aid to Greece and Turkey.

▲ From left to right: British Prime Minister Clement Atlee, U.S. President Harry Truman, and Soviet leader Joseph Stalin at the Potsdam Conference in 1945. The conference contributed to the onset of the Cold War because of disagreements over how to handle postwar Europe.

Effects of the Cold War

Effects in Europe

- U.S. launches the Marshall Plan to rebuild Europe.
- Germany is divided into two separate nations.
- The USSR blockades Berlin; U.S. organizes the Berlin Airlift.
- The U.S. creates NATO; the USSR creates the Warsaw Pact.

Global Effects

- When China falls to communism, the U.S. responds by helping Japan build up its economy and military.
- When Communist North Korea invades South Korea, the U.S. organizes an international force to stop the invasion.

Effects on the United States

- Soviet spies are arrested.
- A new Red Scare leads to laws restricting the Communist Party in the U.S. and to investigations by the House Un-American Activities Committee and Senator Joseph McCarthy.
- Americans practice civil defense; some build bomb shelters.
- President Eisenhower orders the development of new rockets, bombers, and submarines that can carry nuclear weapons.
- Eisenhower uses the CIA to covertly contain communism.

▲ The Soviet Union displays its nuclear capabilities in the form of these short-range missiles during celebrations commemorating the 40th anniversary of the Bolshevik Revolution in 1957. The nuclear arms race was a part of the Cold War for nearly 40 years.

560 Chapter 15 The Cold War Begins

Hands-On Chapter Project

Step 5: Wrap Up

Role-Playing to Demonstrate McCarthyism in Action

Step 5: Wrap Up Essential Question: What was the impact of McCarthyism? How did it shape American history?

Directions Students should draw from each step of the chapter project to write a brief essay that answers the essential question (above). You may want to give students the option of recording their answer to the essential question and submitting it to you as an audio file.

Putting It Together Students will synthesize the information presented and the discussions following each step to summarize the big idea—how McCarthyism impacted the history of the United States. **OL**

STANDARDIZED TEST PRACTICE

TEST-TAKING

When you first start a test, review it completely so that you can budget your time most efficiently. For example, if there are essay questions at the end, you will want to be sure you leave enough time to write complete answers.

Reviewing Vocabulary

Directions: Choose the word or words that best complete the sentence.

1. After World War II, the Soviet Union wanted to establish a buffer zone of _____ on its European border.
   A developing nations
   B capitalist nations
   C satellite nations
   D demilitarization

2. The policy of _____ became the main approach in U.S. foreign policy toward the Soviet Union during the Cold War.
   A democracy
   B limited war
   C free trade
   D containment

3. Once the Soviet Union tested an atomic bomb, Americans began to fear the effects of _____ , assuming they initially survived a nuclear attack.
   A fallout
   B censure
   C subversion
   D duck-and-cover

4. In his farewell address, President Eisenhower warned the American people about the dangers of
   A the Central Intelligence Agency.
   B massive retaliation.
   C the military-industrial complex.
   D brinkmanship.

Reviewing Main Ideas

Directions: Choose the best answer for each of the following questions.

Section 1 *(pp. 532–537)*

5. Which of the following was a major outcome of the Yalta Conference?
   A the division of Germany
   B the terms of Germany's surrender
   C the establishment of satellite nations
   D the establishment of NATO

6. At Potsdam, the main conflict was over which of the following?
   A the United Nations
   B the invasion of Japan
   C German reparations
   D nuclear weapons

Section 2 *(pp. 538–545)*

7. George Kennan first suggested which foreign policy?
   A brinkmanship
   B containment
   C massive retaliation
   D the Marshall Plan

8. Which of the following events set off the Korean War?
   A The Japanese invaded South Korea.
   B Soviet-controlled North Korea invaded South Korea.
   C Chinese-controlled North Korea invaded South Korea.
   D The Soviet Union invaded North Korea.

Need Extra Help?								
If You Missed Questions . . .	1	2	3	4	5	6	7	8
Go to Page . . .	537	538	552–553	559	532–533	536–537	538	543

GO ON

Answers and Analyses
Reviewing Vocabulary

1. C Developing nations are nations that are transforming economically, and are not relevant to the question. Capitalist nations are the opposite of what the USSR would want to set up. Demilitarization is an action, not an object, and does not make grammatical sense.

2. D The United States wanted to stop, or contain, the spread of communism. Democracy is not a foreign policy approach. Free trade does not make sense in the context of the Cold War.

3. A Fallout is the after effects of a nuclear attack. Censure is a political term. Subversion does not make sense in the context of the sentence. Duck and cover was an action that was to be taken during an attack, not after.

4. C Eisenhower issued the warning due to the new relationship that had developed between the military and the defense industry. He was afraid their influence would be too far reaching and warned Americans to be on guard.

5. A At the conference, Germany was divided into four parts, one each controlled by the U.S., Great Britain, France, and the Soviet Union. Berlin was also divided between the four nations. Satellite nations and NATO were not established until after the conference.

6. C Truman and Stalin met at Potsdam to discuss mainly what to do with Germany. Truman believed Germany needed industry to survive and needed money to fuel industry. Stalin wanted reparations from Germany. He was not concerned with the German economy, because the Soviet economy was so devastated.

7. B Kennan's proposal of containment of Communism became the basis for American Cold War foreign policy. Brinkmanship and massive retaliation were later policies instituted by Eisenhower's administration. The Marshall Plan was a plan to help rebuild Europe after WWII.

8. B It is important that students understand the Korean conflict was between North and South Korea, which eliminates *A* and *D*. However, students may have trouble choosing between *B* and *C*. Students should remember that the Korean War involved the two main players in the Cold War: the U.S. and USSR.

9. B The Marshall Plan was aimed at rebuilding Europe after the war. An underlying motivation was to stop the spread of communism—strong European economies would help keep European nations from falling to communism.

10. A Remind students that HUAC stands for House Un-American Activities Committee. Un-American activities are anti-American. During the Red Scare that swept the nation in the years following WWII, Communists or those who were believed to be communist "sympathizers" were considered un-American—a threat to the nation.

11. C Although many local governments, businesses, unions, etc., asked employees to take loyalty oaths, such as the University of California, all government employees did not have to take an oath. The government did not order all Communist Party chapters to disband. The Act did require these organizations to register with the government. The act was passed over Truman's veto.

12. B Students should relate attack to retaliation, which may help them remember the policy of massive retaliation. Containment was the policy under the Truman administration. Subversion is a rebellion or treason, and does not fit. Duck-and-cover was a plan to "survive" a nuclear attack.

13. D The Truman Doctrine offered aid to any nation resisting communism and was connected to the policy of containment. The Eisenhower Doctrine was issued in response to the pan-Arabism movement, which some feared would lead to communism in the Middle East.

14. C Although the map is helpful, the incorrect answers are easily eliminated. The map is labeled East Germany, which eliminates *A*. West

562

---

9. What was the underlying goal of the Marshall Plan?

   A to contain Soviet expansion in the Middle East and Asia

   B to rebuild European economies to prevent the spread of communism

   C to monitor the growth of the military-industrial complex in the United States

   D to Americanize Western European nations

Section 3 *(pp. 546–553)*

10. After World War II, the purpose of HUAC was to

   A hold public hearings on Communist subversion.

   B locate chapters of the Communist Party.

   C administer the loyalty review program.

   D create the McCarran Act.

11. The McCarran Act required

   A every government employee to take a loyalty oath.

   B all Communist Party chapters to disband.

   C all Communist organizations to register with the government.

   D the censure of members of Congress who would not support HUAC.

Section 4 *(pp. 554–559)*

12. Eisenhower's administration developed an approach to foreign policy based on the threat of nuclear attack, known as

   A containment.

   B massive retaliation.

   C subversion.

   D duck-and-cover.

13. The Eisenhower Doctrine extended the Truman Doctrine to which region?

   A Asia

   B Eastern Europe

   C South America

   D the Middle East

Need Extra Help?							
If You Missed Questions . . .	9	10	11	12	13	14	15
Go to Page . . .	540	547	550	554–555	558–559	560–561	560–561

562   Chapter 15   The Cold War Begins

Critical Thinking

Directions: Choose the best answers to the following questions.

Base your answers to questions 14 and 15 on the map below and on your knowledge of Chapter 15.

14. Why was Stalin initially able to control access to West Berlin?

   A West Berlin was in the Soviet Union.

   B West Berlin was ruled by Communists.

   C West Berlin was in the Soviet sector of Germany.

   D West Berlin had been invaded and occupied by the Red Army.

15. Why did Stalin order a blockade of West Berlin?

   A West Berlin was primarily agricultural and would help feed the Soviet army.

   B Stalin wanted to unite Berlin and organize free elections for Germany.

   C Stalin was afraid of the U.S. nuclear technology and wanted a larger buffer zone.

   D Stalin wanted the United States to abandon West Berlin.

GO ON

Berlin included the American, British, and French sectors, according to the map key, so it was not ruled by Communists and not occupied by the Soviet Army. Berlin was, however, in the Soviet sector.

15. D A blockade attempts to keep supplies and food out of a certain area. Keeping food out of West Berlin would not help feed the Soviet army. Stalin wanted to unite Berlin under his own control, and would not want free elections. He wanted the U.S. to leave. West Berlin would not create a significant buffer zone.

16. One historical lesson from the McCarthy era is the realization that

A loyalty oaths prevent spying.

B communism is attractive in prosperous times.

C Communist agents had infiltrated all levels of the U.S. government.

D public fear of traitors can lead to intolerance and discrimination.

Analyze the cartoon and answer the question that follows. Base your answer on the cartoon and on your knowledge of Chapter 15.

"So Russia Launched a Satellite, but Has It Made Cars With Fins Yet?"

17. In this cartoon, the cartoonist is expressing

A pride in America's technological know-how.

B anxiety that America is behind in the space race.

C a wish for larger, more elaborate cars.

D the need to share auto technology with Russia.

Document-Based Questions

Directions: Analyze the document and answer the short-answer questions that follow the document.

Margaret Chase Smith, a Republican senator from Maine, was a newcomer and the only woman in the Senate. Smith was upset by McCarthy's behavior and hoped that her colleagues would reprimand him. When they failed to do so, Smith made her "Declaration of Conscience" speech.

> "As a United States Senator, I am not proud of the way in which the Senate has been made a publicity platform for irresponsible sensationalism. I am not proud of the reckless abandon in which unproved charges have been hurled from this side of the aisle. I am not proud of the obviously staged, undignified countercharges that have been attempted in retaliation from the other side of the aisle . . . I am not proud of the way we smear outsiders from the Floor of the Senate and hide behind a cloak of congressional immunity. . . .
>
> As an American, I am shocked at the way Republicans and Democrats alike are playing directly into the Communist design of 'confuse, divide, and conquer'. . . . I want to see our nation recapture the strength and unity it once had when we fought the enemy instead of ourselves."
>
> —from Declaration of Conscience

18. In the speech, Smith expresses anger with whom? Why?

19. According to Smith, who is really dividing the nation?

Extended Response

20. Many factors contributed to the development of the Cold War, but could it have been avoided? Write a persuasive essay arguing that actions of the United States or the Soviet Union following World War II might have prevented the Cold War, or that it was inevitable.

History ONLINE

For additional test practice, use Self-Check Quizzes—Chapter 15 at glencoe.com.

Need Extra Help?

If You Missed Questions . . .	16	17	18	19	20
Go to Page . . .	549–550	R18	550	550	532–545

---

19. Smith believes the Republicans and Democrats in Senate are dividing the nation, playing into the Soviet plan or "confuse, divide, and conquer."

Extended Response

20. Students must take a position either that the Cold War could have been prevented or could not have been prevented. Students should use evidence from the chapter, and possible topics for discussion include Yalta, the Marshall Plan, the Berlin Airlift, and the formation of NATO. Essays should adhere to the guidelines for writing a persuasive essay and should present a clear and well-reasoned argument.

16. D The Red Scare during the McCarthy era led many people to discriminate and accept poor or legally suspect treatment of people considered to be Communists and subversives. The culture of fear during the era allowed this discrimination to take place.

17. B The car salesman in the cartoon is expressing pride in American know-how, but Uncle Sam looks concerned. Direct students to read the caption. The caption pokes fun at American technology; it says that Americans were making strides in frivolous things like fins on cars while the USSR had already launched a satellite into space.

Document-Based Questions

18. Smith expresses anger with the members of Senate, both Republican and Democrat, who took part in irresponsible charges and accusations against fellow Americans. She also expresses anger at the way they hide behind congressional immunity to do so.

History ONLINE

Have students visit the Web site at glencoe.com to review Chapter 15 and take the Self-Check Quiz.

Need Extra Help?

Have students refer to the pages listed if they miss any of the questions.

563

Chapter 16 | Planning Guide

Levels				Resources		Chapter Opener	Section 1	Section 2	Section 3	Chapter Assess
BL	OL	AL	ELL							
FOCUS										
BL	OL	AL	ELL	🖎	Daily Focus Skills Transparencies		16-1	16-2	16-3	
TEACH										
	OL	AL		📁	Economics and History Activity, URB			p. 7		
BL	OL		ELL	📁	Reading Essentials and Note-Taking Guide*		p. 173	p. 176	p. 179	
	OL			📁	Historical Analysis Skills Activity, URB		p. 124			
BL	OL		ELL	📁	Guided Reading Activities, URB*		p. 150	p. 151	p. 152	
BL	OL	AL	ELL	📁	Content Vocabulary Activity, URB*	p. 129				
BL	OL	AL	ELL	📁	Academic Vocabulary Activity, URB	p. 131				
	OL	AL		📁	Critical Thinking Skills Activity, URB			p. 134		
BL	OL		ELL	📁	Reading Skills Activity, URB			p. 123		
BL			ELL	📁	English Learner Activity, URB		p. 127			
	OL	AL		📁	Reinforcing Skills Activity, URB			p. 133		
BL	OL	AL	ELL	📁	Differentiated Instruction Activity, URB				p. 125	
BL	OL		ELL	📁	Time Line Activity, URB					p. 135
	OL			📁	Linking Past and Present Activity, URB			p. 136		
BL	OL	AL	ELL	📁	American Art and Music Activity, URB					p. 141
BL	OL	AL	ELL	📁	Interpreting Political Cartoons Activity, URB			p. 143		
		AL		📁	Enrichment Activity, URB					p. 147
BL	OL	AL	ELL	📁	American Biographies			✓		
BL	OL	AL	ELL	📁	Primary Source Reading, URB			p. 139	p.137	
BL	OL	AL	ELL	📁	The Living Constitution*	✓	✓	✓	✓	✓
	OL	AL		💿	American History Primary Source Documents Library	✓	✓	✓	✓	✓
BL	OL	AL	ELL	🖎	Unit Map Overlay Transparencies	✓	✓	✓	✓	✓
BL	OL	AL	ELL	📁	Differentiated Instruction for the American High School Classroom	✓	✓	✓	✓	✓
BL	OL	AL	ELL	📀	StudentWorks™ Plus DVD	✓	✓	✓	✓	✓
BL	OL	AL	ELL	💿	Vocabulary PuzzleMaker CD-ROM	✓	✓	✓	✓	✓

Note: Please refer to *Unit 5 Resource Book* for this chapter's URB materials.

* Also available in Spanish

- Interactive Lesson Planner
- Interactive Teacher Edition
- Fully editable blackline masters
- Section Spotlight Videos Launch

- Differentiated Lesson Plans
- Printable reports of daily assignments
- Standards Tracking System

Levels BL	OL	AL	ELL		Resources	Chapter Opener	Section 1	Section 2	Section 3	Chapter Assess
TEACH *(continued)*										
BL	OL	AL	ELL	⦿	American Music Hits Through History CD	✓	✓	✓	✓	✓
BL	OL	AL	ELL	📁	Unit Time Line Transparencies and Activities	✓	✓	✓	✓	✓
BL	OL	AL	ELL	📁	Cause and Effect Transparencies, Strategies, and Activities	✓	✓	✓	✓	✓
BL	OL	AL	ELL	📁	Why It Matters Transparencies, Strategies, and Activities	✓	✓	✓	✓	✓
BL	OL	AL	ELL	📁	American Issues	✓	✓	✓	✓	✓
	OL	AL	ELL	📁	American Art and Architecture Transparencies, Strategies, and Activities	✓	✓	✓	✓	✓
BL	OL	AL		📁	High School American History Literature Library	✓	✓	✓	✓	✓
BL	OL	AL	ELL	🔒	*The American Vision* Video Program DVD	✓	✓	✓	✓	✓
Teacher Resources				📁	Strategies for Success	✓	✓	✓	✓	✓
				📁	Success with English Learner	✓	✓	✓	✓	✓
				📁	Studies Classroom	✓	✓	✓	✓	✓
				🔒	Presentation Plus! DVD	✓	✓	✓	✓	✓
ASSESS										
BL	OL	AL	ELL	📁	Section Quizzes and Chapter Tests*		p. 223	p. 224	p. 225	p. 227
BL	OL	AL	ELL	📁	Authentic Assessment With Rubrics					p. 37
BL	OL	AL	ELL	📁	Standardized Test Practice Workbook					p. 37
BL	OL	AL	ELL	⦿	*ExamView®* Assessment Suite CD-ROM		16-1	16-2	16-3	Ch. 16
BL	OL	AL	ELL	⦿	Interactive Tutor Self-Assessment CD-ROM		16-1	16-2	16-3	Ch. 16
CLOSE										
BL			ELL	📁	Reteaching Activity, URB					p. 145
BL	OL		ELL	📁	Reading and Study Skills Foldables™	p. 77				

Using the Glencoe Web Site

Student Web Activities

Technology Product

The Glencoe Web site provides Web activities to students that reinforce and enrich chapter content. The Student Web Activities

- introduce topic relevant to chapter content, along with link to Web sites that provide information about the topic;
- prompts students to complete tasks specific to the activity;
- assess student comprehension of the material.

Objectives

The Student Web Activities help students

- learn online research and study skills;
- practice reading and comprehension skills.

Steps

Provide students with the following steps to complete the activities:

- Locate the Web page for the textbook being studied on the Glencoe Web site glencoe.com.
- Click on **Student Center** under the textbook title.
- In the Student Center, select a unit from the Unit Resources menu and a chapter from the Chapter Activities menu using the drop-down arrows.
- Click on the **Student Web Activities** link.
- Have students complete the activity on the page, clicking on the featured Web link for the chapter selected and answering the activity questions.

Provide students with an e-mail address to submit their answers for grading.

History ONLINE

	Student	Teacher	Parent
Beyond the Textbook	●	●	●
Chapter Overviews	●	●	●
Time Current Events	●		●
ePuzzles and Games	●		●
Concepts in Motion	●		●
Literature Connections		●	
Multi-Language Glossaries	●		●
Online Student Edition	●	●	●
Self-Check Quizzes	●		●
Student Web Activities	●		●
Study Central™	●		●
Teaching Today		●	
Vocabulary eFlashcards	●		●
Web Activity Lesson Plans		●	

Glencoe Media Center

glencoe.com

❯ **Study-To-Go**
- Vocabulary eFlashcards
- Self-Check Quizzes

❯ **Audio/Video**
- Student Edition Audio
- Spanish Summaries
- Section Videos

- **Timed Readings Plus in Social Studies** helps students increase their reading rate and fluency while maintaining comprehension. The 400-word passages are similar to those found on state and national assessments.

- **Reading in the Content Area: Social Studies** concentrates on six essential reading skills that help students better comprehend what they read. The book includes 75 high-interest nonfiction passages written at increasing levels of difficulty.

- **Reading Social Studies** includes strategic reading instruction and vocabulary support in Social Studies content for both ELLs and native speakers of English.

www.jamestowneducation.com

The following videotape programs are available from Glencoe as supplements to Chapter 16:

- Dwight D. Eisenhower: Commander-in-Chief (ISBN 1-56-501807-9)

- The Class of the 20th Century; Vol. 3 1952–1961 (ISBN 1-56-501049-3)

To order, call Glencoe at 1-800-334-7344. To find classroom resources to accompany many of these videos, check the following home pages:

A&E Television: www.aetv.com

The History Channel: www.historychannel.com

NATIONAL GEOGRAPHIC
Index to National Geographic Magazine:

The following articles relate to this chapter:
- "He Refused to Leave. (Harry Truman)," January 1981.
- "Alone Across the Arctic Crown," by Berge Ousland, November 1993.

National Geographic Society Products To order the following, call National Geographic at 1-800-368-2728:
- *ZipZapMap! USA Windows* (ZipZapMap! USA)

Access National Geographic's new, dynamic MapMachine Web site and other geography resources at:

www.nationalgeographic.com
www.nationalgeographic.com/maps

Reading List Generator CD-ROM

Use this database to search more than 30,000 titles to create a customized reading list for your students.

- Reading lists can be organized by students' reading level, author, genre, theme, or area of interest.
- The database provides Degrees of Reading Power™ (DRP) and Lexile™ readability scores for all selections.
- A brief summary of each selection is included.

Leveled reading suggestions for this chapter:

For students at a Grade 8 reading level:
- *October Sky*, by Homer H. Hickam

For students at a Grade 9 reading level:
- *Plain Speaking: An Oral Biography of Harry S. Truman*, by Merle Miller

For students at a Grade 10 reading level:
- *Elvis Presley*, by Bobbie Ann Mason

For students at a Grade 11 reading level:
- *Harry S. Truman*, by Caroline Evenson Lazo

For students at a Grade 12 reading level:
- *Polio*, by Allison Stark Draper

Focus

MAKING CONNECTIONS
What Does It Mean to Be Prosperous?
Ask students to imagine that each of them just received $10,000 to spend, save, or invest as they choose. Have students brainstorm what they would do with this money and list their ideas on the board. Explain that many Americans had extra money to spend in the 1950s. Discuss with the students how Americans in the 1950s spent this extra money. **OL**

Teach

The Big Ideas

As students study the chapter, remind them to consider the section-based Big Ideas included in each section's Guide to Reading. The **Essential Questions** in the activities below tie in to the Big Ideas and help students think about and understand important chapter concepts. In addition, the Hands-on Chapter Projects with their culminating activities relate the content from each section to the Big Ideas. These activities build on each other as students progress through the chapter. Section activities culminate in the wrap-up activity on the Visual Summary page.

Chapter 16

Postwar America
1945–1960

SECTION 1 Truman and Eisenhower
SECTION 2 The Affluent Society
SECTION 3 The Other Side of American Life

Teens enjoy milkshakes while studying in a 1950's-style diner.

U.S. PRESIDENTS
U.S. EVENTS
WORLD EVENTS

1944
• GI Bill is enacted

Truman 1945–1953

1946
• Strikes erupt across country

1947
• Congress passes Taft-Hartley Act over Truman's veto

1951
• The *I Love Lucy* television show airs its first show

1944   1948   1952

1946
• Churchill gives "Iron Curtain" speech

1948
• South Africa introduces apartheid

1952
• Scientists led by Edward Teller develop hydrogen bomb

564 Chapter 16 Postwar America

Section 1

Truman and Eisenhower
Essential Question: How did Truman and Eisenhower guide the nation after World War II? *(Both presidents worked to keep the nation strong as it returned to a peacetime economy.)* Tell students that in this section they will learn about how the differing policies of presidents Truman and Eisenhower kept the nation's economy strong after World War II. **OL**

Section 2

The Affluent Society
Essential Question: What were the characteristics of affluent Americans in the 1950s? *(Most people had more money to spend; many people moved to the suburbs; leisure time increased.)* Tell students that this section will focus on how many Americans enjoyed their newfound affluence. **OL**

MAKING CONNECTIONS

What Does It Mean to Be Prosperous?

After World War II, the United States experienced years of steady economic growth. Although not everyone bene-fited, the economic boom meant most Americans enjoyed more prosperity than earlier generations.

- *How did Americans spend this new wealth?*
- *How does prosperity change the way people live?*

More About the Photo

Visual Literacy In the 1950s, diners became popular places for young people to gather. The afflu-ence of the 1950s allowed more teenagers to acquire cars, which they drove to school, and then, after school to the local diner or malt shop for milkshakes or soft drinks. Most diners had jukeboxes that played rock and roll music.

FOLDABLES Study Organizer **Dinah Zike's Foldables**

Dinah Zike's Foldables are three-dimensional, interac-tive graphic organizers that help students practice basic writing skills, review vocabu-lary terms, and identify main ideas. Instructions for creat-ing and using Foldables can be found in the Appendix at the end of this book and in the *Dinah Zike's Reading and Study Skills Foldables* booklet.

Eisenhower 1953–1961

1955
- Salk polio vaccine becomes widely available

1956
- Congress passes Federal Highway Act

1957
- Estimated 40 million television sets in use in the United States

1956

1960

1954
- Gamal Abdel Nasser takes power in Egypt

1956
- Suez Canal crisis

1957
- USSR launches *Sputnik I* and *Sputnik II* satellites

FOLDABLES

Categorizing Information Make a Folded-Table Foldable on popular culture in the 1950s and present. List the following for both time periods: data on the types of mass media and size of the audiences for them, characteris-tics of youth cul-ture, and groups represented in the mass media.

Popular Culture	1950s	Present
Mass Media Types		
Youth Culture		
Groups Represented in Media		

History ONLINE Chapter Overview
Visit glencoe.com to preview Chapter 16.

Chapter 16 Postwar America **565**

History ONLINE
Introduce students to chapter content and key terms by having them access the Chapter 16 Overview at glencoe.com.

Section 3

The Other Side of American Life
Essential Question: What groups of Americans did not enjoy the affluence of the 1950s? *(people living in inner cities, people living in Appalachia, minorities, and Native Americans)* Tell students that in Section 3 they will learn about Americans who did not share in the prosperity of the 1950s. **OL**

Focus

Truman and Eisenhower

Bellringer

Daily Focus Transparency 16.1

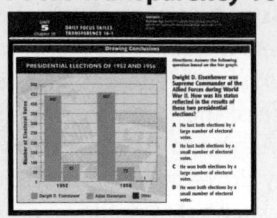

Guide to Reading

Answers:

Characteristics of a Postwar Economy:

increased consumer spending, higher prices, rising inflation, labor unrest

Section Spotlight Video

To generate student interest and provide a springboard for class discussion, access the Chapter 16, Section 1 video at glencoe.com or on the video DVD.

Guide to Reading

Big Ideas

Economics and Society Following World War II, the federal government supported programs that helped the American economy make the transition from wartime to peacetime production.

Content Vocabulary
• closed shop *(p. 566)*
• right-to-work laws *(p. 567)*
• union shop *(p. 567)*
• dynamic conservatism *(p. 570)*

Academic Vocabulary
• legislator *(p. 566)*
• abandon *(p. 568)*

People and Events to Identify
• GI Bill *(p. 566)*
• "Do-Nothing Congress" *(p. 568)*
• Fair Deal *(p. 569)*
• Federal Highway Act *(p. 571)*

Reading Strategy
Complete a graphic organizer similar to the one below by listing the characteristics of the U.S. postwar economy.

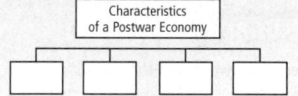

I n the postwar era, Congress limited the power of unions and rejected most of President Truman's plan for a "Fair Deal." When Eisenhower became president, he cut back some government programs and launched the interstate highway system.

Return to a Peacetime Economy

MAIN Idea Despite inflation and strikes, the nation was able to shift to a peacetime economy without a recession.

HISTORY AND YOU Do you know you can get help paying for college if you serve in the military? Read to learn about the origins of the "GI Bill" and how it helped World War II veterans get a college education.

After the war many Americans feared the return to a peacetime economy. They worried that, after military production halted and millions of former soldiers glutted the labor market, unemployment and recession might sweep the country. Despite such worries, the economy continued to grow after the war as increased consumer spending helped ward off a recession. After 17 years of an economic depression and wartime shortages, Americans rushed out to buy the consumer goods they had long desired.

The Servicemen's Readjustment Act, popularly called the **GI Bill,** boosted the economy further. The act provided generous funds to veterans to help them establish businesses, buy homes, and attend college. The postwar economy did have problems, particularly in the first couple of years following the end of the war. A greater demand for goods led to higher prices, and this inflation soon triggered labor unrest. As the cost of living rose, workers in the automobile, steel, electrical, and mining industries went on strike for better pay.

Afraid that the nation's energy supply would be drastically reduced because of the striking miners, Truman ordered government seizure of the mines, while pressuring mine owners to grant the union most of its demands. The president also halted a strike that shut down the nation's railroads by threatening to draft the striking workers into the army.

Labor unrest and high prices prompted many Americans to call for a change. The Republicans seized on these sentiments during the 1946 congressional elections, winning control of both houses of Congress for the first time since 1930.

The new conservative Congress quickly set out to curb the power of organized labor. **Legislators** proposed a measure known as the Taft-Hartley Act, which outlawed the **closed shop,** or the practice of forcing business owners to hire only union members. Under this law,

Resource Manager

R Reading Strategies	**C** Critical Thinking	**D** Differentiated Instruction	**W** Writing Support	**S** Skill Practice
Teacher Edition • Organizing, p. 568 **Additional Resources** • Guided Reading Act., URB p. 150	**Teacher Edition** • Det. Cause/Effect, p. 567 **Additional Resources** • Historical Analysis Skills Act., URB p. 124 • Quizzes/Tests, p. 223	**Teacher Edition** • Interpersonal, p. 568 • Visual/Spatial, p. 570 **Additional Resources** • Eng. Learner Act., URB p. 127 • Academic Vocab. Act., URB p. 131 • Foldables, p. 77	**Teacher Edition** • Personal Writing, p. 569 **Additional Resources** • Content Vocab. Act., URB p. 129	**Teacher Edition** • Evaluating, p. 570 **Additional Resources** • RENTG, p. 173

PRIMARY SOURCE
The GI Bill of Rights

One reason the American economy rebounded so quickly after World War II ended was the Servicemen's Readjustment Act of 1944, popularly called the GI Bill of Rights. The act subsidized college tuition and provided zero down-payment, low-interest loans to veterans to help them buy homes and establish businesses.

Veterans flocked to colleges in large numbers after the war. Among them was William Oskay, Jr., (above) who attended Pennsylvania State University in 1946. By 1947, nearly half of all people attending college were veterans. At the University of Iowa (left), 60 percent of students were veterans in 1947. By 1956, when the GI program ended, 7.8 million veterans had used it to attend college. Another 2.4 million veterans used the program to obtain home loans.

Analyzing VISUALS

1. **Calculating** Based on the graph, what was the increase in college enrollments between 1944 and 1950?

2. **Specifying** About how many new homes were constructed in 1950?

College Enrollment

Source: *Historical Statistics of the United States.*

New Home Construction

Source: *Historical Statistics of the United States.*

states could pass **right-to-work laws,** which outlawed **union shops** (shops in which new workers were required to join the union). The measure also prohibited featherbedding, the practice of limiting work output in order to create more jobs. Furthermore, the bill forbade unions from using their money to support political campaigns.

When the bill reached Truman, however, he vetoed it, arguing that it was a mistake:

PRIMARY SOURCE

". . . [It would] reverse the basic direction of our national labor policy, inject the government into private economic affairs on an unprecedented scale, and conflict with important principles of our democratic society. Its provisions would cause more strikes, not fewer."

—quoted in *The Growth of the American Republic*

The president's concerns did little to sway Congress, which passed the Taft-Hartley Act in 1947 over Truman's veto. Its supporters claimed that the law held irresponsible unions in check, just as the Wagner Act of 1935 had restrained anti-union activities and employers. Labor leaders called the act a "slave labor" law and insisted that it erased many of the gains that unions had made since 1933.

Reading Check **Explaining** Why did Truman veto the Taft-Hartley Act?

Chapter 16 Postwar America **567**

Teach

C Critical Thinking

Determining Cause and Effect Tell students that in the late 1940s nearly half of college students were veterans. **Ask:** What accounted for the high percentage of veterans in college? *(The GI Bill subsidized tuition for veterans.)* **OL**

Analyzing VISUALS

Answers:
1. about 360,000
2. close to 2,000,000

Reading Check

Answer:
He felt that it brought the government into private economic affairs on an unprecedented scale and would cause more strikes without contributing to economic stability and progress.

Hands-On Chapter Project
Step 1

A New Peacetime America

Step 1: Facing the Future Students will focus on the amazing changes that took place in American government and culture following World War II, with their final product being a classroom display of items representing these changes.

Directions Have students review Section 1, noting the new government programs presented by presidents Truman and Eisenhower such as the system of interstate highways and the raising of the minimum wage. Have students meet in small groups to research and discuss these changes and how lasting the impact of each was.

Drawing Conclusions Have students regroup as a class and record what they have found in their research and discussions on the board. After comparing these government programs, then and now, have them draw some conclusions about the effectiveness of the government and the impact it has on their daily lives. **OL**

(Chapter Project continued on page 573)

Truman's Program

MAIN Idea Truman pushed for a "Fair Deal" for Americans, despite the legislative conflicts he had with Congress.

HISTORY AND YOU Do you remember how close the last presidential election was? Read on to learn about Truman's surprise victory in 1948.

The Democratic Party's loss of control in Congress in the 1946 elections did not dampen President Truman's spirits or his plans. Shortly after taking office, Truman had proposed domestic measures seeking to continue the work of Franklin Roosevelt's New Deal. During his tenure in office, Truman worked to push this agenda through Congress.

Truman's Legislative Agenda

Truman's proposals included expansion of Social Security benefits; raising the minimum wage; a program to ensure full employment through aggressive use of federal spending and investment; public housing and slum clearance; and long-range environmental and public works planning. He also proposed a system of national health insurance.

Truman also boldly asked Congress in February 1948 to pass a broad civil rights bill that would protect African Americans' right to vote, abolish poll taxes, and make lynching a federal crime. He issued an executive order barring discrimination in federal employment and ending segregation in the armed forces. Most of Truman's legislative efforts, however, met with little success, as a coalition of Republicans and conservative Southern Democrats defeated many of his proposals.

The Election of 1948

As the presidential election of 1948 approached, most observers gave Truman little chance of winning. Some Americans still believed that he lacked the stature for the job, and they viewed his administration as weak and inept.

Divisions within the Democratic Party also seemed to spell disaster for Truman. At the Democratic Convention that summer, two factions **abandoned** the party altogether. Reacting angrily to Truman's support of civil rights, a group of Southern Democrats formed the States' Rights, or Dixiecrat, Party and nominated South Carolina Governor Strom Thurmond for president. At the same time, the party's more liberal members were frustrated by Truman's ineffective domestic policies and critical of his anti-Soviet foreign policy. They formed a new Progressive Party, with Henry A. Wallace as their presidential candidate.

The president's Republican opponent was New York Governor Thomas Dewey, a dignified and popular candidate who seemed unbeatable. After polling 50 political writers, *Newsweek* magazine declared three weeks before the election, "The landslide for Dewey will sweep the country."

Perhaps the only person who gave Truman any chance to win the election was Truman himself. "I know every one of those 50 fellows," he declared about the writers polled in *Newsweek.* "There isn't one of them has enough sense to pound sand in a rat hole." Ignoring the polls, he poured his energy into the campaign, traveling more than 20,000 miles by train and making more than 350 speeches. Along the way, Truman attacked the majority Republican Congress as "do-nothing, good-for-nothing" for refusing to enact his legislative agenda.

Truman's attacks on the "**Do-Nothing Congress**" did not mention that both he and Congress had passed the Truman Doctrine's aid program to Greece and Turkey, as well as the Marshall Plan. Congress had also enacted the National Security Act of 1947, which created the Department of Defense, the National Security Council, and the CIA; established the Joint Chiefs of Staff as a permanent organization; and made the Air Force an independent branch of the military. The 80th Congress did not "do nothing" as Truman charged, but its accomplishments were in areas that did not affect most Americans directly. As a result, Truman's charges began to stick.

With a great deal of support from laborers, African Americans, and farmers, Truman won a narrow but stunning victory over Dewey. Perhaps just as remarkable as the president's victory was the resurgence of the Democratic Party. When the dust had cleared after election day, Democrats had regained control of both houses of Congress.

Activity: Collaborative Learning

Identifying Organize the class into groups of three or four and have students research the campaign slogans and strategies of the different candidates in the 1948 presidential election. Ask students to write a one-minute radio advertisement for the candidate of their choice. Ads should present the candidate's positions clearly and accurately. Students may incorporate music, dialogue, and sound effects in their radio spot. If possible, students can tape record their spots or simply present them "live" to the class. Encourage the class to discuss how effective the spots are. **Ask:** Did the radio advertisement present accurate information about the candidate? Did the spot influence your opinion of the candidate? How? **OL** **AL**

The Fair Deal

Truman's 1949 State of the Union address repeated the domestic agenda he had put forth previously. "Every segment of our population and every individual," he declared, "has a right to expect from . . . government a fair deal." Whether intentional or not, the president had coined a name—the **Fair Deal**—to set his program apart from the New Deal. In February, he began to send his proposals to Congress.

The 81st Congress did not completely embrace Truman's Fair Deal. Legislators did raise the legal minimum wage to 75¢ an hour. They increased Social Security benefits by 75 percent and extended them to 10 million additional people. Congress also passed the National Housing Act of 1949, which provided for the construction of low-income housing, accompanied by long-term rent subsidies.

Congress refused, however, to pass national health insurance or to provide subsidies for farmers or federal aid for schools. In addition, legislators, led by the same coalition of conservative Republicans and Dixiecrats, opposed Truman's efforts to enact civil rights legislation. His plans for federal aid to education were also not enacted.

✔ **Reading Check** **Summarizing** What did Truman and the Congress accomplish in foreign relations?

PRIMARY SOURCE
The Election of 1948

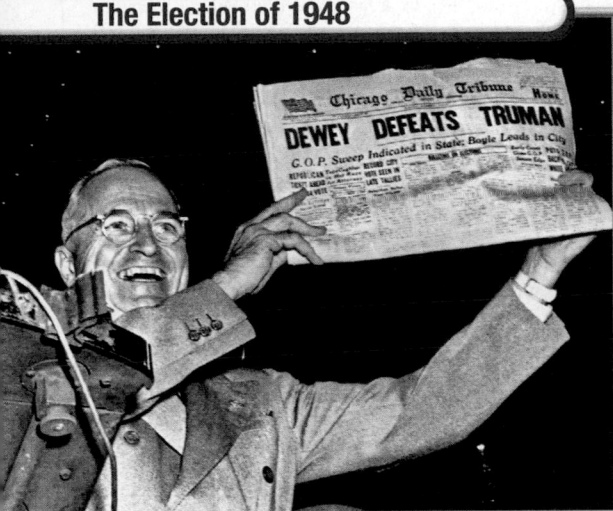

▲ Harry Truman gleefully displays the erroneous Chicago Daily Tribune headline announcing his defeat by Thomas Dewey.

What Was the Fair Deal?

In 1949 Truman outlined in his State of the Union address an ambitious legislative program that became known as the Fair Deal. Some of its main features were:

• the expansion of Social Security benefits
• an increase in the minimum wage
• a program to ensure full employment
• a program of public housing and slum clearance
• a long-range plan for environmental and public works
• a system of national health insurance
• a broad program of civil rights legislation

Presidential Election of 1948

Presidential Candidate	Popular Votes	% of Popular Vote	Electoral Votes
Truman	24,105,695	49.51%	303
Dewey	21,969,170	45.13%	189
Thurmond	1,169,021	2.40%	39
Wallace	1,156,103	2.37%	

*Eleven electors voted for Truman, and one voted for Thurmond.

Analyzing VISUALS

1. **Interpreting** In what regions of the nation did Thomas Dewey receive the most votes?
2. **Calculating** What was the difference in percentage of the popular vote received by Truman and Dewey?

W Writing Support

Personal Writing Truman declared that every citizen has the right to expect a "fair deal" from the government. Ask students to write a few paragraphs expressing their personal feelings about what citizens should expect from government. **OL**

Analyzing VISUALS

Answers:
1. the Northeast and Midwest
2. 4.38%

✔ Reading Check

Answer:
Truman and Congress passed the National Security Act, the Truman Doctrine's aid program to Greece and Turkey, as well as the Marshall Plan.

Additional Support

Activity: Economics Connection

Analyzing Tell students that Bill Clinton's presidential campaign of 1992 famously used the phrase, "It's the economy, stupid!" to underscore the importance of economic concerns for voters. Have students research the economic concerns of the various regions of the United States in 1948. Ask students to make a three-column chart listing the economic considerations of the country's different regions in one column, the presidential candidate's proposals in another column, and, finally, the candidate who got the most votes in each of the different regions. **Ask:** What correlations did you find between the economic concerns of a particular region and the policies of the candidate of its choice? **AL**

Visual/Spatial Organize the class into groups of four. Have each group create two campaign posters for the election of 1952, one for Eisenhower and the other for Adlai Stevenson. Use the posters to discuss the key issues of the 1952 election. **OL**

S **Skill Practice**

Evaluating President Eisenhower used the phrase "middle of the road" to describe his political beliefs. Have students work in pairs to create a table listing Eisenhower's conservative policies in one column, and his liberal policies in the other.
Ask: Do you agree that Eisenhower's political beliefs could be described as "middle of the road?" Why or why not? (Answers will vary.) **OL**

Analyzing GEOGRAPHY

Answers:
1. in the Northeast, because of large population centers
2. It led to suburban sprawl and encouraged travel.

Additional Support

The Eisenhower Years

MAIN Idea President Eisenhower cut federal spending, supported business, funded the interstate highway system, and extended some New Deal programs.

HISTORY AND YOU Do you think it is important for a president to have served in the military? Read to learn how Americans chose a war hero as president in the 1950s.

In 1950 the United States went to war in Korea. The war consumed the nation's attention and resources and effectively ended Truman's Fair Deal. By 1952, with the war at a bloody stalemate and his approval rating dropping quickly, Truman declined to run again for the presidency.

With no Democratic incumbent to face, Republicans pinned their hopes for regaining the White House in 1952 on a popular World War II hero: Dwight Eisenhower, former commander of the Allied Forces in Europe. The Democrats nominated Illinois Governor Adlai Stevenson.

The Republicans adopted the slogan: "It's time for a change!" The warm and friendly Eisenhower, known as "Ike," promised to end the war in Korea. "I like Ike" became the Republican rallying cry. Eisenhower won the election in a landslide, carrying the Electoral College, 442 votes to 89. The Republicans also gained an eight-seat majority in the House, while the Senate became evenly divided between Democrats and Republicans.

Eisenhower Takes Office

President Eisenhower had two favorite phrases. "Middle of the road" described his political beliefs and **dynamic conservatism** meant balancing economic conservatism with activism in areas that would benefit the country. Eisenhower wasted little time in showing his conservative side. The new president's cabinet appointments included several business

GEOGRAPHY AND HISTORY
Effects of the Interstate Highway System

WEST
INTERSTATE
80

Interstate Highway System

Commercial Trucking *Interstate highways made distribution of goods by transport truck fast and efficient. By the 1990s, trucks moved more than 6 billion tons of goods—mostly by interstate.*

Rise of Suburbs *Interstate highways contributed to the growth of suburbs and urban sprawl. Interstates let people commute long distances from home to work.*

Analyzing GEOGRAPHY

1. **Location** Where were most of the interstate highways built? Why do you think that is?
2. **Movement** In what ways did the interstate highway system change daily life?

Road Culture *Interstate travel encouraged the development of cheap hotel chains, roadside convenience stores, and fast food restaurants located near interstate exits.*

570 Chapter 16 Postwar America

Extending the Content

Korea The Korean War sprang from a conflict between factions in Korea. Korean leftists wished to reform Korea's land ownership laws that kept a small group wealthy while many lived in poverty. The right opposed this. Following World War II, Korea was divided: Leftists controlled the North, and rightists controlled the South. Fighting soon broke out along the border, and in 1950 North Korean forces invaded the South. The United States, under the flag of the United Nations, joined the fight on behalf of the South. By the time a cease-fire was established in Korea, on July 27, 1953, the total death toll for both sides had reached 600,000 soldiers and as many as 2 million civilians. The border between North and South Korea was re-established in roughly the same place as before the war. In the early 2000s, it remained the most heavily fortified border in the world.

leaders. Under their guidance, Eisenhower ended government price and rent controls, which many conservatives viewed as unnecessary federal regulation of the economy. Eisenhower's administration believed business growth was vital to the nation. His secretary of defense, formerly the president of General Motors, declared to the Senate that "what is good for our country is good for General Motors, and vice versa."

Eisenhower's conservatism showed itself in other ways as well. In an attempt to cut federal spending, the president vetoed a school construction bill and agreed to slash government aid to public housing. Along with these cuts, he supported some modest tax cuts.

Eisenhower also targeted the federal government's continuing aid to businesses, or what he termed "creeping socialism." Shortly after taking office, the president abolished the Reconstruction Finance Corporation (RFC), which since 1932 had lent money to banks, railroads, and other large institutions in financial trouble. Another Depression-era agency, the Tennessee Valley Authority (TVA), also came under Eisenhower's scrutiny. During his presidency, appropriations for the TVA fell from $185 million to $12 million.

In some areas, President Eisenhower took an activist role. For example, he pushed for two large government projects. During the 1950s, as the number of Americans who owned cars increased, so too did the need for greater and more efficient travel routes. In 1956 Congress responded to this growing need by passing the **Federal Highway Act,** the largest public works program in American history. The act appropriated $25 billion for a 10-year effort to construct more than 40,000 miles (64,400 km) of interstate highways. Congress also authorized construction of the Great Lakes–St. Lawrence Seaway to connect the Great Lakes with the Atlantic Ocean through a series of locks on the St. Lawrence River. Three previous presidents had been unable to reach agreements with Canada to build this waterway to aid international shipping. Through Eisenhower's efforts, the two nations finally agreed on a plan to complete the project.

Extending Social Security

Although President Eisenhower cut federal spending and tried to limit the federal government's role in the economy, he agreed to extend the Social Security system to an additional 10 million people. He also extended unemployment compensation to an additional 4 million citizens and agreed to raise the minimum wage and continue to provide some government aid to farmers.

By the time Eisenhower ran for a second term in 1956, the nation had successfully shifted back to a peacetime economy. The battles between liberals and conservatives over whether to continue New Deal policies would continue. In the meantime, however, most Americans focused their energy on enjoying what had become a decade of tremendous prosperity.

✓ Reading Check **Evaluating** What conservative and activist measures did Eisenhower take during his administration?

Section 1 REVIEW

Vocabulary
1. **Explain** the significance of: GI Bill, closed shop, right-to-work laws, union shop, "Do-Nothing Congress," Fair Deal, dynamic conservatism, Federal Highway Act.

Main Ideas
2. **Identifying** What difficulties could have hindered the return to a peacetime economy?

3. **Analyzing** Why did Congress oppose some of Truman's Fair Deal policies?

4. **Describing** How did Eisenhower describe his approach to politics?

Critical Thinking
5. **Big Ideas** How did President Eisenhower aid international shipping during his administration?

6. **Organizing** Use a graphic organizer like the one below to compare the agendas of the Truman and Eisenhower administrations.

```
        Agendas
          │
    ┌─────┴─────┐
 Truman     Eisenhower
    │           │
 ┌─────┐    ┌─────┐
 │     │    │     │
 └─────┘    └─────┘
```

7. **Analyzing Visuals** Study the map on page 569. In which part of the country did Strom Thurmond receive the most votes? Why do you think this is?

Writing About History
8. **Persuasive Writing** Assume the role of a member of Congress during Truman's administration. Write a speech convincing Congress to pass or defeat Truman's Fair Deal measures.

History ONLINE
Study Central™ To review this section, go to glencoe.com and click on Study Central.

✓ Reading Check

Answer:
He reduced government control over business, cut spending, passed the Federal Highway Act, extended the Social Security System, and increased the minimum wage.

Assess
•••••••••••••••••••••••••
History ONLINE

Study Central™ provides summaries, interactive games, and online graphic organizers to help students review content.

Close
•••••••••••••••••••••••••
Summarizing Ask: In what direction did the federal government take the country after World War II? *(The federal government supported programs such as the GI Bill, Social Security, public works projects, and civil rights.)* **OL**

Section 1 REVIEW

Answers

1. All definitions can be found in the section and the Glossary.
2. Military production had stopped, and millions of former soldiers glutted the labor market.
3. Republicans controlled Congress after 1946 and also formed a coalition with conservative Southern Democrats to defeat many of Truman's proposals.
4. Eisenhower described his approach to politics as "middle of the road" and "dynamic conservatism," meaning balancing eco-

nomic conservatism with activism in those areas that would benefit the country.
5. He pushed for two major projects—the Federal Highway Act and the construction of the St. Lawrence Seaway. Both projects enabled goods to be moved more quickly and efficiently.
6. Truman: increase government involvement in business, expand federal spending, extend civil rights; Eisenhower: limit government involvement in business, curb federal spending

7. Thurmond received the most votes in the South. Thurmond was the candidate of the States' Rights, or Dixiecrat, Party made up of Southern Democrats who opposed federal action on civil rights.
8. Students' speeches will vary but should focus on several components of the Fair Deal.

Focus

The Affluent Society

Bellringer

Daily Focus Transparency 16.2

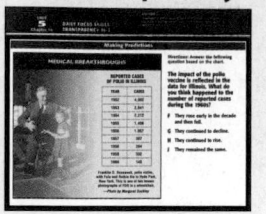

Guide to Reading

Big Ideas
Culture and Beliefs Postwar abundance and new technologies changed American society.

Content Vocabulary
• baby boom (p. 573)
• white-collar job (p. 574)
• blue-collar worker (p. 574)
• multinational corporation (p. 574)
• franchise (p. 574)
• rock 'n' roll (p. 577)
• generation gap (p. 579)

Academic Vocabulary
• phenomenon (p. 572)
• conform (p. 574)

People and Events to Identify
• Levittown (p. 572)
• Jonas Salk (p. 575)
• Elvis Presley (p. 577)
• Jack Kerouac (p. 579)

Reading Strategy
Sequencing Use a time line to record major events of science, technology, and popular culture during the 1950s.

For many Americans, the 1950s was a time of affluence, with many new technological breakthroughs. In addition, new forms of entertainment created a generational divide between young people and adults.

American Abundance

MAIN Idea America entered a period of postwar abundance, with expanding suburbs, growing families, and more white-collar jobs.

HISTORY AND YOU Have you ever noticed that every restaurant in a pizza chain looks alike? Read on to learn about the rise of franchises.

The 1950s was a decade of incredible prosperity. Between 1940 and 1955, the average income of American families roughly tripled. Americans in all income brackets—poor, middle-class, and wealthy—experienced this rapid rise in income. In 1958 economist John Kenneth Galbraith published *The Affluent Society,* in which he claimed that the nation's postwar prosperity was a new **phenomenon.** In the past, Galbraith said, all societies had an "economy of scarcity," meaning that a lack of resources and overpopulation had limited economic productivity. Now, the United States had created what Galbraith called an "economy of abundance." New business techniques and improved technology enabled the nation to produce an abundance of goods and services, thereby dramatically raising the standard of living for Americans.

The economic boom of the 1950s provided most Americans with more disposable income than ever before and, as in the 1920s, they began to spend it on new consumer goods, including refrigerators, washing machines, televisions, and air conditioners. Advertising helped fuel the nation's spending spree. Advertising became the fastest-growing industry in the United States, as manufacturers employed new marketing techniques to sell their products. These techniques were carefully planned to whet the consumer's appetite. A second car became a symbol of status, a freezer became a promise of plenty, and mouthwash was portrayed as the key to immediate success.

The Growth of Suburbia

Advertisers targeted consumers who had money to spend. Many of these consumers lived in new mass-produced suburbs that grew up around cities in the 1950s. **Levittown,** New York, was one of the earliest of the mass-produced suburbs. The driving force behind this planned residential community was Bill Levitt, who mass-produced hundreds of simple and similar-looking homes in a potato field 10 miles east of New York City. Between 1947 and 1951, thousands of

Guide to Reading

Answers:
1946: ENIAC computer developed
1950: Riesman's *The Lonely Crowd* published
1955: Salk polio vaccine widely available
1958: Galbraith's *The Affluent Society* published

Section Spotlight Video

To generate student interest and provide a springboard for class discussion, access the Chapter 16, Section 2 video at glencoe.com or on the video DVD.

Resource Manager

R Reading Strategies	**C** Critical Thinking	**D** Differentiated Instruction	**W** Writing Support	**S** Skill Practice
Teacher Edition • Questioning, p. 574 • Making Connections, p. 576 **Additional Resources** • Pri. Source Reading, URB p. 139 • Guided Reading Act., URB p. 151	**Teacher Edition** • Pred. Conseq., p. 574 • Det. Cause/Effect, p. 578 • Anal. Primary Sources, p. 578 **Additional Resources** • Critical Think. Skills Act., URB p. 134 • Inter. Political Cartoons, URB p. 143 • Quizzes/Tests, p. 224	**Teacher Edition** • Interpersonal, pp. 573, 577 **Additional Resources** • Econ. & Hist. Act., URB p. 7	**Teacher Edition** • Persuasive Writing, p. 577	**Teacher Edition** • Reading Graphs, p. 573 • Evaluating, p. 576 **Additional Resources** • Reading Skills Act., URB p. 123 • Reinf. Skills Act., URB p. 133 • Link. Past/Present Act., URB p. 136 • RENTG, p. 176

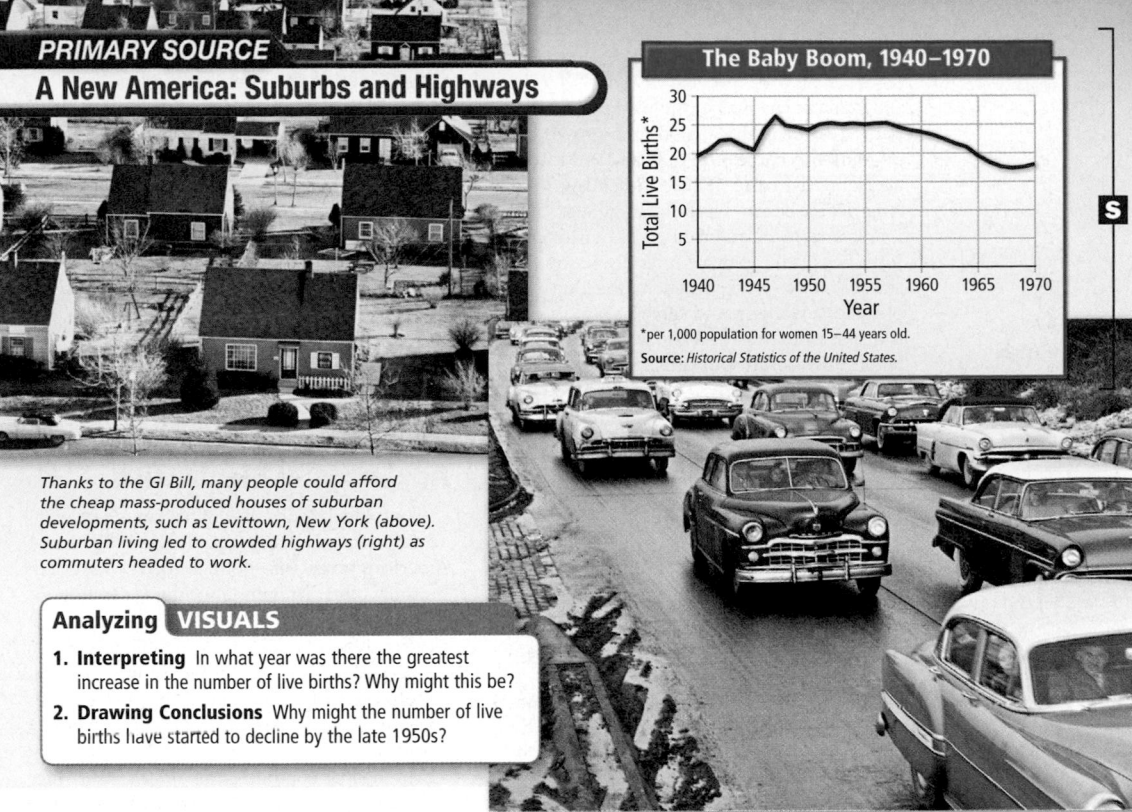

A New America: Suburbs and Highways

The Baby Boom, 1940–1970

Total Live Births*

30
25
20
15
10
5

1940 1945 1950 1955 1960 1965 1970
Year

*per 1,000 population for women 15–44 years old.
Source: *Historical Statistics of the United States.*

Thanks to the GI Bill, many people could afford the cheap mass-produced houses of suburban developments, such as Levittown, New York (above). Suburban living led to crowded highways (right) as commuters headed to work.

Analyzing VISUALS

1. **Interpreting** In what year was there the greatest increase in the number of live births? Why might this be?
2. **Drawing Conclusions** Why might the number of live births have started to decline by the late 1950s?

families rushed to buy the inexpensive homes. These new suburbs multiplied throughout the United States. Suburbs became increasingly popular during the 1950s, accounting for about 85 percent of new home construction. The number of suburban dwellers doubled, while the population of cities rose only 10 percent.

Reasons for the rapid growth of suburbia varied. Some people wanted to escape the crime and congestion of city neighborhoods. Others believed the suburbs would provide a better life for themselves and their children. For millions of Americans, the suburbs came to symbolize the American dream.

Affordability was a key reason that home buyers moved to the suburbs. With the GI Bill providing low-interest loans to veterans, buying a new house was more affordable than at any previous time in American history. The government's decision to give income tax deductions for home-mortgage interest payments and property taxes made owning a home even more attractive. Between 1940 and 1960, the number of Americans who owned their own homes rose from about 41 percent to about 61 percent.

The Baby Boom

The American birthrate exploded after World War II. From 1945 to 1961, a period known as the **baby boom,** more than 65 million children were born in the United States. At the height of the baby boom, a child was born every seven seconds.

Several factors contributed to the baby boom. First, young couples who had delayed marriage during World War II and the Korean War could now marry, buy homes, and begin their families. In addition, the government encouraged the growth of families by offering generous GI benefits for home purchases. Finally, on television and in magazines, popular culture celebrated pregnancy, parenthood, and large families.

Chapter 16 Postwar America **573**

Teach

S Skill Practice

Reading a Graph Ask: Between what years did the birth rate remain steady? *(1950–1958)* **OL**

D Differentiated Instruction

Interpersonal Organize students into groups of three or four. Have them work together to write a one-minute radio spot attracting home buyers to a new suburban development. *(Radio spots will vary but should note affordability, good schools, safety, and more space.)* Invite students to share their advertisements with the class and vote on which one is most convincing. **OL**

Analyzing VISUALS

Answers:
1. 1947; veterans were now able to start a family
2. Most returning GIs had completed their families.

Hands-On Chapter Project
Step 2

A New Peacetime America

Step 2: New Technologies Americans' buying power increased during this boom time following the war.

Directions Have students read Section 2 and remind them that many Americans had new-found wealth in the 1950s and 60s. What did they spend their money on? Have students note all of the new inventions created and discoveries made in postwar America and research others not mentioned in their text.

Putting It Together During their research have them collect photos or drawings of the new developments to be displayed on poster board in their final class presentation. **OL**
(Chapter Project continued in Section 3 on page 583)

C Critical Thinking

Predicting Consequences

Sociologist David Riesman argued that the conformist urge of the 1950s changed people from being "inner-directed" (judging themselves on the basis of their own values) to being "other-directed" (concerned with winning the approval of others). **Ask:** What consequences might this produce for individuals and society? *(Answers will vary.)* **AL**

R Reading Strategy

Questioning Have students brainstorm a list of diseases that affect Americans today for which there are no vaccines, such as cancer, AIDS, diabetes, and so forth. **Ask:** What are reasons why vaccines for these diseases still do not exist? *(Students may note the expense of medical research, mutation of the diseases, and so on.)* **OL**

✓ Reading Check

Answer:
Causes: new business methods and improved manufacturing technology; Effects: average family income tripled and the number of white-collar jobs increased

Differentiated Instruction

Economics and History, URB p. 7

574

The Changing Workplace

Dramatic changes in the workplace accompanied the country's economic growth. The ongoing mechanization of farms and factories accelerated in the 1950s. As a result, more Americans began working in offices. These jobs came to be referred to as **white-collar jobs,** because employees typically wore a white shirt and tie to work, instead of the blue denim of factory workers and laborers. In 1956, for the first time, white-collar workers outnumbered **blue-collar workers.**

Many white-collar employees worked for large corporations. As these businesses competed with each other, some expanded overseas. These **multinational corporations** located themselves closer to important raw materials and benefited from a cheaper labor pool, which made them more competitive.

The 1950s also witnessed the rise of **franchises,** in which a person owns and runs one or several stores of a chain operation. Because many business leaders believed that consumers valued dependability and familiarity, the owners of chain operations often demanded that their franchises present a uniform look and style.

C Like franchise owners, many corporate leaders expected their employees to **conform** to company standards. In general, they did not want free-thinking individuals or people who might speak out or criticize the company. Some observers criticized this trend. In his 1950 book *The Lonely Crowd,* sociologist David Riesman argued that this conformity was changing people. Formerly, he claimed, people were "inner-directed," judging themselves on the basis of their own values and the esteem of their families. Now, however, people were becoming "other-directed"—concerned with winning the approval of the corporation or community.

In his 1956 book, *The Organization Man,* William H. Whyte, Jr., attacked the similarity many business organizations cultivated to keep any individual from dominating. "In group doctrine," Whyte wrote, "the strong personality is viewed with overwhelming suspicion," and the person with ideas is considered "a threat."

✓ Reading Check **Interpreting** Describe two causes and effects of the economic boom of the 1950s.

Scientific Advances

MAIN Idea Computers began a business revolution, and doctors discovered new ways to fight disease.

HISTORY AND YOU Do you own a computer? Read on to learn about the earliest computers.

As the United States experienced many social changes during the postwar era, the nation also witnessed several important scientific advances. In electronics and medicine, American scientists broke new ground during the 1950s.

Advances in Electronics

The electronics industry made rapid advances after World War II. In 1947 three American physicists—John Bardeen, Walter H. Brattain, and William Shockley—developed the transistor, a tiny device that generated electric signals and made it possible to miniaturize radios and calculators. Radios, once a large piece of furniture, became portable and could be easily carried to the beach or other places.

The age of computers also dawned in the postwar era. In 1946 scientists working under a U.S. Army contract developed one of the nation's earliest computers—known as ENIAC (Electronic Numerical Integrator and Computer)—to make military calculations. Several years later, a newer model called UNIVAC (Universal Automatic Computer) would process business data and launch the computer revolution. The computer, along with changes and improvements in communication and transportation systems, allowed many Americans to work more quickly and efficiently.

Medical Miracles

R The medical breakthroughs of the 1950s included the development of new, powerful antibiotics and vaccines to fight infection and the introduction of new techniques to fight cancer and heart disease.

Prior to the 1950s, cancer had been thought to be untreatable. The development of radiation treatments and chemotherapy in the 1950s helped many cancer patients survive. Similarly, treatments for heart disease had eluded

---

Money and the Affluent Society

Objective: Read about money, the money supply, and America's affluence during the 1950s.

Focus: How is money and the money supply important in American society?

Teach: Explain how the money supply is a measure of affluence.

Assess: List the functions of money.

Close: Using evidence from the textbook, show three images of the affluence of the American society in the 1950s.

Differentiated Instruction Strategies

BL List the characteristics of money.

AL Develop an economic system based on something other than money. Does it meet the characteristics of money?

ELL Explain how the money of another country or your native country meets the characteristics of money listed in the reading.

R Reading Strategy

Making Connections Ask:
Why have different types of shows been popular in different periods of television history? *(Students may point out that television shows usually reflect the culture and specific concerns of their time.)* **BL**

S Skill Practice

Evaluating Have students watch a rerun of a program that was popular in the 1950s such as *I Love Lucy* or *The Many Loves of Dobie Gillis*. Tell them to make a list of the styles, slang expressions, attitudes, and behavior that are different from those of today. Discuss the lists and then compile them into a 1950s culture dictionary. **OL**

Analyzing VISUALS

Answers:
1. They were a middle-class family in which the father worked and mom raised the children.
2. a middle-class audience

Additional Support

The New Mass Media

MAIN Idea The rise of television led to changes in the movie and radio industries.

HISTORY AND YOU How many hours of television do you watch weekly? Read to find out about the early days of television broadcasting.

Although regular television broadcasts had begun in the early 1940s, there were few stations, and sets were expensive. There were estimated to be no more than 8,000 sets in use in the entire United States in 1946. By the late 1950s, however, small black-and-white-screened televisions sat in living rooms across the country. Nearly 40 million televisions had been sold by 1957, and more than 80 percent of families had at least one television.

The Rise of Television

R Early television programs fell into several main categories, including comedy, action and adventure, and variety entertainment. In 1953 Lucille Ball and her real-life husband, Desi Arnaz, starred in one of the most popular shows ever to air on American television, a situation comedy (sitcom) called *I Love Lucy*. The episode in which Lucy gave birth (which paralleled Lucille Ball's actual pregnancy) had an audience of 44 million viewers. Fewer people tuned in to watch the presidential inauguration the following day.

Comedy proved popular in other formats. Many early comedy shows, such as those starring Bob Hope and Jack Benny, were adapted from radio programs. Variety shows, such as Ed Sullivan's *Toast of the Town*, provided a mix of comedy, music, dance, acrobatics, and juggling. Quiz shows also drew large audiences after the 1955 debut of *The $64,000 Question*. In this show and its many imitators, two contestants tried to answer questions from separate, soundproof booths.

Television viewers also enjoyed action shows. Westerns such as *Hopalong Cassidy, The Lone Ranger,* and *Gunsmoke* grew quickly in popularity. Viewers also enjoyed police shows

PRIMARY SOURCE

Television in the 1950s

▲ *I Love Lucy,* a comedy about housewife Lucy, husband Ricky, and friends Fred and Ethel was the most popular show of the 1950s.

▲ *Howdy Doody was the first network kids' show ever broadcast in color.*

▲ The Adventures of Ozzie and Harriet *was a comedy featuring the life of Ozzie and Harriet Nelson and their sons in a middle-class American suburb. Their portrayal of family life was idealized—father worked, mother stayed at home raising the children, and there was always plenty of food and consumer goods available.*

Analyzing VISUALS

1. **Explaining** How did *The Adventures of Ozzie and Harriet* reflect an idealized American family?
2. **Making Generalizations** To what type of audience were most of these television programs designed to appeal?

Activity: Interdisciplinary Connection

Language Arts Have students work in small groups to write a short scene in which a character from a 1950s television show, such as Lucy, or Howdy Doody, is magically transported to the present day. Students should begin by borrowing and viewing a tape of a 1950s program from the library. Next, have students select a character from the program they viewed to use in their original scenes. Students should create a scene in which the behaviors and attitudes of today are explained to their 1950s characters. Encourage students to allow their 1950s characters to express how they feel about life in the present versus life in the 1950s. Have groups present their scenes to the class. **Ask:** Which current attitudes and behaviors were most difficult for the 1950s characters to understand? Which 1950s attitudes and behaviors are most difficult to understand today? *(Answers will vary, but should reflect an understanding of section content.)* **AL**

such as *Dragnet,* a hugely successful show featuring Detective Joe Friday and his partner hunting down a new criminal each week. By the late 1950s, television news had also become an important vehicle for information, and televised athletic events had made professional and college sports a popular choice for entertainment.

Hollywood Responds

As the popularity of television grew, movies lost viewers. Weekly movie attendance dropped from 82 million in 1946 to 36 million by 1950. By 1960, when some 50 million Americans owned televisions, one-fifth of the nation's movie theaters had closed.

Throughout the 1950s, Hollywood struggled to recapture its audience. When contests, door prizes, and advertising failed to lure people back, Hollywood tried 3-D films that required the audience to wear special glasses. Viewers soon tired of the glasses and the often ridiculous plots of 3-D movies.

Cinemascope—a process that showed movies on large, panoramic screens—finally gave Hollywood something television could not match. Wide-screen, full-color spectacles like *The Robe, The Ten Commandments,* and *Around the World in 80 Days* cost a great deal of money to produce. These blockbusters, however, made up for their cost by attracting huge audiences and netting large profits.

Radio Draws Them In

Television also forced the radio industry to change in order to keep its audience. Television made radio comedies, dramas, and soap operas obsolete. Radio stations responded by broadcasting recorded music, news, weather, sports, and talk shows.

Radio also had one audience that television could not reach—people traveling in their cars. In some ways, the automobile saved the radio industry. People commuting to and from work, running errands, or traveling on long road trips relied on radio for information and entertainment. As a result, radio stations survived and even flourished. The number of radio stations more than doubled between 1948 and 1957.

✔ **Reading Check Identifying** How did the television industry affect the U.S. economy?

New Music and Poetry

MAIN Idea Young people developed their own popular culture based largely on rock 'n' roll music and literature of the beat movement.

HISTORY AND YOU How do the adults you know feel about your favorite music? Read on to learn of the conflicts over musical taste that began during the 1950s.

Many teens in every generation seek to separate themselves from their parents. One way of creating that separation is by embracing different music. In that respect, the 1950s were no different from earlier decades, but the results were different for two reasons.

For the first time, teens had large amounts of disposable income that could be spent on entertainment designed specifically for them. In addition, the new mass media meant that teens across the country could hear the same music broadcast or watch the same television shows. The result was the rise of an independent youth culture separate from adult culture. The new youth culture became an independent market for the entertainment and advertising industries.

Rock 'n' Roll

In 1951 at a record store in downtown Cleveland, Ohio, radio disc jockey Alan Freed noticed white teenagers buying African American rhythm-and-blues records and dancing to the music in the store. Freed convinced his station manager to play the music on the air. Just as the disc jockey had suspected, the listeners went crazy for it. Soon, white artists began making music that stemmed from these African American rhythms and sounds, and a new form of music, **rock 'n' roll,** was born.

With a loud and heavy beat that made it ideal for dancing, along with lyrics about romance, cars, and other themes that appealed to young people, rock 'n' roll became wildly popular with the nation's teens. Before long, teenagers around the country were rushing out to buy recordings from such artists as Buddy Holly, Chuck Berry, and Bill Haley and the Comets. In 1956 teenagers found their first rock 'n' roll hero in **Elvis Presley,** who became known as the "King of Rock 'n' Roll."

D Differentiated Instruction

Interpersonal Have groups create murals that illustrate the theme "Hollywood in the 1950s." The murals should depict the challenges and changes that defined Hollywood during this era. **OL**

W Writing Support

Persuasive Writing Have students write a paragraph that persuades others about the excellence of a particular style of music, group, or singer. **OL**

✔ **Reading Check**

Answer:
Television drew audiences away from the film and radio industries and forced these industries to change their approaches. Hollywood tried various film processes, and Cinemascope proved to be successful. Radio stations changed their programming from comedies, dramas, and variety shows to sports, news, weather reports, and recorded music.

Additional Support

Extending the Content

Television Television became popular in the 1940s. Viewers could tune into such shows as *The Texaco Star Theater* starring comedian Milton Berle. Many children wouldn't miss *Howdy Doody,* a popular show aimed at youngsters. The television news came to Americans from two news programs lasting only 15 minutes. The 1948 news program *Camel News Caravan* was sponsored by a tobacco company that insisted its news anchor always have a burning cigarette visible when he presented the news. Over the years, Americans began spending more and more time watching television, and some worried that it was taking away from other activities such as reading or socializing. However, by 1960 nearly 90 percent of American families owned at least one TV set. Although the Columbia Broadcasting System presented the first commercial color telecast in 1951, color television remained too expensive during the 1950s for widespread use. Most people watched their shows in black and white.

C1 **Critical Thinking**

Determining Cause and Effect Ask: Why did Ed Sullivan change his mind about allowing Elvis Presley to perform on his television show? *(Elvis appeared on another show, and it received better ratings than the Ed Sullivan Show.)* **BL**

C2 **Critical Thinking**

Analyzing Primary Sources Have students use Internet or library sources to locate the lyrics to a popular rock'n'roll song of the 1950s. Ask students to write one paragraph summarizing some of the key images, ideas, or themes in the song. Then have them write a second paragraph describing how these lyrics represented the concerns of American teenagers of the period. **AL**

Analyzing VISUALS

Answers:
1. They found it shocking and suggestive.
2. Teenagers rebelled against their parents and embraced rock'n'roll.

Additional Support

Elvis Presley was born in rural Mississippi and grew up poor in Memphis, Tennessee. While in high school, Presley learned to play guitar and sing by imitating the rhythm-and-blues music he heard on the radio. By 1956, the handsome young Elvis had a record deal with RCA Victor, a movie contract, and had made public appearances on several television shows. At first, the popular television variety show host Ed Sullivan refused to invite Presley to appear, insisting that rock 'n' roll music was not fit for a family-oriented show. When a competing show featuring Presley upset Sullivan's high ratings, however, he relented. He ended up paying Presley $50,000 per performance for three appearances, more than triple the amount he had paid any other performer.

Presley owed his wild popularity as much to his moves as to his music. During his performances he would gyrate his hips and dance in ways that shocked many in the audience. Not surprisingly, parents—many of whom listened to Frank Sinatra and other more mellow, mainstream artists—condemned rock 'n' roll as loud, mindless, and dangerous. The city council of San Antonio, Texas, actually banned rock 'n' roll from the jukeboxes at public swimming pools.

The rock 'n' roll hits that teens bought in record numbers united them in a world their parents did not share. Thus, in the 1950s,

PRIMARY SOURCE
Rock 'n' Roll Sweeps the Nation

African American singers such as Chuck Berry (left), Little Richard (below left), and Fats Domino (below right) became huge stars in the popular music industry of the 1950s.

Bill Haley and His Comets (above) was one of the first popular rock 'n' roll bands. Elvis Presley (left) became rock 'n' roll's first superstar, but many disapproved of his dance moves.

▲ Little Richard

▲ Fats Domino

Analyzing VISUALS
1. **Explaining** Why did adults disapprove of rock 'n' roll?
2. **Describing** How did this disapproval contribute to the generation gap?

578 Chapter 16 Postwar America

Extending the Content

Hall of Fame The Rock and Roll Hall of Fame Museum opened in Cleveland, Ohio, on September 2, 1995. Artists and musical groups become eligible for induction into the Hall of Fame 25 years after the release of their first records. One of the earliest inductees was Chuck Berry. Named Charles Edward Berry by his parents, he was born in St. Louis on October 18, 1926. In the 1950s, Berry worked as a musician at night leading a popular blues trio. During the

day he worked as a beautician. Berry also played fast, energetic music such as his famous song "Maybellene." It was this music that got him a recording contract. The Rock and Roll Hall of Fame Web site says of Berry, "While no individual can be said to have invented rock and roll, Chuck Berry comes the closest of any single figure to being the one who put all the essential pieces together."

rock 'n'roll helped to create what became known as the **generation gap,** or the cultural separation between children and their parents.

The Beat Movement

If rock 'n' roll helped to create a generation gap, a group of mostly white writers and artists who called themselves beats, or beatniks, highlighted a values gap in 1950s America. The term "beat" may have come from the feeling among group members of being "beaten down" by American culture, or from jazz musicians who would say, "I'm beat right down to my socks."

Beat poets, writers, and artists harshly criticized what they considered the sterility and conformity of American life, the meaninglessness of American politics, and the emptiness of popular culture. In 1956, 29-year-old beat poet Allen Ginsberg published a long poem titled "Howl," which blasted modern American life. Another beat member, **Jack Kerouac,** published *On the Road* in 1957. Although Kerouac's book about his freewheeling adventures with a car thief and con artist shocked some readers, the book went on to become a classic in modern American literature. Although the beat movement remained relatively small, it laid the foundations for the more widespread youth cultural rebellion of the 1960s.

African American Entertainers

African American entertainers struggled to find acceptance in a country that often treated them as second-class citizens. With a few notable exceptions, television tended to shut out African Americans. In 1956 NBC gave a popular African American singer named Nat King Cole his own 15-minute musical variety show. In 1958, after 64 episodes, NBC canceled the show after failing to secure a national sponsor for a show hosted by an African American.

African American rock 'n' roll singers faced fewer obstacles. The talented African Americans who recorded hit songs in the 1950s included Chuck Berry, Little Richard, Fats Domino, and Ray Charles. The late 1950s and early 1960s also saw the rise of several female African American groups, including the Crystals, the Shirelles, and the Ronettes. With their catchy, popular sound, these groups were the musical predecessors of the famous late 1960s groups Martha and the Vandellas and the Supremes.

Over time, the music of the early rock 'n' roll artists had a profound influence on popular music throughout the world. Little Richard and Chuck Berry, for example, provided inspiration for the Beatles, whose music swept Britain and the world in the 1960s. Elvis Presley's music transformed generations of rock 'n' roll bands that followed him and other pioneers of rock.

Despite the innovations in music and the economic boom of the 1950s, not all Americans were part of the affluent society. For many of the country's minorities and rural poor, the American dream remained well out of reach.

✔ **Reading Check** **Summarizing** How did rock 'n' roll help create the generation gap?

Section 2 REVIEW

Vocabulary

1. **Explain** the significance of: Levittown, baby boom, white-collar job, blue-collar worker, multinational corporation, franchise, Jonas Salk, rock 'n' roll, Elvis Presley, generation gap, Jack Kerouac.

Main Ideas

2. **Organizing** Use a graphic organizer like the one below to list the causes and effects of the economic boom of the 1950s.

3. **Listing** What major technological breakthroughs occurred in the 1950s?

4. **Explaining** How did television affect other forms of mass media?

5. **Identifying** How did young people of the 1950s express their own culture?

Critical Thinking

6. **Big Ideas** What were the roots of rock 'n' roll, and how did it reach a mass audience?

7. **Analyzing Visuals** Study the photographs on page 576. These programs have been criticized for presenting a one-sided view of American life. Do you agree? Why or why not?

Writing About History

8. **Expository Writing** Assume the role of a media critic in the 1950s, and use the information in this section to write a critique of one television show, movie, music concert, or piece of literature.

History ONLINE
Study Central™ To review this section, go to glencoe.com and click on Study Central.

✔ **Reading Check**

Answer:
It generated conflict between children and parents based on musical taste and mores of the time, and created a bond among members of the younger generation.

Assess
· ·

History ONLINE

Study Central™ provides summaries, interactive games, and online graphic organizers to help students review content.

Close
· ·

Summarizing Ask: How did American society change after World War II? *(America entered a period of postwar abundance with expanding suburbs, growing families, more white collar jobs, an increased expectation of social conformity, and technological advances.)* **OL**

Section 2 REVIEW

Answers

1. All definitions can be found in the section and the Glossary.

2. Causes: new business techniques, improved technology; Effects: consumerism, suburban growth

3. The transistor was developed, as was the first computer. In medicine, antibiotics and vaccines were created. Also television sets became available to the average American.

4. Television caused changes in radio and film industries. Hollywood tried new film processes, and radio started broadcasting more news, weather, and sports instead of radio dramas and comedies.

5. through rock 'n' roll music and artistic movements such as the Beat movement

6. Its roots were in African American rhythms and sounds. It reached the mass media when a radio DJ in Cleveland, Ohio, named Alan Freed noticed that teenagers were buying African American rhythm and blues records. Freed then received permission to play the music on the air.

7. Student responses will vary but should provide a detailed explanation of opinions.

8. Students' critiques will vary. Critiques should provide a reasoned opinion on a specific television show, movie, musical act, or piece of literature based on the information in this section.

Focus

Tell students that actor James Dean was a favorite with 1950s teenagers. He projected a rebellious image expressing anger, confusion, and hurt. **Ask:** What does the popularity of actor James Dean with teenagers tell you about 1950s youth? What impact do you think his early death had on American youth? *(Answers will vary, but students might say that 1950s teenagers identified with his rebellious image. His early death must have been quite painful for his fans.)* **OL**

Teach

C Critical Thinking

Identifying Central Issues
Have students review the quotes in the Verbatim section and discuss each item as it relates to the people and themes found in the textbook. **OL**

Additional Support

TIME NOTEBOOK

Profile

JAMES DEAN *had a brief but spectacular career as a film star. His role in* Rebel Without a Cause *made him an icon for American youth in the mid-50s. In 1955 Dean was killed in a car crash. He was 24.*

"I guess I have as good an insight into this rising generation as any other young man my age. Therefore, when I do play a youth, I try to imitate life. *Rebel Without a Cause* deals with the problems of modern youth. . . . If you want the kids to come and see the picture, you've got to try to reach them on their own grounds. If a picture is psychologically motivated, if there is truth in the relationships in it, then I think that picture will do good."

—from an interview for Rebel Without a Cause

VERBATIM

❝It will make a wonderful place for the children to play in, and it will be a good storehouse, too.❞
MRS. RUTH CALHOUN,
mother of three, on her backyard fallout shelter, 1951

❝Riddle: What's college? That's where girls who are above cooking and sewing go to meet a man they can spend their lives cooking and sewing for.❞
ad for Gimbel's department store campus clothes, 1952

❝Radioactive poisoning of the atmosphere and hence annihilation of any life on Earth has been brought within the range of technical possibilities.❞
ALBERT EINSTEIN, *physicist, 1950*

❝If the television craze continues with the present level of programs, we are destined to have a nation of morons.❞
DANIEL MARSH, *President of Boston University, 1950*

❝Every time the Russians throw an American in jail, the House Un-American Activities Committee throws an American in jail to get even.❞
MORT SAHL, *comedian, 1950s*

WINNERS & LOSERS

POODLE CUTS Short, curly hairstyle gains wide popularity and acceptance

TV GUIDE New weekly magazine achieves circulation of 6.5 million by 1959

PALMER PAINT COMPANY OF DETROIT Sells 12 million paint-by-number kits ranging from simple landscapes and portraits to Leonardo da Vinci's The Last Supper

Poodle Cut

THE DUCKTAIL Banned in several Massachusetts schools in 1957

COLLIER'S The respected magazine loses circulation, publishes its final edition on January 4, 1957

LEONARDO DA VINCI'S THE LAST SUPPER Now everyone can paint their own copy to hang in their homes

The Ducktail

580 **Chapter 16** Postwar America

Extending the Content

Movie Magazines Americans had always been interested in the movies and the lives of movie stars. The new medium of television gave Americans a whole new medium with which to become fascinated. That medium was television and just as movie magazines had given fans an inside look at the movies, a new magazine did the same for television. That magazine was *TV Guide*. The first issue came out in 1953 and had Lucille Ball on its cover. The magazine let readers know what shows were on their televisions every day and night of the week. It also contained stories on the programs and stars of television. This proved to be exactly what television viewers wanted. Sales soared, and *TV Guide* became the best-selling weekly magazine in the United States.

1950S WORD PLAY

Translation, Please!

Match the word to its meaning.

Teen-Age Lingo
1. cool
2. hang loose
3. hairy
4. yo-yo

a. a dull person, an outsider
b. worthy of approval
c. formidable
d. don't worry

answers: 1.b; 2.d; 3.c; 4.a

American Scene, 1950–1960
(MILLIONS)

Children 5–14
24.3 / 35.5
1950 / 1960

Girl Scouts & Brownies
1.8 / 4.0
1950 / 1960

Bicycle Production
2.0 / 3.8
1950 / 1960

Be Prepared

"Know the Bomb's True Dangers. Know the Steps You Can Take to Escape Them!—You Can Survive."
Government pamphlet, 1950

DIGGING YOUR OWN BOMB SHELTER? Better go shopping. Below is a list of items included with the $3,000 Mark I Kidde Kokoon, designed to accommodate a family of five for a three-to five-day underground stay.

Bomb Shelter
BETTMANN/CORBIS

- air blower
- radiation detector
- protective apparel suit
- face respirator
- radiation charts (4)
- hand shovel (for digging out after the blast)
- gasoline driven generator
- gasoline (10 gallons)
- chemical toilet
- toilet chemicals (2 gallons)
- bunks (5)
- mattresses and blankets (5)
- air pump (blowing up mattresses)
- incandescent bulbs (2) 40 watts
- fuses (2) 5 amperes

- clock—non-electric
- first aid kit
- waterless hand cleaner
- sterno stove
- canned water (10 gallons)
- canned food (meat, powdered milk, cereal, sugar, etc.)
- paper products

NUMBERS 1957

3¢ Cost of first-class postage stamp

19¢ Cost of loaf of bread

25¢ Cost of issue of Sports Illustrated

35¢ Cost of movie ticket

50¢ Cost of gallon of milk (delivered)

$2.05 Average hourly wage

$2,845 Cost of new car

POPPERFOTO/ARCHIVE PHOTO

$5,234 Median income for a family of four

$19,500 Median price of a home

CRITICAL THINKING

1. Predicting If the number of American children continued to grow, how would that affect bicycle production and Scout membership? How could that growth affect the American economy?

2. Hypothesizing How have attitudes towards women changed since the 1952 department store ad for campus clothes? What do you think are some reasons for the change in attitude?

D Differentiated Instruction

Interpersonal Have students interview friends and relatives who lived during the 1950s to learn more about teenage lingo. Make a list of all the words and definitions that students bring in. **BL**

CRITICAL THINKING
Answers:
1. It could lead to greater demand for these things and spur the economy.
2. Women are seen as having lives beyond being wives and mothers; this is partly due to the women's movement.

Assess/Close

Visit the TIME Web site at www.time.com for up-to-date new, weekly magazine articles, editorials, online polls, and an archive of past magazine and Web articles.

Additional Support

Activity: Interdisciplinary Connection

Sociology In the 1950s, the response of citizens to societal dangers such as atomic war was more often an individual rather than a group effort. As early as the 1960s, with efforts such as the civil rights and anti-war movements, this began to change. Ask students to read newspapers and search the Internet for current examples of citizens' response to public concerns such as global warming and war. Have students write a paragraph comparing and contrasting the response of Americans in the 1950s to the threat of atomic war with the responses of Americans to threats today. Have them write a second paragraph expressing their thoughts on the responsibility of citizens to address public concerns and the best ways to do so. **OL**

Focus

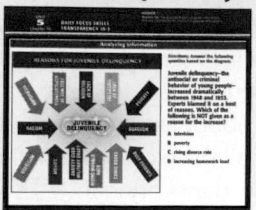

Guide to Reading

Answers:
The Other Side of American Life
I. Poverty Amidst Prosperity
   A. The Decline of the Inner City
   B. African Americans
   C. The Inner City's Ongoing Problems
   D. Hispanics
   E. Native Americans
   F. Appalachia
II. Juvenile Delinquency

Section Spotlight Video

To generate student interest and provide a springboard for class discussion, access the Chapter 16, Section 3 video at glencoe.com or on the video DVD.

Resource Manager

Section 3

The Other Side of American Life

Guide to Reading

Big Ideas
Economics and Society The postwar prosperity did not extend to all Americans. For some groups, poverty and discrimination continued during the apparent abundance of the 1950s.

Content Vocabulary
• poverty line *(p. 582)*
• urban renewal *(p. 583)*
• termination policy *(p. 585)*
• juvenile delinquency *(p. 587)*

Academic Vocabulary
• income *(p. 582)*
• entity *(p. 585)*

People and Events to Identify
• Lorraine Hansberry *(p. 584)*
• Bracero Program *(p. 584)*
• Appalachia *(p. 586)*

Reading Strategy
Taking Notes As you read about social problems in the United States in the 1950s, use the major headings of this section to create an outline similar to the one below.

```
The Other Side of American Life
I. Poverty Amidst Prosperity
   A.
   B.
   C.
   D.
   E.
II.
```

During the 1950s, about 20 percent of the American population—particularly people of color and those living in the inner cities and Appalachia—did not share in the general prosperity. Experts also worried about the rise in juvenile delinquency.

Poverty Amidst Prosperity

MAIN Idea Despite the growing affluence of much of the nation, many groups still lived in poverty.

HISTORY AND YOU Are the pockets of poverty in America today the same as they were in the 1950s? Read on to learn about the people and regions most affected by poverty in the 1950s.

The 1950s saw a tremendous expansion of the middle class. At least one in five Americans, or about 30 million people, however, lived below the **poverty line.** This imaginary marker is a figure the government sets to reflect the minimum **income** required to support a family. Such poverty remained invisible to most Americans, who assumed that the country's general prosperity had provided everyone with a comfortable existence.

The writer Michael Harrington, however, made no such assumptions. During the 1950s, Harrington set out to chronicle poverty in the United States. In his book *The Other America,* published in 1962, he alerted those in the mainstream to what he saw in the run-down and hidden communities of the country:

PRIMARY SOURCE

"To be sure, the other America is not impoverished in the same sense as those poor nations where millions cling to hunger as a defense against starvation. . . . That does not change the fact that tens of millions of Americans are, at this very moment, maimed in body and spirit, existing at levels beneath those necessary for human decency. If these people are not starving, they are hungry, and sometimes fat with hunger, for that is what cheap foods do. They are without adequate housing and education and medical care."

—from *The Other America*

The poor included single mothers and the elderly; minorities such as Puerto Ricans and Mexican immigrants; rural Americans—both African American and white—and inner city residents, who remained stuck in crowded slums as wealthier citizens fled to the suburbs. Many Native Americans endured grinding poverty whether they stayed on reservations or migrated to cities.

R Reading Strategies	**C** Critical Thinking	**D** Differentiated Instruction	**W** Writing Support	**S** Skill Practice
Teacher Edition • Content Vocab., p. 583 • Inferring, p. 585	**Teacher Edition** • Analyzing Info., p. 583 • Drawing Con., p. 585	**Teacher Edition** • Gifted/Talented, p. 584 • Kinesthetic, p. 586	**Teacher Edition** • Expository Writing, p. 584	**Additional Resources** • Authentic Assess., p. 37 • RENTG, p. 179
Additional Resources • Prim. Source Read., URB p. 137 • Guided Reading Act., URB p. 152	**Additional Resources** • Quizzes/Tests, p. 225	**Additional Resources** • Differentiated Act., URB p. 125 • Reteaching Act., URB p. 145 • Enrich. Act., URB p. 147	**Additional Resources** • Am. Art and Music Act., URB p. 141	

PRIMARY SOURCE

The Other America

Amid the prosperity of the 1950s, many lived in terrible poverty. While suburbs boomed, the poor, many of whom were minorities, were relegated to inner-city slums. Native Americans suffered extreme poverty and the breakdown of their culture on reservations, while Mexican migrant workers in the Southwest barely made enough to feed, clothe, and shelter themselves and their children.

▲ A poor Navajo family stands outside their home on an Arkansas reservation in 1948.

▲ Children play in the littered streets of a Chicago slum in 1954.

Analyzing VISUALS

1. **Examining** Based on the photos, what aspect of life does it seem the hardest for the poor in America to obtain?

2. **Hypothesizing** What do you think might account for minorities having a lower average income than whites in the United States in the 1940s and 1950s?

▲ The Cervantes family lived in a one-room shack at a ranch camp near Fresno, California, in 1950.

The Decline of the Inner City

The poverty of the 1950s was most apparent in the nation's urban centers. As middle-class families moved to the suburbs, they left behind the poor and less-educated. Many city centers deteriorated because the taxes that the middle class paid moved out with them. Cities no longer had the tax dollars to provide adequate public transportation, housing, and other services.

C R When government tried to help inner-city residents, it often made matters worse. During the 1950s, for example, **urban renewal** pro-

grams tried to eliminate poverty by tearing down slums and erecting new high-rise buildings for poor residents. These crowded, high-rise projects, however, often created an atmosphere of violence. The government also unwittingly encouraged the residents of public housing to remain poor by evicting them as **R C** soon as they began earning a higher income.

In the end, urban renewal programs actually destroyed more housing space than they created. Too often, the wrecking balls destroyed poor people's homes to make way for roadways, parks, universities, tree-lined boulevards, or shopping centers.

Teach

C Critical Thinking

Analyzing Information Have students conduct additional research on one urban renewal project of the 1950s and the changes this project has undergone from the 1950s to today. They should determine the problems the project created, the steps government undertook to remedy the problems, and any new problems that developed. Have students present their findings in a written report. **OL**

R Reading Strategy

Content Vocabulary Ask: Why was the term *urban renewal* descriptive of the changes in inner cities? (*Old slums were being torn down and new housing was being built.*) **BL**

Analyzing VISUALS

Answers:
1. adequate housing
2. racism; less access to education and good jobs

Hands-On Chapter Project
Step 3

A New Peacetime America

Step 3: Create a Brochure America was bursting with new gadgets after the war years.

Directions Organize students into groups. Have each group select one of the new inventions that appeared in this time period, whether a home device or one used in business or manufacturing. Their task is to create a brochure to sell that product to

whomever their buying audience might be—homemakers, businessmen, choir children, for example. They should write and illustrate their brochures in whatever design they choose. Have the groups present their brochures to the rest of the class, explaining their selling approach and purpose.

Representing Information Give students time to prepare for their presentations. They may role play or use media other than their posters to present the infor-

mation. Encourage students to state the topic clearly, describe it, and summarize the information. **OL**

(Chapter Project continued on the Visual Summary page)

Expository Writing Have students use library or Internet resources to find Langston Hughes's poem "A Dream Deferred," from which Lorraine Hansberry's play *A Raisin In the Sun* drew its name. Instruct students to read the poem and write one-page responses. **Ask:** What key images do you remember from the poem? What does Hughes seem to be saying about dreams that remain unrealized? Why do you think that Lorraine Hansberry chose the phrase "a raisin in the sun" for the title of her play? Invite students to share their responses. **OL**

D **Differentiated Instruction**

Gifted and Talented Tell students that music has long been a way for people to express their emotions. Challenge interested students to take the impressions they have gained while reading the chapter to compose and perform a song expressing the plight of Mexican laborers in the 1950s. **AL**

Additional Support

African Americans

Many of the citizens left behind in the cities were African American. By 1960, more than 3 million African Americans had migrated from the South to Northern cities in search of greater economic opportunity and to escape violence and racial intimidation. For many of these migrants, however, the economic boom of the war years did not continue in the 1950s.

Long-standing patterns of racial discrimination in schools, housing, hiring, and salaries in the North kept many inner-city African Americans poor. The last hired and the first fired for good jobs, they often remained stuck in the worst-paying occupations. In 1958 African Americans' salaries, on average, were only 51 percent of what whites earned. Poverty and racial discrimination also deprived many African Americans of other benefits, such as decent medical care.

In 1959 the play *A Raisin in the Sun* opened on Broadway. Written by African American author **Lorraine Hansberry,** the play told the story of a working-class African American family struggling against poverty and racism. The title referred to a Langston Hughes poem that wonders what happens to an unrealized dream: "Does it dry up like a raisin in the sun?" The play won the New York Drama Critics Circle Award for the best play of the year. Responding to a correspondent who had seen the play, Lorraine Hansberry wrote: "The ghettos are killing us; not only our dreams . . . but our very bodies. It is not an abstraction to us that the average [African American] has a life expectancy of five to ten years less than the average white."

Hispanics

African Americans were not the only minority group that struggled with poverty. Much of the nation's Hispanic population faced the same problems. During the 1950s and early 1960s, the **Bracero Program** brought nearly 5 million Mexicans to the United States to work on farms and ranches in the Southwest. Braceros were temporary contract workers. Many later returned home, but some 350,000 settled permanently in the United States.

These laborers, who worked on large farms throughout the country, lived with extreme poverty and hardship. They toiled long hours, for little pay, in conditions that were often

PAST & PRESENT

The Inner-City's Ongoing Problems

By the end of the 1950s, many major U.S. cities were in decline. "White flight" and lowered tax revenues, as well as racial discrimination and a lack of sympathy for the less fortunate, combined to create islands of decay and poverty in urban centers.

Although numerous programs were launched in the 1960s to try to improve living conditions and eliminate poverty, the problem has proven more difficult than first anticipated. Fifty years separate the two photos of inner-city slums to the right, yet, tragically, the quality of life has barely changed.

Major Cities With High Poverty Rates, 1960

Philadelphia
Detroit
Chicago
Cleveland
New York
Baltimore
St. Louis
Pittsburgh
Los Angeles
San Diego
Dallas
Houston
San Antonio
New Orleans

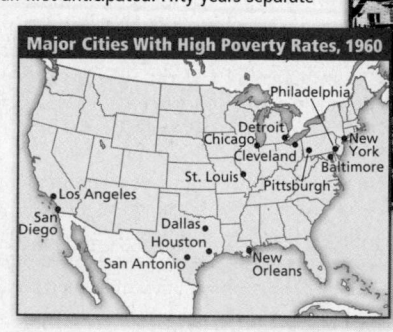

1940

▲ *Even in the 1940s, urban decay was characteristic of many American cities, including Washington, D.C., where people lived in dire poverty within sight of the Capitol.*

Activity: Interdisciplinary Connection

Performing Arts Organize students into small groups and have them discuss what life was like in the 1950s for one of the groups mentioned in this section. Then have students produce a skit depicting one aspect of life for the group they selected. Encourage students to use appropriate music to set the tone for their skits. Make arrangements for students to perform for their classmates. **OL**

unbearable. In *The Other America*, Michael Harrington noted:

PRIMARY SOURCE

"[Migrant laborers] work ten-eleven-twelve hour days in temperatures over one hundred degrees. Sometimes there is no drinking water. . . . Women and children work on ladders and with hazardous machinery. . . . Babies are brought to the field and are placed in 'cradles' of wood boxes."

—from *The Other America*

R Away from the fields, many Mexican families lived in small, crudely built shacks, while some did not even have a roof over their heads. "They sleep where they can, some in the open," Harrington noted about one group of migrant workers. "They eat when they can (and sometimes what they can)." The nation paid little attention to the plight of Mexican farm laborers until the 1960s, when the workers began to organize for greater rights.

Native Americans

Native Americans also faced challenges throughout the postwar era. By the middle of the 1900s, Native Americans—who made up less than one percent of the population—were the poorest ethnic group in the nation. Average annual family income for Native American families, for example, was $1,000 less than that of African American families.

After World War II, during which many Native American soldiers had served with distinction, the United States government launched a program to bring Native Americans into mainstream society—whether they wanted to assimilate or not.

Under the plan, which became known as the **termination policy,** the federal government withdrew all official recognition of the Native American groups as legal **entities** and made them subject to the same laws as white citizens. Native American groups were then placed under the responsibility of state governments. At the same time, the government encouraged Native Americans to blend in with the larger society by helping them move off reservations to cities.

Although the idea of integrating Native Americans into mainstream society began with good intentions, some of its supporters had more selfish goals. Speculators and developers sometimes gained rich farmland at the expense of destitute Native American groups.

C

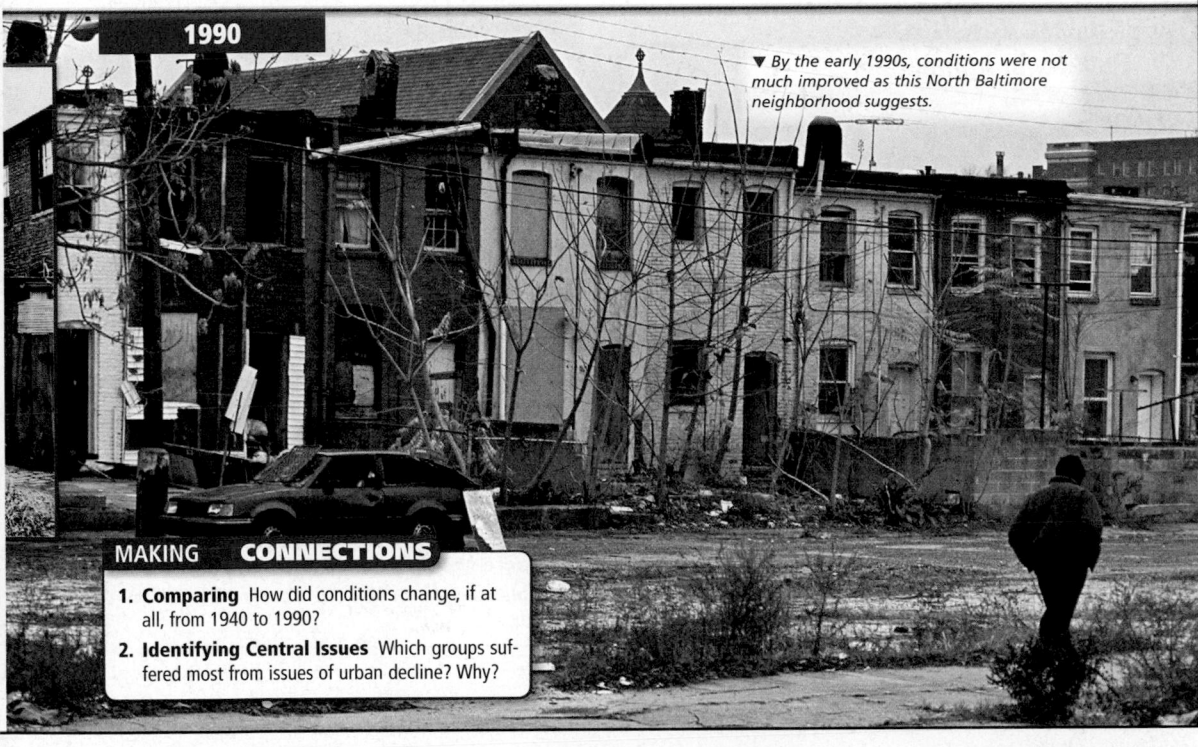

1990

▼ By the early 1990s, conditions were not much improved as this North Baltimore neighborhood suggests.

MAKING CONNECTIONS

1. **Comparing** How did conditions change, if at all, from 1940 to 1990?
2. **Identifying Central Issues** Which groups suffered most from issues of urban decline? Why?

Activity: Interdisciplinary Connection

Daily Life Have students work in groups to research Native American life in the 1950s. Within each group, pairs of students should investigate such aspects of daily life as housing, food, education, religious life, culture, work and leisure. Student pairs should present the results of their research to their groups. Together, each group should then make decisions about how to present the information they have gathered.

Some groups might wish to present their findings in the form of a written report. Others might make an oral presentation. Still others might wish to create an interactive Web site with their findings. Have students present their final products to the class. **Ask:** Did the termination policy change the lives of Native Americans? In what ways? **OL**

D Differentiated Instruction

Kinesthetic Organize students into small groups and have them discuss what life was like in the 1950s for people living in Appalachia. Have students produce skits depicting one aspect of Appalachian life. Encourage them to use appropriate music to set the tone for their skits. Make arrangements for students to perform for their classmates. **OL**

Analyzing VISUALS

Answers:

1. Mississippi, Alabama, Tennessee, Kentucky, Virginia, West Virginia

2. high unemployment in mining communities

✔ Reading Check

Answer:

African Americans, Hispanics, and Native Americans

For most Native Americans, termination was a disastrous policy that only deepened their poverty. In the mid-1950s, for example, the Welfare Council of Minneapolis described Native American living conditions in that city as miserable: "One Indian family of five or six, living in two rooms, will take in relatives and friends who come from the reservations seeking jobs until perhaps fifteen people will be crowded into the space."

During the 1950s, Native Americans in Minneapolis could expect to live only 37 years, compared to 46 years for all Minnesota Native Americans and 68 years for other Minneapolis residents. Similar patterns existed elsewhere. Benjamin Reifel, a Sioux, described the despair that the termination policy produced:

PRIMARY SOURCE

"The Indians believed that when the dark clouds of war passed from the skies overhead, their rising tide of expectations, though temporarily stalled, would again reappear. Instead they were threatened by termination. . . . Soaring expectations began to plunge."

—quoted in *The Earth Shall Weep*

Appalachia

Residents of rural **Appalachia** also failed to share in the prosperity of the 1950s. The scenic beauty of the mountainous region, which stretches from New York to Georgia, often hid desperate poverty. Coal mining had long been the backbone of the Appalachian economy. With mechanization of mining in the 1950s, unemployment soared. With no work to be had, some 1.5 million people abandoned Appalachia to seek a better life in the cities. "Whole counties," wrote one reporter, "are precariously held together by a flour-and-dried-milk paste of surplus foods. . . . The men who are no longer needed in the mines and the farmers who cannot compete . . . have themselves become surplus commodities in the mountains." **D**

Appalachia had fewer doctors per thousand people than the rest of the country. Studies revealed high rates of nutritional deficiency and infant mortality. In addition, schooling in the region was considered even worse than in inner-city slums.

✔ **Reading Check** **Identifying** Which groups were left out of the economic boom of the 1950s?

PRIMARY SOURCE
Poverty in Appalachia

▲ Eight family members lived in this three-room house lined with newspaper in Appalachia in the 1950s.

Appalachia

- Distressed county, 1960
- Other Appalachian county

Albers Equal-Area projection

Analyzing VISUALS **DBQ**

1. **Identifying** Which states had the highest concentration of distressed counties in 1960?

2. **Explaining** What might have accounted for this high number?

586 Chapter 16 Postwar America

Differentiated Instruction

Leveled Activities

BL Reteaching Activity, URB p. 145

OL Academic Vocabulary Activity, URB p. 131

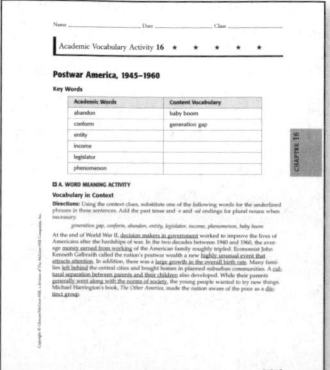

AL Primary Source Reading, URB p. 137

ELL Reinforcing Skills Activity, URB p. 133

Juvenile Delinquency

MAIN Idea Juvenile crime rates rose during the 1950s; a crisis in education occurred when the baby boomers began school.

HISTORY AND YOU Has your school placed a greater emphasis on science and math classes recently? Read to learn about a push in science and math education during the 1950s.

During the 1950s, many middle-class, white Americans found it easy to ignore the poverty and racism that afflicted many of the nation's minorities, since they themselves were removed from it. Some social problems, however, became impossible to ignore.

One problem at this time was a rise in, or at least a rise in the reporting of, **juvenile delinquency**—antisocial or criminal behavior of young people. Between 1948 and 1953, the United States saw a 45 percent rise in juvenile crime rates. A popular 1954 book titled *1,000,000 Delinquents* correctly predicted that in the following year, about 1 million young people would be involved in some kind of criminal activity.

Americans disagreed on what had triggered the rise in delinquency. Experts blamed television, movies, comic books, racism, busy parents, a rising divorce rate, lack of religion, and anxiety over the military draft. Some cultural critics claimed that young people were rebelling against the conformity of their parents. Others blamed a lack of discipline. Doting parents, complained Bishop Fulton J. Sheen, had raised bored children who sought new thrills, such as "alcohol, marijuana, even murder." Still others pointed at social causes, blaming teen violence on poverty. The problem, however, cut across class and racial lines—the majority of car thieves, for example, had grown up in middle-class homes.

Most teens, of course, steered clear of gangs, drugs, and crime. Nonetheless, the public tended to stereotype young people as juvenile delinquents, especially those teens who favored unconventional clothing and long hair, or used street slang.

Concerned about their children, many parents focused on the nation's schools as a possible solution. When baby boomers began entering the school system in the 1950s, enrollments increased by 13 million. School districts struggled to pay for new buildings and hire more teachers.

Americans' education worries only intensified in 1957 after the Soviet Union launched the world's first space satellites, *Sputnik I* and *Sputnik II*. Many Americans felt that the nation had fallen behind its Cold War enemy and blamed what they felt was a lack of technical education in the nation's schools. *Life* magazine proclaimed a "Crisis in Education" and offered a grim warning: "What has long been an ignored national problem, *Sputnik* has made a recognized crisis." In the wake of the *Sputnik* launches, efforts began to improve math and science education. Profound fears about the country's young people, it seemed, dominated the end of a decade that had brought prosperity and progress for many Americans.

✓ Reading Check **Evaluating** What were some suggested explanations of the increase in juvenile crime?

Vocabulary

1. **Explain** the significance of: poverty line, urban renewal, Lorraine Hansberry, Bracero Program, termination policy, Appalachia, juvenile delinquency.

Main Ideas

2. **Evaluating** How did the federal government's termination policy affect Native Americans?

3. **Analyzing** What effects did the baby boomers have on schools?

Critical Thinking

4. **Big Ideas** Why did urban renewal fail to improve the lives of the poor in the inner cities?

5. **Organizing** Use a graphic organizer similar to the one below to list groups of Americans left out of the country's postwar economic boom.

Groups of Low-Income Americans

6. **Analyzing Visuals** Study the photographs on page 583. Why were minority groups hit so hard by poverty, compared to whites, in the 1950s?

Writing About History

7. **Expository Writing** Choose a current social problem that you observe among adolescents. Describe the problem and its causes, and then recommend a solution.

History ONLINE
Study Central™ To review this section, go to glencoe.com and click on Study Central.

587

✓ Reading Check

Answer:
Answers may include: television, movies, comic books, racism, busy parents, a rising divorce rate, lack of religion, anxiety over the military draft, teenage rebellion, lack of discipline, doting parents, boredom, poverty.

Assess

History ONLINE

Study Central™ provides summaries, interactive games, and online graphic organizers to help students review content.

Close

Summarizing Ask: What was the major cause of deteriorating cities in the 1950s? *(The tax base of city governments dropped as middle-class residents moved to the suburbs.)* **OL**

Section 3 REVIEW

Answers

1. All definitions can be found in the section and the Glossary.

2. They lost much of their cultural uniqueness and valuable land, and they were often as poor in the cities as they would have been on the reservations.

3. As the wave of baby boomers entered the education system, school districts had to find the money to build new buildings and hire more teachers.

4. The high-rise projects that were built to replace older buildings were crowded and destroyed more housing space than they created. They also often created an atmosphere of violence.

5. single mothers, the elderly, minority immigrants, inner-city poor, people in Appalachia

6. Minority groups did not have access to the new higher-paying, white-collar jobs that whites did.

7. The social problems and solutions students cover will vary. Students should provide a current problem among juveniles and a relevant, reasoned solution to that problem.

Chapter 16 VISUAL SUMMARY

Drawing Conclusions After World War II, the GI Bill provided generous funds to veterans. **Ask:** What effect did this government spending have on the economy? *(It boosted the economy by putting money in the hands of veterans to start businesses, buy homes and goods, and get an education.)* **OL**

Determining Cause and Effect During the 1950s Americans experienced a baby boom. **Ask:** What were the reasons for the baby boom of the 1950s? *(Young couples who had delayed marriage during the war were now starting families, generous GI benefits helped veterans afford homes in which to raise families, popular culture celebrated large families.)* **OL**

Personal Writing During the 1950s, television did not usually portray women as independent and strong. Minorities were largely absent from television. **Ask:** What impact do you think this may have had on women and minorities in the 1950s? **OL**

The Prosperity of the 1950s

Economy and Society

- The GI Bill provided funds and loans to millions of war veterans.
- Consumer spending increased rapidly.
- More Americans owned homes than ever before.

Population Patterns

- The U.S. population experienced a "baby boom."
- Millions of Americans moved out of cities to the suburbs.

Science, Technology, and Medicine

- Improvements in communication, transportation, and electronics allowed Americans to work more efficiently.
- Medical breakthroughs included the polio vaccine, antibiotics, and treatments for tuberculosis, cancer, and heart disease.

Popular Culture

- New forms of music, radio, cinema, and literature emerged.
- Television replaced movies and radio as the nation's new and most popular form of mass media.

▲ The huge, stylized automobiles of the 1950s, such as this Cadillac convertible, symbolized the good life to many Americans of the time.

The Problems of the 1950s

Economy and Society

- Workers went on strike for higher wages.
- Congress would not pass Truman's civil rights legislation.
- Eisenhower cut back on New Deal programs.

Population Patterns

- Financially able people moved from crowded cities to new suburbs.
- Poverty increased in the inner city and the poor faced ongoing social problems.
- Crime increased among young people.

Science, Technology, and Medicine

- Poor people in inner cities and rural areas had limited access to modern health care.

Popular Culture

- Not everyone could afford to buy the new consumer goods available, such as televisions.
- African Americans and other minorities were, for the most part, not depicted on television.
- Many television programs promoted stereotypical gender roles.

▲ While many prospered in the 1950s, many were excluded from achieving the American Dream.

588 Chapter 16 Postwar America

Hands-On Chapter Project
Step 4: Wrap Up

A New Peacetime America

Step 4: Wrap Up This activity will synthesize the information that students have collected about the society and culture of this time period.

Directions Divide the class into six teams. Each team should select one presenter to take on the role of an individual who lived during this time period. To avoid duplication among the teams, have each team announce which role their presenter will play. If there are duplicates, assign another role to one of the teams.

Analyzing Information Team members will collaboratively write a journal page from the perspective of the presenter. Each journal page should describe vividly the person's life at this time. Presenters will read the group's journal page to the class. The rest of the class may want to ask the presenters questions. To make the presentations more lively and memorable, presenters may wish to carry relevant signs, dress in costumes, or hold up photos. **OL**

ASSESSMENT

STANDARDIZED TEST PRACTICE

TEST-TAKING TIP

Before answering, read the entire question and all answer choices. Then choose the answer that makes the most sense.

Reviewing Vocabulary

Directions: Choose the word or words that best complete the sentence.

1. The Taft-Hartley Act outlawed the _____, opening some industries to nonunion workers.
   - A closed shop
   - B labor unions
   - C right-to-work laws
   - D open shop

2. During the 1950s, the number of _____ grew, as more Americans worked in offices.
   - A computers
   - B blue-collar jobs
   - C franchises
   - D white-collar jobs

3. After World War II, Native Americans suffered from the government policy of _____, which forced them into mainstream society.
   - A urban renewal
   - B termination
   - C migrant work
   - D reservation planning

4. The poem "Howl," by Allen Ginsberg, is a work that came out of the _____ movement.
   - A rock 'n' roll
   - B generation gap
   - C beat
   - D jazz

Reviewing Main Ideas

Directions: Choose the best answer for each of the following questions.

Section 1 *(pp. 566–571)*

5. Which of the following were two characteristics of the U.S. economy after World War II?
   - A high unemployment and scarce goods
   - B abundant goods and low unemployment
   - C low unemployment and scarce goods
   - D abundant goods and high unemployment

6. Which of the following was achieved under Truman's Fair Deal?
   - A a large increase in Social Security benefits
   - B a broad program of civil rights reforms
   - C a decrease in funding for the TVA
   - D a federal highway bill

Section 2 *(pp. 572–579)*

7. One major cause of the growth of the suburbs was the
   - A rise in blue-collar jobs.
   - B Korean War.
   - C affordability of homes.
   - D television.

8. Jonas Salk developed the first vaccine for which illness?
   - A tuberculosis
   - B cancer
   - C heart disease
   - D polio

Need Extra Help?								
If You Missed Questions . . .	1	2	3	4	5	6	7	8
Go to Page . . .	566–567	574	585–586	579	566–567	569	572–573	574–575

 GO ON

Answers and Analyses
Reviewing Vocabulary

1. A The closed shop was an industry that was closed to non-union workers; that is, only union workers could work in the industry. The question states that the act opened some industries to "nonunion" workers. The opposite of the closed shop is the open shop—industries open to all workers.

2. D Computers did not come into popular use in offices until decades after the 1950s. Franchises are a type of business, and usually include retail establishments, not offices. Blue-collar workers worked in factories and as laborers. The name is derived from blue denim work clothes. White collar is derived from white dress shirts. White-collar workers are office workers.

3. B An easy way for students to remember this is to think that the government attempted to "terminate" the Native American way of life by assimilating them into American culture and refusing to recognize tribes as legal entities.

4. C Poetry is an art form associated more with the beat movement than with other movements listed. Rock 'n' roll predated the beat movement. The generation gap was a fact of life, not a movement. Jazz also predated the beat movement.

incorrect choices include at least one negative, and *A* includes two negatives.

6. A Like FDR's New Deal, the Fair Deal was aimed at improving domestic affairs. Have students who answer incorrectly review "What Was the Fair Deal?" on page 569. Listed first is an increase in Social Security benefits.

7. C This is a cause-and-effect question; students must choose the answer that is most likely responsible for growing suburbs. *A* may be tempting for students, because any rise in jobs might equal rise in money for housing. However,

this connection is too tenuous. It is not likely a war would cause suburbs to grow. Nor is it likely that television would cause suburbs to grow. Television grew with suburbs. Affordable homes caused more people to be able to buy homes, which caused suburbs to grow.

8. D Have students who have trouble reread "Medical Miracles" on page 574. All of the answer choices are discussed. Jonas Salk invented the first injected polio vaccine. The other choices discussed are not associated with any single scientist.

Reviewing Main Ideas

5. B The answer choices in this question can confuse students who do not read carefully, because they all contain some combination of "goods" and "unemployment." Remind students that the economy after WWII was good. Therefore, they can eliminate any answer choices that include a negative. All three

9. C This is another cause-and-effect question. The baby boom increased the population. An increase in population would not cause a decrease in housing demand, nor would it cause people to migrate en masse to one part of the nation. Although there is concern for the Social Security system today because of the increasing amount of boomers who are eligible, it is not yet bankrupt.

10. C This question may confuse students, who may be tempted to choose *D*. However, as students read in the chapter, radio stations actually increased after television, because TV forced radio stations to make changes to continue to draw audiences in. The car helped save the radio, because people used the radio for entertainment when driving.

11. B Urban renewal was an action or movement, not an object. Delinquency is criminal behavior or wrongdoing. Income tax does not make sense. An easy way for students to remember this definition is to think of an actual line marking the threshold for poverty.

12. A The Bracero Program began during World War II, when men were brought from Mexico to help harvest crops and work on ranches. They were not citizens of the U.S., they were here on work contracts, but many of their families came over to the U.S. with them and settled. You might tie this in with a current events discussion on Mexican immigration today.

Critical Thinking

13. B The GI Bill was instrumental in helping returning veterans gain access to education, housing, and services. Housing loans helped contribute to the growth of suburbs. Builders, such as William Levitt, developed a system of

590

---

9. How did the post–World War II baby boom affect American society between 1945 and 1960?

   A It decreased the demand for housing.

   B It bankrupted the Social Security system.

   C It increased the need for educational resources.

   D It encouraged people to migrate to the Sun Belt.

10. How did television affect the radio industry?

   A One-fifth of the nation's movie theaters closed.

   B Radio stations started to broadcast soap operas.

   C The number of radio stations increased as the car created a larger audience.

   D Radio stations declined in number as the audience turned to television.

Section 3 (pp. 582–587)

11. The imaginary government marker setting the minimum income required to support a family is called the

   A urban renewal.

   B poverty line.

   C income tax.

   D delinquency.

12. The purpose of the Bracero Program was to

   A bring workers into the United States from Mexico.

   B send workers from the United States to Mexico.

   C find housing for new immigrants.

   D deport illegal immigrants.

Need Extra Help?							
If You Missed Questions . . .	9	10	11	12	13	14	15
Go to Page . . .	573	577	582	584–585	566–567	R16	R16

Critical Thinking

Directions: Choose the best answers to the following questions.

13. The GI Bill boosted the postwar economy by

   A instituting a military draft.

   B providing veterans with generous loans.

   C requiring all veterans to go to college.

   D providing veterans with white-collar jobs.

Base your answers to questions 14 and 15 on the graph below and on your knowledge of Chapter 16.

Suburban Dwellers, 1910–1980

Source: The First Measured Century.

14. What trend in the percentage of suburban dwellers does this graph show?

   A Fewer people were moving from the cities to the suburbs each year.

   B More people lived in the suburbs in 1910 than 1950.

   C More people lived in the cities in 1960 than 1950.

   D More people lived in the suburbs in 1980 than 1970.

15. In what year were there approximately twice the number of suburban residents as there had been in 1910?

   A 1930

   B 1940

   C 1950

   D 1960

GO ON

---

mass-produced housing that took advantage of the fact that the GI Bill made housing affordable to returning veterans.

14. D Study the graph with students. It shows an overall upward trend in the number of suburban dwellers between 1910 and 1980. In 1970, approximately 36 percent of the population lived in suburbs, according to the chart. In 1980, approximately 45 percent of the population lived in suburbs.

15. C There were approximately twice as many suburban residents in 1950.

16. Many Americans responded to the Soviet launching of *Sputnik* by demanding that schools

  A focus more on math and science.

  B offer more physical fitness training.

  C require students to learn a foreign language.

  D require the recitation of the Pledge of Allegiance.

Analyze the cartoon and answer the questions that follow. Base your answers on the cartoon and on your knowledge of Chapter 16.

"He never wastes a minute, J.P.—that's his lunch."

17. The main idea of this cartoon is that 1950s white-collar workers were

  A lazy and useless.

  B unstable and untrustworthy.

  C extremely good at what they did.

  D overly dedicated to their jobs.

Document-Based Questions

Directions: Analyze the document and answer the short-answer questions that follow the document.

George Gallup, one of the nation's first pollsters, spoke at the University of Iowa in 1953 about the importance of mass media in the United States. Below is an excerpt from his remarks:

> "One of the real threats to America's future place in the world is a citizenry which duly elects to be entertained and not informed. From the time the typical citizen arises and looks at his morning newspaper until he turns off his radio or television set before going to bed, he has unwittingly cast his vote a hundred times for entertainment or for education. Without his knowing it, he has helped to determine the very character of our three most important media of communication—the press, radio, and television."
>
> —quoted in *Legacy of Freedom, Vol. 2: United States History from Reconstruction to the Present*

18. According to Gallup, what is a threat to the future of the United States in the world?

19. How do American citizens "cast their votes" to determine what is read, seen, and heard in the mass media?

Extended Response

20. Harry Truman was a Democrat, and Dwight Eisenhower was a Republican. However, the two men did not always act along party lines and, in some cases, took similar approaches to governing. In an expository essay, compare and contrast the domestic agendas of these two presidents of the postwar era. Include an introduction and at least three paragraphs with supporting details that explain how Truman's and Eisenhower's ideas and approaches to domestic issues were different and similar.

For additional test practice, use Self-Check Quizzes—Chapter 16 at glencoe.com.

19. American citizens cast their votes by what they choose to watch, read, and listen to. If most people choose entertainment over education in the mass media, then the mass media will respond by providing more, or only, entertainment.

Extended Response

20. Students' essays will vary, but should make clear and logical comparisons with supporting details from the chapter, between Truman's and Eisenhower's domestic agendas and policies. Essays should include discussion of Truman's Fair Deal and Eisenhower's Dynamic Conservatism.

Need Extra Help?

If You Missed Questions . . .	16	17	18	19	20
Go to Page . . .	587	R18	591	591	566–571

16. A They demanded schools focus more on math and science.

17. D Study the cartoon with students. The man at the desk is working and "eating" lunch. His lunch, though, is being given intravenously. The implication is that he doesn't want to let eating lunch get in the way of his work. This is over dedication. He is not lazy; he is working hard. It appears he never leaves his desk, even to eat lunch, so he is not unstable. He might be good at what he did, but *D* better fits the cartoon.

Document-Based Questions

18. According to Gallup, the threat was that Americans had chosen to be entertained rather than informed or educated. The focus on entertainment and lack of education might cause the U.S. to lag behind in intellectual accomplishments.

Have students visit the Web site at glencoe.com to review Chapter 16 and take the Self-Check Quiz.

Need Extra Help?

Have students refer to the pages listed if they miss any of the questions.

591

UNIT PACING CHART

	Unit 6	Chapter 17	Chapter 18	Chapter 19	Chapter 20	Unit 6
Day 1	Unit Opener	Chapter 17 Opener, Section 1	Chapter 18 Opener, Section 1	Chapter 19 Opener, Section 1	Chapter 20 Opener, Section 1	Wrap-Up/Project, Unit Assessment
Day 2		Section 2	Section 2	Section 2	Section 2	
Day 3		Section 3	Section 3	Section 3	Section 3	
Day 4		Chapter Assessment	Chapter Assessment	Chapter Assessment	Chapter Assessment	

Teacher to Teacher

**Erin Johnston
South Caldwell
High School
Hudson, North
Carolina**

History Music Video Project Have students select a figure, event, or era from world and American history as well as a song. (I generally try to have them use one that is no more than 5 minutes to keep the file size down. You may want them to bring a copy of the lyrics to you so you can determine appropriateness.) If you are uncertain about the choice you should ask students to explain their "vision" to you. Tell them that they are telling a story through images, songs, and quotes to their audience. I have been surprised at how insightful my students have been in selecting their songs.

There are many programs that allow you to make videos, and many students already know how to use this technology and may help demonstrate it in class. The media programs are fairly simple "click and drag" programs that have directions on the screen. I generally have my students save 30–50 images for their projects. These programs allow you to include actual film footage and add quotes/passages as "eyewitness accounts."

These videos have become powerful teaching tools in helping my students understand historical periods such as the civil rights movement.

Author Note

Dear American History Teacher,

The 25 years covered in this unit represented an era of dramatic change in American history. The Cold War served as the backdrop to many of these events and should be reemphasized as you discuss the social and political upheavals of the 1960s and 1970s. The United States emerged from World War II as one of two superpowers, along with the Soviet Union. This fact may help students understand why the United States felt obligated to become immersed in so many foreign policy entanglements.

Indeed, the decades of the 1950s and 1960s witnessed some of the greatest social movements of the twentieth century—the civil rights movement, the student movement, the women's movement, the environmental movement, and the counterculture movement. These movements touched nearly every corner of American society. New leaders emerged on college campuses, in local communities, and on the national stage. American colleges and universities served as forums for many of the movements.

These were years of relative prosperity, rising expectations, and the desire to end poverty and suffering among all Americans, as illustrated in President Lyndon Johnson's Great Society. Historians continue to debate the significance of Johnson's presidency and his Great Society programs, but there is little doubt that many of these programs such as Medicaid, Medicare, Head Start, the Child Nutrition Act, and the Clean Water Act improved the quality of life for millions of Americans.

Students should also, however, get a sense of how deeply the nation divided over American foreign policy, especially U.S. involvement in the Vietnam War. The legacy of that war is still being debated by historians as well. Finally, the struggle for civil rights and racial equality were central to this era, and students are generally excited to learn about the roles of leaders such as Martin Luther King, Jr., Rosa Parks, Thurgood Marshall, and Malcolm X.

Albert S. Broussard

Senior Author

Focus

Why It Matters

Ask students to interview someone who came of age during the 1960s or 1970s. Ask them to focus interview questions on how that era has influenced the person's life and how it has affected national policy. Invite volunteers to share what they learned from the interviews. **OL**

Connecting to Past Learning

In previous units, students have learned about other presidential policies, such as the Square Deal and the New Deal. In this unit, they will learn of the New Frontier and the Great Society. They also learned about other wars. They will learn about the Vietnam War in this unit.

Unit Launch Activity

Write the Scene Have students skim the unit for a photograph that interests them. Then challenge them to write a paragraph describing the photograph or its setting and why they were drawn to it. **OL**

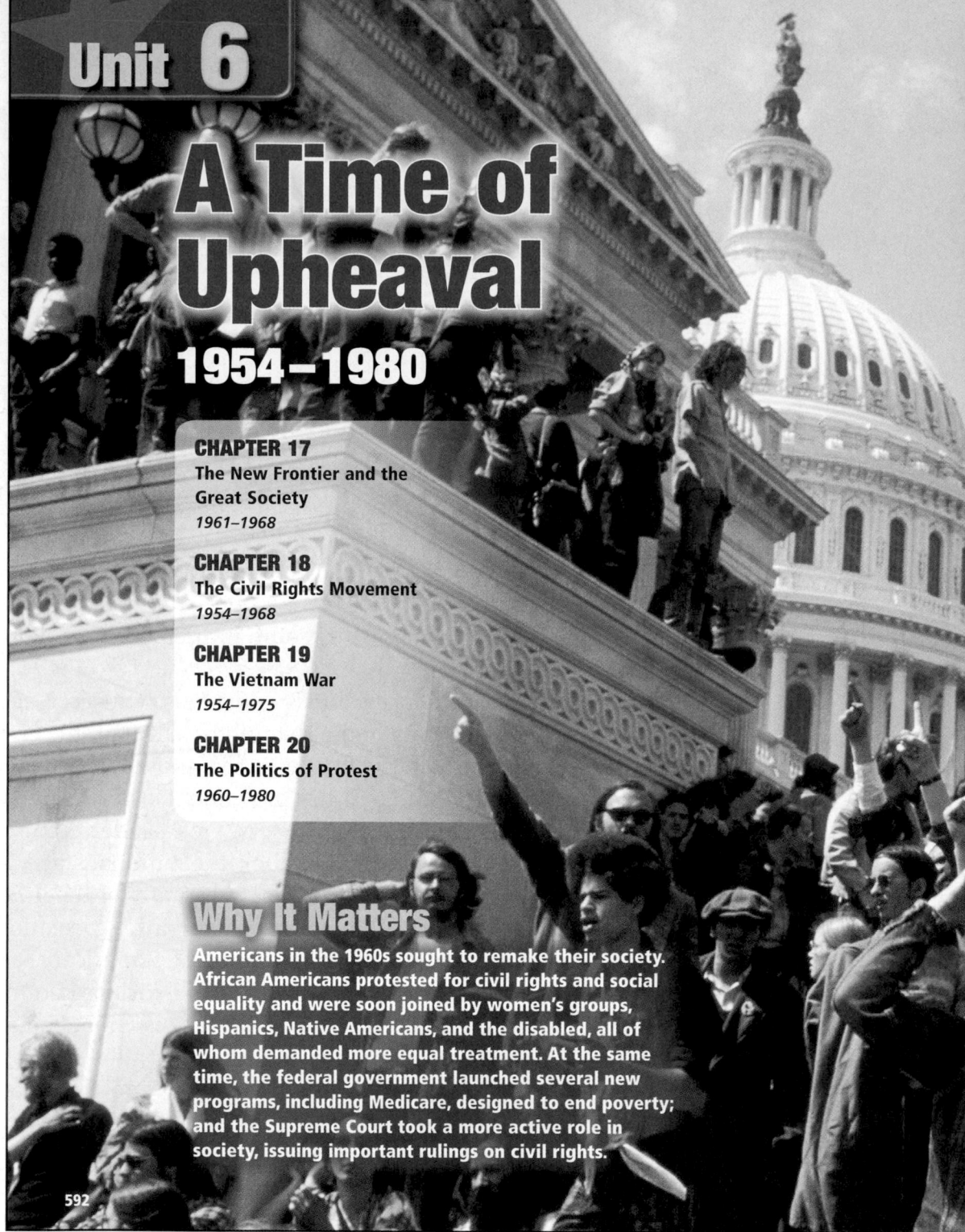

Unit 6

A Time of Upheaval
1954–1980

CHAPTER 17
The New Frontier and the Great Society
1961–1968

CHAPTER 18
The Civil Rights Movement
1954–1968

CHAPTER 19
The Vietnam War
1954–1975

CHAPTER 20
The Politics of Protest
1960–1980

Why It Matters

Americans in the 1960s sought to remake their society. African Americans protested for civil rights and social equality and were soon joined by women's groups, Hispanics, Native Americans, and the disabled, all of whom demanded more equal treatment. At the same time, the federal government launched several new programs, including Medicare, designed to end poverty; and the Supreme Court took a more active role in society, issuing important rulings on civil rights.

592

Team Teaching Activity

Political Science Invite a political science teacher to the class to discuss the impact of visual media on presidential and congressional elections since the 1960 election. Ask him or her to show clips of effective and ineffective use of advertisements, debates, or interviews. Use the clips as background for a discussion on how candidates create positive images for constituents. **OL**

Demonstrators block the entrance to the House of Representatives as part of the "May Day" protest against the Vietnam War, 1971

593

Skill Practice

Using Geography Skills
Ask students to use the world maps in their textbooks to locate Vietnam and its relation to France and to the United States. Have students suggest why its location was significant for the domino theory of the spread of communism. *(Vietnam is near Communist China. The spread of communism could logically extend to the Philippines, in which the United States had a military and economic interest.)* **BL**

Skill Practice

Reading a Time Line Draw students' attention to the time lines of each chapter. Ask them to preview those time lines to prepare for new information they will learn in this unit **OL**

NO CHILD LEFT BEHIND

Teaching Tip The NCLB Act places an emphasis on computer literacy. Assist students doing online research in selecting only reputable sources. For example, Web sites ending in *.gov, .org,* or *.edu* are generally trustworthy. Encourage students to look for historical museum sites and presidential libraries as they do their research for this chapter.

More About the Photo

Visual Literacy Ask students to describe the people who are protesting. *(Most are young and informally dressed; the men wear their hair longer than what was then considered normal.)* Tell them that the early protests were conducted primarily by college students and often on college campuses. At Columbia University in 1968, about 500 students took control of five buildings on campus, including the president's office. Protests increased in other parts of the world as well, notably in Paris, London, and Prague. Protests became more widespread, including many different groups of people, not just college students who did not want to be drafted to fight a war they could not support. One of the most significant ones occurred at the Democratic National Convention in Chicago in 1968, when an estimated 10,000 demonstrators clashed outside the convention center with perhaps 20,000 police and National Guard troops.

Key to Ability Levels	
BL Below Level	**AL** Above Level
OL On Level	**ELL** English Language Learners

Key to Teaching Resources	
📁 Print Material	📀 DVD
💿 CD-ROM	🖨 Transparency

Levels					Resources	Chapter Opener	Section 1	Section 2	Section 3	Chapter Assess
BL	OL	AL	ELL							
					FOCUS					
BL	OL	AL	ELL	🖨	Daily Focus Transparencies		17-1	17-2	17-3	
					TEACH					
	OL	AL		📁	Geography and History Activity, URB	p. 3				
BL	OL	AL		📁	Economics and History Activity, URB					p. 7
	OL	AL		📁	History Simulations and Problem Solving, URB			p. 9		
BL	OL	AL	ELL	📁	Reading Essentials and Note-Taking Guide*		p. 182	p. 185	p. 188	
BL	OL		ELL	📁	Reading Skills Activity, URB				p. 21	
	OL			📁	Historical Analysis Skills Activity, URB			p. 22		
BL	OL		ELL	📁	Guided Reading Activity, URB*		p. 48	p. 49	p. 50	
BL	OL	AL	ELL	📁	Differentiated Instruction Activity, URB			p. 23		
BL	OL		ELL	📁	English Learner Activity, URB			p. 25		
BL	OL	AL	ELL	📁	Content Vocabulary Activity, URB*	p. 27				
BL	OL	AL	ELL	📁	Academic Vocabulary Activity, URB	p. 29				
	OL	AL		📁	Reinforcing Skills Activity, URB		p. 31			
	OL	AL		📁	Critical Thinking Skills Activity, URB			p. 32		
BL	OL		ELL	📁	Time Line Activity, URB					p. 33
	OL			📁	Linking Past and Present Activity, URB					p. 34
BL	OL	AL	ELL	📁	Primary Source Reading, URB			p. 35	p. 37	
BL	OL	AL	ELL	📁	American Art and Music Activity, URB					p. 39
BL	OL	AL	ELL	📁	Interpreting Political Cartoons Activity, URB			p. 41		
		AL		📁	Enrichment Activity, URB			p. 45		
BL	OL	AL	ELL	📁	Differentiated Instruction for the American History Classroom	✓	✓	✓	✓	✓
BL	OL	AL	ELL	🖨	Unit Map Overlay Transparencies	✓	✓	✓	✓	✓
BL	OL	AL	ELL	📁	Unit Time Line Transparencies, Strategies, and Activities	✓	✓	✓	✓	✓
BL	OL	AL	ELL	📁	Cause and Effect Transparencies, Strategies, and Activities	✓	✓	✓	✓	✓
BL	OL	AL	ELL	📁	Why It Matters Chapter Transparencies, Strategies, and Activities	✓	✓	✓	✓	✓

Note: Please refer to the *Unit 6 Resource Book* for this chapter's URB materials.

* Also available in Spanish

TeacherWorks *Plus*
All-In-One Planner and Resource Center

- Interactive Lesson Planner
- Interactive Teacher Edition
- Fully editable blackline masters
- Section Spotlight Videos Launch
- Differentiated Lesson Plans
- Printable reports of daily assignments
- Standards Tracking System

Levels					Resources	Chapter Opener	Section 1	Section 2	Section 3	Chapter Assess
BL	OL	AL	ELL							
TEACH *(continued)*										
BL	OL	AL	ELL		The Living Constitution	✓	✓	✓	✓	✓
BL	OL	AL	ELL		American Issues	✓	✓	✓	✓	✓
	OL	AL	ELL		American Art and Architecture Transparencies, Strategies, and Activities	✓	✓	✓	✓	✓
BL	OL	AL			High School American History Literature Library	✓	✓	✓	✓	✓
	OL	AL			American History Primary Source Documents Library	✓	✓	✓	✓	✓
BL	OL	AL	ELL		American Music: Hits Through History CD	✓	✓	✓	✓	✓
BL	OL	AL	ELL		StudentWorks™ Plus DVD	✓	✓	✓	✓	✓
BL	OL	AL	ELL		Vocabulary PuzzleMaker CD-ROM	✓	✓	✓	✓	✓
BL	OL	AL	ELL		*The American Vision* Video Program DVD	✓	✓	✓	✓	✓
Teacher Resources					Reading Strategies and Activities for the Social Studies Classroom	✓	✓	✓	✓	✓
					Strategies for Success	✓	✓	✓	✓	✓
					Presentation Plus! DVD	✓	✓	✓	✓	✓
					Success With English Learners	✓	✓	✓	✓	✓
ASSESS										
BL	OL	AL	ELL		Section Quizzes and Chapter Tests*		p. 243	p. 244	p. 245	p. 247
BL	OL	AL	ELL		Authentic Assessment With Rubrics					p. 39
BL	OL	AL	ELL		Standardized Test Practice Workbook					p. 39
BL	OL	AL	ELL		*ExamView®* Assessment Suite CD-ROM					Ch. 17
BL	OL	AL	ELL		Interactive Tutor Self-Assessment CD-ROM					Ch. 17
CLOSE										
BL			ELL		Reteaching Activity, URB					p. 43
BL	OL		ELL		Reading and Study Skills Foldables™	p. 78				

Using PuzzleMaker™ 3.1

Online Word Search Puzzles

Technology Product

Glencoe's Vocabulary PuzzleMaker 3.1 CD-ROM is an easy-to-use program that lets you create your own puzzles based on the glossary for classroom use. The PuzzleMaker allows you to

- create word search puzzles based on content vocabulary and academic vocabulary that is specific to what is taught in the classroom;
- create online (LAN-based or local area network) or paper word search puzzles.

Objectives

After students complete the word search puzzles, they will be able to

- recall academic vocabulary terms based on the clues provided for a puzzle;
- reinforce their understanding of the vocabulary.

Steps

- Run PuzzleMaker 3.1. On the main menu, click on **Create a New Puzzle**.
- Select the *Puzzle Database* for the vocabulary.
- The *PuzzleMaker Wizard* will take you through selecting a puzzle type and grid type.
- Then select one or more chapters from the list. Indicate whether you want the words selected randomly or manually.
- Select the language and words you wish to use within the maximum for the puzzle. Click **Finish**.
- Save your word search puzzle to a location that is easily accessible by your students with PuzzlePlayer 3.1, or print copies for your students to complete.
- Use PuzzlePlayer 3.1 to review the puzzles after your students have worked on and saved them.

History ONLINE

	Student	Teacher	Parent
Beyond the Textbook	●	●	●
Chapter Overviews	●	●	●
Time Current Events	●		●
ePuzzles and Games	●		●
Concepts in Motion	●		●
Literature Connections		●	
Multi-Language Glossaries	●		●
Online Student Edition	●	●	●
Self-Check Quizzes	●		●
Student Web Activities	●		●
Study Central ™	●		●
Teaching Today		●	
Vocabulary eFlashcards	●		●
Web Activity Lesson Plans		●	

Glencoe Media Center

glencoe.com

❯ **Study-To-Go**
- Vocabulary eFlashcards
- Self-Check Quizzes

❯ **Audio/Video**
- Student Edition Audio
- Spanish Summaries
- Section Videos

- **Timed Readings Plus in Social Studies** helps students increase their reading rate and fluency while maintaining comprehension. The 400-word passages are similar to those found on state and national assessments.

- **Reading in the Content Area: Social Studies** concentrates on six essential reading skills that help students better comprehend what they read. The book includes 75 high-interest nonfiction passages written at increasing levels of difficulty.

- **Reading Social Studies** includes strategic reading instruction and vocabulary support in Social Studies content for both ELLs and native speakers of English.

  www.jamestowneducation.com

Index to National Geographic Magazine:

The following articles relate to this chapter:

- "Selma to Montgomery: The Road to Equality," by Chuck Stone and Meria Joel Carstarphen, February 2000.

- "A Generation After Sputnik: Are the Soviets Ahead in Space?," by Thomas Y. Canby, October 1986.

National Geographic Society Products To order the following, call National Geographic at 1-800-368-2728:

- *ZipZapMap! USA Windows* (ZipZapMap! USA)

Access National Geographic's new, dynamic MapMachine Web site and other geography resources at:

www.nationalgeographic.com
www.nationalgeographic.com/maps

The following videotape programs are available from Glencoe as supplements to Chapter 17:

- John F. Kennedy: A Personal Story (ISBN 0-76-700010-2)

- Lyndon Johnson: Triumph and Tragedy (ISBN 0-76-700109-5)

To order, call Glencoe at 1-800-334-7344. To find classroom resources to accompany many of these videos, check the following home pages:

A&E Television: www.aetv.com
The History Channel: www.historychannel.com

Reading List Generator CD-ROM

GLENCOE BOOKLINK 3

Use this database to search more than 30,000 titles to create a customized reading list for your students.

- Reading lists can be organized by students' reading level, author, genre, theme, or area of interest.

- The database provides Degrees of Reading Power™ (DRP) and Lexile™ readability scores for all selections.

- A brief summary of each selection is included.

Leveled reading suggestions for this chapter:

For students at a Grade 8 reading level:
- *John Fitzgerald Kennedy: America's Youngest President,* by Lucy Post Frisbee

For students at a Grade 9 reading level:
- *John F. Kennedy,* by Lucia Raatma

For students at a Grade 10 reading level:
- *The First Moon Landing,* by Dale Anderson

For students at a Grade 11 reading level:
- *John F. Kennedy,* by Michael Burgan

For students at a Grade 12 reading level:
- *Footprints on the Moon,* by Alexandra Siy

Focus

MAKING CONNECTIONS
Can Government Fix Society?

Ask students to brainstorm ways in which society needs to be "fixed." Have them suggest ways in which these needs have or have not been met by local, state, or national governments. Remind students of the great changes that the New Deal brought about in terms of providing a social safety net for citizens. Have them identify areas that the New Deal did not address. *(Possible answers include: universal health care, women's issues, and minority issues.)* **OL**

Teach

The Big Ideas

As students study the chapter, remind them to consider the section-based Big Ideas included in each section's Guide to Reading. The **Essential Questions** in the activities below tie in to the Big Ideas and help students think about and understand important chapter concepts. In addition, the Hands-on Chapter Projects with their culminating activities relate the content from each section to the Big Ideas. These activities build on each other as students progress through the chapter. Section activities culminate in the wrap-up activity on the Visual Summary page.

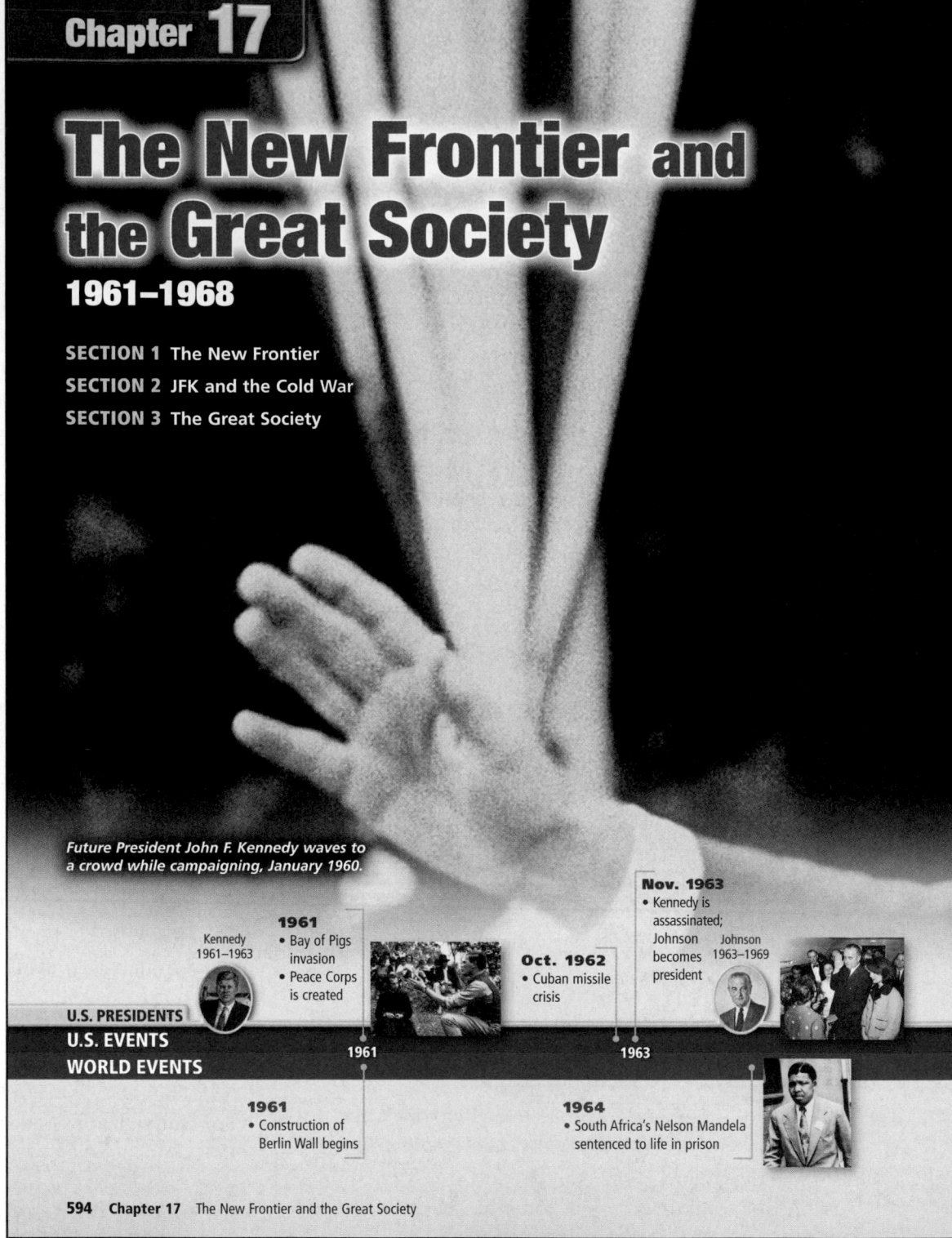

Chapter 17

The New Frontier and the Great Society

1961–1968

SECTION 1 The New Frontier
SECTION 2 JFK and the Cold War
SECTION 3 The Great Society

Future President John F. Kennedy waves to a crowd while campaigning, January 1960.

Kennedy 1961–1963

1961
• Bay of Pigs invasion
• Peace Corps is created

Oct. 1962
• Cuban missile crisis

Nov. 1963
• Kennedy is assassinated; Johnson becomes president

Johnson 1963–1969

U.S. PRESIDENTS
U.S. EVENTS
WORLD EVENTS

1961

1963

1961
• Construction of Berlin Wall begins

1964
• South Africa's Nelson Mandela sentenced to life in prison

594   Chapter 17   The New Frontier and the Great Society

Section 1

The New Frontier
Essential Question: What social issues did the Kennedy administration address? *(affordable housing, minimum wage, women's equality, disability rights)* Tell students that in Section 1 they will learn about Kennedy's domestic agenda and struggles with an unsupportive Congress. **OL**

Section 2

JFK and the Cold War
Essential Question: What efforts to achieve peace did the Kennedy administration follow? *(diplomacy, foreign aid, Peace Corps, expansion of military, space exploration)* Inform students that in this section they will learn about Kennedy's creative efforts to prevent the further spread of communism and war. **OL**

MAKING CONNECTIONS
Can Government Fix Society?

President John F. Kennedy and President Lyndon B. Johnson supported programs intended to end poverty and racism at home and promote democracy abroad. The War on Poverty and the Great Society programs marked the greatest increase in the federal government's role in society since the New Deal. Kennedy's aid programs for developing nations also marked a dramatic shift in American foreign policy towards promoting economic development abroad.

- *How do you think Presidents Kennedy and Johnson changed American society? What programs from the 1960s still exist today?*

More About the Photo

Visual Literacy Kennedy received the Democratic Party's nomination on the first ballot in July 1960. He was the youngest person ever to be elected, a sharp contrast to then-President Dwight Eisenhower, who was, at 70, the oldest person up to that point to serve as president. Kennedy was a son of privilege. His father, Joseph Kennedy, one of the richest men in the United States, nourished and supported the political ambitions of his sons. In 1953 Kennedy had married Jacqueline Bouvier, an elegant and gracious woman whose presence on the campaign trail was an asset.

FOLDABLES

Categorizing Information Make a Four-Door Book Foldable listing the various programs of Lyndon Johnson's Great Society. Sort the programs into these four categories: War on Poverty, Health and Welfare, Education, and Consumer and Environmental Protection. As you read the chapter, list programs inside your Foldable under the four major categories.

FOLDABLES Study Organizer **Dinah Zike's Foldables**

Dinah Zike's Foldables are three-dimensional, interactive graphic organizers that help students practice basic writing skills, review vocabulary terms, and identify main ideas. Instructions for creating and using Foldables can be found in the Appendix at the end of this book and in the *Dinah Zike's Reading and Study Skills Foldables* booklet.

History ONLINE Chapter Overview
Visit glencoe.com to preview Chapter 17.

Timeline

1965
- Congress establishes Medicare and Medicaid

1966
- Congress passes the Child Nutrition Act

1968
- Lyndon Johnson decides not to run for reelection

1965   1967   1968

1966
- Indira Gandhi becomes prime minister of India

1968
- Student riots paralyze France

Chapter 17 The New Frontier and the Great Society **595**

Section 3

The Great Society
Essential Question: What groups of people did Lyndon Johnson's Great Society assist? *(the poor, minorities, the elderly and uninsured, those unable to get an education)* Tell students that in this section they will read about the massive reform efforts the Johnson administration supported. **OL**

History ONLINE
Introduce students to chapter content and key terms by having them access the Chapter 17 Overview at glencoe.com.

Focus

Bellringer
Daily Focus Transparency 17.1

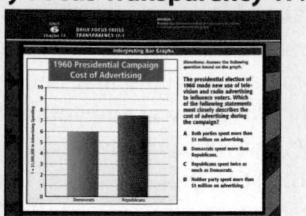

Guide to Reading

Successes	Setbacks
more funds in defense and space exploration	health insurance for senior citizens
some advance in women's rights	a Department of Urban Affairs
economic improvement	federal aid for education
assistance to the disabled	

Section Spotlight Video

To generate student interest and provide a springboard for class discussion, access the Chapter 17, Section 1 video at glencoe.com or on the video DVD.

Resource Manager

Section 1

The New Frontier

Guide to Reading

Big Ideas
Government and Society Under the programs and policies of the Kennedy administration, women, persons with disabilities, and others gained a greater share of civil rights.

Content Vocabulary
• missile gap (p. 596)
• reapportionment (p. 600)
• due process (p. 601)

Academic Vocabulary
• commentator (p. 596)
• arbitrary (p. 601)

People and Events to Identify
• New Frontier (p. 597)
• Earl Warren (p. 600)

Reading Strategy
Categorizing As you read about the presidency of John F. Kennedy, complete a graphic organizer similar to the one below by listing the domestic successes and setbacks of his administration.

Successes	Setbacks

In the presidential election campaign of 1960, John F. Kennedy promised to move the nation into "the New Frontier." After narrowly winning the election, Kennedy succeeded in getting only part of his agenda enacted.

The Election of 1960

MAIN Idea In 1960 a youthful John F. Kennedy narrowly defeated Richard M. Nixon in the presidential election.

HISTORY AND YOU Have you ever watched a televised political debate? Did you pay attention to the candidates' looks and mannerisms? Read on to learn how television changed people's perception of candidates.

On September 26, 1960, at 9:30 P.M. Eastern Standard Time, an estimated 75 million people sat indoors, focused on their television sets, watching the first televised presidential debate. The debate marked a new era of television politics.

During the 1960 presidential race, both parties made substantial use of television. The Democrats spent more than $6 million on television and radio spots, while the Republicans spent more than $7.5 million. Not everyone was happy with this new style of campaigning. Television news **commentator** Eric Sevareid complained that the candidates had become "packaged products" and declared, "the Processed Politician has finally arrived."

The candidates in the first televised debate differed in many ways. The Democratic nominee, John F. Kennedy, was a Catholic from a wealthy and influential Massachusetts family. Richard M. Nixon, the Republican nominee and Eisenhower's vice-president, was a Quaker from California; he had grown up in a family that struggled financially. Kennedy seemed outgoing and relaxed, while Nixon struck many as formal and even stiff in manner.

The campaign centered on the economy and the Cold War. Although the candidates presented different styles, they differed little on these two issues. Both promised to boost the economy, and both portrayed themselves as "Cold Warriors," determined to stop the forces of communism. Kennedy expressed concern about a suspected "**missile gap**," claiming the United States lagged behind the Soviets in weaponry. Nixon warned that the Democrats' fiscal policies would boost inflation, and that only he had the necessary foreign policy experience to guide the nation.

Kennedy's Catholic faith became an issue, as Al Smith's Catholicism had in 1928. The United States had never had a Catholic president, and many Protestants had concerns about Kennedy. Kennedy decided to confront this issue openly in a speech.

R **Reading Strategies**	C **Critical Thinking**	D **Differentiated Instruction**	W **Writing Support**	S **Skill Practice**
Teacher Edition • Act. Prior Know., p. 597 • Inferring, p. 598 • Using Word Parts, p. 601 **Additional Resources** • Guid. Read. Act., URB p. 48 • Foldables, p. 78	**Additional Resources** • Geo. and History Act., URB p. 3 • Quizzes and Tests, p. 243	**Teacher Edition** • Kinesthetic, p. 598 **Additional Resources** • Acad. Vocab. Act., URB p. 29	**Teacher Edition** • Expository Writing, p. 600 **Additional Resources** • Content Vocab. Act., URB p. 27	**Additional Resources** • Reinforcing Skills Act., URB p. 31 • RENTG, p. 182

The Presidential Election of 1960

Presidential Candidate	Popular Votes	% of Popular Vote	Electoral Votes
Kennedy	34,227,096	49.72%	303
Nixon	34,107,646	49.55%	219
Byrd	501,643	0.73%	15

PRIMARY SOURCE

The Election of 1960

▲ *The Kennedy-Nixon debates marked the first televised presidential campaign. Senator Kennedy matched Vice President Nixon's well-known debating skills, grasped facts about the way government worked, and showed he cared about Americans.*

Analyzing VISUALS

1. **Assessing** What region of the nation went most solidly Republican?

2. **Identifying** Which states gave one or more electoral votes to Harry Byrd?

R "I believe in an America where the separation of the church and state is absolute," he said, "where no Catholic prelate would tell the president, should he be a Catholic, how to act."

The four televised debates influenced the election's outcome, one of the closest in American history. Kennedy won the popular vote by 119,000 out of 68 million votes cast, and the Electoral College by 303 votes to 219.

Despite his narrow victory, John F. Kennedy captured the imagination of the American public as few presidents had before him. During the campaign, many had been taken with Kennedy's youth and optimism, and his Inaugural Address reinforced this impression.

In the speech, the new president declared that "the torch has been passed to a new generation" and called on citizens to take a more active role in making the nation better. "My fellow Americans," he exclaimed, "ask not what your country can do for you—ask what you can do for your country."

✓**Reading Check** **Identifying** What were the two main issues of the 1960 presidential election?

Kennedy Takes Office

MAIN Idea Despite an uneasy relationship with Congress, President Kennedy managed to get parts of his domestic agenda passed.

HISTORY AND YOU Do you think there are enough women in top government positions today? Read on to learn how Kennedy's programs were designed to help women.

Upon entering office, President Kennedy set out to implement a legislative agenda that became known as the **New Frontier.** He hoped to increase aid to education, provide health insurance to the elderly, and create a Department of Urban Affairs. He would soon find that transforming lofty ideals into real legislation was no easy task on Capitol Hill.

Although the Democrats had majorities in both houses of Congress, Kennedy was unable to push through many of his programs. Kennedy had trailed Nixon in many Democratic districts and had not helped many Democrats get elected. Those who did win, therefore, did not feel they owed him anything.

Chapter 17 The New Frontier and the Great Society **597**

Teach

R **Reading Strategy**

Activating Prior Knowledge Direct students' attention to the quotation by Senator Kennedy.

Ask: Who had been the first Roman Catholic candidate chosen by a major party to run for president and in what election year did he run for that office? *(Alfred Smith, 1928)*

Analyzing VISUALS

Answers:
1. the West
2. Mississippi, Alabama, Oklahoma

✓**Reading Check**

Answer:
The issues were the economy and the Cold War

Hands-On Chapter Project
Step 1

What Is a Great Society?

Step 1: How Court Decisions Affect Society Today In the first of four activities relating to what makes a great society, students will use information in the section to relate 1960s Supreme Court decisions to modern American life.

Directions Have students review the Court decisions made during the 1960s. Then ask them to research newspaper, library, or Internet sources to find a recent event or legal decision that relates to decisions made by the Supreme Court during the 1960s. Have them explain the connection between the recent event and the original Court decision.

Comparing and Contrasting In their presentations, students will discuss ways in which the current event is similar to or different from an event that led to a 1960s Supreme Court decision. **OL**
(Project continued on page 603)

Inferring Although born into wealth and privilege, Jacqueline Kennedy worked as a photographer and journalist before marrying John Kennedy. As a photographer (the "Inquiring Camera Girl") with the *Washington Times-Herald,* she earned a regular salary. Invite students to consider if her experiences and influence might have shaped Kennedy's push for women's rights. **BL**

D **Differentiated Instruction**

Kinesthetic Ask students to investigate local involvement in the Special Olympics program. Suggest that students help with a local event as part of their community service. **OL**

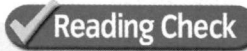 **Reading Check**

Answers:
The legislation was perceived as too expensive and too broad in scope.

Additional Support

Southern Democrats—who were a large part of the Democratic majority in Congress—viewed the New Frontier as too expensive and, together with Republicans, were able to defeat many of Kennedy's proposals. Senator Everett Dirksen, Republican minority leader from Illinois, claimed that Kennedy's efforts to increase the power of the federal government would push the nation down an ominous path.

Successes and Setbacks

Kennedy did achieve some victories, particularly in his efforts to improve the economy. Although the economy had soared through much of the 1950s, it had slowed by the end of the decade. In an effort to increase economic growth and create more jobs, Kennedy advocated deficit spending. The new president convinced Congress to invest more funds in defense and space exploration. Such spending did indeed create more jobs and stimulate economic growth.

In addition, Kennedy asked businesses to hold down prices and labor leaders to hold down pay increases. The labor unions in the steel industry agreed to reduce their demands for higher wages, but several steel companies raised prices sharply. In response, Kennedy threatened to have the Department of Defense buy cheaper foreign steel, and instructed the Justice Department to investigate whether the steel industry was fixing prices. The steel companies backed down and cut their prices, but the victory had strained the president's relations with the business community.

Kennedy also pushed for a cut in tax rates. When opponents argued that a tax cut would help only the wealthy, Kennedy asserted that lower taxes meant businesses would have more money to expand, which would create new jobs and benefit everybody. "A rising tide lifts all boats," Kennedy explained to illustrate how tax cuts would help all Americans.

Congress refused to pass the tax cut because of fears that it would cause inflation. Congress also blocked his plans for health insurance for senior citizens and federal aid to education. However, they did agree to Kennedy's request to raise the minimum wage and his proposal for an Area Redevelopment Act and a Housing Act. These acts helped to create jobs and build low-income housing in poor areas.

Expanding Women's Rights

The issue of women's rights also received attention during the Kennedy administration. In 1961 Kennedy created the Presidential Commission on the Status of Women. The commission called for federal action against gender discrimination and affirmed the right of women to equally paid employment. The commission proposed the Equal Pay Act, which **R** Kennedy signed in 1963. The commission also inspired the creation of similar groups on the state level to study the status of women.

Although he never appointed a woman to his cabinet, a number of women worked in prominent positions in the Kennedy administration, including Esther Peterson, assistant secretary of labor and director of the Women's Bureau of the Department of Labor.

A New View of the Disabled

In 1961 Kennedy convened the President's Panel on Mental Retardation. The panel's first report, containing 112 recommendations, called for funding of research into developmental disabilities and educational and vocational programs for people with developmental disabilities; a greater reliance on residential—as opposed to institutional—treatment centers; and grants to provide prenatal services to women in low-income groups to promote healthy pregnancies.

Responding to the report, Congress enacted the Mental Retardation Facilities and Community Mental Health Centers Construction Act of 1963. This legislation provided grants for construction of research centers; funds to train educational personnel to work with people with developmental disabilities; and grants to states for construction of mental health centers.

In 1962 Eunice Kennedy Shriver, the president's sister, began a day camp at her home for children with developmental disabilities. Camp **D** Shriver, as it was first known, offered people with disabilities a chance to be physically competitive. That effort later grew into the Special Olympics program. The first Special Olympics Games were held in Chicago in 1968.

✔ **Reading Check** **Evaluating** Why did Kennedy have difficulty getting his agenda enacted?

Activity: Economics Connection

Tax Cuts Does a rising tide really lift all boats, as Kennedy suggested? Invite a teacher from the business or economics department to class to discuss the idea of lower taxes helping to create new jobs and thus benefiting everyone. Encourage interested students to track the federal stance on tax cuts for the past two decades and chart the results. Ask them to consider the effect of tax cuts on real wages and gross domestic product. **AL**

ANALYZING SUPREME COURT CASES

Does Each Vote Really Count?

★ *Baker* v. *Carr*, 1962
★ *Reynolds* v. *Sims*, 1964

Background of the Cases

Although many more Americans were living in urban areas, most states had not redrawn their political districts to reflect this shift. This gave rural voters more political influence than urban voters. In *Baker* v. *Carr*, the Supreme Court ruled on whether federal courts had jurisdiction in lawsuits seeking to force states to redraw their electoral districts. In *Reynolds* v. *Sims*, the court decided whether uneven electoral districts violated the equal protection clause of the 14th Amendment.

How the Court Ruled

In *Baker* v. *Carr*, the Supreme Court ruled that federal courts can hear lawsuits seeking to force state authorities to redraw electoral districts. In *Reynolds* v. *Sims*, the Court ruled that the inequality of representation in the Alabama legislature did violate the equal protection clause. These rulings forced states to reapportion their political districts according to the principle of "one person, one vote."

PRIMARY SOURCE

The Court's Opinion

"Legislators represent people, not trees or acres. Legislators are elected by voters, not farms or cities or economic interests. As long as ours is a representative form of government . . . the right to elect legislators in a free and unimpaired fashion is a bedrock of our political system. . . .

And, if a State should provide that the votes of citizens in one part of the State should be given two times, or five times, or 10 times the weight of votes of citizens in another part of the State, it could hardly be contended that the right to vote of those residing in the disfavored areas had not been effectively diluted.

—Justice William Brennan, Jr., writing for the court in
Reynolds v. *Sims*

▲ The 1962 Supreme Court. Seated left to right, Associate Justices Tom Clark and Hugo Black, Chief Justice Earl Warren, Associate Justices William O. Douglas and John Harlan; standing, left to right, Associate Justices Byron White, William Brennan, Potter Stewart, and Arthur Goldberg. Justices Byron White and Arthur Goldberg were appointed by Kennedy.

PRIMARY SOURCE

Dissenting Views

"As of 1961, the Constitutions of all but 11 States . . . recognized bases of apportionment other than geographic spread of population. . . . The consequence of today's decision is that . . . state courts, are given blanket authority and the constitutional duty to supervise apportionment. . . . It is difficult to imagine a more intolerable and inappropriate interference by the judiciary with the independent legislatures of the States. . . . [The Court] says only that 'legislators represent people, not trees or acres,'. . . . But it is surely equally obvious . . . that legislators can represent their electors only by speaking for their interests—economic, social, political—many of which do reflect the place where the electors live. . . . These decisions also cut deeply into the fabric of our federalism."

—Justice John Marshall Harlan dissenting in *Reynolds* v. *Sims*

DBQ | Document-Based Questions

1. **Summarizing** What is the main idea of the majority decision in *Reynolds* v. *Sims*?
2. **Explaining** Why does Justice Harlan disagree with the majority in *Reynolds* v. *Sims*?
3. **Making Inferences** How do you think reapportionment according to "one person, one vote" changed state politics?

More About the Case The notion of "one person, one vote" had already been articulated in the 1963 case *Gray* v. *Sanders* and extended to the legislative and congressional districts in *Wesberry* v. *Sanders* the following year. Over the next decade, the nation's political map was redrawn in response to the many lawsuits subsequently filed on behalf of urban residents.

DBQ | Document Based Questions

Answers:
1. uneven electoral districts violated the equal protection clause.
2. He believes it is a state, not a federal, issue.
3. Students may suggest that urban dwellers gained more influence.

Chapter 17   The New Frontier and the Great Society   **599**

Differentiated Instruction

Leveled Activities

| **BL** Reinforcing Skills Activity, URB p. 31 | **OL** Reading Skills Activity, URB p. 21 | **AL** Linking Past and Present Activity, URB p. 34 | **ELL** English Learner Activity, URB p. 25 |

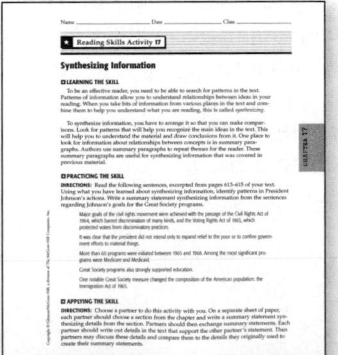

600

W Writing Support

Expository Writing Ask students to investigate the 2002 Texas redistricting case that went to the Supreme Court and the aftermath of the decision. Have them summarize their findings in a short essay agreeing or disagreeing with the Court's ruling. **AL**

Analyzing VISUALS

Answers:

1. *Brown* v. *Board of Education* made segregation of public schools unconstitutional, requiring they be desegregated. *Reynolds* v. *Sims* led to a major restructuring of legislative voting districts.

2. civil rights, due process, and freedom of speech and religion

Additional Support

Warren Court Reforms

MAIN Idea Under Chief Justice Earl Warren, the Supreme Court issued a number of decisions that altered the voting system, expanded due process, and reinterpreted aspects of the First Amendment.

HISTORY AND YOU Do you ever watch cop shows in which police officers read suspects their "Miranda rights"? Read on to learn about the origin of this process.

🏛 For further information on the Supreme Court cases referenced on this page, see pages R58–R61 in **Supreme Court Case Summaries.**

In 1953 President Eisenhower nominated **Earl Warren,** governor of California, to be Chief Justice of the United States. Under Warren's leadership, the Supreme Court issued several rulings that dramatically reshaped American politics and society.

"One Man, One Vote"

W Some of the Warren Court's more notable decisions concerned **reapportionment,** or the way in which states draw up political districts based on changes in population. By 1960, many more Americans resided in cities and suburbs than in rural areas. Yet many states had failed to change their electoral districts to reflect that population shift.

In Tennessee, for example, a rural county with only 2,340 voters had one representative in the state assembly, while an urban county with 133 times more voters had only seven. Thus, rural voters had far more political influence than urban voters. Some Tennessee voters took the matter to court and their case wound up in the Supreme Court. In *Baker* v. *Carr* (1962), the Court ruled that the federal courts had jurisdiction to hear lawsuits seeking to force states to redraw electoral districts.

The Supreme Court subsequently ruled, in *Reynolds* v. *Sims* (1964), that the current apportionment system in most states was unconstitutional. The Warren Court required states to reapportion electoral districts along the principle of "one man, one vote," so that all citizens' votes would have equal weight. The decision was a momentous one, for it shifted political

What Were the Major Decisions of the Warren Court?

Civil Rights	
Brown v. Board of Education (1954)	Declared segregation in public schools unconstitutional
Baker v. Carr (1962)	Established that federal courts can hear lawsuits seeking to force state authorities to redraw electoral districts
Reynolds v. Sims (1964)	Mandated that state legislative districts be approximately equal in population
Heart of Atlanta Motel v. United States (1964)	Upheld the Civil Rights Act of 1964 provision requiring desegregation of public accommodations
Loving v. Virginia (1967)	Forbade state bans on interracial marriage
Due Process	
Mapp v. Ohio (1961)	Ruled that unlawfully seized evidence cannot be used in a trial
Gideon v. Wainwright (1963)	Established suspects' right to a court-appointed attorney if suspects were unable to afford one
Escobedo v. Illinois (1964)	Affirmed right of the accused to an attorney during police questioning
Miranda v. Arizona (1966)	Required police to inform suspects of their rights during the arrest process
Freedom of Speech and Religion	
Engel v. Vitale (1962)	Banned state-mandated prayer in public schools
Abington School District v. Schempp (1963)	Banned state-mandated Bible reading in public schools
New York Times v. Sullivan (1964)	Restricted circumstances in which celebrities could sue the media

Analyzing VISUALS

1. **Interpreting** How did *Brown* v. *Board of Education* and *Reynolds* v. *Sims* affect the nation?

2. **Summarizing** What three major policy areas did the Warren Court's decisions affect?

600 Chapter 17 The New Frontier and the Great Society

Activity: Interdisciplinary Connection

Civics Tell students that Eleanor Roosevelt remained politically active following her husband's death. During the 1960 campaign, she appeared in a television commercial supporting John Kennedy for president. Her appearance signaled to women and traditional Democrats that Kennedy should be elected. Invite a civics teacher to class to discuss with students the pitfalls of such "celebrity" endorsements and their effect on recent elections. **OL**

power from rural and often conservative areas to urban areas, where more liberal voters resided. The Court's decision also boosted the political power of African Americans and Hispanics, who often lived in cities.

Extending Due Process

In a series of rulings, the Supreme Court began to use the Fourteenth Amendment to apply the Bill of Rights to the states. Originally, the Bill of Rights applied only to the federal government. Many states had their own bills of rights, but some federal rights did not exist at the state level. The Fourteenth Amendment states that "no state shall . . . deprive any person of life, liberty, or property without due process of law." **Due process** means that the law may not treat individuals unfairly, **arbitrarily,** or unreasonably, and that courts must follow proper procedures when trying cases. Due process is meant to ensure that all people are treated the same by the legal system. The Court ruled in several cases that due process meant applying the federal bill of rights to the states.

In 1961 the Supreme Court ruled in *Mapp* v. *Ohio* that state courts could not consider evidence obtained in violation of the federal Constitution. In *Gideon* v. *Wainwright* (1963), the Court ruled that a defendant in a state court had the right to a lawyer, regardless of his or her ability to pay. The following year, in *Escobedo* v. *Illinois*, the justices ruled that suspects must be allowed access to a lawyer and must be informed of their right to remain silent before being questioned by the police. *Miranda* v. *Arizona* (1966) went even further, requiring that authorities immediately inform suspects that they have the right to remain silent; that anything they say can and will be used against them in court; that they have a right to a lawyer; and that, if they cannot afford a lawyer, the court will appoint one for them. Today these warnings are known as the Miranda rights.

Prayer and Privacy

The Supreme Court also handed down decisions that reaffirmed the separation of church and state. The Court applied the First Amendment to the states in *Engel* v. *Vitale* (1962). In this ruling, the Court decided that states could not compose official prayers and require those prayers to be recited in public schools. The following year, in *Abington School District* v. *Schempp*, it ruled against state-mandated Bible readings in public schools. Weighing in on another issue, the Court ruled in *Griswold* v. *Connecticut* (1965) that prohibiting the sale and use of birth-control devices violated citizens' constitutional right to privacy.

As with most rulings of the Warren Court, these decisions delighted some and deeply disturbed others. What most people did agree upon, however, was the Court's pivotal role in shaping national policy. The Warren Court, wrote *New York Times* columnist Anthony Lewis, "has brought about more social change than most Congresses and most Presidents."

✓ Reading Check **Examining** What was the significance of the "One Man, One Vote" ruling?

Section 1 REVIEW

Vocabulary
1. **Explain** the significance of: missile gap, New Frontier, Earl Warren, reapportionment, due process.

Main Ideas
2. **Interpreting** In what ways was the 1960 presidential election a turning point in political campaign history?

3. **Summarizing** What progress was made for women's rights during Kennedy's administration?

4. **Describing** Name three decisions of the Warren Court and explain how each protected civil rights.

Critical Thinking
5. **Big Ideas** What were some successes and failures of Kennedy's New Frontier? How did the new programs change the lives of Americans?

6. **Organizing** Use a graphic organizer similar to the one below to list the economic policies of the Kennedy administration.

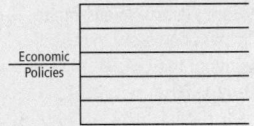

7. **Analyzing Visuals** Look at the election map on page 597. Which states split their electoral votes?

Writing About History
8. **Expository Writing** In his Inaugural Address, President Kennedy asked his fellow Americans to "ask what you can do for your country." Respond to this statement in an essay.

History ONLINE
Study Central™ To review this section, go to glencoe.com and click on Study Central.

R **Reading Strategy**
Using Word Parts Point out to students the academic vocabulary term *arbitrarily*. Ask them to identify the root word (*arbitrary*) and to note the change in spelling when a suffix is added. **EL**

✓ Reading Check

Answer:
All citizens' votes would have equal weight regardless of where they lived.

Assess
• • • • • • • • • • • • • • •
History ONLINE

Study Central™ provides summaries, interactive games, and online graphic organizers to help students review content.

Close
• • • • • • • • • • • • • • •
Summarizing Ask: How was Kennedy's term truly a New Frontier? (*Students may suggest space exploration, court-mandated reforms, and new opportunities for women and people with developmental disabilities.*)

Section 1 REVIEW

Answers

1. All definitions can be found in the section and the Glossary.
2. Television played a more influential role.
3. Presidential Commission on the Status of Women, ending gender discrimination in federal civil service, and the Equal Pay Act
4. Answers should include any of the civil rights decisions listed on page 600 and include explanations of how each influenced civil rights.

5. successes: federal action against gender discrimination, assistance to people with disabilities, development in lower income areas, and raising the minimum wage; failures: no increase in federal aid for education or to senior citizens; changes: more money for cost of living, educational and work opportunities for people with disabilities, and better housing for lower-income families

6. answers may include: a cut in tax rates, an increase in funds for defense and space exploration, an increase in the minimum wage, housing and redevelopment
7. Oklahoma and Alabama
8. Students' essays will vary but should focus on the meaning of Kennedy's statement.

Focus

Bellringer
Daily Focus Transparency 17.2

Guide to Reading

Answers may include:
January 1959: Castro's overthrow of Batista; April 17, 1961: Bay of Pigs; June 1961: Kennedy and Khrushchev meet in Vienna; October 1962: Cuban missile crisis; October 1962: Soviets agree to remove missiles from Cuba; November 1963: Kennedy assassinated

Section Spotlight Video

To generate student interest and provide a springboard for class discussion, access the Chapter 17, Section 2 video at glencoe.com or on the video DVD

Resource Manager

Section 2

JFK and the Cold War

Guide to Reading

Big Ideas
Economics and Society The Kennedy administration used foreign aid to improve relations with Latin American countries and lessen the appeal of left-wing movements.

Content Vocabulary
• flexible response *(p. 602)*
• space race *(p. 604)*

Academic Vocabulary
• conventional *(p. 602)*
• institute *(p. 605)*
• remove *(p. 607)*

People and Events to Identify
• Peace Corps *(p. 604)*
• Berlin Wall *(p. 606)*
• Warren Commission *(p. 607)*

Reading Strategy
Sequencing As you read about the crises of the Cold War, complete a time line similar to the one below to record the major events of the Cold War in the 1950s and early 1960s.

Jan. 1959 — Aug. 1963

During the Kennedy Administration, ongoing tensions with the Soviet Union led to crises over Cuba and West Berlin. To contain communism and stay ahead of the Soviet Union in technology, President Kennedy created aid programs for developing nations and expanded the space program.

Containing Communism

MAIN Idea President Kennedy developed new programs to combat the spread of communism.

HISTORY AND YOU Would you consider joining the Peace Corps and serving in a foreign country? Read on to learn about Kennedy's diplomatic efforts in Latin America.

When John F. Kennedy entered the White House, he had to devote much of his time to foreign policy. The Cold War with the Soviet Union dominated all other concerns at the time, and Kennedy attempted to stop the spread of communism with a range of programs. These included a **conventional** weaponry program to give the nation's military more flexibility, a program to provide economic aid to Latin America, and the creation of the Peace Corps to help developing nations worldwide.

A More Flexible Response

Kennedy took office at a time of growing global instability. Nationalism was exploding throughout the developing world, and the Soviet Union actively supported "wars of national liberation."

Kennedy felt that Eisenhower had relied too heavily on nuclear weapons, which could be used only in extreme situations. To allow for a "**flexible response**" if nations needed help resisting Communist movements, the president pushed for a buildup of troops and conventional weapons. Kennedy also expanded the Special Forces, an elite army unit created in the 1950s to wage guerrilla warfare in limited conflicts, and allowed the soldiers to wear their distinctive "Green Beret" headgear.

Aid to Other Countries

Kennedy wanted to renew diplomatic focus on Latin America. Conditions in many Latin American societies were not good: Governments were often in the hands of the wealthy few and many

---

R Reading Strategies	**C** Critical Thinking	**D** Differentiated Instruction	**W** Writing Support	**S** Skill Practice
Teacher Edition • Act. Prior Know., p. 606 **Additional Resources** • Prim. Source Read., URB p. 35 • Guid. Read. Act., URB p. 49	**Teacher Edition** • Making Inferences, p. 605 **Additional Resources** • Hist. Simulations, URB p. 9 • Interp. Pol. Car. Act., URB p. 41 • Quizzes and Tests, p. 244	**Teacher Edition** • Advanced Learners, p. 604 **Additional Resources** • English Learner Act., URB p. 25 • Enrichment Act., URB p. 45	**Teacher Edition** • Narrative Writing, p. 605	**Teacher Edition** • Visual Literacy, p. 603 • Using Geo. Skills, p. 606 **Additional Resources** • Hist. Analysis Skill, URB p. 22 • RENTG, p. 185

PRIMARY SOURCE
John F. Kennedy's Inaugural Address

▲ John F. Kennedy delivers his inaugural speech, January 20, 1961. He spoke of the obligation of his generation to defend liberty. To his right is incoming Vice President Lyndon Johnson.

PRIMARY SOURCE

"Let the word go forth from this time and place, to friend and foe alike, that the torch has been passed to a new generation of Americans—born in this century, tempered by war, disciplined by a hard and bitter peace, proud of our ancient heritage—and unwilling to witness or permit the slow undoing of those human rights to which this Nation has always been committed. . . . Let every nation know, whether it wishes us well or ill, that we shall pay any price, bear any burden, meet any hardship, support any friend, oppose any foe, in order to assure the survival and the success of liberty. . . .

To those old allies whose cultural and spiritual origins we share, we pledge the loyalty of faithful friends. . . . To those peoples in the huts and villages across the globe struggling to break the bonds of mass misery, we pledge our best efforts to help them help themselves . . . To our sister republics south of our border, we offer a special pledge—to convert our good words into good deeds—in a new alliance for progress—to assist free men and free governments in casting off the chains of poverty. . . .

Now the trumpet summons us again—not as a call to bear arms, though arms we need; not as a call to battle, though embattled we are—but as a call to bear the burden of a long twilight struggle, year in and year out, "rejoicing in hope, patient in tribulation"—a struggle against the common enemies of man: tyranny, poverty, disease, and war itself. . . .

And so, my fellow Americans: ask not what your country can do for you—ask what you can do for your country. My fellow citizens of the world: ask not what America will do for you, but what together we can do for the freedom of man."

—Inaugural Address delivered January 20, 1961

DBQ Document-Based Questions

1. **Expressing** What commitment does Kennedy make with respect to human rights?
2. **Classifying** To what three specific groups does Kennedy promise aid, and what aid is promised?
3. **Finding the Main Idea** What does Kennedy indicate are the common enemies of humankind?

of their citizens lived in extreme poverty. In some countries, these conditions spurred the growth of left-wing movements aimed at overthrowing their governments.

When the United States became involved in Latin America, it usually did so to help existing governments stay in power and to prevent Communist movements from flourishing. Poor Latin Americans resented this intrusion, just as they resented American corporations, whose presence was seen as a kind of imperialism.

The Alliance for Progress To improve relations between the United States and Latin America, Kennedy proposed an Alliance for Progress, a series of cooperative aid projects with Latin American governments. The alliance was designed to create a "free and prosperous Latin America" that would be more stable and less likely to support Communist-inspired revolutions.

Over a 10-year period, the United States pledged $20 billion to help Latin American countries establish better schools, housing, health care, and fairer land distribution. The results were mixed. In some countries—notably Chile, Colombia, Venezuela, and the Central American republics—the alliance did promote real reform. In others, local rulers used the money to keep themselves in power.

Chapter 17 The New Frontier and the Great Society **603**

Teach

S Skill Practice
Visual Literacy
Ask students to look carefully at the photograph of Kennedy giving his Inaugural Address
Ask: How do Kennedy and Johnson differ from the other men in the photograph? *(They are not wearing hats.)* Tell students that this difference in style led to a decline in men wearing hats.

DBQ Document Based Questions

Answers:
1. He is not willing to see or allow the slow undoing of human rights.
2. to old allies: the loyalty of faithful friends; to peoples struggling to break free of misery: our best efforts to help them help themselves; to republics south of our border; to help cast off the chains of poverty
3. tyranny, poverty, disease, and war

Hands-On Chapter Project
Step 2

What Is a Great Society?

Step 2: Motivational Speeches
Students will research memorable speeches made by leaders, writers, and citizens that relate to the building of a great society.

Directions Have students conduct newspaper, library, or Internet research to find speeches made by people throughout history. Speeches may be historical or current. Students may research speeches made by Americans or other citizens of the world.

Encourage students to find a speech that is aimed at the building of an improved or just society. Students should find speeches that are inspirational to them.

Analyzing Primary Sources Students will select the parts of the speech that are most relevant and inspirational to share with the rest of the class, either as oral presentations or in typed papers. **OL**
(Project continued on page 611)

Did You Know?

By the mid-1960s, NASA (National Aeronautics and Space Administration) had about 400,000 people in space programs, with 35,000 focused on the Apollo mission of getting a man to the Moon. Between 1969 and 1972, twelve astronauts walked on the Moon, collected rock samples, set up experiments, and took photographs.

✓ Reading Check

Answer:
the spread of communism, Latin American relations, reducing the threat of nuclear war, and winning the space race

Additional Support

The Peace Corps Another program aimed at helping less-developed nations fight poverty was the **Peace Corps,** an organization that sent Americans to provide humanitarian services in less-developed nations.

D After rigorous training, volunteers spent two years in countries that requested assistance. They laid out sewage systems in Bolivia and trained medical technicians in Chad. Others taught English or helped to build roads. Today, the Peace Corps is still active and remains one of Kennedy's most enduring legacies.

The Cold War in Space

In 1961 Yuri Gagarin (YHOO•ree gah•GAHR•ihn), a Soviet astronaut, became the first person to orbit Earth. Again, as in 1957 when they launched *Sputnik,* the first satellite, the Soviets had beaten the United States in the **space race.** President Kennedy worried about the impact of the flight on the Cold War. Soviet successes in space might convince the world that communism was better than capitalism.

Less than six weeks after the Soviet flight, the president went before Congress and declared: "I believe this nation should commit itself to achieving the goal, before this decade is out, of landing a man on the moon."

Kennedy's speech set in motion a massive effort to develop the necessary technology. In 1962 John Glenn became the first American to orbit Earth. Three years later, the United States sent three men into orbit in a capsule called *Apollo. Apollo* was launched using the Saturn V, the most powerful rocket ever built. The Saturn V was able to give both *Apollo* and the lunar module—which astronauts would use to land on the moon—enough velocity to reach the moon.

On July 16, 1969, a Saturn V lifted off in Florida, carrying three American astronauts: Neil Armstrong, Edwin "Buzz" Aldrin, and Michael Collins. On July 20 Armstrong and Aldrin boarded the lunar module, named *Eagle,* and headed down to the moon. Minutes later, Armstrong radioed NASA's flight center in Texas: "Houston … the *Eagle* has landed."

Armstrong became the first human being to walk on the moon. As he set foot on the lunar surface, he announced: "That's one small step for a man, one giant leap for mankind." The United States had won the space race and decisively demonstrated its technological superiority over the Soviet Union.

✓ Reading Check **Examining** What global challenges did Kennedy face during his presidency?

TECHNOLOGY & HISTORY

Space Technology Cold War tensions between the United States and the Soviet Union fueled the space race. Both countries vied for superiority in aeronautical technology and dominance in space exploration.

▲ American astronaut John Glenn is loaded into his space capsule, named *Friendship 7,* on February 20, 1962, shortly before being launched into orbit.

▲ John Glenn in orbit around Earth

◄ NASA recruited seven astronauts for its first manned space program. Each astronaut would ride in a *Mercury* capsule atop an ICBM reconfigured to lift them into space. The first American astronaut to ride into space in the capsule was Alan Shepard. The first American to orbit Earth was John Glenn.

604 **Chapter 17** The New Frontier and the Great Society

Activity: Collaborative Learning

Investigating Peace Corps Projects
Organize the class into three groups, assigning each group one of the following regions: Africa, Asia, or Latin America. Have each group use library or Internet resources to research and prepare a visual report using charts and maps on the current work of the Peace Corps in their assigned region. Suggest that groups provide both an overview of the work and an in-depth look at one project of special interest. Have groups share their completed reports with the class. **OL**

Crises of the Cold War

MAIN Idea President Kennedy faced foreign policy crises in Cuba and Berlin.

HISTORY AND YOU Do you think the embargo against Cuba should be lifted? Read on to learn about the crises President Kennedy faced over Cuba.

President Kennedy's efforts to combat Communist influence in other countries led to some of the most intense crises of the Cold War. At times these crises left Americans and people in many other nations wondering whether the world would survive.

The Bay of Pigs

The first crisis occurred in Cuba, only 90 miles (145 km) from American shores. There, Fidel Castro had overthrown the corrupt Cuban dictator Fulgencio Batista in 1959. Almost immediately, Castro established ties with the Soviet Union, **instituted** drastic land reforms, and seized foreign-owned businesses, many of which were American. Cuba's alliance with the Soviets worried many Americans. The Communists were now too close for comfort, and Soviet premier Nikita Khrushchev was also expressing his intent to strengthen Cuba militarily.

Fearing that the Soviets would use Cuba as a base from which to spread revolution throughout the Western Hemisphere, President Eisenhower had authorized the CIA to secretly train and arm a group of Cuban exiles, known as *La Brigada*, to invade the island. The invasion was intended to set off a popular uprising against Castro.

When Kennedy became president, his advisers approved the plan. In office less than three months and trusting his experts, Kennedy agreed to the operation with some changes. On April 17, 1961, some 1,400 armed Cuban exiles landed at the Bay of Pigs on the south coast of Cuba. The invasion was a disaster. *La Brigada*'s boats ran aground on coral reefs; Kennedy canceled their air support to keep the United States' involvement a secret; and the expected popular uprising never happened. Within two days, Castro's forces killed or captured almost all the members of *La Brigada*.

The Bay of Pigs was a dark moment for the Kennedy administration. The action exposed an American plot to overthrow a neighbor's government, and the outcome made the United States look weak and disorganized.

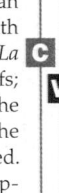

C Critical Thinking

Making Inferences Draw students' attention to the second paragraph of the second column, which alludes to Kennedy's inexperience and his trust of his advisors. Ask students to infer what the text is suggesting in this sentence. *(Students may say that if Kennedy had had more experience or less trust in his experts, the invasion might not have failed.)* **OL**

W Writing Support

Narrative Writing Invite students to imagine an alternative ending to the Bay of Pigs invasion, in which the uprising succeeded as planned. Have them write this alternative ending, considering the effect it would have on U.S.– Latin American relations. **AL**

Analyzing VISUALS

Answers:
1. lots of extra space for fuel
2. gray, barren
3. to carry crew members from the space capsule to the Moon's surface

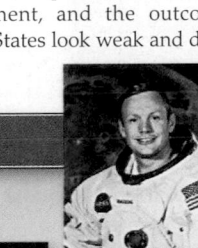

◄ Apollo capsule carried three astronauts.

Lunar Module

▲ Neil Armstrong was the first person to walk on the Moon.

▲ Buzz Aldrin descended to the Moon's surface, July 20, 1969, becoming the second man to walk on the Moon.

▲ To reach the Moon, NASA developed the giant Saturn V rocket, which lifted a three-person capsule, called *Apollo*, and a landing craft, called the Lunar Module, into space. Once *Apollo* and the Lunar Module entered orbit around the Moon, the Lunar Module carried two astronauts from the Apollo capsule down to the Moon's surface.

Analyzing VISUALS

1. **Calculating** What analysis can you make about the size of the space capsules and modules used in space?
2. **Describing** How does the Moon's surface appear in these photos?
3. **Identifying** What was the purpose of the Lunar Module?

Chapter 17 The New Frontier and the Great Society **605**

Additional Support

Activity: Interdisciplinary Connection

Science Organize students into small groups and explain that they will investigate the practical outcomes of the U.S. space program. Ask students to use library or Internet resources to find out how the work of the space program has affected everyday life for all Americans. Suggest that each group select an area such as medicine, robotics, or safety devices on which to focus. Have groups present their findings to the class. **OL**

606

R Reading Strategy

Activating Prior Knowledge

Ask students to recall the division of Germany following World War II as well as the subsequent merging of Allied zones. **OL**

S Skill Practice

Using Geography Skills

Direct students' attention to the map of Cuba and the site of the Bay of Pigs invasion. **Ask:** Why do you think that site was chosen? *(Students may say it was far from Havana and that the CIA hoped the rebels could land unnoticed. Also, there was probably a good harbor there.)* **BL**

Analyzing GEOGRAPHY

Answers:
1. Havana
2. about 250 miles
3. a bay southeast of Havana

Differentiated Instruction

Primary Source Reading, URB p. 35

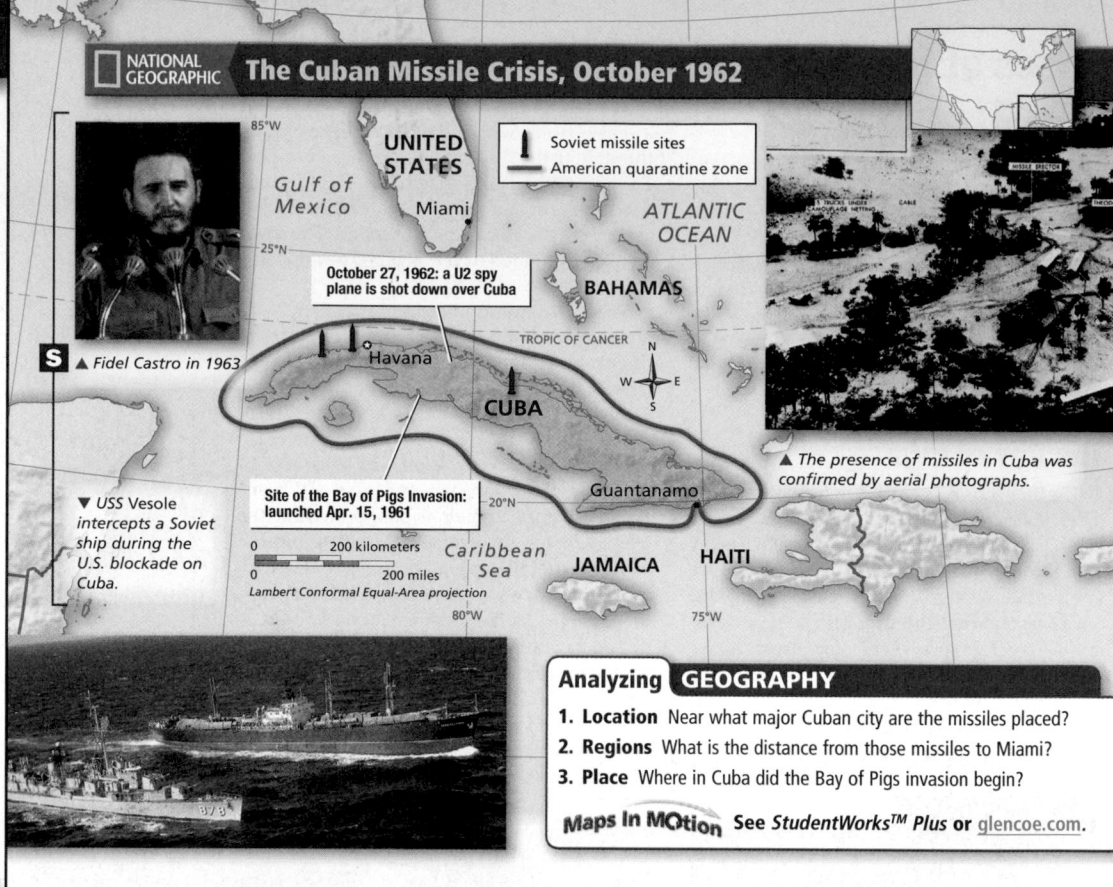

NATIONAL GEOGRAPHIC **The Cuban Missile Crisis, October 1962**

Soviet missile sites
American quarantine zone

October 27, 1962: a U2 spy plane is shot down over Cuba

UNITED STATES
Gulf of Mexico
Miami
ATLANTIC OCEAN
BAHAMAS
TROPIC OF CANCER
Havana
CUBA
Guantanamo
Caribbean Sea
JAMAICA
HAITI

85°W 25°N 20°N 80°W 75°W

▲ Fidel Castro in 1963

▼ USS Vesole intercepts a Soviet ship during the U.S. blockade on Cuba.

Site of the Bay of Pigs Invasion: launched Apr. 15, 1961

0   200 kilometers
0   200 miles
Lambert Conformal Equal-Area projection

▲ The presence of missiles in Cuba was confirmed by aerial photographs.

Analyzing GEOGRAPHY

1. **Location** Near what major Cuban city are the missiles placed?
2. **Regions** What is the distance from those missiles to Miami?
3. **Place** Where in Cuba did the Bay of Pigs invasion begin?

Maps In MOtion See *StudentWorks™ Plus* or glencoe.com.

The Berlin Wall Goes Up

Kennedy faced another foreign policy challenge beginning in June 1961, when he met with Soviet Premier Nikita Khrushchev in Vienna, Austria. Khrushchev wanted to stop the flood of Germans pouring out of Communist East Germany into West Berlin. He demanded that the Western powers recognize East Germany and that the United States, Great Britain, and France withdraw from Berlin, a city lying completely within East Germany. Kennedy refused and reaffirmed the West's commitment to West Berlin.

Khrushchev retaliated by building a wall through Berlin, blocking movement between the Soviet sector and the rest of the city. Guards posted along the wall shot at many of those attempting to escape from the East. For nearly 30 years afterward, the **Berlin Wall** stood as a visible symbol of Cold War divisions.

The Cuban Missile Crisis

By far the most terrifying crisis of the Kennedy era occurred the next year. During the summer of 1962, American intelligence agencies learned that Soviet technicians and equipment had arrived in Cuba and that military construction was in progress. On October 22, President Kennedy announced on television that American spy planes had taken aerial photographs showing that the Soviet Union had placed long-range missiles in Cuba. Enemy missiles stationed so close to the United States posed a dangerous threat.

Kennedy ordered a naval blockade to stop the delivery of more missiles, demanded the existing missile sites be dismantled, and warned that if attacked, the United States would respond fully against the Soviet Union. Still, work on the missile sites continued. Nuclear holocaust seemed imminent.

606 Chapter 17 The New Frontier and the Great Society

Reading Primary Sources: The Cuban Missile Crisis

Objective: Read primary sources to understand key events in history.

Focus: Identify the main issue of the transcript.

Teach: Explain the background of the Cuban Missile Crisis.

Assess: Discuss Kennedy's reaction to the discovery of missiles in Cuba.

Close: Summarize the transcript.

Differentiated Instruction Activities

BL Create a time line sequencing the information Kennedy received.

AL Find out more about the communications between Kennedy and Khrushchev. How are their negotiation strategies similar or different?

ELL Create a list of unfamiliar words, and define the words using a dictionary.

Then, after a flurry of secret negotiations, the Soviet Union offered a deal. It would **remove** the missiles if the United States promised not to invade Cuba and to remove its missiles from Turkey near the Soviet border. The reality was that neither Kennedy nor Khrushchev wanted nuclear war. "Only lunatics . . . who themselves want to perish and before they die destroy the world, could do this," wrote the Soviet leader. On October 28, the leaders reached an agreement. Kennedy publicly agreed not to invade Cuba and privately agreed to remove the Turkish missiles; the Soviets agreed to remove their missiles from Cuba. The world could breathe again.

The Cuban missile crisis forced the United States and the Soviet Union to consider the consequences of nuclear war. In August 1963, the two countries concluded years of negotiation by agreeing to a treaty that banned testing nuclear weapons in the atmosphere.

In the long run, however, the missile crisis had ominous consequences. The humiliating retreat the United States forced on the Soviet leadership undermined the position of Nikita Khrushchev and contributed to his fall from power a year later. The crisis also exposed the Soviets' military inferiority and prompted a dramatic Soviet arms buildup over the next two decades. This buildup contributed to a comparable military increase in the United States in the early 1980s.

Death of a President

Soon after the Senate ratified the test ban treaty, John F. Kennedy's presidency ended shockingly and tragically. On November 22, 1963, Kennedy and his wife traveled to Texas. As the presidential motorcade rode slowly through the crowded streets of Dallas, gunfire rang out. Someone had shot the president twice—once in the throat and once in the head. Horrified government officials sped Kennedy to a nearby hospital, where he was pronounced dead moments later.

Lee Harvey Oswald, the man accused of killing Kennedy, appeared to be a confused and embittered Marxist who had spent time in the Soviet Union. He himself was shot to death while in police custody two days after the assassination. The bizarre situation led some to speculate that the second gunman, local nightclub owner Jack Ruby, killed Oswald to protect others involved in the crime. In 1964 a national commission headed by Chief Justice Warren concluded that Oswald was the lone assassin. The report of the **Warren Commission** left some questions unanswered, and theories about a conspiracy to kill the president have persisted, though none has gained wide acceptance.

In the wake of the assassination, the United States and much of the world went into mourning. Thousands traveled to Washington, D.C., and waited in a line several miles long outside the Capitol to walk silently past the president's flag-draped casket.

Kennedy was president for little more than 1,000 days. Yet he made a profound impression on most Americans. Kennedy's successor, Vice President Lyndon Baines Johnson, set out to promote many of the programs that Kennedy left unfinished.

Reading Check Summarizing How was the Cuban missile crisis resolved?

Section 2 REVIEW

Vocabulary

1. **Explain** the significance of: flexible response, Peace Corps, space race, Berlin Wall, Warren Commission.

Main Ideas

2. **Explaining** What were the goals of the Alliance for Progress?

3. **Discussing** How did Kennedy and Khrushchev reach an agreement to end the Cuban missile crisis? What were the details of this agreement?

Critical Thinking

4. **Big Ideas** What was the role of foreign aid in relations between the United States and Latin America?

5. **Organizing** Use a graphic organizer similar to the one below to list the programs that Kennedy used to reduce the threat of nuclear war and to try to stem communism.

Programs

6. **Analyzing Visuals** Look at the photograph of John Glenn on page 604. What is the name of his craft, and why do you think the name might have been chosen?

Writing About History

7. **Descriptive Writing** Assume the role of an American citizen during the Cuban missile crisis. Write a journal entry describing the mood of the country during that time.

History ONLINE
Study Central™ To review this section, go to glencoe.com and click on Study Central.

607

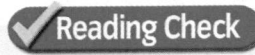

Assess

History ONLINE

Study Central™ provides summaries, interactive games, and online graphic organizers to help students review content.

Close

Summarizing Ask: What difference do you think it might have made if Kennedy had been able to complete a term in office? *(Students may suggest that some of his goals would have been accomplished over time and that he would have found a way to work effectively with Congress and other world leaders.)*

Reading Check

Answer:
Through negotiations, the Soviet Union agreed to remove the missiles, and Kennedy agreed not to invade Cuba and to remove missiles from Turkey.

Section 2 REVIEW

Answers

1. All definitions can be found in the section and the Glossary.

2. The goals were to create cooperative aid projects that helped establish better schools, improve housing, distribute land more equitably, and improve health care in Latin America.

3. They communicated through secret negotiations. The Soviets would remove the missiles from Cuba, while Kennedy promised publicly not to invade Cuba and privately to remove missiles from Turkey.

4. to help governments stay in power and prevent communist revolutions

5. conventional weaponry program, aid to foreign governments, the Peace Corps

6. The craft is called the *Friendship 7*. It may signal a desire to indicate coming in peace.

7. Journal entries will vary but should focus on emotions.

TIME NOTEBOOK

Focus

Introducing TIME Notebook

Inform students that in this speech, given six months after Kennedy's assassination, LBJ set forth his domestic agenda. **Ask:** Why was this speech important to the new president and to the nation? *(Students may suggest that the speech gives hope after the sadness of Kennedy's death and calls on people to do their part toward making a new, richer life.)* Ask students to identify particular phrases they find inspiring. Then **Ask:** What political ideals have recent leaders held out to the nation? How do they compare with Johnson's ideas?

Teach

D Differentiated Instruction

Auditory/Musical Invite interested students to locate recordings of the great hits by the groups listed and to play them for the class. Ask students to compare and contrast the music and lyrics with current hit songs. **BL**

Additional Support

Eyewitness

On May 22, 1964, **PRESIDENT LYNDON JOHNSON** *delivered a speech in Ann Arbor, Michigan, outlining his domestic agenda that would become known as "The Great Society." Speechwriter and policy adviser Richard Goodwin watched the speech on videotape the next morning back in Washington. He recalls his reaction:*

Then, with the cheers, at first muted as if the audience were surprised at their own response, then mounting toward unrestrained, accepting delight, Johnson concluded: "There are those timid souls who say . . . we are condemned to a soulless wealth. I do not agree. We have the power to shape civilization. . . . But we need your will, your labor, your hearts. . . . So let us from this moment begin our work, so that in the future men will look back and say: It was then, after a long and weary way, that man turned the exploits of his genius to the full enrichment of his life."

Watching the film in the White House basement, almost involuntarily I added my applause to the tumultuous acclaim coming from the sound track. . . . I clapped for the President, and for our country.

WHAT IS A PIP, ANYWAY?

Match these rock 'n' roll headliners with their supporting acts.

1. Paul Revere and
2. Martha and
3. Gary Puckett and
4. Gladys Knight and
5. Smokey Robinson and
6. Diana Ross and

a. the Union Gap
b. the Supremes
c. the Miracles
d. the Vandellas
e. the Raiders
f. the Pips

answers: 1. e; 2. d; 3. a; 4. f; 5. c; 6. b

VERBATIM

"Is there any place we can catch them? What can we do? Are we working 24 hours a day? Can we go around the moon before them?"

PRESIDENT JOHN F. KENNEDY,
to Lyndon B. Johnson, after hearing that Soviet cosmonaut Yuri Gagarin had orbited the Earth, 1961

"It was quite a day. I don't know what you can say about a day when you see four beautiful sunsets. . . . This is a little unusual, I think."

COLONEL JOHN GLENN,
in orbit, 1962

"There are tens of millions of Americans who are beyond the welfare state. Taken as a whole there is a culture of poverty . . . bad health, poor housing, low levels of aspiration and high levels of mental distress. Twenty percent of a nation, some 32,000,000."

MICHAEL HARRINGTON,
The Culture of Poverty, 1962

"I have a dream."

MARTIN LUTHER KING JR.,
1963

"I don't see an American dream; . . . I see an American nightmare . . . . Three hundred and ten years we worked in this country without a dime in return."

MALCOLM X,
1964

"The Great Society rests on abundance and liberty for all. It demands an end to poverty and racial injustice."

LYNDON B. JOHNSON,
1964

"In 1962, the starving residents of an isolated Indian village received 1 plow and 1,700 pounds of seeds. They ate the seeds."

PEACE CORPS AD,
1965

Extending the Content

Lyndon Johnson's Rhetorical Skills
LBJ came from a political family; his maternal grandfather was a Texas secretary of state and his father was a member of the Texas legislature. Lyndon was handing out pamphlets and attending political rallies by the time he was six. At ten, he accompanied his father to sessions of the legislature to watch the activity from the gallery. Teaching Mexican-American children in real poverty the year he dropped out of college to earn money, he honed their English skills with recitations, debates, and spelling bees. In college, working as a janitor, he made speeches and told stories to walls and doormats as he worked. One Senate Committee assistant recalled that Johnson "said the only power he had was the power to persuade. That's like saying the only wind we have is a hurricane."

Space Race

Want to capture some of the glamour and excitement of space exploration? Create a new nickname for your city. You won't be the first.

CITY	NICKNAME
Danbury, CT	Space Age City
Muscle Shoals, AL	Space Age City
Houston, TX	Space City, USA
Galveston, TX	Space Port, USA
Cape Kennedy, FL	Spaceport, USA
Blacksburg, VA	Space Age Community
Huntsville, AL	~~Rocket City, USA~~
	~~Space City, USA~~
	~~Space Capital of the Nation~~
	Space Capital of the World

John Glenn, first American to orbit Earth

RALPH MORSE/TIMEPIX

Milestones

PERFORMED IN ENGLISH, 1962. THE CATHOLIC MASS, following Pope John XXIII's Second Vatican Council. "Vatican II... allows the Latin mass to be translated into local languages around the world.

ENROLLED, 1962. JAMES MEREDITH, at the University of Mississippi, following a Supreme Court ruling that ordered his admission to the previously segregated school. Rioting and a showdown with state officials who wished to bar his enrollment preceded Meredith's entrance to classes.

BROKEN, 1965. 25-DAY FAST BY CÉSAR CHÁVEZ, labor organizer. His protest convinced others to join his nonviolent strike against the grape growers; shoppers boycotted table grapes in sympathy.

STRIPPED, 1967. MUHAMMAD ALI, of his heavyweight champion title, after refusing induction into the army following a rejection of his application for conscientious objector status. The boxer was arrested, given a five-year sentence, and fined $10,000.

PICKETED, 1968. THE MISS AMERICA PAGEANT in Atlantic City, by protesters who believe the contest's emphasis on women's physical beauty is degrading and minimizes the importance of women's intellect.

AP

NUMBERS

7% Percentage of African American adults registered to vote in Mississippi in 1964 before passage of the Voting Rights Act of 1965

67% Percentage of African American adults in Mississippi registered to vote in 1969

70% Percentage of white adults registered to vote in 1964, nationwide

90% Percentage of white adults registered to vote nationwide in 1969

57 Number of days senators filibustered to hold up passage of the Civil Rights Bill in 1964

14½ Hours duration of all-night speech delivered by Senator Robert Byrd before a cloture vote stopped the filibuster

72% Percentage of elementary and high school teachers who approved of corporal punishment as a disciplinary measure in 1961

$80–90 Weekly pay for a clerk/typist in New York in 1965

CRITICAL THINKING

1. Determining Cause and Effect Who did the Voting Rights Act of 1965 help more—whites or African Americans? Explain your answer.

2. Speculating Why do you think President Kennedy was eager to best the Soviets in space?

C **Critical Thinking**

Identifying Central Issues
The Miss America Pageant and other beauty contests continue to generate controversy. Ask students to debate the value of such competitions today. **OL**

Assess/Close

Visit the Time Web site at www.time.com for up-to-date news, weekly magazine articles, editorials, online polls, and an archive of past magazine and Web articles.

DBQ Document Based Questions

Answers:
1. Students may suggest that it helped African Americans, since a larger percentage of them were registered to vote, or that it helped whites, because they were the majority, and a 20 percent increase in voter registration would be significant.
2. Students' responses will vary but may conclude that the United States was not used to thinking of itself as less than first in anything.

Additional Support

Activity: Collaborative Learning

Predicting Consequences Ask a volunteer to read the information about Muhammad Ali to the class. **Ask:** What effect do you think Ali's refusal to serve in the army had on others who claimed conscientious objector status? How might it have affected those already serving in the army? *(Ask students to share their responses in a class discussion.)*

Focus

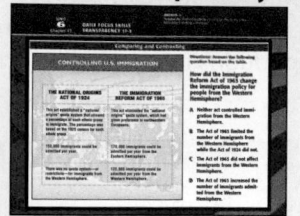

Guide to Reading

Answers:

programs include Higher Education Act, HUD, Job Corps, Medicaid, Medicare, and Project Head Start (see the chart on p. 614 for summary)

Section Spotlight Video

To generate student interest and provide a springboard for class discussion, access the Chapter 17, Section 3 video at glencoe.com or on the video DVD.

Resource Manager

Section 3

The Great Society

Guide to Reading

Big Ideas
Individual Action President Lyndon B. Johnson relied on his experience and persuasiveness to get civil rights and antipoverty bills enacted.

Content Vocabulary
• consensus (p. 611)

Academic Vocabulary
• confine (p.613)
• subsidy (p. 614)

People and Events to Identify
• War on Poverty (p. 611)
• VISTA (p. 612)
• Barry Goldwater (p. 612)
• Great Society (p. 613)
• Medicare (p. 613)
• Medicaid (p. 613)
• Head Start (p. 614)
• Robert Weaver (p. 614)

Reading Strategy
Organizing As you read about Lyndon Johnson's presidency, complete a graphic organizer similar to the one below to list the social and economic programs started during his administration.

Johnson's Programs

Lyndon B. Johnson had decades of experience in Congress and was skilled in getting legislation enacted. When he became president, he moved quickly to push for passage of a civil rights bill and antipoverty legislation.

Johnson Takes the Reins

MAIN Idea President Johnson's experience in Congress helped him push through a civil rights bill and new laws to fight poverty.

HISTORY AND YOU How do you think someone's early life affects his or her career choices? Read on to learn how Lyndon Johnson's early life prepared him for the presidency.

At 2:38 P.M. on November 22, 1963, just hours after President Kennedy had been pronounced dead, Lyndon B. Johnson stood in the cabin of *Air Force One*, the president's plane, with Kennedy's widow on one side of him and his wife, Claudia, known as "Lady Bird," on the other. Johnson raised his right hand, placed his left hand on a Bible, and took the oath of office.

Within days of the assassination, Johnson appeared before Congress and urged the nation to move forward and build on Kennedy's legacy: "The ideas and ideals which [Kennedy] so nobly represented must and will be translated into effective action," he declared. "John Kennedy's death commands what his life conveyed—that America must move forward."

The United States that President Lyndon B. Johnson inherited from John F. Kennedy appeared to be a booming, bustling place. Away from the nation's affluent suburbs, however, was another country, one inhabited by the poor, the ill-fed, the ill-housed, and the ill-educated. Writer Michael Harrington examined the nation's impoverished areas in his 1962 book, *The Other America*. Harrington claimed that, while the truly poor numbered almost 50 million, they remained largely hidden in city slums, in Appalachia, in the Deep South, and on Native American reservations. Soon after taking office, Lyndon Johnson decided to launch an antipoverty crusade.

Johnson's Leadership Style

Lyndon Baines Johnson was born and raised in the "hill country" of central Texas, near the banks of the Pedernales River. He remained a Texan in his heart, and his style posed a striking contrast with Kennedy's. He was a man of impressive stature who spoke directly, convincingly, and even roughly at times.

R Reading Strategies	**C** Critical Thinking	**D** Differentiated Instruction	**W** Writing Support	**S** Skill Practice
Teacher Edition • Academic Vocab., p. 611 • Using Word Parts, p. 614 **Additional Resources** • Read. Skills Act., URB p. 21 • Pri. Source Reading, URB p. 37 • Guid. Read. Act., URB p. 50	**Teacher Edition** • Making Inferences, p. 612 • Analyzing Prim. Sources, p. 613 • Compare. & Contrast., p. 615 **Additional Resources** • Critical Thinking Skills Act., URB p. 32 • Auth. Assess, p. 39 • Quizzes and Tests, p. 245	**Teacher Edition** • Logical/Math., p. 613 • Naturalist, p. 614 **Additional Resources** • Differentiated Instruction, URB p. 23 • Reteach. Act., URB p. 43	**Teacher Edition** • Persuasive Writing, p. 612	**Teacher Edition** • Reading a Chart, p. 611 **Additional Resources** • RENTG, p. 188

When President Johnson launched the War on Poverty in 1964, he wanted programs that would help all impoverished Americans, rural and urban.

▲ *This unemployed miner and his family pose on the porch of their Kentucky home in 1964.*

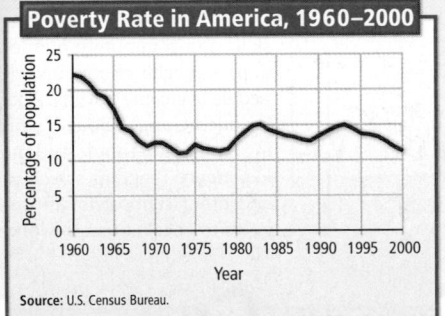

▲ *Low-income residents sweep the front stoops of their row houses in Baltimore, Maryland, in the early 1960s.*

Analyzing VISUALS **DBQ**

1. **Evaluating** Do you find anything hopeful in the photographs shown?
2. **Interpreting** Based on the data in the chart, how successful was Johnson's War on Poverty?

Poverty Rate in America, 1960–2000

(line chart: Percentage of population vs. Year, 1960–2000)

Source: U.S. Census Bureau.

Teach

S Skill Practice

Reading a Chart Direct students' attention to the chart on poverty rates. **Ask:** In what year did the poverty rate begin a climb of nearly 5 percentage points? *(1979)* Encourage students to keep that fact in mind as they continue their study of American history to interpret why the climb might have begun. **BL**

R Reading Strategy

Academic Vocabulary
Remind students that the prefix *con-* means *with*. This knowledge can help them remember the meaning of *consensus*. **BL**

Analyzing VISUALS

Answers:
1. Students' responses will vary.
2. Between 1960 and 1970, the poverty rate dropped 10 percent, a steeper drop than in any subsequent decade. That would be considered a success.

Johnson had honed his style in long years of public service. By the time he became president at age 55, he already had 26 years of congressional experience behind him. He had been a congressional staffer, a member of the House of Representatives, a senator, Senate majority leader, and vice president.

During his career Johnson earned a reputation as a man who got things done. He did favors, twisted arms, bargained, flattered, and threatened. With every technique he could think of, Johnson sought to find **consensus,** **R** or general agreement. His ability to build coalitions had made him one of the most effective and powerful leaders in the Senate's history.

A War on Poverty

Why was this powerful man so concerned about poor people? Although Johnson liked to exaggerate the poor conditions of his childhood for dramatic effect, he had in fact known hard times. He had also seen extreme poverty firsthand in a brief career as a teacher in a low-income area. Johnson believed deeply in social action. He felt that a wealthy, powerful government could and should try to improve the lives of its citizens. Kennedy himself had said of Johnson, "He really cares about this nation." Finally, there was Johnson's ambition. He wanted history to portray him as a great president. Attacking poverty was a good place to begin.

Kennedy had plans for an antipoverty program and a civil rights bill before his death. President Johnson knew that any program linked to the slain president would be very popular. In his State of the Union address in 1964, Johnson told his audience: "Unfortunately, many Americans live on the outskirts of hope, some because of their poverty and some because of their color and all too many because of both." He concluded by declaring an "unconditional **War on Poverty** in America."

Hands-On Chapter Project
Step 3

What Is a Great Society?

Step 3: Creating a Peace Corps or VISTA Work Plan Students will explore responsibilities of citizenship by taking on the role of a Peace Corps or VISTA volunteer.

Directions Discuss why the VISTA and Peace Corps programs are part of a "great society" in terms of a nation's responsibility to its citizens and to other nations. Have students research the types of projects that VISTA and the Peace Corps tackle. Then have each student choose an area of the United States or of another country in which to "volunteer." Ask each student to create a work plan that includes identification of a problem, a specific goal they hope to accomplish, equipment or resources needed, tasks required to achieve the goal, and a schedule for completing the tasks.

Identifying Problems and Solutions By breaking societal problems into achievable steps, students will learn how to find and implement solutions. **OL**

(Project continued on the Visual Summary page)

C Critical Thinking

Making Inferences Ask students to define the word *vista*. ("a distant view") **Ask:** Why do you think this word was chosen as the appropriate acronym for the program? *(Students may suggest that it was offering people a new view of their lives.)* **OL**

W Writing Support

Persuasive Writing Providing adequate day care services for the children of women who work outside the home has continued to be a major challenge. Have students take a position on whether this should be part of federal programs, as it was during World War II. Ask them to write a persuasive essay detailing their arguments. **OL**

✓ Reading Check

Answer: The pockets of extreme poverty in a generally prosperous society; as a former member of Congress, Johnson understood how to play politics to gain consensus on important issues.

Additional Support

By the summer of 1964, Johnson had convinced Congress to pass the Economic Opportunity Act. This legislation attacked inadequate public services, illiteracy, and unemployment as three major causes of poverty. The act established 10 new programs within a new government agency, the Office of Economic Opportunity (OEO). Many of the new programs were directed at young Americans living in inner cities.

The Neighborhood Youth Corps provided work-study programs to help underprivileged young men and women earn a high school diploma or college degree. The Job Corps helped unemployed people ages 16–21 acquire job skills. One of the more dramatic programs introduced was **VISTA** (Volunteers in Service to America), which was essentially a domestic Peace Corps. VISTA put young people with skills and community-minded ideals to work in poor neighborhoods and rural areas to help people overcome poverty. Additional programs included Upward Bound, which offered tutoring to high school students, and a Work Experience Program, which provided day care and other support for those in poor households to enable them to work.

The Election of 1964

In April 1964 *Fortune* magazine observed, "Lyndon Johnson has achieved a breadth of public approval few observers would have believed possible when he took office." Johnson had little time to enjoy such praise, for he was soon to run for the office he had first gained through a tragic event.

The Republican candidate in the 1964 election was Senator **Barry Goldwater** of Arizona. Known for his strong conservatism, he set the tone for his campaign when he accepted his party's nomination, declaring, "Extremism in the defense of liberty is no vice! And let me remind you also that moderation in the pursuit of justice is no virtue!"

Few Americans were ready to embrace Goldwater's message, which seemed too aggressive for a nation nervous about nuclear war. On Election Day, Johnson won in a landslide, gaining more than 61 percent of the popular vote and winning all but six states in the Electoral College.

✓ **Reading Check** **Examining** What inspired the War on Poverty? Why was Johnson able to convince Congress to pass it?

PAST & PRESENT

VISTA Continues the War on Poverty

Volunteers in Service to America (VISTA) began in 1965 as part of President Johnson's War on Poverty. Its focus was to help people help themselves, offering money and programs to low-income communities. Many young people during the idealistic 1960s who weren't able to serve abroad in the Peace Corps program chose instead to work with VISTA. Since the program began, more than 140,000 people have served.

In 1993 VISTA became part of the government agency AmeriCorps. Today, more than 1,200 projects across the nation attempt to make gains in bridging the technology gap, increase housing opportunities, improve health care services, and strengthen community organizations. Volunteers, who must be at least 18, usually work for a year in VISTA-sponsored projects through local, state, or federal agencies or nonprofit, public, or private organizations. In 2006 VISTA had nearly 6,000 volunteers.

1973

▲ In 1973, Leroy Sneed was a VISTA member in his hometown of Mitchellville, South Carolina, where he was involved in home-repair and community organizing. Here he talks with a homeowner about rebuilding or repairing her home.

Activity: Collaborative Learning

Investigate the Work of VISTA Have students work in small groups and use library and Internet sources to find out more about the current work of VISTA. Ask students to present their findings using visual aids, such as maps and charts, to portray the work and its locations.

Have each group select one project or region of the country on which to focus their research. Discuss and compare groups' findings as a class. **OL**

The Great Society

MAIN Idea Great Society programs provided assistance to disadvantaged Americans.

HISTORY AND YOU What reforms do you think might help reduce poverty today? Read on to learn about the antipoverty programs initiated by President Johnson.

After his election, Johnson began working with Congress to create the "**Great Society**" he had promised during his campaign. In this same period, major goals of the civil rights movement were achieved through the Civil Rights Act of 1964, which barred discrimination of many kinds, and the Voting Rights Act of 1965, which protected voters from discriminatory practices.

Johnson's goals were consistent with the times for several reasons. The civil rights movement had brought the grievances of African Americans to the forefront, reminding many that equality of opportunity had yet to be realized. Economics also supported Johnson's goal. The economy was strong, and many believed it would remain so indefinitely. There was no reason to believe, therefore, that poverty could not be significantly reduced.

Johnson elaborated on the Great Society's goals during a speech at the University of Michigan in May of 1964. It was clear that the president did not intend only to expand relief to the poor or to **confine** government efforts to material things. The president wanted, he said, to build a better society "where leisure is a welcome chance to build and reflect, . . . where the city of man serves not only the needs of the body and the demands of commerce but the desire for beauty and the hunger for community."

This ambitious vision encompassed more than 60 programs that were initiated between 1965 and 1968. Among the most significant programs were **Medicare** and **Medicaid.** Health care reform had been a major issue since the days of Harry Truman. By the 1960s, public support for better health care benefits had solidified. Medicare had especially strong support since it was directed at all senior citizens. In 1965 approximately half of all Americans over the age of 65 had no health insurance.

C **Critical Thinking**

Analyzing Primary Sources
Invite a volunteer to read the quotation from Johnson's speech. **Ask:** Why would these words appeal to a college audience? *(Students may say that college students are idealistic.)* Discuss with students whether they feel Johnson's goals for leisure, beauty, and community have been met. **OL**

D **Differentiated Instruction**

Logical/Mathematical Ask students to find out the current statistics on the number of Americans without health insurance. Have them break down the figures by age groups and present their findings in chart or graph form. **OL**

MAKING **CONNECTIONS**

Answers:
1. Students may say that volunteering extends a person's compassion and may enhance useful life skills. The persons being helped are given tangible assistance.
2. Students' responses to both questions will vary.

Additional Support

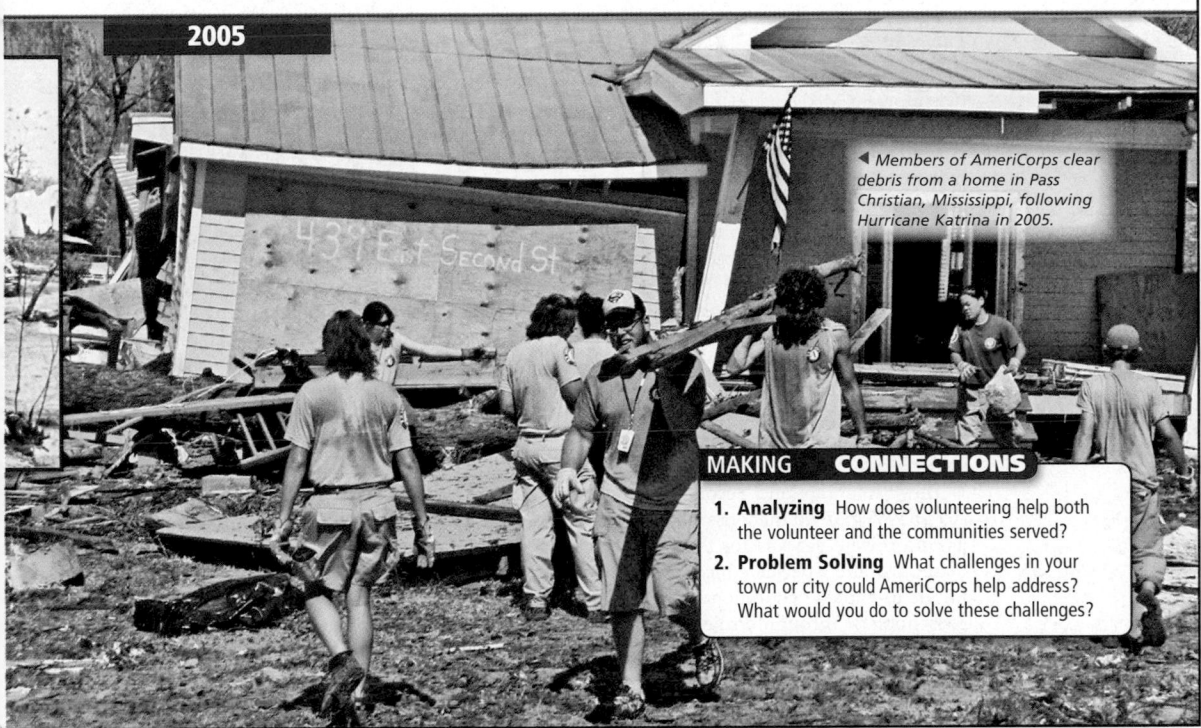

2005

◀ *Members of AmeriCorps clear debris from a home in Pass Christian, Mississippi, following Hurricane Katrina in 2005.*

MAKING **CONNECTIONS**

1. **Analyzing** How does volunteering help both the volunteer and the communities served?
2. **Problem Solving** What challenges in your town or city could AmeriCorps help address? What would you do to solve these challenges?

Extending the Content

Since 1994, more than 400,000 men and women have served in AmeriCorps. Over 50,000 volunteers each year work with nonprofit organizations to provide assistance to other Americans.

Once a person has completed a year of full-time service, he or she receives an education grant of $4725. This can be used for college, graduate school, or to pay back student loans. Those who serve part-time receive a partial award.

R Reading Strategy

Using Word Parts Point out the academic vocabulary term in the second column. **Ask:** What does the prefix *sub-* mean? *(below, under)* Have students come up with other terms using the prefix. (Possible answers include *subatomic, submarine, substandard,* and so on.) **OL**

D Differentiated Instruction

Naturalist Invite interested students to find out how the Water Quality and Clean Air Acts have improved environmental conditions since 1965. Ask them to include information about local efforts on preserving clean water and air. Have them present their findings to the class. **OL**

Analyzing VISUALS

Answers:
1. They supported the development of standards and goals for water and air quality.
2. Students' responses will vary but should be supported.

Additional Support

Health and Welfare

Medicare (1965) established a comprehensive health insurance program for all senior citizens; financed through the Social Security system.

Medicaid (1965) provided health and medical assistance to low-income families; funded through federal and state governments.

Child Nutrition Act (1966) established a school breakfast program and expanded the school lunch and milk programs to improve nutrition.

Education

Elementary and Secondary Education Act (1965) targeted aid to students and funded related activities such as adult education and education counseling.

Higher Education Act (1965) supported college tuition scholarships, student loans, and work-study programs for low- and middle-income students.

Project Head Start (1965) funded a preschool program for disadvantaged children.

The War on Poverty

Office of Economic Opportunity (1964) oversaw many programs to improve life in inner cities, including Job Corps, an education and job training program for at-risk youth.

Housing and Urban Development Act (1965) established new housing subsidy programs and made federal loans and public housing grants easier to obtain.

Demonstration Cities and Metropolitan Development Act (1966) revitalized urban areas through a variety of social and economic programs.

Consumer and Environmental Protection

Water Quality Act and Clean Air Acts (1965) supported development of standards and goals for water and air quality.

Highway Safety Act (1966) improved federal, state, and local coordination and created training standards for emergency medical technicians.

Fair Packaging and Labeling Act (1966) required all consumer products to have true and informative labels.

Analyzing VISUALS

1. **Interpreting** What was the purpose of the Water Quality and Clean Air Acts of 1965?
2. **Evaluating** Which of the Great Society programs do you think had the most effect on American life? Why do you think so?

Johnson convinced Congress to set up Medicare as a health insurance program funded through the Social Security system. Medicare's twin program, Medicaid, financed health care for welfare recipients who were living below the poverty line. Like the New Deal's Social Security program, both programs created what have been called "entitlements," that is, they entitle certain categories of Americans to benefits. Today, the cost of these programs has become a permanent part of the federal budget.

Great Society programs also strongly supported education. For Johnson, who had taught school as a young man, education was a personal passion. Vice President Hubert Humphrey once said that Johnson "was a nut on education.... [He] believed in it, just like some people believe in miracle cures."

The Elementary and Secondary Education Act of 1965 granted millions of dollars to public and private schools for textbooks, library materials, and special education programs. Efforts to improve education also extended to preschoolers through Project **Head Start.**

Administered by the Office of Economic Opportunity, Head Start was directed at disadvantaged children who had "never looked at a picture book or scribbled with a crayon." Another program, Upward Bound, was designed to prepare low-income teenagers for college.

Improvements in health and education were only the beginning of the Great Society programs. Conditions in the cities—poor schools, crime, slum housing, poverty, and pollution—blighted the lives of those who dwelled there. Johnson urged Congress to act on several pieces of legislation addressing urban issues. One created a new cabinet agency, the Department of Housing and Urban Development, in 1965. Its first secretary, **Robert Weaver,** was the first African American to serve in the cabinet. A broad-based program informally called "Model Cities" authorized federal **subsidies** to many cities. The funds, matched by local and state contributions, supported programs to improve transportation, health care, housing, and policing. Since many

Extending the Content

Robert Weaver Although Weaver's great-grandfather had been enslaved, Weaver, born in 1907, graduated from Harvard with a doctorate in economics and served in several government positions nationally and at the state level. He also was a member of Franklin Roosevelt's "Black Cabinet." He served a year as the national chair for the National Association for the Advancement of Colored People. President Kennedy appointed him in 1960 to lead the federal Housing and Home Finance Agency before he became secretary of HUD in 1965. After leaving HUD at the end of 1968, Weaver served as president of Bernard Baruch College and taught at several institutions of higher learning. Weaver is credited with beginning the revitalization of urban centers in the United States, working to pass the Fair Housing Act, and increasing available affordable housing. In 2000 the Department of Housing and Urban Development named their building, which Weaver had opened and dedicated in 1968, in his honor.

urban areas lacked sufficient or affordable housing, legislation also authorized about $8 billion to build houses for low- and middle-income people.

One notable Great Society measure changed the composition of the American population: the Immigration Act of 1965. This act eliminated the national origins system established in the 1920s, which had given preference to northern European immigrants. The new measure opened wider the door of the United States to newcomers from all parts of Europe, as well as from Asia and Africa.

The Great Society's Legacy

The Great Society programs touched nearly every aspect of American life and improved thousands, perhaps millions, of lives. In the years since President Johnson left office, however, debate has continued over whether the Great Society was truly a success.

In many ways, the impact of the Great Society was limited. In his rush to accomplish as much as possible, Johnson did not calculate exactly how his programs might work. As a result, some of them did not work as well as hoped. Furthermore, the programs grew so quickly they were often unmanageable and difficult to evaluate.

Cities, states, and groups eligible for aid began to expect immediate and life-changing benefits. These expectations left many feeling frustrated and angry. Other Americans opposed the massive growth of federal programs and criticized the Great Society for intruding too much into their lives.

A lack of funds also hindered the effectiveness of Great Society programs. When Johnson attempted to fund both his grand domestic agenda and the increasingly costly war in Vietnam, the Great Society eventually suffered. Some Great Society initiatives have survived to the present, however. These include Medicare and Medicaid, two cabinet agencies—the Department of Transportation and the Department of Housing and Urban Development (HUD)—and Project Head Start. Overall, the programs provided some important benefits to poorer communities and gave political and administrative experience to minority groups.

An important legacy of the Great Society was the questions it produced. How can the federal government help disadvantaged citizens? How much government help can a society provide without weakening the private sector? How much help can people receive without losing motivation to fight against hardships on their own?

Lyndon Johnson took office determined to change the United States in a way few other presidents had attempted. If he fell short, it was perhaps that the goals he set were so high. In evaluating the administration's efforts, the *New York Times* wrote, "The walls of the ghettos are not going to topple overnight, nor is it possible to wipe out the heritage of generations of social, economic, and educational deprivation by the stroke of a Presidential pen."

✓ Reading Check **Summarizing** What were the Great Society programs, and what was their impact?

Section 3 REVIEW

Vocabulary

1. **Explain** the significance of: consensus, War on Poverty, VISTA, Barry Goldwater, Great Society, Medicare, Medicaid, Head Start, Robert Weaver.

Main Ideas

2. **Analyzing** How did Johnson's War on Poverty strive to ensure greater fairness in American society?

3. **Describing** Which Great Society programs supported education? How did these programs help?

Critical Thinking

4. **Big Ideas** How did President Johnson carry on the ideals of President Kennedy?

5. **Organizing** Use a graphic organizer similar to the one below to list five of the Great Society initiatives that have survived to the present.

Great Society Initiatives

6. **Analyzing Visuals** Look at the graph on page 611. When was poverty at its lowest in the U.S.?

Writing About History

7. **Descriptive Writing** Assume the role of a biographer. Write a chapter in a biography of Lyndon Johnson in which you compare and contrast his leadership style to that of John Kennedy.

History ONLINE
Study Central™ To review this section, go to glencoe.com and click on Study Central.

615

C Critical Thinking

Comparing and Contrasting Ask students to compare and contrast two major social programs in the twentieth century. They might design graphic organizers to analyze the New Frontier and New Deal, for example. **OL**

✓ Reading Check

Answer: programs for health, housing, jobs, and education that changed the nation

Assess

History ONLINE

Study Central™ provides summaries, interactive games, and online graphic organizers to help students review content.

Close

Summarizing Ask: What programs from the Great Society do you feel had the most lasting significance? Why do you think so? *(Answers will vary.)*

Section 3 REVIEW

Answers

1. All definitions can be found in the section and the Glossary.

2. by offering the less fortunate education, training, and access to jobs

3. Elementary and Secondary Education Act: money to schools for textbooks, library materials, and special education programs; Project Head Start: improved education for preschoolers; Upward Bound: college preparation for low-income teenagers; Higher Education Act: college tuition scholarships, student loans and work-study for low- and middle-income students

4. Johnson pushed through Kennedy initiatives including major civil rights bills and anti-poverty programs.

5. answers may include: Medicare, Medicaid, Department of Transportation, Department of Housing and Urban Development, Project Head Start

6. 1973

7. Chapters should include specific information about the leadership styles of the two men.

Chapter 17 VISUAL SUMMARY

Expository Writing Have students select one of the domestic programs listed and explain why it was important for the Great Society and its legacy for today. **OL**

Taking Notes Have students create graphic organizers to identify the major Supreme Court cases and their provisions. Remind them to use this as a study aid. **OL**

Domestic Programs of the 1960s

- A growing awareness of poverty, as well as concern for women's rights and the rights of various minority groups, leads to a series of new programs known as the War on Poverty and the Great Society.
- The President's Commission on the Status of Women is established and the Equal Pay Act of 1963 is passed.
- New programs aid the developmentally disabled.
- Office of Economic Opportunity is established to fight poverty, illiteracy, unemployment, and disease.
- Civil Rights Act of 1964 prohibits race discrimination and social segregation, and the Voting Rights Act protects universal suffrage.
- Medicare and Medicaid Acts are passed to provide federal medical aid to senior citizens and poor.
- Elementary and Secondary Education Act is passed to increase aid for public schools.

▲ *VISTA volunteers work to curb delinquency by counseling and helping troubled children and their families.*

Foreign Policy of the 1960s

- Kennedy pledges to end Eisenhower's reliance on nuclear weapons and to use new methods to prevent the spread of communism.
- Kennedy introduces the "flexible response" policy—building up both nuclear missiles and conventional forces.
- The United States pledges aid to struggling Latin American nations.
- Peace Corps sends volunteers to help in poor countries.
- The United States aids Cuban exiles trying to overthrow Castro, but their landing at the Bay of Pigs fails.
- Soviet missiles in Cuba lead to the Cuban missile crisis; the United States blockades Cuba and the Soviets remove the missiles.
- The U.S. and Soviet Union sign the Nuclear Test Ban Treaty.

▲ *The U.S. Navy ship, the Vesole, intercepts the missile-carrying Soviet ship Potzunov as it leaves Cuba during the Cuban Missile Crisis.*

Supreme Court Cases of the 1960s

- Led by Chief Justice Earl Warren, the Supreme Court makes a series of decisions that dramatically change American society and the federal government's relationship to citizens.
- In *Reynolds* v. *Sims* the Court requires states to adhere to the principle of one person, one vote.
- In four cases, *Mapp* v. *Ohio*, *Gideon* v. *Wainwright*, *Escobedo* v. *Illinois*, and *Miranda* v. *Arizona*, the Court extends due process, giving more protection to those accused of crimes.
- In *Abington School District* v. *Schemp*, the Court rules that states cannot require prayer and Bible readings in public schools.

▲ *Clarence Earl Gideon was denied counsel during a trial in Florida in 1961. His case eventually went to the Supreme Court.*

616 **Chapter 17** The New Frontier and the Great Society

Hands-On Chapter Project
Step 4

What Is a Great Society?

Step 4: Wrap Up Creating a Great Society Poster Students will discuss what qualities make up a society that can be considered "great" and create a poster illustrating those qualities.

Directions Hang a poster on the wall with the title "A Great Society." Ask the class what societies they have studied—such as ancient Greece—that they consider great. Then ask them to list the qualities that are important in a great society. Use their list as headings for columns on the poster.

Analyzing Information Students will analyze the domestic programs, foreign policies, and court decisions of the 1960s and list below the headings on the poster those items that illustrate each quality. **OL**

ASSESSMENT

STANDARDIZED TEST PRACTICE

TEST-TAKING TIP

To answer vocabulary questions 2–4 below, first look at the terms listed as answers. See if you can mentally define each one. Then read the question to select the right answer.

Reviewing Vocabulary

Directions: Choose the word or words that best completes the sentence.

1. Reapportionment, as ruled on by the Warren Court, is
   A the requirement of separate but equal facilities for schools.
   B the process courts must follow when trying cases to treat individuals fairly.
   C the way in which political districts are drawn based on population changes.
   D the separation of church and state for schools.

2. The policy called _____ helped nations resist Communism by building up conventional troops and weapons.
   A military-industrial complex
   B containment
   C mutual assured destruction
   D flexible response

3. _____ means that the law may not treat individuals unfairly or unreasonably and must treat all individuals equally.
   A Reapportionment
   B Consensus
   C Due process
   D Judicial review

4. President Johnson was successful at building coalitions and finding a _____, or general agreement.
   A discord
   B consensus
   C accord
   D variance

Reviewing Main Ideas

Directions: Choose the best answers to the following questions.

Section 1 *(pp. 596–601)*

5. During the presidential election of 1960, Kennedy focused his campaign message on
   A bridging the "missile gap" between the United States and the Soviet Union.
   B continuing the foreign policy of the current administration.
   C how the Democrats' fiscal policies would boost inflation and harm the economy.
   D how Catholicism would influence his decision-making as president.

6. Congress defeated which of the following proposals of Kennedy's New Frontier?
   A raising the minimum wage
   B investing funds in defense and space exploration
   C health care for senior citizens
   D providing funds to build low-income housing

7. The Warren Court decision requiring that a defendant in a state court had the right to a lawyer, regardless of his or her ability to pay, was
   A *Engel* v. *Vitale.*
   B *Griswold* v. *Connecticut.*
   C *Plessy* v. *Ferguson.*
   D *Gideon* v. *Wainwright.*

Need Extra Help?

If You Missed Questions . . .	1	2	3	4	5	6	7
Go to Page . . .	600	602	601	611	596	598	601

GO ON →

Answers and Analyses

1. C The clue to the correct answer is in the term *reapportionment*. If students spot the prefix *re-*, meaning "again," with the word *changes* in the answer, they can eliminate other distractors.

2. D Students should recall that the flexible response was deemed preferable to the expansion of nuclear weapons that Eisenhower had begun, which led to the military-industrial complex against which he warned. The question asks them to choose the answer that helps resist communism, not contain or destroy it.

3. C By linking the idea of something due to a benefit, students can eliminate the other distractors and select the correct answer.

4. B Students need only a basic knowledge of prefix meanings to see that *dis-* and *con-* are opposing ideas; therefore, one of them must be correct. The other choices can be eliminated. Knowing that *dis-* means "not" can help students select a synonym for *agreement*.

5. A The three incorrect responses are each unlikely to be the work of a Democratic presidential candidate who was also the first Roman Catholic to run in more than three decades. Even without knowing what a missile gap was, students knowing Kennedy's political and religious background could eliminate wrong answers.

6. C Students should recall that Medicaid was a breakthrough program that Johnson succeeded in getting passed after Kennedy had failed. JFK succeeded in the other efforts listed as distractors.

7. D Students should be able to eliminate *Plessy* v. *Ferguson* by recalling the landmark case upholding separate but equal facilities for African Americans and whites. By careful attention to the chart of Supreme Court cases in the Warren years, they can select the correct answer.

8. C None of the other answers proposes an effective solution to reducing nuclear war, even if they may be attractive options for stopping the spread of communism. Students should be able to link creating the Peace Corps with not having war.

9. B Students should be able to eliminate the two options that pertain to Cuba. The Berlin blockade had already occurred, leaving only option B.

10. A The key to the correct answer is for students to link the terms *young people* and *youth,* ignoring the more generic-sounding programs. They may know that AmeriCorps is a current program.

11. D Given chapter content, *A* and *C* can be eliminated at once. To derive the correct answer, students then need only recall that Johnson was able to push through reforms that Kennedy could not.

12. B Students can ignore distractors with negative words such as *eliminating* and *opposing.* Foreign aid to Cuba would not make America a Great Society. The correct answer deals with an increase; students may also recall that the text mentions Johnson's passion for education.

Section 2 *(pp. 602–607)*

8. Kennedy attempted to reduce the threat of nuclear war and stop the spread of communism by

   A withdrawing aid from Latin American countries.

   B withdrawing troops from limited military conflicts.

   C creating the Peace Corps.

   D encouraging growth in the automotive industry to assure that capitalism was superior to communism.

9. How did Soviet Premier Nikita Khrushchev respond when Western powers refused to withdraw from West Berlin?

   A sent long-range missiles to Cuba

   B built a wall through Berlin, blocking movement between the Soviet Union and Western nations

   C enlisted *La Brigada* to invade Cuba and remove Castro from power

   D airlifted food and supplies to Berlin to end a blockade by American forces

Section 3 *(pp. 610–615)*

10. Which Johnson program provided work-study opportunities to help young people earn high school diplomas or attend college?

    A the Neighborhood Youth Corps

    B VISTA

    C the Peace Corps

    D AmeriCorps

11. Medicare and Medicaid were major accomplishments of

    A Franklin Roosevelt's New Deal.

    B John F. Kennedy's New Frontier.

    C Richard Nixon's New Federalism.

    D Lyndon Johnson's Great Society.

12. Which idea was part of Johnson's Great Society?

    A eliminating government-funded health care for senior citizens

    B increasing federal aid for education

    C opposing civil rights legislation

    D increasing foreign aid to Cuba

Need Extra Help?

If You Missed Questions . . .	8	9	10	11	12	13	14
Go to Page . . .	602	606	612	613–614	614	615	R15

618 **Chapter 17** The New Frontier and the Great Society

Critical Thinking

Directions: Choose the best answers to the following questions.

13. How did the Immigration Reform Act of 1965 change the composition of the American population?

    A It set strict limits on the number of immigrants admitted to the United States.

    B It did not allow any immigrants to enter the United States from Eastern Europe.

    C It continued the national origins system, which gave preference to northern European immigrants.

    D It opened the United States to individuals from all over the world, including Asia and Africa.

Base your answer to question 14 on the map below and on your knowledge of Chapter 17.

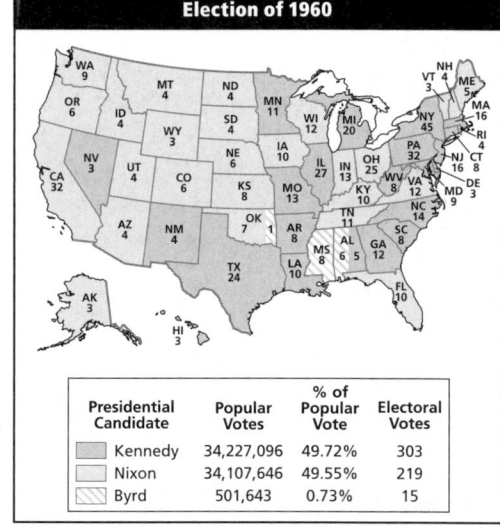

Election of 1960

Presidential Candidate	Popular Votes	% of Popular Vote	Electoral Votes
Kennedy	34,227,096	49.72%	303
Nixon	34,107,646	49.55%	219
Byrd	501,643	0.73%	15

14. Which region of the country gave Kennedy the most electoral votes?

    A Pacific Northwest

    B Northeast

    C Southwest

    D Midwest

GO ON

13. D The key term in the question is the title of the act itself. To reform would be to improve; only opening the country to people from more nations fits that description.

14. B By carefully looking at the map, students can see that simply combining votes from New York and Pennsylvania provided a majority.

ASSESSMENT

15. President Lyndon B. Johnson's Great Society is similar to President Franklin D. Roosevelt's New Deal in that both programs

  A sought ratification of the Equal Rights Amendment to guarantee equality for women.

  B advocated passage of civil rights laws to help African Americans.

  C approved efforts by states to reduce taxes for the middle class.

  D supported federal funding of programs for the poor.

Analyze the cartoon and answer the question that follows. Base your answer on the cartoon and on your knowledge of Chapter 17.

HERBLOCK'S CARTOON

"Kindly Move Over A Little, Gentlemen"

16. According to the cartoon, what is Johnson trying to do?

  A Johnson wants to give more money to the arms race and military establishments.

  B Johnson is trying to give health, education, and welfare programs more money.

  C Military establishments and arms costs are giving money to social programs.

  D Social programs are receiving more money than the military.

Document-Based Questions

Directions: Analyze the document and answer the short-answer questions that follow the document.

Although the standard of living for most Americans rose dramatically throughout the 1960s, some Americans remained mired in poverty. Read the excerpt below in which John Rath discusses his personal experiences with coping with poverty in his sparsely furnished room in Chicago:

> "I come home to an empty room. I don't even have a dog. . . . No, this is not the kind of life I would choose. If a man had a little piece of land or something, a farm, or well . . . anyway, you've got to have something. You sit down in a place like this, you grit your teeth, you follow me? So many of them are doing that, they sit down, they don't know what to do, they go out. I see 'em in the middle of the night, they take a walk. Don't know what to do. Have no home environment, don't have a dog, don't have nothing . . . just a big zero."
> —quoted in *Division Street: America*

17. What does Rath think might help him to have some purpose in his life?

18. What does he mean when he says: "You sit down in a place like this, you grit your teeth . . ."?

Extended Response

19. Discuss why President Johnson proposed the Great Society and how his initiatives were intended to bring about social change. Then evaluate the extent to which the Great Society succeeded in meeting its goals. Write a well-organized essay that includes an introduction, several paragraphs, and a conclusion. Establish a framework that goes beyond a simple restatement of facts and draws a conclusion about the effectiveness of Johnson's programs.

STOP

History ONLINE
For additional test practice, use Self-Check Quizzes— Chapter 17 at glencoe.com.

Need Extra Help?

If You Missed Questions . . .	15	16	17	18	19
Go to Page . . .	614	R18	R19	R19	610–615

---

15. D The question asks students to recall the provisions of the New Deal. By doing so, they will recall that none of the first three items were part of FDR's explicit agenda. *D* is the only common thread.

16. B Johnson is asking the arms race and the military to make way for health, education, and welfare. Johnson is trying to improve these programs by giving them milk (budgetary funds) to help them grow.

17. Rath thinks that owning a piece of land or a farm would give him purpose.

18. He means that the situation is so unpleasant that a person grits his or her teeth to avoid screaming.

19. Students' essays will vary but should include an introduction, several paragraphs, and a conclusion. Essays should address Johnson's Great Society and evaluate its results.

History ONLINE

Have students visit the Web site at glencoe.com to review Chapter 17 and take the Self-Check Quiz.

Need Extra Help?

Have students refer to the pages listed if they miss any of the questions.

Key to Ability Levels

- **BL** Below Level
- **OL** On Level
- **AL** Above Level
- **ELL** English Language Learners

Key to Teaching Resources

- Print Material
- CD-ROM
- DVD
- Transparency

Levels (BL OL AL ELL)					Resources	Chapter Opener	Section 1	Section 2	Section 3	Chapter Assess
					FOCUS					
BL	OL	AL	ELL	🖨	Daily Focus Skills Transparencies		18-1	18-2	18-3	
					TEACH					
	OL	AL		📁	History Simulations and Problem Solving, URB		p. 9			
		AL		📁	American Literature Reading, URB					p. 13
BL	OL		ELL	📁	Reading Essentials and Note-Taking Guide*		p. 191	p. 194	p. 197	
	OL			📁	Historical Analysis Skills Activity, URB		p. 54			
BL	OL		ELL	📁	Guided Reading Activities, URB*		p. 80	p. 81	p. 82	
BL	OL	AL	ELL	📁	Content Vocabulary Activity, URB*	p. 59				
BL	OL	AL	ELL	📁	Academic Vocabulary Activity, URB	p. 61				
	OL	AL		📁	Critical Thinking Skills Activity, URB				p. 64	
BL	OL		ELL	📁	Reading Skills Activity, URB			p. 53		
BL			ELL	📁	English Learner Activity, URB		p. 57			
	OL	AL		📁	Reinforcing Skills Activity, URB		p. 63			
BL	OL	AL	ELL	📁	Differentiated Instruction Activity, URB			p. 55		
BL	OL		ELL	📁	Time Line Activity, URB					p. 65
	OL			📁	Linking Past and Present Activity, URB					p. 66
BL	OL	AL	ELL	📁	American Art and Music Activity, URB	p. 71				
BL	OL	AL	ELL	📁	Interpreting Political Cartoons Activity, URB			p. 73		
		AL		📁	Enrichment Activity, URB			p. 77		
BL	OL	AL	ELL	📁	American Biographies	✓				
BL	OL	AL	ELL	📁	Primary Source Reading, URB			p. 67	p. 69	
BL	OL	AL	ELL	📁	Supreme Court Case Studies		p. 73	p. 97		
BL	OL	AL	ELL	📁	The Living Constitution*	✓	✓	✓	✓	✓
	OL	AL		💿	American History Primary Source Documents Library	✓	✓	✓	✓	✓
BL	OL	AL	ELL	🖨	Unit Map Overlay Transparencies	✓	✓	✓	✓	✓
BL	OL	AL	ELL	📁	Differentiated Instruction for the American High School Classroom	✓	✓	✓	✓	✓

Note: Please refer to the *Unit 6 Resource Book* for this chapter's URB materials.

* Also available in Spanish

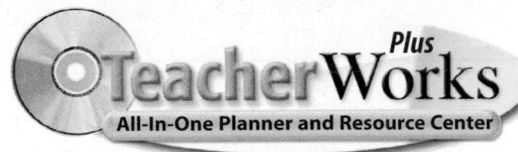

- Interactive Lesson Planner
- Interactive Teacher Edition
- Fully editable blackline masters
- Section Spotlight Videos Launch
- Differentiated Lesson Plans
- Printable reports of daily assignments
- Standards Tracking System

Levels					Resources	Chapter Opener	Section 1	Section 2	Section 3	Chapter Assess
TEACH *(continued)*										
BL	OL	AL	ELL		StudentWorks™ Plus DVD	✓	✓	✓	✓	✓
BL	OL	AL	ELL		Vocabulary PuzzleMaker CD-ROM	✓	✓	✓	✓	✓
BL	OL	AL	ELL		American Music Hits Through History CD	✓	✓	✓	✓	✓
BL	OL	AL	ELL		Unit Time Line Transparencies and Activities	✓	✓	✓	✓	✓
BL	OL	AL	ELL		Cause and Effect Transparencies, Strategies, and Activities	✓	✓	✓	✓	✓
BL	OL	AL	ELL		Why It Matters Transparencies, Strategies, and Activities	✓	✓	✓	✓	✓
BL	OL	AL	ELL		American Issues	✓	✓	✓	✓	✓
	OL	AL	ELL		American Art and Architecture Transparencies, Strategies, and Activities	✓	✓	✓	✓	✓
BL	OL	AL			High School American History Literature Library	✓	✓	✓	✓	✓
BL	OL	AL	ELL		*The American Vision* Video Program DVD	✓	✓	✓	✓	✓
Teacher Resources					Strategies for Success	✓	✓	✓	✓	✓
					Success with English Learner	✓	✓	✓	✓	✓
					Studies Classroom	✓	✓	✓	✓	✓
					Presentation Plus! DVD	✓	✓	✓	✓	✓
ASSESS										
BL	OL	AL	ELL		Section Quizzes and Chapter Tests*		p. 255	p. 256	p. 257	p. 259
BL	OL	AL	ELL		Authentic Assessment With Rubrics					p. 41
BL	OL	AL	ELL		Standardized Test Practice Workbook					p. 42
BL	OL	AL	ELL		*ExamView®* Assessment Suite CD-ROM		18-1	18-2	18-3	Ch. 18
BL	OL	AL	ELL		Interactive Tutor Self-Assessment CD-ROM		18-1	18-2	18-3	Ch. 18
CLOSE										
BL			ELL		Reteaching Activity, URB					p. 75
BL	OL		ELL		Reading and Study Skills Foldables™	p. 79				

Chapter 18 | Integrating Technology

Using the Glencoe Web site

Self-Check Quizzes

Technology Product
Students can assess their comprehension of chapter content with Self-Check Quizzes on the Glencoe Web site. The Web site provides a 10-question quiz for each chapter.

Objectives
The Self-Check Quizzes help students
- assess their comprehension and recall of chapter content;
- build study skills;
- identify areas for additional study and reinforcement.

Steps
Provide students with the following steps to complete the activities:
- Locate the Web page for the textbook being studied on the Glencoe Web site glencoe.com.
- Click on **Student Center** under the textbook title.
- In the Student Center, select a unit from the Unit Resources menu and a chapter from the Chapter Activities menu using the drop-down arrows.
- Click on the **Self-Check Quizzes** link.
- Have students answer the questions in the chapter quiz and review feedback on incorrect answers.
- Provide students an e-mail address to submit their quiz results for analysis and recording.

History ONLINE

	Student	Teacher	Parent
Beyond the Textbook	●	●	●
Chapter Overviews	●	●	●
Time Current Events	●		●
ePuzzles and Games	●		●
Concepts in Motion	●		●
Literature Connections		●	
Multi-Language Glossaries	●		●
Online Student Edition	●	●	●
Self-Check Quizzes	●		●
Student Web Activities	●		●
Study Central™	●		●
Teaching Today		●	
Vocabulary eFlashcards	●		●
Web Activity Lesson Plans		●	

Glencoe Media Center

glencoe.com

❯ **Study-To-Go**
- Vocabulary eflashcards
- Self-Check Quizzes

❯ **Audio/Video**
- Student Edition Audio
- Spanish Summaries
- Section Videos

- **Timed Readings Plus in Social Studies** helps students increase their reading rate and fluency while maintaining comprehension. The 400-word passages are similar to those found on state and national assessments.

- **Reading in the Content Area: Social Studies** concentrates on six essential reading skills that help students better comprehend what they read. The book includes 75 high-interest nonfiction passages written at increasing levels of difficulty.

- **Reading Social Studies** includes strategic reading instruction and vocabulary support in Social Studies content for both ELLs and native speakers of English.

www.jamestowneducation.com

The following videotape programs are available from Glencoe as supplements to Chapter 18:

- Martin Luther King, Jr.: The Man and the Dream (ISBN 0-76-701057-4)
- The Class of the 20th Century; Vol. 4 1961–1968 (ISBN 1-56-501050-7)

To order, call Glencoe at 1-800-334-7344. To find classroom resources to accompany many of these videos, check the following home pages:

A&E Television: www.aetv.com

The History Channel: www.historychannel.com

NATIONAL GEOGRAPHIC

Index to National Geographic Magazine:

The following articles relate to this chapter:

- "On the Civil Rights Trail," by Charles E. Cobb Jr., February 2005.
- "Selma to Montgomery: The Road to Equality," by Chuck Stone and Meria Joel Carstarphen, February 2000.

National Geographic Society Products To order the following, call National Geographic at 1-800-368-2728:

- *Civil Rights* (CD-ROM)

Access National Geographic's new, dynamic MapMachine Web site and other geography resources at:

www.nationalgeographic.com
www.nationalgeographic.com/maps

Reading List Generator CD-ROM

GLENCOE BOOKLINK 3

Use this database to search more than 30,000 titles to create a customized reading list for your students.

- Reading lists can be organized by students' reading level, author, genre, theme, or area of interest.
- The database provides Degrees of Reading Power™ (DRP) and Lexile™ readability scores for all selections.
- A brief summary of each selection is included.

Leveled reading suggestions for this chapter:

For students at a Grade 8 reading level:
- *Neil Armstrong: Young Flyer,* by Montrew Dunham

For students at a Grade 9 reading level:
- *One Giant Leap: The Story of Neil Armstrong,* by Don Brown

For students at a Grade 10 reading level:
- *The Civil Rights Movement,* by Stuart Kallen

For students at a Grade 11 reading level:
- *The Civil Rights Movement,* by Michael Anderson

For students at a Grade 12 reading level:
- *Great African Americans in Civil Rights,* by Pat Rediger

Focus

MAKING CONNECTIONS
What Causes Societies to Change?

Ask students to give suggestions as to why societies change. Students may list economic, political, and social reasons. Have students surmise why the civil rights movement gathered momentum after World War II. Students may recall the effects of the Holocaust on people's views of human rights as well as the fact that the contributions of African Americans in the armed forces during the conflict made American citizens sensitive to the need for social equality. Have students hypothesize whether nonviolent or violent strategies work best in bringing about positive social change. **OL**

Teach

The Big Ideas

As students study the chapter, remind them to consider the section-based Big Ideas included in each section's Guide to Reading. The **Essential Questions** and the activities below tie in to the Big Ideas and help students think about and understand important chapter concepts. In addition, the Hands-on-Chapter Projects with their culminating activities relate the content from each section to the Big Ideas. These activities build on each other as students progress through the chapter. Section activities culminate in the wrap-up activity on the Visual Summary page.

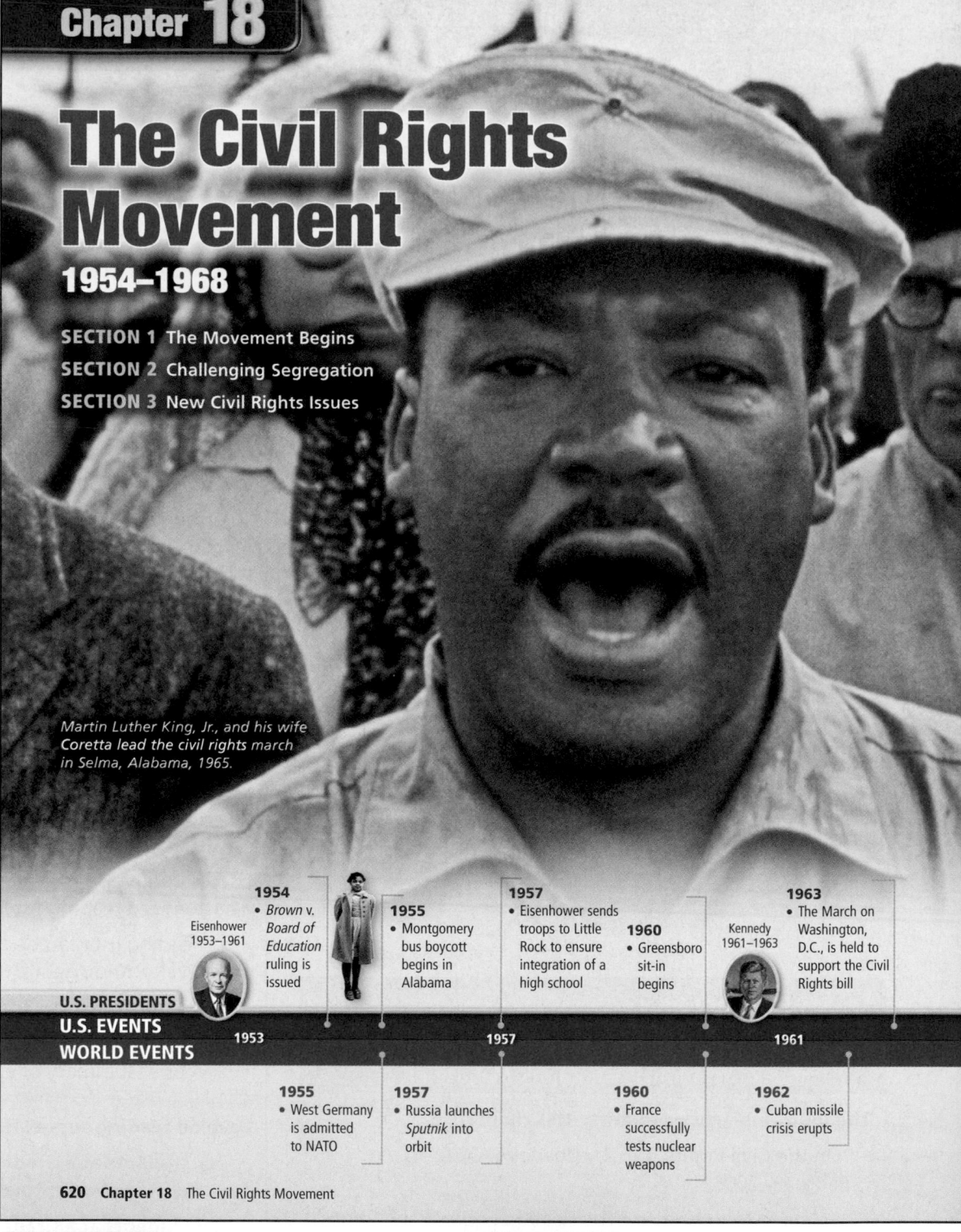

Chapter 18

The Civil Rights Movement
1954–1968

SECTION 1 The Movement Begins
SECTION 2 Challenging Segregation
SECTION 3 New Civil Rights Issues

Martin Luther King, Jr., and his wife Coretta lead the civil rights march in Selma, Alabama, 1965.

U.S. PRESIDENTS
Eisenhower 1953–1961
Kennedy 1961–1963

1954
• *Brown v. Board of Education* ruling is issued

1955
• Montgomery bus boycott begins in Alabama

1957
• Eisenhower sends troops to Little Rock to ensure integration of a high school

1960
• Greensboro sit-in begins

1963
• The March on Washington, D.C., is held to support the Civil Rights bill

U.S. EVENTS
1953   1957   1961

WORLD EVENTS

1955
• West Germany is admitted to NATO

1957
• Russia launches *Sputnik* into orbit

1960
• France successfully tests nuclear weapons

1962
• Cuban missile crisis erupts

620   Chapter 18   The Civil Rights Movement

Section 1

The Movement Begins
Essential Question: How might people work to bring about social change in a democracy? *(People can contact public officials, bring their cases to the courts, vote in elections, and carry out peaceful demonstrations)* Point out that in Section 1 students will learn about the steps taken by African Americans to desegregate public places. **OL**

Section 2

Challenging Segregation
Essential Question: What effect do you think young people can have on the political system? *(Young people can effect change by writing to political leaders, participating in meetings, and going door-to-door to appeal for support.)* Point out in Section 2 students will learn how African American students took part in efforts to end segregation and register voters throughout the South. **OL**

MAKING CONNECTIONS
What Causes Societies to Change?

The civil rights movement gained momentum rapidly after World War II. Decisions by the Supreme Court combined with massive protests by civil rights groups and new federal legislation to finally end racial segregation and disfranchisement in the United States more than 70 years after Southern states had put it in place.

- Why do you think the civil rights movement made gains in postwar America? What strategies were most effective in winning the battle for civil rights?

More About the Photo

Visual Literacy Ask students: What type of activity is taking place in the photo? What people are participating? *(a protest march; African American leaders, such as Martin Luther King, Jr., and Coretta Scott King, as well as some white American citizens)* The main contribution of Martin Luther King, Jr.'s, Southern Christian Leadership Conference (SCLC) to the civil rights movement was a series of highly publicized protest campaigns in Southern cities during the early and mid-1960s. The protests were aimed at forcing white officials and business leaders to end segregation and to allow African Americans to vote. The campaigns involved hundreds, even thousands, of protestors.

FOLDABLES
Study Organizer **Dinah Zike's Foldables**

Dinah Zike's Foldables are three-dimensional, interactive graphic organizers that help students practice basic writing skills, review vocabulary terms, and identify main ideas. Instructions for creating and using Foldables can be found in the Appendix at the end of this book and in the *Dinah Zike's Reading and Study Skills Foldables* booklet.

Johnson
1963–1969

1964
- Civil Rights Act of 1964 passes

1965
- Voting Rights Act passes
- Malcolm X is assassinated

1968
- Civil Rights Act of 1968 is passed
- Martin Luther King, Jr., is assassinated

1965   1969

1965
- China's Cultural Revolution begins

1967
- Arab-Israeli War brings many Palestinians under Israeli rule

FOLDABLES

Sequencing Civil Rights Events Create an Accordion Book Foldable to gather information on a time line about various events of the civil rights movement. As you read the chapter, complete the time line by filling in events for roughly 20 years, starting with Roosevelt's Executive Order 8802 of June 1941. The time line should include brief notes on each event.

History ONLINE Chapter Overview
Visit glencoe.com to preview Chapter 18.

Chapter 18   The Civil Rights Movement   **621**

History ONLINE
Introduce students to chapter content and key terms by having them access the Chapter 18 Overview at glencoe.com.

Section 3

New Civil Rights Issues

Essential Question: How do you think people might respond when their hopes for change are not realized? *(Some people might protest peacefully; others might take a violent course of action.)* Point out to students that in Section 3 they will learn how African Americans responded to the slow pace of change in American society. **OL**

8. A The Selma march was the focal point for the nonviolent Southern Christian Leadership Conference (SCLC) campaign for voting rights. To prevent African Americans from voting, white police and deputized citizens brutally attacked Selma marchers in view of television cameras.

9. D The Civil Rights Act of 1964 gave the U.S. attorney general more power to bring lawsuits to force school desegregation. It also made segregation illegal in most public facilities and required private employers to end job discrimination. The EEOC was established as a permanent agency to monitor the ban on job discrimination.

10. D In 1967 President Johnson set up the Kerner Commission to study the causes of the urban riots and make recommendations to prevent them from happening again. The Commission determined that racism was the root cause, dividing the country into two separate and unequal societies. The Commission recommended efforts to fight de facto segregation and to provide jobs and public housing.

11. B Black Muslims called on African Americans to separate from whites and form their own self-governing communities. They ran their own businesses and schools and had their own publications. Black Muslims did not advocate violence, but they did support self-defense. They also were highly critical of the mainstream civil rights movement and its support of integration.

Section 2 *(pp. 630–639)*

8. "Bloody Sunday" occurred in reaction to which event?

A the Selma march

B the passage of the Civil Rights Act of 1964

C the March on Washington

D the assassination of Dr. Martin Luther King, Jr.

9. How did the Civil Rights Act of 1964 help African Americans?

A The act authorized the U.S. attorney general to send federal employees to register voters.

B The act suspended literacy tests in counties where less than half of all adults had been allowed to vote.

C The act outlawed discrimination in housing sales and rentals.

D The act gave the federal government more power to force school desegregation.

Section 3 *(pp. 642–647)*

10. In response to the race riots in the mid-1960s, the federal government established which of the following?

A SNCC

B EEOC

C Chicago Movement

D Kerner Commission

11. What did the Nation of Islam, or the Black Muslims, advocate?

A African Americans should use nonviolent resistance to fight for civil rights.

B African Americans should separate from whites and form their own government.

C African Americans should use violence to overthrow the government and establish their own nation.

D African Americans should sue the federal government to establish equality among the nation's citizens.

Critical Thinking

Directions: Choose the best answers to the following questions.

12. Which group worked to fight segregation and other inequalities primarily through the courts?

A NAACP   **C** SCLC

B SNCC   **D** CEEO

Base your answers to questions 13 and 14 on the map below and on your knowledge of Chapter 18.

Route of the Freedom Riders, 1961

13. The route of the Freedom Riders focused on which region of the United States?

A the Midwest

B the South

C New England

D the West

14. The final destination of the Freedom Riders was

A Montgomery, Alabama.

B Washington, D.C.

C Selma, Alabama.

D Jackson, Mississippi.

Need Extra Help?							
If You Missed Questions . . .	8	9	10	11	12	13	14
Go to Page . . .	638–639	636–637	643–644	645	622–623	R15	R15

650 **Chapter 18** The Civil Rights Movement

Critical Thinking

12. A The National Association for the Advancement of Colored People (NAACP) supported court cases intended to overturn segregation. It achieved a string of court victories that led to the landmark *Brown* v. *Board of Education* ruling in 1954 that segregation in public schools was unconstitutional.

13. B In 1961, teams of African American and white volunteers known as Freedom Riders rode buses into the South to protest the continued illegal segregation on interstate bus lines. Violence against the Freedom Riders forced President Kennedy to take more action on behalf of civil rights.

14. D The Freedom Ride ended in Jackson, Mississippi, where the Riders were met by an angry mob of segregationists and arrested by local police. Attorney General Robert Kennedy had agreed to the arrests in return for a guarantee of the Riders' safety.

15. Huey Newton, Eldridge Cleaver, and Bobby Seale founded which militant African American group?

A the Black Muslims

B the Black Panthers

C SNCC

D the Chicago Movement

Analyze the cartoon and answer the questions that follow. Base your answers on the cartoon and on your knowledge of Chapter 18.

16. In this cartoon, American cities are represented by

A riots.

B water.

C mines.

D ships.

17. Which of the following describes the main idea of this cartoon?

A American cities are being destroyed by racial issues.

B American cities are much like ships.

C American cities need to change direction.

D American cities should avoid racial issues.

Document-Based Questions

Directions: Analyze the document and answer the short-answer questions that follow the document.

On the evening of July 2, 1964, as he prepared to sign the historic Civil Rights Act of 1964, President Lyndon Johnson made a televised address to the American people. Below is an excerpt:

> "I want to take this occasion to talk to you about what . . . [the Civil Rights Act of 1964] means to every American. . . . We believe that all men are created equal. Yet many are denied equal treatment. . . . We believe that all men are entitled to the blessings of liberty. Yet millions are being deprived of those blessings—not because of their own failures, but because of the color of their skin. The reasons are deeply imbedded in history and tradition and the nature of man. We can understand—without rancor or hatred—how this all happened. But it cannot continue. Our Constitution, the foundation of our Republic, forbids it. The principles of our freedom forbid it. Morality forbids it. And the law I will sign tonight forbids it."
>
> —Lyndon Johnson

18. According to Johnson, what are the origins of racism?

19. What does Johnson say forbids the continuation of racism in the United States?

Extended Response

20. Select one of the African American leaders who advocated a more militant approach to the problems of racism in America than did Martin Luther King, Jr. Write an essay comparing and contrasting the ideas of that figure with King's ideas, providing your views on which approach was more effective and why. Your essay should include an introduction and at least three paragraphs with supporting details from the chapter.

History ONLINE

For additional test practice, use Self-Check Quizzes—Chapter 18 at glencoe.com.

Need Extra Help?

If You Missed Questions . . .	15	16	17	18	19	20
Go to Page . . .	645–646	R18	R18	636–637	636–637	642–647

---

20. Student essays will vary but should coherently compare and contrast the ideas of King with one of the militant African American leaders, and provide a reasoned opinion about the greater efficacy of one of the approaches

15. B The Black Panthers, founded by Huey Newton, Eldridge Cleaver, and Bobby Seale, believed that a revolution by African Americans was necessary to force whites to grant equal rights. Black Panther leaders called for control of major institutions in the African American community, such as schools and housing.

16. D American cities, represented by ships, are threatened by riots, tension, and racial violence, all symbolized as a minefield.

17. A The cartoon states that, in the summer of 1966, cities in the United States were being destroyed by racial issues.

Document-Based Questions

18. The origins of racism are deeply embedded in history, tradition, and human nature.

19. According to President Johnson, the U.S. Constitution, the principles of freedom, morality, and the Civil Rights Act (1964) forbid racism in the United States.

History ONLINE

Have students visit the Web site at glencoe.com to review Chapter 18 and take the Self-Check Quiz.

Need Extra Help?

Have students refer to the pages listed if they miss any of the questions.

Key to Ability Levels	
BL Below Level	**AL** Above Level
OL On Level	**ELL** English Language Learners

Key to Teaching Resources	
Print Material	DVD
CD-ROM	Transparency

Levels					Resources	Chapter Opener	Section 1	Section 2	Section 3	Chapter Assess
BL	OL	AL	ELL		**FOCUS**					
BL	OL	AL	ELL	🖨	**Daily Focus Transparencies**		19-1	19-2	19-3	
					TEACH					
BL	OL	AL	ELL	📁	**Reading Essentials and Note-Taking Guide***		p. 200	p. 203	p. 206	
BL	OL		ELL	📁	**Reading Skills Activity, URB**			p. 85		
	OL			📁	**Historical Analysis Skills Activity, URB**		p. 86			
BL	OL		ELL	📁	**Guided Reading Activity, URB***		p. 112	p. 113	p. 114	
BL	OL	AL	ELL	📁	**Differentiated Instruction Activity, URB**			p. 87		
BL	OL		ELL	📁	**English Learner Activity, URB**				p. 89	
BL	OL	AL	ELL	📁	**Content Vocabulary Activity, URB***	p. 91				
BL	OL	AL	ELL	📁	**Academic Vocabulary Activity, URB**	p. 93				
	OL	AL		📁	**Reinforcing Skills Activity, URB**					p. 95
	OL	AL		📁	**Critical Thinking Skills Activity, URB**		p. 96			
BL	OL		ELL	📁	**Time Line Activity, URB**					p. 97
	OL			📁	**Linking Past and Present Activity, URB**					p. 98
BL	OL	AL	ELL	📁	**Primary Source Reading, URB**		p. 99	p. 101		
BL	OL	AL	ELL	📁	**American Art and Music Activity, URB**					p. 103
BL	OL	AL	ELL	📁	**Interpreting Political Cartoons Activity, URB**					p. 105
		AL		📁	**Enrichment Activity, URB**				p. 109	
BL	OL	AL	ELL	📁	**Differentiated Instruction for the American History Classroom**	✓	✓	✓	✓	
BL	OL	AL	ELL	🖨	**Unit Map Overlay Transparencies**	✓	✓	✓	✓	✓
BL	OL	AL	ELL	📁	**Unit Time Line Transparencies, Strategies, and Activities**	✓	✓	✓	✓	✓
BL	OL	AL	ELL	📁	**Cause and Effect Transparencies, Strategies, and Activities**	✓	✓	✓	✓	✓
BL	OL	AL	ELL	📁	**Why It Matters Chapter Transparencies, Strategies, and Activities**	✓	✓	✓	✓	✓
BL	OL	AL	ELL	📁	**American Biographies**			✓		

Note: Please refer to the *Unit 6 Resource Book* for this chapter's URB materials.

* Also available in Spanish

- Interactive Lesson Planner
- Interactive Teacher Edition
- Fully editable blackline masters
- Section Spotlight Videos Launch
- Differentiated Lesson Plans
- Printable reports of daily assignments
- Standards Tracking System

Levels BL	OL	AL	ELL		Resources	Chapter Opener	Section 1	Section 2	Section 3	Chapter Assess
					TEACH (continued)					
BL	OL	AL		📁	**Supreme Court Case Studies**				p. 109	
BL	OL	AL	ELL	📁	**The Living Constitution**	✓	✓	✓	✓	✓
BL	OL	AL	ELL	📁	**American Issues**	✓	✓	✓	✓	✓
	OL	AL	ELL	📁	**American Art and Architecture Transparencies, Strategies, and Activities**	✓	✓	✓	✓	✓
BL	OL	AL		📁	**High School American History Literature Library**	✓	✓	✓	✓	✓
	OL	AL		💿	**American History Primary Source Documents Library**	✓	✓	✓	✓	✓
BL	OL	AL	ELL	💿	**American Music: Hits Through History CD**	✓	✓	✓	✓	✓
BL	OL	AL	ELL	🔒	**StudentWorks™ Plus DVD**	✓	✓	✓	✓	✓
BL	OL	AL	ELL	💿	**Vocabulary PuzzleMaker CD-ROM**	✓	✓	✓	✓	✓
BL	OL	AL	ELL	🔒	*The American Vision* **Video Program DVD**	✓	✓	✓	✓	✓
Teacher Resources				📁	**Reading Strategies and Activities for the Social Studies Classroom**	✓	✓	✓	✓	✓
				📁	**Strategies for Success**	✓	✓	✓	✓	✓
				🔒	**Presentation Plus! DVD**	✓	✓	✓	✓	✓
				📁	**Success With English Learners**					
					ASSESS					
BL	OL	AL	ELL	📁	**Section Quizzes and Chapter Tests***		p. 267	p. 260	p. 269	p. 271
BL	OL	AL	ELL	📁	**Authentic Assessment With Rubrics**					p. 45
BL	OL	AL	ELL	📁	**Standardized Test Practice Workbook**					p. 45
BL	OL	AL	ELL	💿	*ExamView®* **Assessment Suite CD-ROM**		19-1	19-2	19-3	Ch. 19
BL	OL	AL	ELL	💿	**Interactive Tutor Self-Assessment CD-ROM**		19-1	19-2	19-3	Ch. 19
					CLOSE					
BL			ELL	📁	**Reteaching Activity, URB**					p. 107
BL	OL		ELL	📁	**Reading and Study Skills Foldables™**	p. 80				
BL	OL	AL	ELL	📁	**American History in Graphic Novel**			p. 65	p. 73	

Using the Glencoe Web Site

Chapter Overviews

Technology Product
The Glencoe Web site offers in-depth overviews that summarize the content of each chapter. The overviews consist of brief chapter summaries and separate overviews for each section. The chapter overviews
- summarize and reinforce chapter content;
- provide discussion points to use in class.

Objectives
The overviews help students
- prepare for better understanding chapter content;
- practice reading and comprehension skills.

Steps
- Provide students with the following steps to complete the activities:
- Locate the Web page for the textbook being studied on the Glencoe Web site glencoe.com.
- Click on **Student Center** under the textbook title.

- Once you are in the Student Center, select a unit from the Unit Resources menu and a chapter from the Chapter Activities menu using the drop-down arrows.
- Click on the **Chapter Overviews** link.
- Have students read the chapter overview in preparation for a reading assignment or activity.

History ONLINE

	Student	Teacher	Parent
Beyond the Textbook	●	●	●
Chapter Overviews	●	●	●
Time Current Events	●		●
ePuzzles and Games	●		●
Concepts in Motion	●		●
Literature Connections		●	
Multi-Language Glossaries	●		●
Online Student Edition	●	●	●
Self-Check Quizzes	●		●
Student Web Activities	●		●
Study Central ™	●		●
Teaching Today		●	
Vocabulary eFlashcards	●		●
Web Activity Lesson Plans		●	

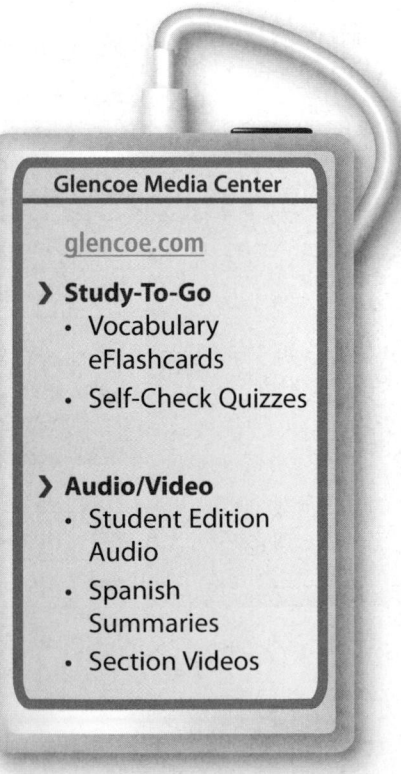

Glencoe Media Center

glencoe.com

❭ **Study-To-Go**
- Vocabulary eFlashcards
- Self-Check Quizzes

❭ **Audio/Video**
- Student Edition Audio
- Spanish Summaries
- Section Videos

READING SUPPORT FROM JAMESTOWN EDUCATION

- **Timed Readings Plus in Social Studies** helps students increase their reading rate and fluency while maintaining comprehension. The 400-word passages are similar to those found on state and national assessments.

- **Reading in the Content Area: Social Studies** concentrates on six essential reading skills that help students better comprehend what they read. The book includes 75 high-interest nonfiction passages written at increasing levels of difficulty.

- **Reading Social Studies** includes strategic reading instruction and vocabulary support in Social Studies content for both ELLs and native speakers of English.

www.jamestowneducation.com

NATIONAL GEOGRAPHIC

Index to National Geographic Magazine:

The following articles relate to this chapter:

- "Hanoi: Shedding the Ghosts of War," by David Lamb, May 2004.

- "Saigon: Fourteen Years After," by Peter T. White, November 1989.

Access National Geographic's new, dynamic MapMachine Web site and other geography resources at:
www.nationalgeographic.com
www.nationalgeographic.com/maps

The following videotape programs are available from Glencoe as supplements to Chapter 19:

- Vietnam: A Soldier's Diary (ISBN 0-76-700772-7)

- War Memorials - Great American Monuments (ISBN 1-56-501643-2)

To order, call Glencoe at 1-800-334-7344. To find classroom resources to accompany many of these videos, check the following home pages:

A&E Television: www.aetv.com
The History Channel: www.historychannel.com

Reading List Generator CD-ROM

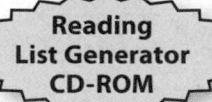

GLENCOE BOOKLINK 3

Use this database to search more than 30,000 titles to create a customized reading list for your students.

- Reading lists can be organized by students' reading level, author, genre, theme, or area of interest.

- The database provides Degrees of Reading Power™ (DRP) and Lexile™ readability scores for all selections.

- A brief summary of each selection is included.

Leveled reading suggestions for this chapter:

For students at a Grade 8 reading level:
- *Young Man in Vietnam,* by Charles Coe

For students at a Grade 9 reading level:
- *Dear America: Letters Home from Vietnam,* by Bernard Edelman

For students at a Grade 10 reading level:
- *Getting to Know the Two Vietnams,* by Fred West

For students at a Grade 11 reading level:
- *Voices from Vietnam,* by Barry Denenberg

For students at a Grade 12 reading level:
- *The Vietnam War,* by Debbie Levy

Focus

MAKING CONNECTIONS
Should Citizens Support the Government During Wartime?
Invite a volunteer to read the paragraph and questions presented. Use the questions provided to begin a discussion about the Vietnam conflict. Have students write the two questions in their notebooks, adding to their answers as they read the chapter. **OL**

Teach
The Big Ideas

As students study the chapter, remind them to consider the section-based Big Ideas included in each section's Guide to Reading. The **Essential Questions** in the activities below tie in to the Big Ideas and help students think about and understand important chapter concepts. In addition, the Hands-on Chapter Projects with their culminating activities relate the content from each section to the Big Ideas. These activities build on each other as students progress through the chapter. Section activities culminate in the wrap-up activity on the Visual Summary page.

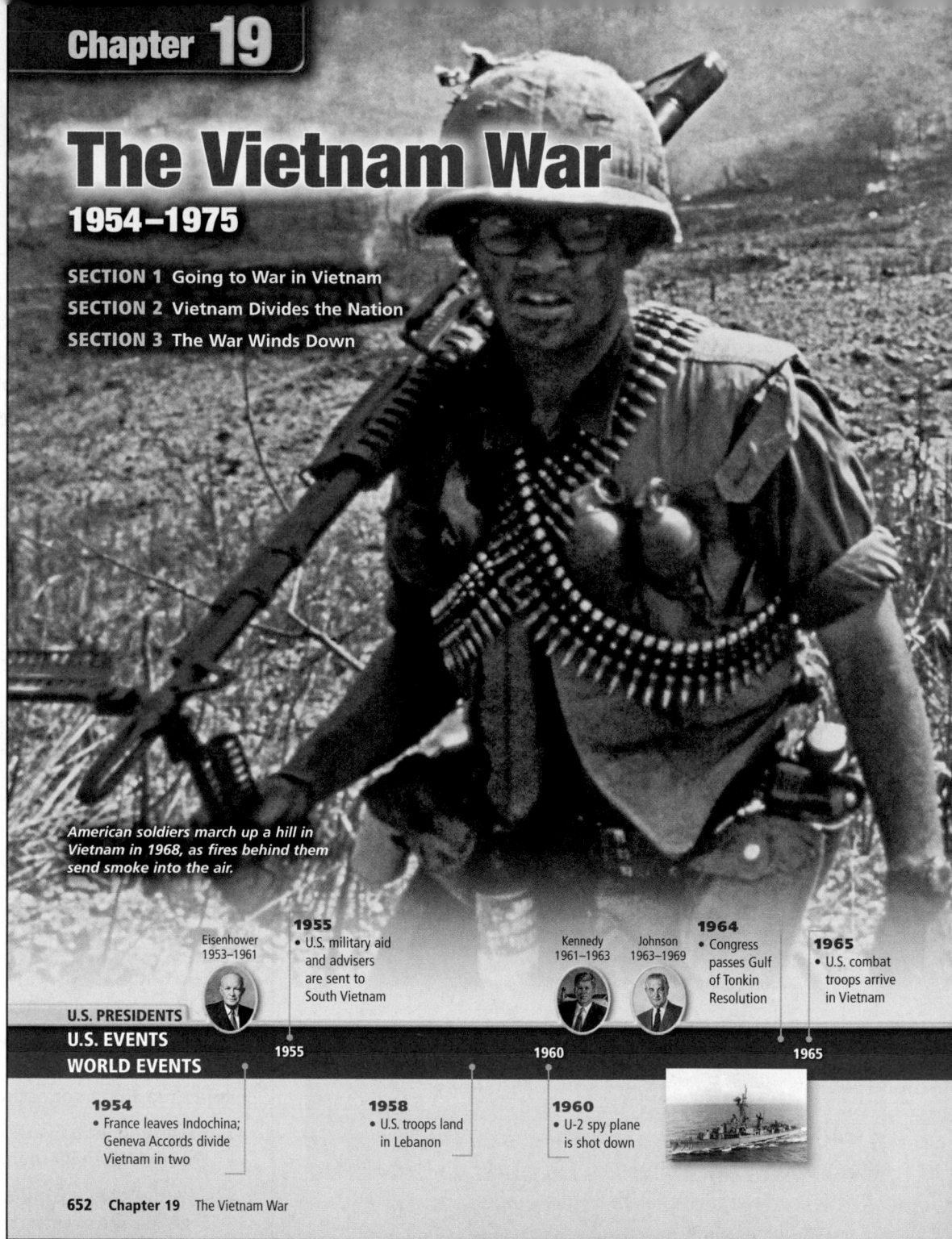

Chapter 19

The Vietnam War
1954–1975

SECTION 1 Going to War in Vietnam
SECTION 2 Vietnam Divides the Nation
SECTION 3 The War Winds Down

American soldiers march up a hill in Vietnam in 1968, as fires behind them send smoke into the air.

U.S. PRESIDENTS
U.S. EVENTS
WORLD EVENTS

Eisenhower 1953–1961

1955
• U.S. military aid and advisers are sent to South Vietnam

Kennedy 1961–1963

Johnson 1963–1969

1964
• Congress passes Gulf of Tonkin Resolution

1965
• U.S. combat troops arrive in Vietnam

1955   1960   1965

1954
• France leaves Indochina; Geneva Accords divide Vietnam in two

1958
• U.S. troops land in Lebanon

1960
• U-2 spy plane is shot down

652   Chapter 19   The Vietnam War

Section 1

Going to War in Vietnam
Essential Question: What created the conflict in Vietnam and how did America become involved? *(The desire for independence from France fueled rebellion. The United States became involved first by aiding the French and later by committing military advisers and troops to prevent the fall of Vietnam to communism.)* Tell students they will learn in this section how the United States began fighting in Vietnam. **OL**

Section 2

Vietnam Divides the Nation
Essential Question: How did Americans protest against the war in Vietnam? *(Teach-ins were held at universities; some men burned draft cards; people held protest marches.)* Inform students that in this section they will read about the protest movement, which helped to change the culture of the United States and its relationship to the federal government. **OL**

MAKING CONNECTIONS
Should Citizens Support the Government During Wartime?

During the Cold War, the United States sent troops to Vietnam to stop the spread of communism. Winning in Vietnam proved to be difficult and, as the war dragged on, many Americans began to protest. Eventually, the United States pulled out of Vietnam.

- *Why do you think the United States sent troops to Vietnam?*
- *Why do you think Vietnam divided Americans?*

1968
- Tet Offensive begins
- Anti-war protest in Chicago

Nixon 1969–1974

1970
- National Guard troops kill student protesters at Kent State

1973
- Last U.S. troops leave Vietnam

1970

1975

1970
- Nixon orders invasion of Cambodia

1975
- Saigon falls to North Vietnamese invasion

FOLDABLES
Defining Vietnam Terminology
Make a Vocabulary Book Foldable to aid your review of the Vietnam War. Select terms for a 10-tab Vocabulary Book. Example terms include: *Ho Chi Minh, Containment,* and *Gulf of Tonkin Resolution.* Define the terms under the appropriate tab.

History **ONLINE Chapter Overview**
Visit glencoe.com to preview Chapter 19.

Chapter 19 The Vietnam War **653**

More About the Photo

Visual Literacy In 1969, the year after this photo was taken, the number of American troops reached their peak of about 540,000. Many of the soldiers were a year or two out of high school. Both civilian and military photographers covered the war, enduring the same hardships and risks as soldiers with some losing their lives. Thousands of the photographs taken by military photographers are housed at the National Archives in Washington, D.C.

FOLDABLES
Study Organizer
Dinah Zike's Foldables

Dinah Zike's Foldables are three-dimensional, interactive graphic organizers that help students practice basic writing skills, review vocabulary terms, and identify main ideas. Instructions for creating and using Foldables can be found in the Appendix at the end of this book and in the *Dinah Zike's Reading and Study Skills Foldables* booklet.

History ONLINE
Introduce students to chapter content and key terms by having them access the Chapter 19 Overview at glencoe.com.

Section 3

The War Winds Down
Essential Question: How did the war end and how did it affect Americans? *(Negotiations dragged on while the military implemented Vietnamization. Ultimately, American troops were withdrawn and South Vietnam fell to communism. Americans became cynical about the war and their government.)* Tell students that this section will describe the end of the war. **OL**

Focus

Bellringer
Daily Focus Transparency 19.1

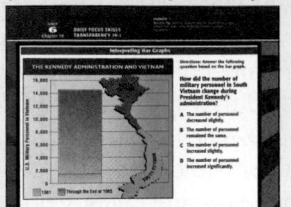

Guide to Reading

Answers: fall of China to communism, the outbreak of the Korean War

Section Spotlight Video

To generate student interest and provide a springboard for class discussion, access the Chapter 19, Section 1 video at glencoe.com or on the video DVD.

Resource Manager

Section 1

Going to War in Vietnam

Guide to Reading

Big Ideas
Trade, War, and Migration American involvement in the war in Vietnam was the result of its Cold War strategy.

Content Vocabulary
• domino theory (p. 655)
• guerrilla (p. 655)
• napalm (p. 661)
• Agent Orange (p. 661)

Academic Vocabulary
• strategic (p. 657)
• traditional (p. 657)

People and Events to Identify
• Ho Chi Minh (p. 654)
• Dien Bien Phu (p. 656)
• Geneva Accords (p. 656)
• Ngo Dinh Diem (p. 656)
• Vietcong (p. 657)
• Gulf of Tonkin Resolution (p. 658)
• Ho Chi Minh trail (p. 661)

Reading Strategy
Organizing Complete a graphic organizer similar to the one below by providing reasons why the United States aided France in Vietnam.

In the late 1940s and early 1950s, most Americans knew little about Indochina, France's colony in Southeast Asia. During the Cold War, however, American officials became concerned the region might fall to communism. Eventually, American troops were sent to fight in Vietnam.

American Involvement in Vietnam

MAIN Idea The Cold War policy of containment led the United States to become increasingly involved in events in Vietnam.

HISTORY AND YOU Have you met anyone who was born in Vietnam? Do you know why he or she left? Read to learn about Vietnam's complicated and tragic history.

In 1940, the Japanese invaded Vietnam. The occupation was only the latest example of foreigners ruling the Vietnamese people. The Chinese Empire had controlled the region for hundreds of years. Then, beginning in the late 1800s and lasting until World War II, France ruled Vietnam as well as neighboring Laos and Cambodia—a region known collectively as French Indochina.

The Growth of Vietnamese Nationalism

The Vietnamese did not want to be ruled by foreigners, and by the early 1900s, nationalism had become a powerful force in the country. The Vietnamese formed several political parties to push for independence or for reform of the French colonial government. One of the leaders of the nationalist movement for almost 30 years was Nguyen Tat Thanh—better known by his assumed name, **Ho Chi Minh.** At the age of 21, Ho Chi Minh traveled to Europe where he lived in London and then Paris. In 1919 he presented a petition for Vietnamese independence at the Versailles Peace Conference, but the peace treaty ignored the issue. Ho Chi Minh later visited the Soviet Union where he became an advocate of communism. In 1930 he returned to Southeast Asia, helped found the Indochinese Communist Party, and worked to overthrow French rule.

Ho Chi Minh's activities made him a wanted man. He fled Indochina and spent several years in exile in the Soviet Union and China. In 1941 he returned to Vietnam. By then, Japan had seized control of the country. Ho Chi Minh organized a nationalist group called the Vietminh. The group united both Communists and non-Communists in the struggle to expel the Japanese forces. Soon afterward, the United States began sending aid to the Vietminh.

R **Reading Strategies**	C **Critical Thinking**	D **Differentiated Instruction**	W **Writing Support**	S **Skill Practice**
Teacher Edition • Act. Prior Know., p. 655 • Making Connections, p. 657 **Additional Resources** • Prim. Source Read, URB p. 99 • Guide Read Act., URB p. 112	**Teacher Edition** • Analyzing, p. 655 • Det. Cause and Effect, p. 657 • Making Generalizations, p. 658 • Contrasting, p. 660 **Additional Resources** • Crit. Think Skills, URB p. 96 • Quizzes and Tests, p. 267	**Teacher Edition** • English Learners, p. 658 • Logical/Math., p. 660 • Naturalist, p. 661 **Additional Resources** • Foldables, p. 80	**Additional Resources** • Content Vocab. Act., URB p. 91 • Academic Vocab. Act., URB p. 93	**Teacher Edition** • Using Geo. Skills, p. 656 **Additional Resources** • Hist. Analysis Skills Act., URB p. 86 • RENTG, p. 200

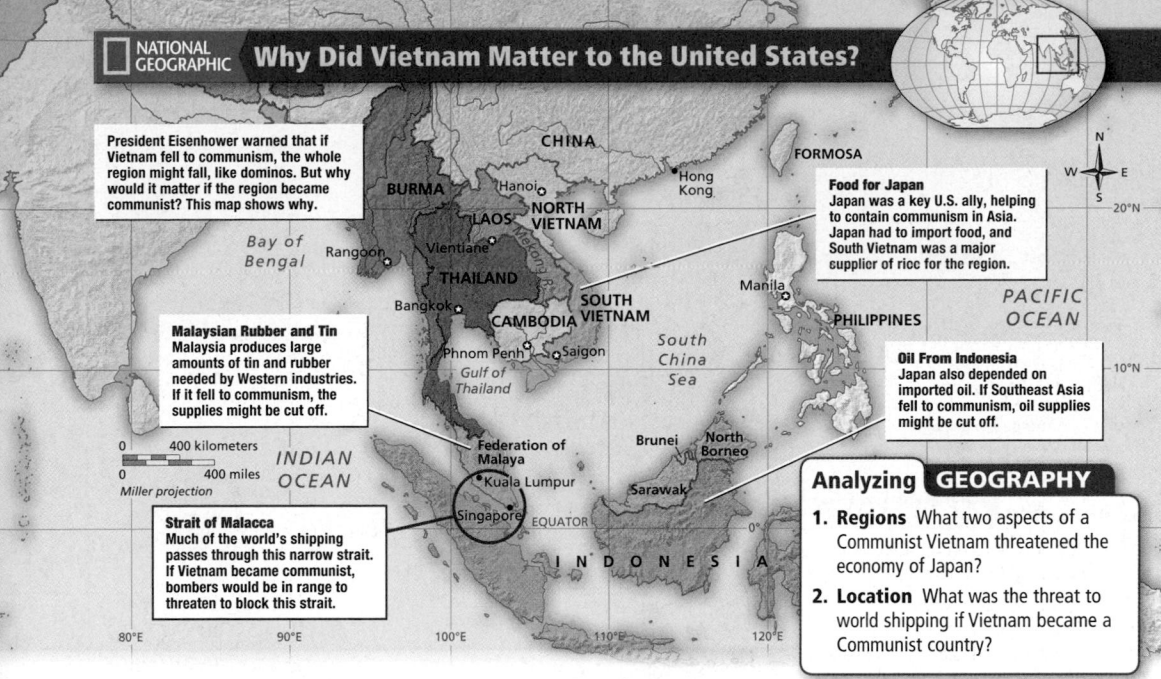

Why Did Vietnam Matter to the United States?

President Eisenhower warned that if Vietnam fell to communism, the whole region might fall, like dominos. But why would it matter if the region became communist? This map shows why.

Food for Japan
Japan was a key U.S. ally, helping to contain communism in Asia. Japan had to import food, and South Vietnam was a major supplier of rice for the region.

Malaysian Rubber and Tin
Malaysia produces large amounts of tin and rubber needed by Western industries. If it fell to communism, the supplies might be cut off.

Oil From Indonesia
Japan also depended on imported oil. If Southeast Asia fell to communism, oil supplies might be cut off.

Strait of Malacca
Much of the world's shipping passes through this narrow strait. If Vietnam became communist, bombers would be in range to threaten to block this strait.

Analyzing GEOGRAPHY
1. **Regions** What two aspects of a Communist Vietnam threatened the economy of Japan?
2. **Location** What was the threat to world shipping if Vietnam became a Communist country?

Teach

C Critical Thinking

Analyzing Invite a volunteer to read the quotation by Eisenhower. **Ask:** What is the "flaw" in this argument? *(It is based on a presupposition that nations act like game pieces. Students should question the validity of Eisenhower's reference to "the certainty that it will go over very quickly.")* **AL**

R Reading Strategy

Activating Prior Knowledge
Ask: What previous experience did Americans have with guerrilla warfare? *(They had fought Filipino guerillas.)* **OL**

Analyzing GEOGRAPHY

Answers:
1. Japan depended on Vietnam for food and a communist Vietnam could threaten its oil supply from Indonesia
2. Vietnam might control the Straits of Malacca.

America Aids the French

When Japan surrendered to the Allies in 1945, it gave up control of Indochina. Ho Chi Minh quickly declared Vietnam to be an independent nation. France, however, had no intention of allowing Vietnam to become independent. Seeking to regain their colonial empire in Southeast Asia, French troops returned to Vietnam in 1946 and drove the Vietminh forces into hiding in the countryside.

The Vietminh fought back against the French-dominated regime and slowly gained control of large areas of the countryside. As the fighting escalated, France appealed to the United States for help. The request put American officials in a difficult position. The United States opposed colonialism. It had pressured the Dutch to give up their empire in Indonesia and supported the British decision to give India independence in 1947. In Vietnam, however, the independence movement had become entangled with the Communist movement. American officials did not want France to control Vietnam, but they also did not want Vietnam to be communist.

Two events convinced President Truman to help France—the fall of China to communism and the outbreak of the Korean War. The latter, in particular, seemed to indicate that the Soviet Union had begun a major push to impose communism on East Asia. Shortly after the Korean War began, Truman authorized military aid to French forces in Vietnam. President Eisenhower continued Truman's policy and defended his decision with what became known as the **domino theory**—the idea that if Vietnam fell to communism, the rest of Southeast Asia would follow:

PRIMARY SOURCE

"You have a row of dominoes set up, you knock over the first one, and what will happen to the last one is the certainty that it will go over very quickly. . . . Asia, after all, has already lost some 450 million of its peoples to Communist dictatorship, and we simply can't afford greater losses." **C**

—President Eisenhower, quoted in *America in Vietnam*

Defeat at Dien Bien Phu

Despite aid from the United States, the French continued to struggle against the Vietminh, who consistently frustrated the French with hit-and-run and ambush tactics. **R** These are the tactics of **guerrillas,** irregular troops who blend into the civilian population and are difficult for regular armies to fight.

Hands-On Chapter Project
Step 1

Create a Documentary of the Vietnam War

Step 1: Determining the Theme
Essential question: What were the milestones in the Vietnam War?

Directions Write the essential question on the board and explain to students that in this first step, different groups will create the basic storyline for a documentary of the Vietnam War. For example, a documentary could describe the battles of the war, the U.S. presidents conducting the war, army life, or life at home during the war.

Putting It Together Later, each group should make a presentation to persuade the others about the merits of their choice. (Students could think about the arguments and style a young filmmaker might use to persuade potential backers about backing his or her project.) **OL**
(Chapter Project continued on page 665)

Using Geography Skills Ask students to calculate the distance from Dien Bien Phu to Hanoi, the North Vietnamese capital, and to Saigon, which had been the French capital. *(about 200 miles to Hanoi and 800 miles to Saigon)* **OL**

Analyzing GEOGRAPHY

Answers:

1. For security reasons, it was better for communist China to have a communist neighbor.

2. Shipping by sea would have been difficult because of American ships guarding the South China Sea; shipping overland through hundreds of miles of jungle was time-consuming and dangerous.

✔ **Reading Check**

Answer: He sought independence for Vietnam.

Additional Support

NATIONAL GEOGRAPHIC **Vietnam, 1959**

▲ *Ho Chi Minh, Communist leader of North Vietnam, was determined to reunite Vietnam and began arming Vietcong guerrillas to seize power in South Vietnam.*

Analyzing GEOGRAPHY

1. **Regions** Why do you think Mao supported North Vietnam?
2. **Human-Environment Interaction** What difficulties would North Vietnam face in sending aid to the Vietcong?

▲ *Mao Zedong, leader of Communist China, supported North Vietnam.*

▲ *Ngo Dinh Diem, South Vietnam's president, accepted American aid to fight the Vietcong.*

The mounting casualties and the inability of the French to defeat the Vietminh made the war very unpopular in France. Finally, in 1954 the struggle reached a turning point when the French commander ordered his forces to occupy the mountain town of **Dien Bien Phu.** Seizing the town would interfere with the Vietminh's supply lines and force them into open battle. Soon afterward, a huge Vietminh force surrounded Dien Bien Phu and began bombarding the town. On May 7, 1954, the French force at Dien Bien Phu fell to the Vietminh. The defeat convinced the French to make peace and withdraw from Indochina.

Geneva Accords

Negotiations to end the conflict were held in Geneva, Switzerland. The **Geneva Accords** divided Vietnam along the 17th parallel, with Ho Chi Minh and the Vietminh in control of North Vietnam and a pro-Western regime in control of the South. In 1956 elections were to be held to reunite the country under a single government. The Geneva Accords also recog-

nized Cambodia's independence. Laos had gained independence in the previous year.

Shortly after the Geneva Accords partitioned Vietnam, the French troops left. The United States became the principal protector of the new government in the South, led by a nationalist leader named **Ngo Dinh Diem** (NOH DIHN deh•EHM). Like Ho Chi Minh, Diem had been educated abroad, but, unlike the North Vietnamese leader, Diem was pro-Western and fiercely anti-Communist. A Catholic, he welcomed the roughly one million North Vietnamese Catholics who migrated south to escape Ho Chi Minh's rule.

The elections mandated by the Geneva Accords never took place. In a special referendum, Diem became president of the new Republic of Vietnam in the South. He then refused to permit the 1956 elections, fearing Ho Chi Minh would win. Eisenhower approved Diem's actions and increased American aid to South Vietnam.

✔ **Reading Check** **Summarizing** Why did Ho Chi Minh lead a resistance movement against France?

Extending the Content

Ngo Dinh Diem Diem's ancestors had converted to Catholicism. They were also a noble family with connections to the imperial family. Frustrated at the French unwillingness to implement legislative reforms he suggested, in 1933 Diem resigned his post as Minister of the Interior.

In 1945 Diem was captured by forces of Ho Chi Minh, who hoped he would join an independent government in the north. Diem refused, however, and lived outside the country for most of the following decade. He returned at the emperor's request to serve as prime minister in 1954; the following year, after a government-controlled referendum, Diem made himself president and staffed his regime with family members. Diem imprisoned and killed hun-

dreds of Buddhists, whom he accused of aiding the Communists. This action in a land primarily Buddhist cost him the support not only of his own people but of the United States.

America Becomes Involved in Vietnam

MAIN Idea Political pressures in the United States led the nation to become deeply involved in the civil war in Vietnam.

HISTORY AND YOU Do you have a relative or family friend who fought in the Vietnam War? Read on to find out why the United States got involved in this complicated conflict.

After Ngo Dinh Diem refused to hold national elections and began to crack down on Communist groups in South Vietnam, Ho Chi Minh and the Communists began an armed struggle to reunify the nation. They organized a new guerrilla army of South Vietnamese Communists, which became known as the **Vietcong.** As fighting began between the Vietcong and South Vietnam's forces, President Eisenhower sent hundreds of military advisers to train South Vietnam's army.

Despite American assistance, the Vietcong continued to grow more powerful because many Vietnamese opposed Diem's government. The Vietcong's use of terror was also effective. By 1961, the Vietcong had assassinated thousands of government officials and established control over much of the countryside. In response Diem looked increasingly to the United States for help.

Kennedy Takes Over

On taking office in 1961, President Kennedy continued the nation's policy of support for South Vietnam. Like Presidents Truman and Eisenhower before him, Kennedy saw the Southeast Asian country as vitally important in the battle against communism.

In political terms, Kennedy needed to appear tough on communism, since Republicans often accused Democrats of having lost China to communism during the Truman administration. From 1961 to late 1963, the number of American military personnel in South Vietnam jumped from about 2,000 to around 15,000.

American officials believed that the Vietcong continued to grow because Diem's government was unpopular and corrupt. They urged him to create a more democratic government and to introduce reforms to help Vietnam's peasants. Diem introduced some limited reforms, but they had little effect.

One program Diem introduced, at the urging of American advisers, made the situation worse. The South Vietnamese created special fortified villages known as **strategic** hamlets. These villages were protected by machine guns, bunkers, trenches, and barbed wire. Vietnamese officials then moved villagers to the strategic hamlets. The program proved to be extremely unpopular. Many peasants resented being uprooted from their villages, where they had worked to build farms and where many of their ancestors lay buried.

The Overthrow of Diem

Diem made himself even more unpopular by discriminating against Buddhism, one of the country's most widely practiced religions. In the spring of 1963, Diem, a Catholic, banned the **traditional** religious flags for Buddha's birthday. When Buddhists took to the streets in protest, Diem's police killed 9 people and injured 14 others. In the demonstrations that followed, a Buddhist monk poured gasoline over his robes and set himself on fire, the first of several Buddhists to do so. Images of their self-destruction horrified Americans as they watched the footage on television news reports. These extreme acts of protest were a disturbing sign of the opposition to the Diem regime.

In August 1963 American ambassador Henry Cabot Lodge arrived in Vietnam. He quickly learned that Diem's unpopularity had so alarmed several Vietnamese generals that they were plotting to overthrow him. When Lodge expressed American sympathy for their cause, the generals launched a military coup. They seized power on November 1, 1963, and executed Diem shortly afterward.

Diem's overthrow only made matters worse. Despite his unpopularity with some Vietnamese, Diem had been a respected nationalist and a capable administrator. After his death, South Vietnam's government grew increasingly weak and unstable. The United States became even more deeply involved in order to prop it up. Coincidentally, three weeks after Diem's death, President Kennedy was assassinated. The presidency, as well as the growing problem of Vietnam, now belonged to Kennedy's vice president, Lyndon Johnson.

C **Critical Thinking**

Determining Cause and Effect Invite students to create graphic organizers showing the cause-and-effect relationships in the segment "Kennedy Takes Over." *(Possible answers include: Cause: Kennedy does not want to appear soft on communism. Effect: number of military personnel in South Vietnam increases. Cause: American officials believe the corruption and unpopularity of Diem's government increased Vietcong growth. Effect: They were sympathetic to his overthrow. Cause: Diem created strategic hamlets. Effect: Program was unpopular among the people.)* **OL**

R **Reading Strategy**

Making Connections Remind students that in the early 2000s some nations, such as France, banned young female Muslims from wearing their traditional head scarves to schools. In the Netherlands, the government proposed banning female Muslims from wearing a burka, a garment that covers both the head and body. Lead a discussion about the rights of religious minorities and majorities. **OL**

Additional Support

Activity: Collaborative Learning

Model a Diplomatic Mission Divide the class into small groups. Ask students to imagine they are the diplomatic team given the task of planning what ought to be done in South Vietnam in 1961 to prevent the nation from collapsing. Have students present their ideas in panel discussion form or as a dialogue between American and South Vietnamese diplomats. **OL**

658

D **Differentiated Instruction**

English Learners Point out the expression "the battle . . . must be joined" in the quotation by President Johnson. Explain to students that in this case the term *joined* does not refer to a putting together of different parts. Rather, it means that the battle must begin. Remind students that every language has its own idioms that must simply be learned and not to be discouraged by the oddities of English. Encourage students to share an example of an idiom in their own language. **ELL**

C **Critical Thinking**

Making Generalizations
Point out the reference to Johnson's sensitivity to accusations of being soft on communism and to Kennedy's equal sensitivity, discussed on page 657. Remind students that these sensitivities were related to earlier accusations against Truman and to the McCarthy era. Lead a discussion on the question of how much the decisions or mistakes of previous administrations influence current foreign or domestic policies. **OL**

Additional Support

Johnson and Vietnam

D   Initially, President Johnson exercised caution and restraint regarding the conflict in Vietnam. "We seek no wider war," he repeatedly promised. At the same time, Johnson was determined to prevent South Vietnam from becoming communist. "The battle against communism," he declared shortly before becoming president, "must be joined . . . with strength and determination."

    Politics also played a role in Johnson's Vietnam policy. Like Kennedy, Johnson remembered that many Republicans blamed the Truman administration for the fall of China to communism in 1949. Should the Democrats also "lose" Vietnam, Johnson feared, it might cause a "mean and destructive debate that would shatter my Presidency, kill my administration, and damage our democracy."

For the text of the Gulf of Tonkin Resolution see R57 in Documents in American History.

C   **The Gulf of Tonkin Resolution** On August 2, 1964, President Johnson announced that North Vietnamese torpedo boats had fired on two American destroyers in the Gulf of Tonkin. Two days later, the president reported that another similar attack had taken place. Johnson was campaigning for the presidency and was very sensitive to accusations of being soft on communism. He insisted that North Vietnam's attacks were unprovoked and immediately ordered American aircraft to attack North Vietnamese ships and naval facilities. Johnson did not reveal that the American warships had been helping the South Vietnamese conduct electronic spying and commando raids against North Vietnam.

    Johnson then asked Congress for the authority to defend American forces and American allies in Southeast Asia. Congress agreed to Johnson's request with little debate. Most members of Congress agreed with Republican representative Ross Adair of Indiana, who defiantly declared, "The American flag has been fired upon. We will not and cannot tolerate such things."

    On August 7, 1964, the Senate and House passed the **Gulf of Tonkin Resolution,** authorizing the president to "take all necessary measures to repel any armed attack against the forces of the United States and to prevent further aggression." With only two dissenting votes, Congress had, in effect, handed its war powers over to the president.

The United States Sends in Troops

Shortly after Congress passed the Gulf of Tonkin Resolution, the Vietcong began to attack bases where American advisers were stationed in South Vietnam. The attacks began in the fall of 1964 and continued to escalate. After a Vietcong attack on a base at Pleiku in February 1965 left eight Americans dead and more than 100 wounded, President Johnson decided to respond. Less than 14 hours after the attack, American aircraft bombed North Vietnam.

    After the air strikes, one poll showed that Johnson's approval rating on his handling of Vietnam jumped from 41 percent to 60 percent. Further, nearly 80 percent of Americans agreed that without American assistance, Southeast Asia would fall to the Communists. An equivalent number believed that the United States should send combat troops to Vietnam

Debates IN HISTORY

Should America Fight in Vietnam?

As the war in Vietnam dragged on, Americans became increasingly divided about the nation's role in the conflict. In January 1966, George W. Ball, undersecretary of state to President Johnson, delivered an address to indicate "how we got [into Vietnam] and why we must stay." George Kennan, a former ambassador to the Soviet Union, testified before the Senate Foreign Relations Committee in that same year, arguing that American involvement in Vietnam was "something we would not choose deliberately if the choice were ours to make all over again today."

Activity: Interdisciplinary Connection

Civics Invite students to find out who voted against the Gulf of Tonkin Resolution and why they voted against it. Students may decide to extend their research to find out who were the other members of Congress who voted against going to war in previous and subsequent clashes. Ask them to see if there is a common thread among these dissenting voters. Suggest they present their findings as a skit or news interview with one of the dissenters. **OL**

to prevent that from happening. The president's actions also met with strong approval from his closest advisers, including Secretary of Defense Robert McNamara and National Security Adviser McGeorge Bundy.

Some officials disagreed, chief among them Undersecretary of State George Ball, who initially supported involvement in Vietnam but later turned against it. He warned that if the United States got too involved, it would be difficult to get out. "Once on the tiger's back," he warned, "we cannot be sure of picking the place to dismount."

Most of the advisers who surrounded Johnson, however, firmly believed the nation had a duty to halt communism in Vietnam, both to maintain stability in Southeast Asia and to ensure the United States's continuing power and prestige in the world. In a memo to the president, Bundy argued:

PRIMARY SOURCE

"The stakes in Vietnam are extremely high. The American investment is very large, and American responsibility is a fact of life which is palpable in the atmosphere of Asia, and even elsewhere. The international prestige of the U.S. and a substantial part of our influence are directly at risk in Vietnam."

—quoted in *The Best and the Brightest*

In March 1965, President Johnson expanded American involvement by beginning a sustained bombing campaign against North Vietnam code-named Operation Rolling Thunder. That same month, the president also ordered the first combat troops into Vietnam. American soldiers would now fight alongside South Vietnamese troops against the Vietcong.

Reading Check Describing How did politics play a role in President Johnson's Vietnam policy?

Debates IN HISTORY

YES

George W. Ball
Undersecretary of State

PRIMARY SOURCE

"[T]he conflict in Viet-Nam is a product of the great shifts and changes triggered by the Second World War.... [T]he Soviet Union under Stalin exploited the confusion to push out the perimeter of its power and influence in an effort to extend the outer limits of Communist domination by force or the threat of force....

The bloody encounters in [Vietnam] ... are thus in a real sense battles and skirmishes in a continuing war to prevent one Communist power after another from violating internationally recognized boundary lines fixing the outer limits of Communist dominion....

In the long run our hopes for the people of South Vietnam reflect our hopes for people everywhere. What we seek is a world living in peace and freedom."

—Speech delivered January 30, 1966

NO

George F. Kennan
Former Diplomat

PRIMARY SOURCE

"Vietnam is not a region of major military-industrial importance.... Even a situation in which South Vietnam was controlled exclusively by the Vietcong, ... would not present, in my opinion, dangers great enough to justify our direct military intervention.

And to attempt to crush North Vietnamese strength to a point where Hanoi could no longer give any support to Vietcong political activity in the South would... have the effect of bringing in Chinese forces at some point....

Our motives are widely misinterpreted; and the spectacle of Americans inflicting grievous injury on the lives of a poor and helpless people... produces reactions among millions of people throughout the world profoundly detrimental to the image we would like them to hold of this country."

—Testimony before the Senate Foreign Relations Committee, February 10, 1966

DBQ Document-Based Questions

1. **Summarizing** Why does Ball believe that the United States is justified in fighting in Vietnam?
2. **Explaining** What are the three main points of Kennan's argument?
3. **Contrasting** What is the fundamental difference between the views of Ball and Kennan?
4. **Evaluating** With which position do you agree? Write a paragraph to explain your choice.

Answers:
1. Ball argues that the United States wants to protect the Vietnamese from communism. He also sees Vietnam as part of the larger Cold War.
2. Vietnam is unimportant; if the U.S. tried to crush North Vietnam, the Chinese would enter the conflict; the war is giving the world a negative view of the U.S.
3. Ball: Vietnam is strategically important in the Cold War, it is the duty of the U.S. to help maintain its freedom; Kennan: Vietnam is not important and that the U.S. is losing good will around the world over it.
4. Students' paragraphs will vary.

Reading Check

Answer: Johnson thought his presidency would be ruined and democracy damaged if the Democrats lost Vietnam.

Additional Support

Extending the Content

The War in Vietnam One of the contentions of those who did not support the war was that it was a civil war in which the United States had no business intervening. Others thought the conflict was one nation, North Vietnam, conducting a war of aggression against another nation, South Vietnam. In a White Paper issued in February 1965, the State Department argued that Vietnam was a new type of war, a covert war of aggression intended to bring about a communist regime. It described the people of South Vietnam as having courageously resisted these efforts for years, which violated the Geneva Accords, the United Nations Charter, and other international agreements. Many felt that in coming to the aid of South Vietnam, without a desire for military bases or territory there, the United States was acting as a friend to the people of that nation.

D Differentiated Instruction

Logical/Mathematical Ask students to use the data on this page and on page 657 to graph the increase of American troops in Vietnam from 1961 to 1966. Tell them to use a bar graph or line graph to chart their findings. **BL**

C Critical Thinking

Contrasting Invite a volunteer to read the quotation by Linda Martin. **Ask:** In what earlier wars might American soldiers have felt they were more certain and safe? Why? *(Students may say that in previous wars the enemy was readily recognizable and that conventional warfare felt safer than guerrilla attacks.)* **OL**

Analyzing GEOGRAPHY

Answers:
1. Laos, Cambodia
2. South Vietnam had a long border with Cambodia and Laos that passed through jungle regions.

Additional Support

A Bloody Stalemate

MAIN Idea The failure of United States forces to defeat the Vietcong and the deaths of thousands of American soldiers led many Americans to question the nation's involvement in Vietnam.

HISTORY AND YOU Have you ever heard people compare a contemporary military conflict to the Vietnam War? Read on to find out why some people fear becoming involved in a similar conflict today.

D By the end of 1965, more than 180,000 American combat troops were fighting in Vietnam. In 1966 that number doubled. Since the American military was extremely strong, it marched into Vietnam with great confidence. "America seemed omnipotent then," wrote Philip Caputo, one of the first marines to arrive. "We saw ourselves as the champions of a 'cause that was destined to triumph.'"

Lacking the firepower of the Americans, the Vietcong used ambushes, booby traps, and other guerrilla tactics. Ronald J. Glasser, an American army doctor, described the devastating effects of one booby trap:

PRIMARY SOURCE

"Three quarters of the way through the tangle, a trooper brushed against a two-inch vine, and a grenade slung at chest high went off, shattering the right side of his head and body.... Nearby troopers took hold of the unconscious soldier and, half carrying, half dragging him, pulled him the rest of the way through the tangle."

—quoted in *Vietnam, A History*

The Vietcong also frustrated American troops by blending in with the general population and then quickly vanishing. "It was a sheer physical impossibility to keep the enemy from slipping away whenever he wished," explained one American general. Journalist Linda Martin noted, "It's a war where nothing is ever quite certain and nowhere is ever quite safe." C

NATIONAL GEOGRAPHIC The Vietnam War, 1965–1973

CHINA

Dien Bien Phu
Hanoi
Gulf of Tonkin

LAOS
Vientiane
NORTH VIETNAM
Mekong R.

February 8–March, 1971: Invasion of Laos

THAILAND

Con Thien 1967
Khe Sanh 1968
Hue 1968
Vinh Huy 1967
Dak To 1967
Cu Nghi 1966
Ia Drang 1965

South China Sea

May 1–June 29, 1970: Invasion of Cambodia

CAMBODIA
SOUTH VIETNAM
Phnom Penh
Saigon

← Major U.S. and South Vietnamese troop movement
← Major North Vietnamese supply line
★ Major battle

0   200 kilometers
0   200 miles
Miller projection

▲ Although helicopters helped American troops cope with Vietnam's jungles and mountains, napalm bombs (right) were also used to counter the thick foliage.

Analyzing GEOGRAPHY

1. **Places** What countries were invaded during the Vietnam War?
2. **Movement** Why was it difficult to seal South Vietnam's border?

Extending the Content

Robert McNamara Robert McNamara's training was in business, with an interest in efficiency. He further developed that interest during World War II, serving in the Air Force's Statistical Control Office, and at the Ford Motor Company, where he became the first non-family member to rise to the presidency of the company. Tapped as Secretary of Defense by John Kennedy, McNamara wanted to streamline both the defense department's bureaucracy and its defense force. An architect of military strategy, he became disillusioned with the progress of the war and resigned in 1966, going on to become president of the World Bank. A 1996 memoir reveals the mistakes McNamara perceives were made in Vietnam.

"Search and Destroy"

To counter the Vietcong's tactics, American troops went on "search and destroy" missions. They tried to find enemy troops, bomb their positions, destroy their supply lines, and force them out into the open for combat.

The Vietcong evaded American forces by hiding out in the thick jungle or escaping through tunnels dug in the earth. To take away the Vietcong's ability to hide, American forces literally destroyed the landscape. American planes dropped **napalm,** a jellied gasoline that explodes on contact. They also used **Agent Orange,** a chemical that strips leaves from trees and shrubs, turning farmland and forest into wasteland. For those South Vietnamese still living in the countryside, danger lay on all sides.

United States military leaders underestimated the Vietcong's strength. They also misjudged the enemy's stamina and the support they had among the South Vietnamese. American generals believed that continuously bombing and killing large numbers of Vietcong would destroy the enemy's morale and force them to give up. The guerrillas, however, had no intention of surrendering, and they were willing to accept huge losses to achieve their goals.

The Ho Chi Minh Trail

In the Vietcong's war effort, North Vietnamese support was a major factor. Although the Vietcong forces were made up of many South Vietnamese, North Vietnam provided arms, advisers, and leadership. As Vietcong casualties mounted, North Vietnam began sending North Vietnamese Army units to fight.

North Vietnam sent arms and supplies south by way of a network of jungle paths known as the **Ho Chi Minh trail.** The trail wound through the countries of Cambodia and Laos, bypassing the border between North and South Vietnam. Because the trail passed through countries not directly involved in the war, President Johnson refused to allow a full-scale attack on the trail to shut it down.

North Vietnam itself received military weapons and other support from the Soviet Union and China. One of the main reasons President Johnson refused to order a full-scale invasion of North Vietnam was his fear that such an attack would bring China into the war, as had happened in Korea. By placing limits on the war, however, Johnson made it very difficult to win. Instead of conquering enemy territory, American troops were forced to fight a war of attrition—a strategy of defeating the enemy forces by wearing them down. This strategy led troops to conduct grisly body counts after battles to determine how many enemy soldiers had been killed. The U.S. military began measuring "progress" in the war by the number of enemy dead.

Bombing from American planes killed as many as 220,000 Vietnamese between 1965 and 1967. By the end of 1966, more than 6,700 American soldiers had been killed. The notion of a quick and decisive victory grew increasingly remote. As a result, many citizens back home began to question the nation's involvement in the war.

✓ Reading Check **Describing** What tactics did the United States adopt to fight the Vietcong?

Section 1 REVIEW

Vocabulary

1. **Explain** the significance of: Ho Chi Minh, domino theory, guerrilla, Dien Bien Phu, Geneva Accords, Ngo Dinh Diem, Vietcong, Gulf of Tonkin Resolution, napalm, Agent Orange, Ho Chi Minh trail.

Main Ideas

2. **Explaining** What convinced the French to pull out of Vietnam?

3. **Determining Cause and Effect** What was the result of the overthrow of Diem in Vietnam?

4. **Analyzing** Why did fighting in Vietnam turn into a stalemate by the mid-1960s?

Critical Thinking

5. **Big Ideas** How did American Cold War politics lead to the United States fighting a war in Vietnam?

6. **Sequencing** Use a graphic organizer similar to the one below to sequence events that led to U.S. involvement in Vietnam.

| August 1963 | → | November 1, 1963 | → | August 2, 1964 |
| August 7, 1964 | ← | February 1965 | → | March 1965 |

7. **Analyzing Visuals** Study the map on page 655. Why is China's location significant in relation to the Cold War struggles in Southeast Asia?

Writing About History

8. **Persuasive Writing** Suppose you are a member of Congress in August 1964. Write a statement supporting or opposing the Gulf of Tonkin Resolution.

History ONLINE
Study Central™ To review this section, go to glencoe.com and click on Study Central.

D Differentiated Instruction

Naturalist Invite interested students to find out more about the effects of napalm and Agent Orange on both Vietnam and American soldiers. Have them present their findings to the class using visual aids. **AL**

Assess

History ONLINE

Study Central™ provides summaries, interactive games, and online graphic organizers to help students review content.

Close

Summarizing Ask: How did America become involved in Vietnam? *(Presidents committed advisers and troops gradually, hoping to prevent the spread of communism.)* **OL**

✓ Reading Check

Answer: search and destroy missions, bombing, the use of napalm and Agent Orange

Section 1 REVIEW

Answers

1. All definitions can be found in the section and the Glossary.

2. The French troops were unable to defeat the Vietminh guerrillas, and casualties made the war increasingly unpopular with the French people. When the French lost Dien Bien Phu to the Vietminh, they decided to make peace and withdraw from Indochina.

3. Diem's overthrow made the situation in South Vietnam more unstable. The U.S. then had to use more resources to keep the government in power.

4. The Vietcong showed no signs of surrendering, and Johnson refused to order a full-scale invasion for fear of involving China in the conflict.

5. As Democrats, both Kennedy and Johnson were concerned about being accused by Republicans of losing Vietnam to Communists. This made them express their clear belief in the Cold War domino theory, and to dedicate more and more forces to efforts against the Vietnamese Communists.

6. August 1963: Henry Cabot Lodge arrives in Vietnam; November 1, 1963: Diem is overthrown; August 2, 1964: Gulf of Tonkin incident; August 7, 1964: Gulf of Tonkin resolution; February 1965: attack on Pleiku base; March 1965: Johnson expands bombing campaign

7. China borders North Vietnam, Laos, and Burma, which all seemed vulnerable to Communist influence.

8. Students' statements should express a clear and reasoned point of view.

Focus

Explain that American pilots could see war supplies, military equipment, and weapons being moved on railroad trains in North Vietnam. For fear of escalating the war, however, Navy and Air Force strikes were rare in North Vietnam. Only after the shipments were divided into small loads moving south on the Ho Chi Minh Trail were bombers allowed to strike.

Teach

C Critical Thinking

Making Inferences Ask: What advantages did the North Vietnamese have in following the natural physical features of the trail? *(They didn't have to build bridges or roads; the tunnels and forest cover helped to hide them.)* **OL**

Additional Support

NATIONAL GEOGRAPHIC

GEOGRAPHY & HISTORY

The Ho Chi Minh Trail

North and South Vietnam were long narrow countries. As a result, the border between them was very narrow and easy to defend. In order to send supplies and troops to the south, the North Vietnamese had to find a way around the border. They achieved this by crossing (illegally) into Laos and Cambodia, two neutral nations to the west, then heading south bypassing South Vietnam's northern border. The mountains and rain forests of the region provided cover for people using the trails and roads that ran south. The Americans referred to the elaborate network of roads, trails, forest paths, bridges, tunnels, and shelters as the Ho Chi Minh Trail.

How Did Geography Influence the Ho Chi Minh Trail?

The Ho Chi Minh Trail followed the topography—or natural physical features—of the region. When viewed from aircraft, the trail often disappeared and blended into the surrounding countryside, making it very difficult to attack. Furthermore, it provided access to multiple points along South Vietnam's long western border, which was much harder for American and South Vietnamese troops to defend. By 1967, an estimated 20,000 Vietnamese soldiers traveled the route each month. The American military tried to disrupt the flow of people and goods, but this proved very difficult to do. By the end of the war, the Ho Chi Minh Trail stretched some 12,000 miles (19,312 km) through the canopied rain forests.

Analyzing GEOGRAPHY

1. **Movement** What diplomatic and international problems were caused by the route of the Ho Chi Minh Trail?

2. **Human-Environment Interaction** What kinds of challenges did the geography of Southeast Asia pose for fighting a war?

662   Chapter 19   The Vietnam War

Extending the Content

The Ho Chi Minh Trail The route that Americans dubbed the Ho Chi Minh Trail was an elaborate patchwork of jungle paths, bridges, and shelters which began in North Vietnam and extended through southern Laos and northeastern Cambodia into South Vietnam. Much of this "trail" existed long before the Vietnam War. Over centuries, the people who lived in this jungle region had carved out the paths as they hunted tigers, elephants, and other prey. In addition the

paths had long been used by caravans of traders who traveled through Southeast Asia.

During the Vietnam War, this web of paths carried soldiers and military supplies from North Vietnam into South Vietnam. In following the trail as it snaked through the rain forests of Southeast Asia, travelers endured leeches, mosquitoes, and attacks by wild animals (in addition to the dangers posed by human enemies).

▲ In an effort to close the trail and ambush enemy troops using it, American troops set up "firebases" on hilltops overlooking part of the trail. Helicopters helped American troops overcome the region's difficult terrain. They could quickly move men and supplies over the rain forest.

American aircraft tried to destroy troops and vehicles on the trail by dropping bombs, including napalm—a jellied gasoline that would catch fire and burn a wide area.

▲ The Vietnamese moved goods along the trail in many ways. Most porters carried goods on their back; others strapped goods to bicycles. Trucks carried supplies and people on wider parts of the trail.

To deprive the enemy of cover, American aircraft sprayed areas near the trail with defoliants that killed all plant life, leaving a barren area. The most famous chemical used was Agent Orange.

GEOGRAPHY & HISTORY

C **Critical Thinking**
Predicting Consequences
Ask students to predict what the effect of napalm and Agent Orange would be on the landscape and economy of Vietnam. *(Students may say that the land would be spoiled through the fires and chemicals used, and would probably not be able to be cultivated for some time.)* **OL**

Assess/Close

. . . .

Analyzing **GEOGRAPHY**

Answers:
1. The Ho Chi Minh Trail went through countries that were supposed to be neutral.
2. Vietnam was a land of mountains and of dense rain forests, which were difficult to penetrate and to see into.

Additional Support

Activity: Economics Connection

Defending the Border The United States shares a border with Mexico to the south. Because this border stretches for 1,900 miles, it is difficult to prevent people and goods from coming illegally into the United States. This flow of people and goods has an enormous effect on the American economy, both in Mexico and in the United States. Have students use library or Internet resources to investigate both the cost of defending the border and the contributions made by people coming from Mexico to work in the United States. Hold a panel discussion focusing on the economic effects of this exchange. **OL**

Section 2

Focus

Bellringer
Daily Focus Transparency 19.2

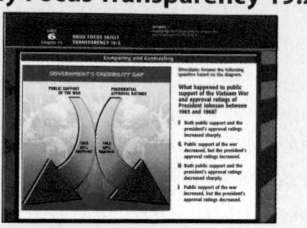

Guide to Reading

Answers: credibility gap, unfair draft system, immorality of defending a corrupt dictatorship in South Vietnam, belief that it was a civil war that was not the business of the United States

Section Spotlight Video

To generate student interest and provide a springboard for class discussion, access the Chapter 19, Section 2 video at glencoe.com or on the video DVD.

Resource Manager

Section 2

Vietnam Divides the Nation

Guide to Reading

Big Ideas
Group Action Many Americans protested to end their country's involvement in the Vietnam War.

Content Vocabulary
- credibility gap *(p. 664)*
- teach-in *(p. 665)*
- dove *(p. 667)*
- hawk *(p. 667)*

Academic Vocabulary
- media *(p. 664)*
- disproportionate *(p. 665)*

People and Events to Identify
- William Westmoreland *(p. 664)*
- Tet Offensive *(p. 667)*

Reading Strategy
Organizing Complete a graphic organizer similar to the one below to list the reasons for opposition to the Vietnam War.

Reasons for Opposition to Vietnam War

A s casualties mounted in Vietnam, many Americans began to protest against the war. Discouraged by domestic conflict over the war, rising violence, and the apparent lack of progress in Vietnam, President Johnson announced he would not seek another term as president.

An Antiwar Movement Emerges

MAIN Idea The Vietnam War produced sharp divisions between Americans who supported the war and those who did not, and the resulting political turmoil led President Johnson to decide not to run again for president.

HISTORY AND YOU Do you know people who did not support the war in Iraq and those who did? Read on to find out how differences over the Vietnam War began to divide the country.

When American troops first entered the Vietnam War in the spring of 1965, many Americans supported the military effort. A Gallup poll published soon afterward showed that 66 percent of Americans approved of the policy in Vietnam. As the war dragged on, however, public support began to drop. Suspicion of the government's truthfulness about the war was a significant reason. Throughout the early years of the war, the American commander in South Vietnam, General **William Westmoreland,** reported that the enemy was on the brink of defeat. In 1967 he confidently declared that the "enemy's hopes are bankrupt" and added, "we have reached an important point where the end begins to come into view."

Contradicting such reports were less optimistic **media** accounts, especially on television. Vietnam was the first "television war," with footage of combat appearing nightly on the evening news. Day after day, millions of people saw images of wounded and dead Americans and began to doubt government reports. In the view of many, a **credibility gap** had developed, meaning it was hard to believe what the Johnson administration said about the war.

Congress, which had given the president a nearly free hand in Vietnam, soon grew uncertain about the war. Beginning in February 1966 the Senate Foreign Relations Committee held "educational" hearings on Vietnam, calling in Secretary of State Dean Rusk and other policy makers to explain the administration's military strategy. The committee also listened to critics, such as American diplomat George Kennan. Although Kennan had helped to create the policy of containment, he argued that Vietnam was not strategically important to the United States.

R Reading Strategies	**C** Critical Thinking	**D** Differentiated Instruction	**W** Writing Support	**S** Skill Practice
Teacher Edition • Using Word Parts, p. 665 • Read. Prim. Sources, p. 666 • Making Connections, p. 666 **Additional Resources** • Prim. Source Read., URB p. 101 • Guide Read Act., URB p. 113	**Additional Resources** • Quizzes and Tests, p. 268	**Teacher Edition** • Verbal/Ling., p. 667 • Adv. Learners, p. 669 **Additional Resources** • Diff. Inst. Act., URB p. 87 • Am. Hist. in Graphic Novel, p. 65	**Teacher Edition** • Expository Writing, p. 667	**Additional Resources** • Read Skills Act., URB p. 85 • RENTG, p. 203

▲ An axe labeled "Vietnam Issue" splits the nation in two.

◄ Ho Chi Minh sends a telegram praising antiwar protesters.

Analyzing VISUALS

1. **Finding the Main Idea** What is the main message of the cartoon on the left?

2. **Making Inferences** The cartoon on the right was drawn before the one on the left. Do you think that differences between the two indicate a change in attitude toward antiwar protests? Explain.

Teach-ins Begin

In March 1965, a group of faculty members and students at the University of Michigan abandoned their classes and joined together in a **teach-in.** They discussed the issues surrounding the war and reaffirmed their reasons for opposing it. The gathering inspired teach-ins at many campuses. In May 1965, 122 colleges held a "National Teach-In" by radio for more than 100,000 antiwar demonstrators.

People who opposed the war did so for different reasons. Some saw the conflict as a civil war in which the United States had no business interfering. Others viewed South Vietnam as a corrupt dictatorship and believed that defending it was immoral and unjust.

Anger at the Draft

Young protesters especially focused on what they saw as an unfair draft system. Until 1969, a college student was often able to defer military service until after graduation. By contrast, young people from working-class families were more likely to be drafted and sent to Viet-

nam because they were unable to afford college. Draftees in the military were most likely to be assigned to combat units where they faced grave dangers. In 1969 draftees made up 62 percent of battle deaths.

The majority of soldiers who served in Vietnam, however, were volunteer enlistees. Holding out the military as an avenue to vocational training and upward social mobility, military recruiters encouraged youth in poor and working-class communities to enlist. Thus, a **disproportionate** number of working-class youths, many of them minorities, were among the volunteers who served in Vietnam.

The Vietnam War coincided with the high tide of the civil rights movement. From early in the war, the treatment of African American soldiers came under scrutiny. Between 1961 and 1966, African Americans constituted about 10 percent of military personnel while African Americans comprised about 13 percent of the total population of the United States. Because African Americans were more likely to be assigned to combat units, however, they accounted for almost 20 percent of combat-related deaths.

Teach

R **Reading Strategy**

Using Word Parts Tell students that taking apart a long word, such as *disproportionate*, may help them reach the word's meaning. By removing the prefix and suffix, they can see the word *proportion*. Recalling that *dis-* means "not" will help them define the word. **BL**

Analyzing VISUALS

Answers:

1. the differing opinions on Vietnam issues threatens to split the nation

2. The cartoon on the right is openly critical of draft card burners, while the one on the left sees the war as dividing all Americans.

Hands-On Chapter Project
Step 2

Create a Documentary of the Vietnam War

Step 2: Planning the Video **Essential question:** What were the key developments in the chosen story and what were the historical results?

Directions Students should use their textbook and other research to outline the basic issue and the chronology. A second team could concentrate on thinking visually. This team would have to collaborate closely with

the first and research photos in magazines and newspapers or video clips of the period.

Putting It Together When the teams meet, they can decide on the "storyboards" for the video—sketches representing each shot in the 10 scenes (or whatever number seems appropriate) so that the topic is covered from beginning to end. **OL**

(Chapter Project continued on page 671)

The high number of African Americans and poor Americans dying in Vietnam angered African American leaders, including Dr. Martin Luther King, Jr. In April 1967 King publicly condemned the conflict:

PRIMARY SOURCE

"I speak for the poor of America who are paying the double price of smashed hopes at home and death and corruption in Vietnam. . . . The great initiative in this war is ours. The initiative to stop it must be ours."

—quoted in *A Testament of Hope*

In response to such criticisms, military officials strived to lower the number of African American casualties. By the end of the conflict, African Americans accounted for about 12 percent of America's dead, roughly equivalent to their presence in the national population.

As the war escalated, American officials increased the draft call, putting many college students at risk. An estimated 500,000 draftees refused to go. Many burned their draft cards or simply did not show up for induction. Some fled the country, moving to Canada, Sweden, or other nations. Others stayed and went to prison rather than fight in a war they opposed.

Between 1965 and 1968, officials prosecuted more than 3,300 Americans for refusing to serve. The draft became less of an issue in 1969 when the government introduced a lottery system, in which only those with low lottery numbers were subject to the draft.

Protests against the war were not confined to college campuses. Demonstrators held public rallies and marches in towns across the country. In April 1965 Students for a Democratic Society (SDS), a left-wing student organization, organized a march on Washington, D.C., that drew more than 20,000 participants. Two years later, in October 1967, a rally at Washington's Lincoln Memorial drew tens of thousands of protesters, as well.

Anger over the draft also fueled discussions about the voting age. Many draftees argued that if they were old enough to fight, they were old enough to vote. In 1971 the Twenty-sixth Amendment to the Constitution was ratified, giving all citizens age 18 and older the right to vote in all state and federal elections.

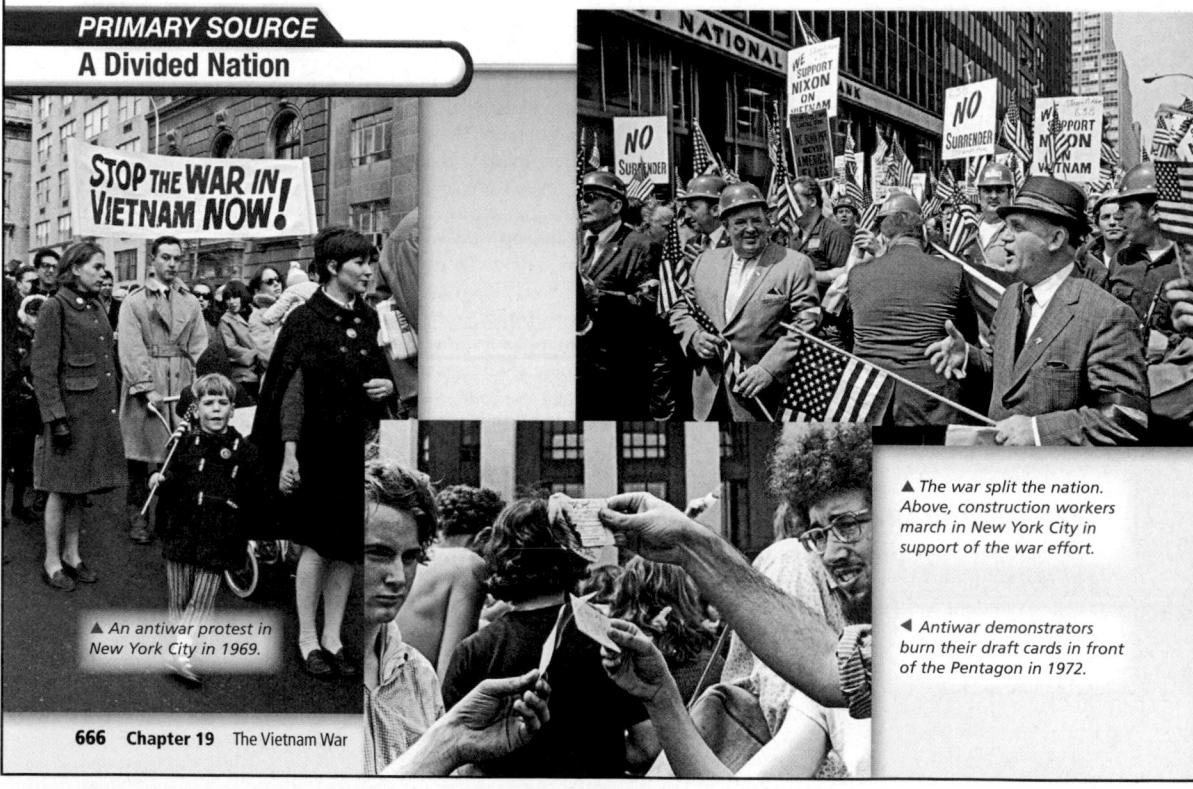

PRIMARY SOURCE
A Divided Nation

▲ An antiwar protest in New York City in 1969.

▲ The war split the nation. Above, construction workers march in New York City in support of the war effort.

◄ Antiwar demonstrators burn their draft cards in front of the Pentagon in 1972.

666 Chapter 19 The Vietnam War

Activity: Collaborative Learning

Investigate Younger Voters Divide the class into small groups. Ask each group to conduct interviews with at least six people between the ages of 18 and 25, three who voted in the last presidential election and three who did not. Have students summarize the participants' answers to questions about why they did or did not vote. Have them also look at and evaluate the work of organizations such as Rock the Vote that attempt to make voting popular among younger people. Have them present their findings to the class as a panel discussion about the question "Have young people effectively used the right to vote?" **OL**

Hawks and Doves

In the face of growing opposition to the war, President Johnson remained determined to continue fighting. He assailed his critics in Congress as "selfish men who want to advance their own interests." He dismissed the college protesters as too naive to appreciate the importance of resisting communism.

The president was not alone in his views. In a poll taken in early 1968, 53 percent of the respondents favored stronger military action in Vietnam, compared to 24 percent who wanted an end to the war. Of those Americans who supported the policy in Vietnam, many openly criticized the protesters for a lack of patriotism.

By 1968 the nation seemed to be divided into two camps. Those who wanted the United States to withdraw from Vietnam were known as **doves.** Those who insisted that the country stay and fight came to be known as **hawks.** As the two groups debated, the war appeared to take a dramatic turn for the worse, and the nation endured a year of shock and crisis.

✔ **Reading Check** **Explaining** What led to the ratification of the Twenty-sixth Amendment?

Opposition to the Vietnam War

First U.S. troops in Vietnam

Tet offensive

Cease-fire signed

First withdrawal of U.S. troops

Source: Statistical Abstract of the United States.

Analyzing VISUALS

1. **Interpreting** During which two years was opposition to the war lowest? What event occurred around that time?

2. **Synthesizing** In what year did opposition to the war peak? How was this sentiment logically related to the withdrawal of American troops?

1968: The Pivotal Year

MAIN Idea The Tet Offensive increased doubt that the United States could win in Vietnam.

HISTORY AND YOU Have you ever participated in a public-opinion poll? Read how Johnson's plummeting approval rating made him decide not to run for re-election in 1968.

The most turbulent year of the chaotic 1960s was 1968. The year saw a shocking political announcement, two traumatic assassinations, and a political convention held amid strident anti-war demonstrations. First, however, the nation endured a surprise attack in Vietnam.

The Tet Offensive

On January 30, 1968, during Tet, the Vietnamese New Year, the Vietcong and North Vietnamese launched a massive surprise attack. In this **Tet Offensive,** guerrilla fighters attacked most American airbases in South Vietnam and most of the South's major cities. Vietcong even blasted their way into the American embassy in Saigon.

Militarily, Tet was a disaster for the Vietcong. After about a month of fighting, the American and South Vietnamese soldiers repelled the enemy troops, inflicting heavy losses on them. President Johnson triumphantly noted that the enemy's effort had ended in "complete failure." Later, historians confirmed that Tet nearly destroyed the Vietcong.

The North Vietnamese, however, had scored a major political victory. The American people were shocked that an enemy supposedly on the verge of defeat could launch such a large-scale attack. When General Westmoreland requested 209,000 troops in addition to the 500,000 already in Vietnam, he seemed to be admitting the United States could not win.

To make matters worse, the media, which had tried to remain balanced in their war coverage, now openly criticized the effort. "The American people should be getting ready to accept, if they haven't already, the prospect that the whole Vietnam effort may be doomed," declared the *Wall Street Journal.* Television newscaster Walter Cronkite announced that it seemed "more certain than ever that the bloody experience in Vietnam is to end in a stalemate."

D **Differentiated Instruction**

Verbal/Linguistic Invite students to hold a debate on the role of protest in a democratic society. Ask them to consider the question of whether the answer changes if that nation is at war. **OL**

W **Writing Support**

Expository Writing Ask students to write brief essays explaining the role of the media in telling unpleasant truths. Have them cite specific examples to support their views. **OL**

✔ **Reading Check**

Answer: Protests concerning the draft led to discussion about the fact that draft-age citizens did not at that time have the right to vote.

Analyzing VISUALS

Answers:
1. 1965, 1966; first U.S. troops arrive
2. 1971; the government did not believe the war could be won.

Extending the Content

Walter Cronkite By the time of the Vietnam War, veteran journalist Walter Cronkite had plenty of experience with war. He had gone ashore with the troops on D-Day and covered the Nuremberg trials as a United Press reporter. In 1950 he joined CBS, becoming news anchor in 1962 and retiring from that position in 1981.

Initially Cronkite was a hawk, and he went to Vietnam after the Tet Offensive. After that trip, he addressed his audience with a changed attitude about the war. In his television broadcast, Cronkite said, "It seems now more certain than ever that the bloody experience of Vietnam is a stalemate." President Lyndon Johnson listened to Cronkite's verdict as did the rest of the nation. According to one of Johnson's aides, the president said, "If I've lost Cronkite, I've lost Middle America."

As media analysts have observed, Cronkite's influence was substantial for two reasons. First, most Americans believed that he was objective, trustworthy, and patriotic. Second, Cronkite worked during an era when the vast majority of Americans regularly tuned in to one of the three major networks.

667

PRIMARY SOURCE
1968: A Year of Turmoil

The election year 1968 was tumultuous. The country was divided over Vietnam. President Johnson chose not to run again. Protesters fought with police at the Democratic National Convention. Race riots erupted in several American cities and both Martin Luther King, Jr., and Robert Kennedy were killed.

▲ Robert Kennedy campaigns for the Democratic nomination (top left) in January 1968. Soon afterward, George Wallace (left) entered the race as an independent. Above, police confront protestors at the Democratic National Convention in August 1968.

Presidential Election of 1968

Nixon   Humphrey

Presidential Candidate	Popular Votes	% of Popular Vote	Electoral Votes
Nixon	31,710,470	43.60%	301
Humphrey	30,898,055	42.48%	191
Wallace	9,906,473	13.62%	46

Analyzing VISUALS

1. **Regions** In what area of the country did George Wallace receive the most votes?
2. **Regions** Do you think Richard Nixon would have won if Wallace had not been in the race?

Public opinion no longer favored the president. In the weeks following the Tet Offensive, the president's approval rating plummeted to a dismal 35 percent, while support for his handling of the war fell even lower, to 26 percent. The administration's credibility gap now seemed too wide to repair.

Johnson Leaves the Race

With the war growing increasingly unpopular and Johnson's credibility all but gone, some Democrats began looking for an alternative candidate to nominate for president in 1968. In November 1967, even before the Tet disaster, a little-known liberal senator from Minnesota, Eugene McCarthy, became the first dove to declare he would challenge Johnson for the Democratic presidential nomination. In March 1968 McCarthy stunned the nation by winning more than 40 percent of the votes in the New Hampshire primary. Realizing that Johnson was vulnerable, Senator Robert Kennedy, who also opposed the war, quickly entered the race for the Democratic nomination.

With both the country and his own party deeply divided, Johnson addressed the public on television on March 31, 1968. He stunned viewers by announcing, "I have concluded that I should not permit the presidency to become involved in the partisan divisions that are developing in this political year. Accordingly, I shall not seek, and I will not accept, the nomination of my party for another term as your President."

Activity: Economics Connection

The Cost of War Lyndon Johnson challenged Congress to fund both "guns and butter" programs, but Congress refused, rendering some of Johnson's Great Society programs all but useless. Have students use the Internet to find out what modern wars cost per day and on what items the money is spent. Suggest that they do a comparative study of the costs of the wars in Vietnam and in Iraq. **OL**

A Season of Violence

Following Johnson's announcement, the nation endured even more shocking events. In April, James Earl Ray was arrested for killing Dr. Martin Luther King, Jr. Just two months later, another assassination rocked the country—that of Robert Kennedy. Kennedy, who appeared to be on his way to winning the Democratic nomination, was gunned down on June 5. The assassin was Sirhan Sirhan, an Arab nationalist angry over the candidate's pro-Israeli remarks a few nights before.

The violence that seemed to plague the country in 1968 culminated with a chaotic and well-publicized clash between antiwar protesters and police at the Democratic National Convention in Chicago. Thousands of protesters surrounded the convention center, demanding that the Democrats adopt an antiwar platform.

Despite the protests, the delegates chose Hubert Humphrey, President Johnson's vice president, as their presidential nominee. Meanwhile, in a park not far from the convention hall, the protesters and police began fighting. As officers tried to disperse demonstrators with tear gas and billy clubs, demonstrators taunted the authorities with the chant, "The whole world is watching!" A subsequent federal investigation of the incident described the event as a "police riot."

Nixon Wins the Presidency

The violence and chaos now associated with the Democratic Party benefited the 1968 Republican presidential candidate, Richard Nixon. Although defeated by John Kennedy in the 1960 election, Nixon had remained active in national politics. A third candidate, Governor George Wallace of Alabama, decided to run in 1968 as an independent. Wallace, an outspoken segregationist, sought to attract Americans who felt threatened by the civil rights movement and urban social unrest.

Public opinion polls gave Nixon a wide lead over Humphrey and Wallace. Nixon's campaign promise to unify the nation and restore law and order appealed to Americans who feared their country was spinning out of control. Nixon also declared that he had a plan for ending the war in Vietnam.

At first Humphrey's support of President Johnson's Vietnam policies hurt his campaign. After Humphrey broke with the president and called for a complete end to the bombing of North Vietnam, he began to move up in the polls. A week before the election, President Johnson helped Humphrey by announcing that the bombing had halted and that a cease-fire would follow.

Johnson's announcement had come too late, however. In the end, Nixon's promises to end the war and restore order at home were enough to sway the American people. On Election Day, Nixon defeated Humphrey by more than 100 electoral votes, although he won the popular vote by a slim margin of 43 percent to 42 percent. Wallace partially accounted for the razor-thin margin by winning 46 electoral votes and more than 13 percent of the popular vote.

Reading Check Explaining Why did President Johnson say he would not run for reelection in 1968?

Section 2 REVIEW

Vocabulary

1. **Explain** the significance of: William Westmoreland, credibility gap, teach-in, dove, hawk, Tet Offensive.

Main Ideas

2. **Explaining** Why did some people view the draft as unfair?

3. **Summarizing** What are three important events that made 1968 such a violent year in the United States?

Critical Thinking

4. **Big Ideas** Why did support of the war dwindle by the late 1960s?

5. **Organizing** Use a graphic organizer similar to the one below to list the effects of the Tet Offensive.

6. **Analyzing Visuals** Study the cartoon on the right on page 665. What is the message of the telegram beyond its literal meaning?

Writing About History

7. **Expository Writing** Suppose that you are living in 1968. Write a letter to the editor of a local newspaper in which you explain your reasons for either supporting or opposing the Vietnam War.

History ONLINE
Study Central™ To review this section, go to glencoe.com and click on Study Central.

669

D Differentiated Instruction

Advanced Learners Invite students to find out how third party candidates have fared in presidential elections since 1900. Ask them to present their findings to the class using visual aids such as graphs or charts. **AL**

Assess

History ONLINE

Study Central™ provides summaries, interactive games, and online graphic organizers to help students review content.

Close

Summarizing Ask: What event eroded public confidence in America's role in Vietnam? *(failure to win the war, especially after the Tet Offensive)* **OL**

Reading Check

Answer: He did not want the presidency to become involved in partisan division.

Section 2 REVIEW

Answers

1. All definitions can be found in the section and the Glossary.

2. Poor men, including a high proportion of minorities, who were unable to afford college, were more likely to be drafted than those who could afford college and thus get deferments.

3. the assassination of Martin Luther King, Jr., the assassination of Robert Kennedy, and the riots at the Democratic National Convention

4. Media coverage of the mounting casualties fueled anger and distrust of government officials' reports on the progress of the war, and many were angry over the unfair draft system.

5. support for the war dropped, the media became critical of the war effort, the president's approval rating plummeted

6. Students may say that the message is that draft card burners were unpatriotic or Communist sympathizers.

7. Students' letters should express a clear and reasoned argument for supporting or opposing the war.

Section 3

Focus

Bellringer
Daily Focus Transparency 19.3

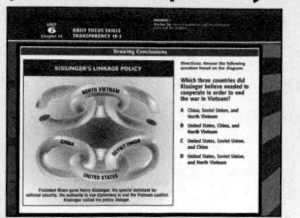

Guide to Reading

Answers may include: Kissinger appointment, linkage policy, Vietnamization, bombing campaign, Cambodian invasion

Section Spotlight Video

To generate student interest and provide a springboard for class discussion, access the Chapter 19, Section 3 video at glencoe.com or on the video DVD.

Resource Manager

Section 3

The War Winds Down

Guide to Reading

Big Ideas
Trade, War, and Migration
The Vietnam War changed the way Americans viewed the government and the military, and led them to question how the armed forces were deployed.

Content Vocabulary
- linkage *(p. 670)*
- Vietnamization *(p. 670)*

Academic Vocabulary
- generation *(p. 671)*
- unresolved *(p. 675)*

People and Events to Identify
- Henry Kissinger *(p. 670)*
- Pentagon Papers *(p. 672)*
- War Powers Act *(p. 675)*

Reading Strategy
Organizing Complete a graphic organizer similar to the one below by listing the steps that President Nixon took to end American involvement in Vietnam.

Steps Nixon Took

S hortly after taking office, President Nixon moved to end the nation's involvement in the Vietnam War. The final years of the conflict, however, yielded more bloodshed and turmoil, as well as a growing cynicism in the minds of Americans about the honesty and effectiveness of the United States government.

Nixon Moves to End the War

MAIN Idea While unrest and suspicion of the government grew, the United States finally withdrew its troops from Vietnam.

HISTORY AND YOU Have you ever protested against something you felt was wrong? Read on to find out how college students reacted to what they viewed as a widening of the Vietnam War.

As a first step to fulfilling his campaign promise to end the war, Nixon appointed Harvard professor **Henry Kissinger** as special assistant for national security affairs and gave him wide authority to use diplomacy to end the conflict. Kissinger embarked upon a policy he called **linkage,** which meant improving relations with the Soviet Union and China—suppliers of aid to North Vietnam—so that he could persuade them to cut back on their aid.

Kissinger also rekindled peace talks with the North Vietnamese. In August 1969 Kissinger entered into secret negotiations with North Vietnam's negotiator, Le Duc Tho. In their talks, which dragged on for four years, Kissinger and Le Duc Tho argued over a possible cease-fire, the return of American prisoners of war, and the ultimate fate of South Vietnam.

Meanwhile, Nixon reduced the number of American troops in Vietnam. Known as **Vietnamization,** this process involved the gradual withdrawal of U.S. troops while the South Vietnamese assumed more of the fighting. On June 8, 1969, Nixon announced the withdrawal of 25,000 soldiers, but he was determined to keep a strong American presence in Vietnam to ensure bargaining power during peace negotiations. In support of that goal, the president increased air strikes against North Vietnam and—without informing Congress or the public— began secretly bombing Vietcong sanctuaries in neighboring Cambodia.

Turmoil at Home Continues

Even though the United States had begun scaling back its involvement in Vietnam, the American home front remained divided and volatile, as Nixon's war policies stirred up new waves of protest.

R Reading Strategies	**C** Critical Thinking	**D** Differentiated Instruction	**W** Writing Support	**S** Skill Practice
Teacher Edition • Act. Prior Know., p. 671 • Making Inferences, p. 672 • Read. Prim. Sources, p. 675 **Additional Resources** • Guide Read Act., URB p. 114 • Am. History in Graphic Novel, p. 73	**Teacher Edition** • Analyzing Prim. Sources, p. 671 **Additional Resources** • Interp. Pol. Cartoons, URB p. 105 • Authentic Assess, p. 45 • Supreme Court Case Studies, p. 109 • Quizzes and Tests, p. 269	**Teacher Edition** • Visual/Spatial, p. 672 **Additional Resources** • English Learner Act., URB p. 89 • Am. Art and Music Act., URB p. 103 • Enrich. Act., URB p. 109	**Additional Resources** • Linking Past/Present, URB p. 98	**Additional Resources** • Reinforcing Skills, URB p. 95 • Time Line Act., URB p. 97 • RENTG, p. 206

PRIMARY SOURCE
Protests and Peace Talks

▲ President Nixon (above) describes the invasion of Cambodia in 1970. Two years later, Secretary of State Henry Kissinger met for peace talks with North Vietnam's representative Le Duc Tho (right).

▲ To convince North Vietnam to settle for a negotiated peace, Nixon ordered troops into Cambodia to destroy North Vietnamese bases there. The invasion led to mass protests in the United States and to the tragic shooting of four students by National Guard troops at Kent State University (above).

Analyzing VISUALS

1. **Determining Cause and Effect** How did the invasion of Cambodia lead to the shootings at Kent State?
2. **Specifying** In what year did the troop level in Vietnam reach its peak?

U.S. Troops in Vietnam, 1964–1974

(Line graph: Number of Troops (thousands) vs. Year. Y-axis from 100 to 600. X-axis years 1964, 1966, 1968, 1970, 1972, 1974. Troops rise to a peak near 1968 at about 540 thousand, then decline sharply to near zero by 1974.)

Source: *Statistical Abstract of the United States.*

Massacre at My Lai In late 1969 Americans learned that, in the spring of 1968, an American platoon under the command of Lieutenant William Calley had massacred unarmed South Vietnamese civilians in the hamlet of My Lai. Most of the victims were old men, women, and children. Calley eventually went to prison for his role in the killings.

Most American soldiers acted responsibly and honorably during the war. The actions of a small group, however, convinced many people that the war was brutal and senseless. Jan Barry, a founder of the Vietnam Veterans Against the War, viewed My Lai as a symbol of the dilemma his **generation** faced in the conflict:

PRIMARY SOURCE

"To kill on military orders and be a criminal, or to refuse to kill and be a criminal is the moral agony of America's Vietnam war generation. It is what has forced upward of sixty thousand young Americans, draft resisters and deserters to Canada, and created one hundred thousand military deserters a year...."

—quoted in *Who Spoke Up?*

The Invasion of Cambodia Sparks Protest Americans heard more startling news when Nixon announced in April 1970 that American troops had invaded Cambodia. The troops were ordered to destroy Vietcong military bases there.

Many viewed the Cambodian invasion as a widening of the war, and it set off many protests. At Kent State University on May 4, 1970, Ohio National Guard soldiers, armed with tear gas and rifles, fired on demonstrators without an order to do so. The soldiers killed four students. Ten days later, police killed two African American students during a demonstration at Jackson State College in Mississippi.

Chapter 19   The Vietnam War   **671**

Teach

C Critical Thinking
Analyzing Primary Sources
Read the quotation aloud. **Ask:** What were the two results of the difficult choices young American men faced? *(about 60,000 went to Canada and another 100,000 deserted the military)* **BL**

R Reading Strategy
Activating Prior Knowledge
Ask students why Nixon's announcement of the invasion of Cambodia was so startling to many. *(The U.S. had invaded a neutral country without a declaration of war.)* **OL**

Analyzing VISUALS

Answers:
1. The protests at Kent State were among many that resulted from the invasion of Cambodia.
2. 1968

Hands-On Chapter Project
Step 3

Create a Documentary of the Vietnam War

Step 3: Creating the Script or Voiceover Essential question: What is the core of the message and how shall it be conveyed with the images?

Directions Students may need to re-assess their storyboards and edit them as they go through them to write the script or "voiceover" for the video or as they create the visuals. The writing will need to be concise and focus on the essential point of what is happening in each scene. Students can divide up in teams to write the voiceover for two or more storyboards.

Putting It Together The teams can meet to review and edit their final script. **OL**
(Chapter Project continued on Visual Summary page)

672

R Reading Strategy

Making Inferences Have students read the first paragraph under the heading "The United States Pulls Out." **Ask:** What can you infer about the timing of Kissinger's announcement? *(it was timed to influence the outcome of the presidential election)* **OL**

D Differentiated Instruction

Visual/Spatial Invite students to make a timeline of the war, showing major events. **BL**

✓ Reading Check

Answer: that the government had not been honest with them

In addition to sparking violence on campuses, the invasion of Cambodia cost Nixon significant congressional support. Numerous legislators expressed outrage over the president's failure to notify them of the action. In December 1970 an angry Congress repealed the Gulf of Tonkin Resolution, which had given the president nearly complete power in directing the war in Vietnam.

The Pentagon Papers Support for the war weakened further in 1971 when Daniel Ellsberg, a disillusioned former Defense Department worker, leaked what became known as the **Pentagon Papers** to the *New York Times*. The documents revealed that many government officials during the Johnson administration privately questioned the war while publicly defending it.

The documents contained details of decisions that were made by the presidents and their advisers to expand the war without the consent of Congress. They also showed how the various administrations had tried to convince Congress, the press, and the public that the situation in Vietnam was better than it really was. The Pentagon Papers confirmed what many Americans had long believed: the government had not been honest with them.

The United States Pulls Out

By 1971, polls showed that nearly two-thirds of Americans wanted to end the Vietnam War as quickly as possible. In April 1972 President Nixon dropped his longtime insistence that North Vietnamese troops had to withdraw from South Vietnam before any peace treaty could be signed. In October, less than a month before the presidential election, Kissinger emerged from his secret talks with Le Duc Tho to announce that "peace is at hand."

A month later, Americans went to the polls to decide on a president. Senator George McGovern, the Democratic candidate, was an outspoken critic of the war. He did not appeal to many middle-class Americans, however, who were tired of antiwar protesters. Nixon was reelected in a landslide, winning 60.7 percent of the popular vote.

Just weeks after the presidential election, the peace negotiations broke down. South Vietnam's president, Nguyen Van Thieu, refused to agree to any plan that left North Vietnamese

troops in the South. Henry Kissinger tried to win additional concessions from the Communists, but talks broke off on December 16, 1972.

The next day, to force North Vietnam to resume negotiations, the Nixon administration began the most destructive air raids of the entire war. In what became known as the "Christmas bombings," American B-52s dropped thousands of tons of bombs on North Vietnamese targets for 11 straight days, pausing only on Christmas Day.

In the wake of the bombing campaign, the United States and North Vietnam returned to the bargaining table. Thieu finally gave in to American pressure and allowed North Vietnamese troops to remain in the South. On January 27, 1973, the warring sides signed an agreement "ending the war and restoring the peace in Vietnam."

The United States promised to withdraw its troops, and both sides agreed to exchange prisoners of war. The parties did not resolve the issue of South Vietnam's future, however. After almost eight years of war—the longest war in American history—the nation ended its direct involvement in Vietnam.

South Vietnam Falls

Two years after the United States pulled its troops out of Vietnam, the peace agreement collapsed. In March 1975 the North Vietnamese army launched a full-scale invasion of the South. Thieu desperately appealed to Washington, D.C., for help.

President Nixon had assured Thieu during the peace negotiations that the United States "[would] respond with full force should the settlement be violated by North Vietnam." Nixon, however, had resigned under pressure following Watergate, a scandal that broke as the war was winding down. The new president, Gerald Ford, asked for funds to aid the South Vietnamese, but Congress refused.

Without American assistance, the South Vietnamese Army was unable to stop the invasion. On April 30, the North Vietnamese captured Saigon, South Vietnam's capital, and united Vietnam under Communist rule. They then renamed the city Ho Chi Minh City.

✓ Reading Check **Evaluating** What did the Pentagon Papers confirm for many Americans?

Differentiated Instruction

Leveled Activities

BL **Historical Analysis Skills Activity, URB p. 86**

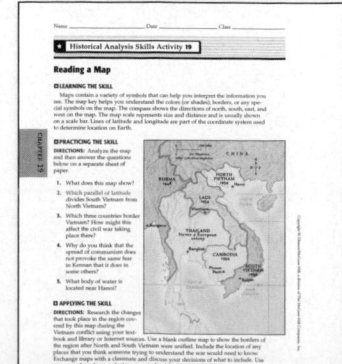

OL **Reinforcing Skills Activity, URB p. 95**

AL **Critical Thinking Skills Activity, URB p. 96**

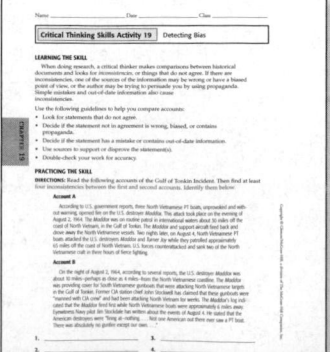

ELL **Content Vocabulary Activity, URB p. 91**

ANALYZING SUPREME COURT CASES

Can the Government Put Limits on the Press?

★ *New York Times* v. *United States*, 1971

Background to the Case

In 1971 Daniel Ellsberg leaked classified documents, known as the Pentagon Papers, to the *New York Times* and the *Washington Post*. When the newspapers attempted to publish these documents, the Nixon administration argued that publication would threaten national security. The case centered on the First Amendment guarantee of a free press.

How the Court Ruled

In a 6-to-3 per curiam opinion—*per curiam* meaning that the decision was issued by the whole Court and not specific justices—the Court found that the Nixon administration had failed to prove that publication of the Pentagon Papers would imperil the nation in any way. The *New York Times* and the *Washington Post* could publish the Pentagon Papers.

PRIMARY SOURCE

Concurring View

"The Government's power to censor the press [via the First Amendment] was abolished so that the press would remain forever free to censure the Government.... And paramount among the responsibilities of a free press is the duty to prevent any part of the government from deceiving the people and sending them off to distant lands to die of foreign fevers and foreign shot and shell. In my view, far from deserving condemnation for their courageous reporting, the *New York Times*, the *Washington Post*, and other newspapers should be commended for serving the purpose that the Founding Fathers saw so clearly. In revealing the workings of government that led to the Vietnam War, the newspapers did precisely that which the Founders hoped and trusted they would do."

—Justice Hugo Black in *New York Times* v. *United States*

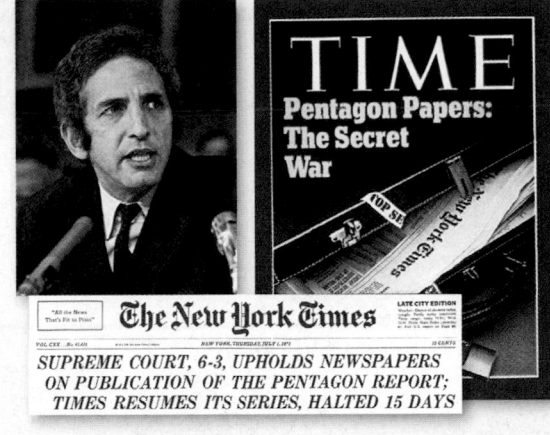

▲ Daniel Ellsberg (above, left) leaked the classified documents known as the Pentagon Papers.

PRIMARY SOURCE

Dissenting View

The First Amendment, after all, is only one part of an entire Constitution. Article II of the great document vests in the Executive Branch primary power over the conduct of foreign affairs and places in that branch the responsibility for the Nation's safety.... What is needed here is a weighing, upon properly developed standards, of the broad right of the press to print and of the very narrow right of the Government to prevent. Such standards are not yet developed. The parties here are in disagreement as to what those standards should be. But even the newspapers concede that there are situations where restraint is in order and is constitutional."

—Justice Harry Blackmun, dissenting in *New York Times* v. *United States*

DBQ Document-Based Questions

1. **Explaining** Why did Justice Black agree with the Court's decision? What did he imply about the government's actions?
2. **Contrasting** Why did Justice Blackmun disagree with the Court's decision?
3. **Assessing** Do you think the government can ever justify media censorship, even based on national security concerns? Explain.

Chapter 19   The Vietnam War   **673**

More About the Case

Daniel Ellsberg, a former bureaucrat working in national security, was unhappy with the course of the war. His leak of the Pentagon Papers did not at first trouble officials in the Nixon administration. Nixon, however, feared that if he did not have control over classified documents, he would later be embarrassed. For his role in the case, Ellsberg was indicted and tried for the leak.

DBQ Document Based Questions

Answers:

1. He feels that the First Amendment guarantees a free press to keep the government from oppressing the people. He implies that the government lied by sending troops off to die for dishonest reasons.
2. He felt the executive branch would know best about issues of national security and thus should be able to restrain the media if necessary.
3. Students' answers will vary.

Differentiated Instruction

Supreme Court Case Study 55

Censorship Prior to Publication

New York Times v. *United States*, 1971

Case Study 55:
New York Times v.
United States, p. 109

Analyzing a Supreme Court Decision

Objective: Learn how the Supreme Court determined whether the government could prevent the publication of materials on the grounds that national security was endangered.

Focus: Identify the central issue of the case.

Teach: Discuss the Court's opinion.

Assess: Explain the importance of the case (interpretation of the First Amendment).

Close: Write a paragraph summarizing the case.

Differentiated Instruction Strategies

BL Explain the role the Vietnam War played in the case.

AL Paraphrase the Court's decision. Read your version to the class.

ELL Explain the First Amendment in your own words.

673

The Legacy of Vietnam

Analyzing VISUALS

Answers:

1. It required the president to consult with Congress before making troop commitments and to inform Congress of any troops committed abroad within 48 hours. Also, unless Congress approved the commitment, troops had to be withdrawn in 60 to 90 days.

2. Students' responses will vary but should be supported by reasons.

The Legacy of Vietnam

MAIN Idea The Vietnam War made a negative impact on the way in which Americans viewed international conflicts, as well as their own government.

HISTORY AND YOU Do you think that leaders at the highest levels of the federal government are trustworthy? Read on to find out how the Vietnam War and other events led Americans to lose some trust in their leaders.

History ONLINE Student Web Activity Visit glencoe.com and complete the activity on the Vietnam Veterans Memorial.

"The lessons of the past in Vietnam," President Ford declared in 1975, "have already been learned—learned by Presidents, learned by Congress, learned by the American people—and we should have our focus on the future." Vietnam had a deep and lasting impact on American society.

The War's Human Toll

The United States paid a heavy price for its involvement in Vietnam. The war had cost the nation over $170 billion in direct costs and much more in indirect economic expenses. It had also resulted in the deaths of approximately 58,000 young Americans and the injury of more than 300,000. In Vietnam, around one million North and South Vietnamese soldiers died in the conflict, as did countless civilians.

PRIMARY SOURCE
The Legacy of Vietnam

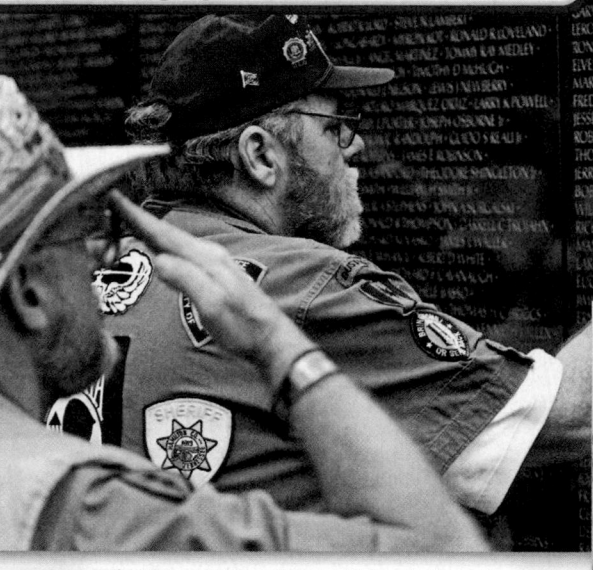

▲ The Vietnam Veterans Memorial is inscribed with the names of the 58,249 people killed or missing in Vietnam.

The War Powers Act

- Requires the president in all cases to consult with Congress before making any troop commitments
- Requires the president to inform Congress of any commitment of troops abroad within 48 hours
- Requires the president to withdraw troops in 60 to 90 days, unless Congress explicitly approves the troop commitment

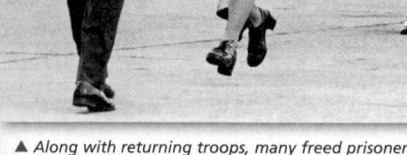

▲ Along with returning troops, many freed prisoners of war, or POWs, such as Lt. Colonel Robert Stirm, were joyfully greeted by their families. Sadly, some did not come home and were labeled as MIAs, or "missing in action," and remain so to this day.

Analyzing VISUALS

1. **Explaining** How did the War Powers Act seek to curb the power of the president?

2. **Assessing** Do you think that the legacy of Vietnam has been a lasting one? Why or why not?

674 Chapter 19 The Vietnam War

Additional Support

Extending the Content

The Vietnam Memorial The names of eight women nurses who died in Vietnam are inscribed on The Wall of the Vietnam Veterans Memorial. Many more women served; a former army nurse began working for a monument to highlight the contributions of women in the war. A sculpture of three women with a soldier, designed by Glenna Goodacre, was dedicated in 1993.

No specific records on women in the military were kept during the war, but it is estimated that as many as 8,000 may have served in Vietnam.

The Vietnam Veterans Memorial was itself controversial. In the fall of 1980, the Vietnam Veterans Memorial Fund sponsored a national competition for the design, to be judged by a panel whose members would

not know the creators of the more than 1400 designs submitted. When 21-year-old Maya Lin, still a student at Yale University, won the competition, many people were dismayed by Lin's youth, gender, and ethnicity, as well as by the design itself, a "black gash of shame," as some called it. The Wall was dedicated in 1982, becoming one of the nation's most-visited public monuments.

Even after they returned home from fighting as in other wars, soldiers found it hard to escape the war's psychological impact. Army Specialist Doug Johnson recalled the problems he faced:

PRIMARY SOURCE

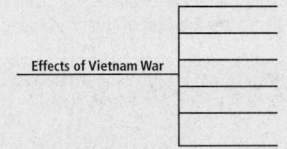 "It took a while for me to recognize that I did suffer some psychological problems in trying to deal with my experience in Vietnam. The first recollection I have of the effect took place shortly after I arrived back in the States. One evening . . . I went to see a movie on post. I don't recall the name of the movie or what it was about, but I remember there was a sad part, and that I started crying uncontrollably. It hadn't dawned on me before this episode that I had . . . succeeded in burying my emotions."

—quoted in *Touched by the Dragon*

One reason why it may have been harder for some Vietnam veterans to readjust to civilian life was that many considered the war a defeat. Many Americans wanted to forget the war. Thus, the sacrifices of many veterans often went unrecognized. There were relatively few welcome-home parades and celebrations after the war.

The war also remained **unresolved** for the American families whose relatives and friends were classified as prisoners of war (POWs) or missing in action (MIA). Despite many official investigations, these families were not convinced that the government had told the truth about POW/MIA policies.

The nation finally began to come to terms with the war almost a decade later. In 1982 the nation dedicated the Vietnam Veterans Memorial in Washington, D.C., a large black granite wall inscribed with the names of those killed and missing in action in the war. "It's a first step to remind America of what we did," veteran Larry Cox of Virginia said at the dedication of the monument.

The War's Impact on the Nation

The war also left its mark on the nation as a whole. In 1973 Congress passed the **War Powers Act** as a way to reestablish some limits on executive power. The act required the president to inform Congress of any commitment of troops abroad within 48 hours, and to withdraw them in 60 to 90 days, unless Congress explicitly approved the troop commitment. No president has recognized this limitation, and the courts have tended to avoid the issue as a strictly political question. Nonetheless, every president since the law's passage has asked Congress to authorize the use of military force before committing ground troops to combat. In general, the war shook the nation's confidence and led some to embrace isolationism, while others began to question the policy of containing communism and instead urged more negotiation with the Soviet Union.

On the domestic front, the Vietnam War increased Americans' cynicism about their government. Many felt the nation's leaders had misled them. Together with Watergate, Vietnam made Americans more wary of their leaders.

Reading Check Describing How did the Vietnam War affect Americans' attitudes toward international conflicts?

Section 3 REVIEW

Vocabulary
1. **Explain** the significance of: Henry Kissinger, linkage, Vietnamization, Pentagon Papers, War Powers Act.

Main Ideas
2. **Explaining** Why was the United States unable to help South Vietnam following the full-scale invasion by North Vietnam in 1975?

3. **Describing** How was the aftermath of the Vietnam War different for its veterans than postwar periods had been for veterans of earlier U.S. wars?

Critical Thinking
4. **Big Ideas** Why did Congress pass the War Powers Act? How did it reflect distrust of the executive branch of government?

5. **Organizing** Use a graphic organizer similar to the one below to list the effects of the Vietnam War on the nation.

Effects of Vietnam War	

6. **Analyzing Visuals** Study the left photo on page 674. Why do you think it is important for society to have war memorials?

Writing About History
7. **Descriptive Writing** Suppose you are a college student in 1970. Write a journal entry expressing your feelings about the events at Kent State University and Jackson State College.

 History ONLINE
Study Central™ To review this section, go to glencoe.com and click on Study Central.

675

R **Reading Strategy**
Reading Primary Sources
Invite a volunteer to read aloud the quotation by Doug Johnson.
Ask: What event triggered Johnson's realization that the war was affecting him emotionally? *(crying uncontrollably at a movie being shown on post)* **BL**

Assess

History ONLINE

Study Central™ provides summaries, interactive games, and online graphic organizers to help students review content.

Close

Summarizing **Ask:** What events led to America pulling out of Vietnam? *(protests over Cambodia, leaking of Pentagon Papers)* **OL**

Reading Check

Answer: They became more reluctant to intervene in other nations' affairs.

Section 3 REVIEW

Answers

1. All definitions can be found in the section and the Glossary.

2. Nixon, who had promised to help, had resigned due to Watergate, and Congress refused to give President Ford the funds.

3. Unlike the periods following other wars, many Americans just wanted to forget the Vietnam War. There was also no sense of having won the conflict, and so there were few welcome-home parades or other celebrations for the returning troops.

4. It wanted to limit executive power. There was a general sense that the presidents had misused the power granted to them in the Gulf of Tonkin Resolution, and it had been found through the Pentagon Papers and other sources that presidents had lied to the American public about the course of the war in Vietnam.

5. Answers may include the following: American cynicism toward government, war dead and casualties, cost, and War Powers Act.

6. Students' responses will vary but may suggest it is important to recall the human costs of war.

7. Students' journal entries should focus on feelings about the events and include descriptive language.

STUDY TO GO — You can study anywhere, anytime by downloading quizzes and flashcards to your PDA from glencoe.com.

Expository Writing Ask students to select one cause or one effect and write a paragraph further explaining the event in its historical context. **OL**

Visual/Spatial Ask students why so many photographs capture people touching the names on the wall. *(Students may say that it is a concrete way to connect with the person whose name is written there.)* **BL**

Causes of the Vietnam War

- During World War II, the United States helps the people of Indochina fight the Japanese, who had invaded the region.
- After World War II, France refuses to give independence to the people of Indochina and sends troops to reestablish control.
- Led by Ho Chi Minh, the Vietminh fight the French. Ho Chi Minh wants Vietnam to be independent but also wants to build a Communist society in Vietnam.
- Concerned about the spread of communism, President Eisenhower sends aid to help the French retain control in Vietnam.
- After losing the battle of Dien Bien Phu, France pulls out of Vietnam. The Geneva Accords create North and South Vietnam.
- Ho Chi Minh becomes the leader of North Vietnam and makes it a Communist nation allied with the USSR and China. North Vietnam begins arming guerrillas to fight the South Vietnamese government.
- American leaders become worried that a "domino effect" might cause all of Southeast Asia to fall to communism if South Vietnam falls.
- President Kennedy sharply increases military aid to South Vietnam.
- President Johnson escalates U.S. involvement and gains war powers after the Gulf of Tonkin incident.

▶ *U.S. troops arrive in Vietnam in 1965 (above). Fighting communist guerrillas proved difficult in the dense jungle terrain (right).*

Effects of the Vietnam War

- Americans applaud President Johnson's response to a Vietcong attack with aggressive air strikes.
- The United States commits over 380,000 ground troops to fighting in Vietnam by the end of 1966.
- American people question the government's honesty about the war, creating the so-called "credibility gap."
- The war casualties and the unfair draft system cause civil unrest.
- The wartime economy hurts domestic spending for programs such as the Great Society.
- President Nixon is elected largely on promises to end the war and unite a divided country.
- Congress passes the War Powers Act to limit the power of the president during wartime.

▲ *The Vietnam Veterans Memorial in Washington, D.C., is a stark reminder of the costs of the Vietnam War.*

676 Chapter 19 The Vietnam War

Hands-On Chapter Project
Step 4

Create a Documentary of the Vietnam War

Step 4: Presenting the Documentaries Ask: What is the message of the documentary?

Directions Allow class time to view the completed documentaries. After each showing, engage the class by asking them to answer the following questions during a class discussion:

- What was the message of the documentary?

- How was the message conveyed? Was it clear?

- What information was "left out" of the documentary?

- What were the best parts of the documentary? Why?

- How could the documentary be improved?

Putting It Together The class should determine as a whole if the documentaries reflected information from the textbook, and if the information was portrayed accurately. **OL**

ASSESSMENT

STANDARDIZED TEST PRACTICE

TEST-TAKING TIP

Do not spend too much time trying to figure out the right answer to a question. Move on, and then come back to that question when you have answered all the questions you do know. If you still do not know the answer, select the one that you think is the most logical.

Reviewing Vocabulary

Directions: Choose the word or words that best complete the sentence.

1. Eisenhower cited the _____ as the reason why the United States had to support South Vietnam.
   A credibility gap
   B self-determination theory
   C domino theory
   D Communist way

2. A person who supported the war effort in Vietnam might be called a
   A hawk.
   B dove.
   C guerrilla.
   D linkage.

3. As the war in Vietnam escalated, a _____ developed as Americans began to find it hard to believe what the Johnson administration said about the conflict.
   A linkage
   B credibility gap
   C domino theory
   D teach-in

4. The Vietcong were Communist _____ located in South Vietnam.
   A elected officials
   B generals
   C diplomats
   D guerrillas

Reviewing Main Ideas

Directions: Choose the best answer for each of the following questions.

Section 1 *(pp. 654–661)*

5. Who was the leader of the North Vietnamese?
   A Mao Zedong
   B Ho Chi Minh
   C Dien Bien Phu
   D Ngo Dinh Diem

6. One reason why President Johnson did not order a full-scale attack on North Vietnam was because
   A he did not think that the United States could win.
   B the military lacked the manpower to launch an assault.
   C he did not want to bring China into the war.
   D he did not want to lose the 1968 election.

7. Which of the following temporarily established North and South Vietnam and recognized Cambodia's independence?
   A the Treaty of Paris
   B Gulf of Tonkin Resolution
   C the Truman Doctrine
   D the Geneva Accords

Section 2 *(pp. 664–669)*

8. Many Americans objected to the draft because they believed it
   A forced young men to flee to Canada.
   B unfairly targeted the poor and minorities.
   C did not include women.
   D did not raise the necessary number of troops.

Need Extra Help?								
If You Missed Questions . . .	1	2	3	4	5	6	7	8
Go to Page . . .	655	667	664	657	654	658	656	665

GO ON

Reviewing Vocabulary

1. C Students may note that two answers are labeled theories, giving a clue that one of those two answers must be correct. By observing that self-determination does not describe the idea of supporting, they can select the domino theory.

2. A Option *D* is easily eliminated, because it is not a term that applies to a person. Because *dove* and *hawk* are contrasting terms, students can also eliminate *C*. Considering the different natures of doves and hawks, students can select the correct answer.

3. B Students with a firm grasp of vocabulary will quickly see that *believe* and *credible* are related words, thus eliminating all false choices.

4. D This question requires simple memorization and identification. There are no real clues in the possible answers themselves, since any of the options could describe Communists.

Reviewing Main ideas

5. B Students should be able to ignore the distraction of Mao Zedong, recalling that he is Chinese. However, this leaves three plausible options. In this case, they will have to resort to basic recall, knowing that Dien Bien Phu is a place and that Ngo Dinh Diem was the leader of South Vietnam.

6. C Knowing that Johnson decided not to run in 1968 will allow students to ignore answer *D*. Options *A* and *B* are also easy to discard as options, since the United States was used to winning wars and the military was at the ready.

7. D Students can eliminate *C* because it is a doctrine and does not sound like a peace treaty. Students should recall that many treaties were signed in Paris, but that this was not one of them. They need to recall as well that the Gulf of Tonkin Resolution was what granted Johnson the power to wage the war. They might also connect the ideas of accord and peace to arrive at the correct answer.

8. B Students can eliminate *A*, which was an unintended effect of the draft. Not including women would not raise an objection, especially in the 1960s. Students should recall that many thousands of military personnel served in the war. They may also recall the objections of Dr. Martin Luther King, Jr., and so choose the correct answer.

9. D The question asks for a turning point against the war. Only *A* and *D* are directly related to the war. None of the other options, although they affected some Americans, influenced public opinion about the war to a great extent. While teach-ins were important in the antiwar movement, they did not turn the majority of public opinion against the war. The Tet Offensive was a major political victory for the North Vietnamese. It led many to believe the war could not be won and widened the credibility gap.

10. D Students should be able to omit Agent Orange, recalling that it was used to deforest Vietnam. Although this leaves three options, they should recall that the suffix *-tion* refers to a process, which aligns it to the idea of a gradual removal.

11. A After abandoning the stalemated war, Americans did not have greater belief in containment as effective nor confidence in their ultimate victory in the Cold War. Within two years the North Vietnamese conquered the South Vietnamese, so there was no need for paranoia about their intentions.

12. B The incorrect options all extend the president's power. Only *B* limits executive power, so it is most likely to be correct.

13. A The resolution gave President Johnson the authority to use force in Vietnam.

14. D If students look carefully at the map, they will see that *D* is the only possible answer.

9. Which of the following events was significant in turning American public opinion against the war in Vietnam?
   A the National Teach-in
   B the 1968 Democratic National Convention
   C the assassination of President Kennedy
   D the Tet Offensive

Section 3 *(pp. 670–675)*

10. The gradual removal of U.S. troops from Vietnam was known as
    A Agent Orange.
    B containment.
    C linkage.
    D Vietnamization.

11. Which of the following was part of the legacy of the Vietnam War?
    A Americans' increased cynicism about their government
    B Americans' belief that the policy of containment worked
    C Americans' confidence that the United States would win the Cold War
    D Americans' paranoia about the intentions of the North Vietnamese government

12. The purpose of the War Powers Act was to ensure that the president would
    A have greater authority over the military.
    B consult Congress before committing troops in extended conflicts.
    C have the authority to sign treaties without Senate approval.
    D have a freer hand in fighting the spread of communism.

Critical Thinking

Directions: Choose the best answers to the following questions.

13. Why is the Gulf of Tonkin Resolution important?
    A It authorized the use of force in Vietnam.
    B It ordered U.S. forces to withdraw from Vietnam.
    C It divided Vietnam into two countries.
    D It required the president to consult Congress before committing troops.

Base your answer to question 14 on the map below and on your knowledge of Chapter 19.

The Vietnam War

14. The Ho Chi Minh trail ran through which two nations?
    A Laos and Japan
    B Laos and Thailand
    C Laos and China
    D Laos and Cambodia

Need Extra Help?						
If You Missed Questions . . .	9	10	11	12	13	14
Go to Page . . .	667–668	670	674–675	675	658	R15

GO ON

15. On which idea is the Twenty-sixth Amendment based?

  A Women should be allowed to serve in the armed forces.

  B The president, not Congress, should decide where and when troops will fight.

  C A person who is old enough to fight is old enough to vote.

  D A draft is an old-fashioned and unworkable system for selecting soldiers.

Analyze the cartoon and answer the questions that follow. Base your answers on the cartoon and on your knowledge of Chapter 19.

16. In this cartoon, the Vietnam War is represented by Johnson and his aides walking through

  A a dark jungle.

  B a minefield.

  C a blinding storm.

  D a dark tunnel.

17. The cartoonist is expressing the opinion that

  A the Johnson administration has no idea of how to get out of Vietnam.

  B President Johnson is being pulled back by his cabinet to stay in the conflict.

  C Vietnam is a conflict with an easy solution.

  D President Johnson is a great leader with a solution to the problems in Vietnam.

Need Extra Help?

If You Missed Questions . . .	15	16	17	18	19	20
Go to Page . . .	666–667	R18	R18	R19	R19	R13

Document-Based Questions

Directions: Analyze the document and answer the short-answer questions that follow the document.

In the 1960s many young Americans enlisted or were drafted for military service. Some believed that they had a duty to serve their country. Many had no clear idea of what they were doing or why. In the following excerpt, a young man expresses his thoughts about going to war:

> "I read a lot of pacifist literature to determine whether or not I was a conscientious objector. I finally concluded that I wasn't. . . .
> The one clear decision I made in 1968 about me and the war was that if I was going to get out of it, I was going to get out in a legal way. I was not going to defraud the system in order to beat the system. I wasn't going to leave the country, because the odds of coming back looked real slim. . . .
> With all my terror of going into the Army . . . there was something seductive about it, too. I was seduced by World War II and John Wayne movies. . . . I had been, as we all were, victimized by a romantic, truly uninformed view of war."
> —quoted in *Nam*

18. What options did the young man have regarding the war?

19. Do you think World War II movies gave him a realistic view of what fighting in Vietnam would be like?

Extended Response

20. The conflict in Vietnam has been called the first "television war." Americans could watch scenes of death and destruction unfold in front of them from their living rooms. Write an expository essay about how television changed the way Americans view war in general and how it contributed to the unpopularity of the Vietnam War specifically. Your essay should include an introduction and at least three paragraphs that explore this issue.

STOP

History ONLINE

For additional test practice, use Self-Check Quizzes—Chapter 19 at glencoe.com.

19. No; the young man realized that the view of war he had from World War II and the movies was romanticized and not at all like what real war would be like.

20. Students' essays will vary but should clearly and logically express the changing effects of television on Americans' perceptions of the Vietnam war and war in general.

15. C Students familiar with the type of content in constitutional amendments will readily eliminate the false possibilities, even if they cannot recall the subject of the Twenty-Sixth Amendment. Other students may remember that protest of the draft also raised questions about the voting age.

16. D By studying the cartoon, students can see that the setting of neither *A* nor *C* makes sense. Given the nature of the background and the etching on the wall, the president and his aides are clearly walking in a tunnel.

17. A The other options are clearly false. No one is pulling on Johnson, who appears to be feeling his way in the dark, thus indicating the lack of easy solutions.

18. He could declare he was a conscientious objector, avoid service in a legal way, leave the country, or become part of the military.

History ONLINE

Have students visit the Web site at glencoe.com to review Chapter 19 and take the Self-Check Quiz.

Need Extra Help?

Have students refer to the pages listed if they miss any of the questions.

679

Levels (BL / OL / AL / ELL)				Resources	Chapter Opener	Section 1	Section 2	Section 3	Chapter Assess
FOCUS									
BL	OL	AL	ELL	Daily Focus Skills Transparencies		20-1	20-2	20-3	
TEACH									
		AL		American Literature Reading, URB			p. 13		
BL	OL		ELL	Reading Essentials and Note-Taking Guide*		p. 209	p. 212	p. 215	
	OL			Historical Analysis Skills Activity, URB				p. 118	
BL	OL		ELL	Guided Reading Activities, URB*		p. 144	p. 145	p. 146	
BL	OL	AL	ELL	Content Vocabulary Activity, URB*	p. 123				
BL	OL	AL	ELL	Academic Vocabulary Activity, URB	p. 125				
	OL	AL		Critical Thinking Skills Activity, URB		p. 128			
BL	OL		ELL	Reading Skills Activity, URB		p. 117			
BL	OL		ELL	English Learner Activity, URB				p. 121	
	OL	AL		Reinforcing Skills Activity, URB			p. 127		
BL	OL	AL	ELL	Differentiated Instruction Activity, URB			p. 119		
BL	OL		ELL	Time Line Activity, URB		p. 129			
	OL			Linking Past and Present Activity, URB			p. 130		
BL	OL	AL	ELL	American Art and Music Activity, URB		p. 135			
BL	OL	AL	ELL	Interpreting Political Cartoons Activity, URB			p. 137		
		AL		Enrichment Activity, URB		p. 141			
BL	OL	AL	ELL	American Biographies			✓	✓	
BL	OL	AL	ELL	Primary Source Reading, URB		p. 131		p. 133	
BL	OL	AL		Supreme Court Case Studies			pp. 111, 115		
BL	OL	AL	ELL	The Living Constitution*	✓	✓	✓	✓	✓
	OL	AL		American History Primary Source Documents Library	✓	✓	✓	✓	✓
BL	OL	AL	ELL	Unit Map Overlay Transparencies	✓	✓	✓	✓	✓
BL	OL	AL	ELL	Differentiated Instruction for the American High School Classroom	✓	✓	✓	✓	✓
BL	OL	AL	ELL	StudentWorks™ Plus DVD	✓	✓	✓	✓	✓
BL	OL	AL	ELL	Vocabulary PuzzleMaker CD-ROM	✓	✓	✓	✓	✓

Note: Please refer to the *Unit 6 Resource Book* for this chapter's URB materials.

* Also available in Spanish

TeacherWorks *Plus*
All-In-One Planner and Resource Center

- Interactive Lesson Planner
- Interactive Teacher Edition
- Fully editable blackline masters
- Section Spotlight Videos Launch

- Differentiated Lesson Plans
- Printable reports of daily assignments
- Standards Tracking System

Levels					Resources	Chapter Opener	Section 1	Section 2	Section 3	Chapter Assess
BL	OL	AL	ELL		**TEACH** *(continued)*					
BL	OL	AL	ELL	●	American Music Hits Through History CD	✓	✓	✓	✓	✓
BL	OL	AL	ELL	📁	Unit Time Line Transparencies and Activities	✓	✓	✓	✓	✓
BL	OL	AL	ELL	📁	Cause and Effect Transparencies, Strategies, and Activities	✓	✓	✓	✓	✓
BL	OL	AL	ELL	📁	Why It Matters Chapter Transparencies, Strategies, and Activities	✓	✓	✓	✓	✓
BL	OL	AL	ELL	📁	American Issues	✓	✓	✓	✓	✓
	OL	AL	ELL	📁	American Art and Architecture Transparencies, Strategies, and Activities	✓	✓	✓	✓	✓
BL	OL	AL		📁	High School American History Literature Library	✓	✓	✓	✓	✓
BL	OL	AL	ELL	📀	*The American Vision* Video Program DVD	✓	✓	✓	✓	✓
BL	OL	AL	ELL	📁	Reading Strategies and Activities for the Social Studies Classroom	✓	✓	✓	✓	✓
Teacher Resources				📁	Strategies for Success	✓	✓	✓	✓	✓
				📁	Success with English Learners	✓	✓	✓	✓	✓
				📀	Presentation Plus! DVD	✓	✓	✓	✓	✓
					ASSESS					
BL	OL	AL	ELL	📁	Section Quizzes and Chapter Tests*		p. 279	p. 280	p. 281	p. 283
BL	OL	AL	ELL	📁	Authentic Assessment With Rubrics					p. 45
BL	OL	AL	ELL	📁	Standardized Test Practice Workbook					p. 47
BL	OL	AL	ELL	●	*ExamView® Assessment Suite* CD-ROM		20-1	20-2	20-3	Ch. 20
BL	OL	AL	ELL	●	Interactive Tutor Self-Assessment CD-ROM		20-1	20-2	20-3	Ch. 20
					CLOSE					
BL			ELL	📁	Reteaching Activity, URB					p. 139
BL	OL		ELL	📁	Reading and Study Skills Foldables™	p. 81				

Using PuzzleMaker™ 3.1

Online Crossword Puzzles

Technology Product

Glencoe's Vocabulary PuzzleMaker™ 3.1 CD-ROM is an easy-to-use program that lets you create your own puzzles based on the glossary for classroom use. The PuzzleMaker allows you to

- create crossword puzzles based on content vocabulary and academic vocabulary that is specific to what is taught in the classroom;
- create online (LAN-based or local area network) or paper crossword puzzles.

Objectives

Completing the crossword puzzles helps students to

- recall vocabulary terms based on the clues provided for a puzzle;
- reinforce their understanding of the vocabulary.

Steps

- Run PuzzleMaker™ 3.1. On the main menu, click on **Create a New Puzzle.**
- From the list of *Puzzle Databases*, select the appropriate database for the vocabulary.
- The *PuzzleMaker Wizard* will take you through selecting a puzzle type and grid type.
- Then select one of the chapters from the list. Indicate whether you want the words selected randomly or manually.
- Select the language and words you wish to use within the maximum for the puzzle. Click **Finish**.
- Save your puzzle to a location that is easily accessible by your students with PuzzlePlayer™ 3.1, or print copies for your students to complete.
- Use PuzzlePlayer™ 3.1 to review the puzzles after your students have worked on and saved them.

History ONLINE

	Student	Teacher	Parent
Beyond the Textbook	●	●	●
Chapter Overviews	●	●	●
Time Current Events	●		●
ePuzzles and Games	●		●
Concepts in Motion	●		●
Literature Connections		●	
Multi-Language Glossaries	●		●
Online Student Edition	●	●	●
Self-Check Quizzes	●		●
Student Web Activities	●		●
Study Central™	●		●
Teaching Today		●	
Vocabulary eFlashcards	●		●
Web Activity Lesson Plans		●	

Glencoe Media Center

glencoe.com

> **Study-To-Go**
- Vocabulary eFlashcards
- Self-Check Quizzes

> **Audio/Video**
- Student Edition Audio
- Spanish Summaries
- Section Videos

- **Timed Readings Plus in Social Studies** helps students increase their reading rate and fluency while maintaining comprehension. The 400-word passages are similar to those found on state and national assessments.

- **Reading in the Content Area: Social Studies** concentrates on six essential reading skills that help students better comprehend what they read. The book includes 75 high-interest nonfiction passages written at increasing levels of difficulty.

- **Reading Social Studies** includes strategic reading instruction and vocabulary support in Social Studies content for both ELLs and native speakers of English.

www.jamestowneducation.com

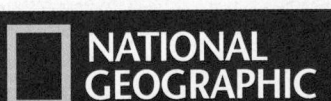

Index to National Geographic Magazine:

The following articles relate to this chapter:

- "Latinos Rise Nationwide: America's New Majority Minority," by A.R. Williams, November 2003.

- "Philadelphia's African Americans: A Celebration of Life," by Roland L. Freeman, August 1990.

Access National Geographic's new, dynamic MapMachine Web site and other geography resources at:

www.nationalgeographic.com
www.nationalgeographic.com/maps

The following videotape programs are available from Glencoe as supplements to Chapter 20:

- Jimmy Carter (ISBN 1-56-501530-4)
- Drive for the American Dream (ISBN 1-56-501221-6)

To order, call Glencoe at 1-800-334-7344. To find classroom resources to accompany many of these videos, check the following home pages:

A&E Television: www.aetv.com
The History Channel: www.historychannel.com

Reading List Generator CD-ROM

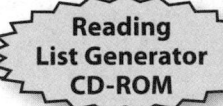

Use this database to search more than 30,000 titles to create a customized reading list for your students.

- Reading lists can be organized by students' reading level, author, genre, theme, or area of interest.
- The database provides Degrees of Reading Power™ (DRP) and Lexile™ readability scores for all selections.
- A brief summary of each selection is included.

Leveled reading suggestions for this chapter:

For students at a Grade 8 reading level:
- *Learning about Justice from the Life of César Chávez*, by Jeanne Strazzabosco

For students at a Grade 9 reading level:
- *Cesar Chavez: Labor Leader*, by Maria E. Cedeno

For students at a Grade 10 reading level:
- *Warriors Don't Cry*, by Melba Pattillo Beals

For students at a Grade 11 reading level:
- *The Beatles*, by Michael Burgan

For students at a Grade 12 reading level:
- *Andy Warhol: Prince of Pop*, by Jan Greenburg & Sandra Jordan

Focus

MAKING CONNECTIONS
Can Protests Bring Change?

Ask students to give examples of why groups today use public protest to achieve change. Have students discuss whether protesters in the 1960s and 1970s might have achieved comparable change using other approaches. Then ask whether the protests of the 1960s and 1970s continue to influence the rights, workplaces, and economic opportunities of students, women, and Latinos today. Students should evaluate their answers after they have completed the chapter. **OL**

Teach
The Big Ideas

As students study the chapter, remind them to consider the section-based Big Ideas included in each section's Guide to Reading. The **Essential Questions** in the activities below tie in to the Big Ideas and help students think about and understand important chapter concepts. In addition, the Hands-on Chapter Projects with their culminating activities relate the content from each section to the Big Ideas. These activities build on each other as students progress through the chapter. Section activities culminate in the wrap-up activity on the Visual Summary page.

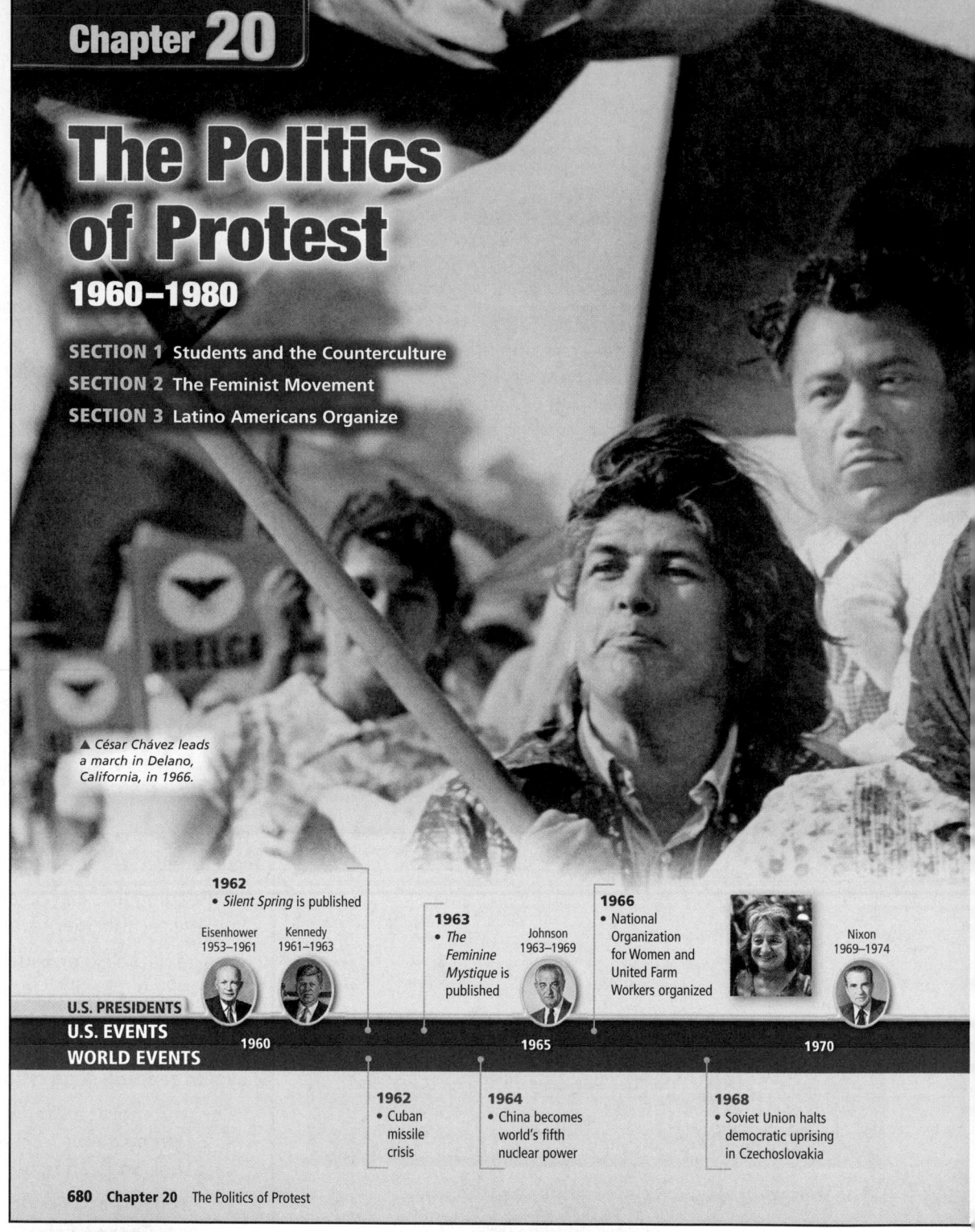

Chapter 20

The Politics of Protest
1960–1980

SECTION 1 Students and the Counterculture
SECTION 2 The Feminist Movement
SECTION 3 Latino Americans Organize

▲ César Chávez leads a march in Delano, California, in 1966.

U.S. PRESIDENTS
U.S. EVENTS
WORLD EVENTS

Eisenhower 1953–1961
Kennedy 1961–1963
Johnson 1963–1969
Nixon 1969–1974

1960

1962
• *Silent Spring* is published

1963
• *The Feminine Mystique* is published

1966
• National Organization for Women and United Farm Workers organized

1965

1970

1962
• Cuban missile crisis

1964
• China becomes world's fifth nuclear power

1968
• Soviet Union halts democratic uprising in Czechoslovakia

680 Chapter 20 The Politics of Protest

Section 1

Students and the Counterculture
Essential Question: How did students and the counterculture want to change society? *(They wanted a society that was free of war, poverty, pressure to conform, and materialism; was tolerant; and offered equal justice and opportunity for all.)* Point out that in Section 1 students will learn about the impact of protest and the counterculture on society. **OL**

Section 2

The Feminist Movement
Essential Question: What were the goals of the feminist movement that began in the 1960s? *(Women wanted equal pay for equal work, better educational and career opportunities, more career choices, and reproductive choice.)* Point out that in Section 2 students will learn about the impact of the renewed women's movement on society. **OL**

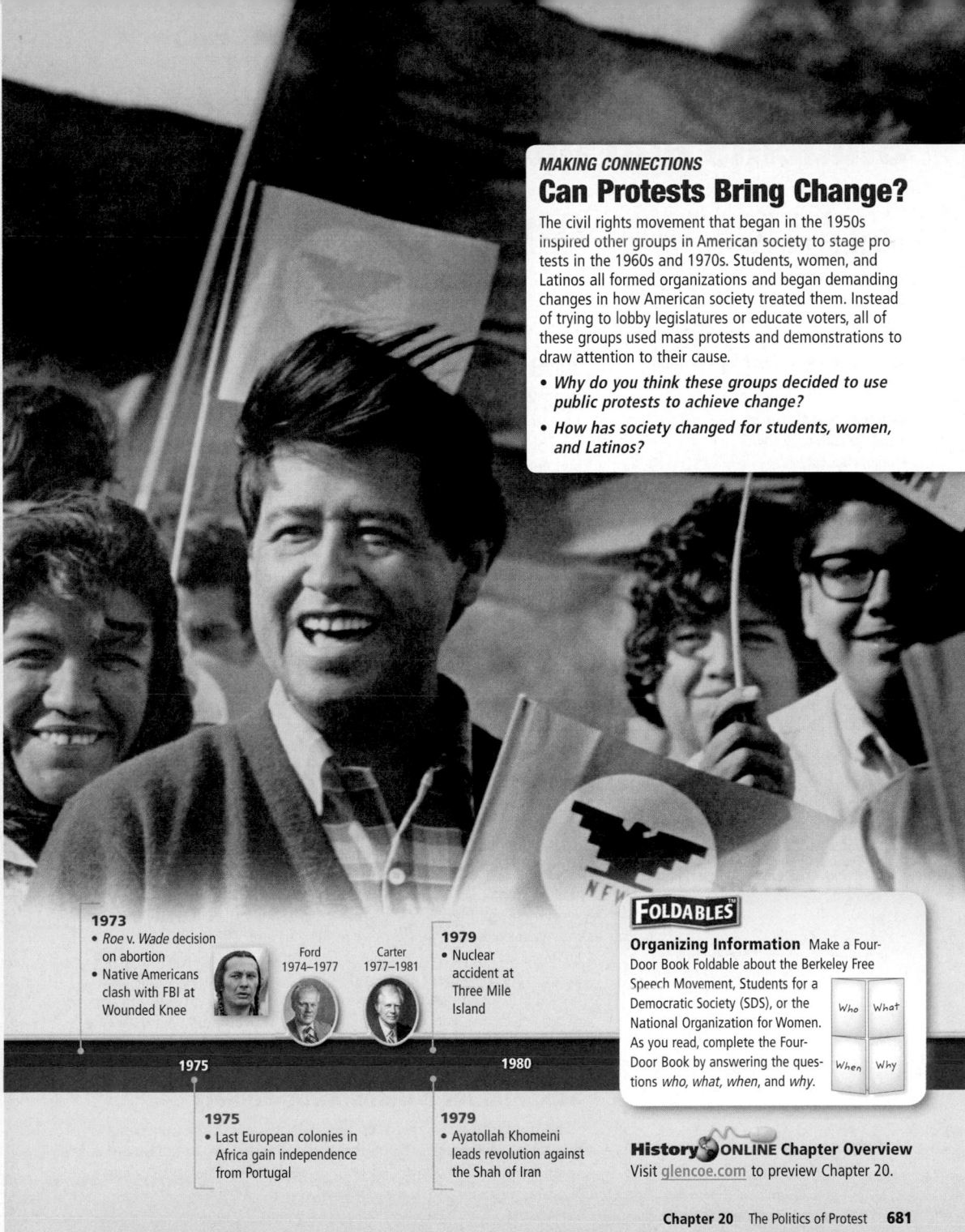

More About the Photo

Visual Literacy César Chávez was born in 1927 on a small farm near Yuma, Arizona. When his father lost his land during the Depression, Chávez began working as a migrant farm worker to help support the family. After serving in the navy during World War II, he returned to farm labor. Soon he became committed to improving the lives of farm workers. For his leadership, he received the Presidential Medal of Freedom.

FOLDABLES **Dinah Zike's**
Study Organizer **Foldables**

Dinah Zike's Foldables are three-dimensional, interactive graphic organizers that help students practice basic writing skills, review vocabulary terms, and identify main ideas. Instructions for creating and using Foldables can be found in the Appendix at the end of this book and in the *Dinah Zike's Reading and Study Skills Foldables* booklet.

History ONLINE
Introduce students to chapter content and key terms by having them access the Chapter 20 Overview at glencoe.com.

MAKING CONNECTIONS

Can Protests Bring Change?

The civil rights movement that began in the 1950s inspired other groups in American society to stage protests in the 1960s and 1970s. Students, women, and Latinos all formed organizations and began demanding changes in how American society treated them. Instead of trying to lobby legislatures or educate voters, all of these groups used mass protests and demonstrations to draw attention to their cause.

- *Why do you think these groups decided to use public protests to achieve change?*
- *How has society changed for students, women, and Latinos?*

1973
- *Roe* v. *Wade* decision on abortion
- Native Americans clash with FBI at Wounded Knee

Ford 1974–1977

Carter 1977–1981

1979
- Nuclear accident at Three Mile Island

1975

1980

1975
- Last European colonies in Africa gain independence from Portugal

1979
- Ayatollah Khomeini leads revolution against the Shah of Iran

FOLDABLES™

Organizing Information Make a Four-Door Book Foldable about the Berkeley Free Speech Movement, Students for a Democratic Society (SDS), or the National Organization for Women. As you read, complete the Four-Door Book by answering the questions *who, what, when,* and *why.*

Who	What
When	Why

History ONLINE Chapter Overview
Visit glencoe.com to preview Chapter 20.

Chapter 20   The Politics of Protest   **681**

Section 3

Latino Americans Organize

Essential Question: What were the goals of the Latinos who organized? *(They wanted an end to discrimination; improved working conditions, and greater pay, especially for farm workers; increased Latino voter participation and more Latino candidates elected.)* Point out that in Section 3 students will learn about the impact of Latino organizations and movements. **OL**

Focus

Bellringer
Daily Focus Transparency 20.1

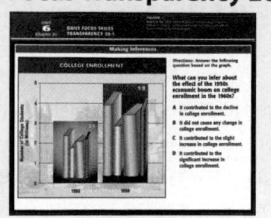

Guide to Reading

Answer to the Graphic:

I. The Rise of the Youth Movement
   A. SDS
   B. The Free Speech Movement

II. The Counterculture
   A. Hippie Culture
   B. The Impact of Counterculture
      1. Fashion
      2. Music

Section Spotlight Video

To generate student interest and provide a springboard for class discussion, access the Chapter 20, Section 1 video at glencoe.com or on the video DVD.

Resource Manager

Section 1

Students and the Counterculture

Guide to Reading

Big Ideas
Struggles for Rights During the 1960s, many of the country's young people raised their voices in protest against numerous aspects of American society.

Content Vocabulary
- counterculture (p. 684)
- hippies (p. 684)
- communes (p. 685)

Academic Vocabulary
- rationality (p. 684)
- conformity (p. 685)

People and Events to Identify
- Port Huron Statement (p. 683)
- Tom Hayden (p. 683)
- Free Speech Movement (p. 683)
- Haight-Ashbury district (p. 685)
- Woodstock (p. 685)
- Bob Dylan (p. 685)

Reading Strategy
Organizing Use the major headings of this section to create an outline similar to the one below.

> **Students and the Counterculture**
> I. The Rise of the Youth Movement
>   A.
>   B.
> II.
>   A.
>   B.

The 1960s was one of the most tumultuous decades in American history. The decade also gave birth to a youth movement that challenged the American political and social system and conventional middle-class values.

The Rise of the Youth Movement

MAIN Idea The youth protest movement of the 1960s included Students for a Democratic Society and the Free Speech Movement.

HISTORY AND YOU Do you know of any groups that work to improve society? Read how the youth of the 1960s protested social injustice.

The roots of the 1960s youth movement stretched back to the 1950s. In the decade after World War II, the country had enjoyed a time of peace and prosperity. Prosperity did not extend to all, however, and some, especially the artists and writers of the beat movement, had openly criticized American society. They believed American society valued conformity over independence and financial gain over spiritual and social advancement.

At the same time, the turmoil of the civil rights movement had raised serious questions about racism in American society, and the nuclear arms race between the United States and the Soviet Union made many of the nation's youth uneasy about the future. For many young people, the events of the 1950s had called into question the wisdom of their parents and their political leaders.

The youth movement originated with the baby boomers, the huge generation born after World War II. By 1970, 58.4 percent of the American population was 34 years old or younger. (By comparison, those 34 or younger in 2000 represented an estimated 48.9 percent.) The early 1960s also saw a rapid increase in enrollment at colleges. The economic boom of the 1950s meant more families could afford to send their children to college. Between 1960 and 1966, enrollment in four-year colleges rose from 3.1 million to almost 5 million. College life gave young people a sense of freedom and independence. It also allowed them to meet and bond with others who shared their feelings about society and fears about the future. It was on college campuses across the nation that youth protest movements began and reached their peak.

Students for a Democratic Society

Some young people were concerned most about the injustices they saw in the country's political and social system. In their view, a small wealthy elite controlled politics, and wealth itself was unfairly

---

R Reading Strategies	**C** Critical Thinking	**D** Differentiated Instruction	**W** Writing Support	**S** Skill Practice
Additional Resources • Pri. Source Read., URB p. 131 • Guid. Read. Act., URB p. 144	**Teacher Edition** • Analyzing Pri. Sources, p. 683 **Additional Resources** • Critical Thinking Skills Activity, URB p. 128 • Quizzes and Tests, p. 279	**Additional Resources** • Am. Art and Music Act., p. 135 • Enrichment Act., URB p. 141	**Teacher Edition** • Descriptive Writing, p. 684 **Additional Resources** • Content Vocab. Act., URB p. 123 • Academic Vocab. Act., URB p. 125	**Additional Resources** • Read. Skills Act., URB p. 117 • Time Line Act., URB p. 129 • RENTG, p. 209

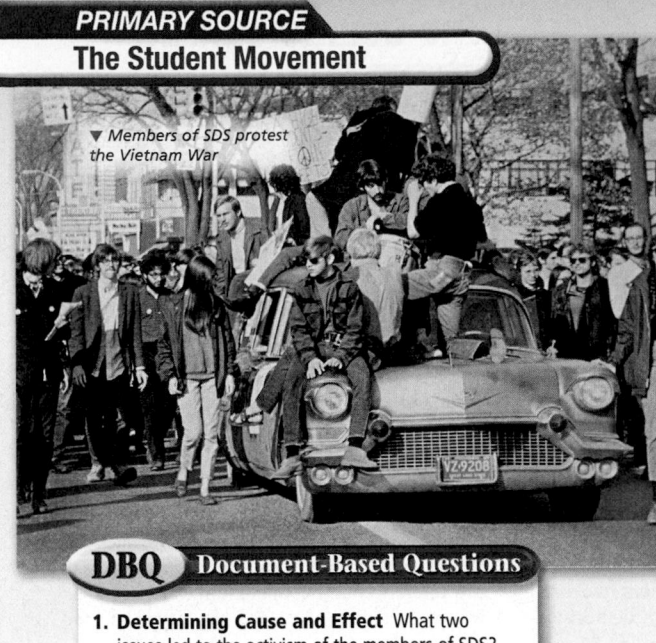

PRIMARY SOURCE
The Student Movement

▼ Members of SDS protest the Vietnam War

PRIMARY SOURCE

In 1962 Students for a Democratic Society issued the Port Huron Statement explaining SDS and the reasons for their actions:

"We are people of this generation, bred in at least modest comfort, housed now in universities, looking uncomfortably to the world we inherit. . . .

When we were kids the United States was the wealthiest and strongest country in the world . . . Freedom and equality for each individual, government of, by, and for the people—these American values we found good. . . .

As we grew, however, our comfort was penetrated by events too troubling to dismiss. First, the permeating and victimizing fact of human degradation, symbolized by the Southern struggle against racial bigotry, compelled most of us from silence to activism. Second, the enclosing fact of the Cold War, symbolized by the presence of the Bomb, brought awareness that we ourselves, and our friends, and millions of abstract 'others' . . . might die at any time.

. . . Our work is guided by the sense that we may be the last generation in the experiment with living. . . . The search for truly democratic alternatives to the present, and a commitment to social experimentation with them, is a worthy and fulfilling human enterprise, one which moves us and, we hope, others today.

—from the *Port Huron Statement,* 1962

C

DBQ Document-Based Questions

1. **Determining Cause and Effect** What two issues led to the activism of the members of SDS?

2. **Summarizing** What were the two goals of the group?

divided. These young people formed what came to be known as the New Left. (The "new" left differed from the "old" left of the 1930s, which had advocated socialism and communism.)

A prominent organization within the New Left was Students for a Democratic Society (SDS), founded in 1959. It defined its views in a 1962 declaration known as the **Port Huron Statement.** Written largely by **Tom Hayden,** editor of the University of Michigan's student newspaper, the declaration called for an end to apathy and urged citizens to stop accepting a country run by big corporations and big government.

SDS chapters focused on protesting the Vietnam War, but they also addressed other issues, including poverty, campus regulations, nuclear power, and racism. In 1968, for example, SDS leaders assisted in an eight-day occupation of several buildings at Columbia University to protest the administration's plan to build a new gym in an area that had served as a neighborhood park near Harlem.

The Free Speech Movement

Another movement that captured the nation's attention in the 1960s was the **Free Speech Movement,** led by Mario Savio and others at the University of California at Berkeley. The movement began when the university decided, in the fall of 1964, to restrict students' rights to distribute literature and to recruit volunteers for political causes on campus. The protesters, however, quickly targeted more general campus matters as well.

Like many college students, those at Berkeley were dissatisfied with practices at their university. Officials divided huge classes into sections taught by graduate students, while many professors claimed they were too busy with research to meet with students. Faceless administrators made rules that were not always easy to obey and imposed punishments for violations. Feeling isolated in this impersonal environment, many Berkeley students rallied to support the Free Speech Movement.

Chapter 20 The Politics of Protest **683**

Teach

C Critical Thinking

Analyzing Primary Sources
Have students read the Primary Source on page 683. **Ask:** How did the American values the students had embraced as children help motivate their later protests? *(Racism and inequality were at odds with these values.)* **BL**

DBQ Document Based Questions

Answers:
1. Accept any two: racism, the Cold War, threat of nuclear attack
2. truly democratic alternatives to the present and social experimentation

Hands-On Chapter Project
Step 1

Presenting a Historical Drama

Step 1: Assigning Groups Small groups of students receive their assignments.

Directions Organize the class into groups and have each prepare a dramatic presentation on one of the situations below or another of their choice. Encourage all students to participate and have each group present their skit to the rest of the class.

• a brother and sister in college trying to explain the counterculture to their parents
• a group of women at the first meeting of the National Organization for Women, setting goals and planning action
• a group of Latino farm workers discussing the benefits and risks of a strike

Putting It Together Encourage students to begin a separate section of their notebooks to take notes on the chapter from the perspective of the Americans they will role-play. **OL**

(Chapter Project continued on page 687)

The struggle between Berkeley's students and administrators peaked on December 2, 1964, with a sit-in and powerful speech by Savio. Early the next morning, 600 police officers entered the campus and arrested more than 700 protesters.

The arrests set off an even larger protest movement. Within days, a campus-wide strike had stopped classes and many members of the faculty also voiced their support for the Free Speech Movement. In the face of this growing opposition, the administration gave in to the students' demands.

Soon afterward, the Supreme Court upheld students' rights to freedom of speech and assembly on campuses. In a unanimous vote, the Court upheld the section of the Civil Rights Act assuring these rights in places offering public accommodations, which, by definition, included college campuses. The Berkeley revolt was one of the first major student protests in the 1960s, and it became a model for others. The tactics the Berkeley protesters had used were soon being used in college demonstrations across the country.

✔ **Reading Check** **Synthesizing** What were three reasons for the growth of the youth movement of the 1960s?

The Counterculture

MAIN Idea Counterculture youths tried to create an alternative to mainstream culture.

HISTORY AND YOU Do you know anyone today who rejects mainstream society? Read on to learn about the ideas of the 1960s counterculture.

While many young Americans in the 1960s sought to reform the system, others rejected it entirely and tried to create a new lifestyle based on flamboyant dress, rock music, drug use, and communal living. They created what became known as the **counterculture** and were commonly called "**hippies.**"

Hippie Culture

Originally, hippies rejected **rationality**, order, and traditional middle-class values. They wanted to build a utopia—a society that was freer, closer to nature, and full of love, empathy, tolerance, and cooperation. Much of this was a reaction to the 1950s stereotype of the white-collar "man in the gray flannel suit" who led a constricted and colorless life.

As the counterculture grew, many newcomers did not understand these ideas. For them, what mattered were the outward signs that

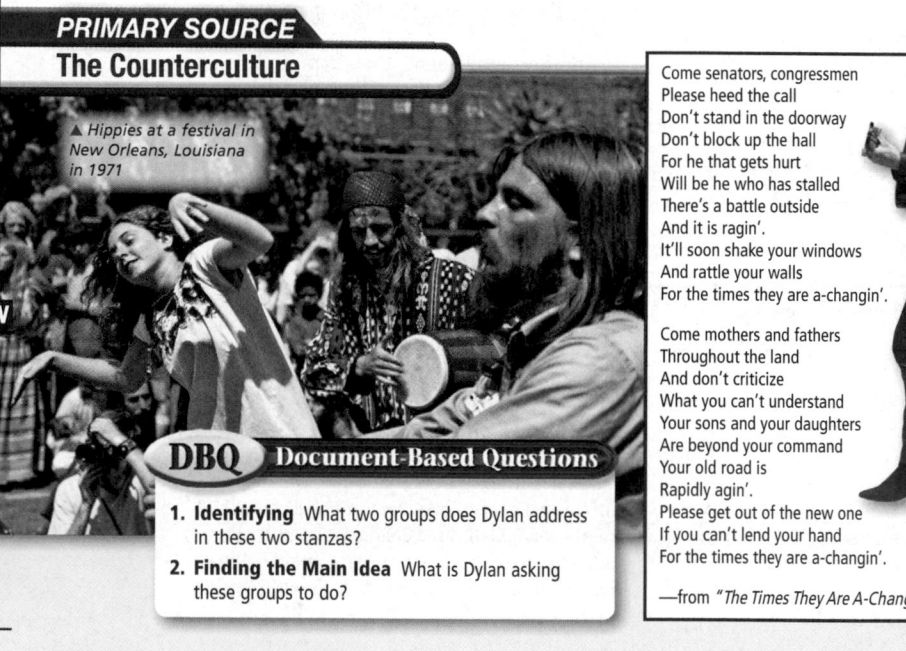

PRIMARY SOURCE
The Counterculture

▲ Hippies at a festival in New Orleans, Louisiana in 1971

Come senators, congressmen
Please heed the call
Don't stand in the doorway
Don't block up the hall
For he that gets hurt
Will be he who has stalled
There's a battle outside
And it is ragin'.
It'll soon shake your windows
And rattle your walls
For the times they are a-changin'.

Come mothers and fathers
Throughout the land
And don't criticize
What you can't understand
Your sons and your daughters
Are beyond your command
Your old road is
Rapidly agin'.
Please get out of the new one
If you can't lend your hand
For the times they are a-changin'.

—from "The Times They Are A-Changin'"

▲ Bob Dylan performs at the Newport Folk Festival in 1965.

DBQ Document-Based Questions

1. **Identifying** What two groups does Dylan address in these two stanzas?
2. **Finding the Main Idea** What is Dylan asking these groups to do?

684   **Chapter 20**   The Politics of Protest

defined the movement—long hair, Native American headbands, cowboy boots, long dresses, shabby jeans, and the use of drugs.

Many hippies wanted to drop out of society by leaving home and living together in **communes**—group living arrangements in which members shared everything and worked together. Some hippies established rural communes, while others lived together in parks or crowded apartments in large cities. One of the most famous hippie destinations was San Francisco's **Haight-Ashbury district.** By the mid-1960s, thousands of hippies had flocked there.

The Impact of the Counterculture

After a few years, the counterculture movement began to decline. Some urban hippie communities became dangerous places where muggings and other criminal activity took place. The glamour of drug use waned as more and more young people became addicted or died from overdoses. In addition, many people in the movement had gotten older and moved on. Although the counterculture declined without achieving its utopian ideals, it did change some aspects of American culture.

Fashion Protesters and members of the counterculture often expressed themselves with their clothing. By wearing cheap surplus clothes recycled from earlier decades and repaired with patches, they showed that they were rejecting both consumerism and the social class structure. Ethnic clothing was popular for similar reasons. Beads and fringes imitated Native American costumes, while tie-dyed shirts borrowed techniques from India and Africa.

Perhaps the most potent symbol of the era was hair. Long hair, beards, and mustaches on young men symbolized defiance of both 1950s **conformity**—when buzz cuts were popular—and the military, which required all recruits to have short hair. School officials at the time debated the acceptable length of a student's hair. Over time, however, longer hair on men and more individual clothing for both genders became generally accepted. What was once the clothing of defiance became mainstream.

Music Counterculture musicians made use of folk music and the rhythms of rock 'n' roll and wrote heartfelt lyrics that expressed the hopes and fears of their generation. At festivals such as **Woodstock,** held in upstate New York in August 1969, and in Altamont, California, later that year, hundreds of thousands of people gathered to listen to the new music.

Major folk singers included **Bob Dylan,** who became an important voice of the movement, as did singers Joan Baez and Pete Seeger. Rock musicians popular with the counterculture included Jimi Hendrix, Janis Joplin, and The Who. These musicians used electrically amplified instruments that drastically changed the sound of rock, and their innovations continue to influence musicians today.

✓ **Reading Check** **Evaluating** What lasting impact did the counterculture have on the nation?

Section 1 REVIEW

Vocabulary

1. **Explain** the significance of: Port Huron Statement, Tom Hayden, Free Speech Movement, counterculture, hippies, communes, Haight-Ashbury district, Woodstock, Bob Dylan.

Main Ideas

2. **Describing** With what issues did SDS concern itself?

3. **Summarizing** What were the core ideals of the members of the counterculture?

Critical Thinking

4. **Big Ideas** How did the U.S. Supreme Court validate the actions of the members of the Free Speech Movement?

5. **Organizing** Use a graphic organizer similar to the one below to list the causes of the youth movement.

Causes

Youth Movement

6. **Analyzing Visuals** Study the image on page 683. Why do you think that older adults were frightened or threatened by the student movement?

Writing About History

7. **Descriptive Writing** Suppose that you are a journalist in the 1960s. Write an article in which you visit a commune and describe the hippie culture of the day.

History ONLINE
Study Central™ To review this section, go to glencoe.com and click on Study Central.

685

✓ Reading Check

Answer: changes in fashion and music and the idea that alternatives to mainstream culture were possible

Assess

History ONLINE

Study Central™ provides summaries, interactive games, and online graphic organizers to help students review content.

Close

Summarizing Ask: What were the goals and accomplishments of the student movement and the counterculture? *(They wanted a society that was free of war, poverty, pressure to conform, and materialism; was tolerant; and offered equal justice and opportunity for all. Students won freedom of speech, assembly, and public protest in general. The counterculture liberalized fashion, influenced music and lessened pressure to conform.)*

Section 1 REVIEW

Answers

1. All definitions can be found in the section and the Glossary.

2. It focused on protesting the Vietnam War, but it also addressed other issues, including poverty, racism, freedom of speech and assembly, and nuclear power, unequal distribution of wealth.

3. They wanted a society that was freer, closer to nature, and full of love, empathy, tolerance, and cooperation.

4. It upheld the rights to freedom of speech and of assembly on campuses.

5. criticism of conformity and materialism, baby boom and increased college enrollments, social and political injustice

6. Possible answer: The students' culture was completely different from the culture of their parents. The young people appeared unkempt, they seemed disrespectful of the values of their parents, and they were vocal and angry.

7. Students' articles will vary. Articles should include descriptions of hippie commune life based on the section and students' prior knowledge.

Focus

Bellringer
Daily Focus Transparency 20.2

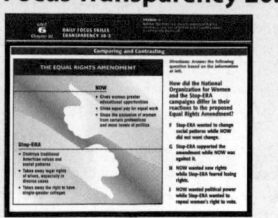

Guide to Reading

Answers: League of Women Voters: promoted laws to protect women and children; National Woman's Party: opposed protective legislation because it reinforced workplace discrimination

Section Spotlight Video

To generate student interest and provide a springboard for class discussion, access the Chapter 20, Section 2 video at glencoe.com or on the video DVD.

Resource Manager

Section 2

The Feminist Movement

Guide to Reading

Big Ideas
Struggles for Rights Women organized to claim their rights and responsibilities as citizens.

Content Vocabulary
• feminism (p. 686)

Academic Vocabulary
• gender (p. 687)
• compatible (p. 691)

People and Events to Identify
• Equal Pay Act (p. 687)
• Betty Friedan (p. 687)
• National Organization for Women (NOW) (p. 688)
• Gloria Steinem (p. 688)
• Equal Rights Amendment (ERA) (p. 689)
• Phyllis Schlafly (p. 690)
• Title IX (p. 690)

Reading Strategy
Categorizing Use a graphic organizer similar to the one below to list the main arguments for and against the Equal Rights Amendment (ERA).

For ERA	Against ERA

By the 1960s, many women had become increasingly dissatisfied with society's perception of women and their place in society. Some women began to join organizations aimed at improving their role in society. The Equal Rights Amendment stirred a national debate.

A Renewed Women's Movement

MAIN Idea Women in the 1960s and 1970s began creating organizations to change society through education and legislative action.

HISTORY AND YOU Have you ever read a book that spurred you to action or got you excited? Read on to learn about a book that helped define and reawaken the women's movement.

African Americans and college students were not the only groups seeking to change American society in the 1960s. By the middle of the decade, a new women's movement had emerged as many women became discontent with their status and treatment in American society. This movement became known as the feminist movement, or the women's liberation movement.

Feminism—the belief that men and women should be equal politically, economically, and socially—had been a weak and often embattled force since the adoption of the Nineteenth Amendment guaranteeing women's voting rights in 1920. Soon after the amendment was ratified, the women's movement split into two camps. For the next 40 years, it had very little political influence.

The onset of World War II provided women with greater opportunity, at least temporarily. With many men enlisted in the army, women became an integral part of the nation's workforce. After the war, however, many women returned to their traditional role of homemaker. Even though 8 million American women had gone to work during the war, the new postwar emphasis on having babies and establishing families discouraged women from seeking employment. Many Americans assumed that a good mother should stay home to raise her children.

Despite the popular emphasis on homemaking, however, the number of women who held jobs outside the home actually increased during the 1950s. Most women who went to work did so in order to help their families maintain their comfortable lifestyles. By 1960, nearly one-third of all married women were part of the paid workforce. Yet many people continued to believe that women, even college-educated women, could better serve society by remaining in the home to influence the next generation of men.

R Reading Strategies	C Critical Thinking	D Differentiated Instruction	W Writing Support	S Skill Practice
Teacher Edition • Taking Notes, p. 688 • Academic Vocab., p. 689 **Additional Resources** • American Lit. Read., URB p. 13 • Guided Read., URB p.145	**Teacher Edition** • Analyzing Prim. Sources, pp. 687, 690 **Additional Resources** • Linking Past and Present, URB p. 130 • Interp. Pol. Cartoons Act., URB p. 137 • Supreme Court Case Studies, pp. 111, 115 • Quizzes and Tests, p. 280	**Additional Resources** • Differentiated Instr. Act., URB p. 119 • Interp. Pol. Cartoons, URB p. 137	**Teacher Edition** • Persuasive Writing, p. 688	**Additional Resources** • Reinforcing Skills Act., URB p. 127 • RENTG, p. 212

PRIMARY SOURCE
What Caused the Women's Movement?

The women's movement was revitalized in the 1960s, partly because of the efforts of the President's Commission on the Status of Women, and partly because writers, such as Betty Friedan, convinced women the time had come to take action.

▲ President Kennedy meets with Eleanor Roosevelt, Representative Edith Green (center) and Esther Peterson, director of the Women's Bureau at the Department of Labor (right) in early 1962 to discuss the findings of the President's Commission on the Status of Women.

PRIMARY SOURCE

▲ Betty Friedan, 1972

In 1963 Betty Friedan tried to describe the feelings that would lead to the rebirth of the women's movement:

"The problem lay buried, unspoken, for many years in the minds of American women. . . . Each suburban housewife struggled with it alone. As she made the beds, shopped for groceries, matched slipcover material, ate peanut butter sandwiches with her children, chauffeured Cub Scouts and Brownies . . . she was afraid to ask even of herself the silent question—'Is this all?'

. . . In the fifteen years after World War II, this mystique of feminine fulfillment became the cherished and self-perpetuating core of contemporary American culture. Millions of women lived their lives in the image of those pretty pictures of the American suburban housewife . . . Words like 'emancipation' and 'career' sounded strange and embarrassing. . . .

But on an April morning in 1959, I heard a mother of four, having coffee with four other mothers in a suburban development . . . say in a tone of quiet desperation, 'the problem.' And the others knew, without words, that she was not talking about a problem with her husband, or her children, or her home. Suddenly they realized they all shared the same problem, the problem that has no name.

. . . Sometimes a woman would say 'I feel empty somehow . . . incomplete.' Or she would say, 'I feel as if I don't exist.'"
—from *The Feminine Mystique*

DBQ Document-Based Questions

1. **Making Inferences** What was the "feminine mystique"?
2. **Drawing Conclusions** What do you think "the problem" was?
3. **Hypothesizing** Why might President Kennedy have wanted Eleanor Roosevelt to head the commission studying the status of women?

Origins of the Movement

By the early 1960s, many women were increasingly resentful of a world where newspaper ads separated jobs by **gender,** banks denied them credit, and, worst of all, they often were paid less for the same work. Women found themselves shut out of higher-paying professions such as law, medicine, and finance. By the mid-1960s, about 47 percent of American women were in the workforce, but three-fourths of them worked in lower paying clerical, sales, or factory jobs, or as cleaning women and hospital attendants.

Workplace Rights One stimulus that invigorated the women's movement was the President's Commission on the Status of Women, established by President Kennedy and headed by Eleanor Roosevelt. The commission's report highlighted the problems faced by women in the workplace and helped create a network of feminist activists who lobbied Congress for women's legislation. In 1963, with the support of organized labor, they won passage of the **Equal Pay Act,** which in most cases outlawed paying men more than women for the same job.

The Feminine Mystique Although many working women were angry about inequality in the workplace, many other women who had stayed home were also discontent. **Betty Friedan** tried to describe the reasons for their discontent in her book *The Feminine Mystique,* published in 1963.

Chapter 20 The Politics of Protest **687**

Teach

C Critical Thinking

Analyzing Primary Sources
Have students read the Primary Source quotation. **Ask:** Do you agree that the only way women in the 1960s could go was up? *(Answers will vary. Some students may point out that they could have lost rights gained earlier, such as the right to vote and own property. Others might point out that these women enjoyed more rights than some women around the world enjoy today.)* **OL**

DBQ Document Based Questions

Answers:
1. The "feminine mystique" was the postwar myth that all women should be completely fulfilled as wives and mothers and not seek professional interests outside the home.
2. "The problem" was that many women felt incomplete and unfulfilled as wives and mothers operating solely in the home.
3. The former First Lady had a history of support for civil rights and human rights.

Hands-On Chapter Project
Step 2

Presenting a Historical Drama

Step 2: Write and Plan the Drama
Students begin to write their scripts, including lines and stage directions. They create any props they might need, such as posters, signs, buttons, or headbands.

Directions Remind students that their dramas should be based on the content of the section. Written scripts can be rough guides, with students free to improvise. Props should be appropriate to protests of the time and the situation they will enact.

Putting It Together Ask students to read each others' drafts and suggest changes for the second draft. **OL**
(Chapter Project continued on page 693)

R Reading Strategy

Taking Notes Have students use the heads of the section to create a study outline. As they complete each subhead, have them write notes about the important points. Then encourage them to discuss their outlines with a partner and make any modifications that would improve their notes. **BL**

W Writing Support

Persuasive Writing Have students write an editorial supporting or challenging the EEOC's decision that jobs and want ads could be gender-specific. Then have them write a letter to the editor arguing against the position taken in the editorial. **OL**

✓ Reading Check

Answer:
the mass protests of ordinary women and the President's Commission on the Status of Women

Additional Support

Friedan had traveled around the country interviewing women who had graduated with her from Smith College in 1942. She found that while most of these women reported having everything they could want in life, they still felt unfulfilled.

Friedan's book became a best-seller. Many women began reaching out to one another, pouring out their anger and sadness in what came to be known as consciousness-raising sessions. While they talked informally about their unhappiness, they were also building the base for a nationwide mass movement.

R The Civil Rights Act and Women

Congress gave the women's movement another boost by including them in the 1964 Civil Rights Act. Title VII of the act outlawed job discrimination not only on the basis of race, color, religion, and national origin, but also on the basis of gender. The law provided a strong legal basis for the changes the women's movement would later demand.

Given the era's attitudes about what kind of work was proper for women, simply having the law on the books was not enough. Even the agency charged with administering the civil rights act—the Equal Employment **W** Opportunity Commission (EEOC)—accepted the idea that jobs could be gender-specific. In 1965 the commission ruled that gender-segregated help-wanted ads were legal.

R The Time Is NOW

By June 1966, Betty Friedan returned to an idea that she and other women had been considering—the need for an organization to promote feminist goals. On the back of a napkin she scribbled that it was time "to take the actions needed to bring women into the mainstream of American society, now . . . in fully equal partnership with men." Friedan and others then set out to form the **National Organization for Women** (NOW).

In October 1966, a group of about 300 women and men held the founding conference of NOW. "The time has come," its founders declared, "to confront with concrete action the conditions which now prevent women from enjoying the equality of opportunity and freedom of choice which is their right as individual Americans and as human beings."

The new organization responded to frustrated housewives by demanding greater edu-

---

cational opportunities for women. The group also focused much of its energy on aiding women in the workplace. NOW leaders denounced the exclusion of women from certain professions and from most levels of politics. They lashed out against the practice of paying women less than men for equal work, a practice the Equal Pay Act had not eliminated.

When NOW set out to pass an Equal Rights Amendment to the Constitution, its membership rose to over 200,000. By July 1972, the movement had its own magazine, *Ms.*, which kept readers informed about women's issues. The editor of the magazine was **Gloria Steinem**, an author who became one of the movement's leading figures.

✓ Reading Check Identifying What two forces helped bring the women's movement to life again?

Debates IN HISTORY

Should the Equal Rights Amendment Be Ratified?

In the 1970s ratification of the Equal Rights Amendment (ERA) was a hotly debated issue. Organizations such as NOW and other supporters of the amendment fought hard for its ratification. One of these was U.S. Representative Shirley Chisholm, who spoke out in support of the ERA in a speech to Congress in 1970. In 1971 conservative activist Phyllis Schlafly formed the group Stop-ERA to fight the legislation.

Extending the Content

Equal Rights Amendment In 1923 the National Woman's Party (NWP) introduced an Equal Rights Amendment to the U.S. Constitution. Some version of the ERA was introduced into every session of Congress between 1923 and 1972, when it was passed. It was sent to the states for ratification with a seven-year time limit, which was extended to 1982. The opposition that defeated the 1973 ERA was similar in many ways to opposition that derailed the earlier amendment. People concerned about women's welfare feared that legal equality threatened laws that protected women.

Successes and Failures

MAIN Idea The women's movement made gains for women in education and employment but has not achieved complete equality for women.

HISTORY AND YOU Have you ever seen men and women treated differently because of their gender? Read to learn how the women's movement tried to get equal treatment for women in the 1960s and 1970s.

During the late 1960s and early 1970s, the women's movement fought to amend the Constitution and enforce Title VII of the Civil Rights Act, lobbied to repeal laws against abortion, and worked for legislation against gender discrimination in employment, housing, and education. The movement had many successes, but also encountered strong opposition to some of the reforms it wanted.

The Equal Rights Amendment

The women's movement seemed to be off to a strong start when Congress passed the **Equal Rights Amendment** (ERA) in March 1972. The amendment specified that "Equality of rights under the law shall not be denied or abridged by the United States or by any State on account of sex." To become part of the Constitution, the amendment had to be ratified by 38 states. Many states did so—35 by 1979—but by then, significant opposition to the amendment had begun to build up.

Opponents of the ERA argued that it would take away some traditional rights, such as the right to alimony in divorce cases or the right to have single-gender colleges. They also feared it would allow women to be drafted into the military and eliminate laws that provided special protection for women in the workforce.

Debates IN HISTORY

YES

Shirley Chisholm
Member of the U.S. House of Representatives

PRIMARY SOURCE

"Discrimination against women . . . is so widespread that it seems to many persons normal, natural and right. . . .

It is time we act to assure full equality of opportunity . . . to women.

The argument that this amendment will not solve the problem of sex discrimination is not relevant. . . . Of course laws will not eliminate prejudice from the hearts of human beings. But that is no reason to allow prejudice to continue to be enshrined in our laws. . . . The Constitution they wrote was designed to protect the rights of white, male citizens. As there were no black Founding Fathers, there were no founding mothers—a great pity, on both counts. It is not too late to complete the work they left undone."

—speech before Congress, August 10, 1970

NO

Phyllis Schlafly
Author and Conservative Activist

PRIMARY SOURCE

"This Amendment will absolutely and positively make women subject to the draft. Why any woman would support such a ridiculous and un-American proposal as this is beyond comprehension. . . . Foxholes are bad enough for men, but they certainly are *not* the place for women—and we should reject any proposal which would put them there in the name of 'equal rights.'. . .

Another bad effect of the Equal Rights Amendment is that it will abolish a woman's right to child support and alimony . . .

Under present American laws, the man is *always* required to support his wife and each child he caused to be brought into the world. Why should women abandon these good laws . . . ?"

—from the *Phyllis Schlafly Report*, February 1972

DBQ **Document-Based Questions**

1. **Summarizing** Why does Chisholm believe that the ERA is necessary?
2. **Explaining** What does Schlafly say was the main flaw in the arguments of the ERA supporters?
3. **Evaluating** With which position do you agree? Write a paragraph to explain your choice.

Chapter 20 The Politics of Protest **689**

Activity: Collaborative Learning

Role Playing Have students work in pairs. One partner in each pair should list what women in 1972 had to lose with the passage of the Equal Rights Amendment, while the other partner lists what women stood to gain. Tell students to draw on chapter content and their own knowledge. Students may also use library or Internet sources to conduct further research. After students have completed their lists, have them share the list with their partner. After partners have studied each other's lists, invite pairs to role-play for the class two state legislators discussing whether or not to vote for ratification. **AL**

C Critical Thinking

Analyzing Primary Sources
Have students study the graphs in the Primary Source feature. **Ask:** What might account for the continuing gap between women's and men's median incomes? *(Answers will vary. Some may say that women are still ending up in lower paid professions. Others may say women's roles as primary parents may exert downward pressure on a self-employed woman's income or the ability of a salaried woman to advance.)* **OL**

Analyzing VISUALS

Answers:
1. from 30% to 60% (a 100% increase between 1950 and 2000)
2. They made no real gains compared to men—the difference between women's and men's median income was still about the same in 2000 as it was in 1970.

Additional Support

One outspoken opponent was **Phyllis Schlafly,** who organized the Stop-ERA campaign. By the end of 1979, four states had voted to rescind their approval. Many people had become worried that the amendment would give federal courts too much power to interfere with state laws. Unable to achieve ratification by three-fourths of the states by the deadline set by Congress, the Equal Rights Amendment finally failed in 1982.

Equality in Education

One major achievement of the movement came in the area of education. Kathy Striebel's experience illustrated the discrimination female students often faced in the early 1970s. In 1971 Striebel, a high school junior in St. Paul, Minnesota, wanted to compete for her school's swim team, but the school did not allow girls to join. Kathy's mother, Charlotte, was a member of the local NOW chapter. Through it, she learned that St. Paul had recently banned gender discrimination in education. She filed a grievance with the city's human rights department, and officials required the school to allow Kathy to swim.

🏛 For further information on the case of *Roe v. Wade*, see page R60 in **Supreme Court Case Summaries.**

Shortly after joining the team, Kathy beat out one of the boys and earned a spot at a meet. As she stood on the block waiting to swim, the opposing coach declared that she was ineligible because the meet was outside St. Paul and thus beyond the jurisdiction of its laws. "They pulled that little girl right off the block," Charlotte Striebel recalled angrily.

Recognizing the problem, leaders of the women's movement lobbied Congress to ban gender discrimination in education. In 1972 Congress responded by passing a law known collectively as the Educational Amendments. One section, **Title IX,** prohibited federally funded schools from discriminating against women in nearly all aspects of its operations, from admissions to athletics.

Roe v. Wade

One of the most important goals for many women activists was the repeal of laws against abortion. Until 1973, the right to regulate abortion was reserved to the states. This was in keeping with the original plan of the Constitution, which reserved all police power—the power to control people and property in the

PRIMARY SOURCE
The Changing Status of Women

Women's roles were changing in society. Although the ERA failed, more women entered the workforce and gender discrimination in schools was banned with the passage of Title IX.

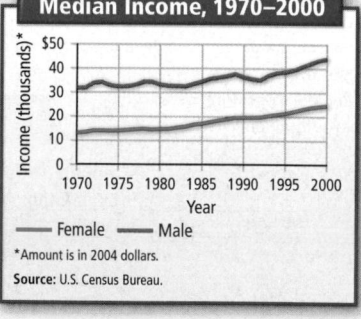

Women in the Workforce

Source: *Historical Statistics of the United States: Earliest Times to the Present, Volume 2.*

Median Income, 1970–2000

— Female   — Male
*Amount is in 2004 dollars.
Source: U.S. Census Bureau.

Analyzing VISUALS
1. **Analyzing** By how much did the percentage of working women increase between 1950 and 2000?
2. **Interpreting** What gains, if any, did women make in median income compared to men?

C

690 Chapter 20   The Politics of Protest

Activity: Technology Connection

Title IX Tell students that Title IX of the 1972 Educational Amendments is still a frequently debated topic. Share these statistics: Girls' participation in high school athletics has increased from fewer than 300,000 in the 1970s to almost 3 million; but girls still receive fewer opportunities to participate than boys do. Male college athletes receive $133 million more in athletic scholarship assistance. Coaches of women's teams receive about 35 percent less than coaches of men's teams. Have students discuss the participation of girls in their school's athletics program and other school activities. **Ask:** How might these activities have been different before the Educational Amendments? *(Answers will vary, but may mention the fact that most schools have women participating on athletic teams that may not have been funded before 1972.)* Ask students to choose a female student athlete and use the Internet to find information for a brief written report. Encourage them to download photographs to illustrate their reports. **OL**

interest of safety, health, welfare, and morals—to the state. Early in the country's history, some abortions were permitted in the early stages of pregnancy, but by the mid-1800s, states had passed laws prohibiting abortion, except to save the life of the mother.

In the late 1960s, some states began adopting more liberal abortion laws. For example, several states allowed abortion if carrying a baby to term might endanger the woman's mental health or if she was a victim of rape or incest. The big change came with the 1973 Supreme Court decision in *Roe v. Wade*. The Supreme Court ruled that state governments could not regulate abortion during the first three months of pregnancy, a time that was said to be within a woman's constitutional right to privacy. During the second three months of pregnancy, states could regulate abortions on the basis of the health of the mother. States could ban abortion in the final three months except in cases of a medical emergency. Those in favor of abortion rights cheered *Roe v. Wade* as a victory, but the issue was far from settled politically. The decision gave rise to the right-to-life movement, whose members consider abortion morally wrong and advocate its total ban.

After the *Roe v. Wade* ruling, the two sides began an impassioned battle that continues today. In the 1992 case *Planned Parenthood v. Casey,* the Supreme Court modified *Roe v. Wade*. The court decided that states could place some restrictions on all abortions, such as requiring doctors to explain the risks and require their patients to give "informed consent." The court also upheld laws that required underage girls to inform their parents before obtaining an abortion. At the same time, the court struck down laws requiring women to notify their husbands before having an abortion. The court also abandoned the rule that states could ban abortion only in the final three months. Technology had now made it possible for the fetus to be viable outside the womb much earlier in a pregnancy. States could now restrict abortion based on the viability of the fetus.

The Impact of the Feminist Movement

Despite the failure of the ERA, the women's movement has brought profound changes to society. Since the 1970s, many more women have pursued college degrees and careers outside the home, and two-career families are much more common than they were in the 1950s and 1960s. Many employers now offer options to help make work more **compatible** with family life, including flexible hours, on-site child care, and job sharing.

Even though the women's movement helped change social attitudes toward women, a significant income gap between men and women still exists. A major reason for the gap is that many working women still hold lower-paying jobs such as bank tellers, administrative assistants, cashiers, schoolteachers, and nurses. It is in professional jobs that women have made the most dramatic gains since the 1970s. By 2000, women made up over 40 percent of the nation's graduates receiving medical or law degrees.

✔ **Reading Check** **Summarizing** What successes and failures did the women's movement experience during the late 1960s and early 1970s?

Section 2 REVIEW

Vocabulary
1. **Explain** the significance of: feminism, Equal Pay Act, Betty Friedan, National Organization for Women (NOW), Gloria Steinem, Equal Rights Amendment (ERA), Phyllis Schlafly, Title IX.

Main Ideas
2. **Explaining** Why did more women work outside the home in the 1950s?

3. **Explaining** Why were some people against passage of the ERA?

Critical Thinking
4. **Big Ideas** What gains have been made in women's rights since the 1960s?

5. **Organizing** Use a graphic organizer similar to the one below to list the major achievements of the women's movement.

Achievements

6. **Analyzing Visuals** Study the bar graph on page 690. What was the first year in which approximately half of all women were in the workforce?

Writing About History
7. **Persuasive Writing** Assume the role of a supporter or an opponent of the ERA. Write a letter to the editor of your local newspaper to persuade people to support your position.

History ONLINE
Study Central™ To review this section, go to glencoe.com and click on Study Central.

691

✔ **Reading Check**

Answer:
Successes: the Educational Amendments/Title IX, abortion rights, and improved working conditions and educational opportunities; Failures: not passing the ERA, lingering income gap, most women still hold low-paying jobs

Assess
· ·
History ONLINE

Study Central™ provides summaries, interactive games, and online graphic organizers to help students review content.

Close
· ·
Summarizing **Ask:** What were the goals and accomplishments of the feminist movement that began in the 1960s? *(Women wanted, and achieved, better educational and career opportunities, more career choices, laws requiring equal pay for equal work, and reproductive choice.)*

Section 2 REVIEW

Answers

1. All definitions can be found in the section and the Glossary.
2. Women worked outside the home to help the family enjoy a more comfortable lifestyle.
3. They were afraid of losing traditional protections and rights, such as the exemption from military combat service, the right to alimony, and the right to have single-gender colleges.

4. More women have achieved equal pay for equal work, better educational opportunities, more career choices, and more political power.
5. Equal Pay Act, Title VII in the Civil Rights Act, Title IX, *Roe v. Wade*, more career possibilities
6. 1980

7. Students' letters will vary but should express a clear and logically reasoned viewpoint.

Focus

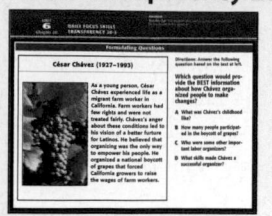
Guide to Reading

Answers may include: 1929: LULAC founded; 1947: *Mendez* v. *Westminster* ends school segregation in California; 1954: *Hernandez* v. *Texas* increases Latino rights in Texas; 1966: Chávez and Huerta form the United Farm Workers; 1967: José Angel Gutiérrez founds MAYO; 1968: Bilingual Education Act passes; 1969: Gutiérrez founds La Raza Unida

Section Spotlight Video

To generate student interest and provide a springboard for class discussion, access the Chapter 20, Section 3 video at glencoe.com or on the video DVD.

Resource Manager

Latino Americans Organize

Guide to Reading

Big Ideas
Struggles for Rights Latinos organized to fight discrimination and to gain access to better education and jobs.

Content Vocabulary
• repatriation *(p. 694)*
• bilingualism *(p. 697)*

Academic Vocabulary
• likewise *(p. 692)*
• adequate *(p. 696)*

People and Events to Identify
• League of United Latin American Citizens *(p. 695)*
• American GI Forum *(p. 696)*
• César Chávez *(p. 697)*
• Dolores Huerta *(p. 697)*
• United Farm Workers *(p. 697)*
• *La Raza Unida* *(p. 697)*
• Bilingual Education Act *(p. 697)*

Reading Strategy
Organizing Complete a time line similar to the one below to record major events in the struggle of Latinos for equal civil and political rights.

Most Mexican Americans and Mexican immigrants lived in the Southwest, where many faced discrimination in jobs and housing. By the mid-twentieth century, more immigrants arrived from various parts of Latin America. Latinos formed civil rights organizations to challenge discrimination.

Latinos Migrate North

MAIN Idea Mexicans, the largest Spanish-speaking immigrant group, faced discrimination and segregation in the West and Southwest.

HISTORY AND YOU Have you ever heard of immigrants getting their "green cards," which permit them to work in the United States? Read on to learn how the Bracero Program allowed some Mexicans to work on a temporary basis.

Americans of Mexican heritage have lived in what is now the United States since before the founding of the republic. Their numbers steadily increased in the 1800s, in part because the United States acquired territory where Mexicans already lived, and in part because Mexicans began migrating north to live in the United States. In the twentieth century, Mexican immigration rose dramatically.

In 1910 the Mexican Revolution began and the resulting turmoil prompted a wave of emigration from Mexico that lasted more than a decade. During the 1920s, half a million Mexicans immigrated to the United States through official channels, and an unknown number entered the country through other means. Precise population estimates are impossible to determine because many Mexicans frequently moved back and forth across the border.

Not surprisingly, persons of Mexican heritage remained concentrated in the areas that were once the northern provinces of Mexico. In 1930, 90 percent of ethnic Mexicans in the United States lived in Texas, California, Arizona, New Mexico, and Colorado. In Texas, the favorite destinations for Mexican immigrants, cities such as San Antonio and El Paso, had large populations of Mexican Americans and Mexican immigrants. As a result of heavy Mexican immigration, the ethnic Mexican population in Texas grew from 71,062 in 1900 to 683,681 in 1930. Southern California, **likewise,** had a large Spanish-speaking population.

Of course, not all Mexican Americans remained in the West and Southwest. In the 1910s and 1920s, along with Americans of other ethnic backgrounds, many Mexican Americans headed for the cities of the Midwest and Northeast, where they found jobs in factories.

R Reading Strategies	**C** Critical Thinking	**D** Differentiated Instruction	**W** Writing Support	**S** Skill Practice
Teacher Edition • Read. Prim. Sources, p. 696 **Additional Resources** • Pri. Source Reading, URB p. 133 • Guid. Read. Act., URB p. 146	**Teacher Edition** • Analyzing Prim. Sources, pp. 694, 695 **Additional Resources** • Quizzes and Tests, p. 281	**Teacher Edition** • Logical/Math, p. 693 **Additional Resources** • English Learner Act., URB p. 121 • Reteaching Act., URB p. 139	**Additional Resources** • Authentic Assess., p. 45	**Additional Resources** • Hist. Skills Analysis, URB p. 118 • RENTG, p. 215

PRIMARY SOURCE
Latinos Arrive in America, 1910–1950

In the twentieth century, Latinos, mainly Mexicans, began to enter the United States in large numbers settling mostly in the West and Southwest. Others, who came from Puerto Rico or Cuba, often settled in the barrios of the large cities in the East.

▲ These refugees, guarded by U.S. troops at Fort Bliss, Texas, were some of the more than 500,000 who came to the United States to escape the turmoil of the Mexican Revolution.

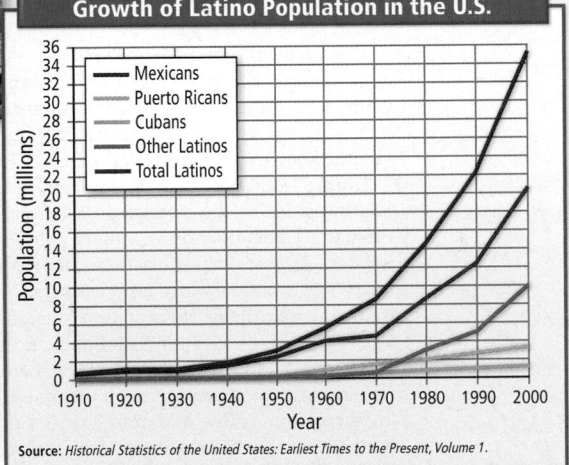

▲ Family of Mexican migrant workers, who came to the United States as part of the Bracero program during World War II

Analyzing VISUALS
1. **Interpreting** The U.S. Latino population is made up of which main groups?
2. **Drawing Conclusions** Why have Latino Americans experienced a growing political influence in recent years?

Growth of Latino Population in the U.S.

Legend:
- Mexicans
- Puerto Ricans
- Cubans
- Other Latinos
- Total Latinos

(y-axis: Population (millions), 0–36; x-axis: Year, 1910–2000)

Source: *Historical Statistics of the United States: Earliest Times to the Present, Volume 1.*

Teach

D Differentiated Instruction

Logical/Mathematical Have students read the figures in the first two lines of the second column. **Ask:** Of the Mexican Americans living in Los Angeles in 1930, what percentage had arrived since 1900? *(97.4)* **OL**

Analyzing VISUALS

Answers:
1. Mexican, Puerto Rican, and Cuban
2. growing numbers and political and labor organizations

Mexicans Face Discrimination

Across the Southwest, most Mexican Americans lived in barrios. Barrios were the product of a combination of the region's history and discrimination against Latinos. Los Angeles, for example, was founded as a Spanish town in 1781. When English-speaking settlers arrived a century later, they built around the older Spanish-speaking district.

Residential segregation, however, also had roots in ethnic discrimination. With heavy Mexican immigration in the early twentieth century, the ethnic Mexican population of Los Angeles grew from 5,000 in 1900 to around 190,000 in 1930. By that time, the Spanish-speaking population was segregated in the eastern part of the city, where most lived in small, dilapidated housing and suffered high rates of infant mortality and disease.

In California and across the Southwest, discrimination in employment meant that most ethnic Mexicans could find work only in low-paying jobs. Many lived in rural areas where they worked as agricultural laborers. Ernesto Galarza was eight years old when his family immigrated to California and settled in Sacramento in 1913. In his autobiography, he recalled the importance of the barrio to new immigrants:

Hands-On Chapter Project
Step 3

Presenting a Historical Drama

Step 3: Present the Drama Students rehearse and present their dramas. They watch the dramas of other groups.

Directions Remind students that scripts can be rough guides. They are free to improvise during the dramatization, as long as any ad-libbed lines are based on the content of the section. Have students rehearse until they are comfortable and ready to present. Students should be attentive during the presentations of other groups.

Putting It Together As students do their presentations ask the class to take notes as to the historical accuracy of the presentation. **OL**

(Chapter Project continued on Visual Summary page)

C Critical Thinking

Analyzing Primary Sources
Direct students to the Primary Source quotation. **Ask:** How did the barrio both help Latino immigrants and hold them back economically? *(The barrio helped them meet basic needs and gave them a supportive community. It also resulted in de facto segregation, which leads to de facto segregation in schools and may have tended to keep Latino immigrants out of areas where better economic opportunities were available. Living in a Spanish-speaking area may have discouraged learning of English, which also restricted economic opportunities.)* **OL**

✓ Reading Check

Answer:
The program sometimes targeted people for "looking Mexican" and often did not distinguish between legal and illegal immigrants.

Additional Support

C "For the Mexicans the *barrio* was a colony of refugees. We came to know families from Chihuahua, Sonora, Jalisco, and Durango. . . . As poor refugees, their first concern was to find a place to sleep, then to eat and find work. In the *barrio* they were most likely to find all three, for not knowing English, they needed something that was even more urgent than a room, a meal, or a job, and that was information in a language they could understand."

—from *Barrio Boy*

During the Great Depression of the 1930s, approximately one-third of the Mexican population in the United States returned to Mexico. Some left voluntarily, believing it would be easier to get by in Mexico. Many Mexican Americans, however, faced increased hostility and discrimination as unemployment rates soared in the early 1930s.

Then, federal officials launched a series of deportations that not only included immigrants from Mexico but often their American-born children as well. This return to Mexico became known as the **repatriation.**

During World War II, labor shortages in the Southwest led to the creation of the Bracero Program. Under this arrangement, Mexican workers entered into short-term labor contracts, mostly as low-wage farm workers.

Meanwhile, illegal immigration increased. In 1954 Eisenhower's administration launched a program intended to deport illegal Latino immigrants. Police swept through barrios seeking illegal immigrants, and more than 3.7 million Mexicans were deported over the next three years. The raids were criticized in the United States and in Mexico for intimidating people for simply looking "Mexican." In addition, the program often failed to distinguish between individuals legally in the country (some of whom were U.S. citizens) and those who had entered illegally.

Other Latinos Arrive

Although Mexicans remained the largest group of Spanish-speaking newcomers in the 1950s, large numbers of Puerto Ricans arrived as well. American citizens since 1917, Puerto Ricans may move freely within American territory. After World War II, economic troubles in Puerto Rico prompted over a million Puerto

Ricans to move to the mainland United States. American factory owners and employment agencies had also begun to recruit in Puerto Rico for workers, and the advent of relatively cheap air travel made immigration easier. The majority of Puerto Ricans settled in New York City. There, they suffered racial discrimination and alarmingly high levels of poverty.

The United States also became home to more than 350,000 Cuban immigrants in the decade after the Cuban Revolution of 1959. Many Cubans fleeing the Communist regime were professionals or business owners who settled in and around Miami, Florida. Most were welcomed in the United States because they were middle class or affluent and viewed as refugees fleeing Communist oppression. In 1960 about 3 million Latinos lived in the United States. By the late 1960s, more than 9 million Latinos lived in the United States.

✓ Reading Check **Summarizing** What were some of the criticisms of Eisenhower's deportation program?

PRIMARY SOURCE
Latinos in the United States

By the late 1960s, approximately 9 million Latinos lived in the United States. Although many were citizens, they still faced segregation, discrimination, and other forms of racial prejudice. However, with their increasing population and through political protest and legal action they began to work to improve conditions.

▲ *Latino dancers in a traditional dance at a fiesta in Taos, New Mexico*

Extending the Content

Puerto Rican Immigrants During the 1940s, Puerto Rico began to industrialize. Many Puerto Ricans moved from rural to urban areas, causing a jump in the urban population. Between 1940 and 1970, the proportion of the Puerto Rican population living in rural areas dropped from 70 percent to 42 percent. With so many people moving from rural areas to cities, the number of workers grew faster than jobs. As a result, migration from Puerto Rico to the mainland United States was extensive from the early 1940s through the 1960s as Puerto Ricans left to find work. Unemployment in Puerto Rico rose again during the 1970s, when worldwide inflation and a recession in the U.S. economy stalled Puerto Rico's economic growth.

Latinos Organize

MAIN Idea Latino civil rights organizations, such as LULAC and the American GI Forum, fought against discrimination.

HISTORY AND YOU Recall what you learned about the decision in the Supreme Court case *Brown v. Board of Education*. Read on to find out how LULAC filed similar lawsuits challenging discrimination against Mexican Americans.

The Latino community in the West and Southwest included American citizens and immigrant noncitizens. Regardless of their citizenship status, however, people of Mexican heritage were often treated as outsiders by the English-speaking majority. Latinos formed several organizations to work for equal rights and fair treatment.

In 1929 a number of Mexican American organizations came together to create the **League of United Latin American Citizens** (LULAC). The purpose of this organization was to fight discrimination against persons of Latin American ancestry. The organization limited its membership to people of Latin American heritage who were American citizens. LULAC encouraged assimilation into American society and adopted English as its official language.

LULAC achieved many advances for Latinos. One of its early crusades ended segregation of public places in Texas where Mexican Americans (along with African Americans) had been barred from "whites only" sections. The organization also ended the practice of segregating Spanish-speaking children in "Mexican schools."

In *Mendez* v. *Westminster* (1947), a group of Mexican parents won a lawsuit that challenged school segregation in California. Two years later, LULAC filed a similarly successful suit in Texas. During the 1950s, the organization was a frequent and vocal critic of the excesses and abuses of deportation authorities. In 1954 the Supreme Court's ruling in *Hernandez* v. *Texas* extended more rights to Latino citizens. The case ended the exclusion of Mexican Americans from juries in Texas.

C **Critical Thinking**

Analyzing Primary Sources
Direct students' attention to the photo of children working in the fields. Ask them how the need for children's labor can deprive future generations of equal opportunity to improve their status. *(Working in the fields can deprive children of the education they need to improve their status. It also isolates them from the larger culture, where they could learn to interact with Americans who enjoy economic opportunities the workers might pursue in the future.)* **BL**

Analyzing VISUALS

Answers:
1. They faced segregation, discrimination, and other forms of racial prejudice.
2. Overcrowded substandard housing; long workdays doing hard, manual labor in fields

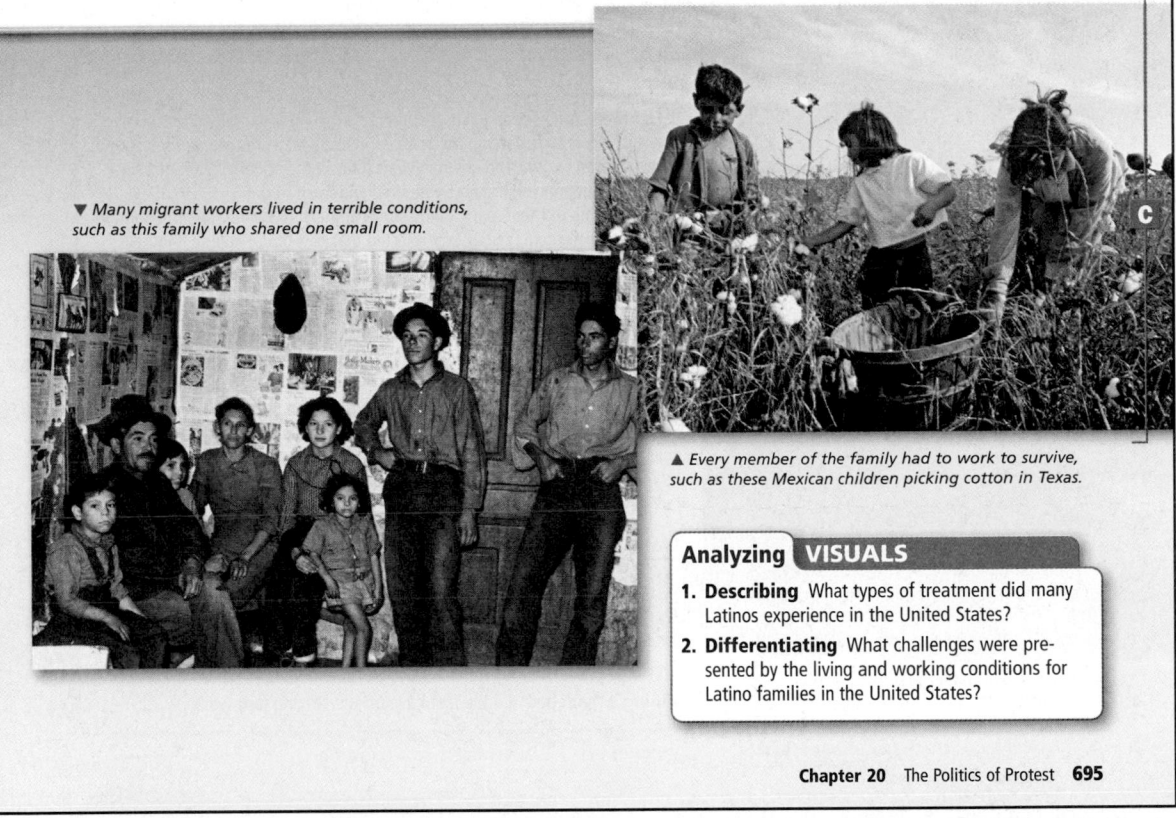

▼ *Many migrant workers lived in terrible conditions, such as this family who shared one small room.*

▲ *Every member of the family had to work to survive, such as these Mexican children picking cotton in Texas.*

Analyzing VISUALS

1. **Describing** What types of treatment did many Latinos experience in the United States?
2. **Differentiating** What challenges were presented by the living and working conditions for Latino families in the United States?

Chapter 20 The Politics of Protest **695**

Additional Support

Activity: Interdisciplinary Connection

Language Arts Give students a copy of the Primary Source Reading 27-2, p. 133, "A Farm Worker's Story" from the Unit 6 URB. Read students this excerpt by Roberto Acuna, in which he explains why he joined United Farm Workers: "I began to see how everything was so wrong. When growers can have an intricate watering system to irrigate their crops but they can't have running water inside the houses of workers. Veterinarians tend the needs of domestic animals but they can't have medical care for the workers. They can have land subsidies for the growers but they can't have adequate unemployment compensation for the workers. They treat him like a farm implement. In fact, they treat their implements better and their domestic animals better. They have heat and insulated barns for the animals but the workers live in beat-up shacks with no heat at all. Illness . . . is 120 percent higher than the average rate for industry. . . . back trouble, rheumatism and arthritis. . . . Tuberculosis is high. And now because of the pesticides, we have many respiratory diseases." **Ask:** What conditions do you think you—and all workers—have a right to expect at a job? *(Students should be able to defend their answers.)* **OL**

History ONLINE
Student Web Activity Visit glencoe.com and complete the activity on protest movements.

Another Latino organization, the **American GI Forum,** was founded to protect the rights of Mexican American veterans. After World War II, Latino veterans were excluded from veterans' organizations and denied medical services by the Veterans Administration.

The GI Forum's first effort to combat racial injustice involved a Mexican American soldier who was killed during World War II. A funeral home refused to hold his funeral because he was Mexican American. The GI Forum drew national attention to the incident and, with the help of Senator Lyndon Johnson, the soldier's remains were buried in Arlington National Cemetery. Initially concerned only with issues directly affecting Latino veterans, the organization later broadened its scope to challenge segregation and other forms of discrimination against all Latinos.

✓ **Reading Check** **Analyzing** How did American society discriminate against Latinos?

Protests and Progress

MAIN Idea Many Latinos worked as poorly paid agricultural laborers; the United Farm Workers tried to improve their working conditions.

HISTORY AND YOU Do you think the United States should have a national language? Read how school districts set up bilingual education classes to teach immigrant students in their own language while they were still learning English.

As the 1960s began, Latino Americans continued to face prejudice and limited access to **adequate** education, employment, and housing. Encouraged by the achievements of the African American civil rights movement, Latinos launched a series of campaigns to improve their economic situation and end discrimination.

One major campaign was the effort to improve conditions for farmworkers. Most Mexican American farm laborers earned little pay, received few benefits, and had no job

PRIMARY SOURCE
César Chávez Promotes Nonviolence

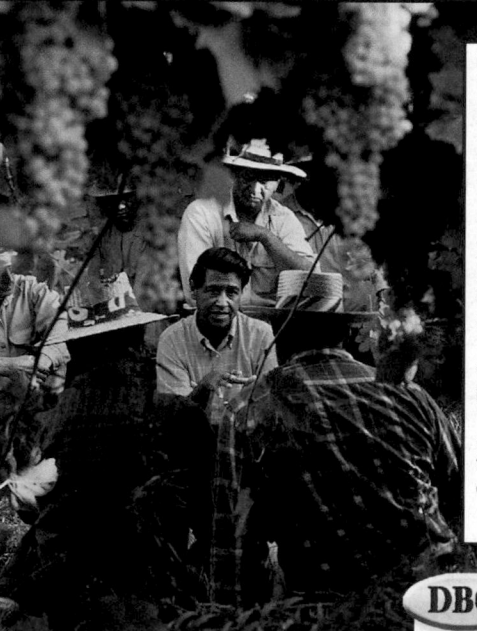

▲ Activist César Chávez was instrumental in improving conditions for Latino migrant workers.

PRIMARY SOURCE

"Farmworkers had been trying to organize a union for more than one hundred years. In 1965 they began a bitter five-year strike against grape growers around Delano, California. Two and one-half years later, in the hungry winter of 1968 with no resolution in sight, they were tired and frustrated.

Among some of them, particularly some of the young men, there began the murmurs of violence. . . . But Cesar rejected that part of our culture 'that tells young men that you're not a man if you don't fight back.' The boycott had followed in the tradition of Cesar's hero, Mahatma Gandhi, whose practice of nonviolence he embraced. And now, like Gandhi, Cesar announced he would undertake a fast. . . .

After twenty-five days, Cesar was carried to a nearby park where the fast ended during a mass with thousands of farmworkers. He had lost thirty-five pounds, but there was no more talk of violence among the farmworkers. . . .

Cesar was too weak to speak, so his statement was read by others in both English and Spanish. 'It is my deepest belief that only by giving our lives do we find life,' they read. 'The truest act of courage . . . is to sacrifice ourselves for others in a totally nonviolent struggle for justice.'"

—Marc Grossman, UFW spokesman, quoted in *Stone Soup for the World*

R

DBQ **Document-Based Questions**

1. **Identifying** Whose ideas inspired César Chávez to begin his fast?
2. **Explaining** What effect did the fast have on the striking farmworkers?

696 **Chapter 20** The Politics of Protest

Extending the Content

The Three-Hundred Mile March In 1965, when grape vineyard owners in Delano, California, cut the already pitiful pay of their workers, farmworker César Chávez called a strike at one of the farms. He knew that, when ripe, grapes do not last long. After attacks on strikers by the grape company, Chávez organized a march of more than three hundred miles from Delano

to the state capitol in Sacramento. There, he would ask for the government's help.

The march began with Chávez and sixty-seven others. For about fifteen miles a day, they marched on blistered and bloody feet. Meanwhile, the unharvested grapes in Delano rotted on the vine.

As the marchers passed, farmworkers fed them and offered places to sleep. Some

joined the march. Every day, more marchers followed Chávez. The marchers arrived in Sacramento on Easter Sunday, and a parade of ten thousand people marched through the streets to the capitol. There, they learned that the grape company had signed a contract with the National Farm Workers Association, promising a pay raise and better conditions.

security. In the early 1960s, **César Chávez** and **Dolores Huerta** organized two groups that fought for farmworkers. In 1965 the groups went on strike in California to demand union recognition, increased wages, and better benefits.

When employers resisted, Chávez enlisted college students, churches, and civil rights groups to organize a national boycott of table grapes, one of California's main agricultural products. An estimated 17 million citizens stopped buying grapes, and industry profits tumbled. In 1966, under the sponsorship of the American Federation of Labor and Congress of Industrial Organization (AFL-CIO), Chávez and Huerta merged their two organizations into one—the **United Farm Workers** (UFW). The new union kept the boycott going until 1970, when the grape growers finally agreed to raise wages and improve working conditions.

During the 1960s and 1970s, a growing number of Latino youths became involved in civil rights. In 1967 college students in San Antonio, Texas, led by José Angel Gutiérrez, founded the Mexican American Youth Organization (MAYO). MAYO organized walk-outs and demonstrations to protest discrimination. In 1968 about 1,000 Mexican American students and teachers in East Los Angeles walked out of their classrooms to protest racism. In Crystal City, Texas, protests organized by MAYO in 1969 led to the creation of bilingual education at the local high school.

MAYO's success and the spread of protests across the West and Southwest convinced Gutiérrez to found a new political party, *La Raza Unida,* or "the United People," in 1969. *La Raza* promoted Latino causes and supported Latino candidates in Texas, California, Colorado, Arizona, and New Mexico. The group mobilized Mexican American voters with calls for job-training programs and greater access to financial institutions. By the early 1970s, it had elected Latinos to local offices in several cities with large Latino populations.

La Raza was part of a larger civil rights movement among Mexican Americans (many of whom began calling themselves Chicanos). This "Brown Power" movement fought against discrimination and celebrated ethnic pride. On September 16, 1969 (Mexican Independence Day), students at the University of California at Berkeley staged a sit-in demanding a Chicano Studies program. Over the next decade, more than 50 universities created programs dedicated to the study of Latinos in the United States.

One issue many Latino leaders promoted in the late 1960s was **bilingualism**—the practice of teaching immigrant students in their own language while they also learned English. Congress supported their arguments, passing the **Bilingual Education Act** in 1968. This act directed school districts to set up classes for immigrants in their own language while they were learning English.

Later, bilingualism became politically controversial. Many Americans worried that bilingualism made it difficult for Latino immigrants to assimilate. Beginning in the 1980s, an English-only movement began, and by the 2000s, legislatures in 25 states had passed laws or amendments making English the official language of their state.

✔ **Reading Check** **Explaining** How did Latino Americans increase their economic opportunities in the 1960s?

Section 3 REVIEW

Vocabulary

1. **Explain** the significance of: repatriation, League of United Latin American Citizens, American GI Forum, César Chávez, Dolores Huerta, United Farm Workers, *La Raza Unida,* bilingualism, Bilingual Education Act.

Main Ideas

2. **Identifying** What are the national origins of the three main groups of Latinos in the United States?

3. **Describing** Under what circumstances did the American GI Forum first take action?

4. **Explaining** Why did some Americans worry about the Bilingual Education Act?

Critical Thinking

5. **Big Ideas** How did the judicial system support Latino civil rights in the last century? Cite two relevant court cases and their decisions.

6. **Categorizing** Use a graphic organizer similar to the one below to identify Latino groups and their achievements.

Civil Rights Group	Achievement

7. **Analyzing Visuals** Study the graph on page 693. What was the total U.S. Latino population in 2000? Which group had the largest population?

Writing About History

8. **Expository Writing** Write a magazine article about the conditions that gave rise to the Latino civil rights movement in the postwar period.

History ONLINE
Study Central™ To review this section, go to glencoe.com and click on Study Central.

✔ Reading Check

Answer:
By forming the UFW and *La Raza Unida* and staging boycotts, they increased their wages, won contracts, improved working conditions, and lobbied successfully to achieve the Bilingual Education Act.

Assess

History ONLINE

Study Central™ provides summaries, interactive games, and online graphic organizers to help students review content.

Close

Summarizing **Ask:** Why did Latino Americans organize? *(They wanted an end to discrimination; improved working conditions and better pay, especially for farmworkers; increased Latino voter participation; more Latino elected officials; and bilingual education in schools.)*

Section 3 REVIEW

Answers

1. All definitions can be found in the section and the Glossary.

2. Mexico, Puerto Rico, Cuba

3. A Latino American soldier was killed during World War II, and a funeral home in Texas refused to hold his funeral.

4. They were concerned that it would make it harder for Latino Americans to assimilate.

5. *Mendez* v. *Westminster*: ended school segregation in California; *Hernandez* v. *Texas*: extended greater rights to Latino citizens, including the right to serve on a jury

6. Answers may include the following: LULAC: brought cases to court that ended many discriminatory practices; American GI Forum: fought for Latino veterans' rights and to end discrimination in general; UFW: fought for improved working conditions and pay for farmworkers; *La Raza Unida*: worked to increase Latino voter participation and got Latino candidates elected; MAYO: held protests against discrimination and got bilingual education added to a high school in Texas

7. about 35 million; Mexicans

8. Students' articles will vary, but should focus on the reasons for and results of the Latino civil rights movement.

Chapter 20 VISUAL SUMMARY

Determining Cause and Effect

Invite students to write at least one cause-and-effect statement for the student protest movement, the feminist movement, and the Latino movement. **Ask:** What was the overall effect of the protest movements that began or gained momentum during the 1960s? **OL**

Expository Writing

Have students select one of the three groups mentioned in the Determining Cause and Effect activity above and write a one-page summary of their achievements during the 1960s and 1970s. **Ask:** Of the movements covered in this chapter, which do you think had the most lasting and important effect? **OL**

Causes of the New Protest Movements

- The earlier beat movement questioned American values.
- The successes of African Americans' fight for civil rights demonstrated to other groups that change was possible if people demanded change.
- Many in the baby boom generation became frustrated with society as they entered college and began to advocate for social reform.
- The Vietnam War and the draft led many students to join protests.
- Women began to question their position in postwar society. Betty Friedan's book *The Feminine Mystique* influenced many young women.
- The Kennedy administration began to pay attention to women's issues, passing the Equal Pay Act and creating the President's Commission on the Status of Women.
- The Latino American population increased through immigration; Latino newcomers, as well as citizens, faced discrimination.

◀ SDS leader Mario Savio speaks at a 1966 sit-in.

▶ Latinos began to fight for improved labor conditions through the work of the United Farm Workers who held rallies such as this one in 1979.

Effects of the New Protest Movements

- New student groups, including Students for a Democratic Society (SDS), were formed. Court cases affirmed student rights to free speech on campus.
- New women's groups, such as the National Organization of Women (NOW), emerged. They fought for equal economic rights in the workplace and in society, and they demanded equal opportunities in education.
- A campaign began for the Equal Rights Amendment, but the amendment was not ratified.
- The *Roe* v. *Wade* decision affirmed a constitutional right to abortion, with some limits.
- New Latino organizations emerged, such as the United Farm Workers (UFW) and *La Raza Unida*, fighting for increased economic opportunity and greater representation in political institutions.
- Latinos made substantial gains politically and economically, and many were elected to positions in Congress and state governments.

▲ Women's rights leaders, such as Bella Abzug (left, in hat) and Betty Friedan (right, in red coat) fought for greater equality for women.

698 Chapter 20 The Politics of Protest

Hands-On Chapter Project

Step 4: Wrap Up

Presenting a Historical Drama

Step 4

Directions Ask groups to write a review of the dramas presented by the other two groups. Have groups share the reviews with each other.

Putting It Together After groups have read the reviews, ask them to make any corrections for accuracy and present the dramas to the class again. **OL**

ASSESSMENT

STANDARDIZED TEST PRACTICE

TEST-TAKING **TIP**

> Read each question carefully to understand exactly what it is asking. Then review all the answer choices before finally choosing the **best** answer to the question.

Reviewing Vocabulary

Directions: Choose the word or words that best complete the sentence.

1. In the 1960s young people known as hippies began the _____ movement.
   A beat
   B counterculture
   C student
   D commune

2. A newly energized belief in _____ led to the fight to pass the Equal Rights Amendment.
   A communism
   B environmentalism
   C fascism
   D feminism

3. In the 1930s U.S. officials began to return Mexican immigrants to Mexico in what became known as the
   A counterculture.
   B barrio.
   C repatriation.
   D *La Raza Unida.*

4. Latinos lobbied successfully for the addition of _____ in public education.
   A bilingualism
   B repatriation
   C feminism
   D legalism

Reviewing Main Ideas

Directions: Choose the best answer for each of the following questions.

Section 1 *(pp. 682–685)*

5. SDS was begun by Tom Hayden at which university?
   A Harvard University
   B University of California at Berkeley
   C Kent State University
   D University of Michigan

6. Which of the following was an outgrowth of hippie culture?
   A SDS
   B rock 'n' roll music
   C communes
   D buzz cuts

Section 2 *(pp. 686–691)*

7. The work of the President's Commission on the Status of Women led to
   A the Equal Employment Opportunity Commission.
   B the Equal Rights Amendment.
   C the Equal Pay Act.
   D the National Organization for Women.

8. Title IX of the Educational Amendments prohibited federally funded schools
   A from paying male teachers more than female teachers.
   B from discriminating against minorities.
   C from providing same-gender education.
   D from discriminating on the basis of gender.

Need Extra Help?								
If You Missed Questions . . .	1	2	3	4	5	6	7	8
Go to Page . . .	684	686–691	694	697	682–683	685	687	690

GO ON

Answers and Analyses
Reviewing Vocabulary

1. B Counter means "against" or "opposing." In essence, hippies were "against" traditional culture. The beat movement was a precursor to the counterculture movement. Communes grew out of the counterculture movement. Student is too general.

2. D The Equal Rights Amendment was specifically intended to give equal rights to women. Feminism is the belief in the need for equal rights for women. Communism and fascism are forms of government. Environmentalism is work to help conserve the environment.

3. C For this vocabulary item, help students break down the word repatriation. Re- is a prefix that means "back" or "again" and comes from Latin. -ation is a suffix that means action or a process. In the middle, "patri" derives from the Latin word *patria* meaning native country. Repatriation = the process of returning someone to their country of origin.

4. A Latinos come from Latin America and usually are Spanish-speakers. Bi- means "two." Lingual means "language." Bilingual means two languages. Latinos sought bilingual education in English and Spanish. The lobbying efforts for bilingual education grew out of the Latino civil rights movement.

6. C Here, students can use the process of elimination. *A* is incorrect, SDS was founded in 1959, before hippie culture had really begun. Rock 'n' roll also predated the hippie culture. Long hair was a symbol of the hippie movement, not a conservative buzz cut. This leaves communes, which were places where hippies practiced communal living.

7. C When the same word appears in more than one answer choice, it is vital that students read each answer choice carefully, to avoid making a careless mistake. Headed by Eleanor Roosevelt, the Commission won the passage of the Equal Pay Act. The Equal Employment Opportunity Commission had to implement the Equal Pay Act. The Equal Rights Amendment was never passed. NOW was an independent group. It was not formed due to a presidential commission.

8. D Title IX today is mostly associated with sports programs. It is somewhat controversial, as the need to have a balance between men's and women's athletic programs sometimes leads to programs simply being cut.

Reviewing Main Ideas

5. D The SDS was an example of a new left movement. Tom Hayden wrote the Port Huron Statement, which stated the goals of SDS. To help remember that SDS began at the University of Michigan, students should relate the Port Huron Statement to Lake Huron, one of the Great Lakes.

9. C *A* and *B* do not make sense. The purpose of the ERA was to gain equal rights for women, not to gain extra advantages, like free schooling. The ERA did not concern abortion. *D* represents a possible opposite effect of the passage of the amendment. *C* correctly represents the fears of some—that full equality would mean no consideration for traditional rights of women.

10. B Remind students to consider the time period; 1959 was in the middle of the Cold War, when communists were the "enemy." This culture created an environment where refugees from communism were welcomed. This was a bit unique, as the 1950s and 1960s saw much discrimination against other Spanish-speaking immigrant groups.

11. C The NAACP experienced much success in the struggle for equality for African Americans through the court system, with cases such as *Brown* v. *Board of Education of Topeka, Kansas*. The LULAC took a similar path, with cases such as *Mendez* v. *Westminster*. An easy way for students to remember that these organizations had similar methods is to think that both are represented by acronyms (and both acronyms have five letters.)

12. C Mexican American veterans of World War II were excluded from the veterans' benefits that other veterans were entitled to, including medical service.

Critical Thinking

13. A The Civil Rights Act supported the right of people to assemble in public places. The Supreme Court ruled that this applied to college campuses. The Equal Rights Amendment was never passed, so it cannot be correct. The educational Amendments is too broad, and would not apply, even though the

9. Why did some people oppose the Equal Rights Amendment?

A It said that state governments could not regulate abortion during the first three months of pregnancy.

B It allowed women to go to college and vocational schools for free.

C People feared that it would take away traditional rights such as receiving alimony and exemption from the military draft.

D People feared that more women would choose to stay at home with their families rather than having a career.

Section 3 *(pp. 692–697)*

10. Cuban immigrants arriving after the Cuban Revolution in 1959 were welcomed by Americans because

A there was a shortage of cheap labor.

B they were considered refugees from communism.

C most of them were fluent in English.

D there was a need for more doctors and other professionals.

11. Using a tactic the NAACP had used to advance the rights of African Americans, LULAC fought discrimination against Latinos mainly through

A lobbying efforts.

B demonstrations and other protests.

C the court system.

D periodicals and other mass media.

12. Who was the American GI Forum founded to protect?

A African American veterans

B women veterans

C Mexican American veterans

D Veterans of Pacific Battles

Critical Thinking

Directions: Choose the best answers to the following questions.

13. The Supreme Court upheld the Free Speech protesters' rights to free speech and assembly under which law?

A the Civil Rights Act of 1964

B the Equal Rights Amendment

C the Educational Amendments

D the Twenty-sixth Amendment

Base your answers to questions 14 and 15 on the map below and on your knowledge of Chapter 20.

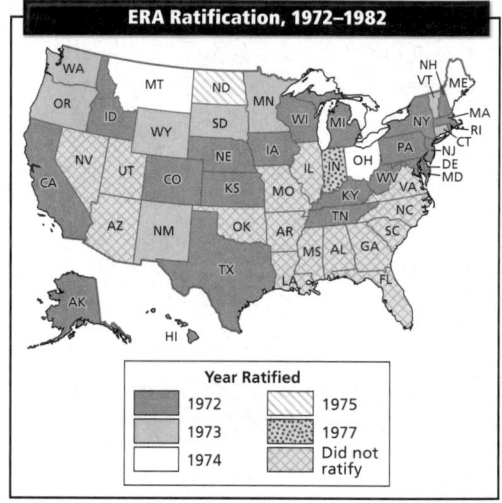

ERA Ratification, 1972–1982

Year Ratified
- 1972
- 1973
- 1974
- 1975
- 1977
- Did not ratify

14. How many states had ratified the ERA by 1977?

A 20   C 30

B 25   D 35

15. In what region did most states fail to ratify the ERA?

A the South   C the West

B New England   D the Midwest

Need Extra Help?							
If You Missed Questions . . .	9	10	11	12	13	14	15
Go to Page . . .	689–690	694–695	695	696	683–684	R15	R15

GO ON

protest took place on a college campus. The Twenty-Sixth Amendment lowered the voting age to 18, and would not apply.

14. D Students may be confused and just look at the states that ratified the ERA in 1977. However, the question asks how many states had ratified it *by* 1977. So, students must count all of the states that match the shading for 1972, 1973, 1974, 1975, and 1977.

15. A The states that did not ratify the ERA are shaded with a crosshatch pattern. From the map, it is apparent that most of the states in the South did not ratify the amendment.

16. The United Farm Workers' boycott against California grape growers was effective because

  A the grape growers gave in so quickly to the union's demands.

  B no one thought that they could organize so well.

  C grapes were a major agricultural product of California.

  D the union had the support of the U.S. government.

17. What did the cartoonist imply with this cartoon?

  A Hippies know a great deal of information.

  B Parents do not listen to their children.

  C Hippies were wrong to question the older generation when they still accepted money from them.

  D The older generation thought hippies were lazy and unintelligent.

Document-Based Questions

Directions: Analyze the document and answer the short-answer questions that follow the document.

On December 2, 1964, Mario Savio, the leader of the Free Speech Movement, led a protest at the University of California at Berkeley. Before the protest, Savio made a speech in reaction to comments by Berkeley's president, Clark Kerr. Kerr had said that he would not speak out in favor of students' demands in opposition to the Board of Regents, in the same way that a manager would not speak out against a board of directors. Savio used Kerr's metaphor of the university as a corporation in the following excerpt from his speech:

> "[I]f this is a firm, and if the Board of Regents are the board of directors, and if President Kerr in fact is the manager, then I'll tell you something: the faculty are a bunch of employees, and we're the raw material! But we're a bunch of raw material[s] that don't mean to have any process upon us, don't mean to be made into any product. . . . We're human beings! . . . you've got to put your bodies upon the gears and upon the wheels, upon the levers, upon all the apparatus, and you've got to make it stop. And you've got to indicate to the people who run it, to the people who own it, that unless you're free, the machine will be prevented from working at all!"
>
> —from Mario Savio's speech to Free Speech Movement demonstrators

18. According to Savio, if the university is a company, then what are the students?

19. What is Savio asking his fellow students to do, both literally and figuratively?

Extended Response

20. Write an expository essay explaining why so many protest movements emerged in the United States during the 1960s and 1970s. Your essay should include an introduction and at least three paragraphs that explore this issue, including facts and examples from the chapter.

STOP

History ONLINE

For additional test practice, use Self-Check Quizzes— Chapter 20 at glencoe.com.

Need Extra Help?

If You Missed Questions . . .	16	17	18	19	20
Go to Page . . .	697	R18	R19	R19	R12

19. Literally: Savio is asking students to protest personally against the problems they see with the university and bring the workings of the university to a halt. Figuratively: Savio is asking them to put themselves "in the works" of the machine. This is a good place to review metaphors with students: the factory as a metaphor for the university.

Extended Response

20. Students' essays will vary, but should clearly and logically express their ideas about why this era was an active period of protest and change. Essays should include at least two examples of protest movements and supporting details from the chapter.

---

16. C Grapes were a major agricultural product in California, therefore, the UFW boycott had a major financial impact. This financial impact is what made the boycott successful, because it forced the growers to negotiate with the UFW. Had the boycott been of a less profitable product, it may not have had as much impact.

17. C Study the cartoon with students. One hippie is chastising/making fun of his father for being old-fashioned, while another in the background reminds the first hippie to "tell him he's late with our allowance." The message is that the hippies had no respect for the older generation, but had no problem being supported by them.

Document-Based Questions

18. The students are the product or material produced by the company. Savio calls the students "raw material" as far as the university is concerned, but asserts that they are in fact, real people.

History ONLINE

Have students visit the Web site at glencoe.com to review Chapter 20 and take the Self-Check Quiz.

Need Extra Help?

Have students refer to the pages listed if they miss any of the questions.

UNIT PACING CHART

	Unit 7	Chapter 21	Chapter 22	Chapter 23	Chapter 24	Unit 7
Day 1	Unit Opener	Chapter 21 Opener, Section 1	Chapter 22 Opener, Section 1	Chapter 23 Opener, Section 1	Chapter 24 Opener, Section 1	Wrap-Up/Project, Unit Assessment
Day 2		Sections 2 & 3	Section 2	Section 2	Section 2	
Day 3		Section 4	Section 3	Section 3	Section 3	
Day 4		Section 5	Section 4	Section 4	Section 4	
Day 5		Chapter Assessment	Chapter Assessment	Chapter Assessment	Chapter Assessment	

Teacher to Teacher

Philip Prale
Oak Park and
River Forest High
School
Oak Park, IL

Into the New Century—The Keeper's Project The purpose of this project is to analyze developments of the 1900s and explain why they are worth keeping in this new twenty-first century.

Ask students to construct a list of five to ten items that are Twentieth Century Keepers. Variations include:

1. Draw keepers from specific categories—Political, Economic, Social, Cultural, Religious, or Environmental.

2. Add one item that you would want to eliminate in this new century.

3. For each item write a description of the item and how it fits into the category.

4. Write an introductory paragraph explaining the general connection, besides time, of the keepers. What is the theme or central idea?

5. Make a poster with images or produce a slide show presentation of the material.

Author Note

Dear American History Teacher:

As you begin to teach this unit, there are themes that recur throughout the chapters that you will want to point out to students.

The last unit in this textbook offers some unique opportunities for connecting students to the major themes of American history. The trends and events that this unit covers occurred during their lifetimes and may have directly affected them. This unit deals with sweeping changes, both nationally and globally, at the end of the twentieth century. It follows political and demographic shifts within the United States, as well as the collapse of the Soviet Union, the end of the Cold War, and the plunge into a war on terrorism.

Vast changes have taken place around us. When I began teaching, essentially the only available equipment was the mimeograph machine. When I went to work at the Capitol in the 1970s, reporters there were writing their stories on typewriters and sending them to their newspapers by telegraph. In short order, equipment that seemed so essential became museum pieces. Personal computers, electronic mail, and the Internet created a communications revolution, in the classroom as well as in the newsroom and the halls of Congress. Digital resources provided instant access to vast amounts of information on a previously unimaginable global scale.

In studying this unit, most students can readily relate to the development of personal computers and the rise of the Internet. They can recall a recent election that was in the news. Most students will have memories of the tragic events on September 11, 2001. Such personal links should enable them to better understand the impact of earlier forms of science and technology, of previous elections, and of other traumatic national events. You might consider teaching the material from the last chapter first to frame the past through students' present experiences.

Donald A. Ritchie

Senior Author

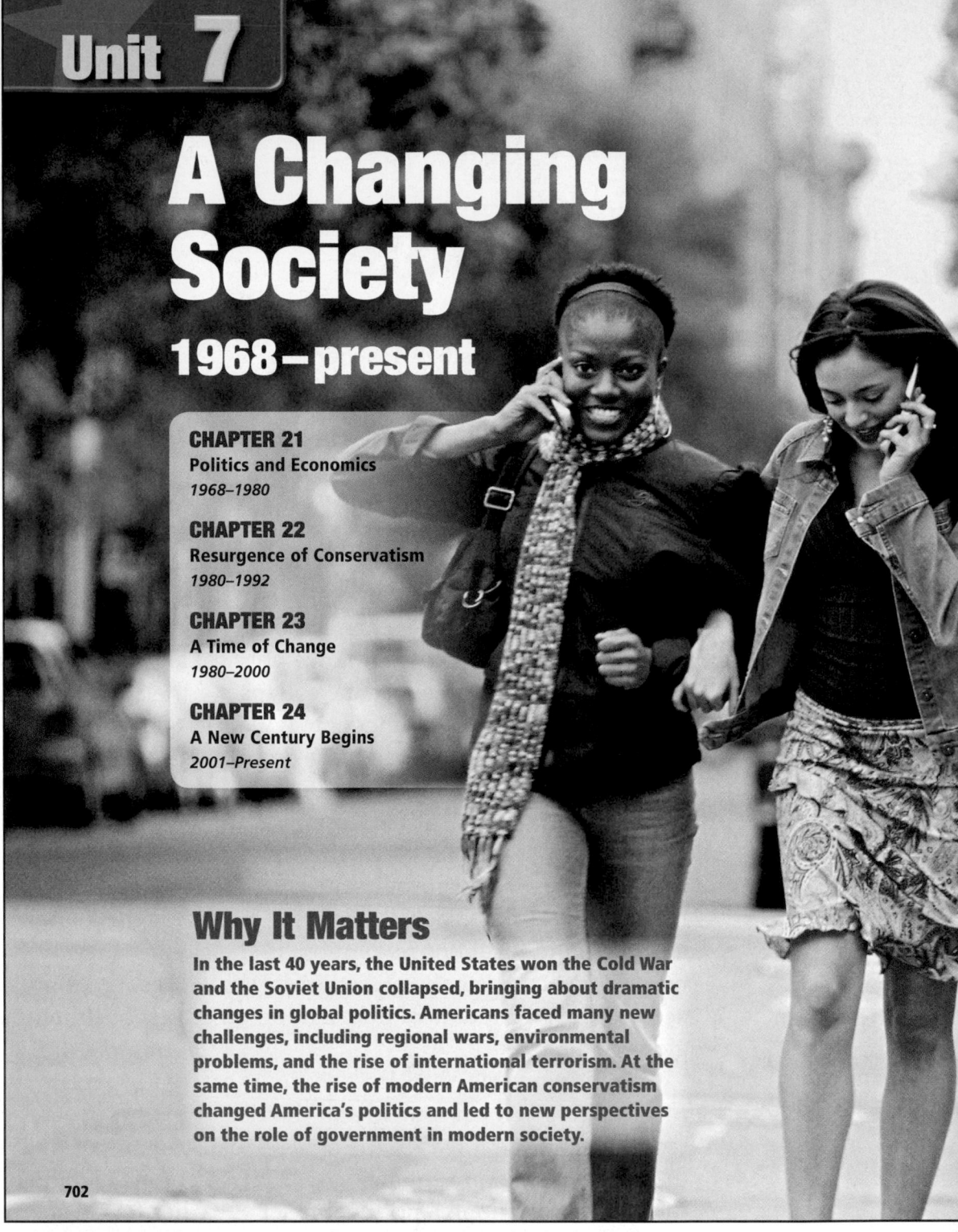

Focus

Why It Matters

Ask students to think about the hot wars that have replaced the Cold War, the globalization of the economy, the issues of global warming, and the political climate today. Have them discuss whether they think Americans are more or less secure economically and politically than they were in 1960 and whether they have more or less personal freedom. **OL**

Connecting to Past Learning

Have students recall the Progressive Era in U.S. history, in which people began to be aware of the environmental damage that industry was causing. **Ask: How did government help correct the environmental problems in the early twentieth century?** *(The government passed new health and safety codes and created national parks.)* Tell students that in this unit they will learn about the changing society in the late twentieth century, the return to conservatism, and the changes caused by terrorism. **AL**

Unit Launch Activity

Making Connections Have students write one fact they know or opinion they hold about each of the following presidents: President Reagan, President George H.W. Bush, President Clinton, and President George W. Bush. Ask volunteers to share their statements, and have the class identify the statement as fact or opinion as they study the unit. **OL**

Unit 7

A Changing Society

1968–present

CHAPTER 21
Politics and Economics
1968–1980

CHAPTER 22
Resurgence of Conservatism
1980–1992

CHAPTER 23
A Time of Change
1980–2000

CHAPTER 24
A New Century Begins
2001–Present

Why It Matters

In the last 40 years, the United States won the Cold War and the Soviet Union collapsed, bringing about dramatic changes in global politics. Americans faced many new challenges, including regional wars, environmental problems, and the rise of international terrorism. At the same time, the rise of modern American conservatism changed America's politics and led to new perspectives on the role of government in modern society.

702

Team Teaching Activity

Economics Invite an economics teacher to the class to discuss how trade agreements, globalization, and technology have affected the economy, employment opportunities, and consumer choices in the last part of the twentieth and the beginning of the twenty-first century. Ask the teacher to include a basic discussion of how microchip technology has affected the economy and society. Encourage students to ask questions to stimulate a class discussion. **OL**

By the early twenty-first century, American society was becoming increasingly diverse even as technology enabled people to become more interconnected.

703

More About the Photo

Visual Literacy Cell phones on the street are a common sight today, but on April 3, 1973, people stared as Martin Cooper walked down the street talking on a portable cellular phone. People knew about cellular phones in cars, but Cooper, general manager of Motorola's Communications Systems Division, was making the first public telephone call from a hand-held portable cell phone. He called his rival at AT&T's Bell Labs. Cooper's cell phone looked like a brick and weighed 30 ounces. Ten years later, his company brought a 16-ounce cell phone to market at a price of $3,500. Today, mobile phones can weigh as little as a few ounces. The cell phone is just one of many advances in communications technology that have brought distant and diverse peoples closer.

Skill Practice

Predicting Consequences
Ask students to consider what they associate with the terms *liberalism* and *conservatism*. As they respond, list their responses on the chalkboard. Clarify the terms briefly, and ask students to predict how a resurgence of conservatism would affect foreign policy, the economy, and daily life. Tell them to verify their predictions as they read. **OL**

Skill Practice

Describing Have students look at the photograph again and describe how the people in the photographs reflect the changing population of the United States. *(Answers may include that the population is more diverse now, that females make up more than 50% of the population, and that young people embrace new technologies.)* **OL**

NCLB — NO CHILD LEFT BEHIND

Teaching Tip The NCLB Act emphasizes reading. One strategy that helps students who are having difficulty understanding information is to have them use graphic organizers, such as flowcharts, to understand the sequence of events in the text. Have students work in groups of four. Each group member should maintain a flowchart showing major events and changes in one of these areas: foreign policy, domestic policy, economy, and society. After they have finished the unit, have them share their charts and discuss the political, economic, and social impacts of these events and changes.

Key to Ability Levels	
BL Below Level	AL Above Level
OL On Level	ELL English Language Learners

Key to Teaching Resources	
Print Material	DVD
CD-ROM	Transparency

Levels					Resources	Chapter Opener	Section 1	Section 2	Section 3	Section 4	Section 5	Chapter Assess
BL	OL	AL	ELL									
					FOCUS							
BL	OL	AL	ELL	🖳	**Daily Focus Transparencies**		21-1	21-2	21-3	21-4		
					TEACH							
	OL	AL		📁	**History Simulations and Problem Solving, URB**			p. 9				
	OL	AL		📁	**American Literature Reading, URB**					p. 13		
BL	OL	AL	ELL	📁	**Reading Essentials and Note-Taking Guide***		p. 218	p. 221	p. 224	p. 227	p. 230	
BL	OL		ELL	📁	**Reading Skills Activity, URB**				p. 21			
	OL			📁	**Historical Analysis Skills Activity, URB**			p. 22				
BL	OL		ELL	📁	**Guided Reading Activity, URB***		p. 48	p. 49	p. 50	p. 51	p. 52	
BL	OL	AL	ELL	📁	**Differentiated Instruction Activity, URB**							p. 23
BL	OL		ELL	📁	**English Learner Activity, URB**		p. 25					
BL	OL	AL	ELL	📁	**Content Vocabulary Activity, URB***	p. 27						
BL	OL	AL	ELL	📁	**Academic Vocabulary Activity, URB**	p. 29						
	OL	AL		📁	**Reinforcing Skills Activity, URB**				p. 31			
	OL	AL		📁	**Critical Thinking Skills Activity, URB**			p. 32				
BL	OL		ELL	📁	**Time Line Activity, URB**			p. 33				
	OL			📁	**Linking Past and Present Activity, URB**							p. 34
BL	OL	AL	ELL	📁	**Primary Source Reading, URB**			p. 35	p. 37			
BL	OL	AL	ELL	📁	**American Art and Music Activity, URB**							p. 39
BL	OL	AL	ELL	📁	**Interpreting Political Cartoons Activity, URB**					p. 41		
		AL		📁	**Enrichment Activity, URB**					p. 45		
BL	OL	AL	ELL	📁	**Differentiated Instruction for the American History Classroom**	✓	✓	✓	✓	✓	✓	✓
BL	OL	AL	ELL	🖳	**Unit Map Overlay Transparencies**	✓	✓	✓	✓	✓	✓	✓
BL	OL	AL	ELL	📁	**Unit Time Line Transparencies, Strategies, and Activities**	✓	✓	✓	✓	✓	✓	✓
BL	OL	AL	ELL	📁	**Cause and Effect Transparencies, Strategies, and Activities**	✓	✓	✓	✓	✓	✓	✓
BL	OL	AL	ELL	📁	**Why It Matters Chapter Transparencies, Strategies, and Activities**	✓	✓	✓	✓	✓	✓	✓

Note: Please refer to the *Unit 7 Resource Book* for this chapter's URB materials.

* Also available in Spanish

TeacherWorks *Plus*
All-In-One Planner and Resource Center

- Interactive Lesson Planner
- Interactive Teacher Edition
- Fully editable blackline masters
- Section Spotlight Videos Launch
- Differentiated Lesson Plans
- Printable reports of daily assignments
- Standards Tracking System

Levels BL OL AL ELL		Resources	Chapter Opener	Section 1	Section 2	Section 3	Section 4	Section 5	Chapter Assess
TEACH *(continued)*									
BL OL AL ELL		American Biographies						✓	
BL OL AL		Supreme Court Case Studies			p. 117		p. 107		
BL OL AL ELL		The Living Constitution	✓	✓	✓	✓	✓	✓	✓
BL OL AL ELL		American Issues	✓	✓	✓	✓	✓	✓	✓
OL AL ELL		American Art and Architecture Transparencies, Strategies, and Activities	✓	✓	✓	✓	✓	✓	✓
BL OL AL		High School American History Literature Library	✓	✓	✓	✓	✓	✓	✓
OL AL		American History Primary Source Documents Library	✓	✓	✓	✓	✓	✓	✓
BL OL AL ELL		American Music: Hits Through History CD	✓	✓	✓	✓	✓	✓	✓
BL OL AL ELL		StudentWorks™ Plus DVD	✓	✓	✓	✓	✓	✓	✓
BL OL AL ELL		Vocabulary PuzzleMaker CD-ROM	✓	✓	✓	✓	✓	✓	✓
BL OL AL ELL		*The American Vision* Video Program DVD	✓	✓	✓	✓	✓	✓	✓
Teacher Resources		Reading Strategies and Activities for the Social Studies Classroom	✓	✓	✓	✓	✓	✓	✓
		Strategies for Success	✓	✓	✓	✓	✓	✓	✓
		Presentation Plus! DVD	✓	✓	✓	✓	✓	✓	✓
		Success With English Learners	✓	✓	✓	✓	✓	✓	✓
ASSESS									
BL OL AL ELL		Section Quizzes and Chapter Tests*		p. 299	p. 300	p. 301	p. 302	p. 303	p. 305
BL OL AL ELL		Authentic Assessment With Rubrics							p. 47
BL OL AL ELL		Standardized Test Practice Workbook							p. 49
BL OL AL ELL		*ExamView®* Assessment Suite CD-ROM		21-1	21-2	21-3	21-4	21-5	Ch. 21
BL OL AL ELL		Interactive Tutor Self-Assessment CD-ROM		21-1	21-2	21-3	21-4	21-5	Ch. 21
CLOSE									
BL ELL		Reteaching Activity, URB							p. 43
BL OL ELL		Reading and Study Skills Foldables™	p. 82						

Presentation Builder

Technology Product

Presentation Builder is a convenient and dynamic McGraw-Hill Learning Network tool to create online presentations. Use the Presentation Builder to

- create your own presentation slides;
- insert graphics from your Glencoe textbook;
- distribute presentations to students using **Assignments** from the *Classroom Tools*.

Steps

- On the McGraw-Hill Learning Network home page (www.mhln.com), log in as a member.
- Choose **Presentation Builder** under **Resources**.
- Click the **New Presentation** button.
- Enter a title in the **Presentation Title** box, then follow the prompts to select colors and fonts.
- Click the **Next** button and select a slide. Follow the prompts to insert information and complete the

slide. The text boxes automatically adjust in size to accommodate the length of each question.

- Click the **Add Slide** button if you have additional presentation information and follow the prompts.
- Click **Review Presentation** when you are done.
- Click **View Presentation** to review the presentation in a pop-up window.
- Click on an underlined slide title to edit slides; use the drop-down keys to change the order of the slides; push the **Delete** button to delete a slide; and press **Insert Slide** to add a slide.
- Click the **Save** button when you are satisfied with your presentation. The presentation is saved to your **File Cabinet** and can be distributed to students through **Assignments**.

History ONLINE

	Student	Teacher	Parent
Beyond the Textbook	●	●	●
Chapter Overviews	●	●	●
Time Current Events	●		●
ePuzzles and Games	●		●
Concepts in Motion	●		●
Literature Connections		●	
Multi-Language Glossaries	●		●
Online Student Edition	●	●	●
Self-Check Quizzes	●		●
Student Web Activities	●		●
Study Central ™	●		●
Teaching Today		●	
Vocabulary eFlashcards	●		●
Web Activity Lesson Plans		●	

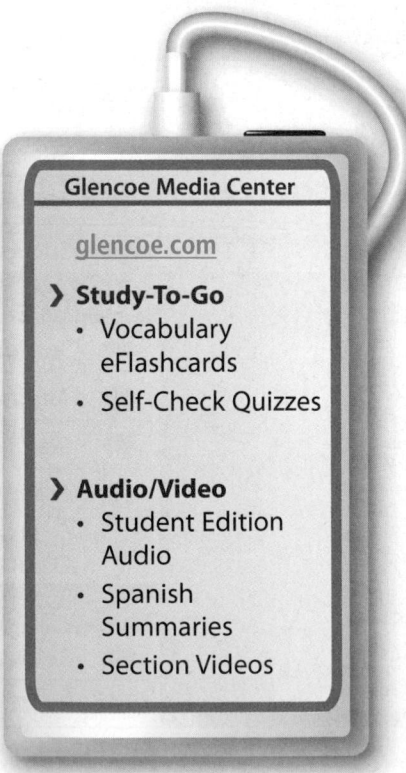

Glencoe Media Center

glencoe.com

› Study-To-Go
- Vocabulary eFlashcards
- Self-Check Quizzes

› Audio/Video
- Student Edition Audio
- Spanish Summaries
- Section Videos

- **Timed Readings Plus in Social Studies** helps students increase their reading rate and fluency while maintaining comprehension. The 400-word passages are similar to those found on state and national assessments.

- **Reading in the Content Area: Social Studies** concentrates on six essential reading skills that help students better comprehend what they read. The book includes 75 high-interest nonfiction passages written at increasing levels of difficulty.

- **Reading Social Studies** includes strategic reading instruction and vocabulary support in Social Studies content for both ELLs and native speakers of English.

www.jamestowneducation.com

The following videotape programs are available from Glencoe as supplements to Chapter 21:

- Richard Nixon: Man and President (ISBN 1-56-501742-0)

- The Secret Service (ISBN 1-56-501521-5)

To order, call Glencoe at 1-800-334-7344. To find classroom resources to accompany many of these videos, check the following home pages:

A&E Television: www.aetv.com
The History Channel: www.historychannel.com

NATIONAL GEOGRAPHIC
Index to National Geographic Magazine:

The following articles relate to this chapter:

- "Widespread as Rain and Deadly as Poison: Our Polluted Runoff," by John G. Mitchell, February 1996.

- "The Great Lakes' Troubled Waters," by Charles E. Cobb Jr., Bob Sacha, and Richard Olsenius, July 1987.

National Geographic Society Products To order the following, call National Geographic at 1-800-368-2728:

- *Civil Rights* (Transparencies)

Access National Geographic's new dynamic MapMachine Web site and other geography resources at:
www.nationalgeographic.com
www.nationalgeographic.com/maps

Reading List Generator CD-ROM

GLENCOE BOOKLINK 3

Use this database to search more than 30,000 titles to create a customized reading list for your students.

- Reading lists can be organized by students' reading level, author, genre, theme, or area of interest.

- The database provides Degrees of Reading Power™ (DRP) and Lexile™ readability scores for all selections.

- A brief summary of each selection is included.

Leveled reading suggestions for this chapter:

For students at a Grade 8 reading level:
- *Andrew Young: Freedom Fighter,* by Naurice Roberts

For students at a Grade 9 reading level:
- *Habitat for Humanity*

For students at a Grade 10 reading level:
- *Andrew Young: A Matter of Choice,* by Jan Simpson

For students at a Grade 11 reading level:
- *All the President's Men,* by Carl Bernstein & Bob Woodward

For students at a Grade 12 reading level:
- *White House Years,* by Henry Kissinger

Focus

MAKING CONNECTIONS
What Stops Government Abuse of Power?

Ask students to give examples from the news of legal and ethical challenges facing individuals in government. Ask them how much people today trust government leaders. Then ask them how they think Watergate affected peoples' attitudes toward government. Students should evaluate their answers after they have completed the chapter. **OL**

Teach

The Big Ideas

As students study the chapter, remind them to consider the section-based Big Ideas included in each section's Guide to Reading. The **Essential Questions** in the activities below tie in to the Big Ideas and help students think about and understand important chapter concepts. In addition, the Hands-On Chapter Projects with their culminating activities relate the content from each section to the Big Ideas. These activities build on each other as students progress through the chapter.

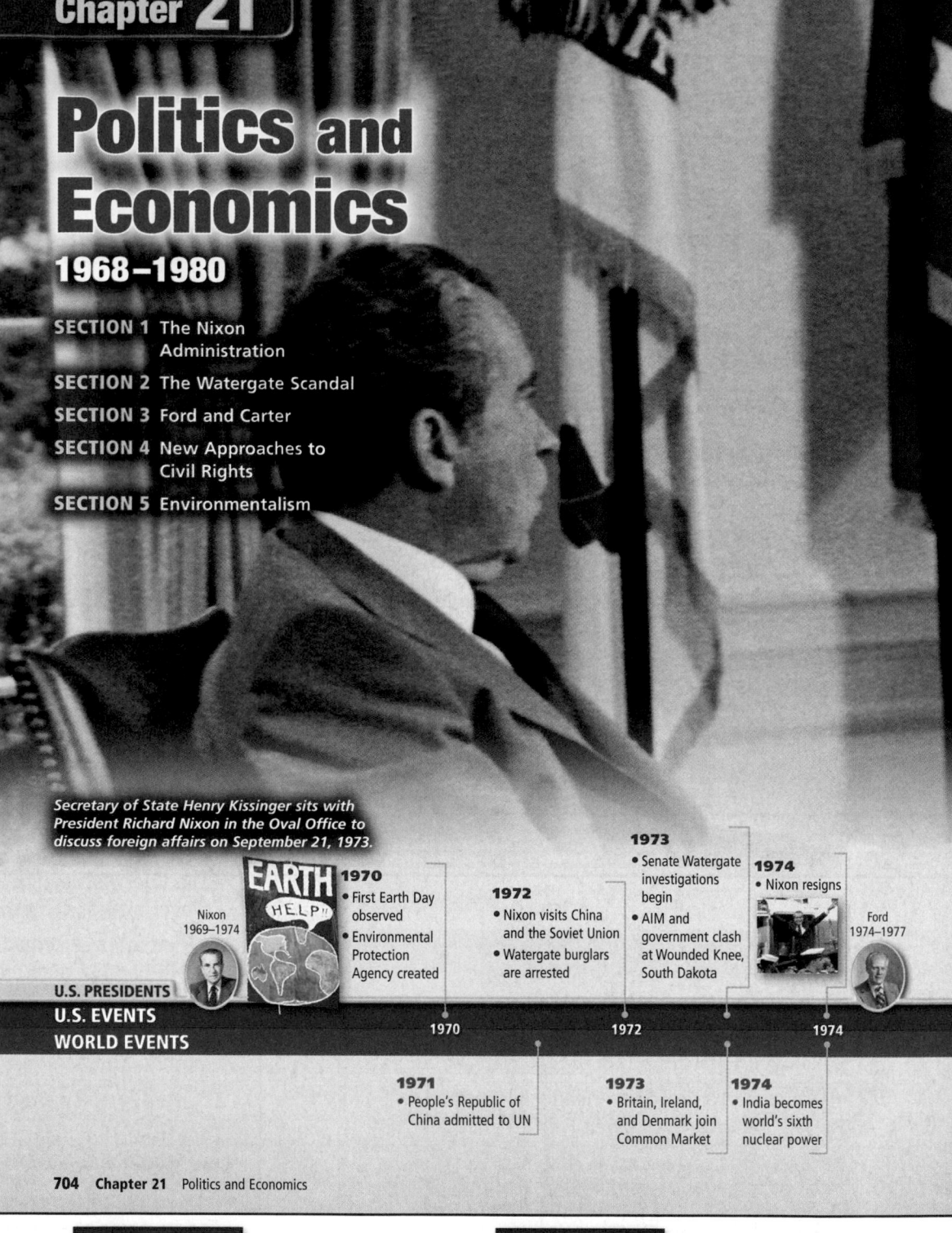

Chapter 21

Politics and Economics
1968–1980

SECTION 1 The Nixon Administration

SECTION 2 The Watergate Scandal

SECTION 3 Ford and Carter

SECTION 4 New Approaches to Civil Rights

SECTION 5 Environmentalism

Secretary of State Henry Kissinger sits with President Richard Nixon in the Oval Office to discuss foreign affairs on September 21, 1973.

U.S. PRESIDENTS
U.S. EVENTS
WORLD EVENTS

Nixon 1969–1974

Ford 1974–1977

1970
- First Earth Day observed
- Environmental Protection Agency created

1972
- Nixon visits China and the Soviet Union
- Watergate burglars are arrested

1973
- Senate Watergate investigations begin
- AIM and government clash at Wounded Knee, South Dakota

1974
- Nixon resigns

1970   1972   1974

1971
- People's Republic of China admitted to UN

1973
- Britain, Ireland, and Denmark join Common Market

1974
- India becomes world's sixth nuclear power

704 Chapter 21 Politics and Economics

Section 1

The Nixon Administration
Essential Question: How did Nixon's presidency change the country and its position in the world? *(He appointed conservative judges, eliminated some of Johnson's programs, and established détente with the Soviet Union and China.)* Tell students that in Section 1 they will learn about the Nixon presidency. **OL**

Section 2

The Watergate Scandal
Essential Question: What were the causes and effects of the Watergate scandal? *(Causes: Nixon's conviction that people were out to get him led to the break-in and cover up. Effects: Nixon's resignation, public distrust of government leaders, new anti-corruption laws.)* Point out that in Section 2 students will learn about the causes and impact of the Watergate scandal. **OL**

Section 3

Ford and Carter
Essential Question: How did Ford and Carter respond to energy and economic challenges? *(Ford cut spending and kept taxes low, while Carter vetoed spending bills, delayed tax cuts, urged the public to curb energy use, created a Department of Energy, and deregulated oil.)* Point out that in Section 3 students will study the Ford and Carter administrations. **OL**

MAKING CONNECTIONS

What Stops Government Abuse of Power?

The Watergate scandal forced Richard Nixon to become the first president to resign from office. The legacy of Watergate, together with the Vietnam War and the economic downturn of the late 1970s, caused many people to distrust the government and worry about the nation's future.

- *How do you think Watergate affected people's attitudes toward government?*
- *Do you think Nixon should have been punished for his role in the scandal?*

1975
- President Ford signs Helsinki Accords

Carter
1977–1981

1979
- Iranian revolutionaries seize U.S. embassy in Tehran

NO GAS

1976

1978

1977
- Human rights manifesto is signed by 241 Czech activists and intellectuals

1979
- Sandinista guerrillas overthrow Nicaraguan dictator Somoza
- Margaret Thatcher becomes prime minister of Great Britain

FOLDABLES

Analyzing Cause and Effect After you have read about the Watergate scandal, create a Shutter Fold Foldable to analyze critical information. Write a summary of Watergate events in the large middle section inside the Shutter Foldable. On the left-hand tab, list the causes of the Watergate scandal. On the right-hand tab, list the effects of Watergate on the political system.

History ONLINE Chapter Overview
Visit glencoe.com to preview Chapter 21.

Chapter 21 Politics and Economics **705**

More About the Photo

Visual Literacy Working together, Henry Kissinger and President Nixon reshaped U.S. foreign policy. They placed limits on U.S. commitments to allies. They also began to rely more heavily on negotiation and building relationships with traditional foes. In his inaugural address, Nixon announced, "After a period of confrontation we are entering an era of negotiation." Nixon relied on Kissinger both as an adviser and a negotiator. Together, Nixon and Kissinger worked to build bridges with the Soviet Union, the People's Republic of China, and Egypt.

FOLDABLES **Dinah Zike's**
Study Organizer **Foldables**

Dinah Zike's Foldables are three-dimensional, interactive graphic organizers that help students practice basic writing skills, review vocabulary terms, and identify main ideas. Instructions for creating and using Foldables can be found in the Appendix at the end of this book and in the *Dinah Zike's Reading and Study Skills Foldables* booklet.

History ONLINE
Introduce students to chapter content and key terms by having them access the Chapter 21 Overview at glencoe.com.

Section 4

New Approaches to Civil Rights
Essential Question: What were the goals of the African Americans, Native Americans, and Americans with disabilities when they organized? *(They wanted an end to discrimination. Native Americans also wanted sovereignty.)* Point out that in Section 4 students will learn about these movements. **OL**

Section 5

Environmentalism
Essential Question: What conditions did the environmental movement address? *(controls on pollution; cleanups; and protection of land, plant, wildlife, air, and water resources)* Tell students that in Section 5 they will learn about the origins of the modern environmental movement. **OL**

1 Focus

Bellringer
Daily Focus Transparency 21.1

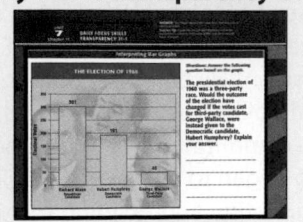

Guide to Reading

Answers:
Students should list Nixon's policies discussed in this section under the appropriate headings.

Section Spotlight Video

To generate student interest and provide a springboard for class discussion, access the Chapter 21, Section 1 video at glencoe.com or on the video DVD.

Resource Manager

The Nixon Administration

Guide to Reading

Big Ideas
Individual Action One of President Nixon's most dramatic accomplishments was changing the United States's relationship with the People's Republic of China and the Soviet Union.

Content Vocabulary
• revenue sharing (p. 708)
• impound (p. 708)
• détente (p. 710)
• summit (p. 711)

Academic Vocabulary
• welfare (p. 708)
• liberal (p. 708)

People and Events to Identify
• Southern strategy (p. 707)
• New Federalism (p. 708)
• Henry Kissinger (p. 709)
• Vietnamization (p. 709)
• SALT I (p. 711)

Reading Strategy
Organizing Complete a graphic organizer similar to the one below by listing Nixon's domestic and foreign policies.

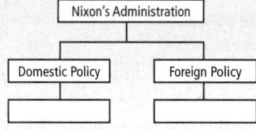

After he won the 1968 presidential election, Richard Nixon sought to restore law and order at home. His greatest accomplishments, however, were in foreign policy, where he worked to ease Cold War tensions with China and the Soviet Union.

Appealing to Middle America

MAIN Idea Nixon won the 1968 election by appealing to a "silent majority" of Americans.

HISTORY AND YOU Do you view your community as politically and socially liberal or conservative? Read on to find out about the strategies Nixon used to convince conservative Southerners to vote for him.

While they did not shout as loudly as the protesters, many Americans supported the government and longed for an end to the violence and turmoil that seemed to be plaguing the nation. The presidential candidate in 1968 who appealed to many of these frustrated citizens was Richard Nixon, a Republican. Nixon aimed many of his campaign messages at these Americans, whom he referred to as "Middle America" and the "silent majority." He promised them "peace with honor" in Vietnam, law and order, a more streamlined government, and a return to more traditional values at home.

Nixon's principal opponent in the 1968 presidential election was Democrat Hubert Humphrey, who had served as vice president under Lyndon Johnson. Nixon also had to wage his campaign against a strong third-party candidate, George Wallace, an experienced Southern politician and avowed supporter of segregation. In a 1964 bid for the Democratic presidential nomination, the former Alabama governor had attracted considerable support.

On Election Day, Wallace captured an impressive 13.5 percent of the popular vote, the best showing of a third-party candidate since 1924. Nixon managed a victory, however, receiving 43.4 percent of the popular vote to Humphrey's 42.7, and 301 electoral votes to Humphrey's 191.

The Southern Strategy

One of the keys to Nixon's victory was his surprisingly strong showing in the South. Even though the South had long been a Democratic stronghold, Nixon had refused to concede the region. To gain Southern support, Nixon had met with powerful South Carolina senator Strom Thurmond and won his backing by promising several things: to appoint only conservatives to the federal

---

R Reading Strategies	**C** Critical Thinking	**D** Differentiated Instruction	**W** Writing Support	**S** Skill Practice
Teacher Edition • Taking Notes p. 708 • Reading Graphs p. 710 **Additional Resources** • Guid. Read. Act., URB p. 48	**Teacher Edition** • Analyzing Visuals pp. 707, 709 **Additional Resources** • Quizzes and Tests, p. 299	**Additional Resources** • English Learner Act., URB p. 25 • Foldables, p. 82	**Teacher Edition** • Expository Writing, p. 708 **Additional Resources** • Content Vocab Act., URB p. 27 • Academic Vocab. Act., URB p. 29	**Additional Resources** • RENTG, p. 218

POLITICAL CARTOONS PRIMARY SOURCE
The Election of 1968

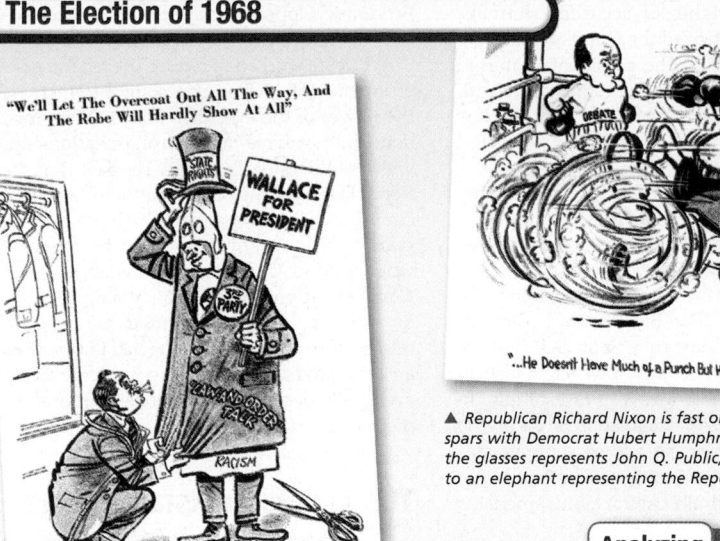

"We'll Let The Overcoat Out All The Way, And The Robe Will Hardly Show At All"

WALLACE FOR PRESIDENT

▲ Third-party presidential candidate George Wallace tailors an overcoat to cover the robe worn by one of his supporters.

"...He Doesn't Have Much of a Punch But He's Awful Fast on His Feet!"

▲ Republican Richard Nixon is fast on his feet as he spars with Democrat Hubert Humphrey. The man with the glasses represents John Q. Public, who is speaking to an elephant representing the Republican Party.

Analyzing VISUALS   DBQ

1. **Identifying** In the cartoon on the left, what is the cartoonist accusing Wallace of doing?
2. **Identifying Points of View** In the cartoon on the right, do you think the cartoonist approves of Nixon? Why or why not?

Teach

C Critical Thinking

Analyzing Visuals Have students study the Political Cartoon on page 707, and think about what they have read about the election. **Ask:** Who is the other person in the ring with Nixon? *(Hubert Humphrey)* **BL**

DBQ Document Based Questions

Answers:
1. Possible answer: He is accusing Wallace of trying to cover up the true nature of his constituency in order to be more attractive as a national presidential candidate.
2. Possible answer: No, the cartoonist does not really approve as he implies that Nixon does not have much of a punch—just fancy footwork.

---

courts, to name a Southerner to the Supreme Court, to oppose court-ordered busing, and to choose a vice presidential candidate acceptable to the South. (Nixon ultimately chose Spiro Agnew, governor of the border state of Maryland.)

Nixon's efforts paid off on Election Day. Large numbers of white Southerners deserted the Democratic Party, granting Humphrey only one victory in that region—in Lyndon Johnson's home state of Texas. While Wallace claimed most of the states in the Deep South, Nixon captured Virginia, Tennessee, Kentucky, and North Carolina. Senator Strom Thurmond's support delivered his state of South Carolina for the Republicans as well.

Following his victory, Nixon set out to attract even more Southerners to the Republican Party, an effort that became known as the **Southern strategy.** Toward this end, he kept his agreement with Senator Thurmond and

took steps to slow desegregation. During his tenure, Nixon worked to overturn several civil rights policies. He reversed a Johnson administration policy, for example, that had cut off federal funds for racially segregated schools.

A Law-and-Order President

During the campaign, Nixon had also promised to uphold law and order. His administration specifically targeted the nation's antiwar protesters. Attorney General John Mitchell declared that he stood ready to prosecute "hard-line militants" who crossed state lines to stir up riots. Mitchell's deputy, Richard Kleindienst, went even further with the boast, "We're going to enforce the law against draft evaders, against radical students, against deserters, against civil disorders, against organized crime, and against street crime."

Chapter 21 Politics and Economics **707**

Hands-On Chapter Project
Step 1

Oral History of the 1970s

Step 1: Researching the Topic Divide the class into small groups. Ask groups to choose one of the following topics: the civil rights movement, the environmental movement, or the Watergate scandal.

Analyzing Visuals Have students use library and Internet sources to find photographs that show a dramatic moment relevant to their topic. (For example, Nixon flashing the "victory" sign after he resigned

or photos of the first Earth Day.) Have students print out the photographs and save them for use later in the project. **OL**
(Chapter Project continued on page 714)

W **Writing Support**

Expository Writing Have students conduct research and write a report describing the ways in which the Burger Court disappointed conservatives. Remind students to include bibliographic references and footnotes in proper style. **AL**

R **Reading Strategy**

Taking Notes For better understanding of the New Federalism and Nixon's proposed Family Assistance Plan, have students use the heads of these sections to create a study outline. **BL**

✔ **Reading Check**

Answer: The New Federalism was an attempt to lessen the power of the federal government by giving money back to the states and asking them to address their problems locally, while the Great Society was a program to alleviate social ills through federal aid. Under the New Federalism, Nixon also attempted to undermine some of the assistance programs of the Great Society.

Differentiated Instruction

President Nixon also went on the attack against the recent Supreme Court rulings that expanded the rights of accused criminals. Nixon openly criticized the Court and its chief justice, Earl Warren. The president promised to fill vacancies on the Supreme Court with judges who would support the rights of law enforcement over the rights of suspected criminals.

W When Chief Justice Warren retired shortly after Nixon took office, the president replaced him with Warren Burger, a respected conservative judge. He also placed three other conservative justices on the Court, including one from the South. The Burger Court did not reverse Warren Court rulings on the rights of criminal suspects. It did, however, refuse to expand those rights further. For example, in *Stone* v. *Powell* (1976), it agreed to limits on the rights of defendants to appeal state convictions to the federal judiciary. The Court also continued to uphold capital punishment as constitutional.

R ## The New Federalism

Nixon had campaigned promising to reduce the size of the federal government by dismantling several federal programs and giving more control to state and local governments. Nixon called this the **New Federalism.** He argued that such an approach would make government more effective.

"I reject the patronizing idea that government in Washington, D.C., is inevitably more wise and more efficient than government at the state or local level," Nixon declared. "The idea that a bureaucratic elite in Washington knows what's best for people . . . is really a contention that people cannot govern themselves." Under the New Federalism program, Congress passed a series of **revenue-sharing** bills that granted federal funds to state and local agencies to use.

Although revenue sharing was intended to give state and local agencies more power, over time it gave the federal government new power. As states came to depend on federal funds, the federal government could impose conditions on the states. Unless they met those conditions, their funds would be cut off.

As part of the New Federalism, Nixon sought to close down many of the programs of Johnson's Great Society. He vetoed funding

for the Department of Housing and Urban Development, eliminated the Office of Economic Opportunity, and tried unsuccessfully to shut down the Job Corps.

While he worked to reduce the federal government's role, Nixon also sought to increase the power of the executive branch. The president did not have many strong relationships with members of Congress. The fact that the Republicans did not control either house also contributed to struggles with the legislative branch. Nixon often responded by trying to work around Congress. For instance, when Congress appropriated money for programs he opposed, Nixon **impounded,** or refused to release, the funds. By 1973, he had impounded an estimated $15 billion. The Supreme Court eventually declared the practice of impoundment unconstitutional.

The Family Assistance Plan

One federal program Nixon sought to reform was the nation's **welfare** system—Aid to Families with Dependent Children (AFDC). The program had many critics, Republican and Democratic alike. They argued that AFDC was structured so that it was actually better for poor people to apply for benefits than to take a low-paying job. A mother who had such a job, for example, would then have to pay for child care, sometimes leaving her with less income than she had on welfare.

In 1969 Nixon proposed replacing the AFDC with the Family Assistance Plan. The plan called for providing needy families a guaranteed yearly grant of $1,600, which could be supplemented by outside earnings. Many **liberals** applauded the plan as a significant step toward expanding federal responsibility for the poor. Nixon, however, presented the program in a conservative light, arguing it would encourage welfare recipients to become more responsible.

Although the program won approval in the House in 1970, it soon came under harsh attack. Welfare recipients complained that the federal grant was too low, while conservatives, who disapproved of guaranteed income, also criticized the plan. Such opposition led to the program's defeat in the Senate.

✔ Reading Check **Evaluating** How did Nixon's New Federalism differ from Johnson's Great Society?

Leveled Activities

BL **Reading Skills Activity 21** URB p. 21	**OL** **Reteaching Activity 21** URB p. 43	**AL** **Reinforcing Skills Activity 21** URB p. 31	**ELL** **English Learner Activity 21** URB p. 25

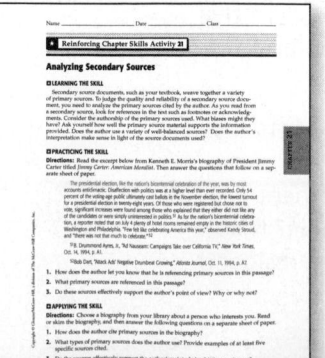

Nixon's Foreign Policy

MAIN Idea With the support of national security adviser Henry Kissinger, Nixon forged better relationships with China and the Soviet Union.

HISTORY AND YOU How should a president balance his efforts between domestic and foreign affairs? Read on to learn about Nixon's strategies for dealing with communist countries.

Despite Nixon's domestic initiatives, a State Department official later recalled that the president had a "monumental disinterest in domestic policies." Nixon once expressed his hope that a "competent cabinet" of advisers could run the country. This would allow him to focus his energies on foreign affairs.

Nixon and Kissinger

In a move that would greatly influence his foreign policy, Nixon chose as his national security adviser **Henry Kissinger,** a former Harvard professor. Kissinger had served under Presidents Kennedy and Johnson as a foreign policy consultant. Although Secretary of State William Rogers outranked him, Kissinger soon took the lead in helping shape Nixon's foreign policy.

The Nixon Doctrine Nixon and Kissinger shared views on many issues. Both believed abandoning the war in Vietnam would damage the United States's position in the world. Thus, they worked toward a gradual withdrawal while simultaneously training the South Vietnamese to defend themselves.

This policy of **Vietnamization,** as it was called, was then extended globally in what came to be called the Nixon Doctrine. In July 1969, only six months after taking office, Nixon announced that the United States would now expect its allies to take care of their own defense. The United States would uphold all of the alliances it had signed, and would continue to provide military aid and training to allies, but it would no longer "conceive all the plans, design all the programs, execute all the decisions and undertake all the defense of the free nations of the world." America's allies would have to take responsibility for maintaining peace and stability in their own areas of the world.

People IN HISTORY

Henry Kissinger
1923–

Born in Germany, Henry Kissinger immigrated to the United States with his family in 1938 to escape Nazi persecution of Jews. During World War II, he served in U.S. military intelligence. After the war, Kissinger attended Harvard University and then joined the faculty there. He held various positions related to government, defense, and international affairs.

After acting as a consultant on national security under Presidents Kennedy and Johnson, Kissinger became President Nixon's national security adviser. In this capacity, he helped to establish the policy of détente with the Soviet Union and China. In 1973 he became secretary of state. Kissinger negotiated the cease-fire with North Vietnam, and along with Le Duc Tho, his co-negotiator, was awarded the Nobel Peace Prize in 1973.

In 1977 Kissinger was awarded the Presidential Medal of Freedom for his services to the nation. Today, he remains an unofficial adviser on international issues to leaders around the world.
How did Henry Kissinger influence foreign policy in the 1970s?

▲ In 1971, Time *magazine celebrated Kissinger as the driving force behind Nixon's trip to China.*

People IN HISTORY

Answer: As Nixon's Assistant for National Security Affairs he established the policy of détente with the Soviet Union and China. As secretary of state under Nixon, he negotiated the ceasefire with North Vietnam and developed the concept of "shuttle diplomacy" when he made numerous trips to the Middle East to broker a peace agreement in that region.

C Critical Thinking

Analyzing Visuals Call attention to the cartoon on the cover of *Time.* **Ask:** What does the cartoon suggest about Nixon's and Kissinger's roles in opening relations with mainland China? *(Nixon is relying on Kissinger's knowledge, skill, and activity to "steer" his foreign policy forward.)* **Ask:** What message does the cartoonist convey with the positions and relative sizes of Nixon and Kissinger? *(Nixon is receiving the recognition for negotiating with Peking. Kissinger remains in the background with less recognition, although he is the power behind Nixon's foreign policy achievements.)* **BL** **OL**

Additional Support

Activity: Collaborative Learning

Comparing Vietnamization with Foreign Policy in Iraq Tell students that the George W. Bush administration announced goals similar to Vietnamization during the Iraq war. Have interested students work in pairs to compare and contrast these policies. One partner should research Vietnamization and its results, while the other partner researches the goals stated by the Bush administration during 2006–2007. Allow time for partners to share their findings. Then have them work together to write a short essay comparing and contrasting these strategies and their results. **Ask:** How does Vietnamization compare to the goals and strategies of the Bush administration during the Iraq war? **OL**

R **Reading Strategy**

Reading Graphs Refer students to the graph in the Primary Source feature. Ask them about what year the Soviets and the United States had the same number of nuclear weapons. *(about 1978–1979)* **OL**

Analyzing VISUALS

Answers:
1. 1965
2. Answers will vary, but students should acknowledge that these two Communist nations had been the enemies of the United States during the Cold War, and still were.

Additional Support

PRIMARY SOURCE
Détente With the Soviet Union and China

The Nuclear Arms Race

Source: *Bulletin of the Atomic Scientists.*

▲ President Nixon meets with Soviet premier Brezhnev to discuss limiting the number of nuclear weapons.

◄ Mao Zedong, leader of China, greets Nixon in Beijing on February 21, 1972.

Analyzing VISUALS

1. **Specifying** In what year did the number of nuclear weapons in the U.S. peak?
2. **Explaining** Why was establishing détente a significant accomplishment?

The New Policy of Détente The Soviet Union was not pleased when Nixon, a man with a history of outspoken anticommunist actions, became president. The Washington correspondent for the Soviet newspaper *Izvestia*, Yuri Barsukov, predicted that Soviet leaders "would have to deal with a very stubborn president."

Things did not turn out that way, however. Nixon was still a staunch anticommunist, but he and Kissinger rejected the notion of a bipolar world in which the superpowers of the United States and the Soviet Union confronted one another. They believed the United States needed to adjust to the growing role of China, Japan, and Western Europe. This emerging "multipolar" world demanded a different approach to American foreign policy.

Both Nixon and Kissinger wanted to continue to contain communism, but they believed that engagement and negotiation with Communists offered a better way for the

United States to achieve its international goals. As a surprised nation watched, Nixon and Kissinger put their philosophy into practice. They developed a new approach called **détente**, or relaxation of tensions, between the United States and its two major Communist rivals, the Soviet Union and China. In explaining détente to the American people, Nixon said that the United States had to build a better relationship with its main rivals in the interest of world peace:

PRIMARY SOURCE

"We must understand that détente is not a love fest. It is an understanding between nations that have opposite purposes, but which share common interests, including the avoidance of a nuclear war. Such an understanding can work—that is, restrain aggression and deter war—only as long as the potential aggressor is made to recognize that neither aggression nor war will be profitable."

—quoted in *The Limits of Power*

Activity: Interdisciplinary Connection

Art Have students work in groups to design a poster that might have been placed in China announcing president Richard M. Nixon's visit in 1972. Posters should include photos, newspaper clippings, and any other visuals that help communicate the Chinese reception of Richard Nixon. Encourage groups to conduct research using the Internet to find information about how the Chinese felt at the time of Nixon's visit. Post completed posters around the room and have each group give a brief summary of its poster. **ELL** **OL**

Nixon Visits China

Détente began with an effort to improve American-Chinese relations. Since 1949, when Communists took power in China, the United States had refused to recognize the Communists as the legitimate rulers. Instead, the American government recognized the exiled regime on the island of Taiwan as the Chinese government. Having long supported this policy, Nixon now set out to reverse it. He began by lifting trade and travel restrictions and withdrawing the Seventh Fleet from defending Taiwan.

After a series of highly secret negotiations between Kissinger and Chinese leaders, Nixon announced that he would visit China in February 1972. During the historic trip, the leaders of both nations agreed to establish "more normal" relations between their countries. In a statement that epitomized the notion of détente, Nixon told his Chinese hosts during a banquet toast, "Let us start a long march together, not in lockstep, but on different roads leading to the same goal, the goal of building a world structure of peace and justice."

In taking this trip, Nixon hoped not only to strengthen ties with the Chinese, but also to encourage the Soviets to more actively pursue diplomacy. Since the 1960s, a rift had developed between the Communist governments of the Soviet Union and China. Troops of the two nations occasionally clashed along their borders. Nixon believed détente with China would encourage Soviet premier Leonid Brezhnev to be more accommodating with the United States.

United States-Soviet Tensions Ease

Nixon's strategy toward the Soviets worked. Shortly after the public learned of American negotiations with China, the Soviets proposed an American-Soviet **summit,** or high-level diplomatic meeting, to be held in May 1972. On May 22, President Nixon flew to Moscow for a weeklong summit, becoming the first American president since World War II to visit the Soviet Union.

During the historic Moscow summit, the two superpowers signed the first Strategic Arms Limitation Treaty, or **SALT I,** a plan to limit nuclear arms the two nations had been working on for years. Nixon and Brezhnev also agreed to increase trade and the exchange of scientific information. Détente profoundly eased tensions between the Soviet Union and the United States.

By the end of Nixon's presidency, one Soviet official admitted that "the United States and the Soviet Union had their best relationship of the whole Cold War period." President Nixon indeed had made his mark on the world stage. As he basked in the glow of his 1972 foreign policy triumphs, however, trouble was brewing on the home front. A scandal was about to engulf his presidency and plunge the nation into one of its greatest constitutional crises.

✓ Reading Check Summarizing What were the results of the 1972 American-Soviet summit?

Section 1 REVIEW

Vocabulary
1. **Explain** the significance of: Southern strategy, New Federalism, revenue sharing, impound, Henry Kissinger, Vietnamization, détente, summit, SALT I.

Main Ideas
2. **Describing** How did President Nixon attempt to increase the power of the presidency?

3. **Explaining** How did Nixon use his visit to China to improve relations with the Soviet Union?

Critical Thinking
4. **Big Ideas** What were the results of Nixon's policy of détente?

5. **Organizing** Use a graphic organizer similar to the one below to describe how President Nixon established détente in the listed countries.

China	
Soviet Union	

6. **Analyzing Visuals** Look at the *Time* cover on page 709. What does the image portray about Nixon's foreign policy?

Writing About History
7. **Expository Writing** Take on the role of a member of President Nixon's staff. Write a press release explaining either Nixon's domestic or foreign policies.

History ONLINE
Study Central™ To review this section, go to glencoe.com and click on Study Central.

✓ Reading Check

Answer: signed SALT I, agreed to increase trade and exchange scientific information

Assess
· · · · · · · · · · · · · · · · · · · ·
History ONLINE

Study Central™ provides summaries, interactive games, and online graphic organizers to help students review content.

Close
· · · · · · · · · · · · · · · · · · · ·
Summarizing Ask: How would you characterize Nixon's domestic and foreign policies? *(Domestic: He increased presidential control, moved the courts and the country in a conservative direction, and eliminated some programs for the disadvantaged. Foreign policy: he found more peaceful ways of waging the Cold War, such as détente with the Soviet Union and improving relations with the People's Republic of China.)* **OL**

Section 1 REVIEW

Answers

1. All definitions can be found in the section and the Glossary.

2. Nixon often tried to work around Congress; for example, he impounded an estimated $15 billion that Congress had earmarked for various programs that the president did not support.

3. He thought that if the United States improved its relations with China, with whom the Soviets had had some friction,

that the Soviets might want to improve U.S.-U.S.S.R. relations, and he was correct.

4. Détente led to more normal relations between the United States and China and eased tensions between the United States and Soviet Union.

5. China: lifted trade and travel restrictions, withdrew Seventh Fleet from Taiwan; Soviet Union: increased trade, signed SALT I, exchanged scientific information

6. Nixon is relying on Kissinger to "steer" his foreign policy.

7. Students' press releases will vary, but should include summaries of Nixon's domestic and foreign policies.

Focus

Section 2

Bellringer
Daily Focus Transparency 21.2

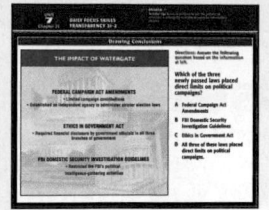

Guide to Reading

Answers:
I. The Roots of Watergate
   A. Mounting a Reelection Fight
   B. The Cover-Up Begins
II. The Cover-Up Unravels
   A. A Summer of Shocking Testimony
   B. The Case of the Tapes
   C. Nixon Resigns
   D. The Impact of Watergate

Section Spotlight Video

To generate student interest and provide a springboard for class discussion, access the Chapter 21, Section 2 video at glencoe.com or on the video DVD.

Resource Manager

Section 2

The Watergate Scandal

Guide to Reading

Big Ideas
Government and Society The Watergate scandal intensified lingering distrust of government that had arisen during the Vietnam War.

Content Vocabulary
• executive privilege (p. 716)
• special prosecutor (p. 716)

Academic Vocabulary
• incident (p. 712)
• challenger (p. 713)

People and Events to Identify
• Sam J. Ervin (p. 714)
• John Dean (p. 714)
• Federal Campaign Act Amendments (p. 715)

Reading Strategy
Taking Notes Use the headings in this section to create an outline similar to the one below by recording information about the Watergate scandal.

The Watergate Scandal
I. The Roots of Watergate
   A.
   B.
II.
   A.
   B.

Despite a successful first term, Richard Nixon and his supporters worried about reelection. The tactics they resorted to led the president to become embroiled in a scandal known as Watergate, one of the United States's great constitutional crises.

The Roots of Watergate

MAIN Idea Tactics used by Nixon's supporters to try to ensure his reelection in 1972 led to the Watergate scandal.

HISTORY AND YOU What do you know about Richard Nixon and the Watergate scandal? Read on to learn how the president became involved in this major governmental crisis.

The Watergate scandal is perhaps the most famous scandal in modern American history. It certainly had momentous consequences, as it led to the only time in the nation's history when the president of the United States was forced to resign from office. As reporter Bob Woodward recounts in his book, *All the President's Men*, the scandal began on the morning of June 17, 1972.

Woodward was a young reporter for the *Washington Post* at that time. His editor had ruined his Saturday by asking him to cover a seemingly insignificant but bizarre **incident**. In the early hours of that morning, five men had broken into the Democratic National Committee (DNC) headquarters in the city's Watergate apartment-office complex. Woodward was ordered to attend the arraignment and see if there was a story worth reporting.

As Woodward sat near the back of the courtroom listening to the bail proceedings for the five defendants, the judge asked each man his occupation. One of the men, James McCord, answered that he was retired from government service.

"Where in government?" asked the judge. "CIA," McCord whispered. Woodward sprang to attention. Why was a former agent of the CIA involved in what seemed to be nothing more than a burglary? Over the next two years, Woodward and another reporter, Carl Bernstein, would investigate this question. In so doing, they uncovered a scandal that helped trigger a constitutional crisis and eventually forced President Nixon to resign.

Mounting a Reelection Fight

The Watergate scandal began when the Nixon administration tried to cover up its involvement in the break-in at the Democratic National Committee headquarters, along with other illegal

---

R Reading Strategies	**C** Critical Thinking	**D** Differentiated Instruction	**W** Writing Support	**S** Skill Practice
Teacher Edition • Taking Notes p. 714 **Additional Resources** • Prim. Source Read., URB p. 35 • Guid Read. Act., URB p. 49	**Teacher Edition** • Analyzing Primary Sources p. 713 **Additional Resources** • Hist. Sim. and Prob. Solve, URB p. 9 • Supreme Court Case Studies, p. 117 • Quizzes and Tests, p. 300	**Teacher Edition** • Visual/Spatial pp. 714, 716		**Additional Resources** • Hist. Analysis Skills, URB p. 22 • Crit. Think. Skills Act., URB p. 32 • Time Line Act., URB p. 33 • RENTG, p. 221

PRIMARY SOURCE

The Watergate Scandal Erupts

In June 1972, five men were arrested attempting to place wiretaps on phones and stealing information from the Democratic National Headquarters at the Watergate Hotel. The subsequent investigation revealed a cover-up that reached to the White House.

▲ James McCord shows Congress the bugging device he installed. E. Howard Hunt (center) and G. Gordon Liddy (right) also testified.

▲ The Watergate Complex gave its name to the resulting scandal. Security guard Frank Willis (right) reported to police evidence of the break-in.

▶ Counsel to the president John Dean testified that Nixon had been directly involved in the cover-up of the Watergate break-in.

Analyzing VISUALS

1. **Speculating** If you had discovered the break-in, what might make you suspicious about the burglars?

2. **Explaining** Why was John Dean's testimony damaging to the president?

---

actions. Although the affair began with the Watergate burglary, many scholars believe the roots of the scandal lay in Nixon's character and the atmosphere that he and his advisers created in the White House.

Richard Nixon had fought hard to become president. He had battled back from numerous political defeats, including a loss to John F. Kennedy in the 1960 presidential election. Along the way, Nixon had grown defensive, secretive, and often resentful of his critics.

Furthermore, Nixon had become president when American society was in turmoil. There were race riots, and protests over the Vietnam War continued to consume the country. In Nixon's view, protesters and other "radicals" were trying to bring down his administration. Nixon was so consumed with his opponents that he compiled an "enemies list" filled with

people—from politicians to members of the media—whom he considered a threat to his presidency.

When Nixon began his reelection campaign, his advisers were optimistic. Nixon had just finished triumphant trips to China and the Soviet Union. Former governor George Wallace, who had mounted a strong campaign in 1968, had dropped out of the race after an assassin's bullet paralyzed him, and the Democratic **challenger,** South Dakota Senator George McGovern, was viewed by many as too liberal.

Nixon's reelection was by no means certain, however. The unpopular Vietnam War still raged, and his staffers remembered how close the 1968 election had been. Determined to win at all costs, they began spying on opposition rallies and spreading rumors and false reports about their Democratic opponents.

Chapter 21 Politics and Economics **713**

Teach

C Critical Thinking

Analyzing Primary Sources
Have students study the photos and captions on page 713. **Ask:** Whose testimony was most damaging to President Nixon? Why? *(Dean's testimony was most damaging, because he implicated Nixon directly in the cover-up.)* **BL**

Analyzing VISUALS

Answers:

1. Students' answers will vary. They may note that the burglars were caught wearing business suits and carrying bugging devices.

2. He was Nixon's lawyer and a White House insider, and he testified that Nixon tried to cover up evidence of the break-in.

Additional Support

Activity: Collaborative Learning

Think/Write–Pair–Share Use this strategy to engage your students in their subject matter through discussion. Tell students to **T**hink silently about what they know of President Nixon and the Watergate scandal. Then ask them to **W**rite three to five ideas down on a piece of paper. Students should then **P**air with another student and **S**hare their ideas. Conclude the activity with a class **S**hare discussion. **OL**

D Differentiated Instruction

Visual/Spatial Have students work in groups to find photos in the library or online and create a photo essay about the Watergate scandal. Encourage students to use photographs and captions to tell how the Watergate scandal started, who was involved, when it happened, and how it concluded. **OL ELL**

R Reading Strategy

Taking Notes Have students use the heads of the section "The Cover-Up Unravels" to create a study outline. As they complete each subhead, have them write notes about the important points. Then encourage them to discuss their outlines with a partner and make any modifications that would improve their notes. **BL**

✓ Reading Check

Answer: They intended to steal sensitive campaign information and place wiretaps.

Hands-on Chapter Project:
Step 2

Oral History of the 1970s

Step 2: Preparing for the Interview Tell students that each of them will be conducting an interview with someone who was a teenager or an adult in the 1970s.

Formulating Questions Have students in groups prepare a list of questions they want to ask interview subjects about their topic. Questions should center on the interviewee's recollections of the events related to the chosen topic. Each student will be con-

714

As part of their efforts to help the president, Nixon's advisers ordered five men to break into the Democratic Party's headquarters at the Watergate complex and steal any sensitive campaign information. They were also to place wiretaps on the office telephones. While the burglars were at work, a security guard making his rounds spotted a piece of tape holding a door lock. The guard ripped off the tape, but when he passed the door later, he noticed that it had been replaced. He quickly called police, who arrived shortly and arrested the men.

History ONLINE Student Web Activity Visit glencoe.com and complete the activity on the 1970s.

The Cover-Up Begins

After the Watergate break-in, the media discovered that one burglar, James McCord, was not only an ex-CIA officer but also a member of the Committee for the Re-election of the President (CRP). Reports soon surfaced that the burglars had been paid from a secret CRP fund controlled by the White House.

At this point, the cover-up began. White House officials destroyed incriminating documents and gave false testimony to investigators. Meanwhile, President Nixon stepped in. The president may not have ordered the break-in, but he did order a cover-up. With Nixon's consent, administration officials asked the CIA to stop the FBI from investigating the source of the money paid to the burglars. The CIA told the FBI that the investigation threatened national security. To combat efforts to block the FBI investigation, the FBI's deputy director, W. Mark Felt, secretly leaked information about Watergate to the *Washington Post.*

Meanwhile, Nixon's press secretary dismissed the incident as a "third-rate burglary attempt," and the president told the American public, "The White House has had no involvement whatever in this particular incident." The strategy worked. Most Americans believed President Nixon, and despite efforts by the media, in particular the *Washington Post,* to keep the story alive, few people paid much attention during the 1972 presidential campaign. On Election Day, Nixon won reelection by one of the largest margins in history with nearly 61 percent of the popular vote, compared to 37.5 percent for George McGovern.

✓ **Reading Check** **Examining** Why did members of the CRP break into the Democratic National Committee headquarters?

The Cover-Up Unravels

MAIN Idea The president's refusal to cooperate with Congress only focused attention on his possible involvement.

HISTORY AND YOU How far do you think that presidents should be able to go in the name of national security? Read on to learn how Nixon tried to invoke national security concerns to thwart an investigation of his involvement in Watergate.

In early 1973, the Watergate burglars went on trial. Under relentless prodding from federal judge John J. Sirica, McCord agreed to cooperate with the grand jury investigation. He also agreed to testify before the newly created Senate Select Committee on Presidential Campaign Activities. The chairman of the committee was Senator **Sam J. Ervin,** a Democrat from North Carolina.

McCord's testimony opened a floodgate of confessions, and a parade of White House and campaign officials exposed one illegality after another. Foremost among the officials was counsel to the president **John Dean,** a member of the inner circle of the White House who leveled allegations against Nixon himself.

A Summer of Shocking Testimony

In June 1973 John Dean testified before Senator Ervin's committee that former Attorney General John Mitchell had ordered the Watergate break-in and that Nixon had played an active role in attempting to cover up any White House involvement. As a shocked nation absorbed Dean's testimony, the Nixon administration strongly denied the charges.

Because Dean had no evidence to confirm his account, for the next month, the Senate committee attempted to determine who was telling the truth. Then, on July 16, the answer appeared unexpectedly. On that day, White House aide Alexander Butterfield testified that Nixon had ordered a taping system installed in the White House to record all conversations. The president had done so, Butterfield said, to help him write his memoirs after he left office. For members of the committee, however, the tapes would tell them exactly what the president knew and when he knew it, but only if the president could be forced to release them.

---

ducting their own interview, but have students discuss amongst themselves who would be the most interesting interviewees. Whenever possible, encourage students to choose interviewees of different backgrounds and ages.

(Chapter Project continued on page 720)

ANALYZING SUPREME COURT CASES

Is Executive Privilege Unlimited?

★ *United States* v. *Nixon*, 1974

Background to the Case

In 1974 Special Prosecutor Leon Jaworski issued a subpoena to gain access to tape recordings President Nixon had made of conversations in the Oval Office. Jaworski believed that the tapes would prove the active involvement of the president in the Watergate cover-up. Nixon filed a motion to prevent the subpoena, claiming executive privilege. The case went to district court, but that court withheld judgment pending the decision of the Supreme Court.

How the Court Ruled

In a unanimous 8-to-0 decision (Justice Rehnquist did not take part), the Supreme Court found that executive privilege did not protect Nixon's tape recordings, stating that while the president has a right to protect military secrets and other sensitive material and has a right to some confidentiality, the needs of a criminal trial must take precedence.

▲ The Senate committee overseeing the Watergate investigation, chaired by Senator Sam Ervin (fourth from left at the table), wanted access to Nixon's tape recordings.

PRIMARY SOURCE

The Court's Opinion

"In this case we must weigh the importance of the general privilege of confidentiality of Presidential communications in performance of such a privilege on the fair administration of criminal justice. The interest in preserving confidentiality is weighty indeed and entitled to great respect. However, we cannot conclude that advisers will be moved to temper the candor of their remarks by the infrequent occasions of disclosure because of the possibility that such conversations will be called for in the context of a criminal prosecution. On the other hand, the allowance of the privilege to withhold evidence that is demonstrably relevant in a criminal trial would cut deeply into the guarantee of due process of law and gravely impair the basic function of the courts. A President's acknowledged need for confidentiality in the communications of his office is general

in nature, whereas the constitutional need for production of relevant evidence in a criminal proceeding is specific and central to the fair adjudication of a particular criminal case in the administration of justice. . . . The President's broad interest in confidentiality of communications will not be vitiated by disclosure of a limited number of conversations preliminarily shown to have some bearing on the pending criminal cases. We conclude that when the ground for asserting privilege as to subpoenaed materials sought for use in a criminal trial is based only on the generalized interest in confidentiality, it cannot prevail over the fundamental demands of due process of law in the fair administration of criminal justice. . . ."

—Chief Justice Warren Burger writing for the Court in *United States* v. *Nixon*

DBQ Document-Based Questions

1. **Finding the Main Idea** What is the main point of the decision in *United States* v. *Nixon*?
2. **Summarizing** What does Burger say that executive privilege in this case would violate?
3. **Expressing** Do you agree with the Supreme Court's decision in this case? Explain.

More About the Case

The Supreme Court's ruling in *United States* v. *Nixon* had two important results. It not only reaffirmed the power of the Court as the final authority in questions of constitutionality, but it also showed that no one, including the president of the United States, was above the law.

DBQ Document Based Questions

Answers:
1. The ruling states that while executive privilege is important and necessary, it cannot be used to impede progress in a criminal proceeding.
2. He says that it would violate due process of law and hinder the activities of the courts.
3. Students' answers will vary; accept all reasoned arguments based on the information in the feature and in Section 2.

Differentiated Instruction

Case Study 59:
United States v. *Nixon*, p. 117

Analyzing a Supreme Court Decision

Objective: Learn how the Supreme Court determined whether the president could refuse to surrender tapes and other information connected to the Watergate break-in.

Focus: Identify the central issue of the case.

Teach: Discuss the Court's opinion.

Assess: Explain the importance of the case (interpretation of executive privilege).

Close: Write a paragraph summarizing the case.

Differentiated Instruction Strategies

BL Explain the role President Nixon played in the case.

AL Paraphrase the Court's decision. Read your version to the class.

ELL Explain the concept of executive privilege in your own words.

D Differentiated Instruction

Visual/Spatial Have students study the Political Cartoons on page 716. **Ask:** Why was a "search dog" necessary during the Watergate investigation? **BL**

Analyzing VISUALS

Answers:

1. a tidal wave
2. Nixon is dressed like a detective, similar to Sherlock Holmes. It may be to signify that the president pretended to try to cooperate with the Watergate investigation, but really was guilty of involvement himself.

Additional Support

POLITICAL CARTOONS PRIMARY SOURCE
The Watergate Scandal

◄ President Nixon clings to his desk as the Watergate scandal crashes like a tidal wave through the Oval Office.

▲ The Watergate investigation takes the form of a search dog who has tracked the evidence directly to the president.

Analyzing VISUALS DBQ

1. **Specifying** What does the cartoon on the left use to symbolize the Watergate scandal?
2. **Explaining** What is the meaning of Nixon's appearance and the magnifying glass in the cartoon on the right?

The Case of the Tapes

At first, Nixon refused to hand over the tapes, pleading **executive privilege**—the principle that White House conversations should remain confidential to protect national security. **Special prosecutor** Archibald Cox, the government lawyer appointed by the president to handle the Watergate cases, took Nixon to court in October 1973 to force him to give up the recordings. Nixon ordered Attorney General Elliot Richardson to fire Cox, but Richardson refused and resigned. Nixon then ordered Richardson's deputy to fire Cox, but the deputy resigned as well. Nixon's solicitor general, Robert Bork, finally fired Cox, but the incident, nicknamed the "Saturday Night Massacre" in the press, badly damaged Nixon's reputation with the public.

The fall of 1973 proved to be a disastrous time for Nixon for other reasons, as well. His vice president, Spiro Agnew, was forced to resign in disgrace after investigators learned that he had taken bribes from state contractors while governor of Maryland and that he had continued to accept bribes while serving in Washington. Gerald Ford, the Republican leader of the House of Representatives, became the new vice president.

Nixon Resigns

In an effort to quiet the growing outrage over his actions, President Nixon appointed a new special prosecutor, Texas lawyer Leon Jaworski, who proved no less determined than Cox to obtain the president's tapes. In July the Supreme Court ruled that the president had to turn over the tapes, and Nixon complied.

Several days later, the House Judiciary Committee voted to impeach Nixon, or officially charge him with misconduct. The committee charged Nixon with obstructing justice in the Watergate cover-up; misusing federal agencies to violate the rights of citizens; and defying the authority of Congress by refusing to deliver tapes and other materials as requested. Before the House of Representatives

---

Activity: Interdisciplinary Connection

Civics Have students use library or Internet resources to conduct research on the order of succession for the president and the process for replacing a vice president who leaves office during his or her term. Have students use their findings to create a poster showing the steps prescribed by the Twenty-fifth Amendment to the Constitution. Remind students that they can review the Twenty-fifth Amendment on page 148 of their textbook. Ask students to share their posters with the class. Then discuss as a class why it is important to have an established procedure for replacing national leaders. **OL**

could vote on whether Nixon should be impeached, investigators found indisputable evidence against the president. One of the tapes revealed that on June 23, 1972, just six days after the Watergate burglary, Nixon had ordered the CIA to stop the FBI's investigation. With this news, even the president's strongest supporters conceded that impeachment by the House and conviction in the Senate were inevitable. On August 9, 1974, Nixon resigned his office in disgrace. Gerald Ford took the oath of office and became the nation's 38th president.

The Impact of Watergate

Upon taking office, President Ford urged Americans to put the Watergate scandal behind them. "Our long national nightmare is over," he declared. On September 8, 1974, Ford announced that he would grant a "full, free, and absolute pardon" to Richard Nixon for any crimes he "committed or may have committed or taken part in" while president. "[This] is an American tragedy in which we all have played a part," he told the nation. "It could go on and on and on, or someone must write the end to it."

The Watergate crisis led to new laws intended to limit the power of the executive branch. The **Federal Campaign Act Amendments** limited campaign contributions and established an independent agency to administer stricter election laws. The Ethics in Government Act required financial disclosure by high government officials in all three branches of government. The FBI Domestic Security Investigation Guidelines Act restricted the Bureau's political intelligence-gathering activities. Congress also established a means for appointing an independent counsel to investigate and prosecute wrongdoing by high government officials.

Despite these efforts, Watergate left many Americans with a deep distrust of their public officials. On the other hand, some Americans saw the Watergate affair as proof that in the United States, no person is above the law. As Bob Woodward observed:

PRIMARY SOURCE

"Watergate was probably a good thing for the country; it was a good, sobering lesson. Accountability to the law applies to everyone. The problem with kings and prime ministers and presidents is that they think that they are above it . . . that they have some special rights, and privileges, and status. And a process that says: No. We have our laws and believe them, and they apply to everyone, is a very good thing."

—quoted in *Nixon: An Oral History of His Presidency*

After the ordeal of Watergate, most Americans attempted to put the affair behind them. In the years ahead, however, the nation encountered a host of new troubles, from a stubborn economic recession to a heart-wrenching hostage crisis overseas.

✔ **Reading Check** **Evaluating** Why did Congress pass new laws after the Watergate scandal?

Section 2 REVIEW

Vocabulary
1. **Explain** the significance of: Sam J. Ervin, John Dean, executive privilege, special prosecutor, Federal Campaign Act Amendments.

Main Ideas
2. **Explaining** How did the Watergate cover-up involve the CIA and the FBI?

3. **Determining Cause and Effect** Why did President Nixon finally resign?

Critical Thinking
4. **Big Ideas** How did the Watergate scandal alter the balance of power between the executive and legislative branches of the federal government?

5. **Organizing** Use a graphic organizer similar to the one below to record the effects of the Watergate scandal.

Effects of Watergate Scandal

6. **Analyzing Visuals** Study the photographs on page 713. How did the Watergate hearings demonstrate the effectiveness of the system of checks and balances?

Writing About History
7. **Descriptive Writing** Take on the role of a television news analyst. Write a script in which you explain the Watergate scandal and analyze the factors that led to it.

History ONLINE
Study Central™ To review this section, go to glencoe.com and click on Study Central.

✔ **Reading Check**

Answer: Congress wanted to put checks on the power of the presidency and the rest of the executive branch of the federal government.

Assess
• • • • • • • • • • • • • • • •

History ONLINE

Study Central™ provides summaries, interactive games, and online graphic organizers to help students review content.

Close
• • • • • • • • • • • • • • • •

Summarizing Ask: How did Nixon's nature and leadership style lead to his downfall? *(Causes: Nixon's distrustful, secretive nature, his need for control, and his conviction that people were out to get him led to the Watergate break-in. His belief that he was above the law led to the cover-up, eventually forcing his resignation.)* **OL**

Section 2 REVIEW

Answers

1. All definitions can be found in the section and the Glossary.

2. Nixon requested that the CIA tell the FBI to cease investigating the Watergate break-in on grounds of national security.

3. The House of Representatives was about to vote to impeach him and everyone felt that if impeached, he would be convicted by the Senate.

4. It led to laws intended to limit the power of the executive branch of the federal government.

5. Nixon's resignation, Federal Campaign Act Amendments, Ethics in Government Act, FBI Domestic Security Investigation Guidelines

6. The hearings demonstrated that the legislative branch could effectively check the power of the executive branch.

7. Students' scripts will vary; encourage students to include suggested visuals in their scripts.

Focus

Bellringer
Daily Focus Transparency 21.3

Guide to Reading

Causes

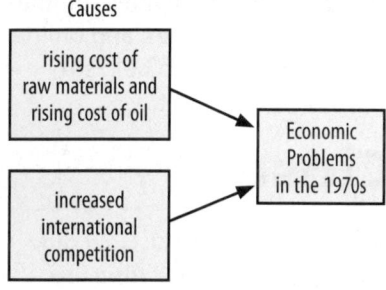

```
┌──────────────────────┐
│ rising cost of       │
│ raw materials and    │──┐
│ rising cost of oil   │  │
└──────────────────────┘  │    ┌──────────┐
                          ├───▶│ Economic │
┌──────────────────────┐  │    │ Problems │
│ increased            │  │    │ in the   │
│ international         │──┘    │ 1970s    │
│ competition          │       └──────────┘
└──────────────────────┘
```

Section Spotlight Video

To generate student interest and provide a springboard for class discussion, access the Chapter 21, Section 3 video at glencoe.com or on the video DVD.

Resource Manager

Section 3

Ford and Carter

Guide to Reading

Big Ideas
Economics and Society A weakening economy and growing energy crisis marred the terms of Presidents Ford and Carter.

Content Vocabulary
• inflation (p. 718)
• embargo (p. 718)
• stagflation (p. 719)

Academic Vocabulary
• theory (p. 719)
• deregulation (p. 721)

People and Events to Identify
• OPEC (p. 718)
• Helsinki Accords (p. 720)
• Department of Energy (p. 721)
• Camp David Accords (p. 723)

Reading Strategy
Organizing Complete a graphic organizer similar to the one below by listing the causes of economic problems in the 1970s.

Causes

By the time Richard Nixon resigned, the boom period Americans had experienced in the previous decades was coming to an end. Through the 1970s, Presidents Gerald R. Ford and Jimmy Carter attempted, with varying levels of success, to lead the United States through both domestic and foreign crises.

The Economic Crisis of the 1970s

MAIN Idea In the 1970s Americans had to face a slowing economy and an end to plentiful, cheap energy.

HISTORY AND YOU Have you ever heard anyone describe their experiences during the energy crisis of the 1970s? Read on to learn how politics and Americans' dependency on oil imports led to a serious crisis.

During the 1950s and 1960s, many Americans enjoyed remarkable prosperity and had come to assume it was the norm. This prosperity rested in large part on easy access to raw materials around the world and a strong manufacturing base at home. In the 1970s, however, the boom years gave way to a decade of hard times.

A Mighty Economic Machine Slows

The nation's economic troubles began in the mid-1960s when President Johnson increased federal deficit spending, to fund both the Vietnam War and the Great Society programs, without raising taxes. This spending spurred **inflation** by pumping large amounts of money into the economy.

The next blow to the economy came in the early 1970s when the price of oil began to rise. By 1970, the United States had become dependent on oil imports from the Middle East and Africa. This was not a problem as long as prices remained low, but in 1973, the **Organization of Petroleum Exporting Countries (OPEC)**—a cartel dominated by Arab countries—decided to use oil as a political weapon. In 1973 a war erupted between Israel and its Arab neighbors. OPEC announced that its members would place an **embargo** on, or prohibit the shipment of, petroleum to countries that supported Israel. OPEC also raised the price of crude oil by 70 percent, and then by another 130 percent a few months later.

Although the embargo ended within a few months, oil prices continued to rise. The price of a barrel of crude oil had risen from $3 in 1973 to $30 in 1980. As oil and gasoline prices rose, Americans had less money for other goods, which contributed to a recession.

R Reading Strategies	C Critical Thinking	D Differentiated Instruction	W Writing Support	S Skill Practice
Teacher Edition • Reading Primary Sources, p. 721 **Additional Resources** • Read. Skills Act., URB p. 21 • Pri. Source Read., URB p. 37 • Guid. Read. Act., URB p. 50	**Teacher Edition** • Comparing and Contrasting, p. 720 • Analyzing Primary Sources p. 722 • Predicting Consequences, p. 723 **Additional Resources** • Quizzes and Tests, p. 301	**Additional Resources** • Reinforcing Skills Act., URB p. 31	**Teacher Edition** • Persuasive Writing, p. 720	**Teacher Edition** • Reading a Graph, p. 719 **Additional Resources** • RENTG, p. 224

PRIMARY SOURCE
The Energy Crisis

OPEC's embargo caused long lines at gas stations and caused inflation to accelerate rapidly. The U.S. government responded by imposing price controls.

▲ The oil embargo and price increases imposed by OPEC, whose members are shown above, severely decreased supply and increased prices in the United States.

Price of Gasoline, 1970–1990

*Price of Leaded Regular Gasoline in Constant 2000 dollars.
Source: Energy Information Administration.

Analyzing VISUALS

1. **Drawing Conclusions** What problems did American consumers face because of the oil embargo?
2. **Specifying** In what year, between 1970 and 1990, did gasoline reach its highest price?

Teach

S Skill Practice
Reading a Graph Ask students to find the years between 1970 and 1990 that gasoline prices were the lowest. *(1972–1973, 1986–1988)*

Analyzing VISUALS

Answers:
1. The embargo led to high gas prices and gas shortages.
2. 1981

Reading Check

Answers: The government cut spending and raised taxes, the Federal Reserve raised interest rates. The president imposed a 90-day freeze on wages and prices and issued regulations to limit future wage and price increases.

A Stagnant Economy

Another economic problem was the decline of manufacturing. By 1970, many American manufacturing plants were old and less efficient than the plants Japan and Germany had built after World War II. In 1971, for the first time since 1889, the United States imported more than it exported. Unable to compete, many factories closed, and millions of workers lost their jobs. Thus, in the early 1970s, President Nixon faced a new economic problem nicknamed **"stagflation"**—a combination of inflation and a stagnant economy with high unemployment.

Economists who emphasized the demand side of economic **theory,** including supporters of Keynesianism, did not think that inflation and recession could occur at the same time. They believed that demand drives prices and that inflation could only occur in a booming economy when demand for goods was high. As a result, they did not know what fiscal policy the government should pursue. Increased spending might help end the recession, but it would increase inflation. Raising taxes might slow inflation, but it would also keep the economy in recession.

Nixon decided to focus on controlling inflation. The government moved first to cut spending and raise taxes. The president hoped that higher taxes would prompt Americans to spend less, which would ease the demand on goods and drive down prices. Congress and much of the public, however, protested the idea of a tax hike. Nixon then tried to reduce consumer spending by getting the Federal Reserve Board to raise interest rates. When this failed, the president tried to stop inflation by imposing a 90-day freeze on wages and prices and then issuing federal regulations limiting future wage and price increases. This too met with little success.

✔ Reading Check **Explaining** How did President Nixon attempt to stop stagflation?

Chapter 21 Politics and Economics **719**

Additional Support

Activity: Interdisciplinary Connection

Economics Ask an economics teacher to present an explanation of cartels, including the fact that OPEC is the most long-lived cartel in history. Then have students use library or Internet sources to research other cartels, either past or present. Students should determine the purpose of cartels, what holds cartels together, and what types of problems bring an end to cartels. Have students report their findings in a three-page research report. Note that students' reports should use one of the cartels of the past or present as an example when discussing the purpose and problems of cartels. **AL**

Did You Know?

After his inauguration, Jimmy Carter and his family chose to walk up Pennsylvania Avenue from the Capitol to the White House instead of riding in the traditional limousine. The gesture symbolized Carter's desire to lead a simple life even while in the White House.

C Critical Thinking

Comparing and Contrasting Ask students to compare and contrast what Carter promised before the election and what he did in office. *(He promised new programs for energy and did address them, but his promises for tax reform, welfare reform, and health care reform were derailed by the need to manage the economic crisis he inherited.)* **OL**

W Writing Support

Persuasive Writing Have students write a campaign handout explaining why the public should vote for either Carter or Ford. **OL**

Hands-on Chapter Project:
Step 3

Oral History of the 1970s

Step 3: Conducting the Interview Students should arrange the interview and be prepared to take notes. (Or, students may ask permission to record the interview.) In addition, students should show interviewees the photographs they selected and ask interviewees to comment on them.

Making Connections After the interview, students should meet back in their groups

---

Ford and Carter Battle the Economic Crisis

MAIN Idea When Gerald Ford failed to solve the nation's problems, Americans turned to political outsider Jimmy Carter to lead the nation.

HISTORY AND YOU Do you think a president should be a Washington insider? Read how being an outsider affected Carter's ability to lead.

When Nixon resigned in 1974, inflation was still high, despite many efforts to reduce prices. Meanwhile, the unemployment rate was over 5 percent. It would now be up to the new president, Gerald Ford, to confront stagflation.

Ford Tries to "Whip" Inflation

By 1975, the American economy was in the worst recession since the Great Depression, with unemployment at nearly 9 percent. Ford responded by launching a plan called WIN—"Whip Inflation Now." He urged Americans to reduce their use of oil and gas, and take steps to conserve energy. The plan had little impact on the economic situation. The president then began cutting government spending and urged the Federal Reserve to raise interest rates to curb inflation. He also sought to balance the budget and keep taxes low. He vetoed more than 50 bills that the Democratic Congress passed during the first two years of his administration. These efforts failed to revive the economy.

Ford's Foreign Policy

In foreign policy, Ford continued Nixon's general strategy. Ford kept Kissinger on as secretary of state and continued to pursue détente with the Soviets and the Chinese. In August 1975, he met with leaders of NATO and the Warsaw Pact to sign the **Helsinki Accords.** Under the accords, the parties recognized the borders of Eastern Europe established at the end of World War II. The Soviets in return promised to uphold certain basic human rights, including the right to move across national borders. The subsequent Soviet failure to uphold these basic rights turned many Americans against détente.

Ford also met with problems in Southeast Asia. In May 1975, soon after Communists seized power in Cambodia, Cambodian forces captured the *Mayaguez,* an American cargo ship traveling near its shores. Calling the seizure an "act of piracy," Ford sent U.S. Marines to retrieve it. Cambodia secretly released the crew shortly before the marines arrived. Unaware the crew was safe, the marines attacked and recaptured the ship, but 41 American servicemen died in the battle.

The Election of 1976

The presidential race pitted Gerald Ford against James Earl Carter, Jr., or Jimmy Carter, as he liked to be called. A former governor of Georgia, Carter had no political experience in Washington. Carter took advantage of his outsider status, promising to restore honesty to the federal government. He also promised new programs for energy development, tax reform, welfare reform, and national health care.

Ford characterized Carter as a liberal whose social programs would produce higher rates of inflation and require tax increases. For many voters, however, Carter's image as a moral and upstanding individual, untainted by Washington politics, made him an attractive candidate. In the end, Carter narrowly defeated Ford with 50.1 percent of the popular vote to Ford's 47.9 percent, while capturing 297 electoral votes to Ford's 240.

Carter's Economic Policies

Most of Carter's domestic policies were intended to fix the economy. At first he tried to end the recession and reduce unemployment by increasing government spending and cutting taxes. When inflation surged in 1978, he changed his mind. He delayed the tax cuts and vetoed the spending programs he had himself proposed. He tried to ease inflation by reducing the money supply and raising interest rates. In the end, none of his efforts succeeded.

Carter believed the nation's most serious problem was its dependence on foreign oil. In one of his first national addresses, he asked Americans to support a "war" against rising energy consumption. "Our decision about energy will test the character of the American people and the ability of the president and Congress to govern this nation," Carter stated.

to discuss and compare what they have learned from the interviews.

(Chapter Project continued on page 725)

PRIMARY SOURCE
The Election of 1976

When President Ford failed to solve the nation's economic problems, voters decided to give Washington outsider Jimmy Carter a chance.

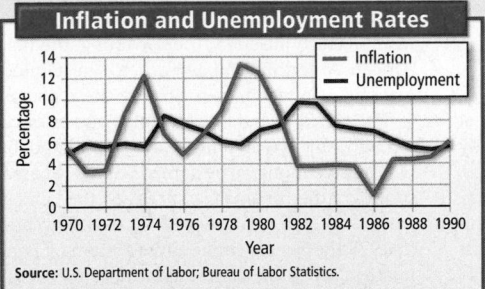

Inflation and Unemployment Rates

— Inflation
— Unemployment

Percentage / Year (1970 1972 1974 1976 1978 1980 1982 1984 1986 1988 1990)

Source: U.S. Department of Labor; Bureau of Labor Statistics.

Analyzing VISUALS

1. **Analyzing** In what areas of the country did Carter receive the most votes? Why do you think this was so?

2. **Interpreting** What was the trend for both unemployment and inflation after 1976?

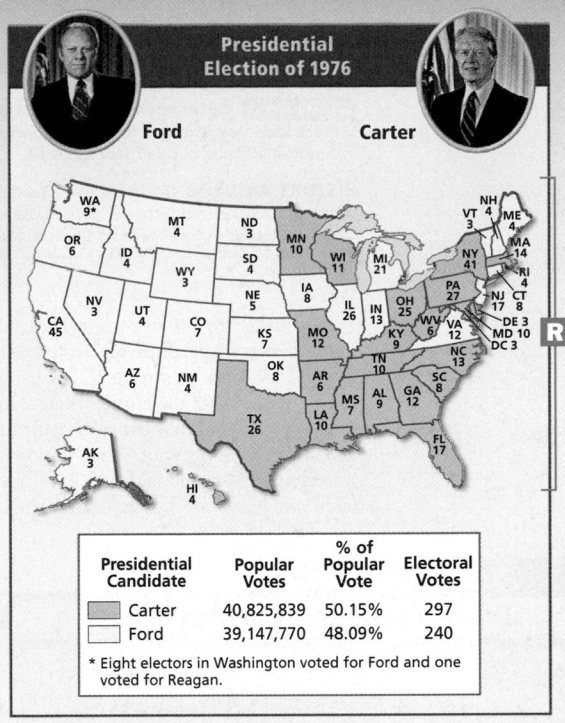

Presidential Election of 1976

Ford   Carter

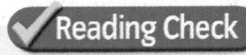

Presidential Candidate	Popular Votes	% of Popular Vote	Electoral Votes
Carter	40,825,839	50.15%	297
Ford	39,147,770	48.09%	240

* Eight electors in Washington voted for Ford and one voted for Reagan.

R

R Reading Strategy
Reading Primary Sources:
Ask: Which candidate carried more states during the election of 1976? *(Ford)* Ask why Carter won, despite carrying fewer states. *(Many of the states Ford carried had very few electoral votes.)* **BL OL**

Analyzing VISUALS

Answers:
1. Carter received the most votes in the East and in the South. This is probably because he is a Southerner, and in the North and East people tended to be more liberal as Carter was more liberal than Ford.
2. inflation increased sharply in the late 1970s, unemployment gradually declined

✓ Reading Check

Answer: His main domestic focus was on the energy crisis.

Carter proposed a national energy program to conserve oil and to promote the use of coal and renewable energy sources such as solar power. He also convinced Congress to create a **Department of Energy,** and asked Americans to reduce their energy consumption.

Meanwhile, many business leaders and economists urged the president and Congress to deregulate the oil industry. They believed that regulations, first imposed as part of President Nixon's price control plan, made it very difficult for oil companies to make a profit. They claimed they lacked the spare capital needed to invest in new domestic oil wells. This in turn kept the nation dependent on foreign oil.

Carter agreed to support **deregulation** but insisted on a "windfall profits tax" to prevent oil companies from overcharging consumers. Critics argued that the tax conflicted with the basic idea of deregulation, which was to free up capital for use in finding new sources of oil.

In the summer of 1979, instability in the Middle East produced a second major fuel shortage and deepened the nation's economic problems. Under increasing pressure to act, Carter made several proposals in a televised address. In the speech, Carter warned about a "crisis of confidence" that had struck "at the very heart and soul of our national will." The address became known as the "malaise" speech, although Carter had not specifically used that word. Many Americans felt that Carter was blaming the people for his failures.

President Carter's difficulties in solving the nation's economic problems lay partly in his inexperience and inability to work with Congress. Carter, proud of his outsider status, made little effort to reach out to Washington's legislative leaders. As a result, Congress blocked many of his energy proposals. The president also failed to set clear goals for the nation. Instead, he followed a cautious middle course that left people confused. By 1979, public opinion polls showed that Carter's popularity had dropped lower than President Nixon's during Watergate.

✓ Reading Check **Summarizing** To what did President Carter devote much of his domestic agenda?

Chapter 21 Politics and Economics **721**

Additional Support

Extending the Content

Life After the White House Carter continued his humanitarian policies after leaving office. He and his wife established a long-standing relationship with Habitat for Humanity, an organization promoting affordable housing in the United States and around the world. The organization builds thousands of houses for low-income families. Each house is built by volunteers, with the families themselves working alongside volunteers to build the homes. Many of the building supplies are donated or are purchased at cost.

C Critical Thinking

Analyzing Primary Sources
Direct students' attention to the captions describing Carter's foreign policy actions. Remind students that Carter negotiated a peace agreement between long-standing enemies Egypt and Israel. Ask them why this major achievement may have weighed less heavily during the election of 1980 than such issues as boycotting the 1980 Summer Olympics or his inability to negotiate the release of the hostages. *(Americans were less directly affected by the peace agreement than by the other issues.)*

Analyzing VISUALS

Answers:
1. the Camp David Accords
2. The Middle East was a major source of oil. The U.S. wanted peace in the region but also U.S.-friendly governments. Good relations with countries in the Middle East would help solve the energy crisis.

Additional Support

Carter's Foreign Policy

MAIN Idea Carter attempted to reestablish the United States as a moral force for good on the international stage but had few successes.

HISTORY AND YOU Do you think a leader's personal morality should shape policy? Read how Carter applied his moral code to foreign policy.

In contrast to his uncertain leadership at home, Carter's foreign policy was more clearly defined. A man of strong religious beliefs, Carter argued that the United States must try to be "right and honest and truthful and decent" in dealing with other nations. Yet it was on the international front that Carter suffered one of his most devastating defeats.

PRIMARY SOURCE
Jimmy Carter and the Middle East

During his administration, Jimmy Carter faced a number of challenges in the Middle East. His foreign policy there met with mixed success.

▲ **The Camp David Accords**
In 1978, Carter helped negotiate a peace treaty between Egypt and Israel. Above, Egyptian President Anwar Sadat, Carter, and Israeli Prime Minister Menachem Begin sign the accords.

Analyzing VISUALS

1. **Specifying** What was Carter's major success in foreign policy?
2. **Theorizing** Why was the Middle East a major focus of Carter's foreign policy?

722 **Chapter 21** Politics and Economics

Morality in Foreign Policy

President Carter set the tone for his foreign policy in his inaugural speech, when he said, "Our commitment to human rights must be absolute. . . . The powerful must not persecute the weak, and human dignity must be enhanced." Along with his foreign policy team—which included Andrew Young, the first African American ambassador to the United Nations—Carter strove to achieve these goals.

The president put his principles into practice in Latin America. To remove a major symbol of U.S. interventionism, he agreed to give Panama control of the Panama Canal, which the United States had built and operated for over 60 years. In 1978 the Senate ratified two Panama Canal treaties, which transferred control of the canal to Panama on December 31, 1999.

▲ **The Soviet Invasion of Afghanistan**
The Soviet invasion of Afghanistan shattered détente. Carter responded by imposing a grain embargo, but it did not force the Soviets to pull back.

▼ **The Iranian Hostage Crisis**
The Ayatollah Khomeini (right) led a revolution in Iran in 1979. Fifty-two Americans were taken hostage. Carter's inability to negotiate their release hurt his reelection campaign.

Activity: Collaborative Learning

Organizing Information Have students work in groups of three, using a graphic organizer similar to the one below to indicate the domestic and foreign policy challenges Nixon, Ford, and Carter faced. Each group member should complete the chart for a different president. *(Answers will vary, but domestic challenges may include the Watergate scandal for Nixon, the pardoning of Nixon by Ford, and stagflation for Carter. Foreign challenges should include détente for Nixon, problems in Southeast Asia for Ford, and the Iranian hostage crisis for Carter.)* **OL**

Challenges	Nixon	Ford	Carter
Domestic			
Foreign			

Most dramatically, Carter singled out the Soviet Union as a violator of human rights. He strongly condemned, for example, the Soviet practice of imprisoning those who protested against the government. Relations between the two superpowers suffered a further setback when Soviet troops invaded the Central Asian nation of Afghanistan in December 1979. Carter responded by imposing an embargo on the sale of grain to the Soviet Union and boycotting the 1980 Summer Olympic Games in Moscow. Under the Carter administration, détente eroded further.

Triumph and Failure in the Middle East

It was in the volatile Middle East that President Carter met both his greatest foreign policy triumph and his greatest failure. In 1978 Carter helped broker a historic peace treaty, known as the **Camp David Accords,** between Israel and Egypt—two nations that had been bitter enemies for decades. The treaty was formally signed in 1979. Most other Arab nations in the region opposed the treaty, but it marked a first step to achieving peace in the Middle East.

Just months after the Camp David Accords, Carter had to deal with a crisis in Iran. The United States had long supported Iran's monarch, the Shah, because Iran was a major oil supplier and a buffer against Soviet expansion in the Middle East. The Shah, however, had grown increasingly unpopular in Iran. He was a repressive ruler and had introduced Westernizing reforms to Iranian society. The Islamic clergy fiercely opposed the Shah's reforms. Opposition to the Shah grew, and in January 1979 protesters forced him to flee. An Islamic republic was then declared.

The new regime, led by religious leader Ayatollah Khomeini, distrusted the United States because of its support of the Shah. In November 1979, revolutionaries stormed the American embassy in Tehran and took 52 Americans hostage. The militants threatened to kill the hostages or try them as spies.

The Carter administration tried unsuccessfully to negotiate for the hostages' release. In April 1980, as pressure mounted, Carter approved a daring rescue attempt. To the nation's dismay, the rescue mission failed when several helicopters malfunctioned and one crashed in the desert. Eight servicemen died in the accident. Hamilton Jordan, President Carter's chief of staff, described the atmosphere in the White House the day after the crash. The president "looked exhausted and careworn. . . . The mood at the senior staff meeting was somber and awkward. I sensed that we were all uncomfortable, like when a loved one dies and friends don't know quite what to say."

The crisis continued into the fall of 1980. Every night, news programs reminded viewers how many days the hostages had been held. The president's inability to free them cost him support in the 1980 election. Negotiations continued right up to Carter's last day in office. On January 20, 1981, the day Carter left office, Iran released the Americans, ending their 444 days in captivity.

✓ Reading Check **Summarizing** What was President Carter's main foreign policy theme?

Section 3 REVIEW

Vocabulary
1. **Explain** the significance of: inflation, OPEC, embargo, stagflation, Helsinki Accords, Department of Energy, Camp David Accords.

Main Ideas
2. **Describing** How did the OPEC embargo affect the U.S. economy?

3. **Specifying** What were two ingredients in Carter's failure to achieve success in his domestic policy?

4. **Identifying** What crisis in the Middle East occurred during the Carter administration?

Critical Thinking
5. **Big Ideas** How did Carter attempt to deal with the nation's energy crisis?

6. **Organizing** Complete a graphic organizer by listing the ways in which President Carter applied his human rights ideas to his foreign policy.

Carter's Human Rights Foreign Policy

7. **Analyzing Visuals** Study the photograph of the hostages on page 722. What effect do you think images such as this one had on Americans who were living or traveling in other countries?

Writing About History
8. **Expository Writing** Write an essay identifying what you believe to be Carter's most important foreign policy achievement. Explain your choice.

History ONLINE
Study Central™ To review this section, go to glencoe.com and click on Study Central.

723

C Critical Thinking
Predicting Consequences
Ask: Who might be affected by the grain embargo other than Soviet leaders? *(Answers will vary, but may include U.S. farmers and Soviet consumers.)* **OL**

✓ Reading Check

Answer: the need for the United States to be honest and decent in foreign relations

Assess

History ONLINE

Study Central™ provides summaries, interactive games, and online graphic organizers to help students review content.

Close

Summarizing Ask: What set Carter's domestic and foreign policy apart from Nixon's and Ford's? *(Domestically he focused on energy. In foreign policy, he made human rights a priority.)* **OL**

Section 3 REVIEW

Answers

1. All definitions can be found in the section and the Glossary.

2. The increase in oil prices caused by the embargo and later price increases accelerated inflation. As prices rose for oil-based products, Americans had less money for other goods, which helped cause a recession.

3. his inexperience and inability to work with Congress

4. the Iranian hostage crisis

5. He proposed a national energy program to conserve oil and promote the use of renewable energy sources, created the Department of Energy, and deregulated the oil industry.

6. Answers should reflect information in the text, particularly about the Soviet Union and Panama.

7. Answers will vary.

8. Students' essays will vary, but should include facts to support the position taken.

Focus

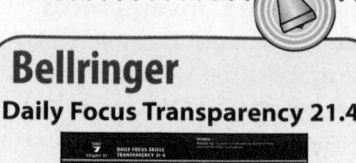

Bellringer
Daily Focus Transparency 21.4

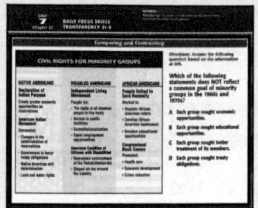

Guide to Reading

1969: AIM took over Alcatraz Island; 1971: PUSH organized voter registration, developed African American businesses, and broadened educational opportunities; CBC focused on African American concerns in Congress; 1973: AIM seized the town of Wounded Knee; 1977: Disability rights activists held a ten-city sit-in and occupied a federal building in San Francisco to force the federal government to enforce Section 504; 1994: Louis Farrakhan organized the Million Man March

Section Spotlight Video

To generate student interest and provide a springboard for class discussion, access the Chapter 21, Section 4 video at glencoe.com or on the video DVD.

Resource Manager

New Approaches to Civil Rights

Guide to Reading

Big Ideas
Struggles for Rights African Americans, Native Americans, and people with disabilities organized to fight discrimination and gain access to better education and jobs.

Content Vocabulary
- busing (p. 725)
- affirmative action (p. 725)

Academic Vocabulary
- criteria (p. 726)
- appropriate (p. 729)

People and Events to Identify
- Allan Bakke (p. 726)
- Jesse Jackson (p. 727)
- Congressional Black Caucus (p. 727)
- Shirley Chisholm (p. 727)
- American Indian Movement (AIM) (p. 727)
- Section 504 (p. 729)

Reading Strategy
Sequencing Complete a time line similar to the one below by recording groups in the civil rights movement and their actions.

Throughout the 1960s and 1970s, reforms took place in many areas of society. In this period, minority groups, such as African Americans, Native Americans, and persons with disabilities, began to develop new ways to expand opportunities and assert their civil rights.

African Americans Seek Greater Opportunity

MAIN Idea During the 1960s and 1970s, African Americans built on the civil rights achievements of the 1950s to advance their social, political, and legal status.

HISTORY AND YOU Does your school district have a program of busing? Read on to learn how such programs originated as a way to integrate public schools.

By the end of the 1960s, many African American leaders felt a growing sense of frustration. Although most legal forms of racial discrimination had been dismantled, many African Americans saw little improvement in their daily lives. Increasingly, the problems facing most African Americans lay in their lack of access to good jobs and adequate schooling. As a result, leaders of the civil rights movement began to focus their energies on these problems.

Equal Access to Education

In the 1970s, African Americans began to push harder for improvements in public education and access to good schools. Although the Supreme Court had ordered an end to segregated public schools in the 1954 case *Brown* v. *Board of Education*, many schools remained segregated because children attended schools near where they lived. As a result many schools, especially in the North, remained segregated, not by law, but because whites and African Americans lived in different neighborhoods.

In many cases where de facto segregation existed, the white schools were superior, as Ruth Baston of the NAACP noted in 1965 after visiting Boston schools:

PRIMARY SOURCE

"When we would go to white schools, we'd see these lovely classrooms with a small number of children in each class. The teachers were permanent. We'd see wonderful materials. When we'd go to our schools, we'd see overcrowded classrooms, children sitting out in the corridors. And so then we decided that

---

R Reading Strategies	**C** Critical Thinking	**D** Differentiated Instruction	**W** Writing Support	**S** Skill Practice
Teacher Edition • Making Connections, p. 725 • Academic Vocabulary, p. 728 **Additional Resources** • Guid. Read. Act., URB p. 51	**Teacher Edition** • Comparing and Contrasting, p. 726 • Making Inferences, p. 727 **Additional Resources** • Supreme Court Case Studies, p. 107 • Quizzes and Tests, p. 302	**Additional Resources** • Enrichment Act., URB p. 45		**Additional Resources** • RENTG, p. 227

Chapter 21 • Section 4

PRIMARY SOURCE

Busing to End Segregation

To end segregation in public schools, state courts ordered the busing of children to schools outside of their neighborhoods. Reaction from parents to forced busing was often violent.

▲ Anger over busing was particularly virulent in some neighborhoods in Boston, Massachusetts, where police often had to escort school buses along their routes.

▲ Supporters of busing took part in the National March on Boston in 1975. The NAACP sponsored the march to mark the anniversary of the *Brown v. Board of Education* decision, which outlawed segregation in schools.

Analyzing VISUALS

1. **Explaining** Why were parents in Boston neighborhoods angry over busing?
2. **Making Inferences** Why are protesters holding signs that read "21 years is too long to wait" in the photograph on the right?

where there were a large number of white students, that's where the care went. That's where the books went. That's where the money went."

—quoted in *Freedom Bound*

To solve this problem, state courts began ordering local governments to bus children to schools outside their neighborhoods to achieve greater racial balance. The practice led to protests and even riots in several white communities, including Boston. The Supreme Court, however, upheld the constitutionality of **busing** in the 1971 case *Swann v. Charlotte-Mecklenburg Board of Education.*

In response, many whites took their children out of public schools or moved to a district where busing had not been imposed. About 20,000 white students left Boston's public system for parochial and private schools. By late 1976, African Americans, Latinos, and other minorities made up the

majority of Boston's public school students. This "white flight" also occurred in other cities. When Detroit tried to bus students from one school district to another in 1974, the Court held in *Miliken v. Bradley* that busing across district lines was unconstitutional unless districts had been deliberately drawn to create segregation.

Affirmative Action

In addition to supporting busing, civil rights leaders in the 1970s began advocating **affirmative action** as a new way to solve economic and educational discrimination. Enforced through executive orders and federal policies, affirmative action called for companies, schools, and institutions doing business with the federal government to recruit African Americans with the hope that this would lead to improved social and economic status. Officials later expanded affirmative action to include other minority groups and women.

🏛 For further information on the case of *Swann v. Charlotte-Mecklenburg Board of Education,* see page R61 in the *Supreme Court Case Summaries.*

Chapter 21 Politics and Economics **725**

Teach

R **Reading Strategy**

Making Connections Ask students how the Primary Source quote that ends on this page explains why courts might order busing. *(With de facto segregation, a greater share of resources went to the schools that served a predominantly white student body. Busing would prevent this injustice by mixing races at schools.)*

Analyzing VISUALS

Answers:
1. They did not want their children bused far from home where they might not be wanted and some probably did not want their children going to school with children of other races.
2. It refers to the 1954 Supreme Court decision *Brown v. Board of Education* that outlawed segregation in public schools and the fact that many schools were still segregated.

Hands-On Chapter Project

Step 4

Oral History of the 1970s

Step 4: Summarizing the Information
Have students in groups collaboratively write an essay about their topic. Encourage students to draw upon information from Chapter 21 as well as their interviews.

Distinguishing Fact from Opinion In their essays, students should clearly delineate between the events that surrounded their topic and the reaction of people to those events at the time.

(Chapter Project continued on page 731)

C Critical Thinking

Comparing and Contrasting

Ask students to compare and contrast the ways Jackson and Chisholm worked for civil rights. *(Answers may vary. Chisholm worked both within and outside the government, while Jackson worked mainly outside it.)* **OL**

People IN HISTORY

Answer: Jesse Jackson He worked with Dr. King, established PUSH and the Rainbow Coalition, ran for president and made African American issues important in the Democratic platform.

Answer: Shirley Chisholm She worked on education and family issues and voted to increase day-care programs.

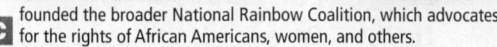

People IN HISTORY

Jesse Jackson
1941–

An ordained Baptist minister, Jesse Jackson first became involved in social causes as an aid to Martin Luther King, Jr. Jackson went on to form Operation PUSH, an organization based in Chicago, which was founded to promote economic opportunities for African Americans. In 1984 he founded the broader National Rainbow Coalition, which advocates for the rights of African Americans, women, and others.

In the 1980s Jackson turned to politics. He ran for the Democratic presidential nomination in 1984 and 1988, placing third and then second to become the most successful African American presidential candidate to that point.

Jackson established the Wall Street Project in 1997 to increase opportunities for minorities in big business. Also in that year, President Clinton selected Jackson as a special envoy to Africa to promote democracy and human rights. In 2000 Jackson received the Presidential Medal of Freedom—the nation's highest civilian honor.

How has Jesse Jackson worked to improve the status of African Americans and promote civil rights for all Americans?

Shirley Chisholm
1924–2005

Shirley Chisholm once remarked, "Of my two 'handicaps,' being female put more obstacles in my path than being black." Her success in challenging both racism and sexism propelled the Brooklyn, New York, native into the national spotlight.

In 1968 Chisholm became the first African American woman to be elected to the United States Congress. There, Chisholm became an ardent defender of several causes, and helped to found the Congressional Black Caucus. She also worked on education and family issues and voted to increase day care programs.

In 1972 Chisholm ran for the Democratic nomination for president. Although she did not win the nomination, she did receive 28 delegates.

After the convention, Chisholm continued her crusade in Congress to help minorities and women for several more terms. She declined to run for re-election in 1982, citing the difficulties of campaigning for liberal issues in an increasingly conservative atmosphere.

On what issues did Shirley Chisholm focus?

Supporters of the policy argued that because so few companies had hired from these groups in the past, they had not necessarily developed the required job skills. If businesses opened their doors wider to minorities, more of them could begin to acquire skills and build better lives.

In one example of affirmative action's impact, Atlanta witnessed a significant increase in minority job opportunities after Maynard Jackson became its first African American mayor in 1973. When Jackson took office, less than one percent of all city contracts went to African Americans, even though they made up about half of Atlanta's population. Jackson used the expansion of the city's airport to redress this imbalance. Through his efforts, small companies and minority firms took on 25 percent of all airport construction work, earning them some $125 million in contracts.

The *Bakke* Case

Affirmative action programs did not go unchallenged, however. Critics viewed them as a form of reverse racial discrimination. They claimed that qualified white male workers and students were kept from jobs, promotions, and places in schools because a certain number of such positions had been set aside for minorities or women.

Affirmative action was addressed by the Supreme Court in 1978. The case began in 1974, after officials at the medical school of the University of California at Davis turned down the admission of a white applicant named **Allan Bakke** for a second time. When Bakke learned that slots had been set aside for minorities, he sued the school. Bakke argued that by admitting minority applicants—some of whom had scored lower than Bakke on their exams—the school had discriminated against him based on his race.

In 1978, in *University of California Regents* v. *Bakke*, the Supreme Court, in a 5 to 4 ruling, declared that the university had violated Bakke's civil rights. It also ruled, however, that schools had an interest in maintaining a diverse student body. Thus, universities could consider race as one part of their admissions **criteria** as long as they did not use "fixed quotas," such as the slots the UC-Davis Medical School had reserved for minority students.

🏛 For further information on the case of *University of California Regents v. Bakke*, see page R60 in the *Supreme Court Case Summaries.*

Activity: Collaborative Learning

Conducting a Debate Organize the class into two groups. Tell the groups that they are to prepare for a debate about affirmative action. Assign one group to concentrate on the pros of affirmative action; the other group should concentrate on the cons. Groups should conduct research using library or Internet sources to identify facts and theories to support their assigned point of view. Once both groups have completed their research, conduct an informal debate in which each side presents its case and rebuts the point of view of the other side. Encourage all students to participate. **OL**

New Political Leaders

New political leaders emerged in the African American community in the 1970s. **Jesse Jackson,** a former aid to Martin Luther King, Jr., was among this new generation of activists. In 1971 Jackson founded Operation PUSH (People United to Save Humanity), an organization dedicated to registering voters, developing African American businesses, and broadening educational opportunities. In 1984 and 1988, Jackson sought the Democratic presidential nomination. Although both attempts were unsuccessful, he won over millions of voters.

African Americans also became more influential in national politics for the first time since Reconstruction. In 1971 African American members of Congress organized the **Congressional Black Caucus** to more clearly represent their concerns. Another prominent leader of the era was **Shirley Chisholm** of New York. Chisholm was a founding member of the Congressional Black Caucus and the first African American woman to serve in Congress. In 1977 another former assistant to Martin Luther King, Jr., U.S. Representative Andrew Young, was selected by President Carter to become the first African American to serve as U.S. ambassador to the United Nations. He went on to become the mayor of Atlanta. By the early 1980s, African American mayors had been elected in Atlanta, Detroit, Chicago, Los Angeles, New Orleans, Philadelphia, and Washington, D.C.

Another leader who emerged in the 1980s was Louis Farrakhan, a prominent minister of the Nation of Islam. He organized the Million Man March, which attracted an enormous crowd in Washington, D.C., on October 16, 1995. Farrakhan had conceived of the march as a way to promote self-reliance and responsibility among African American men. In addition to Farrakhan, the event featured other prominent speakers, including Jesse Jackson and the poet Maya Angelou.

In 1990, voters in Virginia elected L. Douglas Wilder, who became the first African American to serve as governor of a state. In that same year, David Dinkins took office as the first African American mayor of New York City.

✔**Reading Check** **Examining** What were the goals of affirmative action policies?

Native Americans Raise Their Voices

MAIN Idea The most impoverished minority group in America, Native Americans, began organizing for civil rights.

HISTORY AND YOU What do you recall about the Black Power Movement in the 1960s? Read on to learn how some Native Americans formed the American Indian Movement.

In 1970 Native Americans were one of the nation's smallest minority groups, constituting less than one percent of the U.S. population, yet they faced enormous problems. The unemployment rate for Native Americans was ten times the national rate. Their average annual family income was $1,000 less than that of African Americans. Unemployment was very high on reservations, where nearly half of all Native Americans lived. Those living in cities often had little education or training. The bleakest statistic of all showed that the life expectancy for Native Americans was almost seven years below the national average.

A Protest Movement Emerges

In 1961 more than 400 members of 67 Native American groups gathered in Chicago to discuss ways to address their problems. They issued a manifesto, known as the Declaration of Indian Purpose, asking for federal programs to create greater economic opportunities on reservations.

Unlike some groups who wanted to be accepted by mainstream society, many Native Americans wanted more independence from it. They took a step toward this goal in 1968 when Congress passed the Indian Civil Rights Act. The legislation guaranteed reservation residents the protections of the Bill of Rights, but it also recognized local reservation law.

Native Americans who viewed the government's efforts as too modest formed more militant groups, which typically employed a more combative style. One such group, the **American Indian Movement (AIM),** staged a symbolic protest in 1969 by occupying the abandoned federal prison on Alcatraz Island in San Francisco Bay for 19 months, claiming ownership "by right of discovery."

C **Critical Thinking**

Making Inferences What did AIM mean by "right of discovery"? *(They are making a statement about the Europeans who "discovered" Native American lands and claimed them.)* **OL**

✔**Reading Check**

Answer: to improve educational opportunities for African Americans and to actively recruit minorities and women for jobs

Additional Support

Activity: Interdisciplinary Connection

Art Have students design a postage stamp to commemorate progress in the pursuit of equal rights in the United States. The stamp should feature an event, person, or group that made a significant contribution to equal rights. Encourage students to choose a subject they feel is particularly worthy. In addition to a sketch of the stamp, ask students to prepare a short news release announcing the stamp and explaining its significance. Ask students to share their sketches and read their news releases to the class. **OL**

R Reading Strategy

Academic Vocabulary Point out the term *relinquish* in the first paragraph of the second column. Help students define the word as "part with or let go of." Ask them what they or others have relinquished. **ELL**

✔ Reading Check

Answer: high unemployment, limited education and training, discrimination, and poor life expectancy

Analyzing VISUALS

Answers:
1. They struggled for equality in education, employment, and housing. They also worked for equal access to public facilities.
2. There is a ramp and lift on the bus and the sign shows that a spot is for people with disabilities only.

Additional Support

728

The most famous protest by AIM took place at Wounded Knee, South Dakota, where U.S. troops had killed hundreds of Sioux in 1890. In February 1973, AIM members seized the town of Wounded Knee for 70 days. They demanded that the government honor its past treaty obligations to Native Americans and insisted that radical changes be made in the administration of reservations. A brief clash between AIM members and the FBI resulted in two Native Americans dead and several wounded on both sides. Shortly thereafter, the siege came to an end.

Native American Gains

By the mid-1970s, the Native American movement had begun to achieve some of its goals. In 1975 Congress passed the Indian Self-Determination and Educational Assistance Act, which increased funds for Native American education and expanded local control over federal programs. More Native Americans also moved into policy-making positions at the Bureau of Indian Affairs, and the agency pushed for more Native American self-determination.

Native Americans also won several court cases involving land and water rights. The people of the Pueblo of Taos, New Mexico, regained property rights to Blue Lake, a place sacred to their religion. In 1980 a federal court settled a claim of the Passamaquoddy and the Penobscot peoples. The government paid them $81.5 million to relinquish their claim to land in Maine. Other court decisions gave Native American governments the authority to tax businesses on their reservations.

Since Native Americans first began to organize, many reservations have improved their economic conditions by actively developing businesses, such as electric plants, resorts, cattle ranches, and oil and gas wells. More recently, gambling casinos have become a successful enterprise. Because of rulings on sovereignty, Native Americans in some areas are allowed to operate gaming establishments under their own laws even though state laws prevent others from doing so.

✔ Reading Check **Analyzing** What conditions led Native Americans to organize in the 1960s?

PRIMARY SOURCE
The Disability Rights Movement

In the 1970s, people with disabilities struggled for greater rights in education, employment, and housing. They met with success in the passage of legislation such as the Rehabilitation Act of 1973.

▲ On April 5, 1977, the American Coalition of Citizens with Disabilities organized sit-ins demanding equal rights.

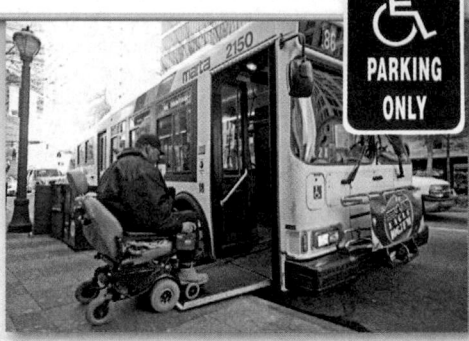

▲ Section 504 of the Rehabilitation Act and, later, the Americans with Disabilities Act specified that disabled people must have equal access to public facilities, such as transportation and parking.

Analyzing VISUALS

1. **Listing** What rights did people with disabilities struggle for in the 1970s?
2. **Specifying** What two accommodations for people with disabilities are shown in the photograph on the right?

728 Chapter 21 Politics and Economics

Activity: Interdisciplinary Connection

Language Arts After students have read the section, have them pose questions such as those below that could be used to interview someone who lived through the civil rights movement. Help students prepare open-ended questions. Then use the responses to evaluate the movement's impact on the American public. **OL**

- When were you first aware that "civil rights" was a broad movement?

- Which forms of protest most impressed you? In which, if any, did you participate?

- How did your life change as a result of the civil rights movement?

- How do you think the civil rights movement should be remembered today?

The Disability Rights Movement

MAIN Idea During the 1970s, people with disabilities fought for greater rights and access to education and jobs.

HISTORY AND YOU Do you or someone you know have a disability? Read on to learn about how people with disabilities achieved new legislation to help protect their civil rights.

The struggle for disability rights had its early expression in the independent living movement begun at the University of California at Berkeley in the early 1970s. The movement advocated for the right of people of all levels of abilities to choose to live freely in society. This was part of a new attitude that encouraged deinstitutionalization of people with disabilities.

People with disabilities also looked to the federal government to protect their civil rights. Access to public facilities and prohibitions on discrimination in employment led their demands. One victory was passage, in 1968, of the Architectural Barriers Act, which mandated that new buildings constructed with federal funds be accessible to disabled persons. The Rehabilitation Act of 1973 was even more significant. According to **Section 504,** "no otherwise qualified individual with a disability . . . shall . . . be excluded from participation in, be denied the benefits of, or be subjected to discrimination under any program or service or activity receiving Federal financial assistance . . ."

Unfortunately passage of the Rehabilitation Act meant little until procedures for enforcing its provisions were established. As of 1977, the Department of Health, Education, and Welfare (HEW) had issued no such regulations. Frustrated, the American Coalition of Citizens with Disabilities, headed by Frank Bowe, organized protests. On April 5, 1977, some 2,000 persons with disabilities in 10 cities began sit-ins at regional HEW offices. Although most protests lasted only a day or two, protesters in San Francisco maintained their sit-in for over three weeks—leaving only when HEW's director signed the regulations banning discrimination.

Changes also occurred in special education. In 1966 Congress created the Bureau for the Education of the Handicapped, which provided grants to develop programs for educating children with disabilities. In 1975 the Education for All Handicapped Children Act required that all students with disabilities receive a free, **appropriate** education. One trend was to mainstream, or bring into the regular classroom, students with disabilities.

In 1990 Congress enacted the Americans with Disabilities Act. This far-reaching legislation banned discrimination against persons with disabilities in employment, transportation, public education, and telecommunications.

Today, new technologies are important assets to people with disabilities. Innovations such as closed-captioned television broadcasts, devices for telephones, and screen readers allow people with disabilities to access information in new ways.

Reading Check **Explaining** Why did the American Coalition of Citizens with Disabilities stage sit-ins in 1977?

Section 4 REVIEW

Vocabulary

1. **Explain** the significance of: busing, affirmative action, Allan Bakke, Jesse Jackson, Congressional Black Caucus, Shirley Chisholm, American Indian Movement (AIM), Section 504.

Main Ideas

2. **Specifying** How did some critics characterize affirmative action?

3. **Identifying Central Issues** What was significant about AIM's claim to Alcatraz Island?

4. **Explaining** What was the significance of the independent living movement?

Critical Thinking

5. **Big Ideas** How did the Supreme Court support civil rights during the 1970s?

6. **Organizing** Use a graphic organizer to identify civil rights leaders and their causes.

Civil Rights Leaders	Causes

7. **Analyzing Visuals** Study the images on page 725 of busing in the 1970s. Why do you think reactions to busing were so strong and at times even violent?

Writing About History

8. **Expository Writing** Write a magazine article about conditions that provoked the Native American protest movement of the 1960s and 1970s. Be sure to discuss the movement's goals and activities.

 History ONLINE
Study Central™ To review this section, go to glencoe.com and click on Study Central.

729

Reading Check

Answer: They were protesting the federal government's inaction over Section 504 of the Rehabilitation Act.

Assess

History ONLINE

Study Central™ provides summaries, interactive games, and online graphic organizers to help students review content.

Close

Summarizing **Ask:** What did African Americans, Native Americans, and Americans with disabilities gain by organizing? *(They all faced less discrimination and gained better employment, educational, and economic opportunities. Native Americans gained more sovereignty and some land and water rights. People with disabilities were supported in their desire to live independently and participate fully in the community.)* **OL**

Section 4 REVIEW

Answers

1. All definitions can be found in the section and the Glossary.

2. as reverse discrimination

3. They claimed ownership "by right of discovery," as Europeans had claimed their lands.

4. It was at the root of the disability rights movement.

5. *Swann v. Charlotte-Mecklenburg Board of Education:* constitutionality of busing; *University of California Regents v. Bakke:* constitutionality of affirmative action

6. Jackson: political power for African Americans; AIM: equal rights and improved conditions for Native Americans; American Coalition of Citizens with Disabilities/Frank Bowe: equal rights for people with disabilities

7. Possible answer: It was forcing integration, which people did not want. Also children were bused out of their own neighborhoods.

8. Students' articles will vary, but should focus on the reasons for the protest movement.

Focus

Bellringer

Daily Focus Transparency 21.5

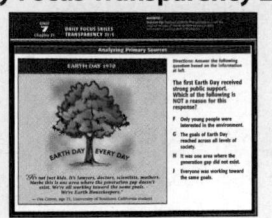

Guide to Reading

Answers: Clean Air Act, Clean Water Act, Earth Day celebration, Endangered Species Act, creation of the Environmental Protection Agency

Section Spotlight Video

To generate student interest and provide a springboard for class discussion, access the Chapter 21, Section 5 video at glencoe.com or on the video DVD.

Resource Manager

Section 5

Environmentalism

Guide to Reading

Big Ideas
Group Action Increased awareness of environmental issues inspired a grassroots campaign to protect nature.

Content Vocabulary
- smog (p. 731)
- fossil fuel (p. 733)

Academic Vocabulary
- intensify (p. 733)
- alternative (p. 733)

People and Events to Identify
- Rachel Carson (p. 730)
- Environmental Protection Agency (p. 732)
- Love Canal (p. 732)
- Three Mile Island (p. 733)

Reading Strategy
Organizing Complete a graphic organizer similar to the one below by including actions taken to combat the nation's environmental problems in the 1960s and 1970s.

Actions Taken

A mericans became increasingly aware of the damage being done to the environment. Soon environmental issues became national concerns, and individuals, local groups, and the government acted to address the damage and protect natural resources.

The Origins of Environmentalism

MAIN Idea Concerns about the effects of a deadly pesticide, the visible signs of pollution in American cities, and an influential book inspired a movement to protect the environment.

HISTORY AND YOU Do you take action personally or with others to preserve and protect the environment? Read on to learn how one woman inspired the environmental movement.

In 1966 Carol Yannacone of Patchogue, a small community on Long Island, New York, learned that officials were using the powerful pesticide DDT as part of a mosquito control operation at a local lake. Alarmed that the pesticide might poison the lake and local streams, Yannacone and her husband Victor, an attorney, contacted several local scientists who confirmed their suspicions.

The Yannacones then successfully sued to halt the use of the pesticide. In so doing, they had discovered a new strategy for addressing environmental concerns. Shortly after the Yannacones' court victory, the scientists involved in the case established the Environmental Defense Fund and used its contributions for a series of legal actions across the country to halt DDT spraying. Their efforts led to a nationwide ban on the use of the pesticide in 1972.

The effort to ban DDT was only one part of a new environmental movement that took shape in the 1960s and 1970s. The person who helped trigger this new movement was not a political leader or prominent academic, but a soft-spoken marine biologist named **Rachel Carson.** Carson's 1962 book *Silent Spring* assailed the increasing use of pesticides, particularly DDT. She contended that while pesticides curbed insect populations, they also killed birds, fish, and other creatures that might ingest them. Carson warned Americans of a "silent spring," in which there would be no birds left to usher spring in with their songs. *Silent Spring* became a best-seller and one of the most controversial and influential books of the 1960s. The chemical industry was outraged and began an intense campaign to discredit Carson and her arguments.

Many Americans believed Carson's warnings, however, largely because of what they were seeing around them and reading in news reports. Rivers across the nation were no longer safe for

R Reading Strategies	**C** Critical Thinking	**D** Differentiated Instruction	**W** Writing Support	**S** Skill Practice
Teacher Edition • Outlining, p. 732 **Additional Resources** • Guid. Read. Act., URB p. 52	**Teacher Edition** • Making Inferences, p. 732 **Additional Resources** • Interp. Pol. Car. Act., URB p. 41 • Quizzes and Tests, p. 303	**Additional Resources** • Differentiated Inst. Act., URB p. 23 • Reteaching Act., URB p. 43 • Auth. Assess., p. 47	**Teacher Edition** • Expository Writing, p. 731 **Additional Resources** • American Art and Music, URB p. 39	**Additional Resources** • Link. Past/Present Act., URB p. 34 • RENTG, p. 230

PRIMARY SOURCE
Origins of the Environmentalist Movement

▲ Industrial pollution in cities like Newark, New Jersey (above) led to thick clouds of smog that caused breathing problems for some people. Tired of the dirty air, many Americans began to demand an end to pollution.

▲ Volunteers work to clean up an oil spill off the coast of California in 1969. News of the spill helped mobilize the new environmentalist movement.

◄ In 1969, the Cuyahoga River in Ohio caught fire. The incident gained national attention and contributed to the passage of the Clean Water Act in 1972.

Analyzing VISUALS

1. **Summarizing** What events raised awareness of the need to protect the environment?
2. **Discussing** Why do you think the fire on the Cuyahoga River convinced many people of the need for action?

---

fishing or swimming. **Smog,** or fog made heavier and darker by smoke and chemical fumes, hung perpetually over many major cities. In the Northwest, timber companies were cutting down acres of forest. In 1969 a major oil spill off Santa Barbara, California, ruined miles of beach and killed scores of birds and aquatic animals. A dike project in Florida's Everglades indirectly killed millions of birds and animals. Pollution and garbage caused nearly all the fish to disappear from Lake Erie. By 1970, many citizens were convinced it was time to do something about protecting the environment.

A Grassroots Effort Begins

Many observers point to April 1970 as the unofficial beginning of the environmentalist movement. That month, the nation held its first Earth Day celebration, a day devoted to addressing environmental concerns. The national response was overwhelming. On 2,000 college campuses, in 10,000 secondary schools, and in hundreds of communities, millions of Americans participated in activities to show their environmental awareness.

After Earth Day, many citizens formed local environmental groups. Long-standing non-profit organizations such as the Audubon Society, the Sierra Club, and the Wilderness Society grew rapidly in membership and political influence. These organizations worked to protect the environment and promote the conservation of natural resources. In 1970 activists started the Natural Resources Defense Council to coordinate a nationwide network of scientists, lawyers, and activists working on environmental issues.

Many communities and businesses responded to these organizations. Many city planners sought to reduce urban sprawl and expand green space. Architects and builders tried to make their structures more energy efficient, and the forestry industry began reforestation programs.

✔ Reading Check **Identifying** What natural resources did environmental groups want to protect?

Teach

Analyzing VISUALS

Answers:
1. oil spills, terrible industrial pollution, fire on the Cuyahoga River
2. If something made of water can catch on fire, that indicates a serious level of pollution.

W Writing Support
Expository Writing Have interested students write a book review of *Silent Spring* by Rachel Carson or a more recent book about the environment. **AL**

✔ Reading Check

Answer: plant, wildlife, air, and water resources

Hands-On Chapter Project
Step 5

Oral History of the 1970s

Step 5: Presenting the Project Visually Students should try to integrate the information presented in this chapter, their research, and their notes based on the interviews.

Illustrating Have students create a poster presenting an overview of their topic using the photographs and excerpts from their interviews.
(Chapter Project continued on the Visual Summary page)

731

The Environmental Movement Blossoms

MAIN Idea Pressure from citizens and activist groups led Congress to pass major environmental legislation.

HISTORY AND YOU Can you think of a recent environmental disaster that has been in the news? Read on to learn about two of the worst environmental disasters in American history.

As the environmental movement gained support, the federal government took action. In 1970 President Nixon signed the National Environmental Policy Act, which created the **Environmental Protection Agency (EPA).** The EPA set and enforced pollution standards, promoted research, and directed anti-pollution activities with state and local governments.

The Clean Air Act also became law in 1970 after Congress overrode President Nixon's veto. This act established emissions standards for factories and automobiles. It also ordered all industries to comply with such standards within five years.

In following years, Congress passed two more pieces of significant environmental legislation. The Clean Water Act (1972) restricted the discharge of pollutants into the nation's lakes and rivers, and the Endangered Species Act (1973) established measures for saving threatened animal and plant species. These laws succeeded in reducing smog, and the pollution of many lakes, streams, and rivers declined dramatically.

Love Canal

Despite the flurry of federal environmental legislation, Americans continued to mobilize on the community level throughout the 1970s. One of the most powerful displays of community activism occurred in a housing development near Niagara Falls, New York, known as **Love Canal.**

POLITICAL CARTOONS PRIMARY SOURCE
A New Focus on the Environment

By the 1970s, the environmental movement was a strong force for change in the nation and around the world. In response, Congress passed a series of laws designed to protect the air, water, and wildlife.

◄ President Ford and others are criticized for supporting industrial interests rather than protecting the environment.

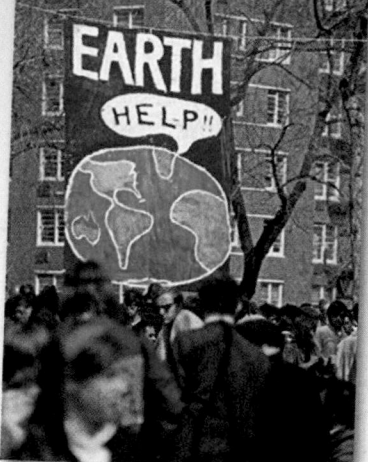

► Events, such as the annual Earth Day celebrations, helped environmentalists increase public awareness of environmental problems.

Analyzing VISUALS DBQ
1. **Identifying** Who does the large figure represent in the cartoon on the left?
2. **Summarizing** What is the main idea being expressed in the Earth Day poster?

732 **Chapter 21** Politics and Economics

Activity: Interdisciplinary Connection

Science Invite a scientist or science teacher to address your class about an environmental issue. Ask the speaker to address how science has helped to create some of the current environmental issues, how science helps prevent other environmental problems, and how science is helping to correct existing problems. For example, the speaker might address how science and technology helped to create many of the disposable products that we use today and how science is being used to help make those products more environmentally friendly. **OL**

During the 1970s, residents of Love Canal began to notice increasingly high incidences of health problems in their community, including nerve damage, blood diseases, cancer, miscarriages, and birth defects. The residents soon learned that their community sat atop a decades-old toxic waste dump. Over time, its hazardous contents had spread through the ground.

Led by a local woman, Lois Gibbs, the residents joined together and demanded that the government take steps to address these health threats. Hindered at first by local and state officials, the residents refused to back down, and by 1978 they had made their struggle known to the entire nation. That year, in the face of mounting public pressure and evidence of the dangers posed by the dump, the state permanently relocated more than 200 families.

In 1980, after hearing protests from the families who still lived near the landfill, President Carter declared Love Canal a federal disaster area and moved over 600 remaining families to new locations. In 1983 Love Canal residents sued the company that had created the dump site and settled the case for $20 million. The site was cleaned up by sealing the waste within an underground bunker and burning homes located above the dumping ground.

Concerns About Nuclear Energy

During the 1970s, a number of citizens also became concerned about the use of nuclear reactors to generate electricity. As nuclear power plants began to dot the nation's landscape, the debate over their use **intensified.** Supporters of nuclear energy hailed it as a cleaner and less expensive **alternative** to **fossil fuels,** such as coal, oil, and natural gas, which are in limited supply. Opponents warned of the risks nuclear energy posed, particularly the devastating consequences of an accidental radiation release into the air.

The debate gained national attention in a shocking fashion in 1979. In the early hours of March 28, one of the reactors at the **Three Mile Island** nuclear facility outside Harrisburg, Pennsylvania, overheated after its cooling system failed. Two days later, as plant officials scrambled to fix the problem, low levels of radiation escaped from the reactor.

Officials evacuated many nearby residents, while others fled on their own. Citizens and community groups expressed outrage at protest rallies. Officials closed down the reactor and sealed the leak. The Nuclear Regulatory Commission, the federal agency that regulates the nuclear power industry, eventually declared the plant safe. President Carter even visited the site in order to allay the public's concerns.

Although no one was hurt, the accident at Three Mile Island had a powerful impact politically. Many people now doubted the safety of nuclear energy. Such doubts have continued. Since Three Mile Island, some 60 nuclear power plants have been shut down or abandoned, and no new facilities have been built since 1973.

✔ Reading Check **Summarizing** What is the environmental movement's main goal?

Section 5 REVIEW

Vocabulary
1. **Explain** the significance of: Rachel Carson, smog, Environmental Protection Agency, Love Canal, fossil fuel, Three Mile Island.

Main Ideas
2. **Summarizing** What were some of the dangers of DDT?

3. **Explaining** Why was Love Canal a dangerous place to live?

Critical Thinking
4. **Big Ideas** What were some groups that lobbied for legislation to protect the environment in the 1960s and 1970s?

5. **Categorizing** Use a graphic organizer similar to the one below to list the environmental laws passed in the 1970s, and explain their purposes.

Environmental Legislation	Purpose

6. **Analyzing Visuals** Study the cartoon on the left-hand side of page 732. What is the meaning of the piece of paper that reads "O.K. Gerald Ford" in the main figure's pocket?

Writing About History
7. **Descriptive Writing** Take on the role of an investigative reporter, and describe the environmental disaster at either Love Canal or Three Mile Island. Explain how community activism brought the issue to the nation's attention.

History ONLINE
Study Central™ To review this section, go to glencoe.com and click on Study Central.

✔ **Reading Check**

Answer: protecting and preserving natural resources

Assess

History ONLINE

Study Central™ provides summaries, interactive games, and online graphic organizers to help students review content.

Close

Summarizing Ask: What did the environmental movement achieve during the 1970s? *(controls on pollution, cleanups; laws such as the Clean Air Act, Clean Water Act, and Endangered Species Act; creation of the Environmental Protection Agency; and establishment of Earth Day)* OL

Section 5 REVIEW

Answers

1. All definitions can be found in the section and the Glossary.
2. It killed many of the birds that ate it and the animals that then ate the birds, and it poisoned some lakes and streams.
3. It was built on a toxic waste dump and caused serious health problems to the people who lived there.
4. Natural Resource Defense Council, Sierra Club, Audubon Society, Wilderness Society
5. Clean Air Act: set emission standards for vehicles and factories; Clean Water Act:

restricted discharge of pollutants into lakes and rivers; Endangered Species Act: established measures to save plant and animal species

6. The cartoonist is implying that President Ford basically gave the strip-mining interests permission to destroy the land and that he is "in their pocket."

7. Students' reports will vary, but should include details about the chosen disaster provided in the section.

Chapter 21 VISUAL SUMMARY

Visual/Spatial Have students make a two-column problem/solution chart matching challenges of the 1970s with solutions attempted. Tell them to list at least two domestic challenges and two foreign policy challenges in the left column and the attempted solutions in the right column. *(Sample entries for domestic might include racial problems and environmental threats in the left column, with affirmative action and creation of the EPA in the right column. Sample entries for foreign policy might include Cold War tensions and conflicts between Israel and neighbors in the left column, with Nixon's détente and Carter's brokered peace treaty in the right.)* **OL**

Expository Writing Have students select a foreign policy or domestic challenge that faced all three presidents. Have them write an essay comparing and contrasting the three presidents' responses to the issue. **OL**

A Era of Challenges

Major Domestic Issues of the 1970s
- A nation is divided and angry over the Vietnam War.
- An energy crisis is triggered by OPEC's raising of oil prices.
- A stagnant economy exists with both inflation and high unemployment.
- Ongoing racial problems occur in major cities.
- Growing awareness of environmental problems including air and water pollution, toxic waste (at Love Canal and other sites), the overuse of pesticides, plus a crisis with the nuclear power plant at Three Mile Island.

Major Foreign Policy Issues of the 1970s
- Cold War tensions continue with the Soviet Union and China.
- The Soviet Union invades Afghanistan.
- War between Israel and its Arab neighbors breaks out in 1973, and ongoing violence occurs in the Middle East.
- A revolution in Iran leads to the taking of American hostages.

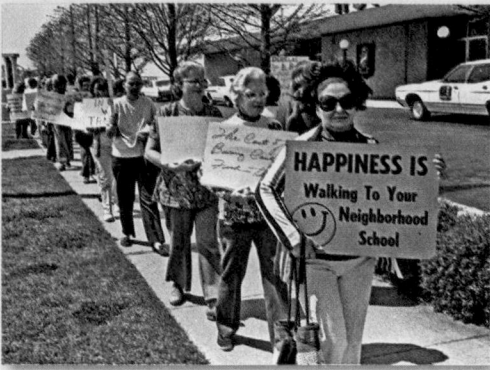

▲ *In the 1970s, state courts order the forced desegregation of public schools through busing, despite protests such as the one above in Memphis, Tennessee.*

▲ *Americans wait in long lines to purchase gasoline during the energy crisis of the 1970s.*

◄ *The first Earth Day in 1970 is often seen as the start of an organized environmentalist movement, which continues to have a major influence on politics and society today.*

New Policies and Activism

Responding to Domestic Issues
- Nixon attempts to win over Southern conservatives, but his administration's determination to win leads to the Watergate cover-up and Nixon's subsequent resignation.
- Ford's WIN campaign fails to overcome inflation.
- Carter urges Americans to conserve energy, creates the Department of Energy, and asks Congress to pass legislation deregulating the oil industry.
- Civil rights leaders propose affirmative action policies to reduce discrimination; the Supreme Court upholds some types of affirmative action in the *Bakke* case.
- Busing begins in northern cities to integrate schools.
- Environmentalist movement begins; Nixon creates the EPA.

Responding to Foreign Policy Issues
- Nixon and Kissinger introduce the policy of détente and begin talks with both the USSR and China.
- Carter mediates negotiations between Israel and Egypt leading to the first Arab-Israeli peace treaty.
- The United States imposes a grain embargo on the USSR for invading Afghanistan and boycotts the Moscow Olympics.
- The hostage crisis with Iran drags on for more than a year; an American rescue attempt fails, and the hostages are not released until Carter leaves office.

Hands-On Chapter Project
Step 6: Wrap Up

Oral History of the 1970s

Step 6: Wrap Up Students should present their final project to the class. They should explain what they learned in their research and interviews. Display final projects in the classroom.

Evaluating Ask students to evaluate their completed projects by answering the following questions in writing:

- Which part of the project was most demanding? Why?
- Which part of the project was the most interesting to me? Why?
- What did I learn from this project about American history? **OL**

STANDARDIZED TEST PRACTICE

TEST-TAKING TIP

Always manage your time during a test so you can go back and review all your answers.

Reviewing Vocabulary

Directions: Choose the word or words that best complete the sentence.

1. Richard Nixon used the _____ to attract more Southerners to the Republican Party.
   A détente
   B revenue sharing
   C Southern strategy
   D Dixiecrats

2. In *United States* v. *Nixon*, the Supreme Court found that President Nixon could not invoke _____ to prevent his tapes from being used as evidence in a criminal trial.
   A revenue sharing
   B habeas corpus
   C détente
   D executive privilege

3. During the 1970s, the U.S. economy was threatened by an oil _____ established by OPEC.
   A embargo
   B boycott
   C importation
   D duty

4. In the 1960s and 1970s, environmentalists began to combat issues such as _____ and other types of air pollution.
   A chemical runoff
   B DDT
   C smog
   D toxic waste

Reviewing Main Ideas

Directions: Choose the best answer for each of the following questions.

Section 1 *(pp. 706–711)*

5. Nixon developed a new program to try to make government more efficient known as
   A New Federalism.
   B the Silent Majority.
   C States' Rights.
   D the Great Society.

Section 2 *(pp. 712–717)*

6. Members of the Committee for the Re-election of the President broke into Democratic Party headquarters at the Watergate to
   A leave incriminating evidence of Democratic wrongdoing.
   B install a tape-recording device so that Nixon could write his memoirs.
   C find information to use in the case *United States* v. *Nixon*.
   D steal sensitive information and install wiretaps.

7. In the wake of the Watergate scandal, Congress passed a series of laws to accomplish which of the following goals?
   A to stop tape recordings in the White House
   B to limit the power of the presidency
   C to pardon Richard Nixon for his part in the cover-up
   D to remove police power from the FBI

Section 3 *(pp. 718–723)*

8. In the early 1970s, OPEC began to use oil as a political weapon against countries that
   A would not join their organization.
   B supported Israel's right to exist.
   C refused to pay the new per-barrel oil price.
   D supported Arab countries' disapproval of Israel.

Need Extra Help?								
If You Missed Questions . . .	1	2	3	4	5	6	7	8
Go to Page . . .	706–707	715	718	731	708	712–714	717	718

 GO ON

Reviewing Vocabulary

1. C This is a good place to reinforce the importance of reading the question carefully. The question asks about Nixon's strategy to attract more *Southerners* to the Republican Party—the Southern strategy.

2. D This question can be answered using the process of elimination. Revenue sharing, or the sharing of profits, does not make sense. Habeas corpus deals with lawful imprisonment. Détente is an easing of tensions. Executive privilege is literally the right of the executive branch to refuse to disclose information it feels would be harmful to the administration.

3. A A boycott is a refusal to buy a certain product. OPEC produced oil, it did not buy it from the U.S., so it would not boycott U.S. oil. Importation does not make sense; the U.S. economy would not be hurt by simple importation of oil. A duty is a tax or tariff, usually on foreign or incoming goods and does not work. OPEC caused economic problems when the OPEC embargo caused an oil shortage.

4. C The key words in the question are "air pollution." Only smog is air pollution. The other answer choices refer to polluted land and water.

Reviewing Main Ideas

5. A Federalism refers to a system of government in which power is shared/divided between the federal government and state governments. New Federalism was Nixon's plan to reduce federal programs and pass them on to the states. The Great Society was LBJ's plan.

6. D During a break-in, something is usually taken. In this case, sensitive information was taken. The break-in was not meant to plant evidence of any kind. It was an attempt to gain information. *B* does not make sense; Nixon would not need to secretly record the Democrats to write his own memoir. *U.S.* v. *Nixon* was a result of the break-in, not the reason for it.

7. B This is a cause-and-effect question. Students must choose the answer that was an effect of the Watergate scandal. Part of the scandal was the liberties taken by the executive branch. New laws affected things like campaign contribution and election laws.

8. B *A* does not make sense; OPEC is an organization of oil-producing nations that used its control of oil supply to try to influence the foreign policies of other nations by withholding product or raising prices. *C* is incorrect because if a nation did not want to buy the oil in the first place OPEC would have no recourse. *D* is the opposite of the correct answer.

735

Chapter 21

9. D Carter did not send troops to Afghanistan. *B* and *C* would not be appropriate actions to take to show displeasure with another nation; they are more like acts to prepare for war. An embargo on grain shipments to the USSR, however, was an attempt to punish the USSR directly for its invasion of Afghanistan.

10. A The case clearly relates to education, so students should be able to immediately eliminate *D*. The fact that the case involved a board of education should tell students that the case dealt with high-school or lower. This eliminates affirmative action, which applied to higher education. Segregation was illegal by 1971, so a case in 1971 would not uphold it.

11. C Section 504 was a landmark because it banned all discrimination on the basis of disability in all federally–funded programs. The Rehabilitation Act was not meant specifically for veterans, nor was it an education bill. The Architectural Barriers Act mandated physical access to new buildings built with federal funds.

12. B Students should associate "beginning" with "first" Earth Day. *A* was a precursor to the first Earth Day. The Clean Air Act was passed after the first Earth Day, and the Love Canal was found to be poisoned after that.

13. B This is another cause-and-effect question. Students who are unsure of the answer should ask themselves what they think is the most likely effect listed in the answer choices. China is a communist nation. The most likely effect is that, if the U.S. improved its relations with China, it would be open to improving its relationship with the USSR, which it did. *B* is the only positive answer choice.

---

9. To protest the Soviet Union's invasion of Afghanistan, President Carter took which of the following actions?

   A He sent U.S. Army troops to fight with the Afghans.

   B He put NATO forces in Europe on high alert.

   C He approved a buildup of U.S. nuclear weapons.

   D He placed an embargo on grain shipments to the USSR.

Section 4 *(pp. 724–729)*

10. The 1971 case *Swann v. Charlotte-Mecklenburg Board of Education* upheld the constitutionality of

   A busing

   B affirmative action

   C segregation

   D revenue sharing

11. Section 504 of the Rehabilitation Act of 1973 was significant because it

   A set aside money for helping injured veterans in their recovery.

   B mandated physical access to federal buildings.

   C banned agencies receiving federal funds from discriminating against people with disabilities.

   D guaranteed all young people a free and appropriately designed education.

Section 5 *(pp. 730–733)*

12. The unofficial beginning of the environmentalist movement occurred

   A when the Yannacones complained about the use of DDT.

   B on the first Earth Day in 1970.

   C when Congress passed the Clean Air Act.

   D after Love Canal was found to be poisoned.

Critical Thinking

Directions: Choose the best answers to the following questions.

13. What effect did the United States's improved relations with China have on its relations with the Soviet Union?

   A Tensions increased between the two nations.

   B The two nations were able to establish détente.

   C The Warsaw Pact began to break up.

   D The Soviet Union began to boycott American goods.

Base your answer to question 14 on the map below and your knowledge of Chapter 21.

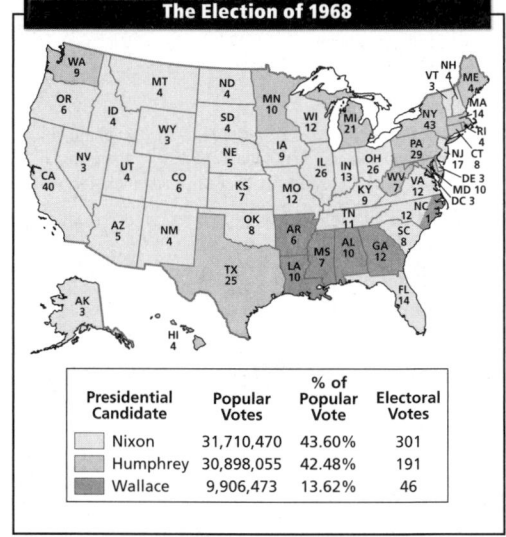

The Election of 1968

Presidential Candidate	Popular Votes	% of Popular Vote	Electoral Votes
Nixon	31,710,470	43.60%	301
Humphrey	30,898,055	42.48%	191
Wallace	9,906,473	13.62%	46

14. In the election of 1968, Nixon received the most support in the

   A North and South.

   B North and Midwest.

   C Midwest and West.

   D South and West.

Need Extra Help?

If You Missed Questions ...	9	10	11	12	13	14
Go to Page ...	723	725	729	730	711	706

GO ON ➤

14. C Nixon carried most of the West and Midwest.

15. In 1961, 67 Native American tribes issued the Declaration of Indian Purpose, which

  A demanded federal programs to create greater opportunities on reservations.

  B demanded that the Bill of Rights be recognized on reservations.

  C established the militant group American Indian Movement (AIM).

  D announced their decision to separate completely from the United States.

16. The result of the environmentalist legislation Congress passed in the 1970s was that

  A many corporations went bankrupt.

  B new renewable energy sources were developed.

  C air and water pollution was greatly reduced.

  D Rachel Carson published *Silent Spring*.

Analyze the cartoon and answer the question that follows. Base your answer on the cartoon and on your knowledge of Chapter 21.

Ranan Lurie, 1970.

17. According to this cartoon, who ultimately suffered over the arms buildup between the United States and the Soviet Union?

  A the military-industrial complex

  B the generals of both nations

  C the politicians of both nations

  D the taxpayers of both nations

Need Extra Help?						
If You Missed Questions . . .	15	16	17	18	19	20
Go to Page . . .	727	732	711	720–721	721	712–717

Document-Based Questions

Directions: Analyze the document and answer the short-answer questions that follow the document.

The following excerpt is from a magazine article that details the growing energy problems in the United States during the 1970s.

> *"Evidence of the full dimensions of the energy crisis in this country is becoming more clear every day.*
> - *As a first step to cut gasoline use, President Nixon was reportedly ready to order closing of service stations nationwide from 9 P.M. Saturday to midnight Sunday. . . .*
> - *Immediate rationing of gasoline and fuel oil is being urged on the President by top oil-industry executives. . . .*
> *One major piece of legislation . . . directs the President to take measures necessary to reduce the nation's energy demands by 25 percent within four weeks.*
>   *Speed limits would be cut nationally; lighting and heating of public and commercial buildings would be curtailed; home-owners would be given tax deductions to winterize their homes. . . .*
>   *Other pending measures would impose year-round daylight saving time and would open naval oil reserves for intense exploration."*
> —from *U.S. News & World Report*, December 3, 1973

18. What proposals did the U.S. government make to deal with the energy crisis?

19. What lessons do you think the United States might have learned from this crisis?

Extended Response

20. In a persuasive essay explain whether the Watergate scandal had a positive or negative effect on U.S. voters' view of politicians. In your essay, include evidence to support your opinion.

History ONLINE

For additional test practice, use Self-Check Quizzes—Chapter 21 at glencoe.com.

Document-Based Questions

18. Proposals included cutting speed limits, curtailing heat and lighting in public buildings, giving tax deductions to homeowners who winterized their homes, imposing year-round daylight savings time, and opening naval oil reserves for exploration. This is a good opener to discuss similarities and differences in energy conservation today.

19. Answers will vary, but students might note that after several years, Americans returned to driving large vehicles and other activities that did not conserve oil.

Extended Response

20. Essays will vary, but should express a clear point of view on the question and support their point of view with reasoned arguments and details from the chapter. Essays should demonstrate an understanding of the events of the Watergate scandal and the political changes it brought about.

15. A Students should remember that the Declaration of Indian Purpose was created by more then 400 members of 67 tribes and represented a moderate stance on Native American affairs. *B* is incorrect because the application of the Bill of Rights to reservations did not happen until 1968, seven years after the Declaration. AIM was a more militant group, and was not formed by the Declaration.

16. C *Silent Spring* was published in 1962; it could not have resulted from legislation in the 1970s. Remind students that the legislation passed in the 1970s included the Clean Air Act and the Clean Water Act, which led to reduction in air and water pollution.

17. D At the bottom of each "pile" in the cartoon, is a Soviet taxpayer and a U.S. taxpayer, being crushed by the piles. They are clearly suffering.

History ONLINE

Have students visit the Web site at glencoe.com to review Chapter 21 and take the Self-Check Quiz.

Need Extra Help?

Have students refer to the pages listed if they miss any of the questions.

Key to Ability Levels

BL Below Level	**AL** Above Level
OL On Level	**ELL** English Language Learners

Key to Teaching Resources

📁 Print Material	🔒 DVD
💿 CD-ROM	📇 Transparency

Levels					Resources	Chapter Opener	Section 1	Section 2	Section 3	Section 4	Chapter Assess
BL	OL	AL	ELL								
FOCUS											
BL	OL	AL	ELL	📇	Daily Focus Skills Transparencies		22-1	22-2	22-3	22-4	
TEACH											
	OL	AL		📁	Geography and History, URB				p. 3		
		AL		📁	American Literature Readings, URB				p. 13		
BL	OL		ELL	📁	Reading Essentials and Note-Taking Guide*		p. 233	p. 236	p. 239	p. 242	
	OL			📁	Historical Analysis Skills Activity, URB				p. 56		
BL	OL		ELL	📁	Guided Reading Activities, URB*		p. 80	p. 81	p. 82	p. 83	
BL	OL	AL	ELL	📁	Content Vocabulary Activity, URB*	p. 61					
BL	OL	AL	ELL	📁	Academic Vocabulary Activity, URB	p. 63					
	OL	AL		📁	Critical Thinking Skills Activity, URB					p. 66	
BL	OL		ELL	📁	Reading Skills Activity, URB					p. 55	
BL			ELL	📁	English Learner Activity, URB			p. 59			
	OL	AL		📁	Reinforcing Skills Activity, URB					p. 65	
BL	OL	AL	ELL	📁	Differentiated Instruction Activity, URB				p. 57		
BL	OL		ELL	📁	Time Line Activity, URB					p. 67	
	OL			📁	Linking Past and Present Activity, URB				p. 68		
BL	OL	AL	ELL	📁	American Art and Music Activity, URB						p. 73
BL	OL	AL	ELL	📁	Interpreting Political Cartoons Activity, URB			p. 75			
		AL		📁	Enrichment Activity, URB					p. 78	
BL	OL	AL	ELL	📁	American Biographies				✓		
BL	OL	AL	ELL	📁	Primary Source Reading, URB			p. 69	p. 71		
BL	OL	AL	ELL	📁	Supreme Court Case Studies				p. 129		
BL	OL	AL	ELL	📁	The Living Constitution*	✓	✓	✓	✓	✓	✓
	OL	AL		💿	American History Primary Source Documents Library	✓	✓	✓	✓	✓	✓
BL	OL	AL	ELL	📇	Unit Map Overlay Transparencies	✓	✓	✓	✓	✓	✓
BL	OL	AL	ELL	📁	Differentiated Instruction for the American High School Classroom	✓	✓	✓	✓	✓	✓
BL	OL	AL	ELL	🔒	StudentWorks™ Plus DVD	✓	✓	✓	✓	✓	✓

Note: Please refer to the *Unit 7 Resource Book* for this chapter's URB materials.

* Also available in Spanish

TeacherWorks Plus
All-In-One Planner and Resource Center

- Interactive Lesson Planner
- Interactive Teacher Edition
- Fully editable blackline masters
- Section Spotlight Videos Launch
- Differentiated Lesson Plans
- Printable reports of daily assignments
- Standards Tracking System

Levels					Resources	Chapter Opener	Section 1	Section 2	Section 3	Section 4	Chapter Assess
BL	OL	AL	ELL		**TEACH** (continued)						
BL	OL	AL	ELL	💿	**Vocabulary PuzzleMaker CD-ROM**	✓	✓	✓	✓	✓	✓
BL	OL	AL	ELL	💿	**American Music Hits Through History CD**	✓	✓	✓	✓	✓	✓
BL	OL	AL	ELL	📁	**Unit Time Line Transparencies and Activities**	✓	✓	✓	✓	✓	✓
BL	OL	AL	ELL	📁	**Cause and Effect Transparencies, Strategies, and Activities**	✓	✓	✓	✓	✓	✓
BL	OL	AL	ELL	📁	**Why It Matters Transparencies, Strategies, and Activities**	✓	✓	✓	✓	✓	✓
BL	OL	AL	ELL	📁	**American Issues**	✓	✓	✓	✓	✓	✓
	OL	AL	ELL	📁	**American Art and Architecture Transparencies, Strategies, and Activities**	✓	✓	✓	✓	✓	✓
BL	OL	AL		📁	**High School American History Literature Library**	✓	✓	✓	✓	✓	✓
BL	OL	AL	ELL	🔒	*The American Vision* **Video Program DVD**	✓	✓	✓	✓	✓	✓
				📁	**Strategies for Success**	✓	✓	✓	✓	✓	✓
				📁	**Success with English Learner**	✓	✓	✓	✓	✓	✓
Teacher Resources				📁	**Studies Classroom**	✓	✓	✓	✓	✓	✓
				🔒	**Presentation Plus! DVD**	✓	✓	✓	✓	✓	✓
					ASSESS						
BL	OL	AL	ELL	📁	**Section Quizzes and Chapter Tests***		p. 313	p. 314	p. 315	p. 316	p. 317
BL	OL	AL	ELL	📁	**Authentic Assessment With Rubrics**						p. 49
BL	OL	AL	ELL	📁	**Standardized Test Practice Workbook**						p. 51
BL	OL	AL	ELL	💿	*ExamView®* **Assessment Suite CD-ROM**		22-1	22-2	22-3	22-4	Ch. 22
BL	OL	AL	ELL	💿	**Interactive Tutor Self-Assessment CD-ROM**		22-1	22-2	22-3	22-4	Ch. 22
					CLOSE						
BL			ELL	📁	**Reteaching Activity, URB**						p. 77
BL	OL		ELL	📁	**Reading and Study Skills Foldables™**	p. 83					
BL	OL	AL	ELL	📁	**American History in Graphic Novel**				p. 87		

Chapter 22 Integrating Technology

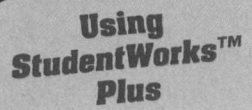

Using StudentWorks™ Plus

Daily Assignments and Grade Log

Technology Product

Glencoe's *StudentWorks™ Plus* CD-ROM contains everything your students need, including the complete Student Edition and access to all student workbooks. *StudentWorks™ Plus* also includes a Daily Assignment and Activity Log that allows students to

- record and track progress on their daily assignments and responsibilities;
- log results achieved, including their grades;
- sort assignments alphabetically or by category;
- view and print the assignment and grade log in a table or calendar format.

Objectives

Using *StudentWorks™ Plus* will help your students

- take responsibility for their individual tasks;
- improve independent study skills.

Steps

Provide students with the following information:
- Launch *StudentWorks™ Plus*.
- Select the **Daily Assignments and Grade Log** button at the bottom of the launch screen.
- Create a new file or open an existing one. The log is organized as a table, with a row of information for each assignment.
- Add information for each assignment, including the date of the assignment, the name, additional comments, the due date, and the grade.
- Edit rows as assignment information is provided or changed. Add a new row to the log for each new assignment.

History ONLINE

	Student	Teacher	Parent
Beyond the Textbook	●	●	●
Chapter Overviews	●	●	●
Time Current Events	●		●
ePuzzles and Games	●		●
Concepts in Motion	●		●
Literature Connections		●	
Multi-Language Glossaries	●		●
Online Student Edition	●	●	●
Self-Check Quizzes	●		●
Student Web Activities	●		●
Study Central™	●		●
Teaching Today		●	
Vocabulary eFlashcards	●		●
Web Activity Lesson Plans		●	

Glencoe Media Center

glencoe.com

❯ **Study-To-Go**
- Vocabulary eFlashcards
- Self-Check Quizzes

❯ **Audio/Video**
- Student Edition Audio
- Spanish Summaries
- Section Videos

- **Timed Readings Plus in Social Studies** helps students increase their reading rate and fluency while maintaining comprehension. The 400-word passages are similar to those found on state and national assessments.

- **Reading in the Content Area: Social Studies** concentrates on six essential reading skills that help students better comprehend what they read. The book includes 75 high-interest nonfiction passages written at increasing levels of difficulty.

- **Reading Social Studies** includes strategic reading instruction and vocabulary support in Social Studies content for both ELLs and native speakers of English.

www.jamestowneducation.com

Index to National Geographic Magazine:

The following articles relate to this chapter:

- "A Broken Empire," by Mike Edwards, March 1993.

- "Persian Gulf Pollution: Assessing the Damage One Year Later," by Sylvia Earle, February 1992.

National Geographic Society Products To order the following, call National Geographic at 1-800-368-2728:

- *ZipZapMap! USA* (ZipZapMap!)

Access National Geographic's new, dynamic MapMachine Web site and other geography resources at:

www.nationalgeographic.com
www.nationalgeographic.com/maps

The following videotape programs are available from Glencoe as supplements to Chapter 22:

- Ronald Reagan: The Role of a Lifetime (ISBN 1-56-501808-7)

- The Class of the 20th Century; Vol. 6 1976–1990 (ISBN 1-56-501052-3)

To order, call Glencoe at 1-800-334-7344. To find classroom resources to accompany many of these videos, check the following home pages:

A&E Television: www.aetv.com
The History Channel: www.historychannel.com

Reading List Generator CD-ROM

Use this database to search more than 30,000 titles to create a customized reading list for your students.

- Reading lists can be organized by students' reading level, author, genre, theme, or area of interest.

- The database provides Degrees of Reading Power™ (DRP) and Lexile™ readability scores for all selections.

- A brief summary of each selection is included.

Leveled reading suggestions for this chapter:

For students at a Grade 8 reading level:
- *The Cold War: An Uneasy Peace: 1945–1980,* by Craig E. Blohm

For students at a Grade 9 reading level:
- *The Persian Gulf War: The War Against Iraq,* by Don Nardo

For students at a Grade 10 reading level:
- *The Iran-Iraq War,* by David Schaffer

For students at a Grade 11 reading level:
- *Challenger,* by Sandra Bricker

For students at a Grade 12 reading level:
- *The Cold War Ends: 1980 to the Present,* by Britta Bjornlund

Focus

MAKING CONNECTIONS
Are There Cycles in American Politics?

Have students read the Making Connections paragraph. Then ask students to think of any other time when voters elected a conservative president. Students may recall the election of 1920, in which voters elected Republican Warren G. Harding after the changes of the Progressive Era and World War I; students may also note that voters elected Republican Dwight D. Eisenhower in 1952 after the traumas of the Great Depression and World War II. In 1980 conservative ideas may have appealed to voters after the Vietnam War, Watergate, and the energy crisis of the early 1970s. **OL**

Teach

The Big Ideas

As students study the chapter, remind them to consider the section-based Big Ideas included in each section's Guide to Reading. The **Essential Questions** in the activities below tie in to the Big Ideas and help students think about and understand important chapter concepts. In addition, the Hands-on Chapter Projects with their culminating activities relate the content from each section to the Big Ideas. These activities build on each other as students progress through the chapter. Section activities culminate in the wrap-up activity on the Visual Summary page.

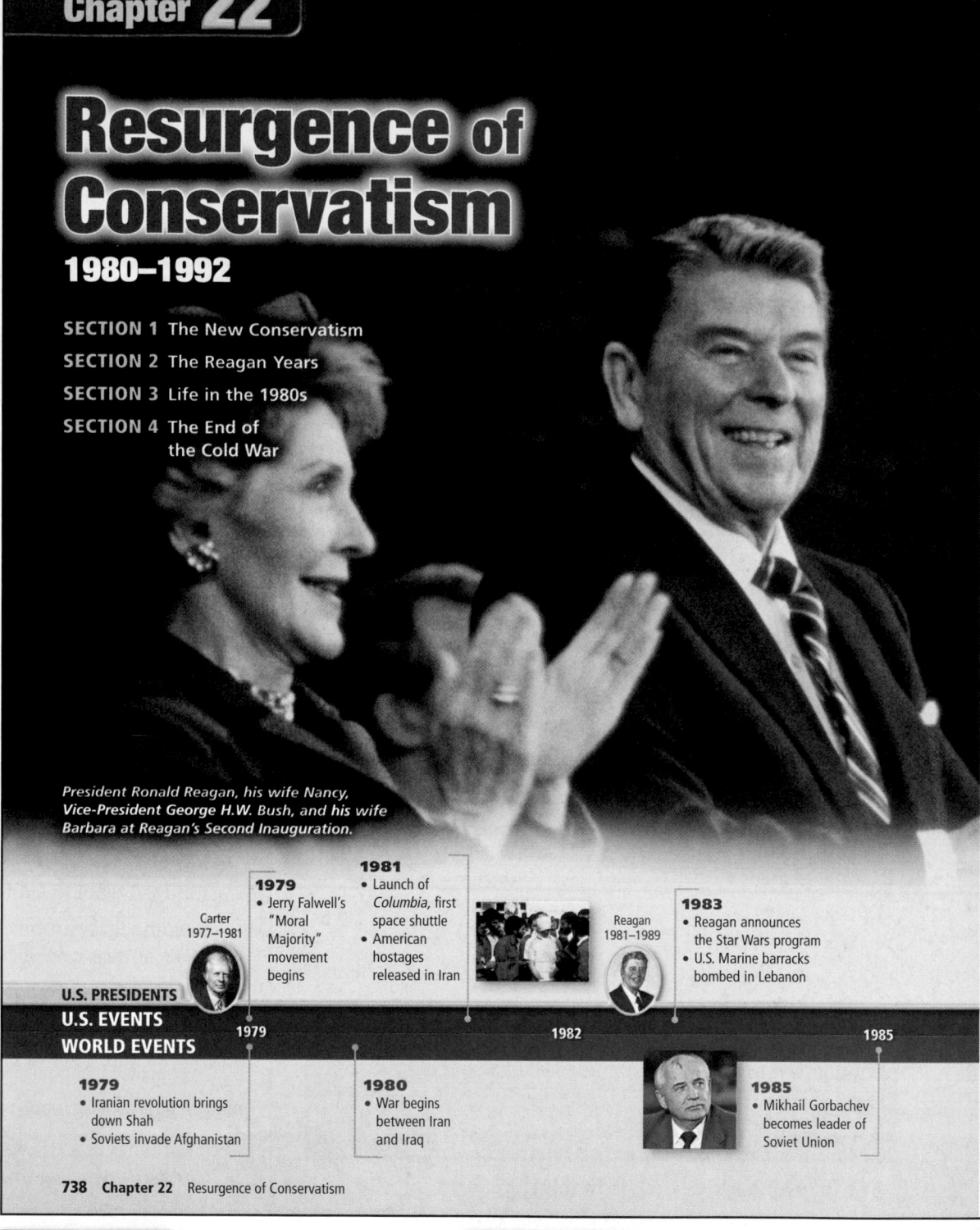

Chapter 22

Resurgence of Conservatism
1980–1992

SECTION 1 The New Conservatism
SECTION 2 The Reagan Years
SECTION 3 Life in the 1980s
SECTION 4 The End of the Cold War

President Ronald Reagan, his wife Nancy, Vice-President George H.W. Bush, and his wife Barbara at Reagan's Second Inauguration.

Carter 1977–1981

1979
• Jerry Falwell's "Moral Majority" movement begins

1981
• Launch of *Columbia*, first space shuttle
• American hostages released in Iran

Reagan 1981–1989

1983
• Reagan announces the Star Wars program
• U.S. Marine barracks bombed in Lebanon

U.S. PRESIDENTS
U.S. EVENTS
WORLD EVENTS

1979   1982   1985

1979
• Iranian revolution brings down Shah
• Soviets invade Afghanistan

1980
• War begins between Iran and Iraq

1985
• Mikhail Gorbachev becomes leader of Soviet Union

738   Chapter 22   Resurgence of Conservatism

Section 1

The New Conservatism
Essential Question: What political changes following World War II supported the growth of political conservatism? *(The focus on defeating the Soviet Union renewed debate about the role and power of the federal government. Some saw the Cold War as a religious fight between good and evil, which increased the influence of conservatives in politics.)* Tell students that Section 1 will discuss the rise of the new conservative coalition in the early 1980s. **OL**

Section 2

The Reagan Years
Essential Question: Are American politics characterized by conflict or cooperation? *(Government is actually designed for both, but excessive conflict makes it run less effectively.)* Tell students that many citizens in the early 1980s were ready to combat a government they believed was increasingly controlling their lives. Section 2 tells how the Reagan presidency brought a different attitude and approach to government. **OL**

Introducing Chapter 22

MAKING CONNECTIONS
Are There Cycles in American Politics?

After several decades where progressive and liberal ideas dominated American politics, conservatism began making a comeback in the 1970s, and in 1980 voters elected the conservative Ronald Reagan president. Reagan's commitment to less government regulation, a stronger military, and uncompromising anticommunism seemed to meet voters' concerns.

- *Why do you think conservative ideas appealed to more Americans in the 1980s?*
- *How do you think conservative ideas have changed society?*

1986
- Iran-Contra scandal enters the news

1987
- INF Treaty between U.S. and USSR

1988
- More than 35,000 cases of AIDS diagnosed for the year

G. Bush 1989–1993

1991
- Persian Gulf War occurs between Iraq and UN coalition

1988

1991

1989
- Tiananmen Square protest in China
- Communist governments in Eastern Europe collapse

1990
- Germany reunites as one nation

1991
- Soviet Union dissolves

FOLDABLES

Analyzing Information Create a Folded Chart Foldable to organize information about the government under Ronald Reagan. List domestic and foreign policy for three eras: before the Reagan era, the Reagan administration, and the post-Reagan years.

The Reagan Revolution	Before Reagan	Reagan Era	After Reagan
Domestic Policy			
Foreign Policy			

History ONLINE Chapter Overview
Visit glencoe.com to preview Chapter 22.

Chapter 22   Resurgence of Conservatism   **739**

More About the Photo

Visual Literacy When the Watergate scandal forced Richard Nixon to resign from the presidency in 1974, most political observers assumed that it would take at least a generation for the Republican Party to restore its integrity in the eyes of American voters. Instead, the election of Ronald Reagan in 1980 reflected the continuing strength of conservatism. Reagan appealed to economic conservatives, social conservatives, and "tough on communism" conservatives.

FOLDABLES Study Organizer Dinah Zike's Foldables

Dinah Zike's Foldables are three-dimensional, interactive graphic organizers that help students practice basic writing skills, review vocabulary terms, and identify main ideas. Instructions for creating and using Foldables can be found in the Appendix at the end of this book and in the *Dinah Zike's Reading and Study Skills Foldables* booklet.

History ONLINE
Introduce students to chapter content and key terms by having them access the Chapter 22 Overview at glencoe.com.

Section 3
Life in the 1980s
Essential Question: What are the greatest social problems in the United States today? Have students list the problems they see as the most important today. *(drugs, AIDS, alcoholism, crime)* Tell students that Section 3 will examine how activists in the 1980s addressed the social issues of the decade. **OL**

Section 4
The End of the Cold War
Essential Question: What areas of problems do presidents face? *(foreign policy: diplomacy, treaties, trade policies, military; domestic policy: homeland security, education, health care, taxes, transportation)* Tell students that as they read Section 4, they will learn how the first President Bush's foreign policy was popular, while his domestic agenda was not. **OL**

739

Focus

Bellringer
Daily Focus Transparency 22.1

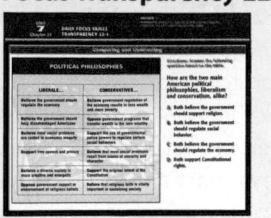

Guide to Reading

Answers:

Students should complete the outline by including all headings in the section.

I. Liberalism and Conservatism
   A. Liberalism
   B. Conservatism
II. Conservatism Revives
   A. The Role of the Cold War
   B. Conservatives Organize
   C. The Rise of the Sunbelt
   D. Sunbelt Conservatism
   E. Suburban Conservatism
   F. The Religious Right
   G. A New Coalition

Section Spotlight Video

To generate student interest and provide a springboard for class discussion, access the Chapter 22, Section 1 video at glencoe.com or on the video DVD.

Resource Manager

Section 1

The New Conservatism

Guide to Reading

Big Ideas
Economics and Society High taxes as well as economic and moral concerns led the country toward a new conservatism.

Content Vocabulary
• liberal (p. 740)
• conservative (p. 740)
• "televangelist" (p. 745)

Academic Vocabulary
• indicate (p. 745)
• stability (p. 745)

People and Events to Identify
• William F. Buckley (p. 743)
• Sunbelt (p. 743)
• Billy Graham (p. 745)
• Jerry Falwell (p. 745)
• "Moral Majority" (p. 745)

Reading Strategy
Taking Notes Use the major headings of this section to outline information about the rise of the new conservatism in the United States.

The New Conservatism
I. Liberalism and Conservatism
   A.
   B.
II.
   A.

By the 1980s, new levels of discontent with government and society had left many Americans concerned about the direction of the nation. Some began to call for a return to more conservative approaches and values.

Liberalism and Conservatism

MAIN Idea Conservatives and liberals disagreed on the role of government.

HISTORY AND YOU Do you consider yourself liberal or conservative? Why? Read on to learn more about conservative and liberal ideas of government.

Midge Decter, a New Yorker and a writer for the conservative publication *Commentary*, was appalled at the violence that hit her city on a hot July night in 1977. On the night of July 13, the power failed in New York City. The blackout left millions of people in darkness, and looting and arson rocked the city. City officials and the media blamed the lawlessness on the anger and despair of youth in neglected areas. Decter disagreed:

PRIMARY SOURCE

"[T]hose young men went on their spree of looting because they had been given permission to do so . . . by all the papers and magazines, movies and documentaries—all the outlets for the purveying of enlightened liberal attitude and progressive liberal policy—which had for years and years been proclaiming that race and poverty were sufficient excuses for lawlessness. . . ."

—quoted in *Commentary*, September 1977

Midge Decter's article blaming liberalism for the New York riots illustrates one side of a debate in American politics that continues to the present day. On one side are people who call themselves **liberals;** on the other side are those who identify themselves as **conservatives.** Liberal ideas had dominated American politics in the 1960s, but conservative ideas regained significant support in the 1970s, and in 1980 Ronald Reagan, a strong conservative, was elected president.

Liberalism

In American politics today, people who call themselves liberals believe several basic ideas. In general, liberals believe that the government should regulate the economy to protect people from the

---

R Reading Strategies	**C** Critical Thinking	**D** Differentiated Instruction	**W** Writing Support	**S** Skill Practice
Teacher Edition • Summarizing, p. 741 **Additional Resources** • Guided Read. Act., URB p. 80	**Teacher Edition** • Making Generalizations, p. 743 **Additional Resources** • Quizzes/Tests, p. 313	**Teacher Edition** • Visual/Spatial, p. 744	**Teacher Edition** • Persuasive Writing, p. 744 • Narrative Writing, p. 743 **Additional Resources** • Cont. Vocab. Act., URB p. 61 • Academic Vocab. Act., URB p. 63	**Teacher Edition** • Analyzing Visuals, p. 741 • Reading a Map, p. 742 **Additional Resources** • RENTG, p. 233

POLITICAL CARTOONS PRIMARY SOURCE
Liberalism vs. Conservatism

▲ Conservatives believe the liberal concern with achieving social equality and alleviating poverty is often taken to excess. They also disapprove of the idea of using the power of government to redistribute wealth from one group to another, preferring that the free market determine the distribution of wealth.

▲ Liberals believe that the conservative concern with keeping taxes low comes at the expense of other social needs and that conservatives who want low taxes are uncaring when it comes to helping the less fortunate.

Analyzing VISUALS

1. **Interpreting** In the cartoon on the left, what is the artist implying about Democratic policies?
2. **Identifying** In the cartoon on the right, what criticisms of tax breaks does the artist illustrate?

---

power of large corporations and wealthy elites. Liberals also believe that the government, particularly the federal government, should play an active role in helping disadvantaged Americans, partly through social programs and partly by putting more of society's tax burden on wealthier people.

Although liberals favor government intervention in the economy, they are suspicious of any attempt by the government to regulate social behavior. They are strong supporters of free speech and privacy, and are opposed to the government supporting or endorsing religious beliefs. They believe that a diverse society made up of different races, cultures, and ethnic groups will be more creative and energetic.

Liberals often support higher taxes on the wealthy, partly because they believe that those with greater assets should shoulder more of the costs of government and partly because it allows the government to redistribute wealth through government programs and thereby make society more equal.

Conservatism

Unlike liberals, conservatives distrust the power of government. They believe governmental power should be divided into different branches and split between the state and federal levels to limit its ability to intrude into people's lives.

Conservatives believe that when government regulates the economy, it makes the economy less efficient, resulting in less wealth and more poverty. They believe that free enterprise is the best economic system, and argue that if people and businesses are free to make their own economic choices, there will be more wealth and a higher standard of living for everyone.

For this reason, conservatives generally oppose high taxes and government programs that transfer wealth from the rich to those who are less wealthy. They believe that taxes and government programs discourage investment, take away people's incentive to work hard, and reduce the amount of freedom in society.

Chapter 22 Resurgence of Conservatism **741**

Teach

S Skill Practice

Analyzing Visuals Have students study the political cartoons on this page. **Ask:** Based on the cartoons, what are two major differences between the liberal and conservative philosophies? *(taxation and the redistribution of wealth)* **OL**

R Reading Strategy

Summarizing Have students write two paragraphs, one summarizing the key beliefs of liberals and one summarizing the key beliefs of conservatives. Encourage students to share their summaries with the class. **OL**

Analyzing VISUALS

Answers:
1. Democrats support the redistribution of wealth through high taxes.
2. Tax breaks negatively affect manufacturing, industry, and welfare.

Hands-On Chapter Project
Step 1

Conducting an Opinion Poll

Step 1: Listing Priorities Tell students they will be conducting an opinion poll on President Ronald Reagan's performance as president.

Organizing Have students review the material presented in Section 1 to compile a list of the issues that were most important to Americans in the 1980s. **OL**

(Chapter Project continued on page 747)

S Skill Practice

Reading a Map Have students study the map. **Ask:** What Sunbelt states did not experience significant growth between 1950 and 1980? *(North Carolina, South Carolina, Tennessee, Alabama, Mississippi, and Arkansas)* **BL**

Analyzing GEOGRAPHY

Answers:
1. California, Texas, and Florida
2. Answers will vary, but students might note that people moved to states that already had a strong infrastructure and a health care system.

✔ Reading Check

Answer:
Liberals often look to government to solve problems and seek government intervention in the economy to protect people from the power of big business; conservatives prefer small government and look to the free enterprise system to guide the economy.

Additional Support

The more the government regulates the economy, conservatives argue, the more it will have to regulate every aspect of people's behavior. Ultimately, conservatives fear, the government will so restrict people's economic freedom that Americans will no longer be able to improve their standard of living and get ahead in life.

Many conservatives believe that religious faith is vitally important in sustaining society. They believe most social problems result from issues of morality and character—issues, they argue, that are best addressed through commitment to a religious faith and through the private efforts of churches, individuals, and communities to help those in need. Despite this general belief, conservatives do support the use of the governmental police powers to regulate social behavior in some instances.

✔ Reading Check **Contrasting** How do liberal and conservative opinions about government differ?

Conservatism Revives

MAIN Idea Geographical regions tend to support either liberal or conservative ideas.

HISTORY AND YOU Politically, how would you define yourself or the region in which you live? Read on to learn about the growing political power of voters in the Southwest.

During the New Deal era of the 1930s, conservative ideas lost much of their influence in national politics. Following World War II, however, conservatism began to revive.

The Role of the Cold War

Support for conservative ideas began to revive for two major reasons, both related to the Cold War. First, the struggle against communism revived the debate about the role of the government in the economy. Some Americans believed that liberal economic ideas

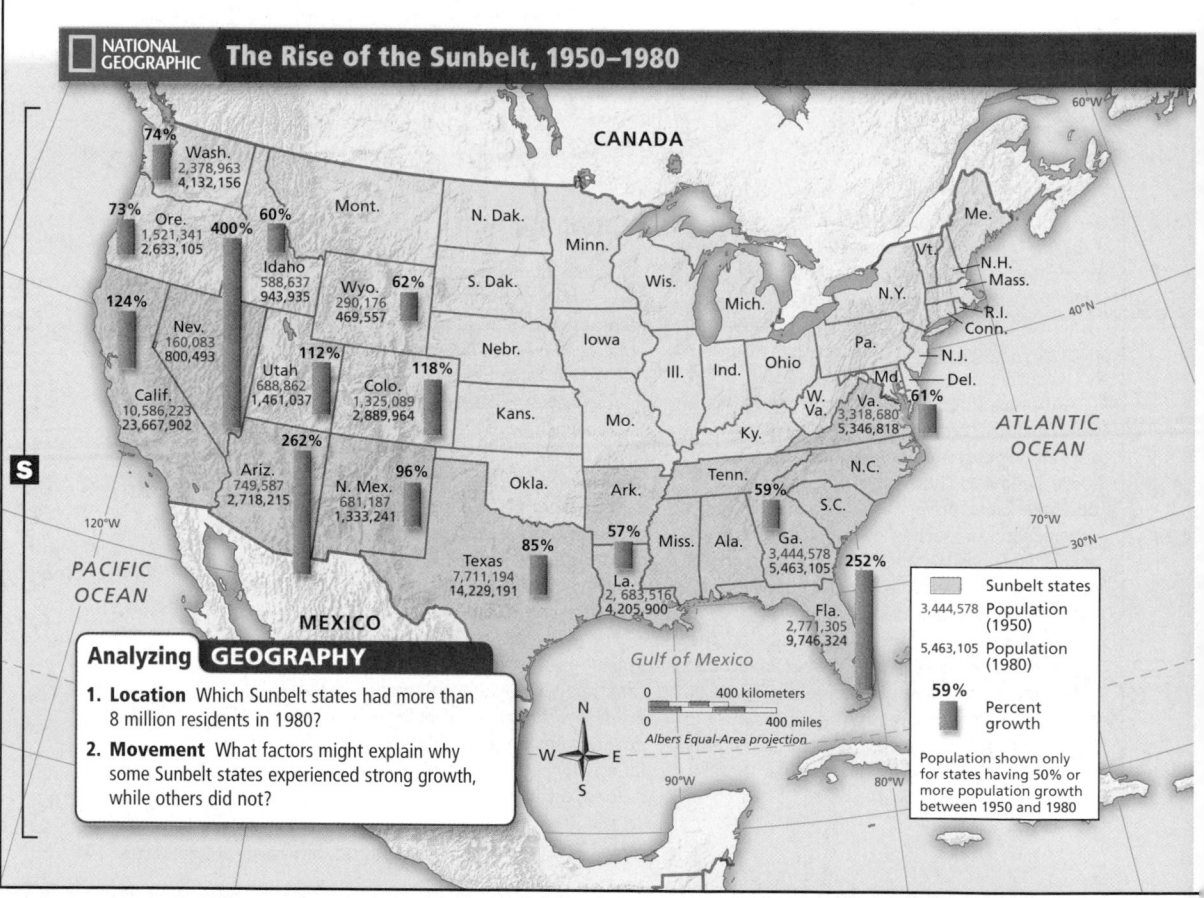

NATIONAL GEOGRAPHIC **The Rise of the Sunbelt, 1950–1980**

Analyzing GEOGRAPHY

1. **Location** Which Sunbelt states had more than 8 million residents in 1980?
2. **Movement** What factors might explain why some Sunbelt states experienced strong growth, while others did not?

Legend:
- Sunbelt states
- 3,444,578 Population (1950)
- 5,463,105 Population (1980)
- 59% Percent growth

Population shown only for states having 50% or more population growth between 1950 and 1980

Activity: Interdisciplinary Connection

Mathematics Provide the population data for the United States and selected Sunbelt states, as shown below. Explain that although you can see that the population of these states increased between 1950 and 1980, the real significance appears when you express each state's population as a percentage of the country's total population. Have students calculate each state's population, in the selected years, as a percentage of the total U.S. population **OL**

	1950	1960		1970	1980
U.S. Total	151,868,000	179,975,000	U.S. Total	203,302,000	226,546,000
Arizona	750,000	1,302,000	Arizona	1,775,000	2,718,000
California	10,586,000	15,717,000	California	19,971,000	23,668,000
Florida	2,771,000	4,952,000	Florida	6,791,000	9,746,000
Texas	7,712,000	9,580,000	Texas	11,199,000	14,229,000

were slowly leading the United States toward communism and set out to stop this trend. They also thought the United States had failed to stop the spread of Soviet power because liberals did not fully understand the need for a strong anticommunist foreign policy.

At the same time, many Americans viewed the Cold War in religious terms. Communism rejects religion and emphasizes the material side of life. To Americans with a deep religious faith, the struggle against communism was a struggle between good and evil. Liberalism, which emphasizes economic welfare, gradually lost the support of many religious Americans, who increasingly turned to conservatism.

Conservatives Organize

In 1955 a young conservative named **William F. Buckley** founded a new magazine called *National Review*. Buckley's magazine helped to revive conservative ideas in the United States. Buckley debated in front of college students and appeared on radio and television shows, spreading conservative ideas to an even wider audience.

Within the Republican Party, conservatives, particularly young conservatives, began to demand a greater role in party decision-making. In 1960 some 90 young conservative leaders met at Buckley's family estate and founded Young Americans for Freedom (YAF), an independent conservative group, to push for their ideas and to support conservative candidates.

By 1964 the new conservative movement had achieved enough influence within the Republican Party to enable the conservative Barry Goldwater to win the nomination for president. To the dismay of the conservatives, however, President Johnson easily defeated Goldwater and won the election in a landslide.

The Rise of the Sunbelt

One of the problems facing conservatives in the 1950s and early 1960s was that their votes were split between the Republicans and the Democrats. Two regions of the country, the South and the West, were more conservative than other areas. Southern conservatives, however, usually voted for the Democrats, while

conservatives in the West voted Republican. This meant that the party that won the heavily populated Northeast would win the election. Since the Northeast strongly supported liberal ideas, both parties were pulled toward liberal policies.

This pattern began to change during World War II, when large numbers of Americans moved south and west to take jobs in the war factories. The movement to the South and West—together known as the **Sunbelt**—continued after the war. As the Sunbelt's economy expanded, Americans living in those regions began to view the federal government differently from people living in the Northeast.

Sunbelt Conservatism

Industry in the Northeast was in decline, leading to the region's nickname—the Rust Belt. This region had higher unemployment than any other, and its cities were congested and polluted. These problems prompted Americans in the Northeast to look to the government for programs and regulations that would help them solve their problems.

In contrast, many Americans in the Sunbelt opposed high taxes and federal regulations that might interfere with their region's growth. Many white Southerners were also angry with the Democrats for supporting civil rights, which they interpreted as an effort by the federal government to impose its policies on the South.

When Barry Goldwater argued in 1964 that the federal government was becoming too strong, many Southerners agreed. For the first time since Reconstruction, they began voting Republican in large numbers. Although Goldwater lost, he showed Republicans that the best way to attract Southern votes was to support conservative policies.

Americans living in the West also responded to conservative criticism of the federal government. Westerners were proud of their frontier heritage and spirit of "rugged individualism." They resented federal environmental regulations that limited ranching, controlled water use, and restricted the development of the region's natural resources. Western anger over such policies inspired the "Sagebrush Rebellion" of the early 1970s—a widespread protest led by conservatives against federal laws that they felt were hindering the region's development.

Writing Support

Narrative Writing Invite students to use library and Internet resources to write a one-page biography of William F. Buckley. Students should include a discussion of his early life and of his successes in organizing the conservative movement. Encourage students to share their biographies with the class. **OL**

Critical Thinking

Making Generalizations Have interested students use library or Internet resources to find out more information about the growth of the Republican Party in the South during the 1960s and 1970s. **Ask:** Do you think racism played a role in the growth of the Republican Party during the 1960s and 1970s? Why or why not? *(Answers will vary, but students should base their answers on their research.)* **AL**

Additional Support

Activity: Interdisciplinary Connection

Civics Have students examine the income, property, and sales tax rate structure in their state. Then have them prepare a visual display of the rates to use during a brief oral presentation in which they either support the state's current tax policies or propose a plan to raise or lower taxes. **OL**

D Differentiated Instruction

Visual/Spatial Have students research the last presidential election to see whether the Sunbelt states followed recent trends by voting for the conservative candidate. Have them create a chart or map showing their results. **OL**

W Writing Support

Persuasive Writing Have students use library or Internet resources to learn more about Howard Jarvis and other proponents of tax cuts. Have them use their findings to decide whether they favor tax cuts or not. Then have them write a letter to their governor persuading him or her to support their point of view. **OL**

Analyzing VISUALS

Answers:
1. They are white; answers will vary.
2. Students might note that those whose primary concern was the Cold War might leave after the Soviet Union collapsed in 1991.

Differentiated Instruction

PRIMARY SOURCE

The Conservative Coalition

The new conservative coalition that emerged in the 1970s was made up of people from the South and West, particularly middle class suburban voters, evangelical Christians, and people concerned about high taxes and resisting the Soviet Union in the Cold War.

▲ Evangelical Christians including supporters of Jerry Falwell (photo left corner) were a major force behind the conservative resurgence.

▲ Voters in the suburbs (top) and rural west (above) increasingly voted conservative in the 1980s.

Analyzing VISUALS

1. **Inferring** What do you notice about the ethnicity of most people in the conservative coalition? Why do you think other groups were not as well represented?
2. **Speculating** What groups in the coalition would be most likely to leave it in the future? Why?

D By 1980, the population of the Sunbelt had surpassed that of the Northeast. This gave the conservative regions of the country more electoral votes. With Southerners also shifting to the Republican Party, conservatives began to build a coalition that could elect a president.

Suburban Conservatism

As riots erupted and crime soared during the 1960s and 1970s, many Americans moved to suburbs to escape the chaos of the cities. Even there, however, they found the quiet middle-class lifestyle they desired to be in danger. The rapid inflation of the 1970s had caused the buying power of middle-class families to shrink while taxes remained high.

W Many Americans resented the taxes they had to pay for New Deal and Great Society programs when they themselves were losing ground economically. In 1978 Howard Jarvis, a conservative activist, launched the first successful tax revolt in California with Proposition 13, a referendum on the state ballot that greatly reduced property taxes.

Soon afterward anti-tax movements appeared in other states, and tax cuts quickly became a national issue. For many Americans, the conservative idea that the government had become too big meant simply that taxes were too high. As conservatives began to call for tax cuts, the middle class flocked to their cause. **W**

The Religious Right

While many Americans turned to conservatism for economic reasons, others were drawn to it because they feared that American society had lost touch with its traditional values. For many Americans of conservative religious faith, the events of the 1960s and 1970s were shocking. The Supreme Court decision in *Roe* v. *Wade,* which established that the right to have an abortion was protected by the Constitution, greatly concerned them. They were also critical of other Supreme Court decisions that limited

744 Chapter 22 Resurgence of Conservatism

Leveled Activities

prayer in public schools and expanded protections for people accused of crimes.

The feminist movement and the push for the Equal Rights Amendment (ERA) also upset some religious Americans because it seemed to represent an assault on the traditional family. Many religious conservatives were shocked by the behavior of some university students in the 1960s, whose contempt for authority seemed to **indicate** a general breakdown in American values and morality. These concerns helped expand the conservative cause into a mass movement.

Although religious conservatives included people of many faiths, the largest group was evangelical Protestants. Evangelicals believe that they are saved from their sins through conversion (which they refer to as being "born again") and a personal commitment to follow Jesus Christ, whose death and resurrection reconciles them to God.

After World War II, a religious revival began in the United States among Protestant evangelicals. Protestant ministers, such as **Billy Graham** and Oral Roberts, built national followings. By the late 1970s, about 70 million Americans described themselves as "born again." Protestant evangelicals owned their own newspapers, magazines, radio stations, and television networks.

Television in particular allowed evangelical ministers to reach a large nationwide audience. These **"televangelists,"** as they were soon called, included Marion "Pat" Robertson, who founded the Christian Broadcasting Network, and **Jerry Falwell,** who used his television show *The Old-Time Gospel Hour* to found a movement that he called the **"Moral Majority."** Using television and mail campaigns, the Moral Majority built up a network of ministers to register new voters who backed conservative candidates and issues. Falwell later claimed to have registered 2 million new voters by 1980.

A New Coalition

By the end of the 1970s, a new conservative coalition of voters had begun to come together. Although the members of this coalition were concerned with many different issues, they were held together by a common belief that American society had somehow lost its way.

The Watergate scandal, high taxes, and special interest politics had undermined many Americans' faith in their government. Rising unemployment, rapid inflation, and the energy crisis had shaken their confidence in the economy. Riots, crime, and drug abuse suggested that society itself was falling apart. The retreat from Vietnam, the hostage crisis in Iran, and the Soviet invasion of Afghanistan seemed to make the nation look weak and helpless internationally. Many Americans were tired of change and upheaval. They wanted **stability** and a return to what they remembered as a better time. For some, the new conservatism and its most prominent spokesperson, Ronald Reagan, offered hope to a nation in distress.

✔ Reading Check **Summarizing** Why did many Americans begin to support the conservative movement?

Section 1 REVIEW

Vocabulary
1. **Explain** the significance of: liberal, conservative, William F. Buckley, Sunbelt, Billy Graham, "televangelist," Jerry Falwell, "Moral Majority."

Main Ideas
2. **Explaining** Why do liberals sometimes support higher taxes on the wealthy?

3. **Determining Cause and Effect** What was the cause of the Sagebrush Rebellion in the 1970s?

Critical Thinking
4. **Big Ideas** What kind of economy do conservatives want?

5. **Organizing** Use a graphic organizer similar to the one below to list conservative beliefs.

Conservative Beliefs

6. **Analyzing Visuals** Study the map of the Sunbelt on page 742. What impact would the migration patterns shown have on representation in the U.S. House of Representatives?

Writing About History
7. **Persuasive Writing** Many conservatives believe that "government that governs least, governs best." Write a paragraph supporting or opposing this statement.

History ONLINE
Study Central™ To review this section, go to glencoe.com and click on Study Central.

745

Assess

History ONLINE

Study Central™ provides summaries, interactive games, and online graphic organizers to help students review content.

Close

Summarizing Ask: Why did many Americans become more conservative in the 1960s and 1970s? *(They believed the federal government was too big and interfering in their lives; they wanted stability and longed for a return to what they remembered as better times.)* **OL**

✔ **Reading Check**

Answer:
They wanted stability and a return to what they remembered as a better time.

Section 1 REVIEW

Answers

1. All definitions can be found in the section and the Glossary.

2. They believe the government should play an active role in helping disadvantaged Americans, partly by putting more of society's tax burden on wealthier people.

3. Westerners believed that government policies were hindering the region's development.

4. Conservatives want a free enterprise system.

5. free enterprise, emphasis on religious values, little government regulation of the economy

6. The number of representatives from the Sunbelt would increase.

7. Paragraphs will vary, but students should use information from the textbook and outside resources as needed.

Focus

Bellringer
Daily Focus Transparency 22.2

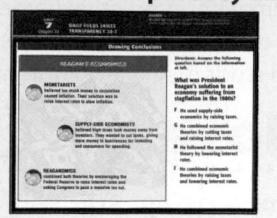

Guide to Reading

Answers may include:
High taxes take away money that could be invested; Cutting taxes will generate capital to make new and larger businesses and new jobs; Larger supply of consumer goods will cause more spending.

Section Spotlight Video

To generate student interest and provide a springboard for class discussion, access the Chapter 22, Section 2 video at glencoe.com or on the video DVD.

Resource Manager

Section 2

The Reagan Years

Guide to Reading

Big Ideas
Trade, War, and Migration During the Cold War, President Reagan reinforced the idea that the United States had to take strong action to resist the spread of Communist influence abroad.

Content Vocabulary
• supply-side economics (p. 748)
• budget deficit (p. 749)
• "mutual assured destruction" (p. 753)

Academic Vocabulary
• confirmation (p. 750)
• visible (p. 751)

People and Events to Identify
• Reaganomics (p. 748)
• Iran-Contra scandal (p. 752)
• Mikhail Gorbachev (p. 753)

Reading Strategy
Organizing Complete a graphic organizer similar to the one below by filling in the major points of the supply-side theory of economics.

In 1980 Americans elected Ronald Reagan president. Reagan cut taxes, deregulated several industries, and appointed conservative justices. He began a massive military buildup that greatly increased the deficit and sent aid to insurgent groups fighting communism.

The Road to the White House

MAIN Idea President Reagan's experiences in Hollywood and as governor of California led to his successful campaign for the presidency.

HISTORY AND YOU How could a previous career as a movie star help someone get elected to public office? Read on to learn more about the way that President Reagan's background helped to make him an attractive presidential candidate.

In 1926, at age fifteen, Ronald Reagan earned $15 a week working as a lifeguard on the Rock River in Illinois. Being a lifeguard, Reagan later wrote, taught him quite a bit about human nature:

PRIMARY SOURCE

"Lifeguarding provides one of the best vantage points in the world to learn about people. During my career at the park, I saved seventy-seven people. I guarantee you they needed saving—no lifeguard gets wet without good reason. . . . Not many thanked me, much less gave me a reward, and being a little money-hungry, I'd done a little daydreaming about this. They felt insulted. . . . I got to recognize that people hate to be saved. . . ."

—from *Where's the Rest of Me?*

The belief that people do not want to be saved by someone else was one of the ideas that Ronald Reagan took with him to the White House. It reflected his philosophy of self-reliance and independence.

Becoming a Conservative

Reagan grew up in Dixon, Illinois, the son of an Irish American shoe salesman. After graduating from Eureka College in 1932, Reagan worked as a sports broadcaster at an Iowa radio station. In 1937 he took a Hollywood screen test and won a contract from a movie studio. During the next 25 years he made more than 50 movies. As a broadcaster and an actor, Reagan learned how to speak publicly and how to project a strong, attractive image—skills that proved invaluable when he entered politics.

In 1947 Reagan became president of the Screen Actors Guild—the actors' union. Soon afterward, he testified about communism in

---

R Reading Strategies	C Critical Thinking	D Differentiated Instruction	W Writing Support	S Skill Practice
Teacher Edition • Act. Prior Know., p. 747 **Additional Resources** • Prim. Source Read., URB p. 69 • Guided Read. Act., URB p. 81	**Teacher Edition** • Analyzing Prim. Sources, p. 747 • Drawing Conclusions, p. 748 **Additional Resources** • Interp. Polit. Cartoon, URB p. 75 • Quizzes/Tests, p. 314	**Teacher Edition** • English Learners, p. 751 • Interpersonal, p. 752 **Additional Resources** • English Learner Act., URB p. 59	**Teacher Edition** • Descriptive Writing, pp. 748, 751 • Persuasive Writing, pp. 749, 750	**Teacher Edition** • Describing, p. 750 • Read. Prim. Sources, p. 751 **Additional Resources** • RENTG, p. 236

POLITICAL CARTOONS PRIMARY SOURCE
The Election of 1980

▲ When Ronald Reagan ran for the Republican presidential nomination, he was still best known to most Americans as an actor. Critics said that while he was scripted and polished, he lacked any real substance.

▼ By 1980, Carter was so unpopular that other Democrats did not want his help in their own campaigns. Reagan soundly defeated Carter in the Election of 1980.

' I PLEDGE TO COME OUT CAMPAIGNING VIGOROUSLY FOR ALL DEMOCRATS !...'

Analyzing VISUALS

1. **Making Inferences** In the cartoon above, what does the artist infer about Reagan's campaign?
2. **Interpreting** What is the artist in the cartoon to the right saying about Carter's place in the Democratic Party?

Hollywood before the House Un-American Activities Committee. Reagan had been a staunch Democrat and a supporter of the New Deal, but dealing with Communists in the union shifted him toward conservative ideas.

In 1954 Reagan became the host of the television show "General Electric Theater" and agreed to be a motivational speaker for General Electric. As he traveled the country speaking to people, he became increasingly conservative. Over and over again, he said later, he heard average Americans describe how high taxes and government regulations made it impossible for them to get ahead.

By 1964 Reagan had become such a popular national speaker that Barry Goldwater asked him to make a televised speech on behalf of Goldwater's campaign. The speech impressed several wealthy entrepreneurs in California. They convinced Reagan to run for governor of California in 1966 and helped finance his campaign. Reagan won the election and was reelected in 1970. Ten years later he won the Republican presidential nomination.

The Election of 1980

Reagan's campaign appealed to Americans who were frustrated with the economy and worried that the United States had become weak internationally. Reagan promised to cut taxes and increase defense spending. He won the support of social conservatives by calling for a constitutional amendment banning abortion. During one debate with President Carter, Reagan asked voters, "Are you better off than you were four years ago?" On Election Day, the voters answered "No." Reagan won nearly 51 percent of the popular vote and 489 electoral votes, easily defeating Carter in the Electoral College. For the first time since 1954, Republicans also gained control of the Senate.

✔ Reading Check **Describing** What event jump-started Ronald Reagan's political career as a conservative leader?

Teach

C Critical Thinking
Analyzing Primary Sources
Reagan once said that "people hate to be saved." **Ask:** How does this quote relate to the conservative political ideology? *(Conservatives believe that people should rely more on themselves to solve problems rather than expect the government to fix their problems for them.* **AL**

R Reading Strategy
Activating Prior Knowledge
In 1947 Ronald Reagan testified before the House Un-American Activities Committee. **Ask:** What was the goal of HUAC? *(to uncover evidence of Communist infiltration in the U.S. government)* **OL**

Analyzing VISUALS

Answers:
1. Reagan's campaign is being run as if it were a movie.
2. Carter is not popular with other members of the Democratic Party.

Hands-On Chapter Project
Step 2

Conducting an Opinion Poll

Step 2: Preparing the Poll Keeping in mind the list of issues they compiled in Step 1, students should review the material presented in Section 2.

Evaluating Ask students to compose five statements that assess President Reagan's job performance on five significant issues of the 1980s.

(Chapter Project continued on page 755)

Descriptive Writing Have students reread the passage about supply-side economics on this page. Then organize the class into three groups and ask each group to write a letter to President Reagan about the impact of his economic policies. One group should represent business, another group should represent workers in manufacturing industries, and the third group should represent people on fixed incomes. **AL**

C Critical Thinking

Drawing Conclusions Discuss in class the question posed by the Debates in History feature. Have students use library or Internet resources to find out more about Reagan's tax cuts and their effects on the nation's economy. **Ask:** Based on your research, what effects did the Reagan tax cuts have? (Answers will vary. Some students might note that the economy grew steadily while others might mention problems such as the savings and loan crisis.) **OL**

Additional Support

Domestic Policies

MAIN Idea Believing that government was part of the problem, President Reagan cut social service programs, sponsored tax cuts, and deregulated industry.

HISTORY AND YOU Do you think that cutting social programs is a good way to help the economy? Read on to learn more about Reagan's economic policies.

Ronald Reagan believed that the key to restoring the economy and overcoming problems in society was to get Americans to believe in themselves again. He expressed this idea in his Inaugural Address:

PRIMARY SOURCE

"We have every right to dream heroic dreams. . . . You can see heroes every day going in and out of factory gates. Others, a handful in number, produce enough food to feed all of us. . . . You meet heroes across a counter. . . . There are entrepreneurs with faith in themselves and faith in an idea who create new jobs, new wealth and opportunity. . . . Their patriotism is quiet but deep. Their values sustain our national life."

—from Reagan's First Inaugural Address

Reagan also told Americans that they should not expect government to help: "In this present crisis, government is not the solution to our problem. Government is the problem."

Reaganomics

History ONLINE
Student Web Activity Visit glencoe.com and complete the activity on the 1980s.

W

Reagan's first priority was the economy, which was suffering from stagflation—a combination of high unemployment and high inflation. According to most economists, the way to fight unemployment was to increase government spending. Increasing spending, however, made inflation worse. Conservative economists offered two competing ideas for fixing the economy. One group, known as monetarists, argued that inflation was caused by too much money in circulation. They believed the best solution was to raise interest rates. Another group supported **supply-side economics.** They argued that the economy was weak because taxes were too high.

Supply-side economists believed that high taxes took too much money away from investors. If taxes were cut, businesses and investors

could use their extra capital to make new investments. Businesses would expand and create new jobs, and the result would be a larger supply of goods for consumers, who would now have more money to spend because of the tax cuts.

Reagan combined monetarism and supply-side economics. He encouraged the Federal Reserve to keep interest rates high, and asked Congress to pass a massive tax cut. Critics called his approach **Reaganomics** or "trickle-down economics." They believed Reagan's policy would help corporations and wealthy Americans, but little wealth would "trickle down" to middle-class or poor Americans.

Reagan made deals with conservative Democrats in the House and moderate Republicans in the Senate. Eventually Congress passed a 25 percent tax cut.

Debates IN HISTORY

Are Tax Cuts Good for the Economy?

Ronald Reagan believed that government regulation of the economy was harmful and that taxes should be as low as possible to promote private spending and investment. During the 1984 presidential campaign, Reagan ran against Jimmy Carter's vice president, Walter Mondale. In these excerpts from the first debate between the two candidates, Reagan and Mondale discuss their fundamentally different approaches to government. Mondale advocated for tax increases and that is often cited as a main reason why he lost the election.

Extending the Content

Presidential Campaigns Political opponents unflatteringly compared Ronald Reagan to Calvin Coolidge, pointing out the similarity between Reaganomics and Coolidge's "trickle-down" economic policies. They also noted that Reagan, like Coolidge, seemed rather detached from the process of government. Far from being insulted, Reagan reveled in the comparison. He hung Coolidge's portrait in a prominent place in the White House and regularly quoted Coolidge's philosophy on business and government.

Cutting Programs Cutting tax rates meant that the government would receive less money, at least until the economy started to grow. This would increase the **budget deficit**—the amount by which expenditures exceed income. To keep the deficit under control, Reagan proposed cuts to social programs. Welfare benefits, including the food-stamp program and the school-lunch program, were cut back. Medicare payments, unemployment compensation, student loans, and housing subsidies were also reduced.

After a struggle, Congress passed most of these cuts. The fight convinced Reagan that he would never get Congress to cut spending enough to balance the budget. He decided that cutting taxes and building up the military were more important than balancing the budget. He accepted a rapidly rising deficit as the price of getting his other programs passed.

Deregulation Reagan believed that excessive government regulation was another cause of the economy's problems. His first act as president was to sign an executive order to end price controls on oil and gasoline. Critics said that ending controls would drive prices up, but in fact they fell. Falling energy prices freed up money for businesses and consumers to spend elsewhere, helping the economy to recover.

Other deregulation soon followed. The Federal Communications Commission stopped trying to regulate the cable television industry. The National Highway Traffic and Safety Administration reduced requirements for air bags and higher fuel efficiency for cars. Carter had already begun deregulating the airline industry, and Reagan encouraged the process, which led to price wars, cheaper fares, and the founding of new airlines.

Writing Support

Persuasive Writing Have interested students use library or Internet resources to find out more information about the Reagan budget cuts of the early 1980s. Based on their research, have them decide whether they favor Reagan's proposals. Then have students write a letter to a member of Congress urging him or her to either support or oppose the president's proposals. Encourage volunteers to read their letters to the class. **AL**

Debates IN HISTORY

Answers:
1. cut taxes
2. the growth in the economy will increase revenues
3. Mondale says the nation will suffer a $263 billion deficit and that some economists are predicting that the nation is moving into a period of very slow growth.
4. Answers will vary, but students should support their answers with examples.

YES

Ronald Reagan
President

PRIMARY SOURCE

"…[T]he plan that we have had and that we are following is a plan that is based on growth in the economy. . . . Our tax cut, we think, was very instrumental in bringing about this economic recovery.

. . . So, we believe that as we continue to reduce the level of government spending…and, at the same time, as the growth in the economy increases the revenues the government gets, without raising taxes, those two lines will meet. . . . The deficit is the result of excessive government spending. . . . I don't believe that Mr. Mondale has a plan for balancing the budget; he has a plan for raising taxes. . . . And for the 5 years previous to our taking office, taxes doubled in the United States, and the budgets increased $318 billion. So, there is no ratio between taxing and balancing a budget."

—from the first presidential debate, Oct. 7, 1984

NO

Walter Mondale
Presidential candidate

PRIMARY SOURCE

"…[E]ven with historically high levels of economic growth, we will suffer a $263 billion deficit. . . . Real interest rates—the real cost of interest—will remain very, very high, and many economists are predicting that we're moving into a period of very slow growth. . . . I proposed over a hundred billion dollars in cuts in federal spending over 4 years, but I am not going to cut it out of Social Security and Medicare and student assistance and things . . . that people need. . . . The rate of defense spending increase can be slowed. . . . And there are other ways of squeezing this budget without constantly picking on our senior citizens and the most vulnerable in American life."

—from the first presidential debate, Oct. 7, 1984

DBQ Document-Based Questions

1. **Specifying** What does Reagan say his administration has done to improve economic growth?

2. **Explaining** How does Reagan propose to balance the federal budget?

3. **Summarizing** How does Mondale respond to Reagan's plan? What effects does he foresee from that course?

4. **Evaluating** Which approach do you feel will be the most effective? Why? Explain your answer.

Chapter 22 Resurgence of Conservatism **749**

Activity: Collaborative Learning

Reaganomics Posters Organize students into five or six groups. Have students prepare posters that explain the assumptions and the results of Reaganomics. Remind the groups that each person should have a part in the project. Group members will need to plan the poster, divide the work fairly, and complete the project. Posters might include charts, graphs, or other visual aids. Some groups may want to explain their posters to the rest of the class. Display all the posters in the classroom. **OL**

W Writing Support

Persuasive Writing Ask students to carefully read the People in History feature about Sandra Day O'Connor. Have them write two-page essays either supporting or opposing O'Connor's nomination to the Supreme Court. Students may use library or Internet resources to find information supporting their arguments. **OL**

S Skill Practice

Describing Have students discuss the impact the Reagan administration had on the make-up of the Supreme Court. *(more conservative justices were appointed; the Court was less willing to continue the reforms of the Warren Court Era)* **OL**

People IN HISTORY

Answer:
because she is a woman

Reading Check

Answer:
Supply-side economics proposes low taxes as an incentive to generate more investment in business.

Additional Support

People IN HISTORY

Sandra Day O'Connor
1930–

When a Supreme Court vacancy opened up in 1981, President Reagan chose Sandra Day O'Connor, an Arizona appeals court judge. Unlike many Supreme Court justices, O'Connor had broad political experience. Appointed to a state senatorial vacancy in 1969, she successfully ran for the seat and became the state senate's first woman majority leader in 1972. O'Connor won election as a superior court judge in 1974 and was later appointed to the court of appeals.

O'Connor's nomination was opposed by the Moral Majority because she had supported the Equal Rights Amendment (ERA), and had refused to back an anti-abortion amendment, or criticize the decision in *Roe v. Wade*. Others, however, praised her legal judgment and conservative approach to the law. As a moderate conservative, she quickly became an important swing vote on the Court, between more liberal and more conservative justices.

Why do you think that O'Connor supported the Equal Rights Amendment?

▲ *(Above photo) From left, front row are Thurgood Marshall; William Brennan, Jr.; William Rehnquist; Byron White; and Harry Blackmun. Back row from left are Antonin Scalia; John Paul Stevens; Sandra Day O'Connor; and Anthony M. Kennedy. (Right photo) Robert Bork failed to be confirmed.*

Reagan's secretary of the interior, James Watt, increased the public land that companies could use for oil drilling, mining, and logging. Watt's actions angered environmentalists, as did the EPA's decision to ease regulations on pollution-control equipment and to reduce safety checks on chemicals and pesticides.

In 1983 the economy began to recover. By 1984, the United States had begun the biggest economic expansion in its history up to that time. The median income of families climbed steadily, rising 15 percent by 1989. Five million new businesses and 20 million new jobs were created. By 1988, unemployment had fallen to 5.5 percent, the lowest in 14 years.

Reagan Wins Reelection By 1984, the economic recovery had made Reagan very popular. Democrats nominated Jimmy Carter's vice president, Walter Mondale. He chose as his running mate Representative Geraldine Ferraro, the first woman nominated to run for vice president for a major party. Instead of arguing issues with his opponent, Reagan emphasized the good economy. In an overwhelming landslide, he won about 59 percent of the popular vote and all the electoral votes except those from Mondale's home state of Minnesota and the District of Columbia.

Shifting the Judicial Balance

Reagan did not apply his conservative ideas only to the economy. He also tried to bring a strict constructionist outlook to the federal judiciary. Reagan wanted judges who followed the original intent of the Constitution. He also changed the Supreme Court by nominating Sandra Day O'Connor, the first woman on the Supreme Court.

In 1986 Chief Justice Warren Burger retired. Reagan chose the most conservative associate justice, William Rehnquist, to succeed him. He then named Antonin Scalia, a conservative, to fill Rehnquist's vacancy. In 1987 his attempt to put Robert Bork on the Court led to a bitter fight in the Senate. Democrats saw Bork as too conservative and blocked his **confirmation.** Reagan then nominated Anthony Kennedy, a moderate, to become the new associate justice.

✓ Reading Check **Explaining** What is supply-side economics?

Activity: Collaborative Learning

Voting Blocs During the 1970s, 1980s, and 1990s, about 55 percent of all qualified voters voted in presidential elections. More women voted than men, and there were more voters in the 55–75 age range than in any other age group. Organize the class into cooperative groups, and have them research why some groups of people vote more than others. How does being from a group that is likely to vote affect a person's clout with politicians? (For example, are politicians careful not to anger senior citizens because they vote in such large numbers?) Students will want to divide up the work and decide on a method of presentation. They may also want to create charts to show differences in voting patterns by region, age, education level, income, and so forth. **OL**

Reagan Oversees a Military Buildup

MAIN Idea President Reagan began a massive military buildup to weaken the Soviet economy and deter Soviet aggression.

HISTORY AND YOU Do you remember President Eisenhower's warning about the military as he left office? Read to learn how President Reagan sought to use military power to defeat the Soviets.

Reagan did not limit his reforms to the domestic scene. He adopted a new foreign policy that rejected both containment and détente. Reagan called the Soviet Union "the focus of evil in the modern world" and "an evil empire." In his view, the United States should not negotiate with or try to contain evil. It should try to defeat it.

"Peace Through Strength"

In Reagan's opinion, the only option open to the United States in dealing with the Soviet Union was "peace through strength"—a phrase he used during his campaign. The military buildup Reagan launched was the largest peacetime buildup in American history. It cost about $1.5 trillion over five years.

Reagan believed that, if the Soviets tried to match the American buildup, it might put so much pressure on their economy that they would be forced to reform their system or it would collapse. In 1982 Reagan told students at Eureka College that Soviet defense spending would eventually cause the Communist system to fall apart:

PRIMARY SOURCE

"The Soviet empire is faltering because rigid centralized control has destroyed incentives for innovation, efficiency, and individual achievement. . . . But in the midst of social and economic problems, the Soviet dictatorship has forged the largest armed force in the world. It has done so by preempting the human needs of its people and in the end, this course will undermine the foundations of the Soviet system."

—from *A Time for Choosing*

The United States also tried to stop nations from supporting terrorism. After Libya backed a terrorist bombing in Berlin, the United States launched an air attack on Libya on April 14, 1986. The raids killed 37 and injured about 200.

Reagan's military buildup created new jobs in defense industries. Supply-side economists had predicted that, despite the spending, lower taxes combined with cuts in government programs would generate enough growth to increase tax revenues and balance the budget. Tax revenues did rise, but other programs were too popular for Reagan to cut significantly. As a result, the annual budget deficit went from $80 billion to over $200 billion.

The Reagan Doctrine

Building up the military was only part of Reagan's military strategy. He also believed that the United States should support guerrilla groups who were fighting to overthrow Communist or pro-Soviet governments. This policy became known as the Reagan Doctrine.

Aid to the Afghan Rebels Perhaps the most **visible** example of the Reagan Doctrine was in Afghanistan. In late December 1979 the Soviet Union invaded Afghanistan to support a Soviet-backed government. The Soviets soon found themselves fighting Afghan guerrillas known as the mujahadeen.

President Carter sent about $30 million in military aid to the Afghan guerrillas, but Reagan sent $570 million more. The Soviets were soon trapped in a situation similar to the American experience in Vietnam. They could not defeat the Afghan guerrillas. As casualties mounted, the war strained the Soviet economy and in 1988 the Soviets decided to withdraw.

Nicaragua and Grenada Reagan was also concerned about Soviet influence in Nicaragua. Rebels known as the Sandinistas had overthrown a pro-American dictator in Nicaragua in 1979. The Sandinistas set up a socialist government and accepted Cuban and Soviet aid. They then began aiding rebels in nearby El Salvador.

In response, the Reagan administration began secretly arming an anti-Sandinista guerrilla force known as the contras, from the Spanish word for "counterrevolutionary." When Congress learned of this policy, it banned further aid to the contras.

D Differentiated Instruction

English Learners Ask students to read the text under the head "Reagan Oversees a Military Buildup" and then, working in pairs, summarize what they have just read. **ELL**

S Skill Practice

Reading Primary Sources
Read aloud Reagan's quote on this page about the Soviet Union. **Ask:** What did Reagan mean when he said the Soviet Union had achieved its military might by "preempting the human needs of its people"? *(The Soviets had denied their citizens basic freedoms.)* **OL**

W Writing Support

Descriptive Writing Have interested students do library or Internet research to find out more about the Reagan administration's policies toward one of the following: the Afghan rebels, Nicaragua, or Grenada. Then have students write a one-page report describing America's policy concerning the nation or group they chose. **OL**

Activity: Interdisciplinary Connection

Geography Organize the class into groups of six to research the island country of Grenada, located in the southeastern Caribbean Sea. It is composed of 8 separate islands, with the island of Grenada being the largest and most populous. Have each group member use library or Internet sources to learn more about one of the following topics: geography, climate, vegetation, history, government, or economy. Then have the groups create a travel poster highlighting the features of the islands and encouraging tourists to visit. Students should illustrate their posters with magazine clippings, drawings, and maps. Have each group present its poster to the class. **OL**

D Differentiated Instruction

Interpersonal As students read "Arms Control," have them work in groups to trace the changes in relations between the Soviet Union and the United States on a time line. Groups should present their time lines to the class. **ELL**

Analyzing VISUALS

Answers:

1. One photograph depicts support of the Afghans against the Soviet Union and the other photograph shows President Reagan talking with Mikhail Gorbachev, the Soviet leader. The photographs indicate that the president was willing to use military power, as well as dialogue, when dealing with the Soviet Union.

2. to clearly state American policy and perhaps to embarrass the other nation; it might be effective because of international pressure

Additional Support

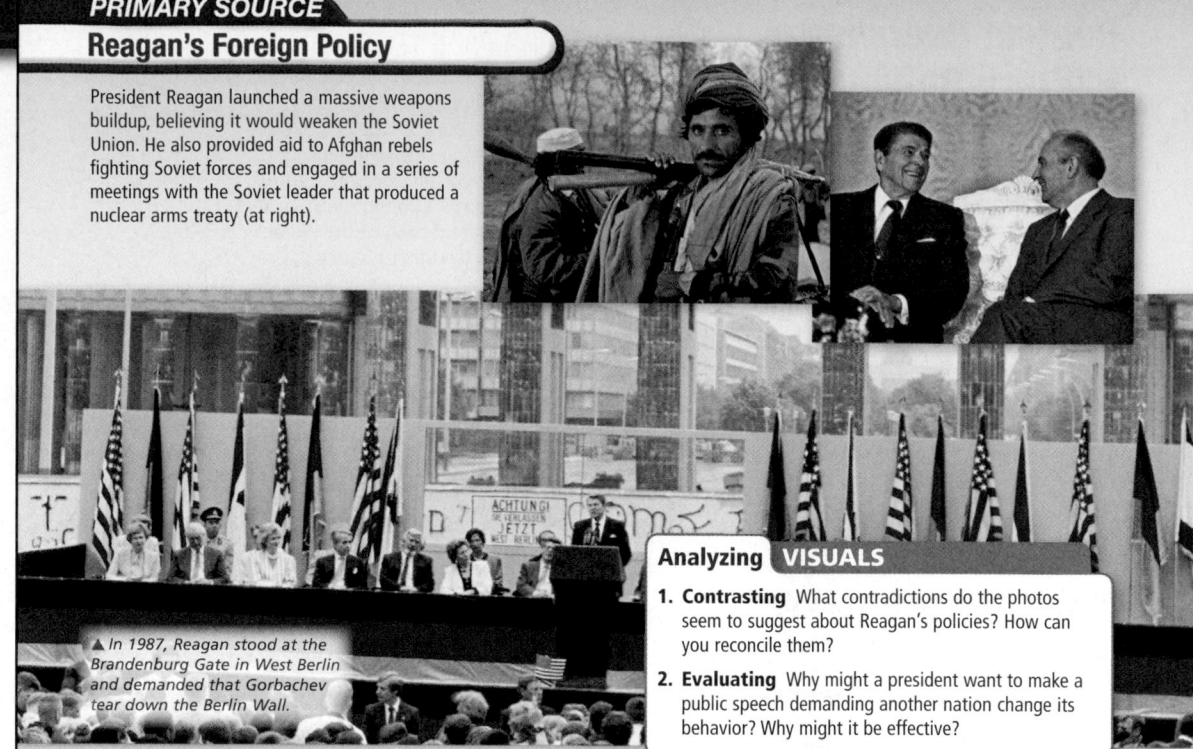

PRIMARY SOURCE
Reagan's Foreign Policy

President Reagan launched a massive weapons buildup, believing it would weaken the Soviet Union. He also provided aid to Afghan rebels fighting Soviet forces and engaged in a series of meetings with the Soviet leader that produced a nuclear arms treaty (at right).

▲ In 1987, Reagan stood at the Brandenburg Gate in West Berlin and demanded that Gorbachev tear down the Berlin Wall.

Analyzing VISUALS

1. **Contrasting** What contradictions do the photos seem to suggest about Reagan's policies? How can you reconcile them?

2. **Evaluating** Why might a president want to make a public speech demanding another nation change its behavior? Why might it be effective?

Aiding the contras was not Reagan's only action in Latin America. In 1983 radical Marxists overthrew the left-wing government on the tiny Caribbean island of Grenada. In October, Reagan sent in American troops. The Cuban and Grenadian soldiers were quickly defeated and a new anti-Communist government was put in place.

The Iran-Contra Scandal Although Congress had prohibited aid to the Nicaraguan contras, individuals in Reagan's administration continued to illegally support the rebels. They secretly sold weapons to Iran, considered an enemy and sponsor of terrorism, in exchange for the release of American hostages being held in the Middle East. Profits from these sales were then sent to the contras.

News of the illegal operations broke in November 1986. One of the chief figures in the **Iran-Contra scandal** was Marine Colonel Oliver North, an aide to the National Security

Council (NSC). He and other senior NSC and CIA officials testified before Congress and admitted to covering up their actions.

President Reagan had approved the sale of arms to Iran, but the congressional investigation concluded that he had had no direct knowledge about the diversion of the money to the contras. To the end, Reagan insisted he had done nothing wrong, but the scandal tainted his second term in office.

Arms Control

As part of the military buildup, Reagan decided to place nuclear missiles in Western Europe to counter Soviet missiles in Eastern Europe. This decision triggered a new peace movement. Tens of thousands of protesters pushed for a "nuclear freeze"—a halt to the deployment of new nuclear missiles.

Reagan offered to cancel the deployment of the new missiles if the Soviets removed their

752 Chapter 22 Resurgence of Conservatism

Extending the Content

Divestment and Apartheid In 1984 an estimated $14 billion was invested in South Africa by multinational corporations; U.S. federal, state, and municipal governments; and American universities. Many college students wanted to support black South Africans' attempts to end apartheid—an official policy of discrimination against non-whites. Between 1977 and 1985, campus protests convinced 150 U.S. universities to divest—or remove—all or part of their investments from South Africa. In 1986 Congress banned new investments in South Africa. By 1991, more than 200 U.S. companies had divested, and 28 states, 24 counties, and 92 cities had imposed sanctions. The divestment movement and economic problems caused by apartheid policies themselves devastated the South African economy. Long imprisoned for his anti-apartheid activities, Nelson Mandela was freed in 1990. In 1994 he helped to craft a new constitution for South Africa that ended white minority rule.

missiles from Eastern Europe. He also proposed Strategic Arms Reduction Talks (START) to cut the number of missiles on both sides in half. The Soviets refused and walked out of the arms control talks.

"Star Wars" Despite his decision to deploy missiles in Europe, Reagan generally disagreed with the military strategy known as nuclear deterrence, sometimes called **"mutual assured destruction."** This strategy assumed that, as long as the United States and Soviet Union could destroy each other with nuclear weapons, they would be afraid to use them.

Reagan believed that mutual assured destruction was immoral because it depended on the threat to kill massive numbers of people. He also knew that if nuclear war did begin, there would be no way to defend the United States. In March 1983 Reagan proposed the Strategic Defense Initiative (SDI). This plan, nicknamed "Star Wars," called for the development of weapons that could intercept and destroy incoming missiles.

A New Soviet Leader In 1985 **Mikhail Gorbachev** became the leader of the Soviet Union and agreed to resume arms-control talks. Gorbachev believed that the Soviet Union had to reform its economic system or it would soon collapse. It could not afford a new arms race with the United States.

Reagan and Gorbachev met in a series of summits. The first of these was frustrating for both, as they disagreed on many issues. Gorbachev promised to cut back Soviet nuclear forces if Reagan would agree to give up SDI, but Reagan refused.

Reagan then challenged Gorbachev to make reforms. In West Berlin, Reagan stood at the Brandenburg Gate of the Berlin Wall, the symbol of divided Europe, and declared: "General Secretary Gorbachev, if you seek peace, if you seek prosperity for the Soviet Union and Eastern Europe . . . tear down this wall!"

Relations Improve By 1987, Reagan was convinced that Gorbachev did want to reform the Soviet Union and end the arms race. While some politicians distrusted the Soviets, most people welcomed the Cold War thaw and the reduction in the danger of nuclear war. In December 1987 the two leaders signed the Intermediate Range Nuclear Forces (INF) Treaty. It was the first treaty to call for the destruction of nuclear weapons.

No one realized it at the time, but the treaty marked the beginning of the end of the Cold War. With an arms control deal in place, Gorbachev felt confident that Soviet military spending could be reduced. He pushed ahead with economic and political reforms that eventually led to the collapse of communism in Eastern Europe and in the Soviet Union.

With the economy booming, the American military strong, and relations with the Soviet Union rapidly improving, Ronald Reagan's second term came to an end. As he prepared to leave office, Reagan assessed his presidency: "They called it the Reagan revolution. Well, I'll accept that, but for me it always seemed more like the great rediscovery, a rediscovery of our values and our common sense."

✓Reading Check **Identifying** What was the Reagan Doctrine?

Section 2 REVIEW

Vocabulary
1. **Explain** the significance of: supply-side economics, Reaganomics, budget deficit, Iran-Contra scandal, "mutual assured destruction," Mikhail Gorbachev.

Main Ideas
2. **Specifying** What political office did Ronald Reagan hold before he was elected president?

3. **Explaining** How did Reagan aim to change the Supreme Court?

4. **Summarizing** What was the goal of the U.S. military buildup under President Reagan?

Critical Thinking
5. **Big Ideas** What was President Reagan's approach to foreign policy?

6. **Organizing** Use a graphic organizer similar to the one below to list the ways in which the Reagan Doctrine was implemented.

7. **Analyzing Visuals** Study the political cartoons on page 747. How do the cartoons portray Reagan and Carter?

Writing About History
8. **Expository Writing** Take on the role of a newspaper editor during the Reagan administration. Write an editorial in which you present your opinion of Reagan's plans for a military buildup.

History ONLINE
Study Central™ To review this section, go to glencoe.com and click on Study Central.

753

✓**Reading Check**

Answer:
The Reagan Doctrine was a policy of supporting guerrilla groups that were fighting to overthrow Communist or pro-Soviet governments.

Assess

History ONLINE

Study Central™ provides summaries, interactive games, and online graphic organizers to help students review content.

Close

Summarizing Ask: How did Ronald Reagan's presidency change the United States? *(taxes were reduced; some social programs were cut; military spending increased; most citizens were optimistic about the future; relations with the Soviet Union eventually improved)* **OL**

Section 2 REVIEW

Answers

1. All definitions can be found in the section and the Glossary.
2. Governor of California
3. Reagan planned to appoint conservative justices.
4. to bring about the fall of the Soviet Union
5. aggressive stance toward Communism everywhere; military buildup to weaken Soviets

6. answers may include: supported Afghan guerrillas and anti-Sandinista guerrillas in Nicaragua, sent American troops to Grenada
7. Reagan is leading a group of filmmakers; Carter is causing other Democrats to run away.
8. Students' editorials will vary.

Focus

Section 3

Bellringer

Daily Focus Transparency 22.3

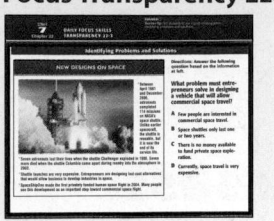

Guide to Reading

Answers may include:
AIDS, alcohol and drug abuse, crime, homelessness, gay and lesbian rights

Section Spotlight Video

To generate student interest and provide a springboard for class discussion, access the Chapter 22, Section 3 video at glencoe.com or on the video DVD.

Resource Manager

Section 3

Life in the 1980s

Guide to Reading

Big Ideas
Science and Technology
Achievements in technology during the 1980s symbolized the optimism many associated with the Reagan era.

Content Vocabulary
• yuppie (p. 754)
• discount retailing (p. 755)

Academic Vocabulary
• via (p. 756)
• orientation (p. 759)

People and Events to Identify
• Mothers Against Drunk Driving (MADD) (p. 758)
• AIDS (p. 759)
• Stonewall Riot (p. 759)
• American Association of Retired Persons (AARP) (p. 759)

Reading Strategy
Organizing Complete a graphic organizer similar to the one below by listing the kinds of social issues that Americans faced in the 1980s.

Social Issues in the 1980s

The 1980s was a period of increased wealth for many, as areas of the economy improved and new technologies came to market. However, cuts in social programs left many Americans in need, leading to a new sense of activism.

A Booming Economy

MAIN Idea Innovation in the retailing and broadcast industries changed American society and generated new businesses and jobs.

HISTORY AND YOU What technological devices are part of your everyday life? Read on to find out about the inventions of the 1980s.

By late 1983, the American economy had revived after the stagflation of the 1970s. Stock prices soared as many companies reported record profits. Stockbrokers, speculators, and real estate developers made multimillion-dollar deals, buying and selling hundreds of companies. Perhaps the most famous real estate developer of the era was Donald Trump, who opened Trump Tower in New York City in 1982. Many of the new moneymakers were young, ambitious, and hardworking. Journalists called them **yuppies,** from "young urban professionals."

The rapid economic growth and emphasis on accumulating wealth in the 1980s was partly caused by the baby boom. By the 1980s, many baby boomers had finished college, entered the job market, and begun building their careers. Young people entering the workforce often placed an emphasis on acquiring goods and getting ahead in their jobs. Because baby boomers were so numerous, their concerns tended to shape the culture.

The strong economic growth of the 1980s mostly benefited middle- and upper-class Americans. As a result, the emphasis on acquiring wealth had another effect on society. From 1967 to 1986, the amount of money earned by the top 5 percent of Americans fluctuated between 15.6 and 17.5 percent of the nation's total income. In the late 1980s, their share of the nation's income began to rise. By the mid-1990s, the top 5 percent of Americans earned well over 21 percent of the nation's income.

A Retail Revolution

In addition to the booming real-estate and stock markets, the economy of the 1980s witnessed a revolution in retail sales. Several entrepreneurs pioneered a new approach to retailing—or selling goods to

---

R Reading Strategies	**C** Critical Thinking	**D** Differentiated Instruction	**W** Writing Support	**S** Skill Practice
Teacher Edition • Summarizing, p. 756 • Setting a Purpose, p. 758 **Additional Resources** • Prim. Source Read., URB p. 71 • Guided Read. Act., URB p. 82	**Teacher Edition** • Det. Cause/Effect, p. 756 **Additional Resources** • Historical Skills Act., URB p. 56 • Supreme Court Case Studies, p. 129 • Quizzes/Tests, p. 315	**Teacher Edition** • Special Ed., p. 755 **Additional Resources** • Differ. Instr. Act., URB p. 57 • American History in Grahic Novel, p. 87	**Additional Resources** • Am. Literature Readings, URB p. 13	**Teacher Edition** • Visual Literacy, p. 757 **Additional Resources** • Geography & Hist., URB p. 3 • Link. Past and Present Act., URB p. 68 • RENTG, p. 239

The Booming Economy of the 1980s

The American economy grew rapidly in the 1980s for several reasons—lower taxes spurred investment and spending while new methods of retailing lowered prices and new technology led to new businesses and the creation of many new jobs.

Security Prices

Source: *Statistical Abstract of the United States, 1995.*

Discount retail stores (above) and cable television (right) took off in the 1980s, helping to further fuel economic growth.

Analyzing VISUALS

1. **Identifying** In what year of the late 1980s did the Dow Jones sharply decline?
2. **Explaining** Examine the photos and then write a brief essay explaining how they demonstrate economic trends of the 1980s.

consumers—that greatly reduced prices for Americans.

This new type of retailing, known as **discount retailing,** had actually begun to emerge in the 1960s—but it did not have a major impact on the economy until the 1980s. Discount retailers sell large quantities of goods at very low prices, trying to sell the goods quickly to turn over their entire inventory in a short period of time. By selling a lot of products at very low prices, they could make more money than traditional retailers who sold fewer products at higher prices. During the 1960s many new discount retail chains were founded, including K Mart, Woolco, Target, and Wal-Mart. Annual sales by discount stores grew from about $2 billion in the mid-1960s to almost $70 billion by 1985.

The most successful discount retailer was Sam Walton, the founder of Wal-Mart. Walton developed a system of distribution centers to rapidly re-supply his stores. He was one of the first retailers to use a computer database to track inventory and sales. By 1985, he was the richest person in the United States.

Others soon copied Walton's approach. By the late 1970s, discount retailers had begun to build huge "superstores" that enabled them to sell large quantities of goods very quickly at low prices. One such entrepreneur was Arthur Blank, who opened Home Depot—a chain of giant home-improvement stores—in 1978. In 1983 Richard Schulze, a former air force officer, used his technical training to found Best Buy, a huge discount retailer of consumer electronics. Dozens of other entrepreneurs started discount stores in other industries. Their innovations created millions of new jobs in the 1980s and helped fuel the era's rapid economic growth.

Chapter 22 Resurgence of Conservatism **755**

Teach

D Differentiated Instruction

Special Education As students read the section, they might encounter text or other information they do not understand, and they should adjust their reading strategies to clarify ideas. Model how this is done by reading part of the section aloud. As you read, ask yourself questions aloud, such as, "What do I think the main focus of the 1980s will turn out to be?" (predicting) and "What discount retail stores have I shopped in or are in my community?" (activating prior knowledge). Modeling how you check your comprehension helps students to think about strategies they can use as they read independently. **BL**

Analyzing VISUALS

Answers:
1. 1988
2. In their essays, students should note economic trends such as discount retailing and the rise of cable television.

Hands-On Chapter Project
Step 3

Conducting an Opinion Poll

Step 3: Conducting the Poll Each student should arrange to interview at least one person who was of voting age in the 1980s. The student should then read each of the statements composed during Step 2 and ask the respondent if he or she agrees or disagrees with the statement.

Classifying Respondents should be given five options, ranked by number: (1) strongly disagree; (2) disagree; (3) neutral; (4) agree;

or (5) strongly agree. Encourage students to ask follow up questions if respondents express a strong opinion on an issue. **OL**

(Chapter Project continued on page 763)

C Critical Thinking

Determining Cause and Effect Discuss with students the changes in television in the 1980s. **Ask:** In what areas of broadcasting or on what new audiences did the new networks focus? *(CNN provided 24-hour news, BET focused on African Americans, MTV focused on youth.)* What do you think are some effects that the new television networks may have had on consumerism and culture in the United States? *(Students may note that new groups were represented more in popular culture with the new networks, but they were also exposed to advertising. CNN created a 24-hour news cycle, which may have led to a huge broadening in the definition of "news" as networks scrambled to fill air time.)* **OL**

R Reading Strategy

Summarizing Dr. Sally Ride became the first American woman to orbit Earth when she flew aboard the space shuttle *Challenger*. **Ask:** What are some innovations that occurred in the nation's space program in the 1980s? *(space shuttle, Hubble Space Telescope, experiments, women astronauts)* **OL**

Additional Support

A Revolution in Media

In the 1980s other entrepreneurs began transforming the news and entertainment industries. Until the late 1970s, television viewers were limited to three national networks, local stations, and the public television network. In 1970 a businessman named Ted Turner bought a failing television station in Atlanta, Georgia. Turner then pioneered a new type of broadcasting by creating WTBS in 1975. WTBS was the first "superstation"—a television station that sold low-cost sports and entertainment programs **via** satellite to cable companies throughout the nation.

The Rise of Cable Television Turner's innovation changed broadcasting and helped spread cable television across the country. Dozens of networks soon appeared. Many of the new networks specialized in one type of broadcasting, such as sports (ESPN), movies (HBO), or news. In 1980 Turner himself founded the Cable News Network (CNN)—the first 24-hour, all-news network.

Other new networks focused on specific audiences, such as churchgoers, shoppers, or minorities. In 1980 entrepreneur Robert Johnson created Black Entertainment Television (BET). Johnson—who had been born into a poor, rural family in Mississippi and gone on to earn a master's degree from Princeton University—was convinced that television had tremendous power to promote African American businesses and culture. BET was the first, and is still the largest, African American-owned network on cable television.

In 1981 music and technology merged when Music Television (MTV) went on the air. MTV broadcast performances of songs and images, or music videos. MTV was an instant hit, though the videos it showed were often criticized for violence and sexual content. Many performers began to produce videos along with each of their new albums. Music videos boosted the careers of artists such as Madonna and Michael Jackson.

Rap music was the new sound of the 1980s. This musical style originated in local clubs in New York City's South Bronx. Emphasizing heavy bass and very rhythmic sounds, rap artists did not usually sing but rather spoke over the music and rhythmic beats. Rap's lyrics frequently focused on the African American expe-

PAST & PRESENT

New Space Technology

After the series of moon landings of the 1970s, NASA concentrated on the space shuttle. Although it looks like a huge airplane, the shuttle is rocketed into space, then glides back to Earth for another flight. Unlike earlier spacecraft, the shuttle was reusable. Astronauts John Young and Roger Crippen made the first space shuttle flight in April 1981.

Between April 1981 and December 2006, shuttle astronauts completed 114 missions. They have placed many satellites in orbit, including the Hubble Space Telescope, and conducted numerous experiments. Tragedy has struck twice during shuttle missions. In 1986, the space shuttle *Challenger* exploded shortly after liftoff. In 2003, the shuttle *Columbia* came apart while reentering the atmosphere. Seven astronauts died in each of these accidents.

As the shuttle nears the end of its service life, both NASA and several independent companies have begun work on vehicles capable of reaching orbit. Shuttle launches are very expensive and many entrepreneurs are seeking to develop low-cost alternatives to the shuttle that will enable business to move into space and develop new industries there.

April 1981

▲ On April 12, 1981, the shuttle Columbia *lifted off on the first space shuttle flight.*

Activity: Interdisciplinary Connection

Science Have students review the history of the space program and research its future goals. Tell students that during times of economic struggle, some have questioned the ongoing usefulness of the space program and have proposed to reduce funding for it. Others see the potential future value to Americans and all humans of continued space exploration. Have students write a persuasive essay either supporting the continued expansion of the space program or call for reduced funding for it. **Ask:** What are the benefits of space exploration to the American public? What are the drawbacks? *(Students' answers will vary, but should be supported with logical reasons.)* **AL**

rience in the inner city. While rap was initially popular among East Coast African Americans, it grew in popularity, becoming a multimillion-dollar industry that appealed to music lovers across the country.

Technology and Media In the 1980s technology also transformed how people accessed their entertainment. Until the 1980s, most people listened to music on large stereo systems in their homes or relied on radio-station programming when they were driving. In the 1980s, the Sony Walkman made music portable. The Sony Walkman played cassette tapes, but it marked the beginning of a new way for people to access music. In the 1990s, portable compact disc (CD) players replaced the Walkman, and in the early 2000s digital audio players, such as the iPod and MP3 players, advanced the technology even further.

Video technology also began to change. Until the 1980s most people had to watch television shows when they aired. By the end of the 1980s, many people had videocassette recorders (VCRs), enabling them to tape television shows or watch taped films whenever they wished. By the 2000s, VCRs were being replaced by digital video disk (DVD) recorders. The growing use of VCRs changed the movie industry, as people increasingly chose to rent taped movies to watch at home rather than go to the theater.

Even as technology changed the music and television industries, it also brought about a new form of entertainment that competed with music and movies—the video game. Early video games grew out of military computer technology. The first video arcade game was a game called *Pong*, released in 1972. Home video games developed quickly. In the early 1980s sales reached about $3 billion with the sale of games such as *Pac-Man* and *Space Invaders*. Video arcades became the new spot for young people to meet. By the mid-1980s, home video games were able to compete with arcade games in graphics and speed. Video games have continued to grow in popularity to the present day and three major companies—Sony, Nintendo, and Microsoft—have emerged as the major developers of video games and game devices.

✔ **Reading Check** **Describing** What forms of entertainment gained popularity in the 1980s?

June 2004

In the early 2000s, many private companies were working on building spaceships. SpaceShipOne (below) was the first privately-built ship to carry a person to space. Another company is working on the Goddard (right)—a ship designed to take off and land vertically, without needing wings.

S

MAKING **CONNECTIONS**

1. **Analyzing** How has the United States benefited from the space program?
2. **Speculating** What kinds of private businesses might benefit from easy, inexpensive space programs?

Chapter 22 Resurgence of Conservatism **757**

S **Skill Practice**

Visual Literacy Have students study the examples of some of the latest spacecraft. **Ask:** What features of *SpaceShipOne* and *Goddard* are similar to and different from the space shuttles? *(All three vehicle types are aerodynamic and are meant to escape Earth's orbit. The newer craft seem to have simpler designs; Goddard does not have any type of wing.)* **OL**

MAKING **CONNECTIONS**

Answers:
1. Students should note that United States benefited from the space program in prestige and also through the many important scientific discoveries that were made and the materials, tools, and machines that were developed for space.
2. possible answer: satellite communications companies

✔ **Reading Check**

Answer:
listening to music such as rap; watching taped movies, cable or satellite TV, and music videos; and playing video games

Differentiated Instruction

Leveled Activities

BL **Guided Reading Activity,** URB p. 82

OL **Linking Past and Present Activity,** URB p. 68

AL **Primary Source Reading,** URB p. 71

ELL **Differentiated Instruction Activity, URB, p. 57**

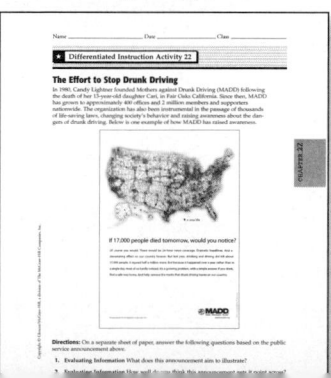

R **Reading Strategy**

Setting a Purpose Point out to students that they can use the Main Idea statements that follow each main heading in a section to help them preview and prepare to read. Instruct students to change the Main Idea statements into a question. For example, the statement on this page could be changed to "What social problems affected many people during the 1980s and what new groups formed to solve them?" Tell students that they should be able to answer the question as they read. **BL**

Analyzing VISUALS

Answers:
1. high interest rates and low food prices
2. low crop prices

Additional Support

New Social Activism

MAIN Idea Social problems affected many people during the 1980s, and new groups formed to try to solve them.

HISTORY AND YOU Does your school have organizations such as Students Against Drunk Driving? Read on to learn more about attempts to limit teen alcohol abuse.

The 1980s was a decade of wealth and prosperity. However, at the same time, many social problems continued to plague the nation, such as drugs, poverty, homelessness, and disease.

Social Problems

Ongoing problems with drug abuse in the 1980s made many neighborhoods dangerous. Drug users often committed crimes to get money for drugs. First Lady Nancy Reagan tried to discourage teen drug use with her "Just Say No" campaign. Drug use also spread from cities to small towns and rural areas.

Fighting Drugs in Schools As part of the effort to reduce drug use among teenagers, some schools began searching student bags and lockers to find concealed drugs. In 1984 one teen who had been arrested for selling drugs challenged the school's right to search her purse without a warrant. In 1985, in the case of *New Jersey* v. *T.L.O.*, the Supreme Court upheld the school's right to search without a warrant if it had reasonable cause to believe a crime was being committed. Although students did have a right to privacy, they did not have the same Fourth Amendment rights as adults. For similar reasons, in the 1995 case of *Vernonia School District* v. *Acton,* the Court held that random drug tests do not violate students' Fourth Amendment rights.

Efforts to Stop Drunk Driving Abuse of alcohol was also a serious concern. In 1980 **Mothers Against Drunk Driving (MADD)** was founded to try to stop underage drinking and drunk driving in general. In 1984 Congress cut highway funds to any state that did not raise the legal drinking age to 21. Within four years, all states complied.

PRIMARY SOURCE

The Farm Debt Crisis of the 1980s

Although the high interest rates of the 1980s helped reduce inflation, when they were combined with the low food prices of the era, they created a crisis for American farmers. Many farmers found themselves deeply in debt. Unable to make enough money to make their loan payments, they were soon forced out of business. By the end of the 1980s, the total number of farms in the United States had sharply declined.

Farm Income and Debt

*In constant 2000 dollars

Source: U.S. Department of Agriculture.

◀ As farmers faced a debt crisis, some began holding demonstrations, such as this one in Washington D.C. in 1984.

Analyzing VISUALS

1. **Hypothesizing** What factors explain why farm debt increased between 1975 and 1980?

2. **Interpreting** What are the farmers at left complaining about?

Activity: Interdisciplinary Connection

Civics Invite someone who works in a mental health facility, free clinic, or other social agency to make a presentation to the class about ways in which students can help address an ongoing social problem, such as drug abuse, AIDS, or drunk driving. Be sure to brief the speaker beforehand on any guidelines your school may have about sensitive subjects. Allow time for students to ask questions of the guest speaker. Conclude with a discussion on civic participation. **Ask:** What are some ways in which you can make a difference in your community? **OL BL ELL**

The AIDS Epidemic Begins In 1981 researchers identified a disease that caused healthy young people to become sick and die. They named it "acquired immune deficiency syndrome," or **AIDS.** AIDS weakens the immune system, lowering resistance to illnesses such as pneumonia and several types of cancer. HIV, the virus that causes AIDS, is spread through bodily fluids.

In the United States, AIDS was first noticed among homosexual men, but it soon spread among heterosexual men and women. Many people were infected by sexual partners. A few got the disease from blood transfusions. Other victims included drug users who shared needles. Between 1981 and 1988, the Centers for Disease Control and Prevention identified more than 100,000 cases in the United States.

New Activist Groups

AIDS increased the visibility of the country's gay and lesbian community, but some homosexuals had been engaged in efforts to defend their civil rights since the 1960s. On June 27, 1969, New York City police raided a nightclub called the Stonewall Inn. The police had often raided the nightclub because of the sexual **orientation** of its patrons. Frustration among the gay and lesbian onlookers led to a riot. The **Stonewall Riot** marked the beginning of the gay activist movement. Soon after, organizations such as the Gay Liberation Front began efforts to increase tolerance of homosexuality.

Rock 'n' Rollers Become Activists Many musicians and entertainers in the 1980s began using their celebrity to raise awareness about social issues. To help starving people in Ethiopia, Irish rocker Bob Geldof organized musicians in England to present "Band Aid" concerts in 1984. In the next year, the event grew into "Live Aid." People in some 100 countries watched benefit concerts televised from London, Philadelphia, and Sydney, Australia. The organization's theme song, "We Are the World," was a best-seller. In the same year, country singer Willie Nelson organized "Farm Aid" to help American farmers who were going through hard times.

Senior Citizens Begin to Lobby Another group that became politically active in the 1980s was senior citizens. Decades of improvements in medicine had resulted in more Americans surviving to an older age. In addition, the birthrate had declined, so younger people represented a comparatively smaller proportion of the population. The fact that more Americans were receiving Social Security payments created budget pressures for the government.

Older Americans became very vocal in the political arena, opposing cuts in Social Security or Medicare. Because they tend to vote in large numbers, senior citizens are an influential interest group. Their major lobbying organization is the **American Association of Retired Persons (AARP),** founded in 1958.

✓ Reading Check **Summarizing** On what issues did some entertainers focus in the 1980s?

Section 3 REVIEW

Vocabulary

1. **Explain** the significance of: yuppie, discount retailing, Mothers Against Drunk Driving (MADD), AIDS, Stonewall Riot, American Association of Retired Persons (AARP).

Main Ideas

2. **Summarizing** How did retailing change in the 1980s?

3. **Listing** What are three social problems that gained focus in the 1980s?

Critical Thinking

4. **Big Ideas** What new innovations occurred in the consumer electronics industry in the 1980s?

5. **Organizing** Use a graphic organizer similar to the one below to list the changes in entertainment in the 1980s.

Changes in Entertainment

6. **Analyzing Visuals** Study the graph of the stock market rise on page 755. How is this graph indicative of what you have read about in this section?

Writing About History

7. **Persuasive Writing** Choose one of the social problems of the 1980s. Write a letter to members of your favorite band asking them to perform a concert to benefit your cause. Your letter should explain why the cause is important.

History ⊙ONLINE
Study Central™ To review this section, go to glencoe.com and click on Study Central.

✓ Reading Check

Answer:
aid to starving people in Africa; aid to American farmers

Assess

History ⊙ONLINE

Study Central™ provides summaries, interactive games, and online graphic organizers to help students review content.

Close

Summarizing Ask: What was life like in the United States in the 1980s? *(The economy was booming, there was a revolution in the media, and there were advances in space technology. However, the decade was also marked by an increase in social problems, such as drug use and the AIDS epidemic, although many groups also began to fight to solve these problems.)* **OL**

Section 3 REVIEW

Answers

1. All definitions can be found in the section and the Glossary.
2. Some companies began to grow in the area of discount retailing.
3. drug abuse, alcohol abuse, AIDS
4. the Sony Walkman, VCRs, video games
5. Innovations include rap music; listening to music on tiny portable cassette players; watching movie and music videos and cable or satellite TV; and playing video games.
6. It indicates a booming economy.
7. Students' letters will vary but should use standard grammar, use correct letter format, and be persuasive.

Focus

Ask students to define basic terms such as urban, rural, and suburban. Explain the meaning of "exurbs." Have students identify the type of community in which they live.

Teach

R Reading Skill

Determining Importance
Ask: What are the possible advantages in several of the high growth areas that have made people and industry move there? *(Students might suggest climate, large labor pool, and infrastructure already in place.)* **BL**

C Critical Thinking

Analyze Information Have students work in teams to create surveys about local community development. Tell students to devise 10 questions that can be answered with a range of responses. *(One example could be: Do you favor increased mass transit options? Sample responses might be Strongly Favor, Favor, Neutral, Oppose, and Strongly Oppose.)* **OL**

Additional Support

NATIONAL GEOGRAPHIC

GEOGRAPHY & HISTORY

Urban America on the Move

R After World War II, cities grew into vast metropolitan areas—a development referred to as "urban sprawl." Inner cities, often inhabited by lower-income people, lost tax revenue, resulting in deteriorating infrastructure and shortages of affordable housing. As the map shows, many high-growth areas are in Southern Sunbelt states.

In response, some cities sought to improve urban neighborhoods and encourage reinvestment in the city core. These policies have had only limited effect, as suburbs and new "exurbs"—communities located in the country beyond the suburbs, continue to grow.

How Has Urban Geography Affected Politics?

C The rapid growth of the suburbs and exurbs plays an important role in American politics. Inner city communities tend to vote for Democrats, while voters in outer suburbs and exurbs tend to vote for Republicans. The reason for this pattern is unclear. In part, it reflects the preference of many minorities who live in the inner city to vote for Democrats. In addition, some political geographers believe that since city-dwellers rely more on government services, they tend to support liberal policies that favor government activism. People in the suburbs and exurbs want more independence and more often distrust government—a conservative perspective. They believe large city governments have done a poor job running schools and controlling crime.

▲ *Urban sprawl, traffic congestion, long commutes, and air pollution are part of the price Atlanta paid for rapid growth.*

Seattle
San Francisco
Los Angeles
San Diego   Phoenix

Existing development as of 1993
Intense
Moderate
Development since 1993
Intense
Moderate

Analyzing GEOGRAPHY

1. **Movement** Which regions experienced the most growth after 1993?
2. **Human-Environment Interaction** How does the urban geography of American cities shape voting patterns and preferences?

760 **Chapter 22** Resurgence of Conservatism

Collaborative Learning

Create an Urban Plan Divide the class into small groups. Challenge each group to imagine that they are a firm of urban planners specializing in "smart growth" and "green building." Have them use the Internet or library resources to find out more about these concepts. Then have them outline a plan with rough sketches for the new community they have designed. Remind them to take climate into account; a development planned for the Sunbelt states will look different than one in northern states.

Atlanta, Georgia was one of the fastest growing cities in the early 1990s. The expansion of Atlanta's suburbs into surrounding counties since 1993 is shown in red and yellow.

Minneapolis

Boston

New York City

Chicago

Denver

Atlanta

Dallas

Austin

Houston

Miami

Like many Sunbelt cities, Austin, Texas, experienced rapid growth in the 1980s and 1990s—much of it fueled by the influx of new high-tech companies. Austin's population was about 465,000 in 1990. By 2007, it had reached 690,000.

Assess/Close

Activity: Top Ten Cities Ask students to use an almanac or other reference source to find the top ten most populous cities in the United States. Have them locate those places on the map. Do they observe any changes or new patterns emerging?

Analyzing GEOGRAPHY

Answers:
1. the south and west
2. Urban voters tend to vote Democratic, while suburban and exurban voters tend to vote Republican. This may reflect the tendency of urban dwellers to rely on and be willing to support government services, while suburban and exurban dwellers tend to distrust government and prefer independence.

Technology Connection

Urban Planning in China Have students working in pairs use the Internet to find reputable sources on the problems of growing industrial cities in China. Ask students to read and summarize at least three articles suggesting ways that China can continue to modernize and still follow the Kyoto Protocols.

Focus

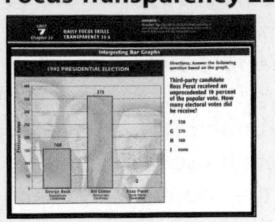
Guide to Reading

Answers:

Soviet Union: cooperated with reform leader Gorbachev; China: halted arms sales and reduced diplomatic contact; Panama: invaded and seized dictator and helped people hold elections and organize a new government; Middle East: imposed economic sanctions against Iraq and carried out Operation Desert Storm

Section Spotlight Video

To generate student interest and provide a springboard for class discussion, access the Chapter 22, Section 4 video at glencoe.com or on the video DVD.

Resource Manager

Section 4

The End of the Cold War

Guide to Reading

Big Ideas
Economics and Society The deficit and an economic slowdown hurt George H.W. Bush's attempt to win reelection in 1992.

Content Vocabulary
- perestroika (p. 763)
- glasnost (p. 763)
- downsizing (p. 766)
- capital gains tax (p. 767)
- grassroots movement (p. 767)

Academic Vocabulary
- initiative (p. 765)
- retain (p. 767)

People and Events to Identify
- Boris Yeltsin (p. 764)
- Tiananmen Square (p. 765)
- Saddam Hussein (p. 765)
- H. Ross Perot (p. 767)

Reading Strategy
Categorizing Complete a graphic organizer similar to the one below by describing U.S. foreign policy in each of the places listed.

Place	Foreign Policy
Soviet Union	
China	
Panama	
Middle East	

In the late 1980s, the United States faced a series of international crises. The Cold War came to an end in Europe, but events in the Middle East soon led the United States into its first major war since Vietnam.

The Soviet Union Collapses

MAIN Idea The Soviet Union's attempts at reforming its social and economic systems failed, leading to the collapse of the Communist eastern bloc.

HISTORY AND YOU What can you recall about the division of Europe after World War II? Read on to learn about the massive changes that took place in Eastern Europe at the end of the 1980s.

When Ronald Reagan left office, few Americans were thinking about foreign policy. Many generally wanted a continuation of Reagan's domestic policies—low taxes and less government action. When Republicans nominated George H. W. Bush for president in 1988, he reassured Americans he would continue Reagan's policies by making a promise: "Read my lips: No new taxes."

The Democrats hoped to regain the White House in 1988 by promising to help working-class Americans, minorities, and the poor. One candidate for the nomination, civil rights leader Jesse Jackson, tried to create a "rainbow coalition"—a broad group of minorities and the poor—by speaking about homelessness and unemployment. Jackson finished second in the primaries, the first African American to make a serious run for the nomination.

The Democrats nominated Massachusetts governor Michael Dukakis. The Bush campaign portrayed him as too liberal and "soft on crime." The Democrats questioned Bush's leadership abilities, but Bush had Reagan's endorsement and, with the economy still doing well, most Americans felt that Bush was the more able candidate. Bush easily defeated Dukakis in the general election, although Democrats kept control of Congress.

Voters had focused on domestic issues during the election campaign, but soon after taking office President Bush had to focus most of his time and energy on foreign policy as change swept through Eastern Europe and the Cold War came to an abrupt end.

Revolution in Eastern Europe

As president, Bush continued Reagan's policy of cooperation with Soviet leader Mikhail Gorbachev. By the late 1980s, the Soviet economy was suffering from years of inefficient central planning and huge expenditures on the arms race. To save the economy,

---

R Reading Strategies	**C** Critical Thinking	**D** Differentiated Instruction	**W** Writing Support	**S** Skill Practice
Teacher Edition • Making Connections, p. 763 • Read. Prim. Sources, p. 764 • Act. Prior Know., p. 765 • Taking Notes, p. 766 **Additional Resources** • Read. Skill Act., URB p. 55 • Guided Read. Act., URB p. 83	**Additional Resources** • Critical Thinking Skills Act., URB p. 66 • Auth. Assess., p. 49 • Quizzes/Tests, p. 316	**Additional Resources** • Reinforcing Skill Act., URB p. 65 • Reteaching Act., URB p. 77	**Teacher Edition** • Narrative Writing, p. 763 **Additional Resources** • Enrichment Act., URB p. 78	**Additional Resources** • Time Line Act., URB p. 67 • RENTG, p. 242

NATIONAL GEOGRAPHIC Revolutions in Eastern Europe

◀ The Berlin Wall fell on November 10, 1989.

4. Germany reunited, 1990

3. Berlin Wall torn down, Nov. 1989

1. Democratic elections, 1989

5. Baltic States became independent, 1991

6. Czechoslovakia separated, 1993

2. Non-Communist governments created, 1989

▲ Boris Yeltsin rallies the crowd against the military coup on August 19, 1991.

Analyzing GEOGRAPHY

1. **Regions** Which Eastern European countries abandoned communism first?

2. **Place** Why was the fall of communism in East Germany significant?

Teach

Analyzing GEOGRAPHY

Answers:

1. Poland, Hungary, Bulgaria, and Romania

2. It was particularly significant because it meant that Germany could be reunified.

R Reading Strategy

Making Connections To help students understand the impact of the Berlin Wall coming down, engage them in this pre-reading activity. Use a large map of your community and draw a line down the center of it. Ask students to look at the map closely and make a list of all the aspects of their lives that would be affected if they could not cross "the wall." **OL**

W Writing Support

Narrative Writing Have students conduct some research about the division and reunification of Germany. Tell them to write a letter that might have been written by a German teenager after the Berlin wall fell. **OL**

Hands-On Chapter Project
Step 4

Gorbachev instituted **perestroika,** or "restructuring," and allowed some private enterprise and profit making.

The other principle of Gorbachev's plan was **glasnost,** or "openness." It allowed more freedom of religion and speech, enabling people to discuss politics openly. With Gorbachev's support, glasnost spread to Eastern Europe. In 1989 revolutions replaced Communist rulers with democratic governments in Bulgaria, Czechoslovakia, Hungary, Poland, and Romania. The tide of revolution then swept over East Germany, and at midnight on November 9, 1989, guards at the Berlin Wall opened the gates.

Within days, bulldozers leveled the hated symbol of Communist repression. Within a year, East and West Germany had reunited to form one nation—the Federal Republic of Germany.

The Soviet Union Collapses

As Eastern Europe abandoned communism, Gorbachev faced mounting criticism from opponents at home. In August 1991 a group of Communist officials and army officers tried to stage a coup—an overthrow of the government. They arrested Gorbachev and sent troops into Moscow.

Chapter 22 Resurgence of Conservatism **763**

Conducting an Opinion Poll

Step 4: Analyzing the Findings Have students return to their groups and compare their poll results.

Identifying Points of View Ask students to calculate the average response to each of their statements and then write a brief paragraph for each in which they attempt to interpret their findings.

(Chapter Project continued on Visual Summary page)

R Reading Strategy

Reading Primary Sources
Ask students where U.S. forces launched attacks before they attacked the invading Iraqis in Kuwait. *(Iraq)* **BL**

Analyzing VISUALS

Answers:
1. Coalition forces most likely chose to launch their invasion from Saudi Arabia because Saudi Arabia, unlike Iran, was an ally, needed some protection anyway, and shared a border with Kuwait, unlike Syria and Turkey.
2. Saudi Arabia and Israel

✓ Reading Check

Answer:
It was intended to save the Soviet economy by allowing some private enterprise and profit-making.

Additional Support

In Moscow, Russian president **Boris Yeltsin** defied the coup leaders from his offices in the Russian Parliament. About 50,000 people surrounded the Russian Parliament to protect it from troops. President Bush telephoned Yeltsin to express the support of the United States. Soon afterward, the coup collapsed, and Gorbachev returned to Moscow.

The defeat of the coup brought change swiftly. All 15 Soviet republics declared their independence from the Soviet Union. Yeltsin outlawed the Communist Party in Russia. In late December 1991 Gorbachev announced the end of the Soviet Union. Most of the former Soviet republics then joined in a federation called the Commonwealth of Independent States (CIS). Although CIS member states remained independent, they agreed to form a common economic zone in 1993.

✓ **Reading Check** **Explaining** Why did Mikhail Gorbachev institute the policy of *perestroika*?

A "New World Order"

MAIN Idea Bush used his foreign policy expertise to deal with crises in China, Panama, and the Persian Gulf.

HISTORY AND YOU Do you remember learning about student protests in the 1960s? Read on to learn about a student protest in China.

After the Cold War, the world became increasingly unpredictable. President Bush noted that a "new world order" was emerging, and with it came several new crises in China, Panama, and the Middle East.

Tiananmen Square

Despite the collapse of communism in Eastern Europe and the Soviet Union, China's Communist leaders were determined to stay in power. China's government had relaxed

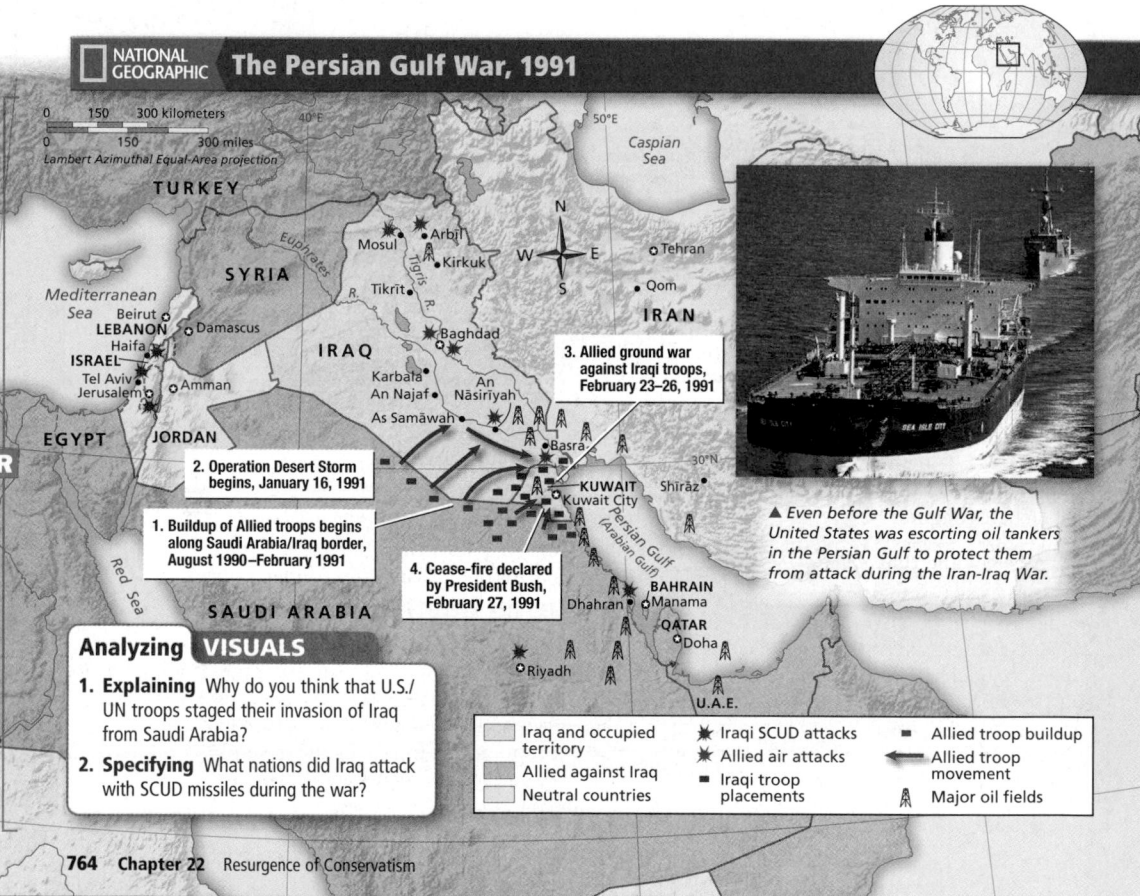

NATIONAL GEOGRAPHIC **The Persian Gulf War, 1991**

3. Allied ground war against Iraqi troops, February 23–26, 1991

2. Operation Desert Storm begins, January 16, 1991

1. Buildup of Allied troops begins along Saudi Arabia/Iraq border, August 1990–February 1991

4. Cease-fire declared by President Bush, February 27, 1991

▲ Even before the Gulf War, the United States was escorting oil tankers in the Persian Gulf to protect them from attack during the Iran-Iraq War.

Analyzing VISUALS

1. **Explaining** Why do you think that U.S./UN troops staged their invasion of Iraq from Saudi Arabia?
2. **Specifying** What nations did Iraq attack with SCUD missiles during the war?

Legend		
Iraq and occupied territory	✹ Iraqi SCUD attacks	▪ Allied troop buildup
Allied against Iraq	✷ Allied air attacks	← Allied troop movement
Neutral countries	▪ Iraqi troop placements	⚒ Major oil fields

---

Extending the Content

Strait of Hormuz The Strait of Hormuz is a narrow shipping lane that connects the Persian Gulf, the Gulf of Oman, and the Arabian Sea. Most of the crude oil produced in the Middle East passes through the Strait of Hormuz. In 1997 about 14 million barrels of crude oil passed through the strait every day. Since the waterway is only about 40 miles (64 km) across at its widest point, it is possible that a country might block or hamper the passage of ships. During the 1980s, the United States began escorting oil tankers through the strait to protect them from Iranian attacks. If the passage were ever closed, oil would have to be shipped overland by pipeline—a much more expensive option.

controls on the economy, but it continued to repress political speech and dissent. In May 1989, Chinese students and workers held demonstrations for democracy. The center of the protests was **Tiananmen Square** in Beijing, China's capital. At first, it appeared as if China were repeating the pattern of Eastern Europe and that communism might be ended peacefully. In early June, however, government tanks and soldiers crushed the protests in Tiananmen Square. Many people were killed and hundreds of pro-democracy activists were arrested. Many were later sentenced to death.

These events shocked the world. The United States and several European countries halted arms sales and reduced their diplomatic contacts with China. The World Bank suspended loans. Some U.S. congressional leaders urged even stronger sanctions, but President Bush resisted these harsher measures, believing that trade and diplomacy would eventually moderate China's behavior.

Panama

While President Bush struggled to deal with global events elsewhere, a crisis developed in Panama. In 1978 the United States had agreed to give Panama control over the Panama Canal by the year 2000. Because of the canal's importance, American officials wanted to make sure Panama's government was both stable and pro-American.

By 1989, Panama's dictator, General Manuel Noriega, had stopped cooperating with the United States. He also aided drug traffickers, cracked down on opponents, and harassed American military personnel defending the canal. In December 1989, Bush ordered American troops to invade Panama. The troops seized Noriega, who was sent to the United States to stand trial on drug charges. The troops then helped the Panamanians hold elections and organize a new government.

The Persian Gulf War

President Bush faced perhaps his most serious crisis in the Middle East. In August 1990 Iraq's dictator, **Saddam Hussein,** sent his army to invade oil-rich Kuwait. American officials feared that the invasion might be only the first step and that Iraq's ultimate goal was to capture Saudi Arabia and its vast oil reserves. American troops rushed to the Middle East and took up positions in Saudi Arabia in response.

President Bush persuaded other UN member countries to join a coalition to stop Iraq. Led by the United States, the United Nations imposed economic sanctions on Iraq and demanded that the Iraqis withdraw. The coalition included troops from the United States, Canada, Europe, and Middle Eastern nations. The UN set a deadline for the Iraqis' withdrawal, after which the coalition would use force to remove them. Congress also voted to authorize the use of force if Iraq did not withdraw.

On October 31, 1990, General Colin Powell, chairman of the Joint Chiefs of Staff, Secretary of Defense Dick Cheney, and other high-ranking officials met with President Bush. It was clear that Iraq would not obey the UN deadline. Powell presented the plan for attacking Iraq. Several advisers gasped at the numbers, which called for over 500,000 American troops. "Mr. President," Powell began, "I wish . . . that I could assure you that air power alone could do it but you can't take that chance. We've gotta take the **initiative** out of the enemy's hands if we're going to go to war." Cheney later recalled that Bush "never hesitated." He looked up from the plans and said simply, "Do it."

On January 16, 1991, the coalition forces launched Operation Desert Storm. Dozens of cruise missiles and thousands of laser-guided bombs fell on Iraq, destroying its air defenses, bridges, artillery, and other military targets. After about six weeks of bombardment, the coalition launched a massive ground attack. Waves of tanks and troop carriers smashed through Iraqi lines and encircled the Iraqi forces defending Kuwait.

The attack killed thousands of Iraqi soldiers, and hundreds of thousands more surrendered. Fewer than 300 coalition troops were killed. Just 100 hours after the ground war began, President Bush declared Kuwait to be liberated. Iraq accepted the coalition's cease-fire terms, and American troops returned home to cheering crowds.

✔ Reading Check **Examining** Why did President Bush take action when Iraqi troops invaded Kuwait?

R Reading Strategy
Activating Prior Knowledge
Before students read, ask them to recall how President Carter responded to human rights abuses around the world. Tell them they will read about how President George H. W. Bush responded to abuses in China. **BL**

Did You Know?

Iraqi leader Saddam Hussein liked to be called by his first name. When pronounced correctly, with the emphasis on the second syllable, *Saddam* means "leader" or "learned one." During the Persian Gulf War, President George H. W. Bush insisted on pronouncing the name with the emphasis on the first syllable. Pronounced this way, *Saddam* means "a boy who fixes or cleans shoes."

✔ Reading Check

Answer:
American officials feared that Iraq's ultimate goal was to capture Saudi Arabia and its vast oil reserves.

Activity: Collaborative Learning

Comparing Invasions In the debate over whether to use force against Saddam Hussein, some who favored military action used the example of Hitler to justify their stance. Those who opposed action used the example of Vietnam. Have students work in pairs. One partner is to review the chapters about World War II; the other, the chapter about the Vietnam war. Ask them to share their information and decide whether each of these historical examples applied to the situation in Kuwait. Then ask students to consider the war that began with Iraq in 2003. **Ask:** Which example best fits that war? *(Students' answers will vary but should be supported with facts.)* **OL**

766

R Reading Strategy

Taking Notes Suggest that students take notes by creating cause-and-effect charts. They should identify the causes and effects of the recession and the causes of the election results in 1992. **BL**

Did You Know?

Many companies began using the term *downsizing* rather than *layoff* because *layoff* sounded too negative. After several years of down-sizing, some companies started to use the term *rightsizing* to imply that cuts were being made to adjust the workforce to the correct size.

Analyzing VISUALS

Answers:

1. They are hurting mainstream parties. The cartoon of Perot is riding Bush, attached like a parasite.
2. The Northeast is a more lib-eral area, and more likely to vote Democratic.

Additional Support

Domestic Challenges

MAIN Idea To reduce the deficit, President Bush raised taxes, an unpopular decision that helped Bill Clinton win the election.

HISTORY AND YOU How are your school and community designed to provide access for people who use wheelchairs? Read on to find out more about the Americans with Disabilities Act of 1990.

President Bush spent much of his time dealing with foreign policy, but he could not ignore domestic issues. He inherited a growing deficit and a slowing economy. With the Persian Gulf crisis, the economy plunged into a recession and unemployment rose.

The Economy Slows

The recession that began in 1990 was partly caused by the end of the Cold War. As the Soviet threat faded, the United States began reducing its armed forces and canceling orders for military equipment. Thousands of soldiers and defense industry workers were laid off.

Other companies also began **downsizing** —laying off workers and managers to become **R** more efficient. The nation's high level of debt made the recession worse. Americans had bor-rowed heavily during the 1980s and now faced paying off large debts.

In addition, the huge deficit forced the gov-ernment to borrow money to pay for its pro-grams. This borrowing kept money from being

---

HISTORY AND GEOGRAPHY
The Election of 1992

The election of 1992 marked the first time since 1968 that no candidate won at least 50 percent of the popu-lar vote and for much the same reason. A strong third party challenger, Ross Perot (below, center), took votes from both major candidates.

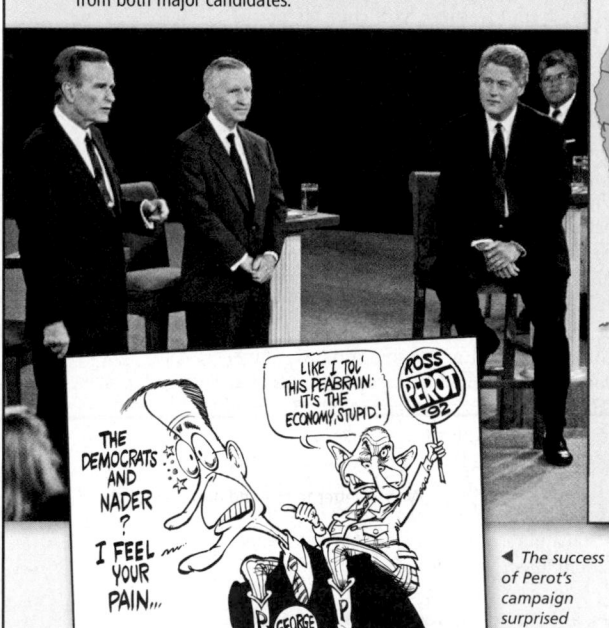

◄ The success of Perot's campaign surprised many Americans.

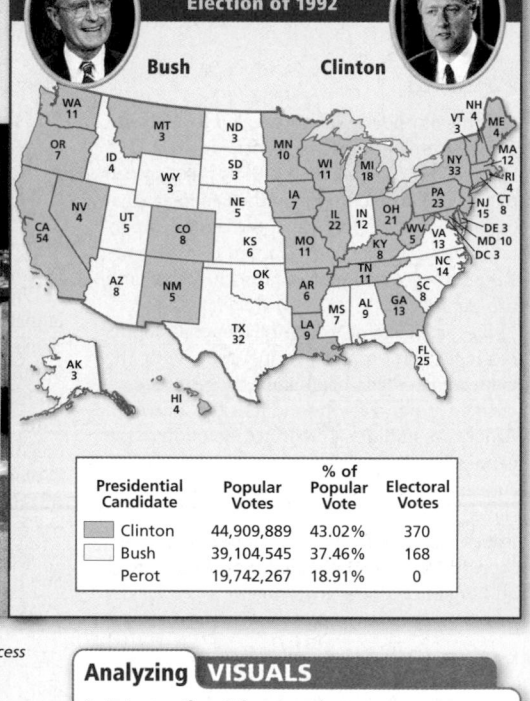

Presidential Election of 1992

Bush   Clinton

Presidential Candidate	Popular Votes	% of Popular Vote	Electoral Votes
Clinton	44,909,889	43.02%	370
Bush	39,104,545	37.46%	168
Perot	19,742,267	18.91%	0

Analyzing VISUALS

1. **Interpreting** What does the cartoon suggest about independent candidates?
2. **Speculating** What factors might explain Clinton's popularity in the Northeast?

766 Chapter 22 Resurgence of Conservatism

Activity: Interdisciplinary Connection

Mathematics Have students use the figures in the map legend above to create a circle graph showing the proportion of total votes for each candidate in 1992. Point out that the percent-ages listed do not total 100 percent. Tell stu-dents to create a category labeled "other" for the remaining votes. Then have students create cir-cle graphs showing the proportion of total votes each candidate received in the west (west of the Mississippi River) and the proportion of total votes each candidate received in the east (east of the Mississippi River). **OL**

available to businesses. The government also had to pay interest on its debt, money that might otherwise have been used to fund programs or boost the economy.

As the economy slowed, hundreds of savings-and-loan institutions collapsed. After President Reagan had allowed them to be deregulated, many had made risky or even dishonest investments. When these investments failed, depositors collected on federal programs to insure deposits. The cost to the public may have reached $500 billion.

Gridlock in Government

Shortly after taking office, Bush tried to improve the economy. He called for a cut in the **capital gains tax**—the tax paid by businesses and investors when they sell stocks or real estate for a profit. Bush believed that the tax cut would encourage businesses to expand. Calling the idea a tax break for the rich, Democrats in Congress defeated it.

Aware that the growing federal deficit was hurting the economy, Bush broke his "no new taxes" campaign pledge. After meeting with congressional leaders, he agreed to a tax increase in exchange for cuts in spending. This decision turned many voters against Bush.

The 1992 Election

Although the recession had weakened his popularity, Bush won the Republican nomination. Bush promised to address voters' economic concerns and he blamed congressional Democrats for the gridlock that seemingly paralyzed the nation's government.

The Democrats nominated Arkansas governor William Jefferson Clinton, despite stories that questioned his character and the fact that he did not serve in Vietnam. Calling himself a "New Democrat" to separate himself from more liberal Democrats, Clinton promised to cut middle-class taxes, reduce government spending, and reform the nation's health care and welfare programs. His campaign repeatedly blamed Bush for the recession.

Some Americans were not happy with either Bush or Clinton. This enabled an independent candidate, billionaire Texas businessman **H. Ross Perot,** to make a strong challenge. Perot stressed the need to end deficit spending. His no-nonsense style appealed to many Americans. A **grassroots movement**—groups of people organizing at the local level—put Perot on the ballot in all 50 states.

Bill Clinton won the election with 43 percent of the popular vote and 370 electoral votes. The Democrats also **retained** control of Congress. Bush won 37 percent of the popular vote, while Perot received 19 percent—the best showing for a third-party candidate since 1912—but no electoral votes.

As the first president born after World War II, the 46-year-old Clinton was the first person from the baby boom generation to enter the White House. It was his task to revive the economy and guide the United States in a rapidly changing world.

✓ Reading Check **Summarizing** Why did President Bush lose popularity as the 1992 election approached?

Section 4 REVIEW

Vocabulary
1. **Explain** the significance of: perestroika, glasnost, Boris Yeltsin, Tiananmen Square, Saddam Hussein, downsizing, capital gains tax, H. Ross Perot, grassroots movement.

Main Ideas
2. **Explaining** How did perestroika and glasnost create conditions that led to the fall of the Soviet Union?

3. **Describing** What actions did the United States take in Panama in 1989?

4. **Determining Cause and Effect** How did the huge deficits from the Reagan years lead to economic problems under George Bush?

Critical Thinking
5. **Big Ideas** How did the economy affect the 1992 election?

6. **Organizing** Use a graphic organizer similar to the one below to list the causes of the recession of the early 1990s.

Budget Problems	Economic Problems	Foreign Developments

7. **Analyzing Visuals** Examine the map on page 764. Which nations have significant oil resources?

Writing About History
8. **Descriptive Writing** Suppose that you are traveling in West Germany in 1989 when the Berlin Wall is being torn down. Write a letter to a friend at home to describe the event and how you think it will affect the United States.

History ONLINE
Study Central™ To review this section, go to glencoe.com and click on Study Central.

767

Assess

History ONLINE

Study Central™ provides summaries, interactive games, and online graphic organizers to help students review content.

✓ Reading Check

Answer:
The economy was failing, and Bush broke his promise not to raise or introduce new taxes.

Close

Summarizing Ask: How did Clinton gain support in the 1992 election? *(He set himself apart from other Democrats by calling himself a "new Democrat." He also promised to cut taxes and spending.)* **OL**

Section 4 REVIEW

Answers

1. All definitions can be found in the section and the Glossary.

2. They created a more open economy and society; people were allowed to discuss politics and to protest, and this led to the overthrow of several Communist regimes in the eastern bloc and, eventually, to the fall of the Soviet Union.

3. U.S. troops invaded Panama, arrested its dictator, Manuel Noriega, and then helped the people hold elections and establish a democratic government.

4. The huge deficit forced the government to borrow money to pay for its programs. This borrowing kept money from being available to businesses. The government also had to pay interest, money that might otherwise have been used to fund programs or boost the economy.

5. The recession hurt Bush's efforts to win reelection.

6. Budget Problems: tax increase; Economic Problems: recession, high consumer debt, federal deficit; Foreign Developments: fall of the Soviet Union, Persian Gulf War

7. Saudi Arabia, Kuwait, Iraq, Iran, and Syria

8. Students' letters will vary but should be descriptive and use standard grammar and punctuation.

Chapter 22 Visual Summary

Activity: Collaborative Learning

Government Priorities As described in this chapter, conservatives and liberals believe in different types of spending, government control, and freedom from government. Have students work in groups. Ask them to discuss what spending, controls, and freedoms are most important. **Ask:** Is it more important for citizens to have personal freedoms or for business to have freedom from control? Should military spending be more or less important than programs that aid citizens personally? Have students make a three-column chart headed "Spending," "Controls," and "Freedoms" and then rank their items in order of priority. Have a member from each group report the results, including disagreements among group members, to the class. **OL**

Narrative Writing Have interested students create a narrative history of U.S. involvement in China, the Middle East, or Latin America during Reagan's and George H. W. Bush's presidencies. **OL**

Causes of the New Conservatism

- The Cold War promotes strong foreign policy and an emphasis on minimal government interference in economics.
- Cold War fears of communism encourage many religious Americans to turn to conservative ideas.
- Many Americans are disturbed by the protests, demonstrations, and violence of the 1960s.
- The population growth in the Sunbelt increases support for conservative politicians.
- The rise of an evangelical movement willing to use politics to change society and defend its values helps mobilize conservative voters.
- Frustration with rising taxes and government regulation, especially in the South and West, turns many voters to conservative ideas.
- Both Western conservatives and Southern conservatives come to see the Republican Party as the more conservative party.

▲ Part of the new conservative movement drew support from Americans who were fed up with high taxes.

The Reagan Administration

- Ronald Reagan is elected president in 1980 and 1984.
- Reagan promotes supply-side economics and pushes large tax cuts through Congress.
- Many industries are deregulated, helping spur a boom in the oil, transportation, and communications industries.
- A political debate over cutting government programs rather than expanding them shapes the domestic politics of the era.
- Reagan's administration takes a strong anti-Communist stance in Latin America, the Caribbean, and the Middle East, providing aid to groups that resist communism.
- The nation begins a sustained military buildup to put pressure on the Soviet economy; in addition the United States begins work on anti-missile "Star Wars" technology.
- The failure to cut domestic programs, combined with increased military spending, drives the growing budget deficit to record levels.
- Energy prices fall, the economy grows rapidly, and stock market values soar.
- The farm debt crisis and deregulation of the banks leads to the collapse of many family farms, and many savings and loan institutions.
- Under great economic stress, the Soviet Union introduces perestroika and glasnost; communism falls across Eastern Europe in 1989, and then the Soviet Union collapses in 1991.

▲ The summit between President Reagan and Mikhail Gorbachev created an easing of tensions between the U.S. and Soviet Union.

768 Chapter 22 Resurgence of Conservatism

Hands-On Chapter Project

Step 5: Wrap Up

Conducting an Opinion Poll

Step 5: Wrap Up Have groups share their results with the rest of the class. Encourage students to discuss why President Reagan scored higher on some students' polls than others.

Putting It Together Have students evaluate the project by answering the following questions:

- What was the most difficult part of the project? Why?
- What was the best part of the project? Why?
- What was the most important thing I learned by completing this project?

Ask students to record their responses in their journal. **OL**

STANDARDIZED TEST PRACTICE

TEST-TAKING TIP

Read each answer choice and eliminate the ones that simply do not make sense for the given question.

Reviewing Vocabulary

Directions: Choose the word or words that best complete the sentence.

1. Political views held by _____ include the belief that the government should regulate the economy to protect people from the power of large corporations.

   A economists

   B liberals

   C conservatives

   D televangelists

2. Reagan based his policies on _____, a philosophy that advocates tax cuts to improve the economy.

   A monetarist economics

   B supply-and-demand economics

   C microeconomics

   D supply-side economics

3. A new business model known as _____ had a major impact on the economy starting in the 1980s.

   A superstations

   B wholesale retailing

   C discount retailing

   D direct mail

4. One part of Mikhail Gorbachev's plan to improve conditions in the Soviet Union was to allow _____, or increased freedom in speech, religion, and political discussion.

   A glasnost

   B perestroika

   C contra

   D rights of assembly

Reviewing Main Ideas

Directions: Choose the best answer for each of the following questions.

Section 1 *(pp. 740–745)*

5. One main difference between liberals and conservatives is that, generally,

   A conservatives believe in government regulation of the economy, while liberals do not.

   B liberals believe in government regulation of the economy, while conservatives do not.

   C conservatives believe that all power should be held by the national government, while liberals do not.

   D liberals believe that all power should be held by the states, while conservatives do not.

6. Which of the following two groups had added their support to conservatives by the 1980s?

   A African Americans and urbanites

   B Northerners and Easterners

   C Democrats and women

   D Sunbelters and suburbanites

Section 2 *(pp. 746–753)*

7. Critics of Reagan's economic policy referred to it as "trickle-down economics" because they

   A believed that the plan would work, allowing wealth to "trickle down" to the middle and lower classes.

   B ridiculed the idea that much wealth would "trickle down" to the middle and lower classes.

   C believed that the plan was messy and would cause a great deal of wasteful government spending.

   D agreed that the richest people would share their wealth with the neediest in society.

Need Extra Help?

If You Missed Questions . . .	1	2	3	4	5	6	7
Go to Page . . .	740–742	748	755	762–763	740–742	743	748

 GO ON

Chapter 22 Resurgence of Conservatism **769**

Answers and Analyses
Reviewing Vocabulary

1. B Review the general differences between liberals and conservatives with students, who will most likely have trouble choosing between *B* and *C*. Economists are people who study economics. They can be liberal or conservative. Televangelists are preachers on television.

2. D Reaganomics was based on supply-side economics. Basically, the theory says that lower taxes lead to more money being spent (including investments), thereby stimulating the economy and leading to economic growth. Basically, supply-side economics seeks to increase the *supply* of capital. Greater money supply = greater investment.

3. C Discount retailing offered goods at a discount. Discount retailers are prevalent today. Ask students to discuss how they think shopping was different in the years before discount retailing.

4. A *Glasnost* means "openness." A way for students to remember its meaning is to think of *glass*, which is clear, and relate it to openness. *Perestroika* dealt with restructuring the economy. To remember this, students should think of the "rest" in *Perest*roika to "restructuring."

Reviewing Main Ideas

5. B Review the sections on liberals and conservatives. Generally, conservatives support a more hands-off government with a laissez-faire approach to economics.

6. D Review "Sunbelt Conservatism" and "Suburban Conservatism" on pages 743–744 with students. The groups/areas listed in *A* and *B in general* tend to be liberals. *C* does not make sense because it includes "Democrats."

7. B Critics believed Reagan's policies would help the wealthy, but that it would not help, or trickle-down to, the middle and lower classes. The question asks about critics' opinions, so *A* and *D* are incorrect, because they are supportive of the plan, not critical.

Chapter 22

8. C The key word in SDI is *defense*. Only *C* includes an action that is a directly defensive maneuver.

9. B VCRs revolutionized the way people watched TV and movies at home. The DVD and the PDA were not available in the 1980s. The digital watch was invented in the 1970s.

10. C Nancy Reagan's "Just Say No" campaign sums up a major focus of 1980s activism. As first lady for most of the decade, Nancy Reagan was able to keep the program in the forefront of public focus. She believed that eliminating drug abuse would lead to a reduction in crime.

11. B Boris Yeltsin was the president of Russia at the time of the coup. He was instrumental in dismantling it. The Berlin Wall had come down in 1989. *D* is irrelevant.

12. B The events in Tiananmen Square sparked protest in the U.S. and other nations, so students can reason that the actions of those nations expressed displeasure with China. Therefore, *A* can be eliminated. Making plans to express their concerns at a meeting would not be harsh enough. The U.S. did not send troops into China.

Critical Thinking

13. A The religious right is conservative in morals and values. Their concern for morals and values led them to join the conservative movement. Liberals generally favor increased social-welfare programs, not conservatives. The religious right was more concerned with the domestic agenda rather than with foreign relations. *D* would not make sense.

8. The Strategic Defense Initiative (SDI) was proposed to strengthen defense by

  A preventing the expansion of Communist countries.

  B re-emphasizing the use of infantry troops in future wars.

  C developing weapons to intercept incoming missiles.

  D severely reducing the number of American troops stationed worldwide.

Section 3 (pp. 754–759)

9. Which technology became available during the 1980s?

  A the digital video recorder

  B the video cassette recorder

  C the personal digital assistant

  D the digital watch

10. A major focus of U.S. social activism in the 1980s was

  A gun control.

  B illiteracy.

  C drug abuse.

  D poverty.

Section 4 (pp. 762–767)

11. The result of the failed Communist coup in Moscow in August 1991 was that

  A Boris Yeltsin became president of the Soviet Union.

  B the Soviet republics declared independence.

  C the Berlin Wall was taken down by bulldozers.

  D the United States sent troops into Saudi Arabia.

12. In response to events in Tiananmen Square in China, the United States and other nations

  A sent weapons and money to the rebels.

  B halted arms sales and reduced their diplomatic contacts with China.

  C made plans for a summit meeting with China to express their concerns.

  D sent in troops to help free the imprisoned protesters.

Critical Thinking

Directions: Choose the best answers to the following questions.

13. The religious right joined the conservative movement because they

  A were concerned about American values and morality.

  B wanted more liberal social welfare programs.

  C felt that the U.S. had been too aggressive with the U.S.S.R.

  D wanted government regulation of local churches.

14. The huge number of baby boomers affected the economy of the 1980s because they

  A were driven to acquire material goods and social success.

  B pushed for increased government spending for the poor.

  C rejected worldly success as members of the Moral Majority.

  D were beginning to draw Social Security benefits.

Base your answer to question 15 on the graph below and your knowledge of Chapter 22.

Military Spending and the Deficit

Sources: Departments of Commerce and Treasury; Office of Management and Budget.

15. How much money was spent on national defense in 1986?

  A approximately 500 billion dollars

  B more than 500 billion dollars

  C approximately 250 billion dollars

  D less than 250 million dollars

Need Extra Help?								
If You Missed Questions . . .	8	9	10	11	12	13	14	15
Go to Page . . .	753	757	758–759	763–764	764–765	764–765	754	R16

GO ON ➡

14. A Choices *C* and *D* can be immediately eliminated. Baby boomers spent money and sought out success, they did not reject it. Baby boomers are *now* affecting the economy because they are becoming eligible for Social Security, but were too young then for this to be a concern.

15. C The bottom line on the graph represents defense spending.

ASSESSMENT

16. The beginning of the collapse of communism in Eastern Europe is most closely associated with the

 A fall of the Berlin Wall.

 B admission of Warsaw Pact nations to the North Atlantic Treaty Organization (NATO).

 C intervention of the North Atlantic Treaty Organization (NATO) in Yugoslavia.

 D formation of the European Union.

Analyze the cartoon and answer the question that follows. Base your answer on the cartoon and on your knowledge of Chapter 22.

'I CAN'T BELIEVE MY EYES!'

17. What is the cartoonist saying about Gorbachev's policies?

 A Marx, Lenin, and Stalin would approve of his policies of glasnost and perestroika.

 B Marx, Lenin, and Stalin would disapprove of restructuring the Soviet economy and allowing some private enterprise.

 C Marx, Lenin, and Stalin would approve of glasnost, or allowing more freedom of religion and speech.

 D Marx, Lenin, and Stalin would disapprove of the expansion of communism to Eastern Europe.

Document-Based Questions

Directions: Analyze the document and answer the short-answer questions that follow the document.

President Ronald Reagan addressed the American people at the end of his presidency in 1988. The following is an excerpt from that address:

> The way I see it, there were two great triumphs, two things that I'm proudest of. One is the economic recovery, in which the people of America created—and filled—19 million new jobs. The other is the recovery of our morale. America is respected again . . . .
>
> Common sense told us that when you put a big tax on something, the people will produce less of it. So, we cut the people's tax rates, and the people produced more than ever before. The economy bloomed. . . . Common sense told us that to preserve the peace, we'd have to become strong again after years of weakness and confusion. So, we rebuilt our defenses, and this New Year we toasted the new peacefulness around the globe. . . .
>
> —from *Speaking My Mind*

18. What did Reagan believe were his greatest accomplishments?

19. How did Reagan feel his administration preserved peace?

Extended Response

20. In the late 1980s, the Cold War came to an end with the disintegration of the Warsaw Pact, the fall of the Berlin Wall, and the collapse of the Soviet Union. In an expository essay trace the events that led to the end of this global conflict and explain why you think the conflict ended when it did. In your essay, include an introduction, a conclusion, and at least three paragraphs with details from the chapter.

History ONLINE

For additional test practice, use Self-Check Quizzes—Chapter 22 at glencoe.com.

Need Extra Help?

If You Missed Questions . . .	16	17	18	19	20
Go to Page . . .	763	R18	R19	R19	762–767

Extended Response

20. Essays must demonstrate a strong understanding of the events that led to the end of the Cold War. Events should be presented with an understanding of their chronological order, and opinions on why the Cold War ended when it did should be supported with well-reasoned arguments.

---

16. A This question does not ask what caused the collapse of communism in Eastern Europe; it asks what event is *associated* with it. The fall of the Berlin Wall was the culmination of a series of revolutions. Students should relate the *collapse* of communism with the *collapse* of the wall.

17. B In the cartoon, Marx, Lenin, and Stalin can be seen peering down with looks of disapproval. They did not believe in private enterprise, so *perestroika* would not please them.

Stalin especially would not approve of greater freedoms of religion and speech.

Document-Based Questions

18. Reagan believed his greatest accomplishments were economic recovery and the recovery of American morale and international respect.

19. Reagan felt his administration preserved peace by becoming strong by rebuilding defenses.

History ONLINE

Have students visit the Web site at glencoe.com to review Chapter 22 and take the Self-Check Quiz.

Need Extra Help?

Have students refer to the pages listed if they miss any of the questions.

Chapter 23 Planning Guide

Key to Ability Levels

BL Below Level **AL** Above Level
OL On Level **ELL** English Language Learners

Key to Teaching Resources

Print Material DVD
CD-ROM Transparency

Levels					Resources	Chapter Opener	Section 1	Section 2	Section 3	Section 4	Chapter Assess
BL	OL	AL	ELL								
FOCUS											
BL	OL	AL	ELL		Daily Focus Transparencies		23-1	23-2	23-3	23-4	
TEACH											
BL	OL	AL			Economics and History Activity, URB		p. 7				
BL	OL	AL	ELL		Reading Essentials and Note-Taking Guide*		p. 245	p. 248	p. 251	p. 254	
BL	OL		ELL		Reading Skills Activity, URB					p. 87	
	OL				Historical Analysis Skills Activity, URB			p. 88			
BL	OL		ELL		Guided Reading Activity, URB*		p. 114	p. 115	p. 116	p. 117	
BL	OL	AL	ELL		Differentiated Instruction Activity, URB		p. 89				
BL	OL		ELL		English Learner Activity, URB			p. 91			
BL	OL	AL	ELL		Content Vocabulary Activity, URB*	p. 93					
BL	OL	AL	ELL		Academic Vocabulary Activity, URB	p. 95					
	OL	AL			Reinforcing Skills Activity, URB			p. 97			
	OL	AL			Critical Thinking Skills Activity, URB				p. 98		
BL	OL		ELL		Time Line Activity, URB		p. 99				
	OL				Linking Past and Present Activity, URB		p. 100				
BL	OL	AL	ELL		Primary Source Reading, URB		p. 101	p. 103			
BL	OL	AL	ELL		American Art and Music Activity, URB						p. 105
BL	OL	AL	ELL		Interpreting Political Cartoons Activity, URB			p. 107			
		AL			Enrichment Activity, URB				p. 111		
BL	OL	AL	ELL		Differentiated Instruction for the American History Classroom	✓	✓	✓	✓	✓	✓
BL	OL	AL	ELL		Unit Map Overlay Transparencies	✓	✓	✓	✓	✓	✓
BL	OL	AL	ELL		Unit Time Line Transparencies, Strategies, and Activities	✓	✓	✓	✓	✓	✓
BL	OL	AL	ELL		Cause and Effect Transparencies, Strategies, and Activities	✓	✓	✓	✓	✓	✓
BL	OL	AL	ELL		Why It Matters Chapter Transparencies, Strategies, and Activities	✓	✓	✓	✓	✓	✓
BL	OL	AL	ELL		American Biographies		✓	✓	✓		

Note: Please refer to the *Unit 7 Resource Book* for this chapter's URB materials.

* Also available in Spanish

- Interactive Lesson Planner
- Interactive Teacher Edition
- Fully editable blackline masters
- Section Spotlight Videos Launch

- Differentiated Lesson Plans
- Printable reports of daily assignments
- Standards Tracking System

Levels					Resources	Chapter Opener	Section 1	Section 2	Section 3	Section 4	Chapter Assess
BL	OL	AL	ELL								
TEACH *(continued)*											
BL	OL	AL		📁	**Supreme Court Case Studies**				p. 157		
BL	OL	AL	ELL	📁	**The Living Constitution**	✓	✓	✓	✓	✓	✓
BL	OL	AL	ELL	📁	**American Issues**	✓	✓	✓	✓	✓	✓
	OL	AL	ELL	📁	**American Art and Architecture Transparencies, Strategies, and Activities**	✓	✓	✓	✓	✓	✓
BL	OL	AL		📁	**High School American History Literature Library**	✓	✓	✓	✓	✓	✓
	OL	AL		💿	**American History Primary Source Documents Library**	✓	✓	✓	✓	✓	✓
BL	OL	AL	ELL	💿	**American Music: Hits Through History CD**	✓	✓	✓	✓	✓	✓
BL	OL	AL	ELL	💾	**StudentWorks™ Plus DVD**	✓	✓	✓	✓	✓	✓
BL	OL	AL	ELL	💿	**Vocabulary PuzzleMaker CD-ROM**	✓	✓	✓	✓	✓	✓
BL	OL	AL	ELL	💾	***The American Vision* Video Program DVD**	✓	✓	✓	✓	✓	✓
Teacher Resources				📁	**Strategies for Success**	✓	✓	✓	✓	✓	✓
				💾	**Presentation Plus! DVD**	✓	✓	✓	✓	✓	✓
				📁	**Success With English Learners**	✓	✓	✓	✓	✓	✓
ASSESS											
BL	OL	AL	ELL	📁	**Section Quizzes and Chapter Tests***		p. 325	p. 326	p. 327	p. 328	p. 329
BL	OL	AL	ELL	📁	**Authentic Assessment With Rubrics**						p. 51
BL	OL	AL	ELL	📁	**Standardized Test Practice Workbook**						p. 53
BL	OL	AL	ELL	💿	***ExamView®* Assessment Suite CD-ROM**		23-1	23-2	23-3	23-4	Ch. 23
BL	OL	AL	ELL	💿	**Interactive Tutor Self-Assessment CD-ROM**		23-1	23-2	23-3	23-4	Ch. 23
CLOSE											
BL			ELL	📁	**Reteaching Activity, URB**						p. 109
BL	OL		ELL	📁	**Reading and Study Skills Foldables™**	p. 84					

Using CyberScout

Research Using Famous Person

Technology Product

CyberScout is a convenient and dynamic search engine that provides several easy ways to locate information outside the McGraw-Hill Learning Network. CyberScout only searches Web sites that have been reviewed by teachers, so the information students find is always appropriate and accurate.

Objectives

After students learn using CyberScout, they will be able to

- research information on famous people in history;
- exercise research and study skills;
- practice writing skills.

Steps

- From the McGraw-Hill Learning Network home page (www.mhln.com), click on **For Students.**
- Choose **CyberScout** below **Homework Help.**

- Enter a name (last, or first and last) in the Famous Person field and click Go.
- The CyberScout page will display a set of results.
- Select the Famous Person's name from the results.
- Click the link to a Web site of interest.
- Students will be redirected to the Web site in a new window.
- Students navigate through the chosen Web site to gain information on their topic and take notes.

History ONLINE

	Student	Teacher	Parent
Beyond the Textbook	●	●	●
Chapter Overviews	●	●	●
Time Current Events	●		●
ePuzzles and Games	●		●
Concepts in Motion	●		●
Literature Connections		●	
Multi-Language Glossaries	●		●
Online Student Edition	●	●	●
Self-Check Quizzes	●		●
Student Web Activities	●		●
Study Central ™	●		●
Teaching Today		●	
Vocabulary eFlashcards	●		●
Web Activity Lesson Plans		●	

Glencoe Media Center

glencoe.com

❯ **Study-To-Go**
- Vocabulary eFlashcards
- Self-Check Quizzes

❯ **Audio/Video**
- Student Edition Audio
- Spanish Summaries
- Section Videos

- **Timed Readings Plus in Social Studies** helps students increase their reading rate and fluency while maintaining comprehension. The 400-word passages are similar to those found on state and national assessments.

- **Reading in the Content Area: Social Studies** concentrates on six essential reading skills that help students better comprehend what they read. The book includes 75 high-interest nonfiction passages written at increasing levels of difficulty.

- **Reading Social Studies** includes strategic reading instruction and vocabulary support in Social Studies content for both ELLs and native speakers of English.

www.jamestowneducation.com

Index to National Geographic Magazine:

The following articles relate to this chapter:

- "Robot Revolution," by Curt Suplee, July 1997.
- "Unveiling the Universe," by Kathy Sawyer, October 1999.

National Geographic Society Products To order the following, call National Geographic at 1-800-368-2728:

- *ZipZapMap! USA (ZipZapMap!)*

Access National Geographic's new, dynamic MapMachine Web site and other geography resources at:
www.nationalgeographic.com
www.nationalgeographic.com/maps

The following videotape programs are available from Glencoe as supplements to Chapter 23:

- Bill Clinton: In the Running (ISBN 1-56-501824-9)
- Yitzhak Rabin (ISBN 1-56-501714-5)

To order, call Glencoe at 1-800-334-7344. To find classroom resources to accompany many of these videos, check the following home pages:

A&E Television: www.aetv.com
The History Channel: www.historychannel.com

Reading List Generator CD-ROM

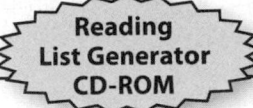

Use this database to search more than 30,000 titles to create a customized reading list for your students.

- Reading lists can be organized by students' reading level, author, genre, theme, or area of interest.
- The database provides Degrees of Reading Power (DRP) and Lexile™ readability scores for all selections.
- A brief summary of each selection is included.

Leveled reading suggestions for this chapter:

For students at a Grade 8 reading level:
- *Bill Clinton: President of the 90s,* by Robert Cwiklik

For students at a Grade 9 reading level:
- *Bill Gates: Helping People Use Computers,* by Charnan Simon

For students at a Grade 10 reading level:
- *Bill Gates: Computer King,* by Josepha Sherman

For students at a Grade 11 reading level:
- *Internet: Electronic Global Village,* by David Jefferis

For students at a Grade 12 reading level:
- *Bill Clinton and His Presidency,* by Elaine Landau

Focus

MAKING CONNECTIONS

How Has Technology Changed Society?
Have students imagine their lives without cell phones, computers, or the Internet. Have them brainstorm how their lives would be different without these technologies. Discuss with students how Americans in the 1990s reacted to new technologies. **OL**

Teach

The Big Ideas

As students study the chapter, remind them to consider the section-based Big Ideas included in each section's Guide to Reading. The **Essential Questions** in the activities below tie in to the Big Ideas and help students think about and understand important chapter concepts. In addition, the Hands-on Chapter Projects with their culminating activities relate the content from each section to the Big Ideas. These activities build on each other as students progress through the chapter. Section activities culminate in the wrap-up activity on the Visual Summary page.

772

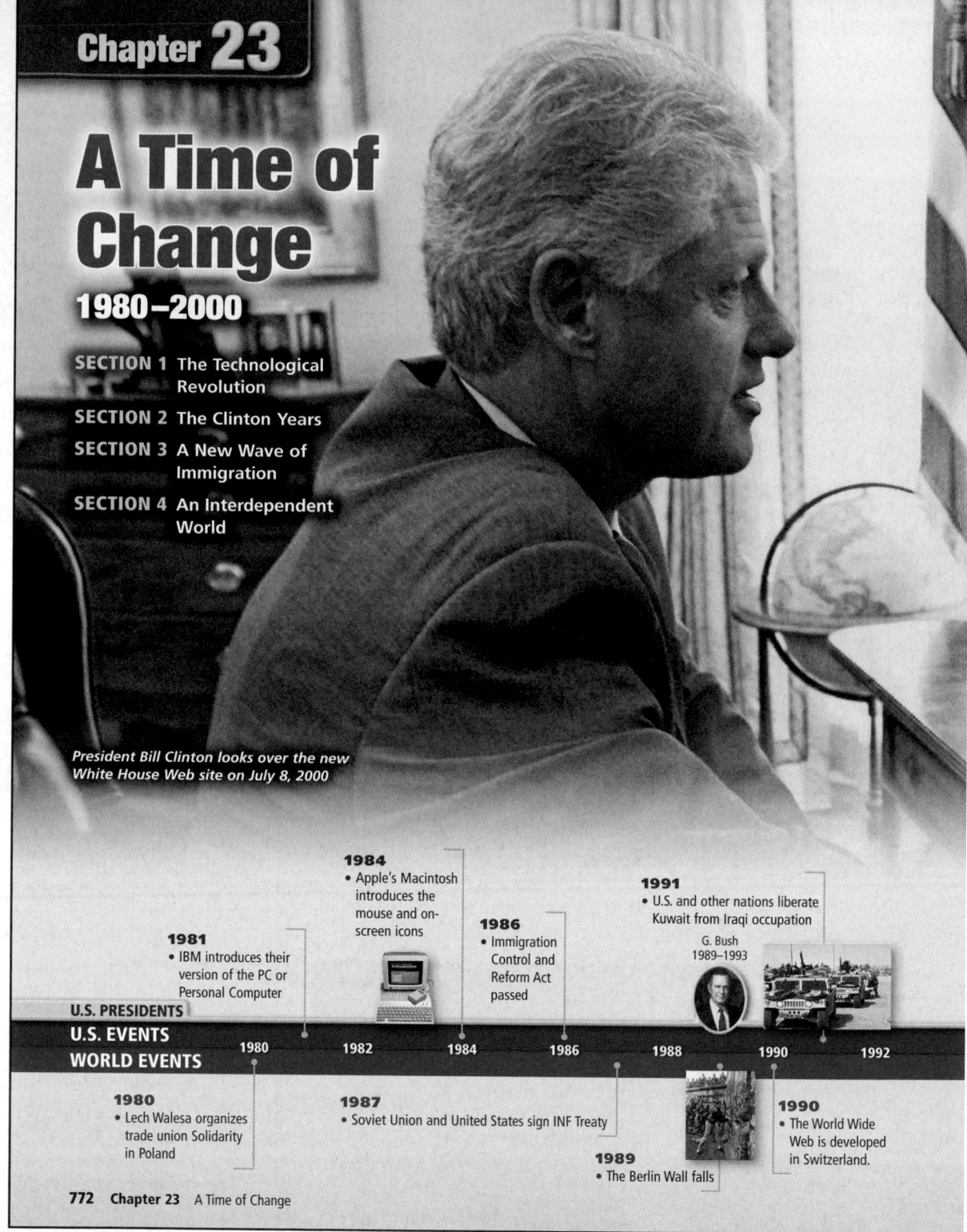

Chapter 23

A Time of Change
1980–2000

SECTION 1   The Technological Revolution

SECTION 2   The Clinton Years

SECTION 3   A New Wave of Immigration

SECTION 4   An Interdependent World

President Bill Clinton looks over the new White House Web site on July 8, 2000

1984
• Apple's Macintosh introduces the mouse and on-screen icons

1981
• IBM introduces their version of the PC or Personal Computer

1986
• Immigration Control and Reform Act passed

1991
• U.S. and other nations liberate Kuwait from Iraqi occupation

G. Bush
1989–1993

U.S. PRESIDENTS
U.S. EVENTS
WORLD EVENTS

1980   1982   1984   1986   1988   1990   1992

1980
• Lech Walesa organizes trade union Solidarity in Poland

1987
• Soviet Union and United States sign INF Treaty

1989
• The Berlin Wall falls

1990
• The World Wide Web is developed in Switzerland.

772   **Chapter 23**   A Time of Change

Section 1

The Technological Revolution
Essential Question: How did the technological revolution change American society? *(Computers became essential in the workplace and common in most homes. Communication became easier with the development of cell phones, e-mail, and instant messaging.)* Tell students that in this section they will learn about the technological revolution of the 1990s and its impact on American society. **OL**

Section 2

The Clinton Years
Essential Question: What were the successes and shortcomings of the Clinton administration? *(Successes: balancing the federal budget; Family Medical Leave Act; Americorps; welfare reform. Shortcomings: failure to get a comprehensive health care package; impeachment; no peace in the Middle East.)* Tell students that this section will focus on the Clinton presidency's successes and failures. **OL**

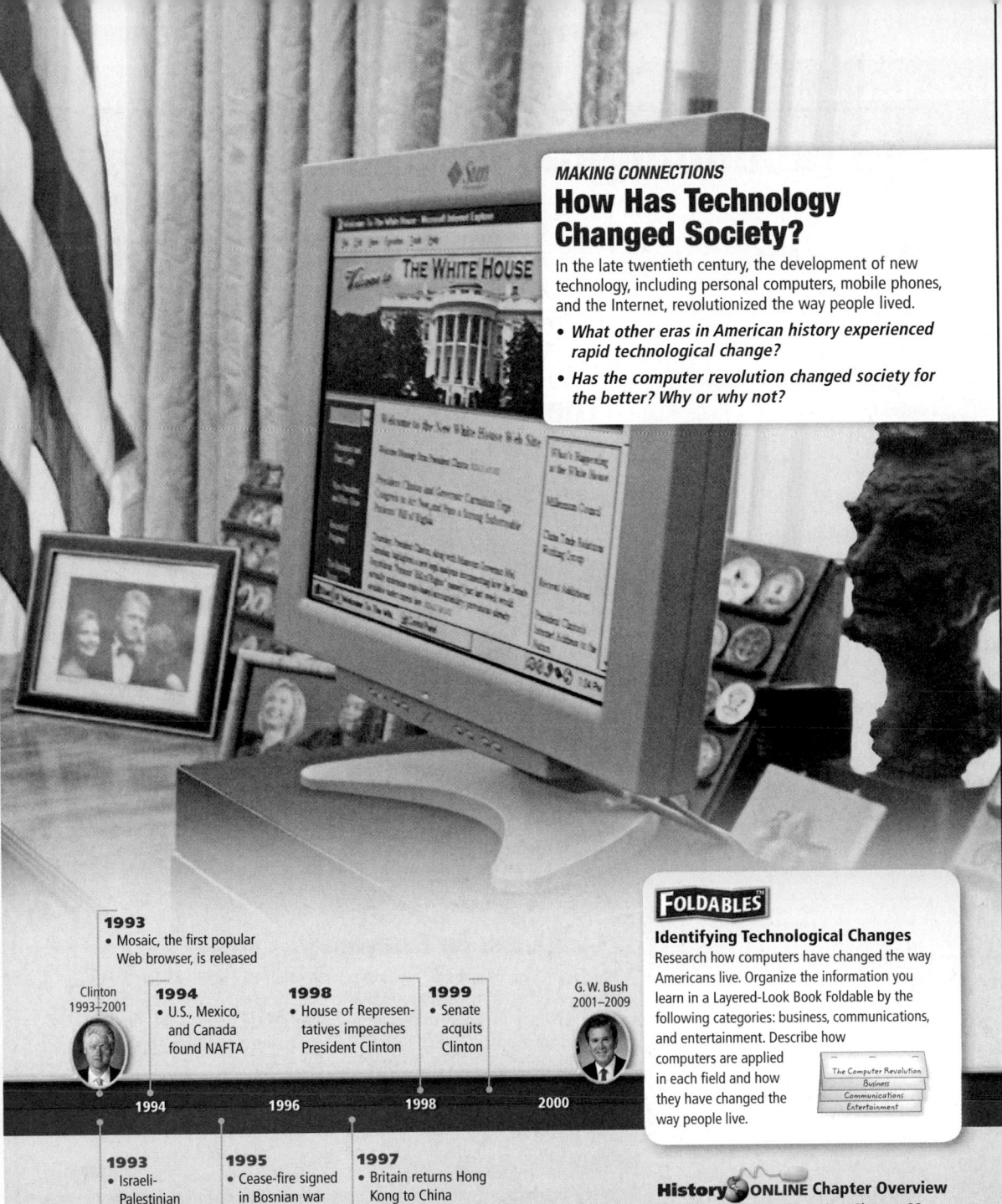

MAKING CONNECTIONS
How Has Technology Changed Society?

In the late twentieth century, the development of new technology, including personal computers, mobile phones, and the Internet, revolutionized the way people lived.

- *What other eras in American history experienced rapid technological change?*
- *Has the computer revolution changed society for the better? Why or why not?*

More About the Photo

Visual Literacy In the 1990s, more and more American homes had desktop computers and Internet access—and this new technology could be found in the Oval Office of the White House. President Clinton had the White House fully wired in 1993.

FOLDABLES Study Organizer — Dinah Zike's Foldables

Dinah Zike's Foldables are three-dimensional, interactive graphic organizers that help students practice basic writing skills, review vocabulary terms, and identify main ideas. Instructions for creating and using Foldables can be found in the Appendix at the end of this book and in the *Dinah Zike's Reading and Study Skills Foldables* booklet.

FOLDABLES

Identifying Technological Changes
Research how computers have changed the way Americans live. Organize the information you learn in a Layered-Look Book Foldable by the following categories: business, communications, and entertainment. Describe how computers are applied in each field and how they have changed the way people live.

The Computer Revolution
Business
Communications
Entertainment

History ONLINE

Introduce students to chapter content and key terms by having them access the Chapter 23 Overview at glencoe.com.

1993
- Mosaic, the first popular Web browser, is released

Clinton 1993–2001

1994
- U.S., Mexico, and Canada found NAFTA

1998
- House of Representatives impeaches President Clinton

1999
- Senate acquits Clinton

G. W. Bush 2001–2009

1994   1996   1998   2000

1993
- Israeli-Palestinian peace accord signed

1995
- Cease-fire signed in Bosnian war

1997
- Britain returns Hong Kong to China

History ONLINE Chapter Overview
Visit glencoe.com to preview Chapter 23.

Chapter 23 A Time of Change **773**

Section 3

A New Wave of Immigration
Essential Question: How did new immigration laws change American society? *(Large numbers of non-European immigrants came to the United States, some legally, some illegally.)* Tell students that in Section 3 they will learn about how immigration laws have changed the ethnic makeup of the United States. **OL**

Section 4

An Interdependent World
Essential Question: Why did the world become more interdependent in the 1990s? *(Computers helped make the world's economies interconnected; the Internet helped link the world together culturally; more people realized that environmental issues are global in nature.)* Tell students that in Section 4 they will learn about how the world grew more interdependent in the 1990s. **OL**

Focus

Bellringer
Daily Focus Transparency 23.1

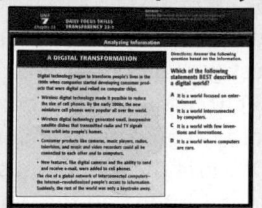

Guide to Reading
Answers:

	How it Revolutionized
Microprocessors	much faster and smaller computers
Apple II	practical, affordable home computers
Macintosh	simplified operating system with mouse-activated, on-screen icons
Windows	enabled PCs to use mouse-activated, on-screen graphic icons

Section Spotlight Video

To generate student interest and provide a springboard for class discussion, access the Chapter 23, Section 1 video at glencoe.com or on the video DVD.

Resource Manager

Section 1

The Technological Revolution

Guide to Reading

Big Ideas
Computers, Telecommunications, and the Internet The introduction of the first electronic digital computer in 1946 launched a technological revolution.

Content Vocabulary
- integrated circuit *(p. 774)*
- microprocessor *(p. 774)*
- telecommute *(p. 775)*
- blogs *(p. 777)*

Academic Vocabulary
- device *(p. 774)*
- refinement *(p. 775)*
- communications *(p. 776)*

People and Events to Identify
- ENIAC *(p. 774)*
- Silicon Valley *(p. 774)*
- Steve Jobs *(p. 774)*
- Bill Gates *(p. 775)*

Reading Strategy
Categorizing As you read about the computer age, complete a chart similar to the one below to describe products that revolutionized the computer industry.

	How It Revolutionized Computer Industry
Microprocessors	
Apple II	
Macintosh	
Windows	

The computers we use today bear little resemblance to the first electronic computers that were built in the 1940s. Since the 1980s, computer technology has advanced dramatically, with the creation of home computers and then the expansion of the Internet.

The Computer Changes Society

MAIN Idea A computer revolution changed the workplace and the way people communicate.

HISTORY AND YOU What computer devices do you use regularly? Read on to learn about the earliest electronic computers.

The development of electronic computers began at the end of World War II. The world's first electronic digital computer, called **ENIAC** (Electronic Numerical Integrator and Computer), went into operation in February 1946. ENIAC weighed over 30 tons and was the size of a small house. In early 1959, Robert Noyce designed the first **integrated circuit**—a complete electronic circuit on a single chip of silicon—which made circuits much smaller and very easy to manufacture. Noyce's company was located south of San Francisco. As new companies sprang up nearby to make products using integrated circuits, the region became known as **Silicon Valley.**

In 1968 Noyce and colleague Gordon Moore formed Intel, for "Integrated Electronics," a company that revolutionized the computer industry by combining on a single chip several integrated circuits containing both memory and computing functions. Called **microprocessors,** these new chips made computers much faster and smaller.

Computers for Everyone

Using microprocessor technology, Stephen Wozniak and his 20-year-old friend **Steve Jobs** set out to build a small computer suitable for personal use. In 1976 they founded Apple Computer and completed the Apple I. The following year they introduced the Apple II, the first practical and affordable home computer.

Apple's success sparked intense competition in the computer industry. In 1981 International Business Machines (IBM) introduced its own compact machine, which it called the "Personal Computer" (PC). Apple responded in 1984 with the revolutionary Macintosh, a new model featuring a simplified operating system using on-screen graphic symbols called icons, which users could manipulate with a hand-operated **device** called a mouse.

R Reading Strategies	**C** Critical Thinking	**D** Differentiated Instruction	**W** Writing Support	**S** Skill Practice
Teacher Edition • Making Connections, p. 775 **Additional Resources** • Prim. Source Reading, URB p. 101 • Guided Reading Act., URB p. 114	**Teacher Edition** • Making Inferences, p. 775 • Compare/ Contrast, p. 776 **Additional Resources** • Economics and History, URB p. 7 • Linking Past/Present, URB p. 100 • Quizzes/Tests, p. 325	**Additional Resources** • Differentiated Instruction, URB p. 89	**Teacher Edition** • Persuasive Writing, p. 777 **Additional Resources** • Content Vocab. Act., URB p. 93 • Academic Vocab. Act., URB p. 95	**Teacher Edition** • Reading Graphs, p. 776 **Additional Resources** • Time Line Act., URB p. 99 • RENTG, p. 245

TECHNOLOGY & HISTORY

Computers Beginning in the late 1970s and continuing to the present, changes in computer and telecommunications technology have transformed how people live and work.

Personal Computer ▶
The Apple Macintosh introduced in 1984 was the first mass-produced personal computer to use a mouse and on-screen icons to help users interact with the software. The new interface made computers far easier to use and encouraged Americans who were not technically trained to begin using computers. The first mouse (shown above) was invented by Douglas Englebart in 1964.

▲ Integrated Circuit
Without the integrated circuit, the computer and telecommunications revolutions would not have been possible. It allowed literally millions of tiny circuits to be mass produced and for manufacturers to greatly reduce the size of computer-based products.

◀ Mobile Phone
Microprocessors and digital technology made small mobile phones (cell phones) possible. Combined with wireless access to the Internet, the cell phone allows people to stay in communication and to view videos, text messages, and photos no matter where they are.

Analyzing VISUALS

1. **Explaining** What aspects of life do computer-based devices make easier?

2. **Inferring** Why do you think it was important for integrated circuits to be so small?

As Jobs and Wozniak were creating Apple, 19-year-old Harvard dropout **Bill Gates** co-founded Microsoft to design PC software, the instructions used to program computers to perform desired tasks. In 1980 IBM hired Microsoft to develop an operating system for its new PC. Gates paid a Seattle programmer $50,000 for the rights to his software, and with some **refinements,** it became MS-DOS (Microsoft Disk Operating System). In 1985 Microsoft introduced the "Windows" operating system, which enabled PCs to use mouse-activated, on-screen graphic icons.

Compact computers soon transformed the workplace, linking employees within an office or among office branches. They became essential tools in almost all businesses. By the late **C** 1990s, workers used home computers and electronic mail (E-mail) to **"telecommute,"** or do their jobs from home via computer.

New Telecommunications

A parallel revolution in telecommunications coincided with the development of personal computers. In the 1970s, the government started deregulating the telecommunications industry. Then, in 1996 Congress passed the Telecommunications Act, which allowed phone companies to compete with each other and to send television signals. It also allowed cable **R** television companies to offer telephone service. This led to much greater competition, and many new technologies were developed.

One major telecommunications technology that became very popular was the cell phone. Cell phones had been invented in the 1940s, and the first large-scale cellular networks were built in the 1980s, but the phones were large and the service was very expensive. All that began to change in the 1990s.

Chapter 23 A Time of Change **775**

Teach

C Critical Thinking
Making Inferences Ask: What is the advantage of linking employees by computer? *(Answers will vary but may include that they can better work together and share ideas and information.)* **BL**

R Reading Strategy
Making Connections Ask: What phone and cable TV options are available locally? *(Answers will vary.)* **OL**

Analyzing VISUALS

Answers:
1. enhanced telecommunications with smaller and more powerful telephones and computers
2. to greatly reduce the size of computer-based products

Hands-On Chapter Project
Step 1

Art Show

Step 1: Researching the History of the Period Essential Question: What events occurred in American history from 1980 to 2000, and how can they be captured in images?

Directions Explain to students that they are going to create an art show of perhaps 10 images that they will hang in the classroom, a school hall or foyer, complete with a title, brief introduction near the beginning and the accompanying explanatory tags that will identify the images. In this step, two teams of students will: a) describe the events occurring in the United States between 1980 and 2000; and b) depict themes of the period. Each team will discuss how to depict the subject using images. (Students may choose to use graphic organizers, maps, charts, paintings, or drawings. Students may create their own images or find historical images online or in the library.)

Putting It Together After the two teams have determined four or five image selections, they should each either obtain the images (photocopies) or sketch them in a rough draft. **OL**
(Chapter Project continued on page 784)

The Rise of the Internet

 C **Critical Thinking**

Comparing and Contrasting
Ask: How are wireless digital cell phones different from older phones? *(They are smaller and portable.)* **BL**

S **Skill Practice**

Reading Graphs **Ask:** Based on the graph, which computer technology developed last? *(broadband Internet)* **ELL**

Reading Check

Answer:
They could be connected to each other and to computers.

Analyzing VISUALS

Answers:
1. E-mail or Instant Messaging
2. accelerating; Answers will vary but may include the idea that more households now have computers.

Additional Support

History ONLINE
Student Web Activity Visit _e_ _coe_ _co_ and complete the activity on the technological revolution.

Wireless digital technology made it possible to miniaturize cell phones, and they quickly became very popular. By the early 2000s, they were in widespread use around the world. Wireless digital technology also made it possible to manufacture small inexpensive satellite dishes that could receive video and radio beamed from orbit into people's homes.

Digital technology rapidly transformed many consumer products. Various companies developed music players, cameras, radios, televisions, and music and video recorders that **C** used digital technology. Because they were digital and relied on computer chips, it became possible to connect them to each other and to computers. Modern cell phones, for example, often have digital cameras built in, and can send and receive E-mail and instant text messages. Computers can play the same videos that can be played on digital television. Further accelerating the interoperability and connections between the technologies was the rise of a global network of interconnected computers that came to be called the Internet.

✓ **Reading Check** **Describing** How did digital technology change consumer products?

The Rise of the Internet

MAIN Idea A computer resource that linked government agencies developed into the Internet.

HISTORY AND YOU Have you ever used the Internet to do research for a class? Read on to learn about the origins of the Internet.

In 1969 the U.S. Defense Department's Advanced Research Project Agency created a system of networked computers known as ARPANET. The system linked computers at government agencies, defense contractors, and several universities, enabling them to communicate with one another.

In 1986 the National Science Foundation built NSFNet, a network connecting several super computer centers across the country. NSFNet was soon linked to ARPANET, and as the connections to other computer networks across the world grew, the system became known as the Internet. The Internet is not the World Wide Web or E-mail. Those are systems that use the Internet. The Internet is the physical network of computers connected together by phone lines, cable lines, and wireless **communications.**

PRIMARY SOURCE
The Rise of the Internet

As the Internet grew in size and people obtained access to faster computers and faster "broadband" connections, people began to use it for almost everything.

Analyzing VISUALS

1. **Classifying** Which category of activities is the Internet used for the most?
2. **Hypothesizing** Is the growth in the use of the internet slowing or accelerating? Why might this be so?

776 **Chapter 23** A Time of Change

Activity: Technology Connection

Organizing an Internet Business **Ask:** How can a company use the Internet to conduct business? *(Answers may include advertising, taking orders, distributing information, communicating with customers, and so on.)* Show students the home page of a dot-com business, such as Amazon.com. Discuss the features of the Web site and the functions they serve. Have students work in groups of five or six to form a mock dot-com business. After groups have chosen a product line, ask them to design a mock-up of an Internet Web site for their business. Remind them to use their Internet sites to inform, persuade, and communicate with customers, as well as sell their products. Encourage creativity with the use of product illustrations and descriptions that will appeal to consumers. Ask groups to share their "Web sites" with the class. **OL**

As personal computers became cheaper and more widely available, more and more people began signing up with Internet Service Providers (ISPs) who could connect their computers to the Internet. By the late 1990s, the Internet had become wildly popular as businesses began experimenting with it to sell goods and services and to improve their productivity and communications. By 2007, more than 1 billion people were regularly using the Internet.

Birth of the World Wide Web

In 1990, researchers at CERN, a physics laboratory in Switzerland, developed a new way to present information on computers linked to the Internet. Known as the World Wide Web, this system used hypertext (what today are referred to as "links" on web pages) and could be accessed with software known as a web browser. The system allowed users to post information in the form of Web pages and click on links to jump from Web site to Web site.

Enthusiasm for the World Wide Web spawned a "dot-com" economy (from the common practice of using ".com" to designate the address of a business Web site). Seemingly rich with promise, a wide variety of dot-com companies made millions of dollars for stock investors without making any actual profits. Internet-related stocks helped fuel the prosperity of the 1990s, but dropped dramatically in 2000—a period that became known as the "dot-com bust" when many unprofitable online companies went out of business.

A few companies have, however, become major success stories. Amazon.com, founded by Jeff Bezos, has become a highly successful online bookseller. The companies Google and Yahoo both created search engines that help people locate information on the web. Many media companies have also found success on the web in the same way that they did in print and on television —by charging fees for advertising. A few have tried making money by offering music files for download, or by selling access to databases of information. Many traditional companies have begun using the Web to take orders from customers and to provide information about their products.

The Internet Changes Society

For many people, the World Wide Web has become more than just a source of information. It has become a way to build a sense of community. People with common interests visit Web sites about those interests and post comments and interact with each other.

Individuals and families share stories and photos about themselves on **blogs**—short for Web logs—Web sites that function as a kind of public diary or notebook. Web sites such as MySpace serve a similar function, while sites such as YouTube enable people to post video clips they want to share with others. Blogs have also led to a renaissance in essay writing and commentary as they enable people to publicly comment on news stories and other events. They have also helped mobilize people for political action. For many, accessing the Web has become a routine and important part of their daily life. **W**

✔ **Reading Check** Analyzing How have the Internet and World Wide Web changed society?

Section 1 REVIEW

Vocabulary
1. **Explain** the significance of: ENIAC, integrated circuit, Silicon Valley, microprocessor, Steve Jobs, Bill Gates, telecommute, blogs.

Main Ideas
2. **Describing** How have personal computers transformed the workplace?

3. **Contrasting** What is the difference between the World Wide Web and the Internet?

Critical Thinking
4. **Big Ideas** How have advances in telecommunications and the rise of the Internet affected the standard of living in the United States?

5. **Organizing** Complete a graphic organizer similar to the one below by listing developments that led to the technological revolution.

Technological Revolution

6. **Analyzing Visuals** Study the photograph of the Apple Computer on page 775. How have computers changed since the 1980s?

Writing About History
7. **Descriptive Writing** Write two paragraphs describing the ways that you and your family use the Internet and how your way of life would be different without it.

History ONLINE
Study Central™ To review this section, go to glencoe.com and click on Study Central.

777

W **Writing Support**
Persuasive Writing
Ask: Should the Internet be censored? Have students write an essay arguing for or against censorship. **AL**

✔ **Reading Check**

Answer:
They built a sense of community, led to more commentary, and helped mobilize people for political action.

Assess

History ONLINE

Study Central™ provides summaries, interactive games, and online graphic organizers to help students review content.

Close

Summarizing Ask: How did computer technology change in the 1970s and 1980s? *(Microprocessors made them smaller and faster; simplified operating systems made them user-friendly.)* **OL**

Section 1 REVIEW

Answers

1. All definitions can be found in the section and the Glossary.
2. They have linked employees within an office or among office branches.
3. The Internet is a physical network of computers connected by phone lines, cable lines, and wireless communications. The World Wide Web is a system that allows Internet users to post information on Web pages and click on links to move from Web site to Web site.

4. People can better communicate; they can share information and interact with others who share common interests. They can publicly comment on news stories and other events and mobilize for political action.
5. Answers may include any of the following: electronic computer, integrated circuit, microprocessor, simplified operating system, cell phone, wireless digital technology, the Internet, the World Wide Web.
6. Answers will vary but may include the following: smaller, optional larger monitors,

different varieties of the mouse device, laptop technology.
7. Paragraphs will vary but should describe students' personal Internet use and its effect on students' lives.

Focus

Ask: What efforts have been made to address the issue of AIDS in the United States? *(Answers will vary but may include education, fund-raising, and government subsidized research.)* Explain that, in late 1990, Congress passed the Ryan White Comprehensive AIDS Resources Emergency Act (CARE), which annually provides about $1.5 billion to care for people living with AIDS/HIV.

Teach

R Reading Strategy

Activating Prior Knowledge

Ask: Why were Africans in need at this time? *(Answers will vary but may include that AIDS, civil unrest, and famine caused great suffering.)* **AL**

S Skill Practice

Reading a Time Line **Ask:** Which event on the time line has most impacted your life? Explain. *(Answers will vary but should relate to one of the advances listed on the time line.)* **OL**

Additional Support

TIME NOTEBOOK

In 1985, **RYAN WHITE** *became a symbol of the intolerance that is inflicted on some people suffering from HIV/AIDS.*

Ryan White was 13 years old when he learned that he had contracted HIV through blood products he was taking for hemophilia, a disease he had since birth. At the time, many people thought the AIDS virus could be passed by casual contact—by shaking hands, sneezing, or coughing. Even though AIDS can't be caught that way, people in Ryan's school in Kokomo, Indiana, were afraid to be near him. School officials banned him from classes, and Ryan had to fight in court to win the right to attend school.

In 1987, his family moved to another Indiana town, Cicero, where he was treated more kindly. Ryan died on April 8, 1990. At his funeral, a family friend, Rev. Ray Probasco, said: "It was Ryan who first humanized the disease called AIDS. He allowed us to see the boy who just wanted, more than anything else, to be like other children and to be able to go to school."

VERBATIM

"Just say no."
—NANCY REAGAN,
in 1983, launching her antidrug campaign

"Show me the money!"
—ACTOR CUBA GOODING, JR.'S CHARACTER,
in the 1996 movie Jerry Maguire

"Mr. Gorbachev, tear down this wall!"
—PRESIDENT RONALD REAGAN,
in 1987 addressing the head of the USSR while standing next to the Berlin Wall, which still divided East and West Berlin.

"Can we all get along?"
—RODNEY KING,
pleading in 1992 with the rioters in Los Angeles and other cities, after violence erupted following a jury's acquittal of the police officer who had beaten him.

"We are the world."
—FORTY-FIVE POP STARS,
including Lionel Richie, Ray Charles, and Bruce Springsteen, known as USA for Africa. The group recorded the song "We Are the World" in 1985 to raise money for Africans in need.

"I do not like broccoli. And I haven't liked it since I was a little kid and my mother made me eat it. And I'm President of the United States and I'm not going to eat any more broccoli."
—PRESIDENT GEORGE H. W. BUSH,
1990

FIRSTS IN TECH

S *Important Dates in the Technology Revolution*

1981	1982	1983	1984	1985	1991	1995	1997
Columbia makes the first space shuttle flight	First use of emoticons in an e-mail: :-) and :-(The first American cell phone system goes into operation	Music CDs go on sale in the United States	Apple Macintosh computer is released	Nintendo Entertainment System comes to America	World Wide Web is created by Tim Berners-Lee of Great Britain	Release of first DVDs (digital video disks)	Dolly the sheep is the first animal made by cloning adult cells

Steve Jobs presents the first Macintosh computer

Extending the Content

Sandra Day O'Connor Justice O'Connor traveled a long way to become the first female U.S. Supreme Court Justice. A top graduate in her Stanford law class, she experienced repeated rejection from law firms who refused to hire women. One firm did offer her employment—as a legal secretary. Determined, O'Connor accepted a position as a deputy county attorney in California.

Later, after moving to Arizona, she served the state as assistant attorney general and state senator, becoming the first woman in any state to hold the office of majority leader in 1972. After her subsequent election to a state judgeship, she served five years before being appointed to the Arizona Court of Appeals. A short two years later, O'Connor replaced Justice Potter Stewart

on the U.S. Supreme Court. On July 1, 2005, she announced her retirement. Justice Samuel Alito was sworn in on Feb. 1, 2006, marking the end of O'Connor's distinguished judicial career.

Time Capsule

In 1992, TIME *magazine ran a short story, "Things to Show How We Live Now," as a way to highlight what was important to the public at the time. Here are 15 items from the list. How do they compare with what you think is important?*

REMOTE CONTROL

GARTH BROOKS CD

8-MM CAMCORDER

CASH-MACHINE CARD

INFLATABLE GLOBE

DISPOSABLE CAMERA

DOLPHIN-SAFE TUNA

BAGGY JEANS

PALMTOP COMPUTER

SPF 15 SUNSCREEN

POCKET T-SHIRT

BOTTLED WATER FROM THE ALPS

IN-LINE SKATES

AIR BAG

BEEPER

JAMES KEYSER/GETTY IMAGES

Milestones

LOST, 1986. THE SPACE SHUTTLE *CHALLENGER* exploded 73 seconds after liftoff. Millions watched in horror as the 25th shuttle mission blew up, killing all seven crew members, including high school teacher Christa McAuliffe.

C

RECONCILED, 1992. U.S. PRESIDENT GEORGE H.W. BUSH AND RUSSIAN PRESIDENT BORIS YELTSIN formally declared an end to the Cold War.

R

RELEASED, 1981. FIFTY-TWO U.S. HOSTAGES IN IRAN were set free after 444 days in captivity. The crisis played a significant part in Jimmy Carter's failure to win a second presidential term.

AIRED, 1981. FORMER RADIO EXECUTIVES CREATED MTV (MUSIC TELEVISION). They knew that advertisers wanted to reach young people, who loved rock music. So they decided to run music videos on a cable channel.

ERUPTED, 1980. MOUNT ST. HELENS IN WASHINGTON STATE erupted after being dormant for 123 years. A stupendous explosion blew the entire top off the volcano.

NAMED, 1981. SANDRA DAY O'CONNOR became the first female justice on the U.S. Supreme Court after being appointed to the position by President Ronald Reagan.

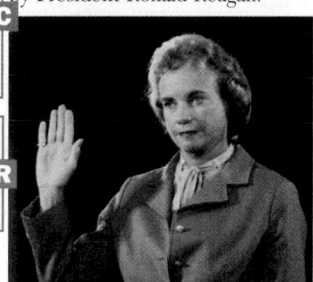

Justice Sandra Day O'Connor

WALLY McNAMEE/CORBIS

HONORED, 1995. BALTIMORE ORIOLES SHORTSTOP CAL RIPKEN, JR. became a national hero just by going to work every day for 13 years. On September 6, 1995, Ripken showed up at his 2,131st game in a row, breaking the 1939 record set by Lou Gehrig.

NUMBERS

168 Number of people killed in the 1995 bombing of Oklahoma City's Federal Building by two Americans, Terry Nichols and Timothy McVeigh

12 Age of Valerie Ambrose, who won a NASA contest in 1997 by coming up with "Sojourner Truth" as the name for a robot explorer to Mars

11,000,000 Number of gallons of crude oil spilled into Prince William Sound by the tanker *Exxon Valdez* in 1989

An oil-soaked whale after the Exxon Valdez *spill*

NATALIE FOBES/CORBIS

20,000,000 Number of albums Michael Jackson's *Thriller* sold, making it the best-selling record of all time as of 1982

Forever Amount of time former player Pete Rose was banned from baseball after the discovery in 1989 that he was gambling on baseball games

CRITICAL THINKING

1. Synthesizing Do you think people's attitudes have changed towards people with HIV/AIDS since 1985? Explain your answer.

2. Hypothesizing Why might celebrities be better able than the "average" citizen to focus public attention on serious global issues and problems?

C **Critical Thinking**

Speculating Ask: How might the Challenger's experience have affected attitudes toward the U.S. space program? *(Answers will vary but may speculate that people began to question the worth or necessity of the program.)* **OL**

R **Reading Strategies**

Activating Prior Knowledge Ask: What was the Cold War? *(Answers may vary but should include the idea of a struggle for power between Communist bloc countries and Western powers.)* **OL**

Critical THINKING

Answers:

1. Answers will vary. Some students may feel attitudes have changed because of the efforts of the government and private groups to educate Americans about HIV/AIDS. Others may feel that people with HIV or AIDS still suffer under a social stigma.

2. Answers will vary but could include the idea that people often emulate the views and actions of celebrities, giving famous people tremendous influence over public opinion and actions.

Activity: Technology Connection

Assessing Ask: What technology is most effective in the classroom? Why? *(Answers will vary but may include videos and DVDs, live TV broadcasts, computers, digital cameras, and CDs.)* Have students form groups. Ask each group to prepare a presentation for a classroom of new immigrants on an event or person from the decades of the 1980s or 1990s. Have students assess and select the forms of technology that will be most appropriate for the audience and the subject of their presentations. Encourage groups to appeal to various senses: sight, hearing, taste, touch, and/or smell. Ask groups to give their presentations to the class. Have audience members list and evaluate the effectiveness of the types of technology each presentation utilizes. **OL**

Focus

Bellringer
Daily Focus Transparency 23.2

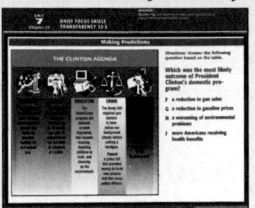

Guide to Reading

Answers:
I. Clinton's Agenda
  A. Raising Taxes, Cutting Spending
  B. Stumbling on Health Care
  C. Families and Education
  D. Crime and Gun Control
II. Republicans Gain Control of Congress
  A. The Contract With America
  B. The Budget Battle
  C. Clinton Wins Reelection
III. Clinton's Second Term
  A. Putting Children First
  B. Clinton Is Impeached
IV. Clinton Foreign Policy
  A. The Haitian Intervention
  B. Bosnia and Kosovo
  C. Peacemaking in the Middle East

Section Spotlight Video

To generate student interest and provide a springboard for class discussion, access the Chapter 23, Section 2 video at glencoe.com or on the video DVD..

Resource Manager

Section 2

The Clinton Years

Guide to Reading

Big Ideas
Government and Society President Clinton pushed through laws to help families and strengthen gun control, but he also raised taxes and failed to reform health care.

Content Vocabulary
• perjury (p. 785)
• ethnic cleansing (p. 787)

Academic Vocabulary
• modify (p.781)
• unprecedented (p.781)
• participant (p. 787)

People and Events to Identify
• AmeriCorps (p. 782)
• Contract with America (p. 783)
• Kenneth Starr (p. 785)
• Dayton Accords (p. 787)

Reading Strategy
Taking Notes As you read about the administration of President Clinton, use the major headings of the section to create an outline similar to the one below.

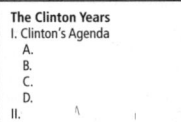

The Clinton Years
I. Clinton's Agenda
  A.
  B.
  C.
  D.
II.

When William Jefferson Clinton was elected in 1992, he became the first Democrat to win the presidency in 12 years. After achieving only part of his agenda, he faced a new Republican Congress that had very different plans. His second term focused on foreign policy and scandal.

Clinton's Agenda

MAIN Idea President Clinton took office in 1993 with plans for improving health care, cutting the federal deficit, aiding families, and increasing gun control.

HISTORY AND YOU Do you know anyone who has worked for AmeriCorps? Read on to learn about the beginnings of this program.

Only 46 years old when he took office, Bill Clinton was the third-youngest person ever to serve as president and the first of the "baby boom" generation to reach the Oval Office. The new president put forth an ambitious domestic program focusing on five major areas: the economy, the family, education, crime, and health care.

Raising Taxes, Cutting Spending

As he had promised in his election campaign, Clinton focused first on the economy. The problem, in his view, was the federal deficit. Under Reagan and Bush, the deficit had nearly quadrupled, adding billions of dollars annually to the national debt. High deficits forced the government to borrow large sums of money, which helped to drive up interest rates. Clinton believed that the key to economic growth was to lower interest rates. Low interest rates would enable businesses to borrow more money to expand and create more jobs. Low rates would also make it easier for consumers to borrow money for mortgages, car loans, and other items, which in turn would promote economic growth.

One way to bring interest rates down was to reduce the federal deficit. In early 1993, Clinton sent Congress a deficit reduction plan. In trying to cut the deficit, however, Clinton faced a serious problem. About half of all government spending went to entitlement programs, such as Social Security, Medicare, and veterans' benefits. These programs are hard to cut because so many Americans depend on them. Faced with these constraints, Clinton decided to raise taxes, even though he had promised to cut them during his campaign. Clinton proposed raising tax rates for middle- and upper-income Americans and placed new taxes on gasoline, heating oil, and natural

---

R Reading Strategies	**C** Critical Thinking	**D** Differentiated Instruction	**W** Writing Support	**S** Skill Practice
Teacher Edition • Activ. Prior Knowledge, pp. 782, 783 • Identifying, p. 784 • Sequencing Info., p. 786 **Additional Resources** • Pri. Source Reading, URB p. 103 • Guided Reading Act., URB p. 115	**Teacher Edition** • Speculating, p. 781 • Drawing Con., p. 783 • Defending, p. 785 • Analyzing Primary Sources, p. 786 • Making Inferences, p. 787 **Additional Resources** • Inter. Political Cartoons, URB p. 107 • Quizzes/Test, p. 326	**Teacher Edition** • Visual/Spatial, p. 784 • Logical/Math., p. 785 **Additional Resources** • English Learner, URB p. 91	**Teacher Edition** • Personal Writing, p. 782	**Teacher Edition** • Analyzing Visuals, p. 781 **Additional Resources** • Hist. Analysis Skills, URB p. 88 • Reinf. Skills, URB p. 97 • RENTG, p. 248

POLITICAL CARTOONS PRIMARY SOURCE
The Debate Over Health Care

During his first term in office, President Clinton launched an ambitious program to reform the nation's health care system. The reforms faced much opposition and never materialized.

▲ President Clinton explains the proposed Health Security card in a speech to Congress in October 1993.

▲ The cartoonist shows President Clinton resolving to be very cautious throughout the rest of his administration.

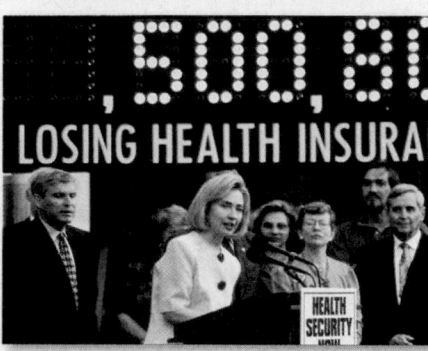

▲ Hillary Clinton speaks about her health care plan in front of a counter showing one person losing health insurance every 1.17 seconds.

Analyzing VISUALS DBQ

1. **Inferring** How does the cartoonist compare Clinton's failed attempt to change health care to an accident?

2. **Analyzing** Why does Clinton resolve to be cautious in the future?

---

gas. The tax increases were very unpopular, and Republicans in Congress refused to support them. Clinton pressured Democrats, and after many amendments, a **modified** version of Clinton's plan narrowly passed.

Stumbling on Health Care

During his campaign, Clinton had promised to reform the health care system. Some 40 million Americans, or roughly 15 percent of the nation, did not have health insurance. The president created a task force and appointed his wife, Hillary Rodham Clinton, to head it—an **unprecedented** role for a first lady. The task force developed a plan to guarantee health benefits for all Americans, but it put much of the burden of paying for the benefits on employers. Small-business owners feared they could not afford it. The insurance industry and doctors' organizations also opposed the plan and mounted a nationwide advertising campaign on television and radio to build public opposition to the plan.

Republicans argued that the plan was too complicated, costly, and relied too much on government control. Democrats were divided. Some supported alternative plans, but no plan had enough support to pass. Faced with public opposition, Clinton's plan died without a vote.

Chapter 23 A Time of Change **781**

Teach

S Skill Practice

Analyzing Visuals Ask: Which frame explains Clinton's first reaction to the failure of his health care reform? *(the embarrassment)* **BL**

C Critical Thinking

Speculating Ask: Why might the insurance industry and doctors' organizations have opposed Clinton's national health care plan? *(Answers will vary but may include that doctors didn't want government regulating care and insurance companies didn't want to be told what to cover.)* **OL**

Analyzing VISUALS

Answers:
1. It shows him having to recover from it in stages.
2. Answers will vary but may include that it took him a long time to recover from his health care mistake.

Additional Support

Extending the Content

Health Insurance According to the Census Bureau, in 2004

- 45.8 million or 15.7 percent of the country's population had no health insurance.

- 11.2 percent of children under the age of 18 were uninsured.

- While 8.4 percent of Americans with incomes over $75,000 were uninsured, about 24.3 percent of those with incomes less than $25,000 lacked insurance.

- African-Americans (19.7 percent) and Hispanics (32.7 percent) were more likely to lack insurance than white, non-Hispanic Americans (11.3 percent).

According to a survey of the time,

- More than one-third of adults, both insured and uninsured, were having problems paying medical bills or accessing medical care.

- Low-income people with chronic health conditions had the most difficulty paying health expenses.

- While company profits rose by 16 percent in 2004, employment-based health insurance fell.

R Reading Strategies

Activating Prior Knowledge

Ask: To what international program is AmeriCorps similar? *(the Peace Corps)* How does it differ from the other program? *(AmeriCorps employs students, rather than adults, and operates domestically, rather than in foreign countries.)* **BL**

W Writing Support

Personal Writing Have students write one or two paragraphs to explain their views on gun control. **OL**

✓ Reading Check

Answers:
Republicans felt it was too costly and heavy on government control; some Democrats supported other plans.

Families and Education

Clinton did manage to push several major pieces of legislation through Congress. During his campaign, he had stressed the need to help American families. His first success was the Family Medical Leave Act. This law gave workers up to 12 weeks per year of unpaid family leave for the birth or adoption of a child or for the illness of a family member.

Clinton also persuaded Congress to create the **AmeriCorps** program. This program put students to work improving low-income housing, teaching children to read, and cleaning up the environment. AmeriCorps incorporated the VISTA program that John F. Kennedy had created. AmeriCorps volunteers earn a salary and are awarded a scholarship to continue their education. In September 1994, the first group of AmeriCorps volunteers—some 20,000 in number—began serving in more than 1,000 communities.

Crime and Gun Control

Clinton had also promised to get tough on crime during his campaign, and he strongly endorsed new gun-control laws. Despite strong opposition from many Republicans and the National Rifle Association (NRA), the Democrats in Congress passed a gun-control law known as the Brady Bill. It was named after James Brady, President Reagan's press secretary who had been severely injured by a gunshot during the assassination attempt on the former president. His wife, Sarah Brady, became an advocate of gun control and lobbied Congress to pass the bill. The Brady Handgun Violence Prevention Act imposed a waiting period before people could buy handguns. It also required gun dealers to have police run a background check for a criminal record before selling someone a handgun.

The following year, Clinton introduced another crime bill. The bill provided extra funds for states to build new prisons, and put 100,000 more police officers on the streets. It banned 19 kinds of assault weapons and provided money for crime prevention programs, such as "midnight" basketball leagues that would get young people off the streets.

✓ Reading Check **Explaining** Why did President Clinton's proposed health care plan fail?

Republicans Gain Control of Congress

MAIN Idea Republican victories in Congress led to conflicts between the executive and legislative branches of the federal government.

HISTORY AND YOU Have you ever refused to back down when you felt sure you were in the right? Read on to learn about a showdown between Congress and the president.

Despite his successes, Clinton was very unpopular by late 1994. He had raised taxes, instead of lowering them as he had promised, and he had failed to fix health care. Although the economy was improving, many companies were still downsizing. Several personal issues involving President Clinton further weakened

Debates IN HISTORY

Is a Balanced Budget Amendment a Good Idea?

One of the ideas that congressional Republicans put forth in the "Contract with America" was a balanced budget amendment to the Constitution. A balanced budget amendment would force Congress to pass a federal budget that balanced projected revenues and expenditures. Would such an amendment force Congress to be more responsible in how it spends the taxpayers' money, resulting in a more efficient, limited government? Or, would it dangerously limit Congress's ability to respond to economic and national security emergencies?

Additional Support

Teacher Tip

Collaborative Learning
Design collaborative projects that allow all members of a group to participate and share ideas. Encourage products that appeal to a variety of learning styles.

782

Activity: Collaborative Learning

Analyzing AmeriCorps Ask: Why might young people sign up for AmeriCorps? *(Answers will vary but could include the idea that it gives young people opportunities to serve the country, earn money for college, and see other parts of the country.)* Have students work in pairs to research AmeriCorps on the Internet at www.americorps.org/. Ask partners to focus on the following aspects: recruiting requirements, types of programs, and service areas. Have student pairs design a poster for one AmeriCorps program. Display the posters in the classroom. Discuss how the various programs contribute to American society and/or the environment. **OL**

public confidence in him. In response, many Americans decided to vote Republican in 1994.

The Contract With America

As the 1994 midterm elections neared, congressional Republicans, led by Newt Gingrich of Georgia, created the **Contract with America.** This program proposed 10 major changes, including lower taxes, welfare reform, tougher anticrime laws, term limits for members of Congress, and a balanced budget amendment. Republicans won a stunning victory—for the first time in 40 years, they had a majority in both houses of Congress.

In their first 100 days in office, House Republicans passed almost the entire Contract with America, but they soon ran into trouble. The Senate defeated several proposals, while the president vetoed others.

The Budget Battle

In 1995 the Republicans clashed with the president over the new federal budget. Clinton vetoed several Republican budget proposals, claiming they cut into social programs too much. Gingrich believed that if Republicans stood firm, the president would back down and approve the budget. Otherwise, the entire federal government would shut down for lack of funds. Clinton, however, refused to budge, and allowed the federal government to close.

By standing firm against Republican budget proposals and allowing the government to shut down, Clinton regained much of the support he had lost in 1994. The Republicans in Congress realized they needed to work with the president to pass legislation. Soon afterward, they reached an agreement with Clinton to balance the budget.

R

C

C Critical Thinking

Drawing Conclusions Ask: What conclusion can be drawn about the Senate from its defeat of several Contract with America proposals? *(Republicans did not vote along party lines.)* **OL**

R Reading Strategies

Activating Prior Knowledge Ask: What concept is illustrated by the presidential veto of proposed legislation? *(checks and balances)* **AL**

Debates IN HISTORY

Answers:
1. Congress has demonstrated a lack of fiscal discipline.
2. Answers may suggest that continued deficit spending could jeopardize the government's ability to make payments such as Social Security.
3. The economy is linked to the federal deficit, so in a weak economy taxes would increase and spending would decrease, possibly causing recession.
4. Answers should be supported with sound reasoning.

YES

Strom Thurmond
U.S. Senator

PRIMARY SOURCE

"While Congress could achieve a balanced budget by statute, past efforts . . . have failed. It is simply too easy for Congress to change its mind. . . . The constitutional amendment is unyielding in its imposition of discipline on Congress to make the tough decisions necessary to balance the federal budget. Over the past half-century, Congress has demonstrated a total lack of fiscal discipline evidenced by an irrational and irresponsible pattern of spending. This reckless approach has seriously jeopardized the Federal government and threatens the very future of this Nation. As a result, I believe we must look to constitutional protection from a firmly entrenched fiscal policy which threatens the liberties and opportunities of our present and future citizens."

—Statement to the Judiciary Committee, February 16, 1994

NO

Bill Clinton
President

PRIMARY SOURCE

"The balanced budget amendment is, in the first place, bad economics. . . . [T]he Federal deficit depends not just on Congressional decisions, but also on the state of the economy. In particular, the deficit increases automatically whenever the economy weakens. If we try to break this automatic linkage by a Constitutional amendment, we will have to raise taxes and cut expenditures whenever the economy is weak. That not only risks turning minor downturns into serious recessions, but would make recovery from recession far more difficult. Let's be clear: This is not a matter of abstract economic theory. . . . A balanced budget amendment could threaten the livelihoods of millions of Americans. I cannot put them in such peril."

—Letter to Congressional leaders, November 5, 1993

DBQ Document-Based Questions

1. **Finding the Main Idea** Why does Senator Thurmond believe that a constitutional amendment, rather than simply a law, is necessary?

2. **Theorizing** How might Congress's "irresponsible pattern of spending" threaten the nation's future?

3. **Specifying** What specific reasons does President Clinton give to explain his opposition to the balanced budget amendment?

4. **Drawing Conclusions** Which argument do you find more convincing? Why?

Chapter 23 A Time of Change **783**

Extending the Content

The Balanced Budget Amendment Under the proposed Balanced Budget Amendment, congressional spending could not exceed revenues, or income. Exceptions could be made if three-fifths of each house approved specific instances of excess spending by a roll call vote. In addition, the national public debt could not be increased without that same three-fifths roll call vote. Finally, the president's annual budget would have had to be balanced when it was submitted to Congress. During years in which the country engaged in a declared war, the provisions of the amendment could be waived. Congress failed to pass this, and other, proposed balanced budget amendments.

D Differentiated Instruction

Visual/Spatial Ask students to make pie graphs to illustrate the popular and electoral voting results of the 1996 election. **ELL**

R Reading Strategies

Identifying **Ask:** What are four accomplishments of Clinton's domestic agenda during his second term? *(child tax credit, Adoption and Safe Families Act, ban on cigarette advertising aimed at children, Children's Health Insurance Program)* **BL**

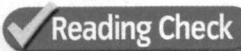
Reading Check

Answers:
Health Insurance Portability Act, Welfare Reform Act

In the months before the 1996 election, the president and the Republicans worked together to pass new legislation. In August Congress passed the Health Insurance Portability Act. This act improved health coverage for people who changed jobs and reduced discrimination against people who had pre-existing illnesses.

Later that month, Congress passed the Welfare Reform Act, which limited people to no more than two consecutive years on welfare and required them to work to receive welfare benefits. The law also increased child-care spending and gave tax breaks to companies that hired new employees who had been on welfare.

Clinton Wins Reelection

As the 1996 campaign began, Clinton took credit for the economy. The economic boom of the 1990s was the longest sustained period of growth in American history. Unemployment and inflation fell to their lowest levels in 40 years. The stock market soared, wages rose, crime rates fell, and the number of people on welfare declined. With the economy booming, Clinton's popularity climbed rapidly.

The Republican Party nominated Senator Bob Dole of Kansas, the Republican leader in the Senate, to run against Clinton. Dole chose as his running mate Jack Kemp, a former member of Congress from New York. Dole promised a 15 percent tax cut and attempted to portray Clinton as a tax-and-spend liberal.

H. Ross Perot also ran again as a candidate as he had in the 1992 election. This time he ran as the candidate of the Reform Party, which he had created. Once again Perot made the deficit the main campaign issue.

President Clinton won reelection, winning a little more than 49 percent of the popular vote and 379 electoral votes. Dole received almost 41 percent and 159 electoral votes, and Perot won about 8.4 percent of the popular vote and no electoral votes. Despite Clinton's victory, Republicans retained control of Congress. Two years later, after the 1998 elections, Republicans kept control of Congress, although the Democrats gained 5 seats in the House of Representatives.

Reading Check **Identifying** What two reforms did Clinton and Congress agree to support?

Clinton's Second Term

MAIN Idea Clinton tried to focus the domestic agenda on the needs of children, but personal problems marred his second term.

HISTORY AND YOU Do you remember learning about the impeachment trial of Andrew Johnson? Read on to learn about the second president ever to be impeached.

During Clinton's second term, the economy continued its expansion. As people's incomes rose, so too did the amount of taxes they paid to all levels of government. At the same time, despite their differences, the president and Congress continued to shrink the deficit. In 1997, for the first time in 24 years, the president was able to submit a balanced budget to Congress. Beginning in 1998, the government began to run a surplus—that is, it collected more money than it spent.

Despite these achievements, Clinton's domestic agenda was less aggressive in his second term. Much of his time was spent on foreign policy and in struggling against a personal scandal.

Putting Children First

During his second term, Clinton's domestic agenda shifted toward helping the nation's children. He began by asking Congress to pass a $500 per child tax credit. He also signed the Adoption and Safe Families Act and asked Congress to ban cigarette advertising aimed at children. In August 1997, Clinton signed the Children's Health Insurance Program—a plan to provide health insurance for children whose parents could not afford it.

Clinton also continued his efforts to help American students. "I come from a family where nobody had ever gone to college before," Clinton said. "When I became president, I was determined to do what I could to give every student that chance." To help students, he asked for a tax credit, a large increase in student grants, and an expansion of the Head Start program for disadvantaged preschoolers.

Clinton Is Impeached

The robust economy and his high standing in the polls allowed Clinton to regain the initiative in dealing with Congress. By 1998, how-

---

Hands-on Chapter Project:
Step 2

Art Show

Step 2: Review and Critique **Essential Question:** Do the selections of the two groups merge well to form a cohesive presentation?

Directions Student teams will share their selected images and see how they fit together. The class as a whole will determine how the pieces work or do not work together to illustrate the topic at hand.

Groups will critique the choices with the goal of presenting a cohesive art show.

Putting It Together Students should create a storyboard or blueprint for the presentation, determining how the selected pieces should be revised to present the whole picture of this period in American history. **OL**
(Chapter Project continued page 790)

PRIMARY SOURCE
Impeaching a President

The Constitution gives Congress the power to remove the president from office "upon impeachment for and conviction of, treason, bribery, or other high crimes and misdemeanors." The House of Representatives has the sole power over impeachment—the formal accusation of wrongdoing in office. If the majority of the House votes to impeach the president, the Senate conducts a trial. A two-thirds vote of those present is needed for conviction. If the president is being impeached, the chief justice of the United States presides. **D**

▲ House Judiciary Committee Chairman, Representative Henry Hyde, stands surrounded by boxes of evidence against President Clinton.

▲ Chief Justice Rehnquist is sworn in for the impeachment trial of President Clinton in the Senate.

Analyzing VISUALS

1. **Hypothesizing** Why do you think the Founders required the House to impeach the president but the Senate to hold the trial?

2. **Theorizing** Why might impeachment only require a majority vote in the House, but conviction requires a two-thirds vote in the Senate?

---

ever, he had become entangled in a serious scandal that threatened to undermine his presidency.

The scandal began in Clinton's first term, when he was accused of arranging illegal loans for Whitewater Development—an Arkansas real estate company—while he was governor of that state. Attorney General Janet Reno **C** decided that an independent counsel should investigate the president. A special three-judge panel appointed **Kenneth Starr,** a former federal judge, to this position.

In early 1998, a new scandal emerged involving a personal relationship between the president and a White House intern. Some evidence suggested that the president had committed **perjury,** or had lied under oath, about the relationship. The three-judge panel directed Starr to investigate this scandal as well. In September 1998, after examining the evidence, Starr sent his report to the Judiciary Committee of the House of Representatives. Starr argued

that Clinton had obstructed justice, abused his power as president, and committed perjury.

After the 1998 elections, the House began impeachment hearings. Clinton's supporters accused Starr of playing politics. Clinton's accusers argued that the president was accountable if his actions were illegal.

On December 19, 1998, the House of Representatives passed two articles of impeachment, one for perjury and one for obstruction of justice. The vote split almost evenly along party lines, and the case moved to the Senate for trial. On February 12, 1999, the senators cast their votes. The vote was 55 to 45 that Clinton was not guilty of perjury, and 50–50 on the charge of obstruction of justice. Although both votes were well short of the two-thirds needed to remove the president from office, Clinton's reputation had suffered.

✔ **Reading Check** **Examining** What events led to the impeachment of President Clinton?

C Critical Thinking

Defending **Ask:** Should a president be investigated for acts committed before he took office? *(Answers will vary.)* **OL**

D Differentiated Instruction

Logical/Mathematical
Ask: What vote in the Senate would have removed Clinton from office? *(67 to 33).* **OL**

Analyzing VISUALS

Answers:
1. The House was closer to the people and more subject to voter passions; the Senate was calmer and more likely to judge fairly.
2. conviction is more serious than charging someone with a crime, so a two-thirds vote is a safeguard against mistakes.

✔ Reading Check

Answer:
Whitewater, Ken Starr's investigation, the House votes on articles of impeachment

Additional Support

Activity: Interdisciplinary Connection

Civics **Ask:** What expectations do you have of the president of the United States? Are they different from your expectations of a neighbor, classmate, or friend? Explain. *(Answers will vary but may include the idea that, because the president has a great deal of power, he or she must be especially honest and trustworthy.)* Have students work in pairs to read the presidential oath of office, which is available on the Internet at memory.loc.gov/ammem/pihtml/pioaths.html.

Ask partners to list the duties of the president as listed in Article II, Sections 2–4 of the U.S. Constitution. Then ask students to rewrite the oath of office, incorporating additional pledges they feel the president should make to the people of the country as he or she takes office. Ask partners to share their oaths with the class. **OL**

R Reading Strategies

Sequencing Information

Ask: What chain of events led the U.S. to send troops to Haiti? *(Aristide is overthrown, U.N. embargo causes economic crisis, Haitian refugees flee to U.S., Clinton orders invasion, Carter convinces Haiti's rulers to step aside.)* **BL**

C Critical Thinking

Analyzing Primary Sources

Ask: How did many Haitians respond to the U.S. presence in their country? *(They seemed happy.)* **ELL**

Analyzing VISUALS

Answers:
1. Answers will vary. Possible problems: overextension of U.S. resources, foreign resentment.
2. Answers will vary but could include the idea that America's democratic system is threatened by the fall of other democracies.

Differentiated Instruction

Clinton Foreign Policy

MAIN Idea During Clinton's second term, the United States worked to end violence in Haiti, southeastern Europe and the Middle East.

HISTORY AND YOU Do you remember when and why NATO was created? Read on to find out how the United States and NATO worked to resolve a crisis in southeastern Europe.

Although Clinton's domestic policies became bogged down in struggles with Congress, he was able to engage in a series of major foreign policy initiatives. On several occasions, President Clinton used force to try to resolve regional conflicts.

The Haitian Intervention

In 1991 military leaders in Haiti overthrew Jean-Bertrand Aristide, the country's first democratically elected president in many decades. Aristide sought refuge in the United States.

Seeking to restore democracy, the Clinton administration convinced the United Nations to impose a trade embargo on Haiti. The embargo created a severe economic crisis in that country. Thousands of Haitian refugees fled to the United States in small boats, and many died at sea. Determined to end the crisis, Clinton ordered an invasion of Haiti. With the troops on the way, former president Jimmy Carter convinced Haiti's rulers to step aside. The American troops then landed to serve as peacekeepers.

Bosnia and Kosovo

The United States also was concerned about mounting tensions in southeastern Europe. During the Cold War, Yugoslavia had been a single federated nation made up of many different ethnic groups under a strong Communist government. In 1991, after the collapse of communism, Yugoslavia split apart.

In Bosnia, one of the former Yugoslav republics, a vicious three-way civil war erupted

PRIMARY SOURCE
Striving for Peace Around the World

With the Cold War over, the Clinton administration focused on bringing stability to the Middle East and southeastern Europe, where religious and ethnic strife had contributed to ongoing violence. In addition, Clinton sent peacekeepers into Haiti to help rebuild the nation's democracy.

▲ *Haitians gather outside the fence of the U.S. camp in Haiti to talk to American peacekeepers.*

▲ *Israeli Prime Minister Yitzhak Rabin and Palestinian leader Yasir Arafat shake hands after signing the 1993 Declaration of Principles.*

▼ *U.S. troops work with Bosnian Serbs in 1996 to set up boundaries between opposing forces.*

Analyzing VISUALS

1. **Predicting** Do you think the United States should intervene in conflicts in the world? What problems can result from such a policy?
2. **Explaining** Why would the United States think intervening in Haiti and Bosnia was important to its own security?

786 Chapter 23 A Time of Change

Leveled Activities

BL Reading Skills Activity, URB p. 87

OL Content Vocabulary Activity, URB p. 93

AL Historical Analysis Skills Activity, URB p. 88

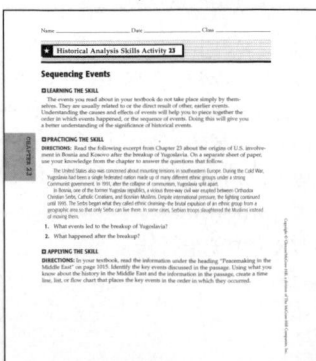

ELL Academic Vocabulary Activity, URB p. 95

between Orthodox Christian Serbs, Catholic Croatians, and Bosnian Muslims. Despite international pressure, the fighting continued until 1995. The Serbs began what they called **ethnic cleansing**—the brutal expulsion of an ethnic group from a geographic area so that only Serbs lived there. In some cases, Serbian troops slaughtered the Muslims instead of moving them.

The United States convinced its NATO allies that military action was necessary. NATO warplanes attacked the Serbs in Bosnia, forcing them to negotiate. The Clinton administration then arranged peace talks in Dayton, Ohio. The **participants** signed a peace plan known as the **Dayton Accords**. In 1996 some 60,000 NATO troops, including 20,000 Americans, entered Bosnia to enforce the plan.

In 1998 another war erupted, this time in the Serbian province of Kosovo. Kosovo has two major ethnic groups—Serbs and Albanians. Many of the Albanians wanted Kosovo to separate from Serbia. To keep Kosovo in Serbia, Serbian leader Slobodan Milosevic ordered a crackdown. The Albanians then organized their own army to fight back. Worried by Serbian violence against Albanian civilians, President Clinton convinced European leaders that NATO should use force to stop the fighting. In March 1999, NATO began bombing Serbia. In response, Serbia pulled its troops out of Kosovo.

Peacemaking in the Middle East

Although Iraq had been defeated in the Persian Gulf War, Iraqi President Saddam Hussein remained determined to hang onto power. In 1996 Iraqi forces attacked the Kurds, an ethnic group whose homeland lies in northern Iraq. To stop the attacks, the United States fired cruise missiles at Iraqi military targets.

Relations between Israel and the Palestinians were even more volatile. In 1993 Israeli Prime Minister Yitzhak Rabin and Palestine Liberation Organization leader Yasir Arafat reached an agreement. The PLO recognized Israel's right to exist, and Israel recognized the PLO as the representative of the Palestinians. President Clinton then invited Arafat and Rabin to the White House, where they signed the Declaration of Principles—a plan for creating a Palestinian government. Opposition to the peace plan emerged on both sides. Radical Palestinians exploded bombs in Israel and in 1995 a right-wing Israeli assassinated Prime Minister Rabin.

In 1998 Israeli and Palestinian leaders met with President Clinton at the Wye River Plantation in Maryland. They hoped to work out details of the withdrawal of Israeli troops from the West Bank and the Gaza Strip. The agreement they reached, however, did not address the ultimate dimensions of the Israeli withdrawal or the contested status of Jerusalem.

In July 2000, President Clinton invited Arafat and Israeli Prime Minister Ehud Barak to Camp David to discuss unresolved issues. Barak agreed to the creation of a Palestinian state in all of Gaza and about 95 percent of the West Bank, but Arafat rejected the deal. Beginning in October, violence again broke out between Palestinians and Israeli soldiers. The region was as far from peace as ever.

Reading Check **Identifying** In what three regions of the world did Clinton use force to support his foreign policy?

Vocabulary

1. **Explain** the significance of: AmeriCorps, Contract with America, Kenneth Starr, perjury, ethnic cleansing, Dayton Accords.

Main Ideas

2. **Identifying** What were two reasons President Clinton's health care plan failed?

3. **Explaining** Why did the federal government shut down in 1995?

4. **Describing** How could Clinton be impeached but remain in office?

5. **Organizing** Complete a chart similar to the one below by explaining the foreign policy issues facing President Clinton in each of the areas listed.

Region	Issue
Latin America	
Southeastern Europe	
Middle East	

Critical Thinking

6. **Big Ideas** What did President Clinton do to help families during his presidency?

7. **Analyzing Visuals** Study the photograph on page 785 of Clinton's impeachment trial. What elements in the photograph reflect the seriousness of the occasion?

Writing About History

8. **Persuasive Writing** Take on the role of a member of Congress. Write a letter in which you attempt to persuade other lawmakers to vote either for or against the impeachment of President Clinton. Provide reasons for your position.

History ONLINE
Study Central™ To review this section, go to glencoe.com and click on Study Central.

C Critical Thinking

Making Inferences Ask: Why did the United States not act on its own? *(Members of treaty organizations, such as NATO, pledge common defense. The Bosnian problem affected all NATO members, not just the United States.)* **OL**

Reading Check

Answers:
Bosnia, Kosovo, northern Iraq

Assess

Study Central™ provides summaries, interactive games, and online graphic organizers to help students review content.

Close

Evaluating Ask: Was Clinton's presidency successful? *(Answers should be supported with information from the text.)* **OL**

Section 2 REVIEW

Answers

1. All definitions can be found in the section and the Glossary.

2. Republicans felt it was too costly and heavy on government control; some Democrats supported other plans.

3. In a clash over the budget, Clinton vetoed some Republican proposals, Republicans stood firm, and Clinton allowed the government to shut down for lack of funds rather than give in.

4. Unless convicted in the Senate, the president remains in office.

5.

Region	Issue
Latin America	military coup in Haiti
Southeastern Europe	civil wars in Bosnia and Kosovo
Middle East	Iraqi attacks on Kurds and volatile relations between Israel and Palestine

6. Answers should include some or all of the following: Family Medical Leave Act, AmeriCorps, child tax credit, Adoption and Safe Families Act, ban on cigarette advertising aimed at children, Children's Health Insurance Program, student tax credit, increased student grants, expanded Head Start

7. Answers will vary but could include the solemn expressions on the faces of people in the photo, the swearing in of the Chief Justice, and the large boxes of information to be presented.

8. Letters will vary.

Focus

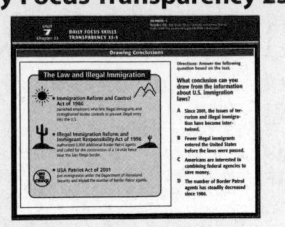
Guide to Reading

Answers:
abolished the national origins quota system; gave preference to skilled persons; established migration chains

Section Spotlight Video

To generate student interest and provide a springboard for class discussion, access the Chapter 23, Section 3 video at glencoe.com or on the video DVD.

Resource Manager

Section 3

A New Wave of Immigration

Guide to Reading

Big Ideas
Trade, War, and Migration A new immigration law allowed more people to immigrate to the United States.

Content Vocabulary
• migration chains (p. 788)
• refugees (p. 789)
• amnesty (p. 789)

Academic Vocabulary
• illegal (p. 789)
• allocate (p. 790)
• resident (p. 790)

People and Events to Identify
• Immigration Act of 1965 (p. 788)
• Immigration Reform and Control Act of 1986 (p. 789)
• Illegal Immigration Reform and Immigrant Responsibility Act of 1996 (p. 790)

Reading Strategy
Determining Cause and Effect
Use a graphic organizer similar to the one below to list the effects of the Immigration Act of 1965.

Effects of the Immigration Act of 1965

In the late twentieth century, the number of immigrants in the United States hit an all time high. Large numbers of non-European immigrants changed the ethnic composition of the United States. Immigration—legal and illegal—emerged as a difficult political issue.

Changes in Immigration Law

MAIN Idea The Immigration Act of 1965 eliminated preferences for certain European immigrants; illegal immigration became a problem.

HISTORY AND YOU Do you remember the controversial elements of the National Origins Act of 1924? Read on to learn how the repeal of the national origins system led to major changes in American society which few people had anticipated.

After the introduction of the national origins quota system in the 1920s, the sources and character of immigration to the United States changed dramatically. For the next few decades, the total number of immigrants arriving annually remained markedly lower. The quota system which gave preference to immigrants from northern and western European countries, although occasionally modified by Congress, remained largely intact until 1965.

In the midst of the flurry of civil rights and antipoverty legislation of the mid-1960s, the **Immigration Act of 1965** received scant attention when it was enacted. The law abolished the national origins quota system. It also gave preference to skilled persons and persons with close relatives who are U.S. citizens—policies which remain in place today. The preference given to the children, spouses, and parents of U.S. citizens meant that **migration chains** were established. As newcomers acquired U.S. citizenship, they too could send for relatives in their home country. Also, for the first time, the legislation introduced limits on immigration from the Western Hemisphere. The act further provided that immigrants could apply for U.S. citizenship after five years of legal residency.

At the time of its passage, few people expected that the new law would radically change the pattern or volume of immigration to the United States. Supporters of the law presented it as an extension of America's growing commitment to equal rights for non-European peoples. As U.S. Representative Philip Burton of California stated, "Just as we sought to eliminate discrimination in our land through the Civil Rights Act, today we seek by phasing out the national origins quota system to eliminate discrimination in immigration to this nation composed of the descendants of immigrants." Supporters of the new law also assumed that the new equal quotas

---

R Reading Strategies	C Critical Thinking	D Differentiated Instruction	W Writing Support	S Skill Practice
Teacher Edition • Activ. Prior Knowledge, p. 791 **Additional Resources** • Guided Reading Act., URB p. 116	**Teacher Edition** • Compare/ Contrast, p. 789 **Additional Resources** • Critical Thinking Skills Act., URB p. 98 • Supreme Court Case Studies, p. 157 • Quizzes/Tests, p. 327	**Teacher Edition** • Visual/Spatial, p. 790 **Additional Resources** • Enrichment Act., URB p. 111	**Teacher Edition** • Persuasive Writing, p. 789	**Teacher Edition** • Analyzing Graphs, p. 790 **Additional Resources** • RENTG, p. 251

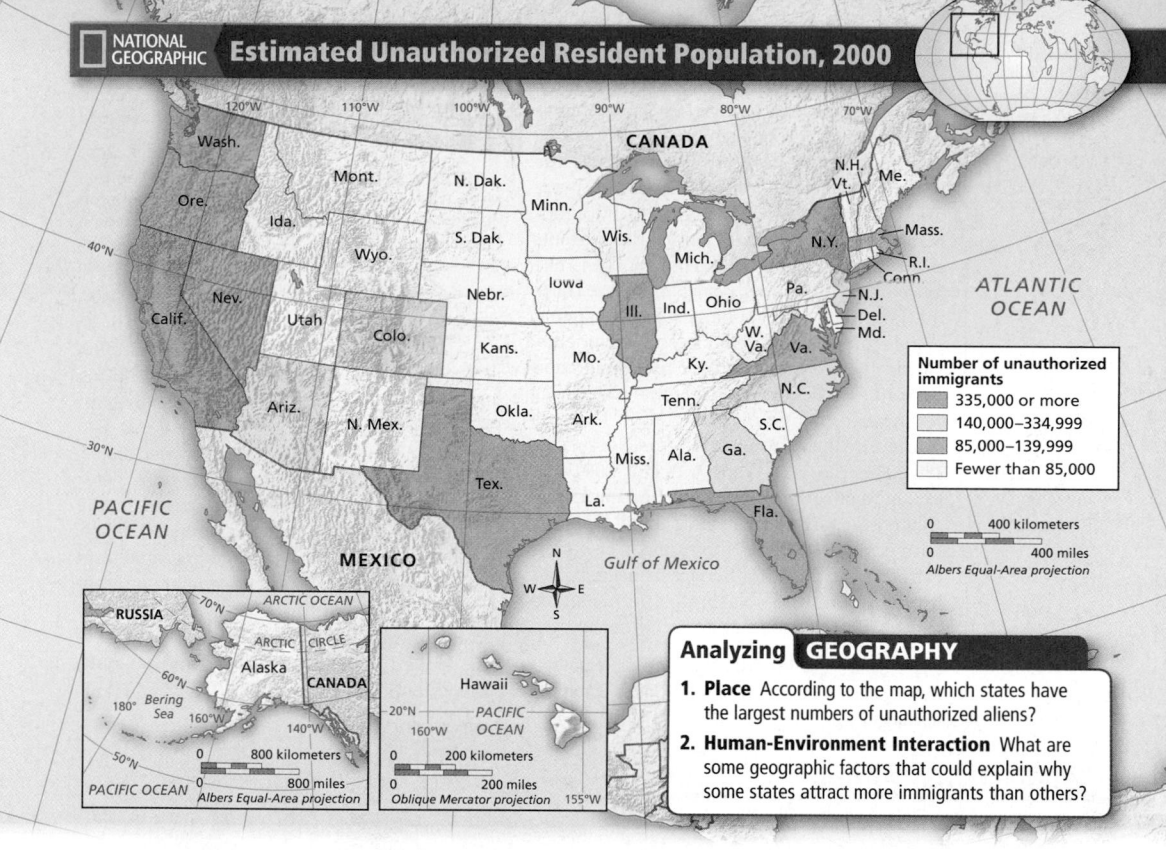

Estimated Unauthorized Resident Population, 2000

Number of unauthorized immigrants

- 335,000 or more
- 140,000–334,999
- 85,000–139,999
- Fewer than 85,000

Albers Equal-Area projection

Analyzing GEOGRAPHY

1. **Place** According to the map, which states have the largest numbers of unauthorized aliens?
2. **Human-Environment Interaction** What are some geographic factors that could explain why some states attract more immigrants than others?

Teach

C Critical Thinking

Comparing and Contrasting
Ask: How did the 1952 and 1980 refugee acts differ? *(The first defined a refugee as one who flees from a communist regime; the second broadened the definition to one who flees from fear of persecution for multiple reasons.)* **BL**

W Writing Support

Persuasive Writing Have students write an editorial supporting or criticizing the granting of amnesty. **AL**

Analyzing GEOGRAPHY

Answers:
1. Florida, Texas, California, Illinois, New York
2. Answers will vary but may state that coastal states offer easier access and warm climates attract farm workers.

for non-European nations would generally go unfilled. In fact, immigration from non-European countries soared in subsequent decades.

In addition to those arriving through traditional immigration channels, some newcomers arrived in the United States as **refugees.** Beginning in 1948, refugees from countries ravaged by World War II were admitted, although they were counted as part of their nation's quota. The Cold War led to another class of refugees. According to the McCarran-Walter Act of 1952, anyone who was fleeing a **C** Communist regime could be admitted as a refugee. Refugee policy was further broadened under the Refugee Act of 1980, which defined a refugee as someone leaving his or her country due to a "well founded fear of persecution on account of race, religion, nationality, membership in a particular group, or political opinion."

The growing problem of **illegal** immigration also prompted changes in immigration law. During the Reagan administration, Congress passed the **Immigration Reform and Control Act of 1986.** This law established penalties for employers who knowingly hire unauthorized immigrants and strengthened border controls to prevent illegal entry into the United States. It also established a process to grant **amnesty** (in other words, a pardon) and legal papers to any undocumented alien who could prove that he or she had entered the country before January 1, 1982, and had resided in the United States since then.

Despite these changes, illegal immigration persisted and the number of unauthorized immigrants continued to grow. By 1990, an estimated 3.5 million unauthorized immigrants resided in the United States. By the mid-1990s, Congress was debating new ways to combat illegal immigration.

Chapter 23 A Time of Change **789**

Additional Support

Activity: Connecting with the United States

Analyzing Visas Tell students that there is no application fee for a visa to enter the United States legally. **Ask:** Why do so many immigrants enter illegally? *(Answers will vary but may include that many immigrants do not qualify for admission.)* Have students form five groups. Ask each group to research the requirements and processes for one of the types of visas available to immigrants who wish to settle permanently in the United States: family immigration, adoption of a foreign child, marriage to a foreign national, Diversity Visa Program, and employment visas. This information is available on the Internet at <u>travel.state.gov/visa/immigrants/types/types_1326.html</u>. Ask groups to create booklets that explain their visa to a prospective immigrant. Encourage students to illustrate their booklets and choose simple language to make information clear and understandable. Ask groups to exchange booklets until everyone has read the information about each visa type. **Ask:** What limitations do these visa types place on immigration? **OL**

D Differentiated Instruction

Visual/Spatial Have students diagram the provisions of the Illegal Immigration Reform and Immigrant Responsibility Act of 1996. **BL**

S Skill Practice

Analyzing Graphs Ask: What year saw the highest number of border deaths? *(2000)* **ELL**

✓ Reading Check

Answers:
a well-founded fear of persecution because of race, religion, nationality, group membership, or political opinion

Analyzing VISUALS

Answers:
1. To identify with the revolutionaries of 1776.
2. Answers will vary but should be supported.

Hands-on Chapter Project:
Step 3

History ONLINE Student Skill Activity To learn how to create and modify spreadsheets, visit glencoe.com and complete the skill activity.

The law that resulted from these debates was the **Illegal Immigration Reform and Immigrant Responsibility Act of 1996,** which made several changes to U.S. immigration law. First, it required families sponsoring an immigrant to have an income above the poverty level. Second, it **allocated** more resources to stop illegal immigration, by authorizing an additional 5,000 Border Patrol agents and calling for the construction of a 14-mile fence along the border near San Diego. Third, the law toughened penalties for smuggling people or providing fraudulent documents. Finally, the law made it easier for immigration authorities to deport undocumented aliens.

Another change in immigration law was spurred by the terrorist attacks of September 11, 2001. The USA Patriot Act of 2001 put immigration under the control of the newly created Department of Homeland Security. Furthermore, it tripled the number of Border Patrol agents, Customs Service inspectors, and Immigration and Naturalization Service inspectors along the Canadian border.

✓ Reading Check Identifying For what reasons may a foreigner be admitted to the United States as a refugee?

PRIMARY SOURCE
Securing the Border

After the attacks of September 11, 2001, many Americans became increasingly concerned about border security. Many agreed on the need for increased border patrols. Others proposed building a continuous wall from Texas to California to prevent illegal immigration. Critics of such proposals, however, claimed such actions would not stop people who were determined to enter the country illegally, but rather force them to take more dangerous risks.

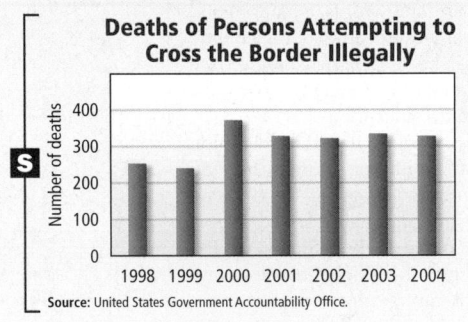

Deaths of Persons Attempting to Cross the Border Illegally

Number of deaths: 1998, 1999, 2000, 2001, 2002, 2003, 2004

Source: United States Government Accountability Office.

Recent Immigration

MAIN Idea In the late twentieth century, immigrants from Latin America and Asia outnumbered European immigrants.

HISTORY AND YOU Do you remember the reasons that some Americans objected to immigration in the late 1800s? Read on to learn how the debate resurfaced in the 1980s and continues today.

Although immigrants headed for all parts of the United States, certain states experienced a larger influx than others. In 1990, California, Texas, New York, Illinois, and Florida had the highest populations of foreign-born **residents.** High numbers of immigrants also increased the ethnic diversity of these states, as their Latino and Asian populations grew. Among the immigrants who arrived in the 1990s, just over 10 percent came from Europe. More than half of new immigrants came from Latin America, while approximately another 25 percent came from Asia. By 2001, the top five countries of origin for legal immigrants to the United States were Mexico, India, China, the Philippines, and Vietnam.

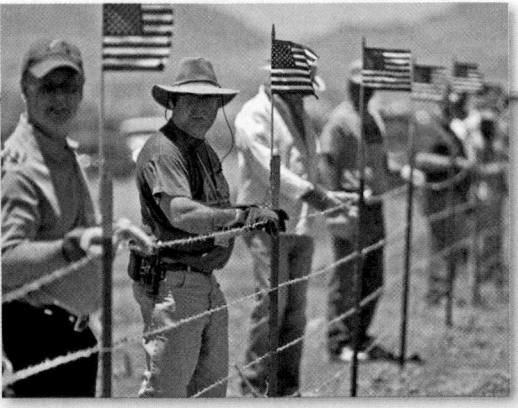

▲ On May 27, 2006, a volunteer organization called the Minutemen Civil Defense Corps built a fence along the Mexican border on private property.

Analyzing VISUALS

1. **Making Connections** Why do you think the organization pictured above decided to call themselves the "minutemen"?
2. **Theorizing** Do you think building a fence along the border would lead to fewer deaths? Why or why not?

Art Show

Step 3: Selecting the Images for the Art Exhibit Essential Question: How do the selected images reflect the period? What is most important about them?

Directions Student teams will continue to create their images. In this step, students will determine which members of their team will create the informational tags that will accompany the images in the art show. The informational tags should be typed

sheets that include the following information:

- Image title
- Brief summary of how the image relates to the historical period
- Media (oil, watercolor, drawing, and so on)
- Date of completion
- Any other pertinent information

Putting It Together In one or two sittings, students should review the submissions

and decide which will be hung in the exhibit. (School policy and space may determine if this ends up being an actual exhibit or a virtual exhibit.) **OL**

(Chapter Project continued on page 796)

Refugees added to the growing immigrant population. In the 25 years following the Cuban Revolution of 1959, more than 800,000 Cubans arrived in the United States. So many of these immigrants settled in the Miami, Florida, area that only the city of Havana, Cuba, is home to more Cubans. In addition, the Vietnam War created refugees. Some 600,000 immigrants from Vietnam, Laos, and Cambodia arrived in the decade after 1974.

In addition to the immigrants entering through legal channels, others arrived without official permission. The largest number of unauthorized immigrants came from Mexico, El Salvador, and Guatemala. The Reagan administration's amnesty program in 1986 had been designed to eliminate the problem of undocumented aliens, but over the next 20 years the number of unauthorized immigrants tripled. American public opinion divided over whether unauthorized immigrants should be able to obtain driver's licenses or send their children to public schools and receive other government services. Some believed that unauthorized immigrants should be deported. Others favored allowing them to apply for temporary work visas so the government could keep track of them, and permitting them to earn permanent residence if they learned English, paid back taxes, and had no criminal record.

In 2006, President George W. Bush made immigration reform a top priority, but members of Congress strongly disagreed over how to solve the problem. A bipartisan majority of the Senate favored legislation that blended tougher enforcement of immigration laws with some form of earned citizenship for the estimated 12 million undocumented aliens living and working in the country. The Senate bill included a provision that undocumented aliens who grew up in the United States and graduated from high school could apply for citizenship. Conservative Republicans who held the majority in the House objected that this would reward illegal behavior. The House rejected any form of amnesty and called for the United States to build a wall along its Mexican border—although the United States had already tripled the size of its border patrol without reducing illegal immigration. As Congress debated a bill that would subject unauthorized aliens to criminal prosecution, Latinos held rallies across the country, carrying signs that read: "We are not criminals."

Advocates of immigration reform promoted alternatives such as expanding quotas through a guest-worker program and establishing a means of legalization for those already in the country. Some undocumented aliens had lived in the United States for years, and had raised families here. Deporting them would mean separating husbands, wives, and children. Some undocumented aliens arrived as children and had lived in the United States most of their lives. Their own children, born in the United States, were native-born citizens even though their parents lacked legal status. Among those who became legal citizens, most wanted other family members to join them, so the reunification of families accounted for three-quarters of all legal immigration.

Reading Check **Explaining** Why did some members of Congress oppose amnesty for undocumented aliens? Why did others support it?

Section 3 REVIEW

Vocabulary
1. **Explain** the significance of: Immigration Act of 1965, migration chains, refugees, Immigration Reform and Control Act of 1986, amnesty, Illegal Immigration Reform and Immigrant Responsibility Act of 1996.

Main Ideas
2. **Summarizing** What problems arose that caused changes in the immigration laws?

3. **Describing** What alternatives to immigration reform did advocates for reform suggest?

Critical Thinking
4. **Big Ideas** What two acts were instrumental in helping refugees?

5. **Organizing** Use a graphic organizer similar to the one below to list the immigration laws and what they intended.

Immigration Law	Intent
Immigration Act of 1965	
Immigration Reform and Control Act of 1986	
Illegal Immigration Reform and Immigrant Responsibility Act of 1996	

6. **Analyzing Visuals** Study the map on page 789. Research the number of unauthorized immigrants in the United States and create a spreadsheet that lists the states where these immigrants settled and the estimated numbers in 2000 and 2005.

Writing About History
7. **Persuasive Writing** After reading about the problem of illegal immigration, write a letter to your representative in Congress explaining what you feel he or she should do about the problem.

History ONLINE
Study Central™ To review this section, go to glencoe.com and click on Study Central.

791

Activating Prior Knowledge
Ask: How were the Cubans' and Southeast Asians' immigrations similar? *(Both fled communism.)* **AL**

Reading Check

Answers:
Some felt amnesty would reward illegal behavior. Supporters felt immigrants who had lived in the U.S. for years deserved to stay.

Assess

History ONLINE

Study Central™ provides summaries, interactive games, and online graphic organizers to help students review content.

Close

Problem-Solving Ask: How has the government tried to regulate immigration? *(by restricting immigrant eligibility, guarding borders, and deportation)* **OL**

Section 3 REVIEW

Answers

1. All definitions can be found in the section and the Glossary.
2. Immigration, both legal and illegal, soared. Terrorists entered the country.
3. expanding quotas through a guest-worker program, establishing a means of legalization for undocumented aliens already in the country
4. the McCarran-Walter Act of 1952 and the Refugee Act of 1980
5. **Immigration Act of 1965:** abolished the national origins quota system, gave preference to skilled persons and persons related to U.S. citizens, limited immigration from the Western hemisphere, let immigrants apply for citizenship after 5 years of legal residency; **Immigration Reform and Control Act:** penalized employers who knowingly hired unauthorized immigrants, strengthened border controls, established amnesty processes for certain immigrants; required sponsor families to have an income above poverty level; **Illegal Immigration Reform and Immigrant Responsibility Act:** allocated more resources to stop illegal immigration; toughened penalties for smuggling people or providing fraudulent documents
6. In addition to creating the spreadsheet, have students give a citation for their source.
7. Letters will vary but should offer a solution to the illegal immigration problem.

Focus

Bellringer
Daily Focus Transparency 23.4

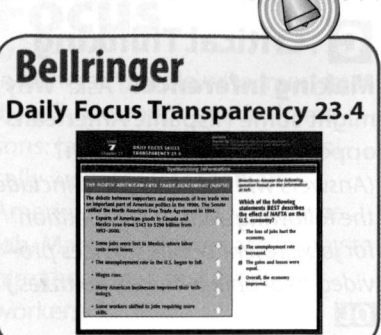

Guide to Reading

Answers:
interdependent economies, international trade, ozone depletion, global warming

Section Spotlight Video

To generate student interest and provide a springboard for class discussion, access the Chapter 23, Section 4 video at glencoe.com or on the video DVD.

Resource Manager

Section 4

An Interdependent World

Guide to Reading

Big Ideas
Economics and Society As the twentieth century drew to a close, world trade and environmentalism became increasingly more important during a period of globalization.

Content Vocabulary
• globalism (p. 794)
• euro (p. 795)
• global warming (p. 797)

Academic Vocabulary
• cited (p. 796)
• awareness (p. 797)

People and Events to Identify
• North American Free Trade Agreement (NAFTA) (p. 795)
• European Union (EU) (p. 795)
• Asia Pacific Economic Cooperation (APEC) (p. 796)
• World Trade Organization (WTO) (p. 796)
• Kyoto Protocol (p. 797)

Reading Strategy
Organizing Complete a graphic organizer like the one below to chart the major political and economic problems facing the world at the turn of the century.

Global Concerns

As the world economy became more interconnected in the 1990s, Americans debated whether the elimination of trade barriers was more beneficial or detrimental for the nation. Concerns about environmental damage led to an international conference in Kyoto, Japan.

The New Global Economy

MAIN Idea Regional trade agreements, such as the North American Free Trade Agreement (NAFTA), reflected the growing interdependence of the global economy.

HISTORY AND YOU Do you remember how tariffs were a hotly debated issue in earlier periods of American history? Read on to learn about NAFTA and the fierce political debate it sparked.

In the 1990s Americans began to realize that their relationship with the rest of the world was changing. The economies of individual countries were becoming much more interdependent, and events in one part of the world could dramatically affect the economy of another country thousands of miles away. Computer technology and the Internet played a big role in forging this new global economy. So too did the conviction of many of the world's political and business leaders that free trade and the global exchange of goods contributed to prosperity and economic growth.

At the same time, the Internet and digital satellite technology helped link the world together culturally. For example, people in the United States could read Australian newspapers on the Web, while Chinese students could download American popular music, and an African doctor could consult a British medical database. This idea that the world is becoming increasingly interconnected is sometimes referred to as **globalism,** and the process is called globalization.

Selling American-made goods abroad had long been important to American prosperity. From World War II to the present, Republican and Democratic administrations have worked to lower barriers to international trade. They reasoned that trade helps the American economy: American businesses make money selling goods abroad, and American consumers benefit by having the option to buy goods that are less expensive than those made in the United States. Importing low-cost goods would also keep inflation and interest rates low.

Opponents warned that embracing the global economy would cause manufacturing jobs to move from the United States to nations where wages were low and there were fewer environmental regulations. They suggested that having cheap imports available to buy

R Reading Strategies	**C** Critical Thinking	**D** Differentiated Instruction	**W** Writing Support	**S** Skill Practice
Teacher Edition • Activ. Prior Knowledge, p. 795 **Additional Resources** • Read. Skills Act., URB p. 87 • Guided Reading Act., URB p. 117	**Teacher Edition** • Drawing Conclusions, p. 795 **Additional Resources** • Quizzes/Tests, p. 328	**Teacher Edition** • Visual/ Spatial, p. 797 **Additional Resources** • American Art/Music, URB p. 105 • Reteaching Act., URB p. 109	**Teacher Edition** • Personal Writing, p. 796 **Additional Resources** • Authentic Assess., p. 51	**Teacher Edition** • Reading Graphs, p. 796 **Additional Resources** • RENTG, p. 254

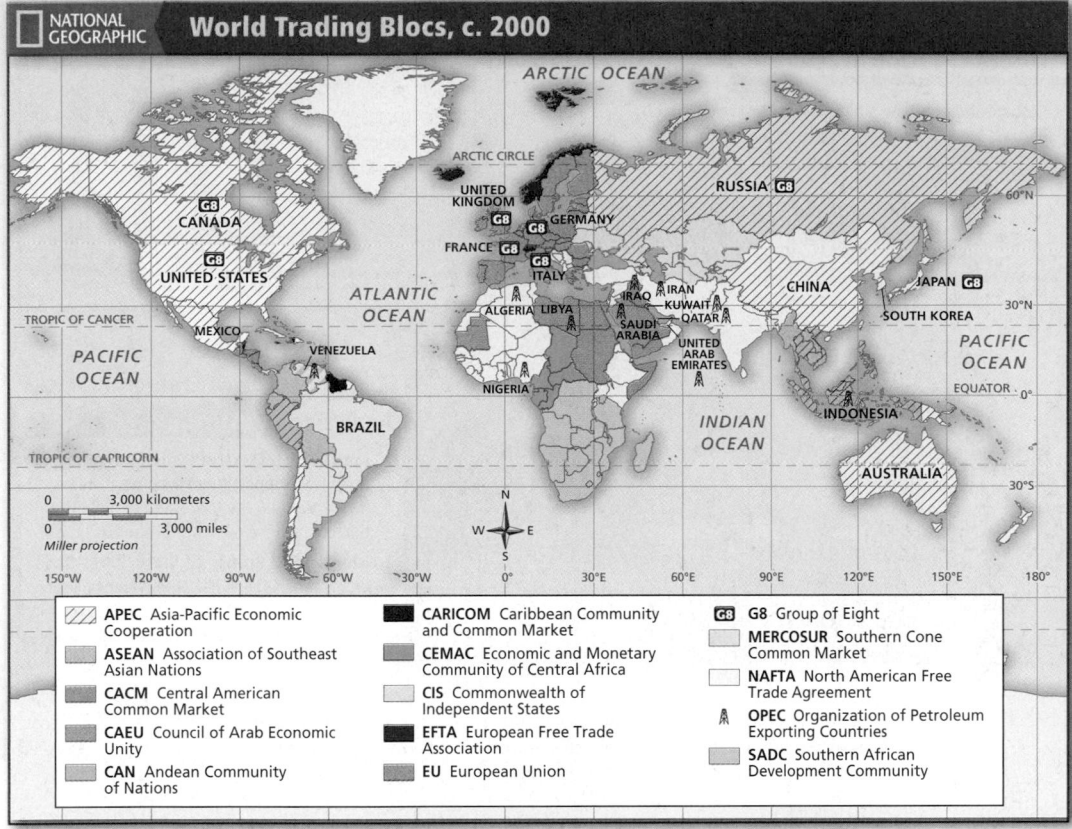

NATIONAL GEOGRAPHIC

World Trading Blocs, c. 2000

APEC Asia-Pacific Economic Cooperation

ASEAN Association of Southeast Asian Nations

CACM Central American Common Market

CAEU Council of Arab Economic Unity

CAN Andean Community of Nations

CARICOM Caribbean Community and Common Market

CEMAC Economic and Monetary Community of Central Africa

CIS Commonwealth of Independent States

EFTA European Free Trade Association

EU European Union

G8 Group of Eight

MERCOSUR Southern Cone Common Market

NAFTA North American Free Trade Agreement

OPEC Organization of Petroleum Exporting Countries

SADC Southern African Development Community

---

would not help those Americans who no longer could find work because their industries had moved overseas. By the 1990s, the debate between supporters of free trade and those who wanted to limit trade had become an important part of American politics.

Regional Blocs

One way to increase international trade was to create regional trade pacts. In 1994 President Clinton convinced the Senate to ratify the **North American Free Trade Agreement** (NAFTA). This agreement joined Canada, the United States, and Mexico in a free-trade zone. With NAFTA in operation, exports of American goods to both Canada and Mexico rose dramatically. From 1993 to 2000, it is estimated that combined exports to those two countries rose from $142 to $290 billion, an increase of 104 percent.

Many Americans feared that NAFTA would cause industrial jobs to move to Mexico, where labor costs were lower. Some jobs were indeed lost, as foreign-owned factories, known as *maquiladoras*, opened in Mexico near the American border. At the same time, however, the unemployment rate in the United States began to fall and wages rose. Many American businesses upgraded their technology, and workers shifted to more skilled jobs or to the service industry.

Regional trade blocs also formed in Europe and Asia. In 1993, the **European Union** (EU) was created to promote economic and political cooperation among many European nations. The EU created a common bank and the **euro,** a common currency for member nations. The organization also removed trade barriers between its members and set policies on imports from nations outside the community.

Chapter 23 A Time of Change **795**

Teach

C Critical Thinking

Drawing Conclusions Ask: Why did the EU create a common bank and currency for member nations? *(to make it easier to trade within the member nations)* **OL**

R Reading Strategies

Activating Prior Knowledge

Ask: What is the term for a trade barrier that taxes imported goods? *(tariff)* **OL**

Differentiated Instruction

Reinforcing Skills Activity, URB p. 97

Reading a Cartogram

Objective: Read a cartogram.

Focus: Define a cartogram.

Teach: What is the purpose of a cartogram?

Assess: Explain why the size of the states are distorted in the cartogram.

Close: Use the cartogram to explain which states have the most popular votes.

Differentiated Instruction Strategies

BL Explain the difference between a cartogram and a thematic map.

AL Create a cartogram on a topic other than an election.

ELL Explain the purpose of the title and key on a cartogram.

S Skill Practice

Reading Graphs Ask: What seems to be the correlation between trade and GDP? *(As trade increases, so does GDP.)* Between what years was there little expansion of trade and GDP? *(2000 and 2001)* **ELL**

W Writing Support

Personal Writing Have students write a personal response to the slogan *Buy American.* **AL**

✓ Reading Check

Answer:
It created global economic interdependence.

Analyzing VISUALS

Answers:
1. Because increased trade increases GDP, countries are more prosperous. However, one country's economic woes can affect other countries.
2. Answers will vary but could include national autonomy and human rights.

Hands-On Chapter Project Step 4

Art Show

Step 4: Hanging the Show Essential Question: How should the images best be presented to illustrate this time of change in American history?

Directions The final job is to hang the show, but this requires decisions about the best order in which to present the images for the audience. Students may choose to hang the images by chronological order, by date of the artwork, by the artists, or by a

---

PRIMARY SOURCE
Debating Free Trade

Globalization and the steady reduction of trade barriers between nations has led to many protests and political debates around the globe.

▲ Demonstrators in Seattle protest a meeting of the WTO on November 30, 1999.

Rise of Global Trade and Global GDP

Source: Australia's Foreign and Trade Policy White Paper.

Analyzing VISUALS

1. **Identifying Central Issues** How does the graph support those who want free trade? How do the protestors of globalization counter the evidence of the bar graph?
2. **Identifying Points of View** If free trade brings prosperity, what other values might opponents be seeking to protect?

Another trade bloc that came together in the early 1990s was the **Asia Pacific Economic Cooperation** (APEC). It includes most nations that have a coastline on the Pacific Ocean, including the United States, Canada, China, Japan, South Korea, Mexico, and Russia. APEC represented the fastest-growing region in the world and controlled 47 percent of global trade in 2001. APEC began as a forum to promote economic cooperation and lower trade barriers, but major political differences kept its members from acting together.

The World Trade Organization

In 1994 some 120 nations formed the **World Trade Organization** (WTO) to administer international trade agreements and help settle trade disputes. President Clinton convinced Congress to pass legislation enabling the United States to participate in the WTO. Supporters of the WTO **cited** benefits for American consumers, including cheaper imports, new markets, and copyright protection for the American entertainment industry. Opponents noted that the United States would be bound to accept the WTO's rulings

in trade disputes even if they hurt the American economy. Despite their concerns, Congress passed the legislation.

Trade With China

China's huge population offered potential as a market for American goods, but many people had reservations about trading with China. These critics cited China's suppression of protests in Tiananmen Square in 1989, its record on human rights, and its threats to invade Taiwan. Despite these concerns, President Clinton argued that expanding trade with China would help bring it into the world community.

After negotiating a new trade agreement, Clinton urged Congress to grant China permanent normal trade relation status. Unions opposed the deal, fearing that inexpensive Chinese goods would flood U.S. markets; conservatives objected to China's military ambitions; and environmentalists worried about pollution from Chinese factories. Over such objections, the bill passed in late 2000.

✓ Reading Check Analyzing How did international trade change the world economy?

---

perceived theme in the images. Another task is to review the informational tags that will accompany the images. Will the tags give the audience enough information to clearly see the topic?

Putting It Together If there is space for the show to actually be hung; getting the materials to hang it is the last step. Students from other classes might view it and review it. **OL**

(Chapter Project continued on the Visual Summary page)

Global Environmentalism

MAIN Idea As scientists learned that certain chemicals could damage the Earth's ozone layer, they worked to ban their use; concern about global warming became a serious political issue.

HISTORY AND YOU Are there groups in your school or community that work to improve the environment? Read on to learn about efforts to reduce damage to the environment.

The rise of a global economy also increased **awareness** of environmental issues. Environmentalists began thinking of the environment as a global system. Increasingly, they began addressing issues that they believed were of global, not just local, concern.

Concern About Ozone

In the 1980s scientists discovered that chlorofluorocarbons (CFCs) had the ability to break down the ozone layer in the Earth's atmosphere. Ozone is a gas that protects life on Earth from the ultraviolet rays of the sun. At that time, CFCs were widely used in air conditioners and refrigerators. Environmental activists began to push for a ban on CFC production. In the late 1980s, public awareness of the issue increased dramatically when scientists documented a large ozone "hole" over Antarctica. In 1987 the United States and 22 other nations agreed to phase out the production of CFCs and other chemicals that might be weakening the ozone layer.

Global Warming

In the early 1990s, another global environmental issue developed when some scientists found evidence of **global warming**—an increase in average world temperatures over time. Such a rise in temperature could eventually lead to more droughts and other forms of extreme weather. A furious debate began over how to measure the Earth's temperature and what the results meant.

Many experts concluded that carbon dioxide emissions from factories and power plants caused global warming, but others disagreed. The issue became very controversial because the cost of controlling emissions would affect the global economy. Industries would have to pay the cost of further reducing emissions, and those costs would eventually be passed on to consumers. Developing nations trying to industrialize would be hurt the most, but economic growth in wealthier nations would be hurt, too.

Concern about global warming led to an international conference in Kyoto, Japan, in 1997. Thirty-eight nations and the EU signed the Kyoto Protocol promising to reduce emissions, but very few have actually complied with its requirements and reduced their emissions. President Clinton did not submit the Kyoto Protocol to the Senate for ratification because most senators were opposed to it. In 2001 President George W. Bush withdrew the United States from the **Kyoto Protocol,** citing flaws in the treaty.

Reading Check **Describing** Why did environmentalists think CFCs were dangerous?

Vocabulary
1. **Explain** the significance of: globalism, North American Free Trade Agreement, European Union, euro, Asia Pacific Economic Cooperation, World Trade Organization, global warming, Kyoto Protocol.

Main Ideas
2. **Explaining** Why was China an important factor in world trade?

3. **Describing** What was the international response to concerns about global warming?

Critical Thinking
4. **Big Ideas** How did NAFTA affect exports of American goods?

5. **Organizing** Complete a graphic organizer by listing and describing the regional trade blocs that formed in the 1990s.

6. **Analyzing Visuals** Examine the image on page 796. Why do some people or groups protest globalization?

Writing About History
7. **Expository Writing** Decide which issue of global concern is the most serious. In an essay, explain why you think it is the most serious problem, and provide some possible solutions.

History ONLINE
Study Central™ To review this section, go to glencoe.com and click on Study Central.

D Differentiated Instruction

Visual/Spatial Have students create posters or cartoons to illustrate the debate over global warming.

✓ Reading Check

Answer:
Environmentalists grew concerned that CFCs may have caused a large ozone "hole" over Antarctica.

Assess

History ONLINE

Study Central™ provides summaries, interactive games, and online graphic organizers to help students review content.

Close

Identifying **Ask:** In what ways is today's world interdependent? *(economically, environmentally)*
OL

Section 4 REVIEW

Answers

1. All definitions can be found in the section and the Glossary.

2. China's huge population offered great potential as a market for U.S. goods.

3. The EU and 38 nations signed the Kyoto Protocol promising to reduce emissions; few have complied, however.

4. With NAFTA in operation, American exports to Canada and Mexico rose dramatically, an estimated 104 percent.

5. NAFTA, EU, APEC

6. Answers will vary but could include that some fear that the U.S. will lose its economic autonomy, that the U.S. economy will be negatively affected by downturns in the economies of other countries, and that jobs will be lost as businesses seek cheaper labor and production costs overseas.

7. Essays will vary but should describe a global problem, provide rationale for the selection, and offer possible solutions.

Chapter 23 VISUAL SUMMARY

Analyzing Visuals Ask: *How did computers change job requirements for American workers?* (Workers had to demonstrate computer proficiency or be willing to learn.) *How might computers have affected work output?* (Answers will vary but could include the ideas that work could be produced and revised more quickly, that employees could share or consult on work, and that uniform appearance was possible.) **ELL**

Drawing Conclusions Ask: *How did increased taxes reduce the federal deficit?* (The increased tax revenues were used to pay off existing debt.) **BL**

A Changing Society

The Technological Revolution

- The invention of the integrated circuit and microprocessors enables small personal computers built by Apple and IBM.
- The telecommunications revolution leads to the development of small portable cell phones, and digital video and audio players.
- The rise of the Internet and World Wide Web provide new ways for people to retrieve information, build communities, and do business.

A New Wave of Immigrants

- New immigration laws in 1965 and 1986 contribute to a rise in Hispanic immigration and an increase in immigrants from Asia, Africa, and the Middle East.
- The American population becomes increasingly culturally diverse.

The Rise of a Global Economy

- Free trade, in combination with the technological revolution, creates a new global marketplace.
- Increasing awareness of the global economy also sparks a new global environmentalist movement.

▲ Today, almost all businesses, such as this public relations firm, rely on computers to help employees perform their day-to-day duties.

The Clinton Years

First-Term Achievements and Failures

- Raised taxes to help cut the deficit
- Proposal for a national health care program fails
- Signed the Family Medical Leave Act into law
- Persuaded Congress to create AmeriCorps
- Signed the Brady Handgun Bill into law
- Worked with Republicans to push the Health Insurance Portability Act and the Welfare Reform Act through Congress

Second-Term Achievements and Failures

- Submits a balanced budget to Congress
- Convinces Congress to pass a new tax credit for children and a children's health insurance program
- Impeached on charges of perjury and obstruction of justice but is acquitted by the Senate

Foreign Policy Achievements

- Dispatched troops to Haiti to restore democracy
- Dispatched troops to Bosnia and bombed Serbia to end the civil war and ethnic cleansing that followed the breakup of Yugoslavia
- Mediated negotiations between Israel and the PLO

▲ President Bill Clinton delivers his State of the Union address to a joint session of Congress on January 24, 1995.

798 Chapter 23 A Time of Change

Hands-On Chapter Project
Step 5: Wrap Up

Art Show

Step 5: Wrap Up After students have hung the presentation, they will acquire feedback and learn from the feedback.

Directions After the audience has had a chance to review the art show, ask them for their feedback. (You may want to put comment cards out for audience members.) As a class, review the comments, as well as discuss your own reactions to the show.

Ask the following questions to start the discussion:

- What was good about the show?

- Did the images illustrate the topics clearly? Why or why not?

- How could the show have been improved?

- What would you do differently if you did this project again?

Putting It Together As a final close to the project, have students write a brief summary of their reactions to the project, explaining how it illustrated the time period. **OL**

ASSESSMENT

STANDARDIZED TEST PRACTICE

TEST-TAKING **TIP**

Consider each answer choice individually and cross out choices you have eliminated. You will save time and stop yourself from choosing an answer you have mentally eliminated.

Reviewing Vocabulary

Directions: Choose the word or words that best complete the sentence.

1. The company Intel revolutionized computers by combining several integrated circuits on a single chip called

   A minicomputer.

   B nanocomputer.

   C microprocessor.

   D microcomputer.

2. Clinton was impeached because he committed

   A perjury.

   B ethnic cleansing.

   C overtaxation.

   D robbery.

3. The Immigration Reform and Control Act of 1986 granted _____ to immigrants who entered the country before January 1, 1982.

   A leniency

   B citizenship

   C a pardon

   D amnesty

4. The process of the world becoming increasingly interconnected is called

   A globalization.

   B internationalism.

   C Americanism.

   D Nationalism.

Reviewing Main Ideas

Directions: Choose the best answer for each of the following questions.

Section 1 *(pp. 774–777)*

5. The government began to deregulate the telecommunications industry in the

   A 1950s.

   B 1960s.

   C 1970s.

   D 1980s.

6. In 1990, researchers at CERN developed a new way to present information known as

   A the Internet.

   B the computer.

   C the Ethernet.

   D the World Wide Web.

Section 2 *(pp. 780–787)*

7. Democrats passed a law during President Clinton's administration that tightened gun control called

   A the Gun Law.

   B the Anti-Gun Bill.

   C the Brady Bill.

   D the NRA Law.

8. The Contract with America was proposed by

   A Hillary Clinton.

   B President Clinton.

   C Al Gore.

   D Newt Gingrich.

Need Extra Help?								
If You Missed Questions . . .	1	2	3	4	5	6	7	8
Go to Page . . .	774	785	789	794	775	777	782	783

 GO ON

Reviewing Vocabulary

1. C The question asks for the name of a computer chip. All of the answer choices except for *C* have prefixes attached to computer, as in minicomputer. A chip is not a computer.

2. A Ethnic cleansing is the attempt to kill off a certain group of people who share a certain ethnicity. Over-taxation is not a crime. Robbery would result in a criminal trial. Clinton was accused of lying under oath, perjury, about his relationship with an intern.

3. D Students may have trouble choosing between *C* and *D*, because amnesty is a type of pardon. However, amnesty is the more precise term.

4. A -ization is a suffix that means an action or a process. Globalization is the process increasing global connections. Internationalism is a tempting choice, but its meaning is slightly different; it is more of an interest in other nations or describes cooperation between nations, but does not describe the process of increasing global connections.

Reviewing Main Ideas

5. C Review "New Communications" on page 775 with students. It states that deregulation began in the 1970s.

6. D The Internet preceded the World Wide Web and began to be developed as early as 1969. The computer was also developed before the 1990s. The Ethernet uses cables to exchange messages between computers.

7. C Remind students that James Brady was shot and injured during the assassination attempt on Reagan. This should help them relate Brady to gun control.

8. D The Contract with America was proposed by congressional Republicans led by Newt Gingrich. Students should remember that the contract was a Republican movement. All answer choices besides *D* are Democrats.

9. B Admittance of refugees fleeing communist regimes was part of the McCarran-Walter Act of 1952. The national origin quota system was introduced in the 1920s. Allocation of more resources was part of the Illegal Immigration Reform and Immigrant Responsibility of 1996.

10. C As mentioned above, the act allocated more resources. *A* is incorrect because the law toughened penalties for smugglers.

11. A Both Republicans and Democrats would most likely support a policy that was beneficial to the U.S. *A* shows the most direct benefit to Americans. It was reasoned that international trade is beneficial because it provides overseas markets for American goods and provides choices for American consumers. *C* is an effect of lowered barriers that some use as an argument against international trade.

12. C It is important that students read the question carefully. All of the answer choices are reasons why people opposed trade with China. However, the question asks why *environmentalists* were concerned. Only *C* relates to the environment.

13. D Newspapers are not digital. They are not even electronic. Therefore, they are not an example of digital technology.

14. C Examine the graph with students. The percentage of Native Americans in 2005 was 1.0%. This is the lowest.

15. D Explain to students that it is important to read all aspects of graphs and tables, especially asterisked or footnoted information.

Section 3 *(pp. 788–791)*

9. The Immigration Reform and Control Act of 1986 established
   A admittance of any refugee fleeing a communist regime.
   B legal papers to any undocumented immigrant who could prove he or she entered the country before 1982.
   C the national origins quota system.
   D allocation of more resources to stop illegal immigration.

10. The Illegal Immigration Reform and Immigrant Responsibility Act of 1996
    A relaxed penalties for smuggling people or providing fraudulent documents.
    B established more schools for immigrant children.
    C allocated more resources to stop illegal immigration.
    D called for a wall to be built at the U.S. border.

Section 4 *(pp. 794–797)*

11. Since WWII, Republicans and Democrats have worked to lower barriers to international trade because
    A it helps the American economy.
    B it supports foreign policy.
    C it moves manufacturing jobs overseas.
    D it helps economically depressed countries.

12. Environmentalists were concerned about trade with China because
    A there was concern about the protests in Tiananmen Square.
    B they believed the goods should be manufactured in the United States.
    C there was concern about pollution from Chinese factories.
    D China had made threats to invade Taiwan.

Critical Thinking

Directions: Choose the best answers to the following questions.

13. Which of the following is not an example of digital technology?
    A cell phones that can receive e-mails
    B MP3 players
    C satellite radio
    D newspapers

Base your answers to questions 14 and 15 on the graph below and your knowledge of Chapter 23.

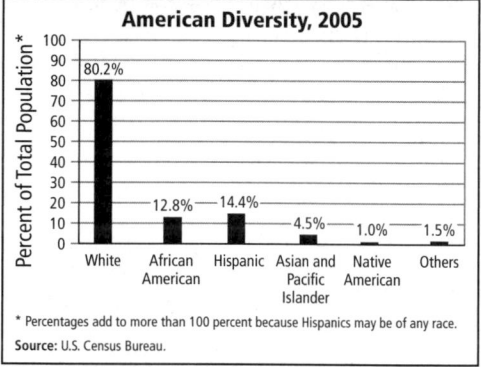

American Diversity, 2005

* Percentages add to more than 100 percent because Hispanics may be of any race.

Source: U.S. Census Bureau.

14. Which group was the smallest percentage of the population in 2005?
    A African American
    B White
    C Native American
    D Multiracial

15. Why do the percentages add up to more than 100 percent?
    A They did not record data carefully.
    B There can be more than 100 percent.
    C There is no way to determine exact numbers of the population.
    D Hispanics may be of any race.

Need Extra Help?							
If You Missed Questions . . .	9	10	11	12	13	14	15
Go to Page . . .	789	789–790	794–795	796	774–777	R16	R16

ASSESSMENT

16. The North American Free Trade Agreement (NAFTA) joined Canada, Mexico, and the United States in a free trade zone. Why was this beneficial?

A Exports to Canada and Mexico increased.

B Jobs were lost to Mexico.

C Unemployment in the United States rose.

D It provided free goods to Canada and Mexico.

Analyze the cartoon and answer the question that follows. Base your answer on the cartoon and on your knowledge of Chapter 23.

17. What is the main idea of this cartoon?

A Clinton needs to raise taxes to decrease the federal deficit.

B Clinton should lower taxes to provide relief to taxpapers.

C Clinton has increased the federal deficit to record levels.

D The taxpayers are taking advantage of the tax cuts.

18. The presence of increased levels of chlorofluorocarbons (CFCs) concerns scientists because

A they make the air hard to breathe.

B they cause global warming.

C they have the ability to break down ozone.

D they can enter the water supply.

Document-Based Questions

Directions: Analyze the document and answer the short-answer questions that follow the document.

Global warming became an important topic during the Clinton administration. It was debated across the country, with many different viewpoints.

> *"The world is getting warmer, and by the end of the 21st century could warm by another 6 degrees Celsius (10.8 degrees Fahrenheit). . . . And climate scientists at the heart of the research are now convinced that human action is to blame for some or most of this warming. . . .*
>
> *Everywhere climatologists look—at tree-ring patterns, fossil succession in rock strata, ocean-floor corings…they see evidence of dramatic shifts from cold to hot to cold again. . . . None of these ancient shifts can be blamed on humans. . . . There is still room for argument about the precise role of the sun or other natural cycles in the contribution to global warming. . . .*
> —from *World Press Review*, February 2001

19. Why are some scientists not convinced humans are to blame for global warming?

20. What evidence do these scientists cite?

Extended Response

21. After the 1992 election, what did President Clinton's domestic agenda include? Explain in detail the successes and failures of the Clinton administration. Your essay should include an introduction, several paragraphs, and a conclusion. Use relevant facts and details to support your conclusion.

STOP

History ONLINE

For additional test practice, use Self-Check Quizzes— Chapter 23 at glencoe.com.

Need Extra Help?						
If You Missed Questions . . .	16	17	18	19	20	21
Go to Page . . .	795	R18	797	797	797	780–782

---

throughout history, so it can still be argued that there are natural causes or cycles of global temperature change.

20. The scientists cite evidence such as tree-ring patterns, fossil succession, and ocean floor corings that show evidence of past dramatic temperature shifts.

Extended Response

21. Students' essays will vary, but should contain a balance between successes and failures, using the text to provide well-reasoned support. Essays should contain a detailed description of Clinton's domestic agenda that is then clearly tied to either a success or failure.

---

16. A The question asks about benefits, so *B* and *C* can be eliminated, because they describe negative effects. *D* does not make sense. The agreement is for free trade, not free goods. Free trade increased exports to Mexico and Canada because it became more economically feasible/ beneficial to U.S. based manufacturers to export.

17. B The cartoon indicates that Clinton should lower taxes to provide relief to taxpayers, even if that means running a deficit.

18. C Students may be tempted to choose *B*, because the weakening of the ozone layer caused by CFCs has been linked to global warming. *C* is the best answer because it is the most specific and directly related to CFCs.

Document-Based Questions

19. Some scientists are not convinced that humans are to blame because there is evidence of dramatic shifts in temperature

History ONLINE

Have students visit the Web site at glencoe.com to review Chapter 23 and take the Self-Check Quiz.

Need Extra Help?

Have students refer to the pages listed if they miss any of the questions.

Levels					Resources	Chapter Opener	Section 1	Section 2	Section 3	Section 4	Chapter Assess
BL	OL	AL	ELL								
FOCUS											
BL	OL	AL	ELL		Daily Focus Skills Transparencies		24-1	24-2	24-3	24-4	
TEACH											
BL	OL		ELL		Reading Essentials and Note-Taking Guide*		p. 257	p. 260	p. 263	p. 266	
	OL				Historical Analysis Skills Activity, URB		p. 122				
BL	OL		ELL		Guided Reading Activities, URB*		p. 148	p. 149	p. 150	p. 151	
BL	OL	AL	ELL		Content Vocabulary Activity, URB*	p. 127					
BL	OL	AL	ELL		Academic Vocabulary Activity, URB	p. 129					
	OL	AL			Critical Thinking Skills Activity, URB				p. 132		
BL	OL		ELL		Reading Skills Activity, URB				p. 121		
BL			ELL		English Learner Activity, URB			p. 125			
	OL	AL			Reinforcing Skills Activity, URB						p. 131
BL	OL	AL	ELL		Differentiated Instruction Activity, URB			p. 123			
BL	OL		ELL		Time Line Activity, URB		p. 133				
	OL				Linking Past and Present Activity, URB				p. 134		
BL	OL	AL	ELL		American Art and Music Activity, URB						p. 139
BL	OL	AL	ELL		Interpreting Political Cartoons Activity, URB		p. 141				
		AL			Enrichment Activity, URB				p. 145		
BL	OL	AL	ELL		American Biographies				✓		
BL	OL	AL	ELL		Primary Source Reading, URB			p. 135	p. 137		
BL	OL	AL	ELL		Supreme Court Case Studies				p. 161		
BL	OL	AL	ELL		The Living Constitution*	✓	✓	✓	✓	✓	✓
	OL	AL			American History Primary Source Documents Library	✓	✓	✓	✓	✓	✓
BL	OL	AL	ELL		Unit Map Overlay Transparencies	✓	✓	✓	✓	✓	✓
BL	OL	AL	ELL		Differentiated Instruction for the American High School Classroom	✓	✓	✓	✓	✓	✓
BL	OL	AL	ELL		StudentWorks™ Plus DVD	✓	✓	✓	✓	✓	✓

Note: Please refer to the *Unit 7 Resource Book* for this chapter's URB materials.

* Also available in Spanish

- Interactive Lesson Planner
- Interactive Teacher Edition
- Fully editable blackline masters
- Section Spotlight Videos Launch
- Differentiated Lesson Plans
- Printable reports of daily assignments
- Standards Tracking System

Levels					Resources	Chapter Opener	Section 1	Section 2	Section 3	Section 4	Chapter Assess
BL	OL	AL	ELL								
TEACH *(continued)*											
BL	OL	AL	ELL	⊙	Vocabulary PuzzleMaker CD-ROM	✓	✓	✓	✓	✓	✓
BL	OL	AL	ELL	⊙	American Music Hits Through History CD	✓	✓	✓	✓	✓	✓
BL	OL	AL	ELL	📁	Unit Time Line Transparencies and Activities	✓	✓	✓	✓	✓	✓
BL	OL	AL	ELL	📁	Cause and Effect Transparencies, Strategies, and Activities	✓	✓	✓	✓	✓	✓
BL	OL	AL	ELL	📁	Why It Matters Transparencies, Strategies, and Activities	✓	✓	✓	✓	✓	✓
BL	OL	AL	ELL	📁	American Issues	✓	✓	✓	✓	✓	✓
	OL	AL	ELL	📁	American Art and Architecture Transparencies, Strategies, and Activities	✓	✓	✓	✓	✓	✓
BL	OL	AL		📁	High School American History Literature Library	✓	✓	✓	✓	✓	✓
BL	OL	AL	ELL	🔒	*The American Vision* Video Program DVD	✓	✓	✓	✓	✓	✓
Teacher Resources				📁	Strategies for Success	✓	✓	✓	✓	✓	✓
				📁	Success with English Learner	✓	✓	✓	✓	✓	✓
				📁	Studies Classroom	✓	✓	✓	✓	✓	✓
				🔒	Presentation Plus! DVD	✓	✓	✓	✓	✓	✓
ASSESS											
BL	OL	AL	ELL	📁	Section Quizzes and Chapter Tests*		p. 337	p. 338	p. 339	p. 340	p. 341
BL	OL	AL	ELL	📁	Authentic Assessment With Rubrics						p. 53
BL	OL	AL	ELL	📁	Standardized Test Practice Workbook						p. 56
BL	OL	AL	ELL	⊙	*ExamView®* Assessment Suite CD-ROM		24-1	24-2	24-3	24-4	Ch. 24
BL	OL	AL	ELL	⊙	Interactive Tutor Self-Assessment CD-ROM		24-1	24-2	24-3	24-4	Ch. 24
CLOSE											
BL			ELL	📁	Reteaching Activity, URB						p. 143
BL	OL		ELL	📁	Reading and Study Skills Foldables™	p. 84					
BL	OL	AL	ELL	📁	American History in Graphic Novel		p. 79				

Using CyberScout

Research Using *Browse Famous People*

Technology Product

CyberScout is a convenient and dynamic search engine that provides several easy ways to locate information outside the McGraw-Hill Learning Network. CyberScout only searches Web sites that have been reviewed by teachers, so the information students find is always appropriate and accurate.

Objectives

After students learn to use CyberScout, they will be able to

- research information on famous people in history;
- exercise research and study skills;
- practice writing skills.

Steps

- From the McGraw-Hill Learning Network home page (www.mhln.com), click on **For Students**.
- Choose **CyberScout** below **Homework Help**.
- Click on a subject area link to narrow the search.
- The CyberScout page will display a set of subcategories.
- Click the **Browse Famous People** button at the bottom of the page.
- The CyberScout page displays a set of names related to the subject area. Click a name.
- The CyberScout page displays a set of results.
- Click the link to a Web site of interest.
- Students will be redirected to the Web site in a new window.
- Students navigate through the chosen Web site to gain information on a topic and take notes.

History ONLINE

	Student	Teacher	Parent
Beyond the Textbook	●	●	●
Chapter Overviews	●	●	●
Time Current Events	●		●
ePuzzles and Games	●		●
Concepts in Motion	●		●
Literature Connections		●	
Multi-Language Glossaries	●		●
Online Student Edition	●	●	●
Self-Check Quizzes	●		●
Student Web Activities	●		●
Study Central™	●		●
Teaching Today		●	
Vocabulary eFlashcards	●		●
Web Activity Lesson Plans		●	

Glencoe Media Center

glencoe.com

❯ **Study-To-Go**
- Vocabulary eFlashcards
- Self-Check Quizzes

❯ **Audio/Video**
- Student Edition Audio
- Spanish Summaries
- Section Videos

- **Timed Readings Plus in Social Studies** helps students increase their reading rate and fluency while maintaining comprehension. The 400-word passages are similar to those found on state and national assessments.

- **Reading in the Content Area: Social Studies** concentrates on six essential reading skills that help students better comprehend what they read. The book includes 75 high-interest nonfiction passages written at increasing levels of difficulty.

- **Reading Social Studies** includes strategic reading instruction and vocabulary support in Social Studies content for both ELLs and native speakers of English.

www.jamestowneducation.com

Index to National Geographic Magazine:

The following articles relate to this chapter:

- "Time to Hit the Panic Button? How We Decide What's Risky," by Joel Achenbach, September 2003.
- "Where Have You Gone New Orleans?," by Ernest J. Gaines, August 2006.

National Geographic Society Products To order the following, call National Geographic at 1-800-368-2728:

- *ZipZapMap! USA* (ZipZapMap!)

Access National Geographic's new, dynamic MapMachine Web site and other geography resources at:

www.nationalgeographic.com
www.nationalgeographic.com/maps

The following videotape programs are available from Glencoe as supplements to Chapter 24:

- Colin Powell: A Soldier's Campaign (ISBN 1-56-501701-3)
- The White House—Great American Monuments (ISBN 1-56-501643-2)

To order, call Glencoe at 1-800-334-7344. To find classroom resources to accompany many of these videos, check the following home pages:

A&E Television: www.aetv.com

The History Channel: www.historychannel.com

Reading List Generator CD-ROM

Use this database to search more than 30,000 titles to create a customized reading list for your students.

- Reading lists can be organized by students' reading level, author, genre, theme, or area of interest.
- The database provides Degrees of Reading Power™ (DRP) and Lexile™ readability scores for all selections.
- A brief summary of each selection is included.

Leveled reading suggestions for this chapter:

For students at a Grade 8 reading level:
- *September 11, 2001: Attack on New York City,* by Wilborn Hampton

For students at a Grade 9 reading level:
- *September 11, 2001: The Day that Changed America,* by Jill C. Wheeler

For students at a Grade 10 reading level:
- *President George W. Bush: Our Forty-Third President,* by Beatrice Gormley

For students at a Grade 11 reading level:
- *Thura's Diary: My Life in Wartime Iraq,* by Thura Al-Windawl

For students at a Grade 12 reading level:
- *Iraq and the Fall of Saddam Hussein,* by Jason Richie

Focus

MAKING CONNECTIONS
How Does the Passage of Time Affect the Way Events are Understood?

Have students reflect on a memorable past event or situation in their lives **Ask:** How was your life permanently changed by the event or situation? What lessons did you learn from the experience? Explain that a nation like the United States can also experience moments when its path in history dramatically alters and when unexpected decisions have to be made. Ask them to name episodes in American history that aroused Americans and suddenly changed the course of the nation's policies and actions. Most students will probably include the 9/11 terrorist attacks and their effect on the nation. Conclude by having students give their ideas about how the United States should respond to terrorism.

Teach

The Big Ideas

As students study the chapter, remind them to consider the section-based Big Ideas included in each section's Guide to Reading. The **Essential Questions** and the activities below tie in to the Big Ideas and help students think about and understand important chapter concepts. In addition, the Hands-on-Chapter Projects with their culminating activities relate the content from each section to the Big Ideas. These activities build on each other as students progress through the chapter. Section activities culminate in the wrap-up activity on the Visual Summary page. **BL** **OL**

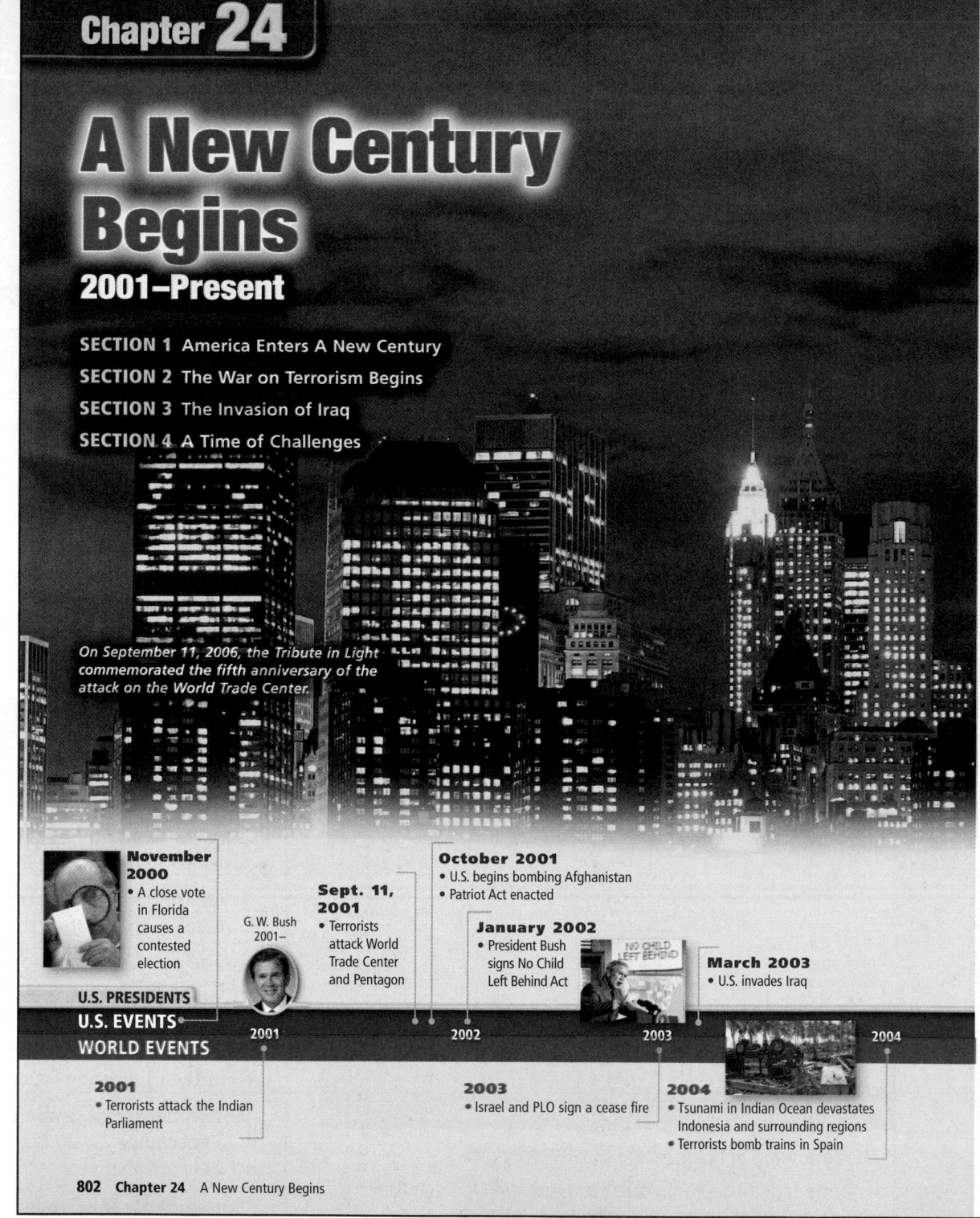

Chapter 24

A New Century Begins

2001–Present

SECTION 1 America Enters A New Century
SECTION 2 The War on Terrorism Begins
SECTION 3 The Invasion of Iraq
SECTION 4 A Time of Challenges

On September 11, 2006, the Tribute in Light commemorated the fifth anniversary of the attack on the World Trade Center.

November 2000
• A close vote in Florida causes a contested election

G. W. Bush 2001–

Sept. 11, 2001
• Terrorists attack World Trade Center and Pentagon

October 2001
• U.S. begins bombing Afghanistan
• Patriot Act enacted

January 2002
• President Bush signs No Child Left Behind Act

March 2003
• U.S. invades Iraq

U.S. PRESIDENTS
U.S. EVENTS — 2001 — 2002 — 2003 — 2004
WORLD EVENTS

2001
• Terrorists attack the Indian Parliament

2003
• Israel and PLO sign a cease fire

2004
• Tsunami in Indian Ocean devastates Indonesia and surrounding regions
• Terrorists bomb trains in Spain

802 Chapter 24 A New Century Begins

Section 1

America Enters a New Century
Essential Question: When an election's results are uncertain or disputed, how do you think the problem should be resolved? *(by compromise, vote counts, the courts, holding run-off elections)* Point out that in Section 1 students will learn about the close presidential election of 2000 and how its outcome was settled peacefully. **OL**

Section 2

The War on Terrorism Begins
Essential Question: What challenges might governments face in fighting terrorism? *(the need to enact tough measures against terrorism that at the same time are respectful of citizens' rights)* Point out in Section 2 students will learn about the terrorist attacks of September 11, 2001 and the response of the Bush Adminstration with the "War on Terror." **OL**

MAKING CONNECTIONS

How Does the Passage of Time Affect the Way Events Are Understood?

As the United States entered the twenty-first century, combating terrorism at home and abroad became a national priority. The attacks on the World Trade Center and the Pentagon resulted in wars in Afghanistan and Iraq. The wars as well as new security policies led to great controversy in American politics.

- *What previous events in American history have forced the nation to dramatically change its policies and actions?*
- *How should the United States respond to terrorism to prevent it from happening again?*

More About the Photo

Visual Literacy Ask students: What city is shown in the photo? What type of event is taking place? *(New York City; a commemoration or memorial using light beams)* The "Tribute in Light" memorial lies near the site of the World Trade Center in lower Manhattan. The two beams of light, which represent the fallen twin towers of the Center, light up the evening sky to remember the people who lost their lives as a result of the terrorist attacks on September 11, 2001.

FOLDABLES Study Organizer **Dinah Zike's Foldables**

Dinah Zike's Foldables are three-dimensional, interactive graphic organizers that help students practice basic writing skills, review vocabulary terms, and identify main ideas. Instructions for creating and using Foldables can be found in the Appendix at the end of this book and in the *Dinah Zike's Reading and Study Skills Foldables* booklet.

November 2004
- George W. Bush defeats John Kerry in the election

August 2005
- Hurricane Katrina devastates Louisiana and Mississippi; levies fail and New Orleans floods

January 2007
- Nancy Pelosi becomes first female Speaker of the House

2005   2006   2007

2005
- Terrorists bomb London subway system

2006
- Israel invades Lebanon to attack Hezbollah
- Over 1 billion people worldwide use the Internet

FOLDABLES

Organizing Information Compile facts about the terrorist attacks at the World Trade Center and Pentagon on September 11, 2001. Then, make a Four-Door Book Foldable that explains what, where, when, and why these events occurred.

Why	What
When	Where

History ONLINE Chapter Overview
Visit glencoe.com to preview Chapter 24.

Chapter 24 A New Century Begins **803**

History ONLINE
Introduce students to chapter content and key terms by having them access the Chapter 24 Overview at glencoe.com.

Section 3

The Invasion of Iraq
Essential Question: How do you think the United States carries out its foreign policy? *(through diplomacy, trade, war, humanitarian aid, public relations)* Explain that in Section 3 students will learn about how the United States became militarily involved in Iraq and Afghanistan and the effects of U.S. actions on these two countries. **OL**

Section 4

A Time of Challenges
Essential Question: How might unexpected events affect a country's politics and government? *(Citizens' votes are based on how well or how badly the government responds to these emergencies.)* Explain that in Section 4 students will learn how scandal and natural disaster weakened Republican control of government and benefited Democrats in congressional elections. **OL**

Focus

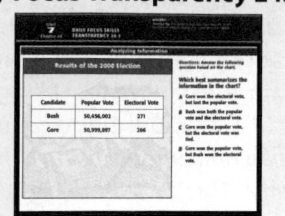
Guide to Reading

Answers:

Fla. recounts; Bush certified winner

Fla. Supreme Court decides for hand recount

U.S. Supreme Court rules in *Bush* v. *Gore* against hand recount

Bush's Victory

Section Spotlight Video

To generate student interest and provide a springboard for class discussion, access the Chapter 24, Section 1 video at glencoe.com or on the video DVD.

Resource Manager

Section 1

America Enters a New Century

Guide to Reading

Big Ideas
Government and Society A very close presidential election saw a shift in power in the White House, as George W. Bush became the forty-third President of the United States.

Content Vocabulary
• chad *(p. 805)*
• strategic defense *(p. 807)*

Academic Vocabulary
• priority *(p. 807)*
• controversial *(p. 807)*

People and Events to Identify
• Al Gore *(p. 804)*
• George W. Bush *(p. 804)*
• Ralph Nader *(p. 805)*

Reading Strategy
Organizing Complete a graphic organizer similar to the one below by charting the key post-election events culminating in George W. Bush's victory.

In the election of 2000, Democrat Al Gore faced Republican George W. Bush. After a dispute over the outcome in Florida, Bush became president. Bush then focused on cutting taxes and introducing health care and education reforms.

The Election of 2000

MAIN Idea In one of the closest presidential races in history, involving vote recounts and the Supreme Court, George W. Bush became president.

HISTORY AND YOU Do you think the Electoral College should be modified or eliminated? Read on to learn how the 2000 election ultimately came down to a decision about Florida's disputed electoral votes.

As he prepared to leave office, President Clinton's legacy was uncertain. He had balanced the budget and presided over a period of rapid economic growth. His presidency was marred, however, by the impeachment trial, which had divided the nation and widened the divide between liberals and conservatives. In the election of 2000, that division led to one of the closest elections in American history.

The Candidates Campaign

The Democrats nominated Vice President **Al Gore** for president in 2000. Gore, a former senator from Tennessee, was regarded as a moderate and his Southern roots were expected to help him win votes in the South. For his running mate, Gore chose Senator Joseph Lieberman from Connecticut, the first Jewish American ever to run for vice president on a major party ticket.

The Republican contest for the presidential nomination came down to two men: Governor **George W. Bush** of Texas, son of former president George H.W. Bush, and Senator John McCain of Arizona, a former navy pilot and prisoner of war in North Vietnam. Most Republican leaders endorsed Bush, who was especially popular with conservatives. He easily won the nomination, despite some early McCain victories in the primaries. Bush chose Richard "Dick" Cheney as his vice presidential running mate. Cheney had served as President George H.W. Bush's Secretary of Defense.

The election campaign revolved around the question of what to do with surplus tax revenues. Both Bush and Gore agreed that Social Security needed reform, but they disagreed on the details. Both promised to cut taxes, although Bush proposed a much larger tax cut than Gore. Both men also promised to improve public education and to support plans to help senior citizens pay for prescription drugs.

R **Reading Strategies**	C **Critical Thinking**	D **Differentiated Instruction**	W **Writing Support**	S **Skill Practice**
Teacher Edition • Summarizing, p. 806 **Additional Resources** • Guided Reading Act., URB p. 148	**Teacher Edition** • Making Inferences, p. 807 **Additional Resources** • Interpret. Political Cartoons, URB p. 141 • Quizzes/Tests, p. 337	**Additional Resources** • Am. History in Graphic Novel, p. 79 • Foldables, p. 84	**Additional Resources** • Hist. Analysis Skills, URB p. 122 • Content Vocab. Act., URB p. 127 • Academic Vocab. Act., URB p. 129	**Teacher Edition** • Interpret. Maps, p. 805 **Additional Resources** • Time Line Act., URB p. 133 • RENTG, p. 257

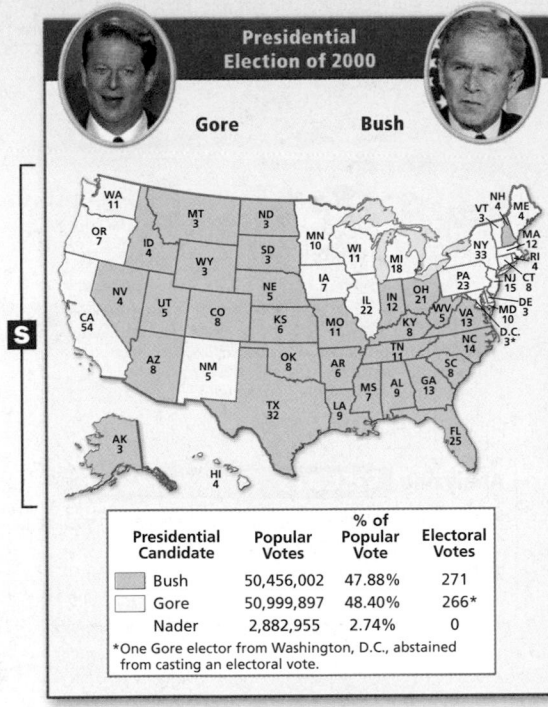

Presidential Election of 2000

Gore   Bush

Presidential Candidate	Popular Votes	% of Popular Vote	Electoral Votes
Bush	50,456,002	47.88%	271
Gore	50,999,897	48.40%	266*
Nader	2,882,955	2.74%	0

*One Gore elector from Washington, D.C., abstained from casting an electoral vote.

▲ The recount of the vote in Florida meant vote counters had to examine ballots individually to determine the intention of the voter.

Analyzing VISUALS

1. **Making Generalizations** What characteristics do the states that voted for Bush share? What characteristics do the states that voted for Gore share?

2. **Assessing** Do you think the Florida ballot was easy to understand or confusing? Why?

Frustrated by what he viewed as the fundamental similarities between Bush and Gore, well-known consumer advocate **Ralph Nader** entered the race as the nominee of the Green Party. Nader was known for his strong environmentalist views and his criticism of the power of large corporations. Nader argued that both Bush and Gore depended on campaign funds from large companies and were unwilling to support policies that favored American workers and the environment.

A Close Vote

The 2000 election was one of the closest in American history. No candidate won a majority of the votes cast, but Gore received the most votes, winning 48.4 percent of the popular vote compared to 47.9 percent for Bush. (Nader won about 3 percent of the vote.) To win the presidency, however, candidates must win 270 electoral votes—not lead in the popular vote.

The election came down to the Florida vote—both men needed its 25 electoral votes to win. The results in Florida were so close that state law required a recount of the ballots using vote-counting machines. There were, however, thousands of ballots that had been thrown out because the counting machines could not read the voting cards. Gore then asked for a hand recount of ballots in several strongly Democratic counties. After the machine recount showed Bush still ahead, a battle began over the manual recounts.

Most Florida ballots required voters to punch a hole. The little piece of cardboard punched out of the ballot is called a **chad.** The problem for vote counters was how to count a ballot if the chad was still partially attached. On some, the chad was still in place, and the voter had left only a dimple on the surface. When looking at the ballots, vote counters had to determine what the voter intended—and different counties used different standards.

Chapter 24 A New Century Begins **805**

Teach

S Skill Practice

Interpreting Maps Point out to students that the 2000 election marked the first election since 1888 in which the candidate who won the popular vote did not win the electoral vote. **Ask:** Which states had more than 20 electoral votes? [California (54), New York (33), Texas (32), Florida (25), Pennsylvania (23), Illinois (22), and Ohio (21)] What candidate won the electoral votes in each of these states? (Bush won Texas, Florida, and Ohio. Gore won California, New York, Pennsylvania, and Illinois.) **OL**

Analyzing VISUALS

Answers:
1. Most Bush states were in the South and Interior West; most Gore states were in the Northeast, upper Midwest, and Pacific Coast.
2. Answers will vary but should focus on the readability and physical appearance of the ballot cards.

Hands-On Chapter Project
Step 1

Exploring the "Blogosphere"

Step 1: Making a Blog Chart Groups of students will use a blog search engine to search the Internet and identify a variety of blogs. They will chart the information.

Directions Tell groups of students to use a blog search engine to find blogs on different topics. Groups will then chart the information they have collected in three columns. The first column will give the name and Web address of the site. The second column will describe the topic of site information. Topics may cover a range of subjects—from politics to pop culture. The third column will cite what kind of blog it is (private, political, or commercial) and its creator's name.

Summarizing Have students share what they learned about how people use the Internet to communicate. Encourage the class to speculate about the goals of each of the blogs on their charts. **OL**

(Project continues on page 811)

POLITICAL CARTOONS PRIMARY SOURCE
The Election of 2000

Summarizing Have students read the first two paragraphs under "Bush v. Gore" and then summarize what they have just read. Remind them that only the main ideas should be included in a summary but that all the main ideas should be included. OL ELL

Analyzing VISUALS

Answers:
1. Answers will vary, but students should support their opinions.
2. The election of 2000 was an extremely close one. Every vote counts in such a close race.

Reading Check

Answer:
The Supreme Court ruled that the hand recounts violated the equal protection clause of the Constitution. Because different vote counters used different standards, the recount did not treat all voters equally.

▲ The candidates are presented as two turkeys arguing over the results with closed captioning provided to translate what they are saying into what they really mean.

▲ The close presidential election of 2000 illustrated clearly how important it is for everyone to exercise the right to vote.

Analyzing VISUALS DBQ

1. **Evaluating** Based on the cartoon on the left, do you think the cartoonist supported Bush or Gore?
2. **Analyzing** Why are the three characters in the cartoon above angry at the man on the right?

Under state law, Florida officials had to certify the results by a certain date. When it became clear that not all of the recounts could be finished in time, Gore went to court to challenge the deadline. The Florida Supreme Court agreed to set a new deadline. At Bush's request, the United States Supreme Court then intervened to decide whether the Florida Supreme Court had acted constitutionally.

While lawyers for Bush and Gore prepared their arguments for the Supreme Court, the hand recounts continued. Despite having more time, not all of the counties where Gore wanted recounts were able to meet the new deadline. On November 26, Florida officials certified Bush the winner by 537 votes.

🏛 For more on *Bush v. Gore* read the case summary on page R58 in **Supreme Court Case Summaries.**

Bush v. Gore

Although Bush had been declared the winner in Florida, Gore's lawyers headed back to court arguing that thousands of ballots were still uncounted. The Florida Supreme Court ordered all Florida counties to begin a hand recount of ballots rejected by the counting machines. As counting began, the United States Supreme Court ordered the recount to stop until it had issued its ruling.

On December 12, in *Bush* v. *Gore*, the United States Supreme Court ruled 7–2 that the hand recounts in Florida violated the equal protection clause of the Constitution. The Court argued that because different vote counters used different standards, the recount did not treat all voters equally.

Both federal law and the Constitution require the electoral votes for president to be cast on a certain day. If Florida missed that deadline, its electoral votes would not count. The Court ruled 5–4 that there was not enough time left to conduct a manual recount that would pass constitutional standards. This ruling left Bush the certified winner in Florida. The next day, Gore conceded the election.

✓ Reading Check **Analyzing** Why did the U.S. Supreme Court stop the manual recounts in Florida?

Differentiated Instruction

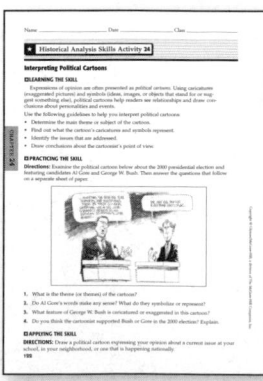

Historical Analysis Skills Activity, URB p. 122

Interpreting Political Cartoons

Objective: Understand how to interpret political cartoons.

Focus: Ask: What is the purpose of political cartoons?

Teach: List the steps to interpreting political cartoons.

Assess: Explain the main idea of this political cartoon.

Close: Find a political cartoon in a recent newsmagazine or newspaper. Bring it to class and interpret it.

Differentiated Instruction Strategies

BL Create a political cartoon on a current national issue.

AL Create a different political cartoon on the same topic.

ELL Explain to a classmate how to interpret a political cartoon.

Bush Becomes President

MAIN Idea George W. Bush supported the enactment of a tax cut, the No Child Left Behind program, and a strategic defense system.

HISTORY AND YOU Have new education policies affected the testing process at your school? Read on to learn more about No Child Left Behind.

On January 20, 2001, George W. Bush became the forty-third president of the United States. In his Inaugural Address, Bush promised to improve the public schools, to cut taxes, to reform Social Security and Medicare, and to build up the nation's defenses.

After taking office, the president's first **priority** was to cut taxes to try to boost the economy. During the election campaign, the stock market dropped sharply, unemployment began to rise, and many new Internet-based companies went out of business. Despite opposition from some Democrats, Congress passed a large $1.35 trillion tax cut to be phased in over 10 years. In the summer of 2001, Americans began receiving tax rebate checks that put about $40 billion back into the economy in an effort to prevent a recession.

Soon after Congress passed the tax cut plan, President Bush proposed two major reforms in education. He wanted public schools to give annual standardized tests, and he wanted to allow parents to use federal funds to pay for private schools if their public schools were doing a poor job. Although Congress refused to give federal funds to private schools, it did vote in favor of annual reading and math tests in public schools for grades 3–8. This law became known as the No Child Left Behind Act.

President Bush also focused on Medicare reform. By the summer of 2002, Congress had introduced a bill adding prescription drug benefits to Medicare. The bill was **controversial.** Some opponents feared it would cost too much, while others argued that it did not go far enough. The program finally became law in November 2003.

Congress also reacted to a rash of corporate scandals—the most famous taking place at a large energy trading company called Enron. Corporate leaders there cost investors and employees billions of dollars before the company went bankrupt. Congress passed a new law—the Public Company Accounting Reform and Investor Protection Act—also known as the Sarbanes-Oxley Act, after the members of Congress who introduced it. The law tightened accounting rules and toughened penalties for dishonest executives.

Shortly after taking office, President Bush also pushed for new military programs designed to meet the needs of the post–Cold War world. One program Bush strongly favored was **strategic defense**—the effort to develop missiles and other devices that could shoot down nuclear missiles. Bush argued that missile defense was needed because many hostile nations were developing long-range missiles.

As the debate about the nation's military programs continued in the summer of 2001, a horrific event changed everything. On September 11, 2001, terrorists crashed passenger jets into the World Trade Center and the Pentagon. A new war had begun.

✔ **Reading Check** **Explaining** What was President George W. Bush's first priority when he took office?

Section 1 REVIEW

Vocabulary

1. **Explain** the significance of: Al Gore, George W. Bush, Ralph Nader, chad, strategic defense.

Main Ideas

2. **Paraphrasing** What did the U.S. Supreme Court decide in *Bush* v. *Gore?*

3. **Describing** What did the No Child Left Behind Act mandate?

Critical Thinking

4. **Big Ideas** What caused the vote-count controversy in Florida in the 2000 election?

5. **Organizing** Use a graphic organizer similar to the one below by listing President Bush's goals when he took office.

6. **Analyzing Visuals** Study the photos on page 805. Explain how you would change the voting process following the controversy of the 2000 election.

Writing About History

7. **Persuasive Writing** Take on the role of a Supreme Court justice. Write a statement explaining how you voted in *Bush* v. *Gore* and why you took this position.

History ONLINE
Study Central™ To review this section, go to glencoe.com and click on Study Central.

807

C Critical Thinking

Making Inferences Ask:
What does the phrase "No Child Left Behind" reveal about Bush's reasons for education reform? *(Students may state that Bush wanted to improve learning and ensure that all students have equal access to good schools)* **OL**

✔ **Reading Check**

Answer:
Bush's first priority was to cut taxes to try to boost the economy.

Assess

History ONLINE

Study Central™ provides summaries, interactive games, and online graphic organizers to help students review content.

Close

Drawing Conclusions
Ask: Why do you think the 2000 presidential election was so close? **OL**

Section 1 REVIEW

Answers

1. All definitions can be found in the section and the Glossary.

2. The Supreme Court decided that hand recounts in Florida were unconstitutional because different voting standards were used that did not treat all voters equally.

3. It mandated annual standardized tests in public schools.

4. Thousands of ballots had been thrown out because the counting machines could not read the voting cards. Then, in the hand recount, different counties used different standards to determine what the voter had intended.

5. Bush's goals were to improve public schools, to cut taxes, to reform Social Security and Medicare, and to build up the nation's defenses.

6. Answers will vary but should focus on simplifying the voting process and ensuring that all votes are counted.

7. Answers will vary but should be supported by reasoned arguments and evidence.

Focus

Guide to Reading

Bellringer

Daily Focus Transparency 24.2

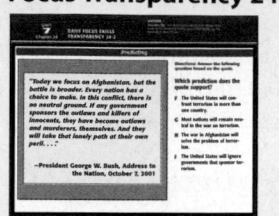

Guide to Reading

Answers:

Causes of Terrorism:
oil wealth and poverty
opposition to Western culture
U.S. support of ruling families
U.S. support of Israel

Section Spotlight Video

To generate student interest and provide a springboard for class discussion, access the Chapter 24, Section 2 video at glencoe.com or on the video DVD.

Resource Manager

Section 2

The War on Terrorism Begins

Guide to Reading

Big Ideas
Government and Society Acts of terrorism against the United States prompted George W. Bush to declare "War on Terror."

Content Vocabulary
• terrorism *(p. 810)*
• state-sponsored terrorism *(p. 811)*
• anthrax *(p. 813)*

Academic Vocabulary
• resolve *(p. 809)*
• interpretation *(p. 810)*
• obtain *(p. 812)*

People and Events to Identify
• Osama bin Laden *(p. 809)*
• al-Qaeda *(p. 809)*

Reading Strategy
Organizing Complete a graphic organizer similar to the one below to show causes of terrorism.

On September 11, 2001, terrorists attacked the United States killing over 3,000 people. The attacks united the nation as Americans worked to help the survivors. President George W. Bush and Congress launched a war on terrorism to prevent such attacks in the future.

September 11, 2001

MAIN Idea The terrorist attacks on the World Trade Center and the Pentagon shocked and alarmed Americans; almost immediately, combating terrorism became the nation's top priority.

HISTORY AND YOU Do you recall learning about the 1919 bombings that triggered government raids and roundups of foreigners? Read on to learn how the United States reacted to the more deadly attacks of 2001.

At 8:45 A.M. Eastern Daylight Time on September 11, 2001, a Boeing 767 passenger jet slammed into the North Tower of the World Trade Center in New York City. As people below gazed in horror, a second plane collided with the South Tower. Soon afterward, a third plane crashed into the Pentagon in Washington, D.C. At 9:50 A.M., the South Tower collapsed in a billowing cloud of dust and debris. The North Tower fell about 40 minutes later. The falling towers killed thousands of people, burying them beneath a vast mound of rubble.

The airplanes did not crash accidentally. Hijackers deliberately crashed them into the buildings. Hijackers also seized a fourth airplane, United Airlines Flight 93, probably hoping to crash it into the White House or the Capitol. Many passengers on Flight 93 had cell phones. After hearing about the World Trade Center, four passengers—Todd Beamer, Thomas Burnett, Jeremy Glick, and Mark Bingham—decided to do something. An operator listening over a cell phone heard Todd Beamer's voice: "Are you ready guys? Let's roll."

Soon afterward, Flight 93 crashed in a field in Pennsylvania. At that moment, Vice President Dick Cheney was in a bunker under the White House. After hearing Flight 93 had crashed, he turned to the others in the room, and said: "I think an act of heroism just took place on that plane."

A National Emergency

The attacks of 9/11, as the day came to be called, killed all 266 passengers and crewmembers on the four hijacked planes. Another 125 people died in the Pentagon. In New York City, nearly 3,000 people died. More Americans were killed in the attacks of September 11,

---

R Reading Strategies	C Critical Thinking	D Differentiated Instruction	W Writing Support	S Skill Practice
Teacher Edition • Academic Vocab., pp. 809, 810 **Additional Resources** • Pri. Source Reading, URB p. 135 • Guided Reading Act., URB p. 149	**Teacher Edition** • Determining Cause/ Effect, p. 810 • Evaluating, p. 811 • Drawing Concl., p. 811 **Additional Resources** • Quizzes/Tests, p. 338	**Teacher Edition** • Visual/Spatial, p. 812 **Additional Resources** • Diff. Inst. Act., URB p. 123 • English Learner Act., URB p. 125	**Teacher Edition** • Narrative Writing, p. 809	**Teacher Edition** • Analyz. a Map, p. 810 **Additional Resources** • RENTG, p. 260

Turning Point

The Attacks of September 11, 2001

The terrorist attacks of September 11, 2001, altered the lives of millions of Americans and shifted the priorities of the federal government. At home the United States launched a new war against terrorists and their supporters. Globally, the United States took aggressive and preemptive steps to stop terrorism. At home, the balance between civil liberties and national security shifted, with passage of the USA Patriot Act, which gave broad new powers to the federal government.

MAKING CONNECTIONS How are the terrorist attacks and their aftermath still affecting American society and foreign policy?

Above, the South Tower of the World Trade Center bursts into flames after being struck by an airliner while the North Tower burns from an attack a few minutes earlier. At left, one side of the Pentagon was badly damaged. Part of the building later collapsed. At right, after the World Trade Center towers collapsed, the resulting debris coated the city with dust.

2001, than died at Pearl Harbor or on D-Day in World War II.

The attacks shocked Americans, but they responded rapidly to the crisis. Medical workers and firefighters from other cities raced to New York to help. Across the nation, Americans donated blood and collected food, blankets, and other supplies. Within weeks, Americans also donated over $1 billion. From around the world came sympathy. "We are all Americans!" wrote one French journalist.

Everywhere across the nation, Americans put up flags to show their unity and **resolve.** They held candlelight vigils and prayer services as they searched for ways to help. If the terrorists had hoped to divide Americans, they failed. As the Reverend Billy Graham noted at a memorial service, "A tragedy like this could have torn our country apart. But instead it has united us and we have become a family."

The American government also responded quickly to the crisis. All civilian airplanes were grounded. The armed forces were put on high alert. Across the nation, Americans in the National Guard left their civilian jobs and reported for duty. The Air National Guard began patrolling the skies over major cities, and Army National Guard troops were deployed to airports to strengthen security.

On September 14, President Bush declared a national emergency. Congress authorized the use of force to fight whoever had attacked the United States. Intelligence sources and the FBI quickly identified the attacks as the work of a man named **Osama bin Laden** and his organization, **al-Qaeda** (al KY•duh).

Chapter 24 A New Century Begins **809**

Teach

W Writing Support

Narrative Writing Have students research the response of American public to the 9/11 attacks. Then have them write a descriptive essay explaining how they think the terrorist attacks united Americans and brought a great sense of patriotism to the country. Have volunteers read their essays to the class. **AL**

R Reading Strategy

Academic Vocabulary Ask students to read the sentence that contains the word *resolve*. Have students list the synonyms and antonyms for the word.

Answer:
Answers will vary but might point out remembrances for those who lost their lives in the 9/11 attacks, the ongoing wars in Afghanistan and Iraq, the effect of the Iraq war on the 2006 congressional elections, and public debate over government intelligence-gathering and citizens' rights.

Additional Support

Activity: Collaborative Learning

Analyzing Information Have students find and bring to class an example of an article that uses both primary and secondary sources to tell the story of the September 11, 2001, terrorist attacks or of the massive relief effort that followed. Have students write a one-page summary of their article identifying the various points of view and explaining how the writer used a variety of source material to paint a picture of the events. As a class, discuss the importance of both types of sources in explaining historical events. **OL**

809

810

S Skill Practice

Analyzing a Map Have the students answer the following questions to help them learn more about current terrorist threats. **Ask:** On what continents have attacks occurred? *(North America, Europe, Africa, and Asia)* What place was attacked twice, and why? *(New York Trade Center; symbol of U.S. economic power)* Why might terrorist attacks have occurred in places other than the United States? *(Countries supporting U.S. policies or having Western residents or visitors)* **OL**

R Reading Strategy

Academic Vocabulary Ask students to read the sentence that contains the word *interpretation.* Then ask them to rewrite the sentence in their own words. **OL**

C Critical Thinking

Determining Cause and Effect **Ask:** Why has U.S. support of Israel angered many people in the Middle East? *(Many Palestinian Arabs claim that Israel, a largely Jewish nation, was founded on land that belongs to them.)* **OL**

Additional Support

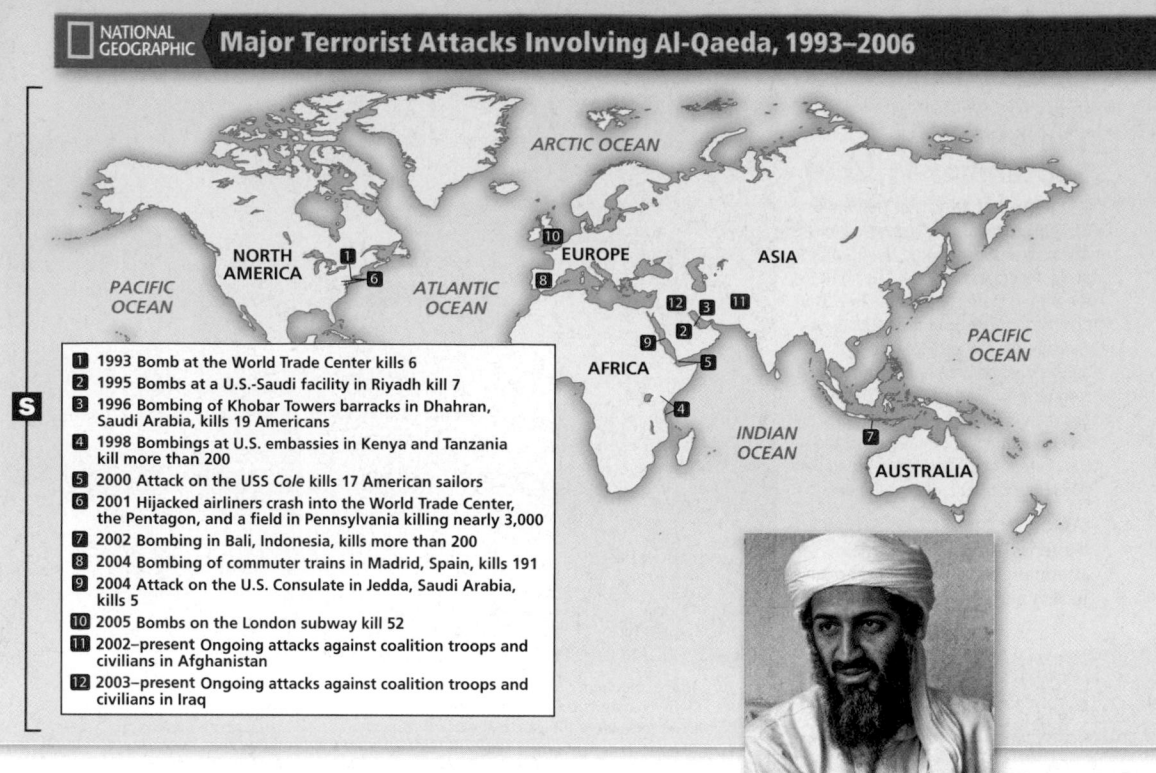

NATIONAL GEOGRAPHIC **Major Terrorist Attacks Involving Al-Qaeda, 1993–2006**

1 1993 Bomb at the World Trade Center kills 6
2 1995 Bombs at a U.S.-Saudi facility in Riyadh kill 7
3 1996 Bombing of Khobar Towers barracks in Dhahran, Saudi Arabia, kills 19 Americans
4 1998 Bombings at U.S. embassies in Kenya and Tanzania kill more than 200
5 2000 Attack on the USS *Cole* kills 17 American sailors
6 2001 Hijacked airliners crash into the World Trade Center, the Pentagon, and a field in Pennsylvania killing nearly 3,000
7 2002 Bombing in Bali, Indonesia, kills more than 200
8 2004 Bombing of commuter trains in Madrid, Spain, kills 191
9 2004 Attack on the U.S. Consulate in Jedda, Saudi Arabia, kills 5
10 2005 Bombs on the London subway kill 52
11 2002–present Ongoing attacks against coalition troops and civilians in Afghanistan
12 2003–present Ongoing attacks against coalition troops and civilians in Iraq

Middle East Terrorism and the United States

The attacks on the World Trade Center and the Pentagon were acts of terrorism. **Terrorism** is the use of violence by nongovernmental groups against civilians to achieve a political goal. Terrorist acts are intended to instill fear in people and to force governments into changing their policies.

Although there have been many acts of terrorism in American history, most terrorist attacks on Americans since World War II have been carried out by Middle Eastern groups. The reason Middle Eastern terrorists have targeted Americans can be traced back to events early in the twentieth century.

As oil became important to the American economy in the 1920s, the United States invested heavily in the Middle East oil industry. This industry brought great wealth to the ruling families in some Middle Eastern kingdoms, but most people remained poor. Some became angry at the United States for supporting the wealthy kingdoms and families.

The rise of the oil industry also led to the spread of Western ideas in the region, and many Muslims feared that their traditional values were being weakened. New movements arose calling for a strict **interpretation** of the Quran—the Muslim holy book—and a return to traditional Muslim religious laws. These Muslim movements wanted to overthrow pro-Western governments in the Middle East and create a pure Islamic society. Muslims who support these movements are referred to as fundamentalist militants. Some militants began using terrorism to achieve their goals.

American support of Israel also angered many in the Middle East. In 1947 the UN divided British-controlled Palestine into two territories to provide a home for Jews. One part became Israel. The other part was to become a state for Palestinian Arabs, but fighting between Israel and the Arab states in 1948 left this territory under the control of Israel, Jordan, and Egypt. In

R

C

Activity: Connecting with the United States

International Response to Terrorism Have students work in groups and use the library or Internet resources to research three of the terrorist attacks that occurred outside of the United States. Have the groups write and present oral reports describing the attacks and the response in the particular countries where the attacks took place. Students' reports should include photos, maps, or other visual aids. Then ask the class to compare these events to those of the attacks of 9/11 in the United States. Discuss how responses vary from country to country. **OL**

the 1950s, Palestinians began staging guerrilla raids and terrorist attacks against Israel. Since the United States gave aid to Israel, it became the target of Muslim hostility. In the 1970s, several Middle East nations realized they could fight Israel and the United States by providing terrorists with money, weapons, and training. This is called **state-sponsored terrorism**. The governments of Libya, Syria, Iraq, and Iran have all sponsored terrorists.

The Rise of Al-Qaeda

In 1979 the Soviet Union invaded Afghanistan. In response, Muslims from across the world headed to Afghanistan to help fight the Soviets. Among them was a 22-year-old named Osama bin Laden. Bin Laden came from one of Saudi Arabia's wealthiest families. He used his wealth to support the Afghan resistance. In 1988 he founded an organization called al-Qaeda or "the Base." Al-Qaeda recruited Muslims and channeled money and arms to the Afghan resistance.

Bin Laden's experience in Afghanistan convinced him that superpowers could be beaten. He also believed that Western ideas had contaminated Muslim society and was outraged by Saudi Arabia's decision to allow American troops to be based on Saudi soil after Iraq invaded Kuwait.

At first, bin Laden ran al-Qaeda from camps in Sudan, but in 1996, he moved back to Afghanistan after the Taliban, a militant Muslim fundamentalist group, took power there. Bin Laden dedicated himself to driving Westerners out of the Middle East. In 1998 he called on Muslims to kill Americans. Soon afterward, his followers set off bombs at the American embassies in Kenya and Tanzania.

After these bombings, President Clinton ordered cruise missiles fired at terrorist camps in Afghanistan and Sudan, but bin Laden was not deterred. In 1999, al-Qaeda terrorists were arrested while trying to smuggle explosives into the United States in an attempt to bomb Seattle. In October 2000, al-Qaeda terrorists crashed a boat loaded with explosives into the *USS Cole*, an American warship, while it was docked in Yemen. Then, on September 11, 2001, al-Qaeda struck again, hijacking four American passenger planes and executing the most devastating terrorist attack in history.

✔ **Reading Check** **Explaining** Why was Osama bin Laden able to create a terrorist organization?

A New War Begins

MAIN Idea The war on terrorism involved halting terrorists' access to funding and launching a war in Afghanistan.

HISTORY AND YOU Does your school have plans for coping with an emergency? Read on to learn about the national response to the terrorist attacks.

In an address to Congress on September 20, 2001, President Bush demanded the Taliban regime in Afghanistan turn over bin Laden and his supporters and shut down all terrorist camps. The president then made it clear that although the war on terrorism would start by targeting al-Qaeda, it would not stop there. "It will not end," the president announced, "until every terrorist group of global reach has been found, stopped, and defeated." While Secretary of State Colin Powell began building an international coalition to support the United States, Secretary of Defense Donald Rumsfeld began deploying troops, aircraft, and warships to the Middle East.

The president also announced that the United States would no longer tolerate states that aided terrorists. "From this day forward," the president proclaimed, "any nation that continues to harbor or support terrorism will be regarded by the United States as a hostile regime." The war would not end quickly, but it was a war the nation had to fight:

PRIMARY SOURCE

"Great harm has been done to us. We have suffered great loss. And in our grief and anger we have found our mission and our moment. . . . Our Nation—this generation—will lift a dark threat of violence from our people and our future."

—President George W. Bush, *Address to Joint Session of Congress*, September 20, 2001

In a letter to the *New York Times*, Secretary of Defense Rumsfeld warned Americans that "this will be a war like none other our nation has faced." The enemy, he explained, "is a global network of terrorist organizations and their state sponsors, committed to denying free people the opportunity to live as they choose." Fighting terrorism would not be easy. Military force would be used, but terrorism had to be fought by other means as well.

For a longer excerpt from this speech read, "President Bush's Address to Joint Session of Congress, September 20, 2001" on page R57 of **Documents in American History.**

C1 **Critical Thinking**

Evaluating Ask students to draw up a list for determining if the United States's war on terror is succeeding. Remind them to look at both short term and long-term success. Have them suggest changes to the nation's policies that may lead to better success. **OL**

C2 **Critical Thinking**

Drawing Conclusions Ask: What did Defense Secretary Rumsfeld mean when he said in 2001 that the war on terror would be "a war like none other our nation has faced"? *(Past wars involved fighting other countries that had standing armies, while the war on terror involves dealing with underground groups, in some cases sponsored by governments, who carry out attacks on civilians.)* **OL**

✔ **Reading Check**

Answer:
He used his personal wealth to build a terrorist organization and relied on fighters trained during the Afghan resistance against the Soviet Union.

Hands-On Chapter Project
Step 2

Exploring the "Blogosphere"

Step 2: Blog Quotes Students will make posters using quotes from blogs selected from the chart they compiled in Step 1.

Directions Write the Big Idea on the board. Have student groups select a quote from three of the blogs found on their charts. Ask students to make a poster for each quote. Each poster should include the quote in large enough type to be easily read. The posters should also include photographs from newspapers, magazines, and the Internet that illustrate the meaning of the quote.

Summarizing Have students present their posters to the class. Ask the class to match the posters to blogs on the chart compiled in Step 1. Have them discuss in what ways, if any, the blogs from which they have quoted strengthen or threaten democracy. **OL**
(Project continued on page 816)

D Differentiated Instruction

Visual/Spatial Have students work in pairs to design a memorial to the victims and heroes of the September 11, 2001, terrorist attacks. Encourage students to use library and Internet resources to learn about the designs of other memorials. Have students note how symbolism is used in the design of many memorials. Have the pairs write a paragraph explaining the symbolism they chose for their memorial. **OL**

Analyzing VISUALS

Answers:
1. They felt a sense of personal loss because the attacks were carried out on innocent people living their everyday lives.
2. Answers will vary but might include more security checks at public places, especially at airports.

Additional Support

PRIMARY SOURCE
Responding to 9/11

After the attacks, Americans held vigils and prayer services to remember and honor those who had died. For months after the attacks, Americans closely followed the efforts of firefighters and rescue workers. Despite increased airport security, the attacks left some Americans wary of air travel.

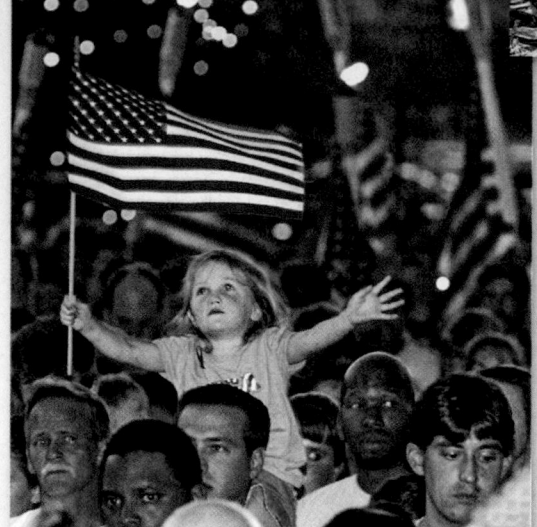

At left, Alana Milawski, waves an American flag during a candlelight vigil in Las Vegas on September 12, 2001. Above, firefighters work in the rubble of the World Trade Center. The attacks led to an increase in airline security (right) resulting in long lines at airports while passengers waited to be screened.

Analyzing VISUALS

1. **Theorizing** Why do you think so many people participated in group vigils and memorials after the attacks?
2. **Evaluating** In what ways were Americans most immediately affected by the attacks of September 11, 2001?

Cutting Terrorist Funding One effective way to fight terrorist groups is to cut off their funding. On September 24, President Bush issued an executive order freezing the financial assets of several individuals and groups suspected of terrorism. As information about terrorist groups increased, more names and organizations were added to the list. President Bush asked other nations to help, and within weeks, some 80 nations had issued orders freezing the assets of the organizations and individuals on the American list.

Homeland Security and the Patriot Act
As part of the effort to protect the American people from further terrorist attacks, President Bush created a new federal agency—the Office of Homeland Security—to coordinate the dozens of federal agencies and departments working to prevent terrorism. He then appointed Pennsylvania governor Tom Ridge to serve as the agency's director.

History ONLINE
Student Web Activity Visit glencoe.com and complete the activity on the war on terrorism.

The president also asked Congress to pass legislation to help law enforcement agencies track down terrorist suspects. Drafting the legislation took time. Congress had to balance Americans' Fourth Amendment protections against unreasonable search and seizure with the need to increase security. President Bush signed the antiterrorist bill—known as the USA Patriot Act—into law in October 2001. In cases involving terrorism, the law permitted secret searches to avoid tipping off suspects and allowed authorities to **obtain** a nationwide search warrant useable in any jurisdiction. The law also made it easier to wiretap suspects and allowed authorities to track Internet communications and seize voice mail.

In the months following the attack, the Office of Homeland Security struggled to coordinate all of the federal agencies fighting terrorism. In June 2002, President Bush asked Congress to combine all of the agencies responsible for the public's safety into a new

Activity: Connecting with the United States

Identifying Ask: Do you know what agencies are included in the Department of Homeland Security? Divide the class into groups, and have each group research the structure of the Department of Homeland Security and the agencies it now includes. Tell the groups to use their findings to create an organizational chart that shows the following directorates of the department: Border and Transportation Security, Emergency Preparedness and Response, Science and Technology, Information Analysis and Infrastructure Protection; describes the general responsibilities of each; and lists the agencies under the umbrella of each. Students' charts also should include agencies in the department that are not part of a directorate. Then ask each student to select an agency and find out how it contributes to the protection of the United States. Have students share what they discover in a class discussion. **AL**

department called the Department of Homeland Security. The plan called for the largest reorganization of the federal government since 1947, when Congress created the Department of Defense, the National Security Council, and the CIA.

The president's proposal led to an intense debate in Congress, and it did not pass until after the midterm elections in November 2002. The new Department of Homeland Security controls the Coast Guard, the Border Patrol, the Immigration and Naturalization Service, the Customs Service, the Federal Emergency Management Agency, and many other agencies. It also analyzes information collected by the FBI, the CIA, and other intelligence agencies.

Bioterrorism Strikes the United States As the nation struggled to cope with the attacks on the Pentagon and the World Trade Center, another terrorist attack began. On October 5, 2001, a newspaper editor in Florida died from an anthrax infection. **Anthrax** is a type of bacteria. Several nations, including the United States, Russia, and Iraq, have used anthrax to create biological weapons. Antibiotics can cure anthrax, but if left untreated, it can quickly become lethal.

Soon after its appearance in Florida, anthrax was found at the offices of news organizations in New York City. In Washington, D.C., a letter containing anthrax arrived at Senator Tom Daschle's office. It was now clear that terrorists were using the mail to spread anthrax. Traces of anthrax were found at several government buildings. Several postal workers who had handled letters containing anthrax contracted the disease, and two workers died. The FBI began investigating the attack, but no suspects were arrested.

The War in Afghanistan Begins

On October 7, 2001, the United States began bombing al-Qaeda's camps and the Taliban's military forces in Afghanistan. In an address to the nation, President Bush explained that Islam and the Afghan people were not the enemy, and that the United States would send food, medicine, and other supplies to Afghan refugees. The president also explained that the attack on the Taliban was only the beginning. The war on terrorism would continue until victory was achieved:

PRIMARY SOURCE

"Today we focus on Afghanistan, but the battle is broader. Every nation has a choice to make. In this conflict, there is no neutral ground. If any government sponsors the outlaws and killers of innocents, they have become outlaws and murderers, themselves. And they will take that lonely path at their own peril. . . . The battle is now joined on many fronts. We will not waver; we will not tire; we will not falter; and we will not fail. Peace and freedom will prevail. Thank you. May God continue to bless America."

—President George W. Bush, Address to the Nation, October 7, 2001

☑ Reading Check **Outlining** What steps did the president take in response to the terrorist attacks?

Section 2 REVIEW

Vocabulary
1. **Explain** the significance of: Osama bin Laden, al-Qaeda, terrorism, state-sponsored terrorism, anthrax.

Main Ideas
2. **Describing** What factors have contributed to the rise of Middle Eastern terrorist groups?
3. **Listing** What major actions marked the beginning of the United States' war on terrorism?

Critical Thinking
4. **Big Ideas** Why do Islamic fundamentalists in the Middle East disagree with U.S. foreign policy?
5. **Categorizing** Use a graphic organizer similar to the one below to list the responses of individual Americans and the federal government to the attacks on September 11, 2001.

Individuals — Response to 9/11 attacks — Government

6. **Analyzing Visuals** Study the map of terrorist attacks on page 810. How would you describe the scope of al-Qaeda's operation?

Writing About History
7. **Persuasive Writing** The Patriot Act gave law enforcement new ways to fight terrorism. Write a letter to a newspaper explaining why you are either for or against giving up some freedoms in exchange for increased security.

History ONLINE
Study Central™ To review this section, go to glencoe.com and click on Study Central.

813

☑ Reading Check

Answer:
He froze financial assets of terrorist groups, created a new federal department to coordinate government efforts to prevent terrorism, signed legislation empowering government officials to hunt down terrorists, and sent the military to overthrow the pro-terrorist Taliban government in Afghanistan.

Assess
· · · · · · · · · · · · · · · · · · ·
History ONLINE
Study Central™ provides summaries, interactive games, and online graphic organizers to help students review content.

Close
· · · · · · · · · · · · · · · · · · ·
Summarizing Ask: How did the United States respond to the terrorist attacks of September 11, 2001? **OL**

Section 2 REVIEW

Answers

1. All definitions can be found in the section and the Glossary.
2. U.S. support of wealthy oil countries and ruling families, Western influences undermining traditional values, and beliefs, and American support for Israel
3. Freezing terrorist assets, expanding government to hunt down terrorists and prevent terrorist attacks, increase of security arrangements to protect the public, and the sending of American forces to the Middle East

4. They resent the use of American power to spread Western political, cultural, and economic influences to the Middle East; they oppose U.S. support for the Jewish nation of Israel.
5. Individuals: medical workers and firefighters helped in New York, citizens donated blood, collected supplies, gave money to relief efforts, and commemorated the dead; Government: froze terrorist funds, reorganized bureaucracy and expanded efforts to hunt down terrorists, mandated security

procedures, and used the military to remove pro-terrorist Taliban government in Afghanistan
6. Answers will vary but might mention the world-wide scope of terrorist operations from North America to Europe and Southeast Asia.
7. Answers will vary but should be supported by reasoned arguments and evidence.

Focus

The Invasion of Iraq

Bellringer

Daily Focus Transparency 24.3

Guide to Reading

Answers:

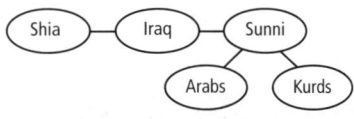

Shia — Iraq — Sunni
Arabs — Kurds

Section Spotlight Video

To generate student interest and provide a springboard for class discussion, access the Chapter 24, Section 3 video at glencoe.com or on the video DVD.

Guide to Reading

Big Ideas
Trade, War, and Migration In an effort to fight terrorism, the United States launched attacks in both Afghanistan and Iraq.

Content Vocabulary
• weapons of mass destruction (WMD) *(p. 816)*

Academic Vocabulary
• inspector *(p. 817)*
• significantly *(p. 818)*
• eliminate *(p. 819)*

People and Events to Identify
• Northern Alliance *(p. 814)*
• Khalid Shaikh Mohammed *(p. 815)*
• "axis of evil" *(p. 816)*
• Saddam Hussein *(p. 817)*

Reading Strategy
As you read this section on the Invasion of Iraq, complete a graphic organizer similar to the one below to show the different groups in Iraq.

Iraq

After the attacks of September 11, 2001, the United States invaded Afghanistan, the Central Asian nation that had sheltered many al-Qaeda members. In March 2003, the United States invaded Iraq and toppled the regime of Saddam Hussein.

The War on Terror Continues

MAIN Idea After forcing Taliban leaders in Afghanistan to flee, the United States and its allies sent more troops as peacekeepers and worked to create a stable and democratic government.

HISTORY AND YOU Can you think of a nation or region today where peacekeepers are stationed while a new government is established? Read on to learn about the role of peacekeepers in Afghanistan.

Less than a month after the September 11 attacks, the United States launched a war in Afghanistan with the goal of bringing down the Taliban regime that had sheltered Osama bin Laden and other members of al-Qaeda. Americans also hoped that bin Laden would be captured and brought back for trial in the United States.

While American warplanes bombed the Taliban's forces, the United States began sending military aid to the **Northern Alliance,** a coalition of Afghan groups that had been fighting the Taliban for several years. U.S. Special Forces also entered Afghanistan to advise the Northern Alliance and identify targets for American aircraft. The American bombing campaign quickly shattered the Taliban's defenses. The Northern Alliance then launched a massive attack. In December 2001, the Taliban government collapsed, and surviving Taliban fled to the mountains of Afghanistan.

Rebuilding Afghanistan

After the Taliban fled, the United States and its allies helped local Afghan leaders create a new government. Meanwhile, thousands of American and allied troops arrived to act as peacekeepers. In 2003 NATO took command of peacekeeping in Afghanistan.

Since 2002 Afghanistan has begun to slowly recover from decades of war. The economy has grown rapidly, although the people remain very poor. The United States and its allies have donated some $24 billion to help rebuild the country. In December 2004, Afghanistan held its first nationwide democratic election, and Hamid Karzai was elected president. One year later, the Afghan people elected a National Assembly. Despite these successes, Afghanistan continues to suffer from violence. Taliban insurgents have staged guerrilla

Resource Manager

R Reading Strategies	**C** Critical Thinking	**D** Differentiated Instruction	**W** Writing Support	**S** Skill Practice
Teacher Edition • Activate. Prior Knowl., p. 816	**Teacher Edition** • Identify Issues, p. 815 • Analyz. Info., p. 816	**Teacher Edition** • Special Education, p. 818	**Teacher Edition** • Persuasive Writing, p. 818	**Teacher Edition** • Reading a Time Line, p. 817
Additional Resources • Guided Reading Act., URB p. 150	**Additional Resources** • Quizzes/Tests, p. 339			**Additional Resources** • RENTG, p. 263

PRIMARY SOURCE

PRIMARY SOURCE
The War in Afghanistan

The United States invaded Afghanistan to overthrow the Taliban regime. Helping to establish a democratic government was the next step.

▲ *American soldiers were sent to act as peacekeepers while the new Afghan government tried to establish order in the mountainous country.*

▲ *The new Afghan constitution granted equal rights to women, including the right to vote.*

▶ *Hamid Karzai was elected president in 2004.*

Analyzing VISUALS

1. **Speculating** What part of their duties do you think these soldiers find most difficult?
2. **Predicting** How may voting rights for women affect the development of the new Afghan government?

---

attacks and suicide bombings. The Afghan government has little control over the mountainous regions of southern Afghanistan and fighting continues between NATO and Taliban forces in the south.

Bin Laden Goes Into Hiding

According to news reports, American intelligence agencies believe Osama bin Laden crossed into Pakistan to hide in the mountainous region of Warizistan where the local people were friendly to al-Qaeda and the Taliban. Between 2002 and 2006, bin Laden released a number of audiotapes and one videotape urging his followers to continue the fight.

Pakistan has not officially allowed American troops to enter its territory to find bin Laden, although news reports suggest U.S. Special Forces may be operating in the area. Pakistan has itself launched several military operations in Warizistan in search of al-Qaeda and Taliban forces. Although many al-Qaeda operatives have been arrested in Pakistan, Osama bin Laden remains at large.

Tracking Down Al-Qaeda

Since 2001, the United States and its allies have continued their worldwide hunt for al-Qaeda members. Hundreds of people have been captured or killed, including several top leaders of al-Qaeda. In November 2002, the CIA used an unmanned remote-controlled flying drone to fire a missile at a car in Yemen killing everyone in the vehicle. The car had been carrying top al-Qaeda leaders who had planned the attack on the USS *Cole* in 1998.

In 2003, Pakistan and the United States captured **Khalid Shaikh Mohammed**—one of the highest ranking members of al-Qaeda, and the man suspected of planning the September 11 attacks. Between 2002 and 2006, the American government believes that at least 10 major attacks by al-Qaeda, including at least three attacks on the United States and two on Great Britain, have been prevented.

✓ Reading Check **Describing** What strategy has the United States used to prevent the Taliban from regaining power?

Chapter 24 A New Century Begins **815**

Teach

C **Critical Thinking**
Identifying Central Issues
Ask: Would the finding of Osama bin Laden bring a significant end to terrorist activities by groups such as al-Qaeda? *(Answers will vary. Some students might state that finding bin Laden would be a severe blow; others might state that other terrorist leaders would arise)* **AL**

Analyzing VISUALS

Answers:
1. Answers will vary but might mention dealing with unexpected terrorist attacks as well as handling cultural differences between Afghan and American ways of life
2. Women will be able to have influence on government policies.

✓ Reading Check

Answer:
The U.S. has helped set up a democratic government, has sent aid to rebuild the country, and contributes military support.

Additional Support

Activity: Interdisciplinary Connection

Geography Provide students with an outline map of Afghanistan. Have students create a series of maps showing the progress of Northern Alliance forces against the Taliban forces. Each map should show major cities and major physical features of Afghanistan. The maps should indicate the approximate areas controlled by opposing sides on each date chosen. Encourage students to create a minimum of five maps, using October 7, 2001 as the date of the first map. Have students display the completed maps in time line fashion. **AL**

Reading Strategy

Activating Prior Knowledge
Remind students that they studied the term *state-sponsored terrorism* in Section 1. Have them explain its relationship to the phrase *axis of evil*. (*Governments, such as those of the axis of evil, sponsor terrorism by supplying arms and funding to terrorist groups to fight wars instead of committing their own military forces.*) **OL**

C Critical Thinking

Analyzing Information Ask:
In what way are weapons of mass destruction more dangerous today than during the Cold War? (*During the Cold War, the threat of counterattack kept the superpowers from using the weapons. Today, the weapons can be spread secretly by nations to terrorists who could use them without being known or located.*) **OL**

Iraq and Weapons of Mass Destruction

MAIN Idea Concern that Iraq might be producing WMDs that could be given to terrorists led to an ultimatum.

HISTORY AND YOU Do you think the UN is an effective mediator of world affairs? Read on to learn about UN actions before the Iraq War.

The terrorist attacks of September 11, 2001 showed that groups such as al-Qaeda were determined to kill as many Americans as possible. President Bush and his advisers were deeply concerned that terrorist groups might acquire **weapons of mass destruction** (WMD). Weapons of mass destruction can kill large numbers of people all at once. Nuclear, chemical, and biological weapons are all examples of weapons of mass destruction.

During the Cold War, very few nations had weapons of mass destruction, and the United States relied upon a policy of deterrence to prevent their use. The United States announced that if any nation used weapons of mass destruction against the United States, the United States would counterattack with its own weapons of mass destruction. Deterrence worked during the Cold War, but the rise of state-sponsored terrorism created a new problem. If a nation secretly gave weapons of mass destruction to terrorists who then used them against the United States, the American military might not know where the weapons came from, or whom to attack in response.

The "Axis of Evil"

In his State of the Union speech in 2002, President Bush warned that an **"axis of evil"** made up of Iraq, Iran, and North Korea posed a grave threat to the world. Each of these nations had been known to sponsor terrorism, and was suspected of developing weapons of mass destruction. The president warned that "The United States of America will not permit the world's most dangerous regimes to threaten us with the world's most destructive weapons."

Of the three nations in the "axis of evil," the president and his advisers believed Iraq to be the most immediate danger. It had used chem-

THE Global War ON Terror, 2001–2007

Oct. 7, 2001
The United States launches attacks on Taliban positions in Afghanistan

March 20, 2003
American and coalition forces begin the invasion of Iraq

2001   **2002**   **2003**

Sept. 11, 2001
Terrorists highjack four planes and attack the World Trade Center and the Pentagon

Nov. 2002
UN Resolution warns Iraq to allow weapons inspectors to return

March 1, 2003
Khalid Shaikh Mohammed, suspected of planning the 9/11 attacks, is captured

Sept. 2003
Eleven countries form the Proliferation Security Initiative to intercept shipments of materials used to make weapons of mass destruction

Hands-On Chapter Project
Step 3

Exploring the "Blogosphere"

Step 3: Blogging Students will work in groups to create their own blog.

Directions Write the Big Idea on the board. Remind students that they have the responsibility to practice free speech in a constructive manner. Any criticism they make should be useful and not abusive. Have student groups use the charts and posters they created in Steps 1 and 2 to brainstorm ideas for a blog topic. Remind students that the content of their blog must meet school standards. When students have selected a topic and a name for their blogs, have them collaborate on writing the first entries for their blogs.

Summarizing Have students read their blog entries to the class. Encourage the class to discuss how they chose their blog topics and how school standards influenced what they wrote. **OL**

(Project continued on page 826)

ical weapons against the Kurds, an ethnic group in northern Iraq, and after the 1991 Gulf War, UN **inspectors** had also found evidence that Iraq had developed biological weapons and had been working on a nuclear bomb.

Between 1991 and 1998, Iraq appeared to be hiding its weapons of mass destruction from UN inspectors. In 1998 the Iraqi government ordered the inspectors to leave the country. In response, President Clinton ordered a massive bombing attack on Iraq to destroy its ability to make such weapons. Despite the attack, intelligence agencies continued to believe Iraq was hiding weapons of mass destruction.

An Ultimatum to Iraq

In 2002 President Bush decided the time had come to deal with Iraq. On September 12, he delivered a speech to the United Nations asking for a new resolution against Iraq. If Iraq's dictator, **Saddam Hussein,** wanted peace he would have to give up Iraq's weapons of mass destruction, readmit the UN weapons inspectors, stop supporting terrorism, and stop oppressing his people. Although he was asking the UN to pass a resolution, the president made it clear that the United States would act with or without UN support.

While the UN Security Council debated a new resolution, President Bush asked Congress to authorize the use of force against Iraq, which it did. With the midterm elections only weeks away, Democrats wanted to focus on the nation's high unemployment rate and the slow economy. Instead, President Bush successfully kept the focus on national security issues. In 2002 Republicans picked up seats in the House of Representatives and regained control of the Senate.

Soon after the American elections, the UN approved a new resolution setting a deadline for Iraq to readmit weapons inspectors. It also required Iraq to declare its weapons of mass destruction, to stop supporting terrorism, and to stop oppressing its people. It threatened "serious consequences" if Iraq did not comply.

✔ **Reading Check** Analyzing Why did the United States think stopping the spread of weapons of mass destruction was linked to the war on terror?

S **Skill Practice**

Reading a Time Line Ask: What was the major report released in October 2004? *(a report on Iraqi weapons of mass destruction)* Who released the report? *(the Iraq Survey Group)* What did the report conclude? *(Iraq did not have weapons of mass destruction at the time the Iraq War began.)* Why were the report's findings important? *(Bush had justified going to war on the basis of intelligence reports claiming that Iraq had weapons of mass destruction. The report cast doubt on this justification.)* **OL**

Analyzing TIME LINES

Answers:
1. Invasion of Afghanistan
2. January 31, 2005

✔ **Reading Check**

Answer:
The U.S. feared the spread of weapons of mass destruction to terrorist groups.

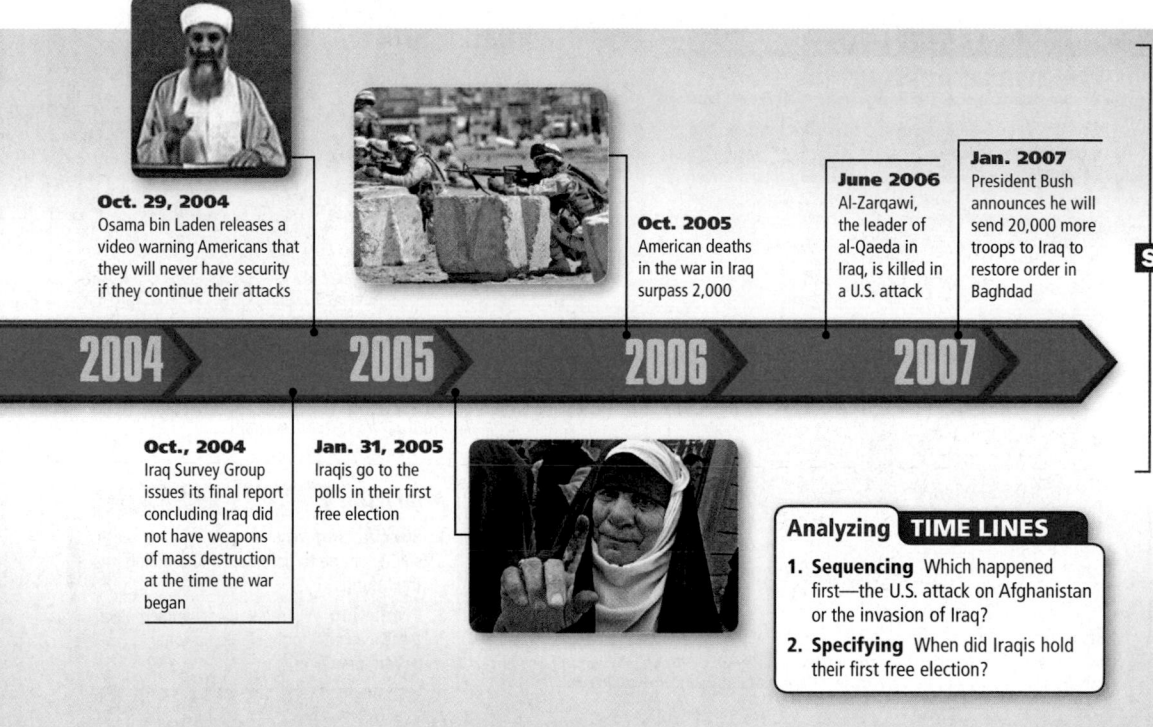

Oct. 29, 2004
Osama bin Laden releases a video warning Americans that they will never have security if they continue their attacks

Oct. 2005
American deaths in the war in Iraq surpass 2,000

June 2006
Al-Zarqawi, the leader of al-Qaeda in Iraq, is killed in a U.S. attack

Jan. 2007
President Bush announces he will send 20,000 more troops to Iraq to restore order in Baghdad

2004 | 2005 | 2006 | 2007

Oct., 2004
Iraq Survey Group issues its final report concluding Iraq did not have weapons of mass destruction at the time the war began

Jan. 31, 2005
Iraqis go to the polls in their first free election

S

Analyzing TIME LINES

1. **Sequencing** Which happened first—the U.S. attack on Afghanistan or the invasion of Iraq?
2. **Specifying** When did Iraqis hold their first free election?

Chapter 24   A New Century Begins   **817**

Differentiated Instruction

Leveled Activities

BL Content Vocabulary Activity, URB, p. 127

OL Reading Skills Activity, URB p. 121

AL Linking Past and Present Activity, URB p. 134

ELL English Learner Activity, URB p. 125

W Writing Support

Persuasive Writing Have students write a newspaper editorial supporting or opposing President Bush's decision to attack Iraq without UN Security Council support. Students should provide reasons for their positions. **AL**

D Differentiated Instruction

Special Education Help students identify the pointers that connect each picture with its caption. Explore what additional information the image teaches about the topic discussed in the caption. **OL**

Analyzing VISUALS

Answers:
1. Answers will vary but might include bringing peace, order, or security to Iraq.
2. Answers will vary but might mention the need for cooperation among Iraq's ethnic groups in order for democracy to work.

Confronting Iraq

MAIN Idea Coalition forces defeated the Iraqi military, but then factions in Iraq took up arms against coalition forces and each other.

HISTORY AND YOU In retrospect, do you believe the invasion of Iraq was justified? Read on to learn more about the different stages of the war.

In November 2002, Iraq agreed to readmit UN weapons inspectors. It then submitted a statement admitting it had weapons of mass destruction before the Gulf War, but denying it currently had weapons of mass destruction. Secretary of State Colin Powell declared that Iraq's declaration contained lies and was in "material breach" of the UN resolution.

As the United States and a coalition of some 30 nations prepared for war with Iraq, others at the UN Security Council argued that the inspectors should be given more time to find evidence of Iraq's WMD programs. By March 2003, the inspectors still had found nothing, and the United States began pressing the UN to authorize the use of force against Iraq.

France and Russia, two Security Council members with veto power, refused to back such a resolution. As war became imminent, world opinion divided between those who supported the United States and those who opposed an attack on Iraq. Around the world antiwar protestors staged rallies and marches. Several nations that had supported the United States in its war on terror, and had sent troops to Afghanistan, including France, Germany, and Canada, refused to join the coalition against Iraq. Saudi Arabia and Turkey—both American allies—refused to allow the United States to attack Iraq from their territories. The only nation bordering Iraq that granted permission to use its territory was Kuwait.

The Invasion Begins

On March 20, 2003, the U.S.-led coalition forces attacked Iraq. Over 150,000 American troops, some 45,000 British troops, as well as a few hundred special forces from Australia and Poland took part in the invasion.

Much of the Iraqi army dissolved as soldiers refused to risk their lives for Hussein. A few fierce battles took place, but the Iraqis were unable to slow the coalition advance **significantly.** On May 1, President Bush declared

PRIMARY SOURCE

The Invasion of Iraq

Overthrowing Saddam Hussein to ensure he could not give WMDs to terrorists was the primary objective of the invasion. Ousting his regime, however, proved easier than establishing a new government.

▲ *U.S. and Iraqi soldiers face the difficult challenge of urban warfare in Iraq where the enemy can be very close, hiding behind walls or in buildings.*

▲ *After decades of sham elections, Iraqi voters get to make real choices when they vote during Iraq's 2005 elections.*

Analyzing VISUALS

1. **Speculating** What do you suppose these soldiers hope to accomplish in fulfilling their duties?
2. **Predicting** Will regularly-scheduled elections lead to a more stable national government?

818 Chapter 24 A New Century Begins

Differentiated Instruction

Primary Source Reading, URB p. 135

Richard Clarke Speaks Out

Objective: To review high-level discussions of foreign policy

Focus: Have students discuss the scene of this excerpt.

Teach: Outline the message of the excerpt.

Assess: Summarize Clarke's warnings.

Differentiated Instruction Strategies

BL Summarize Clarke's warning and the reaction to it.

AL Research to find other primary sources regarding the U.S. government's response to al-Qaeda. Summarize the content to share with the class.

ELL What is the NSC?

that the major combat was over. About 140 Americans and several thousand Iraqis had died. Saddam Hussein was captured in late 2003. After a prolonged trial, an Iraqi court found him guilty of ordering mass executions. He was executed in 2006.

Insurgents and Reconstruction

The quick victory did not end the fighting. Soon after the coalition took control of the country, small groups of Iraqis began staging bombings, sniper attacks, and sporadic battles against coalition forces. Some of the groups carrying out the attacks were former members of Saddam Hussein's military. Others were affiliated with al-Qaeda and other radical Muslim groups who believed the invasion offered a chance to build support in the Muslim world by organizing resistance to the Americans.

Some of the attacks were carried out by militias belonging to the different religious and ethnic groups in Iraq. The majority of Iraq's population is Shia Muslim, but there is a large Sunni Muslim minority as well. The Sunni are themselves divided between Sunni Arabs, who ruled the country under Saddam Hussein's leadership, and Sunni Kurds. The collapse of Hussein's dictatorship renewed old hostilities between these groups, forcing coalition troops to protect them from attacks from each other's militias.

Having gone to war in Iraq to overthrow a tyrant and **eliminate** the possibility of weapons of mass destruction being given to terrorists, the United States found itself trying to suppress an insurgency, prevent a civil war, and establish a new Iraqi government. The United States and its allies spent more than $30 billion to improve Iraq's electrical generating capacity, provide clean water, build schools, and improve health care, but insurgent attacks slowed these efforts. Despite the problems, Iraq's economy began to grow rapidly and a substantial improvement in living standards took place.

Between 2003 and 2006, insurgents killed over 3,000 American soldiers, many more than had died in the initial invasion. Many Americans had expected the war to be over quickly and as the fighting dragged on, support for the war began to decline. The failure to find any weapons of mass destruction also added to the growing controversy as to whether the war was a mistake.

American policy makers now faced a dilemma. If they pulled troops out too soon, Iraq might fall into civil war and provide a safe haven and breeding ground for terrorist groups. At the same time, the longer the United States stayed, the more its presence might stir resentment and support for terrorist groups. The best solution seemed to be to get a functioning and democratic Iraqi government up and running as fast as possible and then train its forces to take over the security of the country. As part of this plan, in January 2005, the Iraqi people went to the polls in huge numbers for the first free elections in their country's history. After much debate, voters then overwhelmingly approved a new constitution in October 2005.

✔ **Reading Check** **Summarizing** Why did it prove so difficult to end the Iraq War quickly?

Section 3 REVIEW

Vocabulary

1. **Explain** the significance of: Northern Alliance, Khalid Shaikh Mohammed, weapons of mass destruction, "axis of evil," Saddam Hussein.

Main Ideas

2. **Explaining** Why did the United States send military aid to the Northern Alliance?

3. **Identifying** Why did Bush choose to focus military attention in Iraq?

4. **Summarizing** Why did fighting continue in Iraq after President Bush declared the major combat was over?

Critical Thinking

5. **Big Ideas** Why did the United States declare war on Afghanistan?

6. **Organizing** Use a graphic organizer to list the reasons why President Bush declared war on Iraq.

> ⟶ War on Iraq

7. **Analyzing Visuals** Examine the photos on page 818. How does the style of warfare in Iraq differ from the fighting in Afghanistan?

Writing About History

8. **Descriptive Writing** Suppose you are an Iraqi who has recently voted in your first election. Write a journal entry that explains how you feel following your vote.

Study Central™ To review this section, go to glencoe.com and click on Study Central.

✔ **Reading Check**

Answer:
Groups of Iraqis opposed to the U.S. invasion attacked American forces; conflicts broke out among Iraq's ethnic groups, adding to the turmoil.

Assess

Study Central™ provides summaries, interactive games, and online graphic organizers to help students review content.

Close

Identifying Central Issues
Ask students to identify the challenges the United States faces in its occupation of Iraq. Ask students to suggest solutions to the challenges. **OL**

Section 3 REVIEW

Answers

1. All definitions can be found in the section and the Glossary.

2. The Northern Alliance had been fighting the Taliban for several years.

3. Bush believed that Iraq was a direct threat because of intelligence reports that Iraq was hiding weapons of mass destruction.

4. Insurgent groups supporting militant causes attacked American forces, and conflict broke out among militias of Iraq's ethnic/religious groups.

5. The Taliban government of Afghanistan had given shelter to the al-Qaeda terrorist movement.

6. He believed Iraq sponsored terrorism and had weapons of mass destruction; also, Iraq had refused to cooperate with the international community and had oppressed its own people.

7. The fighting in Afghanistan took place in mountainous areas; much of the fighting in Iraq occurred in urban areas.

8. Answers will vary but might refer to happiness at having the vote after years of being ruled by kings or dictators.

Focus

Bellringer

Daily Focus Transparency 24.4

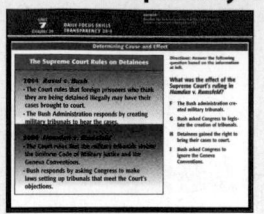

Guide to Reading

Answers:
Student outline notes should follow the major heading structure of the section.

Section Spotlight Video

To generate student interest and provide a springboard for class discussion, access the Chapter 24, Section 4 video at glencoe.com or on the video DVD.

Resource Manager

A Time of Challenges

Guide to Reading

Big Ideas
Government and Society During President Bush's second term, the Republicans faced scandal and a national disaster that led to the Democrats gaining control of Congress in 2007.

Content Vocabulary
• "earmark" (p. 826)

Academic Vocabulary
• monitor (p. 823)
• procedure (p. 824)

People and Events to Identify
• Abu Ghraib (p. 820)
• Guantanamo Bay (p. 822)
• National Security Agency (NSA) (p. 823)
• John G. Roberts, Jr. (p. 824)
• Samuel Alito, Jr. (p. 824)
• Nancy Pelosi (p. 827)

Reading Strategy
Taking Notes As you read about events from the 2004 election to the present day, use the major headings of the section to create an outline.

> A Time of Challenges
> I. The Election of 2004
> II. Security vs. Liberty
>   A.
>   B.

After a close campaign, President Bush won a second term. His administration and the Supreme Court repeatedly clashed over the limits of executive authority in the war on terror. Scandals and frustration over Iraq helped Democrats win control of Congress in 2006.

The Election of 2004

MAIN Idea After a campaign that centered on the war in Iraq and the war on terror, Bush was reelected.

HISTORY AND YOU Have you ever participated in an election at your school? Read on to learn about the election of 2004 in which more voters turned out than had voted in other recent elections.

As the end of President Bush's first term neared, his popularity with Americans began to sink. In the months following the attacks of September 11, 2001, opinion polls showed that more than 80 percent of the public approved of the job he was doing. As the war dragged on in Iraq, and Osama bin Laden remained at large, his approval rating began to fall. The failure of inspectors to find any weapons of mass destruction in Iraq further weakened his support, as did the scandal at the Iraqi prison of **Abu Ghraib** where some Iraqi prisoners of war were abused by their American guards and interrogators. These events provided an opportunity for the Democrats to mount a serious challenge in the 2004 presidential election.

The war on terrorism and the war in Iraq dominated the election. President Bush and Vice President Cheney were renominated by the Republicans. The Democrats nominated Massachusetts Senator John Kerry for president and North Carolina Senator John Edwards for vice president.

Senator Kerry had fought in Vietnam and been decorated for valor, but he had returned from the war convinced of its futility. He joined Vietnam Veterans Against the War and testified before Congress against the war, a stand that angered many veterans and others who supported the war. Opponents used Kerry's actions in the 1970s against him in the 2004 campaign.

The candidates offered the nation a sharp choice. President Bush pledged to continue cutting taxes while building a strong national defense. He opposed abortion, supported limits on stem cell research, and called for a constitutional amendment to ban same-sex marriages. In contrast, Senator Kerry pledged to address domestic issues while pursuing the war on terror. He further promised to raise taxes on the wealthy to fund wider health care coverage, and to strengthen

---

R Reading Strategies	**C** Critical Thinking	**D** Differentiated Instruction	**W** Writing Support	**S** Skill Practice
Teacher Edition • Academic Vocab., p. 823 • Prior Knowl., p. 824 • Make Connect., p. 824 **Additional Resources** • Guided Reading Act., URB p. 151	**Teacher Edition** • Making Inferences, p. 822 • Cause/Effect, pp. 823, 826 • Identify. Issues, p. 825 **Additional Resources** • Prim. Source Reading, URB p. 137 • Supreme Court Case Studies, p. 161 • Quizzes/Tests, p. 340	**Teacher Edition** • Visual/Spatial, p. 821 • Auditory/Musical, p. 825 **Additional Resources** • Reinforcing Skills Act., URB p. 131 • Reteaching Act., URB p. 143 • Enrichment Act., URB p. 145 • Authentic Asses., p. 53	**Additional Resources** • Linking Past/Present, URB p. 134 • Am. Art and Music Act., p. 139	**Additional Resources** • Reading Skills Act., URB p. 121 • Critical Thinking Skills Act., URB p. 132 • RENTG, p. 266

▲ While the war on terror was the central issue of the campaign, Bush and Kerry differed on many issues, including stem cell research, Social Security, health care, and taxes. The two men held three debates during the 2004 campaign.

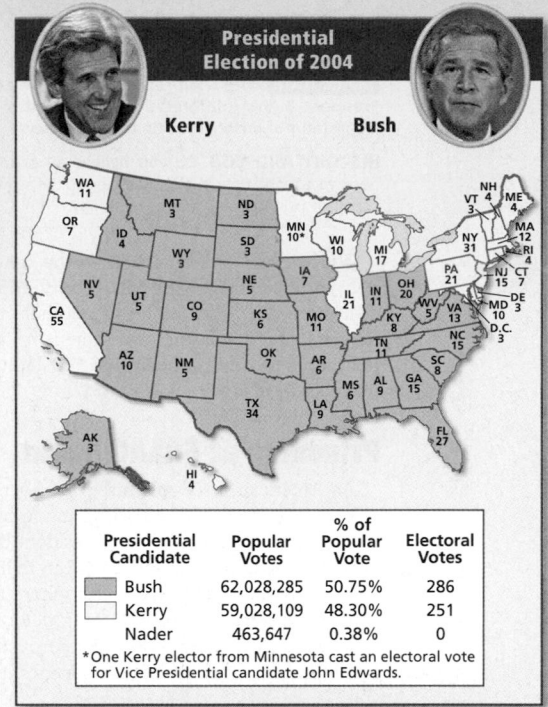

Presidential Election of 2004

Kerry   Bush

Presidential Candidate	Popular Votes	% of Popular Vote	Electoral Votes
▨ Bush	62,028,285	50.75%	286
☐ Kerry	59,028,109	48.30%	251
Nader	463,647	0.38%	0

*One Kerry elector from Minnesota cast an electoral vote for Vice Presidential candidate John Edwards.

Analyzing VISUALS

1. **Formulating Questions** If you had been the moderator of the debate, what questions would you have asked Bush and Kerry? Why?
2. **Theorizing** Why was Kerry more popular than Bush on the West Coast?

Social Security. He took the opposite stand from Bush on most social issues. Bush's campaign portrayed Kerry as an irresolute "flip-flopper" who could not be trusted with the nation's security. Kerry's campaign portrayed Bush as too stubborn and accused him of refusing to admit mistakes or change course when events required it.

Although the events of September 11, 2001, had united the nation emotionally, the country remained as divided politically as it had been in 2000. Bush's support was strongest in the South and on the Great Plains, as well as in rural areas and the outer suburbs of major cities. Kerry's base was in the Northeast and on the West Coast, as well as in cities and inner suburbs. Both candidates focused their efforts on a few key battleground states in the Midwest where voters were narrowly divided.

Both parties saw voter turnout as the key to victory. Election Day witnessed the highest voter turnout since 1968—nearly 61% of eligible voters went to the polls. Democrats won 8 million more votes than in 2000, but the Republicans gained 11.5 million. The election was decided in Ohio whose electoral votes both candidates needed to win. The vote was close enough that Bush was not declared the winner until the following day, having won the state by a little more than 100,000 votes. Nationwide, President Bush won a majority of the popular vote. His victory helped increase the Republican majorities in Congress as well. Despite the problems in Iraq, voters felt it safer to stay the course.

✓ Reading Check **Analyzing** Why did President Bush's popularity decline in the year before the 2004 election?

Chapter 24   A New Century Begins   **821**

Activity: Collaborative Learning

Researching the Candidates Organize the class into six groups. Assign each group one of the following topics: Bush's childhood and family background, Bush's college years and military service, Bush's political background, Kerry's childhood and family background, Kerry's college and military service, or Kerry's political background. Have the groups research their topic. Then have the Bush groups and the Kerry groups work together to prepare a display providing a portrait of the two men. **OL**

C Critical Thinking

Making Inferences Refer students to a map of North America and the Caribbean area that shows the location of Guantanamo Bay in Cuba in relation to the United States. **Ask:** Why might United States officials have selected Guantanamo Bay as a place to hold people suspected of terrorism? *(Students might point out Guantanamo's location outside of the country and beyond the reach of U.S. laws, allowing for secrecy and greater leeway in interrogating suspects.)* **AL**

Analyzing VISUALS

Answers:
1. association with terrorist groups; vocal or financial support for a terrorist cause
2. barbed wire, armed guards, prison cells

Additional Support

Teacher Tip

This activity requires students to do research, to write, and to perform. It allows students with different levels of academic skills and intelligences to work together. As you form groups, consider the needed skills and choose students accordingly.

Security vs. Liberty

MAIN Idea The Supreme Court rejected President Bush's interpretation of the rights and legal status of prisoners at Guantanamo Bay.

HISTORY AND YOU Do you believe all prisoners deserve a right to a trial? Read about the unusual status of prisoners at Guantanamo Bay.

The war on terror heightened the tension between America's national security and its civil liberties. In order to prevent another major terrorist attack, was the government justified in limiting the rights of citizens? Did captured terrorists have any rights at all?

Prisoners at Guantanamo

As American forces captured members of al-Qaeda, a decision had to be made as to what to do with them. In 2004 President Bush decided to hold them at the American military base in **Guantanamo Bay,** Cuba, where they could be interrogated. Establishing detention facilities at Guantanamo proved controversial. Some people argued that the prisoners should have the same rights as Americans taken into custody in the United States, including the right to a lawyer, formal charges, and eventually a proper trial.

Rather than ask Congress for a law setting the rules for handling the detainees, the administration concluded that the president had the right as commander in chief to decide how detainees captured in combat should be treated. The administration insisted that the prisoners were illegal enemy combatants, not suspects charged with a crime, and as such, they did not have the right to appeal their detentions to an American court. The administration also declared that the rules regarding the treatment of prisoners, as specified in the Geneva Conventions, did not apply to terrorists since they were not part of any nation's armed forces.

Hamdan v. Rumsfeld

The Supreme Court disagreed with the administration. In 2004, in the case of *Rasul* v. *Bush,* the Court ruled that foreign prisoners who claimed they were being unlawfully

PRIMARY SOURCE
Abu Ghraib and Guantanamo Bay

The revelation that some American troops had mistreated prisoners at the Abu Ghraib prison in Iraq shocked many people. Photographs of prisoners being abused and humiliated diminished the international image of the United States. Similarly, the lack of judicial proceedings and the secrecy surrounding the detainees at Guantanamo Bay prompted international criticism.

▲ Soldiers escort a detainee at Camp X-Ray at the military base at Guantanamo Bay, Cuba.

▲ A U.S. soldier points to prison cells where high risk detainees are held.

822 Chapter 24 A New Century Begins

Analyzing VISUALS
1. **Interpreting** What might make a detainee "high risk"?
2. **Analyzing** In the photograph above, what elements show the level of security at the detention center?

Activity: Collaborative Learning

Identifying Central Issues Remind students that Americans are strongly divided on many important issues. **Ask:** What are some important national or local issues facing our nation? *(the war in Iraq, illegal immigration, taxes, and so on)* Organize the class into small groups and assign each group a different issue. Ask groups to research their issues. The categories students should research include the nature of the issue, its impact on the public, and at least two different points of view about the issue. Have groups script and perform a mock debate that dramatizes the findings. **AL**

imprisoned had the right to have their cases heard in court. The Bush administration responded by creating military tribunals to hear each detainee's case. In 2006 the Supreme Court struck this plan down in *Hamdan* v. *Rumsfeld,* arguing that the military tribunals at Guantanamo Bay violated both the Uniform Code of Military Justice and the Geneva Conventions regarding the treatment of prisoners of war.

President Bush then asked Congress to pass legislation establishing tribunals that met the Court's objections. In negotiations with Congress, the president agreed that prisoners would have the right to see the evidence against them, and any evidence obtained by torture would be inadmissible. The president also agreed to uphold the Geneva Conventions. Congress then responded with legislation that stated that non-citizens captured as enemy combatants would have no right to file writs of habeas corpus. This meant that as long as the tribunal had determined they were being lawfully held, they could be held indefinitely without trial.

Domestic Surveillance

As part of the war on terror, the **National Security Agency** (NSA) expanded its practice of **monitoring** overseas telephone calls. The NSA began wiretapping domestic calls made to overseas locations in those instances where they had good reason to believe that one party in the call was a member of al-Qaeda or affiliated with al-Qaeda.

When the *New York Times* broke the story of the wiretapping program in late 2005, it created a controversy. Civil rights groups feared the program would be abused and used to violate the privacy and Fourth Amendment rights of American citizens. Congress had created special courts to issue warrants in highly-classified security cases, but President Bush argued the courts were too slow and that he had the authority to expand wiretapping without warrants to help fight the war on terror. In August 2006, a federal judge declared the warrantless wiretapping to be unconstitutional. The federal government immediately appealed the case.

✓**Reading Check** **Explaining** Why did the Bush administration believe detainees at Guantanamo had no right to take their case to a U.S. court?

A Stormy Second Term

MAIN Idea Bush appointed two new Supreme Court justices; his second term was marred by a hurricane, the ongoing war, and scandals.

HISTORY AND YOU Do you remember Hurricane Katrina? Read on to learn how the handling of the crisis hurt the Bush administration.

Having won a second term with a majority of the popular vote, President Bush concluded the American people had given him a mandate to continue his policies. He began his second term by announcing plans to overhaul the Social Security system and to create a prescription drug program for senior citizens.

Debating Social Security

To build support for Social Security reform, President Bush pointed out that the baby boom generation would begin receiving Social Security in 2011. For decades, Congress had been warned that when baby boomers began retiring, the Social Security system would be in danger of collapse. The government would need to raise taxes dramatically, or greatly increase the deficit by borrowing money.

To fix Social Security, President Bush proposed that workers be allowed to put 4 percent of their income in private accounts rather than in Social Security. This money could then be invested in stocks and bonds. The president believed that private accounts would grow rapidly and help cover the expected shortfall in Social Security accounts. Bush's plan generated little enthusiasm in Congress. Democrats argued that the danger to Social Security was overstated and that privatizing any part of Social Security was dangerous. With the American public unenthusiastic, the plan was never brought to a vote in Congress.

Although his plan to reform Social Security failed, President Bush did convince Congress to enact a new prescription drug program for seniors. A major issue during the campaign had been the cost of prescription drugs for retirees living on a fixed income. Under the new program, provided by Medicare, people 65 and older can sign up for insurance that helps cover the cost of prescription drugs.

Chapter 24 A New Century Begins **823**

C **Critical Thinking**

Determining Cause and Effect **Ask:** How did the U.S. Supreme Court ruling in *Hamdan* v. *Rumsfeld* affect Bush administration policy on detainees? How did the administration react to the court ruling? *(The Supreme Court ruled that Bush's creation of military tribunals to hear cases violated U.S. military code and the Geneva Conventions regarding the treatment of prisoners. The Bush administration responded by allowing prisoners the right to see evidence and by agreeing to uphold the Geneva Conventions.)* **OL**

R **Reading Strategy**

Academic Vocabulary Have students read the sentence that contains the word *monitoring.* Then ask a student to define the word. **OL**

✓**Reading Check**

Answer:
The Bush administration held that the detainees were illegal enemy combatants, not suspects charged with a crime, and as such, they did not have a right to appeal their cases to an American court.

Additional Support

Activity: Collaborative Learning

Evaluating **Ask:** How do the government's efforts to protect the nation affect you? *(Answers will vary depending on students' personal experiences and where they live.)* Use the question to elicit ideas and anecdotes from students about ways that they have been affected by measures taken by the government to protect Americans from different kinds of attacks or disasters. Ask students what kinds of disasters have happened or might happen where they live and what they would expect the government to do to help before, during, and after a catastrophic event. Close the activity by discussing the impact of terrorist attacks and other disasters, and why such events matter to everyone in the country. **OL**

823

Conservatives worried that the plan would represent an enormous expansion of Medicare that the government could not afford. Democrats worried that the plan was too complex and did not go far enough in helping poor seniors. Despite the controversy, Congress enacted the plan.

New Supreme Court Judges

Although Republicans had gained four Senate seats in 2004, their majority of 55 still fell short of the 60 votes needed to end Democratic filibusters of President Bush's judicial nominees. Frustrated, Senate Majority Leader Bill Frist developed a plan to ban filibusters of presidential nominees. His plan called for Vice President Cheney, as the presiding officer of the Senate, to rule excessive debate on a nomination out of order. A simple majority of senators could then vote to uphold the vice president's ruling, rather than the 60 votes needed to stop a filibuster.

Worried that the plan would change Senate **procedures** too much, a bipartisan group of senators—the "Gang of 14"—forged a compromise. Under the plan, the seven Democratic members of the group agreed not to support a filibuster of the president's nominees solely because of their conservative ideology. They would support a filibuster only in extraordinary circumstances. In return the seven Republicans agreed not to support Frist if he tried to ban filibusters.

Early in Bush's second term, two vacancies occurred on the United States Supreme Court, enabling him to move the Court in a more conservative direction. First, Justice Sandra Day O'Connor announced her retirement. Although she had been appointed by President Reagan, Justice O'Connor had been a pivotal swing vote on the Court, sometimes siding with conservatives, sometimes with liberals. As her replacement, Bush nominated federal judge **John G. Roberts, Jr.,** who was well regarded in the Senate. Before the Senate could act, however, Chief Justice William Rehnquist died, and the president named Roberts to replace him. Roberts easily won Senate confirmation as chief justice.

Again attempting to fill Justice O'Connor's vacancy, President Bush nominated his White House counselor Harriet Miers. Although some Democrats regarded Miers favorably, conservative Republicans were unhappy with

PRIMARY SOURCE
Hurricane Katrina

Hurricane Katrina was one of the worst natural disasters in the history of the United States. The storm ravaged much of the Gulf Coast region. In New Orleans, the breach of the levies caused even more devastation.

▲ An aerial photograph shows how the flooding in New Orleans ruined entire neighborhoods.

her moderate views and lack of experience as a judge. As Republican opposition mounted, President Bush withdrew Miers' name and nominated federal judge **Samuel Alito, Jr.,** a well-known conservative justice. Democrats worried that Alito's strong views would shift the Court's balance, but the deal crafted by the Gang of 14 meant any filibuster would fail. The Senate voted 58 to 42 to confirm Alito.

Hurricane Katrina

On August 29, 2005, Hurricane Katrina smashed into the Gulf Coast of the United States, spreading devastation from Florida to Louisiana. The hurricane destroyed buildings, roads, and electrical lines, left thousands of people homeless, and cost at least 1,200 lives. Although the news media had given advance warning, many people had not evacuated the storm areas. Some stayed in their homes because they had ridden out previous storms, others because they wanted to protect their property, or because they were elderly and infirm. About 125,000 people in New Orleans had no cars and stayed behind.

Activity: Interdisciplinary Connection

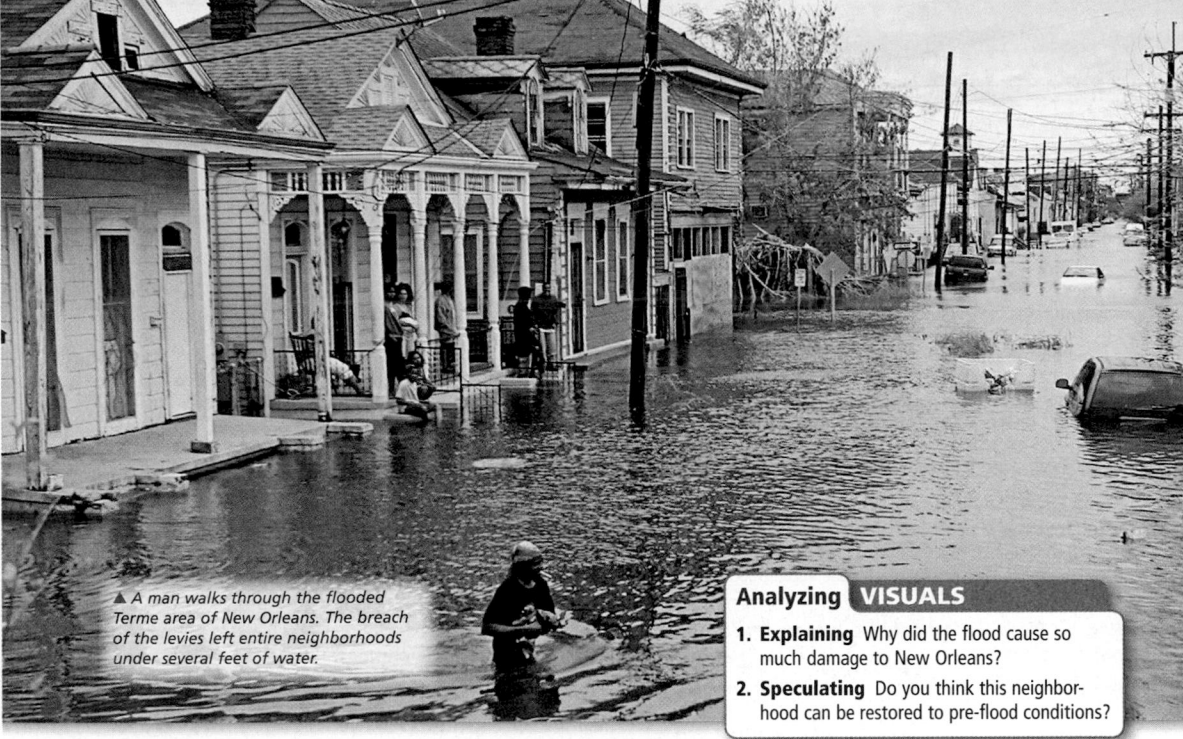

▲ A man walks through the flooded Terme area of New Orleans. The breach of the levies left entire neighborhoods under several feet of water.

1. **Explaining** Why did the flood cause so much damage to New Orleans?

2. **Speculating** Do you think this neighborhood can be restored to pre-flood conditions?

New Orleans Floods The fierce winds, rain, high tides, and storm surges leveled vast coastal areas of Mississippi and Alabama, but initially did only minor damage to New Orleans. Then, after the hurricane had passed, rising waters breached the levees that protected the low-lying city. As water flooded the city, those who had stayed behind were forced to flee onto their roofs, to await rescue.

As the water rose 15 feet in some neighborhoods, many people drowned. Thousands more took shelter in the convention center and at the Superdome, a covered football stadium. There they waited for days without much food, clean water, or information from authorities. City officials promised that buses would evacuate them, but days passed before the buses arrived. Some people began looting neighborhood stores.

The Government's Inadequate Response Television news broadcast scenes of the squalid condition of the survivors, asking why the government was failing to respond more quickly. The mayor of New Orleans was faulted for not issuing a mandatory evacuation until the storm was less than a day away, and for having failed to provide transportation for those who could not leave on their own. The governor of Louisiana engaged in a dispute with federal officials over who should take charge of the state's National Guard units. The Federal Emergency Management Agency (FEMA) seemed unprepared in its response. Only the Coast Guard seemed able to act, as its helicopters and boats began rescuing stranded citizens. Eventually troops and transportation arrived and moved the evacuees to other cities.

As New Orleans remained flooded, President Bush flew over the devastated areas a few days later. Photographs of the president viewing the scene from high above made him appear detached. The public also reacted critically when some members of Congress questioned whether it was worth the expense to rebuild New Orleans at a time when the United States was spending billions to reconstruct Baghdad. With polls showing a sharp drop in public confidence in his administration, President Bush fired the head of FEMA and then traveled to New Orleans to pledge federal funds for rebuilding the city.

Chapter 24 A New Century Begins **825**

C Critical Thinking

Identifying Central Issues Ask: Do you think that the federal government or local government should be more responsible for addressing a disaster like Hurricane Katrina? Why? *(Answers will vary; some students may claim that the responsibility should be shared equally.)* **OL**

D Differentiated Instruction

Auditory/Musical Have students research and prepare a sampling of some of the musicians who performed in benefit concerts for the rebuilding of New Orleans. **OL**

Analyzing VISUALS

Answers:
1. Rising waters breached the levees that protected the low-lying city.
2. Answers will vary but might mention the need for federal funds to rebuild

Additional Support

Activity: Technology Connection

Analyzing Primary Sources Ask: What challenges do people living in areas hit by Hurricane Katrina face today? *(Answers will vary but may include that people are struggling to rebuild or reclaim their homes and businesses and are trying to lead normal lives once again.)* Have students search online news sources for firsthand accounts of life today in New Orleans and other places that were hit by Hurricane Katrina.

Direct students to look for quotations from people who live in the area that tell about conditions there, problems they face, and their thoughts and feelings about the storm and the damage it caused. Tell students to select two quotations to read aloud to the class and explain what each taught them about the hurricane and its aftermath. **OL**

People IN HISTORY

Answers: Rice earned advanced degrees in economics and international studies and was an expert in Eastern and Central Europe. As Speaker of the House, Pelosi has the power to shape legislation, especially regarding government finances and spending. As a talented student, Rice had many interests and was not sure about a future career. She was a skilled pianist and considered majoring in music before finally deciding on international studies. As Speaker of the House, Pelosi ranks second in the line of presidential succession, after Vice President Dick Cheney. No woman has ever been as close in line to the U.S. presidency.

C Critical Thinking

Determining Cause and Effect **Ask:** What factors were responsible for the rapid rise in federal spending by 2005? *(the ongoing costs of the war in Iraq and increased federal funds that members of Congress devoted to special projects in their states and districts)*

Hands-On Chapter Project
Step 4

Exploring the "Blogosphere"

Step 4: Responding to Blogs Student groups respond to blog entries created in Step 3.

Directions Have student groups trade the blogs they created in Step 3. As a group, have students write a response to the blog entry. Remind students that readers contribute to blogs in many ways. They may

826

People IN HISTORY

Condoleezza Rice
1954–

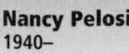

Born in Birmingham, Alabama, the same year as the landmark *Brown* v. *Board of Education* decision, Condoleezza Rice rose to become the first African American female secretary of state.

Before becoming involved in politics, Rice had a distinguished career in academia. She started her college studies at age 15 and went on to earn advanced degrees in economics and international studies. Dr. Rice then became a professor at Stanford University. Due to her expertise in Eastern and Central Europe, Rice served as an adviser on foreign affairs to President Ronald Reagan and President George H.W. Bush. She later returned to her post at Stanford.

When George W. Bush decided to run for president, he asked Rice to be his foreign policy adviser. During his first term, she served as head of the National Security Council and supported the attacks on Afghanistan and the invasion of Iraq. She became secretary of state during Bush's second term.

How did Rice's academic studies prepare her for her future role in politics?

Nancy Pelosi
1940–

Originally from Baltimore, Maryland, Nancy Pelosi's interest in politics began at an early age. Her father was a supporter of Democrat Franklin D. Roosevelt's New Deal and held political office.

Pelosi has spent most of her adult life in the San Francisco area. There, she attracted attention as an effective fund-raiser for the Democratic Party. She became the chair of the California State Democratic Party in 1981 and served for two years.

In 1987 she was elected to Congress in a special election to fill a vacancy caused by the death of her predecessor. The following year she was reelected for a full term and has held that office ever since.

In 2002 Pelosi was elected minority whip and tried to forge greater unity among different factions of her party. In that post, she emerged as one of President Bush's toughest critics. When the Democrats regained control of the House of Representatives after the 2006 elections, she became Speaker, the first woman elected to that post.

Why would Pelosi's position give her a platform from which to criticize the president?

Scandals in Congress

In 2005 Speaker of the House Dennis Hastert pledged that the 109th Congress would be "the Reform Congress." Very quickly, however, many voters grew disenchanted with the Republican majority in the Congress. Federal spending rose rapidly, in part because of the ongoing costs of the war in Iraq and partly because both Republicans and Democrats added **"earmarks"** to spending bills. These earmarks specified spending federal money for particular projects, such as building a bridge, or funding medical research, usually in their sponsors' own states and districts.

Congress also suffered a series of scandals. A prominent lobbyist, Jack Abramoff, pled guilty to bribing members of Congress. House Majority Leader Tom DeLay resigned after being indicted for violating campaign finance laws. California Representative Randy "Duke" Cunningham and Ohio Representative Ralph Ney also resigned after being convicted on corruption charges. Florida Representative Mark Foley gave up his seat after it was revealed that he had sent inappropriate E-mail to former House pages.

As the scandals broke, former Republican majority leader Richard Armey lamented that House Republicans, who had gained the majority in 1994 with big ideas, had descended to what he called "political point-scoring on meaningless wedge issues" such as same-sex marriage and flag burning, rather than getting control of earmarks, government spending, and budget deficits.

The 2006 Midterm Elections

The first two years of President Bush's second term had not gone well for his administration, or for Republicans in Congress. His effort to reform Social Security had failed. The public believed his administration had failed to respond adequately to Hurricane Katrina. Congress seemed awash in corruption scandals and unable to control spending. For many conservatives, Bush's support for a prescription drug plan and his decision to nominate Harriet Miers to the Supreme Court left them disenchanted with his leadership. Some were also angry about his plan to reform the nation's immigration system by creating a guest worker program and a path to citizenship for immigrants who had

---

rebut opinions stated in blogs. They sometimes add helpful information such as links. They may point out errors in information and make corrections. Sometimes, they may simply express admiration for the blog. Have students weigh their rights to free speech with their responsibility to civility as they respond to each other's blogs.

Summarizing Have groups share their blog responses with the class. Encourage

the class to discuss what they learned about the Big Ideas of this chapter as they explored the "blogosphere." **OL**

(Chapter Project continued on the Visual Summary page)

entered the country illegally. For most Americans, however, the single most important reason for their frustration with the government was the grim news coming daily from Iraq.

Problems in Iraq Ongoing suicide bombings, kidnappings, and attacks on American soldiers made Americans increasingly anxious about the situation in Iraq. A year earlier, many Americans had taken heart when large numbers of Iraqis had turned out to vote in democratic elections. The establishment of an Iraqi government gave some hope that the feuding sides might begin to work together. But while the Sunni Kurds and Iraqi Shia generally supported the new constitution, it had much less support among Sunni Arabs. Rather than bring peace, the number of sectarian attacks continued to rise after the elections. In February 2006, the bombing of the Shia Golden Mosque in Samarra set Sunni and Shia militias against each other. Iraq seemed poised on the edge of civil war.

The mounting violence led a majority of Americans to conclude they no longer approved of the president's handling of the war. Democrats in Congress demanded that the Bush administration set a timetable for withdrawing U.S. troops, a policy that President Bush described as "cut and run." When Republicans rejected a timetable and supported the president, they turned the congressional elections of 2006 into a referendum on the war.

The Democrats Gain Control of Congress Voters expressed their unhappiness with both the president and the Republican Congress in 2006. The Democrats won a majority in both the House and the Senate for the first time since 1992. House Democrats then elected California Representative **Nancy Pelosi** to be the first female Speaker of the House of Representatives.

When Democrats won control of Congress, President Bush acknowledged that his party had taken a "thumping" in the election. The day after the election, Secretary of Defense Donald Rumsfeld resigned. Rumsfeld had acknowledged that the administration's strategy in Iraq was not working and a change of course was needed. "In my view it is time for a major adjustment," Rumsfeld wrote. "Clearly what U.S. forces are currently doing in Iraq is not working well enough or fast enough."

President Bush chose Robert Gates to replace Rumsfeld and put a new commander—General David Petraeus—in charge of operations in Iraq. The president then announced a new plan to "surge" some 20,000 more troops to Iraq to restore order in Baghdad where most of the violence was concentrated. Led by Nancy Pelosi, and John Murtha—a Vietnam veteran and long-time opponent of the Iraq war—House Democrats passed a resolution opposing the strategy and began searching for ways to force the president to set a deadline for pulling troops out of Iraq. Whether or not the surge could work was unclear, but by the spring of 2007, what was clear was that Americans remained deeply divided over the war in Iraq and that its ultimate outcome remained uncertain.

✓ **Reading Check** **Analyzing** What events in the first two years of Bush's second term contributed to the Republicans losing control of Congress?

Section 4 REVIEW

Vocabulary

1. **Explain** the significance of: Abu Ghraib, Guantanamo Bay, National Security Agency, John G. Roberts, Jr., Samuel Alito, Jr., "earmarks," Nancy Pelosi.

Main Ideas

2. **Identifying** What issues did President Bush support in his reelection campaign? What did Kerry support?

3. **Explaining** What did the Supreme Court declare unlawful with the *Hamdan v. Rumsfeld* ruling?

4. **Describing** How did Bush propose to fix Social Security?

Critical Thinking

5. **Big Ideas** Why did Donald Rumsfeld resign as secretary of defense? Who did Bush choose to replace Rumsfeld?

6. **Organizing** Use a graphic organizer like the one below to list the reasons for Republican losses in the 2006 election.

> Reasons for Republican Losses in 2006
> I. The Election of 2004
> II. Security vs. Liberty
>   A.
>   B.

7. **Analyzing Visuals** Examine the photo on page 821. Why do you think so many people voted in the 2004 election? Do you think voter turnout will remain high?

Writing About History

8. **Persuasive Writing** Write a journal entry describing current events that will be read by students 50 years in the future. Be clear and concise with your description of these events.

History ONLINE
Study Central™ To review this section, go to glencoe.com and click on Study Central.

827

✓ **Reading Check**

Answers:
Dissatisfaction with the Republican administration's handling of the Iraq war and the Katrina emergency, congressional scandals involving Republicans, and conservative disenchantment with some of Bush's domestic agenda

Assess

History ONLINE

Study Central™ provides summaries, interactive games, and online graphic organizers to help students review content.

Close

Evaluating Ask students what they think are the successes and failures of Bush's second term to date. **OL**

Section 4 REVIEW

Answers

1. All definitions can be found in the section and the Glossary.

2. Bush pledged to continue cutting taxes while building a strong national defense. Kerry favored raising taxes on the wealthy to fund wider health care coverage and strengthen social security.

3. the Bush administration's creation of military tribunals to hear detainees' cases

4. Bush proposed that workers be allowed to put some of their income in private accounts for investment use rather than in Social Security.

5. Rumsfeld acknowledged that the administration's Iraq strategy was not working and a change of course was needed.

6. Answers will vary but should include dissatisfaction with the war, anger at Republican scandals in Congress, and unpopular domestic policies.

7. The candidates offered clear-cut choices reflecting the country's conservative-liberal divide and attracted voter interest. Regarding future voter turnout, answers will vary but should reflect an understanding of the deep divide between conservatives and liberals on many issues.

8. Student journals will vary but should use details from the section and reflect understanding of the key issues presented.

Chapter 24 VISUAL SUMMARY

Identifying Main Idea Ask: Why do you think that 9/11 stunned the country? *(Many students will cite the unexpectedness of 9/11, the sheer scale of the destruction, and the knowledge that the United States was opposed and even hated by some people of the world.)* **OL**

Visual Literacy Ask: Look at the four images on the page. How do the images relate to the causes and effects of 9/11? *(The first two images show al-Qaeda leaders and the training of terrorists at special camps. The last two images show the public response to the loss of life in the 9/11 attacks and the involvement of American forces to eliminate terrorism and allow democracy to develop in Afghanistan and Iraq.)*

Causes of the Attacks of 9/11

- The rise of the oil industry in the Middle East makes many elites wealthy but leaves many people poor and resentful.
- The oil trade with Europe and the United States brings Western ideas and culture into the Middle East; many feel their traditional Muslim values are being undermined, and militant Muslim movements form.
- The founding of Israel in 1948 angers many Arabs, especially Palestinians. European and American support for Israel angers many in the Middle East.
- The Soviets invade Afghanistan in 1979; Muslims from across the Middle East, including Osama bin Laden, go to fight the Soviet troops.
- Osama bin Laden forms al-Qaeda to help drive the Soviets out of Afghanistan and all Westerners out of the Middle East.
- Iraq invades Kuwait leading to the deployment of American troops in Saudi Arabia, angering Muslim militants, including Osama bin Laden.
- The Soviet pullout from Afghanistan leads to a militant group, the Taliban, taking power and offering aid and shelter to bin Laden.
- Al-Qaeda, based in Afghanistan, stages a series of attacks on Americans, culminating in the attack on September 11, 2001.

The Taliban let al-Qaeda train at camps in Afghanistan (above). Osama bin Laden and his second in command, Ayman al-Zawahiri (right), often sent taped messages to Arab television networks.

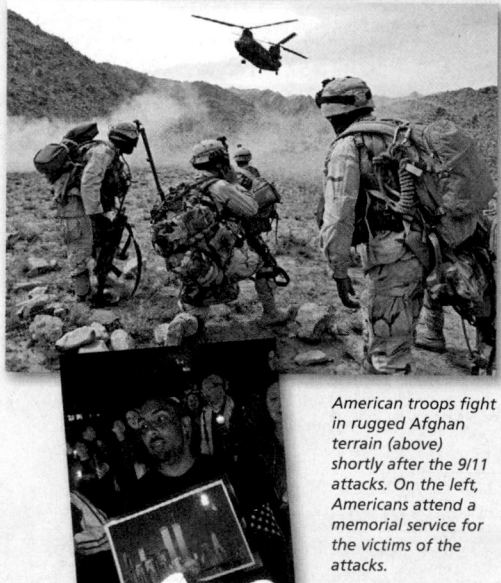

American troops fight in rugged Afghan terrain (above) shortly after the 9/11 attacks. On the left, Americans attend a memorial service for the victims of the attacks.

Effects of the Attacks of 9/11

- Initially, the 9/11 attack unifies Americans and leads to an outpouring of support to the people of New York.
- President Bush declares a global war on terror to put an end to terrorist groups that threaten Americans.
- The United States launches attacks on the Taliban and helps local forces overthrow their regime. NATO troops then enter Afghanistan to serve as peacekeepers.
- Congress passes the Patriot Act giving the FBI additional powers to help prevent another attack in the United States.
- Congress creates the Department of Homeland Security.
- The Bush administration decides that preventing terrorist groups from getting weapons of mass destruction is a high priority.
- The United States, backed by a coalition of allies, invades Iraq to destroy its weapons of mass destruction.
- The invasion of Iraq is controversial; many traditional allies do not support it, and it divides the American people.
- An insurgency begins in Iraq that keeps American troops fighting for several years.

Hands-On Chapter Project
Step 5: Wrap Up

Exploring the "Blogosphere"

Step 5: Wrap Up Students will write an informational essay on blogs.

Directions Direct students to write an essay in which they use what they have learned in Steps 1 through 4 of this project. Student essays should answer the following questions:
- What are blogs?
- What purpose do blogs serve in today's society?
- Are blogs beneficial to American society? Why or why not?
- What other purposes might blogs be used for to benefit society?

Summarizing Students should write and turn in their essays individually, however, you may want to share interesting responses with the entire class. **OL**

STANDARDIZED TEST PRACTICE

TEST-TAKING

If a question involves a table, skim the table before reading the question. Then, read the question and interpret the information from the table.

Review Vocabulary

Directions: Choose the word or words that best complete the sentence.

1. _____ ran for the Green Party in the 2000 presidential election.
   - A Al Gore
   - B Ralph Nader
   - C George W. Bush
   - D Dick Cheney

2. Osama bin Laden heads the terrorist group known as
   - A Al Jazeera.
   - B guerrillas.
   - C Hamas.
   - D al-Qaeda.

3. The majority of Iraq's population is
   - A Shia Muslim.
   - B Sunni Muslim.
   - C Sunni Arabs.
   - D Sunni Kurds.

4. What military base held captured members of al-Qaeda in 2004?
   - A Abu Ghraib
   - B Guantanamo Bay
   - C Pearl Harbor
   - D Geneva

Reviewing Main Ideas

Directions: Choose the best answer for each of the following questions.

Section 1 *(pp. 804–807)*

5. In the 2000 election, Al Gore won
   - A the popular vote.
   - B a majority of electoral votes.
   - C the state of Florida.
   - D a pivotal Supreme Court case.

6. After Bush took office, Congress passed which of the following educational reforms?
   - A federal funding to parents to pay for private schools if their public school was performing poorly
   - B annual standardized testing in reading and math for grades 3–8
   - C prohibiting federally funded schools from discriminating against girls and young women
   - D transporting children to schools outside their neighborhood to achieve a greater racial balance

Section 2 *(pp. 808–813)*

7. After the bombing of American embassies in Kenya and Tanzania, President Clinton
   - A ordered the invasion of Iraq.
   - B created the office of Homeland Security.
   - C ordered the bombing of terrorist camps in Afghanistan.
   - D signed the Patriot Act into law.

Need Extra Help?							
If You Missed Questions . . .	1	2	3	4	5	6	7
Go to Page . . .	805	809	819	822	805	807	811

7. C The bombing of terrorist camps was in response to the embassy bombings. President Bush ordered the invasion of Iraq in the wake of concern that Iraq had WMDs and Iraq's denial of having weapons. The Office of Homeland Security and the Patriot Act were created in response to the September 11 attacks.

Answers and Analyses
Reviewing Vocabulary

1. B Ralph Nader has long been associated with environmentalism. Al Gore was the Democratic candidate. George W. Bush was the Republican Candidate. Dick Cheney was the Republican vice-presidential candidate.

2. D Al Jazeera is a television network in the Middle East. Members of al-Qaeda can be considered to be guerillas, but that is not the name of an organization. Hamas is not headed by bin Laden.

3. A The split between Shia and Sunni Muslims came about after the death of Muhammad. Shia Muslims believed the Muslim leader should be a direct descendent of Muhammad and a religious leader. Sunni Muslims believed the leader could be from Muhammad's tribe and should be a political leader. The majority of Muslims today are Sunni (who are the minority in Iraq).

4. B Abu Ghraib was a former prison, not a military base. Guantanamo Bay in Cuba is a U.S. military base where the captured members of al-Qaeda were held. Pearl Harbor is a naval base in the Pacific. Geneva is a city in Switzerland, not a military base.

Reviewing Main Ideas

5. A This is a good opportunity to review the electoral system with students. Al Gore won the majority of the popular votes, but he did not win the majority of electoral votes. Make sure students understand that some states have more electoral votes than others.

6. B Standardized testing was part of the No Child Left Behind Act. Choice *A* was a reform that President Bush pushed for as part of the education act, but it was rejected by Congress. *C* and *D* are examples of past education reform.

8. B Anthrax was sent through the mail to a number of places, including a newspaper in Florida where one man died. The investigation and contamination shut down several major postal sorting facilities where contaminated mail was suspected or confirmed to have passed through.

9. C Iraq was believed to have WMDs and to be a danger to the U.S. Iraq was not the most vulnerable, nor was it responsible for the September 11 attacks and did not attack the U.S.

10. D Kuwait allowed the U.S. to launch offensives. The other nations were not supportive of the U.S. attacks. Kuwait had been invaded by Iraq in 1990, and the U.S. was instrumental in leading the coalition that expelled Iraq from Kuwait, in Operation Desert Storm.

11. B Students who have trouble remembering this fact will be helped by the map question on this exam, which clearly shows that Bush's support was strongest in the South and the Great Plains.

12. D It is not legal to record phone conversations without a warrant or a ruling from a special court. Thus, the wiretapping was declared unconstitutional. The concern of people who opposed the wiretapping was that it violated civil rights. This is a good opportunity to discuss the issue of civil rights versus national security with students. Tie it in with other suspensions of civil rights during past wars.

Critical Thinking

13. A Discuss the cases in each of the answer choices with students. *A* is correct; the decision resulted in the creation of military tribunals to try the detainees. *C*, *Hamden* v. *Rumsfeld*, struck down the military tribunal plan. *Bush* v. *Gore* dealt with disputed election

830

8. In the fall of 2001, bioterrorists attacked news organizations and political figures with

   A smallpox.

   B anthrax.

   C arsenic.

   D radioactive material.

Section 3 (pp. 814–819)

9. President Bush targeted Iraq, one of the three countries in the "axis of evil," before the other two countries because Iraq

   A was the most vulnerable.

   B was responsible for the September 11 attacks.

   C was believed to pose the most imminent danger to the United States.

   D attacked the United States first.

10. Which country was the only nation bordering Iraq to allow the United States to launch offensives from their territory?

    A Saudi Arabia

    B Turkey

    C Iran

    D Kuwait

Section 4 (pp. 820–827)

11. During the 2004 presidential election, George W. Bush's support was strongest in

    A the Northeast.

    B the South and the Great Plains.

    C the Midwest and Great Lakes.

    D all urban areas.

12. In 2005 the National Security Agency (NSA) expanded its practice of monitoring overseas calls to include domestic calls placed to overseas locations. This resulted in

    A overwhelming public support.

    B the arrest of many terrorists.

    C the NSA director's arrest.

    D a federal court ruling this monitoring unconstitutional.

Need Extra Help?							
If You Missed Questions . . .	8	9	10	11	12	13	14
Go to Page . . .	813	816	818	821	823	822	805

Critical Thinking

Directions: Choose the best answers to the following questions.

13. Which Supreme Court ruling stated that foreign prisoners who claim they were unlawfully imprisoned had the right to have their cases heard in court?

    A *Rasul* v. *Bush*

    B *Bush* v. *Gore*

    C *Hamdan* v. *Rumsfeld*

    D *Gideon* v. *Wainwright*

Base your answer to question 14 on the map below and on your knowledge of Chapter 24.

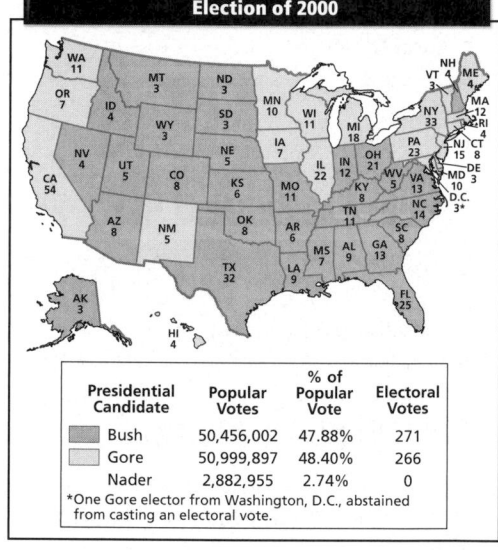

Election of 2000

Presidential Candidate	Popular Votes	% of Popular Vote	Electoral Votes
Bush	50,456,002	47.88%	271
Gore	50,999,897	48.40%	266
Nader	2,882,955	2.74%	0

*One Gore elector from Washington, D.C., abstained from casting an electoral vote.

14. In the election of 2000, George W. Bush won

    A the popular vote.

    B fewer states than Al Gore.

    C a majority of electoral votes.

    D California and New York.

GO ON

results. *Gideon* v. *Wainwright* was decided in 1963. In it, the Court ruled that defendants have the right to a lawyer, and if they cannot afford one, the court should appoint one.

14. C The states that George Bush won are shaded dark gray. Gore's states are light gray. It is clear that Bush won more states. However, the answer can be found in the key/chart that accompanies the map. Bush won 271 electoral votes, and Gore won 266. Therefore, George Bush won the election. Gore won the popular vote and California and New York.

ASSESSMENT

15. Which the following is under the control of the Department of Homeland Security?

   A Central Intelligence Agency (CIA)

   B Defense Intelligence Agency (DIA)

   C Federal Bureau of Investigation (FBI)

   D Federal Emergency Management Agency (FEMA)

Analyze the cartoon and answer the question that follows. Base your answer on the cartoon and your knowledge of Chapter 24.

16. According to the cartoon, what is the artist saying about the 2004 presidential election?

   A The world is excited about another four years with President Bush.

   B The world is disappointed George Bush was reelected.

   C The United States made a mistake reelecting Bush.

   D Kerry was detached from Middle America therefore he lost the election.

17. Why did the United States think stopping the spread of weapons of mass destruction was linked to the war on terror?

   A Saddam Hussein declared an allegiance with al-Qaeda.

   B Bin Laden was believed to be hiding in the mountains of Iraq.

   C Terrorists might buy or steal weapons of mass destruction and use them against the United States.

   D Terrorist groups had already stolen weapons of mass destruction from Iraq.

Document-Based Questions

Directions: Analyze the document and answer the short-answer questions that follow the document.

In October 2001, President Bush signed the highly controversial Patriot Act.

> "If we were to take the position, reflected in provisions in the USA PATRIOT Act, that the government can invade our privacy and gather evidence that can be used against us based on no suspicion whatsoever that we've done anything wrong, but simply because the government wants to gather evidence as part of some generalized, 'anti-terrorism' or 'foreign intelligence' investigation, then we will have rendered that Fourth Amendment principle essentially meaningless."
>
> —Congressman Bob Barr (R-GA),
> "Problems with the USA PATRIOT Act"
>
> "Zero. That's the number of substantiated USA PATRIOT Act civil liberties violations. Extensive congressional oversight found no violations."
>
> —Congressman James Sensenbrenner (R-WI),
> "No rights have been violated"

18. According to Congressman Barr, which constitutional right does the Patriot Act violate and how?

19. What is Congressman Sensenbrenner's response to the accusation that the Patriot Act violates civil rights?

Extended Response

20. The decision to invade Iraq was controversial. Choose to either support a continued U.S. presence in Iraq or immediate troop withdrawal. Write a persuasive essay that includes an introduction and at least three paragraphs that support your position.

STOP

 History ONLINE

For additional test practice, use Self-Check Quizzes—Chapter 24 at glencoe.com.

Need Extra Help?

If You Missed Questions . . .	15	16	17	18	19	20
Go to Page . . .	813	R18	816	R19	R19	826

Document-Based Questions

18. Congressman Barr believes the Patriot Act violates the Fourth Amendment by invading privacy and gathering evidence with no warrant, proof or suspicion of a crime.

19. Congressman Sensenbrenner counters that the Patriot Act does not violate any civil rights and that the congressional committee that investigated it found no violations of civil rights.

Extended Response

20. This is currently a controversial topic. Accept any well-reasoned and reasonable answer. Students' essays should follow the proper format for a persuasive essay and include an acknowledgement and rebuttal of the opposing position.

15. D If students have trouble with this question, review "Homeland Security and Patriot Act" on page 812. It makes sense that FEMA would be under Homeland Security, because the agency would be responsible for helping with rescue and clean up for a domestic disaster.

16. B In the cartoon, the "world" is wearing a suit and watching TV. He is pointing at the TV and looks distraught. His speech bubble says "Oh No!!" On the TV, President Bush is seen holding up his arms making the "V for victory" sign. The world is clearly not happy with the reelection of George W. Bush.

17. C There was no evidence found of an allegiance between Hussein and al-Qaeda. Bin Laden was believed to be hiding in the mountains of Afghanistan. Iraq was not proved to have had WMDs, so *D* is incorrect.

History ONLINE

Have students visit the Web site at glencoe.com to review Chapter 24 and take the Self-Check Quiz.

Need Extra Help?

Have students refer to the pages listed if they miss any of the questions.

Appendix

Contents

Skills Handbook
Table of Contents

Critical Thinking Skills

Social Studies Skills

Teach

. . . .

Introduction

The following **Skills Handbook** offers opportunities to practice individual critical thinking and social studies skills. Students can benefit in multiple ways from completing the lessons. First, being equipped with these skills makes students' reading more meaningful and supports the content of the text. Second, the lessons give students practice in using skills they will need to complete standardized tests successfully since many of these skills are assessed on standardized tests.

You may use these lessons at any point in the text and in any order that you wish. You can also use these lessons as review for students who need extra practice with these skills.

Teach

S Skill Practice

Analyzing Tell students that being able to identify the main idea is a key reading skill whether they are reading fact or fiction. Have students think about a fictional story they have read recently or about a movie they have seen. Have students tell the rest of the class the title of the book or movie and give a two-minute statement that tells what the main idea of the movie or story was. **Ask:** Was the main idea presented at the beginning of the story or did it become apparent at the end of the story? **OL**

Skills Handbook

S

Identifying the Main Idea

Why Learn This Skill?

Finding the main idea in a reading passage will help you see the "big picture" by organizing information and determining the most important concepts to remember.

Migrant mother and children in California, 1936

Learning the Skill

Follow these steps to learn how to make a valid generalization. Then answer the questions below.

2. Skim the material to identify its general subject. Look at headings and subheadings.

In this nation I see tens of millions of its citizens . . . who at this very moment are denied the greater part of what the very lowest standards of today call the necessities of life. I see millions of families trying to live on incomes so meager that the pall of family disaster hangs over them day by day. . . . see one-third of a nation ill-housed, ill-clad, ill-nourished.

3. Notice any details that support a larger idea or issue.

1. Determine the setting of the passage.

It is not in despair that I paint you that picture. I paint it for you in hope—because the Nation, seeing and understanding the injustice in it, proposes to paint it out. We are determined to make every American citizen the subject of his country's interest and concern. . . . The test of our progress is not whether we add more to the abundance of those who have much; it is whether we provide enough for those who have too little.

4. Identify the central issue. Ask: What part of the selection conveys the main idea?

As you read the material, ask yourself: What is the purpose of this passage—why was it written?

—Franklin D. Roosevelt, Second Inaugural Address, January 20, 1937

Practicing the Skill

1. On what occasion was this speech given?

2. When was this speech given?

3. What was the condition of the people mentioned in this passage?

4. What did Roosevelt think should be done about the situation discussed?

Applying the Skill

Bring to class an article about American history from the Internet or another source. Identify the main idea and explain why it is important.

Practicing the Skill: Answers

1. This speech was given by Franklin D. Roosevelt as his Second Inaugural Address.

2. This speech was documented on January 20, 1937.

3. Many citizens are deprived of the basic necessities of human life. They are poor and hungry.

4. Roosevelt proposes that the government (the Nation) help these people.

Determining Cause and Effect

Why Learn This Skill?

Determining cause and effect involves considering *why* an event occurred. That helps you analyze how to encourage or prevent the same event in the future. A *cause* is an action or a situation that produces an event. What happens as a result of a cause is an *effect*.

The effect of pesticides on wildlife

Learning the Skill

To identify cause-and-effect relationships, follow these steps:

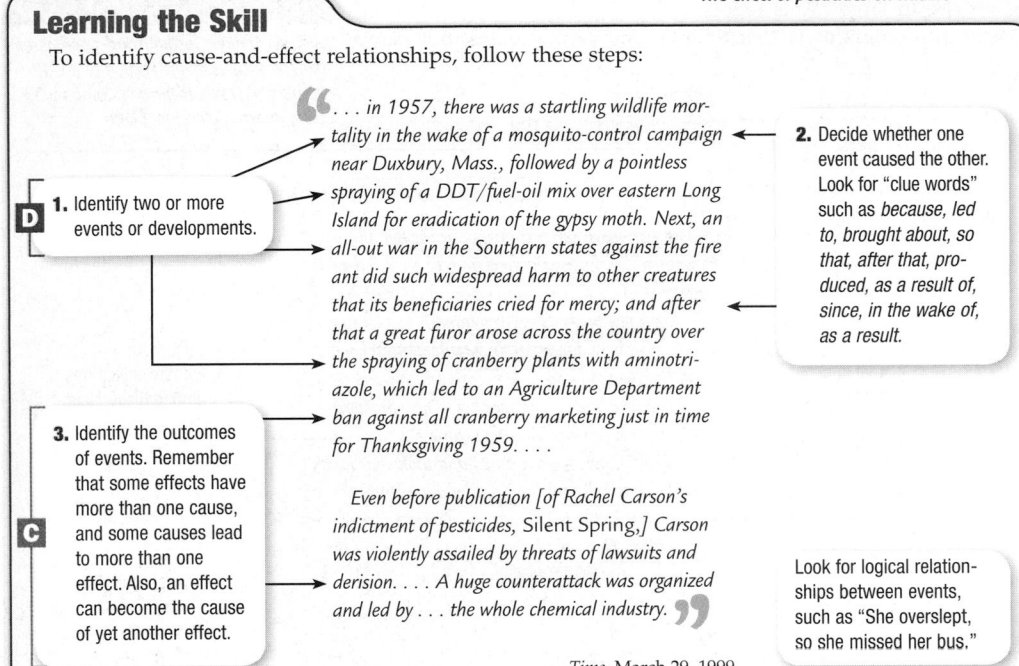

D **1.** Identify two or more events or developments.

" . . . in 1957, there was a startling wildlife mortality in the wake of a mosquito-control campaign near Duxbury, Mass., followed by a pointless spraying of a DDT/fuel-oil mix over eastern Long Island for eradication of the gypsy moth. Next, an all-out war in the Southern states against the fire ant did such widespread harm to other creatures that its beneficiaries cried for mercy; and after that a great furor arose across the country over the spraying of cranberry plants with aminotriazole, which led to an Agriculture Department ban against all cranberry marketing just in time for Thanksgiving 1959. . . .

Even before publication [of Rachel Carson's indictment of pesticides, Silent Spring,*] Carson was violently assailed by threats of lawsuits and derision. . . . A huge counterattack was organized and led by . . . the whole chemical industry.* "

—*Time*, March 29, 1999

2. Decide whether one event caused the other. Look for "clue words" such as *because, led to, brought about, so that, after that, produced, as a result of, since, in the wake of, as a result.*

C **3.** Identify the outcomes of events. Remember that some effects have more than one cause, and some causes lead to more than one effect. Also, an effect can become the cause of yet another effect.

Look for logical relationships between events, such as "She overslept, so she missed her bus."

Practicing the Skill

Categorize the items below as *cause, effect, both,* or *neither.*

1. Rachel Carson published *Silent Spring*, criticizing chemical pesticides.

2. Duxbury's wildlife mortality rate rose significantly in 1957.

3. The gypsy moth is a common insect on Long Island.

4. The Agriculture Department banned cranberry marketing.

5. Southern states used pesticides to eradicate the fire ant.

6. The chemical industry threatened Carson with lawsuits.

Applying the Skill

In a newspaper, read an article describing a current event. Determine at least one cause and one effect of that event, and complete a flowchart like the one below.

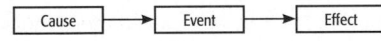

Cause → Event → Effect

Teach

C Critical Thinking

Determining Cause and Effect The statement in item 3 under Learning the Skill states "… an effect can become the cause of yet another effect." This is a cause-and-effect chain. Have students consider such cause-and-effect chains and choose one to research and write about. Tell students that the chain can affect the environment, human population, animal population, or all of the above. Tell them to describe this chain in as much detail as they can. If possible, ask them to create a graphic to illustrate their cause-and-effect chain. **AL**

D Differentiated Instruction

Below Grade Level Ask: What might the effects of the spraying of DDT/fuel-oil mix be? *(The effects could be damage to the population's health, environment, and water systems.)* **BL**

Practicing the Skill: Answers

1. Both
2. Effect
3. Cause
4. Effect
5. Both
6. Effect

R3

Teach

C Critical Thinking

Making Generalizations
Have students research print or online sources to find out more about the roles of women in World War II. Then have them write three paragraphs that make generalizations about women on America's home front during World War II. Ask them to provide evidence from the article to support their generalizations. **OL**

Skills Handbook

Making Generalizations

Why Learn This Skill?

Generalizations are conclusions that are usually accurate, based on the facts at hand. Generalizations are useful in studying history because they help you see trends. If you say, "Most Mexican immigrants to the United States in the early twentieth century worked in agriculture," that's a generalization. To support it, you could mention that federal funding of irrigation projects in the Southwest in 1902 gave rise to large farms requiring thousands of workers. Not all Mexican immigrants at that time became farmworkers, but many did.

Women workers install fixtures and assemblies to a tail fuselage section of a B-17 bomber at Douglas Aircraft Company's, Long Beach, California, plant.

Learning the Skill

To learn how to make a valid generalization, follow these steps:

1. Identify the subject matter.

2. Collect factual information and examples relevant to the topic.

C

The war years had a tremendous impact on women. . . . it was the first time I had a chance to get out of the kitchen and work in industry and make a few bucks. This was something I had never dreamed would happen. In Sapulpa [Oklahoma] all that women had to look forward to was keeping a house and raising families. The war years offered new possibilities. You came out to California, put on your pants and took your lunch pail to a man's job. In Oklahoma a woman's place was in the home, and men went to work and provided. This was the beginning of women's feeling that they could do something more.

—Sybil Lewis,
quoted in *The Homefront: America During World War II*

3. Identify similarities among these facts.

Use these similarities to form some general ideas about the subject.

Practicing the Skill

After reading the excerpt above, determine whether each generalization that follows is valid or invalid. Explain your answers.

1. During World War II, women did not want to work outside the home.

2. Women have careers only so that they can afford luxuries.

3. During the war, women had more choices in California than in Oklahoma.

Applying the Skill

Read three editorials in a newspaper and make a generalization about each.

Practicing the Skill: Answers

1. invalid; Students should note that the excerpt tells of a woman working outside the home for the first time.

2. invalid; There is no information in the excerpt that describes working to afford luxuries.

3. valid; The author compares women's roles in California and Oklahoma in this way.

Distinguishing Fact from Opinion

Why Learn This Skill?

R To make reasonable judgments about what others say or write, it is important to distinguish facts from opinions. Facts can be proved by evidence such as records, documents, or historical sources. Opinions are based on people's differing values and beliefs.

Richard M. Nixon

Learning the Skill

To learn how to separate facts from opinions, follow these steps:

1. Identify the facts. Ask: Which statements can be proved? Where would I find information to verify this statement? If the information is a statistic, it may sound impressive, but you won't know if it's accurate unless you check the source.

❚❚ In speaking of the consequences of a precipitate withdrawal [from Vietnam], I mentioned that our allies would lose confidence in America. Far more dangerous, we would lose confidence in ourselves. . . .

In San Francisco a few weeks ago, I saw demonstrators carrying signs reading: "Lose in Vietnam, bring the boys home."

Well, one of the strengths of our free society is that any American has a right to reach that conclusion and to advocate that point of view. But as President of the United States, I would be untrue to my oath of office if I allowed the policy of this Nation to be dictated by the minority who hold that point of view and who try to impose it on the Nation by mounting demonstrations in the street.

. . . If a vocal minority, however fervent its cause, prevails over reason and the will of the majority, this Nation has no future as a free society. ❚❚

—Richard M. Nixon speech, November 3, 1969

2. Identify opinions by looking for statements of feelings or beliefs. Opinions sometimes contain words like *should, would, could, best, greatest, all, every,* or *always.*

Practicing the Skill

D The excerpt above is from a televised speech given by President Richard M. Nixon in 1969, when a Gallup poll showed that 58 percent of Americans believed the Vietnam War was a mistake. Reread the excerpt and answer the questions that follow.

1. Which statements in the passage are factual?

2. Which statements are opinions? Explain.

3. What was the speaker's purpose?

Applying the Skill

Watch a television interview. Then list three facts and three opinions that you hear.

Teach

R Reading Strategy

Activating Prior Knowledge Have students review the various critical thinking skills they have encountered to determine which skills rely more on facts and which rely on opinion. **Ask:** Which skills utilize facts to form an opinion? *(drawing conclusions, making generalizations, predicting, making inferences)* **AL**

D Differentiated Instruction

Interpersonal Tell students that debates are forums in which facts and opinions are shaped into organized arguments for or against a specific question. Have students work in two groups to gather facts and form opinions about an issue at your school or from your community. Schedule a debate between the two sides. **OL**

Practicing the Skill: Answers

1. The factual statements include:
Demonstrators were carrying signs in San Francisco.
Americans have the right to advocate their point of view.

2. The opinions include:
Our allies would lose confidence in America.
We would lose confidence in ourselves.
He would be untrue to his oath of office.
If a vocal minority prevails, this Nation would not be a free society.

3. Nixon is defending his decision to not withdraw troops from Vietnam.

Teach

Ⓢ Skill Practice

Applying Ask: What do you do when you can't find an answer to your question? *(ask another question)* Have students develop three questions about the critical thinking skill of formulating questions. Tell them to be sure that the questions are not the ones posed in Learning the Skill. The questions should be about asking questions, not about the chart in Practicing the Skill. After students have formed their questions, have them ask the questions for the rest of the class to try to answer. **OL**

Critical Thinking Skills

Formulating Questions

Why Learn This Skill?

Asking questions helps you to understand and remember what you read. Learning increases when you ask yourself what is important about the topic and what you would like to know about the people, places, and events. **S**

Jackie Robinson

Learning the Skill

Follow these steps to formulate questions:

1. Think of questions you would like to have answered.

2. Ask *who, what, when, where, why,* and *how* about the main ideas, people, places, and events.

> *In 1947 life in America . . . was segregation. . . . But Jackie Robinson, God bless him, was bigger than all of that.*
>
> *. . . He had to be bigger than the Brooklyn teammates who got up a petition to keep him off the ball club, bigger than the pitchers who threw at him or the base runners who dug their spikes into his shin, bigger than the bench jockeys who hollered for him to . . . shine their shoes, bigger than the so-called fans who . . . wrote him death threats.*
>
> *. . . Somehow, though, Jackie had the strength to . . . sacrifice his pride for his people's. It was an incredible act of selflessness that brought the races closer together than ever before and shaped the dreams of an entire generation.*

—Henry "Hank" Aaron, holder of major-league career home-run record, *Time*, June 14, 1999

3. Reread the section to be sure all your questions have been answered.

Practicing the Skill

The excerpt above is about the first African American major-league baseball player. After reading it, use a chart like the one below and find the answers in the excerpt.

	Question	Answer
Who?		
What?		
Where?		
When?		
Why?		
How?		

Applying the Skill

Select any section of this textbook to read or reread. Make a question chart to help you ask and answer five or more questions about the section as you read.

Practicing the Skill: Answers

	Question	Answer
Who?	Who is the excerpt about?	Jackie Robinson
What?	What is the main idea of the excerpt?	Jackie overcoming racism
Where?	Where did these events take place?	Jackie played baseball in Brooklyn.
When?	When did the events take place?	1947

Why?	Why did Jackie choose to do this?	He chose to withstand the difficulties to uphold his race and dignity.
How?	How did Jackie overcome segregation?	He had the strength to withstand all those people who threatened and attempted to keep him from playing.

Analyzing Information

Why Learn This Skill?

The ability to analyze information is important in deciding what you think about a subject. For example, you need to analyze the benefits of social services versus the benefits of small government to decide where you stand on the issue of Social Security.

Gloria Steinem (right) with Adelaide Abankwah, a Ghanian asylum-seeker, in 1999

Teach

S Skill Practice

Analyzing Tell students that the Learning the Skill section talks about social issues. Have students work in groups to research issues in various parts of the United States. As students identify an area to be researched, have them analyze the information they find on that area. Tell students to document their research and share it with the class. As students present their research, plot the information on a U.S. map. **Ask:** Does your collective research show that this is a growing problem? **OL**

Learning the Skill

To analyze information, use the following steps:

1. Identify the topic being discussed.

Having spent most of my adult life in social justice movements—from living in post-Gandhian India to working in the civil rights, farm worker and peace movements here, and most of all, in the feminist movement—I've seen constant proof that revolutions are like houses: They can't be built from the top down. Leaders can issue blueprints, which we then adapt to our needs or quietly sabotage. They can prevent us from following our own plan, divide the work force against itself and otherwise slow or stop progress. But what they can't do is create organic and lasting change from the top. Attempts to do so, even in the most authoritarian of systems, eventually end in reversion to old ways, as we see in the countries where Communism and artificial national boundaries were once imposed by Moscow.

—Gloria Steinem, from *The Nation*, July 20–27, 1992

2. Examine how the information is organized. What are the main points?

3. Summarize the information in your own words, and then make a statement of your own based on your understanding of the topic and on what you already know.

W Writing Support

Persuasive Writing Have students write a one-page persuasive argument for or against the need to prevent global warming. **OL**

Practicing the Skill

After reading the excerpt above, answer the following questions:

1. What topic is being discussed?

2. What are the writer's main points?

3. Summarize the information in this excerpt, and then provide your analysis, based on this information and what you already know about the subject.

Applying the Skill

Select an issue that is currently in the news, such as Social Security, oil prices, global warming, or taxation. Read an article or watch a news segment about the issue. Analyze the information and make a brief statement of your own about the topic. Explain your thinking.

Practicing the Skill: Answers

1. social justice movements and how they arise

2. Revolutions cannot be started by governments, they need to be started by people.

3. Students' summaries should include the idea that governments cannot produce lasting change. It must be a grassroots movement. Students' analyses will vary.

Teach

C Critical Thinking

Evaluating a Web Site Point out that virtually anyone can create and post a Web page. There are hosting sites that allow individuals to post Web pages at no charge. This means that when you search for Jimmy Carter, it is likely that your results will include authoritative sites with content developed by historians and a site that showcases a child's third-grade homework assignment. Ask students to search for Web sites about a topic or person in American history. Have students find a site that they consider authoritative. Have them print out the home page of the site and write a brief explanation of why they rate the site as authoritative.
OL

Evaluating Information

Why Learn This Skill?

We live in an information age. Because the amount of information available can be overwhelming, it is sometimes **C** difficult to tell which information is accurate and useful. To do this, you have to evaluate what you read and hear.

Soaring gas prices in the early 2000s frustrated consumers.

Learning the Skill

To figure out how reliable information is, ask yourself the following questions as you read:

The single biggest factor in . . . the increase in the inflation rate last year was from one cause: the skyrocketing prices of OPEC oil. We must take whatever actions are necessary to reduce our dependence on foreign oil—and at the same time reduce inflation.

—former president Jimmy Carter, January 23, 1980

Oil prices are so high, becuz big oil companys are tryng to goug us. Greedy oil executives, are driven up prices to get richer.

—on an individual's Internet "blog"

It's certainly clear that high oil prices aren't dulling demand for energy products. According to the Energy Dept.'s Energy Information Administration (EIA), U.S. demand for gasoline in June was 9.5 million barrels per day, a record.

—*BusinessWeek,* July 7, 2006

1. Is the author or speaker identified? Is he or she an authority on the subject?

2. Is there bias? Does the source unfairly present just one point of view, ignoring any arguments against it?

3. Is the information printed in a credible, reliable publication?

4. Is the information backed up by facts and other sources? Does it seem to be accurate?

5. Is it well written and well edited? Writing filled with errors in spelling, grammar, and punctuation is likely to be careless in other ways, too.

Also notice whether the information is up-to-date.

Practicing the Skill

After reading the statements above, rank them in order of most reliable to least reliable. Explain why you ranked them as you did.

Applying the Skill

Find an advertisement that contains text and bring it to class. In a brief oral presentation, tell the class whether the information in the advertisement is reliable or unreliable, and why.

Practicing the Skill: Answers

1. Students' rankings will vary. Students should be prepared to provide reasons for their rankings.

Making Inferences

Why Learn This Skill?

To *infer* means to evaluate information and arrive at a conclusion. When you make inferences, you "read between the lines," or use clues to figure something out that is not stated directly in the text.

Men read posters at an office of the National Association Opposed to Woman Suffrage.

Learning the Skill

Follow these steps to make inferences:

1. Read carefully for facts and ideas, and list them.

" *Because the suffrage is not a question of right or of justice, but of policy and expediency. . . .*

. . . Because it means simply doubling the vote, and especially the undesirable and corrupt vote of our large cities.

. . . Because the great advance of women in the last century—moral, intellectual and economic—has been made without the vote; which goes to prove that it is not needed for their further advancement along the same lines.

. . . Because our present duties fill up the whole measure of our time and ability, and are such as none but us can perform. Our appreciation of their importance requires us to protest against all efforts to infringe upon our rights by imposing upon us those obligations which can not be . . . performed by us without the sacrifice of the highest interests of our families and our society. "

—from Northern California Association Opposed to Woman Suffrage, 1912

2. Summarize the information.

3. Consider what you may already know about the topic.

4. Use your knowledge and insight to develop logical conclusions.

Practicing the Skill

After reading the statement above, answer the following questions:

1. What points do the authors make?

2. Which points does your experience contradict?

3. What inferences might you draw about the women who wrote the document?

> **Applying the Skill**
>
> **S** Read an editorial printed in today's newspaper. What can you infer about the importance of the topic being addressed? Can you tell how the writer feels about the topic? Explain your answer.

Teach

S Skill Practice

Applying Bring in a copy of a front page of a daily newspaper to class. Put the front page up on the board and have students study it from their seats. Most students will not be able to read more than the headlines of the paper. Have students write a page of inferences they make based on what they can see. After students have had a chance to note their inferences, have them share them with the class. **Ask:** What does this exercise tell you about inferences? *(that much of what a person infers is dependent upon prior knowledge and facts at hand)*

Practicing the Skill: Answers

1. Students should include the following:
Suffrage is not a right.
Woman suffrage would just double the vote.
Women have advanced without suffrage.
Women are too busy to vote.

2. Student answers will vary, but many students will understand that voting is a right and that it enables progress to be made.

3. Students should infer that the authors did not want suffrage, instead seeing it as an unnecessary obligation.

Teach

S **Skill Practice**

Analyzing After students have read the lesson and engaged in practicing the skill, have them study the images on the page. Working with partners, have the students compare and contrast the two images. Possible comparisons include content, topic, style, and colors. As students begin to accumulate data that reflects similarities and differences, have them create a chart or graph that clearly shows their findings. **OL**

Critical Thinking Skills

Comparing and Contrasting

Why Learn This Skill?

When you make comparisons, you determine similarities among ideas, objects, or events. When you contrast, you are noting differences between ideas, objects, or events. Comparing and contrasting are important skills because they help you choose among several possible alternatives.

Learning the Skill

To compare or contrast items, follow these steps:

1. Select the items to compare or contrast.

2. To compare, determine a common area or areas in which comparisons can be drawn, such as topic, style, or point of view. Look for similarities within these areas.

3. To contrast, look for differences that set the items apart from each other.

Practicing the Skill

After studying the paintings above, answer these questions:

1. How are the paintings similar?

2. How are they different?

3. What do the answers to questions 1 and 2 tell you about the two artists' attitudes toward their subject?

Applying the Skill

Survey 10 of your classmates about an issue in the news, and summarize their responses. Then write a paragraph or two comparing and contrasting their opinions.

Practicing the Skill: Answers

1. Students may mention that they are both paintings depicting people.

2. Students should note that the styles are different. Whereas one is realistic, the other is contemporary.

3. Answers will vary. Students should note that whereas the first artist shows a very noble and serious style, the other takes a more abstract approach.

Detecting Bias

Why Learn This Skill?

Most people have a point of view, or bias. This bias influences the way they interpret and write about events and issues.

A politician running for reelection, for example, may claim the economy is strong because 20,000 new jobs were created last month. His or her opponent may say the economy is weak because 40,000 people also lost jobs last month. Recognizing bias helps you judge the accuracy of what you hear or read.

Southerners seize abolitionist literature from a local post office in South Carolina in the 1840s.

Learning the Skill

To recognize bias, follow these steps:

1. Consider the author's identity, location, and motivation. Does the writer or a group he or she represents benefit from an outcome supported in the article?

2. Identify statements of fact, if any.

The great conservative institution of slavery, so excellent in itself, and so necessary to civil liberty and the dignity of the white race, is one of the grand objects of our struggle. It should never be lost sight of, nor under any pressure should we ever take any step incompatible with the relation of master and slave. . . . Our theory is, that he is better off as a slave; and even if he were not, we could not safely have an emancipated class of them amongst us. Much less can we put arms in his hands. . . . Slavery afterwards would become impossible.

—Editorial from the Washington, Arkansas, *Telegraph*, January 13, 1865

3. Identify any expressions of opinion or emotion. Look for words with positive or negative overtones for clues about the author's feelings on a topic.

4. Determine the author's point of view.

5. Notice how the author's point of view is reflected in the work.

Practicing the Skill

Read the passage above and then answer the following questions:

1. What is the purpose of this passage?

2. What statements of fact and/or opinion are presented?

3. What evidence of bias do you find?

4. How does the author attempt to convince the audience?

Applying the Skill

C Find an editorial in the newspaper that deals with a topic of interest to you. Apply the steps for recognizing bias to the editorial. Write a paragraph summarizing your findings.

Teach

C Critical Thinking

Detecting Bias Ask students to find letters to the editor on the editorial page of the newspaper they employ in Applying the Skill. Have students continue their exercise from Applying the Skill to these letters. Have students write a sentence or two summarizing the bias of the writer. **Ask:** Do any of the letters conflict with each other? Do any of the letters conflict with the opinions of the newspaper? *(Answers will vary.)* **AL**

Practicing the Skill: Answers

1. The purpose is to support the institution of slavery.

2. Many opinions are presented—that African Americans are better off as slaves, they cannot live free safely, that we cannot arm them.

3. Students should note that the author sees only one side of slavery.

4. The author uses arguments to justify slavery because, he or she says, it is a better state for African Americans.

Teach

S Skill Practice

Synthesizing Tell students to research the situation in Vietnam starting in the 1960s, apply the critical thinking skill of synthesizing information, and report on what their conclusions are. **Ask:** What are your sources? What did your sources add to your understanding of the situation? What are your conclusions based on your synthesis of information? (Answers will vary.) **OL**

W Writing Support

Personal Have students write a one-page statement that expresses their personal conclusion about the war in Vietnam based on the information they read. Tell them to be sure and support their conclusion with facts. **OL**

Critical Thinking Skills

Synthesizing Information

Why Learn This Skill?

Synthesizing information involves combining information from two or more sources. Each source may shed new light on other information.

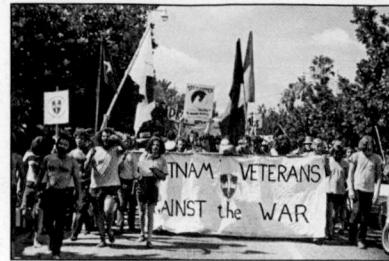

Antiwar rally, Miami Beach, Florida, 1972

Learning the Skill

Follow these steps to learn how to synthesize information:

1. Analyze each source separately to understand its meaning.

2. Determine what information and whose perspective each source adds to the subject.

Source A *We should declare war on North Vietnam. . . . It's silly talking about how many years we will have to spend in the jungles of Vietnam when we could pave the whole country and put parking stripes on it and still be home for Christmas.*

—future president Ronald Reagan, 1965

Source B *Vietnam presumably taught us that the United States could not serve as the world's policeman; it should also have taught us the dangers of trying to be the world's midwife to democracy when the birth is scheduled to take place under conditions of guerrilla war.*

—Jeane Kirkpatrick, future UN ambassador and foreign policy adviser to Ronald Reagan, 1979

Source C *People say we could have won the [Vietnam] war—we know we could not. People say the anti-war movement harassed and betrayed the soldiers . . . the people who supported the war, the folks who favored intervention, the people who sent us crusading against communism—they betrayed us, their own sons and daughters. Anti-war veterans are the witnesses against them . . . we saw the system was not working, we knew the war had to stop.*

—Ben Chitty, member Vietnam Veterans Against the War, April, 2000

3. Identify points of agreement and disagreement among the sources. Ask: Can Source B or C give me new ways of thinking about Source A?

4. Determine how the sources relate to each other.

Practicing the Skill

After reading the passages above, answer the questions that follow.

1. What is the main subject of each source?

2. Does Source B support or contradict Source A? Does Source C support or contradict source A? Explain.

3. Summarize what you learned from the three sources.

4. Which source do you consider the most reliable? Explain why.

Applying the Skill

Find two sources of information on any period of history that interests you. What are the main ideas in the sources? How does each source add to your understanding of the topic?

Practicing the Skill: Answers

1. the Vietnam War

2. Source B contradicts Source A. Whereas Source A states that the war in Vietnam will be quick and easy, Source B refers to the dangers of the war. Source C contradicts Source A. Source C states that the war was not easy; we could not have won it.

3. Answers will vary, but students should conclude that there are many opinions about the war in Vietnam.

4. Students should support their opinions. Be sure that students note the sources of each excerpt.

Drawing Conclusions

Why Learn This Skill?

D₁ A conclusion is a logical understanding that you reach based on details or facts that you read or hear. When you draw conclusions, you use stated information to formulate ideas that are unstated.

Victorian-era house for sale

D₂ Learning the Skill

Follow these steps to draw conclusions:

1. Read the text and labels carefully, looking for facts and ideas.

2. Summarize the information. List trends or important facts.

Homeownership in the U.S.,1890–2005

Post World War II Boom   Declining Real Wages
Great Depression   High Inflation
Roaring '20s
Earliest Data   Highest Immigration

Percentage (y-axis: 0, 10, 20, 30, 40, 50, 60, 70)

Year (x-axis: 1890 1900 1910 1920 1930 1940 1950 1960 1970 1980 1990 1995 2000 2005)

Source: U.S. Bureau of the Census; U.S. Department of Commerce

3. Apply related information that you may already have.

4. Use your knowledge and insight to develop some logical conclusions.

Practicing the Skill

The bar graph above shows the percentage of Americans who owned their own homes during various time periods. Study the graph and answer the following questions:

1. When was the home ownership rate the lowest? Why do you think this was so?

2. During what 20-year period did home ownership rates increase the most? Why do you think this happened?

3. What conclusions can you draw about trends in home ownership?

Applying the Skill

Read one of the People in History profiles in this book. Using the information in the profile, what conclusions can you draw about the life of the person described?

Teach

D₁ Differentiated Instruction

Interpersonal Tell students that people draw conclusions all the time. Ask students to write down three facts (real or hypothetical) about themselves—such as "I've always had pets; I enjoy science; I want to work with animals"—and read them aloud to the class. See if classmates can draw the correct conclusions from the facts provided. **OL**

D₂ Differentiated Instruction

Logical/Mathematical Ask students to research a measurable trend in the United States, then have them explain the topic in terms of numbers and percentages. **Ask:** How can numbers support the conclusion? **OL**

Practicing the Skill: Answers

1. 1940; few people owned homes during this era of the Great Depression.

2. Home ownership increased the most between 1940 and 1950 as Americans moved out of the Depression and to an age of prosperity in the post-war boom.

3. Home ownership increases in times of prosperity.

Teach

C Critical Thinking

Activating Prior Knowledge
Explain to students that predictions are not based on random guesses. Instead, they are based on extending knowledge of facts, events, reactions, patterns, and trends to new circumstances. Ask students to offer examples of how this skill is used in business, government, and personal situations. *(Students' answers will vary. For example, a business has to predict consumer behavior before a product is launched.)* **BL**

Critical Thinking Skills

Skills Handbook

Predicting Consequences

Why Learn This Skill?

Predicting most future events is difficult, but the more information you have, the more accurate your predictions will be. Making good predictions will help you to make better decisions based on their likely outcomes. Using these skills can also help you to understand the outcomes of historical events. **C**

Lois Gibbs

Learning the Skill

To help you make predictions, follow these steps:

1. Gather information about the topic.

2. Use your experience and your knowledge of history and human behavior to predict what consequences could result.

3. Analyze each consequence by asking yourself: How likely is it that this will happen?

> *In the mid-1950s, the Niagara Falls board of education built an elementary school adjacent to a site where Hooker Chemical and Plastics Corporation had dumped more than 22,000 tons of toxic waste. Housing also was built next to the landfill, called Love Canal. Chemicals leached out of the landfill and, by 1976, had shown up in yards and basements.*
>
> *Residents were frequently sick and eventually were found to have extremely high rates of cancer, birth defects, miscarriages, and stillborns. In 1978 Lois Gibbs and other residents began a 3-year battle against Hooker and many levels of government, which claimed the health issues were not related to the chemicals.*
>
> *By 1980, President Jimmy Carter declared Love Canal a federal emergency and more than 1,000 families were relocated and paid for their homes. The tragedy led to "Superfund" legislation that collects taxes from gas and chemical companies, to be used to clean up similar sites.*

Practicing the Skill

1. Do you think the problem described in the passage is likely to reoccur elsewhere?

2. On what do you base your prediction?

3. What are the possible benefits and drawbacks of the "Superfund" legislation described in the passage?

Applying the Skill

Analyze three newspaper articles about an event affecting your community or the nation. Make an educated prediction about what will happen, and explain your reasoning. Then write a letter to the editor, summarizing your prediction. You may want to check back later to see if your prediction came true.

R14 Skills Handbook

Practicing the Skill: Answers

1. Students should recognize that the problem could occur in other places if companies have dumped waste.

2. Students should base their prediction on the cause and effects given in the excerpts and knowledge that some companies produce toxic waste.

3. Students may note the benefits are penalties to companies for dumping waste, which may prevent this practice from occurring in the future. Drawbacks are that if companies can afford the penalties, they may continue the practice.

Reading a Special-Purpose Map

Why Learn This Skill?

Special-purpose maps show more than the location of places. They are useful because they show trends or movements of people or things in a concise, visual way.

Learning the Skill

To read a special-purpose map, follow these steps:

1. Read the title to see what topic is illustrated. If the time period being covered is part of the title, notice that.

2. Read the legend and any other text.

3. Notice the movement shown on the map, if any, including the direction of any arrows, where paths lead, or the concentration of several things in certain places.

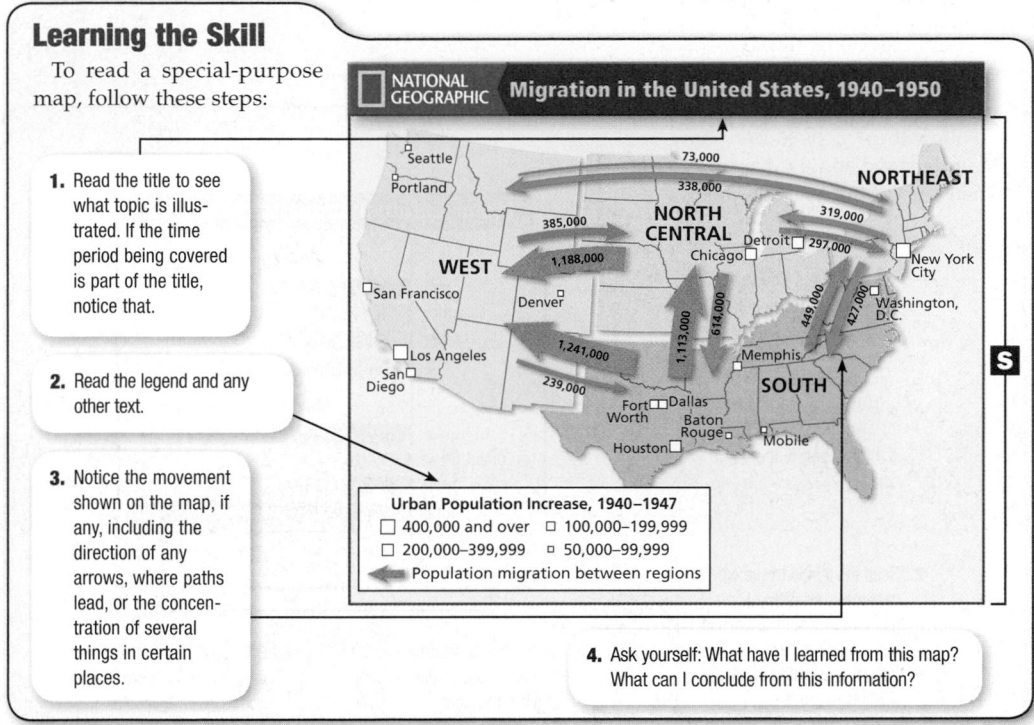

NATIONAL GEOGRAPHIC **Migration in the United States, 1940–1950**

Urban Population Increase, 1940–1947
☐ 400,000 and over   ☐ 100,000–199,999
☐ 200,000–399,999   ☐ 50,000–99,999
⬅ Population migration between regions

4. Ask yourself: What have I learned from this map? What can I conclude from this information?

Practicing the Skill

Answer the following questions about the map above:

1. What period in history does the map cover?

2. Was the U.S. population fairly mobile or stationary during this time?

3. Name two cities that gained 400,000 or more residents.

4. From what part of the country did most immigrants to the West come?

Applying the Skill

Study the map on page 399. Then answer these questions:

1. Name three states through which Chief Joseph traveled in 1877.

2. What part of the country had the largest number of reservations at this time?

3. What does the map tell you about the compromises Native Americans made to the settlers?

Teach

S Skill Practice

Using a Map Looking at a map allows the user to see the big picture, including the physical relationship of the various areas depicted. To take advantage of seeing the big picture, it is important for students to understand the parts of the map. Have students describe what trend this map is showing. *(migration in the United States from 1940 to 1950)*
OL

Practicing the Skill: Answers

1. 1940–1950
2. The U.S. population was mobile at this time.
3. Los Angeles and New York City
4. the South

Teach

S Skill Practice

Applying Have students research the ethnic makeup of their community based on the most recent census. Then, have them show that makeup in the form of a graph of their choosing. **OL**

W Writing Support

Expository After students have developed their graph that shows the ethnic makeup of their community, have them write a one-page expository paper that explains and interprets the graph, its results, and how the data was collected. **AL**

Social Studies Skills

Interpreting Graphs

Bar graphs are often used to compare quantities. By presenting similar categories of information visually, often on a grid, they make it easy to see the relationships among the categories. **S**

Why Learn This Skill?

Being able to read bar graphs makes it easy to understand and analyze data quickly.

Learning the Skill

Follow these steps to learn how to understand and use bar graphs. Then answer the questions below.

1. Read the title to see what topic is being illustrated. Notice whether the period of time covered or other information is included within or just below the title.

2. Read the labels to see what categories are being compared, and what measure is being used; for example, dollars, thousands of people, bushels of grain, etc.

3. Notice the numbers that correlate to the ends of the bars.

4. Compare the lengths of the bars and draw a conclusion about the relationships being shown.

Major Colonial Exports, 1768–1772

New England

	Value (pounds sterling)
Fish	£152,154
Livestock	£73,432
Other	£213,419
Total	£439,005

Middle Colonies

	Value (pounds sterling)
Grain	£381,284
Bread, Meat	£16,726
Other	£127,748
Total	£525,759

Source: *Shipping, Maritime Trade and the Economic Development of Colonial America.*

Practicing the Skill

1. What is the topic of this bar graph?

2. In what currency does the graph measure the products?

3. Which type of exports were the least valuable?

4. If you were going into the export business in 1770, which product would you want to export? Why?

Applying the Skill

Ask five students what their favorite food is. Then create a bar graph showing which foods are the most popular. **W**

Practicing the Skill: Answers

1. major colonial exports from 1768 to 1772
2. British pounds
3. bread and meat
4. grain, because it has the highest value

Sequencing Events

Why Learn This Skill?

Sequencing involves placing facts in the order in which they occurred. Sequencing helps you deal with large quantities of information in an understandable way. In studying history, sequencing can help you understand cause-and-effect relationships among events. This in turn helps analysts to predict outcomes of various events or policies.

John Wilkes Booth escaping Ford's Theatre after shooting President Lincoln

Learning the Skill

To sequence events, follow these steps:

1. Look for dates or clue words: *in 1920, later that year, first, then,* and so on.

2. Arrange facts in the order in which they occurred. Events are not always presented in sequential order. Ask: Would this logically have happened next?

Consider using an organizational tool such as a time line, which makes it easy to see the chronology as well as any cause-and-effect relationships between events.

> This evening [April 14] at about 9:30 P.M., at Ford's Theatre, the President, while sitting in the private box with Mrs. Lincoln . . . was shot by an assassin, who suddenly entered the box and approached behind the President.
>
> The assassin then leaped upon the stage brandishing a large dagger or knife, and made his escape in the rear of the theatre.
>
> . . . It is not probable that the President will live through the night.
>
> . . . Gen. Grant and wife were advertised to be at the theatre this evening, but he started to Burlington at six o'clock this evening.
>
> At a Cabinet meeting, at which Gen. Grant was present, the subject of the state of the country and the prospect of a speedy peace was discussed. The President was very cheerful and hopeful, and spoke very kindly of Gen. Lee and others of the confederacy.

–War Department statement of April 14, 1865, printed in *New York Times*, April 15

Practicing the Skill

Read the passage above and answer the questions that follow.

1. What dates or clue words in this passage help you determine the sequence of the events?

2. Complete a time line such as the one at right to show the sequence of events described in the selection.

Applying the Skill

Find a newspaper or magazine article about a recent event. Sequence the information presented in the article in a time line or chart.

First Event   Final Event

Teach

C Critical Thinking

Sequencing This skill emphasizes the importance of chronological thinking to the study of history. By learning to put things in chronological order, students gain an appreciation for relationships among events. Have students choose several events that occurred in the 1900s. Ask them to write the events down, and then place them in the correct sequence on a time line. **OL**

Practicing the Skill: Answers

1. April 14, around 9:30 PM, then, this evening, six o'clock this evening

2. Students' time lines should show the following sequence of events:

First Event: Cabinet meeting

Second Event: General Grant and his wife started to Burlington

Third Event: President shot

Final Event: Assassin escaped; President not thought to live

Teach

C Critical Thinking

Interpreting Tell students that political cartoons have long been used as an effective means of expressing opinions about events, laws, and political figures. Bring several current political cartoons from local or national newspapers to class. Ask students to identify and interpret the caricatures and symbols used in the cartoons. Have students write a sentence summarizing the point being made by each of the political cartoonists. **OL**

Interpreting Political Cartoons

Why Learn This Skill?

Political cartoons are drawings that express an opinion about public figures, political issues, or economic or social conditions. They appear in newspapers, magazines, books, and on the Internet. They are **C** intended to convince readers of the artist's or the publication's opinion in an amusing way. Knowing how to interpret a political cartoon is useful because it helps you put issues and candidates in perspective.

Learning the Skill

To interpret a political cartoon, follow these steps:

1. Read the title, caption, conversation balloons, and other text to identify the subject of the cartoon.

2. Identify the characters, people, or symbols shown.

3. Ask yourself: What action is occurring? Who is taking the action?

4. Determine the cartoonist's purpose: is it to persuade, criticize, or just make people think? What idea is the cartoonist trying to get across?

5. Ask yourself whether the publication or the cartoonist has a bias that is being expressed in the cartoon.

Practicing the Skill

Study the cartoon. Then use the cartoon and your knowledge of history to answer the questions that follow.

1. What is the topic of the cartoon?

2. Who are the participants, and what are they doing?

3. What point do you think the cartoonist is trying to make? Is the cartoon relevant to any of today's political issues?

Applying the Skill

Bring a newspaper or magazine to class. With a partner, analyze the message and detect any bias in the cartoons you find.

Practicing the Skill: Answers

1. separation of powers between the three branches of government

2. Congress is requesting FBI help from the executive branch (President Truman)

3. Students should note that Congress is overstepping its boundaries by stepping on the executive branch's territory. The separation of powers is an issue that is relevant today.

Analyzing Primary Sources

Why Learn This Skill?

C To determine what happened in the past, historians do some detective work. They comb through bits of written and illustrated evidence from the past to reconstruct events. These bits of evidence are called "primary sources." They include letters, diaries, photographs, newspaper articles, ads, and legal documents.

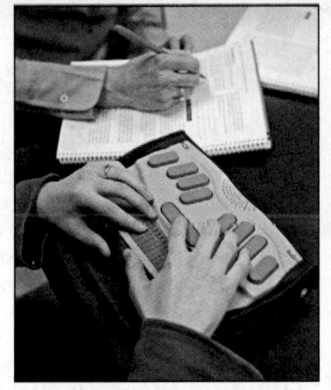

A blind student using a device to take notes in Braille

Learning the Skill

Primary sources yield several important types of information. They often provide details of events or personal perspectives. But remember: any source reflects only one perspective. Before drawing any conclusions, you should examine as many perspectives as possible. To analyze primary sources, follow these steps:

1. Identify the author, the publication, or the document.

2. Determine when and where the document was written or illustrated.

> *No person in the United States shall, on the ground of blindness or severely impaired vision, be denied admission in any course of study by a recipient of Federal financial assistance for any education program or activity; but nothing herein shall be construed to require any such institution to provide any special services to such person because of his blindness or visual impairment.*
>
> —United States Code, Title IX, Education Amendments of 1972

3. Read the document or study the illustration for its content. Try to answer the five "W" questions: Whom is it about? What is it about? When did it happen? Where did it happen? Why did it happen?

Practicing the Skill

The primary source above is a small part of a United States legal document. Read the source and then answer these questions:

1. When was the document written?
2. Who is affected by this document?
3. What is the purpose of this document?
4. Why do you think this document was written?

Applying the Skill

D Find a primary source from your past, such as a photo, a report card, an old newspaper clipping, or your first baseball card. Bring the source to class and explain what it shows about that time in your life.

Teach

C Critical Thinking

Analyzing Primary Sources
Have students use a newspaper or other periodical to identify a current event or news story. After they have identified this news item, have them use an Internet search engine and type in the event. Tell students to choose five entries from the first results page and evaluate the entries for usefulness as primary sources. As the students evaluate their entries, have them keep notes and report to the class what their findings were. **OL**

D Differentiated Instruction

Intrapersonal To help students understand the factor of perspective when reading primary sources, ask students to recall an event in their lives. **Ask:** Would you be able to give a full account of that event to another person? Would someone else give a different account of the event? **BL**

Practicing the Skill: Answers

1. 1972
2. persons in the United States who are blind or have severely impaired vision
3. This document explains legislation enabling persons who are blind to attend universities without discrimination.
4. to halt discrimination

Teach

C Critical Thinking

Analyzing When researching a topic, recommend that students use several secondary sources in order to evaluate all aspects of the topic and to identify various writers' points of view. Assign students various passages from this book. Have students identify the portions of the information that are primary sources and which are secondary sources. Have volunteers share their findings with the class. **OL**

Social Studies Skills

Analyzing Secondary Sources

Why Learn This Skill?

This textbook, like many other history books, is a secondary source. It was written by using primary sources to explain the topics covered. The value of a secondary source depends on how well the author has used those primary sources. Learning to analyze secondary sources will help you figure out whether they are presenting topics completely and accurately.

Painting of Mark Twain by John White

Learning the Skill

Read the passage to the right, which discusses the controversy over the United States's occupation of the Philippines after the Spanish-American War. To analyze secondary sources, ask yourself these questions:

1. Are there references to primary sources in the text? Who are the sources?

2. What insights or biases might these people have?

3. Does the author use the sources effectively to support his or her points?

4. Does the author consider different kinds of sources? Do they represent varying viewpoints?

" . . . [The anti-imperialists] denounced the extension of American rule by force in the Philippines, not because of what it might do to the Filipinos, but because of what they were convinced it was bound to do to American democratic ideals. They saw in the American seizure and retention of the Islands 'the infamy of the doctrine that a people may be governed without their consent.'. . .

. . . The expansionists' reply . . . was the twin slogan: duty and destiny. . . . In the words of the archexpansionist Theodore Roosevelt: 'Peace cannot be had until the civilized nations have expanded in some shape over the barbarous nations.'

. . . Mark Twain was one literary figure who was won over . . . 'I left these shores at Vancouver,' he wrote, 'a red-hot imperialist. I wanted the American eagle to go screaming into the Pacific. . . . Why not spread its wings over the Philippines, I asked myself? . . .' But . . . in 1900 he wrote to Joseph Twichell: 'Apparently we are not proposing to set the Filipinos free and give their islands to them. . . . If these things are so, the war out there has no interest for me.' "

—Harold A. Larrabee, in *Historical Viewpoints*

Practicing the Skill

1. What primary sources does the author use?
2. Does the author cite where the quotations he used first appeared?
3. How reliable do you think these sources are?
4. Which source do you agree with?

Applying the Skill

In a newspaper or online, read an in-depth article about a topic that interests you. Then list the primary sources the article uses and analyze how reliable you think they are.

Practicing the Skill: Answers

1. The author uses writings by Mark Twain and Theodore Roosevelt.
2. No, he does not cite the sources.
3. Students should find that the sources are reliable. They can be verified.
4. Answers should be supported.

Foldables

FOLDABLES **Dinah Zike's Foldables** are three-dimensional, interactive graphic organizers used to help organize and retain information. Every chapter in your text uses a Foldable to help you identify and learn about the Big Ideas discussed in each section. The following pages provide complete folding instructions for the 14 different Foldables used throughout your Student Edition text.

Table of Contents

Basic Foldable Shapes

Taco Fold

Hamburger Fold

Hot Dog Fold

Burrito Fold

Shutter Fold

Valley Fold

Mountain Fold

Foldables

Accordion Book

NOTE: *Steps 1 and 2 should be done only if paper is too large to begin with.*

1. Fold the selected paper into *hamburgers*.

2. Cut the paper in half along the fold lines.

3. Fold each section of paper into *hamburgers*, but fold one side one half inch shorter than the other side. This will form a tab that is one half inch long.

4. Fold this tab forward over the shorter side, and then fold it back away from the shorter piece of paper; in other words, fold it the opposite way.

5. To form an *accordion*, glue a straight edge of one section into the *valley* of another section.

NOTE: *Stand the sections on end to form an accordion to help students visualize how to glue them together. (See illustration.)*

Always place the extra tab at the back of the book so you can add more pages later.

Use this book for time lines, student projects that grow, sequencing events or data, and biographies.

Concept-Map Book

1. Fold a sheet of paper along the long or short axis, leaving a two-inch tab uncovered along the top.

2. Fold in half or in thirds.

3. Unfold and cut along the inside fold line(s) to create two or three flaps.

Folded Table or Chart

1. Fold the number of vertical columns needed to make the table or chart.
2. Fold the horizontal rows needed to make the table or chart.
3. Label the rows and columns.

Remember: Tables are organized along vertical and horizontal axes, while charts are organized along one axis, either horizontal or vertical.

Table

Chart

Four-Tab Book

1. Fold a sheet of paper (8½" × 11") in half like a *hot dog*.
2. Fold this long rectangle in half like a *hamburger*.
3. Fold both ends back to touch the *mountain top* or fold it like an *accordion*.
4. On the side with two *valleys* and one *mountain top*, make vertical cuts through one thickness of paper, forming four tabs.

Use this book for data occurring in fours.

Four-Door Book

1. Make a *shutter fold* using 11" × 17" or 12" × 18" paper.
2. Fold the *shutter fold* in half like a *hamburger.* Crease well.
3. Open the project and cut along the two inside *valley* folds.
4. These cuts will form four doors on the inside of the project.

Use this fold for data occurring in fours. When folded in half like a *hamburger,* a finished *four-door book* can be glued inside a large (11" × 17") *shutter fold* as part of a larger project.

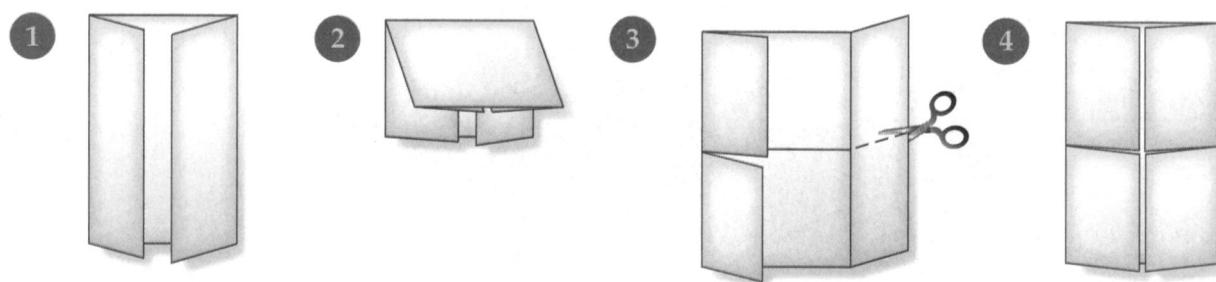

Half-Book

Fold a sheet of paper (8½" × 11") in half.
1. This book can be folded vertically like a *hot dog* or . . .
2. . . . it can be folded horizontally like a *hamburger.*

Use this book for descriptive, expository, persuasive, or narrative writing, as well as for graphs, diagrams, or charts.

Layered-Look Book

1. Stack two sheets of paper (8½" × 11") so that the back sheet is one inch higher than the front sheet.
2. Bring the bottom of both sheets upward and align the edges so that all of the layers or tabs are the same distance apart.
3. When all tabs are an equal distance apart, fold the papers and crease well.
4. Open the papers and glue them together along the *valley*, or inner center fold, or staple them along the *mountain*.

Pocket Book

1. Fold a sheet of paper (8½" × 11") in half like a *hamburger*.
2. Open the folded paper and fold one of the long sides up two inches to form a pocket. Refold along the *hamburger* fold so that the newly formed pockets are on the inside.
3. Glue the outer edges of the two-inch fold with a small amount of glue.
4. **Optional:** Glue a cover around the *pocket book*.

   Variation: Make a multi-paged booklet by gluing several pockets side-by-side. Glue a cover around the multi-paged *pocket book*.

Use 3" × 5" index cards inside the pockets. Store student-made books, such as two-tab books and folded books in the pockets.

Sentence Strips

1. Take two sheets of paper (8½" × 11") and fold into *hamburgers*. Cut along the fold lines making four half sheets. *(Use as many half sheets as necessary for additional pages to your book.)*

2. Fold each sheet in half like a *hot dog*.

3. Place the folds side-by-side and staple them together on the left side.

4. One inch from the stapled edge, cut the front page of each folded section up to the *mountain top*. These cuts form flaps that can be raised and lowered.

To make a half-cover, use a sheet of construction paper one inch longer than the book. Glue the back of the last sheet to the construction paper strip leaving one inch, on the left side, to fold over and cover the original staples. Staple this half-cover in place.

Shutter Fold

1. Begin as if you were going to make a *hamburger* but instead of creasing the paper, pinch it to show the midpoint.

2. Fold the outer edges of the paper to meet at the pinch, or mid-point, forming a *shutter fold*.

Use this book for data occurring in twos. Or, make this fold using 11" × 17" paper and smaller books—such as the half-book, journal, and two-tab book—that can be glued inside to create a large project full of student work.

Three-Tab Book

1. Fold a sheet of paper like a *hot dog*.
2. With the paper horizontal, and the fold of the *hot dog* up, fold the right side toward the center, trying to cover one half of the paper.

   NOTE: *If you fold the right edge over first, the final graphic organizer will open and close like a book.*
3. Fold the left side over the right side to make a book with three folds.
4. Open the folded book. Place your hands between the two thicknesses of paper and cut up the two *valleys* on one side only. This will form three tabs.

Use this book for data occurring in threes, and for two-part Venn diagrams.

Variation A:
   Draw overlapping circles on the three tabs to make a Venn diagram.

Variation B:
   Cut each of the three tabs in half to make a six-tab book.

Trifold Book

1. Fold a sheet of paper (8½" × 11") into thirds.
2. Use this book as is, or cut into shapes. If the trifold is cut, leave plenty of fold on both sides of the designed shape, so the book will open and close in three sections.

Use this book to make charts with three columns or rows, large Venn diagrams, or reports on data occurring in threes.

Foldables

Two-Tab Book

1. Take a *folded book* and cut up the *valley* of the inside fold toward the *mountain top.* This cut forms two large tabs that can be used front and back for writing and illustrations.

2. The book can be expanded by making several of these folds and gluing them side-by-side.

Use this book with data occurring in twos. For example, use it for comparing and contrasting, determining cause and effect, finding similarities and differences, and more.

Vocabulary Book

1. Fold a sheet of notebook paper in half like a *hot dog.*

2. On one side, cut every third line. This results in ten tabs on wide-ruled notebook paper and twelve tabs on college-ruled.

3. Label the tabs.

Presidents of the United States

In this resource you will find portraits of the individuals who served as presidents of the United States, along with their occupations, political party affiliations, and other interesting facts.

**The Republican Party during this period developed into today's Democratic Party. Today's Republican Party originated in 1854.

1 George Washington

Presidential term: 1789–1797
Lived: 1732–1799
Born in: Virginia
Elected from: Virginia
Occupations: Soldier, Planter
Party: None
Vice President: John Adams

2 John Adams

Presidential term: 1797–1801
Lived: 1735–1826
Born in: Massachusetts
Elected from: Massachusetts
Occupations: Teacher, Lawyer
Party: Federalist
Vice President: Thomas Jefferson

3 Thomas Jefferson

Presidential term: 1801–1809
Lived: 1743–1826
Born in: Virginia
Elected from: Virginia
Occupations: Planter, Lawyer
Party: Republican**
Vice Presidents: Aaron Burr, George Clinton

4 James Madison

Presidential term: 1809–1817
Lived: 1751–1836
Born in: Virginia
Elected from: Virginia
Occupation: Planter
Party: Republican**
Vice Presidents: George Clinton, Elbridge Gerry

5 James Monroe

Presidential term: 1817–1825
Lived: 1758–1831
Born in: Virginia
Elected from: Virginia
Occupation: Lawyer
Party: Republican**
Vice President: Daniel D. Tompkins

6 John Quincy Adams

Presidential term: 1825–1829
Lived: 1767–1848
Born in: Massachusetts
Elected from: Massachusetts
Occupation: Lawyer
Party: Republican**
Vice President: John C. Calhoun

7 Andrew Jackson

Presidential term: 1829–1837
Lived: 1767–1845
Born in: South Carolina
Elected from: Tennessee
Occupations: Lawyer, Soldier
Party: Democratic
Vice Presidents: John C. Calhoun, Martin Van Buren

8 Martin Van Buren

Presidential term: 1837–1841
Lived: 1782–1862
Born in: New York
Elected from: New York
Occupation: Lawyer
Party: Democratic
Vice President: Richard M. Johnson

9 William H. Harrison

Presidential term: 1841
Lived: 1773–1841
Born in: Virginia
Elected from: Ohio
Occupations: Soldier,
     Planter
Party: Whig
Vice President: John Tyler

10 John Tyler

Presidential term: 1841–1845
Lived: 1790–1862
Born in: Virginia
Elected as V.P. from: Virginia
Succeeded Harrison
Occupation: Lawyer
Party: Whig
Vice President: None

11 James K. Polk

Presidential term: 1845–1849
Lived: 1795–1849
Born in: North Carolina
Elected from: Tennessee
Occupation: Lawyer
Party: Democratic
Vice President: George M.
     Dallas

12 Zachary Taylor

Presidential term: 1849–1850
Lived: 1784–1850
Born in: Virginia
Elected from: Louisiana
Occupation: Soldier
Party: Whig
Vice President: Millard
     Fillmore

13 Millard Fillmore

Presidential term: 1850–1853
Lived: 1800–1874
Born in: New York
Elected as V.P. from: New York
Succeeded Taylor
Occupation: Lawyer
Party: Whig
Vice President: None

14 Franklin Pierce

Presidential term: 1853–1857
Lived: 1804–1869
Born in: New Hampshire
Elected from: New Hampshire
Occupation: Lawyer
Party: Democratic
Vice President: William R. King

15 James Buchanan

Presidential term: 1857–1861
Lived: 1791–1868
Born in: Pennsylvania
Elected from: Pennsylvania
Occupation: Lawyer
Party: Democratic
Vice President: John C.
     Breckinridge

16 Abraham Lincoln

Presidential term: 1861–1865
Lived: 1809–1865
Born in: Kentucky
Elected from: Illinois
Occupation: Lawyer
Party: Republican
Vice Presidents: Hannibal
     Hamlin, Andrew Johnson

17 Andrew Johnson

Presidential term: 1865–1869
Lived: 1808–1875
Born in: North Carolina
Elected as V.P. from: Tennessee
Succeeded Lincoln
Occupation: Tailor
Party: Republican
Vice President: None

18 Ulysses S. Grant

Presidential term: 1869–1877
Lived: 1822–1885
Born in: Ohio
Elected from: Illinois
Occupations: Farmer, Soldier
Party: Republican
Vice Presidents: Schuyler Colfax, Henry Wilson

19 Rutherford B. Hayes

Presidential term: 1877–1881
Lived: 1822–1893
Born in: Ohio
Elected from: Ohio
Occupation: Lawyer
Party: Republican
Vice President: William A. Wheeler

20 James A. Garfield

Presidential term: 1881
Lived: 1831–1881
Born in: Ohio
Elected from: Ohio
Occupations: Laborer, Professor
Party: Republican
Vice President: Chester A. Arthur

21 Chester A. Arthur

Presidential term: 1881–1885
Lived: 1830–1886
Born in: Vermont
Elected as V.P. from: New York
Succeeded Garfield
Occupations: Teacher, Lawyer
Party: Republican
Vice President: None

22 Grover Cleveland

Presidential term: 1885–1889
Lived: 1837–1908
Born in: New Jersey
Elected from: New York
Occupation: Lawyer
Party: Democratic
Vice President: Thomas A. Hendricks

23 Benjamin Harrison

Presidential term: 1889–1893
Lived: 1833–1901
Born in: Ohio
Elected from: Indiana
Occupation: Lawyer
Party: Republican
Vice President: Levi P. Morton

24 Grover Cleveland

Presidential term: 1893–1897
Lived: 1837–1908
Born in: New Jersey
Elected from: New York
Occupation: Lawyer
Party: Democratic
Vice President: Adlai E. Stevenson

25 William McKinley

Presidential term: 1897–1901
Lived: 1843–1901
Born in: Ohio
Elected from: Ohio
Occupations: Teacher, Lawyer
Party: Republican
Vice Presidents: Garret Hobart, Theodore Roosevelt

26 Theodore Roosevelt

Presidential term: 1901–1909
Lived: 1858–1919
Born in: New York
Elected as V.P. from: New York
Succeeded McKinley
Occupations: Historian, Rancher
Party: Republican
Vice President: Charles W. Fairbanks

U.S. Presidents

27 William H. Taft

Presidential term: 1909–1913
Lived: 1857–1930
Born in: Ohio
Elected from: Ohio
Occupations: Lawyer
Party: Republican
Vice President: James S. Sherman

28 Woodrow Wilson

Presidential term: 1913–1921
Lived: 1856–1924
Born in: Virginia
Elected from: New Jersey
Occupation: College Professor
Party: Democratic
Vice President: Thomas R. Marshall

29 Warren G. Harding

Presidential term: 1921–1923
Lived: 1865–1923
Born in: Ohio
Elected from: Ohio
Occupations: Newspaper Editor, Publisher
Party: Republican
Vice President: Calvin Coolidge

30 Calvin Coolidge

Presidential term: 1923–1929
Lived: 1872–1933
Born in: Vermont
Elected as V.P. from: Massachusetts, Succeeded Harding
Occupation: Lawyer
Party: Republican
Vice President: Charles G. Dawes

31 Herbert C. Hoover

Presidential term: 1929–1933
Lived: 1874–1964
Born in: Iowa
Elected from: California
Occupation: Engineer
Party: Republican
Vice President: Charles Curtis

32 Franklin D. Roosevelt

Presidential term: 1933–1945
Lived: 1882–1945
Born in: New York
Elected from: New York
Occupation: Lawyer
Party: Democratic
Vice Presidents: John N. Garner, Henry A. Wallace, Harry S. Truman

33 Harry S. Truman

Presidential term: 1945–1953
Lived: 1884–1972
Born in: Missouri
Elected as V.P. from: Missouri Succeeded Roosevelt
Occupations: Clerk, Farmer
Party: Democratic
Vice President: Alben W. Barkley

34 Dwight D. Eisenhower

Presidential term: 1953–1961
Lived: 1890–1969
Born in: Texas
Elected from: New York
Occupation: Soldier
Party: Republican
Vice President: Richard M. Nixon

35 John F. Kennedy

Presidential term: 1961–1963
Lived: 1917–1963
Born in: Massachusetts
Elected from: Massachusetts
Occupations: Author, Reporter
Party: Democratic
Vice President: Lyndon B. Johnson

36 Lyndon B. Johnson

Presidential term: 1963–1969
Lived: 1908–1973
Born in: Texas
Elected as V.P. from: Texas
Succeeded Kennedy
Occupation: Teacher
Party: Democratic
Vice President: Hubert H.
    Humphrey

37 Richard M. Nixon

Presidential term: 1969–1974
Lived: 1913–1994
Born in: California
Elected from: New York
Occupation: Lawyer
Party: Republican
Vice Presidents: Spiro T. Agnew,
    Gerald R. Ford

38 Gerald R. Ford

Presidential term: 1974–1977
Lived: 1913–2006
Born in: Nebraska
Appointed as V.P. upon Agnew's
resignation; succeeded Nixon
Occupation: Lawyer
Party: Republican
Vice President: Nelson A.
    Rockefeller

39 James E. Carter, Jr.

Presidential term: 1977–1981
Lived: 1924–
Born in: Georgia
Elected from: Georgia
Occupations: Business, Farmer
Party: Democratic
Vice President: Walter F.
    Mondale

40 Ronald W. Reagan

Presidential term: 1981–1989
Lived: 1911–2004
Born in: Illinois
Elected from: California
Occupations: Actor, Lecturer
Party: Republican
Vice President: George H.W.
    Bush

41 George H.W. Bush

Presidential term: 1989–1993
Lived: 1924–
Born in: Massachusetts
Elected from: Texas
Occupation: Business
Party: Republican
Vice President: J. Danforth
    Quayle

42 William J. Clinton

Presidential term: 1993–2001
Lived: 1946–
Born in: Arkansas
Elected from: Arkansas
Occupation: Lawyer
Party: Democratic
Vice President: Albert Gore, Jr.

43 George W. Bush

Presidential term: 2001–
Lived: 1946–
Born in: Connecticut
Elected from: Texas
Occupation: Business
Party: Republican
Vice President: Richard B.
    Cheney

U.S. Presidents

United States Facts

Washington, D.C.
Population: 572,059
Land area: 61 sq. mi.

The states are listed in the order they were admitted to the Union.

Population figures are based on U.S. Bureau of the Census for 2000. House of Representatives figures are from the Clerk of the House of Representatives. States are not drawn to scale.

U.S. Territories

Puerto Rico
Population: 3,808,610
Land area: 3,425 sq. mi.

Guam
Population: 155,000 (est.)
Land area: 209 sq. mi.

U.S. Virgin Islands
Population: 121,000 (est.)
Land area: 134 sq. mi.

American Samoa
Population: 65,000 (est.)
Land area: 77 sq. mi.

1 Delaware
Year Admitted: 1787
Population: 783,600
Land area: 1,955 sq. mi.
Representatives: 1
★ Dover

2 Pennsylvania
Year Admitted: 1787
Population: 12,281,054
Land area: 44,820 sq. mi.
Representatives: 19
Harrisburg ★

3 New Jersey
Year Admitted: 1787
Population: 8,414,350
Land area: 7,419 sq. mi.
Representatives: 13
Trenton ★

4 Georgia
Year Admitted: 1788
Population: 8,186,453
Land area: 57,919 sq. mi.
Representatives: 13
★ Atlanta

5 Connecticut
Year Admitted: 1788
Population: 3,405,565
Land area: 4,845 sq. mi.
Representatives: 5
★ Hartford

6 Massachusetts
Year Admitted: 1788
Population: 6,349,097
Land area: 7,838 sq. mi.
Representatives: 10
Boston ★

7 Maryland
Year Admitted: 1788
Population: 5,296,486
Land area: 9,775 sq. mi.
Representatives: 8
Annapolis ★

8 South Carolina
Year Admitted: 1788
Population: 4,012,012
Land area: 30,111 sq. mi.
Representatives: 6
Columbia ★

9 New Hampshire
Year Admitted: 1788
Population: 1,235,786
Land area: 8,969 sq. mi.
Representatives: 2
Concord ★

10 Virginia
Year Admitted: 1788
Population: 7,078,515
Land area: 39,598 sq. mi.
Representatives: 11
Richmond ★

11 New York
Year Admitted: 1788
Population: 18,976,457
Land area: 47,224 sq. mi.
Representatives: 29
★ Albany

12 North Carolina
Year Admitted: 1789
Population: 8,049,313
Land area: 48,718 sq. mi.
Representatives: 13
Raleigh ★

13 Rhode Island
Year Admitted: 1790
Population: 1,048,319
Land area: 1,045 sq. mi.
Representatives: 2
★ Providence

14 Vermont
Year Admitted: 1791
Population: 608,827
Land area: 9,249 sq. mi.
Representatives: 1
★ Montpelier

15 Kentucky
Year Admitted: 1792
Population: 4,041,769
Land area: 39,732 sq. mi.
Representatives: 6
Frankfort ★

16 Tennessee
Year Admitted: 1796
Population: 5,689,283
Land area: 41,220 sq. mi.
Representatives: 9
★ Nashville

17 Ohio
Year Admitted: 1803
Population: 11,353,140
Land area: 40,953 sq. mi.
Representatives: 18
★ Columbus

18 Louisiana
Year Admitted: 1812
Population: 4,468,976
Land area: 43,566 sq. mi.
Representatives: 7
★ Baton Rouge

19 Indiana
Year Admitted: 1816
Population: 6,080,485
Land area: 35,870 sq. mi.
Representatives: 9
Indianapolis ★

20 Mississippi
Year Admitted: 1817
Population: 2,844,658
Land area: 46,914 sq. mi.
Representatives: 4
★ Jackson

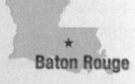

21 Illinois
Year Admitted: 1818
Population: 12,419,293
Land area: 55,593 sq. mi.
Representatives: 19

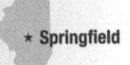
★ Springfield

22 Alabama
Year Admitted: 1819
Population: 4,447,100
Land area: 50,750 sq. mi.
Representatives: 7

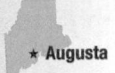
Montgomery
★

23 Maine
Year Admitted: 1820
Population: 1,274,923
Land area: 30,865 sq. mi.
Representatives: 2

★ Augusta

24 Missouri
Year Admitted: 1821
Population: 5,595,211
Land area: 68,898 sq. mi.
Representatives: 9

Jefferson City
★

25 Arkansas
Year Admitted: 1836
Population: 2,673,400
Land area: 52,075 sq. mi.
Representatives: 4

Little Rock
★

26 Michigan
Year Admitted: 1837
Population: 9,938,444
Land area: 56,809 sq. mi.
Representatives: 15

Lansing
★

27 Florida
Year Admitted: 1845
Population: 15,982,378
Land area: 53,997 sq. mi.
Representatives: 25

★ Tallahassee

28 Texas
Year Admitted: 1845
Population: 20,851,820
Land area: 261,914 sq. mi.
Representatives: 32

Austin
★

29 Iowa
Year Admitted: 1846
Population: 2,926,324
Land area: 55,875 sq. mi.
Representatives: 5

★ Des Moines

30 Wisconsin
Year Admitted: 1848
Population: 5,363,675
Land area: 54,314 sq. mi.
Representatives: 8

Madison
★

31 California
Year Admitted: 1850
Population: 33,871,648
Land area: 155,973 sq. mi.
Representatives: 53

Sacramento

32 Minnesota
Year Admitted: 1858
Population: 4,919,479
Land area: 79,617 sq. mi.
Representatives: 8

Saint Paul
★

33 Oregon
Year Admitted: 1859
Population: 3,421,399
Land area: 96,003 sq. mi.
Representatives: 5

★ Salem
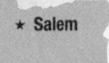

34 Kansas
Year Admitted: 1861
Population: 2,688,418
Land area: 81,823 sq. mi.
Representatives: 4

Topeka ★

35 West Virginia
Year Admitted: 1863
Population: 1,808,344
Land area: 24,087 sq. mi.
Representatives: 3

★ Charleston

36 Nevada
Year Admitted: 1864
Population: 1,998,257
Land area: 109,806 sq. mi.
Representatives: 3

★ Carson City

37 Nebraska
Year Admitted: 1867
Population: 1,711,263
Land area: 76,878 sq. mi.
Representatives: 3

Lincoln ★

38 Colorado
Year Admitted: 1876
Population: 4,301,261
Land area: 103,730 sq. mi.
Representatives: 7

Denver ★

39 North Dakota
Year Admitted: 1889
Population: 642,200
Land area: 68,994 sq. mi.
Representatives: 1

Bismarck
★

40 South Dakota
Year Admitted: 1889
Population: 754,844
Land area: 75,898 sq. mi.
Representatives: 1

Pierre
★

41 Montana
Year Admitted: 1889
Population: 902,195
Land area: 145,556 sq. mi.
Representatives: 1

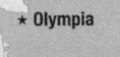
★ Helena

42 Washington
Year Admitted: 1889
Population: 5,894,121
Land area: 66,582 sq. mi.
Representatives: 9

★ Olympia

43 Idaho
Year Admitted: 1890
Population: 1,293,953
Land area: 82,751 sq. mi.
Representatives: 2

★ Boise

44 Wyoming
Year Admitted: 1890
Population: 493,782
Land area: 97,105 sq. mi.
Representatives: 1

Cheyenne
★

45 Utah
Year Admitted: 1896
Population: 2,233,169
Land area: 82,168 sq. mi.
Representatives: 3

★
Salt Lake City

46 Oklahoma
Year Admitted: 1907
Population: 3,450,654
Land area: 68,679 sq. mi.
Representatives: 5

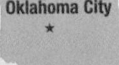
Oklahoma City
★

47 New Mexico
Year Admitted: 1912
Population: 1,819,046
Land area: 121,365 sq. mi.
Representatives: 3

★
Santa Fe

48 Arizona
Year Admitted: 1912
Population: 5,130,632
Land area: 113,642 sq. mi.
Representatives: 8

Phoenix
★

49 Alaska
Year Admitted: 1959
Population: 626,932
Land area: 570,374 sq. mi.
Representatives: 1

Juneau ★

50 Hawaii
Year Admitted: 1959
Population: 1,211,537
Land area: 6,432 sq. mi.
Representatives: 2

Honolulu ★

U.S. Facts

Documents of American History

TABLE OF CONTENTS

(right) Lincoln's drafts of the Gettysburg Address

Magna Carta

Why They Matter

Documents are often public statements by a president or an official body, such as a legislature, on an important issue. They have become documents because they define a particular issue so well that Americans continue to refer to them. Many documents here address fundamental American beliefs, such as the rights of the individual and the proper limits of government. Other documents, such as the Monroe Doctrine or the Truman Doctrine, address the nation's position and responsibilities in the world.

Documents matter because they are guides to American government and values. Sometimes people study them to learn how Americans came to believe in certain principles. Other times people read documents simply because these writings express certain principles passionately.

Signing the Mayflower Compact

Founding Documents of the American Republic

The first seven documents in this collection represent some of the founding documents of American democracy. Each contributed an essential building block for American political principles. Ultimately these principles were embodied in the Declaration of Independence, the Bill of Rights, and the Constitution.

DOCUMENT	WHY IT MATTERS
The Magna Carta In signing this charter in 1215, King John of England granted his subjects certain permanent liberties or rights, such as the right to a fair trial by a jury of their peers.	Over the centuries, English people believed that the Magna Carta gave them certain rights. They took this idea with them when they settled the American colonies. Some provisions of the Bill of Rights reflect ancient Magna Carta liberties.
The Mayflower Compact In 1620 the Pilgrims signed a compact while still aboard the *Mayflower*. This document laid out a plan for self-government the Pilgrims would use once they landed in America.	This document is the first plan for self-government put into effect in the English colonies. It reflected the idea that government should be based on a consensus of the entire community.
The Fundamental Orders of Connecticut Connecticut settlers agreed they would be governed according to a certain set of laws and through certain institutions. All citizens, not only those of a certain religion, could vote.	This document, the first written constitution drawn up in America, strengthened the colonists' beliefs about governing themselves.
The English Bill of Rights In 1689, after the Glorious Revolution, Parliament forced the king to accept this Bill of Rights guaranteeing basic civil rights.	This document clearly established that English subjects had certain rights and that the king could be removed from power for violating those rights.
Second Treatise of Government English philosopher John Locke wrote this document during the 1680s. One of his basic arguments was that government should be based on a contract between a ruler and those who are ruled. Rebellion is justified if a ruler violates the contract.	During the American Revolution, the colonists drew from Locke's theories of government and especially his ideas about the right to rebel.
The Virginia Statute for Religious Freedom This 1786 statute declared that the state of Virginia should not support Anglicanism or any other religious denomination.	The religious clauses of the Bill of Rights protecting the free exercise of religion and prohibiting an official religion were based on this statute.
The Federalist No. 10 In 1787 James Madison wrote this paper, one of a series arguing for stronger central government as reflected in the new Constitution.	The framework for American government today— a representative government with a strong federal government—was laid out in the Federalist Papers.

 *Use the **American History Primary Source Document Library CD-ROM** to find additional primary sources about American heritage.*

Documents

The Magna Carta

The Magna Carta, signed by King John of England in 1215, marked a decisive step forward in the development of English constitutional government. Later it served as a model for the colonists, who carried the Magna Carta's guarantees of political rights to America.

John, by the grace of God, king of England, lord of Ireland, duke of Normandy and Aquitaine, and count of Anjou: to the archbishops, bishops, abbots, earls, barons, justiciaries, foresters, sheriffs, reeves, ministers, and all bailiffs and others his faithful subjects, greeting. . . .

1. We have, in the first place, granted to God, and by this our present charter, confirmed for us and our heirs forever that the English church shall be free. . . .

9. Neither we nor our bailiffs shall seize any land or rent for any debt so long as the debtor's chattels are sufficient to discharge the same. . . .

12. No scutage [tax] or aid shall be imposed in our kingdom unless by the common counsel thereof. . . .

14. For obtaining the common counsel of the kingdom concerning the assessment of aids. . . or of scutage, we will cause to be summoned, severally by our letters, the archbishops, bishops, abbots, earls, and great barons; we will also cause to be summoned generally, by our sheriffs and bailiffs, all those who hold lands directly of us, to meet on a fixed day . . . and at a fixed place. . . .

20. A free man shall be amerced [punished] for a small fault only according to the measure thereof, and for a great crime according to its magnitude. . . . None of these amercements shall be imposed except by the oath of honest men of the neighborhood.

21. Earls and barons shall be amerced only by their peers, and only in proportion to the measure of the offense. . . .

38. In the future no bailiff shall upon his own unsupported accusation put any man to trial without producing credible witnesses to the truth of the accusation.

39. No free man shall be taken, imprisoned, disseised [seized], outlawed, banished, or in any way destroyed, nor will we proceed against or prosecute him, except by the lawful judgment of his peers and by the law of the land.

40. To no one will we sell, to none will we deny or delay, right or justice. . . .

42. In the future it shall be lawful . . . for anyone to leave and return to our kingdom safely and securely by land and water, saving his fealty to us. Excepted are those who have been imprisoned or outlawed according to the law of the land. . . .

61. Whereas we, for the honor of God and the amendment of our realm, and in order the better to allay the discord arisen between us and our barons, have granted all these things aforesaid. . . .

63. Wherefore we will, and firmly charge . . . that all men in our kingdom shall have and hold all the aforesaid liberties, rights, and concessions . . . fully, and wholly to them and their heirs . . . in all things and places forever. . . . It is moreover sworn, as well on our part as on the part of the barons, that all these matters aforesaid will be kept in good faith and without deceit. Witness the above named and many others. Given by our hand in the meadow which is called Runnymede. . . .

Documents

The Mayflower Compact

On November 21, 1620, 41 colonists drafted the Mayflower Compact while still aboard the **Mayflower.** It was the first self-government plan ever put into effect in the English colonies. The compact was drawn up under these circumstances, as described by Governor William Bradford:

"This day, before we came to harbor, observing some not well affected to unity and concord, but gave some appearance of faction, it was thought good there should be an association and agreement that we should combine together in one body, and to submit to such government and governors as we should by common consent agree to make and choose, and set our hands to this that follows word for word."

In the Name of God, Amen. We, whose names are underwritten, the Loyal Subjects of our dread Sovereign Lord King James, by the Grace of God, of Great Britain, France, and Ireland, King, Defender of the Faith, etc.

Having undertaken for the Glory of God, and Advancement of the Christian Faith, and the honor of our King and Country, a Voyage to plant the first Colony in the northern Parts of Virginia, Do by these Presents, solemnly and mutually, in the Presence of God and one another, covenant and combine ourselves together into a civil Body Politick, for our better Ordering and Preservation, and Furtherance of the Ends aforesaid; And by Virtue hereof do enact, constitute, and frame, such just and equal Laws, Ordinances, Acts, Constitutions, and Offices, from time to time, as shall be thought most meet and convenient for the general Good of the Colony; unto which we promise all due Submission and Obedience. In Witness whereof we have hereunder subscribed our names at Cape Cod the eleventh of November, in the Reign of our Sovereign Lord King James of England, France, and Ireland, the eighteenth and of Scotland, the fifty-fourth. Anno Domini, 1620.

Signing of the Mayflower Compact

The Fundamental Orders of Connecticut

In January 1639, settlers in Connecticut, led by Thomas Hooker, drew up the Fundamental Orders of Connecticut—America's first written constitution. It is essentially a body of laws and a compact among the settlers.

Forasmuch as it has pleased the Almighty God by the wise disposition of His Divine Providence so to order and dispose of things that we, the inhabitants and residents of Windsor, Hartford, and Wethersfield are now cohabiting and dwelling in and upon the river of Conectecotte and the lands thereunto adjoining; and well knowing where a people are gathered together the Word of God requires that, to maintain the peace and union of such a people, there should be an orderly and decent government established according to God, . . . do therefore associate and conjoin ourselves to be as one public state or commonwealth. . . . As also in our civil affairs to be guided and governed according to such laws, rules, orders, and decrees as shall be made, ordered, and decreed, as follows:

1. It is ordered . . . that there shall be yearly two general assemblies or courts; . . . The first shall be called the Court of Election, wherein shall be yearly chosen . . . so many magistrates and other public officers as shall be found requisite. Whereof one to be chosen governor . . . and no other magistrate to be chosen for more than one year; provided always there be six chosen besides the governor . . . by all that are admitted freemen and have taken the oath of fidelity, and do cohabit within this jurisdiction. . . .

4. It is ordered . . . that no person be chosen governor above once in two years, and that the governor be always a member of some approved congregation, and formerly of the magistracy within this jurisdiction; and all the magistrates freemen of this Commonwealth. . . .

5. It is ordered . . . that to the aforesaid Court of Election the several towns shall send their deputies.

. . . Also, the other General Court . . . shall be for making of laws, and any other public occasion which concerns the good of the Commonwealth. . . .

7. It is ordered . . . that . . . the constable or constables of each town shall forthwith give notice distinctly to the inhabitants of the same . . . that . . . they meet and assemble themselves together to elect and choose certain deputies to be at the General Court then following to [manage] the affairs of the Commonwealth; . . .

10. It is ordered . . . that every General Court . . . shall consist of the governor, or someone chosen to moderate the Court, and four other magistrates, at least, with the major part of the deputies of the several towns legally chosen. . . . In which said General Courts shall consist the supreme power of the Commonwealth, and they only shall have power to make laws or repeal them, to grant levies, to admit of freemen, dispose of lands undisposed of to several towns or person, and also shall have power to call either Court or magistrate or any other person whatsoever into question for any misdemeanor. . . .

Connecticut settlers on their way to Hartford

The English Bill of Rights

In 1689 William of Orange (pictured at right) and his wife Mary became joint rulers of England after accepting a list of conditions that later became known as the English Bill of Rights. This document assured the English people of certain basic civil rights and limited the power of the English monarchy.

An act declaring the rights and liberties of the subject and settling the succession of the crown. Whereas the lords spiritual and temporal and commons assembled at Westminster lawfully, fully and freely representing all the estates of the people of this realm did upon the thirteenth day of February in the year of our Seal of William and Mary Lord one thousand six hundred eighty-eight [-nine] present unto their majesties . . . William and Mary prince and princess of Orange . . . a certain declaration in writing made by the said lords and commons in the words following viz [namely]:

Whereas the late king James the second, by the assistance of divers evil counsellors, judges, and ministers employed by him did endeavor to subvert and extirpate the Protestant religion and the laws and liberties of this kingdom.

By assuming and exercising a power of dispensing with and suspending of laws and the execution of laws without consent of parliament. . . .

By levying money for and to the use of the crown by pretence of prerogative for other time and in other manner than the same was granted by parliament.

By raising and keeping a standing army within this kingdom in time of peace without consent of parliament and quartering soldiers contrary to law. . . .

By violating the freedom of election of members to serve in parliament. . . .

And excessive bail hath been required of persons committed in criminal cases to elude the benefit of the laws made for the liberty of the subjects.

And excessive fines have been imposed.

And illegal and cruel punishments inflicted. . . .

And thereupon the said lords spiritual and temporal and commons . . . do . . . declare that the pretended power of suspending of laws or the execution of laws by regal authority without consent of parliament is illegal. . . .

That levying money for or to the use of the crown . . . without grant of parliament for longer time or in other manner than the same is or shall be granted is illegal.

That it is the right of the subjects to petition the king and all commitments and prosecutions for such petitioning are illegal.

That the raising or keeping a standing army within the kingdom in time of peace unless it be with consent of parliament is against law. . . .

That election of members of parliament ought to be free. . . .

That excessive bail ought not to be required nor excessive fines imposed nor cruel and unusual punishments inflicted. . . .

The said lords . . . do resolve that William and Mary, prince and princess of Orange, be declared king and queen of England, France, and Ireland. . . .

Second Treatise of Government

English philosopher John Locke (above) wrote "Two Treatises of Government" in the early 1680s. Published in 1690, the "Second Treatise of Government" argues that government should be based on an agreement between the people and their ruler, and that if the ruler violates the agreement, a rebellion by the people may be justified.

Of the State of Nature

To understand Political Power right, and to derive it from its Original, we must consider what State all Men are naturally in, and that is, a State of perfect Freedom to order their Actions, and dispose of their Possessions, and Persons as they think fit, within the bounds of the Law of Nature, without asking leave, or depending upon the Will of any other Man. . . .

Of the Beginning of Political Societies

Men being, as has been said, by Nature, all free, equal and independent, no one can be put out of this Estate, and subjected to the Political Power of another, without his own Consent. The only way whereby any one divests himself of his Natural Liberty, and puts on the bonds of Civil Society is by agreeing with other Men to joyn and unite into a Community, for their comfortable, safe, and peaceable living one amongst another, in a secure Enjoyment of their properties, and a greater Security against any that are not of it. This any number of Men may do, because it injures not the Freedom of the rest; they are left as they were in the Liberty of the State of Nature. . . .

Whosoever therefore out of a state of Nature unite into a Community, must be understood to give up all the power, necessary to the ends for which they unite into Society, to the majority of the Community. . . .

Of the Dissolution of Government

Governments are dissolved from within . . . when the Legislative is altered. . . . First, that when such a single Person or Prince sets up his own Arbitrary Will in place of the Laws, which are the Will of the Society, declared by the Legislative, then the Legislative is changed. . . . Secondly, when the Prince hinders the legislative from . . . acting freely, pursuant to those ends, for which it was Constituted, the Legislative is altered. . . . Thirdly, When by the Arbitrary Power of the Prince, the Electors, or ways of Election are altered, without the Consent, and contrary to the common Interest of the People, there also the Legislative is altered. . . .

In these and the like Cases, when the Government is dissolved, the People are at liberty to provide for themselves, by erecting a new Legislative, differing from the other, by the change of Persons, or Form, or both as they shall find it most for their safety and good. For the Society can never, by the fault of another, lose the Native and Original Right it has to preserve itself. . . .

The Virginia Statute for Religious Freedom

This statute, excerpted below, was the basis for the religion clauses in the Bill of Rights. Thomas Jefferson drafted the statute, and James Madison guided it through the Virginia legislature in 1786. The issue it addresses arose when the new state considered whether citizens should continue to support the Anglican Church, as they had in colonial times, or whether they should support any or all other denominations.

Whereas Almighty God hath created the mind free; that all attempts to influence it by temporal punishments . . . tend only to beget habits of hypocrisy and meanness, and are a departure from the plan of the Holy author of our religion; . . . that the impious presumption of legislators and rulers, civil as well as ecclesiastical, who being themselves but fallible and uninspired men, have assumed dominion over the faith of others, setting up their own opinions and modes of thinking as the only true and infallible, and as such endeavouring to impose them on others, hath established and maintained false religions over the greatest part of the world, and through all time; . . . that to compel a man to furnish contributions of money for the propagation of opinions which he disbelieves, is sinful and tyrannical; . . . that our civil rights have no dependence on our religious opinions, any more than our opinions in physics or geometry; that therefore the proscribing any citizen as unworthy the public confidence by laying upon him an incapacity of being called to offices of trust . . . unless he profess or renounce this or that religious opinion, is depriving him injuriously of those privileges and advantages to which in common with his fellow-citizens he has a natural right; that it tends only to corrupt the principles of that religion it is meant to encourage, by bribing with a monopoly of worldly honours and emoluments, those who will externally profess and conform to it . . . :

Be it enacted by the General Assembly, That no man shall be compelled to frequent or support any religious worship, place, or ministry whatsoever, nor shall be enforced, restrained, molested, or burthened in his body or goods, nor shall otherwise suffer on account of his religious opinions or belief; but that all men shall be free to profess, and by argument to maintain, their opinion in matters of religion, and that the same shall in no wise diminish enlarge, or affect their civil capacities. . . .

Thomas Jefferson

The Federalist No. 10

James Madison (pictured at right) wrote several articles for a New York newspaper supporting ratification of the Constitution. In the excerpt below, he argues for the idea of a federal republic as a guard against factions, or overzealous parties, in governing the nation.

The latent causes of faction are thus sown in the nature of man; and we see them everywhere. . . . A zeal for different opinions concerning religion, concerning government, and many other points; . . . an attachment to different leaders ambitiously contending for preeminence and power . . . have, in turn, divided mankind into parties . . . disposed to vex and oppress each other than to cooperate for their common good. . . . But the most common and durable source of factions has been the various and unequal distribution of property. Those who hold and those who are without property have ever formed distinct interests in society. Those who are creditors, and those who are debtors, fall under a like discrimination. A landed interest, a manufacturing interest, a mercantile interest, a moneyed interest, with many lesser interests, grow up of necessity in civilized nations, and divide them into different classes, actuated by different sentiments and views. The regulation of these various and interfering interests forms the principal task of modern legislation and involves the spirit of party and faction in the necessary and ordinary operations of government. . . .

The inference to which we are brought is that the causes of faction cannot be removed and relief is only to be sought in the means of controlling its effects. . . .

By what means is this object attainable? Evidently by one of two only. Either the existence of the same passion or interest in a majority at the same time must be prevented, or the majority, having such coexistent passion or interest, must be rendered, by their number and local situation, unable to concert and carry into effect schemes of oppression. . . .

From this . . . it may be concluded that a pure democracy, by which I mean a society consisting of a small number of citizens, who assemble and administer the government in person, can admit of no cure for the mischiefs of faction. A common passion or interest will, in almost every case, be felt by a majority of the whole; a communication and concert results from the form of government itself; and there is nothing to check the inducements to sacrifice the weaker party or an obnoxious individual. Hence it is that such democracies have ever been spectacles of turbulence and contention. . . .

A republic, by which I mean a government in which the scheme of representation takes place, opens a different prospect and promises the cure for which we are seeking. . . .

The two great points of difference between a democracy and a republic are: first, the delegation of the government in the latter to a small number of citizens elected by the rest; secondly, the greater number of citizens and great sphere of country over which the latter may be extended.

The Federalist No. 51

The author of this Federalist paper is not known. It may have been either James Madison or Alexander Hamilton. The author argues that the Constitution's federal system and separation of powers will protect the rights of the people.

In order to lay a due foundation for that separate and distinct exercise of the different powers of government, which to a certain extent is admitted on all hands to be essential to the preservation of liberty, it is evident that . . . the great security against a gradual concentration of the several powers in the same department, consists in giving to those who administer each department the necessary constitutional means and personal motives to resist encroachments of the others. . . .

Ambition must be made to counteract ambition. . . . A dependence on the people is, no doubt, the primary control on the government; but experience has taught mankind the necessity of auxiliary precautions. . . . The constant aim is to divide and arrange the several offices in such a manner as that each may be a check on the other. . . . In the compound republic of America, the power surrendered by the people is first divided between two distinct governments, and then the portion allotted to each subdivided among distinct and separate departments. . . .

In a free government the security for civil rights must be the same as that for religious rights. It consists in the one case in the multiplicity of interests, and in the other in the multiplicity of sects. . . . In the extended republic of the United States, and among the great variety of interests, parties, and sects which it embraces, a coalition of a majority of the whole society could seldom take place on any other principles than those of justice and the general good. . . . It is no less certain than it is important . . . that the larger the society, provided it lie within a practical sphere, the more duly capable it will be of self-government.

The Federalist No. 59

In this Federalist paper, Alexander Hamilton explains why Congress, and not the states, should have the final say in how federal elections are conducted.

The natural order of the subject leads us to consider . . . that provision of the Constitution which authorizes the national legislature to regulate, in the last resort, the election of its own members. . . . Its propriety rests upon the evidence of this plain proposition, that every government ought to contain in itself the means of its own preservation. . . . Nothing can be more evident, than that an exclusive power of regulating elections for the national government, in the hands of the state legislatures, would leave the existence of the union entirely at their mercy. They could at any moment annihilate it, by neglecting to provide for the choice of persons to administer its affairs. . . .

It is certainly true that the state legislatures, by forbearing the appointment of senators, may destroy the national government. But it will not follow that, because they have a power to do this in one instance, they ought to have it in every other. . . . It is an evil; but it is an evil which could not have been avoided without excluding the states . . . from a place in the organization of the national government. If this had been done, it would doubtless have been interpreted into an entire dereliction of the federal principle; and would certainly have deprived the state governments of that absolute safeguard which they will enjoy under this provision. . . .

Washington's Farewell Address

Washington never orally delivered his Farewell Address. Instead, he arranged to have it printed in a Philadelphia newspaper on September 19, 1796. Designed in part to remove him from consideration for a third presidential term, the address also warned about dangers the new nation was facing, especially the dangers of political parties and sectionalism.

Washington preparing to leave office

Friends and Fellow Citizens:

The period for a new election of a citizen to administer the executive government of the United States being not far distant . . . I should now apprise you of the resolution I have formed to decline being considered. . . .

The unity of government which constitutes you one people is . . . a main pillar in the edifice of your real independence; the support of your tranquility at home, your peace abroad; of your safety; of your prosperity in every shape; of that very liberty which you so highly prize. But as it is easy to foresee that, from different causes and from different quarters, much pains will be taken, many artifices employed to weaken in your minds the conviction of this truth. . . .

The name of American, which belongs to you, in your national capacity, must always exalt the just pride of patriotism more than any appellation derived from local discriminations. . . .

In contemplating the causes which may disturb our Union, it occurs as matter of serious concern that any ground should have been furnished for characterizing parties by geographical discriminations: Northern and Southern; Atlantic and Western; whence designing men may endeavor to excite a belief that there is a real difference of local interests and views. . . .

Let me now take a more comprehensive view and warn you in the most solemn manner against the baneful effects of the spirit of party generally. . . .The alternate domination of one faction over another, sharpened by the spirit of revenge natural to party dissension . . . is itself a frightful despotism. . . .

Of all the dispositions and habits which lead to political prosperity, religion and morality are indispensable supports. . . . A volume could not trace all their connections with private and public felicity. Let it simply be asked where is the security for property, for reputation, for life, if the sense of religious obligation desert the oaths, which are the instruments of investigation in courts of justice? And let us with caution indulge the supposition, that morality can be maintained without religion. Whatever may be conceded to the influence of refined education on minds of peculiar structure—reason and experience both forbid us to expect that national morality can prevail in exclusion of religious principle.

The great rule of conduct for us, in regard to foreign nations, is in extending our commercial relations to have with them as little political connection as possible. . . .

In offering you, my countrymen, these counsels of an old and affectionate friend, I dare not hope that they will make the strong and lasting impression I could wish. . . . But if I may even flatter myself that they may be productive of some partial benefit. . . .

The Kentucky Resolution

The Alien and Sedition Acts of 1798 made it easier for the government to suppress criticism and to arrest political enemies. This Federalist legislation inspired fierce opposition among Republicans, who looked to the state governments to reverse the acts. Two states, Kentucky and Virginia, passed resolutions stating their right to, in effect, disregard federal legislation. The resolutions laid the groundwork for the states' rights often cited during the Civil War. Thomas Jefferson wrote the Kentucky Resolution, excerpted below, which was adopted in 1799.

RESOLVED, . . . that if those who administer the general government be permitted to transgress the limits fixed by that compact, by a total disregard to the special delegations of power therein contained, annihilation of the state governments, and the erection upon their ruins, of a general consolidated government, will be the inevitable consequence; that the principle and construction contended for by sundry of the state legislatures, that the general government is the exclusive judge of the extent of the powers delegated to it, stop nothing short of despotism; . . . that the several states who formed that instrument, being sovereign and independent, have the unquestionable right to judge of its infraction; and that a nullification, by those sovereignties, of all unauthorized acts done under colour of that instrument, is the rightful remedy; . . .

"The Star-Spangled Banner"

Francis Scott Key

During the British bombardment of Fort McHenry during the War of 1812, a young Baltimore lawyer named Francis Scott Key was inspired to write the words to "The Star-Spangled Banner." Although it became popular immediately, it was not until 1931 that Congress officially declared "The Star-Spangled Banner" as the national anthem of the United States.

O! say can you see, by the dawn's early light,

What so proudly we hail'd at the twilight's last gleaming,

Whose broad stripes and bright stars through the perilous fight,

O'er the ramparts we watch'd, were so gallantly streaming?

And the Rockets' red glare, the Bombs bursting in air,

Gave proof through the night that our Flag was still there;

O! say, does that star-spangled Banner yet wave,

O'er the Land of the free, and the home of the brave?

Fort McHenry flag

The Monroe Doctrine

When Spain's power in South America began to weaken, other European nations seemed ready to step in. The United States was developing trade and diplomatic relations with South America, and it wanted to curb European influence there. The following is a statement President Monroe made on the subject in his annual message to Congress on December 2, 1823.

The occasion has been judged proper for asserting, as a principle in which the rights and interests of the United States are involved, that the American continents, by the free and independent condition which they have assumed and maintain, are henceforth not to be considered as subjects for future colonization by any European powers. . . .

. . . We owe it, therefore, to candor and to the amicable relations existing between the United States and those [European] powers to declare that we should consider any attempt on their part to extend their system to any portion of this hemisphere as dangerous to our peace and safety. With the existing colonies or dependencies of any European power we have not interfered and shall not interfere. But with the Governments who have declared their independence and maintain it, and whose independence we have, on great consideration and on just principles, acknowledged, we could not view any interposition for the purpose of oppressing them, or controlling in any other manner their destiny, by any European power in any other light than as the manifestation of an unfriendly disposition toward the United States. . . .

Our policy in regard to Europe, which was adopted at an early stage of the wars which have so long agitated that quarter of the globe, nevertheless remains the same, which is, not to interfere in the internal concerns of any of its powers; to consider the government de facto as the legitimate government for us; to cultivate friendly relations with it, and to preserve those relations by a frank, firm, and manly policy, meeting in all instances the just claims of every power, submitting to injuries from none.

The Seneca Falls Declaration

One of the first documents to call for equal rights for women was the Declaration of Sentiments and Resolutions, issued in 1848 at the Seneca Falls Convention in Seneca Falls, New York. Led by Lucretia Mott and Elizabeth Cady Stanton, the delegates at the convention used the language of the Bill of Rights to call for women's rights.

We hold these truths to be self-evident: that all men and women are created equal; that they are endowed by their Creator with certain inalienable rights; that among these are life, liberty, and the pursuit of happiness; that to secure these rights governments are instituted, deriving their just powers from the consent of the governed. Whenever any form of government becomes destructive of these ends, it is the right of those who suffer from it to refuse allegiance to it, and to insist upon the institution of a new government. . . .

The history of mankind is a history of repeated injuries and usurpations on the part of man toward woman, having in direct object the establishment of an absolute tyranny over her.

Now, in view of this entire disfranchisement . . . we insist that they have immediate admission to all the rights and privileges which belong to them as citizens of the United States. . . .

Lucretia Mott

The Emancipation Proclamation

On January 1, 1863, President Abraham Lincoln issued the Emancipation Proclamation, which freed all enslaved persons in states under Confederate control. The Proclamation was a significant step toward the passage of the Thirteenth Amendment (1865), which ended slavery in the United States.

Whereas, on the 22nd day of September, in the year of our Lord 1862, a proclamation was issued by the President of the United States, containing, among other things, the following, to wit:

That on the 1st day of January, in the year of our Lord 1863, all persons held as slaves within any state or designated part of a state, the people whereof shall then be in rebellion against the United States, shall be then, thenceforward, and forever free; and the executive government of the United States, including the military and naval authority thereof, will recognize and maintain the freedom of such persons and will do no act or acts to repress such persons, or any of them, in any efforts they may make for their actual freedom.

That the executive will, on the 1st day January aforesaid, by proclamation, designate the states and parts of states, if any, in which the people thereof, respectively, shall then be in rebellion against the United States; and the fact that any state or the people thereof shall on that day be in good faith represented in the Congress of the United States by members chosen thereto at elections wherein a majority of the qualified voters of such states shall have participated shall, in the absence of strong countervailing testimony, be deemed conclusive evidence that such state and the people thereof are not then in rebellion against the United States.

Now, therefore, I, Abraham Lincoln, President of the United States, by virtue of the power in me vested as commander in chief of the Army and Navy of the United States, in time of actual armed rebellion against the authority and government of the United States, and as a fit and necessary war measure for suppressing said rebellion, do, on this 1st day of January, in the year of our Lord 1863, and in accordance with my purpose so to do, publicly proclaimed for the full period of 100 days from the day first above mentioned, order, and designate as the states and parts of states wherein the people thereof, respectively, are this day in rebellion against the United States. . . .

And, by virtue of the power and for the purpose aforesaid, I do order and declare that all persons held as slaves within said designated states and parts of states are, and henceforward shall be, free; and that the executive government of the United States, including the military and naval authorities thereof, will recognize and maintain the freedom of said persons. . . .

And upon this act, sincerely believed to be an act of justice, warranted by the Constitution upon military necessity, I invoke the considerate judgment of mankind and the gracious favor of Almighty God. . . .

Abraham Lincoln

The Gettysburg Address

President Abraham Lincoln delivered the Gettysburg Address on November 19, 1863, during the dedication of the Gettysburg National Cemetery. The dedication was in honor of the more than 7,000 Union and Confederate soldiers who died in the Battle of Gettysburg earlier that year. Lincoln's brief speech is often recognized as one of the finest speeches in the English language. It is also one of the most moving speeches in the nation's history.

There are five known manuscript copies of the address, two of which are in the Library of Congress. Scholars debate about which, if any, of the existing manuscripts comes closest to Lincoln's actual words that day.

National monument at Gettysburg

Four score and seven years ago our fathers brought forth on this continent a new nation, conceived in liberty and dedicated to the proposition that all men are created equal.

Now we are engaged in a great civil war, testing whether that nation or any nation so conceived and so dedicated can long endure. We are met on a great battlefield of that war. We have come to dedicate a portion of that field as a final resting-place for those who here gave their lives that that nation might live. It is altogether fitting and proper that we should do this.

But in a larger sense, we cannot dedicate, we cannot consecrate, we cannot hallow this ground. The brave men, living and dead, who struggled here have consecrated it far above our poor power to add or detract. The world will little note nor long remember what we say here, but it can never forget what they did here. It is for us the living, rather, to be dedicated here to the unfinished work which they who fought here have thus far so nobly advanced. It is rather for us to be here dedicated to the great task remaining before us—that from these honored dead we take increased devotion to that cause for which they gave the last full measure of devotion—that we here highly resolve that these dead shall not have died in vain, that this nation under God shall have a new birth of freedom, and that government of the people, by the people, for the people, shall not perish from the earth.

The Pledge of Allegiance

Students in a New York City school reciting the Pledge of Allegiance

In 1892 the nation celebrated the 400th anniversary of Columbus's landing in America. In connection with this celebration, Francis Bellamy, a magazine editor, wrote and published the Pledge of Allegiance. The words "under God" were added by Congress in 1954 at the urging of President Dwight D. Eisenhower.

I pledge allegiance to the Flag of the United States of America and to the Republic for which it stands, one Nation under God, indivisible, with liberty and justice for all.

President Harrison on Hawaiian Annexation

An early expression of American imperialism came in the annexation of Hawaii. With the support of the American government, a small number of American troops overthrew the Hawaiian monarchy in January 1893. The excerpt below is from President Benjamin Harrison's written message to Congress. He sent the message along with the treaty for annexation to Congress on February 15, 1893.

I do not deem it necessary to discuss at any length the conditions which have resulted in this decisive action. It has been the policy of the administration not only to respect but to encourage the continuance of an independent government in the Hawaiian Islands so long as it afforded suitable guarantees for the protection of life and property and maintained a stability and strength that gave adequate security against the domination of any other power. . . .

The overthrow of the monarchy was not in any way promoted by this government, but had its origin in what seems to have been a reactionary and revolutionary policy on the part of Queen Liliuokalani, which put in serious peril not only the large and preponderating interests of the United States . . . but all foreign interests. . . . It is quite evident that the monarchy had become effete and the queen's government is weak and inadequate as to be the prey of designing and unscrupulous persons. The restoration of Queen Liliuokalani . . . is undesirable . . . and unless actively supported by the United States would be accompanied by serious disaster and the disorganization of all business interests. The influence and interest of the United States in the islands must be increased and not diminished.

Only two courses are now open—one the establishment of a protectorate by the United States, and the other annexation, full and complete. I think the latter course, which has been adopted in the treaty, will be highly promotive of the best interest of the Hawaiian people and is the only one that will adequately secure the interests of the United States. These interests are not wholly selfish. It is essential that none of the other great powers shall secure these islands. Such a possession would not consist with our safety and with the peace of the world. This view of the situation is so apparent and conclusive that no protest has been heard from any government against proceedings looking to annexation.

The American's Creed

In the patriotic fervor of World War I, national leaders sponsored a contest in which writers submitted ideas for a national creed that would be a brief summary of American beliefs. Of the 3,000 entries, the judges selected that of William Tyler Page as the winner. In a 1918 ceremony in the House of Representatives, the Speaker of the House accepted the creed for the United States.

I believe in the United States of America as a Government of the people, by the people, for the people, whose just powers are derived from the consent of the governed; a democracy in a republic; a sovereign Nation of many sovereign States; a perfect union, one and inseparable; established upon those principles of freedom, equality, justice, and humanity for which American patriots sacrificed their lives and fortunes.

I therefore believe it is my duty to my Country to love it; to support its Constitution; to obey its laws; to respect its flag, and to defend it against all enemies.

The Fourteen Points

On January 8, 1918, President Woodrow Wilson went before Congress to offer a statement of war aims called the Fourteen Points. They reflected Wilson's belief that if the international community accepted certain basic principles of conduct and set up institutions to carry them out, there would be peace in the world.

We entered this war because violations of right had occurred. . . . What we demand in this war, therefore, is . . . that the world be made fit and safe to live in. . . .

The only possible programme, as we see it, is this:

I. Open covenants of peace, openly arrived at, after which there shall be no private international understandings of any kind but diplomacy shall proceed always frankly and in the public view.

II. Absolute freedom of navigation upon the seas, outside territorial waters, alike in peace and in war. . . .

III. The removal, so far as possible, of all economic barriers and the establishment of an equality of trade conditions among all the nations. . . .

IV. Adequate guarantees given and taken that national armaments will be reduced to the lowest point consistent with domestic safety.

V. A free, open-minded, and absolutely impartial adjustment of all colonial claims, based upon a strict observance of the principle that in determining all such questions of sovereignty the interests of the populations concerned must have equal weight with the equitable claims of the government whose title is to be determined.

VI. The evacuation of all Russian territory and . . . opportunity for the independent determination of her own political development and national polity. . . .

VII. Belgium . . . must be evacuated and restored. . . .

VIII. All French territory should be freed and the invaded portions restored, and the wrong done to France by Prussia in 1871 in the matter of Alsace-Lorraine should be righted. . . .

IX. A readjustment of the frontiers of Italy should be effected along clearly recognizable lines of nationality.

X. The peoples of Austria-Hungary . . . should be accorded the freest opportunity of autonomous development.

XI. Roumania, Serbia, and Montenegro should be evacuated; occupied territories restored . . . the relations of the several Balkan states to one another determined by friendly counsel along historically established lines of allegiance and nationality. . . .

XII. The Turkish portions of the present Ottoman Empire should be assured a secure sovereignty. . . .

XIII. An independent Polish state should be erected which should include the territories inhabited by indisputably Polish populations. . . .

XIV. A general association of nations must be formed under specific covenants for the purpose of affording mutual guarantes of political independence and territorial integrity. . . .

Discussion of the Fourteen Points at the Versailles peace conference

The Four Freedoms

President Franklin D. Roosevelt delivered this address on January 6, 1941, in his annual message to Congress. In it, Roosevelt called for a world founded on "four essential human freedoms": freedom of speech and expression, freedom of worship, freedom from want, and freedom from fear.

Just as our national policy in internal affairs has been based upon a decent respect for the rights and dignity of all our fellow men within our gates, so our national policy in foreign affairs has been based on a decent respect for the rights and dignity of all nations, large and small. And the justice of morality must and will win in the end.

Our national policy is this:

First, by an impressive expression of the public will and without regard to partisanship, we are committed to all-inclusive national defense.

Second, by an impressive expression of the public will and without regard to partisanship, we are committed to full support of all those resolute peoples, everywhere, who are resisting aggression and are thereby keeping war away from our Hemisphere. . . .

Third . . . we are committed to the proposition that principles of morality and considerations for our own security will never permit us to acquiesce in a peace dictated by aggressors. . . .

Let us say to the democracies, "We Americans are vitally concerned in your defense of freedom. We are putting forth our energies, our resources, and our organizing powers to give you the strength to regain and maintain a free world. We shall send you, in ever increasing numbers, ships, planes, tanks, guns. This is our purpose and our pledge." In fulfillment of this purpose we will not be intimidated by the threats of dictators that they will regard as a breach of international law and as an act of war our aid to the democracies which dare to resist their aggression. . . .

Caricature of President Roosevelt

In the future days, which we seek to make secure, we look forward to a world founded upon four essential human freedoms.

The first is freedom of speech and expression everywhere in the world.

The second is freedom of every person to worship God in his own way everywhere in the world.

The third is freedom from want, which, translated into world terms, means economic understandings which will secure to every nation a healthy peacetime life for its inhabitants everywhere in the world.

The fourth is freedom from fear—which, translated into world terms, means a worldwide reduction of armaments to such a point and in such a thorough fashion that no nation will be in a position to commit an act of physical aggression against any neighbor—anywhere in the world. . . .

The Truman Doctrine

President Harry S. Truman addressed a joint session of Congress on March 12, 1947, to request aid to fight Communist influence in Greece and Turkey. His message that communism had to be contained represents the central idea of American foreign policy during the Cold War.

The United States has received from the Greek Government an urgent appeal for financial and economic assistance. . . .

When forces of liberation entered Greece they found that the retreating Germans had destroyed virtually all the railways, roads, port facilities, communications, and merchant marine. More than a thousand villages had been burned. Eighty-five percent of the children were tubercular. Livestock, poultry, and draft animals had almost disappeared. Inflation had wiped out practically all savings. As a result of these tragic conditions, a militant minority, exploiting human want and misery, was able to create political chaos which, until now, has made economic recovery impossible.

Greece is today without funds to finance the importation of those goods which are essential to bare subsistence. Under these circumstances the people of Greece cannot make progress in solving their problems of reconstruction. Greece is in desperate need of financial and economic assistance to enable it to resume purchases of food, clothing, fuel and seeds. These are indispensable for the subsistence of its people and are obtainable only from abroad. Greece must have help to import the goods necessary to restore internal order and security, so essential for economic and political recovery. . . .

Meanwhile, the Greek Government is unable to cope with the situation. The Greek army is small and poorly equipped. It needs supplies and equipment if it is to restore the authority of the government throughout Greek territory. Greece must have assistance if it is to become a self-supporting and self-respecting democracy.

The United States must supply that assistance. We have already extended to Greece certain types of relief and economic aid but these are inadequate. There is no other country to which democratic Greece can turn. . . .

No government is perfect. One of the chief virtues of a democracy, however, is that its defects are always visible and under democratic processes can be pointed out and corrected.

The Government of Greece is not perfect. Nevertheless it represents eighty-five percent of the members of the Greek Parliament who were chosen in an election last year. . . .

Greece's neighbor, Turkey, also deserves our attention. The future of Turkey as an independent and economically sound state is clearly no less important to the freedom-loving peoples of the world than the future of Greece. The circumstances in which Turkey finds itself today are considerably different from those of Greece. Turkey has been spared the disasters that have beset Greece. And during the war, the United States and Great Britain furnished Turkey with material aid. Nevertheless, Turkey now needs our support.

. . . To ensure the peaceful development of nations, free from coercion, the United States has taken a leading part in establishing the United Nations. The United Nations is designed to make possible lasting freedom and independence for all its members. We shall not realize our objectives, however, unless we are willing to help free peoples to maintain their free institutions . . . against aggressive movements that seek to impose upon them totalitarian regimes. . . .

This is an investment in world freedom and world peace. . . . The seeds of totalitarian regimes are nurtured by misery and want. They spread and grow in the evil soil of poverty and strife. They reach their full growth when the hope of a people for a better life has died. We must keep that hope alive. . . . If we falter in our leadership, we may endanger the peace of the world—and we shall surely endanger the welfare of our own nation.

Documents

Brown v. Board of Education

On May 17, 1954, the Supreme Court ruled in **Brown** *v.* **Board of Education of Topeka, Kansas,** *that racial segregation in public schools was unconstitutional. This decision provided the legal basis for court challenges to segregation in every aspect of American life.*

These cases come to us from the States of Kansas, South Carolina, Virginia, and Delaware. They are premised on different facts and different local conditions, but a common legal question justifies their consideration together in this consolidated opinion.

In each of the cases, minors of the Negro race, through their legal representatives, seek the aid of the courts in obtaining admission to the public schools of their community on a nonsegregated basis. In each instance, they had been denied admission to schools attended by white children under laws requiring or permitting segregation according to race. This segregation was alleged to deprive the plaintiffs of the equal protection of the laws under the Fourteenth Amendment.

The plaintiffs contend that segregated public schools are not "equal" and cannot be made "equal," and that hence they are deprived of the equal protection of the laws. Because of the obvious importance of the question presented, the Court took jurisdiction. . . .

. . . Our decision . . . cannot turn on merely a comparison of these tangible factors in the Negro and white schools involved in each of the cases. We must look instead to the effect of segregation itself on public education.

In approaching this problem, we cannot turn the clock back to 1868 when the Amendment was adopted, or even to 1896 when *Plessy* v. *Ferguson* was written. We must consider public education in the light of its full development and its present place in American life throughout the nation. Only in this way can it be determined if segregation in public schools deprives these plaintiffs of the equal protection of the laws.

Today, education is perhaps the most important function of state and local governments. Compulsory school attendance laws and the great expenditures for education both demonstrate our recognition of the importance of education to our democratic society. . . . In these days, it is doubtful that any child may reasonably be expected to succeed in life if he is denied the opportunity of an education. Such an opportunity, where the state has undertaken to provide it, is a right which must be made available to all on equal terms.

We come then to the question presented: Does segregation of children in public schools solely on the basis of race, even though the physical facilities and other "tangible" factors may be equal, deprive the children of the minority group of equal educational opportunities? We believe that it does.

Linda Brown

. . . We conclude that, in the field of public education, the doctrine of "separate but equal" has no place. Separate educational facilities are inherently unequal. Therefore, we hold that the plaintiff and others similarly situated for whom the actions have been brought are, by reason of the segregation complained of, deprived of the equal protection of the laws guaranteed by the Fourteenth Amendment. . . .

"I Have a Dream"

On August 28, 1963, while Congress was debating broad civil rights legislation, Martin Luther King, Jr., led more than 200,000 people in a march on Washington, D.C. On the steps of the Lincoln Memorial, King gave a stirring speech in which he eloquently spoke of his dreams for African Americans and for the United States.

Martin Luther King, Jr., speaking at the march

Five score years ago, a great American, in whose symbolic shadow we stand, signed the Emancipation Proclamation. This momentous decree came as a great beacon light of hope to millions of Negro slaves who had been seared in the flames of withering injustice. It came as a joyous daybreak to end the long night of captivity.

But one hundred years later, we must face the tragic fact that the Negro is still not free. One hundred years later, the life of the Negro is still sadly crippled by the manacles of segregation and the chains of discrimination. . . .

There are those who are asking the devotees of civil rights, "When will you be satisfied?"

We can never be satisfied as long as the Negro is the victim of the unspeakable horrors of police brutality.

We can never be satisfied as long as our bodies, heavy with the fatigue of travel, cannot gain lodging in the motels of the highways and the hotels of the cities.

We cannot be satisfied as long as the Negro's basic mobility is from a smaller ghetto to a larger one. . . .

We cannot be satisfied as long as a Negro in Mississippi cannot vote and a Negro in New York believes he has nothing for which to vote.

No, no, we are not satisfied, and we will not be satisfied until "justice rolls down like waters and righteousness like a mighty stream." . . .

I say to you today, my friends, so even though we face the difficulties of today and tomorrow, I still have a dream. It is a dream deeply rooted in the American dream.

I have a dream that one day this nation will rise up and live out the true meaning of its creed: "We hold these truths to be self-evident; that all men are created equal."

I have a dream that one day on the red hills of Georgia the sons of former slaves and the sons of former slaveowners will be able to sit down together at the table of brotherhood.

I have a dream that one day even the state of Mississippi, a state sweltering with the heat of injustice and oppression, will be transformed into an oasis of freedom and justice.

I have a dream that my four little children will one day live in a nation where they will not be judged by the color of their skin but by the content of their character. . . .

And when this happens, when we allow freedom to ring, when we let it ring from every village and every hamlet, from every state and every city, we will be able to speed up that day when all of God's children, black men and white men, Jews and Gentiles, Protestants and Catholics, will be able to join hands and sing in the words of the old Negro spiritual, "Free at last! Free at last! Thank God Almighty, we are free at last!"

Gulf of Tonkin Resolution

On August 7, 1964, Congress passed the Gulf of Tonkin Resolution, which stood as the legal basis for the Vietnam War.

Resolved by the Senate and House of Representatives of the United States of America in Congress assembled,

That the Congress approves and supports the determination of the President, as Commander in Chief, to take all necessary measures to repel any armed attack against the forces of the United States and to prevent further aggression.

Section 2. The United States regards as vital to its national interest and to world peace the maintenance of international peace and security in southeast Asia. Consonant with the Constitution of the United States and the Charter of the United Nations and in accordance with its obligations under the Southeast Asia Collective Defense Treaty, the United States is, therefore, prepared, as the President determines, to take all necessary steps, including the use of armed force, to assist any member or protocol state of the Southeast Asia Collective Defense Treaty requesting assistance in defense of its freedom.

President Bush's Address to Joint Session of Congress, September 20, 2001

On September 11, 2001, terrorists crashed airplanes into the World Trade Center in New York City and the Pentagon in Washington, D.C. Thousands of people were killed. In his address, President George W. Bush announced a new kind of war against terrorism.

. . . On September the eleventh, enemies of freedom committed an act of war against our country. . . . Americans have known surprise attacks—but never before on thousands of civilians. All of this was brought upon us in a single day—and night fell on a different world, a world where freedom itself is under attack. . . .

The evidence we have gathered all points to a collection of loosely affiliated terrorist organizations known as al-Qaeda. . . . Our war on terror begins with al-Qaeda, but it does not end there. It will not end until every terrorist group of global reach has been found, stopped, and defeated.

Americans are asking: Why do they hate us? They hate what we see right here in this chamber—a democratically elected government.

Their leaders are self-appointed. They hate our freedoms. . . . By sacrificing human life to serve their radical visions—by abandoning every value except the will to power—they follow in the path of fascism, and Nazism, and totalitarianism. And they will follow that path all the way, to where it ends: in history's unmarked grave of discarded lies.

. . . We will direct every resource at our command—every means of diplomacy, every tool of intelligence, every instrument of law enforcement, every financial influence, and every necessary weapon of war—to the disruption and defeat of the global terror network. . . .

I know there are struggles ahead, and dangers to face. But this country will define our times, not be defined by them. . . . Great harm has been done to us. We have suffered great loss. And in our grief and anger we have found our mission and our moment. . . . Our Nation—this generation—will lift a dark threat of violence from our people and our future. We will rally the world to this cause, by our efforts and by our courage. We will not tire, we will not falter, and we will not fail.

Supreme Court Case Summaries

The following case summaries explain the significance of major Supreme Court cases mentioned in the text.

Abington School District v. Schempp

(1963) struck down a Pennsylvania statute requiring public schools in the state to begin each school day with Bible readings and a recitation of the Lord's Prayer. The Court held that the Constitution's establishment clause leaves religious beliefs and religious practices to each individual's choice and expressly commands that government not intrude into this decision-making process.

Abrams v. United States

(1919) upheld a conviction under the Sedition Act and Espionage Act of 1917. The Court ruled that freedom of speech could be limited if there was a threat to the country.

Baker v. Carr

(1962) established that federal courts can hear suits seeking to force state authorities to redraw electoral districts. In this case, the plaintiff wanted the population of each district to be roughly equal to the population in all other districts. The plaintiff claimed that the votes of voters in the least populous districts counted as much as the votes of voters in the most populous districts.

Brown v. Board of Education

(1954) overruled *Plessy v. Ferguson* (1896) and abandoned the separate-but-equal doctrine in the context of public schools. In deciding this case, the Supreme Court rejected the idea that equivalent but separate schools for African Americans and white students would be constitutional. The Court stated that the Fourteenth Amendment's command that all persons be accorded the equal protection of the law (U.S. Const. amend. XIV, sec. 1) is not satisfied by ensuring that African American and white schools "have been equalized, or are being equalized, with respect to buildings, curricula, qualifications, and salaries, and other tangible factors."

The Court then held that racial segregation in public schools violates the equal protection clause because it is inherently unequal. In other words, the separation of schools by race marks the separate race as inferior. The ruling in this case has been extended beyond public education to virtually all public accommodations and activities.

Bush v. Gore

(2000) found that a manual recount of disputed presidential ballots in Florida lacked a uniform standard of judging a voter's intent, thus violating the equal protection clause of the Constitution. The Court also ruled that there was not enough time to conduct a new manual recount that would meet constitutional standards. The case arose when Republican candidate George W. Bush asked the Court to stop a hand recount. This decision ensured that Bush would receive Florida's electoral votes and win the election.

Chisholm v. Georgia

(1793) stripped the immunity of the states to lawsuits in federal court. The Supreme Court held that a citizen of one state could sue another state in federal court without that state consenting to the suit. The Court's decision created a furor and led to the adoption of the Eleventh Amendment, which protects states from federal court suits by citizens of other states.

Dred Scott v. Sandford

(1857) was decided before the Fourteenth Amendment. The Fourteenth Amendment provides that anyone born or naturalized in the United States is a citizen of the nation and of his or her state. In this case, the Supreme Court held that a slave was property, not a citizen, and thus had no rights under the Constitution. The decision was a prime factor leading to the Civil War.

Engel v. Vitale

(1962) held that the establishment clause (U.S. Const. amend. I, cl. 1) was violated by a public school district's practice of starting each school day with a prayer which began, "Almighty God, we acknowledge our dependence upon Thee." The Supreme Court ruled that religion is a personal matter and that government should not align itself with a particular religion in order to prevent religious persecution.

Escobedo v. Illinois (1964) held that Danny Escobedo's right to counsel, as provided by the Sixth Amendment, had been violated. Throughout police questioning, Escobedo asked repeatedly, but unsuccessfully, to see his attorney. The Supreme Court reversed Escobedo's murder conviction, holding that an attorney could have assisted Escobedo in invoking his Fifth Amendment right against self-incrimination. This case served as a forerunner to *Miranda* v. *Arizona*.

Gibbons v. Ogden (1824) made it clear that the authority of Congress to regulate interstate commerce (U.S. Const. art. I, sec. 8, cl. 3) includes the authority to regulate intrastate commercial activity that relates to interstate commerce. Before this case, it was thought that the Constitution would allow a state to close its borders to interstate commercial activity. This ruling says that a state can only regulate internal commercial activity, but Congress can regulate commercial activity that has both intrastate and interstate dimensions.

Gideon v. Wainwright (1963) ruled that poor defendants in criminal cases have the right to a state-paid attorney under the Sixth Amendment. The ruling in this case has been refined to apply only when the defendant, if convicted, can be sentenced to more than six months in jail.

Griswold v. Connecticut (1965) overturned the conviction of two Planned Parenthood employees charged with violating an 1879 state law banning the use of contraceptives. In deciding this case, the Court went beyond the actual words of the Constitution to protect a right—the right to privacy—which is not listed in the Constitution. The case also served as a forerunner to the *Roe* v. *Wade* decision that legalized abortion on the same basis.

Heart of Atlanta Motel, Inc. v. United States (1964) upheld the Civil Rights Act of 1964, which prohibits racial discrimination by those who provide goods, services, and facilities to the public. The Georgia motel in the case drew its business from other states but refused to rent rooms to African Americans. The Supreme Court explained that Congress had the authority to prohibit such discrimination under both the equal protection clause (U.S. Const. amend. XIV, sec. 1) and the commerce clause (art. I, sec. 8, cl. 3). With respect to the commerce clause, the Court explained that Congress had ample evidence to conclude that racial discrimination by hotels and motels impedes interstate commerce.

Korematsu v. United States (1944) allowed the federal government's authority to exclude Japanese Americans, many of whom were citizens, from designated military areas that included almost the entire West Coast. The government defended the orders as a necessary response to Japan's attack on Pearl Harbor. Yet, in upholding the orders, the Court established that government actions that discriminate on the basis of race would be subject to strict scrutiny.

Loving v. Virginia (1967) ruled that state laws that outlaw interracial marriages are unconstitutional under the Fourteenth Amendment. The Court explained that such laws violated the equal protection clause and deprived "citizens of liberty without due process of law." The Court went on to say, "Marriage is one of the basic civil rights of man, fundamental to our very existence and survival."

Mapp v. Ohio (1961) established that evidence seized in violation of the Fourth Amendment could not be used by the prosecution as evidence of a defendant's guilt at the federal, state, or local level.

Marbury v. Madison (1803) established one of the most important principles of American constitutional law. The Supreme Court held that the Court itself has the final say on what the Constitution means. It is also the Supreme Court that has the final say whether or not an act of government—legislative or executive at the federal, state, or local level—violates the Constitution.

Martin v. Hunter's Lessee (1816) affirmed that the Supreme Court has the authority to review state court decisions and is the nation's final court of appeal. The Supreme Court ruled that section 25 of the Judiciary Act of 1789 was constitutional. This section granted the Supreme Court appellate jurisdiction over state courts in certain situations, such as a state court denying the authority of federal law.

McCulloch v. Maryland (1819) established the basis for the expansive authority of Congress. The Supreme Court held that the necessary and proper clause (U.S. Const. art. I, sec. 8, cl. 18) allows Congress to do more than the Constitution specifically authorizes it to do. This case holds that Congress can enact almost any law that will help it achieve the ends established by Article I, Section 8 of the Constitution. For example, Congress has the power to regulate interstate commerce; the necessary and proper clause permits Congress to do so in ways not specified in the Constitution.

Supreme Court Case Summaries

Miranda v. Arizona (1966) held that a person in police custody may not be held unless reminded of his or her rights. These rights include: 1) the right to remain silent, 2) the right to an attorney (at government expense if the person is unable to pay), and 3) that anything the person says after acknowledging that he or she understands these rights can be used as evidence of guilt at a trial.

The Supreme Court explained that a person alone in police custody may not understand, even if told, that he or she can remain silent and thus might be misled into answering questions. The presence of an attorney is essential.

Morgan v. Virginia (1946) challenged racial segregation in the South. Irene Morgan was convicted for refusing to give up her seat on an interstate bus bound from Virginia to Maryland. The Court ruled that the Virginia law posed an undue burden on interstate commerce and struck down the statute. However, segregation on southern buses continued on an informal basis.

National Labor Relations Board v. Jones and Laughlin Steel Corp. (1937) upheld President Franklin Roosevelt's New Deal legislation, the National Labor Relations Act, which allowed workers to organize unions in businesses operating or affecting interstate commerce. Employers were prohibited from discriminating against their employees because of union membership. Prior to this case, the Supreme Court had ruled much New Deal legislation unconstitutional. This ruling came less than a week after Roosevelt's proposed court-packing plan. The president intended on "packing" the Supreme Court with additional justices in order to obtain a pro-New Deal majority on the Court.

New York Times Co. v. Sullivan (1964) extended the protections afforded to the press by the free press clause (U.S. Const. amend. I). In this case, the Supreme Court held that a public official or public figure suing a publisher for libel (i.e., defamation) must prove that the publisher published a story that he or she knew was false or published the story in "reckless disregard of its truth or falsity," which means that the publisher did not take professionally adequate steps to determine the story's truth or falsity.

Norris v. Alabama (1935) overturned the conviction of Clarence Norris, an African American sentenced to death for a crime in Alabama. The Supreme Court held that the grand jury and trial jury had systematically eliminated African American jurors. Thus, the Court reversed the conviction because it violated the equal protection clause of the Fourteenth Amendment.

Northern Securities Company v. United States (1904) dealt with the application of congressional antitrust legislation. The party involved held three-fourths of the stock in two parallel railroad lines. By a narrow 5–4 decision, the Court upheld the application of the Sherman Antitrust Act. The Court ruled that the holding company clearly intended to eliminate competition between the two railroads, violating the constitutional right of Congress to regulate interstate commerce.

Plessy v. Ferguson (1896) upheld the separate-but-equal doctrine used by Southern states to perpetuate segregation after the Civil War officially ended law-mandated segregation. The decision upheld a Louisiana law requiring passenger trains to have "equal but separated accommodations for the white and colored races." The Court held that the Fourteenth Amendment's equal protection clause required only equal public facilities for the two races, not equal access. This case was overruled by *Brown* v. *Board of Education* (1954).

Regents of the University of California v. Bakke (1978) was the first Supreme Court decision to suggest that an affirmative action program could be justified on the basis of diversity. The Court explained that racial quotas were not permissible under the equal protection clause of the Fourteenth Amendment. However, the justices ruled that the diversity rationale was a legitimate interest that would allow a state medical school to consider an applicant's race in evaluating his or her application for admission. (Recent Supreme Court cases suggest that the diversity rationale is no longer enough to defend an affirmative action program.)

Reynolds v. Sims (1964) extended the one-person, one-vote doctrine announced in *Wesberry* v. *Sanders* to state legislative elections. The Court held that the inequality of representation in the Alabama legislature violated the equal protection clause of the Fourteenth Amendment.

Roe v. Wade (1973) held that women have the right under various provisions of the Constitution—most notably, the due process clause of the Fourteenth Amendment—to decide whether or not to terminate a pregnancy. The Court's ruling in this case was the most significant in a long line of decisions over a period of 50 years that recognized a constitutional right of privacy, even though the word *privacy* is not found in the Constitution.

Schechter Poultry Corporation v. United States

(1935) overturned the conviction of the employers, who were charged with violating the wage and hour limitations of a law adopted under the authority of the National Industrial Recovery Act. The Court held that because the defendants did not sell poultry in interstate commerce, they were not subject to federal regulations on wages and hours.

Schenck v. United States

(1919) upheld convictions under the Federal Espionage Act. The defendants were charged under the act with distributing leaflets aimed at inciting draft resistance during World War I; their defense was that antidraft speech was protected under the First Amendment.

The Supreme Court unanimously rejected the defense, explaining that whether or not speech is protected depends on the context in which it occurs. Because the defendants' antidraft rhetoric created a "clear and present danger" to the success of the war effort, it was not protected.

Stone v. Powell

(1976) reversed a Court of Appeals decision that evidence was seized illegally and should therefore be excluded. The Court ruled that the defendant was provided a fair and legal opportunity to claim a Fourth Amendment violation before a trial jury. The trial jury found that the search was constitutional and the evidence should not be excluded. The Court stated, "Where the state has provided an opportunity for full and fair litigation of a Fourth Amendment claim, a state prisoner may not be granted federal habeas corpus relief."

Swann v. Charlotte-Mecklenburg Board of Education

(1971) established a new plan to ensure that public schools were not segregated. Many school systems were slow to desegregate after *Brown* v. *Board of Education* and used various tactics to appear to be resolving the problem. This case ordered that busing students, reorganizing school boundaries, and racial ratios all be used as methods to obtain desegregated public school systems.

Sweatt v. Painter

(1950) held that it was unconstitutional for African Americans to be denied admission to the University of Texas Law School based on race. An inferior law school established for African Americans did not give the state justification to deny admission to the main school. This act was a violation of the Fourteenth Amendment.

Wabash v. Illinois

(1886) held that states have no authority to regulate railroad rates for interstate commerce. The Supreme Court held that the commerce clause (U.S. Const. art. I, sec. 8, cl. 3) allowed states to enforce "indirect" but not "direct" burdens on interstate commerce. State railroad rates were ruled "direct" burdens and therefore could not be enforced by states. The decision created a precedent by establishing rate regulation of interstate commerce as an exclusive federal power.

Wickard v. Filburn

(1942) indicated how far the Supreme Court had come in complying with President Franklin Roosevelt's economic philosophies. The Court upheld specific parts of the Second Agricultural Adjustment Act. In its ruling, the Supreme Court held that marketing quotas could be applied to wheat that never left the farm. Using the commerce clause (U.S. Const. art. I, sec. 8, cl. 3) as the basis for its decision, the Court ruled that wheat that never left the farm still had an effect on interstate commerce. Farmers growing their own grain depressed the overall demand and market price of wheat. The decision further extended the power of the commerce clause.

Worcester v. Georgia

(1832) overturned the conviction of Samuel A. Worcester, a missionary among the Cherokee. Worcester was imprisoned under a Georgia law forbidding whites to reside in Cherokee country without taking an oath of allegiance to the state and obtaining a permit. The Supreme Court voided the state law, ruling that the Cherokee were an independent nation based on a federal treaty and free from the jurisdiction of the state. Georgia ignored the decision, and President Jackson refused to enforce it, instead supporting the removal of the Cherokee to the Indian Territory.

American Literature Library

TABLE OF CONTENTS

What Is Literature?

Literature is art created with words. Some people use the term "literature" to include anything written—from newspaper articles and how-to books to pamphlets in a doctor's office. On the other hand, some insist that only creative writing can be literature. Still others suggest that some essays, or written opinions, and even speeches are of such high quality that they may be considered literature.

Just as there are many forms of the visual arts, there are many forms and styles of literature. Reading the literature of a certain period of history helps to bring the people and issues of the time to life.

A Good Story

Have you ever created a story to entertain a younger person? That's fiction: a story invented by the author. Writing that describes or explains real events or activities is referred to as "nonfiction."

The most popular type of fiction is the novel, a long story that usually has many people, or characters, and a complex plot, or action. Novels are written in prose, or everyday language, rather than poetry.

Some novels are inspired by actual events the author witnessed or people he or she has known. But a fiction writer is not attempting to report events or describe people accurately.

By telling a good story, the author tries to lead the reader to discover universal truths. Other types of fiction include short stories and novellas, or short novels.

Time and Timelessness

Some writers set their stories in the present; some write historical novels; others write science fiction tales set in the future. All writers hope their work expresses truths that will be valid long after their lifetimes.

Throughout history, writers have addressed major themes such as good and evil, freedom, religion, power, corruption, love, death, and the relationship of humans to the natural world. Works of literature from a specific period of history often reflect their time in several ways:

- the language used
- the form of the work
- the general attitudes of the characters and the issues they face
- the morality expressed by the outcome

Approaching Poetry

Poetry is writing that is intended first and foremost to evoke emotion, not just convey information or tell a story. The first job of poetry is to create feeling—not to stimulate thought. For this reason it often has a rhythm like music, and it is often easier to understand if read aloud.

Eighteenth- and nineteenth-century poets—and some modern ones—wrote in one of many traditional forms. Each form requires a certain rhyme frequency and pattern of accented syllables, or meter. It also requires a specific number of lines of certain lengths.

Modern poetry does not always follow these conventions; words do not always rhyme, and sometimes the rhythm is to be found in how the words are arranged on the page, not how they sound. Despite these modern touches, the poet's goal remains constant—to evoke specific emotions that illuminate some aspect of life.

The Eras of Literature in American History

Writers reflect world events and issues in their work. Some write directly about those events and issues. Others express values or beliefs that were changed by historical events.

The Early National Period During the early years of the United States, authors often wrote about the challenges of settling a new land. They also focused on religion, morality, and the new form of government. Native Americans already had a rich tradition of oral literature.

After the War of 1812, writers such as James Fennimore Cooper and Washington Irving created a uniquely American style of writing with tales of adventures in the New World. Ralph Waldo Emerson and Henry David Thoreau wrote of the spiritual power of nature.

The Civil War Era During the Civil War and in every decade since, the tragedies of that conflict and the nature of race relations in American society have inspired some of America's best writers, from Mark Twain and Harriet Beecher Stowe in the nineteenth century to William Faulkner and Richard Wright in the twentieth century, and contemporary writers such as August Wilson and Toni Morrison.

Naturalism and Realism As industrialization attracted immigrants from around the globe, writers created art out of the attainment—and the failure—of their dreams. In *The Rise of Silas Lapham,* William Dean Howells told the rags-to-riches story of a Northern industrialist. Early in the twentieth century, "realist" writers, such as Theodore Dreiser, aided the work of Progressive reformers by exposing the underside of industry and the lives of laborers. Other major writers of the era included Mark Twain, Henry James, Stephen Crane, and Edith Wharton.

Modernism in the 1920s and 1930s World War I and its aftermath challenged traditional values, family life, and individual identity. Perhaps the best-known writer of this era is Ernest Hemingway, who along with other "lost generation" writers such as John dos Passos, Gertrude Stein, and F. Scott Fitzgerald described their sense of disillusionment with modern life.

The era also witnessed the appearance of several major African American writers and poets, including Langston Hughes and Claude McKay, in what became known as the Harlem Renaissance.

The tragedy of the Great Depression and the struggles of average Americans to survive provided inspiration for many writers. John Steinbeck's novel *The Grapes of Wrath* about Dust Bowl refugees is perhaps best known.

The second world war spawned a flood of war novels as writers reexamined human beings' relationship to evil, religion, and the meaning of life in the wake of the Jewish Holocaust, and what such an event said about human nature and its capacity for evil.

The 1950s and 1960s In the 1950s, beat writers, such as Jack Kerouac and Tom Robbins, shunned the conformity and materialism of affluent postwar America in favor of spontaneity and experimentation. But history had more shocks in store for American society including the social upheaval of the 1960s, the Vietnam War, and the transformation of a society from one based on reading to a mass-media consumer culture.

Postmodern Writers of Today The events of the late twentieth century led to "postmodern" writing. Postmodern writers are skeptical about any single version of reality in the Information Age. Their writing is full of irony and doubt about modern culture.

Unit 1: Creating a Nation

When white settlers arrived in America, the Native Americans living there already had a highly developed civilization dating back thousands of years. They also had their own form of literature—not written, but handed down from generation to generation orally. A theme common to many Native American stories is their relationship to nature. Many are also parables—stories that use symbols or animals to teach lessons. "Bald Eagle Sends Mud-turtle to the End of the World," written down by Jeremiah Curtin, is an example of a parable.

The second selection here is a portion of a famous speech given by Chief Red Jacket (Native American name Sagoyoweha). Red Jacket was an influential leader of the Seneca nation and the Iroquois confederation of tribes from the 1770s until the 1820s. He fought on the side of the British during the American Revolution, but in the War of 1812, he influenced his people to support the United States.

An ardent advocate of the Native American mode of life, he opposed the introduction of white customs, laws, schools, and especially conversion of Seneca to Christianity. In 1820 or 1821 he successfully petitioned Governor Clinton for the removal of missionaries and white teachers from Buffalo Creek reservation near Buffalo, New York. This speech was given at an 1805 meeting to discuss establishment of missions among six Iroquois nations. In it, Red Jacket argues forcefully for the religious freedom that many white settlers had left Europe to enjoy.

forefathers: ancestors

"Bald Eagle Sends Mud-turtle to the End of the World"

Once upon a time, a bald-headed old man lived on the top of a mountain, and his wife and three children lived near a lake about half way to the summit of the same mountain.

Each day the old man went down to fish in the lake. On his way home he stopped and gave some of the fish to his wife, and thus they lived well and happily. After they had passed many years in this manner, the old man became curious to know how large the world is.

Being chief of his people he called a council, and said, "I want to know how large the world is. I wish some man would volunteer to find out."

One young man said, "I will go and find out."

"Very well," said the chief, "How long will you be gone?"

"I can't tell, for I don't know how far I shall have to travel."

"Go," said the chief, "and when you return you will tell us about your journey."

The young man started and after traveling two moons he came to a country where everything was white—the forests, the water, the grass. It hurt his feet to walk on the white ground, so he hurried back. When he reached home he notified the chief. The chief said, "I don't believe that he has been to the end of the world, but I will call a council and we will hear what he has to say."

When the people were assembled, the young man said: "I did not go very far, but I went as far as I was able." And he told all he knew of the White Country.

The chief said, "We must send another man." . . . Many men were sent, one after another, and each returned with a story a little different from that told by others, but still no one satisfied the chief. At last a man said, "I will start and I will go to the end of the world before I come back."

The chief looked at the man and saw that he was very homely, but very strong, and he said, "I think you will do as you promise. You may go." The chief called a council of the whole nation and each man agreed to make a journey by himself . . . The chief and his men went and were gone forty moons. When they came home a council was held and each told what he had seen. When the man came who had promised to go to the end of the world, he said, "I have been to the end of

Chief Red Jacket's Speech

Chief Red Jacket

the world, I have seen all kinds of people, all kinds of game, all kinds of forests and rivers. I have seen things which no one else has ever seen."

The chief was satisfied. He said, "I am chief of all the people, you will be next to me. You'll be second chief." This was the pay the man got for his journey. He took his position as second chief.

The old chief was Bald Eagle. The first man sent out was Deer. His feet were tender, he could not endure the ice and snow of the White Country. The homely man who went to the end of the world was Mud-turtle.

"BROTHER: Our seats were once large and yours were small. You have now become a great people, and we have scarcely a place left to spread our blankets. You have got our country, but you are not satisfied; you want to force your religion upon us. . . . You say that you are right and we are lost. How do we know this to be true? We understand that your religion is written in a book. If it was intended for us as well as you, why has not the Great Spirit given to us, and not only to us, but why did he not give to our **forefathers,** the knowledge of that book, with the means of understanding it rightly? We only know what you tell us about it. How shall we know when to believe, being so often deceived by the white people.

BROTHER: You say there is but one way to worship and serve the Great Spirit. If there is but one religion, why do you white people differ so much about it? Why not all agreed, as you can all read the book?

BROTHER: We do not understand these things. We are told that your religion was given to your forefathers, and has been handed down from father to son. We also have a religion, which was given to our forefathers, and has been handed down to us their children. We worship in that way. It teaches us to be thankful for all the favors we receive, to love each other, and to be united. We never quarrel about religion.

BROTHER: The Great Spirit has made us all, but He has made a great difference between his white and red children. He has given us different complexions and different customs. To you he has given the arts. To these He has not opened our eyes. . . . Since He has made so great a difference between us in other things, why may we not conclude that he has given us a different religion according to our understanding? The Great Spirit does right. He knows what is best for his children; we are satisfied. . . . We do not wish to destroy your religion, or take it from you. We only want to enjoy our own."

Writers of the Young Republic

Sixty years after declaring independence, American culture was still heavily influenced by Europe. In 1836 Ralph Waldo Emerson's groundbreaking essay, "Nature", established a new way for Americans to look at the world. For the first time in history, there was a roadmap showing how to escape from traditional cultures and build a new, American identity. A large part of that identity was the belief in individuality, expressed in another Emerson essay, "Self-Reliance," a portion of which follows.

Born in Boston in 1803, Emerson was descended from a long line of New England clergymen. He began his career as a Unitarian minister, but left the church because of doubts about orthodox doctrine. Still, he spent the rest of his life as a teacher of ethics, through his lectures and his writing.

Emerson wrote against the rising tide of American materialism and conformity in his time—themes that are as relevant today as they were a century ago. As he worded it, "Things are in the saddle/And ride mankind."

Emerson is considered the father of a philosophical, religious, and literary movement called transcendentalism. Along with Walt Whitman, Henry David Thoreau, Margaret Fuller, and other writers of the day, Emerson believed that the divine spirit was present in every man and in all of nature. In nature, man could **intuitively** *discover all universal laws at work. If God is good and just, then so is man. Evil exists only when man has an imperfect awareness of his essential goodness. This belief led some transcendentalists to social activism.*

intuitively: understanding immediately without the need of logic or rational thought

particulars: areas of life

asinine: marked by a failure to use intelligence or good judgment

loath: unwilling

hobgoblin: a mischievous goblin, or ugly sprite

gazetted: announced in a periodical

"Self-Reliance"
Ralph Waldo Emerson

What I must do is all that concerns me, not what the people think. This rule, equally arduous in actual and in intellectual life, may serve for the whole distinction between greatness and meanness. It is the harder, because you will always find those who think they know what is your duty better than you know it. It is easy in the world to live after the world's opinion; it is easy in solitude to live after our own; but the great man is he who in the midst of the crowd keeps with perfect sweetness the independence of solitude.

The objection to conforming to usages that have become dead to you is that it scatters your force. It loses your time and blurs the impression of your character. If you maintain a dead church, contribute to a dead Bible-society, vote with a great party either for the government or against it, spread your table like base housekeepers,—under all these screens I have difficulty to detect the precise man you are. And, of course, so much force is withdrawn from your proper life. But do your work, and I shall know you. Do your work, and you shall reinforce yourself. . . .

Well, most men have bound their eyes with one or another handkerchief, and attached themselves to some one of these communities of opinion. This conformity makes them not false in a few **particulars,** authors of a few lies, but false in all particulars. Their every truth is not quite true. . . . Meantime nature is not slow to equip us in the prison-uniform of the party to which we adhere. We come to wear one cut of face and figure, and acquire by degrees the gentlest **asinine** expression . . . the forced smile which we put on in company where we do not feel at ease in answer to conversation which does not interest us. The muscles, not spontaneously moved, but moved by a low usurping wilfulness, grow tight about the outline of the face with the most disagreeable sensation.

For nonconformity the world whips you with its displeasure. And therefore a man must know how to estimate a sour face. The by-standers look askance on him in the public street or in the friend's parlour. . . . but the sour faces of the multitude, like their sweet faces, have no deep cause, but are put on and off as the wind blows and a newspaper directs.

Ralph Waldo Emerson

and Galileo, and Newton, and every pure and wise spirit that ever took flesh. To be great is to be misunderstood.

. . . I hope in these days we have heard the last of conformity and consistency. Let the words be **gazetted** and ridiculous henceforward. . . . Man is timid and apologetic; he is no longer upright; he dares not say 'I think,' 'I am,' but quotes some saint or sage. He is ashamed before the blade of grass or the blowing rose. These roses under my window make no reference to former roses or to better ones; they are for what they are; they exist with God to-day. There is no time to them. There is simply the rose; it is perfect in every moment of its existence. . . . But man postpones or remembers; he does not live in the present, but with reverted eye laments the past, or, heedless of the riches that surround him, stands on tiptoe to foresee the future. He cannot be happy and strong until he too lives with nature in the present, above time.

. . . The other terror that scares us from self-trust is our consistency; a reverence for our past act or word, because the eyes of others have no other data for computing our orbit than our past acts, and we are **loath** to disappoint them. But why . . . drag about this corpse of your memory . . . ? Suppose you should contradict yourself; what then? It seems to be a rule of wisdom never to rely on your memory alone, scarcely even in acts of pure memory, but to bring the past for judgment into the thousand-eyed present, and live ever in a new day.

. . . A foolish consistency is the **hobgoblin** of little minds, adored by little statesmen and philosophers and divines. With consistency a great soul has simply nothing to do. He may as well concern himself with his shadow on the wall. Speak what you think now in hard words, and to-morrow speak what to-morrow thinks in hard words again, though it contradict every thing you said to-day.—'Ah, so you shall be sure to be misunderstood.'—Is it so bad, then, to be misunderstood? Pythagoras was misunderstood, and Socrates, and Jesus, and Luther, and Copernicus,

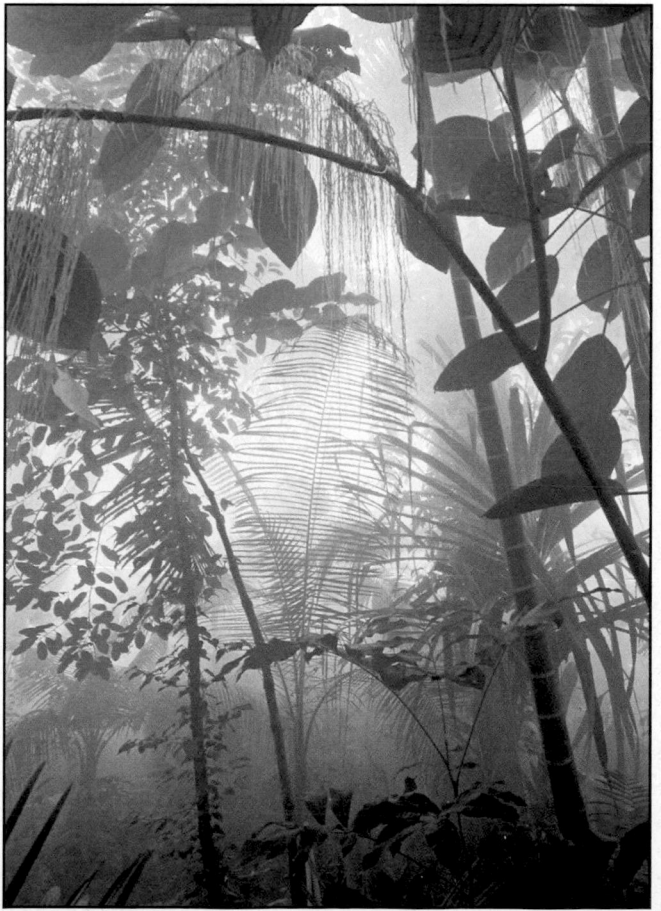

The Crisis of the Union

Harriet Beecher Stowe witnessed the harsh realities of slavery while living in Cincinnati, Ohio, just across the Ohio River from the slave state of Kentucky. Because of these experiences, she became an active abolitionist.

Before the Civil War, many Northerners believed slavery was a constitutionally guaranteed right, and that opposition to it endangered the Union. Even those who agreed with Stowe considered it dangerous to oppose slavery openly and assisted slaveholders in recovering fugitives.

Stowe believed they were able to do this because they did not understand what they were defending. While in church one day in 1851, after she had moved to Brunswick, Maine, she was overcome with a vision of a slave being beaten to death. Sobbing, she ran home and began writing Uncle Tom's Cabin.

The book depicts the life of a long-suffering enslaved person, and the slaveholders and fellow enslaved people in his life. Its 1852 publication attracted threat letters to Stowe, forced closings of bookstores that sold it, and initiated proslavery novels by Southern writers. When Abraham Lincoln met Stowe, he reportedly said, "So this is the little lady who made this big [Civil] war."

In the first year after publication, Uncle Tom's Cabin *sold more than 300,000 copies in the United States. It became the best-selling novel of the nineteenth century, inspired songs and was presented as a play that is still performed today.*

wormwood: A European plant whose leaves yield a bitter oil used to make a liqueur.

dray horse: a horse that hauls heavy loads

Uncle Tom's Cabin
Harriet Beecher Stowe

In this excerpt the enslaved George is visiting his wife, Eliza. They were sold to different slaveholders, but have been allowed to visit each other when not working. George had been hired out to a factory, where he was treated well and had invented a work-saving machine. But when the slaveholder saw George's pride in his accomplishment, he moved George back to the plantation and gave him mindless physical work in order to restore his humility.

Harriet Beecher Stowe

From Chapter 3

You are the handsomest woman I ever saw, and the best one I ever wish to see; but, oh, I wish I'd never seen you, nor you me!"

"O, George, how can you!"

"Yes, Eliza, it's all misery, misery, misery! My life is bitter as **wormwood;** the very life is burning out of me. I'm a poor, miserable, forlorn drudge; I shall only drag you down with me, that's all. What's the use of our trying to do anything, trying to know anything, trying to be anything? What's the use of living? I wish I was dead!"

"O, now, dear George, that is really wicked! I know how you feel about losing your place in the factory, and you have a hard master; but pray be patient, and perhaps something—"

"Patient!" said he, interrupting her; "haven't I been patient? Did I say a word when he came and took me away, for no earthly reason, from the place where everybody was kind to me? I'd paid him truly every cent of my earnings,—and they all say I worked well."

"Well, it *is* dreadful," said Eliza; "but, after all, he is your master, you know."

"My master! and who made him my master? That's what I think of—what right has he to me? I'm a man as much as he is. I'm a better man than he is. I know more about business than he does; I am a better manager than he is; I can read better than he can; I can write a better hand,—and I've learned it all myself, and no thanks to him,—I've learned it in spite of him;

and now what right has he to make a **dray-horse** of me?—to take me from things I can do, and do better than he can, and put me to work that any horse can do? He tries to do it; he says he'll bring me down and humble me, and he puts me to just the hardest, meanest and dirtiest work, on purpose!"

"O, George! George! you frighten me! Why, I never heard you talk so; I'm afraid you'll do something dreadful. I don't wonder at your feelings, at all; but oh, do be careful—do, do—for my sake—for Harry's! . . . O, George, we must have faith. Mistress says that when all things go wrong to us, we must believe that God is doing the very best."

"That's easy to say for people that are sitting on their sofas and riding in their carriages; but let 'em be where I am, I guess it would come some harder. I wish I could be good; but my heart burns, and can't be reconciled, anyhow. You couldn't in my place,—you can't now, if I tell you all I've got to say. You don't know the whole yet."

"What can be coming now?"

"Well, lately Mas'r has been saying that he was a fool to let me marry off the place; that . . . I shall take a wife and settle down on his place . . . or he would sell me down river."

"Why—but you were married to *me* by the minister, as much as if you'd been a white man!" said Eliza, simply.

"Don't you know a slave can't be married? There is no law in this country for that; I can't hold you for my wife, if he chooses to part us. That's why I wish I'd never seen you,—why I wish I'd never been born; it would have been better for us both,—it would have been better for this poor child if he had never been born. All this may happen to him yet!"

"O, but [my] master is so kind!"

"Yes, but who knows?—he may die—and then [our son] may be sold to nobody knows who. What pleasure is it that he is handsome, and smart, and bright? I tell you, Eliza, that a sword will pierce through your soul for every good and pleasant thing your child is or has; it will make him worth too much for you to keep."

The words smote heavily on Eliza's heart; the vision of the trader came before her eyes, and, as if some one had struck her a deadly blow, she turned pale and gasped for breath.

. . . "So, Eliza, my girl," said the husband, mournfully, "bear up, now; and good-by, for I'm going."

"Going, George! Going where?"

"To Canada," said he, straightening himself up; "and when I'm there, I'll buy you; that's all the hope that's left us. You have a kind master, that won't refuse to sell you. I'll buy you and the boy;—God helping me, I will!"

"O, dreadful! if you should be taken?"

"I won't be taken, Eliza; I'll *die* first! I'll be free, or I'll die!"

Eliza flees across the icy Ohio River

Unit 4: The Birth of Modern America

Carl Sandburg was the son of Swedish immigrants who settled in Galesburg, near Chicago. His father worked on the Chicago, Burlington and Quincy railroad at a time when advances in transportation, communications, and manufacturing technology were changing American commerce and life. By the end of the 1800s, the city had become an industrial hub for the lumber, grain, meatpacking, and mail-order businesses.

Sandburg's poem, "Chicago," captures the bustling activity of the city where many African Americans immigrated from the segregated South. It also exposes the evolving urban morality against which many Americans recoiled.

From the time he was a young boy, Sandburg had a variety of jobs—delivering mail, harvesting ice, laying bricks, thrashing wheat, and shining shoes. In 1897 he traveled as a hobo, seeing firsthand the sharp contrast between rich and poor. During his long career, he won two Pulitzer Prizes, one for poetry and another for a five-volume biography of Abraham Lincoln.

Following "Chicago" is a portion of an address by Samuel Clemens to the citizens of another city—his adopted home, San Francisco. It was written in 1866, as he prepared to revisit the town of his youth, Hannibal, Missouri. In this address, Clemens predicts the changes that he sees beginning to occur as San Francisco evolved from a "straggling town" to a modern **mecca** for multicultural immigration.

mecca: a center of activity sought as a goal by people with a common interest

heedlessly: without thinking

hither: here

"Chicago"
Carl Sandburg

Hog Butcher for the World,
  Tool Maker, Stacker of Wheat,
  Player with Railroads and the Nation's Freight Handler;
  Stormy, husky, brawling,
  City of the Big Shoulders:

They tell me you are wicked and I believe them, for I
    have seen your painted women under the gas lamps
    luring the farm boys.
And they tell me you are crooked and I answer: Yes, it
    is true I have seen the gunman kill and go free to
    kill again.
And they tell me you are brutal and my reply is: On the
    faces of women and children I have seen the marks
    of wanton hunger.
And having answered so I turn once more to those who
    sneer at this my city, and I give them back the sneer
    and say to them:
Come and show me another city with lifted head singing
    so proud to be alive and coarse and strong and cunning.
Flinging magnetic curses amid the toil of piling job on
    job, here is a tall bold slugger set vivid against the
    little soft cities;
Fierce as a dog with tongue lapping for action, cunning
        as a savage pitted against the wilderness,
            Bareheaded,
            Shoveling,
            Wrecking,
            Planning,
            Building, breaking, rebuilding,
Under the smoke, dust all over his mouth, laughing with
    white teeth,
Under the terrible burden of destiny laughing as a young
    man laughs,
Laughing even as an ignorant fighter laughs who has
    never lost a battle,
Bragging and laughing that under his wrist is the pulse.
        and under his ribs the heart of the people,
                Laughing!
Laughing the stormy, husky, brawling laughter of
        Youth, half-naked, sweating, proud to be Hog
        Butcher, Tool Maker, Stacker of Wheat, Player with
        Railroads and Freight Handler to the Nation.

Chicago grain elevator, 1900

"Farewell"
Samuel Clemens

"I am now about to bid farewell to San Francisco for a season, and to go back to that common home we all tenderly remember in our waking hours and fondly revisit in dreams of the night—a home which is familiar to my recollection, but will be an unknown land to my unaccustomed eyes. I shall share the fate of many another longing exile who wanders back to his early home to find gray hairs where he expected youth, graves where he looked for firesides, grief where he had pictured joy—everywhere change . . . where he had **heedlessly** dreamed that desolating Time had stood still! . . . And while I linger here upon the threshold of this, my new home . . . I accept the warning that mighty changes will have come over this home also when my returning feet shall walk these streets again.

I read the signs of the times, and I, that am no prophet, behold the things that are in store for you. Over slumbering California is stealing the dawn of a radiant future! The great China Mail Line is established, the Pacific Railroad is creeping across the continent, the commerce of the world is about to be revolutionized. California is Crown Princess of the new dispensation! She stands in the centre of the grand highway of the nations; she stands midway between the Old World and the New, and both shall pay her tribute. From the far East and from Europe, multitudes of stout hearts and willing hands are preparing to flock **hither;** to throng her hamlets and villages; to till her fruitful soil; to unveil the riches of her countless mines; to build up an empire on these distant shores that shall shame the bravest dreams of her visionaries. . . . Half the world stands ready to lay its contributions at her feet! Has any other State so brilliant a future? Has any other city a future like San Francisco?

"This straggling town shall be a vast metropolis; this sparsely populated land shall become a crowded hive of busy men; your waste places shall blossom like the rose, and your deserted hills and valleys shall yield bread and wine for unnumbered thousands; railroads shall be spread hither and thither and carry the invigorating blood of commerce to regions that are languishing now; mills and workshops, yea, and factories shall spring up everywhere, and mines that have neither name nor place to-day shall dazzle the world with their affluence. The time is drawing on apace when the clouds shall pass away from your firmament, and a splendid prosperity shall descend like a glory upon the whole land!

"I am bidding the old city and my old friends a kind, but not a sad farewell, for I know that when I see this home again, the changes that will have been wrought upon it . . . will be brighter, happier and prouder a hundred fold than it is this day."

San Francisco, 1890

Unit 5: Imperialism and Progressivism

Theodore Dreiser and other writers, such as Frank Norris and Upton Sinclair, were Progressive Era "muckrakers." They exposed the scandals and corruption of urban American life at the turn of the twentieth century in a literary **genre** *(ZHAHN•ruh) known as American Realism. In this style, writers present everyday life as it actually is, rather than in a* **romanticized** *style, as many earlier writers had done. Norris and Sinclair were also considered naturalist writers, since they believed that humans had to overcome their environment, their ego, and their "brute instincts."*

Dreiser was born "on the wrong side of the tracks," and learned early that middle-class Americans looked on his impoverished family as outsiders. Because of that, his writing shows a compassionate understanding of life's outcasts and failures, and sympathy for those who desperately crave wealth, love, and power. His famous novel, An American Tragedy, *follows the descent of an ordinary young man who commits a ruthless murder, and the social and political pressures that assail him.*

The life of Madeleine, an impoverished young woman, is the theme of this selection, from the short story "Sanctuary." In it we glimpse some of the urban conditions that inspired the work of many progressive reformers of the day.

genre: a category of artistic composition characterized by form, style, or content

romanticized: presented in a fanciful, imaginative way rather than based on fact

"Sanctuary"
Theodore Dreiser

Primarily, there were the conditions under which [Madeleine] was brought to fifteen years of age: the crowded, scummy tenements; the narrow green-painted halls with their dim gas jets, making the entrance look more like that of a morgue than a dwelling place; the dirty halls and rooms with their green or blue or brown walls painted to save the cost of paper; the bare wooden floors, long since saturated with every type of grease and filth from oleomargarine and suet leaked from cheap fats or meats, to beer and whiskey and tobacco juice. . . .

Theodore Dreiser

And then the streets outside—any of the streets by which she had ever been surrounded—block upon block of other red, bare, commonplace tenements crowded to the doors with human life, the space before them sped over by noisy, gassy trucks and vehicles of all kinds. . . .

In this atmosphere were always longshoremen, wagon drivers, sweepers of floors, washers of dishes, waiters, janitors, workers in laundries, factories—mostly in indifferent or decadent or despairing conditions. And all of these people existed, in so far as she ever knew, upon that mysterious, evanescent and fluctuating something known as the weekly wage.

Always about her there had been drunkenness, fighting, complaining, sickness or death; the police coming in, and arresting one and another; the gas man, the rent man, the furniture man, hammering at doors for their due. . . .

It is not surprising that Madeleine came to her twelfth and thirteenth years without any real understanding of the great world about her and without any definite knowledge or skill. Her drunken mother was now more or less dependent upon her, her father having died of pneumonia and her brother and sister having disappeared to do for themselves. . . .

The child actually went hungry at times. . . . a neighbor perceiving her wretched state and suggesting that some extra helpers were wanted in a department store at Christmastime, she applied there, but so wretched were her clothes by now that she was not even considered. . . . she was able to get a place as a servant in a family.

Those who know anything of the life of a domestic know how thoroughly unsatisfactory it is—the leanness, the lack of hope. . . . she had only the kitchen for her chief chamber or a cubbyhole under the roof. . . .

And then, as was natural, love in the guise of youth, a rather sophisticated gallant somewhat above the world in which she was moving, appeared and paid his all but worthless court to her. . . .

A single trip to Wonderland, a single visit to one of its halls where music sounded to the splash of the waves and where he did his best to teach her to dance, a single meal in one of its gaudy, noisy restaurants . . . were given to hope, a new and seemingly realizable dream of happiness implanted in her young mind. The world was happier than she had thought, or could be made so; not all people fought and screamed at each other. There were such things as tenderness, soft words, sweet words.

But the way of so sophisticated a youth with a maid was brief and direct.

. . . Often in this hour she thought of the swift, icy waters of the river, glistening under a winter moon, and then again of the peace and quiet of the House of the Good Shepherd, its shielding remoteness from life, the only true home or sanctuary she had ever known. And so, brooding and repressing occasional sobs, she made her way toward it . . . thinking of the pathetically debasing love-life that was now over— the dream of love that never, never could be again, for her.

* * *

The stark red walls of the institution stood as before, only dim and gray and cold. . . . She had come a long way, drooping, brooding, half-freezing and crying. More than once on the way the hopelessness of her life and her dreams had given her pause, causing her to turn again with renewed determination toward the river—only the vivid and reassuring picture she had retained of this same grim and homely place, its

restricted peace and quiet, the sympathy of Sister St. Agnes and Mother St. Bertha, had carried her on . . . the face of Mother St. Bertha, wrinkled and aweary, appeared at the square opening.

"What is it, my child?" she asked. . . .

"It is Madeleine. I was here four years ago. I was in the girls' ward. I worked in the sewing room."

She was so beaten by life . . . that even now and here she expected little more than an indifference which would send her away again. . . .

"Of course, my child," said the Mother, moving to the door and opening it. "You may come in. But what has happened, child?. . ."

"Mother," pleaded Madeleine wearily, "must I answer now? I am so unhappy! Can't I just have my old dress and my bed for tonight—that little bed under the lamp?"

"Why, yes, dear. . . . Now, my child," she said, "you may undress and bathe. . . ."

In a kind of dumbness of despair she … entered the warm, clean bath which had been provided. She stifled a sob as she did so, and others as she bathed. . . .

. . . Then she was led along other silent passages, once dreary enough but now healing in their sense of peace and rest, and so into the great room set with row upon row of simple white iron beds, covered with their snowy linen . . . beneath which so many like herself were sleeping.

. . . "Oh, Mother," she sobbed as the Sister bent over her, "don't ever make me go out in the world again, will you? You won't will you? I'm so tired! I'm so tired!"

"No, dear, no," soothed the Sister . . . "You need never go out in the world again unless you wish."

Family outside New York City tenement, 1890

Unit 6: Boom and Bust

Writers sometimes create works of fiction inspired by or based on actual events in the news. The story of Nicola Sacco and Bartolomeo Vanzetti, Italian immigrants convicted of murder in 1921, was the inspiration for this selection by John Dos Passos, written in 1936. Large demonstrations were held in support of Sacco and Vanzetti, who claimed they were convicted for being immigrants and anarchists—not for committing a crime. They were executed in 1927, inspiring this passage, as well as the novel, Boston, *by Upton Sinclair.*

Dos Passos used his wartime experience as an ambulance driver in France as the background for several antiwar novels. In his **trilogy,** U.S.A, *he used an experimental form—fragments of songs, news headlines, monologues, and fragments from the lives of unrelated characters—to depict American* **hypocrisy** *and materialism between the two world wars. Dos Passos often combines separate words into one to shade its meaning and for the flow of a line. His* **impressionistic** *writing influenced several generations of American and European novelists.*

The lines in italics in the following passage from U.S.A. *are from actual letters written by Sacco and Vanzetti.*

trilogy: a work of fiction or nonfiction written in three separately published parts, or books

hypocrisy: acting in a way that contradicts what you say you believe in

impressionistic: using vivid details to create a sensory impression rather than objective reality

wardheeler: a worker for a political boss in a ward or local area

U.S.A., "Sacco and Vanzetti Must Die"
John Dos Passos

*S*hall be the human race.

Much I thought of you when I was lying in the death house— the singing, the kind tender voices of the children from the playground where there was all the life and the joy of liberty—just one step from the wall that contains the buried agony of three buried

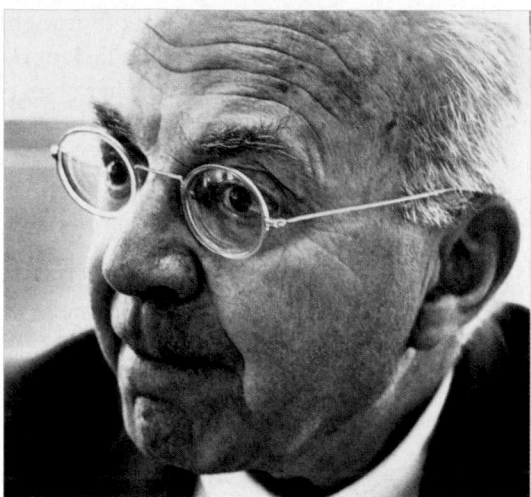

John Dos Passos

souls. It would remind me so often of you and of your sister and I wish I could see you every moment, but I feel better that you will not come to the death house so that you could not see the horrible picture of three living in agony waiting to be electrocuted.

The Camera Eye

they have clubbed us off the streets   they are stronger   they are rich   they hire and fire the politicians the newspapereditors the old judges the small men with reputations the collegepresidents the **wardheelers** (listen businessmen collegepresidents judges   America will not forget her betrayers) they hire the men with guns   the uniforms the policecars the patrolwagons

all right you have won   you will kill the brave men our friends tonight

there is nothing left to do   we are beaten   we the beaten crowd together in these old dingy schoolrooms on Salem Street shuffle up and down the gritty creaking stairs sit hunched with bowed heads on benches and hear the old words of the haters of oppression   made new in sweat and agony tonight

our work is over   the scribbled phrases   the nights typing releases the smell of the printshop the sharp reek of newsprinted leaflets   the rush for Western Union stringing words into wires the search for stinging words to make you feel who are your oppressors America

America our nation has been beaten by strangers who have turned our language inside out who have taken the clean words our fathers spoke and made them slimy and foul

their hired men sit on the judge's bench they sit back with their feet on the tables under the dome of the State House they are ignorant of our beliefs they have the dollars the guns the armed forces the powerplants

they have built the electricchair and hired the executioner to throw the switch

all right we are two nations

America our nation has been beaten by strangers who have bought the laws and fenced off the meadows and cut down the woods for pulp and turned our pleasant cities into slums and sweated the wealth out of our people and when they want to they hire the executioner to throw the switch

but do they know that the old words of the immigrants are being renewed in blood and agony tonight do they know that the old American speech of the haters of oppression is new tonight in the mouth of an old woman from Pittsburgh of a husky boilermaker from Frisco who hopped freights clear from the Coast to come here in the mouth of a Back Bay social-worker in the mouth of an Italian printer of a hobo from Arkansas   the language of the beaten nation is not forgotten in our ears tonight

the men in the deathhouse made the old words new before they died

If it had not been for these things, I might have lived out my life talking at streetcorners to scorning men. I might have died unknown, unmarked, a failure. This is our career and our triumph. Never in our full life can we hope to do such work for tolerance, for justice, for man's understanding of man as now we do by an accident.

now their work is over   the immigrants haters of oppression lie quiet in black suits in the little undertaking parlor in the North End   the city is quiet   the men of the conquering nation are not to be seen on the streets

they have won why are they scared to be seen on the streets? on the streets you see only the downcast faces of the beaten   the streets belong to the beaten nation   all the way to the cemetery where the bodies of the immigrants are to be burned   we line the curbs in the drizzling rain we crowd the wet sidewalks elbow to elbow silent pale looking with scared eyes at the coffins

we stand defeated America

Nicola Sacco and Bartolomeo Vanzetti being arrested

Unit 7: Global Struggles

Many Jews who survived concentration camps during World War II found it too painful to speak or write about their experiences until many years later. Elie Wiesel (vee•ZEHL) waited for 10 years to write the story of his experiences at Auschwitz, where his family was killed. The first passage is from his 1960 novel, Night. *Wiesel was a teenager when the Nazis invaded his town of Sighet in Transylvania in 1944. He became a U.S. citizen in 1963, and won the Nobel Peace Prize in 1986.*

World War II had shown the world an unprecedented scale of conflict. The science, technology, and industrialism—which were supposed to advance humanity—had been used instead for mass killing and devastation. It was not surprising that many postwar writers sought alternatives to traditional ways of thinking and writing.

The Beat Generation—a term coined by Jack Kerouac—was the first modern **subculture,** *or "alternative" culture. It was a group of writers during the late 1950s and early 1960s. Rejecting the intellectual, or mental, focus of traditional writing, the Beats sought spontaneity, emotion, and engagement in real, often gritty experience. Their writing has influenced artists, writers, rock musicians, and popular culture ever since.*

In 1947, Kerouac and a friend took a road trip around the country, which inspired his most famous novel, On the Road. *Published in 1957, it expresses both the quest for experience and the pessimism of the Beats as they struggled to find meaning in the shadow of the atomic bomb.*

subculture: a group that displays behavior different from that of society

Night
Elie Wiesel

And then, one day all foreign Jews were expelled. . . .

Crammed into cattle cars by the Hungarian police, they cried silently. Standing on the station platform, we too were crying. The train disappeared over the horizon; all that was left was thick, dirty smoke.

Behind me, someone said, sighing, "What do you expect? That's war. . . ."

Elie Wiesel

The deportees were quickly forgotten. A few days after they left, it was rumored that they were in Galicia, working, and even that they were content with their fate.

Days went by. Then weeks and months. Life was normal again. A calm, reassuring wind blew through our homes. The shopkeepers were doing good business, the students lived among their books, and the children played in the streets.

One day, as I was about to enter the synagogue, I saw Moishe the Beadle sitting on a bench near the entrance.

He told me what had happened to him and his companions. The train with the deportees had crossed the Hungarian border and, once in Polish territory, had been taken over by the Gestapo. The train had stopped. The Jews were ordered to get off and onto waiting trucks. The trucks headed toward a forest. There everybody was ordered to get out. They were forced to dig huge trenches. When they had finished their work, the men from the Gestapo began theirs. Without passion or haste, they shot their prisoners, who were forced to approach the trench one by one and offer their necks. Infants were tossed into the air and used as targets for the machine guns. This took place in the Galician forest, near Kolomay. How had he, Moishe the Beadle, been able to escape? By a miracle. He was wounded in the leg and left for dead.

On the Road
Jack Kerouac

Later in the afternoon we went out and played baseball with the kids in the sooty field by the Long Island railyard. We also played basketball so frantically the younger boys said, "Take it easy, you don't have to kill yourself." They bounced smoothly all around us and beat us with ease. Dean and I were sweating. At one point Dean fell flat on his face on the concrete court. We huffed and puffed to get the ball away from the boys; they turned and flipped it away. Others darted in and smoothly shot over our heads. We jumped at the basket like maniacs, and the younger boys just reached up and grabbed the ball from our sweating hands and dribbled away. We were like hotrock blackbelly tenorman *Mad* of American back-alley go-music trying to play basketball against Stan Getz and Cool Charlie. They thought we were crazy. Dean and I went back home playing catch from each sidewalk of the street. We tried extra-special catches, diving over bushes and barely missing posts. When a car came by I ran alongside and flipped the ball to Dean just barely behind the vanishing bumper. He darted and caught it and rolled in the grass, and flipped it back for me to catch on the other side of a parked bread truck. I just made it with my meat hand and threw it back so Dean had to whirl and back up and fall on his back across the hedges. Back in the house Dean took his wallet, har-rumphed, and handed my aunt the fifteen dollars he owed her from the time we got a speeding ticket in Washington. She was completely surprised and pleased. We had a big supper. "Well, Dean," said my aunt, "I hope you'll be able to take care of your new baby that's coming and stay married this time."

"Yes, yass, yes."

"You can't go all over the country having babies like that. Those poor little things'll grow up helpless. You've got to offer them a chance to live." He looked at his feet and nodded. In the raw red dusk we said good-by, on a bridge over a superhighway.

"I hope you'll be in New York when I get back," I told him.

"All I hope, Dean, is someday we'll be able to live on the same street with our families and get to be a couple of oldtimers together."

"That's right, man—you know that I pray for it completely mindful of the troubles we both had and the troubles coming, as your aunt knows and reminds me. I didn't want the new baby, Inez insisted, and we had a fight. Did you know Marylou got married to a used-car dealer in Frisco and she's having a baby?"

"Yes. We're all getting in there now." Ripples in the upside-down lake of the void, is what I should have said. The bottom of the world is gold and the world is upside down. He took out a snapshot of Camille in Frisco with the new baby girl. The shadow of a man crossed the child on the sunny pavement, two long trouser legs in the sadness. "Who's that?"

"That's only Ed Dunkel. He came back to Galatea, they're gone to Denver now. They spent a day taking pictures."

Ed Dunkel, his compassion unnoticed like the compassion of saints. Dean took out other pictures. I realized these were all the snapshots which our children would look at someday with wonder, thinking their parents had lived smooth, well-ordered, stabilized-within-the-photo lives and got up in the morning to walk proudly on the sidewalks of life, never dreaming the raggedy madness and riot of our actual lives, our actual night, the hell of it, the senseless nightmare road. All of it inside endless and beginningless emptiness. Pitiful forms of ignorance. "Good-by, good-by." Dean walked off in the long red dusk. Locomotives smoked and reeled above him. His shadow followed him, it aped his walk and thoughts and very being. He turned and waved coyly, bashfully. He gave me the boomer's high-ball, he jumped up and down, he yelled something I didn't catch. He ran around in a circle. All the time he came closer to the concrete corner of the railroad overpass. He made one last signal. I waved back. Suddenly he bent to his life and walked quickly out of sight. I gaped into the bleakness of my own days. I had an awful long way to go too.

Unit 8: A Time of Upheaval

After two world wars many writers began to describe a sense of separateness from nature and a growing sense of personal alienation. The upheaval of societies and cultures brought about by the wars led to a feeling that morality was relative. In other words, what may be immoral in one situation could be considered moral in another situation. These themes, later called modernism by literary critics, showed up in many works of the time.

The early work of poet Adrienne Rich, who was born in 1929, seemed not to be part of this evolving modernist tradition, and wrote in careful, more traditional forms. By the 1960s, her work increasingly confronted themes such as women's role in society, racism, and the Vietnam War, and was written in free verse. In 1973, amid the feminist and civil rights movements, she wrote Diving Into the Wreck, Poems 1971–1972, *which won the National Book Award the next year. The title poem uses the* **metaphor** *of a deep-sea diver to express the goal of looking deeply within to find the truth about ourselves.*

Leroy V. Quintana is a New Mexico native of Mexican ancestry. His poetry draws on his experiences as a Chicano outsider in American society, subject to ethnic and socio-economic discrimination. His poem here, "Natural History," reflects both his sensitivity to nature and the horrors of the Vietnam War, in which he served during 1967 and 1968.

metaphor: a figure of speech in which one word or image is used to mean something else

sundry: miscellaneous

crenellated: notched

"Diving into the Wreck"
Adrienne Rich

First having read the book of myths,
and loaded the camera,
and checked the edge of the knife-blade,
I put on
the body-armor of black rubber
the absurd flippers
the grave and awkward mask.
I am having to do this
not like Cousteau with his
assiduous team
aboard the sun-flooded schooner
but here alone.

There is a ladder.
The ladder is always there
hanging innocently
close to the side of the schooner.
We know what it is for,
we who have used it.
Otherwise
it is a piece of maritime floss
some **sundry** equipment.

I go down.
Rung after rung and still
the oxygen immerses me
the blue light
the clear atoms
of our human air.
I go down.
My flippers cripple me,
I crawl like an insect down the ladder
and there is no one
to tell me when the ocean
will begin.

First the air is blue and then
it is bluer and then green and then
black I am blacking out and yet
my mask is powerful
it pumps my blood with power
the sea is another story
the sea is not a question of power

I have to learn alone
to turn my body without force
in the deep element.

And now: it is easy to forget
what I came for
among so many who have always
lived here
swaying their **crenellated** fans
between the reefs
and besides
you breathe differently down here.

I came to explore the wreck.
The words are purposes.
The words are maps.
I came to see the damage that was done
and the treasures that prevail.
I stroke the beam of my lamp
slowly along the flank
of something more permanent
than fish or weed

the thing I came for:
the wreck and not the story of the wreck
the thing itself and not the myth
the drowned face always staring
toward the sun
the evidence of damage
worn by salt and away into this threadbare
    beauty
the ribs of the disaster
curving their assertion
among the tentative haunters.

This is the place.
And I am here, the mermaid whose dark hair
streams black, the merman in his armored
    body.
We circle silently
about the wreck
we dive into the hold.
I am she: I am he

whose drowned face sleeps with open eyes
whose breasts still bear the stress
whose silver, copper, vermeil cargo lies
obscurely inside barrels
half-wedged and left to rot
we are the half-destroyed instruments
that once held to a course
the water-eaten log
the fouled compass

We are, I am, you are
by cowardice or courage
the one who find our way
back to this scene
carrying a knife, a camera
a book of myths
in which
our names do not appear.

"Natural History"
Leroy Quintana

To cross a river meant leeches.
A company of NVAs crashing toward you
would be a troop of baboons.
A green snake named Mr. Two Step,
for the number you'd last after bitten.
It was said the NVAs carried flashlights.
One night frightening scores of them
turned out to be a swarm of fireflies.
The whir of birds' wings
turned out to be artillery rounds.
Threw stones at a cobra once,
the sun going down.
Fire at it
and the VC would know our position.
A VC moving slowly in the elephant grass
happened to be a water buffalo.
One night they overran the compound.
Loaded down with grenades, AK-47s
from North Vietnam, mines strapped to their
    chests:
these were only the mosquitos.
The VC only a little more than a whisper's
    reach away,
we called in the Cobras. They came in hissing,
cannons twice as fast as the old gunships.
It was also said the VC kept chickens leashed
    to strings.
So easily frightened they were perfect warning.
One night, shivering uncontrollably with fear,
knowing I would have to kill whatever was
    out there,
walking slowly, scratching.

Unit 9: A Changing Society

Dr. Maya Angelou is a poet, historian, author, actress, playwright, civil-rights activist, producer, and director. Born in St. Louis, Missouri, she has lived in many places. She was a newspaper editor in Egypt and Ghana, and has taught at the University of Ghana and, since 1981, at Wake Forest University in Winston-Salem, North Carolina.

*In the 1960s Dr. Martin Luther King, Jr., asked her to be the Northern coordinator for the Southern Christian Leadership Conference. Angelou gained fame in the United States when her **autobiographical** novel,* I Know Why the Caged Bird Sings, *received critical and popular success when it was published in 1969.*

*Like many modern writers, she focuses a harsh spotlight on characters' frailties, failures, and **dilemmas** in today's complex world. Unlike some, however, she also challenges our strengths and human potential. Former president Bill Clinton commissioned her to read her poem "On the Pulse of the Morning" at his 1993 inauguration. Although Angelou wrote her poem in the last decade of the twentieth century, it shows a focus on personal responsibility and peaceful coexistence that have been her lifelong quests and are her hopes for this millennium.*

autobiographical: written about the person's own life

dilemma: problems caused by a person's situation or world conditions

"On the Pulse of the Morning"

Maya Angelou

Maya Angelou

. . . .
You, created only a little lower than
The angels, have crouched too long in
The bruising darkness
Have lain too long
Facedown in ignorance,
Your mouths spilling words
Armed for slaughter.
. . . .
Come, clad in peace,
And I will sing the songs
The Creator gave to me when I and the
Tree and the Rock were one.
Before cynicism was a bloody sear across your brow
And when you yet knew you still knew nothing.
The River sang and sings on.
. . . .
Here, on the pulse of this new day,
You may have the grace to look up and out
And into your sister's eyes,
And into your brother's face,
Your country,
And say simply
With hope—
Good morning.

"Human Family"

Maya Angelou

I note the obvious differences
in the human family.
Some of us are serious,
some thrive on comedy.

Some declare their lives are lived
as true profundity,
and others claim they really live
the real reality.
. . . .

We love and lose in China,
we weep on England's moors,
and laugh and moan in Guinea,
and thrive on Spanish shores.

We seek success in Finland,
Are born and die in Maine.
In minor ways we differ,
In major we're the same.

I note the obvious differences
between each sort and type,
but we are more alike, my friends,
than we are unalike.

We are more alike, my friends,
than we are unalike.
. . . .

"Equality"

Maya Angelou

You declare you see me dimly
through a glass which will not shine
though I stand before you boldly,
trim in rank and marking time.

You do own to hear me faintly
as a whisper out of range,
while my drums beat out the message
and the rhythms never change.

Equality, and I will be free.
Equality, and I will be free.
. . . .

We have lived a painful history,
we know the shameful past,
but I keep on marching forward,
and you keep on coming last.

Equality, and I will be free.
Equality, and I will be free.

Flag Etiquette

For Americans, the flag has always had a special meaning. It is a symbol of our nation's freedom and democracy.

Rules and Customs

Over the years, Americans have developed rules and customs concerning the use and display of the flag. One of the most important things every American should remember is to treat the flag with respect.

- The flag should be raised and lowered by hand and displayed only from sunrise to sunset. On special occasions, the flag may be displayed at night, but it should be illuminated.

- The flag may be displayed on all days, weather permitting, particularly on national and state holidays and on historic and special occasions.

- No flag may be flown above the American flag or to the right of it at the same height.

- The flag should never touch the ground or floor beneath it.

- The flag may be flown at half-staff by order of the president, usually to mourn the death of a public official.

- The flag may be flown upside down only to signal distress.

- When the flag becomes old and tattered, it should be destroyed by burning. According to an approved custom, the Union (stars on blue field) is first cut from the flag; then the two pieces, which no longer form a flag, are burned.

Continental Colors
1775-1777

First Stars and Stripes
1777-1795

Betsy Ross Flag
c. 1790

15-Star Flag
1795-1818

20-Star Flag
1818

Great Star Flag
1818

35-Star Flag
1863-1865

38-Star Flag
1877-1890

48-Star Flag
1912-1959

50-Star Flag
1960

Glossary/Glosario

- Content vocabulary terms in this glossary are words that relate to history content. They are **highlighted** yellow in your text.
- Words below that have an asterisk (*) are academic vocabulary terms. They help you understand your school subjects and are **boldfaced** in your text.

abandon • apparent

<table>
<tr><th>English</th><th>Español</th></tr>
<tr><td colspan="2" align="center">Ⓐ</td></tr>
<tr><td>*abandon to withdraw protection, support, or help (p. 568)</td><td>*abandonar retirar la protección, el apoyo o la ayuda (p. 568)</td></tr>
<tr><td>*academic associated with higher learning at a scholarly institution (p. 308)</td><td>*académico relacionado con los estudios superiores en una institución especializada (p. 308)</td></tr>
<tr><td>*access freedom or ability to obtain or make use of (p. 277)</td><td>*acceso libertad o capacidad de obtener o hacer uso de (p. 277)</td></tr>
<tr><td>*adapt to change in order to meet the demands of a certain environment or circumstance (p. 162)</td><td>*adaptar cambiar para cumplir con las exigencias de cierto entorno o circunstancia (p. 162)</td></tr>
<tr><td>*adequate sufficient for a specific requirement, completed to its minimum requirements (pp. 339, 696)</td><td>*adecuado suficiente para un requisito específico, que se completa con los requisitos mínimos (pp. 339, 696)</td></tr>
<tr><td>*advocate to propose a certain position or viewpoint (p. 299)</td><td>*abogar proponer cierta posición o punto de vista (p. 299)</td></tr>
<tr><td>affirmative action an active effort to improve employment or educational opportunities for minorities (p. 725)</td><td>acción afirmativa un esfuerzo activo para mejorar las oportunidades educacionales y de empleo para las minorías (p. 725)</td></tr>
<tr><td>Agent Orange a chemical defoliant used to clear Vietnamese jungles during the Vietnam War (p. 661)</td><td>Agente naranja defoliante químico utilizado para limpiar las junglas vietnamitas durante la Guerra de Vietnam (p. 661)</td></tr>
<tr><td>*allocate to set apart for something specific (p. 790)</td><td>*asignar diferenciar para algo específico (p. 790)</td></tr>
<tr><td>allotment a plot of land assigned to an individual or family for cultivation (p. 175)</td><td>parcela un terreno asignado a un individuo o familia para su cultivación (p. 175)</td></tr>
<tr><td>*alternative existing or functioning outside the established cultural, social, or economic system (p. 733)</td><td>*alternativo que existe o funciona fuera del sistema cultural, social o económico establecido (p. 733)</td></tr>
<tr><td>Americanization causing someone to acquire American traits and characteristics (p. 239)</td><td>americanización causar que una persona adquiera características y rasgos americanos (p. 239)</td></tr>
<tr><td>amnesty the act of granting a pardon to a large group of people (pp. 140, 789)</td><td>amnistía el acto de otorgar perdón a un número grande de personas (pp. 140, 789)</td></tr>
<tr><td>amphtrac an amphibious tractor used to move troops from ships to shore (p. 514)</td><td>amphtrac un tractor anfibio utilizado para mover tropas desde barcos a la orilla del mar (p. 514)</td></tr>
<tr><td>anarchist person who believes that there should be no government (p. 376)</td><td>anarquista una persona que cree que no debe haber ningún gobierno (p. 376)</td></tr>
<tr><td>annuity money paid by contract on regular intervals (p. 170)</td><td>anualidad dinero pagado por contrato en intervalos regulares (p. 170)</td></tr>
<tr><td>anthrax a bacteria used to create biological weapons (p. 813)</td><td>ántrax bacteria utilizada para crear armas biológicas (p. 813)</td></tr>
<tr><td>*apparent appearing to be fact as far as can be understood (p. 423)</td><td>*aparente que parece ser cierto dentro de lo que puede comprenderse (p. 423)</td></tr>
</table>

Glossary/Glosario

English	Español
appeasement accepting demands in order to avoid conflict (p. 461)	**apaciguamiento** demandas aceptadas a fin de evitar conflictos (p. 461)
***appropriate** (adjective) especially suitable or compatible (p. 729)	***apropiado** (adjetivo) especialmente adecuado o compatible (p. 729)
***approximately** an estimation of a figure close to the actual figure (p. 175)	***aproximadamente** cálculo de un número cercano al número real (p. 175)
***arbitrary** existing or coming about seemingly at random or as an unfair or unreasonable act of will (p. 601)	***arbitrario** que existe u ocurre aparentemente al azar o como un acto de voluntad injusto o irrazonable (p. 601)
arbitration settling a dispute by agreeing to accept the decision of an impartial outsider (p. 204)	**arbitraje** arreglar una disputa acordando aceptar la decisión de una persona imparcial (p. 204)
armistice a temporary agreement to end fighting (p. 341)	**armisticio** acuerdo temporal de paz para terminar con una lucha (p. 341)
assembly line a production system with machines and workers arranged so that each person performs an assigned task again and again as the item passes before him or her (p. 368)	**línea de montaje** sistema de producción con máquinas y trabajadores arreglados para que cada persona haga su trabajo designado una y otra vez mientras el artículo pasa frente a ellos (p. 368)
assimilate to absorb a group into the culture of a larger population (p. 175)	**asimilar** incorporar a un grupo dentro de la cultura de una población más grande (p. 175)
***assume** to take for granted or as true (p. 468)	***suponer** dar algo por sentado o considerarlo verdadero (p. 468)
attrition the act of wearing down by constant harassment or attack (p. 129)	**atrición** acto de desalentar por constantes ataques o acoso (p. 129)
***authorities** those who have control over determining and enforcing what is right or wrong (p. 352)	***autoridades** aquéllas que poseen control sobre la determinación y el cumplimiento de lo que es correcto o incorrecto (p. 352)
autonomy the quality or state of being self-governing (p. 270)	**autonomía** la cualidad o el estado de autogobernarse (p. 270)
***awareness** the state of having or showing realization, perception, or knowledge (p. 797)	***conciencia** estado de poseer o mostrar comprensión, percepción o conocimiento (p. 797)

B

English	Español
baby boom a marked rise in birthrate, such as occurred in the United States following World War II (p. 573)	**auge de nacimientos** aumento marcado en la taza de natalidad, tal como ocurrió en Estados Unidos después de la Segunda Guerra Mundial (p. 573)
bailiff minor officer of the courts (p. 406)	**alguacil** oficial en rango menor de las Cortes (p. 406)
bank holiday closing of banks during the Great Depression to avoid bank runs (p. 424)	**feriado bancario** cierre de bancos durante la Gran Depresión para evitar las corridas bancarias (p. 424)
bank run persistent and heavy demands from a bank's depositors, creditors, or customers (p. 403)	**corrida bancaria** demandas constantes y numerosas por parte de los depositantes, acreedores o clientes de un banco (p. 403)
beats short for "beatniks"; a group of mostly white writers and artists who, in 1950s America, harshly criticized what they considered the sterility and conformity of American life, the meaninglessness of American politics, and the emptiness of popular culture (p. 579)	**beats** nombre corto para "beatniks", un grupo de escritores y artistas en su mayoría blancos quienes en la década de 1950 en Estados Unidos criticaban duramente lo que ellos consideraban la esterilidad y conformismo de la vida estadounidense, el sin sentido de la política estadounidense y el vacío de la cultura popular (p. 579)

*benefit to be useful or profitable (p. 435)

benevolent society an association focusing on spreading the word of God and combating social problems (p. 100)

bilingualism the practice of teaching immigrant students in their own language (p. 697)

Bill of Rights a summary of fundamental rights and privileges guaranteed to a people against violation by the state (p. 78)

binding arbitration process whereby a neutral party hears arguments from two opposing sides and makes a decision that both must accept (p. 438)

black codes laws passed in the South just after the Civil War aimed at controlling freedmen and enabling plantation owners to exploit African American workers (p. 143)

black power the mobilization of the political and economic power of African Americans, especially to compel respect for their rights and to improve their condition (p. 644)

blacklist a list of persons who are disapproved of or who are to be punished or boycotted (p. 201)

blitzkrieg name given to sudden violent offensive attacks the Germans used during World War II; "lightning war" (p. 462)

blockade runner ship that runs through a blockade, usually to smuggle goods through a protected area (p. 130)

blogs online journal where an individual, group, or corporation presents a record of activities, thoughts, or beliefs (p. 777)

blue-collar workers workers in the manual labor field, particularly those requiring protective clothing (p. 574)

blues style of music evolving from African American spirituals and noted for its melancholy sound (p. 390)

bohemian a person (as an artist or writer) leading an unconventional lifestyle (p. 382)

bonanza farm a large, highly profitable wheat farm (p. 169)

*bond a note issued by the government which promises to pay off a loan with interest (p. 242)

*briefly for a short time (p. 512)

brinkmanship the willingness to go to the brink of war to force an opponent to back down (p. 555)

broker state role of the government to work out conflicts among competing interest groups (p. 445)

*beneficiar ser útil o rentable (p. 435)

sociedad de beneficencia una asociación enfocada en llevar la palabra de Dios y combatir problemas sociales (p. 100)

bilingualismo la práctica de enseñar a estudiantes inmigrantes en su propio lenguaje (p. 697)

declaración de derechos resumen de los derechos y privilegios fundamentales que el estado garantiza al pueblo que no se violarán (p. 78)

arbitraje obligatorio proceso por el cual un partido neutral escucha argumentos de dos partidos opositores y toma una decisión que ambos deben aceptar (p. 438)

códigos negros leyes aprobadas en el Sur al terminar la Guerra Civil para controlar a los libertos y permitir a los dueños de plantaciones la explotación de los trabajadores afroamericanos (p. 143)

poder negro movilización del poder económico y político de afroamericanos especialmente para imponer respeto por sus derechos y para mejorar su condiciones (p. 644)

lista negra lista de personas rechazadas o a las que se castigará o boicoteará (p. 201)

guerra relámpago nombre dado a los ataques repentinos ofensivos violentos que los alemanes usaron durante la Segunda Guerra Mundial (p. 462)

forzador de bloqueo un barco que navega a través de un bloqueo, usualmente para pasar contrabando a través de un área protegida (p. 130)

blogs publicación en línea donde un individuo, grupo o empresa presenta un registro de actividades, ideas o creencias (p. 777)

collar azul trabajadors trabajadors de mano de obra, particularmente aquellos que requieren ropa protectora (p. 574)

blues estilo de música que evolucionó de la música espiritual de los afroamericanos, distinguida por su sonido melancólico (p. 390)

bohemio una persona (como artista o escritor) que lleva un estilo de vida poco convencional (p. 382)

granja en bonanza extensa granja de trigo que produce muchas ganancias (p. 169)

*bono una obligación emitida por el gobierno que promete pagar un préstamo con interés (p. 242)

*brevemente por poco tiempo (p. 512)

política arriesgada la buena voluntad para ir al borde de guerra para forzar a un oponente a que se retracte (p. 555)

estado intermediario el papel del gobierno para resolver conflictos entre grupos con intereses competitivos (p. 445)

Glossary/Glosario

Glossary/Glosario

English	Español
budget deficit the amount by which expenses exceed income (p. 749)	**déficit del presupuesto** la cantidad por la cual los gastos exceden los ingresos (p. 749)
bull market a long period of rising stock prices (p. 401)	**bolsa al alza** largo período durante el cual los precios de acciones en la bolsa se incrementan (p. 401)
busing a policy of transporting children to schools outside their neighborhoods to achieve greater racial balance (p. 725)	**traslado** obligatorio la política de transportar estudiantes a escuelas fuera de sus vecindarios para alcanzar un balance racial (p. 725)

C

English	Español
cabinet a group of advisers to the president (p. 78)	**gabinete** grupo de consejeros al presidente (p. 78)
capital gains tax a federal tax paid by businesses and investors when they sell stocks or real estate (p. 767)	**impuestos a las ganancias del capital** impuesto federal pagado por inversionistas y negocios cuando ellos venden acciones y bienes raíces (p. 767)
carpetbagger name given to many Northerners who moved to the South after the Civil War and supported the Republicans (p. 145)	**carpetbagger** nombre dado a muchos norteños que se mudaron al Sur después de la Guerra Civil y apoyaron a los republicanos (p. 145)
censure to express a formal disapproval of an action (p. 550)	**censura** expresar la desaprobación formal sobre una acción (p. 550)
chad a small piece of cardboard produced by punching a data card (p. 805)	**agujereado** pedazo pequeño de cartón producido taladrando una tarjeta de computadora (p. 805)
*challenger one who enters a competition (p. 713)	***contendiente** el que ingresa a una competencia (p. 713)
charter a constitution (p. 525)	**carta de privilegio** una constitución (p. 525)
checks and balances the system in which each branch of government has the ability to limit the power of the other branches to prevent any from becoming too powerful (p. 38)	**control y balances** sistema en el cual cada ramo de gobierno tiene la habilidad para limitar el poder a los otros ramos para que ninguno vuelva a ser demasiado poderoso (p. 38)
*cite to point out as an example in an argument or debate (p. 796)	***citar** señalar como ejemplo en un argumento o debate (p. 796)
*civil of or relating to citizens (p. 109)	***civil** de los ciudadanos o relativo a ellos (p. 109)
closed shop an agreement in which a company agrees to hire only union members (pp. 206, 566)	**taller cerrado** acuerdo en el que una compañía contrata solamente a miembros del sindicato (pp. 206, 566)
cloture a motion which ends debate and calls for an immediate vote, possible in the U.S. Senate by a vote of 60 senators (p. 636)	**clausura** una moción que termina con el debate y requiere un voto inmediato, posible en el Senado de EE.UU. por un voto de 60 senadores (p. 636)
*code a signal or symbol used to represent something that is to be kept secret (p. 496)	***código** señal o símbolo utilizado para representar algo que se mantendrá en secreto (p. 496)
*collapse a sudden loss of force, value, or effect (p. 400)	***colapso** pérdida repentina de fuerza, valor o efecto (p. 400)
*colleague a person who works in the same, or similar, profession (p. 408)	***colega** persona que trabaja en la misma profesión o en una similar (p. 408)
collective a farm, especially in communist countries, formed from many small holdings collected into a single unit for joint operation under governmental supervision (p. 455)	**granja colectiva** una granja, especialmente en los países comunistas, formada por muchas tierras pequeñas reunidas en una sola unidad para operar conjuntamente bajo la supervisión del gobierno (p. 455)

*commentator one who explains, discusses, or reports in an expository manner, especially news on radio or television (p. 596)

*comentarista aquél que explica, discute o informa de manera expositiva, especialmente noticias por radio o televisión (p. 596)

*commissioner the officer in charge of a department or bureau of the public service (p. 145)

*comisionado funcionario a cargo de un departamento o agencia de servicios públicos (p. 145)

committee of correspondence committee organized in each colony to communicate with and unify the colonies (p. 25)

comité de correspondencia comité organizado en cada colonia para comunicar entre las colonias y unificarlas (p. 25)

commune a group living arrangement in which members share everything and work together (p. 685)

comuna un arreglo de vivienda en el cual los miembros de un grupo trabajan juntos y comparten todo (p. 685)

*communications the various media and processes by which information is exchanged between individuals (p. 776)

*comunicaciones los diferentes medios y procesos mediante los cuales se intercambia información entre individuos (p. 776)

*community people with common characteristics living in the same area (p. 413)

*comunidad personas con características comunes que viven en la misma área (p. 413)

*compatible capable of existing in harmony (p. 691)

*compatible capaz de existir en armonía (p. 691)

*concentrate to bring or direct one's powers, efforts, or attention toward a common objective (p. 462)

*concentrar orientar los poderes, esfuerzos o atención hacia un objetivo común (p. 462)

concentration camp a camp where persons are detained or confined (p. 470)

campo de concentración un campamento donde personas están detenidas o encerradas (p. 470)

*conference a meeting of two or more persons for discussing matters of common concern (p. 267)

*conferencia reunión entre dos o más personas para discutir asuntos de interés mutuo (p. 267)

*confine to enclose or restrain (p. 613)

*confinar encerrar o contener (p. 613)

*confirmation the process of supporting a statement by evidence (p. 750)

*confirmación proceso de sustentar una afirmación con evidencia (p. 750)

*conform to change in a way that fits a standard or authority (p. 574)

*adecuarse cambiar para ajustarse a un estándar o autoridad (p. 574)

*conformity agreement in form, manner, or character (p. 685)

*conformidad acuerdo en forma, modo o carácter (p. 685)

consensus general agreement (p. 611)

consenso acuerdo general (p. 611)

conservative a person who believes government power, particularly in the economy, should be limited in order to maximize individual freedom (p. 740)

conservador una persona que cree que el poder del gobierno, particularmente en la economía, debe estar limitado para llevar al máximo la libertad individual (p. 740)

*constitute to be composed of, made up of, or formed from (p. 207)

*constituir estar compuesto de, hecho de o formado por (p. 207)

*constitutional being in accordance with or regulated by a constitution (p. 78)

*constitucional de acuerdo con una constitución o reglamentado por ella (p. 78)

*consumer a person who buys what is produced by an economy (p. 196)

*consumidor persona que compra lo que produce una economía (p. 196)

containment the policy or process of preventing the expansion of a hostile power (p. 538)

contención la política o proceso de prevenir la expansión de un poder hostil (p. 538)

contra Spanish for counterrevolutionary, an anti-Sandinista guerrilla force in Nicaragua (p. 762)

contra contrarevolucionario, la fuerza guerilla anti-Sandinista en Nicaragua (p. 762)

contraband goods whose importation, exportation, or possession is illegal (p. 326)

contrabando artículos de los que la importación, exportación o posesión es ilegal (p. 326)

*controversy a prolonged public dispute (p. 95)

*controversia discusión pública prolongada (p. 95)

*conventional nonnuclear (p. 602)

*convencional no nuclear (p. 602)

Glossary/Glosario

English	Español
*convince to bring to belief, consent, or a course of action (p. 548)	*convencer hacer creer, conseguir el consentimiento o lograr un curso de acción (p. 548)
convoy a group that travels with something, such as a ship, to protect it (p. 339)	convoy un grupo que viaja junto con algo, tal como un barco, para protegerlo (p. 339)
convoy system a system in which merchant ships travel with naval vessels for protection (p. 499)	sistema de convoy un sistema en el cual barcos mercantes viajan con buques navales para protección (p. 499)
cooperative a store where farmers bought products from each other; an enterprise owned and operated by those who use its services (p. 243)	cooperativa tienda donde los granjeros compraban productos el uno del otro; empresa poseída y operada por los que usan sus servicios (p. 243)
cooperative individualism President Hoover's policy of encouraging manufacturers and distributors to form their own organizations and volunteer information to the federal government in an effort to stimulate the economy (p. 365)	individualismo cooperativo política del Presidente Hoover para alentar a los manufactureros y distribuidores a formar sus propias organizaciones y pasar información voluntariamente al gobierno federal en un esfuerzo para estimular la economía (p. 365)
*coordinate to harmonize or bring into common action, movement, or condition (p. 503)	*coordinar armonizar o realizar acciones o movimientos comunes o bien obtener condiciones comunes (p. 503)
corporation an organization that is authorized by law to carry on an activity but treated as though it were a single person (p. 194)	sociedad anónima organización autorizada por ley a montar una actividad, tratada como si fuera una sola persona (p. 194)
cost of living the cost of purchasing goods and services essential for survival (p. 348)	costo de vida el costo de comprar artículos y servicios esenciales para la supervivencia (p. 348)
cost-plus a government contract to pay a manufacturer the cost to produce an item plus a guaranteed percentage (p. 488)	costo más beneficio contrato del gobierno para pagar el costo de fabricación para producir un artículo más un porcentaje garantizado (p. 488)
counterculture a culture with values and beliefs different than the mainstream (p. 684)	contracultura una cultura con valores y creencias diferentes de los de la cultura principal (p. 684)
court-packing the act of changing the political balance of power in a nation's judiciary system whereby a national leader, such as the American president, appoints judges who will rule in favor of his or her policies (p. 442)	recomposición de la corte acto de modificar el equilibrio político de poder en el sistema judicial de una nación mediante el cual un líder nacional, como el presidente estadounidense, nombra jueces que decidirán a favor de las políticas de éste (p. 442)
covert not openly shown or engaged in (p. 557)	secreto no hecho o mostrado abiertamente (p. 557)
creationism the belief that God created the world and everything in it, usually in the way described in Genesis (p. 380)	creacionismo la creencia que Dios creó al mundo y todo lo que hay en él, usualmente como se describe en Génesis (p. 380)
credibility gap lack of trust or believability (p. 664)	barrera de credibilidad falta de confianza (p. 664)
*credit an amount or sum of money placed at a person's disposal by a bank on condition that it will be repaid with interest (p. 372)	*crédito monto o suma de dinero que un banco pone a disposición de una persona con la condición de que se devolverá con intereses (p. 372)
*criteria standards on which a judgment or action may be based (p. 726)	*criterios normas sobre las que puede basarse una opinión o acción (p. 726)
*crucial something considered important or essential (p. 133)	*crucial algo que se considera importante o fundamental (p. 133)
*currency paper money used as a medium of exchange (p. 243)	*moneda dinero en papel que se utiliza como medio de cambio (p. 243)

customs duty a tax on imports and exports (p. 23)

derecho de aduana impuesto sobre importaciones y exportaciones (p. 23)

de facto segregation segregation by custom and tradition (p. 623)

segregación de facto segregación por costumbre y tradición (p. 623)

deficit spending government practice of spending borrowed money rather than raising taxes, usually an attempt to boost the economy (p. 434)

gastos déficits práctica del gobierno de gastar dinero prestado en vez de aumentar impuestos, usualmente una tentativa para levantar la economía (p. 434)

deflation a decline in the volume of available money or credit that results in lower prices, and, therefore, increases the buying power of money (p. 200)

deflación un decremento de la cantidad de dinero o crédito disponible el cual resulta en precios reducidos y por lo tanto aumenta el poder adquisitivo de la moneda (p. 200)

*deny to declare untrue (p. 380)

*negar declarar que algo no es cierto (p. 380)

deport to expel individuals from the country (p. 352)

deportar expulsar del país a individuos (p. 352)

*deregulation the act or process of removing restrictions or regulations (p. 721)

*desregulación acción o proceso de eliminar restricciones o reglamentaciones (p. 721)

*despite in spite of (p. 520)

*a pesar de pese a que (p. 520)

détente a policy which attempts to relax or ease tensions between nations (p. 710)

détente una política que intenta relajar o borrar la tensión entre naciones (p. 710)

developing nation a nation whose economy is primarily agricultural (p. 557)

nación en desarrollo nación en donde la economía es principalmente agrícola (p. 557)

*device a piece of equipment or a mechanism designed to serve a special purpose or perform a special function (p. 774)

*dispositivo pieza de un equipo o mecanismo diseñado para servir un propósito especial o para realizar una función específica (p. 774)

direct primary a vote held by all members of a political party to decide their candidate for public office (p. 294)

elección primaria voto tomado por todos los miembros de un partido político para elegir a su candidato para un puesto público (p. 294)

discount retailing selling large quantities of goods at very low prices and trying to sell the goods quickly to turn over their entire inventory in a short period of time (p. 755)

ventas minoristas de descuento vender grandes cantidades de productos a precios muy bajos e intentar realizar ventas rápidas de productos para la rotación del inventario en un corto período de tiempo (p. 755)

*discrimination to make a difference in treatment or favor on a basis other than individual merit (p. 250)

*discriminación hacer diferencias en el trato o favorecer en base a toda cosa diferente del mérito individual (p. 250)

disenfranchise to deprive of the right to vote (p. 491)

privación civil privar el derecho al voto (p. 491)

*disposable referring to the money remaining to an individual after deduction of taxes (p. 370)

*disponible hace referencia al dinero que le queda a un individuo después de la deducción de impuestos (p. 370)

*disproportionate lacking regularity or symmetry in size, degree, or intensity (p. 665)

*desproporcionado que carece de regularidad o simetría en tamaño, grado o intensidad (p. 665)

*distribution the act or process of being given out or disbursed to clients, customers, or members of a group (p. 194)

*distribución acción o proceso de repartir o desembolsar entre clientes, consumidores o miembros de un grupo (p. 194)

*diverse being different from one another (p. 382)

*diferente ser distinto de otros (p. 382)

dollar diplomacy a policy of joining the business interests of a country with its diplomatic interests abroad (p. 281)

diplomacia del dólar política de juntar los intereses comerciales de un país con sus intereses diplomáticos en el extranjero (p. 281)

Glossary/Glosario

Glossary/Glosario

English	Español
domino theory the belief that if one nation in Asia fell to the Communists, neighboring countries would follow (p. 655)	**teoría dominó** la creencia que si una nación en Asia se derrumbara ante los comunistas, sus países vecinos hubieran caído en seguida (p. 655)
dove a person in favor of the United States withdrawing from the Vietnam War (p. 667)	**paloma** persona a favor de que Estados Unidos se retirara de la guerra en Vietnam (p. 667)
downsizing reducing a company in size by laying off workers and managers to become more efficient (p. 766)	**reducción de personal** reducción del tamaño de una compañía despidiendo gerentes y trabajadores para llegar a ser una empresa más eficiente (pág. 766)
*draft to select a person at random for mandatory military service (p. 332)	***conscripción** selección de una persona al azar para el servicio militar obligatorio (p. 332)
dry farming a way of farming dry land in which seeds are planted deep in the ground where there is some moisture (p. 168)	**cultivo seco** manera de cultivar tierra seca plantando las semillas en la profundidad de la tierra donde hay algo de humedad (p. 168)
due process a judicial requirement that laws may not treat individuals unfairly, arbitrarily, or unreasonably, and that courts must follow proper procedures and rules when trying cases (p. 601)	**proceso justo** requerimiento judicial de que las leyes no deben tratar individuos injusta, arbitraria, o irracionalmente y que las cortes deben de seguir procesos y reglamentos justos al jurar casos (p. 601)
dynamic conservatism policy of balancing economic conservatism with some activism (p. 570)	**conservatismo dinámico** política de alcanzar un balance entre el conservatismo económico y algún activismo (p. 570)

E

English	Español
"earmark" specifications added by both Republicans and Democrats for the expenditure of federal money for particular projects, such as building a bridge or funding medical research, usually in their own states and districts (p. 826)	**destino de fondos** especificaciones que tanto Republicanos como Demócratas añadieron para el gasto del dinero federal en proyectos particulares, por ejemplo, la construcción de un puente o la financiación de investigaciones médicas, generalmente, en sus propios estados y distritos (p. 826)
economies of scale the reduction in the cost of a good brought about especially by increased production at a given facility (p. 194)	**economía a gran escala** reducción del costo de un producto a causa de la producción aumentada en una fábrica de producción (p. 194)
*eliminate to remove or get rid of (p. 819)	***eliminar** quitar o deshacerse de algo (p. 819)
emancipation the act or process of freeing enslaved persons (p. 102)	**emancipación** el proceso de liberar a personas esclavizadas (p. 102)
embargo a government ban on trade with other countries (p. 718)	**embargo** prohibición gubernamental contra el comercio con otros países (p. 718)
*emphasis a special importance given to an object or idea (p. 322)	***énfasis** importancia especial que se le da a un objeto o idea (p. 322)
*enforce to urge or carry out using force (p. 646)	***hacer cumplir** instar o llevar a cabo por medio de la fuerza (p. 646)
*ensure to guarantee or make certain (p. 172)	***asegurar** garantizar o hacer certero (p. 172)
*entity something having independent, separate, or self-contained existence (p. 585)	***entidad** algo que tiene una existencia independiente, separada y autónoma (p. 585)
entrepreneur one who organizes, manages, and assumes the risks of a business or enterprise (p. 187)	**empresario** persona que organiza, dirige y asume el riesgo de un negocio o empresa (p. 187)

enumerated powers powers listed in the Constitution as belonging to the federal government (p. 79)

poderes enumerados poderes nombrados en la Constitución que pertenecen solamente al gobierno federal (p. 79)

***environmental** having to do with the environment; the complex system of plants, animals, water, and soil (p. 304)

***medioambiental** relacionado con el medioambiente; el complejo sistema de plantas, animales, agua y suelo (p. 304)

***equipment** the articles or physical resources prepared or furnished for a specific task (p. 534)

***equipos** artículos o recursos físicos preparados o proporcionados para una tarea específica (p. 534)

***erode** to wear away at something until it fades (p. 326)

***erosionar** desgastar algo hasta que desaparece (p. 326)

espionage spying, especially to gain government secrets (p. 330)

espionaje espiar, especialmente para obtener secretos gubernamentales (p. 330)

***ethnic** relating to large groups of people classed according to common racial, national, tribal, religious, linguistic, or cultural origin or background (p. 216)

***étnico** relativo a grandes grupos de personas clasificadas de acuerdo con características comunes de origen racial, de nacionalidad, tribal, religioso, lingüístico o cultural (p. 216)

ethnic cleansing the expulsion, imprisonment, or killing of ethnic minorities by a dominant majority group (p. 787)

purificación étnica expulsión, encarcelamiento o asesinato de minorías étnicas por un grupo mayoritario dominante (p. 787)

euro the basic currency shared by the countries of the European Union since 1999 (p. 795)

eurodólar moneda básica compartida por los países de la Unión Europea desde 1999 (p. 795)

***evolution** the scientific theory that humans and other forms of life have evolved over time (pp. 231, 380)

***evolución** teoría científica que los humanos y otras formas de vida se han evolucionado tras el tiempo (pp. 231, 380)

executive privilege principle stating that communications of the executive branch should remain confidential to protect national security (p. 716)

privilegio ejecutivo el principio de que las comunicaciones del ramo ejecutivo deben de permanecer confidenciales para proteger la seguridad nacional (p. 716)

***expansion** the act or process of increasing or enlarging the extent, number, volume, or scope (p. 263)

***expansión** acción o proceso de aumentar o ampliar la extensión, número, volumen o alcance (p. 263)

***exposure** the condition of being unprotected, especially from severe weather (p. 99)

***exposición** la condición de estar desprotegido, especialmente del mal tiempo (p. 99)

extermination camp a camp where prisoners were sent to be executed (p. 470)

campo de exterminación campo donde los prisioneros eran enviados para ser ejecutados (p. 470)

***extract** to remove by force (p. 160)

***extraer** quitar algo por la fuerza (p. 160)

***facility** something that is built, installed, or established to serve a particular purpose (p. 622)

***instalación** algo que se construye, instala o establece para servir un propósito especial (p. 622)

fallout radioactive particles dispersed by a nuclear explosion (p. 553)

caída radioactiva partículas radioactivas dispersadas por una explosión nuclear (p. 553)

fascism a political system headed by a dictator that calls for extreme nationalism and racism and no tolerance of opposition (p. 454)

fascismo un sistema político encabezado por un dictador que pide por nacionalismo y racismo extremo y poca tolerancia de la oposición (p. 454)

federalism political system in which power is divided between the national and state governments (p. 37)

federalismo sistema político en el cual el poder está dividido entre los estados y el gobierno federal (p. 37)

feminism the belief that men and women should be equal politically, economically, and socially (p. 686)

feminismo la creencia que los hombres y las mujeres deben ser iguales política, económica y socialmente (p. 686)

filibuster an attempt to kill a bill by having a group of senators take turns speaking continuously so that a vote cannot take place (p. 636)

filibustero un atentado para acabar con un proyecto de ley hablando continuamente a turnos un grupo de senadores para que no pueda haber un voto (p. 636)

***finance** to provide money for a project (p. 436)

***financiar** proporcionar dinero para un proyecto (p. 436)

Glossary/Glosario

Glossary/Glosario

English	Español
fireside chats radio broadcasts made by FDR to the American people to explain his initiatives (p. 425)	**pláticas hogareñas** emisiones de radio transmitidas por FDR al pueblo americano para explicar sus iniciativas (p. 425)
flexible response the buildup of conventional troops and weapons to allow a nation to fight a limited war without using nuclear weapons (p. 602)	**respuesta flexible** formación de tropas y armas convencionales para permitir que un país entre en una guerra limitada sin usar armas nucleares (p. 602)
foreclose to take possession of a property from a mortgagor because of defaults on payments (p. 415)	**ejecutar** una hipoteca tomar posesión de una propiedad por falta de pagos hipotecarios (p. 415)
fossil fuel a fuel formed in the earth from decayed plant or animal remains (p. 733)	**combustible fósil** un combustible formado en la tierra de los restos descompuestos de plantas o animales (p. 733)
*framework a set of guidelines to be followed (p. 35)	***marco** conjunto de pautas por seguir (p. 35)
franchise the right or license to market a company's goods or services in an area, such as a store of a chain operation (p. 574)	**franquicia** derecho o licencia para comercializar los productos o servicios de una empresa en un área, como una tienda de operación en cadena (p. 574)
*fundamental being of central importance (p. 430)	***fundamental** de central importancia (p. 430)

G

English	Español
*gender term applied to the characteristics of a male or female (p. 687)	***género** término aplicado a las características de un ser masculino o femenino (p. 687)
general strike a strike involving all the workers in a particular geographic location (p. 349)	**huelga general** una huelga por todos los trabajadores de un lugar geográfico (p. 349)
*generation a classification of people who share the same experience throughout their lives (p. 671)	***generación** clasificación de personas que comparten las mismas experiencias a lo largo de sus vidas (p. 671)
generation gap a cultural separation between parents and their children (p. 579)	**barrera generacional** una separación cultural entre padres e hijos (p. 579)
glasnost a Soviet policy permitting open discussion of political and social issues and freer dissemination of news and information (p. 763)	**glasnost** política soviética que permitía discusión abierta de temas políticos y sociales y diseminación más libre de noticias e información (p. 763)
globalism the idea that the world is becoming increasingly interconnected (p. 794)	**globalismo** idea de que el mundo se encuentra cada vez más interconectado (p. 794)
global warming an increase in average world temperatures over time (p. 797)	**calentamiento global** aumento en la temperatura promedio mundial tras un período (p. 797)
gold standard a monetary standard in which one ounce of gold equaled a set number of dollars (p. 424)	**patrón oro norma** monetaria en la cual una onza de oro igualaba a un número fijo de dólares (p. 424)
graduated income tax tax based on the net income of an individual or business and which taxes different income levels at different rates (p. 245)	**impuesto graduado** de utilidades impuesto basado en los ingresos netos de un individuo o empresa en el cual la taza del impuesto se diferencia de acuerdo a diferentes niveles de salario (p. 245)
graft the acquisition of money in dishonest ways, as in bribing a politician (p. 227)	**soborno** adquisición de dinero de manera deshonesta tal como el sobornar a un político (p. 227)
grandfather clause a clause that allowed individuals who did not pass the literacy test to vote if their fathers or grandfathers had voted before Reconstruction began; an exception to a law based on preexisting circumstances (p. 250)	**cláusula de abuelo** cláusula que permitió votar a los que no aprobaron el examen de leer si sus padres o sus abuelos habían votado antes de que empezara la Reconstrucción; excepción a una ley basada en circunstancias preexistentes (p. 250)

Glossary/Glosario

grassroots movement a group of people organizing at the local or community level, away from political or cultural centers (p. 767)

movimiento local grupo de personas que se organiza a nivel local y popular lejos de centros políticos o culturales (p. 767)

greenback a piece of U.S. paper money first issued by the North during the Civil War (p. 242)

billete dorso verde billete de papel moneda de EE.UU. expedido por primera vez por el Norte durante la Guerra Civil (p. 242)

gross national product the total value of goods and services produced by a country during a year (p. 182)

producto nacional bruto valor total de bienes y servicios producidos por un país durante un año (p. 182)

*guarantee a statement of assurance (p. 137)

*garantía declaración de seguridad (p. 137)

guerrilla member of an armed band that carries out surprise attacks and sabotage rather than open warfare (pp. 283, 655)

guerrilla banda armada que usa ataques sorpresas o sabotaje en vez de la guerra organizada (pp. 283, 655)

H

habeas corpus a legal order for an inquiry to determine whether a person has been lawfully imprisoned (p. 128)

hábeas corpus orden legal para una encuesta para determinar si una persona ha sido encarcelada legalmente (p. 128)

hacienda a huge ranch (p. 164)

hacienda un rancho extenso (p. 164)

hawk someone who believed the United States should continue its military efforts in Vietnam (p. 667)

halcón persona que creía que Estados Unidos debía continuar sus esfuerzos militares en Vietnam (p. 667)

hedgerow row of shrubs or trees surrounding a field, often on a dirt wall (p. 518)

seto fila de arbustos o árboles cercando un campo a menudo sobre un muro de tierra (p. 518)

hemispheric defense zone national policy during World War II that declared the Western Hemisphere to be neutral and that the United States would patrol this region against German submarines (p. 476)

zona de defensa hemisférica política nacional durante la Segunda Guerra Mundial que declaró que el Hemisferio Oeste fue neutral y que Estados Unidos patrullaría esta región en contra de submarinos alemanes (p. 476)

hippies refers to young Americans, especially during the 1960s, who reject the conventions of established society (p. 684)

hippies se refiere a los jóvenes estadounidenses, especialmente durante la década de 1960, que rechazaban las convenciones de la sociedad establecida (p. 684)

hobo a homeless and usually penniless wanderer (p. 406)

vagabundo persona errante sin hogar y usualmente sin dinero (p. 406)

holding company a company whose primary business is owning a controlling share of stock in other companies (p. 198)

compañía de valores compañía de la cual el negocio principal es poseer el control de acciones en otras compañías (p. 198)

homestead method of acquiring a piece of U.S. public land by living on and cultivating it (p. 167)

posesionar método de adquirir una extensión de tierra pública de EEUU viviendo en ella y cultivándola (p. 167)

horizontal integration combining of many firms engaged in the same type of business into one corporation (p. 197)

integración horizontal asociación do firmas competitivas en una sociedad anónima (p. 197)

hydraulic mining method of mining by which water is sprayed at a very high pressure against a hill or mountain, washing away large quantities of dirt, gravel, and rock, and exposing the minerals beneath the surface (p. 161)

minería hidráulica método de minería mediante el que se pulveriza agua a alta presión contra una colina o montaña, lo que elimina grandes cantidades de suciedad, grava y rocas y expone los minerales que se encuentran debajo de la superficie (p. 161)

*ideology a system of thought that is held by an individual, group, or culture (p. 424)

*ideología sistema de ideas que posee un individuo, grupo o cultura (p. 424)

*illegal not according to or authorized by law (p. 789)

*ilegal que no está de acuerdo con la ley o ésta no lo autoriza (p. 789)

*immigrant one who enters and becomes established in a country other than that of his or her original nationality (p. 214)

*inmigrante aquél que ingresa y se establece en un país que no es su país de origen (p. 214)

Glossary/Glosario

Glossary/Glosario

English	Español
*impact to make a lasting impression upon an individual or group (p. 392)	***impactar** dejar una impresión duradera en un individuo o grupo (p. 392)
imperialism the actions used by one nation to exercise political or economic control over a smaller or weaker nation (p. 262)	**imperialismo** acciones usadas por una nación para ejercer el control político o económico sobre naciones más pequeñas o débiles (p. 262)
*implement to put into action (p. 129)	***implementar** poner en acción (p. 129)
implied powers powers not specifically listed in the Constitution but claimed by the federal government (p. 79)	**poderes implícitos** poderes no nombrados específicamente en la Constitución pero reclamados por el gobierno federal (p. 79)
*imply to express indirectly (p. 558)	***insinuar** expresar indirectamente (p. 558)
impound to take possession of (p. 708)	**confiscar** tomar posesión de (p. 708)
*incentive something that motivates a person into action (p. 222)	***incentivo** algo que motiva a que una persona realice una acción (p. 222)
*incident occurrence of a happening or situation that is a separate unit of experience (p. 712)	***incidente** acontecimiento de un suceso o situación que es una unidad separada de experiencia (p. 712)
*income a gain or recurrent benefit usually measured in money derived from capital or labor (p. 582)	***ingresos** ganancia o beneficio recurrente que generalmente se mide en dinero proveniente de capital o trabajo (p. 582)
income tax a tax based on the net income of a person or business (p. 310)	**impuesto de utilidades** impuesto basado en el ingreso neto de una persona o empresa (p. 310)
indentured servant an individual who contracts to work for a colonist for a specified number of years in exchange for transportation to the colonies, food, clothing, and shelter (p. 12)	**sirviente contratado** individuo contratado para trabajar para un colono durante cierto número de años a cambio de transportación a las colonias, alimento, ropa y refugio (p. 12)
*indicate to point out, point to, or demonstrate the necessity of (p. 745)	***indicar** señalar, describir o demostrar la necesidad de algo (p. 745)
individualism the thought that no matter what a person's background is, he or she can still become successful (p. 230)	**individualismo** el pensamiento de que sin importar el origen de una persona, ésta puede ser exitosa (p. 230)
industrial union an organization of common laborers and craft workers in a particular industry (p. 201)	**sindicato industrial** organización de trabajadores comunes y obreros calificados en una industria (p. 201)
inflation the loss of value of money (pp. 242, 718)	**inflación** pérdida del valor del dinero (pp. 242, 718)
*initial of or relating to the beginning (p. 541)	***inicial** relacionado con el comienzo (p. 541)
initiative the right of citizens to place a measure or issue before the voters or the legislature for approval (p. 295)	**iniciativa** derecho de los ciudadanos de poner una propuesta o tema ante los votantes o la legislatura para su aprobación (p. 295)
injunction a court order whereby one is required to do or to refrain from doing a specified act (p. 205)	**medida cautelar** orden judicial que exige o prohíbe la realización de una acción específica (p. 205)
*innovation a new idea or method (p. 168)	***innovación** nueva idea o método (p. 168)
*insecurity the state of not being confident or sure (p. 538)	***inseguridad** estado de desconfianza o indecisión (p. 538)
*inspector a person appointed to examine foreign facilities, usually in search of weapons (p. 817)	***inspector** persona designada para examinar instalaciones extranjeras, por lo general, en búsqueda de armas (p. 817)

Glossary/Glosario

installment buying an item on credit with a monthly plan to pay off the value of the good (p. 405)

pago a plazos compra de un artículo a crédito con un plan de pago mensual para pagar el valor del artículo (p. 405)

*institute to initiate or establish something (p. 605)

*instituir iniciar o establecer algo (p. 605)

insubordination disobedience (p. 307)

insubordinación desobediencia (p. 307)

*integrate to combine two previously separate things (p. 191)

*integrar combinar dos cosas previamente separadas (p. 191)

integrated circuit a complete electronic circuit on a silicon chip that is small and easy to produce (p. 774)

circuito integrado un circuito electrónico completo en un chip de silicona pequeño y fácil de producir (p. 774)

*intense existing in an extreme degree (p. 512)

*intenso que existe en un grado extremo (p. 512)

*intensify to become more frequent and powerful (p. 733)

*intensificar volverse más frecuente y poderoso (p. 733)

internationalism a national policy of actively trading with foreign countries to foster peace and prosperity (p. 459)

internacionalismo política nacional de intercambio comercial activo con países extranjeros para promover la paz y la prosperidad (p. 459)

*interpret to explain the meaning of complex material (p. 38)

*interpretar explicar el significado de materiales complejos (p. 38)

*interpretation the act or process of explaining or telling the meaning of (p. 810)

*interpretación acción o proceso de explicar o decir el significado de algo (p. 810)

*intervene to get involved in the affairs of another (p. 270)

*intervenir involucrarse en los asuntos de otros (p. 270)

*invest to put money into a company in order to gain a future financial reward (p. 401)

*invertir colocar dinero en una empresa con el fin de obtener una recompensa financiera en el futuro (p. 401)

*investigation a systematic examination or official inquiry (p. 363)

*investigación examen sistemático o indagación oficial (p. 363)

*investor one who puts money into a company in order to gain a future financial reward (p. 192)

*inversor aquél que coloca dinero en una empresa con el fin de obtener una recompensa financiera en el futuro (p. 192)

Iron Curtain the political and military barrier that isolated Soviet-controlled countries of Eastern Europe after World War II (p. 537)

cortina de hierro barrera política y militar que aisló a los países de Europa Oriental controlados por los soviéticos después de la Segunda Guerra Mundial (p. 537)

isolationism a national policy of avoiding involvement in world affairs (p. 366)

aislacionismo política nacional de evitar el involucramiento en asuntos mundiales (p. 366)

J

jazz American style of music that developed from ragtime and blues and which uses syncopated rhythms and melodies (p. 389)

jazz estilo de música americana que se desarrolló de ragtime y blues y que usa melodías y ritmos sincopados (p. 389)

Jim Crow laws statutes or laws created to enforce segregation (p. 250)

Leyes de Jim Crow leyes creadas para reforzar la segregación (p. 250)

jingoism extreme nationalism marked by aggressive foreign policy (p. 271)

patriotismo extremo nacionalismo marcado por la agresiva política extranjera (p. 271)

joint-stock company form of business organization in which many investors pool funds to raise large amounts of money for large projects (p. 8)

compañía por acciones forma de organización de negocios en la cual muchos inversionistas compran acciones para juntar grandes cantidades de dinero para grandes proyectos (p. 8)

judicial review power of the Supreme Court to determine whether laws of Congress are constitutional and to strike down those that are not (p. 83)

revisión judicial derecho de la Suprema Corte para determinar si las leyes del Congreso son constitucionales y para derribar aquellas que no lo son (p. 83)

*justify to prove or to show to be just, right, or reasonable (p. 504)

*justificar probar o demostrar que algo es justo, correcto y razonable (p. 504)

juvenile delinquency antisocial or criminal behavior of young people (p. 587)

delincuencia juvenil comportamiento antisocial o criminal de los jóvenes (p. 587)

Glossary/Glosario

Glossary/Glosario

English	Español

K

kamikaze during World War II, a Japanese suicide pilot whose mission was to crash into his target (p. 515)

kamikase durante la Segunda Guerra Mundial un piloto suicida japonés de quien la misión fue chocar en su objetivo (p. 515)

L

labor union an organization of workers formed for the purpose of advancing its members' interests (p. 92)

sindicato organización de trabajadores formada con el propósito de promover los intereses de sus miembros (p. 92)

laissez-faire policy that government should interfere as little as possible in the nation's economy (p. 186)

laissez-faire política que el gobierno debe interferir tan poco como sea posible en la economía del país (p. 186)

land grant a grant of land by the federal government especially for roads, railroads, or agricultural colleges (p. 192)

concesión de tierras una concesión de terrenos por el gobierno federal especialmente para carreteras, vías de ferrocarril y colegios agrícolas (p. 192)

*legislation a proposed law to be voted on by a governing body (p. 295)

*legislación ley propuesta para que un órgano directivo la vote (p. 295)

*legislator one who makes laws as a member of a political, legislative body (p. 566)

*legislador aquél que elabora leyes como miembro de un órgano político legislativo (p. 566)

*liberal a person who generally believes the government should take an active role in the economy and in social programs but should not dictate social behavior (pp. 708, 740)

*liberal persona que generalmente cree que el gobierno debe desempeñar un papel active en la economía y programas sociales pero que el gobierno no debe dictar el comportamiento social (pp. 708, 740)

*liberate to set free (p. 532)

*liberar dejar en libertad (p. 532)

*likewise in a like manner, similarly (p. 692)

*asimismo de la misma manera, igualmente (p. 692)

limited war a war fought with limited commitment of resources to achieve a limited objective, such as containing communism (p. 545)

guerra limitada guerra peleada con compromisos limitados de recursos para alcanzar un objetivo limitado, tal como la contención del comunismo (p. 545)

linkage policy of improving relations with the Soviet Union and China in hopes of persuading them to cut back their aid to North Vietnam (p. 670)

enlace política de mejorar relaciones con la Unión Soviética y China con la esperanza de persuadirlas a que redujeran su ayuda a Vietnam del Norte (p. 670)

lockout a company tool to fight union demands by refusing to allow employees to enter its facilities to work (p. 202)

cierre patronal práctica de una empresa para rechazar las demandas sindicales negándose a permitir a los empleados a entrar al área de trabajo (p. 202)

long drive driving cattle long distances to a railroad depot for fast transport and great profit (p. 163)

manejo largo conducción de ganado por largas distancias a estaciones de ferrocarril para la transportación rápida y grandes ganancias (p. 163)

loyalty review program a policy established by President Truman that authorized the screening of all federal employees to determine their loyalty to the American government (p. 546)

programa de verificación de la lealtad política que estableció el presidente Truman y que autorizaba la investigación de todos los empleados federales para determinar la lealtad de éstos al gobierno estadounidense (p. 546)

lynching an execution performed without lawful approval (p. 252)

linchamiento ejecución hecha sin aprobación legal (p. 252)

M

mandate authorization to act given to a representative (p. 137)

mandato autorización dado a un representante (p. 137)

*manipulate to operate or arrange manually to achieve a desired effect (p. 547)

margin buying a stock by paying only a fraction of the stock price and borrowing the rest (p. 401)

margin call demand by a broker that investors pay back loans made for stocks purchased on margin (p. 401)

martial law the law administered by military forces that is invoked by a government in an emergency (p. 126)

mass media a medium of communication (as in television and radio) intended to reach a wide audience (p. 385)

mass production the production of large quantities of goods using machinery and often an assembly line (p. 368)

massive retaliation a policy of threatening a massive response, including the use of nuclear weapons, against a Communist state trying to seize a peaceful state by force (p. 555)

*media a means of expression or communication, especially in reference to the agencies of mass communication—newspapers, radio, television, and the Internet (p. 664)

*mediate an attempt to resolve conflict between hostile people or groups (p. 445)

microprocessor a computer processor containing both memory and computing functions on a single chip (p. 774)

*migrate to move from one location to another (p. 330)

migration chain the process by which immigrants who have acquired U.S. citizenship can send for relatives in their home country to join them (p. 788)

militarism a policy of aggressive military preparedness (p. 321)

military-industrial complex an informal relationship that some people believe exists between the military and the defense industry to promote greater military spending and influence government policy (p. 559)

minutemen companies of civilian soldiers who boasted they were ready to fight on a minute's notice (p. 26)

missile gap belief that the Soviet Union had more nuclear weapons than the United States (p. 596)

Model T automobile built by the Ford Motor Company from 1908 until 1927 (p. 368)

*modify to make changes or alter (p. 781)

*monitor to observe, oversee, or regulate (p. 823)

monopoly total control of a type of industry by one person or one company (p. 197)

---

*manipular operar o disponer manualmente para alcanzar un efecto deseado (p. 547)

margen comprar acciones pagando solamente una fracción del precio y pidiendo prestado el resto (p. 401)

llamada de reserva demanda de un accionista a que los inversionistas paguen los préstamos hechos para la compra de acciones al margen (p. 401)

derecho marcial derecho administrado por fuerzas militares que es invocado por un gobierno en una emergencia (p. 126)

medios informativos medios de comunicación (como televisión y radio) con la intención de llegar a la audiencia extensa (p. 385)

fabricación en serie producción de grandes cantidades de productos usando máquinas y a menudo una línea de montaje (p. 368)

represalia masiva una política que amenaza una respuesta masiva, incluyendo el uso de armas nucleares, contra un estado comunista que trata de captar un país pacífico por la fuerza (p. 555)

*medios de comunicación medios de expresión o comunicación, especialmente en referencia a las agencias de comunicación masiva periódicos, radio, televisión e Internet (p. 664)

*mediar intento de resolver un conflicto entre personas o grupos hostiles (p. 445)

microprocesador procesador de computadora que contiene memoria y funciones de computación en un solo chip (p. 774)

*migrar mudarse de un lugar a otro (p. 330)

cadena migratoria proceso mediante el cual los inmigrantes que obtuvieron la ciudadanía estadounidense pueden llamar a sus familiares en sus países de origen para que se les unan (p. 788)

militarismo política de preparación militar agresiva (p. 321)

compejo militar industrial relación informal que algunas personas creen que existe entre lo militar y la industria de defensa para promover mayores gastos militares y para influenciar la política gubernamental (p. 559)

minutemen compañías de soldados civiles que se jactaban de que podrían estar listos para tomar armas en sólo un minuto (p. 26)

diferencia de proyectiles creencia que la Unión Soviética tenía más armas nucleares que Estados Unidos (p. 596)

Modelo T automóvil construido por la Ford Motor Company desde 1908 hasta 1927 (p. 368)

*modificar realizar cambios o alterar (p. 781)

*controlar vigilar, supervisar o regular (p. 823)

monopolio control total de una industria por una persona o una compañía (p. 197)

Glossary/Glosario

English	Español
muckraker a journalist who uncovers abuses and corruption in a society (p. 293)	**muckraker** periodista que revela abusos y corrupción en una sociedad (p. 293)
multinational corporation large corporations with overseas investments (p. 574)	**corporación multinacional** grandes corporaciones de inversión extranjera (p. 574)
"mutual assured destruction" the strategy assuming that, as long as two countries can destroy each other with nuclear weapons, they will be afraid to use them (p. 753)	**destrucción mutua asegurada** estrategia que supone que mientras dos países puedan destruirse mutuamente con armas nucleares, tendrán miedo de utilizarlas (p. 753)

N

English	Español
napalm a jellied gasoline used for bombs (pp. 521, 661)	**napalm** gasolina gelatinosa utilizada para bombas incendiarias (pp. 521, 661)
national self-determination the free choice by the people of a nation of their own future political status (p. 342)	**autodeterminación nacional** es la libre elección que hacen los habitantes de un país sobre su propia situación política futura (p. 342)
nationalism loyalty and devotion to a nation (p. 322)	**nacionalismo** lealtad y devoción a una nación (p. 322)
nativism hostility toward immigrants (p. 376)	**nativismo** sentimientos de hostilidad hacia imigrantes (p. 376)
***network** an interconnected system (p. 336)	***red** sistema interconectado (p. 336)
nomad a person who continually moves from place to place, usually in search of food (p. 170)	**nómada** persona que se mueve de un lugar a otro, generalmente en busca de alimentos o pastos (p. 170)
***nuclear** used in or produced by a nuclear reaction (p. 523)	***nuclear** que se utiliza en una reacción nuclear o que ésta lo produce (p. 523)

O

English	Español
***obtain** to gain possession of (p. 812)	***obtener** lograr posesión de algo (p. 812)
***ongoing** being actually in process, continuing (p. 393)	***continuo** que está en proceso, en curso (p. 393)
Open Door policy a policy that allowed each foreign nation in China to trade freely in the other nations' spheres of influence (p. 277)	**política de Puertas Abiertas** política que permitió a cada nación extranjera en China intercambiar libremente en las esferas de influencia de otras naciones (p. 277)
open range vast areas of grassland owned by the federal government (p. 162)	**terreno abierto** gran extensión de pastos propiedad del gobierno federal (p. 162)
open shop a workplace where workers are not required to join a union (p. 374)	**taller abierto** lugar de trabajo donde los trabajadores no son requeridos de ser miembros del sindicato (p. 374)
***orientation** position relative to a standard (p. 759)	***orientación** posición relativa a un estándar (p. 759)

P

English	Español
***participant** one who takes part or shares in something (p. 787)	***participante** que forma parte de algo o que comparte algo (p. 787)
party boss the person in control of a political machine (p. 227)	**jefe de partido** persona que lleva el control de la maquinaria política (p. 227)
perestroika a policy of economic and government restructuring instituted by Mikhail Gorbachev in the Soviet Union in the 1980s (p. 763)	**perestroika** política de reestructuración económica y gubernamental instituida por Mikhail Gorbachev en la Unión Soviética en los años 1980 (p. 763)

periphery the outer boundary of something (p. 497)

perjury lying when one has sworn under oath to tell the truth (pp. 548, 785)

***phenomenon** an exceptional, unusual, or abnormal person, thing, or occurrence (p. 572)

philanthropy providing money to support humanitarian or social goals (p. 232)

Pilgrim a Separatist who journeyed to the American colonies in the 1600s for religious freedom (p. 8)

pocket veto indirectly vetoing a bill by letting a session of Congress expire without signing the bill (p. 142)

polio abbreviated form of poliomyelitis, an acute infectious disease affecting the skeletal muscles, often resulting in permanent disability and deformity (p. 422)

political machine an organization linked to a political party that often controlled local government (p. 227)

poll tax a tax of a fixed amount per person that had to be paid before the person could vote (p. 250)

pool a group sharing in some activity; for example, among railroad owners who made secret agreements and set rates among themselves (p. 196)

popular sovereignty government subject to the will of the people (p. 168); before the Civil War, the idea that people living in a territory had the right to decide by voting if slavery would be allowed there (pp. 37, 107)

populism political movement founded in the 1890s representing mainly farmers, favoring free coinage of silver and government control of railroads and other large industries (p. 242)

poverty line a level of personal or family income below which one is classified as poor by the federal government (p. 582)

***practice** to do something repeatedly so it becomes the standard (p. 187)

***prior** happening before an event (p. 162)

***procedure** a particular way of conducting or engaging in an activity (p. 824)

***prohibit** to make illegal by an authority (p. 466)

prohibition laws banning the manufacture, transportation, and sale of alcoholic beverages (p. 299)

propaganda the spreading of ideas about an institution or individual for the purpose of influencing opinion (p. 324)

periferia frontera externa de algo (p. 497)

perjurio mentir cuando uno ha jurado decir la verdad (pp. 548, 785)

***fenómeno** persona, cosa o acontecimiento excepcional, inusual o anormal (p. 572)

filantropía proporcionar dinero para apoyar metas humanitarias o sociales (p. 232)

peregrino Separatista que viajó a las colonias americanas durante los años 1600 para libertad religiosa (p. 8)

veto indirecto vetar indirectamente un proyecto de ley permitiendo que una sesión del Congreso expire sin firmar el proyecto (p. 142)

polio abreviatura de poliomielitis, una enfermedad infecciosa aguda que afecta los músculos esqueléticos y a menudo provoca discapacidad y deformidad permanente (p. 422)

maquinaria política organización aliada con un partido político que a menudo controlaba el gobierno local (p. 227)

impuesto de capitación impuesto de cantidad fija por cada persona, el cual tenía que ser pagado antes de que una persona pudiera votar (p. 250)

consorcio grupo compartiendo una actividad; por ejemplo, dueños de ferrocarril que tomaban acuerdos secretos y fijaban tipos entre ellos mismos (p. 196)

soberanía popular teoría política de que el gobierno está sujeto a la voluntad del pueblo (p. 168); antes de la Guerra Civil, la idea de que la gente que vivía en un territorio tenía el derecho de decidir votando si ahí sería permitida la esclavitud (pp. 37, 107)

populismo movimiento político fundado en los años 1890 representando principalmente a los granjeros que favoreció libre acuñación de plata y el control gubernamental de ferrocarriles y otras industrias grandes (p. 242)

línea de pobreza nivel de ingreso individual o familiar bajo del cual uno es clasificado por el gobierno federal como pobre (p. 582)

***práctica** es la realización de algo repetidamente hasta que se convierte en hábito (p. 187)

***previo** que sucede antes de un acontecimiento (p. 162)

***procedimiento** método particular de llevar a cabo una actividad o participar en ella (p. 824)

***prohibir** cuando una autoridad dictamina que algo es ilegal (p. 466)

prohibición leyes que prohibían la manufactura, transportación y venta de bebidas alcohólicas (p. 299)

propaganda diseminación de ideas sobre una institución o individuo con el propósito de influenciar la opinión (p. 324)

Glossary/Glosario

Glossary/Glosario

English	Español
proprietary colony a colony owned by an individual (p. 11)	**colonia propietaria** colonia propiedad de un individuo (p. 11)
*prospective to be likely to, or have intentions to, perform an act (p. 166)	***potencial** que hay probabilidades o se tienen intenciones de realizar una acción (p. 166)
protective tariff tax on imports designed to protect American manufacturers (p. 87)	**arancel protectora** impuesto en importaciones diseñado para proteger a los manufactureros americanos (p. 87)
protectorate a country that is technically independent but is actually under the control of another country (p. 262)	**protectorado** país que es técnicamente independiente pero que en realidad queda bajo el control de otro país (p. 262)
public works projects such as highways, parks, and libraries built with public funds for public use (p. 412)	**obras públicas** proyectos como carreteras, parques y bibliotecas construidos con fondos públicos para uso público (p. 412)
*publish to make a document available to the general public (p. 233)	***publicar** hacer que un documento esté disponible para el público en general (p. 233)
*purchase to gain by paying money or its equivalent (p. 474)	***comprar** adquirir algo pagando dinero o su equivalente (p. 474)

R

English	Español
racism prejudice or discrimination against someone because of his or her race (p. 642)	**racismo** prejuicio o discriminación en contra de alguien por su raza (p. 642)
*rationality the quality or state of being agreeable to reason (p. 684)	***racionalidad** la cualidad o el estado de estar dispuesto a razonar (p. 684)
reapportionment the method states use to draw up political districts based on changes in population (p. 600)	**nueva repartición** método usado por los estados para formar distritos políticos basados en los cambios de población (p. 600)
recall the right that enables voters to remove unsatisfactory elected officials from office (p. 295)	**elección de revocación** derecho que permite a los votantes quitar del cargo a los oficiales elegidos que son inadecuados (p. 295)
*recovery an economic upturn, as after a depression (p. 442)	***recuperación** repunte económico, como sucede después de una depresión (p. 442)
referendum the practice of letting voters accept or reject measures proposed by the legislature (p. 295)	**referéndum** práctica de permitir a los votantes aceptar o rechazar medidas propuestas por la legislatura (p. 295)
*refinement the act or process of improving or perfecting (p. 775)	***refinamiento** acción o proceso de mejorar o perfeccionar (p. 775)
refugee someone leaving his or her country due to a "well-founded fear of persecution on account of race, religion, nationality, membership in a particular group, or political opinion." (p. 789)	**refugiado** persona que abandona su país debido a un "miedo fundado de persecución a causa de su raza, religión, nacionalidad, pertenencia a un grupo en particular u opinión política" (p. 789)
*regime a form of government (p. 460)	***régimen** una forma de gobierno (p. 460)
*register to file personal information in order to become eligible for an official event (p. 631)	***inscribirse** presentar información personal con el fin de ser elegible para un evento oficial (p. 631)
*regulate to govern or direct according to rule (p. 302)	***regular** gobernar o dirigir según las normas (p. 302)
relief aid for the needy, welfare (p. 414)	**asistencia pública** ayuda para los necesitados; beneficencia (p. 414)
*relocate to move to a new place (p. 170)	***trasladar** llevar a un nuevo lugar (p. 170)
*remove to change the location or position (p. 607)	***quitar** cambiar la ubicación o posición (p. 607)

reparations payment by the losing country in a war to the winner for the damages caused by the war (p. 344)

indemnización pago hecho por el país perdedor de una guerra al país ganador por los daños causados por la guerra (p. 344)

repatriation being restored or returned to the country of origin, allegiance, or citizenship (p. 694)

repatriación acción de devolver o regresar a una persona a su país de origen, lealtad o ciudadanía (p. 694)

*resident one who lives in a place for some length of time (p. 790)

*residente que vive en un lugar durante algún tiempo (p. 790)

*resolution a formal expression of opinion, will, or intent voted by an official body or assembly (p. 106)

*resolución expresión formal de una opinión, deseo o intención votada por una asamblea u organismo oficial (p. 106)

*resolve to come to an agreement (pp. 342, 809)

*resolver llegar a un acuerdo (pp. 342, 809)

*resource material used in the production process, such as money, people, land, wood, or steel (p. 182)

*recurso material utilizado en el proceso de producción, como dinero, personas, tierra, madera o acero (p. 182)

*response something said or done as a reaction (p. 559)

*respuesta algo que se dice o hace en reacción a algo (p. 559)

*restraint the act of limiting, restricting, or keeping under control (p. 202)

*restricción acción de limitar, impedir o mantener bajo control (p. 202)

*retain to keep in possession (p. 767)

*retener conservar la posesión (p. 767)

*revelation an act of revealing to view or making known (p. 364)

*revelación acción de divulgar para hacer ver o conocer (p. 364)

revenue sharing federal tax money that is distributed among the states (p. 708)

participación en los ingresos dinero de los impuestos federales que se distribuye entre los estados (p. 708)

revenue tariff tax on imports for the purpose of raising money (p. 87)

arancel de ingresos impuesto en las importaciones con el propósito de recaudar dinero (p. 87)

*revise to make changes to an original document (pp. 39, 474)

*revisar realizar cambios a un documento original (pp. 39, 474)

right-to-work law a law making it illegal to require employees to join a union (p. 567)

derecho a trabajar ley que hace ilegal la demanda que los trabajadores se unan a un sindicato (p. 567)

rock 'n' roll popular music usually played on electronically amplified instruments and characterized by a persistent heavily accented beat, much repetition of simple phrases, and often country, folk, and blues elements (p. 577)

rock 'n' roll música popular que generalmente se toca con instrumentos amplificados electrónicamente y se caracteriza por un ritmo persistente y pesadamente acentuado, muchas repeticiones de frases simples y a menudo elementos del Country, Folk y Blues (p. 577)

safety net something that provides security against misfortune; specifically, government relief programs intended to protect against economic disaster (p. 445)

red de seguridad algo que proporciona seguridad en contra de desgracias, específicamente, programas de beneficencia gubernamentales para proteger en contra del desastre económico (p. 445)

satellite nations nations politically and economically dominated or controlled by another more powerful country (p. 537)

países satélite naciones política y económicamente dominadas o controladas por otro país más poderoso (p. 537)

scalawag name given to Southerners who supported Republican Reconstruction of the South (p. 145)

scalawag nombre dado a los sureños que apoyaron la Reconstrucción republicana del Sur (p. 145)

secede to leave or withdraw (p. 97)

separarse abandonar o retirar (p. 97)

secession withdrawal from the Union (p. 108)

secesión retiro de la Unión (p. 108)

segregation the separation or isolation of a race, class, or group (p. 250)

segregación separación o aislamiento de una raza, clase o grupo (p. 250)

English	Español
separate-but-equal doctrine established by the 1896 Supreme Court case *Plessy* v. *Ferguson* that permitted laws segregating African Americans as long as equal facilities were provided (p. 622)	**separados pero iguales** doctrina establecida por la Suprema Corte en el caso *Plessy* contra *Ferguson* en 1896 que las leyes que segregaron a los afroamericanos fueron permitidas si facilidades iguales fueron proporcionadas (p. 622)
separation of powers government principle in which power is divided among different branches (p. 38)	**separación de poderes** principio de gobierno en el cual el poder está dividido entre diferentes ramos (p. 38)
***series** a number of events that come one after another (p. 412)	***serie** acontecimientos que suceden uno después de otro (p. 412)
settlement house institution located in a poor neighborhood that provided numerous community services such as medical care, child care, libraries, and classes in English (p. 239)	**casa de beneficencia** institución establecida en una vecindad pobre que proveía numerosos servicios comunitarios tal como cuidado médico, cuidado de niños, bibliotecas, e instrucción en inglés (p. 239)
sharecropper farmer who works land for an owner who provides equipment and seed and receives a share of the crop (p. 149)	**aparcero** agricultor que labra la tierra para un dueño que proporciona equipo y semillas y recibe una porción de la cosecha (p. 149)
siege a military blockade of a city or fortified place to force it to surrender (p. 134)	**sitio** bloqueo militar de una ciudad o un recinto fortificado para forzarlo a rendirse (p. 134)
***significantly** to affect something enough to be of some importance (p. 818)	***considerablemente** afectar algo lo suficiente como para que sea de importancia (p. 818)
sit-down strike method of boycotting work by sitting down at work and refusing to leave the establishment (p. 438)	**huelga de brazos caídos** método de boicotear el trabajo por medio de sentarse en el lugar de trabajo y de rehusar a abandonar el establecimiento (p. 438)
sit-in a form of protest involving occupying seats or sitting down on the floor of an establishment (p. 624)	**plantón** forma de protesta ocupando las sillas o sentándose en el piso de un establecimiento (p. 624)
skyscraper a very tall building (p. 222)	**rascacielos** edificio de gran altura (p. 222)
slave code a set of laws that formally regulated slavery and defined the relationship between enslaved Africans and free people (p. 18)	**código de esclavos** leyes aprobadas que regularon formalmente la esclavitud y definieron la relación entre los africanos esclavizados y la gente libre (p. 18)
smog fog made heavier and darker by smoke and chemical fumes (p. 731)	**smog** niebla hecha más pesada y oscura por el humo y vapores químicos (p. 731)
soap opera a serial drama on television or radio using melodramatic situations (p. 409)	**novela** drama en serie de radio o televisión utilizando situaciones melodramáticas (p. 409)
Social Darwinism based on Charles Darwin's theories of evolution and natural selection, states that humans have developed through competition and natural selection with only the strongest surviving (pp. 231, 300)	**Darwinismo social** se basa en las teorías de evolución y de selección natural de Charles Darwin y expresa que los humanos han evolucionado a través de la competencia y de la selección natural, donde sólo sobrevive el más fuerte (pp. 231, 300)
sodbuster a name given to Great Plains farmers (p. 168)	**rompeterrón** nombre dado a los granjeros de las Grandes Planicies (p. 168)
***source** the point at which something is provided (p. 378)	***fuente** punto en el que se proporciona algo (p. 378)
space race refers to the Cold War competition over dominance of space exploration capability (p. 604)	**carrera espacial** se refiere a la competencia durante la Guerra Fría sobre el dominio de la exploración espacial (p. 604)
speakeasy a place where alcoholic beverages are sold illegally (p. 381)	**speakeasy** lugar donde son vendidas clandestinamente bebidas alcohólicas (p. 381)

special prosecutor a lawyer from outside the government appointed by an attorney general or Congress to investigate a government official for misconduct while in office (p. 716)

fiscal especial un abogado externo al gobierno nombrado por un procurador general o congreso para investigar a un funcionario del gobierno por mala conducta durante sus funciones (p. 716)

speculation act of buying stocks at great risk with the anticipation that the price will rise (p. 401)

especulación acciones compradas con alto riesgo con la anticipación que los precios subirán (p. 401)

sphere of influence section of a country where one foreign nation enjoys special rights and powers (p. 276)

esfera de influencia sección de un país donde una nación extranjera tiene derechos y poderes especiales (p. 276)

spoils system practice of handing out government jobs to supporters; replacing government employees with the winning candidate's supporters (p. 97)

sistema de despojos práctica de dar puestos gubernamentales a los partidarios; reemplazando a los empleados del gobierno con los partidarios del candidato victorioso (p. 97)

*stability a state of peace, free from social unrest (p. 745)

*estabilidad estado de paz, libre de inquietud social (p. 745)

stagflation persistent inflation combined with stagnant consumer demand and relatively high unemployment (p. 719)

stagflación inflación persistente combinado con la demanda estancada y una taza de desempleo alta (p. 719)

state-sponsored terrorism violent acts against civilians that are secretly supported by a government in order to attack other nations without going to war (p. 811)

terrorismo patrocinado por el estado actos violentos en contra de civiles que son secretamente apoyados por un gobierno con el motivo de atacar a otras naciones sin entrar en la guerra (p. 811)

steerage cramped quarters on a ship's lower decks for passengers paying the lowest fares (p. 215)

tercera clase cuarteles apretados de las cubiertas bajas de un barco para los pasajeros que pagan los pasajes más bajos (p. 215)

stock money or capital invested or available for investment or trading (p. 194)

reserva dinero o capital invertido o disponible para inversiones u operaciones comerciales (p. 194)

stock market a system for buying and selling stocks in corporations (p. 400)

bolsa de valores sistema para comprar y vender acciones de corporaciones (p. 400)

*strategic necessary to or important in the initiation, conduct, or completion of a military plan (p. 657)

*estratégico necesario o importante para iniciar, realizar o completar un plan militar (p. 657)

strategic defense a plan to develop missiles and other devices that can shoot down nuclear missiles before they hit the United States (p. 807)

defensa estratégica plan para desarrollar proyectiles y otras armas que pueden derribar proyectiles nucleares antes de que estos golpeen en Estados Unidos (p. 807)

strategic materials materials needed for fighting a war (p. 478)

materiales estratégicos materiales necesarios para una guerra (p. 478)

*strategy a plan or method for achieving a goal (p. 244)

*estrategia plan o método para alcanzar una meta (p. 244)

*subsidy money granted by the government to achieve a specific goal that is beneficial to society (p. 614)

*subsidio dinero que otorga el gobierno para alcanzar una meta específica que beneficia a la sociedad (p. 614)

subversion a systematic attempt to overthrow a government by using persons working secretly from within (p. 546)

subversión intento sistemático para derrocar un gobierno utilizando personas que trabajan secretamente desde adentro (p. 546)

*sufficient enough, adequate (p. 127)

*suficiente bastante, adecuado (p. 127)

suffrage the right to vote (p. 296)

sufragio derecho al voto (p. 296)

*sum a specified amount of money (p. 403)

*suma cantidad específica de dinero (p. 403)

summit a meeting of heads of government (p. 711)

cumbre junta de jefes de gobiernos (p. 711)

Sunbelt a new industrial region in southern California and the Deep South developing during World War II (p. 502)

Región Solada nueva región industrial en el sur de California y el Bajo Sur que se desarrolló durante la Segunda Guerra Mundial (p. 502)

Glossary/Glosario

Glossary/Glosario

English	Español
supply-side economics economic theory that lower taxes will boost the economy as businesses and individuals invest their money, thereby creating higher tax revenue (pp. 365, 748)	**economía de oferta teoría** económica de que los impuestos bajos levantarían la economía invirtiendo su dinero los negocios y los individuos, así creando un alto ingreso del impuesto (pp. 365, 748)
*****suspend** to temporarily stop an operation (p. 406)	*****suspender** detener temporalmente una operación (p. 406)
*****symbolize** to represent, express, or identify by a symbol (p. 390)	*****simbolizar** representar, expresar o identificar por medio de un símbolo (p. 390)

T

English	Español
*****target** something or someone fired on or marked for attack (p. 498)	*****objetivo** algo o alguien a quien se dispara o a quien se marca para atacar (p. 498)
teach-in an extended meeting or class held to discuss a social or political issue (p. 665)	**plantón educacional** junta o clase extendida para discutir un asunto político o social (p. 665)
*****technique** a method of achieving a desired task (p. 409)	*****técnica** método para lograr una tarea determinada (p. 409)
telecommute to work at home by means of an electronic linkup with a central office (p. 775)	**viajar electrónicamente** trabajar en casa por medio de conexión electrónica con una oficina central (p. 775)
televangelist an evangelist who conducts regularly televised religious programs (p. 745)	**televangelista** evangelista que transmite regularmente programas evangélicos por televisión (p. 745)
temperance moderation in or abstinence from alcohol (p. 100)	**templanza** moderación o abstinencia del uso del alcohol (p. 100)
tenement multifamily apartments, usually dark, crowded, and barely meeting minimum living standards (p. 225)	**casa de vecindad** apartamentos para varias familias, normalmente obscuros, apretados que apenas cumplen con los estándares mínimos de viviendas (p. 225)
termination policy a government policy to bring Native Americans into mainstream society by withdrawing recognition of Native American groups as legal entities (p. 585)	**política de terminación** política gubernamental para traer a los Nativos Americanos dentro de la sociedad principal retirando el reconocimiento de los grupos Nativos Americanos como entidades legales (p. 585)
terrorism the use of violence by nongovernmental groups against civilians to achieve a political goal by instilling fear and frightening governments into changing policies (p. 810)	**terrorismo** el uso de violencia por grupos no del gobierno en contra de civiles para alcanzar una meta política impartiendo miedo y amenazando gobiernos para que cambien su política (p. 810)
*****theory** a hypothesis meant for argument or investigation (p. 719)	*****teoría** hipótesis pensada para un argumento o investigación (p. 719)
time zone a geographical region in which the same standard time is kept (p. 191)	**huso horario** región geográfica en la cual la misma norma horaria es mantenida (p. 191)
trade union an organization of workers with the same trade or skill (p. 201)	**gremio** organización de trabajadores con el mismo oficio o destreza (p. 201)
*****traditional** relating to cultural continuity in social attitudes, customs, and institutions (p. 657)	*****tradicional** relativo a la continuidad cultural en las actitudes sociales, costumbres e instituciones (p. 657)
*****transport** to convey from one place to another (p. 465)	*****transportar** llevar de un lugar a otro (p. 465)
*****transportation** method of travel from one place to another (p. 86)	*****transporte** método para viajar de un lugar a otro (p. 86)

triangular trade a three-way trade route that exchanged goods between the American colonies and two other trading partners (p. 16)

comercio triangular una ruta comercial de tres ramas para intercambiar productos entre las colonias americanas y otros dos asociados comerciales (p. 16)

*trigger to cause an action that causes a greater reaction (p. 227)

*desencadenar provocar una acción que desencadena una reacción mayor (p. 227)

trust a combination of firms or corporations formed by a legal agreement, especially to reduce competition (p. 198)

cártel combinación de empresas o sociedades anónimas formada por acuerdo legal, especialmente para reducir la competición (p. 198)

U

*unconstitutional not in accordance with or authorized by the constitution of a state or society (p. 312)

*inconstitucional que no está de acuerdo con la constitución de un estado o sociedad o no posee la autorización de ésta (p. 312)

unfair trade practices trading practices which derive a gain at the expense of the competition (p. 311)

prácticas comerciales injustas prácticas comerciales que ganan el beneficio perjudicando a la competencia (p. 311)

*unify to bring a group together with a similar goal or thought pattern (p. 385)

*unificar juntar a un grupo con un objetivo o patrones de pensamiento similares (p. 385)

union shop a business that requires employees to join a union (p. 567)

taller sindicalizado comercio que requiere que los trabajadores se unan al sindicato (p. 567)

*unresolved not cleared up, understandable, or dealt with successfully (p. 675)

*no resuelto no esclarecido, no comprensible o tratado con éxito (p. 675)

urban renewal government programs that attempt to eliminate poverty and revitalize urban areas (p. 583)

renovación urbana programas gubernamentales que intentan eliminar la pobreza y revitalizar las áreas urbanas (p. 583)

V

*vehicle a means of carrying or transporting something (p. 489)

*vehículo medio para llevar o transportar algo (p. 489)

vertical integration the combining of companies that supply equipment and services needed for a particular industry (p. 197)

integración vertical asociación de compañías que abastecen equipo y servicios necesarios a una industria particular (p. 197)

veto power of the chief executive to reject laws passed by the legislature (p. 38)

veto poder del jefe del ejecutivo de rechazar leyes aprobadas por la legislatura (p. 38)

*via to have come by or through (p. 756)

*vía haber llegado mediante o a través de (p. 756)

victory garden gardens planted by American citizens during war to raise vegetables for home use, leaving more for the troops (pp. 328, 507)

huerto de victoria huertos plantados por ciudadanos americanos durante la guerra para cultivar vegetales para usar en casa así dejando más para las tropas (pp. 328, 507)

victory suit a men's suit with no vest, no cuffs, a short jacket, and narrow lapels, worn during World War II in order to save fabric for the war effort (p. 504)

victory suit traje de hombre sin chaleco ni puños, con una chaqueta corta y solapas angostas que se vestía durante la Segunda Guerra Mundial para ahorrar tela para la guerra (p. 504)

Vietnamization the process of making South Vietnam assume more of the war effort by slowly withdrawing American troops from Vietnam (p. 670)

vietnamización el proceso de hacer que el Vietnam del Sur asumiera más de los esfuerzos de la guerra sacando poco a poco a las tropas americanas de Vietnam (p. 670)

vigilance committee group of ordinary citizens formed by local law enforcement officers and tasked with finding criminals and bringing them to justice (p. 159)

comité de vigilancia grupo de ciudadanos comunes formado por funcionarios locales encargados del cumplimiento de la ley, que deben encontrar criminales y ponerlos a disposición de la justicia (p. 159)

Glossary/Glosario

English	Español
*violation the disregard or breaking of the law (p. 460)	*violación ignorar o quebrantar la ley (p. 460)
*virtually almost entirely, nearly (p. 471)	*prácticamente casi por completo, por poco (p. 471)
*visible what can be seen (p. 751)	*visible lo que puede verse (p. 751)

W

English	Español
war on poverty antipoverty program under President Lyndon Johnson (p. 611)	guerra contra la pobreza programa anti-pobreza bajo el Presidente Lyndon Johnson (p. 611)
weapons of mass destruction (WMD) weapons, including nuclear, chemical, and biological, that can kill large numbers of people all at once (p. 816)	armas de destrucción masiva (ADM) armas, incluidas las nucleares, químicas y biológicas, que pueden matar una gran cantidad de personas a la vez (p. 816)
*welfare aid in the form of money or necessities for those in need, especially disadvantaged social groups (p. 708)	*asistencia social ayuda en forma de dinero o necesidades para los necesitados; grupos sociales que se encuentran especialmente en desventaja (p. 708)
welfare capitalism system in which companies enable employees to buy stock, participate in profit sharing, and receive benefits such as medical care common in the 1920s (p. 374)	capitalismo de beneficencia sistema en el cual las compañías permiten a los trabajadores comprar acciones, compartir las ganancias, y recibir beneficios tal como atención médica, común en los años 1920 (p. 374)
white-collar jobs jobs in fields not requiring work clothes or protective clothing, such as sales (p. 574)	collar blanco trabajos trabajos que no requieren ropa de protección o de trabajo, asi como los vendedores (p. 574)
*widespread having influence on or affecting a large group; widely diffused or prevalent (p. 349)	*generalizar influir sobre algo/alguien o afectar a un grupo numeroso (p. 349)

Y

English	Español
yellow journalism type of sensational, biased, and often false reporting for the sake of attracting readers (p. 269)	periodismo amarillista tipo de reportaje sensacional, tendencioso, y a menudo falso con el propósito de atraer a los lectores (p. 269)
yuppie a young college-educated adult who is employed in a well-paying profession and who lives and works in or near a large city (p. 754)	yuppie adulto joven educado en la universidad empleado en una profesión de buen salario y que vive y trabaja en o cerca de una ciudad grande (p. 754)

Z

English	Español
zoot suit men's clothing of extreme cut typically consisting of a thigh-length jacket with wide padded shoulders and peg pants with narrow cuffs (p. 504)	zoot suit vestimenta de hombre de corte extremo que consiste típicamente de una chaqueta a la altura de los muslos con hombreras anchas y pantalón pirata con bocamanga angosta (p. 504)

Index

Italicized page numbers refer to illustrations. The following abbreviations are used in the index:
m = map; c – chart; p – photograph or picture; g = graph; crt = cartoon; ptg = painting; q = quote

Index

Index

Index

Index

Index

Index

Index

Index

Index

Index

Palmer, Potter, 224

Palmer Raids, 352–53

Panama, 280, 765

Panama Canal, 279–80, 722, 765

Pan-Americanism, 267

Pan-Arabism, 558–59

Panic of 1837, 99

Panic of 1873, 147

pardons, Richard Nixon and, 717

Paris, Treaty of (American Revolution), 29

Paris, Treaty of (Spanish-American War), 274

Paris, Treaty of (French and Indian War), 22

Paris Peace Conference, 342–43

Parker, John J., 393

Parks, Rosa, 622, 626, p627

party bosses, 227

patent medicines, 302

Patman, Wright, 415

Patton, George, 498, 509, 518

Paul, Alice, 297

Payne-Aldrich Tariff, 306

Peace Corps, 604, q608

Peace Democrats, 128

Pearl Harbor: attack on, 477, 478, p478, 479, 486, p526; military base at, 266

Pelosi, Nancy, 826, p826, 827

Pendleton Act (1883), 234

Penn, William, 11

Pennsylvania, 11, 34

pension plans, 236, 436, 439

Pentagon, attack on, 808

Pentagon Papers, the, 672

People's Party, the, 245, 246, 247, 249

People United to Save Humanity (PUSH), 727

perestroika, 763

Perkins, Frances, 441, p441

Permanent Court of International Justice. See World Court

Perot, H. Ross, p766, 767, 784

Perry, Matthew C., 264, 265

Pershing, John J., 283, 333, 340

Persian Gulf War, m764, 765, 811

personal computers (PCs), 774–75, p775

Pétain, Henri, 333

Pétain, Philippe, 464

Petersburg, siege of, 136

Peterson, Esther, 598

Petraeus, David, 827

petroleum. See oil industry

philanthropy, 232

Philippine-American war, 275

Philippines, 271–72, m271, 273–74, 275, 494–95, 515

phonographs, p184, 185

photographers, 293, 408, 409

Picasso, Pablo, 457

Pickett, George E., 135

Pickett's Charge, 135, 138–139

Pickford, Mary, p384

Pike, Zebulon, p82

Pilgrims, 8

Pinchot, Gifford, 304, p305, q305, 306–7

Pizarro, Francisco, 6

Planned Parenthood, 379

Planned Parenthood v. Casey (1992), 691

plantations, 12, 13, 18. See also slavery

Platt Amendment, 274–75

Plessy, Homer, 250, 251

Plessy v. Ferguson (1892), 250, 251, crt251, 622, 624, 625

Plunkitt, George W. "Boss," q226, 227

Plymouth Colony, 8

pocket vetoes, 142

poets. See literature

poison gas, 337

Poland, 341, 344, 462, 532

police departments. See law enforcement

police powers, 381

polio, 422, 575, p575

political parties: African Americans and, 392; American Socialist Party, 299; Civil War and, 122–24, 128; election of 1800 and, 81; election of 1824, 96; election of 1948 and, 568; election of 2004, 820–21; Free-Soil Party, 108; La Raza Unida (the United People), 697; Liberty Party, 108; machine politics, crt226, 227; the New Deal and, 434–35; party bosses, 227; the People's Party, 245; Progressive Party, 308; progressivism and, 294; Reconstruction Era and, 145,

147; Reform Party, 784; rise of, 80; sectionalism and, 111–12; Socialist Party, 352; the Sunbelt and, 743; Whig Party, 99, Workingman's Party, 219. See also Democratic Party; Republican Party

politics: African Americans and, 145, 391–93, 623, 727; Civil War and, 128–29; in the Gilded Age, 234–36, crt235; grassroots campaigns, 767; liberalism and conservatism, 740–42; machine politics, 227; Vietnam War and, 657. See also elections

Polk, James K., 105, 106–7

poll taxes, 250

pollution, 227, p731. See also environment

Ponce de León, Juan, 6–7

pools, 196

Poor People's Campaign, 647

popular culture, 233, 553, 576–79

popular sovereignty, 37, 107

population: African American, c392; American colonies and, 16; baby boom, 573, 682; Hispanic Americans, g693; immigration and, 790–91; industrialization and, 183; Native Americans, g171; urbanization and, 222

populism, 242–47, 249

Populist Party. See People's Party, the

Port Huron Statement, 683, q683

postwar era. See 1950s

Potsdam Conference, 536–37, p560

Pound, Ezra, 383

poverty, p584–85, p611, crt643; in the 1950s, 582–87; African Americans and, g646; cities and towns, m584; civil rights movement and, 642–43; poverty rates, g611; War on Poverty, 611–12

poverty line, 582

Powell, Colin, 765, 811

Powhatan Confederacy, 8

prayer in schools, 601

presidency. See elections

presidential debates, 596–97

President's Commission on the Status of Women, 598, 687–88

President's Panel on Mental Retardation, 598

Presley, Elvis, 577–78, p578

price controls, World War II and, 506

Pricoland, Marie, q220

Princip, Gavrilo, 322–23, p323

Principles of Scientific Management, The (Taylor), 294

prisoners of war, p674, 675, 822–23

prison reform, 100

privacy rights, 601, 758, 823

Proclamation Act of 1763, 22–23

Progress and Poverty (George), 237

Progressive Party, 308, 568

progressivism, 290–314, m352, 353

Prohibition, p380, 381, p394. See also temperance movement

prohibition laws, 100

Prohibition movement, 299

Project Venona, 548

property rights: Industrial Revolution and, 91; Native Americans and, 99, 728; Reconstruction Era and, 142; for women, 17

propaganda: World War I and, 324–25, 334–35, p334, p335; World War II and, p506

proprietary colonies, 11

protective tariffs, 87

protectorates, 263

protest movements, 698, p698; in the 1960s, p592–93; anti-globalization movement, p796; farm protests, p758; feminist movement, 686–91; Latinos and, 695–97; student movements, 682–85. See also civil rights movement

Prussia, 320

Public Company Accounting Reform and Investor Protection Act (Sarbanes-Oxley Act), 807

public education. See education

public officials, African Americans as, g646

public opinion: the New Deal and, 434–36, 442, q445; September 11 terrorist attacks, 809; Vietnam War and, 658, 664, 667, 668; World War I and, 330. See also propaganda

Index

Index

Index

Index

Acknowledgments and Photo Credits

TEXT AND ART

317 From *The Century* by Peter Jennings, copyright © 1998 by ABC Television Network Group, a division of Capitol Cities, Inc. Used by permission of Doubleday, a division of Random House, Inc. 383 Reprinted with the permission of Scribner, an imprint of Simon & Schuster Adult Publishing Group, from The Great Gatsby by F. Scott Fitzgerald. Copyright 1925 by Charles Scribner's Sons. Copyright renewed 1953 by Frances Scott Fitzgerald Lanahan. 389 Excerpt from *Dust Tracks on a Road* by Zora Neale Hurston. Copyright 1942 by Zora Neale Hurston, renewed © 1970 by John C. Hurston. Reprinted by permission of HarperCollins Publishers 389 "If we must die" by Claude McKay, courtesy of the Literary Representative for the Works of Claude McKay, Schomburg Center for Research in Black Culture, The New York Public Library, Astor, Lennox and Tilden Foundations. 402 From *1929: the Year of the Great Crash* by William K. Klingman. Copyright © 1989 by William K. Klingman. Reprinted by permission of HarperCollins Publishers. 409 Excerpt from *Dust to Eat: Drought and Depression in the 1930s* by Michael L. Cooper. Copyright © 2004 by Michael L. Cooper. Reprinted by permission of Clarion Books, an imprint of Houghton Mifflin Company. All rights reserved. 432 "Gardiner C. Means" and "Raymond Moley" from *Hard Times* by Studs Terkel. Copyright © 1970, 1986 by Studs Terkel. Reprinted by permission of Donadio & Olson, Inc. 449 Excerpt from *The Autobiography of Eleanor Roosevelt* by Eleanor Roosevelt. Copyright 1937, 1949, © 1958, 1961 by Anna Eleanor Roosevelt. Copyright © 1958 by Curtis Publishing Company. Reprinted by permission of HarperCollins Publishers. 473 "Luther D. Fletcher" from *World War II: From the Battle Front to the Home Front, Arkansans Tell Their Stories,* copyright © 1995 by Kay B. Hall. Reprinted by permission of the University of Arkansas Press. 641 From *Coming of Age in Mississippi* by Anne Moody, copyright © 1968 by Anne Moody. Used by permission of Doubleday, a division of Random House, Inc. 645 Copyright © 1971 by Merlin House, Inc./Seaver Books. Reprinted from *The End of White World Supremacy* by Malcolm X, edited by Imam Benjamin Karim. Published by Seaver Books, New York, New York. 684 from "The Times They Are A-Changin'" by Bob Dylan. Copyright © 1963; renewed 1991 Special Rider Music. All rights reserved. International copyright secured. Reprinted by permission. 687 From The Feminine Mystique by Betty Friedan. Copyright © 1983, 1974, 1973, 1963 by Betty Friedan. Used by permission of W.W. Norton & Company, Inc. 801 from "A Grim Picture" by Tim Radford. *The Guardian,* November, 15, 2000. Copyright Guardian News & Media Ltd, 2000. Reprinted by permission. R7 From "Why I'm Not Running for President" by Gloria Steinem, from the July 20, 1992 issue of *The Nation.* Reprinted by permission. For subscription information call 1-800-333-8536. Portions of each week's Nation magazine can be accessed at http://www.thenation.com. R74 "The Camera Eye (50)" from *The Big Money,* copyright 1933, 1934, 1935, 1936 and © renewed 1963, 1964 by John Dos Passos. Reprinted by permission of Lucy Dos Passos Coggin R77 "Part Four – 1" from On the Road by Jack Kerouac, copyright © 1955, 1957 by Jack Kerouac; renewed © 1983 by Stella Kerouac, renewed © 1985 by Stella Kerouac and Jan Kerouac. Used by permission of Viking Penguin, a division of Penguin Group (USA) Inc.

Glencoe would like to acknowledge the artists and agencies that participated in illustrating this program: American Artists Reps Inc.; Deborah Wolfe Ltd/illustrationOnLine.com; GeoNova LLC.

PHOTO CREDITS

Abbreviation Key: BC: Bettmann/CORBIS; GI: Getty Images; LOC: Library of Congress

Cover (tl)BC, (tc)Bob Adelman/Magnum Photos, (tr)David Turnley/CORBIS, (cl)Catherine Karnow/CORBIS, (c cr) GI, (b)Fine Art Photographic Library, London/Art Resource, NY; vi (t)Boltin Picture Library/Bridgeman Art Library, (b)Painting by Don Troiani, www.historicalartprints.com; vii (t)Lowell Georgia/CORBIS, (c)William Henry Jackson/Cardoza Fine Art Gallery, (b)CORBIS; viii (t)Nagasaki Museum of History and Culture, (c)The Granger Collection, New York, (b)CORBIS; ix (t)Howard A. Thain/Collection of the New York Historical Society/Bridgeman Art Library, (c)Roger-Viollet/Topham/The Image Works, (b)BC; x (t)Mary Evans Picture Library, (c)BC, (b)SuperStock; xi (t)Wally McNamee/CORBIS, (c) Bob Adelman/Magnum Photos, (b)Larry Burrows/Time Life Pictures/GI; xii (t)Eli Reed/Magnum Photos, (c)The White House/Handout/GI, (b)Brooks Kraft/CORBIS; xxiii GI; xxiv (b)Pierce Rafferty/Petrified Collection/GI, (bkgd)Owaki/Kulla/CORBIS; xxv (t)Dynamic Graphics Group/Creatas/Alamy Images, (b)Eric Foltz/iStockphoto, A20 (t)ThinkStock/SuperStock, (cl)Janet Foster/Masterfile, (cr)Mark Tomalty/Masterfile, (bl)Jurgen Freund/Nature Picture Library, (br)age fotostock/SuperStock; GH2 BananaStock/PictureQuest; GH16-1 Boltin Picture Library/Bridgeman Art Library; 2 Galleria degli Uffizi, Florence/Bridgeman Art Library; 2-3 SuperStock; 3 Michael Nicholson/CORBIS; 5 (tl)George Catlin/GI, (tr bl) The Granger Collection, New York, (br)Photograph courtesy of the Schwarz Gallery, Philadelphia; 7 (inset)The Granger Collection, New York, (bkgd)The City of Plainfield, NJ; 9 (tl)Sheffield Galleries and Museums Trust, UK/Bridgeman Art Library, (tr)Adam Woolfitt/Robert Harding World Imagery/CORBIS, (b)National Maritime Museum, London; 10 (l)Kean Collection/GI, (r)Schlesinger Library, Radcliffe Institute, Harvard University/Bridgeman Art Library; 14 (t)CORBIS, (c)PunchStock, (bl)C Squared Studios/GI, (br)Iconotec/Alamy Images; 15 (l to r, t to b) GI, (2 13)LOC, LC-USZ62-242, (3)Ingram Publishing/Alamy Images, (4)Brand X Pictures/PunchStock, (5)Artville/GI, (6)Alan and Sandy Carey/GI, (7)Dynamic Graphics Group/IT Stock Free/Alamy Images, (8)PunchStock, (9)PhotoAlto/GI, (10)CORBIS, (11)GI, (12) C Squared Studios/GI, (14)Creativ Studio Heinemann/GI, (15)Alamy Images, (16)Image Source Pink/GI; 18 The Granger Collection, New York; 19 (l)Ariadne Van Zandbergen/GI, (r)Bridgeman Art Library; 20 GI; 23 (l)LOC, LC-USZC4-5315, (r)LOC; 24 25 BC; 27 (l)National Portrait Gallery/SuperStock, (r)The Granger Collection, New York; 28 35 The Granger Collection, New York; 42 (t)Erich Lessing/Art Resource, NY, (c)SuperStock, (b)The Granger Collection, New York; 45 American Antiquarian Society; 47 Comstock/PunchStock; 51 53 Brooks Kraft/CORBIS; 57 John Aikins/CORBIS; 76-77 akg-images; 81 BC; 82 The Granger Collection, New York; 87 The Landis Valley Museum; 89 The Granger Collection, New York; 90 (l)BC, (r)Underwood & Underwood/CORBIS; 91 (l)Eric Long/National Museum of American History, Smithsonian Institution, (c)The Granger Collection, New York, (r)courtesy of the National Museum of American History, Washington, D.C.; 96 The Granger Collection, New York; 97 (inset)Gary I. Rothstein/Reuters/CORBIS, (bkgd)Monika Graff/The Image Works; 98 SuperStock; 101 Art Archive/Culver Pictures/Napoleon Sarony; 102 (tl)BC, (tc tr) The Granger Collection, New York, (b)Collection of J. Paul Getty Museum; 105 Bridgeman Art Library; 106 LOC; 108 (l)California State Library, Sacramento, (r)LOC; 108-109 The Granger Collection, New York; 109 (t)Bridgeman Art Library, (b)The Granger Collection, New York; 110 (l)Syracuse Newspapers/Dick Blume/The Image Works, (r)BC; 112 Currier and Ives/LOC; 114 The New York Public Library; 115 (tl)BC, (b)Missouri Historical Society, St. Louis; 116 (t)American Textile History Museum, Lowell, MA, (cl cr) BC, (b)Picture History; 119 The New York Historical Society; 120 (l)Museum of the Confederacy, (r)LOC, (LC-DIG-cwpb-06233); 120-121 Minnesota Historical Society/CORBIS; 123 Museum of American Political Life/Photo by Steve Laschever; 124 (tl)BC, (tr b) The Granger Collection, New York; 125 (tl)Henry Horner Lincoln Collection, (tr)Art Archive/Culver Pictures, (b)Bridgeman Art Library; 127 (l)Medford Historical Society Collection/CORBIS; (r)BC; 128 (tl)Collection of David & Kevin Kyle, (tc)Military & Historical Image Bank/Don Troiani, (tr)Medford Historical Society Collection/CORBIS, (b)War Department/National Archives/Time Life Pictures/GI; 131 LOC; 132 (tl)LOC, (tr b)BC; 134 BC; 135 CORBIS; 136 (l)BC, (r)The Granger Collection, New York; 141 (t)CORBIS, (cl)Art Archive/National Archives Washington, DC, (cr b) LOC; 143 (tl)Flip Schulke/CORBIS, (tc)Flip Schulke/Black Star, (tr)AP Images, (bl br)BC; 146 The Granger Collection, New York; 148 CORBIS; 150 (tl)The Granger Collection, New York, (tr)Bridgeman Art Library, (cl)CORBIS, (cr)Kunstler Enterprises, Ltd, (bl)LOC, LC-USZC4-1519, (br)Picture History; 153 LOC; 154-155 William Henry Jackson/Cardoza Fine Art Gallery; 156 The Granger Collection, New York; 156-157 Lowell Georgia/CORBIS; 160 LOC, LC-USZ62-9889; 161 (t)Calvin Larsen/Photo Researchers, (b)Scott T. Smith/CORBIS; 162-163 BC; 164 (l)Art Archive/Bill Manns, (r)GI; 167 Minnesota Historical Society/CORBIS; 168 (l)State Historical Society of Wisconsin, (r)akg-images; 173 (l)GI, (r)CORBIS; 174 (l)CORBIS, (r)The Granger Collection, New York; 176 (t b) The Granger Collection, New

York, (c)CORBIS; **180** National Railway Museum/Science & Society Museum; **180-181** LOC, LC-USZ62-77541; **184** (tl)Mary Evans Picture Library, (bl)The Granger Collection, New York, (bcl)Time Life Pictures/GI, (bcr)BC, (br)Schenectady Museum; Hall of Electrical History Foundation/CORBIS; **185** (tl)BC, (tr)Mary Evans Picture Library, (b)George Eastman House; **186** (l)LOC, LC-USZ62-99122, (r)LOC, LC-USZ62-99407; **189** (tl)Union Pacific Museum, (tr) Private Collection, Peter Newark American Pictures/Bridgeman Art Library, (bl)GI, (bc)Union Pacific Museum, (br)BC; **192** GI; **195** BC; **198** (l)SuperStock, (r)CORBIS; **201** (l tr)CORBIS, (br)Hulton Archive/GI; **206** CORBIS; **208** (tl)Union Pacific Museum, (c)CORBIS, (b)Hulton Archive/GI; **211** Stock Montage/Hulton Archive/GI; **212-213** CORBIS; **213** (t)Shore Line Trolley Museum Library, Sprague Collection, (b)London Stereoscopic Company/GI; **216** (l)Michael Maslan Historic Photographs/CORBIS, (tr)Art Archive/ Culver Pictures, (br)The Granger Collection, New York; **218** The Granger Collection, New York; **220** (t)Picture Research Consultants, (b)Brown Brothers Sterling, PA; **221** OSU Cartoon Research Library; **223** (tl)CORBIS, (tr)Museum of the City of New York/CORBIS, (b)LOC, LC-USZ-54088; **224** Hulton-Deutsch Collection/CORBIS; **225** (tl)CORBIS, (tr)BC, (b)The Granger Collection, New York; **226** The Granger Collection, New York; **231** (l)LOC, LC-USZ62-15566, (r)Frank & Marie Wood/The Picture Bank; **232** Geofferey Clements/CORBIS; **233** Museum of Art, Rhode Island School of Design; Jesse Metcalf and Walter H. Kimball Funds; **235** (l)The Granger Collection, New York, (r)GI; **237** (l)CORBIS, (r)Duke University; **238** (l)The Granger Collection, New York, (r)AP Images; **243** The Everett Collection; **244** The Granger Collection, New York; **246** (tl tr)CORBIS, (b)GI; **249** The Granger Collection, New York; **251** Snark/Art Resource, NY; **252** Brown Brothers; **254** (t)Brown Brothers, (c)Picture Research Consultants, (b)Lewis W. Hine/George Eastman House/GI; **257** Picture Research Consultants; **258-259** Franklin D Roosevelt Library; **260-261** CORBIS; **263** (t)CORBIS, (b)The Mariners' Museum/CORBIS; **265** (l)Nagasaki Museum of History and Culture, (r)James G. Evans/Chicago History Museum (1932.21); **266** (l)Hawaii State Archives, (r)The Granger Collection, New York; **269** (l)LOC, LC-USZ62-99767; (tr)The Granger Collection, New York, (br)Kurz & Allison/The Granger Collection, New York; **270** BC; **271** (l)Hulton Archive/GI, (r)LOC; **273** (l)LOC, LC-USZ62-62631), (r)GI; **274** (l)LOC, LC-USZC4-5392, (r)LOC, LC-USZ62-91465); **277**The Granger Collection, New York; **278** BC; **279** Koichi Kamoshida/GI; **282** The Granger Collection, New York; **285** Morton Beebe/CORBIS; **286** (t)BC, (c b)Time Life Pictures/GI; **289** CORBIS; **290** (t)Museum of the City of New York Print Archives, (b)Key Color/Index Stock Imagery; **290-291** Jessie Beals/Schlesinger Library, Radcliffe Institute, Harvard University/Bridgeman Art Library; **293** (t)BC, (b)Hulton-Deutsch Collection/CORBIS, **294-295** LOC, LC-USZ62-56437; **296** (t)LOC, LC-USZ62-46713, (bl)LOC, LC-USZ62-106109, (br)LOC, LC-ISZ62-28195; **297** BC; **298** (l)Keystone/GI, (r)UNITE HERE Archives, Kheel Center, Cornell University; **301** LOC, LC-USZC4-434; **303** The Granger Collection, New York; **305** (l)BC, (r)The Granger Collection, New York; **306** CORBIS; **309** (t)CORBIS, (b)The Granger Collection, New York; **312** (t)Underwood & Underwood/CORBIS, (b)BC; **314** (t)BC, (c)LOC, Prints & Photographs Division (LC-USZ62-83858), (b)CORBIS; **317** LOC, LC-USZC4-6425; **318** (t)The Mariners' Museum/CORBIS, (b)BC; **318-319** 319 BC; **322** (l)CORBIS, (c r)BC; **323** BC; **325** (l)LOC, LC-DIG-ggbain-05650, (r)CORBIS; **326** (tl b)BC, (tr)CORBIS; **329** (l)Swim Ink 2, LLC/CORBIS, (r)K.J. Historical/CORBIS, (bkgd)BC; **331** BC; **332** (l)LOC, LC-USZ62-116442, (r)LOC, LC-USZC4-2426; **334** (t)LOC, LC-USZC4-1539, (b)LOC, LC-USZ62-91465; **335** UNC University Library; **338** (l)Australian War Memorial Negative Number, E00921, (r)Hulton-Deutsch Collection/CORBIS; **339 341** BC; **344** (l)By Permission of the Marcus Family, (r)LOC/© 1919, The Washington Post. Reprinted with permission; **349** Underwood & Underwood/CORBIS; **350** Brown Brothers; **351** Neville Elder/CORBIS; **352** (l cr)White House Historical Association, (cl)Underwood & Underwood/CORBIS, (r)CORBIS; **354** (t)BC, (c b)CORBIS; **357** Chicago Tribune; **358-359** Howard A. Thain/Collection of the New York Historical Society/Bridgeman Art Library; **360** CORBIS; **360-361** Roger-Viollet/Topham/The Image Works; **361** National Air and Space Museum/Smithsonian Institution; **363 364** The Granger Collection, New York; **369** (tl)Hirz/GI, (tr bl)FPG/Hulton Archive/GI, (cl)Hulton Archive/GI, (cr)Topham/The Image Works, (br)The Granger Collection, New York; **370** (l)Hulton Archive/GI, (cl)The Image Works, (cr)SSPL/The Image Works, (r)Ohio Historical Society; **371** (tl)Mary Evans Picture Library, (tr)LOC, LC-USZ62-119950, (b)Huntington Library/SuperStock, (b)Minnesota Historical Society; **372** The Granger Collection, New York, **373** (l)Frank & Marie-Therese Wood/The Picture Bank, (r)The Granger Collection, New York; **374** Hulton Archive/GI, **377** (l)BC, (r)LOC, LC-USZ62-52584, **378** Underwood & Underwood/CORBIS; **379** (l)Mary

Evans Picture Library, (r)Columbus Dispatch/Ohio Historical Society; **380** (l)LOC/GI, (r)CORBIS, **383** Francis G. Mayer/CORBIS; **384** (tl)Culver Pictures/SuperStock, (tc)National Archives, (tr)Art Archive/Culver Pictures, (b)The Kobal Collection; **389** The Granger Collection, New York; **390** (l)Art Archive/Culver Pictures, (tr br)Frank Driggs Collection/GI; **391** (l)Frank Driggs Collection/GI, (c)Sasha/GI, (r)Underwood & Underwood/CORBIS; **394** (t)Mary Evans Picture Library, (c)Frank Driggs Collection/GI, (b)General Photographic Agency/GI; **397** LOC/© 1925, The Washington Post. Reprinted with Permission; **398-399 399** BC; **401** (l)The Granger Collection, New York, (r)Underwood & Underwood/LOC; **402** Hulton-Deutsch Collection/CORBIS; **403** (l)BC, (r)American Stock/GI; **407** (l)Chicago Historical Society, (r)Hulton Archive/GI; **408** (l)BC, (r)Margaret Bourke-White/Time Life Pictures/GI; **411** Russell Lee/CORBIS; **413** (l)The Granger Collection, New York, (r)GI; **414** (tl)BC, (tr)AP Images, (b)Picture History; **416** (t)Mary Evans Picture Library, (c)BC, (b)Scherl/SVBilderdienst/The Image Works; **419** John T. McCutcheon/The Granger Collection, New York; **420** (t)CORBIS, (b)akg-images; **420-421 421** BC; **423** Underwood & Underwood/CORBIS; **425** BC; **426** (tl)Picture History, (tr)LOC, LC-USF34-032948-D, (b)MPI/GI; **427** (tl b)BC, (tr)Underwood & Underwood/CORBIS; **429** (inset)CORBIS, (bkgd)Tom Brakefield/GI; **430** The Granger Collection, New York; **432** Peter Arno/Conde Nast Art; **433** (l)LOC, LC-DIG-ppmsca-12896, (r)Paolo Garretto/Conde Nast Art; **435** (l c)BC, (r)The Granger Collection, New York; **437** (l)The Granger Collection, New York, (r)CORBIS; **438 441** BC; **443** The Granger Collection, New York; **444** (tl)BC, (tr)courtesy FDIC, (b)courtesy FHA; **446** (t)Underwood & Underwood/CORBIS, (c)U.S. Forest Service,(b)BC; **449 450-451** The Granger Collection, New York; **452** Keystone/GI; **452-453** Mary Evans Picture Library; **453** (l)USHMM, (b)LOC, LC-USZ62-89348; **457** (t)The Granger Collection, New York, (b)BC; **458** BC; **461** CORBIS; **463** (l c) BC, (r)The Granger Collection, New York; **464** (tl)Art Archive, (tr b)Bettmann/ CORBIS; **467** (l r)Mary Evans Picture Library, (bkgd)Roger Foley; **468** (l)Yivo Institute for Jewish Research, (r)Yad Vashem Photo Archives, courtesy of USHMM Photo Archives; **468-469** Roger Foley; **469** (l)AFP/ GI, (r)National Archives: Suitland, courtesy of the United States Holocaust Memorial Museum; **470** USHMM; **472** National Archives; **473** (l)USHMM, (r)David Olere/The Beate Klarsfeld Foundation; **475** (l)The Granger Collection, New York, (r)LOC, LC-USZ62-52601; **476** SuperStock; **478** (t)CORBIS, (bl br)GI; **480** The Granger Collection, New York; **483** Chicago Historical Society; **484 484-485** BC; **485** CORBIS; **487** BC; **488** Time & Life Pictures/GI; **490** BC; **491** (l)US Army Photo, (r)BC; **492** (l)Peter Stackpole/Time Life Pictures/GI, (r)CORBIS; **495** CORBIS; **497** Art Archive/National Archives Washington, DC; **498** (t)CORBIS, (b)Art Archive; **501** (l)LOC, LC-DIG-fsac-1a34953, (c)GI, (r)CORBIS; **502-503** John Vachon/Anthony Potter Collection/GI; **505** GI; **506** (l)United Artists/The Kobal Collection, (c)Walt Disney Pictures/The Kobal Collection, (r)CORBIS; **510** (t) BC, (bl)CORBIS, (br)GI; **511** (t)Art Archive, (b)Ullstein Bild/The Granger Collection, New York; **512-513 514** CORBIS; **520** Digital Stock/CORBIS; **521** (tl b)CORBIS, (tr)Naval Historical Foundation; **523** (l)Art Archive/Culver Pictures, (r)GI; **524** CORBIS; **526** (l)LOC, LC-DIG-fsac-1a35223, (r)LOC, LC-DIG-fsac-1a35297; **529** Dr. Seuss Collection/Mandeville Special Collections Library/University of California, San Diego; **530** (t)BC, (b)Picture Research Consultants; **530-531** BC, **531** Smithsonian Institution; **533** The Granger Collection, New York; **535** (l)BC, (r)Hulton-Deutsch Collection/CORBIS; **539** GI; **541** Time Life Pictures/GI; **543** BC; **544** The Granger Collection, New York; **547** CORBIS; **549** (l)Weber and Beyer/CORBIS, (r)The Granger Collection, New York; **551** BC; **552** (t)LOC, LC-USZC4-4431, (c b)BC; **555** (l c)CORBIS, (r)U.S. Air Force Photo; **556** (t)The Granger Collection, New York, (cl)NSSDC/NASA, (cr)Donald Uhbrock/Time Life Pictures/GI, (b)BC; **558** (tl)NASA, (tr)Time Life Pictures/GI, (b)CORBIS; **560** (t)Picture Research Consultants, (b)BC; **563** Ross Lewis Milwaukee Public Library; **564** (t)FPG/GI, (b)CORBIS; **564-565** SuperStock; **565** Natural Museum of American History/Smithsonian Institution; **567** (l)GI, (r)CORBIS; **569** CORBIS; **570** (tl)Masterfile, (tr)Time Life Pictures/GI, (b)CORBIS; **573** (l)Time Life Pictures/GI, (r)CORBIS; **575** BC; **576** (l)BC, (c)National Museum of American History/Smithsonian Institution, (r)The Kobal Collection; **578** (tl)Brown Brothers, (tr)Michael Ochs Archives/CORBIS, (bl)BC, (bc)Photofest, (br)Michael Ochs Archives/CORBIS; **583** (tl tr)Time Life Pictures/GI, (b)AP Images; **584** BC; **585** Thomas Hoepker/Magnum Photos; **586** National Archives; **588** (t)SuperStock, (b)Time Life Pictures/GI; **591** B. Wiseman/from Hey, Can't You Forget Business? by Charles Preston, ©1953, E.P. Dutton & Co., Inc.; **592-593** Wally McNamee/CORBIS; **594** (tl)Art Resource, NY, (tc)GI, (tr b)AP Images; **594-595** Time Life Pictures/GI; **597 599** BC; **603** George Silk/Time Life Pictures/GI; **604** (l)GI, (c)CORBIS SYGMA, (r)CORBIS; **605** (l)CORBIS SYGMA, (cl)BC, (cr r)

CORBIS; **606** (tl)Rene Burri/Magnum Photos, (tr)AP Images, (b)Carl Mydans/ Time Life Pictures/GI; **611** (l)John Dominis/Time Life Pictures/ GI, (r)CORBIS; **612** Americorps VISTA Archives; **613** Corporation photo by Peter Shifter, Office of Public Affairs/AmeriCorps; **616** (t)AmeriCorps Archive, (c)Carl Mydans/ Time Life Pictures/GI, (b)Flip Schulke/Black Star; **619** LOC; **620** (l)Carl Iwaski/Time Life Pictures/GI, (r)Art Resource, NY; **620-621** Bob Adelman/Magnum Photos; **621** Collection of Janice L. and David J. Frent; **623** Time Life Pictures/GI; **625** Carl Iwasaki/Time Life Pictures/GI; **627** (tl tr br)Don Craven/Time Life Pictures/GI, (bl)Flip Schulke/ CORBIS; **628** (tl tr)CORBIS, (b)BC; **631** (l)CORBIS, (r)AP Images; **632** (t br)BC, (bl)Don Craven/Time Life Pictures/GI; **633** (tl)Charles Moore 1963/Black Star, (tr)Steve Schapiro, (b)BC; **635** Bill Hudson/AP Images; **637** Francis Miller/Time Life Pictures/GI; **638** Flip Schulke/CORBIS; **640** Eve Arnold/ Magnum Photos; **641** The Everett Collection; **643** (l)Atlanta Constitution, 1964, Clifford H. "Baldy" Baldowski Editorial Cartoons. Courtesy of the Richard B. Russell Library for Political Research and Studies, The University of Georgia Libraries, (r)A 1967 Herblock Cartoon, copyright by The Herb Block Foundation; **645** (l) Robert Parent/Time Life Pictures/GI, (c)AP Images, (r)Flip Schulke/CORBIS; **648** (t)Carl Iwasaki/Time Life Pictures/GI, (c)Francis Miller/Time Life Pictures/GI, (b)Flip Schulke/CORBIS; **651** Jon Kennedy/ Arkansas Democrat-Gazette; **652** (t)Art Resource, NY, (b)Naval Historical Foundation; **652-653** Larry Burrows/Time Life Pictures/GI; **656** (tl)BC, (tr)AFP/GI, (b)AP Images; **659** (l)Popperfoto/Alamy Images, (r)CORBIS; **660** (t)MPI/GI, (b)Larry Burrows/Time Life Pictures/GI; **663** (l)BC, (r)AP Images; **665** (l)LOC/Tom Francis Darcy, Newsday/Reprinted with permission from LA Times Reprints, (r)Atlanta Constitution, Oct 18 1965, Clifford H. "Baldy" Baldowski Editorial Cartoons. Courtesy of the Richard B. Russell Library for Political Research and Studies, The University of Georgia Libraries; **666** (l b)Bernard Gotfryd/GI, (c)Hulton Archive/GI, (r)Paul Fusco/ Magnum Photos; **668** (tl)CORBIS, (tr cr)BC, (cl)Bob Gomel/Time Life Pictures/ GI; **671** (l)John Filo, (c)David Kennerly/BC, (r)Dirck Halstead/Time Life Pictures/GI; **673** (tl)BC, (tr)Time Life Pictures/GI, (b)The Granger Collection, New York; **674** (l)Alex Wong/GI, (r)Sal Veder/AP Images; **676** (t)AP Images, (c)Art Archive/Dept Defence Washington, (b)Wally McNamee/CORBIS; **679** Photo by DeAlba/Washington Daily News/Lyndon Baines Johnson Library; **680** (l)Art Resource, NY, (r)Charles Gatewood/The Image Works; **680-681** Take Stock; **681** AP Images; **683** BC; **684** (l)Vince Streano/CORBIS, (r)Andrew DeLory/Hulton Archive/GI; **687** (l)BC, (r)Charles Gatewood/The Image Works; **689** AP Images; **690** BC; **693** CORBIS; **694** LOC; **695** (l)CORBIS, (r)Jim Sugar/CORBIS; **696** Arthur Schatz/Time Life Pictures/GI; **698** (t c)Bettmann/CORBIS, (b)Steve Northup/Time Life Pictures/GI; **701** Jack Knox Estate/OSU Cartoon Research Library; **702-703** Michael Goldman/ Masterfile; **704** (l)Hulton Archive/GI, (r)BC; **704-705** AP Images; **705** Tom Ebenhoh/Black Star; **707** (l)A 1968 Herblock Cartoon, copyright by The Herb Block Foundation, (r)Atlanta Constitution, 1968 Oct 17, Clifford H. "Baldy" Baldowski Editorial Cartoons. Courtesy of the Richard B. Russell Library for Political Research and Studies, The University of Georgia Libraries; **709** (l)BC, (r)Time Life Pictures/GI; **710** (l)Dirck Halstead/Liasion/GI, (r)AFP/GI; **713** (tl cr b) BC, (tr)Robert Maass/CORBIS, (cl)Adam Woolfitt/CORBIS, (c)Dennis Brack/Black Star; **715** Mark Godfrey/The Images Works; **716** (l)A 1973 Herblock Cartoon, copyright by The Herb Block Foundation, (r)Atlanta Constitution, 1973, Clikfford H. "Baldy" Baldowski Editorial Cartoons. Courtesy of the Richard B. Russell Library for Political Research and Studies, The University of Georgia Libraries; **719** (l)Jason Laure/Woodfin Camp/Time Life Pictures/GI, (c r)BC; **721** (l)Brown Brothers, (r)Karl Schumacher/Time Life Pictures/GI; **722** (t)M. Lipschitz/AP Images, (cl)David Rubinger/ CORBIS, (cr)Sergio Gaudenti/Kipa/CORBIS, (b)MPI/GI; **725** (l)AP Images,(r)Scherl/SV-Bilderndienst/The Image Works; **726** (l)PA/Topham/ The Images Works, (r)Charles Gatewood/The Image Works; **728** (l)Wally McNamee/CORBIS, (c)Ed Kashi/CORBIS, (r)Brand X/SuperStock; **731** (l c)BC, (r)Charles E. Rotkin/CORBIS; **732** (l)A 1975 Herblock Cartoon, copyright by The Herb Block Foundation, (r)Hulton Archive/GI; **734** (t)Charles Gatewood/The Image Works, (c)BC, (b)Julian Wasser/Time Life Pictures/ GI; **737** Ranan R. Lurie, Cartoonews International Syndicate, New York City; **738** (t) AP Images, (b)Peter Turnley/CORBIS; **738-739** Eli Reed/Magnum Photos; **739** Lana Harris/AP Images; **741** (l)Gary McCoy/Cagle Cartoons, (r)Chris Slane/Cagle Cartoons; **744** (t)Index Stock Imagery, (bl)Cynthia Johnson/Time Life Pictures/GI, (bc)Annie Griffiths Belt/CORBIS, (br)Joe Raedle/Newsmakers/GI; **747** (l)Atlanta Constitution, 1976 Apr. 6, Clifford H. "Baldy" Baldowski Editorial Cartoons. Courtesy of the Richard B. Russell Library for Political Research and Studies, The University of Georgia Libraries, (b)Atlanta Constitution, 1981 Oct 18, Clifford H. "Baldy" Baldowski Editorial Cartoons. Courtesy of the Richard B. Russell Library for Political Research and

Studies, The University of Georgia Libraries; **749** (l)Wally McNamee/CORBIS, (r)Roger Ressmeyer/CORBIS; **750** (tl)Wally McNamee/CORBIS, (tr)Bob Daughtery/AP Images, (b)BC; **752** (tl)Robert Nickelsberg/Time Life Pictures/ GI, (tr)Dirck Halstead/Time Life Pictures/GI, (b)CORBIS; **755** (l)Eli Reichman/ Time Life Pictures/GI, (r)Bob Krist/CORBIS; **756** NASA/AP Images; **757** (inset)Blue Origin, (bkgd)HANDOUT/epa/CORBIS; **758** BC; **760** AP Images; **763** (l)Stephan Ferry/Liasion/GI, (r)Diane-Lu Hovasse/AFP/GI; **764** Thomas Hartwell/Time Life Pictures/GI; **766** (tl)Owen Franken/CORBIS, (tr)Markowitz Jeffrey/CORBIS SYGMA; (c)Wally McNamee/CORBIS, (b)Mike Lane/Cagle Cartoons; **768** (t)Tony Korody/Time Life Pictures/GI, (c)BC, (b)Alain Nogues/CORBIS SYGMA; **771** LOC, LC-DIG-ppmsc-07930, **772** (tl)Roger Ressmeyer/CORBIS, (tr)Spec. Robert Elliott/CORBIS, (b)David Brauchli/Reuters/CORBIS; **772-773** The White House/Handout/GI; **773** Official White House Photo by Eric Draper; **775** (tl)Ed Young/CORBIS, (tr)Douglas Engelbart/Bootstrap Alliance, (bl)TWPhoto/CORBIS, (br)Roger Ressmeyer/CORBIS; **781** (l)TOLES © 1997 The Washington Post. Reprinted with permission of UNIVERSAL PRESS SYNDICATE. All rights reserved, (tr)Wally McNamee/CORBIS, (br)Markowitz Jeffrey/CORBIS SYGMA; **783** (l)Terry Ashe/Time Life Pictures/GI, (r)SuperStock; **785** (l)Wally McNamee/ CORBIS, (r)Joe Marquette/AP Images; **786** (l)Peter Turnley/CORBIS, (tr)Les Stone/CORBIS SYGMA, (br)Leif Skoogfors/CORBIS; **790** David Kadlubowski/CORBIS; **792** (l) Fred Greaves/Reuters/CORBIS, (r)Carlos Barria/Reuters/CORBIS; **793** (t)Stanley Rogouski, (b)Michael Newman/ PhotoEdit; **796** Hamilton Karie/CORBIS SYGMA; **798** (t)Michael Newman/ PhotoEdit, (b)Ron Edmonds/AP Images; **801** TOLES © 1998 The Washington Post. Reprinted with permission of UNIVERSAL PRESS SYNDICATE. All rights reserved; **802** (l)Alan Diaz/AP Images, (c)Evan Vucci/AP Images, (r)Dimas Ardian/GI; **802-803** Michael Macor/San Francisco Chronicle/ CORBIS; **802** Official White House Photo by Eric Draper; **805** (t)Colin Braley/ Reuters/CORBIS, (bl bc)Ron Sachs/CNP/CORBIS, (br)Najlah Feanny/ CORBIS; **806** Daryl Cagle/Cagle Cartoons; **809** (t)Reuters/Sean Adair/ CORBIS, (bl)Ron Sachs/CNP/CORBIS, (br)Stan Honda/AFP/GI; **810** AP Images; **812** (t)Matthew McDermott/CORBIS, (bl)Reuters/CORBIS, (br)Steve Liss/CORBIS; **815** (t)Alexandra Boulat/VII/AP Images, (bl)Scott Peterson/ GI, (br)David Guttenfelder/AP Images; **816** (t)Ali Haider/AP Images, (b)Reuters/Jeff Christensen/CORBIS; **817** (tl)Al Jazeera via APTN/AP Images, (tr)Lynsey Addario/CORBIS, (b)Wathiq Khuzaie/GI; **818** (l)Lauren Frayer/ AP Images, (r)Khalid al-Mousily/Reuters/CORBIS; **821** (l)Shaun Heasley/ Reuters/CORBIS, (c)Charles W. Luzier/Reuters/CORBIS, (r)Brooks Kraft/ CORBIS; **822** (l)Khampha Bouaphanh/Knight Ridder/Tribune/Pool/ Reuters/CORBIS, (r)Brooks Kraft/CORBIS; **824** Smiley N. Pool/Dallas Morning News/CORBIS; **825** Rick Wilking/Reuters/CORBIS; **826** (l)Wathiq Khuzaie/GI, (r)Nancy Kaserman/ZUMA/CORBIS; **828** (t)AFP/GI, (cl)Kamal Kishore/AP Images, (cr)Al Jazeera/AP Images, (b)Evan Agostini/ ImageDirect/GI; **831** Olie Johannson/Political Cartoons; **R2** LOC, LC-USF34-T01-009095-C; **R3** Art Shay/Time Life Pictures/GI; **R4** LOC, LC-DIG-fsac-1a35337; **R5** Wally McNamee/CORBIS; **R6** Photo File/MLB Photos/GI; **R7** Stan Honda/AFP/GI; **R8** GI; **R9** CORBIS; **R10** (l)Comstock/CORBIS, (r)Art Archive/Reina Sofia Museum, Madrid; **R11** CORBIS; **R12 R13** BC; **R14** Harry Scull Jr./GI; **R17** The Granger Collection, New York; **R18** Clifford K. Berryman/National Archives; **R19** Scott, Lituchy/Star Ledger/CORBIS; R20 Smithsonian Intstitution/CORBIS; **R32 R33** White House Historical Association; **R33** (br)Official White House Photo by Eric Draper; **R36** (tl)National Archives, (tr)Illinois State Historical Library, (b)Private Collection; **R39** Private Collection; **R40** The Wadsworth Atheneum; **R41 R42** Bridgeman Art Library; **R43 R44** National Portrait Gallery, Smithsonian Institution/ Art Resource, NY; **R46** Chicago Historical Society; **R47** (l)Maryland Historical Society, Baltimore, Maryland, (r)National Museum of American History/Armed Forces History Collections/Smithsonian Institution; **R48** Picture Research Consultants; **R49** LOC; **R50** (t)Andre Jenny/Focus Group/PictureQuest, (b)BC; **R52** National Portrait Gallery, Smithsonian Institution, Washington, D.C./Art Resource, NY; **R53** Courtesy Franklin D. Roosevelt Library; **R55** Carl Iwaski/Time Life Pictures/GI; **R56** Francis Miller/Time Life Pictures/GI; **R58 R60** GI; **R61** Picture Research Consultants; **R65** Stock Montage/GI; **R67** (t)Stock Montage/GI, (b)Frans Lanting/CORBIS; **R68** BC; **R69** Collection of the New York Historical Society/Bridgeman Art Library; **R71** (t)Erling Larson/GI, (b)Henry Guttmann/GI; **R72** Keystone/GI; **R73** General Photographic Agency/ GI; **R74** Ray Fisher/Time Life Pictures/GI; **R75** Hulton Archive/GI; **R76** Stephen Jaffe/AFP/GI; **R80** Mitchell Gerber/CORBIS; **Timeline Presidential Paintings** White House Historical Association.

York, (c)CORBIS; **180** National Railway Museum/Science & Society Museum; **180-181** LOC, LC-USZ62-77541; **184** (t)Mary Evans Picture Library, (bl)The Granger Collection, New York, (bcl)Time Life Pictures/GI, (bcr)BC, (br)Schenectady Museum; Hall of Electrical History Foundation/CORBIS; **185** (tl)BC, (tr)Mary Evans Picture Library, (b)George Eastman House; **186** (l)LOC, LC-USZ62-99122, (r)LOC, LC-USZ62-99407; **189** (tl)Union Pacific Museum, (tr) Private Collection, Peter Newark American Pictures/Bridgeman Art Library, (bl)GI, (bc)Union Pacific Museum, (br)BC; **192** GI; **195** BC; **198** (l)SuperStock, (r)CORBIS; **201** (l tr)CORBIS, (br)Hulton Archive/GI; **206** CORBIS; **208** (t)Union Pacific Museum, (c)CORBIS, (b)Hulton Archive/GI; **211** Stock Montage/Hulton Archive/GI; **212-213** CORBIS; **213** (t)Shore Line Trolley Museum Library, Sprague Collection, (b)London Stereoscopic Company/GI; **216** (l)Michael Maslan Historic Photographs/CORBIS, (tr)Art Archive/ Culver Pictures, (br)The Granger Collection, New York; **218** The Granger Collection, New York; **220** (t)Picture Research Consultants, (b)Brown Brothers Sterling, PA; **221** OSU Cartoon Research Library; **223** (tl)Museum of the City of New York/CORBIS, (b)LOC, LC-USZ-54088; **224** Hulton-Deutsch Collection/CORBIS; **225** (tl)CORBIS, (tr)BC, (b)The Granger Collection, New York; **226** The Granger Collection, New York; **231** (l)LOC, LC-USZ62-15566, (r)Frank & Marie Wood/The Picture Bank; **232** Geofferey Clements/CORBIS; **233** Museum of Art, Rhode Island School of Design; Jesse Metcalf and Walter H. Kimball Funds; **235** (l)The Granger Collection, New York, (r)GI; **237** (l)CORBIS, (r)Duke University; **238** (l)The Granger Collection, New York, (r)AP Images; **243** The Everett Collection; **244** The Granger Collection, New York; **246** (tl tr)CORBIS, (b)GI; **249** The Granger Collection, New York; **251** Snark/Art Resource, NY; **252** Brown Brothers; **254** (t)Brown Brothers, (c)Picture Research Consultants, (b)Lewis W. Hine/George Eastman House/GI; **257** Picture Research Consultants; **258-259** Franklin D Roosevelt Library; **260-261** CORBIS; **263** (t)CORBIS, (b)The Mariners' Museum/CORBIS; **265** (l)Nagasaki Museum of History and Culture, (r)James G. Evans/Chicago History Museum (1932.21); **266** (l)Hawaii State Archives, (r)The Granger Collection, New York; **269** (l)LOC, LC-USZ62-99767; (tr)The Granger Collection, New York, (br)Kurz & Allison/The Granger Collection, New York; **270** BC; **271** (l)Hulton Archive/GI, (r)LOC, LC-USZ62-62631), (r)GI; **273** (l)LOC, LC-USZC4-5392, (r)LOC, LC-USZ62-91465); **277** The Granger Collection, New York; **278** BC; **279** Koichi Kamoshida/GI; **282** The Granger Collection, New York; **285** Morton Beebe/CORBIS; **286** (t)BC, (c b)Time Life Pictures/GI; **289** CORBIS; **290** (t)Museum of the City of New York Print Archives, (b)Key Color/Index Stock Imagery; **290-291** Jessie Beals/Schlesinger Library, Radcliffe Institute, Harvard University/Bridgeman Art Library; **293** (t)BC, (b)Hulton-Deutsch Collection/CORBIS, **294-295** LOC, LC-USZ62-56437; **296** (t)LOC, LC-USZ62-46713, (bl)LOC, LC-USZ62-106109, (br)LOC, LC-ISZ62-28195; **297** BC; **298** (l)Keystone/GI, (r)UNITE HERE Archives, Kheel Center, Cornell University; **301** LOC, LC-USZC4-434; **303** The Granger Collection, New York; **305** (l)BC, (r)The Granger Collection, New York; **306** CORBIS; **309** (t)CORBIS, (b)The Granger Collection, New York; **312** (t)Underwood & Underwood/CORBIS, (b)BC; **314** (t)BC, (c)LOC, Prints & Photographs Division (LC-USZ62-83858), (b)CORBIS; **317** LOC, LC-USZC4-6425; **318** (t)The Mariners' Museum/CORBIS, (b)BC; **318-319** BC; **322** (l)CORBIS, (c r)BC; **323** BC; **325** (l)LOC, LC-DIG-ggbain-05650, (r)CORBIS; **326** (tl b)BC, (tr)CORBIS; **329** (l)Swim Ink 2, LLC/CORBIS, (r)K.J. Historical/CORBIS, (bkgd)BC; **331** BC; **332** (l)LOC, LC-USZ62-116442, (r)LOC, LC-USZC4-2426; **334** (t)LOC, LC-USZC4-1539, (b)LOC, LC-USZ62-91465; **335** UNC University Library; **338** (l)Australian War Memorial Negative Number, E00921, (r)Hulton-Deutsch Collection/CORBIS; **339 341** BC; **344** (l)By Permission of the Marcus Family, (r)LOC/© 1919, The Washington Post. Reprinted with permission; **349** Underwood & Underwood/CORBIS; **350** Brown Brothers; **351** Neville Elder/CORBIS; **352** (l cr)White House Historical Association, (cl)Underwood & Underwood/CORBIS, (r)CORBIS; **354** (t)BC, (c b)CORBIS; **357** Chicago Tribune; **358-359** Howard A. Thain/Collection of the New York Historical Society/Bridgeman Art Library; **360** CORBIS; **360-361** Roger-Viollet/Topham/The Image Works; **361** National Air and Space Museum/Smithsonian Institution; **363 364** The Granger Collection, New York; **369** (tl)Hirz/GI, (tr bl)FPG/Hulton Archive/GI, (cl)Hulton Archive/GI, (cr)Topham/The Image Works, (br)The Granger Collection, New York; **370** (l)Hulton Archive/GI, (cl)The Image Works, (cr)SSPL/The Image Works, (r)Ohio Historical Society; **371** (tl)Mary Evans Picture Library, (tr)LOC, LC-USZ62-119950, (c)Huntington Library/SuperStock, (b)Minnesota Historical Society; **372** The Granger Collection, New York; **373** (l)Frank & Marie-Therese Wood/The Picture Bank, (r)The Granger Collection, New York; **374** Hulton Archive/GI, **377** (l)BC, (r)LOC, LC-USZ62-52584, **378** Underwood & Underwood/CORBIS; **379** (l)Mary

Evans Picture Library, (r)Columbus Dispatch/Ohio Historical Society; **380** (l)LOC/GI, (r)CORBIS, **383** Francis G. Mayer/CORBIS; **384** (tl)Culver Pictures/SuperStock, (tc)National Archives, (tr)Art Archive/Culver Pictures, (b)The Kobal Collection; **389** The Granger Collection, New York; **390** (l)Art Archive/Culver Pictures, (tr br)Frank Driggs Collection/GI; **391** (l)Frank Driggs Collection/GI, (c)Sasha/GI, (r)Underwood & Underwood/CORBIS; **394** (t)Mary Evans Picture Library, (c)Frank Driggs Collection/GI, (b)General Photographic Agency/GI; **397** LOC/© 1925, The Washington Post. Reprinted with Permission; **398-399 399** BC; **401** (l)The Granger Collection, New York, (r)Underwood & Underwood/LOC; **402** Hulton-Deutsch Collection/CORBIS; **403** (l)BC, (r)American Stock/GI; **407** (l)Chicago Historical Society, (r)Hulton Archive/GI; **408** (l)BC, (r)Margaret Bourke-White/Time Life Pictures/GI; **411** Russell Lee/CORBIS; **413** (l)The Granger Collection, New York, (r)GI; **414** (tl)BC, (tr)AP Images, (b)Picture History; **416** (t)Mary Evans Picture Library, (c)BC, (b)Scherl/SVBilderdienst/The Image Works; **419** John T. McCutcheon/The Granger Collection, New York; **420** (t)CORBIS, (b)akg-images; **420-421 421** BC; **423** Underwood & Underwood/CORBIS; **425** BC; **426** (tl)Picture History, (tr)LOC, LC-USF34-032948-D, (b)MPI/GI; **427** (tl b)BC, (tr)Underwood & Underwood/CORBIS; **429** (inset)CORBIS, (bkgd)Tom Brakefield/GI; **430** The Granger Collection, New York; **432** Peter Arno/Conde Nast Art; **433** (l)LOC, LC-DIG-ppmsca-12896, (r)Paolo Garretto/Conde Nast Art; **435** (l c)BC, (r)The Granger Collection, New York; **437** (l)The Granger Collection, New York, (r)CORBIS; **438 441** BC; **443** The Granger Collection, New York; **444** (tl)BC, (tr)courtesy FDIC, (b)courtesy FHA; **446** (t)Underwood & Underwood/CORBIS, (c)U.S. Forest Service,(b)BC; **449 450-451** The Granger Collection, New York; **452** Keystone/GI; **452-453** Mary Evans Picture Library; **453** (t)USHMM, (b)LOC, LC-USZ62-89348; **457** (t)The Granger Collection, New York, (b)BC; **458** BC; **461** CORBIS; **463** (l c) BC, (r)The Granger Collection, New York; **464** (tl)Art Archive, (tr b)Bettmann/ CORBIS; **467** (l r)Mary Evans Picture Library, (bkgd)Roger Foley; **468** (l)Yivo Institute for Jewish Research, (r)Yad Vashem Photo Archives, courtesy of USHMM Photo Archives; **468-469** Roger Foley; **469** (l)AFP/ GI, (r)National Archives: Suitland, courtesy of the United States Holocaust Memorial Museum; **470** USHMM; **472** National Archives; **473** (l)USHMM, (r)David Olere/The Beate Klarsfeld Foundation; **475** (l)The Granger Collection, New York, (r)LOC, LC-USZ62-52601; **476** SuperStock; **478** (t)CORBIS, (bl br)GI; **480** The Granger Collection, New York; **483** Chicago Historical Society; **484 484-485** BC; **485** CORBIS; **487** BC; **488** Time & Life Pictures/GI; **490** BC; **491** (l)US Army Photo, (r)BC; **492** (l)Peter Stackpole/Time Life Pictures/GI, (r)CORBIS; **495** CORBIS; **497** Art Archive/National Archives Washington, DC; **498** (t)CORBIS, (b)Art Archive; **501** (l)LOC, LC-DIG-fsac-1a34953, (c)GI, (r)CORBIS; **502-503** John Vachon/Anthony Potter Collection/GI; **505** GI; **506** (l)United Artists/The Kobal Collection, (c)Walt Disney Pictures/The Kobal Collection, (r)CORBIS; **510** (t) BC, (bl)CORBIS, (br)GI; **511** (t)Art Archive, (b)Ullstein Bild/The Granger Collection, New York; **512-513 514** CORBIS; **520** Digital Stock/CORBIS; **521** (tl b)CORBIS, (tr)Naval Historical Foundation; **523** (l)Art Archive/Culver Pictures, (r)GI; **524** CORBIS; **526** (l)LOC, LC-DIG-fsac-1a35223, (r)LOC, LC-DIG-fsac-1a35297; **529** Dr. Seuss Collection/Mandeville Special Collections Library/University of California, San Diego; **530** (t)BC, (b)Picture Research Consultants; **530-531** BC, **531** Smithsonian Institution; **533** The Granger Collection, New York; **535** (l)BC, (r)Hulton-Deutsch Collection/CORBIS; **539** GI; **541** Time Life Pictures/GI; **543** BC; **544** The Granger Collection, New York; **547** CORBIS; **549** (l)Weber and Beyer/CORBIS, (r)The Granger Collection, New York; **551** BC; **552** (t)LOC, LC-USZC4-4431, (c b)BC; **555** (l c)CORBIS, (r)U.S. Air Force Photo; **556** (t)The Granger Collection, New York, (cl)NSSDC/NASA, (cr)Donald Uhbrock/Time Life Pictures/GI, (b)BC; **558** (tl)NASA, (tr)Time Life Pictures/GI, (b)CORBIS; **560** (t)Picture Research Consultants, (b)BC; **563** Ross Lewis Milwaukee Public School; **564** (t)FPG/GI, (b)CORBIS; **564-565** SuperStock; **565** Natural Museum of American History/Smithsonian Institution; **567** (l)GI, (r)CORBIS; **569** CORBIS; **570** (tl)Masterfile, (tr)Time Life Pictures/GI, (bl)J R Eyerman/Time Life Pictures/GI, (br)Marvin Koner/CORBIS; **573** (l)Time Life Pictures/GI, (r)CORBIS; **575** BC; **576** (l)BC, (c)National Museum of American History/Smithsonian Institution, (r)The Kobal Collection; **578** (tl)Brown Brothers, (tr)Michael Ochs Archives/CORBIS, (bl)BC, (bc)Photofest, (br)Michael Ochs Archives/CORBIS; **583** (tl tr)Time Life Pictures/GI, (b)AP Images; **584** BC; **585** Thomas Hoepker/Magnum Photos; **586** National Archives; **588** (t)SuperStock, (b)Time Life Pictures/GI; **591** B. Wiseman/from Hey, Can't You Forget Business? by Charles Preston, ©1953, E.P. Dutton & Co., Inc.; **592-593** Wally McNamee/CORBIS; **594** (tl)Art Resource, NY, (tc)GI, (tr b)AP Images; **594-595** Time Life Pictures/GI; **597 599** BC; **603** George Silk/Time Life Pictures/GI; **604** (l)GI, (c)CORBIS SYGMA, (r)CORBIS; **605** (l)CORBIS SYGMA, (cl)BC, (cr r)

CORBIS; **606** (tl)Rene Burri/Magnum Photos, (tr)AP Images, (b)Carl Mydans/ Time Life Pictures/ GI; **611** (l)John Dominis/Time Life Pictures/ GI, (r)CORBIS; **612** Americorps VISTA Archives; **613** Corporation photo by Peter Shifter, Office of Public Affairs/AmeriCorps; **616** (t)AmeriCorps Archive, (c)Carl Mydans/ Time Life Pictures/GI, (b)Flip Schulke/Black Star; **619** LOC; **620** (l)Carl Iwaski/Time Life Pictures/GI, (r)Art Resource, NY; **620-621** Bob Adelman/Magnum Photos; **621** Collection of Janice L. and David J. Frent; **623** Time Life Pictures/GI; **625** Carl Iwaski/Time Life Pictures/ GI; **627** (tl tr br)Don Craven/Time Life Pictures/GI, (bl)Flip Schulke/ CORBIS; **628** (tl tr)CORBIS, (b)BC; **631** (l)CORBIS, (r)AP Images; **632** (t br)BC, (bl)Don Craven/Time Life Pictures/GI; **633** (tl)Charles Moore 1963/Black Star, (tr)Steve Schapiro, (b)BC; **635** Bill Hudson/AP Images; **637** Francis Miller/Time Life Pictures/GI; **638** Flip Schulke/CORBIS; **640** Eve Arnold/ Magnum Photos; **641** The Everett Collection; **643** (l)Atlanta Constitution, 1964, Clifford H. "Baldy" Baldowski Editorial Cartoons. Courtesy of the Richard B. Russell Library for Political Research and Studies, The University of Georgia Libraries, (r)A 1967 Herblock Cartoon, copyright by The Herb Block Foundation; **645** (l) Robert Parent/Time Life Pictures/GI, (c)AP Images, (r)Flip Schulke/CORBIS; **648** (t)Carl Iwaski/Time Life Pictures/GI, (c)Francis Miller/Time Life Pictures/GI, (b)Flip Schulke/CORBIS; **651** Jon Kennedy/ Arkansas Democrat-Gazette; **652** (t)Art Resource, NY, (b)Naval Historical Foundation; **652-653** Larry Burrows/Time Life Pictures/GI; **656** (tl)BC, (tr)AFP/GI, (b)AP Images; **659** (l)Popperfoto/Alamy Images, (r)CORBIS; **660** (t)MPI/GI, (b)Larry Burrows/Time Life Pictures/GI; **663** (l)BC, (r)AP Images; **665** (l)LOC/Tom Francis Darcy, Newsday/Reprinted with permission from LA Times Reprints, (r)Atlanta Constitution, Oct 18 1965, Clifford H. "Baldy" Baldowski Editorial Cartoons. Courtesy of the Richard B. Russell Library for Political Research and Studies, The University of Georgia Libraries; **666** (l b)Bernard Gotfryd/GI, (c)Hulton Archive/GI, (r)Paul Fusco/ Magnum Photos; **668** (tl)CORBIS, (tr cr)BC, (cl)Bob Gomel/Time Life Pictures/ GI; **671** (l)John Filo, (c)David Kennerly/BC, (r)Dirck Halstead/Time Life Pictures/GI; **673** (tl)BC, (tr)Time Life Pictures/GI, (b)The Granger Collection, New York; **674** (l)Alex Wong/GI, (r)Sal Veder/AP Images; **676** (t)AP Images, (c)Art Archive/Dept Defence Washington, (b)Wally McNamee/CORBIS; **679** Photo by DeAlba/Washington Daily News/Lyndon Baines Johnson Library; **680** (l)Art Resource, NY, (r)Charles Gatewood/The Image Works; **680-681** Take Stock; **681** AP Images; **683** BC; **684** (l)Vince Streano/CORBIS, (r)Andrew DeLory/Hulton Archive/GI; **687** (l)BC, (r)Charles Gatewood/The Image Works; **689** AP Images; **690** BC; **693** CORBIS; **694** LOC; **695** (l)CORBIS, (r)Jim Sugar/CORBIS; **696** Arthur Schatz/Time Life Pictures/GI; **698** (t c)Bettmann/CORBIS, (b)Steve Northup/Time Life Pictures/GI; **701** Jack Knox Estate/OSU Cartoon Research Library; **702-703** Michael Goldman/ Masterfile; **704** (l)Hulton Archive/GI, (r)BC; **704-705** AP Images; **705** Tom Ebenhoh/Black Star; **707** (l)A 1968 Herblock Cartoon, copyright by The Herb Block Foundation, (r)Atlanta Constitution, 1968 Oct 17, Clifford H. "Baldy" Baldowski Editorial Cartoons. Courtesy of the Richard B. Russell Library for Political Research and Studies, The University of Georgia Libraries; **709** (l)BC, (r)Time Life Pictures/GI; **710** (l)Dirck Halstead/Liasion/GI, (r)AFP/GI; **713** (tl cr b) BC, (tr)Robert Maass/CORBIS, (cl)Adam Woolfitt/CORBIS, (c)Dennis Brack/Black Star; **715** Mark Godfrey/The Images Works; **716** (l)A 1973 Herblock Cartoon, copyright by The Herb Block Foundation, (r)Atlanta Constitution, 1973, Clikfford H. "Baldy" Baldowski Editorial Cartoons. Courtesy of the Richard B. Russell Library for Political Research and Studies, The University of Georgia Libraries; **719** (l)Jason Laure/Woodfin Camp/Time Life Pictures/GI, (c r)BC; **721** (l)Brown Brothers, (r)Karl Schumacher/Time Life Pictures/GI; **722** (t)M. Lipschitz/AP Images, (cl)David Rubinger/ CORBIS, (cr)Sergio Gaudenti/Kipa/CORBIS, (b)MPI/GI; **725** (l)AP Images,(r)Scherl/SV-Bilderndienst/The Image Works; **726** (l)PA/Topham/ The Images Works, (r)Charles Gatewood/The Image Works; **728** (l)Wally McNamee/CORBIS, (c)Ed Kashi/CORBIS, (r)Brand X/SuperStock; **731** (l c)BC, (r)Charles E. Rotkin/CORBIS; **732** (l)A 1975 Herblock Cartoon, copyright by The Herb Block Foundation, (r)Hulton Archive/GI; **734** (t)Charles Gatewood/The Image Works, (c)BC, (b)Julian Wasser/Time Life Pictures/ GI; **737** Ranan R. Lurie, Cartoonews International Syndicate, New York City; **738** (t) AP Images, (b)Peter Turnley/CORBIS; **738-739** Eli Reed/Magnum Photos; **739** Lana Harris/AP Images; **741** (l)Gary McCoy/Cagle Cartoons, (r)Chris Slane/Cagle Cartoons; **744** (t)Index Stock Imagery, (bl)Cynthia Johnson/Time Life Pictures/GI, (bc)Annie Griffiths Belt/CORBIS, (br)Joe Raedle/Newsmakers/GI; **747** (t)Atlanta Constitution, 1976 Apr. 6, Clifford H. "Baldy" Baldowski Editorial Cartoons. Courtesy of the Richard B. Russell Library for Political Research and Studies, The University of Georgia Libraries, (b)Atlanta Constitution, 1981 Oct 18, Clifford H. "Baldy" Baldowski Editorial Cartoons. Courtesy of the Richard B. Russell Library for Political Research and

Studies, The University of Georgia Libraries; **749** (l)Wally McNamee/CORBIS, (r)Roger Ressmeyer/CORBIS; **750** (tl)Wally McNamee/CORBIS, (tr)Bob Daughtery/AP Images, (b)BC; **752** (tl)Robert Nickelsberg/Time Life Pictures/ GI, (tr)Dirck Halstead/Time Life Pictures/GI, (b)CORBIS; **755** (l)Eli Reichman/ Time Life Pictures/GI, (r)Bob Krist/CORBIS; **756** NASA/AP Images; **757** (inset)Blue Origin, (bkgd)HANDOUT/epa/CORBIS; **758** BC; **760** AP Images; **763** (l)Stephan Ferry/Liasion/GI, (r)Diane-Lu Hovasse/AFP/GI; **764** Thomas Hartwell/Time Life Pictures/GI; **766** (tl)Owen Franken/CORBIS, (tr)Markowitz Jeffrey/CORBIS SYGMA; (c)Wally McNamee/CORBIS, (b)Mike Lane/Cagle Cartoons; **768** (t)Tony Korody/Time Life Pictures/GI, (c)BC, (b)Alain Nogues/CORBIS SYGMA; **771** LOC, LC-DIG-ppmsc-07930, **772** (tl)Roger Ressmeyer/CORBIS, (tr)Spec. Robert Elliott/CORBIS, (b)David Brauchli/Reuters/CORBIS; **772-773** The White House/Handout/GI; **773** Official White House Photo by Eric Draper; **775** (tl)Ed Young/CORBIS, (tr)Douglas Engelbart/Bootstrap Alliance, (bl)TWPhoto/CORBIS, (br)Roger Ressmeyer/CORBIS; **781** (l)TOLES © 1997 The Washington Post. Reprinted with permission of UNIVERSAL PRESS SYNDICATE. All rights reserved, (tr)Wally McNamee/CORBIS, (br)Markowitz Jeffrey/CORBIS SYGMA; **783** (l)Terry Ashe/Time Life Pictures/GI, (r)SuperStock; **785** (l)Wally McNamee/ CORBIS, (r)Joe Marquette/AP Images; **786** (l)Peter Turnley/CORBIS, (tr)Les Stone/CORBIS SYGMA, (br)Leif Skoogfors/CORBIS; **790** David Kadlubowski/CORBIS; **792** (l) Fred Greaves/Reuters/CORBIS, (r)Carlos Barria/Reuters/CORBIS; **793** (t)Stanley Rogouski, (b)Michael Newman/ PhotoEdit; **796** Hamilton Karie/CORBIS SYGMA; **798** (t)Michael Newman/ PhotoEdit, (b)Ron Edmonds/AP Images; **801** TOLES © 1998 The Washington Post. Reprinted with permission of UNIVERSAL PRESS SYNDICATE. All rights reserved; **802** (l)Alan Diaz/AP Images, (c)Evan Vucci/AP Images, (r)Dimas Ardian/GI; **802-803** Michael Macor/San Francisco Chronicle/ CORBIS; **802** Official White House Photo by Eric Draper; **805** (t)Colin Braley/ Reuters/CORBIS, (bl bc)Ron Sachs/CNP/CORBIS, (br)Najlah Feanny/ CORBIS; **806** Daryl Cagle/Cagle Cartoons; **809** (t)Reuters/Sean Adair/ CORBIS, (bl)Ron Sachs/CNP/CORBIS, (br)Stan Honda/AFP/GI; **810** AP Images; **812** (t)Matthew McDermott/CORBIS, (bl)Reuters/CORBIS, (br)Steve Liss/CORBIS; **815** (t)Alexandra Boulat/VII/AP Images, (bl)Scott Peterson/ GI, (br)David Guttenfelder/AP Images; **816** (t)Ali Haider/AP Images, (b)Reuters/Jeff Christensen/CORBIS; **817** (tl)Al Jazeera via APTN/AP Images, (tr)Lynsey Addario/CORBIS, (b)Wathiq Khuzaie/GI; **818** (l)Lauren Frayer/ AP Images, (r)Khalid al-Mousily/Reuters/CORBIS; **821** (l)Shaun Heasley/ Reuters/CORBIS, (c)Charles W. Luzier/Reuters/CORBIS, (r)Brooks Kraft/ CORBIS; **822** (l)Khampha Bouaphanh/Knight Ridder/Tribune/Pool/ Reuters/CORBIS, (r)Brooks Kraft/CORBIS; **824** Smiley N. Pool/Dallas Morning News/CORBIS; **825** Rick Wilking/Reuters/CORBIS; **826** (l)Wathiq Khuzaie/GI, (r)Nancy Kaserman/ZUMA/CORBIS; **828** (t)AFP/GI, (cl)Kamal Kishore/AP Images, (cr)Al Jazeera/AP Images, (b)Evan Agostini/ ImageDirect/GI; **831** Olie Johannson/Political Cartoons; **R2** LOC, LC-USF34-T01-009095-C; **R3** Art Shay/Time Life Pictures/GI; **R4** LOC, LC-DIG-fsac-1a35337; **R5** Wally McNamee/CORBIS; **R6** Photo File/MLB Photos/GI; **R7** Stan Honda/AFP/GI; **R8** GI; **R9** CORBIS; **R10** (l)Comstock/CORBIS, (r)Art Archive/Reina Sofia Museum, Madrid; **R11** CORBIS; **R12 R13** BC; **R14** Harry Scull Jr./GI; **R17** The Granger Collection, New York; **R18** Clifford K. Berryman/National Archives; **R19** Scott, Lituchy/Star Ledger/CORBIS; **R20** Smithsonian Intstitution/CORBIS; **R32 R33** White House Historical Association; **R33** (br)Official White House Photo by Eric Draper; **R36** (tl)National Archives, (tr)Illinois State Historical Library, (b)Private Collection; **R39** Private Collection; **R40** The Wadsworth Atheneum; **R41 R42** Bridgeman Art Library; **R43 R44** National Portrait Gallery, Smithsonian Institution/ Art Resource, NY; **R46** Chicago Historical Society; **R47** (l)Maryland Historical Society, Baltimore, Maryland, (r)National Museum of American History/Armed Forces History Collections/Smithsonian Institution; **R48** Picture Research Consultants; **R49** LOC; **R50** (t)Andre Jenny/Focus Group/PictureQuest, (b)BC; **R52** National Portrait Gallery, Smithsonian Institution, Washington, D.C./Art Resource, NY; **R53** Courtesy Franklin D. Roosevelt Library; **R55** Carl Iwaski/Time Life Pictures/GI; **R56** Francis Miller/Time Life Pictures/GI; **R58 R60** GI; **R61** Picture Research Consultants; **R65** Stock Montage/GI; **R67** (t)Stock Montage/GI, (b)Frans Lanting/CORBIS; **R68** BC; **R69** Collection of the New York Historical Society/Bridgeman Art Library; **R71** (t)Erling Larson/GI, (b)Henry Guttmann/GI; **R72** Keystone/GI; **R73** General Photographic Agency/ GI; **R74** Ray Fisher/Time Life Pictures/GI; **R75** Hulton Archive/GI; **R76** Stephen Jaffe/AFP/GI; **R80** Mitchell Gerber/CORBIS; **Timeline Presidential Paintings** White House Historical Association.